THINKERS OF THE TWENTIETH CENTURY

THINKERS OF THE TWENTIETH CENTURY

THINKERS OF THE TWENTIETH CENTURY
A Biographical, Bibliographical and Critical Dictionary

Editors
Elizabeth Devine; Michael Held; James Vinson; George Walsh

FIRETHORN PRESS

EDITOR'S NOTE

The selection of twentieth-century thinkers included in this book is based upon the recommendations of the advisers listed on page ix.

The entry for each thinker consists of a biography, a bibliography, a listing of critical studies of the entrant, and a signed critical essay. The bibliographies list all books—with details of original publication in the U.K. and U.S.A. In the case of those entrants who published originally in a language other than English, original foreign language publication is listed as well as, where applicable, subsequent publication in English.

The editors wish to thank the reference librarians of the University of Chicago and the staff of the Reading Room of the British Museum, London, for their assistance in helping us to compile this book.

CONTENTS

ADVISERS

Philip J. Davis
Dale B. Harris
J.H. Hexter
Fred Horne
Dennis J. Hutchinson

Philip Klein
Martin E. Marty
James Redfield
Thomas A. Sebeok
Albert Tsugawa

CONTRIBUTORS

Edward Amend
Harry Ammon
Williard E. Arnett
Frank M. Baglione
Paul Barolsky
Norman P. Barry
Randall Davey Bird
Irving Block
Stephen Botein
Donald F. Bouchard
John E. Bowlt
Charles I. Brooks
Richard A. Brosio
William Bywater
Seymour Cain
Carnegie Samuel Calian
Alex Callinicos
Donald Capps
J.B. Carroll
Victor Cassidy
Robert Cassilo
Myrna Chase
Constance Clark
Sheldon S. Cohen
William H. Coleman
David R. Conrad
Robert D. Cottrell
Robert R. Davis
Hermione de Almeida
John Deedy
Angelo A. De Gennaro
C.F. Delaney
Patricia Devine
William Devine
Ian Duncan
Granville Eastwood
Leonard H. Ehrlich
Bernard Elevitch
Janet Forsythe Fishburn
Ronald C. Fisher
Thomas R. Flynn
N. Fotion
James W. Fowler
Maurice Friedman
Manfred S. Frings
George H. Gilpin
Robert Jerome Glennon
G. Wayne Glick
John Goddeeris
John D. Godsey
James Gouinlock
Donald P. Gray
Walter D. Gray
Geoffrey Green
Sonia F. Guterman
Mauricio Gutierrez

Gary Gutting
Richard Handler
Rollo Handy
Dale B. Harris
H.S. Harris
Irene G. Harvey
Don Hausdorff
Gerard A. Hauser
L.S. Hearnshaw
Steve J. Heims
Mary Henle
Paul L. Holmer
Jackson Lee Ice
David Ingram
Robert E. Innis
R.N. Iyer
James M. Johannes
J. Dines Johansen
Jill Johnston
Michael C. Jordan
Marian Jorgensen
Jack Kaminsky
Philip Kasinitz
Charles W. Kegley
Jacquelyn Ann K. Kegley
George W. Kelling
Douglas Kellner
Joseph M. Kitagawa
E.D. Klemke
Joseph J. Kockelmans
Konstantin Kolenda
Alex Kozulin
Paul Kurtz
John Lange
Nathanial Lawrence
Murray J. Leaf
David E. Leary
Robert T. Lehe
D.L. LeMahieu
R. Bruce Lindsay
Jocelyn Linnekin
Abraham S. Luchins
Christopher Lyon
Henry W. Maier
Stephen Martin
J.M. Massing
B.K. Matilal
George Mauner
C.M.A. McCauliff
Harold G. McCurdy
Sterling M. McMurrin
Chris Milner
Louis O. Mink
J.G. Morawski
Joshua S. Mostow
C. Lynn Munro

Ulric Neisser
Cary Nelson
Jerome Neu
David Newton
Martin Nozick
Norman P. Obst
David O'Connor
David A. Pariser
Stanley L. Paulson
Eugene L. Peters
Robert A. Pois
Philip Pomper
John R. Presley
Michael I. Prochilo
Helena M. Pycior
Terence H. Qualter
John Rajcman
James Redfield
R.W. Rieber
Alexander L. Ringer
Richard C. Roberts
Martin F. Rouse
Michael Ruse
John Paul Russo
Geoffrey Sampson
Warren J. Samuels
Robert P. Scharlemann
Anne-Francoise Schmid
Robert J. Schreiter
Lark Schulze
William T. Scott
Daniel Alan Segal
Thomas Sheehan
Harvey Shepard
Franklin Sherman
Ronald K. Shull

Alan Sica
Seymore Simon
Henryk Skolimowski
R. Margaret Slythe
Charlotte W. Smith
Joseph C. Stevens
Jerome Arthur Stone
Ronald H. Stone
Roland Stromberg
Robert H. Tamarin
Philip Thody
Albert Tsugawa
Bryan S. Turner
Stephen D. Unwin
James O. Urmson
Donald Phillip Verene
Paul L. Ward
Robert D. Warth
Fred E. Wasserman
Alan Waters
Eugene Webb
Linda Wessels
Lorna Bowlby West
Carol A. Whitehurst
Kingsley Widmer
Daniel J. Wilson
Fred Wilson
Kenneth Winetrout
Kenneth I. Winston
Peter Woolstencroft
David J. Wren
Linnea H. Wren
Walter E. Wyman, Jr.
Stephen R. Yarbrough
Harry Zohn

THINKERS OF THE TWENTIETH CENTURY

THINKERS OF THE TWENTIETH CENTURY

Alfred Adler
T.W. Adorno
Kazimierz Ajdukiewicz
Samuel Alexander
Gordon W. Allport
Louis Althusser
Hannah Arendt
Philippe Aries
Rudolf Arnheim
Raymond Aron
Svante Arrhenius
Kenneth Arrow
Antonin Artaud
Erich Auerbach
J.L. Austin
A.J. Ayer

Gaston Bachelard
Karl Barth
Roland Barthes
Frederic Bartlett
Gregory Bateson
George W. Beadle
Charles A. Beard
Monroe C. Beardsley
Carl Becker
Clive Bell
Daniel Bell
Julien Benda
Ruth Benedict
Walter Benjamin
Nicolas Berdyaev
Bernard Berenson
Henri Bergson
Isaiah Berlin
J.D. Bernal
Basil Bernstein
Bruno Bettelheim
Alfred Binet
Hugo L. Black
Max Black
Brand Blanshard
Ernst Bloch
Marc Bloch
Leonard Bloomfield
Franz Boas
Niels Bohr
Dietrich Bonhoeffer
E.G. Boring
Max Born
John Bowlby
Lawrence Bragg
William Bragg
Fernand Braudel
Berthold Brecht
P.W. Bridgman
C.D. Broad
Donald Broadbent
Jacob Bronowski
Johannes Brønsted
L.E.J. Brouwer
Jerome S. Bruner
Léon Brunschvicg
Martin Buber
Karl Bühler
James Burnham
Cyril Burt
Ferruccio Busoni

John Cage
Albert Camus

Benjamin N. Cardozo
Rudolf Carnap
Ernst Cassirer
Carlos Castaneda
Noam Chomsky
Kenneth Clark
Morris Raphael Cohen
R.G. Collingwood
Charles Horton Cooley
F.H.C. Crick
Benedetto Croce

Surendranath Dasgupta
Simone de Beauvoir
Louis de Broglie
Peter Debye
Max Delbrück
Jacques Derrida
Ferdinand de Saussure
Miguel de Unamuno
John Dewey
Paul Dirac
Theodosius Dobzhansky
Emile Durkheim
Ronald Dworkin

A.S. Eddington
Albert Einstein
Sergei Eisenstein
Mircea Eliade
T.S. Eliot
Erik H. Erikson
W.K. Estes
E.E. Evans-Pritchard
H.J. Eysenck

Frantz Fanon
Lucien Febvre
Herbert Feigl
Enrico Fermi
Richard Feynman
J.R. Firth
Raymond Firth
Irving Fisher
Alexander Fleming
Meyer Fortes
Michel Foucault
Jerome N. Frank
Felix Frankfurter
Anna Freud
Sigmund Freud
Milton Friedman
Ragnar Frisch
Erich Fromm
Roger Fry
Lon L. Fuller
R. Buckminster Fuller

Hans-George Gadamer
John Kenneth Galbraith
Mahatma Gandhi
Clifford Geertz
Murray Gell-Mann
Ernest Gellner
Giovanni Gentile
Louis Gernet
Arnold Gesell
James J. Gibson
Etienne Gilson
Kurt Gödel
Erving Goffman

Kurt Goldstein
E.H. Gombrich
Nelson Goodman
Paul Goodman
Pierre Goubert
Antonio Gramsci
H.P. Grice
Walter Gropius
Che Guevara

Jürgen Habermas
Axel Hägerström
J.B.S. Haldane
Elie Halévy
Stuart Hampshire
Oscar Handlin
G.H. Hardy
Harry F. Harlow
H.L.A. Hart
Charles Hartshorne
D.O. Hebb
Martin Heidegger
Werner Heisenberg
Abraham Joshua Heschel
John Hicks
David Hilbert
Ernest Hilgard
Louis Hjelmslev
Wesley N. Hohfeld
Oliver Wendell Holmes, Jr.
Sidney Hook
Max Horkheimer
Karen Horney
Fred Hoyle
Edwin Powell Hubble
Johan Huizinga
Clark Hull
T.E. Hulme
Edmund Husserl
Robert Maynard Hutchins

Ivan Illich
Roman Ingarden
William Ralph Inge
Wolfgang Iser

Francois Jacob
Roman Jakobson
William James
Karl Jaspers
James Jeans
Otto Jespersen
C.G. Jung

Wassily Kandinsky
Sergej Karceveskij
Karl Kautsky
Hans Kelsen
John Kendrew
John Maynard Keynes
Lawrence R. Klein
Frank H. Knight
Kurt Koffka
Wolfgang Köhler
Karl Korsch
H.A. Kramers
Karl Kraus
Hans Krebs
Alfred L. Kroeber
Thomas S. Kuhn
Hans Küng

Simon Kuznets

Jacques Lacan
R.D. Laing
Imre Lakatos
Susanne Langer
K.S. Lashley
Harold Laski
Pierre Lecomte du Noüy
Le Corbusier
V.I. Lenin
Wassily Leontief
Emmanuel Le Roy Ladurie
Claude Lévi-Strauss
Lucien Lévy-Bruhl
Kurt Lewin
C.I. Lewis
C.S. Lewis
Gilbert Newton Lewis
Oscar Lewis
Walter Lippmann
Seymour M. Lipset
Konrad Lorenz
Arthur O. Lovejoy
Georg Lukács
Alexander R. Luria
Salvador Luria
Rosa Luxemburg
Trofim Lysenko

Frederic William Maitland
Norman Malcolm
Bronislaw Malinowski
André Malraux
Karl Mannheim
Mao Tse-tung
Gabriel Marcel
Herbert Marcuse
Jacques Maritain
A.H. Maslow
Garrett Mattingly
Charles Maurras
William McDougall
C.H. McIlwain
Richard McKeon
Marshall McLuhan
William H. McNeill
J. McT. E. McTaggart
George Herbert Mead
Margaret Mead
Friedrich Meinecke
Maurice Merleau-Ponty
Robert K. Merton
C. Wright Mills
Wesley C. Mitchell
Jacques Monod
Maria Montessori
G.E. Moore
Thomas Hunt Morgan
Samuel Eliot Morison
Charles Morris
Gaetano Mosca
O. Hobart Mowrer
Hermann Joseph Muller
Lewis Mumford
Iris Murdoch
Gardner Murphy
Henry A. Murray
Gunnar Myrdal

Ernest Nagel

L.B. Namier
Otto Neurath
H. Richard Niebuhr
Reinhold Niebuhr
Emmy Noether

A.I. Oparin
J. Robert Oppenheimer
José Ortega y Gasset
George Orwell
Charles E. Osgood
Rudolf Otto

Erwin Panofsky
Vilfredo Pareto
Robert E. Park
Talcott Parsons
Wolfgang Pauli
Linus Pauling
Charles Sanders Peirce
Max Perutz
Jean Piaget
Henri Pirenne
John Plamenatz
Max Planck
Henri Poincaré
Michael Polanyi
Karl Popper
Roscoe Pound
Mario Praz

W.V. Quine

A.R. Radcliffe-Brown
Sarvepalli Radhakrishnan
Karl Rahner
Walter Rauschenbusch
John Rawls
Herbert Read
Robert Redfield
Wilhelm Reich
I.A. Richards
Paul Ricoeur
David Riesman
Lord Robbins
D.H. Robertson
Joan Robinson
Carl Rogers
Harold Rosenberg
Bertrand Russell
Ernest Rutherford
Gilbert Ryle

Marshall Sahlins
Paul A. Samuelson
George Santayana
Edward Sapir
Jean-Paul Sartre
Meyer Schapiro
Max Scheler
Edward Schillebeeckx
Moritz Schlick
Arnold Schoenberg
Gershom Scholem
Erwin Schrödinger
Joseph Schumpeter
Albert Schweitzer
Julian Schwinger
John R. Searle
Ernest Sellière
George Bernard Shaw

André Siegfried
Georg Simmel
Herbert A. Simon
B.F. Skinner
Werner Sombart
Susan Sontag
Georges Sorel
Pitirim Sorokin
Charles Spearman
Oswald Spengler
Leo Spitzer
Stanislavsky
Rudolf Steiner
William Stern
S.S. Stevens
Charles L. Stevenson
Adrian Stokes
Lawrence Stone
Leo Strauss
Igor Stravinsky
P.F. Strawson
Henry Stack Sullivan
Louis Sullivan
D.T. Suzuki

R.H. Tawney
Pierre Teilhard de Chardin
William Temple
Lewis M. Terman
W.I. Thomas
E.L. Thorndike
L.L. Thurstone
Paul Tillich
Jan Tinbergen
Edward Bradford Titchener
E.C. Tolman
Stephen E. Toulmin
Charles Townes
Arnold Toynbee
Ernst Troeltsch
Leon Trotsky
A.M. Turing
Frederick Jackson Turner
Victor Turner

Hans Vaihinger
Paul Valéry
Thorsten Veblen
Jean-Pierre Vernant
Eric Voegelin
Max von Frisch
Adolf von Harnack
Friedrich von Hayek
Friedrich von Hügel
John von Neumann
L.S. Vygotsky

Graham Wallas
James D. Watson
J.B. Watson
Sidney and Beatrice Webb
Max Weber
Simone Weil
Max Wertheimer
Edvard Westermarck
Hermann Weyl
Alfred North Whitehead
Benjamin Lee Whorf
Norbert Wiener
Eugene Paul Wigner
Raymond Williams

Edward O. Wilson
Louis Wirth
Ludwig Wittgenstein
Heinrich Wölfflin

C. Vann Woodward
Robert S. Woodworth
Wilhelm Worringer
Frank Lloyd Wright

ADLER, Alfred. Austrian psychologist. Born in Vienna, 7 February 1870. Studied medicine at the University of Vienna, M.D. 1895. Attached to the Austrian Army during World War I. Married Raissa Einstein in 1898; 4 children. Worked in the Vienna General Hospital and Polyclinic, 1895-97, and as a General Practitioner and Nerve Specialist in Vienna, 1897-1927. Lecturer, Pedagogic Institute, Vienna, 1924-27; Lecturer, College of Physicians and Surgeons, Columbia University, New York, 1927-28; Director, Mariahilfer Ambulatorium, Vienna, 1928-32; Visiting Professor of Medical Psychology, Long Island College of Medicine, New York, 1932-37. Organized Child Guidance Centers in Vienna; founded the *Journal of Individual Psychology* in Vienna in 1914 and in New York in 1935. *Died* (in Aberdeen, Scotland) *28 May 1937.*

PUBLICATIONS

Psychology

Studie über die Minderwertigkeit von Organen. Vienna, Urban and Schwarzenberg, 1907; as *Study of Organ Inferiority and Its Psychical Compensation: A Contribution to Clinical Medicine,* New York, Nervous and Mental Diseases Publishing Company, 1917.
Über den nervösen Charakter: Grundzüge einer vergleichenden Individual-Psychologie und Psychotherapie. Munich, Bergmann, 1912; as *The Neurotic Constitution: Outlines of a Comparative Individualistic Psychology and Psychotherapy,* New York, Moffat Yard, 1917; London, Kegan Paul, 1918.
Die andere Seite: Eine massenpsychologische Studie über die Schuld des Volkes. Vienna, Heidrich, 1919.
Praxis und Theorie der Individualpsychologie: Vorträge zur Einführung in die Psychotherapie für Ärzte, Psychologen und Lehrer. Munich, Bergmann, 1920; as *The Practice and Theory of Individual Psychology,* London, Kegan Paul, and New York, Harcourt Brace, 1924.
Menschenkenntnis. Leipzig, Hirzel, 1927; as *Understanding Human Nature,* New York, Greenberg, 1927; London, Allen and Unwin, 1928.
Die Technik der Individualpsychologie: volume 1, *Die Kunst eine Krankengeschichte zu lesen.* Munich, Bergmann, 1928; volume 2, *Die Seele schwererziehbaren Schulkinder,* Munich, Bergmann, 1929; as *The Problem Child: The Life Style of the Difficult Child Analyzed in Specific Cases,* New York, Capricorn Books, 1963.
The Case of Miss R. London, Allen and Unwin, and New York, Greenberg, 1929.
Individualpsychologie in der Schule: Vorlesungen für Lehrer und Erzieher. Leipzig, Hirzel, 1929.
Problems of Neurosis: A Book of Case-Histories. London, Kegan Paul, 1929; New York, Cosmopolitan Book Corporation, 1930.
The Science of Living. New York, Greenberg, 1929; London, Allen, 1930.
The Education of Children. New York, Greenberg, 1930; London, Allen and Unwin, 1957.
The Pattern of Life. New York, Rinehart, 1930; London, Kegan Paul, 1931.
Das Problem des Homosexualität: Erotisches Training und erotischer Rückzug. Leipzig, Hirzel, 1930.
What Life Should Mean to You. Boston, Little Brown, 1931; London, Allen and Unwin, 1932.
The Case of Mrs. A. London, C.W. Daniel, 1931.
Der Sinn des Lebens. Vienna, Rolf Passer, 1933; as *Social Interest: A Challenge to Mankind,* London, Faber, 1938; New York, Putnam, 1939.
Religion und Individualpsychologie: Eine prinzipielle Auseinandersetzung über Menschenführung, with Ernst Jahn. Vienna, Rolf Passer, 1933.
Superiority and Social Interest: A Collection of Later Writings.

Evanston, Illinois, Northwestern University Press, 1965.

*

Critical Studies: *Alfred Adler: A Biography* by Phyllis Bottome, New York, Putnam, 1939; *Alfred Adler: The Man and His Work* by Hertha Orgler, London, Sidgwick and Jackson, 1963.

*   *   *

Throughout his professional life, Alfred Adler consistently advocated that no human being can be comprehended except as a unitive whole; he ardently sought to make the profoundest insights of psychology accessible to all, and courageously confronted the fundamental problems of psychotherapy.

His first work stressed the need to perceive the individual within the context of his environment. Just as a foetus cannot be studied independently of the placenta and the mother, so too the individual cannot be properly understood in isolation. In 1902 Adler accepted Freud's invitation to join his discussion group, but he soon found himself in radical disagreement with many of Freud's basic concepts. Although he accepted the premise that adult psychic dynamics are inherent in the child, he repudiated the conclusion that early sexual experience formed the foundation of psychic development. Sexuality, both in its internal force and in its manifest forms, is, for Adler, the result of deeper factors in the child's growth or retardation. Like Freud, Adler acknowledged the importance of dreams in the psychic life of individuals, but he found Freud's correlation of dream images with (largely sexual) fears and frustrations too mechanical. The same symbol, Adler held, might have a specific function for one person and a rather different significance for another. Adler's strong conviction that Freud's concern to trace adult thought and action chiefly to childhood sexual trauma was a needlessly violent conception of human nature and one that placed an insupportable explanatory burden upon individual sexuality led him to break forever with Freud in 1911.

With *Study of Organ Inferiority and Its Psychical Compensation,* Adler began to propound his original observations, which he would come to call "Individualpsychologie" to distinguish them firmly from theories which too readily subsumed individual conduct under supposedly universal generalizations. Adler placed the problems of psychology within the context of general medicine; he held that from birth each human being is liable through heredity to some organ inferiority (often renal) which commands the attention of the ego as a persisting imperfection in the materials out of which the personality is constructed. The growing child has to compensate for inferiority and may do so in a healthy or a neurotic manner. A person born without a specific limb, for example, cannot simply ignore the fact; rather, the inferior organ becomes the dominant focus of ego-attention. The person may compensate and make the most of what he has to work with, or he may use the inferiority to excuse himself from responsibility or even to manipulate others. This stance implies a teleological view of human nature: the individual is a whole with a central purpose. The holistic dimension of this basic perspective presupposes the inseparability of "psyche" and "soma" in structure and function. The teleological dimension suggests an approach to personality conveyed through a generalized application of the concept of what Adler came to call in 1925 "the inferiority complex."

In *The Neurotic Constitution* Adler offered his theory of individual psychology. Just as in somatic medicine the comparative study of diverse persons allows for the establishment of a "fictive standard of normality" by which deviations may be discerned, so too a similar methodology in the psychic realm reveals that the individual is under the influence of a fictitious idea of personality which can lead to the development of the neurotic character and its symptoms. Since the individual is a teleological unity, every aspect of the psychic life is affected by this dominant urge. The child recognizes its inferiority, and normalcy is marked by his or her compensating for this while growing up as a fully participating member of society; but children can easily tend to overcompensate and thus distort the realities of psycho-physical existence, which results in a range of anti-social attitudes and conduct. The emerging neurotic has an intensified ego-consciousness which posits a simplistic final purpose; it can be formulated as, "I wish to be a complete man." This "masculine protest (Männlichen Protest)" is the chief fiction in neurosis and manifests itself as a will to power or domination which is inherently anti-social. Insofar as neurosis has a sexual content, it arises from the masculine protest cast in terms of an imaginary antithesis of masculine and feminine. Its appearance reveals the distance between subject and goal, which will be reflected in the psychic distance the neurotic puts between himself and others. Infantile wishes, incipient sexuality and dream life, which figure prominently in Freud's thought, were for Adler already subordinate to the all-governing goal. Sexuality itself is expropriated as a tool for domination. This urge to power may take active or aggressive forms, or it may be passive and submissive, but it is all one and reveals itself as the conspicuous inability of the psyche to adapt to society.

There is no element in the neurotic character that cannot also be found in the healthy individual. In the case of the neurotic, however, the universal need to compensate for inferiority has taken an unfortunate turn by being made to serve an imaginary goal, focussed upon heightening the fictitious personality rather than lowering ego-consciousness through social concern or a felt identity with humanity. Given the unattainability of the neurotic's goal, he may make vacillation and doubt a way of life, or he may deify the goal (and move ever closer to full psychosis), or he may pretend to change the goal so that feminine means are used to convey what is in fact masculine protest. Thus, whilst heredity provides the materials for life, the congenital differences between individuals pale into insignificance in the face of the "guiding fiction." Even while the neurotic justifies, explains or excuses his actions and passions in terms of that given material, he is really attempting to abnegate responsibility for being what he is. "Inferior organs and neurotic phenomena are symbols of formative forces which strive to realize a self-constructed life plan by means of intense efforts and expedients." When the dynamics of human nature are understood, striving for power is reduced in favour of energetic pursuit of constructive social interests.

Adler's profound concern that psychology be regarded as a practical science led him to publish *Understanding Human Nature*. It is written for any intelligent reader. In it Adler argues that the immense range of interests and experiences to be found in any life do not indicate alterations in the lines of psychic movement; the "life-plan" remains essentially fixed. All problems of life can be reduced to three broad categories—occupational, social and sexual—and neurosis can develop out of any of them. Therapeutic cures are often adjustments of means, not transformations of goals. When the goal is fictitious or unrealistic, such cures are delusive; the neurotic remains neurotic. While he may cope better with some aspects of the world, neither he nor society has benefitted. Authentic therapy occurs only when the root error, upon which the fictitious goal and deluded life-pattern is based, is fully uncovered. In this the strict determinists are right: the chain of cause and effect is inexorable. Only self-knowledge can make a decisive difference by inserting a new line of causation into the nexus of error. For Adler, parents and schools are crucial, and often negative, influences on the child. In families where the father is leader (the norm in many cultures), masculine protest, the will to power and the implied competitive aggressiveness and its inversions, are enhanced. Teachers are ill-prepared to treat their students in truly human terms, and even when they are, class size and school rules vitiate their efforts. Until parents can draw the fine line between empathy and indulgence, and men and women function on equal terms in the home, and until teachers come to know their students as well as their intellectual disciplines, these basic sources of human health will continue to contribute to the production of weakness and aggression, irresponsibility and disease.

Adler summed up a lifetime of research and reflection in *What Life Should Mean to You*, which he dedicated "to the human family in the hope that its members may learn from these pages to understand themselves better." Pointing out that human beings live in a realm of multiple meanings, he indicated that individuals are bound by a triple tie—to the earth on which one must live, to the human species with which one must interact, and to a sex, since humans "are living in two sexes." From these ties derive the three categories of problems of life, and in their avoidance or solution is found the meaning of life. A true, as contrasted with a fictitious, meaning is sharable with others, and this is so even in regard to genius. "Life means—to contribute to the whole." One meets the problems of life successfully by discerning that the meaning of life is co-operation and sustained interest in one's fellow beings. Individuals are not mere products of their traumas, but may use them as they will. Hence each individual is self-determined through the meaning he assigns to experiences. (This implies, as Adler saw, that eugenic selection is no solution to problems arising out of inferiority.) Neurosis and unsatisfactory life-plans in general result from one's becoming too concerned with the fictitious personality. In work, this leads to tyranny or escape from responsibility; in society, it is revealed in failures of relationship; in sexuality, it is love that turns to oneself. Inferiority may manifest as fear, fatalism or auto-intoxication to the point of feeling superior. Learning to co-operate and to take an interest in the welfare of others involves a sort of self-forgetfulness that is inherently therapeutic. Like Plato, Adler advocated the early training of individuals to take their places in the division of labor, the assumption of responsibility for solving the problems of life co-operatively, and monogamous and equal partnership in love and marriage. In *Social Interest: A Challenge to Mankind*, Adler reiterated these insights with a detailed analysis of superiority in terms of overcompensation for inferiority and turned his attention to the particular problems of the pampered individual and the removal of social obstructions in childhood.

Adler's "Individualpsychologie" was distinguished by its respect for the givens of each individual and its refusal to treat all individuals as psychically intersubstitutable. This was the consequence of Adler's essential respect for the mystery of each human being, inherent in each one's life-plan. Fully aware of the coherence and strength of that line of life, he nevertheless held out the therapeutic possibility of change. The results of experience acquire entirely new values when the power of self-knowledge and self-criticism is still alive and remains a living motif. "The ability to know one's self becomes greater when one can determine the well-springs of his activity and the dynamics of his soul. Once he has understood this, he has become a different man and can no longer escape the inevitable consequences of his knowledge."

—R.N. Iyer

ADORNO, Theodor W(iesengrund). German philosopher, musicologist, and sociologist. Born in Frankfurt, 11 September 1903. Studied at the University of Frankfurt, Ph.D. 1924. Married Gretel Karplus in 1937. Associated with the Institut für Sozialforschung, 1928-69: in Vienna and New York, 1928-38, as Head of Music Study, Institute Office of Radio Research, Princeton, New Jersey, 1938-41, in California, 1941-49, and as Assistant Director, 1950-55, Co-Director, 1955-58, and Director, 1958-69, in Frankfurt; also, Professor of Philosophy and Sociology, University of Frankfurt, 1958-69. Recipient: Arnold Schönberg Medal, 1954; Critics' Prize for Literature, 1959; Goethe Medal, Frankfurt, 1963. *Died* (in Frankfurt) *6 August 1969*.

PUBLICATIONS

Collections

Gesammelte Werke, edited by Rolf Tiedemann. Frankfurt, Suhrkamp, 23 vols., 1970-.

Philosophy, Musicology and Sociology

Kierkegaard: Konstruktion des ästhetischen. Tübingen, Mohr, 1933.
Memorandum: Music in Radio. Princeton, New Jersey, Princeton Radio Research Project, 1938.
Philosophische Fragmente, with Max Horkheimer. New York, Institute for Social Research, 1944; revised edition as *Dialektik der Aufklärung: Philosophische Fragmente*, Amsterdam, Querido, 1947; as *Dialectic of Enlightenment*, New York, Herder, 1972.
Philosophie der neuen Musik. Tübingen, Mohr, 1949; as *Philosophy of Modern Music*, New York, Seabury, 1973.
The Authoritarian Personality, with others. New York, Harper, 1950.
Minima Moralia: Reflexionen aus dem beschädigten Leben. Frankfurt, Suhrkamp, 1951; as *Minima Moralia: Reflections from Damaged Life*, London, New Left Books, 1974.
Versuch über Wagner. Frankfurt, Suhrkamp, 1952; as *In Search of Wagner*, London, New Left Books, and New York, Schocken, 1981.
Die gegängelte Musik: Bemerkungen über die Musikpolitik der Ostblockstaaten. Frankfurt, Eremiten, 1954.
Prismen: Kulturkritik und Gesellschaft. Frankfurt, Suhrkamp, 1955; as *Prisms*, London, Spearman, 1967; Cambridge, Massachusetts, MIT Press, 1982.
Dissonanzen: Musik in der verwalteten Welt. Göttingen, Vandenhoeck und Ruprecht, 1956.
Zur Metakritik der Erkenntnistheorie: Studien über Husserl und die phänomenologischen Antinomien. Stuttgart, Kohlhammer, 1956.
Aspekte der Hegelschen Philosophie. Frankfurt, Suhrkamp, 1957.
Die Funktion des Kontrapunkts in der neuen Musik. Berlin, Akademie der Künste, 1957.
Noten zur Literatur. Frankfurt, Suhrkamp, 4 vols., 1958-74.
Musikalische Schriften: volume 1, *Klangfiguren*; volume 2, *Quasi una fantasia*. Frankfurt, Suhrkamp, 1959-63.
Mahler: Eine musikalische Physiognomik. Frankfurt, Suhrkamp, 1960.
Einleitung in die Musiksoziologie. Frankfurt, Suhrkamp, 1962; as *Introduction to the Sociology of Music*, New York, Seabury, 1976.
Drei Studien zu Hegel. Frankfurt, Suhrkamp, 1963.
Eingriffe: Neun kritische Modelle. Frankfurt, Suhrkamp, 1963.
Der getreue Korrepetitor: Lehrschriften zur musikalischen Praxis. Frankfurt, Fischer, 1963.
Moments musicaux: Neu gedruckte Aufsätze 1928-1962. Frankfurt, Suhrkamp, 1964.
Jargon der Eigentlichkeit: Zur deutschen Ideologie. Frankfurt, Suhrkamp, 1965; as *The Jargon of Authenticity*, London, Routledge, and Evanston, Illinois, Northwestern University Press, 1973.
Negative Dialektik. Frankfurt, Suhrkamp, 1966; as *Negative Dialectics*, New York, Seabury, and London, Routledge, 1973.
Ohne Leitbild: Parva Aesthetics. Frankfurt, Suhrkamp, 1967.
Über einige Relationen zwischen Musik und Malerei: Die Kunst und die Künste. Berlin, Akademie der Künste, 1967.
Berg: Der Meister des kleinsten Übergangs. Vienna, Österreichischer Bundesverlag, 1968.
Impromptus: Zweite Folge neu gedruckter musikalischer Aufsätze. Frankfurt, Suhrkamp, 1968.
Über Walter Benjamin. Frankfurt, Suhrkamp, 1968.

Komposition für den Film, with Hanns Eisler. Munich, Rogner und Bernhard, 1969; as *Composing for the Films*, New York, Books for Libraries Press, 1971.
Stichworte: Kritische Modelle 2. Frankfurt, Suhrkamp, 1969.
Nervenpunkte der neuen Musik. Reinbeck, West Germany, Rowohlt, 1969.
Aesthetische Theorie, edited by Gretel Adorno and Rolf Tiedemann. Frankfurt, Suhrkamp, 1970.
Aufsätze zur Gesellschaftstheorie und Methodologie. Frankfurt, Suhrkamp, 1970.
Erziehung zur Mündigkeit: Vorträge und Gespräche mit Helmut Becker, edited by Gerd Kadelbach. Frankfurt, Suhrkamp, 1970.
Vorlesungen zur Ästhetik, edited by Christof Subik. Rheinstetten, West Germany, Schindel, 1970.
Theodor W. Adorno: Eine Auswahl, edited by Rolf Tiedemann. Frankfurt, Büchergilde Gutenberg, 1971.
Kritik: Kleine Schriften zur Gesellschaft, edited by Rolf Tiedemann. Frankfurt, Suhrkamp, 1971.
Aufsätze zur Literatur des 20. Jahrhunderts: volume 1, *Versuch, das Endspiel zu verstehen*; volume 2, *Zur Dialektik des Engagements*. Frankfurt, Suhrkamp, 1973.
Vorlesungen zur Ästhetik 1967-1968. Zurich, H. Mayer Nachfolger, 1973.
Vorlesung zur Einleitung in die Soziologie. Frankfurt, Junius-Drucke, 1973.
Vorlesung zur Einleitung in die Erkenntnistheorie. Frankfurt, Junius-Drucke, 1973.
Philosophische Terminologie: Zur Einleitung, edited by Rudolf zur Lippe. Frankfurt, Suhrkamp, 1973.
Gesellschaftstheorie und Kulturkritik. Frankfurt, Suhrkamp, 1975.
Against Epistomology (translated from the German). Oxford, Blackwell, 1980.

Other

Briefwechsel: Theodor W. Adorno und Ernst Krenek, edited by Wolfgang Rogge. Frankfurt, Suhrkamp, 1974.

Editor, with Gretel Adorno, *Walter Benjamin: Schriften*. Frankfurt, Suhrkamp, 2 vols., 1955.
Editor, with Gershom Scholem, *Walter Benjamin: Briefe*. Frankfurt, Suhrkamp, 2 vols., 1966.

*

Bibliography: "Vorläufige Bibliographie der Schriften" in *Theodor W. Adorno zum Gedächtnis*, edited by Hermann Schweppenhäuser, Frankfurt, Suhrkamp, 1971.

Critical Studies: *The Dialectical Imagination* by Martin Jay, London, Heinemann, 1973; *Benjamin; Adorno: Zwei Studien* by Gerhard Kaiser, Frankfurt, Fischer, 1974; *The Origin of Negative Dialectics* by Susan Buck-Morss, New York, Free Press, and London, Macmillan, 1977; *Origin and Significance of the Frankfurt School* by Phil Slater, London, Routledge, 1977; *The Frankfurt School* by Zoltan Tar, New York, Wiley, 1977; *Introduction to Critical Theory: Horkheimer to Habermas* by David Held, London, Hutchinson, 1980.

*   *   *

Theodor W. Adorno was a philosopher whose work extended far beyond the traditional boundaries of philosophy. He made original contributions to social psychology, aesthetics, musicology and literary criticism. He returned continually—always in a critical vein—to the works of Kant, Hegel, Marx, Freud, Husserl and Heidegger. His essays, on topics ranging from parataxis in the poetry of Hölderlin to the socio-political function of television, frequently display a subtle literary texture of their own. The breadth of Adorno's knowledge, talents and interests poses a unique and extremely difficult problem for anyone attempting an evaluation of his complete "oeuvre."

Although his name has become closely linked to the Frankfurt Institute for Social Research, Adorno's intellectual orientation and philosophical methods were formulated before he officially joined that organization in 1938. Music had played a decisive role in his cultivated, bourgeois upbringing, and throughout his career it would retain a central place in his philosophical and social scientific work, not just as a recurring subject of analysis but as a model for the organization and presentation of his thought. By the 1920's Adorno had immersed himself equally in classical German philosophy and in the theory of atonal composition in music, and cognitive and aesthetic experience had become inseperable for him. In a series of articles published in the *Zeitschrift für Sozialforschung* in the '30's and in his *Philosophie der neuen Musik* of 1949 Adorno argued that Schoenberg's twelve-tone compositions, in their rigorous exploration of a logic internal to their own musical materials, remained exempt from complete social determination. He devoted so much energy to analyzing cultural products because he believed that under contemporary conditions they alone kept alive the utopian prospects of individual autonomy and happiness. Popular cultural forms, such as jazz and the mass media, were treated under the heading of the "culture industry" and were deemed highly regressive because of the automatic, standardized and passive satisfaction they engender in their audience. Adorno was repeatedly charged with cultural elitism for such statements as: "Popular music is objectively untrue and helps to maim the consciousness of those exposed to it, however hard the individual crippling effects may be to measure."

The most important single influence on Adorno during the '20's and '30's came from the philosophical literary critic Walter Benjamin, who was eleven years his senior. Adorno's assimilation of Marxism as a method of cultural criticism rather than a political program was inspired largely by Benjamin's study of the concept of art criticism in the romantic period (1920) and his essay on seventeenth-century German drama, *Ursprung des deutschen Trauerspiels* (1928). In the "Epistemological-Critical Preface" to this second work Benjamin defined philosophy as a fragmentary, representational mode of discourse given to shattering ossified historical consciousness. The way in which it does so is to cite and arrange concrete details of the phenomenal realm in such a way that a transcendent meaning breaks out from within their configuration. Adorno's Inaugural Lecture to the Philosophy Faculty at Frankfurt University in 1931, "Die Aktualität der Philosophie," eschews a-historical questions concerning reality, appearance, the formal criteria of knowledge and the structure of Being, and instead advocates the construction of verbal images that expose the irrationality of the historical present. The term Adorno takes from Benjamin for such an invention is "constellation." Although he had little if any trust in the proletariat as the bearer of revolutionary social awareness, his own writings were intended to be instrumental in dispelling collective, repressive delusions. Benjamin's theory of figure construction had a lasting effect on Adorno's conception of the emancipatory purpose of philosophy.

Adorno fled Nazism in 1934 for Oxford, England, and then went to the United States in 1938, staying first in New York and then in Los Angeles, where his neighbors included Thomas Mann, Brecht, Schoenberg and his close colleague Max Horkheimer. Adorno's volume of aphorisms from this time, *Minima Moralia*, documents an intense personal effort to analyze totalitarian barbarism. One section bears an epigraph from F.H. Bradley: "When everything is bad it must be good to know the worst." Insinuating themes of insomnia, environmental ugliness, childhood and memory, sexual intimacy, mortality, radical evil and language, Adorno unmasks the presence of awful social conditions in the most private moments of daily experience. Also during this period Adorno co-authored *Dialectic of Enlightenment* with Horkheimer, director of the exiled Institute for Social

Research. This work, which has come to be regarded as a main theoretical statement of the Frankfurt "School" as a whole, traces the historical emergence of reason from myth and the transformation of reason itself into an irrational force dominating both nature and the human subject. They attempt to show that the rationalization of social life has resulted in the virtually complete negation of freedom as embodied in the structures of totalitarian social control. Progress has turned into its opposite. They conclude: "Enlightenment is totalitarian."

Adorno became involved in an empirical study of the psychosocial determinants of anti-semitism sponsored by the Berkeley Public Opinion Study, the Institute for Social Research and the American Jewish Committee. The result of this collective work was the monumental study of *The Authoritarian Personality*. Adorno brought to this project a long-standing interest in psycho-analysis—he'd written his first "Habilitationsschrift" in 1927 on the concept of the unconscious and Kant—and he assisted in devising an ingenious questionnaire (the "F scale") for isolating and quantifying the essential but latent traits of the fascist personality. The underlying assumption of this study was that Fascism was not merely a disastrous political aberration but was rooted in unconscious personality structures conditioned by advanced capitalist society as a whole.

Adorno returned to Frankfurt in 1949 and, with Horkheimer's retirement in 1958, he assumed directorship of the Institute, which had also returned to Europe. During the post-war years Adorno became the leading theoretical voice of the Frankfurt "School" and his microscopic analyses of social and cultural phenomena exerted a strong influence on leftists. He was a central figure in the public controversy known as the "positivist debate," which concerned the conflict between empirical and dialectical methods in sociology. His position was that all observations of discrete social "facts" are necessarily mediated by the social totality and that social science must therefore examine the social whole in order to make truthful investigations of any of its parts. But the polemic mobilized more than views on method. The disagreement was about the kind of knowledge each side was seeking. The "positivist" aim was a unified body of statements explaining that to which they refer, and the critical theorists' aim was a mode of self-awareness consisting of knowledge of one's own true interests.

The major philosophical works of Adorno's later years were *Negative Dialectics* and the *Aesthetische Theorie*. In the first of these Adorno exemplifies a type of discourse in which thought is not inhabited by reality in unperceived ways. This is the main point about Kant, Hegel and Heidegger, the three philosophers discussed in the work—that conceptually their texts reproduce reality in ways uncontrolled either authorially or linguistically. This is why, for Adorno, the aim of philosophy is to criticize ideology without positing yet another conceptual scheme. Adorno was working on the *Aesthetische Theorie* at the time of his death in 1969. This fragmentary and difficult work, to have been dedicated to Samuel Beckett, focuses on the way in which an instance of liberation is built into aesthetic experience precisely in its most formal, non-representational dimensions. This thesis is explored chiefly within the field of modernist art and literature.

In the 1960's German students turned against Adorno and the Institute for Social Research. Although they had found guidelines for political action in his critical theory of society, they themselves had come to be criticized for exhibiting just another form of socially manipulated behaviour. Adorno's career ended with his being held in disfavor by the only social group he ever inspired to action. His thinking had been informed by a fascination with structures of self-deception, a ruthless logicality and a sense of historical helplessness.

—Alan Waters

AJDUKIEWICZ, Kazimierz. Polish logician and philosopher. Born in Tarnopol, Eastern Galacia, now the U.S.S.R., 12 December 1890. Studied at the University of Lvov, Ph.D. 1912. Served in the Polish and Austrian armies during World War I. Married Maria Twardowska in 1919; 2 children. Professor of Philosophy and Logic, University of Warsaw, 1926-39; Professor of Philosophy, 1945-54, and Rector, 1948-52, University of Poznan; Professor of Logic, University of Warsaw, 1954-60. Chief Editor, Studia Logica. *Died 12 April 1963.*

PUBLICATIONS

Philosophy

Główne kierunki filozofii w wyjatkach z dzieł ich klasycznych przedstawicieli: Teoria poznania, logika, metafizyka [Principal Philosophical Theories in the Excerpts from Classics: Theory of Knowledge, Logic, Metaphysics]. Lvov, Poland, 1923.

Zagadnienia i kierunki filozofii: Teoria poznania: Metafizyka. Warsaw, Czytelnik, 1949; as *Problems and Theories of Philosophy,* London, Cambridge University Press, 1973.

Zarys logiki [An Outline of Logic]. Warsaw, Panstwowe Zakłady Wydawnictw Szkolnych, 1953.

Jezyk i Poznanie. Warsaw, PWN, 2 vols., 1960, 1965; selections as *Kazimierz Ajdukiewicz: The Scientific World Perspective and Other Essays 1931-1961,* Dordrecht, The Netherlands, and Boston, D. Reidel, 1978 (contains a bibliography).

Logika pragmatyczna. Warsaw, PWN, 1965; as *Pragmatic Logic,* Dordrecht, The Netherlands, and Boston, D. Reidel, 1974.

Other

Translator, with Maria Ajdukiewicz, *Meditations on First Philosophy,* by Descartes. Warsaw, PWN, 1957.

*

Critical Studies: *The Development of Mathematical Logic and Logical Positivism in Poland Between the Two Wars* by Zbigniew A. Jordan, London, Oxford University Press, 1945; *Polish Analytical Philosophy* by Henryk Skolimowski, London, Routledge, 1967.

*   *   *

The Polish philosopher Kazimierz Ajdukiewicz was a child of his epoch, which was obsessed with precision, logic, semantics, language, an epoch that attempted to give a new expression to philosophy by putting it on a par with science. The ancestry of this philosophy is, on the one hand, Descartes with his quest for the right method to arrive at clear and precise results, and, on the other hand, the German mathematician and logician Gottlob Frege (1848-1925) who initiated the inquiry into the foundations of mathematics and logic. From Frege the line goes to the early work of Bertrand Russell, who was clearly working out Frege's problem: how to secure solid foundations, at least in the realm of mathematics. If mathematics cannot be shown to rest on a secure foundation, then what other branch of knowledge can? From Russell the line goes to the Polish school of logic, especially Lesniewski (1886-1939) and Lukasiewicz (1878-1956) who equally sought to work out a language so clean and precise that it (almost) alone would be able not only to solve complex problems of logic and mathematics, but also to create a universal means to put philosophy on a firm and secure footing—once and for all. The same line of assumptions is continued through other later branches and extensions of analytical philosophy: logical empiricism of the Vienna Circle in the 1930's and 40's; Oxford linguistic philosophy in the 1950's; and then through American analyti-

cal philosophy—Quine, (Carnap during his American period), then Chomsky, then Kripke, and all others of the analytical persuasion; via the refinement of language they all attempted to arrive at lasting philosophical results.

Ajdukiewicz was a part of the same idiom. He was in sympathy with the Vienna Circle. He published his major papers in the early 1930's, which made for him an international reputation, in the official journal of the Vienna Circle called *Erkenntnis.* Yet he clearly separated himself from the one-sidedness and crudity of the Viennese philosophers. He always insisted (like Popper) on the importance of problems and not of techniques.

The main focus of Ajdukiewicz's philosophical endeavours was language and cognition: how do they determine each other; how do they determine the structure of our knowledge and indeed ultimately the structure of our world. The most far reaching result of Ajdukiewicz's insights was the doctrine of "Radical Conventionalism," which claims that the structure of our language—our conceptual apparatus—determines uniquely the world view we hold. Different conceptual apparati lead to different pictures of the "world." The totality of meanings attributed to the expressions of a given language Ajdukiewicz called the conceptual apparatus of this language.

Radical conventionalism was a bold doctrine which incorporated the main insights of 19th century conventionalism and carried these insights to an extreme. While Henri Poincaré (the creator of 19th century conventionalism) suggested that *some* elements of our system of knowledge, be it physics or geometry, can be assumed as a matter of convention, Ajdukiewicz went the whole way and insisted that our entire linguistic apparatus, with which we describe the world, is a matter of convention. The conceptual apparatus is often indistinguishable from language as such. The choice of the conceptual apparatus is not imposed on us by the external reality or our inner experience. It is to a large degree a matter of convention.

This is a fascinating doctrine which has neither been proved nor disproved by "reality." Nor can it be. For it assumes being prior to any reading of reality.

In a profound sense, Radical Conventionalism anticipates the revolution of the New Physics of the 1970's, which maintains (going actually further than Ajdukiewicz) that the notion of reality independent of our knowledge and our minds does not make any sense. We live in a *participatory* universe (J.A. Wheeler), and through our act of participation, through peculiar cognitive faculties we possess and specific concepts of knowledge we have invented, we constitute (or co-create) reality. The epistemological insights of the New Physics are in a perfect accord with Ajdukiewicz's notion of Radical Conventionalism.

Let me emphasize: Radical Conventionalism was not only a semantic or a linguistic doctrine, but also an epistemological one. What Immanuel Kant (1724-1804) attributed to the categories of the mind (shaping reality into appropriate forms), Ajdukiewicz attributed to the conceptual apparatus. Nor was Ajdukiewicz alone in this quest. Concurrently with him, and actually slightly preceding him, was Benjamin Lee Whorf (*Language, Thought and Reality,* 1956) with his Linguistic Relativity Principle, spelling out (though less rigorously) very similar ideas. A bit later came W.V. Quine with his idea of radical conventionalism (see in particular the Introduction to Quine's *Methods of Logic*). Quine's conventionalism was, in my opinion, influenced by Ajdukiewicz's ideas. And later still came Chomsky with his concept of man as language animal. All of them (and many others in the 20th century) attempted to find in language the mediator and indeed determinator of the structure of our knowledge and of reality.

Ajdukiewicz's Radical Conventionalism was born out of his researches into the theory of meaning which, in the 1930's, was the professional preoccupation and obsession of analytical philosophers. To recognize language as such, Ajdukiewicz claimed, implies following the rules of its use. If we do not respect the rules of use (workings of language), we do not operate with the language in question. In a word, meaning is use. This was an important anticipation of Oxford linguistic philosophy, as well as an anticipation of Ludwig Wittgenstein. Indeed, some of the credit that usually goes to Wittgenstein—for grasping the nature of the rules of language in use—should go to Ajdukiewicz.

Ajdukiewicz was a philosopher's philosopher, most rigorous and painstaking in his approach, with a bit of German pedantry thrown into the bargain. He wrote voluminously on all subjects with which analytical philosophers were preoccupied. They all wrote on logic and contributed textbooks to the field. So did Ajdukiewicz. So many of them wanted to salvage empiricism, which was considered a good thing. (This adulation of empiricism among analytical philosophers is to me a strange phenomenon—not justified at all.) Although Ajdukiewicz was a radical conventionalist, he entertained the strange notion of radical empiricism. It was *conceptual* empiricism (really not empiricism in the traditional sense—as language determines it all), not radical empiricism.

Ajdukiewicz studied at Göttingen—philosophy with Husserl and mathematics with Hilbert—in addition to his earlier studies with K. Twardowski in Lwow (Twardowski established the Polish analytical school, often called Lwow-Warsaw School). During the interwar years Ajdukiewicz was one of the handful of Polish philosophers with a truly Renaissance mind: completely at ease with Aristotle in the original as well as with modern formal logic. He also commanded considerable personal respect—to the point of being called, while he was Rector of Poznan University, Casimir the Magnificent. There were at least half a dozen of such individuals in Poland in the interwar period (Lukasiewicz, Kotarbinski, Ajdukiewicz, Witkiewicz, Chwistek, Ingarden): they put Polish philosophy on the map; they also created the legacy of the stubborn independence of the Polish mind not only in the realm of things intellectual but also in the realm of things ideological and political. The spirit of a nation is often determined by the quality of its philosophy.

—Henryk Skolimowski

ALEXANDER, Samuel. British philosopher. Born in Sydney, New South Wales, Australia, 6 January 1859. Educated at Wesley College, Melbourne; Balliol College, Oxford. Fellow of Lincoln College, Oxford, 1882-88; Professor of Philosophy, Owens College, later Victoria University of Manchester, 1893-1924. Gifford Lecturer, University of Glasgow, 1916-18. President, Aristotelian Society, 1908-11. Honorary doctorate: Durham University, 1923; Oxford University, 1924; University of Birmingham, 1924; University of Liverpool, 1925; Cambridge University, 1934. Honorary Fellow, Lincoln College, 1918, and Balliol College, 1925. Fellow of the British Academy, 1913. Order of Merit, 1930. *Died 13 September 1938.*

PUBLICATIONS

Philosophy

Moral Order and Progress: An Analysis of Ethical Considerations. London, Trubner, 1889.
Locke. London, Constable, and New York, Dodge, 1908.
Space, Time, and Diety. London, Macmillan, 2 vols., 1920; New York, Humanities Press, 1950.
Spinoza: An Address. London, Jewish Religious Union, 1927.
Lessons from Spinoza. The Hague, Chronicon Spinozanum, 1927.
Beauty and Other Forms of Value. London, Macmillan, 1933; New York, Crowell, 1968.
Philosophical and Literary Pieces, edited with a memoir by John Laird. London, Macmillan, 1939; Westport, Connecticut,

Greenwood Press, 1970 (contains a complete bibliography).

*

Critical Studies: *Le Systeme d'Alexander* by P. Devaus, Paris, Vrin, 1929; *On the Nature of Value: The Philosophy of Samuel Alexander* by Milton Konvitz, New York, King's Crown Press, 1946; *The Naturalism of Alexander* by John W. McCarthy, New York, King's Crown Press, 1948; *The Philosophy of Samuel Alexander: Idealism in "Space, Time and Diety"* by Bertram D. Brettschneider, New York, Humanities Press, 1964.

*   *   *

Samuel Alexander's aim is to get a synoptic view of the evolving universe which science has depicted and to find in it the place of mind, values and religion. He seeks to "take time seriously" and, as a "naturalist," to understand something without dissolving it away. The relation of mind to body is the clue to how all levels of existence are related. The mind requires a neural basis, and mental processes can be expressed completely in neural terms. But, while the mental process is *also* neural, it is not *merely* neural. For mind to emerge, there is required a constellation of neural conditions not found in vital actions which are not mental. Nor could knowledge of the neural conditions enable us to predict that or explain why it would have a mental quality. Mind is thus something new, even though expressible in neural terms. Mental processes, though they may be reduced to the class of vital processes, are so distinct from the rest of the class that they hold a privileged position in it, just as a king is a man like his subjects but is not one of them. Also, the neural process which carries thought becomes changed into a different one when it ceases to carry thought.

The emergence of a new quality from any level of existence means that at that level there comes into being a constellation of motions belonging to that level with qualities appropriate to that level, which constellation also has a new quality distinctive of the higher complex. The constellation and its qualities are new yet expressible without residue in terms of the processes from the level of which they emerge. Mind, for example, is not merely physiological but is also psychological. The emergent qualities are to be accepted with the "natural piety" of an investigator. It admits of no explanation. The different levels are roughly: motions, physical matter, matter with "secondary qualities" (e.g., color, taste), life, and mind, with possible intermediate levels. Each level is related to the lower as the mind is to the neural processes. They are now emergents, expressible in terms of the lower, but are not merely the lower. This is Alexander's alternative to reductionism and dualism.

It is the job of the scientist to trace the history of things. The philosopher points out the general features of the advance. Philosophy, like science, uses the empirical method: reflective description and analysis of data, making hypothesis to form verifiable connections. Unlike science, its subject matter is comprehensive, the all-pervasive characters of experienced things.

Alexander's ideas about space-time are complex. Each point in space is distinguished by its instant in time and vice-versa. Thus we can speak of space-time and of point-instants. Alexander sees his notion of space-time as somewhat similar to that of Minkowski and Einstein. There is an analogy between time and mind, space and body. This suggests the intimacy of the relationship and also that something like mind was present from the beginning, helping us to see all the forms of existence as a continuous series from Space-Time upwards through matter to mind. The analogy breaks down in that mind, unlike time, is a new emergent. If the past is not to be lost, there must be some continuum to sustain the togetherness of past and present. This is space. This is time. Each plays the part of identity to the other's diversity. Alexander wishes to develop a position distinct from absolute space and from space and time as relationships between things. Space is full of memory and expectation. We always apprehend a bit of duration in the present instant. Even in vision we have both after-images and "before-sensations" when a color sensation is rising to its full intensity. (He spent much time engaged in experimental psychology.)

Space-Time is the infinite matrix of all finites. Whatever substance, electricity, matter or what not there is, must be a fragment of the one stuff of Space-Time. Space-Time, the stuff of all things, is not material. It is not attenuated matter, but material existence is an outgrowth from it. Empirical things are vortices or eddies in the stuff of Space-Time. Alexander calls it "stuff" to avoid confusion with the common idea of matter. All finites are of the same stuff as the Space-Time which connects them. They become in changing, as for example by death, other variations of the same matrix. Space-Time does not grow bigger with the lapse of Time; its Space is always full and it grows older through internal arrangements.

Knower and known are together (compresent) in the world. An object owes to the knowing mind neither its existence nor its qualities, but only that it is known. Even in memory the past event is before my mind, though it bears the stamp of the past.

Some characters of empirical existents ("categories") are pervasive of all reality, some ("qualities") are variable. Categories are pervasive because they are properties of Space-Time. They include traditional philosophical topics like identity, universals and particulars, causality, etc. Alexander's approach and its weakness can be illustrated by his treatment of the category of "relation." All relations between existents (ordinary finite things and point-instants) are spatio-temporal in their simplest expression. In one sense, this is true enough. But to say that relations are the spatio-temporal connections of things seems untrue. For relations between numbers and propositions hardly seem spatio-temporal. His idea of a complex substance as the persistence in time of a contour of space within which occur the motions correlated to the contours of a thing is a fruitful notion. Movement in a straight line is the simplest substance. What changes are compatible with substantial identity is an empirical question.

The self can overflow its boundaries. Damage to my property, or to my country, is like a blow in the face. In certain moods I may feel myself at one with the universe.

Alexander's religious philosophy is surprising. Deity is the next higher empirical quality to the highest we know. We are philosophically assured that the universe is pregnant with deity, although we cannot know what that quality is. The notion of the world striving toward deity is the extension by analogy of the verifiable fact of the drive (nisus) in the world to the generation of fresh empirical qualities. This philosophical notion, which supplies theoretical assurance, is supplemented by religious sentiment, the feeling of going out of ourselves to something greater than ourselves. Deity is thus the next level in process of birth. God, on the other hand, is the universe with its nisus toward deity. "God" thus represents the actual reality, "deity" the new quality being born.

Unvalues are realities which do not persist because they do not fit in with the world. Goodness is a harmony between wills, badness a recalcitrant will ostracised as impracticable. The adapted forms of life, including human goodness, are discovered by experiment. The revolutionary moralist is one who forecasts a social scheme which, if sound, will win acceptance. These adaptations are costly. We must accept this with an incentive to ameliorate effort without expectation that the springs of pain will ever be stopped. Since deity is the outcome of the world's movement, the character of God partly depends on our actions. Man does not merely serve God but helps him and in the measure of his smallness, creates deity.

In his latest work Alexander expanded his theory of values (art, science and morality). Values are relations between objects and mind, not a function of either alone. Values are objective, satisfying the standard judgment of an objective mind. To say, "I think this beautiful," does not mean "beautiful for me alone." It rather expresses tentativeness of judgment or dissent from common opinion.

Significance in art lies in the form and also in the subject matter (if the art is representative). The artist does not conceive and then express. The conception comes through the execution. Mind and material cooperate, like bisexual generation. Double valuations can be made, the second always a matter of degree: in art of the beauty of the form and greatness of the subject, in morality of virtue and the magnitude of the act (the widow's mite is generous but not magnificant), and in science of truth and importance. Alexander studied the visual arts, read autobiographical accounts of creativity, and wrote studies of writers like Austen and Molière. He extends his distinction between poetry and prose, detailed in a study of Pascal and Robert Bridges, to other arts.

The highest values satisfy impulses derived from natural instincts: the search for truth from curiosity, beauty and goodness from the constructive and social impulses (instincts). When these impulses become disinterested, diverted from practical ends, they are desired for their own sakes. There are parallels to values among animals and even physical things, although the three highest values are exclusively human. Thus Alexander sharpened his vision of continuity with difference in the universal process of emergence.

—Jerome Arthur Stone

ALLPORT, Gordon W(illard).   American psychologist.   Born in Montezuma, Indiana, 11 November 1897. Studied at Harvard University, Cambridge, Massachusetts, B.A. 1919, M.A. 1921, Ph.D. 1922; University of Berlin, University of Hamburg, and Cambridge University, 1922-24. Married Ada Lufkin Gould in 1925; 1 son. Instructor in English, Robert College, Istanbul, Turkey, 1919-20; Instructor in Social Ethics, Harvard University, 1924-26; Assistant Professor of Psychology, Dartmouth College, New Hampshire, 1926-30; Assistant Professor of Psychology, 1930-36, Associate Professor, 1937-42, and Professor, 1942-67, Harvard University. Director, National Opinion Research Council. Editor, *Journal of Abnormal and Social Psychology*, 1937-49. President, American Psychological Association, 1939. Recipient: Gold Medal, American Psychological Foundation, 1963. Honorary doctorate: Boston University, 1958; Ohio Wesleyan University, Delaware, 1962; Colby College, Waterville, Maine, 1964; University of Durham, England, 1965. Honorary Member, Italian Psychological Society; Spanish Psychological Society; Deutsche Gesellschaft für Psychologie; and Österreichische Arztegesellschaft für Psychotherapie. Honorary Fellow, British Psychological Association. *Died in October 1967.*

PUBLICATIONS

Psychology

The A-S Reaction Study, with F.H. Allport.   Boston, Houghton Mifflin, 1928.
A Study of Values: A Scale for Measuring the Dominent Interests in Personality: Manual of Directions, with Philip E. Vernon.   Boston, Houghton Mifflin, 1931.
Studies in Expressive Movement, with Philip E. Vernon.   New York, Macmillan, 1933.
The Psychology of Radio, with Hadley Cantril.   New York, Harper, 1935.
Trait-Names: A Psycho-Lexical Study, with others.   Princeton, New Jersey, Psychological Review Company, 1936.
Personality: A Psychological Interpretation.   New York, Holt, 1937; London, Constable, 1938.
The Use of Personal Documents in Psychological Science.   New

York, Social Science Research Council, 1942.

The Roots of Religion: A Dialogue Between a Psychologist and His Student.   New York, National Council of the Protestant Episcopal Church, 1944.

The Psychology of Rumor, with Leo Postman.   New York, Holt, 1947.

The Individual and His Religion: A Psychological Interpretation.   New York, Macmillan, 1950; London, Constable, 1951.

The Nature of Personality: Selected Papers.   Reading, Massachusetts, Addison-Wesley, 1950.

The Resolution of Intergroup Tensions: A Critical Appraisal of Methods.   New York, National Conference of Christians and Jews, 1952.

The Nature of Prejudice.   Reading, Massachusetts, Addison-Wesley, 1954.

Youth's Outlook on the Future, with James M. Gillespie.   New York, Doubleday, 1955.

Becoming: Basic Considerations for a Psychology of Personality.   New Haven, Connecticut, Yale University Press, 1955.

Personality and Social Encounter.   Boston, Beacon Press, 1960.

Pattern and Growth in Personality.   New York, Holt Rinehart, 1961.

Letters from Jenny.   New York, Harcourt Brace, 1965.

The Person in Psychology: Selected Essays.   Boston, Beacon Press, 1968.

Other

Editor, *Controlling Group Prejudice.*   Philadelphia, American Academy of Political and Social Science, 1946.

*

Critical Studies: *Gordon Allport: The Man and His Ideas* by Robert I. Evans, New York, Dutton, 1970; *Humanism in Personology: Allport, Maslow and Murray* by Paul T. Costa and Salvatore Maddi, Chicago, Aldine Atherton, 1972.

*   *   *

Gordon W. Allport's contribution to psychology may be best summed up by saying he was a gadfly. During a period when academic psychology was doing its best to deny the existence of most of what we consider uniquely human, Allport was steadfastly studying the individual and defending the study of the individual person as a legitimate scientific endeavor.

Allport's concept of the "functional autonomy of motives" was a necessary and important antidote to the belief popular in psychology almost from its beginnings (and still very much present now, only slightly diminished in strength) that human behavior springs from a very few basic drives or needs. Psychoanalysis and behaviorism are (incorrectly) viewed by the layman as the two major schools of psychology; both are essentially and basically reductionistic. Asked why a man likes to run marathons, a psychoanalyst would explain in terms of deflections and repressions of the sex drive (the libido) or one of the other basic drives postulated by Freud. A behaviorist would say that somehow running marathons got hooked up or associated with a "primary reinforcer" like food or water or sex, something people will work for no matter what. Allport would say, "That person runs marathons because he likes to." Allport felt that although all our motives may have their origins in primary, basic aspects of the human experience, a liking for X, acquired because of its connection to something basic or primary, may eventually become independent of its origins and continue to function autonomously, whether or not it satisfies, symbolically or in reality, any of the more basic drives. While neither behaviorism nor psychoanalysis is any more sympathetic to functional autonomy now than three or four decades ago, Allport continues to serve as a

reminder to psychologists that man does not live by food and sex alone. And, as important perhaps, Allport has served as an example to the general public that not all psychologists ignore the perfectly obvious fact that most of us engage in a wide variety of activities simply because we like them—that is, because we find them intrinsically rewarding.

Many personality psychologists have studied the "traits" of personality. Among questions they have asked is the following: What are the major traits of human beings—that is, along which important dimensions do they vary? Let us say we all agree that anxiety is one such dimension. Some people are calm; others are anxious. Let us say we have a 25 question anxiety questionnaire, which includes such questions as, "Are you worried about the future?" Presumably, a person who said yes to 20 questions like this would be more anxious than a person who said yes to only 10. And presumably a person who said yes to 20 questions would be *as* anxious as another person who said yes to 20 questions. Allport said no to this presumption. One person's anxiety is not like another's, he said. We can study anxiety in general only if we do not lose sight of this fact. My anxiety is not the same as Joe's. I do not worry about the future, for example, in the same way that Joe does. I have occasional bouts of intense anxiety about the future, while Joe is constantly worried but in a much less extreme way (so that in some sense it averages out and he and I have the same total amount of anxiety). Or, if 10 people are in an airplane that is about to crash, presumably all of them will feel equally anxious; but they will behave in different ways. This notion of the individual trait has not received much serious attention outside of textbooks in personality theory, but it points to one of the many important complexities of human behavior academic psychology has been all too happy to ignore.

Allport will also be remembered for his attitude towards the advanced technology now employed by many psychologists. He was aware at a very early date of the "garbage in/garbage out" problem with computers and mathematical models. One of the few psychologists to concern himself with religion, he commented on a mathematically complex approach to personality that did not find religiosity to be an important trait—that is, it did not find that people varied in the extent to which they were religious, and consequently concluded that the study of personality could dispense with the study of religion. Allport correctly pointed out that if you do not ask people questions about religion—as this study had not—you will invariably find that they have no opinions about religion. Again, that is a point that may seem obvious to the layman, but it is one about which academic psychology has had to be constantly reminded.

Finally, Allport said that if you want to find out something about a person, you should ask him. Again, obvious to the layman. But academic psychology has devoted an enormous amount of energy to developing measurement techniques to circumvent the many distortions that result when you do simply ask people questions—for example, their strong and well-established tendency to present themselves in a socially desirable light. You can't *just* ask a person any question about himself and expect a valid or truthful answer. Allport knew this. He merely wanted psychology to keep in mind that the best source of information about a person is the person himself and that we should utilize that source whenever possible.

—George W. Kelling

ALTHUSSER, Louis.   French political philosopher.   Born in Birmandries, near Algiers, Algeria, 16 October 1918. Educated at Ecole Normal Supérieure, Paris, Diplom Agrégé en Philosophie, 1948. Served in the French Army, 1939-40: captured in 1940 and spent rest of war in German prison-of-war camp. Maître Assistant Agrégé, and Sécretaire, Ecole Normal Supérieure, Paris, since 1948. Director, Collection "Théorie," Editions Maspero, Paris, since 1965. Address: 45 rue d'Ulm, 75005 Paris, France.

PUBLICATIONS

Political Philosophy

Montesquieu: La politique et l'histoire.   Paris, Presses Universitaires de France, 1959; as "Montesquieu: Politics and History" in *Politics and History: Montesquieu, Rousseau, Hegel and Marx,* 1972.
Pour Marx.   Paris, Maspero, 1965; as *For Marx,* London, Allen Lane, and New York, Pantheon, 1969.
Lire le Capital, with E. Balibar and others.   Paris, Maspero, 2 vols., 1965; edition containing only contributions by Althusser and Balibar as *Reading Capital,* London, New Left Books, 1970.
Lénine et la philosophie.   Paris, Maspero, 1969; expanded edition, 1972; as *Lenin and Philosophy and Other Essays,* London, New Left Books, 1971; New York, Monthly Review Press, 1972.
Politics and History: Montesquieu, Rousseau, Hegel and Marx (essays translated from the French).   London, New Left Books, 1972.
Eléments d'autocritique.   Paris, Hachette, 1974; as "Elements of Self-Criticism" in *Essays in Self-Criticism,* 1976.
Philosophie et philosophie spontanée des savants.   Paris, Maspero, 1974.
Essays in Self-Criticism (essays translated from the French).   London, New Left Books, and Atlantic Highlands, New Jersey, Humanities Press, 1976 (contains full bibliography).

*

Critical Studies: *Structuralist Analysis in Contemporary Thought: A Comparison of the Theories of Claude Lévi-Strauss and Louis Althusser* by Miriam Glucksmann, London and Boston, Routledge, 1974; *One-Dimensional Marxism: Althusser and the Politics of Culture* by Simon Clarke and others, London, Allison and Busby, 1980.

*   *   *

Louis Althusser's work represents the most serious and systematic attempt to demonstrate that Marx's thought was fundamentally anti-Hegelian. This distinguishes him from the two other outstanding Marxist philosophers of the twentieth century—Lukács, who sought in *History and Class Consciousness* "to outHegel Hegel," as he later put it, and Adorno, whose relationship with Hegel was, to say the least, ambiguous.

In his most famous essay, "Contradiction and Overdetermination" (1962), Althusser attacked attempts to characterize metaphorically the relation of Marx to Hegel such as Engels's distinction between Hegel's dialectical-materialist method and his idealistic system. Since it is precisely through the dialectical circle of original identity, self-estrangement, and final, enriched reconciliation that Hegel tries to prove that the material world is an emanation of Absolute Spirit, no such distinction between method and system can be made out. The method *is* the system. Marx's dialectic, if it is to be materialist, must be fundamentally different in its structures from that of Hegel.

But what is Marx's materialist dialectic? Althusser in this and later essays considers, and rejects, two ways of conceiving the relationship between economic base and politico-ideological superstructure. The first ("linear causality") is as two discrete substances, the base acting on the superstructure, like one billiard ball hitting another. The second ("expressive causality") treats the economy as the essence of the social whole and the different aspects of the superstructure as expressions of this

hidden core, sharing its structure. The defect of either approach, Althusser argues, is that it is reductionist, in the sense that it denies the superstructure any degree of autonomy, treating it as, in one case, the effect, and, in the other, the epiphenomenon of the economy.

Dismissing both these conceptions, Althusser argues that every social formation is a multiplicity of practices. The chief examples he gives of these practices are economic, political, ideological, and theoretical. Their multiplicity is irreducible, or, as he puts it, "ever-pre-given"—politics, ideology, and theory cannot be collapsed into the economy. However, they are structured by the economy which is "determinant in the last instance." Every social formation possesses a "structure in dominance," a particular hierarchy of different practices with one prevailing over the others, taking what Althusser calls the dominant role. The economy determines which practice is dominant. Economic determination is thus indirect, acting through the allocation of specific roles to different practices. Althusser sought to sum up this conception through the term, borrowed from Freud, of "overdetermination"—the economy never acts alone but only in combination with other practices, with politics, ideology, etc. "The lonely hour of the last instance never sounds."

One implication of this account of economic causality is the "relative autonomy" of the superstructure. Limits are set on the operation of different practices by virtue of the structure in dominance, itself determined by the economy, but within those limits the practices are free of the constraints imposed by production. Of especial importance to Althusser was the proposition that "theoretical practice" is relatively autonomous. He had joined the French Communist Party in 1948 at a time when a "class line in science" was being preached and distinctions were being drawn between "proletarian" and "bourgeois" physics and genetics. The notion of overdetermination slammed the door on this nonsense, providing a respectable Marxist argument for leaving Communist intellectuals free to pursue their own work.

Althusser had independent philosophical arguments for the autonomy of theory. He had been profoundly influenced by the epistemological tradition of Bachelard, Cavaillès and Canguilheim, according to whom scientific theories are systems of concepts rather than accumulations of facts, and scientific revolutions conceptual breakthroughs rather than empirical discoveries. Althusser argues that every science is characterized by an implicit system of questions, or problematic. He describes the point at which such a conceptual structure is formed as an "epistemological break." The most famous application of this epistemology was to Marx. Althusser argues that Marxism was born as a science in 1844-45 when Marx abandoned his earlier humanism for a theory of history as a "process without a subject" in which the class struggle is conceived as the motor of social change. Such changes of problematic are not always obvious, according to Althusser. A special method of "symptomatic reading" analogous to psychoanalysis is necessary to elicit the real structure beneath the surface of the text.

One reason for this "suspicion of language" (Foucault) was that the epistemological break constituting a science is with ideology. One of Althusser's most radical differences with the Marxist tradition lies in his claim that ideology is an inevitable feature of every society, including communism. Human beings, he argues, necessarily live a mystified relation to their conditions of existence; such a situation is a prerequisite of social cohesion. This account of ideology, heavily influenced by Lacan, and later filled out by an analysis of what Althusser called the "ideological state apparatuses" (churches, schools, etc.), is reminiscent of functionalist accounts of religion such as Durkheim's. It underlines a central problem of Althusser's entire system—the status of his own discourse. He claimed to be outside ideology, yet his own writings are clearly philosophical rather than scientific. How could philosophy transcend both science and ideology? Althusser's answer to this question varied. In his early writings, Marxist philosophy was the "theory of theoretical practice," a sort of super-Science of Sciences. Later it became the "class struggle in theory," mediating between science and politics. Neither solution seems satisfactory—a reflection, perhaps, of the difficulties inherent in a Marxist's attempting to render theory autonomous of social practices.

—Alex Callinicos

ARENDT, Hannah. American philosopher and political scientist. Born in Hannover, Germany, 14 October 1906; emigrated to the United States in 1941: naturalized, 1950. Studied at Königsberg University, B.A. 1924; University of Marburg; University of Freiburg; University of Heidelberg, under Karl Jaspers, Ph.D. 1928. Married Günther Stern in 1928 (divorced, 1937); Heinrich Blücher in 1949. Worked with the Youth Aliyah in Paris, 1934-40; Research Director, Conference on Jewish Relations, New York, 1944-46; Chief Editor, Schocken Books, New York, 1946-48; Executive Director, Jewish Cultural Reconstruction, New York, 1949-52. Professor, Committee on Social Thought, University of Chicago, 1963-67; Professor, Graduate Faculty, New School for Social Research, New York, 1967-75. Visiting Professor, University of California, Berkeley, 1955; Princeton University, New Jersey, 1959; Columbia University and Brooklyn College, 1960. Recipient: Guggenheim Fellowship, 1952-54; National Institute of Arts and Letters Award, 1954; Lessing Preis, Hamburg, 1959; Rockefeller Fellowship, 1959-60, 1969-70; Freud Preis, Deutsche Akademie für Sprache und Dichtung, 1967; M. Cary Thomas Prize, Bryn Mawr College, Pennsylvania, 1971; Sonning Prize for Contributions to European Civilization, Denmark, 1975. Honorary doctorate: Bard College, Annandale-on-Hudson, New York, 1959; Goucher College, Baltimore, 1960; Smith College, Northampton, Massachusetts, 1966; York College, University of Toronto, 1968; Loyola University, Chicago, 1970; Yale University, New Haven, Connecticut, 1971; Princeton University, and University of Notre Dame, Indiana, 1972. *Died* (in New York City) *4 December 1975*.

PUBLICATIONS

Philosophy and Political Philosophy

Der Liebesgriff bei Augustin: Versuch einer philosophischen Interpretation. Berlin, Springer, 1929.

Sechs Essays. Heidelberg, Schneider, 1948; reprinted in *Die Verborgene Tradition: Acht Essays*, 1976.

The Origins of Totalitarianism. New York, Harcourt Brace, 1951; as *The Burden of Our Time*, London, Secker and Warburg, 1951; enlarged edition, New York, World, 1958.

Fragwürdige Traditionsbestände im politischen Denken der Gegenwart. Frankfurt, Europäische Verlagsanstalt; reprinted in *Between Past and Future: Six Exercises in Political Thought*, 1968.

The Human Condition. Chicago, University of Chicago Press, 1958.

Karl Jaspers: Reden zur Verleihung des Friedenpreises des Deutschen Buchhandels. Munich, Piper, 1958; reprinted in *Men in Dark Times*, 1968.

Rahel Varnhagen: The Life of a Jewess. London, East and West Library, 1958; as *Rahel Varnhagen: The Life of a Jewish Woman*, New York, Harcourt Brace, 1974.

Die Ungarische Revolution und die totalitäre Imperialismus. Munich, Piper, 1958; reprinted in the enlarged edition of *The Origins of Totalitarianism*, 1958.

Von der Menschlichkeit in finsteren Zeit: Gedanken zu Les-

sing. Hamburg, Hauswedell, 1960; reprinted in *Men in Dark Times*, New York, Harcourt Brace, 1968.

Between Past and Future: Six Exercises in Political Thought. New York, Viking Press, 1961; enlarged edition as *Between Past and Future: Eight Exercises in Political Thought*, New York, Viking Press, 1968; London, Faber, 1971.

Eichmann in Jerusalem: A Report on the Banality of Evil. New York, Viking Press, and London, Faber, 1963; revised edition, New York, Viking Press, 1965.

On Revolution. New York, Viking Press, and London, Faber, 1963.

Men in Dark Times. New York, Harcourt Brace, 1968; London, Cape, 1970.

On Violence. New York, Harcourt Brace, and London, Penguin, 1970.

Crises of the Republic. New York, Harcourt Brace, 1972; London, Pelican, 1973.

Die Verborgene Tradition: Acht Essays. Frankfurt, Suhrkamp, 1976.

The Jew as Pariah: Jewish Identity and Politics in the Modern Age, edited by Ron H. Feldman. New York, Grove, 1978.

The Life of the Mind, edited by Mary McCarthy. New York, Harcourt Brace, 2 vols., 1978.

Lectures on Kant's Political Philosophy, edited and with an interpretative essay by Ronald Beiner. Chicago, University of Chicago Press, 1982.

Other

Editor, *Job's Dungheap*, by Bernard Lazare. New York, Schocken, 1948.

Editor, with Martin Greenberg, *Diaries*, by Frank Kafka. New York, Schocken, 2 vols., 1949.

Editor, *Dichten und Erkennen* and *Essays*, by Hermann Broch. Zurich, Rheinverlag, 1955.

Editor, *The Great Philosophers*, by Karl Jaspers. New York, Harcourt Brace, 2 vols., 1962, 1966.

Editor, *Illuminations*, by Walter Benjamin. New York, Harcourt Brace, 1968.

*

Critical Studies: *The Political Thought of Hannah Arendt* by Margaret Canovan, New York, Harcourt Brace, 1974; *Hannah Arendt: Recovery of the Public World*, edited by Melvyn A. Hill, New York, St. Martin's Press, 1979; *Into the Dark: Hannah Arendt and Totalitarianism* by Stephen Whitfield, Philadelphia, Temple University Press, 1980; *Hannah Arendt and the Search for a New Political Philosophy* by Bhikhu C. Parekh, Atlantic Highlands, New Jersey, Humanities Press, 1981; *Hannah Arendt: For Love of the World* by Elizabeth Young-Breuhl, New Haven, Connecticut, Yale University Press, 1982 (contains a bibliography).

*   *   *

The impressive range of Hannah Arendt's erudition, which spanned such diverse topics as totalitarianism, the nature of evil, the life of mind, Zionism and the Jewish question, revolution, and the crisis of culture in mass society, essentially revolved around her concern for the loss of the public realm in modernity, a loss which coincides with a progressive erosion of freedom and thought. According to Arendt, freedom (spontaneous collective action) and thought (the inner dialogue of conscience and the revelation of meaning) depend upon the separation of political life (the public realm) from social and economic life (the private realm). The Greek polis and, to a lesser extent, workers councils and New England town-hall meetings, were, for her, paradigms of political life in which individual equals, guided by collective ideals, sought to distinguish themselves in service to the community. She felt that the unique success of the polis and the American Revolution could be attributed to the fact that authority was vested in participatory democratic institutions and that the private domain of familial and economic concerns was kept separate from the public realm, thereby providing a sheltered space for thoughtful reflection. With the advent of modern society, the public and private spheres, she argued, were absorbed into the social/economic sphere, depriving thought of its needed privacy and converting political action into economic administration. The reduction of thought and action to the banausic level of utilitarian pragmatism with its attendant concern for the preservation of biological life (production and consumption) in turn contributed to the rise of mass society.

In Arendt's judgement, the atomization, alienation, and anomie of mass society make it extremely vulnerable to totalitarian politics. Totalitarianism, Arendt maintained, is an unprecedented event that defies any analysis in terms of classical despotism and tyranny. Essentially, totalitarianism is definitive of those "movements"—for example, National Socialism under Hitler and Bolshevism under Stalin—in which all aspects of private and public life are subsumed under an all-embracing process of domination. The nucleus of this process is determined by an irresistible pseudo-scientific worldview, or ideology, which compels the movement incessantly to destroy and rebuild society in strict conformity with the "logic" of an "idea," e.g., history as the apocalyptic struggle between races and classes. The result is a complete breakdown of common sense and ordinary utilitarian thinking. Arendt's conception of totalitarianism deviates in important respects from popular belief. For example, instead of conceiving totalitarianism as an authoritarian phenomenon in which power and responsibility are concentrated in the state, she declared that it is basically an amorphous movement in which sources of authority and responsibility are diffuse and conflicting (supreme power usually residing in the secret police rather than in the government) and legality and national sovereignty are rendered all but otiose.

Out of Arendt's striking depiction of totalitarianism emerge two other concerns which later assumed prominence in her thought: the nature of evil and the problem of politically dispossessed pariahs. Totalitarianism represents the epitome of "radical evil" because it engenders a system in which human life is made totally superfluous, meaningless, and therefore worthless. In her coverage of the Eichmann trial, Arendt deepened her understanding of the nature of evil by observing that what makes it so impenetrable to ordinary thought is its utter banality, which is rooted in the "thoughtlessness" of being too absorbed in the task of "doing one's job (i.e., following orders) well." But she also held that "absolute goodness" and the concomitant violence born of extreme idealism (cf. Melville's *Billy Budd*) are almost as pernicious as absolute evil born of banality.

As for the second concern, Arendt contended that what gave totalitarianism its impetus was antisemitism. Antisemitism found its pathetic consummation in the problem of a stateless Jewry, who being deprived of the basic "rights of man" were *ipso facto* reduced to the status of superfluous "outlaws." The problem of stateless persons assumes genuinely tragic proportions in Arendt's philosophy, since she herself could find no way to remedy the insuperable difficulties inherent in the classical doctrine of natural rights.

Arendt's views concerning mass society also led her to espouse a neo-conservative defense of pluralism which, she thought, could best be promoted through a depoliticization of the economic and social sphere—a position that put her in direct conflict with the continental revolutionary tradition. In her treatment of Rousseau and the leaders of the French Revolution she noted that the fateful decision to abandon the quest for political freedom in favor of social justice culminated in the self-consuming violence of a society obsessed with its own humanitarian ideals. As reflected in the inviolate unity of Rousseau's *volonté générale*, the identification of freedom with sovereignty necessarily entailed absolutism at the level of political life. Like-

wise, she reproached Marx for having limited his treatment of political life to the exigencies of class struggle and economic expediency. Marx's construal of communism as a stateless system composed of emancipated administrators—a questionable ideal which, Arendt claimed, was all too easily assimilated to the technocratic dystopia of Soviet bureaucracy—was symptomatic of his general neglect of political thought.

Arendt's discussion of the problem of founding a "new generation of order" convinced her of the importance of tradition and authority in securing political legitimacy. No constitutional committee contains its *raison d'être* within itself but must acquire it by "revolving back" to a prior foundation. Apropos of the above, it was Arendt's conviction that the crisis of the modern age is symptomatic of the decline of the old Roman trinity of religion, tradition, and authority. Again, this decline is due primarily to the process of secularization, whereby the public realm is converted into an appendage of the economic sphere. What arises from this disintegration is an apolitical consumer society in which culture is increasingly debased in servicing the needs of the entertainment industry and the search for meaning is forsaken in exchange for the pragmatic security of scientific truth. In science Arendt perceived an irrepressible "will to power" that lay behind a facade of impartiality—a potential totalitarian impulse which, under the auspices of social engineering, could extend the domination of nature to include human nature as well.

Although Arendt displayed considerable sympathy for the plight of economic underclasses and was sensitive to the social injustices and dark moral tendencies of unregulated capitalism, she never reversed her opinion that the proper function of the state ought to be limited to providing a vehicle for the display of political excellence rather than for the bureaucratic maintenance of the economy. Her favorable estimation of the virtues of Greek political life was, as she herself realized, somewhat anachronistic in view of contemporary realities. With its defense of tradition and authority, her classical outlook was construed by many commentators as indicating a conservative, elitist temperament. What is certainly undeniable is that her own political predilections remained remarkably hidden—an understatement when one considers that she could admire the accomplishments of such diametrically opposed thinkers as the Marxist Rosa Luxemburg and the Federalist John Adams. In the final analysis, Arendt simply abjured prescribing political panaceas for the more modest tasks of teaching others how to think politically. If there is any serious flaw in her work, it is certainly not in her refusal to engage in partisan politics, but rather resides in her tendentious use of historical sources and in her disturbing contempt for any political action undertaken in the service of ameliorating social injustice "for life's sake"—an attitude which is manifestly at odds with her own critique of totalitarianism.

—David Ingram

ARIES, Philippe. French sociologist. Born in Blois, France, 21 July 1914. Studied at the Sorbonne, Paris, diplome d'études supérieures. Director of the Publications and Documentation Center, Institut Français de Recherches Fruitières Outre Mer, France, since 1943. Director, Collection "Civilisations d'hier d'aujourd'hui," at Librairie Plon, Paris; Contributor, *Encyclopedie La Pleiade*, and to *Populations*, *Cahier de l'Institut national d'études demographiques*, and *Foi et vie*. Address: 94 rue Jean Mermoz, Maisons Laffitte 78, Yvelines, France.

PUBLICATIONS

Sociology

Les Traditions sociales dans les pays de France.   Paris, Editions Nouvelle, 1943.

Histoire des populations français et de leurs attitudes devant la vie depuis le XVIIIe siècle.   Paris, SELF, 1948.

Le Temps de l'histoire.   Monaco, Rocher, 1954.

L'Enfant et la vie sous l'ancient regime.   Paris, Plon, 1960; as *Centuries of Childhood: A Social History of Family Life*, New York, Knopf, 1962.

Western Attitudes Toward Death: From the Middle Ages to the Present (translated from the French).   Baltimore, Johns Hopkins University Press, 1974; as *Essais sur l'histoire de la mort en Occident du Moyen-âge à nos jours*, Paris, Seuil, 1975.

Religion populaire et reforme liturgique, with others.   Paris, Cerf, 1975.

L'Homme devant la mort.   Paris, Seuil, 1977; as *The Hour of Our Death*, New York, Knopf, 1980.

Un Historien du dimanche, with Michel Winoch.   Paris, Seuil, 1980.

*   *   *

The writing of history, particularly under the influence of the French Annales school, has been transformed in the last two decades; there has been a major conceptual revision. At a superficial level, it has involved a departure from the conventional view in which history was the history of the people. This shift of emphasis also involves a greater interest in the history of mundane culture than in the history of elite culture. The details of the working-class domestic economy, popular fashion, peasant marriage practices and folklore now provide some of the primary foci of the new history. More importantly, history is now interdisciplinary history. The macro-history of society is now concerned to chart the complex relationship between economy, policy and society through time, and in so doing it has broken down many of the traditional barriers between history and the social sciences. Historians are also now more willing to employ quantitative methods in the analysis of their data than to depend on descriptive, narrative accounts.

The result of these changes in emphasis and direction has been to raise important questions about social change and the nature of historical time. Conventional historians have frequently thought of historical time in terms of taken-for-granted categories. Time was typically measured off in terms of monarchical epochs such as "The Elizabethan Period." Alternatively, Marxist historians conceive history in terms of the dominance of a certain mode of economic production such as "feudalism" or "capitalism." The new history emphasizes the importance of slow but long changes in social arrangements which appear to span both monarchical history and modes of production. The concept of *longue durée* refers to these gradual, deep changes in social structure which cannot be apprehended by traditional methodologies. Philippe Aries' studies of childhood and death are illustrative of this new approach to historical time.

In *Centuries of Childhood* Aries was concerned to trace the slow development of the social category of "the child" from the 10th century to the present day. In pre-modern times there was little differentiation of the population into specialised age groups with their own tasks and social roles. There was little cultural definition of children as a specific category in society, as one separated from adults. In tracing the slow evolution of children, Aries provided a macro-history of European society, because the development of the concept of the child cannot be studied without also examining the evolution of the modern family, education, fashion, sexuality and discipline. In order to provide such a history, Aries employed a diversity of source material—family pictures, biography, school records, manuals of etiquette, memoirs. The book is thus a valuable illustration of the new history.

In mediaeval times a child was simply a small adult and, as such, was not protected from adult society. People were far less sensitive in general to age as a defining characteristic of personal identity. Insofar as the concept of childhood had any currency it was synonymous with dependency, regardless of the actual age of the dependent. The term *enfant* referred to both children and adolescents, while *petit garcon* could embrace both small children and young servants. It was not until the 17th century that a special dress for children developed, signifying their separate status in society. At the same time a new sensibility began to emerge regarding the fragility of the child in adult society. Children were portrayed in the art of the day as outside the family, with their own individuality and consciousness. Children's games were also increasingly specialised and separated from adult pastimes, thus giving special recognition to the needs of children. From the 16th to the 17th century, there was a growing awareness that children should not be exposed to adult sexual life, and a new pedagogic literature developed offering specialised advice on child development. The great turning point in the history of the child, however, took place with the creation of the school. In mediaeval times colleges were not internally graded by age groups, and no special curriculum existed for children. Growing awareness of the particular educational needs of children was thus matched by an institutional differentiation of education both within and between different types of schooling. Children living away from home in boarding schools now needed to be protected both from other pupils and from school masters. A new apparatus of moral discipline was required for an age group that was clearly separated from both adolescence and adulthood.

Centuries of Childhood has achieved classic status in modern social history as a model of inter-disciplinary research; it has spawned debate, criticism and replication. Although Aries has succeeded in breaking down intellectual barriers in the social sciences, his study can be criticised for, among other things, failing to provide a coherent explanation of the emergence of childhood. In particular, he neglected those economic changes in the social structure by which the family became separated from the economy and ceased to be a unit of production. The emergence of the family as a specialized area of human affectivity cannot be analyzed without a detailed inspection of economic changes. Aries has very little to say about the history of child labour and the role of women in the economy, both of which are closely related to the concept of the child. Despite these criticisms, Aries has opened up an important area of debate in relation to biological aging and cultural categories of age groups.

Aries has also produced two major studies of the history of death—*Western Attitudes Toward Death* and *The Hour of Our Death*—which duplicate his approach to childhood in their concern for long-term changes stretching over centuries and for cultural conceptions of death. Just as our notions of the child are relatively recent, so our treatment of death is a departure from patterns which were static for many centuries. Aries has argued that changes in attitudes to death take place extremely slowly or occur between extended periods of immobility. The history of these changing attitudes to death can be seen in a sharp dichotomy between the modern and pre-modern systems of death. Traditional European attitudes and practices towards death had the following characteristics: the death of an individual was typically forewarned or prophesied and was consequently not a surprise. Death occurred in a public setting in which the dying were surrounded by their kinfolk of all ages. There was little stress on the individual and individuality, so that any one death was part of the historical process of the social group. Dying was determined by common rituals and practices, while the dead belonged to the Church, which cared for their bones until the Final Judgment. Aries traces the collapse of this system in which death is familiar and public through the mediaeval period, with its macabre notion of the dance of death, to the modern age when death is secret, private and institutionalized. Death has become a taboo subject, devoid of religious meaning and ritual; it has been medicalized by modern science and secluded within the bureaucratic hospital. Even the elaborate presentation of "the deceased" in the American funeral "parlour" is an attempt to silence death.

Aries' work contains an irony. His research was first published when a silence surrounded the history of childhood and the presence of death. Partly as a result of his work, research on these topics is now voluble. There is now an academic industry focused on childhood and the family, while the study of death has been raised to the level of a science in thanatology. Contemporary fascination with death has rendered some aspects of Aries' argument obsolete, but his historical method and approach have been widely imitated by historians and sociologists.

—Bryan S. Turner

ARNHEIM, Rudolf. German aesthetician and psychologist. Born in Berlin, 15 July 1904; emigrated to the United States, 1940: naturalized, 1946. Studied at the University of Berlin, Ph.D. 1928. Married Mary Elizabeth Frame in 1953; 1 daughter. Associate Editor of Publications, International Institute of Educational Film, League of Nations, Rome, 1933-38. Visiting Professor, New School for Social Research, New York, and Member of the faculty, Sarah Lawrence College, Bronxville, New York, 1943-68; Fulbright Lecturer, Ochanomizu University, Tokyo, 1959-60; Professor of the Psychology of Art, Carpenter Center for Visual Arts, Harvard University, Cambridge, Massachusetts, 1968-74. Since 1974, Emeritus Visiting Professor, University of Michigan, Ann Arbor. Resident, American Academy, Rome, 1978. President, American Society of Aesthetics, 1959-60, 1979-80. Recipient: Guggenheim Fellowship, 1941-42; Distinguished Service Award, National Art Education Association, 1976. Honorary doctorate: Rhode Island School of Design, Providence, 1976. Fellow, American Psychological Association and American Academy of Arts and Sciences. Address: 1133 South Seventh Street, Ann Arbor, Michigan 48103, U.S.A.

PUBLICATIONS

Aesthetics and Psychology

Stimme von der Galerie: 25 kleine Aufsätze zur Kultur der Zeit. Berlin, Benary, 1928.
Film als Kunst. Berlin, Rowohlt, 1932; as *Film*, London, Faber, 1933; as *Film as Art*, Berkeley, University of California Press, 1957.
Radio. London, Faber, 1936; New York, Arno Press, 1971.
Phototips on Children: The Psychology, the Technique and the Art of Child Photography, with Mary Arnheim. London, Focal Press, 1939.
Art and Visual Perception. Berkeley, University of California Press, 1954; London, Faber, 1956.
Picasso's Guernica: The Genesis of a Painting. Berkeley, University of California Press, 1962; London, Faber, 1967.
Toward a Psychology of Art: Collected Essays. Berkeley, University of California Press, 1966; London, Faber, 1967 (contains a bibliography).
Entropy and Art: An Essay on Order and Disorder. Berkeley, University of California Press, 1971.
The Dynamics of Architectural Form. Berkeley, University of California Press, 1977.
The Power of the Center: A Study of Composition in the Visual Arts. Berkeley, University of California Press, 1982.

*

Bibliography: "On Rudolf Arnheim" in *The Canadian Review of Art Education and Research* (Montreal), 6 and 7, 1980-81.

* * *

Rudolf Arnheim's stated goal is to alleviate what he sees as a twofold blight endemic to contemporary culture: the incapacity to see intelligently—that is to say, the inability to look at images and objects with any sense of how formal properties and thematic elements both contribute to the impact of the work, and the unwillingness of most lay people and the majority of psychologists to concede that sensation—most particularly vision—is anything but a handmaiden to the intellect. Much of Arnheim's prolific output is based upon the concept of visual thinking—the idea that vision itself is the primary modality for thought, and that the act of looking is an intelligent process—as complex as any "purely" mental operation:

> My contention is that the cognitive operations called thinking are not the privilege of mental processes above and beyond perception, but the essential ingredients of perception itself. I am referring to such operations as active exploration, selection, grasping of essentials, simplification, abstraction, analysis, synthesis, completion, correction, comparison, problem solving, as well as combining, separating, putting in context... There is no difference in this respect between what happens when a person looks at the world directly and when he sits with eyes closed and "thinks."

He insists that until sensory intelligence is recognized, we will continue to live with the unwieldy notion, bequeathed to us by the associationist psychologists, that our phenomenal world is the sum total of fragmentary impressions painstakingly collected by the senses and "assembled" by the mind.

In addition to "rehabilitating" vision, Arnheim strives also to rebut the philosophical relativism which colors much contemporary aesthetics and psychology. He does not share the belief held by some philosophers that there is a completely arbitrary connection between an image or object and its referent. Semiotician Nelson Goodman, for example, claims that the relationship between image and referent is purely a matter of learned convention. An image can stand for anything one desires it to stand for, says Goodman. Basing his argument on the Gestalt theory of structural isomorphism, Arnheim shows that there are structural affinities between the representation and the thing represented and that these account for the phenomenon of "likeness." Children draw round heads, not because they have been trained to do so, but because there is obvious correspondence between the underlying geometrical structure of that head and the closed form of the circle. The child sees the quality of "roundness" in both head and circle.

The first axiom which governs Arnheim's approach to the arts, then, is that the senses themselves are indispensable to thought: "Perceiving and thinking require each other. They complement each other's functions... Perception would be useless without thinking; thinking without perception would have nothing to think about." Arnheim affirms that language, be it written or spoken, plays some role in the process of thought, but his estimation of this role is limited:

> ...although language is a valuable help in much human thinking, it is neither indispensable nor can it serve as the medium in which thinking takes place. It should be obvious that language consists of sounds or visual signs that possess none of the properties of the things to be manipulated in a problem...productive thinking is done by means of the things to which language refers, referents that in themselves are not verbal but perceptual.

A second basic axiom is that art itself must serve as a rational, illuminating force—one which helps to organize human experience—one which helps to make visible the regularity and orderliness of the natural world. Arnheim defines art in terms of its capacity to elucidate and clarify experience via its sensory organization. In his most recent work, *The Power of the Center*, he offers the following definition: "Art; The ability of perceptual objects or actions, either natural or man-made, to represent, through their appearance, constellations of forces that reflect relevant aspects of the dynamics of human experience. A work of art is a human artifact intended to represent such dynamic aspects by means of ordered, balanced, concentrated form."

Accepting these axioms and the fundamentals of Gestalt psychology, Arnheim comments on a vast range of art-related material. The media he analyzes are dance, mime, film, sculpture, architecture, painting, radio, and conceptual art. He illuminates both artistic successes and failures in these various fields and frequently his observations startle the reader with their freshness. His observations are novel and gripping precisely because Arnheim respects his sensory impressions. In an interview he comments, "the one thing I have tried to do is to take the visual image at its word. I mean, if a picture says it's dark—it means darkness. If, by hiding a person's hands it says this person has no hands, then that person has no hands, and in that sense, seeing things literally is really the basis of my entire work. It deals with spontaneous symbolism." In discussing films with sound tracks, Arnheim maintains that an image of a person talking more often than not fails as cinema, because this kind of image does not express what the film requires. The visual impression of a person speaking, Arnheim points out, is visually incoherent. This is an interesting criticism of the sound film—a form which audiences have come to accept with blind comfort. The observation concerning speech rings true as anyone who has turned off the sound on a television set will attest. The antics of the muted figures are often hilarious and almost never comprehensible. On the other hand, Arnheim points to the numerous instances in silent film when the director is able to convey the visual impressions of an auditory event through visual inventiveness, for example when a flock of pigeons explodes upwards out of a city street in response to a pistol shot. The sudden explosion of white forms is the exact visual analog to the auditory event.

Arnheim's approach, though well substantiated by art historical material, is a-historical. In his discussions of artistic forms from antiquity to the present he shows that no epoch, modern or ancient, has a special claim to artistic excellence. Realism is no more or less privileged a method of representation than cubism, mannerism, or medieval iconography. He does not insist upon any kind of progress in the history of art and believes that the "abstractness" of the work of young children can be profitably compared with that of early stages of "primitive art" in various civilizations. He is adept at showing how each artistic attitude, each set of cultural norms identifies limits within which artists work with greater or lesser success. Each system of representation has its liabilities and its assets. Using Renaissance perspective makes it possible to penetrate the picture plane—but it also makes it much more difficult to emphasize the importance of an object or person through relative size. The use of a projective system, though highly rational, may result in the creation of visual distortions which are perceptually irrational. The 19th-century photographer Muybridge demonstrated by a series of photographs that a galloping horse never reaches the point where front and back legs are stretched out parallel to the ground. Yet artists continue to show running horses in this position. The artists are unwilling to exchange realistic accuracy for visual effectiveness—yet the choice is always there. Arnheim has a large store of such examples which clearly demonstrate the kind of trade-offs which artists of all epochs have had to make. Following the same line of reasoning, when he discusses children's work, Arnheim shows that what the young child's drawings lack in optical accuracy they more than make up for in terms of structural clarity. Conversely, the work of older children may become bogged down in a welter of incidental detail, which may be important to the child, but which confuses the image.

If Arnheim has an aesthetic stance, it is that the art work should respect the integrity of the medium in which it is executed, and that its meaning or content should be clearly articulated through its physical appearance. An example helps to clarify this. In *Art and Visual Perception* Arnheim applauds the intelligence with which Michelangelo succeeded in depicting the creation of Adam for the Sistine Chapel. The artist modified the biblical story so that the creator no longer breathes life into Adam's nostrils (an awkward image to deal with visually), but instead extends His arm to Adam

as though an animating spark, leaping from fingertip to fingertip, were transmitted from the maker to the creature. The bridge of the arm visually connects two separate worlds...Our analysis shows that the ultimate theme of the image, the idea of creation, is conveyed by what strikes the eye first, and continues to organize the composition as we examine its details...Since the pattern of transmitted, life-giving energy is not simply recorded by the sense of vision, but presumably arouses in the mind a corresponding configuration of forces, the observer's reaction is more than a mere taking cognizance of an external object. The forces that characterize the meaning of the story, come alive in the observer and produce the kind of stirring participation that distinguishes artistic experience from the detached acceptance of information.

Ultimately, successful artistry, like the intelligence of vision, goes beyond the simple registration of objects and forms. It serves to make tangible fundamental "universals" which, according to Arnheim, underlie all sensory experiences. Both the subject matter and the formal properties of the art work are subservient to its universal theme.

The kind of connoisseur who looks only for the pattern, does as little justice to the work as the kind of layman who looks for subject matter...Neither the formal pattern nor the subject matter is the final content of the work of art. Both are instruments of artistic form. They serve to give body to an invisible universal.

With examples gleaned from the history of art, psychology, philosophy, and contemporary media, Arnheim persuades his readers that vision and thought are partners in a joint venture. This idea, though it may disturb some, has proven itself a rich source of psychological speculation and experiment. Many researchers are intrigued by the intelligence of perception, and by the way in which media and conventions constrain representation. Arnheim has produced a body of generative ideas and insights which has had an impact on fields as diverse as communications theory, telecommunications, child development, art education, and film criticism. He is a writer who challenges his readers with an electric and persuasive view of what art is, and a striking vision of what art can be at its best.

—David A. Pariser

ARON, Raymond (Claude Ferdinand). French sociologist, philosopher, and political scientist. Born in Paris, 14 March 1905. Studied at the Ecole Normale Supérieure, University of Paris, doctorat des lettres, 1938. Married Suzanne Gauchon in 1933; children: Dominique and Laurence. Lecturer, University of Cologne, 1930-31; member of staff, French Institute, Berlin, 1931-33; Professor of Philosophy, Lycée du Havre, 1933-34;

Secretary, Centre of Social Information, Ecole Normale Supérieure, Paris, 1934-39; Professor of Sociology, University of Toulouse, 1939; Editor, *La France Libre*, London, 1940-44; Professor of Political Science, Institut d'Etudes Politiques, Paris,
1945-55; Professor, Faculté des Lettres, Sorbonne, University of
Paris, 1955-68. Since 1970, Professor of Sociology Collège de
France, Paris, and Professor-at-Large, Cornell University, Ithaca,
New York. Member of staff, *Combat*, 1946; regular contributor
to *Figaro*, 1947-77, and *Express*, since 1977. Recipient: Prix des
Ambassadeurs, 1962; Prix Montaigne, 1968; Prix des Critiques,
1973; Prix Goethe, 1979; Prix Tocqueville, 1979; Prix Aujourd'
hui, 1981; Prix Pour la Liberté et les Droits l'Homme, Berne,
1981. Honorary doctorate: University of Basle, University of
Brussels, Harvard University, Columbia University, University
of Southampton, Hebrew University of Jerusalem, Oxford Uni-
versity, University of Louvain, Seoul University, Brandeis Uni-
versity, University of Chicago, and Cambridge University.
Member, Académie des Sciences morales et politiques, 1963.
Foreign Honorary Member, American Academy of Arts and
Sciences, 1961; Member, American Philosophical Society, and
the British Academy. Officier, Légion d'Honneur, 1974. Address:
87 boulevard Saint-Michel, 75005 Paris, France.

PUBLICATIONS

Sociology, Philosophy and Politics

La Sociologie allemande contemporaine. Paris, Alcan, 1935;
as *German Sociology*, New York, Free Press, 1957.
*Essai sur la théorie de l'histoire dans l'Allemagne contempo-
raine: La Philosophie critique de l'histoire.* Paris, Vrin,
1938; as *La Philosophie critique de l'histoire: Essai sur un
théorie allemande de l'histoire*, 1950.
*Introduction à la philosophie de l'histoire: Essai sur les limites de
l'objectivité historique.* Paris, Gallimard, 1938; as *Introduc-
tion to the Philosophy of History: An Essay on the Limits of
Historical Objectivity*, Boston, Beacon Press, 1961.
L'Homme contre les tyrans. New York, Editions de la Maison
Française, 1944.
De l'armistice à l'insurrection nationale. Paris, Gallimard,
1945.
Les Francais devant la constitution, with F. Clairens. Paris,
Editions Défense de la France, 1946.
L'Age des empires et l'avenir de la France. Paris, Editions
Défense de la France, 1946.
Bilan français depuis la libération. Paris, Editions du Monde
Nouveau, 1948.
Le Grand Schisme. Paris, Gallimard, 1948.
Les Guerres en chaîne. Paris, Gallimard, 1951; as *The Century
of Total War*, New York, Doubleday, 1954.
L'Opium des intellectuels. Paris, Calmann-Levy, 1955; as *The
Opium of the Intellectuals*, New York, Doubleday, 1957.
Polémiques. Paris, Gallimard, 1955.
*Le Développement de la société industrielle et la stratification
sociale.* Paris, Centre de Documentation Universitaire, 2
vols., 1956-57; vol. 1 published separately as *Dix-huit leçons
sur la société industrielle*, Paris, Gallimard, 1963; as *18 Lec-
tures on Industrial Society*, London, Weidenfeld and Nicol-
son, 1967; vol. 2 published separately as *La Lutte des classes:
Nouvelles Leçons sur les sociétés industrielles*, Paris, Galli-
mard, 1964.
The Soviet Economy: A Discussion, with others. London,
Secker and Warburg, 1956.
Espoir et peur du siècle: Essais non partisans. Paris, Calmann-
Levy, 1957; essay published as *On War: Atomic Weapons and
Global Diplomacy*, London, Secker and Warburg, 1958; as
On War, New York, Doubleday, 1959.
*Diversity of Worlds: France and the United States Look at Their
Common Problems*, with August Heckscher. New York,
Reynal, 1957.

La Tragédie algérienne. Paris, Plon, 1957.
L'Unification économique de l'Europe, with others. Boudry-
Neuchâtel, Switzerland, Baconnière, 1957.
L'Algérie et la République. Paris, Plon, 1958.
*Sociologie des sociétés industrielles: Equisse d'une théorie des
régimes politiques.* Paris, Centre de Documentation Uni-
versitaire, 1958; as *Democratie et totalitarisme*, Paris, Galli-
mard, 1975; as *Democracy and Totalitarianism*, London,
Weidenfeld and Nicolson, 1968.
War and Industrial Society. Oxford, Oxford University Press,
1958.
Immuable et changeante: De la IVe à la Ve République. Paris,
Calmann-Levy, 1959; as *France Steadfast and Changing: The
Fourth to the Fifth Republic.* Cambridge, Massachusetts,
Harvard University Press, 1960.
Colloques de Rheinfelden, with others. Paris, Calmann-Levy,
1960; as *World Technology and Human Destiny*, edited by
Aron, Ann Arbor, University of Michigan Press, 1963.
La Démocratie a l'épreuve du XXe Siècle. Paris, Calmann-
Levy, 1960.
*Les Grandes Doctrines de sociologie historique: Montesquieu,
Auguste Comte, Karl Marx, Alexis de Tocqueville; Les Socio-
logues et la révolution de 1848.* Paris, Centre de Documen-
tation Universitaire, 1960; enlarged edition, 1961, as *Les
Etapes de la pensée sociologique: Montesquieu, Comte,
Marx, Tocqueville, Durkheim, Pareto, Weber*, Paris, Galli-
mard, 1967; as *Main Currents in Sociological Thought*: vol. 1,
*Montesquieu, Comte, Marx, Tocqueville: Sociologists and
the Revolution of 1948*, vol. 2, *Durkheim, Pareto, Weber*,
New York, Basic Books, 1965-67.
France, the New Republic. Dobbs Ferry, New York, Oceana,
1960.
Dimensions de la conscience historique (collected essays). Pa-
ris, Plon, 1961; excerpt, "L'Aube de l'histoire univerelle" as
The Dawn of Universal History, New York, Praeger, 1961.
Paix et guerre entre les nations. Paris, Calmann-Levy, 1962; as
Peace and War: A Theory of International Relations. Lon-
don, Weidenfeld and Nicolson, and New York, Doubleday,
1966.
Douze Leçons d'introduction à la stratégie atomique. Paris,
Institut d'Etudes Politiques, University of Paris, 1963.
Le Grand Débat: Initiation à la stratégie atomique. Paris,
Calmann-Levy, 1963; as *The Great Debate: Theories of
Nuclear Strategy*, New York, Doubleday, 1965.
Trois Essais sur l'âge industriel. Paris, Plon, 1965; as *The
Industrial Society: Three Essays on Ideology and Develop-
ment*, New York, Praeger, 1967.
Essai sur les libertés. Paris, Calmann-Levy, 1965; as *An Essay
on Freedom*, New York, World, 1970.
*Progress and Disillusion: The Dialectics of Modern Socie-
ty.* New York, Praeger, 1968.
La Révolution introuvable: Réflexions sur la révolution de mai.
Paris, Fayard, 1968; as *The Elusive Revolution: Anatomy of a
Student Revolt*, London, Pall Mall, and New York, Praeger,
1969.
De Gaulle, Israel et les juifs. Paris, Plon, 1968; as *De Gaulle,
Israel, and the Jews*, New York, Praeger, and London,
Deutsch, 1969.
*D'Une Sainte Famille à l'autre: Essais sur les marxismes imagi-
naires.* Paris, Gallimard, 1969; as *Marxismes imaginaires:
D'Une Sainte Famille à l'autre*, 1970; selected essays published
as *Marxism and the Existentialists*, New York, Harper, 1969.
Le France dans la compétition économique, with others. Paris,
Presses Universitaires de France, 1969.
De la condition historique du sociologue. Paris, Gallimard,
1971.
Etudes politiques. Paris, Gallimard, 1972.
République impériale. Paris, Calmann-Levy, 1973; as *The
Imperial Republic: The United States and the World 1945-
1973*, Englewood Cliffs, New Jersey, Prentice-Hall, 1974.
Histoire et dialectique de la violence. Paris, Gallimard, 1973; as

History and Dialectic of Violence: An Analysis of Sartre's Critique de la raison dialectique, New York, Praeger, 1975.

Penser le guerre, Clausewitz: vol. 1, *L'âge européen*; vol. 2, *L'âge planétaire*.   Paris, Gallimard, 1976.

Plaidoyer pour l'Europe décadente.   Paris, Laffont, 1977.

Les Eléctions de Mars et la Ve République.   Paris, Julliard, 1978.

Politics and History: Selected Essays by Raymond Aron, edited by Miriam Bernheim Conant.   New York, Free Press, 1978.

Other

Raymond Aron, spectateur engagé: Entretiens avec Jean-Louis Missika et Dominique Wolton.   Paris, Julliard, 1981.

Editor, with Daniel Lerner, and contributor, *La Querelle de la C.E.D.: Essais d'analyse sociologique*.   Paris, Colin, 1956; as *France Defeats E.D.C.*, edited by Aron, New York, Praeger, 1957.

Editor, *L'Histoire et ses interpretations: Entretiens autour de Arnold Toynbee*.   The Hague, Mouton, 1961.

Editor, with B. Hoselitz, *Le Développement social*.   The Hague, Mouton, 1965; as *Social Development*, Atlantic Highlands, New Jersey, Humanities Press, 1965.

*

Critical Studies: *La Philosophie historique de Raymond Aron* by Gaston Fessard, Paris, Julliard, 1980.

*   *   *

Political scientist, sociologist, philosopher, historian, professor, journalist, intellectual, Raymond Aron is one of the leading social and political thinkers of the postwar era. French, Jewish, a socialist in his youth, a "liberal" in his adulthood, Aron has a special place in French intellectual life. European in the nature and dimensions of his interests and breadth of his reputation, he has more understanding of and greater contacts with English and American society than most of his compatriots. An Atlanticist— an advocate of cooperation with England and the United States—in foreign policy, he has been anti-fascist, anti-communist, a supporter and a critic of de Gaulle. He is one of the leading controversialists in French and Western European political life, known for brilliant pieces of journalistic analysis such as *The Opium of the Intellectuals* or his analyses of the Algerian war and the events of May 1968.

Aron's intellectual interests, like those of Jean-Paul Sartre, his friend at the Ecole Normale Supérieure, were deeply influenced before the war by currents in German thought. His dissertation was a major contribution to the French understanding of German sociology, particularly the work of Weber, whose major concern Aron has shared. Like those of Weber and Comte, Aron's contribution has been to our understanding of industrial society which he sees as having many similar features whether it is socialist, communist, or capitalist. These similar features arise from technology, from the spirit of innovation and progress that dominates industrial society, and from the bureaucratic and rational organization of the government and economy of industrial society. Aron has never argued the convergence of regimes though many have understood his analysis of different societies moving along comparable tracks as a depiction and prediction of similar evolution determined by technology.

Aron is not a determinist however much he stresses the economic underpinnings of industrial society. For him politics, individual and group action, and history take primacy over technology and structure. He argues the autonomy of the political sphere in many works. As he stressed in *On War* and his Clausewitz study, history continues, technology does not control, only men do. Aron rightly sees himself as a political sociologist in the tradition of Tocqueville and Halévy, a tradition he explicated

masterfully in *Main Currents in Sociological Thought* discussing Montesquieu, Comte, Marx, and Tocqueville.

Aron's relations with Marxism and Marxists (and Marxisant French intellectuals) have been stormy ones. His critique is both political and intellectual and it pre-dates the war and carried into the period when he was an editor of *Les Temps Modernes* together with Sartre, Merleau-Ponty, and Malraux. Like Durkheim, Halévy, and Weber, he has always been critical of Marxist claims to the status of social science, which must seek objectivity and genuine lawfulness. He rejects monistic explanation. He is unsympathetic to attempts to base a non- or anti-positivistic approach to society on the writings of early Marx as opposed to the later Marx. In politics, as opposed to philosophy, he has been hard hitting in his denunciations of *gauchisme* as a pattern of thought among French intellectuals. (His *normalien* friendship with Sartre did not survive the latter's justifications of his steady friendship with the Soviet Union in the 1950's.)

Aron has shown a remarkable capacity to stand outside the mainstream of thought at any particular moment, both in France and in the Atlantic community. He saw the similarities of all industrial societies when the political antagonisms of cold war obscured them for many. And he was a cold warrior speaking out in the Congress for Cultural Freedom, in *Encounter, Preuves*, and daily columns. He took on the unthinkable subject of modern warfare in the 1950's, arguing that the balance of terror mentality had sapped the willingness of many to think of the ends of war, diplomacy, of international relations itself. War is a part of everyday modern life, shaping society just as industrialism does, and must be contemplated in the formulation of policy even under the threat of nuclear holocaust. Anything else is an abdication of politics and of human reason to control our destiny. Issues of national interest remain. It is his belief in human reason, limited as it is, which leads him to describe himself as an "optimist with certain reservations."

Very sympathetic to movements of national self-determination, Aron has not argued that Africans exist in a world apart and should be judged by other than liberal values. He has pointed out that the path of single party or dictatorship in the first steps of industrialization and independence is not so different from France under Napoleon as 20th-century commentators would have it. A state achieves legitimation by a variety of mechanisms and a simple opposition between plan and free market is not Aron's model. Fundamentally, according to him, modern and free societies depend upon self-discipline of their citizenry which can be achieved by religion, patriotism, party loyalty, or a variety of ways, but the level of liberty and prosperity is the criterion of evaluation.

In recent years, since May 1968, Aron's work seems nostalgic and pessimistic as opposed to his earlier realism, skepticism, and vigorous optimism with reservations. He has not stressed changes in the East-West split or the economic changes since the 1970's. He has focused on Europe as a sanctuary for men of traditional values and liberal ideas.

—Myrna Chase

ARRHENIUS, Svante (August).   Swedish chemist and physicist.   Born in Schloss Wijk, 19 February 1859. Studied at the University of Uppsala, Ph.D. 1884. Worked in Germany with Boltzmann and others, 1886-88; Lecturer, 1891-95, and after 1895 Professor of Physics, University of Stockholm (Rector, 1897-1902); Director, Nobel Institute for Physical Chemistry, Stockholm, 1905-27. Visiting Lecturer, University of California, Berkeley, 1904. Recipient: Davy Medal, Royal Society, London, 1902; Nobel Prize in Chemistry, 1903. Member, Swedish Academy of Sciences. Corresponding Member, French Academy of Sciences. Fellow of the Royal Society. *Died* (in Stockholm) *2 October 1927.*

PUBLICATIONS

Chemistry and Physics

Lehrbuch der elektrochemie (from lectures translated from the Swedish). Leipzig, Quandt und Händel, 1901; as *Textbook of Electrochemistry*, New York, and London, Longmans, 1902.

Lehrbuch der kosmischen Physik. Leipzig, Hirzel, 1903.

Die nordlichter in Island und Grönland. Uppsala and Stockholm, Almqvist och Wiksell, 1906.

Die vermutliche Ursache der Klimaschwankungen. Uppsala and Stockholm, Almqvist och Wiksell, 1906.

Untersuchung über die galvanische Leitfähigkeit der Elektrolyte (lecture translated from the Swedish), edited by Otto Sackur. Leipzig, Engelmann, 1907.

Theories of Chemistry: Lectures Delivered at the University of California, in Berkeley, edited by T. Slater Price. London and New York, Longman, 1907.

Immunochemistry: The Application of the Principles of Physical Chemistry to the Study of the Biological Antibodies. New York, Macmillan, 1907.

Das Werden der Welten (translated from the Swedish). Leipzig, Akademische Verlagsgesellschaft, 2 vols., 1907-08; as *Worlds in the Making: The Evolution of the Universe*, New York and London, Harper, 1908.

Über die Schütz'sche Regel bei Reaktionsgeschwindigkeiten. Uppsala and Stockholm, Almqvist och Wiksell, 1908.

Versuche über Hämolyse. Uppsala and Stockholm, Almqvist och Wiksell, 1908.

Die Gesetze der Verdauung und Resorption nach Versuchen von E.S. London. Uppsala and Stockholm, Almqvist och Wiksell, 1909.

Versuch über Fällung von Eiweisskörpern und Agglutination von Erythrocyten. Uppsala and Stockholm, Almqvist och Wiksell, 1909.

The Life of the Universe as Conceived by a Man from the Earliest Ages to the Present Time (translated from the Swedish). New York and London, Harper, 1909.

Theories of Solutions (lectures). New Haven, Connecticut, Yale University Press, 1912.

Quantitative Laws in Biological Chemistry. London, Bell, 1915.

The Destinies of the Stars (translated from the Swedish). New York and London, Putnam, 1918.

Chemistry in Modern Life (translated and revised from the Swedish). New York, Van Nostrand, 1925.

Die Sternenwelt (translated from the Swedish), edited by Knut Lundmark. Leipzig, Akademische Verlagsgesellschaft, 1931.

*   *   *

Svante Arrhenius is best known for his contributions to the theory of electrolytic dissociation. The theory deals with the behavior of certain substances when dissolved in water or other solvents, particularly under the influence of an external electric field.

Two lines of research provide the background for this theory. The first includes studies of conductivity. Some substances, such as sodium chloride (common table salt) do not conduct an electric current when dry, but will do so in a water solution. Hittorf had demonstrated in the 1850's that such substances, when dissolved in water, apparently break apart into two oppositely charged fragments ("ions"). These ions then migrate to the anode and cathode in an electrolysis apparatus at differing speeds. The second line of research involved studies of colligative properties. Colligative properties are those characteristics of a liquid which change when a solute is dissolved in the liquid. For example, the freezing point of a liquid is depressed when a solid is dissolved in that liquid. For many substances, the amount to which the freezing point is depressed is a function only of the amount of solute added and not on the nature of the solute. The major exceptions are electrolytes, those substances whose water solution will conduct an electric current. In the case of electrolytes, the freezing point is lowered two, three, or more times as much as that of comparable amounts of non-electrolytes. The inference seemed to be that each electrolyte particle breaks up into two or more parts in solution.

The empirical work of Hittorf, Kohlrausch, and Raoult and the theoretical speculations of Clausius and Williamson all pointed to the possibility of "charged atoms" in water solutions. Yet, chemists of the late 19th century found this possibility difficult to imagine or interpret. The indivisible Daltonian atom was still regarded as the fundamental particle of matter. Evidence for the existence of sub-atomic particles was still a generation into the future. What meaning, then, could a chemist in the 1880's attach to the event in which an "indivisible atom" separated into charged parts?

Physicists faced a comparable dilemma. For them, the concept of the atom as a fundamental particle had been largely irrelevant to their work. There seemed no reason to adopt this chemical concept of matter to an obviously physical problem in electrical conductance.

In fact, the investigations and speculations of Arrhenius were to constitute one of the first major bridges between chemistry and physics, contributing to the foundation of a new science, physical chemistry. It is hardly surprising that Arrhenius found his greatest support from Ostwald and van't Hoff, two other pioneers in the fledgling science of physical chemistry.

Arrhenius outlined his notions of electrolytic dissociation in his doctoral thesis, submitted in 1884. A more complete and refined version was published three years later. According to the theory, the fundamental particles of which an electrolyte consists are separated in water solution by the action of water molecules. A sodium chloride molecule, for example, breaks apart to form sodium ions and chloride ions. The ions thus formed are similar to atoms, except that they carry electrical charges. Today we know that these charges result from an excess (in anions) or deficiency (in cations) of electrons in the atom/ion. The separation of neutral particles into charged ions in water solution accounted for the conductive properties studied by Hittorf and others.

It also explained the abnormal and unexpected colligative properties of electrolytes. We might, for example, dissolve equal numbers of sodium chloride and sucrose (table sugar, a non-electrolyte) particles in water. But, because of electrolytic dissociation, the number of particles actually in solution would be twice as great for the former as for the latter. The freezing point depression (and other colligative characteristics) would then be twice as great for sodium chloride as for sucrose.

Resistance to the Arrhenius theory diminished rapidly by the turn of the century. Thomson's discovery of the electron provided evidence of the divisible nature of atoms. The concept of a "charged atom," once so inimical to chemical theory, was now a natural and understandable extension of atomic theory. A major stumbling block in the way of chemists' acceptance of the existence of ions had been removed.

—David Newton

ARROW, Kenneth (Joseph). American economist. Born in New York City, 23 August 1921. Studied at the City College of New York, B.S. 1940; Columbia University, New York, M.A. 1941, Ph.D. 1951. Served as a Captain in the United States Army, 1942-46. Married Selma Schweitzer in 1947; 2 sons. Research Associate, Cowles Commission for Research in Economics, 1947-49; Assistant Professor, University of Chicago, 1948-49; Acting Assistant Professor, 1949-50, Associate Professor, 1950-53, Professor, 1953-68, and since 1979 Joan Kenney Professor of Economics, Stanford University, California; Professor, 1968-74, and James Bryant Conant University Professor, 1974-79, Harvard University, Cambridge, Massachusetts. Fellow, Center for Advanced Study in the Behavioral Sciences, Palo Alto, California, 1956-57, and Churchill College, Cambridge, 1963-64, 1970, and 1973. Economist, Council of Economic Advisers, United States Government, 1962. Consultant to the RAND Corporation. Vice-President, 1955, and President, 1956, Econometric Society; Vice-President, American Academy of Arts and Sciences, 1979-81; President, 1963, and Chairman of the Council, 1964, Institute of Management Sciences; Member, Executive Committee, 1967-69, and President, 1973, American Economics Association; President, Western Economic Association, 1980-81. Recipient: Social Science Research Fellowship, 1952; John Bates Clark Medal, American Economic Association, 1957; Nobel Prize in Economics, 1972; Guggenheim Fellowship, 1972-73. Honorary M.A.: Harvard University, 1968; honorary doctorate: University of Chicago, 1967; University of Vienna, 1971; City University of New York, 1972; Columbia University, 1973; Yale University, New Haven, Connecticut, and Université René Descartes, Paris, 1974; Hebrew University of Jerusalem, 1975; University of Pennsylvania, Philadelphia, and University of Helsinki, 1976. Foreign Honorary Member, Finnish Academy of Sciences; Corresponding Member, British Academy. Address: Department of Economics, Stanford University, Stanford, California 94305 U.S.A.

PUBLICATIONS

Economics

Methodological Problems in Airframe Cost-Performance Studies, with Selma G. Arrow. Santa Monica, California, RAND, 1950.

Cost Quality Relations in Bomber Airframes, with others. Santa Monica, California, RAND, 1951.

On Mandelbaum's Study of The Industrialization of Backward Areas, with Selma G. Arrow. Santa Monica, California, RAND, 1951.

Social Choice and Individual Values. New York, Wiley, 1951.

The Combination of Time Series and Cross-Section Data in Interindustry Flow Analysis. Santa Monica, California, RAND, 1956.

Studies in Linear and Non-Linear Programming, with others. Stanford, California, Stanford University Press, 1958.

Studies in the Mathematical Theory of Inventory and Production, with others. Stanford, California, Stanford University Press, 1958.

Dynamic Shortages and Price Rises: The Engineer-Scientist Case, with William M. Capron. Santa Monica, California, RAND, 1958.

A Time Series Analysis of Interindustry Demands. Amsterdam, North-Holland, 1959.

Quasi-Concave Programming, with Alain C. Enthoven. Santa Monica, California, RAND, 1959.

Constraint Qualifications in Maximization Problems, II, with Hirofumi Uzawa. Stanford, California, Stanford University Press, 1960.

Economic Welfare and the Allocation of Resources for Invention. New York, National Bureau of Economic Research, 1960.

The Economic Implications of Learning by Doing. Stanford, California, Stanford University Press, 1961.

Optimal Advertising Policy under Dynamic Conditions, with Marc Nerlove. Stanford, California, Stanford University Press, 1961.

Control in Large Organizations. Stanford, California, Stanford University Press, 1963.

Aspects of the Theory of Risk-Bearing (lecture). Helsinki, Yrjö Jahnssonin Säätiö, 1965.

Statistical Requirements for Greek Economic Planning (lecture). Athens, Center of Planning and Economic Research, 1965.

Optimal Capital Policy with Irreversible Investment. Stanford, California, Stanford University Press, 1966.

Uniqueness of the Internal Rate of Return with Variable Life of Investment, with David Levhari. Stanford, California, Stanford University Press, 1968.

Essays in the Theory of Risk-Bearing. Amsterdam, North-Holland, 1970.

Public Investment, the Rate of Return, and Optimal Fiscal Policy, with Mordecai Kurz. Baltimore, Johns Hopkins University Press, 1970.

General Competitive Analysis, with F.H. Hahn, San Francisco, Holden-Day, 1971.

Some Models of Racial Discrimination in the Labor Market. Santa Monica, California, RAND, 1971.

Cost- and Demand-Theoretical Approaches to the Theory of Price Determination, with David A. Starrett. Cambridge, Massachusetts, Harvard University Press, 1971.

The Theory of Discrimination (lecture). Princeton, New Jersey, Princeton University Press, 1971.

Gifts and Exchanges. Cambridge, Massachusetts, Harvard University Press, 1972.

Information and Economic Behavior. Cambridge, Massachusetts, Harvard University Press, 1973.

Optimal Insurance and Generalized Deductibles. Santa Monica, California, RAND, 1973.

Theoretical Issues in Health Insurance. Colchester, England, University of Essex, 1973.

Welfare Analysis of Changes in Health Coinsurance Rates. Santa Monica, California, RAND, 1973.

The Limits of Organization. New York, Norton, 1974.

Two Notes on Inferring Long Run Behavior from Social Experiments. Santa Monica, California, RAND, 1975.

Energy, the Next Twenty Years: A Report, with others. Cambridge, Massachusetts, Ballinger, 1979.

Petroleum Price Regulation: Should We Decontrol?, with Joseph P. Kalt. Washington, D.C., American Enterprise Institute for Public Policy Research, 1979.

Other

Editor, *Mathematical Methods in the Social Sciences: Proceedings of the Stanford Symposium on Mathematical Methods in the Social Sciences*. Stanford, California, Stanford University Press, 1960.

Editor, with others, *Studies in Applied Probability and Management Science*. Stanford, California, Stanford University Press, 1962.

Editor, *Readings in Welfare Economics*. Homewood, Illinois, Irwin, 1969.

Editor, *Selected Readings in Economic Theory from Econometrica*. Cambridge, Massachusetts, and London, M.I.T. Press, 1971.

Editor, with Leonard Hurwicz, *Studies in Resource Allocation Processes*. New York and Cambridge, Cambridge University Press, 1977.

Editor, with others, *Applied Research for Social Policy: The United States and the Federal Republic of Germany*. Cambridge, Massachusetts, Abt Books, 1979.

Editor, with Michael D. Intriligator, *Handbook of Mathematical Economics*. New York and Amsterdam, North-Holland, 1981.

*

Critical Studies: *Kenneth Arrow's Contribution to Economic Science* by Carl Christian von Weizacker, Rheda, Germany, Institut für Mathematische Wirtschaftsforschung an der Universität Bielefeld, 1972.

*   *   *

Kenneth Arrow is one of the most active and influential mathematical economists and theorists of the last half of this century. While some scholars are recognized for a singularly important result or discovery, others for the breadth of their work, and still others for articulating some fundamental concepts that inspire new paths of research, Arrow deserves recognition for contributions in all of these ways.

Arrow is probably most widely known for his General Impossibility Theorem, the result of inquiring whether it is possible to discover a collective choice rule to transform individual preferences into a social ordering that satisfies certain axioms. The theorem proves that if the social ordering is to be universal, complete and transitive, nondictatorial, and consistent with the concept of Pareto optimality and the principle of independence of irrelevant alternatives, then no such collective choice rule exists. While each of Arrow's axioms is subject to some criticism, the theorem suggests that there are serious potential difficulties with every collective choice mechanism. Arrow's 1951 seminar paper in which the theorem was first proved, along with some earlier work by Bergson, led to the development of a new body of economic research, public choice economics. This field has grown tremendously in the last 30 years exploring both theoretical issues about collective choice rules and social welfare as well as more practical issues about election rules and voting behavior.

For many economists, Arrow's most important contribution to the theory is his work in general equilibrium and welfare economics, rather than the Impossibility Theorem. Arrow was among the first of the modern mathematical economists (along with Debreu and McKenzie) who, using new mathematical techniques, provided simpler and more general proofs of the existence and uniqueness of general competitive equilibrium. Arrow, using the theory of convex sets, also formulated a precise mathematical meaning for the general efficiency of competitive systems (a notion that dates at least to Adam Smith) and proved, again in the most general terms of the time, the fundamental theorems of welfare economics, that all competitive equilibria are optimal and that all optimal states can be achieved through the competitive market process. These proofs were very important because some crucial, limiting assumptions previously necessary were relaxed without cost to the theorems. The techniques used in this path-breaking work have become standard among economic theorists and have been used, by Arrow and many others, to explore the effects of uncertainty, externalities, and various market structures on the theorems.

Arrow was also a pioneer in developing and applying the concepts of uncertainty and risk to economic analysis. He articulated the theory in a series of lectures in 1963 and in subsequent papers applied those concepts to economic analysis of medical care, insurance, organizational control, public investment, the role of information costs in market failure, and the formation of expectations, among others. He noted that lack of information, or differential information among economic agents, is a source of uncertainty and risk and was therefore led to examine how economic information is defused and why some markets to reduce this uncertainty exist while others do not. In his presidential address to the American Economic Association in 1973 Arrow argued that "the uncertainties about economics are rooted in our need for a better understanding of the economics of uncertainty; our lack of economic knowledge is, in good part, our difficulty in modelling the ignorance of the economic agent." Much of Arrow's work in the last decade has been directed toward this difficulty while at the same time other economists, some spurred by Arrow's insights or suggestions, worked to improve the theory to encompass imperfectly informed economic agents.

The questions posed in Arrow's work are among the most fundamental in economics. Can the economic system achieve an equilibrium and, if so, how should it be evaluated in terms of social welfare? Can nonmarket choice rules be used instead of or as an addition to the market, and, if so, how do these collective choice rules perform? Can the economic system function smoothly with uncertainty and imperfect information and how might economic institutions be changed in the face of that uncertainty. It is certain that Arrow's contributions to these issues will endure and form, as they have already, the foundation for much additional, productive economic research.

—Ronald C. Fisher

ARTAUD, Antonin. French actor, playwright and theorist of the drama. Born in Marseilles, 4 September 1896. Became addicted to drugs with first period of hospitalization, 1915. Medical discharge after nine months of military service, 1915. Hospitalized frequently, 1916-20. Worked as an actor and designer for the theater companies of Charles Dullin and Georges Pitöeff, Paris, 1921-24; joined the Surrealist movement, 1924 (expelled, 1926); founded the Théâtre Alfred Jarry in Paris, with Roger Vitrac and Robert Aron, 1926; worked as an actor in films by Abel Gance, Carl Dreyer and others, 1924-35. Lectured on the theater at the Sorbonne, Paris, 1928, 1931 and 1933. Traveled in Mexico and Ireland, 1937. Confined in various asylums, 1937-46 (released, 1946). Recipient: Prix Sainte-Beuve for *Van Gogh, le suicidé de la société*, 1948. *Died 8 March 1948.*

PUBLICATIONS

Collections

Oeuvres complètes. Paris, Gallimard, 16 vols., 1956-81; revised edition, 1970-.
Collected Works. London, Calder and Boyars, 4 vols., 1968-75.
Artaud Anthology, edited by Jack Hirschman. San Francisco, City Lights Books, 1965.
Antonin Artaud: Selected Writings, edited with an introduction by Susan Sontag. New York, Farrar Straus, 1976.

Theatre

Le Théâtre Alfred Jarry et l'hostilité du publique, with Roger Vitrac. Paris, Nouvelle Revue Française, 1930.
Le Théâtre de la cruauté. Paris, Denoël, 1933.
Le Théâtre de Séraphin. Paris, Belmont, 1936; as "The Theater of the Seraphim," in *Selected Writings*.
Le Théâtre et son double. Paris, Gallimard, 1938; as *The Theater and Its Double*, New York, Grove Press, 1958; London, Calder and Boyars, 1970.

Plays and Scenarios

"Le Jet de sang," in *L'Ombilic des limbes.* Paris, Nouvelle Revue Française, 1925; as "The Jet of Blood," in *Selected Writings*.
"Le Dix-huit Secondes" (scenario). Paris, Les Cahiers de la Pléiade, 1949; as "Eighteen Seconds," in *Collected Works*, vol. 3.
"Deux Nations sur les confins de la Mongolie" (scenario), in *Oeuvres complètes*, vol. 3; as "Two Nations at the Border of Mongolia," in *Collected Works*, vol. 3.
"La Coquille et la clergyman" (film scenario, produced 1927), in *Oeuvres complètes*, vol. 3; as "The Seashell and the Clergyman," in *Collected Works*, vol. 3.
"Les 32" (scenario), in *Oeuvres complètes*, vol. 3; as "Thirty-Two" in *Collected Works*, vol. 3.
"La Révolte du Boucher" (scenario), in *Oeuvres complètes*, vol.

3; as "The Butcher's Revolt," in *Collected Works*, vol. 3.
"Le Maître de Ballantrae" (scenario), in *Oeuvres complètes*, vol.
3; as "The Master of Ballantrae," in *Collected Works*, vol. 3.
"Les Cenci" (produced 1935), in *Oeuvres complètes*, vol. 4; as
"The Cenci," in *Collected Works*, vol. 4, and New York,
Grove Press, 1970.
Pour le finir avec le jugement de Dieu (recorded but not broadcast, 1947). Paris, K Editeur, 1948; as "To Have Done with
the Judgment of God: A Radio Play," in *Selected Writings*.

Other

Tric-trac du ciel (poems). Paris, Galerie Simon, 1923.
L'Ombilic des limbes (prose poems). Paris, Nouvelle Revue
Française, 1927; as "The Umbilicus of Limbo," in *Selected
Writings*.
Correspondence avec Jacques Rivière. Paris, Nouvelle Revue
Française, 1927; as "Correspondence with Jacques Rivière,"
in *Selected Writings*.
Le Pèse-nerfs (reflections). Paris, Collection "Pour vos beau
yeux," 1925; with *Fragments d'un journal d'enfer*, Marseilles,
Cahiers du Sud, 1927; as "The Nerve Meter" and "Fragments
of a Diary of Hell," in *Selected Writings*.
L'Art et la mort (prose poems). Paris, Denoël, 1929; as "Art
and Death," in *Selected Writings*.
Héliogabale ou l'anarchiste couronné (historical study). Paris,
Denoël and Steele, 1934; selections as "Heliogabalus, or The
Anarchist Crowned," in *Selected Writings*.
Les Nouvelles Révélations de l'être (prophetic writings). Paris,
Denoël, 1937; selections as "The New Revelations of Being,"
in *Selected Writings*.
D'un voyage au pays de Tarahumaras (essays and letters). Paris, Fontaine, 1945; selections as "A Voyage to the Land of the
Tarahumara," in *Selected Writings*.
Lettres de Rodez. Paris, GLM, 1946; as "Letters from Rodez,"
in *Selected Writings*.
Artaud le mômo (poems). Paris, Bordas, 1947; as *Artaud the
Momo*, Santa Barbara, California, Black Sparrow Press,
1976.
Ce-gît, précédé de la culture indienne (poems). Paris, K Editeur, 1947; as "Indian Culture" and "Here Lies," in *Selected
Writings*.
Van Gogh, le suicidé de la société (essay). Paris, K Editeur,
1947; as "Van Gogh, the Man Suicided by Society," in
Selected Writings.
Supplément aux Lettres de Rodez suivi de Coleridge le traître
(additional letters from Rodez and an essay "Coleridge the
Traitor"). Paris, GLM, 1949.
Lettre contre la Cabbale. Paris, Haumont, 1949.
Lettres d'Antonin Artaud à Jean-Louis Barrault. Paris, Bordas, 1952.
La Vie et mort de Satan le feu. Paris, Arcanes, 1953; as *The
Death of Satan and Other Mystical Writings*, London, Calder
and Boyars, 1974
Les Tarahumaras (letters and essays). Déclines, Isère, L'Arbalete, 1955.
Galapagos, les îles du bout du monde (travel). Paris, Brodeur,
1955.
Autre chose que l'enfant beau. Paris, Brodeur, 1957.
Voici un endroit. Paris, PAB, 1958.
Mexico (travel). Mexico City, Universidad Nacional Autonoma de Mexico, 1962.
Lettres à Anaïs Nin. Paris, Editions du Seuil, 1965.
Lettres à Génica Athanasiou. Paris, Gallimard, 1970.
Nouvelles écrits de Rodez (letters and essays). Paris, Gallimard, 1977.
Lettres à Anie Besnard. Paris, Le Nouveau Commerce, 1978.

Translator, *The Monk*, by G.M. Lewis. Paris, Denoël and
Steele, 1931.

Translator, *The Case of Mr. Crump*, by Ludwig Lewisohn. Paris, Denoël, 1932.

*

Critical Studies: *The Dramatic Concepts of Antonin Artaud* by
Eric Sellin, Chicago, University of Chicago Press, 1968; *Antonin
Artaud: Poet Without Words* by Naomi Greene, New York,
Simon and Schuster, 1970; *Antonin Artaud et le théâtre* by Alan
Vrimaux, Paris, Seghers, 1970 (contains an extensive bibliography); *Antonin Artaud* by Jean-Louis Brau, Paris, La Table
Ronde, 1971; *Artaud and After* by Ronald Hayman, London
and New York, Oxford University Press, 1977.

* * *

On April 7th, 1939, during his period of internment as a
psychiatric patient in the Hôpital de Sainte-Anne, in Paris,
Antonin Artaud wrote to Jacqueline Breton, wife of the famous
surrealist poet, a letter in which he stated that he was "a fanatic
and not a madman." The distinction is sometimes a fine one to
make, since he also told Breton himself that he believed in a
Christ who "called men towards the absolute, because he recognised that Life is Evil and Death the ultimate Good," and Artaud
did spend some nine years of his unhappy life in lunatic asylums.
He is best known for the book *Le Théâtre et son double* in which
he denounced the way in which the theatre had developed from
Aeschylus to Ibsen. Instead of giving primacy to language and to
the clear analysis and representation of character and plot, the
theatre ought, in Artaud's view, to concentrate on physical
movement and incantatory noise. Its object should be to strike
terror into the soul of the spectator by essentially irrational
means, and to thus destroy the confidence in a rational universe
which, in his view as in that of his admirers, provided a basis for
the smug bourgeois self-confidence which was so absolute an
enemy of Art. What Martin Esslin describes as the "truly prophetic" nature of his utterances was realised to some extent in the
productions of the plays of Fernando Arrabal, Jean Genet, and
René de Obadia as well as in Peter Brook's 1966 version of Peter
Weiss's *Marat-Sade*. His idea of the "Theatre of Cruelty" can
also be seen as related to the cult of the "Happening" which
characterised the American and French theatre in the 1970's,
while the production in the cinema of Fellini's *Sado Sadom* in
1978 can be regarded as the logical if perhaps unconscious apotheosis of his ideas.

Although—like most people—Artaud was officially excluded
from the Surrealist movement, much of the very extensive writing about him comes from authors and critics sympathetic to the
general aims of that movement, such as Maurice Blanchot and
J.H. Matthews. He is also greatly admired by many current
cultural commentators, including Philippe Sollers, Susan Sontag, and Jacques Derrida.

—Philip Thody

AUERBACH, Erich. German philologist and critic. Born in
Berlin, 9 November 1892; emigrated to Turkey, 1936, to the
United States, 1947; naturalized, 1953. Studied at the University
of Berlin; University of Freiburg; University of Munich; University of Heidelberg, Dr.jur. 1913; University of Greifswald, Ph.D.
1921. Married Marie Mankiewicz in 1933; 1 son. Librarian,
Prussian State Library, Berlin, 1923-29. Professor of Romance
Philology, University of Marburg, 1929-35; Professor, Turkish
State University, Istanbul, 1936-47; Visiting Professor, Pennsylvania State University, State College, 1948-49; Member, Institute for Advanced Study, Princeton, New Jersey, 1949-50; Professor of French and Romance Philology, 1950-57, and Sterling

Professor, 1956-57, Yale University, New Haven, Connecticut. *Died 13 October 1957.*

PUBLICATIONS

Philology and Literary Criticism/Theory

Zur Technik der Frührenaissancenovelle in Italien und Frankreich. Heidelberg, Winter, 1921.
Dante als Dichter der irdischen Welt. Berlin, de Gruyter, 1929; as *Dante, Poet of the Secular World,* Chicago, University of Chicago Press, 1961.
Das franzöische Publikum des 17. Jahrhunderts. Munich, Hueber, 1933.
Mimesis: dargestellte Wirklichkeit in der abendländischen Literatur. Berne, Francke, 1946; as *Mimesis: The Representation of Reality in Western Literature.* Princeton, New Jersey, Princeton University Press, 1953.
Introduction aux études de philologie romane. Frankfurt, Klosterman, 1949; as *Introduction to Romance Languages and Literature,* New York, Capricorn Books, 1961.
Vier Untersuchungen zur Geschichte der franzöischen Bildung. Berne, Francke, 1951.
Typologische Motive in der mittelalterlichen Literatur. Krefeld, West Germany, Scherpe, 1953.
Literatursprache und Publikum in der lateinischen Spätantike und im Mittelalter. Berne, Francke, 1958; as *Literary Language and Its Public in Late Latin Antiquity and in the Middle Ages,* London, Routledge, and New York, Bollingen, 1965.
Scenes from the Drama of European Literature: Six Essays. New York, Meridian Books, 1959.
Gesammelte Aufsätze zur romanische Philologie, edited by Gustav Konrad. Berne, Francke, 1967.

Other

Die Teilnahme in den Vorarbeiten zu einem neuen Strafgesetzbuch. Berlin, Frensdorf, 1913.

*

Critical Studies: "Auerbach's Special Realism" by René Wellek in *Kenyon Review* (Gambier, Ohio), 16, 1954; "Philosophy or Philology: Auerbach and Aesthetic Historicism" by Charles Breslin in *Journal of the History of Ideas* (New York), 22, 1961; "Erich Auerbach's Critical Theory and Practice: An Assessment" by Wolfgang Fleischman in *Modern Language Notes* (Baltimore), 81, 1966; "Erich Auerbach as European Critic" by Arthur R. Evans, Jr. in *Romance Philology* (Berkeley, California), 25, 1971; "Auerbach's 'Mimesis': Aesthetics as Historical Understanding" by Wolfgang Holdheim in *Clio* (Fort Wayne, Indiana), 10, 1980; *Literary Criticism and the Structures of History: Erich Auerbach and Leo Spitzer* by Geoffrey Green, Lincoln, Nebraska and London, University of Nebraska Press, 1982.

*   *   *

The explicit goals of Erich Auerbach's literary scholarship were quite different from what he achieved. He practiced the discipline of Romance philology, that careful examination of the language and imagery of literature in order to note peculiarities and developments among the European national cultures descended from imperial Rome. And yet, in the process of carrying forth such apparently narrow and restricted investigations of Italian, French, Latin, and related literary languages, Auerbach gave a panoramic account of human self-understanding in Europe from the epics of the ancients to the artistic revolutions of the modern novel.

In particular, Auerbach's major studies covered: 1) changes that occurred between medieval story traditions and those of the Renaissance novelle; 2) how the language and imagery of Dante's *Divine Comedy* reflected not only theological subjects and artistic ideals but also an appreciation of the earthly circumstances of human life; 3) narrative style and referential imagery from antiquity to the latest centuries, and especially the "breakdown" of the classical rhetorical doctrine that "levels of style" were to be more or less sublime according to the subject matter of works; 4) the transformation which resulted from a particular form of Christian imagery connecting concrete narrative materials with the Biblical interpretation of past and future events and types; 5) the relationship between medieval literary language and the public it epitomized; and 6) many other aspects of writers, their relationship to society, and the peculiarities by which their works influenced the general history of Western literature and civilization.

These highly specialized studies of Auerbach were very dependent upon concepts of German Romantic aesthetics and especially its legacy in *Geistesgeschichte* that preserved notions such as the "spirit" of a people or an age, historical "forces," and "inner" and "outer" realities. His use in *Mimesis* of the principle of "style-separation" appears to have been primarily a negative springboard for his positive studies and, therefore, more doctrinaire than persuasive as evidence for his comparisons and contrasts among texts. Throughout his scholarly career Auerbach was reluctant to specify the philosophical underpinning of his scholarly methods, at least in the terms of contemporary philosophers whose concerns and insights greatly paralleled Auerbach's own, such as Dilthey, Husserl, Heidegger, and even the later Sartre. Clearly he was trying to reconcile, in his mind if not in his published work, 19th-century historicism with 20th-century existentialism. He did acknowledge his indebtedness to Hegel as the latter provided a description of the processes of history and a key for Auerbach's own interpretations of Dante. Auerbach also repeatedly turned attention to the 18th-century Italian philosopher, Giambattista Vico; he regarded Vico's observations about history and human creativity as a major source of his own "historical perspectivism."

Yet, given the apparently fragmented nature of Auerbach's *explications des textes* and the philosophical reluctance to which he seemed prone, his achievements in literary and cultural history are nothing less than spectacular. Through his enormously sensitive intuition and the breadth of his vision, Auerbach was able to identify the special contribution of Christianity to the development of Western literature. It was a "figural" view of mankind that conferred transcendent meaning upon ordinary characters and their temporal existence. The story of Christ in the gospels provided Auerbach an almost sacred source for that revolutionary concept of the human condition. Dante's great *Comedy* had both perfected and "eclipsed" this highly original feature of Christian realism. Auerbach also identified the historicity which came to replace Christian eschatology as a dynamic structure of the modern realism of Stendhal, Balzac, Flaubert, and Zola. These French novelists used their art to display how ordinary life was a focal point of the giant movements of social, political, and economic change. Consequently, Auerbach's research offered a vivid account of the modern legacy of the Christian literary imagination as well as its secularization.

The avowed intentions of Auerbach's scholarship concealed, therefore, what its results could not. His was a quest, admittedly at times with rather inexact categories, for ethical and even religious qualities in the literature of Europe, what Auerbach most often called its "seriousness." Avoiding philosophy, he was nonetheless a philosopher of literature, and perhaps even, more profoundly, a perceptive theologian of culture in the traditions of Hegel and Schleiermacher, of Troeltsch and Tillich. As Auerbach said both early in the Dante book and quite late in his *Literary Language and its Public* and as he so eminently showed in *Mimesis,* he wanted to preserve "a lucid and coherent picture" of the "living reality" of Western civilization "and its unity." For ultimately his scholarly tasks and their results were the accomplishments of one who felt bound to "love our epoch for the sake of its abundance of life and the incomparable historical vantage point which it affords" as well as for one whose scholarship was an attempt to "achieve a proper love of the world." Auerbach's selfless dedication and ever sympathetic intuition shaped his interpretations of literary seriousness into acts of love towards the mankind he wished to represent and understand.

—Edward W. Amend

AUSTIN, J(ohn) L(angshaw). British philosopher. Born in Lancaster, 26 March 1911. Educated at the Shrewsbury School; studied at Oxford University, 1929-33 (Fellow of All Souls College, 1933). Served as a Lieutenant-Colonel in the Intelligence Corps, 1939-45; Croix de Guerre, 1951; O.B.E. (Officer, Order of the British Empire), 1945; Officer, Legion of Merit, 1945. Married Jean Coutts in 1941; 4 children. Fellow and Tutor in Philosophy, Magdalen College, Oxford, 1935-39; Junior Proctor, Oxford University, 1949-50; White's Professor of Moral Philosophy, Fellow of Corpus Christi, and Delegate to the University Press, Oxford, 1952-60. William James Lecturer, Harvard University, Cambridge, Massachusetts, 1955; Visiting Professor, University of California, Berkeley, Autumn 1958. Fellow of the British Academy, 1958. *Died 10 February 1960.*

PUBLICATIONS

Philosophy

Philosophical Papers, edited by J.O. Urmson and G.L. Warnock. London, Oxford University Press, 1962.
Sense and Sensibilia: Reconstructed from the Manuscript Notes by G.L. Warnock. London, Oxford University Press, 1962.
How to Do Things with Words: The William James Lectures Delivered at Harvard University, edited by J.O. Urmson. London, Oxford University Press, 1962.
" 'Agathon' and 'Eudaimonia' in the 'Ethics' of Aristotle," in *Aristotle: A Collection of Critical Essays,* edited by J.M.E. Moravcsik. New York, Doubleday, 1967.

Other

Translator, *The Foundations of Arithmetic: A Logico-Mathematical Enquiry into the Concept of Number,* by Gottlob Frege. Oxford, Blackwell, 1950.

Critical Studies: *Symposium on J.L. Austin,* edited by K.T. Fann, London, Routledge, and New York, Humanities Press, 1969 (contains a complete bibliography); *Saving and Meaning: A Main Theme in J.L. Austin's Philosophy* by Mats Furberg, Oxford, Blackwell, 1971; *Essays on J.L. Austin* by Sir Isaiah Berlin and others, Oxford, Clarendon Press, 1973; *J.L. Austin: A Critique of Ordinary Language Philosophy* by Keith Graham, Atlantic Highlands, New Jersey, Humanities Press, 1977.

*   *   *

John Langshaw Austin was a leading figure in the Language Analysis Movement. Austin conceived the central task of philosophy to be the careful analysis of the forms and concepts of ordinary language. He believed not only that language in itself was of sufficient interest for study, but that the subtle distinctions and concepts embedded and already operating in language, having survived the test of time, would give insights into important aspects of the world.

Austin's method of analysis consisted of three basic steps. First, the collection of all the linguistic idioms and expressions which are relevant to the particular area of concern. The second stage of analysis involves imagining as precisely and in as much detail as possible different situations in which expressions could be said to be appropriately used. Austin saw this step as providing data, which was then explained in the third step: giving an account of the meanings of the terms and their interrelationships by the use of the methods of agreement and difference, that is, distinguishing what is present in those cases where we do say, e.g., "deliberately," and what is absent when we don't say "deliberately."

Austin used this technique to examine a number of expressions and to get proper data before making any philosophical generalizations. Thus, in "A Plea for Excuses," he discussed subtle distinctions between "mistake," "accident," and "inadvertence," and in "If's and Can's" dwelt on the meaning of "I can if I can." In "Other Minds," his concern was with what sort of things actually happened when ordinary people are asked "How Do You Know?" In *Sense and Sensibilia,* in a sustained attack on A.J. Ayer and the logical positivists, Austin contrasts the actual complexities and differences in our uses of "looks," "appears," and "seems" and shows that "reality" takes its significance from the implied contrast with "artificial," "fake," "bogus," and "synthetic," as well as "illusion" and "apparent."

Austin also takes language as his subject matter and when he does he is able to formulate some important theories about concrete speech acts and actual utterances in a social context. Thus, in *How to Do Things with Words,* he investigates how saying something can also be doing something, that is, the fact that when someone says anything he performs a number of distinguishable acts. There is the *phonetic act* of making certain noises and the *phatic act* of uttering words in conformity with grammar. Austin discusses three additional acts. The *locutionary* act is using an utterance with a more or less definite sense and reference. The *illusionary act* has to do with how an utterance is to be taken, i.e., asking or answering a question, giving a warning, making an appeal. The *prelocutionary* act has to do with the fact that you may bring about certain effects with your utterance, e.g., convince or persuade. Austin also discusses various kinds of illocutionary forces such as the commissive force which is to promise, bet, vow, adopt, or consent.

Austin was brilliant in his analytic and critical work, but some fault him for his conservatism and his too great attention to minutiae. As his method is no longer in sustained use, it is unlikely to be of lasting influence.

—Jacquelyn Ann K. Kegley

AYER, A(lfred) J(ules). British philosopher. Born in London, 29 October 1910. Educated at Eton College (King's Scholar); studied at Christ Church, Oxford, 1929-32, B.A. (first class honours) 1932, M.A. 1936. Enlisted, then commissioned in the Welsh Guards, 1940, rising to the rank of Captain, 1943; served as Attaché, British Embassy, Paris, 1945. Married Grace Isabel Renée Lees in 1932 (divorced); 1 son, 1 daughter; married Alberta Chapman (journalist Dee Wells) in 1960; 1 son. Lecturer in Philosophy, 1932-35, and Research Lecturer, 1935-44, Christ Church, Oxford; Fellow, 1944-46, and Dean, 1945-46, Wadham College, Oxford (Honorary Fellow, 1957); Grote Professor of the Philosophy of Mind and Logic, University College, University of London, 1946-59; Wykeham Professor of Logic, Oxford University, and Fellow of New College, Oxford, 1959-78. Since 1978, Fellow of Wolfson College, Oxford. Visiting Professor, New York University, 1948-49, and City College of New York, 1961-62; William James Lecturer, Harvard University, Cambridge, Massachusetts, 1970; John Dewey Lecturer, Columbia

University, New York, 1970; Gifford Lecturer, University of St. Andrews, Scotland, 1972-73; Visiting Professor, University of Surrey, 1978. Member, Central Advisory Council for Education (U.K.), 1963-66; President, Humanist Association, 1965-70, and Modern Languages Association, 1966-67; Chairman, Booker Prize Committee, 1978. Honorary doctorate: University of Brussels, 1962; D.Litt.: University of East Anglia, Norwich, 1972; University of London, 1978. Fellow of the British Academy, 1952. Honorary Member, American Academy of Arts and Sciences, 1963; Foreign Member, Royal Danish Academy of Sciences and Letters, 1976; Chevalier de la Légion d'Honneur, 1977; Member, Order of Cyril and Methodius, First Class, Bulgaria, 1977. Knighted, 1970. Address: Wolfson College, Oxford OX2 6UD, England.

PUBLICATIONS

Philosophy

Language, Truth and Logic. London, Gollancz, 1936.
The Foundations of Empirical Knowledge. London and New York, Macmillan, 1940.
Thinking and Meaning: University College London Inaugural Lecture. London, Athlone Press, 1947.
Philosophical Essays. London, Macmillan, and New York, St. Martin's Press, 1954.
"Philosophical Scepticism," in *Contemporary British Philosophy,* edited by H.D. Lewis. London, Allen and Unwin, 1956.
The Problem of Knowledge. London, Macmillan, and New York, St. Martin's Press, 1956.
Philosophy and Language: Oxford University Inaugural Lecture. London, Oxford University Press, 1960.
The Concept of a Person and Other Essays. London, Macmillan, and New York, St. Martin's Press, 1963.
"What I Believe," in *What I Believe.* London, Allen and Unwin, 1966.
The Origins of Pragmatism: Studies in the Philosophy of Charles Saunders Peirce and William James. London, Macmillan, and San Francisco, Freeman Cooper, 1968.
Metaphysics and Common Sense. London, Macmillan, and San Francisco, Freeman Cooper, 1969.
Russell and Moore: The Analytical Heritage: 1970 William James Lectures at Harvard University. Cambridge, Massachusetts, Harvard University Press, and London, Macmillan, 1971.
Probability and Evidence: John Dewey Lectures for 1970 at Columbia University. New York, Columbia University Press, and London, Macmillan, 1972.
The Central Questions of Philosophy. London, Weidenfeld and Nicolson, and New York, Holt Rinehart, 1973.
Hume. London, Oxford University Press, and New York, Hill and Wang, 1980.
Philosophy in the Twentieth Century. London, Weidenfeld and Nicolson, and New York, Random House, 1982.

Other

Part of My Life. London, Collins, 1977; as *Part of My Life: The Memoirs of a Philosopher,* New York, Harcourt Brace, 1974.

Editor, with R. Winch, *British Empirical Philosophy.* London, Routledge, 1952.
Editor, *Logical Positivism.* London, Allen and Unwin, and Glencoe, Illinois, Free Press, 1959.

*

Critical Studies: *Perception and Identity: Essays Presented to*

A.J. Ayer, with His Replies, edited by G.F. Macdonald. London, Macmillan, and Ithaca, New York, Cornell University Press, 1979 (contains a bibliography).

*   *   *

A.J. Ayer's first and most famous book, *Language, Truth and Logic,* was published when he was only 26 years old. As an undergraduate at Oxford he had Gilbert Ryle as his tutor and had conceived a great admiration for Hume and Russell; he had then spent a year in Vienna studying the work of the Vienna Circle. So it is not surprising that this first book was an uncompromising empiricist manifesto. The main tenets are: The Verification Principle, according to which only such statements as are to some degree verifiable or falsifiable empirically have any literal meaning; the claim that speculative metaphysics is impossible since it attempts to go beyond the limits of sense-experience; phenomenalism—the doctrine that all talk about the physical world is reducible to talk of the immediate data of sense; extreme behaviorism about other persons; the doctrine that all moral and other evaluative judgments are non-empirical, and therefore have no literal meaning but are merely expressions of emotion. All this was propounded with the cock-sureness of youth, but also with great intelligence, clarity, and literary grace, so that the book had large sales and wide influence.

Everything had been made too simple, as Ayer himself soon saw. His later work has largely consisted of treatments of the same problems as he had discussed in *Language, Truth and Logic* from the same basic viewpoint, but with far greater recognition of the difficulties and complexities of the issues. Thus his second book, *The Foundations of Empirical Knowledge,* is almost entirely devoted to the problems of perception and the development of a sophisticated version of phenomenalism as an answer to them, whereas in the earlier book these problems had been dismissed in a few dogmatic pages. Ayer has frequently reverted to these problems, especially to defend the terminology of sense-data as being both sound and useful, though not theoretically essential, against the attacks of J.L. Austin and others. But Ayer's treatment of the problem not only became more elaborate; it also became less dogmatic. He became less confident that even a sophisticated phenomenalism could yield all that a robust common sense requires.

Ayer also became less satisfied with the Verification Principle. Stated as a slogan: "the meaning of a statement is its method of verification" it was attractive; but Ayer had to admit that his first attempt to state it precisely was a failure and the still more elaborate version in the introduction to the second edition of *Language, Truth and Logic* also failed; either too much or too little was always admitted to the realm of significant discourse. So Ayer abandoned the search for a single general test of significance in favor of a careful examination of various forms of discourse from an empiricist point of view. Thus the possibility of a metaphysical ontology, once brushed aside, was later queried more carefully on the ground that reality had to be determined against the background of a conceptual system and an area of discourse, while the metaphysician attempted to give an absolute account of reality for which no criteria were available.

Ayer's re-examination of many other problems can be found in *The Problem of Knowledge,* where many of the dogmatic claims of earlier years are replaced by more careful and detailed studies. In later years he has also shown an interest in the history of philosophy which was less conspicuous in earlier years.

—J.O. Urmson

BACHELARD, Gaston (Louis Pierre). French philosopher. Born in Bar-sur-Aube, 27 June 1884. Educated at the Collège de Sézanne, 1902-03, and the University of Paris, licence in mathematics 1912, licence in philosophy 1920, Docteur-ès-lettres 1927. Served in the French Army during World War I. Worked for the postal service in Remiremont, 1903-05, and in Paris, 1907-13. Professor of Physics, Collège de Bar-sur-Aube, 1919-30; Faculté des Lettres, University of Dijon, 1930-40; Professor of History and of the Philosophy of Science, Sorbonne, Paris, 1940-54. Director, Institut d'Histoire des Sciences. Recipient: Grand Prix National aux Lettres, 1961. Honorary doctorate: University of Brussels. Commandeur, Légion d'Honneur, 1951. Member, Académie des Sciences Morales et Politiques, 1955. *Died 10 October 1962.*

PUBLICATIONS

Philosophy of Science and Art

Essai sur la connaissance approchée.   Paris, Vrin, 1927.
Etude sur l'évolution d'un problème de physique: la propagation thermique dans les solides.   Paris, Vrin, 1927.
La Valeur inductive de la relativité.   Paris, Vrin, 1929.
Le Pluralisme cohérent de la chimie moderne.   Paris, Vrin, 1932.
L'Intuition de l'instant: étude sur le Siloë de Gaston Roupnel. Paris, Stock, 1932.
Les Intuitions atomistiques.   Paris, Boivin, 1933.
Le Nouvel Esprit scientifique.   Paris, Alcan, 1934.
La Dialectique de la durée.   Paris, Boivin, 1936.
L'Expérience de l'espace dans la physique contemporaine.   Paris, Alcan, 1937.
La Formation de l'esprit scientifique: contribution à une psychanalyse de la connaissance objective.   Paris, Vrin, 1937.
Le Psychanalyse du feu.   Paris, Gallimard, 1938; as *The Psychoanalysis of Fire,* Boston, Beacon Press, and London, Routledge, 1964.
Lautréamont.   Paris, Corti, 1939.
La Philosophie du "non": essai d'une philosophie du nouvel esprit scientifique.   Paris, Presses Universitaires de France, 1940; as *The Philosophy of No: A Philosophy of the New Scientific Mind,* New York, Orion Press, 1968.
L'Eau et les rêves: essai sur l'imagination de la matière.   Paris, Corti, 1942.
L'Air et les songes: essai sur l'imagination du mouvement.   Paris, Corti, 1943.
La Terre et les rêveries de la volonté.   Paris, Conti, 1948.
La Terre et les rêveries du repos.   Paris, Conti, 1948.
La Rationalisme appliqué.   Paris, Presses Universitaires de France, 1949.
L'Activité rationaliste de la physique contemporaine.   Paris, Presses Universitaires de France, 1951.
Le Matérialisme rationnel.   Paris, Presses Universitaires de France, 1953.
La Poétique de l'espace.   Paris, Presses Universitaires de France, 1957; as *The Poetics of Space,* New York, Orion Press, 1964.
La Poétique de la rêverie.   Paris, Presses Universitaires de France, 1959; as *The Poetics of Reverie,* New York, Orion Press, 1969.
La Flamme d'une chandelle.   Paris, Presses Universitaires de France, 1961.
Le Droit de rêver.   Paris, Presses Universitaires de France, 1970; as *The Right to Dream,* New York, Grossman, 1971.
On Poetic Imagination and Reverie: Selections from the Works of Gaston Bachelard, translated, with an introduction, by Colette Gaudin.   Indianapolis, Bobbs Merrill, 1971.
L'Engagement rationaliste.   Paris, Presses Universitaires de France, 1972.
Etudes.   Paris, Vrin, 1972.

*

Bibliography: "Gaston Bachelard: une bibliographie" by Jean Rummens in *Revue internationale de philosophie* (Brussels), 19, 1964.

Critical Studies: *Hommage à Gaston Bachelard: études de philosophie et d'histoire des sciences* by G. Bouligano and others, Paris, Presses Universitaires de France, 1957; *Gaston Bachelard* by Pierre Quillet, Paris, Seghers, 1964; *Gaston Bachelard, sa vie, son oeuvre, avec un résumé de sa philosophie* by Francois Dagognet, Paris, Presses Universitaires de France, 1965; *Gaston Bachelard ou la conversion à l'imagination* by Jacques Gagey, Paris, Rivière, 1969; *La Révolution de Gaston Bachelard en critique littéraire, ses fondements, ses techniques, sa portée* by Vincent Therrien, Paris, Editions Klincksick, 1970; *Bachelard ou l'concept contre l'image* by Jean-Pierre Roy, Montreal, Les Presses de l'Université de Montréal, 1977.

*   *   *

Gaston Bachelard's work centers around two basic themes, science and art, and thus developed in two different directions, in the direction of philosophy of science and in the direction of "poetics." At first sight these two aspects of his work seem to be completely unrelated. In Bachelard's view, however, both flow from the same source in man himself, namely his creative imagination, whose activities stretch over these two opposite domains; and both must furthermore be related "dialectically." Using ideas taken from psychoanalysis Bachelard tries to show how man time and again suppresses himself mysteriously in these two frameworks of meaning in which he continuously finds himself in a new way, almost like someone else, but then in a purer and richer form.

Bachelard's philosophy of science can be characterized by saying that he tried to develop further the basic ideas of the movement in philosophy of science known in France as "la critique de la science"; that in his own thought he was influenced by Boutroux, Bergson, and Brunschvicg; and that he finally came to views which are rather close to those defended by Gonseth. Yet this characterization, although correct, in no way specifies the uniqueness of Bachelard's own ideas. Perhaps his philosophy can best be described as "dialectic," provided this term is not taken in the sense of the speculative, a priori dialectic of Hegel. According to Bachelard both philosophy and science must be understood as continuous processes. The decisive moment in both is the actual situation, taken not as a final stage, but rather as a phase in which the past is still present and the future is already indicated. In the actual situation in which both philosophy and science find themselves in each case one can distinguish various views that must be transcended in the direction of a rational "system" which employs a dialectic built not on the principle of contradiction, but on the principle of complementarity.

In these ideas Bachelard claims to have been influenced by Kant; but he develops Kant's ideas in a completely different way. For Kant the basic categories are a priori and independent of all experience; for Bachelard there are no basic scientific categories which are a priori in regard to the scientific activities of man. Scientific thought produces its own basic categories by means of its theoretical concern with what is empirically given. In this process the scientist is oriented toward and guided by "what is true," but the latter expression cannot be understood in the traditional sense. For in science one cannot take the truth to refer to a complete, exhaustive, and definitive agreement between the claims made by science and the actual "state of affairs." Scientific truths are always partial and provisional. They continue to turn against the scientists who formulated them, and compel them time and again to take cognizance of the fact that the most obstinate obstacle to the enunciation of a new truth consists in what the scientists themselves have already discovered. This explains why scientific revolutions are so difficult and rare. From this it is also understandable why genuine science is basically method, and why it never can develop into a complete system. To engage in philosophy of science and to reflect critically on science today means that one tries to comprehend the process by which science developed: the correction of the "errors" over time; it also means that one learns to perceive the "truths" which science now offers as being just the last point in a long history of wandering; it finally means that one realizes that our understanding of tomorrow will have to go through the negation of the scientific discourse that takes place today. In the domain of practice, to know something means to be able to foresee it; in the domain of scientific theory, on the other hand, one can never claim that to know means to be able to foresee; in scientific theory, what-is-true is always beyond our scientific claims so that one can never predict the road to be followed in the future.

The most important trait of contemporary science for Bachelard is the continuous interchange of rational and experimental elements, of the a priori and the a posteriori, of "rationalism" and "empiricism" within actual scientific practice. What is truly characteristic of contemporary science is that it tries to understand the empiricism of the "facts," while applying the rationalism of the principles which it itself has developed. This is why philosophy and science develop dialectically in the continuous interchange of rational and empirical elements, without ever reaching a final or absolute point.

Bachelard's philosophy of art, his poetics, is closely related to his philosophy of science. As we have seen already, although science and art seem to be completely different from one another, and often even seem to be in conflict with each other, they nonetheless find their origin in a common root; and, in their mutual dialectical relationship, they need one another because they must "purify" each other. The opposition between science and poetry in content and method, in the final analysis, does not refer back to different basic principles but rather to the different ways in which they flow from the same source. The "substructure" of science is work, whereas that of poetry is dream. Now work and dream are but the two faces of the same "contradiction" which runs through each man's life: to have to be himself by means of what is alien from him, namely the "products" of his work and the fabulous phantasms of his dreams. This is why, by means of its oppositions, our imagination as it were joins us together with ourselves through the detour of work and dream.

In the domain of language this "contradiction" is developed further and articulated, and it is reborn time and again in our scientific claims and our poems. Hyppolite has rightly pointed out that the very core of Bachelard's philosophy is to be found in the fact that he wants to elucidate man's creativity in science and in art, a creativity which is finite and thus continually finds itself opposite an insurmountable obstacle, namely the contingent world, which it transcends but which it can never leave completely behind.

—Joseph Kockelmans

BARTH, Karl. German theologian. Born in Basle, 10 May 1886. Educated at the University of Berne, 1904 and 1907; University of Berlin, 1906; University of Tübingen, 1907, and at the University of Marburg, 1909; ordained, 1909. Married Nelly Hoffmann in 1913; 5 children. Pastor, Reformed Church, Geneva, 1909-11, and Reformed Church, Safenwil, Switzerland, 1911-21; Professor of Reformed Theology, University of Göttingen, 1921-25; Professor of Dogmatics and New Testament Exegetics, University of Münster, 1925-30; Professor of Systematic Theology, University of Bonn, 1930-35 (expelled by the Nazis); Professor of Theology, University of Basle, 1935-62. Gifford Lecturer, University of Edinburgh, 1937-38; Visiting Lecturer, University of Chicago and Princeton University, New Jersey,

1962. Recipient: Sonning Prize, Denmark, 1963; Freud Prize, 1968. Honorary doctorate: University of Münster, 1922; University of Glasgow, 1931; University of Utrecht, 1936; Oxford University, 1938; University of Edinburgh, 1956; University of Strasbourg, 1959; University of Chicago, 1962; the Sorbonne, 1963. Associate Member, Académie des Sciences Morales et Politiques de l'Institut de France. *Died* (in Basle) *10 December 1968.*

PUBLICATIONS

Collections

Gesamtausgabe. Zurich, Evangelischer Verlag, 1971—.

Theology

Suchet Gott, so werdet ihr leben!, with Eduard Thurneysen. Berne, Bäschlin, 1917.
Der Römerbrief. Berne, Bäschlin, 1919; as *The Epistle to the Romans,* Oxford, Oxford University Press, 1935.
Komm, schöpfer Geist!, with Eduard Thurneysen. Munich, Kaiser, 1924; as *Come, Holy Spirit,* New York, Round Table Press, 1933; Edinburgh, Clark, 1934.
Das Wort Gottes und die Theologie (lectures). Munich, Kaiser, 1924; as *The Word of God and the Word of Man,* London, Hodder and Stoughton, 1928; New York, Harper Torchbooks, 1957.
Die Auferstehung der Töten. Munich, Kaiser, 1924; as *The Resurrection of the Dead.* London, Hodder and Stoughton, and New York, Revell, 1933.
Erklärung des Philipperbriefes. Munich, Kaiser, 1926; as *The Epistle to the Phillipians,* London, SCM Press, and Richmond, Virginia, John Knox Press, 1962.
Prolegomena zur christlichen Dogmatik: Die Lehre vom Worte Gottes. Munich, Kaiser, 1927.
Die Theologie und die Kirche. Munich, Kaiser, 1928; as *Theology and Church,* London, SCM Press, 1962.
The Christian Life. London, SCM Press, 1930.
Fides quaerens intellectum: Anselms Beweis der Existenz Gottes. Munich, Kaiser, 1931; as *Anselm: Fides quaerens intellectum,* London, SCM Press, and Richmond, Virginia, John Knox Press, 1960.
Die kirchliche Dogmatik I, 1: Die Lehre vom Worte Gottes. Munich, Kaiser, 1932; as *Church Dogmatics I, 1: The Doctrine of the Word of God,* Edinburgh, Clark, and New York, Scribner, 1936.
Theologische Existenz heute. Munich, Kaiser, 1933; as *Theological Existence Today,* London, Hodder and Stoughton, 1933.
Offenbarung, Kirche, Theologie. Munich, Kaiser, 1934; as *God in Action,* New York, Round Table Press, 1936; Edinburgh, Clark, 1937.
Ein theologischer Briefwechsel, with G. Kittel. Stuttgart, Kohlhammer, 1934.
Nein! Antwort an Emil Brunner. Munich, Kaiser, 1934; as "No!" in *Natural Theology,* London, Bles, 1946.
Credo. Munich, Kaiser, 1935; as *Credo,* New York, Scribner, 1936; London, Hodder and Stoughton, 1937.
Die grosse Barmherzigkeit, with Eduard Thurneysen. Munich, Kaiser, 1935; as *God's Search for Man,* New York, Round Table Press, 1935.
Not und Verheissung im deutschen Kirchenkampf. Berne, BEG, 1938; as *Trouble and Promise in the Struggle of the Church in Germany,* Oxford, Clarendon Press, 1938.
The Knowledge of God and the Service of God, According to the Teaching of the Reformation (lectures). London, Hodder and Stoughton, 1938.
The Holy Ghost and the Christian Life. London, Muller, 1938.
Cross and Swastika: The Ordeal of the German Church. London, SCM Press, 1938.

Die kirchliche Dogmatik I, 2: Die Lehre vom Worte Gottes. Zurich, Evangelischer Verlag, 1939; as *Church Dogmatics I, 2: The Doctrine of the Word of God*, Edinburgh, Clark, and New York, Scribner, 1956.

The Church and the Political Problem of Our Day. London, Hodder and Stoughton, and New York, Scribner, 1939.

Church and State. London, SCM Press, 1939.

Die kirchliche Dogmatik II, 1: Die Lehre von Gott. Zurich, Evangelischer Verlag, 1940; as *Church Dogmatics II, 1: The Doctrine of God*, Edinburgh, Clark, and New York, Scribner, 1957.

La Confession de foi de l'église. Neuchâtel, Switzerland, Delachaux and Niestlé, 1940; as *The Faith of the Church*, New York, Meridian Books, 1958; London, Collins, 1960.

A Letter to Great Britain from Switzerland. London, Sheridan Press, and New York, Macmillan, 1941.

Die kirchliche Dogmatik II, 2: Die Lehre von Gott. Zurich, Evangelischer Verlag, 1942; as *Church Dogmatics II, 2: The Doctrine of God*, Edinburgh, Clark, and New York, Scribner, 1957.

Die kirchliche Lehre von der Taufe. Zurich, Evangelischer Verlag, 1943; as *The Teaching of the Church Regarding Baptism*, London, SCM Press, 1943.

Eine schweitzer Stimme 1938-1945. Zurich, Evangelischer Verlag, 1945.

Die kirchliche Dogmatik III, 1: Die Lehre von der Schöpfung. Zurich, Evangelischer Verlag, 1945; as *Church Dogmatics III, 1: The Doctrine of Creation*, Edinburgh, Clark, and New York, Scribner, 1958.

The Germans and Ourselves. London, Nisbet, 1945.

The Christian Churches and Living Reality. London, Hutchinson, 1946.

Natural Theology. London, Bles, 1946.

Die protestantische Theologie im 19. Jahrhundert: Ihre Geschichte und Vorgeschichte. Zurich, Evangelischer Verlag, 1947; abridged version as *Protestant Thought: From Rousseau to Reitschl*, London, SCM Press, and New York, Harper, 1959; complete work as *Protestant Theology in the Nineteenth Century*, London, SCM Press, and Valley Forge, Pennsylvania, Judson Press, 1972.

Dogmatik im Grundriss. Munich, Kaiser, 1947; as *Dogmatics in Outline*, London, SCM Press, and New York, Philosophical Library, 1949.

The Only Way: How Can the Germans be Saved? New York, Philosophical Library, 1947.

Die kirchliche Dogmatik III, 2: Die Lehre von der Schöpfung. Zurich, Evangelischer Verlag, 1948; as *Church Dogmatics III, 2: The Doctrine of Creation*, Edinburgh, Clark, and New York, Scribner, 1961.

Prayer. Philadelphia, Western Press, 1949.

Die kirchliche Dogmatik III, 3: Die Lehre von der Schöpfung. Zurich, Evangelischer Verlag, 1950; as *Church Dogmatics III, 3: The Doctrine of Creation*, Edinburgh, Clark, and New York, Scribner, 1961.

Die kirchliche Dogmatik III, 4: Die Lehre von der Schöpfung. Zurich, Evangelischer Verlag, 1951; as *Church Dogmatics III, 4: The Doctrine of Creation*, Edinburgh, Clark, and New York, Scribner, 1961.

Rudolf Bultmann: Ein Versuch, ihn zu verstehen. Zurich, Evangelischer Verlag, 1952.

Christus und Adam nach Römer 5. Zurich, Evangelischer Verlag, 1952; as *Christ and Adam: Man and Humanity in Romans 5*, Edinburgh, Oliver and Boyd, 1956; New York, Harper, 1957.

Die kirchliche Dogmatik IV, 1: Die Lehre von der Versöhnung. Zurich, Evangelischer Verlag, 1953; as *Church Dogmatics IV, 1: The Doctrine of Reconciliation*, Edinburgh, Clark, and New York, Scribner, 1956.

Against the Stream: Shorter Post-War Writings 1946-52. London, SCM Press, and New York, Philosophical Library, 1954.

Die kirchliche Dogmatik IV, 2: Die Lehre von der Versöhnung. Zurich, Evangelischer Verlag, 1955; as *Church Dogmatics IV, 2: The Doctrine of Reconciliation*, Edinburgh, Clark, and New York, Scribner, 1958.

Die Menschlichkeit Gottes. Zurich, Evangelischer Verlag, 1956; as *The Humanity of God*, London, Collins, and Richmond, Virginia, John Knox Press, 1961.

Kurze Erklärung des Römersbriefes. Munich, Kaiser, 1956; as *A Shorter Commentary on Romans*, London, SCM Press, and Richmond, Virginia, John Knox Press, 1956.

Den Gefangenen Befreiung. Zurich, Evangelischer Verlag, 1959; as *Deliverance to the Captives*, London, SCM Press, and New York, Harper, 1961.

Die kirchliche Dogmatik IV, 3, 1: Die Lehre von der Versöhnung. Zurich, Evangelischer Verlag, 1959; as *Church Dogmatics IV, 3, 1: The Doctrine of Reconciliation*, Edinburgh, Clark, and New York, Scribner, 1963.

How to Serve God in a Marxist Land. New York, Association Press, 1959.

God, Grace and the Gospel. Edinburgh, Oliver and Boyd, 1959.

Die kirchliche Dogmatik IV, 3, 2. Zurich, Evangelischer Verlag, 1960; as *Church Dogmatics IV, 3, 2*, Edinburgh, Clark, and New York, Scribner, 1965.

Der Götze wackelt. Zurich, Evangelischer Verlag, 1961.

Community, State and Church. New York, Doubleday, 1961.

Church Dogmatics: A Selection. New York, Harper, 1962.

Theology and Church: Shorter Writings 1920-1928. London, SCM Press, and New York, Harper, 1962.

Einführung in die evangelische Theologie. Zurich, Evangelischer Verlag, 1962; as *Evangelical Theory: An Introduction*, London, Weidenfeld and Nicolson, and New York, Holt, 1963.

Karl Barth's Table Talk, edited by John Godsey. Richmond, Virginia, John Knox Press, 1963.

The Great Promise. New York, Philosophical Library, 1963.

The Heidelberg Catechism for Today. Richmond, Virginia, John Knox Press, 1964

God Here and Now. New York, Harper, 1964.

Revolutionary Theology in the Making: Barth-Thurneysen Correspondence 1914-1925. Richmond, Virginia, John Knox Press, 1964.

Selected Prayers. Richmond, Virginia, John Knox Press, 1965.

Rufe mich an! Zurich, Evangelischer Verlag, 1965; as *Call for God*, London SCM Press, and New York, Harper, 1967.

The German Church Conflict. Richmond, Virginia, John Knox Press, 1965.

How I Changed My Mind. Richmond, Virginia, John Knox Press, 1966.

Homiletik. Zurich, Evangelischer Verlag, 1966.

Ad limina apostolorum. Zurich, Evangelischer Verlag, 1967; as *Ad Limina Apostolorum: An Appraisal of Vatican II*, Richmond, Virginia, John Knox Press, 1968.

Law and Gospel. Philadelphia, Fortress Press, 1967.

Die kirchliche Dogmatik IV, 4 (fragments). Zurich, Evangelischer Verlag, 1968; as *Church Dogmatics IV, 4*, Edinburgh, Clark, and New York, Scribner, 1969.

Letzte Zeugnisse. Zurich, Evangelischer Verlag, 1969; as *Final Testimonies*, Grand Rapids, Michigan, Eerdmans, 1969.

Action in Waiting. London, Hodder and Stoughton, and New York, Plough Press, 1969.

Fragments Gay and Grave, edited by Martin Rumscheidt. London, Collins, 1971.

Karl Barth-Rudolf Bultmann: Letters, edited by Bernd Jaspert. Grand Rapids, Michigan, Eerdmans, 1981.

Karl Barth Letters 1961-1968, edited by Jürgen Fangmeier and Hinrich Stoevesandt. Grand Rapids, Michigan, Eerdmans, 1981.

The Christian Life: Church Dogmatics IV, 4 (lecture fragments). Grand Rapids, Michigan, Eerdmans, 1981.

Ethics, edited by Dietrich Braun. New York, Seabury Press,

1981.

The Theology of Schleiermacher, edited by Dietrich Ritschl. Grand Rapids, Michigan, Eerdmans, 1982.

Letters of Karl Barth: A Late Friendship (letters of Barth and Carl Zuckmayer). Grand Rapids, Michigan, Eerdmans, 1982.

*

Critical Studies: *Antwort: Karl Barth zum siebzigsten Geburtstag am 10 May 1956*, Zurich, Evangelischer Verlag, 1956 (contains a bibliography); *The Theology of Karl Barth: An Introduction* by Herbert Hartwell, Philadelphia, Westminster Press, 1964; *Karl Barth: His Life from Letters and Autobiographical Texts*, Philadelphia, Fortress Press, 1976; *Introduction to the Theology of Karl Barth* by Geoffrey W. Bromiley, Grand Rapids, Eerdmans, 1979.

*   *   *

Karl Barth is widely acknowledged to be the most prominent and productive Christian theologian of the 20th century. Barth was a young pastor of the Swiss Reformed Church when he burst upon the theological scene with the publication in 1919 of *The Epistle to the Romans*. This commentary, in which he interpreted the message of Paul the Apostle for a generation of Europeans shocked by World War I, was a prophetic statement that marked a turning from the liberal theology of German cultural Protestantism to a fresh theological movement which during the 1920's was known as "dialectical theology" or "theology of crisis."

Barth's theological concern arose from his experience in the pastoral ministry, where each week he faced the task of preaching the Word of God to an expectant congregation. But, he asked, how can a mere *human* speak the Word of *God*? After all, there is an infinite qualitative difference between the eternal God and temporal human beings, between the Holy One and sinful creatures. Barth claimed to find the answer to this dilemma within "the strange new world of the Bible," where God is depicted as the one who has taken the initiative to overcome the distance and estrangement by speaking his Word through the prophets of Israel and finally by coming to humanity in Jesus Christ, the Word made flesh. When this Word, which is attested by Scripture, is faithfully proclaimed in the preaching of the church, God through an act of grace speaks to humans today through the power of the Holy Spirit.

Barth opposed liberal theology because he believed it had become too anthropocentric and had lost the Bible's awesome sense of the deity of God, of the "wholly Other" whose self-revelation in the history of Israel and in Jesus Christ has brought reconciliation to the world. Liberal theology, in his estimation, had accommodated itself too much to the idealistic philosophy and bourgeois ethics of the 19th century. It centered attention on the psychological and historical study of human religious experience, assumed the basic goodness of humanity and the inevitability of social progress, reduced theology to philosophy of religion, and depicted Christianity as the highest form of world religion. Such a theology, contended Barth, could no longer address the urgent issues of a 20th century world torn by war. It lacks the realism and power of the biblical view, which is centered not on human religion but on divine revelation, not on the human search for the divine but on the marvelous way God has taken to come and save sinful humanity, not on the word of man but on the Word of God.

By recalling the church to its true foundation in the event of divine revelation, Barth helped to revitalize its life and thought. Church theology must be a theology of the Word of God, he insisted, which for him meant that it must also be a dialectical theology. By "dialectical" Barth meant that in its endeavor to speak the Word of God, the church would always have to say both yes and no. Humanly speaking, the task is impossible, because only God can speak God's Word; and yet God in an act of grace chooses to speak through human language to those who hear by faith. Barth's point was that the church never *controls* divine revelation, as if it could capture it in an infallible Bible or orthodox doctrines or supernatural dogmas or mystical experiences. Rather, revelation is an *event* which God causes to happen, and the church must be aware of its own limitation and depend utterly upon the promise of God to be present when obedient testimony is given to Jesus Christ as God's incarnate Word.

From 1921 until 1935 Barth was a professor of theology in Germany, first at Göttingen, then at Münster, and finally at Bonn. During this period he worked to develop a theology that was Christ-centered and eschewed any acknowledgement of the validity of so-called natural theology, that is, a theology whose knowledge of God allegedly stems from human rationality independent of the divine revelation in Christ. With the rise of Nazism in Germany, Barth's theology became a bulwark against the attempt of "German Christians" to see in the rise of Hitler God's "new revelation" in history. Barth's opposition to Nazi interference in the affairs of the churches in Germany and his refusal to swear an unconditional loyalty oath to Hitler resulted in his expulsion in 1935. He then returned to Switzerland, where he was appointed to the chair of systematic theology at the University of Basle, a position he held with distinction until his retirement in 1962.

Though his bibliography exceeded 600 items during his lifetime, Barth's major theological contribution consisted of his multi-volumed *Church Dogmatics*, the first volume of which appeared in 1932. In this monumental work, which had progressed to 13 volumes but which was still unfinished at his death, Barth conducted a critical inquiry into the truth of the message of the church by examining it in the light of God's Word attested in Holy Scripture. Undertaking his task in the spirit of Anselm of Canterbury, who defined theology as "faith in search of understanding," Barth set forth his own interpretation of the various Christian doctrines in constant dialogue with the witness of Scripture and church tradition. By a method of continuous questioning under the normative authority of the Word of God Barth believed the truth of God would emerge. Since God's truth is a *living* truth that can never be captured in propositional form, Barth wanted above all to avoid the appearance that his theology was controlled by a philosophical system or was deduced from a rational principle or set of principles.

According to Barth, God's Word is none other than God's own self who meets us in the act of revelation as the one Lord who exists in the triune form of Father, Son, and Holy Spirit. For Barth, the doctrine of the Trinity attempts to do justice to the unity of God, that is, to account for the fact that it is the same God who creates us and all things, who reconciles us in Jesus of Nazareth, and whose indwelling Spirit guides our life to final redemption. The one God exists in three distinguishable yet mutually interrelated modes of being: as Creator, Reconciler, and Redeemer.

Barth defined the triune God revealed in Christ as "the One who loves in freedom." God is love in himself, stressed Barth, and thus it is a sign of the overflowing of divine love that God freely decided from all eternity to create the world and to enter into a covenant of grace with humankind. Humans are elected to be God's covenant-partners. It is in this sense of divine purpose that Barth could speak of God's everlasting covenant with all humanity in Jesus Christ, who in his historical life and death and resurrection fulfilled the covenant on behalf of and in the place of a sinful humanity that had rebelled and broken the covenant. Jesus Christ restores the covenant and calls humans to a life of responsive love as God's partners. In Barth's view, creation is the external basis of the covenant, just as the covenant is the internal basis of creation.

Although Barth conceded that much worthwhile knowledge about human beings could be obtained through the human and physical sciences, he insisted that their true nature is revealed only in their relationship to God, that is, in their determination to be God's covenant-partners. Barth interpreted the biblical view that humans are created in the image of God to mean that they are created male and female to be in a loving relationship with each other. This relationship is analogous to the relationship between Father and Son in the Godhead and finds its proper fulfillment in the relation between Christ and the church.

Barth developed his doctrine of reconciliation (God with us!) in a way that integrates christology (Jesus Christ as truly God, truly man, and God-man), hamartiology (sin as pride, sloth, and falsehood), soteriology (human-kind's justification, sanctification, and vocation), ecclesiology (the Spirit's gathering, upbuilding, and sending of the church), and the Christian life (in faith, in love, and in hope).

If in his early theology Barth emphasized the uniqueness and transcendence of God, his theology in *Church Dogmatics* focuses increasingly on what he called the "humanity of God." By this he meant that in Jesus Christ there is no isolation of God from humanity or of humanity from God. Rather, in him we encounter the history and dialogue in which God and humanity meet and are together. In him we find the true God as man's loyal partner and true man as God's loyal partner. Thus Jesus Christ is the Mediator, the Reconciler, between God and humanity. Jesus Christ attests to humanity God's free grace and to God humanity's free gratitude, and as such he is the Revealer of both God and man. This affirmation was the center of Barth's theology and thus the key to understanding him as a theologian.

—John D. Godsey

BARTHES, Roland (Gérard).   French critic.   Born in Cherbourg, 12 November 1915. Educated at the Lycée de Bayonne, 1916-24, Lycée Montaigne, Paris, 1924-30, and the Lycée Louis-le-Grand, Paris, 1930-34, baccalaureate 1933, 1934; also studied at the Sorbonne, Paris; licence in classical letters, 1939; diplôme d'études supérieures in Greek tragedy, 1941; licence in grammar and philology, 1943. Reader at Debreczen, Hungary, 1937; Professor of Literature and Rectoral Delegate, Third and Fourth Forms, Lycée de Biarritz, 1939-40; Professor and Rectoral Delegate, Lycées Voltaire and Carnot, Paris, 1940-41; Assistant Librarian, then Professor, Institute Français, Bucharest, and Reader, University of Bucharest, 1948-49; Reader, University of Alexandria, 1949-50; Member, Instruction Branch, Direction Général des Affaires Culturelles, Ministry of Foreign Affairs, Paris, 1950-52; Officer of Instruction and Researcher in Lexicography, 1952-54, and Research Attaché in Sociology, 1955-59, Centre National de la Recherche Scientifique, Paris; Chairman, 1960-62, and Director of Studies and Professor of the Sociology of Signs, Symbols and Collective Representations, 1962-76, VI Section, Social and Economic Sciences, Ecole Pratique des Hautes Etudes, Paris; Member, Collège de France, Paris, 1975: Professor of Literary Semiology, 1976-80. Visiting Professor, Johns Hopkins University, Baltimore, 1967-68. Founder, Groupe de Théâtre Antique, University of Paris, 1936; Co-Founder, *Théâtre Populaire*, 1953, and *Arguments*, 1956. Member of the Jury, Prix Medicis, 1973-80. Chevalier des Palmes Académiques. *Died* (in Paris) *26 March 1980*.

PUBLICATIONS

Criticism/Semiology

Le Degré zéro de l'écriture.   Paris, Le Seuil, 1953; as *Writing Degree Zero [and] Elements of Semiology*, London, Cape,

1967, and New York, Hill and Wang, 1968.
Michelet par lui-même.   Paris, Le Seuil, 1954.
Mythologies.   Paris, Le Seuil, 1957; selections as *Mythologies*, London, Cape, 1972, and New York, Hill and Wang, 1973.
Sur Racine.   Paris, Le Seuil, 1963; as *On Racine*, New York, Hill and Wang, 1964.
Essais critiques.   Paris, Le Seuil, 1964; as *Critical Essays*, Evanston, Illinois, Northwestern University Press, 1972.
Eléments de sémiologie avec Le Degré zéro de l'écriture.   Paris, Gonthier, 1965.
Critique et vérité.   Paris, Le Seuil, 1966.
Système de la Mode.   Paris, Le Seuil, 1967.
S/Z.   Paris, Le Seuil, 1970; as *S/Z*, London, Cape, and New York, Hill and Wang, 1975.
L'Empire des signes.   Geneva, Skira, 1970; as *The Empire of Signs*, New York, Hill and Wang, 1982.
Sade, Fourier, Loyola.   Paris, Le Seuil, 1971; as *Sade/Fourier/Loyola*, New York, Hill and Wang, 1976.
Nouveaux essais critiques.   Paris, Le Seuil, 1972; as *New Critical Essays*, New York, Hill and Wang, 1980.
Le Plaisir du texte.   Paris, Le Seuil, 1972; as *The Pleasure of the Text*, London, Cape, 1975, and New York, Hill and Wang, 1976.
Leçon inaugurale.   Paris, Collège de France, 1977.
Image, Music, Text (essays selected and translated by Stephen Heath).   London, Fontana, and New York, Hill and Wang, 1977.
Fragments d'un discours amoureux.   Paris, Le Seuil, 1977; as *A Lover's Discourse*, New York, Hill and Wang, 1978.
The Eiffel Tower and Other Mythologies.   New York, Hill and Wang, 1979.
Le Chambre claire.   Paris, Le Seuil, 1980; as *Camera Lucida*, New York, Hill and Wang, 1981.

Other

Exégèse et herméneutique, with others.   Paris, Le Seuil, 1971.
Analyse structurale et exégèse biblique, with others.   Paris, Le Seuil, 1973; as *Structural Analysis and Biblical Exegesis: Interpretation and Essays by Roland Barthes and Others*, Pittsburgh, Pennsylvania, Pickwick Press, 1974.
Roland Barthes par Roland Barthes.   Paris, Le Seuil, 1975; as *Roland Barthes by Roland Barthes*, New York, Hill and Wang, 1977.

*

Critical Studies: *Nouvelle Critique ou nouvelle imposture* by Raymond Picard, Paris, Pauvert, 1965, as *New Criticism or New Fraud?*, Pullman, Washington State University Press, 1969; *Vertige du déplacement: lecture de Barthes* by Stephen Heath, Paris, Fayard, 1974; *Roland Barthes: A Conservative Estimate* by Philip Thody, London, Macmillan, 1977; *Comprendre Roland Barthes* by J.B. Fages, Paris, Privat, 1979; "Reflections: Writing Itself: On Roland Barthes" by Susan Sontag in *The New Yorker*, 28 April 1982.

*   *   *

Roland Barthes's most important work is based on the idea first developed by the Swiss philologist Ferdinand de Saussure (1857-1913) in his *Cours de Linguistique générale* in 1913: that all signs are arbitrary, and that there is no such thing as the "natural" expression of a thought, an emotion, or an attitude. Saussure himself had dealt primarily with language, and exploited in a linguistic context the implications of the fact that the words *vache* and *cow* mean the same thing by virtue of their place in the structure of French or English and not because of a mysterious link between the word and the animal. It was Barthes who carried out Saussure's own ambition to develop what the *Cours de Linguistique générale* called "semiology," and defined as "a science which studies the way signs behave in social life."

After the publication of a short book of critical essays called *Le Degré zéro de l'écriture*, it was in 1957, with the appearance of *Mythologies*, that Barthes was recognised as one of the most original commentators on how we communicate with one another through language, clothes, and gesture. It is not, as the famous essay on all-in wrestling observed, because the nature of our thoughts and feelings produced spontaneous words and gestures which naturally express our innermost essence. It is because we live in a society dominated by codes, and the way the all-in wrestlers exploit these codes is a kind of paradigm case for how communication works in general. For when they make grandiose gestures expressing intense pain or anger, they are not really expressing what is happening either inside or outside them. If they did everything they pretended to do, they would kill one another. They are exploiting the conventions which say that anger is expressed by raising one's hands to heaven, or despair by hammering on the canvas. But the fact that there is nothing real behind the gestures illustrates how, in fiction or in the theatre, writers communicate with their audience. They do so not by describing what really happened but by constructing an elaborate network of signs, and these signs work because of the system of codes and conventions already in the mind of the people who read the novel or watch the play.

Barthes described his own ambition as that of "totally destroying the idea that signs are natural," and there are those who have seen him as pushing an open door. He himself always considered that it was nevertheless characteristic of bourgeois, middle-class society to cling to the notion that since content determines form, there is only one way of saying something, which is the "natural" way. Barthes attacked this notion in his most influential work on fiction, the essay *S/Z*, an analysis of a Balzac short story, not long after he had caused a major literary row with his essay on Racine in 1963. This book was violently attacked by a leading Racinian scholar, Raymond Picard, who strongly objected to the mixture of Freudianism and structuralism which Barthes had used in his analysis of Racinian tragedy. Barthes's reply in 1966, *Critique et vérité*, contained an impassioned appeal to readers to break loose from ready-made ideas of what Racine was like and look at his plays not only in the terms of modern ideologies but also as examples of how literature is always first and foremost made up of a struggle of language with itself.

Barthes analysed clothes as instruments of communication in *Système de la Mode*, insisting on how the way we dress expresses, in terms of the conventions of our times, the vision which we have of the kind of person we would like to be. He expressed another aspect of his personality in his hedonistic approach both to literature and to sex in *Le Plaisir du Texte* and *Fragments d'un discours amoureux*. He made little secret of his homosexuality, and in spite of his election in 1975 to the prestigious Collège de France, always felt something of an outsider in French society. His opponents criticize the frequent obscurity of his language, his attribution to unnamed opponents of impossibly naïve ideas on language and literature, and his unmotivated opposition to "bourgeois" society. His admirers see him as opening the way to the vision of literature as primarily text, the use of words to create patterns which are to be appreciated not for what they tell us about society or about the author himself but for the light they throw on the functioning of language itself.

—Philip Thody

BARTLETT, Frederic (Charles). British psychologist. Born in Stow-on-the-Wold, Gloucestershire, 20 October 1886. Studied at the University of London, B.A. 1909, M.A. 1911; St. John's College, Cambridge, 1st class honours in moral sciences 1914. Married Emily Mary Smith; 2 sons. Assistant to the Director, 1914-22, and Director, 1922-52, of the Psychological Laboratory, and Professor of Experimental Psychology, 1931-52, Cambridge University. Huxley Lecturer, University of Birmingham, 1957-58. Editor, *British Journal of Psychology*, 1924-48. President, British Psychological Society, 1950. Recipient: Baly Medal, 1943; Huxley Medal, 1943; Royal Medal, 1952; Longacre Award, Aero Medical Association, 1952; Gold Medal, International Academy of Aviation and Space Medicine, 1964. Honorary doctorate: University of Athens, 1937; Princeton University, New Jersey, 1947; University of Louvain, 1949; University of London, 1949; University of Edinburgh, 1961; Oxford University, 1962; University of Padua, 1965. Fellow of the Royal Society, 1932. Foreign Associate Member, French Psychological Society, 1930; Member, American Philosophical Association, 1946; Foreign Associate Member, American National Academy of Sciences, 1947; Honorary Member, Swedish Psychological Society, 1952, Spanish Psychological Society, 1955, Swiss Psychological Society, 1956, Turkish Psychological Society, 1957, and International Association for Applied Psychology, 1958; Foreign Honorary Member, American Academy of Arts and Sciences, 1959; Honorary Member, Experimental Psychological Society, 1960, and Italian Psychological Society, 1963. C.B.E. (Commander, Order of the British Empire), 1941; knighted, 1948. *Died 30 September 1969.*

PUBLICATIONS

Psychology

Exercises in Logic.   London, W.B. Clive, 1913.
Psychology and Primitive Culture.   Cambridge, Cambridge University Press, and New York, Macmillan, 1923.
Psychology and the Soldier.   Cambridge, Cambridge University Press, 1927.
Remembering: A Study in Experimental and Social Psychology.   Cambridge, Cambridge University Press, and New York, Macmillan, 1932.
Two Studies in the Psychological Effects of Noise, with others.   London, H.M. Stationers Office, 1932.
The Problem of Noise.   Cambridge, Cambridge University Press, 1934.
Political Propaganda.   Cambridge, Cambridge University Press, 1940.
Religion as Experience, Belief, Action (lectures).   London and New York, Oxford University Press, 1950.
Planned Seeing: Some Psychological Experiments, with N.H. Mackworth.   London, H.M. Stationery Office, 1950.
The Mind at Work and Play.   London, Allen and Unwin, 1951.
Some Recent Developments in Psychology in Great Britain (lecture).   Istanbul, Baha Matbaasi, 1957.
Thinking: An Experimental and Social Study.   London, Allen and Unwin, and New York, Basic Books, 1958.

Other

Editor, with others, *The Study of Society: Methods and Problems.*   London, Kegan Paul, 1932.

*   *   *

Frederic Bartlett will be remembered primarily for two things: his classic work *Remembering* and his stimulating leadership of the Cambridge school of psychology, which he directed for 30 years, and which he continued to inspire up to his death in 1969. His personal influence on British psychology in general, and Cambridge psychology in particular, was very great.

Remembering was notable both for the methods of experimentation that Bartlett employed, and for the conclusions he arrived at. Experimentation on memory processes began in 1885 with the work of the German psychologist Ebbinghaus who endeavoured to arrive at an understanding of the basic processes of memorizing by using the simplest material without overtones of meaning or emotional significance, which he regarded as disturbing factors. His findings were enormously interesting, but Bartlett believed that they did not throw much light on memory as it actually operated in conditions of real life. His own experiments were designed to overcome this by employing material "which any normal individual deals with constantly in his daily activities." So he used picture material and stories, and explored the way in which these were distorted and changed in the course of repeated reproduction over intervals of time. And, as Bartlett had always been interested in social situations (an interest he acquired while studying with W.H.R. Rivers, who was both psychologist and social anthropologist), he conducted a series of studies designed to throw light on how memories were changed when passed on through a group of people. In all this work Bartlett's experimental techniques were simple. He employed neither elaborate equipment, nor abstruse quantification and statistics. Nevertheless his experiments yielded some remarkably interesting results. This was partly because Bartlett never forgot that "The psychologist, whether he uses experimental methods, or not, is dealing not simply with reactions, but with human beings."

Remembering was a function which in real life was always linked with other aspects of the individual's make-up. It could not be divorced from perceiving, imaging and constructive thinking. It was subject to the influence of attitudes, moods, and personality. All this came out clearly in Bartlett's experimental results. His first experiments were on perception. He exposed simple diagrams and drawings for very short intervals of time in a special exposure apparatus, and asked his subjects to report what they saw. The process of perception, which at first sight seemed to be so simple and direct, was shown to be exceedingly complex and to involve previous experience and constructive processes, as well as to be affected by idiosyncracies of attitude and temperament. A great deal of what is said to be perceived is actually inferred. Similarly, in the reproduction of material from memory there is a great deal of rationalization, what Bartlett termed, in one of his most quoted phrases, "an effort after meaning." The subject aimed, he maintained, "to render material acceptable, understandable, comfortable, straightforward, to rob it of all puzzling elements." Accurate recall was the exception rather than the rule. It was the constructive—rather than the purely reproductive—aspects of memory on which Bartlett laid most stress.

There is no doubt that Bartlett's work when it was first published opened up new territory and suggested new problems. Although he probably overestimated the constructive side of memory, and underestimated the routine, mechanical aspects, his work was a valuable corrective to the unduly mechanistic slant of many experimental, particularly behaviouristic, psychologists. His own theoretical explanations in terms of "schemata" (dynamic, organised structures) were somewhat less successful. Nevertheless the influence of his work is far from exhausted half a century later. It still lives, not only in many of his pupils, but further afield.

None of Bartlett's other published work had so epoch-making an impact as *Remembering*. Many of his books, though stimulating and suggestive, were fairly popular in style, and his one other major piece of research, *Thinking*, revealed his limitations rather than his strengths. There was a certain naive simplicity about the book: the experimental tools consisted mainly of paper and pencil; the methodology was primitive; and there was an almost total neglect of the work of other psychologists working in the area. Yet the book still had some of the usual Bartlett qualities of appeal and freshness.

Apart from *Remembering* Bartlett's main memorial must be the Cambridge school of psychology together with its many brilliant pupils, and the Applied Psychology Unit (also located in Cambridge), which he was largely responsible for founding, and which under a series of able directors has over the last 40 years produced a stream of valuable work on problems closely related to real life issues. Both in the Cambridge department of psychology, and in the Applied Psychology Unit, in spite of their growing sophistication, the core of Bartlett's outlook has tended to prevail. Bartlett was essentially an empiricist. His mind was singularly uncluttered, and he was capable of looking at real life problems without too heavy a load of theoretical preconceptions. Indeed he positively distrusted theory; and he eschewed elaborate methodology, particularly statistical methodology, which he regarded as rather a shoddy makeshift, and a substitute for experimental exploration. The Applied Psychology Unit, established in 1944, grew directly out of Bartlett's involvement with wartime problems. The need to operate complex equipment, often under stress and difficult environmental conditions, demanded a study of the human factors involved in maintaining adequate performance. Early in the war special committees, such as the Flying Personnel Research Committee, were set up to study problems such as skill fatigue, which was liable to affect pilots in flights of long duration and danger. Bartlett was deeply involved in his work, which led to the focussing of his interest on the topic of skill, and particularly the element of timing in high level performance. The work of the unit broadened out to include such topics as vigilance, fatigue, man-machine control problems, visual search, the effects of environmental noise, the application of information theory to psychology, and various aspects of stress. Though primarily guided by practical considerations and the problems of human performance and adjustment, the work of the unit has also been of great theoretical and academic interest. Almost until his death Bartlett remained in close touch with the group, and continued to be a stimulating background influence.

—Leslie Hearnshaw

BATESON, Gregory. American anthropologist. Born in Grantchester, England, 9 May 1904; emigrated to the United States, 1940; naturalized, 1956. Educated at Charterhouse School, London, 1917-21; studied at St. John's College, Cambridge (Entrance Scholar, 1922; Foundation Scholar, 1924; Anthony Wilkin Student, 1927-29), B.Sc. in biology 1925, M.A. in anthropology 1930. Married the anthropologist Margaret Mead in 1936 (divorced, 1950); 1 daughter; Elizabeth Sumner in 1951 (divorced, 1958); 1 son; Lois Cammack in 1961; 1 daughter. Engaged in anthropological field work, in New Britain, 1927-28, in New Guinea, 1928-33 and 1939, and in Bali, 1936-38. Lecturer in Linguistics, University of Sydney, Australia, 1928; Fellow, St. John's College, Cambridge, 1931-37; Anthropological Film Analyst, Museum of Modern Art, New York, 1942-43; Lecturer, Naval School of Government and Administration, Columbia University, New York, 1943-44; Regional Specialist, United States Office of Strategic Services, Washington, D.C., 1944-47; Visiting Professor of Anthropology, New School for Social Research, New York, 1946-47, and Harvard University, Cambridge, Massachusetts, 1947-48; Research Associate in Psychiatry and Communications, Langley-Porter Clinic, San Francisco, 1949-51; Ethnologist and Researcher on Alcoholism, Veterans Administration Hospital, Palo Alto, California, and Visiting Professor of Anthropology, Stanford University, Palo Alto, 1951-62; Associate Research Director in Ethnology, Communications Research Institute, Virgin Islands, 1962-64; Chief, Biological Relations Division, Oceanic Institute, Waimanalo, Hawaii, 1964-72; Professor of Anthropology and Ethnology, University of California at Santa Cruz, 1972-78 (Member, University of California Board of Regents, 1976-78); Scholar-in-Residence,

Esalen Institute, Big Sur, California, 1978-80. Recipient: Guggenheim Fellowship, 1946-47; Frieda Fromm-Reichmann Award for Research in Schizophrenia, 1962; Career Development Award, National Institutes of Mental Health, 1964. D.Sc.: Northwestern University, Evanston, Illinois, 1972. Fellow, American Association for the Advancement of Science. *Died* (in San Francisco) *4 July 1980.*

PUBLICATIONS

Anthropology

Naven: A Survey of the Problems Suggested by a Composite Picture of the Culture of a New Guinea Tribe Drawn from Three Points of View. Cambridge, Cambridge University Press, 1936; revised edition, Stanford, California, Stanford University Press, 1958.
Balinese Character: A Photographic Analysis, with Margaret Mead. New York, National Academy of Sciences, 1943.
Communication: The Social Matrix of Psychiatry, with Jürgen Ruesch. New York, Norton, 1951.
Steps to an Ecology of the Mind. San Francisco, Chandler, and London, Intertext, 1972.
Mind and Nature: A Necessary Unity. New York, Dutton, 1978; London, Wildwood House, 1979.

*

Critical Studies: *Our Own Metaphor* by Mary Catherine Bateson, New York, Knopf, 1972; *Blackberry Winter* by Margaret Mead, New York, Morrow, 1972; *About Bateson: Essays on Gregory Bateson,* edited by John Brockman, New York, Dutton, 1977; *The Legacy of a Scientist* by David Lipset, Englewood Cliffs, New Jersey, Prentice-Hall, 1980 (contains a bibliography); *Rigor and Imagination: Essays on the Legacy of Gregory Bateson,* edited by C. Wilder-Mott and John H. Weakland, New York, Praeger, 1981.

*   *   *

To a diverse range of subjects, from animal communication to Iatmul ritual, from schizophrenia to biological evolution, Gregory Bateson brought an unflagging interest in examining the basic presuppositions of how we think about things, as well as an informing vision of the systemic nature of experience. The first of these features was actually a particular manifestation of the second: he examined the terms we use to think about things precisely because he believed them to be the least examined part of the *system* that constitutes our experience and knowledge. Throughout his remarkably diverse work, we find a consistent account of how systems of relationships establish the features of their parts.

One of Bateson's favorite illustrations of his approach was an engine:

> Imagine a machine in which we distinguish, say, four parts, which I have loosely called "flywheel," "governor," "fuel," and "cylinder." In addition, the machine is connected to the outside world in two ways, "energy input" and "load,"... The machine is circular in the sense that the flywheel drives governor which alters fuel supply which feeds cylinder which, in turn, drives flywheel.
> *Because the system is circular, effects of events at any point in the circuit can be carried all around...* (emphasis added).

Bateson's work focussed on how such systems respond to input from their environment. For instance, a decrease in the load on an engine might cause the flywheel to move faster, but how would this affect the system as a whole? If the engine were constructed with positive feedback between the flywheel and the governor, an increase in the rate of the flywheel would cause an increase in the fuel supply to the cylinder, making the flywheel go faster, and so on. Thus, the system would continuously accelerate, quite likely causing some part to wear out and the system to stop. By contrast, engines are usually built with a negative feedback between the rate of the flywheel and the governor's regulation of the fuel supply, and such systems maintain a relatively constant operation. In both cases, the system's environment can be thought of as information that is taken as input to one part, transformed, and passed on to the next part.

In developing his analyses of systems, Bateson built upon Norbert Wiener's work on cybernetics, the mathematical study of the flow and control of information. Bateson applied these concepts to a wide range of problems, demonstrating relationships between topics usually separated by the boundaries of academic disciplines. This multi-disciplinary quality gives Bateson's writing a sense of discovery rarely found in such sophisticated academic work. As a result, Bateson achieved an unusually large "underground" audience, even though he never gained a place in the established canon of any academic discipline.

Trained as an anthropologist, Bateson did his first field work with the Baining of New Britain, but this project was, by his own account, "a failure." His next field work, among the Iatmul of New Guinea, resulted in *Naven,* a hidden classic in the history of ethnography. *Naven* epitomizes the general process of learning which Bateson described at length in his later works: he tries out a number of different approaches within the text itself, then provides an epilogue offering a more integrated formulation of his analysis, and in the second edition, offers yet another critique of his earlier work. This willingness to reconsider his own work should not distract from his consistent interest in analyzing Iatmul rituals (the Naven ceremonies of the book's title) as messages and responses between inter-related parts of the larger social system: messages between men and women, initiates and elders, and one community and another. *Naven* differed from the functionalist orthodoxy of the anthropology and sociology of its time in a number of ways: perhaps most importantly, Bateson recognized that the Iatmul social system not only constructed the means of its operation, but also constructed its ends. Thus, although Bateson provided a synchronic account, he did not assume that the Iatmul social system functioned in an unchanging manner due to psychological and economic exigencies.

In his work on schizophrenia, which has greatly influenced the recent "Family Therapy" movement, Bateson argued that schizophrenia results when a child is raised in a family system that both encourages and penalizes alternative conceivable responses to input from the environment. In brief, if a child does "x," he is told to do "not-x," and if he responds by following this advice, he receives an opposite message. Since no coherent response is possible, the child swings between alternative modes of interacting with the world, caught in "a double-bind." Bateson's work on schizophrenia (which he conducted as an official "Ethnologist" at a Veterans Administration hospital) demonstrated Bateson's anthropological commitment to field work: he not only interviewed patients at the hospital, but he joined them for visits to their families.

In his later work, Bateson applied his interest in the behavior of systems to the problems of biological evolution and learning. He developed a unified approach to these two phenomena as "stochastic systems," or systems that "combine a random component with a selective process." In Bateson's view, continuation of a species requires an ability to respond to changes in the input from the environment, but such a response must not be total: a species must maintain the capacity to adapt to future changes in the environment. Thus, at the level of the organism, changes in the environment may quickly eliminate ill-adapted individuals, but at the level of the gene pool, the possibility for diverse alternatives (generated by the random recombination of genes) is maintained. Not only are unexpressed genes preserved, but acquired adaptations do not directly alter the gene pool: a learned pattern for finding food does not become a programmed instruction in the next generation.

Learning, in Bateson's view, follows a similar pattern of elimination from a range of conceivable responses to a new input. For instance, a rat in a maze will try many paths to find food, and will eventually eliminate wrong paths, thus learning the correct path to the food. Such learning is a more flexible response to environmental conditions than alterations to the gene pool, but organisms also exhibit an even more flexible response, learning to learn, or "deutero-learning." To continue our example, the amount of time it takes a rat to learn a new maze decreases as the rat is exposed to more and more different mazes: the rat learns something about how to "solve" mazes. This more general level of learning allows a great flexibility in responding to change, and allows a decreasing reliance on fixed patterns of behavior.

Fundamentally, Bateson's own research was an attempt not to learn, nor even to learn to learn, but to learn to learn to learn... Always seeking a greater freedom from the fixity of established patterns of knowing the world, while continuing to respect the diversity of patterns as part of a rich human resource.

—Daniel Alan Segal

BEADLE, George W(ells). American geneticist. Born in Wahoo, Nebraska, 22 October 1903. Studied at the University of Nebraska, Lincoln, B.S. 1926, M.S. 1927; Cornell University, Ithaca, New York, Ph.D. 1931. Married Marion Cecile Hill in 1928 (divorced, 1953); 1 son; married Muriel Barnett in 1953. Teaching Assistant and Experimentalist, Cornell University, 1926-31; National Research Council Fellow, 1931-33, and Instructor, 1933-35, California Institute of Technology, Pasadena; Guest Investigator, Institut de Biologie, Paris, 1935; Assistant Professor of Genetics, Harvard University, Cambridge, Massachusetts, 1936-37; Professor of Biology and Chairman of the Division of Biology, California Institute of Technology, 1946-60; Acting Dean of the Faculty, 1960-61, President, 1961-68, William E. Wrather Distinguished Service Professor, 1969-75, and since 1968 President Emeritus and since 1975 Professor Emeritus, University of Chicago. George Eastman Visiting Professor, Oxford University, 1958-59. President, American Association for the Advancement of Science, 1946, Genetics Society of America, 1955, and Chicago Horticultural Society, 1968-71; Member of the Council, National Academy of Sciences, 1969-72. Trustee, Pomona College, 1958-61, and Museum of Science and Industry, Chicago, 1967-68. Recipient: Lasker Award, American Public Health Association, 1950; Dyer Award, 1951; Emil C. Hansen Prize, Denmark, 1953; Albert Einstein Commemorative Award in Science, 1958; Nobel Prize in Medicine and Physiology, with E.L. Tatum and J. Lederberg, 1958; National Award, American Cancer Society, 1959; Kimber Genetics Award, National Academy of Sciences, 1960; Priestley Memorial Award, 1967; Edison Award, with Muriel B. Beadle, 1967; Donald Forsha Jones Medal, 1972. Honorary M.A.: Oxford University, 1958; honorary doctorate: Yale University, New Haven, Connecticut, 1947; University of Nebraska, 1949; Northwestern University, Evanston, Illinois, 1952; Rutgers University, New Brunswick, New Jersey, 1954; Kenyon College, Gambier, Ohio, 1955; Wesleyan University, Middletown, Connecticut, 1959; Oxford University, 1959; University of Birmingham, England, 1959; Pomona College, California, 1961; Lake Forest College, Illinois, 1962; University of California at Los Angeles, 1962; University of Miami, 1963; Brandeis University, Waltham, Massachusetts, 1963; University of Rochester, New York, 1963; University of Illinois, Urbana, 1963; Brown University, Providence, Rhode Island, 1963; Kansas State University, Manhattan, 1964; University of Pennsylvania, Philadelphia, 1964; Jewish Theological Seminary

of America, New York, 1966; Wabash College, Crawfordsville, Indiana, 1966; Johns Hopkins University, Baltimore, 1966; Beloit College, Wisconsin, 1966; Syracuse University, New York, 1966; De Paul University, Chicago, 1969; University of Chicago, 1969; Canisius College, Buffalo, New York, 1969; Knox College, Galesburg, Illinois, 1969; University of Michigan, Ann Arbor, 1969; Loyola University, Chicago, 1970; Ohio Northern University, Ada, 1970; Carroll College, Waukesha, Wisconsin, 1971; Roosevelt University, Chicago, 1971; Hanover College, Indiana, 1971; Eureka College, Illinois, 1972; Butler University, Indianapolis, 1973; Gustavus Adolphus College, St. Peter, Minnesota, 1975; Indiana State University, Terre Haute, 1976. Foreign Member, Royal Society, London, 1960. Address: Department of Biology, University of Chicago, Chicago, Illinois 60637, U.S.A.

PUBLICATIONS

Genetics

An Introduction to Genetics, with A.H. Sturtevant.   Philadelphia, Saunders, 1939.
The Place of Genetics in Modern Biology.   Cambridge, Massachusetts Institute of Technology, 1959.
Science and Resources: Prospects and Implications of Technological Advance, with others, edited by Henry Jarrett.   Baltimore, Johns Hopkins University Press, 1959.
Genetics and Modern Biology.   Philadelphia, American Philosophical Society, 1963.
The Language of Life: An Introduction to the Science of Genetics, with Muriel Beadle.   New York, Doubleday, 1966.

*   *   *

George W. Beadle, geneticist, Nobel laureate, former president of the University of Chicago, helped found the field of biochemical genetics by showing that genes regulate certain biochemical processes. Beadle's earliest scientific work was influenced by an important line of investigation begun during the first decade of this century by Sir Archibald Garrod. Garrod and his co-workers were interested in the underlying cause of a group of congenital metabolic diseases in man. One of these diseases was alcaptonuria (a condition in which homogentisic acid appears in urine—an extremely abnormal clinical finding), the cause of which Garrod attributed to the inactivity of the enzyme which metabolizes homogentisic acid. He hypothesized that the lack of the necessary enzyme was due to a mutant gene. Thus Garrod had articulated the concept of a gene-enzyme reaction system in which the two components were interrelated in specific fashions. It would be several decades before his brilliant insight would be demonstrated experimentally by Beadle and his close associates.

One attempt at solving the mystery surrounding the interactions between genes and enzymes began around 1933 when Boris Ephrussi and Beadle collaborated in developing an organ transplantation technique in the fruit fly (*Drosophila*), which was genetically the best understood organism of the time. Beadle joined Ephrussi in Paris where they transplanted eye buds from *Drosophila* of one genetic constitution into the body of larvae of different genetic constitutions. From these transplantation experiments Beadle and Ephrussi observed that the color of a transplanted eye varied according to the genetic make-up of both the original bud and the host. They explained this observation by hypothesizing that certain genes on the *Drosophila* chromosome controlled certain steps in a biochemical pathway leading eventually to an end product—in this case, eye pigment. They elaborated on their hypothesis by stating that a mutant gene blocked a certain step in a biochemical pathway thus preventing the completion of the production of an end product. If there were many steps contributing to the synthesis of a product, Beadle and

Ephrussi proposed that each step might be controlled by the action of a single gene. For example, during the reaction A—B—C if all the genes were normal then an end-product "C" would be metabolized. But, if the genes governing the second step (...B—C) was mutant, "C" could not be produced, leaving only the synthesis of product "B." Their transplantation experiments led Beadle and Ephrussi to believe that genes control certain steps in a biochemical pathway, but neither of them hypothesized at the time *how* genes acted as controllers.

After completing his transplantation experiments Beadle collaborated with Edward L. Tatum (a microbiologist and biochemist whom Beadle lured to Stanford University) and began working with a simple organism, *Neurospora* (a bread fungus). There were many advantages of *Neurospora* over *Drosophila* for laboratory study of biochemical genetics. Specifically, *Neurospora* generated offspring in a relatively short period of time; it was easy to grow and maintain; and its biochemical mutants could be identified with ease.

In order to discover the secret of *how* genes effected the control of biochemical pathways Beadle and Tatum designed a simple but elegant experiment. Since the nutritional requirements of *Neurospora* were such that it could grow on a "minimal" medium of sugar plus only one vitamin (biotin), Beadle and Tatum assumed that the fungus synthesized all other nutrients necessary for its growth. They began their experiment by exposing *Neurospora* to radiation (X-rays), which would increase the rate of mutation of genes responsible for triggering the synthesis of certain nutrients. They predicted that the mutant genes would result in the blockage of certain steps in a biochemical pathway necessary for the synthesis of nutrients. Since certain nutrients were no longer being synthesized, the fungus could not grow on a "minimal" medium. For example, spores with a mutant gene might grow only on a "complete" medium supplemented with amino acids and vitamins.

The preparation of thousands of single spore cultures demonstrated beautifully the truth behind Beadle's and Tatum's prediction. Spores known to contain mutations were grown on a number of "modified" media (each lacking specific nutrients, but containing all the others). If a certain spore could grow on all media except the one lacking, for example, Vitamin "B", then it was reasoned that this spore had a mutant gene which blocked the biochemical pathway for the synthesis of that certain Vitamin "B." More specifically, since it was known that each step in a biochemical pathway was catalyzed by a specific enzyme, Beadle and Tatum concluded that gene mutations must cause enzymatic changes. This became a fundamental concept in genetics, namely, during biochemical reactions each step is facilitated by an enzyme produced by a single gene. This concept became known as the "one gene-one enzyme" hypothesis—a landmark in the history of modern genetics.

Perhaps the most important contribution to genetics made by Beadle was his use of an organism in which gene function (at a biochemical level) could be studied experimentally. The introduction of *Neurospora* in biology did for biochemical genetics what *Drosophila* had done for classical chromosomal genetics. Beadle and Tatum shared the 1958 Nobel Prize for their work on *Neurospora*. In a speech delivered at the award ceremony, Beadle said, "In this long, roundabout way, we had rediscovered what Garrod had seen so clearly many years before." Indeed, they had demonstrated experimentally what Garrod had stated. But through their demonstration of the "one gene-one enzyme" concept they also had opened a new path of biological research by conclusively unlocking the secret of *how* genes act as "controllers" in biochemical pathways.

—Randall Davey Bird

BEARD, Charles A(ustin). American historian. Born near Knightstown, Indiana, 27 November 1874. Studied at De Pauw University, Greencastle, Indiana, Ph.B. 1898; Oxford University, 1898-99; Cornell University, Ithaca, New York, 1899-1901; Columbia University, New York, M.A. 1903, Ph.D. 1904. Married Mary Ritter in 1900; 1 daughter, 1 son. Adjunct Professor, 1907-10, Associate Professor, 1910-15, and Professor, 1915-17, Columbia University; Director, Training School for Public Service, New York Bureau of Municipal Research, 1917-22; Adviser, Institute of Municipal Research, Tokyo, 1922; Adviser to Viscount Geto, Japanese Minister of Home Affairs, 1923; Visiting Professor of Government, Columbia University, 1939 and 1941; Professor, Johns Hopkins University, Baltimore, 1940-41. President, American Political Science Association, 1926, Association of History Teachers of the Middle States and Maryland, 1932, and National Association for Adult Education, 1936. Recipient: Gold Medal of National Institute of Arts and Letters in History, 1948. Honorary doctorate: De Pauw University, 1917; Columbia University, 1944. Member, National Institute of Arts and Letters, 1939; American Academy of Arts and Letters, 1946. *Died 1 September 1948.*

PUBLICATIONS

History and Political Science

The Industrial Revolution. London, S. Sonnenschein, 1901; New York, Macmillan, 1906.
The Office of Justice of the Peace in England in Its Origin and Development. New York, Columbia University Press, and London, P. King, 1904.
An Introduction to the English Historians. New York, Macmillan, 1906.
The Development of Modern Europe: An Introduction to the Study of Current History, with James Harvey Robinson. Boston, Ginn, 2 vols., 1907-08; enlarged edition, 1929-30.
European Sobriety in the Presence of the Balkan Crisis. New York, American Branch of the Association for International Conciliation, 1908.
Lectures on Science, Philosophy, and Art, 1907-08. New York, Columbia University Press, 1908.
Politics: A Lecture Delivered at Columbia University in the Series on Science, Philosophy and Art, February 12, 1908. New York, Columbia University Press, 1908.
Readings in Modern European History: A Collection of Extracts from the Sources Chosen with the Purpose of Illustrating some of the Chief Phases of the Development of Europe During the Last Two Hundred Years, with James Harvey Robinson. Boston, Ginn, 2 vols., 1908-09.
American Government and Politics. New York, Macmillan, 1910.
American City Government: A Survey of Newer Tendencies. New York, Century, 1912; London, Unwin, 1913.
Outlines of European History, with James Harvey Robinson. Boston, Ginn, 2 vols., 1912-14; enlarged edition, 1927.
The Supreme Court and the Constitution. New York, Macmillan, 1912.
An Economic Interpretation of the Constitution of the United States. New York, Macmillan, 1913.
American Citizenship, with Mary R. Beard. New York, Macmillan, 1914.
Contemporary American History, 1877-1913. New York, Macmillan, 1914.
Economic Origins of Jeffersonian Democracy. New York, Macmillan, 1915.
Six Years' Experience with the Direct Primary in New Jersey. New York, 1917.
The History of the American People, with William C. Bagley. New York, Macmillan, 1918; with an additional chapter by Maximo M. Kalaw, 1932.

The History of the American People, for Grammar Grades and Junior High Schools, with William C. Bagley. New York, Macmillan, 1918.

How American Citizens Govern Themselves. New York, Education Bureau, National War Work Council of Young Men's Christian Association, 1919.

A Manual to Accompany The History of the American People, with William C. Bagley. New York, 1919; revised edition with a chapter on the Philippines by Maximo M. Kalaw, 1932.

National Governments and the World War, with Frederic A. Ogg. New York, Macmillan, 1919.

Public Service in America. Philadelphia, Municipal Court, 1919.

Report of Reconstruction Commission to Governor Alfred E. Smith on Retrenchment and Reorganization in the State Government, October 10, 1919, with others. Albany, New York, J.B. Lyon, 1919.

The Traction Crisis in New York. New York, Bureau of Municipal Research and Training School for Public Service, 1919.

A First Book in American History, with William C. Bagley. New York, Macmillan, 1920.

History of Europe, Our Own Times: The Eighteenth and Nineteenth Centuries, the Opening of the Twentieth Century, the World War, and Recent Events, with James Harvey Robinson. Boston, Ginn, 1921.

History of the United States, with Mary R. Beard. New York, Macmillan, 1921.

Cross Currents in Europe To-day. Boston, Marshall Jones, 1922; London, Harrap, 1923.

The Economic Basis of Politics. New York, Knopf, 1922; enlarged edition, 1945.

Our Old World Background, with William C. Bagley. New York, Macmillan, 1922.

The Administration and Politics of Tokyo: A Survey and Opinions. New York, Macmillan, 1922.

A Collection of Lectures (in Japanese). Tokyo, Shisei Chosakai, 1923.

My Views Regarding the Reconstruction of Tokyo (in Japanese). Tokyo, Shisei Chosa-kai, 1924.

Government Research, Past, Present and Future. New York, Municipal Administration Service, 1926.

The Rise of American Civilization, with Mary R. Beard: volume 1, The Agricultural Era, New York, Macmillan, and London, Cape, 1927; volume 2, The Industrial Era, New York, Macmillan, and London, Cape, 1927; volume 3, America in Midpassage, New York, Macmillan, and London, Cape, 1939; volume 4, The American Spirit: A Study of the Idea of Civilization in the United States, New York, Macmillan, 1942.

The American Party Battle. New York, Macmillan, 1928.

The Balkan Pivot: Yugoslavia: A Study in Government and Administration, with George Radin. New York, Macmillan, 1929.

The Outline of the Capital Reconstruction Work. Tokyo, Sanshusha, 1929.

The Constitution and Social Issues. New York, Council for Social Action, 193?

The American Leviathan: The Republic in the Machine Age, with William Beard. New York, Macmillan, 1930; London, Cape, 1931.

The Myth of Rugged American Individualism. New York, Day, 1931.

A Charter for the Social Sciences in the Schools. New York, Scribner, 1932.

Elementary World History: A Revised and Simplified Edition of Our Old World Background, with William C. Bagley. New York, Macmillan, 1932.

Issues of Domestic Policy. Chicago, University of Chicago Press, 1932.

Issues of Foreign Policy. Chicago, University of Chicago Press, 1932.

The Navy: Defense or Portent? New York and London, Harper, 1932.

The Future Comes: A Study of the New Deal, with George H.E. Smith. New York, Macmillan, 1933.

The Open Door at Home: A Trial Philosophy of National Interest, with George H.E. Smith. New York, Macmillan, 1933.

Conclusions and Recommendations of the Commission, with the Commission on Social Studies in the Schools. New York, Scribner, 1934.

Hitlerism and Our Liberties: Text of Address given by Professor Charles A. Beard at the New School for Social Research, Tuesday, April 10, 1934. New York, 1934?

The Idea of National Interest: An Analytical Study in American Foreign Policy, with George H.E. Smith. New York, Macmillan, 1934.

The Nature of the Social Sciences in Relation to Objectives of Instruction. New York, Scribner, 1934.

The Recovery Program (1933-34): A Study of the Depression and the Fight to Overcome It, with George H.E. Smith. New York, Macmillan, 1934.

The Presidents in American History. New York, J. Messner, 1935.

Schools in the Story of Culture, with William G. Carr. Washington, D.C., National Education Association, 1935.

Cumulative Annual Guide to American Government and Politics. New York, Macmillan, 1935-38.

A Correlated Curriculum. New York, Appleton, 1936.

The Devil Theory of War: An Inquiry into the Nature of History and the Possibility of Keeping out of War. New York, Vanguard Press, 1936.

The Discussion of Human Affairs: An Inquiry into the Nature of the Statements, Assertions, Allegations, Claims, Heats, Tempers, Distempers, Dogmas, and Contentions which Appear when Human Affairs Are Discussed and into the Possibility of Putting Some Rhyme and Reason into Processes of Discussion. New York, Macmillan, 1936.

Jefferson, Corporations, and the Constitution. Washington, National Home Library Foundation, 1936.

The Making of American Civilization, with Mary R. Beard. New York, Macmillan, 1937; enlarged edition, 1939.

Our Own Age, with others. Boston, Ginn, 1937.

The Unique Function of Education in American Democracy. Washington, D.C., Educational Policies Commission, National Education Association of the United States and the Department of Superintendent, 1937.

America Today, with others. New York, Macmillan, 1938.

America Yesterday, with others. New York, Macmillan, 1938.

America Yesterday and Today, with others. New York, Macmillan, 1938.

Giddy Minds and Foreign Quarrels: An Estimate of American Foreign Policy. New York, Macmillan, 1939.

Philosophy, Science and Art of Public Administration: Address Delivered Before the Annual Conference of the Governmental Research Association, Princeton, New Jersey, September eighth, 1939. Princeton, New Jersey, Governmental Research Association, 1939.

A Foreign Policy for America. New York, Knopf, 1940.

The Lincoln of Carl Sandburg: Some Reviews of "Abraham Lincoln: The War Years," with others. New York, Harcourt Brace, 1940?

The Old Deal and the New, with George H.E. Smith. New York, Macmillan, 1940.

Our Own Age, with others. Boston, Ginn, 1940.

Public Policy and the General Welfare. New York, Farrar and Rinehart, 1941.

The Republic: Conversations on Fundamentals. New York, Viking Press, 1943.

A Basic History of the United States, with Mary R. Beard. New York, Doubleday, 1944.

American Foreign Policy in the Making, 1932-1940: A Study in Responsibilities. New Haven, Connecticut, Yale University Press, 1946.

President Roosevelt and the Coming of the War, 1941: A Study in Appearance and Realities. New Haven, Connecticut, Yale University Press, 1948.

The Economic Basis of Politics and Related Writings, edited by William Beard. New York, Vintage Books, 1957.

Other

Editor, *Readings in American Government and Politics.* New York, Macmillan, 1909.

Editor, *Loose Leaf Digest of Short Ballot Charters: A Documentary History of The Commission Form of Municipal Government.* New York, The Short Ballot Organization, 1911.

Editor, *Documents on the State-Wide Initiative, Referendum and Recall,* with Birl E. Schultz. New York, Macmillan, 1912.

Editor, *Whither Mankind: A Panorama of Modern Civilization.* New York, Longman, 1928.

Editor, *Toward Civilization.* New York, Longman, 1930.

Editor, *America Faces the Future.* Boston, Houghton Mifflin, 1932.

Editor, *A Century of Progress.* New York and London, Harper, 1933.

Editor, *A Charter for the Social Sciences in the Schools.* New York, Scribner, 1932.

Editor, *Current Problems of Public Policy: A Collection of Materials,* with George H.E. Smith. New York, Macmillan, 1936.

Editor, *The Enduring Federalist.* New York, Doubleday, 1948.

*

Critical Studies: *The Influence of Charles A. Beard upon American Historiography* by Maurice Blinkoff, Buffalo, New York, Committee on Publications of the Roswell Park Publication Fund, 1936; *Beard and the Constitution: The History of an Idea* by Richard Hofstadter, Indianapolis, Bobbs Merrill, 1950; *Charles A. Beard: An Appraisal,* edited by Howard Kennedy Beale, Lexington, University of Kentucky Press, 1954; *The Making of Charles A. Beard: An Interpretation* by Mary R. Beard, New York, Exposition Press, 1955; *Charles Beard and the Constitution: A Critical Analysis of "An Economic Interpretation of the Constitution"* by Robert Eldon Brown, Princeton, New Jersey, Princeton University Press, 1956; *The Historical Thinking of Charles A. Beard* by Elias Berg, Stockholm, Almqvist and Wiskell, 1957; *The Pragmatic Revolt in American History: Carl Becker and Charles Beard* by Cushing Strout, New Haven, Connecticut, Yale University Press, 1958; *Turner and Beard: American Historical Writing Reconsidered* by Lee Benson, Glencoe, Illinois, Free Press, 1960; *The Political and Social Thought of Charles A. Beard* by Bernard C. Borning, Seattle, University of Washington Press, 1962 (contains an extensive bibliography); *The Progressive Historians: Turner, Beard, Parrington* by Richard Hofstadter, Chicago, University of Chicago Press, 1968; *Charles A. Beard and the Social Studies: A Book of Readings,* edited by Raymond A. Ducharme, Jr., New York, Teachers College Press, 1969; *Charles A. Beard and American Foreign Policy* by Thomas C. Kennedy, Gainesville, University Presses of Florida, 1975; *Charles A. Beard: An Observance of the Centennial of His Birth, De Pauw University, Greencastle, Indiana, October 11-12, 1974,* Greencastle, Indiana, De Pauw University Press, 1976.

*   *   *

No historian of the United States has had a more enduring influence upon the interpretation of the American past than Charles A. Beard. He received his doctorate from Columbia University in 1904 after several years of post-graduate study at Oxford, and then joined Columbia's political science department. Although he supported American entry into the first

World War, he resigned in 1917 in protest over the dismissal of colleagues who had opposed American participation. His resignation marked a life-long public commitment to the principle of academic freedom. He never again held an academic appointment, embarking on a successful career of historical writing, publishing some 50 volumes before his death.

His most significant scholarly work and the one which has had the most lasting impact was *An Economic Interpretation of the Constitution,* a work which won scholarly approval but shocked popular commentators. Beard depicted the framers of the Constitution as self-interested men of property whose primary concern at Philadelphia was to protect their interests to the disadvantage of the common man. He viewed the Constitution as an essentially undemocratic document arguing that the vast majority of Americans were unable to participate in its ratification because of restrictive property qualifications on the suffrage. According to Beard, if the small farmer had been able to vote, the Constitution would have been rejected. In drawing these conclusions Beard was reflecting the influence both of the critical atmosphere of the Progressive movement and of economic concepts presented in the work of a Columbia colleague, E.R.A. Seligman's *The Economic Interpretation of History.* In this book Seligman formulated in a modified way the Marxist interpretation of history. Beard's application of Marxian concepts was highly ambiguous alternating between a strict economic determinism and a limited economic interpretation which merely accepted economic motivation as one factor in the historical process. Beard utilized the then unusual methodology of collective biography basing many of his conclusions on the fact that all the framers were men of property and that some of them were public security holders. It is in this last aspect that Beard has been severely criticized for having relied upon much too small a sample of biographical sketches to justify such rigid conclusions. He also assumed that very small security holders had a vested interest akin to that of the largest holders, who were, in fact, not numerous at the convention. Another serious defect has been exposed in the last quarter century as modern researchers have demonstrated that the property qualification was not as restrictive as Beard assumed.

Although much of the data used by Beard is now considered inadequate, his basic point of view has been accepted; namely, that the Constitution was the work of men of property who were deeply concerned about the creation of a stable political order. However, his conclusion that they were indifferent to the libertarian goals of the Revolution has not been sustained. Since Beard's work no American historian can ignore the role of economics as a potent, although not necessarily the sole, factor in historical developments. Beard continued the exploration of the role of economics in a second, less influential, monograph, *The Economic Origins of Jeffersonian Democracy* in which he analyzed the first party conflict in terms of a capitalist-agrarian struggle. While historians now agree that this was an element in the party battles, it is apparent that he gave too much weight to the disagreement over Alexander Hamilton's fiscal program and insufficient attention to the impact of ideological issues aroused by the French Revolution. Beard also failed to consider the question of why, if economic factors were central, the victory of the Jeffersonian Republicans did not result in a real change of economic policy.

While his influence upon scholars was enormous, Beard enjoyed an even greater popular success with *The Rise of American Civilization,* written with his wife Mary. This narrative history, which sold more than 12,000,000 copies, was written in a florid rhetorical style contrasting to the austere tone of Beard's scholarly works. He continued to place primary stress on economic factors, and his analysis of the Civil War as a conflict between the industrial North and the agricultural South was widely accepted by the public as well as by scholars. He gave little weight to the moral issue of slavery as a factor in the conflict, an aspect now regarded as central by students of this era.

In his work in the 1930's Beard drifted from his earlier insistence upon economic interpretation to a position of historical relativism, noting that the historian was a product of his own age, reflecting its issues and its attitudes. Hence, there could be no absolutely objective scientific history—a position well illustrated in his own career. In the books published during the last two decades of his career he demonstrated a more eclectic interpretation and, indeed, a certain scepticism. While the distinction of his early work was acknowledged, his later publications brought a decline in his reputation as he manifested a powerful strain of isolationism in such books as *The Idea of National Interest* and *The Devil Theory of War*. In these books he advocated a program of national self-sufficiency and withdrawal from European concerns as a means of avoiding war. It was his contention that wars, such as World War I, had been welcomed by politicians as a means of evading serious domestic crises. This sceptical view erupted in full force in his last two books, *American Foreign Policy in the Making* and *President Roosevelt and the Coming of the War*, in which he portrayed Roosevelt as deliberately leading the nation into war as a means of seeking a solution to the domestic crisis. These books were less works of scholarship than briefs in behalf of a narrow interpretation of national interest. They were widely criticized for their bias and distortions and added nothing to the solid fame which he had enjoyed as a pioneer in opening new fields of historical interpretation.

—Harry Ammon

BEARDSLEY, Monroe C(urtis). American philosopher and aesthetician. Born in Bridgeport, Connecticut, 10 December 1915. Studied at Yale University, New Haven, Connecticut, B.A. 1936, Ph.D. 1939. Married Elizabeth Lane in 1940; 2 sons. Instructor, 1940-44, and Assistant Professor, 1946-47, Yale University; Assistant Professor, Mt. Holyoke College, South Hadley, Massachusetts, 1944-46; Assistant Professor, 1947-52, Associate Professor, 1952-59, and Professor of Philosophy, 1959-69, Swarthmore College, Pennsylvania. Since 1969, Professor of Philosophy, Temple University, Philadelphia. Editor, with Elizabeth Beardsley, Foundations of Philosophy series, Prentice Hall, from 1964. Trustee and President, American Society for Aesthetics, 1967-68. Recipient: Guggenheim Fellowship, 1950-51. Fellow, American Academy of Arts and Sciences. Address: Department of Philosophy, Temple University, Philadelphia, Pennsylvania 19122, U.S.A.

PUBLICATIONS

Philosophy and Aesthetics

Practical Logic. New York, Prentice Hall, 1950.
Aids to Study for Theme and Form: An Introduction to Literature, with Robert Daniel and Glenn Leggett. Englewood Cliffs, New Jersey, Prentice Hall, 1956.
"The Intentional Fallacy" and "The Affective Fallacy," with William K. Wimsatt, Jr., in *The Verbal Icon: Studies in the Meaning of Poetry*. Lexington, University of Kentucky Press, 1954; London, Methuen, 1970.
Aesthetics: Problems in the Philosophy of Criticism. New York, Harcourt Brace, 1958.
Philosophical Thinking, with Elizabeth Lane Beardsley. New York, Harcourt Brace, 1965.
Aesthetics from Classical Greece to the Present: A Short History. New York, Macmillan, 1966.
Literature and Aesthetics. Indianapolis, Bobbs Merrill, 1968.
The Possibility of Criticism. Detroit, Wayne State University Press, 1970.

From an Aesthetic Point of View. Ithaca, New York, Cornell University Press, 1982.

Other

Thinking Straight: A Guide for Readers and Writers. New York, Prentice Hall, 1950.
Writing with Reason: Logic for Composition. Englewood Cliffs, New Jersey, Prentice Hall, 1976.
History as a Tool in Critical Interpretation: A Symposium, with others, edited by Thomas F. Rugh and Erin R. Silva. Provo, Utah, Brigham Young University Press, 1978.

Editor, *The European Philosophers from Descartes to Nietzsche*. New York, Modern Library, 1960.
Editor, with Herbert Schueller, *Aesthetic Inquiry: Essays on Art Criticism and the Philosophy of Art*. Belmont, California, Dickenson, 1967.
Editor, *Modes of Argument*. Indianapolis, Bobbs Merrill, 1967.

*   *   *

Monroe C. Beardsley's writings are chiefly in the philosophy of art and criticism. His earliest studies, written in collaboration with W.K. Wimsatt, Jr., already take up topics that recur in his later work. In their diagnosis of two forms of fallacies, the intentional and the affective, the authors present an account of the critical relevance of creative origins and reader responses.

The intentional fallacy is the confusion of "the poem and its origins." The term "origins" includes incitement, inspiration, and occasion. Thus the authors attach more to the term "intention" than we ordinarily do when we say that "X's intention was Y in saying or doing Z." The fallacy adduces evidence about motives, purposes, and goals as well as psychological causes to explicate the work. The affective fallacy confuses what the poem is with what it does, the latter including not only affects but any form of psychological consequences and associations. The authors give a semantical formulation to the problem. According to A.J. Ayer and C.L. Stevenson, there are two kinds of meanings, descriptive or cognitive meaning and emotive meaning. They are technically independent since the former is in principle verifiable while the latter is not. Thus the habitual connections of certain thoughts to feelings are "quasi-dependent." Such a view, brought to bear on literary texts, would, aside from ontological problems about imaginative discourse, lead to skepticism or relativism about the "proper" emotive response to them. Common sense must close up the "great divide" between thought and feeling by reasserting the incontrovertible fact that a text displays a pattern of thought and associated with it in a veridical fashion is the different but equally important structure of emotions. (An account of this relationship is formulated more precisely below in the discussion of the semantical theory of literature.) Proper critical talk will keep the poem intact, not dissolving it among its sources and consequences, especially since what the poem says can differ from what was "intended" and how readers are affected. Only the object can be a safe guide.

In this manner, Beardsley reaffirms the doctrine of the autonomy of art which functions as a presupposition to his subsequent delineations of artistic creation, aesthetic experience, and literary theory, writings that stretch over more than quarter of a century.

Artistic creation: Beardsley notices two typical ways of structuring a theory of creation: the propulsive theory that emphasizes the impetus that activates the artist, e.g., a strong emotion or a memorable experience; or the finalist theory that pinpoints the ends and goals set up by the artist. In either case, one would expect the initial impulse or activating goal to color the ensuing activity. Yet in actual practice as reported by artists, the situation is varied, some works strongly retaining the original affective color or intention but others scarcely recognizable as related to its origins. Contrary to both theories, artistic creation is a "self-correcting activity." After each artistic move, the object is a "new individual," and the artist must decide "whether he wants to mean what he is saying." On the propulsive theory, artistic creation stops on the exhaustion of the moving impulse and on the finalist view when the object and the initiating purpose match. For the autonomist, the *artist* is finished when he can no longer improve on the work, but the artistic *work* is done when the result can stand on its own as an object of aesthetic enjoyment. The creativity lies "in the operation of the work itself."

Aesthetic experience: Skeptical criticism of the concept of the aesthetic, Beardsley finds, is directed at reductionist theories that attempt to relate the aesthetic to a specific sort of thing, property or sets of psychological affects. A work of art, objectively, is constituted by a complex of perceptual qualities. Concomitantly, there are affective responses in the perceiver which are conditioned ("caused") by these objective properties. As a third factor, there is the aesthetic experience which is constituted by these affective factors. Under favorable circumstances, each of these may be said to be coherent, complete, etc. A complex of affective responses often displays the characteristics of gestalt-closure, these being just the phenomena of integration, balance, harmony, etc., that are subjective yet prominent in critical language. Aesthetic experience can be, thus, defined in terms of the unities that characterize the perceiver's mental activity. The *degrees* of aesthetic quality (e.g., better, best) have reference to the pleasurable aspect of this experience, some aesthetic experiences encompassing more vivid, more intense, richer pleasures than others.

Literary theory: The term "literature" is equivocal. It has both neutral and evaluative usages. Further, it can function narrowly to mean "imaginative literature" ("the central concept of literature" being poetry and prose fiction), or more widely to include forms such as diaries, letters, histories, and discursive treatises. Beardsley's discussion is confined to the neutral and restricted senses. 1) A taxonomy of meaning: A speaker's utterance has the capacity to affect the listener, either in his beliefs (cognitive import) or feelings (emotive import). The utterance also conveys information about the speaker's beliefs (cognitive purport) or his feelings (emotive purport); and the listener can also infer other things about the speaker, his social status, his religious or political convictions (general purport). Strictly, "meaning" refers to the cognitive import and purport but the import of utterances depends on the wider emotive and general purport as well, there being mutual dependence of thought and feeling. 2) Moreover, not only declarative sentences but other forms of sentences also convey information. 3) One can alternatively divide the taxonomy above into primary meanings—what utterances state and evoke, and secondary meanings—what they suggest by way of general purport. Secondary meanings include choices among alternative words and syntax, sentence and topical order, repetition, parallel structures, figures of speech, contextual connotations—i.e., all the rhetorical and compositional devices used in speech. 4) Summarily, then, "a literary work is a discourse in which an important part of the meaning is implicit." In such discourse, secondary meaning is not fully realized. By contrast, some types of writing, e.g., legal and technical reports, restrict the communication to explicit, primary meanings. 5) To explicate an utterance in a specific context is "to declare its meaning," contrasting explication with definition which abstractly formulates the general meaning of a word, its designation. Explicatory statements are part of the description of a poem. This is the "semantical theory of literature" developed in *Aesthetics*.

(For a brief period, Beardsley advocated another account of literary discourse, that it was, as he wrote in *The Possibility of Criticism*, "a complex imitation of a compound illocutionary act." On either view, "poems are distinguished by their complexity of meaning." Beardsley now seems to be diffident about this later formulation.)

Theory of criticism: The following observations of critical

phenomenon presuppose its objectivity: individuals, critics as well as laymen, act as if there were real disagreements in aesthetic responses and evaluations; they argue and present considerations pro and con and attempt to build up cases. In Beardsley's diagnosis of the veridicality of criticism, all the topics discussed previously converge: that authorial intentions cannot reliably or relevantly function as the source of meaning; that although critics refer to all sorts of interesting things, the ground of their talk is the judging of "an object (that is the poem)—in terms of its actual or possible effects"; that in an interpretation, the critic does not bring a prior and often external schema to the object. Instead, he elucidates the local meanings (i.e., micro-meaning) of a text and interrelates them in the light of larger, regional meanings (i.e., macro-meaning). The atoms of micro-meanings and their compounds include not only cognitive meaning but emotive import and purport (connotations) and general purport (suggestions); and the latter two are not merely something psychological and personal but also rank among the stubborn data for the interpreter. A poem as a whole is a complex of various types of utterances and this complex constitutes "public semantic fact."

—Albert Tsugawa

BECKER, Carl (Lotus). American historian. Born in Lincoln Township, Blackhawk County, Iowa, 7 September 1873. Studied at Cornell College, Mt. Vernon, Iowa, 1892-93; University of Wisconsin, Madison, B.Litt. 1896, Ph.D. 1907; Fellow in Constitutional Law, Columbia University, New York, 1898-99. Married Maude Hepworth Ranney in 1901; 1 son. Instructor, Pennsylvania State College, College Park, 1899-1901, and Dartmouth College, Hanover, New Hampshire, 1901-02; Assistant Professor, 1902-07, Associate Professor, 1907-08, and Professor, 1908-16, University of Kansas, Lawrence; Professor, University of Minnesota, Minneapolis, 1916-17; Professor, 1917-22, John Stambaugh Professor of History, 1922-41, and Professor Emeritus and University Historian, 1941-45, Cornell University, Ithaca, New York. Editor, *Journal of Social Philosophy*, 1935-42. President, American Historical Association, 1934-35. Honorary doctorate: Yale University, New Haven, Connecticut, 1932; University of Rochester, New York, 1938; Columbia University, 1939. Member, American Academy of Arts and Sciences. *Died 10 April 1945.*

PUBLICATIONS

History and Political Science

The History of Political Parties in the Province of New York, 1760-1776. Madison, Wisconsin, 1909.
Beginnings of the American People. Boston, Houghton Mifflin, 1915.
The Eve of the Revolution: A Chronicle of the Breach with England. New Haven, Connecticut, Yale University Press, 1918.
The United States: An Experiment in Democracy. New York and London, Harper, 1920; as *Our Great Experiment in Democracy: A History of the United States*, New York, Harper, 1920.
The Declaration of Independence: A Study in the History of Political Ideas. New York, Harcourt Brace, 1921.
The Spirit of '76 and Other Essays, with others. Washington, D.C., Robert Brookings Graduate School of Economics and Government, 1927.
Modern History: The Rise of a Democratic, Scientific, and Industrial Civilization. New York, Silver Burdett, 1931.

The Heavenly City of the Eighteenth-Century Philosophers.
New Haven, Connecticut, Yale University Press, 1932.

Everyman His Own Historian: Essays on History and Politics.
New York, Appleton Century, 1935.

Progress and Power (lectures). Stanford, California, Stanford
University Press, and London, Oxford University Press, 1936.

*Story of Civilization, Showing How, from Earliest Times, Men
Have Increased Their Knowledge and Mastery of the World,
and Thereby Changed Their Ways of Living in It,* with Frederic Duncalf. New York, Silver Burdett, 1938.

Modern Democracy. New Haven, Connecticut, Yale University Press, and London, Oxford University Press, 1941.

New Liberties for Old. New Haven, Connecticut, Yale University Press, and London, Oxford University Press, 1941.

Cornell University: Founders and the Founding (lectures).
Ithaca, New York, Cornell University Press, 1943.

Freedom and Responsibility in the American Way of Life (lectures). New York, Knopf, 1945.

*How New Will the Better World Be? A Discussion of Post-War
Reconstruction.* New York, Knopf, 1944; as *Making a Better World,* London, Hamish Hamilton, 1945.

*History of Modern Europe: A Self-Teaching Course Based on
Modern History,* with others. New York, Silver Burdett,
1944.

Safeguarding Civil Liberties, with others. New York, P. Smith,
1949.

The Past That Lives Today, with others. New York, Silver
Burdett, 1952.

*Detachment and the Writing of History: Essays and Letters of
Carl L. Becker,* edited by Phil L. Snyder. Ithaca, New York,
Cornell University Press, 1958.

Other

Benjamin Franklin: A Biographical Sketch (reproduced from
Dictionary of American Biography, volume VI). Ithaca,
New York, Cornell University Press, 1946.

*"What Is the Good of History?" Selected Letters of Carl L.
Becker, 1900-45,* edited by Michael Kammen. Ithaca, New
York, Cornell University Press, 1973.

*

Critical Studies: *Carl Becker: On History and the Climate of
Opinion* by Charlotte Watkins Smith, Ithaca, New York, Cornell University Press, 1956; *Carl Becker's Heavenly City Revisit-
ed,* edited by Raymond Oxley Rockwood, Ithaca, New York,
Cornell University Press, 1958; *The Pragmatic Revolt in Ameri-
can History: Carl Becker and Charles Beard* by Cushing Strout,
New Haven, Connecticut, Yale University Press, 1959; *Carl
Becker: A Biographical Study in American Intellectual History*
by Burleigh Wilkins Taylor, Cambridge, Massachusetts, M.I.T.
Press, 1961; *Carl Becker on History and the American Revolution* by Robert Eldon Brown, East Lansing, Michigan, Spartan
Press, 1970.

*   *   *

Although a number of Carl Becker's delightful essays and
sections of his books have passed by way of anthologies into the
realm of literature, his academic renown rests less on the history
that he wrote than on what he wrote about how and why history
should be written. What is remembered and said about his role
among the historians and philosophers of the first half of the 20th
century is sometimes contradictory, but that could hardly surprise him.

To begin with, he is almost always listed as one of the leading
Progressive or "New" historians, dedicated to using history "as a
weapon for reform." His activist students, however, used to be
disappointed that he was not enough of a reformer. Of course
Becker could hardly have failed to be influenced by the Progres-

sive Movement. He grew up in Iowa in the midst of the long
agricultural depression following the Civil War, and in the 1890's
he attended the University of Wisconsin, the very source of much
of the Progressive gospel. Most conscientious young professionals of the Progressive era were eager to take part in the betterment of society. The question for historians was how to make
knowledge of the past serve the present.

Some historians thought they should either intensify the
efforts to be objective which had characterized the previous
generation or they should borrow the methods of the newer
social sciences, especially psychology and sociology. The main
body of the New historians, however, sought improvement in
another direction. History could do some work in the world if
historians would ask useful questions of the past, and if they
would stop pretending they didn't care what answers they found.
They should ask questions they did care about. Becker's teacher,
the noted historian of the frontier, Frederick Jackson Turner,
thought history might "hold the lamp for conservative reform."

Carl Becker's name was, and still is, usually coupled with that
of Charles A. Beard, the best known (rightly) of all the Progressive historians. This pairing of names is conveniently alliterative,
but otherwise a mismatch in almost every way. Temperamentally
Becker was always inclined toward observation, analysis, and
reflection. His services to the Progressive historians were largely
negative ones. He disposed of their most serious critics by refuting the claim that history could be truly objective, but to turn and
"exploit the past in the interest of advance" was another thing.
First one had to have a conviction about which way was advance.
On that question Becker was stopped. He thought and wrote
about the idea of progress all his life, but he never gained the
necessary certitude—so typical of Beard—that any current campaign of reform was necessarily in the right direction.

As Richard Hofstadter wrote in 1958, "The pivotal idea of the
Progressive historians was economic and political conflict." For
them leaders and movements of the past could all be divided into
two kinds: one humane, democratic, liberal, agrarian; the other
conservative, acquisitive, and commercial. In his frequent reviews
Becker defended some extremely biased history written in that
dualistic vein, often on the ground that anything provoking
thought and discussion must do good. He did not himself, however, believe much in heroes or villains—particularly not in
villains conspiring to oppress the human race. His notes and his
comments to students express the conviction that motivation is
complex and seldom primarily economic. Conflict between men
with differing visions of the public good was the situation he
usually portrayed. His chapter on Thomas Hutchinson and
Samuel Adams in *The Eve of the Revolution* is a prime example.
History should "deepen the sympathies," and "prepare us to live
more humanely in the present," he wrote. To do this the historian
needed "a flair for the unconscious influences that activate the
human animal."

No one doubted Becker's flair or denied the felicity of his
prose. Some, however, found such felicity suspect. His older
critics, believing that the historian's only duty was to establish
what really happened, grumbled that he spent too much time
polishing his phrases—time that should be spent digging in the
sources. Later critics accused him of being too eager to turn a
phrase to resist some witty but dubious observations about the
meaning of the Enlightenment. Refuting Becker's aphorisms
about the American Revolution and about the Heavenly City of
the 18th century philosophers has been big business in the world
of historical research for over half a century.

The flair for catching the atmosphere of a period, Becker
found, could not come from following any set of rules for assessing and arranging piles of note cards. None of the rules for
judging the accuracy of witnesses or the importance of their
testimony really worked. Something deeper entered into the
historian's judgment. Speculation about that something, about
the nature of historical knowledge, led Becker to radical conclusions years before even the New historians saw any need for
accepting them. He became convinced that historical truth was

no more exempt from modern Pragmatic redefinition than any other truth. The Pragmatics said that truth is not absolute, that there is no objective standard by which to verify any proposition. Their contention that knowledge is relative to the mind of the knower, and may vary from individual to individual and from time to time, made nonsense of the professional historian's attempt to collect the facts-and-only-the-facts. In "Detachment and the Writing of History" (*Atlantic Monthly*, October 1910), Becker first attacked the basic tenets of the orthodox, scientific historian: first, that a fact is a thing purely objective which can be established, once for all, by proper scientific analysis of evidence; and second, that the historical account (the synthesis) which links the facts together is a wholly different thing—something which historians have not yet learned to construct with complete objectivity, but something which will emerge of itself once the facts are all in and allowed to "speak for themselves."

Becker denied this distinction between analysis and synthesis. He denied that facts could be uncovered by "cultivating mental detachment." Facts are not hard or cold or tangible; facts are but "images in the mind" and they "do not exist for any historian until he creates them," he argued. These images in the mind are not single elements: facts are not "pebbles to be gathered in a cup; there is in truth no unit fact in history." Every fact is a compound of smaller facts. Not only that, every fact that forms itself in the mind of the historian is partly made up of the historian's inferences from his own experience. If he has had no experience of this world at all, the words he finds in his sources will form no images at all. Each fact is in itself, then, a small synthesis to which the mind of the historian has contributed something. In short, real detachment, if we had it, would be a fatal gift. We would be unable to understand or to evaluate the evidence. Our own experience of reality "is actually the final court of appeal in evaluating the sources themselves." Neither two witnesses nor two hundred can establish a miracle as a fact for a modern historian. He will always disqualify the witnesses, however trustworthy on other matters, as "self-deceived" because he cannot escape his own preconceived idea of "the nature of the world and the kind of occurrences that can take place in it."

Since men cannot be detached from the climate of opinion of their time, there is no use in trying to pile up facts in cold storage, waiting for an objective synthesis to emerge. Nothing will emerge. Facts do not speak for themselves. "The perceiving mind of the historian" must speak. Let him tell a story that his generation is interested in, and tell it well enough so that it will be read.

This 1910 message was the message to historians that Becker repeated in many forms and with differing emphases for the rest of his life, while also following his own advice. By 1931 when he made his presidential address to the American Historical Association ("Everyman His Own Historian"), most historians were prepared to accept some form of relativism if not the more radical subjectivism that Beard shortly adopted. In fact, the cruder forms of pragmatism and relativism were soon all too prevalent among those "not out to understand the world but to change it." Becker became more and more pessimistic as the depression deepened and as Hitler and Stalin grew in power. During those years his rather melancholy temperament, his increasing ill health, and his sceptical convictions often combined to make his essays and books sound bleak. Appalled by the moral and political effects of relativism, he still could not help thinking that truth was "in some sense relative." The question "relative to what?" left him in a logical bind which he admitted bluntly in his private papers, with charming self-deprecation in his public ones.

It was only after the worst had happened, and World War II began, that Becker emerged from his disillusion with Wilson and World War I, and, freed from his philosophical inhibitions, attacked the threat to everything he held dear. "Some Generalities That Still Glitter" (*Yale Review*, 1940) proclaimed that "in the long run all values are inseparable from the love of truth and the disinterested search for it." If we have clearly found that truth is relative and reason limited, he reminded us that it was reason

that found it out. "The fallacy is to suppose that because truth is in some sense relative it cannot be distinguished from error." Here he professed the faith that he had always taken for granted in practice: that truth is relative to something else besides "the needs of the time." What that something is, reason cannot show; *that* it is we must take on faith or reason has no purpose.

The years of American participation in World War II coincided with Becker's years of retirement. They were years of improved health for him after drastic surgery for ulcers, and were productive and optimistic years in which he finally was able to fight wholeheartedly for a cause. It was perhaps ironic that the cause entailed supporting war, the most irrational and barbaric activity of man, but irony was, after all, his chosen medium. He wrote prolifically and, except for his commitment to write the history of Cornell University, entirely on public affairs until his death in 1945. He tried valiantly to prevent the romantic disillusionment he thought was sure to occur when the defeat of the Axis powers failed to bring about the new and better world always hoped for during times of effort and sacrifice. He tried to create a climate of opinion that would encourage clearer thought, more reasonable expectations.

These essays were widely read as they came out, and exerted an influence on public opinion—or at least on the molders of public opinion such as editors, teachers, and theologians. If he never upset the whole tenor of opinion as Beard's *An Economic Interpretation of the Constitution* once did, that was appropriate also. A mild sort of humanizing influence is undoubtedly all Becker would have wished to be responsible for.

—Charlotte W. Smith

BELL, (Arthur) Clive (Heward).   British art critic and aesthetician.   Born in East Shefford, Bedfordshire, 16 September 1881. Educated at Marlborough and Trinity College, Cambridge (Exhibitioner and Earl of Derby Student), 1889-92. Married Vanessa Stephen in 1907: 3 children. Organized the first exhibition of Post-Impressionist art in London with Roger Fry, 1910. Art Critic, *New Statesman and Nation*, London, 1933-43. Chevalier, Légion d'Honneur. *Died 19 September 1964.*

PUBLICATIONS

Art History and Aesthetics

Art. London, Chatto and Windus, and New York, Stokes, 1974.
Since Cezanne. London, Chatto and Windus, and New York, Harcourt Brace, 1922.
Landmarks in Nineteenth-Century Painting. London, Chatto and Windus, and New York, Harcourt Brace, 1927.
An Account of French Painting. London, Chatto and Windus, 1931; New York, Harcourt Brace, 1932.
Enjoying Pictures: Meditations in the National Art Gallery and Elsewhere. London, Chatto and Windus, and New York, Harcourt Brace, 1934.
Victor Passmore. London, Penguin, 1945.
Modern French Painting: The Cone Collection. Baltimore, Johns Hopkins University Press, 1951.
The French Impressionists: With Fifty Plates in Full Colour. London, Phaidon, and New York, New York Graphic Society, 1952.

Other

Peace at Once (essay).   Manchester, National Labour Press, 1915.

Ad Familiares (poems). London, Pelican Press, 1917.
Pot-Boilers (essays). London, Chatto and Windus, 1918.
The Legend of Monte della Sibilia; or, le Paradis de la reine Sibille (poem). Richmond, Surrey, Hogarth Press, 1923.
Civilization: An Essay. London, Chatto and Windus, and New York, Harcourt Brace, 1928.
Proust. London, Hogarth Press and New York, Harcourt Brace, 1928.
Warmongers (essay). London, Peace Pledge Union, 1938.
Old Friends: Personal Recollections. London, Chatto and Windus, 1956; New York, Harcourt Brace, 1957.

*

Critical Studies: *British Journal of Aesthetics* (London), 5, 1965 (contains essays on Bell by Herbert Read, R.K. Elliott, R. Meager, H. Osborne and G.T. Dickie); *The Interpretation of Art: Essays on the Art Criticism of John Ruskin, Walter Pater, Clive Bell, Roger Fry and Herbert Read* by Solomon Fishman, Berkeley, University of California Press, 1963; *Clive Bell's Eye* by William Bywater, Detroit, Wayne State University Press, 1975 (contains a bibliography by Donald A. Laing).

*   *   *

Clive Bell, English art critic and aesthetician, is perhaps most widely known as a central figure in the Bloomsbury Group. He was the husband of the painter Vanessa Bell and brother-in-law of the novelist Virginia Woolf. His most enduring work has been the book *Art*, published in 1914. This work has been taken as an early manifesto of formalist theory in the visual arts. Bell's love of art, clearly manifest in the verve with which he presented his theory, was rooted in a stay in Paris in 1904 and blossomed after he met Roger Fry in 1909. Fry was the mentor whose appreciation for the post-impressionists (a name coined by Fry) freed Bell to voice his deep response to the revolutionary painters, and especially to Cézanne. Bell introduced the expression "significant form" into the vocabulary of aesthetics in order to express his understanding of the post-impressionist revolution. He saw the post-impressionists as moving away from painting which was representational, and away from the kind of space required for representational painting, toward painting which derives its values as art solely from the presence in it of certain combinations of lines and colours which in turn articulate a dynamic space—a space completely inappropriate for story telling and moralizing. Bell gave the name significant form to the complex of color, line, and space in which all the elements dynamically interact with one another to maintain a balance of planes where there is no fixed foreground or background. He claimed that any painting which can be truly called a work of art will have significant form. Significant form is *the* property which all true works of visual art have in common. This formalism reaches its full expression when Bell tells us that to appreciate visual art we need only a sense of form and color together with a familiarity with three-dimensional space. Representational aspects of a painting are *at best* neutral (and usually detrimental) to that painting's achieving the status of real art.

To prove his point about significant form Bell turns to the history of art. Post-impressionism, he argues, is a return to great art in the tradition of Giotto and the sixth-century mosaics at Ravenna. Post-impressionism raises itself from the "sea-level of nasty naturalism" of the 19th century toward the mountain peaks of pure art. This art has admixed none of the emotions of life but, rather, transports us from worldly concerns to more noble realms. According to Bell the history of art contains many "slopes" which fall from the high mountains of art's "primitive morning," in various parts of the world, down to the flats of naturalism. The fall of the slope is uneven for they contain peaks and valleys as they drop. In examining post-impressionism, Bell is interested in what he calls the "Christian Slope." The summit of this slope is sixth-century Byzantine art. It is in this art, Bell

feels, that the spirituality which gave rise to Christianity finds its full and most immediate expression. From its height the slope falls through the notable points of Giotto, Rembrandt, Poussin, Chardin, and French impressionism as it descends to the near death of art in the 19th century when scientific accuracy is taken to be the goal of painting. Bell poses the question: Is post-impressionism simply a momentary rise in the general descent of the Christian slope or is it a new dawn for art—a new spiritual awakening? He refuses to answer this question, but his enthusiasm for post-impressionism leaves no doubt that Bell hopes for the latter alternative.

This brief description of Bell's approach to art history introduces two aspects of his theory which throw into doubt claims that he is a formalist. A strict formalism focuses upon the work of art, deliberately excluding any concern with audience reaction or with the artist's creative experience, both of which are regarded as irrelevant to aesthetic value. Bell, however, holds that there is an aesthetic emotion (as opposed to the emotions of life) which transports art's audience out of the everyday. The experience is a sure indication of the presence of significant form. Bell has been accused of circularity when he appears to say that it is the presence of significant form which yields an aesthetic emotion and it is the presence of an aesthetic emotion which yields other forms of spirituality. It is one of the indicators that "man does not live by bread alone," he says. The point of this formalism is not art for art's sake, but art for the sake of spiritual elevation. Thus, Bell sees the summit of the Christian slope at the point when spirituality, and not accuracy is most apparent in art.

The second unusual feature of Bell's formalism is the "metaphysical hypothesis." This is Bell's suggestion (which is not properly part of aesthetic theory, he says) that aesthetic emotion occurs as a response to significant form because art which exhibits significant form is an expression of its creator's vision of, or response to, reality (or ultimate reality, as Bell sometimes calls it). It appears that the artist's vision of ultimate reality—the formal structure of nature—is entwined with an emotional response (a response very much like, if not the same as, an aesthetic emotion) so that what is expressed in the work is both the artist's seeing of and feeling for this reality. When we join this expressive element with the formalistic and evocative aspects of Bell's theory, the situation is this. A person with an emotional vision of the underlying formal structure of nature (and with the requisite abilities and skills) imbeds that vision in the formal structure of a visual work. An appropriately educated and sensitive viewer responds to this work with an aesthetic emotion (something very similar to the artist's original emotion) and, as a result, the work is experienced as art. Its creator is an artist. In the larger society art functions to produce a spiritual community, or at least to provide a spirituality which is an antidote to our society's materialism. Bell's hope must have been that post-impressionism would be a summit in a new slope whose appearance would mark a new (but secular) emergence of spirituality in the West.

Bell published books and articles of aesthetics and art criticism until the early 1950's. This work reveals that he personally was committed to formalism in neither critical theory nor practice. He continued to be an enthusiastic spokesman for the good he saw in art, and he used a variety of critical techniques to get his audience to share his view. His commitment was always first to expand and educate vision. In the preface to the new edition of *Art* (1948), for example, Bell admits that the book impertinently belittles the work of the renaissance and the 18th century, and that he generalizes too quickly. His comments, however, do little to defend against the theoretical objections to *Art*. In one way or another these objections point out that the formal, evocative, and expressive aspects of the theory do not cohere, and at some points contradict one another. Bell's focus on issues of formalism—an understandable choice given his historical position—created a statement which did not accurately reflect the full range and coherence of his interest in art.

—William Bywater

BELL, Daniel. American sociologist. Born in New York, 10 May 1919. Educated at City College, New York, B.S. 1939; Columbia University, New York, Ph.D. 1960. Married Nora Potashnick in 1943; daughter: Jordy; married Elaine Graham in 1949 (divorced); married Pearl Kazin in 1960; son: David. Staff writer, 1939-41, and Managing Editor, 1941-44, *The New Leader*, New York; Managing Editor, *Common Sense*, 1945; Instructor to Assistant Professor of Social Sciences, University of Chicago, 1945-48; Labor Editor, *Fortune*, 1948-58; Lecturer in Sociology, 1952-58, and Professor, 1958-69, Columbia University. Professor of Sociology, 1969-80, and since 1980 Henry Ford II Professor of Social Sciences, Harvard University, Cambridge, Massachusetts. Member, Board of Directors, American Civil Liberties Union, 1957-61; U.S. Representative, D.E.C.D. Interfutures Project, 1976-79. Member, President's Commission on Technology, Automation and Economic Progress; Member, President's Commission for Agenda for the 1980's; Trustee, Institute for Advanced Study, Princeton, New Jersey. Has served as Member of the Editorial Board, *American Scholar*; Editor, *Daedalus*; Co-Editor, *Public Interest*. Recipient: Center for Advanced Study in the Behavioral Sciences Fellowship, 1958-59; Borden Medal, American Council on Education, 1966. Fellow, American Sociological Association. Member, American Academy of Arts and Sciences. Address: 65 Francis Avenue, Cambridge, Massachusetts 02138, U.S.A.

PUBLICATIONS

Sociology

History of Marxian Socialism in the United States. Princeton, New Jersey, Princeton University Press, 1952.
Work and Its Discontent. Boston, Beacon, 1956.
The End of Ideology: On the Exhaustion of Political Ideas in the Fifties. Glencoe, Illinois, Free Press, 1960.
The Reforming of General Education: The Columbia College Experience in Its National Setting. New York, Columbia University Press, 1966.
The Coming of Post-Industrial Society. New York, Basic Books, 1973; London, Heinemann, 1974.
The Cultural Contradictions of Capitalism. New York, Basic Books, 1976.
The Winding Passage: Essays and Sociological Journeys 1960-1980. Cambridge, Massachusetts, Abt Associates, 1980.
England: The Future That Never Was. New Brunswick, New Jersey, Transaction Books, 1980.
Sociological Journals. London, Heinemann, 1980.

Other

Editor, *The New American Right*. New York, Criterion, 1955; revised edition as *The Radical Right*, New York, Doubleday, 1963.
Editor, *Towards the Year 2000: Work in Progress*. Boston, Houghton Mifflin, 1967.
Editor and Contributor, with Irving Kristol, *Confrontation: The Student Rebellion and the Universities*. New York, Basic Books, 1969.
Editor, with Irving Kristol, *Capitalism Today*. New York, Basic Books, 1976.
Editor, with Irving Kristol, *The Crisis in Economic Theory*. New York, Basic Books, 1981.

*   *   *

Daniel Bell is one of the leading American sociologists, a prolific writer, a man of catholic interests and erudition. A moralist, he is liberal and social democratic in his political and economic views and culturally conservative; personally independent, he is attacked and praised in America by both conservatives and radicals. He has made several important contributions to sociological analysis, which have shaped debate on such issues as the "end of ideology," "the post-industrial society," and the "cultural contradictions of capitalism" and which have sparked inquiries into such areas as future studies. He is particularly strong as a sociological theorist and as a social thinker who draws on and adds to the sociological tradition. He has educated, through teaching and writing, two generations of sociologists and has reached a large non-academic public in the United States and Western Europe.

Bell's earliest writings were those of a young socialist—anti-fascist, anti-Stalinist—concerned with labor questions and American capitalism, warning of the potential for corporate control of American society and government, particularly if the war economy were made permanent. In the post-war period, he wrote in a mood of greater optimism with regard to democratic society than was common among intellectuals oppressed by the thoughts of totalitarianism and mass culture. He too responded to the Holocaust and the Moscow trials, to anti-semitism in American labor, to racism in American society, but nonetheless his writings indicate hope for a welfare state, for American politics, for democratic socialism abroad. He contrasted fascism and authoritarianism with American populism and anti-intellectualism. His tone shifted from that of a critical socialist tracing the inexorable logic of economic institutions to a reformer convinced of the complexity of American society and of the importance of political decisions and choices.

Bell's post-war studies culminated in the enormously influential and controversial *The End of Ideology*, a collection of essays, written across a decade, which called for a new, stronger, more pragmatic social science and social theory. Intellectuals could no longer, or ought not again, accept the ideologies of the 1930's. An intellectually rigorous approach to the role of interest groups, the nature of bargaining and consensus in liberal society, and to the problems of the welfare state was essential. As "the post-industrial society," as he would name it, developed in both "socialist" and "capitalist" states, its realities cut across the ideological analyses of the past, much the same as Max Weber's concept of "bureaucracy" did. There was nothing controversial in the call for greater rigor and science, but the rejection of the "vulgar Marxism" of the 1930's and the emphasis on the intellectual's role within the system, as analyst, reformer, and manager, was. Bell's assumption that the modern democratic welfare state could and ought to manage a consensus and to moderate conflicting powers and interests, rejected the view of both classic liberalism and socialism. Furthermore, Bell was an outspoken opponent of totalitarianism and of intellectuals who habitually rationalized the policies of the Soviet Union as if they were the positions of the "Left."

In the 1950's Bell's work shared many of the concerns of the French sociologist Raymond Aron, both men emerging as leading social thinkers of the era immediately following. Both attacked the treason of those intellectuals who served an ideology rather than truth; both defended social science, though they did not idealize it as a "calling" for intellectuals; both resurrected the key concept of the industrial society, particularly the economically advanced society, and argued that it had important common structural and cultural features despite political and traditional differences; both denied primacy to economic structure in determining the evolution of modern society and asserted the ultimately political nature of choice and of social science itself. Both were attacked for underplaying the place of conflict, class or race conflict, in capitalist welfare states; both were accused of technocratic thought, of preaching government by an elite of managers, and of neglecting political values in estimating the present and hypothesizing the future. Reflecting the preoccupations of their native countries, Bell was more sensitive to problems of race, education, and social stratification and Aron to the problems of war, war economies, and developing nations; Bell perhaps was more convinced of the ability of post-industrial society to manage social ills and the likelihood of democratic success in production and adaptation competing with totalitarian states. Both men responded to the conflicts of the 1960's, particularly the attack on the universities and liberal learning, with a deep cultural pessimism that was not characteristic of their previous work.

Out of this profound cultural pessimism, rather than the technocratic optimism critics accused him of when they commented on *The Coming of Post-Industrial Society*, Bell wrote *The Cultural Contradictions of Capitalism*. He depicted the destruction of the value system (the ethic of hard, meaningful work, deferred gratification, a sense of calling and social responsibility) which had traditionally cemented the capitalist system. The polity today is organized according to the assertion of varying interests; individuals feel both insatiably needy *and* entitled. Technological society is structured by rationalized production and rewards those whose merits contribute to that process; such a society pulls in another direction from political life which balances interests. The segregation of culture (understood as the arts and literature), which is now used merely as a leisure time activity, threatens to pull society further apart. Bell is impressed, as was Lionel Trilling, with the power of modernist culture and sees it as debased from avant-garde to merely counter-culture, politicized perhaps and also trivialized. Having refrained from the critique of mass culture so popular among intellectuals in the decade following World War II, Bell is now much less convinced that the protestant ethic can cement society. He despairs for the wealth of culture a more integrated society was capable of supporting.

—Myrna Chase

BENDA, Julien. French political and social philosopher. Born in Paris, 26 December 1867. Educated at Lyceum St. Louis, Litt.B. 1884, Sc.B. 1886; Ecole Centrale, Paris, Lic.Litt. 1894. Essayist. Contributor, *La Revue Blanche, La Nouvelle Revue Français, Mercure de France, Divan,* and *Figaro.* Member, Société des Gens de Lettres. Commandeur, Légion d'Honneur, 1938. *Died* (in Fontenay-Aux-Roses, France) *7 June 1956.*

PUBLICATIONS

Political and Social Philosophy

Dialogues à Byzance. Paris, Editions Revue blanche, 1900.
Mon premier testament. Paris, Cahiers de la Quinzaine, 1910 (dated 1908).
Dialogue d'Eleuthère. Paris, Cahiers de la Quinzaine, 1911.
Le Bergsonisme: ou, Un Philosophie de la mobilité. Paris, Editions Mercure de France, 1912.
Sur le succès du Bergsonisme. Paris, Editions Mercure de France, 1914.
Une Philosophie pathétique. Paris, Cahiers de la Quinzaine, 1913.
Les Sentiments de Critias. Paris, Emile-Paul, 1917.
Belphégor: Essai sur l'esthétique de la présente société français. Paris, Emile-Paul, 1918; as *Belphegor,* London, Faber, and New York, Payson and Clarke, 1929.
Le Bouquet de Glycère. Paris, Emile-Paul, 1918.
Billets de Sirius. Paris, Le Divan, 1925.
Lettres à Melisande pour son éducation philosophique. Paris, Le Livre, 1925.

Pour les vieux garçons. Paris, Emile-Paul (private printing), 1926.
La Trahison des clercs. Paris, Les Cahiers verts, Grasset, 1927; as *The Treason of the Intellectuals,* New York, Morrow, 1928; as *The Great Betrayal,* London, Routledge, 1928; as *The Betrayal of the Intellectuals,* Boston, Beacon, 1955.
Cléanthis: ou, Du beau et de l'actuel. Paris, Grasset, 1928.
Properce: ou, Les Amants de Tibur. Paris, Collection Les Heures antiques, Grasset, 1928.
La Fin de l'éternel. Paris, Gallimard, 1928.
Supplément à De l'esprit du faction de Saint-Evremond. Paris, Editions du Trianon, 1929.
Appositions. Paris, Gallimard, 1930.
Essai d'un discours cohérent sur les rapports de Dieu et du Monde. Paris, Gallimard, 1931.
Esquisse d'une histoire des Français dans leur volonté d'être une nation. Paris, Gallimard, 1932.
Discours à la nation européenne. Paris, Gallimard, 1933.
Délice d'Eleuthère. Paris, Gallimard, 1935.
La Jeunesse d'un clerc. Paris, Gallimard, 1936.
Un Régulier dans le siècle. Paris, Gallimard, 1937.
Précision (1930-1937). Paris, Gallimard, 1937.
La Grande Epreuve des démocraties. New York, Editions de la Maison Française, 1942.
Le Rapport d'Uriel. Paris, Editions de Minuit, 1943.
Un Antisémite sincère. Toulouse, Comité National des Ecrivains, Centre des Intellectuels, 1944.
La France byzantine: ou, Le Triomphe de la littérature pure: Mallarmé, Gide, Proust, Valéry, Alain, Giraudoux, Suarès, les surréalistes. Paris, Gallimard, 1945.
Exercice d'un enterré vif. Geneva and Paris, Editions Trois Collines, 1946.
Non Possumus. Paris, Editions de la Nouvelle Revue Critique, 1946.
Du poétique. Paris, Editions Trois Collines, 1946.
Tradition de l'existentialisme: ou, Les Philosophies de la vie. Paris, Grasset, 1947.
Du style d'idées. Paris, Gallimard, 1948.
Trois idoles romantiques: Le Dynamisme, l'existentialisme, la dialectique materialiste. Geneva, Collection Internationales, Mont-Blanc, 1948.
Deux croisades pour la paix, juridique et sentimentale. Neuchatel, Switzerland, Editions du Griffon, and Brussels, Editions du Temple, 1948.
Les Cahiers d'un clerc (1936-1949). Paris, Emile-Paul, 1949.
Songe d'Eleuthère. Paris, Grasset, 1949.
De quelques constantes de l'esprit humain: Critique du mobilisme contemporaine. Paris, Gallimard, 1950.
Mémoires d'infra-tombe. Paris, Collection "La Nef," Editions René Julliard, 1952.

Novels and Short Stories

L'Ordination. Paris, Cahiers de la Quinzaine, 2 vols., 1911-12; as 1 vol., Paris, Emile-Paul, 1913; as *The Yoke of Pity,* London, Unwin, and New York, Holt, 1913.
Les Amorandes. Paris, Emile-Paul, 1922.
La Croix des roses (short stories). Paris, Les Cahiers verts, Grasset, 1923.

Other

Entretien avec Julien Benda, with F. Lefevre. Paris, Le Livre, 1925.

*

Critical Studies: *Julien Benda* by Robert J. Niess, Ann Arbor, University of Michigan Press, 1956; *Treason, Tradition, and the Intellectual: Julien Benda and Political Discourse* by Ray Nichols, Lawrence, Regents Press of Kansas, 1978; *The Spec-*

trum of Political Engagement: Mounier, Benda, Nizan, Brasill-ach, Sartre by David L. Schalk, Princeton, New Jersey, Princeton University Press, 1979.

*   *   *

In the course of a long literary career the eccentric erudite Julien Benda wrote about 50 books, mostly of literary and social criticism, but he is chiefly remembered for one of them, *La Trahison des clercs* published in 1927 when he was 60 years old. It is unjust to say that Benda was anti-intellectual, but throughout his career he displayed hostility to prevailing fashions in French literature and thought, especially those that looked in a subjectivist or irrationalist direction: Symbolism in literature, Bergsonian intuition, Surrealism, Existentialism. A Voltairean polemicist, he stood in the tradition of French rationalism, the classicists, Cartesians, and *philosophes*.

The Treason of the Intellectuals was a timely work which appealed to post-World War I moods of re-evaluation in assailing Western intellectuals for deserting "eternal principles" to run after the false gods of political partisanship. There was some apparent confusion in Benda's argument, critics pointed out, for he himself was a fervent French patriot who fiercely supported his country in both world wars against the hated Germans, on whom he tended to place blame for the romanticism and mysticism he scorned. Those whom he condemned for deserting eternal truth were mainly people of the Right, especially the Italian Fascists. He became a Communist sympathizer in the 1930's, though claiming that the intellectuals' first loyalty was to truth not party. Students of Benda have noted that his message was frequently misinterpreted, the "treason of the clerks" being regarded (e.g., by Senator Joseph McCarthy) as the *failure* to become "committed" political activists, whereas Benda's point was very nearly the exact opposite. But his own career as a passionate pamphleteer, patriot, and man of the Left belies the message of elevation above the battle which Benda seemed to preach. Paul Nizan observed that "Benda changes eternities," though he refused to admit this. Benda sought to distinguish between service to a cause and service to a party, and rejected the Marxist as well as other types of totalitarian claims which would destroy the autonomy of the intellectual life. But by the late 1930's he had decided that "the *clerc* must now take sides."

The German Nazis destroyed Benda's notes and library in Paris in 1941, but, though Jewish, he escaped arrest by the Gestapo. After 1945, at an advanced age, he returned to prolific journalistic production. In a new edition of the *Treason* in 1947 he retracted nothing, flaying the intellectuals for serving either the Nazis during the Occupation years or the Communist Party. Austere and disinterested thought, by a mind free from any social or political system, remained his ideal.

His masterpiece continues to find readers, but as an unrepentant rationalist in the century of Freud, Bergson, and Sartre, Benda was a doughty anomaly. He tended to reject almost the whole of European thought since the Enlightenment. He saw in Hegel's dialectic the beginning of the insidious trend to regard truth as something other than fixed and certain; 19th-century nationalism and historicism had relativized knowledge and destroyed standards. "Pure" literature such as became the vogue in the 20th century had in fact led writers away from the search for objective truth into murky depths of sentiment and feeling.

The call to "relevance" in studies which was so fashionable in the 1960's would have incited Benda's scorn. We need Benda, Lewis Coser wrote in 1973, "as antidote against the 'with it' intellectuals, the Sartres, Marcuses and Mailers of the age." This is not say that according to Benda the true intellectual abjures his responsibilities and retires to the ivory tower; on the contrary, he fights as a participant in the public arena. But he is a partisan for truth, not for any particular nation, class, dogma, or interest. The distinction raises issues Benda was perhaps not fully

equipped to resolve, but he did raise them with unusual verve and energy.

—Roland Stromberg

————————

BENEDICT, Ruth. American anthropologist. Born Ruth Fulton in New York City, 5 June 1887. Educated at Vassar College, Poughkeepsie, New York, A.B., 1909; New School for Social Research, New York, 1918-19; Columbia University, New York, Ph.D. 1923. Married Stanley R. Benedict in 1914 (died, 1936). Lecturer in Anthropology, 1923-30, Assistant Professor, 1930-36, Executive Officer of the Department, 1936-39, Associate Professor, 1936-48, and Professor, 1948, Columbia University, New York. Served with the Office of War Information as Head of Basic Analysis Section, Bureau of Overseas Intelligence, 1943-45, and as Social Science Analyst, Foreign Morale Division, 1944-45. Visiting Lecturer, Bryn Mawr College, Pennsylvania, 1941, and Washington School of Psychiatry, 1944-45. Director, Research in Contemporary Cultures, Office of Naval Research, 1947-48. Editor, *Journal of American Folklore*, 1925-39, and *Columbia University Contributions to Anthropology*, 1936-40; Member of Editorial Board, *The American Scholar*, 1942-44; Assistant Editor, *Psychiatry*, 1946. President, American Ethnological Society, 1927-29; Vice-President, American Psychopathological Association, 1946; President, American Anthropological Association, 1947. Recipient: Washington School of Psychiatry Fellowship, 1945; American Association of University Women Achievement Award, 1946. D.Sc.: Russell Sage College, Troy, New York, 1947. Fellow, American Academy of Arts and Sciences, 1947. *Died* (in New York City) *17 September 1948*.

PUBLICATIONS

Anthropology

The Concept of the Guardian Spirit in North America (monograph).   New York, American Anthropological Association, 1923.

Tales of the Cochiti Indians (monograph).   Washington, D.C., Bureau of American Ethnology, Smithsonian Institution, 1931.

Patterns of Culture.   Boston, Houghton Mifflin, 1934; London, Routledge, 1935.

Zuni Mythology.   New York, Columbia University Press, 2 vols., 1935.

Race, Science, and Politics.   New York, Viking Press, 1940.

The Chrysanthemum and the Sword.   Boston, Houghton Mifflin, 1946.

An Anthropologist at Work: Writings of Ruth Benedict, edited by Margaret Mead.   Boston, Houghton Mifflin, 1949.

*

Critical Studies: *Ruth Fulton Benedict: A Memoir* (contains a full bibliography), New York, Viking Fund, 1949; *Ruth Benedict* by Margaret Mead, New York, Columbia University Press, 1974; *Ruth Benedict: Patterns of a Life* by Judith Schachter Modell, Philadelphia, University of Pennsylvania Press, 1983.

*   *   *

Ruth Benedict is one of the major figures in the development of American cultural anthropology. In her two great works, *Patterns of Culture* and *The Chrysanthemum and the Sword*, she elaborated one of the first and most influential theories of cultural integration.

Benedict was first taught anthropology by students of Franz Boas and, as a graduate student, was trained by Boas himself. Her early essays, "The Vision in Plains Culture" and "The Concept of the Guardian Spirit in North America," focused on the distribution of culture "elements" or "traits" among native North American groups. This work led logically to the issue that Benedict's mature writings address: the nature of cultural wholes. Distributional studies showed that culture elements could not be understood, or even defined, without reference to the specific cultural contexts in which they were found. The guardian-spirit concept, for example, differed from group to group because in each it "associated itself" with different phenomena—with totemism among one people, with secret societies among another, with black magic among a third, and so on. In each case, in order to understand the guardian-spirit concept one had to see how it related to the cultural whole. How, then, were anthropologists to talk about whole cultures and the combination of disparate traits out of which they were built? This question had been implicit in Boas's development of the culture concept, but it was only in the work of his students that answers were developed.

Patterns of Culture grew out of Benedict's field experiences in the American Southwest, where she was struck by the cultural differences that separated geographically contiguous groups. In "Psychological Types in the Cultures of the Southwest" she borrowed Nietzsche's terms—"Dionysian" and "Apollonian"— to characterize "two diametrically different ways of arriving at the values of existence." This concern with the patterning of values is central to *Patterns of Culture*, which presents a complete theory of culture as well as illustrative accounts of three cultures, Zuni (American Southwest), Dobu (Melanesia), and the Northwest Coast of America. Benedict begins *Patterns of Culture* by defining anthropology as "the science of custom" and pointing out, first, that the apparently trivial details of customary behavior and thought fundamentally shape each person's understanding of reality:

No man ever looks at the world with pristine eyes. He sees it edited by a definite set of customs and institutions and ways of thinking. Even in his philosophical probings he cannot go behind these stereotypes; his very concepts of the true and the false will still have reference to his particular traditional customs.

Second, the facts of custom, of culture, are diverse, or locally variable. Because the possibilities for a viable way of life are almost limitless, each human group has had to select a specific cultural pattern, and this pattern makes it unique. Third, this selection of cultural material becomes, in the course of history, "integrated": disparate culture traits are woven together in a fundamental pattern such that any one of them can be understood only in terms of its relationship to all the others:

The significance of cultural behaviour is not exhausted when we have clearly understood that it is local and manmade and hugely variable. It tends also to be integrated. A culture, like an individual, is a more or less consistent pattern of thought and action. Within each culture there come into being characteristic purposes not necessarily shared by other types of society. In obedience to these purposes, each people further and further consolidates its experience, and in proportion to the urgency of these drives the heterogeneous items of behaviour take more and more congruous shape. Taken up by a well-integrated culture, the most ill-assorted acts become characteristic of its peculiar goals, often by the most unlikely metamorphoses.

These major assumptions about culture entail others. Culture is an historical rather than a racial product: to explain human diversity in terms of biology is fallacious. Other determinisms—those of geography, environment, or technology—are equally fallacious: for Benedict a culture is, like an established style in art, a product of the human imagination. This means that culture is open-ended: particular cultures can change, and no definitive typology of cultures can be established. This last point has been obscured by Benedict's use of such terms as those taken from Nietzsche and from the psychoanalytic literature—she characterized Northwest Coast culture, for example, as paranoid and megalomaniacal. However, as she herself stated, each term that she chose was meant only as "an empirical characterization." Finally, because cultural wholes are patterns of values in terms of which human beings understand the world, people tend to (mis)understand other cultures by interpreting them in terms of their own. Different cultures

are oriented as wholes in different directions. They are travelling along different roads in pursuit of different ends, and these ends and these means in one society cannot be judged in terms of those of another society, because essentially they are incommensurable.

The incommensurability of different value systems has an important bearing on the anthropological attempt to understand other cultures, for people will orient their reading of another culture in terms of their own. This fundamental fact of cultural translation is brilliantly demonstrated in *The Chrysanthemum and the Sword*, where Benedict develops an analysis of Japanese culture by beginning with those aspects of it that seem most strange, contradictory, or inexplicable to Americans. In other words, her interpretation of Japanese culture grows out of a dialectical juxtaposition of two world views: what appears strange when seen from one perspective must be made sense of in its own terms; apparently exotic traits must be replaced in, or explicated in terms of, the cultural context in which they are implicit, ordinary. Thus *The Chrysanthemum and the Sword* begins with a discussion of Japanese conceptions of hierarchy and indebtedness, for these contradict the crucial American values of equality and freedom:

Much of what Westerners name ancestor worship is not truly worship and not wholly directed toward ancestors: it is a ritual avowal of man's great indebtedness to all that has gone before. Moreover, he is indebted not only to the past; every day-by-day contact with other people increases his indebtedness in the present. From this debt his daily decisions and actions must spring. It is the fundamental starting point. Because Westerners pay such extremely slight attention to their debt to the world and what it has given them in care, education, well-being or even in the mere fact of their ever having been born at all, the Japanese feel that our motivations are inadequate. Virtuous men do not say, as they do in America, that they owe nothing to any man. They do not discount the past. Righteousness in Japan depends upon recognition of one's place in the great network of mutual indebtedness that embraces both one's forebears and one's contemporaries.

Once we understand that Japanese value hierarchy—"taking one's proper station"—as highly as we value egalitarianism, we can understand many initially confusing aspects of Japanese culture. For example, because Japanese understand family relationships to be grounded in indebtedness, they accept both filial and parental duties that to us seem overly severe and lacking in "love." Similarly, civic duty in Japan is understood as the repayment of debt to the supreme authority, the figurehead—for example, the Emperor—at the apex of the social hierarchy. A person's self-respect is bound to his fulfillment of this duty. By contrast, American self-respect depends largely on individual freedom and initiative, hence Americans tend to view governmental regulation as a violation of their dearest values. Each culture misunderstands the other because apparently similar traits take on fundamentally different significances in each:

> The Japanese judge...that we are a lawless people. We judge that they are a submissive people with no ideas of democracy. It would be truer to say that the citizens' self-respect, in the two countries, is tied up with different attitudes; in our country it depends on his management of his own affairs and in Japan it depends on repaying what he owes to accredited benefactors.

As her study of Japanese culture demonstrates, Ruth Benedict sought intercultural understanding, but, as Margaret Mead has pointed out, she did not thereby advocate an unlimited cultural relativism. She believed that anthropology, by helping people to see their own institutions in a new light, could lead them to change customs that would appear irrational or harmful in comparative perspective. She also believed that people could learn from other cultures, provided they were allowed to learn new values in their own way rather than forced to accept the beliefs of the powerful. She herself accepted individual freedom and equality, and social cooperation rather than irresponsible privilege, as the most worthy of human values. This led to her dignified criticism of what she saw as the great evils of her own culture—racism and poverty.

—Richard Handler

BENJAMIN, Walter. German critic and essayist. Born in Berlin, 15 July 1892. Educated at the University of Freiburg, 1912; University of Berlin, 1913; University of Munich, 1915-17; University of Berne, Ph.D. 1919. Married Dora Sophie Pollak in 1917 (divorced, 1930); 1 son. Worked as a journalist and translator in Berlin and Paris. Member, in Paris, of the New School for Social Research, Frankfurt, 1934-35. *Died* (committed suicide) *27 September 1940.*

PUBLICATIONS

Collections

Gesammelten Schriften. Frankfurt, Suhrkamp, 1972—.
Schriften. Frankfurt, Suhrkamp, 1955.
Illuminationen: Ausgewählte Schriften, edited by Siegfried Unseld. Frankfurt, Suhrkamp, 1961.
Illuminations, edited and with an introduction by Hannah Arendt. New York, Harcourt Brace, 1968; London, Fontana, 1973.
Reflections: Essays, Aphorisms, Autobiographical Writings, edited and with an introduction by Peter Demetz. New York, Harcourt Brace, 1979.
One-way Street and Other Writings, with an introduction by Susan Sontag. London, New Left Books, 1979.

Criticism

Der Begriff der Kunstkritik in der deutschen Romantik. Berne, Francke, 1920.
Ursprung des deutschen Trauerspiels. Berlin, Rowohlt, 1928; as *The Origin of German Tragic Drama,* London, New Left Books, 1977.
Goethes Wahlverwandtschaften (essay). Frankfurt, Insel-Verlag, 1964.
Zur Kritik der Gewalt und andere Aufsätze (essays). London, Suhrkamp, 1965.

Versuche über Brecht (essays), edited by Rolf Tiedemann. Frankfurt, Suhrkamp, 1966.
Über Literatur. Frankfurt, Suhrkamp, 1969.
Charles Baudelaire: Ein Lyriker im Zeitalter des Hochkapitalismus (essays), edited by Rolf Tiedemann. Frankfurt, Suhrkamp, 1969; as *Charles Baudelaire: A Poet in the Era of High Capitalism,* London, New Left Books, 1973.
Lesezeichen: Schriften zur deutschsprachigen Literatur (essays), edited by Gerhard Seidel. Leipzig, Reclam, 1970.
Drei Hörmodelle (essays). Frankfurt, Suhrkamp, 1971.
Über Haschisch: Novellistiches, Berichte, Materialien, edited by Tillman Rexroth. Frankfurt, Suhrkamp, 1972.
Understanding Brecht, with an introduction by Stanley Mitchell. London, New Left Books, 1973.

Other

Einbahnstrasse (aphorisms). Berlin, Rowohlt, 1928.
Berliner Kindheit um Neunzehnhundert (reminiscences). Berlin, Suhrkamp, 1950.
Briefe, edited by Gershom Scholem and T.W. Adorno. Frankfurt, Suhrkamp, 2 vols., 1965.
Berlin Chronik (essays). Frankfurt, Suhrkamp, 1970.
Walter Benjamin: Gershom Scholem: Briefwechsal 1933-1940, edited by Gershom Scholem. Frankfurt, Suhrkamp, 1980.

Editor, as Detlef Holz, *Deutsche Menschen: Eine Folge von Briefen.* Lucerne, Vita Nova, 1936.

Translator, *Charles Baudelaire: Tableaux Parisiens.* Heidelberg, Weissbach, 1923.
Translator, *Ursule Mirouet,* by Balzac, as *Ursula Mirouet.* Berlin, Rowohlt, 1925.
Translator, with Franz Hessel, *A l'ombre des jeunes filles en fleurs,* by Proust, as *Im Schatten der jungen Mädchen.* Berlin, Die Schmiede, 1927.
Translator, with Franz Hessel, *Le Côté des Guermantes,* by Proust, as *Die Herzogin von Guermantes.* Munich, Piper, 2 vols., 1930.
Translator, *Charles Baudelaire: Ausgewählte Gedichte.* Frankfurt, Suhrkamp, 1970.

*

Critical Studies: *Studieren zur Philosophie Walter Benjamins* by Rolf Tiedemann, Frankfurt, Europäische Verlagsanstalt, 1965; *Zur Aktualität Walter Benjamins,* edited by Siegfried Unseld, Frankfurt, Suhrkamp, 1972 (contains an extensive bibliography); *Walter Benjamin: Zwischen den Stühlen: Eine Biographie* by Werner Fuld, Munich, Hauser, 1979; *Walter Benjamin; or, Towards a Revolutionary Criticism* by Terry Eagleton, London, New Left Books, 1981.

*   *   *

Walter Benjamin, who as translator, critic, and man of letters, established himself early on as a master of German prose, is today chiefly renowned for his views concerning the nature of language. At the beginning of his career, Benjamin held that language was neither a conventional system of signs that are adventitiously related to their objects nor a mystical identity of word and reality, but was rather the medium that mediates the original, creative word of God, of which it is but an imperfect reflection, and human knowledge. Language ontologically elevates the lower, uncommunicative strata of creation to the level of meaningful existence by the activity of naming, which, according to Benjamin, is prior to that of speech and communication. This theological conception of language, though eventually rejected by Benjamin, anticipated two important facets of his later thought, namely his interest in semiotics (the interpretation of textual meanings which reside in unspoken, unwritten "expressions," such as contained, for example, in the detritus of cities) and his attitude concerning the intertranslatability of languages and sign systems as reflections of one and the same *logos*. Benjamin's thought at this stage also presages a dialectical tension between his mature belief that language, and sign systems generally, display a textual wholeness linking spirit and matter— the pre-established harmony of economics, technology, and public life—and his view that the disclosure of truth and significance presupposes a corresponding rupture with the context of meaning.

As for the former view, Benjamin was inspired not only by Hegel, but by the French Symbolists, most notably Baudelaire, whose *correspondences* provided him with a motif for analyzing the phenomenon of remembrance. In Benjamin's opinion, each artifact or thing (e.g., Proust's *madeleine*) possesses an "aura" of meaningfulness—literally a nexus of associated images concentrated in a single, unified whole—that implicitly contains the totality of past, present, and future experience. Benjamin's early fragment on the mimetic faculty already suggests that language is more like writing than speaking, more like a static tableau of non-sensuous "resemblances" linking words and things than a dynamic process of communication. However, this notion (the timeless ideality of language as the repository of revealed truth) was later abandoned by him. In its place he substituted the contrary notion of a corrupted text whose evanescent meanings continually dissolve and reconstitute themselves within the temporal "continuum" of a broken narrative. Proust's *mémoire involuntaire*, Benjamin realized, is also a tapestry woven from the remnants of a tattered, i.e., forgotten, past.

In his later Marxist phase, Benjamin became increasingly fascinated with the dissolution of tradition wrought by the technological age and he himself sought to incorporate this development in his aesthetic theory. Contrary to orthodox Marxist literary criticism, Benjamin maintained that materialist hermeneutics should not causally relate cultural artifacts to forces and relations of production so much as show how the latter operate within the former. The introduction of photography and cinema as well as the mass reproducibility of works of art shatters traditional aesthetic categories and modes of perception by destroying the timeless authority and legitimating context of cultural artifacts. Thus liberated, art, Benjamin felt, could enter the practical arena of everyday political life. Though he hoped that such liberation would lead to the democratization of culture, he balefully observed that almost all of the avant garde art movements spawned by technical innovations, such as Dadaism, Futurism, Expressionism, and *Neue Sachlichkeit*, were either assimilated to bourgeois culture or enlisted in the service of Fascism. He was nevertheless favorably impressed with the Surrealists and their "profane illumination" of reality, which he attributed to their imaginative decontextualization and recombination of everyday use-objects in shocking montages. It was precisely the capacity of such revolutionary juxtapositions to stimulate critical reflection that most attracted Benjamin. For this reason, Kraus's method of quoting out of context and Brecht's epic theatre, with its anti-Aristotelian neglect of plot, character, and catharsis in favor of exposing the "conditions of life" through episodic presentation, alienation, surprise, and "coarse thinking," especially appealed to him. He himself strongly identified with the causal urban stroller/observer (the Parisian *flâneur*) who flows along the mainstream of crowded boulevards without really being absorbed into it.

The violence that Benjamin believed was necessary to stimulate critical reflection and that figured so predominantly in his own apocalyptic vision of a world redeemed through proletarian revolution is nowhere more evident than in his theory of interpretation. As a young Hegelian, Benjamin believed that the truth-content of a text—its ideal, ultimately incommunicable significance—was only revealed to critical reflection after temporal distance had dimmed its connection to the historical context wherein it originated. In later life, however, Benjamin came to regard interpretation more as a confrontation between the interpreter's practical standpoint and traditional authority in which

meaning fragments are violently wrested from their context. In the final analysis, it must be conceded that for Benjamin, it was always the isolated word/name and never the sentence, text, or socio-historical environment that constituted the alpha and omega of revealed meaning.

—David Ingram

BERDYAEV, Nicolas (Alexandrovich).   Russian religious philosopher.   Born in Kiev, 6 March 1874. Entered the University of Kiev but was expelled for Marxist activities and exiled to Vologda, 1901-03. Married Lydia Troucheva in 1904. Professor of Philosophy and History, University of Moscow, 1920-22 (exiled). Helped to found the Academy of Philosophy and Religion in Berlin (later in Paris), 1922; lived in Paris after 1924; founded and edited the Russian review *Put* ("The Way"), 1925-40. Honorary doctorate: Cambridge University, 1947. *Died 23 March 1948.*

PUBLICATIONS

Religious and Social Philosophy

Sub"ektivizm i individualizm v obshchestvennoi filosofii: Kriticheskii etiud o N.K. Mikhailovskom [Subjectivism and Individualism in Social Philosophy: A Critical Study of N.K. Mikhailovskii].   St. Petersburg, O.N. Popova, 1901.
Sub Specie Aeternitatis: Opyty filosopkie, sotsial'nye i literaturnye, 1900-1906 [Sub Specie Aeternitatis: Philosophical, Social and Literary Essays, 1900-1906].   St. Petersburg, M.V. Pirozhkov, 1907.
Novoe religioznoe sozdanie i obshchestvennost' [The New Religious Work and the Public].   St. Petersburg, M.V. Pirozhkov, 1907.
Dukhovnyi krizis intelligentsii [The Religious Crisis of the Intelligentsia].   St. Petersburg, Public Benefit Publishing House, 1910.
Filosofiia svobody [The Philosophy of Freedom].   Moscow, Put', 1911.
Aleksei Stepanovich Khomiakov.   Moscow, Put', 1912.
Dusha Rossii [The Soul of Russia].   Moscow, I.D. Sytin, 1915.
Smysl tvorchestva: Opyt opravdaniia cheloveka.   Moscow, Leman and Sakharov, 1916; as *The Meaning of the Creative Act*, New York, Harper, 1954; London, Gollancz, 1955.
Nationalizm i imperializm [Nationalism and Imperialism].   Moscow, Leman and Sakharov, 1917.
Nationalizm i messianizm [Nationalism and Messianism].   Moscow, Leman and Sakharov, 1917.
Sud'ba Rosii: Opyty po psikhologii voiny i natsional'nosti [The Fate of Russia: Attempts at a Psychology of War and Nationality].   Moscow, Leman and Sakharov, 1918.
Krizis iskusstva [The Crisis in Art].   Moscow, Leman and Sakharov, 1918.
Filosofiia Dostoevskogo.   Petrograd, Epokha, 1921; as *Dostoevskii: An Interpretation*, London, Sheed and Ward, 1926.
Konets renessansa [The End of the Renaissance].   Petrograd, Epokha, 1922.
Smysl istorii: Opyt filosofii cheloveckestkoi sud'by.   Berlin, Obelisk, 1923; as *The Meaning of History*, London, Bles, and New York, Scribner, 1936.
Filosofiia neravenstva: Pis'ma k nedrugam po sotsial'noi filosofii [The Philosophy of Inequality: Letters to my Foes on Social Philosophy].   Berlin, Obelisk, 1923.
Novoe srednevekov'e. Razmyshlenie o sud'be Rossii i evropy. Berlin, Obelisk, 1924; as *The End of Our Time, Together with*

an Essay on the "General Line" of Soviet Philosophy, London and New York, Sheed and Ward, 1933.

Konstantin Leont'ev. Paris, YMCA Press, 1926; as *Leontiev*, London, Bles, 1940; Orono, Maine, Academic International, 1968.

Filosofiia svobodnogo dukha. Paris, YMCA Press, 2 vols., 1927-28; as *Freedom and the Spirit*, London, Bles, and New York, Scribner, 1935.

O dostoinstve krhistianstva i nedostoinstve khristian [On the Virtue of Christianity and the Unworthiness of Christians]. Paris, YMCA Press, 1928.

Marksizm i religiia. Religiia, kak orudie gospodstva i ekpluatatsii [Marxism and Religion: Religion as an Instrument of Domination and Exploitation]. Paris, YMCA Press, 1929.

The Russian Revolution: Two Essays on Its Implications in Religion and Philosophy. London, Sheed and Ward, 1931; Ann Arbor, University of Michigan Press, 1961.

O samoubiistve. Psikhologicheskii etiud [On Suicide: A Psychological Study]. Paris, YMCA Press, 1931.

O naznachenii cheloveka: Opyt paradoksal'noi etiki. Paris, Sovremennye Zapiski, 1931; as *The Destiny of Man*, London, Bles, and New York, Harper, 1937.

Russkaia religioznaia psikhologiia i kommunisticheskii ateizm [Russian Religious Psychology and Communist Atheism]. Paris, YMCA Press, 1931.

Krhistianstvo i klassovaia bor'ba. Paris, YMCA Press, 1931; as *Christianity and Class War*, London and New York, Sheed and Ward, 1933.

Vital Realities, with others. New York, Macmillan, 1932.

Ia i mir ob"ektov: Opyt filosofii odinochestva i obshcheniia. Paris, YMCA Press, 1934; as *Solitude and Society*, London, Bles, and New York, Scribner, 1938.

Sud'ba cheloveka v sovremennom mire. Paris, YMCA Press, 1934; as *The Fate of Man in the Modern World*, London, SCM Press, and Milwaukee, Morehouse, 1935.

The Bourgeois Mind, and Other Essays. London, Sheed and Ward, 1934.

Dukh i real'nost'. Osnovy bogochelovecheskoi dukhovnosti. Paris, YMCA Press, 1937; as *Spirit and Reality*, New York, Scribner, 1939; London, Bles, 1946.

O rabstve i svobode cheloveka: Opyt personalisticheskoi filosofii. Paris, YMCA Press, 1939; as *Slavery and Freedom*, London, Bles, and New York, Scribner, 1939.

Russkaia ideia: Osnovnye problemy russkoi mysli XIX veka i nachala XX veka. Paris, YMCA Press, 1946; as *The Russian Idea*, London, Bles, 1947; New York, Macmillan, 1948.

Opyt eskhatologicheskoi metafiziki: Tvorchestvo i ob"ektivatsiia. Paris, YMCA Press, 1947; as *The Beginning and the End: An Essay on Eschatological Principles*, London, Bles, and New York, Harper, 1952.

Au seuil de la nouvelle époque. Neuchâtel, Switzerland, Delachaux and Niestlé, 1947; as *Towards a New Epoch*, London, Bles, 1949.

Tsarstvo Dukha i isarstvo kesaria. Paris, YMCA Press, 1949; as *The Realm of Spirit and the Realm of Caesar*, London, Gollancz, and New York, Harper, 1952.

Samopoznanie: Opyt filosofskoi avtobiografii. Paris, YMCA Press, 1949; as *Dream and Reality: An Essay in Autobiography*, London, Bles, 1950; New York, Macmillan, 1951.

Ekzistentsiial'naia dialektika bozhestvennago i chelovecheskogo. Paris, YMCA Press, 1952; as *The Divine and the Human*, London, Bles, 1949.

Istoki i smysl russkogo kommunizma. Paris, YMCA Press, 1955; as *The Origin of Russian Communism*, London, Bles, 1955; Ann Arbor, University of Michigan Press, 1960.

Istina i otkrovenie: Prolegomeny k kritike otkroveniia (unedited text), as *Truth and Revelation*, London, Bles, and New York, Harper, 1953.

Christian Existentialism: A Berdiaev Anthology, edited by Donald A. Lowrie. London, Allen and Unwin, and New York, Harper, 1965.

*

Bibliography: *Bibliographie des oeuvres de Nicolas Berdiaev* by Tamara Klépinine, Paris, Institut d'Études Slaves, 1978.

Critical Studies: *Introduction to Berdyaev* by O. Fielding Clarke, London, Bles, 1950; *Berdyaev's Philosophy of Hope: A Contribution to Marxist-Christian Dialogue* by C.S. Calian, Leiden, Brill, 1968.

*   *   *

Nicolas Alexandrovich Berdyaev, ranks as one of the outstanding Christian philosophers of the 20th century. Berdyaev is remembered for his many writings on the themes of freedom, creativity, and hope. Most of his works are still in print, testifying to the enduring value of his impact upon society.

Berdyaev was a creative and restless individual. Freedom was not only one of his favorite themes, it also characterized his life. He placed his concern for freedom within the Christian context of hope, to which he often referred as an "eschatological philosophy." Berdyaev was in many respects an intellectual "Zorba," which explains in large measure why his writings and behavior were never easy to categorize or predict. History for Berdyaev was the stage on which God's creative force seeks fulfillment. Berdyaev's vision of the eschaton pointed to the final overcoming of time. As he described it in *The Beginning and the End*, "the central thought of eschatological philosophy is connected with the interpretation of the Fall as objectification, and of the end as the final and decisive victory over objectification." Berdyaev found himself always trying to resolve the tensions caused by the constraints and limitations of our world. He sought to transcend this world through the principles of another world, the kingdom of God. Thus, for him, eschatology was mainly what the Judeo-Christian heritage names the doctrine of "last things." This doctrine more positively is described as an outlook of openness and hope toward the future.

Berdyaev's hope is accomplished when this world of "objects" that we know is destroyed and replaced by the true kingdom of God. "The end," he wrote, "is not merely the destruction of the world, and judgment, it is also the illumination and transformation of the world, the continuation, as it were, of creation, the entry upon a new aeon." Therefore, "at each moment of one's living, what is needed is to put an end to the old world and to begin the new. In that is the breadth of the Spirit. The aeon of the end is the revealing of the Spirit." The goal of human history is the completed revelation of the Spirit.

From his early youth Berdyaev tended to regard the world about him as illusory. He considered himself a part of another, "real" world. The child's consciousness of spiritual apartness—this eschatological germ—was expressed in his principal works. He spoke of his early outlook on the first page of his autobiography: "I cannot remember my first cry on encountering the world, but I know for certain that from the very beginning I was aware of having fallen into an alien realm. I felt this as much on the first day of my conscious life as I do at the present time. I have been a pilgrim."

Berdyaev's life was divided into three quarter-centuries: the years in Kiev where he was born in 1874; the years of activity in Vologda, St. Petersburg, and Moscow; and the years abroad in exile, almost entirely in Paris. He never realized his desire to return to his homeland. In spite of his indebtedness to the West, Berdyaev was first and always a Russian. He saw himself as an heir to the tradition of Dostoevsky, Tolstoy, Solovyev, Fyodorov, and the Slavophils. His insistence on being a Russian also enabled him to claim a certain universalism in outlook.

It was Berdyaev's regard for universalism that attracted him to Marxism. Marxism, he thought, was sensitive to the forces moving below the surface of history, aware of the importance of certain events in the perspective of universal history. At first, Berdyaev saw Marxism as a living and universal form of eschatology. Later, on closer examination, he rejected it. In the preface to his *Christianity and Class War* he referred to his experience with Marxism: "I dedicate this book to the memory of Karl Marx who was the social master of my youth and whose opponent in ideas I have now become."

Berdyaev, in the beginning, approved of Lenin's revolution and was in fact installed as professor of philosophy of Moscow University following the revolution. His disillusionment with Lenin's restrictive rule and interpretation of marxism soon followed, leading to his exile. This was also a time in which his religious consciousness grew and his Christian commitments deepened.

Berdyaev's understanding of Christianity and Eastern Orthodoxy was basically eschatological. He found in Eastern Orthodox tradition a greater emphasis upon mystery, the Spirit, and the vision of a future changed by God. Therefore, Berdyaev wrote, "I was led to the conclusion that Orthodoxy is less susceptible of definition and rationalization than either Catholicism or Protestantism. For me this was significant of greater freedom, and hence evidence of the pre-eminence of Orthodoxy." Berdyaev's eschatological understanding of Christianity let him be comfortable within an Orthodox tradition. Until his death, he was a faithful member of the Russian Orthodox Church, even though he was thought at times to be less than orthodox. Berdyaev's pilgrimage from atheism to Christianity and from Marxism to the Orthodox church was a major part of his intellectual and emotional development. In *Dream and Reality* he wrote, "My original religious impulse was bound up with a bitter feeling of discontent with and dissent from the world with its evil and corruption. And this was a first indication of my subsequent conviction that the existence of evil is not so much an obstacle to faith in God as a proof of God's existence, a challenge to turn towards that in which love triumphs over hatred, union over division and eternal life over death." As Berdyaev turned from Marxism, a new emphasis upon the importance of the individual emerged.

Berdyaev rejected Marxism because of Marx's subordination of individuality and freedom to the collective. Marxism, he found, limited reality to a worldly-materialistic plane that denied the existence of another world. This was unacceptable to an eschatologically inclined person like Berdyaev. He wrote: "Living only in one (world), would make life flat...To my finite and limited consciousness there is given a striving toward the unlimited and the infinite. Recognizing only the realm of Caesar is shutting oneself up in the finite." He wanted instead to reach out for a larger destiny found in a Christian eschatological future.

His view of this destiny shifted. At first he saw it in terms of a classless society, but eventually he looked for a Christian end which promises to restore all life through a transforming and creative process. In Berdyaev's ethic, past and present are in the nature of stewardship, responsible for continuous creativity toward the future. He saw Marxism as a legalistic ethic that is neither redemptive nor creative.

Berdyaev called for an ethic open to the future wherein individuals realize their rightful destiny as the sons and daughters of God entrusted with the Father's creation. As he wrote in *The Destiny of Man*, his ethical attitude was "directed towards the aeon which lies between time and eternity, between this world and the world beyond, in which the hard-set limitations of our existence are melted down."

The content of Berdyaev's ethic of redemption is the good news of the coming of the kingdom of God. The gospel is revolutionary, but it points to another world. It has eschatological dimension and is based on love, rather than on rights and rules. Berdyaev strongly felt that the kingdom of God cannot be expressed by any social and historical forms. In other words, he rejected the idea that there could be a Christian state, Christian economics, Christian family, Christian learning, Christian social life. For him, the kingdom of God was more than state, economics, family, learning, or any social life determined by law and rules. His vision of the kingdom pictures a freedom in the Spirit in which worldly restrictions are removed.

—Carnegie Samuel Calian

BERENSON, Bernard. American art historian and aesthetician. Born in Butremanz, Lithuania, 26 June 1865; emigrated to the United States, 1875, and subsequently naturalized. Educated at the Boston Latin School, 1881-83; Boston University, 1883-84; Harvard University, Cambridge, Massachusetts, B.A. 1887. Married Mary Pearsall Smith Costelloe, 1909. Travelled and lived abroad, beginning in 1887; settled at I Tatti, Settignano, Italy. Adviser and purchaser of works of art for Isabella Stewart Gardner; Duveen Brothers, 1907-36; Georges Wildenstein Gallery, Paris; Henry Clay Frick, and others. Recipient: Serena Medal for Italian Studies, British Academy. Honorary doctorate: University of Florence; University of Paris. Honorary Citizen of Florence, 1949. Member, American Academy of Arts and Letters. Honorary Member, American Academy of Arts and Sciences, 1958. Associate of the Belgian Academy; Foreign Member, Norwegian Academy; Italian Lincei; and Venetian Ateneo. *Died 6 October 1959* (bequeathed I Tatti to Harvard University, now the Center for Italian Renaissance Studies).

PUBLICATIONS

Art History and Aesthetics

The Venetian Painters of the Renaissance. New York and London, Putnam, 1894.
Lorenzo Lotto: An Essay in Constructive Art Criticism. New York and London, Putnam, 1895.
The Florentine Painters of the Renaissance. New York and London, Putnam, 1896.
The Central Italian Painters of the Renaissance. New York and London, Putnam, 1897.
The Study and Criticism of Italian Art. London, Bell, 1901.
The Study and Criticism of Italian Art: Second Series. London, Bell, 1902.
Drawings of the Florentine Painters, Classified, Criticized and Studied as Documents in the History and Appreciation of Tuscan Art with a Copious Catalogue Raisonné. London, Murray, 2 vols., 1903.
The North Italian Painters of the Renaissance. New York and London, Putnam, 1907.
A Sienese Painter of the Franciscan Legend. London, Dent, 1909.
Catalogue of a Collection of Paintings and Some Art Objects. Philadelphia, John G. Johnson, 1913.
Venetian Paintings in America: The Fifteenth Century. New York, Frederick Fairchild Sherman, and London, Bell, 1916.
The Study and Criticism of Italian Art: Third Series. London, Bell, 1916.
Pictures in the Collection of P.A.B. Widener at Lynnewood Hall, Elkins Park, Pennsylvania: Volume III: Early Italian and Spanish School, with Biographical and Descriptive Notes. Philadelphia, privately printed, 1916.
Essays in the Study of Sienese Painting. New York, Frederick Fairchild Sherman, 1918.
Three Essays in Method: Nine Pictures in Search of an Attribution: A Neglected Altarpiece by Botticelli: A Possible and an Impossible "Antonello da Messina." Oxford, Clarendon Press, 1926.
Speculum Humanae Salvationis: Being a Reproduction of an Italian Manuscript of the Fourteenth Century. Oxford, Clarendon Press, 1926.

Studies in Medieval Painting. New Haven, Connecticut, Yale University Press, and London, Oxford University Press, 1930.

The Italian Painters of the Renaissance. Oxford, Clarendon Press, 1930.

Italian Pictures of the Renaissance: A List of the Principal Artists and Their Works with an Index of Places. Oxford, Clarendon Press, 1932.

Aesthetics and History in the Visual Arts. New York, Pantheon, 1948; London, Constable, 1950.

Seeing and Knowing. London, Chapman and Hall, 1953.

Caravaggio, His Incongruity and Fame. London, Chapman and Hall, 1953.

Piero Della Francesca; or, the Ineloquent in Art. London, Chapman and Hall, 1954.

The Arch of Constantine; or, the Decline of Form. London, Chapman and Hall, 1954.

Essays in Appreciation. London, Chapman and Hall, and New York, Macmillan, 1958.

The Bernard Berenson Treasury: A Selection from the Works, Unpublished Writings, Letters, Diaries, and Journals of the Most Celebrated Humanist and Art Historian of Our Time, 1887-1958, edited by Hanna Kiel. New York, Simon and Schuster, and London, Methuen, 1962.

Homeless Paintings of the Renaissance, edited by Hanna Kiel. London, Thames and Hudson, and Bloomington, Indiana University Press, 1969.

Other

Sketch for a Self-Portrait. London, Constable, and New York, Pantheon, 1949.

Rumour and Reflection, 1941-44. London, Constable, and New York, Simon and Schuster, 1952.

Colloqui con Berenson, with Umberto Morra. Milan, Garzanti, 1963; as *Conversations with Berenson,* Boston, Houghton Mifflin, 1965.

Selected Letters of Bernard Berenson, edited by A.K. McComb. Boston, Houghton Mifflin, 1964; London, Hutchinson, 1965.

One Year's Reading for Fun, 1942. New York, Knopf, and London, Weidenfeld and Nicolson, 1960.

The Passionate Sightseer: From the Diaries, 1947-1956, edited by Nicky Mariano. London, Thames and Hudson, and New York, Simon and Schuster, 1960.

Sunset and Twilight: From the Diaries of 1947-58, edited by Nicky Mariano. New York, Harcourt Brace, 1963; London, Hamish Hamilton, 1964.

The Berenson Archive: An Inventory of Correspondence. Cambridge, Massachusetts, Harvard University Press, 1965.

*

Bibliography: *Bibliografia di Bernard Berenson* by William Mostyn-Owen, Milan, Electa, 1955.

Critical Studies: *Berenson: A Biography* by Elizabeth Sprigge, London, Allen and Unwin, and Boston, Houghton Mifflin, 1960; *Forty Years with Berenson* by Nicky Mariano, London, Hamish Hamilton, 1966; *Bernard Berenson: The Making of a Connoisseur* by Ernest Samuels, Cambridge, Massachusetts, Belknap Press, 1979; *Being Bernard Berenson* by Meryl Secrest, New York, Holt Rinehart, 1979, London, Weidenfeld and Nicolson, 1980.

*   *   *

The most distinguished and influential of all American art critics, Bernard Berenson is best known as an historian and connoisseur of Italian Renaissance painting. His four volumes *The Venetian Painters, The Florentine Painters, The Central Italian Painters,* and *The North Italian Painters* were reprinted in 1930 as *The Italian Painters of the Renaissance.* A milestone in the study of Renaissance art, they are regarded as classic works in art history. These books originally included Berenson's "lists" of attributions which were subsequently published in greatly amplified and revised form as *Italian Pictures of the Renaissance.* Following the method of attributing pictures devised by Giovanni Morelli, Berenson brought great order to the study of Italian art by identifying the artists of a vast number of paintings, many of which had been previously misattributed or whose creators were unknown. Of related importance is Berenson's early, monumental book on Florentine drawings which was the first synthetic study of a large body of drawings from the Renaissance. Berenson's fame rests in part on the fact that—despite the vicissitudes of connoisseurship—a remarkably high percentage of his attributions are still adhered to today by scholars. Through his activities as an artistic adviser to dealers and collectors he was also responsible for the acquisition of a large number of masterpieces of Italian painting by American collectors.

Influenced by various philosophers, psychologists, art historians, critics, and theorists—including Jacob Burckhardt, Hippolyte Taine, Walter Pater, Vernon Lee, Adolf Hildebrand, and William James—Berenson outlined the history of Italian painting in evocative, descriptive essays the judgments of which still profoundly influence our perception of Renaissance art today. Closely following the aesthetics of Pater, Berenson insisted that the essential values of art depend on its "form" or what he called "decoration"—that is, color, tactile values, movement, and space-composition. Although Berenson distinguished "decoration" from "illustration" (the literary content or iconography of art), he acknowledged that this distinction is a "necessary fiction," since in a work of art form and content are indissolubly united. Not formalist in the narrow sense in which this word is often employed, Berenson's writings are always sensitive to the intellectual milieu in which art was created and to its reflections and resonances of literature—for example, his appreciation of the idyllic character of Perugino's and Raphael's landscapes, his depiction of Pisanello's courtly and chivalric themes, his descriptions of Mantegna's romantic enthusiasm for archeology and his evocations of Raphael's Hellenism.

No writer after Vasari (whose *Lives* of the artists was first published in 1550) has influenced our understanding of the specific qualities of Renaissance painters as has Berenson; what he in fact succeeded in accomplishing, in large measure, was to read Vasari with exceptional intensity and clarity of mind, both sharpening one's sense of Vasari's seminal, still undervalued judgments and creatively expanding them. For example, Berenson's description of the "energy" of "movement" in Pollaiuolo and the "hyperaesthesia" it induces in us (which has been assimilated in scholarship) is a creative embellishment of Vasari's account of the painter's *forza* or energy; his influential celebration of Mantegna's statuesque grandeur is a reworking of Vasari's criticism of the painter's obsession with sculpture, in which Berenson modifies Vasari's negative judgment. Whereas 19th-century critics still treated Fra Angelico as a medieval artist, Berenson, paying close attention to Vasari's observation that Angelico studied Masaccio's work, characterized Angelico's modernity for the first time, and his view of the artist, popularized by Langton Douglas, is the dominant one in Renaissance studies today. Recognizing that Vasari's observations on Castagno's brutal personality were at bottom a commentary on his art, Berenson illuminated the "brutality" of the painter's style in an interpretation that has come to be fundamental in scholarship on the painter.

In addition, his characterizations of Duccio's gifts as a narrative artist and of Giotto's tactility of form have played an important role in art history, as have his appreciations of Masaccio's heroic powers, of Tura's exoticism of form, and of Bassano's dazzling colors. Berenson was also the first critic to identify the essential role of line in Botticelli's painting and to elevate the "impersonal" art of Piero della Francesca to a place of great importance in the history of quattrocento painting.

In a more general way, Berenson's brief characterization of the "scientific" character of Florentine painting and of its analogy to Renaissance scientific inquiry introduced a major topic that has since been widely discussed, especially by scholars in the great Warburgian tradition. It has also been observed that Berenson was the first scholar to date the advent of Mannerism at about 1520; he recognized the decorative qualities, charm, and playfulness of the first Mannerists in an interpretation that foreshadows more recent scholarship. It goes unnoticed in the vast historiography on Mannerism that Berenson also identified one of the important sources of Mannerism in the quattrocento when he discussed the tendency of 15th-century Florentine artists toward "dexterity," the showing off of skill for its own sake. He saw that such a self-conscious cultivation of dexterity inevitably leads to "academic" art. Finally, Berenson was the first scholar to associate the formal qualities of Renaissance painting with original art; his comparison has become commonplace in art history, especially in writings on Sienese art. Berenson's influences on the history of art are too extensive to chart systematically; but one can observe the special importance of his writings for Roger Fry, Roberto Lorghi, Richard Offner, Kenneth Clark, John Pope-Hennessy, Sydney Freedberg, and Frederick Hartt.

—Paul Barolsky

BERGSON, Henri (Louis). French philosopher. Born in Paris, 12 October 1859. Educated at the Lycée Fontane and at the École Normale Supérieure, 1878-81; University of Paris, docteur-ès-lettres, 1889. Married Louise Neuberger in 1891. Professor, Lycée d'Angers, 1881-83; Lycée Blaise Pascal, Clermont-Ferrand, 1883-88; Lycée Henri-IV, 1889-98; École Normale Supérieure, 1899-1900; Collège de France, 1901-40. Diplomatic missions to America, 1912-13, 1917, 1918, and to Spain, 1915. Recipient: Grand-Croix, Légion d'Honneur; Nobel Prize for Literature, 1928. Member, Académie des Sciences Morales et Politiques, 1901; Académie Française, 1914. *Died* (in Paris) *3 January 1941.*

PUBLICATIONS

Collections

Oeuvres complètes. Geneva, Skira, 3 vols., 1945-46.

Philosophy

Quid Aristotle de loco senserit. Paris, Alcan, 1889.
Essai sur les donées immédiates de la conscience. Paris, Alcan, 1889; as *Time and Free Will: An Essay on the Immediate Data of Consciousness,* London, Sonnenschein, and New York, Macmillan, 1910.
Matière et mémoire: Essai sur la relation du corps avec l'esprit. Paris, Alcan, 1896; as *Matter and Memory,* London, Allen, 1910; New York, Macmillan, 1911.
Le Rire: Essai sur la signification du comique. Paris, Alcan, 1900; as *Laughter: An Essay on the Meaning of the Comic,* London and New York, Macmillan, 1911.
"Le Rêve," in *Bulletin de l'Institut Général Psychologique* (Paris), 3, 1901; as *Dreams,* London, Unwin, and New York, Huebsch, 1914.
"Introduction à la métaphysique," in *Revue de Métaphysique et de Morale* (Paris), 29, 1903; as *Introduction to Metaphysics,* New York, Putnam, 1912; London, Macmillan, 1913.
L'Évolution créatrice. Paris, Alcan, 1907; as *Creative Evolu-*

tion, New York, Holt, 1911; London, Macmillan, 1964.
La Perception du changement (lectures). Oxford, Clarendon Press, 1911.
Choix de textes. Paris, Louis Michaud, 1911.
L'Intuition philosophique. Paris, Colin, 1911.
Le Matérialisme actuel, with others. Paris, Flammarion, 1913.
La Signification de la guerre. Paris, Bloud and Gay, 1915; included in *The Meaning of War, Life and Matter in Conflict,* 1915.
The Meaning of War, Life and Matter in Conflict. London, Unwin, and New York, Macmillan, 1915.
L'Énergie spirituelle: Essais et conférences. Paris, Alcan, 1919; as *Mind-Energy: Lectures and Essays,* London, Macmillan, and New York, Holt, 1920.
Durée et simultanéitié, à propos de la théorie d'Einstein. Paris, Alcan, 1922; as *Duration and Simultaneity,* Indianapolis, Bobbs Merrill, 1965.
Réflexions sur le temps, l'espace et la vie. Paris, Payot, 1929.
Les Deux Sources de la morale et de la religion. Paris, Alcan, 1932; as *The Two Sources of Morality and Religion,* London, Macmillan, and New York, Holt, 1935.
La Pensée et le mouvant: Essais et conférences. Paris, Alcan, 1934; as *The Creative Mind,* New York, Philosophical Library, 1946.
Le Bon Sens et les études classiques. Clermont-Ferrand, France, Épervier, 1947.
Ecrits et paroles, edited by R.-M. Mossé-Bastide. Paris, Presses Universitaires de France, 3 vols., 1957-59.
Mélanges. Paris, Presses Universitaires de France, 1972.

Other

Translator and editor, *Extraits de Lucrèce: Avec un commentaire des notes et une étude sur la poésie, la philosophie et la langue de Lucrèce.* Paris, Delagrave, 1883; selections as *The Philosophy of Poetry: The Genius of Lucretius,* New York, Wisdom Library, 1959.

*

Bibliography: *Henri Bergson: A Bibliography* by P.A.Y. Gunter, Bowling Green, Ohio, Philosophy Documentation Center, 1974.

Critical Studies: *Henri Bergson: Essais et temoignages,* edited by A. Béguin and P. Thévenaz, Neuchâtel, Switzerland, La Baconnière, 1942; *Bergson: Philosopher of Reflection* by Ian W. Alexander, London, Bowes and Bowes, and New Haven, Connecticut, Yale University Press, 1957; *The Bergsonian Heritage,* edited by Thomas Hanna, New York, Columbia University Press, 1962.

* * *

In the contemporary philosophy Henri Bergson's place is a paradoxical one. He is a thinker of wide, indeed, in the case of French philosophy and letters, of near ubiquitous, influence, yet a thinker too whose work, taken on its own terms, is now largely in eclipse. He is a philosopher who addressed himself to some of the basic problems of Western philosophy, for example, the problems of mind-body relation, of freedom and determinism, of the ultimate nature of the whole of reality, and who proposed radical solutions to those problems. Now to the extent that his issues are those of the mainstream of the tradition in his field, he can rightly be said to belong to that tradition, to be, in relation to it, an insider. Yet, in a more dominant sense, so far as that same tradition is concerned, Bergson is a outsider. This is due to his repudiation of the conception of philosophy handed down through and by the mainstream of the Western tradition and his seeking to substitute for it a fundamentally different conception. The traditional notion of philosophy in question is that of an intellectual discipline, the whole *modus operandi* of which is ratiocination, directed towards the solution of the kinds of problems listed above. In Bergson's view, however, the basic puzzles about the nature of man and of the world around him which perennially have vexed the philosopher cannot be solved, or even adequately formulated, in intellectual terms. In place of the orthodox primacy of intellect in philosophy Bergson proposes intuition, a kind of self-verifying instinct for the concrete. This emphasis on concreteness in Bergson's thought is deliberately set in contrast to the abstractions of the intellect. In fine, Bergson is offering nothing less than a revolution in the conception of what sort of enterprise philosophy is to be.

In keeping with his view of philosophy as, at its core, intuitive, Bergson's writing does not much resemble the argumentative, hypothetico-deductive tracts so typical of his fellow philosophers. And, given that his philosophical *métier* is not principally argument, anything else would be surprising. Bergson's writing is often imagistic, aimed at making points and unfolding positions metaphorically and through simile. He seeks to give to his readers a vision of the world and their place in it, of philosophy and science, and of how those basic philosophical puzzles listed above are properly to be approached and solved. In regard to his literary qualities he can, as a writer of philosophical prose, be ranked with Plato and Augustine and his having been chosen as Nobel laureate in literature in 1927 testifies to his power as a writer.

Dividing philosophers into the admittedly broad and imprecise categories of visionaries and technicians, we can see Bergson as unquestionably a visionary. And, more than any other single factor, it is this that forms the basis for his being regarded, especially by analytical philosophers, as something of a curiosity and also as a philosopher for whose work they feel both a professional and temperamental antipathy. But the question about the identity of philosophy that his work forces upon us is an important philosophical question and so we ought briefly to look into it here.

One of the first points to note is that philosophers seem to be unique among academicians in being so easily moved to disquiet about the nature—by which I do not just mean the state at any particular point in time—of their discipline. A focus on this doubt can be achieved here through consideration of those other undertakings that philosophy is sometimes said to resemble, namely, science and literature. If philosophy is like science, indeed if it is itself a kind of science, then it has fairly definite fields of study over which its proprietorial claims are justified and generally conceded, and it has methods of inquiry and canons of success and failure in investigation upon which there is also significant consensus, particularly within the discipline itself. Furthermore, if philosophy is like science, then it has progress to show for its efforts, or, at the least, promise of progress. On the other hand, if philosophy is less like science than it is like literature (within which I include poetry) then none of the above yardsticks seems to be relevant. Now a fundamental question is which, if either, is it like and how do we tell?

In Bergson's eyes, philosophy usually has tried to be like science and has failed, for precisely that reason, to find solutions to any of its basic problems. For Bergson, intellect will never be able to answer the question of the ultimate nature of reality, whether it be intellect manifested as the pure reasoning of the philosopher or the theory-and-text approach of his scientific colleague. Yet Bergson does not see philosophy as just another part of literature either, for he believes that once it is reformed to heed intuition (hence, to *that* extent, being like poetry and literature) it can make progress in discovery. In this context, his conception of his own role is that of one who would expose the errors in philosophy's past and present, the main error of which is the belief that in the abstractions and formulae of the philosophers and the scientists the ultimate secrets of the universe can be captured, and, having identified those mistakes, point to the future of philosophy based on intuition.

In rejecting Bergson's view of philosophy his critics sometimes forget that, supposing the point that the philosopher is he who seeks for the most general understanding of things to be granted, the form which philosophy takes is contingent and something decided upon by philosophers themselves. Hence there is no self-evidence or a priori disqualification of Bergson's proposal. In a related point, it can be seen too that in the criticisms of Bergson made by a philosopher such as Bertrand Russell, and by others (such as myself below) influenced by him, there is a disturbing taint of *petitio principii* involved in faulting Bergson's theses for not passing the test of rational argument and proof. Another way of looking at this point is, perhaps, this: that Bergson, in this respect at least like the great philosophers in the Western tradition, Plato, Aristotle, Kant, Wittgenstein and others, dictates the terms in which is work is fairly to be appraised.

In addition to his contribution to articulating philosophy's self-conscious puzzlement over the question of its own true nature and identity, let us look at Bergson's views on some of philosophy's other perennial problems.

In a famous phrase, Wilfrid Sellars has depicted philosophy as "an attempt to see how things, in the broadest possible sense of the term, hang together, in the broadest possible sense of the term." It is just such a large-scale program of philosophy that Bergson is offering us. Traditionally, metaphysics, the effort to give a systematic account of the whole of reality, has been erected on the shoulders of an epistemology which, in its turn, has taken its start from a theory of perception. Also traditionally, perception has been interpreted in cognitivist terms and this sets in train a like approach to philosophy generally, resulting in, in effect, the notion of philosophy as non-experimental science. Now, in Bergson's scheme of things, psychology replaces epistemology and in place of intellect and cognition are put intuition and instinct. This sets the basic framework of his proposed revolution in philosophy.

In specific terms, this proposed change has Bergson categorizing the metaphysics of Plato and Aristotle and their respective progenies as so many futile efforts to make sense of the world built on the erroneous basic presupposition that the world is, at bottom, a network of substances related together in various ways. This view of the world is so deeply ingrained in our outlook that we forget that it is not a necessary view, that there is no contradiction in denying it, that it is a product of a particular kind of logic and thinking. And this logic, the logic philosophers and scientists alike take for granted, Bergson maintains is "pre-eminently a logic of solids." In passing, it might be mentioned here that, on this line of criticism of the Western philosophical tradition Heidegger's debt to Bergson can, in part, be measured. Bergson repudiates substance theories in metaphysics and science and he rejects too the logic which permeates them. The ground of this double rejection is his repudiation of an even more basic presupposition that he claims to detect at the heart of both, namely, the concept of space as either the surface extension of a thing or as the extension between things. In modern thought such a view has been most forcefully advocated by Descartes, but it is a position which, in one form or another, long pre-dates the 17th century. Bergson's conviction is that if he can successfully show the shortcomings of this concept of space the whole philosophical-*cum*-scientific edifice of theory standing on it will fall and he will then have cleared the way for a new and more adequate theory of reality.

In Bergson's eyes the substance theorist posits a world essentially static and accounts for change and movement in terms of relations of before and after. Such relations reflect a linear view of time. On this view the present is here, the past back there and the future up ahead. For Bergson, this view of time as linear, a view common to science, philosophy, and common sense, is essentially a spatial view, hence one whose true character is to be grasped through mathematics. According to it, time is really a function of space. Change, then, is accounted for as a property of relations between stages on the line of time. But change, Bergson insists, basing his insistence upon an appeal to intuition, is not like that at all. Change is what Heraclitus said it was—pure flux. And furthermore, again on the strength of intuition, the world is not a network of individual things or substances; rather it is, as Heraclitus also said, ceaseless becoming, perpetual flux. In order to be clear on the magnitude of Bergson's counter-proposal to the metaphysical traditions tracing back to Plato and Aristotle, it is important to note that his point is not that those traditional ways of doing metaphysics failed to give sufficient place to the phenomenon of change in their respective substance-views. His point is the more radical one that the very idea of change embedded in Western thought from, Heraclitus excepted, the ancient Greeks on down is irredeemably false, that change and hence, by extrapolation, the world itself is not in the least the sort of place portrayed in the realisms or idealisms of the great philosophers or, in science, in the physical systems of the Galileos and the Newtons. In his own memorable words: "...things and states are only views, taken by our mind, of becoming. There are no things, there are only actions." His fundamental point is that, in effect, the concept of a thing, so central to traditional science and philosophy, is a theoretician's abstraction, one which Bergson finds seriously misguided and misguiding, and he argues too that the conception of the world as a vast complex of things is a further intellectual construct and one incapable of being correct because of the error of its core idea, that of a substance, an individual, self-identifiable thing.

What is the evidence for so radically a different view? As I remarked earlier, this new metaphysics stands on an account of psychology, in particular the psychology of the investigator himself from the perspective of his own introspective intuition, not from the clinical viewpoint of an outside theorist. In effect what Bergson is offering as the starting-point of philosophy and science is a phenomenological self-psychology. The testimony of such intuition, Bergson tells us, is first of all that persons are not substances, whether physical or mental substances, but rather currents of life-forces and, secondly, that we directly intuit the "flow" of life. Intuition further testifies, Bergson claims, that time is quite unlike the mathematical face put upon it by the mathematicians, and via them the philosophers, scientists, and, ultimately, plain men of common sense, that time itself, real time, is experienced as "real duration."

In the context of those points, consider Bergson's thoughts on two closely related issues: the problem of mind-body relation and the problem of freedom and determinism. The former is the problem of how theoretically to reconcile what ordinarily we take for granted as two distinct ontological spheres, the mental and the physical. In contemporary thought two major competing theories, the materialist identity theory on the one hand and, on the other, some version of the dualism proposed in the 17th century by Descartes, together set both the stage for and the dimensions of the mind-body debate. According to the identity theory the concept of mind is, in principle, capable of being translated, without loss of scientific predictability or explanatory power, into the terminology of electro-chemical processes in the central nervous system. The dualist denies it, maintaining, typically, that mind is a distinct kind of thing from matter, that it is spiritual substance and not subject to any law of any physical science, hence that, also in principle, mind is forever beyond the comprehension of science. While the identity theorist hopes to account for such things as thinking, remembering, wishing, deciding, feeling and so on in terms of patterns of neural activity, the dualist seeks for a theory which will be adequate to what he regards as the interaction of two different kinds of substances, different in the very basic sense of having no common properties whatsoever. In fine, the competition between these theories is that between, on the one hand, a one-substance metaphysics and, on the other, a two-substance metaphysics.

For Bergson the question, posed as that of the rivalry of substance theories, is impossible and its impossibility is due to its being, as formulated by materialists and mentalists alike, a pseudo-question. This rivalry is predicated upon mutual endorsement of the concept of substance, of the spatial world (which the materialist then seeks to extend to include mind too), of change and time as both relative to substance. Bergson's claim is that,

with his attunement to intuition, he has decomposed the base presuppositions of identity and dualist theories alike, thus divorcing both from reality.

In the case of the dispute between determinists and advocates of the view that (some at least) human actions are free in the sense of being uncaused, Bergson offers a similarly radical approach. Determinists, he believes, fail the test of experience because, for Bergson in *Time and Free Will*, we actually experience our own freedom. His claim is that freedom is phenomenologically given to us. But, even more than this, the conceptual basis of determinism, Bergson argues, is fundamentally unsound. One main reason for this is that the serial view of the mind, which Bergson believes is indigenous to determinism, is predicated upon the linear conception of time discussed earlier. Operating on the basis of such views of time and the mind, the determinist believes that choices are, at bottom, steps in this direction or that on the line of time, which, he supposes, stretches predictably into the future. And, Bergson's position allows, if the mind and time were constituted the way the determinist believes, then, in principle, all future choices could be foretold and determinism would be vindicated. But, he argues, they are not so constituted and his opposition to determinism issues at the fundamental level of denying the very conceptual ground on which it stands.

What are we to make of Bergson and his theories, including his repudiation, again on the basis of intuition, of two basic and related tenets of the Darwinist conception of evolution, namely: first, the theory that evolution is not finalistic, that is, is not the progressive undertaking of a journey to some pre-ordained goal and, second, the theory that the development and adaptation to their environment of organisms is explicable wholly in terms of random, natural selection? I noted already the difficulty that a commentator, not sharing Bergson's view of philosophy, faces in criticizing Bergson's work. For, as a whole system, it is proposing to change the rules by reference to which philosophical theories traditionally are assessed. But, even with the large issue involved in that set to one side as not appropriate subject-matter for criticism in a piece the length of the present one, several significant problems remain with Bergson's thought. In the first place there seems to be, on the basic issue of his accounts of space, time, and substance, a circularity in his position. This can be seen as follows: real time, real duration, he tells us, is felt as the confluence of past and present and not as a line on which past and present are stretched out; however, and without denying that this *is* real duration, it can be pointed out that those very distinct notions, past and present, which Bergson insists are not really distinct at all, are needed for his description of what time is experienced to be. A further line of criticism might be developed in the following way: even supposing it were to be granted to Bergson that there is something to be said for his criticisms of rival philosophical theories, there yet remains the need for him to work out much more thoroughly than he has done the precise and full positive content of his own views. A particular case in point would be his affirmation of the reality, in experience, of freedom without any adequate theoretical account of the nature of that freedom subsequently being offered. Criticism has also been directed against his version of theism and in particular his conception of God as a "supra-consciousness," a concept which, as explained by Bergson, implies that God is neither a being nor perfect, this latter because God is portrayed as perpetual becoming with becoming regarded by Bergson as always goal-oriented. Finally, the biologists maintain that there is no empirical evidence for, nor explanatory need of, his progress-imbued idea of evolution as essentially creative and according to which "(it is man), or some other being of like significance, which is the purpose of the entire process of evolution."

—David O'Connor

BERLIN, Isaiah. British philosopher and historian of ideas. Born in Riga, Latvia, now in the Soviet Union, 9 June 1909; emigrated to England, 1920. Educated at St. Paul's School, London; studied at Corpus Christi College, Oxford, 1st Class Honours in Humane Letters and Modern Greats. Served in the British Ministry of Information, New York, 1941-42; First Secretary, British Embassy, Washington, D.C., 1942-46, and British Embassy, Moscow, 1945-46: C.B.E. (Commander, Order of the British Empire), 1946. Married Aline de Gunzbourg in 1956. Lecturer in Philosophy, New College, Oxford, 1933; Fellow, 1932-38, 1950-66, and Honorary Fellow, since 1975, All Souls College, Oxford; Chichele Professor of Social and Political Theory, Oxford University, 1957-67; President, 1966-75, and Honorary Fellow, since 1975, Wolfson College, Oxford. Visiting Professor, Harvard University, Cambridge, Massachusetts, 1949, 1951, 1953, 1962; Bryn Mawr College, Pennsylvania, 1952; University of Chicago, 1955; Princeton University, New Jersey, 1965; City College of New York, 1966-71 (Distinguished Professor of Humanities, since 1971). Northcliffe Lecturer, University of London, 1953; Mellon Lecturer, National Gallery of Art, Washington, D.C., 1963; Danz Lecturer, University of Washington, Seattle, 1971. Member, Board of Directors, Royal Opera House, Covent Garden, London, 1954-65 and since 1974; Trustee, National Gallery, London, since 1975; also, Member, Board of Governors, Hebrew University of Jerusalem. Fellow, 1957, Vice-President, 1959-61, and President, 1974-78, British Academy; President, Aristotelian Society, 1963-64. Honorary doctorate: University of Hull, 1965; University of Glasgow, 1967; University of East Anglia, Norwich, 1967; Brandeis University, Waltham, Massachusetts, 1967; Columbia University, New York, 1968; Cambridge University, 1970; University of London, 1971; Hebrew University of Jerusalem, 1971; University of Liverpool, 1972; Tel Aviv University, 1973; Harvard University, 1979; University of Sussex, Brighton, 1979. Foreign Member, American Academy of Arts and Sciences, and American Institute of Arts and Letters. Knighted, 1957; Order of Merit, 1971. Address: All Souls College, Oxford, England.

PUBLICATIONS

History of Ideas and Philosophy

Karl Marx: His Life and Environment. London, Butterworth, 1939; New York, Oxford University Press, 1948.
"Lev Tolstoy's Historical Scepticism," in *Oxford Slavonic Papers*, 2, 1951; as *The Hedgehog and the Fox: An Essay on Tolstoy's View of History.* London, Weidenfeld and Nicolson, and New York, Simon and Schuster, 1953.
Historical Inevitability (lecture). London, Oxford University Press, 1953; reprinted in *Four Essays on Liberty*, 1969.
Two Concepts of Liberty (lecture). Oxford, Clarendon Press, 1958; reprinted in *Four Essays on Liberty*, 1969.
John Stuart Mill and the Ends of Life (lecture). London, Council of Christians and Jews, 1959; reprinted in *Four Essays on Liberty*, 1969.
Four Essays on Liberty. London and New York, Oxford University Press, 1969.
Fathers and Children: Turgenev and the Liberal Predicament (lecture). Oxford, Clarendon Press, 1972; reprinted in *Russian Thinkers*, 1978.
"Austin and the Early Beginnings of Oxford Philosophy," in *Essays on J.L. Austin.* Oxford, Clarendon Press, 1973; reprinted in *Personal Impressions*, 1980.
The Divorce Between the Sciences and the Humanities (lecture). Urbana, University of Illinois Press, 1974; reprinted in *Against the Current*, 1979.
Vico and Herder: Two Studies in the History of Ideas. London, Hogarth Press, and New York, Viking Press, 1976.
Russian Thinkers, edited by Henry Hardy. London, Hogarth Press, and New York, Viking Press, 1978.

Concepts and Categories: Philosophical Essays, edited by Henry Hardy. London, Hogarth Press, and New York, Viking Press, 1979.
Against the Current: Essays in the History of Ideas, edited by Henry Hardy. London, Hogarth Press, and New York, Viking Press, 1980 (includes bibliography).
Personal Impressions, edited by Henry Hardy. London, Hogarth Press, and New York, Viking Press, 1981.

Other

Chaim Weizmann (lecture). London, Weidenfeld and Nicolson, and New York, Farrar Straus, 1958; reprinted in *Personal Impressions*, 1980.
The Life and Opinions of Moses Hess (lecture). Cambridge, Heffer, 1959; reprinted in *Against the Current*, 1979.
Mr. Churchill in 1940. London, Murray, 1964; reprinted in *Personal Impressions*, 1980.

Editor, *The Age of Enlightenment: The Eighteenth Century Philosophers.* Boston, Houghton Mifflin, 1958; London, Oxford University Press, 1979.

Translator, *First Love*, by Turgenev. London, Hamish Hamilton, 1950.

*   *   *

Sir Isaiah Berlin is undoubtedly one of the most distinguished political philosophers of the post-war period and has been especially influential on a generation of writers concerned with the philosophical and political problems of liberty. However, he has written, surprisingly, little directly on political theory and the bulk of his published work is in the history of ideas and the philosophy of history, general philosophy, world affairs, and literary criticism. His work in these areas, especially in the history of ideas, however, is not merely exegetical; his interpretation and evaluation of past writers informs his own political philosophy.

Of lasting significance in the history of ideas are his intellectual biography *Karl Marx*, *Vico and Herder*, and *Russian Thinkers*. Not only did he rescue Vico and Herder from obscurity but he also showed the permanent importance of their anti-scientistic and quintessentially humanist philosophies of history. His essay, "Historical Inevitability," (1954) is an important critique of the attempt to apply mechanistic methods to historical explanation and discover predictive laws. In his studies of Tolstoy, Herzen, Bakunin, and Belinsky he brought out the remarkable complexity of pre-Revolutionary Russian thought and shows how these thinkers were both attracted and repelled by absolutist and utopian systems of values.

Although he was associated at Oxford with the analytic and linguistic philosophers, Berlin never accepted their somewhat narrow view of philosophy. For him, philosophy is concerned with those abiding questions to which neither the tools of observation and empirical investigation nor the methods of formal logic can formulate satisfactory answers. These questions concern knowledge and belief, the nature of history and politics and the description of those intransient characteristics of man and the world. We examine these fundamental issues through the use of certain explanatory categories rather than by the methods of empirical science.

The whole of Berlin's thought is coloured by his distinction between the *monist* and *pluralist* visions of the world. While these concepts pertain to explanations of all phenomena, Berlin's unparalleled contribution to knowledge is his exploration of their significance in ethics, history, and politics. The monist seeks to impose on social phenomena a uniform explanation in which all divergences are reconciled, all conflicts resolved, and individual ends and purposes subordinated to an over-all social purpose. In ethics, all values form a hierarchy under a single supreme value, so that those disagreements, such as the tensions between, say, freedom and equality, utility and justice, and the collective good and individual rights, which seem to characterize the moral life can be removed once the nature of this value is understood. In monism, reason, instead of being a human faculty, becomes itself the objective principle of the good life. It is Berlin's novelty as an historian of ideas to have exposed monism as the prevailing feature of European thought, from the objective idealism of Plato through to Hegel and the rigid determinism of Marxist-inspired social doctrines.

In contrast, pluralism as a doctrine describes the world in terms of an ineradicable divergence of men's interests and purposes. There is in ethics and politics a variety of competing values which are in perpetual disharmony and these logically cannot be integrated and subsumed under a single unifying principle: "Everything is what it is: liberty is liberty, not equality or fairness or justice or culture, or human happiness...." Furthermore, these ends are not only incompatible but, ultimately, cannot be rationally argued about because they are the categories with which political argument is itself conducted. Nevertheless, Berlin maintains that a recognition of this necessary pluralism is essential for civilization and the preservation of those values and institutions that have contributed to man's well being. Since Berlin defines *man* in terms of autonomy, rationality, and freedom, to deny him the opportunity of choosing between values and purposes, as the application of a rigid monism appears to do, is to subvert his essence as a man.

It is Berlin's contention, however, that pluralism has only rarely prevailed in European history. This is because it appears to be a feature of the human condition that men seek the security of fixed, orderly systems of values and fear the responsibility of making ultimate choices that pluralism imposes on them. In some respects, aspects of the English classical liberal tradition display pluralism, while in Russian thought Berlin shows how Alexander Herzen rebelled against the systematizing of his monist contemporaries on behalf of an admirable uncertainty concerning ultimate truth.

It is in his 1958 lecture *Two Concepts of Liberty* (included in *Four Essays on Liberty*, 1969) that Berlin brings to bear these philosophical principles on the political theory of freedom. Here he makes a crucially important distinction between "negative" and "positive" liberty. Theorists of negative liberty define freedom in terms of the absence of coercion: freedom exists when there is an area around the individual within which he can choose, whether his choices be good or bad, rational or irrational. On the other hand, positive liberty theorists define freedom in terms of self-control or self-mastery: a person is free not simply when he is unconstrained but when he is pursuing his rational ends. Thus a person can be constrained by irrational desires and his "lower self." Freedom and reason, therefore, become coterminous so that, for example, coercion, when used to remove an irrational desire, does not count as a restriction on liberty since its purpose is to maximize a higher freedom. For positive libertarians, a law, *rightfully* constructed, can never impede liberty.

Berlin claims that this form of liberty, this "despotic vision," exemplifies monism because it re-defines all competing values in terms of "rational freedom": it becomes totalitarian because the only genuine freedom is identified with certain collective ends or purposes so that individual choices are obliterated. Negative liberty is associated with pluralism because it treats freedom as one principle among many and allows it to be expanded or contracted in accordance with the demands of other values such as equality or utility. Because it recognizes conflict and choice, and the necessity of trade-offs between values, Berlin claims that the political theory of negative liberty has been associated with free societies, and has also advanced those elements of autonomy and a minimal morality that are contained in his concept of man.

Berlin's critique of monism, utopianism, and the totalitarian implications of positive liberty has been more influential than his pluralism or his conceptual analysis of freedom. His scepticism about the ultimate truth of moral principles leaves him powerless to adjudicate between rival values, and it is by no means obvious that the pluralism of values guarantees his version of liberalism since there is, in principle, no limit to how much liberty may be traded away for increases in, say, equality or social justice. Regardless of this, his contributions to the history of ideas are of permanent importance, not only for their scholarly qualities but also because he clearly exposes the anti-humanistic consequences that flow from that pursuit of abstractions which characterizes much of Western thought. Equally important is his philosophy of history which attacks both the logical foundations of a *natural* science of history and the immorality implicit in the idea that there can be temporal laws or social processes that can have values higher than the ends of each individual.

—Norman Barry

BERNAL, J(ohn) D(esmond). British physical scientist. Born in Nanagh, Ireland, 10 May 1901. Educated at Stonyhurst College, Bedford School, and at Emmanuel College, Cambridge. Married; 2 sons. Researcher, Davy Faraday Laboratory, 1923-37, and Lecturer, and later Assistant Director of Research in Crystallography, 1934-37, Cambridge University; Professor of Physics, 1937-63, Professor of Crystallography, 1963-68, and Professor Emeritus, 1968-71, Birkbeck College, University of London. Honorary Professor, Moscow University, 1956. Helped to organize For Intellectual Liberty, 1936, Rassemblement Universelle pour la Paix, Brussels, 1936, the World Federation of Scientific Workers, 1946 (Vice-President, 1946-71), the Association of Scientific Workers, 1947 (President, 1947-49), and the World Peace Council, Wroclaw, 1948 (Chairman, 1959-60). Recipient: Royal Medal, Royal Society, London, 1945; American Medal of Freedom with Palms, 1945; Lenin Peace Prize, 1953; Grotius Medal, 1959. Fellow of the Royal Society, 1937. Member, Hungarian Academy of Sciences, 1954; Polish Academy of Sciences, 1955; Rumanian Academy of Sciences, 1957; Bulgarian Academy of Sciences, 1958; Czechoslovak Academy of Sciences, 1960; Academy of Sciences, Norway, 1966. Corresponding Member, German Academy of Sciences, Berlin, 1962; Foreign Member, Academy of Sciences, U.S.S.R., 1958. *Died 15 September 1971.*

PUBLICATIONS

Science

The World, the Flesh and the Devil: An Enquiry into the Future of the Three Enemies of the Rational Soul. London, Kegan Paul, 1929.
Aspects of Dialectical Materialism, with others. London, Watts, 1935.
The Frustration of Science, with others. New York, Norton, 1935.
The Social Function of Science. London, Routledge, and New York, Macmillan, 1939.
Le Rôle de la science dans la solution des problèmes économiques modernes. Paris, Les Conférences du Palais de la Découverte, 1948.
Science for Peace and Socialism, with Maurice Cornforth. London, Birch Books, 1949.
The Freedom of Necessity. London, Routledge, 1949.
The Physical Basis of Life. London, Routledge, 1951.
Marx and Science. London, Lawrence and Wishart, and New York, International Publishers, 1952.

Science and Industry in the Nineteenth Century. London, Routledge, 1953.
Science in History. London, Watts, 1954; New York, Hawthorne Books, 1965.
World Without War. London, Routledge, 1958.
The Origin of Life. London, Weidenfeld and Nicolson, and Cleveland, World, 1967.
The Extension of Man: A History of Physics Before 1900. London, Weidenfeld and Nicolson, 1972; as *The Extension of Man: A History of Physics Before the Quantum*, Cambridge, Massachusetts Institute of Technology, 1972.

*

Critical Study: *Three Scientists Face Social Responsibility: Joseph Needham, J.D. Bernal, F. Joliot-Curie* by Maurice Goldsmith, New Delhi, Centre for the Study of Science, Technology and Development, CSIR, 1976.

*   *   *

J.D. Bernal was one of the most outstanding and at the same time most controversial figures in British science. A man of great learning, he possessed an amazing talent for incorporating within his sphere of knowledge any new subject that intrigued him. Bernal's research began after he won a post in the laboratory that Sir William Bragg had organized at the Royal Institution in London. There Bernal joined a group of young enthusiastic crystallographers all of whom collaborated on and succeeded at perfecting X-ray diffraction technique. He employed X-ray diffraction to determine the structure of inorganic crystals, most specifically graphite. The tedious and often painstaking procedure associated with X-ray crystallography caused Bernal to look for simpler methods, the result of which led to his first publication of major importance—on the technique of single cotation photography. The major significance of this work was the creation of standard diagrams for indexing and interpreting X-ray photographs. These diagrams are now known as the Bernal Charts.

Bernal was never one to stay with any single area of research for long periods of time. He was gifted with an extraordinary ability to amass and synthesize copious amounts of information from almost any branch of science. This is well illustrated by his work on the chemical properties of metals. He pointed out that bonds between transition metals in the periodic table increase in strength until the 18th element, after which bonds decrease in strength. His findings proved to be quite novel; they were presented well before quantum mechanical study of resonance of valence bonds had been developed. The breadth of Bernal's activities and interests is further illustrated by his investigations on the structure and properties of liquid water. These efforts led to the formulation of a detailed geometrical theory of liquids.

Bernal's continued involvement in crystallography as well as his close association with the Biochemistry Department at Cambridge University sparked his interest in the structure of biological molecules—his major pioneer work. He was one of the very first physical scientists of the 20th century to delve into the biological make-up of organisms. Bernal began to take X-ray photographs of biologically important molecules, beginning with sterols, turning to crystalline proteins, and moving on to viruses. These works contained ingenious speculations about the shapes of molecules and the intermolecular forces that cause them to arrange themselves in fashions suggested by the physical dimensions of living cells. His study of sterols demonstrated that the already held molecular formula for one of the compounds was quite incorrect: the size of the molecule, which was determined by Bernal's X-ray techniques, was much smaller than the size proposed by the molecular formula.

Closely following his work on sterols came Bernal's investigations on the crystalline protein, pepsin. Up until the time of his work the results gained from X-ray photographs of proteins gave little evidence of a highly organized or regular molecular architecture, although most scientists theorized that such a sound structure existed. Bernal solved this dilemma by taking photographs of wet rather than dry crystals. He found that the resulting X-ray photographs had enough detail present to warrant a complete structural determination of the pepsin molecule. This innovation made possible several advances in understanding the structure of proteins. Much of Bernal's pathbreaking research on crystalline proteins was followed by the work of others, such as Max Perutz and John Kendrew, on complex proteins, including hemoglobin and myoglobin.

Bernal was a pioneer in yet another branch of biology, the study of viruses. He carried out experiments on the tobacco mosaic virus, which resulted in the determination of the virus particles and demonstrated that the virus has a regular internal structure composed of patterns of small protein molecules. Despite Bernal's great contribution to the study of viruses as well as other aspects of structural chemistry he never failed to comprehend the more profound implications of his work. He constantly sought to apply the results of his research to the grandest questions in the field of the life sciences at that time, namely, how did life begin and how does life continue to develop? Bernal intuited that answers to these questions were to be found in the geometry and physical structure of macromolecules. His hunch was certainly realized with the announcement of the structure of DNA. In many ways Bernal can be said to have been one of the founders of molecular biology.

Bernal's scientific work in the laboratory often occupied a much less important position in his life than did the more immediate problems of society. Such problems were, to his way of thinking, inseparable from science as a whole. As a scientist he was extremely concerned about the deleterious function that advances in science and technology were beginning to have on society. His best-known book is a direct response to the potential dangers of science: *The Social Function of Science* is a highly-charged criticism of the non-use and mis-use of scientific resources in capitalist societies. In his book, Bernal described the change from a science that led to continuous improvement of life, to a science that was being used for destructive and wasteful purposes such as the production of weaponry. He attributed this change to the rise of Fascism, which because of its single-minded dedication to creating fear and destruction, had removed the freedom of scientists to carry out their work for the maximum benefit to human welfare. It was the scientist's task to recognize his or her own social responsibility and to see to it that science was utilized productively. Bernal also believed that the scientific process consisted of much more than isolated individuals in search for solutions to particular problems: he maintained that science developed in the context of pressing socio-economic concerns. Thus, it was no accident that both chemistry and physics were set as priorities during the times of social upheaval and war since they were the sciences that were the most readily applicable to the production of weapons of destruction. In short, the impact of science on society and society on science was a reciprocal one.

Politically, Bernal was not only a Marxist but also a communist, an open feature of his life which caused him some professional harm, but which guided his analysis of both the history and present-day development of science. He strongly supported the communist experiment in the Soviet Union, following closely the development of events there in both the political and scientific spheres. Unlike many British intellectuals Bernal tried deeply to follow the events of the Stalin era, particularly the rise of Lysenko's peculiar theory of the inheritance of acquired characters. However, he was not naive or blindly following a Marxist "line." His faith in communism in general gave him the strength of resolve not to abandon the cause in response to isolated events. At the same time, he often did not focus on the severe problems of communist practice that engaged his more cynical colleagues. To the end of his life Bernal was a supporter of the general communist movement, though he became more critical of later developments such as the suppression of the Hungarian uprising in 1956 and the invasion of Czechoslovakia in 1968.

As a totally committed Marxist, Bernal knew that the only way to bring about change was to organize and take direct action. With the rise of Nazism he became especially active in anti-Fascist organizations in England. During the German strikes against Great Britain, Bernal devoted considerable time to teaching civilians how to protect themselves from air raids and took valiant steps to disarm bombs on his own. He undertook a great deal of research on the physics of building and dropping bombs, an accomplishment that won him fame among the leaders of the allied forces. Bernal eventually became a top military adviser to Lord Mountbatten. Despite the controversial aspects of his political life, he was, nonetheless, revered, loved and respected.

—Randall Davey Bird

BERNSTEIN, Basil (Bernard). British sociologist. Born in London, 1 November 1924. Studied at the University of London, at London School of Economics and Political Science, B.Sc.; and University College London, Ph.D. Married Marion Black in 1955; 2 sons. Teacher, City Day College, Shoreditch, London, 1954-60. Honorary Research Assistant, 1960-62, Head of Sociological Research Unit since 1963, Senior Lecturer in Sociology of Education, 1963-65, Reader, 1965-67, Professor, 1967-69, and since 1979 Karl Mannheim Professor of Sociology, University of London. D.Litt.: University of Leicester; Fil.H.Dr.: University of Lund, 1980. Address: 90 Farquhar Road, Dulwich, London SE19 1LT, England.

PUBLICATIONS

Sociology

Class, Codes and Control: vol. 1, *Theoretical Studies Towards a Sociology of Language:* vol. 2, *Applied Studies Towards a Sociology of Language*; vol. 3, *Towards a Theory of Educational Transmission.* London, Routledge, 1971-75; vol. 1 published separately, New York, Schocken, 1975.
Selection and Control: Teachers' Ratings of Children in Infant School, with Walter Brandis. London, Routledge, 1974.

*

Critical Studies: *Language Management in Education: The Australian Context* by William Peter Robinson, Sydney and Boston, Allen and Unwin, 1978.

*   *   *

Basil Bernstein, a major and somewhat controversial British social psychologist, emerged into prominence during the 1960's with a series of important research articles in the field of sociolinguistics which had a dramatic impact on educational policies in both England and America. Credited with doing pioneer research in the description of varieties of speech within a language community, Bernstein concentrated on dialect studies and explored the ramifications to the question of how the language dialect one speaks is, among other things, an indicator of one's cognitive abilities.

His research rests on a key assumption: language learning is determined by social environment and by the verbal and non-verbal experiences of speakers. In "Language and Social Class" (1960), he contends that many (British) children are raised in culturally disadvantaged environments and are exposed to non-standard dialects, to modes and styles of language significantly different from the middle and upper classes, which in turn can stunt their cognitive abilities. His major research centered on studying the characteristics of the language dialects of two groups of London teenage boys from the working and middle classes.

In "Aspects of Language and Learning in the Genesis of the Social Process" (1964), in "Social Class, Linguistics Codes, and Grammatical Elements" (1962), and in "Elaborated and Restricted Codes..." (1964), Bernstein examined clear-based variabilities and their implications for language fluency and learning. Revising his earlier concepts of formal and public speech, he reformulated his concepts and, based on his continuing research, put forth in these major articles the terms "elaborated code" and "restricted code." He showed that middle class boys used both codes with facility and ease, while working class boys tended to use only the "restricted code," and thus were restricted in their language and thinking behavior. Middle class boys were fluent in the "elaborated code," which exhibited a wide range of syntactic and lexical alternatives. This code exhibited verbal dexterity, the ability to manipulate language, the use of accurate grammatical order and syntax to regulate what is spoken, i.e., a fluency with conjunctions and subordinate elements in sentences, an ease with prepositions (often the less common ones) to indicate logical relationships, a frequent use of indefinite and third person pronouns, a wide range of adverbs and adjectives, and the use of expressive symbolism to discriminate meaning within speech sequences. These, and other characteristics of the "elaborated code," were to show the direction of a higher organization of thinking and reasoning power.

On the other hand, the "restricted code" of the working class boys was less fluent and highly static. This code manifested a narrower range of language alternatives, often tended to the predictably formulaic, and exhibited highly individuated utterances. Characteristics of this code included a simplified grammatical system, often poor syntactic form, repetitive use of common conjunctions, little use of subordination, a rigid and limited selection of adjectives and adverbs, reinforcement statements following what was immediately said, and a tendency to confound reason and conclusion in statements. Where the elaborated code was characterized as open and liberating and taking full range of language possibilities, the restricted code was inhibiting and restrictive. Further, Bernstein's work gravitated to the notion that each code had psychological implications and social functions which indicated not just class distinction but also distinctions in cognitive abilities. Restricted code language was described as concrete, highly narrative and descriptive, while elaborated code language embraced this, and more importantly was analytical and abstract, plus an indicator of a higher order of thinking.

Bernstein's publications and research, especially his notion of predictability, raised a storm of controversy. Some linguists argued that, though dialects often correlate with class, the differences are linguistically unimportant. Others argued that any heterogeneous community will have dialectical variability. To suggest that one's dialect was connected to cognitive abilities drew strong negative reactions. Some questioned his conclusions as too extreme and based on limited observations; others simply rejected the anti-egalitarian notion of social class.

Despite this controversy, his work did have enormous impact on education in the 1960's and early 1970's His ideas strongly influenced many educational programs, notably Head Start in America, especially the creation of programs for the culturally disadvantaged. In America and England, intensive language and cultural experiences found themselves firmly rooted in the new curricula as ways to reduce the distance between a child's language and the standard dialect of the teacher. To many, the dialect of the culturally disadvantaged prevented them from learning the standard dialect and from developing their full potential psychologically, socially, and cognitively. For Bernstein, this indicates that a child must know how to use a language as a learning tool in order to succeed in any educational system. His data and research raised prickly questions for education policy-planners, with specific attention aimed toward the elements responsible for language differences that separate individuals and social groups.

To that end, his work continues to stir action and reaction from those researchers who still search for hard linguistic data to confirm or negate Bernstein's particular view of class differences and their implications in language.

—Michael I. Prochilo

BETTELHEIM, Bruno. American psychologist. Born in Vienna, Austria, 28 August 1903; emigrated to the United States in 1939: naturalized, 1944. Educated at schools in Germany and Austria, and at the Reform Realgymnasium, Vienna, graduated 1921; studied at the University of Vienna, Ph.D. 1938. Married Gertrud Weinfeld in 1941; 3 children. Prisoner in Dachau and Buchenwald concentration camps, 1938-39. Research Associate, Progressive Education Association, University of Chicago, 1939-41; Associate Professor of Psychology, Rockford College, Illinois, 1942-44; Assistant Professor, 1944-47, Associate Professor, 1947-52, Professor of Educational Psychology, 1952-73, Stella M. Rowley Distinguished Service Professor of Education and Professor of Psychology and Psychiatry, 1963-73 (Head of the Sonia Shankman Orthogenic School, 1944-73), University of Chicago. Fellow, Center for Advanced Study in the Behavioral Sciences, Stanford, California, 1971-72. Honorary doctorate: Cornell University, Ithaca, New York. Founding Member, American Academy of Education. Fellow, American Psychological Association; American Orthopsychiatric Association. Member, American Academy of Arts and Sciences. Address: 1 Sierra Lane, Portola Valley, California 94025, U.S.A.

PUBLICATIONS

Psychology

Love Is Not Enough: The Treatment of Emotionally Disturbed Children. Glencoe, Illinois, Free Press, 1950.
Dynamics of Prejudice: A Psychological and Sociological Study of Veterans, with Morris Janowitz. New York, Harper, 1950; expanded edition as *Social Change and Prejudice, Including Dynamics of Prejudice*, New York, Free Press, and London, Collier Macmillan, 1964.
Overcoming Prejudice. Chicago, Science Research Associates, 1953.
Symbolic Wounds: Puberty Rites and the Envious Male. Glencoe, Illinois, Free Press, 1954; London, Thames and Hudson, 1955.
Truants from Life: The Rehabilitation of Emotionally Disturbed Children. Glencoe, Illinois, Free Press, 1955.
The Informed Heart: Autonomy in a Mass Age. Glencoe, Illinois, Free Press, 1960; London, Thames and Hudson, 1961.
Paul and Mary: Two Cases from "Truants from Life.". New York, Doubleday Anchor Books, 1961.
Youth: Challenge and Change, with others. Boston, American Academy of Arts and Sciences, 1961.
Child Guidance—A Community Responsibility: An Address, with a Summary of Public Provisions for Child Guidance Services to Michigan Communities. East Lansing, Michigan State University, 1962.

Dialogues with Mothers. New York, Free Press, 1962.
The Empty Fortress: Infantile Autism and the Birth of the Self. New York, Free Press, 1967.
Mental Health in the Slums: Preliminary Draft. Chicago, University of Chicago Center of Policy Study, 1968.
The Children of the Dream. New York, Macmillan, and London, Thames and Hudson, 1969.
Food to Nurture the Mind. Washington, D.C., Children's Foundation, 1970.
Obsolete Youth: Toward a Psychograph of Adolescent Rebellion. San Francisco, San Francisco Press, 1970.
Moral Education: Five Lectures, with others. Cambridge, Massachusetts, Harvard University Press, 1970.
A Home for the Heart. New York, Knopf, and London, Thames and Hudson, 1974.
The Uses of Enchantment: The Meaning and Importance of Fairy Tales. New York, Knopf, 1976; London, Penguin, 1978.
Surviving, and Other Essays. New York, Knopf, and London, Thames and Hudson, 1979.
On Learning to Read: The Child's Fascination with Meaning, with Karen Zelan. New York, Knopf, 1982.

*   *   *

Bruno Bettelheim is best-known for his successful treatment and teaching of children with serious emotional disturbances. He has been especially successful with the autistic—those who disregard the real world and withdraw into hallucinations and daydreams. Bettelheim is also the author of a classic analysis of human behavior in extreme situations.

A knowledge of his personal background helps one to understand Bettelheim's early work. Born, raised, and educated in Vienna, he received a doctorate in psychology and philosophy from the university there in 1938. During that same year, the Nazis annexed Austria. Bettelheim was arrested, sent to Germany, and imprisoned in Dachau and Buchenwald, the notorious concentration camps. Released in 1939, he moved to the United States and found academic employment.

While he was imprisoned in Dachau and Buchenwald, Bettelheim attempted to analyze the mental processes of his fellow prisoners and the effect upon them of incarceration and Nazi propaganda. In order to ensure objectivity he allowed three years to elapse between being released from the camps and writing down his conclusions. Late in 1943, he published the article "Individual and Mass Behavior in Extreme Situations." Bettelheim wrote that his purpose was to examine "the concentration camp as a means of producing changes in the prisoners which will make them more useful subjects of the Nazi state." He described how human minds and spirits adapted to live in the camps and how personalities were affected by totalitarian terrorism. Bettelheim's article was reprinted in another scholarly journal, reprinted again as a pamphlet, and then distributed to all American military officers as required reading.

In 1944 Bettelheim became assistant professor of psychology at the University of Chicago and head of the university's Sonia Shankman Orthogenic School. This live-in laboratory institution has a small student body of children ranging in age from six to fourteen. The students, whose intelligence ranges from normal to above-normal, have severe emotional disturbances that private physicians, child guidance clinics, and child analysis have been unable to treat. The autistic are among the school's most notable students. Bettelheim has described his work at the Sonia Shankman Orthogenic School in many books and articles. *Truants from Life* consists of four case histories of children who were utterly unable to cope in the real world when they arrive at the school. Bettelheim explains his therapeutic approach and details his experiences, showing how he led his patients toward normal lives. This hopeful book has found readers far outside of academic and professional circles.

Love is Not Enough describes Bettelheim's professional experiences at the school. He tells how children are taught there and how the staff deals with their emotional problems from day to day. Bettelheim states that his observations of abnormal children and their reactions to the surrounding environment can be applied to the normal as well—by parents, teachers, social agency staff, and other professionals who work with the young. Normal children often undergo mild versions of the experiences that cause severe disturbance in others. The most conscientious and affectionate of parents often make needless mistakes in rearing their children. Bettelheim concludes that parents should not only love their children but also must work to "create a setting in which both their own legitimate needs and the needs of their children can be satisfied with relative ease." This, he hopes, will lead everyone toward "a socially useful and emotionally satisfying life."

Bettelheim focuses on autism in *The Informed Heart* and *The Empty Fortress*. His *Children of the Dream* describes young people and the way they are reared and taught in kibbutzim, the communal agricultural settlements of Israel. This latter investigation caused Bettelheim to suggest that the kibbutz may in some ways be a better place to rear children than the traditional family.

Social prejudice—anti-Semitism in particular—has also engaged Bettelheim's interest. He has written in the American journal *Commentary* that Jews confronted by anti-Semitism must react calmly. "If we are to fight anti-Semitism effectively," he writes, "the struggle must be based on the realities of human character and behavior rather than on fictitious group stereotypes. It must concern itself with the living individual on both sides of the fence, seen fully as human beings, and not as stock figures in a melodrama or a cartoon." More general work in this field was published as *Dynamics of Prejudice*, in collaboration with Morris Janowitz. In this study, Chicago-area veterans were interviewed and their prejudices were analyzed from a psychological and sociological point of view.

—Victor M. Cassidy

BINET, Alfred. French psychologist. Born in Nice, 11 July 1857. Educated at the Lycée Louis-le-Grand, Paris, 1872-75; licence in law, 1878. Married Laure Balbiani in 1884; 2 children. Worked at the Laboratory of Physiological Psychology, the Sorbonne, Paris, as Associate Director, 1892, and after 1894 as Director. Founded and edited the first French psychological journal, *L'Année Psychologique*, in 1894. *Died* (in Paris) *in 1911*.

PUBLICATIONS

Psychology

La Psychologie du raisonnement. Paris, Alcan, 1886; as *The Psychology of Reasoning*, Chicago, Open Court, 1886.
Le Magnétisme animal, with Charles Féré. Paris, Alcan, 1887; as *Animal Magnetism*, New York, Appleton, 1892.
"La Vie psychique des micro-organismes," in *Revue Philosophique* (Paris), 24, 1887; as *The Psychic Life of Microorganisms*, Chicago, Open Court, 1889.
On Double Consciousness. Chicago, Open Court, 1889.
Les Altérations de la personnalité. Paris, Alcan, 1892; as *Alterations of Personality*, New York, Appleton, 1896.
La Psychologie des grands calculateurs et joueurs d'échecs, with L. Henneguy. Paris, Hachette, 1894.
Introduction à la psychologie expérimentale, with others. Paris, Alcan, 1894.

La Fatigue intellectuelle, with Victor Henri. Paris, Schleicher, 1898.
La Suggestibilité. Paris, Schleicher, 1900.
L'Étude expérimentale de l'intelligence. Paris, Schleicher, 1903.
L'Âme et le corps. Paris, Flammarion, 1905; as *The Mind and the Brain*, London, Kegan Paul, 1907.
Les Révélation de l'écriture a'après un contrôle scientifique. Paris, Alcan, 1906.
"Le Développement de l'intelligence chez les enfants," in *L'Année Psychologique* (Paris), 14, 1908; as *The Development of Intelligence in Children*, Vineland, New Jersey, Vineland Press, 1916.
Les Idées modernes sur les enfants. Paris, Flammarion, 1909.
"L'Intelligence des imbéciles," with Théodore Simon, in *L'Année Psychologique* (Paris), 15, 1909; as *The Intelligence of the Feeble-minded*, Vineland, New Jersey, Vineland Press, 1916.

*

Critical Studies: *Alfred Binet et son oeuvre* by François L. Bertrand, Paris, Alcan, 1930; *Alfred Binet* by Theta H. Wolf, Chicago, University of Chicago Press, 1973 (contains a full bibliography of Binet's scientific papers).

*   *   *

Alfred Binet, along with his collaborator Théodore Simon, developed the first intelligence test. They did so at the request of the French government and in response to a practical need. With the advent of compulsory education, something needed to be done about the substantial numbers of pupils who were not able to do the work. Were they sick? Were they simply too ignorant? Or were they deficient in the mental ability required to perform adequately at school? If the last, a special school would be appropriate. Concrete decisions of this sort needed to be made, and that is why Binet and Simon constructed their intelligence test. It required the child to perform a wide variety of tasks of differing difficulty—repeating strings of numbers, copying drawings, vocabulary, math problems, making change, discovering absurdities. The scores for the various tasks were combined to create a composite score indicating mental ability.

Binet had to make an initial assumption, one for which he is sometimes criticized. He assumed that intelligence was a *general* attribute, that is, that a child who does well in one area will tend to do well in another. This is the proper assumption to make for several reasons, the most important of which is that it appears to be true. David Wechsler argued several decades after Binet's test appeared that Binet's tests stressed verbal skills, and that there were other intellectual skills his tests did not measure. Wechsler's tests have a verbal score and a performance score. The latter is based on performance on a variety of spatial tasks, such as reassembling decomposed objects. It is true that there are stable individual differences on the performance part of Wechsler's intelligence test—that is, that there *are* abilities Binet did not tap. But it is also true that, generally, people who have a high verbal score have a high performance score, while people who have a low verbal score have a low performance score (that is, the verbal and the performance scores are *correlated*). This is so much the case that psychologists who use Wechsler's tests often diagnose psychopathology or brain damage when there is a substantial difference between the verbal and the performance score. While research has not supported the psychopathology diagnosis, there is growing support for the brain damage diagnosis in some cases.

There has also been a concern that basic intelligence testing in the Binet tradition emphasizes ordinary verbal and mathematical skills at the expense of verbal or mathematical creativity. A wide variety of tests have been constructed to remedy this deficiency. For example, a child—or adult—may be asked to think of as many uses as he can for a brick, or to solve problems for which there is no right answer, which require imagination and inventiveness. Such tests also manifest stable individual differences. Nevertheless, over the broad range of the population, people tend to do about as well on intelligence tests as they do on creativity tests—that is, the scores are correlated.

So Binet was correct in his assumption—in fact, far more correct than he knew. And the composite score created by summing the scores from the separate tests correlated with school grades and with teachers' assessments of intellectual ability. It would seem, then, that he had got close to the notion of ability.

Critics charged, however—and still do—that one cannot manifest ability on his tests without prior knowledge, so that they are tests of knowledge rather than ability. Despite the fact that this criticism of intelligence testing is venerable, little attention will be given to it, for it is quite silly. Of course ability cannot exist in a vacuum—of course you can't make change if you don't know what money is, or define a word if you don't know the word (or what a word is). But if everyone knows what money is, then some people can make change well and others poorly; if everyone has had exposure to the language, some will have picked up more words (and better) than others. Binet attempted to use materials everyone could be expected to have been exposed to. Insofar as he achieved this goal, his tests were surely tests of ability. No doubt some intelligence tests have *not* used universally known materials, but this criticism has been sufficiently mindless and broad in its application that a standard parody in the early 1970's had intelligence test questions for slum children beginning, "If Johnny stole 8 hubcaps and Fred only 4, how many...."

A related criticism of intelligence testing is that it is unfair to minorities because it does not take into account the fact that minorities may be insufficiently motivated to do well on tests and in school, because of low expectations of reward from society. This may in fact be true of minority group members, but it does not invalidate intelligence tests as measures of intellectual ability, particularly as we use that term in daily life. A person who, for whatever reasons of whatever excellent validity, does not attempt to take part in intellectual endeavors is not manifesting intellectual ability. Given an increase in motivation, his ability may increase, and that would be reflected on test scores, school grades, and general appearance of having intellectual ability.

Binet's next major problem was dealing with the fact that four year olds cannot do as many tests as can eight year olds. Binet handled this by making the obvious assumption that intelligence increases gradually and at a continuous rate with age. A child who could pass the tests the average four year old could pass—as determined by taking a sample of four year olds and testing them—was said to possess a *mental age* (MA) of 4—no matter how old the child was. An eight year old with an MA of 4 was obviously retarded, or at least "slow." A two year old with an MA of 4 was very smart.

This assumption has been challenged by the work of Jean Piaget, who argues for something like a quantum theory of intelligence. Children go through various stages. In a given stage, there are certain things the child cannot do and cannot be taught to do. Then, relatively suddenly, the child can do these things. Here is an example. Consider these two sets of dots: . . . . Up until a certain age, the child does not say that the two sets have the same number of dots. Either he says the first set has more because it is longer or the second set has more because they're close together. Then, rather suddenly, he realizes that both sets have five dots.

Research has indicated that the discontinuity is not as great as Piaget originally stated, and that children differ in the extent to which they switch stages at the predicted times. So Piaget's concept of the development of intelligence is not completely at odds with Binet's. Still, he has added still another range of tasks to the domain of such tasks considered necessary to encompass intelligence. As you might expect, children who do well on Piagetian tasks tend to do well on Binet-type tasks—correlation is found again. Intelligence is indeed a general attribute.

Brief mention should be made of the I.Q. (Intelligence Quotient), even though this was not proposed by Binet, as is often supposed, but by William Stern, a German psychologist. I.Q. =

Mental Age divided by Chronological Age (CA) times 100. Thus a person with an MA equal to his CA has the average I.Q. score of 100. This index is not very satisfactory. If, for example, your mental age is constantly two years ahead of your chronological age, at 2 your I.Q. will be 200, but by 10 it will have "dropped" to 120. I.Q. is now calculated differently.

—George W. Kelling

BLACK, Hugo L(afayette). American jurist. Born in Harlan, Alabama, 27 February 1886. Studied at the University of Alabama, LL.B. 1906. Served in United States Army, 1917-1919. Married Josephine Foster in 1921; 1 daughter, 2 sons; married Elizabeth Seay DeMeritte in 1957. Practiced law in Ashland, Alabama, 1906-07, and Birmingham, Alabama, 1907-10, 1919-27; Police Judge, Alabama, 1910-22; Solicitor (Prosecuting Attorney), Jefferson County, Alabama, 1915-17; United States Senator from Alabama, 1927-37; Associate Justice, United States Supreme Court, Washington, D.C., 1937-71. *Died 25 September 1971.*

PUBLICATIONS

Law

Investigation of Air Mail and Ocean Mail Contracts: Preliminary Report. Washington, D.C., U.S. Government Printing Office, 1935.
Investigation of Lobbying Activities: Partial Report. Washington, D.C., U.S. Government Printing Office, 1935.
Revenue Bill of 1936: Report and Minority Views. Washington, D.C., U.S. Government Printing Office, 1936.
Civilian Conservation Corps: Conference Report. Washington, D.C., U.S. Government Printing Office, 1937.
Creating a United States Housing Authority: Report. Washington, D.C., U.S. Government Printing Office, 1937.
Fair Labor Standards Act: Report. Washington, D.C., U.S. Government Printing Office, 1937.
Federal Aid to the States for the Support of Public Schools: Report. Washington, D.C., U.S. Government Printing Office, 1937.
Making the Civilian Conservation Corps a Permanent Agency: Report. Washington, D.C., U.S. Government Printing Office, 1937.
Dissents in the United States Supreme Court, with others. New York, Emergency Civil Liberties Committee, 1959.
We Dissent: Supreme Court Justice Hugo Black's Ringing Declaration of His Faith in Freedom. Los Angeles, Citizens Committee to Preserve American Freedoms, 1959.
The Bill of Rights (lecture). New York, New York University School of Law, 1960.
Workmen's Compensation. Anniston, University of Alabama, 1960.
"A Fateful Moment in Our History": Dissenting Opinion of Hugo L. Black in the McCarran Act Decision. Chicago, Committee to Defend the Bill of Rights, 1961.
One Man's Stand for Freedom: Mr. Justice Black and the Bill of Rights: A Collection of His Supreme Court Opinions, edited by Irving Dilliard. New York, Knopf, 1963.
A Constitutional Faith. New York, Knopf, 1968.

Other

"Sincerely Your Friend": Letters of Mr. Justice Hugo L. Black to Jerome A. Cooper. University, University of Alabama Press, 1973.

*

Critical Studies: *Mr. Justice Black: The Man and His Opinions* by John P. Frank, New York, Knopf, 1949; *Hugo Lafayette Black: A Study in the Judicial Process* by Charlotte Williams, Baltimore, Johns Hopkins Press, 1950; *Justices Black and Frankfurter: Conflict in the Court* by Wallace Mendelson, Chicago, University of Chicago Press, 1961; *The Vision and the Dream of Justice Hugo L. Black: An Examination of a Judicial Philosophy* by Howard Ball, University, University of Alabama Press, 1975; *Hugo Black and the Judicial Revolution* by Gerald T. Dunne, New York, Simon and Schuster, 1977; *Justice Hugo Black and the First Amendment: " 'No Law' Means No Law,"* edited by Everette E. Dennis, Donald M. Gillmor, David L. Grey, Ames, Iowa State University Press, 1978; *Mr. Justice Black: Absolutist on the Court* by James T. Magee, Charlottesville, University Press of Virginia, 1980.

*   *   *

Throughout his 34-year tenure on the United States Supreme Court, from the Presidency of Franklin D. Roosevelt to the Presidency of Richard Nixon, Hugo L. Black maintained that the Constitution's primary function was to safeguard human rights, not to defend abstract propositions or to defend property interests. The First Amendment specified that Congress could pass no law abridging the freedom of speech or the press, and that, said Black, meant NO LAW.

It is ironic, considering Black's civil rights record, that he was sharply criticized back in 1937 for once having belonged to the Ku Klux Klan. That information, never really a secret, was widely publicized shortly after his confirmation to the Supreme Court. Black had joined the KKK in 1923 in Alabama, but had soon left and disavowed his action. The criticisms in 1937 were transparently political and even absurd: one of the sitting Justices, James McReynolds, was a notorious bigot who pointedly ignored two of his colleagues, Louis Brandeis and Benjamin Cardozo, because they were Jewish.

The real point of the attack on Black was his strong liberal record in the Senate, which was why Roosevelt had named him to the Court. The appointment of Black was the first step to transforming the Court, as its older members began to die or retire.

Black was a solid and productive New Dealer. He had been the Senate's most effective investigator of corruption by big business and of collusion between business and government agencies. His culminating effort was a massive indictment of the entire lobbying industry, with its enormous expenditures, false fronts and phony telegram campaigns. Black also had sponsored important minimum-wage and maximum-hour bills (sometimes with Frank Murphy, who later joined him on the Supreme Court).

As a Justice, Black fulfilled Roosevelt's expectations. He was instrumental in the Court's approving an ever-expanding mandate for Congressional legislation in economic affairs. For decades, the Court had been resisting governmental intervention in business affairs, often claiming that the Fourteenth Amendment to the Constitution protected them. Nonsense, said Black; the Fourteenth Amendment was designed to protect people from discriminatory laws—it did not imply that corporations were "legal persons" who should be rendered immune to government regulation. Black's presence on the Court helped to form a majority that lifted its economic thinking out of the 19th century.

Which did not mean, in Black's estimate, that the government could do whatever it wished with the economy. In 1952, President Truman, by executive order, literally took control of the steel industry. Such Presidential arrogance was flagrantly unconstitutional, ruled Black in a major decision (*Youngstown Sheet & Tube v. Sawyer*) that nullified the seizure. Presidents, like Congresses and corporations, were held accountable to the people and to the Constitution.

Today, Black is best remembered for his spirited defense of First Amendment freedoms, even to the point of framing them in "absolute" terms. He said that he did not believe, for example, that *any* law aimed at curbing obscenity could pass a Constitutional test. He thought that the greatest danger would arise when the government, for political reasons, would seek to suppress the free expression of ideas. During the Cold War years of the late 1940's and early 1950's, that precise danger arose.

Two of Black's staunch liberal colleagues, Frank Murphy and Wiley Rutledge, both died in 1949. This left Black and a fellow liberal William O. Douglas, in lonely dissent on a Court that was not particularly sensitive to civil liberties. When Congress, with the implicit support of President Truman, moved to abrogate rights of speech, press and assembly for persons accused of Communist (or "un-American") leanings, the Supreme Court complied in the name of "national security." In such cases as *American Communications Assn. v. Dowds*, 1950, and *Dennis v. United States*, 1951, Black and Douglas dissented vigorously, arguing that there was no war on, and no emergency existed that could justify trampling on First Amendment freedoms.

In the Barenblatt case a decade later, Black was still dissenting, upholding the right of a person to refuse to respond to questions from a hostile Congressional committee. A Congressional hearing was not a court of law, Black pointed out; the key question was whether we should try "to preserve democracy by adopting totalitarian methods, or whether in accordance with our traditions and our Constitution we will have the confidence and courage to be free."

Black's liberal thinking encompassed much more than a defense of free expression. In his very first case as a lawyer, he had successfully defended a black convict in Alabama who had been treated almost like a slave. As a prosecuting attorney and judge in Birmingham, Black had been active in curbing police brutality and in securing justice for workers who filed injury claims against callous employers. He was already building a reputation for protecting the rights of persons who had been accused of crimes.

When Black joined the Supreme Court, he found himself in dissent when he argued that Constitutional "rights of the accused," primarily embodied in the Fifth and Sixth Amendments, should be protected in state as well as federal courts. But after Earl Warren became Chief Justice, the tide turned. Black now had the satisfaction, as Anthony Lewis details in his book *Gideon's Trumpet*, of writing majority opinions that overturned old precedents. In a string of dramatic cases in the 1960's, including *Gideon v. Wainright*, *Malloy v. Hogan*, *Miranda* and *Escobedo*, the Court proceeded to "federalize" much of the Bill of Rights; the guarantees of adequate counsel, fair procedures, etc., were ruled applicable to all levels of the legal process.

In protecting religious rights too, Black was active. When children of the Jehovah's Witnesses sect refused to salute the United States flag in school exercises (they cited the Biblical injunction against "graven images"), Black and a majority of Justices ultimately held that these religious beliefs were worthy of Constitutional protection. He and Douglas wrote that the nation hardly needed to "compel little children" to engage in this "patriotic formula."

In a case that would have continuing repercussions in later years, Black penned the decision that outlawed prayers in the public schools (*Engel v. Vitale*, 1962). Citing the Constitution's concept of the "wall of separation" between church and state, Black argued successfully that the state of New York had no business prescribing any religious observance.

He also put his weight solidly behind the Warren Court's desegregation decisions, beginning with the first Brown case of 1954. In one case, Black indicated his impatience with a school system's foot-dragging route to compliance with the law. He'd had enough with "all deliberate speed," he stormed; the time for compliance was *now*.

The one glaring exception to Black's brilliant civil rights record on the Court was his concurrence with the majority in the Japanese Exclusion Cases during World War II. The Court, under the banner of "national security," sanctioned the forced re-location of 112,000 Japanese-Americans to detention camps. In this instance Black's civil libertarianism yielded to the widespread fear of sabotage. (Fellow Justice Frank Murphy dissented angrily from "this legalization of racism.") For Black, Pearl Harbor and, of course, Hitler, made World War II a "just war." It was the only war, he said in 1968 to a national television audience, "that I thoroughly approved."

In his final Supreme Court decision, Black found the opportunity to combine his intense dislike of the Vietnam War with his lifelong reverence for the Bill of Rights. In 1971, shortly before he died, he wrote the majority decision upholding the *New York Times'* free press rights against the United States government—while President Nixon's Chief Justice Warren Burger sputtered in dissent. This was the Pentagon Papers case and the Constitutional issue, according to Black, was whether the people had a right to know. For him, the answer was never in doubt.

—Don Hausdorff

BLACK, Max. American philosopher. Born in Baku, Russia, 24 February 1909; emigrated to the United States, 1940; naturalized, 1948. Educated at Queens College, Cambridge, B.A. 1930; University of London, Ph.D. 1939. Married Michal Landsberg in 1933; 2 children. Lecturer and Tutor, Institute of Education, University of London, 1936-40; Professor of Philosophy, University of Illinois, Urbana, 1940-46; Professor of Philosophy, 1946-54, Susan Linn Sage Professor of Philosophy and Humane Letters, 1954-77, and since 1977 Professor Emeritus, Cornell University, Ithaca, New York. Visiting Professor, University of Washington, Seattle, 1951-52, and University of Kyoto, Japan, 1957; United States State Department Lecturer in India, 1962; Visiting Member, Institute for Advanced Study, Princeton, New Jersey, 1970-71; Visiting Fellow, St. John's College, Oxford, and Clare Hall, Cambridge, 1978. Tarner Lecturer, Trinity College, Cambridge, 1976. Co-Editor, *Journal of Symbolic Logic*, 1945-51. Editor, *Philosophical Review*, since 1946. President, American Philosophical Association, 1958; Director, Society for the Humanities, Cornell University, 1965-70; Vice-President, International Institute of Philosophy, 1970. Recipient: Guggenheim Fellowship, 1950. D.Litt.: University of London, 1955. Fellow, American Academy of Arts and Sciences. Address: 408 Highland Road, Ithaca, New York 14850, U.S.A.

PUBLICATIONS

Philosophy

The Nature of Mathematics: A Critical Survey. London, Kegan Paul, and New York, Harcourt Brace, 1933.
Critical Thinking: An Introduction to Logic and Scientific Method. New York, Prentice Hall, 1946.
Philosophical Studies: Essays in Memory of L. Susan Strebbing, with others. London, Allen and Unwin, 1948.
Language and Philosophy: Studies in Method. Ithaca, New York, Cornell University Press, 1949.
Problems of Analysis: Philosophical Papers. Ithaca, New York, Cornell University Press, and London, Routledge, 1954.
Models and Metaphors: Studies in Language and Philosophy. Ithaca, New York, Cornell University Press, 1962.
A Companion to Wittgenstein's Tractatus. Ithaca, New York, Cornell University Press, 1964.
The Raison d'Etre of Inductive Argument. Stanford, California, Center for the Behavioral Sciences, 1965.

The Labyrinth of Language. New York, Praeger, and London, Pall Mall, 1968.
Margins of Precision: Essays in Logic and Language. Ithaca, New York, Cornell University Press, 1970.
Art, Perception and Reality, with others. Baltimore, Johns Hopkins University Press, 1972.
Caveats and Critiques: Philosophical Essays on Language, Logic and Art. Ithaca, New York, Cornell University Press, 1975.
Prevalence of Humbug and Other Essays. Ithaca, New York, Cornell University Press, 1983.

Other

The Teaching of Mathematics: A Bibliography. London, Christophers, 1938.

Editor, *Philosophical Analysis: A Collection of Essays*. Ithaca, New York, Cornell University Press, 1950.
Editor, with Peter Geach, *Translations from the Philosophical Writings of Gottlob Frege*. New York, Philosophical Library, 1952; Oxford, Basil Blackwell, 1960.
Editor, *The Sociological Theories of Talcott Parsons: A Critical Examination*. Englewood Cliffs, New Jersey, Prentice Hall, 1961.
Editor, *Philosophy in America: Essays by William P. Alston and Others*. Ithaca, New York, Cornell University Press, and London, Allen and Unwin, 1965.
Editor, with others, *The Morality of Scholarship*. Ithaca, New York, Cornell University Press, 1967.
Editor, with Morton Bloomfield, *In Search of Literary Theory*. Ithaca, New York, Cornell University Press, 1972.
Editor, *Problems of Choice and Decision*. Ithaca, New York, Cornell University Program on Science, Technology and Society, 1975.

*   *   *

One of the most prominent of American philosophers, Max Black represents the analytic tradition at its very best. Trained in the logico-linguistic approach of Wittgenstein and the precision analysis of G.E. Moore, and with a strong reliance on scientific methodology and common sense examples, Black has made novel and provocative examinations of most of the traditional and contemporary issues in philosophy. In Wittgensteinian fashion he argues that many such issues arise out of ignorance about sentential presuppositions, about verbal usages, and about the importance of context in understanding expressions. Thus, for example, it is assumed that there can be no genuine way of justifying induction since there can be no good reason for believing the future will be like the past. But Black asks whether it is legitimate to use "good reason" with such abstruse concepts as the future and the past. We can use "on top of" to state meaningfully "The man is on top of the table" but not "The man is on top of the universe." In ordinary and scientific contexts good reason, credibility, reliability, and probability function in accordance with specific rules that make induction a perfectly proper procedure. "Given our present language and the system of concepts that it embodies, we are logically unable to imagine wholesale deviation from (the inductive rules we use.)" Similarly, Zeno's paradox arose because he argued that space is infinitely divisible. But was he talking about space or about the mathematics he was applying to space? Necessarily true statements such as "All bachelors are unmarried men" are continuing soures of philosophical perplexity. But what we have here is a confusion of reporting with rule-making. We are not reporting a fact. We are merely making it a rule that "bachelor" can, in most contexts, be replaced by "unmarried man."

The nature of rules has as much interest for Black as it had for Wittgenstein. But he avoids the extremes of Wittgenstein who made rules all important in the *Tractatus* and of little importance in the *Investigations*. In some contexts, e.g. much of mathematics, logic, and science, precision concerning terms and inferences is a requirement. But in other contexts, such as political and social ones, vagueness might be preferable. In fact, Black has been foremost in pointing out the often ill-defined nature of many so-called sets and classes, and this has led to the development of a mathematics dealing with fuzzy sets. Finally, there are contexts in which we can only speak of rules in a very relativistic way. Various cultural changes and the use of metaphor, a figure of speech closely examined by Black in much of his writing, can change the meanings and, therefore, the semantic and syntactic rules governing words. It is important to note that for Black the problem of meaning does not exist. Many definitions of meaning have been proposed, but all have been found to be defective. Perhaps the only way to be sufficiently clear about "meaning" is simply to investigate how words actually function, i.e. how they are coordinated and interrelated to the functions of other words. Meaning may "prove to be more like a handclasp than like a crystal."

Perhaps Black's major work is his definitive commentary on Wittgenstein's *Tractatus*. The commentary is not only a clarification and criticism of Wittgenstein's views, but also a series of essays on the major controversies in contemporary philosophy. Negation, analyticity, logical truth, propositions, and necessity are only a few of the notions examined.

Black's interests are not restricted solely to the technical questions of philosophy. He has written extensively on education, the humanities and liberal arts in general, medicine, the social and physical sciences, psychology, and art. He is highly critical of B.F. Skinner who is constantly involved in "endemic ambiguity" and "unwarranted generalizations." Noam Chomsky's work is stimulating, but it contains unsound influences from mathematical grammar to psychological and epistemological conclusions. Other critical articles and reviews relate to such diverse figures as F.P. Ramsey, R. Carnap, G.E. Moore, Bertrand Russell, G. Frege, C.D. Broad, Karl Popper, John Dewey, Aldous Huxley, Benjamin Lee Whorf, Alonzo Church, Nelson Goodman, W.V. Quine, and Talcott Parsons.

—Jack Kaminsky

BLANSHARD, Brand. American philosopher. Born in Fredericksburg, Ohio, 27 August 1892. Studied at the University of Michigan, Ann Arbor, B.A. 1914; Columbia University, New York, M.A. 1918; Oxford University (Rhodes Scholar, 1913-15, 1919-20), B.Sc. 1920; Harvard University, Cambridge, Massachusetts, Ph.D. 1921. Served with the United States Army in France, 1918-19. Married Frances Bradshaw in 1918 (died, 1966); Roberta Yerkes in 1969. Assistant Professor, University of Michigan, 1921-25; Associate Professor, 1925-28, and Professor, 1928-45, Swarthmore College, Pennsylvania; Professor of Philosophy, 1945-61, and Chairman of the Department, 1959-61, Yale University, New Haven, Connecticut. Fellow, Wesleyan University Center for Advanced Studies, Middletown, Connecticut, 1961-62; Visiting Professor, University of Minnesota, Minneapolis, 1962. Dudleian Lecturer, 1945, Noble Lecturer, 1948, and Whitehead Lecturer, 1961, Harvard University, Cambridge, Massachusetts; Gifford Lecturer, University of St. Andrews, Scotland, 1952-53; Hertz Lecturer, British Academy, 1952; Adamson Lecturer, University of Manchester, 1953; Howison Lecturer, University of California, Berkeley, 1954; Matchette Lecturer, Wesleyan University, 1957; Carus Lecturer, American Philosophical Association, 1959. President, American Theological Society, 1955-56. Recipient: Guggenheim Fellowship, 1929-30; Senior Award, American Council of Learned Societies, 1958; Medal of Honor, Rice Institute, Houston, 1962. Honorary doc-

torate: Swarthmore College, 1947; Bucknell University, Lewiston, Pennsylvania, 1954; Oberlin College, Ohio, 1956; Colby College, Waterville, Maine, 1956; Trinity College, Hartford, Connecticut, 1957; Roosevelt University, Chicago, 1959; University of St. Andrews, 1959; Kenyon College, Gambier, Ohio, 1961; Simpson College, Indianola, Indiana, 1961; Concord College, Athens, West Virginia, 1962; Albion College, Michigan, 1966; University of New Mexico, Albuquerque, 1968. Corresponding Fellow, British Academy; Honorary Member, Aristotelian Society, London; Honorary Fellow, Merton College, Oxford. Member, American Academy of Arts and Sciences. Address: 4 St. Ronan Terrace, New Haven, Connecticut 06511, U.S.A.

PUBLICATIONS

Philosophy

The Nature of Thought, 2 volumes. London, Allen and Unwin, 1939; New York, Macmillan, 1940.
Philosophy in American Education, Its Task and Opportunities, with others. New York, and London, Harper, 1945.
The Uses of a Liberal Education. New Haven, Connecticut, Hazen Foundation, 1951.
On Philosophical Style. Bloomington, Indiana University Press, and Manchester, Manchester University Press, 1954.
The Impasse in Ethics, and A Way Out. Berkeley, University of California Press, 1955.
Education in the Age of Science. New York, Basic Books, 1959.
Reason and Goodness. New York, Macmillan, and London, Allen and Unwin, 1961.
On Sanity in Thought and Art (lecture). Tucson, University of Arizona Press, 1962.
Reason and Analysis. La Salle, Illinois, Open Court, and London, Allen and Unwin, 1962.
The Life of the Spirit in a Machine Age (lecture). Northampton, Massachusetts, Smith College, 1967.
The Uses of a Liberal Education, and Other Talks to Students, edited by Eugene Freeman. La Salle, Illinois, Open Court, 1973; London, Alcove Press, 1974.
Reason and Belief. London, Allen and Unwin, 1974; New Haven, Connecticut, Yale University Press, 1975.
The Philosophy of Brand Blanshard, with others, volume XV of "The Library of Living Philosophers," edited by Paul Arthur Schilpp. La Salle, Illinois, Open Court, 1980. (Includes complete bibliography of Blanshard's publications; Blanshard's intellectual autobiography; critical essays on his philosophy; and his replies to his critics).

*

Bibliography: in *The Philosophy of Brand Blanshard*, 1980.

*   *   *

The American philosopher Brand Blanshard was born in Fredericksburg, Ohio, in 1892. He was educated at the University of Michigan, Merton College, Oxford, and Harvard. In his philosophical thought he was influenced at Oxford especially by F.H. Bradley and H.H. Joachim; and at Harvard, where he received his doctorate in 1921, he studied especially with Hocking and Perry. His major faculty positions were at the University of Michigan, Swarthmore College, and Yale University, from which he retired in 1961. In his intellectual autobiography, published in 1980 in *The Philosophy of Brand Blanshard*, edited by Paul Arthur Schilpp, Blanshard recognized the strong influence of British philosophers on his thought, especially Henry Sidgwick, F.H. Bradley, and G.E. Moore.

Blanshard has lived through the era of the rise of logical empiricism and analytical philosophy, and his writings express very strong opposition to the conception of philosophy as an activity directed quite exclusively to the "sharpening of the tools of thought." Those tools, he insists, should be employed in the more traditional functions of philosophy—the search for truth, the extension of substantive knowledge, and the pursuit of values—functions that follow from the rationality of human nature.

In general Blanshard's philosophy is idealistic but with characteristics that distinguish him from many idealists, as that he does not employ his logic or metaphysics in support of religion, or religion in support of ethics. Nor does he set free will in opposition to determinism, but rather defines moral freedom and responsibility as compatible with a system of general causality.

It is his rationalism, however, rather than idealism, that most clearly characterizes Blanshard's thought, not simply the rationalistic method and the coherence theory of truth which he has brought to a most refined form, but more especially his conception of the world as a rationally integrated whole and his aggressive advocacy of reasonableness in practical as well as theoretical matters. Indeed, Blanshard has centered his efforts not only upon rationality in ethics, religion, and the philosophy of education, as well as metaphysics and the philosophy of science. More often than not they are direct attacks upon those philosophical positions which he regards as the enemies of rationality, such as existentialism, neo-orthodoxy in religion, and emotivism in ethics. Blanshard's conception of reason reaches far beyond the confines of logical inferences, embracing the entire quest for knowledge and the determination of truth. It includes as well the practical virtues of common sense, wisdom in judgment, and intelligent, informed decision in action.

In *The Nature of Thought*, a work devoted to the analysis of knowledge and its implications for methodology, logic, and the nature of reality, Blanshard analyzed the structure of logical empiricism and constructed a basic critique of the entire positivistic position as a defense in principle of metaphysics and the objective meaning of value judgments, a defense grounded in his view that nature conforms to the structure of logic. His refinement of the coherence definition of truth that has been widely accepted by rationalists was related to the doctrine of the internal relatedness of the totality of reality traditional among metaphysical idealists. "Truth," wrote Blanshard, "is the approximation of thought to reality....at any given time the degree of truth in our experience as a whole is the degree of system it has achieved. The degree of truth of a particular proposition is to be judged in the first instance by its coherence with experience as a whole, ultimately by its coherence with that further whole, all comprehensive and fully articulated, in which thought can come to rest."

More recently, as reported in the Schilpp volume, Blanshard has indicated that he now (published in 1980) has a "disposition" to "include correspondence along with coherence as a component of truth." He holds, nevertheless, especially against Tarski's semantic theory and Wittgenstein's earlier picture theory, that despite its status in common sense, correspondence is elusive and ambiguous in meaning and perhaps undefinable. In admitting a degree of correspondence, however, Blanshard does not abandon the ground of his rigorously rationalistic metaphysics, that causal relationships are entirely necessary.

Blanshard's 1959 Carus Lectures, *Reason and Analysis*, while apparently less committed to idealism than his earlier work, continued his attack upon the philosophic threats to the rationalism of which he had become the most distinguished exponent. Realism, naturalism, and pragmatic instrumentalism were identified as enemies of the rationalistic, idealistic tradition—realism for undermining idealism in both epistemology and metaphysics, naturalism especially for its propensity for behaviorism, and instrumentalism, which treated thought as an instrument of action, for its distortions of the proper function of reason, which for Blanshard was logical inference and the achievement of factual knowledge.

But logical empiricism, linguistic analysis, and existentialism were regarded by Blanshard as the chief culprits. He saw the

deterioration of rationality over the past several decades as a characteristic not only of philosophy but also of the culture generally, to be seen clearly in theology, psychology, art, and morals. His critique of logical positivism, with its basis in logical atomism, its radically empirical criterion of cognitive meaning, and its strong physicalistic inclinations, was a lengthy and thorough examination of the problem of meaning. "There is no reason," Blanshard insisted, "why we should not think and speak meaningfully of the self, of other minds, and, whether or not it exists, of a divine mind. We can freely think of non-sensible relations—of implication, of likeness and difference, of time, of causality.... We can still debate the meaning of goodness and justice without fear that they will be ruled out as senseless because non-sensible."

Blanshard's 1952-53 Gifford Lectures at St. Andrews resulted in two volumes, *Reason and Goodness*, and *Reason and Belief*, which with *Reason and Analysis* were a defense of reason that is one of the more impressive philosophical arguments of this century. Blanshard had long shown strong interests in ethical theory as well as in practical morality, and his defense of rationalism and rationality was directed in part against irrationality, subjectivism, and relativism in ethics. In the tradition of idealism he was committed to the possibility of both reasonableness and knowledge in both morals and art and was intensely critical of the hedonism prompted by sensory empiricism and the emotivism that thrived in the wake of positivism and linguistic analysis. He examined the history of the tension between reason and feeling from the early Greek moralists and Christian beginnings. He criticized instrumentalism for identifying the "good" with the "desired," and for describing moral judgments as proposals for action, and ethical emotivism for its failure to recognize that at least some moral judgments are not simply expressions of feeling but are concerned objectively with goodness and badness. For Blanshard moral judgments are statements that have objective meaning concerning which rational argument and knowledge are appropriate. Those who hold that moral judgments are only expressions of emotion, Blanshard insisted, belie their own theory in their moral actions, which are directed to duty or to the good. There is, he held, the possibility of treating the good, as objective and intrinsic, within the context of knowledge.

In *Reason and Belief*, Blanshard critically examined both Catholicism and Protestantism in keeping with his ideal of rationality and his concept of religion as "the attitude of the whole man including his thought, his feelings, and the commitments of his will—toward what he takes to be ultimately true and good." He did not find historical Christianity acceptable. Although his treatment of religion was essentially positive, he made a most vigorous attack upon the irrationalism of Luther and the Neo-orthodox, with some of his sharpest barbs aimed at Kierkegaard, "that twisted genius, who provides so ill a model of either thought or conduct.

—Sterling M. McMurrin

BLOCH, Ernst.   German philosopher.   Born in Ludwigshafen, 8 July 1885. Educated at the University of Munich and at the University of Würzburg, Ph.D. 1908. Married Elsa von Stritzky in 1913 (died, 1921); Karola Piotrkowska in 1934; 1 son. Pacifist during World War I; lived in Switzerland, 1915-18. Worked as a free-lance writer in Berlin and for the *Frankfurter Zeitung* and *Voissichen Zeitung*. Joined the Communist Party during the 1920's and left Germany in 1933. Lived in Paris and Zurich and emigrated to the United States in 1938. Worked in New York, and in Cambridge, Massachusetts, as a free-lance writer and for Aurora Verlag, New York, and the newspaper, *Freies Deutschland*. Returned to East Germany in 1949. Professor of Philosophy, University of Leipzig, 1949-61 (Director of the Institute of

Philosophy, 1949-56). Denounced as a reactionary and revision-ist and applied for political asylum in the Federal Republic, 1961. Guest Professor of Philosophy, University of Tübingen, 1961-77. Editor, *Deutsche Festschrift für Philosophie*, 1953. Honorary doctorate: University of Zagreb, Yugoslavia, 1969; University of Paris (I), 1975; University of Tübingen, 1975. Recipient: Natio-nalpreis, German Democratic Republic, 1955; Culture Prize, Deutscher Gewerkschaftsbund, 1964; Peace Prize, German Book Trade, 1967; Bayreuth Medal, 1974; Sigmund Freud Prize, Akademie fur Spräche und Dichtung, 1975. Honorary Member, Berlin Akademie der Künste, 1975. Member, Deutsche Akade-mie der Wissenshcaft, Berlin. *Died* (in Tübingen) *4 August 1977*.

PUBLICATIONS

Collections

Gesamtausgabe. Frankfurt, Suhrkamp, 17 vols., 1958-78.

Philosophy

Kritische Erörterungen über Rückert und das Problem der modernen Erkenntnistheorie. Ludwigshafen, 1909.
Geist der Utopie. Munich, Duncker and Humblot, 1918.
Thomas Münzer als Theologe der Revolution. Munich, Wolff, 1921.
Durch die Wüste: Kritische Essays. Berlin, Cassirer, 1923.
Spuren. Berlin, Cassirer, 1930.
Erbschaft dieser Zeit. Zurich, Oprecht and Helbling, 1935.
Freiheit und Ordung: Abriss der Sozial-Utopien. New York, Aurora, 1946.
Subjekt-Objekt: Erläuterungen zu Hegel. Berlin, Aufbau, 1951.
Avicenna und die aristotelische Linke. Berlin, Rütten and Loening, 1952.
Christian Thomasius: Ein deutscher Gelehrter ohne Misere. Berlin, Aufbau, 1953.
Das Prinzip Hoffnung. Berlin, Aufbau, 3 vols., 1954-59; selec-tions as *On Karl Marx*, New York, Herder, 1970.
Differenzierungen im Begriff Fortschritt. Berlin, Akademie, 1956.
Naturrecht und menschliche Würde. Frankfurt, Suhrkamp, 1961.
Philosophische Grundfragen. Frankfurt, Suhrkamp, 1961.
Verfremdungen. Frankfurt, Suhrkamp, 2 vols., 1962-64.
Tübinger Einleitung in die Philosophie. Frankfurt, Suhrkamp, 2 vols., 1963-64; vol. 1 as *A Philosophy of the Future*, New York, Herder, 1970.
Literarische Aufsätze. Frankfurt, Suhrkamp, 1965.
Atheismus im Christentum: Zur Religion des Exodus und das Reiches. Frankfurt, Suhrkamp, 1968; as *Atheism in Chris-tianity: The Religion of the Exodus and Kingdom*, New York, Herder, 1972.
Philosophische Aufsätze zur objektiven Phantasie. Frankfurt, Suhrkamp, 1969.
Man on His Own: Essays in the Philosophy of Religion. New York, Herder, 1970.
Über Methode und System bei Hegel. Frankfurt, Suhrkamp, 1970.
Vorlesungen zur Philosophie der Renaissance. Frankfurt, Suhr-kamp, 1972.
Das Materialismusproblem, seine Geschichte und Substanz. Frankfurt, Suhrkamp, 1972.
Experimentum Mundi. Frankfurt, Suhrkamp, 1974.
Zur Philosophie der Musik. Frankfurt, Suhrkamp, 1974.

Other

Schadet oder nützt Deutschland eine Niederlage seiner Militärs. Berne, Freie Verlag, 1918.

Vademecum für heutige Demokraten. Berne, Freie Verlag, 1970.
Politische Messungen, Pestzeit, Vormärz. Frankfurt, Suhr-kamp, 1970.
Widerstand und Freiheit: Aufsätze zur Politik. Frankfurt, Suhrkamp, 1970.
Im Christentum steckt die Revolte: Ein Gespräch mit Adelbert Reif. Zurich, Die Arche, 1971.
Vom Hasard zur Katastrophe: Politische Aufsätze 1934-1939. Frankfurt, Suhrkamp, 1972.
Tagträume vom aufrechten Gang: Sechs Interviews mit Ernst Bloch, edited by Arno Münster. Frankfurt, Suhrkamp, 1977.

*

Critical Studies: *Uber Ernst Bloch*, Frankfurt, Suhrkamp, 1968; *Ernst Blochs Wirkung: Ein Arbeitsbuch zum 90. Geburtstag*, Frankfurt, Suhrkamp, 1975; *The Marxist Philosophy of Ernst Bloch*, New York, St. Martin's Press, 1982.

*   *   *

On the occasion of Ernst Bloch's 90th birthday in summer 1975, he was celebrated in Germany as "one of the most impor-tant philosophers of our epoch." Yet Bloch's work is relatively unknown in the English-speaking world. Although several col-lections of his writings were translated during the last years of his life, his main works have not yet been translated into English. This is unfortunate for there are few bodies of 20th-century thought as complex, fascinating and challenging as the writings of Ernst Bloch. Although Bloch has generally been interpreted as a "Marxist Romantic," or as a mediator in a Christian-Marxist dialogue, in my opinion his work is best read as a highly original version of Marxist philosophy which avoids mechanistic, reduc-tionistic versions of dogmatic Marxism, as well as the "negative dialectics" of the Frankfurt school which frequently avoids posit-ing social alternatives or attempting to construct visions of an emancipated future.

Bloch's philosophy is grounded in a philosophical vision of an emancipated humanity and is described by himself as a "philo-sophy of Hope." Bloch, following the young Marx, sees the human being as a species-being, containing as yet unsatisfied needs and unrealized potentialities which for Bloch are the motors of human self-activity. Art, philosophy and religion are the repository of needs and potentialities struggling for expres-sion, hence they give us clues as to what the human being is and can be. Bloch's work is a magnificent project of decoding our cultural heritage to restore us to our human potential. His con-cept of the "not-yet" militates against the notion of an innate, ahistorical human essence, for our species has not-yet become what it can be and thus has not yet realized its humanity. At bottom, the human being is a problem and a mystery. In a 1975 *Die Zeit* interview, Bloch argues that the human being is an "X of determinateness" and an "X of indeterminateness." Further, "We really do not know at all who and what the human being is; we do not even know if we are humans in the old sense of the word. I would like to say that we are an experimental expression."

Bloch proposes an experimental anthropology which sees the human adventure as a series of experiments whose outcome is unknown in advance. Like the world (see Bloch's *Experimentum Mundi*), human life is a venture, a series of risks, that is radically open to an indefinite future without a certain conclusion. Bloch advocates a revolutionary humanism that sees the human being first realizing its potentialities through a process of revolutionary struggle and social transformation (as opposed to what he calls "bourgeois humanism" which glorifies the human being as it is in bourgeois society). For Bloch, the human being is "not-yet" because at present we are trapped and held back by a set of social-historical conditions and institutions that prevent us from realizing our full potential. The categorical imperative of humanist-revolutionary morality is, Bloch constantly reiterates, hearkening back to the explosive dicta of the young Marx: "to overthrow all conditions in which the human being is a degraded, enslaved, abandoned, and wretched creature." For Bloch and Marx, the transformation to the free society and liberated humanity involves a project of revolution. Bloch's anthropology is directed toward the "release of the richness of human nature" that will in the future achieve the fulfillment of the human being: a future which will come about when men and women join together and overthrow those relations which inhibit and prevent the realization of humanity.

For Bloch, Marxist philosophy is a "philosophy of the future" which calls for "what is not, building into the blue that lines all edges of the world; this is why we build ourselves into the blue and search for truth and reality where mere facticity vanishes—*incipit vita nova*." Bloch posits the task of philosophy to interpret "what is not-yet-realized" and to change the world in accordance with what could be. Bloch calls the ontological foundation of his theory "Left-Aristotelianism." Aristotle's concept of matter as activity and potentiality suggests an ontological priority of possibility over actuality and necessity: reality is conceived as a dynamic process latent with possibility directed toward the realization of its potentialities which provide its telos and entelechia. But all is not fullness and ripeness in this metaphysical scenario for the not-yet is permeated with a constitutive not: "The not is the lack of something and the flight from this lack: hence, it is drives toward that which is lacking. With the not, drives are modelled in the living being: as drive, need, striving, and primarily as hunger." For Bloch, we are needy, hungering beings who are driven to fill our emptiness, our lacks, our needs and our hungers.

Bloch's major work *Das Prinzip Hoffnung*, as yet untranslated into English, contains his most brilliant explorations of the hopes, fantasies and cultural artifacts that he believes contain clues to human potentialities and "outlines of a better world." He believes that our cultural heritage points to socialism as the hoped for realization of humanity's hopes and dreams. Bloch, almost alone among contemporary Marxists, call himself a "utopian philosopher." He describes socialism as a "concrete utopia" rooted in historical possibilities, which to be truly emancipatory must be conceived and constructed with the goal of human emancipation in sight. Bloch seeks to infuse the socialist project with the revolutionary humanism of the early Marx and wishes to infuse contemporary Marxism with the most emancipatory and utopian elements of the young Marx. His unique blend of utopian Marxism won him the wrath of communist ideologues and the affection of the New Left, especially in West Germany.

Bloch often talked of the "unclaimed heritage" of emancipatory ideas in the bourgeois cultural heritage and looking back on Bloch's work in the light of his contemporary neglect, it is fitting to characterize his own immense corpus of writings as an "unclaimed heritage" that contains a treasure house of philosophical, political, and aesthetic writings. Bloch's thought continues to resonate with relevance and importance: will he finally be discovered in the English-speaking world, or will his appropriation be a task for the next generation?

—Douglas Kellner

BLOCH, Marc (Léopold Benjamin). French historian. Born in Lyons, 6 July 1886. Educated at Lycée Louis-le-Grand, Paris, 1900-04, and the Ecole Normale Supérieure, Paris, 1904-08; Agrégation in History and Geography, 1908; studied at the Universities of Leipzig and Berlin, 1908-09; Docteur-ès-Lettres, Sorbonne, Paris, 1920. Served in the French Army, 1914-19 (Croix de Guerre) and 1939-40. Married Simone Vidal in 1919; 6 children. Professor, Lycée, Montpellier, 1912-13, Lycée, Amiens, 1913-14, and University of Strasbourg, 1919-36; Professor of Economic History, Sorbonne, from 1936; Professor, University of Clermont-Ferrand, until 1941; University of Montpellier, 1941-43. Co-Founder, with Lucien Febvre, *Annales d'histoire économique et sociale*, 1929 (Co-Editor, 1929-38); Co-Founder, with Lucien Febvre, *Annales d'histoire sociale*, 1939 (Co-Editor, 1939-41); Editor, *Cahiers politiques*, during World War II. Member, Légion d'honneur. *Died* (executed by the Gestapo at Les Rousilles) *16 June 1944*.

PUBLICATIONS

History

L'Île-de-France (les pays autour de Paris). Paris, L. Cerf, 1913; as *L'Ile-de France: The Country around Paris*, Ithaca, New York, Cornell University Press, and London, Routledge, 1971.
Rois et Serfs: Un Chapitre d'Histoire Capétienne. Paris, E. Champion, 1920.
Les Rois Thaumaturges: Étude sur le Caractère surnaturel attribué à la Puissance royale, particulièrement en France et en Angleterre. Strasbourg, Librarie Istra, London and New York, Oxford University Press, 1924; as *The Royal Touch: Sacred Monarchy and Scrofula in England and France*, London, Routledge, 1973.
Les caractères originaux de l'histoire rurale française. Oslo, Aschehoug, 1931; as *French Rural History: An Essay on its Basic Characteristics*, Berkeley, California, University of California Press, 1966.
La Société féodale. Paris, A. Michel, 1939; as *Feudal Society*, Chicago, University of Chicago Press, and London, Routledge, 1961.
L'Etrange défaite: Témoignage écrit en 1940. Paris, Société des Éditions Franc-tireur, 1946; as *Strange Defeat: A Statement of Evidence Written in 1940*, London and New York, Oxford University Press, 1949.
Apologie pour le métier d'un historien. Paris, Colin, 1949; as *The Historian's Craft*, New York, Knopf, 1953; Manchester, Manchester University Press, 1954.
Esquisse d'une Histoire monétaire de l'Europe. Paris, Colin, 1954.
La France sous les derniers Capétiens 1223-1328. Paris, Colin, 1958.
Seigneurie française et Manoir anglais. Paris, Colin, 1960.
Mélanges historiques. Paris, 1963; selections as *Land and Work in Medieval Europe: Selected Papers*, Berkeley, University of California Press, 1967; selections as *Slavery and Serfdom in the Middle Ages: Selected Papers by Marc Bloch*, Berkeley, University of California Press, 1975.
Souvenirs de Guerre, 1914-15. Paris, Colin, 1969; as *Memoirs of War, 1914-15*, Ithaca, New York, Cornell University Press, 1980.

*

Critical Studies: *Hommages solennel de l'Université et la Résistance à la mémoire de Marc Bloch, professeur d'histoire économique à la Sorbonne, fusillé par les Allemands le 16 juin 1944: Cérémonie du 26 juin 1944 au grand amphithéatre de la Sorbonne sous la présidence de M. le Ministre de l'Education Nationale; Marc Bloch, grand historien, heros et martyr de la Résistance; l'homme et l'oeuvre* by Lucien Febvre and Georges Altman, Paris, Enterprise de Press, 1946; *Marc Bloch* by Oscar Mourat, Montevideo, Universidad de la Republica, 1969; *Le instituzioni della società feudale nell'opera di Marc Bloch: Lezioni di storia medioevale alla Facoltà di magistero raccolte da M. Lazzarin e Magl* by Giorgio Picasso, Milan, CELUC, 1971.

*   *   *

Marc Bloch is certainly the most distinguished French medieval and economic historian of the period before the Second World War. The son of a distinguished professor of ancient history at the Ecole Normale and later the Sorbonne, Bloch was from birth a member of the Third Republic's intellectual elite. The events and persons which influenced the young Marc Bloch are varied and interrelated. The milieu in which he grew to maturity was marked by the aftermath of the Dreyfus Affair. In his own words, Bloch and his classmates at the Ecole Normale were "the last generation of the Dreyfus Affair." His national feeling was heightened at an early age by the significance which his father placed upon the disastrous French defeat in 1870-71. His own long military service in the First World War also deepened his already fervent nationalism. Among the major influences which resulted from his formal education were his study of Durkheim's spirit and method, Henri Berr's historical views, as well as the irrational in politics and life as it was experienced in the Dreyfus Affair. His formal training in Paris and Berlin as well as his preliminary researches were completed before the outbreak of the War in 1914. The main body of the works of the mature Marc Bloch was published in the period between the two world wars and posthumously.

After the War he became a faculty member at the University of Strasbourg in Alsace, a province which had been reannexed to France in 1918. His senior colleague at Strasbourg was Lucien Febvre and the two became not only close friends but also intellectual companions. In 1929 they cooperated in founding the journal, *Annales d'histoire économique et sociale*, a journal that has had a significant effect on 20th-century historical writing.

Bloch's dissertation, *Les Rois Thaumaturges*, deals with rural history of the Ile de France and the psychological bases of kingship. Specifically, the book considers the alleged healing powers of the French medieval kings to cure scrofula. He drew upon the medical expertise of his brother who was a physician as well as on more traditional sources. The work represents an attempt to understand medieval man's belief in the miraculous. In short, in Bloch's terms, a "collective illusion" took place: "what created faith in a miracle was the idea that a miracle was going to take place." Bloch saw this belief in the miraculous as a means whereby royalty held sway over its people. He also noted that once a phenomenon in history had lost the rational function to which it owed its origin it no longer held sway "over the minds of men" and it came to be without influence or significance. In describing a "collective illusion," Bloch develops the collective mentality of the annaliste historians.

In his masterpiece, *Les caractères originaux de l'histoire rurale française*, Bloch attempted to reconstruct a social history of the Middle Ages. In this work he traced the continuity and development of agriculture and rural life from the Middle Ages to the present. Rather than relying on such traditional sources as legal documents and institutional relationships, Bloch examined field crop systems, cropping systems, and various farming techniques. Central to Bloch's method was to determine the causation of historical change. It was because of this major contribution to historical method and medieval studies that Bloch was appointed to the chair of economic history at the Sorbonne in 1936.

In his third major work, *La Société féodale*, Bloch departed once again from traditional approaches to the subject by his efforts at reconstitution of what he termed "a total social ambiance" or milieu. In an attempt to examine the decline of a social structure, he engages in fascinating discussions of place names, means of transportation, and differences in experiencing the sense of time. His research for this work was based on an astonishing number of sources such as legal documents, epic poems, literature, theological writings, and chronicles. In his attempt to recreate the milieu of feudalism he did not restrict himself to any particular country nor did he feel constrained to follow a rigid chronological order. His conclusions, however, caused medievalists to revise or rethink their views on feudal

society. By writing *The Feudal Society* Bloch demonstrated his interest as well as his competence in rural history, an interest that was to influence many succeeding historians including Pierre Goubert.

With the outbreak of the Second World War, Bloch once more returned to military service. During the war years he wrote three works or testaments, all of which were published after his tragic death in 1944. They are *L'Etrange défaite*, *Apologie pour le métier d'un historien*, and a fragmentary spiritual testament published in the *Annales* in 1946. In *L'Etrange défaite* (translated as *Strange Defeat*) Bloch showed a grasp of the military reasons for France's defeat as well as a thorough knowledge of French geography which was gleaned from his previous historical studies. He was harsh in his criticism of both the French military leadership and the civilian and business leadership of the country. He argued that the governmental and financial leaders did not sacrifice their personal interests and rally to the "patrie en danger." It was one of the first books published on the defeat, and one of the most widely read.

His *Apologie pour le métier d'un historien* (published in English as *The Historian's Craft*) was left unfinished at the time of his death and was prepared for publication by his colleague and friend, Lucien Febvre. In this work Bloch sets forth his views on history, especially, his notion of retrogressive history, that is, a technique of starting with the present and going backward into the past, a technique he employed in his work on feudalism. He advocates the comparative history that is central to his major works, asserting that to restrict history to a single nation or area or class would result in distortion. Underscoring all of his views was the necessity of an historical explanation. He wrote, "What a curious contradiction there is in the successive attitudes of so many historians: when it is a question of ascertaining whether or not some human act has really taken place, they cannot be sufficiently painstaking. If they proceed to the reasons for that act, they are content with the merest appearance, ordinarily founded upon one of those maxims of commonplace psychology which are neither more nor less true than their opposites." Thus for Bloch, discovering and describing the reasons behind an act is the most important work of the historian. Bloch succeeded in pointing out what was wrong with the historical conclusions of his contemporaries, but premature death prevented him from finishing those sections of his work in which he might have shown the way to what he would have considered proper conclusions.

In the years after Bloch's death by a Nazi firing squad in 1944, Lucien Febvre undertook the task of publishing his friend and colleague's works. Febvre's moving eulogy to his younger colleague published in 1946 epitomizes the esteem in which he held Bloch. The Annales School, which they founded, has refashioned historical writing in the western world just as Bloch refashioned medieval studies.

—Walter D. Gray

BLOOMFIELD, Leonard. American philologist. Born in Chicago, 1 April 1887. Studied at Harvard University, Cambridge, Massachusetts, B.A. 1906; University of Wisconsin, Madison, 1906-08; University of Chicago, Ph.D. 1909; University of Leipzig, 1913-14; University of Göttingen, 1914. Married Alice Sayers in 1909; 2 sons. Instructor, University of Cincinnati, 1919-10; Instructor, 1910-13, and Assistant Professor, 1913-21, University of Illinois, Urbana; Professor, Ohio State University, Columbus, 1921-27, and University of Chicago, 1927-40; Sterling Professor of Linguistics, Yale University, New Haven, Connecticut, 1940-49. President, Linguistic Society of America, 1935. Member, Permanent International Committee of Linguists, Royal Danish Academy of Sciences. *Died 18 April 1949.*

PUBLICATIONS

Linguistics

An Introduction to the Study of Language. New York, Holt, and London, Bell, 1914; enlarged edition as *Language*, New York, Holt, 1933, and London, Allen and Unwin, 1935; selections as *Language History*, edited by Harry Hoijer, New York, Holt, Rinehart and Winston, 1965.
Tagalog Texts with Grammatical Analysis. Urbana, University of Illinois, 3 vols., 1917.
First German Book. New York and London, Century, 1923.
Menomini Texts. New York, Stechert, 1928.
Sacred Stories of the Sweet Grass Cree. Ottawa, Acland, 1930.
Linguistic Aspects of Science. Chicago, University of Chicago Press, 1939.
Outline Guide for the Practical Study of Foreign Languages. Baltimore, Linguistic Society of America, 1942.
Colloquial Dutch. Baltimore, Linguistic Society of America, 1944; as *Spoken Dutch*, New York, Holt, 1944.
Eastern Ojibwa: Grammatical Sketch, Texts, and Word List. Ann Arbor, University of Michigan Press, 1957.
Let's Read: A Linguistic Approach, with Clarence L. Barnhart. Detroit, Wayne State University Press, 1961.
The Menomini Language. New Haven, Connecticut, Yale University Press, 1962.
A Leonard Bloomfield Anthology, edited by Charles F. Hockett. Bloomington, Indiana University Press, 1970.
Menomini Lexicon, edited by Charles F. Hockett. Milwaukee, Milwaukee Public Museum Press, 1975.

Other

Translator, *Before Dawn: A Social Drama* by Gerhart Hauptmann. Boston, Badger, 1909.

Editor, *Plains Cree Texts.* New York, Stechert, 1934.

*

Critical Studies: *Mentalism and Objectivism in Linguistics: The Sources of Leonard Bloomfield's Psychology of Language* by Erwin Allen Esper, New York, American Elsevier, 1968.

*   *   *

Leonard Bloomfield was largely responsible for the emergence of linguistics as a recognized, independent academic discipline, and for placing it on a sounder scientific basis than it had previously possessed.

Linguistics in America before Bloomfield had drawn on two main traditions. On one hand there were strong links with the historical philology of the German-speaking world; this had attained a high level of rigour and intellectual sophistication, but issues of scientific method concerning the relationship between observable speech-behaviour and internal linguistic structure did not arise, because these studies dealt mainly with the early history of languages whose contemporary forms are exhaustively documented. On the other hand there was the anthropological approach pioneered by Franz Boas, which aimed to record the empirical facts about the numerous (in many cases dying) languages of the American Indian and had little time for philosophical considerations.

Leonard Bloomfield had a foot in both of these camps. He studied in Germany and taught Germanic philology for many years, and his substantive linguistic research was largely concerned with the Algonquian languages of North America and with certain languages of the Philippines. But Bloomfield differed from most members of the two intellectual traditions just mentioned in that he saw language primarily as an aspect of human behaviour and treated its study as a branch of psychology. Bloomfield's views about psychology changed markedly during his career. In his youth he was influenced by the introspectionism of the Würzburg school; but, as J.B. Watson's "behaviourism" came to dominate the thinking of English-speaking psychologists, Bloomfield switched to become its chief advocate within the field of linguistic studies.

Probably the most important implication of behaviourism for the linguist was the idea that speakers of a language have no specially privileged access to the facts about the language's structure. The descriptive linguist must free himself from all traditional or instinctive beliefs about the language he investigates and base his description exclusively on observation of the language in use: he must "accept everything the native speaker says in his language and nothing he says about it." In Bloomfield's version of linguistic method, the familiar European languages are not the easiest but the most difficult languages to deal with, since the linguistic scientist has more ingrained assumptions to rid himself of than in the case of unwritten languages like those of the Americas or Africa. Bloomfield's precepts led to work such as Charles Fries's influential description of American English which dispensed entirely with terms such as "verb" and "noun".

Behaviourism had implications not only for methodology but for substantive beliefs about human nature. Many people felt that, if introspection is invalid as a scientific technique, this must mean that there is nothing to introspect: human behaviour is wholly a matter of direct associations between external stimuli impinging on the individual and his externally-observable responses, unmediated by anything that one could call a "mind". There is a fallacy in this reasoning, and some psychologists did not accept it; but Bloomfield did. He argued that the meanings of linguistic forms were stateable wholly in terms of the stimuli which cause them to be uttered and/or the effects they have on their hearers' behaviour. This may be a satisfactory approach for cases such as the shout of *Fire!* in a crowded theatre; it is hard to see how it can have any application to a large proportion of uses of language, for instance the various statements on the page which you are now reading.

The practical consequence of this aspect of Bloomfield's teaching was that a generation of linguists ignored the fact that people speak in order to communicate, and concentrated exclusively on analysis of the formal structure of languages.

Whatever the objections to behaviourism as a theory about human nature, its methodological prescriptions seem admirable. However, at present linguists pay as little attention to Bloomfield's ideas about research method as they do to his views on the nature of meaning. Bloomfield's intellectual authority has been eclipsed by that of Noam Chomsky, who regards introspective techniques as essential to linguistics and suggests that worthwhile linguistic research can be carried out only on one's mother tongue. In the long run it is probably fair to say that Bloomfield's greatest influence over the discipline of linguistics has concerned organizational rather than purely intellectual issues. He was the prime mover in the establishment of the Linguistic Society of America, founded in 1924 and still the leading professional body for the discipline in the world, and he did much in other ways to promote linguistics as a distinctive province of the map of learning.

—Geoffrey Sampson

BOAS, Franz. American anthropologist. Born in Minden, Germany, 9 July 1858; emigrated to the United States, 1888; subsequently naturalized. Educated at the Universities of Heidelberg, Bonn and Kiel, Ph.D., 1881. Married Marie A.E. Krackowizer in 1887; 3 children. Explored Baffin Land, 1883-84; Assistant, Royal Ethnology Museum, Berlin, and Docent in Geography, University of Berlin, 1885-86; made investigations in North America, Mexico and Puerto Rico, 1886-1931; Docent in Anthropology, Clark University, 1888-92; Chief Assistant in Anthropology, *Chicago Exposition*, 1892-95; Lecturer in Physical Anthropology, 1896-99, Professor of Anthropology, 1899-1937, and from 1937 Professor Emeritus, Columbia University, New York. Assistant Curator, 1896, and Curator, 1901-05, Department of Anthropology, American Museum of National History, New York; Honorary Philologist, Bureau of American Ethnology, 1901-19; Founder, International School of American Archeology and Ethnology, Mexico, 1910; Honorary Professor, National Museum of Archaeology, Mexico, 1910-12. Editor, *Publications of the Jesup North Pacific Expedition*, New York, 1900-30, *Publications of the American Ethnological Society*, 1907-42, *Journal of American Folk-Lore*, 1908-24, *Handbook of American Indian Languages*, 1911-42, and *Columbia University Contributions to Anthropology*, 1913-1936; Founder and Editor, *International Journal of American Linguistics*, 1917-39. Vice-President, 1895 and 1907, and President, 1931, American Association for the Advancement of Science; President, American Anthropological Society, 1907 and 1908; President, New York Academy of Sciences, 1910; Corresponding Secretary, Germanistic Society of America, 1914; President, Emergency Society of German and Austrian Science, 1927; National Chairman, 1929-40, and Honorary Chairman, from 1940, Committee for Democracy and Intellectual Freedom. Member, National Academy of Sciences; American Academy of Arts and Sciences; and Deutsche Akademie, Munich; Honorary Member, Anthropological Society, Vienna; Société des Américanistes, Paris; Senckenbergische Gesellschaft, Frankfurt; Geographical Societies of Gothenburg, Hamburg and Würzburg; Anthropological Institute of Great Britain and Ireland; and the Folk Lore Society of London; Corresponding Member, Institute for History of Civilization, Oslo; Anthropological Societies of Berlin, Brussels, Florence, Moscow, Paris, Rome, Stockholm and Washington; American Numismatic Society, German Anthropological Society; Prussian, Munich, Danish and Vienna Academies of Science; Leopoldina Academy, Halle; and Society for Oriental Languages, Frankfurt. *Died* (in New York City) *21 December 1942*.

PUBLICATIONS

Anthropology

Beiträge zur Erkenntnisse der Farbe des Wassers. Kiel, Schmidt und Klaunig, 1881.
Kwakiutl Tales (vol. 1, texts and translations, 1910; vol. 2, translations, 1935; vol. 2, texts, 1943). New York, Columbia University Press, 2 vols., 1910-43.
Changes in Bodily Form of Descendants of Immigrants. Washington, D.C., U.S. Government Printing Office, 1911.
The Mind of Primitive Man (lectures). New York, Macmillan, 1911; revised edition as *Kultur und Rasse*, Leipzig, Veit, 1914.
Primitive Art. Oslo, Institutt for Sammenlignende Kulturforskning, and Cambridge, Massachusetts, Harvard University Press, 1927.
Anthropology and Modern Life. New York, W.W. Norton, 1928; London, Allen and Unwin, 1929; revised edition, 1932.
Rasse und Kultur (speech). Jena, Fischer, 1932.
General Anthropology, with others. Boston, D.C. Heath, 1938.
Race, Language and Culture (selected writings). New York, Macmillan, 1940.
Dakota Grammar, with Ella Deloria. Washington, D.C.,

National Academy of Sciences, 1941.

Other

Ethnography of Franz Boas: Letters and Diaries of Franz Boas Written on the Northwest Coast from 1886-1931, edited by Ronald Rohner. Chicago, University of Chicago Press, 1969.

Editor and Contributor, *General Anthropology*. Boston, Heath, 1938.

*

Bibliography: "Bibliography of Franz Boas" by H.A. Andrews and others in *American Anthropologist* (New York), July-September, 1943.

Critical Studies: *Franz Boas* by Melville Herskovits, New York, Scribner, 1953.

*   *   *

Franz Boas is the central figure in the early history of academic anthropology in North America. He began the first teaching program in anthropology in the United States, at Clark University in 1892, and awarded the first Doctorate. After 1899, at Columbia, he trained a group of scholars who dominated the discipline from the first decades of this century through the 1950's. In 1910, he founded the International School of American Archeology and Ethnology in Mexico, and in the same year served as President of the New York Academy of Sciences. Boas himself did important work in all four branches of anthropology: ethnology, linguistics, physical anthropology, and archeology, yet his leadership was based less on these several accomplishments than on a vision of an exact and rigorous social science that unified them.

Boas's intellectual background lay in a widespread and very important scholarly and social movement in 19th century Germany, grounded ultimately in the critical philosophy, legal theory, geography, and anthropology of Immanuel Kant and the related earlier social theories of Montesquieu. By Boas's time, threads of this movement ran through linguistics, the "historical jurisprudence" of Savigny, the psychophysics of Fechner and the "folk psychology" of Wundt deriving from it. One theme Boas drew from this tradition was a very specific and rigorously defined "comparative method" of historical inference, first perfected in linguistics and comparative law. Another was a broad democratic and pluralistic political outlook he sometimes characterized as the spirit of the revolution of 1848.

Although Boas's 1881 doctoral dissertation *Contributions on Cognition of the Color of Waters* was in geography, its central problem derived from psychophysics. Its most basic concern was with "thresholds of perception," the subject of six other articles through 1883. Thresholds of perception were then widely seen as basic building blocks of human consciousness, and as a possible foundation of thought itself. One important open question about them was whether they varied from group to group. If they did, a further question was why.

Boas's dissertation convinced him that they did indeed vary. There were then three possibilities to consider as the basis of the variation: race, geography, or culture. In 1883, he undertook a trip among the Eskimo of Baffinland in pursuit of a "plan to regard as my life's task the investigation: how far may we consider the phenomenon of organic life, and especially those of the psychic life, from a mechanistic point of view, and what conclusions may be drawn from such an investigation?" "Mechanistic" meant mainly geographic determinism. By 1887, he had concluded that the answer to "how far?" was "not very," and the conclusion he drew was that the most important influences lay in the basic ideas that appeared to be developed in different ways in different cultures. The explanation of the forms of these ideas lay mainly in the historical development of that culture. The influences of geography, while real, were relatively trivial.

Boas's ethnological work after 1883 consisted in a very large number of studies of cultural artifacts of all kinds, from needlecases to folk-stories. The general pattern was to consider the variations among a clearly circumscribed set of such artifacts along with their geographical distribution in order to reconstruct the way the observed pattern developed and, almost always, to reject one or more alternative views of general developmental processes (usually evolutionary views) then current.

Boas's view that the basic ideas in any culture reflected its unique historical development has recently been labelled "historical particularism," and construed as the idea that one explains each *culture* only by looking at *its* unique history, and that there are no general laws. Boas's actual view was quite different. He always traced the histories of specific cultural elements not whole cultures, and always grounded his explanations in a general theoretical conception of human action and thought that was sometimes called, in his tradition, "the psychic unity of man." This assumed freedom of choice, a common human ability to recognize what was rational across cultural boundaries, and recognition that all communicable perceptions had a basis in categories that were inherently shared and thus could be learned. Choice thus necessarily drew upon culture, but was never determined by it, and culture in turn was shaped by choices.

Boas's linguistic analyses, mainly in the Pacific Northwest and Mexico, had three major aims. The first was to describe and classify the languages, and Boas was among the first to recognize the extreme linguistic diversity in North America. The second was to provide access to the ideas of those in the culture through their established lore, and to record that lore before the communities changed any further. He developed a consistent system for recording spoken language and transcribed faithfully many texts of traditional stories, myths, and the like. The third was to help with cultural history. Boas's counterparts in Europe had used European texts to provide data on the development of social and ethical ideas within Europe from Roman times to the 19th century. Boas evidently intended that the Indian texts he collected would serve the same purpose, and in a sense they did, although they led to quite different substantive results. All European languages except Basque were of the single Indo-European language family, and have been as far back as texts go. As this came to be known through the 19th century, it naturally seemed to support fairly simple evolutionary models of cultural development that assumed the all or most of the important changes occur by an internal genetic process. By contrast, Boas's work quickly showed him that in the Pacific Northwest alone (quite apart from the rest of North America and even excluding Eskimo) there were at least four absolutely unrelated language families—as distinct as any old world languages. Yet the languages had many vocabulary items in common. More importantly, the communities that spoke them had many common cultural traits, and clearly formed a single regional system. This naturally precluded any justified attempt to treat the modern languages as simple genetic growths from their early roots, and led Boas to a more complex view of cultural development, involving many distinct processes and the possibilities of movements in many directions. One of the processes to which Boas assigned great stress, as compared with his European predecessors, was "diffusion," the borrowing of traits from one community by another. He also stressed that development of a trait over time need not be "progressive." Traits could become more elaborated and complex; they could equally become simpler and seemingly more primitive. Exactly the same points were made in his ethnology.

Boas's consideration of race paralleled and expanded his considerations of geography and culture history. He consistently argued against those who held intelligence and character to be racially based, or even to vary according to heredity. Boas's attack was basic, and involved showing that the physical features then most commonly taken as indicating "race" were not in fact stable over long periods of time and were indeed not even demonstrably based on biological inheritance. His best known and largest research project was undertaken in response to a request from the United States Immigration Commission and submitted to the Congress in 1911. This involved studying a large number of families of several European nationalities who had migrated to the United States, comparing the immigrants to each other and to their relatives who had not migrated. The results were, first, that all the groups changed their physical form. Those who migrated to this country as children were different from their parents, and those born here were even more different. Children were increasingly different as their length of residence increased. The differences were sometime great enough to class parents and children as different races by the established criteria. Second, the changes were always in the direction of the American norms. The conclusion was that human plasticity was so great that attempts to divide people into numerous races and "admixtures" were inherently unwarranted. There was only one race, the human race, and all else were local varieties greatly influenced by environment (clearly including culture).

Overall, Boas stressed the variety within cultures more than the differences between them, and saw each community and each individual as the custodian of not just one but many traditions. In 1911 he had emphasised that people cannot be "classified" the same way by physical type, language, or culture traits—meaning that language cannot be predicted from race nor race from language, and so on. Each of these kinds of things has a separate history, and the histories come together not in the "the culture" or society but in each person.

Boas's stern and factual arguments concealed a liberal and romantic conception of man in the tradition of Goethe. The value of the individual and freedom of choice and thought were basic values for him as well as basic facts. He consistently exposed the weaknesses of theories of racial superiority or inferiority and opposed attempts to subordinate science to politics. In 1918 he publicly criticized President Wilson and several American scholars who had used their positions to engage in wartime spying in Latin America. In the furor that followed he was removed from the Presidency of the American Anthropological Association and even stripped of his membership—though later reinstated.

—Murray J. Leaf

BOHR, Niels (Henrik David). Danish physicist. Born in Copenhagen, 7 October 1885. Educated at the Gammelholm School and the University of Copenhagen, Ph.D. 1911. Married Margrethe Nörlund in 1912; 4 children. Worked at the Cavendish Laboratory, Cambridge University, 1911-12; Lecturer, University of Copenhagen, 1913; Reader in Mathematical Philosophy, University of Manchester, 1914-16; Professor of Theoretical Physics, University of Copenhagen, 1916-62, and Founder and Director, Institute for Theoretical Physics, Copenhagen (now the Niels Bohr Institute), 1920-62. Advisor, Scientific Staff, Los Alamos atom bomb project, New Mexico; Chairman, Danish Atomic Energy Commission. Recipient: Nobel Prize in Physics, 1922; Atoms for Peace Prize, 1957; Sonning Prize, Denmark, 1961. Honorary doctorate: Cambridge University, 1923; University of Liverpool, 1923; University of Manchester, 1925; Oxford University, 1926; University of Edinburgh, 1929; University of Kiel, 1929; Technical University of Denmark, 1929; Brown University, Providence, Rhode Island, 1933; University of California, Berkeley, 1937; University of Oslo, 1938; University of Birmingham, 1938; University of London, 1938; University of Paris, 1945; Princeton University, New Jersey, 1946; McGill University, Montreal, 1946; University of Glasgow, 1951; University of Aberdeen, 1952; University of Athens, 1953; University of Lund,

Sweden, 1953; Columbia University, 1954; University of Basle, 1955; University of Aarhus, 1956; University of Zagreb, 1958; University of Bombay, 1960; University of Calcutta, 1960; University of Warsaw, 1960; University of Brussels, 1961; Harvard University, Cambridge, Massachusetts, 1961; Rockefeller University, New York, 1962. Foreign Member, Royal Institution, and Royal Society, London. Member, Order of the Elephant, Denmark. *Died* (in Carlsberg) *18 November 1962.*

PUBLICATIONS

Physics

Abhandlungen über Atombau aud den Jahren 1913-1916. Braunschweig, Germany, Vieweg, 1921.
The Effect of Electric and Magnetic Fields on Spectral Lines. London, Physical Society, 1922.
The Theory of Spectra and Atomic Constitution. Cambridge, Cambridge University Press, 1922.
Drei Aufsätze uber Spektren und Atombau. Braunschweig, Germany, Vieweg, 1922.
Über die Quantentheorie der Linienspektren. Braunschweig, Germany, Vieweg, 1923.
Über den Bau der Atome. Berlin, Springer, 1924.
Atomtheorie und Naturbeschreibung. Berlin, Springer, 1931; as *Atomic Theory and the Description of Nature,* Cambridge, Cambridge University Press, 1934.
Atomfysik og menneskelig erkenkelse. Copenhagen, Schultz, 1957; as *Atomic Physics and Human Knowledge,* New York, Wiley, 1958.
Essays, 1958-1962, on Atomic Physics and Human Knowledge. New York, Interscience Publishers, 1963.

*

Critical Studies: *Neils Bohr: The Man, His Science, and the World They Changed,* by Ruth E. Moore, New York, Knopf, 1966; *Niels Bohr: His Life and Work as Seen by His Friends and Colleagues,* edited by S. Rozental, Amsterdam, North Holland Publishing Company, and New York, Wiley, 1967; article by Leon Rosenfield in *Dictionary of Scientific Biography,* New York, Scribners, 1970.

*   *   *

The greatest contribution of Niels Bohr to science was his invention of the quantum theory of atomic structure, enshrined in three famous papers in the *Philosophical Magazine* in 1913. In these he inaugurated a way of looking at atomic problems that revolutionized atomic physics, leading to the development 12 years later of quantum mechanics, which has dominated the subject for the balance of the 20th century.

To understand the significance of Bohr's contribution, it is essential to review earlier attempts at a theory of atomic structure. After the identification of the electron as a fundamental atomic particle by J.J. Thompson in 1897, it became apparent that all atoms must contain electrons. But their negative charges must be neutralized by an appropriate distribution of positive charges. The relative distribution of the two kinds of charges must satisfy not only the requirements of the chemical interaction of atoms, but also the dynamical properties of the atomic constituents leading to the observed atomic optical spectra, whose regularities had been extensively studied since the middle of the 19th century. Earlier attempts to explain these phenomena were not particularly successful. Thus it had proved impracticable to account for the spectral regularities by any reasonable assumptions concerning the electromagnetic radiation from the electrons moving in an atom. Moreover, the atom could not be stable if the electrons were assumed to be at rest.

The picture changed radically when Ernest Rutherford introduced in 1911 the nuclear atom model, in which the positive charge of the atom is concentrated in a small massive particle called the nucleus, about which the electrons can revolve in appropriate orbits. This picture fascinated Bohr, who worked in Rutherford's laboratory in the University of Manchester while it was being developed. Bohr's earlier doctoral dissertation on the electron theory of metals may well have predisposed him to provide a theory of the behavior of the electrons in the Rutherford atom model.

Bohr realized at the outset that two fundamental problems confronted him. The first was to insure the dynamical stability of the Rutherford model. From the standpoint of classical mechanics and electromagnetic theory the electrons revolving about the nucleus would be expected to radiate energy in the form of electromagnetic radiation as long as they remain in motion. The resultant loss would cause their orbits to shrink in size until eventually the electrons would all fall into the nucleus. Some special assumption of a non-classical character would have to be made to avoid this result. The second problem concerned the radiation itself. According to classical theory this would have to have a frequency equal to or closely connected with the frequency of revolution of the electrons in their revolutions about the nucleus. But as the orbits shrink this frequency would increase continuously, leading to continuous spectra. However, spectroscopic observations were in disagreement with this result. The emission spectrum of hydrogen, for example, consists in part, at least, of separated lines of sharply defined frequency. Bohr felt that this must have its origin in a quantized character of the radiation. Hence he had to seek an answer to the problem in the quantum theory that had been invented in 1900 by Max Planck. In order to make his theory as general as possible, Bohr based it on two fundamental postulates: 1) Every atom (independently of the precise model adopted) in equilibrium with its surroundings can exist only in certain stationary states in which the energy remains constant (i.e., no radiation is emitted); and 2) the energy of the atom can change only through a transition from one stationary state to another and hence in discrete amounts equal to the energy difference of the two states in question. If this energy change is connected with the absorption or emission of electromagnetic radiation, the frequency of the radiation will be equal to the energy difference divided by the Planck constant of action, h (a quantity equal in magnitude to 6.6256×10^{-27} erg sec.). This second postulate is referred to as the "Bohr frequency condition".

In order to test his theory Bohr had to apply it to an atomic model; he chose the Rutherford nuclear model. Since the model for hydrogen is the simplest, with a singule electron (in the normal unionized state) circling the nucleus, Bohr decided to make this his test case. His first problem was the identification of the stationary states. Here he had to make an arbitrary assumption essentially dictated by the result he hoped to find, a common enough tactic in the development of any scientific theory. For the sake of simplicity, he assumed that the electron can move only in a circular orbit and that its moment of momentum (momentum multiplied by the radius of the circle) must take only discrete values equal to an integral multiple of Planck's constant, h, divided by 2π. Such an integer he called a quantum number. This enabled him at once to evaluate from ordinary mechanics the electron's energy in each stationary state in terms of its charge and mass, quantities already known. Application of the Bohr frequency condition then provided the frequency values for the spectral lines emitted when the hydrogen atom makes a transition from a higher energy stationary state to one of lower energy. These frequencies were found to agree very closely with the experimentally measured ones, thus providing a verification of the theory.

Bohr also observed that the frequency of the radiation resulting from transitions between states of very high energy and corresponding to very large quantum numbers approaches in the limit the actual frequency of revolution of the electron, that is, the frequency that would be expected from the classical theory of electromagnetic radiation. This suggested the existence of a principle, called by Bohr the "correspondence principle", according to which every quantum transition in the atom leading to the radiation corresponds to a classical radiation frequency, even if it is not identical with it.

Bohr's success with the hydrogen atom provoked considerable interest, mingled indeed with some skepticism, since his postulates seemed to be a curious mixture of classical and quantum ideas. He strengthened his position considerably by showing that the spectrum of singly ionized helium, i.e., helium that has lost an electron from its normal quota of two extra nuclear electrons, could be successfully accounted for by his theory. He also showed how certain small discrepancies between his theory and experiment could be explained by taking into account the very small motion of the atomic nucleus, neglected in his first calculations.

However, substantial difficulties began to appear when the attempt was made to apply the theory to polyelectronic atoms, i.e., those with more than one electron in the normal unionized state, e.g., 3 for lithium, 4 for beryllium, and so on (numbers which are referred to as atomic numbers). Many models were suggested, but because of interactions of various electrons it became impossible to calculate the quantized energy states with enough accuracy to make a reasonable comparison with the precise experimental values, though in certain cases order of magnitude agreement was achieved. Bohr ultimately decided that it was more practical to devote his attention to the way his theory indicated the buildup of the constitution of the elements in the periodic system as originally mapped out by the Russian chemist Mendeleev and later elaborated by the Danish chemist Hans Thomsen. Here Bohr was successful in assigning the proper physical and chemical properties to certain elements whose position in the periodic system was uncertain. Thus he predicted the properties of the element with the atomic number 72, which was ultimately named hafnium in honor of the City of Copenhagen. This result became known in 1922, the year in which Bohr received the Nobel Prize in physics. The development of Bohr's fundamental ideas into the theory of quantum mechanics was the work of men like Werner Heisenberg, Louis de Broglie, Erwin Schrödinger, Max Born, and P.A.M. Dirac, most of whom greatly profited from association with Bohr, whose critical and catalytic comments played a profound role for the rest of his life.

One particularly important development in the late 1920's led to Bohr's invention of a philosophical principle of far reaching importance. In this connection it should be emphasized that in all Bohr's researches he ever sought for the most general point of view, and in this sense he ranks as a great philosopher. When Heisenberg developed the indeterminacy principle in quantum mechanics in 1927 and discussed the whole problem in detail with Bohr, the latter saw it almost at once as a special case of a more fundamental philosophical principle he called "complimentarity". The indeterminacy principle emphasizes that it is impossible to measure the position and velocity of an atomic particle like an electron simultaneously with the highest degree of precision. The highly precise measurement of position excludes the highly precise measurement of velocity and vice versa. Bohr saw these two measurements as complementary in the sense that though they are both necessary for the complete description of the behavior of the electron, the precise measurement of the one precludes the precise simultaneous measurement of the other. Bohr was able to extend this complementary idea to the other aspects of experience. For example, in the attempt to understand the nature of life, the analytical study of all the component parts of what is thought to be a living organism finally winds up with the organism dead, whereas the external observational study of the organism as a whole excludes the detailed study of its parts and their role. The two methods are complementary aspects of experience related to life.

During the vast development of nuclear physics subsequent to 1930 Bohr was able to make one very significant contribution. This was his analogy between a nucleus and a liquid drop. This

ingenious point of view contributed greatly to the understanding of nuclear fission, the phenomena at the basis of practical atomic energy and the atomic bomb.

During his later years Bohr's chief role in science was that of a friendly but decisive critic of all ideas in atomic physics. Though always basically concerned with the effective development of physics as a science, he also sought to direct its applications into peaceful uses. He was one of the most profound philosophers of science of our time.

—R. Bruce Lindsay

BONHOEFFER, Dietrich. German theologian. Born in Breslau, 4 February 1906. Studied at the University of Tübingen and the University of Berlin, Licentiate in Theology, 1927 (revoked, 1940); Union Theological Seminary, New York, 1930 (Sloane Fellow). Taught at the University of Berlin, 1931-36; Director, Seminary of the Confessing Church, Zingst and later Finkenwalde, 1934-37. Arrested by the Nazis in 1943, imprisoned at Tegel, Buchenwald, Schönberg, and Flossenbürg, and hanged 9 April 1945.

PUBLICATIONS

Collections

Gesammelte Schriften. Munich, Kaiser, 6 vols., 1958-74; selections as *Christology,* London, Collins, and *Christ the Center,* New York, Harper, 1966; as *No Rusty Swords,* London, Collins, and New York, Harper, 1966; as *The Way to Freedom,* London, Collins, and New York, Harper, 1966; and as *True Patriotism,* London, Collins, and New York, Harper, 1973.

Theology

Sanctorum Communio: Eine dogmatische Untersuchung zur Soziologie der Kirche. Berlin, Trowitzsch, 1930; as *The Community of Saints,* London, Collins, and New York, Harper, 1963.
Akt und Sein: Transzendentalphilosophie und Ontologie in der systermatischen Theologie. Gütersloh, Bertelsmann, 1931; as *Act and Being,* London, Collins, and New York, Harper 1962.
Schöpfung und Fall: Theologische Auslegung von Genesis 1-3. Munich, Kaiser, 1933; as *Creation and Fall,* London, SCM Press, and New York, Macmillan, 1959.
Nachfolge. Munich, Kaiser, 1937; as *The Cost of Discipleship,* London, SCM Press, 1948; New York, Macmillan, 1949.
Gemeinsames Leben. Munich, Kaiser, 1939; as *Life Together,* London, SCM Press, and New York, Harper, 1955.
Das Gebetbuch der Bibel: Eine Einführung in die Psalmen. Bad-Salzuflen, MKB, 1940; as *Psalms: The Book of Prayer of the Bibel.* Minneapolis, Augsburg, 1970.
Auf dem Wege zur Freiheit: Gedichte und Briefe aus der Haft. Berlin, Haus und Schule, 1946; as *Prayers from Prison: Prayers and Poems,* London, Collins, 1977; Philadelphia, Fortress Press, 1978.
Ehtik, edited by E. Bethge. Munich, Kaiser, 1949; as *Ethics,* London, SCM Press, and New York, Harper, 1955.
Widerstand und Ergebung: Briefe und Aufzeichnungen aus der Haft, edited by E. Bethge. Munich, Kaiser, 1951; as *Letters and Papers from Prison,* London, SCM Press, 1953; as *Prisoner for God: Letters and Papers from Prison,* New York Macmillan, 1955.

Versuchung, edited by E. Bethge. Munich, Kaiser, 1953; as *Temptation*, London, SCM Press, and New York, Macmillan, 1955.

Ich habe dieses Volk geliebt: Zeugnisse der Verantwortung, edited by Hans Rothfels, as *I Loved These People: Testimonies of Responsibility*, London, S.P.C.K., 1966.

Beten mit der Bibel. Hamburg, Fruche, 1970.

Das Wesen der Kirche, edited by Otto Dudzus. Munich, Kaiser, 1971.

*

Bibliography: "Bibliographie Dietrich Bonhoeffer," in *Die Mündige Welt II*, Munich, Kaiser, 1956.

Critical Studies: *The Theology of Dietrich Bonhoeffer* by John D. Godsey, Philadelphia, Westminister Press, 1960; *The Place of Bonhoeffer: Problems and Possibilities in His Thought*, edited by Martin E. Marty, New York, Association Press, 1962; *Dietrich Bonhoeffer: Man of Vision, Man of Courage*, by Eberhard Bethge, New York, Harper, 1970.

* * *

Dietrich Bonhoeffer was one of the leading Lutheran theologians in Germany during the Nazi period. After his death his work became not only one of the deepest and most inspiring but also one of the most controversial sources of modern Christianity in that it directly addresses issues which pertain to the Church as it finds itself confronted with a growing secularization of most Western societies, with social sciences which lay claim to autonomy and revelance, and with the general dislocation of a culture that is threatened by an abundance of means and a secret nihilism as far as goals are concerned.

As a theologian, Bonhoeffer tried to reconcile sociological ideas concerning the Church, taken as a human organization, with his theological conception of the Church, as the divine society on earth. His doctoral dissertation, *Communio Sanctorum*, was devoted to this complex theme. His inaugural dissertation, *Akt und Sein*, was mainly concerned with the philosophical presuppositions of this theological conception; in this work, Bonhoeffer tried to find his own way in philosophy by carefully comparing basic ideas from Kant and Heidegger; in applying the result of these investigations to theology, he was guided mainly by Grisebach and Barth. His letters from prison made him famous. In these letters he returns time and again to the question of how the Christ can become the Lord of people who have no need for innerness and metaphysics, and who have lost sense for and interest in religion. Can there be Christians without religion? (April 30, 1944). The questions raised here are related to Bonhoeffer's view on the meaning of the incarnation and his conviction concerning the basic "this-worldliness" of Christianity. Bonhoeffer made important contributions to the ecumenical movement and its theology, to social theology through his view of Christianity's role in a secular world, and to dogmatic theology in general, and ecclesiology in particular.

His first works show the influence of the theologian Barth, the sociologist of religion Troeltsch, and the philosophers Hegel and Heidegger. In his ecclesiology Bonhoeffer tries to portray the Church as the revelation of a collective design on the part of God and as the place where the knowledge of God becomes manifest. For him Jesus is not an isolated historical figure who founded Christianity as a particular religion; rather, he is a collective person who is more the foundation than the founder of the Church. It is clear that in these works Bonhoeffer tried to combine theological with sociological ideas in order to overcome the individualism of Protestant theology and help sociology of religion avoid becoming a science of purely formal structures only. For Bonhoeffer the Church is not an institution that more or less falls short of an ideal that it can never materialize, but rather the manifestation of the restructuring of the world in Christ.

After 1933, when Bonhoeffer became deeply involved in the battle of the Confessing Church with national socialism, he focussed more and more on the earthly dimension of the Church and its responsibility in the political arena. The Church can no longer limit itself to man's inner life; the entire world must restructure itself in Christ; at the same time the Church must give up its one-sided clericalism. In 1937, he published *Nachfolge* (The Cost of Discipleship) and in 1938 *Gemeinsames Leben* (Life Together). These works, which show some similarity with the theological works of Kierkegaard, demand that the Christian imitates the Christ with respect to obedience, penance, and discipline in order that the Church may save the world and the society in which it finds itself. Such an apprenticeship of the Lord can develop fruitfully only within the community of the Church and under the guidance of the Holy Spirit.

During his stay in prison Bonhoeffer completed his *Ethics* which appeared posthumously with his *Letters and Papers from Prison*. The latter show a growing feeling of complete abandonment in a world without God. Bonhoeffer speaks here of the "weakness" of God which in his opinion has a twofold positive meaning; first of all, God himself approves of the autonomy of this world; secondly, there is the companionship with the crucified Jesus who, before God, lived the "without-God" of his total abandonment. Instead of speaking about an omnipotent God who overcomes the misery of man, Bonhoeffer portrays here a suffering God in agony (Pascal) and an emancipated, autonomous man who is capable of responsibility.

It is very difficult to interpret Bonhoeffer's theological writings; in part this is due to the fragmentary character of his major works and the fact that his last works remained incomplete. There is a substantial difference between the interpretations given by Ebeling, Robinson, and Müller. Where Robinson describes Bonhoeffer as a forerunner of a theology without God, Ebeling and Müller stress typical Lutheran concerns in Bonhoeffer's work, namely the doctrine of the two kingdoms, and that of salvation by faith.

In his *Ethics*, Bonhoeffer rejects the commonly accepted view that ethics aims at the knowledge of good and evil; he wanted to write a Christian ethics whose first task it would be to invalidate this thesis. He was fully aware of the fact that a Christian ethics is affected by many basic problems; yet, at the same time, he was also convinced that in principle they can be solved. Thus a genuinely Christian ethics is possible, and it "claims to discuss the origin of the whole problem of ethics, and this professes to be a critique of all ethics simply as ethics." When a man claims that he knows good and evil, then he has already fallen away from his origin. According to the Christian view, man's true origin is God; and at his origin he knows only one thing: God. All other things he knows in God and he only knows God in all things. Now in the knowledge of good and evil, man no longer understands himself from the destiny that is implied in his origin, but rather from his own possibilities, i.e., his possibility of being good or evil. "He knows himself now as something apart from God, outside God, and this means that he now knows only himself and no longer God at all.... The knowledge of good and evil is therefore separation from God. Only against God can man know good and evil." By conceiving of himself as the source of good and evil, man attempts to become like God and makes himself his own creator and judge. When a man reflects on what has taken place here, he finds himself in shame. For shame is man's indelible recollection of his estrangement from his genuine origin. The world of disunion with God, conflict, and moral problems, which his conscience shows him, must be overcome in a reconciliation with his true origin; this can be brought about only by Christ (Christian ethics). As soon as man is reunited with God through Christ the law becomes of minor importance; then man is concerned with God's will only, and that is something new and different in each different situation. This view brings Bonhoeffer close to the so-called situation ethics of Kierkegaard and Grisebach.

—Joseph Kockelmans

BORING, E(dwin) G(arrigues). American psychologist. Born in Philadelphia, Pennsylvania, 23 October 1886. Studied at Cornell University, Ithaca, New York, M.E. 1908, Ph.D. 1918. Served in the United States Army, 1918: Captain. Married Lucy May Day in 1914; 4 children. Worked for Bethlehem Steel Company, 1908-09; Teacher, Moravian Parochial School, Bethlehem, Pennsylvania, 1909-10. Instructor, Cornell University, 1914-18; Professor of Experimental Psychology and Director, Psychology Laboratory, Clark University, Worcester, Massachusetts, 1919-22; Associate Professor, 1922-28, Professor, 1928-56, and Professor Emeritus, 1956-68, Harvard University, Cambridge, Massachusetts (Director, Psychology Laboratory, 1924-49; Chairman, Psychology Department, 1936-38 and again after the war; Lowell TV Lecturer and Edgar Peirce Professor, 1956-57). President, American Psychological Association, 1929. Editor, *Contemporary Psychology*, 1956-61. Honorary M.A.: Harvard University, 1942; honorary doctorate: University of Pennsylvania, Philadelphia, 1946; Clark University, 1956. Fellow, American Academy of Arts and Sciences; Society of Experimental Psychologists. Honorary Member, British Psychological Society; French Psychological Society; Spanish Psychological Society; and Italian Psychological Society. Honorary President, XVII International Congress of Psychology, 1963. *Died 1 July 1968.*

PUBLICATIONS

Psychology

Learning in Dementia Praecox. Princeton, New Jersey, Psychological Monographs, 1913.
A History of Experimental Psychology. New York and London, Century, 1929.
The Physical Dimensions of Consciousness. New York and London, Century, 1933.
A Manual of Psychological Experiments, with others. New York, Wiley, and London, Chapman and Hall, 1937.
Sensation and Perception in the History of Experimental Psychology. New York, Appleton Century, 1942.
Psychology for the Fighting Man, with others. Washington, D.C., Infantry Journal, 1943.
Psychology for the Armed Services, with others. Washington, D.C., Infantry Journal, 1944.
Psychologist at Large: An Autobiography and Selected Essays. New York, Basic Books, 1961 (contains a bibliography).
History, Psychology, and Science: Selected Essays, edited by Robert I. Watson and Donald T. Campbell. New York, Wiley, 1963.

Other

Editor, with others, *Psychology: A Factual Textbook.* New York, Wiley, 1935.
Editor, with others, *Introduction to Psychology.* New York, Wiley, 1939.
Editor, with others, *Foundations of Psychology.* New York, Wiley, 1948.
Editor, with Gardner Lindzey, *A History of Psychology in Autobiography*, vol. 4. Worcester, Massachusetts, Clark University Press, 1952; vol. 5, New York, Appleton Century, 1967.
Editor, with Richard J. Herrnstein, *A Source Book in the History of Psychology.* Cambridge, Massachusetts, Harvard University Press, 1965.
Editor, with Davis H. Howes, *Elements of Psychophysics*, by Gustav Fechner. New York, Holt Rinehart, 1966.

*   *   *

E.G. Boring graduated from Cornell University in 1908 with an M.E. in electrical engineering. He spent the year following his graduation working for the Bethlehem Steel Company, where he discovered his enthusiasm for engineering quickly waning. After teaching for a year, he decided to return to Cornell and work towards an A.M. in physics. He was sidetracked, however, by Madison Bentley who engaged him in work on animal psychology.

In 1905, during his undergraduate career at Cornell, Boring took a course in elementary psychology with E.B. Titchner. Now that he was a formal student of psychology Boring began to work on his thesis, of visceral sensibility, with Titchner as his advisor. In 1912, Titchner began working on re-establishing the lecture course in systematic psychology which he had once taught. He decided that the lectures—200 of them, three a week for two years—would be handled by his instructors and assistants, including Boring, and they set about translating the German works on experimental psychology into workable lectures.

At about this same time Boring did work in a number of other areas. He studied the behavior of flatworms with Madison Bentley, protopathic and epicritic sensibility in nerve-regeneration with Sutherland Simpson, and the fidelity of report on moving-picture incidents with G.M. Whipple. In the summer of 1912 he worked with S.I. Franz at the Government Hospital for the Insane, in Washington, where he produced a monograph on learning in schizophrenics.

In 1918 Boring was appointed a captain in the United States Army Medical Department, and he reported to Camp Upton on Long Island where Joseph W. Hayes was Chief Psychological Examiner. Boring was named second in command; he later took over the post when Hayes was called away. After the war ended Boring joined R.M. Yerkes in Washington to help him complete a report on intelligence testing in the army.

In 1919, Boring was appointed Professor of Experimental Psychology at Clark University where he remained until 1922 when he went to Harvard as an associate professor. At that time psychology at Harvard was a part of the Department of Philosophy and Psychology. When H.S. Langfield left Harvard for Princeton in 1924 Boring became the "head" of the psychology division, and he began working to separate the two departments.

During the 1920's, Boring was involved for the most part with teaching, administration, writing, and directing research, which prevented him from accomplishing much original research of his own. He had carried the 200-lecture course he helped Titchner create on to Clark and continued with it at Harvard until 1932. In 1925 Boring, along with Madison Bentley and Margaret Washburn, took over the editorship of the *American Journal of Psychology*. In 1927, upon Titchner's death, Boring was offered his post at Cornell, but he turned it down. In 1929 he published his book *A History of Experimental Psychology*.

In 1936 a separation of philosophy and psychology was finally effected at Harvard, and Boring was named first chairman of the department. He resigned the position two years later, however, in favor of G.W. Allport. In 1939 he became interested in problems of apparent visual size, and published extensively on the moon illusion with A.H. Holway and D.W. Taylor. In the late 1930's Boring began revising his *History of Experimental Psychology* as *Sensation and Perception in the History of Experimental Psychology*.

In 1942 Boring was appointed by the National Research Council's Emergency Committee on Psychology to a committee to prepare a textbook of military psychology. The committee produced two volumes, *Psychology for the Fighting Man* and *Psychology for the Armed Services*. Working with R.M. Yerkes and several others, Boring also prepared proposals for the Emergency Committee which eventually led to the merger of the American Psychological Association and the Association for Applied Psychology. Boring served as first chairman of the Policy and Planning Board of the new group.

Following the war, the Harvard Department of Psychology was divided into two sections, with social psychology and clinical psychology forming part of a new Department of Social Relations, separate from experimental and physiological psychology. At this point Boring found himself appointed chairman of the department again, and he continued his career at Harvard as an experienced administrator and director in the field.

—R.W. Rieber

BORN, Max. German physicist. Born in Breslau, 11 December 1882; emigrated to England in 1933; returned to Germany in 1953. Studied at the University of Berlin, University of Heidelberg, University of Zurich, and at the University of Göttingen, Ph.D. 1907. Married Hedwig Ehrenberger in 1913; 3 children. Lecturer, 1909-21, and Professor, 1921-33, University of Göttingen; Guest Professor, Indian Institute of Science, 1935-36; Professor of Natural Philosophy, 1936-53, and Professor Emeritus, 1953-70, University of Edinburgh. Visiting Lecturer, University of Chicago, 1912; University of Berlin, 1915; Frankfurt University, 1919; Massachusetts Institute of Technology, Cambridge, 1925; Stokes Lecturer, Cambridge University, 1933. Recipient: Stokes Medal, Cambridge University, 1934; Macdougall-Brisbane and Gunning-Victoria Jubilee Prize, Royal Society of Edinburgh, 1945, 1950; Max Planck Medal, Germany, 1948; Hughes Medal, Royal Society of London, 1950; Freedom of the City of Göttingen, 1953; Nobel Prize, 1954; Grotius Medal, Munich, 1956. Honorary doctorate: Bristol University, 1928; Cambridge University, 1933; Bordeaux University, 1948; Oxford University, 1954; University of Freiburg, 1957; University of Edinburgh, 1957; Stuttgart Technical University, 1960; Oslo University, 1961; Brussels University, 1961; Frankfurt University, 1964; University of Berlin. Member, Berlin Academy; Göttingen Academy; Copenhagen Academy; Stockholm Academy; Moscow Academy; Dublin Academy; American Academy of Arts and Sciences; National Academy of Sciences. Fellow, Royal Society of Edinburgh; Royal Society of London. *Died 5 January, 1970.*

PUBLICATIONS

Physics

Untersuchungen über die Stabilität der elastische Linie in Ebene und Raum unter verscheidenen Grenzbedingungen. Göttingen, Kaestner, 1906.

Dynamik der Kristallgitter. Berlin, Teubner, 1915.

Die Relativitätstheorie Einsteins. Berlin, Springer, 1920; as *Einstein's Theory of Relativity*, London, Methuen, 1924; New York, Dover, 1962.

Der Aufbau der Materie: Drei Aufsätze über moderne Atomik und Elektonentheorie. Berlin, Springer, 1920; as *The Constitution of Matter, Modern Atomic and Electron Theories*, New York, Dutton, 1923.

Vorlesungen über Atommechanik. Berlin, Springer, 2 vols., 1925, 1930; as *The Mechanics of the Atom*, New York, Ungar, 1960.

Problems of Atomic Dynamics (lectures). Cambridge, Massachusetts Institute of Technology, 1926.

Optik: Ein Lehrbuch der elektromagnetischen Lichttheorie. Berlin, Springer, 1933; revised and enlarged version, with Emil Wolf, as *Principles of Optics: Electromagnetic Theory, Interference and Diffraction*, London and New York, Pergamon Press, 1959.

Moderne Physik: Sieben Vorträge über Materie und Strahlung. Berlin, Springer, 1933; as *Atomic Physics*, London, Blackie, 1935; New York, Hafner, 1946.

The Restless Universe. London, Blackie, 1935; New York, Harper, 1936.

Experiment and Theory in Physics. Cambridge, Cambridge University Press, 1943; New York, Dover, 1956.

Atomic Energy and Its Use in War and Peace. Cairo, Fouad University Press, 1947.

A General Kinetic Theory of Liquids, with H.S. Green. Cambridge, Cambridge University Press, 1949.

Dynamic Theory of Crystal Lattices, with Hun Huang. Oxford, Clarendon Press, 1954.

Continuity, Determinism, and Reality. Copenhagen, I Komission hos Munksgaard, 1955.

Physics in My Generation: A Selection of Papers. London and New York, Pergamon Press, 1956.

Der Realitätsbegriff in der Physik. Cologne, Westdeutscher Verlag, 1958.

Physik un Politik. Göttingen, Vandenhoeck and Ruprecht, 1960; as *Physics and Politics*, Edinburgh, Oliver and Boyd, and New York, Basic Books, 1962.

Zur Begründung der Matrizenmechanik. Stuttgart, Battenberg, 1962.

Zur statistischen Deutung der Quantentheorie. Stuttgart, Battenberg, 1962.

Ausgewählte Abhandlungen. Göttingen, Vandenhoeck and Ruprecht, 2 vols., 1963.

Natural Philosophy of Cause and Chance (lectures). London, Oxford University Press, and New York, Dover, 1964.

Von der Verantwortung des Naturwissenschaftlers: Gesammelte Vorträge. Munich, Nymphenburger, 1965.

Erinnerungen an Einstein, with Leopold Infeld. Berlin, Union, 1968.

Die Luxus des Gewissens: Erlebnisse und Einsichten im Atomzeitalter, with Hedwig Born, edited by Armin Hermann. Munich, Nymphenburger, 1969.

Problems of Atomic Dynamics. Cambridge, Massachusetts Institute of Technology, 1970.

Other

Briefwechsel 1916-1955 Albert Einstein Max Born. Munich, Nymphenburger, 1969; as *The Born-Einstein Letters: Correspondence Between Albert Einstein and Max and Hedwig Born from 1916 to 1955.* New York, Walker, 1971.

My Life: Recollections of a Nobel Prize Winner. New York, Scribner, 1978.

Translator, *Klecksel the Painter*, by Wilhelm Busch. New York, Ungar, 1965.

*   *   *

Max Born was more successful at participating in and indeed shaping modern physics than any other physicist of his generation. Born's was a transition generation. Its members were trained before 1910, when 19th century theories still determined what counted as interesting problems and as acceptable solutions. Behind most of those theories was a general assumption about the aims and methods of physics: physics seeks to explain phenomena in terms of the distributions of bodies and fields in space, and this is done by uncovering deterministic laws governing the interactive forces among these bodies and fields, and governing the way these distributions and interactions change over time. Just as Born and his contemporaries were attempting to launch their careers in physics, this assumption was challenged. According to Einstein's theories of relativity, developed in 1905-1915, bodies and fields are no longer conceived as distributed in space and moving about over time, but rather as regions in and attributes of an abstract four dimensional space-time manifold. The atomic theory proposed by Niels Bohr in 1913 allowed atomic electrons to make instantaneous and uncaused leaps from orbit to orbit. While the theory described orbital paths, no description of the path during a leap was provided, and indeed Bohr argued that no such description could possibly be given. Quantum mechanics, created in the mid-1920's to replace Bohr's theory, went even farther in discarding the 19th century assumption. It was first conceived as a theory that purposely avoids any attempt to describe even the orbital paths of atomic electrons, and then was subsequently interpreted in a way that denies the possibility of any spatio-temporal descriptions of objects or processes at the sub-microscopic level. By 1930, when the physicists of Born's generation were entering middle age and becoming the leaders and keepers of their profession, the 19th century view of the aims and methods of physics had been left behind.

Born was more successful than most of his generation at making the transition to the new physics. He recognized earlier than most the importance of Einstein's relativity theory, of Bohr's atomic theory and of the new quantum mechanics, and made innovative and often extremely significant contributions to each. Though Einstein's first paper on the special theory of relativity was published in 1905, it was not until 1910 that its full significance was generally recognized. In 1909, as a new Ph.D., Born published a paper that was one of the first contributions to the development of the special theory that took proper account of its revolutionary character. In the teens and early 1920's, he turned to a typical 19th century problem: how are the molecules of a crystal lattice arranged and what forces between the molecules account for the structural and dynamic properties of crystalline matter? During the First World War he finished the first of several books on crystal theory that would establish him as "the founder and undisputed master of lattice dynamics," in the works of the physicist Nevill Mott, works which "themselves are of Nobel prize caliber." When Born was awarded the prize it was not for crystal theory, however, but for his work on quantum mechanics.

Born took his first step toward quantum mechanics near the end of the war, when he tried to use Bohr's atoms as the building blocks of crystals. This led him to an examination of the Bohr theory itself. Working with his young assistant, Werner Heisenberg, Born showed that even in the simple case of helium atoms, Bohr's theory gave incorrect results. Born's diagnosis was that Bohr had not gone far enough in rejecting 19th century physics. Bohr still assumed that the orbital motions of atomic electrons could be described using classical mechanics. A new mechanics for electrons must be found, Born urged, one that would not give spatio-temporal descriptions of the unobservable orbits, but would include only laws governing the observable properties of the atom. In 1924, he offered a specific though schematic prescription for the mathematical form of the new mechanics, and gave the still undiscovered theory its name: quantum mechanics. In 1925 Heisenberg attempted to follow out Born's prescription. When he showed his first results to Born, Born recognized immediately that this was what he had been looking for. He worked with Heisenberg and a new assistant, Pascual Jordan, to generalize Heisenberg's ideas, and to place the new quantum mechanics on a firm mathematical foundation. At the same time an Austrian physicist of Born's generation, Erwin Schrödinger, was busy constructing yet another new atomic theory that was completely different in form and intuition from that of Heisenberg, Born and Jordan. Schrödinger then proceeded to show that the two new theories were mathematically equivalent. Born was one of the first to appreciate and make use of this startling fact. He saw a way of applying Schrödinger's version to a problem that the Heisenberg, Born and Jordan version seemed unable to solve, the problem of predicting the outcome of a collision between an electron and an atom. The result was a quantum theory of collisions that is still a standard and frequently used tool of experimental and theoretical physics today.

The Nobel Prize went to Max Born for this work not because it solved the problem of collisions, but because in the course of solving that problem Born had been led to develop a radical new interpretation of quantum mechanics itself, one that called for an even more drastic break from the 19th century world view than even he had envisioned. For Born found that his theory of collisions did not predict uniquely the motions of the atom and electron after the collision, as one might have expected. It only determined a whole set of possible outcomes. Born saw that certain parts of his formulae for collisions could be interpreted as giving the probabilities for each of these possible outcomes, however, and within a month he was able to generalize this identification of probabilities to cover cases other than collisions. Following Born's lead, Jordan and another former Born assistant, Wolfgang Pauli, generalized the statistical interpretation even further. The result was a new, unified interpretation of the two different versions of quantum mechanics. Though Schrödinger had shown the versions to be formally equivalent, it was only with the development of Born's statistical interpretation that the versions could be seen as different formulations of a single coherently interpreted quantum theory.

The statistical interpretation raised an obvious question. Doesn't the fact that quantum mechanics gives only probabilities indicate that yet another theory must be sought, one that delves deeper into the sub-microscopic world to find the causes on which we can again build deterministic laws? Born took a tentative stand on this question in his first paper on the quantum theory of collisions: "I myself am inclined to give up determinism in the atomic world." His inclination turned to conviction as he saw the rest of the physics community give up determinism too. Born then watched in surprise as Bohr and Heisenberg went on to develop, on the basis of his statistical interpretation, the even more revolutionary Copenhagen interpretation. Not only must we relinquish causality and determinism, said this interpretation, but we must relinquish all hope of providing any spatio-temporal descriptions of the atomic world. Born did not argue against the Copenhagen interpretation, but in his own writings he continued to focus primarily on the rejection of causality and determinism. No 19th style theory will ever be found to replace quantum mechanics, he argued, since quantum mechanics has shown that there are no deterministic causes that act at the micro level. Born found it difficult to give up the spatio-temporal model of matter with which he had started his work in physics, however. A corner stone of the Copenhagen interpretation is the claim that neither the wave model nor the particle model is appropriate for matter, but both must be used in a complementary way. In spite of this Born boldly stated, "I am emphatically for the retention of the particle idea," and then added, "Naturally it is necessary to redefine what is meant." Even a revolutionary is limited in how far he can move beyond his own conceptual roots. Born was one of the first to see the need for drastic change, he worked consciously and eagerly for it and took some of the first steps that brought it about; the young physicists he had helped train went on from there.

—Linda Wessels

BOWLBY, (Edward) John (Mostyn). British psychologist. Born in London, 26 February 1907. Educated at the Royal Naval College, Dartmouth; Trinity College, Cambridge, B.A. 1928, M.A. 1932; University Hospital Medical School, Cambridge, M.D. 1939. Served as a psychiatrist in the British Army, 1940-45: Lieutenant-Colonel. Married Ursula Longstaff in 1938; 4 children. Staff psychologist, London Child Guidance Clinic, 1937-40. Associated with the Tavistock Clinic, London, since 1946: now Senior Research Fellow and Psychiatrist Emeritus. Consultant, World Health Organization, since 1950. Fellow, Center for Advanced Study in the Behavioral Sciences, Stanford, California, 1957-58; Visiting Professor of Psychiatry, Stanford University, California, 1968; H.B. Williams Traveling Professor, Australian and New Zealand College of Psychiatrists, 1973; **Frend**

Memorial Visiting Professor, University College, London, 1980. President, International Association for Child Psychology and Allied Professions, 1962-66. Recipient: Sir James Spence Medal, British Paediatric Association, 1974; G. Stanley Hall Medal, American Psychological Association, 1974; Distinguished Scientific Contribution Award, Society for Research in Child Development, 1981. Honorary doctorate: University of Leicester, 1971; Cambridge University, 1977. Fellow, British Psychological Association, 1945; Royal College of Physicians, 1964; Royal College of Psychiatrists (Foundation Fellow, 1971, and Honorary Fellow, 1980). Foreign Honorary Member, American Academy of Arts and Sciences, 1981. C.B.E. (Commander, Order of the British Empire), 1972. Address: Wyldes Close Corner, Hampstead Way, London NW11 7JB, England.

PUBLICATIONS

Psychology

War and Democracy: Essays on the Cause and Prevention of War, with others. London, Kegan Paul, 1938.
Personal Aggressiveness and War, with E.F.M. Durbin. London, Kegan Paul, 1939.
Personality and Mental Health: An Essay in Psychiatric Diagnosis. London, Kegan Paul, 1940; New York, Emerson Books, 1942.
Forty-four Juvenile Thieves: Their Characters and Home Life. London, Ballière, Tindall and Cox, 1946.
Maternal Care and Mental Health. Geneva, World Health Organization, 1951; abridged edition as *Child Care and the Growth of Love*, edited by Margery Frye. London, Penguin, 1953.
The Roots of Parenthood (lecture). London, National Children's Home, 1953.
Can I Leave My Baby? (lecture). London, National Association for Mental Health, 1958.
Attachment and Loss. London, Hogarth Press and Institute of Psychoanalysis, and New York, Basic Books, 3 vols., 1969, 1973, 1980.
The Making and Breaking of Affectional Bonds. London, Tavistock Publications, 1979.

* * *

John Bowlby, Senior Research Fellow and Psychiatrist Emeritus at London's Tavistock Clinic, has devoted his career to research on child rearing practice and the effects on human development of the pattern of attachment a child makes with his mother. His lifetime work is reflected in his magnum opus *Attachment and Loss*, three volumes which present his scientific challenge to traditional child psychiatry and psychoanalysis. His theories have affected the hospital care of children all over the world.

He is humble in describing his work, but rigorously self-disciplined in his principles: "I have developed a new conceptual framework, and that's not popular; it never is. I received an awful clobbering for it in the 50's and 60's. I experienced great resistance from some of my colleagues at the Tavistock initially, and the shift towards treating a child as an integral part of his family unit developed only slowly over 20 years".

Bowlby's "holistic" theoretical framework is based on ethological principles, and has been much influenced by the biologist Robert Hinde, who has long been a close friend and critical adviser. Bowlby's research on attachment, separation, and loss of the mother views personality development in the context of the child's real experiences within his family in contrast to the previous feeding model of maternal child bonding and the emphasis given to phantasy. A "Bowlby child" has become a common expression that recognizes the cause of emotional damage in adolescents and adults, for Bowlby holds that prolonged deprivation of maternal care in childhood may cause extreme damage to self-esteem and inability to trust others for fear of abandonment. The longer a young child has experienced separation or deprivation of care, he believes, the more devoted care he will need to repair the loss.

Bowlby's study, *Forty-four Juvenile Thieves*, and his WHO monograph *Maternal Care and Mental Health*, were among the first to describe the symptoms and effects of maternal deprivation. The monograph, later abridged as *Child Care and the Growth of Love*, presents evidence that prolonged separations of a child from his mother (or mother substitute) during the first five years of life, and frequent changes of mother-figure, are principal causes of a chronically delinquent character development. His book includes his concern for future generations: "The difficulty deprived children have becoming successful parents is perhaps the most damaging of all the effects of deprivation."

Bowlby's interest in child development and child care began in his college years at Cambridge, which led him to take a year off to work in a school for maladjusted children in Norfolk. "That gave me first-hand experience of children that became indelibly printed on my mind. For instance, there was an illegitimate child of well-to-do parents who had been chucked out of one of the public schools for persistent stealing and who was a very, very emotionally frozen character. His problems were attributed to his emotionally deprived early years. At that time there was very little in the way of a coherent theory about child development. The prevalent attitude was that the more affection and attention you gave a child, the more he'd grow up to be a selfish brat— which of course is the exact opposite of the truth."

Bowlby's work has consistently pointed to a child's basic need for security, love, and trust from the primary care-giver, the parent. In an interview with Geraldine Carro in 1981, John Bowlby was asked this question: "Can we, in today's changing world raise happy and well-adjusted children?" "Yes," Dr. Bowlby answered, "but it's not easy. There is a great deal of evidence that happy, healthy children generally come from stable homes where both parents give them lots of love and time and attention. They live in families that stay put rather than in ones that move around a lot. They have friends and know other children and families in the neighbourhood. All this is old-fashioned stuff. It happens to be true."

John Bowlby's family life is an example of his beliefs; he and his wife live in an extended family system, his elder son, daughter-in-law and two grandchildren live next door, his younger daughter and her family nearby. He delights in spending time with his grandchildren at their summer retreat on the Isle of Skye, Scotland.

—Lorna Bowlby West

BRAGG, (William) Lawrence. British physicist. Born in Adelaide, Australia, 31 March 1890, son of the physicist William Bragg, *q.v.* Studied at Adelaide University, 1908, and at Trinity College, Cambridge (Allen Scholar). Married Alice Grace Jenny Hopkinson in 1921; 4 children. Fellow and Lecturer, Trinity College, 1914; Technical Adviser on Sound Ranging, General Headquarters, Paris, 1915-19; Military Cross; C.B.E. (Commander, Order of the British Empire), 1918. Langworthy Professor of Physics, Victoria University of Manchester, 1919-37; Director, National Physical Laboratory (U.K.), 1937-38; Cavendish Professor of Experimental Physics, Cambridge University, 1938-53; Fullerian Professor and Director, Royal Institution, London, 1953-66. Recipient: Nobel Prize in Physics, with William Bragg, 1915; Hughes Medal, 1931, and Royal Medal, 1946, Royal Society, London; Roebling Medal, Minerological Society of America, 1948; Copley Medal, Royal Society, 1966. Honorary doctorate: University of Dublin; University of Leeds; University of Manchester; University of Lisbon; University of Paris; University of Brussels; University of Liège; University of Durham; University of Cologne; St. Andrews University, Scotland. Fellow of the Royal Society. Member, American Philosophical Society; Associate Member, Royal Academy of Belgium; Foreign Member, Dutch Academy of Sciences; Honorary Member, Royal Irish Academy; Institute of Metals; Foreign Honorary Member, American Academy of Arts and Sciences; Honorary Fellow, Institute of Physics; Royal Institute of Chemistry; Royal Society of Edinburgh. Commander, Order of Leopold, Belgium. Knighted, 1941; C.H. (Companion of Honour), 1967. *Died 1 July 1971.*

PUBLICATIONS

Physics

X-Rays and Crystal Structure, with William Bragg. London, Bell, 1915.
The Structure of Silicates. Leipzig, Akademische Verlagsgesellschaft, 1930.
The Crystalline State: A General Survey. London, Bell, 1934.
Atomic Structure of Minerals. London, Oxford University Press, and Ithaca, New York, Cornell University Press, 1937.
The Structure of Alloys (lecture). London, Oxford University Press, 1938.
The History of X-Ray Analysis. London, Longman, 1943.
A Review of Recent Advances in X-Ray Analysis, with *The Impact of Radioactivity on Inorganic Chemistry*, by H.J. Eméleus. Cambridge, Heffer, 1950.
The Crystal Structures of Minerals, with G.F. Claringbull. London, Bell, 1965.
Ideas and Discoveries in Physics. London, Longman, 1970.

Other

Artillery Service in the First World War, with others. Elstree, England, Field Service Association, 1971.
Advice to Lecturers: An Anthology Taken from the Writings of Michael Faraday and Lawrence Bragg, edited by Sir George Porter and James Friday. London, Royal Institution, 1974.

Editor, with William Bragg, *Stereoscopic Photographs of Crystal Models.* London, Hilger, 2 parts, 1929-30.
Editor, with William Bragg, *The Crystalline State.* London, Bell, 4 vols., 1933-53.
Editor, with Sir George Porter, *Physical Sciences.* Barking, England, Elsevier, 1970.

*   *   *

BRAGG, William (Henry). British physicist. Born in Wigton, Cumberland, 2 July 1862. Educated at King William College, Isle of Man; studied at Trinity College, Cambridge, 1st class honours 1885. Married Gwendoline Todd in 1889; 1 son (the physicist Lawrence Bragg, *q.v.*) and 1 daughter. Professor, Adelaide University, Australia, 1888-1908; Cavendish Professor, Leeds University, 1909-15; Quain Professor of Physics, University of London, 1915-23; Fullerian Professor of Chemistry, Royal Institution, London, 1923-42, and Director of Davy-Faraday Research Laboratory, 1937-42. Recipient: Nobel Prize in Physics, with Lawrence Bragg, 1915; Rumford Medal, 1916, and Copley Medal, 1930, Royal Society, London; Franklin Gold Medal, Franklin Institute, Philadelphia, 1930; Faraday Medal, Institution of Electrical Engineers, 1936; John Cartney, National Academy of Sciences, 1939. Honorary doctorate: University of Manchester, 1914; Brown University, Providence, Rhode Island, 1914; University of Leeds, 1919; Trinity College, Dublin, 1920; Oxford University, 1926; University of Bristol, 1937; University of Glasgow, 1928; University of Sheffield, 1931; University of Pennsylvania, Philadelphia, 1924; University of Durham, 1924; St. Andrews University, Scotland, 1925; Cambridge University, 1932; University of Wales, Bangor, 1934; University of London, 1936; University of Edinburgh, 1937; University of Birmingham, 1939. Fellow of the Royal Society (President, 1935-40). Member, Royal Danish Academy of Science; Royal Academy of Science, Turin; Academy of Sciences, Paris; Dutch Academy of Science; Norwegian Academy of Sciences; Academy of Science, Madrid; Honorary Member, New York Academy of Science. Honorary Fellow, Trinity College, 1920. C.B.E. (Commander, Order of the British Empire), 1917; knighted, 1929; O.M. (Order of Merit), 1931. *Died 12 March 1942.*

PUBLICATIONS

Physics

Studies in Radioactivity. London, Macmillan, 1912.
X-Rays and Crystal Structure, with Lawrence Bragg. London, Bell, 1915.
Electrons and their Waves (lecture). London, Oxford University Press, 1921.
Concerning the Nature of Things. London, Bell, 1924.
The Crystalline State (lecture). Oxford, Clarendon Press, 1925.
Old Trades and New Knowledge: Six Lectures Delivered Before a "Juvenile Auditory". London, Bell, 1926; as *Creative Knowledge: Old Trades and New Science*, New York, Harper, 1927.
Introduction to Crystal Analysis. London, Bell, 1928.
The Universe of Light. London, Macmillan, 1933.
Scientific Progress, with others. New York, Macmillan, 1936.
Science and Faith (lecture). London, Oxford University Press, 1941.

Other

Editor, with Lawrence Bragg, *Stereoscopic Photographs of Crystal Models.* London, Hilger, 2 parts, 1929-30.
Editor, with Lawrence Bragg, *The Crystalline State.* London, Bell, 4 vols., 1933-53.

*

Critical Study: *William Henry Bragg, 1862-1942: Man and Scientist*, by G.M. Caroe, London, Cambridge University Press, 1978.

*   *   *

At the age of 40, the senior member of the famous father-son team of William and Lawrence Bragg had given little indication of a record of achievement that would earn him a Nobel Prize and fame in the community of scientists. William Bragg had published nothing of note and appeared committed to a career of teaching at the little known University of Adelaide. But, like so many of his contemporaries, Bragg was swept up in the excitement of the Roentgen and Becquerel discoveries of the middle 1890's and turned his attention to a study of X-rays and radioactivity.

The first problem in which he became interested was the identification of X-rays. Roentgen's discovery of this highly energetic form of radiation had resulted in a classic wave-particle controversy about their composition. Were they truly a form of electromagnetic radiation, like visible light, or were they streams of particles? Bragg was inclined toward the latter view, arguing that an X-ray consisted of a beam of electrons (beta particles) in close association with neutrons. The production of *X-rays by electrons* and the ultimate production of *electrons in matter by*

X-rays led him to suspect a structural connection between these two forms.

(The resolution of this question came some years later in Max Laue's studies on the wave properties of X-rays, research which, interestingly enough, was to stimulate the studies for which Bragg himself was to become most famous.)

The second problem to which Bragg turned his attention was the nature of alpha radiation. In a 1904 review of research on the properties of radiation, Bragg had been highly critical of both methodology and the theoretical basis for much previous experimentation on radioactive materials. In his efforts to remedy that situation, he chose to study the energetics of alpha particles. He found that radiation from alpha emitters did not consist of a continuous spectrum, with alpha rays of all possible energies produced. Instead, the radiation contained particles moving with specific and discrete amounts of energies. This finding proved to be of great value in supporting the Rutherford-Soddy theory of nuclear disintegration. The unique energies observed for specific alpha rays were attributed to different radioactive isotopes produced in a nuclear decay family. In a direct application of this finding, the energy of emergent alpha rays was thereafter used as an identifying characteristic of the isotopes in an unknown sample of radioactive material.

The work for which the Braggs are best known took place after the elder Bragg had returned to England in 1909. The question of the nature of X-rays had been solved by Laue, Friedrich, and Knipping in 1912. Passing X-rays through a crystal, Laue's team had found that the radiation was diffracted in much the same way that light is diffracted from a grating. The results were taken as compelling evidence of the wave nature of X-rays.

The Braggs immediately became interested in the Laue phenomenon and began to consider possible variations. One way to analyze the Laue event, they suggested, was to think of the planes of atoms that make up a crystal as rows of mirrors. X-rays striking the atomic planes, then, might be expected to reflect from them much as light reflects from glass mirrors. From this assumption, the Braggs were able to derive a mathematical expression relating the wavelength of incident X-rays to the spacing between planes of atoms within a crystal. That relationship is now known as Bragg's Law.

The younger Bragg first used this principle to study the nature of X-rays reflected from a crystal. Soon, however, he and his father became interested in studying the inverse relationship, calculating the spacing between atoms in a crystal by using X-rays of known wavelength. Thus, when X-rays of known wavelength are caused to fall on a crystal and the angle of reflection measured, all variables in Bragg's Law are known except one, the interatomic spacing. This application of the law has, in the long run, had the most extensive application. It is still used as a research tool for studying the atomic structure of crystalline materials and, especially, of complex organic molecules which are otherwise resistant to exact detailed molecular analysis.

—David Newton

BRAUDEL, Fernand. French historian. Born in Luméville, 24 August 1902. Educated at Lycée Voltaire, Paris; studied at the Sorbonne, Paris, Agrégé 1923, Docteur-ès-Lettres 1947. Married Paule Pradel in 1933; 2 daughters. Professor, University of Algiers, 1924-32; Lycée Condorcet and Lycée Henri IV, Paris, 1932-35; University of São Paulo, Brazil, 1935-37; and Collège de France, Paris, 1949-72 (since 1972, Honorary Professor). Director, Section VI, l'École Pratique des Hautes Études, since 1937; Administrator, Maison des Sciences de l'Homme, since 1963. Member, Commission of Diplomatic Archives, since 1975. Co-Editor, *Cahiers de l'Institut de Sciences Économiques*

Appliquées, Revue annales E.S.C., Paris, until 1968; Co-Editor until 1956, Editor since 1957 of the series *Destins du Monde*. Honorary doctorate: Oxford University; University of São Paulo; University of Brussels; University of Cologne; University of Geneva; University of Madrid; University of Warsaw; University of Chicago; University of Padua; University of Florence; Cambridge University. Corresponding Member, Academy of Sciences of Poland; British Academy; Academy of History (Madrid); Academy of History (Buenos Aires); Bavarian Academy; American Philosophical Society; Academy of Sciences of Belgrade; Academy of Sciences of Heidelberg. Address: Maison des Sciences de l'Homme, 54 Boulevard Raspail, 75270 Paris, France.

PUBLICATIONS

History

La Méditerranée et le monde méditerranéen à l'époque de Philippe II. Paris, Colin, 1949; as *The Mediterranean and the Mediterranean World in the Age of Philip II*, London, Collins, 1972-73.

Leçon inaugural, faite le 1er decembre, 1950, au Collège de France pour la chaire d'Histoire de la Civilisation moderne. Paris, Collège de France, 1951.

Navires et marchandises à l'entrée du port de Livourne (1547-1611), with Ruggiero Romano. Paris, Colin, 1951.

Le Monde actuel: Histoire et civilisations: Classes terminales propédeutiques, classes préparatoires aux grandes écoles, with others. Paris, Belin, 1963.

Civilisation materielle et capitalisme, XVe-XVIIIe siècle. Paris, Colin, 1967; reprinted as volume 1 of *Civilisation materielle, économie et capitalisme: XVe-XVIIIe siècle*, 3 vols., 1979; as *Capitalism and Material Life, 1400-1800*, London, Weidenfeld and Nicolson, and New York, Harper, 1973.

Écrits sur l'Histoire. Paris, Flammarion, 1969; as *On History*, Chicago, University of Chicago Press, 1980.

Au Siècle des Lumières. Paris, Service d'Édition et de Vente des Publications de l'Education Nationale, 1970.

Conjoncture économique, structure sociales: Hommage à Ernest Labrousse, with others. Paris, Mouton, 1974.

Afterthoughts on Material Civilization and Capitalism. Baltimore, Johns Hopkins University Press, 1977.

The Structures of Everyday Life. New York, Harper, 1982.

Other

Translator, with others, *Mouvements monétaires dans l'État de Milan (1580-1700)*, by C.M. Cipolla. Paris, Collection Monnaie, 1952.

Editor, *Temas de historia economica hispanoamericana, ensayos de A. Jara, et al.* Paris, Mouton, 1965.

Editor, with C. Ernest Labrousse, *Histoire Économique et sociale de la France.* Paris, Presses Universitaires de France, 4 vols., 1977-80.

Editor, *Storia e le altre scienze sociale.* Rome, Laterza, 1974.

Editor, *Méditerannée: l'Espace et l'histoire.* Paris, Arts et metiers graphiques, 1977.

*

Critical Studies: *Der historiographische Ansatz Fernand Braudel und die gegenwärtige Krise der Geschichtswissenschaft* by Jörg Schmidt, Munich, 1971; *Histoire économique du monde Méditerraneen, 1450-1650: Mélanges en l'honneur de Fernand Braudel*, Toulouse, Privat, 1973; *Méthodologie de l'histoire et des sciences humaines: Mélanges en l'honneur de Fernand Braudel*, Toulouse, Privat, 1973 (contains an extensive bibliography).

* * *

Fernand Braudel published what is in all probability the most influential historical work written in the 20th century. This 1,175 page seminal work, *La Méditerranée à l'époque de Philippe II*, was published in 1949 and was the outgrowth of his doctoral dissertation. Braudel, who was then 47 years old, had done research on this massive study for decades, especially while teaching at a lycée in Algiers. The book was written in a Nazi prison during the Second World War. A second and revised edition was published in 1966 to be followed by an English edition in 1972. All of these publication dates were major events and touched off extensive reviews in most historical journals. For example, the prestigious *Journal of Modern History* devoted a special issue to Braudel, and the journal's editor, William H. McNeill, termed the book a "majestic monument of 20th century historiography," and H.R. Trevor-Roper said in the same issue, "No group of scholars has had a greater impact, or more fertilizing effect, on the study of history in this century than the French historians of 'the Annales School.'"

As Braudel himself said, he drew inspiration for his approach to history from the work of the Annales School in the 1930's, especially Lucien Febvre, his mentor, and Marc Bloch. He also acknowledges Henri Pirenne and Henri Berr who edited *Revue de Synthèse*. The dominant influence in his intellectual formation was undoubtedly Lucien Febvre who directed Braudel's doctoral dissertation and who did his own dissertation on an aspect of Philip II's reign. Later Braudel would succeed Febvre not only as editor of the *Annales* but also as Director of the Section VI of the *École Pratique des Hautes Études* whose extensive publications (more than 800) reflect the work of the Annalistes and "le monde Braudellien." Febvre, himself, in a glowing tribute to his pupil, said Braudel's work was the "embodiment" of the Annaliste "image of history."

The importance of Braudel's view of history is that he has attempted to determine the basic layer or *structure* of an historical epoch or geographical area, in this case the Mediterranean, by using a three-tiered or layered approach. In Braudel's terms the *structures* are the *mentalités*, that is, the mind sets, the points of view, and the paradigms that are imbedded in institutions. They are the durable organisms that provide the coherence and totality of an historical epoch.

The structure of his own book aids in understanding the layered approach: the work is divided into a first section on the role of the environment of the entire Mediterranean area, a second section on "Collective Destinies and General Trends," and a final section on "Events, Politics, and People." According to Braudel these divisions represent three kinds of time: geographical, social, and individual. Three kinds of history correspond to these three kinds of time: a "geohistory" which seeks to grasp "an almost immobile history of man's relations with the milieu surrounding him;" "a slowly rhythmic history...of groups and groupings;" and a "history of short, rapid, nervous oscillations" of "traditional" or "eventful history" (for Braudel the inter-relationship between political and military history). Braudel did not slavishly follow the paths chartered by Febvre and Bloch, but he was clearly influenced by their attempts to synthesize history and the social sciences and drew some influence, no doubt, from Levi-Strauss who was his colleague during the two years they taught in Brazil. Rarely has an historian used the findings of the social sciences as evidence in research leading toward "the totality of history" as Braudel has.

Braudel is a self-proclaimed structuralist in his approach to history. However, this statement should not be taken as an indication that he is a structuralist in the most current avatar of the term, that is, that all meaning is arbitrary. On the contrary, Braudel's aim is to determine meaning, points of view, and *mentalités*. Braudel represents the Annaliste School in its fullest development with stress upon the totality of history, *histoire totale*, illuminated by the human forces which motivate and animate it. He believes that history, at least in part, is also determined by forces external to man, such as geography and climate, or social structures such as religious and intellectual

traditions. He is also willing to use statistical, mathematical, and economic data in appropriate cases. The result is that Annaliste historians must usually deal with a mass of statistical data from the social and mathematical sciences. The synthesis and interpretation of the data from all these sources is considered by the Annaliste and Braudel to be *histoire totale*.

Braudel has devoted his most recent writing to a three-volume *Civilisation materielle, économie et capitalisme*, which one writer characterizes as "Braudel's Triptych on Modern Economic History." Here again he eschews writing a traditional economic history. Instead, following the earlier three-fold approach of his *La Méditerranée* he traces the development of the capitalist economy. He calls his first two volumes "typological" and the final volume "chronological." Here once more he draws on material from the social sciences, most particularly from economics and sociology, significantly enlarging the scope of his previous study of the Mediterranean world to include the material civilization of Europe. His goal now is to write *histoire globale*. His study is enormously ambitious and, consequently, has drawn criticism as well as approval.

Braudel's other publications include *Navires et marchandises à l'entrée du port de Livourne* and *Écrits sur l'histoire*, which contains an incisive group of essays on his method, and is a recent version of Lucien Febvre's *Combats pour l'histoire*. Also he has hundreds of reviews and numerous articles which have usually been published in the *Annales*. Braudel retired as editor of the *Annales* in 1968, and he passed on his legacy to a trinity of younger men who stand now at the center of the historical stage, Jacques Le Goff, Le Roy Ladurie, and Marc Ferro, a medievalist, a modernist, and a specialist in Russian history. Probably the best summation of Braudel's thought is in the concluding sentence of the Preface to the first edition of *La Méditerranée*: "'It is the fear of great history which has killed great history,' wrote Edmond Faral, in 1942. May it live again!"

—Walter D. Gray

BRECHT, (Eugen) Bertholt (Friedrich). German playwright, poet and dramatic theorist. Born in Augsburg, 10 February 1898. Educated at the Realgymnasium, Augsburg, 1908-17. Began pre-medical studies at Munich University in 1917 and served as a medical orderly in World War I. Married Marianne Zoff in 1922 (divorced, 1927), 1 daughter; married the actress Helene Weigel in 1928, 1 son, 1 daughter. Dramaturg, Munich Kammerspiel, 1922; dramatist and producer in Berlin, 1924-33; left Germany in 1933 and lived in Denmark, Finland and Sweden, 1933-40; lived in America and worked as a script-writer in Hollywood, California, 1941-47. Subpoenaed by the House Committee on Un-American Activities in 1947; returned to Europe in 1947 and settled in East Berlin in 1949; founded the Berliner Ensemble, 1949. Recipient: Stalin Peace Prize, 1955. *Died 14 August 1956.*

PUBLICATIONS

Collections

Bertolt Brecht: Plays, Poetry, and Prose, edited by Ralph Manheim and John Willett. London, Eyre Methuen, and New York, Pantheon, 1960.
Works of Bertolt Brecht: The Grove Press Edition, edited by Eric Bentley. New York, Grove Press, 1964-.
Gesammelte Werke. Frankfurt, Suhrkamp, 24 vols., 1967-82.

Theater and Literary Criticism

Brecht on Theater: The Development of an Aesthetic, edited by John Willett. London, Methuen, and New York, Hill and Wang, 1964.
The Messingkauf Dialogues. London, Methuen, 1965.
Schriften zum Theatre and Schriften zur Literatur und Kunst. Frankfurt, Suhrkamp, 5 vols., 1967 (vols. 15-19 of the *Gesammelte Werke*).

Dramatic Works

Plays. London, Methuen, 2 vols., 1960-62.
Stücke. Frankfurt, Suhrkamp, 7 vols., 1967 (vols. 1-7 of the *Gesammelte Werke*).
Texte für Filme. Frankfurt, Suhrkamp, 2 vols., 1969 (supplemental volumes I and II of the *Gesammelte Werke*).
Collected Plays. London, Eyre Methuen, and New York, Pantheon, 1970-.

Poetry

Selected Poems. New York, Reynal and Hitchcock, 1947; London, Calder, 1959.
Poems on the Theater. London, Scorpion Press, 1961.
Selected Poems, edited by K. Wölfel. London, Oxford University Press, 1965.
Gedichte. Frankfurt, Suhrkamp, 3 vols., 1967 (vols. 8-10 of the *Gesammelte Werke*).
Poems 1913-1956, edited by Ralph Manheim and John Willett. London, Eyre Methuen, 1976.
Gedichte aus dem Nachlass. Frankfurt, Suhrkamp, 2 vols., 1982 (supplemental volumes III and IV of the *Gesammelte Werke*).

Other

A Penny for the Poor (novel). London, Hale, 1937; New York, Curl, 1938 (later editions as *The Threepenny Novel*).
Tales from the Calendar. London, Methuen, 1961.
Die Hauspostille / Manual for Piety (German and English texts). New York, Grove Press, 1966.
Kriegsfibel. Berlin, Eulenspiegel, 1967.
Prosa and *Schriften zur Politik und Gesellschaft*. Frankfurt, Suhrkamp, 5 vols., 1967 (vols. 11-14 and 20 of the *Gesammelte Werke*).
Arbeitsjournal, edited by Werner Hecht. Frankfurt, Suhrkamp, 3 vols., 1973.
Tagebücher 1920-22. Frankfurt, Suhrkamp, 1975; as *Bertolt Brecht Diaries 1920-22*, New York, St. Martin's Press, 1979.
Briefe, edited by Günther Glaeser. Frankfurt, Suhrkamp, 1981.

*

Bibliographies: "Bertolt-Brecht-Bibliographie", by Walter Nubel in *Sinn und Form* (Berlin), 1957; *Bertolt Brecht* by Reinhold Grimm, Stuttgart, 3rd revised edition, 1971; *Bibliographie Bertolt-Brecht* by Gerhard Seidel, Berlin, Aufbau, 1975-.

Critical Studies: *The Theatre of Bertolt Brecht: A Study from Eight Aspects* by John Willett, New York, New Directions, 1959; *Bertolt Brecht: His Life, His Art, and His Times* by Frederic Ewen, New York, Citadel, 1967; *Brecht: The Man and His Work* by Martin Esslin, New York, Doubleday Anchor Books, revised edition, 1971; *Bertolt Brecht: Eine Biographie* by Klaus Völker, Munich, Hanser, 1976; *Brecht-Handbuch: Theater* by Jan Knopf, Stuttgart, Metzler, 1980.

*   *   *

Bertolt Brecht was an aesthetic revolutionary who sought the total reformation of the arts and of their place in contemporary society. His primary importance arises from his recognition that artistic decisions reflect fundamental moral choices and that in the 20th century those choices are necessarily socio-political in nature. His contribution to modern aesthetic thought lies above all in his attempts to formulate a pragmatic philosophy of art to guide the artist in making morally responsible choices within a given socio-political context. Although in his wealth of writings Brecht touches upon virtually every art form, it is in his approach to theatre that he tried most consistently and most successfully to articulate his aesthetic, and it is for this work that he is best known.

Brecht defines theatre as the production of "living images of reported or imagined occurrences among human beings...for purposes of enjoyment." The principles of this theatre proceed from the Marxist assumption that human beings are social animals which utilize tools in order to produce the goods necessary to their common survival and betterment. The degree to which one is allowed to fulfill one's productive potential and thus to meet one's needs depends upon one's relationship to the means of production. Where these means are controlled by the few, the masses labor but do not receive full benefit from their labor.

To change these conditions, Brecht proposes

a theatre which not only makes possible the sensations, insights and impulses allowed by the particular historical field of human relations in which the action takes place, but which also encourages those thoughts and feelings which play a role in the transformation of the field itself.

Brecht's epic or dialectical theatre, then, is a revolutionary social act. Its ultimate goal is the radical reassignment of the means of production. Its immediate goal is the radicalization of the audience's way of viewing the world, such that its members perceive their own productive potential. Indeed, the source of enjoyment in Brecht's theatre is to be productivity itself, i.e., the creation of socially valuable items, and it is productivity which is thematicized in the drama and in the drama's presentation on the stage. In short, Brecht's theatre seeks to free the productive potential of its audience by being itself an exemplary act of human productivity.

The principal means of accomplishing this goal is one which demonstrates the possibility of productive action. Brecht calls this means *Verfremdung*, i.e., "estrangement."

To estrange an event or a character means simply to remove from the event or character that which is self-evident, known, apparent, and to induce amazement and curiosity about it.... Estrangement, then, means historization, i.e., the presentation of events and persons as historical, transient.

Through estrangement Brecht seeks "to remove from socially modifiable incidents the stamp of trusted familiarity which today protects them from our intervention". The defamiliarization of events and characters in the dramatic world allows Brecht to show that world as a result of and alterable through human action. At the same time, Brecht estranges the dramatic world itself and its presentation upon the stage. That is, he exposes both the drama and its presentation as human constructs and offers their producers' moral choices for critical attention. The auditors are thereby encouraged to view their own world as subject to change through their own productive action.

The most important means by which Brecht accomplishes estrangement are:

On the dramatic level—
Language: Brecht's dramatic figures speak a fabricated argot in which physical gesture is implicit and which exposes—often ironically—the characters' moral choices and attitudes. Simul-

taneously, the language calls attention to itself as a fabrication of the playwright.

Episodic structure: Scenes and moments within scenes are presented as self-contained units and separated from one another by scenic, musical or narrative interruptions which allow the auditor to reflect upon the *Gestus* of the preceding moment and to recognize the dramatic structure as a human construction.

Gestus: Each moment within the drama is informed by a specific *Gestus*, i.e., a set of verbal, gestural, pictorial, and/or musical acts which define concretely the social relations inherent in the dramatic moment.

Commentary: Through printed scenic titles, songs, and narrative, the *Gestus* of dramatic events and the playwright's attitude toward those events are made explicit.

On the theatrical level—

Separation of the elements: All the "sister arts" of the theatre join together in relating the plot or story of the drama, but they do not thereby lose their autonomy as independent arts. Indeed, each art must be free to "take a position" on the events of the dramatic world.

Anti-illusionistic method of presentation: The presentation of the dramatic world by theatrical means is to be perceived not as an illusory reality in its own right but as a human creation. To facilitate this perception, the means by which the presentation is produced are to be visible throughout the performance.

Anti-illusionistic acting: The actors are not to "become" the characters but are to "demonstrate" the characters' behavior and, at the same time, to show the audience that they are engaged in the act of demonstrating that behavior. They are, thereby, to engender a critical attitude toward the behavior rather than an emotional identification with it.

All the techniques of Brecht's theatre are designed to confront accepted notions of art as removed from everyday social reality. They aim at eliciting a morally critical response to dramatic events and to the presentation of these events on the stage. That Brecht's efforts in this vein have spawned an overwhelming body of scholarly literature and a growing number of productions of his plays pays tribute to his success. Indeed, whether or not one accepts Brecht's fundamental assumptions, one must confront his work when considering the function of theatre. This confrontation leads to the examination of the moral, social and political foundations of one's own aesthetic for which Brecht strived.

—Ronald K. Shull

BRIDGMAN, P(ercy) W(illiams). American physicist. Born in Cambridge, Massachusettes, 21 April 1882. Studied at Harvard University, Cambridge, Massachusettes, B.A. 1904, M.A. 1905, Ph.D. 1908. Married Olive Ware in 1912; 2 children. Fellow, 1908-10, Instructor of Physics, 1910-13, Assistant Professor, 1913-19, Professor, 1919-26, Hollis Professor of Mathematics and Natural Philosophy, 1926-50, Higgins University Professor, 1950-54, and Professor Emeritus, 1954-61, Harvard University. President, American Physical Society, 1942. Recipient: Rumford Medal, American Academy of Arts and Sciences, 1917; Cresson Medal, Franklin Institute, 1932; Roozenbloom Medal, Netherlands Royal Academy, 1933; Comstock Prize, National Academy of Sciences, 1933; Research Corporation of America Award, 1937; Nobel Prize in Physics, 1946; Bingham Medal, Society of Rheology, 1951. Honorary doctorate: Brooklyn Polytechnic Institute, 1934; Harvard University, 1939; Stevens Institute of Technology, Hoboken, New Jersey, 1941; Prince-

ton University, New Jersey, 1950; University of Paris, 1950; Yale University, New Haven, Connecticut, 1951. Corresponding Member, Academia Nacional de Ciencias, Mexico; Foreign Member, Indian Academy of Science, and Royal Society, London; Honorary Fellow, Physical Society, London. Member, American Academy of Arts and Sciences. *Died* (committed suicide) *20 August 1961.*

PUBLICATIONS

Physics

Dimensional Analysis. New Haven, Connecticut, Yale University Press, 1922.

A Condensed Collection of Thermodynamic Formulas. Cambridge, Massachusettes, Harvard University Press, 1925.

The Logic of Modern Physics. New York, Macmillan, 1927.

The Physics of High Pressure. London, Bell, 1931.

The Thermodynamics of Electrical Phenomena in Metals. New York, Macmillan, 1934.

The Nature of Physical Theory. Princeton, New Jersey, Princeton University Press, 1936.

The Intelligent Individual and Society. New York, Macmillan, 1938.

The Nature of Thermodynamics. Cambridge, Massachusetts, Harvard University Press, 1941.

Reflections of a Physicist. New York, Philosophical Library, 1951.

The Nature of Some of Our Physical Concepts. New York, Philosophical Library, 1952.

Studies in Large Plastic Flow and Fracture, with Special Emphasis on the Effects of Hydrostatic Pressure. New York, McGraw Hill, 1952.

The Way Things Are. Cambridge, Massachusetts, Harvard University Press, 1959.

A Sophisticate's Primer of Relativity. Middletown, Connecticut, Wesleyan University Press, 1962.

Collected Experimental Papers. Cambridge, Massachusetts, Harvard University Press, 7 vols., 1964.

*

Critical Study: in *Dictionary of Scientific Biography*, New York, Scribners, 1970.

* * *

The principal contributions of P.W. Bridgman to physical science may be summarized as his extraordinary development of the physics of high pressure on the one hand and on the other his searching inquiry into the nature of theorizing in physics, with the adoption of a point of view that came to be called operational.

Bridgman's interest in the problem of producing very high pressures and the study of the properties of substances subjected to such pressure began shortly after he received his doctorate at Harvard University in 1908. From that time on, scarcely a year passed without the appearance of one or more publications in this field; the last one came out in 1959, two years before his death. A general article on the physics of high pressure appeared posthumously in 1963. In all Bridgman published somewhat more than 200 articles on this subject along with two influential books: *The Physics of High Pressure* and *Studies in Large Plastic Flow and Fracture, with Special Emphasis on the Effects of Hydrostatic Pressure.*

Bridgman was singularly skillful with his hands and displayed unusual mental and manual coordination. He once reported that the most influential single discovery he ever made was a successful method of producing high hydrostatic pressure without a leak. This goal was attained by assuring that the sealing gasket of his pressure vessel was always compressed to a higher pressure than that in the vessel, so that effectively the latter is used to tighten the packing. The ultimate pressure limitation then becomes the strength of the metal parts used. Using such equipment, Bridgman embarked in 1915 on a 40-year research program that saw the maximum pressure limit gradually raised from 20,000 kg/cm^2 to 400,000 kg/cm^2. He also devised methods for the precise measurement of such pressures. He studied the effect of high pressure on practically all measurable properties of substance, including, for example, elasticity, viscosity, and electrical and thermal conductivities. He was able to produce never before achieved polymorphic transformations of substances. For the first time it was possible to observe in the laboratory properties of matter under the extreme pressure conditions prevailing deep within the earth. This inevitably led to increased interest in geophysical research.

Bridgman had a rather light teaching load at Harvard, mainly devoted to advanced courses. These along with his research stimulated him to think much about the fundamentals of thermodynamics, electrodynamics, relativity, and the properties of matter in general. The result was a succession of thought provoking articles and books, such, for example, as his study of dimensional analysis in a book with that title and his volume *The Nature of Thermodynamics*. Bridgman was fortunate that his professional position allowed him to devote all his time to teaching, research and writing. He was able to stay clear of involvement with university administration. One exception to his general tendency to avoid administrative work was his long continued service to the American Academy of Arts and Sciences of whose Rumford Award Committee he was a member from 1919 to 1952. The Academy did provide some financial support for his research, and a large number of his papers on high pressure were published in the Academy Proceedings.

Bridgman had a very restless mind and was not inclined to devote all his professional attention to experimental research. Rather early in his career he felt the urge to investigate the meanings of physical concepts and the nature of physical theory; he felt that the common attitude toward such matters in conventional theoretical physics could lead to serious misconceptions, which could only be avoided by associating the real significance of physical concepts with actual experimental operations. This was not too surprising a view on the part of an experimentalist! Bridgman first presented his views in this field in a book entitled *The Logic of Modern Physics*. This was followed at intervals by further books and articles devoted to elaboration of what came to be called the operational approach to the meaning of concepts like mass, force, energy, electric field intensity, etc. In its original and rather extreme form this approach maintained that the ultimate precise meaning of every physical concept is secured only through actual experimental operation by which it is observed and/or measured. Bridgman's attitude was soon characterized as "operationalistic", though he frequently expressed his dislike of this tag, insisting that he was not advocating a new philosophical system. In any case, his views excited much interest among both scientists and philosophers.

To many they came as a breath of fresh air in a rather foggy region. But others objected that strict adherence to Bridgman's operationalism would render much of theoretical physics untenable in spite of its generally admitted success in the explanation of physical experience. Probably as a result of such objections Bridgman relaxed his viewpoint somewhat and admitted "mental" or "paper and pencil" operations among those he demanded. This satisfied many of his critics; however, some still felt through a close inspection of his later writings that he would never take other than a dim view of a concept like the quantum mechanical state function, which is the dependent variable in the fundamental Schrödinger equation and is certainly not directly observable in any experiment, but from which average charge distribution in atoms can be computed, leading ultimately to the evaluation of quantities like ionization potentials which can be measured in the laboratory. Yet the main thrust of Bridgman's

ideas—namely that all results of the theorizing in physics must be brought into very close relationship with actual physical experience in order to have any satisfactory meaning—has had during the 20th century a very salutary effect on what may be called the methodology of physics.

In his later years Bridgman sought to apply his operational point of view to the problems of social experience, with questionable success; yet his attempt never failed to arouse interest. Though he was by no means the clear and inspiring lecturer one might have expected from his profound insight into difficult problems, conversations with him were always rewarding, for he had an effective way of getting down to basics and dismissing vague and wishy-washy ideas. His complete intellectual integrity and sincerity were evident in everything he said and did. He lived and died a thoroughly honest empiricist.

—R. Bruce Lindsay

BROAD, C(harlie) D(unbar). British philosopher. Born in London, 30 December 1887. Educated at Dulwich College, London, 1900-06; studied at Trinity College, Cambridge, 1906-10, 1st Class Honours. Fellow of Trinity College, 1911-17; Assistant to the Professor of Logic, University of St. Andrews, Scotland, 1911-14; Lecturer on Logic, University College of Dundee, Scotland, 1914-20; Professor of Philosophy, University of Bristol, 1920-22; Fellow and Lecturer in Moral Science, Trinity College, 1922-33; Knightsbridge Professor of Moral Philosophy, Cambridge University, 1933-53. Tarner Lecturer, Trinity College, 1923-24; Donnellan Lecturer, Trinity College, Dublin, 1929; Sidgwick Lecturer, Cambridge University, 1931. Visiting Professor, University of Michigan, Ann Arbor, 1953-54; Flint Professor of Philosophy, University of California at Los Angeles, 1954; Visiting Professor, Columbia University, New York, 1960. President, Aristotelian Society, 1927-28, 1954-55; President, Society for Physical Research, 1935-36. Honorary doctorate: University of Aberdeen; University of Bristol; University of Dublin; Cambridge University; University of Uppsala, Sweden. Fellow of the British Academy. Fellow, Swedish Academy of Science, and the American Academy of Arts and Sciences. *Died 11 March 1971.*

PUBLICATIONS

Philosophy

Perception, Physics, and Reality: An Enquiry into the Information That Physical Science Can Supply about the Real. Cambridge, Cambridge University Press, 1914.
Scientific Thought. London, Kegan Paul, and New York, Harcourt Brace, 1923.
The Mind and Its Place in Nature. London, Kegan Paul, and New York, Harcourt Brace, 1925.
The Philosophy of Francis Bacon (lecture). Cambridge, Cambridge University Press, 1926; New York, Octagon Books, 1976; reprinted in *Ethics and the History of Philosophy*, 1952.
Five Types of Ethical Theory. London, Kegan Paul, and New York, Harcourt Brace, 1930.
Examination of McTaggert's Philosophy. Cambridge, Cambridge University Press, 2 vols., 1933, 1938.
Determinism, Indeterminism, and Libertarianism (lecture). Cambridge, Cambridge University Press, 1934; reprinted in *Ethics and the History of Philosophy*, 1952.
Ethics and the History of Philosophy. London, Routledge, 1952; Westport, Connecticut, Hyperion Press, 1979.
Religion, Philosophy and Psychical Research. London, Routledge, and New York, Harcourt Brace, 1953.

Human Personality and the Possibility of Its Survival (lecture). Berkeley, University of California Press, 1955.

Personal Identity and Survival. London, Society for Psychical Research, 1958.

Lectures on Psychical Research, Incorporating the Perrott Lectures Given in Cambridge in 1959 and 1960. London, Routledge, and New York, Humanities Press, 1962.

Induction, Probability, and Causation: Selected Papers. Dordrecht, The Netherlands, D. Reidel, 1968.

Religion, Philosophy and Psychical Research: Selected Essays. New York, Humanities Press, 1969.

Broad's Critical Essays on Moral Philosophy, edited by David Cheyney. London, Allen and Unwin, 1971.

Leibniz: An Introduction, edited by C. Lewy. London, Cambridge University Press, 1975.

Berkeley's Argument About Material Substance. New York, Haskell House, 1975.

Kant: An Introduction, edited by C. Lewy. London and New York, Cambridge University Press, 1978.

Other

"Autobiography" and "A Reply to My Critics", in *The Philosophy of C.D. Broad*, 1959.

Editor, *The Nature of Existence*, vol. 2, by John McTaggert. Cambridge, Cambridge University Press, 1927; Grosse Pointe, Michigan, Scholarly Press, 1968.

*

Bibliography: by C. Lewy in *The Philosophy of C.D. Broad*, 1959.

Critical Studies: *The Philosophy of C.D. Broad*, edited by Paul Arthur Schilpp, New York, Tudor, 1959.

*   *   *

Meticulous and indefatigable in his treatment of philosophical problems, C.D. Broad brought considerable analytical acumen to bear on a wide range of topics, including the theory of perception, the philosophy of mind, the philosophy of science, ethics, and the philosophical aspects of physical research. Broad also wrote extensively on a variety of figures from the history of philosophy and science. With each problem he tackled Broad could see advantages and disadvantages of a number of different solutions, and he frequently offered only tentative support for his own views. Much of the value in Broad's work lies in his incomparably thorough analysis of problems, alternative theories, arguments, and counter-arguments.

Three of Broad's first four books are concerned with the theory of perception and the problem of our knowledge of the external world. Broad defends a version of the sense data theory, wherein a distinction is drawn between physical objects and what Broad calls a *sensa*, the immediately sensed objects of perception. When I look at a circular penny from an oblique angle, what I actually sense is elliptical. Since the same object cannot be both circular and elliptical, Broad concludes that the object immediately sensed must be distinct from the physical object. The directly sensed object is made up of the sensa—the colored patches, sounds, odors, etc., which, according to Broad, are neither physical nor mental objects, but, having some characteristics of each, serve as intermediaries between our minds and the physical world. Broad concludes that no sensum is identical to a part of a physical object, that therefore we can never immediately sense physical objects.

The epistemological difficulty raised by Broad's theory is that of explaining how the physical world can be known. Broad's reply is that while knowledge of the existence of physical objects cannot be justified by direct experience or by inference, we may postulate the existence of physical objects as the best hypothesis to account for the order of experience.

Throughout his career Broad maintained an interest in psychical research, and he took its philosophical implications seriously. When writing on such topics as causality, time, and the nature of mind, Broad tried to develop and defend theories which would allow for the possibility of psychic phenomena. For instance, his theory of mind, which he called the compound theory, was an attempt to reconcile the apparent dependence of consciousness on the activity of the brain and nervous system with the possibility of the persistence of mental activity after death. The mind, according to Broad, is a compound of a psychic factor and a bodily factor, only the latter—the brain and nervous system—having substantial ontological status. The psychic part of the mind is not a separable substance which can survive the death of the body, but remnants of the psychic factor may persist for a time after death in the form of fleeting, disassociated sensations and feelings which are sometimes communicated to mediums.

Broad's reluctance to commit himself to philosophical theories is especially marked in his ethical writings. In *Five Types of Ethical Theory*, Broad assumes that moral terms, such as "good", "bad", "right", "wrong", "ought", and "duty", refer to properties, and he is concerned with the question whether the properties denoted by moral terms are unique and peculiar, or rather definable in terms of words denoting natural or non-moral properties. Since he did not think ethical disputes could be settled by argument or observation, Broad hesitatingly leaned toward the view that moral properties are unique and intuited by a special moral sense.

After 1934 Broad no longer assumed that ethical terms refer to properties or that moral judgements are true or false. In the inaugural lecture, *Determinism, Indeterminism, and Libertarianism*, published in 1934, Broad argues that moral judgements probably imply categorical obligation, which in turn probably entails libertarianism, which is self-evidently impossible. From this he concludes that the notion of categorical obligation is probably delusive. This conclusion would imply an extreme moral skepticism, but in subsequent writings Broad continues to discuss and find sympathy for three kinds of ethical theory—naturalism, nonnaturalism, and emotivism—without committing himself to any of them. In a personal confession at the close of his autobiography Broad states—inconsistently with the inaugural lecture and his emotivist sympathies—that there were things which he had not done which he should have done, and in an important sense could have done, and that he deserves moral blame because he did not. Thus in his personal reflections Broad assumes a robust sense of moral freedom and categorical obligation.

C.D. Broad was an honest and fair-minded inquirer—a scientifically oriented philosopher whose undogmatic temperament permitted him to avoid the antimetaphysical prejudices of some of his contemporaries. He is admired for the elegance and clarity of his writing, and the thoroughness, rigor and lucidity of his thought.

—Robert T. Lehe

———————

BROADBENT, Donald (Eric). British psychologist. Born 6 May 1926. Educated at Winchester College; studied at Pembroke College, Cambridge, Moral Sciences Tripos, 1st Class, 1949. Served in the Royal Air Force during World War II. Married Margaret Elizabeth Wright in 1949, 2 daughters; married Margaret Hope Pattison Gregory in 1972. Member, Scientific Staff, 1949-58, and Director, 1958-74, Applied Psychology Research Unit, Cambridge, and Fellow, Pembroke College, 1965-74. Since 1974, Member, External Staff, Medical Research

Council, and Fellow, Wolfson College, Oxford. Visiting Fellow, All Souls College, Oxford, 1967-68. Lister Lecturer, British Association; Gregynog Lecturer, University of Aberystwyth; Pilsbury Lecturer, Cornell University, Ithaca, New York; Fitts Lecturer, University of Michigan, Ann Arbor; William James Lecturer, Harvard University, Cambridge, Massachusetts; Fairey Lecturer, University of Southampton; Fletcher-Stevens Lecturer, University of Utah, Provo; Bartlett Lecturer, Experimental Psychology Association. President, Section J, British Association for the Advancement of Science, 1967. Recipient: Distinguished Scientist Award, American Psychological Association, 1975. Honorary doctorate: University of Southampton, 1974; York University, 1979. Fellow and Council Member, Royal Society. Foreign Associate Member, United States Academy of Science, 1971. C.B.E. (Commander, Order of the British Empire), 1974. Address: Department of Experimental Psychology, 1 South Parks Road, Oxford OX1 3UD, England.

PUBLICATIONS

Psychology

Perception and Communication. London, and New York, Pergamon Press, 1958.
Behaviour (lectures). London, Eyre and Spottiswoode, and New York, Basic Books, 1961.
Decision and Stress. London and New York, Academic Press, 1972.
In Defence of Empirical Psychology. London, Methuen, 1973.

Other

Editor, with Karl H. Pribram, *Biology of Memory*. London and New York, Academic Press, 1970.

*   *   *

Donald Broadbent is the leading and most eminent member of the Cambridge school of experimental psychologists who followed in Sir Frederic Bartlett's footsteps and were largely inspired by his example.

Broadbent was just old enough to get called up for service in the Royal Air Force towards the end of the Second World War, and he took a short course in engineering in Cambridge under Air Force auspices before crossing the Atlantic for training as a pilot in Florida. It was while still in the Air Force, just after the termination of the war, that Broadbent got interested in psychology through contact with the personnel selection branch of the service. On his demobilisation in 1947 he decided to undertake a university course in the subject; he was lucky to find in the Cambridge department precisely the outlook and the inspiration that he needed. Bartlett's approach to psychology was experimental and practical, and was closely tied to the psychological issues raised by real life situations. At that time, too, Cambridge psychology was much influenced by the cybernetic ideas of the brilliant young psychologist Kenneth Craik, who had unfortunately been killed in a road accident two years before Broadbent entered the department. Most of Broadbent's subsequent work has in a sense been derived from these two sources, but he has been much less insular than his teacher, Sir Frederic Bartlett, and with him Cambridge psychology can be said to have merged with the main stream of psychology.

After graduating Broadbent joined the staff of the Medical Research Council's Applied Psychology Unit in Cambridge, and on the departure of its Director, Dr. N.H. Mackworth, for America in 1958, he was appointed Director of the Unit, a post he held for 16 years. He began his research career by investigating the effects of noise on the performance of tasks involving vigilance. It was during the course of these experiments that he became interested in the effects of the interaction between two or more stimuli. On the basis of the dichotic listening experiment devised by Colin Cherry, in which different messages were delivered simultaneously to the two ears, Broadbent developed an explanatory model which has proved the source for much further work. He expounded this in some detail in his first book, *Perception and Communication*. The model proposed a short-term store in which information from the senses is held; a selective filter, which passes on some of the incoming information (how this filter operates was an important aspect of further research); and a limited capacity channel which is only capable of dealing with information at a certain rate. What Broadbent was in effect providing was a new approach to the old problem of attention, which in the behaviourist period had practically disappeared from the psychological landscape. His work was a major influence in the revival of studies on attention, which has since become an important research area.

Broadbent's second substantial research publication, *Decision and Stress*, elaborated the theoretical model proposed in his earlier work and dealt with developments in the study of vigilance, selective perception, and reaction time with particular reference to the effects of stress. The limited channel capacity stage of information processing he now referred to as the "categorizing" stage in which information is grouped or "pigeonholed".

In his method of approach to psychological problems Broadbent is experimental and behaviouristic. In two of his more popular books, *Behaviour* and *In Defence of Empirical Psychology*, he has defended his adherence to Anglo-Saxon empiricism with its concern for practicality and manageable problems and its avoidance of high-flown theory. "The proper road for psychology," he wrote, "is by way of more modest theorizing." Nevertheless, Broadbent cannot be called a behaviourist in the more extreme sense of the term. He can better be described as a cognitive psychologist, because he speaks in terms of internal representations, structures and processes, and, as his 1972 William James lectures showed, he is concerned with such matters as choices, decisions, and strategies. He always attempts, however, to treat these topics in a down-to-earth manner and to formulate them in ways that can be handled experimentally. "Human action is not like clockwork," he has said; "(but) it does not require some mysterious causality.... The key point in voluntary action is the occurrence of a command signal." The old problems of psychology are thus phrased in new ways more amenable to experimental treatment.

In 1974 Broadbent gave up his Directorship of the Applied Psychology Unit and moved to Oxford. He did this to give himself more time for his personal research. In Oxford he continues to work on problems of attention, the way in which long sequences are controlled, and the various strategies people employ to achieve their goals. Although now working in an academic environment, Broadbent still believes that theoretical psychology needs the stimulus of practical problems, above all the urgent problems raised by the stresses resulting from the complexity of modern life. Broadbent's work is marked at the same time by technical excellence and concern for people.

—Leslie Hearnshaw

BRONOWSKI, Jacob. British scientist and man of letters. Born in Poland, 18 January 1908; emigrated to England (naturalized), and in 1964 to the United States. Studied mathematics at Cambridge University, M.A. 1930, Ph.D. 1933. Married Rita Coblentz in 1941; 4 children. Senior Lecturer, University College, Hull, 1934-42; Researcher, British Ministry of Home Security, 1942-45; served with the Joint Target Group, Washington, D.C., and as Scientific Deputy, British Joint Chiefs of Staff mission to Japan, 1945; Statistical Researcher, British Ministry of Works, 1946-50; Director of Coal Research Establishment, 1950-59, and Director-General, Process Development Department, 1959-63, National Coal Board of Great Britain; Commentor for the British Broadcasting Corporation, 1949-59; Research Professor, Fellow, and Director, Council for Biology in Human Affairs, Salk Institute for Biological Studies, San Diego, California, 1964-74. Carnegie Visiting Professor, Massachusetts Institute of Technology, Cambridge, 1953; Eastman Memorial Visiting Professor, University of Rochester, 1965. Condon Lecturer, Oregon State University, Eugene, 1965; Silliman Lecturer, Yale University, New Haven, Connecticut, 1967; Bampton Lecturer, Columbia University, New York, 1969; Mellon Lecturer, National Gallery of Art, Washington, D.C., 1969. Recipient: Thornton Medal; Italia Prize, 1950-51. Fellow, Royal Society of Literature, London. Honorary Fellow, Jesus College, Cambridge. Foreign Honorary Member, American Academy of Arts and Sciences. *Died 22 August 1974.*

PUBLICATIONS

Scientific and Critical Writings

The Poet's Defence. Cambridge, Cambridge University Press, 1939; as *The Poet's Defence: The Concept of Poetry from Sidney to Yeats*, Cleveland, World, 1966.
William Blake, 1757-1827: A Man Without a Mask. London, Secker and Warburg, 1943; revised version as *William Blake and the Age of Revolution*, New York, Harper, 1965.
The Common Sense of Science. London, Heinemann, 1951; Cambridge, Massachusetts, Harvard University Press, 1953.
Lessons Of Science (lecture). London, Gollancz, 1951.
The Face of Violence: An Essay with a Play. London, Turnstile Press, 1954; New York, Braziller, 1955.
The Dilemma of the Scientist. London, National Peace Council, 1955.
Science and Human Values. New York, Messner, 1956; London, Hutchinson, 1961; revised version as *Science and Human Values and The Abacus and the Rose* (radio play), New York, Harper, 1965.
The Western Intellectual Tradition: From Leonardo to Hegel, with Bruce Mazlish. New York, Harper, 1960; London, Penguin Books, 1963.
Imagination and the University, with others. Toronto, University of Toronto Press, 1964.
Insight. New York, Harper, and London, Macdonald, 1964.
Biography of an Atom, with M.E. Selsam (juvenile). New York, Natural History Press, 1965.
The Identity of Man. New York, Natural History Press, 1965; London, Heinemann, 1966.
On Being an Intellectual. Baltimore, Maryland, Barton Gillet, 1968.
Nature and Knowledge: The Philosophy of Contemporary Science. Eugene, Oregon State System of Higher Education, 1969.
The Ascent of Man. London, British Broadcasting Corporation, 1973; Boston, Little Brown, 1974.
A Sense of the Future: Essays in Natural Philosophy, edited by Piero E. Ariotti and Rita Bronowski. Cambridge, Massachusetts Institute of Technology, 1977.
The Visionary Eye: Essays in the Arts, Literature, and Science, edited by Piero E. Ariotti and Rita Bronowski. Cambridge, Massachusetts Institute of Technology, 1978.
The Origins of Knowledge and Imagination. New Haven, Connecticut, Yale University Press, 1978.
Magic, Science, and Civilization. New York, Columbia University Press, 1978.

Other

For Wilhelmina, Queen of the Netherlands (poem). Cam-

bridge, Heffer, 1929.
Spain 1939: Four Poems. Hull, Yorkshire, Andrew Marvell Press, 1939.

Editor, with John Morris Reeves, *Songs for Sixpence.* Cambridge, Heffer, 6 Parts, 1929.
Editor, *William Blake: A Selection of Poems and Letters.* London, Penguin, 1958.
Editor, with others, *Science: Chemistry, Physics, Astronomy.* New York, Doubleday, and London, Macdonald, 1960.
Editor, with others, *Technology: Man Remakes His World.* London, Macdonald, 1966; revised version, Englewood Cliffs, New Jersey, Prentice Hall, 1966.

*   *   *

Jacob Bronowski's remarkably wide range of intellectual interests was well matched by the comprehensiveness and overall consistency of his ideas. While it may seem odd to discover that the first major publications of a research mathematician were books on poets and poetry, the intimate connection between art and science as the twin expressions of the human imagination was one of Bronowski's fundamental themes and one to which he returned in almost all of his published works.

Born in Poland in 1908, Bronowski moved first to Germany and then to England where he studied mathematics at Cambridge University. Remaining there after graduation, he continued his research. During his years in Cambridge, he also served as editor of the literary magazine, *Experiment*, which brought him into contact with a variety of contemporary authors. Dissatisfied with what he saw of critical appraisals of poetry, which he felt merely reflected the analyses of outsiders, he turned to a study of the criticism written by poets themselves, being particularly concerned to discover what their self-appraisal of the significance of poetry might be. His conclusion, expressed in his book, *The Poet's Defence*, was that the best poets believed that they had access to a truth that was unique, direct and absolute and that literature was therefore to be considered a form of universal knowledge.

While the book was widely discussed, Bronowski himself acknowledged its lack of influence. Those who denied the universality of literature and saw it as a product of its immediate social environment found his argument unpersuasive. It was for this reason that he turned to a study of the poetry of William Blake, whom he saw as representing a suitable test of the relationship of literature and its immediate social and political surroundings. Blake, who came to represent all artists to Bronowski, is marked by the gift of being able to catch the universal themes that sound in the particularities of his time. While he is not unshaped by his age, he is most certainly not determined by it. Blake's timeless importance lay, for Bronowski, in his ability to penetrate the true meaning of his time by the special gift of the imagination.

It was the theme of imagination and its foundational status for all forms of knowledge that marked the rest of Bronowski's work. To this point, he had concentrated on the role of the imagination in the kind of knowledge that is brought to us in the arts. In his later works, Bronowski became an equally vigorous advocate of the role of imagination in science. But this was a shift of emphasis rather than a shift of position. He made equally clear in his later works that science and art must be looked at together. He described them as the two threads that run continuously through every human culture. To appreciate this was, in his view, to come to see that an understanding of human imagination must be central to any full understanding of human nature.

In 1942, Bronowski left a teaching position at Hull to play an active part in the British war effort. He put his particular training to use conducting statistical analyses of the effects of bombing, and subsequently he was sent to Japan to report on the effects of the atomic bombing of Hiroshima and Nagasaki. It was this latter experience, coupled with a deep sense of the failures of

German culture which had permitted the rise of Hitler, that led him to the ideas expressed in *Science and Human Values*. His reflections led him to the conclusion that these great failures of our civilization were tied in substantial part to the popular but fatally flawed notion of a value-free science. He argued that this idea reflected a confusion between the way in which the results of research are expressed with the actual methods employed in arriving at those results. Bronowski argued that science was as much as an act of the imagination as any art and proceeded to explore the consequences of this view. Rather than simply provide a generalization to cover a set of facts, a scientific theory, according to Bronowski, shows these facts to flow from an inner order and from an imaginative arrangement of a few deep conclusions. He firmly rejected the naive positivist view of science as being true in so far as it was an accurate representation of the world and argued instead that science constructed visions of the world which gained their validity in the same way as does a metaphor. Furthering these echoes of the philosopher Kant, Bronowski suggested that science does not tell us about the way the world is but about the way we see the world. Thus, he allied himself to a tradition, represented by many philosophers but unsympathetic to many scientists, that denies immediate access to the world unshaped by perception. If he was right, then the idea of a neutral value-free science is of course an impossibility. Bronowski also reflected on the implications of this view of science would have for ethics. Where the individual act of the imagination is so important for our knowledge, then the appropriate conditions that make this possible must be fostered. For him this meant an ethical code that stressed the importance of truth, trust and freedom to dissent.

In 1964, Bronowski moved to the Salk Institute in California to pursue his research into what he called "human specificity." By this he meant the attempt to define those particular biological and behavioural characteristics which are expressions of human uniqueness. This research lay at the basis of the achievement for which Bronowski became most widely known: the television series, and subsequent book, *The Ascent of Man*. His argument here, and in a number of posthumously published collections of lectures and papers, is once again the centrality of imagination to the development of human culture. This distinctive ability, possessed uniquely by the human species, to hold in mind for long periods what is not immediately present to the mind is the clue to understanding human nature. Without imagination, therefore, there could be no knowledge, no culture, no science, no art, no humanity in any real sense of the term. Bronowski's passionate plea, conflicting with the popular image of the scientist almost as much as his variety of interests might seem to, serves to provide us with a clear dramatization of his fundamental views on the actual nature of scientific knowledge. While it has not gone undisputed, his position is given considerable weight by the force of both Bronowski's argument and example.

—David Wren

BRØNSTED, Johannes (Nicolaus). Danish chemist. Born in Varde, 22 February 1879. Studied at the Polytechnical Institute and University of Copenhagen, Ph.D. 1908. Assistant, 1905-08, and after 1908 Professor of Chemistry, University of Copenhagen; Director, Physio-Chemical Institute, 1930-47. *Died* (in Copenhagen) *17 December 1947.*

PUBLICATIONS

Chemistry

Underøgelser over racemiske omdamelsers affenitet [Research into the Affinity of Changes in Racemization]. Copenhagen,

A.F. Høst, 1915.
Om syre- og basekatalyse [On Acid and Base Catalysis]. Copenhagen, B. Lunos, 1926.
On the Definition of the Gibbs Potential. Copenhagen, Levin og Munksgaard, 1933.
On the Use of Osmotic Pressure in Chemical Thermodynamics: The Solubility Curve of Slightly Soluble Substances. Copenhagen, Levin og Munksgaard, 1933.
Om realtionen mellen varme og arbejde [On the Relationship Between Heat and Work]. Copenhagen, Levin og Munksgaard, 1937.
Laerebog i fysisk kemi. Copenhagen, Levin og Munksgaard, 1936; as *Physical Chemistry*, London, Heinemann, 1937; New York, Chemical Publishing Company, 1938.
De thermodynamiske hovedsaetningers grundlag og formulering. [The Foundation and Formulation of Thermodynamic Principles]. Copenhagen, E. Munksgaard, 1939.

* * *

Acids were among the earliest classes of compounds to be studied by chemists. In fact, the existence of a group of substances—the acids—with a common set of physical and chemical properties was recognized for centuries before the rise of modern chemistry. The first effective explanation for the chemical behavior of acids was not formulated, however, until Arrhenius proposed his theory of electrolytic dissociation in 1884. According to that theory, an acid is any substance which releases hydrogen ions (protons) in water solution, while a base is any substance that releases hydroxide ions in water solution. The acidic properties of a solution are assumed to be, then, a function of the hydrogen ions present rather than the compound from which they were released.

One disadvantage of the Arrhenius theory—largely an aesthetic incongruity—was its failure to relate the definitions of acid and base. Empirically, the two classes of compounds appear to have some clear association, the properties of one being the opposite of the properties of the other. In a neutralization reaction, for example, an acid reacts with a base to produce two neutral substances, a salt and water. The acid and base appear to have "canceled out" each other's properties.

Johannes Brønsted suggested redefining acids and bases in such a way as to make this connection more clear. He proposed defining an acid as a proton donor and a base as a proton acceptor. The acid definition is essentially the same as that formulated by Arrhenius. A water solution of hydrogen chloride is still an acid, for example, because hydrogen chloride molecules ionize in water to produce hydrogen ions (protons) and chloride ions. Bases are defined somewhat more broadly, however. A water solution of sodium hydroxide is to be regarded as a base, for example, because in water solutions the totally dissociated sodium hydroxide consists of sodium ions and hydroxide ions. It is the hydroxide ion that is regarded as the base because it has the tendency to combine with (accept) protons: $OH^- + H^+ \rightarrow HOH$. The mechanisms by which hydrogen chloride ionizes and sodium hydroxide dissociates are no different, of course, but the way in which we regard them *is* different under the Arrhenius and Brønsted theories.

One consequence of the Brønsted theory is to provide that close connection between acids and bases lacking in the Arrhenius theory. That is, the very existence of an acid *implies* a related (or "conjugated") base. Consider the reaction between hydrogen chloride and ammonia: $HCl + NH_3 \leftrightarrow NH_4^+ + Cl^-$. In this reaction, hydrogen chloride molecules have donated protons to the ammonia molecule. Hydrogen chloride is, then, by Brønsted's definition, an acid. Similarly, ammonia, which has received protons from the hydrogen chloride, must be a base.

This reaction is obviously reversible also. The ammonium ion (NH_4^+) may donate a proton to the chloride ion, producing hydrogen chloride and ammonia molecules. In this case, the ammonium ion is the acid and the chloride ion the base. The close association of all species in this equilibrium condition is highlighted by designating the chloride ion as the *conjugate base* of hydrogen chloride. That is, when hydrogen chloride molecules have *lost* their protons, they become chloride ions which then have the ability to *accept* protons. Similarly, the ammonium ion is the *conjugate acid* of the base ammonia.

An additional benefit of the Brønsted definition is its ability to refer to acids and bases in non-aqueous conditions. For example, the reaction described above need not take place in water. Under suitable conditions, not involving water, hydrogen chloride may still donate protons to ammonia molecules, allowing us to define the former as an acid and the latter a base. This broadens the definitions of acids and bases and permits us to use those terms for substances that would not have been so regarded under the Arrhenius system.

—David Newton

BROUWER, L(uitzen) E(gbertus) J(an). Dutch mathematician. Born in Overschie, 27 February 1881. Educated at high school in Hoorn, and at the Gymnasium, Haarlem; studied at the University of Amsterdam, 1897-1904, Ph.D. 1907. Privat-docent from 1909, Professor, 1912-51, and Professor Emeritus from 1951, University of Amsterdam. Honorary doctorate: University of Oslo, 1929; Cambridge University, 1955. Member, Royal Dutch Academy of Sciences, 1912; German Academy of Science, Berlin, 1919; American Philosophical Society, Philadelphia, 1943; and the Royal Society of London, 1948. Knight, Order of the Dutch Lion, 1932. *Died* (in Blaricum, Netherlands) *2 December 1966.*

PUBLICATIONS

Collections

Collected Works, edited by A. Heyting. Amsterdam and Oxford, North-Holland, and New York, American Elsevier, 1975-.

Mathematics and Philosophy

Leven, Kunst, en Mystiek [Life, Art, and Mysticism]. Delft, 1905.
Over de Grondslagen der Wiskunde [On the Foundations of Mathematics]. Amsterdam and Leipzig, Maas and van Suchtelen, 1907.
Wiskunde, Waarheid, Werkelijkheid [Mathematics, Truth, Reality]. Groningen, P.N. Noordhoff, 1919.

Other

Editor, with others, *Studies in Logic and the Foundation of Mathematics.* Amsterdam, North-Holland, 1951.

*

Critical Studies: *Introduction to Topology* by S. Letschetz, Princeton, New Jersey, Princeton University Press, 1949; *Intuitionism: An Introduction* by Arend Heyting, Amsterdam, North-Holland Publishing Co., 1956; *The Foundations of Intuitionistic Mathematics* by S.C. Kleene and R.E. Vesley, Amsterdam, North-Holland, 1965.

*   *   *

L.E.J. Brouwer was a Dutch mathematician who led the school of mathematical thought called Intuitionism and made major contributions to the branch of mathematics called Topology.

Since antiquity, scholars have investigated the concepts from which mathematics springs and the assumptions made about them. In the late 19th and early 20th centuries, there was much active controversy over these questions: Brouwer took an important part. At that time there were three schools of thought about the foundations of mathematics: Logicism, led by the English mathematician and philosopher Bertrand Russell; Formalism, associated with the German mathematician David Hilbert; and Brouwer's Intuitionism.

Logicism states that mathematicians examine abstractions such as lines and points, the existence of which are independent of the mathematician. Mathematical ideas can all be reduced to abstract properties. Mathematics flows from basic logical principles about properties.

According to Formalism, mathematicians manipulate finite configurations of symbols, following certain rules as they do so. Pragmatism customarily dictates the choice of rules, although it is best to have results justify this choice.

Brouwer's Intuitionist school contends that mathematicians work with mental constructions which are governed by self-evident primitive notions (primordial intuition). Brouwer's thinking led to considerable redevelopment of mathematics to eliminate aspects which could not withstand his analysis. Overall, the controversy over Logicism, Formalism, and Intuitionism led to substantial development of mathematical logic so that positions could be more clearly defined, studied, and argued.

Though some Intuitionist principles were developed during the 18th and early 19th centuries, it was Brouwer who laid out the philosophy in its full modern form. He is thus considered the father of Intuitionism.

Brouwer said that the starting point of mathematics is an intuitive understanding of the generation and sequence of positive integers—the duplication in abstract terms of a single entity (x, xx, xxx, xxxx, etc.). Human beings derive this from their basic inner awareness of time.

Brouwer went on to declare that mathematical knowledge is limited to that which can be known about mental constructions and proofs. A given proposition must have a proof in order to be known; its negation must have a non-proof in order to be known. This non-proof is a demonstration that the proposition leads to contradiction.

Brouwer's analysis results in rejection of the law of the excluded middle which causes many fundamental arguments and definitions in mathematics to collapse and requires their complete re-examination. The law of the excluded middle, which was generally accepted before Brouwer's time, states that for any proposition p, p is either true or it is false. The Intuitionist cannot, however, accept this statement since he cannot be sure that for every p a proof or a disproof can be found.

Brouwer began as a destructive critic of other schools of thought, moved on to a reconstruction of mathematics according to Intuitionist tenets, and then, late in his career, introduced new theories.

Brouwer's redevelopment of mathematics took place during the decade following 1915. Applying the principles of Intuitionism, he developed a new theory of real numbers and real functions, a new theory of sets, and a theory of ordinals. In doing this, he took major steps toward redevelopment of classical algebra, geometry, analysis, and topology. In spite of this effort, Brouwer made few converts during his lifetime, and Intuitionism has only a tiny number of adherents today. Brouwer's writings were in part the cause of this. They were often antagonistically argumentative or obscure. In some essays, he employed familiar terminology but gave it unexpected new meanings, confusing the reader and making the argument hard to follow.

Brouwer is also considered one of the founders of modern topology. This branch of mathematics, which originated from geometry during the 19th century, involves the study of those properties retained by an object under deformation (e.g., bending, stretching, squeezing) but not breaking, tearing, or pasting parts together. A topologist would investigate, for example, how a triangle drawn on a balloon changes as the balloon bends, stretches, or is squeezed. The triangle can be shaped into a circle which is thus its topological equivalent. Triangles and straight lines are not similarly equivalent. By the same token, a cube of clay can be bent and squeezed into a sphere, which is the cube's topological equivalent. Not equivalent, however, is a ring which might be made by piercing the clay or shaping it into a cylinder, bending the two ends together, and joining them.

A key concept in topology is the homeomorphism—a continuous two-way transformation of one geometric object or set of points (p) into another geometric object or set of points (p'). There are limits to topological deformation, depending upon the way the problem is defined. Two circles of different size with the smaller internally tangent to the larger can be topologically transformed into a figure with the two circles externally tangent by moving one or the other of the circles through the third dimension. Some problems involving deformation of three-dimensional figures can only be solved by making use of a fourth dimension. The fourth dimension does not present any particular difficulties mathematically, but it is impossible to visualize.

Brouwer's name is associated with the fixed point theorem in topology. To understand it, one must begin by conceiving of a figure in topological terms as a set of points or point set, as it is commonly called. Brouwer proved that every homeomorphism of a round spherical surface onto itself leaves at least one point fixed. This can also be stated as follows: any orientation that preserves topological mapping (i.e., one-to-one continuous mapping) of a two-dimensional sphere into itself leaves at least one point invariant (i.e., the fixed point that gives the theorem its name). Brouwer was able to prove this theorem for three-dimensional spheres and for some of higher dimensions. One of his successors later generalized the theorem to apply to continuous mapping of n-dimensional balls.

—Victor M. Cassidy

BRUNER, Jerome S. American psychologist. Born in New York City, 1 October 1915. Studied at Duke University, Durham, North Carolina, B.A. 1937; Harvard University, Cambridge, Massachusetts, M.A. 1939, Ph.D. 1941. Served in the United States Army Intelligence Corps, 1941-44. Married Katherine Frost in 1940 (divorced), 2 children; married Blanche Marshall McLane in 1960. Lecturer, 1945-48, Associate Professor, 1948-52, and Professor of Cognitive Studies, 1957-72 (Director, Center for Cognitive Studies, 1961-72), Harvard University; since 1972, Watts Professor of Psychology, Oxford University. Associate Director, Office of Public Opinion Research, 1942-44, Princeton, New Jersey; Visiting Member, Institute for Advanced Study, Princeton, 1951-52; Lecturer, Salzburg Seminar, 1952; Bacon Professor, University of Aix-en-Province, 1965. Editor, *Public Opinion Quarterly*, 1943-44. President, American Psychological Association, 1964-65. Recipient: Guggenheim Fellowship, 1955-56; Distinguished Science Contribution Award, American Psychological Association, 1962; Joint Award, American Educational Research Association and American Educational Publishers Institute, 1969; Citation from the Merrill-Palmer Institute, 1970. Honorary doctorate: Lesley College, Cambridge, Massachusetts, 1964; Temple University, Philadelphia, 1965; Northwestern University, Evanston, Illinois, 1965; University of Cincinnati, 1966; Duke University, 1969; Northern Michigan University, Marquette, 1969; University of New Brunswick, 1969; University of Sheffield, 1970; Sorbonne, Paris, 1974; University of Bristol, 1975; University of Louvain, 1976;

University of Ghent, 1977. Fellow, American Academy of Arts and Sciences; American Association for the Advancement of Science; National Academy of Education (Founding Fellow). Honorary Fellow, Federation Suisse de Psychologie; Puerto Rican Academy of Arts and Sciences. Address: 916 Washington Street, Gloucester, Massachusetts 01930, U.S.A.

PUBLICATIONS

Psychology

Public Thinking and Post-War Problems. Washington, D.C., National Planning Association, 1943.
Mandate from the People. New York, Duell Sloan, 1944.
A Study of Thinking, with Jacqueline J. Goodnow and George A. Austin. New York, Wiley, 1956.
Opinions and Personality, with others. New York, Wiley, 1956.
Contemporary Approaches to Cognition, with others. Cambridge, Massachusetts, Harvard University Press, 1957.
Logique et perception, with others. Paris, Presses Universitaires de France, 1958.
On Knowing: Essays for the Left Hand. Cambridge, Massachusetts, Belknap Press, 1962.
Man: A Course of Study. Cambridge, Massachusetts, Educational Services, 1965.
Studies in Cognitive Growth, with others. New York, Wiley, 1966.
Towards a Theory of Instruction. Cambridge, Massachusetts, Belknap Press, 1966.
Learning About Learning: A Conference Report. Washington, D.C., Government Printing Office, 1966.
The Growth of the Mind. Cambridge, Massachusetts, Educational Services, 1966.
A Look at Incongruity. Cincinnati, University of Cincinnati Press, 1966.
Processes of Cognitive Growth: Infancy (lectures). Worcester, Massachusetts, Clark University Press, 1968.
Poverty and Childhood. Detroit, Merrill-Palmer Institute, 1970.
Education of the Infant and Young Child, with others. New York, Academic Press, 1970.
Dare to Care/Dare to Act: Racism and Education. Washington, D.C., Association for Supervision and Curriculum Development, 1971.
The Application of Learning Principles to Classroom Instruction, with others. Bellingham, Western Washington State College, 1971.
The Relevance of Education, edited by Anita Gil. New York, Norton, 1971; London, Penguin, 1974.
Beyond the Information Given: Studies in the Psychology of Knowing. New York, Norton, 1973.
Patterns of Growth (lecture). Oxford, Clarendon Press, 1974.
Entry into Early Language: A Spiral Curriculum (lecture). Swansea, University College of Swansea, 1975.
Under Five in Britain. London, Grant McIntyre, 1980.

Other

Editor, *Perception and Personality: A Symposium.* Durham, North Carolina, Duke University Press, 1950.
Editor, *The Growth of Competence.* London and New York, Academic Press, 1974.
Editor, *Play: Its Role in Development and Evolution.* London, Penguin, and New York, Basic Books, 1976.
Editor, with Alison Garton, *Human Growth and Development.* Oxford, Clarendon Press, 1978.

*

Critical Studies: *Invention and Discovery of Reality: The Acquisition of Conservation of Amount*, by E.J. Peill, London and New York, Wiley, 1975.

*   *   *

Jerome S. Bruner must be considered one of the fathers of what is now being called the cognitive revolution in psychology. *A Study of Thinking*, by Bruner and two associates, was published in 1956, a year often cited as the beginning of the revolution. By current standards, it is technically and conceptually simple, yet it has that broad sweep, that willingness to theorize, that characterize early works in a movement. Later, complexity—often excessive—and specialization set in.

What is the cognitive revolution in psychology? James Joyce said that history was a nightmare from which he was trying to awake. Many psychologists would say that Behaviorism is the historical nightmare from which they are trying to awake; the cognitive revolution is what one sees when one opens one's eyes. The avowed goal of Behaviorism was to produce a psychology with an "empty organism," a psychology that did not need to deal with internal factors. Behaviorism hoped to prove hypothetical fictions such concepts as thought, emotion, consciousness, and mind. The goal was to predict an organism's behavior solely from knowledge of the stimuli the organism was presented with and the organism's learning history. Nothing about the organism's internal state need be known—in fact, it was nonsense to even speak of internal states.

Why presumably intelligent people would pursue such a goal is an interesting question that would take us far from our topic. Suffice it to say that for decades, a radical behavioristic approach was the dominant force in academic psychology. The cognitive approach is different in two ways. It does not postulate an empty organism—it does not assume it is possible not to take internal factors into account and it does assume that such factors exist. Second, it sets up as an important object of study the behavior of organisms as they react to stimuli.

Perhaps the most elementary and important concept of cognitive psychology is "mediation." A stimulus impinges upon the organism, which then processes it in some way and responds. Thus, for example, my dog and Joe's dog are both presented with the same stimulus—me. My dog recognizes me and wags its tail. Joe's dog feels threatened by me and barks. A behaviorist would try to specify the learning histories of the two dogs. My dog has been rewarded often by me, and associates me, therefore, with the "primary reinforcer" food. Joe's dog has somehow learned that strangers are dangerous. A cognitive psychologist would study the mediational aspects of the same situation. How do dogs—and humans—recognize other organisms? That is a major topic in cognitive psychology. This example, however, does not allow further exploration of the approach of cognitive psychology; it is too simple. It is an example of a situation where the behaviorist approach is adequate for dealing with most aspects of the situation. Part of the reason behaviorism appeared potentially successful is that it dealt in such simple situations.

Here is another example. Joe and I are riding on a bus from New York to Washington. Buses leave New York for Washington every hour on the hour; buses leave Washington for New York every hour on the hour. The trip takes four hours. Counting buses that arrive just as we depart or depart just as we arrive, how many buses will Joe and I pass heading for New York as we head for Washington?

Suppose Joe and I consider this problem. It is likely that one of us will get it wrong; it is not an easy problem, it appears. And there are two ways of looking at it which yield the correct answer. If we are leaving at noon, the 8 A.M. bus will be arriving in New York just as we depart; when we arrive at 4 P.M., the 4 P.M. bus will just be departing. That makes nine buses. Or you can solve the problem in a more intuitive way. You can think, "Buses arrive in New York at the rate of one per hour, but we are approaching these buses as rapidly as they are approaching New York. So we

should meet them about every half hour, so about eight."

What does behaviorism have to say about this situation? Not much. If Joe thoughtlessly blurts out "four," while I think about the problem and get it right, a behaviorist might hypothesize that I had been rewarded in the past for solving problems. But if, which seems more likely, Joe and I are equally motivated, behaviorism has nothing to say. Cognitive psychology investigates problem solving, however—the strategies people employ to solve this kind of problem, and ones more difficult.

This writer thought of this problem while on a bus from New York and got it wrong (which is one reason he knows it is not as easy as it seems). He had some difficulty remembering the problem and some difficulty believing he actually has the right answer, since when he finally got it right, it seemed as if he had made a breakthrough, whereas this time it seemed obvious. What would a behaviorist have to say about all this? Absolutely nothing. A cognitive psychologist, on the other hand, would be very interested in how my memory operated to retrieve the problem and in the mechanisms I employed to assure that the answer presented as correct is in fact correct.

In general, when one thinks of real life situations and of what behaviorism has to say about them, the answer generally is, "Not much." Cognitive psychology usually has something to say, is working on it, or is willing to work on it. Jerome Bruner was at the center of the cognitive revolution when it began and is still making important contributions. His goal appears to be a psychology which is responsive to real life and to real life problems. He is an outstanding educational theorist in his own right, which further testifies to his real life goals. The cognitive revolution is an important step for a field which until recently has had its head in the sand, and it is a testimony to Bruner's courage and independence that it has developed.

—George W. Kelling

BRUNSCHVICG, Léon. French philosopher. Born in Paris, 10 November 1869. Educated at the Lycée Condorcet and the Ecole Normale Supérieure, Paris, 1888-91; license in letters and sciences; Docteur-ès-Lettres, the Sorbonne, 1897. Served in the French Army, 1914-18. Married Cécile Kahn in 1899; 4 children. Professor of Philosophy, Lycée de L'Orient, Paris, 1891-93; Lycée Descartes, Tours, 1893-95; Lycée Corneille, Rouen, 1895-1900; Lycée Condorcet, 1900-03; and Lycée Henri IV, Paris, 1903-09; Maître de Conférences, Faculté des Lettres, 1909-14, 1918-27, and Professor of the History of Modern Philosophy, 1927-40, University of Paris. Honorary doctorate: University of Durham, 1923. Member, Académie des Sciences Morales et Politiques, 1919 (President, 1932). Officier, Légion d'Honneur. Member of the Royal Academies of Denmark, Lincei (Naples) and Rumania. *Died 4 February 1944.*

PUBLICATIONS

Philosophy

Spinoza. Paris, Alcan, 1894.
La Modalité du jugement. Paris, Alcan, 1897.
La Vertu métaphysique du syllogisme selon Aristotle. Paris, Alcan, 1897.
Introduction à la vie de l'esprit. Paris, Alcan, 1900.
L'Idéalisme contemporain. Paris, Alcan, 1905.
Les Etapes de la philosophie mathématique. Paris, Alcan, 1912.
Nature et liberté. Paris, Flammarion, 1921.
L'Expérience humaine et la causalité physique. Paris, Alcan, 1922.

Spinoza et ses contemporains. Paris, Alcan, 1923.

La Génie de Pascal. Paris, Hachette, 1924.

Le Progrès de la conscience dans la philosophie occidentale. Paris, Alcan, 1927.

De la connaissance de soi. Paris, Alcan, 1931.

Pascal. Paris, Rieder, 1932.

Les Ages de l'intelligence. Paris, Alcan, 1934.

La Physique du XXᵉ siècle et la philosophie. Paris, Hermann, 1936.

Le Role du pythagorisme dans l'évolution des idées. Paris, Hermann, 1937.

Descartes. Paris, Rieder, 1937.

L'Actualité des problèmes platoniciens. Paris, Hermann, 1937.

La Raison et la religion. Paris, Alcan, 1939.

Descartes et Pascal, lecteurs de Montaigne. Neuchâtel, Baconnière, 1942.

Héritage de mots, héritage d'idées. Paris, Presses Universitaires de France, 1945.

L'Esprit européen. Neuchâtel, Baconnière, 1947.

Agenda retrouvé, 1892-1942. Paris, Minuit, 1948.

La Philosophie de l'esprit. Paris, Presses Universitaires de France, 1949.

De la vraie et de la fausse conversion, suivi de La Querelle de l'athéisme. Paris, Presses Universitaires de France, 1950.

Écrits philosophiques. Paris, Presses Universitaires de France, 3 vols., 1951-58.

Blaise Pascal. Paris, Vrin, 1953.

Other

Un Ministère de l'éducation nationale. Paris, Plon-Nourrit, 1922.

Editor, *Blaise Pascal.* Paris, Hachette, 1897.

Editor, with Pierre Boutroux and Felix Gazier, *Oeuvres complètes de Blaise Pascal.* Paris, Hachette, 14 vols., 1904-14.

Editor, *Reproduction en phototypie du manuscrit des Pensées de Pascal.* Paris, Hachette, 1905.

Editor, *Pensées de Pascal.* Paris, Cluny, 1934.

Editor, *Pensées et opuscules* by Pascal. Paris, Hachette, 1950.

*

Critical Studies: *La Philosophie de Léon Brunschvicg,* by Marcel Deschoux, Paris, Presses Universitaires de France, 1949; *Léon Brunschvicg ou l'idéalisme à hauteur d'homme,* Paris, Seghers, 1969 (contains an extensive bibliography); *La Philosophie de Léon Brunschvicg,* by O.P. Messaut, Paris, Presses Universitaires de France, 1937; *Brunschvicg, sa vie, son oeuvre avec un exposé de sa philosophie,* by René Boirel, Paris, Presses Universitaires de France, 1964.

*   *   *

Léon Brunschvicg, French idealist philosopher, was born in Paris and educated in science, classics and philosophy at the Lycée Condorcet, l'Ecole Normale Supérieure and the Sorbonne. As long-time president of the jury supervising the *concours d'agrégation*—comprehensive examinations for a degree and teaching position—Brunschvicg extended his influence to a generation of younger scholars who accepted his idealist reading of the history of philosophy. Those who did not (notably Sartre, Beauvoir, Merleau-Ponty) regarded his idealism as philosophically and politically reactionary, tending to legitimize the principles on which the Third Republic claimed to be founded.

"Critical idealism" recalls Kant's analysis of the conditions of knowledge, but Brunschvicg defended an historical rather than deductive method; through a close analysis of major texts in mathematics, science and philosophy, he endeavored to trace the mind's activity as asserting and constituting the primacy of ideas over being. In general perspective, he may be seen as heir to two currents in 19th-century French philosophy: the tradition of epistemological idealism descending through Charles Renouvier from Kant and Antoine Cournot, and the metaphysical idealism of Maine de Biran, Félix Ravaisson, Jules Lachelier and Jules Lagneau. Indeed, Brunschvicg's major theme may be seen as a response to the question he attributed to Cournot: Is the ideal of reason "satisfied spontaneously by the positive sciences" insofar as they express the values of simplicity, order and harmony, or does the ideal reflect a higher norm, "like a kind of superior sense that captures in itself its own criterion and its own certitude"?

Brunschvicg read the history of philosophy (favoring Plato, Descartes and Kant) as evidencing a tendency he called "the progress of consciousness" (*le progrès de la conscience*). The double meaning of this expression—referring to conscience as well as consciousness—suggests the moral dimension of his idealism. For the individual, the process is a conversion from naive realism to idealism in recognition of mind's constitution of intelligible order. At the same time the advance of moral intelligence is acknowledged as progressively refining the capacity for conscientious judgment and choice. Viewed historically, an imminent process is recognized on behalf of humanity as a whole; it is oriented toward spiritual values, of which unity is said to be the highest. In concrete terms, Brunschvicg envisioned a community of rational beings: "All the forms of human genius, genius of science and of art, genius of justice and of friendship... move toward the same goal: to overturn the barriers that separate men from one another."

The critique of this process, Brunschvicg asserted, excludes a priori assumptions as well as the premises of ideology; these are seen as falsifying the mind's essential freedom and inventiveness. Derivation of categories or functions of thought is ruled out on the same grounds. The emphasis on creative spontaneity suggests a relationship with Bergson that Brunschvicg was proud to admit, but not to the extent that he supported Bergson's intuitionism. Deeply concerned with the historical interdependence of philosophy, mathematics and science, he remained closer than Bergson to the rational values of the French intellectual tradition.

Brunschvicg rejected any imputation of Hegelian absolutism, insisting that his reading of essential texts owed nothing to metaphysics. He held that metaphysics is reducible to theory of knowledge, that judgment as a synthesizing or unifying activity autonomously advances knowledge in all areas. In respect to physical science, where judgment is determined in part by evidence of lawful regularities, one may speak tentatively of a collaboration between mind and nature. But ultimately the limiting conditions of natural phenomena are conceived (apparently following Fichte) as restraints imposed by mind on its own freedom. Thus Brunschvicg attempted to maintain an unqualified idealism while extolling natural science as the highest expression of intellect and of mankind's developing self-awareness. In this intellectualist sense he defended a "spiritual" conception of science as opposed to positivist or conventionalist notions. A similar position, very likely influenced by Brunschvicg, was held by Gaston Bachelard—see, for example, *La Formation de l'esprit scientifique*—who is still widely appreciated in France. Brunschvicg, by contrast, is in eclipse, although he deserves to be remembered as an interpreter of the French philosophical tradition and as a spokesman for the life of reason and the value of science.

—Bernard Elevitch

BUBER, Martin. German theologian. Born in Vienna, Austria, 8 February 1878. Studied at the University of Leipzig, the University of Zurich, and at the University of Vienna, Ph.D 1904. Married the novelist Paula Winkler ("Georg Munk") in

1899; 2 children. Editor of the Zionist journal, *Die Welt*, 1901; helped to found the *Jüdischer Verlag* in 1902; founder of the periodical, *Der Jude*, 1916. With Franz Rosenzweig founded and taught at the Freis Judisches Lehrhaus, Frankfurt, 1920-33; Honorary Professor, University of Frankfurt, 1920-33; Professor of the Sociology of Religion, Hebrew University, Jerusalem, from 1938. Recipient, Hanseatic Goethe Prize, 1951; Peace Prize of the German Book Trade, 1953; Erasmus Prize, 1963. Honorary doctorate: University of Heidelberg, 1964. *Died* (in Jerusalem) *13 June 1965.*

PUBLICATIONS

Collections

Werke. Munich, Kösel, and Heidelberg, Schneider, 3 vols., 1962-64.

Theology

Die Geschichten des Rabbi Nachman. Frankfurt, Rütten and Loening, 1906; as *Tales of Rabbi Nachman*, New York, Horizon Press, 1956.

Die Legende des Baalschem. Frankfurt, Rütten and Loening, 1908; as *Jewish Mysticism, and the Legends of the Baal-Schem*, London, Dent, 1931; *The Legend of the Baal-Shem*, London, East and West Library, and New York, Harper, 1955.

Ekstatische Konfessionen. Jena, Diedrichs Verlag, 1909.

Chinesische Geister- und Liebesgeschichten. Frankfurt, Rütten and Loening, 1911.

Drei Reden uber das Judentum. Frankfurt, Rütten and Loening, 1911.

Buberheft. Berlin, Neue Blatter, 1913.

Daniel: Gespräche von der Verwirklichung. Leipzig, Insel, 1913; as *Daniel: Dialogues on Realization*, New York, Holt Rinehart, 1964.

Reden und Gleichnisse des Tschuang-Tse. Leipzig, Insel, 1914.

Die jüdische Bewegung: Gesammelte Aufsätze und Ansprachen. Berlin, Jüdischer Verlag, 2 vols., 1916, 1921.

Vom Geist des Judentums. Leipzig, Wolff, 1916.

Ereignisse und Begegnungen. Leipzig, Insel, 1917.

Völker, Staaten und Zion. Vienna, Löwit, 1917.

Mein Weg zum Chassidismus: Erinnerungen. Frankfurt, Rütten and Loening, 1918.

Cheruth: Eine Rede über Jugend und Religion. Vienna, Löwit, 1919.

Der heilige Weg. Frankfurt, Rütten and Loening, 1919.

Worte an die Zeit: vol. 1, *Grundsätze*, and vol. 2, *Gemeinschaft.* Munich, Dreiländer Verlag, 1919.

Die Rede, die Lehre, and das Lied. Leipzig, Insel, 1920.

Der Grosse Maggid und seine Nachfolge. Frankfurt, Rütten and Loening, 1922.

Ich und Du. Leipzig, Insel, 1922; as *I and Thou*, Edinburgh, Clark, 1937; New York, Scribner, 1958.

Reden uber das Judentum. Frankfurt, Rütten and Loening, 1923.

Das verborgene Licht. Frankfurt, Rütten and Loening, 1924.

Rede uber das Erzieherische. Berlin, Schneider, 1926.

Des Baal-Schemp-Tow Unterweisung im Umgang mit Gott. Hellerau, Hegner, 1927.

Die chassidischen Bücher: Gesamtausgabe. Hellerau, Hegner, 1928.

Hundert chassidische Geschichten. Berlin, Schocken, 1930.

Das Kommende: Untersuchungen der Entstehungsgeschichte des messianischen Glaubens. Berlin, Schocken, 1932; as *Kingship of God*, New York, Harper, 1967.

Zwiesprache. Berlin, Schocken, 1932.

Kampf um Israel: Reden und Schriften (1921-1932). Berlin, Schocken, 1933.

Erzählungen von Engeln, Geistern und Dämonen. Berlin, Schocken, 1934; as *Tales of Angels, Demons and Spirits*, New York, Hawk's Well Press, 1958.

Deutung des Chassidismus. Berlin, Schocken, 1935.

Die Frage an den Einzelnen. Berlin, Schocken, 1936; as *Between Man and Man*, London, Kegan Paul, 1947; Boston, Beacon Press, 1955.

Die Schrift und ihre Verdeutschung, with Franz Rosenzweig. Berlin, Schocken, 1936.

Die Stunde und die Erkenntnis: Reden und Aufsätze, 1933-1935. Berlin, Schocken, 1936.

Zion als Ziel und Aufgabe. Berlin, Schocken, 1936.

Die Forderung des Geistes and die geschichtliche Wirklichkeit. Leipzig, Schocken, 1938.

Worte an die Jugend. Berlin, Schocken, 1938.

Torat haneviim. Jerusalem, Mosad Bialik, 1942.

Bfardes hachasidut. Tel Aviv, Mosad Bialik, 1945.

Bein Am learzo. Jerusalem, Schocken, 1945.

Darko shel Adam (meolam hahassidut). Jerusalem, Mosad Bialik, 1945.

For the Sake of Heaven. Philadelphia, Jewish Publication Society, 1945.

Moshe. Jerusalem, Shocken, 1945; as *Moses: The Revelation and the Covenant*, Oxford, East West Library, 1946; New York, Harper Torchbooks, 1958.

Mamre: Essays in Religon. Melbourne, University Press, 1946.

Netivot beutopia. Tel Aviv, Am Oved, 1947; as *Paths in Utopia*, London, Routledge, 1949; Boston, Beacon Press, 1958.

Tales of the Hasidim: The Early Masters. New York, Schocken, 1947.

Ten Rungs: Hasidic Sayings. New York, Schocken, 1947.

Dialogisches Leben: Gesammelte philosophische und pädagogische Schriften. Zurich, Müller, 1947.

Das Problem des Menschen. Heidelberg, Schneider, 1945.

Israel and the World: Essays in a Time of Crisis. New York, Schocken, 1948.

Hasidism. New York, Philosophical Library, 1948; new translations as *Hasidism and Modern Man*, New York, Horizon Press, 1958, and *The Origin and Meaning of Hasidism*, New York, Horizon Press, 1960.

Tales of the Hasidim: The Later Masters. New York, Schocken, 1948.

Der Weg des Menschen, nach der chassidischen Lehre. Jerusalem, n.p., 1948; as *The Ways of Man, According to the Teachings of Hasidism*, London, Routledge, and Chicago, Wilcox and Follett, 1950.

The Prophetic Faith. New York, Macmillan, 1949.

Die Erzählungen der Chassidim. Zurich, Manesse, 1950.

Israel und Palästina: Zur Geschichte einer Idee. Zurich, Artemis, 1950; as *Israel and Palestine: The History of an Idea*, London, East and West Library, and New York, Farrar Straus, 1952.

Hazedek vehaavel al pi Zror mismorei tehillim. Jerusalem, Magnes Press, 1950.

Two Types of Faith. London, Routledge, 1951; New York, Macmillan, 1952.

At the Turning: Three Addresses on Judaism. New York, Farrar Straus, 1952.

Images of Good and Evil. London, Routledge, 1952.

Die chassidische Botschaft. Heidelberg, Schneider, 1952.

Eclipse of God: Studies in the Relation Between Religion and Philosophy. New York, Harper, 1952; London, Gollancz, 1953.

Right and Wrong: An Interpretation of Some Psalms. London, SCM Press, 1952; expanded version as *Good and Evil: Two Interpretations*, New York, Scribner, 1953.

Einsichten: Aus den Schriften gesammelt. Wiesbaden, Insel, 1953.

Hinweise: Gesammelte Essays (1909-1953). Zurich, Manesse, 1953.

Reden über Erziehung. Heidelberg, Schneider, 1953.

Die Schriften über das dialogische Prinzip. Heidelberg, Schneider, 1954.

Der Mensch und sein Gebild. Heidelberg, Schneider, 1955.

Sehertum: Anfang und Ausgang. Cologne, Hegner, 1955.

The Writings of Martin Buber, edited by Will Herberg. New York, Meridian Books, 1956.

Pointing the Way: Collected Essays, edited by Maurice Friedman. London, Routledge, and New York, Harper, 1957.

Das Buch der Preisungen. Cologne, Hegner, 1958.

Bücher und Kündung. Cologne, Hegner, 1958.

Schuld und Schuldgefühle. Heidelberg, Schneider, 1958.

To Hallow This Life: An Anthology, edited by Jakob Trapp. New York, Harper, 1958.

Logos: Zwei Reden. Heidelberg, Schneider, 1962.

Der Jude und sein Judentum: Gesammelte Aufsätze und Reden. Cologne, Melzer, 1963.

Elija: Ein Mysterienspiel. Heidelberg, Schneider, 1963; as "Elijah: A Mystery Play", in *Martin Buber and the Theater*, edited by Maurice Friedman, New York, Funk and Wagnalls, 1969.

Nachlese. Heidelberg, Schneider, 1964.

The Knowledge of Man, edited by Maurice Friedman. London, Allen and Unwin, 1965; New York, Harper, 1966.

Addresses on Judaism. New York, Schocken, 1966.

The Way of Response, edited by Nahum Glatzer. New York, Schocken, 1966.

On Judaism, edited by Nahum Glatzer. New York, Schocken, 1967.

A Believing Humanism: My Testament 1902-1965, edited by Maurice Friedman. New York, Simon and Schuster, 1967.

On the Bible. London, MacDonald, 1968; as *Biblical Humanism: Eighteen Studies*, edited by Nahum Glatzer, New York, Schocken, 1968.

Meetings, edited by Maurice Friedman. La Salle, Illinois, Open Court, 1973.

Other

Briefwechsel aus sieben Jarhzehnten. Heidelberg, Schneider, 3 vols., 1972-75.

Translator, *The Psalms*, from Hebrew into German. Berlin, Schocken, 1936.

Translator, with Franz Rosenzweig, *The Bible*, from Hebrew into German. Berlin, Schneider, 15 vols., 1937.

Editor, *Die Gesellschaft: Sammlung sozialpsychologischer Monographien.* Frankfurt, Rütten and Loening, 40 vols., 1906-12.

Editor, *Kalevala* (Finnish epic). Munich, Müller, 1914.

Editor, *Die vier Zweige des Mabinogi.* Leipzig, Insel, 1914.

Editor, *Der Jude: Eine Monatsschrift.* Berlin, Löwit 8 vols., 1916-24.

Editor, *Meister Eckharts mystische Schriften*, by Gustav Landauer. Berlin, Schanbel, 1920.

Editor, *Der wederne Mensch*, by Gustav Landauer. Potsdam, Kiepenheuer, 1921.

Editor, *Beginnen*, by Gustav Landauer. Cologne, Marcan-Block, 1924.

Editor, with others, *Die Kreatur.* Berlin, Schneider, 3 vols., 1926-30.

Editor, with Ina Britschgi-Schimmer, *Gustav Landauer: Sein Lebensgang in Briefen.* Frankfurt, Rütten and Loening, 2 vols., 1929.

Editor, *Entsiklopedyah Hainochit.* Jerusalem, Misrad Hahinuk vHatarbut, 1959.

*

Critical Studies: *Martin Buber: The Life of Dialogue*, by Maurice Friedman, Chicago, University of Chicago Press, 1955,

revised editions, 1960, 1976 (contains a bibliography); *The Philosophy of Martin Buber*, edited by Paul Arthur Schilpp and Maurice Friedman, La Salle, Illinois, Open Court, 1967; *The Hebrew Humanism of Martin Buber* by Grete Schaeder, Detroit, Wayne State University Press, 1973; *Martin Buber*, by Werner Manheim, New York, Twayne, 1974; *Martin Buber's Life and Work*, by Maurice Friedman, New York, Dutton, 3 vols., 1982-84.

*   *   *

Martin Buber is not concerned with theology, the word *about* God, but with the word that points to man's relation to the God whom he can never know as he is in himself apart from that relation. "God," says Buber in his classic work *I and Thou*, "is the Being that is directly, most nearly, and lastingly over against us, that may properly only be addressed and not expressed." God is the "Absolute Person" who is met whenever we meet our fellow man or the world as "Thou." He is the "eternal Thou" who cannot become an "It." The true God can never be an object of our thought, not even the "Absolute" object from which all others derive. Man becomes aware of the address of God in everything that he meets if he remains open to that address and ready to respond with his whole being. Religion is not philosophy, which seeks to know the absolute as an object of contemplation. Religious knowledge is "mutual contract,...the genuinely reciprocal meeting in the fullness of life between one active existence and another," and faith is entering into this reciprocity, binding oneself in relationship "with an undemonstrable and unprovable, yet even so, in relationship, knowable Being, from whom all meaning comes." The religious essence of every religion is found, says Buber, in "the certainty that the meaning of existence is open and accessible in the actual lived concrete, not above the struggle with reality but in it." This meaning must be confirmed in one's life, verified and authenticated by one's own commitment and response.

Human existence is *either* the direct, reciprocal, present relationship of two persons each of whom enters the relationship with the whole of his person, or even the faithful relationship of one person with the non-human reality that faces him—a tree, a cat, a symphony. *Or* it is the indirect, non-reciprocal, essentially already categorized and fixed relation of active knowing and using subject to passive, known, and used object. Without this latter, "I-It" relation man could not live, for through it he orders his world and builds his economies. Yet one who lives in this relation alone is not truly human. I become a person, an "I," through being called into existence in an "I-Thou" relationship and through responding to this call. "I-Thou" must ever again become "I-It" for me, but this It can be taken up and interpenetrated by the Thou, and it is through this ever-renewed act of entering into reciprocal relationship that I authenticate my humanity.

The real opposition for Buber is not between religion and philosophy but between that philosophy which sees the absolute in universals and hence removes reality into the systematic and the abstract and that which means the bond of the absolute with the particular and hence points man back to the reality of the lived concrete—the immediacy of real meeting with the beings that one encounters. Human truth is participation in Being, not conformity between a proposition and that to which the proposition refers. It cannot claim universal validity, yet it can be exemplified and symbolized in actual life. The meaning of the religious symbol is found not in its universality, but in the fact that it points to a concrete event which witnesses just as it is, in all its concreteness, transitoriness, and uniqueness, to the relation with the Absolute. The religious reality of the meeting with God knows no image of God, nothing comprehensive as object. "It knows only the presence of the Present One."

Man is the completer of God's creation and the initiator of his redemption. He has real independence, accordingly, and "takes part with full freedom and spontaneity" in the dialogue with God that forms the essence of his existence. But he must enter this dialogue with his whole being; for God claims the whole of his personal existence—his social and political life as well as his private relations, his inner intentions as well as his outer acts. The Holy is not a separate and secluded sphere of being. It is open to all spheres of being and it is that through which they find their fulfillment. Only in responsibility to the claim of situations does the soul achieve unification, and, conversely, only as a whole being can man attain the fullness of dialogue.

Only, too, through the wholeness of the person in fulness of response does man become aware of his personal direction—the special way to God that he can realize in his relations with the world and men. Every person in the world represents a created uniqueness given to him not for mere existence but for the fulfillment of a purpose that only he can fulfill. Everything that affects one participates in the realization of this uniqueness. Each moment's new direction is *the* direction if reality is met in lived concreteness. Revelation, correspondingly, is the address that comes to us from the unique present when we become aware that *we* are the person addressed. What we can know of God when we are addressed by these signs of life is never accessible apart from that address. Yet from a succession of such "moment Gods" there may arise for us with a single identity "the Lord of the Voice." Each new Thou renews in all presentness the past experiences of Thou, so that the moments of the past and the moment of the present become simultaneously present and joined in living unity.

The biblical dialogue finds its most significant expression, in Buber's opinion, in the concept of the kingship of God. Israel must make real God's kingship through becoming a holy people, a people that brings all spheres of life under God's rule. There can be no split here between the "religious" and the "social," for Israel cannot become the people of YHWH without faith between human beings. The prophets renewed the Sinai covenant in their rejection of any merely symbolic fulfillment of the divine commission, their fight against the division of community life into a "religious" realm of civic and economic laws. YHWH demands righteousness and justice of the people for the sake of the completion of his work. He seeks not "religion" but community.

The way of the kingship is the way from failure to failure in the dialogue between the people and God. As the failure of the judge leads to the king and the failure of the king to the prophet, so the failure of the prophet in his opposition to the king leads to the conception of two new types of leader who will set the dialogue aright—the Immanuel of Isaiah and the "suffering servant" of Deutero-Isaiah. Isaiah's Messiah is the king of the *remnant* from which the people will renew itself, hence not a divine figure who brings about a redemption which man has merely to accept and enter into but the "perfected one" who, arising from the nucleus that upholds the living connection between God and people, through his word and life leads Israel to turn to God and serve as the beginning of his kingdom. The Messiah, the righteous one, must rise out of the historic loam of man. The core of the messianic hope does not belong to the margin of history but to everywhere and all times, yet a state of redemption exists nowhere and never. "A drop of messianic consummation must be mingled with every hour; otherwise the hour is godless, despite all piety and devoutness."

In *Two Types of Faith* Buber identifies faith as trust (*emunah*) with biblical and Pharisaic Judaism and with the teachings of Jesus, faith in the truth of a proposition (*pistis*) with Greek thought and Paulinism. Whatever was the case with Jesus' "messianic consciousness," he did not summon his disciples to have faith in Christ but preached the unconditional trust in God. Paul and John, in contrast, made faith in Christ the one door to salvation. This meant the abolition of the immediacy between God and man which had been the essence of the biblical covenant and the kingship of God. *Emunah* also precludes the acceptance of the Jewish Law as a separate, objective reality divorced from the dialogue with God whose *Torah*, even when it takes the

form of the commanding word, is not essentially law but God's instruction in his way.

Martin Buber's approach to religion is based not only upon his philosophy of dialogue and his translation and interpretation of the Hebrew Bible, but also upon a lifetime of work retelling the tales and interpreting the teachings of Hasidism, that popular communal mysticism of East European Jewry that Buber almost singlehandedly made a part of the heritage of the Western world. The emphasis on ecstasy that dominated much of Buber's early interpretation of Hasidism gave way in time to an emphasis on the hallowing of the everyday in ordinary life. On the other hand, his understanding of "the true zaddik...who hourly measures the depth of responsibility with the sounding lead of his words" deepened throughout the years as his remarkable characterizations of the early and later masters in the introductions to his two-volume *Tales of the Hasidim* bear witness.

Although recognizing that Hasidism derived its formal teaching entirely from the Zohar and the Lurian Kabbala, Buber contrasts that Kabbalistic gnosis that attempts to see through the contradictions of existence by schematizing the mystery with the "holy insecurity" of Hasidism which stops short and cowers before the reality that outstrips all ready-made knowledge and acquired truth. The passion, alien thoughts, and "evil" urges that seek to take possession of us must be transformed into the substance of real life by giving them direction in genuine dialogue with the world. Only thus can the contradictions which distress us be endured and redeemed. Although he does not bring it out explicitly except in his Hasidic chronicle-novel *For the Sake of Heaven*, Buber is well aware of the double strain that continued and interacted in the succession of Hasidic leaders— the emphasis on hallowing the everyday and sanctifying the profane and the mystical-gnostic teaching of nullifying the particular in order to reach the spiritual essence. In his well-known essay on Buber's interpretation of Hasidism (*The Messianic Idea in Judaism*), Gershom Scholem censures Buber's stress on the hallowing of the everyday and claims that only the gnostic and neo-Platonic elements are essential to Hasidism. In his reply to Scholem, Buber recognizes the presence of *both* streams but justifies his emphasis on the former because of his own role as a "filter" for needs of faith of today. To Scholem the formal teachings of the masters represent the true heart of Hasidism, whereas Buber sees it in the "legendary anecdotes" told by inspired but stammering witnesses which give us insight into the actual communal life of the Hasidim as well as into the host of unique zaddikim who led them.

Buber points to Hasidism as a living antidote to the modern Western crisis that has split the world into spiritual ideals that have no binding power or connection with everyday life. This "concentrated degree of inauthenticity" Buber counters with the Hasidic recognition that the wretchedness of present-day man is founded on the fact that he does not become "humanly holy" in the measure and manner of his personal resources and in the structures of community. Whether in the ambience of Hasidism, the Hebrew Bible, or the "I-Thou" relationship, Buber is concerned about the "eclipse of God" that arises through our refusal to recognize any otherness that transcends human subjectivity:

In our age the I-It relation, gigantically swollen, has usurped, practically uncontested, the mastery and the rule. The I of this relation, an I that possesses all, makes all, succeeds with all, this I that is unable to say Thou, unable to meet a being essentially, is the lord of the hour. This selfhood that has become omnipotent, with all the It around it, can naturally acknowledge neither God nor any genuine absolute which manifests itself to men as of non-human origin. It steps in between and shuts off from us the light of heaven.

—Maurice Friedman

BÜHLER, Karl. German psychologist. Born in Meckesheim, 27 May 1879; emigrated to the United States in 1940. Studied at the University of Freiburg, M.D. 1903; University of Strasbourg, Ph.D. 1904. Served in the German Army during World War I. Married Chalotte Malachowski in 1916; 2 children. Worked with the psychologist Oswald Külpe in Würzburg; Associate Professor, University of Bonn, 1909-13, and University of Munich, 1913-18; Professor of Psychology, Technische Hochschule, Dresden, 1918-22; Professor of Psychology and Head of the Psychological Institute, University of Vienna, 1922-38 (removed and imprisoned by the Nazis); Professor of Psychology, Scholastica College, Duluth, Minnesota, 1939-40, and St. Thomas College, St. Paul, Minnesota, 1940-45. Visiting Professor, Stanford University, California, Johns Hopkins University, Baltimore, and Harvard University, Cambridge, Massachusetts, 1927-28; University of Chicago, 1929. President, German Psychological Association, 1929. Honorary President, International Congress of Psychology, 1960. Recipient: ten year research grant from the Rockefeller Foundation, for the Psychological Institute, Vienna, 1926; Special Prize, City of Vienna, 1962. Honorary doctorate: Wittenberg College, Springfield, Ohio, 1927. *Died 24 October 1963.*

PUBLICATIONS

Psychology and Language Theory

Beiträge zur Lehre von der Umstimmung des Sehorgans. Freiburg, n.p., 1903.
Der Einfluss niederer Temperaturen auf die Funktion der Froschnerven. Strassburg, n.p., 1904.
Studien über Henry Home. Bonn, Bach, 1905.
Die Gestaltwahrnehmungen: Experimentelle Untersuchungen zur psychologischen und ästhetischen Analyse der Raum- und Zeitanschauung. Stuttgart, Spemann, 1913.
Die Geistige Entwicklung des Kindes. Jena, Fischer, 1918.
Abriss der geistigen Entwicklung des Kindes. Leipzig, Quelle and Meyer, 1919; as *The Mental Development of the Child: A Summary of Modern Psychological Theory.* London, Kegan Paul, and New York, Harcourt Brace, 1930.
Handbuch der Psychologie. Jena, Fischer, 1922.
Die Krise der Psychologie. Jena, Fischer, 1927.
Ausdruckspsychologie. Jena, Fischer, 1934.
Sprachtheorie: Die Darstellungsfunktion der Sprache. Jena, Fischer, 1934.
Die Zukunft der Psychologie und die Schule. Vienna, Deutscher Verlag für Jugend und Volk, 1936.
Die Gestaltprinzip im Leben der Menschen und Tiere. Berne, Huber, 1960.
Die Axiomatik der Sprachwissenschaften, edited by Elizabeth Ströker. Frankfurt, Klostermann, 1969; as "The Axiomatization of the Language Sciences," in *Karl Bühler: Semiotic Foundations of Language Theory*, by Robert E. Innis, New York and London, Plenum Press, 1982.

Other

Editor, *Vorlesungen über Psychologie*, by Oswald Külpe. Leipzig, Herzel, 1922.

*

Critical Studies: "Symposium on Karl Bühler's Contributions to Psychology," in *Journal of General Psychology* (Provincetown, Massachusetts), 75, 1966; *Karl Bühler: Semiotic Foundations of Language Theory* by Robert E. Innis, New York and London, Plenum Press, 1982; *Bühler-Studien* edited by Achim Eschbach, Frankfurt, Suhrkamp, 1983.

*   *   *

Karl Bühler was arguably the greatest psycholinguist and psychologically-oriented language theorist of the first half of the 20th century. His work displays, from the very beginning, a marvelous combination of synthesis and original thought, and he has wielded, primarily through his great book on language theory, an enormous influence on later thinkers of divers provenience, such as Karl Popper (one of his students in Vienna), E.H. Gombrich, Jan Mukařovský, Roman Jakobson, Susanne Langer, and Michael Polanyi. His writings represent a goldmine of unexploited insights for psychology, epistemology, linguistics, and semiotics in general, as well as for their various points of intersection. Bühler's early research, which concentrated, though not exclusively, on perceptual and developmental problems and which had a fundamentally Gestalt theoretical orientation, gradually gave way to a semiotic approach, culminating in three books written when he was at the height of his powers, in the late 1920's and 1930's, and which constitute a kind of semiotic trilogy. They contain the most mature and complete exposition of Bühler's ideas on a wide range of issues and problems and establish his permanent place in 20th century thought.

In his *Die Krise der Psychologie* of 1927 Bühler utilized the Saussurian thesis of the double-faced nature of the sign—that it is both a material structure and a *Sinngebilde* or meaning-structure—and the distinction between signals, indexes, and symbols to show how it was possible to thematize and to reconcile the three autonomous object domains and methodologies of psychological theory. The signal, which steered externally verifiable and correlated social behavior, became the key to behaviorism, a position echoed in the lectures of the American philosopher and social psychologist G.H. Mead. The index, discovered in the analysis of perception, became the key to introspective psychology which was concerned with the problems of sensations and with the experiential phenomena of consciousness. The symbol, as an ideal sense-bearing structure, became the key to the culturally-oriented approach of Dilthey, Simmel, Spranger, and others. This turning to the sense-functions of signs and away from their material embodiment as such made it possible to show the complex unified structure of a psychology conceived in the semiotic key and to build psychological theory around the concept of sense (*Sinn*) or meaning.

The distinction between indexes, signals, and symbols allowed Bühler to establish his famous trichotomy of linguistic functions—or, more generally, of sign functions and of "semantic directions"—which became the foundation of Roman Jakobson's expansion to a sixfold functional matrix in his classic essay "Linguistics and Poetics." The expressive function, manifested in indexes, was directed toward and revealed the interiority of the speaker or sender of linguistic signs. The appellative function, manifested in signals, was directed toward steering the bahavior of the addressee. The representational function, manifested in symbols as bearers of articulate content, was directed toward "things and states of affairs" whose intelligibility they were meant to delineate. These three functions were abstract "moments read off from a concrete speech-event, though usually only one was dominant at any one time. To these three functions, using them explicitly as his own basis, Jakobson added the phatic, the poetic, and the metalingual.

At the heart of Bühler's approach to psychological, linguistic, and expression theory lay the principle of abstractive relevance, derived from phonology's distinction between phones and phonemes. Imminent in de Saussure's work, made explicit in that of Trubetzkoy and Sapir, the point of this principle is that a sign functions not by reason of its material character but by virtue of socially constituted abstract characteristics, ideal properties or marks. Bühler was one of the first to understand the immense theoretical importance of phonology and of the abstractive procedures underlying the grasp of phonemes not just for language theory but also for psychology, expression theory, and especially for the theory of knowledge. The grasp of phonemes became the model for the grasp of sense, meaning, and intelligibility as such and the key to the thorny and long standing problem of abstraction in traditional epistemology, for the tacit selectivity built into our grasp of diacritical features of phonic units was a paradigm for cognitional processes quite generally and not just in the domain of sign perception.

Phonological theory also relied upon Gestalt characteristics and Gestalt theoretical procedures, which were similarly crucial in determining the sense of a sign or system of signs. While these Gestalt components were important for Bühler's work in many respects—a topic to which he returned at the end of his life—it was in his theory of metaphor that the emergent, non-summative character of metaphorical perception and expression was most fruitfully discussed. The perceptual fusion of disparate data into novel foci is potentiated in metaphor, where two or more autonomous semantic spaces are joined together on the basis of certain shared abstract characteristics. Bühler anticipated by decades the later so-called interaction theory of metaphor of Black, Beardsley, and others, rooting it more securely in general epistemological and psychological principles.

Bühler's language theory, developed most fully in his masterwork *Sprachtheorie*, was built around the irreducible distinction between pointing and symbolizing, giving rise to his famous two-field theory. The index-field—later called the field of shifters by Jakobson, Benveniste and others—is a linguistic species of pointing and involves the intuitive, perceptual sharing of a common spatial or temporal framework. The symbol-field carries the concepts and abstract schemata of intelligible content which do not demand perceptual fulfillment. The dialectic between these two fields and their inseparable joining together make up—along with the irreducible distinction between words and sentences—the specificity of language as a representational instrument, the aspect of language in which Bühler was most interested. The segmentation of experience, and hence of the "world", through linguistic signs is creative and selective for Bühler, and in his discussion of linguistic fields and of linguistic schemata Bühler continued, set within a proper context, and refined the linguistic field theories of the German tradition originating primarily with von Humboldt; he also contributed to the linguistic relativity problem in a way that has still not been adequately explored.

For Bühler language was not a form of abstract algebra, an independent system of signifiers. Not only was it a species of primarily social action—a notion that contrasts with Husserl's act-theory of meaning and language, which Bühler accepted in modified form, and that anticipates the later work of Wittgenstein, Austin, and Searle—but the factual or material knowledge (*Sachwissen*) of the language users was a permanent necessary supplement to our understanding of language structures on both the syntactic and semantic levels. The linguistic autonomism of much of contemporary language theory is directly opposed by Bühler's work. All throughout this work there is a constant attempt to balance the psychological, the abstract, and the social dimensions of language as well as to draw many interesting parallels with other non-linguistic sign and symbol systems such as film and graphs. Indeed Bühler's book on expression theory, which remains unexploited for later work in paralinguistic phenomena, uses the model developed in his "The Axiomatization of the Language Sciences" to construct a semiotic analysis of the complex field of expressions.

Bühler's heuristic fertility is immense. His focussing on the interrelations between signs, language, and perception and his methodological sophistication join him to that oft-remarked, but even now still inadequately understood, current of reflection that characterized Viennese thought in the early 20th century, represented by such names as Sigmund Freud, Karl Kraus, Ludwig Wittgenstein, and many others, comparison with whom in no way diminishes the originality and power of his work.

—Robert E. Innis

BURNHAM, James. American social philosopher and journalist. Born in Chicago, Illinois, 22 November 1905. Studied at Princeton University, B.A. 1927; Oxford University, B.A. 1929, M.A. 1932. Married Marcia Lightner in 1934; 3 children. Professor of Philosophy, New York University, 1929-53. Editor, with Philip E. Wheelwright, *The Symposium*, 1930-33. Member, Editorial Board, *National Review*, since 1955. Address: Kent, Connecticut, 06757, U.S.A.

PUBLICATIONS

Social Philosophy

Introduction to Philosophical Analysis, with Philip E. Wheelwright. New York, Holt, 1932.
The People's Front: The New Betrayal. New York, Pioneer, 1937.
How to Fight the War: Isolation, Collective Security, Relentless Class Struggle (pamphlet). New York, Socialist Workers Party, 1938.
The Managerial Revolution: What Is Happening in the World. New York, Day, 1941; London, Cape, 1942.
The Machiavellians, Defenders of Freedom. New York, Day, and London, Putnam, 1943.
The Struggle for the World. New York, Day, and London, Cape, 1947.
The Case for De Gaulle: A Dialogue between André Malraux and James Burnham. New York, Random House, 1948.
The Coming Defeat of Communism. New York, Day, and London, Cape, 1950.
Containment or Liberation: An Inquiry into the Aims of United States Foreign Policy. New York, Day, 1953.
The Web of Subversion: Underground Networks in the United States Government. New York, Day, 1954.
Congress and the American Tradition. Chicago, Regnery, 1959.
Suicide of the West. New York, Day, 1964.
Dialectic of American Foreign Policy. Johannesburg, University of Witwatersrand, 1966.
The War We Are In. New York, Arlington House, 1967.

Other

Editor, *What Europe Thinks of America*, by Julian Amery and others. New York, Day, 1953.

*   *   *

James Burnham is one of the leading intellectuals of the American political Right. As resident commentator on international relations for the *National Review* since the 1950s when he was a major cold warrior, his columns have influenced the thinking of the entire spectrum of the Right, including numerous American politicians. Burnham was a disciple of Trotsky in his youth, but the apparent political inconsistency of his shift from Left to Right is a superficial one; underlying his politics then and now is a consistent distaste for the liberal consensus in America, an intense hatred of Stalinism, and a suspicion of democracy.

Burnham's most noted work, *The Managerial Revolution*, developed from his confrontation with Trotsky. Burnham saw an inexorable trend toward managerial rule in advanced industrial societies because they depended upon technological authority and rational bureaucratic organization of the political system and the economy. He argued that the Soviet Union under Stalin partook of that inexorable trend just as capitalist states did. The technological necessities of advanced industrial societies created a new class with new power imperatives but with control of the mode of production which made the realization either of socialism or of liberal democracy impossible. Trotsky had argued that the Bolshevik Revolution, though betrayed by Stalin and his bureaucrat-henchmen, was nonetheless a genuine proletarian movement and had laid the foundations of socialism in Russia. The proletariat would rise, under the duress of war, throw off Stalin and regenerate socialism. For Trotsky in 1940 the Soviet Union could exert a positive and progressive revolutionary force in foreign affairs (in Eastern Europe and Asia) despite the fact that it was a regime of repression and chauvinism. Others rejected Stalinism on empirical grounds of its domestic and foreign policies, but Burnham devised a social theory, which has been popularized and criticized until many have forgotten its origins in the Burnham-Trotsky debate on the Left. (The theory was itself a popularization of the criticism levelled at Marxism by Weber and Michels. A theory of bureaucracy as an alternative source of power, neither capitalist nor socialist, but a phenomenon of "modern" society, was impossible for orthodox marxists.)

During the Second World War Burnham published *The Machiavellians* which presented modern elitist theory (Michels, Mosca, Pareto and Sorel) to an American audience in a two-pronged attack on socialism and democracy. Michels' "iron law of oligarchy", Mosca's theory of elites, Sorel's belief in the activating power of myth and of violence and Pareto's view of politics as the habits and prejudices of human beings and the ideologies which justify them were all joined in a new Burnham thesis that liberty was best preserved by an elite which could divorce ethics from politics and could perpetuate the necessary myths to hold society together and enable it to act. The question of the temper and talent of the elite became an essential issue for Burnham in the post-war period, and his judgment of the temper and talent of the American liberal democratic elite was a negative one.

American liberal democracy was likely to fail to meet the challenge of aggressively expansionist Stalinism. Burnham saw the world as faced with total war, the outcome of which would be the domination of the world by a single state which possessed the technological capacity (weaponry and industry) and an elite willing to use that capacity. In his mind, the communists were a monolithic movement, committed to world domination and to that threat Americans responded with mere defensive and defeatist tactics, the Marshall Plan or containment. In 1950 Burnham advocated the United States take advantage of the balance of terror of nuclear weapon superiority and wage economic and propoganda warfare on Russia and her satellites. He advocated the "liberation" of Eastern Europe.

Burnham's Machiavellianism might have led him to the conservative position of a Churchill or Walter Lippmann which separated the ideology of communism from Russian *realpolitik*. Conservatives argued Russian national interests and traditional foreign policy aims could be met and countered by traditional diplomacy, by power politics. Burnham, however, denied the cold war was fundamentally a power struggle, that the aims of the United States and the Soviet Union could have a common basis. Ideology drives the totalitarian state in an unending conflict with all other regimes, and here Burnham seems to have turned Marx around and made ideology the driving force rather than the reflection of the class conflict. For Burnham there are many tactics in the war waged by the communists, including deStalinization, coexistence and permanent revolution, but there are merely differences in tactics, not in fundamentals or ultimate goal. Tracing or responding to these changes in tactics over the last 30 years, Burnham has not added to his social theory. Though his ideas may be widely held in certain segments of American society, he has not maintained the celebrity of the late 1940s and early 1950s.

—Myrna Chase

BURT, Cyril (Ludovic). British psychologist. Born in London, 3 March 1883. Educated at Christ's Hospital, 1894-1901; studied at Jesus College, Oxford, M.A. 1906, D.Sc. 1916; Postgraduate Research Scholar, Würzburg University, 1908; John Locke Scholar in Mental Philosophy, Oxford University, 1908. Married Joyce Woods in 1931. Lecturer in Experimental Psychology, University of Liverpool, 1909-13; Assistant Lecturer, Psychological Laboratory, Cambridge University, 1913-14; Psychologist, Department of Education, London County Council, 1913-32; Professor of Educational Psychology, 1924-31, Professor of Psychology, 1932-50, and Professor Emeritus, 1950-71, University of London. Consulting Editor, *Encyclopaedia Britannica*; Editor, *British Journal of Statistical Psychology*. Member, Advisory Committee on Personnel Selection, British War Office; National Institute of Industrial Psychology; Industrial Health Research Board; British Psychological Society (President, 1940); and Mensa (President, 1960-70); Chairman, Psychological Committee, Industrial Health Research Board, Medical Research Council; Governor and Almoner, Christ's Hospital. Honorary doctorate: University of Aberdeen; University of Reading. Honorary Fellow, Jesus College. Knighted, 1946. *Died* (in London) *10 October 1971*.

PUBLICATIONS

Psychology

The Distribution and Relations of Educational Abilities. London, King, 1917.
Mental and Scholastic Tests. London, King, 1921.
Report of an Investigation upon Backward Children in Birmingham. Birmingham, City of Birmingham Education Committee, 1921.
Handbook of Tests for Use in School. London, King, 1923.
The National Institute Group Test of Intelligence. London, National Institute of Industrial Psychology, 1923.
The Young Delinquent. London, University of London Press, and New York, Appleton, 1925.
The Northumberland Standardized Tests: Test I, Arithmetic, Test II, English; Test III, Intelligence; Manual of Instructions. London, University of London Press, 1925.
A Study of Vocational Guidance, with others. London, H.M. Stationers Office, 1926.
The Measurement of Mental Capacities (lecture). London, Oliver and Boyd, 1927.
How the Mind Works, with others. London, Allen and Unwin, 1933.
The Subnormal Mind. London, Oxford University Press, 1935.
The Backward Child. London, University of London Press, 1937.
The Factors of the Mind. London, University of London Press, 1940.
Intelligence and Fertility. London, Hamish Hamilton, 1946.
The Causes and Treatment of Backwardness (lecture). London, National Children's Home and University of London Press, 1952.
A Psychological Study of Typography. London, Cambridge University Press, 1959.
Psychology and Psychical Research (lecture). London, Society for Psychical Research, 1968.
The Gifted Child. London, Hodder and Stoughton, 1975.
E.S.P. and Psychology, edited by Anita Gregory. London, Weidenfeld and Nicolson, 1975.

Other

"Autobiography," in *History of Psychology in Autobiography, IV,* edited by E.G. Boring and H.S. Langfield. Worcester, Massachusetts, Clark University Press, 1951.

Critical Studies: *Stephnaos: Studies in Psychology Presented to Cyril Burt*, edited by Charlotte Banks and P.L. Broadhurst, London, University of London Press, 1965; *Cyril Burt: Psychologist* by L.S. Hearnshaw, Ithaca, New York, Cornell University Press, 1979.

*   *   *

Cyril Burt was one of the pioneers in Great Britain in the development of psychology as an applied scientific discipline. He may be regarded essentially as a follower and disciple of the eminent Victorian scientist, Sir Francis Galton. Galton was one of the founders of differential psychology, which stresses the individual variability of human beings, and in particular the role of heredity in causing these variations. Burt, like Galton, was especially interested in differences in general ability, or intelligence, and its study constituted the central theme of his professional life.

Burt first contacted Galton during boyhood, as his father, a country physician, was medical adviser to the Galton family. This was one of the factors that decided Burt to take up psychology. At Oxford he studied the subject under William McDougall, and shortly after graduation assisted McDougall in an investigation on intelligence. The results of this enquiry were published in 1909 and set the pattern for much of Burt's subsequent work. Burt concluded, and he always continued to maintain, that there was a "general factor" of intelligence and that the level of an individual's ability was largely determined by heredity.

Burt's first post was at the University of Liverpool, where he worked as a psychologist in the department of physiology directed by Sir Charles Sherrington. In Liverpool he continued and extended his work on intelligence, and devised a number of tests for its measurement, in particular his well-known reasoning tests.

In 1913 Burt left Liverpool on being appointed psychologist to the Education Department of the London County Council. This was a notable appointment, as it was the first official post for a psychologist in Great Britain outside the walls of the universities. During the 19 years he worked as L.C.C. psychologist Burt carried out, quite apart from a great deal of routine testing and clinical work, a number of highly influential investigations. He made a detailed survey of the distribution of educational abilities among the school population of a large area of central London with a view to determining the number of subnormal pupils requiring special educational treatment and also the number of extremely bright children suitable for the award of scholarships. He devised a whole series of mental and scholastic tests for measuring educational abilities, tests which were extensively used for at least a generation. He made special investigations into the problems of juvenile delinquency, and educational backwardness, and his books on both these topics became classics. In behalf of the National Institute of Industrial Psychology, which had been set up in London after the end of the First World War, he established a system of vocational guidance which remained in use for nearly half a century. He was also largely instrumental in promoting child guidance on the American model in Great Britain. During this period Burt's reputation steadily increased, and he was frequently called on for advice by government bodies. In particular the Board of Education, as it was then termed, relied very largely on his advice in drawing up the plan of selective education, which, with some modifications, was finally incorporated in the Education Act of 1944. This involved the separation of children at the age of eleven into separate secondary schools on the basis of their intelligence and general educational abilities. Later, during the Second World War, Burt's advice was again called upon by the armed services, particularly in connection with the use of psychological methods of personnel selection and placement. There is no doubt that Burt's years at the London County Council were highly productive. He estab-

lished the pattern of psychological work in the fields of education and child guidance, and he greatly improved the tests which constituted the basic tools of the psychologist. He collected a great deal of research data himself and created a lively school of research students at the London teachers' training college where he was Professor of Educational Psychology.

In 1932 Burt resigned from his London County Council post on his appointment to the chair of psychology at University College, London, recently vacated by Charles Spearman. The centre of Burt's interest now moved from data collection to statistical methods of analysis. In particular he devoted himself to developing the technique of factor analysis, originally devised by his predecessor, Spearman. Burt had used this technique in several of his earlier investigations; he now went much more fully into its theoretical and mathematical foundations, and his methods and his conclusions began to diverge from those of Spearman. His mathematics became much more sophisticated, and he arrived at a hierarchical scheme of factors, general, group, and specific, which gained wide support from British psychologists, though not so much in America. After the war, in collaboration with Godfrey Thomson of Edinburgh, he founded and edited the *British Journal of Statistical Psychology*.

Burt retired in 1950, but remained actively writing up to the time of his death 21 years later. During this period, partly as a result of illness, and partly as a result of personal set-backs, Burt became increasingly alienated from his fellow psychologists, and his views, particularly on educational selection and the influence of heredity on ability, came more and more under attack. Burt, who always strove to be pre-eminent, struck back vigorously. He was constantly involved in controversy. It was during this period that he published his now notorious work on twins. The study of identical twins is an extremely important source of material for determining the influence of heredity, and Burt claimed to have collected the largest number of separated identical twins ever recorded. On the basis of this alleged study he calculated that heredity played a predominant part in determining the level of intelligence. His results were widely quoted in literature, and were regarded as a main plank of the hereditarian case. It was not till after his death in 1971 that serious anomalies were discovered in Burt's results. For a time there was some uncertainty as to whether these anomalies were the result of carelessness or were fraudulent. An examination of Burt's correspondence and diaries, however, showed beyond doubt that Burt had not carried out the research on twins that he claimed to have carried out, and that he was not in contact with the assistants whom he alleged were helping him. There remained no question that during the latter period of his life Burt did fake his results. His reputation, therefore, suffered a catastrophic decline. Nevertheless, the valuable work that Burt did in the early part of his career in establishing applied psychology as a profession still deserves recognition. He was in many ways an extremely talented person, and his downfall was a tragedy.

—Leslie Hearnshaw

BUSONI, Ferruccio (Dante Michelangeliolo Benvenuto). Italian pianist, composer, and theorist of music. Born in Empoli, 1 April 1866. Gave his first piano recitals in Trieste, 1873, and in Vienna, 1876; studied with Wilhelm Mayer in Graz, 1880-81; elected to the Reale Accademia Filarmonica of Bologna, 1882; studied in Leipzig and began his career as a recitalist in 1888. Married Gerda Sjöstrand in 1890; 2 sons. Professor of Piano at the Conservatoire, Helsingfors, Finland, 1889-90; lived and concertized in America, 1891-94: taught at the New England Conservatory, 1892; settled in Berlin, giving master classes, teaching composition and making extensive concert tours until 1913;

Director, Liceo Rossini, Bologna, 1913-14; lived in Switzerland during World War I and returned to Berlin in 1920 as Professor at the Akademie der Künste. Recipient: Rubinstein Prize, 1890. Honorary doctorate: University of Zurich, 1919. *Died* (in Berlin) *27 July 1924.*

PUBLICATIONS

Music Theory

Lehre von der Übertragung von Orgelwerken auf das Klavier. Leipzig, Breitkopf und Härtel, 1904; reprinted in *Bach-Busoni gesammelte Ausgabe,* 1920.

Entwurf einer neuen Ästhetik der Tonkunst. Trieste, 1907; as *Sketch of a New Esthetic of Music,* New York, Schirmer, 1911.

Versuch einer organischen Klavier-Notenschrift. Leipzig, Breitkopf und Härtel, 1910; reprinted in *Bach-Busoni gesammelte Ausgabe,* 1920.

Von der Einheit der Musik. Berlin, Hesse, 1922.

Über die Möglichkeit der Oper und über die Partitur des "Doktor Faust." Leipzig, Breitkopf und Härtel, 1926; reprinted in *Wesen und Einheit der Musik,* 1956.

Scritti e pensieri sulla musica, edited by Luigi Dallapiccola and Guide Gatti. Florence, Monnier, 1941.

Ferruccio Busoni: Wesen und Einheit der Musik, edited by Joachim Herrmann. Leipzig, Hesse, 1956.

The Essence of Music and Other Papers. London, Rockliff, and New York, Philosophical Library, 1957.

Other

Briefe an seine Frau, edited by Frederich Schnapp. Zurich, Rotapfel, 1935; as *Letters to His Wife,* New York, Da Capo Press, 1975.

Editor, *Bach-Busoni gesammelte Ausgabe.* Leipzig, Breitkopf und Härtel, 8 vols., 1920.

*

Critical Studies: *Ferruccio Busoni: A Biography,* by Edward J. Dent, Oxford, Clarendon Press, 1933; *Down Among the Dead Men,* by Bernard van Dieren, London, Oxford University Press, 1935; *Ferruccio Busoni,* by Hans Heinz Stuckenschmidt, London, Calder and Boyars, 1970.

*

MUSICAL WORKS

Busoni's major works include an opera, *Doktor Faust* (1916-24, completed by Philipp Jarnach, 1925); four Orchestral Suites (1888, 1895, 1911, 1917); a Concerto for Violin and Orchestra (1897); a Concerto for Piano, Orchestra, and Male Chorus (1904); *Six Sonatinas* (1910-20), *Six Elegies* (1910-19), and the *Fantasia Contrappuntistica* (1912) for solo piano, and numerous transcriptions including the Bach *Chaconne* from the *Violin Partita #2* transcribed for the piano. For detailed listings of Busoni's original works and transcriptions, see *Ferruccio Busoni: A Biography,* by Edward J. Dent, Oxford, Clarendon Press, 1933, and "Ferruccio Busoni" by Helmut Wirth in *The New Grove Encyclopedia of Music and Musicians,* edited by Stanley Sadie, London, Macmillan, 1980.

*   *   *

Anyone who studies Ferruccio Busoni's biography can not fail to apply to his life the truth of his own comment on introducing a chorus into the last movement of his *Piano Concerto* (1903-04): "it resembles rather some original inborn quality of a person which in the course of years comes out again in him purified and matured as he reaches the last phase of his transformations." The inborn quality of Busoni is an intense and purifying idealism. It informed his aesthetic theories which in turn explain his compositional practices and attempt to justify them. It was spoken of by his many students. It should be related to his particular style of concertizing. One of the two or three foremost pianists at the turn of the century, Busoni impressed equally by his intellect, emotional intensity, matchless virtuosity, and objectivity. The word "monumental," as Paul Jacobs notes, was often used to describe his style.

The key to all of Busoni's ideas is that of the "oneness" of music. By this term he meant that music has an absolute integrity in and of itself. Busoni holds that there is no exclusively church, concert, or operatic music, for the forms of music are constantly being appropriated by the various musical genres. This concept represents an attempt to liberate music from its conventional forms and to relocate it within a universal sphere, without dehumanizing it by exclusive attention to form. Although he was a profound interpreter of Beethoven, Chopin, and Lizst, Busoni returned for major examples to Bach and Mozart. Thus, in Bach's works, the "little deviations of expression and style are most frequently to be traced back to the instrument assigned to play it". Otherwise, the musical form could have been designated for any genre and scored for any instrument. This emphasis on the objectivity of the musical form led Stravinsky to call Busoni "the first of the neo-Classicists", and indeed Busoni is himself the inventor of the term "Young Classicism". Busoni pursued his ideas of oneness and objectivity with an almost mystical fervor. At the end of his life, in very ill health, he contemplated the essence of music: "even though every single one of these examples *[*a performance, a theory of harmony, a song*]* contains a tiny seed of the supreme whole, in so far as music includes all the elements, it is just because they do fall into sections that they will again be subdivided, as if the vault to heaven were to be torn up into little strips".

A second idea of Young Classicism is the "definite departure from what is thematic and the return to melody again as the ruler of all voices and all emotions". In part, Busoni was reacting to 19th century programme music—he has an uneasy, though by no means uncharitable, relation to Wagner—and to the "hysteria" of neo-expressionism. Also, Busoni wanted to secure "absolute" melody united with an accompanying harmony and "later melted with it into oneness"; "out of this oneness the continually progressive poly-harmony aims to free and liberate itself".

Third, Busoni rejects "subjectivity" in music; he wants to cast off what is "sensuous" and idiosyncratic, a theoretical imperative shared widely in the arts in the first twenty years of the 20th century, from Stravinsky and T.E. Hulme to Pound and Eliot. Busoni described the necessity of an author's "standing back from his work," of taking "a purifying road, a hard way...and the re-conquest of serenity".

Finally, Busoni's Young Classicism looks backward as well as forward in its quest for universality: "It is not through inventing new resources or through individual cleverness that the distance will gradually be reduced, but through an unremitting effort to accumulate all previous achievements and those yet to be achieved; and at the same time we must continue to move away from that which is merely of individual importance and make it give way to the increasingly expansive and inexhaustible development of that which is of more general value." His transcriptions of earlier composers as well as his extensive *Klavierübung* (1918, 1925) reveal an intense preoccupation with the history of music. Busoni's notes and lectures on composers—for he often wrote his programs and taught extensively—are invaluable. His "Mozart Aphorisms" constitute a landmark in the understanding of the composer: "His never-clouded beauty disconcepts"; "Together with the riddle he gives the solution"; "Architecture is next of kin to his art"; "He is universal through his dexterity";

"His smile, which was so human, still shines on us transfigured." Then, there are Busoni's numerous notes on piano playing, where one requirement, as he noted, is foremost: "Anyone who will master the language of art must have nurtured his life through the soul."

Busoni's theories and compositions exerted a potent influence over Varèse, Weill, Vogel, Jarnach, and the modern Italian tradition. His theory of harmony anticipated Hindemith's. His style in concertizing style points forward to that of Arturo Benedetti Michelangeli, whose recording of the Bach-Busoni *Chaconne* is one of the musical peaks of 20th-century performance.

—John Paul Russo

CAGE, John (Milton, Jr.)   American composer and theorist of music.   Born in Los Angeles, California, 5 September 1912. Studied at Pamona College, Claremont, California, 1928-30; studied and travelled abroad, 1930-31; studied with Henry Cowell in New York, and with Richard Bühlig and Arnold Schönberg in California, 1933-34. Married Xenia Kashevaroff in 1935 (divorced, 1945). Composer-accompanist at the Cornish School, Seattle, Washington, 1936-37; taught at the Institute of Design, Chicago, 1941; accompanist and later Musical Director, Merce Cunningham Dance Company, New York, 1944-66; taught at Black Mountain College, North Carolina, summer 1948, 1952, and New School for Social Research, New York, 1956-60; Fellow, Center for Advanced Studies, Wesleyan University, Middletown, Connecticut, 1960-61, 1970; Research Professor and Associate, Center for Advanced Studies, University of Illinois, Urbana, 1967-69; Composer-in-Residence, University of Cincinnati, Ohio, 1967; Artist-in-Residence, University of California at Davis, 1969. Recipient: Guggenheim Fellowship, 1949; National Academy of Arts and Letters award for having "extended the boundaries of musical art", 1949; First Prize, *Woodstock Art Film Festival*, 1951; People to People Committee on Fungi Award, 1964; Thorne Music Fund grant, 1968. Works commissioned by the Boston Symphony Orchestra, Ballet Society, Donaueschinger Musiktage, Montreal Festivals Society, and other groups. Founding Honorary Member, New York Mycological Society, 1962. Member, National Institute of Arts and Letters; American Academy of Arts and Sciences. Address: 101 West 18th Street, New York, New York 10010, U.S.A.

PUBLICATIONS

Music

Virgil Thompson: His Life and Music, with Kathleen Hoover. New York, Yoseloff, 1959.
Silence: Lectures and Writings.   Middletown, Connecticut, Wesleyan University Press, 1961; London, Calder and Boyars, 1968.
A Year from Monday: New Lectures and Writings.   Middletown, Connecticut, Wesleyan University Press, 1967; London, Calder and Boyars, 1968.
Liberations: New Essays on the Humanities in Revolution, with others.   Middletown, Connecticut, Wesleyan University Press, 1971.
M: Writings, '67-72.   Middletown, Connecticut, Wesleyan University Press, 1973.
Empty Words: Writings, 73-78.   Middletown, Connecticut, Wesleyan University Press, 1980.
For the Birds.   London and Salem, New Hampshire, Marion Boyars, 1981.

Other

Diary: Part III.   New York, Something Else Press, 1967.
Diary: Part IV.   New York, S.M.S. Press, 1968.
Notations, with Alison Knowles.   New York, Something Else Press, 1969.
Mushroom Book, with Lois Long and Alexander H. Smith. New York, Hollanders Workshop, 1972.
Writings Through Finnegans Wake.   Tulsa, University of Oklahoma Press, 1978.

*

Critical Studies: *John Cage*, edited by Richard Kostelanetz, New York, Praeger, 1970, and London, Allen Lane, 1971; *Experimental Music: Cage and Beyond* by Michael Nyman, London, Studio Vista, 1974; *Glosses sur John Cage* by Daniel Charles, Paris, Union Générale d'Editions, 1978; *Cage* by Paul Griffiths, London and New York, Oxford University Press, 1981; "Looking Myself in the Mouth" by Yvonne Rainer in *October* (Cambridge, Massachusetts), Summer, 1981.

*

MUSICAL WORKS

Cage's compositions include: *Music for Wind Instruments* (1939); a ballet, *The Seasons* (1947); *Sonatas and Interludes for Prepared Piano* (1947-48); *Music of Changes*, for piano (1950); *4'33"*, tacit for any instruments (1952); *Fontana Mix*, for tape (1958); *HPSCHD* for amplified harpsichord and tape, with Lejaren Hiller (1957-59), etc. For extensive listings of Cage's music, see *John Cage*, edited by Richard Kostelanetz, New York, 1970, London, 1971, and Charles Hamm, "John Cage", in *The New Grove Dictionary of Music and Musicians*, edited by Stanley Sadie, London, Macmillan, 1980.

*   *   *

John Cage's distinction as a "thinker" in this century has been to convince large numbers of American and Western European artists, especially composers, that Eastern philosophies, Zen in particular, are more relevant to contemporary aesthetic interests than Western traditions of thought and art. Almost single-handedly, it seems, Cage has created an important diversionary trend away from Western musical tradition and reinvigorated the intermedia avant-garde movement inherited from Europe. All of Cage's work since the 1950's springs essentially from one idea: the abdication of authority, which translates in Zen terms as transcendence of ego and in aesthetic terms as removal of personal taste and choice from the making of art. Cage has mounted his unique assault on authority (hierarchy, causality, teleology, rules governing harmony and unity and sequence and climax, on necessary connections or logical development, on materials considered intrinsically proper to any medium, etc.) not by working within, through alternative or innovative modes which rework the conventions, as in reform politics, but by seceding from the main body and operating like a separatist or a kind of artist/thinker guerilla.

For Cage the ego exists only to be discarded or transcended; he begins evidently from the position of having an ego which one can *afford* to reject, at least for the purpose of creation, but the conditions that might allow for this (social, psychological, economic, etc.) are never articulated. His position is that the ego and all its trappings get in the way of enjoying life as it is. He urges "an affirmation of life, not an attempt to bring order out of chaos nor to suggest improvements on creation, but simply...waking up to the very life we're living which is so excellent once one gets one's mind and one's desires out of its way and lets it act of its own accord."

But Cage of course is a naturalist (his hobbies are plants and mushrooms, and his favorite author for a decade or more has been Thoreau), and the life he recommends accepting is the ab-cultural one: whatever is left that man has not touched or destroyed or polluted or created in his own image. Not surprisingly, his social/political thought is purely utopian, a field he leaves to Buckminster Fuller, whom he believes has the best or only blueprint for an ideal world. Cage's quarrel with culture is that it separates people, through power mongering (exclusive structures which reflect political realities), from the phenomenal world. "Music," he has said, "has never existed as a separate entity, except in the imagination of 'professional' musicians. It has always opened into nature (the working together or playing together of all the elements) even when it was structured in the opposite direction. The problem was that people paid all their attention to its construction." Cage has avowed over and over that he does not want power (for) himself, and that he wants to destroy it. "When I really began making music...it was to involve myself in noise, because noises escape power, that is, the laws of counterpoint and harmony."

In assessing Cage's thought and influence it should be possible to make sense out of the rationales he developed for his work by linking them with more autobiographical statements, which in turn might suggest some bearing on his early life, for example: "...I don't have absolute pitch. I can't keep a tune. In fact, I have no talent for music. The last time I saw her, Aunt Phoebe said, 'You're in the wrong profession.' "—and, "After I had been studying with him for two years, Schoenberg said, 'In order to write music you must have a feeling for harmony.' I then explained to him that I had no feeling for harmony. He then said that I would always encounter an obstacle, that it would be as though I came to a wall through which I could not pass. I said, 'In that case I will devote my life to beating my head against that wall.' "

Cage's appeal to a higher (or the highest) authority—nature in her manner of operation—leaves worldlier manifestations of authority ironically intact. Put differently, he fled the field of contest, the paternal stake-out, which he might criticize from afar but leave unperturbed in its value schemes and relations of hierarchial identity, just as he wishes to be left free in his own—where "noise" flattens out all distinctions but permits a certain sovereignty of the lone ideologue. Only Cage's psychological naiveté and political idealism grants him this curious privilege. He is certainly the most recent flower and white hope of the entire counter-tradition of the avant-garde, in which the denial of authority has provided an occasion for the most eccentric and outrageous reputations. A pose of egolessness belied by a strong individuality is the subtlest, perhaps most powerful projection of the inner character of the avant-garde. Promising not to try and change anything or go anywhere in particular ("the highest purpose is no purpose at all"), the avant-garde Zen master carves out a kingdom on the far side of the Western mountain.

—Jill Johnston

CAMUS, Albert. French novelist and philosopher. Born in Mondovi, Algeria, 7 September 1913. Studied at the University of Algiers, licence in philosophy and diplôme d'études supérieure, 1936. Married Simone Hié in 1933 (divorced): Francine Faure in 1940; 2 children. Founded the Théâtre du Travail, Algiers, 1936. Worked as a journalist for the *Alger-Républicain*, 1938-40, and *Paris-Soir*, 1942-44. Worked with the Resistance during World War II; Co-Founder and Editor of the newspaper *Combat*, Paris, 1945-47. Reader for Gallimard, Paris, 1947-60. Lectured in the United States, 1946-47, and South America, 1949. Founder, Committee to Aid the Victims of Totalitarian States. Recipient: Medal of the Liberation; Prix de la Critique, for *La Peste*, 1947; Nobel Prize for Literature, 1957. *Died* (killed in an automobile accident) *4 January 1960*.

PUBLICATIONS

Collections

Oeuvres complètes. Paris, Imprimerie Nationale Sauret, 2 vols., 1961-62.
Resistance, Rebellion and Death. London, Hamish Hamilton, and New York, Knopf, 1961.
Théâtre, récits, nouvelles, edited by Roger Quilliot. Paris, Gallimard, Bibliothèque de la Pléiade, 1962.
Essais, edited by Roger Quilliot. Paris, Gallimard, Bibliothèque de la Pléiade, 1965.
Lyrical and Critical, edited by Philip Thody. London, Hamish Hamilton, 1967; as *Lyrical and Critical Pieces*, New York, Knopf, 1968.
Le Premier Camus, suivi des ecrits de jeunesse d'Albert Camus, edited by Paul Viallaneix. Paris, Gallimard, 1973; as *Youthful Writings of Albert Camus*, New York, Knopf, 1976.

Philosophy

L'Envers et l'Endroit. Algiers, Charlot, 1937; as "The Wrong Side and the Right Side," in *Lyrical and Critical*, 1967.
Noces. Algiers, Charlot, 1938; as "Nuptials," in *Lyrical and Critical*, 1967.
Le Mythe de Sisyphe. Paris, Gallimard, 1943; as *The Myth of Sisyphus*, London, Hamish Hamilton, and New York, Knopf, 1955.
Lettres à un ami allemand. Paris, Gallimard, 1945; as "Letters to a German Friend," in *Resistance, Rebellion and Death*, 1961.
Prométhée aux enfers. Paris, Palimurge, 1947; as "Prometheus in the Underworld," in *Lyrical and Critical*, 1967.
Le Minotoure ou la halte d'Oran. Algiers, Charlot, 1950; as "The Minotaur, or Stopping in Oran," in *Lyrical and Critical*, 1967.
Actuelles: Chroniques 1944-48. Paris, Gallimard, 1950; selections in *Resistance, Rebellion and Death*, 1961.
L'Homme révolté. Paris, Gallimard, 1951; as *The Rebel*, London, Hamish Hamilton, 1953; New York, Knopf, 1954.
Actuelles II: Chroniques, 1948-53. Paris, Gallimard, 1953; selections in *Resistance, Rebellion and Death*, 1961.
L'Eté. Paris, Gallimard, 1954; as "Summer," in *Lyrical and Critical*, 1967.
Actuelles: Chronique algérienne, 1939-1958. Paris, Gallimard, 1958; selections in *Resistance, Rebellion and Death*, 1961.
"Reflexions sur la guillotine," in *Reflexions sur la peine capitale*, with Arthur Koestler. Paris, Calmann-Levy, 1957; as "Reflections on the Guillotine," in *Resistance, Rebellion and Death*, 1961.
L'Intelligence et l'échafaud. Liège, Dynamo, 1958; as "Intelligence and the Scaffold," in *Lyrical and Critical*, 1967.
Méditation sur le théâtre et la vie. Liège, Dynamo, 1961.

Fiction

L'Etranger. Paris, Gallimard, 1942; as *The Outsider*, London, Hamish Hamilton, and as *The Stranger*, New York, Knopf, 1946.
La Peste. Paris, Gallimard, 1947; as *The Plague*, London, Hamish Hamilton, and New York, Knopf, 1948.
La Chute. Paris, Gallimard, 1956; as *The Fall*, London, Hamish Hamilton, and New York, Knopf, 1957.
L'Exil et le royaume (short stories). Paris, Gallimard, 1957; as *Exile and the Kingdom*. London, Hamish Hamilton, and New York, Knopf, 1958.
La Mort heureuse (early novel). Paris, Gallimard, 1971; as *A Happy Death*, London, Hamish Hamilton, and New York, Knopf, 1973.

Dramatic Works

La Révolte dan les Asturies: Essai de creation collective.   Algiers, Charlot, 1936.
"Le Malentendu" suivi de "Caligula."   Paris, Gallimard, 1944; as *Caligula and Cross-Purpose*, London, Hamish Hamilton, 1947; New York, New Directions, 1948.
L'Etat de siège.   Paris, Gallimard, 1948; as "State of Siege," in *Caligula and Three Other Plays*, London, Hamish Hamilton, and New York, Knopf, 1958.
Les Justes.   Paris, Gallimard, 1950; as "The Just Assassins," in *Caligula and Three Other Plays*, London, Hamish Hamilton, and New York, Knopf, 1958.
"Le Vie d'artiste: Mimodrame en deux parties," in *Simoün* (Oran), 2, 1953.

Stage adaptations of *Les Esprits*, by Pierre de Larivey (Paris, Gallimard, 1953); *Requiem pour une nonne*, by William Faulkner (Paris, Gallimard, 1957); and *Les Possédés*, by Dostoevsky (Paris, Gallimard, 1959).

Other

Discours de Suède et "L'artist et son temps."   Paris, Gallimard, 1958; as "Speech of Acceptance upon the Award of the Nobel Prize for Literature," in *Resistance, Rebellion and Death*, 1961.
Carnets: mai 1935-février 1942.   Paris, Gallimard, 1962; as *Carnets 1935-1942*, London, Hamish Hamilton, and as *Notebooks Volume I, 1935-1942*, New York, Knopf, 1963.
Carnets II: jan. 1942-mars 1951.   Paris, Gallimard, 1964.
Lettre à Bernanos.   Paris, Manard, 1963.

Translator, *The Last Flower*, by James Thurber, as *La Dernière Fleur*.   Paris, Gallimard, 1952.
Translator, *La Devoción de la Cruz*, by Caldéron, as *La Dévotion à la croix*.   Paris, Gallimard, 1953.
Translator, *Un Caso clinico*, by Dino Buzzati, as *Un Cas intéressant*, in *L'Avant-scène No. 4* (Paris), 1955.

*

Bibliography: *Albert Camus: Essai de bibliographie* by Simone Crespin, Brussels: Commission Belge de Bibliographie, 1960; *Camus: A Bibliography*, by Robert F. Roeming, Madison, University of Wisconsin Press, 1968.

Critical Studies: *Camus*, by Germaine Brée, New Brunswick, New Jersey, Rutgers University Press, revised edition, 1961; *Albert Camus, 1930-1960*, by Philip Thody, London, Hamish Hamilton, 1961.

*   *   *

Albert Camus was born in Mondovi, in what was then French Algeria, in 1913. In August 1914, his father, Lucien Camus, an itinerant agricultural labourer, was killed in the first battle of the Marne. His mother, née Catherine Sintès, of Majorcan descent, went out to work as a charwoman to provide for Camus and his elder brother Lucien, born in 1909. The fact of sharing a three-room flat in the French working class area of Belcaut with five other people but no books did not prevent Camus from winning a scholarship to the lycée in Algiers, and in 1957, when he became the youngest French writer to win the Nobel Prize for Literature, he dedicated his *Discours de Suède* to Louis Germain, the primary school teacher who had given him special lessons. Illness added itself to poverty when Camus fell ill of tuberculosis in 1930. He almost died. He had a number of relapses throughout his life, but it was in a car accident, on January 4th, 1960, that he actually died, with the ticket for the journey he was to have taken by rail in his pocket.

The theme of the absurdity of human life, which runs through the whole of his early work, was thus reinforced in an extraordinarily dramatic manner by his death; and it was as the painter of a world without hope or meaning that he made his immediate reputation, in 1942 and 1943, with the short novel *L'Etranger* and the philosophical essay, *Le Mythe de Sisyphe*. But as he himself wrote, "life will be lived all the more fully because it has no meaning," and the books by which he imposed himself as the most original writer to emerge in the France of the German occupation took up the paganistic themes of his early essays, *Noces* and *L'Envers et l'Endroit*. The inevitability of death, for the early Camus, only heightens the intensity of the pleasures of this life, and his early work is, paradoxically, a hymn to happiness.

In the "second cycle" of his work, with *La Peste* and *L'Homme révolté*, Camus assumes a more humanistic stance, asserting the importance of the individual life against left as well as right-wing totalitarianism and rejecting all political as well as all religious absolutes. His attack on Communism in *L'Homme révolté* led to a famous quarrel with Jean-Paul Sartre in 1952, and the apparently more conservative tenor of his thought emerged when, from 1954 onwards, he seemed to ally himself increasingly with the million or so French settlers in Algeria who were seeking to remain French in face of the demand for independence and armed rebellion of the nine million Arabs. His short novel *La Chute* contained both a brilliantly ironic self-portrait and an apparently greater sympathy for Christianity than the defiant agnosticism of his first and second cycles. The short stories in *L'Exil et le Royaume* showed more of Camus the dedicated literary artist, an aspect of his character reflected by his proclaimed desire to write prose as Mozart wrote music. It was this ambition which he had in mind in devoting his Nobel Prize speeches to the theme of the artist in the modern world, and he expressed his attitude towards the problem of political commitment by saying that it was not the struggle which made men into artists but art itself, and its need for freedom, which forced men into the political struggle.

For his critics, Camus was one of the great betrayers, the working-class lad who became a cold-war warrior, the man who began by denying that the world had any meaning and ended up with a series of humanistic reassurances about the creation, through revolt, of the values of art and moderation. For his admirers, he was a man who celebrated the physical life with the same vigour and for some of the same reasons as D.H. Lawrence; showed himself a shrewder political thinker than Sartre or Simone de Beauvoir; reinvented the technique of story-telling in *L'Etranger*; provided in *La Peste*, some of the best arguments against Christianity; and wrote the clearest French of his generation.

—Philip Thody

CARDOZO, Benjamin N(athan).   American jurist. Born in New York City, 24 May 1870. Studied at Columbia University, New York, B.A. 1889. M.A. 1890; admitted to New York Bar, 1891. Justice of the New York Court of Appeals, 1914-32 (Chief Judge, 1927-32); Associate Justice, Supreme Court of the United States, Washington, D.C., 1932-38. Honorary doctorate: Columbia University, 1915; Yale University, New Haven, Connecticut, 1921; New York University, 1922; University of Michigan, Ann Arbor, 1923; Harvard University, Cambridge, Massachusetts, 1927; St. John's College, New York, 1928; St. Lawrence University, Canton, New York, 1932; Williams College, Williamstown, Massachusetts, 1932; Princeton University, New Jersey, 1932; University of Pennsylvania, Philadelphia, 1932; Brown University, Providence, Rhode Island, 1933; University of Chicago,

1933; Yeshiva University, New York, 1935; University of London, 1936. *Died 9 July 1938.*

PUBLICATIONS

Law

The Jurisdiction of the Court of Appeals of the State of New York. Albany, New York, Banks, 1903.

The Nature of the Judicial Process. New Haven, Connecticut, Yale University Press, and London, Oxford University Press, 1921.

The Growth of the Law (lectures). New Haven, Connecticut, and London, Yale University Press, 1924.

The Paradoxes of Legal Science. New York, Columbia University Press, 1928.

What Medicine Can Do for Law (lecture). New York, Harper, 1929; London, Harper, 1930.

John G. Milburn (lecture). New York, Carnegie Corporation, 1931.

Law and Literature and Other Essays and Addresses. New York, Harcourt Brace, 1931.

Mr. Justice Holmes, with others, edited by Felix Frankfurter. New York, Coward McCann, 1931.

Law Is Justice: Notable Opinions of Mr. Justice Cardozo, edited by A.L. Sainer. New York, Ad Press, 1938.

Selected Writings of Benjamin Nathan Cardozo, edited by Margaret E. Hall. New York, Fallon, 1947.

*

Critical Studies: *The Influence of Judge Cardozo on the Common Law* by Irving Lehman, New York, Doubleday, 1942; *Five Jewish Lawyers of the Common Law,* by Sir Arthur Goodhart, London and New York, Oxford University Press, 1949; *Mr. Justice Cardozo: A Liberal Mind in Action,* by Joseph Percival Pollard, Westport, Connecticut, Greenwood Press, 1970.

* * *

Benjamin N. Cardozo served on the United States Supreme Court for less than six years, from 1932 to 1938, but no other Justice has made such an indelible imprint on the Court in such a short time. His razor-sharp mind, his acknowledged powers of persuasion, and his demonstrated "legal realism" all contributed vitally to the Court during the crucial years of the New Deal.

Cardozo's reputation preceded him to the Supreme Court. When Oliver Wendell Holmes, Jr., the revered elder statesman of American law, retired in 1932, Cardozo was the popular choice to succeed him. He had been serving with great distinction for eighteen years on the prestigious New York Court of Appeals, the last five as Chief Judge; and he was the author of *The Nature of the Judicial Process,* already considered a classic of judicial thinking. President Hoover was reluctant to appoint him because he perceived Cardozo as too "liberal"; furthermore, he would become the second Jew (joining Louis Brandeis) and the third New Yorker on the Supreme Court. But western politicians and journalists pressured the President as much as easterners did. He finally acceded and named Cardozo.

Cardozo's "liberalism," unlike that of Brandeis, had never been overtly political. Rather, it was in the tradition of his predecessor and idol Holmes. For many years, mostly in Court dissents, Holmes had charged that the judiciary had fossilized the legal process: they had become obsessed with logic-chopping, and they adhered slavishly to anachronistic precedents. Holmes' demand for "realism" on the bench echoed sentiments that had been expressed in different ways by Justice John Marshall Harlan in the 1890's and by Chief Justice Roger Taney in the Charles River Bridge case of 1937. In the 20th century, the idea of judicial "realism" paralleled the philosophical pragmatism of William James and John Dewey; in the hands of Louis Brandeis, it was amplified by an insistence on the relevance of economic and social data.

Cardozo's major contribution to the literature of judicial realism was outlined in a series of lectures he delivered at Yale University, subsequently published as *The Nature of the Judicial Process.* In strikingly thought-out and shrewdly documented analysis, he proceeded to de-mystify the Courts, by explaining how judges actually arrive at their decisions.

In a majority of instances, he said, the case and the law are so clear that only one decision is possible. In a lesser number of cases, the law is quite clear, and only the direct application to the particular circumstance is in question. In a still smaller number of cases (but perhaps the most crucial ones), a decision either way might be plausible. In this last-named group, he said, "balancing of judgment," and "testing and sorting of considerations of analogy and logic and utility and fairness" all come into play. These are the cases where the decision will have implications for the future, and "the process in its highest reaches is not discovery, but creation."

In short, judges have no secret access to ultimate Truth; they need hard work, imagination and open minds. This realistic appraisal of how law is generated and interpreted was tantamount to blowing a current of fresh air into the musty temples of Justice.

Cardozo's expertly balanced judgment and astute scholarship had been apparent on the New York Court. Now in 1932 he was joining a bitterly divided Supreme Court at a time of severe crisis. Franklin Roosevelt's New Deal soon began producing a flood of innovative and controversial legislation. Much of it was challenged in lower courts and ultimately would arrive at the Supreme Court. Of the eight sitting Justices, four were extreme conservatives; two voted consistently liberal; and two, including Chief Justice Charles Evans Hughes, were "swing men" who might vote either way.

The first New Deal measure to be voided was a minor portion of the National Industrial Recovery Act. The Court ruled that the President had unconstitutionally delegated administrative powers to Congress, violating the "balance of powers" concept. That argument sounded persuasive, but Cardozo alone dissented, correctly pointing out that the Constitution actually contained no such injunction.

Then the Court, with Cardozo and others dissenting, killed the Railroad Retirement Act, an action that wiped out workers' pensions. "Swing man" Owen Roberts, in his majority decision, relied on familiar conservative interpretations of two Constitutional clauses: that the "interstate commerce clause" did not give Congress regulatory power in this instance (or almost anywhere else), and that the "Due Process" clause of the Fifth Amendment militated against legislative control over business.

Next, and most dramatically, the Court threw out the entire NIRA, which Roosevelt had called the keystone of the New Deal. The Supreme Court was dubbed the "nine old men" and widely ridiculed for stonewalling any efforts at economic recovery. But all nine were not obstacles—only the implacable conservatives ("the four horsemen") and the mercurial, politically ambitious Owen Roberts. Cardozo and his other colleagues were backing most of the New Deal measures. When the conservative majority wiped out the maximum hours-minimum hours provisions of the Guffey Coal Act, Cardozo wrote a lucid and stinging dissent, ridiculing the familiar mechanical interpretations of "interstate commerce" and "Due Process."

In addition to his trenchant analysis of the particulars of each case, Cardozo was demanding flexibility. He deplored the court's attitude that any item of novel legislation was automatically an abdication of "principle" and the Court's acceptance of businessmen's assumptions that any "interference" with existing business practices would have deleterious results.

After the reports surfaced about Roosevelt's "court-packing" plan, and then his resounding re-election in 1936, the balance on the Court suddenly shifted. The "swing men" swung to the other side, giving majority assent to New Deal legislation. Deaths and retirements altered the Court's composition further, and thereafter the old resistance to innovative lawmaking largely vanished. Cardozo found his views congenial to an increasingly large majority, and he wrote some of the strongest opinions in some of the most complex cases—particularly those involving the interstate commerce clause.

Among the most important, couched in Cardozo's idiosyncratic, occasionally florid, prose, were his two decisions sustaining the unemployment insurance and old-age pension provisions of the Social Security Act. The Constitutional bedrock underlying his complicated discussion of Congressional taxing powers was the "general welfare" clause.

Understandably during those New Deal years, economic issues preoccupied Cardozo, and in fact they had dominated Supreme Court activity through much of American history. But the passage of the Espionage and Sedition Acts (and similar state legislation) during World War I spurred new concern about civil rights and began to draw more Court attention. In this area, too, Cardozo made important contributions.

In 1922, when the New York Court of Appeals sustained the conviction of Benjamin Gitlow for violating the New York Criminal Anarchy Act, Cardozo dissented, holding that Gitlow's pamphleteering did not fall under the scope of the act. Three years later, when a conservative Supreme Court upheld the conviction, Justice Edward Sanford injected an interesting aside that later would have momentous consequences. The First Amendment prohibits Congress from abridging the rights of free speech, press and assembly, but it is silent about actions by *state* legislatures. "It is assumed," said Sanford almost casually, that the Fourteenth Amendment, with its guarantees of equal protection to all citizens, means that state laws abridging fundamental freedoms also are unconstitutional.

Cardozo already had staked his ground on the paramount importance of First Amendment freedoms. In an article published before he was appointed to the Supreme Court he wrote: "There shall be no compromise of the freedom to think one's thoughts and speak them, except at those extreme borders where thought merges into action."

In several important cases in 1936 and 1937, Cardozo reiterated this belief. Only in extreme circumstances should there be any governmental intrusion upon the basic liberties of speech, press and assembly: "neither liberty nor justice would exist if they were sacrificed," he said.

Cardozo was not convinced that the other civil liberties outlined in the Bill of Rights came under the same umbrella of protection. In *Hamilton v. Regents*, by convoluted analysis, he upheld a university's right to prescribe military training for all of its male students. In *Palko v. Connecticut* he refused to extend protection against "double jeopardy" when state laws differed.

From hindsight, after the sweeping changes enacted by the Earl Warren Court, Cardozo's position seems no more than moderate. Very clear about the First Amendment freedoms, he was unable to extend that recognition to encompass the significance of other vital rights. But in his own time, Cardozo's approach to civil rights was among the most advanced on any court; he surely was charting the path to the future. In regard to the Court's transformation to economic realities, he already was the future.

—Don Hausdorff

CARNAP, Rudolf.   German philosopher.   Born in Ronsdorf, now Wuppertal, 18 May 1891; emigrated to the United States, 1935: naturalized, 1941. Studied at the University of Freiburg; University of Jena, 1910-14, Ph.D. 1921. Served in the German Army, 1914-18. Married Elizabeth Ina von Stöger in 1933; 4 children. Lecturer in Philosophy, University of Vienna, 1926-30; Professor of Natural Philosophy, German University, Prague, 1931-35; Professor of Philosophy, University of Chicago, 1936-52; Fellow, Institute for Advanced Study, Princeton, New Jersey, 1952-54; Professor of Philosophy, 1954-62, and Research Professor, 1962-70, University of California at Los Angeles. Visiting Professor, Harvard University, Cambridge, Massachusetts, 1936, 1940-41; University of Illinois, Urbana, Spring, 1950. Editor, with others, *Erkenntnis*, 1930-37. Recipient: Rockefeller Fellowship, 1942-44. Honorary doctorate: Harvard University, 1936; University of California, 1963; University of Michigan, Ann Arbor, 1965; University of Oslo, 1969. Fellow, American Academy of Arts and Sciences. Corresponding Fellow, British Academy. *Died 14 September 1970.*

PUBLICATIONS

Philosophy

Der Raum: Ein Beitrag zur Wissenschaftslehre.   Berlin, Reuther and Reichard, 1922.

Physikalische Begriffsbildung.   Karlsruhe, Braun, 1926.

Der logische Aufbau der Welt.   Berlin, Weltkreis, 1928; as *The Logical Structure of the World and Pseudo-Problems in Philosophy*, Berkeley, University of California Press, and London, Routledge, 1967.

Scheinprobleme in der Philosophie: Das Fremdpsychische und der Realismusstreit.   Berlin, Weltkreis, 1928; as *Pseudo-Problems in Philosophy*, 1967.

Abriss der Ligistik, mit besonderer Berücksichtigung der Relationstheorie und ihrer Anwendungen.   Vienna, Springer, 1929.

Die Aufgabe der Wissenschaftslogik.   Vienna, Gerold, 1934.

The Unity of Science.   London, Kegan Paul, 1934.

Logische Syntax der Sprache.   Vienna, Springer, 1934; as *The Logical Syntax of Language*, London, Kegan Paul, and New York, Harcourt Brace, 1937.

Philosophy and Logical Syntax.   London, Kegan Paul, 1935; Cleveland, Bell and Howell, 1963.

Foundations of Logic and Mathematics.   Chicago, University of Chicago Press, 1939.

Introduction to Semantics.   Cambridge, Massachussetts, Harvard University Press, 1942.

Formalization of Logic.   Cambridge, Massachusetts, Harvard University Press, 1943.

Meaning and Necessity: A Study in Semantics and Modal Logic.   Chicago, University of Chicago Press, 1947.

Logical Foundations of Probability.   Chicago, University of Chicago Press, 1950.

The Continuum of Inductive Methods.   Chicago, University of Chicago Press, 1952.

An Outline of a Theory of Semantic Information, with Yehoshua Bar-Hillel.   Cambridge, Massachusetts, Research Laboratory of Electronics, Massachusetts Institute of Technology, 1952.

Einfürhung in die symbolische Logik, mit besonderer Berücksichtigung ihrer Anwendungen.   Vienna, Springer, 1954.

"Intellectual Autobiography" and "Replies and Systematic Expositions," in *The Philosophy of Rudolf Carnap*, edited by Paul Arthur Schilpp.   La Salle, Illinois, Open Court, and London, Cambridge University Press, 1963.

The Philosophical Foundations of Physics: An Introduction to the Philosophy of Science, edited by Martin Gardner.   New York, Basic Books, 1966.

Studies in Inductive Logic and Probability, edited by Richard C. Jeffrey.   Berkeley, University of California Press, 2 vols., 1971, 1980.

Two Essays on Entropy, edited by Abner Shimony.   Berkeley, University of California Press, 1977.

Other

Editor, with Hans Reichenbach, *Erkenntnis, zugleich Annalen der Philosophie*. Leipzig, Meiner, 1930-37; The Hague, W.P. van Stockum and Zoon, 1938-40.

Editor, with others, *Einheitswissenschaft*. Vienna, Gerold, 1933-35; The Hague, W.P. van Stockum and Zoon, 1939-46.

Editor, with others, *Library of Unified Science*. The Hague, W.P. van Stockum and Zoon, 1939-46.

Editor, with others, *International Encyclopedia of Unified Science*. Chicago, University of Chicago Press, 1955.

*

Critical Studies: *The Philosophy of Rudolf Carnap*, edited by Paul Arthur Schilpp, La Salle, Illinois, Open Court, and London, Cambridge University Press, 1963; (contains a complete bibliography); *Die Philosophie Carnaps* by Lothar Krauth, Vienna, Springer, 1970; *Rudolf Carnap, Logical Empiricist: Materials and Perspectives*, edited by Jaakko Hintikka, Dordrecht, The Netherlands, and Boston, D. Reidel, 1975.

*   *   *

His parents were deeply religious, but Rudolf Carnap gradually, and without inner crises, moved away from those beliefs. This was accompanied by a growing enthusiasm for, and faith in, modern science. Carnap studied at Jena with Herman Nohl (a student of Dilthey) and with Gottlob Frege, and also at Feiburg im Breisgau (where Martin Heidegger was a fellow-student). Neo-Kantianism was the main trend, but it was the New Logic of Frege and of Russell and Whitehead that proved decisive: in it Carnap was to find for the rest of his life an inexhaustible source for satisfying his needs for clarity of concepts and precision of methods. His life-work was to use this New Logic to further the progress of science.

For Carnap the outbreak of war in 1914 was an incomprehensible catastrophe. It led him to recognize his latent cosmopolitanism and pacifism, though he completed his military service as part of his felt duty. Neither the war, nor the terrible post-war years, led him to despair or irrationalism, as they did Heidegger. To the contrary, they made even more clear to him that what the world needed was not less but more rationality: the war confirmed him in his commitment to the Enlightenment values of science (including the science of man) and rationality.

From Nohl and Dilthey Carnap had learned of a non-theoretical or non-cognitive component in any world-view. It became one of Carnap's main tasks to try to separate the non-cognitive component—the ethical, moral, poetical components—from the scientific or cognitive component, in order to free the latter from encumbrances which do not belong to it, and which hinder its progress. Traditional metaphysics he saw as consisting for the most part of non-cognitive issues disguised as cognitive. The "riddle of death," for example, consists in the shock through death of a fellow man or in the fear of one's own death. Its solution is not cognitive—this sort of question about death can be answered by biology—but rather is the practical task of "getting over" the shock and perhaps even making it fruitful for one's later life. In the latter the self-knowledge provided by a psycho-therapy based on a genuine science of man might well be useful—as a knowledge of physiology might be useful in learning a sport. But as in the latter, so in the case of the "riddle of death": the primary task is practical, and not cognitive—even though some have deceived themselves into the belief that there is a cognitive issue at the core of the "riddle". It is such self-deception that is at the core of traditional metaphysics.

Carnap aimed to use the tools provided by the New Logic to separate science from non-science, the cognitive or what admits of empirical test from the non-cognitive; and then to use the same tools to clarify the logical structure of the science that has been thus defined. In the late 1920's and early 30's, as Europe slipped

ever deeper into irrationalism, Carnap defended his position with a strongly anti-metaphysical rhetoric. Even so, his actual analyses of the errors of metaphysical discourse (most notoriously, of Heidegger's "Das Nichts nitchet") remain sketchy. It was Carnap's position that it was better by far to get on with the tasks of defining science and clarifying its logic. In fact, Carnap does not even provide a general defence of his own, positivist, position. In his view, his work ought to be judged by its fruitfulness in furthering the ends of science and enlightenment. An *a priori* defence is as inappropriate for his own work as it is for metaphysics. Since Carnap was never enamoured of metaphysics, he felt no loss over its disappearance. After he moved to the United States in 1935, and its more tolerant atmosphere, Carnap's anti-metaphysical rhetoric lost its stridency: his later work is more appropriately characterized as ametaphysical than as anti-metaphysical.

Carnap's earliest published work concerned the logical structure of relativity theory. It showed a neo-Kantian influence. The latter was soon replaced by a positivist turn, inspired by Moritz Schlick, who formed the Vienna Circle with Carnap and Otto Neurath, among others. Schlick's positivism insisted upon a phenomenalistic basis for the language of science. Since phenomena are private, public knowledge is of structure alone. In his first major work, *Der logische Aufbau der Welt*, Carnap proceeded on this basis, but formally, using the New Logic, to present in logical order a hierarchy of concepts rising from the phenomenal level to physical objects and the entities of physics. As his primitive basis, Carnap selected cross-sections of the stream of experience rather than sense-data (he acknowledges a debt here to the gestalt psychologists). What we ordinarily regard as ingredients within such a cross-section—e.g., colours—must be constituted out of them. Carnap uses that part of the New Logic, developed by Peirce and Russell, concerning *relationships*, that is, *structure*. The primitive relation Carnap uses is "recognition of similarity," and, inventing a number of ingenious technical devices, Carnap relates segments of experience, on the ground of their recognized similarity, into quality-classes, and these in turn into sense-classes. He then goes on to outline in general terms a procedure by which "things," as distinct from "qualities," can be "formally constituted"; but this latter part of the book is merely a sketch.

Carnap never completed the programme. Persuaded by arguments of Neurath, he came to accept the view that the language of science is best constructed on a physicalistic, rather than a phenomenalistic basis. But for Carnap, in contrast to Schlick and Neurath, the question of which basis to choose was not a matter of philosophic argument but rather of decision: which was the most convenient sort of language for the purpose at hand? This "conventionalist" tendency in Carnap's thought becomes explicit in his *Logical Syntax of Language*, where he espouses the "principle of tolerance": "In logic there are no morals. Everyone is at liberty to build up his own logic, i.e. his own form of language, as he wishes."

In any language, Carnap argued, sentences could be divided into those that are necessary or analytic and those that are contingent. The former are those the acceptability of which can be decided by appeal to the syntax of the language. The latter are those that are not necessary. Ontological claims, insofar as they have cognitive content, are not claims about the world, but claims about syntax. For example, "there are numbers" is more properly construed as "Language contains number terms."

The status of contingent claims remained obscure, however: how is their truth to be decided? Commonsensically we say that it is by comparing them to the facts. But "fact" is a term of ontology and when explicated syntactically means "statement of fact," i.e., "contingent sentence." So sentences are compared only to sentences! This paradox was accepted by Neurath, but Carnap learned from Tarski a way to avoid it by formalizing not just syntax but also the semantical, word-world, dimension of language. Several studies in the 1940's were devoted to the study of semantics. A semantical system is a linguistic framework; e.g., we may have phenomenalistic or physicalistic linguistic frameworks, and frameworks with number concepts and those without. Ontological questions Carnap now took to be *external* questions about the existence or reality of the framework, in contrast to *internal* questions concerning the existence of entities within the framework which introduces them. For example, given a framework with number concepts, one can ask within it whether the number five exists. External questions, such as whether numbers exist in some sense absolutely, are, he claims, pseudo-questions, non-cognitive: they concern the choice of a framework, and are to be decided not by argument but by a decision based on such considerations as those of simplicity and convenience.

The analytic was still explicated as the syntactically decidable. In any language, terms were construed as either primitive observation terms or explicitly defined on the basis of these primitives. For example, we define: "x is soluble" if and only if "x is in water then x dissolves." Now, in the New Logic, an "if-then" statement is usually construed as false if the antecedent is true and the consequent false, and otherwise true. Since an "if-then" statement is true if the antecedent is false, matches never placed in water turn out to be soluble. Some positivists such as G. Bergmann argued that this is not a problem, since the special status of disposition terms such as "soluble" can be construed as deriving from the context in which they occur in theories. But Carnap held to a more formalistic position, and suggested ("Testability and Meaning," 1936) introducing disposition terms by means of sentences like "if x is in water then x is soluble if and only if x dissolves" (called "reduction sentences"). Syntactically such a sentence is contingent, and does not permit the elimination of the new term by means of definitions. This term is in effect a new primitive term, but Carnap held that its logical dependence on the observation terms could be secured by construing reduction sentences as analytic in a broader, non-syntactical, sense. No clear linguistic criterion for this category was provided, however, save decision based on convenience—Carnap construed it as a non-cognitive external question—so that the category of the analytic eventually expanded to include many other kinds of sentence. It became a special problem to delimit this class so as to include the terms of science but exclude such metaphysical concepts as that of "God." Eventually Carnap took the scientific theory itself as analytic in the broad sense, so that its acceptance was no longer a cognitive decision but a non-cognitive framework decision.

This seems odd to many empiricists, but it fit in well with another of Carnap's concerns. After coming to America he had attempted not only to separate science from non-science but also to lay down rules for separating good science from bad, that is, Carnap claimed, those theories that are more probable from those that are less. For this Carnap developed a notion of *logical* or *a priori probability* defined in terms of certain *syntactical* features of language. But it was a paradoxical feature of this that all general statements, including all laws and theories, turned out to have *zero* probability, no matter what the evidence. Carnap resolved this problem by arguing on the one hand that for its predictive purposes science need not resort to general statements, and on the other hand that what was essential to theories could be captured by construing them as analytic in the broad sense.

Moreover, it turned out that an infinite number of satisfactory probability functions could be defined. A choice among them could be made on grounds of convenience, Carnap suggested. Besides, once the initial choice of language was made, all these probability functions were determined automatically, so it was not clear how such probabilities could be useful in answering internal questions. And since they could not be used to answer non-cognitive external questions, many wondered if this aspect of Carnap's work was as fruitful as he believed.

Many questions can be raised about Carnap's work on probability, and others such as W. Quine have criticized Carnap's broad notion of analyticity. Many wonder whether Carnap does not misconstrue many cognitive issues as mere decisions. Certainly, he says nothing about the kind of languages used in stages preparatory to a judicious choice of framework, nor about the frameworks of such languages. None of these specific criticisms calls into question, however, Carnap's standards of clarity and exactitude, and his Enlightenment ideal of scientific rationality, to which today we have more need than ever to make our commitment.

—Fred Wilson

CASSIRER, Ernst.   German philosopher.   Born in Breslau, Silesia, Germany, 28 July 1874. Educated at the Universities of Berlin, Leipzig and Heidelberg, 1892-96, and the University of Marburg, Ph.D. 1899. Married in 1902; 3 children. Had private means; wrote, then eventually taught at the University of Berlin (Privatdozent), until World War I; drafted into civilian work for the duration of the war; taught at the University of Hamburg from 1919: Rector of the University, 1930 until he resigned, 1933; lectured at Oxford University, 1933-35; taught at the University of Gothenburg, 1935-41; Visiting Professor, Yale University, New Haven, Connecticut, 1941-44, and Columbia University, New York, 1944-45. *Died* (in New York) *13 April 1945.*

PUBLICATIONS

Philosophy

Descartes' Kritik der mathematischen und naturwissenschaftlichen Erkenntnis.   Marburg, 1899; reprinted in *Leibniz' System*, 1902.
Leibniz' System in seinen wissenschaftlichen Grundlagen.   Marburg, Elwert, 1902.
Das Erkenntnisproblem in der Philosophie und Wissenschaft der neueren Zeit.   Berlin, Cassirer, 3 vols., 1906, 1907, 1920.
Substanzbegriff und Funktionsbegriff: Untersuchungen über die Grundfragen der Erkenntniskritik.   Berlin, Cassirer, 1910; included in *Substance and Function and Einstein's Theory of Relativity*, Chicago and London, Open Court, 1923.
Freiheit und Form: Studien zur deutschen Geistesgeschichte.   Berlin, Cassirer, 1916.
Kants Leben und Lehre.   Berlin, Cassirer, 1918; as *Kant's Life and Thought*, New Haven, Connecticut, and London, Yale University Press, 1981.
Zur Einsteinschen Relativitätstheorie.   Berlin, Cassirer, 1921; in *Substance and Function*, 1923.
Idee und Gestalt: Fünf Aufsätze.   Berlin, Cassirer, 1921.
Die Begriffsform im mythischen Denken.   Leipzig, Teubner, 1922.
Philosophie der symbolischen Formen.   Berlin, Cassirer, 3 vols., 1923, 1925, 1929; as *The Philosophy of Symbolic Forms*, New Haven, Connecticut, and London, Yale University Press, 3 vols., 1953-57.
Sprache und Mythos: Ein Beitrag zum Problem der Götternamen.   Leipzig, Teubner, 1925; as *Language and Myth*, New York, Harper, 1946.
Die Philosophie der Griechen von den Anfängen bis Platon.   Berlin, Ullstein, 1925.
Individuum und Kosmos in der Philosophie der Renaissance.   Leipzig, Teubner, 1927; as *The Individual and the Cosmos in Renaissance Philosophy*, Oxford, Basil Blackwell, 1963; New York, Harper, 1964.
Die Platonische Renaissance in England und die Schule von Cambridge.   Leipzig, Teubner, 1932; as *The Platonic Renaissance in England*, Austin, University of Texas Press, and Edinburgh, Nelson, 1953.

Die Philosophie der Aufklärung. Tübingen, Mohr, 1932; as *The Philosophy of the Enlightenment*, Princeton, New Jersey, Princeton University Press, 1951.

Goethe und die geschlichtliche Welt: Drei Aufsätze. Berlin, Cassirer, 1932.

Determinismus und Indeterminismus in der modenernen Physik. Gothenburg, Göteborgs Högskolas Arsskrift XLII, 1936; as *Determinism and Indeterminism in Modern Physics: Historical and Systematic Studies of the Problem of Causality*, New Haven, Connecticut, Yale University Press, 1956.

Descartes: Lehre—Persönlichkeit—Wirkung. Stockholm, Bermann-Fischer, 1939.

Axel Hägerström: Eine Studie zur schwedischen Philosophie der Gegenwart. Gothenburg, Göteborgs Högskolas Arsskrift XLV, 1939.

Zur Logik der Kulturwissenschaften: Fünf Studien. Gothenburg, Wettergren and Kerbers, 1942; as *The Logic of the Humanities*, New Haven, Yale University Press, 1961.

An Essay on Man: An Introduction to a Philosophy of Human Culture. New Haven, Connecticut, Yale University Press, and London, Oxford University Press, 1944.

Rousseau, Kant, Goethe: Two Essays. Princeton, New Jersey, Princeton University Press, 1945.

The Myth of the State. New Haven, Connecticut, Yale University Press, and London, Oxford University Press, 1946.

The Problem of Knowledge: Philosophy, Science, and History since Hegel. New Haven, Connecticut, Yale University Press, 1950.

Symbol, Myth, and Culture: Essays and Lectures of Ernst Cassirer 1935-1945, edited by Donald Phillip Verene. New Haven, Connecticut, Yale University Press, 1979.

Other

Editor, *Philosophische Werke*, by G.W. Leibniz. Leipzig, Dürrsche, 1904-06.

Editor, with others, *Immanuel Kants Werke*. Berlin, Cassirer, 10 vols., 1912.

Editor, with others, *The Renaissance Philosophy of Man*. Chicago, University of Chicago Press, 1948.

*

Critical Studies: *The Philosophy of Ernst Cassirer*, edited by Paul Arthur Schilpp, Evanston, Illinois, The Library of Living Philosophers, 1949, and New York, Tudor, 1958; *Symbol and Reality: Studies in the Philosophy of Ernst Cassirer* by Carl H. Hamburg, The Hague, Martinus Nijhoff, 1956; *Ernst Cassirer: Scientific Knowledge and the Concept of Man* by Seymour W. Itzkoff, Notre Dame, Indiana, University of Notre Dame Press, 1971; *Ernst Cassirer: Philosophy of Culture* by Seymour W. Itzkoff, Boston, Twayne, 1977; *Ernst Cassirer: The Dilemma of a Liberal Intellectual in Germany 1914-1933* by David R. Lipton, Toronto, University of Toronto Press, 1978; *Mein Leben mit Ernst Cassirer* by Toni Cassirer, Hildesheim, Gerstenberg, 1981.

*   *   *

Ernst Cassirer was both an original philosopher and an historian of philosophy. He also wrote literary criticism, particularly on Goethe. Few readers of Cassirer realize the extent of his writings which span almost half a century. Cassirer's approximately 125 published works are nearly as large in volume as the Prussian Academy Edition of Kant's works.

Cassirer's works in the history of philosophy concentrate on the development of modern philosophy from Nicholas Cusanus to Kant, and German idealism from Kant through Hegel to Cassirer's own day. Cassirer has special works on the Renaissance and Enlightenment and on such thinkers as Descartes, Leibniz, Kant, and Rousseau. Cassirer's historical research focuses on the problem of knowledge. He shows how philosophical views of knowledge are related to scientific understandings and specialized fields of thought in various historical periods.

Cassirer's original philosophy is often described as Neo-Kantian, partly because of Cassirer's origins in the Marburg School of Neo-Kantianism and partly because Kant is for Cassirer the pivotal figure in the development of modern philosophy. Cassirer's inaugural dissertation was written at the University of Marburg under the Neo-Kantian Hermann Cohen. The Marburg School was part of the "back to Kant" movement of German universities at the turn of the century, and Marburg was known for its narrow focus on Kantian philosophy of science.

Cassirer's first work of original philosophy, *Substance and Function*, reflects this interest in science. This work contrasts concepts constructed on the Aristotelian idea of substance with those constructed on the mathematical idea of function. Cassirer shows that only a logic derived from function explains the type of thinking present in modern science. This work contains the roots of Cassirer's notion of functional form that was later to be the basis of his conception of the symbol.

Hermann Cohen had doubts that this work was orthodox to the Marburg position, and rightly so, in that Cassirer's later works develop views well beyond Kantian philosophy of science and are more than a simple extension of Kant. Cassirer's later conception of a phenomenology of knowledge is based on Hegel's sense of form as developmental, and his philosophy of culture is influenced by Hegel's view that culture must be understood as a whole. Cassirer did not give up his specific interest in science. In *Einstein's Theory of Relativity* and *Determinism and Indeterminism in Modern Physics* he sought to resolve the discoveries and thought of modern physics with Kantian epistemology.

The central idea of Cassirer's philosophy and the one special term with which it is identified is "symbolic form" (*symbolische Form*). It is the title of Cassirer's three volume work, *The Philosophy of Symbolic Forms* (1923-1929), treating language, myth, and phenomenology of knowledge respectively. Cassirer's notion of the symbol is based on his view that there are three functions of consciousness. There is first the expressive function (*Ausdrucksfunktion*) in which symbols are used to present an object directly. We find this in the mythic image or ritual where, for example, the dancer is apprehended as actually the god whose mask he wears. Expression can be transformed into the representational function (*Darstellungsfunktion*) when the symbol is used to refer to objects that are apprehended apart from the symbol. We find this function in the power of natural languages to form words that refer to objects that we perceive apart from language as, for example, the way "chair" is used as a word that refers to a particular object or class of objects having a certain perceptual character.

Representation can be transformed into the significative function (*Bedeutungsfunktion*) when symbols are used to freely and systematically create their own world of meanings. We find an approximation of this in natural languages when they formulate meanings that can be defined only by the meanings of other words and that do not refer back to some specific perception of an object. But we find this in its purest form in the systems of symbols of modern mathematics, symbolic logic, and scientific thought. In these spheres man's symbolic ability builds reflectively on itself. New meanings are reached purely through the systematic extension of symbols. Here, for example, the meaning of one set of symbols can be in another set of symbols that are on either a higher or lower logical level.

For Cassirer all thought and all of human consciousness is symbolic. There is not a part of thought that is symbolic and a part that is not. In his late work, *An Essay on Man*, written in English to describe and extend his theory of symbolic forms, Cassirer defines man as *animal symbolicum*. Man is an *animal rationale* but the form of his rationality is the symbol. Man always approaches experience through his power to symbolize it—to form it as an immediate image, or to refer to it with a word, or to construct its meaning as a system of notations. Man gives form to perceptual experience through his power of the symbol.

For Cassirer the forms of symbolizing are writ large in the major areas of human cultural activity. Cassirer often gives a list of "symbolic forms" in terms of culture. Most often included are myth and religion, language, art, history, and science; but Cassirer also mentions the possibility of ethics, law, economics, and technology. Man lives within the circle of his symbolizing activity, the product of which is culture. Culture is the unity of the various symbolic forms. Human nature is defined through man's activity as a cultural animal.

The most original element of Cassirer's philosophy is his theory of myth. It is the basis of his conception of knowledge and culture. Cassirer is the only major philosopher of the 20th century to formulate a theory of myth as the basis of total philosophy. All man's cultural activity originates in mythical consciousness, and myth as the form of the expressive function of symbolizing is a moment in any of our acts of apprehending the world. Cassirer sees only two precursors to the philosophical theory of myth—Vico's *New Science* and Schelling's *Philosophie der Mythologie*. Without an understanding of myth, philosophy can offer no understanding of the origin of either culture or knowledge. Cassirer first formulated his logic of mythical thought in the second volume of *The Philosophy of Symbolic Forms*, and in his last work, *The Myth of the State*, he applied his logic of primitive mythical thought to a theory of modern political myths as the basis of the modern state, particularly totalitarian states.

In one of the most interesting confrontations in 20th century philosophy, Cassirer and the existential philosopher, Martin Heidegger, met during an academic short course held in Davos, Switzerland in the spring of 1929. Their debate is often characterized as a debate over Neo-Kantianism, perhaps because Heidegger begins by asking Cassirer about his Neo-Kantian origins. But the deeper level of the exchange concerned Heidegger's notion of *Dasein*, "existence," "being-there," and the possibility of human freedom in Heidegger's philosophy. Heidegger had previously written a review of Cassirer's volume on myth and ended this with the doubt as to whether it could give us a true understanding of *Dasein*, of the fundamental condition of human existence. Cassirer's doubts at Davos, which he later turns into an explicit criticism in *The Myth of the State*, concern whether Heidegger has any room in his theory of man for acts of human freedom.

In *The Myth of the State* Cassirer shows how the logic of primitive myths is substituted for the rational basis of the state in modern political life. He accuses Heidegger and the philosopher of history, Oswald Spengler, of reducing philosophizing to mythologizing. Their form of thought precludes the critical function of consciousness necessary for a sense of political freedom. In modern political life, Cassirer claims, as in Nazi Germany, myth is joined to technique such that man is enveloped in a mythical interpretation of his existence and understands himself as in a state of *Geworfenheit*, of "being-thrown", where his traditional faculties of rational thought and ethical freedom are no longer present for him. Cassirer sees Heidegger's thought as ethically dangerous as it supports an understanding of man and culture that corresponds to a mythical rather than a rational basis for the state. Cassirer's theory of myth is the crucial element that lies at the basis of his conception of knowledge and the symbol, considered purely as philosophical problems, and that is the ground of the ethical thrust of his thought that emerges in his last works.

—Donald Phillip Verene

CASTANEDA, Carlos. Brazilian anthropologist. Born in Sao Paulo, 25 December 1931. Educated at the University of California at Los Angeles, B.A. 1962, M.A. 1964, Ph.D. 1970. Anthropologist: lived in Mexico for 10 years as apprentice to a Yaqui Indian sorcerer. Address: c/o Simon and Schuster, 1230 Avenue of the Americas, New York, New York 10020, U.S.A.

PUBLICATIONS

Anthropology

The Teachings of Don Juan: A Yaqui Way of Knowledge.   Berkeley and London, University of California Press, 1968.
A Separate Reality: Further Conversations with Don Juan. New York, Simon and Schuster, and London, Bodley Head, 1971.
Journey to Ixtlan: The Lessons of Don Juan. New York, Simon and Schuster, 1972; London, Bodley Head, 1973.
Tales of Power.   New York, Simon and Schuster, 1974; London, Hodder and Stoughton, 1975.
The Second Ring of Power.   New York, Simon and Schuster, 1977; London, Hodder and Stoughton, 1979.
The Eagle's Gift.   New York, Simon and Schuster, and London, Hodder and Stoughton, 1981.

*

Critical Studies: *Reading Castaneda: A Prologue to the Social Sciences* by David Silverman, London, Routledge, 1975; *Castaneda's Journey: The Power and the Allegory* by Richard De Mille, Santa Barbara, California, Capra Press, 1976; *Seeing Castaneda: Reactions to the "Don Juan" Writings of Carlos Cantaneda*, edited by Daniel C. Noel, New York, Putnam, 1976.

*   *   *

Carlos Castaneda has now written six books about his experiences with Don Juan, a Yaqui Indian sorcerer from northern Mexico. Beginning with *The Teachings of Don Juan*, Castaneda's gradual movement away from the detached, objectivist stance of a cultural anthropologist and his increasing involvement with a new-found "way of knowledge" highlight the basic contradiction between the role of observer/scientist and that of participant/apprentice. The dry, qualified jargon which characterized the appendix of his first book has given way to an amalgamation of introspection, revelation, parody and fantasy. However, this shift in style has been accompanied by a more fundamental change in substance.

During Castaneda's ten-year apprenticeship to Don Juan, he experiences certain inexplicable events which lead him to discard the rationale for a detached, objective attitude. Earlier, he treats sorcery as one system of knowledge (as rational and pragmatically-inspired as his own) among many which attempt to explain a uniform and objective reality. Now he sees all such "attempts" as *constitutive* of reality. He makes his position clear in *Journey to Ixtlan*: we take for granted that version of reality produced by our efforts to "describe" it. Thus, Castaneda's earlier work at abstracting the invariant properties of Don Juan's system of knowledge in order to draw comparisons with his own has been followed by a new focus on the unique—and untranslatable—properties of the sorcerer's world.

It is simpler to assess Castaneda as a writer than it is to understand Don Juan. First, there is a reliance on the use of psychotropic plants as a device to enable the neophyte to break out of one reality and to perceive another. Second, there is the relationship between Don Juan and Carlos. At one time it resembles that between master and apprentice with the title "man of knowledge" being conferred upon the completion of training. At other times, the interaction between the two reads like a yogi scolding his disciple for some weakness of spirit. Indeed, some have even seen convergences between Don Juan's teachings and various forms of mysticism. If this is true, Castaneda's experiences are less an apprenticeship than a conversion. Third, there are the techniques that Don Juan uses to enable Castaneda to perceive the special characteristics of "nonordinary reality". The same artfulness that a con artist might employ is used by Don Juan in order to "manipulate cues": to separate those features of the environment that were safe to ignore from those that had meaning. Don Juan is portrayed as a man of knowledge, uniquely capable of creating the "special consensus" that would collapse without his participation. His success in creating an alternative reality is guaranteed by the force of his personality and the sense of drama he gives to the situation.

This last point has created some problems for Castaneda and fueled a controversy about the veracity of his writing. The basis for this alternate reality is Don Juan, yet "Don Juan" is a mystery. As the anthropologist Edward H. Spicer put it, "the teachings of Don Juan exist in a cultural limbo". There seems to be no connection between Don Juan's way of life and what we already know about Yaqui Indian culture. The various aspects of Don Juan's teachings create an aura of plausibility. When viewed in their entirety, his statements exhibit their own logic: they appear to be based on a *systematic* body of knowledge. The possibility that he and Castaneda are one and the same raises insurmountable obstacles to understanding Don Juan's teachings as an *authentic* body of knowledge.

—Martin Rouse

CHOMSKY, (Avram) Noam. American theoretical linguist. Born in Philadelphia, Pennsylvania, 7 December 1928. Studied at the University of Pennsylvania, Philadelphia, B.A. 1949; M.A. 1951; Ph.D. 1955. Married Carol Doris Schatz in 1949; 3 children. Member of the Faculty, 1955-61, Professor, 1961-66, Ferrari P. Ward Professor of Modern Languages and Linguistics from 1966, and Institute Professor from 1976, Massachusetts Institute of Technology, Cambridge. Research Fellow, 1951-55, and American Council of Learned Societies Fellow, 1964-65, Harvard Cognitive Studies Center, Cambridge, Massachusetts; Visiting Professor, Columbia University, New York, 1957-58; National Science Foundation Fellow, Institute for Advanced Studies, Princeton, New Jersey, 1958-59; Linguistic Society of America Professor, University of California at Los Angeles, 1966; Beckman Professor, University of California, Berkeley, 1966-67; John Locke Lecturer, Oxford University, 1969; Sherman Lecturer, University of London, 1969. Honorary doctorate: University of Chicago, and University of London, 1967; Loyola University, Chicago, and Swarthmore College, Pennsylvania, 1970; Bard College, Annandale-on-Hudson, New York, 1971; Delhi University, India, 1972; University of Massachusetts, Amherst, 1973; Visva-Bharati University, Santiniketan, West Bengal, 1980. Fellow, American Academy of Arts and Sciences. Corresponding Fellow, British Academy. Address: Massachusetts Institute of Technology, 77 Massachusetts Avenue, Cambridge, Massachusetts 02139, U.S.A.

PUBLICATIONS

Linguistics

Syntactic Structures. The Hague, Mouton, 1957.
A Transformational Approach to Syntax. Cambridge, Massachusetts, 1958.
The Transformational Basis of Syntax. Cambridge, Massachusetts, 1959.
Current Issues in Linguistic Theory. The Hague, Mouton, 1964.
Aspects of the Theory of Syntax. Cambridge, Massachusetts, M.I.T. Press, 1965.
Cartesian Linguistics: A Chapter in the History of Rationalist

Thought. New York and London, Harper, 1966.
Topics in the Theory of Generative Grammar. The Hague, Mouton, 1966.
Language and Mind. New York, Harcourt Brace, 1968.
Remarks on Nominalization. Bloomington, Indiana University Press, 1968.
The Sound Pattern of English, with Morris Halle. New York and London, Harper, 1968.
Chomsky: Selected Readings, edited by J.P.B. Allen and Paul Van Buren. London and New York, Oxford University Press, 1971.
Problems of Knowledge and Freedom. New York, Pantheon Books, 1971; London, Collins, 1972.
Studies on Semantics in Generative Grammar. The Hague, Mouton, 1972.
Essays on Form and Interpretation. New York, North Holland, 1977.
Language and Responsibility: Based on Conversations with Mitsou Ronat. New York, Pantheon Books, 1979.
Language and Learning: The Debate Between Jean Piaget and Noam Chomsky, edited by Massimo Piattelli-Palmarini. Cambridge, Massachusetts, Harvard University Press, 1980.
Rules and Representations. New York, Columbia University Press, and Oxford, Blackwell, 1980.
Some Concepts and Consequences of the Theory of Government and Binding. Cambridge, Massachusetts, M.I.T. Press, 1982.

Other

American Power and the New Mandarins. New York, Pantheon Books, and London, Chatto and Windus, 1969.
At War with Asia. New York, Pantheon Books, 1970; London, Fontana, 1971.
Two Essays on Cambodia. Nottingham, Bertrand Russell Peace Foundation, 1970.
The Backroom Boys. London, Fontana, 1973.
For Reasons of State. London, Fontana 1973.
Peace in the Middle East: Reflections on Justice and Nationhood. New York, Vintage Books, 1974; Glasgow, Fontana/Collins, 1975.
Chomsky on Carter. Nottingham, Spokesman, 1977.
"Human Rights" and American Foreign Policy. Nottingham, Spokesman, 1978.
Intellectuals and the State. Baarn, Holland, Wereldvenster, 1978.
The Political Economy of Human Rights, with Edward S. Herman. Montreal, Black Rose Books, 2 vols., 1979.
Towards a New Cold War: Essays on the Current Crisis and How We Got There. New York, Pantheon Books, 1982.

Editor, with Howard Zinn, *The Pentagon Papers. Vol. 5: Critical Essays.* Boston, Beacon Press, 1971.

*

Critical Studies: *Noam Chomsky* by John Lyons, New York, Viking Press, 1970; *On Noam Chomsky: Critical Essays*, edited by Gilbert Harman, New York, Anchor Press, 1974; *Noam Chomsky: A Philosophic Overview* (lectures) by Justin Leiber, Boston, Twayne, 1975; *Language and Creativity: An Interdisciplinary Essay on Chomskyan Humanism* by Bernard D. den Ouden, Lisse, Holland, Peter de Ridder Press, 1975; *The New Grammarian's Funeral: A Critique of Noam Chomsky's Linguistics* by Ian Robinson, Cambridge and New York, Cambridge University Press, 1975; *Modern Linguistics: The Results of Chomsky's Revolution* by Neil Smith and Dierdre Wilson, Bloomington, Indiana University Press, 1979; *Liberty and Language* by Geoffrey Sampson, Oxford and New York, Oxford University Press, 1979; *Linguistics and Theology: The Significance of Noam Chomsky for Theological Construction* by Irene Lawrence, Metuchen, New Jersey, Scarecrow Press, 1980; *Hel-*

lenistic Greek Grammar and Noam Chomsky: Nominalizing Transformations by Daryl Dean Schmidt, Chico, California, Scholars Press, 1981.

* * *

Noam Chomsky's intellectual contributions fall into two categories: his "professional" writings on linguistics, psychology, and the philosophy of the mind, and his writings and activities as a concerned citizen in the political arena. There is little doubt that the popularity of Chomsky's political stance had much to do with the widespread attention accorded to his often highly technical professional work during the late 1960's and 1970's. However, it is open to question how far Chomsky's "professional" and "political" ideas are intrinsically related.

The pivot of Chomsky's thought is the thesis that the cognitive, intellectual aspects of human life are as much a part of our biology as the physiological, anatomical aspects.

Commonly, the man in the street recognizes that his physical development is governed by heredity (he cannot choose to grow a pair of wings, he cannot prevent himself going bald); but he supposes that his mental life, by contrast, does not have the same constraints—we seem to be able to invent and develop ideas freely, even in a prison cell. The "behaviourist" doctrine which dominated North American academic psychology in the mid-20th century claimed that this appearance of mental freedom was illusory, and that, insofar as it was legitimate to speak of human beings as having "thoughts" or "ideas" at all, these were produced purely mechanically by the impact of environment on individual. Chomsky rejects this view. However, he replaces the doctrine of environmental determination of cognition, not with the view that humans are intellectually creative, but with a doctrine of hereditary determination of cognition.

We are not conscious of genetic constraints on our mental life because we operate wholly within these constraints, and nothing alerts us to the possibility of other kinds of thinking. Nevertheless, according to Chomsky, the evidence suggests our mental development is predetermined by the mechanisms of biological inheritance, with the result that the differences between various individuals' structures of thought are almost trivial by comparison to their resemblances: "...our systems of belief are those that the mind, as a biological structure, is designed to construct." For instance, Chomsky argues that the scientific theories which have been developed during human history have been drawn from a limited stock of potential theories made available to us by our genes. This stock may well be approaching exhaustion, now that the world contains many people to whom society grants the leisure and facilities necessary for scientific research, and where a particular topic is not yet well understood it may be that it is destined never to be understood because the truth about it happens to lie outside the range of theories biologically available to man. Chomsky has similar ideas about developments in the arts and in other cognitive domains.

Chomsky sees this hereditarian approach as constituting a far more optimistic view of man than the behaviourist or empiricist view which emphasizes the role of environment. Chomsky draws heavily on the rhetoric of freedom in explaining his theory of mind; the notion that our thoughts are restricted to a definite range of possibilities laid down in our genes is, for him, not antagonistic to but actually a necessary pre-condition of the thesis that man is intellectually creative. The widely held assumption that genetic limitations are even less congenial (because less open to modification) than environmental constraints is summarily dismissed. Chomsky associates environmental determination of mind with the exploitation of man by man; inherited constraints are acceptable to him because they come from within.

The evidence that Chomsky uses to support his nativist theory of mind is drawn mainly from linguistics. There are essentially two lines of argument.

First, the process by which each child acquires his mother-tongue is too rapid, effortless, and efficient to be explained as a case of learning from scratch. When people learn to drive a car, we find that some individuals take to the task naturally but others find it challenging and painful, and a few never succeed despite prolonged effort and careful tuition. On the other hand, all children master the language of their community (which involves a system of rules very much more complex than those underlying the skill of driving) at about the same early age, without apparent strain and without formal teaching, simply through exposure to a random sample of the often slipshod speech of their elders. The best analogy for language-acquisition, Chomsky suggests, is physiological processes such as the replacement of milk teeth by adult teeth, or the bodily changes of puberty, which unfold automatically at a set age under the control of a genetic program.

Chomsky's second argument appeals to the fact that all human languages share certain common structural features. As students of foreign languages we naturally tend to notice the differences between languages rather than their similarities, because it is the differences which pose learning-problems. However, the fact that languages differ in certain respects should not blind us to the fact that in other, deeper respects they are alike. According to Chomsky the resemblances between languages are far more extensive than we have any reason to expect *a priori*, and the best explanation for the "linguistic universals" is that they are imposed by the structure of the intellectual apparatus which is encoded in the genetic inheritance shared by all Mankind. (Chomsky's notion that abstract, logical features of our patterns of speech and thought are contingent but independent of experience echoes the philosophy of Kant—though Chomsky more commonly cites Plato and Descartes as intellectual ancestors.) The contemporary discipline of theoretical linguistics, which has been heavily shaped by Chomsky's ideas, is in large part concerned with extending and refining the theory of linguistic universals by investigating different structural aspects of a wide range of human languages.

Of Chomsky's two arguments the former is harder to take seriously than the latter. The claim that children acquire their mother-tongue far quicker than would be possible unless they began life with innate "knowledge of language" invites the reply "How long would they take without innate knowledge?" Chomsky never hints at an answer to this question, and until he does so we have no good reason to agree that children are surprisingly fast at language-acquisition. It is difficult to avoid the conclusion that popular acceptance of this leg of Chomsky's thesis owes something to our instinctive willingness to cherish small children and exalt their achievements. (The differential success-rate as between language-acquisition and learning to drive may be adequately explained by reference to the very different strength of motive in the respective cases.)

If, on the other hand, it is true that all languages spoken by human communities share common features which are not necessary properties of any efficient vehicle of communication, then some explanation for these linguistic universals must be given, and Chomsky's explanation in terms of genetic inheritance is clearly a reasonable contender. However, the persuasiveness of Chomsky's nativist account of the linguistic universals depends wholly on whether or not satisfactory alternative explanations for the same facts are available. A number of scholars have reached the conclusion that Chomsky's linguistic universals are best explained in terms of theories which do not require, or which even contradict, the postulate of inherited cognitive structure.

Turning to political issues, Chomsky is an advocate both of anarchism and of equalitarian socialism. He is of course far from alone in embracing both of these apparently antagonistical political ideals; Chomsky tries to resolve the paradox by arguing that in the 20th century the chief threat to personal freedom comes not from the State but from large commercial organizations, and his recipe for a better world involves a version of syndicalism. But Chomsky is vague about ultimate political goals; he concentrates rather on analysis of the ills of the contemporary world.

During the years around 1970 he was one of the leaders of opposition to the American war in Vietnam. A well as campaigning in practical ways against U.S. government policy (e.g. by organizing a taxpayers' revolt), he documented at great length what he regarded as the hypocrisy and dishonesty of official accounts of the American involvement in S.E. Asia. These were the years when the danger of being called up to fight in a bloody war on behalf of a distant and alien people weighed heavily upon every male American college student's mind, and enthusiasm for Chomsky's role as a leader of resistance to the war and the draft won many readers for Chomsky's professional work. After the Vietnam War was over, Chomsky broadened his critique of U.S. foreign policy to portray America as the chief sponsor of vicious, repressive government throughout the world.

There are clear intellectual links between Chomsky's philosophical views and his brand of socialism. A standard objection to socialism is that it requires an impossible level of detailed knowledge of human needs and potentialities; satisfactory solutions to the problems posed by economic life can be achieved only by releasing unpredictable human creativity via the continuing discovery-procedure of the free market. But, if human potential is genetically limited as Chomsky believes, then it becomes more plausible to suppose that economic problems may be solved by calculation rather than experiment. Indeed, Chomsky's claim that free creativity presupposes a framework of rigid constraints, though discussed in the context of linguistics, suggests a solution to the *prima facie* contradiction between socialism and anarchism which other libertarian socialists have left unresolved.

However, Chomsky has usually avoided linking the two sides of his thought explicitly. Indeed, he has on occasion denied the validity of such links; and others' attempts to draw them have been rejected with some heat. For his part, though, Chomsky has not hesitated to link the empiricist philosophy which he opposes with unpopular political attitudes such as racialism and imperialism.

Within the discipline of linguistics Chomsky's position of dominance has waned gradually, as his arguments for innate knowledge of language ceased to seem convincing to those who were interested in them, while the profession as a whole moved on to focus most of its attention on new issues. In the political arena Chomsky lost his influence more abruptly, as a result of specific actions on his part. Having supported communist insurgency in Cambodia before it was successful, he reacted to the unprecedented atrocities which followed the Khmer Rouge takeover with a series of polemics in questionable taste disputing the precise numbers killed. Then in 1980 Chomsky contributed a preface to a book (which he admitted he had not read) by a Frenchman who argued that Nazi concentration-camp gas chambers were a myth invented by postwar Zionism for its own ends; and he reacted to the furore which this occasioned in France by describing it as a symptom of the lower standards of French intellectual life by comparison with that of America. Through such moves Chomsky has forfeited much of the audience which his analyses of the politics of his own country doubtless deserve.

—Geoffrey Sampson

CLARK, Kenneth (Mackenzie); Lord Clark of Saltwood. British art historian and critic. Born in London, 13 July 1903. Educated at Winchester College; studied at Trinity College, Oxford. Married Elizabeth Martin in 1927 (died, 1976); 2 sons and 1 daughter; married Nolwen de Janze-Rice in 1977. Worked with Bernard Berenson on the revision of *Florentine Painters,* 1926-28; Keeper, Department of Fine Arts, Ashmolean Museum, Oxford, 1931-33; Surveyor of the King's Pictures, 1934-44, and Director of the National Gallery, London, 1934-45; Director of Film Division, later Controller, Home Publicity, U.K. Ministry of Information, 1939-41; Slade Professor of Art, Oxford Univer-

sity, 1946-50, 1961-62; Chairman, Arts Council of Great Britain, 1953-60; Chairman, Independent Television Authority (U.K.), 1954-57; Professor of the History of Fine Art, Royal Academy, London, 1977-83. Presented the television series *Civilisation,* 1969, and *Romantic Versus Classic Art,* 1973. Chancellor, University of York, 1969-79. Recipient: Serena Medal for Italian Studies, British Academy, 1955; United States National Gallery of Art Medal, 1970. Honorary Fellow, Trinity College, Oxford, 1968; honorary doctorates: Universities of Oxford, Cambridge, London, Glasgow, Liverpool, Sheffield, York, Warwick, and Bath; Columbia University, New York; Brown University, Providence, Rhode Island. Fellow, British Academy, 1949; Member, French Academy, 1973. K.C.B. (Knight Commander of the Bath), 1938; C.H. (Companion of Honour), 1959; created Life Peer (Baron Clark of Saltwood), 1969; O.M. (Order of Merit), 1976. *Died 21 May 1983.*

PUBLICATIONS

Art History and Criticism

The Gothic Revival: An Essay in the History of Taste. London, Constable, and New York, Scribner, 1929.
A Catalogue of the Drawings of Leonardo da Vinci in the Collection of His Majesty the King at Windsor Castle. Cambridge, Cambridge University Press, 2 vols., 1935; revised edition, with Carlo Pedretti, as *A Catalogue of the Drawings of Leonardo da Vinci in the Collection of Her Majesty the Queen at Windsor Castle,* London, Phaidon, 3 vols., 1968.
Leonardo da Vinci: An Account of His Development as an Artist. Cambridge, Cambridge University Press, 1939.
Ruskin at Oxford (lecture). Oxford, Clarendon Press, 1946.
The Idea of a Great Gallery (lecture). Melbourne, Specialty Press, 1949.
Landscape into Art. London, Murray, 1949; as *Landscape Painting,* New York, Scribner, 1950.
Pierro della Francesca. London, Phaidon, 1951.
Moments of Vision (lecture). Oxford, Clarendon Press, 1954; reprinted in *Moments of Vision and Other Essays,* 1981.
The Nude: A Study of Ideal Art. London, Murray, and New York, Pantheon, 1956.
Looking at Pictures. London, Murray, and New York, Holt Rinehart, 1960.
Provincialism (lecture). London, The English Association, 1962; reprinted in *Moments of Vision and Other Essays,* 1981.
The Blot and the Diagram: An Historian's Reflection on Modern Art (lecture). Wellesley, Massachusetts, Wellesley College, 1962.
Rembrandt and the Italian Renaissance (lecture). London, Murray, and New York, New York University Press, 1966.
A Failure of Nerve: Italian Painting 1520-1535 (lecture). Oxford, Clarendon Press, 1967.
Civilisation: A Personal View. London, Murray, 1969; New York, Harper, 1970.
The Concept of Universal Man (lecture). Ditchley Park, England, Ditchley Foundation, 1972; reprinted in *Moments of Vision and Other Essays,* 1981.
The Artist Grows Old (lecture). London, Cambridge University Press, 1972; reprinted in *Moments of Vision and Other Essays,* 1981.
Blake and Visionary Art (lecture). Glasgow, University of Glasgow Press, 1973.
The Romantic Rebellion: Classic Versus Romantic Art. London, Murray, and New York, Harper, 1973.
Animals and Men: Their Relationship as Reflected in Western Art from Prehistory to the Present Day. London, Thames and Hudson, 1977.
An Introduction to Rembrandt. London, Murray, and New York, Harper, 1978.
Happiness (lecture). Birmingham, University of Birmingham

Press, 1978.

What is a Masterpiece? (lecture).   London, Thames and Hudson, 1979.

Moments of Vision and Other Essays.   London, Murray, and New York, Harper, 1981.

The Art of Humanism.   London, Murray, 1983.

Other

Another Part of the Wood: A Self-Portrait.   London, Murray, 1974; New York, Harper, 1975.

The Other Half: A Self-Portrait.   London, Murray, and New York, Harper, 1977.

Editor, *The Renaissance*, by Walter Pater.   London, Collins, 1961.

Editor, *Ruskin Today.*   London, Murray, and New York, Holt Rinehart, 1964.

*

Bibliography: *Kenneth Clark: Lord Clark of Saltwood: Guides to the Published Works of Art Historians No. 1* by R. Margaret Slythe, Bournemouth, Bournemouth and Poole College of Art, revised edition, 1971.

*   *   *

For many years, Kenneth Clark considered that his upbringing in a rich, philistine, godless environment had disadvantaged his development as an aesthete, but gradually he came to understand that isolation and the disciplined use of time spent alone had provided an opportunity to contemplate, uninterrupted, things of natural beauty, and to form a visual memory which was to become as acute and impressive as his sense of tactile values. Humoured by self-indulgent and neglectful parents, Clark discovered the challenge of performance, of holding the attention of those who felt unwilling to be attracted. Aged 13, he encountered the power of the human mind through *King Lear*. The Suffolk punches, carthorses on his father's estate, provided the basis for his sense of form, and the splendours of the Gothic architecture of Winchester, where he was at school, contributed permanent influences. Exposure to realistic art favoured by the bourgoisie of his childhood, together with an early hunger for information, was followed by a need to record what he saw, nourished by what he read. By these means the Kenneth Clark who left Winchester College to take up a scholarship at Oxford, disappointed at not having talent enough to be a painter, could evaluate quality in all forms of the arts and literature and took pleasure in translating such for others. His Oxford friends, concerned mostly with philosophy and the past, were astounded by his awareness of change, motivation and forward direction.

The Ashmolean Museum and the tasks set for Kenneth Clark by C.F. Bell as keeper of Fine Arts, a job Clark later took over from him, provided an incomparable training ground. Bell's taste and knowledge stopped short at 1810, but his advice was sought on English watercolours by scholars and dealers everywhere. Within the limitations of many prejudices, Charles Bell provided a valuable insight into the world of museums and scholarship. At the same time Kenneth Clark had discovered with excitement the London commercial galleries which were showing the post-Impressionist painters to a bewildered public. When this era of a century of French Art collapsed suddenly, he was the first to interpret why and to evaluate what remained and what could be provoked to follow.

After Oxford, he went immediately to Italy where he assisted Bernard Berenson with listing a new edition of his *Florentine Painters*. There he had access to one of the great libraries on the history of art, Berenson's fame as a connoisseur, an authenticator, was at its height, and Kenneth Clark witnessed first hand, from a centre of international power, the mania for attribution.

Certificates signed by Bernard Berenson involved a phenomenal feat of memory as well as critical judgement. Although Kenneth Clark complained that Bernard Berenson rarely spoke to him about art, the opportunity to work with him and to share the company of endless visitors involved with their work, and, perhaps most important of all, the many hundreds of letters they wrote to one another in later years, established a bond which was of permanent influence in ways which was revealed in both Kenneth Clark's work and in his manner of living. Of great value, too, whilst in Italy, Logan Pearsall Smith taught him to write English prose.

On his return to England, Kenneth Clark interrupted his Italian Art studies to write his first book, *The Gothic Revival*. By the time he had completed it, he felt that he had missed a great chance, that it might have been a pioneering work, resurrecting some reputations, repudiating less deserved ones. Much of the book is regarded highly still, and, importantly, it established within Kenneth Clark the appetite to communicate, to teach, to interpret. He returned to Italian Art, concentrating upon Leonardo da Vinci, whose vast body of written works had remained largely unrelated to his drawings and paintings. An article on Leonardo published in *Life and Letters* in 1929, relating Leonardo to the intellectual life of his time, led to an offer to catalogue the Leonardo drawings in the Royal Library at Windsor Castle. In 1930, Kenneth Clark was one of the organisers of the highly successful exhibition of Italian Art in Burlington Place, an event that revealed all the animosities of the Art world. From this moment, he accepted invitations to lecture, and these remained an important feature of his life, until, in his mid-70's, he felt that he had lost the necessary physical relationship with an audience. Collecting he considered to be largely a physical impulse too; the appeal of both collecting and lecturing left him with his own lessening of physical energy.

"Philosophy," he wrote, "has for me the fascination of the unattainable," yet he read all he could with admiration and, in spite of his claim, digested much of it and argued his way through the subject with philosopher friends. Their world was too removed from the centre of things, which Kenneth Clark had almost unwillingly come to enjoy.

His years as Director of the National Gallery were successful in terms of the Collection, less so where staff, for whom he was responsible, were concerned. By now his friends were in seats of the highest power, a generation sooner than would have been possible but for the carnage of the First World War. He blended this world and family life together with an impressive social one. To live through two world wars, first as a child and secondly as a high ranking public servant, strengthened his assertion of eternal values. He appointed War Artists to record buildings which might be destroyed and events of lasting national interest. If this provided little of great art, an encyclopedic visual backcloth of social history remains, distributed among provincial galleries throughout the Commonwealth. The search for the truly exceptional became his constant pre-occupation. When he found artists doing work which he felt close to being that of rare quality, he remained supportive, directive, watchful, putting his own resources, values and energies at their disposal.

At the Ministry of Information, the Arts Council of Great Britain, the Independent Television Authority, the National Theatre and the British Museum, in addition to major national art galleries in many countries, he suffered committees for the decisions he realised he wanted to influence. He declared a dislike of men of action, but in his way he became one. Kenneth Clark enjoyed the arena, and by his unique blend of knowledge, charm, humour and authority more often than not was at the centre of it.

After he resigned from public commitments, the subsequent generation of directors continually sought his advice and opinions, and he remained informed and influential. A few months after leaving the National Gallery in 1945, Kenneth Clark was offered the job of Slade Professor in Oxford, a visiting lectureship of high prestige, founded at the instigation of John Ruskin. For many years Ruskin became the most significant influence on Kenneth Clark's mind. His first Slade lecture, entitled "Ruskin in Oxford" preluded several series of lectures delivered to packed lecture halls. "To enjoy," he maintained, "one must first understand," and he certainly gave his audience an opportunity to do so. Themes of his lectures involved man's response to landscapes, motivations, or to particular paintings. His enthusiasm was intoxicating, and undergraduates of those days consider his lectures still the high point of their time at Oxford. Kenneth Clark worked on a premise that an artist with a long-standing reputation must deserve it, and one must examine how and why that reputation had been established. By now Rembrandt was interesting him deeply as was the conflict between classic and romantic art. Piero della Francesca was his intense concern, and he declared that, while much of his work was inexplicable, we must surrender to an imagination far beyond our normal experience.

The height of Kenneth Clark's powers as a communicator came with the Mellon Lectures in Washington in 1951, which were published as *The Nude* and must remain his most outstanding work. Critics were astounded at its breadth and treatment of an almost inspired knowledge and understanding and declared the book to be too full, leaving nothing more to say in the future. Indeed, Kenneth Clark found this magnificent study almost impossible to follow, comparing always what he was achieving to *The Nude* and often despairing at the comparison. Even so, many of the lectures delivered on both sides of the Atlantic were impressive, and some of these have become the basis for *Moments of Vision*, the first of his collected essays published in 1981. The title essay was the Romanes Lecture delivered in Oxford in 1954. It was written in Italy without the interruptions of London daily life, and Kenneth Clark regarded it as one of his best lectures and essays.

He wanted to follow *The Nude* with a series of "Motives"—where form and content are so closely connected that they have a recurring fascination for artists and are used repeatedly in the illustration of quite different subjects. "Motives" became the subject of the Slade lectures in 1961, but sadly the audience found them extremely difficult to understand, so Clark abandoned the idea of a book.

It was inevitable that television performing should have followed television administration, and Kenneth Clark had much success in this field. In the early days he talked about a particular painting which was propped against an easel. At the other extreme came *Civilisation* 13 programmes produced at great cost and shown in every country transmitting television throughout the world. The scripts of the series represented the length of pieces of work he was happiest with, developed from the obligatory weekly essay of his Oxford days. More recent books have related also to television programmes.

Kenneth Clark was conscious always of the huge gap between popular and informed taste, and he endeavoured to attract both extremes. "Roger Fry" he declared, "taught our generation how to look"; one might say that for the next 30 years he took over that role. Unlike many of those who influenced him, he gave expression to all forms of art with a personal dignity that cannot have been surpassed.

—Margaret Slythe

COHEN, Morris Raphael. American philosopher and legal theorist. Born in Minsk, Russia, 25 July 1889; brought to the United States in 1892. Studied at the College of the City of New York, B.S. 1900; Harvard University, Cambridge, Massachusetts, Ph.D. 1906. Married Mary Ryshpan in 1906; 3 children. Taught at the American Educational Alliance, 1899-1900, Davidson Collegiate Institute, 1900-01, and the public schools of New York, 1901-02; teacher of mathematics, 1902-04, 1906-12, and Professor of Philosophy, 1912-38, City College of New York;

Professor of Philosophy, University of Chicago, 1938-47. Visiting Lecturer, Columbia University, New York, 1906-07, 1914-15, 1918; Johns Hopkins University, Baltimore, 1921, 1925; University of Chicago, 1923; New School for Social Research, New York, 1923-38; Columbia Law School, 1927; and Law School of St. John's College, Annapolis, Maryland, 1928-31; Visiting Professor, Yale University, New Haven, Connecticut, 1929-31, and Harvard University, 1938-39. President, Thomas Davidson Society, 1899, 1901-02, 1906-08; Organizer, Conference on Legal and Social Philosophy, 1913; President, American Philosophical Association, 1929; President, 1933-41, and Honorary President, 1941-47, Conference on Jewish Relations; President, Jewish Organizational Conference, 1939-47. Fellow, American Association for the Advancement of Science. *Died 24 January 1947.*

PUBLICATIONS

Philosophy and Legal Theory

Reason and Nature: An Essay on the Meaning of Scientific Method. New York, Harcourt Brace, 1931.
Law and Social Order: Essays in Legal Philosophy. New York, Harcourt Brace, 1933.
An Introduction to Logic and Scientific Method, with Ernest Nagel. New York, Harcourt Brace, 1934.
Preface to Logic. New York, Holt, 1944.
The Faith of a Liberal. New York, Holt, 1946.
The Meaning of Human History (lectures). La Salle, Illinois, Open Court, 1947.
Studies in Philosophy and Science. New York, Holt, 1949.
American Thought: A Critical Sketch. Glencoe, Illinois, Free Press, 1954.

Other

A Source Book in Greek Science, with Israel E. Drabkin. New York, McGraw-Hill, 1948.
A Dreamer's Journey: The Autobiography of Morris Raphael Cohen. Boston, Beacon Press, and Glencoe, Illinois, Free Press, 1949.
Reflections of a Wondering Jew. Boston, Beacon Press, and Glencoe, Illinois, Free Press, 1950.
King Saul's Daughter: A Biblical Dialogue. Glencoe, Illinois, Free Press, 1951.

Editor, with Felix S. Cohen, *Selected Readings in the Philosophy of Law.* New York, privately printed; expanded version as *Readings in Jurisprudence and Legal Philosophy*, New York, Prentice Hall, 1951.

*

Bibliography: *Morris Raphael Cohen: A Bibliography*, by Martin A. Kuhn, New York, City College of New York Library, 1957.

Critical Studies: *Freedom and Reason: Studies in Philosophy and Jewish Culture in Memory of Morris Raphael Cohen*, edited by Salo W. Baron, Glencoe, Illinois, Free Press, 1951; *Portrait of a Philosopher: Morris Raphael Cohen in Life and Letters*, by Leonora Davidson Rosenfeld, New York, Harcourt Brace, 1962; *Mind and Nature: A Study of the Naturalistic Philosophies of Cohen, Woodbridge, and Sellars*, by Cornelius F. Delaney, Notre Dame, Indiana, University of Notre Dame Press, 1969; *Morris R. Cohen and the Scientific Ideal* by David A. Hollinger, Cambridge, Massachusetts, Massachusetts Institute of Technology Press, 1975.

*   *   *

Both as an original philosopher and as a charismatic teacher,

Morris Raphael Cohen was one of the most influential figures on the American philosophic scene in the 1920's and 1930's. His philosophical investigations spanned the areas of philosophy of science, metaphysics, philosophy of history and the philosophy of law; and some of the leading American philosophers of the next generation began as his students. The American philosophical scene in the 20's and the 30's was dominated first by pragmatism and then by logical positivism. Both of these traditions, although in very different ways, were heirs of classical empiricism and characterized by an instrumentalist (or conventionalist) view of scientific laws and theories and a disdain for rationalistic metaphysical speculation. In this philosophical milieu, Morris Cohen stood for a realistic interpretation of science and a metaphysics of reason.

Cohen viewed the inductivism of the empiricist tradition and the deductivism of the rationalist tradition as obviously inadequate accounts of scientific method. In an attempt to construct a mean between these extremes, he saw scientific theorizing as an effort of creative reason, but viewed this effort of reason as having its origin and confirmation in experience. Scientific theories emerge from human insight into felt difficulties in ordinary experience, and these theories then are systematically elaborated to reveal what they imply. The central role of reason in scientific method is systematization, a systematization which makes possible specific prediction. This having been secured, the scientific theory is directed again to the realm of experience for possible verification. Cohen construed scientific method as involving the interplay of reason and experience in such a way as to enable us progressively to understand the order of nature.

The project of metaphysics for Cohen was to explore the conditions of possibility of scientific method so understood. From his point of view there must be an ontological correlate of logical principles, scientific laws and the brute facticity which necessitates the moment of verification. Accordingly, he developed a relational theory of reality wherein real relations both logical and physical were constituents of but did not exhaust the actually existing individuals of our world. The nature of anything, therefore, is rational and can be revealed by our logical principles and scientific laws; but there is a brute facticity of things that escapes our rational understanding.

While it may be fairly said that Cohen's principal philosophical contributions were in the area of philosophy of science, he was much more than a narrow specialist. He wrote a history of American thought, numerous papers in social and political philosophy, a classic work on the philosophy of history and was a major figure in the development of philosophy of law in America. The same spirit that informed his philosophy of science informed his philosophy of law. Law was both a principle of stability and a principle of dynamism, a bridge between tradition and the emerging demands of society. As such it had to be informed by reason and the norms reason dictated, but it also had to be grounded in the actual facts of human nature and conduct historically understood. Like those of Kant and Peirce before him, the cornerstone of Cohen's philosophical orientation was the belief that experience without reason is blind and reason without experience is empty.

—C.F. Delaney

COLLINGWOOD, R(obin) G(eorge). British philosopher. Born in Cartmel Fell, Lancashire, 22 February 1889. Educated at Rugby School, and at University College, Oxford, B.A. 1912 (first class honours). Served in the Admiralty Intelligence Division, London, 1915-1918. Married Ethel Winifred Graham in 1918 (divorced, 1942), 2 children; married Kathleen Frances Edwardes in 1942, 1 daughter. Fellow, Tutor and Librarian of Pembroke College, and University Lecturer in Philosophy and

Roman History, 1912-35, and Waynflete Professor of Metaphysical Philosophy, 1935-41, Oxford University. Honorary doctorate: St. Andrews University, Scotland, 1938. Fellow of the British Academy, 1934. *Died 9 January 1943.*

PUBLICATIONS

Philosophy

Religion and Philosophy. London, Macmillan, 1916.
Ruskin's Philosophy (lecture). Kendal, T. Wilson, 1920.
Speculum Mentis; or, The Map of Knowledge. Oxford, Clarendon Press, 1924.
Outlines of a Philosophy of Art. London, Oxford University Press, 1926; reprinted in *Essays in the Philosophy of Art,* 1964.
Faith and Reason. London, Benn, 1928; Chicago, Quadrangle Books, 1968.
The Philosophy of History. London, Bell, 1930.
An Essay on Philosophical Method. Oxford, Clarendon Press, 1933.
The Historical Imagination (lecture). Oxford, Clarendon Press, 1935.
Human Nature and Human History (lecture). London, Oxford University Press, 1936.
The Principles of Art. Oxford, Clarendon Press, 1938.
An Essay on Metaphysics. Oxford, Clarendon Press, 1940; Chicago, Regnery, 1972.
The Three Laws of Politics (lecture). London, Oxford University Press, 1941.
The New Leviathan; or, Man, Society, Civilization and Barbarism. Oxford, Clarendon Press, 1942; New York, Crowell, 1971.
The Idea of Nature. Oxford, Clarendon Press, 1945.
The Idea of History, edited by T.M. Knox. Oxford, Clarendon Press, 1946.
Essays in the Philosophy of Art, edited by Allen B. Donagen. Bloomington, Indiana University Press, 1964.
Essays in the Philosophy of History, edited by William Debbins. Austin, University of Texas Press, 1965.

Other

Roman Britain. London, Oxford University Press, 1923.
Ambleside Roman Fort. Ambleside, St. Oswald Press, 1924.
The Roman Signal Station on Castle Hill, Scarborough. Scarborough, Yorkshire, Scarborough Corporation, 1925.
A Guide to the Roman Wall. Newcastle upon Tyne, Reid, 1926.
A Guide to the Chesters Museum. Newcastle upon Tyne, Reid, 1926.
Roman Eskdale. Whitehaven, Whitehaven News, 1929.
The Archaeology of Roman Britain. London, Methuen, 1930.
The Book of the Pilgrimage of Hadrian's Wall, July 1st to 4th, 1930. Newcastle upon Tyne, Society of Antiquaries and Cumberland and Westmorland Antiquarian and Archaeological Society, 1930.
Roman Britain. Oxford, Clarendon Press, 1932.
Roman Britain and the English Settlements, with J.N.L. Myres. Oxford, Clarendon Press, 1936; Baltimore, Johns Hopkins University Press, 1937.
An Autobiography. London, Oxford University Press, 1939.
The First Mate's Log of a Voyage to Greece in the Schooner Yacht Fleur de Lys in 1939. London, Oxford University Press, 1940.

Translator, *The Philosophy of Gianbattista Vico,* by Benedetto Croce. London, Allen and Unwin, and New York, Macmillan, 1913.
Translator, *Modern Philosophy,* by G. de Ruggiero. London,

Allen and Unwin, and New York, Macmillan, 1921.
Translator, *The History of European Liberalism*, by G. de Ruggiero. London, Oxford University Press, 1927.
Translator, *An Autobiography*, by Benedetto Croce. Oxford, Clarendon Press, 1927.

*

Bibliography: "Notes on Collingwood's Philosophical Work with a Bibliography" by T.M. Knox in *Proceedings of the British Academy* (London), 29, 1943.

Critical Studies: *The Later Philosophy of R.G. Collingwood* by Allen Donagen, Oxford, Clarendon Press, 1962; *The Formative Years of R.G. Collingwood* by William M. Johnston, The Hague, Nijhoff, 1967; *Mind, History, and Dialectic* by Louis O. Mink, Bloomington, Indiana University Press, 1969; *Critical Essays on the Philosophy of R.G. Collingwood*, edited by Michael Krausz, Oxford, Clarendon Press, 1972.

*   *   *

R.G. Collingwood was F.J. Haverfield's pupil and successor as an archaeologist of Roman Britain, and also a philosopher who became Oxford's Waynflete Professor of Metaphysical Philosophy. Many of his contemporaries succumbed to temptation to regard him as either a philosopher who dabbled in history or an historian who encroached on philosophy. He was also often misperceived as Benedetto Croce's "English disciple"; although he had general sympathy with the Italian philosopher's ideas and translated his book on Vico, there is little in Collingwood's ten philosophical books of Crocean derivation. Since Collingwood's death and the posthumous publication of two of his best-known books, his work has come into clearer focus as an independent and essentially systematic synthesis of British empiricism and post-Kantian idealism. The single concern which runs through all of his books is the study of mind and the levels of mental activity which enter into "forms of experience," particularly art, religion, science, history, and philosophy—as foreshadowed in his early book *Speculum Mentis*.

Collingwood sharply rejected the "realism" of his Oxford colleagues in the 1920's and 1930's but also refused to consider himself an "idealist" in the tradition of Bradley and Bosanquet. Especially but not only in the case of historical understanding, he regarded the problem of knowledge as insoluble either on the realist principle of the independence of the cognitive object or on the idealist principle that acts of thought cannot be identical in different mental contexts. However, with the transposition of the ancient opposition of realism and idealism into new forms, especially in philosophy of science, phenomenology, and hermeneutics, Collingwood has come to be regarded as a neo-idealist, not incorrectly in view of his emphasis on mental activity as constitutive of different forms of experience and their interrelations.

From among Collingwood's best-known views, three can be singled out as especially characteristic: in philosophy of history, his claim that historical knowledge is the re-enactment of past acts of thought; in philosophy of art, his definition of art as consisting of expressive uses of language; and in metaphysics his Theory of Presuppositions.

(1) Anticipating more recent analyses of the nature of human actions, Collingwood held that history is the reconstruction of *res gestae*, human actions performed in the past, and that every action is a unity of "outside," or how it is perceived, and "inside," or how it is intended. Thus all historical reflection seeks to re-enact the "thought" of historical agents on the basis of evidence about their behavior; re-enactment is neither a mere representation of the past nor a pure reconstruction of it in the historian's imagination. Historical understanding is therefore narrative in form rather than theoretical (which would make history a branch of "science"). Critics have often failed to recognize that Collingwood's concept of thought is broad enough to encompass mental processes other than the purely ratiocinative and also the trans-individual conceptual systems which enter into political, economic, and social institutions. The "re-enactment" of thought, in fact, is the only access which individual agents can have to the understanding or explanation of their own actions. In Collingwood's view, his philosophy of history accounts for historical explanations ranging from archaeology to the history of ideas, and in fact beyond historiography to the self-understanding of all experience.

(2) Collingwood distinguished "art proper" from all forms of pseudo-art by locating it in the imaginative experience of artists (and audiences), only secondarily in created physical objects or events, and by denying that such imaginative experience can plan its form or effects before actually coming into existence. The nature of all art is the conversion of indeterminate feeling into determinate emotion in the very process of expressing that emotion. Feeling can be physically discharged (as in, say, the physiological symptoms of anger), but *having* an emotion and expressing it are identical, and, like thought, emotion itself is an activity which can succeed or fail. The "corruption of consciousness," in both art and everyday life, is the failure to bring feeling to consciousness as an emotion. The link between imagination and expression Collingwood found in "language," including gesture as well as speech, the "intellectualized" form of language. Thus he concluded not only that poetry precedes prose but also that "dance is the mother of all languages." As in his philosophy of history, he concentrates on the continuities between the activity as specialized by the historian or artist and its occurrence as a feature of everyday life, and on the identity between the experience of the historian or artist and that of the audience, although he nowhere explains clearly how that identity can be known or tested.

(3) Collingwood introduced his Theory of Presuppositions ostensibly to support his bold hypothesis that metaphysics is (and always has been) nothing other than the analysis of the absolute presuppositions of current natural science. In fact, he uncannily anticipated T.S. Kuhn's notion (or notions) of "paradigms" and how the latter enter into scientific revolutions; but the Theory of Presuppositions can be understood as an account of conceptual frameworks which define any culture or historical epoch in its diverse forms of expression: science, art, religion, politics, philosophy—even fashion. Every statement actually made or entertained, Collingwood claimed, has meaning only as an answer to a question; and every question in turn derives from one or more presuppositions. Presuppositions which themselves are answers to other questions are "relative" and those which are not are "absolute"; the latter resemble Kantian synthetic a priori concepts, although they are not universal but subject to change. Absolute presuppositions combine into "constellations" which underlie the styles of thought characteristic of an historical epoch. Never quite complete or compatible, constellations of absolute presuppositions are subject to strains which when severe enough result in the painful abandonment of the constellation for a new one. Understanding of such an historical transition requires a clearer identification of the absolute presuppositions involved than was possible when they were simply taken for granted.

Underlying these and other views of Collingwood is a theory of levels of mind which locates forms of practical consciousness, such as appetite, desire, and will, and forms of cognitive consciousness such as imagination, perception, and discursive thinking, in their dialectical development from pure feeling to rational self-consciousness. Explicitly stated only in Collingwood's last book, *The New Leviathon*, and there in briefest outline, this theory is more evident in Collingwood's unpublished writings than in his published works; but it clarifies the unity and development of his thought, and it partially answers the objections of many critics who have seen in his thought from about 1936 an abrupt and unjustified conversion to "historicism": the abandonment, that is, of belief in the possibility of truth in favor of the view that beliefs cannot be evaluated as true or false and can be understood only in terms of how they came to be held.

Although there has never been a Collingwood school, his influence has been as great in philosophy of history as that of any philosopher since Marx. In philosophy of art, philosophy of religion, philosophy of culture, and the philosophy of philosophy itself, his influence has been more diffuse and harder to estimate; as in his own lifetime, his writings have attracted more attention outside the U.K. than within it, and at least as much interest among people who are not professional philosophers as among professional philosophers themselves. Additions to the literature interpreting and assessing various aspects of his thought show no signs of diminishing.

—Louis O. Mink

COOLEY, Charles Horton. American sociologist. Born in Ann Arbor, Michigan, 17 August 1864. Educated at the University of Michigan, Ann Arbor, Ph.D. 1894. Married Elsie Jones in 1890; 3 children. Worked for the Interstate Commerce Commission and then the Census Bureau, Washington, D.C., 1889-91. Assistant in Political Science and Economics, 1892-95, Instructor of Sociology, 1895-99, Assistant Professor, 1899-1904, and Professor, 1904-29, University of Michigan, Ann Arbor. President, American Sociological Society, 1918. *Died* (in Ann Arbor) 8 May 1929.

PUBLICATIONS

Sociology

The Theory of Transportation. Baltimore, American Economic Association, 1894.
Human Nature and the Social Order. New York, Scribner, 1902; expanded edition, 1922; in *Two Major Works: Social Organization and Human Nature, and the Social Order,* Glencoe, Illinois, Free Press, 1956.
Social Organization: A Study of the Larger Mind. New York, Scribner, 1909; in *Two Major Works: Social Organization, and Human Nature and the Social Order,* Glencoe, Illinois, Free Press, 1956.
Social Process. New York, Scribner, 1918.
Life and the Student: Roadside Notes on Human Nature, Society, and Letters. New York and London, Knopf, 1927.
Sociological Theory and Social Research: Selected Papers of Charles Horton Cooley, edited and with an introduction by Robert Cooley Angell. New York, Holt, 1930.
Introductory Sociology, with Robert Cooley Angell and Lowell Juillard Carr. New York, Scribner, 1933.
Two Major Works: Social Organization and Human Nature and the Social Order. Glencoe, Illinois, Free Press, 1956.

*

Critical Studies: *Charles Horton Cooley: His Life and Social Theory* by Edward Jandy, New York, Dryden, 1942; *Cooley and Sociological Analysis,* edited by Albert J. Reiss, Jr., Ann Arbor, Michigan, University of Michigan Press, 1968; *Charles Horton Cooley and the Social Self in American Thought* by Marshall J. Cohen, New York, Garland, 1982.

*   *   *

From the age of 18 Charles Horton Cooley kept a journal which has provided us with access to his thinking and to those ideas which most influenced him. He was much impressed by certain thinkers of his time, among them especially Goethe,

Thoreau and Emerson. As his own nature was serious and somewhat introverted, he was attracted particularly to philosophers of idealism, introspection and reflectiveness. He was generally unimpressed with the work of the early sociologists, although he shared an interest in the organic view of society with Herbert Spencer. However, Darwin's theoretical and empirical work did impress him, and from this influence he developed his own interests in process and evolution. The pragmatic psychologist and philosopher William James helped to shape his own ideas about the self as object and the pluralism of the self.

As Cooley began to hit his stride as a sociologist, he turned away from his training in statistics and his interest in a demographic approach to an interest in social psychology. His first important work, *Human Nature and the Social Order,* was the first of his trilogy on social theory. *Human Nature and the Social Order* introduces themes which were to pervade all his later work. In his organic view all in society are interdependent, parts of a whole: neither the individual nor the group is basic. Human nature to Cooley meant those "sentiments" and impulses that belong to human beings alone, and at all times, acquired only through interactions with others, such as sympathy, love, resentment, ambition, vanity, the feeling of social right and wrong, etc. This developed through the all-important medium of the primary group.

To Cooley, human beings communicate and interact through the mind, or ideas, as embodied in gestures, symbols and language. The self is developed only through interaction and through a process Cooley referred to as the reflected or looking-glass self: the self-idea has three elements, including "the imagination of our appearance to the other person, the imagination of his judgment of that appearance; and some sort of self-feeling, such as pride or mortification." Thus Cooley was concerned with three aspects of consciousness: self-consciousness, or what I think of myself; social consciousness, or what I think of other people; and public consciousness, or a collective view of the foregoing as organized in a communicative group.

Cooley based a considerable amount of his theorizing about human nature, communication, and the development of the self on careful observation of his own young children. Although he had empirical interests, he did no systematic research outside his own home, except to use information obtained from such sources as articles, contemporary novels, student autobiographies, and books in many fields. Although trained in measurement techniques, he distrusted measurement and preferred instead to use his own experience to interpret the experience of those under study, in what has variously been called trained sympathy or introspection. He arrived at his theoretical conclusions, not by systematic hypothesis testing, but through what he referred to as "brooding."

His great trilogy on social theory also included *Social Organization,* which dealt with social structure or society, held together by communication. In this he further developed the important notion of primary groups. Cooley's emphasis, out of phase with his times, was that of the individual's responsibility to the community, and he clearly admired the values of small primary communities. His faith in communication, growth and progress are most completely dealt with in the third of the trilogy, *Social Process,* in which he developed his notion of gradual, continuous, linear societal change. He held to the belief, based on his faith in American democracy which he used as a model, that change was in the direction of progress, and that catastrophic changes were abnormal and undesirable. Cooley's sociology was also his social philosophy, for values and morals were part of his analysis, and led to recommendations for the social order. For Cooley, mature and committed participation in social life and the setting of standards were necessary and of the highest order of importance. Values or ideals learned in the primary group—loyalty, truth, service, kindness—became the basis for interactions within the institutions of the larger society.

—Carol Whitehurst

CRICK, F(rancis) H(arry) C(ompton). British biophysicist and geneticist. Born in Northampton, 8 June 1916. Studied at University College, London, B.Sc. 1938; Caius College, Cambridge, Ph.D. 1954. Married Ruth Doreen Dodd in 1940, 1 son; Odile Speed in 1949, 2 daughters. Scientist, British Admiralty, 1940-47, and Strangeways Research Laboratory, Cambridge University, 1947-49; Member, Research Council Laboratory of Biology, Cambridge University, 1949-77; also worked with the protein structure project, Brooklyn Polytechnic, New York, 1953-54; Non-Resident Fellow, 1962-73, Fernkauf Foundation Visiting Professor, 1976-77, and since 1977 W. Kieckhefer Distinguished Professor, Salk Institute for Biological Studies, University of California at San Diego. Visiting Professor of Chemistry, 1959, and Visiting Professor of Biophysics, 1967, Harvard University, Cambridge, Massachusetts; Visiting Lecturer, Rockefeller Institute, New York, 1959; Bloor Lecturer, University of Rochester, New York, 1959; Triennial Lecturer, with J.D. Watson, Boston University, 1959; Korkes Memorial Lecturer, Duke University, Durham, North Carolina, 1960; Herter Lecturer, Johns Hopkins School of Medicine, Baltimore, 1960; Franklin Harris Lecturer, Mt. Zion Hispital, New York, 1962; Holme Lecturer, University of London, 1962; Henry Sidgwick Memorial Lecturer, Cambridge University, 1963; Harveian Lecturer, University of London, 1963; Graham Young Lecturer, Glasgow University, 1963; Robert Boyle Lecturer, Oxford University, 1963; Elisha Mitchell Memorial Lecturer, University of North Carolina, Chapel Hill, 1964; Vanuxem Lecturer, Princeton University, New Jersey, 1964; Charles West Lecturer, University of London, 1964; William T. Sidgwick Memorial Lecturer, Massachusetts Institute of Technology, 1965; A.J. Carlson Memorial Lecturer, University of Chicago, 1965; Failing Lecturer, University of Oregon, Eugene, 1965, 1977; Robbins Lecturer, Pomona College, California, 1965; Telford Memorial Lecturer, University of Manchester, 1965; Kinnard Lecturer, Regent Street Polytechnic, London, 1965; John Danz Lecturer, University of Washington, Seattle, 1966; Sumner Lecturer, Cornell University, Ithaca, New York, 1966; Royal Society Croonian Lecturer, 1966; Cherwill-Simon Memorial Lecturer, Oxford University, 1966; Genetical Society Mendel Lecturer, 1966; Rickman Lecturer, University College, London, 1968; Shell Lecturer, Stanford University, California, 1969; Gehrmann Lecturer, University of Illinois, Urbana, 1973; Cori Lecturer, University of Buffalo, New York, 1973; Jean Weigle Memorial Lecturer, California Institute of Technology, Pasadena, 1976; John Stauffer Distinguished Lecturer, University of Southern California, Los Angeles, 1976; Smith Kline and French Lecturer, University of California at San Francisco; Paul Lund Lecturer, Northwestern University, Evanston, Illinois, 1977; Steenbeck Lecturer, University of Wisconsin, Madison, 1977; Sir Hans Krebs Lecturer, University of Copenhagen, 1977; Lynen Lecturer, University of Miami, 1978; Dupont Lecturer, Harvard University, 1979; Ferguson Lecturer, University of Missouri, Columbia, 1980. Recipient: Lasker Award (jointly), 1960; Prix Charles Léopold Mayer, Académie des Sciences, 1961; Research Corporation Award, with James D. Watson, 1961; Gairdiner Foundation Award, Toronto, 1962; Nobel Prize for Medicine, with James D. Watson and Maurice H.F. Wilkins, 1962; Royal Medal, 1972, and Copley Medal, 1976, Royal Society, London. Member, Royal Irish Academy; Associate Foreign Member, Académie des Sciences; Foreign Honorary Member, American Academy of Arts and Sciences, and National Academy of Sciences; Fellow, American Association for the Advancement of Science, and Royal Society of Edinburgh; Honorary Fellow, Churchill College, Cambridge. Address: The Salk Institute for Biological Studies, Post Office Box 85800, San Diego, California 92138, U.S.A.

PUBLICATIONS

Science

Of Molecules and Men (lectures). Seattle, University of Wash-

ington Press, 1966.

* * *

F.H.C. Crick, British biophysicist and geneticist, who shared the 1962 Nobel Prize in Physiology and Medicine with Maurice H.F. Wilkins and James D. Watson, dominated the so-called "dogmatic" era (1950-1965) of biochemical genetics by deducing the actual structure of DNA (deoxyribonucleic acid) and from that inferring a number of its functional properties. Crick's earliest work in physics consisted of studies on the viscosity of water at temperatures exceeding 100° C. With the outbreak of World War II the physics laboratory in which he worked was closed and he soon joined the Admiralty Research Laboratory at Teddington. For the next eight years Crick contributed to the war effort by working closely with military teams that developed systems which would detect and detonate enemy mines. When peace returned he was intent of going into bench research either in particle physics or biophysics. Upon reading Erwin Schrödinger's new book, *What is Life?*, which emphasized the fact that fundamental biological problems could be thought about in precise terms, using concepts borrowed from physics and chemistry, Crick was convinced more than ever that great prospects were just around the corner in the field of biophysics.

Crick joined a group of X-ray crystallographers at the Cavendish Laboratory at Cambridge University. He worked closely with Max Perutz who at the time was working on the X-ray crystallography of hemoglobin—iron containing protein that carries oxygen and carbon dioxide in the blood. Although Crick taught himself almost everything he knew about crystallography, he did not hesitate to challenge some of the basic techniques and modes of interpretation adopted by his collegues at Cambridge. He felt that the hemoglobin molecule was much more complex than the simple model that was then being proposed. Remaining critical of traditional ideas about crystallography, Crick set out to force some of his collegeagues to rethink some of the fundamental issues about molecular structure. Perhaps it was Crick's uninhibited manner of challenging established ideas that attracted James Watson (a young American molecular geneticist) to him shortly after Watson arrived at the Cavendish in 1951. To Watson's extreme delight he had found in Crick someone who was interested in the same problem—finding out the "secret" of the gene. Both Watson and Crick realized that the discovery of this "secret" would be possible only if the molecular structure of the gene were determined.

From the time Crick joined the Cavendish group he had been searching for some way to relate gene structure to protein structure. He was certain that the specificity of proteins lay in the sequence of their amino acids and that this sequence was somehow related to the specific ordering of the hereditary material. At first Crick was unconvinced that DNA (thought to be the major component of the gene) was an important molecule to study because of the difficulty of interpreting its X-ray diffraction patterns. However, by 1951, a number of molecular biologists felt that DNA "smelled" like the essential genetic material: it was evident that DNA actually transmitted genetic information in some instances. It was in the context of Crick's inability to grasp the importance of DNA that Watson, a biologist anxious to discover *how* the gene worked at a molecular level and convinced that DNA was the answer, proved to be an invaluable co-worker for Crick. On the other hand, Crick's extensive knowledge of physics and crystallography, as well as his primary interest in relating gene structure to biological function, were equally invaluable assets for Watson. In 1951, both scientists decided to work on DNA. Their mutual effort turned out to be one of the most exciting and zealous pursuits in the history of biology.

When Watson and Crick began working on the structure of DNA its chemical composition had already been determined. The problem they faced was to devise a molecular model that would not only be in agreement with X-ray diffraction data but also would account for the regularity of the molecule's structure.

its chemical stability, and, above all, how the molecule could replicate itself faithfully. This meant that they had to determine what physical arrangement was geometrically possible and search for known molecular forces that could hold the parts of the molecule together. As a result of endless days of building numerous possible structural models of DNA and piecing together essential data obtained from the research of several scientists—including Maurice Wilkins, Rosalind Franklin, John Griffith, Erwin Chargaff, Linus Pauling, and Jerry Donohue, to name only a few—Watson and Crick announced their model of DNA in a short article in *Nature* (1953). Their model consisted of two helices (double helix) wound around each other, appearing very much like a spiral staircase, with steps composed of paired bases, and with a sugar-phosphate backbone spiraling around the outside. This model accounted beautifully for the major genetic, structural, and biochemical aspects of hereditary material. On the biochemical and structural level, it explained the data obtained from X-ray diffraction studies of DNA and the climbing pattern of bases at regular intervals. On a genetic level, it explained how the hereditary material duplicated itself and suggested how DNA stores genetic information. In short, Crick's collaboration with Watson had resulted in the single most important development in biology of the present century. The "secret" of life, that is, the nature of the gene had been found out!

Once the double helical structure of DNA was established, Crick's main interest became studying the specific mechanisms by which DNA codes, translates, and carries genetic information for the synthesis of proteins. To account for these problems he proposed the theory that amino acids were first attached to adapter molecules before being attracted to a nucleic acid molecule. He further hypothesized that the genetic code was a triplet: for every three bases on DNA there was a corresponding amino acid. Crick's studies coincided with other scientists' discoveries of "messenger" and "transfer" RNA (ribonucleic acid), which in simple molecular and biochemical language explained *how* genes replicate and carry information to form proteins. He later contributed greatly to working out the myriad of details of coding and carrying processes. In particular, he was concerned with the elucidation of the specific structure of a number of proteins, including collagen. He was also interested in showing the relationship between the mutation of genes and the resulting structural irregularity in a corresponding protein chain.

Perhaps the most important contribution to biology made by Crick was his insistence on relating every structural feature of DNA to the requirements of its biological function. In essence, Crick and his co-workers had pulled together the once separate disciplines of classical genetics, biochemistry, and molecular genetics to form a unified biology.

—Randall Davey Bird

CROCE, Benedetto. Italian philosopher and historian. Born in Pecasseroli, 25 February 1866. Studied law at the University of Rome, 1883-86. Married Adele Rossi in 1914; 4 daughters. With Giovanni Gentile founded the review *La Critica* (Editor, 1903-43). Made lifetime Senator of the Kingdom of Italy in 1910; served as Minister of Education, 1920-21; President of the Italian Liberal Party, 1943-47; Member of the Constituent Assembly, 1946-47; founded the Istituto Italiano per gli Studi Storici, Naples, 1947; Senator of the Republic after 1948. Recipient: Gold Medal, Columbia University, New York, 1923. Honorary doctorate: Oxford University, 1923; University of Marburg, Germany; University of Freiburg, Germany. *Died* (in Naples) *20 November 1952.*

PUBLICATIONS

The following list is based in part on Appendix 2, "Crocean Bibliography," in Gian Orsini's *Benedetto Croce: Philosopher of Art and Literary Critic*, Carbondale, Southern Illinois University Press, 1961, and gives the titles of Croce's works as they now appear in the complete edition published by Laterza Brothers of Bari.

Philosophy

Materialismo storico ed economia marxistica. Bari, Laterza, 1900; as *Historical Materialism and the Economics of Karl Marx*, London, Latimer, 1914.
Estetica come scienza dell'espressione e linguistica generale. Bari, Laterza, 1902; part one as *Aesthetic as Science of Expression and General Linguistic*, London, Macmillan, 1909; revised version with part two, London, Macmillan, 1922, and New York, Noonday Press, 1953.
Logica come scienza del concetto puro. Bari, Laterza, 1909; as *Logic as the Science of Pure Concept*, London, Macmillan, 1917.
Filosofia della pratica, economia ed etica. Bari, Laterza, 1909; as *Philosophy of the Practical, Economic and Ethic*, London, Macmillan, 1913; New York, Bilbo and Tanner, 1967.
Problemi di estetica. Bari, Laterza, 1910.
La filosofia di Giambattista Vico. Bari, Laterza, 1911; as *The Philosophy of Giambattista Vico*, London, Latimer, 1931; New York, Russell and Russell, 1964.
Saggio sullo Hegel, seguito da altri scritti di storia della filosofia. Bari, Laterza, 1913; selection as *What Is Living and What Is Dead in the Philosophy of Hegel*, London, Macmillan, 1915.
Cultura e vita morale. Bari, Laterza, 1914.
Teoria e storia della storiografia. Bari, Laterza, 1917; as *Theory and History of Historiography*, London, Harrap, 1921; and as *History, Its Theory and Practice*, New York, Harcourt Brace, 1921.
Nuovi saggi di estetica. Bari, Laterza, 1920; selection as "The Breviary of Aesthetic," in *The Book of the Opening of the Rice Institute*, vol. 2, Houston, Texas, 1912; and as *The Essence of Aesthetic*, London, Heinemann, 1921.
Etica e politica. Bari, Laterza, 1922; selections as *The Conduct of Life*, New York, 1924; as *An Autobiography*, Oxford, Clarendon Press, 1927; and as *Politics and Morals*, London, Allen and Unwin, 1946.
Ultimi saggi. Bari, Laterza, 1935; selection as *The Defence of Poetry: Variations on a Theme of Shelley* (lecture), Oxford, Clarendon Press, 1933.
La poesia: Introduzione alla critica e storia della poesia e della letteratura. Bari, Laterza, 1936; as *Poetry and Literature*, Carbondale, Southern Illinois University Press, 1981.
La storia come pensiero e come azione. Bari, Laterza, 1938; as *History as the Story of Liberty*, London, Allen and Unwin, and New York, Norton, 1941.
Il carattere della filosofia moderna. Bari, Laterza, 1941.
Discorsi di varia filosofia. Bari, Laterza, 2 vols., 1945; selections as *My Philosophy and Other Essays on the Moral and Political Problems of Our Time*, London, Allen and Unwin, 1949; New York, Collier Books, 1962.
Filosofia e storiografia. Bari, Laterza, 1949.
Storiografia e idealità morale. Bari, Laterza, 1950.
Filosofia, poesia, storia: Pagine tratte da tutte le opere, a cura dell'autore. Milan, Ricciardi, 1951; as *Poetry, Philosophy, History: An Anthology of Essays by Benedetto Croce*, London and New York, Oxford Universiry Press, 1966.
Indagini su Hegel e schiarimenti filosofici. Bari, Laterza, 1952.

History and Politics

La rivoluzione napoletana del 1799. Bari, Laterza, 1897.
La Spagna nella vita italiana durante la Rinascenza. Bari,

Laterza, 1917.

Storie e leggende napoletane. Bari, Laterza, 1919.

Storia della storiografia italiana nel secolo XIX. Bari, Laterza, 2 vols., 1928.

Storia del regno di Napoli. Bari, Laterza, 1925; as *History of the Kingdom of Naples,* Chicago, University of Chicago Press, 1970.

Uomini e cose della vecchia Italia. Bari, Laterza, 2 vols., 1927.

Storia d'Italia dal 1871 al 1915. Bari, Laterza, 1928; as *A History of Italy 1871-1915,* Oxford, Clarendon Press, 1929; New York, Russell and Russell, 1963.

Storia dell'età barocca in Italia. Bari, Laterza, 1929.

Storia d'Europa nel secolo decimonono. Bari, Laterza, 1932; as *History of Europe in the Nineteenth Century,* London, Allen and Unwin, 1934; New York, Harcourt Brace, 1963.

Vite di avventure, di fede e di passione. Bari, Laterza, 1936.

Per la nuova vita dell'Italia. Milan, Ricciardi, 1944.

Pagine politiche. Bari, Laterza, 1945.

Pensiero politico e politica attuale. Bari, Laterza, 1946.

Due anni di vita politica italiana. Bari, Laterza, 1948.

Quando l'Italia era tagliata in due (estratto di un diario). Bari, Laterza, 1948; as *Croce, the King and the Allies: Extracts from a Diary by Benedetto Croce, July 1943-June 1944,* London, Allen and Unwin, 1950.

Scritti e discorsi politici (1943-1947). Bari, Laterza, 1963.

Essays on Marx and Russia, edited by Angelo De Gennaro. New York, Ungar, 1966.

Discorsi parlamentari. Rome, Bardi, 1966.

Criticism and History of Literature

I teatri di Napoli dal Rinascimento alla fine del secolo decimottavo. Bari, Laterza, 1891.

Saggi sulla letteratura italiana del Seicento. Bari, Laterza, 1911.

La letteratura della nuova Italia. Bari, Laterza, 6 vols., 1914-40.

Conversazioni critiche. Bari, Laterza, 5 vols., 1918-39.

Goethe. Bari, Laterza, 1919; enlarged edition, 2 vols., 1946; original edition as *Goethe,* London, Methuen, 1923.

Una famiglia di patrioti ed altri saggi storici e critici. Bari, Laterza, 1919.

Ariosto, Shakespeare e Corneille. Bari, Laterza, 1920; as *Ariosto, Shakespeare and Corneille,* London, Allen and Unwin, 1920; New York, Russell and Russell, 1966.

La poesia di Dante. Bari, Laterza, 1921; as *The Poetry of Dante,* London, Allen and Unwin, and New York, Holt, 1922.

Poesia e non poesia. Bari, Laterza, 1923; as *European Literature in the Nineteenth Century,* London, Chapman and Hall, 1924; New York, Haskell House, 1969.

Nuovi saggi sulla letteratura italiana del Seicento. Bari, Laterza, 1931.

Poesia popolare e poesia d'arte. Bari, Laterza, 1933.

Poeti e scrittore del pieno e tardo Rinascimento. Bari, Laterza, 3 vols., 1945-52.

La letteratura italiana del Settecento: Note critiche. Bari, Laterza, 1949.

Aneddoti di varia letteratura. Bari, Laterza, 4 vols., 1953.

Other

Gli scritti di Francesco de Sanctis e la loro varia fortuna, Saggio bibliografico. Bari, Laterza, 1917.

Primi saggi. Bari, Laterza, 1919.

Pagine sulla guerra. Bari, Laterza, 1919.

Pagine sparse. Milan, Ricciardi, 4 vols., 1919-27.

An Autobiography. Oxford, Clarendon Press, 1927 (original Italian text now reprinted as "Contributo alla critica di me stesso," in *Etica e politica,* Bari, Laterza, 1922).

Nuove pagine sparse. Milan, Ricciardi, 2 vols., 1948.

Carteggio Croce-Vossler. Bari, Laterza, 1951.

Terze pagine sparse. Bari, Laterza, 2 vols., 1955.

Perche non possiamo non dirci "Cristiani.". Bari, Laterza, 1959.

Il Croce Minore, edited by Fausto Nicolini. Milan, Ricciardi, 1963.

Epistolario. Naples, Istituto Italiano Studi Storici, 1967.

Carteggio Croce-Valgimigli. Bibiopolis, 1976.

Carteggio Croce-Omodio. Naples, Istituto Italiano Studi Storici, 1978.

Carteggio Croce-Torraca. Galatina, Congedo, 1979.

Lettere a Giovanni Gentile (1896-1924), edited by Alda Croce. Milan, Mondadori, 1981.

For a complete listing of works edited and translated and series directed by Croce, see the Borsari bibliography listed below.

*

Bibliography: *L'Opera di Benedetto Croce* by Silvano Borsari, Naples, Istituto Italiano per gli Studi Storici, 1964.

Critical Studies: *Benedetto Croce,* by Cecil Sprigge, London, Bowes and Bowes, 1952; *The Philosophy of Benedetto Croce* by Angelo De Gennaro, New York, Citadel Press, 1961; *Benedetto Croce, Philosopher of Art and Literary Critic* by Gian Orsini, Carbondale, Southern Illinois University Press, 1961; *Rivista di Studi Crociani* (Naples), 1964-; *Croce: L'Uomo e l'opera,* by Italo De Feo, Milan, Mondadori, 1975.

*   *   *

Benedetto Croce's thought is the result of his original mind as well as the product of the philosophical speculation of Vico and other thinkers of the 19th century: Hegel, Herbart, Francesco De Sanctis and Antonio Labriola.

In his early twenties Croce had already established himself as a renowned writer of local Neapolitan history, and in his historical research he began to meditate on the nature of history. Is history an art or a science? The result was Croce's idea that history is the "knowledge of the individual," that is, art. Thus, in Croce's view, there is no difference between the world of Shakespeare and that of Gibbon. This view was the outright rejection of the Aristotelian concept of art and a restatement of the Vicoan position.

It was Giambattista Vico who fascinated Croce. Vico had spoken of the history of mankind as the recurrent passage from *fantasia* or creative imagination to rationality, from brutal force to morality. Croce took up this idea and transformed it: *fantasia* or intuition, reason, selfishness and morality are not recurrent historical epochs but eternal manifestations of the human soul or spirit.

But if Croce felt the influence of Vico, he was not indifferent to the philosophy of Herbart with his theory of the "distincts." For Croce there is thought without action, but there is no action without thought. There is art without concepts, but there is no concept or thought without expression, art or language—terms which are synonymous in Croce. There is selfishness without morality, but there is no morality without selfishness, hedonism or personal utility. The effect of this view was the complete re-evaluation of Machiavelli. For Croce Machiavelli was a genius because he divorced politics or selfishness from morality.

This theory of the "distincts" which Croce upheld in his *Aesthetics, Logic,* and *Philosophy of the Practical* provoked a great deal of criticism. Is it possible for a man to poetize or to feel without reasoning? Does not Croce divide the human soul or spirit into separate compartments? Aware of this difficulty, Croce began to speak of the "circularity of the spirit" in his *Guide to Aesthetics.* In this beautifully written small book Croce asserted the "cosmic" view of art: there is no great poetry without a philosophy of life. It is an idea which Croce further elaborated in his *Poetry* in stressing the difference between popular poetry and great poetry. "Popular poetry expresses emotions which are not based on great travail of thought and passions...great poetry moves and evokes in us great masses of remembrances, experiences and thoughts."

Croce had expounded his idealistic system in *Aesthetics*. In his well known work *What is Living and What is Dead in the Philosophy of Hegel*, Croce then began to examine and elaborate on the thought of Hegel. In this work Croce recognized Hegel's contribution to the world of philosophy: the rediscovery of reality as the synthesis of the opposites. The negative is the spring of development: opposition is the soul itself of reality. An example. "The lack of any contact with error is neither thought nor truth, but it is the absence itself of thought and, therefore, of reality."

Croce admired and subscribed to Hegel's theory of the synthesis of the opposites: beauty is the unity of beauty and ugliness; truth is the unity of truth and error; goodness is the unity of goodness and evil. Yet Croce could not help criticizing Hegel for applying the dialectic theory to the philosophy of nature. Croce was equally irritated at Hegel's extension of his dealectic theory to beauty and truth: Croce preferred the application of his theory of the "distincts." Hegel treated beauty or art as the thesis and philosophy or truth as the synthesis of the Absolute Spirit. Croce viewed them as "distincts": art can exist without philosophy, but philosophy cannot exist without art, expression or language. Thus Croce, in the tradition of Baumgarten, Vico and Kant asserted the principle that the logic of beauty or imagination has to be distinguished from the logic of rational and logical thought.

How did Croce view the world of the natural sciences? He stated that philosophy is cognitive but that the natural sciences are essentially utilitarian. They measure, calculate, classify and formulate laws and show how a fact is derived from another, but they find themselves helpless before the world of beauty, truth and goodness: the true reality. If philosophy grasps the essence of reality, natural sciences only create useful abstractions. "The natural concepts are very useful but they are incapable of knowing the essence of the spirit or reality." It goes without saying that Croce belongs to the economic-scientific school whose representatives are Bergson, Poincaré, Boutroux, Rickert, Le Roy, Avenarius and Mach.

The Crocean system was already well conceived and constructed by the year 1908: a system in which his *Logic* stressed the identification of history with philosophy.

For Croce there is no history without philosophy. How can a historian narrate a historical event without the use of concepts or thought? But philosophy is also history. Would, for example, Kant's philosophy be possible without the geographical discoveries which preceded him, capitalistic society and Hume's thought? "These events are in the philosopher's bones, and he must consider them, that is, he must know them historically, and the breadth of his philosophy is in proportion of his historical knowledge."

The identification of history with philosophy is one of the main themes of Croce's *Logic* but he was still dissatisfied with it. Croce examined it more closely and developed it in his *Theory and History of Historiography*.

This important book stressed the distinction between "chronicle" and "history." For Croce "chronicle" is dead history; "history" is contemporary history. If, in the historian, the feeling of Christianity and the love for democracy are dormant, he will not succeed in representing the true spirit of the Gospel or of the French Revolution. The historian will write "chronicle" but not a "history." It is this Crocean thesis—history as contemporary history—that leads, therefore, to a complete identification of history with philosophy.

This identification of history with philosophy reveals Croce's idealism: as there is no objective reality outside me, so there is no history unless my soul or spirit makes history speak or makes the reader empathize with the historical event. This identification also illuminates the fact that Croce was a philosopher interested in aesthetics, economics, and ethics, as well as a professional historian of politics and literature. Benedetto Croce certainly

lived his theory in the unity of his mental and practical life.

—Angelo A. De Gennaro

DASGUPTA, Surendranath. Indian philosopher and historian of religion. Born in Calcutta, October 1887. Studied at Calcutta University and Cambridge University, Ph.D. Married. Senior Professor of Sanskrit, Chittagong College, 1911-20; Lecturer, Cambridge University, 1920-22; Professor of European Philosophy, Indian Education Service Presidency College, Calcutta, 1924-31; Principal, Sanskrit College, Calcutta, 1933-42; King George V Professor of Philosophy, Calcutta University, 1942-45; Life Professor of Philosophy, Benares Hindu University, 1945-52. Harris Foundation Lecturer, University of Chicago, 1926; Stephanos Nirmalendu Ghosh Lecturer, Calcutta University, 1941. Secretary, Bengal Sanskrit Association, 1931-42. Honorary doctorate: Calcutta University; Cambridge University; University of Rome. Commander, Order of the Indian Empire, 1941. *Died 18 December 1952.*

PUBLICATIONS

Philosophy and Religion

A Study of Pantañjali.   Calcutta, University of Calcutta, 1920.
A History of Indian Philosophy.   Cambridge, Cambridge University Press, 5 vols., 1922-55.
Yoga as Philosophy and Religion.   London, Kegan Paul, and New York, Dutton, 1924.
Hindu Mysticism (lectures).   Chicago, Open Court, 1927.
Yoga Philosophy in Relation to Other Systems of Indian Thought.   Calcutta, University of Calcutta, 1930.
Indian Idealism.   Cambridge, Cambridge University Press, 1933.
Philosophical Essays.   Calcutta, University of Calcutta, 1941.
Rabindranath, the Poet and Philosopher.   Calcutta, Mitra and Ghosh, 1947.
Religion and Rational Outlook.   Allahabad, Law Journal Company, 1954.

Other

A Glimpse into the System of Education in Ancient India Through an Old Sanskrit Institution of Modern Bengal.   Chittagong, De, 1920.
Fundamentals of Indian Art.   Bombay, Bharatiya Vidya Bhavan, 1952.
The Vanishing Lines (poems).   Calcutta, Thacker Spink, 1956.

Editor, *A History of Sanskrit Literature, Classical Period*, with S.K. De.   Calcutta, University of Calcutta, 1947.

*

Critical Studies: *An Ever-Expanding Quest of Life and Knowledge*, by Surama Dasgupta, Bombay, Orient Longman, 1971 (contains a bibliography and list of Dasgupta's works in Bengali).

*   *   *

Surendranath Dasgupta was both a Sanskritist and a philosopher. If he had written nothing else but his 5-volume *A History of Indian Philosophy* as well as editing *A History of Sanskrit Literature: Classical Period*, he would still be remembered today by scholars of both Sanskrit and Indian Philosophy. He had in him the rare combination of Sanskritic learning and philosophical acumen.

Quite early in his career he wrote his Ph.D. dissertation at the University of Calcutta on Patañjali's Yoga system, and his interest in Yoga and its philosophy of mysticism remained alive throughout his life. Several volumes were to appear later dealing with this subject, such as *A Study of Patañjali, Yoga as Philosophy and Religion, Yoga Philosophy in Relation to Other Systems of Indian Thought*, and *Hindu Mysticism*. In *Hindu Mysticism* he argued that not only are there types of religious and mystical experience other than that of an intimate communion with God, but also that there can be no true mysticism without real moral progress. The latter point was meant to allay the "fears" of some religious thinkers who wanted to connect amoral behaviour with the mystical by a causal tie. The six chapters deal with the six types of mysticism found in the Indian tradition, ranging from the "Sacrificial mysticism" of the Vedic ritualists to Yoga, Buddhist mysticism, and popular mysticism of the Bhakti movement. His book in *Yoga Philosophy* is a very comprehensive survey of Samkhya and Yoga, dealing with metaphysical and ethical doctrines âs well as the Yoga practice. He was a teacher of another important 20th century thinker, Mircea Eliade, who wrote his *Yoga: Immortality and Freedom*, while he was studying with him in Calcutta. Dasgupta's *Indian Idealism* was published in 1933. Here, after devoting the first two chapters to Vedic and Upanishadic idealism, he wrote two long chapters to cover Buddhist idealism. The last chapter was devoted to Vedanta and kindred forms of idealism. This was rather an ambitious project of compressing the vast field of Indian idealistic thought within a small compass, and as a result, it suffers from a few shortcomings. But here, probably for the first time, he showed his awareness of the vastness of Buddhist philosophical literature and its implication for the rest of Indian philosophy.

His *magnum opus*, the 5-volume *A History of Indian Philosophy*, is unique of its kind, and will no doubt be an indispensable aid to researchers in Indian classical philosophical ideas for a long time to come. The merit of the work lies primarily in the fact that Dasgupta invariably consulted original Sanskrit texts as well as a large number of unpublished Sanskrit manuscripts before he summarized them for the volumes. He was a very painstaking scholar, and his deep knowledge of the Sanskritic tradition constituted a fruitful component of this work. There is some imbalance in his distribution of space to each individual school and each system, but in a pioneering work of this kind such imbalances are bound to happen. He was aiming at comprehensiveness, which was probably a near-impossible task. We may ask today as to why he devoted only 94 pages of volume I to the combined school of Nyaya and Vaiśesika but more than three entire volumes, covering about 1,700 pages, to Vedanta. But such imbalances need not detract from the unquestionable excellence of this work.

A philosopher's own inclination and philosophic preference is usually reflected in what he finds most important and interesting in the history of philosophy. In the case of Dasgupta, this was obviously so. In his philosophic endeavour, he was inclined towards a synthetic approach to Patañjala Yoga and Sankara's Advanta Vedanta. This is why he found *pramana* epistemology and methodology of Nyaya, Mimamsa, Buddhism and Jainism uninteresting and philosophically less significant. He was unable to see Buddhism independently of his Vedantic outlook, and thus he lent support to the general (and often true) accusation by Western Buddhist scholars that modern Indian scholars are incapable of presenting Buddhism without a Vedantic bias.

Dasgupta's contribution to the history of Sanskrit literary criticism and Sanskrit (classical) literature was also significant. He tried to analyse the periods of the history of Sanskrit literature using an independent criterion for decadence and revival. He made a comparative study of B. Croce and Indian aesthetics in a few Bengali publications. He also left behind a number of books written on literary criticism and aesthetics in his mother tongue, Bengali, and thus enriched the Bengali literature on these subjects.

—B.K. Matilal

---

de BEAUVOIR, Simone (Lucie Ernestine). French novelist and philosopher. Born in Paris, 9 January 1908. Educated at the Cours Désir, Paris, 1913-25; Institut Sainte-Marie, Neuilly; Ecole Normal Supérieure, Paris, agrégation de philosophie, 1929. Began lifelong relationship with Jean-Paul Sartre, 1929. Taught at the Lycée Victor Duruy, Paris, 1929-31; Lycée Montgrand, Marseilles, 1931-32; Lycée Jean d'Arc, Rouen, 1932-36; Lycée Molière, Paris, 1936-39; and Lycée Camille-Sée and Lycée Henri VI, Paris, 1939-43. Editor, with Sartre, *Les Temps Modernes*, Paris, from 1945. Member, Consultative Committee, Bibliothèque Nationale, 1969. President, Choisir, 1972. Recipient, Prix Goncourt, for *Les Mandarins*, 1954; Jerusalem Prize, 1975; State Prize, Austria, 1978. Honorary doctorate: Cambridge University. Address: 11 bis rue Schoelcher, 75014 Paris, France.

PUBLICATIONS

Philosophy

Pyrrhus et Cinéas.   Paris, Gallimard, 1944.
Pour un morale de l'ambiguité.   Paris, Gallimard, 1947; as *The Ethics of Ambiguity*, New York, Philosophical Library, 1948.
L'Existentialisme et la sagesse des nations.   Paris, Nagel, 1948.
Que peut la littérature? with others.   Paris, Union Générale d'Éditeurs, 1965.

Fiction

L'Invitée.   Paris, Gallimard, 1943; as *She Came to Stay*, London, Secker and Warburg, 1949; Cleveland, World, 1954.
Le Sang des autres.   Paris, Gallimard, 1945; as *The Blood of Others*, London, Secker and Warburg, and New York, Knopf, 1948.
Tous les hommes sont mortels.   Paris, Gallimard, 1946; as *All Men Are Mortal*, Cleveland, World, 1956.
Les Mandarins.   Paris, Gallimard, 1954; as *The Mandarins*, London, Collins, 1957, and Cleveland, World, 1960.
Les Belles Images.   Paris, Gallimard, 1966; New York, Putnam, 1968, and London, Fontana, 1969.
La Femme rompue, with *Monologue* and *L'Age de discrétion*. Paris, Gallimard, 1968; as *The Woman Destroyed, with The Monologue and The Age of Discretion*, London, Collins, 1969.
Quand prime le spirituel (short stories).   Paris, Gallimard, 1979; as *When Things of the Spirit Come First: Five Early Tales*, New York, Pantheon, 1982.

Other

Les Bouches inutiles (play).   Paris, Gallimard, 1945.
L'Amérique au jour de jour (travel).   Paris, Morihien, 1948; as *America Day by Day*, London, Duckworth, 1948; New York, Grove, 1953.
Le Deuxième Sexe (essay).   Paris, Gallimard, 2 vols., 1948; as *The Second Sex*, London, Cape, and New York, Knopf, 1953.
Must We Burn Sade?   London, Peter Neville, 1953; reprinted in *Privilèges*, 1955.
Privilèges (essays).   Paris, Gallimard, 1955.
La Longue Marche: Essai sur la Chine.   Paris, Gallimard, 1957; as *The Long March*, London, Deutsch, and Cleveland, World, 1958.

Mémoires d'une jeune fille rangée. Paris, Gallimard, 1958; as *Memoirs of a Dutiful Daughter.* London, Deutsch and Weidenfeld and Nicolson, and Cleveland, World, 1959.
La Force de l'âge (memoirs). Paris, Gallimard, 1960; as *The Prime of Life*, London, Deutsch and Weidenfeld and Nicolson, and Cleveland, World, 1962.
Brigitte Bardot and the Lolita Syndrome (essay). London, Deutsch and Weidenfeld and Nicolson, and New York, Reynal and Hitchcock, 1960.
La Force des choses (memoirs). Paris, Gallimard, 1963; as *Force of Circumstance*, New York, Putnam, 1964; London, Deutsch and Weidenfeld and Nicolson, 1965.
Une Mort très douce (essay). Paris, Gallimard, 1964; as *A Very Easy Death*, London, Deutsch and Weidenfeld and Nicolson, and New York, Putnam, 1964.
La Vieillesse (essay). Paris, Gallimard, 1970; as *Old Age*, London, Deutsch and Weidenfeld and Nicolson, and New York, Putnam, 1972.
Tout compte fait (memoirs). Paris, Gallimard, 1972; as *All Said and Done*. London, Deutsch and Weidenfeld and Nicolson, and New York, Putnam, 1974.

*

Critical Studies: *La Nature chez Simone de Beauvoir* by Claire Cayron, Paris, Gallimard, 1973 (contains an extensive bibliography); *Simone de Beauvoir* by Robert D. Cottrell, New York, Ungar, 1975; *Simone de Beauvoir* by Konrad Bieber, Boston, Twayne, 1979; *Simone de Beauvoir and the Limits of Commitment* by Anne Whitmarsh, London, Cambridge University Press, 1981; *Simone de Beauvoir: A Life of Freedom* by Carol Ascher, Boston, Beacon, 1981.

*   *   *

Simone de Beauvoir has often declared that her principal purpose in writing has been not to convey a body of knowledge but rather to communicate the feeling of her own existence as she lived it in a particular historical context. In none of her works does she realize this purpose more directly than in the four volumes of her memoirs (*Mémoires d'une jeune fille rangée;La force de l'âge*; *La force des choses*; and *Tout compte fait*), which, together with her two major novels (*L'invitée* and *Les Mandarins*), and her *récit*, or narrative, on her mother's death agony in a modern hospital (*Une mort très douce*) constitute both a chronicle of the intellectual, social, and political currents in Europe from the 1930's to the 1970's and an account of the growth and evolution of a brilliant French intellectual whose development was determined largely by two factors: that she was female and that she had rejected at an early age the religious and social values of the upper-middle-class family into which she had been born.

Forming an intimate and intellectual relationship in the 1930's with philosopher and writer Jean-Paul Sartre, whose theorizing about existentialism provides the philosophical substructure of much of her own work, Beauvoir emerged in the years following World War II as a dynamic member of a group of left-wing, atheistic writers who exerted considerable influence on opinions and beliefs in France and abroad. Like many post-war intellectuals, she rejected the ethics of individualism she advocated in the 1930's and embraced an ethics of political commitment, drawing closer to Marxist ideology and seeing increasingly in economic factors the determinant cause of human misery and distress.

Propelled by a desire to confront fundamental questions of good and evil, happiness and suffering, life and death, and to present them to as wide an audience as possible, Beauvoir was led to explore two issues that have become particularly important in the 20th century: the status of old people in modern society (*La Vieillesse*) and the status of women (*Le deuxième sexe*). Both of these volumes contain a great deal of sociological, psychological, and anthropological information, which Beauvoir amasses in an attempt to raise the consciousness of her readers. Both are elaborate and passionately argued indictments of society. With considerable vigor, Beauvoir condemns the callous contempt with which society often treats its elderly, who are judged to be useless, she maintains, because of their limited productive capacity. *Le deuxième sexe* is a mammoth edifice that rests on two postulates: first, that man, conceiving of himself as the essential being, the subject, has made woman into the unessential being, the object, the Other; second, that there is no such thing as feminine nature and that all notions of femininity are therefore artificial. Both postulates are derived from Sartre's *L'être et le néant*. As Beauvoir announces in the introduction to *Le deuxième sexe*, her perspective is that of existentialist ethics. The importance of this book was not fully recognized when it was first published. But with the advent of the women's liberation movement in the late 1960's, it became clear that Beauvoir's two-volume treatise provided a theoretical framework within which questions relating to women in society and culture could be seriously discussed. *Le deuxième sexe* is the most widely-read and influential of Beauvoir's texts, the work in which she fulfilled her wish to provoke social change and to leave her mark on the world.

—Robert D. Cottrell

de BROGLIE, Louis (Victor Pierre Raymond). French physicist. Born in Dieppe, 15 August 1892. Studied at the University of Paris, Licencié ès lettres, 1910, Licencié ès sciences, 1924, and Docteur ès sciences, 1924. Instructor, 1924-32, and Professor, Faculty of Sciences, 1932-62, University of Paris. Recipient: Nobel Prize in Physics, 1929; Henri Poincaré Medal, 1929; Grand Prize, Monaco, 1932; Kalinga Prize, UNESCO, 1952. Member, Académie Française, 1944. Foreign Member, National Academy of Sciences, 1948; American Academy of Arts and Sciences, 1958; Fellow of the Royal Society, London, 1953. Address: 94 Rue Perronet, 92200 Neuilly-sur-Seine, France.

PUBLICATIONS

Physics

Ondes et mouvements. Paris, Gauthier-Villars, 1926.
Selected Papers on Wave Mechanics, with Léon Brillouin. London, Blackie, 1928.
La Mécanique ondulatoire. Paris, Gauthier-Villars, 1928.
Recueil d'exposés sur les ondes et corpuscules. Paris, Hermann, 1930.
Introduction à l'étude de la mécanique ondulatoire. Paris, Hermann, 1930; as *Introduction to the Study of Wave Mechanics*, London, Methuen, 1930.
Théorie de la quantification dans la nouvelle mécanique. Paris, Hermann, 1932.
Conséquences de la relativité dans le developpment de la mécanique ondulatoire. Paris, Hermann, 1932.
Sur une forme plus restrictive des relations d'incertitude de après MM. Landau Peierls. Paris, Hermann, 1932.
Une Nouvelle Conception de la lumière. Paris, Hermann, 1934.
L'Électron magnétique (théorie de Dirac). Paris, Hermann, 1934.
Nouvelle Recherches sur la lumière. Paris, Hermann, 1936.
Matière et lumière. Paris, Michel, 1937; expanded edition as *Matter and Light: The New Physics*, London, Allen and Unwin, and New York, Dover, 1939.

La Physique nouvelle et les quanta.   Paris, Flammarion, 1937;
  as *The Revolution in Physics: A Non-Mathematical Survey of
  Quanta*, New York, Noonday Press, 1953.
*Le principe de correspondance et les interactions entre la matière
  et le rayonnment.*   Paris, Hermann, 1938.
Le Mécanique ondulatoire des systèmes de corpuscules.   Paris,
  Gauthier-Villars, 1939.
*Une Nouvelle Théorie de la lumière: La Mécanique ondulatoire
  du photon.*   Paris, Hermann, 2 vols., 1940, 1942.
*Problèmes de propagations guidées des ondes électromagnéti-
  ques.*   Paris, Gauthier-Villars, 1941.
Continu et discontinu en physique moderne.   Paris, Michel,
  1941.
De la Mécanique ondulatoire a la théorie du noyan.   Paris,
  Hermann, 1943.
Théorie génerale des particules à spin (méthode de fusion).
  Paris, Gauthier-Villars, 1943.
Ondes, corpuscules, mécanique ondulatoire.   Paris, Michel,
  1945.
Physique et microphysique.   Paris, Michel, 1947; as *Physics
  and Microphysics*, London, Hutchinson, and New York, Pan-
  theon, 1955.
*Mécanique ondulatoire du photon et théorie quantiques des
  champs.*   Paris, Gauthier-Villars, 1949.
Optique électronique et corpusculaire.   Paris, Hermann, 1950.
La Mécanique ondulatoire des sytèmes de corpuscules.   Paris,
  Gauthier-Villars, 1950.
Savants et découvertes.   Paris, Michel, 1951.
La Théorie des particulaes de spin 1/2: Électrons de Dirac.
  Paris, Gauthier-Villars, 1952.
Élements de théorie des quanta et de mécanique ondulatoire.
  Paris, Gauthier-Villars, 1953.
La Physique quantique restera-t-elle indeterministe?   Paris,
  Gauthier-Villars, 1953.
*Une tentative d'interpretation causale et non lineaire de la méca-
  nique ondulatoire (la théorie de la double solution).*   Paris,
  Gauthier-Villars, 1956; as *Non-Linear Wave Mechanics: A
  Causal Interpretation*, Amsterdam and New York, Elsevier,
  1960.
Nouvelles Perspectives en microphysique.   Paris, Michel, 1956;
  as *New Perspectives in Physics*, Edinburgh, Oliver and Boyd,
  and New York, Basic Books, 1962.
*Le Théorie de la mésure en mécanique ondulatoire: Interpréta-
  tion usuelle et interprétation causale.*   Paris, Gauthier-Villars,
  1957.
Seminaire des théories physiques.   Paris, Secretariat Mathema-
  tique, 1958.
Sous les sentiers de la science.   Paris, Michel, 1960.
*Introduction à la nouvelle théorie des particules de M. Jean-
  Pierre Vigier et ses collaborateurs.*   Paris, Gauthier-Villars,
  1961; as *Introduction to the Vigier Theory of Elementary
  Particles*, Amsterdam and New York, Elsevier, 1963.
*Étude critique des bases de l'interprétation actuelle de la méca-
  nique ondulatoire.*   Paris, Gauthier-Villars, 1963; as *The
  Current Interpretation of Wave Mechanics: A Critical Study*,
  Amsterdam and New York, Elsevier, 1964.
*Le Thermodynamique de la particule isolée; ou, thermodyna-
  mique cachée des particules.*   Paris, Gauthier-Villars, 1964.
Certitudes et incertitudes de la science.   Paris, Michel, 1966.
Louis de Broglie, edited by M.A. Tonnelat (selections).   Paris,
  Seghers, 1966.
Ondes électromagnétiques et photons.   Paris, Gauthier-Villars,
  1968.
La Réinterprétation de la mécanique ondulatoire, with J.A.
  Andrade e Silva.   Paris, Gauthier-Villars, 1971.
Recherches d'un demi-siècle.   Paris, Michel, 1976.

Other

Editor, *Wave Mechanics and Molecular Biology.*   Reading,
  Massachusetts, Addison-Wesley, 1966.

*   *   *

Louis de Broglie's study of "electron waves" provided the final
link in our modern understanding of the relationship of matter
and energy.

The theoretical foundation for this work had been laid by
Einstein at the turn of the century. In his general theory of
relativity, Einstein had demonstrated the intraconvertability of
mass and energy. His now famous equation predicted that mass
could be changed into energy and vice versa. The notion was
certainly a revolutionary one and, if shown to be true, would
modify the most fundamental presuppositions of the physical
sciences.

One line of confirmation for the theory eventually came from
the study of radioactivity. Precise measurements showed that the
mass of products formed during radioactive decay were slightly
less than that of the original radioactive isotope. The loss in mass
could be equated with the energy released during decay. The
Einstein relationship actually predicted quite accurately the correspondence of the *mass defect* in radioactive decay with the
energy released.

A second line of research arose within efforts to study the
momentum of photons, the ultimate "particles" of energy postulated by Einstein. As early as 1900, studies demonstrated that
light waves appear to possess momentum in their interaction
with matter. This discovery was surprising since momentum was
regarded classically as uniquely a property of matter, a function
of the mass and velocity of a particle. How a massless form of
energy like light waves could possess momentum was not clear.

The problem was resolved in 1923 in a series of experiments by
the American physicist, A.H. Compton. Compton bombarded
matter with a beam of X-rays and found that the radiation was
deflected by electrons. He was able to calculate the scattering of
the X-rays and the recoil of electrons with great precision and
found that the event followed the model of billiard-ball collisions
traditionally used to demonstrate the conservation of momentum. Momentum was conserved in the X-ray-electron interaction, just as it would have been in a particle-particle interaction. Compton had demonstrated that a beam of energy had the
same properties as a beam of particles.

De Broglie saw the implications of this discovery for the
evolving concept of the atom. If energy can have the properties of
matter, then might not matter also possess the characteristics of
energy? In particular, might not the electrons in an atom travel in
paths that could be described by and analyzed as *waves*? Consequently, de Broglie suggested that the motion of an electron in an
atom would be determined by the wave which accompanies it. He
predicted that the wavelength of this "electron wave" (he called it
a "pilot wave") would be a function of the electron's momentum
and could be expressed by the function: $\lambda = h/p$, where λ is the
wavelength of the pilot wave, p the momentum of the electron,
and h Planck's constant.

De Broglie further suggested that the only stable electron
orbits in an atom were those in which "standing waves" could
exist. This provided a restriction on the possible values of λ,
satisfying the conditions of quantum theory and providing the
specified orbital paths which, since Bohr's original model, had
become accepted as part of atomic theory.

The predicted wavelengths for orbiting electrons are comparable in magnitude to the wavelengths of X-rays and are, therefore, measurable in a fairly straight-forward manner. In 1928,
electron waves were observed in two independent studies by C.J.
Davisson of the United States and G.P. Thomson of Great
Britain. The evidence for the complete complimentarity of matter and energy, particles and waves, had thereby been demonstrated.

De Broglie's analysis of electron waves was applied most effectively by Erwin Schrödinger in 1926. Schrödinger's wave analysis
of electron orbits solved some long-standing problems in atomic

theory and provided the theoretical basis for our current mathematical model of the atom.

—David Newton

DEBYE, Peter (Joseph William). Dutch physical chemist. Born in Maastricht, 24 March 1884; emigrated to the United States in 1940. Studied at the University of Aachen, degree in electrical engineering, 1905; University of Munich, Ph.D. 1908. Married Mathilde Alberer in 1913; 2 children. Taught in Zurich, 1911-12, and Utrecht, 1912-14; Professor, University of Zurich, 1919-27; Professor, University of Leipzig, 1928-35; Professor, University of Berlin, 1935-40 (Director, Kaiser Wilhelm Institute of Physics); Professor of Chemistry and Head of Department, 1940-50, and Professor Emeritus, 1950-66, Cornell University, Ithaca, New York. Recipient: Nobel Prize in Chemistry, 1936; William Gibbs Medal, 1949, Nichols Award, 1961, and Priestley Medal, 1963, American Chemical Society; American Physical Society High Polymer Prize, 1965; National Medal of Science, 1965. Honorary doctorate: Harvard University, Cambridge, Massachusetts; Brooklyn Polytechnic, New York; St. Lawrence University, Canton, New York; Colgate University, Hamilton, New York; Oxford University; University of Brussels; University of Liège. Fellow of the Royal Society, London, 1933. Member, Royal Society of Amsterdam; Pontifical Society, Rome; Royal Irish Academy; Royal Danish Academy; Academy of Sciences, Berlin; Academy of Sciences, Göttingen; Academy of Sciences, Munich; Academy of Sciences, Brussels; Academy of Sciences, Liège; U.S. National Academy of Sciences; Franklin Institute, Philadelphia; Royal Institution, London; Hungarian Academy of Sciences; Academy of Sciences, Argentina; American Philosophical Society; Reale Sociedad Española de Fisica y Quimica, Madrid. *Died 2 November 1966.*

PUBLICATIONS

Physics and Chemistry

Polar Molecules. New York, Chemical Catalog Company, 1929.
Struktur der Materie: Vier Vorträge. Leipzig, Hirzel, 1933; as *The Structure of Matter: Four Lectures,* Albuquerque, University of New Mexico, 1934.
Kernphysik. Leipzig, Hirzel, 1935.
Methoden zur Bestimmung der elektrischen und geometischen Struktur von Molekülen (Nobel lecture). Leipzig, Hirzel, 1937.
Collected Papers. New York, Interscience Publishers, 1954.
Topics in Chemical Physics, Based on the Harvard Lectures of Peter J.W. Debye. Amsterdam and New York, Elsevier, 1962.
Molecular Forces, Based on the Baker Lectures of Peter J.W. Debye. New York, Interscience Publishers, 1967.

Other

Editor, *Dipolmoment und chemische Struktur.* Leipzig, Hirzel, 1929; as *The Dipole Moment and Chemical Structure,* London, Blackie, 1931.
Editor, *Elektroneninterferenzen,* Leipzig, Hirzel, 1930, as *The Interference of Electrons,* London, Blackie, 1931.
Editor, *Molekülstruktur,* Leipzig, 1931; as *The Structure of Molecules,* London, Blackie, 1932.
Editor, *Magnetismus.* Leipzig, Hirzel, 1933.

*   *   *

Peter Debye's research spanned an enormous range of topics. His earliest work evolved out of his initial interests in electrical phenomena, as applied to molecular structure. This research involved the measurement of dipole moments for a variety of substances. In many covalently bonded molecules, the distribution of charge is not symmetrical within the molecule. One atom or another displays a greater attraction for electrons, and the region of that molecule containing this atom is somewhat more negatively charged than other parts of the molecule. When placed within an electric field, this molecule will experience a coulombic force tending to orient it parallel to the external field. The force needed to rotate the molecule is related to the relative separation of charges within the molecule and, hence, to the character of the bond in the molecule. Debye's work in this field is honored by the selection of the *debye* as the unit of dipole moment in the SI system of measurement.

A significant portion of Debye's research was concerned with a variety of topics from theoretical physics to thermodynamics. In 1926, for example, he independently verified the conservation of linear momentum during interactions between photons and electrons, a phenomenon known as the Compton effect for its somewhat earlier discoverer. His interest in low temperature physics led to useful suggestions for achieving temperatures very close to absolute zero. And he extended the techniques of crystallographic analysis, developed by the Braggs, to powdered substances.

It is somewhat ironic, then, that Debye's Nobel Prize in 1936 was awarded in the field of chemistry. The Prize recognized his work in the area of solutions. The earliest modern explanation of solutions had been developed by Arrhenius in the 1880's. The Arrhenius theory left unsolved a number of questions, however. Of special interest was the relationship between solution concentration and certain solution properties. The inference from the Arrhenius theory was that the number of ions in a solution was directly proportional to the concentration of that solution. As more and more solute particles are added to water, they ionize and produce a proportionately greater number of ions. Properties dependent on the number of solute particles should, therefore, show a linear relationship to solution concentration.

In fact, Arrhenius himself knew that this was not the case. Electrical conductance, for example, does not change linearly with solution concentration. His explanation of this phenomenon was that not all particles of the solute ionize in water. As solution concentration increases, the degree of ionization becomes less, he said. This explanation proved unsatisfactory for Debye. He argued that many common solutes already exist as ions in the solid state. Crystallographic data confirmed that a salt such as sodium chloride would almost inevitably dissociate completely in water solutions.

Debye's explanation for this discrepancy was that ionic solids *do* dissociate completely in water solution. The result is masked, however, by the interaction among ions of opposite charges within the solution. Each positively charged ion, for example, is surrounded by a "cloud" of negatively charged ions, and vice versa. Although dissociated, then, the ions are not *effectively* independent of each other.

By 1923, Debye and his colleague, Erich Hückel, had developed mathematical expressions describing the effect of this "drag" of ions on each other. The *activity coefficient* which can be calculated from Debye-Hückel equations now provides an effective method for predicting the properties of solutions.

—David Newton

DELBRÜCK, Max. American geneticist. Born in Berlin, Germany, 4 September 1906; emigrated to the United States in 1937; naturalized, 1945. Studied at the University of Göttingen,

Ph.D. 1930. Married Mary Bruce in 1941; 4 children. Rockefeller Foundation Fellow in Physics, University of Zurich and University of Copenhagen, 1931; Assistant, Kaiser Wilhelm Institute for Chemistry, Berlin, 1932-37; Rockefeller Foundation Fellow in Biology, California Institute of Technology, Pasadena, 1937-39; Instructor in Physics, Vanderbilt University, Nashville, Tennessee, 1940-45; Assistant Professor, 1945-46, Albert Billings Rudock Professor of Biology, 1947-77, and Professor Emeritus, 1977-81, California Institute of Technology. Recipient: Nobel Prize in Physiology and Medicine (jointly), 1969. Member, National Academy of Sciences. *Died 10 March 1981.*

PUBLICATIONS

Scientific Writings

Der Aufbau natürliche und künstliche Kernumwandlungen, with Lise Meitner. Berlin, Springer, 1935.
Statistische Quantenmechanik im Thermodynamik, with Gert Molière. Berlin, De Gruyter, 1936.
Über Verebungschemie. Cologne, Westdeutscher Verlag, 1963.
Anfänge der Wahrnehmung. Weisbaden, Steiner, 1974.

Other

Editor, *Conference on the Similarities and Dissimilarities Between Viruses, Animals, Plants and Bacteria.* Pasadena, California Institute of Technology, 1950.

*   *   *

Max Delbrück came to the field of genetics at a time when the occurrence of genes throughout the plant and animal kingdoms and the extensive linkage of genes were clearly established. However, the chemistry and function of genes were entirely unknown, and the genetic studies of the time were unsuccessful at resolving these problems. That we now have detailed molecular answers to basic questions concerning gene structure, function, replication and mutation is due to the brilliant success of the field of microbial genetics, of which Max Delbrück was one of the founding fathers and the conceptual and spiritual guide.

Delbrück was a student of the physicist Niels Bohr, thus he was schooled in the quantum nature of radiation, in atomic structure, and in mathematical examination of natural phenomenon. A paper published in 1935 by Timofeyev-Ressovsky, Zimmer and Delbrück in a mathematical-physical journal of the University of Göttingen suggested analyzing the gene as a target for radiation. This paper introduced a rational approach to attacking problems of gene size, replication and mutability, and suggested use of target theory and radiation dose response as tools for obtaining answers. A subsequently outdated notion described in this paper, that a gene in one form might be distinguished from that in another form by a transient alteration of energy state, was publicized in the book *What Is Life?* by Erwin Schrödinger. Schrödinger's book, published in 1944, was widely read and exerted a major influence on many scientists who had emigrated to the United States to escape Nazi persecution. These scientists were thus interested in Delbrück's experiments, at the California Institute of Technology, using bacterial viruses as the simplest life form and a model for gene function and replication.

Delbrück chose bacterial viruses (bacteriophage) as an experimental system since these were known to be composed of protein and DNA, components that constitute the chromosomes of higher organisms. Genes had been shown to be located on chromosomes. DNA was discovered in 1868, however early hypothesis for the structure of DNA described a molecule of simple predictability that was incapable of housing the vast informational content of an organism. The correct structure of DNA was not elucidated until 1953, by Watson and Crick.

The life cycle of the bacteriophage was also obscure as a result of conflicting data arising from use of many different phage strains and bacterial host species. Delbrück suggested limiting the choice to concentrate on the virulent T phage strains that infect the human gut bacterium *Escherichia coli,* and suggested standardizing growth temperature and medium. As a result, much progress was made concerning the sequence of events that characterize a phage infection and successful production of progeny. Most important, these studies defined an "eclipse" period immediately following the phage infection during which no progeny could be detected, and the infected unit took on the characteristics of the host cell. Extension of this "latent period" before the first appearance of progeny was shown by Delbrück in 1940 to result in an increase in the yield of total progeny. Phage morphology was examined in early electron microscopes, and the characteristic size of the phage particles of each of several strains was shown to be independent of the yield of progeny. Heritable variants or mutants of viruses were discovered in the mid-1940's, and co-infection of *E. coli* by mutationally marked phage parents led to demonstration of linkage, recombination, and a genetic map of phage genes.

These studies and the results of experiments by other members of the phage group led to a paradigm which could be used to examine other host-virus relationships. Delbrück and his disciples had cut through the obscurity of diversity of different organisms to get at the nugget of gene replication and function. Delbrück's development of the bacteriophage system was described by Theodore Puck as "a device, capable of rapid and exquisitely precise answers to specific questions dealing with biological replication and its associated processes...whose usefulness continues to expand after more than 25 years."

Delbrück attracted phage workers from all parts of the world together to a laboratory in Cold Spring Harbor, New York, each summer to exchange ideas in the form of seminars, laboratory courses and intensive discussions of recent data. André Lwoff described his visit to Cold Spring Harbor with the words, "I thus discovered America, Delbrück, and the powerful 'phage church'." The issues raised at Cold Spring Harbor interested James Watson to learn more about the structure of DNA, since the central role of DNA in the life cycle of phage was quite apparent from data accumulated by 1950. Another concept raised at a Cold Spring Harbor Meeting, in 1951, was Delbrück's perceptive question concerning the nature of conditional mutations in *Neurospora crassa*: could mutations of essential functions be observed? The approach suggested at this meeting has been the basis of subsequent analyses of genes coding for essential functions. Another product of Delbrück's efforts during these years was the establishment of the animal virus program at Cal Tech, and his early perspicacity remains evident as continuing breakthroughs with animal viruses provide much current excitement in the biological sciences.

The response of living matter to radiation retained Delbrück's curiosity, and he pursued this interest by studying the growth response to light of the mold *Phycomyces.* He showed in 1976 that the physics of the mold's response to light corresponded to the triplet state of the intracellular compound riboflavin. Delbrück's promotion of this system provoked a number of *E. coli* geneticists and many younger scientists to turn their attention to the molecular biology of fungi.

The scientific and social attitudes of many of the early phage workers surrounding Delbrück set a style that has been basic to molecular genetics since that time. The approach consisted of rigorous quantitative analysis in a generous and optimistic environment. Many of the leaders in a wide variety of biological areas acknowledge Delbrück's inspiration. James Watson wrote that "in the presence of Delbrück I hoped I might someday participate just a little in some great revelation." As described by Salvador Luria, Delbrück offered scientists an invitation to "the feast table of microbial genetics."

—Sonia Guterman

DERRIDA, Jacques. French philosopher. Born in El Biar, Algiers, in 1930. Studied at the Ecole Normale Supérieure, Paris, and Harvard University, Cambridge, Massachusetts, 1956-57. Taught at the Sorbonne, 1960-64. Since 1965, Professor of the History of Philosophy, Ecole Normale Supérieure, Paris. Lives in Paris.

PUBLICATIONS

Philosophical Works

Le Voix et le phénomène: Introduction au problème du signe dans la phénoménologie de Husserl. Paris, Presses Universitaires de France, 1967; as *Speech and Phenomena, and Other Essays on Husserl's Theory of Signs*, Evanston, Illinois, Northwestern University Press, 1973.
L'Ecriture et la différence. Paris, du Seuil, 1967; as *Writing and Difference*, Chicago, University of Chicago Press, 1978.
De la grammatologie. Paris, Minuit, 1967; as *Of Grammatology*, Baltimore, Johns Hopkins University Press, 1976.
La Dissémination. Paris, du Seuil, 1972; as *Dissemination*, Chicago, University of Chicago Press, 1981.
Marges de la philosophie. Paris, Minuit, 1972; as *Margins of Philosophy*, Chicago, University of Chicago Press, 1982.
Positions: Entretiens avec Henri Ronse, Julia Kristeva, Jean-Louis Houdebine, Guy Scarpetta. Paris, Minuit, 1972; as *Positions*, Chicago, University of Chicago Press, 1981.
Glas. Paris, Galilée, 1974.
Eperons: Les Styles de Nietzsche. Paris, Flammarion, 1978; as *Spurs: Nietzsche's Styles*. Chicago, University of Chicago Press, 1979.
La Vérité en peinture. Paris, Flammarion, 1978.
La Carte postale: de Socrate à Freud et au-dela. Paris, Flammarion, 1980.

*

Critical Studies: *The Prison House of Language* by Fredric Jameson, Princeton, New Jersey, Princeton University Press, 1972; "Jacques Derrida: His 'Difference' with Metaphysics" by Lionel Abel in *Salmagundi* (Saratoga Springs, New York), 25, 1974; "Translator's Preface" by Gayatri Chakravorty Spivak in *Of Grammatology*, Baltimore, Johns Hopkins University Press, 1976; "The Problem of Textuality: Two Exemplary Positions" by Edward W. Said in *Critical Inquiry* (Chicago), 4, 1978; "Philosophy as a Kind of Writing: An Essay on Derrida" by Richard Rorty in *New Literary History* (Charlottesville, Virginia), 10, 1978; "Jacques Derrida" by Jonathan Culler in *Structuralism and Since: From Lévi-Strauss to Derrida*, edited by John Sturrock, London and New York, Oxford University Press, 1979; *Marxism and Deconstruction* by Michael Ryan, Baltimore, Johns Hopkins University Press, 1982.

*   *   *

From his earliest published article Jacques Derrida has been concerned with questions of origin, of structure, of closure, and of writing, in particular as they relate to history, truth, scientific objectivity generally, and the constitution of meaning itself. The conditions of the possibility of a given structure, he has argued, can never be understood from within that structure. From this array of issues Derrida gradually generated a set of principles which were first formulated as such in 1967 in his monumental early work *De la grammatologie*. These principles provide the framework for all of his subsequent work, and although much elaboration and expansion of their problematics has been done in the subsequent 15 years, Derrida's work as a whole (to date) has the striking characteristic of a remarkable consistency of focus, direction, orientation and ultimately of formulation, despite its apparent variations.

These principles adhere to a strategy of textual analysis singularly developed and originated by Derrida which he calls *deconstruction*. It involves the following aims and tasks in its operation: (i) to reveal the economy of the written text; (ii) to undo "onto-theology"; and (iii) to show the law of the relationship between what a writer commands and what he does not command of the patterns of language that he uses. Ultimately, Derrida aims towards the "deconstruction of metaphysics" and the "destruction of the Aufhebung" upon which Hegel's system essentially hinges.

This strategy is an "empirical" approach to the text of any genre—e.g. philosophy, literature, linguistics, etc.—which in a certain respect applies the text's own principles to itself. Derrida's analyses of Husserl and of Rousseau are particularly exemplary in this respect. In his detailed examination of Husserl in *La Voix et le phénomène*, Derrida aims to reveal the hidden level of metaphysical presuppositions and assumptions which animate the former's phenomenology at the very moment in which he claims to perform an epochè on those same assumptions. The key issue here for Derrida is the role of the sign, indeed of language itself and hence of a certain spacing, a certain absence which "allows for the possibility" of the presencing of "presence" itself *as* immediate in Husserl's phenomenology. Suffice it to say that Derrida concludes in this study that perception as such, as traditionally understood within philosophy, can no longer be said to exist.

With the deconstruction of Rousseau, Derrida aims to show once again precisely how, where and why the explicit claims made by Rousseau are undercut by the very phenomena which he has, albeit invisibly to himself, described. This relation between that which Rousseau "declares" and that which he "describes" which entails a non-unifiable differing and deferring Derrida calls *the logic of the supplement*. It is such a process which characterizes textuality itself, Derrida insists, and which paradoxically: (i) allows for the constitution of metaphysics itself in and through writing or textuality (the necessary prerequisite for scientific objectivity, Husserl insisted) and yet, (ii) unravels all claims to the constitution of an object due to the differing and displacing process of textuality and its cohort, contextuality itself. Thus ultimately Derrida insists not that objectivity is no longer possible (and within this philosophy, metaphysics, and science itself) due to this formative/deformative double structure of textuality, but rather that this process has always already been the foundation of all that we take to be knowledge, science and truth. The name for such a process he terms *différance*.

The more radical and indeed apparently more threatening side of Derrida's early work—the deconstruction of metaphysics and the destruction of the Aufhebung—began to flourish and to develop within Derrida's work in the 1970's. At this time he began to engage in what might be called a certain experimental writing in addition to the continuation of various deconstructive projects. These projects include the following: *Marges de la philosophie* (concerning Hegel, Heidegger, Beneveniste, Husserl, and Valéry, for instance); *La Dissémination* (concerning Hegel, Plato, Mallarmé and Sollers); *Eperons: Les Styles de Nietzsche* (concerning Nietzsche, Heidegger and Lacan principally); and *La Vérité en peinture* (concerning Kant, Hegel and Heidegger). The more radical side, however, appeared in the form of *Glas* and that of *La Carte Postale*.

In *Glas*, which is undoubtedly his magnum opus to date, Derrida sets up a double text: each page entails (at least) two columns which face each other and to a large extent parallel each other thematically yet which deal explicitly with somewhat different subject matter. The left column entails an analysis of Hegel, in particular with respect to his early writings, his philosophy of religion, his treatment of the Jews, of women, his aesthetics and also various significant biographical data. The right column is a critical analysis of Jean Genet's writings and seems to leap from theme to theme, from text to meta-text, statement to meta-statement, etc. The labyrinth Derrida sets up in this text has its forerunners in several earlier essays (including "Tympan," for example) and its follow-up in *La Carte Postale*, where the "other text" is absent explicitly. With *Glas*, however, one cannot simply subsume its approach within the process of deconstruction. Instead it seems that Derrida is experimenting with the process of *différance* itself. In addition, it would seem that *Glas* is a text most highly resistant to any form of totalization, synthetic understanding or hermeneutic interpretation. On the other hand, the text does not simply fall apart into disparate fragments without any apparent continuities. Precisely the type of framework needed for the analysis of such a text is a question which as yet has no answer in or beyond the work of Derrida.

Derrida's most recent work once again sustains his original principles and adheres to the projects he so early on seems to have set for himself. The subject matter with which he now seems concerned, however, involves the relation of the law to literature. The law here is both institutionalized and institutionalizing and thus entails both juridico-political as well as metaphysical and traditional philosophic dimensions. Such recent studies include work on Kafka, Benjamin, Nietzsche and Blanchot.

These comments do not sum up Derrida's work as a whole, but they do suggest two crucial dimensions of his projects. First, it seems clear that Derrida has sustained a consistent, coherent and explicitly defined program in his writing which is concerned with the revelation of the conditions of the possibility of metaphysics itself. Second, and equally as important, it is also evident that Derrida's development of this same problematic has taken on radically original formats of textuality such as (a) have never before been attempted within philosophy as such, and (b) have yet to be thoroughly analysed, understood or appropriated by that same tradition. It is, of course, this appropriation, in the Hegelian sense, that Derrida himself is concerned to examine, place in question, and indeed keep his own work always "at the limits" of. It remains to be seen, however, whether or not his own principles can (or indeed must) in the name of rigorous analysis be applied to Derrida's work as well as a whole.

—Irene E. Harvey

---

de SAUSSURE, Ferdinand. Swiss philologist. Born in Geneva, 26 November 1857. Studied at the University of Geneva, 1875-76; University of Leipzig, 1876-80; Ph.D. (summa cum laude), 1880; University of Berlin, 1878-79. Married; 2 sons. Maitre de Conférences, Ecole pratique des hautes études, Paris, 1881-91; Professor, University of Geneva, 1891-1912. Secretary, Linguistic Society of Paris, 1882. Corresponding Member, Institut de France. Chevalier, Légion d'Honneur. *Died 22 February 1913*.

PUBLICATIONS

Linguistics

Mémoire sur le système primitif des voyelles dans les langues indo-européennes. Leipzig, B.G. Teubner, 1878.
De l'emploi du génitif absolu en sanscrit. Geneva, J.G. Fick, 1881.
Cours de linguistique générale, edited by Charles Bally, Albert Sechehaye and Albert Riedlinger. Lausanne, Payot, 1916; as *Course in General Linguistics*, New York, Philosophical Library, 1959; London, P. Owen, 1960.
Recueil des publications scientifiques de Ferdinand de Saussure. Geneva, Droz, 1921.

*

Critical Studies: *A General School Reader in Linguistics*, edited by Robert Godel, Bloomington, Indiana University Press, 1969; *Bibliographia Saussureana 1870-1970: An Annotated, Classified Bibliography of the Background, Development, and Actual Relevance of Ferdinand de Saussure's General Theory of Language* by E.F.K. Koerner, Metuchen, New Jersey, Scarecrow Press, 1972; *Ferdinand de Saussure: Origin and Development of His Linguistic Thought: A Contribution to the History and Theory of Linguistics* by E.F.K. Koerner, Brunswick, Germany, Vieweg, 1973; *Studi saussuriani* by René Amacker and others, Bologna, Il Molino, 1974; *Linguistique Saussurienne* by René Amacker, Geneva, Droz, 1975; *Ferdinand de Saussure* by Jonathan D. Culler Glasgow, Fontana/Collins, 1976; *Words upon Words: The Anagrams of Ferdinand de Saussure* by Jean Starobinski, New Haven, Connecticut, Yale University Press, 1979; *Ferdinand de Saussure: Rezeption v. Kritik* by Thomas M. Scheerer, Darmstadt, Wissenschaftliche Buchgesellschaft, 1980.

*   *   *

Ferdinand de Saussure is commonly acknowledged as the father of 20th-century linguistics in Europe and of the general intellectual movement known as "structuralism".

In his lifetime de Saussure was principally a historical linguist in the German "neogrammarian" tradition; at the age of 21 he reconstructed the sound-system of the hypothetical "Proto-Indo-European" ancestor of the contemporary European languages in a monograph which has been described as "the most splendid work of comparative philology ever written." The very different kind of thinking about language for which Saussure is now famous seems to have played a rather small role in his career; the book, *Cours de linguistique générale*, in which it has been transmitted to us was compiled after de Saussure's death on the basis of courses of lectures he gave in two of the last years of his life.

19th-century philology had viewed a language as a collection of elements—words, grammatical suffixes, letters or sounds—each of which endures through time, sometimes changing its nature and perhaps eventually dropping out of the language altogether, but quite capable while it lasts of being identified as a unit without reference to the other elements included in the language as a whole. A central part of de Saussure's argument in the *Cours* was that it makes only a limited amount of sense to think of the units of a language as having independent existence. Sounds, words, and other linguistic units should be seen as essentially relational items like husband and wife, or beginning, middle, and end, for which the existence of one presupposes the existence of the others.

To the reader unversed in phonetics it may seem odd to suggest that the sound of the vowel *e*, say, as in *pet* or *weld*, has no existence apart from the other sounds in the language: we can certainly pronounce an *e* sound in isolation. But for that matter we can meet a husband apart from his wife: nevertheless he *is* a husband only by virtue of the existence, somewhere, of a woman who is his wife. Likewise the English sound *e* can be identified as an individual sound-unit, or "phoneme," of the language only because it contrasts with other sounds which, in turn, derive their identity from their contrast with *e*. If the vowel-sound of *pet* is compared with those of *pit* and *pat* we find that there is no natural physical line of demarcation between them; they represent different stages on a single continuum, and while English happens to cut that continuum up into just three segments another language may divide it into more or fewer phonemes— French makes a four-way distinction between *i, é, è, a*. Conversely, the vowel-sounds of English *pet* and *weld* are, physically, rather different from one another, yet in English they function as the same phoneme; another language might use them contrastively.

The point is perhaps more easily understood with reference to the meaning side of language. If we consider the words for colours, for instance, we find that Nature does not impose any particular set of colour-concepts on us: different languages divide the spectrum up in different ways, so that while Welsh makes no distinction corresponding to English "green" v. "blue", Russian conversely distinguishes two colour-words which both translate as "blue" in English. The value of any one term in English or another language derives from its opposition to the other terms in the system: "green" is what is not "blue" on the one hand, not "yellow" on the other.

de Saussure saw a language as a whole as a structured system of "signs"—pairings of a phonetic form with a semantic content—which in this way derive their various values from their positions in a very complex network of mutual relationships. He uses the image of a game of chess, where in a given state of play the potential of any one piece depends crucially on the positions of the other pieces on the board, and the movement of any piece will alter not just its own value but that of the other pieces too. de Saussure argued that as well as the "diachronic" linguistics of the 19th century, which had studied the changes that languages undergo through time, there was room for a logically-prior discipline of "synchronic" linguistics, which would describe languages as systems of signs at a particular point in time. Since de Saussure the linguistics of the 20th century has been predominantly concerned with synchronic description.

Another key component of de Saussure's doctrine, which was novel within linguistics although the idea was familiar (in other terms) to philosophers of science, was the distinction between *langue* and *parole*: between a language as a general system and the individual acts of speech which are the observable manifestations of that system. We encounter particular examples of a language, and the examples we encounter are determined by all sorts of considerations having to do with speakers' momentary needs and wishes; from these the linguist aims to reconstruct general rules defining a language which includes many kinds of utterance that we are never likely to encounter in practice—rather as an astronomer, from a limited set of observations of a comet while it is near the Earth, aims to reconstruct its entire orbit, much of which lies too far away for observation.

In fact the *langue/parole* concepts ran together two separate distinctions in one pair of terms. Apart from the fact that linguists' observations are particular while their theories are general, de Saussure had the notion that an individual's speech will often be in some sense imperfect while the linguist aims to describe the ideal language of a society, from which individuals' personal "languages" deviate in different ways. Here de Saussure seems (although this is a matter of debate) to be influenced by the theories of Emile Durkheim, according to whom elements of culture were ideas in the mind of society viewed as a living, intelligent agent, which controls the lives of its members while they understand it only partially.

The notion that the average adult member of a society is less than fully competent as a user of its language is a very French one. In the English-speaking world it has been usual to think of language as primarily a property of the individual and to regard the rules by which purists attempt to standardize usage as artificial inventions of no interest to the scientific linguist. Accordingly, the American schools of linguistics which have come to dominate the discipline during most of this century have ignored this latter aspect of the *langue/parole* distinction and have seen linguistics as a branch of psychology rather than of sociology. The principle that observed linguistic performance is a poor guide to the underlying rules of linguistic competence, on the other hand, has become a central axiom of recent theorizing.

The most original of de Saussure's insights was the idea of a language as a system of signs whose identities and values depend wholly on their mutual relationships (although even here de Saussure's originality lay only in explicit conceptualization—as a guiding principle of linguistic analysis the idea was already clearly implicit in the work of Franz Boas before the end of the 19th century). This idea has continued to mould subsequent linguistic description, although those linguists influenced by

Roman Jakobson and Noam Chomsky have come to believe that Nature imposes more constraints on the ways in which languages articulate phonetic and semantic reality than de Saussure supposed.

de Saussure's current fame, however, derives less from his influence within linguistics itself that from his adoption as a cult figure by the French "structuralist" movement. The term "structuralism" is confusing—within linguistics it usually refers to a group of mid-century American linguists who were not especially interested in de Saussure's ideas. In France, however, "structuralism" is an approach to the understanding of a wide range of aspects of culture—anthropology, literature, cinema, and so on—which claims that all these subjects must be understood in terms of relationships between contrasting elements whose individual properties have no significance. Since in France philosophy is part of popular culture rather than a specialized professional discipline as it is in the English-speaking world, de Saussure's name has come to be revered by many who would be hard put to it to expound his views in any detail.

—Geoffrey Sampson

---

de UNAMUNO (y Jugo), Miguel. Spanish philosopher, novelist, dramatist and poet. Born in Bilbao, 29 September 1864. Studied at the University of Salamanca, Ph.D. 1884. Married Concha Lizárraga Ecénarro in 1891; 9 children. Professor of Greek and the History of the Spanish Language, University of Salamanca, 1891-1924, 1930-34 (Rector, 1901-14, Lifetime Rector, 1934). Exiled to the Canary Islands in 1924 for his criticism of the Primo de Rivera dictatorship; lived in Paris, 1924, and Hendaye, 1925-30; returned to Salamanca in 1930; placed under house arrest in 1936 for his criticism of the Franco dictatorship. Recipient: Cross of the Order of Alfonso XII, 1905. *Died* (in Salamanca) *31 December 1936.*

PUBLICATIONS

Collections

Obras completas, edited by Manuel García Blanco.   Madrid, Escelicer, 9 vols., 1966-71.

Philosophy and Writings about Spanish Life and Culture

En torno al casticismo.   Madrid, La España Moderna, 1895.
De la enseñanza superior en España.   Madrid, Revista Nueva, 1899.
Tres ensayos.   Madrid, Rodríguez Serra, 1900.
Paisajes.   Salamanca, Colección Calón, 1902.
De mi país: Descripciones, relatos y artículos de costumbres.   Madrid, Fernando Fe, 1903.
Vida de Don Quijote y Sancho según Miguel de Cervantes Saavedra, explicada y comentada.   Madrid, Fernando Fe, 1905; as *The Life of Don Quixote and Sancho,* New York, Knopf, 1927; as *Our Lord Don Quixote and Sancho with Related Essays,* Princeton, New Jersey, Princeton University Press, 1967.
Recuerdos de niñez y de mocedad.   Madrid, Suarez, 1908.
Mi religión y otros ensayos breves.   Madrid, Renacimiento, 1910; as *Perplexities and Paradoxes,* New York, Philosophical Library, 1956.
Por tierras de Portugal y de España.   Madrid, Renacimiento, 1911.
Soliloquios y conversaciones.   Madrid, Renacimiento, 1911.
Contra esto y aquello.   Madrid, Renacimiento, 1912.

El porvenir de España, with Ángel Ganivet.   Madrid, Renacimiento, 1912.

Del sentimiento trágico de la vida en los hombres y en los pueblos.   Madrid, Renacimiento, 1913; as *The Tragic Sense of Life in Men and in Peoples,* London, Macmillan, 1926; as *The Tragic Sense of Life in Men and in Nations,* Princeton, New Jersey, Princeton University Press, 1972.

Ensayos.   Madrid, Residencia de Estudiantes, 8 vols., 1916-18.

Sensaciones de Bilbao.   Bilbao, n.p., 1922.

Andanzas y visiones españolas.   Madrid, Renacimiento, 1922.

La agonía del cristianismo.   Paris, Editorial Excelsior, 1925; as *The Agony of Christianity,* New York, Payson and Clarke, 1928; as *The Agony of Christianity and Essays on Faith,* Princeton, New Jersey, Princeton University Press, 1974.

Essays and Soliloquies.   New York, Knopf, 1925.

Cómo se hace una novela.   Buenos Aires, Editorial Alba, 1927.

Dos artículos y dos discursos.   Madrid, Historia Nueva, 1930.

La ciudad de Henoc: Comentario 1933.   Mexico City, Séneca, 1941.

Cuenca Ibérica: Lenguaje y paisaje.   Mexico City, Séneca, 1943.

Temas argentinos.   Buenos Aires, Institución Cultural Española, 1943.

Viejos y jóvenes.   Buenos Aires, Espasa-Calpe, 1944.

El caballero de la triste figura.   Buenos Aires, Espasa-Calpe, 1944.

Paisajes del alma.   Madrid, Revista de Occidente, 1944.

La enormidad de España: Comentarios.   Mexico City, Séneca, 1945.

Algunos consideraciones sobre la literatura hispano-americana.   Madrid, Espasa-Calpe, 1947.

Visiones y comentarios.   Buenos Aires, Espasa-Calpe, 1949.

De esto y de aquello.   Buenos Aires, Sudamericana, 4 vols., 1950-54.

Madrid.   Madrid, Afrodisio Aguado, 1950.

Vida literaria.   Buenos Aires, Sudamericana, 1951.

España y los españoles.   Madrid, Afrodisio Aguado, 1955.

Inquietudes y meditaciones.   Madrid, Afrodisio Aguado, 1956.

En el destierro.   Madrid, Pegaso, 1957.

Almas jóvenes.   Madrid, Espasa-Calpe, 1957.

Libros y autores españoles contemporáneos.   Madrid, Espasa-Calpe, 1972.

Fiction

Paz en la guerra.   Madrid, Fernando Fe, 1897.

Amor y pedagogía.   Barcelona, Heinrich, 1902.

El espejo de la muerte.   Madrid, Renacimiento, 1913.

Niebla.   Madrid, Renacimiento, 1914; as *Mist: A Tragicomic Novel,* New York, Knopf, 1928.

Abel Sánchez, una historia de pasión.   Madrid, Renacimiento, 1917; as *Abel Sanchez,* New York, Dryden Press, 1947; as *Abel Sanchez and Other Stories,* Chicago, Regnery, 1956.

Tulio Montalbán y Julio Macedo.   Madrid, La Novela Corta, 1920.

Tres novelas ejemplares y prólogo.   Madrid, Calpe, 1920; as *Three Exemplary Novels,* New York, Boni, 1930.

La tía Tula.   Madrid, Renacimiento, 1931.

San Manuel Bueno, mártir y tres historias más.   Madrid, Espasa-Calpe, 1933; as "St. Emanuel the Good Martyr," in *Abel Sanchez and Other Stories,* Chicago, Regnery, 1956.

Plays

La Venda. La Princesa Doña Lambra.   Madrid, El Libro Popular, 1913.

Fedra.   Madrid, La Pluma, 1924.

Sombras de sueño.   Madrid, El Teatre Moderno, 1931.

El otro.   Madrid, Espasa-Calpe, 1932.

El hermano Juan o el mundo es teatro.   Madrid, Espasa-Calpe, 1934.

Teatro completo.   Madrid, Aguilar, 1959.

Poetry

Poesías.   Bilbao, Rojas, 1907.

Rosario de sonetos líricos.   Madrid, Fernando Fe, 1911.

El Cristo de Velázquez.   Madrid, Calpe, 1920; as *The Christ of Velasquez,* Baltimore, Maryland, Johns Hopkins University Press, 1951.

Rimas de dentro.   Valladolid, privately printed, 1923.

Teresa.   Madrid, Renacimiento, 1924.

De Fuerteventura a París.   Paris, Excelsior, 1925.

Romancero del destierro.   Buenos Aires, Editorial Alba, 1928.

Poems of Miguel de Unamuno.   Baltimore, Maryland, Johns Hopkins University Press, 1952.

Cancionero: Diario poético.   Buenos Aires, Losada, 1953.

Cincuenta poesías inéditas.   Madrid, Ediciones Papeles de Son Armadans, 1958.

The Last Poems of Miguel de Unamuno.   Rutherford, New Jersey, Fairleigh Dickinson University Press, 1974.

Other

Mi Salamanca.   Bilbao, Miñambres, 1950.

Epistolario entre M. de Unamuno y Juan Maragall.   Barcelona, Edimar, 1951.

Autodiálogos.   Madrid, Aguilar, 1959.

Mi vida y otros recuerdos personales.   Buenos Aires, Losada, 1959.

Pensamiento político, edited by Elias Diaz.   Madrid, Editorial Tecnos, 1965.

Diario íntimo.   Madrid, Alianza Editorial, 1970.

Cartas, 1903-1933.   Barcelona, Aguilar, 1972.

Escritos socialistas.   Madrid, Arguso, 1976.

Unamuno "agitador de espíritus" y Giner: Correspondencia inédita.   Madrid, Narcea, 1977.

*

Bibliography: "Bibliografía de Miguel de Unamuno" by Federico de Onís in *La Torre* (San Juan, Puerto Rico), 9, 1961.

Critical Studies: *Unamuno* by José Ferrater-Mora, Berkeley, University of California Press, 1962; *The Lone Heretic: A Biography of Miguel de Unamuno* by Margaret Thomas Rudd, Austin, University of Texas Press, 1963; *Miguel de Unamuno: The Rhetoric of Existence* by Allen Lacy, The Hague, Mouton, 1967; *Unamuno* by Martin Nozick, New York, Twayne, 1971.

*   *   *

"God is silent," said Miguel de Unamuno, the master of paradox, "because He is an atheist." Since, in the words of Kierkegaard, Unamuno's spiritual ancestor, God is the "Wholly Other," neither theological exegesis can prove His existence nor can positivistic reasonings disprove Him. Unamuno was a supreme intellectual: Professor of Greek and the History of the Spanish Language at the University of Salamanca where he became rector; reader of French, English, German, Italian, Portuguese, Catalan, and the Scandinavian languages; student of philosophy, various literatures, politics, and history. But he was also a God-hungry man longing for the unsophisticated Catholicism that marked his early years. Consequently, he was caught between the extremes of ecclesiastical opposition to free examination in a monolithically Catholic Spain, and the equally fanatical anti-religious posture of dogmatic non-believers. His own conception was of a Deity that escaped analysis since He is the Pascalian *Deus abscoditus sensible au coeur.*

An emphatic personalist, de Unamuno could find no comfort within the prescriptions of a hierarchical Church closely allied to the monarchy, nor could he derive any sense of liberation from the ratiocinations of the materialists, and in an endless stream of essays, novels, plays, short-stories, and poems, he frantically acts out the pain of that impasse which is the tragic sense of life or the insoluble stuggle between logic and desire, Spencerian agnosticism and the Spinozian axiom that the very essence of man is the desire to persist forever in his self.

The validity of intellectual arguments is counter-balanced by the affective needs of the total man who longs for satisfactions far more encompassing and transcendental than those of logic or coherence. "Christendom," Kierkegaard declared, "does not lie in the sphere of the intellect." The dogmas and doctrines of Christianity, as Adolf von Harnack demonstrated in his monumental *Dogmengeschichte* (another of de Unamuno's major sources), are an amalgam of Hebrew metaphysics, Greek speculation and Roman law, and consequently too earth-bound. And the priests (especially the Jesuits) who explicate such laws to the faithful are far more interested in the letter than the spirit, thus encouraging passive compliance in their flock.

A living Christianity must, for de Unamuno, be the affirmation of belief against doubt, an imperative overcoming of scepticism (the Jamesian "will to believe"); it must be a continuous "agon," struggle and anguish. Indeed, the difference between "*Creer*" or "to believe" and "*Crear*", to create, is simply one letter, and what thinkers cannot supply each one must create for himself. de Unamuno, the existentialist concerned with the *whole* man of flesh and blood and longing, as against the partial, fragmented, *ens cogitans*, is also de Unamuno the voluntarist who wishes God into existence as guarantor of more than the paltry life of three score and ten.

The entire prolix opus of de Unamuno, in all genres, adapted to his own ex-centric views (the anti-Socialist socialist, the believer in hopes rather than in convictions, the anti-monarchist republican, the anti-Republican under the Republic, the lay preacher doubting his own sincerity) dramatizes the multiple dilemmas of the author himself. Strident, repetitious, often deliberately perverse, his works reflect the over-stocked mind at loggerheads with the lyrical, explosive writhing spirit of the unanchored *homo religiosus* wandering through a maze of contradictions, always "against this and that", never at ease within any structure, system or programme: ("I am rarely of my own opinion;" "If there were a de Unamuno party, I would be against it"). If he had a motto, it would be Tertullian's "*Credo quia absurdum*", a total challenge to the *homme moyen sensuel*. If we were sometimes exasperated by his conceptual acrobatics, we must understand that if we seek de Unamuno the thinker, we find de Unamuno "the feeler" ("sentidor"). With each reading we expect to find a book, but we find a man, the paradigm of the free-believer rather than the free-thinker.

—Martin Nozick

DEWEY, John. American philosopher, psychologist and educator. Born in Burlington, Vermont, 20 October 1859. Studied at the University of Vermont, Burlington, B.A. 1879; Johns Hopkins University, Baltimore, Ph.D. 1884. Married Alice Chipman in 1886 (died, 1927), 6 children; married Roberta Grant in 1946. High School Teacher, Oil City, Pennsylvania, 1879-81; Assistant Professor, 1886-88, and Professor of Philosophy, 1889-94, University of Michigan, Ann Arbor; Professor of Philosophy, University of Minnesota, Minneapolis, 1888-89; Professor of Philosophy and Chairman of the Department of Philosophy, Psychology and Education, University of Chicago, 1894-1904 (Director of the School of Education, 1902-04); Professor of Philosophy, 1904-30, Professor Emeritus in Residence, 1930-39, and Professor Emeritus, 1939-52, Columbia University, New York. Lecturer, Imperial University of Tokyo, 1919, and National

Universities of Peking and Nanking, 1919-21. Clifford Lecturer, University of Edinburgh, 1929; William James Lecturer, Harvard University, Cambridge, Massachusetts, 1930; Dwight Harrington Terry Lecturer, Yale University, New Haven, Connecticut, 1934. Conducted surveys of education in Turkey, 1924, Mexico, 1926, and the Soviet Union, 1928. Chairman, Commission of Inquiry into the Charges Made Against Leon Trotsky in the Moscow Trials, 1937. President, American Philosophical Association, 1905-06; a Founder and first President, American Association of University Professors, 1915. Honorary doctorates: University of Wisconsin, Madison, 1904; University of Vermont, 1910; University of Michigan, 1913; Johns Hopkins University, 1915; University of Peking, 1920; University of St. Andrews, Scotland, 1929; Columbia University, 1929; University of Paris, 1930; Harvard University, 1932; University of Pennsylvania, Philadelphia, 1946; University of Oslo, 1946; Yale University, 1951. Member, National Academy of Sciences, 1910. *Died* (in New York City) *1 June 1952.*

PUBLICATIONS

Collections

John Dewey: The Early Works, 1882-1898, edited by Jo Ann Boydston. Carbondale, Southern Illinois University Press, 5 vols., 1967-72.

John Dewey: The Middle Works, 1899-1924, edited by Jo Ann Boydston. Carbondale, Southern Illinois University Press, 1976-.

John Dewey: The Later Works, 1925-52, edited by Jo Ann. Boydston. Carbondale, Southern Illinois University Press, 1981-.

Philosophy, Psychology and Education

Psychology. New York, Harper, 1887.

Leibniz's New Essays Concerning the Human Understanding: A Critical Exposition. Chicago, C.S. Griggs, 1888.

The Ethics of Democracy (lecture). Ann Arbor, Michigan, Andrews, 1888.

Applied Psychology: An Introduction to the Principles and Practices of Education, with J.A. McLellan. Boston, Educational Publishing, 1889.

Outlines of a Critical Theory of Ethics. Ann Arbor, Michigan, Register Publishing, 1891.

The Study of Ethics: A Syllabus. Ann Arbor, Michigan, Register Publishing, 1894.

The Psychology of Number and Its Application to Methods of Teaching Arithmetic, with J.A. McLellan. New York, Appleton, and London, Arnold, 1895.

My Pedagogic Creed. New York, Kellog, 1897.

Psychology and Philosophic Method (lecture). Berkeley, University of California Press, 1899.

The School and Society (lectures). Chicago, University of Chicago Press, 1899; London, P.S. King, 1900.

The Educational Situation. Chicago, University of Chicago Press, 1902.

Studies in Logical Theory, with others. Chicago, University of Chicago Press, 1903; London, Fisher and Unwin, 1909.

Logical Conditions of a Scientific Treatment of Morality. Chicago, University of Chicago Press, 1903.

Ethics (lecture). New York, Columbia University Press, 1908.

Ethics, with James H. Tufts. New York, Holt, 1908; London, G. Bell, 1909.

Moral Principles in Education. Boston, Houghton Mifflin, 1909; London, Calder, 1959.

How We Think. Boston, Heath, and London, Harrap, 1910.

The Influence of Darwin on Philosophy and Other Essays in Contemporary Thought. New York, Holt, and London, G. Bell, 1910.

Educational Essays by John Dewey, edited by J.J. Findlay. London, Blackie, 1910.

Interest and Effort in Education. Boston, Houghton Mifflin, 1913.

German Philosophy and Politics. New York, Holt, 1915.

Schools of Tomorrow, with Evelyn Dewey. New York, Dutton, and London, Dent, 1915.

Democracy and Education: An Introduction to the Philosophy of Education. New York, Macmillan, 1916.

Essays in Experimental Logic. Chicago, University of Chicago Press, and Cambridge, Cambridge University Press, 1916.

Creative Intelligence: Essays in the Pragmatic Attitude, with others. New York, Holt, 1917.

Reconstruction in Philosophy. New York, Holt, 1920; London, University of London Press, 1921.

Human Nature and Conduct: An Introduction to Social Psychology. New York, Holt, 1922; London, Allen and Unwin, 1922.

Experience and Nature (lectures). Chicago and London, Open Court, 1925.

The Public and Its Problems. New York, Holt, and London, Allen and Unwin, 1927.

The Philosophy of John Dewey, edited by Joseph Ratner. New York, Holt, 1928; London, Allen and Unwin, 1929.

Characters and Events: Popular Essays in Social and Political Philosophy, edited by Joseph Ratner. New York, Holt, 2 vols., 1929.

Art and Education, with others. Merion, Pennsylvania, Barnes Foundation, 1929.

The Quest for Certainty. New York, Minton Balch, 1929; London, Allen and Unwin, 1930.

The Sources of a Science of Education (lectures). New York, Liveright, 1929.

Individualism, Old and New. New York, Minton Balch, 1930; London, Allen and Unwin, 1931.

Construction and Criticism (lecture). New York, Columbia University Press, 1930.

Philosophy and Civilization. New York, Minton Balch, 1931; London, Putnam, 1933.

The Way Out of Educational Confusion (lecture). Cambridge, Massachusetts, Harvard University Press, 1931.

American Education Past and Future (lecture). Chicago, University of Chicago Press, 1931.

The Place of Minor Parties in the American Scene (lecture). Chicago, University of Chicago Press, 1932.

The Educational Frontier, with others. Chicago, University of Chicago Press, 1933.

Art as Experience. New York, Minton Balch, and London, Allen and Unwin, 1934.

A Common Faith (lectures). New Haven, Connecticut, Yale University Press, and London, Oxford University Press, 1934.

Liberalism and Social Action (lectures). New York, Putnam, 1935.

The Teacher and Society, with others. New York, Appleton-Century, 1937.

Logic: The Theory of Inquiry. New York, Holt, 1938; London, Allen and Unwin, 1939.

Experience and Education (lectures). New York, Macmillan, 1938.

Democracy and Education in the World of Today (lecture). New York, Society for Ethical Culture, 1938.

Intelligence in the Modern World: John Dewey's Philosophy, edited by Joseph Ratner. New York, Modern Library, 1939.

Freedom and Culture. New York, Putnam, 1939; London, Luzac, 1955.

Theory of Valuation. Chicago, University of Chicago Press, 1939.

Education Today, edited by Joseph Ratner. New York, Putnam, 1940; abridged edition, London, Allen and Unwin, 1940.

Problems of Men. New York, Philosophical Library, 1946.

Knowing and the Known, with Arthur F. Bentley. Boston, Beacon, 1949.

Other

Letters from China and Japan, with Alice Chipman Dewey. New York, Dutton, and London, Dent, 1920.

The Case of Leon Trotsky: Report of the Hearings of the Charges Made Against Him in the Moscow Trials, with others. New York, Harper, 1937.

Not Guilty: Report of the Commission of Inquiry into the Charges Made Against Leon Trotsky in the Moscow Trials, with others. New York, Harper, 1938.

John Dewey and Arthur Bentley: A Philosophical Correspondence, 1932-1951, edited by Sidney Ratner and Julie Altman. New Brunswick, New Jersey, Rutgers University Press, 1964.

Editor, *The Living Thoughts of Jefferson.* New York, Longman, 1940.

*

Bibliography: *John Dewey: A Centennial Bibliography* by Milton Halsey Thomas, Chicago, University of Chicago Press, 1962.

Critical Studies: *John Dewey: An Intellectual Portrait* by Sidney Hook, New York, Day, 1939; *The Philosophy of John Dewey*, edited by Paul Arthur Schilpp, Evanston, Illinois, Northwestern University Press, 1939; *The Logic of Pragmatism* by H.S. Thayer, New York, Humanities Press, 1952; *Guide to the Works of John Dewey*, edited by Jo Ann Boydston, Carbondale and Edwardsville, Southern Illinois University Press, 1970; *John Dewey's Philosophy of Value* by James Gouinlock, New York, Humanities Press, 1972; *The Life and Mind of John Dewey* by George Dykhuizen, Carbondale and Edwardsville, Southern Illinois University Press, 1973.

*   *   *

John Dewey was the author of one of the two or three most adequate world views formulated in the last hundred years. His reflections on a multiplicity of philosophic issues are remarkably innovative; and they are coherent with each other, with new developments in the natural and behavioral sciences, and with human experience. They came to a focus in the concern with human well-being—in moral philosophy, broadly conceived. Accordingly, it is best to understand Dewey's philosophy as an endeavor to understand man and the world in a way that illuminates and enriches the human striving for a better life.

Dewey set himself in opposition to what he called the classical tradition, which he regarded as the dominant mode of thought in the history of the western world. It originates with Plato (if not earlier) and was represented in Dewey's formative years by absolute idealism. The classic tradition, in his view, comprehended much of classical empiricism as well. The cardinal assumption of the classic tradition was that the universe in its essential nature is fixed and changeless. The world of change—insofar as it was acknowledged at all—was consigned to an inferior realm of being. It was written off as non-being, mere appearance, or nothing but a construction of private and subjective mind. Insofar as it was subject to judgment at all, the realm of change was to be both known and evaluated by reference to the rationally apprehended verities of the eternal order. The moral life of man consisted in conforming to this order. Plato, for example, tells us of a world of pure forms: perfect, eternal, and unchanging. By means of unaided reason we may apprehend the forms; this sort of apprehension is knowledge. The world of change is unknowable in itself, but it may be known in a derivative sense insofar as its events are classified according to the forms. Likewise, evaluation of changing things is a matter of classification. With knowledge of the forms of the good and the just, we may perceive what events in the changing world of ordinary experience are good and just. The good for man consists in realizing the divine order in the earthly city and in the individual soul. There is also fixed essence, then, of the state and of human nature. Ideas similar in import are found in idealism. The inherent order of the universe is the changeless standard of perfection. It is known by an exclusively rational logic, and the good of man is to conform to the absolute order as it manifests itself in time. Self-realization is perfect conformity to this order. In the final analysis, error, evil, and change are unreal according to this scheme.

There are many variations on these themes found, e.g., in Christianity, theories of natural law, Kantianism, and anywhere that processes of change are found inherently deficient and must be arrested to conform to antecedently fixed standards. Utilitarianism, too, fails by demanding a fixed end and criterion. The complement of the classic tradition is the assumption that moral values are subjective and arbitrary: if absolute norms are lacking, we are left with nothing but caprice or blind custom.

In contrast to all this, Dewey insists on the reality of change. He found the assumptions of fixed essences or principles to be groundless. The division of existence into a heaven of perfect being radically set off against a fallen and earthly condition was unsupportable and pernicious. The universe shows constant change and novelty that are not to be deprived of reality by a "trick of logic."

Dewey's analyses also led him to deny the Cartesian dualism of man and nature, with all its implications. He treated man and nature (organism and environment) as wholly continuous with each other; the individual and his surroundings function as a unitary organic system. With the rejection of the dualism of being and becoming as well as that of man and nature, Dewey adopted "nature" as the most inclusive philosophic conception.

Faithful to the evidence of experience, he argued that nature's processes generate precious values. The manifold properties of experience are neither "in the subject" nor "in the object" as subject and object are conceived dualistically. They are eventual functions of nature conceived inclusively. The traits of things we cherish, esteem, love, admire, fear, detest, and so on are real traits of nature. We find numberless occasions of great value, and there is no need to justify them at large by reference to absolutes. The need is to discriminate the conditions of their occurrence so that they can be deliberately secured and enriched.

Although Dewey was extremely critical of the notion of a realm of changeless perfection, he did not deny the notions of permanence and fixity altogether; but he gave them a notably different ontological status. What seems to be constant in the nature of things is the correlation between processes of change. There is, for example, a definite correlation between the pressure and temperature in an enclosed volume of gas. Likewise there is a correlation between mass and distance in the measurement of gravity. Variations in one process are correlated with changes in another. As the constituent variables are altered, so, too, the nature of processes and their outcomes. According to this analysis, permanence and change are not traits of separate realms. They are functions of the same natural processes; and the practical task of life is, generally, to learn how to function effectively with these changes, giving them intelligent direction.

In a world of change, inquiry and knowledge must be conceived on a different model. Inquiry is not a passive beholding but an active participation in processes of change to determine how variations in them are correlated, and the object of knowledge is precisely this correlation. Hence Dewey's pragmatism—or instrumentalism, as he preferred to call it. According to instrumentalism, knowing requires deliberate manipulation of objects to find out what they are and how they change relative to other events. Inquiry is guided by hypotheses that predict specific variations in a subject matter contingent upon the introduction of specific changes. Tests are performed to see whether the object actually functions as predicted; if it does, the proposition is verified. Dewey emphasizes the creative character of inquiry. A hypothesis proposes that a particular reconstruction of present conditions will have certain consequences. Thus a novel reordering of natural processes is undertaken. It might be predicted, for example, that if educational institutions are altered in a certain way, the performance of the students will show certain improvements. The hypothesis directs a definite plan of action. By specifying conditions to be introduced in existing circumstances, hypotheses guide conduct through processes of change from the present to the future. This is experimental logic as distinguished from classificatory logic.

The good, as Dewey conceives it, is not a static condition but a certain kind of activity. This activity he calls growth. It is conduct in which the individual interacts with his environment to transform initially troubling circumstances in a way to convert them into instrumentalities for reunified behavior. In this process the powers of the individual are engaged and united with those of the environment and are fulfilled in ongoing activity. Ends, Dewey argues, are for the sake of means—for the sake of activity. Properly selected ends unite hitherto disparate desires and abilities and facilitate intrinsically satisfying experience. For example, a person might particularly enjoy family activities, and he might also have the skills of a builder. Thus the building of a house for his family would be a valuable end for such a person, for it would allow him to unify and consummate his interests in activity. Ideally, he would share his endeavors with his family, thereby enriching his experience still more. As an individual engages in various kinds of conduct, he refines and enlarges his powers to transform and unify problematic situations. Thus human nature undergoes change and continually grows to adapt to varying conditions of life.

In his analysis of human nature, Dewey's most crucial concept is that of habit. Habit is a function of organism and environment, and Dewey analyzes all phases of human nature in these terms. The social environment is especially important in the formation and development of our habits of thought and action. The very existence of mind requires the habits of language; and language, Dewey argues, is a product—not a precondition—of social behavior. Hence variations in the social environment are all-important in the process of growth; so it is of urgent importance to determine the correlations between variations in social life and variations in habit. It is impossible in Dewey's terms to conceive the individual and society to be inherently antithetical to each other, for the individual is not a separate substance nor does he possess a changeless nature. Personal growth need not be at the expense of society. Indeed, Dewey proclaims that "shared experience is the greatest of human goods." Growth, accordingly, incorporates the enrichment of one's powers to participate in associated life.

Growth is the norm for all human activity. Whether we are evaluating education, politics, production of goods and services, artistic activity, or group behavior, we should seek ways in which such conduct can be ordered into a harmonious and integral process, rather than arrested to conform to an antecedently fixed end. The act of evaluation, Dewey continues, is not one of classification, but criticism. Criticism is the application of instrumentalism to problems of conduct. It is the process of inquiry by which one determines which activity will succeed in transforming a situation from a problematic to an integrated condition. Agents must inquire into the relations of change in which they are immersed and try to conceive of ways to reconstruct them to provide intrinsically satisfying activity.

Dewey's systematic dismantling of the classic tradition includes a critique of the notion that knowledge is an achievement of the solitary individual. Inquiry is a social process, and knowledge claims become reliable only when they are a product of a community of experimental inquirers. Dewey adapted this notion with special effect to the problem of moral discourse. The classic tradition had been individualistic in the sense that it treated the determination of what to do as the province of individual reason or intuition, typically cognizing absolute values. Dewey, on the other hand, advocates that the resolution of moral problems be conceived as a social process, as a method of intelligent communication. In other words, the process of criticism should be social; deliberation about means to transform socially problematic situations should be a shared activity. Through consultation and sharing of information and ideas for action, it might be possible for individuals to adjust and unite their activities. The moral absolutist cannot, by definition, revise his standards; and given the plurality of alleged absolutes, absolutism makes cooperative resolution of conflict impossible. A deliberately social and experimental mode of moral discourse, Dewey pleaded, would take us much further towards a harmonious way of life than any of the methods tried hitherto. Much of his social philosophy is a sustained argument for the establishment of the conditions for such a moral community, and his voluminous writings on education are largely a specification of many of those conditions.

In a steady flow of articles and books, Dewey criticised the classic tradition with all its trappings. Incisively and passionately, he analyzed prevailing institutions as embodiments of an antiquated scheme of thought, and in their place he urged arrangements that would liberate human powers and enrich the social bond. Dewey's philosophy is exemplary of that mode of thought that goes beyond a mere series of technical exercises to provide an integrated vision of human existence.

—James Gouinlock

DIRAC, Paul (Adrien Maurice). British physicist. Born in Bristol, 8 August 1902. Studied at Bristol University, B.Sc. 1921; Cambridge University, Ph.D. 1926. Married Margit Wigner in 1937. Lucasian Professor of Mathematics, 1932-69, and since 1969 Professor Emeritus, Cambridge University; since 1971, Professor of Physics, Florida State University, Tallahassee. Visiting Lecturer, University of Wisconsin, Madison, and University of Michigan, Ann Arbor, 1929; Princeton University, New Jersey, 1931. Member, Institute for Advanced Study, Princeton, 1934-35, 1947-48, and 1958-59. Recipient: Nobel Prize in Physics, with Erwin Schrödinger, 1933; Royal Medal, 1939, and Copley Medal, 1952, Royal Society, London. Fellow, Royal Society. Foreign Associate, National Academy of Sciences, 1949. Address: Department of Physics, Florida State University, Tallahassee, Florida 32306, U.S.A.

PUBLICATIONS

Physics

The Principles of Quantum Mechanics. Oxford, Clarendon Press, 1930.
Quantum Electrodynamics. Dublin, Institute for Advanced Studies, 1943.
Developments in Quantum Electrodynamics. Dublin, Institute for Advanced Studies, 1946.
Lectures on Quantum Mechanics and Relativistic Field Theory. Bombay, Tata Institute of Fundamental Research, 1956.
Lectures on Quantum Mechanics. New York, Belfer Graduate School of Science of Yeshiva University, 1964.
Lectures on Quantum Field Theory. New York, Belfer Graduate School of Science of Yeshiva University, 1966.
The Physical Interpretation of Quantum Electrodynamics. Vatican City, Pontificia Academia Scientarum, 1968.
The Scientific Work of George Lemaître. Vatican City, Pontificia Academia Scientarum, 1968.
Spinors in Hilbert Space. Coral Gables, Florida, Center for Theoretical Studies of the University of Miami, 1970.

The Development of Quantum Theory (lecture). New York, Gordon and Breach, 1971.
General Theory of Relativity. New York, Wiley, 1975.
Directions in Physics (lectures). New York, Wiley, 1978.

*　　*　　*

Paul Dirac is among the handful of men during the early part of the 20th century whose capacity for abstract and original thought spawned a revolution in our view of the physical world. Although quantum mechanics, developed in quite distinct forms by Werner Heisenberg and Erwin Schrödinger, cast the earlier atomic model of Niels Bohr in a new light, precluding many of the difficulties that arose in his semi-classical approach, certain new problems had become evident. It was recognized that in order to obtain more precise agreement between the experimental observation and the theoretical prediction of atomic spectral emissions, the latter would have to account for relativistic effects in accordance with Albert Einstein's special theory. Schrödinger's attempts to incorporate such modifications in 1926, however, were without success, resulting in relativistic corrections that diverged from observation. Dirac's mathematical description of the electron, published in 1928, not only offered a solution to the problem of the relativistic atom but also led to a profound review of the nature of matter.

From innovative work of great mathematical elegance and economy, he deduced the inherent spin of the electron and presented a relativistic description of the atom in sound theoretical form, in conformity with spectroscopic observation. Three years earlier, in response to experimental evidence but without theoretical foundation, Samuel Goudsmit and George Uhlenbeck had conjectured that the electron was endowed with a form of internal angular momentum, or spin, despite the fact that it was considered to be point-like and hence incapable of rotation. Dirac's definition of spin was of a more abstract nature, yet it ascribed to the electron a property analogous to that of inherent rotation.

This was but the first surprise that the Dirac equation held for physicists in their understanding of matter, and the second was no less exciting. In 1930 Dirac produced a paper pertaining to a particular aspect of the equation that now bears his name, and thus was born the concept of antimatter.

His previous work had suggested that there may exist electrons of negative energy, and hence a problem arose which Dirac addressed in an intriguing manner. The difficulty was this: it is a well established aspect of classical physics that matter seeks to attain its lowest possible potential energy level—and similarly in the quantum situation: if a state of negative energy is accessible to an electron, then calculations reveal that it will jump down (in a metaphorical sense) to such a state within an extremely small fraction of a second. Indeed, the availability of states with unbounded lower energies would ensure that all electrons tumble down to infinitely low levels of energy, a prediction which is clearly inconsistent with our observations of the real world. The solution was this: Dirac proposed that what we observe as a vacuum, where no particles are detected, is the situation in which all the negative-energy electron states are occupied. Now the exclusion principle, due to Wolfgang Pauli, stipulates that no more than one electron may occupy a given state, that is, no two electrons may be ascribed exactly the same properties. Hence, an electron of positive energy existing in vacuum may not make a transition down to any negative-energy state, since each one already contains its permitted quota. If occupied negative-energy states are unobservable, Dirac asked further, what would be the manifestation of such a state that is unoccupied?

Before relating his conclusion, let us consider an analogous situation which comprises a row of seats, each being occupied with the exception of that on the far right. The occupant of the seat adjacent to that which is vacant now relocates himself one seat to the right; the unoccupied seat becomes the second from the right. The person to the left of this newly vacated seat moves one seat to the right and this procedure continues until, finally, it is the seat on the far left that is vacant. We have described this process in terms of the motions of the seats' occupants and a net flow of people to the right. There is, of course, an alternative manner in which to construe the events which have occurred, and that is to view the procedure as the net movement of a vacant seat to the left. We now return to Dirac's negative energy states, all of which are occupied but one. An observer who considers the situation in which all negative-energy states are occupied to be a vacuum will view this "hole" in the negative-energy sea as an object of positive energy (since the zero energy of a hole relative to negative energy is positive). As in the analogy the motion of people to the right could be interpreted as the movement of a vacant seat to the left, so the net flow of negative-energy electrons in one direction may be viewed as the movement of a hole in the opposite direction. Further, since such a hole in the vacuum is observed as a positive-energy particle, Dirac had predicted the existence of anti-electrons, or positrons, which, indeed, were experimentally observed two years later in 1932.

Imagine a situation in which an electron falls into a hole, thus relinquishing its positive energy to become part of the negative-energy sea. To an observer, this process would be viewed as an electron-positron collision and subsequent mutual annihilation, with the resultant release of energy in the form of radiation. Similarly, the radiation-induced jump of an electron from the negative-energy sea to leave behind a hole would be viewed as the generation by photons, the quanta of radiation, of an electron-positron pair. So was born the branch of physics known as "quantum field theory," describing the creation and annihilation of particles. This development in theoretical physics was of monumental significance, and, indeed, most subsequent theories seeking to describe fundamental processes and to absorb the particles and forces of nature into a grand unified scheme, are based upon the concept of quantum fields.

Quite apart from his formulation of the now famous equation which describes not only the electron-positron pair but also many other fundamental particle-antiparticle pairs, Dirac's contributions to the development of quantum theory have been extensive. In particular, his powerful sense of mathematical aesthetics has allowed him both to cast earlier quantum mechanical ideas in compact and general form and to develop methods which have found application in many diverse branches of modern physics.

Included amongst his innovations was, in 1931, the first theoretical description of the magnetic monopole. A particle, be it fundamental or a piece of metal, may possess an overall electric charge, yet the same is not true of magnetic charge. Take a magnet which has a north and a south pole (the word "pole" rather than "charge" being associated with magnetism for historical reasons) and cut it in two. The result is not two objects, one of which is endowed with just a north magnetic charge and the other a south, but two smaller magnets, each with its full complement of two poles. Magnets, therefore, may appear as dipoles, but it would seem impossible to construct an object with only a single pole, that is, a magnetic monopole. Dirac demonstrated, however, that in principle a particle endowed with a net single magnetic charge may exist. Since that time there have been several refinements in the mathematical description of the magnetic monopole, though to date there has been no absolute experimental confirmation of their existence.

Dirac's contributions to theoretical physics have not been confined to the realms of quantum theory. The mathematical structure of theoretical cosmology and Einstein's general theory of relativity also have been enriched greatly as a consequence of his work. The "Hamiltonian formulation" of Einstein's theory, for example, where certain classical methods are extended to accommodate the subtleties of general relativity, was due initially to Dirac.

In 1938, Dirac brought attention to a rather curious property of the universe in which we live and proposed his so-called "large numbers hypothesis." He observed that the electromagnetic, divided by the gravitational, force between an electron and a proton results in a number that is of the order 10^{39} (1 followed by thirty nine zeros), its largeness being due to the relative weakness of gravity. Also, if one measures the age of the universe, not in years since such a unit is artificial, merely being associated with the properties of our own solar system, but in units of time determined by the atom, then that age is of the order 10^{39}. Dirac suggested that such a correlation between these enormous numbers could hardly be attributed to coincidence and that there exists a fundamental relationship between the two that ensures their perpetual, approximate equality. However, the age of the universe, clearly, is not constant, and in accordance with Dirac's hypothesis, so that the equality of the numbers is preserved, we must conclude that neither is the ratio of electromagnetic to gravitational forces between a proton and an electron constant. Such a situation may be interpreted as demanding that the Newtonian gravitational constant, usually denoted as G, which is a component of equations measuring the force of gravity between objects, is *not* in fact a constant but gradually diminishes as the universe grows older. Further, Dirac proposed that any quantity which results from a fundamental theory and is described by a large, pure number will vary in time.

While certain modern physical theories include ideas incorporating a varying G, the status of such models is considered by many to be spurious. Einstein's theory of gravitation, for example, demands that G be constant, and our knowledge of the creation of nuclear material subsequent to the big bang would appear to cast Dirac's hypothesis in a poor light.

There are few scientists of this or any other century to whom one might attribute contributions to the understanding of nature more significant and numerous than those of Paul Dirac. Just as we seldom reflect upon the origins of arithmetic when employing its powerful theorems to sum a sequence of numbers, it is a measure of Dirac's profound influence upon today's physicists that his techniques and ideas are incorporated, continually, into modern works with a thought rarely spared for their roots.

—Stephen Unwin

DOBZHANSKY, Theodosius. American geneticist. Born in Nemirov, Russia, 25 January 1900; emigrated to the United States in 1927: naturalized, 1937. Studied at the University of Kiev. Married Natalie Sivertzev in 1924; 1 daughter. Assistant Professor of Zoology, Polytechnic Institute, Kiev, 1921-24; Lecturer in Genetics, University of Leningrad, 1924-27; Rockefeller Foundation Fellow, Columbia University, New York, and California Institute of Technology, Pasadena, 1928-29; Assistant Professor of Genetics, California Institute of Technology, 1930-36; Professor, 1936-40, Professor of Zoology, 1940-58, and DaCosta Professor of Zoology, 1958-62, Columbia University; Professor, Rockefeller Institute, New York, 1962-71; Adjunct Professor, University of California at Davis, 1971-75. Exchange Professor, University of Brazil, São Paulo, 1943, 1948-49. Served as President, American Philosophical Society, and American Society of Zoologists. Recipient: Elliott Prize and Medal, 1946, and Kimber Prize, 1958, National Academy of Sciences; Guggenheim Fellowship, 1959; National Medal of Science, 1964; Addison Emery Verrill Medal, 1966; Distinguished Achievement in Science Award, American Museum of Natural History, New York, 1969. Honorary doctorate: University of Brazil, 1943; Wooster College, Ohio, 1945; University of Munster, Germany, 1958; University of Montreal, 1958; University of Chicago, 1959; University of Sydney, 1960; Oxford University, 1964; Columbia University, 1964; University of Louvain, 1965; Kalamazoo College, Michigan, 1965; Clarkson College of Technology, Potsdam, New York, 1965; University of Michigan, Ann Arbor, 1966; University of Syracuse, New York, 1967;

University of California, Berkeley, 1968; University of Padua, 1968; Northwestern University, Evanston, Illinois, 1968; Wittenberg College, Springfield, Ohio, 1970. *Died 19 December 1975.*

PUBLICATIONS

Genetics

Contributions to the Genetics of Certain Chromosome Anomalies in Drosophila Melanogaster, with A.H. Sturtevant. Washington, D.C., Carnegie Institute of Washington, 1931.
Genetics and the Origin of Species. New York, Columbia University Press, 1937.
The Raw Materials of Evolution (lecture). Washington, D.C., Carnegie Institute of Washington, 1938.
Beetles of the Genus Hyperaspis Inhabiting the United States. Washington, D.C., Smithsonian Institution, 1941.
Contributions to the Genetics, Taxonomy, and Ecology of Drosophila Melanogaster and Its Relatives. Washington, D.C., Carnegie Institute of Washington, 1944.
Heredity, Race, and Society, with L.C. Dunn. New York, Penguin Books, 1946.
Evolution, Genetics, and Man. New York, Wiley, 1955.
The Biological Basis of Human Freedom (lectures). New York, Columbia University Press, 1956.
Radiation, Genes, and Man, with Bruce Wallace. New York, Holt, 1959.
Mankind Evolving: The Evolution of Human Species (lectures). New Haven, Connecticut, Yale University Press, 1962.
Heredity and the Nature of Man. New York, Harcourt Brace, 1964.
The Genetic Effects of Radiation, with Isaac Asimov. Washington, D.C., United States Atomic Energy Commission, Division of Technical Information, 1966.
The Biology of Ultimate Concern. New York, New American Library, 1967.
Genetics and the Evolutionary Process. New York, Columbia University Press, 1970.
Genetic Diversity and Human Equality (lecture). New York, Basic Books, 1973.
The Roving Naturalist: Travel Letters of Theodosius Dobzhansky, edited by Bentley Glass. Philadelphia, American Philosophical Society, 1980.
Dobzhansky's Genetics of Natural Populations I-XLIII, edited by R.C. Lewontin and others. New York, Columbia University Press, 1981.

Other

Translator, *Heredity and Its Variability*, by Trofim Lysenko. New York, King's Crown Press, 1946.

Editor, with José Ayala, *Studies in the Philosophy of Biology: Reduction and Relation Problems.* Berkeley, University of California Press, 1974.

*   *   *

Theodosius Dobzhansky was born and educated in Russia. He emigrated to America before the age of 30 and worked until the end of his life at universities in New York and California. He was the most important figure in evolutionary studies in this century, being the chief architect of the "synthetic theory of evolution," otherwise known as "Neo-Darwinism." He was also a naturalist in the best Darwinian sense, loving the organic world for its own sake. Student after student speaks of the sheer joy of going with Dobzhansky to South America on collecting trips.

Dobzhansky's earliest work, in Russia between 1918 and 1927, was primarily on *Coccinellidae* (ladybird beetles), emphasizing classification and systematics. It was a fortunate time to be a Russian biologist, for—given Marx's praise of Darwin—one could explore evolutionary ideas with a freedom from ideological constraints not possible before the Revolution, or (indeed) much after 1930, when Lysenko's Lamarckism rose in prominence. Also, since biology (compared to physics) is relatively cheap, the new communist government strongly encouraged biological studies. Although Dobzhansky was to do his greatest work later, in America, his homeland surely deserves some credit for his later achievements.

The greatest of the Russian biologists in the 1920's was Sergei Chetverikov, who was moving evolutionary studies ahead significantly. Although Dobzhansky never formally became one of Chetverikov's students, the influence through writings and discussions was great. Dobzhansky turned more and more to evolutionary problems, and one can see clearly that Dobzhansky took up where Chetverikov and others left off.

Essentially, the situation in evolutionary studies at the beginning of the second quarter of the 20th century was as follows. In the *Origin of Species* (1859), Darwin had argued for evolution through the mechanism of natural selection, the differential reproduction of the "fittest." What Darwin did not have was an adequate theory of heredity, and, as many 19th century biologists realized, without such a confirmed theory, natural selection could have little or no lasting effect.

At the beginning of the 20th century such a theory of heredity, to be called "Mendelian genetics," was discovered and articulated. Unfortunately, because early "geneticists" concentrated on major, clearcut, physical features, the conclusion tended to be drawn that—far from vindicating natural selection—the new genetics made it redundant! All evolutionary change supposedly came through "macromutations": the spontaneous change of the units of heredity, the genes, which thus causes major new organic features.

Then in the 1920's, thanks to the (mainly theoretical) work of Chetverikov, together with Sir Ronald Fisher and J.B.S. Haldane in Britain and Sewell Wright in the U.S., it was realized that Darwinism and Mendelism can *together* tell the full tale. Evolution is a matter of natural selection working on small new variations, caused by ordinary mutations. Darwin's difficulties are thus overcome, and yet his seminal contributions preserved.

But, it is one thing to have mathematical models showing that these ideas are viable. It is another to give them empirical flesh, and to make them understandable and acceptable to working biologists. This was Dobzhansky's task, and one which he performed nobly. With a firm background in insect systematics, and fired by Chetverikov's evolutionary speculations, Dobzhansky went to America. Here, he worked first in the genetics laboratory of T.H. Morgan, much increasing his knowledge of contemporary work on heredity. He also began his studies on the little animal with which the name of "Dobzhansky" will always be linked: *Drosophila* (so-called, "fruitflies"). The importance of the right organism for the evolutionist cannot be over-emphasized. Unless one has something rapidly breeding and fully manipulatable, like the fruit-fly, all hope of successful experimentation is lost.

Dobzhansky's inquiries culminated in a series of lectures he gave in 1936, which were subsequently published as his deservedly famous book: *Genetics and the Origin of Species*. It is no exaggeration to say that this is the second-most important work in the evolutionary *corpus*, after *On the Origin of Species*. In it, he established the dominant paradigm in evolutionary thought, which holds right down to this day.

The first part of Dobzhansky's work deals with the units of heredity, the genes, as they function in breeding groups. What sorts of distributions does one find, how do they get passed on, how do they get changed, what internal and external factors affect distributions? This is so-called "population genetics." A corner-stone of Dobzhansky's thinking is the Hardy-Weinberg law: this states that gene ratios stay constant, if there are no external forces. For Dobzhansky, the law operates rather as

Newton's first law of motion operates for physicists: it guarantees a background of stability. Dobzhansky then felt able to introduce his disruptive factors, like mutation and selection. These lead initially to small changes—"microevolution." Large changes, "macroevolutions," are just the summations of small changes. Anticipating certain modern thinkers, Dobzhansky argues that a species is more than just a set of organisms with common features. By virtue of the links which exist between members, it is itself a kind of individual: a super-organism.

At all stages through the work Dobzhansky refers to empirical evidence, both that gathered from nature and (most particularly) that gained in experiments. One point after another is made by reference to actual fruitflies or to butterflies or to the like. Thanks to Dobzhansky, the "synthetic" theory—a synthesis of Darwin and Mendel—became a reality. And it was immediately picked up and elaborated on by others. Ernst Mayr applied the theory to problems of biogeography and classification (*Systematics and the Origin of Species*, 1942), George Gaylord Simpson to paleontology (*Tempo and Mode in Evolution*, 1944), and George Ledyard Stebbins to botany (*Variation and Evolution in Plants*, 1950).

Genetics and the Origin of Species went through three editions, and by the time of the last one (1951) it was clear that Dobzhansky had made an even-stronger commitment to Darwinism than before. No one has ever claimed that natural selection is the only mechanism of evolutionary change. In the 1930's, a popular supplement was "genetic drift." Sewell Wright had pointed out that in small populations, gene ratios might fluctuate randomly, due to the vagaries of interbreeding. Selection might not be effective. In the first edition of *Genetics and the Origin of Species*, drift played a larger role than it did later. By the 1950's natural selection had become almost all-powerful for Dobzhansky. He was more Darwinian than ever before.

However, there is a major problem that a Darwinian faces. If natural selection is nearly all-powerful, how can it get to work, given that its raw materials are the rare changes in the genes, "mutations," which Mendelism supposes are always "random" in the sense that change is not in the direction of the needs of the organism? Surely, selection will not have time to be effective?

Dobzhansky thought he had the answer to this problem. He emphasized that selection itself can hold variation (*i.e.* many different genes) in populations through balance. Suppose, for instance, there is an advantage in being rare (say that a predator has to learn to recognize your form). Different forms will balance each other, for if any one form starts to decline it will become rare and thus favoured by selection. Dobzhansky believed that, in fact, populations of organisms are full of variation maintained by selection. Thus, whenever an organism feels a new stress, hence setting up new selective pressures, there is no need to wait for appropriate mutations. Needed variation is probably already present!

This balance view of populations led Dobzhansky and his followers into an acrimonious dispute with the geneticist Hermann J. Muller and his followers. Muller argued that populations are basically genetically uniform, with just the occasional mutant form. His vision of populations—and of the workings of selection—was fundamentally different from that of Dobzhansky. Unfortunately, for many years not a great deal of progress was made in settling the dispute between the rival positions. However, at last, in the late 1960's new techniques of measuring intra populational variation were developed. These techniques, relying on molecular biology, showed definitively that Dobzhansky was right. There is always lots of variation in natural populations. Dobzhansky's extreme Darwinism was saved.

As often is the case when scientists fall out, there were factors in the Dobzhansky/Muller dispute which went beyond science in the strictest sense. Muller was a eugenicist, believing that one should strive for perfect human forms. Dobzhansky's view of populations made Muller's position scientifically untenable. There is no such thing as a Platonic idea of human, against which we should be judged. Humans, like members of other species, differ.

Dobzhansky likewise had more at stake than just some technical problem in population genetics. Although he did very little formal work on human biology, the nature of man occupied his thought increasingly as he grew older. This culminated in a brilliant survey given in the Silliman lectures at Yale University, published as *Mankind Evolving: The Evolution of Human Species*. In this work, Dobzhansky spoke of our own evolution, and of the biological similarities and differences between humans as we find them today. In certain respects Dobzhansky foreshadowed today's "sociobiologists," like E.O. Wilson, for he was certainly not beyond supposing that major human behavioural features are controlled (in part, at least) by the genes. For instance, he speculated that homosexuality might have a biological basis.

However, it was clear in this discussion of humans, as it was in his other publications, that Dobzhansky considered humans to be far more than just biological automata. Indeed, to the contrary, Dobzhansky thought that biology guarantees a human freedom and capacity for moral worth. And with this, he stressed the value of each and every individual. Thus, with reason, Dobzhansky's approach to intra-population variability was felt to be a crucial underpinning to his conception of humankind.

> Although all men now living are members of a single biological species, no two persons, except identical twins, have the same genetic endowment. Every individual is biologically unique and nonrecurrent. It would be naive to claim that the discovery of this biological uniqueness constitutes a scientific proof of every person's existential singularity, but this view is at least consistent with the fact of biological singularity. (*Mankind Evolving*, p. 219)

This ethical stance on humans was, in turn, connected to a growing feeling and sympathy for religion, a subject which came to occupy more and more of Dobzhansky's thought. Somewhat to the horror of his more materialistically minded fellow evolutionists, Dobzhansky responded warmly to the Christian/metaphysical speculations of the French Jesuit paleontologist, Teilhard de Chardin. Dobzhansky quoted with approbation Teilhard's belief that man is in some sense the culmination of evolution, and that evolution points to the "Omega Point"—the incarnate Jesus Christ. Dobzhansky realised that at this point he and Teilhard went beyond science, but like Teilhard he felt that unless one goes beyond science the picture remains incomplete.

Whether Teilhard made lasting contributions to either science or religion is perhaps a moot point. What is not a moot point is Dobzhansky's solid contribution to biological science. It is true that, in recent years, the synthetic theory of evolution has come under attack. Some population geneticists think that, in fact, drift does play a major role in evolution. Some paleontologists think that evolution sometimes goes in jumps, the causes of which cannot be accounted for in traditional population biology. These are still contentious issues, and neo-Darwinism has yet many defenders. But, Dobzhansky would have been the first to admit that his was not the last word on evolution. Like Charles Darwin, Dobzhansky's lasting achievement was to write one very important chapter in the unfolding story of organic origins, of how we descended with modification by a natural process of evolution.

—Michael Ruse

DURKHEIM, Emile. French sociologist. Born in Epinal, Lorraine, 15 April 1858. Educated at Ecole Normale, Paris, agregation 1882; studied under German psychologist Wilhelm Wundt, 1885-86. Married Louise Dreyfus in 1887; 2 children.

Taught philosophy in provincial lycées, 1882-85; Lecturer in Education and Sociology, 1887-96, and Professor of Sociology (first professorship in sociology in France), 1896-1902, University of Bordeaux; Professor of Sociology and Education, University of Paris, Sorbonne, 1902 until his death, 1917. Founder, *Année sociologique*, to promote specialization and collective work within the field of sociology, 1897. *Died* (in Paris) *15 November 1917.*

PUBLICATIONS

Sociology

Quid Secundatus politicae scientiae instituendae contulerit. Bordeaux, Gounouilhou, 1892; expanded as *Montesquieu et Rousseau, précurseurs de la sociologie,* Paris, M. Rivière, 1953; as *Montesquieu and Rousseau: Forerunners of Sociology,* Ann Arbor, Michigan, University of Michigan Press, 1960.
De la division du travail social: Etude sur l'organisation des sociétés supérieures. Paris, Alcan, 1893; as *The Division of Labor in Society,* New York, Macmillan, 1933.
Les Règles de la methode sociologique. Paris, Alcan, 1895; as *The Rules of the Sociological Method,* edited by George E.G. Catlin, Chicago, University of Chicago Press, 1938.
Le Suicide: Etude de sociologique. Paris, Alcan, 1897; as *Suicide: A Study in Sociology,* edited by George Simpson, Glencoe, Illinois, Free Press, 1951; London, Routledge, 1952.
Les Formes élémentaires de la vie religieuse: Le système totémique en Australie. Paris, Alcan, 1912; as *The Elementary Forms of Religious Life,* London, and New York, Allen and Unwin, 1915.
Qui a voulu la guerre?: Les origines de la guerre d'après les documents diplomatiques / Who Wanted War?: The Origin of the War According to Diplomatic Documents, with E. Denis. Paris, Armand Colin, 1915.
"L'Allemagne au-dessus de tout": La mentalité allemande et la guerre/"Germany above All": The German Mental Attitude and the War. Paris, Armand Colin, 1915.
Education et sociologie. Paris, Alcan, 1922; as *Education and Sociology,* Glencoe, Illinois, Free Press, 1956.
Sociologie et philosophie. Paris, Alcan, 1924; as *Sociology and Philosophy,* Glencoe, Illinois, Free Press, 1953.
L'Education morale (lectures, 1902-03). Paris, Alcan, 1925; as *Moral Education: A Study in the Theory and Application of the Sociology of Education,* edited by Everett K. Wilson, New York, Free Press of Glencoe, 1961.
Le Socialisme: Sa définition, ses débuts, la doctrine Saint-Simonienne (lectures, 1895-96), edited by M. Mauss. Paris, Alcan, 1928; as *Socialism and Saint-Simon,* edited by Alvin W. Gouldner, Yellow Springs, Ohio, Antioch Press, 1958; London, Routledge, 1959.
L'Evolution pédagogique en France: vol. 1, *Des origines à la renaissance;* vol. 2, *De la renaissance à nos jours* (lectures, 1904-05). Paris, Alcan, 1938.
Leçons de sociologie: Physique des moeurs et du droit (lectures, 1890-1900). Istanbul, l'Université d'Istanbul, and Paris, Presses Universitaires de France, 1950; as *Professional Ethics and Civic Morals,* London, Routledge, 1957.
Emile Durkheim 1858-1917: A Collection of Essays with Translations and a Bibliography, edited by Kurt Wolff. Columbus, Ohio University Press, 1960.
Primitive Classifications (translated from the French), edited by Rodney Needham. Chicago, University of Chicago Press, and London, Cohen and West, 1963.
Incest: The Nature and Origin of the Taboo (translated from the French). New York, Lyle Stuart, 1981.

*

Bibliography: *The Durkheimian School: A Systematic and Comprehensive Bibliography* by Hash Nandon, Westport, Connecticut, Greenwood Press, 1977.

Critical Studies: *Emile Durkheim and His Sociology* by Harry Alpert, New York, Columbia University Press, 1939; *Emile Durkheim* by Robert Bierstedt, London, Weidenfeld and Nicolson, 1966; *Durkheim: Morality and Milieu* by Ernest Wallwork, Cambridge, Massachusetts, Harvard University Press, 1972 (contains a full bibliography); *Emile Durkheim: A Historical and Critical Study* by Steven Lukes, New York, Harper, 1972 (contains a full bibliography); *Durkheim's Suicide: A Classic Analyzed* by Whitney Pope, Chicago, University of Chicago Press, 1976; *Durkheim et le politique* by Bernard La Croix, Paris, Presses de la Fondation Nationale des Sciences Politique, and Montreal, University of Montreal, 1981.

*   *   *

There were two major themes which provided an underlying coherence to Durkheim's sociology. The first focused on the problem of social order in societies in which there was an extensive division of labour, conflicts between social classes and an absence of general consensus over values and moral principles. Durkheim thought that sociology had an important role to play in the search for a new basis of social coherence in modern society. To some extent, this issue was specifically relevant to French society which, in the late 19th century, was being transformed by the secularisation of religious values, the industrialisation of an agrarian economy and urbanisation. For Durkheim, the crisis of the Franco-Prussian War clearly indicated the urgent need for social reorganisation in French social life. However, the problem of social order was not simply an issue peculiar to France; it was endemic to industrial society as such. The second organising theme of Durkheim's sociology focused on the problem of establishing sociology as an independent academic discipline within the university system and more profoundly of establishing sociology as a viable science of society with an adequate epistemological and methodological foundation. In particular, Durkheim sought to distinguish sociology clearly from social philosophy which involved speculative evaluation of social arrangements and social psychology which explained social institutions in terms of the characteristics of individuals. By contrast, sociology was not evaluative and aimed to explain social phenomena in terms of social causes.

These two features of Durkheim's sociology—the problem of order and the problem of science—were in fact intimately related. The social reorganisation of France could only be achieved on the basis of an adequate analysis of the causes and effects of rapid social change. The specific task of sociology was to provide a body of scientific analysis and evidence upon which adequate social legislation could be based. In more general terms, sociology was a type of consciousness appropriate to modern society and, according to Durkheim, to a modern culture profoundly influenced by Cartesian rationalism. In this respect, Durkheim can be regarded as the representative of the French positivist tradition which had its roots in the social philosophy of Henri Comte de Saint Simon and Auguste Comte. Just as the scientific development of positive medicine promised to provide a radical therapy for diseases in the human body, so sociology as a *physique sociale* would cure the illness within the social body. While Durkheim was critical of Comte, he was securely within the Comtean tradition which regarded sociology as a positivist science seeking to understand the social pathology of modern society.

The central themes of Durkheim's sociology were clearly present in his first major work, *The Division of Labour in Society,* in which he argued against the English sociologist Herbert Spencer that social order in industrial society could not be explained as the consequence of social contracts between individuals motivated by self interest. The pursuit of self interest would result in social chaos and individual social contracts could not be guaranteed without social restraint in the form of law. Having rejected utilitarian perspectives on social order, Durkheim distinguished between the forms of social order found in traditional and modern societies. In the former, social cohesion was based on mechanical solidarity and the *conscience collective*, namely a system of common beliefs, attitudes and rituals. The modern conception of "the individual" as a self-motivated free agent with a private conscience was absent from such societies. Deviation from the *conscience collective* was savagely punished by social exclusion and retributive laws. With the social changes brought about by population growth, urbanisation and industrialisation, mechanical solidarity declined, and the *conscience collective* was undermined with the decline of a common religion and the growth of individualism. However, a new form of social order would emerge on the basis of organic solidarity. While the increasing division of labour resulted in the differentiation and specialisation of the individual, it also increased reciprocal ties between individuals who could no longer be socially or economically self-sufficient. Traditional religious values, common rituals and coercive legal practices gradually disappeared and society became organised on a new basis. The coherence of modern society is explained by economic reciprocity within the division of labour, the presence of redistributive justice in exchange relations, the growth of occupational associations such as guilds linking the individual to the state and the development of professional or occupational ethics which control individual behaviour within these associations.

Debates about Durkheim's analysis of the division of labour hinge on two issues. Durkheim's study was implicitly an illustration of scientific procedure in sociology in which one social fact ("the organic solidarity of modern society") was explained by another social fact ("the social division of labour") without recourse to causal factors which were not social (for example, individual psychology). However, the cause of the division of labour was demographic expansion which forced social groups to specialise in order to survive. Durkheim has to assume that demographic facts ("population density") are social rather than features of the biological structure of human groups and offers no account of the theoretical relationship between demographic and sociological explanations. The second issue is whether a modern society can exist without any, or at least minimal, *conscience collective*, that is, without any consensus over general values. Most commentators on Durkheim's sociology of social order suggest that in his later work he was less concerned with economic reciprocity as the basis of social cohesion and more concerned with the development of alternatives to traditional religion as the root of a contemporary *conscience collective*. One possible basis for such a common belief system was nationalism, and this assumption was clearly present in Durkheim's popular pamphlets written during the First World War.

The middle period of Durkheim's intellectual development was dominated by the problem of establishing sociology as a separate and autonomous science. For example, in *The Rules of Sociological Method* he gave more detailed consideration to the methodological slogan that "social facts explain social facts." The point of this principle was to deny the notion that society is simply an aggregation of individuals and to rule out psychological reductionism in which social reality is regarded as ultimately determined by individual psychology. Social facts have the following characteristics: they exist independently of the subjective awareness of individuals; they are exterior to the individual; they exercise constraint over behaviour; and they are general and collective. In less formal terms, Durkheim argued that the culture and structure of social groups existed independently of the individuals who happen at any given time to be members of such groups. For example, the structure and culture of a tribe may exist for decades, irrespective of the birth and death of successive tribal members. We can detect the same methodological and philosophical themes in *Suicide*. While suicide was traditionally regarded as simply a feature of abnormal psychology, Durkheim, through an analysis of the suicide statistics of different societies and different groups within them, attempted to demonstrate that the suicide rate had social causes. Durkheim identified four types of suicide—egoistic, altruistic, anomic and fatalistic—and his thesis was that in modern society the suicidal drives of individuals are unleashed as social regulation of group life declines. In the transition to organic solidarity, secularisation and urbanisation effectively undermine the system of social regulation based on common culture, group personality, religious rituals and repressive law. There were no longer any adequate checks on the *courants suicidogenes* in society, and hence there was a sharp rise in the suicide rate. However, Durkheim also pointed to differences between groups within society to confirm his thesis; for example, the higher incidence of "egoistic suicides" among Protestants than Catholics reflected an individualist ethos in theology and the curtailment of group solidarity. "Anomic suicides" were characteristic of individuals isolated from social life who experienced normlessness as a consequence. Other types of suicide were more common in primitive societies and were the product of excessive rather than declining social regulation. "Fatalistic suicide" among slaves was an illustration of the argument. While Durkheim's positivistic philosophy of social science has been seriously questioned by modern sociologists, his study of suicide remains a monumental classic within the discipline.

In his last major works, Durkheim was preoccupied with the role of belief and knowledge, particularly in religious systems, in social life. In *The Elementary Forms of Religious Life* Durkheim criticised existing interpretations of religion as the false beliefs of individuals in the existence of God. Durkheim's sociology of religion rested on four basic assertions. Ritual practice is more important than formal beliefs in the organisation and continuity of religious systems. Furthermore, sociologists are not concerned with the truth of religious propositions but with the functions of religion in society. Religion is not a feature of individual behaviour but an essential dimension of collective life. Finally, the belief in God is not a universal feature of religious systems; it in the separation between the profane and the sacred world which is essential to religion. Durkheim defined religion as a system of beliefs and practices relative to sacred reality which unite believers into a moral community as a result of their involvement in collective rituals. On the basis of anthropological data collected by anthropologists on aboriginal tribes in Australia, Durkheim argued that social solidarity was generated and sustained by collective rituals which were the vehicles of social symbols, collective memory and the *conscience collective*. The truth or falsity of totemism was not an issue. The sociological importance of totemism was its functional contribution to the survival of group life. This theory of religion was not specific to Australian aboriginal societies; Durkheim had identified the "elementary" structures of all religious systems.

If religion was so important to the survival of social groups as the principal fountain of social solidarity, how could modern secular society survive? Durkheim's answer was that, while the "old gods were dead," a new *conscience collective* would emerge from the associational structure of modern industrial societies. Furthermore, sociology had an important part to play in the birth of the modern consciousness. The emphasis on common beliefs as the basis of social cohesion appeared to contradict his earlier argument that economic reciprocity was the root of organic solidarity in contemporary society and it seems doubtful that, for example, occupational guilds could produce a "religion" of any collective vitality. At the end of his life, Durkheim observed in nationalism a new source of collective rituals, symbols and myths which could provide a social cement for modern societies.

Durkheim's sociology, which can be seen as an attempt to create a science of moral life, has been subjected to extensive and penetrating criticisms, three in particular. First, it has been argued that Durkheim's attempt to exclude individual consciousness and subjectivity from sociology was unsuccessful.

Beliefs and values cannot be regarded as "things" existing outside subjective awareness. Furthermore, to become effective values have to be internalised as part of the consciousness and the conscience of the individual. To assert the importance of subjectivity for social life is not necessarily to argue that sociology depends on psychology. Secondly, his sociology has been criticised as conservative and normative, because it involves a prescriptive commitment to social order as a value. Thirdly, it is argued that Durkheim's theoretical commitment to the problem of social order precluded any successful treatment or explanation of social change and social conflict. For Durkheim, the notion of "constraint" always involved the moral constraint of social custom, collective practices and legal arrangements, and neglected the importance of economic, political and military coercion. Despite these criticisms, Durkheim's influence on subsequent sociology in Europe and, to a lesser extent, in North America was profound. His emphasis on the autonomy of social structure and culture played an important part in the theoretical development of functionalism as a perspective in both sociology and anthropology. The Durkheimian approach to social phenomena remains one of most cogent and coherent statements of sociology as an independent, scientific discipline within the social sciences.

—Bryan S. Turner

DWORKIN, Ronald (Myles). American jurist. Born in Worcester, Massachusetts, 11 December 1931. Studied at Harvard University, Cambridge, Massachusetts, B.A. 1953, LL.B. 1957; Oxford University, B.A. 1955, M.A.; admitted to the bar, 1959. Married Betsy Ross in 1958; 2 children. Law Clerk for Judge Learned Hand, 1957-58; Associate, Sullivan and Cromwell, 1958-62; Member of the Faculty, from 1962, and Hohfeld Professor of Jurisprudence, 1968-69, Yale University Law School, New Haven, Connecticut. Professor of Jurisprudence, Oxford University, since 1969; Professor of Law, New York University, since 1976. Visiting Professor, Princeton University, New Jersey, 1963 and 1974-75, and Stanford University, California, 1967; Professor at Large, Cornell University, Ithaca, New York, 1976-82; Visiting Professor of Law and Philosophy, 1977, and Visiting Professor of Philosophy, 1979, Harvard University. Rosenthal Lecturer, Northwestern University, Evanston, Illinois, 1975; Academic Freedom Lecturer, University of Witwatersrand, South Africa, 1976; Roscoe Pound Lecturer, University of Nebraska, Lincoln, 1979. Honorary doctorate: Williams College, Williamstown, Massachusetts, 1981. Fellow, British Academy and American Academy of Arts and Sciences. Address: New York University Law School, Washington Square, New York, New York 10012, U.S.A.

PUBLICATIONS

Law

Taking Rights Seriously. Cambridge, Massachusetts, Harvard University Press, and London, Duckworth, 1977.

Other

Editor, *The Philosophy of Law.* London and New York, Oxford University Press, 1977.

*   *   *

Ronald Dworkin is one of the major figures in contemporary jurisprudence and social philosophy. His *Taking Rights Seriously* is a complex and subtle attempt to refute the prevailing "positivist" model of law, exemplified in the work of H.L.A. Hart, his predecessor at Oxford: this and his general essays on social philosophy constitute an impressive statement of contemporary American "liberalism". It is a feature of Dworkin's thought that in it no rigid separation is made between its descriptive and prescriptive elements.

In his formal jurisprudence Dworkin challenges a number of "positive" assumptions about law: namely, that the description of a legal system is exhausted by a description of its rules, that a logical distinction can be made between law and morality and that judges must "legislate" in a discretionary manner when a given structure of rules is inadequate in difficult cases. The crux of Dworkin's argument turns on a logical distinction he makes between "principles" and "rules". In "hard" or controversial cases where lawyers dispute about legal rights and obligations, and where no rule may be applicable, Dworkin claims that appeal has to be made to principles. Although principles are legal phenomena, they differ from rules in that whereas the latter can be precisely delineated and have the characteristic of being "all or nothing" in application, principles may be balanced and weighed against one another, they may not always apply and cannot be easily enumerated. A famous example of a principle is that which holds that a man "should not profit from his own wrong" (which has been invoked to prevent a murderer benefiting from his victim's will).

In fact, on analysis, Dworkin's principles turn out to be *rights*, which are embedded in the community, and judges must always uphold them against the state. The law cannot abrogate principles based on rights in order to advance *policies*, since these latter are concerned only with the advancement of collective goals. Dworkin, therefore, maintains that the positivist's distinction between law and morality is untenable precisely because judges have to use political and moral arguments in determining what the law is; that is, in determining what rights to uphold.

Furthermore, and somewhat paradoxically, Dworkin maintains that, despite the apparently controversial nature of principles, there is always one right answer to any legal dispute, even though judges may often be mistaken in their decisions. This extreme rationalism is used to counter the argument that judges exercize strong discretion in difficult cases by, in effect, legislating new rules where there appear to be gaps in the law. If this were so, argues Dworkin, judges would be frequently creating *retroactive* rules. Finally, Dworkin's stress on principles leads him to reject the view that there is ultimately one "master" rule that determines validity in a legal system.

Dworkin's own social philosophy (see his "Liberalism", in *Public and Private Morality*, ed. S. Hampshire) is linked to his jurisprudential thesis about rights. Rights are "political trumps" held by individuals against governments; they are based on the idea that each person is entitled to equal concern and respect, and they over-ride any utilitarian or welfarist public policy. Furthermore, Dworkin's liberalism is claimed to be ethically neutral in that it prohibits the state legislating a particular conception of the good life; therefore, Dworkin accepts that a market allocation of resources is a better protector of this neutrality than paternalist socialist planning. However, inequalities, for example, those that derive from traditional property structures, and even from differential rewards that accrue to the most talented, may be altered without disturbing liberal neutrality. Thus Dworkin's liberalism turns out to be highly radical indeed since it sanctions economic redistribution, reverse discrimination to favour minorities (even if this means denying equal opportunities to others) in education and employment and special protection for suspects in the criminal process; also it encourages a tolerant attitude towards disobedience to laws that appear to be in breach of fundamental rights.

As regards jurisprudence, positivists have accepted that Dworkin has highlighted a weakness in their standard model of law; that is, that it did not take proper account of the importance of legal principles. However, they have rejected his description of rules as "all or nothing" things and maintained that a broader conception of rules can account for the difficulties of hard cases. It is maintained that to admit ultimate moral and political principles into the process of legal validation is to confuse political theory and ethics with law. The idea that there is always one correct answer to every case is rejected, as is the thesis that it is necessarily harmful for judges to appeal to public policy, rather than philosophical statements about rights, in deciding difficult cases. Dworkin's thesis not only demands extraordinary qualities of judges but also presupposes agreement on the rights that he claims must be at the foundation of a system of law.

Dworkin's social philosophy of liberalism is a vigorously independent one and not a half-way house between socialism and conservatism; nor does it consist of a pluralist trade-off between the ideals of liberty and equality. However, the strongly activist role for the state implied in the protection of the fundamental but vague right to equal concern and respect threatens the liberty principle implicit in the more traditional versions of liberalism. In fact, Dworkin does not recognize a *general* right to liberty, and is, despite his professed anti-utilitarianism, prepared to override individualist economic and property rights if they conflict with the general welfare.

—Norman Barry

EDDINGTON, A(rthur) S(tanley). British astronomer and philosopher. Born in Kendal, Westmoreland, 28 December 1882. Studied at Owens College, Manchester, B.Sc. 1902, and at Trinity College, Cambridge (Fellow, 1907). Chief Assistant, Royal Observatory, Greenwich, 1906-13; Pulmian Professor of Astronomy and Director of the Observatory, Cambridge University, 1913-44. Romanes Lecturer, Cambridge University, 1922; Gifford Lecturer, University of Edinburgh, 1927. President, Royal Astronomical Society, 1921-23, International Physical Society, 1930-32, and International Astronomical Union, 1938-44. Recipient: Royal Medal, Royal Society, London, 1928. Honorary B.Sc.: University of London; honorary M.Sc.: University of Manchester; honorary doctorate: University of Manchester; Oxford University; University of Dublin; University of Bristol; University of Leeds; University of Witwatersrand, Johannesburg, South Africa; University of Durham; University of Edinburgh; Harvard University, Cambridge, Massachusetts; Allahabad University and Benares Hindu University, India; University of Calcutta. Fellow of the Royal Society, 1914. Knighted, 1930; O.M. (Order of Merit), 1938. *Died 22 November 1944.*

PUBLICATIONS

Astronomy and Physics

Stellar Movements and the Structure of the Universe. London, Macmillan, 1914.
Report on the Relativity Theory of Gravitation. London, Fleetway Press, 1918.
Space, Time and Gravitation: An Outline of the General Relativity Theory. Cambridge, Cambridge University Press, 1921.
The Theory of Relativity and Its Influence on Scientific Thought (lecture). Oxford, Clarendon Press, 1922.
The Mathematical Theory of Relativity. Cambridge, Cambridge University Press, 1923.
The Internal Constitution of the Stars. Cambridge, Cambridge University Press, 1926.
Stars and Atoms. London, Oxford University Press, and New Haven, Connecticut, Yale University Press, 1927.
The Nature of the Physical World. Cambridge, Cambridge

University Press, and New York, Macmillan, 1928.
Science and the Unseen World (lecture). London, Allen and Unwin, and New York, Macmillan, 1929.
The Rotation of the Galaxy (lecture). Oxford, Clarendon Press, 1930.
The Expanding Universe. Cambridge, Cambridge University Press, and New York, Macmillan, 1933.
New Pathways in Science (lectures). Cambridge, Cambridge University Press, 1935.
Relativity Theory of Protons and Electrons. Cambridge, Cambridge University Press, and New York, Macmillan, 1936.
The Philosophy of Physical Science (lectures). Cambridge, Cambridge University Press, and New York, Macmillan, 1939.
Fundamental Theory. Cambridge, Cambridge University Press, 1946.

*

Critical Studies: *The Sources of Eddington's Philosophy* by Herbert Dingle, Cambridge, Cambridge University Press, 1954; *The Philosophy of Science of A.S. Eddington* by John W. Yolton, The Hague, Nijhoff, 1960.

*   *   *

The first decade of A.S. Eddington's career gave scant indication of the ultimate contributions he was to make to astronomy. His early work at the Royal Observatory and Cambridge focused on observational studies, monitoring solar eclipses, measuring transits for a new zodiacal catalogue, and determining the longitude of a geodetic station in Malta. By 1916, however, he had turned his attention to the first of many theoretical questions which were to occupy his attention for the remaining three decades of his life. This was the question of the internal composition of stars.

The question Eddington attacked was how the sun (and, by extension, other stars) maintained its structure. The gravitational forces within a body of this size are so great that it would seem inevitable that the body would collapse in upon itself. Explaining why this did not happen was Eddington's task. He began by suggesting that heat and radiation generated at the sun's center is transported to its surface by radiation, not, as currently believed, by convection. Then, he calculated the radiation pressure that would result from this assumption. He found that the magnitude of the expansive force of radiation pressure was great enough to balance the contractive force of gravitation and, hence, to account for the stability of the sun.

Other valuable results came about as a result of this analysis. The most important was his discovery that the luminosity of a star is dependent almost entirely upon its mass. The more massive a star, the greater its internal pressure, temperature, and radiation pressure, and, hence, its absolute brightness. This *mass-luminosity relationship* proved to be of enormous value in later astronomical research.

Eddington also demonstrated that the mass-luminosity relationship implies an upper limit to the size a star might attain. The force of radiation pressure increases so rapidly with mass, he showed, that stars much more massive than our own sun would have a strong tendency to blow themselves apart. Few stars, in fact, would have 10 times the sun's mass, and many fewer would have 50 times its mass. The behavior of stars near these limits, Eddington found, was much like that observed for the Cepheid variables: their energy output pulsates regularly at the verge of explosiveness.

The announcement of Einstein's general theory of relativity marked a turning point in Eddington's career. Few scholars of the time so completely threw themselves into a study and application of Einstein's ideas. In a pair of expeditions to study solar eclipses in 1919 and 1920, Eddington obtained crucial **data** needed for one of the empirical tests of the general theory, the bending of light rays as they pass massive (in this case, stellar) objects. His speculations also led him to propose another test for the general theory, namely that the frequency of light would show a shift toward the red end of the spectrum when it was emitted from a body of very high density. Confirmation for this test was obtained by W.S. Adams in 1924.

Eddington also became intensely interested in finding a way to integrate the two great theoretical discoveries of the 20th century: general relativity and quantum mechanics. To this end, he devoted a major part of his energy for the rest of his life. His most significant achievement in this direction was to show the relationship among ordinary units of length, gravitational force, curvature of space, and the linear dimensions of atoms, expressed in wave mechanical form. This accomplishment allowed him to derive the fundamental constants of nature (the mass and charge of an electron, the velocity of light, the Planck and Rydberg constants and the gravitational constant) from purely theoretical considerations.

His efforts at reaching a "grand synthesis", his "Fundamental Theory," were probably premature. Too much about atomic and nuclear physics and astrophysics was yet to be learned. As a result, his text on the subject, published posthumously in 1946, has met with considerable controversy and limited acceptance.

Beyond his theoretical research and writings, Eddington was a great popularizer of Einstein's ideas. At the same time he was producing profound papers on the Fundamental Theory, he was writing popular expositions that made the ideas of relativity more accessible to the general public than any other literary works of his time.

—David Newton

EINSTEIN, Albert. American physicist and philosopher. Born in Ulm, Germany, 14 March 1879; renounced German citizenship, 1894; became Swiss citizen, 1900; emigrated to England in 1933 and to the United States in 1935: naturalized, 1940. Educated at the Luitpold Gymnasium, Munich, 1889-95; the Gewerbeabteilung, Aarau, Switzerland, 1895-96; Federated Institute of Technology, Zurich, 1896-1901; University of Zurich, Ph.D. 1905. Married Mileva Maric in 1903, 2 sons; married Elsa Einstein Löwenthal in 1919. Technical Assistant, Berne Patent Office, 1902-09; Lecturer, University of Berne, 1908-09; Associate Professor, University of Zurich, 1909-11; Professor, Karl-Ferdinand University, Prague, 1911-12; Professor, Federated Institute of Technology, Zurich, 1912-14; Professor, University of Berlin, 1914-32; Professor and Life Member, Institute for Advanced Study, Princeton, New Jersey, 1932-55. Herbert Spencer Lecturer, Oxford University, 1933. Recipient: Nobel Prize in Physics, 1922; Gold Medal, Royal Astronomical Society, London, 1926; Franklin Institute Medal, Philadelphia, 1935. Honorary doctorate: University of Geneva; University of Zurich; University of Rostock; University of Madrid; University of Brussels; University of Buenos Aires; Sorbonne, Paris; University of London; Cambridge University; Oxford University; University of Glasgow; University of Leeds; University of Manchester; Harvard University, Cambridge, Massachusetts; Princeton University, New Jersey; New York State University at Albany; Yeshiva University, Jerusalem. First Honorary Citizen, Tel Aviv, 1923. Offered the Presidency of Israel in 1952 (declined). Fellow of the Royal Society, London, and of the French Academy of Sciences, Paris. *Died* (in Princeton) *18 April 1955.*

PUBLICATIONS

Physics

Eine neue Bestimmung der Moleküldimensionen. Berne, Wyss, 1905.

Entwurf einer verallgemeinerten Relativitätstheorie und eine Theorie der Gravitation, with Marcel Grossman. Leipzig, Teubner, 1913.

Grundlage der allgemeinen Relativitätstheorie. Leipzig, Barth, 1916; included in *The Principle of Relativity,* 1920.

Über die spezielle und die allgemeine Relativitätstheorie, gemeinverständlich. Brunswick, Germany, Vieweg, 1917; as *Relativity, the Special and the General Theory: A Popular Exposition,* London, Methuen, 1920; New York, Holt, 1921.

The Principle of Relativity: Original Papers by A. Einstein and H. Minkowski. Calcutta, University of Calcutta, 1920.

Äther und Relativitätstheorie (lecture). Berlin, Springer, 1920; included in *Sidelights on Relativity,* 1922.

The Meaning of Relativity: Four Lectures Delivered at Princeton University. Princeton, New Jersey, Princeton University Press, 1921; London, Methuen, 1922.

Sidelights on Relativity: I. Ether and Relativity. II. Geometry and Experience. London, Methuen, and New York, Dutton, 1922.

Untersuchungen über die Theorie der Brownschen Bewegungen, edited by R. Fürth. Leipzig, Akademische Verlagsgesellschaft, 1922; as *Investigation on the Theory of Brownian Movement,* London, Methuen, and New York, Dutton, 1926.

Grundgedanken und Probleme der Relativitätstheorie. Stockholm, Imprimerie Royale, 1923.

On the Method of Theoretical Physics (lecture). Oxford, Clarendon Press, 1933; reprinted in *The World As I See It,* 1934.

Origins of the General Theory of Relativity (lecture). Glasgow, Jackson, 1933; reprinted in *The World As I See It,* 1934.

The Evolution of Physics: The Growth of Ideas from Early Concepts to Relativity and Quanta, with Leopold Infeld. New York, Simon and Schuster, 1938.

Other

About Zionism: Speeches and Letters, edited by Sir Leon Simon. London, Soncino Press, 1930.

Cosmic Religion, with Other Opinions and Aphorisms. New York, Covici-Friede, 1931.

Why War?, with Sigmund Freud. Paris, International Institute of Intellectual Cooperation, League of Nations, 1933.

The Fight Against War, edited by Alfred Lief. New York, John Day, 1933.

The World As I See It. New York, Covici-Friede, and London, Lane, 1934.

Test Case for Humanity. London, Jewish Agency for Palestine, 1944.

The Arabs and Palestine, with E. Kahler. New York, Christian Council on Palestine and American Palestine Committee, 1944.

Out of My Later Years. New York, Philosophical Library, 1950.

Ideas and Opinions, edited by Carl Seelig. New York, Crown, 1954.

Lettres à Maurice Solovine. Paris, Gauthier-Villars, 1956.

Einstein on Peace, edited by Otto Nathan and Heinz Norden. New York, Simon and Schuster, 1960.

Letters on Wave Mechanics: Schrödinger, Planck, Einstein, Lorentz, edited by K. Przibram. New York, Philosophical Library, 1967.

*

Bibliography: *A Bibliographical Checklist and Guide to the Published Writings of Albert Einstein* by Nell Boni and others, Paterson, New Jersey, Pageant Books, 1960.

Critical Studies: *Albert Einstein: Philosopher-Scientist*, edited by Paul Arthur Schilpp, Evanston, Illinois, Library of Living Philosophers, and London, Cambridge University Press, 1949; *Albert Einstein, His Work and Its Influence on Our World* by Leopold Infeld, New York, Scribner, 1950: *Einstein, His Life and Times* by Philipp Frank, New York, Knopf, 1953; *Einstein: The First Hundred Years*, edited by Maurice Goldsmith and others, Oxford and New York, Pergamon Press, 1980; *"Subtle is the Lord..."*: *The Science and the Life of Albert Einstein* by Abraham Pais, Oxford, Clarendon Press, and New York, Oxford University Press, 1982.

*   *   *

Albert Einstein transformed our most fundamental beliefs about the nature of the physical universe and thereby shook our faith in the possibility of achieving certainty in any intellectual domain. His theories are difficult, partly because they require one to discard patterns of thinking which are so basic that they seem an integral part of our human nature. The theories also have the popular reputation of being extremely abstruse, in the sense that they concern only out-of-the-way phenomena alien to the experience of all but a handful of scientists in laboratories. This is wrong: for instance, a fact as crucial to ordinary human life as the ability of the Sun to give off heat and light was incomprehensible before Einstein.

The Newtonian approach to physics which was regarded as axiomatic up to the beginning of the 20th century might be described as treating the universe as a stage (three-dimensional space enduring through regularly-unfolding time) on which various players (lumps of matter) act upon one another (by transmitting and re-transmitting energy). Einstein abolished this distinction between fixed stage and changing players; within his theories, the properties of space and time are themselves governed by the matter and energy in the universe, and these properties are by no means as austerely simple as the Newtonian picture suggests.

Already at the age of 16 Einstein was puzzled by a problem about light. Light waves moved at a fixed, experimentally-discoverable speed, which happens to be almost exactly 300,000 kilometres per second. Within the physics of Einstein's childhood this figure had no other special significance. In principle there was no bar to a material body in outer space travelling this fast, or faster. Suppose a space traveller kept pace with a light-ray, Einstein wondered: what would he observe? Logically, he should observe "a spatially oscillatory electromagnetic field at rest"; but this notion seemed to make no sense.

Einstein's Special Theory of Relativity resolved such paradoxes by postulating that the speed of light is constant for all observers: anyone who times a light-beam will always find it to be moving at 300,000 km/s, even if observer and light-source are rushing away from or towards one another at great speed. However, this postulate implies that motion affects the observed size of an object. Suppose a mile-long rod is rushing past us at high speed; in principle we can measure its length by placing a long ruler parallel to the track of the rod and noting which two marks on the ruler are opposite the two ends of the rod at any one moment. Clearly the two readings must be simultaneous. But simultaneity is not a straightforward concept, when the events in question are distant from one another; we have to test for simultaneity by comparing the arrival times of light-waves transmitted from the different events, and the assumption about constancy of the speed of light has implications for the results of such tests. Suppose we are standing by the zero mark on the ruler. Then we will see the trailing end of the rod pass this mark at a moment which, by our tests of simultaneity, coincides with the moment at which the distant leading end of the rod passes a point on the ruler rather nearer to us than the one-mile mark. In other words, we will measure the length of the rod as falling short of one mile, by an amount which depends on its speed; while, conversely, a rider on the rod who measures our "one-mile ruler" will find that

from his point of view our ruler is less than one mile long.

Now, one might respond to this by arguing that it merely shows the shortcomings of measurement using moving light-beams; but Einstein would reply that we have no better method. *Any* measurement technique used by observers located in "frames of reference" which are moving relative to one another will show to each observer that the contents of the other frame have shrunk along the direction of movement, by comparison with measurements taken at rest. In this situation it would be merely superstitious, as it were, to insist that moving objects are "really" as long as ever: we must accept that size is dependent on speed. And not merely size: similar arguments show that movement of a frame of reference slows the flow of time in that frame, and increases the mass of its material contents. (The last point ensures that no material thing can ever surpass the speed of light: as objects move faster they become more massive and hence need more force to accelerate them, and the forces required approach the infinite as the speed of light is reached.)

Even the laws of Euclidean geometry are affected by motion. Consider an observer standing at the centre of a large disc which begins to spin. As it spins faster he will measure its circumference as changing in length; but its diameter remains unaffected, since relativistic shrinking happens only in the direction of motion. Thus the circumference and diameter are no longer related by the quantity *pi*, even though the disc remains a disc. In general, Einstein's theories imply that the Euclidian axioms must be taken as defining, not "geometry" as a unique, universal system, but merely as "a" geometry among others, and one which happens to be invalid in many real situations. As a pure mathematical system, Euclidean geometry is of course self-contained and impervious to empirical disproof; but we commonly interpret it as telling us factual things about the world we live in, by equating its "straight lines" with real things such as taut strings or light-rays—what Einstein shows is that these real things do not always obey Euclid's rules.

The disturbance to the geometry of the spinning disc has to do with the fact that it involves accelerated motion (unaccelerated motion occurs in straight lines, but the various parts of the disc move in circles). Einstein's "Special Theory" considered only motion without acceleration (in which tha laws of geometry are unaffected). The General Theory deals with accelerated motion, which does deform geometry; and, since acceleration is indistinguishable in its effects from gravitational attraction, we are led to the conclusion that matter, by exerting gravitational force, shapes the geometry of the spacing around it. It is thought probable that the universe is spatially finite, in the sense that a straight line projected in any direction will ultimately return to its origin; the instinctive reaction "If the universe is finite, what lies outside it?" does not apply, because there is no direction that leads "outside".

The significance of Einstein's thought lies not only in its intrinsic interest but in the status of the theories which he overthrew. Newton had been revered in the 18th and 19th centuries as the first man to have produced new knowledge not known in classical antiquity. His physics was seen as the paradigm example of the ability of empirical scientific method to derive unassailable theoretical truths from quantities of individual observations. Einstein showed that even this most apparently secure of all scientific advances, while it certainly embodied a worthwhile approximation to the truth, must ultimately be regarded as mistaken. This has been central to the new understanding of science (expressed most forcefully by Sir Karl Popper) according to which science does not establish reliable conclusions but only proposes fallible "conjectures," which can be refuted by counter-evidence but can never be decisively confirmed. Before Einstein, no-one seriously entertained the possibility that Newton's theory might prove false. Since Einstein, it has been generally understood that sooner or later Einstein's theory, like any other, will be shown to be false.

Einstein calls into question not only the reliability of science but also the degree to which it depends on observation. He worked out his theories almost wholly by aprioristic reasoning about how the universe must be organized, given the assumption that its laws were as elegant as possible. As Einstein himself put it, "What I'm really interested in is whether God could have made the world in a different way; that is, whether the necessity of logical simplicity leaves any freedom at all." Empirical testing came afterwards. There have been many experiments to adjudicate between Newton's and Einstein's physics (which have constantly favoured the latter), but when he worked out his theories Einstein was probably unaware of, and certainly uninfluenced by, the relevant experimental findings that were readily available.

This is not meant to imply that Einstein's theoretical intuitions were infallible. Having spent much of his earlier career elaborating his very successful theories of relativity, Einstein devoted his later years to a lonely and ultimately fruitless attempt to construct an alternative to another novel physical theory, the principle of indeterminacy. This principle, associated with the name of Werner Heisenberg, asserts that matter at the very fine-grained, subatomic level exhibits an impenetrable vagueness: at any given instant a particle does not occupy a definite position and move in a definite direction; rather, its location and velocity must be described as a blurred cloud of probability. One might feel that this notion is scarcely more mind-bending than the concepts of relativity. But to Einstein indeterminacy was intuitively unacceptable; there must be something definite hidden within the probabilistic cloud: "God does not play at dice." However, Einstein's repeated attempts over almost 30 years to explain away the arguments for indeterminacy were never successful, and Heisenberg's principle is now an established axiom of physics.

—Geoffrey Sampson

EISENSTEIN, Sergei (Mikhailovich). Russian film-maker and theorist. Born in Riga, Latvia, now the Soviet Union, 23 January 1898. Studied at the University of Petrograd, 1914-18. Served in the Red Army, 1918-20. Worked in Moscow with the Meyerhold Theater and as Director of the Proletkult Theater, 1920-24; began making films in 1925, and lectured in film in London, and in Paris at Sorbonne, 1929-30; went to Hollywood in 1931 to work on several projects, none of which was realized; worked in Mexico on *Que Viva Mexico!*, 1931-32; returned to Moscow in 1932 and began teaching film courses at the Institute of Cinematology; became Artistic Director of Mosfilm in 1939. Officially censured for his uncompleted film, *Bezhin Meadow*, 1937, but later awarded the Order of Lenin, and the Stalin Prize First Class, for *Ivan the Terrible, Part I*. Died 10 February 1948.

PUBLICATIONS

Collections

Izbrannye proizvedeniia v shesti tomakh [Collected Works]. Moscow, "Iskusstvo," 6 vols., 1964-71. (Vol. 1: Autobiographical writings; vol. 2: Theoretical essays; vol. 3: Theoretical research; vol. 4: Stage-directing; vol. 5: Critical essays; vol. 6: Scenarios).

Film

The Soviet Screen. Moscow, Foreign Languages Publishing House, 1939.
The Film Sense, edited by Jay Leyda. New York, Harcourt Brace, 1942; London, Faber, 1943.

Notes of a Film Director, edited by R. Yurenev. Moscow, Foreign Languages Publishing House, 1947; New York, Dover, 1970.
Film Form: Essays in Film Theory, edited by Jay Leyda. New York, Harcourt Brace, 1949; London, Dobson, 1951.
Film Essays with a Lecture, edited by Jay Leyda. London, Dobson, 1968; New York, Praeger, 1970.

Screenplays

Que Viva Mexico! London, Vista, 1951.
Ivan the Terrible: A Screenplay, edited by Ivor Montagu. New York, Simon and Schuster, 1962; London, Secker and Warburg, 1963.
The Battleship Potemkin. London, Lorimer, 1968; as *Potemkin,* New York, Simon and Schuster, 1968.
Battleship Potemkin, October and Alexander Nevsky. London, Lorimer, 1974; as *Three Films,* edited by Jay Leyda, New York, Harper, 1974.
The Complete Films of Eisenstein, Together with an Unpublished Essay by Eisenstein. New York, Dutton, 1974.

*

Bibliography: "The Published Writings (1922-1964) of Sergei Eisenstein with Notes on Their English Translations," in *Film Essays with a Lecture,* 1968.

Critical Studies: *The Making and Unmaking of Que Viva Mexico* by Harry M. Geduld and Ronald Gottesman, Bloomington, Indiana University Press, and London, Thames and Hudson, 1970; *Eisenstein* by Yon Barna, Bloomington, Indiana University Press, 1973; *Sergei M. Eisenstein: A Biography* by Marie Seton, London, Dobson, revised edition, 1978.

*

FILMS

Strike (silent film, released in 1925); *Battleship Potemkin* (silent film, released in 1926); *October* (in the West as *Ten Days that Shook the World;* silent film, released in 1928); *Old and New* (silent film, released in 1929); *Que Viva Mexico!* (silent film, shot but not edited by Eisenstein in 1931-32; unauthorized cut version as *Thunder Over Mexico,* 1933; version edited by Marie Seton, as *Time in the Sun,* 1939); *Alexander Nevsky* (sound film, released in 1938); *Ivan the Terrible, Part I* (sound film with colour sequences, released in 1944); *Ivan the Terrible, Part II* (filmed in 1946 but suppressed until 1958).

*   *   *

Sergei Eisenstein wrote prolifically on film theory at the same time he was making films, and it is tempting to read the one in terms of the other, if at the risk of facility. Certainly a major crisis in Eisenstein's career can be identified in the mid-30's. The experimental innovator of "the first half decade of Soviet cinema," with his roots in the European Futurism that dominated the post-revolutionary avant-garde, was the Modernist, anti-naturalist Eisenstein of *Strike, Potemkin, October,* the formulator of montage, the most influential term of his aesthetic. The Eisenstein who returned in the 1930's from the failure of his American projects had to come to terms with the conforming pressures of Socialist Realism: he formally recanted his early "leftist excesses," paid lip-service to Socialist Realism, and restored narrative as the vehicle for a "correct" ideology in the patriotic-historical *Alexander Nevsky;* his aesthetic research was henceforth devoted to grandiose, erudite, and (as it now seems to us) historically irrelevant versions of the Romantic-Symbolist *Gesamtkunstwerk*—cinema as "synthesis of all the arts," operating through a totalizing "synchronization of the senses" to provide a transcendental experience of "organic unity" for the viewing subject, sanctioned by a Marxist-Hegelian dialectic model.

Eisenstein's main theoretical strategy was always toward the description of a psychological-affective base for the formal and semantic principles of film practice. In 1923 he coined the term "montage of attractions" to locate theatrical-cinematic practice within a psychological formalism to which, in its various guises, Eisenstein remained committed. Montage—the juxtaposition of photographic images to reproduce the impression of movement in time—is no mere technical device but the principle of filmic signification: meaning and affect are generated by the dynamic structures of this juxtaposition, do not reside in the inert and pictorial image-in-itself. Montage emerges from a Futuristic matrix of the "dynamic instance" and image-in-process as a rhythmic counterpoint of movements in collision—shot lengths, frame to frame, within frame, line and volume—in polemical opposition to Pudovkin's description of montage as the mere "linking" of inert, given signifieds (1929). Despite the eclectic assumption of certain Freudian terms and concepts, the defining base of Eisenstein's psychological model remained Pavlovian. A 1929 description of filmic signification in musical terms—the image-sign as a cluster of connotative "overtones" around a regulating, "dominant" signifier—depends on a Pavlovian provision of signifiers as "stimuli" for the viewing subject, according to the conditions of the specific system of representations constructed by the artist. As late as 1945 Eisenstein reviewed the "montage of attractions" as "a theory of artistic stimulants," systematizing the impressions of the spectator according to a "common denominator" set by the artist: the principle of systematic over-determination prepares the way for the "synchronization of the senses" as logical end of the Pavlovian model of a conditioned-reflex aesthetic psychology. Eisenstein drew on Freudian discourse to define the relationship between montage signification—juxtaposition and superimposition of signifiers—and "universal" psychic processes of condensation and displacement: montage foregrounds signification as process, "construction of a chain of representations" (1939). A Freudian distinction between primary and secondary processes allows Eisenstein to propose a pre-logical psychic level of "sensual and imagist thought-processes" with its own "clear-cut laws and structural peculiarities," which montage is uniquely privileged to tap: montage will aim to reproduce these "primitive," "emotional" structures, the "syntax of inner speech." The potential subversiveness of these formulations—liberation of the signifying chain—is undercut, however, by retention of the traditional dualism between social language and a transcendental "pre-linguistic" level of origin. Eisenstein's claim for montage as access to a transcendental "primary" provides in fact the model for a totalization of control over the viewer's reflexes through the overdetermination of sensory input.

Yet there was a shift. The 1920's "montage of attractions" asserted a Brechtian program of inducing "contradictions" within the social-symbolic affect of the viewing subject, jolting him by the collision of signifiers, by a refusal of synchronization, out of the "illusion" of coherence (the refuge of the imaginary) provided by the crafted sound-image unities of, for example, the Hollywood sound film (1928). Nevertheless, montage as assertion of the imaginary—integration of the subject through a cinema of "organic synthesis"—is not so much a late formulation as, within the pressures of Socialist Realism, a late emphasis. The resolving theoretical strategy was declared as early as 1929: the dynamic, "cellular" conflictuality of Futurist discourse was appropriated within a Hegelian-Marxist dialectical model. He resorted to this model increasingly as authority for the obsessive, detailed forays in quest of the *Gesamtkunstwerk*; informing it, a stubborn attempt to assert consistency, to rehabilitate montage and salvage the psychological formalism under other terms. The "secret of the very nature of affective form" now became a convenient transcendental, an organic synchronization of affect.

Futurist formulations of the displacement of emotional energies into gesture and acrobatics were translated into terms of pathos and ecstasy, the affective flow in the service of the dialectic: the collision of signifiers translated to dialectical "tensions" which resolve to an organic "higher unity"; thus, the montage of over-tones/conflicts plays upon the neurological/emotional/intellectual complex of the viewing subject and raises him beyond himself to an integrating "synthesis." This model conveniently accommodates the ontological plenitudes proposed by the new Soviet State, as (after all) transcendental resolution of the dynamic contradictions of history. If it seems to us now so much (perhaps strategic) confusion and evasion, we must remember that Eisenstein was still able to work on his disturbing late masterpiece, *Ivan the Terrible*.

—Ian Duncan

ELIADE, Mircea. Rumanian historian of religions and novelist. Born in Bucharest, 9 March 1907; emigrated to the United States in 1956. Studied at the University of Bucharest, Ph.D. 1935; also studied with Surandranath Dasgupta in India, 1928-30. Married Nina Mares in 1935; Christinel Cottesco in 1950. Taught at the University of Bucharest, 1933-39; Cultural attaché, Rumanian Royal Legation, London, 1941, and Lisbon, 1941-45; Lecturer, Sorbonne, Paris, 1945, and at the Universities of Rome, Lund, Marburg, Frankfurt, Uppsala and Strasbourg, 1948-56; Visiting Professor, 1956, Professor and Chairman of the History of Religions Department, 1957-64, and since 1964 Sewell L. Avery Distinguished Service Professor, University of Chicago. Founded the journal *Zalmoxis*, in Paris, 1938; with Ernst Jünger founded the journal *Antaios* in 1960; and with Joseph M. Kitagawa and Charles Long founded the journal *History of Religions* in Chicago, 1961. President, Centre Roumain de Recherches, 1950-55. Recipient: Bollingen Foundation grant, 1951; Christian Culture Award Gold Medal, University of Windsor, Ontario, 1968. Honorary Professor, Universidad de San Salvadore, 1969. Honorary doctorate: Yale University, New Haven, Connecticut, 1966; Universidad de la Plata, Argentina, 1969; Ripon College, Wisconsin, 1969; Loyola University, Chicago, 1970; Boston College, 1971; La Salle College, Philadelphia, 1972; Oberlin College, Ohio, 1972; University of Lancaster, 1975; Sorbonne, 1976. Member, Royal Academy of Belgium; Corresponding Member, Austrian Academy of Sciences; Corresponding Fellow, British Academy. Member, American Academy of Arts and Sciences, 1966. Address: Swift Hall, University of Chicago, Chicago, Illinois 60637, U.S.A.

PUBLICATIONS

Myth, Science and Religion

Alchimia Asiatica [Asiatic Alchemy]. Bucharest, Editura Cultura Porporului, 1934.
Yoga: Essai sur les origines de la mystique indienne. Paris, Geuthner, 1936.
Cosmologie si Alchimie babiloniana [Babylonian Cosmology and Alchemy]. Bucharest, Editura Vremea, 1937.
Metallurgy, Magic, and Alchemy. Paris, Geuthner, 1938.
Mitul Reintegrarii [The Myth of Reintegration]. Bucharest, Editura Vremea, 1938.
Comentarii la legenda Mesterului Manole [Commentaries on the Legend of Master Manole]. Bucharest, Editura Publicom, 1943.
Insula lui Euthanasius [The Island of Euthanasius]. Bucharest, Editura Fundatia Regala pentru Arta si Literatura, 1943.
Techniques du Yoga. Paris, Gallimard, 1948.

Traité d'histoire des religions.   Paris, Payot, 1949; as *Patterns in Comparative Religion*, London and New York, Sheed and Ward, 1958.

Le Mythe de l'eternel retour.   Paris, Gallimard, 1949; as *The Myth of the Eternal Return*, London, Routledge, and New York, Pantheon, 1955; as *Cosmos and History*, New York, Harper Torchbooks, 1959.

Le Chaminisme et les techniques archaïques de l'Extase.   Paris, Payot, 1951; as *Shamanism: Archaic Techniques of Ecstasy*, London, Routledge, and New York, Pantheon, 1964.

Images et symboles: Essais sur le symbolisme magico-religieux.   Paris, Gallimard, 1952; as *Images and Symbols: Studies in Religious Symbolism*, London, Harvill Press, and New York, Sheed and Ward, 1961.

Le Yoga: Immortalité et Liberté.   Paris, Gallimard, 1954; as *Yoga: Freedom and Immortality*, London, Routledge, and New York, Pantheon, 1958.

Forgerons et Alchimistes.   Paris, Flammarion, 1956; as *The Forge and the Crucible*, London, Ridder, and New York, Harper, 1962.

Mythes, Rêves et Mystères.   Paris, Gallimard, 1957; as *Myths, Dreams and Mysteries*, London, Harvill Press, and New York, Harper, 1960.

Das Heilige und das Profane: Vom Wesen des Religiösen.   Munich, Rowohlt, 1957; as *The Sacred and the Profane: The Nature of Religion*, New York, Harper, 1959.

Birth and Rebirth: The Religious Meaning of Initiation in Human Culture.   London, Harvill Press, and New York, Harper, 1958.

Méphistophélès et l'Androgyne.   Paris, Gallimard, 1962; as *Mephistopheles and the Androgyne: Studies in Religious Myth and Symbol*, New York, Sheed and Ward, and as *The Two and the One*, London, Harvill Press, 1965.

Pantañjali et le yoga.   Paris, Seuil, 1962; as *Pantanjali and Yoga*, New York, Funk and Wagnalls, 1969.

Aspects du Mythe.   Paris, Gallimard, 1963.

From Primitives to Zen: A Thematic Sourcebook on the History of Religions.   London, Collins, and New York, Harper, 1967.

The Quest: History and Meaning in Religion.   Chicago, University of Chicago Press, 1969.

De Zalmoxis à Gengis-Khan: Études comparatives sur les religions et le folklore de la Dacie et de l'Europe orientale.   Paris, Payot, 1970; as *Zalmoxis: The Vanishing God*, Chicago, University of Chicago Press, 1972.

Religions australiennes: I. Religions primitives.   Paris, Payot, 1972; as *Australian Religions: An Introduction*, Ithaca, New York, Cornell University Press, 1973.

Histoire des croyances et des idées religieuses: I. De l'âge de la pierre aux mystères d'Eleusis; II. De Gautama Bouddha au triomphe du christianisme.   Paris, Payot, 1976, 1978; as *A History of Religious Ideas: I. From the Stone Age to the Eleusinian Mysteries; II. From Gautama Buddha to the Triumph of Christianity*, Chicago, University of Chicago Press, 1978, 1981.

Myths, Rites, Symbols: A Mircea Eliade Reader, edited by W.C. Beane and W.G. Doty.   New York, Harper, 1976.

Occultism, Witchcraft, and Cultural Fashions: Essays in Comparative Religion.   Chicago, University of Chicago Press, 1978.

Novels

Isabel si Apele Diavolului [Isabel and the Devil's Waters].   Bucharest, Editura Nationala Ciorne, 1930.

Maitreyi [Maitreyi].   Bucharest, Editura Cultura Nationala, 1933.

Intoarcerea din Rai [The Return from Paradise].   Bucharest, Editura Nationala-Ciornei, 1934.

Lumina ce se stinge [The Light Which Fails].   Bucharest, Editura Cartea Româneasca, 1934.

Huliganii [The Hooligans].   Bucharest, Editura Nationala-Ciornei, 2 vols., 1935.

Domnisoara Christina [Mademoiselle Christina].   Bucharest, Editura Cultura Nationala, 1936.

Sarpele [The Snake].   Bucharest, Editura Nationala-Ciornei, 1937.

Nunta în Cer [Marriage in Heaven].   Bucharest, Editura Cugetarea, 1938.

Secretul Doctorului Honigberger [The Secret of Dr. Honigberger].   Bucharest, Editura Socec, 1940.

La forêt interdite.   Paris, Gallimard, 1955; as *The Forbidden Forest.*   Notre Dame, University of Notre Dame Press, 1978.

Pe strada Mântuleasa [Mantuleasa Street].   Paris, Caietele Inorugului, II, 1968.

Die Pelerine.   Frankfurt, Suhrkamp, 1970.

Short Stories

Nuvele.   Madrid, Editura Destin, 1963.

La Tiganci si alte povestiri [At the Gypsies and Other Short Stories].   Bucharest, Editura Pentru Literatura, 1968.

Fantastic Tales, with A. Niculescu (English and Rumanian texts).   London, Dillon's University Bookstore, 1969.

Two Tales of the Occult.   New York, Herder and Herder, 1970.

Other

Soliloquii [Soliloquies] (aphorisms).   Bucharest, Editura Cartea ce Semne, 1932.

Intr'o mânastire din Himalaya [In a Himalayan Monastery] (autobiographical).   Bucharest, Editura Cartea Româneasca, 1932.

India (autobiographical).   Bucharest, Editura Cugetarea, 1934.

Oceanografie (essays).   Budapest, Editura Cultura Porporului, 1934.

Santier [Work in Progress] (autobiographical).   Bucharest, Editura Cugetarea, 1935.

Fragmentarium (essays).   Bucharest, Editura Vremea, 1939.

Salazar si revolutia in Portugalia [Salazar and the Revolution in Portugal].   Bucharest, Editura Gorjan, 1942.

Os Romenos, Latinos do Oriente [The Rumanians, Latins of the East].   Lisbon, Livraria Clássica Editora, 1943.

Iphigenia (play).   Valle Hermoso, Editura Cartea Pribegiei, 1951.

Amintiri: I. Mansarda.   Madrid, Editura Destin, 1966.

Témoignages sur Brancusi, with others.   Paris, Arted, 1967.

Fragments d'un journal.   Paris, Gallimard, 1973; selections as *No Souvenirs: Journal, 1957-1969*, New York, Harper, 1977; London, Routledge, 1978.

L'Epreuve du labyrinthe: Entretiens avec Claude-Henri Rocquet.   Paris, Belfond, 1978; as *Ordeal by Labyrinth: Conversations with Claude-Henri Rocquet*, Chicago, University of Chicago Press, 1982.

Translator, into Rumanian, *Revolt in the Desert*, by T.E. Lawrence.   Bucharest, Editura Fundatia Regala pentru Literatura si Arta, 2 vols., 1934.

Translator, into Rumanian, *Fighting Angel*, by Pearl Buck.   Bucharest, Editura Fundatia Regala pentru Literatura si Arta, 1939.

Editor, *Roza Vânturilor*, by Nae Ionescu.   Bucharest, Cultural Nationala, 1936.

Editor, *Scrieri literare, morale si politice de B.P. Hasdeu.*   Bucharest, Editura Fundatia Regala pentru Arta si Literatura, 2 vols., 1937.

Editor, with Joseph M. Kitagawa, *History of Religions: Essays in Methodology.*   Chicago, University of Chicago Press, 1959.

*

Bibliography: *Mircea Eliade: An Annotated Bibliography* by Douglas Allen and Dennis Doeing, London and New York, Garland Press, 1980.

Critical Studies: *Myths and Symbols: Studies in Honor of Mircea Eliade*, edited by Joseph M. Kitagawa and Charles Long, Chicago, University of Chicago Press, 1969; *Religion on Trial: Mircea Eliade and His Critics* by G. Dudley, Philadelphia, Temple University Press, 1977; *Structure and Creativity in Religion: Hermeneutics in Mircea Eliade's Phenomenology and New Directions* by Douglas Allen, The Hague, Mouton, 1978.

*   *   *

Mircea Eliade is an influential Rumanian-born historian of religions, Orientalist, and novelist whose works (which number well into the hundreds) have been translated into most of the major languages of the world. Born in Bucharest, Eliade left Rumania during the Second World War and since that time has lived in self-imposed exile in London, Lisbon, Paris, and Chicago. His writings reveal his interest in the religious intuitions and aspirations that he feels have been expressed in myths and symbols in all cultures throughout history. Maintaining that the sacred is an irreducible and universal dimension of human existence, and that religious experiences lie at the base of culture itself, Eliade senses that the history of religious expression is the history of the human spirit, of humanity's understanding of the meaning of its existence. In his studies of the history of religions, Eliade calls for a "new humanism" which, like the humanism of the European Renaissance, seeks to extend the cultural horizon of its studies as it considers humanity's existential and historical situations from a wide perspective. However, Eliade's new humanism is larger than that of the Renaissance, which he feels was modeled too much on Mediterranean literary, artistic, and philosophical classicism: he finds a wealth of religious meaning in the larger world of magical and alchemical practices, in Asian religious systems, and in myths, legends, and symbols of peasant societies and archaic folk cultures around the world.

Throughout his scholarly and literary works, Eliade expresses fascination with the religious significance of humanity's experience of time, history, and three-dimensional space. He finds the most articulate expressions of these experiences in various cultures' mythic and symbolic expressions. One senses that, for Eliade, myth is a narration of sacred history, an account of the way things were before the beginning of time and beyond the structures and limitations of historical existence. Eliade discerns in his studies of myths the transcendent models that people use to guide their actions in the world and to interpret the meaning of their lives. He tends to see the paradigmatic myth to be that of the creation of the universe, for in cosmogonic narratives Eliade sees a culture's understanding of the relationship between the present world—and humanity's place in that world—and the cosmos as it was in primordial time (*illud tempus*). Eliade uses the term *hierophany* to describe the irruption of the sacred into the profane realm. The most common mode of hierophany is the symbol, something that exists in the profane world but at the same time reveals the perceived reality of the sacred world. In his book *Traité d'histoire des religions* Eliade presents a phenomenological study of several of the major types of hierophany in the world's religions (sky epiphanies, water symbolism, vegetation and Goddess-worship, and so on). The book is considered a classic in the field. In this and his other works, Eliade discusses other mythic and symbolic themes that he has found in the world's religious systems: the *axis mundi*, a mountain at the center of the world, a cosmic tree, a ritual post, or other type of pathway that connects the various layers of the vertical universe and along which communications between the residents of those universes travel; the notion of *hierosgamos*, or the marriage between Heaven and Earth; the patterns of ritual and mythic initiation of a human being into different modes of existence; the alteration or reversal of time and the related "nostalgia for paradise" that he sees exhibited in many religious systems. In all of his works Eliade firmly maintains that the religious experience has its own autonomy and cannot be reduced to a variation of other modes of experience. According to Eliade, religion must be understood on its own terms and not merely on those of sociology, psychology, or political economy.

Eliade's research into the religious forms of various cultures began when he was a young man. While in Rome writing his baccalaureate thesis on the philosophies of the Italian Renaissance (he was especially interested in alchemical thought), Eliade became increasingly fascinated by the Greek Orphic religions, and, more so, by the religions of India. He saw a pervasive link between Eastern European folklore, medieval Italian occultism, Mediterranean mystery religions, and Asian yogic thought and practice. Drawn Eastward by his interests, and dedicated to the idea that the Orient held unlimited resources for his humanistic study of religions, Eliade went to Calcutta in 1928 at the age of 20, perhaps the first Rumanian to study at first hand the religions of India. Eliade's main resource in India lay in the metaphysics, physiology, and religious practices of Tantrism and Yoga. Out of his studies came his doctoral dissertation, which was later published as *Le Yoga: immoralité et liberté*. The book remains today the most thorough and comprehensive study of the subject.

Returning to Bucharest in 1931, Eliade directed more of his interests to the larger systematic study of religions around the world. He continued his research on alchemy and cosmology, concentrating during the 1930's on Asian and Babylonian examples. In 1938, he founded the journal, *Zalmoxis: A Review of Religious Studies*. At the outbreak of the Second World War, he was sent by the Rumanian government to London as a cultural attaché. He was transferred in 1941 to Lisbon, where he held a similar position; here he completed *Traité d'histoire des religions* as well as *Le Myth de l'eternel retour*, a study in which he summarizes his notions of the way myths and symbols both regenerate sacred time and free people from the confines of historical existence.

At the end of the war, Eliade chose to stay in Paris, where he was associated with the École des Hautes Études and there wrote *Le Chaminisme et les techniques archaïques de l'extase*, a comparative study of the symbols, practices, and ideologies of shamanic experiences in Asia, the Indo-European cultural sphere, the Americas, and Oceania.

Eliade was invited to the University of Chicago in 1956. He founded *History of Religions: An International Journal of Comparative and Historical Studies*. His *The Sacred and the Profane* appeared in 1959 and *The Quest: History and Meaning in Religion* was published in 1969. The former summarizes his notions of the religious importance of myths, symbols, and rituals; the latter is a statement of ideals for the academic discipline of History of Religions and a discussion of the role that humanity's experience of the sacred plays both in religious and secular societies. As of 1983, Eliade has completed and published two volumes of a projected three-volume set, *Histoire des croyances et des idées religieuses*. He also is the editor of the international 16-volume *Encyclopedia of Religion*, scheduled for publication in 1985.

While Eliade is known in the English-reading world primarily as a scholar, in Western and Eastern Europe he is also widely respected as a novelist, essayist, and journalist. In fact, his first international fame came with the publication in 1933 of his semi-autobiographical novel, *Maitreyi*. His creative works, including *Secretul Doctorului Honigberger*, *La forêt interdite*, and *Pe strada Mântuleasa*, all tend to express in fictional narratives the major themes of the rediscovery of forgotten mythic truths, the alteration and obliteration of time, and the transformative experiences of an extraordinary universe emerging into the structures of the mundane world.

—Joseph M. Kitagawa/ W. Mahoney

ELIOT, T(homas) S(tearns). British poet, playwright and critic. Born in St. Louis, Missouri, U.S.A., 26 September 1888; emigrated to England, 1914: naturalized, 1927. Educated at Smith Academy, St. Louis, 1898-1905, and Milton Academy, Massachusetts, 1905-06; studied at Harvard University, Cambridge, Massachusetts (Editor, *Harvard Advocate*, 1909-10; Sheldon Fellowship, for study in Munich, 1914), 1906-11, 1911-14, B.A. 1909, M.A. 1910; the Sorbonne, Paris, 1910-11; Merton College, Oxford, 1914-15. Married Vivienne Haigh-Wood in 1915 (died, 1947); Esmé Valerie Fletcher in 1957. Taught at High Wycombe Grammar School, Buckinghamshire, and Highgate School, London, 1915-17; clerk, Lloyds Bank, London, 1917-25; Editor, later Director, Faber and Gwyer, later Faber and Faber, publishers, London, 1926-65. Assistant Editor, *The Egoist*, London, 1917-19; Founding Editor, *The Criterion*, London, 1922-39. Clark Lecturer, Trinity College, Cambridge, 1926; Charles Eliot Norton Professor of Poetry, Harvard University, 1932-33; Page-Barbour Lecturer, University of Virginia, Charlottesville, 1933; Theodore Spencer Memorial Lecturer, Harvard University, 1950. President, Classical Association, 1941, Virgil Society, 1943, and Books Across the Sea, 1943-46. Resident, Institute for Advanced Study, Princeton, New Jersey, 1950. Honorary Fellow, Merton College, and Magdalene College, Cambridge. Recipient: *The Dial* Award, 1922; Nobel Prize for Literature, 1948; New York Drama Critics Circle Award, 1950; Hanseatic Goethe Prize, 1954; Dante Gold Medal, Florence, 1959; Order of Merit, Bonn, 1959; American Academy of Arts and Sciences Emerson-Thoreau Medal, 1960. Honorary doctorate: Columbia University, 1933; University of Edinburgh, 1937; Cambridge University, 1938; University of Bristol, 1938; University of Leeds, 1939; Harvard University, 1947; Princeton University, New Jersey, 1947; Yale University, New Haven, Connecticut, 1947; Oxford University, 1948; University of London, 1950; Washington University, St. Louis, 1953; St. Andrews University, Scotland, 1953; University of Rome, 1958; University of Sheffield, 1959; University of Aix-Marseille, 1959; University of Rennes, 1959; University of Munich, 1959. Officier, Légion d'Honneur. Honorary Member, American Academy of Arts and Letters; Foreign Member, Accademia dei Lincei, and Akademie der Schönen Künste. O.M. (Order of Merit) 1948. *Died* (in London) *4 January 1965.*

PUBLICATIONS

Criticism

Ezra Pound: His Metric and Poetry. New York, Knopf, 1918; reprinted in *To Criticize the Critic and Other Writings,* 1965.
The Sacred Wood: Essays on Poetry and Criticism. London, Methuen, 1920; New York, Knopf, 1921; reprinted in part in *Selected Essays,* 1932.
Homage to John Dryden: Three Essays on Poetry of the Seventeenth Century. London, Hogarth Press, 1924; included in *The Hogarth Essays,* New York, Doubleday, 1928; reprinted in *Selected Essays,* 1932.
Shakespeare and the Stoicism of Seneca (lecture). London, Oxford University Press, 1927; reprinted in *Selected Essays,* 1932.
For Lancelot Andrewes: Essays on Style and Order. London, Faber and Gwyer, 1928; New York, Doubleday, 1929; reprinted in part in *Selected Essays,* 1932.
Dante. London, Faber, 1929; reprinted in *Selected Essays,* 1932.
Selected Essays 1917-1932. London, Faber, and New York, Harcourt Brace, 1932; revised edition, Harcourt Brace, 1950; Faber, 1951.
John Dryden: The Poet, The Dramatist, The Critic. New York, Terence and Elsa Holliday, 1932.
The Use of Poetry and the Use of Criticism: Studies in the Relation of Criticism to Poetry in England. London, Faber,

and Cambridge, Massachusetts, Harvard University Press, 1933.
After Strange Gods: A Primer of Modern Heresy. London, Faber, and New York, Harcourt Brace, 1934.
Elizabethan Essays. London, Faber, 1934; reprinted in part as *Essays on Elizabethan Drama,* New York, Harcourt Brace, 1956; as *Elizabethan Dramatists,* Faber, 1963.
Introduction to *Selected Poems,* by Marianne Moore. New York, Macmillan and London, Faber, 1935.
Essays Ancient and Modern. London, Faber, and New York, Harcourt Brace, 1936; reprinted in part in *Selected Essays,* 1950.
Introduction to *Nightwood,* by Djuna Barnes. New York, Harcourt Brace, 1937; London, Faber, 1950.
"A Note on Two Odes of Cowley", in *Seventeenth Century Studies Presented to Sir Herbert Grierson.* Oxford, Clarendon Press, 1938.
Points of View, edited by John Hayward. London, Faber, 1941; Westport, Connecticut, Hyperion Press, 1979.
The Classics and the Man of Letters (lecture). London and New York, Oxford University Press, 1942.
The Music of Poetry (lecture). Glasgow, University Press, 1942; reprinted in *On Poetry and Poets,* 1957.
What Is a Classic? (lecture). London, Faber, 1945; reprinted in *On Poetry and Poets,* 1957.
On Poetry (lecture). Concord, Massachusetts, Concord Academy, 1947.
Milton (lecture). London, Oxford University Press, 1947; reprinted in *On Poetry and Poets,* 1957.
From Poe to Valéry (lecture). New York, Harcourt Brace, 1948; reprinted in *To Criticize the Critic and Other Writings,* 1965.
The Aims of Poetic Drama (lecture). London, Poets' Theatre Guild, 1949.
Poetry and Drama (lecture). Cambridge, Massachusetts, Harvard University Press, and London, Faber, 1951.
American Literature and the American Language (lecture). St. Louis, Washington University, 1953; reprinted in *To Criticize the Critic and Other Writings,* 1965.
The Three Voices of Poetry (lecture). London, Cambridge University Press, 1953; New York, Cambridge University Press, 1954; reprinted in *On Poetry and Poets,* 1957.
Religious Drama, Mediaeval and Modern (lecture). New York, House of Books, 1954.
The Literature of Politics (lecture). London, Conservative Political Centre, 1955; reprinted in *To Criticize the Critic and Other Writings,* 1965.
The Frontiers of Criticism (lecture). Minneapolis, University of Minnesota Press, 1956; reprinted in *On Poetry and Poets,* 1957.
On Poetry and Poets. London, Faber, and New York, Farrar Straus, 1957.
Introduction to *The Art of Poetry,* by Paul Valéry. New York, Pantheon Books, and London, Routledge, 1958.
George Herbert. London, Longman, 1962; in *British Writers and Their Work 4,* Lincoln, University of Nebraska Press, 1964.
To Criticize the Critic and Other Writings. London, Faber, and New York, Farrar Straus, 1965.

Religion and Culture

Thoughts after Lambeth. London, Faber, 1931.
Charles Whibley: A Memoir (lecture). London, Oxford University Press, 1931.
The Idea of a Christian Society. London, Faber, 1939; New York, Harcourt Brace, 1940.
Reunion by Destruction: Reflections on a Scheme for Church Union in South India, Addressed to the Laity. London, Council for the Defence of Church Principles, 1943.
Die Einheit der Europäischen Kultur. Berlin, Clark Habel,

1946.

A Sermon Preached in the Magdalene College Chapel. Cambridge, privately printed, 1948.

Notes Towards the Definition of Culture. London, Faber, 1948; New York, Harcourt Brace, 1949.

The Value and Use of Cathedrals in England Today (lecture). Chichester, Sussex, Friends of Chichester Cathedral, 1952.

Poetry

Prufrock and Other Observations. London, The Egoist, 1917.

Poems. Richmond, Surrey, Hogarth Press, 1919.

Ara Vos Prec. London, Ovid Press, 1920; as *Poems*, New York, Knopf, 1920.

The Waste Land. New York, Boni and Liveright, 1922; Richmond, Surrey, Hogarth Press, 1923.

Poems 1909-1925. London, Faber and Gwyer, 1925; New York, Harcourt Brace, 1932.

Journey of the Magi. London, Faber and Gwyer, and New York, William Edwin Rudge, 1927.

A Song for Simeon. London, Faber and Gwyer, 1928.

Animula. London, Faber, 1929.

Ash-Wednesday. New York, Foundation Press, and London, Faber, 1930.

Marina. London, Faber, 1930.

Triumphal March. London, Faber, 1931.

Sweeney Agonistes: Fragments of an Aristophanic Melodrama. London, Faber, 1932.

Words for Music. Bryn Mawr, Pennsylvania, privately printed, 1935.

Two Poems. Cambridge, privately printed, 1935.

Collected Poems 1909-1935. London, Faber, and New York, Harcourt Brace, 1939.

Old Possum's Book of Practical Cats. London, Faber, and New York, Harcourt Brace, 1939.

The Waste Land and Other Poems. London, Faber, 1940; New York, Harcourt Brace, 1955.

East Coker. London, New English Weekly, 1940.

Later Poems, 1925-1935. London, Faber, 1941.

The Dry Salvages. London, Faber, 1941.

Little Gidding. London, Faber, 1942.

Four Quartets. New York, Harcourt Brace, 1943; London, Faber, 1944.

A Practical Possum. Cambridge, Massachusetts, privately printed, 1947.

Selected Poems. London, Penguin, 1948; New York, Harcourt Brace, 1967.

The Undergraduate Poems of T.S. Eliot. Cambridge, Massachusetts (unauthorized edition), 1949.

Poems Written in Early Youth, edited by John Hayward. Stockholm, privately printed, 1950; London, Faber, and New York, Farrar Straus, 1967.

The Cultivation of Christmas Trees. London, Faber, 1954; New York, Farrar Straus, 1956.

Collected Poems 1909-1962. London, Faber, and New York, Harcourt Brace, 1963.

The Waste Land: A Facsimile and Transcript of the Original Drafts Including the Annotations of Ezra Pound, edited by Valerie Eliot. London, Faber, and New York, Farrar Straus, 1971.

Plays

The Rock: A Pageant Play. London, Faber, and New York, Harcourt Brace, 1934.

Murder in the Cathedral. London, Faber, and New York, Harcourt Brace, 1935; revised edition, as *The Film of Murder in the Cathedral*, with George Hoellering, 1952.

The Family Reunion. London, Faber, and New York, Harcourt Brace, 1939.

The Cocktail Party. London, Faber, and New York, Harcourt Brace, 1950; revised edition, 1950.

The Confidential Clerk. London, Faber, and New York, Harcourt Brace, 1954.

The Elder Statesman. London, Faber, and New York, Farrar Straus, 1959.

Collected Plays: Murder in the Cathedral, The Family Reunion, The Cocktail Party, The Confidential Clerk, The Elder Statesman. London, Faber, 1962; as *The Complete Plays*, New York, Harcourt Brace, 1969.

Other

The Complete Poems and Plays. London, Faber, and New York, Harcourt Brace, 1952.

An Address to Members of the London Library. London, London Library, 1952; Providence, Rhode Island, Providence Atheneum, 1953.

Selected Prose, edited by John Hayward. London, Penguin, 1953.

Geoffrey Faber 1889-1961 (address). London, Faber, 1961.

Knowledge and Experience in the Philosophy of F.H. Bradley (doctoral dissertation). London, Faber, and New York, Farrar Straus, 1964.

Selected Prose, edited by Frank Kermode. London, Faber, and New York, Harcourt Brace, 1975.

Translator, *Anabasis: A Poem*, by St.-John Perse. London, Faber, 1930; revised edition, New York, Harcourt Brace, 1938, 1949, Faber, 1959.

Editor, *Selected Poems*, by Ezra Pound. London, Faber and Gwyer, 1929; revised edition, Faber, 1949.

Editor, *A Choice of Kipling's Verse.* London, Faber, 1941; New York, Scribner, 1943.

Editor, *Introducing James Joyce.* London, Faber, 1942.

Editor, *Literary Essays of Ezra Pound.* London, Faber, and New York, New Directions, 1954.

Editor, *The Criteriŏn 1922-1939.* London, Faber, and New York, Barnes and Noble, 18 vols., 1967.

*

Bibliography: *T.S. Eliot: A Bibliography* by Donald Gallup, London, Faber, 1952, revised edition, Faber, and New York, Harcourt Brace, 1969.

Critical Studies: *The Achievement of T.S. Eliot: An Essay on the Nature of Poetry* by F.O. Matthiessen, London and New York, Oxford University Press, 1935, revised edition, 1947; *Notes on Some Figures Behind T.S. Eliot* by Herbert Howarth, Boston, Houghton Mifflin, 1964; *T.S. Eliot's Intellectual Development, 1922-1939* by John D. Margolis, Chicago, University of Chicago Press, 1969; *Eliot's Early Years* by Lyndall Gordon, New York, Oxford University Press, 1977.

*   *   *

T.S. Eliot was the dominant poetic voice of the 1920's and he lost scarcely nothing of his appeal when younger writers such as W.H. Auden introduced a more consciously political, progressive note into English poetry in the 1930's. His celebration of Christian mysticism in *The Four Quartets* also had a wide appeal to young American and English intellectuals in the 1940's, coinciding as it did with the popularising of other, more eclectic forms of mysticism by Aldous Huxley, and carrying the promise of a revival of religious feeling and Christian belief in the English-speaking world. His use of verse as a dramatic form in *Murder in the Cathedral* and in later plays such as *The Cocktail Party* also coincided with the popularity of Christopher Fry and seemed to show that the English stage might bring back to life an older, poetic and almost sacramental form of drama.

As a poet, Eliot was much influenced by the French symbolist writers of the late 19th century, as well as by his fellow American Ezra Pound. His first major poem, *The Waste Land* used an essential allusive and elliptical technique to put across the view, highly attractive to many at the time, that modern Western, urban civilization was sterile and unsatisfying. The economy of Eliot's poetic style, together with his deliberate avoidance of personal emotion, offered a welcome and salutary contrast to the more romantic effusions of the Georgian poets, and traces of his liking for emotional understatement, like his ability to evoke the atmosphere of the modern city, recur in younger poets such as Kingsley Amis and Philip Larkin.

Eliot's criticism also showed a distaste for romanticism, a desire to treat the poem in isolation from the poet, and a cult of traditional, classical values that often went hand in hand with a dislike of the modern world which now seems almost pathological. Thus he proclaimed himself, in religion and political matters, a royalist and an Anglican; and did not exclude from his poetry a number of anit-semitic remarks which read oddly after Auschwitz. The anti-progressive temper of his mind is also visible in his admiration for Baudelaire, Dante and Pascal, on whom he wrote with great sympathy and admiration, while in the field of literary taste, he is largely responsible for the shift in preference among many young people from Shelley and Wordsworth to Donne and Herbert.

—Philip Thody

ERIKSON, Erik H(omburger). American psychoanalyst. Born in Frankfurt, Germany, 15 June 1902; emigrated to the United States in 1933; naturalized, 1939. Graduate, Vienna Psychoanalytic Clinic, 1933; Certificate from the Montessori School; studied with Anna Freud and at the Harvard University Psychological Clinic, Cambridge, Massachusetts. Married Joan Mowat Serson in 1930; 3 children. Practicing psychoanalyst since 1933; training psychoanalyst, since 1942. Teacher and Researcher, Department of Neuropsychiatry, School of Medicine, Harvard University, 1934-35; Teacher and Researcher, School of Medicine, Yale University, New Haven, Connecticut, 1936-39, University of California at Berkeley and San Francisco, 1939-50, and San Francisco Psychoanalytic Institute and Menninger Foundation, Topeka, Kansas, 1944-50; Senior Staff Member, Austen Riggs Center, Stockbridge, Massachusetts, 1951-60; Professor of Human Development and Lecturer in Psychiatry, 1960-70, and since 1970 Professor Emeritus, Harvard University. Senior Consultant in Psychiatry, Mt. Zion Hospital, San Francisco, since 1972. Trustee, Radcliffe College, Cambridge, Massachusetts. Recipient: National Book Award and Pulitzer Prize, for *Gandhi's Truth*, 1970; Foneme Prize, Milan, 1971; Aldrich Award, American Academy of Pediatrics, 1971; Montessori Medal, American Montessori Society, 1973; McAlpin Research Award, National Association for Mental Health, 1974. Honorary Master's degree: Harvard University, 1960; honorary doctorate: University of Calfornia, 1968; Loyola University, Chicago, 1970; Yale University, 1971; Brown University, Providence, Rhode Island, 1972; Harvard University, 1978; University of Lund, Sweden, 1980. Member, National Academy of Education (Emeritus); American Psychoanalytic Association (Life Member). Fellow, American Academy of Arts and Sciences. Address: 1705 Centro West, Tiburon, California 94920, U.S.A.

PUBLICATIONS

Psychology

Observations on the Yurok: Childhood and World Image.

Berkeley, University of California Publications in American Archaeology and Ethnology, 1943.
Childhood and Society.   New York, Norton, 1950; enlarged edition, 1963; London, Penguin, 1965.
Young Man Luther: A Study in Psychoanalysis and History. New York, Norton, 1958; London, Faber, 1959.
Identity and the Life Cycle: Selected Papers.   New York, International Universities Press, 1959.
Insight and Responsibility: Lectures on the Ethical Implications of Psychoanalytic Insight.   New York, Norton, 1964; London, Faber, 1966.
Dialogues with Erik Erikson, with Richard I. Evans.   New York, Harper, 1967.
Identity: Youth and Crisis.   New York, Norton, and London, Faber, 1968.
Insight and Freedom (lecture).   Cape Town, South Africa, University of Cape Town, 1968.
Gandhi's Truth: On the Origins of Militant Non-Violence.   New York, Norton, 1969; London, Faber, 1970.
In Search of Common Ground: Conversations with Erik Erikson and Huey P. Newton.   New York, Norton, 1973.
Dimensions of a New Identity: The 1973 Jefferson Lectures. New York, Norton, 1974.
Life History and the Historical Moment.   New York, Norton, 1975.
Toys and Reasons: Stages in the Ritualization of Experience.   New York, Norton, 1977; London, M. Boyars, 1978.
Adulthood, with others, edited by Erikson.   New York, Norton, 1978.
The Life Cycle Completed.   New York, Norton, 1982.

Other

Editor, *Youth: Challenge and Change.*   New York, Basic Books, 1963.
Editor, with Neil J. Smelser, *Themes of Work and Love in Adulthood.*   Cambridge, Massachusetts, Harvard University Press, 1980.

*

Critical Studies: *Erik H. Erikson: The Growth of His Work* by Robert Coles, Boston, Little Brown, 1970; *Erik H. Erikson: The Power and Limits of a Vision* by Paul Roazen, New York, Free Press, 1976; *Encounter with Erikson: Historical Interpretation and Religious Biography*, edited by Donald Capps, Walter H. Capps and M. Gerald Bradford, Missoula, Montana, Scholars Press, 1977 (contains a bibliography).

*   *   *

In *Young Man Luther* and *Gandhi's Truth*, Erik H. Erikson uses a biographical method that has some value for exploring his own professional career. Through careful psychological analysis of selected "critical events" in the lives of Luther and Gandhi, he shows how the two men met crises in their lives and managed to emerge the stronger for it. In probing these events, he suggests that Luther and Gandhi were willing to take risks with their professional identities. But, by allowing themselves to become vulnerable, they were able to shape a professional identity that was more reflective of their true selves, and more responsive to the aspirations of those who looked to them for leadership.

One could cite a number of critical events in Erikson's life, but the most crucial for his professional career was the confluence of two major events in 1950: his resignation as Professor of Psychiatry at the University of California in Berkeley (June 1), and the publication of his first book, *Childhood and Society*, four months later. His resignation was in protest of a special loyalty oath imposed by the University Board of Regents. In his letter of resignation, Erikson denounced this oath as "a vague, fearful, and somewhat vindictive gesture designed to ban an evil in some magic way—an evil which must be met with much more searching and concerted effort." His resignation left him professionally vulnerable; it was not choice, but concern for his professional integrity, that led him to resign. But the publication of *Childhood and Society* on the heels of this "debacle" was to bring him great prominence as a developmental theorist. Since the publication of this major work, he has been the most widely acclaimed and most widely quoted developmental theorist in America, if not the world. (Jean Piaget was his only peer.)

In this classic work, Erikson put forward his theory that the human life cycle consists of eight stages. He called them *Basic Trust Vs. Basic Mistrust* (infancy), *Autonomy Vs. Shame and Doubt* (early childhood), *Initiative Vs. Guilt* (play age), *Industry Vs. Inferiority* (school age), *Identity Vs. Role Confusion* (adolescence), *Intimacy Vs. Isolation* (young adulthood), *Generativity Vs. Stagnation* (adulthood), and *Ego Integrity Vs. Despair* (old age). Each stage represents a "crisis" in the developmental process, with a new strength accompanied by a new vulnerability (hence, the stages each have a positive and negative pole). Each stage is "psycho*social*" because the crisis is acted out in encounter with other humans, beginning with the mother in stage 1, and then following a "widening radius of social relations" through the remaining seven stages.

This conception of the human life cycle had a revolutionary effect on developmental theory. Its immediate impact was the rediscovery of the adolescent period, which had been neglected since G. Stanley Hall's famous study of adolescence in 1905. The term, "identity crisis," which Erikson used to describe the developmental problems of adolescence, soon became a household word. His second book, *Young Man Luther*, sustained this interest in adolescence. While it centered more on Luther's young adulthood than his adolescence, it was concerned with his crisis of identity, and thus served as a dramatic "case study" of how one gifted young man worked through his severe identity problems in a highly innovative fashion.

In more recent years, especially since the mid-1960's, the adult stages of Erikson's life cycle theory have received much greater attention, and his own work has centered increasingly on issues of adult maturity. One effect of this emphasis is the extension of his life cycle theory in two new and significant directions. In an important essay in *Insight and Responsibility* entitled "Human Strength and the Cycle of Generations," he proposed a "schedule of virtues" to correspond to the eight stages of the life cycle. In order, the virtues are: *Hope, Will, Purpose, Competence, Fidelity, Love, Care,* and *Wisdom.* These virtues are not acquired traits or special gifts reserved for the moral elite, but "strengths" inherent in the human organism. They are there to be fostered by hospitable social environments, and thwarted by inhospitable ones. This formulation placed the life cycle in a moral context, making clear that Erikson was concerned with moral as well as psychological health; that, in fact, he considered psychological growth and the formation of moral character two sides of the same coin.

Two years later, he published an article in which he proposed stages in the ritualization of human experience, also corresponding to the eight psychosocial stages of the life cycle. (This article was subsequently expanded into his book *Toys and Reasons*.) By ritualization, Erikson meant the "creative formalization" of everyday life in human society. The ritual forms are, in order, the *numinous, judicious, dramatic, formal, convictional, affiliative, generational,* and *integral.* This developmental perspective on the ritualization of everyday life was another important expansion of the original life cycle theory. It offered the thesis that every society orients its members to its way of construing the world through a set of universal ritual elements. This socialization process begins with the ritualized encounters between mother and infant (numinous) and culminates in old age, when the old person becomes a living testimony to the wisdom of the society's ritual process (integral).

These expansions of Erikson's original life cycle theory indicate that his stage theory is more than a descriptive account of psychological development. It is also a moral vision, one that places particular stress on the moral obligation of adults to provide the young with a social environment conducive to the realization of their "inherent strengths." Much of his work since the initial formulation of his schedule of virtues and stages in the ritualization of human experience has centered on his concern for the "generative" role of adults toward the younger generation. In moral terms, this means learning to *care* and learning *how* to care. In terms of ritualization, it means becoming the "ritualizer" who takes responsibility for conducting the whole ritualization process, and doing so in an authoritative, not authoritistic, fashion. This concern for the generative role of adults toward younger generations led Erikson to address the major social issues of the day, including the revolt of *humanistic* (as opposed to *technological*) youth in the 1960's, the use of militant nonviolence in redressing social grievances, the problems of birth control and arms control, and especially the need of humankind to overcome its tribalisms (its tendency toward "pseudospeciation") and to work toward wider, more inclusive identities.

In the period between 1950-1965, Erikson was generally referred to as a "psychoanalyst," who specialized in work with children and adolescents, and as an "educator," who spent the bulk of his career as a university professor. But, in more recent years, these professional labels would no longer suffice. He was more than a psychoanalyst, and more than a professor. But what was he? Erikson likes to characterize himself as a man whose professional life was spent "on the boundaries" between academic disciplines and professional groups, for "throughout my career I worked in institutional contexts for which I did not have the usual credentials." He believes that his own early years as a wandering artist predisposed him to be "enamored with the aesthetic order of things," and confesses that he has had to make a "virtue out of a constitutional necessity by basing what I have to say on representative description rather than theoretical argument." To critics who contend that his life cycle theory is more impressionistic than scientific, he makes no defense, but also no apology: "I find it hard to put up a good argument, because I am more at home in observation and illustration." Hence, Erikson the "artist." Since 1950, developmental psychology has had an artist in its midst and, ironically, the result is that it now enjoys much greater respect as a *scientific*-enterprise.

In addition to his appreciation for the aesthetic order of things, Erikson has also demonstrated an ethical, even religious, concern for the *moral* order. Besides his artistic powers of observation and illustration, he has stressed the need for moral wisdom in addressing contemporary social problems. In *Young Man Luther*, he points out that Luther's mentor, Staupitz, handled his protege with "therapeutic wisdom." Throughout his own professional career, but especially in the past two decades, Erikson has reflected a similar appreciation for the therapeutic wisdom that enables individuals and groups to find their place in the moral order of things. Hence, Erikson the "respecter of wisdom." In describing "wisdom," the virtue of old age, he says that it is not something one evolves for oneself, but rather a "comradeship with men and women of distant times and of different pursuits who have created orders and objects and sayings conveying human dignity and love." Now in his early eighties, Erikson has been devoting himself to the study of the "sayings" of Jesus, thus affirming his comradeship with a young man who, in spite of his youth, addressed "the last problems" of life. Erikson would strenuously resist the claim that he is a "wise man," a "modern sage." But he would perhaps agree that he knows where to *look* for wisdom, and can recognize it when he *sees* it. Hence, artist and respecter of wisdom as two integral elements of a single professional identity.

—Donald Capps

ESTES, W(illiam) K(aye). American psychologist. Born in Minneapolis, Minnesota, 17 June 1919. Studied at the University of Minnesota, Minneapolis, B.A. 1940, Ph.D. 1943. Served in the United States Army, 1944-46. Married Katherine Walker in 1942; 2 sons. From Instructor to Professor of Psychology, Indiana University, Bloomington, 1946-62; Professor of Psychology, Stanford University, California, 1962-68; Professor of Psychology, Rockefeller University, New York, 1968-79. Since 1979, Professor of Psychology, Harvard University, Cambridge, Massachusetts. Visiting Professor, Northwestern University, Evanston, Illinois, Spring 1959; University of London, 1961. Social Science Research Council faculty research fellow, 1952-55; Fellow, Center for Advanced Study in the Behavioral Sciences, Stanford, California, 1955-56. Associate Editor, *Journal of Experimental Psychology*, 1958-62; Editor, *Journal of Comparative and Physiological Psychology*, 1962-68. Since 1977, Editor, *Psychological Review*. President, Midwestern Psychology Association, 1956-57. Recipient: Distinguished Science Contribution award, American Psychological Association, 1962; Warren Medal, Society of Experimental Psychologists, 1963. Fellow, American Psychological Association. Member, National Academy of Sciences, and American Academy of Arts and Sciences. Address: 620 W. James Hall, 33 Kirkland Street, Cambridge, Massachusetts 02138, U.S.A.

PUBLICATIONS

Psychology

Modern Learning Theory: A Critical Analysis of Five Examples, with others. New York, Appleton Century, 1954.
Learning Theory and Mental Development. New York, Academic Press, 1970.

Other

Editor, with Robert R. Bush, *Studies in Mathematical Learning Theory*. Stanford, California, Stanford University Press, 1959.
Editor, with E. Niemark, *Stimulus Sampling Theory*. San Francisco, Holden Day, 1967.
Editor, *Handbook of Learning and Cognitive Processes*. Hillsdale, New Jersey, Lawrence Erlbaum, 5 vols., 1975-78.

*   *   *

The theoretical and empirical contributions of William Kaye Estes began some 40 years ago. Since that time, the range and depth of his research has had a profound influence on a generation of psychologists and has established him as a major figure in experimental psychology.

Estes's early work was in the S-R behavioristic tradition of his mentor, B.F. Skinner. In 1944, he published his doctoral dissertation dealing with punishment (shock) in the rat in which he confirmed Skinner's prior finding that punishment affected only the momentary rate of responding and not the overall tendency to make a response. Estes also found, however, that the total number of responses made following punishment was diminished if the shock intensity or its duration was increased. He also reported that the depressed rate of responding persisted if punishment was administered intermittently rather than on every trial. This work thus suggested some of the variables that could prolong the inhibitory effects of punishment.

A classic 1950 paper entitled "Toward a Statistical Theory of Learning" provided the foundation for contemporary work in mathematical learning theory. In this paper, Estes attempted to quantify Guthrie's contiguity theory by formalizing its assumptions and recasting its terminology into a framework referred to as stimulus sampling theory (SST). The intent of SST was to predict the numerical values of given experimenter-chosen statistics (e.g., mean number of errors) and to examine how well the predicted values matched the ones actually obtained.

According to SST, the stimuli in a learning environment comprise a hypothetical population of elements, only some of which are sampled or active at a given time. Each active element becomes associated in all-or-none fashion with a particular response, so that response probability on a given trial depends simply on the proportion of conditioned elements sampled. Reinforcers function either to protect newly-formed associations or to change these associations when the reinforcer is paired with an alternative response. In the latter instance, we would say that the original response had been extinguished by its replacement with the alternate response. Subsequent extensions of the theory allow for the sampling of stimulus patterns rather than individual elements, and for changes in the stimulus environment with the passage of time ("stimulus fluctuation").

An important consequence of SST was to provide an integrated and testable framework for studying a number of problems in learning theory, including stimulus and response generalization, short- and long-term memory, probability learning (predicting which of two or more events will occur), and concept learning. An equally important result was to stimulate other investigators to learn the techniques of mathematical theory construction so that they could apply the methods to their own work. Mathematical modeling in areas such as classical and instrumental conditioning, human learning and memory, psychophysics, and social psychology can be traced, in part, to the early work of Estes on SST.

Estes's research has also included work on all-or-none learning, the effects of repeated tests on retention, serial learning, and visual information processing. He developed the so-called RTT (study-test-test) paradigm to investigate whether associations are formed on a single trial, the reasoning being that the "state" of an association (i.e., whether it is learned or unlearned) should remain the same from one unreinforced test trial to the next. Thus, under a one-trial learning assumption, responses given correctly on an initial test trial should also be correct on an immediately following test trial, whereas responses given incorrectly on an initial test trial should be incorrect on a subsequent test trial. The paradigm was later extended to include additional unreinforced test trials, the finding being that, within limits, retention was directly related to the number of such tests.

More recently, Estes has developed an associative coding theory to account for item and order information in the processing of visual materials such as words. The theory proposes a hierarchical memory structure with higher-order codes or control elements which allow access to subordinate components, e.g., words allow access to syllables, syllables allow access to letters, etc. Estes has demonstrated how such a system can explain the so-called word-letter phenomenon, the finding that it is more difficult to process a letter alone than in the context of a word.

Estes's contributions extend to numerous chapters in texts, edited volumes, monographs, journal editorships, and the training of an influential number of graduate students. His impact on 20th century psychology has been truly impressive.

—Seymore Simon

EVANS-PRITCHARD, E(dward) E(van). British anthropologist. Born in Crowborough, Sussex, 21 September 1902. Educated at Winchester College, Oxford; studied at Exeter College, Oxford, B.A. 1924; London School of Economics, University of London, Ph. D. 1927. Served in the British Army, in Ethiopia, Sudan and Syria, 1940-45. Married Ioma Gladys Heaton Nicholls in 1939 (died, 1959); 5 children. Made six major and several minor anthropological expeditions to Central, East and North Africa, 1926-39. Lecturer in Anthropology, London

School of Economics, 1928-31; Professor of Sociology, Fuad I University (now the Egyptian University), Cairo, 1932-34; Research Lecturer in African Sociology, Oxford University, 1935-40; Reader in Anthropology, Cambridge University, 1945-46; Fellow of All Souls College (Sub-Warden, 1963-65) and Professor of Social Anthropology, Oxford University, 1946-70. Visiting Professor, University of Chicago, 1950; Fellow, Center for Advanced Study in the Behavioral Sciences, Stanford, California, 1957-58; Honorary Fellow, School of Oriental and African Studies, University of London, 1963; Honorary Professor, University of Wales, 1971. Founder, with Meyer Fortes, and Life President, Association of Social Anthropologists, 1946; President, Royal Anthropological Institute, 1949-51. D.Sc.: University of Chicago, 1967; University of Bristol, 1968; D.Litt., University of Manchester, 1969. Fellow, British Academy. Chevalier, Légion d'Honneur, 1971. Honorary Member, American Academy of Arts and Sciences. *Died* (in Oxford) *11 September 1973.*

PUBLICATIONS

Anthropology

Witchcraft, Oracles, and Magic among the Azande. Oxford, Clarendon Press, 1937; revised edition, 1958.

The Nuer: A Description of the Modes of Livelihood and Political Institutions of a Nilotic People. New York, Oxford University Press, 1937; Oxford, Clarendon Press, 1940.

The Political System of the Anuak of the Anglo-Egyptian Sudan. London, Lund Humphries, 1940.

The Divine Kingship of the Shilluk of the Nilotic Sudan. Cambridge, Cambridge University Press, 1948.

Social Anthropology (lecture). Oxford, Clarendon Press, 1948.

The Sansusi of Cyrenaica. Oxford, Clarendon Press, and New York, Oxford University Press, 1949; revised edition, 1963.

Kinship and Marriage among the Nuer. Oxford, Clarendon Press, and New York, Oxford University Press, 1951.

Social Anthropology (broadcast talks). London, Cohen and West, 1951; New York, Free Press, 1952; revised edition, 1956.

The Institutions of Primitive Society (broadcast talks). Oxford, Blackwell, 1954; New York, Free Press, 1956; revised edition, 1961.

Nuer Religion. Oxford, Clarendon Press, and New York, Oxford University Press, 1956.

Anthropology and History (lecture). Manchester, Manchester University Press, 1961.

Essays in Social Anthropology. London, Faber, 1962; New York, Free Press, 1963.

The Comparative Method in Social Anthropology (lecture). London, Athlone Press, 1963.

Zande Texts. Oxford and New York, Oxford University Press, 1963.

The Zande State: The Huxley Memorial Lectures 1963. London, Royal Anthropological Institute, 1963.

Social Anthropology and Other Essays. New York, Free Press, 1965.

Theories of Primitive Religion. Oxford and New York, Oxford University Press, 1965.

The Sociology of Comte: An Appreciation (lecture). Manchester, Manchester University Press, 1970.

The Azande: History and Political Institutions. Oxford, Clarendon Press, 1971.

Man and Woman among the Azande. New York, Free Press, 1974.

A History of Anthropological Thought, edited by André Singer. New York, Basic Books, 1981.

Other

Co-Editor, *Essays Presented to C.G. Seligman.* London, Kegan Paul, 1934.

Editor, with Meyer Fortes, *African Political Systems.* Oxford, Oxford University Press, 1940.

Editor, *The Zande Trickster* (collection of folktales). Oxford, Oxford University Press, 1967.

Editor, *Peoples of the World.* Suffern, New York, Danbury Press, 3 vols., 1972.

*

Bibliography: *A Bibliography of the Writings of E.E. Evans-Pritchard,* compiled by E.E. Evans-Pritchard, London, Tavistock, 1974.

Critical Studies: *Studies in Social Anthropology: Essays in Memory of E.E. Evans-Pritchard,* edited by J.H.M. Beattie and R.G. Lienhardt, Oxford, Clarendon Press, 1975; *Edward Evans-Pritchard* by Mary T. Douglas, New York, Viking Press, and Brighton, England, Harvester Press, 1980.

* * *

E.E. Evans-Pritchard is a principle formulator of modern social anthropology, known principally for reformulation of social structural theory to include recognition that organizations include patterns of ideas and values as well as patterns of objective behavior.

He took his B.A. in modern history at Exeter College, Oxford (1924), and his Ph.D. in anthropology at LSE, under C.G. Seligman, in 1927. His thesis incorporated the results of his first field work among the Azande of southern Sudan. From 1928 to 1940 he held a series of academic posts in England and Egypt. He also conducted further field work on the Azande, the Nuer and the Anuak of the southern Sudan, the Luo of Kenya, and other groups. He served in the British army from 1940-1945 in Ethiopia, the Sudan, and Libya. He served as Reader in Anthropology at Cambridge in 1945, and from 1946 to 1970 held the chair of Professor of Social Anthropology at Oxford, building one of the most cohesive and influential anthropological schools anywhere.

Apart from C.G. and Brenda Seligman, Evans-Pritchard's intellectual background has to be described as lying primarily in the work of Bronislaw Malinowski, A.R. Radcliffe-Brown, and Lucien Lévy-Bruhl. The latter two each represent an alternative "sociological" view of society as a single organic whole that determines individual behavior and an alternative concept of scientific method. Malinowski had pioneered the modern ethnographic monograph, reporting first hand field-work organized by a theoretical problem. Evans-Pritchard adapted this to his own "organic" assumptions, which had been radically at variance with the individualistic and pluralistic perspective Malinowski had drawn out of European ethnology, folk-psychology, and pragmatism.

Evans-Pritchard's two most influential works continue to be *Witchcraft, Oracles, and Magic among the Azande* and *The Nuer.* The first is still considered a landmark study of an exotic system of ideas; the latter is a classic study of an entire "social structure," and remains one of the fullest and most coherent attempts to say what such a structure is and what it reflects.

Evans-Pritchard was often oblique in stating his theoretical goals, but at one point he describes what he learned among the Azande as "thinking black," which clearly suggests that he was describing all of "Azande thought," not just one set of ideas out of many that were used in the community. Like Lévy-Bruhl, he emphasised that this pattern of thought was internally coherent and correct, although it had features we would regard as magical. Specifically, he argued that Azande thought included concepts of cause and effect like our own, but went further to provide an account of what we would regard as chance associations. They realized, he argued, that a granary fell because termites ate its supports, but considered it also important to explain why it fell exactly when it did and why it fell on so-and-so. The Azande themselves did not promulgate their ideas as a single system, but this was not considered a problem. Like Lévy-Bruhl, Evans-Pritchard obtained his characterization of Azande thought from many particular observations, integrated by a process of theoretically informed logical inference. There was no attempt to seek indigenous ideas based on different assumptions and thereby to test empirically the implication that no other system of Azande was of equal or greater importance.

The Nuer remains the most comprehensive argument for the sociological determinism of thought by a comprehensive analysis of a single society. The argument was complex and often oblique, but began with the claim that Nuer behavior is dominated by a single overriding value, "interest in cattle." By describing the way this interest ran though Nuer activities and contrasting the Nuer with the Dinka who lived nearby and even among them in the same ecological setting, Evans-Pritchard argued that this interest directly reflected and maintained the Nuer social organization, a system of segmentary clans in dynamic equilibrium.

Evans-Pritchard's arguments had numerous technical flaws and internal contradictions. Probably no one today would regard his major theses as having been proven, although many of his specific characterisations of institutions and usages are widely accepted. Yet few alternative perspectives have been developed with as much thoroughness, and many anthropologists are still trying to carry out his program.

—Murray J. Leaf

EYSENCK, H(ans) J(urgen). British psychologist. Born in Berlin, Germany, 4 March 1916; emigrated to England in 1934. Educated at the University of London, B.Sc. 1938, Ph.D. 1940; University of Dijon and University of Exeter. Married Margaret Malcolm Davies in 1938, 1 son; married Sybil Bianca Giuletta Rostal in 1950; 4 children. Senior Research Psychologist, Mill Hill Emergency Hospital, London, 1942-45. Since 1946, Director, Psychology Department, Maudsley Hospital, London; Reader in Psychology, 1950-54, and since 1955 Professor of Psychology, Institute of Psychiatry, University of London. Visiting Professor, University of Pennsylvania, Philadelphia, 1949-50; University of California at Berkeley, 1954. Since 1963, Editor-in-Chief, *Behaviour Research and Therapy*; since 1980, Editor, *Personality and Individual Differences*. Honorary doctorate: University of London, 1962. Fellow, British Psychological Society, and American Psychological Association. Address: 10 Dorchester Drive, London SE24, England.

PUBLICATIONS

Psychology

Dimensions of Personality: A Record of Research, with others. London, Routledge, 1947; New York, Macmillan, 1948.
The Scientific Study of Personality. London, Routledge, and New York, Macmillan, 1952.
The Structure of Human Personality. London, Methuen, and New York, Wiley, 1953.
Uses and Abuses of Psychology. London, Penguin, 1953.
The Psychology of Politics. London, Routledge, 1954; New York, Praeger, 1955.
Psychology and the Foundations of Psychiatry (lecture). London, H.K. Lewis, 1955.
Perceptual Processes and Mental Illness, with others. London, Chapman and Hall, and New York, Basic Books, 1957.
Sense and Nonsense in Psychology. London, Penguin, 1957.
The Dynamics of Anxiety and Hysteria: An Experimental Application of Modern Learning Theory to Personality.

London, Routledge, and New York, Praeger, 1957.
Manual of Maudsley Personality Inventory. London, University of London Press, 1959.
The Language of the Gene, with others. London, University of London Press, 1961.
Know Your Own I.Q. London, Penguin, 1962.
Manual of Eysenck Personality Inventory, with Sybil Bianca Eysenck. London, University of London Press, 1964.
Crime and Personality. London, Routledge, and Boston, Houghton Mifflin, 1964.
The Causes and Cures of Neuroses: An Introduction to Modern Behaviour Therapy Based on Learning Theory and the Principles of Conditioning, with Stanley Rachman. London, Routledge, and San Diego, California, Robert R. Knapp, 1965.
Fact and Fiction in Psychology. London, Penguin, 1965.
Smoking, Health and Personality. London, Weidenfeld and Nicolson, and New York, Basic Books, 1965.
Check Your Own I.Q. London, Penguin, 1966; New York, Bell, 1979.
The Effects of Psychotherapy. New York, International Science Press, 1966.
The Biological Basis of Personality. Springfield, Illinois, C.C. Thomas, 1967.
Personality Structure and Measurement, with Sybil Bianca Eysenck. London, Routledge, and San Diego, California, Robert R. Knapp, 1969.
Race, Intelligence and Education. London, Temple Smith, 1971; as *The I.Q. Argument: Race, Intelligence and Education*, New York, Liberty Press, 1971.
Psychology Is About People. London, Lane, and New York, Liberty Press, 1972.
The Experimental Study of Freudian Theories, with Glenn D. Wilson. London, Methuen, 1973.
Eysenck on Extraversion. New York, Wiley, 1973.
The Inequality of Man. London, Temple Smith, 1973; San Diego, California, EDITS, 1975.
Know Your Own Personality, with Glenn D. Wilson. London, Temple Smith, 1975; New York, Barnes and Noble, 1976.
The Future of Psychiatry. London, Methuen, 1975.
Psychoticism as a Dimension of Personality, with Sybil Bianca Eysenck. London, Hodder and Stoughton, 1976.
Sex and Personality. London, Open Books, and Austin, Texas, University of Texas Press, 1976.
Reminiscence, Motivation, and Personality: A Case Study in Experimental Psychology, with C.D. Frith. New York, Plenum, 1977.
You and Neurosis. London, Temple Smith, 1978.
Sex, Violence, and the Media, with D.K.B. Nias. London, Temple Smith, and New York, St. Martin's Press, 1978.
The Psychological Basis of Ideology, with G.A. Wilson. Lancaster, Medical and Technical Publishers, 1978.
The Structure and Measurement of Intelligence, with David W. Fulker. New York, Springer, 1979.
The Psychology of Sex, with Glenn D. Wilson. London, Dent, 1979.
The Causes and Effects of Smoking. London, Temple Smith, 1980.
The Intelligence Controversy: H.J. Eysenck Versus Leon Kamin. New York, Wiley, 1981.
Mindwatching, with Michael Eysenck. London, Joseph, 1981.

Other

Editor, *Handbood of Abnormal Psychology: An Experimental Approach*. London, Pitman, 1960; New York, Basic Books, 1961.
Editor, *Experiments in Personality*. London, Routledge, 2 vols., 1960; New York, Humanities Press, 2 vols., 1961.
Editor, *Behaviour Theory and Neurosis: Readings in Modern Methods of Treatment Derived from Learning Theory.* Ox-

ford and New York, Pergamon Press, 1960.

Editor, *Experiments with Drugs: Studies in the Relation Between Personality, Learning Theory and Drug Action*. New York, Macmillan, 1963.

Editor, *Experiment in Motivation*. Oxford and New York, Pergamon Press, 1964.

Editor, *Experiments in Behaviour Therapy: Readings in Modern Methods of Treatment Derived from Learning Theory*. New York, Macmillan, 1964.

Editor, *Readings in Extraversion-Introversion*. London, Staples, 3 vols., 1970; New York, Wiley, 3 vols., 1972.

Editor, with J. Wankowski, *Personality Dimensions of Students*. Birmingham, University of Birmingham Press, 1970.

Editor, with others, *Encyclopedia of Psychology*. London, Search Press, 3 vols., 1972; New York, Seabury Press, 3 vols., 1979.

Editor, *The Measurement of Intelligence*. Lancaster, England, Medical and Technical Publishing Company, and Baltimore, University Park Press, 1973.

Editor, *Case Studies in Behaviour Therapy*. London, Routledge, 1976.

Editor, *The Measurement of Personality*. Baltimore, University Park Press, 1976.

Editor, *A Textbook of Human Psychology*, with Glenn D. Wilson. Lancaster, England, Medical and Technical Publishing Company, and Baltimore, University Park Press, 1976.

Editor, *Advances in Behaviour Research and Therapy*, with Stanley Rachman. Oxford and New York, Pergamon Press, 2 vols., 1977, 1979.

Editor, *Die Grundlagen des Spätmarxismus*. Stuttgart, Bonn Aktuell, 1977.

Editor, with Glenn D. Wilson, *The Psychological Basis of Ideology*. Baltimore, University Park Press, 1978.

*

Critical Studies: *Dimensions of Personality: Papers in Honor of H.J. Eysenck*, edited by Richard Lynn, Oxford and New York, Pergamon Press, 1981; *Hans Eysenck: The Man and His Work* by H.B. Gibson, London, Peter Owen, 1981.

*   *   *

Hans Eysenck was born in Berlin, but he left the country of his birth at the age of eighteen because of his dislike of the Nazi regime which had come into power the year previously. He came to England in 1934, and it has been his home ever since. Shortly after his arrival he enrolled at University College, London, to study psychology under Cyril Burt. His first journal publication dates from 1939, and since then he has produced a steady stream of books, journal articles and compendiums. He is highly and diversely talented, scientifically, artistically and also athletically, and is a man of considerable courage and uncompromising convictions. His influence has been great; but he has also aroused a good deal of hostility and distrust. Influenced by Burt, Eysenck's work has been focussed on the central, but at the same time most complex, problems of psychology, the problems of personality, and he has endeavoured to bring to bear upon these problems the rigorous methods of science, quantitative and experimental.

After graduating, Eysenck commenced his career under wartime conditions at the Mill Hill Emergency Hospital under the distinguished psychiatrist, Aubrey Lewis. The fruits of this work were published in 1947 in his first book, *Dimensions of Personality*. This book showed many of the qualities which have marked Eysenck's subsequent work. It was bold and comprehensive in its theorizing, well-documented, based on experimental evidence statistically analysed, and it arrived at simple and testable conclusions. Eysenck found two main personality dimensions, or factors—the neuroticism factor, and the introversions factor—to which he later added a third factor, psychoticism. The quantita-

tive, dimensional, approach based on factor analysis, the statistical method developed by Eysenck's teachers at London University, was intended to replace the categorial classification of personality disorders commonly employed in psychiatry. Eysenck went on to employ the same factorial method to a study of social and political attitudes, and arrived at rather similar results. There were, he concluded, two main dimensions, conservatism vs. radicalism, and tough-minded vs. tender-minded, on which social and political attitudes could be located. Thus the fascist was a combination of conservative and tough, while the communist was radical and tough.

Eysenck has always attempted to link conclusions based on statistical analysis with physiological and behavioural data. He has been particularly influenced by the work of Pavlov and the behaviourist school of psychology. He proposed that an individual's location on the extraversion-introversion dimension was a function of the balance between excitatory and inhibitory processes. This proposal generated testable conclusions, for example, that extraverts would condition less easily than introverts, a conclusion which has received some experimental support. In the department which he built up at the Maudsley Hospital, London, Eysenck has promoted a great deal of research into the biological basis of psychological functioning, particularly in the field of behaviour genetics. This has partly been based on work with animals, but has also involved large scale human studies. Eysenck has fearlessly maintained the importance of genetic influences on personality and behaviour, not only in such matters as intelligence, but also in connection with such aspects of human behaviour as crime, smoking, drug addiction and racial differences. This has brought upon him a great deal of obloquy, and even physical assault.

The main focus of work at the Maudsley Hospital, which is a psychiatric institution, has been in the clinical area, and here Eysenck has built up what is undoubtedly the leading department of clinical psychology in Great Britain. It has played a major part in establishing clinical psychology as a profession and in winning a role for clinical psychologists which is to some extent independent of medicine. The basis of Eysenck's work has been the development of behaviour therapy, a field in which he has been one of the leading pioneers. His advocacy of behaviour therapy has been founded on scientific grounds, and also on his scepticism as to the value of psychotherapeutic, and particularly psychoanalytic, modes of treatment. His campaign against the pretensions of psychoanalysts has been long-standing.

Eysenck is a gifted writer whose many popular books on psychology have deservedly had a wide readership. He has never hesitated to speak on the most contentious issues, such as race, crime, sex, heredity and politics, backing up his views with hard evidence, or to further unpopular causes. In his latest book, for example, he has provided some factual support for the practice of astrology. He has been criticised by psychologists for over-ambitious theorizing and for a too facile faith in quantification. Nevertheless it would be ungenerous not to recognise that his aim of bringing the central and most complex topics of psychology within the ambit of science is a worthy one, and that his contributions to this end have been both numerous and stimulating. He is indeed among the most fertile of living psychologists.

—Leslie Hearnshaw

FANON, Frantz. French psychiatrist and social philosopher. Born in Martinique, French Antilles, 20 July 1925. Educated in Martinique and France; studied medicine and psychiatry, University of Lyons, M.D. 1951. Served in the French Army, in Europe, 1944. Married in 1953. Head, Psychiatric Department, Blida-Joinville Hospital, Algeria, 1953-56; aided Algerian rebels in Algerian Revolution, 1954-56; worked for the Algerian liberation movement (FLN), as an editor for *El Moudjahid*, from 1956; attended inter-African Congress at Bamako and Cotonou, 1958; seriously injured by a mine on the Algerian-Moroccan frontier, 1959; appointed Ambassador of the Algerian Provisional Government to Ghana, 1960; travelled to Mali to explore southern supply routes to Algeria, and evaded several attacks on his life, 1960; travelled to the U.S.S.R. for leukemia treatment, 1960, and then to Washington, D.C., 1961. *Died* (in Washington, D.C.) *6 December 1961.*

PUBLICATIONS

Social Philosophy

Peau noire, masques blancs. Paris, Seuil, 1952; as *Black Skin, White Masks*, New York, Grove, 1965; London, Paladin, 1970.
L'An V de la Révolution Algérienne. Paris, Maspero, 1959; as *Sociologie d'une révolution*, 1966; as *Studies in a Dying Colonialism*, New York, Monthly Review Press, 1965; as *A Dying Colonialism*, New York, Grove, 1967; London, Penguin, 1970.
Les damnés de la terre. Paris, Maspero, 1961; as *The Damned*, Paris, Présence Africaine, 1963; as *The Wretched of the Earth*, New York, Grove, and London, MacGibbon and Kee, 1965.
Pour la Révolution Africaine, écrits politiques. Paris, Maspero, 1964; as *Towards the African Revolution*, New York, Monthly Review Press, 1967; London, Penguin, 1970.

*

Critical Studies: *Kolonialismus und Entfremdung: Zur politischen Theorie Frantz Fanons* by Renate Zahaı, Frankfurt, Europäische Verlagsanstalt, 1959; *Frantz Fanon* by David Caute, New York, Viking Press, and London, Collins/Fontana, 1970; *Fanon* by Peter Geismar, New York, Dial Press, 1971; *Frantz Fanon: A Critical Study* by Irene L. Gendzier, New York, Pantheon, 1973; *Frantz Fanon: Social and Political Thought* by Emmanuel Hanser, Columbus, Ohio State University Press, 1977; *Frantz Fanon: Language as the God Gone Astray in the Flesh* by Chester J. Fontenot Jr., Lincoln, University of Nebraska Press, 1979.

*   *   *

Frantz Fanon gained a global reputation not merely for his open plea for armed violence in the Algerian struggle for independence, but even more because of his devastating exposure of the psychic traumas and social disruption of modern colonialism. Poet, humanist and psychiatrist, he wrote as a black man who was deeply sensitive to the psychological wounds and spiritual privations of large masses of mute victims to alien rule, cultural imperialism and racial prejudice. He insisted that his ultimate aim was the authentic liberation of all peoples. This requires the affirmation of the essential humanity of all persons as well as deliberate choices by oppressed individuals seeking self-realization. He discerned a dialectical interaction between concealed concepts, actual experience and distinct levels of reality.

Fanon perceived colonialism to be a pervasive structure of oppression which served the economic interests of capitalism, masked by the deceptive rhetoric of racial and cultural superiority. As an economic system, colonialism organized the exploitation of land and resources by white settlers and the less visible trading enterprises which supported them. Until the native regains effective control of these material resources, there can be no release from psychological and political dominance. Dominant racism, vitiating all social relations and penetrating to the psychic core of all persons, white and black, must be fully grasped before it can be completely eradicated.

In his first book, *Black Skin, White Masks*, Fanon stressed the Manichean psychology engendered by colonial cultures and internalized to the point where members of each race lived under the continual tension of neurotic responses to the behaviour of the "Other." White racism spawned the Negro. The visible fact of a black skin was transmogrified into a psychological reality reeking of the assumption that black men are primitive savages without any redeeming culture in the "darkest night of humanity." Behind the enormity of this expedient rationalization for colonial authority, the white man masked his cowardly fears and his sexual obsessions with the alleged "genital power" of blacks. Fanon found that individuals who experimented with mixed liaisons did not enjoy authentic or lasting experiences: it was as if they were playing with the fires which fed racial discrimination. The obliteration of pre-colonial history and culture was achieved by a colonial structure of institutions, rules and roles which idealized the "mother country" whilst enforcing a tight system of social differentiation. Through education in language and literature, as well as by social custom and severe punishment, the black became what the Other expected of him, yet continued to carry the irremovable stigma of inescapable inferiority. The psychological effects of this shameful livery put together by centuries of incomprehension were dramatically illustrated by Fanon and became the basis for all his subsequent statements on political action.

Sealed in his blackness, whilst vainly striving to become white, the black man developed an aberration of over-sensitivity, "overdetermined from without" and alienated from his essential identity as man. Shame and self-hatred sank into the core of his psyche and paralyzed his human power to make choices. No amount of assimilation and success in the colonial culture could bring escape from the paranoiac vulnerability to being "dissected by white eyes." This abnormal state of existence was aggravated by the constant manifestation of "negro phobia genesis" that even well-meaning whites would display in daily contacts. The condition became endemic for the native intellectual belonging to an urban elite, with material interests interlocked with the persistence of the colonial economy. Less vulnerable, Fanon stated in a later work, was the rural peasant whose traditional institutions and concrete focus on the need for land, appropriated by the white settler, provided a foundation for resistance to racism.

Fanon concluded this initial study of colonial relationships with a personal testament of liberation. Just as there is no white man's burden, so too there is no Negro mission. "I find myself suddenly in the world, and I recognize that I have one right alone: that of demanding human behaviour from the other.... One duty alone: that of not renouncing my freedom through my choices."

The possibility of escape from the psychological slavery imposed by white men was considered by Fanon in a collection of essays, *Towards the African Revolution*, and in his report on the Algerian War of Liberation, *Studies in a Dying Colonialism*. Writing in the midst of his active ideological participation in the Algerian war—"the most hallucinatory war that any people has ever waged to smash colonial aggression"—Fanon proclaimed ultimate victory because the struggle had already transformed the Algerian people. He gave special attention to the ways in which Algerian women destroyed the pseudo-truths of field studies by transcending traditional Muslim roles without violating their self-respect. He responded to the charge that the rebels were bloodthirsty by asserting that an underdeveloped people must prove itself by its fighting power, its ability to set itself up as a nation, and by the purity of its acts, even to the smallest detail. Although this is very difficult, the idea of the nation provided the unity needed to channel the dynamism of the revolution, released by the self-liberation of myriads of individuals.

Fanon provided a broad perspective of national liberation movements in *The Wretched of the Earth*, completed a few months before he died. His analysis of the sources and pitfalls of liberation movements was merged into one sustained, passionate, defiant negation. *Not* the urban middle class, *not* a return to

African culture, *not* a call for negritude. African unity cannot come through a one-party dictatorship enthroning the desire for personal enrichment, and certainly not through the reforms and concessions proposed by colonial powers. Both the urban élite and the rural peasant were susceptible to the offer of concessions, but the urban dwellers would settle for even less, such as seats in the home parliament or qualified political independence. With less to lose, the rural native and his urban counterpart from the *lumpenproletariat* were more likely to erupt spontaneously in violent reaction to colonial oppression.

Such spontaneity must be wisely guided by committed revolutionaries, who established contact with the peasants. A strong driving force of intellect channelled through an effective political organization was needed, but it must be an intellect which watches for the lessons of partial truths revealed in specific applications and which induces the peasants to further their understanding of the wider discipline of nation-building. The rural native was more accustomed to discipline and self-sacrifice than the urban intellectual, who could be enticed by the self-seeking individualism offered by colonialism. Given the psychological and material vulnerability of the colonized to the colonizer, violence becomes a necessary means of purgation, liberation and revolution. "Collective catharsis" could be achieved through the cleansing power of confrontation.

Fanon could not lend his support to the defenders of *negritude*. "The Negro is disappearing," he wrote, and cultural societies were being set up by urban intellecuals to cope with the psychic trauma of discovering their complicity in a dying colonialism. Each new nation must be constructed by realistic political action, not emotional involvement in cultural myths. Nation-building must be undertaken in the context of sociogenetic diversity; generic claims about African culture and African unity have no reality.

There was a global dimension to Fanon's work in that he prophesied that the cumulative effect of national liberation movements throughout Africa, Asia and Latin America would eventually initiate a new era in human evolution. Proclaiming that humanity is waiting for something other than an imitation of European blueprints, Fanon concluded that the Third World today faces Europe like a colossal mass whose aim should be to try to resolve the problems to which Europe had not been able to find the answers. New blueprints should be developed and all humanity would benefit by creative applications of revolutionary theory that truly developed the personality of a new man. National liberation could provide the social context in which individuals could help each other to find themselves. "For Europe, for ourselves, and for humanity, comrades, we must turn over a new leaf, we must work out new concepts, and try to set afoot a new man."

—R.N. Iyer

FEBVRE, Lucien (Paul Victor). French historian. Born in Nancy, 22 June 1878. Educated at Lycée, Nancy, Lycée Louis-le-Grand, Paris, and École Normale Supérieure, Paris, 1898-1902; Agrégé, Docteur-ès-lettres, 1911. Served in French Army, 1914-18: Croix de Guerre. Professor, Lycée, Bar-le-Duc; Lycée, Besançon; and University of Dijon, 1912-14; Chair of Modern History, University of Strasbourg, after World War I for 12 years; Chair of History of Modern Civilization, Collège de France, Paris, from 1933; Director, Section of Economic and Social Sciences, l'École des Hautes Études, Paris from 1948. Co-Founder and Co-Editor, with Marc Bloch, *Annales d'histoire économique et sociale*, 1929-39; Editor, *Encyclopédie française permanente*, 1935-40; Co-Founder and Co-Editor, with Marc Bloch, 1939-41, and Editor, 1941-45, *Annales d'histoire sociale*; Editor, *Mélanges d'histoire sociale*, 1942-44; *Annales:*

économies, sociétés, civilisations, from 1946; and *Cahiers d'histoire mondiale (Journal of World History)*, from 1951. Founder, *Revue d'histoire de la guerre mondiale*, 1950. President, Comité d'Histoire de la Guerre Mondiale, from 1946. French delegate to Unesco. Member, Institut de France (Académie des Sciences morales et politiques). Commandeur, Légion d'honneur, 1956. *Died 27 September 1956.*

PUBLICATIONS

History

Ordonnances des rois de France: Règne de François Ier.   Paris, Imprimerie nationale, 1902.
La Franche-Comté.   Paris, Cerf, 1905.
Un secrétaire d'Erasme, Gilbert Cousin, et la réforme en Franche-Comté.   Fontenay-aux-Roses, France, Bellenand, 1907.
Notes et documents sur la Réforme et l'Inquisition en Franche-Comté: Extraits des archives du Parlement de Dole.   Paris, Champion, 1911.
Philippe II et la Franche-Comté: Étude d'histoire politique, religieuse et sociale.   Paris, Champion, 1911.
Histoire de Franche-Comté.   Paris, Boivin, 1912.
Ducs de Valois de Bourgogne et les idées politiques de leur temps (lecture).   Dijon, 1913.
La Terre et l'evolution humaine: Introduction géographique à l'histoire, with Lionel Bataillon.   Paris, Michel, 1922; as *A Geographical Introduction to History*, London, Routledge, 1924; New York, Knopf, 1925.
Un destin: Martin Luther.   Paris, Rieder, 1928; as *Martin Luther: A Destiny*, New York, Dutton, 1929; London, 1930.
Civilisation: Le Mot et l'idée, with others.   Paris, La Renaissance du livre, 1930.
Ce qu'est l'Encyclopédie française.   N.p., Arbelot et du Droit, 1933.
Le Rhin: Problèmes d'histoire et d'économie, with Albert Demangeon.   Paris, Colin, 1935.
Origene et Des Périers: Ou, l'énigme du "Cymbalum mundi."   Paris, Droz, 1942.
La Problème de l'incroyance au XVIe siècle: La Religion de Rabelais.   Paris, Michel, 1942; as *The Problem of Unbelief in the Sixteenth Century: The Religion of Rabelais*, Cambridge, Massachusetts, Harvard University Press, 1983.
Autour de l'Heptaméron: Amour sacré, amour profane.   Paris, Gallimard, 1944.
Hommage solonnel de l'Université et la Résistance à la mémoire de Marc Bloch, professeur d'histoire économique à la Sorbonne: Marc Bloch, grand historien, héros et martyr de la Résistance: l'Homme et l'oeuvre, with Georges Altman.   Paris, Enterprise de Press, 1945.
International Origins of a National Culture: Experimental Materials for a History of France, with François Crouzet.   Paris, Unesco, 1951.
Combats pour l'histoire.   Paris, Colin, 1953.
Le Nouveau Monde et l'Europe: Texte des conférences et des entretiens organisés par les Recontres internationales de Genève et des conférences prononcées aux Recontres intellectuelles de São Paulo, 1954, with others.   Brussels, Office de publicité, 1955.
Au coeur religieux de XVIe siècle.   Paris, Service d'éditions de vente des publications de l'Éducation nationale, 1957.
L'Apparition du livre, with Henri Jean Martin.   Paris, 1958; as *The Coming of the Book: The Impact of Printing, 1450-1800*, London, NLB, 1976.
Pour une histoire à part entière.   Paris, Service d'éditions de vente des publications de l'Éducation nationale, 1962; selections as *Life in Renaissance France*, Cambridge, Massachusetts, Harvard University Press, 1977.
A New Kind of History, from the Writings of Febvre, edited by

Peter Burke. London, Routledge, and New York, Harper, 1973.

Other

Editor, *Michelet, 1798-1874*. Geneva, Traits, 1946.

*

Critical Studies: *Eventail de l'histoire vivante, hommage à Lucien Febvre offert par l'amité d'historiens, linguistes, géographes, économistes, sociologues, ethnologues*, Paris, Colin, 2 vols., 1953; *Lucien Febvre: La Pensée vivante d'un historien* by Hans Dieter Mann, Paris, Colin, 1971; *Strasbourg au coeur religieux du XVIe siècle: Hommage à Lucien Febvre*, edited by Georges Livet and Francis Rapp, Strasbourg, Istra, 1977.

*   *   *

Lucien Febvre, France's premier historian of the years 1922-1956, ranks with Fustel de Coulanges and Jules Michelet in his influence on French historical writing. In addition to numerous books, articles, and reviews, he is remembered as one of the co-founders of the Annales School and of its journal which first appeared in 1929. Febvre, whose academic training and career began before the First World War, rejected the traditional academic approach to historical writing of the academic historians, Charles Langlois, Ernest Lavisse, and Charles Seignobos. Their *histoire événementiel* was considered by Febvre as not recounting the totality of history. In seeking this totality of history Febvre was strongly influenced by the eminent geographer Vadal de la Blache, the sociologist Emile Durkheim, the historian Henri Berr, and he also drew inspiration from two historians, Jules Michelet and Henri Pirenne. From Berr he received support and encouragement and also the opportunity to publish his first articles in the *Revue de Synthèse* which Berr edited. Berr also edited the monograph series *L'Évolution de l'Humanité*, in which the factors essential to the evolution of the world were studied with a view to finding a coherent explanation. Berr rejected the notion of history as a mere chronicling of facts and his disciple, Febvre, who published in this series, agreed with him. Febvre, however, carried Berr's views much further.

Febvre, a native of the Franche-Comté in Eastern France, came from a provincial intellectual household where he was encouraged as a youth to pursue serious study. Later, true to his Burgundian antecedents, he chose as the subject of his doctoral dissertation the Franche-Comté during the reign of Philip II. In this work he devoted an enormous amount of space to the geography of the region in order to illustrate his major theme, namely, the social conflict in that region during the later 16th century. This work, which was published in 1911, established his reputation as a historian who wrote the totality of history and not just a series of facts. To illustrate his points he drew upon political, economic, geographic, sociological, religious, and cultural phenomena as well as material from the social sciences. This was in sharp contrast to the sources used by the traditional historians, Lavisse, Seignobos, and Langlois, who were committed to narrative political history. Febvre's view of history was not readily accepted by the French historical establishment. In fact, it was only after the Second World War that Febvre's views gained wide acceptance.

Febvre left his post at the University of Dijon in 1914 to serve as an officer in the French army. His military service was significant in that it underscored and heightened his intense Burgundian patriotism and his devotion to France. He emerged from the war a captain. In 1919, with his appointment to the chair of history at the University of Strasbourg, he entered the mature phase of his academic career. His arrival in Strasbourg coincided with the reestablishment of the French University after the reannexation of Alsace to France in 1918. Febvre joined a select but significant group of French scholars at Strasbourg, "the most

brilliant university our history has known." (Fernand Braudel). His colleagues, chosen by the French government as representatives of the best in French culture, were a stimulus to him, especially, a young maitre assistant in medieval history, Marc Bloch.

In 1922 Febvre published a pioneer work on historical geography in Berr's *L'Évolution de l'Humanité* series and later in 1935 a work on the historical geography of the Rhine. During the 1920's he was a regular contributor to the *Revue de Synthèse* edited by Berr, and in these books and articles he carried forward his attempts to synthesize human knowledge. Perhaps the decisive event in his intellectual life was meeting Marc Bloch with whom he developed a productive collaboration and deep friendship. Both shared similar views on the nature of history and Febvre encouraged and praised his younger colleague's writing on medieval history. In 1929 they jointly founded the *Annales d'histoire économique and sociale*, a journal still published today that was to have a decisive influence on historical studies throughout the western world and one that would challenge traditional views of history such as those held at the Ecole de Chartes. Only after the Second World War, however, could it be said that the *Annales* view prevailed. In 1933 Febvre was rewarded for his extensive and influential publications by being elected to the chair of history of modern civilization at the Collège de France, a position he held until his retirement in 1950. In his inaugural address, "he called attention to the fact that it was in effect a restoration of the professorship which Michelet had held and which had been abolished in 1892. The lesson was manifest: four decades of compartmentalized, 'positivist' history had come to an end; France was ready once more to listen to the voice of the general historian."

During the wartime years Febvre devoted himself primarily to a study of religious sentiment in the Sixteenth Century. His earlier work on Martin Luther, which was published in 1928 to refute the tendentious work of Denifle, served as an inspiration for his other books. These books: *L'Incroyance au xvie siècle, la religion de Rabelais* (1942), *Origène et des Periers et l'énigme du "Cymbalum Mundi"* (1943), and *Autour de l'Héptameron* (1944) provide us with insights into his method as well as the variety of sources used to describe the political, religious, economic, and social climate in which the events of the Sixteenth Century unfolded.

In the period after the War he not only continued his editorial duties at the *Annales* but also edited and published the posthumous work of Marc Bloch, and headed the VIth Section of the École Pratique des Hautes Études which published and gave financial support to members of the Annales School.

Eschewing a straight factual approach to history, Febvre sought to determine the underlying theme or structure of past events and of economic and social phenomena. He was extremely interested in determining, or at least speculating about, the psychological motivation of historical figures. It is no exaggeration to say that he prepared the way for the structuralist approach to history and also the present widespread interest in psychohistory. Febvre's versatility and insatiable historical curiosity also led him to advocate and study rural history. After 1945 Febvre's eminence in the historical profession was so great that H. Stuart Hughes terms it a "pontificate." This is largely true, as his combat for history, his persuasiveness, and his prestige placed him on Clio's lofty eminence, and upon his death in 1957 the torch was passed to his pupil, Fernand Braudel.

—Walter D. Gray

FEIGL, Herbert. American philosopher of science. Born in Reichenberg, Austria, now Czechoslovakia, 14 December 1902; emigrated to the United States in 1930: naturalized, 1937. Studied at the University of Munich, 1921-22, and at the University of Vienna, 1922-26, Ph.D. 1927. Married Maria Kasper in 1931; 1 son. Lecturer, People's Institute, Vienna, 1927-30, Harvard University, Cambridge, Massachusetts, 1930, and University of Iowa, Iowa City, 1931-32; Assistant Professor, 1932-38, Associate Professor, 1938-40, and Professor of Philosophy, 1940-67, Regents Professor, 1967-71, and since 1971 Professor Emeritus, University of Minnesota, Minneapolis; since 1953, Director, Minnesota Center for the Philosophy of Science. Visiting Professor, University of California, 1946; University of Puerto Rico, 1957; and University of Hawaii, Honolulu, 1958; Fulbright Visiting Professor, Austria and Australia, 1964-65. President, American Philosophical Association, 1962-63. Recipient: Rockefeller Fellowship, 1930-31 and 1940; Guggenheim Fellowship, 1947. Fellow, American Association for the Advancement of Science (Vice-President, 1959). Member, American Academy of Arts and Sciences. Address: 5601 Dupont Avenue South, Minneapolis, Minnesota 55419, U.S.A.

PUBLICATIONS

Philosophy of Science

Theorie und Erfahrung in der Physik.   Karlsruhe, Braun, 1929.

Other

Editor, with Wilfrid Sellars, *Readings in Philosophical Analysis.* New York, Appleton Century, 1949.

Editor, with Max Brodbeck, *Readings in the Philosophy of Science.* New York, Appleton Century, 1953.

Editor, *Minnesota Studies in the Philosophy of Science.* Minneapolis, University of Minnesota Press, 3 vols., 1956-58.

Editor, with Grover Maxwell, *Scientific Explanation, Space, and Time.* Minneapolis, University of Minnesota Press, 1962.

Editor, with Wilfrid Sellars and Keith Lehrer, *New Readings in Philosophical Analysis.* New York, Appleton Century, 1972.

*

Critical Study: *Mind, Matter and Method: Essays in Philosophy and Science in Honor of Herbert Feigl,* edited by Paul K. Feyerabend and Grover Maxwell, Minneapolis, University of Minnesota Press, 1966 (contains a bibliography).

*   *   *

Herbert Feigl was born in Reichenberg, in the old Austria-Hungary. He was educated at the Universities of Munich and Vienna, 1921-26, specializing in the philosophy of science. From 1925 to 1930 he took part in informal meetings with several philosophers who were later called "The Vienna Circle." The stimulus and friendship of Wittgenstein, Waismann, Schlick, Carnap, Reichenbach, Frank and others made Feigl a debtor to both Berlin and Vienna and also honed his enthusiasms and skills. From them and with them, Feigl brought to America and to Anglo-American philosophy in 1930 a zest for so-called "logical positivism."

Something of a zealot for this new outlook, Feigl combined the new logics (the symbolic logics of Tarski, Russell, Frege) with a kind of radical empirical stance (which made him advocate scientific knowing rather than intuition, introspection, revelation or even insight). This is what he renamed "logical empiricism." He became to American philosophers and students the chief popular spokesman for a kind of lively positivism and a science-oriented philosophy. Feigl became a controversial figure because he stated his philosophical outlook in such polemical terms. He was quick to define himself against metaphysicians and moralists, taking advantage always of the obscurities, the

pseudo-profundities, and the perennial problems of older philosophies, insisting that he had only modesty and clarity on his side. Though not a logician in a technical sense, he used modern logicism to state a plausible diatribe against the sanctities of rationalism, of Aristotle, of deduction, of laws of thought, invoking instead ideas about convention, decision, knowledge, commonsense, and science being the foundation for all thought. For Feigl, there was real progress in philosophy. It had been hinted at by the British empiricists like Hume and Locke, adumbrated by the French skeptics of the 18th Century, but finally given cogency by persons as diverse as Comte, the French founder of sociology, and Mach, the German prototype of physicist-philosopher.

With the examples and help of Bertrand Russell's numerous books, of Wittgenstein's *Tractatus,* and the ferment of Vienna, Feigl also declared himself against what he thought were the pretensions of the poets, of the notion that the arts "said" something, of the theologians who claimed another kind of knowing. Feigl's ideas were accessible, partly because they impinged so painfully of what so many humanists and earnest advocates had seldom had challenged, fundamental notions of where truth, meaning and human dignity really lay. Feigl's negations were blunt, plausible, yet articulated with a courtly elegance. His affirmations were with Einstein and others, that the sciences give the description and explanations of the facts of nature, man, and society. Here we have the foundation of rationality, the occasion for awe and deep emotions, and all that we need to be moral and humane.

His thought always was that the new philosophy was dependent upon actual increments in technical prowess, in logical acuity, and in sheer advance of discursive knowledge. Feigl wanted to free philosophy of dependence upon attitude, upon emotional needs, and of anything else that was subjective, fortuitous, or of a pontifical or partisan quality. It was as if the empirical criteria of meaning were a discovery, not a point of view; as if modern logicians were seeing logical factors for the first time, not enunciating an alternative to older logics; as if current physics simply was finally value-free and more stringently bound by what is what. When these latter general views were challenged, not only from without but also within the movement—by followers of Wittgenstein, by Ryle, by those who declared that these platform views were dubious—the so-called "analytic movement" and "positivism" began also to break into partisan camps and the unity of science and philosophy seemed to fade.

Feigl, however, was resolute in the defense and enlargement of his own thought. His later reflections and writings seem like an effort to refine those foundational views. He modifies his views of "meaning"; he tries to rethink a host of issues about minds, bodies, causality, the concepts "philosophy," "science," and "verification," etc. Increasingly that erstwhile factual case for his philosophy requires even more detail, subtle argumentation, and a formidable technical vocabulary. As this went on, the more dramatic polemical features of his thought became more muted and seemed far less plausible.

Feigl's later philosophizing became less a pronouncement and more of an inquiry. He also, with others, edited numerous collections of essays, in which his essays played a more customary and supplemental role in on-going philosophical work. His brief essay "Logical Empiricism" (1943); his "The Mental and the Physical" (1958); his "The Philosophy of Science" (1969)—these show his views and methods over his mature years.

—Paul Holmer

FERMI, Enrico. American physicist. Born in Rome, Italy, 29 September 1901; emigrated to the United States in 1939:

naturalized, 1945. Studied at the University of Pisa, 1918-22. Married Laura Capon in 1928; 2 children. Lecturer, University of Florence, 1924-26; Professor of Theoretical Physics, University of Rome, 1927-38; Professor of Physics, Columbia University, New York, 1939-42; researcher on the development of the atom bomb (Manhattan Project), 1942-46, and Professor of Physics, 1946-54, University of Chicago. President, American Physical Society, 1953. Recipient: Premio Matteucci, 1926; Nobel Prize, 1938; Hughes Medal, Royal Society, London, 1942; Lewis Prize, American Philosophical Society, 1946; Congressional Medal for Merit, 1946; Transenster Medal, University of Liège, Belgium, 1947; Franklin Medal, Franklin Institute, Philadelphia, 1947; Medaglia Donegani per la Chimica, 1948; Barnard Medal, Columbia University, 1950; Dr. Bimala Law Gold Medal, Indian Association for the Advancement for the Cultivation of Science, 1951; Rumford Medal, American Academy of Arts and Sciences, 1953; Gold Medal, Italian-American Charitable Society, 1954; Award of Merit, President of the United States, and Atomic Energy Commission, 1954. Honorary doctorate: University of Heidelberg, 1936; University of Utrecht, 1936; Columbia University, 1946; Washington University, St. Louis, 1946; Yale University, New Haven, Connecticut, 1946; Rockford College, Illinois, 1947; Harvard University, Cambridge, Massachusetts, 1948; University of Rochester, New York, 1952. Member, Reale Accademia d'Italia; Accademia Gioenia di Scienze Naturali; Società Italiana della Scienze o dei XL; Imperiale Accademia del Naturalisti di Halle; Indian Academy of Sciences; Wiener Akademia der Wissenschaften; Academia Rumena; U.S. National Academy of Sciences; Franklin Institute; Order of Sons of Italy in America; Fondazione Angelo della Riccia (Honorary President, 1946); Società Italiana di Fisica; and the Royal Academy. Fellow, American Academy of Arts and Sciences and the Royal Society of Edinburgh. *Died 28 November 1954.*

PUBLICATIONS

Physics

Introduzione alla fisica atomica. Bologna, Zanichelli, 1928.
Fisica per i licei. Bologna, Zanichelli, 1929.
Molecole e cristalli. Bologna, Zanichelli, 1934; included in *Molecules, Crystals, and Quantum Statistics,* edited by Lloyd Motz, New York, Benjamin, 1966.
Thermodynamics. New York, Prentice Hall, 1937.
Fisica per istituti tecnici commerciali. Bologna, Zanichelli, 1938.
Fisica per i licei scientifici. Bologna, Zanichelli, 1938.
Elementary Particles (lectures). New Haven, Connecticut, Yale University Press, 1951.
Notes on Quantum Mechanics: A Course Given at the University of Chicago (facsimile reproduction). Chicago, University of Chicago Press, 1961.
Collected Papers (Note e Memorie). Chicago, University of Chicago Press, 2 vols., 1962, 1965.
Notes on Thermodynamics and Statistics. Chicago, University of Chicago Press, 1966.

*

Critical Studies: *Atoms in the Family: My Life with Enrico Fermi* by Laura Fermi, Chicago, University of Chicago Press, 1954; *Enrico Fermi, Physicist* by Emilio Segrè, Chicago, University of Chicago Press, 1970.

*   *   *

Enrico Fermi's professional career was unusual in many ways. For one thing, he was the rare modern physicist who was equally at home in theoretical and empirical research. His theoretical

analysis of the nature of degenerate gases (gases in which atoms have lost all or most of their electrons) was fundamental in later explanations of stellar phenomena. He also developed the mathematical theory of beta transformation, the process by which a neutron in the nucleus of an atom is transformed into a proton and an electron, with the emission of the latter as a beta particle. Some years earlier, Pauli had postulated that beta transformation would result in the release not only of the beta particle but also of a massless, chargeless particle which was later named (by Fermi) the *neutrino.* Fermi's mathematical analysis of the beta decay process showed that Pauli's theory explained precisely the empirical data on beta decay.

But perhaps the most curious and fascinating aspect of Fermi's professional career was its continuous involvement with studies of a single nuclear particle: the neutron. Fermi became interested in the neutron almost immediately upon its discovery by James Chadwick in 1932. At first, the possibilities of using the neutron in nuclear reactions seemed particularly attractive. Physicists had known how to induce nuclear transformations by firing sub-atomic particles (for example, protons and electrons) at nuclei since the first artificial transformation had been achieved by Rutherford in 1919. But prior to Chadwick's discovery the technology required for bringing about nuclear transformations was extremely difficult. The electric charge on all known "bullets" meant that they would be repelled by the cloud of orbital electrons around a nucleus (if electrons were used as bullets) or by the nucleus itself (if positively charged bullets, such as alpha particles or protons, were used as bullets). Interactions between atomic nuclei and sub-atomic particle bullets could be achieved only, therefore, by using powerful, sophisticated, expensive particle accelerators ("atom-smashers") such as the cyclotron.

Fermi realized that, having no charge, the neutron would make an ideal bullet with which to initiate nuclear changes. In fact, his early research indicated that slow neutrons had a higher probability of reacting with nuclei than did faster ones. Those which move at room temperature ("thermal neutrons") apparently had a greater opportunity of being captured by nuclei than did those moving at higher speeds. Fermi attempted to utilize this principle to convert uranium to elements of higher atomic number. Since uranium is the naturally-occurring element with the highest atomic number, this would have meant the creation of a new transuranic element that does not exist in nature.

His results proved to be inconclusive and unsatisfactory. The mixture of products obtained in the neutron/uranium reaction could not be unambiguously identified. Fermi suspected that he might have produced his sought-after transuranic element, but the evidence was too equivocal for him to make that claim.

Within a matter of five years, the proper interpretation of Fermi's work had become apparent. His thermal neutrons had initiated fission reactions in uranium, resulting in a mixture of fission products that had confounded his efforts to identify the products of the change. By the time Fermi heard of Lise Meitner's paper on fission (1939), he had received the Nobel Prize for his research on thermal neutrons and emigrated to the United States.

When President Roosevelt decided to subsidize research on nuclear fission through the Manhattan Project, Fermi was a logical choice for a leadership position in the project. He was appointed director of the research arm of the Project with the task of developing a mechanism for creating a self-sustaining nuclear fission chain reaction.

By the early 1940's, it had become apparent that such a chain reaction might be theoretically possible. The particles needed to initiate a nuclear fission reaction are just those which are also produced in the reaction. Given an adequate supply of fissionable material, then, there appeared to be no reason the reaction could not, once started, be self-sustaining.

Fermi's team at the University of Chicago was charged with the task of testing this hypothesis and determining the conditions under which a chain reaction could be made to occur. The project involved the construction of a "pile" of materials: uranium ore (the fissionable material), a moderator (to slow down the neutrons moving through the pile), and control rods (metallic bars with high affinity for neutrons, providing a way of controlling the rate at which neutrons are made available to fission uranium). The objective was to produce a "pile" of dimensions and composition such that the ratio of neutrons produced to neutrons used up would be almost exactly 1:1. This would assure a chain reaction that was "under control," that is, in which energy is released at a moderate rate. All of this was, of course, in preparation for the design and production of a nuclear chain reaction which was permitted to take place *without* control, i.e., a nuclear bomb. On December 2, 1942, Fermi's team achieved its objectives. The world's first controlled nuclear fission chain reaction took place in an abandoned squash court under the University of Chicago.

—David Newton

FEYNMAN, Richard (Philipps). American physicist. Born in New York City, 11 May 1918. Studied at the Massachusetts Institute of Technology, Cambridge, B.S. 1939, and Princeton University, New Jersey, Ph.D. 1942. Staff member, atomic bomb project, Princeton, 1942-43, and Los Alamos, New Mexico, 1943-45; Associate Professor of Theoretical Physics, Cornell University, Ithaca, New York, 1945-50. Since 1950, Professor of Theoretical Physics, California Institute of Technology, Pasadena. Recipient: Einstein Award, 1954; Nobel Prize in Physics, with J.S. Schwinger and S. Tomonaga, 1965; Oersted Medal, 1972; Niels Bohr International Gold Medal, 1973. Foreign Member, Royal Society. Address: Department of Physics, California Institute of Technology, Pasadena, California 91125, U.S.A.

PUBLICATIONS

Physics

Quantum Electrodynamics. New York, Benjamin, 1961.
Theory of Fundamental Processes: A Lecture Note Volume. New York, Benjamin, 1961.
The Feynman Lectures on Physics, with others. Reading, Massachusetts, Addison Wesley, 3 vols., 1963-64.
Quantum Mechanics and Path Integrals, with A.R. Hibbs. New York, McGraw Hill, 1965.
The Character of Physical Law (lectures). London, British Broadcasting Corporation, 1965; Cambridge, Massachusetts, Institute of Technology, 1967.
Photon-hadron Interactions. Reading, Massachusetts, Benjamin, 1972.
Statistical Mechanics (lectures). Reading, Massachusetts, Benjamin, 1972.

*   *   *

Richard Feynman shared the 1965 Nobel Prize in Physics with Sin-itiro Tomonaga and Julian Schwinger "for their fundamental work in quantum electrodynamics, with deep-ploughing consequences for the physics of elementary particles." Q.E.D. (Quantum Electrodynamics) is the theory which combines the principal theories of 20th-century physics, relativity and quantum mechanics, into a description of the interaction of electromagnetic radiation with matter. That is, it is the mathematical description of how charged particles, such as the electron, interact with other charged particles and with photons, the light quanta of the electromagnetic field. This theory, which was

developed during the 1940's, is the most accurate and precisely tested theory in physics.

Feynman's approach to Q.E.D. was radically different from that of Schwinger or Tomonaga (whose early work in Japan was unknown to Feynman and Schwinger). Feynman's approach grew out of the work begun in his Princeton Ph.D. thesis (under John Wheeler) which led to a totally new formulation of quantum mechanics. Formally, it looks quite different from the original quantum theory developed in the 1920's by Schrödinger and Heisenberg, but it is mathematically and physically equivalent.

Feynman's "space-time" view is a global (integral) rather than local (differential) description in which the fundamental quantity is the "amplitude" for a complete space-time path. Feynman has written (in his Nobel Prize speech): "The behavior of Nature is determined by saying her whole space-time path has a certain character." Amplitudes for the different ways that a particle can go from one space-time point to another are added together (superposed) and may interfere when the total amplitude sum is squared to produce a predicted probability for the particle to "propagate" between two space-time points. The basic physical quantity in Feynman's theory is the "action" (which is the integrated Lagrangian). Feynman's quantum mechanics is in the tradition of the least-action principles of classical mechanics and optics (Fermat's principle of least time).

In devising his computational scheme for quantum electrodynamics, Feynman used the space-time quantum path method applied to a version of the electrodynamics he had developed with Wheeler at Princeton. The principal difficulty which Feynman (and Schwinger) faced was to find a relativistically invariant way to remove the unphysical "divergent" (infinite) parts of the calculation, leaving finite results for the physical quantities. Recent experimental results had indicated that the energy levels of the hydrogen atom and the magnetic moment of the electron were not correctly given by the existing Dirac theory of the electron, and it was mainly these quantities which were the focus of the new Q.E.D. calculations.

It was believed (correctly) that the divergences would be removed if the computations properly incorporated the notions of mass and charge renormalization which had been developed by Kramers, Heisenberg, and Weisskopf. Feynman discovered a non-rigorous intuitive diagrammatic solution to the problem, and he gave the rules and techniques for systematically doing any calculation in Q.E.D. The diagrams enabled one to visualize the terms (arranged by magnitude) which corresponded to a perturbation series expansion of the theory. They are a pictorial representation of the elementary processes responsible for particle interactions.

"Feynman diagrams" and the accompanying calculational techniques can be applied to other theories besides Q.E.D., and they have become a basic tool for the study of almost all field theories of the elementary particles and many-particle systems.

In the early 1950's, Feynman applied his space-time quantum-mechanical approach to the problem of understanding the behavior of liquid He^4 near absolute zero. Below the so-called λ-point (2.17° K) liquid He^4 has many unusual properties, the most striking being "superfluidity," the ability to flow through small holes without resistance. From the microscopic properties of Helium atoms, Feynman showed that at the λ-point, He^4 undergoes a phase transition which is the analog of the condensation in an ideal Bose-Einstein gas, where all the particles in the system collapse into the lowest energy state. He also deduced the qualitative features of the spectrum of the low energy collective excitations ("phonons" and "rotons") of the system which are responsible for its superfluidity and the change in its behavior as the temperature is varied. During the 1950's and early 60's, Feynman also applied his path integral approach to the motion of an electron as it propagates through a polar crystal lattice. Such an electron in equilibrium with the surrounding lattice is known as a polaron; as it moves it distorts the ions in the crystal, thereby lowering its energy and increasing its effective mass.

Working with his Caltech colleague, Murray Gell-Mann,

Feynman proposed in 1958 the Conserved Vector Current hypothesis for the weak interactions. This theory has been confirmed by many experiments, including the decay of the pi-meson.

In the late 1960's Feynman proposed a simple intuitive picture—the parton model—to describe the behavior of very high energy scattering of hadrons, which are strongly interacting particles (like the proton and neutron). By viewing each hadron as composed of point constituents, called partons, Feynman was able to explain observed experimental results on electron-proton and proton-proton scattering. Feynman has made important contributions to other problems, including the still unsolved question of how to quantize gravity—that is, unite quantum mechanics with Einstein's Theory of Gravitation (the General Theory of Relativity).

Feynman is a dynamic, exciting and extroverted lecturer. Several books have been developed from edited versions of his transcribed lectures. During the early 1960's, he lectured to the freshmen and sophomores at Caltech and the resulting three volumes, *The Feynman Lectures on Physics*, are read with delight and enormous profit by all physicists—from freshmen to professors.

The main characteristic of Feynman's contributions is their striking originality. Each problem was attacked in a way radically unlike other existing approaches. He succeeded in finding a unique intuitive way of thinking about the physical situation. And with each approach he developed special techniques for calculating the important physical quantities. His new point of view and methods of calculation have found myriads of applications far from their original use. In his Nobel Lecture, Feynman has written that "the special viewpoint gives one a power and clarity of thought," and "furthermore, in the search for new laws, you always have the psychological excitement of feeling that possibly nobody has yet thought of the crazy possibility you are looking at right now."

—Harvey Shepard

FIRTH, J(ohn) R(upert). British philologist. Born 17 June 1890. Studied at Leeds University, B.A. 1911 (first class honours in history), M.A. 1913. Served in the British Army, 1914-18. Lecturer in History, City of Leeds Training College, before 1914; Professor of English, University of Punjab, Lahore, India, 1920-28; Senior Lecturer, Department of Phonetics, University College, London, 1928-37; Senior Lecturer in Linguistics and Indian Phonetics, School of Oriental and African Studies, University of London, 1938-40; Reader, 1940-44, Chair of General Linguistics, 1944-56, and Professor Emeritus, 1956-60, University of London. Leverhulme Fellow, 1937-38; Visiting Professor, University of Alexandria, Egypt, 1947; Visiting Lecturer, University of Edinburgh, 1958. President, 1954-57, and Vice President, 1957-60, Philological Society of Great Britain. Honorary doctorate: University of Edinburgh, 1959. Honorary Fellow, School of Oriental and African Studies, University of London. *Died 14 December 1960.*

PUBLICATIONS

Linguistics

Speech. London, Benn, 1930.
The Tongues of Men. London, Watts, 1937.
Papers in Linguistics, 1934-1951. London and New York, Oxford University Press, 1957.
Selected Papers of J.R. Firth, 1952-59, edited by F.R. Palmer. Bloomington, Indiana University Press, 1968.

Other

Editor, with A.H. Harley, *Teach Yourself Hindustani* by Thomas G. Bailey. London, English Universities Press, 1950.

*

Critical Studies: *In Memory of J.R. Firth,* edited by Charles Ernest Bazell, London, Longmans, 1966; *Principles of Firthian Linguistics* by T.F. Mitchell, London, Longmans, 1975.

* * *

J.R. Firth inaugurated linguistics as a separate, recognized academic discipline in Britain and founded the one distinctively British approach to the subject (commonly called the "London School" and represented today by M.A.K. Halliday and R.A. Hudson).

Firth's linguistic theories were chiefly concerned with phonological analysis. His approach to phonological description was "polysystemic" and "prosodic." The term "polysystemic" refers to the idea that the range of alternative possibilities at any one place in a phonological structure will not in general be in a one-to-one correspondence with the range of alternatives at another place in the structure. For instance, the possible syllable-initial consonants in a given language may be quite different in number and in quality from the possible syllable-final consonants—in which case it would be artificial to try to link pairs of initial and final consonants (as was usual in contemporary American linguistics) as "allophones" of single "phonemes." Prosodic analysis involved another departure from phoneme theory: rather than treating a linguistic form as a linear sequence of units like beads on a chain, with "suprasegmental" phenomena playing an uneasy peripheral role, Firth saw an utterance as a strand made up of simultaneous and overlapping phonological units of many different sizes: some "prosodies" extend over a consonant cluster, others over a syllable, and others again (e.g. in vowel-harmony languages) may extend over entire words.

Firth, like his colleagues at the School of Oriental and African Studies, was influenced by familiarity with exotic, non-European languages, and he regarded American phoneme theory as unduly swayed by prejudices deriving from the particular type of writing-system which happens to be used for European languages, namely linear alphabetic notation. Firth was undoubtedly correct in suggesting that the linear model of phonology distorts the intuitions of speakers of languages which are not written alphabetically.

Another aspect of Firth's linguistics is less easy to agree with. Firth saw sound and meaning in language as related quite directly. He did not accept André Martinet's doctrine of the "double articulation" of language, according to which the way a language is organized into meaningful elements is independent of, and only indirectly related to, the articulation imposed by the language on the vocal medium. Firth came close to suggesting that a phonological analysis of a language in his style constituted an analysis of the *whole* of the structure of the language: a phonological system is a set of choices between alternatives, and wherever we have choice we have meaning. Yet the fact is that the choice of a *p* rather than a *b* or *t* as the first sound in a word has no particular implications, in isolation, for the meaning of the word.

Firth's difficulty arose in part because, under the influence of his friend Bronislaw Malinowski—and in harmony with the behaviourist philosophical atmosphere of his day—Firth held rather strange, reductivist views about the nature of meaning. He sometimes suggested, for instance, that the meaning of a word could be identified with the set of linguistic contexts in which the word occurs—which has the advantage of making "meaning" a thoroughly objective concept, but one that loses almost all connexion with its pre-theoretical use.

The discipline of linguistics expanded greatly in Britain (for extraneous reasons) in the late 1960's, at a time when American linguistics was particularly dynamic and in consequence a period of study in the U.S.A. became a high priority for young British linguists. As a result, Firthian linguistics has virtually ceased to exist as an independent tradition, and, when Firthian approaches to phonology have been introduced into American linguistics, those responsible for introducing these concepts have appeared to be unaware of their British antecedents.

—Geoffrey Sampson

FIRTH, Raymond (William). British social anthropologist. Born in Auckland, New Zealand, 25 March 1901. Studied at Auckland University College, B.A. 1921, M.A. 1922, Diploma in Social Science 1923, and at London School of Economics, Ph.D. 1927. Served in the Naval Intelligence Division of Admiralty, 1941-44. Married Rosemary Upcott in 1936; 1 son. Conducted field research in anthropology, British Solomon Islands, 1928-29, and in Kelantan, Malaysia, 1939-40; social research surveys in West Africa, 1945, in Malaya, 1947 and 1963, in New Guinea, 1951, and in Tikopia, 1952, 1966 and 1973. Lecturer in Anthropology, 1930-31, and Acting Professor, 1931-32, University of Sydney; Lecturer in Anthropology, 1933-35, Reader, 1935-44, Professor of Anthropology, 1944-68, and since 1968 Professor Emeritus, London School of Economics. Visiting Professor, University of Chicago, 1955, 1971, University of Hawaii, Honolulu, 1968-69, University of British Columbia, Vancouver, 1969, Cornell University, Ithaca, New York, 1970, City University of New York, 1971, Australian National University, Canberra, 1972-73, University of California at Davis, 1974, University of California at Berkeley, and University of Auckland, 1978. Secretary, Colonial Social Science Research Council, 1944-45; Fellow, Center for Advanced Studies in the Behavioral Sciences, Stanford, California, 1958-59. Honorary Secretary, 1936-39, and President, 1953-55, Royal Anthropological Institute; Life President, Association of Social Anthropologists of the Commonwealth. Recipient: Leverhulme Research Fellowship, 1939-40; Viking Fund Medal, 1959; Huxley Memorial Medal, Royal Anthropological Institute, 1959. D.Ph.: University of Oslo, 1965; LL.D.: University of Michigan, Ann Arbor, 1967; Litt.D.: University of East Anglia, 1968; D.H.L.: University of Chicago, 1968; D.Letters: Australian National University, 1969; D.Sc.: University of British Columbia, 1970; D.Litt: University of Exeter, 1972; D.Litt: University of Auckland, 1978. Fellow, British Academy. Foreign Honorary Member, American Academy of Arts and Sciences, and Royal Society of New Zealand; Foreign Member, American Philosophical Society, and Royal Danish Academy of Sciences and Letters. Knighted, 1973. Address: 33 Southwood Avenue, London N6, England.

PUBLICATIONS

Social Anthropology

The Kauri-Gum Industry: Some Economic Aspects. Auckland, W.G. Skinner, 1924.
Primitive Economics of the New Zealand Maori. New York, Dutton, 1929; as *Economics of the New Zealand Maori,* Atlantic Highlands, New Jersey, Humanities Press, 1959.
Art and Life in New Guinea. Ipswich, Suffolk, Studio Publications, 1936.
We the Tikopia: A Sociological Study of Kinship in Primitive Polynesia. London, Allen and Unwin, 1936; New York, Barnes and Noble, 1961.
Human Types: An Introduction to Social Anthropology.

London, Thomas Nelson, 1938; revised edition, London, Sphere, 1975.
Primitive Polynesian Economy. London, Routledge, 1939.
The Work of the Gods in Tikopia. London, Lund Humphries, 2 vols., 1940; Atlantic Highlands, New Jersey, Humanities Press, 1 vol., 1967.
Malay Fishermen: Their Peasant Economy. London, Kegan Paul, 1946.
Elements of Social Organization. London, Watts, 1951; Boston, Beacon, 1963.
The Fate of the Soul: An Interpretation of Some Primitive Concepts. Cambridge, Cambridge University Press, 1955.
Social Anthropology as Science and as Art. Dunedin, New Zealand, University of Otago Press, 1958.
Social Change in Tikopia: A Re-Study of a Polynesian Community After a Generation. London, Macmillan, 1959.
History and Traditions of Tikopia. New Zealand, Polynesian Society, 1961.
A Study in Ritual Modification: The Work of the Gods in Tikopia in 1929 and 1952, with James Spillius. London, Royal Anthropological Institute, 1963.
Essays on Social Organization and Values. London, Athlone Press, 1964; Atlantic Highlands, New Jersey, Humanities Press, 1969.
Tikopia Ritual and Belief. Boston, Beacon, 1967.
Rank and Religion in Tikopia. Boston, Beacon, 1970.
The Sceptical Anthropologist? Social Anthropology and Marxist Views on Society. London, Oxford University Press, 1972.
Symbols: Public and Private. Ithaca, New York, Cornell University Press, 1973.

Other

Editor, with E.E. Evans-Pritchard and others, *Essays Presented to C.G. Seligman.* London, Kegan Paul, 1934.
Editor and Contributor, *Two Studies of Kinship in London.* London, Athlone Press, 1956.
Editor and Contributor, *Man and Culture: An Evaluation of the Work of Bronislaw Malinowski.* Atlantic Highlands, New Jersey, Humanities Press, 1957.
Editor, with B.S. Yamey, and Contributor, *Capital, Saving, and Credit in Peasant Societies from Asia, Oceania, The Caribbean, and Middle America.* London, Aldine, 1964.
Editor and Contributor, *Themes in Economic Anthropology.* London, Tavistock, 1967.
Editor and Commentator, *Kinship and Social Organization,* by William Halse Rivers. Atlantic Highlands, New Jersey, Humanities Press, 1968.
Editor, with Jane Hubert and Anthony Forge, *Families and Their Relatives: Kinship in a Middle-Class Sector of London—An Anthropological Study.* Atlantic Highlands, New Jersey, Humanities Press, 1969.

*   *   *

Raymond Firth pointed British social anthropology toward its characteristic concern with "on-the-ground" behavior, and continued the tradition of empiricism begun by his mentor, Bronislaw Malinowski. A scholar of tremendous breadth, Firth has been an influential teacher to several generations of students. He has written major works on religion, symbolism, and social change, and, with the London Kinship Project, pioneered the study of kinship in complex society. Yet Firth is best known for his work in primitive economics and social organization. *We, The Tikopia* is an anthropological classic, one of the first expert analyses of kinship and rank in a Polynesian society. Firth used the term "ramage" to describe the "branching" quality of the Polynesian ranked lineage, which segments along the lines of senior/junior siblings. But in the name of empiricism, Firth has consistently rejected the concept of "social structure" as a reified abstraction. His work stresses the dynamic aspects of social life.

Firth's analyses of primitive and peasant economies mark the emergence of economic anthropology. Like Malinowski, Firth assumes that economic acitivity "is at root the response of man to certain primary physical needs." In keeping with his early training as an economist, he holds that the assumptions of Western economics are applicable to primitive societies:

> The basic aspects of the Tikopia economy do correspond to the data of ordinary economic analysis, and can be covered by the same general propositions. There is a scarcity of the means available for satisfying wants,... and on the whole choice is exercised in a rational manner....

Primitive man too responds to "the logic of scarcity," and is not immune from considerations of "economic advantage": "the notion of economy and of economizing are *not* basically separate [his italics]." The principle of maximization is cross-culturally valid if one broadens it to include "status and prestige" as well as material wealth. But characteristically, Firth eschews overly theoretical discussions: "the issue in this abstract form is not highly relevant." His economic analyses are always firmly tied to ethnographic description.

It is important to note that, in the early 1920's and 1930's, Firth was asserting the humanity of primitive man in the face of the evolutionist school's derogatory labels of "savagery" and "barbarism." By applying the concepts of Western economics to subsistence-level societies, Firth intended to show that primitive and "civilized" men were not fundamentally different and were guided by similar motives. He denied that primitive man is "concerned solely with the food quest," and lives "by a day-to-day satisfaction of his needs." Firth's economic anthropology is not a crude material determinism, but is eminently social in nature; he everywhere stresses that "economic relationships are also explicitly social relationships." When applying the concept of "rational choice," one must remember that such choice is "largely dictated by the traditional pattern of the institutions and values of the culture." Firth is not interested in technology and environment as such; he sees economic anthropology as focusing on "relationships between persons rather than between persons and things."

Firth's work on religion bears the stamp of functionalism. He admittedly is not concerned with beliefs *per se*, but with the social organization of ritual and the relation of religion to other spheres of social life. He is not so much interested in the content of ritual as in "the *when* and *how*" of its performance. Here he reveals the functionalist premise that "by consideration of what a thing *does*...one is likely to best understand what it *is* [his italics]." In his description of the Tikopia ritual cycle, Firth stresses the effect, or function, of social integration: "the Work of the Gods was performed as much for the sake of society as for that of religion." Ritual "expresses social status by reaffirmation," and in Tikopia served to reinforce the social hierarchy.

The influence of Malinowski's empiricism is apparent in Firth's rejection of abstract models, which he makes explicit in his major theoretical work, *Elements of Social Organization*. For Firth, the anthropologist's object of study is behavior: "The anthropologist above all sees at first hand what people actually do." Firth's theoretical hesitancy follows from the premise that only physical phenomena are objectively real:

> Social anthropologists are usually said to study a society, a community, a culture. But this is not what they *observe*. The material for their observation is human activity. They do not even *observe* social relationships; they infer them from physical acts [italics in original].

Voicing nominalist objections, Firth is reluctant to attribute any precedence to "social" phenomena, which he sees as epiphenomena of human acitivity. Radcliffe-Brown's definition of social structure as "the network of actually existing social rela-

tions" is a useful metaphor, but Firth cautions that "social relations" is, after all, an abstraction. Structure is an aspect of "social action," and is deduced after the fact from observed bits of behavior. It is the activity that is real; structure is a generalization from that reality, a "heuristic tool rather than a substantial social entity."

Firth sees "structure" as a label for regularity, "the persistence or repetition of behavior." These antecedent patterns serve as a "framework for action" for members of a society. In contrast, social organization includes actions outside "the structural framework" and not determined by structural precedents. The notion of organization "involves that more spontaneous, decisive activity which does not follow from role-playing." The determinant of this "decisive activity" is individual motivation, which Firth describes in economistic terms. Given unexpected contingencies, individuals effect structural change by pursuing their several goals, and by not repeating behavior:

> ...circumstances provide always new combinations of factors. Fresh choices open, fresh decisions have to be made.

> ...choice is exercised in a field of available alternatives, resources are mobilized and decisions are taken in light of probable social costs and benefits.

> Ultimately, the social structure may have to give way through a concatenation of organizational acts.

Thus in Firth's paradigm, social organization is more significant than "structure" for understanding human behavior, which is ultimately explicable in terms of "choice-making and decision-taking" from a limited set of alternatives. Even primitive man faces the dilemma of scarce means. One of Firth's "principles of social organization" is "economy of effort," which he says relies on the perception of the "limited character" of resources. Applying the assumptions of Western economics to social organization, he states: "We can follow the economists, and say that the *fact* of decision is the most important thing." Firth's teachings, emphasizing empirical discovery and the dynamic aspects of human activity, form the basis of the "action theory" that underlies much British social anthropology today.

—Jocelyn Linnekin

FISHER, Irving. American economist. Born in Saugerties, New York, 17 February 1867. Studied at Yale University, New Haven, Connecticut, B.A. 1888, Ph.D. 1891; also studied in Berlin and Paris, 1893-94. Married Margaret Hazard in 1893; 3 children. Tutor in Mathematics, 1890-93, Assistant Professor, 1893-95, Assistant Professor of Political Economy, 1895-98, Professor, 1898-1935, and Professor Emeritus, 1935-47, Yale University. Hitchcock Lecturer, University of California, Berkeley, 1917; Visiting Lecturer, London School of Economics and Political Science, 1921, and Geneva School of International Studies, 1927. Editor, *Yale Review*, 1896-1910. Vice-President and Director, Gotham Hospital, Gotham Medical Center; Chairman of the Board and Director, Check Master Plan, Inc.; Gyrobalance Corporation; and Automatic Signal Corporation; Director and Member of Executive Committee, Remington Rand; Director, Cowles Commission for Economic Research; Buffalo Electric Furnace Corporation; Sonotone Corporation; Latimer Laboratory; and the Life Extension Institute. President, American Association of Labor Legislation, 1915-17; Citizen's Commission on War-Time Prohibition, 1917; Committee of Sixty on National Prohibition, 1917; National Institute of Social Sciences, 1917; American Economic Association, 1918; Eugenics Research Association, 1920; Pro-League Independents, 1920;

Econometric Society, 1931-33; and the American Statistics Association, 1932; Founder and First President, American Eugenics Society, 1923-26. Honorary doctorate: Rollins College, Winter Park, Florida, 1932; University of Athens, 1937; University of Lausanne, 1937. Member, Royal Economic Society; Reale Accademia dei Lincei, Rome; Norwegian Academy of Science and Letters; Instituto Lombardo, Milan. Fellow, Royal Statistics Society, A.A.A.S. *Died 29 April 1947.*

PUBLICATIONS

Economics, Mathematics and Social Comment

Essentials of Analytical Trigonometry. New York, Macmillan, 1890.

Appreciation and Interest: A Study of the Influence of Monetary Appreciation and Depreciation on the Rate of Interest, with Application to the Bimetallic Controversy and the Theory of Interest. New York, Macmillan, 1896.

Logarithms of Numbers, with Andrew W. Phillips. New York, Harper, 1896.

A Brief Introduction to the Infinitesimal Calculus. New York and London, Macmillan, 1897.

Elements of Geometry, with Andrew W. Phillips. New York, Harper, 1897-98.

The Nature of Capital and Income. New York and London, Macmillan, 1906.

The Rate of Interest: Its Nature, Determination and Relation to Economic Phenomena. New York, Macmillan, 1907; enlarged edition as *The Theory of Interest as Determined by Impatience to Spend Income and Opportunity to Invest,* New York, Macmillan, 1930.

Introduction to Economic Science. New York, Macmillan, 1910; enlarged edition as *Elementary Principles of Economics,* New York, Macmillan, 1911.

The Purchasing Power of Money: Its Determination and Relation to Credit, Interest and Crises, with Harry G. Brown. New York, Macmillan, 1911.

How to Invest When Prices Are Rising: A Scientific Method of Providing for the Increasing Cost of Living, with others. Scranton, Pennsylvania, G.L. Sumner, 1912.

Instability of Gold (lectures). New York, Alexander Hamilton Institute, 1912.

What an International Conference on the High Cost of Living Could Do. Vienna, F. Jasper, 1913.

Why Is the Dollar Shrinking? A Study in the High Cost of Living. New York, Macmillan, 1914.

The "Ratio" Chart for Plotting Statistics. New Haven, Connecticut, Yale University, 1917.

The New Price Revolution (lecture). Washington, D.C., Government Printing Office, 1919.

Money and Credit. Boston, American Institute of Finance, 1920.

Stabilizing the Dollar: A Plan to Stabilize the General Price Level without Fixing Individual Prices. New York, Macmillan, 1920.

The Making of Index Numbers: A Study of their Varieties, Tests, and Reliability. Boston, Houghton Mifflin, 1922.

Fluctuations in Price Levels. Newton, Massachusetts, Pollak Foundation for Economic Research, 1923.

Stabilization of Purchasing Power of Money: Hearings Before the Committee on Banking and Currency of the House of Representatives. Washington, D.C., Government Printing Office, 1923.

Unstable Money and the Farmer (lecture). Springfield, Illinois, Illinois Farmers' Institute, 1926.

The Money Illusion (lectures). New York, Adelphi, 1928.

The Stock Market Crash—and After. New York, Macmillan, 1930.

Booms and Depressions: Some First Principles. New York,

Adelphi, 1932.

After Reflation What?, with Herbert W. Fisher. New York, Adelphi, 1933; as *Mastering the Crisis,* London, Allen and Unwin, 1934.

Inflation?, with Herbert W. Fisher. New York, Adelphi, 1933.

Stamp Scrip, with others. New York, Adelphi, 1933.

The Debt-Inflation Theory of Great Depressions. Boston, National Economic League, 1934.

Stable Money: A History of the Movement, with Hans R.L. Cohrssen. New York, Adelphi, 1934; as *Stabilised Money: A History of the Movement,* London, Allen and Unwin, 1935.

100% Money: Designed to Keep Checking Banks 100% Liquid; to Prevent Inflation and Deflation; Largely to Cure or Prevent Depressions; and to Wipe Out Much of the National Debt. New York, Adelphi, 1935.

Constructive Income Taxation: A Proposal for Reform, with Herbert W. Fisher. New York and London, Harper, 1942.

Other

The Modern Crusade against Tuberculosis. Chicago, State Association for Prevention of Tuberculosis, 1908.

Bulletin 30 of the Committee of One Hundred on National Health. Being a Report on National Vitality, Its Wastes and Conservation. Washington, D.C., Government Printing Office, 1909.

The Costs of Tuberculosis in the United States and Their Reduction (lecture). New Haven, Connecticut, Committee of One Hundred on National Health, 1909.

Economic Aspect of Lengthening Human Life (lecture). New York, 1909.

Movements to Lengthen Life, with Dr. Burnside Foster. New York, Association of Life Insurance Presidents, 1909.

Statement of Professor Fisher Before the Committee on Interstate and Foreign Commerce, House of Representatives, on National Health Legislation. Washington, D.C., Government Printing Office, 1909.

Memorial Relation to the Conservation of Human Life as Contemplated by Bill (S. 1) Providing for a United States Public Health Service, with Emily F. Robbins. Washington, D.C., Government Printing Office, 1912.

Sale of Intoxicating Liquors: Statement of Prof. Irving Fisher Before a Subcommittee on Excise and Liquor Legislation of the Committee on the District of Columbia. Washington, D.C., Government Printing Office, 1912.

Eugenics. New York, Life Extension Institute, 1915.

How to Live: Rules for Healthful Living, Based on Modern Science, with Eugene Lyman Fisk. New York and London, Funk and Wagnalls, 1915; selections as *Health for the Soldier and Sailor,* New York and London, Funk and Wagnalls, 1918.

How to Live Long. New York, Metropolitan Life Insurance Co., 1915.

Life Extension (lecture). Poughkeepsie, New York, Vassar College, 1917.

Public Health as a Social Movement. Chicago, National Conference of Social Work, 1917.

A Clear Answer to Ex-President Taft, the Most Prominent Anti-National Prohibitionist. Boston, Massachusetts Anti-Saloon League, 1918.

The Effect of Diet on Endurance. New Haven, Connecticut, Yale University Press, 1918.

Independents, You Are to Decide this Election. Read, Think, Then—Vote! New York, Pro-League Independents, 1920.

League or War? New York and London, Harper, 1923.

America's Interest in World Peace. New York and London, Funk and Wagnalls, 1924.

Prohibition at Its Worst. New York, Macmillan, 1926.

Prohibition Still at Its Worst, with H. Bruce Brougham. New York, Alcohol Information Committee, 1928.

The "Noble Experiment", with H. Bruce Brougham. New York, Alcohol Information Committee, 1930.

What Are the People Thinking? New York, League of Nations Association, 1932.

World Maps and Globes, with O.M. Miller. New York, Essential Books, 1944.

Editor, *Bibliographies of the Present Officers of Yale University: Together with the Bibliography of the Late President Porter.* New Haven, Connecticut, Tuttle Morehouse and Taylor, 1893.

*

Bibliography: *A Bibliography of the Writings of Irving Fisher* by Irving Norton Fisher, New Haven, Connecticut, Yale University Library, 1961.

Critical Studies: *My Father, Irving Fisher* by Irving Norton Fisher, New York, Comet Press, 1956; *Ten Economic Studies in the Tradition of Irving Fisher* by William Fellner and others, New York and London, Wiley, 1968.

*   *   *

Irving Fisher's achievements in economics include landmark contributions to abstract theory, applied theory and empirical analysis.

Fisher's advancement of pure theory started with his Ph.D. dissertation. In 1947 Ragnar Frisch, the Norwegian econometrician and Nobel laureate, would remark that "It will be hard to find any single work that has been more influential than Fisher's dissertation." Fisher used mathematical analysis to investigate general equilibrium theory and value theory. He generated utility theory in a way which enabled him to compute cardinal utility (although he recognized that only ordinal utility was required for value theory development). His cardinal approach was designed to apply the theory to answer social questions by computing utility gains and losses.

It was Fisher's later contributions, however, that were to increase his contemporary popularity and fame. *The Purchasing Power of Money* was considered a classic. In it he produced an analysis of the "transition period" between the initial and final equilibrium following a monetary disturbance which is as current today as when it was written. Using the framework of the Quantity Theory of Money, Fisher described causes of the credit cycle. His presentation of the effects of sluggish interest rate and price adjustment was so insightful and timeless that on reading today it seems to have been written to depict the severe recession of 1981-82.

The relation between interest and inflation rates was actually first studied by Fisher in his book *Appreciation and Interest*. Although previously defined, Fisher's complete analysis of the relation between real and nominal interest rates was totally accurate and, in ways, novel.

The *Rate of Interest* contained many sophisticated empirical tests scientifically analyzing the effect of *rising* prices as well as *high* prices on the interest rate. He found, among other items, that interest rates are affected by prior events of as long as 30 years.

From a theoretical standpoint, some today regard Fisher's contributions to the theory of interest as his most important. His general equilibrium presentation antedates later classic works. Samuelson calls Fisher's interest theory "modern".

Perhaps Fisher's most important *application* of theory, however, was his advocacy of a monetary stabilization policy to eliminate the effects of changes in the quantity of gold on the price level. In *Stabilizing the Dollar* Fisher proposed varying the gold content of the dollar to maintain its purchasing power. To the extent that such a policy would have prevented large decreases in the quantity of money, the Great Depression could possibly have been avoided. Fisher was advocating a non-discretionary activist monetary policy which would use feedback

based on a price index. Fifty years later empirical work would support the use of feedback rules to stabilize the economy.

Fisher's theoretical applications and empirical work was not limited to interest rates. His *The Making of Index Numbers* was an attempt to create better measures of macroeconomic variables. These would be used for, among many things, his feedback stabilization rule.

Fisher also studied speculation and, in particular, the stock market. He created several indices, and described the immediate causes of the 1929 stock market crash. His reputation suffered when his stock market predictions did not include the 1929 drop nor the later severe drops of 1931 and 1932.

Fisher's contributions to economics and economic statistics were many and were substantial. He was able to examine economic data to understand the fundamental causes of the phenomena he observed. It was the combination of scientific technique in both theory and empirical work together with an intuitive understanding of the economy that led to his successes. It is a mistake to judge Fisher's accomplishments solely on the basis of any incorrect stock market predictions, for he was, without doubt, one of the greatest scientific American economists.

—Norman Obst

FLEMING, Alexander. British bacteriologist. Born in Lochfield, Darvel, Scotland, 6 August 1881. Studied at the University of London, B.S., and St. Mary's Hospital Medical School, London, M.B. 1906. Served in the Royal Medical Corps during World War I: Captain (mentioned in despatches). Married Sarah Marion McElroy in 1915; 1 son; married Dr. Amalia Koutsouri-Voureka in 1953. Faculty Member, St. Mary's Hospital Medical School, 1908-14, 1918-28; Professor of Bacteriology, 1928-48, and Professor Emeritus, 1948-55, University of London. Hunterian Professor, 1919, and Arris and Gale Lecturer, 1929, Royal College of Surgeons, London; William Julius Mickle Fellowship, London University, 1942; Charles Mickle Fellowship, University of Toronto, 1944; Cutter Lecturer, Harvard University, Cambridge, Massachusetts, 1945. Rector, University of Edinburgh, 1951-54. Recipient: John Scott Medal, City Guild, Philadelphia, 1944; Cameron Prize, University of Edinburgh, 1945; Nobel Prize in Medicine, with E.B. Chain and H.W. Florey, 1945; Moxon Medal, 1945, and Honorary Gold Medal, 1946, Royal College of Physicians, London; Albert Gold Medal, Royal Society of Arts, London, 1946; Gold Medal, Royal Society of Medicine, London, 1947; Medal for Merit, U.S.A., 1947; Grand Cross of Alphonse X the Wise, Spain, 1948. Fellow of the Royal Society, Royal College of Physicians, and Royal College of Surgeons. Member, French Academy of Sciences. Knighted, 1944. *Died 11 March 1955.*

PUBLICATIONS

Medicine

Studies in Wound Infections, with others. London, H.M. Stationery Office, 1929.
Recent Advances in Vaccine and Serum Therapy, with G.F. Petrie. Philadelphia, Blakiston, 1934.
Chemotheraphy: Yesterday, Today, and To-morrow (lecture). Cambridge, Cambridge University Press, 1946.

Other

Editor, *Penicillin, Its Practical Application.* London, Butterworth, and Philadelphia, Blakiston, 1946.

*

Critical Studies: *Fleming: Discoverer of Penicillin* by L.J. Ludovici, London, Dakers, 1952 (contains a full bibliography); *The Life of Sir Alexander Fleming, Discoverer of Penicillin* by André Maurois, New York, Dutton, 1959.

*   *   *

Alexander Fleming was a physician whose career was devoted primarily to the investigation of the human body's defense mechanisms against infectious agents, especially bacteria. His earliest work as a doctor was centered in a research laboratory attached to St. Mary's Hospital in London. At St. Mary's Fleming modified existing diagnostic techniques for the detection of syphilis. His work in this area made it possible for physicians to carry out tests for syphilis using only 1/10 the amount of blood required previously.

With the onset of World War I Fleming's research shifted its focus to medical problems of a different nature. Physicians knew that many lives were being lost due to infections resulting from explosive-related wounds. Fleming and his mentor, Almroth Wright, quickly set off to France where they organized the first war-time laboratory for medical research. Fleming found that, while many war wounds were infected with many kinds of microbes, blood stream infection was always associated with a specific microbe, namely streptococcus. From these observations he concluded that wound infection was caused primarily by the deep penetration of clothing infected with streptococcus into the tissue and bone. He figured that the penetration was caused by the force imparted by projectiles traveling at extremely high velocities. Fleming also found that the use of antiseptics either on the front line or at the base hospitals was ineffective, a discovery which went against the current practice of military surgeons. His explanation of the surgeons' failures was twofold: 1) the antiseptics did not usually reach the microbes, which were often found deep within the bone, muscle or other tissue; and 2) the potency of antiseptics was reduced by the formation of pus. Since Fleming was puzzled by the second explanation, he quickly turned his attention to the anti-bacterial action of pus. He learned that certain cells contained in the pus were able to kill large numbers of bacteria. Thus, the introduction of highly concentrated antiseptic drugs directly into the blood stream interfered with the "microbe-killing" cells contained in the pus. Fleming continued to perform experiments to demonstrate the fact that germicides actually interfered with the body's natural ability to fight harmful bacteria. Ironically, the continued use of antiseptics was doing more harm than good.

Fleming's interest in physiological defense mechanisms of the human body led him down the road to yet another significant discovery—an enzyme found in nasal secretions that dissolved bacteria. He called this enzyme "lysozyme," which means dissolving enzyme. At the time of this discovery bacteriologists throughout Europe were studying nasal secretions with the hope of finding the bacterium responsible for the "common cold." Thus, the significance of Fleming's discovery was that he provided an explanation for the inability to locate bacteria in nasal secretions. The "lysozymes" were destroying all the evidence. Although Fleming (or any other bacteriologist) was unsuccessful at discovering the cause of the "common cold," he was able to show the bactricidal actions of extracts from sweat, sputum, tears, and many tissues found in the body. The discovery of "lysozyme" provided the first glimpse at how enzymes ward off bacterial infection, which in effect opened up a new field of investigation focussing on the immunological properties of enzymes.

In 1928, while he continued his work on bactricidal agents, Fleming noticed that some of the bacterial cultures were growing in the company of contaminating mold. Fleming's superb observational skills served him well once again. He saw that those bacteria surrounded by mold were becoming translucent. Fleming linked the translucence to the same process he observed during his experiments on lysozymes, that is, that the mold was dissolving the bacteria. He decided at once to grow the mold (now called *Penicillium notatum*) on a nourishing culture medium. He soon discovered that the culture medium had antibacterial effects three times more powerful than the antiseptics used up to that time. Upon further investigation, "penicillin" proved to have other properties of considerable importance, that it was readily diffused and, most importantly, that it demonstrated few harmful effects on normal tissue or on the cells that naturally fight off bacteria. Fleming had arrived at a viable therapeutic solution for the treatment of infection. At one and the same time "penicillin" proved to be a powerful bactricide that also had no deleterious effects on the body's natural defense mechanisms.

Unfortunately, it was extremely difficult to preserve the bactricidal effect of "penicillin" because it appeared to deteriorate rapidly. This fact placed a damper on any immediate hope of purifying the substance. Consequently, Fleming never seriously followed through with developing penicillin as a drug that could be used in a clinical setting. He did, however, apply his discovery as a laboratory aid by showing that it was extremely useful for suppressing the growth of undesired bacteria. This innovation made a marked improvement on bacteriologists' abilities to obtain pure cultures of bacteria.

Fleming's discovery of penicillin began a stream of investigations, all of which resulted in the preparation of an extract of "penicillin" (Howard Florey and Ernst Chain, 1940) that was not subject to fast decomposition and was an active anti-bacterial agent. By 1944 penicillin's unique position in therapeautic medicine was fully recognized. Physicians were now armed with a remedy against a variety of infectious maladies, including staphloccal septicemia, pneumonia, infections of wounds and burns, gas gangrene, syphilis and gonorrhea.

—Randall Davey Bird

FORTES, Meyer. British social anthropologist. Born in Britstown, Cape, South Africa, 25 April 1906. Studied at the University of Cape Town (Roderick Noble Scholar, 1926, and Willem Hiddingh Scholar, 1927-30); University of London (Ratan Tata Scholar, 1930-31, and Rockefeller Fellow, 1933-34, both at London School of Economics), Ph.D. Served with the National Service, in West Africa, 1942-44. Married Sonia in 1928 (died, 1956); one daughter; married Doris Y. Mayer in 1960. Fellow, International African Institute, 1934-38; conducted field research, in Northern Territories, Gold Coast, 1934-37, in Nigeria, 1941-42, in Ashanti Gold Coast, 1945-46, and in Bechuanaland, 1948. Lecturer, London School of Economics, 1938-39; Research Lecturer, Oxford University, 1939-41; Head of Sociological Department, West African Institute, Accra, Gold Coast, 1944-46; Reader in Social Anthropology, Oxford University, 1946-50; Fellow of King's College, Cambridge, 1950-78, and William Wyse Professor of Social Anthropology, Cambridge University, 1950-73. Visiting Professor, University of Chicago, 1954, 1973; University of Ghana (Leverhulme Fellow), 1971; Australian National University, Canberra, 1975; University of California at Santa Cruz, 1977; Northwestern University, Evanston, Illinois (M.J. Herskovits Fellow), 1978; and University of Manchester, 1980. Fellow, Center for Advanced Study in Behavioral Science, Stanford, California, 1958-59, 1967-68; and University College, London, 1975. Lectureships: Josiah Mason, University of Birmingham, 1949; Frazer, University of Glasgow, 1956; Henry Myers, Royal Anthropological Institute, 1960; Lewis Henry Morgan, University of Rochester, New York, 1963; Munro, University of Edinburgh, 1964, 1973; Emanuel Miller Memorial, Association of Child Psychology and Psychiatry, 1972; Ernest Jones Memorial, British Psychonanalytical Society,

1973; Marett, Oxford University, 1974; Huxley Memorial, Royal Anthropological Institute, 1977. President, Royal Anthropological Institute, and Honorary Editor, Journal of the Royal Anthropological Institute, 1947-53; Member, Executive Committee, British Sociological Association, 1952-55; President, Section H, British Association for the Advancement of Science, 1953; Chairman, Association of Social Anthropologists, 1970-73; President, Section 25, Australian and New Zealand Association for the Advancement of Science, 1975. Recipient: Rivers Medal, Royal Anthropological Institute, 1973. D.H.L.: University of Chicago, 1973; D.Litt.: University of Belfast, 1975. Foreign Honorary Member, American Academy of Arts and Sciences, 1964; Foreign Member, American Philosophical Association, 1972; Honorary Fellow, London School of Economics, 1979. *Died 27 January 1983.*

PUBLICATIONS

Social Anthropology

The Dynamics of Clanship among the Tallensi: The First Part of an Analysis of the Social Structure of a Trans-Volta Tribe. Oxford, Oxford University Press, 1945.
The Web of Kinship among the Tallensi: The Second Part of an Analysis of the Social Structure of a Trans-Volta Tribe. Oxford, Oxford University Press, 1949.
Social Anthropology at Cambridge since 1900 (lecture). Cambridge, Cambridge University Press, 1953.
Oedipus and Job in West African Religion. Cambridge, Cambridge University Press, 1959.
African Systems of Thought: Studies Presented and Discussed at the Third International African Seminar in Salisbury, December 1960, with Germaine Dieterlen and others. Oxford, Oxford University Press, 1965.
Kinship and the Social Order: The Legacy of Lewis Henry Morgan. Chicago, Aldine, 1969.
Time and Social Structure and Other Essays. London, Athlone Press, and Atlantic Highlands, New Jersey, Humanities Press, 1970.
The Plural Society in Africa (lecture). Johannesburg, South African Institute of Race Relations, 1970.

Other

Editor, with E.E. Evans-Pritchard, *African Political Systems.* Oxford, Oxford University Press, 1940.
Editor, *Social Structure: Studies Presented to A.R. Radcliffe-Brown.* Oxford, Clarendon Press, 1949.
Editor, *Marriage in Tribal Societies.* Cambridge, Cambridge University Press, 1962.
Editor, with S. Patterson, *Studies in African Social Anthropology.* Oxford, Oxford University Press, 1975.

Translator, *The Gestalt Theory and the Problem of Configuration*, by Bruno Petermann. London, Kegan Paul Trench Trubner, 1932.

*

Critical Studies: *The Character of Kinship*, edited by Jack Goody, New York and London, Cambridge University Press, 1973 (contains a full bibliography).

*   *   *

Meyer Fortes is the main formulator of "descent theory" in British social anthropology.
Fortes took his Ph.D. at the University of London as a student of Malinowski, but early in his career he repudiated Malinowski's theoretical guidance and affiliated himself with A.R. Radcliffe-Brown and E.E. Evans-Pritchard (whom he characterized as his "elder brother"). From Radcliffe-Brown, Fortes accepted a rather literal and contractual construction of the much older idea that the legal "constitution" of a community lay in the entire system of social rules and relations. From Evans-Pritchard, he accepted the idea that it was nevertheless a conceptual system, more specifically an intellectual construct of the analyst on the basis of theoretically informed intepretations of the goals thought to underlie observed behaviors. From both, and from the broader continental sociological tradition they both drew upon, he accepted the idea that society was a single "organic whole" that existed apart from individuals and determined their actions through determining the categories of their thought. Fortes' distinctive ideas lay in his construction of primitive society as a system of kinship relations in such a way that it would have both types of theoretical properties, conceptual and juridical.

Fortes began field work among the Tallensi in the Trans-Volta in 1934. His first publication, in cooperation with Radcliffe-Brown and Evans-Pritchard, set out the general division of tribal societies between "segmentary" and "centralized" systems. Their approach henceforth was to be to describe both types through the distribution, in a "territorial framework," of the "balance between power and authority on the one hand and obligation and responsibility on the other." These were to be the "constituted arrangements, not...how they work in practice."

Fortes' own first major work was *The Dynamics of Clanship among the Tallensi*, followed by *The Web of Kinship among the Tallensi*. The argument of *Clanship*, drawing heavily on interpretations of rituals, myths, and stereotyped statements of behavior, is that the patrilineal clans are the "corporate" constituents in an equilibrium of balanced opposition that make up the tribal segmentary system. Each clan corporately holds a unit of territory and represents a community of interests among its members.

Evans-Pritchard's very similar previous description of the Nuer had created a major theoretical problem by forcing him to hold that social structure did not include family organization. This is because the marriage rule in these societies required clan or lineage exogamy. Thus some members (the wives) of every family group necessarily were not of whatever clan was considered local. Moreover, families, not clans, actually worked land. Hence one could not include families and clans together in the "structure" so long as one held that structure was organized as only one system of actual corporate groups.

Fortes' *Web* attempted to include families without raising the fatal contradictions. It introduced a number of technical ideas of great subsequent importance in African ethnography, including the idea that domestic groups went through several forms in a fixed "developmental cycle." The theoretical argument was based mainly on the claim that a woman who marries a man marries "into" his lineage and clan in a very literal sense, eventually becoming part of it. A second argument was that the woman became corporate property, the clan as whole acquiring an "interest" in her. Problems remained. For example, it was clear in *Clanship* that in native opinion an out-married woman's tie to her natal group was never completely broken. Conversely, people in domestic groups draw upon relations through their mother as well as their father; how could they do so if the mother was regarded only as property of her husband's clan?

Fortes' subsequent work continued to defend and develop the idea of an organic system of corporate descent groups, advancing an elaborate system of distinctions between overt rights and latent or residual rights of various sorts.

Descent theory continues to command adherents, especially in Britain, and its vocabulary of quasi-legal terms has come into rather general use among Africanists and some others. Fortes' monographs and articles continue to be regarded as models of clear and comprehensive argument, even by those who reject his theoretical outlook.

—Murray J. Leaf

FOUCAULT, Michel (Paul). French philosopher, psychologist, and historian. Born in Poitiers, 15 October 1926. Educated at the École Normale Supérieure and University of Paris, licence in philosophy, 1948, licence in psychology, 1950, diplôme de psycho-pathologie, 1952, Doctorat d'état, 1960. Head of the Department, 1960-62, and Professor of Philosophy, 1964-68, University of Clermont-Ferrand; Professor, University of Paris-Vincennes, 1968-70. Since 1970, Professor of the History and Systems of Thought, Collège de France, Paris. Address: c/o Gallimard, 5 rue Sébastien-Bottin, 75007 Paris, France.

PUBLICATIONS

Philosophy, Psychology and History

Maladie mentale et personnalité. Paris, Presses Universitaires de France, 1954; revised edition as *Maladie mentale et psychologie*, 1962; as *Mental Illness and Psychology*, New York, Harper, 1976.
Folie et déraison: Histoire de la folie à l'âge classique. Paris, Plon, 1961; shortened edition as *Histoire de la folie*, Paris, U.G.E., 1961; as *Madness and Civilization*, New York, Pantheon, 1965; London, Tavistock, 1967.
Naissance de la clinique: Une Archéologie du regard médical. Paris, Presses Universitaires de France, 1963; as *The Birth of the Clinic: An Archaeology of Medical Perception*, New York, Pantheon, and London, Tavistock, 1973.
Raymond Roussel. Paris, Gallimard, 1963.
Les Mots et les choses: Une Archéologie des sciences humaines. Paris, Gallimard, 1966; as *The Order of Things: An Archaeology of the Human Sciences*, New York, Pantheon, and London, Tavistock, 1970.
L'Archéologie du savoir. Paris, Gallimard, 1969; as *The Archaeology of Knowledge*, New York, Pantheon, and London, Tavistock, 1972.
Moi, Pierre Rivière, ayant égorgé ma mère, ma soeur et mon frère... Un Cas de parricide au XIXe siècle, with others. Paris, Gallimard, 1973; as *I, Pierre Riviere, having slaughtered my mother, my sister and my brother... A Case of Parricide in the 19th Century*, New York, Pantheon, 1975; London, Peregrine, 1978.
Surveiller et punir. Paris, Gallimard, 1975; as *Discipline and Punish*, New York, Pantheon, and London, Allen Lane, 1977.
Les Machines à guérir (aux origines de l'hôpital moderne), with others. Paris, Institut de l'Environnement, 1976.
Histoire de la sexualité, vol. 1, *La Volonté de savoir*. Paris, Gallimard, 1976; as *The History of Sexuality*, New York, Pantheon, and London, Allen Lane, 1979.
Language, Counter-Memory, Practice: Selected Essays and Interviews, edited by Donald F. Bouchard. Ithaca, New York, Cornell University Press, and Oxford, Blackwell, 1977.
Power/Knowledge: Selected Interviews and Other Writings 1972-1977, edited by Colin Gordon. Brighton, Sussex, Harvester Press, and New York, Pantheon, 1980.

Other

Ceci n'est pas une pipe. Montpellier, Fata Morgana, 1973.

Translator, *Le Rêve et l'existence*, by Ludwig Binswanger. Paris, Desclée de Brouwer, 1954.
Translator, with others, *Études de style*, by Leo Spitzer. Paris, Gallimard, 1962.
Translator, *Anthropologie du point de vue pragmatique*, by Kant. Paris, Vrin, 1964.

*

Critical Studies: *Foucault* by Annie Guédez, Paris, Editions Universitaires, 1972; *Foucault* by Angèle Kremer-Marietti,

Paris, Seghers, 1974; *Michel Foucault: The Will to Power* by Alan Sheridan, London, Tavistock, 1980.

*   *   *

A basic imperative has guided the intellectual tradition in which one locates the works of Michel Foucault: the necessity to historicize everything. Such thinkers as Hegel, Marx and Nietzsche are seen as inaugural figures in this tradition because (1) they wrote histories and (2) they linked historical reflection to the most challenging aspects of their thought. They issued the challenge of history to the formulation of any thought in the present, and of the present. Further, they exemplified the manner of transforming the act of thinking into an intrepid adventure of activist erudition that can effect the active possibility of life and action in the present.

Foucault has recently declared that his objective has been to write "the history of the present." Through numerous concrete and local histories, he has wanted to map the emergence and specific nature of modern forms of rationality; he has done so by distinguishing both the level at which such forms start to take shape and the variety of reasons and conditions that account for the forms that modern knowledge has assumed. In the *Archaeology of Knowledge* Foucault defines his level of analysis as the "historical a priori," as the determining "archive" immanent to intellectual practices. These general concepts are, perhaps, better understood in terms of the explicit orientation that Foucault first announces in *Madness and Civilization*. His purpose in investigating the beginnings of psychopathology is to see how "reason" (at a certain time and on the basis of practical historical conditions) was able to distance itself from "non-reason." On this basis, two questions immediately arise: what was "non-reason" before it became "madness" and, due to this transformation, the knowledge of a fledgling science, and what tactics and alliances gave power to a barely articulated science, so that it could erect itself in the place held by "truth"? By the end of the 1960's, when Foucault specifies the nature of his archaeological approach, the questions of *Madness and Civilization* undergo the following mutation and elaboration: to determine how objects are delimited within a given field of knowledge; to discover how a particular discursive constellation accommodates and defines the legitimate role of an agent of knowledge; and to find how an intellectual practice fixes the norms for developing concepts and theories.

During the period of the 1960's, the linchpin of Foucault's analyses is found in *The Order of Things* and the operational concept of *episteme*. The *episteme* is a transindividual tool to deploy the anonymous operation of discourse in the production of knowledge. Necessarily, it rejects such notions as a major author or of a book, an *oeuvre* or of a discipline as the essential ingredients to the constitution of a field of knowledge; it also denies, from a philosophical perspective, the founding role of the subject as argued by phenomenology and the so-called *Weltanschauung*, the mentality or world view that characterizes an era. The *episteme* sets out Foucault's conviction that systems of knowledge do not "progress" in relation to a stable, universal object; rather, it characterizes a situated knowledge (in time and place) that produces objects to satisfy its practical needs and sense of order. It is a "code of knowledge" as well as that which limits the statements and thoughts of a period. Foucault's inaugural lecture at the Collège de France in 1970, translated as "The Discourse on Language," comes full circle in linking the concept of *episteme* to the practical constraints addressed in *Madness and Civilization*. ("The Discourse on Language" is perhaps the single clearest exposition of Foucault's perspective.) For any culture, Foucault maintains, it is never enough simply to speak the "truth," if one wishes to be heard; one must be "within the truth" and embody its "regime." Consequently, the *episteme* not only stands for the multiple conditions activated in the production of "truthful" statements, but serves as a threshold concept to establish exclusions and discriminations. Knowledge, it can now be seen, always implies taking sides.

"When I think back now," Foucault said in a 1977 interview, "I ask myself what else it was that I was talking about, in *Madness and Civilization* or *The Birth of the Clinic*, but power?" Aside from showing the new, all-pervasive, technical, and strategic nature of power in the modern framework and the inability of the older juridical form of sovereignty to explain this new phenomenon, Foucault wishes to know how one form gives way to another. In short, he poses the problem of the genealogist, the problem of *descent* and *emergence*, the problem of one "who listens to history" and who finds that the things that have come down to us in the present were "fabricated in a piecemeal fashion from alien forms." Thus, the birth of the prison and its new "microphysics of power" were made possible by adopting the more efficient "economy of power" first formulated by monarchies in the Classical period in the context of the army, the police and fiscal administration. As for modern sexuality, it too is the product of a refashioning of an older purpose and "alien form," in this instance that found in the Catholic confessional. The view of history proposed by Foucault as genealogist is one of countless "invasions, struggles, plundering, disguises, ploys," at the level of forms as well as that of historical documents. Here, it is possible to see the nature of discourse as an "event" in time, since it is not only that which represents "struggles or systems of domination, but the object through which and with which we struggle, the power we seek to possess."

Through his works, Foucault has re-established an uneasy connection between history and philosophy and also a redefinition of the new role of "resistance" for the intellectual. The classic philosophical question, "What is the surest path to the Truth?" has been refashioned, first through Nietzsche, into a new basis for historical interrogation: "what is the hazardous career that Truth has followed?"—the question of genealogy for which the will to truth, in Western culture, is the most deeply enmeshed historical phenomenon. In Foucault's works, truth is no longer an unchanging, universal essence, but the perpetual object of appropriation, domination. Foucault's stance and practice in the 1960's were extremely ambiguous, largely defined in negative terms, but the publication of *Discipline and Punish* marked a new-found certainty, one that supports his involvement in the historical problem of the present: "what's effectively needed is a ramified, penetrative perception of the present, one that makes it possible to locate the lines of weakness, the strong points.... In other words, a topological and geological survey of the battlefield—that is the intellectual's role."

—Donald F. Bouchard

FRANK, Jerome N. American jurist. Born in New York, 10 September 1889. Studied at the University of Chicago, Ph.B. 1909, J.D. 1912; admitted to Illinois Bar, 1912. Married Florence Kiper in 1914; 1 daughter. Practiced law in Chicago, 1912-28, and in New York, 1928-33 and 1936-37. Research Associate, Yale Law School, New Haven, Connecticut, 1932; General Counsel, Agricultural Adjustment Administration, Washington, D.C., 1933-35, and Federal Surplus Relief Corporation, Washington, D.C., 1933-35; Special Counsel, Reconstruction Finance Corporation, Washington, D.C., 1935; Commissioner, 1937-41, and Chairman, 1939-41, Securities and Exchange Commission, Washington, D.C.; Judge, U.S. Court of Appeals for 2nd Circuit, from 1941. Visiting Lecturer, Yale University, from 1947; New School for Social Research, New York, 1946-47; and Brandeis University, Waltham, Massachusetts, 1954-55. Honorary doctorate: University of Chicago, 1953. *Died 13 January 1957.*

PUBLICATIONS

Law

Law and the Modern Mind. New York, Brentano's, 1930.
Save America First: How to Make Our Democracy Work. New York and London, Harper, 1938.
If Men Were Angels: Some Aspects of Government in a Democracy. New York and London, Harper, 1942.
Fate and Freedom: A Philosophy for Free Americans. New York, Simon and Schuster, 1945; selections as *The Place of the Expert in a Democratic Society* (lecture), Philadelphia, Brandeis Lawyers' Society, 1945.
Courts on Trial: Myth and Reality in American Justice. Princeton, New Jersey, Princeton University Press, 1949.
Not Guilty, with others. New York, Doubleday, and London, Gollancz, 1957.
Censorship and Freedom of Expression: Essays on Obscenity and the Law, with others, edited by Harry M. Clor. Chicago, Rand McNally, 1971.

Other

A Man's Reach: The Philosophy of Judge Jerome Frank, edited by Barbara Frank Kristein. New York, Macmillan, 1965.

*

Critical Studies: *The Legal Realism of Jerome N. Frank: A Study of Fact-Skepticism and the Judicial Process*, by Julius Paul, The Hague, Nijhoff, 1959; *The Passionate Liberal: The Political and Legal Ideas of Jerome Frank*, by Walter E. Volkomer, The Hague, Nijhoff, 1970; *Jerome Frank's Impact on American Law: The Iconoclast as Reformer* by Robert Jerome Glennon, Ithaca, New York, Cornell University Press, 1984.

*   *   *

Jerome N. Frank pioneered American legal realism, a movement which began in the 1930's and remains influential. "Realism" drew on William James's pragmatism but was never a technical philosophical term. Instead, realism was used, as in art, to describe fidelity to nature or an accurate representation of things as they are, not as one wishes them to be.

Frank's influence began with the publication in 1930 of *Law and the Modern Mind*, his first and most important book. Describing as a myth the concept that law is fixed and predictable, he attacked the conventional wisdom that judges discover pre-existing law and use formal logic to reach the correct result. Frank reasoned that a syllogism provides only a logical structure not the premises, and, since courts select the premises, judges may decide cases any way they choose and camouflage their preferences behind flawless logic. To Frank, legal rules play a very limited role in determining judicial decisions. Instead, judges begin with the desired conclusion and then rationalize their decisions by finding facts and selecting rules which justify the desired conclusion. Frank thought that "the personality of the judge is the pivotal factor in law administration." He thus identified unfettered judicial discretion, rather than legal rules and *stare decisis*, as the real explanation for court decisions.

Law and the Modern Mind attempted both to expose the basic myth of legal predictability and to explain its remarkable persistence. For a partial explanation of the source of this widespread illusion, Jerome Frank turned to the nascent discipline of psychology. In early life each child comes to rely on a seemingly omniscient and omnipotent father who personifies certainty and infallibility. However, as evidence of the father's fallibility slowly accumulates, the child becomes disillusioned. Yet the urge to find certainty and security continues. The law "inevitably becomes a partial substitute for the Father-as-Infallible-Judge." To overcome the blindness of legal uncertainty, adults must relinquish their childish need for an authoritative father. Jerome Frank's "modern mind is a mind free of childish emotional drags, a mature mind."

A hallmark of Frank's legal realism was his bold and innovative use of sources outside the law. He sought to understand how law works by looking beyond narrow legal rules and drawing creatively on the insights of other disciplines. Psychology had special utility as the best instrument available for the study of human nature: Freudian concepts permeate Frank's father-substitute theory, and Piaget's child psychology also influenced him. In addition, Frank relied on the philosophic writings of Plato and Aristotle, the work in logic of F.C.S. Schiller and John Dewey, the linguistic theories of Ogden and Richards, and the anthropology of Malinowski.

Frank pioneered in introducing social science analysis in the law, but his effort never took hold. A problem in interdisciplinary study is to select among competing methodologies from the companion field. Frank's eclectic style led him to borrow from conflicting approaches, such as Freudian and gestalt psychology, without appreciating that each theory had its own coherence and demands. Frank's effort to engage in social science analysis was primitive and incomplete. Yet he lent credibility to psychology as a serious discipline at an early critical stage in its development, and he generally encouraged the subsequent use of social science methodology to analyze legal problems.

Law and the Modern Mind exaggerated the degree of judicial discretion and unpredictability in the legal system. By concentrating only on court-made law, Frank slighted the role of the legislature in enacting statutes and thereby circumscribing judicial discretion. Because he could demonstrate that rules do not translate into absolutely predictable court decisions, Frank assumed the legal rules had negligible value. He ignored how probability guides human behavior as men and women adapt their behavior to comply with legal rules. The law affects people not merely by litigation producing a court order but also by shaping people's expectations of what will probably, or even possibly, occur if a rule is violated.

Law and the Modern Mind challenged central tenets of the American legal system. Conventional wisdom portrays the common law system as one of slow growth guided by *stare decisis*. Reasoning from past experience to present problems, judges apply the law. The democratic system prides itself as a government of laws not of men, remembering the maxim that "where law ends, tyranny begins." Under the American system of separation of powers, the legislature makes the law and the judiciary applies it. In rejecting these ideas *Law and the Modern Mind* presented a potentially explosive attack on the political status quo. By exploding the myth of the role of *stare decisis* and by exposing judicial power and discretion, Jerome Frank tried to disabuse both the profession and the public of the idea that judges follow the law. But if judges do not obey the law, then why do people obey the judges? Frank raised a serious challenge to the legitimacy not only of court decisions but also of law generally. If the law does not embody principles of natural law and if it is not the expression of democratic sovereignty, then from where does law derive its legitimacy? If law depends on "the personality of the judge," on an act of will of very human and biased men, then its arbitrary character deprives it of any rightful claim to allegiance and obedience. By exposing the political aspect of law Jerome Frank revealed law's inevitable role in the distribution of wealth and power.

During the 1930's and 1940's Frank published a steady stream of books and articles on philosophy, jurisprudence, legal education, and law reform, culminating in 1949 with the publication of *Courts on Trial*. A major jurisprudential work, it carved out for Frank a unique niche in the realist movement as a "fact skeptic." In *Courts on Trial* Frank turned his focus to the trial courts and exposed the frailty of the fact-finding process. At trial a witness reports his or her memory of events occurring in the past. Assuming a completely honest witness, memory may be faulty, the

original observation erroneous, or the present recollection misstated. Conscious and/or unconscious partisanship make the "facts" even less certain. In addition, "facts" depend on accurate documentation, often unavailable due to missing letters or witnesses. Finally, "facts" are found by the presentation of testimony to a judge or jury, but the judge and jury are witnesses as well and suffer similar human weaknesses. Findings of fact, then, are the opinion of the judge or jury about the opinions of witnesses.

Frank's skepticism had changed from *Law and the Modern Mind* to *Courts on Trial*. Instead of focusing on the ambiguity of legal rules and the breadth of judicial discretion to select between and among competing doctrines and precedent, Frank now located the source of uncertainty in the fact-finding process. He now thought the rules had "great importance" but were often skewed by defective fact-finding. The application of any legal rule depends on the facts, and the "facts are guesses."

Courts on Trial sparkled with the inimitable style of Jerome Frank. Witty and didactic, contentious and unsettling, the book displayed extraordinarily broad knowledge. It drew on philosophy and psychology, history and historiography, literature and literary criticism, science and medicine, sociology and anthropology, classical music and aesthetics. Basically optimistic, it exhibited concern for justice and confidence that people have good will, and will act justly, if their psychological fetters are removed.

Courts on Trial turned away from the broad political implications of *Law and the Modern Mind*. Although Frank still recognized the enormous discretion of judges, he concentrated on concrete reforms which would improve the performance of trial courts and not on exposing the political power of judges. Yet the issues he first raised in *Law and the Modern Mind* have never been resolved. Legal rules continue to be pliable instruments in the hands of the judiciary whose political power remains unhampered.

—Robert Jerome Glennon

FRANKFURTER, Felix. American jurist. Born in Vienna, Austria, 15 November 1882; emigrated to the United States in 1894; later naturalized. Studied at College of the City of New York, B.A. 1902, and Harvard University, Cambridge, Massachusetts, LL.B. 1906. Served in United States Army, as Assistant to the Secretary of War, and as Counsel to the President's Mediation Commission, during World War I. Married Marion A. Denman in 1919. Assistant United States Attorney, Southern District of New York, 1906-10; Law Officer, Bureau of Insular Affairs, War Department, Washington, D.C., 1911-14; Professor, Harvard Law School, 1914-39; George Eastman Visiting Professor, Oxford University, 1933-34; Associate Justice, United States Supreme Court, Washington, D.C., 1939-62. Honorary doctorate: Oxford University, 1939; Amherst College, Massachusetts, 1940; College of the City of New York, 1947; University of Chicago, 1953; Brandeis University, Waltham, Massachusetts, 1956; Harvard University, 1956; Yale University, New Haven, Connecticut, 1961. Honorary Master of the Bench, Grays Inn, London, 1952. *Died 22 February 1965.*

PUBLICATIONS

Law

The Case for the Shorter Work Day, with Josephine Goldmark. New York, National Consumers' League, 2 vols., 1916.
Oregon Minimum Wage Cases: Supreme Court of the United States, October Term, 1916, with Josephine Goldmark. New

York, National Consumers' League, 1917.

District of Columbia Minimum Wage Case, with Mary W. Dawson. New York, C.P. Young, 1921; enlarged edition, New York, Steinberg Press, 2 vols., 1923.

Helen Gainer, Plaintiff and Appellant, vs. A.B.C. Dohrman, Katherine Philips Edson, and Others: Brief on Behalf of Amici Curiae, with Mary W. Dawson. New York, 1924.

Power of Congress Over Procedure in Criminal Contempts in "Inferior" Federal Courts—A Study in Separation of Powers, with James M. Landis. Cambridge, Massachusetts, Harvard Law Review Association, 1924.

State Minimum Wage Laws in Practice, with others. New York, National Consumers' League, 1924.

The Compact Clause of the Constitution: A Study in Interstate Adjustment, with James M. Landis. New Haven, Connecticut, Yale University Press, 1925.

The Business of the Supreme Court: A Study in the Federal Judicial System, with James M. Landis. New York, Macmillan, 1927.

The Case of Sacco and Vanzetti: A Critical Analysis for Lawyers and Laymen. Boston, Little Brown, 1927.

Mr. Justice Holmes and the Constitution: A Review of His Twenty-Five Years on the Supreme Court. Cambridge, Massachusetts, Dunster House Bookshop, 1927.

The Case for the Jews, with others. New York, Zionist Organization of America, 1930.

The Labor Injunction, with Nathan Greene. New York, Macmillan, 1930.

The Public and Its Government. New Haven, Connecticut, Yale University Press, and London, Oxford University Press, 1930.

The Commerce Clause Under Marshall, Taney and Waite. Chapel Hill, University of North Carolina Press, 1937.

Mr. Justice Holmes and the Supreme Court. Cambridge, Massachusetts, Harvard University Press, 1938.

Law and Politics: Occasional Papers of Felix Frankfurter, 1913-1938, edited by Archibald MacLeish and E.F. Prichard, Jr. New York, Harcourt Brace, 1939.

The Permanence of Jefferson (lecture). Washington, U.S. Government Printing Office, 1943.

Some Reflections on the Reading of Statutes. New York, Association of the Bar of the City of New York, 1947.

The Constitutional World of Mr. Justice Frankfurter: Some Representative Opinions, edited by Samuel J. Konefsky. New York, Macmillan, 1949.

Some Observations on Supreme Court Litigation and Legal Education. Chicago, University of Chicago Law School, 1954.

Of Law and Men: Papers and Addresses, 1939-1956, edited by Philip Elman. New York, Harcourt Brace, 1956.

Of Law and Life and Other Things That Matter: Papers and Addresses of Felix Frankfurter, 1956-63, edited by Philip B. Kurland. Cambridge, Massachusetts, Belknap Press, 1965.

Felix Frankfurter on the Supreme Court: Extrajudicial Essays on the Court and the Constitution, edited by Philip B. Kurland. Cambridge, Massachusetts, Belknap Press, 1970.

Mr. Justice Frankfurter and the Constitution, edited by Philip B. Kurland. Chicago, University of Chicago Press, 1971.

Other

Felix Frankfurter Reminisces. New York, Reynal, and London, Secker and Warburg, 1960.

Roosevelt and Frankfurter: Their Correspondence, 1928-45, edited by Max Freedman. Boston, Little Brown, 1968.

From the Diaries of Felix Frankfurter, edited by Joseph P. Lash, with Jonathan Lash. New York, Norton, 1975.

Editor, *A Selection of Cases Under the Interstate Commerce Act*. Cambridge, Massachusetts, Harvard University Press, 1915.

Editor, with Roscoe Pound, *Criminal Justice in Cleveland*. Cleveland, Cleveland Foundation, 1922.

Editor, with Wilber G. Katz, *Cases and Other Authorities on Federal Jurisdiction and Procedure*. Chicago, Callaghan, 1931; enlarged edition, 1937.

Editor, *Mr. Justice Holmes*, by Benjamin N. Cardozo and others. New York, Coward McCann, 1931.

Editor, with J. Forrester Davison, *Cases and Other Materials on Administrative Law*. New York, Commerce Clearing House, 1932.

*

Critical Studies: *Felix Frankfurter: Scholar on the Bench* by Helen Shirley Thomas, Baltimore, Johns Hopkins Press, 1960; *Justice Frankfurter and Civil Liberties* by Clyde Edward Jacobs, Berkeley, University of California Press, 1961; *Justices Black and Frankfurter: Conflict in the Court* by Wallace Mendelson, Chicago, University of Chicago Press, 1961; *Essays in Legal History in Honor of Felix Frankfurter*, edited by Morris D. Forkosch, Indianapolis, Bobbs-Merrill, 1966; *Louis D. Brandeis, Felix Frankfurter, and the New Deal* by Nelson S. Dawson, Hamden, Connecticut, Archon Books, 1980; *The Enigma of Felix Frankfurter* by H.N. Hirsch, New York, Basic Books, 1981; *The Brandeis-Frankfurter Connection: The Secret Political Activities of Two Supreme Court Justices* by Bruce Allen Murphy, New York, Oxford University Press, 1982.

*   *   *

Any discussion of Felix Frankfurter limited to his contributions to American jurisprudence is inherently flawed, not only because it overlooks a vast part of his life's work but also because these extra-judicial activities informed his work with the Supreme Court. By the time he was appointed to the Supreme Court by President Franklin Roosevelt in 1939, Frankfurter was well known as a civil libertarian, social policy advocate, and legal scholar. The traditional wisdom is that Frankfurter repudiated his civil libertarian views once on the bench, but that view is too narrow. The key to Frankfurter's judicial career is his commitment to procedure. Commitment to procedure is premised on the assumption that proper observance of procedure is the best guarantor of the fairness which Frankfurter sought to foster through his extra-judicial activities. That commitment to procedure also dictated the judicial self-restraint which characterized his work on the Supreme Court.

In 1940 the Court considered whether public schools could require children of Jehovah's Witnesses to salute the flag. Frankfurter wrote for the Court, concluding that the state's interest in fostering citizenship outweighed the individual's interest in not violating his religious beliefs. *Minersville School District* vs. *Gobitis*, 310 U.S. 586 (1940). Attacked for betraying his civil libertarian views, Frankfurter defended his position three years later in a dissent from the majority's reversal of the *Gobitis* decision, *Virginia State Board of Education* vs. *Barnette*, 319 U.S. 624 (1943). Frankfurter stated that he shared the majority view that it was reprehensible that a state would force children to violate their religious beliefs by compelling them to salute the flag, but he could not conclude that the Constitution required the result reached by the majority. He continued:

> As a member of this Court, I am not justified in writing my private notions of policy into the Constitution, no matter how deeply I may cherish them or how mischievous I may deem their disregard.... It can never be emphasized too much that one's own opinion about the wisdom or evil of a law should be excluded altogether when one is doing one's duty on the bench. The only opinion of our own, even looking in that direction, that is material is our opinion whether legislators could in reason have enacted such a law.

The *Barnette* dissent made it clear that Frankfurter would respect what he saw as constitutional limitations on judicial power. When examining challenged legislation, the only permissible inquiry is whether there is some rational basis for the enactment. Judicial self-restraint does permit, however, a more searching inquiry when the challenged legislation involves a right protected by the Constitution. For example, in the flag salute cases, it was not sufficient that the legislation was rationally based; it must also further some compelling state interest. Frankfurter weighed the children's interest in not being forced to salute the flag and their First Amendment right to exercise their religion freely against the state's interest in inculcating patriotism; he concluded that the latter interest was sufficiently compelling to justify this minimal—in Frankfurter's view—infringement of the children's constitutional rights.

This balancing approach to First Amendment issues is in sharp contrast to that of Roosevelt appointees Hugo Black and William O. Douglas who regarded the prohibitions of the First Amendment as absolute. Black and Douglas argued that "Congress shall make no law" meant that no state interest could justify infringement of a right protected by the First Amendment.

The balancing approach to issues of free speech and assembly is illustrated by Frankfurter's opinion for the Court in *Dennis* vs. *United States*, 391 U.S. 494 (1951), upholding the conviction of Communist leaders under the Smith Act which made it unlawful to conspire "to advocate and teach" the violent overthrow of the Government. Recognizing that the Act did restrict the right of free speech, Frankfurter reasoned that some speech has a greater claim to constitutional protection. The degree of protection afforded a particular type of speech is determined by weighing the value of that speech against the interests the legislature seeks to safeguard. Frankfurter concluded that Congress' interest in national security is greater than an individual's interest in advocating violence.

Two observations about Frankfurter's approach to the First Amendment are appropriate. First, the Supreme Court has never adopted the absolute approach to the First Amendment advocated by Justices Black and Douglas, but instead has balanced the right at issue against the interest advanced by the state as justification for a particular piece of legislation. In this respect, Frankfurter's *Dennis* opinion is representative of the modern Court's approach. Second, in other cases Frankfurter joined Black in striking down loyalty oaths and security checks and in protecting the rights of teachers to keep their jobs despite charges of subversive affiliations. In these cases, however, Black would base his decision on First Amendment grounds, while Frankfurter would rely on procedural or jurisdictional grounds, thereby avoiding the constitutional question. Again, Frankfurter is firmly in the mainstream, for it is a commonplace of constitutional law that the Court must resolve issues on other than constitutional grounds whenever possible.

Unlike his approach to First Amendment issues, which did not add significantly to constitutional interpretation, Frankfurter's view of Fourteenth Amendment due process arguably enabled the Warren Court to find that a number of rights not specifically enumerated in the Constitution are in fact covered by the constitutional umbrella. The Fourteenth Amendment guarantees that no *state* "shall deprive any person of life, liberty, or property, without due process of laws." Determining exactly what process is due under the Fourteenth Amendment has been a central concern of the Court for more than 40 years. In the early part of this century the Court contended that in the absence of a violation of a specific Federal statute or constitutional provision, its review of legislation would be limited to inquiring whether there was some minimum rational basis for enacting the legislation. The Bill of Rights restricted only the Federal government—not those of the states—and thus did not protect individuals against state infringement of rights enumerated in the first ten Amendments. The Fourteenth Amendment due process guarantee was not considered sufficiently specific to justify more searching judicial review.

Justice Cardozo stated in 1937 that due process applied to any right "so rooted in the tradition and conscience of our people as to be ranked as fundamental" and thus "inherent in the concept of ordered liberty." *Palko* vs. *Connecticut*, 302 U.S. 319, 325 (1937). Rejecting the view that due process protects only those rights which can be determined to be fundamental, Justice Hugo Black and others argued that the Fourteenth Amendment was intended to make all of the Bill of Rights applicable to the states; that is, that the Fourteenth Amendment incorporated the first ten Amendments. Frankfurter demonstrated with impressive scholarship that the authors of the Fourteenth Amendment had no such intention. Forced to identify some other way of defining due process, Frankfurter elaborated upon the Cardozo test, stating that "disinterested inquiry...duly mindful of reconciling the needs both of continuity and of change in a progressive society" would enable identification of those fundamental rights essential to an open society. That inquiry would be based upon "considerations deeply rooted in reason and in the compelling, traditions of the legal profession." *Rochin* vs. *California*, 342 U.S. 165 (1942).

Application of this test was, however, difficult. In *Rochin*, the Court reserved the conviction of a man whom the police had forced to vomit up two capsules containing morphine that were admitted into evidence at trial. Frankfurter wrote for the Court that such procedures violated due process of law because such police conduct "shocks the conscience." Black, who argued that the Fourteenth Amendment incorporated all of the rights guaranteed by the Bill of Rights but no more, quickly pointed out such a test is essentially subjective and thus provides the Court with no guidelines in determining what rights are protected by the due process guarantee. Ironically, given Frankfurter's reservations about judge-made law, the Cardozo-Frankfurter due process analysis was capable of expansion far beyond those rights enumerated in the first ten Amendments. Frankfurter had left the bench when the Court struck down a state law which made it a crime for married couples to use birth control, *Griswold* vs. *Connecticut*, 381 U.S. 479 (1965). That law violated due process, stated the Court, because it impinged upon the right of privacy protected by the "penumbras" of the Bill of Rights, that is, by the shadows created by the first ten Amendments. Whether or not one agrees with the result in *Griswold*, it is apparent that Frankfurter's due process approach permits locating constitutionally protected rights between the lines—or in the penumbras—of the Constitution.

That Frankfurter's belief in judicial self-restraint did not absolutely preclude judicial activism was demonstrated by his role in insuring unanimity in the historic case of *Brown* vs. *Board of Education*, 347 U.S. 483 (1954), in which the Court held that segregating children in public schools on the basis of race even though the facilities are equal, deprives minority children of the equal protection of the laws guaranteed by the Fourteenth Amendment. *Brown* is unabashed judicial activism, and yet Frankfurter never regretted his part in that case. The judicial restraint of the flag salute cases and judicial activism of *Brown* appear irreconcilable. Yet Frankfurter never doubted that even if the doctrine of judicial self-restraint were carried to the extreme, ultimately a justice had to rely on his own judgement. In a 1947 lecture on Cardozo, Frankfurter stated that "The only sure safeguard against crossing the line between adjudication and legislation is an alert recognition of the necessity not to cross it and instinctive, as well as trained, reluctance to do so."

Frankfurter is usually placed in the Holmes-Brandeis line of justices articulating the position of judicial self-restraint. In Frankfurter's case, the restraint probably can be traced to his understanding of the Court's history and his belief that the individual justice must not allow his personal opinion of the merits of the particular case to supplant the role of the Court as the guardian of legal process. Nevertheless, as his approach to due process and his support in *Brown* indicate, Frankfurter's restraint was tempered by recognition that on rare occasions the only proper role for the Court was to make—not merely interpret—the law.

—Nancy Elizabeth Lark Schulze

FREUD, Anna.   British psychoanalyst.   Born in Vienna, Austria, 3 December 1895; daughter of Sigmund Freud, *q.v.*; emigrated to England in 1938, later naturalized. Educated at the Cottage Lyceum, Vienna. Chairman, Vienna Institute of Psycho-Analysis until 1938. Member, London Institute of Psycho-Analysis, from 1938; worked with the Hampstead War Nursery during World War II and in 1952 founded the Hampstead Child Therapy Course and Clinic, London. Recipient: Grand Decoration of Honour in Gold, Austria, 1975. Honorary doctorate: Clark University, Worcester, Massachusetts, 1950; University of Sheffield, 1966; Jefferson Medical College, Philadelphia, 1964; University of Chicago, 1966; Yale University, New Haven, Connecticut, 1968; University of Vienna, 1972; Columbia University, New York, 1978; Harvard University, Cambridge, Massachusetts, 1980. *Died* (in London) *9 October 1982*.

PUBLICATIONS

Collections

The Writings of Anna Freud.   London, Hogarth Press and Institute of Psycho-Analysis, and New York, International Universities Press, 1966-.

Psychology

Einführung in die Technik der Kinderanalyse: Vier Vorträge. Leipzig, Internationaler Psychoanalytischer Verlag, 1927; as *Introduction to the Technique of Child Analysis*, New York, Nervous and Mental Diseases Publishing Company, 1928.
Einführung in der Psychoanalyse für Pädagogen: Vier Vorträge. Stuttgart, Hippokrates, 1930; as *Psycho-Analysis for Teachers*, London, Allen and Unwin, 1931, as *Psychoanalysis for Teachers and Parents: Introductory Lectures*, New York, Emerson, 1935.
Das Ich und die Abwehrmechanismen.   Vienna, Internationaler Psychoanalytischer Verlag, 1936; as *The Ego and the Mechanisms of Defense*, London, Hogarth Press and Institute of Psycho-Analysis, 1937; New York, International Universities Press, 1946.
Young Children in War Time: A Year's Work in a Residential War Nursery, with Dorothy Burlingham.   London, Allen and Unwin, 1942.
War and Children, with Dorothy Burlingham.   New York, Medical War Books, 1943.
Infants Without Families: The Case for and Against Residential Nurseries, with Dorothy Burlingham.   London, Allen and Unwin, 1943.
Psycho-Analytic Treatment of Children: Technical Lectures and Essays.   London, Imago Press, 1946.
Safeguarding the Emotional Health of Our Children: An Inquiry into the Concept of the Rejecting Mother.   New York, Child Welfare League of America, 1955.
The Enrichment of Children (lectures), with W.D. Wall.   London, Nursery School Association of Great Britain and Northern Ireland, 1961.
Normality and Pathology in Childhood: Assessments and Developments.   London, Hogarth Press and Institute of Psycho-Analysis, and New York, International Universities Press, 1966.
Children in the Hospital, with Thesi Bergmann.   New York, International Universities Press, 1966.
Indications for Child Analysis, and Other Papers, 1945-1956.

New York, International Universities Press, 1968; London, Hogarth Press and Institute for Psycho-Analysis, 1969.
Difficulties in the Path of a Psychoanalysis: A Confrontation of Past with Present Viewpoints (lecture).   New York, International Universities Press, 1969.
Research at the Hampstead Child Therapy Clinic, and Other Papers, 1956-1965.   New York, International Universities Press, 1969; London, Hogarth Press and Institute for Psycho-Analysis, 1970.
Problems of Psychoanalytic Training, Diagnosis and the Technique of Therapy, 1966-1970.   New York, International Universities Press, 1971; as *Problems of Psychoanalytic Technique and Therapy*, London, Hogarth Press and Institute of Psycho-Analysis, 1972.
Beyond the Best Interests of the Child, with others.   New York, Free Press, and London, Collier Macmillan, 1973.
Introduction to Psychoanalysis: Lectures for Child Analysts and Teachers, 1922-1935.   London, Hogarth Press and Institute for Psycho-Analysis, and New York, International Universities Press, 1974.
Infants Without Families and Reports on the Hampstead Nurseries, 1939-1945, with Dorothy Burlingham.   London, Hogarth Press and Institute of Psycho-Analysis, and New York, International Universities Press, 1974.
Studies in Child Psychoanalysis, Pure and Applied.   New Haven, Connecticut, Yale University Press, 1975.
Before the Best Interests of the Child, with others.   New York, Free Press, 1979; London, Burnett Books, 1980.
The Technique of Child Psychoanalysis: Discussions with Anna Freud, Hansi Kennedy, Robert L. Tyson.   Cambridge, Massachusetts, Harvard University Press, 1980.
Psychoanalytical Psychology of Normal Development, 1970-1980.   New York, International Universities Press, 1981.

Other

Editor, with others, *The Standard Edition of the Complete Psychological Works of Sigmund Freud*.   London, Hogarth Press, and New York, Macmillan, 24 vols., 1953-56.
Editor, with others, *The Origins of Psycho-Analysis: Letters to Wilhelm Fliess, Drafts and Notes, 1889-1902*, by Sigmund Freud.   London, Imago Publishing Company, and New York, Basic Books, 1954.
Editor, with others, *Gesammelte Werke*, by Sigmund Freud. Frankfurt, Fischer, 1961-.
Editor, with Ilse Grunbrich-Simitis, *Werkausgaben in zwei Bänden*, by Sigmund Freud.   Frankfurt, Fischer, 2 vols., 1978.

Translator, with Sigmund Freud, *Topsy, Chow-Chow au poil d'or*, by Marie Bonaparte.   Amsterdam, n.p., 1939.

*

Bibliography: in *Difficulties in the Path of a Psychoanalysis*, 1969.

Critical Study: *Anna Freud: Ein Leben für das Kind*, by Uwe Henrick Peters, Munich, Kindler, 1979.

*   *   *

One of the areas with which Anna Freud was most concerned throughout her career was the relationship between theory construction and phenomenology. Yet, because she so rarely addressed this matter directly, this important area of her work also has been perhaps the least attended to and the least appreciated. This is unfortunate since it may well be that her constant focus on the connection between the life of the mind and theoretical descriptions of that life will prove to be one of her most important and enduring contributions to the field of psychology. In the sciences, one of the most important goals of a theory is to break down and simplify (without oversimplifying) the phenomenon that it describes, creating an ordered foundation out of a chaotic whole. This breaking down facilitates data collection and presents a viable means of approaching hierarchical organization. Moving on, the investigator begins a reintegration of the parts into an ordered whole. The utility of a theory depends on the paths it opens up for investigators following in the footsteps of the theoretician. Without this continual flow of new insights the whole process of breaking down and building up reaches a dead end.

With time a good theory comes more and more to resemble the phenomenon it describes as succeeding investigators fine tune it with the conceptions of their own. It is possible, however, for us to forget that we are dealing with concepts which had authors, rather than life as it is lived. When this happens, theories harden, taking on a reality of their own divorced from the world of experience.

Anna Freud was continually aware of this possible split, and she always struggled to maintain a connection between her ideas and the world she was trying to describe. From her first efforts to help teachers, on through her response to war-torn families and their children, to her most abstract level of theory building, there remained for her a deep commitment to developing psychoanalysis to help the development of children, and using this material to help the development of psychoanalysis. This effort led Anna Freud to pioneer in the development and use of additional research techniques to supplement and compliment classical psychoanalytic methods. These extend from the development of child analysis and the use of the nursery school, residential care center, day care center, and hospital, to the investigation of the developmental impact of such sensory deprivations as blindness and deafness.

What appears in Anna Freud as practicality is not fortuitous. It is a calculated but rare combination of lucidity, humanism, and science, and a remarkable appreciation and utilization of the reciprocal relationship between theory and phenomenology. Speaking at Yale University in 1966, she addressed just this matter:

It is serious that the division between theory and practice is widespread. There are many people who work on the theory of child development, and there are many other people who work practically with children, but not enough people have the opportunity to apply their theories or to be taught developmental theory while the practical work with children goes on. I may say that in this last respect, I have been especially fortunate all my life.

From the very beginning I was able to move back and forth between practice and theory. I started as an elementary school teacher. I changed from there into the field of analysis and therapy; and then, from then on I changed constantly back from the theoretic study of these problems to their practical application.

This openness to new experiences gave Anna Freud a wider perspective of the world and a resiliency and flexibility that allowed her to build anew without relinquishing the hard-won knowledge of the past. This, combined with an unfettered and articulate intellect, allowed her to cut through a mass of complexities and organize troublesome material into a coherent whole.

In her developmental Profile schema, Anna Freud was aware of these complexities, arising from the difficulty of dealing theoretically with many factors. Her concern was with presenting a useable organizational model which would facilitate the gathering, storage, and assessment of data. Such an instrument imposes balance, completeness, and comparability, not only for individual cases but also for comparisons between analysts. This is an instrument with many potential uses, including the assessment of change over time, compilation of similar cases, comparison of differing ones, and as a training aid.

It was in coming to grips with this question of data colection, storage, and analysis that Anna Freud came to the concept of developmental lines. Before this, psychoanalytic methods rested primarily on the conceptualizations of the structural model, which was an attempt to disentangle and articulate individual functions. Although concerns with interrelationships were present, they were not the primary focus at that time. With the concept of developmental lines, Anna Freud forcefully reintroduced organization and hierarchy as major concepts.

Few within or without psychoanalysis have contributed so large a body of theoretical propositions so pertinent and useful to the field as Anna Freud.

—R.W. Rieber

FREUD, Sigmund. Austrian psychoanalyst. Born in Freiberg, Moravia, 6 May 1856; emigrated to England in 1938. Studied at the University of Vienna, 1874-79, M.D. 1881; studied under Jean Charcot in Paris, 1885-86. Married Martha Bernays in 1886; 6 children, including the psychoanalyst Anna Freud, q.v. Worked at the Brücke Institute, 1881-82, and General Hospital, Vienna, 1882-85; Lecturer, University of Vienna, 1885; began private practice in Vienna in 1886. Visiting Lecturer, Clark University, Worcester, Massachusetts, 1909; Huxley Lecturer, University of London, 1931. Founder, with others, of the Vienna Psycho-Analytic Society, 1902, the International Psycho-Analytic Congress, 1908, the *Zeitschrift für Psychoanalyse und Imago*, the *Jahrbuch der Psychoanalyse*, and the Internationaler Psychoanalytischer Verlag. Recipient: Goethe Prize, 1930. Honorary doctorate: Clark University, Worcester, Massachusetts, 1909. Honorary Member, Gesellschaft der Ärtze, 1931; American Psychiatric Association, 1931; American Psychoanalytic Association, 1931; New York Neurological Society, 1931; French Psychoanalytic Society, 1931; and Royal Medico-Psychological Association, 1931. Fellow, Royal Society of Medicine, London, 1935. Corresponding Member, Royal Society, London, 1936. *Died* (in London) *23 September 1939.*

PUBLICATIONS

Collections

Sammlung kleiner Schriften zur Neurosenlehre. Vienna, 5 vols., 1906-22 (vols. 1-3, Deuticke; vol. 4, Heller; vol. 5, Internationaler Psychoanalytischer Verlag).
Gesammelte Schriften. Vienna, Internationaler Psychoanalytischer Verlag, 12 vols., 1924-34.
Collected Papers. London, Hogarth Press, and New York, Basic Books, 5 vols., 1924-50.
The Basic Writings of Sigmund Freud, edited by A.A. Brill. New York, Random House, 1938.
Gesammelte Werke. London, Imago Publishing Company, 17 vols., 1940-52; after 1960, Frankfurt, Fischer.
The Standard Edition of the Complete Psychological Works of Sigmund Freud, James Strachey, general editor. London, Hogarth Press, and New York, Macmillan, 24 vols., 1953-74.

Psychology and Medicine

Zur Auffassung der Aphasien: Eine kritische Studie. Leipzig, Deuticke, 1891; as *On Aphasia: A Critical Study,* London, Imago Publishing Company, and New York, International Universities Press, 1953.
Studien über Hysterie, with Josef Breuer. Leipzig, Deuticke, 1895; selections in *Selected Papers on Hysteria,* 1909; com-

plete text as "Studies in Hysteria," in *The Standard Edition of the Complete Psychological Works of Sigmund Freud*, vol. 2.

Die infantile Cerebrallähmung. Vienna, Hölder, 1897; as *Infantile Cerebral Paralysis*, Coral Gables, Florida, University of Miami Press, 1968.

Die Traumdeutung. Leipzig, Deuticke, 1900; as *The Interpretation of Dreams*, London, Allen and Unwin, and New York, Macmillan, 1913; 8th revised edition, 1954.

Zur Psychopathologie des Alltagslebens (Über Vergessen, Versprechen, Vergreifen, Aberglaube und Irrtum). Berlin, Karger, 1904; as *Psychopathology of Everyday Life*, London, Fisher Unwin, and New York, Macmillan, 1914.

Der Witz und seine Beziehung zum Unbewussten. Leipzig, Deuticke, 1905; as *Wit in Its Relation to the Unconscious*, New York, Moffat Yard, 1916; London, Fisher Unwin, 1917; as *Jokes and Their Relation to the Unconscious*, New York, Norton, 1960.

Drei Abhandlungen zur Sexualtheorie. Leipzig, Deuticke, 1905; as *Three Contributions to the Sexual Theory*, New York, Journal of Nervous and Mental Disease Publishing Company, 1910; as *Three Essays on the Theory of Sexuality*, London, Imago Publishing Company, 1949.

Der Wahn und die Träume in W. Jensens Gradiva. Leipzig, Heller, 1907; as *Delusion and Dream*, New York, Moffat Yard, 1917; London, Allen and Unwin, 1921.

Selected Papers on Hysteria and Other Psychoneuroses. New York, Journal of Nervous and Mental Disease Publishing Company, 1909.

Über Psychoanalyse: Fünf Vorlesungen gehalten zur zwanzigjährigen Gründungsfeier der Clark University in Worcester, Massacusetts, September 1909. Leipzig, Deuticke, 1910; as "The Origin and Development of Psychoanalysis," in *Lectures and Addresses Delivered Before the Departments of Psychology and Pedagogy in Celebration of the Twentieth Anniversary of the Opening of Clark University*, Worcester, Massachusetts, Clark University Press, 1910; selections in *A General Selection from the Works of Sigmund Freud*, edited by J. Rickman, London, Hogarth Press and Institute of Psycho-Analysis, 1937.

Eine Kindheitserinnerung des Leonardo da Vinci. Leipzig, Deuticke, 1910; as *Leonardo da Vinci: A Psychosexual Study of Infantile Reminiscence*, New York, Moffat Yard, 1916; London, Kegan Paul, 1922.

Über den Traum. Weisbaden, Bergmann, 1911; as *On Dreams*, London, Heinemann, and New York, Rebman, 1914.

Totem und Tabu: Über einige Übereinstimmungen im Seelenleben der Wilden und der Neurotiker. Leipzig, Heller, 1913; as *Totem and Taboo: Resemblances Between the Psychic Drives of Savages and Neurotics*, New York, Moffat Yard, 1917; London, Routledge, 1919.

"Zeitgemässes über Krieg und Tod," in *Imago* (Vienna), 4, 1915; as *Reflections on War and Death*. New York, Moffat Yard, 1918; as "Thoughts for the Times on War and Death," in *Collected Papers*, vol. 4.

Vorlesungen zur Einführung in die Psychoanalyse. Leipzig, Heller, 3 vols., 1916; as *A General Introduction to Psychoanalysis*, New York, Boni and Liveright, 1920; as *Introductory Lectures on Psycho-Analysis*, London, Allen and Unwin, 1922.

Jenseits des Lustprinzips. Leipzig, Internationaler Psychoanalytischer Verlag, 1920; as *Beyond the Pleasure Principle*, London, International Psychoanalytic Press, 1922; New York, Boni and Liveright, 1924.

Massenpsychologie und Ich-Analyse. Leipzig, Internationaler Psychoanalytischer Verlag, 1921; as *Group Psychology and the Analysis of the Ego*, London, International Psychoanalytic Press, 1922; New York, Liveright, 1940.

Das Ich und das Es. Leipzig, Internationaler Psychoanalytischer Verlag, 1923; as *The Ego and the Id*, London, Hogarth Press and Institute of Psycho-Analysis, 1927.

Eine Teufelneurose im siebzehnten Jahrhundert. Leipzig,

Internationaler Psychoanalytischer Verlag, 1924; as "A Neurosis of Demoniacal Posession in the Seventeenth Century," in *Collected Papers*, vol. 4.

Zur Technik der Psychoanalyse und zur Metapsychologie. Leipzig, Internationaler Psychoanalytischer Verlag, 1924; translated in various volumes of the *Standard Edition*.

Psychoanalytische Studien an Werken der Dichtung und Kunst. Leipzig, Internationaler Psychoanalytischer Verlag, 1924; translated in various volumes of the *Standard Edition*.

Kleine Beiträge zur Traumlehre. Leipzig, Internationaler Psychoanalytischer Verlag, 1925; translated in various volumes of the *Standard Edition*.

Hemmung, Symptom und Angst. Leipzig, Internationaler Psychoanalytischer Verlag, 1926; as *Inhibition, Symptom and Anxiety*, Stamford, Connecticut, Psychoanalytic Institute, 1927; as *Inhibitions, Symptoms and Anxiety*, London, Hogarth Press and Institute of Psycho-Analysis, 1936.

Die Frage der Laienanalyse: Unterredung mit einem Unparteiischen. Leipzig, Internationaler Psychoanalytischer Verlag, 1926; as *The Problem of Lay-Analysis*, New York, Brentano, 1927; as *The Question of Lay-Analysis: An Introduction to Psycho-Analysis*, London, Imago Publishing Company, 1947.

Die Zukunft einer Illusion. Leipzig, Internationaler Psychoanalytischer Verlag, 1927; as *The Future of an Illusion*, London, Hogarth Press and Institute of Psycho-Analysis, and New York, Liveright, 1928.

Das Unbehagen in der Kultur. Vienna, Internationaler Psychoanalytischer Verlag, 1930; as *Civilization and Its Discontents*, London, Hogarth Press and Institute of Psycho-Analysis, and New York, Cape and Smith, 1930.

Theoretische Schriften. Vienna, Internationaler Psychoanalytischer Verlag, 1931; translated in various volumes of the *Standard Edition*.

Schriften zur Neurosenlehre und zur psychoanalytischen Technik (1913-1926). Vienna, Internationaler Psychoanalytischer Verlag, 1931; translated in various volumes of the *Standard Edition*.

Kleine Schriften zur Sexualtheorie und zur Traumlehre. Vienna, Internationaler Psychoanalytischer Verlag, 1931; translated in various volumes of the *Standard Edition*.

Vier psychoanalytische Krankengeschichten. Vienna, Internationaler Psychoanalytischer Verlag, 1932; translated in various volumes of the *Standard Edition*.

Neue Folge der Vorlesungen zur Einführung in die Psychoanalyse. Vienna, Internationaler Psychoanalytischer Verlag, 1933; as *New Introductory Lectures on Psycho-Analysis*, London, Hogarth Press and Institute of Psycho-Analysis, and New York, Norton, 1933.

Why War?, with Albert Einstein. Paris, International Institute of Intellectual Cooperation, 1933; London, Peace Pledge Union, 1939.

Der Mann Moses und die monotheistiche Religion: Drei Abhandlungen. Amsterdam, Allert de Lange, 1939; as *Moses and Monotheism*, London, Hogarth Press and Institute of Psycho-Analysis, and New York, Knopf, 1939.

An Outline of Psycho-Analysis. London, Hogarth Press and Institute of Psycho-Analysis, and New York, Norton, 1949.

Dreams in Folklore, with D.E. Oppenheim. New York, International Universities Press, 1958.

The Cocaine Papers. Vienna, Dunquin Press, 1963; New York, Stonehill, 1975.

Thomas Woodrow Wilson, Twenty-Eighth President of the United States: A Psychological Study, with William C. Bullitt. London, Weidenfield and Nicolson, and Boston, Houghton Mifflin, 1967.

Other

Selbstdarstellungen. Leipzig, Meiner, 1925; as "An Autobiographical Study," in *The Problem of Lay-Analysis*, New York, Brentano, 1927; as *An Autobiographical Study*, London, Hogarth Press and Institute of Psycho-Analysis, 1935.

The Origins of Psycho-Analysis: Letters to Wilhelm Fleiss, Drafts and Notes, 1889-1902, edited by Anna Freud and others. London, Imago Publishing Company, and New York, Basic Books, 1954.

Briefe 1873-1939, edited by E.L. Freud. Frankfurt, Fischer, 1960; as *The Letters of Sigmund Freud*, New York, Basic Books, 1960.

Sigmund Freud/Oskar Pfister: Briefe 1909 bis 1939, edited by E.L. Freud and H. Meng. Frankfurt, Fischer, 1963; as *Psychoanalysis and Faith: Dialogues with the Reverend Oskar Pfister*, London, Hogarth Press, and New York, Basic Books, 1963.

Sigmund Freud/Karl Abraham: Briefe 1907 bis 1926, edited by H.C. Abraham and E.L. Freud. Frankfurt, Fischer, 1965; as *A Psychoanalytic Dialogue: The Letters of Sigmund Freud and Karl Abraham, 1907-1926*, New York, Basic Books, 1965.

Sigmund Freud/Lou Andreas-Salomé, Briefwechsel, edited by E. Pfeiffer. Frankfurt, Fischer, 1966; as *Sigmund Freud and Lou Andrea-Salomé*, New York, Harcourt Brace, 1972.

Briefwechsel von Sigmund Freud und Arnold Zweig, 1927-1939, edited by E.L. Freud. Frankfurt, Fischer, 1968; as *The Letters of Sigmund Freud and Arnold Zweig, 1927-1939*, London, Hogarth Press and Institute of Psycho-Analysis, and New York, Harcourt Brace, 1970.

Briefwechsel, with Carl Jung, edited by William McGuire and Wolfgang Sauerländer. Frankfurt, Fischer, 1974; as *The Freud/Jung Letters: The Correspondence Between Sigmund Freud and C.G. Jung*, London, Hogarth Press and Routledge, and Princeton, New Jersey, Princeton University Press, 1974.

Translator, *Leçons sur les maladies du système nerveux*, Vol. III, by Jean-Martin Charcot. Vienna, Deuticke, 1886.

Translator, *De la suggestion et des applications à la thérapeutique*, by Hippolyte-Marie Bernheim. Vienna, Deuticke, 1888.

Translator, *Leçons du mardi à la Salpêtrière (1887-1888)*, by Jean-Martin Charcot. Vienna, Deuticke, 1892.

Translator, *Hypnotisme, suggestion et psychothérapie: Etudes nouvelles*, by Hippolyte-Marie Bernheim. Vienna, Deuticke, 1892.

Translator, with Anna Freud, *Topsy, Chow-Chow au poil d'or*, by Marie Bonaparte. Amsterdam, n.p., 1939.

*

Bibliography: *Sigmund Freud's Writings: A Comprehensive Bibliography* by Alexander Grinstein, New York, International Universities Press, 1977.

Critical Studies: *The Life and Work of Sigmund Freud* by Ernest Jones, London, Hogarth Press, and New York, Basic Books, 3 vols., 1953-57; *Freud: The Mind of the Moralist* by Philip Rieff, New York, Viking Press, 1959, London, Gollancz, 1960; *Freud: Political and Social Thought* by Paul Roazen, New York, Knopf, 1968, London, Hogarth Press, 1969; *Freud and Philosophy* by Paul Ricoeur, New Haven, Connecticut, Yale University Press, 1970; *Freud: A Collection of Critical Essays*, edited by Richard Wollheim, New York, Anchor Books, 1974; *Freud and Modern Society* by Robert Bobock, London, Nelson, 1976; *Freud, Biologist of the Mind* by Frank J. Sulloway, New York, Basic Books, 1970, London, Burnett Books, 1980; *Freud: The Man and the Cause* by Ronald W. Clark, New York, Random House, 1980; *Freud's Odyssey* by S. Draenos, New Haven, Connecticut, Yale University Press, 1982.

*   *   *

If no greater influence on 20th century thought exists than that of Sigmund Freud, the answer lies partly in the unusual amalgamation of science and humanism that marked the Viennese physician-author. Freud practiced as a clinical psychiatrist all his life, and his famous theory of psychoanalysis claimed to be scientific, in rationally understanding and treating the sicknesses of the mind. Freud's general spirit was adverse to metaphysics, mysticism, religion or anything except the empirically verifiable hypotheses of scientific method. In this respect he shared in the vogue for scientific positivism which characterized the last decades of the 19th century, and he reminds us of Charles Darwin or Bertrand Russell. At the same time, Freud was steeped in the classics and made use of concepts drawn from literature (which he influenced enormously); he was in many ways an obviously imaginative writer. Few major intellectual figures have so successfully straddled the two cultures which are both essential to modern man but which have so often been antagonistic.

Freud's influence stems also from the vigor and clarity of his prose, but it is chiefly the daring originality of his thought which captures the imagination. Like the works of Marx, Freud's theories have sometimes been vulgarized by being reduced to a simple set of propositions when in fact they are much richer than such popular formulations indicate; and Freud shares with his fellow Jewish social theorist a certain intolerant dogmatism: he definitely wished to father a "movement" that would bear his name. Freud worked out his key ideas between 1885 and 1905, then co-founded the International Psychoanalytical Association, which disseminated his views widely and survived the notable schisms besetting the movement. He added significantly to his corpus of writing after 1920 despite a painful cancer that afflicted him through the last 15 years of his life. The 1920's saw a world-wide reception of his ideas; Freudian terms such as the unconscious, repression, Oedipus complex, Id and Ego became household words. Freud's theories, along with those of Albert Einstein, seemed the most exciting and radical of the ideas changing the world in that iconoclastic period. Psychoanalysis developed into a major profession, especially in America. (Its vogue in the United States as a gadget to fix your hangups did not please Freud, whose aristocratic Old-World temperament strongly disliked American culture.)

Essential Freudian concepts, in the formulation of which he was highly original, even when transforming older ideas, included the "Unconscious" which Freud thought played a large part in human life (Freud said he found the Unconscious in poets and novelists, but made it scientific); the idea of mental illness as traceable to traumatic events which are repressed and buried in the subconscious; the sexual nature of most of these traumatic events, involving infantile experiences (Freud, it is said, slew the Victorian myth of innocent childhood); the therapy for neurosis in a dialogue between patient and physician which aims at uncovering the buried and repressed memory; the interpretation and therapeutic use of dreams, which offer clues to the unconscious; and the application of theories of the Unconscious to everyday life, in explaining jokes, dreams, "Freudian slips" of the tongue.

Freud sketched theories of early sexual development, wrote up his most interesting cases, and applied his theories to the explanation of works of art (*Hamlet*, Leonardo's "Mona Lisa"). After World War I he added aggression to sex as a basic drive, and wrote of the death instinct as well as the erotic force. *Id, Ego, and Superego* presented a dramatic picture of conflict between antisocial and authoritarian pressures bearing on the divided self; the later Freud, more speculative and philosophical, visualized man as tragically torn between these irreconcilable claims of society and the individual.

In *Totem and Taboo* Freud attempted to relate his theory of individual behavior to human history, postulating a primeval rebellion of the sons against the father on grounds of sexual jealousy, which was the social counterpart of the Oedipal complex. In *The Future of an Illusion* Freud scornfully rejected the crutch of religion, the "collective neurosis", and placed his faith in science while conceding that man's lot on earth is a harsh one. Along with his anti-religious stance, Freud regarded art as a neurotic illusion, a retreat from reality through fantasy. Yet, paradoxically, during the postwar years his ideas blended with revivals of traditional Christianity and Judaism on the common ground of a gloomy view of human nature; and a veritable swarm of novels, plays, and paintings registered the role of Freud as ringmaster in a renaissance of the arts. To the creative writer and artist he had opened up the fascinating realm of the unconscious, of forces from the mysterious depths of the self; he touched on hitherto tabooed themes of sexual perversion, incest, homosexuality. The new novel of Proust, Joyce, Lawrence and Kafka intersected with Freudian themes of deep subjectivity even as these writers criticized Freud on theoretical grounds for attempting to eliminate the sources of creativity, rather than tap them.

Freud had no message of social salvation; he "refused to play the prophet," and wanted only to strengthen the individual personality for whatever goals it might wish to pursue. There was an element of conservatism in Freud's later view of humanity's inevitable imperfections. Aggressive, anti-social impulses exist in human nature and can be curbed only at the price of neurosis; if uncurbed, these impulses make civilized existence impossible.

Suspicious of all utopian political schemes, Freud was sceptical about the new Communism of the Soviet Union. He was proud of his Jewishness though scornful of traditional religious Judaism, and he was an admirer of Herzl's Zionism. Freud was forced to flee from his lifelong home in Vienna in the last year of his life when Hitler's Nazis seized Austria in 1938.

"You cannot nowadays open a novel, read a modern history or biography, discuss a painting or sculpture, attend a sociological lecture, or even wonder why your next door neighbor's children are so badly behaved" without encountering Freudian ideas. Freud's vast impact was partly the result of his coinciding with major cultural changes, the liberation of sexual subjects from earlier taboos being the most obvious. Freud has not escaped severe criticism. It has been said that Freudianism is a pseudoscience consisting of speculative ideas never adequately supported by clinical evidence. Its major tenets such as the Oedipus complex (male child's sexual jealousy of his father) when tested empirically do not seem to bear the weight he put on them. Freud was one-sided and overly dogmatic in stressing sexual motives to the exclusion of others. Psychoanalytic therapy has largely failed as a means of treating the great bulk of serious mental disturbances. Freudian interpretations of biography and history are usually unproven and unproveable, though interesting. Some urge that Freud provided a new myth for modern man, not a new science. The undeniable influence of Freudian methods on literary criticism, and Freudian metaphors on creative writing and the arts, may be deplored. Violently controversial from the beginning, Freud saw most of his early disciples break with him to set up their own rival theories and schools; of these erstwhile disciples at least one, Carl Jung, appears to some a more impressive figure than the Master. Radical feminists have reproached Freud for his views about women's nature, which they claim are demeaning to them; and today's professional, academic psychology makes little room for Freud or any of the other psychoanalytic schools.

Yet against such cavils stands the fact of Freud's continuing influence on our ways of thinking about human behavior. Like Marx and other prophetic figures, Freud has been much reinterpreted and revised. Jacques Lacan combined his thought with structural linguistics and radical politics, leading a significant neo-Freudian revival recently in France. Apart from the "system", which like all systems in human sciences proves inadequate to its subject, there is the rich lode of Freud's particular studies, letters, etc. which only now is being thoroughly mined, and which yields the insights of a keenly perceptive and highly civilized mind. Freudianism has followed the familiar process of being diffused and absorbed so that it disappears as a monolithic doctrine but becomes a part of intellectual culture as a whole. Freud continues to count as one of the towering figures of the century, and a maker of the modern mind.

Comparing himself to Copernicus and Darwin, Freud once remarked that his revolution was the last of the three that had humbled man, and thought his the greatest blow. Man was first dethroned from his place at the center of the physical universe, then lost his distinctiveness from other forms of life; Freud, finally, had shown that man was not even master of his own actions and mental processes, which arise from unconscious sources over which he has no control. Freud hoped to found a science which would provide such rational mastery of the unconscious. Whether he did so or not has yet to be decided.

—Roland Stromberg

FRIEDMAN, Milton. American economist. Born in Brooklyn, New York, 31 July 1912. Studied at Rutgers University, New Brunswick, New Jersey, B.A. 1932; University of Chicago, M.A. 1933; Columbia University, New York, Ph.D. 1946. Associate Director, Statistical Research Group, Division of War Research, Columbia University, 1943-45. Married Rose Director in 1938; 1 daughter, 1 son. Associate Economist, National Resources Committee, Washington, D.C., 1935-37, and National Bureau of Economic Research, New York, 1937-45 (on leave 1940-45) and from 1948; Visiting Professor, University of Wisconsin, Madison, 1940-41; Principal Economist, Tax Research Division, U.S. Treasury Department, 1941-43; Associate Professor, University of Minnesota, Minneapolis, 1945-46; Associate Professor, 1946-48, Professor, 1948-62, and Paul Snowden Russell Distinguished Service Professor of Economics, University of Chicago, from 1962. Senior Research Fellow, Hoover Institution, Stanford University, California, since 1977. Fulbright Lecturer, Cambridge University, 1953-54; Fellow, Center for Advanced Study in Behavioral Science, Palo Alto, California, 1957-58; Visiting Wesley Clair Mitchell Research Professor of Economics, Columbia University, 1964-65; Visiting Scholar, Federal Reserve Bank, San Francisco, 1977. Member, President's Council of Economic Advisors, from 1981. President, American Economic Association, 1967, and Mont Pelerin Society, 1970-72. Recipient: John Bates Clark Medal, American Economic Association, 1951; Nobel Prize in Economics, 1976; Private Enterprise Exemplar Medal, Freedoms Foundation, 1978. Honorary doctorate: St. Paul's University, Rikkyo, Japan, 1963; Kalamazoo College, Michigan, 1968; Rutgers University, 1968; Lehigh University, Bethlehem, Pennsylvania, 1969; Rockford College, Illinois, 1969; Loyola University, Chicago, 1971; University of Rochester, New York, 1971; Roosevelt University, Chicago, 1975; University of New Hampshire, Durham, 1975; Hebrew University, Jerusalem, 1977; Francisco Marroquin University, Guatemala, 1978; Harvard University, Cambridge, Massachusetts, 1979; Brigham Young University, Provo, Utah, 1980; Dartmouth College, Hanover, New Hampshire, 1980. Member, National Academy of Sciences, American Enterprise Institute, and Royal Economic Society. Fellow, Mathematical Statistics Association, American Statistics Association, and Econometric Society. Address: Hoover Institution, Stanford University, Stanford, California, U.S.A.

PUBLICATIONS

Economics

Taxing to Prevent Inflation: Techniques for Estimating Revenue Requirements, with others. New York, Columbia University Press, 1943.

Income from Independent Professional Practice, with Simon Kuznets. New York, National Bureau of Economic Research, 1945.

Roofs or Ceilings? The Current Housing Problem, with George

J. Stigler. Irvington-on-Hudson, New York, Foundation for Economic Education, 1946.

Essays in Positive Economics. Chicago, University of Chicago Press, 1953.

A Theory of the Consumption Function. Princeton, New Jersey, Princeton University Press, 1957.

A Program for Monetary Stability. New York, Fordham University Press, 1959.

The Demand for Money: Some Theoretical and Empirical Results. New York, National Bureau of Economic Research, 1959.

Capitalism and Freedom, with Rose D. Friedman. Chicago, University of Chicago Press, 1962.

Price Theory: A Provisional Text. Chicago, Aldine, 1962.

Inflation: Causes and Consequences. Bombay and New York, Asia Publishing House, 1963.

A Monetary History of the United States, 1867-1960, with Anna Jacobson Schwartz. Princeton, New Jersey, Princeton University Press, 1963; selections as *The Great Contraction 1929-1933,* 1965.

Post War Trends in Monetary Theory and Policy (lecture). Athens, Center of Economic Research, 1963.

The Balance of Payments: Free Versus Fixed Exchange Rates, with Robert V. Roosa. Washington, D.C., American Enterprise Institute for Public Policy Research, 1967.

Dollars and Deficits: Living with America's Economic Problems. Englewood Cliffs, New Jersey, Prentice Hall, 1968.

Monetary vs. Fiscal Policy: A Dialogue Between Milton Friedman and Walter W. Heller, with Walter W. Heller. New York, Norton, 1969.

The Optimum Quantity of Money and Other Essays. Chicago, Aldine, 1969.

The Counter-Revolution in Monetary Theory (lecture). London, Institute of Economic Affairs, 1970.

Monetary Statistics of the United States: Estimates, Sources, Methods, with Anna Jacobson Schwartz. New York, National Bureau of Economic Research, 1970.

A Theoretical Framework for Monetary Analysis. New York, National Bureau of Economic Research, 1971.

An Economist's Protest: Columns in Political Economy. Glen Ridge, New Jersey, T. Horton, 1972; as *There's No Such Thing as a Free Lunch,* La Salle, Illinois, Open Court, 1975.

Social Security: Universal or Selective?, with Wilbur J. Cohen. Washington, D.C., American Enterprise Institute for Public Policy Research, 1972.

A Theoretical Framework for Monetary Analysis. New York, National Bureau of Economic Research, 1972.

Money and Economic Development (lecture). New York and London, Praeger, 1973.

Monetary Correction: A Proposal for Escalator Clauses to Reduce the Costs of Ending Inflation. London, Institute of Economic Affairs, 1974.

Free Markets for Free Men. Chicago, University of Chicago Graduate School of Business, 1974.

Milton Friedman in Australia, 1975. Sydney, Constable and Bain and the Graduate Business School Club, 1975.

Unemployment Versus Inflation? An Evaluation of the Phillips Curve. London, Institute of Economic Affairs, 1975.

Milton Friedman Speaks to CEDA: A Report on the Visit of Professor Milton Friedman to the Committee for Economic Development of Australia. Melbourne, CEDA, 1975.

Friedman on Galbraith, and on Curing the British Disease. Vancouver, Fraser Institute, 1977; as *From Galbraith to Economic Freedom,* London, Institute of Economic Affairs, 1977.

The Nobel Prize in Economics (lecture). Stanford, California, Hoover Institution, 1977.

Tax Limitation, Inflation and the Role of Government. Dallas, Fisher Institute, 1978.

Free to Choose: A Personal Statement, with Rose D. Friedman. New York, Harcourt Brace, 1980.

Market Mechanisms and Central Economic Planning (lectures). Washington, D.C., American Enterprise Institute for Public Policy Research, 1981.

Other

Editor, *The Ethics of Competition and Other Essays,* by Frank Hyneman Knight. London, Allen and Unwin, 1935.

Editor, *Studies in the Quantity Theory of Money.* Chicago, University of Chicago Press, 1956.

*

Critical Studies: *Milton Friedman's Monetary Framework: A Debate with His Critics,* edited by Robert J. Gordon, Chicago, University of Chicago Press, 1974; *Capitalism and Freedom: Problems and Prospects: Proceedings of a Conference in Honor of Milton Friedman,* edited by Richard T. Selden, Charlottesville, University Press of Virginia, 1975; *Die Neubegrundung der Quantitatstheorie durch Milton Friedman* by Petros A. Gemtos, Tübingen, Germany, Mohr, 1975.

*   *   *

Milton Friedman was the first and most famous disciple of the "Chicago school" of economic thought to be honored with the Nobel Prize in Economics. When Friedman received the award in 1976 after thirty years on the University of Chicago staff, only John Maynard Keynes and Paul Samuelson could rival Friedman among 20th century economists in combined impact on secular and academic thought. Arguably, his ascension since the mid-1960s has eclipsed both of his competitors.

Friedman's remarkable advocacy and influence has resulted not only from intellectual prowess, but also from a uniform and robust analytical approach which is applied with seemingly equal effect to social and political problems as well as those which are purely economic. He undoubtedly owes much to his graduate training at the University of Chicago and Columbia University. Frank Knight intoned the philosophical beauty of laissez-faire liberalism, Jacob Viner provided the foundation in economic theory, Henry Simon illustrated the importance of macroeconomic policy, Harold Hotelling and Henry Schultz provided the mathematical and statistical tools, and Wesley Clair Mitchell instilled an appreciation for institutional arrangements and facts. However, it may be Friedman's self-reliance, and an appreciation of the potential for free markets to reward mankind for self-reliant effort, that ultimately explains the depth and success of Friedman's vision.

For an economist to have such a large impact both within and outside his profession requires great powers of persuasion. Indeed, Paul Samuelson remarked that he "would bet that any two persons in the same room with Milton Friedman for ten minutes will come out on the same side, at least temporarily." However, Friedman's reputation does not depend on the "black art" of debate. In the preface to *Free to Choose,* he recognizes that "anyone who is persuaded in one evening...is not really persuaded. He can be converted by the next person of opposite views with whom he spends an evening.... You must...consider the many arguments, let them simmer, and after a long time turn your preferences into convictions." To this end, Friedman has made a career of converting sharp debates into elegant essays and studied empirical investigations, ranging from his popular policy analyses in *Newsweek* to the monumental *A Monetary History of the United States, 1867-1960,* co-authored with Anna Schwartz.

Friedman's contributions to economic theory and policy are predicated on his belief in "doctrines relating to a 'free man' which are diametrically opposed to the modern day concept which stresses 'welfare' and equality over freedom." Not surprisingly, in the introduction to *Free to Choose* Friedman traces the success of western economic and social advancement to the ideas embodied in two works which appeared in 1776, Adam Smith's *The Wealth of Nations* and Thomas Jefferson's *Declaration of Independence*. The *Wealth of Nations* identified market forces, powered by individuals' desires to enter mutually advantageous trade, as a superior coordinator of human action for the general benefit of society. Through the market economy, individuals with different tastes and values can find accommodation and develop a consensus, thereby avoiding much costly conflict that might occur otherwise. Friedman feels that coercion is the biggest threat to mankind, and, as Jefferson did, finds that government produces the most debilitating coercion of all. Moreover, he states that "economic freedom is an essential requisite for political freedom. By enabling people to cooperate with one another without coercion or central direction, it reduces the area over which political power is exercised. In addition, by dispersing power, the free market provides an offset to whatever concentration of political power may arise. The combination of economic and political power in the same hands is a sure recipe for tyranny."

Friedman's erudite arguments were among the most important elements of an evolution of public sentiment during the 1970's away from the belief that government solutions necessarily are superior solutions. With these changes in sentiment have come changing political objectives in several countries, notably the United States and the United Kingdom, the longevity of which remain to be seen. However, it is popularly recognized that even well-introduced government actions often produce inferior outcomes, both because the lagged effects of plodding government processes frequently impact the economy after the problem to be addressed has been resolved by other means, and because central control or coercion hinders the socially beneficial effects of mutually advantageous exchange. Hence, Friedman's free market alternatives continue to be debated in the political arena. These include limits on government's power to tax and spend, removal of tariffs and quotas in foreign trade, easing of controls on entry to occupations by licensure, abolition of price and wage controls, and the removal of other impediments to free choice. His influence has spurred progress toward restoring the view "that government's role is to serve as an umpire to prevent individuals from coercing one another," rather than "that government's role is to serve as a parent charged with the duty of coercing some to aid others."

Friedman tends to look at all the universe with a single methodological approach, failing to make the distinctions that Frank Knight made between moral problems and economic problems. However, Friedman follows the lead of Knight in clearly distinguishing between "positive" analysis and "normative" judgments. Compelled by the belief that man's normative preferences for desired outcomes are less diverse than the disagreements over optimal means of reaching these outcomes, he set out to discover what was indisputable fact.

Friedman's most well known and valuable contributions to economic science are encompassed within what is popularly called monetarism. The modern version of monetarism, or the quantity theory of money, states that: 1) there is a stable relationship between the amount of money supplied to an economy and the amount of spending generated; 2) the money/spending relationship will vary in a predictable manner in response to a few variables such as interest rates and inflationary expectations; 3) changes in spending generated by changes in money supply will induce temporary changes in economic output; 4) changes in money supply ultimately affect only the price level; 5) interest rates, after adjustment for inflationary expectations, are determined by time preference, productivity, and the physical return on capital; and 6) the money supply is an independently targetable policy objective of government. Regarding the power of the modern quantity theory, the 20th century's most prominent monetarist stated, "There is no other empirical relation in economics that has been observed to recur so uniformly under so wide a variety of circumstances as the relationship between substantial changes over short periods in the stock of money and

prices."

A Monetary History of the United States is probably Milton Friedman's single most important work. In this volume, he and Anna Schwartz make a convincing case that the Great Depression was not caused by a failure of free markets which implied the need for government intervention, but was caused by a sharp and sustained decline in the money supply for which the government was largely responsible. The historical evidence confirmed his earlier belief that "...the central problem is not to construct a highly sensitive instrument that can continuously offset instability introduced by other factors, but rather to prevent monetary arrangements from themselves becoming a primary source of instability."

Friedman believes that "the most remarkable feature of the record is the adaptability and flexibility that the private economy has so frequently shown under such extreme provocation." Consequently, he has called for a non-discretionary monetary policy that maintains a constant, predictable, non-inflationary money growth rate so that destabilizing changes from monetary policy are eliminated. In developing support for such a policy over the years, Friedman's research has exploded the Keynesian view of monetary policy that prescribed an expansive monetary growth to lower interest rates. Alternatively, monetarists maintain that low interest rates indicate that money growth and inflation are low, and that high rates of money growth and inflation will generate high interest rates. "These considerations ...explain why interest rates are such a misleading indicator of whether monetary policy is 'tight' or 'easy.' For that, it is far better to look at the rate of change in the quantity of money."

In addition to his pioneering work to restore and extend monetarist doctrine, Friedman has made substantial contributions in other areas of economics. These include introduction of the concept of human capital to the field of labor economics, analysis of the different effects of permanent and transitory changes in income on consumption decisions, and development of a theory of unemployment which established the futility of policies designed to lower unemployment below its equilibrium or "natural" rate. In spite of these remarkable academic achievements, Milton Friedman's greatest influence has been as a teacher and mentor who has taken for his audience not just students and fellow academicians, but the whole world.

—Robert R. Davis

FRISCH, Ragnar (Anton Kittil). Norwegian economist. Born in Oslo, 2 March 1895. Studied at University of Oslo, M.A. 1919; Ph.D. 1926. Married Marie Smedal in 1920; 1 daughter; married Astrid Johannessen in 1953. Member of the Faculty, 1925-31, and Professor, 1931-65, University of Oslo; also, Professor of Economics, 1931-71, and Director of Research, 1932-65, University Institute of Economic Foundations. Visiting Professor, Yale University, New Haven, Connecticut, 1930, and Sorbonne, Paris, 1933. Editor, *Econometrica*, 1933-65. Chairman, United Nations Economic and Employment Commission, 1947. Recipient: Nobel Prize in Economics, with Jan Tinbergen, 1969. Honorary doctorate: Handelshogskolan i Stockholm and Copenhagen University, 1959; Stockholm University, 1966; Queens' College, Cambridge, 1967. Fellow, Econometric Society and Institute of Mathematical Statistics; Honorary Fellow, Royal Statistics Society; Corresponding Fellow, British Academy; Honorary Member, American Economics Association and American Academy of Arts and Sciences; Corresponding Member, Royal Economic Society; Foreign Member, American Philosophic Society. *Died* (in Oslo) *31 January 1973.*

PUBLICATIONS

Economics

New Methods of Measuring Marginal Utility. Tübingen, Mohr,
1932.
*Pitfalls in the Statistical Construction of Demand and Supply
Curves.* Leipzig, Buske, 1933.
*Statistical Confluence Analysis by Means of Complete Regres-
sion Systems.* Oslo, Universitetets Økonomiske Institutt,
1934.
Etterspørselen efter melk i Norge [The Demand for Milk in
Norway], with Trygve Haavelmo. Oslo, 1938.
*Notater til grunnkursus i økonomisk teori: Etter forelesninger av
Ragnar Frisch* [Notes to an Elementary Course in Economic
Theory: From the Lectures of Ragnar Frisch]. Oslo, Trykk,
1939.
*En byggekostnadsindeks grunnlagt på de faktiske byggeforhold
til enhever tid: Prinsipiell utredning og data for A/S Storm-
bulls indeks for totale byggekostnader for trevilla i Aker 1932-
1938* [An Index of the Construction-Costs Based upon the
Actual Construction Conditions at Any Given Time: Funda-
mental Budgeting and Data for A/S Storbull's Index of the
Total Construction Costs of Wooden Housing in Aker 1932-
1938], with others. Oslo, Universitetets Socialøkonomiske
Institutt, 1943.
Innledning til produksjonsteorien (7th to 9th editions). Oslo,
Trykk, 1946; as *Theory of Production*, Dordrecht, D. Reidel,
and Chicago, Rand McNally, 1965.
*Noen trekk av konjunkturlaeren, med et tillegg om levestandard
og prisindeks.* [Some Aspects of the Concept of Supply and
Demand Curves, with an Appendix on Living Standard and
Price Index]. Oslo, H. Aschehoug, 1947.
Notater til økonomisk teori [Notes on Economic Theory] (4th
edition). Oslo, Universitetets Socialøkonomiske Institutt,
1947.
Planning for India: Selected Explorations in Methodology.
London, Statistical Publications Society, and New York, Asia
Publishing House, 1960.
Maxima and Minima: Theory and Economic Applications
(translated from the Norwegian), with A. Nataf. Dordrecht,
D. Reidel, and Chicago, Rand McNally, 1966.
*Cooperation Between Politicians and Econometricians on the
Formalization of Political Preferences.* Stockholm, Federa-
tion of Swedish Industries, 1971.
Economic Planning Studies: A Collection of Essays, edited by
Frank Long. Dordrecht and Boston, D. Reidel, 1976.

Other

Editor, *Socialøkonomiske utsnitt: originaltekster ugitt med
innføriner og forklaringar* [Socio-Economic Aspects: Original
Texts with Introductions and Explanations], with Wilhelm
Keilhau. Oslo, H. Aschehoug, 1940.

*   *   *

The Norwegian Ragnar Frisch was a pioneer econometrician,
a founder of the Econometric Society, and recipient in 1969, with
Jan Tinbergen, of the first Nobel Prize in Economics. He coined
the term "econometrics" to denominate an approach to economic study represented by the combination of theory, mathematics, and statistics.

Frisch sought an exact, quantitative economic science which
integrated both theory and empirical data, especially one which
was useful in formulating and administering economic policy.
He was one of the first economists to use the axiomatic method
to produce conclusions intended to be amenable to tests using
empirical data and refined techniques of computation and conceptual manipulation. He was perhaps the foremost econometrician who had a deep sense of the epistemological limits of statis-

tical and econometric techniques, including the dangers of
empty, mathematical formalism. Frisch did pioneer work on
numerous computational methods and on the identification
problem and other complexities of complex, multi-determinant
systems.

Early in his career Frisch, following the lead of Irving Fisher,
attempted what most economists have come to believe is an
impossible, if not also an unnecessary, task, namely, the empirical measurement of cardinal utility. In that attempt he assumed
independent utility functions. Much later, he incorporated cross-
elasticities of demand in models with less emphasis on the measurement of utility per se and more on the interactive consequences of demand functions on macroeconomic planning and
forecasting.

Frisch is probably best known among English-speaking economists for his work in production theory in which he undertook
early, refined, and thorough efforts on the estimation of empirical production functions. In this work, among other things, he
distinguished between technological and economic elements.

Frisch's most dedicated work was undertaken in business cycle
analysis and general macroeconomics. He was very much concerned about instability and unemployment. He worked on the
clarification of such important distinctions as between equilibrium and disequilibrium and between statics and dynamics. He
developed dynamic macroeconomic models some of which
focused on the phenomenon of reinvestment, random shocks
and their consequences, and what came to be called the acceleration principle. He was a leading developer of large-scale macroeconomic decision models for use as tools of economic policy
and development planning, especially with regard to the relation
of goals and means and the necessity for adopting an explicit
strategy. Among other characteristics, these planning models
used input-output analysis and mathematical programming and
emphasized optimization.

Other work of Frisch's marks him as a precursor of modern
activity analysis, linear programming, and game theory, work
useful to both private and public institutions.

Frisch's work was characterized as being more comprehensive
and more refined than most other comparable models, due in
part to his sense of detail and the niceties and complexities of
computation. He was a prolific worker, only a fraction of whose
work found its way into formal publications, much circulating in
working papers and mimeographed lecture notes; and of his
publications only a fraction were translated into languages
accessible to most economists. Nonetheless, he had a significant
impact on the technical practice of econometrics and on substantive developments in several important areas of economics.

—Warren J. Samuels

FROMM, Erich. American psychologist and social critic.
Born in Frankfurt, Germany, 29 March 1900; emigrated to the
United States in 1934: naturalized, 1940. Studied at the University of Heidelberg, Ph.D. 1922; University of Munich, 1923-24;
Institute of the German Psychoanalytic Society, 1928-31. Married Frieda Reichmann in 1926 (divorced); Henny Gurland in
1944 (died); Annis Freeman in 1952. Lecturer, Psychoanalytic
Institute of Frankfurt and Institute for Social Research, University of Frankfurt, 1929-32; worked with the International Institute of Social Research, Geneva, 1933-34, and New York, 1934-
38; Lecturer, Columbia University, New York, 1940-41, and
American Institute for Psychoanalysis, 1941-42; Member of the
faculty of Bennington College, Vermont, 1941-50; after 1945,
Member of the faculty, William Allanson White Institute of
Psychiatry, Washington, D.C. (chairman of the faculty after
1947), and after 1951, Professor of Psychoanalysis, National
Autonomous University of Mexico (head of department after

1955); Professor, Michigan State University, East Lansing, 1957-61; after 1962, Adjunct Professor of Psychology, New York University, and Director, Mexican Institute for Psychoanalysis, Mexico City. Terry Lecturer, Yale University, New Haven, Connecticut, 1949-50. Fellow, National Academy of Sciences. *Died* (in Muralto, Switzerland) *18 March 1980.*

PUBLICATIONS

Psychology

Die Entwicklung des Christusdogmas. Vienna, Internationaler Psychoanalytischer Verlag, 1931; as "The Development of the Dogma of Christ," in *The Dogma of Christ and Other Essays in Religion, Psychology and Culture,* 1963.
Escape from Freedom. New York, Holt Rinehart, 1941; as *The Fear of Freedom,* London, Kegan Paul, 1942.
Man for Himself: An Inquiry into the Psychology of Ethics. New York, Holt Rinehart, 1947; London, Routledge, 1948.
Psychoanalysis and Religion. New Haven, Connecticut, Yale University Press, 1950; London, Gollancz, 1951.
The Forgotten Language: An Introduction to the Understanding of Dreams, Fairy Tales, and Myths. New York, Holt Rinehart, 1951; London, Gollancz, 1952.
The Sane Society. New York, Holt Rinehart, 1955; London, Routledge, 1956.
The Art of Loving. New York, Harper, 1956; London, Allen and Unwin, 1957.
Sigmund Freud's Mission: An Analysis of His Personality and Influence. New York, Harper, and London, Allen and Unwin, 1959.
May Man Prevail? An Inquiry into the Facts and Fictions of Foreign Policy. New York, Doubleday, 1961; London, Allen and Unwin, 1962.
Beyond the Chains of Illusion: My Encounter with Marx and Freud. New York, Simon and Schuster, 1962.
War Within Man: A Psychological Inquiry into the Roots of Destructiveness. New York, American Friends Service Committee, 1963.
The Dogma of Christ and Other Essays on Religion, Psychology and Culture. New York, Holt Rinehart, and London, Routledge, 1963.
The Heart of Man: Its Genius for Good and Evil. New York, Harper, 1964; London, Routledge, 1965.
You Shall Be as Gods: A Radical Interpretation of the Old Testament and Its Traditions. New York, Holt Rinehart, 1966; London, Cape, 1967.
The Revolution of Hope: Toward a Humanized Technology. New York, Harper, 1968.
Social Character in a Mexican Village: A Sociopsychoanalytical Study, with Michael Maccoby. Englewood Cliffs, New Jersey, Prentice Hall, 1970.
The Crisis of Psychoanalysis: Essays on Freud, Marx and Social Psychology. New York, Holt Rinehart, 1970; London, Cape, 1971.
The Anatomy of Human Destructiveness. New York, Holt Rinehart, 1973; London, Cape, 1974.
To Be or To Have? New York, Harper, 1976; London, Cape, 1978.
Greatness and Limitation of Freud's Thought. New York, Harper, 1980.
On Disobedience and Other Essays. New York, Seabury Press, 1982.
Erich Fromm: Materialien zu seinem Werk, edited by Adelbert Reif. Vienna, Europverlag, 1982.

Other

Dialogue with Erich Fromm, with Richard Evans. New York, Harper, 1966.

In Namen des Lebens: Ein Protrait im Gespräch mit Hans Jürgen Schultz. Stuttgart, Deutsche Verlagsanstalt, 1974.

Editor, with D.T. Suzuki and Richard De Martino, *Zen Buddhism and Psychoanalysis.* New York, Harper, 1960.
Editor, with Hans Herzfeld, *Der Friede: Idee und Verwirklichung.* Heidelberg, Schneider, 1961.
Editor, *Marx's Concept of Man.* New York, Ungar, 1963.
Editor, *Socialist Humanism: An International Symposium.* New York, Doubleday, 1965.
Editor, with Ramon Xirau, *The Nature of Man.* New York, Macmillan, and London, Collier Macmillan, 1968.

*

Critical Studies: *Escape from Authority: The Perspectives of Erich Fromm* by John H. Schaar, New York, Harper, 1961; *In the Name of Life: Essays in Honor of Erich Fromm,* edited by Bernard Landis and others, New York, Holt Rinehart, 1971; *Erich Fromm* by Don Hausdorff, New York, Twayne, 1972 (contains a bibliography).

*　　*　　*

Erich Fromm envisaged psychology as a continuation of humanity's age-old effort to understand itself. Whilst employing the insights of anthropology and sociology to expand knowledge gained through clinical, psychoanalytical and psychiatric studies, Fromm drew substantially upon the history of ideas, reminding his readers that ethical thinkers of the past were philosophers *and* psychologists. As a Freudian in his basic perspective, he showed the scope and strength of Freud's insights while stressing the open texture of his thought, thus avoiding dogmatism and remaining free to move significantly beyond the sources of his initial inspiration.

Though Fromm was the author of many volumes, *Escape from Freedom* is his best known book. Therein he argued that just as one cannot comprehend the individual without taking his cultural context into account, so too one cannot grasp the social process without knowing the psychological processes at work in the individual. "Pre-individualistic society" gave man security but severely limited his freedom for development. Since the collapse of the medieval feudal order, man has been freed from traditional constraints, but he has not gained freedom in the positive sense of realization of his individual self. The historical development of individuality has furnished many blessings, but the individual today must generate the inner courage to activate his full potentials, or he will seek to escape from his freedom into new forms of self-limiting dependency. The eradication of external restraints is insufficient to make man positively free: freedom *from* may be a precondition, but freedom *to* is essential for human growth. The rise of fascist governments cannot be satisfactorily explained by invoking inadequate experience in democratic methods, economic disorders or political knavery, but is rooted in internal attitudes found in all populations. Unless the sources of those attitudes are recognized and transformed—unless the individual accepts and uses his freedom in a positive way—various kinds of deadening authoritarianism (the label *e.g.*, Fascism or anti-Fascism, hardly matters) will continue to plague humanity. The problem is not, as Freud mistakenly thought, the satisfaction of instinctual needs *per se,* but rather the way an individual relates to the world. Human inclinations are not fixed through biological drives, but are the result of social endeavors, some suppressive, others creative. Society moulds man, but man in turn moulds the social process.

The freedom from socio-cultural restraint which is the experience of modern man isolates him. Physical aloneness by itself is not unbearable, but contemporary isolation from ideas, values and social patterns, from a feeling of communion, constitutes a "moral aloneness" which is intolerable and which leads, in extreme cases, to schizophrenia. Moral communion allows the individual to transcend the insignificance he feels in the face of his knowledge of the cosmos. This means he must unite himself with the world through spontaneous love and productive work or else seek security through modes of interaction that impair his freedom and undermine his integrity as an individual self. Escape from freedom may take an authoritarian turn, involving a fatalistic standpoint manifest as dominance and submission (sadism and masochism). Escape may follow a destructive route, aimed at the removal of threatening objects—ultimately the world itself. A third attempt to escape is withdrawal from the world so that it cannot harm one, and this may end in psychosis. A fourth is the inflation of self to such a point that the world diminishes to insignificance. The first two modes of escape have serious implications for society and its future. Positive freedom, on the other hand, arises from the spontaneous activity of the integrated personality. Spontaneity requires the elimination of the artificial split between reason and nature, and its chief component is love as the affirmation of others, a love which is neither self-dissolution nor possession of another.

Man for Himself elaborated these ideas in terms of ethics. Fromm held that psychology must not only debunk false ethical judgments but also provide the basis for objective and valid norms of conduct. Neurosis is a symptom of moral failure, whilst mere adjustment cannot be considered a symptom of moral achievement. Curing is removing obstacles to an active and effective life. Objectively valid ethics are possible if they are not confused with absolutist ethics and are based on principles that aid man in unfolding his powers according to the laws of human nature. Good in humanistic ethics is the affirmation of life. Virtue is responsibility toward one's own existence. "Evil constitutes the crippling of man's powers; vice is irresponsibility toward himself." Ethical significance is not found in temperament but is located in character, the relatively permanent form in which human energy is channelled. Fromm distinguished four nonproductive character orientations in terms of assimilating the world and being socialized: receiving-masochistic, exploiting-sadistic, hoarding-destructive, and marketing-indifferent, all of which are ideal types found in various combinations in individuals. The productive characterological orientation assimilates the world through work and manifests its socialization in love and reason. A key problem in engendering a productive orientation lies in selfishness, which is the product of a lack of authentic self-love. When one truly loves oneself, altruism will radiate naturally through care, respect, responsibility and knowledge. Hedonism is not enough because people can crave that which is harmful to the total personality; happiness involves the whole being, and is virtue in the sense which Fromm gave the concept.

Fromm's later writings apply these basic themes to specific topics. *Psychoanalysis and Religion*, in which he maintained that science does not threaten religion though authoritarianism undermines it, affirms the universality of religious experience independent of the forms it takes. In *The Forgotten Language* he suggested that archetypal symbols in dreams point to a universal inheritance, with intimations of immortality. *The Sane Society* elaborately shows that technological growth without social maturation will throw humanity back to crude self-worship and worship of things and images, a form of idolatry that fails to grasp reality. *The Art of Loving* reiterates the role of love in Fromm's psychology. His contribution to *Zen Buddhism and Psychoanalysis* correlates Zen thought and practice with making the unconscious conscious and with compelling the ego to be true to itself by confronting its "contradictions." *You Shall Be as Gods* portrays the Old Testament as a radical document encouraging men to free themselves from authoritarian idolatry through the recognition of an attributeless deity before which each one is responsible for himself and for the whole. Fromm began to put forth a comprehensive psychoanalytic theory in *The Anatomy of Human Destructiveness*, in which he distinguishes aggression (which is innate) from destructiveness (which is a wish to control through destruction) as a basis for analyzing competing and complementary psychological theories.

To Be or To Have summarizes Fromm's thought in terms of two modes of existence, one focussed on material possession, power and dominance, the other on love, sharing and creative productivity. Much of the contemporary crisis in human life is symptomatic of the failure of the "having" mode to help humanity attain its full potential. Fromm's prolific writing has without exception been a summons to reflective persons to recognize the gravity of the human condition and the untapped potential of all mankind. "It is the task of the ethical thinker to sustain and strengthen the voice of human conscience, to recognize what is good or what is bad for *man*, regardless of whether it is good or bad for society at a special period of its evolution. He may be the one who 'crieth in the wilderness,' but only if this voice remains alive and uncompromising will the wilderness change into fertile land."

—R.N. Iyer

FRY, Roger(Eliot). British painter and aesthetician. Born in London, 14 December 1866. Studied at King's College, Cambridge, 1887-88, first class degree, parts I and II of Natural Science Tripos; studied painting with Francis Bate, 1888, and travelled abroad, 1889-92. Married the painter Helen Coombe in 1896; 1 daughter. Gave Extension Lectures on Renaissance Art, 1894; became art critic for the *Athenaeum*, London, 1900; helped to re-establish the *Burlington Magazine*, London, 1903; Curator of Paintings, Metropolitan Museum, New York City, 1906-10; organized the first London exhibitions of Post-Impressionist art, 1910 and 1912; founded the Omega Workshops, 1913-19; Slade Professor of Fine Art, Cambridge University, 1933-34. Honorary Fellow of King's College, 1927. Honorary doctorate: University of Aberdeen, Scotland, 1929. *Died 9 September 1934.*

Publications

Art History and Aesthetics

Giovanni Bellini. London, At the Sign of the Unicorn, 1899; New York, Longman, 1901.
Vision and Design. London, Chatto and Windus, 1920; New York, Brentano's, 1921.
Architectural Heresies of a Painter (lecture). London, Chatto and Windus, 1921.
The Artist and Psycho-Analysis (lecture). London, Hogarth Press, 1924.
Art and Commerce (lecture). London, Hogarth Press, 1926.
Transformations: Critical and Speculative Essays on Art. London, Chatto and Windus, 1926; New York, Brentano's, 1927.
Flemish Art: A Critical Survey. London, Chatto and Windus, and New York, Brentano's, 1927.
Cézanne: A Study of His Development. London, Hogarth Press, and New York, Macmillan, 1927.
Henri Matisse. London, Zwemmer, and New York, Weyhe, 1930.
The Arts of Painting and Sculpture. London, Gollancz, 1932.
Characteristics of French Art. London, Chatto and Windus, 1932; New York, Brentano's, 1933.
Art-History as an Academic Study (lecture). Cambridge, Cambridge University Press, and New York, Macmillan, 1933.
Reflections on British Painting. London, Faber, and New York, Macmillan, 1934.
Last Lectures, edited by Kenneth Clark. Cambridge, Cambridge University Press, and New York, Macmillan, 1939.

French, Flemish and British Art. • London, Chatto and Windus, and New York, Coward McCann, 1951.

Other

Goldsworthy Lowes Dickinson 6 August 1962-3 August 1932: Fellow of the College: 1887-1932. Cambridge, King's College, 1933.
Sermons by Artists, with others. London, Golden Cockerel Press, 1934.
Letters of Roger Fry, edited by Denys Sutton. London, Chatto and Windus, 2 vols., 1972; New York, Random House, 2 vols., 1973.

Editor, *The Discourses of Sir Joshua Reynolds.* London, Seeley, 1905.

Translator, *Men of Europe*, by P.J. Jouve. London, Omega Workshops, 1915.
Translator, *The Nature of Beauty in Art and Literature*, by Charles Mauron. London, Hogarth Press, 1927.
Translator, *Aesthetics and Psychology*, by Charles Mauron. London, Hogarth Press, 1935.
Translator, *Poems*, by Stéphane Mallarmé. London, Chatto and Windus, 1936; New York, New Directions, 1951.

*

Bibliography: *Roger Fry: An Annotated Bibliography of the Published Writings* by Donald A. Laing, New York and London, Garland, 1979.

Critical Studies: *Roger Fry: A Biography* by Virginia Woolf, London, Hogarth Press, and New York, Harcourt Brace, 1940; *The Interpretation of Art: Essays on the Art Criticism of John Ruskin, Walter Pater, Clive Bell, Roger Fry, and Herbert Read* by Solomon Fishman, Berkeley, University of California Press, 1963; *Roger Fry* (lecture) by Quentin Bell, Leeds, University of Leeds Press, 1964.

*   *   *

R.G. Collingwood may well have had Roger Fry in mind when, in *The Principles of Art* published three years after Fry's death, he distinguished between philosopher-aestheticians such as himself and artist-aestheticians: "People who interest themselves in the philosophy of art fall roughly into two classes: artists with a leaning towards philosophy and philosophers with a taste for art. The artist-aesthetician knows what he is talking about. He can discriminate things that are art from things that are pseudo-art.... This is art-criticism, which is not identical with the philosophy of art, but only with the first of the two stages that go to make it up. It is a perfectly valid and valuable activity in itself; but the people who are good at it are not by any means necessarily able to achieve the second stage and offer a definition of art. All they can do is to recognize it. This is because they are content with too vague an idea of the relations in which art stands to things that are not art: I do not mean the various kinds of pseudo-art, but things like science, philosophy, and so forth. They are content to think of these relations as mere differences. To frame a definition of art, it is necessary to think wherein precisely these differences consist."

Such an extensive quote from Collingwood will perhaps be allowed since he has here, in a straightforward way, explained the virtues and limitations of the type of thinker represented by Roger Fry. Fry participated in the consolidation of the theory of the aesthetic that emerged during the 18th and 19th centuries from the theory of beauty. Specifically, he is associated with the theory of art as "significant form," a term first expounded by his Bloomsbury group colleague Clive Bell in *Art* (1914), though Fry had already used the term in a review of Cézanne in 1911. This early formalism found a much wider audience in 1920 with the publication of Fry's influential *Vision and Design*, a collection of essays and occasional pieces that is the primary source for a study of the evolution of Fry's thought.

The importance of Fry's writings, thin and tentative as they must seem now, can hardly be overstated in art historical terms. He is credited with originating the idea of the integrity of the picture plane, derived from his awareness of the tension between a flat surface and a three-dimensional image, an idea which dominated serious art criticism after World War II and until very recently. He is equally well-known as the first champion in the English-speaking world of the Post-Impressionists, a term he coined at the time of his revolutionary Grafton Galleries exhibition of 1911, "Manet and the Post-Impressionists." Perhaps most significantly, he helped free art from judgments of morality and demands that it should mean something in terms other than purely artistic ones. As Kenneth Clark has written, "In so far as taste can be changed by one man, it was changed by Roger Fry."

The sources of Fry's thought can be derived from the many roles he played in the art world of his time. Already in 1885, Whistler had asserted in his *Ten O'Clock Lecture* that those who haven't experienced creative activity are bound to misrepresent the work of art. A key prerequisite for a practitioner of the theory of significant form is that he possess, in Bell's words, "artistic sensibility" as well as "a turn for clear thinking." Fry, as a life-long painter of more than modest ability, met this requirement.

It is a peculiarly modern paradox that this requirement both serves to support the position of an aesthetic elite such as the Bloomsbury circle against the Philistines, and to democratize the appreciation of art. One result of Fry's activities as an organizer of exhibitions that challenged conventional taste was to realize the class basis of "aesthetic" judgments among the upper classes who had long been the audience of his art criticism. ("...their special culture was one of their social assets.") He writes: "It was felt that one could only appreciate Amico di Sandro when one had acquired a certain considerable mass of erudition and given a great deal of time and attention, but to admire a Matisse required only a certain sensibility. One could feel fairly sure that one's maid could not rival one in the former case, but might by a mere haphazard gift of Providence surpass one in the second."

This passage naturally leads to the third of Fry's roles, that of connoisseur and curator. He claimed in 1920 that the work of the Impressionists which had initially interested him lacked "structural design" and that this "drove me to the study of the Old Masters." With the initial encouragement of Bernard Berenson, who soon viewed him as a rival, Fry made a thorough study of Renaissance art which led, in 1906, to his appointment as a curator at New York's Metropolitan Museum. Fry's central role in setting the direction of this great collection, and that of the Johnson Collection now in the Philadelphia Museum of Art, has apparently not received the scholarly attention it deserves.

It would be very hard to demonstrate just what Fry learned about "structural design" from the Old Masters. What they seem to have provided him with, besides great pleasure and a critical vocation, was historical validation for his aesthetic instincts. It was in this spirit that he compared the rise of Post-Impressionism to the triumph of Byzantine art over Graeco-Roman "impressionism."

As a critic Fry achieved his greatest influence. His aim, as he writes in "An Essay in Aesthetics" (1909) is to "arrive at...conclusions as to the nature of the graphic arts, which will...explain our feelings about them [or] will at least put them into some kind of relation with the other arts...." He begins by seeking affinities between art and music or architecture "in which the imitation of objects is a negligible quantity."

Before he can attempt a formal explanation of how art affects our feelings, he must divorce the content of a work of art from its apparent subject. The way he chooses to do this is radically to devalue the art object and what it represents, throwing emphasis over onto the relationship between the artist and the viewer. (He was fond of quoting the statement in Kakuzo's *Book of Tea*:

"The canvas upon which the artist paints is the spectator's mind.") He divides life into actual and imaginative spheres and draws distinctions between them:

> Art, then, is an expression and a stimulus of this imaginative life, which is separated from actual life by the absence of responsive action. Now this responsive action implies in actual life moral responsibility. In art we have no such moral responsibility—it represents a life freed from the binding necessities of our actual existence.

Such a stance will continue to present ethical difficulties to many persons or at least violate the common sense of those who see art as a cultural or ideological construction serving many vital "actual" functions in the world of commerce, for example, or communications. On the other hand, recent aesthetic philosophers, such as Arthur Danto, have proposed rather sophisticated versions of Fry's autonomous art world.

The key concepts for understanding what art expresses and how are implied by the title of Fry's *Vision and Design*. In "The Artist's Vision," an essay in that volume, Fry elaborates on the idea that the artist's function is to look at things we don't ordinarily see. He creates a hierarchy of vision with mere seeing (identifying) at the bottom and aesthetic vision (disinterested contemplation of form and harmony) and creative vision, which artists possess, at the top, a capacity for utterly ignoring meaning in favor of pure appearances.

The creative vision organizes appearances for the delectation of the aesthetic vision, it seems, by means of design, and by use of "significant form." Fry didn't go so far as Bell in denying a role to representation, or to something, in providing that significance. In a review of Bell's *Art* he wrote: "...is it not just the fusion of this something with form that makes the difference between the finest pattern-making and a real design?... We should have to admit that this something, this X in the equation was quite inconstant, and might be of almost any inconceivable nature."

Fry's rather inchoate theories might best be considered protoformalist in that they prefigure much later formalist criticism and yet lack certain essential features. For example, his lack of commitment to the constructivist implications of formalism that would now be taken for granted is revealed in the activities of his Omega Workshop. Instead of deriving designs for furniture or fabrics from properties of materials or from manufacturing methods, the Omega artists, having received a commission, frequently bought commercially-produced objects and simply repainted them.

Fry seemed aware of the limitations of his approach. In his 1920 essay "Retrospect", he wrote: "In my work as a critic of art I have never been a pure Impressionist.... I have always had some kind of aesthetic.... But, on the other hand, I have never worked out for myself a complete system, such as the metaphysicians deduce from *a priori* principles. I have never believed that I knew what was the ultimate nature of art. My aesthetic has been a purely practical one...."

—Christopher Lyon

FULLER, Lon L(uvois). American jurist. Born in Hereford, Texas, 15 June 1902. Studied at the University of California, Berkeley, 1919-20; Stanford University, California, B.A. 1924, J.D. 1926. Married Florence Gail Thompson in 1926 (deceased); 1 daughter, 1 son; married Marjorie D. Chapple in 1960. Instructor, University of Oregon Law School, 1926-28; University of Illinois College of Law, 1928-31; Professor, Duke University Law School, 1931-40; Visiting Professor, 1939-40, Professor, 1940-48, Carter Professor of General Jurisprudence from 1948, and later Professor Emeritus, Harvard Law School, Cambridge,

Massachusetts. Associate, Ropes, Gray, Best, Coolidge, and Rugg, Boston, 1942-45. Recipient: Phillips Award, American Philosophical Society, 1935. Member, American Academy of Arts and Sciences. *Died 8 April 1978.*

PUBLICATIONS

Law

The Law in Quest of Itself (lectures). Evanston, Illinois, Northwestern University Press, 1940.
Reason and Fiat in Case Law. New York, American Book-Stratford Press, 1943.
Basic Contract Law. St. Paul, Minnesota, West Publishing Company, 1947; 2nd edition, with Robert Braucher, 1964; 3rd and 4th editions, with Melvin Aron Eisenberg, 1972, 1981.
The Morality of Law (lectures). New Haven, Connecticut, and London, Yale University Press, 1964; revised edition, 1969.
Legal Fictions. Stanford, California, Stanford University Press, 1967.
Anatomy of the Law. Chicago, Britannica Perspectives, and London, Praeger, 1968.
The Principles of Social Order: Selected Essays of Lon L. Fuller, edited by Kenneth I. Winston. Durham, North Carolina, Duke University Press, 1981.

Other

Editor, *The Problems of Jurisprudence: A Selection of Readings.* Brooklyn, Foundation Press, 1949.

*   *   *

Lon L. Fuller reached his intellectual maturity in the 1930's by coming to terms with American legal realism. The relationship was complex, involving neither an undeviating adherence to the movement nor a complete rejection of it. It is useful to begin with the revolt against formalism, for from that most everything follows. Fuller shared the view that previous legal scholars, such as Langdell, had a conception of law based, inappropriately, on a mathematical model. The law was regarded as an axiomatic system with its central concepts known intuitively by properly-trained lawyers and its specific rules inferred deductively from those concepts. In place of this model, Fuller adopted the instrumentalist theory of William James and John Dewey, according to which concepts are understood functionally as a product of the creative power of the intellect, marking off and organizing areas of experience so that they may be dealt with systematically, and assessed in terms of their utility in accomplishing this task. Fuller made his first extended use of the instrumentalist conception in a series of three papers on legal fictions (1930-31), in which judicial employment of fictions is viewed as an intellectual tool for achieving structure and coherence in legal argument, bridging gaps between established precedents and unfamiliar questions posed for resolution.

If legal concepts do not possess *a priori* validity, but are only heuristic devices for accomplishing the judge's task, attention moves to the practical significance of the judicial process; the choice of remedies for resolving specific disputes. Fuller shared with the legal realists an emphasis on the primacy of remedies. This was the basis of his innovative casebook on contracts, the first chapter of which is devoted solely to questions about remedies. Students are introduced to statements of contractual obligation in terms of their concrete meaning. Of course, Fuller did not declare that the law is only what judges do. He believed, as did most realists, that the reasoning by which a judge arrives at the choice of a remedy is equally central to the law. But, again like the realists, Fuller remarked on the thinness of the explanations judges actually offer for their decisions. He distrusted their own accounts of what they were doing when they appealed only to prior cases and previously formulated rules. He saw judicial decisionmaking as profoundly influenced by perceptions of social reality and continually searched for the latent rules or implicit law underlying explicit statements.

Fuller thought of this as a quest for "the law behind the law," and he employed what he called the natural law method to uncover it. This consisted in bringing to explicit consciousness the policy decisions and shared purposes shaping the development of the law over time and then evaluating specific judicial outcomes in terms of their contribution to or detraction from these aims. Fuller employed this method most brilliantly in two essays on contracts, one on the reliance interest (1936-37) and one on the doctrine of consideration (1941). However, in his conception of "the law behind the law" Fuller made his most decisive break with the legal realists. For while they shared the view that legal rules are only the most visible manifestations or most articulate expressions of underlying social conventions and practices, the realists took this conception as an invitation to employ the latest social science approaches in understanding law. This led them to a variety of commitments that Fuller firmly rejected, especially a behaviorist analysis of human action (in which its purposive character seems to disappear), an emotivist analysis of valuation (in which reason plays no role), and treatment of the existence of law as a theory-independent fact or datum. Fuller rejected each of these tenets on the single ground that they distort the relation between law and morality. Like traditional natural law theorists, Fuller saw "the law behind the law" as having an essential moral component; the central aim of his jurisprudential writing was to explain that connection.

Fuller distinguished three important ways in which law and morality intersect. First are the moral attitudes of citizens, whose support is necessary for the effective operation of legal institutions. Mere acquiescence or obedience will not do. Citizens must regard the law as conforming, on the whole, to their own moral views. And what they regard as morally correct is not independent of what actually is morally correct, since the former notion is parasitic on the latter. The second way in which law and morality necessarily intersect is through the official roles that constitute legal institutions. These roles—such as that of legislator, judge, administrator—are defined in part by responsibilities that occupiers of the roles have toward citizens. Fuller's most famous jurisprudential work, *The Morality of Law*, is devoted principally to characterizing the duties of legislators: to promulgate general rules that are clear, typically prospective, possible to obey, relatively constant over time, and so on. These requirements compose what Fuller called the internal morality of legislation. Finally, the third way in which law and morality intersect is through the substantive moral ends embodied in law and legal institutions. For Fuller, no particular substantive end is necessarily implicated in the law, but he offered an explicitly normative argument (especially in the essays of 1955 and 1968) to suggest that the design of legal institutions should be assessed predominantly in terms of their contribution to human freedom, to enabling individual choice to become socially effective. For this reason, Fuller argued (1978) that the most fruitful way of characterizing legal institutions is in terms of the individual's manner of participating in them.

—Kenneth I. Winston

FULLER, R(ichard) Buckminster. American inventor, philosopher, architect and environmentalist. Born in Milton, Massachusetts, 12 July 1895. Educated at Milton Academy, 1904-13; Harvard University, Cambridge, Massachusetts, 1913-15, and the United States Naval Academy, Annapolis, Maryland, 1917. Served in the United States Navy, 1917-19: Lieutenant. Married Anne Hewlett in 1917; 2 daughters. Assistant Export Manager,

Armour and Company, New York, 1919-21; National Accounts Sales Manager, Kelly-Springfield Truck Company, 1922; President, Stockade Building System, Chicago, 1922-27; Founder and President, 4D Company, Chicago, 1927-32; Editor and Publisher, *Shelter* magazine, Philadelphia, 1930-32; Founder, Director, and chief Engineer, Dymaxion Corporation, Bridgeport, Connecticut, 1932-36; Assistant to the Director of Research and Development, Phelps Dodge Corporation, New York, 1936-38; Technical Consultant on the staff of *Fortune* magazine, New York, 1938-40; Vice-President and Chief Engineer, Dymaxion Company Inc., Delaware, 1940-50; Chief Mechanical Engineer, United States Board of Economic Warfare, Washington, D.C., 1942-44, and Special Assistant to the Deputy Director of the United States Foreign Economic Administration, Washington, 1944; Chairman and Chief Engineer, Dymaxion Dwelling Machine Corporation, Wichita, Kansas, 1944-46; Chairman, Fuller Research Foundation, Wichita, 1946-54; President, Geodesics Inc., Forest Hills, New York, 1949-83, Synergetics Inc., Raleigh, North Carolina, 1954-59, and Plydomes Inc., Des Moines, Iowa, 1957-83; Chairman, Tetrahelix Corporation, Hamilton, Ohio, 1959-83. Research Professor, 1959-68, University Professor, 1968-75, Distinguished Service Professor, 1972-75, and University Professor Emeritus, 1975-83, Southern Illinois University, Carbondale. Charles Eliot Norton Professor of Poetry, Harvard University, 1962-63; Harvey Cushing Orator, American Association of Neuro-Surgeons, 1967; Nehru Lecturer, New Delhi, 1969; Hoyt Fellow, Yale University, New Haven, Connecticut, 1969; Fellow, St. Peter's College, Oxford, 1970; World Fellow in Residence, Consortium of the University of Pennsylvania, Swarthmore College, Bryn Mawr College, and the University City Science Center, Philadelphia, and Consultant to the Design Science Institute, Philadelphia, 1972-75; Tutor in Design Science, International Community College, Los Angeles, 1975. Editor-at-large, *World Magazine*, New York, 1972-75. President, Triton Foundation, Cambridge, Massachusetts, 1967; International President, MENSA, Paris, 1975, and World Society for Ekistics, Athens, 1975. Recipient: Award of Merit, American Institute of Architects, New York Chapter, 1952; Grand Prize, *Triennale*, Milan, 1954-1957; Award of Merit, United States Marine Corps, 1955; Gold Medal, National Architectural Society, 1958; Gold Medal, AIA, Philadelphia Chapter, 1960; Franklin P. Brown Medal, Franklin Institute, Philadelphia, 1962; Allied Professions Gold Medal, 1963, Architectural Design Award, 1968, and Gold Medal, 1970, national AIA; Plomado de Oro Award, Society of Mexican Architects, 1963; Delta Phi Delta Gold Key, 1964; Creative Achievement Award, Brandeis University, Waltham, Massachusetts, 1965; First Award of Excellence, Industrial Designers Society of America, 1966; Order of Lincoln Medal, Lincoln Academy, Illinois, 1967; Gold Medal for Architecture, National Institute of Arts and Letters, 1968; Royal Gold Medal for Architecture, Royal Institute of British Architects, London, 1968; Citation of Merit, United States Department of Housing and Urban Development, 1969; Citation of Excellence, National Institute of Steel Construction, 1969; Humanist of the Year Award, American Association of Humanists, 1969; McGraw-Hill Master Designer in Product Engineering Award, 1969; Alpha Rho Chi Master Architect Life Award, 1970; President's Award, University of Detroit, 1971; Salmagundi Medal, Salmagundi Club, 1971; Annual Award of Merit, Philadelphia Art Alliance, 1973; Honorary Citizenship Award, City of Philadelphia, 1973; Planetary Citizens Award, United Nations, 1975. Honorary doctorate: North Carolina State University, Raleigh, 1954; University of Michigan, Ann Arbor, 1955; Washington University, St. Louis, 1957; Southern Illinois University, 1959; Rollins College, Winter Park, Florida, 1960; University of Colorado, Boulder, 1964; Clemson University, South Carolina, 1964; University of New Mexico, Albuquerque, 1964; Monmouth College, West Long Branch, New Jersey, 1965; California State Colleges, 1966; Long Island University, Greenvale, New York, 1966; California State College of Arts and Crafts, Oakland, 1966; Clarkson College of

Technology, Potsdam, New York, 1967; Dartmouth College, Hanover, New Hampshire, 1968; University of Rhode Island, Kingston, 1968; New England College, Henniker, New Hampshire, 1968; Ripon College, Wisconsin, 1968; Bates College, Lewiston, Maine, 1969; Boston College, 1969; University of Wisconsin, Madison, 1969; Brandeis University, 1970; Columbia College, Chicago, 1970; Park College, Parkville, Missouri, 1970; Minneapolis School of Art, 1970; Wilberforce University, Ohio, 1970; Southeastern Massachusetts University, North Dartmouth, 1971; University of Maine, Orono, 1972; Grinnell College, Iowa, 1972; Emerson College, Boston, 1972; Nasson College, Springvale, Maine, 1973; Rensselaer Polytechnic Institute, Troy, New York, 1973; Beaver College, Glenside, Pennsylvania, 1973; Pratt Institute, Brooklyn, New York, 1974; McGill University, Montreal, 1974; St. Joseph's College, Philadelphia, 1974; University of Pennsylvania, Philadelphia, 1974; University of Notre Dame, Indiana, 1974; Hobart and William Smith Colleges, Geneva, New York, 1975. Member, National Academy of Design; Fellow, American Institute of Architects, and of the Building Research Institute of the National Academy of Sciences; Life Fellow, American Association for the Advancement of Science. Member, National Institute of Arts and Letters; Fellow, American Academy of Arts and Sciences. R. Buckminster Fuller Chair of Architecture established at the University of Detroit, 1970. Member, Mexican Institute of Architects; Honorary member, Society of Venezuelan Architects, Israel Institute of Engineers and Architects, Zentralvereiningung der Architekten Österreichs, and Royal Society of Siamese Architects; Benjamin Franklin Fellow, Royal Society of Arts; Honorary Fellow, Royal Institute of British Architects. *Died* (in Los Angeles) *1 July 1983*.

PUBLICATIONS

Society and Environment

The Time Lock. Privately printed, 1928; reprinted as *4D Time Lock*, Corrales, New Mexico, Lama Foundation, 1970.
Nine Chains to the Moon. Philadelphia, Lippincott, 1938; London, Cape, 1973.
Designing a New Industry: A Composite of a Series of Talks. Wichita, Kansas, Fuller Research Institute, 1945-46.
Earth, inc. (lecture). New York, Fuller Research Foundation, 1947.
Design for Survival—Plus. Ann Arbor, Michigan, 1949.
Untitled Epic Poem on the History of Industrialization. Millerton, New York, Jargon Books, 1962.
Education Automation: Freeing the Scholars to Return to Their Studies (lecture). Carbondale, Southern Illinois University Press, 1962.
Ideas and Integrities: A Spontaneous Autobiographical Discourse, edited by Robert W. Marks. Englewood Cliffs, New Jersey, Prentice Hall, 1963.
No More Secondhand God, and Other Writings. Carbondale, Southern Illinois University Press, 1963.
World Design Science Decade Documents. Carbondale, World Resources Inventory, Southern Illinois University, 6 vols., 1963-67.
Comprehensive Thinking, selected and edited by John McHale. Carbondale, World Resources Inventory, Southern Illinois University, 1965.
What I Am Trying to Do. London, Cape Goliard, 1968.
Reprints and Selected Articles. Belfast, Maine, Bern Porter, 1969.
Operating Manual for Spaceship Earth. Carbondale, Southern Illinois University Press, 1969.
Utopia or Oblivion: The Prospects for Humanity. New York, Bantam Books, 1969; London, Penguin Books, 1970.
Fifty Years of Design, Science, Revolution and the World Game. Carbondale, World Resources Inventory, Southern Illinois University, 1969.
Planetary Planning (lecture). New Delhi, India, 1969.

Approaching the Benign Environment, with others. University, University of Alabama Press, 1970.
The Buckminster Fuller Reader, edited by James Meller. London, Cape, 1970.
I Seem to Be a Verb, with Jerome Agel and Quentin Fiore. New York, Bantam Books, 1970.
The World Game: Integrative Resource Civilization Planning Tool. Carbondale, World Resources Inventory, Southern Illinois University, 1971.
Old Man River: An Environmental Domed City. St. Louis, Parsimonious Press, 1972.
Intuition (poems). New York, Doubleday, 1972.
Buckminster Fuller to Children of Earth. New York, Doubleday, 1972.
Synergetics: Explorations in the Geometry of Thinking, with E.J. Applewhite. New York, Macmillan, 1975.
And It Came to Pass—Not to Stay. New York, Macmillan, 1976.
Pound, Synergy, and the Great Design. Moscow, University of Idaho Press, 1977.
R. Buckminster Fuller on Education, edited by Peter H. Wagschal and Robert D. Kahn. Amherst, University of Massachusetts Press, 1979.
Critical Path. New York, St. Martin's Press, 1982.
Tetrascroll: Goldilocks and the Three Bears: A Cosmic Fairy Tale. New York, St. Martin's Press, 1982.

*

Critical Studies: *Buckminster Fuller* by John McHale, New York, Braziller, 1962; *The Dymaxion World of Buckminster Fuller* by Robert W. Marks, New York, Reinhold, 1959; *Bucky: A Guided Tour of Buckminster Fuller* by Hugh Kenner, New York, Morrow, 1973.

*   *   *

Visionary, architect, inventor, metaphysician, poet, scientist, engineer, and evolutionary technologist, R. Buckminster Fuller was called by Marshall McLuhan "the 20th-century Leonardo da Vinci."

The effect of technology on society is a central concern in the thought of Buckminster Fuller. Humanity is moving forward logically, and self-destruction is not an inevitability. Technology can be harnessed; resources are both available and sufficient. Malthus and Darwin were wrong. Survival is not merely for the fittest. "I've got news for you," Fuller said. "I know what I'm talking about. I now know that we have the capability to take care of all humanity."

Fuller, then 87 years old, spoke in Washington, D.C. in 1982 to the Fourth General Assembly of the World Future Society. "In 1927," he said, "I conducted an experiment to see what, if anything, an unknown, penniless human being could do with a wife and a child. I came to the conclusion that, quite clearly, the political system locally is not interested in the world at all. I had no competition in thinking about the whole world."

In *Synergetics: Explorations in the Geometry of Thinking* Fuller applied the principles of his "comprehensive anticipatory design science" to the human situation. Synergetics (viewing the part in relation to the whole) understands the universe as an infinitely various repetition of simple forms related to the tetrahedron. This science resulted in a series of revolutionary designs for practical structures, his goal being to "find ways of doing more with less to the end that all people, everywhere, can have more and more of everything." Human nature will never change, he asserted, so man's environment must be altered. To this end, Fuller contributed a line of Dymaxion inventions. "Dymaxion," a trade name, is derived from the words "dynamic," "maximum," and "ion." He created Dymaxion Dwelling Machines (inexpensive, self-sufficient, lightweight homes); Dymaxion Insulation Shields, designed to prevent heat loss in buildings; the

Dymaxion dye-stamped bathroom unit, mobile and capable of being assembled in minutes; and the ill-fated, streamlined Dymaxion car, a sturdy, three-wheeled vehicle which was precursor of today's aerodynamic automobile. The Dymaxion car could attain speeds of one-hundred-and-twenty miles an hour.

Fuller entered the world of popular culture in 1967 as a result of his design for the United States pavilion at *Expo 67*. The self-ventilating geodesic dome (250 ft. in diameter, containing 6.7 million cu. ft. of space) combined a series of tetrahedron skeletons (open, three-dimensional pyramid shapes) in a self-supporting, spherical form. Based on principles he discovered in the 1940's while working on the science of geodesics (defined by Fuller as "the most economical momentary relationship among a plurality of points and events"), the dome first attracted the attention of the American military, and has been used as a design for housing units, radar shelters in Alaska, portable "foxholes" in wartime, sports arenas, botanical gardens, restaurants, and auditoriums. The potential of geodesic structures for container domes over cities is of particular interest to visionaries and futurists, groups dedicated to insuring a high quality of life in centuries to come.

Resources, which are ample, Fuller insisted, must be shared. His method for sharing resources, and thereby insuring a decent quality of life in the future, he put forth in the Dymaxion Air-Ocean World Map (which projects a spherical world as a flat surface with no visible distortion) and the accompanying World Game. The map is the size of a basketball court. The World Game, a sort of Fuller computer, gives up-to-date information about world resources. Together, these tools can be used to guarantee an equitable division of bounty. Fuller's game principle is "no-one wins if anyone loses." Because he believed that we must eventually evolve to a liberated state of non-nationhood, Fuller said, "As long as you have nations, you're not going to use resources and knowledge and energy in a logical manner to make everything work for everybody. Nations are going to look out for themselves. Evolution is integration of humanity." A pacifist, Fuller urged youth, during the Vietnam War, to "turn from preoccupation with killingry to preoccupation with livingry."

Expelled from Harvard University on two separate occasions (1913 and 1915), once for "irresponsible conduct" (a lavish spending spree in New York), and once again for "lack of sustained interest in the processes within the university," Buckminster Fuller ended his formal education prematurely. He even set out upon a formal process of "unlearning" whatever he could not prove from his own experience, fearing that he might have acquired misinformation. In the last three decades of his life, however, Fuller taught and lectured at the most prestigious American universities, including Harvard, where, in his capacity as a poet, he occupied the Charles Eliot Norton chair of poetry in 1961-62.

"Spaceship Earth" is Fuller's conceit for our planet, and our spaceship is hurtling through the universe at 60,000 miles an hour. It is impossible to "leave home," he said, because "You take off! You look down! There's home. My backyard is a spherical yard." Spaceship Earth will continue its progress in time and space. We will not run out of energy. Ultimate solutions lie in world-connected power grids, wind-powered generators and harnessing the force of the ocean tides. "We do not have an energy crisis," Buckminster Fuller insisted. "We just have a crisis of ignorance." But we are evolving. We will be omni-integrated, freely intercirculating, and omni-literate. The voice of R. Buckminster Fuller was a voice of hope.

—Marian Jorgensen

GADAMER, Hans-Georg. German philosopher. Born in Marburg, 11 February 1900. Studied at the University of Munich and at the University of Marburg. Married Kaete Lekebusch in 1950; 1 daughter. Professor of Philosophy, University of Marburg, 1937-39; University of Leipzig, 1939-47 (Rector, 1946-47); University of Frankfurt, 1947-49; and University of Heidelberg, 1949-68, now Professor Emeritus. Visiting Professor, McMaster University, Hamilton, Ontario, fall terms 1972-75; Boston College, 1976. Recipient: Reuchlin-Preis, Pforzheim, 1971; Hegel-Preis, Stuttgart, 1979. Honorary doctorate: University of Ottawa, 1977. Member, Academy of Leipzig, 1942; Academy of Heidelberg, 1950; Academy of Athens; Academy of Rome; Academy of Darmstadt; Boston Academy. Address: Philosophisches Seminar, University of Heidelberg, Heidelberg, West Germany.

PUBLICATIONS

Philosophy

Platos dialektische Ethik: Phänomenologische Interpretationen zum "Philebus". Leipzig, Meiner, 1931.
Plato und die Dichter. Frankfurt, Klostermann, 1934.
Regards sur l'histoire, with others. Paris, Sorlot, 1941.
Volk und Geschichte im Denken Herders (lectures). Frankfurt, Klostermann, 1942.
Bach und Weimar (lecture). Weimar, Böhlau, 1946.
Goethe und die Philosophie. Leipzig, Volk und Buch Verlag, 1947.
Über die Ursprünglichkeit der Wissenschaft (lecture). Leipzig, Barth, 1947.
Über die Ursprünglichkeit der Philosophie (lectures). Berlin, Chronos, 1948.
Vom Geistigen Lauf des Menschen: Studien zu unvollendeten Dichtungen Goethes. Godesberg, West Germany, Küpper, 1949.
Gedächtnisrede auf Oskar Schürer. Darmstadt, Neue Darmstädter Verlagsanstalt, 1952.
Wahrheit und Methode: Grundzüge einer philosophischen Hermeneutik. Tübingen, Mohr, 1960; as *Truth and Method*, London, Sheed and Ward, and New York, Seabury Press, 1975.
Le Problème de la conscience historique (lectures). Louvain, Publications Universitaires de Louvain, 1963.
Dialektik und Sophistik im siebenten platonischen Briefe. Heidelberg, Winter, 1964.
Kleine Schriften. Tübingen, Mohr, 4 vols., 1967-77 (vol. 4 contains a bibliography); selections as *Philosophical Hermeneutics*, Berkeley, University of California Press, 1976.
Platos dialektische Ethik und andere Studien zur platonischen Philosophie. Hamburg, Meiner, 1968.
Werner Scholz. Recklinghausen, West Germany, Bongers, 1968.
Hegel, Hölderlin, Heidegger, with others (lectures). Karlsruhe, Bademia, 1971.
Die Begriffsgeschichte und die Sprache der Philosophie. Opladen, West Germany, Westdeutscher Verlag, 1971.
Hegels Dialektik: Fünf hermeneutische Studien. Tübingen, Mohr, 1971; as *Hegel's Dialectic: Five Hermeneutical Studies*, New Haven, Connecticut, Yale University Press, 1976.
Wer bin ich und wer bist du? Ein Kommentar zu Paul Celans Gedichtfolge "Atemkristall". Frankfurt, Suhrkamp, 1973.
Idee und Wirklichkeit in Platos "Timaios" (lecture). Heidelberg, Winter, 1974.
Vernunft in Zeitalter der Wissenschaft: Aufsätze. Frankfurt, Suhrkamp, 1976; as *Reason in the Age of Science*, Cambridge, Massachusetts, MIT Press, 1981.
Rhetorik und Hermeneutik (lecture). Göttingen, Vanderhoeck und Ruprecht, 1976.
Poetica: Ausgewählte Essays. Frankfurt, Insel-Verlag, 1977.
Die Aktualität des Schönen: Kunst als Spiel, Symbol und Fest. Stuttgart, Reclam, 1977.
Philosophische Lehrjahre, with E. Ruckschau. Frankfurt, Klostermann, 1977.

Heidegger: Freiburger Universitätsvorträge zu seinem Gedenken,
with others. Munich, Alber,1977.
Die Idee der Guten zwischen Plato und Aristoteles (lecture).
Heidelberg, Winter, 1978.
Dialogue and Dialectic: Eight Hermeneutical Studies on Plato. New Haven, Connecticut, Yale University Press, 1980.

Other

Editor, *Grundriss der algemeinen Geschichte der Philosophie,*
by Wilhelm Dilthey. Frankfurt, Klostermann, 1949.
Editor, *Platonismus und christliche Philosophie,* by Ernst Hoffmann. Zurich, Artemis, 1960.
Editor, *Beiträge zur Deutung der Phänomenologie des Geistes.*
Bonn, Bouvier, 1966.
Editor, *Hegel-Tage, Royaumont, 1964.* Bonn, Bouvier, 1966.
Editor, *Deutscher Kongress für Philosophie: Das Problem der Sprache.* Munich, Fink, 1967.
Editor, *Idee und Zahl.* Heidelberg, Winter, 1968.
Editor, *Hegel-Tage, Urbino, 1965.* Bonn, Bouvier, 1969.
Editor, *Hermeneutik und Dialektik.* Tübingen, Mohr, 1970.
Editor, *Parmenides,* by Kurt Riezler. Frankfurt, Klostermann, 1970.
Editor and translator, with commentary, *Metaphysics, Book XII,* by Aristotle. Frankfurt, Klostermann, 1970.

*

Critical Studies: *Hermeneutics: Interpretation Theory in Schleiermacher, Dilthey, Heidegger and Gadamer* by Richard E. Palmer, Evanston, Illinois, Northwestern University Press, 1969; *The Critical Circle: Literature, History and Philosophical Hermeneutics* by D.C. Hoy, Berkeley, University of California Press, 1978; *Contemporary Hermeneutics: Hermeneutics as Method, Philosophy and Critique* by Josef Bleicher, London, Routledge, 1980.

* * *

Hans-Georg Gadamer's work is uniformly concerned with the problem of hermeneutics, which for him is not merely a task defined by the interpretation of temporally distant texts, although that is the situation which first prompts hermeneutic thinking. "I will maintain," says Gadamer, "that the hermeneutical problem is universal and basic for all interhuman experience, both of history and of the present moment, precisely because meaning can be experienced even where it is not intended."

This last statement, that "meaning can be experienced even where it is not intended," is Gadamer's often repeated summary of the foundational assumption of his philosophy. As such, it shows Gadamer's heavy reliance on Heidegger's ontological analytic, especially in its conclusion that the "distinction between the judgment of fact and the judgment of value is problematic." Thus, in Gadamer's formulation of the hermeneutic circle, "everything that is said and is there in the text stands under anticipations." Negatively, this means that we can never find a prejudice-free standpoint from which to make assertions about any text. Much of Gadamer's writing therefore seeks to undermine interpretive theories which attempt to establish such standpoints. Aestheticism, for example, by virtue of specific alienating acts, disengages texts and artifacts from the worlds from which they arose and from the world of the critic in order to describe their formal unity or disunity. But, says Gadamer, the artwork offers more than its formal perfection:

...is it not also true that these artistic creations, which come down through the millennia, were not created for such aesthetic acceptance or rejection? No artist of the religiously vital cultures of the past ever produced his work of art with any other intention than that his creation should be received in terms of what it says and presents and that it should have its place in the world where men live together. The consciousness of art—the aesthetic consciousness—is always secondary to the immediate truth-claim that proceeds from the work of art itself.

Alienating acts of aesthetic consciousness prevent the artwork from saying what it has to say. Set up over against the beholder or reader, the artwork is silent, except insofar as the beholder or reader supplies it with something to say.

Similarly, the historical consciousness at work in all theories of historicity alienates the historian from his documents. Much as Nietzsche criticized all attempts to understand past worlds by entering the spirit of the time, Gadamer criticizes all attempts to eliminate present prejudices from historical analyses of the past. The stricture against prejudice is itself prejudiced, for every misunderstanding induced by prejudice presupposes "a deep common accord," and interpretive theories which attempt to exclude methodologically all prejudices merely cover over the continuity of tradition which in fact proceeds through prejudice and precedent. For Gadamer, then,

Prejudices are not necessarily unjustified and erroneous, so that they inevitably distort the truth. In fact, the historicity of our existence entails that prejudices, in the literal sense of the word, constitute the initial directedness of our whole ability to experience.

Thus Gadamer's working assumption—"Everything that is said and is there in the text stands under anticipations"—means, positively, that "only what stands under anticipation can be understood at all...." One can only understand what one might misunderstand. That is to say, there must be *some* continuity between the world of the text and the world of the interpreter or else the interpreter would never know that he did not understand in the first place.

Gadamer's understanding of prejudices as constituting the continuity of tradition leads him to assert the impossibility of the idea of absolute reason: "Reason exists for us only in concrete, historical terms, i.e. it is not its own master, but remains constantly dependent on the given circumstances in which it operates." Discarding the subject-object model of knowledge, Gadamer describes the event of understanding as a "fusion of horizons." In his terminology, the horizons that must be fused are those of the interpreter's world and the world of the text he tries to interpret. A world is not the totality of objects of which the intrepreter is aware. Rather, a world is a totality of relations the text does not make explicit but from which the objects of concern arise. The hermeneutic task is for the interpreter to expand the horizon of his own world so that it includes the horizon of the foreign text.

Thus the hermeneutic circle is not described, as it was in the 19th century, within the formal relation of the part and the whole and its subjective reflex. Now it describes the interplay of the movement of tradition and the movement of the interpreter. The anticipation of meaning necessary for gaining any understanding is no longer regarded in terms of the subjective act of throwing a framework about an object but in terms of the communality that binds the interpreter and the text to the same tradition. Tradition here is not a precondition that must be overcome by method; tradition is the very product of our acts of understanding.

This, of course, should not be understood as a re-emergence of subjectivism. Understanding "happens to us," just as we never know how a conversation will turn out until it is completed, because the whole hermeneutic process is linguistic. Language itself speaks to us. It is not a tool, not a system of signs. On the contrary, since language discloses our world, without language, we would have no world:

The fundamental relation of language and world does not...mean that world becomes the object of language. Rather, the object of knowledge and of statements is already enclosed within the horizon of language.

Language, in effect, is universal, extending beyond the surface of what is said or presented. This is easily seen in the fact that "Every dialogue has an inner infinity and no end." One can always break off when enough has been said, but a dialogue can always resume, since every assertion is motivated. As Gadamer says, "...one can sensibly ask of everything that is said, 'Why do you say that?' And only when what is not said is understood along with what is said is an assertion understandable." Everything that we can understand is ultimately expressible in language: "Everything that is is language."

—Stephen R. Yarbrough

GALBRAITH, John Kenneth. American economist. Born in Iona Station, Ontario, Canada, 15 October 1908; emigrated to the United States in 1931; naturalized, 1937. Studied at Ontario Agricultural College, Canada, B.S. 1931; University of California, Berkeley, M.S. 1933, Ph.D. 1934; Cambridge University, England, 1937-38. Married Catherine Atwater in 1937; 3 sons. Instructor and Tutor, 1934-39, Lecturer, 1948-49, Professor, 1949-59, Paul M. Warburg Professor of Economics, 1959-75, and since 1975 Professor Emeritus, Harvard University, Cambridge, Massachusetts; also, Fellow, Social Science Research Council, 1937-38; Assistant Professor, Princeton University, New Jersey, 1939-42. BBC Reith Lecturer, 1966. Economic Adviser, National Defense Advisory Committee, 1940-41; Assistant Administrator, 1941-42, and Deputy Administrator, 1942-43, Office of Price Administration; Member, Board of Editors, *Fortune* Magazine, 1943-48; Director, U.S. Strategic Bombing Survey, 1945, and Office of Economic Security Policy, U.S. Department of State, 1946; U.S. Ambassador to India, 1961-63. President, American Economic Association, 1972. Recipient: Medal of Freedom, 1946. Honorary doctorate: Bard College, Annandale-on-Hudson, New York; University of California; Miami University, Oxford, Ohio; University of Massachusetts, Amherst; University of Mysore, India; Brandeis University, Waltham, Massachusetts; University of Toronto; University of Guelph, Canada; University of Saskatchewan; University of Michigan, Ann Arbor; University of Durham, England; Rhode Island College, Providence; Boston College, Chestnut Hill, Massachusetts; Hobart and William Smith Colleges, Geneva, New York; Albion College, Michigan; Tufts University, Medford, Massachusetts; Adelphi University, Garden City, New York; Suffolk College, Boston; Michigan State University, East Lansing; University of Louvain, Belgium; Cambridge University, England; University of Paris; Carleton College, Northfield, Minnesota; University of Vermont, Burlington; Queen's University, Kingston, Ontario. Member, National Institute of Arts and Letters; Fellow, American Academy of Arts and Sciences. Honorary Professor, University of Geneva, and Fellow, Trinity College, Cambridge. Address: 107 Littauer Center, Harvard University, Cambridge, Massachusetts, U.S.A.

PUBLICATIONS

Economics

Economic Aspects of the Bee Industry, with others. Berkeley, University of California Press, 1933.
Honey Marketing in California, with others. Berkeley, California, University of California Press, 1933.
California County Expenditures. Berkeley, California, University of California Press, 1934.
Modern Competition and Business Policy, with H.S. Dennison. New York, Oxford University Press, 1938.
The Economic Effects of the Federal Public Works Expendi-

tures, 1933-38, with G.G. Johnson, Jr. Washington, D.C., U.S. Government Printing Office, 1940.
Recovery in Europe. Washington, D.C., National Planning Association, 1946.
Beyond the Marshall Plan. Washington, D.C., National Planning Association, 1949.
Can Europe Unite? New York, Foreign Policy Association, 1950.
America and Western Europe. New York, Public Affairs Committee, 1950.
American Capitalism: The Concept of Countervailing Power. Boston, Houghton Mifflin, and London, Hamish Hamilton, 1952.
A Theory of Price Control. Cambridge, Massachusetts, Harvard University Press, 1952.
Economics and the Art of Controversy (lecture). New Brunswick, New Jersey, Rutgers University Press, 1955.
The Great Crash, 1929. Boston, Houghton Mifflin, and London, Hamish Hamilton, 1955.
Marketing Efficiency in Puerto Rico, with others. Cambridge, Massachusetts, Harvard University Press, 1955.
Economic Planning in India: Five Comments. Calcutta, Indian Statistical Institute, 1956.
Inequality in Agriculture—Problem and Program. Guelph, Canada, Ontario Agricultural College, 1956.
The Affluent Society. Boston, Houghton Mifflin, and London, Hamish Hamilton, 1958.
Journey to Poland and Yugoslavia. Cambridge, Massachusetts, Harvard University Press, 1958.
The Liberal Hour. Boston, Houghton Mifflin, and London, Hamish Hamilton, 1960.
The Causes of Poverty: A Clinical View (lecture). Ahmedabad, India, Gujarat University, 1962.
Economic Development in Perspective. Cambridge, Massachusetts, Harvard University Press, 1962; enlarged edition as *Economic Development*, Boston, Houghton Mifflin, 1964.
Economic Policy since 1945: The Nature of Success (lecture). New York, New York University School of Business Administration, 1963.
How Keynes Came to America. Stamford, Connecticut, Overbrook Press, 1965.
The Underdeveloped Country (lectures). Toronto, Canadian Broadcasting Company, 1965.
Underdevelopment: An Approach to Classification. Rehovoth, Israel, Segal, 1965.
The New Industrial State. Boston, Houghton Mifflin, and London, Hamish Hamilton, 1967.
A Contemporary Guide to Economics, Peace, and Laughter. Boston, Houghton Mifflin, and London, Deutsch, 1971.
Economics and the Public Purpose. Boston, Houghton Mifflin, 1973; London, Deutsch, 1974.
Money: Whence It Came, Where It Went. Boston, Houghton Mifflin, and London, Deutsch, 1975.
Socialism in Rich Countries and Poor (lecture). Ahmedabad, India, Ajit Bhagat Memorial Trust, 1975.
The Age of Uncertainty. Boston, Houghton Mifflin, and London, Deutsch, 1977.
The Galbraith Reader: From the Works of John Kenneth Galbraith, edited by the Editors of Gambit. Ipswich, Massachusetts, Gambit, 1977.
Almost Everyone's Guide to Economics, with Nicole Salinger. Boston, Houghton Mifflin, 1978.
Annals of an Abiding Liberal, edited by Andrea D. Williams. Boston, Houghton Mifflin, 1979.
Galbraith Reader. New York, Bantam Books, 1979.
The Nature of Mass Poverty (lectures). Cambridge, Massachusetts, Harvard University Press, 1979.

Other

The McLandress Dimension (as Mark Epernay). Boston,

Houghton Mifflin, 1963; London, Hamish Hamilton, 1964.
The Scotch. Boston, Houghton Mifflin, 1964; as *Made to Last*, London, Hamish Hamilton, 1964.
A Beginner's Guide to American Studies (lecture). Welwyn Garden City, Hertfordshire, Broadwater Press, 1967.
How to Get Out of Vietnam: A Workable Solution to the Worst Problem of Our Time. New York, New American Library, 1967.
The Triumph: A Novel of Modern Diplomacy. Boston, Houghton Mifflin, and London, Hamish Hamilton, 1968.
Indian Painting: The Scenes, Themes and Location, with Mohinder Singh Randhawa. Boston, Houghton Mifflin, and London, Hamish Hamilton, 1968.
Ambassador's Journal: A Personal Account of the Kennedy Years. Boston, Houghton Mifflin, and London, Hamish Hamilton, 1969.
How to Control the Military. New York, Doubleday, 1969.
Who Needs the Democrats, and What It Takes To Be Needed. New York, Doubleday, 1970.
The American Left and Some British Comparisons. London, Fabian Society, 1971.
A China Passage. Boston, Houghton Mifflin, 1973.
A Life in Our Times. Boston, Houghton Mifflin, 1981.

*

Critical Studies: *The Economists* by Leonard Silk, New York, Basic Books, 1976; *From Galbraith to Economic Freedom* by Milton Friedman, London, Institute of Economic Affairs, 1977; *The Economics of John Kenneth Galbraith: A Study in Fantasy* by Frank Scott McFadzean, London, Centre for Policy Studies, 1977; *The Galbraithian Vision: The Cultural Criticism of John Kenneth Galbraith* by C. Lynn Munro, Washington, University Press of America, 1979; *Galbraith and Market Capitalism* by David A. Reisman, New York, New York University Press, 1980; *Tawney, Galbraith, and Adam Smith: State and Welfare* by David A. Reisman, New York, St. Martin's Press, 1982.

*   *   *

In the course of his career, John Kenneth Galbraith has established himself as one of the most preeminent and persuasive writers of the 20th century; he has attracted a wide international audience, introduced numerous neologisms into the language and influenced the thinking of countless generations. Whether as an economist, journalist, adviser or statesman, Galbraith has relentlessly challenged both the assumptions and models advanced by more orthodox thinkers and has insisted upon the need to revise theoretical constructs in accordance with the march of events.

While many take exception to his depiction of the structure of the advanced industrial state, few deny his pronounced influence upon contemporary intellectual history or his ability to translate esoteric concepts into terms comprehensible to the layman. His books have been widely read and translated, and in 1977 he was afforded the rare opportunity of conducting what was tantamount to a multi-national university course in the history of economic ideas when the BBC produced his series of lectures entitled "The Age of Uncertainty." Were this not enough to raise the cackles of his brethren, the following year he and Nicole Salinger co-authored *Almost Everyone's Guide to Economics*, a primer of sorts in which Galbraith deftly explains economic terminology and demystifies contemporary economic issues.

Galbraith's ability to explain complex phenomena and to clarify arcane economic theories and concepts so as to make them readily accessible to the general public is complemented by his sardonic wit and his prescient vision. Unlike many of his colleagues, Galbraith has refused to pay obeisance to the conventional wisdom. His theoretical formulations are always informed by a humanistic philosophy which underscores the moral and ethical ramifications of various ideas and policies; his vision is

synthetic and marked by a distinct preference for qualitative rather than quantitative analysis. In each of his major works, he presents a convincing and compelling socio-economic model which reveals the ways in which the various components of the system are interrelated. In short, his is a heterodox perspective which takes into account the cultural and historical context of the phenomena he is analyzing and recognizes the impacts of social and technological change, especially as they influence the ways in which various actors perform their economic and political roles.

Galbraith is perhaps best known for the concern he has expressed over social imbalance and uneven economic development. Both phenomena stem, in his estimation, from the exaggerated importance which economists and politicians attach to growth as measured by the GNP. What such an indicator ignores is the disparate performance of the various sectors of the economy. Long before most, Galbraith anticipated the very real human and social costs of allowing market forces, such as they were, to dictate what goods and services would be available to whom and at what price. The coincidence of public squalor amidst affluence alerted him to the risks of relying on the private sector to enhance the quality of life, a point which he convincingly argued in *The Affluent Society*.

His study of the systemic roots of poverty led Galbraith to a host of related considerations which lie at the heart of both *The New Industrial State* and *Economics and the Public Purpose*. While recognizing a continuum, Galbraith has argued that the modern industrial economy is essentially bimodal. On the one hand, there is the planning sector composed of mature corporations which wield power over such basic factors of production as costs, prices and consumer demand. On the other hand, there is the market sector consisting of the thousands of entrepreneurial firms which not only lack the prerogatives of the mature corporation, but also fall victim to the economic policies which serve the ends of the more influential members of the planning sector.

Galbraith's analysis of the power available to the mature corporations has generated the most heated debate; orthodox economists have been aroused because the power which Galbraith ascribes to the planning sector cannot be objectively measured. Further, Galbraith's analysis challenges almost all of the cornerstones upon which the neo-classical model rests. Among his targets are the notions of consumer sovereignty, the competitive market and profit maximization; in their stead, he argues that the mature corporation has both the need and the ability to effect demand and to transcend market forces, and that those who run the large corporations, the members of the technostructure, have little to gain from profit maximization and are guided by a different motivational scheme. He has further averred that the ostensible differences between the capitalist and socialist economies have been canceled out by the imperatives of large-scale production and technological development. As a result, he argues, the capitalist corporation and the socialist *combinat* are on a broadly convergent path despite ideological disclaimers.

Galbraith's identification of the convergence of two seemingly antithetical systems is in keeping with his longstanding contention that circumstances, rather than belief systems, are the final arbiters of economic and political policies. This is not to say that Galbraith believes that the appropriate decisions are made as a matter of course but, rather, that he is convinced that in time even the staunchest defenders of a paradigm which has become outmoded due to social and technological change will be forced to endorse decisions they would once have dismissed as heretical. It is this belief which leads Galbraith in *Economics and the Public Purpose* to advance a number of policy prescriptions which constitute what he terms "the new socialism" and which evoked a predictable response from his more orthodox colleagues. Rereading his proposals in the midst of the economic malaise of the early 1980's causes one to wonder whether events may not yet force his critics to reconsider his arguments.

Galbraith is a tireless reformer bent upon improving rather than overthrowing the free enterprise system. In the course of his career he has used many mediums in order to contribute to the emancipation of belief and appeal to the public cognizance; his primary aim has been to explain the system in such a way as to demonstrate the inherent contradictions between the priorities established by the planning sector and the needs and desires of the public at large. That he places his faith in the people is in keeping with his steadfast defense of education as a means of freeing people from their own sense of powerlessness.

While he has worn many hats in the course of his career, he is first and foremost an educator in the truest sense of the term. No matter what his official role or title at any particular juncture, he has never abdicated the responsibility of the intellectual to become an active participant in the cultural dialogue, to challenge the assumptions, raise the difficult issues and propose the unfashionable solutions. *A Life in Our Times*, a truly fascinating memoir, demonstrates the range of Galbraith's accomplishments and contributions as well as the sincerity of his conviction that the individual who is open to ideas and willing to risk criticism can indeed make a difference.

—C. Lynn Munro

GANDHI, Mohandâs (Karamchand), Mahatma. Indian philosopher, politician and social thinker. Born in Porbandar, Kathiawar, 2 October 1869. Educated at Samaldas College, Kathiawar; studied law in London, 1887-91. Married Kasturbai in 1883 (died, 1944). Practiced law, Bombay, 1891-93; moved to South Africa where he opposed discriminatory legislation against Indians, 1893-1914; aided Britain by forming Indian Ambulance Corps during Boer War, 1899; led Indians in nursing European victims of Black Plague, Johannesburg, South Africa, formed another Ambulance Corps during the Zulu rebellion, and made possible the compromise with General Smuts over taxes imposed on Indians coming out of indenture, 1908; returned to India and supported British in World War I, 1914; took interest in Home Rule movement (Swaraj), became President of the Congress organization, and formed Satyagraha League, 1919; civil disobedience campaign of 1920 caused violent disorder and led to his imprisonment for conspiracy, 1922-24; led 200-mile march to the sea (Dandi Salt-March) to collect salt as a symbolic defiance of Government monopoly, 1930; negotiated truce between Congress and the Government and attended London Round Table Conference on Indian Constitutional Reform, 1931; on return to India renewed civil disobedience campaign and was again arrested, 1931; maintained a pattern of arrests and fasts, 1931-37; resigned as President and member of Congress, 1934; settled in Sevagram, near Wardha, 1936; assisted in adoption of constitutional compromise under which Congress ministers accepted office in new provincial legislatures, 1937; induced Congress to offer co-operation in British war effort, if British Government agreed to set up immediate provisional government, 1940; arrested and jailed for civil disobedience in obstruction of war effort for urging Indian independence, 1942-44; negotiated with British Cabinet Mission which recommended new constitutional structure, resulting in India's independence, 1947; conducted fasts to shame instigators of communal strife between Hindus and Moslems, making last fast in Delhi, 1948. *Died* (assassinated by Hindu fanatic) *30 January 1948.*

PUBLICATIONS

Collections

Collected Works. Delhi, Publications Division of the Government of India, 80 vols., 1958-.

Political and Social Philosophy

Speeches and Writings. Madras, Natesan, 1918.
Swaraj and Non-Co-operation (speeches and writings). Mymensing, Chakravartty, 1920.
Swaraj in One Year. Madras, Ganesh, 1921.
Mahatma Gandhi on Spinning, compiled by Manoranjan Bhattacharya. Calcutta, Bhattacharya, 1921.
Freedom's Battle: Being a Comprehensive Collection of Writings and Speeches on the Present Situation. Madras, Ganesh, 1922.
Non-Co-operation: Recent Speeches and Writings. Madras, Ganesh, 1922.
India on Trial. Madras, Ahimsa Ashram, 1922.
Mahatma Gandhi's Jail Experiences. Madras, Tagore, 1922.
The Tug of War (articles and letters). Calcutta, Book Club, 1922.
Young India: vol. 1, *1919-1922*; vol. 2, *1924-1926*; vol. 3, *1927-1928* (articles published in the *Young India* weekly). Madras, Ganesan, 1922-35.
A Guide to Health. Madras, Ganesan, 1923.
Hindu-Muslim Tension: Its Cause and Cure. Ahmedabad, Young India Office, 1924.
Is India Different?: The Class Struggle in India. London, Communist Party, 1927.
Satyagraha in South Africa (translated from the Gujarati). Ahmedabad, Navajivan, 1928.
Ethical Religion (translated from the Hindi). Madras, Ganesan, 1930.
How to Compete with Foreign Cloth. Calcutta, Calcutta Book Company, 1931.
India's Case for Swaraj: Being Selected Speeches, Writings, Interviews, etc., of Mahatma Gandhi in England and India, September 1931-January 1932. Bombay, Yeshanand, 1932.
My Soul's Agony: Being Statements Issued from Yeravda Prison about the Removal of Untouchability. Bombay, Servants of Untouchables Society, 1932.
Views on Untouchability: Being Extracts from Speeches and Writings, edited by Mukut Beharilal. Kashi, privately printed, 1932.
Self-Restraint Versus Self-Indulgence. Ahmedabad, Navajivan, 2 vols., 1933-39.
To the Students, edited by Anand T. Hingorani. Karachi, Hingorani, 1935.
Cent Percent Swadeshi or the Economics of Village Industries. Ahmedabad, Navajivan, 1938.
Hind Swaraj or Indian Home Rule (translated from the Gujarati). Ahmedabad, Navajivan, 1939.
Swadeshi: True or False. Poona, Chandrashankar, Shukla, 1940.
Birth Control Versus Self Control, edited by Dewan Ram Parkash. Lahore, Dewan, 1941.
Christian Missions: Their Place in India. Ahmedabad, Navajivan, 1941; revised edition, 1957.
Constructive Programme: Its Meaning and Place. Ahmedabad, Navajivan, 1941.
Economics of Khadi. Ahmedabad, Navajivan, 1941.
The Indian States' Problems (articles). Ahmedabad, Navajivan, 1941.
To the Women (articles), edited by Anand T. Hingorani. Karachi, Hingorani, 1941.
Quit India, edited by R.K. Prabhu and U.R. Rao. Bombay, Padma, 1942.
To the Hindus and Muslims (articles), edited by Anand T. Hingorani. Karachi, Hingorani, 1942.
To the Princes and Their People (articles), edited by Anand T. Hingorani. Karachi, Hingorani, 1942.
Women and Social Injustice. Ahmedabad, Navajivan, 1942.
Our Language Problem. Karachi, Hingorani, 1942.
Conquest of Self: Being Gleanings from His Writings and Speeches, compiled by R.K. Prabhu and U.R. Rao. Bom-

bay, Thacker, 1943.

I Ask Every Briton (articles).   London, Baines and Scarsbrook, 1943.

The Wisdom of Gandhi, edited by Roy Walker.   Calcutta, Calcutta Book Company, 1943.

Ethics of Fasting, edited by Jag Parvesh Chander.   Lahore, Indian Printing Works, 1944.

Unseen Power, edited by Jag Parvesh Chander.   Lahore, Indian Printing Works, 1944.

From Yeravda Mandir: Ashram Observances (translated from the Gujarati).   Ahmedabad, Navajivan, 1945.

The Mind of Mahatma Gandhi, compiled by R.K. Prabhu and U.R. Rao.   Oxford, Oxford University Press, 1945.

Swaraj Through Charkha, compiled by Kanu Gandhi.   Sevagram, All India Spinners' Association, 1945.

Daridranarayan (collection of articles on food and cloth shortage), edited by Anand T. Hingorani.   Karachi, Hingorani, 1946.

Communal Unity.   Ahmedabad, Navajivan, 1947.

Gandhigrams, compiled by S.R. Tikeker.   Bombay, Hind Kitabs, 1947.

Gita the Mother (articles), edited by Jag Parvesh Chander.   Lahore, Indian Printing Works, 1947.

India of My Dreams, compiled by R.K. Prabhu.   Bombay, Hind Kitabs, 1947.

Ramanama: The Infallible Remedy, edited by Anand T. Hingorani.   Karachi, Hingorani, 1947.

Teachings of Mahatma Gandhi.   Lahore, Indian Printing Works, 1947.

To the Protagonists of Pakistan (articles), edited by Anand T. Hingorani.   Karachi, Hingorani, 1947.

Delhi Diary: Prayer Speeches from 10-9-1947 to 30-1-1948.   Ahmedabad, Navajivan, 1948.

Mahatma Gandhi's Sayings, compiled by Priyaranjan Sen.   Calcutta, Orient Book Company, 1948.

Fellowship of Faiths and Unity of Religions, edited by Abbul Majid Khan.   Madras, Natesan, 1948.

Precious Pearls, compiled by R.S. Kausbala.   Delhi, Clifton, 1948; as *Gandhian Gems*, Ambala, Standred, 1954.

Key to Health (translation).   Ahmedabad, Navajivan, 1948.

Non-Violence in Peace and War.   Ahmedabad, Navajivan, 2 vols., 1948-49.

Selection from Gandhi, compiled by N.K. Bose.   Ahmedabad, Navajivan, 1948.

Why the Constructive Programme.   New Delhi, All India Congress Committee, 1948.

Diet and Diet Reform (articles).   Ahmedabad, Navajivan, 1949.

Food Shortage and Agriculture.   Ahmedabad, Navajivan, 1949.

For Pacifists.   Ahmedabad, Navajivan, 1949.

The Mahatma and the Missionary: Selected Writings, edited by Clifford Manshardt.   Chicago, Regnery, 1949.

Mohanmala: A Gandhian Rosary: Being a Thought for Each Day of the Year Gleaned from the Writings and Speeches of Mahatma Gandhi, compiled by R.K. Prabhu.   Bombay, Hind Kitabs, 1949.

Ramanama.   Ahmedabad, Navajivan, 1949.

Hindu Dharma.   Ahmedabad, Navajivan, 1950.

Health, Wealth and Happiness.   New Delhi, Bharatiya Karmayogi Samaj, 1950.

Thus Spake Mahatma.   Bangalore, Vichar Sahitya, 1950.

A Day Book of Thoughts, edited by K.T. Narasimha Char.   Calcutta, Macmillan, 1951.

Selected Writings of Mahatma Gandhi, edited by Ronald Duncan.   London, Faber, 1951.

Ruskin's Unto This Last: A Paraphrase (translated from the Gujarati).   Ahmedabad, Navajivan, 1951.

Satyagraha: Non-Violent Resistance.   Ahmedabad, Navajivan, 1951.

Towards Non-Violent Socialism, edited by Bharatan Kumarappa.   Ahmedabad, Navajivan, 1951.

The Wit and Wisdom of Gandhi, edited by Homer A. Jack.   Boston, Beacon, 1951.

Drink, Drugs and Gambling, edited by Bharatan Kumarappa.   Ahmedabad, Navajivan, 1952.

Rebuilding Our Villages, edited by Bharatan Kumarappa.   Ahmedabad, Navajivan, 1952.

To the Students, edited by Bharatan Kumarappa.   Ahmedabad, Navajivan, 1953.

Towards New Education, edited by Bharatan Kumarappa.   Ahmedabad, Navajivan, 1953.

For Workers Against Untouchability.   Ahmedabad, Navajivan, 1954.

Goan Struggle for Freedom.   Ahmedabad, Navajivan, 1954.

How to Serve the Cow, edited by Bharatan Kumarappa.   Ahmedabad, Navajivan, 1954.

Linguistic Provinces, edited by Bharatan Kumarappa.   Ahmedabad, Navajivan, 1954.

Medium of Instruction, edited by Bharatan Kumarappa.   Ahmedabad, Navajivan, 1954.

Nature Cure (articles and extracts), edited by Bharatan Kumarappa.   Ahmedabad, Navajivan, 1954.

The Removal of Untouchability, edited by Bharatan Kumarappa.   Ahmedabad, Navajivan, 1954.

Sarvodaya: The Welfare of All, edited by Bharatan Kumarappa.   Ahmedabad, Navajivan, 1954.

Untouchability, edited by Bharatan Kumarappa.   Ahmedabad, Navajivan, 1954.

Ashram Observances in Action (translation from the Gujarati).   Ahmedabad, Navajivan, 1955.

Gokhale: My Political Guru.   Ahmedabad, Navajivan, 1955.

Khadi [Hand-Spun Cloth]: Why and How, edited by Bharatan Kumarappa.   Ahmedabad, Navajivan, 1955.

My Religion (articles), edited by Bharatan Kumarappa.   Ahmedabad, Navajivan, 1955.

On Removal of Untouchability.   Bombay, Director of Publicity, 1956.

Thoughts on National Language.   Ahmedabad, Navajivan, 1956.

Towards Lasting Peace, edited by Anand T. Hingorani.   Bombay, Bharatiya Vidya Bhavan, 1956.

God Is Truth, edited by Anand T. Hingorani.   Bombay, Bharatiya Vidya Bhavan, 1957.

Economic and Industrial Life and Relations, edited by V.B. Kher.   Ahmedabad, Navajivan, 3 vols., 1957.

Food for the Soul, edited by Anand T. Hingorani.   Bombay, Bharatiya Vidya Bhavan, 1957.

The Law of Love, edited by Anand T. Hingorani.   Bombay, Bharatiya Vidya Bhavan, 1957.

The Science of Satyagraha, edited by Anand T. Hingorani.   Bombay, Bharatiya Vidya Bhavan, 1957.

Socialism of My Conception, edited by Anand T. Hingorani.   Bombay, Bharatiya Vidya Bhavan, 1957.

All Men Are Brothers: Life and Thoughts of Mahatma Gandhi as Told in His Own Words.   Calcutta, Longman, 1958.

Evil Wrought by the English Medium, edited by R.K. Prabhu.   Ahmedabad, Navajivan, 1958.

The Gandhi Reader, edited by Homer Jack.   London, Dobson, and New York, Grove, 2 vols., 1958.

Hindi and English in the South (India), edited by M.P. Desai.   Ahmedabad, Navajivan, 1958.

Homage to the Departed (includes tributes to Gandhi by others), edited by V.B. Kher.   Ahmedabad, Navajivan, 1958.

Women.   Ahmedabad, Navajivan, 1958.

Birth Control: The Right Way and the Wrong Way, compiled by R.K. Prabhu.   Ahmedabad, Navajivan, 1959.

Character and Nation Building, edited by V.G. Desai.   Ahmedabad, Navajivan, 1959.

Communism and Communists, compiled by R.K. Prabhu.   Ahmedabad, Navajivan, 1959.

Co-operative Farming, edited by Shirman Narayan.   Ahmedabad, Navajivan, 1959.

The Message of the Gita, compiled by R.K. Prabhu. Ahmedabad, Navajivan, 1959.

The Moral Basis of Vegetarianism, compiled by R.K. Prabhu. Ahmedabad, Navajivan, 1959.

My Socialism, compiled by R.K. Prabhu. Ahmedabad, Navajivan, 1959.

Non-Violent Way to World Peace, compiled by R.K. Prabhu. Ahmedabad, Navajivan, 1959.

Panchayat Raj, compiled by R.K. Prabhu. Ahmedabad, Navajivan, 1959.

What Jesus Means to Me, compiled by R.K. Prabhu. Ahmedabad, Navajivan, 1959.

Women's Role in Society, compiled by R.K. Prabhu. Ahmedabad, Navajivan, 1960.

Congress and Its Future, compiled by R.K. Prabhu. Ahmedabad, Navajivan, 1960.

Discourses on the Gita (translation from the Gujarati). Ahmedabad, Navajivan, 1960.

India's Food Problem, compiled by R.K. Prabhu. Ahmedabad, Navajivan, 1960.

Jawaharlal Nehru: The Jewel of India, edited by Anand T. Hingorani. Bombay, Pearl, 1960.

My Non-Violence, compiled and edited by Sailesh Kumar Bandyopadhyaya. Ahmedabad, Navajivan, 1960.

The New Indian States, compiled by R.K. Prabhu. Ahmedabad, Navajivan, 1960.

Prohibition at Any Cost, compiled by R.K. Prabhu. Ahmedabad, Navajivan, 1960.

Village Industries, compiled by R.K. Prabhu. Ahmedabad, Navajivan, 1960.

Wit and Wisdom of Mahatma Gandhi, edited by N.B. Sen. New Delhi, New Book Society, 1960.

Writings and Speeches of Gandhi Relating to Bihar 1917-1947, edited by K.K. Datta. Patna, Government of Bihar, 1960.

The Art of Living, edited by Anand T. Hingorani. Bombay, Bharatiya Vidya Bhavan, 1961.

Democracy: Real and Deceptive, compiled by R.K. Prabhu. Ahmedabad, Navajivan, 1961.

The Gospel of Renunciation, compiled by R.K. Prabhu. Ahmedabad, Navajivan, 1961.

My Philosophy of Life, edited by Anand T. Hingorani. Bombay, Pearl, 1961.

Search of the Supreme, edited by V.B. Kher. Ahmedabad, Navajivan, 3 vols., 1961-62.

Strikes, compiled by R. Kelekar. Ahmedabad, Navajivan, 1961.

The Task Before Indian Students, compiled by R.K. Prabhu. Ahmedabad, Navajivan, 1961.

Voluntary Poverty, compiled by R. Kelekar. Ahmedabad, Navajivan, 1961.

All Religions Are True, edited by Anand T. Hingorani. Bombay, Pearl, 1962.

Birth Control, edited by Anand T. Hingorani. Bombay, Bharatiya Vidya Bhavan, 1962.

The Law and the Lawyers, edited by S.B. Kher. Ahmedabad, Navajivan, 1962.

My God, compiled by R.K. Prabhu. Ahmedabad, Navajivan, 1962.

The Problem of Education (articles). Ahmedabad, Navajivan, 1962.

The Teachings of the Gita, edited by Anand T. Hingorani. Bombay, Bharatiya Vidya Bhavan, 1962.

The Thought of Mahatma Gandhi: A Digest, compiled by Mirabehn. Ahmedabad, Navajivan, 1962.

True Education. Ahmedabad, Navajivan, 1962.

Varnashramadharma, compiled by R.K. Prabhu. Ahmedabad, Navajivan, 1962.

Village Swaraj, compiled by H.M. Vyas. Ahmedabad, Navajivan, 1962.

Co-operation, compiled by H.M. Vyas. Ahmedabad, Navajivan, 1963.

The Essential Gandhi: An Anthology, edited by Louis Fischer. London, Allen and Unwin, 1963.

The Message of Jesus Christ, edited by Anand T. Hingorani. Bombay, Bhartiya Vidya Bhavan, 1963.

The Supreme Power, edited by Anand T. Hingorani. Bombay, Bharatiya Vidya Bhavan, 1963.

The Way to Communal Harmony, edited by U.R. Rao. Ahmedabad, Navajivan, 1963.

All Are Equal in the Eyes of God (selections). Delhi, Publications Division of the Government of India, 1964.

Caste Must Go and the Sin of Untouchability, compiled by R.K. Prabhu. Ahmedabad, Navajivan, 1964.

The Law of Continence: Brahmacharya, edited by Anand T. Hingorani. Bombay, Bharatiya Vidya Bhavan, 1964.

The Role of Women, edited by Anand T. Hingorani. Bombay, Bharatiya Vidya Bhavan, 1964.

Stone Walls Do Not a Prison Make, compiled and edited by V.B. Kher. Ahmedabad, Navajivan, 1964.

Through Self-Control, edited by Anand T. Hingorani. Bombay, Bharatiya Vidya Bhavan, 1964.

Fasting in Satyagraha: Its Use and Abuse, compiled by R.K. Prabhu and Ravindra Kelekar. Ahmedabad, Navajivan, 1965.

Gandhiji Expects: What the Father of the Nation Expected of People's Representatives, compiled by H.M. Vyas. Ahmedabad, Navajivan, 1965.

Gita My Mother, edited by Anand T. Hingorani. Bombay, Bharatiya Vidya Bhavan, 1965.

Glorious Thoughts of Gandhi, edited by N.B. Sen. New Delhi, New Book Society, 1965.

The Hindu Muslim Unity, edited by Anand T. Hingorani. Bombay, Bharatiya Vidya Bhavan, 1965.

My Picture of the Free India, edited by Anand T. Hingorani. Bombay, Bharatiya Vidya Bhavan, 1965.

None High, None Low, edited by Anand T. Hingorani. Bombay, Bharatiya Vidya Bhavan, 1965.

Industrialize and Perish, compiled by R.K. Prabhu. Ahmedabad, Navajivan, 1966.

The Nature Cure, edited by Anand T. Hingorani. Bombay, Bharatiya Vidya Bhavan, 1966.

The Doctrine of the Sword: The Law of Suffering, Modern Politics. London, Peace Pledge Union, n.d.

Great Thoughts of Mahatma Gandhi. Madras, Ganesh, n.d.

The Good Life, edited by Jag Parvesh Chander. Second edition. Lahore, Indian Printing Works, n.d.

Thought Currents: A Selection from Mahatma Gandhi's Writings and Speeches. Baroda, Harilal M. Desai, n.d.

Untouchability, edited by Dewan Ram Parkash. Lahore, Gandhi Publications League, n.d.

Epigrams from Gandhiji, compiled by S.R. Tikekar. New Delhi, Publications Division of the Government of India, 1971.

Pathway to God, compiled by M.S. Deshpande. Ahmedabad, Navajivan, 1971.

Why Fear or Mourn Death, edited by Anand T. Hingorani. Bombay, Bharatiya Vidya Bhavan, 1971.

Gandhi and Haryana: A Collection of His Speeches and Writings Pertaining to Haryana, edited by J. Chandra. New Delhi, Usha, 1977.

Other

Autobiography or the Story of My Experiments with the Truth (translated from the Gujarati). Ahmedabad, Navajivan, 1927.

My Early Life (1869-1914), arranged and edited by M. Desai. New Delhi, Oxford University Press, 1932.

Songs from Prison (translation of lyrics made in jail by Gandhi), edited by John S. Hoyland. London, George Allen, 1934.

Correspondence Between Gandhiji and P.C. Joshi. Bombay, People's Publishing House, 1945.

Gandhi's Correspondence with the Government 1942-1944. Ahmedabad, Navajivan, 1945.

Letters from Prison, compiled by R.M. Khanna.   Lahore, Allied Indian Publishers, 1946.

Famous Letters of Mahatma Gandhi, compiled and edited by R.L. Khipple.   Lahore, Indian Printing Works, 1947.

Selected Letters (translation).   Ahmedabad, Navajivan, 2 vols., 1949-62.

Bapu's Letters to Mira 1924-1948.   Ahmedabad, Navajivan, 1949; New York, Harper, 1950.

(Letters) to a Gandhian Capitalist: Correspondence Between Gandhi and Jamnalal Bajaj and Members of His Family, edited by Kaka Kalelkar.   Wardha, Jamnalal Seva Trust, 1951.

(Letters) to Ashram Sisters (6-12-26 to 30-12-29), edited by Kaka Kalelkar.   Ahmedabad, Navajivan, 1952.

The Story of My Life (for use in schools).   Ahmedabad, Navajivan, 1955.

My Dear Child: Letters to Esther Faering, edited by Alice M. Barnes.   Ahmedabad, Navajivan, 1959.

Letters to Raj Kumari Amrit Kaur (1931-1947).   Ahmedabad, Navajivan, 1961.

Letters to Manibahen Patel (translation).   Ahmedabad, Navajivan, 1963.

*

Bibliographies: *Gandhiana: A Bibliography of Gandhian Literature* by P.G. Deshpande, Ahmedabad, Navajivan, 1948 (lists books in Hindi, Gujarati, Marathi, Bengali, Urdu, Kannad, Sanskrit and Sindhi); *Gandhi Bibliography* by Dharma Vir, Nidhi, Punjab, Haryana and Himachel Pradesh, 1967.

Critical Studies: *Mahatma* by D.G. Tendulkar, Bombay, Pradesh, 8 vols., 1951-54; *Gandhi and Modern India* by Penderel Moon, New York, Norton, 1969; *Gandhi's Social Philosophy: Perspective and Relevance* by B. Ganguli, New York, Wiley, 1973; *Mahatma Gandhi and His Apostles* by Ved Mehta, New York, Viking Press, 1976; *Gandhi and Civil Disobedience: The Mahatma in Indian Politics 1928-1938* by Judith M. Brown, Cambridge, Cambridge University Press, 1973; *Gandhi: A Memoir* by William L. Shirer, New York, Simon and Schuster, 1979.

*   *   *

In order to grasp Gandhi's moral and political thought, one need not necessarily come to a firm view about Gandhi's personality as a saintly politician or a political saint. It is, however, necessary to accept his profound integrity as a thinker and as a seeker of truth. Gandhi's concepts of conscience and heroism, tolerance and civility, *satya* and *asatya*, *ahimsa* and *himsa*, *moksha* and *tapas*, *satyagraha*, *sarvodaya*, *swaraj* and *swadeshi* are based upon metaphysical presuppositions, but they have important ethical and political implications. Some of his writings, which will fill 90 volumes when published in their entirety, are inconclusive and fragmentary, but among them there are important essays embodying his political thought. He thought that his central convictions and crucial statements would come to be accepted in the decades after his death.

Gandhi's standpoint as a political moralist was expressed early in life in *Hind Swaraj*, in which he spoke out strongly against modern civilization. He saw a contradiction between our deepest moral values as individuals and the materialistic criteria by which we tend to judge our institutions and our collective progress. He thought that the "sickness" of modern civilization is reflected in our "soulless" politics, owing to a segregation between religion and politics and the prevalent doctrine of double standards. He redefined both "religion" and "politics" so as to emphasize the distinction between sectarian beliefs and spiritual commitment, between power politics and *sattvic* or "pure" politics. Politics is corrupted by power-seeking, and it could be puri-

fied by introducing the monastic ideal into the sphere of political activity and social science. All men and women must come to accept certain moral values as absolute, especially *satya*—truth—and *ahimsa*—nonviolence. At least, some votaries must pledge themselves by vows to upholding these absolute values in public life. The reason for such drastic remedies is that human nature is so constituted that it must either soar or sink, and it will increasingly connive at untruth and violence if the quest for self-perfection is abandoned. Individuals should not abdicate from social responsibilities in their search for personal salvation. It is possible to combine an appeal to conscience with heroic action in the midst of society, to yoke freedom with commitment.

The word *satya* does not correspond exactly to what we normally mean by truth or veracity. It has a variety of connotations, of which the most important are: real, sincere, existent, pure, good, effectual, valid. *Satya* is derived from *sat*, which means being. *Sat* also means abiding, actual, right, wise, self-existent essence, as anything really is, as anything ought to be. The derivation of *satya* from *sat* was taken by Gandhi to imply that nothing exists in reality except Truth; everything else is illusory. Beyond and behind the illusory flux of fleeting phenomena there is an eternal substratum of noumenal reality, a single bedrock of supernal Truth. In the Indian tradition, *SAT* in its highest sense stands for absolute, archetypal Reality and for the absolute, archetypal Truth. Although a clear distinction was made between knowledge and being, between epistemology and ontology, this distinction was said to be transcended at the height of the human quest, when the knower and the known are united in a state of mystical communion owing to their essential identity with a single, if unknowable, Reality.

Although Gandhi regarded *satya*, or truth, as the highest value, his name is commonly identified with the concept of *ahimsa*, or nonviolence. The word *ahimsa* literally means non-injury, or, more narrowly, non-killing, and, more widely, harmlessness, the renunciation of the will to kill and of the intention to hurt any living thing, the abstention from hostile thought, word and act. Gandhi inflated the term *ahimsa* to include all the moral virtues; he equated it with humility, forgiveness, love, charity, selflessness, fearlessness, strength, non-attachment, meekness and innocence. Similarly, he stretched *himsa* or violence far beyond its ordinary usage to include all unfair and foul means. Gandhi held that although *ahimsa* is universally applicable, its daily exercise must be exemplified by a few votaries who take vows and undergo a comprehensive moral and spiritual discipline. The relationship between *satya* and *ahimsa* may be put in the form of three propositions. First of all, the pursuit of *satya* gives us the humility to accept the need for *ahimsa* in our relationship with our fellow men, who are also truth-seekers in their own way. *Satya* implies *ahimsa*. Secondly, the pursuit of *ahimsa* shows that *himsa* is rooted in fear which can be removed only by the strength that comes from *satya*. *Ahimsa* presupposes *satya*. Thirdly, *ahimsa* is the means to *satya*, but as the end ever eludes us, the means become supremely important. Thus, although *satya* is higher than *ahimsa*, *ahimsa* is in practice more important than *satya*. As a working rule, the degree of *ahimsa* we display is a measure of the degree of *satya* we possess.

In order to understand Gandhi's view of the connection between *satya* and *ahimsa*, it would be useful to inflate these notions to *moksha* and *tapas*, which are basic to Hindu thought. *Moksha* for Gandhi signified the vision of Absolute Truth, to be attained by means of *tapas* or "self-suffering," and the relation between *moksha* and *tapas* was mirrored in the relation between *satya* and *ahimsa*. Gandhi regarded the aim of human life as *moksha*, liberation from impure thought, and the total elimination of impure thought is possible only as a result of much *tapasya*. The utter extinction of egoism is *moksha* and those few who have achieved this will be the very image of Truth or God. Government over self is the truest *swaraj* (freedom); it is synonymous with *moksha* or salvation. He also said that "*ahimsa* means *moksha* and *moksha* is the realization of Truth." The test of love is *tapasya*, and this means self-suffering. Self-realization is impossible without service of, and identification with, the poorest. The quest of Truth involves *tapas*—self-suffering, sometimes even unto death. *Satya* requires the *tapas* of *ahimsa*, which implies self-suffering and self-sacrifice in the midst of society.

Gandhi's concepts of *satya* and *ahimsa* lie at the heart of his entire social and political philosophy. He nurtured his own vision of the radical transformation of the existing social order and political system, but he was even more concerned to evolve a revolutionary approach to political action and social change within the limits of the prevailing conditions of politics and society. Immediate resistance to injustice and coercion as well as a long-term program of social and political reconstruction must alike be legitimated in terms of the twin absolutes of truth and nonviolence. His concept of *satya*, with *ahimsa* as the means, determined his doctrine of *satyagraha* or active resistance to authority, while the concept of *ahimsa*, with *satya* as the common end, enabled him to formulate his doctrine of *sarvodaya* or nonviolent socialism. The doctrine of *satyagraha* was meant to show how the man of conscience could engage in heroic action in the vindication of truth and justice against all tyranny, social abuse and sectional interest. Gandhi challenged the conventional notions of authority, law and obligation by appealing to his conceptions of natural law or *dharma* and self-suffering or *tapas*.

When Gandhi entered Indian politics, he restored the term *swaraj* to its older meaning of self-rule whilst retaining its new sense of political independence. He reinterpreted the term *swadeshi*—patriotism and self-dependence—and pointed to the close connection between *swaraj* and *swadeshi*, between individual self-rule and individual self-reliance, between national self-government and national self-dependence. He derived the notion of communal self-reliance from his doctrine of individual self-rule, and showed how the pursuit of *swaraj* must necessarily involve the acceptance of *swadeshi*, and yet the former must be taken as logically and morally prior to the latter. He achieved this result by basing *swaraj* upon *satya*, i.e., linking the notions of freedom and of truth; secondly by deriving the doctrine of *swadeshi* from his concept of *ahimsa* (emphasizing its positive rather than its negative connotation); and thirdly, by basing the connection between *swaraj* and *swadeshi* upon the relationship between *satya* and *ahimsa*.

Gandhi seems to stand almost alone among social and political thinkers in his firm rejection of the rigid dichotomy between ends and means and in his extreme moral preoccupation with the means to the extent that they, rather then the ends, provide the standard of reference. Gandhi was led by his metaphysical belief in the law of *Karma*—the law of ethical causation that links all the acts of interdependent individuals—to the view that the relationship between means and ends is organic, the moral quality of the latter being causally dependent upon that of the former. The psychology of human action in a morally indivisible community of apparently isolated units demands that the means-end relationship must be seen in terms of the consistent growth in moral awareness of individuals and communities and not in relation to the mechanical division of time into arbitrary and discrete intervals.

Gandhi's concepts of *satya*, *ahimsa* and *satyagraha*, of *tapas* and, above all, of the *satyagrahi*, are ideal constructions—"Euclidean" models as he himself called them. In constructing these, Gandhi was in the oldest political tradition that goes back to classical Chinese and Indian thinkers, and to Plato in the West. They could serve in the serious task of civic education (*paideia*) provided they are not taken to represent decisively the political realities of the future. Every society must choose its own mode of transmission of this ethic into the detailed experience which it sums up in its past. In seeing beyond the confinements of past creeds and present *isms*, Gandhi drew from the reservoirs of the untapped moral energies of mankind, and pointed to the spiritual formulations of the civilization of the future.

—R.N. Iyer

GEERTZ, Clifford (James). American anthropologist. Born in San Francisco, California, 23 August 1926. Studied at Antioch College, Yellow Springs, Ohio, B.A. 1950; Harvard University, Cambridge, Massachusetts, Ph.D. 1956. Served in the United States Navy, 1943-45. Married Hildred Storey in 1948; 2 children. Research Associate, Laboratory of Social Relations, and Instructor in Social Relations, Harvard University, Cambridge, Massachusetts, 1956-57; Research Associate, Center for International Studies, Massachusetts Institute of Technology, in Indonesia, 1957-58; Fellow, Center for Advanced Study in the Behavioral Sciences, Stanford, California, 1958-59; Assistant Professor of Anthropology, University of California, Berkeley, 1959-60; Assistant Professor of Anthropology, 1960-61, Associate Professor, 1961-64, and Professor, 1964-70, University of Chicago. Since 1970, Professor of Social Science, Institute for Advanced Study, Princeton, New Jersey. Eastman Professor, Oxford University, 1978-79. Member, 1960-70, and Chairman, 1968-69, Committee for the Comparative Study of New Nations. Recipient: Social Science Prize, American Academy of Arts and Sciences, 1974; Sorokin Prize, American Anthropological Association, 1974. LL.D.: Harvard University, 1974; L.H.D.: North Michigan State University, 1975; University of Chicago, 1979; and Bates College, 1980. Fellow, American Academy of Arts and Sciences; American Philosophical Society; and National Academy of Sciences. Address: Department of Social Science, Institute for Advanced Study, Princeton, New Jersey 08540, U.S.A.

PUBLICATIONS

Anthropology

The Rotating Credit Association: An Instrument for Development. Cambridge, Massachusetts Institute of Technology Center for International Studies, 1956.
The Development of the Javanese Economy: A Socio-Cultural Approach. Cambridge, Massachusetts Institute of Technology Center for International Studies, 1956.
The Social Context of Economic Change: An Indonesian Case Study. Cambridge, Massachusetts Institute of Technology Center for International Studies, 1956.
Modjokuto: Religion in Java. Cambridge, Massachusetts Institute of Technology Center for International Studies, 1958; part published separately as *The Religion of Java*, New York, Free Press, 1960.
Agricultural Involution: The Process of Ecological Change in Indonesia. Berkeley, University of California Press, 1963.
Peddlers and Princes: Social Change and Economic Modernization in Two Indonesian Towns. Chicago, University of Chicago Press, 1963.
The Social History of an Indonesian Town. Cambridge, Massachusetts, MIT Press, 1965.
Person, Time, and Conduct in Bali: An Essay in Cultural Analysis. New Haven, Connecticut, Yale University Press, 1966.
Islam Observed: Religious Development in Morocco and Indonesia. New Haven, Connecticut, Yale University Press, 1968.
The Interpretation of Cultures. New York, Basic Books, 1973.
Kinship in Bali, with Hildred Geertz. Chicago, University of Chicago Press, 1975.
Meaning and Order in Moroccan Society, with L. Rosen and Hildred Geertz. Cambridge, Cambridge University Press, 1979.
Negara: The Theatre State in Nineteenth-Century Bali. Princeton, New Jersey, Princeton University Press, 1980.

Other

Editor, *Old Societies and New States.* New York, Free Press, 1963.
Editor, *Myth, Symbol and Culture.* New York, Norton, 1974.

*   *   *

In "Blurred Genres," a recent essay that he published in *The American Scholar*, Clifford Geertz writes of a "refiguration of social thought" that involves a turning away from natural-scientific models and a turning toward the discourse of the humanities: "society is less and less represented as an elaborate machine or a quasi-organism than as a serious game, a sidewalk drama, or a behavioral text." This reorientation of the social sciences stems from the increasing realization that "order in collective life" depends upon the fact that human activity is "organized in terms of symbols...whose meaning...we must grasp if we are to understand that organization and formulate its principles." In short, the social sciences are becoming "interpretive," and "interpretive explanation," according to Geertz,

> trains its attention on what institutions, actions, images, utterances, events, customs, all the usual objects of social-scientific interest, mean to those whose institutions, actions, customs, and so on they are. As a result, it issues not in laws like Boyle's, or forces like Volta's, or mechanisms like Darwin's, but in constructions like Burckhardt's, Weber's, or Freud's: systematic unpackings of the conceptual world in which *condottiere*, Calvinists, or paranoids live.

Geertz himself has been perhaps the leading contemporary exponent of this approach, providing both elegant case studies and a sophisticated theoretical discourse with which to talk about them. But his influence rests on more than this. In the topics that he has treated—religion, art, economics, politics—and the fora in which he has treated them—a wide variety of intellectual journals, general as well as specialized—he has consistently addressed himself to an audience far wider than one composed only of his fellow anthropologists. Furthermore, he has drawn on an unusually broad range of thinkers—from Aristotle to Jeremy Bentham to Wittgenstein and Kenneth Burke—as sources for the theoretical underpinnings and analogies of his work. Thus, for example, *Agricultural Involution*, a study of the effects of colonialism on the Javanese economy, takes its leading idea of "involution" from Alexander Goldenweiser's discussion of aesthetic styles; the image of "deep play," developed in an essay on Balinese cockfighting, comes from Bentham's discussion of the immorality of gambling; and "Thick Description: Toward an Interpretive Theory of Culture," a seminal essay arguing for an interpretive social science, borrows its leading trope from an essay by Gilbert Ryle on the nature of thinking. In each case Geertz has been able both to broaden and refocus these borrowed ideas, creating in the process a social-scientific discourse that has been original and persuasive.

At the heart of Geertz's program has been a persistent concern for what he once called, simply, "the role of thought in society." He has approached this issue by way of the macrosociological theories of Max Weber and, following Weber, Talcott Parsons. Geertz has used Parsons' model of a "human action system," which posits a clear analytic distinction between "culture" and "social structure," as a jumping-off point for the study of culture. Geertz has consistently worked to develop a concept of culture seen as "interdependent" with social structure rather than as derivative of or dominant over it. In practice this has meant serious attention to the role of thought—of "symbols," of intersubjective "meanings"—in society—that is, as a crucial element in the construction of social action. In such celebrated works as "Religion as a Cultural System," "Deep Play: Notes on the Balinese Cockfight," and *Islam Observed*, Geertz has drawn on his field experiences in Java, Bali, and Morocco to present both thickly descriptive accounts of "exotic" ways of life, and elegant analyses which at once illuminate the ethnography and contribute to the development of a theory of culture.

For Geertz, culture is

> an historically transmitted pattern of meanings embodied in symbols, a system of inherited conceptions expressed in symbolic forms by means of which men communicate, perpetuate, and develop their knowledge about and attitudes toward life.

By contrast, "social structure" refers to the human activity that is patterned in terms of such knowledge and attitudes:

> Culture is the fabric of meaning in terms of which human beings interpret their experience and guide their action; social structure is the form that action takes, the actually existing network of social relations.

Geertz's conception of culture is thus dual: "knowledge about" and "attitudes towards," "interpret" and "guide." In other words, for the people who live within it, a cultural system is a frame of reference that defines reality: their knowledge about the world is couched in terms of—indeed, created from—a particular cultural discourse. At the same time, their understanding of the world influences their attitudes towards it, hence their actions in it. Believing the world to be constructed in a particular (culturally defined) fashion, they believe also that particular attitudes and actions (also culturally defined) are appropriate in such a world. Finally, culture is continually recreated in or by human action: as people act out their lives in terms of the reality that their culture defines for them, they create that very reality and maintain its believability. In sum, culture is "at once a product and a determinant of social interaction."

Culture, then, is the human means to understand and experience the world. This position has led Geertz to reject so-called functional explanations in the study of culture. He has argued that the relationship between cultural institutions and the functional imperatives of human existence is "loose and indeterminate:"

> Not only does almost any institution serve a multiplicity of social, psychological, and organic needs (so that to say marriage is a mere reflex of the social need to reproduce, or that dining customs are a reflex of metabolic necessities, is to court parody), but there is no way to state in any precise and testable way the interlevel relationships that are conceived to hold.

Geertz further contends that since culture is inherently meaningful, "the thing to ask" about cultural phenomena is not what they "do" but what they mean—"what their import is," "what it is...that, in their occurrence and through their agency, is getting said." In short, culture cannot be reduced to assumed biological, psychological, or social functions. If anything, the "function" of culture is to impose meaning on the world, to make it understandable. And for man, the animal that depends for its survival upon symbolically mediated cultural patterns rather than upon specific innate capacities, "the drive to make sense out of experience, to give it form and order, is evidently as real and as pressing as the more familiar biological needs."

The "function" of culture is thus interpretive, as is the science that studies it. In "Thick Description: Toward an Interpretive Theory of Culture," Geertz spells out the implications of this (at least) doubly interpretive aspect of the science of culture. If culture is itself an "acted document"—"written not in conventionalized graphs of sound but in transient examples of shaped behavior"—then anthropological research is a process of reading, of interpretation. Furthermore, though terms such as "ethnographic facts" and "observation" suggest an objective reality that is merely noted, anthropologists may be said to create their "data" as they construct a reading of the lives of the people they study:

> In finished anthropological writings...this fact—that what we call our data are really our own constructions of other people's constructions of what they and their compatriots are up to—is obscured because most of what we need to

comprehend a particular event, ritual, custom, idea, or whatever is insinuated as background information before the thing itself is directly examined.... There is nothing particularly wrong with this, and it is in any case inevitable. But it does lead to a view of anthropological research as rather more of an observational and rather less of an interpretive activity than it really is. Right down at the factual base, the hard rock, insofar as there is any, of the whole enterprise, we are already explicating....

In short, anthropologists do not merely note down facts of what they observe; rather, they construct accounts of their experience of other people's experience. And these accounts

are, thus, fictions; fictions, in the sense that they are "something made," "something fashioned"—the original meaning of *fictio*—not that they are false, unfactual, or merely "as if" thought experiments.

If, finally, anthropological research is interpretive rather than observational, can anthropology be considered a science? Geertz argues that it can, but that the role of theory in interpretive science differs from its role in the natural sciences. First, cultural theory must "stay rather closer to the ground than tends to be the case in sciences more able to give themselves over to imaginative abstraction." This is because the general concepts of cultural theory take us into the world of the people we study—"so that we can, in some extended sense of the term, converse with them"—rather than away from it—by subsuming the aspects of that world (the "data" that it offers us) under laws or generalizations. Second, cultural theory is not predictive: "conceptualization is directed toward the task of generating interpretations of matters already in hand, not toward projecting outcomes...or deducing future states...." However, this does not mean that theory and interpretation are unchallengeable: "the theoretical framework in terms of which...an interpretation is made must be capable of continuing to yield defensible interpretations as new social phenomena swim into view." In the end, Geertz tells us, "cultural analysis is intrinsically incomplete." We can refine our understanding of culture and cultures, substituting what seem to be better interpretations for those that have become unsatisfactory, but we will never exhaust our material.

—Richard Handler

GELL-MANN, Murray. American physicist. Born in New York City, 15 September 1929. Studied at Yale University, New Haven, Connecticut, B.S. 1948; Massachusetts Institute of Technology, Cambridge, Ph.D. 1951. Married J. Margaret Dow in 1955; 2 children. Member, Institute for Advanced Study, Princeton, New Jersey, 1951; Instructor, 1952-53, Assistant Professor, 1953-54, and Associate Professor, 1954-55, University of Chicago; Associate Professor of Theoretical Physics, 1955-56, and since 1956 Professor and later Robert A. Millikan Professor of Physics, California Institute of Technology, Pasadena. Visiting Professor, Collège de France and University of Paris, 1959-60. Member, President's Science Advisory Committee, 1969-72. Regent, Smithsonian Institution, Washington, D.C., since 1974. Recipient: Dannie Heineman Prize, American Physical Society, 1959; E.O. Lawrence Memorial Award, Atomic Energy Commission, 1966; Franklin Medal, 1967; Carty Medal, National Academy of Sciences, 1968; Nobel Prize in Physics, 1969. Fellow, American Physical Society. Member, National Academy of Arts and Sciences; American Academy of Arts and Sciences. Address: Department of Physics, California Institute of Technology, Pasadena, California 91125, U.S.A.

PUBLICATIONS

Physics

Lectures on Weak Interactions of Strongly Interacting Particles. Bombay, Tata Institute of Fundamental Research, 1961.
The Eightfold Way: A Review with a Collection of Reprints, with Yuval Ne'eman.   New York, Benjamin, 1964.

*   *   *

Murray Gell-Mann received the 1969 Nobel Prize in Physics "for his contributions and discoveries concerning the classification of elementary particles and their interactions." His most important work involves the discovery and mathematical description of symmetries which characterize the internal structure of elementary particles. These symmetries allowed known particles to be organized in natural groupings or families, called multiplets, and also led to the prediction of new particles which were subsequently found by experiment. The specific form of the theories also determines the behavior of particles when they interact with each other, for example in high energy particle accelerator experiments or in processes occurring naturally when cosmic rays collide with matter.

Since the 1930's the basic forces of nature have been classified as being of four types: gravitational, electromagnetic, strong (or nuclear), and weak. Each force is distinguished by several properties, including its range, strength (or rate), and the nature of the particles which transmit the force. Some particles, known as leptons (such as the electron and neutrino), have no strong interactions. Baryons and mesons (such as the neutron, proton, pion, and K-meson), which do have strong interactions, have been the focus of much of Gell-Mann's most significant work.

In 1953 he proposed a solution to the puzzling behavior of the recently discovered "strange particles" which were produced copiously in the strong interaction scattering of pions from nucleons but decayed very slowly with times typical of the weak rather than strong interactions. Extending an idea of Pais, Gell-Mann (and independently also Nishijima) proposed that the isotopic-spin classification scheme (which is a generalization of the fact that the neutron and proton are identical as far as the nuclear-strong force is concerned) be extended to the strange particles. The resulting selection rules for the production and decay of these particles can be summarized by introducing a new internal property, "strangeness," which is additively conserved in strong and electromagnetic interactions but not in the weak interactions. Thus, the strange particles can be produced rapidly in pairs (with one particle of positive and one of negative strangeness such that the total strangeness equals zero) by strong interaction processes, but when they decay individually, violating strangeness conservation in the process, it must be due to the much slower weak interaction force. With his theory, Gell-Mann could explain all the existing experimental results on strange particles, and he also predicted the existence of new particles, which were eventually found with the required properties.

In the following years, many new unstable particles were discovered as accelerator scattering experiments were performed with higher energy and greater beam intensity. Something was clearly needed if physicists were to make sense of the growing elementary particle "zoo." In 1961, Gell-Mann (and independently also Ne'eman) proposed a new classification scheme for the baryons and mesons. This theory, which Gell-Mann called the "Eightfold Way" (the name was inspired by the Buddha's Eightfold Path for self-realization), is based on the symmetry which is described mathematically by the continuous Lie group SU (3). (Sophus Lie was a Norwegian mathematician who lived from 1842-1899.) It is a generalization of the group SU(2), which is used to describe isotopic spin and intrinsic spin angular momentum. If SU(3) were an exact underlying symmetry of nature, then multiplets of eight and ten particles all with the same mass and spin (and the space-reflection property of parity) would be observed. Instead, groups of particles with the same intrinsic spin-parity, but somewhat unequal masses, are found experimentally. Thus, physicists call SU(3) a broken, or approximate, symmetry. Gell-Mann described the pattern of symmetry breaking and predicted the existence (and masses) of several new particle states, which were needed to complete multiplets. The 1964 discovery of one of these, the omega-minus, convinced physicists of the basic truth of the SU(3) symmetry scheme.

The Eightfold Way gradually became more established, and in 1964 Gell-Mann (and also Zweig) took another bold step. As the name indicates, the symmetry group SU(3) can be thought of in terms of a basic triplet of objects. Gell-Mann proposed that it would be fruitful to think of all baryons and mesons as being composed of these fundamental entities. He named them "quarks," after a line in James Joyce's, *Finnegan's Wake*: "Three Quarks for Master Mark!" Among the most striking predicted properties of quarks is that they carry an electric charge only one-third or two-thirds as big as that of the charge on the electron or proton. Previously, the negative (positive) charge of the electron (proton) was believed to be the smallest charge which a particle could carry. Although no free quarks have yet been conclusively observed experimentally (and there are theoretical arguments for believing that they will never will, because they are so tightly bound to other quarks), the quark hypothesis has proven to be enormously productive and has been used as the basis for later successful models.

In addition to the work described above, Gell-Mann has made important contributions to quantum field theory, nuclear physics, the development of dispersion theory and the S-matrix theory for the strong interactions, and to the theory of weak interactions. His approach has been flexible and eclectic rather than wedded to a single predetermined point of view. In fact, he has argued that there are seemingly different approaches to relativistic quantum mechanics and the theory of elementary particles which will ultimately turn out to be equivalent.

In a sense, Gell-Mann's discoveries were the next great step after Einstein in the use of invariance and symmetry principles in physics. In developing his special and general theories of relativity, Einstein exploited the invariance of physical laws under physical space-time transformation, while Gell-Mann used continuous symmetry groups to discover the rich internal structure of the elementary particles. The search for underlying symmetries (both exact and broken) has dominated all subsequent theoretical work in elementary particle physics and led to major new advances, including the Weinberg-Salem model of the combined weak-electromagnetic interaction and the recently proposed unified gauge theories for the strong, weak and electromagnetic interactions.

—Harvey Shepard

GELLNER, Ernest (André). British philosopher and social anthropologist. Born in Paris, 9 December 1925. Studied at Balliol College, Oxford, M.A. 1947; University of London, Ph.D. 1961. Served in the Czechoslovak Armoured Brigade, 1944-45. Married Susan Ryan in 1954; 4 children. Assistant, University of Edinburgh, 1947-49. Lecturer, 1949-62, and since 1962 Professor, London School of Economics and Political Science, University of London. Member, Royal Anthropological Institute; Fellow, British Academy. Address: Old Litten Cottage, Froxfield, Hampshire, England.

<small>PUBLICATIONS</small>

Philosophy, Anthropology and Social Theory

Words and Things: A Critical Account of Linguistic Philosophy and a Study in Ideology. London, Gollancz, and Boston, Beacon, 1959; as *Words and Things: Examination of and an Attack on Linguistic Philosophy.* London, Routledge, 1979.
Thought and Change. London, Weidenfeld and Nicolson, and Chicago, University of Chicago Press, 1965.
Saints of the Atlas. London, Weidenfeld and Nicolson, and Chicago, University of Chicago Press, 1969.
Cause and Meaning in the Social Sciences, edited by I.C. Jarvie and Joseph Agassi. London, Routledge, 1973.
Contemporary Thought and Politics, edited by I.C. Jarvie and Joseph Agassi. London, Routledge, 1974.
The Devil in Modern Philosophy, edited by I.C. Jarvie and Joseph Agassi. London, Routledge, 1974 (contains bibliography).
Legitimation of Belief. Cambridge, Cambridge University Press, 1975.
Patrons and Clients. London, Duckworth, 1977.
Spectacles and Predicaments: Essays in Social Theory. Cambridge, Cambridge University Press, 1980.
Muslim Society. Cambridge, Cambridge University Press, 1981.

Other

Editor, with Ghita Ionescu, *Populism: Its National Characteristics.* London, Weidenfeld and Nicolson, and Chicago, University of Chicago Press, 1969.
Editor, with Charles Micaud, *Arabs and Berbers.* London, Duckworth, 1973.

* * *

Ernest Gellner has made significant contributions to the critique of linguistic philosophy, anthropological theory and the sociology of industrial societies. His philosophical anthropology is addressed to the issue of cultural relativism, while his sociological inquiry is focused on the question of legitimacy. In both areas, Gellner's approach involves a rationalist critique of subjectivist relativism in modern thought.

The central themes of Gellner's philosophical critique were first outlined in *Words and Things,* in which he attacked the assumptions of linguistic philosophy characteristic of the Oxford school. In brief, linguistic philosophy has claimed that the meaning of a word is defined by its use in everyday discourse. To discover the meaning of concepts like "justice" or "freedom," we must examine their conversational employment in everyday social contexts. Since meaning varies according to context, meaning is relative. Philosophy can have no critical role, since criticism presupposes that there are standards which are not context-dependent. The task of philosophy is to describe the rules which govern the use of words in their context. In noting the implicit conservatism of this perspective, Gellner has argued that philosophy must evaluate the world as well as describing it, and that philosophy must add to human knowledge as well as preserve it.

Gellner has been equally critical of the philosophical relativism in anthropology which regards any attempt at evaluating beliefs and institutions in other cultures as philosophically suspect and morally inappropriate. For the majority of modern anthropologists, it is not possible to evaluate the beliefs and practices of other cultures by reference to any universal standards of truth or rationality. Such standards do not exist, and furthermore the meaning of, for example, a magical belief in a traditional society can only be understood in terms of assumptions which are indigenous to that culture. Gellner has attacked such "contextual charity" on the grounds that (1) beliefs which are indigenous to social groups may often be confused or contradictory even in terms of indigenous criteria; (2) contextual charity blinds us to the important functions which false beliefs may have in any society; (3) since most human societies are bound to some degree of industrialization and the acceptance of affluence as a value, this fact implies a conscious criticism of poverty which was the general condition of traditional societies; and (4) anthropologists in fact require certain implicit assumptions about valid, general knowledge. For example, anthropologists require some understanding of human reproduction in order to evaluate beliefs about "fictive fatherhood." For Gellner, both anthropology and philosophy have to be evaluative and not just descriptive.

Gellner's other major publications have been concerned with certain paradoxes which are inescapable in modern society. In *Thought and Change* he argued that the legitimacy of modern society depends on its ability to produce affluence and on government by co-nationals. These two conditions can be secured only by industrialisation and nationalism, but these conditions may be incompatible with other forms of progress. Industrialisation often undermines political democracy and individual liberty by requiring some degree of state control and intervention. Similarly cultural nationalism is often destructive of local traditions and minority customs. In *Legitimation of Belief* Gellner was also critically aware of the crisis of knowledge and personal disenchantment which appear to accompany industrialisation. The growth of science has meant that we can longer regard ourselves as the centre of the world or enjoy any stable cognitive certainty. The paradox of science is that, in making the world intelligible, it renders it meaningless. Gellner has rejected most attempts at the "re-endorsement" of thought in evolutionism, relativism and modern critical theory. His own involves a "truncated evolutionism," namely a commitment to the development of an industrial civilization and to rational criticism of modern illusions.

The characteristic feature of Gellner's work is its use of anthropological field-work to criticise the ethnocentrism of philosophy and the use of philosophy to criticise the intellectual limitations of anthropology. In pursuit of both, Gellner has made a major contribution to the sociological analysis of Islam, especially in North Africa. In *Saints of the Atlas* and *Muslim Society* he explored the traditional conflict in Islamic society between sedentarised urban populations and nomadic, tribal society in terms of philosophical and social issues in Ibn Khaldun and David Hume. Gellner's collected essays in *Cause and Meaning in the Social Sciences*, *Contemporary Thought and Politics* and *The Devil in Modern Philosophy* also illustrate his ability to combine diverse philosophical and anthropological interests. The result is that Gellner has emerged as one of the most provocative and influential thinkers in both anthropology and philosophy.

—Bryan S. Turner

GENTILE, Giovanni. Italian philosopher and educational reformer. Born in Castelvetrano, Sicily, 30 May 1875. Studied at the University of Pisa, Ph.D. 1897. Taught at secondary schools in Campobasso, 1898-1901, and Naples, 1901-03; Lecturer, University of Naples, 1903-07; Professor of the History of Philosophy, University of Palermo, 1907-14; Professor of Philosophy, University of Pisa, 1914-17; Professor of the History of Philosophy, University of Rome, 1917-44; also, Director, Scuola Normale Superiore, Pisa, 1936-43. With Benedetto Croce founded the review *La Critica* in 1903; founded the *Giornale Critico della Filosofia Italiana* in 1920. Senator after 1922; Minister of Public Instruction under Mussolini, 1922-24; President of the National Fascist Institute of Culture after 1925. Directing Editor, *Enciclopedia Italiana*, 1925-37; director of the *Collezione Scolastica di Testi Filosofici*, the *Collana di Studi Filosofici*, and other series published by Le Monnier and Laterza. Corresponding Member, Accademia dei Lincei. Member, Italian Academy (President, 1943-44). *Died* (assassinated by Italian communist partisans in Florence) *15 April 1944.*

PUBLICATIONS

Collections

Opere complete. Florence, Sansoni, 55 vols., 1947-

Philosophy, Education and Italian Culture

Rosmini e Gioberti. Pisa, Nistri, 1898.
La filosofia di Marx: Studi critici. Pisa, Spoerri, 1899.
L'insegnamento del filosofia nei Licei: Saggio pedagogico. Palermo, Sandron, 1900.
Polemica hegeliana. Naples, Pierro, 1902.
Dal Genovesi al Galluppi: Ricerche storiche. Naples, Edizione della "Critica," 1903; enlarged edition as *Storia della filosofia italiana dal Genovesi al Galluppi,* Milan, Treves, 2 vols., 1930.
La rinascita dell'idealismo. Naples, n.p., 1903.
Studi sullo stoicismo romano del primo secolo d. Cristo. Trani, Vecchi, 1904.
La filosofia. Milan, Vallardi, 1904-15.
Il figlio di G.B. Vico. Naples, Pierro, 1905.
Le varie redazioni del "De sensu rerum" di Tommaso Campanella. Naples, Giannini, 1906.
Giordano Bruno nella storia della cultura. Palermo, Sandron, 1907.
Per la scuola primaria di Stato. Palermo, Sandron, 1907.
Scuola e filosofia: Concetti fondamentali e saggi di pedagogie sulla scuola media. Palermo, Sandron, 1908.
Il modernismo e i rapporti tra religione e filosofia: Saggi. Bari, Laterza, 1909.
Bernardino Telesio. Bari, Laterza, 1911.
La riforma della dialettica hegeliana. Messina, Principato, 1913.
I problemi della scolastica e il pensiero italiano. Bari, Laterza, 1913.
Sommario di pedagogie come scienza filosofica. Bari, Laterza, 2 vols., 1913, 1914.
La filosofia della guerra. Palermo, n.p., 1914.
Studi vichiani. Messina, Principato, 1915.
L'esperienza pura e la realtà storica. Florence, La Voce, 1915.
Teoria generale dello spirito come atto puro. Pisa, Mariotti, 1916; as *The Theory of Mind as Pure Act,* London, Macmillan, 1922.
Sistema di logica come teoria del conoscere. Pisa, Spoerri, 1917.
Le origini della filosofia contemporanea in Italia. Messina, Principato, 3 vols., 1917-23.
Il carattere storico della filosofia italiana. Bari, Laterza, 1918.
Il tramonto della cultura siciliana. Bologna, Zanichelli, 1919.
Guerra e fede: Frammenti politici. Naples, Ricciardi, 1919.
Il problema scolastico del dopoguerra. Naples, Ricciardi, 1919.
Mazzini. Caserta, Marino, 1919.
Discorsi di religione. Florence, Vallecchi, 1920.
La riforma dell'educazione. Bari, Laterza, 1920; as *The Reform of Education,* New York, Harcourt Brace, 1922; London, Benn, 1923.
Giordano Bruno e il pensiero del Rinascimento. Florence, Vallecchi, 1920.
Dopo la vittoria: Nuovi frammenti politici. Rome, La Voce, 1920.
Frammenti di estetica e letteratura. Lanciano, Carabba, 1921.
Educazione e scuola laica. Florence, Vallecchi, 1921.
Saggi critici: Serie prima. Naples, Ricciardi, 1921.
Il concetto moderno della scienza e il problema universitario. Rome, Libreria di Cultura, 1921.
Gino Capponi e la cultura toscana nel secolo decimonono. Florence, Vallecchi, 1922.
Studi sul Rinascimento. Florence, Vallecchi, 1923.
Albori della nuova Italia: Varietà e documenti. Lanciano, Carabba, 2 vols., 1923.

I profeti del Risorgimento.   Florence, Vallecchi, 1923.
Dante e Manzoni, con un saggio su arte e religione.   Florence, Vallecchi, 1923.
Preliminari allo studio del fanciullo.   Rome, De Alberti, 1924.
Bertrando Spaventa.   Florence, Vallecchi, 1924.
Il fascismo al governo della scuola.   Palermo, Sandron, 1924.
La riforma della scuola.   Bari, Laterza, 1924.
Il fascismo e la Sicilia.   Rome, De Alberti, 1924.
Vincenzo Cuoco.   Rome, De Alberti, 1924.
La nuova scuola media.   Florence, Vallecchi, 1925.
Che cosa e il fascismo: Discorsi e polemiche.   Florence, Vallecchi, 1925.
Frammenti di storia della filosofia.   Lanciano, Carabba, 1926.
L'eredità di Vittorio Alfieri.   Venice, La Nuova Italia, 1926.
Saggi critici: Serie seconda.   Florence, Vallecchi, 1927.
Vincenzo Cuoco: Studi e appunti.   Venice, La Nuova Italia, 1927.
Manzoni e Leopardi: Saggi critici.   Milan, Treves, 1928.
Il pensiero italiano del secolo XIX.   Milan, Treves, 1928.
Fascismo e cultura.   Milan, Treves, 1928.
Origini e dottrina del fascismo.   Rome, Libreria del Littorio, 1929.
La filosofia dell'arte.   Milan, Treves, 1931; as *The Philosophy of Art*, Ithaca, New York, Cornell University Press, 1972.
Introduzione alla filosofia.   Milan, Treves, 1933.
La profezia di Dante.   Rome, Casa Editrice Novissima, 1933.
Memorie italiane e problemi della filosofia e della vita.   Florence, Sansoni, 1936.
La tradizione italiana.   Florence, Sansoni, 1936.
Giambattista Vico.   Florence, Sansoni, 1936.
Dottrina politica del fascismo.   Padua, Cedam, 1937.
Poesia e filosofia di G. Leopardi.   Florence, Sansoni, 1939.
Giuseppe Pitrè (1841-1916).   Florence, Sansoni, 1940.
Il pensiero di Leopardi.   Florence, Sansoni, 1941.
La filosofia italiana contemporanea: Due scritti.   Florence, Sansoni, 1941.
Vittorio Alfieri uomo.   Asti, Casa d'Alfieri, 1942.
La mia religione.   Florence, Sansoni, 1943.
Genesi e struttura della società: Saggio di filosofia pratica.   Florence, Sansoni, 1946; as *Genesis and Structure of Society*, Urbana, University of Illinois Press, 1960 (contains a bibliography).
Storia della filosofia.   Florence, Sansoni, 1964.

Other

Epistolario.   Florence, Sansoni, 1969-.

For a complete list of works translated and edited by and series directed by Gentile, see the bibliography listed below.

*

Bibliography: *Bibliografia degli Scritti di Giovanni Gentile* by Vito A. Bellezza, Florence, Sansoni, 1950.

Critical Studies: *The Idealism of Giovanni Gentile* by Roger W. Holmes, New York, Macmillan, 1937; *The Philosophy of Giovanni Gentile* by P. Romanell, New York, S.F. Vanni, 1938; *The Social Philosophy of Giovanni Gentile* by H.S. Harris, Urbana, University of Illinois Press, 1960; *Gentile on the Existence of God* by William Smith, Louvain, Nauwelaerts, 1970.

*   *   *

Giovanni Gentile shared with Benedetto Croce the leadership of the great resurgence of Hegelian idealism that dominated Italian intellectual life in the first half of the 20th century. He was also a prominent political figure in the period of the Fascist regime in Italy (1922-43); the main architect of a major reform in the Italian school system (the "Riforma Gentile", 1922-4); and the general editor of the *Italian Encyclopedia*.

His "actual idealism" (founded on a "reform of the Hegelian dialectic") took shape in a series of essays written between 1908 and 1912; and it was first fully expounded in his *Summary of Educational Theory as Philosophic Science*. His first systematic theoretical statement of his views (*General Theory of the Spirit as Pure Act*) was soon translated into English (1922); but the most fruitful approach to his thought is through its educational application (see especially *The Reform of Education*). This is because, being the most extreme form of subjective idealism yet produced, it is only properly intelligible as a theory of moral responsibility.

This "reform of the Hegelian dialectic"—which Gentile replaced by what he called "the method of absolute immanence"—makes it possible to identify the "finite spirit" of the individual thinking consciousness (*pensiero pensante*) with the "absolute spirit" of Hegel's ultimate triad of the philosophical Idea: art, religion, and philosophy. Thus the "act of thinking" upon which all subjective consciousness depends becomes the "pure act" by which the whole world of ordinary reality is created. Gentile did not, of course, deny that for ordinary finite consciousness the world is *already there*, or that it goes its own way regardless of what an individual may think about it. But he insisted that in *this* aspect—as nature theoretically or convention practically—the world is only the necessary but abstract *content* (*pensiero pensato*) of the *act* of thinking. His theory focusses upon the problem of *self-constitution* that any *free* self must face in striving to interpret the world in order to act both intelligently and autonomously.

The problem of "self-construction" imposed itself upon Gentile as the truly focal problem of philosophy, because he was fervently committed (in opposition to Croce) to the view that there must be no fundamental division or separation between theory and practice. One might also put this the other way around, but the errors of Gentile's social philosophy are more easily comprehended if we see "self-constitution" thus as a *duty*. For in this perspective we can see how the problem of the nascent self in relating to others becomes the problem of the internalization of *authority*. Absolute insistence on the unity of theory and practice leads to the conclusion that any form of authoritative action or influence that is effective (recognized and accepted) is thereby validated. This essentially *backward* interpretation of his theory made it possible for Gentile to support the institution of open dictatorship by the Fascist party in 1925. The immediate result of this decision was that 30 years of collaborative and productive dispute with Croce gave way to 20 years of hostile and fruitless polemic. In the end his quixotic persistence in loyalty to the ideal, which he believed Mussolini personified, brought Gentile to his death at the hands of Communist partisans, because he publicly supported the puppet Republic of Salò.

This authoritarian tendency in Gentile's work sprang from his *religious* concern—religion being for him, the awareness of an absolute *authority*. The real primacy of freedom and spontaneity in his theory is fully evident in his *Philosophy of Art*. But it was only in his last work, *Genesis and Structure of Society*, that Gentile finally discovered in the internally social character of the Hegelian theory of "Spirit" a way of overcoming the opposition between freedom and authority that is valid for every one, not just for the philosophically educated elite. Many of the ambiguities of his earlier books are repeated here, but the conception of the act of thinking as a collaborative *dialogue* makes it possible to resolve them. Thus Gentile's idealism emerges here, at last, in its properly moral form.

Gentile's influence among Italian thinkers during his own lifetime was enormous. Among English intellectuals between the two world wars he had a small but still quite noteworthy following, headed by J.A. Smith at Oxford. But the most important English thinker to be seriously influenced by him was R.G. Collingwood, who chose partly on political grounds, to conceal—

and even to deny—the existence of any affiliation between them.

—H.S. Harris

GERNET, Louis. French sociologist. Born in 1882. Studied at the Ecole Normale, Paris, agrégation de grammaire, 1907. Engaged in research at the Foundation Thiers, 1907-19; taught at La Flèche, near Tours, 1911-17; Professor, University of Algiers, 1917-47; Professor of Sociology, Ecole Pratique des Hautes Etudes, Paris, 1948-62. Associated with Durkheim school of sociology. Contributor, *Notes critiques*, 1903-05; contributor, 1906-c. 1920, and General Secretary and Chief Editor, 1948-62, *Année Sociologique. Died* (in Paris) *in 1962.*

PUBLICATIONS

Sociology

"L'Approvisionnement d'Athènes en blé au Ve et au IVe siècle," in *Mélanges d'histoire ancien.* Paris, Alcan, 1909; published separately, New York, Arno Press, 1979.
Recherches sur le développement de la pensée juridique et morale en Grèce. Paris, Leroux, 1917.
Le Génie grec dans la religion, with André Boulanger. Paris, Renaissance du livre, 1932.
Sur les actions commerciales en droit athénien. Paris, Leroux, 1938.
Droit et société dans la Grèce ancienne. Paris, Recueil Sirey, 1955.
Anthropologie de la Grèce antique. Paris, Maspero, 1968.

Other

Editor and Translator, *Demosthenes: Plaidoyers civils.* Paris, Société d'édition "Les Belles lettres," 1954-57.
Editor and Translator, with Marcel Bizos, *Lysias: Orationes.* Paris, Société d'édition "Les Belles lettres," 1961.
Editor and Translator, with Marcel Bizos, *Lysias: Discours.* Paris, Société d'édition "Les Belles lettres," 2 vols., 1962-64.
Editor and Translator, *Discours,* by Antiphon (orator). Paris, Société d'édition "Les Belles lettres," 1965.

*

Critical Studies: *Hommage à Louis Gernet,* Paris, Presses Universitaires de France, 1966; "The Work of Louis Gernet" by S.C. Humphreys, in *History and Theory* (Middletown, Connecticut), vol. 10, 1971.

*   *   *

Louis Gernet is a link between the Année Sociologique school around Emile Durkheim and the Paris School of Greek studies around J-P. Vernant. He was educated in Paris as a younger contemporary and colleague of Durkheim's successor Marcel Mauss and in his old age was Vernant's most important teacher. But his work is not reducible to the history of intellectual schools; if it has a slightly hermetic quality, that is perhaps because Gernet spent half his adult life in North Africa, personally and intellectually somewhat isolated.

Gernet produced no big book; his publications were essays, suggestive and mostly quite brief, overlapping in topic and theme; much of his work was literally footnotes, in his editions of the Greek texts of Athenian law-court speeches. He nowhere gives an extensive statement of his intellectual method; it must be deduced from his practice. He wrote mostly about archaic and classical Greece, and about patterns of social action; characteristically, he is concerned with concrete institutions, with stateable rules and legal forms—and at the same time with the meaning of these forms for the actors who used them, with the collective aspirations and life-orientations they embody. Very often he has recourse to mythology, which for him states schematically and paradigmatically concepts and values held by the society at large. In all this he is much like Durkheim; many of the particular themes of his work, also, reflect the concerns of the Année Sociologique school. He is interested in initiations, in gift-exchange, in the social functions of the sacred, and in collective definitions of legitimacy, especially in relation to authority and property. Gernet approaches all these themes, however, as an historian and a Hellenist; he does not attempt general social theory, but rather lets his theoretical interests guide him toward the discernment of underlying patterns in the life of a particular society.

Gernet is interested in early Greece as one of the several historical moments in which the West became western; the rise of the city-state is for him a kind of first modernization, in terms of which we can better understand certain things about ourselves. Our own society, relative to others, is intellectually de-mythologized, socially rationalized, and economically monetized; none of these things happened accidentally or instantaneously, and all of them began in early Greece. Gernet asks always: how did this happen? and also: what were things like before? He is most concerned, not with some more-or-less hypothetical "primitive" condition, but with the transitional phase from which modern forms emerge. He has a special eye for the magical origins of rational behavior; he shows us, for instance, that science originated in archaic philosophy, which while secular remained inspired knowledge, revealed only to the initiate. Similarly rational law originated in rites and ordeals, and money originated in the pre-rational exchange of gifts and prizes.

For Gernet social development and intellectual change do not happen of themselves, but as aspects of a struggle for power wherein specific groups seek to establish their claims to moral authority and material advantages. Greek legality, for instance, does not reflect a concern for the natural rights of mankind in general; it was rather the mode whereby those adult free males who defined themselves as citizens asserted their control of the state and their superior position in society. We can thus understand how the rise of legality entailed the supression of women and of those within the society now legally defined as slaves or strangers. In all this Gernet is a materialist; he asks always the hardnose question: *cui bono?* People in all periods pursue their interests; at the same time Gernet sees that interests are not fixed: he is not one of those who presume that the driving force of history is competition for scarce resources defined as valuable by some unchanging standard of natural utility. Rather, for him, interests are historically conditioned by culturally variable aspirations, by values which themselves are proper only to particular periods and places. For him, as for Max Weber, the social action of others can be understood by us only to the degree that we are able imaginatively to stand with the actor, to grasp the standards and aspirations of that time and place.

Therefore, for Gernet, as for Weber, the inner meaning of history is in a sense religious, in that action in history is shaped by a continually transformed collective understanding of the higher and better, of the standard against which mankind should properly measure itself. His own formulation of this question is characteristically Greek: "What is of particular interest in an anthropological study is the question of the barrier between human and divine reality: what separated the human from the divine, and, conversely, what brings them together?"

—James Redfield

GESELL, Arnold (Lucius). American child psychologist. Born in Alma, Wisconsin, 21 June 1880. Studied at the University of Wisconsin, Madison, Ph.B. 1903; Clark University, Worcester, Massachusetts, Ph.D. 1906; Yale University, New Haven, Connecticut, M.D. 1915. Married Beatrice Chandler in 1909; 2 children. Teacher, Department of Psychology, Los Angeles Normal School, 1908-10; Founder-Director, Clinic of Child Development, 1911-1948, Assistant Professor of Education, 1911-15, Professor of Child Hygiene, 1915-48, Research Associate, Child Vision Research, 1948-50, Research Consultant, Gesell Institute of Child Development, 1950-58, and after 1950. Lecturer, School of Social Research—all Yale University. School Psychologist, Connecticut State Board of Education, 1915-19; Attending Pediatrician, New Haven Hospital, 1928-48. Member, National Research Council, 1937-40; President, American Academy for Cerebral Palsy, 1952-53. Honorary doctorate: Clark University, 1930; University of Wisconsin, 1953. Fellow, American Academy of Arts and Sciences. *Died 29 May 1961.*

PUBLICATIONS

Child Psychology

What Can the Teacher Do for the Deficient Child? A Manual for Teachers in Rural and Graded Schools. Hartford, Connecticut, State Board of Education, 1918.

The Normal Child and Primary Education, with Beatrice Chandler Gesell. Boston, Ginn, 1921.

Exceptional Children and Public School Policy. New Haven, Connecticut, Yale University Press, 1921.

The Kindergarten and Health, with Julia Wade Abbott. Washington, D.C., Government Printing Office, 1923.

The Pre-School Child from the Point of View of Public Hygiene. Boston, Houghton Mifflin, 1923.

The Mental Growth of the Pre-School Child: A Psychological Outline of Normal Development from Birth to the Sixth Year, Including a System of Diagnosis. New York, Macmillan, 1925.

Social Aspects of Mental Hygiene, with others. New Haven, Connecticut, Yale University Press, 1925.

The Influence of Puberty Praecox upon Mental Growth. Worcester, Massachusetts, Clark University Press, 1926.

Psychological Guidance in Child-Adoption. Washington, D.C., Government Printing Office, 1926.

Infancy and Human Growth. New York, Macmillan, 1928.

Learning and Growth in Identical Infant Twins, with Helen Thompson. Worcester, Massachusetts, Clark University Press, 1921.

The Guidance of Mental Growth in Infant and Child. New York, Macmillan, 1930.

The Growth of the Infant Mind (lecture). Chicago, University of Chicago Press, 1931.

An Atlas of Infant Behavior: A Systematic Delineation of the Forms and Early Growth of Human Behavior Patterns. London, Oxford University Press, 1934; New Haven, Connecticut, Yale University Press, 1936.

Feeding Behavior of Infants: A Pediatric Approach to the Mental Hygiene of Early Life, with Frances Ilg. Philadelphia, Lippincott, 1937.

The Psychology of Early Growth, Including Norms of Infant Behavior and a Method of Genetic Analysis, with others. New York, Macmillan, 1938.

The Retarded Child: How to Help Him. Bloomington, Illinois, Public School Publishing Company, 1938.

Biographies of Child Development: The Mental Growth Careers of Eighty-four Infants and Children. New York and London, Hoeber, 1939.

The First Five Years of Life: A Guide to the Study of the Pre-School Child. New York, Harper, 1940.

Twins T and C from Infancy to Adolescence. Provincetown, Massachusetts, Journal Press, 1941.

Wolf Child and Human Child: The Life History of Kamala, the Wolf Girl, Based on the Diary Account of a Child Who was Raised by a Wolf and Who then Lived for Nine Years in the Orphanage of Mindapore, in the Province of Bengal, India. New York, Harper, 1941.

Developmental Diagnosis: Normal and Abnormal Child Development, Clinical Methods and Practical Applications, with Catherine S. Amatruda. New York and London, Hoeber, 1941.

Infant and Child in the Culture of Today: The Guidance of Development in Home and Nursery School. New York, Harper, 1943; London, Hamish Hamilton, 1945.

The Embryology of Behavior: The Beginnings of the Human Mind, with Catherine S. Amatruda. New York, Harper, 1945.

How a Baby Grows: A Story in Pictures. New York, Harper, 1945.

The Child from Five to Ten, with others. New York, Harper, 1946.

Studies in Child Development. New York, Harper, 1948.

Child Development: An Introduction to the Study of Human Growth, with others. New York, Harper, 2 vols., 1949.

Vision: Its Development in Infant and Child, with others. New York and London, Hoeber, 1949.

Infant Development: The Embryology of Early Human Behavior. New York, Harper, 1952.

Youth: The Years from Ten to Sixteen, with others. New York, Harper, and London, Hamish Hamilton, 1956.

Infant Behavior: Its Genesis and Growth, with others. New York, McGraw Hill, 1959.

Other

"Autobiography," in *A History of Psychology in Autobiography, Volume 4.* Worcester, Massachusetts, Clark University Press, 1952.

*

Critical Study: "Arnold Lucius Gesell" by Walter Richard Miles, in *National Academy of Sciences: Biographical Memoirs, Volume XXXVIII,* New York, National Academy of Sciences, 1964.

*   *   *

Although the scientific study of child growth and development in North America dates from the conferences sponsored by the Laura Spelman Rockefeller Memorial Fund in the 1920's, there were notable pioneers in the preceding two decades. G.S. Hall is usually recognized as the founder of child study, and his student Arnold Gesell must be acknowledged as one of the first to establish a center for the study of infants and children prior to the impetus of the Rockefeller grants.

His early intellectual interests and professional experiences (including public school and normal college teaching and social welfare activities) foreshadowed the applied science he later embodied in his career. He was early convinced that a thoroughgoing study of the developmental stages of childhood must be undergirded by an understanding of the physical and physiological bases of life and growth. Accordingly, when he was called to Yale University as Assistant Professor of Education in 1911 he began medical studies in the Yale School of Medicine.

By 1920 he was engrossed in comparative studies of behavioral development in young normal children, conducted in the psychoclinic he established at Yale in 1911, the precursor of the famed Yale Clinic of Child Development. His interest in the origins of behavior led him to the study of infants in particular. Lecture-demonstrations in the clinical amphitheater using pairs of normal infants, disparate in age, seated on their mother's laps and addressing a variety of small objects placed before them, was the precursor to filming these behaviors, begun in 1924. The publication in 1925 of *Mental Growth of the Preschool Child* established Gesell as a notable contributor to the nascent field of child development.

A Rockefeller grant at this time enabled Gesell to design his photographic dome, a one-way observation device permitting cinematography from various angles while preserving a modicum of normalcy for the infant subject and his mother. From this device came miles of film recording infant behavior in the circumstances of feeding, bathing, dressing and social play. His research program by this time had also developed the co-twin control method, whereby one member of an identical twin pair was given special training while the other member remained under conditions of typical care, as a "control," to estimate the immediate and long-term advantage of special tuition. The studies were limited to relatively short periods of training and fairly simple skills and not surprisingly gave no permanent advantage to the trained twin. These findings strengthened Gesell's growing conviction that "cultural factors inflect but they do not generate the basic progressions and ontogenetic patterning of behavior."

The Yale Clinic of Child Development was by 1930 housed in new and enlarged quarters and was serving some 50 social agencies. Gesell considered that the concept of development was extremely useful in studying normal individual differences and applying the insights of maldevelopment. The 1930's saw Gesell continuing the publication of profusely illustrated works on the development of motor, adaptive, language, and personal-social patterns through 34 progressive age levels to 11 years.

Gesell's later work embraced major studies of vision and visual perceptual skills, feeding behavior of infants, "rooming-in" and "self-regulation" in newborn and infant care, and fetal behavior studies. Physical proximity to the Yale Medical School and the establishment in the medical school of a Department of Child Development under Gesell's guidance led to an increasing emphasis on the pediatric and child guidance aspects of his program.

Gesell's basic method was observation in laboratory settings contrived as naturalistically as possible, description and comparison of behaviors, with the induction of principles. His concept of development was founded upon concepts derived from experimental embryology. He characterized the infant as "a growing action system," mind as well as body having morphology which changes according to definite principles. He identified five major behavioral principles expressed in an organismic, phenomenological language, which incorporate intrinsic growth tendencies oscillating between polarities and along gradients to produce cyclical developmental "spirals". Gesell interpreted these principles as guaranteeing that the development of behavior follows species-specific patterns, yet assuring also that each individual assumes a unique expression of these patterns. He concluded that individuality as well as similarity of growth patterns has a constitutional base. Although he conducted many finely graded analyses of the development of particular reflexes (e.g., the tonic neck reflex) and intentional movements (e.g., grasping)—based on frame-by-frame study of his cinematographic records—he emphasized their ubiquitous organization and integration into complex patterns.

This strong affirmation of constitutional base for all behavior led behavioristic contemporaries to reject Gesell's notions of development as expressing a "simple unfolding" of predetermined patterns. It is true that Gesell stressed the stabilities and continuities in development rather than focusing on instability and discontinuity. Yet he anticipated Jean Piaget's more explicit emphasis on the joint and reciprocal action of both intrinsic and extrinsic factors in modulating development, and he emphasized repeatedly that the individual can adapt "prodigiously".

As an outgrowth of his interest in the development of the embryo and of his studies of self-regulation in the vital cycles of infancy, he came to stress the "hidden developmental reserves" which he affirmed to be present in some measure in defective as well as all normal individuals. Though difficult to estimate, these reserves, he believed, serve to counter to some extent the effects of stress and adversity.

Such a stress on individuality and autonomy had a marked effect on a generation of pediatricians. Gesell advanced substantially the concern of that profession with the maintenance of health and the supervision of development as contrasted with merely treating illness. "The protection of mental health, beginning with infancy," he said, "should be based primarily on a science of normal human growth and only secondarily on psychopathology"; this science he expected to be a "clinical science of child development."

However, as the interdisciplinary field of child development came to be dominated by an academic psychology which more and more embraced rigorous experimental methods and concepts of behavior change through conditioning and reinforcement, Gesell's clinical method and his thinking came to be neglected. Nor did his use of the term "mind" as virtually synonymous with "behavior" and a certain Olympian attitude toward the work of others endear him to psychologists. Yet his profusely illustrated and engagingly written books on the "ages and stages" of childhood and early adolescence markedly influenced parents and those engaged professionally in child care and the nursery school movement through the second quarter of the century. Although he deplored the public's tendency to interpret his descriptions of age characteristics as stereotypes, his writing style and positive affirmations undoubtedly encouraged such oversimplification. But to researchers who are influenced by physical growth concepts, or are biologically oriented, and to many practical workers with children, his descriptive principles still have appeal.

—Dale B. Harris

GIBSON, James J(erome).   American psychologist.   Born in McConnelsville, Ohio, 27 January 1904. Studied at Princeton University, New Jersey, B.S. 1925, M.A. 1926, Ph.D. 1928. Served in the United States Army Air Force, 1942-46 (Director, Research Unit, Army Air Force Aviation Psychology Program): from Captain to Lieutenant-Colonel. Married Elanor Grier Jack in 1932; 2 children. Instructor to Associate Professor, Smith College, Northampton, Massachusetts, 1928-49; Professor of Psychology, Cornell University, Ithaca, New York, 1949-72 (Chairman of the Department, 1961-64). Research Associate, Yale University, New Haven, Connecticut, 1935-36; Visiting Professor, University of California, Berkeley, 1954-55; Senior Fulbright Research Scholar, Oxford University, 1955-56; Member, Institute for Advanced Study, Princeton, New Jersey, 1958-59; Fellow, Center for Advanced Study in the Behavioral Sciences, Stanford, California, 1963-64; Visiting Professor, Massachusetts Institute of Technology, Cambridge, 1973, and University of California at Davis, 1978; Visiting Scientist, Salk Institute, La Jolla, California, 1979. President, Eastern Psychological Association, 1959-60. Recipient: Howard Crosby Warren Medal, 1952; Distinguished Science Contribution Award, American Psychological Association, 1961; National Institute of Health Career Development Award, 1964, 1972. Honorary doctorate: University of Edinburgh, 1973; Uppsala University, 1976. Fellow, American Psychological Association. Member, National Academy of Sciences, and American Academy of Arts and Sciences. *Died 11 December 1979.*

PUBLICATIONS

Psychology

The Perception of the Visual World.   Boston, Houghton Mifflin, 1950.

The Senses Considered as Perceptual Systems.   Boston, Houghton Mifflin, 1966; London, Allen and Unwin, 1968.
The Ecological Approach to Visual Perception.   Boston, Houghton Mifflin, 1979.
Reasons for Realism: Selected Essays of James J. Gibson, edited by Edward Reed and Rebecca Jones.   Hillsdale, New Jersey, Lawrence Erlbaum Associates, 1982.

Other

Editor, *Studies in Psychology from Smith College.*   Princeton, New Jersey, Psychological Review Company, 1935.
Editor, *Motion Picture Testing and Research.*   Washington, D.C., Government Printing Office, 1947.

*

Critical Studies: *Perception: Essays in Honor of James J. Gibson,* Ithaca, New York, Cornell University Press, 1974.

*   *   *

James J. Gibson was an experimental psychologist whose theory of perception led him to a radical epistemology. His assertion that perception is "direct," requiring no processing of sensory fragments and no inferential steps, presents a serious challenge to prevailing views in cognitive science and philosophy.

Unlike other theorists, Gibson did not begin his analysis of vision with the image on the retina of the eye. His starting point was the structured "optic array" that is formed by the reflection of light from the surfaces of objects and from the ground. The optic array exists independently of any observer, and its structure accurately specifies the layout and properties of the surfaces themselves. The visual systems of men and animals have evolved to pick up that structure, especially during movement: it is not accessible from any one point of observation or at any one instant. When observers are permitted to explore their environment in a natural way, they perceive it without error. The illusions that play such a prominent part in most theories of perception appear only in artificial laboratory displays or under reduced viewing conditions. Gibson insisted that the study of perception must be conducted with these ecological considerations in mind. Traditional forms of research are often misleading: to present immobilized observers with simple line drawings or flashes of light is to eliminate much of the information on which vision normally depends.

It was not until 1961 that Gibson coined the term "ecological optics" for the study of the aspects of optical structure that are significant for behaving organisms. He had already been engaged in that study for a number of years, and had made a series of fundamental contributions to it. His research demonstrated the functional importance of (1) optical microstructure, and especially of texture gradients; (2) the occlusions and disocclusions of surfaces and textures that appear when objects move relative to one another; (3) the optical flows and transformations produced by movements of the observer; and (4) the invariant optical structures that remain unchanged during those transformations. Gibson's first analysis of these forms of information, based primarily on his experience in the U.S. Air Force during the Second World War, appeared in his book *The Perception of the Visual World.* He deliberately chose the term "visual world" to contrast with the "visual field" emphasized by other perception psychologists and by philosophers. In his view, the transient, shifting, illusion-packed "field" of visual sensations is simply irrelevant to perception. We may occasionally attend to it, as we may notice an after-image or a toothache, but normal perceiving depends on the pickup of higher-order invariants that specify the world around us much more directly and consistently.

The systematic implications of these ideas were spelled out in Gibson's later book, *The Senses Considered as Perceptual Systems,* in which he applied them to every sense modality and every

form of perceiving. He presented a more detailed analysis of vision later in *The Ecological Approach to Visual Perception;* the philosophical implications of his ideas are stressed in a posthumous collection of essays called *Reasons for Realism.* In Gibson's view, perception does not depend on the processing of sensations as supplemented by memory but on the direct pickup of invariants and transformations. The available information usually specifies not only the physical layout of the environment but also the possibilities for action that it affords. Gibson defined "affordances" as properties of things taken with reference to the actions of particular organisms: for people, floors afford walking and small objects afford grasping. Affordances need not be inferred; like other objective aspects of the environment, they can be directly seen. Because the environment and the information in the light are indefinitely rich in structure, no one can see everything there is to see. Experience enables people to perceive more and more adequately, in more sophisticated and economical ways. Such learning reflects the increasingly fine tuning of the perceptual systems to objectively available information.

Gibson's hypothesis that perception is based on information structures rather than on transient inputs led him to some surprising conclusions. *Visual proprioception:* people can directly see their own movements in the environment and their own path of locomotion, because these are specified "in the light." Experimental studies have confirmed this hypothesis, demonstrating the importance of visual proprioception in the control of coordinated movement. *Pictorial perception:* Gibson had his own definition of a picture, as a surface treated to present some of the optical information that would also be yielded by a particular layout of objects. Because optical information can be abstract, pictures need not simply copy the objects they represent. Thus while Gibson firmly rejected the suggestion that pictures are based on an arbitrary "code" or "language," his theory can provide a sensible interpretation of caricature and other forms of selective or abstract depiction. *Amodal invariants:* perhaps the most remarkable consequence of these assumptions is that perception can be entirely independent of sensory quality. It is based on information structures that may be equally available to several perceptual systems. How a thing looks, how it sounds, and how it feels can all have something in common; the same structure can reappear in every case. Shape, rigidity of substance, texture of surface, and pattern of movement are among the objective characteristics of objects that may be specified through more than one modality. Recent studies of very young infants confirm the existence of this form of perception, supporting Gibson's interpretation of perceiving as based on abstract, amodal invariants. He insisted that those invariants make it possible to acquire perceptual knowledge directly, effectively, and without illusion.

—Ulric Neisser

GILSON, Étienne (Henri).   French philosopher and theologian.   Born in Paris, 13 June 1884. Educated at the Petit Seminaire de Notre-Dame-des-Champs and the Sorbonne, Paris, 1895-1906, Ph.D. 1913. Served in the French Army during World War I; prisoner of war, 1915-18; awarded Croix de Guerre. Married Caroline Rainaud in 1908; 3 children. Professor, University of Lille, 1913-19, and University of Strasbourg, 1919-21; Professor of the History of Philosophy, Sorbonne, 1921-32; Professor of the History of Medieval Philosophy, Collège de France, Paris, 1932 until he resigned, 1951; also, Founder and Director of Studies, Pontifical Institute of Medieval Studies, St. Michael's College, University of Toronto, 1928-56. Visiting Professor, 1926-29, and William James Lecturer, 1936, Harvard University, Cambridge, Massachusetts; Clifford Lecturer, University of Aberdeen, 1929-30; Richards Lecturer, University of

Virginia, Charlottesville, 1937; Powell Lecturer, University of Indiana, Bloomington, 1940; Visiting Professor, University of Notre Dame, Indiana, 1950; Mellon Lecturer, National Gallery, Washington, D.C., 1955. President, Scientifique Institut Franco-Canadien, Montreal. Recipient: Christian Culture Medal, Assumption College, Windsor, Ontario, 1949; Serena Medal for Italian Studies, British Academy, 1952; Cardinal Spellman Thomas Aquinas Medal, 1952. Honorary doctorates: universities of Paris; Oxford; Aberdeen; Glasgow; Montreal; Harvard; Columbia, New York; Laval, Quebec; Pennsylvania, Philadelphia; and St. Andrews, Scotland. Grand Officier, Légion d'Honneur; Counseiller de la Republique, 1947-48; Member, Ordre pour le Mérite; Member, Académie Française, 1947. Honorary Member: British Academy; Royal Academy of Denmark; Royal Academy of the Netherlands; Polish Academy; American Academy of Arts and Sciences; Royal Society of Canada; Roman Academy; and Academy of Moral Sciences. *Died 19 September 1978.*

PUBLICATIONS

Philosophy and Theology

Index Scolastico-cartésien. Paris, Alcan, 1912-13.
La Liberté chez Descartes et la théologie. Paris, Alcan, 1913.
Le Thomisme: Introduction au système de saint Thomas d'Aquin. Strasbourg, Vix, 1919; as *The Philosophy of Saint Thomas Aquinas,* Cambridge, Heffer, 1924; as *The Christian Philosophy of Saint Thomas Aquinas,* New York, Random House, 1956.
Études de philosophie médiévale. Strasbourg, Université de Strasbourg, 1921.
La Philosophie au moyen âge. Paris, Payot, 2 vols., 1923.
La Philosophie de saint Bonaventure. Paris, Vrin, 1924; as *The Philosophy of Saint Bonaventure,* London and New York, Sheed and Ward, 1938.
René Descartes: Discours de la méthode: Texte et commentaire. Paris, Vrin, 1925.
Saint Thomas d'Aquin. Paris, Garbalda, 1925; as *Moral Values and the Moral Life: The Ethical Theory of St. Thomas Aquinas,* London, Herder, 1931.
Introduction à l'étude de saint Augustin. Paris, Vrin, 1929; as *The Christian Philosophy of Saint Augustine,* New York, Random House, 1960.
Études sur le rôle de la pensée médiévale dans la formation du système cartésien. Paris, Vrin, 1930.
L'Ésprit de la philosophie médiévale (lectures). Paris, Vrin, 2 vols., 1932; as *The Spirit of Mediaeval Philosophy,* London, Sheed and Ward, and New York, Scribner, 1934.
Les Idées et les lettres. Paris, Vrin, 1932.
Pour un ordre catholique. Paris, Desclée de Brouwer, 1934.
La Théologie mystique de saint Bernard. Paris, Vrin, 1934; as *The Mystic Theology of Saint Bernard,* London and New York, Sheed and Ward, 1940.
Le Réalisme méthodique. Paris, Tequi, 1935.
Christianisme et philosophie. Paris, Vrin, 1936; as *Christianity and Philosophy,* London and New York, Sheed and Ward, 1939.
The Unity of Philosophical Experience (lectures). New York, Scribner, 1937.
Héloise et Abélard. Paris, Vrin, 1938; as *Heloise and Abelard,* Chicago, Regnery, 1951.
Reason and Revelation in the Middle Ages (lectures). New York, Scribner, 1938.
Dante et la philosophie. Paris, Vrin, 1939; as *Dante the Philosopher,* London and New York, Sheed and Ward, 1948.
Réalisme thomiste et critique de la connaissance. Paris, Vrin, 1939.
God and Philosophy (lectures). New Haven, Connecticut, Yale University Press, 1941.

Philosophie et incarnation selon saint Augustin. Montreal, Institut Albert le Grand, 1947.
L'Être et l'essence. Paris, Vrin, 1948.
History of Philosophy and Philosophical Education (lecture). Milwaukee, Marquette University Press, 1948.
Being and Some Philosophers. Toronto, Pontifical Institute of Mediaeval Studies, 1949.
L'École des muses. Paris, Vrin, 1951; as *The Choir of Muses,* London, Sheed and Ward, 1953.
Wisdom and Love in Saint Thomas Aquinas (lecture). Milwaukee, Marquette University Press, 1951.
Jean Duns Scot: Introduction à ses positions fondamentales. Paris, Vrin, 1952.
Les Métamorphoses de la cité de dieu. Louvain, Publications Universitaires de Louvain, 1952.
The Church Speaks to the Modern World: The Social Teachings of Pope Leo XIII. New York, Doubleday, 1954.
History of Christian Philosophy in the Middle Ages. New York, Random House, 1955.
Painting and Reality (lectures). New York, Bollingen, 1957.
A Gilson Reader: Selected Writings of Étienne Gilson, edited by Anton C. Pegis. New York, Doubleday, 1957.
Peinture et réalité: Problèmes et controverses. Paris, Vrin, 1958. (A companion volume to, and not a translation of, *Painting and Reality,* 1957.)
Elements of Christian Philosophy. New York, Doubleday, 1960.
La Philosophie et la théologie. Paris, Fayard, 1960; as *The Philosopher and Theology,* New York, Random House, 1962.
Introduction à la philosophie chretienne. Paris, Vrin, 1960.
St. Thomas Aquinas and Philosophy (lecture). West Hartford, Connecticut, St. Joseph College, 1961.
Modern Philosophy: Descartes to Kant, with Thomas Langan. New York, Random House, 1963.
Introduction aux arts du beau. Paris, Vrin, 1963; as *The Arts of the Beautiful,* New York, Scribner, 1965.
Matières et formes: Poétiques particulières des arts majeurs. Paris, Vrin, 1964; as *Forms and Substances in the Arts,* New York, Scribner, 1966.
The Spirit of Thomism. New York, P.J. Kenedy, 1964.
Recent Philosophy: Hegel to the Present, with Thomas Langan and Armand A. Maurer. New York, Random House, 1966.
In Search of Saint Thomas Aquinas (lecture). West Hartford, Connecticut, St. Joseph College, 1966.
Les Tribulations de Sophie. Paris, Vrin, 1967.
La Société de masse et sa culture. Paris, Vrin, 1967.
Linguistique et philosophie: Essai sur les constantes philosophique de langage. Paris, Vrin, 1969.
D'Aristotle à Darwin et retour: Essai sur quelques constantes de la biophilosophie. Paris, Vrin, 1971.
Dante et Béatrice: Études dantesque. Paris, Vrin, 1974.

Other

Editor, *Saint Bernard: Textes choisis et présentés.* Paris, Plon, 1949.

*

Bibliography: "The Writings of Étienne Gilson Chronologically Arranged," in *Mélanges offerts à Étienne Gilson de l'Académie Française,* Toronto, Pontifical Institute of Mediaeval Studies, and Paris, Vrin, 1959.

*   *   *

Two things, closely related in his thought throughout his long career, are dominant in Étienne Gilson's vast literary output. These are: 1) his scholarly work on the history of modern and medieval philosophy; and 2) his efforts, as a philosopher, to defend the legitimacy and specify the precise nature of what he called Christian philosophy.

Gilson's first work was on the thought of Descartes. Then, in the mid-1920's, at the suggestion of Lucien Lévy-Bruhl, Gilson began to read medieval philosophy, and it is upon his work in that field that his reputation as an historian primarily rests. Coming to the study of scholastic thought from a background in cartesianism, Gilson was able to detect important influences upon Descartes of scholasticism, in particular the influence exerted by the metaphysics of Thomas Aquinas. However, Gilson's work on medieval philosophy was not confined to tracing its impact upon the ideas of Descartes, and his considerable reputation as a medievalist rests no less upon his contribution to the overthrow of the perception, common in the early decades of this century, of scholasticism as a homogeneous body of thought. In a succession of books and articles he argued that while, as theologians, the leading intellectual figures of the Middle Ages—say Anselm, Bonaventure, Albert, Aquinas and Scotus—all subscribed to essentially the same views, this uniformity of thought did not extend to their work in philosophy. By arguing for important differences between the philosophical positions of those men, Gilson went a long way towards establishing, for a contemporary audience, first of all the scholastics' reputations as philosophers and secondly their identities as *individual* philosophers. Yet, different philosophically as he argued the major figures of scholasticism to be, Gilson maintained that, when taken together and compared to the philosophical blocs we call ancient and modern philosophy respectively, the work of these men constitutes a distinctive and important philosophical epoch. That is to say, Gilson argued against the notion that, between the ancient and the modern worlds, philosophy was barren. The distinctiveness of philosophy in that long middle period, Gilson maintained, was due to its specifically Christian character, the central place in that philosophy of the basic Christian idea—that of a benevolent, creator God in a salvationist relationship to mankind.

Viewed as a philosopher in his own right, as opposed to his being regarded as an historian of philosophy, Gilson is a thomist. His work is marked by its fidelity to what he takes to be the actual ideas of the historical Thomas Aquinas. In other words, Gilson's is no revisionist neo-thomism brought to address, often on their own terms, the epistemological and metaphysical puzzlements articulated for Western philosophy by the thinkers of the Enlightenment and since. To Gilson, many of the presuppositions upon which the post-cartesian tradition stands are foreign to the mentality of the medieval philosophers, and so problems reflecting those presuppositions are not problems for thomism. The fundamental of these diverging preconceptions concerns the nature of philosophy itself, or at least philosophy regarded through thomistic eyes. To Gilson's mind, thomistic philosophy cannot exist as such apart from its moorings in theology, and post-Enlightenment philosophy's rejection of such a status for itself bring us, so far as Gilson is concerned, to what is the central divide between medieval and modern philosophy.

An important element of the cartesian legacy is the view of philosophy common to most contemporary philosophers, that is, a perception of their own discipline as independent of religious belief and in fact as no more tied to a faith or its theology than, say, physics or biology are. By contrast, in keeping with the views of Aquinas, as with those of the other schoolman on this topic, Gilson's philosophy is avowedly Christian and this entails two things: 1) the acceptance, as a governing precept, of the idea of a creator and redeemer God; and 2) the perception of philosophy as self-consciously contributing to a theological view of the world. Hence, for Gilson, there is little common ground of importance on which medieval and modern philosophy can meet, and so fusion or basic alignment of the two does not seem possible.

In response to those critics and commentators, and in the ranks of contemporary philosophers there are many, who regard the expression "Christian philosophy" as oxymoronic, Gilson seeks to belie the apparent contradiction by citing, as evidence for the legitimate conjunction of philosophy and Christian faith, the medieval scholastics whose work, he argues, was, despite its home in theology, genuinely philosophy, genuinely free investigation. For Gilson, as for them, acceptance of certain views ascribed to divine revelation is a bedrock position providing the framework within which his philosophical questions arise and then reside. It is a framework too which, like any basic regulative frame of reference, is immune to repudiation from within.

However, even supposing it be granted to Gilson and the scholastics that no basic conceptual system can be repudiated from the inside, for that would seem to involve one simultaneously in affirming and denying it, and furthermore that all inquiry operates within some general frame of reference which that inquiry itself takes for granted, the question yet remains of whether philosophy, properly speaking, can give prior allegiance to a substantive framework as opposed to a methodological one, that is to say, to a set of basic views about the nature of reality as opposed to a set of views about canons of investigation, confirmation and disconfirmation. Gilson's affirmative answer to this question is one which most contemporary philosophers would be disposed to reject, or at least to accept as no more than, theoretically speaking, a provisional point of departure.

—David O'Connor

GÖDEL, Kurt. American mathematician. Born in Brünn, Austria-Hungary, now Brno, Czechoslovakia, 28 April 1906; emigrated to the United States in 1940: naturalized, 1948. Studied at the University of Vienna, Ph.D. 1930. Privatdocent, University of Vienna, 1933-38; Member, 1933, 1935, 1938-52, and Professor, 1953-76, Institute for Advanced Study, Princeton, New Jersey. Recipient: Einstein Award, 1951; National Medal of Science, 1975. Honorary doctorate: Yale University, New Haven, Connecticut, 1951; Harvard University, Cambridge, Massachusetts, 1952; Amherst College, Massachusetts, 1967; Rockefeller University, New York, 1972. Member, National Academy of Sciences, American Academy of Arts and Sciences, Royal Society of London; Corresponding Member, Académie de Science Morale et Politique, Paris, and the British Academy; Honorary Member, London Mathematical Society. *Died 14 January 1978.*

PUBLICATIONS

Mathematics

"Über formal unentscheidbare Sätze der Principia Mathematica und verwandter Systeme I," in *Monatshefte für Mathematik und Physik*, vol. 38, 1931; as *On Formally Undecidable Propositions of Principia Mathematica and Related Systems*, Edinburgh, Oliver and Boyd, and New York, Basic Books, 1962.
The Consistency of the Axiom of Choice and of the Generalized Continuum-Hypothesis with the Axioms of Set Theory. Princeton, New Jersey, Princeton University Press, 1940.

*

Critical Studies: *On Undecidable Propositions of Formal Mathematical Systems: Notes on Lectures by Kurt Gödel, February-May, 1934* by S.C. Kleene and J.B. Rosser, Princeton, New Jersey, Institute for Advanced Study, 1934; *Sentences Undecidable in Formalized Arithmetic: An Exposition of the Theory of Kurt Gödel* by A. Mostowski, Amsterdam, North-Holland, 1952; *Gödel's Proof* by Ernest Nagel and J.R. Newman, London, Routledge and Kegan Paul, 1959; *The Undecida-*

ble: *Basic Papers on Undecidable Propositions, Unsolvable Problems and Computable Functions*, edited by M. Davis, Hewlett, New York, Raven, 1965; *Büchi's Monadic Second Order Successor Arithmetic* by D. Siefkes, New York, Springer-Verlag, 1970; *Ontology and the Vicious-Circle Principle* by Charles S. Chihara, Ithaca, New York, Cornell University Press, 1973; *Gödel, Escher, Bach: An Eternal Golden Braid* by Douglas R. Hofstadter, New York, Basic Books, and Hassocks, Sussex, Harvester Press, 1979.

*   *   *

Kurt Gödel's logical results shook the very foundations of early-20th-century mathematics. His most famous paper, published in 1931, refuted both the long-standing assumption that the basic systems of mathematics (such as arithmetic) are complete (contain no undecidable statements, or statements which can be neither proved nor disproved) and David Hilbert's belief that the consistency (freedom from contradiction) of such systems can be demonstrated through proofs constructed within the systems themselves. Later Gödel reached important conclusions concerning the continuum hypothesis and the axiom of choice.

Throughout all this major mathematical work, Gödel was responding to issues raised in the first and second of the famous 23 problems offered by Hilbert in 1900 for the special attention of his fellow mathematicians. Gödel's answers to these problems, however, were largely unanticipated by and even inimical to Hilbert and his formalist school of mathematics. Hilbert's address to the International Congress of Mathematicians, in which the problems were outlined, was based on assumption of the completeness of mathematics. "This conviction of the solvability of every mathematical problem," Hilbert had declared, "is a powerful incentive to the worker....in mathematics there is no *ignorabimus*." Yet Gödel showed that incompleteness is fundamental to rich mathematical systems. Similarly, while Hilbert's second problem asked for a proof of the consistency of arithmetic, Gödel showed the impossibility of supplying it.

Hilbert's questions and Gödel's answers can most easily be understood as aspects of the 20th-century reconstruction of mathematics necessitated by major 19th-century developments in the field. The discovery of the non-Euclidean geometries had been particularly disruptive of traditional mathematics. For centuries, Euclidean geometry was thought to be a body of truths based on self-evident postulates. Then, in the early 19th century Carl Friedrich Gauss and others developed a non-Euclidean (hyperbolic) geometry with a postulate set consisting of Euclid's first four postulates and a fifth postulate contrary to Euclid's fifth. Consistency then became a major concern of mathematicians. Since, despite extensive use over a long period of time, Euclidean geometry had generated no contradictions, mathematicians felt reasonably sure that it was consistent. But was the new geometry—with its contrary fifth postulate and strange resulting theorems—also consistent? And, how could consistency be assured? By the end of the century, Eugenio Beltrami and Henri Poincaré had demonstrated that hyperbolic geometry is consistent if Euclidean geometry is consistent; others had proved that the Riemannian or elliptic (additional non-Euclidean) geometries are also as consistent as Euclidean geometry.

In 1900 Hilbert gave the question of consistency of Euclidean geometry priority among mathematical problems of the new century. Hilbert's formalist approach to mathematics lay behind the importance he attached to the question. The non-Euclidean geometries and other mathematical creations of the preceding century led Hilbert to treat mathematics as a game based on meaningless symbols governed by axioms of the mathematician's making. He then viewed geometry as a deductive system dealing with undefined terms—such as "point," "line," and "plane"— which take on "meaning" only through the assigned rules governing their use. Thus devoid of inherent meaning, Hilbert's geometry seemed to demand some other form of justification. For it Hilbert turned to consistency, making the latter synonymous

with mathematical existence: "If contradictory attributes be assigned to a concept...*mathematically the concept does not exist*.... But if it can be proved that the attributes assigned to the concept can never lead to a contradiction by the application of a finite number of logical processes,...the mathematical existence of the concept...is thereby proved." Reducing the question of the consistency of geometry to the question of the consistency of arithmetic, Hilbert called—in his second problem—for a proof of the absolute consistency of arithmetic.

Gödel's major mathematical breakthrough came in response to Hilbert's second problem. In his paper of 1931 ("On Formally Undecidable Propositions of *Principia Mathematica* and Related Systems I"), once described as an "amazing intellectual symphony," Gödel proved that fertile mathematical systems (such as arithmetic developed by Bertrand Russell and Alfred North Whitehead in their *Principia Mathematica*) contain undecidable propositions. In other words, there can be formulated in these systems statements which can be neither proved nor disproved. Perhaps even more disturbing from Hilbert's formalist perspective, consistency is among these undecidable questions. As Gödel showed, there cannot be formulated within arithmetical calculus a proof of the consistency of arithmetic.

Gödel's so-called "incompleteness theorem" dealt a serious blow to Hilbert's formalism and left mathematicians in a quandary concerning the foundations of mathematics. Thus the distinguished Hermann Weyl captured the frustration of mathematicians when he remarked that God exists because mathematics is consistent and the devil exists because mathematicians cannot prove its consistency. The theorem also gave impetus to alternative non-formalist approaches to mathematics, including L.E.J. Brouwer's intuitionism.

Gödel's second set of major results was stimulated by Hilbert's first problem, which stemmed from Georg Cantor's work on the infinite and actually involved two related questions. First, is there a cardinal number between N_0 and c? (The cardinal number of a finite set is the number of elements in the set. But some sets, such as that of the whole numbers and that of the real numbers, are infinite. Infinite sets are said to have transfinite cardinal numbers, and any two infinite sets have the same cardinal number provided they can be put into one-to-one correspondence with each other.) N_0 is the cardinal number of the set of whole numbers; c is the cardinal number of the set of all real numbers (the latter set's popular designation being the "continuum"). c is clearly greater than N_0. Thus Hilbert asked if there was a set with cardinal number greater than N_0 and yet less than c. More specifically, he directed mathematicians to try to prove the continuum hypothesis—that there is no such intermediate transfinite number. The second part of Hilbert's first problem was: can the continuum be considered a well-ordered set? (A well-ordered set is the set with an ordering relation such that each of its subsets has a first element with respect to that relation.) The continuum, in its natural order, is not well-ordered. Consider, for example, the segment (0,1], or the subset of the continuum containing all real numbers greater than 0 but less than or equal to 1. It does not have a least or first number. Thus Hilbert now asked for a reordering of the real numbers to assure that each of its subsets had a first element.

Work on the latter part of Hilbert's first problem led to additional mathematical questions. As early as 1904 Ernst Zermelo proved that for any set whatever there is a dyadic relation with respect to which the set is well-ordered. Thus, as a corollary, the set of all real numbers can be well ordered. Zermelo's proof, however, assumed the controversial axiom of choice, according to which, given any collection of mutually exclusive nonempty sets, there exists a set which contains one and only one element from each of the original sets. Zermelo's well-ordering theorem was, in fact, eventually shown to be the equivalent to the axiom of choice.

In his later years Gödel studied the relationship of the continuum hypothesis and the axiom of choice to basic set theory as formulated by Zermelo and Abraham Fraenkel. In 1940 he showed that both the continuum hypothesis and the axiom of choice are consistent with the axioms of set theory. More precisely, he demonstrated that if the Zermelo-Fraenkel system without the axiom of choice is consistent, then the Zermelo-Fraenkel system with the axiom of choice is consistent, and that the continuum hypothesis is consistent with the Zermelo-Fraenkel system. Gödel's work was continued and superseded in 1963 by Paul Cohen's proof that both the axiom of choice and the continuum hypothesis are independent of the Zermelo-Fraenkel postulates—that is, neither can be proved from the postulates. As a result of the combined efforts of Gödel and Cohen, then, mathematicians realized that in developing set theory they were free to adopt or deny the axiom of choice and the continuum hypothesis.

—Helena M. Pycior

GOFFMAN, Erving. Canadian sociologist. Born in Manville, Alberta, 11 June 1922; emigrated to the United States in 1945. Studied at the University of Toronto, B.A. 1945; University of Chicago, M.A. 1949, Ph.D. 1953. Married Angelica Schuyler Choate in 1952 (died, 1964); 1 son. Member, Shetland Field Research, University of Edinburgh, 1949-51; Assistant, Division of Social Sciences, 1952-53, and Resident Associate, 1953-54, University of Chicago; Visiting Scientist, National Institute of Mental Health, Bethesda, Maryland, 1954-57; Assistant Professor, 1958-59, Associate Professor, 1959-62, and Professor of Sociology, 1962-68, University of California, Berkeley; Benjamin Franklin Professor of Anthropology and Sociology, University of Pennsylvania, Philadelphia, 1968 until his death in 1982. President, American Sociological Society, 1981-82. Recipient: MacIver Award, 1961; In Medias Res Award, 1978. LL.D.: University of Manitoba, 1976; L.H.D.: University of Chicago, 1979. Fellow, American Academy of Arts and Sciences. *Died* (in Philadelphia) *19 November 1982.*

PUBLICATIONS

Sociology

The Presentation of Self in Everyday Life. New York, Doubleday, 1959; London, Allen Lane, 1969.
Encounters: Two Studies in the Sociology of Interaction. Indianapolis, Bobbs-Merrill, 1961; London, Allen Lane, 1972.
Asylums: Essays on the Social Situation of Mental Patients and Other Inmates. New York, Doubleday, 1961; London, Penguin, 1968.
Stigma: Notes on the Management of Spoiled Identity. Englewood Cliffs, New Jersey, Prentice Hall, 1963; London, Penguin, 1968.
Interaction Ritual: Essays on Face-to-Face Behaviour. New York, Doubleday, 1967; London, Allen Lane, 1972.
Strategic Interaction. Philadelphia, University of Pennsylvania Press, 1969; Oxford, Blackwell, 1970.
Where the Action Is: Three Essays. London, Allen Lane, 1969.
Relations in Public: Microstudies of the Public Order. New York, Basic Books, and London, Allen Lane, 1971.
Frame Analysis: An Essay on the Organization of Experience. New York, Harper, 1974; London, Penguin, 1975.
Gender Advertisements. New York, Harper, and London, Macmillan, 1979.
Forms of Talk. Philadelphia, University of Pennsylvania Press, 1981.

Critical Studies: *The View from Goffman,* edited by Jason Ditton, London, Macmillan, 1980 (contains a bibliography).

*   *   *

Erving Goffman was a sociologist specializing in the analysis of the face-to-face interactions of people in public. His general position was a familiar one in sociology—it is most helpful to analyze such interactions as if they were performances by an actor. In daily life, we distinguish between real and false performances. Goffman says that false performances are merely bad ones. People intend to put on good performances, so that we cannot see the actor behind the mask. When we do, we say it is a false performance and that the actor is "insincere." The actor has merely failed—no doubt he has tried as hard as anyone, and perhaps too hard, to give a convincing performance.

All of us in society collaborate with each other to present the selves we wish to present. I have an interest in your being able to successfully present your chosen self, for *my* chosen self very probably cannot exist unless yours does. A teacher would rather not hear that the reason a student missed a test was that he is so bored with the class that he never comes and so did not know a test was scheduled. So lies are gratefully accepted—the teacher's identity as a teacher depends upon it. The student is likely to help the teacher out. Goffman calls this tact. But tact exists to help the tactful too. The student cannot remain a student if the teacher considers himself and his class a failure, for his role as a student—that is, someone interested in the pursuit of knowledge—requires teachers who believe that they are successfully disseminating knowledge. We all participate together in sewing the social fabric, and we all must participate together, for it exists only by consensus.

Having said this, one must add that the interesting and truly original aspects of Goffman's work are his analyses of situations where bizarre complexities are introduced into the daily round of impression management. Goffman is at his best with specifics.

For example, expressions of love are obviously extremely important in a developing relationship. And so you would expect people to practice such expressions, in front of a mirror or close friends. They do—in fictional performances, e.g., in plays. They are funny and embarrassing, for expressions of love are just not the kind of thing that should be practiced. So while we long to, as evidenced by our embarrassed laughter when we see such practice fictionally portrayed, we rarely do. A teacher, on the other hand, is supposed to practice, at least to the extent of having notes. And so a female student asking a male professor where his notes are would be just as affronted, would feel the social fabric just as rippled, to be told that he always talked off the top of his head as she would be if he declared his love for her while continuously casting his eyes down to a piece of paper.

Goffman analyzes human existence into two main regions—front, when one is on stage, fostering the impressions one needs in order to maintain one's definition of oneself; and back, where one relaxes with members of one's team and expresses the sentiments one cannot express while on stage. Thus behind the swinging doors to a restaurant kitchen waiters make fun of customers, and when the mortuary closes funeral directors talk about "stiffs." This is well known. Goffman's original contribution to this analysis comes from his refusal to make the assumption that ordinary people do, that back stage is where the "true self" resides. To prove that the true self is a fiction, Goffman makes a variety of points. For one thing, we tend to reserve our best, our energy and our wit, for the front region. Back stage may be a place for jovial, earthy joking and intimacy, but it is also the place for silence, sullenness, and irritation. We do not have a difficult performance to put on backstage, that is the only thing that is always the case back there. We may blow off steam with our teammates or we may blow off steam at our teammates. It is interesting to note that marriage has traditionally marked the point in a relationship between a man and a woman when they go from being in the front region with each other to being in a common back region, where apathy and general slackness often prevail. It is not that marriage kills romantic love, but that romantic love is a front region performance.

There is another limitation to the equation of the back region with the true self. Back regions have traditions, just as do front regions, and, to the extent that the performer lacks the energy or desire to live up to that tradition, he will experience all the strain that any front region performer will. Males are not "really" hearty, back-slapping, hard-drinking dirty-jokers when back stage with each other. They are *required* to be, and it is not an easy act. A newspaper account of life in Moscow written by an American who had lived and worked among Russians provides an interesting twist to this theme. This man found the back stage in Moscow impossibly hard. There were social gatherings every night, which lasted well into the night and required the consumption of much vodka. He did not want to miss them, as the conversations were energetic and wide-ranging, but he did not know how he could work too—his job was as a translator in an important news agency, the sort of job that in the States requires a concentrated front stage performance. What he had to learn was that working in Russia for almost all jobs is a back region. People feel free to wander off to wait in line for hours for scarce goods, sleep during lectures on communism, and in general follow the common Russian joke, "they pretend to pay us; we pretend to work." All sorts of variations suggest themselves—imagine the strain on a typically ambitious American who first had to reverse his front and back regions and then had to pretend to be lazy and bored during work hours.

Often the need to maintain an impression interferes with the actual doing of what one is trying to pretend one is doing. For example, a person reading in a library or other public place may need to spend so much time and energy appearing to be engrossed that he will be unable to concentrate. But one *must* always maintain a distance from one's performance, lest one's enthusiasm destroy it. A novice teacher may, for example, get so carried away by what he is talking about that he goes off on a tangent and gets lost and confused. Goffman could point out here that such "evidences" of confusion are usually endearing and may well be used to foster the impression of being enthusiastic.

Just as only a sampling of Goffman's work may be given in a brief essay, so can only a sampling of a full critique be offered. The last example will provide the occasion for this. Goffman implies that spontaneity is a fiction—it is a concept we use in daily life, but it is really just a good performance. But surely there is a difference between really being carried away and faking it. Even Goffman himself recognizes this when he says that the good performer must be careful not to get carried away—he recognizes that one *can* get carried away. Thus his description of social behavior has a limited range of applicability. How limited? Does it fit what most of us would feel free to call true love or true friendship? Social scientists rarely engage in criticism of this variety, so no good answer can be given. In any event, Goffman's enormous output is always interesting and provocative, and he seems to have been allowed to break the basic commandment of psychology and sociology, "Thou shalt not be original, individual, or powerful."

—George W. Kelling

GOLDSTEIN, Kurt. American psychologist. Born in Kattowitz, Upper Silesia, 6 November 1878; emigrated to the United States in 1935: naturalized, 1940. Studied at the University of Heidelberg and the University of Breslau, M.D. 1903. Married Eva Rothmann. Assistant to Ludwig Edinger, Senckenbergische Neurologische Institut, Frankfurt, 1904; Staff Member, Psychiatric Clinic, University of Königsberg, 1906-14; First Assistant,

Neurological Institute, Frankfurt, 1914-19; Professor of Neurology, University of Frankfurt, 1919-30; taught neurology and psychiatry at the University of Berlin, 1930-33 (removed by the Nazis); lived in Amsterdam, 1933-34; in private practice, New York City, and Clinical Professor of Neurology and Lecturer in Psychopathology, Columbia University, New York, 1935-40; Clinical Professor of Neurology, Tufts College Medical School, Medford, Massachusetts, 1940-45; after 1945 taught at City College, New York, the New School for Social Research, New York, and Brandeis University, Waltham, Massachusetts. William James Lecturer, Harvard University, Cambridge, Massachusetts, 1938. Founding Editor, *Psychologische Forschung*, 1922; Co-Founder, International Society for Psychotherapy, 1927. Honorary doctorate: University of Frankfurt, 1958. *Died* (in New York City) *19 September 1965.*

PUBLICATIONS

Psychology and Medicine

Die Zusammensetzung der Hinterstränge: Anatomische Beiträge und kritische Übersicht. N.p., 1903.
Über das Realitätsurteil halluzinatorischer Warhnehmungen. Privately printed, 1908.
Über Rassenhygiene. Berlin, Springer, 1913.
Schemata des Neurologischen Institutes zu Frankfurt a. M. zum Einzeichen von Kopf- und Gehirnverletzungen. Wiesbaden, Bergmann, 1916.
Die Behandlung. Fürsorge und Begutachtung der Hirnverletzten. Leipzig, Vogel, 1919.
Diagnostik der Hirngeschwülste, with H. Cohen. Berlin, Urban und Schwarzenber, 1932.
Der Aufbau des Organismus: Einführung in die Biologie unter besonderer Berücksichtigung der Erfahrungen am kranken Menschen. The Hague, Nijhoff, 1934; as *The Organism: A Holistic Approach to Biology Derived from Pathological Data in Man,* New York, American Book Company, 1939.
Human Nature in the Light of Psychopathology. Cambridge, Massachusetts, Harvard University Press, 1940.
Abstract and Concrete Behavior: An Experimental Study with Special Tests, with M. Scheerer. Evanston, Illinois, American Psychological Association, 1941.
Aftereffects of Brain Injuries in the War: Their Evaluation and Treatment. New York, Grune and Stratton, 1942.
Case Lanuti: Extreme Concretization of Behavior Due to Damage of the Brain Cortex, with others. Evanston, Illinois, American Psychological Association, 1944.
The Goldstein-Scheerer Tests of Abstract and Concrete Thinking, with M. Scheerer. New York, Psychological Corporation, 1945.
A Case of "Idiot Savant": An Experimental Study of Personality Organization, with others. Evanston, Illinois, American Psychological Association, 1945.
Language and Language Disturbances: Aphasic Symptom Complexes and their Significance for Medicine and Theory of Language. New York, Grune and Stratton, 1948.
Selected Papers, edited by Aron Gurwitsch and others. The Hague, Nijhoff, 1971.

Other

Editor, with A. Gelb, *Psychologische Analysen hirnpathologischer Fälle.* Leipzig, Barth, 1920.
Editor, with A. Wallenberg, *Einführung in die Lehre vom Bau und den Verrichtungen des Nervensystems,* by Ludwig Edinger. Leipzig, Vogel, 1921.

*

Critical Studies: *The Reach of Mind: Essays in Memory of Kurt*

Goldstein, edited by Marianne L. Simmel, New York, Springer, 1968 (contains a bibliography).

*   *   *

Although his major background was in neurology, Kurt Goldstein contributed a great deal to current psychological theory. His first area of study was philosophy. He entered Breslau University intending to study philosophy, but, after a short time at Heidelberg, he turned to medicine, with an emphasis on mental disease. He worked closely with Karl Weinicke (in the field of neuroanatomy) and graduated in 1903. In 1904 he went to the Senckenbergische Neurologische Institut in Frankfurt, where he worked with Ludwig Edinger. After working in Königsberg, he returned to Frankfurt in 1914 to serve as Edinger's assistant at the Neurological Institute. While in this position, he founded a research hospital to investigate brain injury in soldiers. His studies here evolved from an original base of cortical injuries and sensory defects into the area of perceptual problems and cerebellar function. He also had developed an interest in aphasia, which he studied under Weinicke, and in psychotherapy.

Goldstein's career was interrupted when Hitler came to power in 1933 (Goldstein was Jewish). He was jailed briefly and then went into exile for a year in Amsterdam. During this year he wrote his magnum opus *The Organism*. In this book he develops his theory of "self-actualization" as the motivational force of the organism and accentuates the need to view behavior in the context of the whole organism.

Goldstein came to the United States in 1935 and set up a private practice in New York City; he also held a number of academic appointments in New York and Boston. From 1940-45 he taught at Tufts College Medical School where he further developed his theory of concrete vs. abstract thinking. Goldstein believed that brain damaged patients lost their ability to think abstractly, which was manifested in their inability to perform certain tasks.

Kurt Goldstein made two major contributions to psychology. The first, organismic psychology, rejects both Freudian and Gestalt theory but lies between them. Goldstein believes that the organism can only be analyzed as a whole and that the fundamental human behavior motivation is "self-actualization." "Self-actualization" involves the need to fulfill the capacities of the organism rather than simply to satisfy needs. Goldstein believes three concepts are involved in motivation: "self-actualization", "coming to terms" with the environment, and maintaining constancy in the face of environmental change. Of these, "self-actualization" is the dominant motivation. Thus, Goldstein sees the individual as being motivated from within toward a goal rather than pushed by external drives.

Goldstein's other major work involves the differentiation between abstract and concrete conceptual ability. Goldstein believed that brain injured patients retained the ability to think concretely but lost the ability for abstract thought. Goldstein, in collaboration with Scheerer, postulated eight modes of thinking in which brain-damaged individuals were defective: 1) the ability to detach the ego from external or interior experiences; 2) the ability to assume a certain mental set; 3) the ability to explain spatial relationships; 4) the ability to shift a mental set from one task to another; 5) the ability to keep in mind two tasks simultaneously; 6) the ability to synthesize parts into an integrated whole; 7) the ability to abstract out the common properties embedded in a variety of test situations; 8) the ability to plan ahead. These incapacities may not all be present in every brain-damaged individual, depending on the extent and location of the injury.

Goldstein also emphasized that it was not possible to localize particular brain functions (such as speech, walking, etc.) to a specific area of the brain, although it might be possible to localize specific injuries. This emphasis was in contradiction to earlier neurologists who actually attempted such localization. Goldstein's attitude is consistent with his emphasis on the need to view the organism as a whole.

—R.W. Rieber

GOMBRICH, E(rnst) H(ans) (Josef).   British aesthetician and art historian.   Born in Vienna, Austria, 30 March 1909; emigrated to Great Britain and later naturalized. Educated at the University of Vienna, Ph.D. Served with the British Broadcasting Corporation Monitoring Service, 1939-45. Married Ilse Heller in 1936; 1 son. Research Assistant, 1936-39, Senior Research Fellow, 1946-48, Lecturer, 1948-54, Reader, 1954-56, Senior Lecturer, 1956-59, and Professor of the History of Classical Tradition and Director, 1959-76, Warburg Institute, University of London; also, Durning-Lawrence Professor of the History of Art, University College, University of London, 1956-59. Slade Professor of Fine Art, Oxford University, 1950-53, and Cambridge University, 1961-63; Lethaby Professor, Royal College of Art, London, 1967-68; Visiting Professor, Harvard University, Cambridge, Massachusetts, 1967-68; Andrew White Professor-at-Large, Cornell University, Ithaca, New York, 1970-77. Trustee of the British Museum, London, 1974-79. Recipient: W.H. Smith Literary Award, 1964; Medal for Distinguished Visitors, New York University, 1970; Austrian Cross of Honour for Science and Art, 1975; Erasmus Prize, 1975; Hegel Prize, 1976; Medal, Collège de France, Paris, 1977. Honorary doctorate: University of Belfast, 1963; University of Leeds, 1965; University of St. Andrews, Scotland, 1965; Oxford University, 1969; Cambridge University, 1970; University of Manchester, 1974; University of Chicago, 1975; University of London, 1976; Harvard University, 1976; University of Essex, 1977; University of Pennsylvania, Philadelphia, 1977; Brandeis University, Waltham, Massachusetts, 1981. Fellow, British Academy, 1960; Society of Antiquaries, 1961; Royal Society of Literature, 1969; and Royal Institute of British Architects, 1971. Honorary Fellow, Royal College of Art, 1961; Jesus College, Cambridge, 1963. Corresponding Member, Academy of Science, Turin, 1962; Royal Academy of Arts and Sciences, Uppsala, Sweden, 1970; Royal Netherlands Academy of Arts and Sciences, 1973; Bavarian Academy of Science, 1979; Foreign Honorary Member, American Academy of Arts and Sciences, 1964; Foreign Member, American Philosophical Society, 1968. C.B.E. (Commander, Order of the British Empire), 1966; knighted, 1972. Address: 19 Briardale Gardens, London NW3 7PN, England.

PUBLICATIONS

Aesthetics and Art History

Weltgeschichte von der Urzeit bis zur Gegenwart (for children). Vienna, Steyremühl, 1936.
Caricature, with Ernst Kris. London, Penguin, 1940.
The Story of Art. London and New York, Phaidon, 1950.
Raphael's Madonna della sedia (lecture). London and New York, Oxford University Press, 1956.
Art and Scholarship (lecture). London, H.K. Lewis, 1957.
Lessing (lecture). London, Oxford University Press, 1957.
Art and Illusion: A Study in the Psychology of Pictorial Representation. London, Phaidon, and New York, Pantheon, 1960.
The Cartoonist's Armory (lecture). Durham, North Carolina, Duke University Press, 1963.
Meditations on a Hobby Horse and Other Essays on the Theory of Art. London and New York, Phaidon, 1956.
In Search of Cultural History (lecture). Oxford, Clarendon Press, 1969.

The Ideas of Progress and Their Impact on Art (lecture). New York, Cooper Union School of Art and Architecture, 1971.

Norm and Form: Studies in the Art of the Renaissance. London and New York, Phaidon, 1971.

Art, Perception and Reality, with others. Baltimore, Johns Hopkins University Press, 1972.

Symbolic Images: Studies in the Art of the Renaissance. London, Phaidon, and New York, Praeger, 1975.

Anna Mahler: Ihr Werk. Stuttgart, Belser, 1975.

Art History and the Social Sciences (lecture). Oxford, Clarendon Press, 1975.

Means and Ends: Reflections on the History of Fresco Painting (lecture). London, Thames and Hudson, 1976.

The Heritage of Apelles. London, Phaidon, and Ithaca, New York, Cornell University Press, 1976.

The Sense of Order: A Study in the Psychology of Decorative Art. London, Phaidon, and Ithaca, New York, Cornell University Press, 1979.

Ideals and Idols: Essays on Values in History and Art. London, Phaidon, 1979; Ithaca, New York, Cornell University Press, 1982.

Other

Aby Warburg: An Intellectual Biography. London, Warburg Institute, 1970.

Myth and Reality in German War-time Broadcasts (lecture). London, Athlone Press, 1970.

Editor, *Essays in Honor of Hans Tietze, 1880-1954.* Paris and New York, Gazette des Beaux-Arts, 1958.

Editor, with R.L. Gregory, *Illusion in Nature and Art.* New York, Scribner, 1973.

*   *   *

"No cultural historian starts from scratch. The traditions of his own culture, the bias of his teacher, the questions of the moment can all stimulate his curiosity and his questioning." This quotation from Sir Ernst Gombrich's lecture *In Search of Cultural History* exemplifies the author's basic belief that we are the heirs to culture and traditions and that we react according to them. Such a standpoint, and the belief in inherited cultural values, is hardly surprising for the former Professor of the History of the Classical Tradition and Director of the Warburg Institute. Gombrich's own method, after all, and his preoccupations, reflect the deep respect for primary sources that he learned from Julius von Schlosser in Vienna, and the interest in the psychology of form inspired by Wolfgang Koehler in Berlin.

The range of Gombrich's interests, and his achievements, can hardly be summarized; the general reader will find his *The Story of Art* one of the most lucid and intelligent introductions to the field, while the student will read, and re-read, his studies on Renaissance art theory and iconographic problems, and in his *Aby Warburg: An Intellectual Biography* will be given insights into the mind of a great scholar. In his studies, Gombrich's final aim is often philosophical. To account for historical change and for the development of art, he rejects the notions of an organic unity explained by an independent supra-individual collective mind, like the Hegelian Spirit of Age. Rather, he follows Sir Karl Popper's theory of the growth of scientific knowledge as a continuous process of trial and error. "The undeniable subjectivity of vision does not preclude objective standards of representational accuracy"; this observation leads Gombrich, in *Art and Illusion*, to examine the psychology of pictorial representation to show why art, or rather naturalistic art, has a history, "why different ages and different nations have represented the visible world in...different ways." In this book, Gombrich showed clearly that the artist cannot reproduce what he sees and that he is limited by the techniques and the conventions that he knows and masters. Gombrich does not accept the Romantic idea of the artist painting from his mind. "The forms of art, ancient and modern, are not duplications of what the artist has in mind any more than they are duplications of what the artist sees in the outer world. In both cases they are rendering within an acquired medium, a medium grown up through tradition and skill—that of the artist and that of the beholder." This leads him to explain the evolution of art, both through the combination of technical developments of new formulae and skills and through sociological factors. The process itself follows Popper's "trial and error" theory. Gombrich describes his "making and matching" as the slow and systematic modification of schematic images to match the motif. "Without some starting point, some initial schema, we could never get hold of the flux of experience. Without categories we could not sort our impressions." The problem, in fact, is inherent to our perception, which Gombrich stresses by studying the beholder's share; he selects evidence from classical authors and experimental psychology to show that we see, in fact, what we know or rather what follows our expectations. Even linear perspective, or photography, which we tend to accept as a perfect representation of a three-dimension space, is only a conventional rendering; there is, as Gombrich writes, no innocent eye.

Gombrich's approach breaks down barriers between disciplines. Throughout his career he has dealt with all the aspects of modern art history, discussing, sometimes even questioning, notions of style, iconography, patronage or taste. His study of Renaissance symbolism includes the "Neo-Platonic notion of images as instruments of a mystical revelation" and "the influential teachings of Aristotelian philosophy which link the visual image to the didactic theory of metaphor"; he stresses the impact of such ideas on Freud and on Jung. A methodological intent is emphasized in his introduction to *Symbolic Images*, a collection of articles on Renaissance art. Using D.E. Hirsch's terminology found in *Validity in Interpretation*, Gombrich defines the original meaning of a work, its implications and also the possibility of a different significance given to it. To find the intended meaning, what is central to iconography, he stresses the primacy of genre—the category to which a work belongs—and the importance of decorum—appropriateness or "what is fitting". Gombrich's aim is to set standards and safeguards but also to correct the habit of overinterpreting images that has given such a bad name to iconology.

For his scholarly method, his theoretical approach and his defence of cultural values, Gombrich will be remembered as one of the leading art historians of this century. Through his study of the psychology of perception, he is also one of the very few to have widened our understanding of the visible world.

—J.M. Massing

GOODMAN, (Henry) Nelson. American philosopher. Born in Somerville, Massachusetts, 7 August 1906. Studied at Harvard University, Cambridge, Massachusetts, B.S. 1928, Ph.D. 1941. Served in the United States Army, 1942-45. Married Katharine Sturgis in 1944. Art dealer in Boston, 1929-41. Instructor, Tufts College, Medford, Massachusetts, 1945-46; Associate Professor, 1946-51, and Professor, 1951-64, University of Pennsylvania, Philadelphia; Henry Austryn Wolfson Professor, Brandeis University, Waltham, Massachusetts, 1964-67; Director, Project Zero, Graduate School of Education, 1967-71, and Professor of Philosophy, 1968-77 (now Professor Emeritus), Harvard University. Visiting Lecturer, 1951, and Whitehead Lecturer, 1956, Harvard University; Special Lecturer, University of London, 1956; Visiting Lecturer, Princeton University, New Jersey, 1958; John Locke Lecturer, Oxford University, 1962; Distinguished Visiting Professor, C.W. Post College, Long Island, New York, 1968; Immanuel Kant Lecturer, Stanford University, California, 1976. Vice-President, Association for Symbolic Logic, 1951-52; President, Eastern Division, American Philosoohical Association, 1967. Recipient: Guggenheim Fellowship, 1946-47. Fellow, British Academy. Address: Emerson Hall, Harvard University, Cambridge, Massachusetts 02138, U.S.A.

PUBLICATIONS

Philosophy

The Structure of Appearance. Cambridge, Massachusetts, Harvard University Press, 1951.
Fact, Fiction, and Forecast. Cambridge, Massachusetts, Harvard University Press, 1955.
The Languages of Art: An Approach to a Theory of Symbols. Indianapolis, Bobbs Merrill, 1968.
Problems and Projects. Indianapolis, Bobbs Merrill, 1972.
Ways of Worldmaking. Indianapolis, Hackett, and Hassocks, Sussex, Harvester Press, 1978.

*

Critical Studies: *Carnap and Goodman: Two Formalists* by Alan Hausman and Fred Wilson, Iowa City, University of Iowa Press, 1967; *Logic and Art: Essays in Honor of Nelson Goodman*, edited by Richard Rudner and Israel Scheffler, Indianapolis, Bobbs Merrill, 1972 (contains a bibliography).

*   *   *

One of the most distinguished and influential of contemporary American philosophers, Nelson Goodman has made a substantial contribution to a number of fields, including logic, epistemology, philosophy of science and aesthetics.

Goodman's books and articles are notable both for a distinctively witty personal style and for the rigorous application of logical analysis to the various problems of philosophy. While he stands firmly in the analytic tradition of modern philosophy and while some of his conclusions seem complementary to those of Wittgenstein, his method is in striking contrast. Rather than proceeding by the examination of narrow and limited issues on a case by case basis, Goodman follows in the tradition of system building typified by the early Carnap. Goodman likens the construction of a philosophical system to the production of a map of a landscape. He points out that while it is possible to give satisfactory directions on a case-by-case basis without the aid of a map, a map may nonetheless prove its worth by exhibiting connections that could not have been seen just from a clear view of the landscape. These philosophical maps are called by Goodman "constructional systems," and their aim is the building by logical analysis, on the foundation of a set of explicit formal definitions, a representation of reality that is consistent, comprehensive and connected.

The major emphasis in Goodman's early work is on the formal issues involved in creating such constructional systems. His later work raises the wider epistemological implications of such system building and focusses on some important consequences of its inherent limitations.

Goodman's first book, *The Structure of Appearance*, was a substantially revised version of his doctoral dissertation, "A Study of Qualities." In the first part of the book, he discusses the nature and methods of constructional philosophy. Concerned with setting out the criteria for determining the adequacy of such systems, he argues that the individual definitions within the system cannot be tested on the basis of any one-to-one relationship to reality. Rather, the complete system under analysis must be tested against the newly constructed system which is the product of analysis. When certain weak extensional correspondences can be shown to exist, the accuracy of the analysis is demonstrated. Constructional systems can also be judged according to the criterion of simplicity, particularly the simplicity of their predicate base. The latter part of the book contains the

construction of his own systematic analysis of phenomenal concepts. While he makes quite clear that he has no overriding commitment to a phenomenological stance, he does contend that a nominalist position is required by his commitment to simplicity in predicate structures.

Goodman's second book, *Fact, Fiction and Forecast*, is perhaps the most influential of his works. Dealing with concerns that had occupied him for a number of years, the book begins with an early paper on the problem of counterfactual conditionals. Goodman argues that no satisfactory account of them can be given without raising the whole question of inductive validity and of the nature and confirmation of scientific laws. He argues that the real issue is not the justification of induction in general but the establishment of criteria which can separate valid and invalid instances of induction. Particular inductive inferences are to be validated by appeal to rules of induction and these rules by reference to specific accepted practices. To predict on the basis of past observations is, in Goodman's terms, to project an hypothesis. And there is clearly some distinction between those hypotheses which can justifiably be projected and those which ought not to be. Goodman finds the essence of this distinction to lie, not in any logical feature, but in terms of a pragmatic and historical distinction which gives preference to the hypothesis whose predicates are better "entrenched" in our past practice.

Goodman's concern in *The Languages of Art* is far wider than specifically aesthetic concerns. His object is to give an account in general terms of symbolic systems. Thus he focusses on the similarities between representation in pictures and description in language rather than the differences between them. Goodman argues that the internal structure of a symbol is of no importance in its functioning; representation cannot be accounted for in terms of resemblance nor language on structural similarity between it and the world. While he does touch on some aesthetic issues, such as the distinction between arts in which forgery is possible (autographic) and those in which it is not (allographic), Goodman consciously avoids questions involving judgements of value. Elsewhere, he suggests that attention to the question of excellence in art obscures more important purposes of aesthetics. Judgements of value ought to be seen as a means of inspiring closer analysis and the discovery of specific qualities in the work of art. They lead to a more careful observation and not vice versa.

One of the most important themes in *The Languages of Art* appears in the first chapter, in which Goodman argues that there is not one right way of describing, seeing or picturing the world, a judgement that he sees as affecting science equally with art. It is this theme that is elaborated in *Ways of Worldmaking*. Goodman contends that there is no possibility of speaking about the world apart from some particular frame of reference. Each description of an event functions as part of some system, and there is no possibility of an independent evaluation of the many functioning systems. These world-versions, as Goodman calls them, cannot be reduced, combined or neutrally appraised. He does not argue that we are merely dealing with different conventional versions of the same underlying fact in some "real" world, because he believes that facts themselves only function within conventions. He argues that we are genuinely dealing with different worlds. But this does not lead him to complete relativism. He does contend that there is a difference between true and false world versions, but this distinction resides in what he calls permanent credibility. This obtains when a world version is shown to be internally consistent and not incompatible with any unyielding beliefs, but even this, he reminds us in a final irony, is world dependent. Which is perhaps the clue to the most accurate understanding of Goodman's ultimate philosophical position.

—David J. Wren

GOODMAN, Paul. American. Born in New York City, 9 September 1911. Studied at the City College of New York, B.A. 1931; University of Chicago, Ph.D. 1940 (received, 1954). Married twice; 3 children. Reader for Metro-Goldwyn-Mayer, 1931; Instructor, University of Chicago, 1939-40; Teacher of Latin, physics, history, and mathematics, Manumit School of Progressive Education, Pawling, New York, 1942; also taught at New York University, 1948; Black Mountain College, North Carolina, 1950; and Sarah Lawrence College, Bronxville, New York, 1961; Knapp Professor, University of Wisconsin, Madison, 1964; taught at the Experimental College of San Francisco State College, 1966; and University of Hawaii, Honolulu, 1969, 1971. Editor, *Complex* magazine, New York; Film Editor, *Partisan Review*, New Brunswick, New Jersey; Television Critic, *New Republic*, Washington, D.C.; Editor, *Liberation* magazine, New York, 1962-70. Recipient: American Council of Learned Societies Fellowship, 1940; Harriet Monroe Memorial Prize (*Poetry*, Chicago), 1949; American Academy grant, 1953. Fellow, New York Institute for Gestalt Therapy, 1953; Institute for Policy Studies, Washington, D.C., 1965. *Died 3 August 1972.*

PUBLICATIONS

Social Criticism

Communitas: Means of Livelihood and Ways of Life, with Percival Goodman. Chicago, University of Chicago Press, and London, Cambridge University Press, 1947; revised edition, New York, Knopf, 1960.
Gestalt Therapy: Excitement and Growth in the Human Personality, with Frederick Perls and Ralph Hefferline. New York, Julian Press, 1951.
Censorship and Pornography on the Stage, and Are Writers Shirking Their Political Duty? New York, Living Theatre, 1959.
Growing Up Absurd: Problems of Youth in the Organized Society. New York, Random House, 1960; London, Gollancz, 1961.
Drawing the Line. New York, Random House, 1962.
The Community of Scholars. New York, Random House, 1962.
Utopian Essays and Practical Proposals. New York, Random House, 1962.
The Society I Live in Is Mine. New York, Horizon Press, 1963.
Compulsory Mis-Education. New York, Horizon Press, 1964; revised edition, London, Penguin, 1971.
People or Personnel: Decentralizing and the Mixed System. New York, Random House, 1965.
The Moral Ambiguity of America (lectures). Toronto, Canadian Broadcasting System, 1966; revised edition, as *Like a Conquered Province: The Moral Ambiguity of America*, New York, Random House, 1967.
Mass Education in Science (lecture). Los Angeles, University of California, 1966.
The Open Look. New York, Funk and Wagnalls, 1969.
New Reformation: Notes of a Neolithic Conservative. New York, Random House, 1970.
Little Prayers and Finite Experience. New York, Harper, 1972.
Drawing the Line: The Political Essays of Paul Goodman, edited by Taylor Stoehr. New York, Free Life Editions, 1977.
Nature Heals: The Psychological Essays of Paul Goodman, edited by Taylor Stoehr. New York, Free Life Editions, 1977.
The Black Flag of Anarchism. London, Kropotkin's Lighthouse Publication, 1978.

Novels

The Grand Piano; or, The Almanac of Alienation. San Francisco, Colt Press, 1942.

The State of Nature. New York, Vanguard Press, 1946.
The Dead of Spring. Glen Gardner, New Jersey, Libertarian Press, 1950.
Parents Day. Saugatuck, Connecticut, 5 x 8 Press, 1951.
The Empire City. Indianapolis, Bobbs Merrill, 1959; London, Wildwood House, 1978.
Making Do. New York, Macmillan, 1963.
Don Juan; or, The Continuum of the Libido, edited by Taylor Stoehr. Los Angeles, Black Sparrow Press, 1979.

Short Stories

The Facts of Life. New York, Vanguard Press, 1945; London, Editions Poetry London, 1946.
The Break-Up of Our Camp and Other Stories. New York, New Directions, 1949.
Our Visit to Niagara. New York, Horizon Press, 1960.
Adam and His Works: Collected Stories. New York, Random House, 1968.
The Collected Stories and Sketches of Paul Goodman, edited by Taylor Stoehr. Los Angeles, Black Sparrow Press, 4 vols., 1978-80.

Plays

Childish Joke: Crying Backstage. New York, 5 x 8 Press, 1938.
The Tower of Babel, in *New Directions in Prose and Poetry* 5. New York, New Directions, 1940.
Stop-Light: 5 Dance Poems (5 Noh plays: *A Noh Play, The Birthday, The Three Disciples, The Cyclist, The Stop Light*). Harrington Park, New Jersey, 5 x 8 Press, 1941.
Three Plays: The Young Disciple, Faustina, Jonah. New York, Random House, 1965.
Tragedy and Comedy: Four Cubist Plays (includes *Structure of Tragedy, After Aeschylus; Structure of Tragedy, After Sophocles; Structure of Pathos, After Euripides; Little Hero, After Molière*). Los Angeles, Black Sparrow Press, 1970.

Verse

Ten Lyric Poems. New York, 5 x 8 Press, 1934.
12 Ethical Sonnets. New York, 5 x 8 Press, 1935.
15 Poems with Time Expressions. New York, 5 x 8 Press, 1936.
Homecoming and Departure. New York, 5 x 8 Press, 1937.
A Warning at My Leisure. Harrington Park, New Jersey, 5 x 8 Press, 1939.
Pieces of Three, with Meyer Liben and Edouard Roditi. Harrington Park, New Jersey, 5 x 8 Press, 1942.
Five Young American Poets, with others. New York, New Directions, 1942.
The Copernican Revolution. Saugatuck, Connecticut, 5 x 8 Press, 1946; revised edition, 1947.
Day and Other Poems. Privately printed, 1954 (?).
Red Jacket. Privately printed, 1955.
Berg Goodman Mezey: Poems. Philadelphia, New Ventures Press, 1957.
The Well of Bethlehem. Privately printed, 1957 (?).
Ten Poems. Privately printed, 1961.
The Lordly Hudson: Collected Poems of Paul Goodman. New York, Macmillan, 1962.
Hawkweed. New York, Random House, 1967.
North Percy. Los Angeles, Black Sparrow Press, 1968.
Homespun of Oatmeal Gray. New York, Random House, 1970.
Two Sentences. Toronto, Coach House Press, 1970.
Collected Poems, edited by Taylor Stoehr. New York, Random House, 1974.

Other

Art and Social Nature. New York, Vinco, 1946.

Kafka's Prayer. New York, Vanguard Press, 1947.
The Structure of Literature. Chicago, University of Chicago Press, and London, Cambridge University Press, 1954.
Five Years: Thoughts During a Useless Time. New York, Brussel, 1966.
Speaking and Language: Defence of Poetry. New York, Random House, 1972.
Creator Spirit Come! The Literary Essays of Paul Goodman, edited by Taylor Stoehr. New York, Free Life Editions, 1977.

Editor, *Seeds of Liberation.* New York, Braziller, 1964.

*

Bibliography: *Adam and His Work: A Bibliography of Sources by and about Paul Goodman (1911-1972)* by Tom Nicely, Metuchen, New Jersey, Scarecrow Press, 1979.

Critical Studies: *The Literary Rebel* by Kingsley Widmer, Carbondale, Southern Illinois University Press, 1965; *Toward an Effective Critique of American Education* by James E. MacLellan, Philadelphia, Lippincott, 1968; *The Party of Eros: Radical Socialist Thought and the Realm of Freedom* by Richard King, Chapel Hill, University of North Carolina Press, 1972; *Paul Goodman et le reconquête du présent* by Bernard Vincent, Paris, Seuil, 1976; *Paul Goodman* by Kingsley Widmer, Boston, Twayne, 1980.

*   *   *

With some appropriateness, Paul Goodman variously described himself as an "Enlightenment Man of Letters," a "utopian sociologist," and a "conservative anarchist." He functioned as a prolific literary radical-bohemian in New York intellectual circles in the period from around World War II through the American Vietnam War, achieving a national dissident role of considerable notoriety and influence in the dozen years from 1960 to his death. Largely because of an emphatic and distinctive libertarian social criticism and protest role, he remains, in spite of intellectual fracturing and much bad writing, a provocative figure.

His early, and recurring, identification, and work, was as a literary critic and a vanguardist poet and fictionist. The literary studies went in several antithetical directions: minor neo-Aristotelianism (as in his published doctoral thesis, *The Structure of Literature*); rather idiosyncratic psychoanalytic ruminations (as in *Kafka's Prayer,* and various essays on writing therapy); and ragged but earnest defenses of literary humanism against scientism (as in the late *Speaking and Language*). None of this writing was particularly rigorous, subtle, or important. Nor are half a hundred stories and sketches. "The Facts of Life" (an anecdote about Jewish ambivalence), "Our Visit to Niagara" and "A Statue of Goldsmith" (self-satiric personal anecdotes) are probably the best. But most suffer badly from garbled forms and tones, exceptionally infelicitous language, and woodenly ponderous quaintness. So do his five novels, three later combined in the unreadable ruminative-picaresque *The Empire City,* the other two (*Parents' Day* and *Making Do*) crude half-dramatized autobiographies around homosexual dilemmas and collapsing bohemian communities. His many volumes of verse-jottings have a few admirers, less for the awkward imitations in a muddled style of antiquarianism and slang than for the inchoate crude candor of homoerotic and other laments. The dozens of literary volumes probably have only a curiosity value.

Yet the fervent self-identification on the literary margins did provide a distinctive perspective, aesthetically and morally dissident, for the Man of Letters turned social critic. In the mid-1940's the bohemian writer started to combine the aesthetic and anarchist theories (as in the essays in *Art and Social Nature*). This culminated in one of his best books (co-authored with his archi-

tect brother Percival), *Communitas,* a sophisticated primer for thinking about city planning and the deeper issues of "human scale" and aesthetic environment. Besides historically surveying some modern planning issues, *Communitas* ironically juxtaposed three utopias: the city as super-department store of compulsive consumption, as welfarist-competivist society exaggerating the mid-20th century dilemmas, and as the better social-moral choice of humanely aesthetic decentralized urban sub-communities.

Continuing such imaginative sociology, Goodman applied anarchist theory (especially indebted to the Kropotkin tradition) to much of the American scene, as in his fervent but often commonsensical critique of dehumanizing centralism and giganticism in organization, as in *People or Personnel.* In a variety of ragged but often suggestive essays, he also argued for abolishing censorship, banning automobiles from cities, sexually freeing the young, debureaucratizing science, and protesting the war and other political passivity. He propounded more direct democracy, including new rural communities, education in the streets, participatory media, and other de-hierarchicalized initiatives for doing and living.

An early defender of sexual revolutionary Wilhelm Reich, and for some years a lay-therapist, he wrote (with Fritz Perls) a rather abstractly tendentious bio-social psychological theory, *Gestalt Therapy,* a forerunner of the "humanistic psychology" movement. He saw it as part of a larger utopian-pragmatic therapeutics for unblocking an increasingly stultifying society. This was continuous with the earnest polemic which made him famous, *Growing Up Absurd,* a rough essay in pop-sociology in which he adapted an anarchist critique to reformist demands around the social discontents of the American young. Better polemics, such as *Like a Conquered Province,* an attack on American centralism, militarism, and repressive lifestyles, followed in his self-conscious role as prophet and scold of generational discontent.

Probably Goodman's most persuasive and influential radical stance was as libertarian critic of American education. Strikingly, he combined open "progressive" schooling for children (*Compulsory Mis-Education*) with an "intellectualist" argument for autonomous universities (*The Community of Scholars*). With acute insistence, he urged (*New Reformation*) the abolition of high schools and their replacement with youth corps, apprenticeships, public service engagements, and other "natural learning" over bureaucratized indoctrination. He was a major voice and impetus for the "de-schooling society" movement.

Though not a rigorous libertarian theorist, Goodman significantly applied its principle that "voluntary association has yielded most of the values of civilization" to a variety of mid-20th century American institutions. He played a provocative role as a bohemian-artist dissenter and anarchopacifist in the statist warfare-welfare ordering, and left a legacy of some import: the new abolitionism of radically unschooling American evolution; enlarged sexual and other freedom for young, and homoerotic, males; the broad negation of bureaucracy and power and domination in our technocracy; and a revived libertarian advocacy of socioeconomic decentralization, democratic community, and utopian efforts for greater human autonomy.

—Kingsley Widmer

GOUBERT, Pierre (Marie Jean). French historian. Born in Saumur, 25 January 1915. Educated at École Normale d'Instituteurs, Angers, and École Normale Supérieure, Saint-Cloud; Agrégé, 1948; Docteur-ès-lettres, 1958. Married Odette Boulonzac; 2 children. Taught at various secondary schools, 1937-51; Détaché, Centre National de la Recherche Scientifique, 1951-55; Directeur d'Études, l'École Pratique des Hautes Études, from 1955; Professor, Faculté des Lettres, Rennes, 1958; Paris-

Nanterre, 1965; and the Sorbonne, Paris, from 1969. Address: 5 rue Francis-que-Sarcey, 75016 Paris, France.

PUBLICATIONS

History

Familles marchandes sous l'Ancien régime: Les Danse et les Motte, de Beauvais.   Paris, Service d'éditions et de vente des publications de l'Éducation nationale, 1959.
Beauvais et le Beauvaisis de 1600 à 1730: Contribution à l'histoire sociale de la France du XVIIe siècle.   Paris, Service d'éditions et de vente des publications de l'Éducation nationale, 1960; first half as *Cent mille provinciaux au XVIIe siècle, Beauvais et le Beauvaisis de 1600 à 1700*, Paris, Flammarion, 1968.
Louis XIV et vingt millions de Français.   Paris, Fayard, 1966; as *Louis XIV and Twenty Million Frenchmen*, London, Allen Lane, and New York, Pantheon, 1970.
L'Ancien Régime.   Paris, Colin, 2 vols., 1969-73; vol. 1 as *The Ancien Regime: French Society, 1600-1750*, London, Weidenfeld and Nicolson, and New York, Harper, 1973.
Des derniers temps de l'âge seigneurial aux préludes de l'âge industriel (1660-1789), with others.   Paris, Presses Universitaires de France, 1970.
Clio parmi les hommes: Recueil d'articles.   The Hague, Mouton, 1976.
Jane Austen: Étude psychologique de la romancière.   Paris, Presses Universitaires de France, 1976.
La vie quotidienne des paysans français au xviie siècle.   Paris, Hachette, 1982.

Other

Editor, with Michel Denis, *Les Français ont la parole: Cahiers de doléances des États generaux.*   Paris, Julliard, 1964.

*   *   *

Pierre Goubert, a professor at the Sorbonne and a director of studies at the prestigious École Pratique des Hautes Études, is a leading French historian of the early modern period, notably the 17th Century. His works, written in the tradition of the Annales School, demonstrate in addition to the Annales method a versatility and extreme competence with quantitative data, demographic research, and skill in concentrating on a local area. His work is representative of what Traian Stoianovich calls the third generation of the Annales School.

In his masterpiece, *Beauvais et le Beauvaisis*, a lengthy two volume study which is an outgrowth of his doctoral dissertation, Goubert concentrates on a relatively small area, the region of Le Beauvaisis, which contained perhaps 100,000 people and comprised about 150,000 to 200,000 hectares in the 17th century. The city of Beauvais, which is included in this region, had only 13,000-14,000 inhabitants. Although Goubert can be said to be studying the microcosm of 17th-century France he, nevertheless, stated that this work was the "total history" of the Beauvaisis but in a limited period of time. Goubert's work is often compared to the work of his colleague and fellow *annaliste*, Emmanuel Le Roy de Ladurie, who concentrated on the region of Languedoc in his *Les Paysans de Languedoc*. Historians have since disagreed on the question of whether "total history" can be said to apply to a small region. Goubert and Le Roy Ladurie answer in the affirmative.

In his study of the *Beauvais et le Beauvaisis* Goubert charted new paths for historical methodology. Instead of following the traditional approach of applying quantitative methods to prices, he embarked upon an exhaustive study of parish registers and applied quantitative methods to them. He enjoyed a particular success in examining the parish registers of the Parish of Auneuil and its 400 families. The result of this study of parish registers gave us a completely new picture of family life in 17th-century France. What also emerges is a description of the geographic, social, and economic structures of the region as well as their conjunctures.

In reviewing Goubert's masterpiece in the *Annales*, his mentor, Fernand Braudel, although generally approving of the work of his pupil, did not hesitate to criticize certain aspects of Goubert's method, particularly the fact that he restricted his study to such a small area. Nevertheless, he approves of his fellow *annaliste* Pierre Chaunu's observation that the work is written in a style that can be compared only to Michelet, that to quote Chaunu, Goubert "has been able to present the work as one worthy of the great masters of history," and that "all the rules of the historian's craft have been respected." One thing is certain: Goubert's masterpiece touched off a spate of studies on French local history and demography. Not all measured up to the standards set by the master, but they drew inspiration from his seminal work.

Since completing his masterpiece on Beauvais, Goubert has continued to publish in two broad categories: studies of demography and local history and works of *haute vulgarisation* on such subjects as Louis XIV and the French Revolution. In the first he has extended his methodology to become a major authority on demographic techniques and their interpretation. He has collaborated on a multi-volume economic and social history of France as well as a multi-volume collaborative work on French demography. Goubert is also the author of several seminal articles on the importance of local history and of the quantitative methods which should be used in studying it. He is now considered one of the foremost authorities on local history. In the second category of works, namely his work of *haute vulgarisation* (the term is not pejorative in French but refers to works of a broader interest than specialized monographs), the most famous is *Louis XIV and Twenty Million Frenchmen*. In this work he incorporates the ideas and the findings of the Annales School in his analysis of the 17th Century. For Goubert, the average Frenchman is the hero of the century: by concentrating on the life of the ordinary Frenchman, he revises the traditional views of Louis XIV and his times. More recently he has published *La vie quotidienne des paysans français au xviie siècle*, in which he again uses knowledge gleaned from parish registers, memoirs, public and private documents, and statistics collected by computer. "Le grand siècle de Louis XIV," becomes, after Goubert, "Le petit siècle de Louis XIV."

—Walter D. Gray

———————

GRAMSCI, Antonio.   Italian political philosopher.   Born in Ales, Province of Cagliari, Sardinia, in 1891. Studied at the University of Turin, 1911-14 (studies broken off because of ill health). Married Giulia Schucht; 1 son. Worked in local registry office, Ghilarza, 1903-05; made first contacts with the Italian Socialist Party, Turin, 1913; contributor, Socialist paper *Il Grido del Popolo*, from 1914; contributor, Socialist paper *Avanti*, from 1916; helped to organize Russian Soviet delegates' visit to Turin, 1917, and thereafter became increasingly active in the Socialist Party; Co-Founder, and regular contributor, *L'Ordine nuovo*, from 1919; active in Turin Factory Councils, and participated in the occupation of factories during widespread strikes, 1919-20; attended Livorno Congress of the Italian Socialist Party: party split occurred and Communist Party was formed in which he became member of Central Committee, 1921; visited Moscow as member of Executive Council of Communist International, 1922; sent by Comintern to Vienna, 1923; elected Deputy in Veneto constituency and participated in parliamentary secession to Aventine, 1924 (after several months Communist deputies decided to return to Chamber and confront Fascists who had come into power under Mussolini in 1922); visited Moscow for meeting of Comintern Executive Council, and on return to Italy spoke in Chamber against law banning secret associations, 1925; spoke at National Congress of Italian Communist Party, Lyons, France, 1926; arrested in Rome and sent to camp for political prisoners at Ustica, 1926; transferred to prison in Milan, 1927; brought to trial in Rome, condemned to 20 years' imprisonment, and sent to special penal establishment, Bari, 1928; suffered serious hemorrhage, 1931; after further serious illness transferred to private clinic in Formia, 1933, then to Quisiana Clinic in Rome, 1935. *Died* (in Rome) *27 April 1937.*

PUBLICATIONS

Collections

Opere di Antonio Gramsci. Turin, Einaudi, 12 vols., 1947-72.

Political Theory

Lettere del Carcere. Turin, Einaudi, 1947; revised edition, edited by Elsa Fubini and Sergio Caprioglio, 1965 (*Opere*, vol. 1.)
Quaderni del Carcere: vol. 1, *Il Materialismo storico e la filosofia di Benedetto Croce*; vol. 2, *Gli Intellettuali e l'organizzione della cultura*; vol. 3, *Il Risorgimento*; vol. 4, *Note sul Machiavelli, sulla politica e sullo Stato moderno*; vol. 5, *Letteratura e vita nazionale*; vol. 6, *Passato e Presente.* Turin, Einaudi, 1948-51; critical edition as *Quaderno del Carcere: Edizione Critica dell'Istituto Gramsci*, edited by Valentino Gerratana, Turin, Einaudi, 4 vols., 1975. (*Opere*, vols. 2-7.)
L'Ordine Nuovo (1919-1920). Turin, Einaudi, 1955. (*Opere*, vol. 9.)
The Open Marxism of Antonio Gramsci (selection translated from *Quaderni del Carcere*, vol. 1). New York, Cameron Associates, 1957.
Scritti Giovanili 1914-1918. Turin, Einaudi, 1958. (*Opere*, vol. 8.)
The Modern Prince and Other Writings (limited selection translated from *Quaderno del Carcere*, vols. 1, 2 and 4). New York, International Publishers, 1959.
Sotto la Mole 1916-1920. Turin, Einaudi, 1960. (*Opere*, vol. 10.)
La Questione Meridionale (selected writings on problem of Southern Italy). Rome, Riuniti, 1966.
Scritti Politici (selected political writings), edited by Paolo Spriano. Rome, Riuniti, 1967.
Socialismo e Fascismo; L'Ordine Nuovo 1921-1922. Turin, Einaudi, 1967. (*Opere*, vol. 11.)
Scritti 1915-1921. Milan, Quaderni de Il Corpo, 1968.
La Costruzione del Partito Comunista 1923-1926. Turin, Einaudi, 1971. (*Opere*, vol. 12.)
Selections from the Prison Notebooks of Antonio Gramsci (selection translated from *Quaderni del Carcere*), edited by Q. Hoare and G.N. Smith. New York, International Publishers, 1971.
Letters from Prison (selection translated from *Lettere del Carcere*), edited by Lynne Lawner. New York, Harper Colophon, 1973.
History, Philosophy and Culture in the Young Gramsci (selection of translated articles from 1914-1918), edited by P. Cavalcanti and P. Piccone. St. Louis, Telos, 1975.
Selections from Political Writings: vol. 1, *1910-1920*; vol. 2, *1921-26*, edited by Q. Hoare. New York, International Publishers, 1977-78.

*

Critical Studies: *Antonio Gramsci and the Origins of Italian Communism* by J.M. Cammett, Stanford, California, Stanford University Press, 1967; *Antonio Gramsci: Towards an Intellectual Biography* by A. Davidson, Atlantic Highlands, New Jersey, Humanities Press, 1977; *Gramsci and Marxist Theory*, edited by C. Mouffe, London, Routledge, 1979; *Gramsci and the State* by Christine Buci-Glucksmann, London, Lawrence and Wishart, 1980; *Hegemony and Revolution: Antonio Gramsci's Political and Cultural Theory* by W.L. Adamson, Berkeley, University of California Press, 1980.

*   *   *

Antonio Gramsci's great intellectual accomplishments cannot be fully understood independent from his commitment to political struggle. He is admired by many people specifically because his life and work are classic examples of action which is informed by theory (praxis). The title of his most famous work, *Prison Notebooks* (*Quaderni del Carcere*) dramatically informs us what the consequences of political conviction, and action, can be. While in a fascist prison (1926-1937), Gramsci wrote that the intellectual's error lies in thinking that one can know without understanding, or without feeling and passion. Gramsci is considered important, and attractive, by Western Marxists, among others, because of his defense of human freedom in a world that seemingly has been dominated by various kinds of determinism.

Gramsci's epistemology is Hegelian: knowing is never merely a passive reflection of the given, but instead is an act which can change the given. His training in idealist philosophy, including a mastery of Croce, caused him to believe in the tenacious will of man. Unlike deterministic Marxists, who have subscribed to iron laws of economic development, Gramsci argued that individuals can, and do, act alone and collectively in order to make their own history. Gramsci posits the existence of man as an actor—one who can understand the data which comprise the physical and social worlds, and who can then act in a politically effective manner to create an order which makes the good and just life possible. Although conscious human intervention is at the center of Gramsci's thought, the actor(s) does not create from nothing, nor can he move in a void. Men and women make history, but not under conditions of their choosing. Gramsci's historical actor studies in order to establish the facts of a particular society and period in order to discern what the opportunities are for transformation. As Gramsci said: socialism will not arrive in the shape of a royal decree, countersigned by two ministers.

In his insistence that man was a product of history, and not merely of physical nature, Gramsci belonged to an Italian tradition going at least as far back as Giambattista Vico. Gramsci wrote to his son that the boy should like the study of history because it was an account of how humanity has struggled for a better life. For Gramsci, Marxism was a philosophy of praxis, not an unerring insight into immutable laws. *La Città futura* is a summary of his university experiences in Turin and within the socialist movement. It proclaims a belief in: the power of the will; the ability dialectically to analyze physical and social reality; and man's ability to act collectively in order to realize his legitimate plans. The Italian Marxist agreed with Lenin that it was possible to achieve socialism without waiting for a bourgeois revolution and a long period of bourgeois hegemony.

Idealist philosophy had taught Gramsci that seemingly utopian hopes could be converted into reality; i.e., the discrepancy between painful necessity (is), and a normative (ought) could be bridged. As a Marxist, Gramsci went beyond idealism; moreover, in his role of a political activist and leader he sought to give his philosophical insight political body. Gramsci's historical actor, who has the intellectual ability to recognize the discrepancy between is and ought, would act through agencies of the party, and the factory councils (*consigli di fabrica*).

It is to the Italian soviets, or *consigli*, that we turn in our description and analysis of Gramsci's importance. Gramsci believed that the party could serve as an agent of the working-class, but that the workers (*operai*) themselves were the embodiment of revolutionary transformation. Gramsci's central insight was that all workers—all of the active persons in the society—should become masters of production. The *consigli di operai* were conceptualized and formed to take in all of the workers, not just the skilled ones, in order to educate and organize the whole proletariat. The workers would become aware of their powers and responsibilities as historical actors through their involvement in the *consigli*. Gramsci, and the other young communists, who edited *L'Ordine nuovo* provided theoretical leadership for the worker councils within the developed industrial factories of Turin. The relationship between the intellectuals of *L'Ordine nuovo* and their worker (*operai*) allies is a classic example of praxis: Gramsci and his comrades provided theoretical leadership on a familiar and day-to-day basis for the Turin workers; furthermore, the action outcomes caused the *ordinovisti* to rethink the fluid series of obstacles which they and their allies confronted. The *consigli* were not unions which fought for bread and butter issues, but were instead organizations wherein the workers were to learn how to become the ruling class. Gramsci was convinced that the communist worker would relate to the factory, and other work sites, in the same way that the bourgeois citizen related to the electoral district. The term comrade would replace citizen, and the *consigli* would replace the state (*stato dei consigli*).

In the meantime, the *consigli* were to help prepare workers to become autonomous producers who were aware of their position in the productive process. Gramsci believed that only through education within the *consigli*, the movement, and the party would workers attain the maturity to seize and then to exercise power. He knew that the workers would have to develop a *Weltanschauung* of their own, or else they would be relegated to living within bourgeois hegemony.

Because Gramsci was Italian and did his early work in highly industrialized Turin, a city which already had a long history of skilled and radical workers, he came to realize that a frontal attack on the state (as was done in Russia) was not the proper strategy for victory. Gramsci described the state in the West as an outer ditch behind which there stands a powerful system of fortresses and earthworks. The bourgeois civilization which controlled the workers, and other subaltern classes, could do so because its leaders controlled the very definitions of what was considered real, commonsensical, good, etc. Bourgeois hegemony meant that a class could rule a highly developed society without the flagrant, or regular, use of naked force. Hegemonic classes lead their allies and dominate their enemies. Control of the economic apparatus was in bourgeois, or capitalist, hands, of course; however, hegemony is more than economic control. Gramsci has taught us that hegemony (*egemonia*) consists of a group or class creating a state of affairs in which their leadership and privileged positions seem natural. It consists too of ways of living, thinking, speaking, habits, hopes, fears, and underlying assumptions.

Gramsci's originality as a Marxist lies in his conception of bourgeois rule in which the real strength is not to be found in violence, or the coerciveness of state machinery, but in the acceptance by the ruled subaltern groups, and classes, of a system of meanings and habit which serves the interests of a powerful few. Gramsci sought to understand how the rulers accomplished this feat: how they made their domination seem commonsensical and seemingly anchored to a preordained universal nature of things. He also wished to learn how historical actors, in this case the proletariat, could come to recognize this hegemony, resist it, defeat it, and then build a just social order comprising a new world view, *lingua franca*, collective symbols, and common meanings.

Antonio Gramsci saw Marxism as the most recent synthesis of the Western tradition. His goal can be described as securing the consummation of what this tradition has been aiming for: the free social person described by Marx, who can be traced back through the best of Christian and Greek civilizations. Gramsci believed that a communist society was needed in the 20th century

to realize this old Western promise. This realization would be made possible by the abolition of class divisions based upon greatly unequal wealth and economic power—divisions which have prevented men and women from becoming human beings in the richest and most complete sense of the term.

—Richard A. Brosio

GRICE, H.P. American philosopher. Professor Emeritus of Philosophy, University of California, Berkeley. Address: Department of Philosophy, University of California, Berkeley, California, U.S.A. *Died August 1988*

PUBLICATIONS

Philosophy

Various essays, including

"Utterer's Meaning, Sentence-Meaning, and Word-Meaning," in *Foundations of Language* (Dordrecht, Netherlands), 4, 1968; reprinted in *The Philosophy of Language*, edited by John Searle. London, Oxford University Press, 1971.
"Vacuous Names," in *Words and Objections: Essays on the Work of W.V. Quine*, edited by Donald Davidson and Jaakko Hintikka. Dordrecht, Netherlands, Reidel, 1969.

*

Critical Studies: "Professor Grice's Theory of Meaning" by Alfred F. MacKay, in *Mind* (Oxford), 81, 1972; "Meaning and Intention: An Examination of Grice's Views" by Max Black, in *New Literary History* (Charlottesville, Virginia), 4, 1973.

*   *   *

H.P. Grice's work aims at a philosophy of language. His investigations place speech among other forms of human action, and the various aspects of language, including its chief element "meaning," are initially examined as particular occurrences; their time-less aspects to be formulated only at a later stage. Philosophers usually divide meanings into two types: natural meanings (signals) and nonnatural ones. An example of the former: "The spots on his skin mean he has measles (the spots are symptoms of measles)"; of the latter: "The three rings of the bell mean the bus is full." Nonnatural meanings, we commonly say, are based on convention in some sense, but Grice chooses to avoid this concept at the start. Another difference between the two types of meanings is that with regard to nonnatural meanings, we can say "The three rings mean the bus is full, but in fact it isn't; the conductor made a mistake;" that is, "X means that P" need not entail P. This cannot be with natural meanings. (In the discussion, there are several other differences, here omitted.) Grice confines further discussion to nonnatural meanings. On his account, "A meant something by X" is roughly equivalent to "A intended the utterance of X to produce some effect in the audience by means of the recognition of this intention." To ask what A meant is to ask for a specification of the intended effect; and, as a first shot, Grice suggests that the effect be a "belief that such-and-such is the case."

The above formulation in an essay of 1957 received a great deal of attention and exerted much influence. One line of criticism was evoked by the account's intensionality, for there is an irreducible, nonpublic aspect to intentions, and the definition seems circular, for the "meanings" we want to have clarified have to do just with the intention of a speaker—his understanding of what e said. Grice answered that one at least had to start somewhere with a free hand in forming a theory. And "intensionality seems to be embedded in the very foundation" of the theory of language. Moreover, he was not "sympathetic towards my methological policy" which ruled out intensional terms altogether at the start. Another line of comment: a listener need not believe or act as a consequence of what was said to him, even though he grasped the words addressed to him and caught the speaker's intention to have him believe or do what the speaker said or commanded. Clearly the connection in Grice's account between the intention and the uptake is too close, for he identifies the apprehension of the speaker's meaning with the listener's belief (or action). As a result of this criticism, in an essay published in 1968, "the intended effect of the utterance" becomes the fact that 'the hearer should think the speaker believed something (wants something done, etc.)."

One can begin to appreciate the force of Grice's account of "meaning" by taking note of his later contributions to the on-going discussion about the varieties of meaning. Since the middle of the last century, logicians have been working at the varieties of logical connections—implies, materially implies, yields, entails, equivalence and synonymy. In less formal contexts, conversational ploys convey meanings indirectly in innuendo and suggestion. Grice called these last examples "implicatures" and discussed them in his 1967 William James Lectures at Harvard University, "Logic and Conversation." The give-and-take of conversations is guided by the relevance of contributions, and each utterance has a point. The rule of relevance shows the implicit discipline of the "Principle of Cooperation": that each speaker make his contribution as it is required at the stage of the contribution, to fit the accepted purpose and direction of the talk exchange. (Talking is a special case of purposive and thus rational behavior, and analogous principles work in nonverbal contexts.) The Cooperative Principle is divided into four maxims which, in the light of traditional logic and Kant's table of judgments, Grice labels the maxims of quantity, quality, relation and manner: *Quantity*: (1) Make your contribution as informative as required; (2) Do not make your contribution more informative than required; *Quality*: First stated as a supermaxim, "Try to make your contribution one that is true;" then divided into two sub-maxims: (1) Do not say what you know to be false; (2) Do not say that for which you lack adequate evidence; *Relation*: Be relevant. (In operation, this maxim tends to fuse with the cooperative principle itself); *Manner*: Stated as a supermaxim, "Be perspicuous" with four, and possibly more, sub-maxims: (1) Avoid obscurity of expression; (2) Avoid ambiguity; (3) Be brief (avoid unnecessary prolixity); (4) Be orderly.

A conversation proceeds smoothly because these maxims are implicitly operative. Speakers, for example, do not interrupt or change the topic without appropriate signaling, nor should they ramble on or say obscure or unsuitable things. When a maxim is violated, this fact is first noticed as a vague misgiving, but on diagnosis, it reduces to one of four kinds: (1) a simple mistake, the speaker being misinformed, confused, unaware of a damaging ambiguity, etc.; (2) a conflict in maxims, the speaker, for example, in order to avoid a lie, forced to take a more circuitous approach to the topic than a listener might wish—or, (3) a speaker may simply opt out: e.g., refuse to say anything, pretend incomprehension, say "no comment", etc.; or (4) He may flout a maxim, that is, blatantly violate it, the obviousness signalizing to the listener his awareness of the violation of the maxim and his intention to have the listener know that he is aware of it. The point of such utterances follows from the shared awareness that what is said in one plain sense of "say" (a sense that Grice leaves inexplicit) but evolved indirectly. An example: X is told that Y got the job he wanted for which his qualifications were known to be mixed. X says, "Y's new employer must be a philanthropist." The comment seems irrelevant, not being about Y's new job. Yet we

readily understand the negative assessment of Y contained in the retort. To formulate the connection, a listener asks what must be the case if the retort is to have point. Philanthropists perform acts of charity and X *presupposes* that to hire Y is to do just that. He believes that Y's abilities for the job are less than mixed; his employer is wasting money since Y is a loser. Still, if X were later accused by Y of having *said* that he was unfit for the job, X can reply that he merely said the new employer must be a philanthropist (a bit disingenuous but common enough, for this is the use of innuendo in everyday talk). Implicatures in this manner exploit the maxims, and Grice's method explicitly shows us the connection of what is "said" and what is implicated. At the same time, we see that we can make such catty remarks only by flouting the maxim and that no direct way will do. Thus implicatures cannot be detached from what is said and put in some other way.

Grice's typology of implicatures is varied and include such topics as metaphor, meiosis, hyperbole, deflation, irony and certain sorts of stresses in speech. The four maxims order this diversity. Whether the logic of conversation is need to supplement the concepts of illocution and perlocution in speech act theory (e.g., as developed by John Searle) is still an open issue. Linguists and related specialists have applied the concept of implicature to their study of everyday semantics and pragmatics, on topics such as satire, literary and narrative discourse and fiction. Success in these further areas will go a long way in deciding questions about the status of the logic of conversation.

—Albert Tsugawa

GROPIUS, Walter. American architect. Born in Berlin, Germany, 18 May 1883; emigrated to England, 1934; emigrated to the United States, 1937. Studied at the Humanistisches Gymnasium, Berlin, 1903; Technische Hochschule, Munich 1903-04; and Technische Hochschule, Charlottenburg, Berlin, 1905-07. Served as an officer in the German Army, 1904-05, 1914-18: Iron Cross (first and second class); Bavarian Military Medal; Royal Austrian Decoration. Married Alma Schindler Mahler (widow of the composer) in 1916 (divorced), 1 daughter; married Ilse Frank in 1923, 1 daughter. Worked in the office of the architects Solf and Wichards, Berlin, 1904; travelled in Europe, 1906-07; Chief Assistant in the office of the architect Peter Behrens, Berlin, 1907-10; in private practice, Berlin, 1910-14; Director, Grand Ducal Academy of Arts, Wiemar, and Grand Ducal Saxon School of Applied Arts, Wiemar, 1915-19; merged the two schools under the name Das Staatliche Bauhaus, 1919: Director of the Bauhaus at Weimar, 1919-25, and Dessau, 1925-28; in private practice, Berlin, 1928-33; in partnership with E. Maxwell Fry, London, 1934-36, and with Marcel Breuer, Cambridge, Massachusetts, 1937-41; Founder, and Partner with seven associates, in TAC: The Architects' Collaborative, Cambridge, 1945-69. Professor of Architecture, 1937-52, Chairman of the Department of Architecture, 1938-52, and Professor Emeritus, 1952-69, Graduate School of Design, Harvard University, Cambridge. Founder Member and President, 1928, and Vice-President, 1929-57, CIAM (Congrès Internationaux d'Architecture Moderne); Vice-President, Institute of Sociology, London, 1937. Recipient: Gold Medal, *World's Fair*, Ghent, 1913; First Prize, Dammerstock District Development Competition, Karlsruhe, 1928; First Prize, Spandau-Haselhorst Experimental District Competition, Berlin, 1929; Gold Medal of Honor, The Architectural League of New York, 1951; Grand Prix d'Architecture, Sao Paulo, 1953; Royal Gold Medal, Royal Institute of British Architects, London, 1956; Hanseatic Goethe Prize, University of Hamburg, 1956; Ernst Reuter Medal, City of Berlin, 1957; Gold Medal, American Institute of Architects, 1959; Grand State Professor of Architecture Award, Germany, 1960; Prince Albert Gold Medal, Royal Society of Arts, London, 1961;

Goethe Prize, Frankfurt, 1961; Kaufmann International Design Award, 1961; Cornelius Gurlitt Medal, German Academy for City and Regional Planning, 1962. Honorary M.A.: Harvard University, 1942. Honorary doctorate: Technische Hochschule, Hannover, 1929; Western Reserve University, Cleveland, 1951; Harvard University, 1953; North Carolina State College, Raleigh, 1953; University of Sydney, 1954; University of Brazil, 1955; Pratt Institute, New York, 1961; Columbia University, New York, 1961; Williams College, Williamstown, Massachusetts, 1963; Free University of Berlin, 1963. Fellow, American Institute of Architects, 1954; Member, National Institute of Arts and Letters; Associate, National Academy of Design, 1967. Honorary Member, Royal Institute of British Architects, London, 1937; Honorary Fellow, Royal Society of Arts, London, 1946; Fellow of the Society of Industrial Artists and Designers, London, 1950; Honorary Senator, Hochschule für Bildende Künste, Berlin, 1962; Honorary Royal Academician, London, 1967. Grand Cross of Merit with Star, Germany, 1958. *Died* (in Boston) *5 July 1969.*

PUBLICATIONS

Architecture

Idee und Aufbau des Staatlichen Bauhauses. Weimar, Bauhaus, 1923.
Die Bühne im Bauhaus. Munich, Langen, 1924.
Neue Arbeiten der Bauhauswerkstätten, with L. Moholy-Nagy. Munich, Langer, 1925.
Internationale Architektur. Munich, Langer, 1925.
Bauhausbauten, Dessau. Munich, Langer, 1930.
The New Architecture and the Bauhaus. London, Faber, 1935; Boston, Bradford, n.d.
Rebuilding Our Communities (lecture). Chicago, P. Theobald, 1945.
The Scope of Total Architecture. New York, Harper, 1955; London, Allen and Unwin, 1956.
Arquitectura y Planeamiento. Buenos Aires, Ediciónes Infinito, 1958.
Katsura: Tradition and Creation in Japanese Architecture, with others. New Haven, Connecticut, Yale University Press, 1960.
Apollo in der Demokratie. Mainz, Kupferberg, 1967; as *Apollo in the Democracy: The Cultural Obligation of the Artist,* edited by Ilse Gropius, New York, McGraw-Hill, 1968.
The Vertical City (lecture). Urbana, University of Illinois Press, 1968.

Other

Editor, with others, *Bauhaus, 1919-1928.* New York, Museum of Modern Art, 1938.
Editor, *The Architects' Collaborative 1945-1967.* New York, Architectural Book Publishing Company, and London, Tiranti, 1966.

*

Critical Studies: *Walter Gropius: Work and Teamwork* by Sigfried Giedion, New York, Reinhold, 1954; *The Synthetic Vision of Walter Gropius* by Gilbert Herbert, Johannesburg, South Africa, Witwatersrand University Press, 1959; *Walter Gropius* by James Morton Fitch, New York, Braziller, 1960; *Walter Gropius and the Creation of the Bauhaus in Wiemar: The Ideals and Artistic Theories of Its Founding Years* by Marcel Franciscono, Urbana, University of Illinois Press, 1971.

*

For a full listing of Gropius' buildings, projects and exhibitions, see *Contemporary Architects,* edited by Muriel Emanuel, London, Macmillan, and New York, St. Martin's Press, 1980.

*   *   *

Walter Gropius made a profound impact on modern architecture both through his work as a practising architect and, more importantly, through his work as a theorist and teacher.

Like Le Corbusier, Gropius worked as an assistant to Peter Behrens and, at an early stage in his career, developed an unswerving commitment to the realization of the practical and aesthetic potential of the new building materials and construction methods made possible by modern technology. This commitment is evident in his design for the Fagus Shoe Factory at Alfeld-an-der-Leine (1911), which was designed in co-operation with Adolph Meyer shortly after Gropius had established his independent architectural practice in Berlin. A steel frame forms the structural support for the building, while the external walls are clearly recognized as non-structural in nature. Consisting of a sheathing of plate glass surfaces which continue without interruption around the corner supports, the transparent walls admit a maximum of light and reduce the distinction between indoor and outdoor spaces. The style of the structure is free of any historicism and derives instead from Gropius' utilization of the visual effects made possible by industrial processes and from his belief that architecture should be treated as an empirical science free from the personal idiosyncrasies of a single designer. Gropius collaborated with Meyer again in the designs for a machine workshop and administration building for the *Werkbund Exhibition* at Cologne in 1914. Like their predecessor, these buildings employed a steel frame supporting a system of continuous fenestration.

Profound as the impact on modern architecture of these early works proved to be, Gropius was to wield an even greater influence through his appointment in 1915 as director of two schools of art in Weimar, soon united to form the Bauhaus. As architect, Gropius designed a four-story workshop which consisted of a glass screen wrapped around a post and slab structure; for decades it was to remain one of the most progressive examples of the transparent curtain wall. As director, Gropius welcomed representatives of all the arts, including painters, printmakers, technicians, artisans and craftsmen, as well as architects. As teacher, he urged the Bauhaus participants first to find forms of art appropriate to the context of contemporary life; second, to exploit the aesthetic possibilities of industrial production; and third, to seek an approach that endowed every man-made object with artistic value and that united all objects into a "total art." The Bauhaus, under Gropius' leadership, became a creative educational institution without parallel. Its faculty included Joseph Albers, Marcel Breuer, Lyonel Feininger, Wassily Kandinsky, Paul Klee, Adolph Meyer and Laszlo Moholy-Nagy. While stressing the importance of collaboration, Gropius also encouraged variety, dissent and individual expression.

Adverse public reaction to avant-garde art forced Gropius to resign from the Bauhaus in 1928. Six years later, he emigrated from Germany, settled briefly in England, then moved to the United States. Still motivated by his belief in teamwork, Gropius formed The Architects Collaborative (TAC) with a group of former students and younger partners. TAC was responsible for such major projects as the Harvard University Graduate Center, Temple Oheb Shalom in Baltimore, and the Pam Am Building in New York City. In addition, Gropius designed private residences, which demonstrate the consistency of his concerns. A housing project designed with Adolph Meyer in 1922-23 explores the possibility of utilizing prefabricated standardized building units that could be mass-produced in factories with speed and economy but assembled at the site according to individual family needs. The Aluminium City housing estate in Pittsburgh (1943) designed with Marcel Breuer, places blocks of terrace houses in irregular terrain in order to permit maximum sunlight in domestic buildings.

Innovative in his use of materials developed by modern technology and progressive in his acceptance of the physical forms and aesthetic effects resulting from industrial processes, Gropius was an architect motivated by a lofty social vision. In his practice and in his teaching, he called for the development of a modern architectural style that would be more than the expression of the individual taste of contemporary architects, and he urged the creation of architectural forms that would achieve a cultural integration between the aesthetic, social and economic needs of a community. During his years at the Bauhaus and later in America, Gropius came as close as has been possible in the 20th century to realizing these ideals.

—Linnea H. Wren

GUEVARA, "Che."   Argentinian revolutionary.   Born Ernesto Guevara Serna in Rosario, Argentina, 14 June 1928. Studied at the University of Buenos Aires, M.D. 1953. Married Hilda Gadea (marriage dissolved); married Aleida March in 1959; 3 children. Political observer and activist in Bolivia, Guatemala and Mexico, 1953-55; joined Fidel Castro and fought in the Cuban Revolution, 1956-59; Director, National Bank of Cuba, 1959, then Ministry of Industry, 1961; left Cuba to engage in revolutionary activities in Bolivia, 1965. *Died* (captured and shot by Bolivian forces at La Higuera, Bolivia) *9 October 1967.*

PUBLICATIONS

Collections

Obras completas.   Buenos Aires, Ediciónes de la Plata, 1968.
Venceremos!: The Speeches and Writings of Che Guevara, edited by John Gerassi.   New York, Macmillan, and London, Weidenfeld and Nicolson, 1968.
Obras 1957-1967.   Havana, Casa de las Americas, 2 vols., 1970.
Escritos y Discursos.   Havana, Editorial de Ciencias Sociales, 9 vols., 1977.

Political Theory

La Guerra de guerrillas (training manual).   Havana, Cuban Government, 1960; as *Guerrilla Warfare,* New York, Monthly Review Press, 1961.
Pasajes de la Guerra Revolucionaria.   Havana, Unión de Escritores y Artistas de Cuba, 1963; as *Reminiscences of the Cuban Revolutionary War,* New York, Monthly Review Press, and London, Allen and Unwin, 1968.
El socialismo y el hombre en Cuba.   Havana, Ediciónes R, 1965; as *Socialism and Man,* New York, Young Socialist Alliance, and London, Stage 1, 1968.
Che Guevara Speaks, edited by George Lanvan.   New York, Grove, 1967.
Diaria de Che en Bolivia.   Havana, Instituto del Libro, 1968; as *Diary of Che Guevara,* edited by Robert Scheer, New York, Bantam, 1968; as *Bolivian Diary of Ernesto "Che" Guevara,* London, Lorrimer, 1968.
Che Guevara on Revolution: A Documentary Overview, edited by Jay Mallin.   Coral Gables, Florida, University of Miami Press, 1969.
Che Guevara (selected works).   Havana, Instituto del Libro, 1969.
Che: Selected Works of Ernesto Guevara, edited by Rolando Bonachea and Nelson P. Valdes.   Cambridge, Massachusetts, and London, MIT Press, 1970 (contains a bibliography).

*

Critical Studies: *Che: The Making of a Legend* by Martin Ebon, New York, Universe, 1969; *Che Guevara* by Andrew Sinclair, New York, Viking Press, 1970; *The Marxism of Che Guevara: Philosophy, Economics and Revolutionary Warfare* by Michael

Lowy, New York and London, Monthly Review Press, 1973; *The Latin American Revolution* by Donald C. Hodges, New York, Morrow, 1974; *The Legacy of Che Guevara,* edited by Donald C. Hodges, London, Thames and Hudson, 1977.

*   *   *

Che Guevara has had a significant impact on 20th century thought and politics both as a revolutionary theorist and political activist. His theoretical writings present a strongly activist type of Third World Marxism, quite different from the orthodox Marxism dominant in Soviet or Chinese Communism and most Marxist-Leninist political movements. Che's major theoretical writings emphasize revolutionary will and the subjective factors of revolutionary consciousness. There are uncanny similarities to the thought of Herbert Marcuse, which may in part help explain Che's popularity with sectors of the New Left influenced by Marcuse. For instance, Che insists that revolutionary struggle has "the happiness of the people as the basis of our struggle."

Like Marcuse, Che argued that the goal of socialism is to create new, more complete human beings and a new way of life. In his most famous theoretical article, "Notes on Man and Socialism in Cuba," Che argues that "to build communism, you must build new men as well as the new economic base." He puts special emphasis on the need for moral education and the need to create a society where moral incentives would replace material incentives as forces which motivate human action. Che claims that the goal of socialism is the overcoming of alienation and that socialist societies must create institutions that would make possible the creation of more complete and more developed human beings. This goal requires developing new technologies, a new organization of labor, new political institutions, and a new culture. About this kind of socialism he asserts: "This is not a matter of how many pounds of meat one might be able to eat, nor of how many times a year someone can go to the beach, nor how many ornaments from abroad you might be able to buy with present salaries. What is really involved is that the individual feels more complete, with much more internal richness and much more responsibility."

After his presentation of his vision of socialism, quite similar to the concept of socialism in the early Marx, Che makes the surprising claim that "the true revolutionary is guided by a great feeling of love." Like Mao, Che writes constantly of the need for revolutionaries to serve the people, to join and work with popular forces, and to struggle actively on the people's behalf. However, in addition to this stream of revolutionary humanism and idealism in his thought, there is also a strong current of "revolutionary realism." Che wrote many articles and speeches on tactics of guerilla warfare and constantly defended armed struggle and revolutionary war as the primary force in eliminating imperialism on a world-wide scale. In his last article, "Vietnam and World Struggle," Che outlined his global, internationalist, anti-imperialist perspective and stressed the dual role of hate and love, revolutionary will and proletarian internationalism as the key forces in producing revolutionary struggle.

Although nine volumes of published writings are collected in the Cuban edition of Che's *Escritos y Discursos,* and while translations of his writings appear in every major language, Che's continued impact on contemporary thought and politics probably stems as much from his image as a revolutionary internationalist as from his writings or speeches. As a revolutionary icon, Che represents the selfless, devoted revolutionary internationalist. Born in Argentina, he involved himself in the revolutionary politics of several Latin American countries, most notably the Cuban revolution, in which he became the closest associate of Fidel Castro and one of the most powerful figures in the Cuban government. In addition, Che travelled extensively through Africa and died in a struggle in Boliva. Third World revolutionary governments hold Che up to their citizens and youth as a model of the new socialist man, and thus he has been immortalized as the model of the revolutionary activist.

—Douglas Kellner

HABERMAS, Jürgen. German social scientist. Born in Dusseldorf, 18 June 1929. Studied at the University of Göttingen; University of Bonn, Ph.D. 1954; University of Marburg, 1961. Married Ute Wesselhoeft in 1955; 3 children. Lecturer in Philosophy, University of Heidelberg, 1962-64; Professor of Philosophy and Sociology, 1964-71, and since 1974 Honorary Professor, University of Frankfurt; Director, Max-Planck-Institut zur Erforschung der Lebensdingungen der wissenschaftlich-technischen Welt, Starnberg, West Germany, 1971-82; resumed teaching at Frankfurt, 1983. Recipient: Hegel Prize, Stuttgart, 1974; Sigmund Freud Prize, 1976. Address: Riemerschmidstrasse 7, 8130 Starnberg, West Germany.

PUBLICATIONS

Philosophy and Social Theory

Das Absolut und die Geschichte: Von der Zwiespaltigkeit in Schellings Denken. Bonn, University of Bonn, 1954.
Student und Politik, with others. Neuwied, Luchterhand, 1961.
Strukturwandel der Offentlichkeit. Neuwied, Luchterhand, 1962.
Theorie und Praxis (essays). Neuwied, Luchterhand, 1963; revised and expanded edition, Frankfurt, Suhrkamp, 1971; abridged as *Theory and Practice*, Boston, Beacon Press, 1973; London, Heinemann, 1974.
Zur Logik der Sozialwissenschaften. Tübingen, Siebeck und Mohr, 1967; revised and with related essays, Frankfurt, Suhrkamp, 1970.
Erkenntnis und Interesse. Frankfurt, Suhrkamp, 1968; as *Knowledge and Human Interests*, London, Heinemann, and Boston, Beacon Press, 1971.
Technik und Wissenschaft als "Ideologie" (essays). Frankfurt, Suhrkamp, 1968; selected essays in *Toward a Rational Society*, 1970.
Protestbewegung und Hochschulreform (essays). Frankfurt, Suhrkamp, 1969; selected essays in *Toward a Rational Society*, 1970.
Arbeit, Erkenntnis, Fortschritt (essays). Amsterdam, Verlag de Munter, 1970.
Toward a Rational Society: Student Protest, Science and Politics (translations of essays written in the 1960's). Boston, Beacon Press, 1970; London, Heinemann, 1971.
Theorie der Gesellschaft oder Sozialtechnologie: Was Leistet die Systemforschung?, with Niklas Luhmann. Frankfurt, Suhrkamp, 1971.
Philosophisch-politische Profile (essays). Frankfurt, Suhrkamp, 1971.
Legitimationsprobleme im Spätkapitalismus. Frankfurt, Suhrkamp, 1973; as *Legitimation Crisis*, London, Heinemann, and Boston, Beacon Press, 1976.
Kultur und Kritik (essays). Frankfurt, Suhrkamp, 1973.
Zwei Reden, with Dieter Henrich. Frankfurt, Suhrkamp, 1974.
Zur Rekonstruktion des historischen Materialismus (essays). Frankfurt, Suhrkamp, 1976; selected essays in *Communication and the Evolution of Society*, 1979.
Communication and the Evolution of Society (translations of essays). London, Heinemann, and Boston, Beacon Press, 1979.

Theorie des kommunikatives Handelns I-II. Frankfurt, Suhrkamp, 1982.

*

Critical Studies: *The Critical Theory of Jürgen Habermas* by Thomas McCarthy, Cambridge, Massachusetts, MIT Press, and London, Hutchinson, 1978; *Introduction to Critical Theory: Horkheimer to Habermas* by David Held, London, Hutchinson, 1980; *Habermas: Critical Debates*, edited by John B. Thompson and David Held, Cambridge, Massachusetts, MIT Press, and London, Macmillan, 1982.

*   *   *

Jürgen Habermas, German philosopher and social scientist, is presently the most important and influential representative of the so-called Frankfurter-School of critical theory within philosophy.

His first work to break new ground was *Strukturwandel der Offentlichkeit*, in which Habermas studies the development of the idea of public opinion and democratic will-formation. He shows that these ideas are contemporary with the rise of capitalism (late 18th and 19th centuries) and that the liberalistic idea of democracy is modelled on the relation between buyer and seller in the market. Despite its origin and despite the fact that political discussion never became a reality throughout society, since its participants were members of the ruling classes, Habermas nevertheless regards public opinion as a norm for political will-formation and an anticipation of a good society. Habermas shows furthermore that these ideas, central to the enlightenment, degenerate in modern times, because political decisions become the result of compromise between powerful interests (e.g., organizations) and not the outcome of rational discussion, and because the media (e.g., the press) no longer serve informative and argumentative purposes but purposes of commercial interests and entertainment.

In his major work, *Erkenntnis und Interesse*, Habermas undertakes a study of the presuppositions and foundations of knowledge, claiming that different types of scientific inquiry are linked with different kinds of human interests. He distinguishes between three types of scientific inquiry: 1) The *empirical-analytic* (e.g., physics) aiming at the formulation of general laws that can lead to reliable predictions. The interest linked with this kind of inquiry is called *technical*: this attitude implies an objectification of the object of study in order to manipulate it according to the goals of *purpose-rational action*. The natural sciences are bound up with the technical interest of control. 2) The *historical-hermeneutic* sciences analysing texts and human action. Since this approach involves understanding communicative action, an analysis of the agent's self-understanding and of the norms and communicative rules according to which they act is necessary. The interest that guides this type of inquiry is called *practical* (cf. Kant). 3) The so-called *critically oriented sciences* and *philosophy* are or ought to be guided by the *emancipatory interest*. Among these sciences Habermas mentions psychoanalysis and the critique of ideology (cf. Marx). Their objective is to lay bare the forces and private interests that distort communication and the possibility of reaching a true consensus not disturbed by outer and inner compulsion.

Habermas's concept of interest has a quasi-transcendental status since the three interests express three aspects of man's relation to his natural and social environment and to their development through history. The claim that there exists a quasi-transcendental relation between knowledge and interest is directed against the ideal of objectivism and value-neutrality of positivism. This critique, however, does not imply either a rejection of the empirical analytic inquiry as such or a general technophobia. It is an attempt to show the limits of the applicability of this type of inquiry and an attack of the use of instrumental rationality (e.g., technocratic solutions) within the social sciences and within politics (cf. the book *Technik und Wissenschaft als Ideologie* and his discussion with the sociologist N. Luhmann in *Theorie der Gesellschaft oder Sozialtechnologie*).

By stressing the role of intersubjective understanding, norms, and values within the social sciences and the humanities Habermas must show that: 1) a distinction between distorted and non-distorted communication is possible—by seeing through the self-understanding of the agents and by revealing the compulsions distorting their speech; 2) furthermore, he must show that norms and values admit of a rational consensus.

With regard to the first issue Habermas claims that psychoanalysis shows it is possible to go behind the self-understanding of the patient and explain his distorted conception of self and others. The German hermeneutic philosopher H.-G. Gadamer objected that even if this might be true for individual neurosis, it will not be possible to liberate oneself completely from the historically-given tradition of interpretation, since even reflection is context-bound. This challenge is one reason why Habermas developed his theory of *universal pragmatics*, in which he (inspired by Austin and Searle) attempts to reconstruct the preconditions and presuppositions of communication and understanding of utterances. According to Habermas every utterance implies four validity-claims: 1) *comprehensibility* for the linguistic expression; 2) *truth* for the propositional content; 3) *truthfulness* (veracity) for the stated intentions of the utterer; 4) The claim that the utterance is *right* or *appropriate* in relation to a normative context recognized by speaker and hearer.

Without presupposing that these four conditions are met, it would not be meaningful to engage in communication in order to reach intersubjective understanding. Obviously, these conditions are not always fulfilled (false statements, lies). Habermas's point, however, is that even factual deviation from these claims presupposes them, and that the ideal speech situation free of any constraints is anticipated in actual communication. If the implied validity-claims are questioned, communication is changed to the meta-communicative level of *discourse*, i.e. the level on which the validity of the theories and norms implied are scrutinized. Habermas concentrates on two kinds of discourse: *theoretical discourse* in which truth claims are analysed (he is a proponent of a version of the consensus theory of truth), and *practical discourse* in which the rightfulness of norms is discussed. While communicative action is integrated in action in general, at the level of discourse no pressure for immediate action exists. This "virtualization of the constraints of action" is one of the fundamental preconditions of reaching a rational consensus. Equally fundamental are the following: a suspension of the use of force and of motives other than the interest in a rationally-grounded agreement, and the symmetrical distribution of chances of all participants to choose their speech acts freely. Thus no argument should be left out, and the only force should be that of the better argument; consequently, no time limit should be imposed. This ideal speech situation is seldom or never reached in reality, but just as the four validity-claims are presupposed in communicative action, so is their possible redemption on the level of discourse.

The second problem—how to argue that norms and values can be rationally discussed—Habermas claims must be answered within the framework of *communicative ethics* connected with practical discourse. He claims that only interests that admit of universalization can be discursively redeemed, i.e., the participants interpret and communicate their needs, and only those interests that are generalizable will survive rational argumentation.

The theory of *universal pragmatics*, the concept of *discourse*, and the idea of *communicative ethics* are central to Habermas's philosophy. They only constitute, however, one part of his objective, the attempt to establish a formal framework defining the necessary preconditions of a rational will-formation. At the same time Habermas has continued to write sociological works. In addition to the influence of classical German philosophy and modern analytic philosophy, the inspiration from Marx has been

decisive for his thought. It has been much discussed whether Habermas can be regarded as a marxist. If he is, he is certainly not orthodox, since he has constantly criticized what he has called Marx's scienticism and marxist dogmatism. According to Habermas, one of Marx's errors is to describe historical change as a function of the *forces of production* and to regard *labor* as the only basic category and force in social evolution. In addition to labor and the forces of production, which Habermas admits are decisive, he adds the categories *language* and *interaction*, which he accuses Marx of having neglected in his later writings (e.g. *Capital*).

In *Legitimationsprobleme im Spätkapitalismus* Habermas supplements marxist sociological analysis with system theory, and in addition to *economic crisis* analyzes three other but related forms of crisis: *rationality crisis* (steering problems within the state and other systems); *legitimation crisis* (the impossibility of administratively maintaining effective normative structures within late capitalist societies); and *motivation crisis*. In contemporary capitalist societies these crises constitute a hierarchy. Economic crisis is the basic one, but the complexity of the societies permits its displacement to other levels, with the result that crisis becomes manageable within certain limits, although fundamental problems remain unsolved. A more or less permanent state of crisis has been substituted for a periodic and violent economic crisis.

Habermas's relation to marxism is the subject of his *Zur Rekonstruktion des historischen Materialismus*. To explain social evolution, Habermas claims, it is necessary to study the development of learning capacities and that of normative structures and world pictures in addition to the study of the development of the forces of production, since changes in the organization of society need not be the result of the development of the forces of production but can be triggered off by steering problems within other social systems. With regard to the development of these capacities, norms, and world pictures, Habermas suggests the use of ontogenetic studies of cognitive and moral development (e.g., Piaget and L. Kohlberg) to develop a theory of the impact of these factors on social evolution. Habermas is well aware of the problems in applying a model of individual development to a collective phenomenon like social organization and its development, and until now he has only presented a sketch.

No doubt Habermas's work is eclectic, but he himself claims that "the appearance of eclecticism will be unavoidable so long as a complex and powerful theory is still in *statu nascendi*." That work is, however, at the same time unified, since it is bound together by some recurrent and interconnected themes: 1) the epistemological problem of the relation of knowledge to outer nature, society and inner nature; 2) the difference in validity-claims and applicability of three different types of inquiry; 3) the claim that human interaction constitutes a specific area, the study of which demands the incorporation of the hermeneutic understanding that the researcher possesses by participating as subject in a life-world. On the other hand, he asserts, in opposition to traditional hermeneutics, that it is possible to surpass the limits that the tradition imposes upon man by reconstructing the conditions and presuppositions of communication directed towards understanding and those of theoretical and practical discourse. He avows the possibility of founding a communicative ethics on universal pragmatics, since needs and interests can be subjected to a rational consensus. Furthermore, Habermas thinks that it will be possible to reconstruct the logic of social evolutionary structure, homologous to that of genetic development, and that this reconstruction can help to inform the aims of political action by bridging the gap between theory and praxis. All these themes are united in his latest book *Theorie des kommunikatives Handelns*, a major work in post-war continental philosophy.

As a philosopher Habermas is perhaps best characterized as a 20th century version of a representative of the Enlightenment, since he shares a deep concern for the question of public will-formation, the relation between state and society, and the belief in reason with philosophers of that time. His own statement, that his theoretical work is faithful to "the insight that the truth of statements are linked in last analysis to the intention of the true and good life," seems to sum up his principal philosophical endeavour.

—J. Dines Johansen

HÄGERSTRÖM, Axel (Anders Theodor). Swedish philosopher. Born in Vireda in 1868. Educated at Jönköping, 1879-86; studied at the University of Uppsala, Ph.D. 1893. Married Esther Nyander in 1899; 2 daughters. Assistant Professor, 1893-1911, and Chair of Practical Philosophy, 1911-33, University of Uppsala. Inspector, Östgöta Nation, Uppsala, 1925-33. *Died* (in Uppsala) *7 July 1939.*

PUBLICATIONS

Philosophy and Law

Aristoteles etiska grundtankar och deras teoretiska förutsättningar [Aristotle's Fundamental Concepts of Ethics and Their Theoretical Basis]. Uppsala, Berling, 1893.

Om den moraliska känslan och driften säsom förnuftiga i den moderna rationalismens hufvudformer [On Ethical Feelings and Drives as Revealed in the Fundamental Forms of Modern Rationalism]. Uppsala, Berling, 1895.

Undersökning af den empiriska etikens mojlighet med särskild hänsyn till dess moderna hufvudformer [An Examination of the Possibilities of Empirical Ethics with Emphasis on Their Principal Modern Forms]. Uppsala, Berling, 1895.

Om filosofiens betydelse för människan [On the Importance of Philosophy to Mankind]. Uppsala, Almqvist och Wiksell, 1898.

Kants Ethik im Verhältnis zu seinen Erkenntnistheoretischen Grundgedanken, systematisch dargestellt. Uppsala, Almqvist och Wiksell, 1902.

Stat och rätt: En rättsfilosofisk undersökning [State and Justice: A Legal-Philosophical Examination]. Uppsala, Almqvist och Wiksell, 1904.

Das Prinzip der Wissenschaft: Eine logisch-erkenntnistheoretische Untersuchung. Uppsala, Almqvist och Wiksell, 1908.

Social teleologi i Marxismen [Social Teleology in Marxism]. Uppsala, Berling, 1909.

Botanisten och filosofen [The Botanist and the Philosopher]. Stockholm, Bonnier, 1910.

Kritiska punkter i värdepsykologien [Critical Points in the Psychology of Value]. Uppsala, Appelberg, 1910.

Till analysen af det empiriska själfmedvetandet: En psykologisk och filosofisk undersökning [About the Analysis of Empirical Self-Consciousness: A Psychological and Philosophical Examination]. Uppsala, Berling, 1910.

Om moraliska förestallningars sanning [On the Truths of Ethical Concepts]. Stockholm, Bonnier, 1911.

Till frågan om den objektiva rättens begrepp [About the Question of the Concept of Objective Justice]. Uppsala, Berling, 1917.

Der römische Obligationsbegriff im Lichte der allgemeinen römischen Rechtsanschauung. Uppsala, Almqvist och Wiksell, 2 vols., 1927-41.

Das magistratische ius in seinem Zusammenhang mit dem römischen Sakralrechte. Uppsala, Lundequist, 1929.

Socialfilosofiska uppsatser [Social-Philosophical Dissertations]. Stockholm, Bonnier, 1939.

De socialistiska ideernas historia [The History of the Concepts of Socialism]. Stockholm, Natur och Kultur, 1946.

Religionsfilosofi. Stockholm, Natur och Kultur, 1949; as *Philosophy and Religion*, London, Allen and Unwin, and Atlantic Highlands, New Jersey, Humanities Press, 1964 (contains a bibliography).

Moralpsykologi [The Psychology of Ethics]. Stockholm, Natur och Kultur, 1952.

Inquiries into the Nature of Law and Morals (translations from the Swedish). Stockholm, Almqvist och Wiksell, 1953.

Filosofi och vetenskap [Philosophy and Science], edited by Martin Fries. Stockholm, Ehlins, 1957.

Rätten och staten: Tre föreläsningar om rätts- och statsfilosofi [Justice and the State: Three Lectures on Justice- and State-Philosophy]. Stockholm, Almqvist och Wiksell, 1963.

Recht, Pflicht und bindende Kraft des Vertrages nach römischer und naturrechtlicher Anschauung, edited by Karl Olivecrona. Stockholm, Almqvist och Wiksell, 1965.

Jesus: En karaktärsanalys [Jesus: A Character Analysis]. Stockholm, Natur och Kultur, 1968.

Other

Doc. Nyman's "Erinringar": Ett genmäle [Doctor Nyman's "Memoirs": A Biography]. Uppsala, Almqvist och Wiksell, 1929.

Vad jag varit med om: Minnen från ofärdsåren och frihetskampen [Events in Which I Participated: Memories from the War and the Resistance Movement]. Helsinki, Söderström, 1936.

*   *   *

Axel Hägerström is an enigmatical figure; on the one side, he is a proto-type of the somewhat tedious and pedantic scholar, writing books almost too big either to hold or to read; on the other side, he was an affectionate teacher, father, and friend, and, besides, became a major force in general Swedish and northern European cultural and intellectual life. Hence, his ideas, though conceived in striking independence of the main movements of thought in continental Europe and in England, bear the same weight and do the same things. Besides, they have resemblances to both the positivism associated with the Vienna Circle and the analytic philosophy centering in British universities during the 1930's and 40's. The odd thing is that Hägerström preceded both in time, and, thus, he made these two movements seem almost redundant to later Swedish thinkers. Besides, the force and learning with which he argued, gave a thrust to his thoughts and a social use that neither of the other movements quite evinced.

What accounts for his power and role as an exceedingly abstract thinker? Seemingly three factors. One, his thought had a power because it was directed against a highly conventionalized and widely-accepted form of philosophical idealism, that of C.J. Boström. Hägerström simply showed by essays and lectures that general culture, religion, law, and morals were not dependant upon that idealistic scheme of thought. There were many Swedish practitioners who were ready to hear the diatribes against the notion of the necessity of philosophical orthodoxy in order to justify other activities and thoughts. Secondly, Hägerström made an appeal because he was so adamantly anti-metaphysical. His arguments here are very technical and refined, but they lead to a repudiation of certain strands of Kant's thought, to the negation of the charm of the concept, "being," and to a strong advocacy of empirical and ordinary ways of knowing. Here he is a kind of champion of plain thinking and of science in its more mundane aspects.

Thirdly, Hägerström refounded both morals and law. In effect, he admitted "feeling" to major status; he gave authority to the actual modes of living that produced law; and he discounted the more elaborate notions of natural rights, of natural law, of a general imperative kind of duty, and other philosophical notions that shroud laws and morals. Part of this he did by long studies of Kant's philosophy, another part tempered accounts of the origins and nature of Roman law. But all of these factors together allowed Hägerström to stimulate legal theorists, to cause theologians to re-think the roots of faith, and to give Sweden a genuine pride in a thinker who was relevant, clear-headed, and who had anticipated European and English philosophy. Two volumes in English give access to Hägerström's main themes: *Inquiries into the Nature of Law and Morals* and *Philosophy and Religion*. The first is translated by C.D. Broad, the eminent Cambridge philosopher, and his essay introduces the second volume.

—Paul L. Holmer

HALDANE, J(ohn) B(urdon) S(anderson). British geneticist. Born in Oxford, 5 November 1892. Educated at Eton College; studied at New College, Oxford, 1911-14. Served in the Black Watch in France and Iraq, 1914-19: Captain. Married Charlotte Franken in 1926; Helen Spurway in 1945. Fellow, New College, 1914-22; Reader in Biochemistry, Cambridge University, 1922-32; Fullerian Professor of Physiology, Royal Institution, London, 1930-32; Professor of Biometry, University College, London, 1937-57; Research Professor, Indian Statistical Institute, Calcutta, 1957-61; Head of Genetics and Biometry Laboratory, Government of Orissa, India, 1962-64. Chairman, Editorial Board, *Daily Worker*, 1940-49. President, Genetical Society, London, 1932-36. Recipient: Darwin Medal, Royal Society, 1953; Darwin-Wallace Medal, Linnean Society, 1958; Kimber Medal, National Academy of Sciences, 1961; Feltrinelli Prize, Accademia dei Lincei, 1961. Honorary doctorate: University of Gröningen, 1946; University of Paris, 1949; University of Edinburgh, 1956; Oxford University, 1961. Fellow of the Royal Society, London, 1932. Member, German Academy of Sciences, Berlin; National Institute of Science, India; Royal Danish Academy of Science; Honorary Member, Moscow Academy of Sciences. Chevalier, Légion d'Honneur, 1937. *Died* (in Bhudaneswar, India) *1 December 1964*.

PUBLICATIONS

Genetics and Social Commentary

Daedalus; or, Science and the Future. London, Kegan Paul, 1923.
Callinicus—A Defence of Chemical Warfare. London, Kegan Paul, and New York, Dutton, 1925.
Animal Biology, with J.S Huxley. Oxford, Clarendon Press, 1927.
Possible Worlds and Other Essays. London, Chatto and Windus, 1927; New York, Harper, 1928.
Enzymes. London, Longman, 1930.
The Inequality of Man and Other Essays. London, Chatto and Windus, 1932.
The Causes of Evolution. London, Longman, 1932.
Fact and Faith. London, Watts, 1934.
The Outlook of Science. London, Kegan Paul, 1935.
Science and the Supernatural: A Correspondence Between Arnold Lunn and J.B.S. Haldane. London, Eyre and Spottiswoode, and New York, Sheed and Ward, 1935.
Science and Well-Being. London, Kegan Paul, 1935.
My Friend Mr. Leakey. London, Cresset Press, 1937.
The Chemistry of the Individual (lecture). London, Oxford University Press, 1938.
A.R.P. London, Gollancz, 1938.
The Marxist Philosophy and the Sciences. London, Allen and Unwin, 1938; New York, Random House, 1939.
Heredity and Politics. London, Allen and Unwin, and New York, Norton, 1938.

Science in Peace and War. London, Lawrence and Wishart, 1940.
Science in Everyday Life. New York, Macmillan, 1940.
Keeping Cool and Other Essays. London, Chatto and Windus, 1940; as *Adventures of a Biologist*, New York, Harper, 1940.
New Paths in Genetics. London, Allen and Unwin, 1941; New York, Harper, 1942.
A Banned Broadcast and Other Essays. London, Chatto and Windus, 1946.
Science Advances. London, Allen and Unwin, and New York, Macmillan, 1947.
What is Life? New York, Boni and Gaer, 1947.
Is Evolution a Myth? A Debate, with D. Dewar and C.M. Davies. London, Watts and The Paternoster Press, 1949.
Everything Has a History. London, Allen and Unwin, 1951.
The Biochemistry of Genetics. London, Allen and Unwin, 1954; New York, Macmillan, 1960.
The Unity and Diversity of Life. New Delhi, Government of India Publications Division, 1957.
Science and Life: Essays of a Rationalist. London, Barrie and Rockliff, 1968.

*

Critical Studies: *JBS: The Life and Work of J.B.S. Haldane* by Ronald W. Clark, New York, Coward McCann, 1958 (contains a bibliography); *Haldane and Modern Biology*, edited by K.R. Dronamraju, Baltimore, Johns Hopkins University Press, 1968.

*   *   *

J.B.S. Haldane was one of those rare individuals who made important contributions in many diverse fields, including genetics, evolutionary theory, mathematics, statistics, ethology, religion and social thought. In the field of genetics Haldane was particularly adept at providing numerous critical analyses of data. His analyses often contained novel statistical methods that provided new ways of pulling together information once thought to be unconnected. These statistical studies contributed greatly to our understanding of the patterns of inheritance of many plants and animals, especially man. Since laboratory experiments were out of the question as a means of studying genetics, Haldane's statistical analyses were of particular value as a way of extracting the maximum amount of information from the minimum amount of data (and often inaccurate data) contained in family pedigrees.

Between 1920 and 1935 Haldane's work in genetics was extremely specialized. He carried out experiments on mice, rats, locusts and mosquitos in order to illuminate a phenomenon observed when two or more genes are located on the same chromosome, such that the two characteristics are passed together. Haldane was one of the first geneticists to recognize this process, which is known today as "linkage." His vast knowledge of biochemistry and physiology enabled him also to explore the gene as a biochemically functioning unit. Even though his contributions to this area remained theoretical, he stressed the importance of the so-called "one gene, one enzyme" hypothesis long before it became one of the central dogmas of experimental genetics. In general, Haldane's work in biochemical genetics has become a significant part of evolutionary theory in the past half-century.

Perhaps Haldane's greatest contribution to the fields of genetics and evolution was his mathematical theory of natural and artificial selection. He maintained that a satisfactory theory of natural and artificial selection must be quantitative. At the time Haldane attempted to quantify selection, the precise effect of the process of selection on the genetic makeup of populations had been revealed in only the simplest of cases. He began by investigating the most straightforward examples and then moved on to studying the effects of selection on systems of multiple interacting factors. In its most simplified form, Haldane carried out his selection studies by assigning selective values to each gene or in some cases to several interacting genes located at certain positions on the chromosome. From this information he deduced the number of generations required to change the frequency of genes, which would result in the appearance of new or modified characters. Haldane's work in this area was of particular importance to the development of evolutionary theory, which had lacked established demonstration that natural selection could cause a species to change at a rate that complied with the record of past and present transmutation of species. Haldane highlighted his work on natural and artificial selection by publishing a series of papers on a number of evolutionary topics, such as the evolution of dominance, loss of fitness due to the recurrence of mutant genes, and conditions when mutant genes actually become advantageous. All of the works above were summarized in his book *The Causes of Evolution*.

It is regrettable that in recent years Haldane's work has been dismissed by some evolutionists as nothing more than a sophisticated version of classical "beanbag genetics." Though the period in which he worked may be called classical, he nevertheless made a giant step toward breaking from that very tradition by introducing new statistical techniques for dealing with many interacting evolutionary factors. These statistical concepts made it possible to treat the changes in gene frequencies from one generation to the next in a quantifiable fashion, which was quite unlike any genetics done before his time. Haldane's work also provided the seedbed from which the synthesis of evolutionary theory, natural history and genetics grew to fruition.

Haldane was well aware of the possible applications to human evolution of his work on quantifying evolution. He sought to explain the evolutionary development of human traits such as hemophilia, Rh-positive and Rh-negative, and sickle-cell anemia. He hypothesized that the prevalence of many diseases affecting man might be due to selection factors producing a state of equilibrium among the genes' coding for certain diseases. Haldane was also one of the first geneticists to analyze formally the relation between heredity and the environment and the effect that this relation might have on the proliferation of human diseases.

Haldane's contribution to mathematics and statistics was naturally linked to his work on genetics. He is best known for working out algebraic details on non-linear equations. This extremely detailed work allowed him and others to deal with the important statistical problem of applying large-sample theory to actual samples of a necessarily more moderate size.

As in mathematics and statistics, Haldane made small, but significant ventures into applied physiology. During World War II the British Navy was concerned about the physiological changes that occur in the body as a result of extreme pressure to which both submariners and frogmen were exposed. The Navy was also interested in finding alternative gas mixtures for underwater work that did not induce unwanted symptoms such as hallucinations or deterioration of manual and mental skills. Haldane ran a series of experiments in which he exposed himself to mixtures of different gases and measured their pharmacological effects. He also placed himself inside chambers that contained gases under different pressures. As a result of once undergoing too rapid a decompression process, Haldane was left partially disabled. His fearless attempts at self-experimentation for the war cause did, however, provide some viable alternatives as to what gases could be inhaled by men and under what pressures those gases were safe. Toward the end of his life Haldane became interested in the evolution of behavior of animals and man. He was one of the first of his generation to drive hard at the point that the study of behavior, known as ethology, was a topic for scientific inquiry, not mere speculation. Though his contributions to ethology amounted to nothing more than a dabbling, he initiated serious discussions of the manners of inheritance in song and other forms of communication among different species of birds, the rhythms of breathing in fish, and food gathering habits in birds.

Like so many scientists of his generation, Haldane was fascinated by the question: how did life originate on earth? He outlined a process, which he called chemosynthesis, by which life might have begun on earth. Quite independently of, but quite similar to, the work of the Russian biophysicist A.I. Oparin, Haldane maintained that life originated from organic chemicals in the ancient waters of the earth. Like Oparin, he held that the earth's atmosphere contained little oxygen but had a plentiful supply of hydrogen. It was thus a "reducing" atmosphere in which hydrogen atoms were constantly donating their electrons to other atoms and molecules. Energy from volcanic activity and lightning helped to combine different atoms to form simple organic compounds. Little droplets of basic chemical building blocks, such as amino acids, carbohydrates and purines reached a certain size and broke into two parts. Some of these parts became self-replicating molecules and began to guide the reproductive process of simple cells. Life was "born"! Throughout his life Haldane suggested stimulating additions to his original chemosynthetic outline.

Like a number of other British scientists in the 1920's and 1930's, Haldane had strong leftist leanings. He joined the Communist Party soon after the outbreak of the Spanish Civil War and advised both the Republican Government in Spain and, a few years later, the British Government after the outbreak of World War II. Originally a supporter of the theories of Lysenko in Russia, Haldane later broke with the official Communist Party policy and became one of the staunch attackers against the Lysenkoist movement (1949).

Haldane pioneered work in a number of fields and was able, through his broad background and interests, to generate new insights by applying the concepts developed in one area of biology to problems in another. For him, as one biographer, Ronald Clark, has written, "the cross-fertilization of ideas really worked." Haldane's life provides a clear example of the advantages of uniting various approaches and styles of work—the theorist and the experimenter, the intellectual and the political activist, the biochemist and the geneticist—in the mind and visions of one individual.

—Randall Davey Bird

HALÉVY, Elie. French historian. Born in Étretat, 6 September 1870. Educated at Lycée Condorcet, Paris; École Normale Supérieure, Paris; Agrégé, 1892; Docteur-ès-lettres, 1900. Married Florence Noufflard in 1901. Professor, Écoles des Sciences Politiques, Paris, 1892-1937. Co-Editor, 1893-1935, and Editor, 1935-37, *Revue de Metaphysique et de Morale*. Co-Founder, Société Française de Philosophie. Honorary doctorate: Oxford University, 1926. *Died 21 August 1937.*

PUBLICATIONS

History

La Théorie platonicienne des sciences. Paris, Alcan, 1896.
La Formation du radicalisme philosophique: La Revolution et la doctrine de l'utilité (1789-1815). Paris, Alcan, 1900; reprinted as vol. 2 of *La Formation du radicalisme philosophique*, Paris, Alcan, 3 vols., 1901-04; as *The Growth of Philosophic Radicalism*, London, Faber, and New York, Macmillan, 1928.
De Concatenatione quae inter affectiones mentis propter similitudinem fieri dicitur. Paris, Alcan, 1901.
Thomas Hodgskin (1787-1869). Paris, Société Nouvelle de Librairie et d'Édition, 1903; as *Thomas Hodgskin*, London, Benn, 1956.
L'Angleterre et son empire. Paris, "Pages Libres," 1905.

"La Naissance du methodisme en Angleterre," in *Revue de Paris*, 1906; as *The Birth of Methodism in England*, edited by Bernard Semmel.   Chicago, University of Chicago Press, 1971.

Histoire du peuple anglais au XIXᵉ siècle.   Paris, Hachette, 6 vols., 1912-32; as *A History of the English People in the Nineteenth Century*, London, Benn, 6 vols., 1912-47; New York, Harcourt Brace, 6 vols., 1924-51.

La Part de la France: Lettre ouverte d'un soldat français aux soldats américains.   Paris, Attinger Frères, 1917 (published anonymously).

The World Crisis of 1914-18: An Interpretation (lecture).   Oxford, Clarendon Press, 1930.

Sismondi.   Paris, Alcan, 1933.

L'Ère des tyrannies: Études sur le socialisme et la guerre.   Paris, Gallimard, 1938; as *The Era of Tyrannies: Essays on Socialism and War*, New York, Anchor Books, 1965; London, Allen Lane, 1967.

Histoire du socialisme européen: Redigée d'après des notes de cours par un groupe d'amis et d'élèves.   Paris, Gallimard, 1948.

Other

Correspondance avec Élie et Florence Halévy, by Emile Chartier.   Paris, Gallimard, 1958.

Editor, with Celestin Bougle, *La Doctrine de Saint-Simon: Exposition, Premiere Année, 1829.*   Paris, Rivière, 1924.

*

Bibliography: *Bibliography of Signed Works by Élie Halévy* by Melvin Richter, Middletown, Connecticut, Wesleyan Unversity Press, 1967.

Critical Studies: *Portrait d'Élie Halévy* by Michele Bo Bramsen, Amsterdam, B.R. Grüner, 1978; *Élie Halévy, an Intellectual Biography* by Myrna Chase, New York, Columbia University Press, 1980 (contains a bibliography).

*   *   *

Élie Halévy, French historian of the English people, was one of the most distinguished historians of this century and one of the Third Republic's foremost educators. By birth, education, social standing and intellectual capacities one of the elite of the republic of professors, Halévy was passionately committed to the republic, as he was to rationalism, secularism, to individual liberty and justice. A Dreyfusard, he defined his commitment as an intellectual—he founded the *Revue de Metaphysique et de Morale*, trained the elite of administration and diplomacy at the Ecole Libre des Sciences Politiques, and interpreted English history and politics and modern socialism for his countrymen.

His six volume *History of the English People in the Nineteenth Century* is a classic study, its interpretations still sparking controversy and shaping our view of the English past more than a half century after its publication. Undertaken to answer a theoretical question—what, in a modern state, are the preconditions for liberty, justice and progress?—Halévy's achievement was not a history to prove a general theory but a sustained narrative of the complex interaction of social and economic forces, institutions, individuals and ideas which shaped and continues to shape a culture both liberal and stable. The famous "Halévy thesis"—that the socially and politically stabilizing influence of evangelical Protestantism, particularly Methodism, shaped the culture of all levels of English life in the 18th and 19th century, modifying the impact of industrialization, liberalization and ultimately democratization—is the most influential of many interpretations contained in this work.

His work on the Benthamite utilitarians, *The Growth of Philosophic Radicalism*, pointed to the common projects for reform

between the utilitarians and the evangelicals which provided both progress and conservation, unlike France where enlightened ideas very similar to those of Jeremy Bentham's had inspired radical revolution. The Philosophic Radicals and the Evangelicals were two sets of reformers whose inspiration differed more than their aspirations on issues such as emancipation of slaves, education, prison and penal reform.

The Growth of Philosophic Radicalism stressed an inherent contradiction in radicalism between the desire to liberate man from the obstacles of an economic, social, political and legal system which hampered his activities and the desire to organize efforts to greater productivity and efficiency. The currents which swept the classical economists to their triumphs in the first part of the 19th century and those which brushed aside the early critics of the industrial system, the first socialists, were the same currents. The conflicts between them would become more apparent as the century progressed. This work, which is in great part definitive and where it is not is seminal, develops the thought of the school of reformers around Bentham, tracing the development of economic ideas from the predecessors of Smith through Ricardo and his working class critics, the legal ideas from their Enlightenment origins through the Benthamite jurists and the constitutional ideas of Bentham and James Mill.

From this work in the history of ideas and through the *History* Halévy makes the argument for the revolution in government, that is, in the midst of the laissez-faire Victorian era the instruments of a powerful state were developed. He was keenly aware of the ambivalence toward liberty in Benthamite thought, in the desire to organize, but his final judgement was that the epoch was nonetheless the triumph of liberty, that the English were capable of living with paradoxes of liberty and organization.

The first volume of the *History* begins with a masterpiece which is Halévy's estimation of *England in 1815*, in fact a survey of the institutions of the 18th century with the explicit question: why in view of so much chaos, disorder and political and economic mishap did England avoid the revolution which France met at the end of the century? That question of revolution, which for that time he answered with his "thesis," was raised again with regard to the emergence of an industrial society. His work can be seen as a sustained effort to offer an alternative explanation to a Marxist materialistic history because of the weight he gives to the necessities of the particular situation and the power of ideas and culture.

The *History* omits the period from 1851 to 1895, the age of Gladstonian liberalism, which Halévy found congenial but which he was not able to finish writing, and picks up the narrative in the *Epilogue*, two volumes on the age of imperialism and democracy, both written after the First World War and detailing forces leading to that holocaust for Western civilization. The war deepened his philosophic pessimism, perhaps providing the motive for the shift to his own era. He saw a decline in British confidence, which threatened the liberal society he had chronicled to the mid-19th century. Stimulated by the war he advanced ideas on the twin themes of socialism and nationalism. Here again he saw British socialism as made more democratic and more liberal by its native culture than Continental varieties.

All the evils of state power of which he had seen the implications in his narratives of socialism (again an idea suffering from an inherent contradiction between the desire to emancipate and the ambition to organize) were multiplied many times over in the actual centralization and control which had taken place among the belligerents. Halévy thought he saw in the fear of socialism on the eve of the war the impetus for the ruling elite in many states to be willing to risk war to save their regime. Then the actual process of the war strengthened state power and drew into the state the trade unions and socialist parties. The breakdown of Russian and indeed of the state system in Eastern and parts of Central Europe brought about social uprisings, some in the guise of socialism, some as national revolutions. These thoughts he brought together in an essay on the "World Crisis."

In the 1930s, the last few years of his life, he warned of a new phenomenon in European civilization, a phenomenon which we have come to designate as totalitarianism but which he called the "Era of Tyrannies," using the designation tyranny for the new regimes in Italy, Germany and the Soviet Union, regimes which had no obvious end, which organized the life of their citizenry around ideologies which combined nationalism and increased state power in an unprecedented fashion and which he felt in 1936 were bound to lead to yet another war. He was sharply criticized at the time for comparing Bolshevism with fascism, something a man of the Left did not do. His analysis of the tyrannies and of the origins of and nature of total warfare have influenced many Western scholars and statesmen since that era.

—Myrna Chase

HAMPSHIRE, Stuart (Newton). British philosopher. Born in Healing, Lincolnshire, 1 October 1914. Educated at Repton; studied at Balliol College, Oxford, 1st class honours, 1936. Served in the British Army, 1940-45 (Assistant to Minister of State, Foreign Office, 1945). Married Renée Lees in 1961. Fellow, All Souls College, and Lecturer, Oxford University, 1936-40; Lecturer in Philosophy, University College, London, 1947-50; Fellow, New College, Oxford, 1950-55; Research Fellow and Domestic Bursar, All Souls College, Oxford, 1955-60; Grote Professor of Philosophy of Mind and Logic, University of London, 1960-63; Professor of Philosophy, Princeton University, New Jersey, 1963-70. Since 1970, Warden of Wadham College, Oxford. Member, Arts Council of Great Britain, since 1972. Fellow, British Academy, 1960. Knighted, 1979. Address: Wadham College, Oxford, England.

PUBLICATIONS

Philosophy

Spinoza. London, Penguin, 1951.
Thought and Action. London, Chatto and Windus, 1959; New York, Viking Press, 1967.
Feeling and Expression (lecture). London, H.K. Lewis, 1960.
Freedom of the Individual (lecture). London, Chatto and Windus, and New York, Harper, 1965; expanded version, Princeton, New Jersey, Princeton University Press, 1975.
The Morality of Scholarship, with others. Ithaca, New York, Cornell University Press, 1967.
Modern Writers and Other Essays. London, Chatto and Windus, 1969; New York, Knopf, 1970.
Freedom of Mind and Other Essays. Princeton, New Jersey, Princeton University Press, 1971; Oxford, Clarendon Press, 1972.
Morality and Pessimism (lecture). London, Cambridge University Press, 1972.
Knowledge and the Future (lecture). Southampton, University of Southampton Press, 1977.
Two Theories of Morality (lecture). London, Oxford University Press, 1977.

Other

Editor, *The Age of Reason: The Seventeenth Century Philosophers.* Boston, Houghton Mifflin, 1956.
Editor, *Philosophy of Mind.* New York, Harper, 1966.
Editor, with Leszek Kolakowski, *The Socialist Idea: A Reappraisal.* London, Weidenfeld and Nicolson, 1974.
Editor, *Public and Private Morality.* London and New York, Cambridge University Press, 1978.

*   *   *

Stuart Hampshire's work, while ranging over politics, morality, psychology, and aesthetics, has centered on issues of freedom. Writing in the Oxford tradition of precise philosophical analysis, but with the sort of comprehensive vision epitomized by Spinoza, he has subtly explored the conditions and implications of reflexive knowledge in an effort to understand the distinctively human possibilities of freedom of mind.

From his earliest work in the theory of perception he has emphasized the interdependence of two kinds of knowledge: self-knowledge and knowledge of the external world. The two types of knowledge have different sources, require different types of support, and are open to different types of error, but each is necessary to the other. In application, our shared vocabulary for the description and criticism of psychological states and action is also subject to the division. The two kinds of knowledge are associated with two different points of view from which we can understand our own mental states and attitudes and the mental states and attitudes of others. It is in the interplay of the two points of view (that of an agent and that of a spectator) that the paradoxes and potentials of freedom emerge. How are we to reconcile the notion that our changing mental states are the effects of assignable causes with our sense of freedom in the formation of our beliefs, desires, and intentions?

Starting from Spinoza's insight that in the realm of the mental our beliefs about causes can modify their effects (causal beliefs themselves being constitutive, discriminatively important, parts of our mental states), some of Hampshire's most provocative and influential claims (in *Thought and Action, Freedom of the Individual,* and *Freedom of Mind and Other Essays*) have concerned illuminating peculiarities of reflexive knowledge; for example: the difficulties in the dual stance involved in attempting to predict one's own decisions—the unavoidability of stepping back from any prediction or self-prediction for further consideration if one is to maintain one's view of oneself as a responsible agent; the inherent role of rational standards and other constraints in commitments to belief and other self-ascriptions of psychological states—the natural reflective application of critical standards of defensibility or desirability to our beliefs and sentiments that follows from their lack of independence from our beliefs about their causes, the element of assessment that gets built into self-description; the complications and different prospects for the human sciences, as opposed to the physical sciences, that result from their operating in a realm where knowing can affect the thing known; and the need for self-conscious self-examination in order to achieve ideals of sincerity and freedom (ideals sometimes mistakenly connected with unthinking spontaneity in speech and action). Throughout, Hampshire eschews the narrow confinement of empiricist models to the passive position of the spectator, while also avoiding the exaggerated claims of some existentialists on behalf of freedom. In philosophy of mind, Hampshire has been searching for a middle way between Cartesian dualism and reductionist behaviorism: seeking to give a proper place to the embodied character of human thought and action while rejecting assimilations of that which is distinctively mental to its overt behavioral expression, and seeking to give sense to the special authority and significance of first-person claims about one's own mental states while rejecting incorrigibility as the mark of the mental.

Hampshire's appreciation of the less transparent, more hidden and confused, aspects of our self-understanding carries over to his writings on moral theory. From his first paper in that area ("Fallacies in Moral Philosophy"), Hampshire has been concerned with the relation of practical and theoretical reasoning, rescuing for moral seriousness the particular (distinctively moral) intuitions and arguments too often dismissed in the name of unremitting demands for explicitness, computational rationality, and non-conflicting abstract principles. He recognizes that moral life is inevitably full of conflict, and he writes of the varieties of reason and the different requirements of theoretical articulateness in public and private morality. In moral theory, Hampshire attempts to embrace both the Aristotelian sensitivity to the perception of particular cases, with its reciprocal influence on general principle, and the more radical Spinozist demand for systematic coherence. Maintaining the two together presents difficulties, but along the way Hampshire manages to restore to consideration the more neglected, complex features of emotion, desire, intention, and belief—seeing the historically conditioned character of human nature and the importance of alternative classifications and descriptions in practical reasoning and the moral life.

Hampshire pays (un-Spinozist) attention to the imagination. Over the years, in brief essays and reviews (many collected in *Modern Writers and Other Essays*), Hampshire has explored reflections of his philosophical concerns in literature and literary temperaments. Beyond criticizing particular beliefs, there is an importance in criticizing our categories of belief that becomes manifest once one appreciates the power of our inherited vocabulary to set limits on our experience. Creative writers provide resources for description and understanding that (because of the character of reflexive knowledge) can be liberating, can transform our lives. This gives a special urgency and power to Hampshire's remarkable brief literary studies.

Hampshire's own writing style is urbane and flowing, perhaps concealing the precision and rigor of his thought and its fruitfully systematic character. In linking freedom and knowledge he brings epistemology, philosophy of mind, and moral philosophy closer together. In exploring wider alternative visions, he reveals the assumptions and arguments needed for a self-critical understanding of human powers and valued ways of life.

—Jerome Neu

HANDLIN, Oscar. American historian. Born in Brooklyn, New York, 29 September 1915. Studied at Brooklyn College, A.B. 1934; Harvard University, Cambridge, Massachusetts, M.A. 1935, Ph.D. 1940. Married Mary Flug in 1937; 3 children; married Lilian Bombach in 1977. Instructor, Brooklyn College, 1938-39; Instructor, 1939-44, Assistant Professor, 1944-48, Associate Professor, 1948-54, Professor, 1954-62, Winthrop Professor of History, 1962-65, Charles Warren Professor of History, 1965-72, and since 1972 Carl Pforzheimer University Professor, Harvard University. Harmsworth Professor, Oxford University, 1972-73. Director, Center for Study of Liberty in America, 1958-66; Charles Warren Center for Studies in American History, 1965-72; and Harvard University Library, since 1979. Vice-Chairman, 1962-65, and Chairman, 1965-66, U.S. Board of Foreign Scholarships. Recipient: History Prize, Union League Club, 1934; J.H. Dunning Prize, American Historical Association, 1941; Award of Honor, Brooklyn College, 1945; Pulitzer Prize for History, 1952; Guggenheim Fellowship, 1954; Christopher Award, 1958; Brooklyn College Alumni Award, 1958; Brandeis University Fellowship, 1965; Robert H. Lord Award, 1972. Honorary doctorate: Colby College, Waterville, Maine, 1962; Hebrew Union College, New York, 1967; Oakland University, Rochester, Michigan, 1968; Northern Michigan University, Marquette, 1969; Brooklyn College, 1972; Seton Hall University, South Orange, New Jersey, 1972; Boston College, Massachusetts, 1975; University of Cincinnati, 1981. Fellow, American Academy of Arts and Sciences. Address: 18 Agassiz Street, Cambridge, Massachusetts, U.S.A.

PUBLICATIONS

History

Boston's Immigrants, 1790-1865: A Study in Acculturation.
Cambridge, Massachusetts, Harvard University Press, and London, Oxford University Press, 1941.

Commonwealth: A Study of the Role of Government in the American Economy: Massachusetts, 1774-1861, with Mary Flug Handlin. New York, New York University Press, 1947.

Danger in Discord: Origins of Anti-Semitism in the United States, with Mary Flug Handlin (pamphlet). New York, Anti-Defamation League of B'nai B'rith, 1948.

A Century of Jewish Immigration to the United States, with Mary F. Handlin. New York, American Jewish Committee, 1949.

The Uprooted: The Epic Story of the Great Migrations That Made the American People. Boston, Little Brown, 1951; London, Watts, 1953; enlarged edition, Little Brown, 1973.

Israel and the Mission of America (lecture). Brookline, Massachusetts, Hebrew Teachers College Press, 1953.

Adventure in Freedom: Three Hundred Years of Jewish Life in America. New York, McGraw Hill, 1954.

The American People in the Twentieth Century. Cambridge, Massachusetts, Harvard University Press, 1954.

Harvard Guide to American History, with others. Cambridge Massachusetts, Belknap Press, 1954.

Chance or Destiny: Turning Points in American History. Boston, Little Brown, 1955.

Race and Nationality in American Life. Boston, Little Brown, 1957.

Al Smith and His America. Boston, Little Brown, 1958.

American Jews: Their Story. New York, Anti-Defamation League of B'nai B'rith, 1958.

Theodore Roosevelt Centennial: Suggestions for Colleges. New York, Theodore Roosevelt Association, 1958.

The Newcomers: Negroes and Puerto Ricans in a Changing Metropolis. Cambridge, Massachusetts, Harvard University Press, 1959.

John Dewey's Challenge to Education: Historical Perspectives on the Cultural Context (lecture). New York, Harper, 1959.

The Dimensions of Liberty, with Mary Handlin. Cambridge, Massachusetts, Belknap Press, 1961.

The American People: A New History. London, Hutchinson, 1963.

Fire-Bell in the Night: The Crisis in Civil Rights. Boston, Little Brown, 1964.

A Continuing Task: The American Jewish Joint Distribution Committee, 1914-1964. New York, Random House, 1965.

The American People: The History of a Society. London, Penguin, 1966.

The History of the United States. New York, Holt Rinehart, 2 vols., 1967-68.

America: A History. New York, Holt Rinehart, 1968.

Dissent, Democracy, and Foreign Policy: A Symposium, with others (pamphlet). New York, Foreign Policy Association, 1968.

The American College and American Culture: Socialization as a Function of Higher Education, with Mary F. Handlin. New York, McGraw Hill, 1970.

The American University as an Instrument of Republican Culture (lecture). Leicester, England, Leicester University Press, 1970.

Facing Life: Youth and the Family in American History, with Mary F. Handlin. Boston, Little Brown, 1971.

Statue of Liberty, with others. New York, Newsweek, 1971.

A Pictorial History of Immigration. New York, Crown, 1972.

One World: The Origins of an American Concept (lecture). Oxford, Clarendon Press, 1974.

The Wealth of the American People: A History of American Affluence, with Mary F. Handlin. New York, McGraw Hill, 1975.

Abraham Lincoln and the Union, with Lilian Handlin. Boston, Little Brown, 1980.

Truth in History. Cambridge, Massachusetts, Belknap Press, 1980.

The Distortion of America. Boston, Little Brown, 1981.
A Restless People: Americans in Rebellion, 1770-1787, with Lilian Handlin. New York, Anchor Press, 1982.

Other

Occasions for Love, and Other Essays at Recollection. Lunenburg, Vermont, Stinehour Press, 1977.

Editor, *This Was America: True Accounts of People and Places, Manners and Customs, as Recorded by European Travelers to the Western Shore in the Eighteenth, Nineteenth and Twentieth Centuries.* Cambridge, Massachusetts, Harvard University Press, 1949.
Editor, *Readings in American History.* New York, Knopf, 1957.
Editor, *Immigration as a Factor in American History.* Englewood Cliffs, New Jersey, Prentice Hall, 1959.
Editor and Translator, with John Olive, *Journey to Pennsylvania* by Gottlieb Mittelberger. Cambridge, Massachusetts, Belknap Press, 1960.
Editor, *American Principles and Issues: The National Purpose.* New York, Holt Rinehart, 1961.
Editor, with Mary Handlin, *The Popular Sources of Political Authority: Documents on the Massachusetts Constitution of 1780.* Cambridge, Massachusetts, Belknap Press, 1966.
Editor, with John Burchard, *The Historian and the City.* Cambridge, Massachusetts, M.I.T. Press, 1967.
Editor, *Children of the Uprooted.* New York, Grosset and Dunlap, 1968.
Editor, *Slave and Citizen: The Life of Frederick Douglass* by Nathan Irvin Huggins. Boston, Little Brown, 1980.
Editor, *Elizabeth Cady Station: A Radical for Woman's Rights* by Lois W. Banner. Boston, Little Brown, 1980.
Editor, *John Marshall: Defender of the Constitution* by Francis N. Stites. Boston, Little Brown, 1981.
Editor, *Louis D. Brandeis and the Progressive Tradition* by Melvin I. Urofsky. Boston, Little Brown, 1981.

*

Critical Studies: *Oscar Handlin's The Uprooted: A Critical Commentary* by Frederick C. Jaher, New York, American R.D.M., 1966; *Uprooted Americans: Essays to Honor Oscar Handlin*, edited by Richard L. Bushman, Boston, Little Brown, 1979.

*   *   *

By 1952, a Pulitzer prize-winner while still in his 30's, Oscar Handlin had contributed as much as anyone to the definition of an agenda for the writing of American history in the third quarter of the 20th century. Three decades and some 25 books later, he had become a curiously isolated and controversial figure, often bitterly critical of his own profession and more generally of the modern academic establishment in America.

Early in his career, encouraged by Harvard's Arthur M. Schlesinger, Sr., Handlin began to study the history of immigration from Europe to America. He soon expanded the methods and themes of his doctoral research into a comprehensive understanding of the American past that drew inspiration from the work of Marcus Lee Hansen and from Hansen's mentor Frederick Jackson Turner. The son of immigrant Ukrainian Jews, Handlin was immune to the Anglophilia of most scholars previously concerned with his subject. In his efforts to recreate the experience of "ordinary" as well as "exceptional" people, he anticipated the enthusiasm of the 1960's for "history from the bottom up." Using census data to reveal patterns of social activity in Boston and other American cities, he laid a foundation for the "new urban history" espoused by such students of his as Sam Bass Warner, Jr., and Stephan Thernstrom. And Handlin identi-

fied a powerful metaphor for interpreting the larger significance of his story. Having been "uprooted" from peasant European backgrounds, according to Handlin, immigrants were disoriented by the strange circumstances of their new American world and so found themselves in a "prolonged state of crisis." Adapting the insights of such urban sociologists as Robert E. Park and the Lynds, whose community studies from the 1920's and 1930's brought Durkheim to the attention of American historians, Handlin wrote feelingly of anxious people forced by social upheaval to abandon familiar settings and navigate through vast anonymous environments. Their "alienation" was an exaggerated version of a typically modern plight.

Variations on this basic theme surfaced repeatedly as the range of Handlin's work widened to include such topics as slavery and anti-Semitism and such genres as economic history and political biography. Starting in the early 1950's, too, he attempted self-consciously to reach a popular audience that assumed historians could read the past for wisdom regarding "problems" of the present and future. Handlin was quite prepared to supply that wisdom. If migration was the essence of American historical experience, as he perceived it, then "liberty" was the essential American value to be derived from that experience. People in flight should learn to live with danger or uncertainty and seize opportunities to enhance their individuality and personal dignity. From this perspective, perhaps better called Emersonian than "existentialist," Handlin was predictably scornful of suburbanites in the 1950's for their preoccupation with "security" and "adjustment." In the 1960's he also emerged as an outspoken opponent of what he charged was "infantile leftism" rampant among college students, intellectuals, and other affluent elites out of touch with reality. Like many of his generation on their way to becoming neo-conservatives, Handlin believed that the "new left" in America had shamelessly distorted the progressive heritage of Dewey, Holmes, and Brandeis.

The shrillness of Handlin's political commentary during and after the Vietnam War may have resulted from a certain unease that he sometimes betrayed in playing the role of an academic statesman. He had broken into an exclusive genteel world of scholarship in the 1930's, only to watch higher education in America change pell-mell following World War II. Student populations grew immense and heterogeneous; overspecialized professors no longer shared a general culture. Although intermittently disdainful of the new intelligentsia establishing itself in the post-war American universities, Handlin had been an "outsider" himself and so was implicated in the very trends that he tended to deplore. He knew how unrealistic it was to emulate Robert M. Hutchins in campaigning for a return to old ways that in any case had never been positively good. The contradictions between Handlin's rhetoric and practice entertained his critics, and exasperated many admirers. While castigating historians on the left for their chronic eagerness to politicize the past, he not only did much the same himself but outdid them all by experimenting with potentially popular forms of historical prose.

Handlin's ambiguous professional experience seemed of a piece with his ironical vision of voluntaristic modern society. Though inclined to belittle social-scientific theory and technique, not only did he use both himself but he educated a long line of talented interdisciplinary historians. Having supervised more than 70 dissertations at Harvard, where he also developed a program of research fellowships, he never claimed to preside over a "school" of historical scholarship. His students noted the rather mischievously unsystematic quality of his mind when they recalled that he taught by asking Delphic questions. He was too much an American, as he expounded the complex meaning of that term, to insist on asserting the prerogatives of a "master" historian.

—Stephen Botein

HARDY, G(odfrey) H(arold).   British mathematician.   Born in Cranleigh, Surrey, 7 February 1877. Educated at Winchester College; studied at Trinity College, Cambridge, from 1896, M.A. Fellow, Trinity College, from 1900; Lecturer, 1906-14, Cayley Lecturer in Mathematics, 1914-19, Cambridge University; Savilian Professor of Geometry, 1919-31, and Fellow, New College, from 1920, Oxford University; Sadleirian Professor of Pure Mathematics, Cambridge University, 1931-42. Visiting Professor, Princeton University, New Jersey, and California Insitute of Technology, Pasadena, 1928-29. President, Mathematical Association, 1924-26; National Union of Scientific Workers, 1924-26; and London Mathematical Society, 1926-28, 1939-41. Recipient, Royal Medal, 1920, Sylvester Medal, 1940, and Copley Medal, 1947, Royal Society, London; De Morgan Medal, London Mathematical Society, 1929; Chanevent Prize, American Mathematical Association, 1933. Honorary doctorate: University of Athens; Harvard University, Cambridge, Massachusetts; University of Sofia; University of Birmingham; University of Edinburgh; Marburg University, Germany; Oslo University. Fellow, Royal Society; Royal Astronomical Society; and Cambridge Philosophical Society. Associé Étranger, Paris Academy of Sciences, 1947. *Died* (in Cambridge) *1 December 1947*.

PUBLICATIONS

Mathematics

The Integration of Functions of a Single Variable.   Cambridge, Cambridge University Press, 1905.
A Course of Pure Mathematics.   Cambridge, Cambridge University Press, 1908; New York, Macmillan, 1945.
Orders of Infinity: The 'Infinitärealcül' of Paul Du Bois-Reymond.   Cambridge, Cambridge University Press, 1910.
Examinations for Mathematical Scholarships at Oxford and Cambridge.   London, His Majesty's Stationery Office, 1912.
The General Theory of Dirichlet's Series, with Marcel Riesz.   Cambridge, Cambridge University Press, 1915; New York, Stechert-Hafner, 1964.
Mr. S. Ramanujan's Mathematical Work in England: Report to the University of Madras.   Cambridge, Cambridge University Press, 1916.
Some Famous Problems of the Theory of Numbers and in Particular Waring's Problem (lecture).   Oxford, Clarendon Press, 1920.
A Theorem Concerning Series of Positive Terms, With Application to the Theory of Functions, with J.E. Littlewood.   Copenhagen, A.F. Høst, 1925.
The Case Against the Mathematical Tripos (lecture).   London, G. Bell, 1926.
Inequalities, with others.   Cambridge, Cambridge University Press, 1934.
Lectures by Godfrey H. Hardy on the Mathematical Work of Ramanujan.   Ann Arbor, Michigan, Edwards, 1937.
An Introduction to the Theory of Numbers, with E.M. Wright.   Oxford, Clarendon Press, 1938.
Ramanujan: Twelve Lectures on Subjects Suggested by His Life and Work.   Cambridge, Cambridge University Press, 1940; New York, Chelsea Publishing, 1959(?).
Fourier Series, with W.W. Rogosinski.   Cambridge, Cambridge University Press, and New York, Macmillan, 1944.
Divergent Series.   Oxford, Clarendon Press, 1949.
Collected Papers of G.H. Hardy: Including Joint Papers with J.E. Littlewood and Others, edited by a Committee Appointed by the London Mathematical Society.   Oxford, Clarendon Press, 1966-.

Other

A Mathematician's Apology.   Cambridge, Cambridge University Press, 1940.

Bertrand Russell and Trinity: A College Controversy of the Last War.   Cambridge, Cambridge University Press, 1942; New York, Arno Press, 1977.

Editor, with others, *Collected Papers of Srinivasa Ramanujan*. Cambridge, Cambridge University Press, 1927; New York, Chelsea Publishing, 1962.

*   *   *

G.H. Hardy was a British mathematician who made numerous fundamental contributions to his field, often through collaboration with other scholars. Rather casually, he discovered and published what is now called the Hardy-Weinberg law—a statement of central importance to the study of genetics.

In 1908, Hardy wrote a letter to *Science*, the scholarly journal, in which he commented upon a controversy related to genetics and provided algebraic calculations to settle it. He was then a lecturer in mathematics at Cambridge University, at work every day with highly complex equations. His letter and his calculations did not seem particularly important to him. Hardy had, in fact, found a way to state in algebraic terms the genetic equilibrium of a population. Since W. Weinberg, a German physician, independently made this discovery during the same year, the equation is known today as the Hardy-Weinberg law.

Generally speaking, the Hardy-Weinberg law states that in a large population where mating is random, the proportion of dominant and recessive genes remains constant in succeeding generations unless some outside force disturbs the equilibrium. Rare traits do not disappear as one might expect. There is no evolution. Selection, mutation, and migration are the outside forces that can transform the population.

The Hardy-Weinberg law is important for its affirmation of natural selection as the primary mechanism of evolution. If mating is random, the rate of evolution is zero. If mating is selective, however, the population changes over time in the direction of the characteristics favored in selection and away from those not favored. The Hardy-Weinberg law is used by medical scientists to predict the probability of defective offspring from human matings. It is valuable in the study of genetic problems including Rh blood group distribution and hemolytic disease. The law also helps to determine whether there are harmful mutations among human beings as a result of radioactivity in the environment.

Hardy had two major professional collaborators. The first of these was J.E. Littlewood, a fellow professor, with whom Hardy co-authored many papers starting in 1912. Hardy also teamed with Srinivasa Ramanujan, a self-taught Indian mathematician who mailed Hardy specimens of his work, received encouragement, arrived in England one year later, and remained until 1919. Ramanujan and Hardy wrote papers together during this period. Hardy published a memorial volume after his colleague's early death in 1920.

Working with Littlewood, Hardy made major contributions to number theory, the branch of mathematics that concerns itself with integers or whole numbers and their properties. (Typical whole numbers are $\pm 1, \pm 2, \pm 3$, etc.) Number theory is one of the oldest fields in mathematics. Its history begins with the ancients.

Hardy and Littlewood made contributions to Diophantine analysis. This is a group of problems in numbers theory that is named after the Greek mathematician Diophantes of Alexandria (*fl.* 250 AD). A Diophantine equation is one whose solutions are required to be integers. The best-known equation of this kind—$ax + by = c$—involves the first powers of x and y. Diophantine equations stand among the oldest problems in analytic number theory, the branch that deals with the effects of analysis upon number theory. Analysis is used to prove certain properties of integers (both ordinary and algebraic) and to express results quantitatively.

Hardy was involved in the use of analysis to establish quantitative results in number theory. He and Littlewood worked on the sequence of primes. Prime numbers are integers greater than one which have no positive divisors other than one and themselves. The sequence of primes begins 2, 3, 5, 7, 11 and goes on to infinity. Hardy studied the function $\pi(x)$ associated with the sequence of primes: $\pi(x)$ = the number of primes equal to or less than x; thus $\pi(10)$ = 4 (standing for the primes 2, 3, 5, and 7); and $\pi(20)$ = 8 (standing for the primes 2, 3, 5, 7, 11, 13, 17, and 19). This function too can proceed to infinity.

Hardy and Littlewood tried but failed to solve a major problem in numbers theory: the proof of Goldbach's conjecture. In 1742, the Prussian-born mathematician Christian Goldbach had declared that every number greater than or equal to 4 can be written as the sum of two primes. Thus: $12 = 5 + 7$ or $20 = 17 + 3$, etc. This hypothesis is simple enough, but its proof cannot be approached without extensive and intricate analysis. Hardy was not alone in his failure to prove Goldbach's conjecture. It took until 1937 for a partial solution to be published. At that time, Ivan Matveyevich Vinogradov, a Soviet mathematician, demonstrated that large odd numbers can be written as the sum of three primes.

In his work on the distribution of prime numbers, Hardy was concerned with a major topic that still engages the attention of mathematicians: the theory of the Riemann zeta-function. This function, which is used in numbers theory to help with investigations of prime numbers, is the infinite sum: $\zeta(x) = 1 + (1/2)^x + (1/3)^x + (1/4)^x + ...$, where $x = u + iv$. When $x = 1$ the sum is called a harmonic series; its solution is infinite; when x is less than 1, the sum is also infinite; when x is greater than 1, the sum is finite. The major student of this function was Bernhard Riemann, the 19th century German mathematician. In 1859, Riemann elaborated upon his original zeta-function, proposing a hypothesis (today called the Riemann hypothesis) which mathematicians have been trying to prove ever since. Hardy was one of those who investigated this problem, making a contribution to its solution; specifically, Hardy proved that when the Riemann zeta-function equals zero, an infinite number of values of u are equal to 1/2 when $v \neq 0$. He also stated that not all values of u are necessarily equal to 1/2 when $v \neq 0$. Riemann had hypothesized that all u equals 1/2 when $v \neq 0$.

Hardy worked with Ramanujan (in 1917) and later with Littlewood to develop what is called the Circle method. Subsequently refined by other investigators, the Circle method is used to solve additive problems in number theory. This method has been employed in a partial demonstration of the Goldbach conjecture—proving that almost all even numbers are the sum of two primes.

Hardy was considered the leading English mathematician of his time. Though a thorough grasp of higher mathematics is requisite to comprehensive understanding of his significance, any layperson can appreciate Hardy's wide-ranging curiosity, his original turn of mind, and his uncompromising insistence upon rigorous thinking.

—Victor Cassidy

HARLOW, Harry F(rederick). American psychologist. Born in Fairfield, Iowa, 31 October 1905. Studied at Stanford University, California, B.A. 1927, Ph.D. 1930. Married Clara Mears in 1932 (divorced; remarried in 1972); married Margaret Kuenne in 1948; 4 children. Assistant Professor, 1930-39, Associate Professor, 1939-44, Professor, 1944-56, George Cary Comstock Research Professor of Psychology and Director of Primate Laboratory, 1956-74, and Professor Emeritus, 1974-81, University of Wisconsin, Madison; Honorary Research Professor of Psychology, University of Arizona, Tucson, 1974-81. Carnegie Fellow in Anthropology, 1939-40. Messenger Lecturer, Cornell University, Ithaca, New York, 1961; Harris Lecturer, Northwestern

University, Evenston, Illinois, 1971; Martin Rehfuss Lecturer, Jefferson Medical College, Philadelphia, 1972. Head, Human Resources Research Branch, Department of the Army, 1950-52; Head, Division of Anthropology and Psychology, National Research Council, 1953-55; Consultant, Army Scientific Advisory Panel, 1956-65; Director, Wisconsin Regional Primate Research Center, 1961-71. President, Midwest Psychological Association, 1947-48, and American Psychological Association, 1958-59. Recipient: Howard Crosby Warren Medal, 1956; Distinguished Psychologist Award, 1960; National Medal of Science, 1967; Gold Medal, American Psychological Foundation, 1973; Annual Award, Society for the Scientific Study of Sex, 1974; Von Gieson Award, New York State Psychiatric Institute, 1975; International Award, Kittay Scientific Foundation, 1975. Member, National Academy of Sciences; Fellow, American Psychological Association, and American Academy of Arts and Sciences. Affiliate, Royal Society of Medicine. *Died 6 December 1981.*

PUBLICATIONS

Psychology

Performance of Macaque Monkeys on a Test of the Concept of Generalized Triangularity, with Gwen Andrew. Berkeley, University of California Press, 1948.
Learning to Love. San Francisco, Albion Publishing Company, 1971.
Psychology, with others. San Francisco, Albion Publishing Company, 1971.
The Human Model: Primate Perspectives, with Clara Mears. Washington D.C., V.N. Winston, 1979.

Other

Editor, with Clinton N. Woolsey, *Biological and Biochemical Bases of Behavior.* Madison, University of Wisconsin Press, 1958.
Editor, with others, *Behavior of Nonhuman Primates: Modern Research Trends.* New York, Academic Press, 1965.

*   *   *

As a graduate student at Stanford Harry F. Harlow held assistantships teaching social psychology for Paul Farnsworth and conducting rat-research for C.P. Stone. His dissertation, which he wrote under the guidance of Stone, left him disenchanted with both rats and parametric research. At the same time, however, he was becoming strongly interested in the history of psychology, and it was this point of view that helped him to revolutionize the fields of animal learning and motivation.

Shortly after becoming a member of the faculty at the University of Wisconsin, Harlow began working with an orangutang; it died several months later, but shortly after that the university provided him with a monkey laboratory in which to work. Harlow's original interest was in cortical localization of higher learning. In order to carry out this work he needed a standard set of measures of discrimination and other visual-perceptual processes; this led him to construct the Wisconsin General Test Apparatus. While he was developing this standard battery, however, his observations of monkey learning behavior led him to discover the "learning set"—the process of learning to learn.

After Harlow had completed his tenure as Head of the Human Resources Branch of the U.S. Army, he returned to Wisconsin where, working with his wife, he did extensive work studying the love relationship between mother and child and among peers. His first observations were accidental. In attempting to establish a breeding colony of monkeys he separated them from their mothers, who had brought back germs from India when they were imported, and isolated them in a germ-free environment.

The infants grew physically, but emotionally they proved to be severely retarded and would not mate. Observing how the young monkeys clung to their diapers like security blankets, Harlow inferred that their diapers served as surrogate mothers. From this observation he developed the "cloth mother" and the "wire mother," which led him to the discovery of contact comfort.

According to the behaviorists, the incentive value of neutral objects resulted from their association with primary drive reduction. Harlow's monkeys, while they were well-fed and cared for, did not, however, develop strong attachments for the artificial mothers. Even though the cloth mother was modified several times so that it served as a source of feeding, warmth, and motion, the young monkeys did not develop strong attachments to the surrogates.

The Harlows distinguished five types of love in the monkeys: maternal love for the child; infant love for the mother; peer love; adult heterosexual love; and paternal love for the child. It became obvious to them that the parent-child relationship was vital to the development of stable peer relationships and that both were necessary for the development of adult and paternal love. When young monkeys were isolated, their emotional growth was stunted, so that they became autistic and behaved as many schizophrenic human children do, rocking and huddling. They also became badly depressed. The Harlows found that the peer relationship could be reasonably well-activated when the monkey raised in isolation was introduced to a younger, less aggressive monkey, who was just at the age of starting his or her own peer interaction.

Harlow's career spanned half a century, and he was responsible for contributing notably to understanding of both monkey and human behavior.

—R.W. Rieber

HART, H(erbert) L(ionel) A(dolphus). British jurist. Born 18 July 1907. Educated at Cheltenham College, and Bradford Grammar School; studied at New College, Oxford, first class honors 1929. Served in the War Office, 1940-45. Married Jenifer Williams in 1941; 4 children. Practiced at the Chancery Bar, 1932-40; Fellow and Tutor in Philosophy, New College, 1945; University Lecturer, 1948, and Professor of Jurisprudence, 1952-68, Oxford University; Fellow, 1952-68, and Resident Fellow, 1969-73, University College, Oxford; Senior Resident Fellow, Nuffield Foundation, 1969-73; Principal, Brasenose College, Oxford, 1973-78. Visiting Professor, Harvard University, Cambridge, Massachusetts, 1956-57, and University of California at Los Angeles, 1961-62. President, Aristotelian Society, 1959-60. Honorary doctorate: University of Stockholm, 1960; University of Glasgow, Scotland, 1966; University of Chicago, 1966; Cambridge University, 1978; National University of Mexico, 1979. Honorary Master of the Bench, London, 1963. Fellow, British Academy, 1962 (Vice-President, 1976-77), Academy of Science, Turin, 1964; Commonwealth Prestige Fellow (Government of New Zealand), 1971. Foreign Member, American Academy of Arts and Sciences, 1966. Honorary Fellow, New College, 1968; University College, 1973; and Brasenose College, 1978. Address: University College, Oxford, England.

PUBLICATIONS

Law

Definition and Theory in Jurisprudence (lecture). Oxford, Clarendon Press, 1953.
Causation in the Law, with A.M. Honoré. Oxford, Clarendon Press, 1959.
The Concept of Law. Oxford, Clarendon Press, 1961.

Punishment and the Elimination of Responsibility (lecture). London, Athlone Press, 1962.
Law, Liberty, and Morality (lectures). London, Oxford University Press, 1963.
The Morality of the Criminal Law (lectures). London, Oxford University Press, 1964.
Punishment and Responsibility: Essays in the Philosophy of Law. Oxford, Clarendon Press, and New York, Oxford University Press, 1968.
Essays on Bentham. Oxford, Clarendon Press, 1982.

Other

Editor, *Knowledge and the Good in Plato's Republic*, by Horace William Brindley Joseph. London, Oxford University Press, 1948.
Editor, with J.H. Burns, *An Introduction to the Principles of Morals and Legislation*, by Jeremy Bentham. London, Athlone Press, 1970.
Editor, *Of Laws in General*, by Jeremy Bentham. London, Athlone Press, 1970.
Editor, with J.H. Burns, *A Comment on the Commentaries and A Fragment on Government*, by Jeremy Bentham. London, Athlone Press, 1977.

*

Critical Studies: *Symposium: The Philosophy of H.L.A. Hart*, Chicago, University of Chicago Law School, 1967; *Fundamental Change in Society: Hart and Sartre on Revolution* by William L. MacBride, The Hague, Mouton, 1970; *Law, Morality, and Society: Essays in Honour of H.L.A Hart*, edited by P.M.S. Hacker and J. Raz, Oxford, Clarendon Press, 1977; *H.L.A. Hart* by Neil MacCormick, London, Arnold, 1981.

*   *   *

Unquestionably H.L.A. Hart is the most distinguished legal philosopher in the English-speaking world. His academic background in philosophy and his practical experience as a barrister have combined to form a powerful intellectual apparatus for the study of jurisprudence, a subject that was in something of a decline for much of this century.

His inaugural lecture on becoming Professor of Jurisprudence in Oxford, *Definition and Theory in Jurisprudence*, introduced the methods of linguistic philosophy to legal theory. In this lecture Hart objected to the tendency of legal philosophers to search for exact terms such as "right," "intention," "duty" and "law." These words do not stand for real entities; rather, their meaning is to be discovered in a close analysis of their use in typical legal discourse. However, legal philosophy is not merely about words for it is the *social context* of legal language that gives words their sense.

This approach was typified in Hart's next major work, *Causation in the Law*, jointly written with A.M. Honoré. In this book the authors show how the ordinary uses of "causality" are handled in the legal process, and explore the relationship between causal explanations of events and the familiar notions of criminal and civil liability. It was followed in 1961 by the major statement of Hart's jurisprudence, *The Concept of Law*. His other work in technical jurisprudence consists of essays on various aspects of the theory and justification of punishment, on the criminal law and the theory of legal rights. Also his work as an editor (especially *Of Laws in General*) in the Bentham series has contributed to the revival of interest in that author.

Hart's work in social philosophy, however, has not been limited to the technical aspects of the philosophy of law. In shorter books and essays he has constructed a normative philosophy of liberal-utilitarianism: this combines a plea for the relaxation of the role of state and positive law in the field of personal morality (see *Law, Liberty and Morality*) with a justification for a modest degree of intervention in welfare and the economy.

In methodology, Hart may be described as a legal positivist, but with some important qualifications. Against traditional natural lawyers he maintains that there is a logical distinction between law and morality so that the criteria for the validity of a purported law cannot be those that derive from an alleged objective morality. He maintains this not only for the purpose of intellectual clarity but also because in his view ethical evaluation of the law is possible only when such a distinction has been made. However, unlike some positivists, he did not believe that law may have any content to be formally valid: a system of rules must be consistent with some fairly basic features of the human condition if it is to be called "law."

Hart, furthermore, departs from orthodox positivism with the distinction he makes between the "external" and the "internal" points of view in the explanation of the fundamentals of a legal order. Those who understand law from the external point of view, often under the influence of extreme empiricist social science, try to identify law by some hard objective criteria, such as the habit of obedience to a sovereign's command, or reduce law to predictions of judicial decisions; but Hart argues that this is to distort systematically the nature of a legal system. The internal point of view, which embodies a methodology now known as "hermeneutics," asks us to consider law as a system of normative rules which guides people's conduct and sets standards to which they *ought* to conform. Unlike habitual behavior, rule-governed behavior is behavior characterized by a "critical reflective attitude," such that the breach of a rule is followed by criticism and pressure for conformity. Unless enough people in a community "internalize" rules in this way, the continuity of a legal system is hard to envisage; though, of course, Hart acknowledges that legal rules are distinguished from other sorts of social rules by the fact that certain obligations are enforceable.

An important limitation in the "Command" theory of law (as formulated by Bentham and Austin) is that it tries to reduce all legal phenomena to one type of law—the duty-imposing type. While Hart concedes that criminal law may look like a set of duties that are imposed on people through fear of sanctions, he insists that there are other legal rules, which he calls "power-conferring" rules; these rules have an entirely different logical structure. They do not compel citizens to do anything but enable them to do certain things, such as marry, leave wills and convey property. Also, these rules may confer powers on public bodies as well as private individuals. Hart's stress on the social function of rules distinguishes his jurisprudence from the abstract formalism of say, Kelsen, and justifies his own description of *The Concept of Law* as an essay in "descriptive sociology."

Although Hart does not attempt an exact definition of law, he does describe a mature legal system as a "union of primary and secondary rules." Hart's account is not without ambiguities, but primary rules can be said to consist of the "content" of a legal system, the substance of the criminal and civil law which tells people what they may and may not do; secondary rules are rules of adjudication, alteration and recognition. These latter rules are not concerned with the conduct of individuals but with the way primary rules may be enforced and interpreted through the courts, altered by new legislation and tested for validity by reference to an ultimate constitutional rule. In other words, secondary rules are "rules about rules." It is to be noted that the distinction between primary and secondary rules is not identical to that between duty-imposing and power-conferring rules because the secondary rule of recognition imposes a *duty* upon officials of a legal order to validate claims to law according to that rule.

The rule of recognition is crucially important for Hart's jurisprudence because it gets over certain difficulties in the Command theory. This held that a law was valid if it emanated from the will of a determinate sovereign. But this did not explain how legal authority is passed from one sovereign to another. This can only be accounted for by the notion of a fundamental rule that confers authority on a sovereign body. In other words, rules must pre-cede sovereignty. A rule of recognition may be simple, such as that in the British system of parliamentary sovereignity, or complex, such as in federal systems.

In his evaluative social philosophy Hart has pursued a cautious liberal-utilitarianism. While he envisages some positive role for government in maximizing happiness he, as a pluralist, holds that this should be limited by the logically independent principles of justice and individual rights.

Hart's normative ethics were cogently expressed in his well-publicized debate with Patrick (Lord) Devlin over the relationship between law and morality. In reply to Devlin's argument that abstract philosophical principles could not be used to determine how much personal liberty could be held against the claims of organized society, that the state had an interest in preventing immorality (even where this appeared to cause no assignable harm) and that the social order would collapse if its moral order were undermined, Hart, in *Law, Liberty and Morality* revived the argument of John Stuart Mill that there ought to be a protected area around the individual into which the law should not reach and that reason could determine how large this area should be. However, unlike Mill, Hart believes that paternalist legislation, for example, to prevent people consenting to their own murder or taking dangerous addictive drugs, can be justified on liberal grounds. In fact, Hart has to defend paternalism because his belief in a compulsory welfarist role for the State necessitates an element of paternalism.

His argument for a wide area of personal liberty for the individual in choosing life styles and experimenting with different moralities is based on the liberal belief that the law should be ethically neutral; it should not uphold the dominant morality but protect individuals from injury. Thus, for example, the only regulation of sexual conduct which is morally permissible is that which prevents violence and exploitation. Hart, on utilitarian grounds, argues that much of the moralistic legislation concerning personal conduct was objectionable precisely because it caused considerable pain to individuals. However, Hart's principles could be used to justify some controls on, say, obscene publications if the *public* display of them was offensive: but not on the grounds that they were immoral because this would logically prohibit their *private* consumption.

Some of Hart's best work in analytical social philosophy is in his essays on *Punishment and Responsibility*. Here, in addition to his analysis of concepts, he contributes to the general question of the justification of punishment. His arguments are consistent with his ethical pluralism since he rejects an exclusive commitment to either utilitarianism or retributivism. In his view the "general justifying aim" of punishment must be a utilitarian one, since he can see no moral value in punishing the guilty merely because they are guilty, but in the question of *distribution* of punishment he accepts the relevance of the typically retributivist notions of "desert" and "responsibility." Furthermore, Hart's own commitment to rights, personal responsibility and individual freedom makes him highly sceptical of those social reformers who would replace conventional forms of punishment by "treatment" or "reform."

Criticism of Hart's jurisprudence has centred on his account of a legal system in terms of primary and secondary rules. It is contended that his formulation here is confused, that he ignores the role of legal principles which are not reducible to rules and that the existence of a legal system does not depend on the existence of a rule of recognition. Also, it is argued that despite his claim to have written about the theory of law in the context of a broad social theory, his description of a legal system in terms of rules is still heavily formalistic. Nevertheless, all the criticisms have been constructive and endorse his lasting contribution to jurisprudence.

—Norman P. Barry

HARTSHORNE, Charles. American philosopher. Born in Kittanning, Pennsylvania, 5 June 1897. Studied at Haverford College, Pennsylvania, 1915-17; Harvard University, Cambridge, Massachusetts, B.A. 1921, Ph.D. 1923; and at the Universities of Marburg and Freiburg, 1923-25. Served in the United States Army, 1917-19. Married Dorothy Eleanore Cooper, 1928; 1 daughter. Instructor and Research Fellow, Harvard University, 1925-28; Instructor to Professor of Philosophy, University of Chicago, 1928-55; Professor of Philosophy, Emory University, Atlanta, 1955-62; Ashbel Smith Professor, 1962-76, and since 1976 Professor Emeritus, University of Texas at Austin. Visiting Professor, Stanford University, California, 1937; New School for Social Research, New York, 1941-42; Goethe University, Frankfurt, 1948-49; University of Washington, Seattle, 1958; Banaras Hindu University, India, 1966; Colorado College, Colorado Springs, 1977 and 1979; University of Louvain, Belgium, 1978. Fulbright Professsor, Melbourne, Australia, 1952, and Kyoto, Japan, 1958 and 1966. Terry Lecturer, Yale University, New Haven, Connecticut, 1947; Matchette Lecturer, Wesleyan University, Middletown, Connecticut, 1964; Dudleian Lecturer, 1964, and Lowell Lecturer, 1979, Harvard University; Morse Lecturer, Union Theological Seminary, New York, 1964. President, Western Division, American Philosophical Association, 1949; Charles Peirce Society, 1950-51; Metaphysical Society of America, 1954-55; Southern Society for Philosophy of Religion, 1963; and Southern Society for Philosophy and Psychology, 1965. Recipient: Lecomte de Noüy Award, for *The Logic of Perfection*, 1963. Honorary doctorate: Haverford College, 1967; Emory University, 1969; University of Louvain, 1978. Fellow, American Academy of Arts and Sciences. Address: 313 Waggener Hall, University of Texas, Austin, Texas 78712, U.S.A.

PUBLICATIONS

Philosophy and Theology

The Philosophy and Psychology of Sensation. Chicago, University of Chicago Press, 1934.
Beyond Humanism: Essays in the New Philosophy of Nature. Chicago, Willett Clark, 1937.
Man's Vision of God and the Logic of Theism. Chicago, Willett Clark, 1941.
The Divine Relativity: A Social Conception of God (lectures). New Haven, Connecticut, Yale University Press, 1948.
Whitehead and the Modern World: Science, Metaphysics, and Civilization: Three Essays on the Thought of Alfred North Whitehead, with others. Boston, Beacon Press, 1953.
Reality as Social Process: Studies in Metaphysics and Religion. Glencoe, Illinois, Free Press, 1953.
The Logic of Perfection. La Salle, Illinois, Open Court, 1962.
Anselm's Discovery: A Re-Examination of the Ontological Proof for God's Existence. La Salle, Illinois, Open Court, 1965.
Aquinas to Whitehead: Seven Centuries of Metaphysics of Religion. Milwaukee, Marquette University Publications, 1970.
Creative Synthesis and Philosophical Method. London, S.C.M. Press, and La Salle, Illinois, Open Court, 1970.
Whitehead's Philosophy: Selected Essays 1935-1970. Lincoln, University of Nebraska Press, 1972.
Whitehead's View of Reality, with Creighton Peden. New York, Pilgrim Press, 1981.

Other

Born to Sing: An Interpretation and World Survey of Bird Song. Bloomington, Indiana University Press, 1973.

Editor, with Paul Weiss, *Collected Papers of Charles Sanders Peirce*. Cambridge, Massachusetts, Harvard University Press, 6 vols., 1931-35.

Editor, with William L. Reese, *Philosophers Speak of God*. Chicago, University of Chicago Press, 1953.

*

Critical Studies: *The Hartshorne Festschrift: Process and Divinity: Philosophical Essays Presented to Charles Hartshorne*, edited by William L. Reese and Eugene Freeman, La Salle, Illinois, Open Court, 1964 (contains a bibliography); *The Concrete God: A New Beginning for Theology: The Thought of Charles Hartshorne* by Ralph E. James, Indianapolis, Bobbs Merrill, 1967; *Hartshorne and Neoclassical Metaphysics* by Eugene H. Peters, Lincoln, University of Nebraska Press, 1970; *Charles Hartshorne* by Alan Gragg, Waco, Texas, Word Books, 1973.

*   *   *

Charles Hartshorne is an American-born metaphysician who like the classical metaphysicians is concerned with the great perennial issues of philosophy. Yet he departs from most in the classical tradition by making change, not permanence, the underlying principle of reality. Accordingly, Hartshorne's thought has been classified with "process philosophy." Permanence or being has a place in the system, but its place is that of an aspect or dimension of the processive.

The relation of the two categories can be seen in Hartshorne's doctrine of God. One of the few who in the 20th century has boldly defended the ontological argument of St. Anselm, Hartshorne nonetheless holds that the argument is weakened by Anselm's adherence to the classical vision of God as sheer immutability. In fact, the existence of God is inalienable just because God in his concrete states is capable of infinite flexibility or adaptability. Whatever occurs God possesses as a datum within his omniscient awareness. Thus, there is a dipolarity in deity, God's existence being the abstract truth that the divine essence is actualized in *some* concrete state or states. The distinction between existence and actuality, the first an abstract feature or character of the second, is one of Hartshorne's novel contributions.

Clearly, Hartshorne's theism is unique in introducing potentiality into the life and constitution of deity. As ground of possibility, God is not one of the possible options—even if actual. God is rather the basis for and accompaniment of any and all possibilities, on both sides of every alternative, as Hartshorne says. It is God's relation to possibility as such which explains his universal functioning as the creative source of every concrete entity.

It is basic in Hartshorne that God not only enables creatures to be realized but also possesses and preserves them, just as they are, in his own concrete experience. God then is all-inclusive, each entity in the world being predictable of God as something possessed in his experience. The world is dynamic, and God continually adds new elements to his experience and in this sense is self-surpassing while remaining the surpasser of all others.

God's omniscience, to which Hartshorne is committed, does not entail God's knowledge of future events. The future consists not of actualities but of possibilities, which of course God knows as such and possesses. Hence, God knows the future as determinable, though the less remote future is known to deity with its various likelihoods and probabilities.

Even the most general features of nature, its laws, are subject to change. Every change introduces some novel determination into being. Though such determinations are not contained in the antecedent states of affairs, nor in the laws governing phenomena, creative additions always arise from causal conditions. So there can never be some contingency x which is simply uncaused. The point is that Hartshorne, while repudiating determination, affirms that every event is a resolution, by its self-determination, of the potentialities given by its causal conditions. Nor is any contingency x ever without origin, as though it might always have existed, while being at every moment capable of failing to exist. For Hartshorne, any contingent thing was once future, even the natural laws. Otherwise, we lack any principle for explaining that thing, and face a sheer, inexplicable fact. The universe consists of creations within contexts given by divine and worldly antecedent conditions.

The laws of nature are, says Hartshorne, dependent on divine decisions. The laws coordinate the world and limit the freedom of creatures. A decision taken in the past, whether by God or creature, is subsequently a causal factor for at least some entities, which are obliged to make that decision a datum in and for their own self-determinations. In turn, those self-determinations become causal data for creativity subsequent to themselves.

The temporal process furnishes the various modalities, the past being fixed and necessary, given the present, the future being possibility, and deity being, as existent, common to all possibilities and hence unconditionally necessary. Each concrete event, emergent from its causal conditions, is a new deposit of actuality, in a limited but genuine sense a creation. Not even the proximate possibility of the event contains its precise and definite qualities. The appearance of those qualities constitutes the event a reality. It should be evident that the actual is for Hartshorne the metaphysical locus to which all else is relative and subservient. Possibilities, for example, do not hang suspended in a semi-autonomous region beyond space and time. They are resident in the actual as its future, as the incomplete and determinable features of the present.

Now the concrete entities of which the universe is composed are each individual or singular things, not because they lack parts or merely because they are unified by their functions and organization, but because they are sentient unities. One must not of course confuse the mere aggregate with the concrete singular. The former may (and in fact does) consist of sentient members, yet itself lack sentience. Hartshorne's commitment to psychicalism (or panpsychism) is based in part on the contention that absence of feeling in concrete singulars would represent a purely negative fact, one for which no available, positive evidence could be adduced. In short, the absence of feeling or awareness in particular entities cannot be a known fact. Hence, it is arbitrary and groundless to parcel the world into minds and mindless bodies. Hartshorne of course intends no simple extension of human psychical categories to the nonhuman world of entities. What he insists on is a kinship of feeling among all individual creatures, however simple or remote from man. Nothing is so flexible and various as experience itself.

The sensitivity of all entities helps explain how the divine influence is exercised over the cosmos. For God is not only the universal subject—for whom all entities are data—but also the universal object—for all entities a datum. By constituting himself an appropriate datum God provides a suasion over all entities. This suasion is not the full and exhaustive control of events. It may be conceived rather as the setting of optimal limits to the possible acts of creatures, minimizing risks of discord and evil, and maximizing opportunities for harmony and good.

The divine inspiration of the creatures in turn enables them to furnish God data of interest and value, however humble they may be, data which God receives and treasures immortally. It is then the aesthetic qualities creatures provide which enrich the life of God in perhaps minor yet unique ways.

Hartshorne, one of the most prolific of philosophic writers, is retired from teaching (Chicago, Emory, Texas) and lives in Austin, Texas. In addition to philosophy, his interest in bird song is one he has cultivated over many years. He enjoys followers in Europe and Asia as well as America, and in theology as well as philosophy.

—Eugene H. Peters

HEBB, D(onald) O(lding). Canadian psychologist. Born in Chester, Nova Scotia, 22 July 1904. Educated at Dalhousie University, Halifax, Nova Scotia, B.A. 1925; McGill University, Montreal, M.A. 1932; University of Chicago, 1934; Harvard University, Cambridge, Masschusetts, Ph.D. 1936. Married Marion Isabel Clark; Elizabeth Nichols Donovan in 1937; Margaret Doreen Wright in 1966; 2 daughters. Fellow, Montreal Neurological Institute, 1937-39; Lecturer and Assistant Professor, Queen's University, Kingston, Ontario, 1939-42; Research Associate, Yerkes Laboratory, Orange Park, Florida, 1942-47; Professor of Psychology, 1947-72, Chancellor, 1970-74, and since 1975 Professor Emeritus, McGill University; since 1977, Honorary Research Associate in Psychology, Dalhousie University. President, Canadian Psychological Association, 1952, and American Psychological Association, 1960. Recipient: Medal, Society of Experimental Psychology, 1958; Award, American Psychological Association and Association for Research in Nervous and Mental Disease, 1962. Honorary doctorate: University of Chicago, 1951; University of Waterloo, Ontario, 1963; Northeastern University, Boston, 1963; Dalhousie University, 1965; York University, Toronto, 1966; McMaster University, Hamilton, Ontario, 1967; Queen's University, 1967; University of Western Ontario, London, 1968; McGill University, 1975. Member, American Academy of Arts and Sciences, and the Royal Society of Canada. Address: RR 1, Chester Basin, Nova Scotia, Canada.

PUBLICATIONS

Psychology

The Organization of Behavior: A Neuropsychological Theory. New York, Wiley, 1949.
A Textbook of Psychology. Philadelphia, Saunders, 1958.
Essay on Mind. Hillsdale, New Jersey, Lawrence Erlbaum, 1980.

*

Critical Studies: *The Nature of Thought: Essays in Honor of D.O. Hebb,* edited by Peter Jusczyk and others, Hillsdale, New Jersey, Lawrence Erlbaum, 1980.

* * *

D.O. Hebb received his Ph.D. from Harvard in 1936; in his thesis he compared the perceptions of rats raised in darkness with normally-reared rats. In two papers published in 1937 based on this research, Hebb came to the conclusion that perceptive ability was not based on experience, that it was innate. From 1937 to 1939 he worked at the Montreal Neurological Institute with Wilder Penfield, where he studied the status of Penfield's patients following brain surgery. There he found that large lesions may in some cases have little effect on intelligence-test performance. Eventually he began edging toward the conclusion that intelligence itself, and not just the ability to do well on intelligence tests, was a result of experience. This was a conclusion that ran counter not only to Hebb's own assumptions but also to the general theories of the time. Yet he remained baffled about how to explain this matter neurologically.

In 1942 Hebb joined K.S. Lashley, with whom he had studied at the University of Chicago, at the Yerkes Laboratories of Primate Biology in Florida. Lashley's original plan was to train chimpanzees in a set of habits and then make brain lesions, conducting pre- and post-operative examinations to determine the effects of the lesions. The plan was seriously delayed, however, when they discovered that the initial training of the monkeys took an extremely long time. But this time spent training the chimpanzees proved useful to Hebb, for it led him to consider the nature of emotion and behavior in them and, by extension, in people. Hebb also considered the matter of recognition of emotion in the monkeys by the staff members at the laboratories. Eventually he came to the conclusion that this recognition involved perception of the present behavior informed by that which had been usual in the past.

In 1944 he returned to the problem of thought and the brain which he had earlier considered while working with Penfield. Recent work by Rafael Lorente de Nó led Hebb to formulate the neurological explanation of a concept, which he had earlier been lacking. According to Hebb, a concept is "a group of cortical neurons exciting and re-exciting each other."

Hebb was now looking at thought as a sequence of brain events, each excited jointly by the preceding event and by the sensory stimulation of the moment, and approaching the conclusion that experience was an important factor in the nature of thought and behavior. This conclusion seemed to imply, however, that thought would be disrupted in a strange environment with unfamiliar contingencies. But as Hebb put it, even if things should fall up rather than down, would it not still be possible to think clearly about what was going on? At this point he remembered how the chimpanzees would become terrified at seeing a model of a portion of chimp anatomy. He concluded that such disturbances resulted from the lack of the usual contingencies (a head without a body) rather than a conflict.

In 1947 Hebb was appointed Professor of Psychology at McGill University. It was during this time that he worked on his book *The Organization of Behavior*, which was published in 1949. The book was an immediate—and, for Hebb, an astonishing—success. Though certain physiological aspects of the book were inexact, the overall theory—that experience, among other things, played a key role in determining behavior, a refutation of the conclusion he had come to 12 years earlier—remains fairly stable.

During the 1950's and 60's Hebb continued to produce important work, such as studies of the early-environment of children that were instrumental in persuading psychologists that IQ was not innate, which was a major factor in the founding of the Head Start program.

—R.W. Rieber

HEIDEGGER, Martin. German philosopher. Born in Messkirch, 26 April 1889. Studied at the University of Freiburg, Ph.D. 1914. Married Elfride Petri in 1917; 3 children. Lecturer and later assistant to Edmund Husserl, 1916-23, and Associate Professor, 1923-28, University of Marburg; Professor 1928-45 (Rector, 1933-34), and Professor Emeritus, 1951-57, University of Freiburg (removed from teaching by the Occupation Forces, 1945-51). Recipient: Hebel Prize, 1960. Member, Academy of Fine Arts, Berlin; Academy of Sciences, Heidelberg; Bavarian Academy of Fine Arts. Honorary Citizen of Messkirch, 1959. *Died 26 May 1976.*

PUBLICATIONS

Collections

Gesamtausgabe. Frankfurt, Klostermann, 1975-.
Martin Heidegger: Basic Writings: From Being and Time (1927) to The Task of Thinking (1964), edited by David Farrell Krell. New York, Harper, 1976.

Philosophy

Die Lehre vom Urteil im Psychologismus: Ein kritisch-positiver Beitrag zur Logik. Leipzig, Barth, 1914.
Die Katagorien- und Bedeutungslehre des Duns Scotus. Tü-

bingen, Mohr, 1916.
Sein und Zeit: Erste Hälfte. Halle, Germany, Niemeyer, 1927; as *Being and Time,* New York, Harper, and London, SCM Press, 1962.
Kant und das Problem der Metaphysik. Bonn, Cohen, 1929; as *Kant and the Problem of Metaphysics,* Bloomington, Indiana University Press, 1962.
"Vom Wesen des Grundes," in *Festschrift für Edmund Husserl.* Halle, Germany, Niemeyer, 1929; as *The Essence of Reasons,* Evanston, Illinois, Northwestern University Press, 1969.
Was ist Metaphysik? Bonn, Cohen, 1929; as "What is Metaphysics?" in *Existence and Being,* edited by Werner Brock, Chicago, Regnery, 1949.
Vom Wesen der Wahrheit. Frankfurt, Klostermann, 1943; as "On the Essence of Truth," in *Existence and Being,* edited by Werner Brock, Chicago, Regnery, 1949.
Erläuterungen zu Hölderlins Dichtung. Frankfurt, Klostermann, 1944; selection as "Hölderlin and the Essence of Poetry," in *Existence and Being,* edited by Werner Brock, Chicago, Regnery, 1949.
Platons Lehre von der Wahrheit: Mit einem Brief über den "Humanismus." Berne, Francke, 1947; as "Plato's Doctrine of Truth" and "Letter on 'Humanism,' " in *Philosophy in the Twentieth Century,* edited by William Barrett and Henry D. Aiken, New York, Random House, vol. 2, 1962.
Holzwege. Frankfurt, Klostermann, 1950; selection as "The Origin of the Work of Art," in *Poetry, Thought, Language,* New York, Harper, 1971.
Der Feldweg. Frankfurt, Klostermann, 1953.
Einführung in die Metaphysik. Tübingen, Niemeyer, 1953; as *An Introduction to Metaphysics,* New Haven, Connecticut, Yale University Press, and London, Oxford University Press, 1959.
Aus der Erfahrung des Denkens. Pfullingen, Germany, Neske, 1954.
Vorträge und Aufsätze. Pfullingen, Germany, Neske, 3 vols., 1954.
Was heisst Denken? Tübingen, Niemeyer, 1954; as *What Is Called Thinking?,* New York, Harper, 1968.
Was ist das—die Philosophie? Pfullingen, Germany, Neske, 1956; as *What Is Philosophy?* New York, Twayne, and London, Vision Press, 1958.
Zur Seinsfrage. Frankfurt, Klostermann, 1956; as *The Question of Being,* New York, Twayne, 1958; London, Vision Press, 1959.
Der Satz vom Grund. Pfullingen, Germany, Neske, 1957.
Identität und Differenz. Pfullingen, Germany, Neske, 1957; as *Identity and Difference,* New York, Harper, 1969.
Hebel—Der Hausfreund. Pfullingen, Germany, Neske, 1957.
Gelassenheit. Pfullingen, Germany, Neske, 1959; as *Discourse on Thinking,* New York, Harper, 1966.
Unterwegs zur Sprache. Pfullingen, Germany, Neske, 1959; as *On the Way to Language,* New York, Harper, 1971.
Nietzsche. Pfullingen, Germany, Neske, 2 vols., 1961; as *Nietzsche,* New York, Harper, 4 vols., 1979.
Kants These über das Sein. Frankfurt, Klostermann, 1962.
Die Technik und die Kehre. Pfullinger, Germany, Neske, 1962; in *The Question Concerning Technology and Other Essays,* New York, Harper, 1976.
Die Frage nach dem Ding: Zu Kants Lehre von den transzendentaler Grundsätzen. Tübingen, Niemeyer, 1962.
Wegmarken. Frankfurt, Klostermann, 1967.
Zur Sache des Denkens. Tübingen, Niemeyer, 1969; selections in *The End of Philosophy,* New York, Harper, 1973; London, Souvenir Press, 1975.
Heraklit: Seminar Wintersemester 1966/67. Frankfurt, Klostermann, 1970; as *Heraclitus Seminar, 1966-67,* University, University of Alabama Press, 1979.
Phänomenologie und Theologie. Frankfurt, Klostermann, 1971.
Frühe Schriften. Frankfurt, Klostermann 1971.
Die Grundprobleme der Phänomenologie. Frankfurt, Klos-

termann, 1975; as *The Basic Problems of Phenomenology*, Bloomington, Indiana University Press, 1982.

Early Greek Thinking (selected essays). New York, Harper, 1975.

Logik: Die Frage nach der Wahrheit. Frankfurt, Klostermann, 1976.

The Piety of Thinking: Essays by Martin Heidegger. Bloomington, Indiana University Press, 1976.

*

Bibliographies: *Heidegger-Bibliographie* by Hans-Martin Sass, Meisenheim am Glan, Hain, 1968; *Materialen zur Heidegger-Bibliographie 1917-1972* by Hans-Martin Sass and others, Meisenheim am Glan, Hain, 1975; *Martin Heidegger: Bibliography and Glossary*, Bowling Green, Ohio, Philosophical Documentation Center, 1982.

Critical Studies: *Martin Heidegger* by Marjorie Green, London, Bowes and Bowes, and New Haven, Connecticut, Yale University Press, 1957; *Heidegger: Through Phenomenology to Thought* by William J. Richardson, The Hague, Nijhoff, 1963; *Heidegger's Philosophy: A Guide to His Basic Thought* by Magda King, New York, Macmillan, and Oxford, Blackwell, 1964; *Martin Heidegger: A First Introduction to His Thought* by Joseph Kockelmans, Pittsburgh, Duquesne University Press, 1965; *The Philosophy of Martin Heidegger* by J.L. Mehta, New York, Harper, 1971; *Martin Heidegger: An Illustrated Study* by Walter Biemel, New York, Harcourt Brace, 1976; *Martin Heidegger* by George Steiner, London, Collins, and New York, Viking Press, 1978.

*   *   *

In the opinion of many, Martin Heidegger is one of the most important philosophers of the 20th century. In his early works Heidegger had been concerned mainly with logical and epistemological issues, and in both instances his attention had also gone out to language. But in these works he had been unable to transcend the classical metaphysical framework to which he had been introduced during his studies in Freiburg. *Being and Time*, on the other hand, was a truly innovative work, and it was immediately recognized as such. According to many, it may very well be the most important contribution to philosophy written in the 20th century.

The book was supposed to have had two major parts, both subdivided into three major divisions. Yet the book was published in an incomplete form, partly due to time pressures, partly as a consequence of difficulties which Heidegger had been unable to solve at that time. In its present form the book contains only the first major subdivisions of the first part.

In *Being and Time* Heidegger attempts to apply "hermeneutic phenomenology" to an analytic of man's Being, and carefully explains the sense in which hermeneutic phenomenology is to be understood. In his opinion philosophy's main concern is to be found in the question concerning the meaning of Being. This question is to be dealt with in ontology; yet such an ontology is to be prepared by a *fundamental* ontology which must take the form of an existential analytic of man's Being which is to be understood as Being-in-the-world. It is particularly in this fundamental ontology that the hermeneutic phenomenological method is to be employed. At the outset Heidegger makes it quite clear that what is to be understood by hermeneutic phenomenology is not identical with Husserl's transcendental phenomenology. He explicitly claims the right to develop the idea of phenomenology in his own way, beyond the stage to which it had been brought by Husserl himself. On the other hand, it is clear also that Heidegger sees the indispensable foundation for such a further development in Husserl's phenomenology. The reason why Heidegger was unable to follow Husserl more closely is to be found in Husserl's conception of the transcendental reduction

and his idea that the ultimate source of all meaning consists in transcendental subjectivity which as such originally is world-less. This explains why Heidegger tries to conceive man's Being as Being-in-the-world.

As the title of the book suggests, the concept of time occupies an important place in Being and Time. In the brief preface to the book Heidegger indicates how Being and Time are to be related: "Our aim in the following treatise is to work out the question concerning the meaning of Being.... Our provisional aim is the interpretation of time as the possible horizon for any understanding whatsoever of Being."

In the first division of Part I Heidegger takes as his guiding clue the fact that the essence of man consists in his ek-sistence; that toward which man stands out is the world; thus one can also say that the essence of man is Being-in-the-world. The main task of this first division now is to unveil the precise meaning of this compound expression; but in so doing the final goal remains the preparation of an answer for the question concerning the meaning of Being. Heidegger justifies this approach to the Being question by pointing out that man taken as Being-in-the-world is the only being who can make himself transparent in his own mode of Being. The very asking of this question is one of this being's modes of Being; and as such it receives its essential character from what is inquired about, namely Being itself. "This entity which each of us is himself and which includes inquiring as one of the possibilities of its Being we shall denote by the term *Dasein*." Thus the technical term *Dasein*, which usually is left untranslated, refers to man precisely insofar as he essentially relates to Being.

The preparatory analysis of *Dasein's* mode of Being can serve only to *describe* the essence of this being; it cannot *interpret* its meaning ontologically. The preparatory analysis merely tries to lay bare the horizon for the most primordial way of interpreting Being. Once this horizon has been reached, the preparatory analysis is to be replaced by a genuinely ontological interpretation. The horizon referred to here is temporality, which thus determines the meaning of the Being of *Dasein*. This is the reason why all the structures of man's Being exhibited in the first division are to be re-interpreted in the second as modes of temporality. But even in interpreting Dasein as temporality, the question concerning the meaning of Being is not yet answered; only the ground is prepared here for later obtaining such an answer. *Being and Time* was thus meant to lay the foundations for an ontology (metaphysics) and with Kant to stress the finitude of man in any attempt to found metaphysics.

In *Being and Time* Heidegger uses the phenomenological method. For him phenomenology (*legein ta phainomena*: to let what shows itself be seen from itself) is that method by means of which we let that which of its own accord manifests itself, reveal itself as it is. The "thing itself" to be revealed in *Being and Time* is man taken as *Dasein*. *Being and Time* attempts to let *Dasein* reveal itself in what and how it is, and the analysis shows concretely that the genuine self of *Dasein* consists in the process of finite transcendence whose ultimate meaning is time.

Characteristic for *Dasein* is its comprehension of Being, and this is the process by which *Dasein* transcends beings in the direction of Being and comprehends all beings, itself included, in their Being. This explains why the essence of *Dasein* can also be defined as transcendence. It should be stressed here at once that the process of transcendence is inherently finite. For, first of all, *Dasein* is not master over its own origin; it simply finds itself thrown among beings (thrownness). Secondly, thrown among beings, *Dasein* must concern itself with these beings and, thus, has the tendency to lose itself among them (fallenness), and to forget its ontological "destination." Finally, transcendence is a process which inherently is unto *Dasein's* end, death. The ground of the negativity which manifests itself in these modalities is what Heidegger calls "guilt," which is here thus not to be understood in a moral sense.

The basic structure of finite transcendence consists of comprehension (*Verstehen*), i.e., the component in and through which

Dasein projects the world, ontological disposition or mood (*Befindlichkeit*), i.e., the component through which *Dasein*'s thrownness, fallenness, and the world's non-Being are disclosed, and *logos (Rede)*, i.e., the component through which *Dasein* can unfold and articulate "in language" what comprehension and original mood disclose. These components constitute a unity insofar as transcendence essentially is care (*Sorge*): ahead of itself Being already in the world as Being alongside beings encountered within the world. When this unity is considered as a totality, it is understood as coming to its end, i.e. death. Finally, that which gives *Dasein* to understand its transcendence as well as its finitude and "guilt" and thus calls it to achieve its own self is what Heidegger calls the voice of conscience. To achieve itself *Dasein* must let itself be called toward its genuine self, i.e., the process of finite transcendence. The act in and through which *Dasein* achieves authenticity is called resolve (*Entschlossenheit*).

Heidegger finally shows how care itself is founded in time insofar as the basic components of care, namely ek-sistence, thrownness, and fallenness, inherently refer to the three ekstases of time, future, past, and present. By transcending beings toward Being *Dasein* comes to its true self (*Zu-kunft*, future), but this self is always already as having been thrown forth (past), and concerning itself with beings, thus making them manifest and present (present). Interpreted from the perspective of temporality, resolve manifests itself as retrieve (*Wiederholung*); it lets the process of finite transcendence become manifest as historical. By fetching itself back time and again, *Dasein* lets its own self be in terms of its authentic past; in addition, it also is as constantly coming toward its authentic self. It is thus in this complex process that *Dasein* hands over to itself its own heritage and thus "finds" its true self.

In his later works (1935-1976), i.e., the period of the "turn" (*Kehre*), Heidegger continues to think the basic relationship between Being and man, but whereas in *Being and Time* he seems to give the privileged position in this relation to *Dasein*, the later works grant this to Being itself. Being, which originally was described in terms of world, is now shown primarily as the process of the coming-to-pass of the truth (*a-leteia*). Being is shown as sending itself towards *Dasein*; it sends itself in different epochs in different ways which consign *Dasein* to its privileged destiny, which is to be the "shepherd of Being." In each individual epoch, Being both reveals itself and conceals itself. As intrinsically finite, Being itself can reveal itself only by revealing being; thus it can never be grasped by itself, in view of the fact that it itself is not a being; thus it must also somehow conceal itself in the beings which it makes manifest. The finitude of Being also explains why Being must send itself in each epoch in a different way and why no single sending can ever exhaust the power of Being to reveal itself. The totality of these different ways in which Being sends itself and to which different epochs of thinking correspond, is what we call "history."

The function of thought consists in this, that it must bring the relation between Being and man to fulfillment; in so doing thought brings Being to language and *Dasein* to its proper and authentic self. Heidegger tries particularly to explain precisely how, in the relation between being and man, in each epoch the ontological difference between being and Being, thing and world, comes to pass and how it is brought into language. This explains his constant concern with the great thinkers of the past from Parmenides and Heraclitus to Hegel and Nietzsche. It also explains why he is led time and again to meditate on our current condition, the era of technicity and the atomic age. It should be evident that a thinking which tries to do just this, and thus has the character of a meditative recollection, has nothing in common with the calculating way of thinking we encounter in modern science and technology. Rather, it is intrinsically poetizing in its docile response to the language of Being.

—Joseph J. Kockelmans

HEISENBERG, Werner. German physicist. Born in Würzburg, 5 December 1901. Studied at the University of Munich, Ph.D. 1923; University of Göttingen, 1924. Married Elisabeth Schumacher in 1937; 7 children. Professor of Theoretical Physics, University of Leipzig, 1927-41; Director, Kaiser Wilhelm Institute for Physics, and Professor of Physics, University of Berlin, 1941-45; Director, Max Planck Institute for Physics, and Professor of Physics, University of Göttingen, 1946-58; Director, Max Planck Institute for Physics and Astrophysics, and Professor of Physics, University of Munich, 1958-70. Recipient: Barnard Medal, Columbia University, New York, 1929; Matteucci Medal, 1929; Nobel Prize in Physics, 1932; Max Planck Medal, 1933; Pour le Mérite für Wissenschaften und Kunste, 1957; Kultur-Ehrenpreis, Munich, 1958; Bronze Medal, National Academy of Sciences, 1964; Niels Bohr Gold Medal, Copenhagen, 1970; Sigmund Freud Preis, Deutsche Akademie für Spräche und Dichtung, 1970. Honorary doctorate: University of Brussels, 1961; Technische Hochschule, Karlsruhe, 1961; University of Budapest, 1964; University of Copenhagen, 1965; Technical University, Athens, 1966; University of Zagreb, Yugoslavia, 1969. Member, Norwegian Academy of Sciences; Götingen Academy of Sciences; German Academy of Sciences; Roumanian Academy of Sciences; Accademia Nazionale dei Lincei; Spanish Academy of Sciences; National Institute of Sciences, India; Royal Society, London; American Academy of Arts and Sciences; Royal Institution, London; U.S. National Academy of Sciences; New York Academy of Sciences; Royal Irish Academy; Japanese Academy. *Died 1 February 1976.*

PUBLICATIONS

Physics

Die physikalischen Prinzipien der Quantentheorie. Leipzig, Hirzel, 1930; as *The Physical Principles of the Quantum Theory*, Chicago, University of Chicago Press, 1930.
Die moderne Atomtheorie, with others. Leipzig, Hirzel, 1934.
Wandlungen in den Grundlagen der Naturwissenschaft. Leipzig, Hirzel, 1935; enlarged and revised editions, 1936-73; as *Philosophical Problems of Nuclear Science*, London, Faber, and New York, Pantheon, 1952.
Neuere Fortschritte in den exakten Wissenschaften (lecture). Leipzig, Deiticke, 1936.
Die Physik der Atomkerne. Brunswick, Vieweg, 1943; as *Nuclear Physics*, London, Methuen, and New York, Philosophical Library, 1953.
Two Lectures. Cambridge, Cambridge University Press, 1949.
Das Naturbild der heutigen Physik. Hamburg, Rowohlt, 1955; as *The Physicist's Conception of Nature*, London, Hutchinson, and New York, Harcourt Brace, 1958.
Physics and Philosophy. New York, Harper, 1958; London, Allen and Unwin, 1959.
On Modern Physics, with others. New York, Potter, 1961.
Introduction to the Unified Field Theory of Elementary Particles. London, Wiley, 1966.
Der Teil und das Ganze: Gespräche im Umkreis der Atomphysik. Munich, Piper, 1969; as *Physics and Beyond: Encounters and Conversations*, New York, Harper, 1974.
Schritte über Grenzen: Gesammelte Reden und Aufsätze. Munich, Piper, 1971; as *Across the Frontiers*, New York, Harper, 1974.
Tradition in der Wissenschaft. Munich, Piper, 1977.

*

Critical Studies: *Werner Heisenberg und die Philosophie* by Herbert Hörz, Berlin, Deutsche Verlag der Wissenschaften, 1966; *Denken und Umdenken: Zu Werk und Wirkung von Werner Heisenberg*, edited by Heinrich Pfeiffer, Munich, Piper,

1977 (contains a full bibliography of Heisenberg's scientific papers).

* * *

Though Werner Heisenberg made major contributions to theoretical atomic physics throughout the middle half of the 20th century, his most noteworthy work was done in the 1920's with his invention of an important form of quantum mechanics and the pronouncement of the famous indeterminacy principle.

In order to appreciate the significance of Heisenberg's achievement, one must recall the difficulties encountered by Bohr in the Application of his quantum theory of atomic structure to atoms with more than a single extranuclear electron in the normal state. Though Bohr's frequency condition and his quantum conditions sufficed to predict correctly the energy states of the neutral hydrogen atom and the frequencies in its optical spectrum, it proved impossible to devise models for polyelectronic atoms for which the theory would lead to precise agreement with experiment. It is true that Bohr could predict in a general way the variation in the properties of the elements in the various groups in the periodic system. Moreover, by the use of Bohr's correspondence principle, connecting his quantum theory calculations rather closely with those of classical mechanics and electrodynamics in the case of atoms excited to very high frequency states, it proved possible to compute the intensities and polarizations of many spectral lines to a fair approximation. By the use of the so-called self-consistent field method, one could also make approximate calculations of the sizes of Bohr orbits and the magnitude of energy levels in polyelectronic atoms in fair order of magnitude agreement with experimental values. But the precise kind of agreement demanded by a really successful theory was lacking. Moreover, many physicists, including Bohr himself, felt that Bohr's application of his fundamental ideas, involving as it did a curious mixture of classical concepts and the non-mechanical quantum idea, was philosophically unsatisfactory.

A move in a new direction came with the publication in 1926 of a joint paper by H.A. Kramers and Heisenberg on the scattering and dispersion of light by atoms. This led Heisenberg to conclude that a really successful quantum theory of atomic structure should be based on the use in the theory of only observable quantities in place of those like position and angular velocity of electrons, which are not subject to observation. This meant conferring theoretical significance exclusively on quantities like the frequencies and intensities of spectral lines in the radiation emitted by atoms.

Heisenberg was then faced with the problem of deciding on the most plausible relations he might assume connecting with observables, which would lead to the correct energy states of the atom. He tried out his idea first on the one dimensional harmonic and anharmonic oscillators, feeling that the hydrogen atom would be too difficult on a first attempt. He found it desirable in his theory to represent classical observables by aggregates of quantities rather than single quantities. He was guided in his choice by Bohr's correspondence principle. His quantum mechanical quantities turned out to be rather peculiar mathematically in the sense that when two were multiplied they did not always follow the commutative rule. The first paper by Heisenberg on his new theory was published in the *Zeitschrift für Physik* in 1925, with the title (English translation) "On the Quantum Theory Reinterpretation of Kinematical and Mechanical Relations." When this paper came to the attention of the German physicists Max Born and Ernst Pascual Jordan they immediately saw that the quantum mechanical quantities introduced by Heisenberg behave like matrices, whose mathematical properties had long been well known. Born and Jordan then prepared a long article systematizing Heisenberg's concepts and expressing them in matrix notation. This was the beginning of a form of quantum mechanics that came to be called matrix mechanics. With its use it ultimately proved possible to calculate correctly the quantized energy levels of the hydrogen atom and other atomic systems.

In the meantime the German theoretical physicist Erwin Schrödinger had developed a different version of quantum mechanics based on the earlier (1924) work of French physicist Louis de Broglie, connecting the motion of atomic particles with wave motion. The Schrödinger version was called wave mechanics; his first paper on the subject was published in 1926. It was soon shown that his approach is fully compatible with Heisenberg's matrix mechanics, but is on the whole much easier to use in actual calculations.

Some critics objected to Heisenberg's emphasis on the need to develop quantum mechanics solely on the basis of the use of "observable" quantities. It was emphasized by experimentalists, for example, that atomic physics has to deal with the identification and localization of atomic particles, as in the Wilson cloud chamber. In answer to this criticism Heisenberg decided to introduce "anschaulichkeit" into his theory and did so in a famous paper (*Zeitschrift für Physik*, 1927) with the title (in English translation) "On the Intuitive Content of Quantum Kinematics and Mechanics." Here he showed how quantum mechanical meaning can be given to quantities like the position and momentum (or velocity) of an electron. But he emphasized that a price has to be paid for this, namely that two so-called canonically conjugate quantities like position and momentum can be determined simultaneously only with a characteristic indeterminacy. More precisely, the product of the average uncertainty in the measured value of the position of a particle and the average uncertainty in the simultaneously measured value of its momentum cannot be less in order of magnitude than Planck's constant of action $h(6.63 \times 10^{-27}$ erg sec) divided by 4π. This is a theorem of quantum mechanics which has been named the indeterminacy principle. It impressed Heisenberg so much that he tried to demonstrate it phenomenologically by a "thought" experiment in which the position of an electron is measured by shining on it light of suitable wave length so that it can be "seen." The higher the frequency of the light, the more precisely is the position defined. But at the same time the higher the frequency the greater the disturbing push which the light gives to the electron, providing it with an uncontrolled increase in its momentum and hence making the possible simultaneous measurement of its momentum (or velocity) highly uncertain. This "explanation" helped to clarify the meaning of the indeterminacy principle, but it has been criticized, especially by Neils Bohr, as overlooking some important factors concerning measurement. In any case the principle has proved to be of great value in applications of quantum mechanics. For example, when applied to the attempted simultaneous measurement of the variables of energy and time, it provides a method of estimating the breadth of spectral lines.

During Heisenberg's professorship at the University of Leipzig he developed a very active institute of theoretical physics, which attracted students from all over the world. Among his own researches during that period may be mentioned his successful quantum mechanical explanation of ferromagnetism (the magnetism of iron and iron-like substances). Here he used the Pauli exclusion principle to show that the phenomenon is due mainly to the interaction of the electrons in the atom in metals in which each atom is surrounded by at least eight near neighbors.

Heisenberg's last attempt at an important theoretical problem was quantum field theory, which endeavors to understand the radiation emitted and absorbed by an atom. He made a definite contribution to the severe mathematical problems connected with this theory through his introduction of the so-called "S-matrix," a development of his early ideas about the use of "observable" quantities in theory. Unfortunately his endeavors have not led to a definite result.

Heisenberg preferred to remain in Germany during World War II. There is some ambivalence in the record of his war research activities. It seems clear that he was in some way involved in the German effort to produce an atomic bomb, but the evidence is not definite. Heisenberg's principle post-war research was devoted to the attempt to introduce some theoretical order into the interpretation of the various types of "elemen-

:ary" particles turned up by nuclear experimentation. He introduced the notion of a single field through which it ought to be
possible to explain the existence and properties of all the "elementary" particles. It's not surprising that here success eluded
him.

—R. Bruce Lindsay

HESCHEL, Abraham Joshua. American theologian. Born
in Warsaw, Poland, in 1907; emigrated to the United States in
1940; naturalized, 1945. Studied at the University of Berlin,
Ph.D. 1933; Hochschule für die Wissenschaft des Judentums,
Berlin, 1934. Married Sylvia Straus in 1945; 1 daughter. Instructor, Hochschule für die Wissenschaft des Judentums, 1932-33;
Lecturer, Mittelstelle für Jüdische Erwachsenenbildung, Frankfurt, 1937-38; Lecturer in Philosophy, Institute for Judaistic
Studies, Warsaw, 1938-39; Founder, Institute of Jewish Learning, London, 1940; Instructor, 1940-43, and Assistant Professor
of Jewish Philosophy and Rabbinics, 1943-44, Hebrew Union
College, Cincinnati, Ohio; Professor of Jewish Ethics and Mysticism, Jewish Theological Seminary of America, New York,
1945-72. Visiting Professor, University of Iowa, Iowa City, and
University of Minnesota, Minneapolis, 1961; Raymond Fred
West lecturer, Stanford University, California, 1963; Harry
Emerson Fosdick Visiting Professor, Union Theological Seminary, New York, 1965-66. Recipient: Guggenheim Fellowship;
Frank L. Weil Medal. Honorary doctorate: St. Michael's College, Winooski, Vermont, 1966; University of Notre Dame, Indiana, 1967; Park College, Parksville, Missouri, 1969; Upsala College, East Orange, New Jersey; Spertus College of Judaica,
Chicago. Fellow, American Academy of Arts and Sciences. *Died
23 December 1972.*

PUBLICATIONS

Theology

Maimonides: Eine Biographie. Berlin, Reiss, 1935; as *Maimo-
    nides: A Biography,* New York, Farrar Straus, 1982.
Die Prophetie. Cracow, Polish Academy of Sciences, 1936;
    revised as *The Prophets,* New York, Harper, 1962.
Don Jizchak Abravanel. Berlin, Reiss, 1937.
The Quest for Certainty in Saadia's Philosophy. New York,
    Feldheim, 1944.
Pikkuah Neshamah [The Control of the Soul]. New York,
    Baronial Press, 1949.
*The Earth is the Lord's: The Inner Life of the Jew in East
    Europe.* New York, Schuman, 1950; revised edition, Cleve-
    land, World, 1963.
Man is Not Alone: A Philosophy of Religion. New York,
    Farrar Straus, 1951.
The Sabbath: Its Meaning for Modern Man. New York, Far-
    rar Straus, 1951; expanded edition with *The Earth Is the
    Lord's: The Inner Life of the Jew in East Europe,* Cleveland,
    World, 1963.
Man's Quest for God: Studies in Prayer and Symbolism. New
    York, Scribner, 1954.
God in Search of Man: A Philosophy of Judaism. New York,
    Farrar Straus, 1955.
*Between God and Man: An Interpretation of Judaism from the
    Writings of Abraham J. Heschel,* edited by Fritz Rothschild.
    New York, Harper, 1959.
Torah min ha-shamayim be-ispaklaryah shel ha-dorot [Theol-
    ogy of Ancient Judaism]. London and New York, Socino
    Press, 2 vols., 1962, 1965.
Who is Man? Stanford, California, Stanford University Press,
    1965.

The Insecurity of Freedom: Essays on Human Existence. New
    York, Farrar Straus, 1965.
Israel: An Echo of Eternity. New York, Farrar Straus, 1969.
A Passion for Truth. London, Secker and Warburg, and New
    York, Farrar Straus, 1973.
The Wisdom of Heschel. New York, Farrar Straus, 1975.

*

Critical Studies: *The Promise of Heschel* by Franklin Sherman,
Philadelphia, Lippincott, 1970; *Abraham Joshua Heschel* by
Byron L. Sherwin, Atlanta, John Knox Press, 1979.

*   *   *

Abraham Joshua Heschel, Jewish philosopher of religion of
Polish origin who flourished as a writer and religious leader in
the United States after his emigration in 1940, made significant
contributions in Biblical and Talmudic studies and in the interpretation of the Jewish mystical tradition. He was best known to
the public, however, as a social critic and activist in movements
working for justice and peace, and as an exponent of the fundamentals of religious belief. His writing, whether in English, German or Hebrew, has an evocative quality and is at times close to
poetry.

The prerequisite for the knowledge of God, says Heschel in his
basic work *Man is Not Alone,* is "the sense of the ineffable" (the
indescribable). Elsewhere, Heschel speaks of this as the dimension of "mystery" or the "sublime." The sense of the ineffable, he
asserts, involves the recognition that "what is intelligible to our
minds is but a thin surface of the profoundly undisclosed." The
knowledge of God, therefore, involves not the gaining of new
information, but the learning of a new way of seeing. "The
ineffable inhabits the magnificent and the common, the grandiose and the tiny facts of reality alike," Heschel declares. At the
root of religion is this sense of mystical awareness of the divine,
but in Jewish tradition it is a "this-worldly" mysticism which
seeks, in Heschel's words, to "ennoble the common" rather than
flee from it.

In his work on the Hebrew prophets, expressed in an early
monograph in German and then in his massive English work *The
Prophets,* Heschel further expounds his understanding of God
and the divine-human relation. A prophet, he writes, "is a man
who feels fiercely. God has thrust a burden upon his soul, and he
is bowed and stunned at man's fierce greed."

> Frightful is the agony of a man; no human voice can
> convey its full terror. Prophecy is the voice that God has
> lent to the silent agony, a voice to the plundered poor, to
> the profaned riches of the world.... God is raging in the
> prophet's words.

Central to the prophetic consciousness is what Heschel calls
"the divine pathos," God's "transitive concern" for human
beings, and especially for the poor and oppressed. The medium
of revelation is the prophet's sympathy with this divine pathos.
God is not the "unmoved mover"; rather, he is the "most moved
mover." The *imitatio dei* thus implies a deep concern for and
involvement with human suffering. Yet it also, paradoxically,
implies an intense capacity for joy.

In his book *The Earth is the Lord's: The Inner Life of the Jew
in East Europe,* Heschel pays tribute to a now vanished world
from which he himself had sprung. East European Judaism had
been deeply influenced by Hasidism, the movement founded by
the Baal Shem Tov (1699-1761) and sometimes called "Jewish
Pietism," of which Heschel and Buber have been the greatest
modern interpreters. It was the Baal Shem, says Heschel, who
"banished melancholy from the soul and uncovered the infinite
delight of being a Jew." To obey the precepts of the Torah was
felt not as a burden but as a joy, indeed as a foretaste of heaven.
Especially in the observance of the Sabbath, the genius of Juda-

ism was shown as "the art of significant forms in time," the *architecture of time.*

In his book, *God in Search of Man: A Philosophy of Judaism,* Heschel deals with questions of Jewish observance, polemicizing against "religious behaviorism," a mere outward obedience to the law, while urging those estranged from the tradition to undertake a "leap of action" in order to experience its meaning from within. He also devoted major studies to the subject of prayer and the renewal of religious worship (*Man's Quest for God*); a biographical study of Maimonides; a comparative study of the Hasidic leader Reb Mendl of Kotzk and the Christian philosopher Søren Kierkegaard (*A Passion for Truth*); an essay on human nature from a religious perspective (*Who is Man?*); an exposition of the religious significance of the State of Israel (*Israel: An Echo of Eternity*), and a two-volume study (in Hebrew) of types of rabbinic theology.

Heschel was deeply involved in inter-religious dialogue, and his work has had great influence in Christian as well as Jewish circles, possibly more so in the former than in the latter. Always aware of the Holocaust, from which he himself had only narrowly escaped, he repeatedly warned of the fragility of human civilization, and called for repentance and renewal out of the well-springs of religious faith.

—Franklin Sherman

HICKS, John (Richard). British economist. Born in Warwick, 8 April 1904. Educated at Clifton College and Balliol College, Oxford. Married Ursula K. Webb in 1935. Lecturer, London School of Economics, 1926-35; Fellow, Gonville and Caius College, Cambridge, 1935-38; Professor, University of Manchester, 1938-46; Fellow, Nuffield College, Oxford, 1946-52; Drummond Professor of Political Economy, Oxford University, 1952-65; Fellow, All Souls College, Oxford, since 1952. Recipient: Nobel Prize in Economics, 1972. Fellow, British Academy, 1942. Honorary Fellow, London School of Economics, 1969; Gonville and Caius College, Cambridge, 1971. Knighted, 1964. Address: All Souls College, Oxford, England.

PUBLICATIONS

Economics

The Theory of Wages. London, Macmillan, 1932; New York, P. Smith, 1948.
Value and Capital: An Inquiry into Some Fundamental Principles of Economic Theory. Oxford, Clarendon Press, 1939.
The Taxation of War Wealth, with others. Oxford, Clarendon Press, 1941.
The Social Framework: An Introduction to Economics. Oxford, Clarendon Press, 1942; revised edition as *The Social Framework of the American Economy: An Introduction to Economics,* with Albert Gailord Hart, New York, Oxford University Press, 1945.
The Beveridge Plan and Local Government Finance (lecture), with U.K. Hicks. Manchester, Norbury Lockwood, 1943.
Standards of Local Expenditure: A Problem of the Inequality of Incomes, with U.K. Hicks. Cambridge, Cambridge University Press, 1943.
The Problem of Valuation for Rating, with others. Cambridge, Cambridge University Press, 1944.
The Incidence of Local Rates in Great Britain, with Ursula K. Hicks. Cambridge, Cambridge University Press, 1945.
The Problem of Budgetary Reform. Oxford, Clarendon Press, 1948.
A Contribution to the Theory of the Trade Cycle. Oxford,

Clarendon Press, 1950.
Report on Finance and Taxation in Jamaica, with U.K. Hicks. Kingston, Jamaica, Government Printer, 1955.
A Revision of Demand Theory. Oxford, Clarendon Press, 1956.
The Future of the Rate of Interest. Manchester, Manchester Statistical Society, 1958.
Essays in World Economics. Oxford, Clarendon Press, 1959.
Capital and Growth. Oxford, Clarendon Press, and New York, Oxford University Press, 1965.
After the Boom: Thoughts on the 1966 Economic Crisis. London, Institute of Economic Affairs, 1966.
Critical Essays in Monetary Theory. Oxford, Clarendon Press, 1967.
Monetary Theory and Policy: A Historical Perspective. Perth, Australia, University of Western Australia Press, 1967.
A Theory of Economic History. Oxford, Clarendon Press, 1969.
Capital and Time: A Neo-Austrian Theory. Oxford, Clarendon Press, 1973.
The Crisis in Keynesian Economics (lectures). Oxford, Blackwell, 1974; New York, Basic Books, 1975.
Economic Perspectives: Further Essays on Money and Growth. Oxford, Clarendon Press, 1977.
Causality in Economics. Oxford, Blackwell, 1979.
Collected Essays in Economic Theory, Volume I. Oxford, Blackwell, 1981; as *Wealth and Welfare,* Cambridge, Massachusetts, Harvard University Press, 1981.

Other

Editor, with others, *Bibliography in Economics for the Honour School of Philosophy, Politics and Economics.* Oxford, Oxford University Press, 1948.
Editor, with Wilhelm Weber, *Carl Menger and the Austrian School of Economics.* Oxford, Clarendon Press, 1973.

*

Critical Studies: *Value, Capital and Growth: Papers in Honour of Sir John Hicks,* edited by J.N. Wolfe, Edinburgh, Edinburgh University Press, 1968; *Das Hickssche Konjunkturmodel und Seine Monetare Problematik* by Dieter Romheld, Berlin, Duncker and Humbolt, 1972.

*   *   *

John Hicks's Nobel Prize was in recognition of his work in general equilibrium and welfare analysis. However, few economists can claim as strong a contribution to economics, in originality, in synthesising the works of others, and in assisting the teaching of the subject in so many and varied fields. His work has had a profound impact not only on general equilibrium analysis and utility theory but also upon monetary theory, the treatment of uncertainty in economics, the development of Keynesian theory, and stability analysis. More recently, in the 1970's, he developed further the Keynesian liquidity preference theory and the portfolio analysis which he had first introduced in 1935; in addition, he has extended his treatment of Capital and Growth, although this has not been favourably received in some quarters; his latest work explores causality in economics, distinguishing between static, contemporaneous and sequential causal relationships.

Economists have grown to appreciate Hicks's work in economics; his explorations and discoveries in the subject have not dated; indeed, the importance of his work grows as we move on in time, perhaps indicating that he may well have been ahead of his contemporaries in many areas of economics. Leijonhufvud (1979) wrote "Hicks...was supremely successful...in constructing the moulds into which 40 years of subsequent theoretical developments were to be cast." This is no more apparent than his interpretation of Keynes's *General Theory* and his reconciliation of Keynes and the Classics via IS/LM curve analysis in 1937. This particular piece of graphical analysis and the clear exposition given by Hicks has formed the backbone of most macroeconomics texts since that date; it has been the apparatus employed for most modern debates on Keynesianism and monetarism and the framework within which economic policy has been worked out. But it was more than a convenient teaching device; it demonstrated the relevance and validity of general equilibrium analysis, showing, amongst other things, that income and the rate of interest are simultaneously determined. The partial equilibrium approach of Keynes and the Classics had given rise to inaccurate conclusions. The former appeared to argue that an increase in the productivity of investment would change only income; the Classics argued that only the rate of interest would change. Hicks demonstrated that both would be affected outside of the liquidity trap region.

Equally Hicks has altered the course which welfare economics took from 1934 onwards. He was responsible, with R.G.D. Allen, for establishing the ordinal utility approach to optimisation and through the introduction of indifference curve analysis was able to differentiate between the income and substitution effects of price changes. Even earlier, in 1932, he had introduced the concept of elasticity of substitution which led to much controversy and debate, particularly in relation to the question of income distribution.

Even now, some of his work in the 1930's remains undervalued. There is no better example of this than his contribution to monetary theory. In 1935 he used marginal utility analysis to examine the decision to hold money or buy securities. He not only anticipated Keynes's theory of liquidity preference but also provided the origins of the theory of portfolio adjustment which has appeared in post-war literature. In commenting upon Hicks's approach, Keynes expressed (in 1934) his approval, regarding liquidity preference as the essential concept for monetary theory.

The pinnacle of Hicks's contribution in the 1930's came with *Value and Capital*. This was full of new ideas. It not only extended his work in general equilibrium analysis but also clarified the possibility of temporary equilibrium and introduced the influence of expectations upon current decisions on production and consumption. Few would dispute Leijonhufvud's contention that: "to this day there have been few works so grand in conception or so pregnant with new ideas about the basic structure of economic theory."

It may be too early to judge Hicks's later work; certainly it may well mature like a good wine. In ten or twenty years time the discussion of the growth process may centre around the concept of the Traverse—the process of change from one growth path to another and the concept of impulse (1977) rather than upon the equilibrium growth. Time alone will tell.

—John R. Presley

HILBERT, David. German mathematician. Born in Königsberg, 23 January 1862. Studied at the University of Königsberg, 1880-1884, Ph.D. 1885. Married Käthe Jerosch in 1892. Privatdozent, 1886-92, Extraordinary Professor, 1892, and Professor, 1893-95, University of Königsberg; Chair, University of Göttingen, Germany, 1895-1930. *Died* (in Göttingen), *14 February 1943*.

PUBLICATIONS

Collections

Gesammelte Abhandlungen, edited by Ernst Hellinger, Paul Bernays and Otto Blumenthal. Berlin, Springer, 3 vols., 1932-35.

Mathematics

Über die invarianten Eigenschaften spezieller binärer Formen, insbesondere der Kugelfunctionen. Königsberg, R. Leupold, 1885; as "On the Invariant Properties of Special Binary Forms, Especially Spherical Functions" in *Hilbert's Invariant Theory Papers*, 1978.
"Grundlagen der Geometrie" in *Festschrift zur Feier der Enthüllung des Gauss-Weber-Denkmals in Göttingen*. Leipzig, Teubner, 1899; as *The Foundations of Geometry*, Chicago, Open Court, and London, Kegan Paul, 1902.
Über das Dirichlet'sche Princip. Berlin, Weidmann, 1901.
Grundzüge einer allgemeinen Theorie der linearen Integralgleichungen. Leipzig, Teubner, 1912.
Die Grundlagen der Mathematik, with supplementary material by H. Wehl and P. Bernays. Leipzig, Teubner, 1928.
Methoden der mathematischen Physik, with R. Courant and D. Milbert. Berlin, Springer, 1931; revised edition as *Methods of Mathematical Physics*, New York, Interscience, 1953.
Grundzüge der theoretischen Logik, with W. Ackermann. Berlin, Springer, 1928; as *Principles of Mathematical Logic*, New York, Chelsea, 1950.
Anschauliche Geometrie, with S. Cohn-Vossen. Berlin, Springer, 1932; as *Geometry and the Imagination*, New York, Chelsea, 1952.
Mathematische Probleme: Die Hilbertschen Probleme (lecture, translated from the Russian), edited by Hans Wussing. Leipzig, Geest and Portig, 1971.
Hilbert's Invariant Theory Papers, with commentary by R. Hermann (translations from the German). Brookline, Massachusetts, Math Sci Press, 1978.

Other

Editor, *Gesammelte Abhandlungen von Hermann Minkowski.* Leipzig and Berlin, Teubner, 1911.

*

Critical Studies: "David Hilbert and His Work," by H. Weyl, in *Bulletin of the American Mathematical Society*, vol. 50, 1944; *Hilbert: Gedenkband*, edited by K. Reidemeister, Berlin and New York, Springer, 1971.

*   *   *

In 1944, H. Weyl wrote an appreciation of David Hilbert for the *Bulletin of the American Mathematical Society*. Although Hilbert had died only one year before, Weyl was able to give a panoramic view of his work and influence to the expert reader. Normally this is difficult, and at least a few years are needed to give the author and readers some distance to appreciate a man and the influence of his ideas. Not so in this case; when Hilbert died he was already a legend, and some of his most spectacular contributions were more than 40 years old. In 1943 a great deal of mathematics, its methods and its problems, were the result of Hilbert's work.

His famous 23 problems were stated in 1900. Instantly they became central, and those who settled any of them won great fame. The third problem was settled almost immediately, and by 1940 six more had been solved. Since then another 7 or so have been settled, and much progress has been made on all of them. Indeed, the most influential of them have been those that are either too difficult or too vague. Just as the alchemist's quest for the philosophical stone yielded methods to produce pure alcohol and sulphuric acid, and in many ways gave rise to modern chemistry, these unsolved problems led mathematicians to develop entire new theories and even branches of the science.

It is natural that this program attracted so much attention. By 1900 Hilbert's work, mostly in algebra, was already famous. In 1898, to his students' and colleagues' surprise, he turned his interest into the logical foundations of geometry, and later, of mathematics. This was not Hilbert's last interest, for at the same time he became very interested in analysis (an advanced form of the more familiar calculus), where today the so-called Hilbert spaces are a common tool, and after 1910 physics occupied a good part of his attention.

Hilbert's work in geometry and foundations is both his most influential and most accessible.

Geometry deals with figures, and as such it relies on intuition. Euclid recognized that intuition was insufficient and sometimes deceiving, and he introduced an axiomatic approach. In Euclid's original conception one starts with certain objects, such as points, lines, etc., and certain "compelling truths" which are the axioms. "Compelling" was a key word, and by the 19th century this became difficult to sustain. For example, in our familiar plane geometry, given a line and a point not in the line, it is possible to draw exactly one line through the point and parallel to the line. This is the axiom of parallels. On the other hand, on the surface of Earth, assumed perfectly spherical, the shortest path between two points is part of a great circle which lies on the plane formed by these two points and the center of the Earth. Longitudes are such lines, but the so-called "parallels" are not—with the exception of the Equator. Clearly any two such lines meet (any two longitudes meet at the poles). This, of course, forced on mathematicians a re-evaluation of the idea of an axiom as an obvious "truth". Hilbert's own approach, accepted today as a matter of course, was to strip both the concepts (point, line, etc.) and the axioms of any intrinsic meaning: "it must be possible to replace in all geometric statements the words point, line, plane by table, chair, mug." In this approach to mathematics (termed "formalist"), we use the axioms, which are grammatical sentences involving the fundamental concepts (as nouns and verbs), and the rules of logic (syllogisms, etc.) to prove theorems. We can add or delete axioms according to certain rules and obtain new "Geometries." For instance, if the axiom of the parallels is removed, we can draw triangles whose angles are all right (think of longitude $0°$, longitude $90°$ W and the equator), which is not possible in traditional plane geometry where the angles of any triangle add up to exactly $180°$.

Beyond geometry Hilbert concentrated on the axiomatic method itself. A system of axioms must be *consistent* (not give rise to contradictions), *complete* (yield all possible theorems) and *independent* (no axiom is a consequence of the remaining ones). Hilbert also stressed the necessity of making all conclusions through finite processes. All this was very unclear, indeed debatable, in 1898. A great deal is owed to Hilbert for laying down these foundations and for his efforts to prove the consistency of the axioms of geometry.

The axioms of geometry turn out to be consistent provided that those governing our familiar real numbers are consistent. On the negative side, Hilbert's program was set back by later results (of Kurt Gödel) which showed that axioms of arithmetic may not be proved consistent within arithmetic. This is not for lack of trying; it is simply not possible. This was, and remains, a serious setback, and mathematical logic has been dealing with the consequences ever since. To the rest of the mathematical world, particularly to algebraists and geometers, the legacy of the axiomatic method is fundamental.

Hilbert's 23 problems have been a source of inspiration and results in the last 80 years. A description of a few of them will give the reader a feeling for the direction taken by mathematics in this century. Problem 2 questioned the consistency of the axioms of arithmetic. It cannot be answered within arithmetic. Problem 3 asked: is it possible to find a formula for the volume of a pyramid by using only the axioms of planar congruence? The answer, found in 1900, was no. Problem 8, unsolved and famous, asks for a description of the way prime numbers are scattered among the whole numbers. For instance, many small integers tend to be prime: 2, 3, 5, 7, 11,...but as they get larger, primes get scarcer. Is there a systematic behavior?

Problem 18: Here is a problem which is both interesting, unsolved and inspiring (to algebraists): what are the possible shapes for tiles that will permit us to cover the whole plane? For example square tiles will do, and so will certain triangular ones. Circular tiles, of course, will not work. We can ask the same question about solid bricks to fill up our three-dimensional space.

—Mauricio Gutierrez

_____

HILGARD, Ernest (Ropiequet). American psychologist. Born in Belleville, Illinois, 25 July 1904. Studied at the University of Illinois, Urbana, B.S. 1924; Yale University, New Haven, Connecticut, Ph.D. 1930. Civilian, Office of War Information and War Production Board, 1942-44. Married Josephine Rohrs in 1931; 2 children. Instructor in Psychology, Yale University, 1928-33; Assistant Professor to Professor of Psychology, 1933-69, and since 1969 Professor Emeritus, Stanford University, California (Dean of the Graduate Division, 1951-55). Member, National Institute of Mental Health, 1952-56; Fellow, Center for Advanced Study in the Behavioral Sciences, Stanford, 1956-57. President, American Psychological Association, 1948-49, and International Society of Hypnosis, 1974-77. Recipient: Warren Medal, Society of Experimental Psychologists, 1940; Distinguished Science Contribution Award, American Psychological Association, 1968; Wilbur Cross Medal, Yale University, 1971. Member, National Academy of Sciences, and National Academy of Education. Address: Department of Psychology, Stanford University, Stanford, California 94305, U.S.A.

PUBLICATIONS

Psychology

Student Counseling, with Richard H. Edwards. Ithaca, New York, Cayuga Press, 1928.
Conditioned Eyelid Reactions to a Light Stumulus, Based on the Reflex Wink to Sound. Princeton, New Jersey, Psychological Publishing Company, 1931.
Conditioning and Learning, with Donald G. Marquis. New York, Appleton Century, 1940.
Theories of Learning. New York, Appleton Century, 1948; London, Methuen, 1959.
Psychoanalysis as Science: The Hixon Lectures on the Scientific Status of Psychoanalysis, with others. Stanford, California, Stanford University Press, 1952.
Introduction to Psychology. New York, Harcourt Brace, 1953.
Unconscious Processes and Man's Rationality (lecture). Urbana, University of Illinois Press, 1958.
Stanford Hypnotic Susceptibility Scale, Forms A and B, with André Weitzenhoffer. Palo Alto, California, Consulting Psychologists Press, 1959.
The Distribution of Suggestibility to Hypnosis in a Student Population, with others. Washington, D.C., American Psychological Association, 1961.
Hypnotic Susceptibility. New York, Harcourt Brace, 1965.
A Basic Reference Shelf on Learning Theory. Stanford, California, ERIC Clearing House on Educational Media and Technology, Institute for Communication Research, 1967.
The Experience of Hypnosis, with Josephine R. Hilgard. New York, Harcourt Brace, 1968.
Hypnosis in the Relief of Pain, with Josephine R. Hilgard. Los Altos, California, Kaufmann, 1975.
Divided Consciousness: Multiple Controls in Human Thought and Action. New York, Wiley, 1977.

Other

Editor, with others, *Theories of Learning and Instruction.* Chicago, University of Chicago Press, 1964.

Editor, *American Psychology in Perspective: Addresses of the Presidents of the American Psychological Association 1892-1977.* Washington, D.C., American Psychological Association, 1978.

*   *   *

Ernest Hilgard's career as a research scientist and theoretician is roughly divisible into two periods. During the first of these periods, Hilgard concerned himself with analyzing and synthesizing behavioristic theories of learning and with conducting experimental research into the differences between voluntary and involuntary responses to selective reinforcements. The second period, beginning in the late 1940's, was one during which Hilgard increasingly moved away from the behavioristic model of personality as a set of "habits" or conditioned responses and moved toward a more phenomenological, psychodynamic perspective on human nature. In *Psychoanalysis as Science*, he observed:

The topics of psychodynamics are not side issues for psychology. They lie at the very heart of psychological subject matter, for we cannot understand motivation, learning and forgetting, perceiving, personality development, or social behavior until we understand the issues of psychodynamics. The renewed interest in the concept of the self in contemporary psychology stems in part from the concern of psychoanalysis to understand the role of self-knowledge, and to understand the devices of self-deception. The tasks of psychodynamics cannot be left solely to those specialists within psychology and psychiatry concerned with treating the mentally or emotionally disturbed. They are tasks that belong to all of psychological science.

Here Hilgard touches upon a theme which was to become characteristic of all his subsequent work, namely the notion that psychology must strike a rapprochement between the experimental laboratory and the psychiatric clinic. In other words, if psychology is to advance as a science and contribute to a more profound understanding of human behavior, there must be greater collboration between research scientists with all their strategies of experimental control and measurement and clinical workers with their knowledge of personality dynamics and idiographic techniques.

The extent to which Hilgard himself sought a rapprochement between the experimental and clinical paradigms is evidenced by the fact that he increasingly devoted his attention to the study of a topic which provided an unusually rich and complex intersection of those paradigms, the topic of hypnosis.

Working principally in collaboration with his wife, Josephine, a psychoanalyst, Hilgard established the Stanford Laboratory of Hypnosis Research, where he conducted a wide array of investigations into the nature of hypnotic phenomena. These investigations represent one of the most careful and extensive attempts to integrate statistical and psychometric assessments with subject self-reports and psychiatric interviews.

Of Hilgard's many contributions to a scientific understanding of hypnosis, two have special significance. The first of these contributions is a methodological one, the development and standardization of an instrument for measuring a person's responsiveness to hypnotic suggestions. The device, now known as the Stanford Hypnotic Susceptibility Scale (SHSS), consists of an hypnotic induction followed by a series of 12 suggestions to the subject. Each of the suggestions instructs the subject to engage in some specific task, ranging from a very simple motoric task (e.g., to move the hands together) to a very complex psychological one (e.g., to experience post-hypnotic amnesia). A subject is assigned a score for his or her performance on each of these tasks, and the total score for all tasks is regarded as a measure of the subject's hypnotizability. Though Hilgard's scale is by no means the first of its kind, it is probably the most reliable and well researched such measure yet to be constructed.

Hilgard's other great contribution is his theory of the nature of hypnosis, a theory which he terms "developmental-interactive." Most essentially, the theory construes hypnotic phenomena as a complex interplay of three sets of factors: 1) factors in the individual subject's developmental history; 2) factors in the interaction between the subject and the hypnotist; and 3) factors which distinguish hypnosis from other states of consciousness.

In regard to the developmental factors in hypnosis, Hilgard posits that all human beings are born with an innate capacity to experience profound hypnotic trance and that this capacity may be significantly diminished or enhanced during the course of a person's childhood. If, for example, parents actively involve a child in such pleasurable imaginative activities as reading, tale-telling, and music listening, there is a tendency for hypnotic susceptibility to be sustained into later life. Conversely, when children are encouraged to engage in activities which require a high degree of vigilance and reality-orientation, such as certain forms of competitive sport, there is a tendency for hypnotic susceptibility to be reduced.

Whereas developmental factors account for why certain individuals are more hypnotizable than others, interactive factors concern how the relationship between the hypnotist and the subject actualizes the subject's latent susceptibility to trance. In general, Hilgard theorizes that the subject-hypnotist relationship bears strong affiliations with psychoanalytic transference. For example, trance is like transference not only in that its "success" depends more on the readiness of the subject than on any specific personality attributes of the hypnotist but also in that its nature varies widely according to the subject's preferred style of coping and defense.

In discussing the nature of hypnotic consciousness, Hilgard rejects the notion that trance is a state of regressive hyper-suggestibility and maintains instead that it involves a dissociation of various information processing functions. In other words, certain mental processes—some perceptual, some evaluative, and some strategic—which are complexly interwoven in waking consciousness become, in the state of trance, somewhat dissociated or compartmentalized from one another. Thus it is that a hypnotized subject who has been instructed to become temporarily deaf can at one moment be totally unresponsive to a sound as loud as a gunshot and, at the next, successfully follow the paradoxical suggestion to describe in detail every sound that he did *not* hear.

Hilgard's work, more than that of any other contemporary psychologist, has revivified interest in hypnosis as both a clinical tool and a research topic. Moreover, his work serves as a model for those who see a need to reconcile psychology's disparate images as a healing art and a science of behavior.

—William Devine

HJELMSLEV, Louis (Trolle). Danish linguist. Born in Copenhagen, 3 October 1899. Studied at the University of Copenhagen from 1916; also studied in Paris, 1926-27. Member of the faculty, University of Aarhus, Denmark, 1934-37; Professor of Comparative Philology, University of Copenhagen, from 1937. Founder, Cercle Linguistique de Copenhague, 1931; Founder, with Viggo Brøndal, *Acta Linguistica*, 1939. *Died* (in Copenhagen) *in 1965.*

PUBLICATIONS

Linguistics

Principes de grammaire générale. Copenhagen, Høst, 1929.
Det litauiske folk og dets sprog [The Lithuanian People and
   Their Language]. Copenhagen, Koppels Forlag, 1930.
Études baltiques. Copenhagen, Levin og Munksgaard, 1932.
*Indledning til sprogvidenskaben: Forelaesning ved tiltraedelsen
   af professoratet i sammenlignende sprogvidenskab ved
   Kobenhavns universitet den 14. september 1937* [Introduction
   to Linguistics: Inaugural Lecture upon Accession as the
   Chairman to the Department of Comparative Linguistics at
   the University of Copenhagen, 14 September 1937]. Copen-
   hagen, Levin og Munksgaard, 1937.
Omkring sprogteoriens grundlaeggelse. Copenhagen, Munksgaard, 1943; as *Prolegomena to a Theory of Language*, Baltimore, Waverly Press, 1953; revised edition, Madison, University of Wisconsin Press, 1963.
Sur l'indépendance de l'épithète. Copenhagen, Munksgaard,
   1956.
*Outline of Glossematics: A Study in the Methodology of the
   Humanities with Special Reference to Linguistics*, with H.J.
   Uldall. Copenhagen, Nordisk Sprog- og Kulturforlag, 1957.
Essais linguistiques. Copenhagen, Nordisk Sprog- og Kultur-
   forlag, 1959 (contains a full bibliography).
Sproget: En Introduktion. Copenhagen, Berlingske Forlag,
   1963; as *Language: An Introduction*, Madison, University of
   Wisconsin Press, 1970.
Sprogsystem og sprogforandring [Language System and Lan-
   guage Change]. Copenhagen, Nordisk Sprog- og Kulturfor-
   lag, 1972.
Résumé of a Theory of Language, edited and translated by
   Francis J. Whitfield, vol. xvi of *Travaux du Cercle Linguistique de Copenhague* (Copenhagen), 1975.

Other

Editor, *Rasmus Rask: Udvalgte afhandlinger/ Rasmus Rask:
   Ausgewählte Abhandlungen.* Copenhagen, Levin og Munks-
   gaard, 1932.
Editor, *Breve fra og til Rasmus Rask*: vol. 1, *1805-1819*; vol. 2,
   1820-1832 [Correspondence from and to Rasmus Rask].
   Copenhagen, Munksgaard, 2 vols., 1941.
Editor, *Mélanges linguistiques offerts à m. Holger Pedersen à
   l'occasion de son soixante-dixième anniversaire 7 avril 1937.*
   Aarhus, Universitetsforlaget, 1937.
Editor, with Axel Sandal, *H.C. Andersen: Kejserens nye klaeder,
   paa femogtyve sprog/ Les habits neufs de l'empereur, en vingt-
   cinq langues.* Copenhagen, Munksgaard, 1944.
Editor, *Knut Hagberg: Saedernes Bog* [Knut Hagberg: A Book
   on Manners]. Copenhagen, Munksgaard, 1947.

*   *   *

The Danish linguist and semiotician Louis Hjelmslev, founder
of the glossematic theory of language, studied comparative philology with the Danish philologist Holger Pedersen at Copenhagen University, and succeeded him as Professor of Comparative Philology in 1937. In 1929 he published *Principes de grammaire générale*, giving in this book a formal description of
grammar as an abstract system trying to cover all grammatical
forms in the natural languages. This study was primarily concerned with the syntagmatic aspect of language, whereas his next
theoretical study, "La catégorie des cas, étude de grammaire
générale," mainly focused on the paradigmatic and semantic
aspects of language and was based on a combinational analysis
which resulted in 216 possible cases.
   The second period in Hjelmslev's scientific development was
decisive and the most fruitful. In 1931 he and other young Danish
linguists founded the Cercle linguistique de Copenhague (cf. the

series *Traveaux du Cercle linguistique de Copenhague* (TCLC),
1944-), and about the same time he started a collaboration with
another young Danish linguist and phonetician, Hans Jørgen
Uldall (1907-1957). Together they formulated a new theory
called phonematics. The central idea is (in opposition to Prague
School linguistics) that phonemes ought not to be described
according to their inherent properties (e.g., distinctive features)
but according to their function, i.e., the rules for their combination in the speech chain.
   Uldall and Hjelmslev were separated by World War II, and
consequently Hjelmslev worked out glossematics in his own way
during the early 1940's, and the result was three highly important
manuscripts within a few years. In 1941 he wrote his short
introduction to linguistics, *Sproget* (Language), which was not
published until 1963. It is not a book intended for specialists, but
the point of view is glossematic so it can serve as an introduction
to his theory.
   Omkring sprogteroiens grundlaeggelse [*Prolegomena to a
Theory of Language*] is Hjelmslev's most famous work. It is an
attempt to define both what uniquely characterizes natural languages and to describe the necessary prerequisites for the foundation of linguistics as an exact science. Hjelmslev claims that
even if language from the point of view of its purpose may
primarily be regarded as a sign system, it is made up of two
systems of figurae from the point of view of its immanent structure. This follows from the double dichotomy between form vs.
substance, and expression vs. content: Hjelmslev defines language as consisting of two planes, the expression plane and the
content plane. Within each plane he makes a distinction between
form and substance, e.g., the sound chain of actual speech is
considered to be one of the substances of the expression plane,
and the system of phonemes is the form (in precise glossematic
terminology: taxemes of expression). On the content plane, the
form is constituted by the specific divisions made within a given
language, whereas the content substance is regarded as amorphous meaning. The sign function is a solidarity between expression form and content form, and the minimal formal units on
both planes are found by using the commutation test, which
establishes the number of invariants within the categories of both
planes. Glossematics is defined as a deductive theory of language; Hjelmslev was aiming to formulate an algebraic calculus
to describe the system behind the language process, the text, i.e.,
finite sets of elements, functives, and rules for their combination
both within the system and within the text. Three general combi-
natory possibilities are mentioned: determination, interdependence, and constellation. The first principle of the theory is the
so-called empirical principle, according to which the description
must bee commutation test, consists in continuous partition of
each plane separately until the text is completely analyzed and
the minimal units on each plane are found. But the subject matter
of linguistics is, in Hjelmslev's opinion, only the two forms, the
expression form and the content form, because they alone, and
the sign function established by the solidarity between them,
constitute language as a structure *sui generis*, whereas the substance should be the subject matter of other sciences (e.g., physics
and psychology).
   This procedure is initially applied to natural languages, which
are defined as consisting of two planes neither of which are
languages themselves (but systems of figurae), but Hjelmslev
widens the scope of the theory by taking into account languages
in which either the expression plane is itself a language, the
so-called connotative language, or the content plane is itself a
language, a meta-language. In this way a hierarchy of semiolo-
gies is established.
   The third work written during this period is *Sprogteori.
Résumé*, which was not published until 1975, when Francis J.
Whitfeld edited an English translation, *Résumé of a Theory of
Language*. Whereas *Prolegomena* gave the general outline of the
glossematic way of thinking and theory of language (Hjelmslev
called it a "work of popularization"), the *Résumé* is, despite its
280 pages, a highly-concentrated exposition of what Hjelmslev

considered to be the principles and procedures of a glossematic description of language. It is formalized throughout, based on principles, rules, and definitions (amounting to 454), and a special notation. It was never completely finished, and the last part is reconstructed by the editor on the basis of Hjelmslev's manuscript, but it is important for the understanding of Hjelmslev's conception of language description and suggests he would have developed glossematics.

In the third period from 1943 to his death, Hjelmslev did not write any general work and glossematics, but he expounded and applied it partially in a series of papers (collected in *Essais linguistique*). In the important paper "Pour une semantique structurale" (1957), the structural analysis of the content form is sketched. In "La stratification du langage" (1954) Hjelmslev tries to give a complete description of language by distinguishing between four strata: content substance, content form, expression form, and expression substance, and both the expression substance and the content substance are further divided into three levels: the apperceptive, the social-biological, and the physical, with the apperceptive (i.e., concerning the content plane, the meaning generally accepted within a society) as the primary. This paper also gave a valuable definition of the concepts parole, usage, norm, and scheme (schéma) relative to the four strata, and the scheme (language system) is said to relate immanent functions on each separate plane, whereas usage is defined to cover interstratic relations (c.f. Hjelmslev's definition of language as system of figure in *Prolegomena*).

Although Hjelmslev did not complete the exposition of the glossematic theory, which in his opinion would have turned linguistics and semiotics into exact, formal sciences, and although it is doubtful whether all of this very elaborate system building would have been used by other linquists in describing language, it is certain that his general approach to the study of language, and to semiotics, and his claim that language must be seen as a system of immanent dependencies, has had great influence on linguistics. In this respect he follows Saussure, by whom he was very much influenced from the late 1930's, but he is more consistent, and he develops the implicit possibilities in Saussure's thinking into a set of explicit principles, definitions, and rules for description. Furthermore, his insistence on the isomorphism of the language sign, and his sketch of a structural theory of semantics, has been very influential. Owing to his consistency and originality, he was a leading figure in the shaping of modern structural linguistics and of modern semiotics.

—J. Dines Johansen

HOHFELD, Wesley N(ewcomb). American jurist. Born in Oakland, California, 8 August 1879. Studied at University of California, Berkeley, graduated, 1901; Harvard Law School, Cambridge, Massachusetts, graduated *cum laude*, 1904. Practised with Morrison, Cope and Brobeck, San Francisco, 1904; Professor, Stanford University, California, 1905-14, and Yale University, New Haven, Connecticut, 1914-18. *Died* (in Alameda, California) *21 October 1918*.

PUBLICATIONS

Law

Fundamental Legal Conceptions as Applied in Judicial Reasoning, and Other Legal Essays, edited by Walter Wheeler Cook. New Haven, Connecticut, Yale University Press, 1919.

*

Critical Studies: *Structure of Laws as Represented by Symbolic Methods* by Ward Waddell, San Diego, California, 1961.

* * *

Wesley N. Hohfeld's remarkable contribution was chiefly in the area of analytic jurisprudence. Although he focussed upon the analysis of fundamental legal relations between individuals, his singular approach was applied to diverse aspects of general jurisprudence. He constantly drew attention to the confusion, conflation and ambiguity imported into legal analysis by the careless usage of crucial terms. In order to mitigate these tendencies, he devised an exhaustive scheme of dyadic relations and used it as a heuristic device to reveal deficiencies in statutes, litigation and analytic jurisprudence itself. Hohfeld's method was not meant to solve problems of social or juristic policy. But, as Arthur Corbin acknowledged, "it does much to define and clarify the issue that is in dispute and thus enables the mind to concentrate on the interests and policies that are involved, and increases the probability of an informed and sound conclusion." His method is relevant to basic principles of political philosophy.

Hohfeld developed his system of classification early in this century, in the context of an extended debate concerning the pertinence of due process to the Fourteenth Amendment. He thought that the more immediate issues in this debate—centered upon human and property rights, the nature of corporations and trusts, the scope of the commerce clause and of taxation—obscured older historical problems in relation to common law and equity. He preferred to use the term "jural relations" instead of "legal relations" to highlight the distinction between legal and equitable interests. He argued that various legal fictions, especially those referring to corporations and trusts, were the direct result of efforts to maintain common law usages, through metaphorical devices, under ascendant equity law. Not only did this lead to avoidable confusion, according to Hohfeld, but it also impeded the teleological function of legal policy in meeting the changing needs of society. When Hohfeld commended analysis in terms of "ultimates," in terms of the relations of "natural persons," he employed formal criticism for more than formal reasons. He never disputed the *de facto* predominance of equity, but, as his analysis of legal and equitable interests showed, he could not share the sanguine view of F.W. Maitland that equity emerged not to destroy the law, but to fulfil it.

Hohfeld's endeavour to construct a comprehensive and discriminating analysis of jural relations was part of a broader attempt to render an account of the legal elements that enter into all types of jural interests. He castigated the prevailing tendency to oversimplify a specific problem and held that if analysis started from fundamentals, a compelling simplicity would be revealed. It becomes possible not only to discover essential similarities and illuminating analogies in the midst of what seems superficially to be infinite and hopeless variety, but also to discern common principles of justice and policy underlying diverse jural problems. The deeper the analysis, the greater one's perception of fundamental unity and harmony in the law.

Hohfeld divided his account of legal elements into three sections. First of all, he stressed the importance of differentiating purely legal relations from the physical and mental facts that call them into being. The tendency to conflate the legal and non-legal qualities of a problem arises through the association of ideas involved in the two sets of relations, and also through the ambiguity and looseness of legal terminology. Terms like "property" are variously employed to indicate the physical objects to which legal terms relate, the aggregate of legal relations appertaining to such objects, or even both. Similarly discussions of corporeal and incorporeal "hereditaments" fail to recognize that only legal interests as such can be inherited. Since all legal interests are "incorporeal"—consisting of aggregates of abstract *legal* relations—the contrast itself is misleading. Similarly, legal discussions of "transfer," "power," "liberty," "obligation" and so on become obscure owing to the metaphorical use of words largely borrowed from the physical world. For example, the physical or mental capacity to do a thing connoted in the ordinary use of the term "power" is quite different from the connotation of the term "legal power." The latter has to do with the volitional control of operative facts which, under the general rules applicable, suffice to change legal relations through creation, extinction or both.

The term "operative fact" is employed by Hohfeld in setting out the second component of his account of legal elements. The facts important in relation to a given jural transaction may be either *operative* facts or *evidential* facts. The former are facts which are constitutive, causal or dispositive with regard to jural relations, under existing rules. Evidential facts, on the other hand, allow some logical though non-conclusive basis for inferring other facts, operative or evidential. Operative facts may be either affirmative (e.g., that the parties are human beings), or negative (e.g., that a matter has not been wilfully misrepresented). The totality of operative facts bearing upon a dispute determines the complex of jural relations between the contending parties. Hohfeld stressed the more or less generic nature of operative facts alleged by pleadings (more in the case of negligence and less in the case of fraud), and exposed the fallacy of regarding the specific operative facts established in a case as "evidence" of the alleged generic facts. He also pointed to the potential error of regarding the presentation of an instrument to a tribunal as a single operative fact, whereas the piece of paper, together with other evidential facts, merely tends to show various operative facts from the past.

With these cognitives and existential criteria in mind, Hohfeld proceeds to the third, the most extensively worked out, portion of his account. This is the comprehensive set of jural relations between individuals. By setting forth the nature and interconnections of the members of this set, he sought to lay the basis for lucid analysis of the most complex legal interests, including trusts, options, escrows, future interests and corporate interests, as encountered in single and multi-jurisdictional contexts. Each jural relation is a dyadic relation between two individual natural persons, together describable in terms of a set of relevant and ascertainable operative facts. Each relation has two correlative designations, one from each of the standpoints of the two individuals. Through eight terms Hohfeld generated four correlative pairs: *right* and *duty, privilege* and *no-right, power* and *liability, immunity* and *disability*. A right is one's affirmative claim against another. A privilege is one's freedom from the right or claim of another. A power is one's affirmative control over a given legal relation as against another. An immunity is one's freedom from the legal power or control of another in regard to some legal relation. If A has a right, privilege, power or immunity with respect to B, then B has a corresponding duty, "no-right" (Hohfeld apologized for the term), liability or disability, respectively, with regard to A. Further, from the standpoint of a single individual, it is impossible to be in both of certain pairs of relations, in respect to the same issue. Thus, four opposite or mutually exclusive pairs of terms are generated: right and "no-right," privilege and duty, power and disability, immunity and liability. This has been called by J.R. Lucas "The Square of Obligations."

Combining correlatives and opposites, a given privilege is the negation of a duty having a content or term precisely opposite to that of the privilege in question. Similarly, a given immunity is the negation of a liability having a content or term precisely opposite to that of the immunity in question. Hohfeld developed each of those eight terms and objections. He amply illustrated the subtle intricacies and permutations of these correlative and opposite concepts in specific cases over a wide range of legal interests. It was Hohfeld's aim to apply this overall scheme of analysis, with its strictures against confusion and its positive matrix of relations, to several major classifications of judicial reasoning. Before his untimely death, he was able to make substantial progress in the classification of legal relations as *in rem* and *in personam*, and the classification of relations as concurrent and exclusive with regard to common law and equity.

Hohfeld's subtle and complex ideas are comparatively unknown today among contemporary political philosophers and legal theorists. Nonetheless, his perceptive analysis can still provide a tool in clarifying the issues involved in any rigorous treatment of reciprocal obligations. His original and pioneering contribution can be fruitfully employed by those who are actively committed to the reform or refinement of the judicial system. His work can certainly benefit all who seek a better understanding of the complex functions of law and government in modern societies. Hohfeld is also relevant to any serious consideration of international law and world government.

—R.N. Iyer

HOLMES, Oliver Wendell, Jr. American jurist. Born in Boston, Massachusetts, 8 March 1841; son of American man of letters Oliver Wendell Holmes. Studied at Harvard University, Cambridge, Massachusetts, B.A. 1861, LL.B. 1866; admitted to Massachusetts Bar, 1867. Served with 20th Massachusetts Volunteers, 1861-64. Married Fanny Dixwell in 1872. Practiced law in Boston, 1867-82, with firm Shattuck, Holmes and Munroe, from 1873; Instructor, Harvard College, 1870-71; University Lecturer, Harvard University, 1871-72; Lecturer, 1872-73, and Professor, 1882, Harvard Law School; Lecturer, Lowell Institute, Massachusetts, 1880; Associate Justice, 1882-99, and Chief Justice, 1899-1902, Supreme Judicial Court of Massachusetts, Boston; Associate Justice, United States Supreme Court, Washington, D.C., 1902-32. Editor, *United States Law Review*, from 1866; *American Law Review*, 1870-73; *New York Law Review*, from 1897. Recipient: Roosevelt Medal, Roosevelt Memorial Association, 1924. Honorary doctorate: Yale University, New Haven, Connecticut, 1886; Harvard University, 1895; Oxford University, 1909; University of Berlin, 1910; Williams College, Williamstown, Massachusetts, 1912. Member, Harvard University Board of Overseers, 1876-82. Corresponding Fellow, British Academy. *Died* (in Washington, D.C.) *6 March 1935.*

PUBLICATIONS

Law

The Common Law. Boston, Little Brown, and London, Macmillan, 1881.
Dead, Yet Living: An Address Delivered at Kenne, N.H., Memorial Day, May 30, 1884. Boston, Ginn Heath, 1884.
Speeches by Oliver Wendell Holmes, Junior. Boston, Little Brown, 1891; enlarged editions, 1896-1934.
The Soldier's Faith: An Address by Oliver Wendell Holmes. Boston, Little Brown, 1895.
Address Delivered at the Dedication of the New Hall of the Boston University School of Law, January 8, 1897. Boston University Offices, 1897.
Decision of the Supreme Court of the United States in the Case of Paine Lumber Company et al. vs. Elbridge H. Neal. New York, American Anti-Boycott Association, 1917.
Collected Legal Papers. New York, Harcourt Brace, and London, Constable, 1920.
The Dissenting Opinions of Mr. Justice Holmes, edited by

Alfred Lief. New York, Vanguard Press, 1929.

Representative Opinions of Mr. Justice Holmes, edited by Alfred Lief. New York, Vanguard Press, 1931.

The Black Book of Oliver Wendell Holmes. Boston, John G. Palfrey, 1936.

The Judicial Opinions of Oliver Wendell Holmes: Constitutional Opinions, Selected Excerpts, and Epigrams. Buffalo, New York, Dennis, 1940.

The Mind and Faith of Justice Holmes: His Speeches, Essays, Letters and Judicial Opinions, edited by Max Lerner. Boston, Little Brown, 1943.

The Holmes Reader: The Life, Writings, Speeches, Constitutional Decisions, etc., of the Late Oliver Wendell Holmes, edited by Julius J. Marke. New York, Oceana, 1955.

Justice Holmes, Ex Cathedra, edited by Edward J. Blander. Charlottesville, Virginia, Michie, 1966.

Other

Justice Holmes to Doctor Wu: An Intimate Correspondence, 1921-32. New York, Central Book Company, 1935.

Some Table Talk of Mr. Justice Holmes and "the Mrs." Boston, A.C. Getchell, 1935.

Justice Oliver Wendell Holmes: His Book Notices and Uncollected Letters and Papers, edited by Harry C. Shriver. New York, Central Book Company, 1936.

Holmes-Pollock Letters: The Correspondence of Mr. Justice Holmes and Sir Frederick Pollack, 1874-1932, edited by Mark De Wolfe Howe. Cambridge, Massachusetts, Harvard University Press, 2 vols., 1941; as *The Pollock-Holmes Letters: Correspondence of Sir Frederick Pollock and Mr. Justice Holmes, 1874-1932*, Cambridge, England, Cambridge University Press, 2 vols., 1942.

Touched with Fire: Civil War Letters and Diary of Oliver Wendell Holmes, Jr., 1861-64, edited by Mark De Wolfe Howe. Cambridge, Massachusetts, Harvard Univesity Press, 1946.

Holmes-Laski Letters: The Correspondence of Mr. Justice Holmes and Harold J. Laski, 1916-1935, edited by Mark De Wolfe Howe. Cambridge, Massachusetts, Harvard University Press, 2 vols., 1953.

The Wit and Wisdom of Oliver Wendell Holmes, Father and Son, edited by Lester Eugene Denonn. Boston, Beacon Press, 1953.

Occasional Speeches, edited by Mark De Wolfe Howe. Cambridge, Massachusetts, Belknap Press, 1962.

The Holmes-Einstein Letters: Correspondence of Mr. Justice Holmes and Lewis Einstein, 1903-1935, edited by James Bishop Peabody. London, Macmillan, and New York, St. Martin's Press, 1964.

Holmes-Sheehan Letters: The Letters of Justice Oliver Wendell Holmes and Canon Patrick Augustus Sheehan, edited by David H. Burton. Port Washington, New York, Kennikat Press, 1976.

Progressive Masks: Letters of Oliver Wendell Holmes, Jr., and Franklin Ford, edited by David H. Burton. London and East Brunswick, New Jersey, Associated University Presses, 1982.

Editor, *Commentaries on American Law by James Kent*, 12th edition. Boston, Little Brown, 4 vols., 1873.

*

Bibliography: *What Justice Holmes Wrote, and What Has been Written About Him: A Bibliography, 1866-1976*, edited by Harry Clair Shriver, Potomac, Maryland, Fox Hills Press, 1978.

Critical Studies: *Mr. Justice Holmes and the Supreme Court* by Felix Frankfurter, Cambridge, Massachusetts, Harvard University Press, 1938; *Yankee from Olympus: Justice Holmes and His Family* by Catherine Drinker Bowen, Boston, Little Brown,

1944; *The Legacy of Holmes and Brandeis: A Study in the Influence of Ideas* by Samuel Joseph Konefsky, New York, Macmillan, 1956; *Justice Oliver Wendell Holmes: The Shaping Years, 1841-1870* by Mark De Wolfe Howe, Cambridge, Massachusetts, Belknap Press, 1957; *Justice Holmes, Natural Law and the Supreme Court* by Francis Beverley Biddle, New York, Macmillan, 1961; *Justice Holmes on Legal History* by James Willard Hurst, New York, Macmillan, 1964.

* * *

Like Chief Justice John Marshall a century earlier, Oliver Wendell Holmes, Jr. became almost a legendary figure on the United States Supreme Court. He was hailed as a judge who effortlessly fused erudition with eloquence, a Boston patrician who became "the champion of the common man." In 1931 Benjamin Cardozo, who shortly would succeed Holmes on the Court, called him "the greatest of our age in the domain of jurisprudence, and one of the greatest of the ages." Such was Holmes's awesome reputation during his lifetime.

But Holmes frequently could not persuade his own colleagues on the Court to agree with his opinions. Unlike Marshall, whose opinions totally dominated the Supreme Court from 1801 to 1835, many of Holmes's most memorable opinions were issued in dissent—and thus had no legal standing whatever. Even in the years 1916-1932, when he and Louis Brandeis jointly dissented from majority decisions, their conclusions rose from very different premises; the tone and substance of their thinking were often poles apart. For much of his career, despite the adulation, Holmes stood alone.

Holmes had been a great legal historian and scholar. His comprehensive study *The Common Law* was widely celebrated not only in the United States but also in England, where he was acclaimed "the classical successor to Blackstone and Kent." After a brief stint as a Professor of Law at Harvard, he was named to the Massachusetts Supreme Court, where his reputation was further enhanced. Twenty years later, in 1902, President Theodore Roosevelt tapped him for the highest bench. Roosevelt recognized his talents, and he believed Holmes to be a kindred spirit who would help win judicial approval for his "trust-busting" and generally "Progressive" policies.

At this time, Holmes was already 61, and the thrust of his judicial philosophy had long been clear. The eloquent opening lines of *The Common Law* were a direct challenge to the stuffy legalism of his day: "The life of the law has not been logic; it has been experience. The felt necessities of the time, the prevalent moral and political theories, intuitions of public policy, avowed or unconscious, even the prejudices which judges share with their fellow-men, have had a good deal more to do than the syllogism in determining the rules by which men should be governed."

In this spirit Holmes, who had been a friend and intellectual associate of philosophical pragmatists Charles Sanders Peirce and William James, examined and interpreted the vast body of common law materials, making them more comprehensible and accessible. The same spirit prevailed during his tenure on the Massachusetts court.

Some critics thought him "radical" when he was first appointed to the Supreme Court, but he was far from that. In one sense, he really was conservative, believing that change should be gradual, evolutionary, and always linked firmly to the past. "The provisions of the Constitution are not mathematical formulas having their essence in their form," he once wrote; "they are organic living institutions transplanted from English soil." His understanding of modern economics in no way compared with that of Brandeis; he surely was closer in his thinking to Adam Smith than to Karl Marx. His personal politics were such that he voted for Harding, Coolidge, and Hoover twice.

But Holmes was a liberal in a very important *judicial* sense, and therein lay his significance. He rejected the rigid judicial style that pretended to arrive at Truth through precedent and linguistic manipulation, but which in practice was stifling any attempt to bring about needed social change. He might disagree with the rationale behind a particular piece of legislation, but he did not believe it was the judicial function to determine the "rightness" or "wrongness" of the law. This view was not widely shared on the Supreme Court of his time.

Although he disappointed Roosevelt by his dissent in the *Northern Securities* case, the first successful prosecution of a trust, Holmes quickly made it clear that he supported "Progressive" attempts to reform corrupt and unfair business practices. He joined with the majority decision to break up the Standard Oil Company (although that action turned out to be largely ineffectual).

In 1905, in the *Lochner* case, the Court considered a New York law which imposed limits on the daily and weekly hours that bakers could work. Ignoring factual considerations of health and safety, as well as popular support for the measure, the Court ruled it unconstitutional; the law violated "liberty of contract," the Justices decided.

Holmes dissented vigorously: "This case is decided upon an economic theory which a large part of the country does not entertain. If it were a question whether I agreed with that theory, I should desire to study it further.... But I do not conceive that to be my duty, because I strongly believe that my agreement or disagreement has nothing to do with the right of a majority to embody their opinions in law.... The Fourteenth Amendment does not enact Mr. Herbert Spencer's Social Statics."

His dissent was lucid and memorable. It was also, perhaps, somewhat detached, lacking the substantive economic and social force of the dissent written by his colleague John Marshall Harlan. But Holmes's argument was a powerful one nevertheless: it embraced the democratic principle that the people, through their elected representatives, had a right to seek improvements in the general welfare. That position would achieve full judicial sanction 30 years later, during the New Deal.

Holmes returned to his theme again and again. He dissented when the Court approved "yellow-dog contracts" that effectively prevented workers from joining unions. He dissented when the Court threw out minimum wage laws for women. He dissented when the Court voided laws that restricted exploitative child labor. Perhaps the clearest statement of what Holmes was against was expounded pompously by Chief Justice William Howard Taft, in *Truax v. Corrigan* (1921): "The Constitution was intended, its very purpose was, to prevent experimentation with the fundamental rights of the individual." Holmes' exactly opposed sentiments appeared in another context: "Our Constitution...is an experiment, as all life is an experiment."

With this declaration, as happened so often in his writings, Holmes seemed to partake of the old New England tradition of Jonathan Edwards, Ralph Waldo Emerson, Henry David Thoreau, and Holmes's own father, the physician-poet Oliver Wendell Holmes, Sr., all of whom delighted in blending cosmic generalizations with everyday realities. When Virginia passed a law permitting the sterilization of feeble-minded patients, Holmes's opinion translated his general theory about "the right to experiment" into the hard facts of the situation: "Three generations of imbeciles is enough" (*Buck v. Bell*, 1927).

Nobody ever questioned Holmes's eloquence (he had, incidently, been class poet at Harvard). What was perhaps his most famous phrase occurs in this sentence: "The question in every case is whether the words used are used in such circumstances and are of such a nature as to create a clear and present danger that they will bring about the substantive evils that Congress has a right to prevent." "Clear and present danger" is so quotable that it is widely believed to be part of the Constitution itself. And many people consider it a classic defense of free speech.

But there are several ironies here. For one thing, Holmes's words appeared in his opinion upholding a conviction that *denied* free speech (*Schenck v. United States*, 1919). Holmes was sanctioning a dubious law (the Espionage Act) and an even more questionable application of the law. *Schenck* was an unfortunate judicial contribution to the repressive "Red Scare" activity after World War I.

Additionally, the phrase "clear and present danger" subsequently was adopted, and sometimes distorted, by other Justices to justify suppression of free speech and association. In 1919 and in 1925, Holmes found himself in uncomfortable dissent when a majority of the Court cited "clear and present danger" to silence alleged "radicals." And during the Cold War period of the 1950's, Holmes's phrase was trotted out once more, and misquoted, for the same purpose. It had become clear that every judge has his own idea of when a danger was "clear" or "present"; as Justice Hugo Black noted, Holmes's classic test for free speech was totally unworkable.

Despite the sad fate of his famous phrase, Holmes's own devotion to civil liberties was solid and lifelong. When Chief Justice Taft wrote the majority opinion approving wire-tap evidence in a federal case, Holmes roared against his violation of the Fourth Amendment, calling wire-tapping "dirty business." When the Supreme Court upheld the conviction of a conscientious objector who refused to take an oath to bear arms in future wars, Holmes strongly dissented: "Quakers have done their share to make the country what it is...they believe more than some of us do in the teachings of the Sermon on the Mount."

To the end, Holmes remained magisterial, with a faith in the power of ideas and in the democratic tradition, that was always tempered by a healthy skepticism. "The best test of truth," he wrote, "is the power of the thought to get itself accepted in the competition of the market.... That at any rate is the theory of our Constitution.... Every year if not every day we have to wager our salvation upon some prophecy based upon imperfect knowledge." At 91, with his mind still keen but his hands shaking, he retired from the Supreme Court.

—Don Hausdorf

HOOK, Sidney. American philosopher and social critic. Born in New York City, 30 December 1902. Studied at the City College of New York, B.S. 1923; Columbia University, New York, M.A. 1926, Ph.D. 1927. Married Carrie Katz in 1924 (divorced); 1 son; married Ann E. Zinken in 1935; 1 son and 1 daughter. Public school teacher in New York, 1923-28; Instructor, 1927-32, Assistant Professor, 1932-34, Associate Professor, 1934-39, and Professor of Philosophy, 1939-72 (Head of the Graduate Department of Philosophy, 1949-55, and all-university Department, 1957-72), and since 1972 Professor Emeritus, New York University. Lecturer, New School for Social Research, New York, from 1931. Fellow, Center for Advanced Study in the Behavioral Sciences, Stanford, California, 1961-62. Visiting Professor, Harvard University, Cambridge, Massachusetts, 1961; Regents Professor, University of California at Santa Barbara 1966; Visiting Professor, University of California at San Diego 1975. Organizer, with others, Americans for Intellectual Freedom; American Committee of Cultural Freedom; Conference on Methods in Science and Philosophy; New York University Institute of Philosophy; Conference on Scientific Spirit and Democratic Faith; University Centers for Rational Alternatives; and Committee Against Academic Discrimination and for Academic Integrity. Member, International Committee for Academic Freedom; International Committee for the Rights of Man; John Dewey Society. Council Member, American Association of University Professors. Vice-President, Eastern Division, 1958, and President, 1959-60, American Philosophical Association. Recipient: Guggenheim Fellowship, 1928-29 and 1961-62; Nicholas Murray Butler Silver Medal of Columbia University, for *The Hero in History*, 1945; Ford Foundation Travelling Fellowship, 1958. Honorary doctorate: University of Maine, Orono, 1960; University of California, 1966; University of Utah, Provo, 1970; Rockford College, Illinois, 1971; University of Florida, Gainesville, 1971; Hebrew Union College, Cincinnati, Ohio; University of Vermont, Burlington. Fellow, American Academy of Arts and Sciences, 1965; National Academy of Education, 1966. Address: Hoover Institute, Stanford, California 94305, U.S.A.

PUBLICATIONS

Philosophy and Social Commentary

The Metaphysics of Pragmatism.   Chicago, Open Court, 1927.
Towards the Understanding of Karl Marx: A Revolutionary Interpretation.   New York, John Day, 1933.
The Meaning of Marx, with others.   New York, Farrar and Rinehart, 1934.
The Democratic and Dictatorial Aspects of Communism.   Worcester, Carnegie Endowment for International Peace, 1934.
Christianity and Marxism, with others.   New York, Polemic Publications, 1935.
From Hegel to Marx: Studies in the Intellectual Development of Karl Marx   New York, Reynal and Hitchcock, 1935.
John Dewey: An Intellectual Portrait   New York, John Day, 1936.
Reason, Social Myths and Democracy.   New York, John Day, 1940.
The Hero in History: A Study of Limitation and Possibility.   New York, John Day, 1943.
Education for Modern Man.   New York, Dial Press, 1946; enlarged edition, New York, Knopf, 1963.
Democracy and Desegregation.   New York, Tamiment Institute, 1952.
Heresy, Yes—Conspiracy, No!   New York, John Day, 1953.
Modern Education and Its Critics.   New York, American Association of Colleges for Teacher Education, 1954.
Marx and the Marxists: The Ambiguous Legacy.   Princeton, New Jersey, Van Nostrand, 1955.
Dialectical Materialism and Scientific Method.   Manchester, Manchester University Press, 1955.
Common Sense and the Fifth Amendment.   New York, Criterion Books, 1957.
Political Power and Personal Freedom: Critical Studies in Democracy, Communism, and Civil Rights.   New York, Criterion Books, 1959.
John Dewey: His Philosophy of Education and Its Critics.   New York, Tamiment Institute, 1959.
The Quest for Being and Other Studies in Naturalism and Humanism.   New York, St. Martin's Press, 1961.
Paradoxes of Freedom (lecture).   Berkeley, University of California Press, 1962.
The Fail-Safe Fallacy.   New York, Stein and Day, 1963.
Man's Quest for Security: A Symposium, with others, edited by E.J. Faulkner.   Lincoln, University of Nebraska Press, 1966.
Religion in a Free Society (lecture).   Lincoln, University of Nebraska Press, 1966.
Social Justice and the Problems of the Twentieth Century, with others.   Raleigh, University of North Carolina Press, 1968.
Academic Freedom and Academic Anarchy.   New York, Dell Books, 1969.
Education and the Taming of Power.   La Salle, Illinois, Open Court, 1973.
Pragmatism and the Tragic Sense of Life.   New York, Basic Books, 1975.
Philosophy and Public Policy.   Carbondale, Southern Illinois University Press, 1980.

Other

Translator, with David Kvitko, *Collected Works of Vladimir Ilich Lenin,* vol. 13.   New York, International Publications, 1927.

Editor, with Horace M. Kallen, *American Philosophy Today and Tomorrow.*   New York, Furman, 1935.
Editor, with Milton Konvitz, *Freedom and Experience: Essays Presented to Horace M. Kallen.*   Ithaca, New York, Cornell University Press, 1947.
Editor, *John Dewey: Philosopher of Science and Freedom: A Symposium.*   New York, Dial Press, 1950.
Editor, *American Philosophers at Work: The Philosophic Scene in the United States.*   New York, Criterion Books, 1956.
Editor, *Determinism and Freedom in the Age of Modern Science.*   New York, New York University Press, 1958.
Editor, *Psychoanalysis, Scientific Method and Philosophy.*   New York, New York University Press, 1959.
Editor, *Dimensions of Mind.*   New York, New York University Press, 1960.
Editor, *Religious Experience and Truth.*   New York, New York University Press, 1961.
Editor, *World Communism: Key Documentary Material.*   Princeton, New Jersey, Van Nostrand, 1962.
Editor, *Philosophy and History.*   New York, New York University Press, 1963.
Editor, *Law and Philosophy.*   New York, New York University Press, 1964.
Editor, *Art and Philosophy.*   New York, New York University Press, 1966.
Editor, *Human Values and Economic Policy.*   New York, New York University Press, 1967.
Editor, *Language and Philosophy.*   New York, New York University Press, 1969.
Editor, *The Essential Thomas Paine.*   New York, New American Library, 1969.
Editor, with E. Chalfant, *In Defense of Academic Freedom.*   New York, Pegasus, 1971.
Editor, with Paul Kurtz, *The Idea of a Modern University.*   Buffalo, New York, Prometheus Books, 1974.
Editor, with others, *The Philosophy of the Curriculum: The Need for General Education.*   Buffalo, New York, Prometheus Books, 1975.
Editor, with others, *The Ethics of Teaching and Scientific Research.*   Buffalo, New York, Prometheus Books, 1977.
Editor, with others, *The University and the State: What Role for Government in Higher Education.*   Buffalo, New York, Prometheus Books, 1978.

*

Critical Studies: *Knowledge and Freedom in Sidney Hook* by John Dennis Crowley, Rome, Pontifical Gregorian University, 1966; *Sidney Hook and the Contemporary World: Essays on the Pragmatic Intelligence,* edited by Paul Kurtz, New York, John Day, 1968 (contains a bibliography); *Sidney Hook,* edited by Paul Kurtz, Buffalo, New York, Prometheus Books, 1983 (contains a bibliography).

*   *   *

Sidney Hook is the chief heir in the later part of the 20th century to the pragmatic tradition in American thought. A student of John Dewey, he illustrates, perhaps better than any other contemporary philosopher, the application of the pragmatic intelligence to ethical, social, and political issues. His main contribution has been his use of analytic methods in dealing with concrete problems of praxis. Hook's basic interest is normative: he constantly seeks to test ideas experimentally by reference to their observed consequences in behavior.

Influenced by his early reading of Marx, he attempted to reinterpret Marxism in pragmatic terms. Indeed, he was one of the first in America to treat Marx in a serious scholarly vein (see *Towards the Understanding of Karl Marx* and *From Hegel to Marx*). He has dealt at length with the practical results of Marxist theory in real life, and has been a leading critic of the contradictions and failures of totalitarian forms of Marxism, e.g., Leninism, Stalinism, and later-day varieties of the New Left.

Democracy plays a central role in Hook's normative position. Calling himself a democratic socialist (or social democrat), he has consistently defended freedom as a basic value. Democracy is grounded, he says, upon the ethical principle of equality, and "equality of concern." This principle is not a description of fact about human nature, but a prescription of how to treat men. It states that individuals should be provided with the opportunities to fulfill their own unique dimensions of freedom and growth; and, where necessary and available, the means to satisfy their basic economic and cultural needs should be supplied. Political democracy, including civil liberties and majority rule, are necessary pre-conditions of any viable democracy and cannot be sacrificed at the altar of egalitarian ends. Hook believes that democracy is empirically justified by its benefit to the common man and is in no way derived from any metaphysical premises or natural rights doctrine (*Political Power and Personal Freedom*). It achieves more freedom, security, cooperative diversity, and voluntary creativity than alternative systems.

Hook, like Dewey, argues that a key goal of education in a democracy is the development of critical intelligence and an appreciation of the arts of negotiation and mediation. He has consistently defended the important role public schools have played in achieving a democratic society (*Education for Modern Man*). Hook has devoted much attention to defining academic freedom and integrity in the universities and colleges. We must resist any efforts to politicize institutions of higher education or lower their qualitative standards of excellence by introducing extraneous political criteria, such as quotas of admissions and employment. These detract from the primary function of the university: teaching and the search for truth.

Hook has defended a form of naturalistic ethics, arguing that ethical principles, norms, and values grow out of individual and social reflection and must be tested by their consequences in conduct. Although relative to human interests and needs, these values entail some rational criteria of scientific objectivity and need not be subjective. Factual knowledge pertaining to situations helps to shed light on alternative courses of action; our principles need to be constantly modified by the crucible of experience.

Hook is a secular humanist. A critic of theology, he has argued that there is insufficient evidence for the existence of God or a divine purpose to reality. In *The Quest for Being*, he is skeptical concerning the search for ultimate Being or the development of an existential ontology. Even those who were humanists do not escape his skeptical eye. But he is also critical of Dewey and Tillich for misusing language and for attempting to redefine the term "God" in naturalistic terms. Hook criticizes any effort to derive ethical conclusions from theological premises. From the fatherhood of God different moral and political prescriptions can and have been drawn. Humanism for him is primarily an ethical position, in the sense that ethical judgements are autonomous, growing out of human experience and reflection, and do not need any reference to ultimate first principles for their validation.

A scientific naturalist, Hook maintains that the method of science is the most reliable method for establishing truth claims, but this is continuous with the use of critical intelligence in ordinary life. He holds that we should draw upon the sciences for our understanding of the universe and man's place within it. Although nature is materialistic in foundation, Hook is a non-reductionist; for he allows that there are various qualitative dimensions of nature as revealed by art, culture, history, and other forms of human experience.

In *Pragmatism and the Tragic Sense of Life* he criticizes any pessimistic retreat from the world. Pragmatism, he says, is not insensitive to the tragic, which arises primarily from the conflict of moral ideas, goods, rights and duties. Pragmatism is for Hook "the theory and practice of enlarging human freedom in a precarious and tragic world by the arts of intelligent social control."

The great challenge for human beings is to use their creative intelligence in order to resolve problems, not seek to escape into a world of theological salvation or an ideology of messianic utopianism. Hook believes that with the cultivation of the humanist virtues of intelligence and courage, and the development of a free, democratic, and open society, it is possible for humans to resolve many, if not all, of their problems and to achieve a better life.

—Paul Kurtz

HORKHEIMER, Max. German philosopher and social scientist. Born in Stuttgart, 14 February 1895; emigrated to the United States in 1934; returned to Germany in 1949. Studied at the University of Frankfurt, Ph.D. 1922, Habilitation 1925. Married Rose Christine Riekher in 1926. Assistant, under Hans Cornelius, 1922-25; Privatdozent in Social Philosophy, 1926-30; Professor, 1930-33, President of University, 1951-53, and Professor Emeritus from 1959, University of Frankfurt. Director, Institut für Sozialforschung (Institute for Social Research), in Frankfurt, 1930; established branches of the Institute in Geneva and London, 1931; fled to Switzerland, relinquishing teaching post; then emigrated to the United States where he established the Institute at Columbia University, New York, 1934-48; returned to the University of Frankfurt, and re-established the Institut in Frankfurt, 1949-58. Visiting Professor, University of Chicago, 1954-59. Founder and Editor, *Zeitschrift für Sozialforschung*, published in Leipzig, 1932, Paris, 1933, and New York, 1934 until publication ceased, 1940. Director, Scientific Section, American Jewish Committee, 1943-44. Recipient: Goethe Medal, City of Frankfurt, 1953; Citizen Medal, Stuttgart, 1970; Lessing Prize, Hamburg, 1971. *Died* (in Nuremberg) 7 July 1973.

PUBLICATIONS

Philosophy and Social Theory

Kants Kritik der Urteiskraft als Bindeglied zwischen theoretischer und praktischer Philosophie. Stuttgart, Kohlhammer, 1925.

Anfänge der bürgerlichen Geschichtsphilosophie. Stuttgart, Kohlhammer, 1930.

Dämmerung: Notizen in Deutschland (as Heinrich Regius). Zurich, Oprecht und Helbling, 1934; revised and expanded edition as *Notizen 1950-1969 und Dämmerung*, Frankfurt, Fischer, 1974; as *Dawn and Decline: Notes 1926-1931 and 1950-1969*, New York, Seabury, 1978.

Philosophische Fragmente, with Theodor Adorno. New York, Institute for Social Research, 1944; revised edition as *Dialektik der Aufklärung: Philosophische Fragmente*, Amsterdam, Querido, 1947; as *Dialectic of Enlightenment*, New York, Herder, 1972.

Eclipse of Reason. New York, Oxford University Press, 1947.

Zur Kritik der instrumentellen Vernunft. Frankfurt, Fischer, 1967; as *Critique of Instrumental Reason*, New York, Seabury, 1974.

Kritische Theorie: Eine Dokumentation, edited by Alfred Schmidt. Frankfurt, Fischer, 2 vols., 1968; partial translation as *Critical Theory: Selected Essays*, New York, Herder, 1972.

Die Sehnsucht nach dem ganz Anderem (interview with Helmut Gumnior). Hamburg, Furche, 1970.

Traditionelle und kritische Theorie: Vier Aufsätze. Frankfurt, Fischer, 1970.

Vernunft und Selbsterhaltung (1942). Frankfurt, Fischer, 1970.

Gesellschaft im Übergang: Aufsätze, Reden und Vorträge 1942-

1970, edited by Werner Brede.   Frankfurt, Fischer Taschenbuch, 1972.

Sozialphilosophische Studien: Aufsätze, Reden und Vorträge 1930-1972, edited by Werner Brede.   Frankfurt, Fischer Taschenbuch, 1972.

Aus der Pubertät: Novellen und Tagebuchblätter.   Munich. Kösel, 1974.

*

Critical Studies: *Max Horkheimer in Selbstzeugnissen und Bilddokumenten* by Helmut Gumnior and Rudolph Ringguth, Hamburg, Rowohlt, 1973; *The Origin of Negative Dialectics: Theodor W. Adorno, Walter Benjamin, and the Frankfurt Institute* by Susan Buck-Morss, New York, Free Press, 1977; *Origin and Significance of the Frankfurt School: A Marxist Perspective* by Phil Slater, London and Boston, Routledge, 1977; *The Frankfurt School: The Critical Theories of Max Horkheimer and Theodor W. Adorno* by Zoltan Tar, New York, Wiley, 1977; *Introduction to Critical Theory: Horkheimer to Habermas* by David Held, London, Hutchinson, 1980.

*   *   *

Max Horkheimer was a philosopher and social theorist who served as director of the Frankfurt Institute for Social Research (later, the International Institute for Social Research), from 1930 to 1958. His writings and research, already well-known among philosophers and sociologists, came to have a decisive influence on the New Left in the 1960's. He was born into the family of a wealthy Jewish businessman but clearly wanted an intellectual career from an early age. He studied philosophy under Hans Cornelius and wrote his doctoral thesis on Kant's third *Critique*. Also while a student he formed a life-long friendship with Freidrich Pollock, the political economist, who would become one of the Institute's most active members. As a young man Horkheimer wrote a series of novels which have remained unpublished. Although Marx's theory of social relations remained a constant ingredient of his thinking, Horkheimer was permanently influenced by Schopenhauer, Bergson, Nietzsche, Dilthey and Freud as well. He opposed philosophical systemization, and he published a volume of aphorisms, *Dammerung, Notizen in Deutschland* under the pseudonym Heinrich Regius. Many have observed that Horkheimer brought to his philosophic work a sensibility closer to that of an artist than that of a scientist.

The Institute for Social Research was founded by Felix Weil in 1923 as an independent academy for the Marxist study of society. Initially most of the work of Institute members concerned the history of the German labour movement and the empirical analysis of capitalist production. In the late 1920's, however, with the growing involvement of Horkheimer, Theodor Adorno and Leo Lowenthal in the activities of the Institute, a reorientation of the research interests of its members took place in the direction of social philosophy and the theory of cultural criticism. Political engagement was never among the purposes of the Institute. Horkheimer, as director, also served as editor of the Institute's publication, the *Zeitschrift für Sozialforschung*, which began appearing in 1932 and which included articles and monographs by Raymond Aron, Erich Fromm, Walter Benjamin and Ernst Krenek. Horkheimer was an efficient and tireless administrator, both in Europe and during the Institute's period of exile in the United States (1934-49).

During the 1930's Horkheimer wrote a series of essays for the *Zeitschrift* (collected in *Kritische Theorie*) on such topics as authoritarianism and the family, historical materialism, mass culture and logical positivism. The unifying theme of these essays is the definition of theory as the criticism of ideology in the interest of a free and rational society. In "Traditional and Critical Theory" (1937), a seminal statement of method from this period, Horkheimer juxtaposes the attempt of modern philosophy to indicate reality through the elaboration of metaphysical schemes,

to the project of a critical theory which takes a negative stance in relation to present social reality by attempting to articulate people's hidden and unfulfilled needs. Horkheimer argues, in a vein close to that of Lukács's *History and Class Consciousness* (1923), that the detachment of thought—theory, science, philosophy—from its material situation is merely apparent and that this self-deception on the part of thought is really a form of complicity with massively repressive social institutions. Horkheimer realized that the proletariat could no longer be regarded as the historical carrier of a progressive, undistorted consciousness simply by virtue of its position in the productive process. Thus, the acknowledged lack of a collective human agent that could actualize freedom and reason turns the critical theory into a wholly negative debunking of patterns of false consciousness. The theory itself becomes the scene of liberation, or at least the last stronghold in an otherwise deteriorating situation. Horkheimer evaluated society by considering the real happiness of its members. He remained a Marxist, even through the pessimism and moralism of his later years, to the extent that he maintained that theories of society were to be judged according to whether they clarify or obscure the rational needs of people. A deep sense of unfulfilled human potential is evident in all his writings.

While living in the United States during the 1940's Horkheimer wrote *Dialectic of Enlightenment* with Theodor Adorno. Their friendship and collaboration was to become so close that they each declared a number of times that their own ideas were indistinguishable from the other's. The *Dialectic of Enlightenment* criticizes the concept of historical progress. The authors claim that the increased rationalization of social relations in the modern period has brought about a decrease in individual autonomy and has ultimately resulted in the horrors of anti-semitism and totalitarianism. Capitalism transformed the ideals of the Enlightenment into the reality of the concentration camps. This book led an underground existence until the '60's during which time it influenced the thinking of the nascent New Left in Europe.

Horkheimer returned to Frankfurt and re-established the Institute there in 1949. In a collection of essays from the post-war period, *Critique of Instrumental Reason*, Horkheimer discusses the failure of European socialism, the bureaucratic liquidation of the individual, the influence of society on marriage and education, and the meaning of the holocaust for Jews. He retired to Switzerland with Pollock in 1958 and produced essays on Schopenhauer and Marx as well as a second volume of aphorisms *Notizen, 1950-1969* (1974). One fragment of this work, entitled "On Critical Theory," says:

> The Jewish prohibition against portraying God, or Kant's against straying into the noumenal world, both recognize the absolute whose determination is impossible. This also applies to Critical Theory when it states that evil, primarily in the social sphere, but also in individuals, can be identified, but that the good cannot.... The critical analysis of society points to the prevailing injustice. The attempt to overcome it has repeatedly led to greater injustice. To torture a person to death is purely and simply an outrage; to save him, if possible, a human duty. If one wishes to define the good as the attempt to abolish evil, it can be determined. And this is the teaching of the Critical Theory.

In his work as a director of the Institute for Social Research, and in his writings and lectures, Horkheimer asserted the need for theory always to pit itself *against* the status quo and to lay hold of whatever kernel of hope for a better future it could find.

—Alan Waters

HORNEY, Karen. American psychoanalyst. Born Karen Clementine Theodore Danielssen in Hamburg, Germany, 16 September 1885; emigrated to the United States in 1932; naturalized, 1938. Studied at the University of Freiburg, the University of Göttingen, and the University of Berlin, M.D. 1915. Married Dr. Heinrich Horney in 1909; 3 daughters. Worked at the Berlin-Lankwitz Sanatorium, 1915-18; after 1920, training analyst and lecturer, Berlin Psychoanalytical Institute and Society. Associate Director, Chicago Institute for Psychoanalysis, 1932-34; after 1934, in private practice, lecturer, and training analyst, Washington-Baltimore Institute of Psychoanalysis, New York Institute for Psychoanalysis, and the New School for Social Research, New York, Member, New York Psychoanalytic Association, 1935-41. Co-Founder, Association for the Advancement of Psychoanalysis, 1941. *Died* (in New York) *4 December 1952.*

PUBLICATIONS

The Neurotic Personality of Our Time. New York, Norton, and London, Routledge, 1937.
New Ways in Psychoanalysis. New York, Norton, and London, Routledge, 1939.
Self-Analysis. New York, Norton, and London, Routledge, 1942.
Our Inner Conflicts: A Constructive Theory of Neurosis. New York, Norton, 1945; London, Routledge, 1946.
Neurosis and Human Growth: The Struggle Toward Self-Realization. New York, Norton, 1950; London, Routledge, 1951.
Feminine Papers, edited by Harold Kelman. New York, Norton, and London, Routledge, 1967.

Other

The Adolescent Diaries of Karen Horney. New York, Basic Books, 1980.

Editor, *Are You Considering Psychoanalysis?* New York, Norton, 1946.

*

Critical Studies: *Helping People: Karen Horney's Psychoanalytic Approach* by Harold Kelman, New York, Science House, 1971 (contains a bibliography); *Karen Horney: Gentle Rebel of Psychoanalysis* by Jack L. Rubins, New York, Dial Press, 1978.

*   *   *

Karen Horney's writings show the steady growth that she saw as vital to the well-integrated individual. Starting with her clinical training in psycho-analysis under Karl Abraham, an early Freudian, she soon outgrew Freud's concepts, adopted principles similar to those of Adler, and eventually helped to prepare the ground for humanistic psychology. Best known for her trenchant analysis of the male chauvanist bias in the Freudian analysis of women, Horney observed marked discrepancies between many theories of Freud and the psychological logic revealed by her patients. She radically reorganized prevailing explanations of neuroses and patiently revised therapeutic practices.

Horney's elaborate criticism of Freud's analysis challenged the assumption that neurotic disturbances are internal disorders of instinctual drives. She contended that neuroses are generated by disturbances in human relationships caused by cultural and environmental factors. Allegedly feminine psychopathologies are evident reactions to the psychic pressures inherent in a male-dominated culture. Horney concluded that therapy designed to help the patient cope with the destructive power of instincts is insufficient. The capacity for self-directed and creative integration should be nurtured, and all human beings could benefit from

self-analysis. Furthermore, Freud's concepts of the *id, ego* and *super-ego* as well as his *libido* theory of compulsive drives are too general to explain the diversity and existential relativity of specific neuroses and too vague to delineate the complex and interacting development over a lifetime of inner conflicts.

Horney maintained that neuroses have a power of continuous growth that cannot be explained exclusively in terms of past experiences and childhood traumas. Human relationships cannot be understood by reducing them to sexual relationships—symbolic or erotic—and psychology cannot be subsumed under anatomy or biology. The ego, developed by Horney into the comprehensive concept of the Real Self, is capable of becoming a self-conscious, self-determining agent engaged in a process of self-realization. The choices of the ego are potentially integrated parts of a "morality of evolution." The inner development of healthy, happy, affectionate human beings could consciously draw upon a large potential for goodness and raise the general level of collective well-being, negating any adventitious "death instinct." Citing Albert Schweitzer's distinction between "world and life affirmation" and "world and life negation," Horney declared herself an optimist in contrast to Freud's ingrained pessimism.

Our Inner Conflicts and *Neurosis and Human Growth* gave full expression to Horney's mature thought. Neuroses are rooted in a basic anxiety induced by fearsome and hostile experience, often but not exclusively part of childhood. To cope with a hostile environment, a person may develop a neurotic tendency, a compulsive pattern of behaviour unconsciously designed to avoid a functional crisis. Among neurotic trends, each with a diverse constellation of desires, three are pervasive: *moving towards people*, arising from a desire to win affection through compliance; *moving against people*, wherein an aggressive effort to dominate and manipulate others persists; and *moving away from people*, which leads to a self-protective isolation and an obsessive concern for one's own perfection. More than one trend can develop in the same personality, and the inherent incompatibility of divergent neurotic trends inevitably results in neurosis. Inner conflicts are spawned by contradictory qualities, attitudes towards self and others, and unstable sets of values. The resulting complex character structure, if not understood, produces an expanding web of compulsions which vitiate typical reactions to one's environment. A neurotic may attempt to cope with these inner conflicts by developing an idealized self, a fantasy portrait which expresses every desired quality, so that a fundamental alienation develops between the fantasy portrait and the Real Self. The neurotic personality is threatened by the existence of the Real Self and may retreat into increasingly delusive images. Sadism develops when the neurotic "gives up" on the possibility of discovery and achieving a firm capacity for self-control and mutual self-help. Moral decay is the sad outcome of psychological alienation.

The goal of therapy is to help the neurotic confront inner contradictions to release the potential for an integrated personality. The therapist may have to engage the patient (challenging, demanding, encouraging) if the critical resistance to facing contradictions is to be overcome. The structure of alienation is complex and must be dissolved if "psychic growth" is to become possible. The alienated personality has nurtured a deep-seated neurotic pride which requires a "system of avoidances" to prevent feared and anticipated pain. "The pride system" seeks actualization of the idealized self—entirely divorced from the Real Self—and also involves self-hate, the characteristic mark of false pride. To avoid having to confront this contradictory neurotic structure, the individual has encouraged compartmentalization (holding different aspects of selfhood out of relationship to one another), streamlining (radically suppressing some aspects entirely), resignation (withdrawing from psychic life). However thoroughly the dynamics of a particular neurosis is understood, the aim is always its dissolution. The individual must come to assume responsibility for himself as an active force in his own life and to accept responsibility in respect to others. He must achieve self-dependence through establishing his own hierarchy of values and applying them in his own life. Generating spontaneity of feeling is requisite for authentic expression as well as voluntary control. The most comprehensive therapeutic goal is whole-heartedness, living without pretence, wholly sincere and fully engaged. These goals are feasible ideals which can replace the false idea of the neurotic precisely because progressive fulfill-ment is possible.

In conditions of warmth, cordiality and civility, the Real Self serves as a stable center of self-directed cognitive and construc-tive change, leading to inner unity and peace as well as spontane-ous and confident relationships free of compulsions. Reciprocal love can replace submissive demands to be loved. However great human tendencies for becoming destructive, the history of man-kind also shows an untiring striving toward greater knowledge about self and world, toward deeper religious experiences, spir-itual powers and moral courage, greater achievement in all fields, and better ways of living. "By dint of his intellect and the power of his imagination, man can visualize things not yet existing. He reaches beyond what he is or can do at any given time. He has limitations but they are not fast and final."

—R.N. Iyer

HOYLE, Fred. British astronomer and novelist. Born in Bingley, Yorkshire, 24 June 1915. Educated at Bingley Grammar School; studied at Emmanuel College, Cambridge (Mayhew Prizeman, 1936, Smith's Prizeman, 1938, Goldsmith's Exhibi-tioner, and Senior Exhibitioner of the Royal Commission for the Exhibition of 1851), Mathematical Tripos 1936, M.A. 1939. Served in the Admiralty, London, 1939-45. Married Barbara Clark in 1939; 1 son (the writer, Geoffrey Hoyle) and 1 daughter. Research Fellow, St. John's College, 1939-72, University Lec-turer in Mathematics, 1945-58, Plumian Professor of Astronomy and Experimental Philosophy, 1958-72, and Director of the Institute of Theoretical Astronomy, 1966-72, Cambridge Uni-versity. Visiting Professor, 1953, 1954, 1956, Fairfield Scholar, 1974-75, and since 1963 Associate in Physics, California Institute of Technology, Pasadena. Staff Member, Mount Wilson and Palomar Observatories, California, 1957-62; Professor of Astronomy, Royal Institution, London, 1969-72; White Profes-sor, Cornell University, Ithaca, New York, 1972-78. Honorary Research Professor, University of Manchester, since 1972, and University College, Cardiff, since 1975; Honorary Fellow, St. John's College, Cambridge, since 1975. Member, Science Research Council, 1968-72. President, Royal Astronomical Society, 1971-73. Recipient: Gold Medal, Royal Astronomical Society, 1968; Kalinga Prize, Unesco, 1968; Bruce Medal, 1970, and Klumpke-Roberts Award, 1977, Astronomical Society of the Pacific; Royal Society Medal, 1974. Guest of Honor, Frontiers of Astronomy Symposium, Venice, 1975. Honorary doctorate: University of East Anglia, Norwich, 1967; University of Leeds, 1969; University of Bradford, 1975; University of Newcastle, 1976. Fellow of the Royal Society. Foreign Associate Member, American Academy of Arts and Sciences. Knighted, 1972. Address: c/o Royal Society, 6 Carlton House Terrace, London SW1Y 5AG, England.

PUBLICATIONS

Astronomy and Cosmology

Some Recent Researches in Solar Physics. Cambridge, Cam-bridge University Press, 1949.
The Nature of the Universe: A Series of Broadcast Lectures. Oxford, Blackwell, 1950; New York, Harper, 1951.

A Decade of Decision. London, Heinemann, 1953.
Frontiers of Astronomy. London, Heinemann, and New York, Harper, 1955.
Man and Materialism. New York, Harper, 1956; London, Allen and Unwin, 1957.
Astronomy. London, Macdonald, and New York, Doubleday, 1962.
A Contradiction in the Argument of Malthus (lecture). Hull, University of Hull, 1963.
Star Formation. London, H.M. Stationery Office, 1963.
Of Men and Galaxies. Seattle, University of Washington Press, 1964; London, Heinemann, 1965.
Nucleosynthesis in Massive Stars and Supernovae, with William A. Fowler. Chicago, University of Chicago Press, 1965.
Encounter with the Future. New York, Simon and Schuster, 1965.
The Asymmetry of Time (lecture). Canberra, Australian National University, 1965.
Galaxies, Nuclei, and Quasars. New York, Harper, 1965; Lon-don, Heinemann, 1966.
Man in the Universe. New York, Columbia University Press, 1966.
The New Face of Science. Cleveland, World, 1971.
From Stonehenge to Modern Cosmology. San Francisco, Freeman, 1972.
Nicolaus Copernicus: An Essay on His Life and Work. Lon-don, Heinemann, and New York, Harper, 1973.
Action-at-a-Distance in Physics and Cosmology, with J.V. Nar-likar. San Francisco, Freeman, 1974.
Astronomy and Cosmology: A Modern Course. San Fran-cisco, Freeman, 1975.
Astronomy Today. London, Heinemann, 1975; as *Highlights in Astronomy*, San Francisco, Freeman, 1975.
Ten Faces of the Universe. London, Heinemann, and San Francisco, Freeman, 1977.
On Stonehenge. London, Heinemann, and San Francisco, Freeman, 1977.
Energy or Extinction? The Case for Nuclear Energy. London, Heinemann, 1977.
The Cosmogony of the Solar System. Cardiff, University Col-lege Press, and Short Hills, New Jersey, Enslow, 1978.
Lifecloud: The Origin of Life in the Universe, with Chandra Wickramasinghe. London, Dent, 1978; New York, Harper, 1979.
Diseases from Space, with Chandra Wickramasinghe. Lon-don, Dent, 1979; New York, Harper, 1980.
The Physics-Astronomy Frontier, with J.V. Narlikar. San Francisco, Freeman, 1980.
Steady-State Cosmology Revisited. Cardiff, University Col-lege Press, 1980.
Commonsense in Nuclear Energy. London, Heinemann, and San Francisco, Freeman, 1980.
The Relation of Astronomy to Biology. Cardiff, University College Press, 1980.

Novels

The Black Cloud. London, Heinemann, and New York, Harper, 1957.
Ossian's Ride. London, Heinemann, and New York, Harper, 1958.
A for Andromeda, with John Eliot. London, Souvenir Press, and New York, Harper, 1962.
Fifth Planet, with Geoffrey Hoyle. London, Heinemann, and New York, Harper, 1963.
Andromeda Breakthrough, with John Eliot. London, Sou-venir Press, and New York, Harper, 1964.
October the First is Too Late. London, Heinemann, and New York, Harper, 1966.
Rockets in Ursa Major, with Geoffrey Hoyle. London, Heine-mann, and New York, Harper, 1969.

Seven Steps to the Sun, with Geoffrey Hoyle. London, Heine-
mann, and New York, Harper, 1970.
The Molecule Men: Two Short Novels, with Geoffrey Hoyle.
London, Heinemann, and New York, Harper, 1971.
The Inferno, with Geoffrey Hoyle. London, Heinemann, and
New York, Harper, 1973.
Into Deepest Space, with Geoffrey Hoyle. London, Heine-
mann, 1974; New York, Harper, 1975.
The Incandescent Ones, with Geoffrey Hoyle. London, Heine-
mann, and New York, Harper, 1977.
The Westminster Disaster, with Geoffrey Hoyle. London,
Heinemann, and New York, Harper, 1978.

Short Stories

Element 79. New York, New American Library, 1967.

*   *   *

Fred Hoyle's contributions to astronomical thought have been
primarily in the areas of stellar evolution and cosmology. In the
early 1940's he proposed an explanation for the presence of
heavy elements in stars. Hans Bethe had, in 1938, initiated efforts
to rationalize the chemical composition of stars and to show how
this composition was related to energy production in stars. He
outlined a sequence of nuclear fusion reactions in which, essentially, four hydrogen atoms are converted to a single helium
atom, with the loss of a minute quantity of mass. The conversion
of this mass to energy, Bethe argued, accounts for the energy
released by stars. Bethe was able to obtain a close match between
the predicted amount of energy produced in this sequence of
fusion reactions and the amount actually observed in our own
sun.

The Bethe theory offered no suggestions, however, about the
presence of atoms heavier than helium. Yet, many stars contain
appreciable concentrations of such heavier elements. Hoyle
attempted to clarify this situation by outlining other possible
fusion cycles, each of which is possible at higher and higher
temperatures. He showed that when the amount of hydrogen
falls below a certain critical level, the hydrogen-to-helium fusion
cycle comes to an end. At that point, energy production is
reduced, and the star begins to collapse in upon itself. Gravitational energy is released in this event, and the interior of the star
is heated to even higher temperatures than those produced in the
hydrogen-to-helium cycle. At these higher temperatures, a new
nuclear fusion cycle is initiated. In this cycle, helium atoms are
fused to produce carbon and oxygen atoms. At a still later point,
this cycle terminates, the star collapses again, and yet another
fusion cycle begins.

This sequence of fusion cycle and termination, stellar collapse,
energy release, and new fusion cycle continues until atoms of iron
are formed. At this point, the energetics of further fusion cycles
are such that no heavier atoms are formed through such cycles.
Gravitational forces cause the star to collapse to a white dwarf
and outer portions of the star are blown off as a supernova.

Such a stellar explosion releases into space a complex mix of
stellar matter, containing atoms ranging from the lightest (hydrogen) to the heaviest (iron). These atoms become part of the
interstellar matter from which new stars are later built. The
theory provides, therefore, an explanation of the varying composition of stars, a fact that is presumably due to their difference in
ages. Observational evidence in support of some points in
Hoyle's theory are lacking, so that the above scheme must still be
regarded as logical and possible, but speculative.

The context in which Hoyle's name is probably most familiar
has been his espousal of the continuous creation or "steady-
state" theory of cosmology. Originally developed by Bondi and
Gold in 1948, the theory has been most widely and effectively
explained and popularized by Hoyle. The continuous creation
theory evolved out of Bondi, Gold, and Hoyle's efforts to extend
a fundamental principle of cosmology, namely that "the universe

looks very much the same from any location and in all directions." The principle claims that there is no privileged *position* in
the universe from which observations can be made. Bondi and
Gold argued that this principle should be extended to include
time, so that we are not justified in arguing that the universe we
study today is different in any way from the form in which it has
existed at all times in the past or the form in which it will exist at
all times in the future. They referred to this modification as the
perfect cosmological principle. The answer posed by continuous
creation to the fundamental question of cosmogony—"How was
the universe created?"—is: It wasn't. It is now as it always has
been and always will be.

Working from this fundamental assumption, Bondi, Gold and
Hoyle derived some rather startling notions about the nature of
the universe. It is clear from observations that the universe is
continually expanding. But the perfect cosmological principle
requires that the *density* of the universe *not* change. The only way
both of these conditions can be met simultaneously is for matter
to be created continuously. As stars recede from each other, new
hydrogen atoms must be created at a constant rate to fill the
space left between stars.

This theory creates some obviously serious problems. Since
matter is constantly being created out of nothing, it violates one
of the most fundamental physical laws: the conservation of mass.
Bondi, Gold, and Hoyle's response to this objection is that the
conservation law may, in fact, not be correct when phenomena of
cosmologic proportions are considered. Like other physical
laws, conservation of mass is nothing other than a tentative
human description based on a vanishingly small sample of the
total universe: our earth. The amount of matter which must be
created to satisfy the conditions of the steady state theory is
actually so small (about 500 hydrogen atoms per cubic kilometer
of space per year) as to be beyond our powers of detection.

In recent years, the theory of continuous creation has lost
favor among most astronomers. Empirical tests are available to
choose among this theory and others that have been proposed for
the creation of the universe. The final evidence is by no means in
on the question, but existing studies seem to suggest that the Big
Bang theory, rather than the steady state theory, may be a more
useful method for describing the origin of the universe.

—David Newton

HUBBLE, Edwin Powell. American astronomer. Born in
Marshfield, Missouri, 20 November 1889. Studied at the University of Chicago, B.Sc. 1910, Ph.D. 1917; Rhodes Scholar,
Oxford University, B.A. in Jurisprudence, 1912; admitted to the
Kentucky Bar in 1913. Served in the United States Infantry,
1917-19: Major; Chief Ballistician and Director of Supersonic
Wind Tunnels Laboratory, Ballistics Research Laboratory, Uni-
ted States War Department, 1942-46. Married Grace Burke in
1924. Researcher, Yerkes Observatory, University of Chicago,
1914-17; Astronomer, Mount Wilson Observatory, Pasadena,
California, 1919-53: Chairman, Research Committee, Mount
Wilson and Palomar Observatories. Silliman Lecturer, Yale
University, New Haven, Connecticut, 1935; Rhodes Memorial
Lecturer, Oxford University, 1936; Hitchcock Lecturer, Univer-
sity of California, 1948. Recipient: Barnard Medal for Scientific
Achievement, Columbia University, 1935; Bruce Medal, 1938;
Franklin Medal, Franklin Institute, 1939; Royal Astronomical
Society Medal, 1940. Honorary doctorate: Oxford University,
1934; Princeton University, New Jersey, 1936; Occidental Col-
lege, Los Angeles, 1936; University of Brussels, 1937; University
of California, 1949. Member, National Academy of Sciences.
Fellow of the Royal Astronomical Society, London. Honorary
Fellow, Queen's College, Oxford. *Died* (in San Marino, Califor-
nia) *28 September 1953*.

PUBLICATIONS

Astronomy

Photographic Investigations of Faint Nebulae.   Chicago, University of Chicago Press, 1920.
Red-Shifts in the Spectra of Nebulae (lecture).   Oxford, Clarendon Press, 1934.
The Realm of the Nebulae (lectures).   New Haven, Connecticut, Yale University Press, and London, Oxford University Press, 1936.
Our Sample of the Universe (lecture).   Washington, D.C., Carnegie Institution of Washington, 1937.
The Observational Approach to Cosmology (lecture).   Oxford, Clarendon Press, 1937.
The Nature of Science and Other Lectures.   San Marino, California, Huntington Library, 1954.

*   *   *

Edwin Powell Hubble's career marks a watershed between classical astronomy, with its emphasis on our own solar system, and modern astronomy, concerned to a far greater extent with our Milky Way galaxy and other extra-galactic phenomena. In fact, the term "extra-galactic" would have had little meaning in the early 1920's when Hubble began his career at Mt. Wilson. The general consensus among astronomers was that our Milky Way was all that there was to the universe. Many believed that nothing existed beyond the outermost cloud of stars that make up our galaxy.

This opinion was not unanimous, however. Some astronomers argued that other universes like our own existed beyond the Milky Way. The crucial issue on which this debate focused in the early 1920's was the existence of "planetary nebulae." These blurry objects had been observed and studied as early as 1745, but their exact character had still not been determined more than 150 years later. Telescopes available before the early 1900's were simply not powerful enough to examine the nebulae in sufficient detail. Thus, the controversy over whether they were intra- or extra-galactic objects.

Making full use of the powerful new 100-inch Hooker telescope at Mt. Wilson, Hubble studied the great nebula in Andromeda. In the arms of the nebula, he discovered a Cepheid variable which allowed him to estimate the distance of the nebula from the earth. The use of Cepheid variables as astronomical measuring sticks had been proposed by Henrietta Leavitt in 1904. Leavitt had observed that the variations of luminosity for a Cepheid variable star are proportional to the distance of that star from the earth. If we can determine the period of luminosity for a star of this category, then, we can estimate its distance from us.

Using this relationship, Hubble calculated the distance to the Cepheid variable in the Andromeda nebula at about 900,000 light years. Since the diameter of the Milky Way was already well known to be only about a tenth that size, it was obvious that the Andromeda structure was well beyond the boundaries of our own galaxy. The very real likelihood that many other nebulae might also exist beyond the Milky Way could no longer be questioned. The science of extra-galactic astronomy was born.

Within a short time, our understanding of "extragalactic nebulae" had advanced significantly. It had become obvious that these "nebulae" were, in fact, galaxies of stars not unlike our own Milky Way. The studies of galaxies proceeded rapidly but in a somewhat haphazard, disorganized way. In an effort to rationalize this new field of astronomy, Hubble proposed a system for classifying galaxies. The first level of classification distinguished between those with a recognizably ordered shape (the "regular" galaxies) and those with an apparently random appearance (the "irregular" galaxies). The former group constitutes by far the greatest fraction of galaxies observed so far.

At the next level, Hubble subdivided the regular galaxies into "spirals" and "ellipticals" based on their similarities to these geometric shapes. Finally, he further divided these two groups into sub-classes (E_0 through E_7 and S_a, S_b, and S_c) depending on a particular galaxy's degree of ellipticity or tightness of spiral. This classification scheme was a purely empirical exercise, based on the desire to bring order to the study of galaxies rather than on any theoretical construct.

By far Hubble's major achievement was to come in 1929. His ongoing research on galaxies was producing data on a host of characteristics. One which caught his attention in particular was the relationship between distance of a galaxy and its radial velocity (the velocity at which the galaxy moves away from the earth). He observed that, in general, the more distant a galaxy was from the earth, the more rapidly it receded from us. This relationship has come to be known as Hubble's Law and can be expressed mathematically as: $V = Hx$—where H, the constant of proportionality, is called Hubble's Constant. The value of Hubble's constant, based on current data, is 17 kilometers per second per million light years. This means that a galactic system 1,000 light years from us is receding at a velocity of 17,000 kilometers per second. One 3,000 light years distant is receding at a velocity of 51,000 kilometers per second.

Althouh *H* is a constant, its value could conceivably change over very long periods of time. For example, suppose that the universe we see today is exactly the same now as it always has been. In that case, we would expect the relationship between *x* and *v* to be the same forever, and *H* would be an infinitely invariant quantity. But suppose that the universe has *not* always been the same. Suppose that at one time the relationship between *v* and *x* was greater or less than it is now. Then *H* would have different values throughout cosmologic history.

This argument illustrates the crucial role of Hubble's constant in cosmologic theory. At present, there are at least three possible explanations for the origin of the universe. One of these, the Steady State Theory, claims that matter is constantly being created throughout the universe, and the conditions we see today are the same as they have always been. In this case, measured values of *H* would be the same throughout the history of the universe. The Big Bang theory, however, argues that the universe was created at some specific moment (about ten billion years ago) in history and has been expanding outward ever since. The rate of expansion, however has slowed under the influence of gravitational factors, so that the value of *H* would be different for various periods in cosmologic history. Since methods are available for the measurement of *H* over billions of years of history, it should be possible to use this constant to choose among competing theories of cosmology.

—David Newton

HUIZINGA, Johan.   Dutch historian.   Born in Groningen, 7 December 1872. Studied at the University of Groningen, Ph.D. 1896. Taught high school in Haarlem, 1897-1905; Lecturer in the literature of India, University of Amsterdam, 1903-05; Professor of History, University of Groningen, 1905-15; Professor of History and Geography, Leiden University, 1915-40; taken hostage by the German occupation forces and imprisoned (released, 1942). Editor, *De Gids,* 1916-32. Honorary doctorate: Oxford University; University of Tübingen. Member, International Committee of Intellectual Cooperation with the League of Nations (Vice-President, 1938); Royal Netherlands Academy of Sciences (President, Humanities Section, 1929-42). *Died* (in De Steeg) *1 February 1945.*

PUBLICATIONS

Collections

Verzamelde werken.   Haarlem, Tjeenk Willink, 9 vols., 1948-53 (vol. 9 contains a full bibliography).

History

De Vidûsaka in het Indisch toneel [The Vidûsake in Indian Comedy]. Groningen, Noordhoff, 1897.

Mensch en mengte in Amerika. Haarlem, Tjeenk Willink, 1918; included in *America: A Dutch Historian's Vision from Afar*, New York, Harper, 1972.

Herfsttij der middeleeuwen: Studie over levens- en gedachten-vormen en vijftiende in Frankrijk en de Nederlanden. Haarlem, Tjeenk Willink, 1919; as *The Waning of the Middle Ages: A Study in the Forms of Life, Thought and Art in France and the Netherlands in the 14th and 15th Centuries,* London, Arnold, 1924.

Erasmus. Haarlem, Tjeenk Willink, 1924; as *Erasmus,* London and New York, Scribner, 1924.

Tien studien [Ten Studies]. Haarlem, Tjeenk Willink, 1926.

Amerika Leven en Denkend. Haarlem, Tjeenk Willink, 1927; as *America: A Dutch Historian's Vision from Afar*, New York, Harper, 1972.

Leven en werk van Jan Veth [The Life and Works of Jan Veth]. Haarlem, Tjeenk Willink, 1927.

Cultuurhistorische verkenningen [Explorations in Cultural History]. Haarlem, Tjeenk Willink, 1929.

In de schaduwen van morgen. Een diagnose van het geestelijk lijden van onzen tijd. Haarlem, Tjeenk Willink, 1935; as *In the Shadow of Tomorrow: A Diagnosis of the Spiritual Distemper of Our Time,* London, Heinemann, and New York, Norton, 1936.

De wetenschap der geschiedenis [The Science of History]. Haarlem, Tjeenk Willink, 1937.

Homo Ludens: Proeve eener bepaling van het spel-element der cultur. Haarlem, Tjeenk Willink, 1938; as *Homo Ludens: A Study of the Play-Element in Culture,* London, Routledge, 1949.

Nederlands beschaving in de zeventiende eeuw: Een schets. Haarlem, Tjeenk Willink, 1941; as *Dutch Civilization in the Seventeenth Century,* New York, Ungar, 1968; as *Dutch Civilization in the Seventeenth Century and Other Essays,* London, Collins, 1968.

Geschonden wereld: Een beschouwing over de kanses op herstel von onze beschaving [A Shattered World: Studies in the Possibility of Reviving World Culture]. Haarlem, Tjeenk Willink, 1945.

Men and Ideas: History, the Middle Ages, the Renaissance: Essays. New York, Meridian Books, 1959; London, Eyre and Spottiswoode, 1960.

De Nederlandse natie: Vijf opstellen [The Dutch Nation: Five Essays]. Haarlem, Tjeenk Willink, 1960.

*

Critical Studies: *Visions of Culture: Voltaire, Guizot, Burck-hardt, Lamprecht, Huizinga, Ortega y Gasset* by Karl J. Weintraub, Chicago, University of Chicago Press, 1966.

*   *   *

Johan Huizinga's father was a baptist minister and, although the great historian was never religious in the formal sense of the word, a basic respect for the spiritual aspects of life informed virtually all of his works. Huizinga completed his university training at Groningen, doing his work, not in history, but in language and literature. When he obtained his doctorate in 1896, it was in the field of philology, with particular emphasis upon Sanskrit. At the same time, Huizinga had acquired a strong background in history, and, on this basis—and that provided by several publications on aesthetics and local Netherlands history—he was appointed to a teaching post at the University of Groningen in 1905. In 1915, he moved to Leiden, which would remain his formal academic post until the institution was essentially closed down by the Nazi occupation.

Although his first "historical" work appeared as early as 1905, the piece which established Huizinga as an historian of genius did not emerge until 1919. Five years later this work would appear in English as *The Waning of the Middle Ages: A Study in the Forms of Life, Thought and Art in France and the Netherlands in the 14th and 15th Centuries.* In this book, Huizinga revealed his quite conscious tendency to work with (and within) that putatively frustrating dialectic between a more or less formally established "history of ideas" and "popular history." In a word, Huizinga, eschewing the social historian's concern with the masses as representing the most important object for historical reflection, emphasized the role of prevailing ideas, obviously, during the period under consideration, generated by relatively few people. At the same time, Huizinga attempted—and rather successfully, by most standards—to establish an ideational relationship between certain prevailing "ideas," proffered by the few, presumably in their own self interest, and much broader social needs and interests. From this point on, an interest in intellectual history, which some would deem hide-bound and parochial, would exist in fascinating proximity with an interest in mass symbolism quite congruent with more recent concerns.

Beginning with his 1919 work and in his equally distinguished 1924 work on Erasmus, Huizinga placed great emphasis on the historian's ability to achieve an intuitive grasp of an age and of those figures who embodied its salient characteristics. While he adhered to no formal historical "school," there can be little doubt that, in his emphasis upon intuitive understanding of historical events and upon the singular importance of historical individualists, Johan Huizinga was an "historicist," differing from his German counterparts only in his relative lack of interest in matters of state.

Huizinga, at least formally, rejected those socio-economic interpretations of history often identified with the Marxist approach, and, in his emphasis upon the powerful, creative individual, he appeared to be "conservative" in spirit and methodology. Huizinga also was quite adamant in rejecting Freud and thus efforts to apply the Freudian method to history. Yet, in his 1938 work, *Homo Ludens: A Study of the Play-Element in Culture*, he placed a great deal of emphasis upon symbolism in mass society, effectively fusing those concerns which, to no small degree, have informed both the Marxist and psycho-historical approaches. In this regard, it is perhaps of some significance that one of the individuals most admired by Huizinga was Max Weber, an adamant anti-Marxist and certainly no psychohistorian, who nonetheless was strongly committed to the study of both contemporary and historical societies and who, for deeply personal reasons, was interested in the role of the irrational in human affairs. Huizinga also displayed interest in that approach which would become associated with the *Annales* school.

In many respects, then, Huizinga foreshadowed contemporary interests in mass culture and mass symbolism (the latter, of course, being a central concern of psychohistory), while adhering to a method which was in many ways historicist in nature. There was a tension in this most difficult of syntheses. In a sense, this tension was resolved by Huizinga's increasingly pronounced tendency to assume the role of cultural critic rather than historian. This can be seen in *Homo Ludens* and in several other works of the 1930's. Huizinga, to be sure, never abandoned his interest in history; his 1942 work, "Im Bann der Geschichte: Betrachtungen und Darstellungen," testified to that. Furthermore, his most important essay on historiography, which first appeared in 1934, and was translated in 1956 as "Historical Conceptualization," pointed to an interest in *historiography* which remained with Huizinga until the end of his life. Nevertheless, there can be little doubt that, from the mid-1930's on, a most palpable break with the historicist principle of studying the past "for the sake of studying the past" was noticeable. It would appear that, much as in the case of Jacob Burckhardt, to whom Huizinga bore somewhat of a resemblance, certain deeply felt psychological needs which found resonance in historical speculation, eventually had to be expressed in terms of social criticism. With Burckhardt, this can be seen in his essays translated as *Force and Freedom*. With regard to Huizinga, works such as *In the Shadow of Tomorrow: A Diagnosis of the Spiritual Distemper of our Time*, which first appeared in English in 1936, some earlier works on America, and the above-mentioned *Homo Ludens*, served the same purpose. Huizinga died in 1945. It was, perhaps, no accident that the biographer of Burckhardt, Werner Kaegi, wrote the most significant memorial essay to him, one which appeared in a 1946 issue of the, in this case, most appropriately and poignantly named journal, *Historische Meditationen*.

—Robert A. Pois

HULL, Clark (Leonard). American psychologist. Born in Akron, Ohio, 24 May 1884. Studied at the University of Michigan, Ann Arbor, B.A. 1913; University of Wisconsin, Madison, Ph.D. 1918. Married Bertha Iutzi in 1911; 2 children. Public School Principal, Sickels, Michigan, 1909-11; Acting Professor of Psychology, Eastern Kentucky State Normal School, Richmond, 1913-14; Instructor in Psychology, 1916-20, Assistant Professor, 1920-22, Associate Professor, 1922-25, and Professor of Psychology, 1925-29, University of Wisconsin; Professor of Psychology, Institute of Human Relations, 1929-47, and Sterling Professor of Psychology, 1947-52, Yale University, New Haven, Connecticut. President, American Psychological Association, 1935-36. Member, National Academy of Sciences. Fellow, American Academy of Arts and Sciences. *Died 10 May 1952*.

PUBLICATIONS

Psychology

Quantitative Aspects of the Evolution of Concepts: An Experimental Study.   Princeton, New Jersey, Psychological Monographs, 1920.
The Influence of Tobacco Smoking on Mental and Motor Efficiency: An Experimental Investigation.   Princeton, New Jersey, Psychological Monographs, 1924.
Aptitude Testing.   Yonkers, New York, World Book Company, 1928.
Hypnosis and Suggestibility: An Experimental Approach.   New York, Appleton Century, 1933.
Mathematico-deductive Theory of Rote Learning: A Study in Scientific Methodology, with others.   New Haven, Connecticut, Yale University Press, 1940.
Principles of Behavior: An Introduction to Behavior Theory.   New York, Appleton Century, 1943.
Essentials of Behavior.   New Haven, Connecticut, Yale University Press, 1951.
A Behavior System: An Introduction to Behavior Theory Concerning the Individual Organism.   New Haven, Connecticut, Yale University Press, 1952.

*   *   *

Clark Hull was the leading theoretician of the new learning psychology in America in the 1930's and 1940's. His theory considered the basic phenomena of classical conditioning (first studied by Pavlov) and instrumental conditioning (first studied in Thorndike). The majority of his hypotheses and propositions concerning learning were derived from and tested in laboratory studies using these conditioning methodologies.

Hull's method of theorizing is associated with the term *hypothetico-deductive method*, where basic postulates are subjected to empirical verification. More precisely, however, Hull's theory may be labelled an *intervening variable* one. The intervening variable is a verbal label representing an inferred organismic process occurring between some antecedent stimulus event and the response of the organism. When Hull introduced these intervening labels, he was precise in relating each one mathematically to specific, measurable antecedent conditions and to specific measurable responses of the organism. The variable *Drive*, for instance, was tied to deprivation-producing operations (e.g., hours without food) at the antecedent end and to response intensity at the consequent end. Such assumptions led to a specific prediction which could be empirically tested: a food-deprived organism would give a larger startle response to a loud noise than a non-food deprived organism. Food deprivation increases drive, and drive energizes behavior.

Hull's theorizing centered primarily around four basic intervening variables. (1) The most fundamental was *Habit*, the basic unit of behavior representing a permanent receptor-effector connection in the nervous system. (2) Biological need states were represented by the *Drive* concept. Hull's theory was ultimately a biological one, based on the Darwinian survival model. Conditions of need arise, and the purpose of learning is to enable the organism to satisfy those needs. Hence, only those responses which lead to a *reduction in drive* will be learned. (3) The actual goal objects (reinforcers) which produced such drive reduction were represented by the intervening variable *Incentive*. (4) Finally, Hull developed a set of postulates concerning *Inhibition*. This concept represented organismic states based on aversive experiences like non-reward which served to decrease the probability of a response.

Hull's theory is characterized by a number of clear and precise positions on a variety of issues in learning. He maintained that learning occurred only when a response was reinforced; practice alone was not sufficient. Hull also said that only goal objects which reduced the organism's drive could function as reinforcers. He stated that drive states energize all habits of the organism in a general, non-specific manner. This hypothesis was summarized in his equation, $E = H \times D$ (where E = Behavior, H = Habit, and D = Drive). This multiplicative assumption led to several empirical predictions that were generally supported by the literature. Hull further maintained that learning was a gradual process, where habits (H) grow as a positive growth function of the number of reinforcements (N): $H = 1 - 10^{-aN}$. Finally, and perhaps most importantly, Hull firmly believed that complex behavior would ultimately be explained by behavioral laws uncovered in simple laboratory situations, especially those utilizing conditioning methodologies which offered a good degree of experimental control and precise behavioral measurement.

The clarity of the above positions, and Hull's allegiance to laboratory methodology, stimulated a prodigious quantity of research in learning psychology well into the 1960's. Hull's insistence on tying his concepts directly to antecedent and consequent events made his theory an exceptionally testable one. Naturally, many of his hypotheses did not receive empirical verification, but Hull himself never considered his theory "final." His system was designed with revisions in mind, and indeed, his later theoretical statements showed changes in certain areas (reflecting new experimental findings) compared to earlier statements. And even though many of his hypotheses did not withstand the rigors of experimental analysis, the fact remains that Hull's position on basic learning phenomena like acquisition, extinction, motivation, reinforcement, generalization, and discrimination are the starting point for any consideration of these and other topics.

—Charles I. Brooks

HULME, T(homas) E(rnest).   British philosopher and poet. Born in Endon, 16 September 1883. Studied at St. John's College, Cambridge, 1902-04; University College, London, 1904-05. Travelled in Canada and abroad, 1906-07; returned to London in 1908 and worked as a journalist for *The New Age* and other publications. Founded *The Poets' Club* in 1908. Member, Aristotelian Society, 1910-12. Enlisted in the Honourable Artillery Company in 1914. *Killed in action, September 1917.*

PUBLICATIONS

Philosophy

Speculations, edited by Herbert Read.   London, Kegan Paul, 1924; New York, Harcourt Brace, 1936.
Further Speculations, edited by Sam Hynes.   Minneapolis, University of Minnesota Press, 1955.

Verse

"The Complete Poetical Works of T.E. Hulme," in *Ripostes* by Ezra Pound, London, Stephen Swift, 1912; New York, Small Maynard, 1913; reprinted and edited by Alun R. Jones, in *The Life and Opinions of T.E. Hulme*, London, Gollancz, and Boston, Beacon Press, 1960.

Other

Translator, *Introduction to Metaphysics*, by Bergson.   New York and London, Putnam, 1912.
Translator, *Reflections on Violence*, by Georges Sorel.   London, Allen and Unwin, 1916; New York, P. Smith, 1941.

*

Critical Studies: *T.E. Hulme* by Michael Roberts, London, Faber, 1938; "Hulme and the Tragic View," by Dixon Wecter, in *Southern Review* (Baton Rouge, Louisiana), 5, 1939; "The Ambiguous Anti-Romanticism of T.E. Hulme," by Murray Krieger, in *English Literary History* (Baltimore), 20, 1953; *The Life and Opinions of T.E. Hulme* by Alun R. Jones, London, Gollancz, and Boston, Beacon Press, 1960 (contains a bibliography).

*   *   *

T.E. Hulme saw the chaos and conceit of pre-1914 Europe as signifying the last degenerate phase of Renaissance Humanism. An intrepid and unabashed iconoclast, Hulme located the ultimate source of decay in the rejection of original sin by Pico, Bruno, Montaigne and many others. He traced the traumatic consequences of this error in philosophy and religion, politics and the arts, down to his own time. By drawing attention to the deep malaise of European civilisation, as well as to contemporary counter-instances, he sought to bring about a shift in attitudes toward a more sober, if less sanguine, view of human nature and social institutions. Neither a sectarian nor a sentimentalist, Hulme held that the concern with human perfection was a persistent if delusive tendency in many societies, and looked to Egyptian and Indian cultures for examples of the denial of perfectionism through the principle of renunciation. By acknowledging the irreducible moral and intellectual limitations of mankind, through an admission of the vanity of all desires, and by accepting the essential difference between the human and the divine, Hulme hoped to restore a sense of objectivity in ethical and religious values, a true creativity in the arts, and an authentic, if tragic, heroism in individual conduct.

Hulme distinguished three regions or levels of reality which are radically separate in kind, not degree: *the divine*, perfect in itself and the realm of absolute values; *conscious life*, the relative realm of thought and memory; and chaotic "cindery" *objective physical existence*, the ash heap region of physical sensation. Er-

ror and distortion arise, on the one side, when one claims continuity between the divine and the human, which is the aberration of humanists, and, on the other side, when one claims continuity between the human and the physical, which is the mistake of materialists. Humanists confuse life with the divine, producing pantheism in religion, idealism in metaphysics, rationalism in epistemology, utopianism in politics, romanticism in literature and personalism in psychology. All alike rest upon an impermissible importation of perfection into human nature, a misappropriation of the absolute and infinite into the region of limit and uncertainty. Materialists confuse life with physical existence, producing either extreme ethical relativism or the nightmare of mechanistic determinism, depending upon whether the chaotic flux of the physical is imposed on life (Hume, Rousseau and Russell), or the formal fixity of rationality is forced upon the physical (Spinoza, LaPlace and T.H. Huxley). Hulme found humanists and materialists alike culpable by being obsessed with rational intellect and by misapplying it variously to indefinable perfection or disordered chaos. All such theories were unwitting rationalisations of vain desires for impossible satisfactions. Philosophy itself is at best an art, not a science. While he admired G.E. Moore's attempts to find objectivity in moral values, his suspicion of intellectualism made him even more sympathetic to Nietzsche.

Hulme's positive views centered largely on poetry and the visual arts, wherein he was considered an *avant-garde* critic, and he made periodic forays into social and political polemic. As an admirer and exponent of Bergson, he adopted a distinction between extensive manifolds—subject to spatial analysis by reason—and intensive manifolds—formed of inextricably interpenetrating elements and apprehensible only by intuition. Intensive life and consciousness gain unity by intuition alone, not by the algebraic "counter-language" of reason, which only serves to distort the endless disordered variety of "cindery" physical existence whilst denying the particularity of concrete experience. The poet must strive to intuit fresh analogies from experience and express them so vividly that a sustained physical image is presented to the reader's mind. There is no place for any romantic musical enthusiasm for the infinite apprehended by imagination, such as infects Coleridge and Shelley, Ruskin and Whitman. Hulme insisted that the play of verbal fancy in creating images regenerates language, pointing to Horace, Keats and Pound as exemplars of such "imagism." In painting and sculpture, an apt recognition of the vanity of human desire should lead to an austere rejection of vitalism and realism. Instead, the use of geometric abstraction should reflect the tragic insignificance of the human form before the immensity of divine space and duration. Hulme found serene truth in the geometric forms of Byzantine mosaics, the stylized abstractions of Egypt and India, and the simple designs of African art. He rejected both Greek and post-Renaissance naturalism, finding in Giotto and Michelangelo the precursors of the romantic decadence of Turner and Constable. In Picasso and Bomberg, Epstein and Gaudier, he found the harbingers of a resurgence of the geometric mode which used machine-like motifs to convey the stark emptiness of human pretension.

Man's primary need is action and not knowledge, Hulme argued in "Bergson's Theory of Art." Subjugated to human need, sense awareness is only accidentally fresh: we tend to see not unique particulars but types which fit into pre-established patterns of need fulfillment. The artist is not so rigidly attached to the necessities of action and is thus able to see things as they are. Freshness of perception is the basis of art, but since this "accident of Nature" which is impossible of manufacture occurs in a single sense or in consciousness alone, there is a rich diversity among the arts. In "Notes on Language and Style" Hulme asserted that thought is prior to language and consists of the juxtaposition of images. Language reflects this process feebly, and as the juxtaposition can become mechanical, language largely consists of dead analogies. Poetry is the expression of fresh juxtapositions, attempting to get at things in themselves and not merely as types.

It is the advance guard of language, the momentary emancipation of man from the driving necessity of action and the liberation of expressed thought. Analogy is not decorative, but the thing in itself. Ideas are dead pretensions artificially built from mouldy analogies.

Socially and politically, Hulme castigated Rousseau for the romantic view that human nature will improve through the removal of external fetters. He traced a line from Pico to Turgot and Condorcet, through Rousseau, to Saint-Simon and the Webbs, accusing all alike of fostering the false doctrine of automatic progress based upon a mistaken affirmation of human malleability. Extolling the wisdom of the doctrine of original sin as an essentially correct assessment of human nature, he preferred Aristotle to Plato, Augustine to Pelagius, Pascal to Goethe. He strongly held that no good can be got out of human beings except through discipline, authority and institutions that conserve the recognition of a hierarchy of absolute values against the inherent imperfection of man and the persistence of physical chaos. He dismissed democratic socialism as a romantic delusion and endorsed Sorel's pragmatic justification of violence and of economic reform. He rejected utilitarian schemes as rooted in subjectivist hedonism or as a misreading of evolution based upon the facile assumption of continual progressive improvement.

In a sharp interchange with Bertrand Russell during World War I, Hulme spurned pacifism as a romantic attachment to life, and argued for a hierarchy of heroic and objective values in which life is not always ranked above other obligations. What these values were Hulme did not explain before his death in Flanders. Even this event he would not have romanticised. He called the War a great and useless sacrifice, "as negative barren, and as *necessary* as the work of those who repair sea-walls...which in this actual 'vale of tears' becomes from time to time necessary merely in order that bad may not get worse."

—R.N. Iyer

HUSSERL, Edmund.   German philosopher.   Born in Prossnitz, Moravia, 8 April 1859. Studied at the University of Berlin, Ph.D. 1881 (in mathematics). Married Charlotte Steinscheider in 1887; 3 children. Worked with Franz Brentano, 1884-86. Lecturer, University of Halle, 1887-1901; Professor, University of Göttingen, 1901-16, and University of Freiburg, 1916-29. *Died (in Freiburg) 27 April 1938.*

PUBLICATIONS

Collections

Husserliana.   The Hague, Nijhoff, 1950-.

Philosophy

Über den Begriff der Zahl.   Halle, Germany, Niemeyer, 1887.
Philosophie der Arithmetik: I. Psychologische und logische Untersuchungen.   Halle, Germany, Pfeiffer, 1891.
Logische Untersuchungen.   Halle, Germany, Niemeyer, 2 vols., 1900, 1901; as *Logical Investigations, I-II*, London, Routledge, and New York, Humanities Press, 1970.
Ideen zu einer reinen Phänomenologie und phänomenologischen Philosophie.   Halle, Germany, Niemeyer, 2 vols., 1913, 1928; as *Ideas: General Introduction to Pure Phenomenology*, New York, Macmillan, 1931; London, Allen, 1952.
Erfahrung und Urteil: Untersuchungen zur Genealogie der Logik, edited by Ludwig Landgrebe.   Prague, Academia-Verlag, 1939; as *Experience and Judgment: Investigations in Genealogy of Logic*, Evanston, Illinois, Northwestern University Press, 1973.

The Paris Lectures.   The Hague, Nijhoff, 1964 (translation of part of *Husserliana*, vol. 1).
The Idea of Phenomenology.   The Hague, Nijhoff, 1964 (translation of *Husserliana*, vol. 2).
The Phenomenology of Internal Time-Consciousness.   The Hague, Nijhoff, 1964 (translation of *Husserliana*, vol. 10).
Phenomenology and the Crisis of Philosophy.   New York, Harper, 1965 (selections from *Husserliana*).
Cartesian Meditations: An Introduction to Phenomenology.   New York, Humanities Press, 1966 (translation of part of *Husserliana*, vol. 1).
Formal and Transcendental Logic.   The Hague, Nijhoff, 1969 (translation of *Husserliana*, vol. 17).
The Crisis of European Sciences and Transcendental Phenomenology: An Introduction to Phenomenological Philosophy.   Evanston, Illinois, Northwestern University Press, 1970 (translation of *Husserliana*, vol. 6).
Phenomenological Psychology.   The Hague, Nijhoff, 1975 (translation of *Husserliana*, vol. 9).
Edmund Husserl's "Origin of Geometry," with a commentary by Jacques Derrida.   Stony Brook, New York, Hays, 1978 (translation of "Die Frage nach dem Ursprung der Geometrie," in *Revue Internationale de Philosophie* [Brussels], 1, 1938-39).

Other

Briefe an Roman Ingarden.   The Hague, Nijhoff, 1968.

Editor, with others, *Jahrbuch für Philsophie und Phänomenologische Forschung*.   Halle, Niemeyer, 10 vols., 1913-29.

*

Bibliography: *Edmund Husserl and His Critics: An International Bibliography (1894-1979) Preceded by a Bibliography of Husserl's Writings* by Francois M. Lapointe, Bowling Green, Ohio, Philosophy Documentation Center, 1980.

Critical Studies: *A First Introduction to Husserl's Phenomenology* by Joseph Kockelmans, Pittsburgh, Duquesne University Press, 1967; *Husserl: An Analysis of His Philosophy* by Paul Ricoeur, Evanston, Illinois, Northwestern University Press, 1967; *Edmund Husserl: Philosopher of Infinite Tasks* by Maurice Natanson, Evanston, Illinois, Northwestern University Press, 1973; *Husserl-Chronik: Denk- und Lebensweg Edmund Husserls* by Karl Schuhmann, The Hague, Nijhoff, 1977; *Husserl: Expositions and Appraisals*, edited by Frederick A. Elliston and Peter McCormick, South Bend, Indiana, University of Notre Dame Press, 1977.

*   *   *

Edmund Husserl is undoubtedly one of the most important philosophers of the 20th century. This is true not only because of the profundity, breadth, and rigor of his own philosophical thinking, but also because of the influence he has exerted on a great number of other leading thinkers of the 20th century such as Scheler, Hartmann, Heidegger, Sartre, Merleau-Ponty, Levinas, Ingarden, Fink, Gadamer, Ricoeur, de Waelhens, and many others. His influence has been vast and deep not only in philosophy proper, but also in the social sciences, the historical disciplines, the arts, literary criticism, and other fields of study.

Husserl's contributions to philosophy can perhaps be divided into three major areas: (1) his early work in philosophy of mathematics and logic, research which gradually led him to the discovery of the phenomenological method; (2) investigations which were meant to develop, articulate, and justify this new method from a transcendental point of view; and finally (3) numerous manuscripts and lecture courses in which this method was applied in different areas, such as problems of perception, imagination, memory, space, time, intersubjectivity, etc., but also problems of philosophy of science, ethics, the social world, history, etc. It is well to concentrate on Husserl's conception of philosophy and on the phenomenological method, because they more than anything else can explain the enormous influence he has exerted during the past 80 years.

For Husserl the goal of philosophy still is, as it was for the Greeks, to prepare man for a truly philosophical form of existence in and through which man gives himself, his whole life, a rule through pure reason. Today philosophy consists of different "disciplines;" but one should realize that they all are fundamentally one in their basic aim: they all concern themselves with the great problems of reason. Thus reason is the explicit theme in the disciplines of knowledge, in the disciplines concerned with man's valuation which aims at genuine values as values of reason, and in the disciplines of ethical and social action which flow from practical reason. Throughout the centuries philosophy has tried in different ways to achieve this multiple goal, sometimes more or less succeeding, mostly however failing. Husserl was convinced that one would come closer to this great ideal if one were to discover and apply the proper method. He thought that phenomenology was this method. What he wanted to achieve by the development and application of his phenomenological method can thus best be described as follows: To bring latent reason to the understanding of its own possibilities and to bring to insight the possibility of philosophy as a genuine means; for this is the only way to put philosophy on the difficult road to realization. It is the only way to decide whether the goal which was inborn in Western man at the birth of Greek philosophy is merely a factual, historical delusion, or whether the Greek conception of man was not rather the first breakthrough to what is essential to humanity as such. To be human at all is essentially to be a genuine human being in a social world whose life is guided by reason. For man is a rational being only to the degree that his whole world is a rational world and his entire civilization a rational civilization, that is, one with a latent orientation toward reason or one openly oriented toward this goal. Although these ideas were for the first time formulated only in Part One of *The Crisis of European Sciences (1936)*, they nonetheless give guidance to Husserl's concern throughout his entire career as a philosopher.

In Husserl's opinion, since its beginning in Greece, philosophy has always aspired to be an all-encompassing, intellectually fully-justified knowledge of all that is. In every epoch of its long history, thinkers have tried to realize this aim of philosophy in their own way; Husserl wished to attain this goal by means of phenomenology, whose essential aim it is to attain absolutely valid knowledge of things and events. In so doing philosophy, contrary to the sciences, does not want to leave anything unsolved; rather, it wants to reduce everything to primary "presuppositions" which do not need to be clarified because they are immediately evident and cannot be clarified further. It is only in this sense that philosophy as the science of ultimate grounds is a strictly rigorous science.

Although in some sense it is natural for man to philosophize, one should realize that in our everyday life we are mainly guided by opinion and *doxa*. Thus it is necessary to make a clear distinction between the natural and the philosophical attitudes, just as it is necessary to make a distinction between "natural" and philosophical sciences. As compared with the empirical sciences, philosophy lies in an entirely different dimension; it needs entirely new starting points and an entirely new method, one which is in principle different from those used in the "natural" sciences. Its aim as philosophy, thus, implies a radicalism of foundation, a reduction to absolute presuppositionlessness, and a fundamental method through which the philosopher at the beginning secures an absolute foundation for himself.

Husserl seeks this ultimate foundation of all our rational assertions and positions in an immediate vision, an original intuition of "the things themselves." Thus the "principle of all principles" for phenomenology states that every primordially given intuition is a legitimate source of knowledge; whatever presents itself in intuition in primodial form is simply to be accepted as it presents itself and to be accepted within the limits in which it there presents itself. Accordingly, Husserl does not see the radical and absolute starting point of philosophy in any single basic intuition or concept, in any one single fundamental principle, in one simple *cogito*, but rather in an entire field of original experiences. Within this enormous field there is no room for induction or deduction, but only for intuition; yet this intuition is obviously to be prepared by carefully articulated methodical steps (reductions, analysis, description). For intuition implies that "subject" and "object" are present to each other on the same level, so that the one can directly "see" the other. Thus the intuition of the "true beginnings" demands that we first try to arrive at the "lowest field of work" in which these foundations are immediately present to the ego. In Husserl's view a set of reductions can lead us to this field. By reduction is meant here any methodic procedure by which one places himself in the "transcendental" sphere, the sphere in which one can see things as they are in themselves, independently of any prejudice or false assumption. Husserl then distinguishes two types of reductions, the eidetic reduction and the set of reductive processes to which one usually refers with the term "the phenomenological reductions." The *eidetic reduction* is to lead us from the realm of concrete things and events, i.e., from the "facts," to that of general essences, i.e., the sphere of "ideas." By essences or ideas Husserl does not mean the empirical generalities which provide us with types encountered in experience, but rather "pure generalities," which are pure possibilities and whose validity is independent of ordinary experience. The *phenomenological reductions*, on the other hand, make us pass from the world of "realities" to that of their ultimate presuppositions. Sometimes one distinguishes the following methodical steps: 1) the step which leads us from our cultural world to the world of our immediate experiences; 2) the step through which we take distance from the conceptions of former philosophers whose opinions we do not deny but merely put between brackets, so to speak; 3) the step through which we move from a concern with ontic things to the concern with their meaning; this step is often called the "bracketing of being;" 4) the transcendental reduction which leads from the empirical and mundane ego to the transcendental subjectivity as the ultimate source of all meaning. As for the latter, Husserl was inspired here by Kant's conception of transcendental consciousness, which he however interpreted in a new way. To engage in philosophy means for Husserl to return to the transcendental subjectivity as the foundation where all meaning ultimately is constituted. Only when we have reached this ground can we achieve the insight which makes us understand how meaning really comes to pass. Husserl continued to work on the clarification of the meaning and function of the transcendental reduction until the very end of his life.

That which these reductions opens up for us is a field of original experiences, all of which have in common that they are intentional. Husserl borrowed the concept of intentionality from Brentano who in turn had derived it from the Aristotelian tradition. But just as Brentano changed the meaning of the original, Aristotelian conception of intentionality, so Husserl reinterpreted Brentano's conception. For Husserl intentionality means that in all pure experiences there is found inherently a being-directed-toward; perceiving is perceiving something, judging is judging about something, hoping is hoping for something, etc. The phenomenological analysis and description must examine the different forms of intentionality in a critical and reflective attitude, because it is precisely through these different forms of intentionality that each domain of objects becomes accessible to us. Now the large majority of all intentional acts performed by an adult human being are not original and primordial, but rather derived acts. Thus if one is to arrive at the sphere in which things appear to us primordially, he is to find a way which leads from what manifests itself actually in these derived acts to the original objects of our most primordial acts. Husserl speaks of "intentional analysis" to refer to the method to be used when one goes back in his questioning from his derived acts and their correlates to the original lived experiences, in which any kind of being whatsoever primordially appears as itself in its immediate givenness.

The dominant tradition of science, in which we are educated, has imposed on us a number of prejudices regarding the alleged original objects of experience. Science claims that the original object is the object as it manifests itself through the description and determination of the sciences. In fact, however, these objects are really abstractions and idealizations of the things given in original experience. Thus if we want to discover the truly original structures of the objects in the various regions of being, we must abandon the prejudices of the sciences and return to the world as it manifests itself in our primordial experiences; in other words, we must return from the world of the sciences to the original life-world.

—Joseph J. Kockelmans

HUTCHINS, Robert Maynard. American educationist and lawyer. Born in Brooklyn, New York, 17 January 1899. Studied at Oberlin College, Ohio, 1915-17; Yale University, New Haven, Connecticut, A.B. (honors) 1921, LL.B. 1925. Served in the United States Army Ambulance Service, in Italy, 1917-19: Croce di Guerra. Married Maude Phelps McVeigh in 1921 (divorced, 1948), 3 children; married Vesta Sutton Orlick in 1949. English and history teacher in a private school in Lake Placid, New York, 1921-23; Lecturer, 1925-27, Professor of Law, 1927-29, Acting Dean, 1927-28, and Dean of the Law School, 1928-29, Yale University; President of the University, 1929-45, and Chancellor, 1945-51, University of Chicago. Associate Director, Ford Foundation, New York, 1951-54; Chief Executive Officer, Fund for the Republic, New York, from 1954; also, Chief Executive Officer, Center for the Study of Democratic Institutions, Santa Barbara, California, and Member of the Board of Directors, *Encyclopaedia Britannica* and Encyclopaedia Britannica Films, Chicago. Regional Chairman, National Labor Board, 1933; Chairman, Commission on International Economic Relations, 1933-36; Member, Commission on the Freedom of the Press, 1947; Chairman, Goethe Bicentennial Foundation, 1949. Member, Board of Directors, St. John's College, Annapolis, Maryland. Recipient: Goethe Medal, City of Frankfurt, 1948; Aspen Founders Award, 1960. LL.D.: Oberlin College, Ohio, 1929; Williams College, Williamstown, Massachusetts, 1930; Harvard University, Cambridge, Massachusetts, 1936; Tulane University, New Orleans, 1938; University of Copenhagen, 1946; University of Illinois, Urbana, 1947; University of Frankfurt, 1948; University of Stockholm, 1949; University of Chicago, 1951; Colby College, Waterville, Maine, 1956; University of Rochester, New York, 1958; D.Litt.: Georgetown University, Washington, D.C., 1964. Officier, Légion d'Honneur. *Died* (in Santa Barbara) *14 May 1977.*

PUBLICATIONS

Education, Sociology and Law

No Friendly Voice. Chicago, University of Chicago Press, 1936.
The Library. Chicago, American Library Association, 1936.
The Higher Learning in America. New Haven, Connecticut, Yale University Press, 1936; revised edition, 1962.
Education and the Social Order. Los Angeles, Modern Forum, 1936.
Education for Freedom. Baton Rouge, Louisiana State University Press, 1943.

The Atomic Bomb Versus Civilization. Chicago, Human Events Inc., 1945.
The Atom Bomb and Education. London, National Peace Council, 1947.
The Constitutional Foundations for World Order. Denver, Colorado, Social Science Foundation of the University of Denver, 1947.
Saint Thomas and the World State. Milwaukee, Marquette University Press, 1949.
Morals, Religion, and Higher Education. Chicago, University of Chicago Press, 1950.
The Great Conversation: The Substance of a Liberal Education. Chicago, Encyclopaedia Britannica, 1952; as *Great Books: The Foundation of a Liberal Education*, New York, Simon and Schuster, 1954.
The Democratic Dilemma. Stockholm, Almqvist och Wiksell, 1952.
The Conflict in Education in a Democratic Society. New York, Harper, 1953.
The University of Utopia. Chicago, University of Chicago Press, 1953.
Some Observations on American Education. Cambridge, Cambridge University Press, 1956.
Freedom, Education, and the Fund: Essays and Addresses 1946-1956. New York, Meridian, 1956.
The Bill of Rights, Yesterday, Today, Tomorrow (speech). New York, Fund for the Republic, 1956.
What's a College For, with others. Washington, D.C., Public Affairs Press, 1960.
The Nurture of Human Life. Santa Barbara, California, Center for the Study of Democratic Institutions, 1961.
Two Faces of Federalism: An Outline of an Argument about Pluralism, Unity, and Law. Santa Barbara, California, Center for the Study of Democratic Institutions, 1961.
The Political Animal: A Conversation, with Joseph P. Lyford. Santa Barbara, Center for the Study of Democratic Institutions, 1962.
Addresses on the Role of Government in Education, with Arthur S. Fleming. Houston, Rice University, 1963.
A Conversation on Education: Robert M. Hutchins Answers Questions from the Floor. Santa Barbara, California, Center for the Study of Democratic Institutions, 1963.
Science, Scientists, and Politics, with others. Santa Barbara, Center for the Study of Democratic Institutions, 1963.
Dialogues in Americanism, with others. Chicago, Regnery, 1964.
Dr. Zuckerkandl! (from the film). New York, Grove, 1968.
The Learning of Society. New York, Praeger, 1968.
The Future of International Education. New York, United Nations Institute for Training and Research, 1970.

Other

The Britannica: An Exchange of Letters, with Harvey Einbinder. Privately printed, 1960.

Editor, with Mortimer Adler, *The Great Ideas of Today.* Chicago, Encyclopaedia Britannica, 1961.

*

Critical Studies: *Court of Reason: Robert Hutchins and The Fund for the Republic* by Frank K. Kelly, New York, Free Press, and London, Collier Macmillan, 1981.

*   *   *

Robert Maynard Hutchins championed the ideals and aims of true education. His trenchant criticism of conventional pretensions, technological excess and institutional inversions were anchored in his richly-endowed vision of ancient educational philosophy. The reforms instituted during his chancellorship at the University of Chicago provided an educational paradigm in the liberal arts. No revision in college curricula could thereafter avoid encountering the humane educational goals which Hutchins expounded and exemplified. *The Higher Learning* and *No Friendly Voice*, written in the Depression amidst devastated educational budgets and stereotypes of college students as the spoiled sons of the irresponsible wealthy, foresaw the emerging role of the junior college and unwaveringly supported the American dream of education for all.

The goal of authentic education is the development of *human* power—intellectual, moral, aesthetic and spiritual. From such strength flows understanding, the arts of deliberation, judgment and moral choice, a sense of values, creativity and mature responsibility. Drawing upon the timeless themes of great thinkers, Hutchins spoke of a "new classicism" focussed upon the examination of ideas—how to recognize, analyze, develop and apply them. Ideas stir the universally-shared potential of human beings who can be educated in a Socratic sense to transcend the mindless habits and material modes of modern life. With a broadened vision, individuals can know more, do more, enjoy more and share more than pragmatic or positivist theories suggest. A liberal education is essential to free men. If all men were to be free, all men must have this education.

The task of "helping people to become human" is, according to Hutchins, the same in every age and society. It must be undertaken even when there is no agreement on the nature of man or the aims of living. "We believe that the voices that may recall the West to sanity are those which have taken part in the Great Conversation." The tendency to confine great books to formal education is calamitous for adults who can no longer appreciate the value of liberal education for the individual and for society. "The rising generation has been deprived of its birthright." Human lives which are comparatively rich in material comforts have become impoverished morally, intellectually and spiritually. Participation in the Great Conversation—the essence of mature thinking over millennia—should be sought by all; its absence in any generation is an aberration. Without it, the ideal of democracy is vitiated in practice by a population unknowingly hypnotized by ceaseless propaganda. Individual growth is stunted by putting a closure on thoughtful self-education. Joining in the Great Conversation includes walking and talking with poets and philosophers, and also with great scientists and mathematicians. Its chief aim is learning to think, to discern and to draw conclusions.

In *The Conflict in Education* Hutchins criticized doctrines of educational adjustment, curricula designed to meet immediate needs and broader theories of social reform through educational goals. Such views are only rationales of democratic necessity used to justify educational systems that are inefficient and unphilosophical. Theories and institutions nurtured by pragmatism and positivism become rooted in a parasitical relationship to "facts" and the so-called "pressing needs" of society. They contain no assessment of values, no standards and therefore no power to generate and apply an educational philosophy. Without this, there are no ideals, there is only purposelessness—the hallmark of contemporary educational systems.

Vocational or career goals are not an effective substitute for a genuine educational philosophy. Technological society requires education for anything, not education for a specific skill likely to become obsolete. Schools should not compete with on-the-job training but should concentrate their resources on the more fundamental task of developing flexibility for human survival in the dynamic and cosmopolitan diversity of technological and urban societies. The training of the mind rather than the discipline of the hands was a favoured theme of Hutchins, but it was not an elitist view vitiating his egalitarian philosophy.

Innovations aimed to reduce the custodial and service station approaches to education should concentrate on the central purpose. While new forms could not guarantee effective communication, they could provide opportunities for developing the

capacity to think, speak and write. Articulate individuals could learn to share ideas uncluttered by special languages and restrained only by the civility and tolerance of true humanity. (*University of Utopia*.) Communication is the pathway to positive community. Hutchins used the word "community" in many senses as he came to understand the complex social context in which educational institutions operate. Sobered by the experiences of the McCarthy era and a witness to student protests of the 1960's, he came to speak of political community as the most important and encompassing. His later writings call for education for citizenship. Nonetheless, educational institutions cannot control social appetites and cultural proclivities: society asks for and receives what it wants from educational systems. Majority opinion is a persuasive factor, no matter how distasteful the result. Unhealthy and disintegrative demands can be checked by affecting the culture through individuals with noble vision who can serve as the yeast of effective leadership. "The good society is not just a society we happen to like or be used to; it is a community of good men."

In his post-1960's assessments, Hutchins spoke of his vision of America as a learning society. The freedom of discussion guaranteed by the First Amendment and the constitutional plan of the founding fathers authorizes this vision. "Civilization is the deliberate pursuit of a common ideal." The republic of learning is the archetype by which all actual political republics are measured. A world community can emerge from an authentic effort to understand the needs and potentials of all mankind. The goal towards which mankind has moved over 25 centuries is a world-wide political republic of mutual support. "The civilization we seek will be achieved when all men are citizens of the world republic of law and of the republic of learning all their lives long." (*The Conflict in Education*.)

Hutchins lived with the painful recognition that modern man remains highly vulnerable to the imagery of mass media. The satirical pessimism in *Zuckerkandl* highlighted the absurd complacency of man in a mass consumer society ignorant of what philosophy and science could teach. When corporate technological power seizes control of cultural and political life, then the Jeffersonian ideal of yeomen participation in constitutional democracy is reduced to a delusive myth. Free rein would be given to the "four horsemen of the philosophical apocalypse"—relativism, scientism, skepticism and intellectualism—ending in the moral disintegration of the West.

—R.N. Iyer

ILLICH, Ivan. American social critic and theorist. Born in Salzburg, Austria, 4 September 1926; emigrated to the United States in 1951; subsequently naturalized. Studied at the University of Florence; University of Rome; University of Munich; Gregorian University, Licentiate in Philosophy, 1946, Licentiate in Theology, 1951; University of Salzburg, Ph.D. 1951; ordained Roman Catholic priest, 1951. Assistant Pastor, Incarnation Church, New York, 1951-56; Vice-Rector, Catholic University of Puerto Rico, Ponce, 1956-60; Monsignor, 1957; subsequently resigned priestly functions. Co-Founder and Director, Center for Intercultural Documentation (CIDOC), Cuernavaca, Mexico, 1961-76. Lecturer in Political Science and Sociology since 1968, and Researcher since 1973, Fordham University, Bronx, New York. Visiting Professor of Medieval History, University of Kassel, West Germany, 1979-80. Address: c/o Centro Intercultural de Documentacion, Apartado 479, Cuernavaca, Mexico.

PUBLICATIONS

Social Criticism

Metamorfosi del clero. Vicenza, Italy, La Locusta, 1968.

Celebration of Awareness: A Call for Institutional Awareness. New York, Doubleday, 1970; London, Calder and Boyars, 1971.

The Church: Change and Development. London, Herder and Herder, 1970.

The Dawn of Epimethean Man and Other Essays. Cuernavaca, Mexico, Centro Intercultural de Documentacion, 1970.

De-Schooling Society. New York, Harper, 1971; London, Calder and Boyars, 1972.

Ensayos sobre la transcendencia. Cuernavaca, Mexico, Centro Intercultural de Documentacion, 1971.

The Breakdown of Schools. Cuernavaca, Mexico, Centro Intercultural de Documentacion, 1971.

Education Without School: How It Can Be Done. Cuernavaca, Mexico, Centro Intercultural de Documentacion, 1971.

Retooling Society III. Cuernavaca, Mexico, Centro Intercultural de Documentacion, 1973.

En América Latina para qué sirve le escuela? Buenos Aires, Búsqueda, 1973.

After De-Schooling, What?, with others. New York, Harper, 1973 .

Tools for Conviviality. New York, Harper, and London, Calder and Boyars, 1973.

Energy and Equity. New York, Harper, and London, Calder and Boyars, 1974.

Medical Nemesis: The Expropriation of Health. London, Calder and Boyars, 1975.

The Right to Useful Unemployment and Its Professional Enemies. London, Boyars, 1978.

Toward a History of Needs. New York, Pantheon, 1978.

Shadow-Work. London, Boyars, 1981.

Other

Editor, *Spiritual Care of Puerto Rican Migrants.* Cuernavaca, Mexico, Centro Intercultural de Documentacion, 1970.

*

Critical Studies: *Ivan Illich and His Antics*, by Peter Lund, Denby Dale, England, SLD, 1978.

* * *

Ivan Illich, from a wealthy middle-European background and broadly sophisticated higher education, was for some years an American Catholic priest (early a Monsignor, later resigned). Paradoxically, he achieved note as a pungent institutional critic and radical reformer who was yet theologically conservative and pious. As a New York parish priest, Vice-Rector of the Catholic University in Puerto Rico, scholar-critic of Latin-American religion, founder and director of a famous research and educational institute (Center of Intercultural Documentation of Cuernavaca, Mexico), and learned polemicist, he became a personally and intellectually influential gadfly within the Catholic establishment.

But from the late-1960s on, Illich's greatest concern and influence was with sweeping polemical-theoretical critiques of dominant secular institutions: schooling, medical care, transportation, development of impoverished societies, professionalism, work, and the underlying technocratic-consumer ideologies. The early essays on recognizing contemporary social-moral dilemmas (*Celebration of Awareness*) were vigorously extended in radical dialectical polemics. Probably the best known, and justifiably so, was the broad attack on educational institutionalization in *De-Schooling Society* and related essays. The argument, a sardonic extension of such libertarian American education critics as Paul Goodman, emphatically proposes the longterm disestablishment of schooling. At issue are not only the anti-intellectual, custodial, inegalitarian, bureaucratic, and absurdly expensive (especially for less developed areas) schooling systems, but the ideological pieties towards them. Such institutionaliza-

tion enforces limited access, arbitrary certification, class domination and submission, and massive meritocratic exploitation. The "hidden curriculum" of much contemporary schooling comes out as pervasive technocratic-consumer indoctrination and invidious control. Prolonged subservience to schooling operates as the religiosity of our time, and heretic Illich insists that "schools have alienated man from his learning." Truly free learning must have no state or other compulsion, no "discrimination on the basis of prior attendance," no institutional (only individual) control of public funding for education, and no direct correlation with certification, employment, marketing, status, or power.

In *De-Schooling Society*, and elsewhere (such as *Tools for Conviviality*, which might be translated as: means for authentically free and equal community), Illich argues that all must have entirely self-determining, easy access to the "tools" of learning (all equipment, records, information, skills, resource persons). This libertarian utopia is not visualized in much detail, nor are the likely dilemmas in attempting it, such as the replacement of schooling by more efficiently vicious institutions. But the radical, rather than reformist, critique stimulates.

Illich develops a number of parallel issues in other areas. For example, in the free-wheeling little book *Energy and Equity*, he argues, on the premise that "high quanta of energy degrade social relations just as inevitably as they destroy the physical milieu," for the moral necessity of a low-energy and low-capital (and therefore unmonopolistic) dominant transportation mode. By a striking dialectical reach, the "tool" most compatible with egalitarian and participatory democracy would be the bicycle with its distance-speed ordering of twelve miles an hour. Any other transportation pattern in contemporary conditions will tend to be elitist, exploitative, disproportionate, destructive of natural and social relations—dehumanizing.

Medical Nemesis and related essays elaborate characteristic Illich paradoxes about current health-care ideologies, such as "the medical establishment has become a major threat to health." This nemesis comes not only from rising medically induced illness, dehumanizing mechanistic specialism, and excessive medical intervention; it also comes from gross misallocation of health resources for the few, exploitation by the medical-technocratic priesthood, and obfuscating evasion of many of our real malaises caused by a wrong social-industrial order. Individual autonomy and social justice require drastically deprofessionalizing and detechnocratizing health care in order to equalize and humanize it. Medical intervention in life should be minimized. Throughout the arguments appears an ancient ethical insistence on the recognition of human limitations, the underlying requirement for a simpler, more balanced, more decent, institutional ordering. The restoration of a "healthy attitude toward sickness," pain, and death, would require a drastic moral as well as institutional change.

"Useful Employment and Its Professional Enemies" (in *Toward a History of Needs*) extends the issue to a yet broader deprofessionalization—not only a reduction of control by specialist hierarchies but generally reducing the division of labor. Professionalism is analyzed as enforcing commodity/market standardization of needs which "paralyzes the autonomous creation of use-values." Less subservience to technocratic affluence means more richly humane life. The worldwide "frenzied pursuit of impoverishing wealth" expands controlling hierarchies which destroy freedom, equality, and community.

The later *Shadow-Work* provides a preliminary (and not very cogently developed) analysis of the loss of vernacular, subsistence, leisure, and other autonomous activities. Most such values suffer increasing oppression by the dominance of the mass technocratic institutions and our religiosity about them.

Illich may be understood as essentially a radical religious philosopher about social institutions. The curiously reactionary elements in his sensibility—an aristocratic eccentricity, traditional Christianity, a conservative-romantic belief in neolithic man, a sweeping rage against late-modernity—give unusual resonance to his essentially libertarian critiques. He may be one of the most provocative, though often frustratingly abstract, radical critics of our dehumanizing order and its ideology.

—Kingsley Widmer

INGARDEN, Roman (Witold). Polish philosopher. Born in Cracow, 5 February 1893. Studied at the University of Göttingen and at the University of Freiburg, under Edmund Husserl, Ph.D. 1918. Taught mathematics at secondary schools in Lublin, Warsaw and Toruń; Lecturer, 1925-32, and Professor of Philosophy, 1933-41, University of Lvov; Professor of Philosophy, University of Cracow, 1945-50, 1958-63. Recipient: Herder Prize, University of Vienna, 1968. *Died 14 June 1970.*

PUBLICATIONS

Philosophy

Über die Stellung der Erkenntnistheorie im System der Philosophie. Halle, Germany, Niemeyer, 1925.
Das literarische Kunstwerk: Eine Untersuchung aus dem Grenzgebiet der Ontologie, Logik und Literaturwissenschaft. Halle, Germany, Niemeyer, 1931; enlarged edition, 1960; as *The Literary Work of Art: An Investigation on the Borderlines of Ontology, Logic, and Theory of Literature, with an Appendix on the Functions of Language in the Theater,* Evanston, Illinois, Northwestern University Press, 1973.
O poznawaniu dzieła literackiego. Lvov, Poland, Ossolineum, 1937; enlarged version as *Vom Erkennen des literarischen Kunstwerk,* Tübingen, Niemeyer, 1968; as *The Concept of the Literary Work of Art,* Evanston, Illinois, Northwestern University Press, 1973.
O budowie obrazu: Szkic z teorii sztuki [The Structure of Painting: A Sketch from the Theory of Art]. Cracow, Polish Academy of Science, 1946.
Spór o istnienie świata [The Controversy Over the Existence of the World]. Cracow, Polish Academy of Sciences, 2 vols., 1947, 1948; selections from vol. 1 as *Time and Modes of Being,* Springfield, Illinois, Charles C. Thomas, 1964.
Szkice z filozofii literatury [Essays on the Philosophy of Literature]. Lodz, Spółdzielnia Wydawnicza "Polonista," 1947.
Studia z estetyki [Studies in Aesthetics]. Warsaw, Polish Scientific Publishers, 3 vols., 1957-70.
Untersuchungen zur Ontologie der Kunst: Musikwerk, Bild, Architektur, Film. Tübingen, Niemeyer, 1962.
Z badań nad filozofia współczesna [Investigations in Contemporary Philosophy]. Warsaw, Scientific Publishers, 1963; selection as *On the Motives Which Led Husserl to Transcendental Idealism,* The Hague, Nijhoff, 1975.
Der Streit um die Existenz der Welt. Tübingen, Niemeyer, 3 vols., 1964-65 (vols. 1 and 2 are translations of *Spór o istnienie świata;* vol. 3 appears in German only).
Przeżycie—dzieło—wartość [Experience—Work of Art—Value]. Cracow, Wdawnictwo Literackie, 1966; as *Erlebnis, Kunstwerk und Wert,* Tübingen, Niemeyer, 1969.
Über die Verantwortung: Ihre ontische Fundamente. Stuttgart, Reclam, 1970.
U podstaw teorii poznania, Cześć pierwsza [The Basis of Cognitive Theory, Part I]. Warsaw, Polish Scientific Publishers, 1971.
Ksiażeczka o człowieku [A Little Book About Man]. Cracow, Wdawnictwo Literackie, 1972.
Z teorii jezyka filozoficznych podstaw logiki [From the Theory of Language and the Philosophical Foundations of Logic].

Warsaw, Polish Scientific Publishers, 1972.
Gegenstand und Aufgaben der Literaturwissenschaft (1937-1964), edited by Rolf Fieguth. Tübingen, Niemeyer, 1976.

*

Critical Studies: *Szkice filozoficzne. Romanowi Ingardenowi w darze* [Philosophical Studies in Honor of Roman Ingarden], Warsaw, Polish Scientific Publishers, 1962 (contains a bibliography); *The Poetics of Roman Ingarden* by Eugene H. Falk, Chapel Hill, University of North Carolina Press, 1981; "Roman Ingarden" by René Wellek, in *Four Critics: Croce, Valéry, Lukács, Ingarden,* Seattle, University of Washington Press, 1981.

*   *   *

Throughout his philosophic work Roman Ingarden strove to direct himself fully to the objects of his inquiries—including objects that correspond to acts of thought, imagination, and feeling—and to discover the approach that would allow him to grasp the objects in all the particulars of their natures. Underlying Ingarden's inquiries in the diverse fields of ontology, epistemology, aesthetics, and philosophy of values (axiology) is an abiding interest in the nature of the human person. It is in part due to this interest that he vigorously opposed various modern movements such as positivism in philosophy, "psychologism" and "historicism" in the study of literature and art, and relativism and subjectivism in questions pertaining to values. Those who hold such positions, he thought, attain a complacent illusion of possessing the truth because their theories—their scepticism and reductionist principles—gradually impose a blindness upon them which is then itself held to be a virtue. As a result, the true objects of thought, imagination, and feeling (especially values) are distorted or disappear from sight, and the human world is diminished by their loss.

Ingarden acquired his philosophic orientation from the phenomenology of Edmund Husserl, whose call for philosophy to return "to the things themselves" was heard eagerly by a talented group of students. However, a number of these students, among them Ingarden, eventually opposed what they considered to be Husserl's turn to "transcendental idealism." We can therefore say that Ingarden belongs to a philosophic tradition that has been called "phenomenological realism," and which also includes Max Scheler, A. Reinach, Dietrich von Hildebrand, and Hedwig Conrad-Martius.

Ingarden's early works argue that epistemology does not form a necessary foundation for philosophy, a position that contradicts common philosophic opinion since the time of Kant. In his view philosophy needed to be shifted away from the critique of our capacity for knowing and back to a careful study of the objects of thought themselves.

Ingarden then sought to clarify the nature of some of the most important objects of philosophic knowledge. Husserl had described his phenomenology as an "inquiry into essences," but Ingarden concluded that several concepts were being combined equivocally when Husserl spoke of "essence" and that they needed to be separated. In his own investigations he developed clear distinctions among the concepts of the essence of an individual object, general and particular ideas, and pure or essential qualities; he was then able to determine the necessary relations among these concepts. Ingarden's studies begun in "Essential Questions" and later expanded in *The Controversy over the Existence of the World* provide penetrating analyses of these concepts and of the concepts of form, matter, objects, relations, causality, time, and modes of existence, among many others. His writings exhibit the rare combination of careful and rigorous expression with rich, intuitive insight.

The central theme of Ingarden's ontological investigations is the recurrent philosophical controversy concerning the relation between objects encountered in the world and human consciousness. According to Ingarden, Husserl in his turn to transcendental idealism believed that the real world, given to us in experience, is dependent for its existence on the being and constitutive activities of pure consciousness. Now for Ingarden this position was particularly troublesome because it meant that the human person, as well as its center of existence, the personal "I," would be nothing other than an object that is self-constituted in a determinate course of pure experiences. If the human person, along with all other objects experienced in the world, is ultimately dependent for its existence on pure consciousness, then one would have to deny the autonomous existence of the human soul as a real object existing in time with determinant properties that are expressed so to speak, in acts of consciousness. There are strong indications that in Ingarden's view such a denial would contradict certain fundamental human experiences in the world.

The concept of "existential moments" is the key to Ingarden's ontological inquiries. (The word "existential" in Ingarden's writings has nothing in common with the sense of that term in Heidegger and the French existentialists.) These are the moments (elements) that together determine the mode of existence of an object, for instance whether it is real, ideal, or fictive ("purely intentional" in Ingarden's terms). Since each of the existential moments identified by Ingarden necessarily excludes coexistence with some of the others, he was able to state a limited number of possible solutions to the controversy concerning the modes of existence of the real world and of consciousness, and to provide a clear description of the various possible modes of existence.

Ingarden began his studies in aesthetics as part of his critique of transcendental idealism. He hoped to bring to light the essential differences between real objects encountered in the world and objects such as the characters in a novel that come into existence only through the acts of consciousness that create them. His book *The Literary Work of Art* goes far beyond this original purpose and provides a foundation for literary aesthetics because it presents a clear concept of the essential nature of literary works of art. Ingarden shows that every literary work of art is a multi-layered, schematic formation which has a sequential extension. The four layers are: sound formations: meaning-units; the modes of appearance or "aspects" in which the characters and objects are presented; and the presented objects such as characters and events that are determined by the other three layers. The presented objects constitute a kind of "world" existing on the foundations of the meaning-units; this world cannot be completely identified with the actual worlds of the author and reader. When the reader becomes absorbed in the contemplation of the configurations of qualities that exist on the basis of the presented world, he undergoes an aesthetic experience in which he may gain a deeper awareness and knowledge of the qualitative nature of his own life. This experience may sometimes culminate in the revelation of a "metaphysical quality" such as the tragic, the holy, or the sublime, which is usually founded in the interpersonal situations presented by the work. Experiencing these qualities provides an insight into human life which fulfills a deeply rooted human desire to grasp the sense of life. Such qualities provide a certain type of knowledge that can be obtained in full vividness for the most part only through works of art.

At the heart of Ingarden's writings on the mode of existence of works of art is the insight that the cultural world, although necessarily built upon real objects (the marble of a statue, the sound or printed page of a poem), is nevertheless essentially different from its material foundation because it is dependent for its existence also upon the human acts that endow that world with its meaning and significance. However, the cultural world is not an arbitrary creation with a merely conventional meaning. Acts of human "creation" are intended to actualize values, and the process of making a work of art, or for that matter of drafting a constitution for a republic, is guided by the attempt to provide a secure foundation for actualized values. Values are "objective" when they possess a sufficient foundation in the objects that carry them. Cultural values such as aesthetic or ethical values are not derived from personal dispositions or social conventions, although such dispositions and conventions play a role in our attainment of knowledge of values.

The recognition of the objectivity of cultural values is one necessary condition for the concept of responsibility, as Ingarden shows in *Über die Verantwortung*. The other condition is the identity of the human person throughout the various phases of life. Conscious individuals in acts of recollection, retention, and anticipation attain a certain kind of projection above the ceaseless flow of time and possess the capability of achieving a degree of unification through time that is not possible for any other kind of object. This projection above time is achieved above all in the cultural world that man builds for himself and in which he comes to know himself.

We perceive the deepest significance of Ingarden's writings in the confluence of the concepts of the objectivity of values, the mode of existence of the cultural world, and the identity of the human person in time. Human beings exist in time, subsisting in the material world but called upon by their essences to transcend it. In the cultural world they learn to recognize their responsibility to actualize positive values and to atone for negative values. Only in the light of this cultural world and the values actualized in it can the human being fulfill the faculties belonging to the core of human existence and attain the freedom that is yearned for as part of the human essence. Only through the continual striving for the responsible production of goodness, beauty, and truth can the human person fully exist.

—Michael C. Jordan

INGE, William Ralph. British theologian. Born in Crayke, Yorkshire, 6 June 1860. Educated at Eton College and at King's College, Cambridge (Bell Scholar and Porson Prizeman, 1880; Porson Scholar, 1881; Craven Scholar and Browne Medalist, 1882; Senior Chancellor's Medalist, 1883; Hare Prizeman, 1885). Married Mary Catharine Spooner in 1904; 3 children. Assistant Master, Eton College, 1884-88; Fellow and Tutor, Hertford College, Oxford, 1888-1904; Vicar, All Saints, Knightsbridge, London, 1905-07; Lady Margaret Professor of Divinity, and Fellow of Jesus College, Cambridge University, 1907-11; Dean of St. Paul's Cathedral, London, 1911-34. Bampton Lecturer, Oxford University, 1899; Paddock Lecturer, General Seminary, New York, 1906; Gifford Lecturer, University of St. Andrews, Scotland, 1917-18; Romanes Lecturer, Oxford University, 1922; Rede Lecturer, Cambridge University, 1922; Lyman Beecher Lecturer, Yale University, New Haven, Connecticut, 1925; Hulsean Lecturer, Cambridge University, 1926; Herbert Spencer Lecturer, Oxford University, 1934. Trustee, National Portrait Gallery, London; President, Classical Association, 1933. Honorary doctorate: University of Aberdeen, 1905; University of Durham, 1920; University of Edinburgh, 1923; University of Sheffield, 1924; Oxford University, 1928; University of St. Andrews, Scotland, 1930, Fellow, British Academy. Honorary Fellow, Jesus College and King's College, Cambridge; Hertford College, Oxford. Commander, 1918, and Knight Commander, 1930, of the Royal Victorian Order. *Died 26 February 1950.*

PUBLICATIONS

Religion and Society

Society in Rome Under the Caesars. London, Murray, and New York, Scribner, 1888.
Christian Mysticism (lectures). London, Methuen, and New York, Scribner, 1899.

Faith and Knowledge. Edinburgh, Clark, 1904.

Studies of English Mystics (lectures). London, Murray, and New York, Dutton, 1906.

Truth and Falsehood in Religion (lectures). London, Murray, and New York, Dutton, 1906.

Personal Idealism and Mysticism (lectures). London and New York, Longman, 1907.

All Saints' Sermons, 1905-1907. London, Macmillan, 1907.

Faith and Its Psychology. London, Duckworth, 1909; New York, Scribner, 1910.

Speculum Animae. London and New York, Longman, 1911.

The Church and the Age. London and New York, Longman, 1912.

Types of Christian Saintliness. London and New York, Longman, 1915.

The Philosophy of Plotinus (lectures). London and New York, Longman, 2 vols., 1918.

Outspoken Essays: First Series. London, Putnam, 1919.

Outspoken Essays: Second Series. London and New York, Longman, 1922.

Personal Life and the Life of Devotion. London and New York, Longman, 1924.

The Platonic Tradition in English Religious Thought (lectures). London and New York, Longman, 1926.

Lay Thoughts of a Dean. London and New York, Putnam, 1926.

England. London, Benn, and New York, Scribner, 1926.

The Church in the World: Collected Essays. London and New York, Longman, 1927.

Protestantism. London, Benn, 1927; New York, Doubleday, 1928.

Assessments and Anticipations. London, Cassell, 1929; as *Labels and Libels,* New York, Harper, 1929.

Christian Ethics and Modern Problems. London, Hodder and Stoughton, 1930.

More Lay Thoughts of a Dean. London and New York, Putnam, 1931.

Things Old and New (sermons). London and New York, Longman, 1933.

God and the Astronomers (lectures). London and New York, Longman, 1933.

Vale. London and New York, Longman, 1934.

The Gate of Life (sermons). London and New York, Longman, 1935.

The Bible and How to Read It. London and New York, Longman, 1935.

A Rustic Moralist. London and New York, Putnam, 1937.

Our Present Discontents. London and New York, Putnam, 1938.

A Pacifist in Trouble. London and New York, Putnam, 1939.

The Fall of the Idol. London and New York, Putnam, 1940.

Talks in a Free Country. London, Putnam, 1942.

Mysticism in Religion. London, Hutchinson, 1947.

The End of an Age and Other Essays. London, Putnam, 1948.

Diary of a Dean: St. Paul's, 1911-1934. London and New York, Hutchinson, 1949.

Goodness and Truth (sermons), edited by A.F. Judd. London, Mowbray, 1958; as *The Things That Remain,* New York, Mowbray, 1958.

The Awakening of the Soul: Lectures on Mysticism, edited by A.F. Judd. London, Mowbray, 1959.

Other

Editor, *Life and Love: Selections from the German Mystics of the Middle Ages.* London, Library of Devotion, 1904.

Editor, *Freedom, Love, and Truth: An Anthology of the Christian Life.* London and New York, Longman, 1936.

*

Critical Study: *Dean Inge* by Adam Fox, London, Murray, 1960.

* * *

William Ralph Inge, an erudite exponent of Christian Platonism, was also a well-known commentator on world events for three decades. His *Christian Mysticism* (The Bampton Lectures, 1899) set forth the fundamental standpoint and essential religious outlook that he elaborated over half a century. In it he pleaded that his preoccupation with mystical writers arose out of his intense intellectual and spiritual needs in seeking a philosophy *and* rule of life that could satisfy both his mind and conscience. Rejecting both the supernaturalism of Roman Catholic mysticism and psychic research as religion—it was for him a legitimate science—Inge invoked the Johannine Logos-doctrine to find a pathway between pantheism, acosmism, subjective idealism and deism.

Inge defined mysticism as the attempt to realize, in thought and feeling, the immanence of the temporal in the eternal, and of the eternal in the temporal. He traced mysticism to the Greek mysteries through later Neoplatonism which passed almost entirely into Christianity. Indeed religion has its origin in mysticism, but the symbols engendered by thought encountering profound experience soon petrify or evaporate and, repudiating their source, lose their content. However, if it is to nourish spiritual aspirations and remain relevant to the world, religion must be freshly infused with the mystical impulse.

Mysticism rests on four presuppositions: the soul can perceive, man cannot know God unless he partakes of the divine nature, without holiness no man may see God, and the true hierophant of the mysteries is supremely disinterested love. He who tries to be holy in order to be happy or owing to concern with his own holiness, will realize neither happiness nor holiness, for eternal happiness is mental attunement with God. Thus the mystic seeks to transform himself gradually and by degrees into the likeness of God in whose image he was created. This *scala perfectionis* has three phases—purgative, illuminative, and unitive, the state of perfect contemplation being the goal. The rule of life begins with negative ethnics which prescribe order and limit, proceeds to exemplify positive ethics through concentration of all the faculties (will, intellect, feeling) upon Deity, and passes to a pure contemplation which ever more closely approaches God face to face. This goal, like a mathematical limit, can only be approximated (consummation would also be annihilation), but the process of gaining nearness gives religion its vitality and significance.

The individual must seek to unify the faculties of reason and intuition—for when the eye is single, the whole body is full of light. When authority for intuition lies wholly beyond reason, the essential unity in the ideas of God, the world and mankind is destroyed. Revelation cannot fully transcend reason, for then religion would be merely a matter of feeling.

Mysticism is not philosophy or religion, but sustains both. In religion it is the enemy of dry formalism and cold rationality; in philosophy it takes the field against materialism and scepticism. The test of truth is straightforward: whatever view of reality deepens our sense of the tremendous issues of life in the world wherein we move, is for us nearer the truth than any view which diminishes that sense. Absolute reality is thought and will of God expressed through the forms of space and time, and everything reflects Deity in some degree. The human soul is the clearest mirror of divinity when it is not tainted.

Here mysticism divides into two branches, one looking to nature and humanity for intimations of Deity, the other plunging into the depths of innermost consciousness in search of direct communion with God. Both are necessary, for they are the "systole and diastole of the spiritual life." Man is the microcosm in two ways: the soul partakes of the divine (Plotinus and Proclus), and each individual life recapitulates the spiritual history of humanity (Eckhart and the Cambridge Platonists). Medieval mysticism was predominantly introspective, but mystics since the Renaissance have stressed the religious observation of nature, the search for harmony underlying seeming discord. In both movements, the fact that love leads human beings to the heart of life is proof that man is rightly bound up in the world even while looking beyond it.

In *Studies of English Mystics*, Inge reiterated these ideas and added detailed discussions of the *Ancren Riwle*, Julian of Norwich, Hilton, William Law, Wordsworth and Browning. *Faith and Its Psychology* sought to restore dignity to faith through a critical analysis of different conceptions of faith (as feeling, as authority, as act of will, as practicality and as aesthetic sensibility). Inge held that faith seeks to unify experience so that authority becomes internal and involves the whole being. What is faith in the human dimension is grace in the divine; faith for the mind is revelation, and for the heart redemption. Faith for the will is moral freedom and moral energy, and reason gives harmony to all expressions of faith. Two series of *Outspoken Essays* contained topical lectures on religion, classical thought and the Victorian age. Inge called himself a Christian Platonist and claimed that this tradition constitutes a "third school" as legitimate and productive as Catholicism and Protestantism. In *Lay Thoughts of a Dean*, a collection of sermons and articles, he showed the limits of psychology as a tool for supporters of religion. *Protestantism* praised the Quakers for coming closest to achieving the intentions of Jesus, even though Inge could not agree with them on many issues. He reiterated this view in *The Church in the World*, a collection of essays which called for serious dialogue between religion and science.

His topical *Labels and Libels*, taking its title from the view that every label constitutes some degree of libel against its object, showed concern about the decline of the English public school, but looked to the state schools to revitalize a society becoming degenerate through snobbery and classicism. *The Philosophy of Plotinus* (The Gifford Lectures, 1917-18) offered an exposition of Plotinus for the modern age. Plotinian evolution occurs against a timeless background, a perspective that can welcome science without secularizing religion, if one recognizes that *amor intellectualis dei* alone leads up the pathway of reality. On this path, one can see the importance of reincarnation when the soul and its liabilities (and not personalities) are considered. Suffering is a symptom, not the disease. It shows the moral ugliness of a civilization immersed in hedonism and false conceptions of happiness which impel individuals to sentimentalism, "ultimately the most cruel of all moods." For Dean Inge, Christianity, western civilization and Platonism rise or fall together.

Throughout his life, Dean Inge commented on world affairs. He anticipated increased Asian competition with industrialised Europe, and he warned that over-mechanization of life could lead to human retrogression. In 1929 he predicted that the United States would become unassailable, while Canada would remain independent even though its society would become thoroughly Americanized. He saw Russia becoming a power intent upon Eastern Europe; he hoped for a United States of Europe, since Great Britain would inevitably cease to be a great power, though it too would remain independent.

In later life, Dean Inge wrote on a broad range of subjects—the reconciliation of science and religion without facile claims of agreement (*God and the Astronomers*), the problem of Christian pacifism on the brink of World War II, the impending war between Germany and Russia despite pretensions to the contrary, and the saintliness of the atheist and scientist Madame Curie (*A Pacifist in Trouble*), dialogues on war and society, in which he called himself "a Victorian fossil" and "a rustic moralist" (*Talks in a Free Country*). As his final books show, Inge was steadfast in his conviction that the individual endures through his awareness of the inner light which is true spiritual authority. In *Mysticism in Religion* he pointed to the wisdom of the East as a source of sustenance, stating that Christians have almost as much to learn from Hindus and Buddhists as the reverse. *The End of an Age* discerned underlying reasons for optimism despite the probability that the second half of the twentieth century would be difficult and dangerous. Dean Inge's concern to learn and to grow, awakening to ever greater degrees of the spiritual life and the needs of humanity, pervades all his work. "The

Neoplatonic mystic must be prepared to outgrow many early enthusiasms, and to break every mould in which his thought threatens to crystallize. The danger of arrested development is always present. Life is a *schola animarum*; and we must be learners to the end." (*The Philosophy of Plotinus*.)

—R.N. Iyer

ISER, Wolfgang. German aesthetician and critic. Born in Marienberg, 22 July 1926. Studied at the University of Leipzig, 1946; University of Tübingen, 1946-47; and the University of Heidelberg, Ph.D. 1950. Married Lore Reichert in 1952. Instructor in English, University of Heidelberg, 1951-52; Assistant Lecturer in German, University of Glasgow, 1952-55; Assistant Professor, 1955-57, and Associate Professor, 1957-60, University of Heidelberg; Professor of English and Comparative Literature, University of Würzburg, 1960-63; Professor of English and Comparative Literature, University of Cologne, 1963-67. Since 1967, Professor of English and Comparative Literature, University of Constance. Address: University of Constance, Constance, Germany.

PUBLICATIONS

Aesthetics and Literature

Die Weltanschauung Henry Fieldings. Tübingen, Niemeyer, 1952.
Walter Pater: Die Autonomie der Ästhetischen. Tübingen, Niemeyer, 1960.
Der Appellstruktur der Texte: Unbestimmtheit als Wirkungsbedingung literarischer Prosa. Constance, University of Constance, 1970; as "Indeterminacy and the Reader's Response in Prose Fiction," in *Aspects of Narrative*, edited by J. Hillis Miller, New York, Columbia University Press, 1971.
Spensers Arkadien: Fiktion und Geschichte in der englischen Renaissance. Krefeld, West Germany, Scherpe, 1970.
Der implizite Leser: Kommunikationsinformen des Romans von Bunyan bis Beckett. Munich, Fink, 1972; as *The Implied Reader: Patterns of Communication in Prose Fiction from Bunyan to Beckett*, Baltimore, Johns Hopkins University Press, 1974.
Der Akt des Lesens: Theorie ästhetischer Wirkung. Munich, Fink, 1976; as *The Act of Reading: A Theory of Aesthetic Response*, Baltimore, Johns Hopkins University Press, 1978.

Other

Editor, *Immanente Ästhetik, ästhetische Reflexion: Lyrik als Paradigma der Moderne*. Munich, Fink, 1966.
Editor, *Dargestellte Geschichte in der europäischen Literatur des 19. Jahrhunderts*. Frankfurt, Klostermann, 1970.

*   *   *

Wolfgang Iser is an historian of English literature who has turned his attention to developing a theory of aesthetic response or effect. His theory is based upon the insight that the meaning of a literary work comes into existence only during an act of reading, so that literary theory must investigate the text, the reader, and their interrelation.

A literary text must be considered primarily as a means of communication, according to Iser. Communication requires the transmission of a message from the author to the reader using a code which is conditioned by the author's and reader's worldviews. In non-literary (i.e., non-artistic) communication, the code has a referential function, pointing to a state of affairs that exists within the author's world. Communication is artistic (literary) when the text elicits from the reader an imaginative response that brings into existence something that cannot be found in the author's historical world. Such a text is what we usually call "fiction."

The material from which the text is constructed is called the "repertoire" by Iser. The author selects from the prevailing worldview of his time certain social and historical norms (e.g., the Calvinist doctrine of predestined salvation) and transforms them by removing them from their familiar, stable positions within the worldview. He may also select references and allusions to elements and traditions of past literature, which may be used to project solutions to certain problems as a background for his own work. The elements of the repertoire are always presented from a certain perspective and only through certain points of view or aspects, and so must be regarded as textual "schemata." There are in general four perspectives through which the pattern of the repertoire emerges: the perspectives of the narrator, the characters, the plot, and the role textually predetermined for the reader. The mutual interactions of these diverse perspectives establish discontinuity, contradictions, and indeterminateness between textual schemata. Whenever the connection between textual schemata is not explicitly determined by the text, a "blank" or "gap" is said to exist.

These blanks stimulate the imagination of the reader, whose appropriate responses are necessary to fulfill the intentions of the text. The reader has his own worldview, and brings his pre-suppositions and expectations to the text. But these presuppositions and expectations are frustrated because the blanks and gaps prevent him from combining the schemata into a representation of a world that is identical with his own. The reader must therefore suspend his habitual frame of reference and use imagination to constitute a new object on the basis of the textual directives. He thus achieves a fresh insight into his own habitual worldview which the text has persuaded him to suspend temporarily, and through his active participation is made to experience for himself the meaning of the text which he has helped to bring into existence.

Such meanings are primarily ways of overcoming some of the deficiencies of the worldview from which the repertoire was drawn. For instance, in eighteenth-century England the empiricism of John Locke was predominant. This view taught that all knowledge was derived from experience, so that moral standards derived from reason or tradition were questionable. Locke's empiricism thereby implicitly raised new problems for discovering the foundations for proper human conduct and relations. In response to this problem, eighteenth-century English novels were intensely preoccupied with questions of morality; through the juxtaposition of various norms of human behavior presented from diverse perspectives, the reader is encouraged to perceive the deficiencies of each norm by itself and to construct a new image of human nature that is better able to capture the complexity of human experience. Iser, then, views literature as a counterbalance to other cultural systems within any historical period.

Iser acknowledges his indebtedness to the literary theory of Roman Ingarden, who first explored the ways in which a reader "concretizes" an aesthetic object on the basis of a schematically determinate text. However, Iser and Ingarden belong to radically different traditions. Iser's fundamental orientation is derived from the philosophical hermeneutics of Hans-Georg Gadamer, who himself owes much to Martin Heidegger. Iser sees all meaning and truth as inseparable from history and time. Consequently the meaning of a literary text is seen as a historical response to a prevailing worldview; the twentieth-century reader can observe in an eighteenth-century novel only an outdated response to a worldview that he does not share. Iser's theory shows how literature participates in the transformations of worldviews in time, but one must decide for oneself whether the essential function of literature is to be found in the history of mankind's changing views of the world.

—Michael C. Jordan

JACOB, François.   French biologist.   Born in Nancy, 17 June 1920. Educated at the Lycée Carnot, Paris; studied at the Faculty of Medicine, Paris, M.D. 1947, and the Faculty of Sciences, Paris, D.Sc. 1954. Served with the Free French Forces, 1940-45: Compagnon de la Libération. Married Lysiane Bloch in 1947; 4 children. Assistant, 1950-56, Head of Laboratory, 1956-60, since 1960 Head of the Department of Cellular Genetics, and since 1982 President, Institut Pasteur, Paris; also since 1965 Professor of Cellular Genetics, Collège de France, Paris. Recipient: Charles Léopold Mayer Prize, 1962; Nobel Prize in Physiology and Medicine, with A. Lwoff and Jacques Monod, 1965; Grand Croix, Légion d'Honneur. Honorary doctorate: University of Chicago, 1965. Member, Académie des Sciences; Royal Academy of Medicine, Belgium; U.S. National Academy of Sciences; New York Academy of Sciences; American Academy of Arts and Sciences; American Philosophical Society; and the Royal Society, London. Grand Officier de l'Ordre National du Mérite. Address: Institut Pasteur, 28 rue du Docteur-Roux, 75006 Paris, France.

PUBLICATIONS

Biology

Les Bactéries lysogènes et la notion de provirus.   Paris, Masson, 1954.
La Sexualité des bactéries, with Élie L. Wollman.   Paris, Masson, 1959; as Sexuality and the Genetics of Bacteria, New York, Academic Press, 1961.
Viruses and Genes, with Élie Wollman.   San Francisco, Freeman, 1961.
La Logique du vivant: Une Histoire de l'hérédité.   Paris, Gallimard, 1970; as The Logic of Life: A History of Heredity, New York, Pantheon, 1974, and as The Logic of Living Systems, London, Allen Lane, 1974.
Le Jeu des Possibles.   Paris, Fayard, 1981; as The Possible and the Actual, New York, Pantheon, 1982.

*   *   *

François Jacob was an essential member of a core of scientists who initiated and contributed to the revolution in biology during the 1950's and 1960's. These molecular biologists (as they came to be called) added new insights to understanding the biochemistry of life and changed forever mankind's way of studying life forms.

Jacob's approach to experimentation was rooted in the science of genetics, and his earliest major contributions were made in this area. With Élie Wollman he discovered polarity of bacterial mating (conjugation). Bacterial strains which demonstrated a higher rate of recombination were found to be either donor (male) or recipient (female) of genetic information. This information was followed by identifying certain genetic markers. For example, bacteria requiring various nutrients were isolated, and they could easily be identified through nutritional experiments. In this way, characteristics of one strain would be incorporated into a second, different strain of the same bacterial species. Furthermore, Jacob and his colleagues followed the time of transfer of this genetic information from donor to recipient cell. Recombination of donor DNA with recipient DNA occurs, permitting construction of genetic maps of the characteristics examined. Furthermore, this understanding of bacterial conjugation provided a precise experimental tool for examining the expression of a "new" gene or genes placed in a cell. Before cell division restored the original single chromosome per cell in the culture, the cell contained two sets of genes. During this time, questions associated with higher plant and animal cells could be examined in bacteria. For example, dominance of one gene over another in its expression and the mechanisms of recombination of genetic material could be studied in detail for the first time.

After examining genetic maps of different bacterial strains, Jacob concluded that the chromosome of the bacterium used,

Escherichia coli, was circular. Although this idea, based solely on deductions from genetic experiments, was at first opposed, it was confirmed by electron microscope observation some years later.

Very early in his career, Jacob showed an interest in the control of metabolic processes. Using the techniques of bacterial conjunction, he and his colleagues examined the phenomenon of the prophage, a hidden form of bacterial virus within a host bacterium, which is then called a lysogenic bacterium. When a lysogenic male (donor) bacterium was crossed with a non-lysogenic female (recipient) bacterium, a large proportion of the female (recipient) bacteria burst open (lysed) and produced viruses (bacteriophages). However, no viruses were produced when the reciprocal type of conjugation experiment was performed. Therefore the control factor which prevented the lysis of the bacterium and the production of bacteriophages was *not* transferred along with the genes for determining the bacteriophage structure and synthesis.

This control factor was postulated as a result of a series of brilliant experiments which examine another system: the synthesis of an enzyme in the bacterium *E. coli*. The enzyme studied was β-galactosidase. Mutants were isolated and characterized. Inducible strains synthesized the enzyme only when an appropriate chemical substrate ("inducer") was present. Constitutive strains synthesized the enzyme whether an inducer was present or not. Furthermore, a cluster of genes relating to the synthesis and control of β-galactosidase were mapped close together on the chromosome. Jacob and his colleagues showed that these clusters of genes were expressed together when induced. Such coordinated units of gene expression were called operons. The effect of an inducer on this system was to unblock the repressed operon. What was postulated, then, was that a protein called a repressor protein was deactivated by an inducer or substrate molecule. When the inducer and the repressor protein combined, the repressor protein was no longer able to bind to the operator locus of the operon, and the genetic message could be transcribed. The phenomenon of induction, in this case, could be called depression. The control of other metabolic pathways was due to an activation of the specific repressor protein by substrates. In all cases, a repressor protein was a vital part of the control of enzyme synthesis.

With remarkable insight, Jacob realized that the repressor hypothesis could also explain the control of the expression of bacteriophage genes in host bacterial cells. Such viral repressors were active in lysogenic bacteria, and the expression of virus genes was prevented. The induction of lysis in a lysogenic culture paralleled the destruction or the loss of the repressor proteins. Some of these proteins have since been isolated and studied, thus proving this hypothesis.

Furthermore, Jacob postulated the concept of messenger RNA in the papers which presented and discussed the operon theory. This was undoubtedly a vital stimulus for the discovery of this species of RNA which is central to our understanding of cell molecular processes.

Jacob and his colleagues (most notably Jacques Monod) continued their extraordinary contributions with the concept of *allostery*. Literally meaning "other site," this explains that enzyme activity can be controlled by the binding of a chemical structurally unrelated to the substrate to a site other than the active site for that substrate on the enzyme protein. Any metabolic pathway could be connected with any other pathway in the cell by this process. With this concept, Monod and Jacob show they are generalists, as biological thinkers: allostery explains a wide variety of protein activity control mechanisms including oxygen-hemoglobin binding, hormonal control of enzyme activity and even repressor proteins.

—William H. Coleman

JAKOBSON, Roman. American philologist and critic. Born in Moscow 11 October 1896; emigrated to the United States in 1941: naturalized, 1952. Studied at the Lazarev Institute of Oriental Languages, Moscow, B.A. 1914; University of Moscow, M.A. 1918; and the University of Prague, Ph.D. 1930. Married Krystyna Pomorska in 1962. Research Associate, University of Moscow, 1918-20; Professor, Masaryk University, Brno, Czechoslovakia, 1933-39; Professor, École Libre des Hautes Études, New York, 1942-46; Visiting Professor, 1943-46, and T.G. Masaryk Professor of Czech Studies, 1946-49, Columbia University, New York; S.H. Cross Professor of Slavic Language and Literature, 1949-67, and Professor Emeritus, 1967-82, Harvard University, Cambridge, Massachusetts; Institute Professor, 1957-67, and Professor Emeritus, 1967-82, Massachusetts Institute of Technology, Cambridge. Visiting Professor, Yale University, New Haven, Connecticut, 1967, 1971; Princeton University, New Jersey, 1968; Brown University, Providence, Rhode Island, 1969-70; Brandeis University, Waltham, Massachusetts, 1970; Collège de France, Paris, 1972; University of Louvain, Belgium, 1972; New York University, 1973; Bergen University, Norway, 1976. Founder and Chairman, Cercle Linguistique, Moscow, 1915-20; Co-Founder, and Vice-President, 1927-38, Cercle Linguistique, Prague; Co-Founder, and Vice-President, 1943-49, Linguistic Circle of New York; President, Linguistic Society of America, 1956. Recipient: Gold Medal, Slovak Academy of Science, 1962; American Association for the Advancement of Scavic Studies Award, 1970; American Council of Learned Societies Award, 1970; International Feltrinelli Prize for Philology and Linguistics, 1980. Honorary doctorate: Cambridge University, 1960; University of Chicago, 1961; University of Oslo, 1961; University of Uppsala, Sweden, 1963; University of Michigan, Ann Arbor, 1963; University of Grenoble, 1966; University of Nice, 1966; University of New Mexico, Albuquerque, 1966; University of Rome, 1967; Yale University, 1967; Charles University, Prague, 1968; University of Brno, 1968; Clark University, Worcester, Massachusetts, 1969; Zagreb University, Yugoslavia, 1969; Ohio State University, Columbus, 1970; University of Louvain, 1972; University of Tel Aviv, 1975; Columbia University, 1976; University of Liège, Belgium, 1979; University of Copenhagen, 1979; Ruhr University, 1980; Georgetown University, Washington D.C., 1980; Brandeis University, 1981; Oxford University, 1981. Member, American Academy of Arts and Sciences. Honorary Member, New York Academy of Sciences; Philological Society, London; Royal Anthropological Institute of Great Britain and Ireland; International Committee of Slavists; Cercle Linguistique, Copenhagen; and International Phonetic Association; Foreign Member, Royal Netherlands Academy of Science; Polish Academy of Science; Danish Academy of Science; Serbian Academy of Science; Irish Academy of Science; Italian Academy of Science, Bologna; British Academy of Science; Finnish Academy of Science; and the Bohemian Royal Society; Honorary Foreign Member, Royal Society of Letters, Lund, Sweden; Finno-Ugric Society. Chevalier, Légion d'Honneur. *Died* (in Boston) *18 July 1982*.

PUBLICATIONS

Language and Literature

O cesskom stixe preimuscestvenno v sopostavlennii s russkim [About Czech Poetry, Mainly in Comparison with Russian Poetry]. Berlin, Society for the Study of Poetical Language, 1923.
Základy ceského verse [Foundations of Czech Versification]. Prague, Odeon, 1926.
Spor duse s telem: O nebezpecném casu smrti [Dispute Between Body and Soul: The Dangerous Time of Dying]. Prague, L. Kuncir, 1927.
Nejstarsí ceské pisne duchovní [The Oldest Czech Ritual Songs]. Prague, L. Kuncir, 1929.

Remarques sur l'évolution phonologique du russe comparée à celle des autres langues slaves. Prague, Association of Czech Mathematicians and Physicists, 1929.

K kharakteristike evraziiskogo jazykogo souza [The Characteristic of Eurasian Linguistic Unity]. Paris, Navarre, 1931.

Kindersprache, Aphasie und allgemeine Lautgesetze. Uppsala, Almqvist och Wiksell, 1941; as *Child Language, Aphasia and Phonological Universals,* The Hague, Mouton, 1968.

Moudrost starých Cechu [The Wisdom of Old Czechs]. New York, Czechoslovak Cultural Circle, 1943.

Preliminaries to Speech Analysis, with others. Cambridge, Massachusetts Institute of Technology Press, 1952.

Slavic Languages. New York, Columbia University Press, 1949; revised edition as *Slavic Languages: A Condensed Survey,* 1955.

Fundamentals of Language, with M. Halle. The Hague, Mouton, 1956.

Paleosiberian Peoples and Languages: A Bibliographical Guide, with others. New Haven, Connecticut, Yale University Press, 1957.

Selected Writings: Phonological Studies. The Hague, Mouton, 1962.

Selected Writings: Slavic Epic Studies. The Hague, Mouton, 1966.

Lingüística, Poética, Cinema. São Paulo, Editora Perspectiva, 1970.

Selected Writings: Word and Language. The Hague, Mouton, 1971.

Studies in Verbal Art. Ann Arbor, Michigan, Czechoslovak Society of Arts and Sciences in America, 1971.

Selected Writings: Phonological Studies. The Hague, Mouton, 1971.

Questions de poétique. Paris, Seuil, 1973.

Main Trends in the Science of Languages. New York, Harper, 1973.

Pushkin and His Sculptural Myth. The Hague, Mouton, 1975.

Hölderlin, Klee, Brecht: Zur Wortkunst dreier Gedichte, edited by Elmar Holmstein. Frankfurt, Suhrkamp, 1976.

Yeats' Sorrow of Love Through the Years, with Stephen Rudy. Lisse, Peter de Ridder, 1977.

Jakobson/Avant-propos de Roland Barthes. Lausanne, L'Âge d'Homme, 1978.

Six Lectures on Sound and Meaning. Cambridge, Massachusetts Institute of Technology Press, and Brighton, Sussex, Harvester, 1978.

The Sound and Shape of Language, with Linda R. Waugh. Bloomington, Indiana University Press, 1979.

Other

Editor, with others, *Description and Analysis of Contemporary Standard Russian.* The Hague, Mouton, 3 vols., 1959-61.

Editor, *Structure of Language and Its Mathematical Aspects.* New York, American Mathematical Society 1961.

Editor, with others, *Tönnies Fenne's Low German Manual of Spoken Russian-Pskov 1607.* Copenhagen, Royal Danish Academy of Sciences, 2 vols., 1961-1970.

Editor, with D. Worth, *Sofonija's Tale of the Russian-Tatar Battle on the Kulikovo Field.* The Hague, Mouton, 1963.

Editor, with others, *Form and Substance: Phonetic and Linguistic Papers.* Copenhagen, Akademisk Forlag, 1971.

Editor, *Slavic Poetics.* The Hague, Mouton, 1973.

*

Bibliography: *Roman Jakobson: A Bibliography of His Writings,* The Hague, Mouton, 1971.

Critical Studies: *Roman Jakobson's Science of Language* by Linda R. Waugh, Lisse, Peter de Ridder, 1976; *Roman Jakobson: Echoes of His Scholarship,* edited by Daniel Armstrong and C.H. Van Schooneveld, Lisse, Peter de Ridder, 1977.

*   *   *

Roman Jakobson was the intellectual channel through which a number of Continental European ideas about language and literature entered the mainstream of American thought. Apart from making very numerous and diverse contributions of his own to the academic literature, he acted as the catalyst for the creation by others of a body of theory which has dominated thinking about language and the human mind in the Western world over much of the last two decades.

As a young man Jakobson was one of the founders of the Russian "Formalist" literary movement, being influenced particularly by the futurist poet Velimir Khlebnikov; and formalism—the notion that humanistic, literary topics can fruitfully be approached in the spirit of the mathematician, abstracting away from the complexities of content to lay bare the bones of structural relationships—was a keynote of Jakobson's work throughout his career. The flavour of Jakobson's thought is neatly encapsulated in the title of one of his influential articles: "Poetry of Grammar and Grammar of Poetry." As this title suggests, there were two aspects to the *rapprochement* Jakobson effected between literary and mathematical thinking. Part of his achievement lay in making formally-minded American linguists rather more conscious than they had previously been of the humanistic dimensions of their subject-matter. But the converse aspect, which promoted the use of mathematical techniques of thought in areas to which they had previously been alien, was the one which predominated in Jakobson's work. Jakobson was always most interested in examining those facets of literature in which "structure" was relatively salient: in poetry, theories of metre; in prose, traditional folk-tale genres characterized by strong parallelism between successive sentences; and, by concentrating on them, Jakobson perhaps made such features appear somewhat more pervasive in literature generally than is truly the case.

In his emphasis on structural approaches to literature and language Jakobson was typical enough of his Moscow and Prague milieux in particular and of post-Saussurean Continental scholarship in general, though for Americans Jakobson was the chief personal link with that tradition. (Significantly, Jakobson was a close associate of the structuralist anthropologist Claude Lévi-Strauss when the two were both working in New York in the 1940s.) For that matter, American linguists too had an indigenous tradition of structural analysis of the sound-patterns of language, though a tradition which differed in detail from that of the Prague School. The most original aspect of Jakobson's thought lay in his notion of structural invariance. Even here he had precursors, notably the folklorist Vladimir Propp who uncovered complex patterning common to all members of a genre of Russian tales which are superficially quite diverse. But Jakobson took this idea much further, applying it not merely to different examples of a single literary genre but across diverse cultures. For Jakobson, different cultures all reflected the same constants of human mental structure; hence the apparent differences between the cultures of separate societies are relatively superficial, and mask underlying invariants.

This notion could scarcely have been more alien to American linguists of the mid-twentieth century, who were working within the relativistic paradigm established by the anthropologist Franz Boas according to whom there were no bounds to the diversity of languages. It was an axiom of American linguistics, for instance, that languages differ without limit in respect of which particular phonetic parameters they exploit in order to encode linguistic information, among the wealth of such parameters that are physically available. Already in the early 1940s Jakobson was arguing against this. Observation of the development of speech in children, he claimed, shows that there is a universal hierarchy of more-basic and less-basic phonetic distinctions: children in all societies begin with the same most-basic phonetic skills and develop along the same lines (and people unfortunate enough to lose the power of speech because of brain injury or disease regress down the same phonetic path that children climb). Languages differ from one another only in terms of how far their adult speakers ultimately proceed along each particular branch of the ramified universal hierarchy. As the new subject of information theory, linking mathematics and electronic engineering, emerged in the years following the Second World War, Jakobson and his collaborators sought to relate linguistics to it, arguing that the innumerable physically-distinct phonetic contrasts used by the thousands of languages spoken in the world can all be reduced to a universal set of twelve psychologically-significant binary oppositions.

Lying behind this somewhat technical difference of opinion between Jakobson and the American linguistic tradition was concealed a more philosophical contrast of views. American linguists—like English-speaking scholars in general—tended to be empiricists, holding that men's cognitive achievements were determined principally by interaction with their environment, so that there was no mechanism which could induce uniformity between separate cultures. Many of them were influenced by behaviourist psychology, which in at least some of its versions implied that men scarcely possess any internal arrangements complex enough to be identified with the traditional notion of "mind": according to this view we are mere bundles of stimulus/response associations. Jakobson's instincts, by contrast, were rationalist: he saw men as bringing subtle, well-defined mental organization into the world with them from birth, and he treated culture as more the product of our cognitive structure than its cause.

Jakobson, with his rhetorical skill, charm, and sophisticated mastery of several European cultures, was able after his move to America to dazzle the scholars who surrounded him there into acceptance of the validity of the rationalist approach to human sciences. Ultimate responsibility for broad changes in intellectual climate is never easy to assign unambiguously, but it seems fair to identify Jakobson as the initiator of what has been one of the major switches in outlook to have occurred in our age. Among those who came to scholarly maturity within Jakobson's ambit in Massachusetts was Noam Chomsky; Chomsky and his associates and followers took Jakobson's notion of cultural universals derived from innate cognitive structure and developed it into an intellectual system which has radically transformed modern philosophy, psychology, and many other disciplines.

Jakobson's influence on the work of others was highly significant. Arguably, his own scholarly output was less so. His published writings are extremely numerous, but in almost all cases they are short, even somewhat dilettantish articles rather than full-length monographs. Furthermore, when Jakobson did elaborate complex theories, these were often very speculative and based on quite meagre evidence, and their ability to survive has proved to be low. Within linguistics, even those who identified themselves as proponents of Jakobson's phonological theory soon modified it into something which is difficult to recognize as related to the theory that Jakobson himself stated. Nevertheless, his role as intellectual *accoucheur* alone would suffice to make him one of the most important figures in twentieth-century language studies.

—Geoffrey Sampson

JAMES, William. American philosopher and psychologist. Born in New York City, 11 January 1842; brother of the novelist Henry James. Educated abroad, 1857-60, and at Lawrence Scientific School and Harvard Medical School, Cambridge, Massachusetts, M.D. 1869. Married Alice Howe Gibbons in 1878; 5 children. Instructor in Anatomy and Physiology, 1873-

76, Assistant Professor of Physiology, 1876-80, Assistant Professor of Philosophy, 1880-85, and Professor of Philosophy and Psychology, 1885-1907, Harvard University. Gifford Lecturer, University of Edinburgh, 1901-02; Lowell Institute Lecturer, Boston, 1906; Hibbert Lecturer, Manchester College, Oxford, 1908. *Died* (in Chocorua, New Hampshire) *26 August 1910.*

PUBLICATIONS

Collections

The Works of William James. Cambridge, Massachusetts, Harvard University Press, 1975-.

Philosophy and Psychology

The Principles of Psychology.   New York, Holt, 2 vols., 1890.
Psychology (Briefer Course). New York, Holt, 1892.
Is Life Worth Living? (lecture). Philadelphia, S.B. Weston, 1896.
The Will to Believe, and Other Essays in Popular Philosophy. New York and London, Longman, 1897.
Human Immortality: Two Supposed Objections to the Doctrine. Boston, Houghton Mifflin, 1898.
Talks to Teachers on Psychology, and to Students on Some of Life's Ideals. New York, Holt, and London, Longman, 1899.
The Varieties of Religious Experience: A Study in Human Nature (lectures). New York and London, Longman, 1902.
Pragmatism: A New Name for Some Old Ways of Thinking (lectures). New York and London, Longman, 1907.
The Energies of Men (Religion and Medicine Series). New York, Moffat Yard, 1908.
The Meaning of Truth: A Sequel to "Pragmatism". New York and London, Longman, 1909.
A Pluralistic Universe: Hibbert Lectures at Manchester College on the Present Situation in Philosophy. New York and London, Longman, 1909.
Some Problems of Philosophy: A Beginning of an Introduction to Philosophy. New York and London, Longman, 1911.
Memories and Studies. New York and London, Longman, 1911.
Essays in Radical Empiricism. New York and London, Longman, 1912.
Collected Essays and Reviews. New York and London, Longman, 1920.
Essays on Faith and Morals, edited by Ralph Barton Perry. New York, Longman, 1943.
William James on Psychical Research, edited by Gardner Murphy. New York, Viking Press, 1960.

Other

Letters of William James. Boston, Atlantic Monthly Press, and London, Longman, 2 vols., 1920.
The Selected Letters of William James, edited by Elizabeth Hardwick. New York, Farrar, 1961.

Editor, *The Literary Remains of the Late Henry James.* Boston, Houghton Mifflin, 1884.

*

Bibliography: "Annotated Bibliography of the Writings of William James" by John J. McDermott, in *The Writings of William James: A Comprehensive Edition,* Chicago, University of Chicago Press, 1977.

Critical Studies: *The Thought and Character of William James* by Ralph Barton Perry, Boston, Little Brown, 2 vols., 1935; *The*

Thirteen Pragmatisms and Other Essays by Arthur O. Lovejoy, Baltimore, Johns Hopkins University Press, 1963; *William James: A Biography* by Gay Wilson Allen, New York, Viking Press, 1967; *Freedom and the Moral Life: The Ethics of William James* by John K. Roth, Philadelphia, Westminster Press, 1969; *The Radical Empiricism of William James* by John Wild, New York, Doubleday, 1969; *Purpose and Thought: The Meaning of Pragmatism* by John E. Smith, New Haven, Connecticut, Yale University Press, 1978.

* * *

William James (1842-1910), an extraordinarily many-sided thinker, played a conspicuously creative role in the development of twentieth-century thought. His work in psychology is uniformly recognized as giving massive impetus to the emergence of scientific experimental inquiry in that field. In philosophy he was a powerful influence on Husserl and the phenomenological movement. The philosophy of American naturalism (above all, that of Dewey) is deeply indebted to James; he also had a great effect in process philosophy and earned the profound respect of Alfred North Whitehead. His *The Varieties of Religious Experience* was a pioneering effort in the psychology of religion, and he also exerted influence on literature: He formulated the expression "stream of consciousness" and elaborated the nature of the stream. His brother Henry, the novelist, experimented with stream of consciousness as a literary form, which in due course was used by the leading novelists of this century.

James is responsible above all others for the criticisms leading to the demise of absolute idealism, the reigning philosophy in England, Europe, and America at the turn of the century. Something of this philosophy must be understood in order to appreciate James fully. According to absolute idealism, the universe is a unitary system of relations whose very being is constituted by the knowledge of an absolute mind—the Absolute. The system is perfect and unchanging, and each part in it is determined by nothing less than the whole. Monistic idealism is apologetic. It claims that evil and error are mere appearance, and it denies to human agency any possibility of introducing genuine change into the order of events.

James found this view illogical and repulsive. It excludes from reality all the changing, imperfect, incomplete, on-going and plural forms of existence that are so obvious to experience and so vital to human life. For himself, James was sworn to uphold a philosophy that would be faithful to the realities of human experience. His empiricism consists in this commitment above all.

James is perhaps best known as one of the founders (along with C.S. Peirce) of pragmatism. Pragmatism for James was a theory of the nature of meaning and truth. The meaning of a conception or proposition is simply the summation of the consequences that are believed to follow from the state of affairs denoted by the concept or proposition. James uses the example of "paper." There is no fixed and inherent essence of paper, but the meaning of "paper" is all of the functions of the stuff called paper: If something is paper, it can be written upon, pasted to the wall, consumed by fire, disintegrated by water, folded around packages, and so on. To determine the meaning of a term, we must perform operations on what the term refers to and/or observe the functions of the referent in relation to other events. Likewise, the truth of "This is a piece of paper" would be found not by intuiting an essence but by performing operations suitable to the meaning of paper and observing whether the alleged paper actually behaves as predicted. In this, James's pragmatism reflects the actual procedures of experimental science and anticipates what later became known as the operationist philosophy of science.

The important point for James is that the determination of both meaning and truth requires attention to the future. Meanings and propositions must have implications for future experience. Empty talk—the scourge of so much metaphysics and theology—would be banished by recourse to the pragmatic method. All talk of the Absolute, for example, is meaningless unless it leads to predictable experiences. Ideas are anticipations of future events contingent upon specified present conditions. Thus they are crucial in guiding us from present to future experiences.

James goes on to say that when a proposition cannot yet be established as true or false by scientific procedures, we have a right to believe it if it accords with our "passional" nature. For James, many religious beliefs fall into this category, as well as beliefs about free will and a moral world order. He was particularly concerned to indicate the consequences of our beliefs for moral experience. If we believe in freedom, for example, our efforts will be inspired by the assumption that conduct really can make a difference in the course of events, while a belief that the future is "foredoomed" leads to apathy and resignation.

One of the most conspicuous themes in James's pragmatism is the notion that our ultimate beliefs are tempered by deep personal disposition. Similarly, while he insisted on being scientific, he urged that pure scientific objectivity is a myth. The nature of scientific theory is necessarily qualified by the fact that it is a product of human intention and selectivity in the face of incomplete and ambiguous data.

James did not take anything in his pragmatism as reason to be intellectually complacent. He was striving to give a clear sense of the nature of our cognitive resources and limitations. He conceived pragmatism as a demand for never-ceasing inquiry and a scrupulous regard for the evidences of experience.

His interest in religious experience was characteristically directed to its consequences. The worth of such experience depends on its effects, not its source; he was incisive in showing how different types of religious experience lead to corresponding changes in one's spirit and behavior. He believed that the renewed energy that such experiences bring might originate in the unconscious and possibly also in a cosmic "mother sea" of consciousness, of which we are all partakers. We are all "compounded" with it. He held that empirical inquiry tends to such a conclusion but cannot yet establish it. God for James is, or includes, this "mother sea." God is nevertheless finite, limited, and must contend with an environment. Otherwise, James thought, there is no accounting for evil and no accounting for the possibility of real change. James conceived of man and God as immediately united in moral struggle against the deficiencies of the universe.

It is evident that James was preoccupied with the various ways in which human personality is related to the universe. In this context he always found unsatisfactory the notion that mind and matter are distinct and separate substances with no intelligible relation between them. That is, he found Cartesian dualism repugnant. Showing the influence of Darwin's theory of evolution, James's *The Principles of Psychology* initiated a fundamental attack on Cartesian assumptions. Even while accepting certain dimensions of the dualistic legacy, James went far to put the basic questions about the relation between man and nature in completely different terms. In place of the thinking substance that operates only by an internal and self-complete law, James broke ground in understanding the individual and its environment as functioning together as one inclusive system. According to this new direction, human nature is a function of the biological organism striving to adapt to its environment. All thinking, James said, is for the sake of acting. Mind is "a fighter for ends," engaged in a process of discriminating and selecting events in its surroundings that are organic to its behavior. Effective thinking (as noted earlier) is for the sake of directing conduct from present to future experiences. (James's pragmatism is clearly rooted in a conception of human nature contending and collaborating with processes of change tending towards uncertain outcomes.)

In the epochal essay "Does 'Consciousness' Exist" (included in *Essays in Radical Empiricism*), James denies the existence of consciousness as an entity. He characterizes it as a *function* of an underlying process (called, unhappily, pure experience). Likewise, what we know as material objects are a function of the same process. Consciousness is always consciousness *of* events of pure experience. "Does 'Consciousness' Exist" is the most important single article written in the twentieth-century onslaught on Cartesian philosophy.

Another radical departure from antecedent traditions is found in James's analysis of experience. He made a devastating critique of the virtually universal notion in philosophy that experience is comprised of inherently unrelated and meaningless bits and pieces. These were thought to be somehow united by a power wholly independent of the properties of experienced objects. In contrast to this view, James pointed out that we experience relations as directly and immediately as the things related. We experience things-in-their-relations. The atomistic view of the world was primarily the result of a seriously deficient analysis of experience. Events of experience are, then, inherently meaningful. They are portentous of the events to which they are related; and the need to contrive elaborate postulates to account for relations becomes gratuitous. At the same time, James insisted that the universe is not an integral system of internal relations—not the "block universe" of the idealists. Thus his theory of relations finds a mean between the conception of the universe as wholly pulverized on the one hand or wholly systematic on the other.

As James argued throughout his life, the universe is open and pluralistic. It is not constituted of independent substances; it is not held rigid by fixed essences; it is not reducible to a monistic system of relations. All such "intellectualist" reductions fail the test of experience. The universe is a process of change and development; and the novelties that occur in it are genuine. Changes in one part, however, might be effective in initiating changes in another. Human effort can be efficacious in bringing about a new and better future. James celebrated a living universe to which we are organically related, which is open to creative initiatives on our part. It is a universe in which intelligence and aspiration can play a vital part and can find intimate relation with the universe in return.

Such ideas were expressed in the liveliest and most engaging prose of any philosophical writer of this century; but his writing alone hardly accounts for James's popularity and honor. His philosophy is distinguished more for its guiding spirit and for its initiatives than for its finalities. The resurgence of his spirit and the elaboration of so many of his initiatives in succeeding generations are testimony to the abiding fecundity and appeal of his thought.

—James Gouinlock

JASPERS, Karl (Theodor). German-Swiss philosopher. Born in Oldenburg, 23 February 1883. Studied at the University of Heidelberg, University of Munich, University of Berlin, and at the University of Göttingen, M.D. 1909. Married Gertrud Mayer in 1910. Assistant, Psychiatric Clinic, University of Heidelberg, 1910-13; Lecturer, 1913-21, and Professor of Philosophy, 1921-37 (removed by the Nazis), 1945-48, University of Heidelberg; after 1948, Professor of Philosophy, University of Basel. Recipient: Goethe Prize, 1947; German Bookdealers' Peace Prize, 1958; Erasmus Prize, 1959; Oldenburg Prize, 1963. Honorary doctorate: University of Lausanne, 1947; University of Heidelberg, 1953; University of Geneva, 1959; Sorbonne, 1959. Honorary Citizen, City of Oldenburg, 1963. *Died 26 February 1969.*

PUBLICATIONS

Philosophy and Psychology

Allgemeine Psychopathologie: Ein Leitfaden für Studierende, Ärzte und Psychologen. Berlin, Springer, 1913; as *General*

Psychopathology, Chicago, University of Chicago Press, 1963.

Psychologie der Weltanschauungen. Berlin, Springer, 1919.

Max Weber (lecture). Tübingen, Mohr, 1921.

Die Idee der Universität. Berlin, Springer, 1923; as *The Idea of the University*, Boston, Beacon Press, 1959; London, Peter Owen, 1960.

Die geistige Situation der Zeit. Berlin, de Gruyter, 1931; as *Man in the Modern Age*, London, Routledge, 1933; New York, Doubleday, 1957.

Philosophie. Berlin, Springer, 3 vols., 1932; as *Philosophy*, Chicago, University of Chicago Press, 3 vols., 1969-71.

Max Weber: Deutsches Wesen im politischen Denken, im Forschen und Philosophieren. Oldenburg, Germany, Stalling, 1932; as "Max Weber," in *Three Essays: Leonardo, Descartes, Max Weber*, New York, Harcourt Brace, 1964.

Vernunft und Existenz (lectures). Groningen, Wolters, 1935; as *Reason and Existence*, London, Routledge, and New York, Noonday Press, 1955.

Nietzsche: Einführung in das Verständnis seines Philosophierens, Berlin, de Gruyter, 1936; as *Nietzsche: An Introduction to the Understanding of His Philosophical Activity*, Tucson, University of Arizona Press, 1965.

Descartes und die Philosophie. Berlin, de Gruyter, 1937; as "Descartes," in *Three Essays: Leonardo, Descartes, Max Weber*, New York, Harcourt Brace, 1964.

Existenzphilosophie (lectures). Berlin, de Gruyter, 1938; as *Philosophy of Existence*, Philadelphia, University of Pennsylvania Press, 1971.

Die Schuldfrage. Heidelberg, Schneider, 1946; as *The Question of German Guilt*, New York, Dial Press, 1947.

Vom europäischen Geist (lecture). Munich, Piper, 1947; as *The European Spirit*, London, SCM Press, 1948; New York, Macmillan, 1949.

Von der Wahrheit: Philosophische Logik, vol. 1. Munich, Piper, 1947; selection as *Tragedy Is Not Enough*, Boston, Beacon Press, 1952; selection as *Truth and Symbol*, New York, Twayne, and London, Vision Press, 1959.

Der philosophische Glaube (lectures). Zurich, Artemis, 1948; as *The Perennial Philosophy*, New York, Philosophical Library, 1949; London, Routledge, 1950.

Unsere Zukunft und Goethe (lecture). Bremen, Storm, 1949.

Philosophie und Wissenschaft (lecture). Zurich, Artemis, 1949; included in *Way to Wisdom*, 1951.

Vom Ursprung und Ziel der Geschichte. Zurich, Artemis, 1949; as *The Origin and Goal of History*, London, Routledge, and New Haven, Connecticut, Yale University Press, 1953.

Einführung in die Philosophie (radio lectures). Zurich, Artemis, 1950; as *Way to Wisdom*, London, Gollancz, and New Haven, Connecticut, Yale University Press, 1951.

Rechenschaft und Ausblick: Reden und Aufsätze. Munich, Piper, 1951; selections as *Existentialism and Humanism: Three Essays by Karl Jaspers*, New York, Russel F. Moore, 1952.

Vernunft und Widervernunft in unserer Zeit (lectures). Munich, Piper, 1952; as *Reason and Anti-Reason in Our Time*, London, SCM Press, and New Haven, Connecticut, Yale University Press, 1952.

Nietzsche und das Christentum (lecture). Munich, Piper, 1952; as *Nietzsche and Christianity*, Chicago, Regnery, 1961.

Lionardo als Philosoph. Berne, Francke, 1953; as "Leonardo," in *Three Essays: Leonardo, Descartes, Max Weber*, New York, Harcourt Brace, 1964.

Die Frage der Entmythologisierung, with Rudolf Bultmann. Munich, Piper, 1954; as *Myth and Christianity*, New York, Noonday Press, 1958.

Schelling, Grösse und Verhängnis. Munich, Piper, 1955.

Die grossen Philosophen: Erster Band, Die massgebenden Menschen: Sokrates, Buddha, Konfuzius, Jesus; Die fortzeugenden Gründer des Philosophierens: Plato, Augustin, Kant; Aus dem Ursprung denkende Metaphysiker: Anaximander,

Heraklit, Parmenides, Plotin, Anselm, Spinoza, Laotse, Nagarjuna. Munich, Piper, 1957; as *The Great Philosophers: The Foundations, The Paradigmatic Individuals: Socrates, Buddha, Confucius, Jesus; The Seminal Founders of Philosophical Thought: Plato, Augustine, Kant,* edited by Hannah Arendt, New York, Harcourt Brace, 1962; and as *The Great Philosophers: The Original Thinkers: Anaximander, Heraclitus, Parmenides, Plotinus, Anselm, Nicholas of Cusa, Spinoza, Lao-Tzu, Nagarjuna,* edited by Hannah Arendt, New York, Harcourt Brace, 1966.

Die Atombombe und die Zukunft des Menschen: Politisches Bewusstein unserer Zeit. Munich, Piper, 1958; as *The Future of Mankind,* Chicago, University of Chicago Press, 1961.

Philosophie und Welt: Reden und Aufsätze. Munich, Piper, 1958; as *Philosophy and the World: Selected Essays and Lectures,* Chicago, Regnery, 1963.

Freiheit und Wiedervereinigung: Über Aufgaben deutscher Politik. Munich, Piper, 1960.

Der philosophische Glaube angesichts der Offenbarung. Munich, Piper, 1962; as *Philosophical Faith and Revelation,* Chicago, University of Chicago Press, 1967.

Über Bedingungen und Möglichkeiten eines neuen Humanismus (lectures). Stuttgart, Reclam, 1962.

Gesammelte Schriften zur Psychopathologie. Berlin, Springer, 1963.

Kleine Schule des philosophischen Denkens. Munich, Piper, 1965; as *Philosophy is for Everyman: A Short Course in Philosophical Thinking,* New York, Harcourt Brace, 1967.

Aneignung und Polemik: Gesammelte Reden und Aufsätze zur Geschichte der Philosophie, edited by Hans Saner. Munich, Piper, 1968.

Chiffren der Transzendenz, edited by Hans Saner. Munich, Piper, 1970.

Notizen zu Martin Heidegger, edited by Hans Saner. Munich, Piper, 1978.

Die grossen Philosophen, Nachlass 1, Darstellungen und Fragment, edited by Hans Saner. Munich, Piper, 1981.

Die grossen Philosophen, Nachlass 2, Fragment, Anmerkungen, Inventar, edited by Hans Saner. Munich, Piper, 1981.

Weltgeschichte der Philosophie, Einleitung, edited by Hans Saner. Munich, Piper, 1982.

Other

Wohin treibt die Bundesrepublik? Tatsachen-Gefahren-Chancen. Munich, Piper, 1966; as *The Future of Germany,* Chicago, University of Chicago Press, 1967.

Antwort: Zur Kritik meiner Schrift "Wohin treibt die Bundesrepublik?" Munich, Piper, 1967.

Schicksal und Wille: Autobiographische Schriften, edited by Hans Saner. Munich, Piper, 1967.

Provokationen: Gespräche und Interviews, edited by Hans Saner. Munich, Piper, 1969.

*

Critical Studies: *The Philosophy of Karl Jaspers,* edited by Paul Arthur Schilpp, New York, Tudor, 1957 (contains a bibliography); *Karl Jaspers: An Introduction to His Philosophy* by Charles F. Wallraff, Princeton, New Jersey, Princeton University Press, 1970; *Reason Revisited: The Philosophy of Karl Jaspers* by Sebastian Samay, South Bend, Indiana, University of Notre Dame Press, 1971; *Existence, Existenz, and Transcendence: An Introduction to the Philosophy of Karl Jaspers* by Oswald O. Schrag, Pittsburgh, Duquesne University Press, 1971; *Karl Jaspers in der Diskussion,* edited by Hans Saner, Munich, Piper, 1973; *Karl Jaspers: Philosophy as Faith* by Leonard H. Ehrlich, Amherst, University of Massachusetts Press, 1975.

*   *   *

It is impossible to assign Jaspers a place in philosophy. In an age of the professionalization of philosophy down to its training regimen, he came to it after a career in scientific research. While philosophers of the 20th century tend to group themselves according to methodological orientation, Jaspers deliberately moved from one method of thought to another according to his need. He rejected followers and does not have any. He demanded that one think independently. Philosophical thought was for him as much, and even more, at home in the everyday concerns of life as in the scholar's study or the seminar room. Thus ultimately he meant to direct himself as much to the plain man, the man of action, the conscience of the doer and mover, as to their teachers at the university. His idiom, however, is not popular. To hear its limpid verve requires considerable schooling, and the patience to listen to one who makes man's finitude and the consequent limitation of the scope of truth a principle of his thinking. The watchword is 'freedom,' the freedom of man in his singular potential to decide his own destiny; it is not an easy freedom, but full of travail and risk. Yet Jaspers does not absolutize man or his freedom. Thus, while he originated the 'existential' turn in the philosophy of man, he was not an 'existentialist.' Jaspers's abode is in the infinite reaches of Being illumined by the infinitesimal beacon of man's busy and communicative realization.

Jaspers considered modern science to have preempted the realm of truth that is equally valid for all by virtue of investigative procedures where one investigator is, in principle, replaceable by any other. However, truths by which a human being lives require the validation of his commitment and the testimony of his action. It is the task of philosophy to clarify such truth in its distinctness from science.

Basic to that clarification is Jaspers's distinction of 'Existenz' from 'existence' (*Dasein*). Existence is the human being regarded as one among other beings in the world and as potentially an object of scientific investigation. Regarded as Existenz the human being participates essentially in deciding what he is to be. Every actual man is thus unique; philosophically we cannot give a description but merely an 'illumination' of 'possible' Existenz. Accordingly Jaspers sees man as exercising his freedom with respect to the challenges of situations, and within the bounds of ineluctible 'limit-situations' (chance, guilt, failure, death). Though decisions are made at a moment, man bears responsibility for them beyond the moment ('historicity'); moreover, in his works and actions man shows the truth out of which he lives (the 'absolute consciousness' of love and faith). Man is not alone, however, but essentially with and with respect to others ('communication'). Also, though man in his authentic selfhood is regarded as Existenz, he requires the concreteness of existence as the means of his actualization.

Inasmuch as the risk of faith is personal, the truth of which it is a factor cannot require the sort of universal assent which science is able to claim for its truths. Men may be bound to each other by virtue of a common tradition or commitment to the same purpose, but traditions differ, and adherents to the same tradition differ as to its meaning and demands. In this disparateness of fundamental truths I cannot require as a confirmation for my truth that the other assent to it as well, but I have to live with the other as one whose truth is not my truth. Jaspers's conception of reason is responsive to this task. Reason is thought that is directed toward unity. But for man in time unity is not achieved, but rather a goal whose realization is the task of human beings involved in the here-and-now of their concerns, encounters and conflicts. Communication for Jaspers is a vying for the truth of one's ultimate commitments face to face with that of the other. The realization of truth as communication is a struggle, and it is truth to the degree that the struggle is loving and not destructive.

In his periechontology (doctrine of the Encompassing) Jaspers addresses the problem of how men of diverse basic truth-beliefs can meet in their communicative struggle. He proposed that human realization of truth takes place within and is "encompassed" by the open horizon of Being and its modes. In this "radical theory of Being" he tries to identify the spaces in which

Being and its truth become manifest in rich diversity to man in time, and he does so with reference to the testimony of mankind's hitherto achieved realization whether in philosophy, religion, art, literature, science, mythology, the practical realm, etc. Encompassing Being is primordially divided into the following modes which in turn are 'encompassing.' The modes of what man "is or could be" are: (a) and (b) existence and Existenz, mentioned above; (c) consciousness-as-such, the thinking whose prime articulation is logic and whose main fulfillment is science; (d) spirit, which, as in Hegel, is the unifying activity animated by ideas. The modes of the Encompassing "that is Being itself" are (e) world and (f) transcendence, which is the ground of freedom insofar as man is independent of the world, and, being finite, cannot be the source of his own being. Finally, (g) reason is the "bond within us of all the modes".

On this basis Jaspers presents a new and elaborate theory delimiting the ways truth manifests itself to man in time. Untruth is a vehicle of truth, as in symbols or in political compromise. Truth in its wholeness transcends human realization and will burst into human lives and history in the form of authorities and exceptions. It is a basic decision for man whether to keep the horizon open for the travail of reason, or to serve an all-embracing authority ('catholicity'). For man what is truth in its completeness is a matter of a person's free risk of faith and a life-long task of communicative realization. Ultimate truths as envisaged by man are 'ciphers' of transcendence whose 'reading' by man is personal and neither objective nor scientific.

Jaspers sees the great promise of the age in the yearning for freedom, and the great dangers in the potential for totalitarian power and the threat of nuclear annihilation. To Jaspers the cause of freedom depends on the inner liberation of the individual. These motives led him to take up philosophical battle with respect to fundamental political questions of the age. Whether it concerned Germany's nazi past, or her frail commitment to democracy, or the chances of peace in the confrontation of the super-powers under the threat of nuclear war—the aim to Jaspers was peace, not at any price, but peace in freedom grounded on open and uncompromising integrity. It led him to reexamine the meaning of history and to call mankind to bring the force of reason attained during the 'axial period' (1st millennium B.C.) to bear on the problems facing mankind today. And—recognizing revelation as a source of truth distinct from philosophy and science—Jaspers challenges Western religions as regards their dogmatic absolutizations and claims of exclusiveness. Similarly he directs himself against the dangers to freedom that consist of demonology, the deification of man and nihilism.

—Leonard H. Ehrlich

JEANS, James (Hopwood). British astronomer and physicist. Born in Ormskirk, Lancashire, 11 September 1877. Studied at Trinity College, Cambridge, B.A. 1899, M.A. 1903. Married Charlotte Tiffany Mitchell in 1907, 1 daughter; married Susi Hock in 1935, 3 children. Fellow of Trinity College, 1901, and University Lecturer in Mathematics, 1904, Cambridge University; Professor of Applied Mathematics, Princeton University, New Jersey, 1905-09; Stokes Lecturer in Applied Mathematics, Cambridge University, 1910-12; Secretary of the Royal Society, London, 1919-29; Research Associate, Mount Wilson Observatory, California, 1923-44; Professor of Astronomy, Royal Institution, London, 1935-46. President, Royal Astronomical Society, 1925-27, and British Association for the Advancement of Science, 1934. Recipient: Adams Prize, Cambridge University, 1917; Royal Medal, Royal Society, 1919; Gold Medal, Royal Astronomical Society, London, 1922; Franklin Medal, Franklin Institute, Philadelphia, 1931; Mukerjee Medal, Indian Associa-

tion for the Cultivation of Science, 1937; Calcutta Medal, Royal Asiatic Society of Bengal, 1938. Honorary doctorate: Oxford University; University of Manchester; Benares Hindu University, India; University of Aberdeen; Johns Hopkins University, Baltimore; St. Andrews University, Scotland; University of Dublin; University of Calcutta. Fellow of the Royal Society. Honorary Fellow of Trinity College, Cambridge, 1942. Knighted, 1928; O.M. (Order of Merit), 1939. *Died 16 September 1946.*

PUBLICATIONS

Astronomy and Physics

The Dynamical Theory of Gases.   Cambridge, Cambridge University Press, 1904.
An Elementary Treatise on Theoretical Mechanics.   Boston, Ginn, 1906.
The Mathematical Theory of Electricity and Magnetism.   Cambridge, Cambridge University Press, 1908.
Report on Radiation and the Quantum Theory.   London, The Electrician, 1914.
Problems of Cosmogony and Stellar Dynamics.   Cambridge, Cambridge University Press, 1919.
The Nebular Hypothesis and Modern Cosmogony (lecture).   Oxford, Clarendon Press, 1923.
Atomicity and the Quanta (lecture).   Cambridge, Cambridge University Press, 1926.
Astronomy and Cosmogony.   Cambridge, Cambridge University Press, 1928.
The Universe Around Us.   Cambridge, Cambridge University Press, and New York, Macmillan, 1929.
Eos; or, The Wider Aspects of Cosmogony.   London, Kegan Paul, and New York, Dutton, 1929.
The Mysterious Universe (lecture).   Cambridge, Cambridge University Press, and New York, Macmillan, 1930.
The Stars in Their Courses.   Cambridge, Cambridge University Press, and New York, Macmillan, 1931.
The New Background of Science.   Cambridge, Cambridge University Press, and New York, Macmillan, 1933.
Through Space and Time.   Cambridge, Cambridge University Press, and New York, Macmillan, 1934.
Science and Music.   Cambridge, Cambridge University Press, and New York, Macmillan, 1937.
The Origin of the Planets (lecture).   Calcutta, Indian Association for the Cultivation of Science, 1938.
An Introduction to the Kinetic Theory of Gases.   Cambridge, Cambridge University Press, 1940.
Physics and Philosophy.   Cambridge, Cambridge University Press, 1942; New York, Macmillan, 1943.
The Astronomical Horizon (lecture).   Oxford, Clarendon Press, 1945.
The Growth of Physical Science.   Cambridge, Cambridge University Press, 1947; New York, Macmillan, 1948.

*

Critical Study: *Sir James Jeans: A Biography* by E.A. Milne, Cambridge, Cambridge University Press, 1952 (contains a full bibliography).

*   *   *

James Jeans' intellectual interests ranged over a wide variety of subjects, including molecular physics, rotating bodies, cosmology, stellar dynamics, and the science of music. In the last twenty years of his life, he became a widely effective popularizer of science.

Jeans' earliest studies involved the analysis of the distribution of energy in collections of molecules. Among the problems he examined was that of black-body radiation. By the early 1900's it had become obvious that classical efforts to predict the distribution of frequencies emitted by a radiating black-body were unsuccessful. Wien had developed an empirical relationship which worked well for this problem at high frequencies and Rayleigh had achieved a similar success for radiation of low frequencies. But neither law could be applied over the complete range of radiated frequencies.

Jeans attempted to correct and modify Rayleigh's law. His modification is now known as the Rayleigh-Jeans Law. However, a totally satisfactory analysis of the black-body problem was not achieved until Max Planck applied the principles of quantum mechanics to it. Jeans doubted that quantum theory was as dramatic a departure from classical physics as it appeared to be to many physicists at the time, and he attempted to demonstrate that the Planck conclusions were a special case that could be accounted for by means of a classical analysis. In this effort he was unsuccessful and, by 1914, he acknowledged the revolutionary character of quantum theory.

It was about this time that Jeans' interests turned to astronomical questions. One of the earliest problems he pursued evolved out of a second topic from physics of longstanding interest: the nature of revolving bodies. Even before completing his master's degree, Jeans had shown an interest in this subject. The question he attacked was one about which physicists and astronomers had argued for a number of years: what was the final, degenerate condition of a rotating body. Earlier workers had shown that a rotating spherical body evolves gradually through various ellipsoidal shapes until it assumes a pear-shaped form. The question was whether this form was then stable, or whether it degenerated further until the body flew apart. By 1928, Jeans had demonstrated that the latter is the most likely case.

The significance of this problem in astronomy is its relevance to cosmology. Over a hundred years earlier, Laplace had proposed a "nebular" hypothesis for the formation of the solar system. He had suggested that the sun and planets might have been formed out of a giant revolving cloud (nebula) of gas. As the nebula revolved more and more rapidly, Laplace argued, clumps along its outer edge broke off, condensed, and formed planets. The nucleus of the nebula also condensed, forming the sun.

Based on his studies of revolving bodies, Jeans demonstrated that the Laplace model was dynamically not possible. The angular momentum of the solar system is located almost entirely in the planets, whereas the nebular hypothesis would demand that much of it be retained in the sun. Jeans proposed, therefore, an alternative explanation for the formation of the solar system. It was based on the possible near-collision of another star with our own sun. This close encounter would, Jeans tried to show, pull small masses of matter from the sun, masses that could later condense to form the planets.

The fatal flaw in Jeans' theory is the low probability of such a near encounter between two stars. The unlikelihood of such an event would suggest that planetary systems like our own are rare events indeed. Jeans himself had written that "the calculation shows that even after a star had lived its life of millions of millions of years, the chance is still about a hundred thousand to one against its being surrounded by planets." In fact, it is now clear that this is not the case at all in the universe. Instead, astronomers believe that the number of planetary systems like our own numbers in the millions and upwards. This raises very serious doubts about the validity of the Jeans' encounter theory.

Jeans' other research in astronomy covered an impressive array of topics including the formation of galaxies, the creation and evolution of stars, the internal composition of stars, the formation and nature of binary stars, and the properties of spiral nebulae. In a 1904 paper on radioactivity, he anticipated Einstein's prediction that matter might be convertible into energy and that this change might be the source of all stellar energy.

—David Newton

JESPERSEN, (Jens) Otto (Harry). Danish philologist. Born in Randers, Denmark, 16 July 1860. Studied at the University of Copenhagen, Ph.D. Married Ane Marie Djoerup in 1897. Professor of English Language and Literature, University of Copenhagen, from 1893 (Rector, 1920-21). Editor, *Dania: Tidskrift for dansk sprog*, 1890-98. Honorary doctorate: Columbia University, New York; St. Andrews University, Scotland; Sorbonne, Paris. Fellow, British Academy. Member, Academy of Copenhagen; Academy of Oslo; Academy of Lund, Norway; Academy of Helsinki; Academy of Ghent, Belgium; Academy of Prague; Academy of Amsterdam. *Died 30 April 1943.*

PUBLICATIONS

Language

The Articulations of Speech Sounds Represented by Means of Analphabetic Symbols. Marburg, Elwert, 1889.
Studier over Engelske kasus, med en indledning: Fremskridt i sproget. Copenhagen, Kleins, 1891; revised and expanded edition as *Progress in Language, with Special Reference to English*, London, Sonnenschein, and New York, Macmillan, 1894.
Fonetik: En systematisk fremstilling af laeren om sproglyd [Phonetics: A Systematic Presentation of the Principles of Phonetics]. Copenhagen, Schubothe, 1897-99.
Kortfattet Engelsk grammatik for tale- og skriftsproget [Concise English Grammar for Speech and Writing.] Copenhagen, Schubothe, 1897.
Ergänzungsheft zu Spoken English. Leipzig, Reisland, 1899.
Sprogundervisning. Copenhagen, Schubothe, 1901; as *How to Teach a Foreign Language*, London, Sonnenschein, and New York, Macmillan, 1904.
Growth and Structure of the English Language. Leipzig, Teubner, and New York, Stechert, 1905; 9th revised edition, New York, Doubleday, 1956; Oxford, Blackwell, 1958.
Modersmålets fonetik [Phonetics of Our Native Language]. Copenhagen, Schubothe, 1906.
John Hart's Pronunciation of English (1569-1570). Heidelberg, Winter, 1907.
Folkesprog og Verdenssprog [Native Language and World Language]. Copenhagen, Universitetsudvalget, 1908.
A Modern English Grammar on Historical Principles. Heidelberg, Winter, and London, Allen and Unwin, 7 vols., 1909-49.
Elementarbuch der Phonetik. Berlin, Teubner, 1912.
Engelsk fonetik til brug for laerere og studerende [English Phonetics: A Guide for Teachers and Students], with H. Helweg-Möller. Copenhagen and Christiana, Gyldendal, 1912; revised edition, 1921.
Sprogets logik [The Logic of Language]. Copenhagen, Universitetsbogtrykkeriet, 1913.
Nutidssprog hos börn og voxne [Contemporary Language Among Children and Grown-Ups]. Copenhagen and Christiana, Gyldendal, 1916; revised edition as *Börnesprog: En bog for foraeldre* [Children's Language: A Book for Parents], 1923.
Negation in English and Other Languages. Copenhagen, Høst, 1917.
Historio di nia linguo / History of Our Language, and Artificala lingui pos la mondmilito / Artificial Languages after the World War. London, Baxter, 1921.
De to hovedarter av grammattiske forbindelser [The Two Principal Kinds of Grammatical Connections]. Copenhagen, Høst, 1921.
Language: Its Nature, Development and Origin. New York, Holt, 1921; London, Allen and Unwin, 1922.
The Philosophy of Grammar. London, Allen and Unwin, and New York, Holt, 1924.
Menneskehed, nasjon og individ i sproget. Oslo, Aschehong, and Cambridge, Massachusetts, Harvard University Press,

1925; as *Mankind, Nation and Individual from a Linguistic Point of View*, Oslo, Aschehong, and Cambridge, Massachusetts, Harvard University Press, 1925; London, Allen and Unwin, 1946.

Sprogets udvikling og opstäen [The Origin and Progress of Language]. Copenhagen, Pios, 1926.

Et Verdenssprog: et forsøg på sporsmålets løsning [A World Language: An Attempt to a Solution of the Question]. Copenhagen, Pios, 1928.

An International Language. London, Allen and Unwin, 1928; New York, Norton, 1929.

Novial lexike/International Dictionary/Dictionnaire international/Internationales Wörterbuch. Heidelberg, Winter, and London, Allen and Unwin, 1930.

Tanker og studier [Thoughts and Studies]. Copenhagen, Gyldendal, 1932.

Essentials of English Grammar. London, Allen and Unwin, and New York, Holt, 1933.

Linguistica: Selected Papers in English, French and German. Copenhagen, Levin og Munksgaard, 1933.

The System of Grammar. London, Allen and Unwin, 1933.

Selected Writings. London, Allen and Unwin, 1934.

Discussion pri international lingue [Discussion on an International Language], with E. Wahl. Copenhagen, Munksgaard, 1935.

Analytic Syntax. Copenhagen, Levin og Munksgaard, 1937.

Efficiency in Linguistic Change. Copenhagen, Munksgaard, 1941.

Sproget: Barnet, kvinden, slaegten [Language: The Child, the Woman, the Family]. Copenhagen, Gyldendal, 1941.

Other

Dr. J. Stéfanssons bog om Robert Browning [Dr. J. Stéfansson's Book on Robert Browning]. Copenhagen, Klein, 1893.

Chaucers liv og digtning [The Life and Writings of Chaucer]. Copenhagen, Klein, 1893.

Engelsk begynderbog [Elementary English]. Copenhagen, Schubothe, 1895.

Engelske laesestykker, med øvelser [Textbook in English, with Exercises], 6th edition. Copenhagen, Gyldendal, 1914.

Rasmus Rask: I hundredåret efter hans hovedvaerk [Rasmus Rask: On the Centenary of His Principal Work]. Copenhagen, Gyldendal, 1918.

En sprogmands levned [The Life of a Linguist]. Copenhagen, Gyldendal, 1938.

Editor, *The England and America Reader*. Copenhagen, Schubothe, 1903; *Notes to the England and America Reader*, 1903; revised edition as *A British Reader, with Notes*, 1928.

Editor, *Engelsk läsebok för realskolan* [An English Reader for Junior High School]. Stockholm, Fritz, 1907.

Editor, *Fransk laesebog for begyndere* [A French Reader for Beginners], with V. Stigaard, 4th edition. Copenhagen, Gyldendal, 1915.

*   *   *

Otto Jespersen is one of the very few Continental linguists who have been widely read in Britain in the twentieth century, thanks to the fact that he wrote on the English language and wrote even his general linguistic works in English. Jespersen's description of Modern English, of which the first volume appeared in 1909 and the seventh and last a few years after his death, is only now beginning to be superseded by work drawing on computer-aided research.

Jespersen's theoretical writings, as opposed to the purely descriptive work just referred to, are not in the very highest class of linguistic scholarship. Nevertheless they played a unique role in the English-speaking linguistics of the inter-war decades, advocating views which were alien to British and American readers both geographically and also chronologically—Jespersen's books on general linguistic topics, which gained a large readership outside the professional discipline thanks to their accessible style, were written when the author was in his sixties and seventies and they represented a generation of scholarship which was otherwise largely forgotten. Jespersen never came to terms with the structural approach inaugurated by Ferdinand de Saussure several decades before Jespersen's death; on the other hand, he kept alive an evolutionary view of language which was almost extinct by the end of the nineteenth century and has only recently been taken seriously once again.

Jespersen's linguistic interests were always tied to practical issues. In his twenties, with a Swedish and a Norwegian collaborator he founded an association to promote what was then a revolutionary approach to language-teaching, which stressed the primacy of natural, spoken language over polished written style and the importance of informal, "direct" teaching methods. His early scholarly work was largely in the related area of phonetics. When the idea of creating a simple artificial language for international communication gathered momentum, having been initiated by Pastor Martin Schleyer's invention of Volapük in 1880, Jespersen became probably the most eminent academic linguist to throw his weight behind the movement; he was a leading member of the committee which in 1907 promulgated the language Ido (a reformed version of the better-known Esperanto), and in 1928 he claimed to have improved on Ido by inventing a language of his own called Novial.

In his purely theoretical writings Jespersen's concern with questions of utility and efficiency manifested itself in his emphasis on the notion of progress. Language, for Jespersen, was a tool, which had originally been produced and which was still being improved by the processes of cultural evolution. One reason why the English language in particular attracted Jespersen was that he saw its grammatical simplicity, its fewness of inflected forms by comparison with other European languages, as representing an especially advanced stage of linguistic evolution. This point of view (while no doubt widely shared by English-speaking laymen) was near-unique among academic linguists. German philologists of the nineteenth century had seen languages as evolving in a constant direction, but on the whole they had taken the direction of evolution, at least in the historical period, to be a downward one: they saw languages as having decayed from the logical sophistication of Greek and Latin to the crude grammar of contemporary European languages. By the end of the nineteenth century, however, when a wider range of the world's languages was accessible to European scholarship, most linguists no longer believed that there was *any* constancy in the direction of linguistic evolution: one language would be developing from type A into type B at the same time as another language was changing from type B to type A. For American linguists influenced by the relativism of Franz Boas and his school, it was an article of faith that no language could be described as "superior" to any other; languages of diverse societies might be adapted to different needs of their respective speakers, but the adaptation was assumed to be perfect in each case.

It is unlikely that Jespersen would have maintained his views about universal trends of linguistic evolution if he had known more about non-European languages, and his portrayal of English as uniquely efficient seems naive today (our language is simple in some relatively salient respects, but highly complex in other, less obvious, ways). But in his view of languages as tools which serve their users better or worse and which may be highly imperfect, Jespersen is being vindicated by recent developments in linguistic thought. While he was writing Jespersen seemed to be a survival from a largely-superseded past, but forty years after his death his work appears well in advance of its time in a number of respects. His analysis of grammar in terms of aprioristic logical categories has been claimed as a precursor of the recent Chomskyan approach. His interest in child language and in speculating about the origins of human language likewise anticipate recent developments in linguistics. Late-twentieth-century linguistics is in many ways returning to the preoccupations of its nineteenth-century youth, and Jespersen can now be seen as a solitary bridge-figure linking earlier and later periods.

—Geoffrey Sampson

JUNG, C(arl) G(ustav). Swiss psychologist. Born in Kesswil, Canton Thurgau, 26 July 1875. Studied at the University of Basel, 1895-1900, M.D. 1902; studied under Pierre Janet in Paris, 1902-03. Married Emma Rauschenbach in 1903; 5 children. Worked at the Burghölzli Psychiatric Clinic, Zurich, 1900-09 (Clinical Director and Senior Physician, 1903-09); Lecturer in Psychiatry, University of Zurich, 1905-13; began private practice in 1909; Professor of Psychology, Federal Polytechnical University, Zurich, 1933-41; after 1944, Professor of Medical Psychology, University of Basel. Honorary doctorate: Clark University, Worcester, Massachusetts, 1909; Fordham University, New York, 1920; Harvard University, Cambridge, Massachusetts, 1936; University of Allahabad, and Benares Hindu University, India, 1937; Oxford University, 1938; University of Calcutta, 1938; University of Geneva, 1945. Honorary Associate, Kaiserlich Deutschen Akademie der Naturforscher, 1934. Honorary Fellow, Royal Society of Medicine, London, 1939. *Died 6 June 1961.*

PUBLICATIONS

Collections

Die gessamelten Werke von C.G. Jung, edited by Marianne Niehus-Jung, Lena Hurwitz-Eisner, Franz Riklin, Lily Jung-Merker and Elizabeth Rüff. Zurich, Rascher, 1958-70, and Olten, Walter, 1971-.
The Collected Works of C.G. Jung, edited by Herbert Read, Michael Fordham, Gerhard Adler and William McGuire. London, Routledge, New York, Pantheon, and Princeton, New Jersey, Princeton University Press, 19 vols., 1953-79.

Psychology

Zur Psychologie und Pathologie sogenannter occulter Phänomene: Eine psychiatrische Studie. Leipzig, Mutze, 1902; as "On the Psychology and Pathology of So-called Occult Phenomena," in *Collected Papers on Analytical Psychology*, 1916.
Über die Psychologie der Dementia praecox: Ein Versuch. Halle, Marhold, 1907; as *The Psychology of Dementia Praecox*, New York, Journal of Nervous and Mental Disease Publishing Company, 1909.
Der Inhalt der Psychose (lecture). Vienna, Deuticke, 1908.
Wandlungen und Symbole der Libido: Beiträge zur Entwicklungsgeschichte des Denkens. Leipzig, Deuticke, 1912; as *Psychology of the Unconscious: A Study of the Transformation and Symbolism of the Libido: A Contribution to the History of the Evolution of Thought*, London, Kegan Paul, and New York, Moffat Yard, 1916.
Psychotherapeutische Zeitfragen: Ein Briefwechsel mit Dr. C.G. Jung, edited by Dr. R. Loÿ. Leipzig, Deuticke, 1914; as "On Some Crucial Points in Psychoanalysis," in *Collected Papers on Analytical Psychology*, 1916.
The Theory of Psychoanalysis. New York, Journal of Nervous and Mental Disease Publishing Company, 1915.
Collected Papers on Analytical Psychology, edited by Constance Long. London, Baillière, Tindall and Cox, and New York, Moffat Yard, 1916; revised edition, 1917.
VII Sermones ad Mortuos: Die sieben Belehrungen der Toten.

Privately Printed, 1916; as *VII Sermones ad Mortuos: The Seven Sermons of the Dead*, Edinburgh, Neill, 1925.
Über Konflikte der kindlichen Seele. Leipzig, Deuticke, 1916.
Die Psychologie der unbewussten Prozesse: Ein Überblick über die moderne Theorie und Methode der analytischen Psychologie, Zurich, Rascher, 1917; as "The Psychology of the Unconscious Processes," in *Collected Papers on Analytical Psychology*, revised edition, 1917.
Psychologische Typen. Zurich, Rascher, 1921; as *Psychologie Types; or, The Psychology of Individuation*, London, Routledge, and New York, Harcourt Brace, 1959.
Analytische Psychologie und Erziehung (lectures). Heidelberg, Kampmann, 1926.
Die Beziehungen zwischen dem Ich und dem Unbewussten. Darmstadt, Reichl, 1928; as "The Relation of the Ego to the Unconscious," in *Two Essays on Analytical Psychology*, 1928.
Two Essays on Analytical Psychology. London, Baillière, Tindall and Cox, and New York, Harcourt Brace, 1928.
Über die Energetik der Seele. Zurich, Rascher, 1928; selection as "On Psychical Energy," in *Contributions to Analytical Psychology*, 1928.
Contributions to Analytical Psychology. London, Kegan Paul, and New York, Harcourt Brace, 1928.
Die Frau in Europa. Zurich, Verlag der Neuen Schweitzer Revue, 1929; as "Woman in Europe," in *Collected Works*, vol. 10.
Das Geheimnis der goldenen Blüte: Ein chinesisches Lebensbuch, with Richard Wilhelm. Munich, Dorn, 1929; as *The Secret of the Golden Flower*, London, Routledge, and New York, Harcourt Brace, 1955.
Seelenprobleme der Gegenwart. Zurich, Rascher, 1931; selections translated in various volumes of the *Collected Works*.
Die Bezeihung der Psychotherapie zur Seelsorge (lecture). Zurich, Rascher, 1932; as "Psychotherapists or the Clergy," in *Modern Man in Search of a Soul*, 1933.
Modern Man in Search of a Soul. London, Kegan Paul, and New York, Harcourt Brace, 1933.
Allgemeines zur Komplextheorie (lecture). Aarau, Sauerländer, 1934.
Wirklichkeit der Seele: Anwendungen und Fortschritte der neueren Psychologie, with others. Zurich, Rascher, 1934; selections translated in various volumes of the *Collected Works*.
Psychology and Religion: The Terry Lectures. London, Oxford University Press, and New Haven, Connecticut, Yale University Press, 1938.
The Integration of the Personality. London, Kegan Paul, and New York, Farrar and Rinehart, 1939.
Die psychologische Diagnose des Tatbestandes. Zurich, Rascher, 1940; as "The Psychological Diagnosis of Evidence," in *Collected Works*, vol. 2.
Das göttliche Kind in mythologischer und psychologischer Beleuchtung, with K. Kerényi. Amsterdam, Pantheon, 1941.
Das göttliche Mädchen: Die Hauptgestalt der Mysterien von Eleusis in mythologischer und psychologischer Beleuchtung, with K. Kerényi. Amsterdam, Pantheon, 1941.
Einführung in das Wesen der Mythologie, with K. Kerényi. Amsterdam, Pantheon, 1941; as *Essays on a Science of Mythology*, New York, Pantheon, 1949; as *Introduction to a Science of Mythology*, London, Routledge, 1950.
Paracelsica (lectures). Zurich, Rascher, 1942; selections translated in *Collected Works*, vols. 13 and 15.
Über die Psychologie des Unbewussten. Zurich, Rascher, 1943; as "The Psychology of the Unconscious," in *Collected Works*, vol. 7.
Psychologie und Alchemie. Zurich, Rascher, 1944; as *Psychology and Alchemy, Collected Works*, vol. 12.
Psychologische Betrachtungen, edited by Jolande Jacobi. Zurich, Rascher, 1945; as *Psychological Reflections: An Anthology of the Writings of C.G. Jung*, London, Routledge, and New York, Pantheon, 1953.
Aufsätze zur Zeitgeschichte. Zurich, Rascher, 1946; selections

translated in various volumes of the *Collected Works.*

Psychologie und Erziehung.   Zurich, Rascher, 1946; selections translated in *Collected Works,* vol. 17.

Die Psychologie der Übertragung.   Zurich, Rascher, 1946; as "The Psychology of the Transference," in *Collected Works,* vol. 16.

Essays on Contemporary Events.   London, Kegan Paul, 1947.

Symbolik des Geistes, with Riwkah Schärf.   Zurich, Rascher, 1948; selections translated in various volumes of the *Collected Works.*

Über psychische Energetik und das Wesen der Träume.   Zurich, Rascher, 1948; selections translated in various volumes of the *Collected Works.*

Die Bedeutung des Vaters für das Schicksal des Einzelnen.   Zurich, Rascher, 1949; as "The Significance of the Father in the Destiny of the Individual," in *Collected Works,* vol. 4.

Gestaltungen des Unbewussten, with Aniela Jaffé.   Zurich, Rascher, 1950; selections translated in various volumes of the *Collected Works.*

Aion: Untersuchungen zur Symbolgeschichte, with Marie-Louise von Franz.   Zurich, Rascher, 1951; as *Aion: Researches into the Phenomenology of the Self, Collected Works,* vol. 9, pt. 2.

Antwort auf Hiob.   Zurich, Rascher, 1952; as *Answer to Job,* London, Kegan Paul, and New York, Pastoral Psychology Book Club, 1954.

Naturklärung und Psyche, with W. Pauli.   Zurich, Rascher, 1952; as *The Interpretation of Nature and Psyche,* London, Kegan Paul, and New York, Harcourt Brace, 1955.

Paracelsus.   St. Gallen, Switzerland, Tschudy, 1952; as "Paracelsus," in *Collected Works,* vol. 15.

Symbole der Wandlung: Analyse des Vorspiels zu einer Schizophrenie.   Zurich, Rascher, 1952; as *Symbols of Transformation: An Analysis of the Prelude to a Case of Schizophrenia, Collected Works,* vol. 5.

Von den Wurzeln des Bewusstseins: Studien über den Archetypus.   Zurich, Rascher, 1954; selections translated in various volumes of the *Collected Works.*

Welt der Psyche: Eine Auswahl zur Einführung, edited by A. Jaffé and G.P. Zacharias.   Zurich, Rascher, 1954; selections translated in various volumes of the *Collected Works.*

Spirit and Nature, with others.   London, Routledge, and New York, Pantheon, 1954.

Mysterium coniunctionis: Untersuchung über die Trennung und Zusammensetzung der seelischen Gegensätze in der Alchemie, with Marie-Louise von Franz.   Zurich, Rascher, 2 vols., 1955, 1956; as *Mysterious Conjunctions: An Inquiry into the Separation and Synthesis of Psychic Opposites into Alchemy, Collected Works,* vol. 14.

Versuch einer Darstellung der psychoanalytischen Theorie.   Zurich, Rascher, 1955; as "The Theory of Psychoanalysis," in *Collected Works,* vol. 4.

Bewusstes und Unbewusstes: Beiträge zur Psychologie, edited by A. Jaffé.   Frankfurt, Fischer, 1957.

Gegenwart und Zukunft.   Zurich, Rascher, 1957; as *The Undiscovered Self,* London, Routledge, and Boston, Little Brown, 1958.

Ein moderner Mythus: Von Dingen, die am Himmel gesehen werden.   Zurich, Rascher, 1958; as *Flying Saucers: A Modern Myth of Strange Things Seen in the Skies,* London, Routledge, and New York, Harcourt, 1958.

Psyche and Symbol: A Selection from the Writings of C.G. Jung, edited by Violet S. de Laszlo.   New York, Doubleday Anchor Books, 1958.

Errinerungen, Träume, Gedanken, edited by A. Jaffé.   Zurich, Rascher, 1962; as *Memories, Dreams, Reflections,* New York, Pantheon, 1962; London, Routledge, 1963.

Analytical Psychology: Its Theory and Practice: The Tavistock Lectures.   London, Routledge, and New York, Pantheon, 1968.

On the Nature of the Psyche (selections from the *Collected Works*).   Princeton, New Jersey, Princeton University Press, 1969.

Psychology and Education (selections from the *Collected Works*).   Princeton, New Jersey, Princeton University Press, 1969.

The Psychology of the Transference (selection from the *Collected Works*).   Princeton, New Jersey, Princeton University Press, 1969.

Four Archetypes: Mother, Rebirth, Spirit, Trickster (selections from the *Collected Works*).   Princeton, New Jersey, Princeton University Press, 1970.

Psychological Reflections: A New Anthology of His Writings 1905-1961, edited by Jolande Jacobi.   London, Routledge, and Princeton, New Jersey, Princeton University Press, 1970.

The Portable Jung, edited by Joseph Campbell.   New York, Viking Press, 1971.

Mandala Symbolism (selections from the *Collected Works*).   Princeton, New Jersey, Princeton University Press, 1972.

Synchronicity: An Acausal Connecting Principle (selections from the *Collected Works*).   London, Routledge, and Princeton, New Jersey, Princeton University Press, 1973.

Dreams (selections from the *Collected Works*).   Princeton, New Jersey, Princeton University Press, 1974.

Other

Briefe, edited by A. Jaffé.   Olten, Walter, 3 vols., 1972-73; as *Letters,* edited by A. Jaffé and Gerhard Adler, London, Routledge, and Princeton, New Jersey, Princeton University Press, 2 vols., 1973, 1976.

Briefwechsel, with Sigmund Freud, edited by William McGuire and Wolfgang Sauerländer.   Frankfurt, Fischer, 1974; as *The Freud/Jung Letters: The Correspondence Between Sigmund Freud and C.G. Jung,* London, Hogarth Press and Routledge, and Princeton, New Jersey, Princeton University Press, 1974.

Editor, *Diagnostische Assoziationsstudien: Beiträge zur experimentallen Psychopathologie.*   Leipzig, Barth, 2 vols., 1906, 1909; selections as *Studies in Word-Association: Experiments in the Diagnosis of Psychopathological Conditions Carried Out at the Psychiatric Clinic of the University of Zurich, under the Direction of C.G. Jung,* London, Heinemann, and New York, Moffat Yard, 1918.

*

Bibliography: *General Bibliography of C.G. Jung's Writings* by Lisa Ress and others, London, Routledge, and Princeton, New Jersey, Princeton University Press, 1979, *Collected Works,* vol. 19.

Critical Studies: *The Psychology of C.G. Jung: An Introduction* by Jolande Jacobi, New Haven, Connecticut, Yale University Press, 1962; *What Jung Really Said* by E.A. Bennet, New York, Schocken, 1967; *C.G. Jung* by Anthony Storr, London, Collins, and New York, Viking Press, 1973; *Jung in Context: Modernity and the Making of a Psychology* by Peter Homans, Chicago, University of Chicago Press, 1979; *Jungian Psychology in Perspective* by Mary Ann Mattoon, New York, Free Press, and London, Collier-Macmillan, 1981.

*   *   *

Carl Gustav Jung was a major contributor in the development of psychology. Although, he at first considered studying archaeology, he became interested in the natural sciences and decided to study medicine at the University of Basle. He received his M.D. in 1900. In 1902, while studying psychology under Janet in Paris, he developed his "word association" test, which he used to investigate emotional and subconscious problems of his patients. He also developed the concept of the "complex" at this time.

Jung met Freud in 1907 and worked closely with him until 1913, when their growing differences caused a breach in their relationship.

In 1912, Jung gave a series of lectures at Fordham University in New York that revealed the real depth of the breach between Freud and himself. Criticizing Freud's theory of sexual trauma, which Freud had not yet fully abandoned, Jung insisted that neurotic phenomena are much too complicated to understand in terms of a single trauma long past. To arrive at a fuller understanding of such phenomena one must consider hereditary predispositions and environmental factors in all their complexity, Jung said.

Jung also criticized Freud's limiting of the term "libido" strictly to sexual want. Pointing out that long before Freud the term libido was used as a description of all passionate desires, Jung wished to revive this meaning and extend it even further to refer to all of the various energetic processes of the human psyche.

He rejected too Freud's theory of infantile sexuality on the grounds that the nutritional and growth processes, rather than the sexual processes, are the important processes of childhood. In contrast to Freud's view that the period before puberty, what Freud called the latency period, is the period in which sexuality is repressed, Jung said that he believed it was during this period that sexuality begins. By rejecting Freud's view of infantile sexuality Jung also rejected his view of childhood amnesia. Whereas Freud attributed this to the patient's repression of their infantile sexuality, Jung considered the general amnesia to be simply due to immaturity and not analogous to the amnesia of neurosis. The failure to recall the events of childhood, he said, is due not only to repression but also to the inability in the early years to formulate events in a way that makes them available for memory and recall later. We are best able to recall that which we can formulate for ourselves at the time. If we cannot organize an experience in our own mind we cannot remember it later; it can only be recalled as isolated fragments of sensations and images.

Jung differed sharply with Freud's view that the determining cause of neurosis is the conflict between ego instincts and sexual instincts. He stressed, instead, the conflict resulting from the failure of a person's emotional development to keep pace with his physical and chronological development as the determining factor. The person whose emotional development has been arrested at some earlier stage is unable to meet the demands made on persons of his physical and chronological age. The resulting disharmony lays the foundation for the dissociation of personality seen in a neurosis. In neurosis, according to Jung, psychic energy is taken up by childish fantasies ill-suited for adaptation to adult life. Jung called this state "introversion." Introverted patients, he said, live in a world that belongs mostly to their past, a world in which the personalities of their parents play the most important determining part.

In his emphasis on the unconscious influence of the members of the family on each other, Jung anticipated the interpersonal conception of mental illness as something that develops between people, rather than as a walled-off intra-psychic occurrence in an isolated individual. The parent, he believed, is a far more important factor than the Oedipus complex in the development of psychopathology. In this context, Jung reinterpreted the Oedipus complex by seeing it not as the wish for sexual intercourse with the mother but as a wish by children of either sex for the exclusive possession of this protective and comforting being.

In contrast to Freud's emphasis on the patient's early history, Jung emphasized the actual present in the cause of neuroses, insisting that it also played a large part in the development of neurotic illnesses. His criticism of Freud's theory of regression is closely linked with this view. Freud regarded regression entirely in terms of the earlier pregenital instincts, describing it as the release of dammed-up libido—frustrated sexual excitement— along the pathways of early fixation or constitutional predisposition. Jung regarded it as a pathological way of dealing with a present situation by replacing a real action with a childish illu-

sion; it is a form of self-deceit that the person employs to preserve his self-esteem by hiding from a knowledge of his limitations.

In his work, Jung emphasized the unconscious insight of individuals into the social and ethical reality of their times. People are more in touch, he said, with the social and ethical problems of their community than they are conscious of. And, to a considerable extent, neurosis is an expression of the individual's genuine attempt to solve these problems as they are manifest in his own life. According to Jung, the symptoms of the neurotic illness express not only the false answers but the creative struggle of the individual for a true solution.

In 1913 Jung first presented his theory of personality types which he termed "introverted" (motivated by internal feelings) and "extroverted" (motivated by external factors). He later developed this theory further to say that the personality types were made up of four functions of mental activity: thinking, feeling, sensation, and intuition. These activities are seen as pairs of opposites: thinking and feeling, sensation and intuition. According to Jung, the tendency for one aspect of the pair to dominate the ego limits the ability of the individual to achieve self-realization. He also believed that the subconscious mind tends to complement the conscious. Thus, an introverted ego would indicate an extroverted unconscious.

It was also during this period that Jung developed an interest in myths, legends, and cultural history and the influence of these on the unconscious mind. For this reason he began to study the mental processes of primitive peoples, doing field work in North America in 1921 and Kenya in 1926. He also investigated the symbols and myths involved in alchemy, which he viewed as an attempt to understand nature. Out of this work he developed his theory of "archetypes," the inherited tendency to respond to situations which are present in all cultures in a way which resembles the response of man's ancestors. He believed that archetypes in the subconscious represent a collective personality manifesting itself in dreams, myths, and religions, and also in the fantasies of the psychotic, whose individual psyche has been overcome by the collective subconscious.

Like his former teacher, Pierre Janet, Jung regarded neurosis as essentially a form of self-division or a dissociation of the self. The moral part of a person as well as the immoral may be represented in the unconscious, he asserted, and lead to the development of autonomous complexes. Not only hate and lust are buried there; creativity, love, and truth may also be repressed. Jung, more than anyone else, pointed up to the creative, positive effort that the neurotic person makes to deal with the real problems of his life. He was also among the first to stress moral values in his theory. Where Freud, because of his particular biophysical bent, attempted to reduce moral issues to infantile narcissistic strivings, Jung emphasized love and respect as goals to achieve in the treatment of mental illness. These goals exist not only in relation to one's own nature, he said, but also in relation to others; in order to have love and respect for others, one must have love and respect for oneself.

—R.W. Rieber

KANDINSKY, Wassily. French artist and theorist of art. Born in Moscow, 4 December 1866; emigrated to Germany in 1921; naturalized, 1928; emigrated to France in 1933; naturalized, 1939. Educated at primary schools in Odessa; studied law and economics at Moscow University, 1886-92; studied painting at Anton Azbe's School of Art, Munich, 1897-99, and at the Kunstakademie, Munich, under Franz Stuck, 1900. Married Nina Andreevsky in 1917. Lecturer in Law, Moscow University, 1893-96; Professor, Free State Art Studios, Moscow, 1918; worked at various art research institutes in Moscow, 1920-21; Deputy Director and Professor at the Bauhaus, Wiemar and

Dessau, 1922-23. Founder, with others, 1902, and President, 1902-04, Phalanx group, Munich (later the Phalanx school); Founder, with others, Neue Künstler Vereinigung, Munich (President, 1909); Founder, with Franz Marc, Der Blaue Reiter, Munich, 1911; Co-Founder, Institute of Artistic Culture, Moscow, 1920, and Russian Academy of Artistic Sciences, Moscow, 1921; Founder, with von Jawlensky, Paul Klee and Lyonel Feininger, Die Blaue Vier, 1924. Co-Editor, *Bauhaus Zeitung für Gestaltung*, 1926-31. Member, Deutscher Kunstlerbund, 1905; Union International des Beaux-Arts et des Lettres, Paris, 1906; Vice-President, Société Anonyme, New York, 1923. *Died* (in Neuilly-sur-Seine) *13 December 1944.*

PUBLICATIONS

Collections

Les Écrits de Kandinsky.   Paris, Denöel et Gonthier, 2 vols., 1970; as *Kandinsky: Complete Writings on Art*, edited by Kenneth C. Lindsay and Peter Vergo, Boston, Hall, 2 vols., 1982 (contains a bibliography).

Art

Über das Geistige in der Kunst.   Munich, Piper, 1912; as *The Art of Spiritual Harmony*, London, Constable, 1914; as *Concerning the Spiritual in Art*, New York, Guggenheim Foundation, 1946, and Wittenborn, 1947.
Der Blaue Reiter, with others, edited by Franz Marc and Wassily Kandinsky.   Munich, 1912; as *The Blue Rider Almanach*, New York, Viking Press, 1974.
Punkt und Linie zu Flache: Beitrag zur Analyse der malerischen Elemente.   Munich, Langen, 1926; as *Point and Line to Plane: Contributions to the Analysis of the Pictorial Elements*, New York, Guggenheim Foundation, 1947.

Other

Klänge (prose poems).   Munich, Piper, 1912; as *Sounds*, New Haven, Connecticut, Yale University Press, 1980.
Arnold Schönberg [and] Wassily Kandinsky: Briefe, Bilder und Dokumente einter aussergewönnlichen Begegnung.   Vienna, Residenz Verlag, 1980.

*

Critical Studies: *Wassily Kandinsky: Life and Work* by Will Grohmann, New York, Abrams, 1958; *Kandinsky in Munich: The Formative Jugendstil Years* by Peg Weiss, Princeton, New Jersey, Princeton University Press, 1979; *Kandinsky: The Development of an Abstract Style* by Rose-Carol Washton Long, Oxford, Clarendon Press, 1980.

*   *   *

Like many of his colleagues in the Russian avant-garde, especially Kazimir Malevich, Wassily Kandinsky regarded art as much more than a formal or esthetic exercise, and imbued the creative process with a deeply philosophical, even messianic, significance. In other words, Kandinsky saw art as part of a universal system, as an instrument that could foresee and even transform concrete reality. Kandinsky's concentration on what he called the "inner sound" (i.e. on the philosophical and often mystical content of the artifact) remained an important component of his approach to painting, even during the 1920s, a period of more calculated, more objective formulations. Kandinsky took great pains to elucidate his artistic system in theoretical terms, and his essays, especially "On the Spiritual in Art" (1910-12), are major contributions to artistic thinking in the 20th century.

Kandinsky came to art late in life, enrolling in a formal art course in Munich only in 1896 when he was thirty years old. Consequently, he brought to his new found profession a substantial experience as a Moscow lawyer, ethnographer and essayist— something that contributed much to the intellectual maturity and sense of equilibrium that we associate with his work. However, although his decision to become an artist was a conscious one, there were a number of impressions from his earlier life that made him acutely aware of the potentials of artistic expression. One of these came in 1889 when he was taking part in an anthropological expedition through the Vologda Region: Kandinsky entered a peasant hut there and felt at once that he had walked into a painting, so brightly decorated was the interior. He later recalled: "It was here that I learned not to look at the picture from the side, but to revolve in the picture myself, to live in it." Kandinsky's apprehension of this total art form remained with him throughout his life, and one of his recurrent concerns was with the notion of synthetic art, with the *Gesamtkunstwerk.*

Kandinsky's experience of the peasant hut emphasizes certain other features of his worldview and the intellectual climate in which he lived. It is not by chance that Kandinsky made his discovery of peasant art in the 1880s, the very decade when the Russian Neo-Nationalist movement, supported by Savva Mamontov and his Abramtsevo art colony, was gaining momentum. With their creative interest in Russian folklore, fairytales, and the traditional handicrafts, the Abramtsevo artists thought a great deal about the application of "art" to "life" and the idea of a universal style. There is a direct connection between this impulse and the general renaissance of the Russian decorative arts from the 1890s onwards, and, no doubt, this revival coupled with Munich *Jugendstil*, accounted for the essential ingredients in Kandinsky's early stylizations.

This reference to "total art" and the Russian decorative arts just before and after 1900 connects Kandinsky's painting to another sphere of inquiry—Russian and European Symbolism and its relation to Kandinsky's development of an abstract style of painting. Indeed, it is becoming increasingly clear that the pioneers of abstraction, such as Kupka, Malevich and Mondrian, started their careers as "Symbolists," and Kandinsky was no exception. Kandinsky was exposed to many of the social, esthetic and philosophical ideas of *fin de siècle* Russia and Germany and there are particular ones that he assimilated and reprocessed. For example, an important point for investigation is the comments on art by Andrei Bely, Nicholas Berdiaev and Dmitrii Merezhkovsky: when Bely wrote in 1907 that he feared Impressionism because it was too "subjectless" and too full of "individualization," he was anticipating what Kandinsky said about the dangers of mere decorativism in 1911 and 1912. Also in the Symbolist context, a common interest was in Theosophy, which also relates immediately to Kandinsky's entry into abstraction. The ideas of clairvoyance, spiritual purity, and prescience find clear reflections in Kandinsky's own theory and practice of ca. 1912, not least in "On the Spiritual in Art." When Kandinsky affirmed that life was like a triangle with the true artist at the apex and the vulgar masses at the base, when he emphasized the religious meaning of art, when he invoked the principle of music in his discussion of painting, he was repeating Theosophical lessons.

Like the Symbolists, Kandinsky felt that music undermined and destroyed the ritual and cult of physical objects. Confronted by the "new harmony" of contemporary art and philosophy, the object "diffused," just as it did amidst the exuberant, rhythmical ornamentation on the Vologdian artifacts that Kandinsky had seen in 1889. Like the Symbolists, too, Kandinsky gained access to this inner sound or music of the spheres at moments of supersensory and abnormal perception. This was one reason, therefore, why the conditions of intuition, spontaneity and inspiration were of vital importance to Kandinsky's artistic outlook.

Kandinsky propagated his views in many ways—through his paintings, his theories, his exhibitions and his groups, particularly through the Blaue Reiter group that he founded in Munich in 1911. The *Blaue Reiter Almanac*, in fact, is now considered a pioneer document in the history of 20th century art. As indices to subsequent developments in Expressionist and abstract art, the written contributions by Kandinsky and Franz Marc, in particular, present important ideas and tendencies manifest concurrently in Germany and Russia. Of course, the almanac reflects the editors' personal choices and the texts are diverse and sometimes contradictory in subject and tone. Mikhail Kuzmin's poem, "The Wreath of Spring", for example, affirms rather than undermines the material world, whereas the extract from Vasilii Rozanov's *Italian Impressions* is a curious echo of the God-seeking initiated by the poet and philosopher Vladimir Soloviev in the late 19th century. Still, the articles by Kandinsky's friend Nikolai Kulbin ("Free Music"), and colleague David Burliuk ("The 'Savages' of Russia") are of more immediate relevance to the evolution of the new painting, including Kandinsky's own series of abstract or abstracted *Improvisations* and *Compositions*.

Kandinsky's most important theoretical elucidation was his essay "On the Spiritual in Art" that first appeared in German in 1912 under the title *Über das Geistige in der Kunst. Inbesondere in der Malerei*. Kandinsky's thesis here was that art, specifically painting, was to be liberated from mere external, mechanical denotation and that the "inner, emotional necessity" was to be revealed through the appropriate choice of form. The new art would thus differ profoundly from the art of Realism and also from Impressionism which, according to Kandinsky, was only the "organic culmination of the naturalist trend in art." In the new art a "spiritual aroma" was to replace the "outward experience....devoid of soul." Just as scientific experiment had resulted in the splitting of the atom and the pulverization of the world of appearances (a moment of "deep shock" to Kandinsky), so, by the mid-1900s, artistic experiment was also revealing the inner sound. An immediate conclusion to this could have been the establishment of a self-sufficient kind of painting, but, actually, Kandinsky was cautious in his approach to this phase and even warned that "at the moment the artist cannot confine himself to abstract forms." For Kandinsky, especially in the early years of "abstraction," art was still a representational medium, a vehicle of communication and prophecy.

Although in infusing art with sacred powers Kandinsky was maintaining a long tradition in Russian art, his association with his artist colleagues in Moscow and St. Petersburg was an uneasy one. When he returned to Russia in 1914, he did not establish wide and fruitful connections with the avant-garde there. Certainly, he was active in education, administration and museum reform between 1918 and 1921 under the new government, but he never gained popularity in the Soviet Union. So when, towards the end of 1921, a time of great material hardship in Russia, Kandinsky received the offer of a post at the Bauhaus, he could have had no second thoughts. Kandinsky enjoyed a much greater patronage in Germany, at least until 1933 when he moved to Paris, but even so his art always remained closed to the masses, accessible only to the initiated. However, for Kandinsky this was the real sign of spiritual elevation: as he wrote in "On the Spiritual in Art":

It seems at times that the path has been lost forever and that it can never be followed again. At such moments a certain person always comes upon the scene. He is just like one of us, he looks the same as everyone else, but upon him has been bestowed the secret gift of "seeing." And in seeing, he reveals. There are times when he would refuse this noble gift, for it can become a cross to bear. But he does not have the power to do this. Surrounded by malice and derision, he drags behind him the heavy burden of mankind, ever forwards, ever upwards.

—John E. Bowlt

KARCEVSKIJ, Sergej. Russian philologist. Born in Tobolsk, Siberia, 28 August 1884; emigrated to Switzerland in 1907. Studied at the University of Geneva, Ph.D. 1907. Lecturer, University of Strasbourg, 1920-21; after 1927, Lecturer, and later Professor, University of Geneva. *Died 7 November 1955.*

PUBLICATIONS

Language

Iazyk, voina i revoliutsiia [Language, War, and Revolution]. Berlin, Russkoe Universal'noe Izdatel'stvo, 1923.
Russkii iazyk. Ch. 1: Grammatika [The Russian Language. Part 1: Grammar]. Prague, Plamja, 1925.
Système du verbe russe: Essai de linguistique synchronique. Prague, Plamja, 1927.
Povtoritel'nyi kurs russkogo iazyka [Recapitulatory Course of the Russian Language]. Moscow, Gosizdat, 1928.
Notes de morphologie russe. Geneva, Droz, 1948.
Manuel pratique et théoretique de russe. Geneva, Droz, 1956.
Language as Process: The Selected Writings of Sergej Karcevskij, edited and translated, with an introduction, by Joshua S. Mostow. Philadelphia, University of Pennsylvania Press, 1984.

*

Critical Studies: "Language as Process: Sergej Karcevskij's Semiotics of Language" by Wendy Steiner in *Sound, Sign and Meaning*, edited by Ladislav Matjeka, Ann Arbor, University of Michigan, 1978; "The Axes of Poetic Language" by Peter and Wendy Steiner in *Language, Literature and Meaning I: Problems of Literary Theory*, edited by John Odmark, Amsterdam, John Benjamins B.V., 1979.

*   *   *

At the conclusion of his 1955 obituary for Sergej Karcevskij in *Cahiers Ferdinand de Saussure*, Roman Jakobson wrote: "One may repeat about Karcevski what he himself said when analyzing the Russian perfective present: 'Pour lui, le passé et l'avenir se rejoignent facilement' ['For it/him, the past and future are easily joined']. And thus, when returning to his work, which at present belongs to the past, 'on empiète sur l'avenir' ['we encroach upon the future']." These words were perhaps more prophetic than Jakobson himself realized, for in the last few years Karcevskij's work has gained international attention and the value of his contributions to the field of semiotics and the philosophy of language has begun to be more fully appreciated.

Karcevskij's foremost contribution to semiotics was his concept of the "asymmetric dualism" of the sign. For his teacher, Saussure, a sharp division between synchronic and diachronic linguistics—that is, between the study of a language as it is properly spoken at any one time and the study of that language's historical evolution—precluded an explanation for change within the synchronic system—any change could only be catastrophic, as it would disrupt the mutually-defining relationships between the linguistic elements. It was this precise problem in Saussure's thinking that Karcevskij addressed. For Karcevskij, there is no absolute one-to-one correspondence between a signifier and a signified, for instance, between a word and the concept it designates. Every application of a word to reality requires an adjustment, a broadening, of that word to fit the unique historical circumstance. At the same time, several other words could be properly used instead of the one actually chosen. These two possibilities give rise to the concepts of homonymity and synonymity which "constitute the two most important relational coordinates of language because they are the most dynamic, flexible, and adequate to concrete reality." Every use of language is for Karcevskij to some extent metaphorical—an assertion on the speaker's part that the terms or construction used in a particular case are analogous to a previous series of applications. Based as this is within a synchronic, semiotic system, Karcevskij's model for communication is a balanced compromise between the linguistic theory of Vossler, where language is unbridled creativity, and the narrow Saussurian dogma of language as impervious to influence from individuals. Karcevskij believed that even individual speech-acts form some sort of system, and that they should not be ignored as accidental or fortuitous. Throughout his life, Karcevskij demonstrated the importance and primacy of asymmetric slippage, both in the evolution of language and in its daily usage, at all linguistic levels: morphological, lexical, syntactical, and pragmatic.

Within the philosophy of language, Karcevskij's other chief contribution was his conceptualization of dialogue as the basis of discourse. The ramification of this was his definition of the sentence as an intonational unit, having nothing to do with grammar. This he rigorously distinguished from, on the one hand, a predicate clause and, on the other, an utterance, in which a speaker unites both the rising tone of a question and the falling tone of a response in the intonational curve of one sentence. This was the work that in Karcevskij's own lifetime drew the greatest attention, and it provided Jan Mukarovský with a framework with which to distinguish prose from verse.

For current scholars, however, Karcevskij's work appears as a sound synthesis, *avant la lettre*, of several important theories of the day. His insistence on language as goal-directed, whether as a reasoned exchange of theses, an elicitation of a response, or a "duel" where a speaker attempts to impose his will on another, pre-dates the speech-act theories of Austin and Searle. His concept of sign usage as a compromise between an individual's consciousness and societal ideology and of dialogue as the basis of discourse is strikingly similar to Volosinov's theory of language, though Karcevskij applies this idea in a more concrete and semiotically rigorous fashion. Finally, his argument for the continual "slippage" of signs bears a marked similarity to Derrida's notion of the trace. As Jakobson indicated, all this was a result of Karcevskij's unremitting attention to the most dynamic aspects of language, whether verbs, derivation, syntagmatics, or discourse, and of his lifelong fascination with how man, at all levels of society, attempts to adapt the language bequeathed him to his own individual reality.

—Joshua S. Mostow

KAUTSKY, Karl (Johann). German political and social philosopher. Born in Prague, 16 October 1875. Educated at the Latin School and University of Vienna. Married Luise Tonsperger in 1890; 1 son. Joined the Austrian Social Democratic Party (SPD), 1875; worked under Eduard Bernstein on *Der Sozialdemokrat*, Zurich, 1880; Founder and Editor, *Die Neue Zeit*, 1883-1917; helped to draft the Erfurt Program of the German Social Democratic Party, 1891; broke with majority of Social Democrats and drafted founding statement of new pacifist Independent Social Democratic Party (USPD), 1917; edited the German Foreign Office archives, 1918-1919. *Died* (in Amsterdam) *17 October 1938*.

PUBLICATIONS

Politics, History and Philosophy

Der Einfluss der Volksvermehrung, auf den Fortschritt der Gesellschaft untersucht. Vienna, Bloch und Hasbach, 1880.
Karl Marx' ökonomische Lehren: Gemeinverständlich dargestellt und erläutert. Stuttgart, Dietz, 1887; as *The Economic Doctrines of Karl Marx*, London, Black, 1925.

Thomas More und seine Utopie. Stuttgart, Dietz, 1888; as *Thomas More and His Utopia*, London, Black, and New York, International Publishers, 1927.
Die Klassengegensätze von 1789: Zum hundertjährigen Gedenktag der grossen Revolution. Stuttgart, Dietz, 1889.
Der Arbeiterschutz, besonders die internationale Arbeiterschutzgesetzgebung und der Achtstundentag. Nuremberg, Wörlein, 1890.
Das Erfurter Programm in seinem grundsätzlichen Teil erläutert. Stuttgart, Dietz, 1892; as *The Class Struggle*, Chicago, Kerr, 1910.
Das Parlamentarismus, die Volksgesetzgebung und die Sozialdemokratie. Stuttgart, Dietz, 1893.
Die Vorläufer des neueren Sozialismus. Stuttgart, Dietz, 2 vols., 1895; vol. 2 as *Communism in Central Europe in the Time of the Reformation*, London, Fisher and Unwin, 1897.
Friedrich Engels: Sein Leben, sein Wirken, seine Schriften. Berlin, Vorwärts, 1895; as *Friedrich Engels: His Life, His Work and His Writings*, Chicago, Kerr, 1899.
Die Agrarfrage: Eine Übersicht über die Tendenzen der modernen Landwirtschaft und die Agrarpolitik der Sozialdemokratie. Stuttgart, Dietz, 1899.
Bernstein und das sozialdemokratische Programm: Eine Anti-Kritik. Stuttgart, Dietz, 1899.
Die soziale Revolution: Sozialreform und soziale Revolution, [and] Am Tage nach der Revolution. Berlin, Vorwärts, 2 vols., 1902; as *The Social Revolution, and On the Morrow of the Social Revolution*, London, The 20th Century Press, and Chicago, Kerr, 1903.
Ethik und materialische Geschichtsauffassung: Ein Versuch. Stuttgart, Dietz, 1906; as *Ethics and the Materialist Conception of History*, Chicago, Kerr, 1907.
Sozialismus und Kolonialpolitik. Berlin, Vorwärts, 1907.
Der Ursprung des Christentums: Eine historische Untersuchung. Stuttgart, Dietz, 1908; as *Foundations of Christianity*, New York, Boni and Liveright, 1917; London, Allen and Unwin, 1925.
Der Weg zur Macht: Politische Betrachtungen über das Hineinwachsen in die Revolution. Berlin, Vorwärts, 1909; as *The Road to Power*, Chicago, Progressive Woman Publishing Company, 1909.
Vermehrung und Entwicklung in Natur und Gesellschaft. Stuttgart, Dietz, 1910.
Der politische Massenstreik: Ein Beitrag zur Geschichte der Massenstreikdiskussionen innerhalb der deutschen Sozialdemokratie. Berlin, Vorwärts, 1914.
Die Dikatur des Proletariats. Vienna, Wiener Volksbuchhandlung, 1918; as *The Dictatorship of the Proletariat*, Manchester, The National Labour Press, 1919.
Sozialdemokratische Bemerkungen zur Übergangswirtschaft. Leipzig, Leipziger Buchdruckerei, 1918.
Terrorismus und Kommunismus: Ein Beitrag zur Naturgeschichte der Revolution. Berlin, Neues Vaterland, 1919; as *Terrorism and Communism: A Contribution to the Natural History of Revolution*, London, National Labour Press, 1921; as *Proletarian Dictatorship and Terrorism*, Detroit, Marxian Educational Society, 1921.
Von der Demokratie Staatssklaverei: Eine Auseinandersetzung mit Trotzki. Berlin, Freiheit, 1921.
Die proletarische Revolution und ihr Programm. Stuttgart, Dietz, 1922; as *The Labour Revolution*, London, Allen and Unwin, and New York, Dial Press, 1925.
Die materialistische Geschichtsauffassung. Berlin, Dietz, 2 vols., 1927.
Der Bolschewismus in der Sackgasse. Berlin, Dietz, 1930; as *Bolshevism at a Deadlock*, London, Allen and Unwin, 1931.
Krieg und Demokratie: Eine historische Untersuchung und Darstellung ihrer Wechselwirkungen in der Neuzeit. Berlin, Dietz, 1932.
Sozialisten und Krieg: Ein Beitrag zur Ideengeschichte des Sozialismus von den Hussiten bis zum Völkerbund. Prague,

Orbis, 1937.
Karl Kautsky, Selected Political Writings, edited by Patrick Goode. New York, St. Martin's Press, 1983.

Other

Aus der Frühzeit des Marxismus: Engels' Briefwechsel mit Kautsky. Prague, Orbis, 1935.
Erinnerungen und Erörterungen, edited by Benedikt Kautsky. The Hague, Mouton, 1960.

Editor, *Die deutschen Dokumente zum Kriegsausbruch.* Charlottenburg, Deutsche Verlagsgesellschaft für Politik und Geschichte, 1919; as *The Outbreak of the World War*, New York, Oxford University Press, 1924.

*

Bibliography: *Karl Kautskys literarisches Werk: Eine bibliographische Übersicht* by Werner Blumenberg, The Hague, Mouton, 1960.

Critical Studies: *Karl Kautsky 1854-1938: Marxism in the Classical Years* by Gary P. Steenson, Pittsburgh, University of Pittsburgh Press, 1978; *Karl Kautsky and the Socialist Revolution 1880-1938* by Massimo Salvadori, London, New Left Books, 1979.

*   *   *

Before the watershed of socialism in the First World War and the Russian Revolution, Karl Kautsky was, after Marx and Engels, the leading theorist of orthodox Marxism and the German Social Democratic Party (SPD). Through his editing of the SPD's *Die neue Zeit* from 1883 to 1917, works like *The Economic Doctrines of Karl Marx* (1887), and his drafting of the theoretical section of the SPD's *Das Erfurter Programm* in 1891, Kautsky summarized, explained and fashioned the abstract theories and obscure political ideas of Marx into the doctrine of a mass political party.

Kautsky repeated the basic tenets of Marxism: Capitalism produces but maldistributes great wealth leading to the concentration of capital in a few hands while the proletariat grows larger and more miserable. Eventually the proletariat, led by the socialist party, would overthrow the bourgeoisie and take over the means of production.

In several works Kautsky attempted to apply Marxian concepts to the past. In *Thomas More and His Utopia* (1888) he saw the first socialist work to predict the demise of capitalism, even as it was just emerging, and sketch a communistic society. In *Die Vorläufer des neueren Sozialismus* (1895) he portrayed religious heretics of the Middle Ages as heretical communists, and in *Foundations of Christianity* (1908) he identified the early faith as the doctrine of the urban poor and the early Church as instrumental in the transition from a slave to a feudal economy.

Kautsky's interpretation of the Marxian class struggle emphasized its political aspects. The goal of the workers' movement was a political revolution, and this had to precede the social revolution. His view was both deterministic—fully developed capitalism inevitably led to socialism—and voluntaristic—the political transformation prior to socialism could be prompted by acts of will by the workers.

On tactics Kautsky held that an independent working class party was necessary. This party could, at times, support liberal-bourgeois candidates in a temporary alliance against conservatives. Indeed, he stressed that traditional bourgeois freedoms and representative government were so important to the workers that the need to defend democracy could temporarily take precedence over the class struggle. And although he had written in *Die Klassengegensätze von 1789* (1889) that peasant uprisings and urban violence had been important in sustaining and promoting the French revolution, Kautsky did not believe that violence and bloodshed were necessary for the socialist revolution, only "vigorous action" on the part of the workers.

Given these ideas Kautsky's role in the Revisionist controversy which began in 1898 was surprising. Eduard Bernstein, Kautsky's friend until that time, pointed out that the objective conditions of capitalist development no longer supported many Marxist concepts, like the immiserization of the workers, and argued for the SPD to stop talking revolution and seek to accomplish its goals as a parliamentary, reformist party.

Although he had expressed comparable ideas, Kautsky objected to abandoning orthodox Marxian theory in favor of parliamentary or trade unionist activity. And he argued that while power might be achieved through democratic means in countries like England, it was not possible in Germany where there were no democratic classes besides the workers and no genuinely democratic institutions through which the SPD could function as a reformist party.

On the question of the general strike, which was raised by the Russian Revolution of 1905, Kautsky argued that it could be useful as a threat and as an organizational tool under firm party control. Though not enthusiastic about the general strike, he maintained that socialists could not renounce force.

The socialist debate on the new imperialism, following the appearance of J.A. Hobson's *Imperialism: A Study* (1902), showed Kautsky's weakening position on matters of theory. While most socialists came to accept the interpretation of Rudolf Hilferding, linking imperialism to finance capitalism, and Lenin's "highest stage of capitalism" theory, Kautsky held to the view that imperialism represented an alliance between commercial-industrial capitalism and the old land-holding aristocracy seeking the control of increasingly larger agrarian regions. Kautsky's position separated imperialism from capitalism and emphasized its political aspects.

In the First World War Kautsky was able to join in neither the regular SPD's support of the war nor the Spartacist left's call for revolution. He joined the left-moderate Independent SPD in support of a defensive war but not Germany's war aims, and as a result lost both influence and, in 1917, the editorship of *Die neue Zeit*.

Kautsky's reputation was further damaged by his dispute with the new socialist rulers of Russia in 1918. Two decades earlier, in the Revisionist controversy, he had argued that in Germany the proletarian revolution took precedence over democratic reform. But in his *Dictatorship of the Proletariat* (1918) Kautsky scolded the Bolsheviks for attempting to introduce socialism in a backward society by violent and undemocratic means. According to Kautsky, Marx's concept of the dictatorship of the proletariat described a political condition, not a form of government, for a class could rule but it could not govern. What the Bolsheviks had created was in reality the dictatorship of one faction of the workers over the others.

Kautsky charged that the Bolsheviks had allowed their revolutionary will to outstrip the objective conditions in Russia, a petit bourgeois state with an especially prominent peasantry. A peasant-worker alliance might hasten Russia's development from feudalism to capitalism, but only then would normal economic development lead to the struggle between the workers and the bourgeoisie. The peasantry itself, a reactionary force obsessed with private property, would always be destroyed as capitalism developed. Agrarian trade unions could be used for the transition from private property to collectivization, but land, the most important means of production, had to be held collectively in a socialist state.

Interest in Kautsky's work declined dramatically after the First World War. His interpretation of Marxism had always stressed its more deterministic and less violent implications, but the leadership of the socialist movement had been seized by those who followed its more voluntaristic and violent implications to their logical conclusion.

—Frank M. Baglione

KELSEN, Hans. American jurist and philosopher. Born in Prague, 11 October 1881; raised and educated in Vienna; emigrated to the United States, 1940: naturalized, 1945. Married Margarethe Bondi in 1912; 2 daughters. Professor, University of Vienna, 1919-30; Judge, Austrian Constitutional Court, 1921-30; Professor, University of Cologne, 1930-33, University of Geneva, 1933-40; and German University of Prague, 1936-37; Oliver Wendell Holmes Lecturer, Harvard Law School, Cambridge, Massachusetts, 1940-41; Guest Lecturer and Professor, 1942-45, Professor, 1945-52, and Professor Emeritus, 1952-73, University of California, Berkeley. Honorary Professor, University of Rio de Janeiro, National University of Mexico, and University of Vienna. Honorary doctorate: University of Vienna, 1966; Harvard University; University of Utrecht, Belgium; University of Chicago; National University of Mexico, Free University of Berlin, New School for Social Research, New York, University of Paris, and University of Salzburg. Member, American Academy of Arts and Sciences, Belgian Royal Academy of Science, Letters and the Arts, Austrian Academy of Sciences, Dutch Royal Academy of Sciences, Academy of Science, Turin, and Accademia Nazionale dei Lincei, Rome. Hans Kelsen Institute, Vienna, founded by Austrian Federal Government, 1972. *Died 19 April 1973.*

PUBLICATIONS

Law and Philosophy

Die Staatslehre des Dante Alighieri. Vienna and Liepzig, Deuticke, 1905.
Hauptprobleme der Staatsrechtslehre entwickelt aus der Lehre vom Rechtssatze. Tübingen, Mohr, 1911.
Über Grenzen zwischen juristischer und soziologischer Methode (lecture). Tübingen, Mohr, 1911.
Das Problem der Souveränität und die Theorie des Völkerrechts: Beitrag zu einer reinen Rechtslehre. Tübingen, Mohr, 1920.
Sozialismus und Staat: Eine Untersuchung der politischen Theorie des Marxismus. Leipzig, Hirschfeld, 1920; expanded edition, 1923.
Vom Wesen und Wert der Demokratie. Tübingen, Mohr, 1920; expanded edition, 1929.
Rechtswissenschaft und Recht: Erledigung eines Versuches zur Überwindung der "Rechtsdogmatik." Vienna and Leipzig, Deuticke, 1922.
Der soziologische und der juristische Staatsbegriff: Kritische Untersuchung des Verhältnisses von Staat und Recht. Tübingen, Mohr, 1922.
Österreichisches Staatsrecht: Ein Grundriss entwicklungsgeschichtlich dargestellt. Tübingen, Mohr, 1923.
Allgemeine Staatslehre. Berlin, Springer, 1925.
Das Problem des Parlamentarismus. Vienna, Braumüller, 1925.
Der Staat als Übermensch: Eine Erwiderung. Vienna, Springer, 1926.
Die philosophischen Grundlagen der Naturrechtslehre und des Rechtspositivismus. Charlottenburg, Heise, 1928; as "Natural Law Doctrine and Legal Positivism" in an appendix to *General Theory of Law and State*, 1945.
Rechtsgeschichte gegen Rechtsphilosophie? Eine Erwiderung. Vienna, Springer, 1928.
Der Staat als Integration: Eine prinzipielle Auseinandersetzung. Vienna, Springer, 1930.
Staatsform und Weltanschauung. Tübingen, Mohr, 1933.
Reine Rechtslehre: Einleitung in die Rechtswissenschaftliche Problematik. Leipzig and Vienna, Deuticke, 1934.
Legal Technique in International Law: A Textual Critique of the League Covenant. Geneva, Geneva Research Centre, 1939.
Vergeltung und Kausalität: Eine soziologische Untersuchung. The Hague, van Stockum, 1941; as *Society and Nature: A Sociological Inquiry*, Chicago, University of Chicago Press, 1943; London, Kegan Paul, 1946.

Law and Peace in International Relations. Cambridge, Massachusetts, Harvard University Press, 1942.
Peace Through Law. Chapel Hill, The University of North Carolina Press, 1944.
General Theory of Law and State. Cambridge, Massachusetts, Harvard University Press, 1945.
The Political Theory of Bolshevism: A Critical Analysis. Berkeley, University of California Press, 1948.
The Law of the United Nations: A Critical Analysis of Its Fundamental Problems. London, Stevens, and New York, Praeger, 1950; *Supplement: Recent Trends in the Law of the United Nations*, London, Stevens, and New York, Praeger, 1951.
Principles of International Law. New York, Rinehart, 1952; revised edition, edited by Robert U. Tucker, 1966.
The Communist Theory of Law. London, Stevens, and New York, Praeger, 1955.
Collective Security under International Law. Washington, D.C., U.S. Government Printing Office, 1957.
What Is Justice? Justice, Law and Politics in the Mirror of Science: Collected Essays. Berkeley, University of California Press, 1957.
Reine Rechtslehre, completely rewritten and expanded second edition, with an appendix "Das Problem der Gerechtigkeit." Vienna, Deuticke, 1960; as *Pure Theory of Law*, Berkeley, University of California Press, 1967.
Aufsätze zur Ideologiekritik, edited by Ernst Topitsch. Neuwied am Rhein, Luchterhand, 1964.
Demokratie und Sozialismus: Ausgewählte Aufsätze, edited by Norbert Leser. Vienna, Wiener Volksbuchhandlung, 1967.
Die Wiener rechtstheoretische Schule: Ausgewählte Schriften von Hans Kelsen, Adolf Merkl und Alfred Verdross, volumes 1-2, edited by Hans Klecatsky, René Marcic, and Herbert Schambeck. Vienna, Europa, 1968.
Essays in Legal and Moral Philosophy (selected essays translated from the German), edited by Ota Weinberger. Dordrecht and Boston, Reidel, 1973.
Allgemeine Theorie der Normen, edited by Kurt Ringhofer and Robert Walter. Vienna, Manz, 1979.
Rechtsnormen und logische Analyse: Ein Briefwechsel 1959 bis 1965 [Hans Kelsen-Ulrich Klug]. Vienna, Deuticke, 1981.

*

Critical Studies: *The Pure Theory of Law* by William Ebenstein, Madison, University of Wisconsin Press, 1945; *Hans Kelsen: Leben und Werk* by Rudolf A. Métall, Vienna, Deuticke, 1969 (contains biography and full bibliographies of primary and secondary material); *Festschrift für Hans Kelsen zum 90. Geburtstag*, edited by Adolf J. Merkl, René Marcic, Alfred Verdross, and Robert Walter, Vienna, Deuticke, 1971 (selected essays and supplement to Métall's bibliography); *A Tribute to Hans Kelsen*, special issue of the *California Law Review*, volume 59, 1971; *Der Aufbau der Rechtsordnung* by Robert Walter, Vienna, Manz, 2nd edition, 1974; *Die Reine Rechtslehre in wissenschaftlicher Diskussion* ("Schriftenreihe des Hans Kelsen-Instituts," volume 7), Vienna, Manz, 1982 (selected essays and a further supplement to Métall's bibliography).

*   *   *

Roscoe Pound, the American legal theorist and for many years Dean of the Harvard Law School, wrote in 1934 that Hans Kelsen was "unquestionably the leading jurist of the time," that his ideas were being "discussed in all languages," that his followers were "probably the most active group in contemporary jurisprudence." As the impact of Kelsen's Pure Theory of Law over the past fifty years has shown, Pound's confidence was not misplaced. Legal theorists in England, among them H.L.A. Hart and Joseph Raz, both philosophers in their own right, have been profoundly influenced by Kelsen's Pure Theory. Jurists in Latin

America and Japan have written as Kelsenites for a generation. In Poland, where analytical jurisprudence has been a lively and productive field since the last world war, the most substantial work reflects tenets of the Pure Theory. And in Austria, where Kelsen's position until 1930 was comparable to that of the Founding Fathers, John Marshall, and Oliver Wendell Holmes rolled up into one, legal philosophy and the theory of public law remain decidedly Kelsenian.

Kelsen conceives of the law as a norm or, more precisely, as a system of norms, a normative order. He puts the question: If one person directs another to do something, is the act of will expressed by the directive simply a demand—which could be made by anyone, including, say, a thief—or does it qualify as a legal norm? Kelsen's view is that the act, more precisely, its meaning, is properly regarded as a legal norm if the act has been authorized by a legal norm. The authorizing norm, in turn, is a legal norm because it has been authorized by a legal norm, and so on. The result is a chain of authorizing norms, terminating in what Kelsen calls the basic norm. Unlike the authorizing norms in the chain, each of which is the meaning of an act of will, Kelsen's basic norm is a presupposed norm, representing a cognitive element. An aggregate of norms is a normative order if the norms can all be traced to a single, basic norm.

Why does Kelsen's basic norm represent an element of cognition rather than another act of will? Would not the first constitutional norm insure the unity of the normative order just as well as the presupposed basic norm? To be sure, if the unity of the normative order were the only consideration, the basic norm would be dispensable. Kelsen's primary concern, however, lies elsewhere, with an explication of the normative character of the law apart from the natural law theory.

In the history of jurisprudence two legal philosophies have competed for favor: legal positivism and natural law. The first is known mainly for its separability thesis, the notion, roughly, that there is no noncontingent link between law and morality, that the validity of legal norms in no way turns on the satisfaction of conditions imposed by moral precepts. The second philosophy, natural law, rejects the separability thesis, affirming at some level of abstraction a noncontingent link between law and morality. Given this characterization of the competing philosophies, a certain assumption respecting their scope comes as no surprise— namely, that they are mutually exclusive and jointly exhaustive of the possibilities. In other words, no third type of philosophical theory is possible.

While defending the separability thesis, Kelsen rejects both traditional theories, arguing that the tacit assumption that they are together exhaustive is mistaken. As long as legal positivism and natural law theory are characterized in terms of an affirmation and a denial, respectively, of the separability thesis, these philosophies do indeed appear to be jointly exhaustive of the possibilities. But, as Kelsen correctly points out, traditional legal positivism is a reductionistic theory; the putatively normative material of the law—rights, obligations, powers—is thought to be reducible, without remainder, to concatenations of fact. And since reductionism is not entailed by the separability thesis, two legal philosophies are in fact possible apart from natural law theory: traditional or reductionistic legal positivism and normative or nonreductionistic legal positivism.

Kelsen's rejection of the assumption of exhaustability is his first step in making a case for the normative character of the law apart from natural law theory. A rejection, on the merits, of reductionistic legal positivism is his second. Consider, Kelsen says, a normative relation in the law, that represented by an obligation. If my claim that you are legally obligated to pay me $1,000 is reducible, say, to the chance that you will pay me (reducible, then, to a concatenation of fact), then the normative concepts of right, obligation, and the like simply vanish. They can be preserved, Kelsen argues, only by rejecting reductionism.

Having rejected traditional or reductionistic legal positivism, what sort of case does Kelsen make for the alternative, for normative legal positivism? The problem in its defense is that

there can be no appeal to a version of natural law theory, for that would entail the rejection of the separability thesis, which Kelsen accepts. The solution to the problem, Kelsen believes, lies with the presupposed basic norm.

The key to the basic norm is a version of the Kantian transcendental argument, which Kelsen adopts from the neo-Kantian philosopher Hermann Cohen. Following the form of the transcendental argument, one takes as one's starting point (i) some feature of experience that is claimed to be beyond question and then moves to (ii) some less obvious tenet without which the phenomenon at (i) would not be possible. Since the phenomenon at (i) is in fact the case, the tenet at (ii) must be the case. Applying the transcendental argument to the normative character of the law, it is the case that we distinguish between lawful and unlawful directives, that we interpret inter-personal relations normatively, as legal relations, that is, as legal rights, obligations, and powers. Kelsen argues that such distinctions presuppose a basic norm, an assumption to the effect that states of affairs so interpreted are recognized as normative relations. Without the basic norm, so-called normative relations in the law would be nothing but power relations, governed by the law of causation. But, since we do in fact interpret inter-personal relations normatively, it must be the case that the basic norm is presupposed.

The philosophical significance of the basic norm and of Kelsen's normative legal positivism generally is the prospect it offers of explicating the normative character of the law apart from natural law theory. In short, Kelsen's theory, an enduring contribution, has redrawn the boundaries of legal philosophy.

—Stanley L. Paulson

KENDREW, John (Cowdrey). British molecular biologist. Born in Oxford, 24 March 1917. Educated at the Dragon School, Oxford; Clifton College, Bristol; Trinity College, Cambridge, B.A. 1939, M.A. 1939, Ph.D. 1949. Worked with the Ministry of Aircraft Production, 1940-45; Fellow of Peterhouse, Cambridge, 1947-75; Department Chairman, Medical Research Council Laboratory for Molecular Biology, Cambridge, 1947-75; also, Reader, Davy-Faraday Laboratory, Royal Institution, London, 1954-68; Director General, European Molecular Biology Laboratory, 1975-82. Since 1982, President, St. John's College, Oxford. Herbert Spencer Lecturer, Oxford University, 1965; Crookshank Lecturer, Faculty of Radiologists, 1967; Procter Lecturer, International Society of Leather Chemists, 1969; Fison Memorial Lecturer, Guy's Hospital, London, 1971; Mgr. de Brún Lecturer, University of Galway, 1979; Saha Memorial Lecturer, University of Calcutta, 1980. Since 1959, Editor-in-Chief, *Journal of Molecular Biology*. Member, Council for Scientific Policy, 1965-72 (President, 1970-72); President, International Union for Pure and Applied Biophysics, 1969-72; Secretary-General, European Molecular Biology Conference, 1970-74; Chairman, Defence Scientific Advisory Council, 1971-74; President, British Association for the Advancement of Science, 1973-74. Secretary-General, International Council of Scientific Unions, 1974-80. Trustee, British Museum, 1974-79, and International Foundation for Science, 1975-78. Recipient: Nobel Prize for Chemistry, with Max Perutz, 1962; Royal Medal, Royal Society, London, 1965; Order of Madara Horseman, 1st Degree, Bulgaria, 1980. Honorary doctorate: Cambridge University, 1962; University of Reading, 1968; University of Keele, 1968. Fellow of the Royal Society. Corresponding Member, Heidelberg Academy of Sciences; Foreign Associate, U.S. National Academy of Sciences; Foreign Member, Bulgarian Academy of Science; Honorary Member, American Society of Biological Chemists; and Royal Irish Academy; Foreign Honorary Member, American Academy of Arts and Sciences; and the Leopoldina Academy. Honorary Fellow, Institute of

Biology, 1966; Weizmann Institute, 1970; Peterhouse, Cambridge, 1975. C.B.E. (Commander, Order of the British Empire), 1963; knighted, 1974. Address: President's Lodgings, St. John's College, Oxford OX1 3JP, England.

PUBLICATIONS

Molecular Biology

The Thread of Life: An Introduction to Molecular Biology. London, British Broadcasting Corporation, 1963; Cambridge, Massachusetts, Harvard University Press, 1966.

Other

Editor, with F.J.W. Roughton, *Haemoglobin: A Symposium Based on a Conference Held at Cambridge in June 1948 In Memory of Sir John Barcroft.* London, Butterworth, and New York, Interscience Publishers, 1949.

*   *   *

John Kendrew's research was strongly influenced by that of Max Perutz, whom he joined at the Cavendish Laboratory in 1946. Both were engaged in the analysis of the molecular architecture of proteins. The properties of these large, complex macromolecules depend on two distinct characteristics: the way in which amino acids are combined to make up the molecule and the three-dimensional, geometric form of the resulting polypeptide chain of amino acids formed. The first of these factors, called the primary structure of a protein, is subject to analysis by traditional chemical methods. Particular enzymes are available for cleaving the polypeptide chain at specific points. The repeated use of these enzymes in a carefully monitored, but very complex, sequence of reactions, permits the eventual determination of the amino acid sequence in the chain. The process is so laborious that only a small fraction of relatively simple proteins have so far yielded to this analysis.

The primary structure of a protein is not, of itself, sufficient to describe its behavior. Higher levels of structure, involving the coiling, folding, or twisting of the polypeptide chain, are also necessary if the protein is to function properly. This fact is demonstrated by the familiar process of denaturation, in which these higher levels of organization may be destroyed even though the primary structure is left unaltered. Denaturation renders the protein incapable of carrying out its normal functions, clear evidence of the essential role of higher (secondary, tertiary and quaternary) levels of structure.

It was to the determination of the geometric configuration of protein molecules that Perutz and Kendrew set themselves in the late 1940's. The task was an imposing one indeed. What was needed was a "picture" of the molecule that showed what shape the polypeptide chain assumed in any particular protein. There was, however, no very effective way of "photographing" large, complex molecules like proteins. More than thirty years earlier, the Braggs had shown that X-rays could be used to produce diffraction patterns ("shadow pictures") of simple molecules. The Bragg technique had been useful in determining the structures of crystals and other simple structures. But when used with larger organic molecules, the patterns produced were so complex and physically unclear that they could not be interpreted.

In 1953, Perutz showed that the substitution of a heavy metal atom, such as gold, in a protein molecule greatly enhanced the X-ray diffraction pattern obtained from that protein. Some parts of the molecule stood out more clearly, while others faded into the background. The method is known as isomorphous replacement.

Kendrew immediately applied this technique to the study of myoglobin from sperm whales. Thousands of exposures were required before a clear picture of the molecule evolved. By 1958,

Kendrew had recognized that the polypeptide chain of which the myoglobin molecule is composed is twisted around itself in a spiral shape known as an alpha helix. This structure had been predicted in 1951 by Pauling, Corey and Branson.

—David Newton

KEYNES, John Maynard.   British economist.   Born in Cambridge, 5 June 1883. Educated at Eton College, from 1897; King's College, Cambridge, from 1902, M.A. Married Lydia Lopokova in 1925. Served in India Office, British Government, 1906-08; Lecturer, 1908, Fellow, from 1909, and Bursar, from 1924, King's College. Member, Royal Commission on Indian Finance and Currency, 1913-14; Staff Member, 1915-17, Principal Clerk, 1917-19, Principal Representative at Peace Conference, 1919, and Representative to Supreme Allied Economic Council, 1919, British Treasury; Member, Committee on Finance and Industry, 1929-31, and Economic Advisory Council, 1930-39; Adviser to Chancellor of the Exchequer, from 1940. Editor, *Economic Journal*, 1911-44; Chairman, Board of *Nation* (later *New Statesman and Nation*). Member of the Board, Provincial Insurance Company, from 1923; Director, Bank of England, from 1941. President, Cambridge Union Society, 1905, and Royal Economic Society. Chairman, Arts Theatre Cambridge, and Committee for the Encouragement of Music and the Arts (later the Arts Council), from 1942. Trustee, National Gallery, from 1941. Honorary doctorate: Columbia University, New York, 1934; University of Manchester, 1942; University of Edinburgh, 1945; Sorbonne, Paris, 1946; Cambridge University, 1946. Fellow, British Academy, 1929, and Royal Society, 1946. Awarded Order of Leopold (Belgium), and Order of St. Sava, Fourth Class (Serbia). Created First Baron of Tilton in 1942. O.M. (Order of Merit), 1946. *Died* (at Tilton, Sussex), *21 April 1946.*

PUBLICATIONS

Economics

Indian Currency and Finance.   London, Macmillan, 1913; New York, B. Franklin, 1971.
The Economic Consequences of the Peace.   London, Macmillan, 1919; New York, Harcourt Brace, 1920; selection as *Mr. Lloyd George's General Election*, London, Liberal Publication Department, 1920.
A Treatise on Probability.   London, Macmillan, 1921; New York, Harper, 1962.
A Revision of the Treaty: Being a Sequel to The Economic Consequences of the Peace.   London, Macmillan, and New York, Harcourt Brace, 1922.
A Tract on Monetary Reform.   London, Macmillan, 1923; as *Monetary Reform*, New York, Harcourt Brace, 1924.
A Short View of Russia.   London, Leonard and Virginia Woolf, 1925.
The Economic Consequences of Mr. Churchill.   London, Leonard and Virginia Woolf, 1925.
The End of Laissez-Faire (lecture).   London, Leonard and Virginia Woolf, 1926.
Laissez-Faire and Communism.   New York, New Republic, 1926.
Can Lloyd George Do It? An Examination of the Liberal Pledge, with H.D. Henderson.   London, The Nation and Athenaeum, 1929.
A Treatise on Money.   London, Macmillan, and New York, Harcourt Brace, 2 vols., 1930.
Unemployment as a World Problem (lectures), edited by Quincy Wright.   Chicago, University of Chicago Press, 1931.

Essays in Persuasion. London, Macmillan, 1931; New York, Harcourt Brace, 1932.

The World's Economic Crisis and the Way of Escape, with others. New York, Century, 1932.

The Means to Prosperity. London, Macmillan, and New York, Harcourt Brace, 1933.

The General Theory of Employment, Interest and Money. London, Macmillan, and New York, Harcourt Brace, 1936.

How to Pay for the War: A Radical Plan for the Chancellor of the Exchequer. London, Macmillan, and New York, Harcourt Brace, 1940.

Speech by Lord Keynes on the International Monetary Fund Debate, House of Lords, May 23, 1944. New York, Economists' National Committee on Monetary Policy, 1944.

The Collected Writings of John Maynard Keynes, edited by Elizabeth Johnson and D.E. Moggridge. London, Macmillan, and New York, St. Martin's Press, 29 vols., 1971-81.

Other

Essays in Biography. London, Macmillan, and New York, Harcourt Brace, 1933; enlarged edition, edited by Geoffrey Keynes, London, Hart-Davis, and New York, Horizon Books, 1951.

Two Memoirs: Dr. Melchior, a Defeated Enemy, and My Early Beliefs. London, Hart-Davis, and New York, A.M. Kelley, 1949.

Editor, *Official Papers*, by Alfred Marshall. London, Macmillan, 1926.

Editor, with P. Sraffa, *An Abstract of a Treatise of Human Nature 1740*, by David Hume. Cambridge, Cambridge University Press, 1938.

*

Critical Studies: *The Keynesian Revolution* by Lawrence R. Klein, New York, Macmillan, 1947, London, Macmillan, 1949; *The Life of John Maynard Keynes* by R.F. Harrod, London, Macmillan, 1951; *Keynes: Aspects of the Man and His Work: The First Keynes Seminar Held at the University of Kent at Canterbury, 1972*, edited by D.E. Moggridge, London, Macmillan, 1974; *Essays on John Maynard Keynes*, edited by Milo Keynes, London and New York, Cambridge University Press, 1975; *John Maynard Keynes* by Hyman P. Minsky, New York, Columbia University Press, 1975; *Keynes and International Monetary Relations: The Second Keynes Seminar Held at the University of Kent at Canterbury*, edited by A.P. Thirlwall, London, Macmillan, 1976; *Keynes' Monetary Thought: A Study of Its Development* by Don Patinkin, Durham, North Carolina, Duke University Press, 1976; *Keynes* by D.E. Moggridge, London, Macmillan, 1976; *The Shadow of Keynes: Understanding Keynes, Cambridge, and Keynesian Economics* by Elizabeth S. Johnson and Harry S. Johnson, Chicago, University of Chicago Press, 1978; *Keynes and Laissez-Faire: The Third Keynes Seminar Held at the University of Kent at Canterbury, 1976*, edited by A.P. Thirlwall, London, Macmillan, 1978.

* * *

John Maynard Keynes is without doubt the most seminal economist of the twentieth century. However, he did not accomplish the Keynesian Revolution single-handedly; others made important coordinate empirical and analytical contributions, including the development of national income accounting. Nevertheless, his *General Theory of Employment, Interest, and Money* (1936) provided both a paradigmatic and theoretical breakthrough of the highest order.

Keynes is important for several reasons, each of them critical. Most important, he provided a theory of income determination. Indeed, prior to his epochal work, there was no field of macro-economics of which economists were clearly conscious. Economics was microeconomics—value theory or price theory—the theory of how markets allocate resources under conditions of scarcity. Although some economists investigated business cycles and other disturbances or perturbations, for most purposes the general level of income, output, and employment was assumed to be stable at the economy's full employment level. Accordingly, there was no felt need to develop a theory of the level of income determination, and no theory was developed, Say's Law's reasoning (that supply constituted its own demand) did provide some deductive if not also ideological comfort that there woud be equilibrium at full employment but its assumptions were increasingly questioned. Perhaps more important, the Great Depression (the latest and the worst episode of cyclicality) suggested that the presumption of full employment equilibrium was dubious and that disequilibrium and less-than-full-employment were more realistic descriptions. Keynes took the determination of the level of income, as a dependent variable requiring explanation, to be a central problem of economics, and he provided a general model of income determination. Henceforth, it would appear, macroeconomics would have to be analytically coordinate with microeconomics as the twin foci of technical economic theory.

Keynes's other important contributions are in one sense derivative of the first and in another supportive and elaborative of it. He reoriented economists' analysis of saving: Instead of greater saving being presumptively better than less saving for the larger investment it might support, Keynes showed that not only was investment financed by bank credit in advance of saving but that saving could be, *vis-a-vis* investment, excessive. In general, saving and investment were analytically different categories (one relating to the disposition of income and the other to the origin of income), and the level of actual equilibrium income depended upon their relationship. Far from saving being automatically equal to investment independent of income, if saving were greater than investment, income would fall and with it, oddly and unfortunately but no less truly, saving and probably investment as well.

Keynes also reoriented analysis with regard to the rate of interest. Instead of the interest rate automatically equating saving and investment (as under Say's Law), the interest rate had a much narrower, if still important, role. Keynes's theory of the interest rate has been reformulated and absorbed in a quite different theory, for most economists, but the interest rate is still subordinate to the other macroeconomic forces governing spending and thereby income (see below).

Keynes also altered seriously economists' views of price and wage rate changes as equilibrium-creating mechanisms. In addition to calling attention to the lack of realism in assuming price and wage flexibility, Keynes showed that a fall in the price level does not guarantee greater spending and thereby income; individuals may prefer to hold money balances, fearful of the future. Similarly, cutting wages would not necessarily engender greater employment if lowered wage incomes meant lowered effective demand, that is, less spending due to less income. Closely related to both of these points, Keynes's analysis led to a new view of unemployment. Instead of locating its cause in individual failures to perform adequately on the job or to accept lower wages, he saw unemployment as a systematic problem, the solution to which could not rest necessarily with individual adjustments.

Further, Keynes is important, for good or ill depending on one's point of view, in his effect on both the theory and practice of the economic role of government. His analysis provided a clearer understanding of the macroeconomic consequences of government taxing and spending and, further, of the possibilities of compensatory government policy to counter instability generated either in the private sector or by untoward past government policies. Moreover, the burden of these compensatory government policies was located in fiscal policy, quite a considerable revolution in itself.

The basic logic of Keynes's macroeconomics rests upon the complex relationships he envisioned between spending and income. Income, in the Keynesian system, is a product of the spending which gives rise to it; that is, income in the Gross National Product sense of new goods and services produced during a period (a year) is said to equal the spending which gave rise to it. Changes in spending, then, generate changes in income. But income is not necessarily equal to spending: While spending for year one will necessarily equal the income for year one that it produces, income for year one will not necessarily equal the spending which gives rise to the income for year two. The heart of Keynes's analysis thus becomes the spending decisions which make spending for year two less than or greater than the spending for year one, and thereby make year two's income less than or greater than year one's income. In this context, there is no guarantee, no mechanism, by which equilibrium income for any year will be at the full employment level; if spending is deficient, there will be less than full employment; if spending is excessive, there will be inflation. Keynes's analysis is thus one of gaps: gaps between income and spending and between actual and full employment.

The basic variables in Keynes's model consisted of the principal avenues which spending takes: consumption, investment and government spending (C + I + G) as well as exports, and the independent determinants which governed their respective levels or magnitudes. Consumption, to Keynes, was a function of the propensity to consume; investment, of the expected rate of profit being greater enough than the interest rate (a proxy for non-real investment uses of funds and their returns) which is itself a function of the quantity of money in the economy and the desire to hold money (liquidity preference); and government spending was a product of the concatenation of forces entering into the making of the annual budget. It will be noticed that the principal independent determinants—propensity to consume, expected rate of profit, and liquidity preference—are psychological and expectational in nature. They relate to Keynes's fundamental insight that decision making under uncertainty, in a world (of radical indeterminacy) which is made in part through individual and collective choice, precludes tight mechanistic and automatic determinations of income levels.

Keynes's analysis included a number of tools, not the least of which was the multiplier, which indicates that the ultimate total effect on income of a given initial change in a category of spending, for example, investment, likely will be greater than the initial change, in part because of the impact, through intermediate changes in income, on other spending variables, for example, consumption. The multiplier also is particularly useful in the fourth area of income determination through spending, namely, foreign trade.

Keynes came to this seminal contribution in a complex manner. During the 1920's he was both a leading orthodox economist and a leading critic of monetary and financial orthodoxy. He accepted the basically Marshallian microeconomics developed at Cambridge but he was part of a considerable intellectual ferment there and elsewhere involved in the rethinking of monetary theory. Keynes was a critic of the gold standard and its illusory automaticity and benevolence and of the idea that greater government spending *ipso facto* meant less private investment. Already by the late twenties he advocated public sector investment to combat unemployment, opposed deliberate deflationary policies, and advocated deliberate and continuous monetary management of the economy (as opposed, for example, to passively meeting the needs of trade).

Although his *Treatise on Money* (1930) seemed a landmark orthodox statement of monetary theory, one sees in it (and in even earlier work) breaks with traditional theorizing and understanding. He was not so preoccupied with inflation as *the* crucial problem. He questioned the automatic equality of savings and investment, held by Say's Law to provide stable full employment; increasingly, he recognized disequilibrium between savings and investment and saw it as fundamental to instability. He directed attention to the factors governing the holding and the spending of money, rather than to the quantity of money alone. The

innovations are halting and incomplete and the road is tortuous but eventually Keynes came to see that employment, output, and income were dependent variables of greater analytical importance than the relation between the quantity of money and the price level.

The precise meaning and significance of Keynes's *General Theory*, however, depends on the uses to which it is put. Consequently, later economists either have seen in the book quite different things to emphasize or have put its ideas to quite different uses, sometimes in quite different contexts. Some have refocused Keynes's technical analysis to place greater weight on the interest rate, particularly as the connection between the goods and money markets. Some have stressed structural factors in the macroeconomy having effects on income determination and price level behavior that have not been elicited in other approaches. Some have stressed the fiscal-policy implications of Keynes's spending analysis; other have restressed the role of monetary policy.

In sum, Keynes's contribution has been so immense and so complex that it can be interpreted in many ways, some of which are evidently incongruent with others. Accordingly, there has been both a (left-right) spectrum of interpretations of Keynes's *General Theory* and a conservative counter-revolution against his ideas. But it is indicative of the overriding importance of Keynes that the substance of both the spectrum and the counter-revolution is profoundly influenced by Keynes. Whether Keynes be seen as a conservative innovator seeking to strengthen the market economy or as a radical threat to the system, he has been *the* economist to be reckoned with.

—Warren J. Samuels

KLEIN, Lawrence R(obert). American economist. Born in Omaha, Nebraska, 14 September 1920. Educated at University of California, Berkeley, B.A. 1942; Massachusetts Institute of Technology, Cambridge, Ph.D. 1944; Lincoln College, Oxford, M.A. 1957. Married Sonia Adelson in 1947; 4 children. Member of the Faculty, University of Chicago, 1944-47; Research Associate, National Bureau of Economic Research, 1948-50; Member of the Faculty, University of Michigan, Ann Arbor, and Research Associate, Survey Research Center, 1949-54; at Oxford Institute of Statistics, 1954-58; Professor, 1958-64, University Professor from 1964, and Benjamin Franklin Professor from 1968, University of Pennsylvania, Philadelphia. Ford Visiting Professor, University of California, Berkeley, 1968. Visiting Professor, Osaka University, Japan, 1960; University of Colorado, Boulder, 1962; City University of New York, 1962-63; Hebrew University of Jerusalem, 1964; Princeton University, New Jersey, 1966; Institute for Advanced Studies, Vienna, 1970 and 1974; University of Copenhagen, 1974. Editor, 1959-65, and Associate Editor, from 1965, *International Econometric Review*; Member of the Editorial Board, *Empirical Economics*, from 1976. Consultant, Canadian Government, 1947; UNCTAD, 1966, 1967, 1975, 1977, and 1980; McMillan Company, 1965-74; E.I. du Pont de Nemours, 1966-68; State of New York, 1969; American Telephone and Telegraph, 1969; Federal Reserve Board, 1973; UNIDO, 1973-75; Congressional Budget Office, from 1977; Council of Economic Advisors, 1977-80. Chairman, Board of Trustees, 1969-80, and Professional Board, from 1980, Wharton Econometric Forecasting Associates. Principal Investigator, Econometric Project, Brookings Institution, 1963-72, and Project LINK, from 1968. President, Eastern Economic Society, 1974-76, and American Economics Society, 1977. Recipient: William P. Butler Award, New York Association of Business Economists, 1975; President's Medal, University of Pennsylvania, 1980; Nobel Prize for Economics, 1980. Honorary doctorate: Bonn University, Germany, 1974; University of Michigan, Ann Arbor, 1977; Widener College, Chester, Pennsylvania, 1977; University of Vienna, 1977; Villanova University, Pennsylvania, 1978; Free University of Brussels, 1979; University of Paris, 1979; University of Madrid, 1980. Member, National Academy of Sciences. Fellow, American Academy of Arts and Sciences; Association of Business Economists; Econometric Society; and Social Science Research Council. Address: University of Pennsylvania, Philadelphia, Pennsylvania, 19104, U.S.A.

PUBLICATIONS

Economics

The Keynesian Revolution. New York, Macmillan, 1947; London, Macmillan, 1949.

Economic Fluctuations in the United States, 1921-1941. New York, Wiley, 1950.

A Textbook of Econometrics. Evanston, Illinois, Row Peterson, 1953.

An Econometric Model of the United States, 1929-1952, with A.S. Goldberger. Amsterdam, North-Holland, 1955.

An Econometric Model of the United Kingdom, with others. Oxford, Blackwell, 1961.

An Introduction to Econometrics. Englewood Cliffs, New Jersey, Prentice Hall, 1962.

Stochastic Nonlinear Models, with R.S. Preston. Philadelphia, University of Pennsylvania, 1965.

The Wharton Econometric Forecasting Model, with Michael K. Evans. Philadelphia, University of Pennsylvania, 1967.

The Wharton Index of Capacity Utilization, with Robert Summers. Philadelphia, University of Pennsylvania, 1967.

An Essay on the Theory of Economic Prediction (lecture). Helsinki, Yrjö Jahnssonin Säätiö, 1968; Chicago, Markham, 1971.

Expanding the Benefits of Manpower Research. Tucson, University of Arizona, 1973.

Techniques of Model Building for Developing Economies, with Stefan Schleicher. Vienna, Institut f. Höhere Studien, 1975.

An Introduction to Econometric Forecasting and Forecasting Models, with Richard M. Young. Lexington, Massachusetts, Lexington Books, 1980.

Econometric Models as Guides for Decision-Making (lectures). New York, Free Press, 1981.

Other

Editor, *Contributions of Survey Methods to Economics,* by George Katona and others. New York, Columbia University Press, 1954.

Editor, with J. Duesenberry, G. Fromm and E. Kuh, *The Brookings Quarterly Econometric Model of the United States.* Chicago, Rand McNally, 1965.

Editor, *Readings in Business Cycles.* Homewood, Illinois, Irwin, 1965; London, Allen and Unwin, 1966.

Editor, *Economic Growth.* Homewood, Illinois, Irwin, 1968.

Compiler, with M.K. Evans and M. Hartley, *Econometric Gaming: A Kit for Computer Analysis of Macroeconomic Models.* New York, Macmillan, 1969.

Editor, with G. Fromm, *The Brookings Model: Perspective and Recent Developments.* Amsterdam, North-Holland, 1975.

Editor, with Edwin Burmeister, *Econometric Model Performance: Comparative Simulation Studies of the U.S. Economy.* Philadelphia, University of Pennsylvania Press, 1976.

Editor, with M. Nerlove and S.C. Tsiang, *Quantitative Economics and Development: Essays in Memory of Ta-chung Lui.* New York, Academic Press, 1980.

* * *

Lawrence R. Klein has made numerous contributions to eco-

nomics. Three of these contributions stand out for they helped shape the development of modern day economics. First, he popularized the construction and practical use of mathematical/statistical (econometric) models of the economy for which he received the Nobel Prize in Economics in 1980. Second, the success of his work on econometric models helped educate the economics profession to the potential benefits of quantitative economic methods and thereby served as a catalyst for the development of the quantitatively oriented subdiscipline of economics known as econometrics. Third, his work in the 1940's on Keynes' *General Theory* helped clarify the real revolutionary contribution of Keynes' seminal work.

Klein is most widely recognized for his work popularizing and constructing large scale econometric models of business fluctuations. His endeavors in this area are significant, not because he was the founding father of econometric modelling nor because he was the only economist of his time to work on models, but because it was he who successfully championed the practical and beneficial use of econometric models to a rather skeptical economics profession. This was no minor feat since most economists at that time were uneducated in statistical methods and the few who were generally believed practical problems of data availability, handling and computation made practical modelling infeasible. Despite these hurdles, Klein managed to convince people both in and out of the economics profession, through persistent modelling efforts unequaled by his contemporaries, that econometric models were feasible and useful. He did this in part by demonstrating the accuracy of forecasts from his own models, in particular through a forecast, which later proved accurate (to the chagrin of many economists who felt that it was a bad forecast), that the U.S. economy would not stagnate after World War II. Since the time of his early successes with models Klein has worked on numerous modelling projects, the best known being the Klein-Goldberger model, the Wharton model and Project Link, which is an attempt to integrate models of several economies to better understand and forecast international economic conditions. While some economists remain skeptical of econometric models, especially of forecasting with such models, the degree of skepticism in the 1980s pales in comparison to what it was forty years earlier. Indeed, econometric models have been so widely received that they are used in all sectors of the economy for forecasting economic conditions and assessing the effects of alternative government policies and programs. This popularity is in large part due to the persistent and pioneering efforts of Klein.

Less widely recognized, but perhaps just as important, is the impact that Klein's model building efforts had on the development of economics as a science. In the days before Klein and the other modern model builders, when modelling was generally considered impossible and/or impractical, economics was primarily a theoretical discipline. As Klein exploited new data sources and breakthroughs in computer technology to demonstrate the feasibility and usefulness of large scale empirical models, considerable attention turned to the general application of quantitative methods to solving other economic problems. This spillover of quantitative methods to other areas, occasioned in large part by Klein's successes with large models, has been so widespread that today quantitative work in economics is as or more prevalent than theoretical work and the subdiscipline of economics devoted to quantitative methods, known as econometrics, has grown considerably. It is worth noting that the way econometrics has grown has been influenced by Klein's work. An inspection of the leading econometrics texts (including Klein's own text) of the past three decades indicates that while the development of econometrics might have taken several different paths it took the path whose first step centered on the estimation of large econometric models using time series data. There is little doubt that this was in response to the demand for better models of the type popularized by Klein.

Klein's other great contribution was his interpretation of Keynes' *General Theory* in the 1940's. This work put him in a small group of individuals who attempted to make Keynes' *mag-*

num opus clear to the entire economics profession. This helped demonstrate the potential value of Keynesian economics and, therefore, contributed to the ultimate popularity of Keynesian economics.

Klein's overall contribution to economics might best be characterized as a publicist for existing, and a catalyst for further, work in economics, especially quantitative work. One thing is clear: economics today is what it is in no insignificant part because of the work of Lawrence Klein.

—James M. Johannes

KNIGHT, Frank H(yneman). American economist. Born in White Oak Township, Illinois, 7 November 1885. Studied at American University, Harriman, Tennessee, 1905-07; Milligan College, Tennessee, Ph.B. 1911; University of Tennessee, B.S., M.A. 1913; Cornell University, Ithaca, New York, Ph.D. 1916. Married Minerva O. Shelburne in 1911: 4 children; Ethel Verry in 1929: 2 children. Instructor, Cornell University, 1916-17; Instructor, 1917-19, Professor, 1927-46, Morton D. Hall Distinguished Service Professor, 1946-51, and Professor Emeritus, 1951-72, University of Chicago. Associate Professor, 1919-22 and Professor, 1922-28, University of Iowa, Iowa City. Fellow, Center for Behavioral Study, Palo Alto, California, 1957. President, American Economics Association, 1950. Recipient: Walker Medal, 1957. Honorary doctorate: Princeton University, New Jersey, 1946; Northwestern University, Evanston, Illinois, 1951; University of Glasgow, 1951; University of Rochester, New York, 1954; Columbia University, New York, 1954; University of Illinois, Champaign, 1967. Fellow, American Academy of Arts and Sciences. Member, Royal Economic Society, London, and Accademia Nazionale dei Lincei, Rome. *Died 15 April 1972.*

PUBLICATIONS

Economics

Risk, Uncertainty and Profit. Boston, Houghton Mifflin, 1921.
The Economic Organization. Chicago, University of Chicago Press, 1933.
The Ethics of Competition. New York and London, Harper, 1935.
The Economic Order and Religion, with Thornton W. Merriam. New York and London, Harper, 1945.
Freedom and Reform: Essays in Economics and Social Philosophy. New York and London, Harper, 1947.
Economic Freedom and Social Responsibility: An Essay in Economics and Ethics. Atlanta, Georgia, Emory University, 1952.
On the History and Method of Economics: Selected Essays. Chicago, University of Chicago Press, 1956.
Intelligence and Domestic Action (lecture). Cambridge, Massachusetts, Harvard University Press, 1960.

Other

Translator, *General Economic History* by Max Weber. New York, Greenberg, 1927.

*   *   *

Economic thought in the last 100 years can be divided into three overlapping and often contentious stages. First, the "marginal revolution," which contended that the costs and benefits associated with incremental changes were the motivating factors behind economic action, was codified by Alfred Marshall into neoclassical economic thought. Second, men such as Thorstein Veblen, Arthur Cecil Pigou, and John Maynard Keynes cast the laissez-faire prescriptions of neoclassical economics into doubt, and the "Keynesian revolution" provided the basis of public economic policy for most of the post-war period. However, during the late 1960s the neoclassical counterrevolution began to overtake the Keynesian revolution in economics. This counterrevolution had a long period of gestation and many skilled proponents, but the man probably most responsible for its philosophical underpinnings and ultimate success was Frank Knight.

Frank Knight's first and most important published work, *Risk, Uncertainty and Profit,* appeared in 1921, effectively answering the critics of the competitive, neoclassical framework, who claimed that open competition did not produce an efficient allocation of resources. The critics' arguments were supported by the observation that competition did not drive business profits to zero, as predicted by neoclassicists, and were bolstered by the claim that businessmen did not respond to consumers' desires. By introducing uncertainty into decision theory for the first time, Knight demonstrated that profits should exist in competitive equilibrium as payment to entrepreneurs. After production is sold and labor and capital expenses are paid, the residual revenue (profit) is the reward for organizing production and bearing uncertainty. Moreover, consumer sovereignty is maintained because revenues from production depend on satisfying consumers' desires. Those entrepreneurs who most closely anticipate uncertain consumer wishes will reap the greatest profit, while those who inefficiently organize resources to produce less desirable goods will experience losses.

Frank Knight was primarily a teacher and essayist who set straight the inconsistent and erroneous conclusions of others. He rehabilitated neoclassical economic thought, improved theory through such innovations as allowance for uncertainty, and provided the most complete outline and definition of the competitive framework. Besides developing a theory of profit and restoring the importance of consumer sovereignty, he rejuvenated laissez-faire principles as a means of efficient resource allocation, developed a theory of capital based on marginal productivity and opportunity cost, and clarified the assumptions behind "economic man," the stylized actor present in all economic models. In so doing, Knight became the most important contributor to the development of the now renowned "Chicago School" of economic thought. Moreover, contemporary economists working in such important areas as the impact of expectations on economic activity and the formulation of growth policies based on competitive principles bear a direct debt to Knight.

Early in his career, Knight recognized that many so-called failures of economic theory were in fact not failures of theory at all, but failures to account for certain costs and benefits that are generated as externalities of the actions of others. When these external costs and benefits are recognized and distributed, there is no conflict with principles of economic efficiency. When such externalities are not recognized, the loss of welfare results not from a failure of economic theory, but from a failure of social institutions accurately to assign property rights to the resources in question. It is in the area of externalities and property rights that Knight first integrated the implications of economic theory with the broader problems of social organization and development.

Frank Knight's work as a social and moral philosopher is less well known than his work as an economist, although both were equally important to Knight and his students. In the preface to the 1957 reprint of *Risk, Uncertainty and Profit,* he stated that "economics, in a practical reference, must be 'welfare' economics, and that most pointedly calls for cooperation between disciplines." He reaffirmed that economics "is by far the most scientific of the disciplines dealing with motivated human behavior, and the most usable in guiding social action," but emphasized that "abstractly rational economic principles are in fact much 'corrupted' in action by individuals and social interests...All this does not invalidate the economic laws, or destroy their usefulness; but it enormously complicates the interpretation and limits the application."

Frank Knight developed and refined a useful economic system on which much of modern economics is based. However, he cautioned that man's greatest problems are moral rather than economic. The implications of economic models must be interpreted in light of the social contracts that also govern human action, and the evolution of social institutions is inevitably a process of compromise. Knight concludes in his 1957 preface that "to act intelligently men must curb their romantic propensity to jump to conclusions on desirable changes and to 'do something.' Especially, they must learn to respect the most solid knowledge there is, the simple truisms of economics, while recognizing their limitations."

—Robert R. Davis

KOFFKA, Kurt. German psychologist. Born in Berlin, 18 March 1886; emigrated to the United States in 1928. Studied at the University of Edinburgh, 1903-04; University of Berlin, Ph.D. 1908; University of Würzburg, 1909-10. Married Elisabeth Ahlgrimm in 1923. Assistant, University of Würzburg, 1909-10, and University of Frankfurt, 1910-11; Lecturer, 1911-18, and Assistant Professor, 1918-27, University of Giessen; William Allan Neilson Research Professor, 1927-32, and Professor of Psychology, 1932-41, Smith College, Northampton, Massachusetts. Visiting Professor, Cornell University, Ithaca, New York, 1924-25; University of Wisconsin, Madison, 1926-27. Co-Founder of *Psychologische Forschung*, 1922 (Editor, 1922-35); Editor, *Smith College Studies in Psychology*. Died 22 November 1941.

PUBLICATIONS

Psychology

Experimentaluntersuchungen zur Lehre vom Rhythmus. Leipzig, 1908.
Zur Analyse der Vorstellungen und ihrer Gesetze: Eine experimentelle Untersuchung. Leipzig, Quelle und Meyer, 1912.
Die Grundlagen der psychischen Entwicklung. Osterwieck am Harz, A.W. Zickfeldt, 1921; as *The Growth of the Mind: An Introduction to Child Psychology*, London, Kegan Paul, and New York, Harcourt Brace, 1924.
On the Influence of Transformation and Contrast on Colour- and Brightness-Thresholds, with Alexander Mintz. Northampton, Massachusetts, Smith College, 1931.
Art: A Bryn Mawr Symposium, with others. Bryn Mawr, Pennsylvania, Bryn Mawr College, 1931.
Principles of Gestalt Psychology. London, Kegan Paul, and New York, Harcourt Brace, 1935.

*   *   *

Kurt Koffka was one of the three original Gestalt psychologists. He met the other two, Max Wertheimer and Wolfgang Köhler in 1910 when they all came to the Psychological Institute in Frankfurt am Main. The three collaborated closely; in fact, Koffka and Köhler were subjects in Wertheimer's experiments on the perception of movement. The 1912 publication on the results of the experiments officially launched Gestalt Psychology.

The ideas presented in Wertheimer's paper and developed in the many discussions of the three Gestalt psychologists needed to be tested, defended, and extended to new areas. Koffka went vigorously to work on all three tasks. In 1911, at the University of Giessen, he established a laboratory, of which he once remarked

to a friend: "Small as it is, it is my own. I made it and with me it got its tradition."

The first work to come out of Koffka's laboratory extended Wertheimer's work on the perception of movement. A notable example of this kind of research was Korte's; his laws formulated the intensity, space, and distance relations of visual objects needed to produce optimal phi phenomena. Gamma movement was also investigated; and soon Koffka and his students and collaborators were doing experimental work on other problems of visual perception: for example on color, brightness, and form perception, as well as on memory and thinking.

In the way of polemics, Koffka engaged in a discussion with V. Benussi, whose production theory (introduced by Meinong) was representative of those theories that Gestalt psychology was put forward to displace. Koffka's 1915 article, which is generally regarded as deriving as much from Wertheimer (who hesitated to write his ideas) as from Koffka, is the first formulation by a Gestalt psychologist of the new theory. It attacks the traditional atomism on the levels of phenomena, correlated stimuli, and psychophysical relationships, substituting molar concepts for them. Another example of a notable polemical article by Koffka is his response, in 1938, to a series of articles by William McDougall critical of Gestalt psychology. This paper—the very model of a polemical article—is not only a fair and friendly reply to McDougall's sometimes immoderate criticisms, but it is appreciative of McDougall's own contributions, and it advances the problems under consideration. It emphasizes one of the themes of Gestalt psychology, the way to avoid the pitfalls of both vitalism and mechanism.

Koffka's greatest achievements, however, lay in the extension of Gestalt ideas to new areas and in the systematization of Gestalt psychology. In two books he undertook these tasks. *The Growth of the Mind*, whose subject is developmental psychology, attempts, as the author puts it, "to give a new and wider application to certain principles of psychological theory and research which have recently been advanced under the name of the *Gestalt-Theorie*."

Principles of Gestalt Psychology (1935) is a still bolder attempt to systematize the findings and principles of Gestalt psychology and to extend this approach to new fields. Koffka includes strong chapters on perception, the major area of his own experimental contributions and the area of his greatest erudition. His question: "Why do things look as they do?" has been described as itself a brilliant achievement; it interested many psychologists in a question they had not known needed an answer. Another major clarification is Koffka's distinction between proximal and distal stimuli, which raises the neglected question of the nature of the stimulus. Beyond perception, the *Principles* attempts to bring the facts of learning and memory under the concept of Gestalt. The book includes a theory of the Ego and applies the Gestalt approach to social psychology and to personality. Its emphasis on value reflects a central concern of Gestalt psychology.

—Mary Henle

KÖHLER, Wolfgang. German psychologist. Born in Reval, Estonia, 21 June 1887; emigrated to the United States in 1935. Studied at the University of Tübingen, the University of Bonn, and at the University of Berlin, Ph.D. 1909. Assistant, Psychological Institute, Frankfurt, 1909-13; Director, Anthropoid Station, Prussian Royal Academy of Science, Tenerife, Canary Islands, 1913-20; Acting Director, 1920-22, and Director, 1923-35, Psychological Institute, and Professor, 1923-35, University of Berlin (resigned); Professor of Psychology and later Research Professor, Swarthmore College, Pennsylvania, 1935-58; Research Professor, Dartmouth College, Hanover, New Hampshire,

1958-67. Member, Institute for Advanced Study, Princeton, New Jersey, 1955-56. Visiting Professor, Clark University, Worcester, Massachusetts, 1925-26, and the University of Chicago, 1935. William James Lecturer, Harvard University, Cambridge, Massachusetts, 1934-35; Page-Barbour Lecturer, University of Virginia, Charlottesville, 1935; Gifford Lecturer, University of Edinburgh, 1958; Langfeld Lecturer, Princeton University, Princeton, New Jersey, 1966. Co-Founder, *Psychologische Forschung*. President, Deutsche Gesellschaft für Psychologie, and American Psychological Association, 1959. Recipient: Distinguished Science Contribution Award, American Psychological Association, 1956. Honorary doctorate: University of Chicago; University of Pennsylvania; Swarthmore College; Kenyon College, Gambier, Ohio; University of Freiburg; University of Münster; Uppsala University, Sweden. Member, National Academy of Sciences. Ehrenbürger, Free University of Berlin. *Died 11 June 1967.*

PUBLICATIONS

Psychology

Akustische Untersuchungen. Leipzig, Barth, 1909.

Optische Untersuchungen am Schimpansen und am Haushuhn. Berlin, Prussian Royal Academy of Science, 1915.

Intelligenzprüfungen an Anthropoiden. Berlin, Prussian Royal Academy of Science, 1917; expanded edition as *Intelligenzprüfungen an Menschenaffen*, Berlin, 1921; as *The Mentality of Apes*, London, Kegan Paul, 1924; New York, Harcourt Brace, 1925.

Nachweis einfacher Strukturfunktionen beim Schimpansen und bei Haushuhn; Über eine neue Methode zur Untersuchung des bunten Farbensystems. Berlin, Prussian Royal Academy of Science, 1918.

Die physischen Gestalten in Ruhe und in stationären Zustand: Eine naturphilosophische Untersuchung. Braunschweig, Vieweg, 1920.

Gestalt Psychology. New York, Liveright, 1929; London, Bell, 1930; enlarged edition as *Psychologische Probleme*, Berlin, Springer, 1933.

The Place of Value in a World of Facts. New York, Liveright, 1938.

Dynamics in Psychology. New York, Liveright, 1940.

The Task of Gestalt Psychology (lectures). Princeton, New Jersey, Princeton University Press, 1969.

The Selected Papers of Wolfgang Köhler, edited by Mary Henle. New York, Liveright, 1971 (contains a bibliography).

*

Critical Studies: *Gestalt Psychology: Its Nature and Significance* by David Katz, New York, Ronald Press, 1950; London, Methuen, 1951.

*   *   *

Wolfgang Köhler made important contributions in two areas of psychology. The first was in the area of learning theory with his studies at the Anthropoid Station on Tenerife. There he developed his theory of insight learning, studying the ability of apes to solve several types of problems. Köhler used five types of problems: 1) detour problems; 2) problems involving the use of available implements; 3) problems involving the making of implements; 4) building problems; and 5) problems involving imitation. Köhler found that the solving of most problems involved some trial and error behavior and some degree of insight (the ability to see the relationship between all parts of the problem). Köhler also found that different species of animals and different individuals within a species had different abilities to use insight in solving a problem.

The second area of work by Köhler involves the Gestalt theory of isomorphism and cortical brain fields. Most of his work was in the area of perception. Köhler hypothesized that electro-mechanical processes in the brain create fields in response to the observed image. Although it is impossible to prove this theory directly, Köhler has been able to demonstrate phenomena which support his theory, both by measuring brain activity and by using figural after-effects to demonstrate that some pathways in the brain have become saturated by overexposure to some visual stimulus.

His ideas on the subject were highlighted in a difficult but very significant book, which has yet to be translated into English, entitled *Die physischen Gestalten in Ruhe und in stationären Zustand: Eine naturphilosophische Untersuchung* (1920). In it he describes how the physical gestalt operates in chemistry, electricity, and biology, and then attempts to explain how these same gestalt fields that operate in the physical world can be shown to occur in brain functioning too. He continued in trying to elaborate further on this doctrine of isomorphism in much of his later work, emphasizing the similarity of the gestalt processes in psychological phenomena and the brain processes underlying the phenomena. Systematic developments of his gestalt position were reflected in such books as *Gestalt Psychology* (1929), *The Place of Value in a World of Facts* (1938), and *Dynamics in Psychology* (1940). He also published experimental material on his work in figure aftereffects which is a class of perceptual illusions stemming from his isomorphic theory.

During the early decades of this century the Gestalt psychologists were mistakenly referred to as "nativists" because they opposed the strong empirical approach of the behaviorists. In particular they were accused of believing that certain elements of the human organism, e.g. neural organization, could be explained in terms of inherited mechanisms. The nativists would claim that particular chromosomes cause the organism to exhibit certain histological structures because the entire organism is, in fact, a product of evolution.

This is not what the Gestalt psychologists said about evolution and in fact it is in total opposition to their position, which of course means that nativism can in no way be equated with Gestalt psychology. Köhler made this position very clear throughout his whole life. In his last book, published in 1950 and entitled *The Task of Gestalt Psychology* he states clearly that "Gestalt psychologists are not nativists." Although evolution can be pictured in terms of chance or variance there is another part which can only be thought of through principles of invariance. Because organisms develop from inorganic nature they must have common determinants which cannot contribute to evolution. Invariant dynamics does not allow the organism to acquire any new kind of action; constraints are the only contributions of evolution.

At his retirement "headquarters" of Dartmouth College, Köhler continued to write and conduct research while also spending several semesters teaching at several different universities throughout Europe.

—R.W. Rieber

———————

KORSCH, Karl. German political and social philosopher. Born in Toştedt, Lüneburger Heide, Germany, 15 August 1886. Studied at the universities of Munich, Geneva, and Jena, State Exam in Law, 1910, Promotion, 1911, Habilitation, 1919. Served briefly in the German Army, 1914: wounded 3 times as result of refusal to bear arms. Married Hedda Gagliardi in 1913. Assistant to E. Schuster, London, 1912; joined Fabian Nursery and Socialist Party of Germany (SPD), 1911; began intensive interest in Marxism, 1919; Contributor, *Praktischer Sozialismus*, 1919-21; joined independent Socialist Party (USPD) following split with SPD, 1919, and then the Communist Party (KPD), until expelled as result of bolshevization of international communist movement, 1926; active in Marxist politics, from 1920; Editor, KPD journal *Die Internationale*, 1924-25; participated in various Left-opposition political groups, from 1926; active in organizing resistance to Hitler, 1933; fled to England, 1933, and to the United States, 1936: unable to secure steady employment as a result of his politics. Privatdozent, 1920-23, and Professor of Law, Jena University, 1923-24: stripped of professorship, but regained it in 1925, although he did not resume teaching duties; barred from teaching by Nazi government, 1933; associated with the Institute for Social Research, New York, from 1936; Lecturer, State College of Washington, Pullman, 1942; Visiting Assistant Professor of Sociology, Tulane University, New Orleans, 1943-45. *Died* (in Belmont, Massachusetts) *21 October 1961.*

PUBLICATIONS

Collections

Gesamtausgabe, edited by Michael Buckmiller. Frankfurt, Europäische Verlagsanstalt, 1980-.

Political and Social Theory

Die Anwendung der Beweislastregeln im Zivilprozess und das qualifizierte Geständnis. Bonn, Marcus und Webers, 1911.
Was ist Sozialisierung? Hannover, Freies Deutschland Verlagsgesellschaft, 1919.
Quintessenz des Marxismus: Eine gemeinverständliche Darlegung. Berlin and Leipzig, Frankes, 1922.
Arbeitsrecht für Betriebsräte. Berlin and Leipzig, Frankes, 1922.
Kernpunkte der materialistischen Geschichtsauffassung: Eine quellenmässige Darstellung. Berlin, Frankes, 1922.
Marxismus und Philosophie. Leipzig, Hirschfeld, 1923; enlarged edition, with "Der gegenwärtige Stand des Problems 'Marxismus und Philosophie': Zugleich eine Antikritik," edited by E. Gerlach, Frankfurt, Europäische Verlagsanstalt, 1966; as *Marxism and Philosophy*, London, New Left Books, 1970; New York, Monthly Review Press, 1971.
Der Weg der Komintern: Diskussionsrede des Gen. Korsch auf der Konferenz der politischen Sekretäre und Redakteure der KPD. Berlin, KPD, 1926.
Um die Tariffähigkeit: Eine Untersuchung über die heutigen Entwicklungstendenzen der Gewerkschaftsbewegung. Berlin, Prager, 1928.
Die materialistische Geschichtsauffassung: Eine Auseinandersetzung mit Karl Kautsky. Leipzig, Hirschfeld, 1929.
Karl Marx (translated from German manuscript). London, Chapman and Hall, and New York, Wiley, 1938; revised edition, 1947.
Schriften zur Sozialisierung, edited by Erich Gerlach. Frankfurt, Europäischer Verlagsanstalt, 1969.
Three Essays on Marxism (translated from the German). London, Pluto, 1970; New York, Monthly Review Press, 1972.
Die materialistische Geschichtsauffassung und andere Schriften, edited by Erich Gerlach. Frankfurt, Europäischer Verlagsanstalt, 1971.
Kommentare zur deutschen "Revolution" und ihrer Niederlage. Giessen, Prolit-Buchvertrieb, 1972.
Revolutionärer Klassenkampf. Berlin, Kollektiv Verlag, 1972.
Zusammenbruchstheorie des Kapitalismus oder Revolutionäres Subjekt, with Paul Mattick and Antonie Pannekoek. Berlin, Kramer, 1973.
Politische Texte, edited by Erich Gerlach and Jürgen Seifert. Frankfurt, Europäischer Verlagsanstalt, 1974.
Gesammelte Aufsätze, edited by Erich Gerlach and Jürgen Seifert. Frankfurt, Europäischer Verlagsanstalt, 1974.

Karl Korsch: Revolutionary Theory (translations from the German), edited, with an introduction, by Douglas Kellner. Austin, University of Texas Press, 1977.

*

Bibliography: "Bibliographie der Schriften Karl Korschs" by Michael Buckmiller in *Über Karl Korsch*, edited by Claudio Pozzoli, Frankfurt, Fischer, 1973.

Critical Studies: *Karl Korsch: A Study in Western Marxism* by Patrick Goode, London, Macmillan, 1979.

*   *   *

Karl Korsch's contributions to contemporary social theory are somewhat difficult to appraise today. Korsch was neither as prolific a writer nor as profound a thinker as those other members of his generation of "Western Marxists" (i.e. Georg Lukács, Ernst Bloch, Walter Benjamin, or the Frankfurt School). He is not as consistent as some of the other theorists of the heroic age of Western Marxism and he underwent sharp and often surprising political and theoretical metamorphoses. Yet Korsch was one of the most solid Marxist theorists of his generation, as well as one of the most active and dedicated political militants. He was a clear and often provocative interpreter of Marx and made many contributions to Marxian theory and practice.

In retrospect, Korsch's chief contributions to contemporary social theory include his theory of the workers' councils as the authentic organ of socialist society; his critiques of Social Democratic revisionism and Leninism; his analysis of the crisis of Marxism; his theory of fascism and counterrevolution; his proposals for new working class political strategies and new models of socialism; his recognition of the so-called "Third World" as a likely site of the sort of revolutionary politics advocated by Marxists; and his interpretations of Marxism and meta-theoretical reflections on the mixture of science and dialectics, theory and practice, which in his view constitutes the specificity of the Marxian theory.

Korsch consistently argued that "socialization of the means of production" meant workers' control of labor and society. He advocated what he called "practical socialism" and believed that the workers' councils (i.e. what were called "soviets" in Russia and "Arbeiterräte" in Germany) were the institutional organ that made possible socialist democracy where the workers would really control production and their own lives. He criticized anarchists and syndicalists for their unrealistic neglect of the necessity to have a planned economy and criticized Social Democrats (and later Soviet Marxists) for putting too strong an emphasis on state planning and control and not enough emphasis on workers' democracy. The main contradiction of "socialist socialization," in his view, involved satisfying dual demands for nationalization of the means of production in a planned economy and the demand for workers' control in a socialist democracy. His writings in the early 1920's were concerned with solving what remains a central problem in the construction of socialism today.

Korsch generally took a "left communist" position criticizing more gradualist Social Democratic politics. Korsch argued against Bernstein's "evolutionary socialism" claiming that "true socialization requires a radical break with capitalism and change in direction." Korsch would never countenance any compromises with capitalism and sharply criticized Social Democratic reformism—especially Bernstein and Kautsky who were subject to Korschian polemics. Hence, for Korsch, there could be no genuine socialism without "the *complete* elimination of the private property owner from the social process of production."

Yet Korsch was also one of the first Marxian critics of Leninism and what he perceived as the distortions of genuinely Marxian socialism in the Soviet Union. He was one of the first intellectuals to be driven out of the Communist Party in Germany and in his last speech to the Communists as a party member he attacked the "degeneration" of revolutionary politics and harshly criticized Stalin's thesis of "socialism in one country" as a falsification of Marxian proletarian internationalism and an attempt by the Soviet leadership to put the interests of the Soviet state before all else.

After his expulsion from the communist movement, Korsch developed a critique of Marxism-Leninism and continually reflected on Marxism and the political movements which used Marxism as their ideology. In the late 1920's Korsch urged "breaking the umbilical cord" of Leninism which he came to perceive as a fetter on the working class movement and socialist politics. He also analyzed what he called "the crisis of Marxism" in the face of what he saw as the failure to realize genuinely Marxian socialism and the rise of "counterrevolutionary forces" in fascism, Stalinism and the Western democracies. Korsch sought new models of social change in the Spanish anarchist communes and in revolutionary struggles in the Third World after what he perceived as the failure of Marxian revolutionary movements in the West.

Despite his many critiques of various Marxists and the crisis of Marxism, Korsch continued to his death to identify himself as a Marxist. His book *Marxism and Philosophy* (1923) contains an original interpretation of the stages of development of the Marxian theory and is one of the first attempts to apply the theory of historical materialism to Marxism itself. His book *Karl Marx* (1938), written in exile from his native Germany, contains one of the clearest presentations of the Marxian theories of society, political economy and history. But some of his most interesting work is found in various articles which contain original and stimulating critiques of Marxism and a wealth of ideas on a variety of topics—which are collected in *Karl Korsch: Revolutionary Theory.* Korsch's strong activist tendencies were frustrated by the course of history, and his failure to develop a revolutionary version of Marxism for his time is bound up with the failure of the European and American working classes to develop successful socialist-revolutionary movements. Yet despite a string of defeats for the working class and revolutionary movements through which he lived, Karl Korsch continued to develop revolutionary theory and tried to reconstitute Marxism as a theory and practice of revolution for the contemporary era.

—Douglas Kellner

KRAMERS, H(endrik) A(nthony). Dutch physicist. Born in Rotterdam, 17 December 1894. Studied at the University of Leiden, M.A. 1916. Married; 4 children. Assistant, 1920-24, and Lecturer, 1924-26, Institute for Theoretical Physics, Copenhagen; Chair of Theoretical Physics, University of Utrecht, 1924-36; Professor, University of Leiden, 1934-52. Chairman, Scientific and Technological Committee, United Nations Atomic Energy Commission, 1946; President, International Union of Pure and Applied Physics, 1951. Honorary doctorate: University of Oslo; University of Lund, Sweden; Stockholm University; Sorbonne, Paris. *Died* (in Oegstgeest) *24 April 1952.*

PUBLICATIONS

Physics

Intensities of Spectral Lines: On the Application of the Quantum Theory to the Problem of the Relative Intensities of the Components of the Fine Structure and of the Stark Effect of the Lines of the Hydrogen Spectrum. Copenhagen, Höst, 1919.
Bohrs atomteori almenfattelig fremstillet, with Helge Holst. Copenhagen, Gyldendal, 1922; as *The Atom and the Bohr Theory of Its Structure: An Elementary Presentation,* London, Gyldendal, 1923.

Die Grundlagen der Quantentheorie [and] *Quantentheorie des Elektrons und der Strahlung.* Leipzig, Akademische Verlagsgesellschaft, 1938; as *Quantum Mechanics,* Amsterdam, North Holland, and New York, Interscience Publishers, 1957; abridged edition as *The Foundations of Quantum Theory,* 1957.
De bouw der atomen en moleculen [Atomic and Molecular Structure], with Helge Holst, edited by H.C. Brinkman. Amsterdam, D.B. Centen, 1949.
Collected Scientific Papers. Amsterdam, North Holland, 1956.

*

Critical Study: article by H.B.G. Casimir in *Dictionary of Scientific Biography,* New York, Scribners, 1973.

*   *   *

The contributions of H.A. Kramers (usually known as Hans by his friends and colleagues) to modern theoretical physics during his all-too-short lifetime were numerous and important. He was the author or co-author of sixty-six scientific articles and wrote as well many popular papers on scientific and related subjects. His 1938 textbook on quantum mechanics was very influential in twentieth-century higher education in physics.

Kramers' most significant contributions to physics probably were made during his stay with Niels Bohr in Copenhagen from 1916 to 1926. Here he used his outstanding mathematical ability in the application of Bohr's correspondence principle to the calculation of the polarization and relative intensities of the lines in the optical spectrum of hydrogen. This involved the evaluation of the harmonic oscillations into which the electron motions in the various energy stationary states of the atom can be resolved (1919). This was the basis of the dissertation he presented to the University of Leiden for his doctorate. In the same paper and in a subsequent one (1920), he calculated the effect on the fine structure of the spectral line of hydrogen of an external electric field (Stark effect) and found satisfactory agreement with experiment of the theoretical results in both papers.

Kramers wrote an elaborate 1923 article on the application of the Bohr theory to the most plausible model of the helium atom (the next simplest to that of hydrogen); through its inability to yield the correct experimental value for the ionization potential of helium it served to emphasize the essential difficulties involved in applying Bohr's quantum theory postulates to polyelectronic atoms. This encouraged the search for a more fundamental quantum mechanics. In 1924 Kramers collaborated with Bohr and John C. Slater in a paper introducing the concept of virtual oscillators as a way of describing the radiation corresponding to the energy transitions between stationary states in an atom. Though this paper did not achieve the hoped-for goal and one of its fundamental assumptions (that energy conservation in atomic phenomena is purely statistical in character) was shortly disproved by experiment, it proved to be an important milestone on the way to the development of the new quantum mechanics. Further progress in this direction was made by Kramers' attempts at a new quantum theory of the dispersion and scattering of light by atoms. In a notable paper (1925), co-authored by Werner Heisenberg, the problem of the scattering of radiation by an atom was studied. This included a prediction of the later-discovered Raman effect, in which the frequency and phase of the incident radiation is changed by the scattering process. This paper was also an immediate forerunner of Heisenberg's first article on his matrix theory of quantum mechanics.

After Kramers' return to the Netherlands in 1926, he worked on a great variety of theoretical problems in quantum mechanics. A notable example was his contribution to the development of the so-called W.K.B. (Wentzel, Kramers and Brillouin) method for securing approximate solutions of the Schrödinger wave equation for systems of one degree of freedom (1926). This served to stress the relation between quantum mechanics and classical mechanics in the light of Bohr's correspondence principle.

In the 1930's Kramers turned his attention to paramagnetism in crystals and to the theory of ferromagnetism. This was followed by important contributions to the kinetic theory of gases, in which Kramers introduced an improvement in the original theory of Maxwell by showing that when there is a gas concentration gradient near a wall of the containing vessel there must be a diffusion slip along the wall. This was successfully applied to diffusion through a capillary tube.

All Kramers' papers demonstrated an unusually competent grasp of powerful mathematical techniques, indicating that he was a talented applied mathematician as well as an outstanding theoretical physicist. His lectures were clear and graceful in delivery, as the present writer can testify, from a course he took under Kramers in Copenhagen in 1922-23 (in Danish!). Kramers had a flair for clearly elucidating difficult ideas. His (1922) book with Helge Holst: *Bohrs Atomteori* was a decided success in facilitating popular understanding of Bohr's fundamental ideas.

Kramer was also devoted to the extension of international cooperation in science, serving as chairman of an important committee of the United Nations Atomic Energy Commission (1946) and from 1946-1949 as President of the International Union of Pure and Applied Physics.

—R. Bruce Lindsay

KRAUS, Karl. Austrian journalist, poet and social critic. Born in Jicin, Bohemia, 28 April 1874. Attended classes at the University of Vienna, 1892-98. Contributed critiques and satirical sketches to the *Neue Freie Presse* and other Vienna papers and founded his own periodical, *Die Fackel*, in 1899 (Kraus wrote virtually all of the 922 issues by himself). Between 1892 and 1936 gave 700 public recitals in Vienna and other cities of his own works and the works of other writers. *Died* (in Vienna) *12 June 1936.*

PUBLICATIONS

Collections

Worte in Versen. Leipzig, Verlag der Schriften von Karl Kraus, 5 vols., 1916-20.
Worte in Versen. Vienna, Die Fackel, 4 vols., 1922-30.
Werke. Vols. 1-10, Munich, Kösel, 1952-61; vols. 11-14, Munich, Albert Langen-Georg Müller, 1962-67.
Die Fackel. Munich, Kösel, 37 vols., 1968.

Journalism, Poetry and Plays

Die demolirte Literatur. Vienna, Bauer, 1897.
Eine Krone für Zion. Vienna, Frisch, 1898.
Sittlichkeit und Kriminalität. Vienna, Rosner, 1908.
Sprüche und Widersprüche. Munich, Langen, 1909.
Heine und die Folgen. Munich, Langen, 1910.
Die chinesische Mauer. Munich, Langen, 1910.
Pro domo et mundo. Munich, Langen, 1912.
Weltgericht. Leipzig, Verlag der Schriften von Karl Kraus, 2 vols., 1919.
Ausgewählte Gedichte. Leipzig, Verlag der Schriften von Karl Kraus, 1920; selections as *Poems*, Boston, Four Seas, 1930.
Literatur oder Man wird doch da sehn. Vienna, Die Fackel, 1921.
Die letzten Tage der Menschheit. Vienna, Die Fackel, 1922; abridged version as *The Last Days of Mankind: A Tragedy in Five Acts*, New York, Ungar, 1974.
Untergang der Welt durch schwarze Magie. Vienna, Die Fackel, 1922.

Traumstück. Vienna, Die Fackel, 1923.
Wolkenkuckucksheim. Vienna, Die Fackel, 1923.
Traumtheater. Vienna, Die Fackel, 1923.
Epigramme. Vienna, Die Fackel, 1927.
Die Unüberwindlichen. Vienna, Die Fackel, 1928.
Literatur und Lüge. Vienna, Die Fackel, 1929.
Zeitstrophen. Vienna, Die Fackel, 1931.
Die Sprache, edited by Philipp Berger. Vienna, Die Fackel, 1937.
Half-Truths and One-and-a-Half-Truths: Selected Aphorisms, edited by Harry Zohn. Montreal, Engendra Press, 1976.
In These Great Times: A Karl Kraus Reader, edited by Harry Zohn. Montreal, Engendra Press, 1976.

Other

Briefe an Sidonie Nádherný von Borutin: 1913-1936. Munich, Kösel, 1974.

For a complete listing of Kraus' numerous adaptations and radio versions of works by Shakespeare, Nestroy, Offenbach and others, see Otto Kerry, *Karl-Kraus-Bibliographie*, Munich, Kösel, 1970.

*

Bibliography: *Karl-Kraus-Bibliographie mit einem Register der Aphorismen, Gedichte, Glossen und Satiren* by Otto Kerry, Munich, Kösel, 1970.

Critical Studies: *The Last Days of Mankind: Karl Kraus and His Vienna* by Frank Field, New York, St. Martin's Press, 1967; *Karl Kraus: A Viennese Critic of the Twentieth Century* by Wilma Iggers, The Hague, Nijhoff, 1967; *Karl Kraus* by Harry Zohn, New York, Twayne, 1971; *Karl Kraus und der Sozialismus: Eine politische Biographie* by Alfred Pfabigan, Vienna, Europaverlag, 1976; *Geist und Geschlecht: Karl Kraus und die Erotik der Wiener Moderne* by Nike Wagner, Frankfurt, Suhrkamp, 1982.

*   *   *

Karl Kraus, the vitriolic Viennese who haled the powerful and the pitiful alike before his tribunal of satire was a legend in his lifetime, adored or vilified by many of his contemporaries, and he still makes tempers run high almost five decades after he stopped writing.

Quotation is the hallmark of his satire, and in keeping with his conviction that what was most unspeakable about his age could be spoken only by the age itself, he set out to fashion the imperishable profile of his time from such perishable materials as newspaper reports. Kraus's monumental documentary drama *Die letzten Tage der Menschheit* (The Last Days of Mankind), written during World War I and as powerful a pacifistic statement as has ever been made, presents the "acoustical masks" of hundreds of characters in a sort of phonomontage as "a world literally talks its way to perdition" (Max Spalter). *Die Fackel* (The Torch), the journal that Kraus edited from 1899 to his death and wrote himself from 1911 on, contains most of his essays, poems, and plays. It is both an enormous pillory and a unique personal chronicle. Since Kraus's mode of thinking and writing was essentially theatrical, *Die Fackel* may be regarded as a world stage on which Kraus dramatized himself as well as his ethical, didactic, aesthetic, and, above all, satiric mission. His 700 public readings (of his own writings and those of others, including spellbinding one-man performances of Shakespeare plays, Nestroy comedies, and Offenbach operettas in his translation or adaptation) were an integral part of his creativity.

In 1919 Kraus indicated the compass of his themes as follows: "Sex and untruth, stupidity, abuses, cadences and clichés, printer's ink, technology, death, war and society, usury, politics, the insolence of office...art and nature, love and dreams." Kraus lived a life that oscillated between love and hate ("Hate must make a person productive; otherwise one might as well love"), and—like Sigmund Freud, whose teachings he opposed—he had a love-hate relationship with Vienna, the city in which he spent almost his entire life. He regarded Habsburg Austria in its dying decades as a "proving ground for world destruction," and his marked apocalyptic sense and stance as a "late" warner derive from his epoch's *Zeitgeist*: overripeness, transitoriness, inner insecurity, and disintegration.

The key to Kraus's work is his relationship to language. As Erich Heller put it, "Karl Kraus did not write 'in a language,' but through him the beauty, profundity, and accumulated moral experience of the German language assumed personal shape and became the crucial witness in the case this inspired prosecutor brought against his time." The man who once said "Word and substance—that is the only combination I have striven for in my life" saw an absolute congruity between word and world, language and life; the unworthiness of his "language-forsaken" age was for him defined by its treatment of language. Kraus never tired of emphasizing the connection between language and morality; for him language was the moral criterion and accreditation for a writer or speaker. J.P. Stern has described this equation of linguistic incompetence, obtuseness, or dishonesty with moral torpor or degeneracy as Kraus's "moral-linguistic imperative." To Kraus, language is the mother of thought, not its handmaiden. But despite the fact that Kraus raised language to an almost apocalyptic significance, he never developed a theory or philosophy of language, being essentially an unsystematic and anti-philosophical thinker. Yet the Vienna Circle of logical positivists and the group around Ludwig von Ficker's periodical *Der Brenner* (Innsbruck) were greatly interested in Kraus's view of language, and there are certain parallels between Kraus and Ludwig Wittgenstein—for example, their insight into the fundamental connection between, or even identity of, aesthetics and ethics. Wittgenstein learned from Kraus how to think in and through language, yet he thought *against* language—which, for him, was an obstacle to thought that had to be painstakingly surmounted—while Kraus fought *for* language, striving to keep it inviolate and mystically uncovering thought through it. He saw himself as being midway between *Ursprung* and *Untergang*, the origin or source of all things and the end of the world (or of the human spirit) as conjured up by his satiric vision, and he viewed language as the only means of going back to the origin—the origin that was forever the goal.

"My readers think that I write for the day because my writings are based on the day. So I shall have to wait until my writings are obsolete. Then they may acquire timeliness." This seemingly paradoxical *Spruch* (dictum) or *Widerspruch* (contradiction) is coming true, and now that the translation barrier has finally been broken, at least to a minor extent, and a representative sampling of Kraus's work is available in serviceable English translation, the universality and enduring significance of his writings are beginning to be appreciated.

—Harry Zohn

KREBS, Hans (Adolf). British biochemist. Born in Hildesheim, Germany, 25 August 1900; emigrated to England in 1933; later naturalized. Studied at the University of Göttingen; University of Freiburg; University of Munich; University of Berlin; University of Hamburg, M.D. 1925; Cambridge University, M.A. 1934. Married Margaret Cicely Fieldhouse in 1938; 3 children. Assistant to O.H. Warburg, Kaiser Wilhelm Institute of Biology, Berlin, 1926-30; Instructor in Medicine, University of Freiburg, 1932; Rockefeller Research Student, 1933-34, and Demonstrator in Biochemistry, 1934-35, Cambridge University;

Lecturer in Pharmacology, 1935-38, and in Biochemistry, 1938-45, University of Sheffield; Professor, 1945-54, and Whitley Professor of Biochemistry and Fellow of Trinity College, 1954-67, Oxford University. Since 1967, Research Scientist in the Nuffield Department of Clinical Medicine, Radcliffe Infirmary and Supernumerary Fellow of St. Cross College, Oxford, and Visiting Professor of Biochemistry, Royal Free Hospital School of Medicine. Recipient: Nobel Prize for Medicine and Physiology, with F.A. Lipmann, 1953; Royal Medal, Royal Society, London, 1954; Gold Medal of the Netherlands Society for Physics, Medicine, and Surgery, 1958; Copley Medal, Royal Society, 1961; Gold Medal, Royal Society of Medicine, London, 1965. Honorary doctorate: University of Chicago; University of Freiburg; University of Glasgow; University of Paris; University of Sheffield; University of London; Humboldt University, Berlin; University of Jerusalem; University of Leicester; University of Leeds; University of Granada and University of Valencia, Spain; University of Pennsylvania, Philadelphia; University of Wales; University of Bordeaux; University of Bristol; University of Hannover; Cambridge University; Indiana University, Bloomington; University of Göttingen. Foreign Associate, U.S. National Academy of Sciences; Foreign Member, Académie Nationale de Médecine, Paris; Honorary Member, Belgium Royal Academy of Science; American Association of Physicians; German Institute of Medicine; and Société de Biologie, Paris, 1973. Honorary Fellow, National Institute of Sciences, India; and Weizmann Institute of Science. Knighted, 1958. Address: Nuffield Department of Clinical Medicine, Radcliffe Infirmary, Oxford, England.

PUBLICATIONS

Biochemistry

The Advent of Biochemistry (lecture).   Sheffield, University of Sheffield, 1946.
Energy Transformations in Living Matter: A Survey, with H.L. Kornberg.   Berlin and New York, Springer, 1957.

Other

Otto Warburg: Zellphysiologie, Biochemiker, Mediziner, 1883-1970. Stuttgart, Wissenschaftliche Verlagsgesellschaft, 1979.

Editor, with others, *The Creative Process in Science and Medicine.* New York, American Elsevier, 1975.

*   *   *

Two of the most fundamental questions in biochemistry are the following: (1) How do cells produce energy? and (2) How do cells get rid of potentially toxic waste products? Hans Krebs made major contributions to the solution of both problems; his work on the former earned him the Nobel Prize in 1953.

The problem of amino acid catabolism attracted Krebs' attention first, in research that began in the early 1930's. Amino acids are nitrogen-containing compounds from which proteins are built. The degradation of proteins in cells produces amino acids which must, in turn, be reduced to even simpler forms for excretion from the body. The removal of nitrogen in amino acids constitutes a significant problem for cells since most nitrogen compounds are highly toxic. Ammonia, one of the simplest nitrogen compounds and a logical waste product of cell catabolism, is toxic in very small concentrations.

Since the early 1900's, biochemists had recognized that cells solve the problem of nitrogen elimination by converting amino acids to urea, a relatively harmless derivative of ammonia. The mechanism by which the transformation takes place, however, was not understood. And it was this question to which Krebs turned his attention after leaving Warburg's laboratory in 1930.

Krebs' approach was to introduce various amino acids into

living liver tissue and measure the production of urea. He found that in nearly all cases, the amino acid studied was converted quantitatively into urea. The two striking exceptions were arginine and ornithine, both of which produced much larger yields of urea than would have been predicted stoichiometrically. From this, Krebs concluded that arginine and ornithine played a special role in amino acid metabolism and that the former probably played a catalytic role in this conversion.

In 1932, he proposed a complete mechanism for the catabolism of any amino acid. The process is a cyclic one in which ammonia, carbon dioxide, water, and phosphate combine to form a compound called carbamoyl phosphate, which reacts with a molecule or ornithine. This complex is converted to a second amino acid, citruline, and eventually to arginine. When the arginine molecule cleaves, a molecule of urea and a molecule of ornithine are formed. The ornithine is then available to repeat the cycle with a new molecule of carbamoyl phosphate.

Krebs turned his efforts next to an even more complex biochemical riddle: How do cells extract the energy stored in the chemical bonds in glucose during the process of metabolism? Elements in the solution of that question had already been explicated by a variety of researchers. Embden and Meyerhof, for example, had shown in the 1910's that glycogen, a polymeric form of glucose, was converted to lactic acid in muscle tissue. The details of this process were elucidated by Gerty and Carl Cori two decades later. The series of steps by which this anaerobic metabolic process occurs is now referred to as the Embden-Meyerhof pathway, or glycolysis. The pathway is a relatively inefficient method of extracting energy from carbohydrates, and is used only by simpler organisms and in muscle cells under special circumstances. As Krebs later showed, however, it constitutes the first stages in the more efficient aerobic process by which other cells obtain their energy.

The details of the far more complex aerobic process were also studied in a number of laboratories. Albert von Szent-Györgyi, Martius and Knoop, and Lipmann all demonstrated the relationships among a number of carboxylic acids which had been found in cells. By 1940, Krebs had been able to show how an intermediary product of the Embden-Meyerhof pathway (later identified as acetyl coenzyme A) was the precursor of a cyclic series of reactions involving these same carboxylic acids. The key intermediary in the intraconversion of these acids was citric acid. Acetyl coenzyme A, produced during glycolysis, reacts with a four carbon compound, oxaloacetic acid, to yield the six carbon citric acid. The citric acid is then transformed in a series of reactions to other six, five, and four carbon carboxylic acids. Two molecules of carbon dioxide, the gaseous waste product of cell metabolism, are released in the series. Hydrogen atoms are also removed from certain acid molecules and are transferred to another complex series of reactions known as the electron transport chain. There they combine with molecular oxygen to produce water and more energy. At the conclusion of the citric acid transformations, oxaloacetic acid is regenerated and the cycle is ready to be repeated with the introduction of another molecule of acetyl coenzyme A.

The cycle sequence of reactions outlined here is now referred to as the Krebs cycle (in honor of its founder), the citric acid cycle (because of the special role of that compound), or the tricarboxylic acid cycle.

—David Newton

KROEBER, Alfred L(ouis). American anthropologist. Born in Hoboken, New Jersey, 11 June 1876. Studied at Columbia University, New York, M.A. in English 1897, Ph.D. in Anthropology (under Franz Boas) 1901. Married Henrietta Rothschild in 1906 (died, 1913); Theodora Kracaw Brown in 1926; 4 children. Conducted anthropological expeditions, 1899-1901, in New Mexico, 1915-20, in Mexico, 1924 and 1930, and in Peru, 1925, 1926 and 1942; ethnological exploration of California, from 1900. Instructor in Anthropology (first member of department), 1901-06, Assistant Professor, 1906-11, Associate Professor, 1911-19, and Professor, 1919 until his retirement, 1946, University of California at Berkley; also, Curator, 1908-25, and Director, 1925-46, Anthropological Museum, University of California at Berkeley. Curator of Anthropology, 1900, and 1903-11, California Academy of Sciences; Research Associate, Museum of Natural History, Chicago, from 1925. Visiting Professor, Harvard University, Cambridge, Massachusetts, 1947-48; Columbia University, New York, 1948-52; Brandeis University, Waltham, Massachusetts, 1954; and Yale University, New Haven, Connecticut, 1958; Fellow, Center for Advanced Study in the Behavioral Sciences, Stanford, California, 1955-56. President, American Folklore Society, 1906; Founder and President, American Anthropological Association, 1917; President, Linguistic Society of America, 1940. Recipient: Huxley Medal, Royal Anthropological Institute, London, 1945; Viking Medal, 1946. Sc.D.: Yale University, 1946; LL.D.: University of California at Berkeley, 1951; D.H.L.: Harvard University, 1952; Columbia University, 1953. *Died* (in Berkeley, California) 5 October 1960.

PUBLICATIONS

Anthropology

Sourcebook in Anthropology, with Thomas T. Waterman. Berkeley, University of California Press, 1920; revised edition, New York, Harcourt Brace, 1931.
Three Essays on the Antiquity and Races of Man. Berkeley, University of California Press, 1920.
Anthropology. New York, Harcourt Brace, 1923; with supplement for 1923-33, 1933; revised edition, 1948.
Handbook of the Indians of California. Washington, D.C., Bureau of American Ethnology, 1925.
Cultural and Natural Areas of Native North America. Berkeley, University of California Press, 1939.
Configurations of Culture Growth. Berkeley, University of California Press, 1944.
Peruvian Archaeology in 1942. New York, Viking Fund, 1944.
The Ancient "oikoumene" as an Historic Culture Aggregate (Huxley Memorial Lecture for 1945). London, Royal Anthropological Institute, 1946.
The Nature of Culture. Chicago, University of Chicago Press, 1952.
Style and Civilization. Ithaca, New York, Cornell University Press, 1957.

*

Bibliography: "A Bibliography of the Publications of Alfred Louis Kroeber" in *American Anthropologist* (Washington, D.C.), vol. 63, 1961.

Critical Studies: *Alfred Kroeber: A Personal Configuration* by Theodora Kroeber, Berkeley, University of California Press, 1970; *Alfred Kroeber* by Julian Haynes Steward, New York, Columbia University Press, 1973.

*   *   *

Alfred L. Kroeber was a leading figure in the history of the Department of Anthropology at the University of California at Berkeley and in California ethnology, and he was a principal formulator of a set of ideas that characterized American cultural anthropology in the middle part of this century and distinguished it both from the earlier ethnological traditions in North

America and from British and continental social anthropology and sociology.

Kroeber's reputation rests on several hundred concrete studies of diverse topics in American Indian ethnography, mainly California ethnography, and also on a large number of short critical articles on theoretical topics or popular ideas that exhibit a very broad view of anthropology and anthropological predispositions in relation to ideas anthropologists opposed.

By the 1950's Kroeber had come to be very widely accepted as representing the broad mainstream of American anthropology that had developed continuously out of the work of Franz Boas, and this is precisely what has made it difficult for recent commentators to characterize his views. In fact, Kroeber agreed with Boas more in what they opposed than in what they proposed. He was not a "Boasian" either in his own view or Boas's.

Kroeber's most distinctive theoretical argument was his advocacy of "history" rather than "science," a paradoxical position in view of the strong proclivity of the vast majority of anthropologists to see anthropology as a "natural science" of some sort, and if anything to see history as particularistic and unscientific. Yet, as in several other cases, Kroeber's oddness was oddness mainly in his language.

Kroeber's basic assumptions were those of the American diffusionists associated with Clark Wissler and, later, Robert Lowie, also a former student of Boas and his long-term colleague at Berkeley. He shared the diffusionist's concern with "cultures" as entities that occupied geographical space, rather than with "culture" as a process of development. As a corollary, he agreed with the diffusionists (among others) that culture was unique and could not be explained by reducing it to anything else, such as race or individual psychology. Only culture could explain culture. Like the other diffusionists, Kroeber saw "culture areas" as having a specific type of organization: a central "culture climax" where the characteristic traits were most fully developed and peripheries where they were more attenuated until the characteristic features of one area began to blend into the characteristic features of the next. For the American diffusionists, these culture areas were generally the areas occupied by Indian tribal/ linguistic groups just before "contact," and were hence reconstructions. Kroeber had begun using this idea 1904. His most substantial work was a comprehensive mapping of the *Cultural and Natural Areas of Native North America* (1939), delineating six major American Indian cultural/linguistic areas. It remains the most extensive and systematic application of the culture area concept.

The diffusionist assumptions made it necessary to identify cultural "traits," and especially those traits which were the "basic units" of culture. In this context Kroeber and Lowie instituted the massive "culture element survey" at Berkeley, wherein literally dozens of doctoral students in the Department of Anthropology went out with a fixed list of "culture elements" and noted whether any given culture either had or did not have each item. The volumes of the survey became a fixture of anthropological libraries, but they never proved very useful, even in Kroeber's view.

The second major problem of diffusionist theory was to show how the traits managed to form into cultural wholes. This was broken into two sub-problems: movement and combination. The explanation of movement was "diffusion," a term deliberately borrowed from Chemistry. The suggestion was that traits simply spread over time from areas of high concentration to areas of low concentration, like molecules in chemical concentrations. All the diffusionists used the metaphor, but none actually defended it.

The main problem was considered to be that of integration of traits into "cultural wholes." Why, given diffusion, was there one and only one kinship system in a tribal community between two tribal groups each of whom had two very different kinds of kinship systems? The main answer, barring recourse to human psychology, was the principle of the "limitation of possibilities"—that there were, somehow, just a limited number of ways

cultural traits could combine. Kroeber sometimes called this "the principle of order." Kroeber's important 1909 treatment of kinship classifications as reflecting everywhere a limited number of linguistic "discernments" that were simply grouped or divided in different ways supported this idea, although the principle wasn't specifically named. The paper is generally cited as the starting point of modern componential analysis.

The limitation of possibilities was closely related, for Kroeber, to the idea of "style." This he explored in several efforts to show first that style was a researchable topic and secondly (in a widely cited 1919 paper "On the Principle of Order in Civilization as Exemplified by Changes of Fashion," describing style changes in women's clothing) that styles were themselves based on simple and constant elements combined in accordance with definite cyclical trends that the stylists themselves were not aware of.

The diffusionist's predilection for mechanistic explanations of culture, molding the idea that only culture explains culture into a zealous cultural determinism, reflected the epistemological conviction that one simply could not have a science that recognized free will in its subject matter—a position in radical opposition to Boas' tradition whose program was the compilation of a scientific account of the development of culture though human choice and action. The determinism was supported by several psychological arguments which Kroeber did not offer himself, but which he indirectly supported. Wissler, Radin, and Lowie had all argued for what they called "primitive uninventiveness" and/or the predominance of "irrational motives" among primitive peoples. They argued that the thinking of people in primitive communities was itself dominated by culture, so that free choice or rationality could not exist as a significant independent explanatory variable. Kroeber's version of the argument, spelled out in an important article in 1917, was that all psychological theorizing was beyond the scope of anthropology because anthropology dealt with the "superorganic" and psychology was "organic." A related argument, aimed mainly at Boas, was at the heart of Kroeber's rejection of "science" in favor "history."

Franz Boas had always defined his anthropological work as both scientific and historical. After 1905 Boas increasingly attacked the diffusionists' methods and results. Kroeber responded to the criticism in an important article titled "History and Science in Anthropology" (1937). He first repeated the then fashionable assertion that the method of history and the method of science were different. Then he argued that while Boas was indeed scientific, and while his method also conformed to all the "thou-shalt-nots" of the best historical method, he nevertheless "does not *do* history" (p. 544). Boas produced tightly reasoned experimental analyses that showed particular social processes, which took place over time, but process in Kroeber's view was not history. He argued that "the historic approach, as distinct from merely historical technique," "was not the dealing with time sequences...but an endeavor at descriptive integration" (p. 545). An important aside expanded the ideas:

> ...the essential quality of the historical approach is an integration of phenomena, and therefore ultimately an integration in term of the totality of phenomena, it is obvious that the time relations...enter into the task. I am not belittling the time factor; I am only taking the stand that it is not the most essential criterion of the historic approach. Space relations can and sometimes must take its place (p. 547).

The bulk of what followed was an evaluation of current theoretical schools that made Kroeber's own alignments perfectly clear.

Obviously, Kroeber was saying that even though the kinds of reconstructions of pre-contact Indian cultures he and his colleagues were producing did not meet Boas's standards of scientific rigor, and did not indeed produce conclusions about cultural process, they were as legitimate as what Boas did—not despite these deficiencies but because of them—especially because they showed a pattern in space. The important underlying implication was that scientific methods could not, in principle, yield descriptions of pattern: one had to choose between scientific method and history, between understanding process and seeing cultural integration. By the 1950's, Boas's strictures were widely held to be too restrictive to permit one to describe human cultures.

It should immediately be added that Kroeber's arguments did not create a trend so much as they codified and reinforced one already started in an especially acceptable way. Wissler had already offered similar arguments, and Lowie's *History of Ethnological Theory* (1937), expanded them. Some preferred to think that a concern with total patterns was scientific rather than historical. Some held that the important total pattern was "social structure" and not culture, but the underlying import was the same. All in all, Kroeber's arguments contributed to the eclipse of the tradition Boas represented, and to the rise to a dominant position of quite a different tradition, centering on cultural determinism and the separation of cultural processes from individual psychology. Diffusionism has long since passed out of fashion, but these more basic positions are still widely accepted.

—Murray J. Leaf

KUHN, Thomas S(amuel). American philosopher and historian of science. Born in Cincinnati, Ohio, 18 July 1922. Studied at Harvard University, Cambridge, Massachusetts, B.S. 1943, M.A. 1946, Ph.D. in physics, 1949. Married Kathryn Louise Muhs in 1948 (divorced, 1978); 3 children. Civilian Employee, United States Office of Scientific Research and Development, 1943-45. Junior Fellow, 1948-51, Instructor, 1951-52, and Assistant Professor of General Education and the History of Science, 1952-56, Harvard University; Assistant Professor of Philosophy and the History of Science, 1956-58, Associate Professor, 1958-61, and Professor of the History of Science, 1961-64, University of California, Berkeley; Professor of the History of Science, 1964-68, and M. Taylor Pyne Professor of the History of Science, 1968-78, Princeton University, New Jersey. Since 1978, Professor of Philosophy and the History of Science, Massachusetts Institute of Technology, Cambridge. Fellow, Center for Advanced Study in the Behavioral Sciences, Stanford, California, 1958-59; Member, Institute for Advanced Study, Princeton, New Jersey, 1972-79. President, History of Science Society, 1968-70. Honorary degree: Linköpking University, Sweden; honorary doctorate: University of Notre Dame, Indiana, 1973; Rider College, Trenton, New Jersey, 1978; Bucknell University, Lewisburg, Pennsylvania, 1979. Member, American Academy of Arts and Sciences. Address: Department of Linguistics and Philosophy, Massachusetts Institute of Technology, Cambridge, Massachusetts 02139, U.S.A.

PUBLICATIONS

History and Philosophy of Science

The Copernican Revolution: Planetary Astronomy in the Development of Western Thought. Cambridge, Massachusetts, Harvard University Press, 1957.
Sources for History of Quantum Physics: An Inventory and Report, with others. Philadelphia, American Philosophical Society, 1967.
The Structure of Scientific Revolutions. Chicago, University of Chicago Press, 1962; enlarged edition, 1970.
The Essential Tension: Selected Studies in Scientific Tradition and Change. Chicago, University of Chicago Press, 1977.

Black-Body Theory and the Quantum Discontinuity, 1894-1912. New York, Oxford University Press, 1978.

*

Critical Studies: *Criticism and the Growth of Knowledge,* edited by Imre Lakatos and Alan Musgrave, London, Cambridge University Press, 1970; *Paradigms and Revolutions: Appraisals and Applications of T.S. Kuhn's Philosophy of Science,* edited by Gary Gutting, Notre Dame, Indiana, University of Notre Dame Press, 1980; *T.S. Kuhn and Social Science* by Barry Barnes, New York, Columbia University Press, 1982.

*   *   *

Thomas S. Kuhn is an historian and philosopher of science best known for his work on the nature of scientific revolutions. This work, which emphasizes both the need to understand science through its history and the social character of scientific knowledge, has had a significant impact in numerous disciplines. Indeed, it is likely that Kuhn's major work, *The Structure of Scientific Revolutions,* has been the most widely influential academic book of the last twenty years. Kuhn has also written important studies of specific episodes in the history of science (from the Copernican revolution to the development of quantum mechanics); but his greatest significance derives from the general view of science he articulates in *The Structure of Scientific Revolutions* and a number of subsequent articles (most reprinted in *The Essential Tension*).

The central concept in Kuhn's view of science is that of a *paradigm.* Critics have found this an elusive notion, but, in its basic meaning, it refers to a particular scientific achievement (e.g., what Newton did in his *Principia*) that provides a model for subsequent scientific activity. It does this, first, by specifying a set of problems, along with standards and methods for their solution, and, second by being accepted by virtually all those competent in a given scientific discipline as the proper basis for its development. When a discipline is dominated by a paradigm, work in it takes the form of what Kuhn calls *normal science.* This consists in the deployment of the paradigm's resources to solve various problems (e.g., extending the approach of the paradigm to new areas, refining results already obtained). One main spur to the development of normal science is the occurrence of what Kuhn calls *anomalies;* namely, observed facts about the world that we did not expect on the basis of our understanding of the paradigm. Ordinarily, anomalies are resolved by improving our grasp of the paradigm as it applies to particular cases. But sometimes they persist and accumulate to the point that we question the correctness of the paradigm's basic approach. Then we have a *crisis,* during which scientists search for possible new paradigms. If a crisis is resolved by replacing the old paradigm with a new one, then Kuhn says there has been a *scientific revolution.* The new paradigm defines a new version of normal science, and the cycle continues.

Much discussion of Kuhn's view has focused on the process whereby the scientific community abandons one paradigm in favor of another. Kuhn emphasizes the radical differences (incommensurability) of different paradigms and argues that there is no independent body of evidence or methodological rules that can rationally compel a change in paradigm. Rather, he views scientific revolutions as analogous to perceptual Gestalt switches or religious conversions, whereby we come to see the world in new ways but without being forced to do so by evidence or argument. Philosophical critics have strongly objected to Kuhn's ideas here on the grounds that they undermine the rationality of science by making scientific revolutions the results of psychological and social causes. Imre Lakatos, for example, said that Kuhn makes scientific change a matter of "mob psychology." On the other hand, some readers of Kuhn (especially some social scientists) have welcomed his work for dismantling science's pretensions to rationality and opening the door to the study of science is just another social phenomenon. Kuhn himself is not happy with either of these reactions. He sees his view of science as undermining not its rationality but rather the viability of certain entrenched conceptions of rationality (especially those associated with logical positivism). What we need, he maintains, is a conception of rationality that will show how it is rooted not in appeals to theory-free observation reports or changeless methodological rules but rather in the shared judgments of the scientific community.

Kuhn's work was importantly influenced by historians of science such as Alexandre Koyré and has some important affinities to the work of contemporary philosophers of science such as N.R. Hanson, Paul Feyerabend, Stephen Toulmin, and Michael Polanyi. There are also more distant but possibly important affinities to the views of Continental thinkers such as Michel Foucault.

—Gary Gutting

KÜNG, Hans. German theologian. Born in Lucerne, Switzerland, 19 March 1928. Studied at the Pontifical Gregorian University, Rome, Licenciate in Theology, 1955; Institut Catholique and the Sorbonne, Paris, Dr. of Theology, 1957; ordained as a Roman Catholic priest, 1954. Pastoral work, Lucerne, 1957-59; Assistant in Dogmatics, University of Münster, 1959-60; Professor of Dogmatic Theology, 1963-80 (removed and censured by the Vatican), and since 1963 Professor of Ecumenical Theology and Director, Institute for Ecumenical Research, University of Tübingen. Visiting Professor, Union Theological Seminary, New York, 1968; University of Basel, 1969; University of Chicago, 1981. Recipient: Ludwig Thoma Medal, Hamburg, 1975. Editor of the series *Theologische Meditationen* since 1964; founded, with others, the series *Ökumenische Forschung*, 1967. Appointed Official Theological Consultant by Pope John XXIII, Second Vatican Council, 1962. Honorary doctorate: St. Louis University, 1963; Pacific School of Religion, Berkeley, California, 1966; Loyola University, Chicago, 1966; University of Glasgow, 1971. Address: Faculty of Catholic Theology, Institute of Ecumenical Research, University of Tübingen, Tübingen, Federal Republic of Germany.

PUBLICATIONS

Theology and Society

Rechtfertigung: Die Lehre Karl Barths und eine katholische Besinnung. Einsiedeln, Johannes-Verlag, 1957; as *The Doctrine of Karl Barth and a Catholic Reflection,* New York, Nelson, 1964; London, Burns and Oates, 1965.

Konzil und Wiedervereinigung: Erneuerung als Ruf in die Einheit. Vienna, Herder, 1960; as *The Church and Reunion,* London, Sheed and Ward, 1961; as *The Council, Reform and Reunion,* New York, Sheed and Ward, 1961.

Damit die Welt glaube: Briefe an junge Menschen. Munich, Pfeiffer, 1962; as *That the World May Believe: Letters to Young People,* London, Sheed and Ward, 1963; as *That The World May Believe,* New York, Sheed and Ward, 1963.

Strukturen der Kirche. Freiburg, Herder, 1962; as *Structures of the Church,* New York, Nelson, 1964; London, Burns and Oates, 1965.

Kirche im Konzil. Freiburg, Herder, 1963; as *The Living Church,* London, Sheed and Ward, 1963; as *The Council in Action,* New York, Sheed and Ward, 1963.

Freiheit in der Welt: Sir Thomas More. Einsiedeln, Benziger, 1964; as *Freedom in the World: Sir Thomas More,* London, Sheed and Ward, 1965; included in *Freedom Today,* New York, Sheed and Ward, 1966.

Theologe und Kirche. Einsiedeln, Benziger, 1964; as *The Theologian and the Church,* London, Sheed and Ward, 1965; included in *Freedom Today,* New York, Sheed and Ward, 1966.

Kirche in Freiheit. Einsiedeln, Benziger, 1964; as *The Church and Freedom,* London, Sheed and Ward, 1965; included in *Freedom Today,* New York, Sheed and Ward, 1966.

Christenheit als Minderheit: Die Kirche unter den Weltreligionen. Einsiedeln, Benziger, 1965; included in *Freedom Today,* New York, Sheed and Ward, 1966; included in *Christian Revelation and World Religions,* edited by J. Neuner, London, Burns and Oates, 1967.

Gott und das Leid. Einsiedeln, Benziger, 1967.

Die Kirche. Freiburg, Herder, 1967; as *The Church,* London, Burns and Oates, and New York, Sheed and Ward, 1971.

Wahrhaftigkeit: Zur Zukunft der Kirche. Freiburg, Herder, 1968; as *Truthfulness: The Future of the Church,* London and New York, Sheed and Ward, 1968.

Menschwerdung Gottes: Eine Einführung in Hegels theologisches Denken als Prolegomena zu einer künftigen Christologie. Freiburg, Herder, 1970.

Unfehlbar? Eine Anfrage. Zurich, Benziger, 1970; as *Infallible? An Inquiry,* London, Collins, and New York, Doubleday, 1971.

Was ist Kirche? Freiburg, Herder, 1970.

Wozu Priester? Eine Hilfe. Zurich, Benziger, 1971; as *Why Priests?* London, Collins, 1972; as *Why Priests? A Proposal for a New Church Ministry,* New York, Doubleday, 1972.

Freiheit des Christen. Zurich, Ex Libris, 1971.

Was in der Kirche bleiben muss. Zurich, Benziger, 1973; as *What Must Remain in the Church,* Glasgow, Collins, 1977.

Fehlbar? Eine Bilanz. Zurich, Benziger, 1973.

Christ sein. Munich, Piper, 1974; as *On Being a Christian,* New York, Doubleday, 1976; London, Collins, 1977.

Was ist Firmung? Zurich, Benziger, 1976; included in *Signposts for the Future,* 1978.

Jesus im Widerstreit: Ein jüdisch-christlicher Dialog mit Pinchas Lapide. Stuttgart, Calwer-Kösel, 1976; as *Brother or Lord? A Jew and a Christian Talk Together About Jesus,* Glasgow, Collins, 1977; included in *Signposts for the Future,* 1978.

Gottesdienst—warum? Zurich, Benziger, 1976; included in *Signposts for the Future,* 1978.

20 Thesen zum Christsein. Munich, Piper, 1977; included in *Signposts for the Future,* 1978.

Heute noch an Gott glauben? Munich, Piper, 1977.

Signposts for the Future. New York, Doubleday, 1978.

Existiert Gott? Antwort auf die Gottesfrage der Neuheit. Munich, Piper, 1978; as *Does God Exist? An Answer for Today,* New York, Doubleday, 1980.

Consensus in Theology? A Dialogue with Hans Küng, Edward Schillebeeckx and David Tracy. Philadelphia, Westminster Press, 1980.

The Church, Maintained in Truth: A Theological Meditation. New York, Seabury Press, 1980.

Kunst und Sinnfrage. Zurich, Benziger, 1980; as *Art and the Question of Meaning,* New York, Crossroad, 1981.

Other

Editor, with others, *Konzilsreden.* Einsiedeln, Benziger, 1964; as *Council Speeches of Vatican II,* London, Sheed and Ward, 1964.

Editor, with others, *Toward Vatican III: The Work That Needs to Be Done.* New York, Seabury Press, 1978.

*

Critical Studies: *Hans Küng: Weg und Werk,* edited by Hermann Häring and Karl-Josef Kuschel, Munich, Piper, 1978; *Küng in Conflict,* edited by Leonard Swidler, New York, Doubleday, 1981.

* * *

Father Hans Küng's theology has moved over twenty-five years from study of the institutional structures of Roman Catholicism, to examination of basic doctrinal tenets of Catholic Christianity, to finally probing the very existence of God. Küng came to prominence in the early 1960s with a style as lecturer and international traveler that seemed to fit a jet setter rather than a theologian, and a book (*The Council, Reform and Reunion*), which proved to be a virtual blueprint for Vatican Council II.

In a Church still essentially rooted in the Council of Trent (1545-63), he arrested attention with calls for internationalization of the Roman Curia (the United Nations Secretariat, he alleged, was more catholic than the Curia), and for democratization of the Church through such steps as ending precensorship of religious books and lifting the Index of Forbidden Books. He linked freedom of Catholic believers to the very nature of the Church, and he described freedom as an essential element for ecumenical progress between the Christian faiths. "The more the Catholic Church makes freedom a reality within her, freedom of thought, of speech, of writing and of action, the more this freedom and order of hers will represent an advance towards the Christians separated from her, who are seeking for order and freedom," said Küng. He held that blind obedience without knowledge and freedom was for Catholics, as any others, not only unnatural, but unChristian and immoral.

When Küng passed to examination of central convictions of historical, traditional Roman Catholicism, he was equally provocative. "The gospels," he wrote in *The Church*, "do not report any public announcement by Jesus of his intention to found a Church." On apostolic succession, he maintained that "Apostolicity can never mean power through which the Church might rule," and on papal succession he declared that "it is difficult to see how Peter could have had a monarchical bishop as his successor." In the early Church, he contended, there were no signs that anyone seriously thought of a connection between the passage in Matthew, "Thou art Peter...." (16:18ff) and Rome. Küng, in sum, aligned himself with the concept of the Pauline, non-hierarchical communities of the New Testament, which were quite different from the hierarchical Church that evolved with Rome at the apex.

If Küng seemed on a collision course with Rome, he was. The collision came with the book *Infallible? An Inquiry*, and Küng's proposition that there are no serious exegetical, historical or theological grounds for the doctrine of papal infallibility, a dogmatic constitution of Vatican Council I, 1867-70; that infallibility belongs only to God; and that the Church's legitimate spiritual claim is rather to "indefectibility or perpetuity in the truth." Küng's postulates that "the Church remains in the truth and this is not annulled by the sum total of individual errors." In other words, the Church can indeed err through the popes, and has—e.g., on Galileo, on usury and currently, in Küng's view, on birth control. But the Church remains the community of the faithful, assured of surviving all upheavals. The message of Christ will endure, says Küng, and Christ will remain "with her in the Spirit and thus keep her through all errors and confusions in the truth."

Küng's proposition hit Rome with special impact, for not only does it strike at the dogmatic basis of papal authority, but it opens up for reevaluation broad areas of the Catholic faith, whose legitimacy rests heavily on the fact of papal promulgation. Conceivably vulnerable under the Küng proposition would be such teachings as the Virgin Birth, the Assumption of Mary into heaven, and the divinity of Jesus Christ.

Küng launched into his own reevaluation of traditional Catholic belief in *On Being a Christian*, the closest he has come to offering a comprehensive, systematic theology. The book is complex, sometimes abstruse, and once again thoroughly controversial. Küng concedes the two natures of Jesus Christ, the human and the divine, but the divinity of Jesus, he says, is to be understood in the sense that the offer of freedom and love made to the people of God through Jesus is unique and unsurpassable. With respect to the incidents of Easter, Küng discounts literal understanding of the empty tomb and the post-Resurrection appearances, and advances the view that "the Crucified lives" through being "taken up by that incomprehensible and comprehensive ultimate reality which we designate by the name of God." The Resurrection of Jesus, therefore, is not an event in human space and time, but rather the passing over of Jesus into God's life. It follows that individuals must be wary about identifying Jesus *tout court* with God. That Jesus sits at the right hand of God is to be understood as metaphor for the notion that Jesus "is nearest to the Father in authority and exercises it vicariously with the same dignity and status." Many details of traditional Catholic creed are thus to be regarded as more symbolic than real. Included among them would be the doctrine of Virgin Birth.

Küng proceeded to the ultimate theological question, the existence of God, in his 1978 book *Does God Exist?* He decides in the affirmative, but characteristically with a logic that confronts traditional biblical and dogmatic suppositions. For instance, Küng believes that the existence of God cannot be proved absolutely on rational grounds and so is not validated by arguments but rather by practice and trust. Küng affirms to these bases for belief and accordingly to the God of the Bible and of Jesus Christ. But he enters a critical qualification: this God is not to be thought of as exclusively masculine. The "feminine-maternal" element must be recognized in God as well as the "masculine paternal."

Küng's consistently adventurous and, for Rome, unorthodox theologizing have cost him his designation as a specifically Catholic theologian at the University of Tübingen, where he may still teach but where he may no longer be involved in examining candidates for the Catholic priesthood. He continues however to write and to lecture on theological topics, and he has lost none of the flair of the young, handsome, media-oriented priest, who burst upon international consciousness in the 1960s. Rome does not like his theology, and perhaps not his style either. Still, he seems very much at home in the post-Vatican II Church, which he helped shape. His theology remains infused with an explicit loyalty to Catholic Christianity, and his following is large, particularly among progressive and liberal Catholics.

—John Deedy

KUZNETS, Simon (Smith). American economist. Born in Kharkov, Russia, 30 April 1901; emigrated to the United States; later naturalized. Studied at Columbia University, New York, B.S. 1923, M.A. 1924, Ph.D. 1926. Married Edith Handler in 1929; 2 children. Social Science Research Council Fellow, 1925-27; Staff Member, National Bureau of Economic Research, New York, 1927-61; Assistant Professor, 1930-34, Associate Professor, 1934-35, and Professor, 1936-54, University of Pennsylvania, Philadelphia; Professor, Johns Hopkins University, Baltimore, 1954-60; Frank W. Taussig Research Professor of Economics, 1958-59, and Professor, 1960-71, Harvard University, Cambridge, Massachusetts. Associate Director, War Production Board, Washington, D.C., 1942-44. Economic Advisor, National Resources Commission of China, 1946, and National Income Committee of India, 1950-51. President, American Statistics Association, 1949, and American Economic Association, 1954. Recipient: Nobel Prize in Economics, 1971. Honorary doctorate: Princeton University, New Jersey, 1951; Columbia University, 1954; University of Pennsylvania, 1956 and 1976; Harvard University, 1959; Hebrew University of Jerusalem, 1965; University of New Hampshire, Durham, 1972; Brandeis University, Waltham, Massachusetts, 1975. Fellow, American Association for the Advancement of Science, American Statistical Association, and Econometric Society. Corresponding Fellow, British Academy; Honorary Fellow, Royal Statistical Society, London; Member, Royal Academy of Sciences, Sweden. Member, American Academy of Arts and Sciences, and U.S. National Academy of Sciences. Address: 67 Francis Avenue, Cambridge, Massachusetts 02138, U.S.A.

PUBLICATIONS

Economics

Cyclical Fluctuations: Retail and Wholesale Trade, United States, 1919-1925. New York, Adelphi, 1926.

Secular Movements in Production and Prices: Their Nature and Their Bearing on Cyclical Fluctuations. Boston, Houghton Mifflin, 1930.

Seasonal Variations in Industry and Trade. New York, National Bureau of Economic Research, 1933.

Current Problems in Measurement of National Income, with Wesley Clair Mitchell. The Hague, Institut International de Statistique, 1934.

Gross Capital Formation, 1919-1933. New York, National Bureau of Economic Research, 1934.

National Income, 1929-1932. New York, National Bureau of Economic Research, 1934.

Income Originating in Nine Basic Industries, 1919-1934. New York, National Bureau of Economic Research, 1936.

National Income and Capital Formation, 1919-1935: A Preliminary Report. New York, National Bureau of Economic Research, 1937.

Commodity Flow and Capital Formation. New York, National Bureau of Economic Research, 1938.

National Income and Its Composition, 1919-1938, with others. New York, National Bureau of Economic Research, 2 vols., 1941.

Uses of National Income in Peace and War (lecture). New York, National Bureau of Economic Research, 1942.

National Product, War and Prewar. New York, National Bureau of Economic Research, 1944.

Income from Independent Professional Practice, with Milton Friedman. New York, National Bureau of Economic Research, 1945.

National Product in Wartime. New York, National Bureau of Economic Research, 1945.

National Income: A Summary of Findings. New York, National Bureau of Economic Research, 1946.

National Product since 1869, with others. New York, National Bureau of Economic Research, 1946.

Shares of Upper Income Groups in Income and Savings. New York, National Bureau of Economic Research, 1950; enlarged edition, with Elizabeth Jenks, 1953.

Income and Wealth of the United States: Trends and Structure, with Raymond Goldsmith. Cambridge, England, Bowes and Bowes, 1952.

Economic Change: Selected Essays in Business Cycles, National Income, and Economic Growth. New York, Norton, 1953; London, Heinemann, 1954.

International Differences in Capital Formation and Financing. New York, National Bureau of Economic Research, 1953.

Quantitative Aspects of the Economic Growth of Nations. Chicago, University of Chicago Press, 1956.

Toward a Theory of Economic Growth (lecture). Baltimore, Johns Hopkins University Press, 1956.

Analyses of Economic Change, with others. Philadelphia, American Philosophical Society, 1960.

Six Lectures on Economic Growth. Glencoe, Illinois, Free Press, 1960.

Capital in the American Economy: Its Formation and Financing, with Elizabeth Jenks. Princeton, New Jersey, Princeton University Press, 1961.

Postwar Economic Growth: Four Lectures. Cambridge, Massachusetts, Belknap Press, 1964.

Economic Growth and Structure: Selected Essays. New York, Norton, 1965; London, Heinemann, 1968.

Modern Economic Growth: Rate, Structure, and Spread. New Haven, Connecticut, Yale University Press, 1966.

Toward a Theory of Economic Growth, With Reflections on the Economic Growth of Modern Nations. New York, Norton, 1968.

Lectures on: Methodological Problems in the Study of Economic Growth. Functions of Economists in Public Service. Taipei, Academia Sinica, 1969.

Economic Growth of Nations: Total Output and Production Structure. Cambridge, Massachusetts, Belknap Press, 1971.

Data for Quantitative Economic Analysis: Problems of Supply and Demand (lecture). Stockholm, Federation of Swedish Industries, 1972.

Economic Structure of U.S. Jewry: Recent Trends. Jerusalem, Hebrew University of Jerusalem, 1972.

Income-Related Differences in Natural Increase: Bearing on Growth and Distribution of Income. New Haven, Connecticut, Yale University, 1972.

Quantitative Economic Research: Trends and Problems. New York, National Bureau of Economic Research, 1972.

Population, Capital, and Growth: Selected Essays. New York, Norton, 1973; London, Heinemann Educational, 1974.

Demographic Components in Size-Distribution of Income. New Haven, Connecticut, Yale University, 1975.

Growth, Population and Income Distribution: Selected Essays. New York, Norton, 1979.

Other

Immigration and the Foreign Born, with Ernest Rubin. New York, National Bureau of Economic Research, 1954.

Editor, with others, *Economic Growth: Brazil, India, Japan.* Durham, North Carolina, Duke University Press, 1955.

Editor, with Dorothy Swaine Thomas, *Population Redistribution and Economic Growth: United States, 1870-1950.* Philadelphia, American Philosophical Society, 3 vols., 1957-64.

Editor, with Abram Bergson, *Economic Trends in the Soviet Union.* Cambridge, Massachusetts, Harvard University Press, 1963.

*   *   *

Simon Kuznets was awarded the 1971 Nobel Prize in Economic Science for his work on the comparative study of the economic growth of nations. This work represented the culmination of certain distinctive lifelong efforts: his approach to economic research, the development of national income accounting, the study of economic fluctuations, and the analysis of economic growth.

Kuznets has a deserved reputation as a cautious investigator concerned about spurious mathematical and quantitative precision (although he is a preeminent user of quantitative data), the historical relativity of economic theory (although he seeks patterns of relationships and continuity), the limits of determinate deductive reasoning, and the narrow scope of technical economic theory. He is an advocate of the cautious blending of careful definition, theory, and empirical analysis in the use of wide ranging—but to him relevant—material. He is willing to consider alternative hypotheses, unwilling to manipulate data to reinforce preconceived theories and ideas, and willing to reach only tentative conclusions—even speculations—in the absence of material enabling him to dispose of an issue conclusively.

If he had accomplished little else, Kuznets would have earned a distinguished reputation for his work as a (perhaps the) principal developer of the U.S. national income accounting system, the results of which have been the statistical basis of much subsequent empirical work in economics. Among other things, he has been a creator, systematizer, and user of historical income and wealth time series. He has been concerned with data generation but also with the coherence of the concepts and terms used in the accounts and thereby underlying the data, as well as with the technical limits of the statistical series. Some of his specialized work has focused on the identification of capital stock, depreciation, and intermediate products.

One of the earliest purposes for which Kuznets sought national income data was to use in his landmark studies of economic fluctuations. Here he studied seasonal variations, cyclical fluctuations, and secular movements. Some of his work was a forerunner of modern studies relating consumption, saving, and income, largely defining a good part of the field. Other economists have designated as the Kuznets Cycle his finding of a fifteen to twenty year pattern of perturbations centering on variations in the growth rate.

Kuznets's later work has centered on the causes, characteristics, and consequences of economic growth. Here he has dealt with both U.S. and comparative national experiences. In all cases he has used quantitative historical national income data, for whose production he has often been directly or indirectly responsible. His work emphasizes population, other demographic variables, and structural relationships, as well as the interrelationships between these and other variables. His work also is characterized by a long term (multi-century) perspective; the treatment of population, technology, structural variables, and market forms as endogenous variables; the quality of economic growth; and a focus on the specific interrelationships between growth rate, population, business cycles, productivity, income distribution, consumption, and saving and credit creation. In his view, the complexity of these materials requires cautious interpretation, a consideration reinforcing his antipathy to extreme *a priori* theorizing and extreme empiricism.

—Warren J. Samuels

LACAN, Jacques (Marie Émile). French psychoanalyst. Born in Paris, 13 April 1901. Studied at the Collège Stanislas and the Faculté de Médecine de Paris, M.D. 1932. Married Marie-Louise Blondin in 1934, 3 children; married Sylvia Maklès in 1953, 1 daughter. Head of the Clinic, Faculté de Médecine de Paris, 1932-36; after 1936, Médecin des Hôpitaux Psychiatriques, Paris; after 1953, Professor, St. Anne's Hospital, Paris; after 1963, Chargé de Conférences, L'École Pratique des Hautes Études, Paris. Director, Editions du Seuil, 1963-81. Founded L'École Freudienne de Paris in 1964 (disbanded by Lacan in 1980 for its failure to adhere strictly to Freudian principles). *Died* (in Paris) *9 September 1981.*

PUBLICATIONS

Psychology

Écrits (essays, 1937-66). Paris, Seuil, 1966; selections as *Écrits: A Selection,* London, Tavistock, and New York, Norton, 1977, and as *The Language of the Self: The Function of Language in Psychoanalysis,* Baltimore, Johns Hopkins University Press, 1978.
Le Séminaire: Livre XI: Les Quatre Concepts fondamentaux de la psychanalyse, edited by Jacques-Alain Miller. Paris, Seuil, 1973; as *The Four Fundamental Concepts of Psychoanalysis,* London, Hógarth Press, and New York, Norton, 1978.
La Télévision. Paris, Seuil, 1974.
De la psychose paranoïque dans ses rapports avec la personnal-

ité, suivi de premiers écrits sur le paranoïa. Paris, Seuil, 1975.
Le Séminaire: Livre I: Les Écrits techniques de Freud 1953-54, edited by Jacques-Alain Miller. Paris, Seuil, 1975.
Le Séminaire: Livre XX: Encore, edited by Jacques-Alain Miller. Paris, Seuil, 1975.
Le Séminaire: Livre II: Le Moi dans le théorie de Freud et dans la technique de la psychanalyse, edited by Jacques-Alain Miller. Paris, Seuil, 1978.
Le Séminaire: Livre III: Les Psychoses, edited by Jacques-Alain Miller. Paris, Seuil, 1981.
The Talking Cure: Essays in Psychoanalysis and Language, edited by Colin MacCabe. London, Macmillan, 1981.

*

Critical Studies: *Jacques Lacan* by Anika Lemaire, Brussels, Dessart, 1970, as *Jacques Lacan,* London, Routledge, 1977; *Comprendre Jacques Lacan* by Jean-Baptiste Fages, Paris, Privat, 1971; *Returning to Freud: Clinical Analysis in the School of Lacan* edited by Stuart Schneiderman, New Haven, Connecticut, Yale University Press, 1980; *Lacan and Language: A Reader's Guide to Écrits* by John P. Muller and William J. Richardson, New York, International Universities Press, 1982.

* * *

Jacques Lacan advocated a major rethinking of psychoanalysis, its theoretical orientation and its therapeutic aims. Trained in the 1930's as a psychiatrist, Lacan was drawn to Freudian theory and contributed to its introduction into France. In the Surrealist journals of the period, he also published on such topics as psychopathological crime and the linguistic analysis of the writings of schizophrenics. But his influence came largely after the war, when he decisively shaped French psychoanalysis both intellectually and institutionally. For more than a generation he offered an image of what it means to "do" an analysis, and of how analytic theory might be developed; he lived to witness a spectacular growth in each area. Lacan also founded his own "school" of analysis that flourished independently of the I.P.A. which refused to recognize it. At the same time, his theoretical work made him a leading "structuralist" thinker, and was widely discussed by writers, literary and cinema critics, feminists, philosophers, anthropologists, and historians as well as by psychiatrists. Outside France Lacan's institutional approach has taken root in Italy and in Latin America, and his theoretical work has been discussed internationally and translated into many languages, including English.

Lacan was fiercely independent and polemical even towards his own followers. He apparently could abide no enduring allegiance, and his career is a story of stormy "breaks" with all the associations or groups to which he belonged, including the one he himself founded and directed. Moreover, he perfected a unique style; he spurned both an accessible and a technical way of writing, preferring a wilfully arcane and highly literary manner. His writings (or *Écrits*) are exceptional in analytic writing for their involuted rhetoric, their range of erudition, their philosophical sophistication, and for the almost complete lack of concrete case-material. Apart from the *Écrits,* there are some twenty transcripts of the oral *Séminaire* which he delivered to various audiences over as many years, and which provides the principle vehicle of his teaching. Five of these transcripts, edited by his son-in-law, Jacques-Alain Miller, have been published, and the others are to follow.

Two basic aims inform Lacan's work. First, he tried to replace the corrective medical model of analysis he associated with the New York ego-psychological school with analysis as an ethics of speech (*parole*). Fundamentally analysis deals with a subject's relation to the analytic "truth" in his discourse, and analytic theory should be seen as a theory about that relation. Accordingly Lacan attempted to introduce the study of language (linguistics, philosophy, poetics, and rhetoric) into psychoanalytic theory. For example, he held that the primary processes of condensation and displacement, which Freud had identified in dreams, jokes, and symptoms, may be formally described in terms of the tropes of metaphor and metonomy, and that, more generally, "the unconscious is structured like a language." He also adopted the anti-psychologist attitude of the modern study of language, employing Emile Benveniste's distinction between the "I" as a formal element of speech and the "me" as an imagistic or psychological entity. He held that we have in fact no real psychological selves, there being no more to our self-images than the results of the various identifications in our lives, and the inter-relations that grow out of them. All self-images, including those that comprise the ego, are basically fantasmatic; they may be analyzed by postulating a "mirror-stage" between 6 and 18 months in which a child jubilantly assumes a total image of his body, and then, by deriving certain aggressive or self-mutilating results from this "alienation" in the child's later relations with self and others. As distinct from this "imaginary" kind of identification Lacan recognized a "symbolic" kind, associated with the acquisition of language, and with the adoption of the various symbolic positions prescribed by the inherited forms of a culture. He argued that the New York school, in making a reinforcement of the ego the central goal of an analysis, had hopelessly confused the "I" with the "me," and, thus, the imaginary with the symbolic. The distinction between imaginary and symbolic dimensions became central; Lacan used it to reformulate Freud's view on the various kinds of identification and their role in the Oedipal Complex. Claiming to have thus discovered Freud's original message, Lacan presented his own work as a "return to Freud."

Second, Lacan promoted a view of the cultural position of psychoanalysis. Freud was neither a doctor of the mind nor a priest of interpretation but the originator of a more fundamental revolution. For psychoanalysis doesn't just provide knowledge about ourselves; it changes our very conception of knowledge and of ourselves, and of the relation between the two. Thus it supplies the framework for a post-Enlightenment literary and philosophical culture. At first Lacan sought the vocabulary for this new culture in modern linguistics, philosophy, anthropology, and more generally in the structuralist turn in thought. Later, however, he became more impressed by what distinguishes analysis from those disciplines. In his last years, he stressed that psychoanalysis, in its discoveries of the Symbolic dimension, of the relation of the subject to the truth of his own discourse, and of the centrality of the position of woman, both continues, and helps to analyze, truths developed in the Judeo-Christian tradition which the Enlightenment had misunderstood.

Thus Lacan opened analysis to many new fields. He linked the Symbolic dimension in analysis with the Symbolic Order Lévi-Strauss claimed as an organizing principle of the systems of myth, language, kinship, and economic exchange in a culture. Analysis studied how such an order unconsciously determines the lives of men. Lacan was also influenced by the seminal interpretations of Hegel by Alexander Kojève; thus he argued with Sartre about the concept of the Other, and with Merleau-Ponty over the concept of the Body. He translated some late Heidegger into French, and absorbed that philosopher's late views on language, poetry, and truth. He vacillated between the view that psychoanalysis is a new science and the view that it helps to identify the pathologies and limits of a culture dominated by science. The first view influenced Althusser, and the second, Foucault and Derrida—all prominent French philosophers. Finally Lacan drew attention to the complex sorts of linguistic analysis Freud had employed in his interpretations, and demonstrated how they resembled those which modernist literature discovered when it turned to the examination of its own medium, for example, in Mallarmé and Joyce. Lacan was thus acclaimed by literary theorists who employed analytic theory not for culturalist or psychobiographical interpretation but to answer more basic questions about the nature of literary discourse, and the relation of the subject to it.

Starting with his thesis on an erotomaniac woman whose "involuntary poetry" was published by Paul Eluard, Lacan devoted particular attention to the topic of women within analytic theory. Defending Freud's view against the objections of the English School, that it is symbolic castration that determines sexual identity, Lacan developed his own account of the female Oedipal Complex. Further he developed the idea that Freud's discovery of the unconscious grew out of his contact with the discourse of the hysterical women he first treated. He offered an original re-interpretation of Freud's early Dora case, and attempted to spell out the structure of hysterical discourse. Lacan's views were taken up by an influential group of French feminists, and, in later years, Lacan himself became increasingly preoccupied with the theme of sexual difference. He worked with the notion that there is a basic femininity which, far from being a gender identity deriving from castration, defies the process of symbolic identification as such.

—John Rajcman

LAING, R(onald) D(avid). British psychologist. Born in Glasgow, Scotland, 7 October 1927. Studied at Glasgow University, M.B. 1951; West of Scotland Neurosurgical Unit. Served in the British Army as a neurosurgical intern and psychiatrist, 1951-53. Married twice; 7 children. Worked at the Department of Psychological Medicine, Glasgow University, 1953-56, Tavistock Clinic, London, 1956-60, and Tavistock Institute of Human Relations, 1960-67; now in private practice as a psychoanalyst. Fellow, Foundations Fund for Research in Psychiatry, 1960-67. Director, Langham Clinic, London, 1962-65. Founded the Philadelphia Association in 1965 and the Institute of Phenomenological Studies in 1967. Address: 2 Eton Road, London NW3, England.

PUBLICATIONS

Psychology

The Divided Self: A Study of Sanity and Madness. London, Tavistock, and Chicago, Quadrangle, 1960.
The Self and Others: Further Studies in Sanity and Madness. London, Tavistock, 1961; Chicago, Quadrangle, 1962; revised version as *Self and Others,* London, Tavistock, 1969; New York, Pantheon, 1970.
Reason and Violence: A Decade of Sartre's Philosophy 1950-60, with David G. Cooper. London, Tavistock, and New York, Pantheon, 1964.
Sanity, Madness, and the Family: Families of Schizophrenics, with Aaron Esterson. London, Tavistock, 1964; New York, Basic Books, 1965.
Interpersonal Perception: A Theory and a Method of Research, with others. London, Tavistock, and New York, Springer, 1966.
The Politics of Experience and The Bird of Joy. London, Penguin, 1967; as *The Politics of Experience,* New York, Pantheon, 1967.
The Politics of the Family. Toronto, Canadian Broadcasting Company, 1969.
Intervention in Social Situations. London, Association of Family Caseworkers and Philadelphia Association, 1969.
Knots. London, Tavistock, and New York, Pantheon, 1970.
The Politics of the Family and Other Essays. London, Tavistock, and New York, Pantheon, 1971.
The Facts of Life. London, Allen Lane, 1976; as *The Facts of Life: An Essay in Feelings, Facts, and Fantasy,* New York, Pantheon, 1976.

Conversations with Adam and Natasha. New York, Pantheon, 1977.
Conversations with Children. London, Allen Lane, 1978.
The Voice of Experience. New York, Pantheon, 1982.

Other

Do You Love Me? An Entertainment in Conversation and Verse. New York, Pantheon, 1976.
Sonnets. London, Joseph, 1979.

*

Critical Studies: *R.D. Laing: The Man and His Ideas* by Richard I. Evans, New York, Dutton, 1976; *The Schizoid World of Jean-Paul Sartre and R.D. Laing* by Douglas Kirsner, St. Lucia, University of Queensland Press, 1976; *R.D. Laing: The Philosophy and Politics of Psychotherapy* by Andrew Collier, New York, Pantheon, 1977; *R.D. Laing: His Work and Its Relevance for Sociology* by Martin Howarth-Williams, London, Routledge, 1977.

*   *   *

R.D. Laing, the British existential psychiatrist, has a rather radical view of schizophrenia. A schizophrenic, he claims, suffers from "ontological insecurity." It is best to introduce this concept in his own words (from *Self and Other*): "The schizophrenic does not take for granted his own person (and other persons) as being an adequately embodied, alive, real, substantial, and continuous being, who is at one place at one time and at a different place at a different time, remaining 'the same' throughout."

Laing is a sufficiently unclear writer, or the notion of "ontological insecurity" is sufficiently difficult, that in the perhaps twenty accounts of Laing this writer has encountered in textbooks, no mention has been made of the concept, and Laing in general is seriously misrepresented. Therefore, a bit more time should be spent attempting to explicate ontological insecurity. Some points: 1.) All of us behave differently in different situations. It is sometimes shocking to us to find, for example, that we are a model of linguistic propriety with our mothers but swear like a longshoreman with our peers. "Where does the filthy language come from?" and "Why am I so prissy?" are equally valid questions. To be overcome by similar and less banal juxtapositions and to doubt that one has a stable self as a result is to be ontologically insecure. 2.) Most of us have had the experience of looking at someone we love and trust and momentarily seeing an emptiness in that someone's face. And then we wonder if we really are loved, and what love is. To be constantly overcome by such doubts is to be ontologically insecure. Note that we can and often do look at ourselves and wonder if we really love someone, or care about the things people care about, and so on. This is an even more frightening experience of ontological insecurity. 3.) The reader interested in excellent literary accounts of ontological insecurity should read the opening parts of Dostoevsky's *Underground Man* and Sartre's *Nausea*.

The ontologically insecure person often sees behind the masks all of us present the world with and *freezes* or becomes petrified, to use Laing's terms. What such a person—a schizophrenic—needs is a place to explore himself, in the hopes of finding himself in some sense or of making an adaptation or of using his ontological insecurity to some purpose. To promote such searches, Laing founded the Tavistock Institute. A textbook describes these searches as "psychedelic trips," and Laing is often accused of glorifying schizophrenia. One gets no hint of glorification from his books. He thinks of schizophrenics as *people*, it is true, and that is exceptionally rare in the field of psychopathology, but he does not consider them better than people who do have both feet on the ground. He does consider them different, and they are. Any description of what schizophrenics think about when left alone is likely to sound psychedelic to an accountant.

Laing is also criticized for finding the family to be the origin of schizophrenia, mainly because a large body of empirical evidence, mostly collected in America, has found no evidence that any of the theories that suggest familial interaction is of etiological significance in schizophrenia have any validity. It is difficult to decide if the empirical evidence is adequate reason to dismiss Laing's theory of familial etiology, for the British system of diagnosing schizophrenia is more precise, restricted, and narrow. Thus a large number of the people included in the American studies would not be considered schizophrenic by the British. In any event, it does not seem crucial to the theory of the etiological significance of ontological insecurity that this insecurity come directly from the family.

Laing is also criticized for his suggestion that these "retreats" he offers schizophrenics at the Tavistock Institute are valuable to them. The basis of this criticism is also empirical. Schizophrenics, especially those with poor premorbid adjustments (that is, for example, those who have had few friends prior to becoming schizophrenic), do not tend to do well in life. About half who leave a mental hospital (and many never do leave) return. This criticism may be answered in part as follows: The schizophrenic who suffers from ontological insecurity may be frozen so deeply by, for example, a state mental institution, that he would never be expected to come out of it. And most of this research is also American. Schizophrenia in America has been a wastebasket diagnostic category, and no doubt includes many unfortunates who could profit from nothing.

In any event, it seems plausible that there is a subset, small in America and larger in Geat Britain, of all people diagnosed as schizophrenic who do indeed suffer from the kind of problem Laing describes, and his ideas deserve more respect than they receive. However, as suggested, this is in large part due to the difficult and obscurity of Laing's writings. The reader wishing to further explore Laing would do well to read some moderately clear existential writing first. The passages from Dostoevsky and Sartre mentioned above are very good. Kierkegaard is less directly to the point, but he is very clear. *Fear and Trembling* is a good introduction.

—George W. Kelling

LAKATOS, Imre. Hungarian philosopher of science and mathematics. Born Imre Lipschitz in Hungary, 9 November 1922; changed name to Imre Molnar during the Nazi occupation; changed it to Imre Lakatos after World War II. Studied at the University of Debrecen, graduated 1944; University of Budapest, 1945-46; University of Moscow, 1949; Cambridge University, 1956-58, Ph.D. Member of the Anti-Nazi resistance in Hungary during World War II. Secretary, Hungarian Ministry of Education, Budapest, 1947-49; imprisoned as dissident, 1950-53; worked as a translator at the Mathematical Research Institute of the Hungarian Academy of Science, Budapest, 1954-56; fled to Vienna and later England after the Hungarian uprising of 1956; taught at the London School of Economics, 1960-74; Professor of Logic, 1969-74. *Died* (in London) *2 February 1974.*

PUBLICATIONS

Philosophy of Science and Mathematics

Proofs and Refutations: The Logic of Mathematical Discovery, edited by J. Worrall and G.P. Currie. London, Cambridge University Press, 1976.
The Methodology of Scientific Research Programmes: Philosophical Papers, Volume I, edited by J. Worrall and G.P. Currie. London, Cambridge University Press, 1977 (contains a bibliog-

raphy).

Mathematics, Science and Epistemology: Philosophical Papers, Volume II, edited by J. Worrall and G.P. Currie.   London, Cambridge University Press, 1977.

Other

Editor, *Problems in the Philosophy of Mathematics.*   Amsterdam, North Holland, 1967.
Editor, *The Problem of Inductive Logic.*   Amsterdam, North Holland, 1968.
Editor, with Alan Musgrave, *Problems in the Philosophy of Science.*   Amsterdam, North Holland, 1968.
Editor, with Alan Musgrave, *Criticism and the Growth of Knowledge.*   London, Cambridge University Press, 1970.

*

Bibliography: in *Essays in Memory of Imre Lakatos* edited by R.S. Cohen, Paul Feyerabend, and M.W. Wartofsky, Dordrecht, Reidel, 1976.

*   *   *

Imre Lakatos has been described as "the foremost philosopher of mathematics in his generation," and as "the best philosopher of science of our strange and uncomfortable century." In our greyly professional age, which has turned "emotion" into a pejorative term in academic life, Lakatos was remarkable for combining passion in intellectual matters with logical rigour and deep scholarship. He was a bitter foe of authoritarianism; hatred of the authority-principle, which had been fuelled by his experiences at the hands of Nazis and Stalinists, manifested itself in his attitude to orthodox styles of mathematical and scientific discourse (as well as to the anti-rationalism of radical Western political movements of the 1960's).

Lakatos broke down the barrier which is commonly taken to divide mathematics rigidly from empirical science. Karl Popper had shown that science was an affair of fallible conjectures followed by refutations which led to improved conjectures, in a continuing process that never yielded final truths. Lakatos argued that the history of mathematics, likewise, was a process of "proofs and refutations"—a notion which flew in the face of the orthodox view that treats a mathematical proof as a logical deduction whose validity is established for all time. Lakatos urged his case in a brilliant essay, chiefly concerned with an example from topology (Euler's relationship between the number of faces, edges, and vertices of polyhedra), which is at once an extended philosophical argument and a "rational reconstruction" of an important chapter in the history of mathematics: that is, a reconstruction in which the various false or obscure moves actually made by the individual participants are shunted into footnotes in order to allow the main text to display the logic of the dialectic process by which the community of mathematicians gradually improved their understanding of their subject. (Lakatos's book is surely unique in the philosophy of mathematics also in being a work of literary value which laymen can read with pleasure.)

Having assimilated mathematics to empirical science, Lakatos went on to improve on Popper's account of the latter. Popper was manifestly wrong, according to Lakatos, in suggesting that a scientific hypothesis is overthrown by an observation inconsistent with its predictions. Practising scientists have almost never abandoned their theories so readily. Logic does not require them to do so: as had already been pointed out by earlier writers such as P.M.M. Duhem, it is always possible to preserve a given theory from refutation by making adjustments elsewhere in one's total system of beliefs in order to reconcile the theory with any amount of *prima facie* counter-evidence. (For instance, if the theory of gravity predicts that a given planet should be at a particular location, then rather than giving up the theory when

we observe the planet to be elsewhere we may postulate that it is subject to perturbation by another, previously unknown planet; if the latter cannot be found when we search the area of sky where it should be, we still need not abandon the theory of gravity because we can suppose that a cloud of dust is obscuring the second planet's light and so on.) Lakatos argued that scientists not only constantly do make such moves but are often right to do so. Indeed, if Popper's falsification test were taken seriously, every theory we hold would have to be given up.

Lakatos's "methodology of scientific research programmes" represents a criterion for distinguishing good from bad scientific practice which finds a satisfying middle ground between the barren scepticism that results from strict application of Popper's principle and the immature frivolity of Paul Feyerabend's intellectual anarchism (which, like the anarchism of 1960's political movements, Lakatos saw as a front for a particularly intransigent form of authoritarianism). For Lakatos, there were no rules by which one could decide whether any particular move by a scientific thinker was legitimate rather than objectionably *ad hoc*; but individual steps of scientific thought take place within wider traditions of theorizing—"research programmes"—which retain their identity over time, and it is possible to make objective judgments between rival research programmes although not between particular theories taken in isolation from their intellectual background. With hindsight we can say that some research programmes have been "progressive" while others have "degenerated," although instinct alone can tell the participant scientist whether he is helping his intellectual tradition to progress rather than to degenerate.

The significance of Lakatos's philosophy lies not solely in the new understanding it gives us of the nature of mathematics and science, but also in its implications for the spirit in which these activities ought to be conducted. Particular theories or results can be understood only against the intellectual background in which they were produced, and they should be understood only as temporary steps on a continuing journey. Lakatos saw the guild mentality of 20th-century scholarship as conspiring to obscure these truths, by encouraging—if not requiring—a style of discourse in which the presentation of results is purged of references to the "problem-situation" from which they sprang or to the dialectic process which shaped their current form. This style serves no purpose other than that of bolstering the position of established scholars; "present mathematical and scientific education is a hotbed of authoritarianism and is the worst enemy of independent and critical thought". Scientists not only are, but must be seen to be, limited and fallible human beings. Little since Lakatos's untimely death suggests that we are less in need of this teaching today than when he offered it.

—Geoffrey Sampson

LANGER, Susanne (Katerina, née Knauth).   American philosopher.   Born in New York City, 20 December 1895. Studied at Radcliffe College, Cambridge, Massachusetts, B.A. 1920, M.A. 1924, Ph.D. 1926; University of Vienna, 1921-22. Married William L. Langer in 1921 (divorced, 1942); 2 sons. Tutor in Philosophy, Radcliffe College, 1927-42; Assistant Professor, University of Delaware, Newark, 1943; Lecturer in Philosophy, Columbia University, New York, 1945-50; Professor of Philosophy, 1954-61, and since 1961 Professor Emerita and Research Scholar in Philosophy, Connecticut College, New London. Visiting Professor, New York University, 1945; Northwestern University, Evanston, Illinois, 1950; Ohio State University, Columbus, 1950; University of Washington, Seattle, 1952-53; and University of Michigan, Ann Arbor, 1954. Recipient: Radcliffe Alumnae Achievement Medal, 1950. Honorary doctorate: Wilson College, Chambersburg, Pennsylvania, 1954; Mt. Holyoke College, South

Hadley, Massachusetts, 1962; Western College, Oxford, Ohio, 1962; Wheaton College, Norton, Massachusetts, 1962; Columbia University, 1964; Philadelphia College of Fine Arts, 1966; Clark University, Worcester, Massachusetts, 1968. Member, American Academy of Arts and Sciences. Address: Neck Road, Old Lyme, Connecticut 06371, U.S.A.

PUBLICATIONS

Philosophy

The Practice of Philosophy. New York, Holt, 1930.
An Introduction to the Study of Symbolic Logic. Boston, Houghton Mifflin, and London, Allen and Unwin, 1937.
Philosophy in a New Key: A Study in the Symbolism of Reason, Rite, and Art. Cambridge, Massachusetts, Harvard University Press, 1942.
Feeling and Form: A Theory of Art. New York, Scribner, and London, Routledge, 1953.
Problems of Art: Ten Philosophical Lectures. New York, Scribner, and London, Routledge, 1957.
Philosophical Sketches. Baltimore, Johns Hopkins University Press, and London, Oxford University Press, 1962.
Mind: An Essay on Human Feeling. Baltimore, Johns Hopkins University Press, 3 vols., 1967-82.

Other

The Cruise of the Little Dipper and Other Fairy Stories. New York, Norcross, 1923.

Editor, *Reflections on Art: A Source Book of Writings by Artists, Critics, and Philosophers.* Baltimore, Johns Hopkins University Press, 1958.

*

Critical Study: *Aesthetic Theory and Art: A Study in Susanne Langer* by Ranjan Kuman Ghosh, Delhi, Ajanta, 1979.

*   *   *

Susanne Langer is important in part because she has attempted to construct a philosophic system—i.e., in the words of A.N. Whitehead, who was an early influence on her philosophical thinking, "to frame a coherent, logical, necessary system of ideas in terms of which every element of our experience can be interpreted"—in which the arts (music, painting, poetry, dance, etc.) are no less important as forms of knowledge than mathematics and physics. From one perspective it might be said that Langer attempts to give a more adequate account than any previous theory or philosophy of "our serious attitude towards the arts," or for the enormous cultural and educational or intellectual significance which the arts assume in practically every culture. From a slightly different perspective, it is equally true to say that her interest in the arts, as a philosopher, is due essentially to the conviction that the arts in fact provide the most promising clues to puzzles about the nature and origin of experience, the mind, and knowledge. Because the arts are notoriously *symbolic*, this in turn suggests that from another perspective it may be said that Langer, following Ernst Cassirer especially but also several other illustrious contemporary philosophers, is persuaded that *symbolism* is the common key to the most difficult problems in understanding the distinctive forms of human experience. If we can only discover the origin and nature of symbol-making, she suggests, we shall be well on our way to understanding the functions, limits, and importance of myth, religion, art, and science. Certain of her claims suggest that she does not fully agree with Cassirer when he says that the human world is wholly a symbolic world. Perhaps she recognizes this tendency in herself

when she acknowledges that "Sheer observation is hard to contradict, for sense data have an inalienable semblance of 'fact.'" Certainly she often writes as if observation does indeed disclose facts. Yet she also says that "empiricism in science is jeopardized by the surprising truth that our sense data are primarily symbols," and that "What is directly observable is only a sign of the 'physical fact.'" Thus, although she is not completely unambiguous on the point, she seems to be committed, as Cassirer was, to the view that no one ever experiences *what is* directly but always in terms of a *symbolic transformation,* which is "a natural activity, a high form of nervous response, characteristic of man among the animals."

Langer has emphasized that the importance of symbolism has been widely recognized among contemporary philosophers and other scholars. She claims no distinction for herself in this respect. What she has attempted which others have not—at least not so systematically and at such great length—is to understand the arts as a symbolism which is continuous with the symbolism of language, science, and mathematics, to show how symbolism may be conceived as a development of *feeling* when feeling itself is "regarded as a phase of a physiological process" and how even "the greater concept of mind" may be described "as a phenomenon in terms of the highest physiological processes, especially those which have physical phases." Thus she has attempted a unified theory or account of all mythical, artistic, and scientific phenomena on the assumption that the most materialistic versions of modern science "are essentially sound."

The shape and trend of Langer's thought can perhaps best be briefly indicated by her treatment of music. The fact that music is central and paradigmatic in her theory is, in her own mind, one of its greatest achievements and strengths. The great significance of music is probably due in part, she claims, to the fact that musical forms share certain characteristics with language. Like language, music is made of separable items which are easily produced and easily combined in a variety of ways which finally assume a significance that is not merely sensuous but also semantical, in spite of the fact that music in the strictest sense has no vocabulary. Music, she suggests, can be best conceived as an "unconsummated symbol" which "can actually reflect...the morphology of feeling." Because musical forms resemble human feelings more than do the forms of language, music "can reveal the nature of feelings with a detail and truth that language cannot approach" and can in fact "present emotions and moods we have not felt, passions we did not know before." Viewing music as a semantic which negotiates insight into feeling, she suggests, accounts for both the intellectual and the emotional appeal of music. Music, like all art, is primarily symbolic, an illusion created by the artist but which also arises out of and expresses or negotiates insight into the form of human feeling. Even as the physical *stuff* of language is essentially irrelevant—though not dispensable—so in music and all art, according to Langer, the thingness of the work of art disappears into the illusion or symbol, and a work of art is "not, in any relevant way, a thing at all, but a symbol." Somewhat oddly, however, Langer concludes that because feeling is "a phase of a physiological process" and art negotiates insight into the forms of feeling, art is not concerned with anything actual. "Poetic statements are no more actual statements than the peaches in a still life are actual dessert." *Mutatis mutandis* the same may be said of all the arts. "Art...has no consequences."

—Willard E. Arnett

LASHLEY, K(arl) S(pencer). American psychologist. Born in Davis, West Virginia, 7 June 1890. Studied at the University of West Virginia, Morgantown, B.A. 1910; University of Pittsburgh, Pennsylvania, M.S. 1911; Johns Hopkins University,

Baltimore, Ph.D. 1914. Married Ann Baker in 1918; married Claire Schiller in 1957. Instructor, 1917-18, Assistant Professor, 1920-21, Associate Professor, 1921-24, and Professor of Psychology, 1924-26, University of Minnesota, Minneapolis; Research Psychologist, Behavior Research Fund, Institute for Juvenile Research, Chicago, 1927-29; Professor of Psychology, University of Chicago, 1929-35; Professor of Psychology, 1935-37, Research Professor in Neuropsychology, 1937-55, and Professor Emeritus, 1955-58, Harvard University, Cambridge, Massachusetts. Hughlings Jackson Memorial Lecturer, Montreal Neurological Clinic, 1937; Vanuxem Lecturer, Princeton University, New Jersey, 1952. Investigator, United States Interdepartmental Hygiene Board, 1919-20. Director, 1937-55, and Director Emeritus, 1955-58, Yerkes Laboratories of Primate Behavior, Orange Park, Florida. Associate Editor, *Journal of Genetic Psychology, Quarterly Review of Biology, Genetic Psychology Monographs*, and *Journal of Psychology*. President, American Psychological Association, 1929, and Society of American Naturalists, 1947. Recipient: Howard Crosby Warren Medal, Society of Experimental Psychologists, 1937; Daniel Giraud Elliot Medal, National Academy of Sciences, 1943; William Baly Medal, Royal College of Physicians, London, 1953. Honorary M.A.: Harvard University, 1942. Honorary doctorate: University of Pittsburgh, 1936; University of Chicago, 1941; Western Reserve University, Cleveland, 1951; Johns Hopkins University, 1953; University of Pennsylvania, Philadelphia, 1954. Member, National Academy of Sciences; American Academy of Arts and Sciences. Foreign Member, British Psychological Association; Royal Society. *Died 7 August 1958.*

PUBLICATIONS

Psychology

Brain Mechanisms and Intelligence. Chicago, University of Chicago Press, 1929.
The Neuropsychology of Lashley: Selected Papers, edited by Frank O. Beach and others. New York, McGraw Hill, 1960 (contains a full bibliography).

*   *   *

After completing his doctorate on cortical learning in rats, K.S. Lashley worked with Shepherd Franz at the Government Hospital for the Insane in Washington, D.C. In 1917 the two of them published work on the effects of cerebral destruction on habit-formation and retention in rats. Lashley soon took over this work from Franz and produced an important series of studies on the effects of cortical lesions on sensory discrimination and speed and ability in learning mazes in rats.

It was during this time that Lashley created the jump stand, an apparatus used in studying opperant conditioning. A rat is placed on a small stand and forced to jump through one of two doors, each of which is marked with a stimuli, such as vertical and horizontal lines. If he jumps through the correct door the rat finds some food or other reinforcement behind it. If he attempts to jump through the incorrect door he finds it locked, bumps his nose, and falls down into a net. In order to avoid the possibility that the rat is learning a position preference—that is, jumping through the right or left door—Lashley switched the doors back and forth at random.

Lashley summed up his general conclusions in a monograph entitled *Brain Mechanisms and Intelligence* in 1929. In this work, Lashley plotted the number of errors rats made in learning a maze against the amount of destruction of cortical tissue and against the difficulty of the maze. Lashley found that the more difficult the maze and the more extensive the cortical destruction, the more rapid was the increase in the number of errors the rats made. From this work Lashley laid down his principle of mass action, which stated that the more cortical area available

the more rapid and accurate the rat's learning. Lashley was unable to discover whether any specific area of the cortex was responsible for any specific function, and he determined that in general it was the size of the lesion, rather than its location, which impaired the rat's learning abilities. Although all of the lesions had some effect, none of them completely obliterated the rat's capabilities. Some years later, surveying the work he had done over the years, Lashley said facetiously that he was tempted to conclude that learning was impossible.

Lashley developed the principle of equipotentiality from this work. Equipotentiality stresses the complexity of habit-formation. According to this principle, which is an extension of the principle of mass action, the cortex is able to substitute new areas for control in performing a task when the old areas are destroyed.

Nonetheless, Lashley concluded that there were certain tasks where specific areas of the cortex were responsible for learning. For instance, the visual area is necessary for the rat to discriminate visual patterns; they are not, however, necessary to discriminate brightness. Thus, while more difficult learning tasks may indeed require extensive cortical use, simpler tasks, such as pattern discrimination, may after all have only one specific area of control available for use.

As early as 1929, Lashley raised a number of questions involving this matter of specific versus general areas of control. How do you put a relationship between two stimuli on a common path which carries the report of what is discriminated? How especially can this be done when the two stimuli are simultaneous? When they are successive? And how do you get temporal organizations within the cortex which take account of order?

Lashley's research shows just how it is possible for a physiological psychologist to study the neural bases of learning and discrimination, both of which can be measured through behavioral techniques, without resorting to the concept of consciousness.

—R.W. Rieber

LASKI, Harold (Joseph). British political and social scientist. Born in Manchester, England, 30 June 1893. Educated at Manchester Grammar School; New College, Oxford (Beit Prize, 1913), B.A. in modern history 1914. Married Frida Kerry in 1911; 1 daughter. Lecturer in History, McGill University, Montreal, 1914-16; Lecturer in Politics, Harvard University, Cambridge, Massachusetts, 1916-20; Lecturer, 1920-26, and Professor of Political Science, 1926-50, London School of Economics. Henry Ward Beecher Lecturer, Amherst College, Massachusetts, 1917; Harvard Lecturer, 1919-20, and Visiting Professor, 1931-33, Yale University, New Haven, Connecticut; Lecturer in Political Science, Magdalene College, Cambridge, 1922-25; Lecturer, Institute of Soviet Law, Moscow, 1934; Donnellun Lecturer, Trinity College, Dublin, 1936. Member, from 1920, and Member of Executive Committee, 1936-49, British Labour Party; Vice-Chairman, British Institute of Adult Education, 1921-30; Member, Fabian Society Executive, 1922-36; helped trade unions in strikes and participated in industrial arbitrations as member of Industrial Court, from 1926; Member, Lord Chancellor's Committee in Delegated Legislation, 1929-31, Departmental Committee in Local Government, 1931-32, Departmental Committee on Legal Education, and Council of the Institute for Public Administration, from 1932. LL.D.: University of Athens, 1937. *Died* (in London) *24 March 1950.*

PUBLICATIONS

Political and Social Philosophy

On the Correlation of Fertility with Social Value, with others.

London, Dulau, 1913.

Studies in the Problem of Sovereignty. New Haven, Connecticut, Yale University Press, and London, Oxford University Press, 1917.

Authority in the Modern State. New Haven, Connecticut, Yale University Press, and London, Oxford University Press, 1919.

Political Thought in England: From Locke to Bentham. New York, Holt, and London, Williams and Norgate, 1920.

The Foundations of Sovereignty and Other Essays. New York, Harcourt Brace, 1921; London, Allen and Unwin, 1922.

Karl Marx: An Essay. London, Allen and Unwin, 1922; New York, League for Industrial Democracy, 1933.

A Grammar of Politics. London, Allen and Unwin, and New Haven, Connecticut, Yale University Press, 1925.

On the Study of Politics (lecture). London, Oxford University Press, 1926.

Communism. New York, Holt, and London, Williams and Norgate, 1927.

The Dangers of Obedience and Other Essays. New York, Harper, 1930.

Liberty in the Modern State. New York, Harper, and London, Faber, 1930; revised edition, London, Allen and Unwin, 1948; New York, Viking, 1949.

The Relation of Justice to Law (lecture). London, Ethical Union, 1930.

The Socialist Tradition in the French Revolution. London, Fabian Society, 1930.

An Introduction to Politics. London, Allen and Unwin, 1931; as *Politics*, Philadelphia, Lippincott, 1931.

Nationalism and the Future of Civilisation (lecture). London, Watts, 1932.

Studies in Law and Politics. New Haven, Connecticut, Yale University Press, and London, Allen and Unwin, 1932.

Democracy in Crisis. Chapel Hill, University of North Carolina Press, and London, Allen and Unwin, 1933.

The Labour Party and the Constitution. London, Socialist League, 1933.

The State in Theory and Practice. New York, Viking, and London, Allen and Unwin, 1935.

The Rise of European Liberalism. London, Allen and Unwin, 1936; as *The Rise of Liberalism*, New York, Harper, 1936.

The Spirit of Co-operation (lecture). Manchester, Co-operative Union, 1936 (?).

Parliamentary Government in England. New York, Viking, and London, Allen and Unwin, 1938.

The Labour Party, The War, and the Future. London, Labour Party, 1939.

The American Presidency. New York, Harper, and London, Allen and Unwin, 1940.

The Danger of Being a Gentleman and Other Essays. New York, Viking, and London, Allen and Unwin, 1939.

The Decline of Liberalism (lecture). London, Oxford University Press, 1940.

Is This an Imperialist War? London, Labour Party, 1940.

Labour's Aims in War and Peace, with others. London, Labour Party, 1940.

Political Offences and the Death Penalty (lecture). London, E.G. Dunstan, 1940.

Where Do We Go from Here? New York, Viking, and London, Penguin, 1940.

Freedom of the Press in Wartime. London, National Council for Civil Liberties, 1941.

The Germans—Are They Human? London, Gollancz, 1941.

The Strategy of Freedom. New York, Harper, 1941; London, Allen and Unwin, 1942.

Marx Today. London, Gollancz-Fabian Society, 1943.

Reflections on the Revolution of Our Time. New York, Viking, and London, Allen and Unwin, 1943.

Faith, Reason, and Civilization. New York, Viking, and London, Gollancz, 1944.

Will Planning Restrict Freedom? Cheam, Surrey, Architectural Press, 1944.

The Place of the Scientist in Post-War Administration (lecture). London, n.p., 1945.

The Webbs and Soviet Communism (lecture). London, Fabian Society, 1947.

The American Democracy. New York, Viking, 1948; London, Allen and Unwin, 1949.

Communist Manifesto: Socialist Landmark. London, Allen and Unwin, 1948.

Socialism as Internationalism. London, Fabian Society, 1949.

Trade Unions in the New Society. New York, Viking, 1949; London, Allen and Unwin, 1950.

Reflections on the Constitution. New York, Viking, and Manchester, Manchester University Press, 1951.

The Dilemma of Our Times. London, Allen and Unwin, 1952.

Other

Holmes-Laski Letters: Correspondence of Mr. Justice Holmes and Harold J. Laski 1916-1935, edited by Mark DeWolfe Howe. Cambridge, Massachusetts, Harvard University Press, 2 vols., 1953.

Editor, *Collected Legal Papers of Oliver Wendell Holmes.* New York, Harcourt Brace, 1920.

Editor, *Letters of Edmund Burke: A Selection.* London, Oxford University Press, 1922.

Editor, *The Library of European Political Thought.* London, Benn, 1926-28.

Translator, with Frida Laski, *Law in the Modern State*, by Léon Duguit. New York, Huebsch, 1919.

*

Critical Studies: *Harold Laski* by Kingsley Martin, New York, Viking Press, and London, Gollancz, 1953; *Harold Laski* by Granville Eastwood, London, Mowbrays, 1977.

*　　*　　*

While some of Harold Laski's activities and writings were of short-term interest (concerned as they were with day-to-day affairs), most of his books have had a longer vogue and some a lasting value. One, *A Grammar of Politics*, has been described as "a milestone on the road from Plato," Laski explaining that the volume's purpose is "to construct a theory of the place of the State in the great Society." In some of his earlier books he had been largely critical or had discussed technical issues in political philosophy; in "The Grammar" (as it is affectionately called) he discussed the objections of those who had criticised his earlier volumes.

Laski attempted in his writings to find the answer to the question "Since government is necessary who is to give orders to whom and upon what terms." Over the years, in the course of his articles and books, he returned to the basic questions of States and Government. Making the proposition that the State is "an organization for enabling the mass of men to realise social good on the largest possible scale" Laski asserted that political power, too, will be found there. In *The State in Theory and Practice* he claimed that the true end of the State was the "creation of those conditions under which the members of the State may attain the maximum satisfaction of their desires." And he asserted that "any State in which the instruments of property are in private hands is, by that fact, biased in its incidence."

In his *Parliamentary Government in England* Laski discusses the question as to whether the Parliamentary method can be used to transform the social foundation on which it rests and can continue after such a transformation. He argues that if the House of Commons were to be refashioned to correspond with the way the electorate voted it would not be in a position to present to the nation a strong and effective administration.

Contributing to a volume published under the title *I Believe*, Laski set out the reasons for his accepting the basic truth of the Marxist philosophy which he developed in his writings. He said that during his comparatively brief stay, as a young man, in America, he had seen more nakedly than in Europe the significance of the struggle between capital and labour and "how little meaning there can be in an abstract political liberty which is subdued to the control of economic plutocracy." He said he came back to England from the United States convinced that liberty had no meaning save in the context of equality, adding that "and I had begun to understand that equality also has no meaning unless the instrument of production is socially owned."

At the height of the 1939-45 war Laski wrote two books on the theme that a world revolution was taking place and that while Russia had achieved one form of socialism the Western world should also progress towards another type, non-violently if at all possible and without loss of the liberty of the individual. The books were *Reflections on the Revolution of Our Time* and *Faith, Reason, and Civilization*; of the latter a *Times* newspaper reviewer commented that it was a scintillating book and went on: "It is not to everybody's political and economic taste but everybody will be the better for having read and—still more—having digested it."

In his book *Communism* (1927), Laski had said that whatever the shortcomings of Marxism it was "far more important to grasp the truth it emphasises than to be merely denunciatory of the methods by which it seeks its ends." And when in 1948 the Labour Party celebrated the centenary of the "Communist Manifesto" by the publication of a new edition Laski wrote an introduction. It occupied more than half the volume and, claiming that Marx's desire for justice for the mass of people was one of the main driving forces of his life, Laski summed it up as "the desire to take from the shoulders of the people the burden by which it is oppressed.... He transformed the fears of the workers into hope, he translated their efforts from interest in political mechanisms to interest in social foundations.... He was often wrong, he was rarely generous, he was always bitter; yet when the roll of those to whom the emancipation of the people is due comes to be called, few will have a more honourable and none a more eminent role."

—Granville Eastwood

LECOMTE DU NOÜY, Pierre (-André-Léon). French biophysicist and philosopher. Born in Paris, 20 December 1883. Educated at the Lycée Carnot, Paris; studied at the Sorbonne, Ph.B. 1901, Ph.D. 1905, Sc.D. 1916; Faculté de Droit, Paris, LL.B. 1905. Served in the French Army, 1914-19. Married Jeanne Double in 1911 (divorced, 1922), 1 son; married Mary Harriman Bishop in 1923. Practiced law in Paris and served as private secretary to the Minister of Justice, 1909; worked in the Research Laboratory, Hôpital du Front, No. 21, Compiègne, 1916-19; Associate Member, Rockefeller Institute of Medical Research, New York, 1920-27; Director, Department of Biophysics, Pasteur Institute, Paris, 1927-36; lived and lectured in America, 1943-47. Recipient: Certificate of Merit, Franklin Institute of Pennsylvania, 1922; Grand Prix des Sciences, 1923; Prix Vitet, French Academy; Prix Arnold Raymond, 1944. Member, German Academy of Sciences; Romanian Academy of Sciences. Fellow, American Association for the Advancement of Science. *Died* (in New York City) *22 September 1947.*

PUBLICATIONS

Biological Sciences and Philosophy

Surface Equilibria of Biological and Organic Colloids. New York, Reinhold, 1926.
Methodes physiques en biologie et en médecin. Paris, Baillière, 1933.
Le Temps et la vie. Paris, Gallimard, 1936; as *Biological Time,* London, Methuen, 1936; New York, Macmillan, 1937.
La Température critique du serum. Paris, Hermann, 1936; as *The Critical Temperature of Serum,* New York, Reinhold, 1945.
L'Homme devant la science. Paris, Flammarion, 1939; as *The Road to Reason,* New York, Longman, 1948.
L'Avenir de l'esprit. Paris, Gallimard, 1941.
La Dignité humaine. New York, Brentano, 1944.
Human Destiny. New York and London, Longman, 1947.
Entre savoir et croire. Paris, Hermann, 1967; as *Between Knowing and Believing,* New York, McKay, 1967.

*

Bibliography: in *Evolution in Perspective: Commentaries in Honor of Pierre Lecomte du Noüy,* edited by George N. Shuster and Ralph E. Thorson, Notre Dame, Indiana, University of Notre Dame Press, 1970.

Critical Studies: *Pierre Lecomte du Noüy: De l'agnosticisme à la foi* by Mary Lecomte du Noüy, Paris, La Colombe, 1955; *De quelques apprentis-sorciers: Gandhi, Jean XXIII, Teilhard de Chardin, Lecomte du Noüy, C.G. Jung* by Carlo Suarès, Brussels, Être Libre, 1956.

* * *

While the intellectual development of most thinkers may be seen as the progressive elaboration of initial insights, the protracted thinking of Pierre Lecomte du Noüy was an unbroken line of meditation that attained its climactic statement only at the end. *Human Destiny,* which rapidly spawned dozens of editions in twenty-three languages, was first published in 1947, a few months before its author died. During World War I, Lecomte du Noüy had studied the cicatrization of wounds, the healing process involving the formation of new connective tissue, in order to predict the healing time for injuries. At first assuming that the area of the wound would be the chief determinant in healing time, he soon discovered that the age of the victim is equally relevant, so that, for example, a wound that would cicatrize within a month in a person of twenty will take 78 days in a person of fifty. His formula for predicting initial recovery allowed for accurate assessment of hospital needs in the battlefield. While constituting an original contribution to the mathematical treatment of biological problems, Lecomte du Noüy conceived in these early studies the concept of biological time. Ageing and healing processes operate in terms of a biological time intrinsic to the organism and quite at variance with sidereal time. In *Biological Time* he argued that given the unity of mind and body in an individual, biological time implies psychological time in which both mind and body experience time in contrast to projecting it abstractly on the actual infinity of the cosmos as sidereal time.

Lecomte du Noüy then turned his attention to the application of physical concepts and techniques to biology and cognate fields. His research into serum led to better understanding of the basis of immunity and also of antigen activity. He invented several instruments for ascertaining the surface tensions of liquids and for circulating serum slowly without contamination, and he showed how to establish molecular size in biological fluids containing proteins. As a pioneer in biophysics, he set up a model biophysical laboratory at the Pasteur Institute in Paris, where he developed an infrared spectrograph. Throughout his life as a theoretical and especially as an applied scientist, Lecomte du Noüy viewed scientific endeavor as an avenue for exploring ultimate questions concerning the meaning of human existence and the future of mankind.

In *The Road to Reason* he contended that in science complex phenomena are analyzed into simpler elements with consequent changes in the scale of observation (*e.g.*, looking at a molecule is not the same as looking at a visible piece of an object composed of such molecules). When the observer crosses a certain threshold in the scale, the unity of the phenomenon is lost. One will not discover a pointillist painting by examining isolated dots of paint. Unity of knowledge is a seductive dream; only continuity of experimental research will show if it corresponds to reality. Since phenomena are arbitrarily isolated for study, they are assigned beginnings and endings. From the standpoint of universal evolution, life and death may be arbitrarily starting and stopping points assumed by human beings. Statistical laws can provide some understanding of phenomena the real causes of which are unknown, but they do not provide a proper perspective for raising ultimate questions. The problem for science is critical distance, the point on the scale of observation that allows access to worthwhile considerations. Knowledge must be supported by imagination, a promising proclivity of youth too often stifled by formal education and "artificial life." Given the need for an imaginative perspective and the inherent weakness of statistical laws to explain the emergence of life in inorganic matter, finalism (later called telefinalism) bridges the gap between the enigma of evolution and the failure of crude determinism to account for it. *Telefinalism* posits a goal in all evolution without presupposing a single mechanism for achieving it. This entelechy is not mathematically expressible or conceivable by the mere intellect, a paradigm perplexing to many scientists although no more problematic than the intellect itself which creates science. Scientific endeavor points to an unknown goal and a presiding principle often called God, but the crises confronting mankind are ultimately moral, not scientific, and cannot be solved solely by narrowly conceived scientific means.

In *Human Destiny* Lecomte du Noüy reiterated and elevated this line of thinking into a rich perspective on human life. Biological evolution shows that a species which becomes stable in its ecological niche may survive for an enormous time, but it has reached a dead end. Nature prefers emerging possibilities to stable antecedents. Only unstable species promise evolutionary advancement. The role of individuals in evolution is unclear because statistical laws—adequate for inorganic sciences—cannot take individuals into account. Telefinalism manifests itself as the will to liberty through unstable species; in this sense, the human brain was the goal of purely physical evolution. Once man became conscious of choice he was emancipated from the laws governing unconscious nature. The capacity to decide marks the emergence of conscience in man, and in order to evolve he must no longer obey Nature. Insofar as biological problems remain for the human being, they are not worked out through morphological adaptation, but rather a trial on the biological plane transforms itself into a test on the psychological plane. The degree of humanness in any individual is revealed not by method or result, but by the effort put forth to be liberated from material bondage and blind desire. "Liberty is not only a privilege; it is a test." Man is fundamentally responsible for his future evolution.

For Lecomte du Noüy, man need not visualize God any more than he need visualize the electron. No image of God can prove God's existence, but the effort made to formulate an image is proof enough. Intelligence has not evolved over time—the ancient Greeks were as intelligent as modern man—but there is growth in spirituality. Spiritual thought was exemplified by Jesus, the eloquent prototype of human destiny. Yet man can choose to retreat into savagery as well as advance toward his destiny. Since moral evolution—the consequence of man's liberation from physical evolution—depends upon choice, humanity advances through its noblest individuals. The struggle for life has been replaced by the struggle for morality and spirituality, with

conscience as the key to the conflict. In order to progress humanity must avoid purposelessness in science and superstition in religion. The unity of religions cannot be discovered by looking for what is human in their doctrines but should be sought in what is universal and divine in man. Pride hinders the fanatic and the unbeliever, for the former denies intelligence, the latter intuition.

Beyond the parameters of science based on statistical laws and outside of received tradition, each individual must concentrate his will on the construction of an unshakeable faith, at least in human dignity and destiny. From this standpoint, present tragedies may be viewed in a larger whole: rather than being pessimistic, in the evolving realm of human spirit where effort is more important than immediate results, one may affirm that humanity can undergo major changes toward true unity, ultimate knowledge, and irradiating love within the next few thousand years. Lecomte du Noüy combined his contagious optimism with practical inventiveness, scientific interest, and philosophical concern to delineate possibilities for humanity that preclude regret for the past or indulgent gloom in the present. "We must therefore turn toward the future and model a new youth—rich in ideals, liberated from pseudophilosophical impostures, strengthened by an unalloyed science, respectful of its mission, and capable of transmitting the flickering torch to future generations" (*The Road to Reason*).

—R.N. Iyer

LE CORBUSIER. French architect and theorist. Born Charles-Edouard Jeanneret in La Chaux-de-Fonds, Switzerland, 6 October 1887; emigrated to France in 1917: naturalized, 1930; adopted the pseudonym Le Corbusier in 1920. Studied engraving at the School of Applied Arts, La Chaux-de-Fonds, 1900-05. Married Yvonne Gallis in 1930. Worked in the office of the architect Josef Hoffmann, Vienna, 1907, Auguste Perret, Paris, and with Walter Gropius and Mies van der Rohe in the office of Peter Behrens, Berlin, 1910; Founder and Director, L'Atelier d'Art Réunis, La Chaux-de-Fonds, 1909-14, and Instructor, l'Eplattenier's Nouvelle Section de l'Ecole d'Art, La Chaux-de-Fonds, 1911-14; also worked as a painter and lithographer from 1912. In private practice as an architect, Paris, 1917-65: in partnership with his cousin Pierre Jeanneret, 1922-40; collaborated with the architect Charlotte Perriand, 1927-29; Practised at ATBAT (Atelier des Bâtisseurs), from 1942; developed Modulor System, with Hanning and Elisa Maillard, 1943-48; Chief Planner, La Rochelle-Pallice, France, 1945; Architectural Adviser, Capital City, Chandigarh, India, 1951-59. Founder and Editor, with Amédée Ozenfant and Paul Dermée, *L'Esprit Nouveau*, Paris, 1919-25. Founder and Member, CIAM (Congrès Internationaux d'Architecture Modern), 1928; Founder, ASCORAL (Assemblée de Constructeurs pour une Renovation Architecturale), Paris, 1942. Lectured extensively at universities in Europe and the United States, 1921-56. Recipient, Medal, *Exposition International d'Art Décoratif*, Turin, 1902; First Prize, with Pierre Jeanneret, League of Nations Competition, Geneva, 1927; Gold Medal, Royal Institute of British Architects, 1959. Honorary doctorate: University of Zurich, 1933; Eidgenössische Technische Hochschule, Zurich, 1955; Cambridge University, 1959. Chevalier, 1937, Commandeur, 1952, and Grand Officier, 1963, Légion d'Honneur. *Died* (at Cap Martin, France) *27 August 1965.*

PUBLICATIONS

Art, Architecture and City Planning

Étude sur le mouvement d'art décoratif en Allemagne (as

Charles Edouard Jeanneret).   La Chaux-de-Fonds, Switzerland, Haefeli, 1912.

Après le cubisme (as Edouard Jeanneret), with Amédée Ozenfant.   Paris, Éditions des Commentaires, 1918.

Vers une architecture.   Paris, Crès, 1923; as *Towards a New Architecture*, London, Rodker, and New York, Etchells Warren and Putnam, 1927.

La Peinture moderne (as Edouard Jeanneret), with Amédée Ozenfant.   Paris, Crès, 1925.

L'Art décoratif d'aujourd'hui.   Paris, Crès, 1925.

Urbanisme.   Paris, Crès, 1925; as *The City of Tomorrow and Its Planning*, New York, Etchells Payson and Clarke, 1927; London, Rodker, 1929.

Almanach d'architecture moderne.   Paris, Crès, 1926.

Une Maison, un palais.   Paris, Crès, 1928.

Vers le Paris de l'epoque machiniste.   Paris, Le Redressement Français, 1928.

Précisions sur un état présent de l'architecture et de l'urbanisme.   Paris, Crès, 1930.

Croisade; ou, Le Crépuscule des académies.   Paris, Crès, 1932.

La Maison de verre.   Geneva, L'Art en Suisse, 1933.

La Ville radieuse: Éléments d'une doctrine d'urbanisme pour l'équipement de la civilisation machiniste.   Paris, Éditions de l'Architecture d'Aujourd'hui, 1935; as *The Radiant City*, New York, Orion Press, 1965.

Quand les cathédrales étaient blanches: Voyage au pays des timides.   Paris, Plon, 1937; as *When the Cathedrals Were White: A Journey to the Country of Timid Souls*, New York, Reynal and Hitchcock, 1947.

Les Tendances de l'architecture rationaliste en rapport avec la peinture et de la sculpture.   Rome, Reale Accademia d'Italia, 1937.

Des canons, des munitions? Merci! des logis, s.v.p.   Paris, Éditions de l'Architecture d'Aujourd'hui, 1938.

Air Craft.   London and New York, The Studio, 1935.

Le Lyrisme des temps nouveaux et l'urbanisme.   Colmar, Le Point, 1939.

Oeuvre plastique, peintures, et dessins.   Paris, Morance, 1939.

Destin de Paris.   Paris, Sorlot, 1941.

Sur les quatre routes.   Paris, Gallimard, 1941; as *The Four Routes*, London, Dobson, 1947.

La Maison des hommes, with François de Pierrefou.   Paris, Plon, 1942; as *The Home of Man*, London, Architectural Press, 1949.

Les Constructions "Muroundin."   Paris, Chiron, 1942.

La Charte d'Athènes.   Paris, Plon, 1943.

Entretiens avec les étudiants des écoles d'architecture.   Paris, Denöel, 1943; as *Talks with Students from the Schools of Architecture*, New York, Orion Press, 1961.

Les Trois Établissements humains, with others.   Paris, Denöel, 1946.

Propos d'urbanisme.   Paris, Bourrelier, 1945; as *Concerning Town Planning*, London, Architectural Press, and New Haven, Connecticut, Yale University Press, 1948.

Manière de penser l'urbanisme.   Paris, Éditions de l'Architecture d'Aujourd'hui, 1946.

Lettre 27 juin 1945 (sur le role du bâtisseur).   Paris, Les Nouvelles Épîtres, 1947.

United Nations Headquarters.   New York, Reinhold, 1947.

New World of Space.   New York, Reynal and Hitchcock, 1948.

Le Modulor: Essai sur une mesure harmonique à l'échelle humain applicable à l'architecture et à la méchanique.   Paris, Éditions de l'Architecture d'Aujourd'hui, 1950; as *The Modulor: A Harmonious Measure to the Human Scale Universally Applicable to Architecture and Mechanics*, London, Faber, and Cambridge, Massachusetts, Harvard University Press, 1954.

Le Problème de la normalisation.   Paris, Presses Universitaires de France, 1950.

Poésie sur Alger.   Paris, Editions Falaize, 1950.

L'Unité d'habitation de Marseille.   Mulhouse, Le Point, 1950; as *The Marseilles Block*, London, Harvill Press, 1953.

Y a-t-il une crise de l'art?   Venice, Société Européenne de Culture, 1951.

Une Petite Maison.   Zurich, Editions Girsberger, 1954.

Modulor II: La Parole est aux usagers.   Paris, Éditions de l'Architecture d'Aujourd'hui, 1955; as *Modulor 2: Let the User Speak Next*, London, Faber, 1958.

L'Urbanisme est une clef.   Paris, Editions Forces Vives, 1955.

Architecte du bonheur.   Paris, Presses de l'Ile-de-France, 1955.

Le Poème de l'angle droit.   Paris, Tériade, 1955.

Les Plans de Paris.   Paris, Editions de Minuit, 1956.

L'Urbanisme des trois établissements humains, edited by Jean Petit.   Paris, Éditions de Minuit, 1959.

L'Atelier de la recherche patient.   Paris, Frèal, 1960; as *My Work*, London, Architectural Press, 1960, and as *Creation Is a Patient Search*, New York, Praeger, 1960.

Orsay Paris.   Paris, Éditions Forces Vives, 1961.

Textes et dessins pour Ronchamp.   Paris, Éditions Forces Vives, 1965.

Le Voyage d'orient.   Paris, Éditions Forces Vives, 1966.

Les Maternelles.   Paris, Gonthier Denöel, 1968.

*

Critical Studies: *Le Corbusier and the Tragic View of Architecture* by Charles Jencks, Cambridge, Massachusetts, Harvard University Press, 1973; *Le Corbusier in Perspective* by Peter Serenyi, Englewood Cliffs, New Jersey, Prentice Hall, 1974; *The Open Hand: Essays on Le Corbusier* edited by Russell Walden, Cambridge, Massachusetts, M.I.T. Press, 1977.

*

For a complete listing of Le Corbusier's buildings, plans and exhibitions, see *Contemporary Architects*, edited by Muriel Emanuel, London, Macmillan, and New York, St. Martin's Press, 1980.

*   *   *

Le Corbusier, "the builder," was the pseudonym by which one of the most influential architects of the 20th century, Charles Edouard Jeanneret, chose to be known. The Swiss-born Le Corbusier entered the art school in La Chaux-de-Fonds at the age of 14. His first important teacher, Charles L'Eplattenier, directed Le Corbusier to architecture and, thereafter, the artist pursued the practice of architecture and painting. In 1907 Le Corbusier began an extended period of travel and study. He visited northern Italy; in Vienna, he met Josef Hoffmann; in Lyons, he met Tony Garnier; in Paris, he spent 15 months in the office of Auguste Perret; in Berlin, he was employed by Peter Behrens. His experiences exposed him to the problems of architecture posed by industrialism, to the potentialities of modern materials, especially steel and re-inforced concrete, and to theories of functionalism. In 1911 he traveled through Italy, the Balkans, and Asia Minor where he was impressed by the geometric clarity of classical and modern vernacular buildings and by the distinction maintained between the natural environment and man-made structures.

In 1917 Le Corbusier settled in Paris. The urban environment, with its reordering of the patterns of contemporary life, became the chief preoccupation of Le Corbusier's career. He addressed the issues raised by the growth of modern cities in a variety of ways. He collaborated with the painter Amédée Ozenfant in initiating the Purist Movement (1918) and in founding the review, *L'Esprit Nouveau*, which, in combination with later writings, became a vehicle for his ideas on architecture. He was one of the principal organizers of the first International Congress of Modern Architecture (1928). He developed architectural projects of major significance, including the Citrohan houses, "Immeubles-Villas," and the designs for a city of 3,000,000 inhabitants. Finally, he built structures which utilized modern building materials and techniques while retaining what Le Corbusier considered to be the principles of visual clarity and harmonic proportions fundamental to all great architecture.

Le Corbusier was concerned with both private and public forms of architecture. He redefined the family dwelling as the "machine for living." Seeking to find a rational solution to the problem of providing mass housing, Le Corbusier incorporated in the Dom-ino project (1914) a system of building a skeleton consisting of two horizontal concrete slabs supported by columns and which was capable of being mass-produced. The Villa Savoye, in Poissy-sur-Seine (1929), demonstrates the masterly manipulation of these simple elements of which Le Corbusier was capable. Planned as a perfect square, the house is raised above the ground on pilotis. Parts of the cubic structure are hollowed out to create outdoor spaces. Elongated ribbon windows permit a view of the surrounding landscape. Exterior and interior surfaces are carefully finished, ironically with skilled craft labor to suggest the precision of machined surfaces. In Unité d'Habitation, Marseilles, (1945-52), Le Corbusier tackled the problem of social housing. The structure consists of a reinforced concrete cage with 337 structurally independent dwelling units designed in 23 different types to accommodate the widest possible range of individual family needs. In addition, Le Corbusier sought to provide for collective needs by placing a shopping street in the middle of the slab-like building and by designing playgrounds and a gymnasium on the roof.

Le Corbusier also considered the problems of the city as a whole. In his projects of urban renovation, he admitted the need for the concentration of population in densely occupied areas, and he recognized the impact of the automobile on the city. His plans called for the construction of skyscrapers as residential units, for the multiplication of green areas as recreational centers and for the separation of traffic areas. In the 1950's Le Corbusier was commissioned to plan the city of Chandigarh, the new capital of Punjab, and to construct a monumental ensemble of buildings. Both the general plan and the individual structures demonstrate Le Corbusier's life-long concerns.

The early work of Le Corbusier is characterized by the same desire to define simple volumes and to achieve geometric order that can be seen in his paintings and in Cubism. Later works by Le Corbusier, such as the Ronchamp Chapel (1950-53) are more plastic in form. The sweeping curves of the walls and roof, the dramatic use of light and the roughly textured use of concrete are laden with a multiplicity of meaning. But despite the contrast in appearance between Le Corbusier's early Purist work and the more evocative work of the 1950's, an underlying continuity of approach can be traced. While never sacrificing beauty to utility, Le Corbusier created modern architectural forms appropriate to contemporary life. While designing structures ranging from single family dwellings to entire cities, Le Corbusier consistently placed all plans on a harmonic system of proportions, which he called the "Modular." Finally, whether constructing straight smooth surfaced buildings or rough textured flowing structures, Le Corbusier considered architecture to be a form of sculpture, a sculpture which both reflected and shaped modern life.

—Linnea H. Wren

LENIN, V(ladimir) I(l'ich). Russian revolutionary theorist and political leader. Born Vladimir Il'Ich Ul'ianov in Simbirsk, now Ulianovsk, 10 April 1870. Studied law at the University of Kazan (expelled for political reasons in 1887); external student, St. Petersburg University; passed law examinations in 1891. Married Nadezhda Krupskaia in 1898. Worked with Marxist groups and was arrested and exiled to Siberia, 1897-1900.

Founded the periodical *Iskra* ("The Spark") in Munich in 1901, and the Bolshevik Party in 1903. Lived abroad, 1900-1905, 1907-17, and returned to Russia in 1917 to lead the Bolshevik overthrow of the Provisional Government. Founded the Communist International in 1919 and introduced the New Economic Policy in 1921. Suffered a stroke in 1921. *Died* (in Gor'kii) *21 January 1924.*

PUBLICATIONS

Collections

Sobranie sochinenii [Collected Works]. Moscow, Gosudarstvennoe izd-vo, 20 vols. in 26 parts, 1921-23; 5th revised and expanded edition as *Polnoe sobranie sochinenii* [Complete Works] 55 vols., 1958-65; 4th Russian edition as *Collected Works*, Moscow, Foreign Languages Publishing House, and London, Lawrence and Wishart, 45 vols., 1960-68.

Leninskie sborniki [The Lenin Collections]. Moscow, Gospolitizdat, 37 vols., 1924-70.

Selected Works. New York, International Publishers, 3 vols., 1967.

Social and Political Theory

Ekonomicheskie etiudy: stat'i [Studies in Economics]. St. Petersburg, Leiferta, 1899.

Razvite kapitalizma v Rossii: protsess obrazovaniia vnutrenniago rynka dlia krupnoi promyshlennosti Vladmir Il'in. St. Petersburg, Leiferta, 1899; as *The Development of Capitalism in Russia*, Moscow, Foreign Languages Publishing House, 1958.

Chto dielat'?: Nabolevshie voprosy nashego dvizheniia. Stuttgart, Dietz, 1902; as *What Is To Be Done?: Burning Questions of Our Movement*, London, Lawrence, and New York, International Publishers, 1929.

K derevenskoi biednotie: ob''iasnenie dlia krest'ian, chego khotiat sotsial'demokraty [The Village Poor: The Explanation for the Peasant of What the Social-Democrats Want]. Geneva, Izd. Zagranichnoi Ligi Russk. Revoliutsionnoi Sotsial'demokratii, 1903.

Shag vpered dva shaga nazad: kriziz v nashei partii. Geneva, Partii, 1904; as "One Step forward, two steps back," in *The Essentials of Lenin*, London, Lawrence and Wishart, 1947.

Dve taktiti sotsial'demokratii v demokraticheskoi revoliutsii. Geneva, Izd. TSentr. Kom. R.S.D.R.P., 1905; as *Two Tactics of Social-Democrats in the Democratic Revolution*, New York, International Publishers, 1935.

Pobeda kadetov i zadachi rabochei partii [The Kadets' Victory and the Tasks of the Workers Party]. St. Petersburg, Nasha mysl', 1906.

Agrarnaia programma sotsial-demokratii v pervoi russkoi revoliutsii 1905-1907 godov [Agrarian Problems of Social-Democrats in the First Russian Revolution of 1905-1907]. St. Petersburg, Zerno, 1908.

Za 12 liet: Sobranie statei [For 12 Years: A Collection of Articles]. St. Petersburg, Zerno, 1908.

Materializm i empiriokrititsizm: Kriticheskiia zamietki ob odnoi reaktsionnoi filosofii. Moscow, Zveno, 1909; as *Materialism and Empirio-Criticism: Critical Notes Concerning a Reactionary Philosophy*, London, Lawrence, 1927; New York, International Publishers, n.d.

Imperializm, kak novieishii etap kapitalizma: populiarnyi ocherk. Petrograd, Zhizn' i znanie, 1917; as *Imperialism, The Last Stage of Capitalism*, London, Communist Party of Great Britain, 1917; as *Imperialism, The Latest Stage in the Development of Capitalism*, Detroit, Marxian Educational Society, 1924.

Novyia dannyia o zakonakh razvitiia kapitalizma v zemledielii. Vypusk 1. Kapitalizm i zemledielie v Soed. Shtatakh Ameri-

ki. Petrograd, Zhizn' i znanie, 1917; as *Capitalism and Agriculture in the United States of America*, New York, International Publishers, 1934.

Iz istorii sotsial-demokraticheskoi agrarnoi programmy: Stat'i 1901-1906 [From the History of the Social-Democratic Agrarian Program: Articles of 1901-1906]. Petrograd, Zhizn' i znanie, 1917.

Agrarnyi vopros v Rossii k kontsu XIX vieka [Agrarian Questions in Russia at the End of the XIX Century]. Moscow, Zhizn' i znanie, 1918.

Protiv techeniia: Sbornik statei iz "Sotsial-demokrata," "Kommunista" i "Sbornika Sotsial-demokrata," with G. Zino'ev [Against the Current: A Collection of Articles from "Social-Democrat," "Kommunist" and "Sbornik Sotsial-Demokrata"]. Petrograd, Petrogradskii Soviet rabochikh i soldatskikh deputatov, 1918.

Proletarskaia revoliutsiia i renegat Kautskii. Moscow, Knigoizd-vo, "Kommunist," 1918; as *The Proletarian Revolution and Kautsky the Renegade*, New York, Contemporary Publishers Association, 1920.

Gosudarstvo i revoliutsiia: Uchenie marksizma o gosudarstvie i zadachi proletariata v revoliutsii. Petrograd, Zhizn' i znanie, 1918; as *The State and Revolution*, N.p., United Communist Party of America, 1917.

Detskaia bolezn' "levizny" v ₖommunizme. Petersburg, Gosudarstvennoe izd-vo, 1920; as *"Left Wing" Communism: An Infantile Disorder*, Detroit, Marxian Educational Society, 1921.

Novyi kurs: rechi i stat'i [The New Course: Speeches and Articles]. Ekaterinaburg, Uralgosizdat, 1921.

Starye stat'i na blizkie k novym temy: k voprosu o "novoi ekonomicheskoi politike": dve stat'i i odna rech' 1918 [Old Articles on Topics That Are Nearly New: On the Question of the "New Economic Policy"]. Moscow, Gosizdat, 1922.

Stat'i: Stranichki iz dnevnika, Kak nam reorganizovat' Rabkrin, Luchshe men'she, da luchshe, Doklad XI s"ezdu RKP [Articles: Pages from the Diary, How We Should Re-organize the Rabkrin, Better less, But Better: Report to the 11th Congress of the RKP]. Moscow, Gosizdat, 1923.

K kharakteristike ekonomicheskogo romantizma: Sismondi i nashi otechestvennye sismondisty [Towards the Characterization of Romanticism in Economic Theory: Sismondi and Our Home-grown Sismondians]. Moscow, Gosudarstvennoe izd-vo, 1923.

Ekonomicheskoe soderzhanie narodnichestva i kritika ego v knige g. Struve: Otrazhenie marksizma v burzhuaznoi literature [Economic Contents of Populism and Its Criticism in Mr. Struve's Book: Reflection of Marxism in Bourgeois Literature]. Moscow, Gosudarstvennoe izd-vo, 1923.

Taktika bol'shevizma: izbrannye stat'i i rechi 1905-1923 gg. [Tactics of Bolshevism: Selected Articles and Speeches, 1905-23]. Moscow, Moskovskii rabochii, 1923.

Izbrannye stat'i po natsional'nomu voprosu [Selected Articles on the Question of Nationality]. Moscow, Gosudarstvennoe izd-vo, 1923.

Aprel'skie tezisy. Moscow, Partiinoe izdatel'stvo, 1934 (first book edition); as *The April Conference*, London, Lawrence, and New York, International Publishers, 1932.

Other (selection)

The Letters of Lenin. New York, Harcourt Brace, 1937.

Translator, *The Theory and Practice of British Trade-Unionism*, by Beatrice and Sidney Webb. St. Petersburg, Izd. O. Popovoi, 1901.

*

Bibliography: *Khronologivhesky ukazatel proizvedeny V.I. Lenina* [Chronological Index to the Works of V.I. Lenin], Moscow, Institute of Marxism-Leninism, 3 vols., 1959-63.

Critical Studies: *Leninism* by Alfred G. Meyer, Cambridge, Massachusetts, Harvard University Press, 1957; *The Life of Lenin* by Louis Fischer, New York, Harper, 1964; *Lenin* by Robert D. Warth, New York, Twayne, 1972.

*   *   *

Lenin's thought can be seen as a synthesis of two distinctive traditions, classical Marxism and Russian revolutionary populism. The first, at least as expounded by the Marxists of the Second International (1889-1914), conceived history to be a succession of modes of production rising and falling in response to the development of the productive forces. Plekhanov, for example, argued that socialism would only arise in Russia after the Tsarist regime had been overthrown and capitalism had been permitted to develop along Western European lines, creating the material conditions for the conquest of power of the working class. Till then the Russian socialist movement should conduct themselves as a loyal opposition to the liberal bourgeoisie.

The Russian populist revolutionaries of the latter part of the 19th century had also read their *Capital*, but they took it as an awful warning of a fate Russia could still avoid. They saw the peasant *mir*, or commune, as the basic of a socialist revolution which would cut short Russia's progress towards the horrors of industrial capitalism. And they organized a succession of revolutionary conspiracies in the hope, as one of them put it, of "giving history a push."

Lenin was always firmly in the Marxist camp, but rejected the quietism and fatalism characteristic of the Second International's politics. His early economic writings sought to demonstrate that Russia was already a long way down the road to capitalism: there could be no return to the rural past. However, works such as *The Development of Capitalism in Russia* go far beyond those of Plekhanov, revealing, with considerable theoretical subtlety and a wealth of empirical detail, less the inevitability of Russia following a Western path than the complex class structure by the advent of capitalism in town and country alike. Such a stress on class relations and class struggle distinguished Lenin's Marxism from the start.

Lenin's political strategy, especially as it evolved during and after the revolution of 1905, reflected his theoretical differences with "orthodox" Marxism in Russia as represented by Plekhanov and the Mensheviks. He continued to believe that Russia would inevitably pass through a period of bourgeois development, but argued that the nature of this development would depend on the outcome of the class struggle. If the Tsarist regime survived, then a "Prussian" solution was most likely—a gradual symbiosis of landowners and industrial bourgeoisie. On the other hand, if the monarchy was overthrown, then Russia would take the "American road," based on the political and economic primacy of the small producers, and permitting a rapid progress on the part of the labour movement towards socialism.

Which of these alternatives actually took place would depend, according to Lenin, on the role of the numerically small but economically and socially cohesive and powerful working class. The liberal bourgeoisie were already too closely integrated in Tsardom to pursue a revolutionary strategy, but the workers, in alliance with the peasantry, could provide the drive and leadership for a radical settling of accounts with absolutism. Thus, while Plekhanov feared and despised the "dark folk" of Russia's villages, regarding them as a potentially reactionary force, Lenin agreed with the populists to the extent of seeing the peasantry as an essential factor in the overthrow of the monarchy.

This schema accorded a central part to the working class. It is here he made his most important contribution to Marxism. Marx and Engels had believed that the working class would naturally and inevitably develop revolutionary consciousness in the course of their struggle against exploitation. Lenin rejected this doctrine, denying that the working class would "automatically gravitate to socialism." At best what could emerge from the economic class struggle was "trade-union consciousness," a sharp sense of the conflicts of interest between capital and labour lacking any strategy for achieving socialism. *What Is to Be Done?* is famous for its stress on the role of a centralized organization of revolutionaries in overcoming the limits of trade-union consciousness.

Undoubtedly Lenin drew here on the conspiratorial traditions of Russian populism, partly because of the exigencies of underground organization. But while the revolutionary populists created closed secret societies which acted on behalf of, but in isolation from, the masses, Lenin's party was to develop in constant interaction with the working class. In 1905 Lenin argued that the Bolsheviks should "throw open their doors" to the workers, and abandon many of the secretive and undemocratic practices imposed on them by Tsarist repression. He pursued the same course during 1912-14, when the Russian workers' movement revived after the defeat of the 1905 revolution.

Until 1914 Lenin operated mainly as a Russian Marxist, applying what he mistakenly believed to be the strategy of the Second International in a backward and despotically ruled country. The outbreak of the First World War, and the support given by the chief parties of the International to their respective governments forced Lenin to reappraise this attitude. Typically, he saw the war less as a catastrophe than as an opportunity for world revolution, coining the slogan "Turn the imperialist war into a civil war." At the same time as he adopted this uncompromisingly revolutionary stance, Lenin threw himself into an intensive study of Hegel's *Logic*. He emerged with a deeper sense of reality's complex and contradictory structures, of the uneven development between different societies, and of how they nevertheless formed a unified system. These insights informed his pamphlet on imperialism, where Lenin drew on Hilferding, Hobson, Bukharin, and others to give a comprehensive account of the manner in which the development of capitalism into a set of competing imperialist powers had laid the basis for the world war.

This theoretical recasting of Lenin's Marxism is crucial to understanding his subsequent political conduct. Thus, when revolution broke out in Russia in February 1917, Lenin approached it from an international perspective. Russia was not simply a specific social formation, possessing the class-structure he knew so well; it was also the weak link in the imperialist chain. By the time he returned to Petrograd in April 1917 Lenin no longer believed that revolution in Russia need confine itself to bourgeois limits: the workers and peasants could, by taking power, stimulate revolution in the great industrial centres of Europe.

Reflecting on the revolution shortly before his death, Lenin quoted Napoleon: "You commit yourself, and then you see." The Bolshevik gamble failed, despite the revolutionary upsurge which convulsed central Europe at the end of the First World War. The result was, inevitably, the degeneration of the Soviet state into a bureaucratic monster, as Lenin recognized in the last two years of his life. His legacy was *The State and Revolution*, written in the months before the Bolshevik seizure of power in October 1917. It showed how far Lenin had gone beyond both populism and Second International Marxism, and how profoundly he differed from his totalitarian successors. Socialist revolution could succeed, he argued, only by dismantling the structures of the capitalist state, and replacing them with workers' councils. Socialism, then, meant the radical extension of democracy, not its abolition or restriction. This vision of workers' power informed Lenin's Marxism, providing its objective. He combined this commitment of principle with great realism and tactical flexibility in selecting the means by which the goal should be attained. This "revolutionary *Realpolitik*," as Lukács called it, died with Lenin. Later Marxists have tended either to surrender to utopianism, or to prostitute their socialism to *raison d'état*.

—Alex Callinicos

LEONTIEF, Wassily (W.) American economist. Born in St. Petersburg, now Leningrad, Russia, 5 August 1906; emigrated to the United States, 1931; later naturalized. Studied at University of Leningrad, 1921-25, graduated in economics; University of Berlin, Ph.D. 1928. Married Estelle Helena Marks in 1932; 1 daughter. Research Economist, University of Kiel Economic Research Institute, 1927-28, 1930; Economic Adviser to the Chinese government, Nanking, 1929; with National Bureau of Economic Research, New York, 1931; Instructor, 1931, Assistant Professor, 1933-39, Associate Professor, 1939-46, Professor, 1946-75, Director of Economics Project, 1948-72, and Henry Lee Professor of Economics, 1973-75, Harvard University, Cambridge, Massachusetts; Professor since 1975, and Director of the Institute of Economic Analysis since 1978, New York University. Consultant, Department of Labor, 1941-47; Office of Strategic Services, 1943-45; United Nations, 1961-62 and from 1980; Department of Commerce, from 1966; and Environmental Protection Agency, from 1975. Senior Fellow and Chairman, Section F, British Association for the Advancement of Science, 1976. Recipient: Guggenheim Fellowship, 1940, 1950; Bernhard-Harms Prize in Economics (Germany), 1970; Nobel Prize in Economics 1973. Honorary doctorate: University of Brussels, 1962; University of York, 1967; University of Louvain, Belgium, 1971; University of Paris, 1972; University of Pennsylvania, Philadelphia, 1976; University of Lancaster, 1976. Member, American Academy of Arts and Sciences, and the National Academy of Sciences. Fellow, Econometric Society. Honorary Member, Japanese Economic Research Center; Royal Irish Academy; Corresponding Member, British Academy, and French Academy of Sciences; Honorary Fellow, Royal Statistical Association. Corresponding Fellow, Institut de France. Address: Institute of Economic Analysis, New York University, Room 203, 269 Mercer Street, New York, New York 10003, U.S.A.

PUBLICATIONS

Economics

Die Wirtschaft als Krieslauf. Berlin, 1928.
The Structure of American Economy, 1919-1929: An Empirical Application of Equilibrium Analysis. Cambridge, Massachusetts, Harvard University Press, 1941; enlarged edition, 1960.
Studies in the Structure of the American Economy: Theoretical and Empirical Explorations in Input-Output Analysis, with others. New York, Oxford University Press, 1953.
Essays in Economics: Theories and Theorizing. New York, Oxford University Press, 1966.
Input-Output Economics. New York, Oxford University Press, 1966.
The New Outlook in Economics. (lecture). York, University of York, 1967.
Struktureller Ansatz zur Analyse internationaler ökonomischer Interdependenzen. Kiel, University of Kiel, 1971.
The Economic System in an Age of Discontinuity: Long-Range Planning or Market Reliance? New York, New York University Press, 1976.
The Future of the World Economy: A United Nations Study, with others. New York, Oxford University Press, 1977.
Essays in Economics: vol. 2: Theories, Facts and Policies. Oxford, Blackwell, 1977; White Plains, New York, M.E. Sharpe, 1978.

*

Critical Studies: *Genese, contens, et prolongements de la notion de reproduction du capital selon Karl Marx, Boisguillebert, Quesnay, Leontiev* by Jacques Nagels, Brussels, Free University of Brussels, 1970; *Proceedings of the Fourth International Conference on Input-Output Techniques, Geneva, 8-12 January*

1968: Published in Honour of Wassily Leontief edited by A.P. Carter and A. Brody, Amsterdam and London, North-Holland, 2 vols., 1970.

* * *

Most economists would associate Wassily Leontief with one topic only—namely input-output or inter-industry economics. This first, significant attempt to model an economy empirically in a genuine, general equilibrium manner has certainly been a major contribution to the discipline, and is Leontief's outstanding accomplishment.

Leontief, much more than most other economists of such standing, has continued to work on the subject matter for which he originally established his reputation. It is not surprising, therefore, that he has not been particularly prolific compared with many of the other Nobel Prize winners in economics. Leontief has tackled the time-consuming problems of collecting, processing, and simplifying actual data. Solving practical problems with the use of analytical tools has been more important to him than involvement with theoretical controversy. The widespread use of input-output techniques by governments, business, and other academics involved in empirical research in several disciplines besides economics is the reward for this commitment to a problem-solving view of the role of economics. This commitment has not been shared sufficiently by economists in general, who, in Leontief's view, display a "continued preoccupation with imaginary, hypothetical rather than observable reality." The dominant theme in Leontief's work is the view that the only valid test of economic research is its empirical significance and practical implications. This was the basis of his attack on Keynes and the Cambridge economists in his 1937 paper (*Quarterly Journal of Economics*), and it motivated his warning during his presidential address to the American Economic Association in 1970 about the drift in the discipline away from facts to abstruse theorizing.

The narrowness of Leontief's contribution to economics is therefore more apparent than real. He has written widely on the development of economics and on economic policy, and for a wider audience than the economics profession. Academic economists in general, however, only tend to be acquainted with his technical writings on input-output methods of representing the interdependencies between various sectors or industries within an economy. At the most basic level this representation is merely an accounting statement of the destination of the gross output of each industry, whether it be as inputs to other industries (intermediate outputs) or as goods for final consumption. The idea of interdependencies between different segments of the economy goes back to Quesnay, who published his Tableau Economique in 1758. Similarly Leontief did not invent the mathematics of input-output analysis. What economists call "Leontief matrices" had long been known to mathematicians. Leontief's innovatory contribution was to operationalise the model with actual numbers; to calculate input-output coefficients from recorded data and to provide answers to practical questions in business and national economic planning via the necessary algebraic manipulations.

Despite this desire to operationalise, it does not mean that Leontief has not made a significant contribution to economic theory itself. Despite his scepticism about the application of mathematics to economics, he had a thorough mathematical training, and most of his research papers deal with the interpretation and application (proper and improper) of mathematical formulations used in economic theory. His earliest papers in the early 1930's were on the statistical estimation of demand and supply curves, and a still widely used exposition of the use of indifference curves in the analysis of foreign trade. These papers foreshadowed his continuing concern with adapting theoretical constructs to empirical reality. In input-output models themselves some consolidation or aggregation of separate activities into sectors is necessary. Leontief has been concerned with identifying when and what aggregation is and is not justified. It is a recurring problem in economics. The 1936 paper (*Econometrica*) on indices of the general price level and two 1947 papers (*Bulletin of the American Mathematical Society* and *Econometrica*) on the restrictive conditions for aggregation have contributed to an important literature, and have stimulated other important developments and debates within economics. Demand theorists have been encouraged to investigate the demand for commodity groups (grouped according to the purposes they serve) rather than for individual commodities. The restrictive conditions for aggregation have formed the basis of the controversy about neo-classical capital and distribution theories based on production functions in which capital appears as a single aggregate.

Thus Leontief has published papers on international trade theory, non-competitive markets, Marxian economics, the estimation of demand curves, aggregation problems, and Keynesian macro-economics. But from 1934 onwards, his major efforts were devoted to the development of input-output and its applications, and to the direction of the Harvard Economic Research Project, which he founded and headed. The first papers announcing his discovery appeared in 1936 and 1937, but the definitive statement is found in *The Structure of American Economy, 1919-1929*, first published in 1941. The subsequent refinements (incorporation of the foreign sector) and extensions (temporal and spatial) of the approach, which have been aided by the arrival of the electronic computer, are to be reflected in his subsequent major monographs. Leontief has remained at the forefront of this area of analysis. Indeed, Leontief's most recent and ambitious input-output model is one for the world economy prepared for the United Nations. He has used the model to investigate the future of the world economy! Clearly the technique has great potentiality and practical relevance. Its usefulness depends critically, however, upon the assumption of the fixity or proportionality of input-output relationships. For Leontief the validity of this assumption is an empirical problem. Paradoxically it has been Leontief's empirical work which has frequently been the stimulus for many of the developments in economic theory of which he himself has been critical. Following his application of input-output analysis to the resource content of United States foreign trade in papers in 1954 and 1956 (*Proceedings of the American Philosophical Society* and *Review of Economics and Statistics*), he concluded in complete contradiction to the received theoretical belief of the day that U.S. exports were more labour-intensive than U.S. imports. This result, known as the "Leontief paradox" has induced many attempts to revise the traditional theory. But there is, of course, no paradox in empirically refuting the conclusions of an abstract model. Leontief has merely sought to bridge the gap between theoretical concepts in economics and observable phenomena more satisfactorily. He has been more successful than most.

—Chris Milner

LE ROY LADURIE, Emmanuel. French historian. Born in Moutiers-en-Cinglais, 19 July 1929. Educated at Collège Saint-Joseph, Caen; Lycée Henri-IV, Paris; Lycée Lakanal, Sceaux; École Normale Supèrieure, Paris; Faculté des Lettres, Paris, Agrégé, Docteur-ès-Lettres. Married Madeleine Pupponi in 1955; 2 children. Taught at the Lycée Montpellier, 1953-57; Attaché de Recherche, Centre National de la Recherche Scientifique, 1957-60; Assistant, Faculté des Lettres, Montpellier, 1960-63; Maitre-Assistant, 1963-65, and since 1965, Directeur d'Études, l'École Pratique des Hautes Études, Paris; Maitre de Conferences, Faculté des Lettres, Paris, 1969; Professor, L'Unité d'Enseignement et de Recherches de Geographie et Sciences, Société de l'Université de Paris-VII, since 1970; Chaire d'Histoire de la Civilisation Moderne, Collège de France, since 1973. Chevalier,

Légion d'Honneur. Address: Collège de France, 11 place Marce-lin-Berthelot, 75005 Paris, France.

PUBLICATIONS

History and Geography

Histoire du Languedoc. Paris, Presses Universitaires de France, 1962.

Les Paysans de Languedoc. Paris, Service d'Éditions et de Vente des Publications de l'Education Nationale, 2 vols., 1966; as *The Peasants of Languedoc*, Urbana, University of Illinois Press, 1974.

Introduction cartographique à une écologie quantitative de la France traditionelle, XVII-XIX siècles. N.p., 1966(?).

Histoire du climat depuis l'an mil. Paris, Flammarion, 1967; as *Times of Feast, Times of Famine: A History of Climate since the Year 1000*, New York, Doubleday, 1971; London, W.H. Allen, 1972.

Anthropologie du conscrit français d'après les comptes numériques et sommaires du recrutement de l'armée, 1819-26: Présentation cartographique, with others. Paris, Mouton, 1972.

Médecins, climat, et épidémies à la fin du 18e siècle, with others. Paris, Mouton, 1972.

Le Territoire de l'historien. Paris, Gallimard, 1973; selections as *The Territory of the Historian*, Hassocks, Sussex, Harvester Press, 1978; Chicago, University of Chicago Press, 1979; and *The Mind and Method of the Historian*, Hassocks, Sussex, Harvester Press, and Chicago, University of Chicago Press, 1981.

Leçon inaugurale. Paris, Collège de France, 1974.

Montaillou, village occitan de 1294 à 1324. Paris, Gallimard, 1975; as *Montaillou: The Promised Land of Error*, New York, Braziller, 1978; as *Montaillou: Cathars and Catholics in a French Village, 1294-1324*, London, Scolar Press, 1978.

Paysannerie et croissance, with Michel Morineau. Paris, Presses Universitaires de France, 1977.

Le Carnaval de Romans: De la Chandeleur au mercredi des cendres, 1579-80. Paris, Gallimard, 1979; as *Carnival: A People's Uprising at Romans, 1579-80*, New York, Braziller, 1979; London, Scolar Press, 1980.

L'Argent, l'amour, et la mort en pays d'oc. Paris, Seuil, 1980; as *Love, Death, and Money in the Pays d'Oc*, London, Scolar, 1982.

Other

Editor, with Joseph Goy, *Les Fluctuations du produit de la dime: Conjoncture decimale et dominale de la fin du moyen âge au 18e siècle.* Paris, Mouton, 1972; as *Tithe and Agrarian History from the Fourteenth to the Nineteenth Centuries: An Essay in Comparative History*, Cambridge and New York, Cambridge University Press, 1982.

Editor, *L'Âge classique des paysans, 1340-1789.* Paris, Seuil, 1975.

*   *   *

"In the last 20 years Emmanuel Le Roy Ladurie has been one of the most—if not the most—original, versatile and imaginative historians in the world," Professor Lawrence Stone of Princeton wrote in 1979. Described as "the most fashionable living historian in the world" after the success of his *Montaillou*, a runaway best-seller in France and much-publicized in its (abridged) American translation, the maestro seemed to have the rare gift of pleasing both the professional specialists and the general public. *Montaillou* was not universally acclaimed, however; if the British historian Keith Thomas called it the best historical work of recent decades, another reviewer (in the *Christian Science Monitor*) found its style "leaden academic prose leavened by clichés"

and its methods questionable. But this was decidedly a minority opinion.

Le Roy Ladurie is a scholar of enormous erudition, with technical skills including those of sophisticated quantitative research. He is a member of the distinguished French historical school associated with the name of the *Annales*, a journal founded in the 1920's by Marc Bloch and Lucien Febvre, and now in its third generation of historians (Bloch, Febvre, and Fernand Braudel are covered in other articles in this volume). The *Annales* historians have boasted of achieving a wholly new kind of history, which (a) is a *histoire totale* drawing on many disciplines—geography, anthropology, economics included—to give a picture of the whole society, (b) brings history down from the centers of elite power and culture to mingle with the common folk, (c) focuses on the long, slow processes which are more important than mere "events." Drawing on demography, local archives, and the technical resources of computers, this kind of social history has employed new sources and new methodologies. Its critics claim it is dehumanizing and dull, reproducing tables of statistics rather than real people. But Le Roy Ladurie usually avoids this vice. Indeed, his most celebrated books deal with very specific subjects. Based on a document in the papal archives, *Montaillou* brings to vivid life a village in the Pyrenees during ten years of the later Middle Ages. *Carnival* tells of two weeks in 1580 in a town in the Dauphiné when a festival turned into bloody rioting. Le Roy Ladurie quite successfully makes these particular episodes microcosms for the larger issues of social history.

His first major work, *The Peasants of Languedoc*, established Le Roy Ladurie's basic interest in southern France and in rural society. (Again, the English translation is far shorter than the two-volume French original; Le Roy Ladurie is a historian of fecund abundance who overwhelms the reader with a mass of details.) In one of his essays, on the Rouergue region, he confesses that "My wish for our planet is...a rural and probably impossible one." An impossible wish, perhaps, but also a fashionable one in an ecological generation filled with rejections of the technological society and nostalgia for vanished communities; Le Roy Ladurie's popularity certainly owes something to this orientation toward a non-urban past. Yet he does not portray an arcadian past; the picture he draws of pre-modern France (roughly 13th to 18th century) is one where plague, epidemic, and famine operated cruelly as a check on population; where poverty and vagabondage were endemic, life was cheap, and the struggle for survival acute.

This was also a period when, looked at from the point of view of "the solid rural mass" rather than "the elite," nothing much changed basically; "History stood still." The structuralist instincts of these anti-historical historians of the *Annales* school can concentrate on the analysis of a society complex but essentially static. Apparent "events" like famines and plagues are recurrent, predictable. The tendency to be interested in impersonal forces is reflected in Le Roy Ladurie's history of climate, translated as *Times of Feast, Times of Famine*. This has been a persisting interest, as also has been the histories of plagues and epidemics. *Les Paysans de Languedoc* is crammed with details about foods, diet, agricultural methods, as well as disease, medicine, hygiene (or the lack of it), and a host of economic data.

Le Roy Ladurie shows signs of some discontent with the tradition of which he is the finest flower; that historiography "in the last few decades has virtually condemned to death the narrative history of events and the individual biography" seems to him "a pity" (*The Territory of the Historian*). For explanations of political behavior, one is, however reluctantly, "obliged to turn to the past." Structure must sometimes take account of event. Such reflections and much of the recent work of Le Roy Ladurie suggests that he is on the way to overcoming the sectarian narrowness of *Annales* dogma, to re-absorb "events" and continuities of the traditional sort into a higher synthesis of narrative and structural history that will be truly total.

—Roland Stromberg

LÉVI-STRAUSS, Claude. French social anthropologist. Born in Brussels, Belgium, 28 November 1908. Studied at the Sorbonne, Paris, Agrégé de Philosophie, 1932, Doctorat ès Lettres, 1948. Married Dina Dreyfus in 1932 (divorced); married Rosemarie Ullmo in 1946; 1 son; married Monique Roman in 1954; 1 son. Professor, University of Sao Paulo, 1935-39; Visiting Professor, New School for Social Research, New York, 1942-45; Cultural Counsellor, French Embassy, Washington, D.C., 1946-47; Associate Curator, Musée de l'Homme, Paris, 1948-49. Since 1950, Director of Studies, Ecole Pratique des Hautes Etudes, Paris; Professor of Social Anthropology, 1959-83, and since 1983, Honorary Professor, Collège de France, Paris. Recipient: Viking Fund Medal, Wenner-Gren Foundation, 1966; Erasmus Prize, 1975. Honorary doctorate: University of Brussels, 1962; Oxford University, 1964; Yale University, New Haven, Connecticut, 1965; University of Chicago, 1967; Columbia University, New York, 1971; Stirling University, 1972; Université Nationale de Zaïre, 1973; University of Uppsala, 1977; Laval University, Quebec, 1979; Universidad Nacional Autonoma de Mexico, 1979. Member, Académie Française, 1973; National Academy of Sciences; American Academy and Institute of Arts and Letters; British Academy; American Academy of Arts and Sciences; Norwegian Academy of Letters and Sciences; and New York Academy of Sciences; Foreign Member, Royal Academy of the Netherlands; and Academy of Norway; Honorary Fellow, Anthropological Institute of Great Britain; Fellow, American Museum of Natural History. Commandeur de l'Ordre Nationale du Mérite, 1971; Commandeur de la Légion d'Honneur, 1976; Commandeur de l'Ordre des Palmes Académiques; Commandeur des Arts et des Lettres; Commandeur de la Coronne de Belgique. Address: 2 rue des Marronniers, 75016 Paris, France.

PUBLICATIONS

Anthropology

La Vie familiale et sociale des Indiens Nambikwara. Paris, Société des Américanistes, 1948.
Les Structures élémentaires de la parenté. Paris, Presses Universitaires de France, 1949; as *The Elementary Structures of Kinship*, Boston, Beacon, 1969.
Race et histoire. Paris, UNESCO, 1952.
Tristes Tropiques. Paris, Plon, 1955; partial translation as *A World on the Wane*, London, Hutchinson, 1961; as *Tristes Tropiques*, New York, Criterion, 1961; complete translation, London, Cape, 1973; New York, Atheneum, 1974.
Anthropologie structurale. Paris, Plon, 2 vols., 1958-73; as *Structural Anthropology*, New York, Basic Books, 2 vols., 1963-76.
Le Totemisme aujourd'hui. Paris, Presses Universitaires de France, 1962; as *Totemism*, Boston, Beacon, 1963.
Le Pensée sauvage. Paris, Plon, 1962; as *The Savage Mind*, Chicago, University of Chicago, 1966.
Mythologiques: vol. 1, *Le cru et le cuit*; vol. 2, *Du Miel aux cendres*; vol. 3, *L'Origine des manières de table*; vol. 4, *L'Homme nu.* Paris, Plon, 1964-71; as *Introduction to the Science of Mythology:* vol. 1, *The Raw and the Cooked*; vol. 2, *From Honey to Ashes*; vol. 3, *The Origin of Table Manners*; vol. 4, *The Naked Man*, New York, Harper, 1969-81; vols. 3 and 4 published separately, London, Cape, 1973-81.
The Scope of Anthropology (address). London, Cape, 1968.
La Voie des masques. Geneva, Skira, 2 vols., 1975.
Myth and Meaning: Five Talks for Radio. Toronto, University of Toronto Press, and London, Routledge, 1978; New York, Schocken, 1979.

Other

Entretiens avec Claude Lévi-Strauss, edited by Georges Charbonnier. Paris, Plon-Julliard, 1961; as *Conversations with*

Claude Lévi-Strauss, London, Cape, 1969.
Discours de reception a l'Académie française. Paris, Institut de France, 1974.

*

Bibliography: *Claude Lévi-Strauss and His Critics: An International Bibliography of Criticism (1950-1976) Followed by a Bibliography of the Writings of Claude Lévi-Strauss* by François Y. LaPointe and Claire C. LaPointe, New York, Garland, 1977.

Critical Studies: *Lévi-Strauss* by Edmund Leach, London, Fontana, 1970, revised edition, London, Penquin, 1976; *Structural Models in Folklore and Transformational Essays* by Elli Kongas Maranda and Pierre Maranda, Paris and The Hague, Mouton, 1971; *From Symbolism to Structuralism: Lévi-Strauss in a Literary Tradition* by James A. Boon, Oxford, Blackwell, and New York, Harper, 1972; *The Quest for the Mind: Piaget, Lévi-Strauss, and the Structuralist Movement* by Howard Gardner, New York, Knopf, 1973; *The Foundations of Structuralism: A Critique of Lévi-Strauss and the Structuralist Movement* by Simon Clarke, Brighton, Sussex, Harvester, and Totowa, New Jersey, Barnes and Noble, 1981.

*   *   *

Some thinkers are influential, a few create schools, a very few characterize a period. It is hard to predict the fate of current work but it is possible that, just as we speak of the age of Aquinas or of Goethe, later ages will speak of our time as the age of Lévi-Strauss. It would already be possible to write a good book about the works written about and against his work. He is a maker of the modern mind, and has influenced many who have never read him, and some who have quite mistaken ideas about what he says.

The charm of Lévi-Strauss's work lies partly in its complexity; it does not lend itself to summary. Neither does it lend itself to quotation; he expresses himself with lucid French dogmatism, behind which, however, lurks an irony which is almost perverse and equally French. Lévi-Strauss is a dialectical thinker; he most frequently establishes a position only to reject it in the next section, and we have no reason to suppose that his last section is in any instance his last word. This is dialectic of the Socratic kind, full of jokes and teasing, of plain statements made with (as it were) a malicious smile. The power of the intellect is used not so much to clarify a position as to establish the writer's superiority to his audience, to fascinate and exasperate, to challenge us to contradiction and thereby draw us into the process of thought.

Lévi-Strauss's work is best begun in the middle, with *Tristes Tropiques*. This is not a work of anthropology, but rather the intellectual autobiography of an anthropologist, told not in chronological order but as a retrospect in which the author tries to come to terms with the meaning of his life as a whole, arguing from later moments to earlier as well as in the other order. The centerpiece of the book is an account of a trip across central Brazil made for the purpose of studying the natives; in this sense *Tristes Tropiques* is a book about fieldwork. It becomes clear that Lévi-Strauss dislikes fieldwork; in the course of his career he has done as little of it as possible and that (from the point of view of the professional ethnographers) to a very low standard. He does not learn the languages and he does not stay with any people long enough to acquire that immersion in their culture which is the basis of participant observation. Lévi-Strauss's anthropology involves maintaining some distance from the savages, and is best carried on in a library. *Tristes Tropiques* is in a sense a book about that distance, about the question: why, if we do not enjoy the company of these savages, are we interested in them at all? Why leave Paris even for a time and go to central Brazil?

This turns out to be a question about the modern mind. We are the first people who have been drawn to study other peoples, because we are the first to define ourselves, not merely in contrast to the others, but in terms of the others. We are the exception to be explained, and we know it; we are interested in the varieties of culture because we are interested in culture, because we want to know what makes sense of cultural life, and this because we have a well-grounded suspicion that our own culture makes no sense.

Tristes Tropiques is thus an extended meditation on modernism; the anthropologist places his personal story within a vision of the totality of human history. In the process he defines anthropology as the most characteristic and the most necessary of modern activities; our interest in Culture, while symptomatic of the problem, is also potentially the solution. Our distaste for our own culture liberates us from its contingent particularities, and makes possible an aspiration to a culture which would be founded on an understood reality, whereby mankind for the first time in history would be at home in nature. This is the (somewhat messianic) task of the anthropologist, who is thus the authentic modern hero, best exemplified, of course, by Lévi-Strauss himself.

Those who go to Lévi-Strauss for humility and an accomodating temper are likely to be disappointed. *Tristes Tropiques* is the most accessible of his books, but it must be read with care before the unity of its argument becomes apparent. Furthermore many readers are disappointed to find nothing in it about structuralism, the method with which Lévi-Strauss is identified. *Tristes Tropiques*—"the best book ever written by an anthropologist" as Clifford Geertz (*q.v.*) called it—is a book about the place of the intellect in history, and avoids limiting itself to any particular intellectual method.

Lévi-Strauss's structuralism is to be found in his other work, which may be roughly divided into two phases. In his early books on kinship and on totemism he took on central textbook problems of anthropological theory and proposed new solutions. His method was to discern behind the apparent weltering variety of cultural rules a simple set of elementary relations which give rise to endless complex recombination but whose underlying simplicity can be revealed by the analytic anthropologist. His fundamental question is this: how is it that cultural systems are intelligible to those who (quite unreflectingly) use them? The fundamental model of analysis is drawn from the phonemics of Ferdinand de Saussure (*q.v.*) and Roman Jakobson (*q.v.*). These linguists had asserted that we understand one another's speech because we (unreflectingly) interpret the enormous variety of sounds produced in actual articulation in terms of a few contrasting features. We hear phonetic variety (the "etic" level) but we experience intelligible speech because we immediately interpret this variety in terms of a phonemic system (the "emic" level).

In structuralist analysis the fundamental element of the underlying system is seen as a triangle, consisting of two contrasting elements and a mediator. The structural triangle has been compared by Edmund Leach (*q.v.*) to a traffic light. Red means stop and green means go; these are opposite. Between them is yellow, which means that the light is about to change. Yellow is the mediator because it is both midway between the opposites and at the same time in contrast to the two of them taken together, since they both signal a continuing state—motion or station—while yellow signals change of state. Lévi-Strauss similarly analyses the varieties of kinship systems in terms of such a triangle—but this is not the place to summarize the result.

It is often said (by Lévi-Strauss himself, among others) that structuralism is about "the structure of the human mind." This formulation is confusing because it seems to suggest that there could be some kind of mind, differently structured. Such a mind, if it existed, would be literally unthinkable by us, and therefore of no interest. We might better say that structuralism attempts to make sense of the way in which human things make sense. The structuralist operates with abstractions, whereas most thought is on the level of the concrete, but he abstracts contrasts which must be present on the concrete level if thinking is to take place at all. Merely to decide to get up in the morning requires that we have in mind a set of features which characterise "up" and opposed to "in bed"—and that we have in mind a process for getting from one to

the other. Getting up in the morning thus has a logical structure. The fundamental structural triangle is metaphysical; it is the contrast between being and not-being, where the mediator, "becoming," united coming-to-be with passing-away. Lévi-Strauss sees all cultural life as consisting of logical operations within metaphysical categories. Such an analysis may seem farfetched (and is intended to), but it restores a certain dignity to the quotidian—and to the primitive—since it reminds us that all human action involves thinking.

Transitional in Lévi-Strauss's work is *Le Pensée Sauvage*. The title, like so many of Lévi-Strauss's titles, is ironic (the original French edition displayed on the jacket a picture of a wild pansy) since this book among other things shows that the sort of thinking we rather patronisingly attribute to savages is still very much with us. The kind of classification represented by totemism, for instance, corresponds in our world to the meaningfulness of proper names. The book is partly a polemic against Lucien Lévy-Bruhl (*q.v.*) and partly against Jean-Paul Sartre (*q.v.*); both, in their different ways, are accused of denying full humanity to the pre-urban, pre-literate peoples of the world.

Lévi-Strauss himself describes *Le Pensée Sauvage* as the completion of his work on totemism; it appears to us rather as a preface to his masterpiece, *Mythologiques*. This work, in four extraordinarily difficult volumes, is a book which has been read in its entirety by few, and with full understanding by still fewer. Formally it is an analysis of some Brazilian myths; since, however, this analysis is conducted by putting and reputting the question: with what categories is it possible for a myth to be constructed? (which is really the question: how is the world thinkable?) this is really a book about human nature—if we understand that "nature" here means the mind, which is to say, the sense that things make. The fundamental terms are drawn from music, since in music the forming capacities of the mind come to their purest results, both lucid and beautiful; the structural triangle here early takes the form of a contrast between noise (a continuous variation of frequencies) and the diatonic scale, with chromaticism as the mediator. The first stages of the argument are an application of this triangle to cultural forms; from here the work proliferates into a unified vision of the nature and fate of mankind. This book has not yet had its influence; it is a labyrinth which remains to be explored.

—James Redfield

LÉVY-BRUHL, Lucien. French philosopher and sociologist. Born in Paris, 10 April 1857. Educated at Lycée Charlemagne, Paris; studied at the École Normale Supérieure, Paris, Dr.-ès-Lett. 1884. Served in the Ministry for Munitions, 1915-19, and the Ministry of Foreign Affairs, 1919. Married; 3 sons. Taught at schools in Poitiers, 1879-82, and Amiens, 1882-83; taught philosophy at Lycée Louis-Le-Grand, Paris, 1883-95; taught at the Sorbonne, Paris, from 1896: Professor of Philosophy, 1904-27. Professor at Harvard University, Cambridge, Massachusetts, 1919-20, Johns Hopkins University, Baltimore, 1926, and the University of California, Berkeley, 1926. American Academy of Arts and Literature Lecturer, 1930; Herbert Spencer Lecturer, Oxford, 1931. Administrator, *Revue philosophique*, from 1917. Founder, Institut d'Ethnologie, 1925. *Died 13 March 1939.*

PUBLICATIONS

Philosophy and Sociology

L'Idée de responsabilité. Paris, Hachette, 1885.
L'Allemagne depuis Leibniz: Essai sur le devéloppement de la conscience national en Allemagne 1700-1848. Paris, Hachette, 1889.
La Philosophie de Jacobi. Paris, Alcan, 1894.

History of Modern Philosophy in France. Chicago, Open Court, and London, Kegan Paul, 1899.

La Philosophie d'Auguste Comte. Paris, Alcan, 1900; as *The Philosophy of Auguste Comte*, London, Sonnenschein, and New York, Putnam, 1903.

La Morale et la Science des moeurs. Paris, Alcan, 1903; revised edition, 1910; as *Ethics and Moral Science*, London, Constable, 1905.

Les Fonctions mentales dan les sociétés inférieures. Paris, Alcan, 1910; as *How Natives Think*, New York, Knopf, 1925; London, Allen and Inwin, 1926.

La Conflagration européene: Les Causes économiques et politiques. Paris, Alcan, 1915.

Jean Juarès: Essai biographique. Paris, Rieder, 1916.

La Mentalité primitive. Paris, Alcan, 1922; as *Primitive Mentality*, London, Allen and Unwin, and New York, Macmillan, 1923.

L'Âme primitive. Paris, Alcan, 1927; as *The "Soul" of the Primitive*, London, Allen and Unwin, and New York, Macmillan, 1928.

Le Surnaturel et la nature dans la mentalité primitive. Paris, Alcan, 1931; as *Primitives and the Supernatural*, New York, Dutton, 1935; London, Allen and Unwin, 1936.

La Mentalité primitive (lecture). Oxford, Clarendon Press, 1931.

La Mythologie primitive: Le Monde mythique des Australiens et des Papous. Paris, Alcan, 1935.

L'Expérience mystique et les symboles chez les primitifs. Paris, Alcan, 1938.

Les Carnets de Lévy-Bruhl. Paris, Presses Universitaires de France, 1949; as *The Notebooks on Primitive Mentality*, Oxford, Blackwell, 1975.

Other

Editor, *Lettres inédites de John Stuart Mill à Auguste Comte.* Paris, Alcan, 1899.

Editor, *Essais*, by Emile Meyerson. Paris, Vrin, 1936.

*

Critical Study: *Lucien Lévy-Bruhl* by Jean Cazeneuve, Oxford, Blackwell, 1972.

*   *   *

Lucien Lévy-Bruhl, a close associate of Emile Durkheim and one of the main founders of French academic sociology, is credited by modern sociologists with having been among the first to argue that human morals ought to be made the object of a truly scientific study, and that such a study would have to recognize relativity.

Lévy-Bruhl took his undergraduate and graduate training in philosophy with minor work in psychopathology and strong avocational interest in music. He taught in provincial universities and took his Doctorate in 1884. In 1904 he was appointed Professor of the History of Modern Philosophy at the Sorbonne. He cooperated in several major publishing ventures in philosophy, the arts, literature, and sociology, and in 1925 created the Institute of Ethnology.

Lévy-Bruhl's writings mainly deal with history of philosophy and "primitive mentality." For him, these were closely related and represented two different ends of the spectrum of human development: the thought of civilized men and of "primitive" man.

The philosophical writings, following his courses, touched on the immediate precursors of Kant: Descartes, Leibniz, Schopenhauer, Hume, F.H. Jacobi, J.S. Mill, and Auguste Comte. His main starting points, however, are mostly directly in Comte and Jacobi. Jacobi had agreed that Kant's criticisms of the earlier philosophers had shown the inadequacies of *a priori* idealist and materialist approaches to mind, but had misconstrued Kant's position as having been that knowledge of God was inherently beyond human limits. In response, Jacobi had argued that knowledge was not merely cognitive but also intuitive and affective, and that therefore God could indeed be known not so much as something directly given in consciousness but as something felt. Lévy-Bruhl accepted most of the Jacobi's argument, but recognized that this did not respond to a basic Kantian point, that the basic perceptual categories under which people make judgements about the "objective" world, regardless of how fully conscious they may be, are not just matters of private conviction but are also *shared.* It was at this point that philosophy turned to sociology.

The link between Lévy-Bruhl's philosophy and his sociology is most fully explained in *La Morale et la science des moeurs.* The first of three major threads of its argument is an attempt to demonstrate the impossibility and uselessness of what he called "theoretical moralities." By this he evidently meant attempts to derive universal ethical systems from absolute *a priori* premises, such as in the schemes of Locke, Hegel, and Mill. Such schemes, he held, rested on two erroneous postulates. The first was that human nature was always and everywhere the same, but just developed in different ways in different civilizations. The second was that "the moral conscience" was always a single harmonious whole. In reality, for Lévy-Bruhl, human nature was not everywhere the same, and the moral conscience, far from being a harmonious whole, was consistently full of internal contradictions.

The second theme was the development of Lévy-Bruhl's own alternative approach: a "positive science" of "practical morality." In this he is generally understood as including the study of "sentiments" as well as "representations," but he held that the physiological aspect of sentiments was controlled by their social forms. Man "living in society (and above all in primitive societies) is determined in his action not by sentiments as distinct from ideas and from representations, but by complex physiological states, dominated by energetic and imperative representations." The idea of sentiments being complex states "dominated" by representations was linked back to the original idea that there was no constant human nature to form the basis of his proposed study: the idea that morality was shaped by society and in order to study one studied its varying social forms. To get at these forms, he argued that one began by determining the "motive," which was also the "goal" of specific acts, and then built up to ever more general principles, the dominant goals or motives of the society. Thus Lévy-Bruhl's relativism is not individualistic (as in the Kantian tradition) but social. His concept of human behavior is deterministic, and ignores free will and choice.

The third theme of Lévy-Bruhl's argument was an attack on Wundt's concept of a "normative science." Wundt's was the major psychological representative of the Kantian tradition at the time, and hence the major alternative to what Lévy-Bruhl was proposing. Lévy-Bruhl's attack seriously misrepresented what Wundt was doing. He held that what was normative (deductive, legislative) could not be a science (inductive, theoretical), suggesting erroneously that Wundt had been attempting to produce the same kind of ethical system as Locke and Mill, among others, but had been claiming to do so inductively. Actually, Wundt was proposing a strictly descriptive science of morality that was experimental rather than inductive, that included the idea of choice, and that was based on the idea that mentality was grounded in physiology and that, in this, human nature was indeed everywhere the same.

Lévy-Bruhl's concept of science did not require direct observation, and his descriptions of primitive mentality were based entirely on secondary sources. He argued first that people in primitive societies were more uniformly dominated by their social representations than people in civilized societies (as suggested by the above quote); he then proceeded to describe the qualities of mind itself that such domination presupposed. This is his famous concept of "pre-logical" mentality. Here, he mainly opposed E.B. Tylor's view that human thought was the same everywhere but that primitive thought was simply in error. Instead, he argued, primitive thought was equally correct (the relativism), but operated by its own rules and it was these themselves that were different. Primitive thought was "mythopoeic," metaphoric, and poetical. There were a characteristic lack of abstract conceptualization, an acceptance of contradiction, and a direct mystical identification of things we would regard as natural with things we would regard as supernatural forces and powers. A second argument was against the idea of "pure" thought. As also suggested in the above quote (and following the ideas of Jacobi), Lévy-Bruhl argued that thought, especially primitive thought, was inherently mixed with emotions. Thus, in his view, primitive man did not merely see a raven and attribute magical powers, he saw a raven with magical powers; primitive man did not merely transgress a rule and expect a punishment, he transgressed the rule and felt the punishment, even unto death.

In the modern period, Lévy-Bruhl's philosophy of science has been considerably more important than his substantive view of primitive mentality. His concept of the method of social science as inductive generalization from particular "representations" was the fullest statement of sociological method apart from Durkheim's statistical procedure. Generally, Lévy-Bruhl's statements of method have been adopted more by academic ethnologists, while Durkheim's formulations have been more important among academic sociologists. Among the most important modern schools of thought directly built upon Lévy-Bruhl's base are the social anthropology of E.E. Evans-Pritchard and the "structuralism" of Claude Lévi-Strauss and Louis Dumont.

—Murray J. Leaf

LEWIN, Kurt. German psychologist. Born in Mogilno, 9 September 1890; emigrated to the United States in 1933. Studied at the University of Freiburg, 1908; University of Munich, 1909; University of Berlin, Ph.D. 1914. Served in the German Army, 1914-18; Lieutenant. Married Gertrud Weiss in 1918; 4 children. Assistant, Psychological Institute, Berlin, 1921; Lecturer, 1921-26, and Professor of Psychology and Philosophy, 1926-33, University of Berlin; Visiting Professor of Psychology, Cornell University, Ithaca, New York, 1933-35; Professor of Child Psychology, Child Welfare Research Station, University of Iowa, Iowa City, 1935-41; Director, Research Center for Group Dynamics, Massachusetts Institute of Technology, Cambridge, 1944-47. Visiting Professor, Harvard University, Cambridge, 1938, 1939, 1940; University of California, Berkeley, 1939. Counsellor, United States Department of Agriculture, 1944-47; Office of Strategic Services, 1944-45; and Commission on Community Interrelations, New York, 1944-47. Member, American Academy of Arts and Sciences. *Died 12 February 1947.*

PUBLICATIONS

Collections

Werkausgabe, edited by Carl Friedrich Graumann. Bern, Huber 1981-.

Psychology

Der Begriff der Genese in Physik, Biologie, und Entwicklungsgeschichte. Berlin, Springer, 1922.
Vorsatz, Wille, und Bedurfnis (mit Vorbemerkungen über die psychischer Krafte und Energien und die Struktur der Seele). Berlin, Springer, 1926.
Gesetz und Experiment in der Psychologie. Berlin, Weltkris,

1927.
Die Entwicklung der experimentellen Willenpsychologie und die Psychotherapie. Leipzig, Herzel, 1929.
Die psychologische Situation bei Lohn und Strage. Leipzig, Herzel, 1931.
A Dynamic Theory of Personality. New York, McGraw Hill, 1935.
Principles of Topographical Psychology. New York, McGraw Hill, 1936.
Psychological Problems in Jewish Education. New York, Jewish Education Committee, 1946.
Resolving Social Conflicts. New York, Harper, 1948.
Field Theory in Social Science: Selected Theoretical Papers, edited by Dorwin Cartwright. New York, Harper, 1951.
Group Decision and Social Change, edited by G.E. Swanson and others. New York, Holt, 1952.
Autocracy and Democracy: An Experimental Inquiry, with R. Lippitt and R. White. New York, Harper, 1960.

*

Critical Study: *The Practical Theorist: The Life and Work of Kurt Lewin* by Alfred J. Marro, New York, Basic Books, 1969.

*   *   *

Kurt Lewin brought to his mature work enduring influences from both his early personal and intellectual experiences, which he freely acknowledged. Among these is the childhood and later experience of membership in a Jewish family and community, as well as the overt institutionalized anti-Semitism in Germany. In 1910, while still a student, he heard Ernst Cassirer lecture on the philosophy of science, and subsequently made Cassirer's views on the methodology of science and concept-formation his own, or more precisely, extended and adapted them to his own needs as a scientific psychologist. A third major influence derived from his close early association as researcher and Privatdozent with Wolfgang Köhler and Max Wertheimer, and the ideas of Gestalt psychology which they were developing at the Psychological Institute in Berlin. However deeply rooted in central European concerns, after his immigration to the United States (1933) he found a new stimulus in American political and social styles and attracted a large following of talented students and colleagues. He in turn became one of the major influences in the United States on the social psychology of his day.

The importance of Cassirer's philosophy of science for Lewin was that he used Cassirer's "analysis of the methodology and concept-formation of the natural sciences" as a guide to his own approach in developing theory for the social sciences. Lewin contrasted Aristotelian with Galilean modes of thought, be it in physics or in psychology (*Journal for General Psychology 5*, 1931), and concluded that most of the social science of his day was mired in the Aristotelian mode. But in some of the work of the Gestalt school in cognitive psychology, and especially in his own work in social psychology he saw the beginnings of psychology in the Galilean mode: his theories were deliberately systemic in approach rather than developmental (unlike Freud's, Piaget's, or Darwin's theories); they were mathematical so as to permit precision of concept, but they were not statistical—laws were to be expressed not by finding correlations between observations, but by identifying intervening connections which revealed the inner structure of personality and social phenomena (or, using the idiom of biology, the laws were in terms of genotypes not phenotypes). The laws would describe constancies of relations, not constancy of elements. The concepts would not be limited to validity or reference to any particular culture, historic time, or geographic location; they would furthermore have to apply in all branches of psychology and the social sciences. The types of laws Lewin had in mind would not merely be statistically valid, but by their very nature could have no exceptions. In any application of the concepts, Lewin specified, it would be essential that "the whole concrete situation must be represented," for only then could one expect "exceptionless" laws. The function of experiments in the social sciences would, according to Lewin's philosophy, be to set up "pure cases" in which structural relations become clearly evident. Lewin's students in Berlin indeed carried out experiments to refine and to some extent test his theories dealing with such concepts as "level of aspiration," "tension systems," "frustration," and "satiation." In all, his was a bold and optimistic program for the social sciences.

Lewin's own "field theory," which made use of the mathematical language of topology and vectors in representing concrete situations, and introduced the "life space" and "social field" concepts as means for including "the whole situation," demonstrated the possibility of psychological theory in the Galilean mode. Although Lewin's ambitious field theory has not become the beginning of a major development in psychology, and has failed in the sense of not having survived in a prominent way, it is nevertheless an extraordinary effort in devising a scheme in the human sciences which incorporates the subjective and the objective, including the subject's contexts perceived or surmised by the observer making the description. Especially since it is grounded in an explicit meta-psychology, his field theory is of interest to philosophers of science.

One of the enduring innovations by Lewin and his younger associates was the development of very carefully designed experiments with small groups. Lewin initiated the study of "group dynamics," which was explored further by his students, who became influential in social psychology in later decades. His experiments with co-workers Wright, Barker, and Dembo pertaining to frustration, regression, and development are now classics. Similarly his experimental studies with Lippitt and White on the influence of autocratic or democratic leadership respectively on a group of children in various situations are justly famous. Again Lewin's style, which he imparted to students, was to use theory as a guide to experiment in social psychology. The extent and manner in which conclusions from laboratory experiments in "pure situations" are to be transferred to help understand actual, tangled, historical circumstances remains a topic of controversy.

Aside from functioning as an academic psychologist and as a meta-theorist, Kurt Lewin was an original thinker about the process of social change, who implemented his thoughts by social action. The avowed purpose of a portion of his work was to "build a better world." Some of his research and social action dealt with the situation of minority groups within society. In particular he recommended various kinds of action to the victims or potential victims of racial and religious prejudice, types of action which should enhance the strength and integrity of the individual victim, as well as alter discriminatory practices. It is characteristic of Lewin's style of objectivity that he discussed the issue of minority groups with equal empathy and clarity from the viewpoint of a member of the minority group, as well as from the viewpoint of the manager of a project designed to ameliorate the conditions effecting the minority. He predicted verifiable qualitative consequences resulting from the behavior patterns which he recommended to Jews in Nazi Germany, as well as to minority group members in the United States.

In his later efforts, while acting as a consultant to numerous institutions seeking to improve intergroup relations, Lewin emphasized efficient methods for social engineering, although in his work for the American Jewish Congress he encouraged legal actions and face-to-face confrontation. In his capacity as consultant and social engineer, he found it difficult to implement his awareness that an improvement in the situation of the Black minority must come from below, and must involve sharp conflict and disruption of the smooth machinery of society. Indeed the civil rights and liberation movements of the Black minority in the 1960's exemplify many aspects of the description of and prescription for an abused minority, which Lewin had devised in the 1930's and 1940's. Especially since the social action research of Lewin, and the younger co-workers who outlived him, had

become increasingly identified with efficient management to resolve social conflicts, it is not surprising that his work did not effectively connect with the social movement which it had all but anticipated. Leaders of that movement obtained their theoretical understanding and information from far different sources. During World War II, Lewin considered the problem of how one might change a whole culture, i.e., alter the characteristic attitudes and patterns of action of either a small group or a whole society. A particular case for which he prepared a blueprint was the application of social science to reform the character structure of the defeated Nazi-trained German population, once the War was over. He thus envisioned social scientists as effecting the course of history on a large scale.

In surveying Lewin's published work, what is particularly striking is its span: From philosophy of science to action research, from formal theory to ingenious experiment, and each of these activities was carried out in depth, with original and clear thought and forms a natural part of a unity.

—Steve J. Heims

LEWIS, C(larence) I(rving). American philosopher. Born in Stoneham, Massachusetts, 12 April 1883. Studied at Harvard University, Cambridge, Massachusetts, B.A. 1906, Ph.D. 1910. Served in the United States Army, 1918. Married Mabel Maxwell Graves in 1907; 3 children. Instructor in English, University of Colorado, Boulder, 1906-08; Instructor and Assistant Professor of Philosophy, University of California, Berkeley, 1911-20; Professor and later Peirce Professor of Philosophy, Harvard University, 1920-53. Hibben Research Fellow in Philosophy, Princeton University, New Jersey, 1953-54; Visiting Lecturer in Philosophy, Stanford University, California, 1954-58. President, Eastern Division, American Philosophical Association, 1923. Recipient: Butler Medal, 1950; American Academy of Learned Societies Award, 1961. Honorary doctorate: University of Chicago, 1941. Corresponding Member, British Academy. Member, American Academy of Arts and Sciences. *Died 3 February 1964.*

PUBLICATIONS

Philosophy

A Survey of Symbolic Logic. Berkeley, University of California Press, 1918.
Mind and the World-Order: Outline of a Theory of Knowledge. New York, Scribner, 1929.
Symbolic Logic, with C.H. Langford. New York, Appleton Century, 1932.
An Analysis of Knowledge and Valuation. La Salle, Illinois, Open Court, 1946.
The Ground and Nature of the Right. New York, Columbia University Press, 1955.
Our Social Inheritance. Bloomington, Indiana University Press, 1957.
Values and Imperatives: Studies in Ethics, edited by John Lange. Stanford, California, Stanford University Press, 1969.
Collected Papers, edited by John Goheen and John L. Mothershead, Jr. Stanford, California, Stanford University Press, 1970.

*

Critical Studies: *The Philosophy of C.I. Lewis* edited by Paul Arthur Schilpp, La Salle, Illinois, Open Court, and London, Cambridge University Press, 1968 (contains a bibliography).

*   *   *

It is incontestable that C.I. Lewis is one of the major philosophers in the 20th century. It is also generally conceded that he is one of the soundest. He lacked the dramatic erraticisms of the several Bertrand Russells, so to speak, and the cataclysmic polar reversals of a Ludwig Wittgenstein. Indeed, outside the philosophic community itself, in which he worked and published for better than fifty years, he is almost unknown. There are three major reasons for this. First, it is difficult to read certain of the major works of Lewis unless one possesses a certain amount of philosophical aptitude and expertise. Similarly, an investment of time and effort is required. This type of limitation characterizes the work of innovative professionals in many fields. Secondly, Lewis was the sort of man who would have regarded the founding of a school as preposterous, the initiation of a movement as presumptuous, and the recruitment of disciples as embarrassing. As well might one found a "school" of chemistry or physics. The point is truth, neither vanity nor war. Lastly, Lewis's work, once understood, has a tendency to strike one as being so plausible, so sensible, as to seem almost familiar. He is so close to "right," it seems, that the reader sometimes gets the impression that he is being told what he already knows. And, indeed, in a sense, that is Lewis's avowed intention, to undertake and carry through the reflective analysis of humanity's common sense, in matters of knowledge, evaluation, and morality.

The human being, following Lewis, is an active and self-governing organism. It must decide the direction of its own behavior. Significant then for such a creature are attendance to empirical realities, current and projected; a commitment to ends to be sought; and an allegiance, implicit or explicit, to directives. Indissolubly intertwined in the nature of the organism are knowledge, evaluation, and the rational recognition of obligation.

In knowledge there are two central, interrelated factors: the *given* and its *conceptualization*. The given in experience is that which thought cannot create or alter; it is that, fundamentally, which is conceptualized. Concepts, on the other hand, are alterable. They are subject to replacement and revision; indeed, they may be the product of cognitive reconstruction and creation. The human world, the experiential world, is a function of both given and concept. Accordingly, inasmuch as *human* reality is a partial function of conceptualization, it follows that the *human* reality is malleable, that it is responsive to human design, to human values, intentions, and purposes. Our classificatory schemes, so to speak, are houses men build, architectures in virtue of which men may significantly improve the human reality in which they have their habitation. To be sure, most familiar categories and conceptualizations today have broad social and historical warrants. We must not confuse, however, a useful tool of tradition with an inalterable fixture of reality. Intelligible experience presupposes an interpretative conceptual structure; without such a conceptual structure we could not have intelligible experience. In this sense one may think of the conceptual structure as being *logically* prior to experience; that is the sense in which the conceptual structure may be thought of as *a priori*. In Lewis's views the *a priori* is neither dictated by the nature of the given nor the result of inalterable structures in the human mind. It is a creative product of the human mind, to which conceivable alternatives exist. Its formation, like that of language, to which it is logically prior but with which it is intimately intertwined, is subject to development in the light of such considerations as simplicity and utility. It is in this sense that Lewis may be thought of as having a *pragmatic* conception of the *a priori*. In a similar sense, his general position, with respect to the theory of knowledge, may be characterized as "conceptual pragmatism."

Once the unification of the given and the conceptual structure is effected, knowledge becomes possible. One form of knowledge, for Lewis, is valuation. Valuations, for Lewis, may be as true or false as measurements and weather predictions. This follows from his analysis of the complex conceptual structures pertaining to "good." In brief, a division is drawn between the values of objects and the values of experiences, and another division between extrinsic and intrinsic goods. The distinction between objects and experiences, at this point, is a commonsense distinction, for example, between a saw and the pleasures of using the saw. Objects have value in two modes. One object may have value in both modes. The saw, for example, may have instrumental value in achieving a desired end, say, the sawing of a board; it may have inherent value in the sense that it pleases the workman to look upon it; works of art, in this sense, might have inherent value. The values of experiences may be contributory, immediate and nonimmediate, or distributively immediate. Training for a race, for example, might be contributory to the *felt* good of having done well in the race. The basic and root sense of "good" for Lewis is a felt quality of experience, not analyzable into other qualities. This is "intrinsic good," that which is good in itself; it may be immediate or nonimmediate. All other goods, following Lewis, whether of objects or experiences, are "extrinsic goods," goods which are not good in themselves, *simpliciter*, but which obtain their value by being directly or indirectly conducive to the attainment of intrinsic good, immediate or nonimmediate. Intrinsic good is, in effect, a hedonic tone which can characterize experience. Difficult as it is to discuss it, it is presumably a felt quality of experience with which we are all familiar, and could only pretend otherwise. It is not to be identified with simple pleasure, any more that the glories of the spectrum could properly be identified with a particular shade of blue. It could range from the comfort of warm boots on a cold day to the delights of mathematics and chess, to the ecstasy of the entranced mystic, to the emotional fulfillments of the morally righteous. To be sure, the sacrifice of an immediate good in the present may be conducive to the flourishing of more immediate good in the future. We thus come to the notion of nonimmediate good; this is the quantity and quality of *immediate* good considered temporally distributed and, ultimately, one supposes, over the course of an individual lifetime. Here one would be concerned with the enjoyableness or satisfaction of a life as a whole. On this analysis, which Lewis regards not as a proposal, but as a reflective analysis of *de-facto* common-sense notions, implicit in the actual conceptual structure governing our considerations in these matters, it is clear that valuations would become empirical hypotheses and, accordingly, like other empirical hypotheses, would involve confirmable and disconfirmable predictions of future experience. They, too, then, like other empirical hypotheses, would be true or false. On this analysis, then, valuation, like chemistry and physics, is a form of empirical knowledge.

Just as Lewis's work in the theory of knowledge can be regarded as a mediation between rationalism and empiricism, in which comparable weights are assigned to the inalterable empirical elements in experience and the activity of the mind, as a condition of experience, so, too, his work in ethics may be regarded as a mediation between naturalism and rationalism. His analysis of the good in terms of a detectable, verifiable property of human experience is *naturalistic* to the core. In his conception of the right, on the other hand, he is uncompromisingly rationalistic. He distinguishes among various species of the right, such as the logically, technically, prudentially and morally right. Associated with these species of right are rational imperatives, imperatives the validity of which is recognized by the informed, rational mind, concerned with ends to be sought and consistency in its goals, beliefs, and behaviors. The basic datum here is the active, self-governing organism. On Lewis's views such a creature cannot rationally repudiate allegiance to imperatives, and, among them, moral imperatives. It cannot rationally except itself from ideal universalities of conduct which it recognizes as appropriate to all such creatures. Such imperatives are non-repudiable by the rational organism; it cannot repudiate them without betraying its rational nature, its recognition of the imperativeness of consistency. Such a repudiation, in Lewis's view, further, generates a "pragmatic contradiction." In its broadest sense, a pragmatic contradiction is a self-frustrating or self-contravening act. Such a contradiction, or behavioral inconsistency, would be involved in arguing logically against logic. Similarly, he who would seriously argue against an objective morality seems to presuppose, in the act of his argumentation, that an auditor, if the argumentation be cogent, would be *morally* bound, and objectively so, in all honesty, to accept his conclusions. Such a line of argumentation, thus, while it may be logically consistent, involves behavioral inconsistency, or pragmatic contradiction. In this sense it is self-refuting, or self-defeating, and one is again returned to the original thesis, that of the objectivity of morality, its nonrepudiability vindicated anew.

A rationalism whose dictates of the right were supposedly independent of man's actual nature would presumably be misguided, irrelevant, and fruitless. On the other hand, a naturalism which does not recognize the right, and imperatives and obligation, would be, in Lewis's opinion, a naturalism which surely falls far short of human nature as it exists, and as we are familiar with it. Allegiance to imperatives, and rational respect for them, comes with the human territory, as much as prehensile appendages and binocular vision. We have thus returned to where we began, completing the circuit, to the rational animal, which some men are. And Lewis was one of them.

—John Lange

LEWIS, C(live) S(taples). British theologian, critic and novelist. Born in Belfast, Northern Ireland, 29 November 1898. Educated at Wynyard School, Hertfordshire, 1908-10; Campbell College, Northern Ireland, 1910; Cherbourg School, Malvern, 1911-13; studied privately, 1914-17, and at University College, Oxford (Scholar; Chancellor's English Essay Prize, 1921), 1917, 1919-23, B.A. 1922. Served in the Somerset Light Infantry, 1917-19; First Lieutenant. Married Joy Davidman Gresham in 1956. Tutor in Philosophy, 1924, and Lecturer in English, 1924, University College, Oxford; Fellow and Tutor in English, Magdalen College, Oxford, 1924-54; Professor of Medieval and Renaissance English, Cambridge University, 1954-63. Riddell Lecturer, University of Durham, 1943; Clark Lecturer, Cambridge University, 1944. Recipient: Gollancz Prize for Literature, 1937; Library Association Carnegie Medal, 1957. Honorary doctorate: St. Andrews University, Scotland, 1946; Laval University, Quebec, 1952; University of Manchester, 1959; University of Dijon, 1962; University of Lyons, 1963. Honorary Fellow: Magdalen College, Oxford, 1955; University College, Oxford, 1958; Magdalene College, Cambridge, 1963. Fellow, Royal Society of Literature, 1948; British Academy, 1955. *Died 22 November 1963.*

PUBLICATIONS

Religion and Culture

The Pilgrim's Regress: An Allegorical Apology for Christianity, Reason and Romanticism. London, Dent, 1933; New York, Sheed and Ward, 1935; revised edition, London, Bles, 1943; Sheed and Ward, 1944.
The Problem of Pain. London, Bles, 1940; New York, Macmillan, 1943.
The Weight of Glory. London, S.P.C.K., 1942.
The Screwtape Letters. London, Bles, 1942; New York, Macmillan, 1944; revised edition, Bles, 1961.
Broadcast Talks: Right and Wrong: A Clue to the Meaning of the Universe, and What Christians Believe. London, Bles, 1942; as *The Case for Christianity,* New York, Macmillan, 1943; reprinted in *Mere Christianity,* 1952.
Christian Behaviour: A Further Series of Broadcast Talks. London, Bles, and New York, Macmillan, 1943; reprinted in *Mere Christianity,* 1952.

The Abolition of Man; or, Reflections on Education with Special Reference to the Teaching of English in the Upper Forms of School. London, Oxford University Press, 1943; New York, Macmillan, 1947.
Beyond Personality: The Christian Idea of God. London, Bles, 1944; New York, Macmillan, 1945; reprinted in *Mere Christianity,* 1952.
The Great Divorce: A Dream. London, Bles, 1945; New York, Macmillan, 1946.
Miracles: A Preliminary Study. London, Bles, and New York, Macmillan, 1947.
Vivisection. London, Anti-Vivisection Society, 1948.
Transpositions and Other Addresses. London, Bles, 1949; as *The Weight of Glory and Other Addresses,* New York, Macmillan, 1949.
The Literary Impact of the Authorized Version (lecture). London, Athlone Press, 1950; Philadelphia, Fortress Press, 1963.
Mere Christianity. London, Bles, and New York, Macmillan, 1952.
Hero and Leander (lecture). London, Oxford University Press, 1952.
Surprised by Joy: The Shape of My Early Life. London, Bles, 1955; New York, Harcourt Brace, 1956.
Reflections on the Psalms. London, Bles, and New York, Harcourt Brace, 1958.
Shall We Lose God in Outer Space? London, S.P.C.K., 1959; reprinted in *The World's Last Night and Other Essays,* 1960.
The Four Loves. London, Bles, and New York, Harcourt Brace, 1960.
The World's Last Night and Other Essays. New York, Harcourt Brace, 1960.
A Grief Observed (as N.W. Clerk; autobiography). London, Faber, 1961; Greenwich, Connecticut, Seabury Press, 1963.
Beyond the Bright Blur (letters). New York, Harcourt Brace, 1963.
Letters to Malcolm, Chiefly on Prayer. London, Bles, and New York, Harcourt Brace, 1964.
Screwtape Proposes a Toast and Other Pieces. London, Collins, 1965.
Of Other Worlds: Essays and Stories, edited by Walter Hooper. London, Bles, 1966; New York, Harcourt Brace, 1967.
Letters, edited by W.H. Lewis. London, Bles, and New York, Harcourt Brace, 1966.
Christian Reflections, edited by Walter Hooper. London, Bles, and Grand Rapids, Michigan, Eerdmans, 1967.
Letters to an American Lady, edited by Clyde S. Kilby. Grand Rapids, Michigan, Eerdmans, 1967; London, Hodder and Stoughton, 1969.
Mark vs. Tristram: Correspondence Between C.S. Lewis and Owen Barfield, edited by Walter Hooper. Cambridge, Massachusetts, Lowell House Printers, 1967.
A Mind Awake: An Anthology of C.S. Lewis, edited by Clyde S. Kilby. London, Bles, 1968; New York, Harcourt Brace, 1969.
God in the Dock: Essays on Theology and Ethics, edited by Walter Hooper. Grand Rapids, Michigan, Eerdmans, 1970; as *Undeceptions: Essays on Theology and Ethics,* London, Bles, 1971.
The Humanitarian Theory of Punishment. Abingdon, Berkshire, Marcham Books Press, 1972.
Fern-Seed and Elephants and Other Essays on Christianity, edited by Walter Hooper. London, Fontana, 1975.
The Joyful Christian: 128 Readings, edited by William Griffin. New York, Macmillan, 1977.
They Stand Together: The Letters of C.S. Lewis to Arthur Greeves 1914-1963, edited by Walter Hooper. London, Collins, and New York, Macmillan, 1979.

Criticism

The Allegory of Love: A Study in Medieval Tradition. Oxford,

Clarendon Press, and New York, Oxford University Press, 1936.

Rehabilitations and Other Essays. London and New York, Oxford University Press, 1939; reprinted in part in *Selected Literary Essays*, 1969.

The Personal Heresy: A Controversy, with E.M.W. Tillyard. London and New York, Oxford University Press, 1939.

A Preface to "Paradise Lost." London and New York, Oxford University Press, 1942.

Commentary in *Arthurian Torso, Containing the Posthumous Fragment of "The Figure of Arthur,"* by Charles Williams. London and New York, Oxford University Press, 1948.

English Literature in the Sixteenth Century, Excluding Drama. Oxford, Clarendon Press, 1954. (Vol. 3 of The Oxford History of English Literature)

De Descriptione Temporum (lecture). London, Cambridge University Press, 1955; reprinted in *Selected Literary Essays*, 1969.

Studies in Words. London, Cambridge University Press, 1960; revised edition, 1967.

An Experiment in Criticism. London, Cambridge University Press, 1961.

They Asked for a Paper: Papers and Addresses. London, Bles, 1962; reprinted in part in *Selected Literary Essays*, 1969.

The Discarded Image: An Introduction to Medieval and Renaissance Literature. London, Cambridge University Press, 1964.

Studies in Medieval and Renaissance Literature, edited by Walter Hooper. London, Cambridge University Press, 1966.

"Christianity and Literature," in *Christian Reflections*, edited by Walter Hooper. London, Cambridge University Press, 1967.

Spenser's Images of Life, edited by Alastair Fowler. London, Cambridge University Press, 1967.

Selected Literary Essays, edited by Walter Hooper. London, Cambridge University Press, 1969.

Verse

Spirits in Bondage: A Cycle of Lyrics (as Clive Hamilton). London, Heinemann, 1919.

Dymer (as Clive Hamilton). London, Dent, and New York, Macmillan, 1926.

Poems, edited by Walter Hooper. London, Bles, 1964, New York, Harcourt Brace, 1965.

Narrative Poems, edited by Walter Hooper. London, Bles, 1969, New York, Harcourt Brace, 1972.

Novels

Out of the Silent Planet. London, Lane, 1938; New York, Macmillan, 1943.

Perelandra. London, Lane, 1943; New York, Macmillan, 1944; as *Voyage to Venus*, London, Pan, 1960.

That Hideous Strength: A Modern Fairy-Tale for Grown-Ups. London, Lane, 1945; New York, Macmillan, 1946; abridged edition as *The Tortured Planet*, New York, Avon, 1958.

The Lion, the Witch, and the Wardrobe (juvenile). London, Bles, and New York, Macmillan, 1950.

Prince Caspian: The Return to Narnia (juvenile). London, Bles, and New York, Macmillan, 1951.

The Voyage of the "Dawn Treader" (juvenile). London, Bles, and New York, Macmillan, 1952.

The Silver Chair (juvenile). London, Bles, and New York, Macmillan, 1953.

The Horse and His Boy (juvenile). London, Bles, and New York, Macmillan, 1954.

The Magician's Nephew (juvenile). London, Lane, and New York, Macmillan, 1955.

The Last Battle (juvenile). London, Lane, and New York, Macmillan, 1956.

Till We Have Faces: A Myth Retold. London, Bles, and New York, Harcourt Brace, 1957.

Short Stories

The Dark Tower and Other Stories, edited by Walter Hooper. London, Collins, and New York, Harcourt Brace, 1977.

Other

Editor, *Arthurian Torso, Containing the Posthumous Fragment of "The Figure of Arthur,"* by Charles Williams. London, and New York, Oxford University Press, 1948.

Editor, *George MacDonald: An Anthology.* London, Bles, 1946; New York, Macmillan, 1962.

*

Bibliography: *C.S. Lewis: An Annotated Checklist of Writings about Him and His Works* by Joe R. Christopher and Joan K. Ostlin, Kent, Ohio, Kent State University Press, 1975.

Critical Studies: *C.S. Lewis: A Biography* by Roger Lancelyn Green and Walter Hooper, London, Collins, and New York, Harcourt Brace, 1974, and *Past Watchful Dragons: The Narnian Chronicles of C.S. Lewis* by Hooper, New York, Macmillan, 1979; *Light on C.S. Lewis* edited by Jocelyn Gibb, London, Bles, 1965 (includes bibliography by Walter Hooper); *The Lion of Judah in Never-Never Land: The Theology of C.S. Lewis Expressed in His Fantasies for Children* by Kathryn Ann Lindskoog, Grand Rapids, Michigan, Eerdmans, 1973; *The Secret Country of C.S. Lewis* by Anne Arnott, London, Hodder and Stoughton, 1974, Grand Rapids, Michigan, Eerdmans, 1975; *The Longing for Form: Essays on the Fiction of C.S. Lewis*, edited by Peter J. Schakel, Kent, Ohio, Kent State University Press, 1977, and *Reading with the Heart: The Way into Narnia* by Schakel, Grand Rapids, Michigan, Eerdmans, 1979; *The Literary Legacy of C.S. Lewis* by Chad Walsh, New York, Harcourt Brace, and London, Sheldon Press, 1979; *The Taste for Order: The Social and Ethical Thought of C.S. Lewis* by Gilbert Meilander, Grand Rapids, Michigan, Eerdmans, 1979; *C.S. Lewis* by Margaret Patterson Hannay, New York, Ungar, 1981.

* * *

C.S. Lewis was talking at two and giving evidence of his brilliance even at this age. The world-famous Oxford Don and professor wrote 15 major books, first in literary criticism but then chiefly on religion, two books of poetry, four of fiction, and seven for children. In all of these categories, and as teacher, philosopher, leader in university life he not only excelled but merits the rare adjective genius.

Lewis went through the typical adolescent and university age of questioning and rejecting his religious background until his early days at Oxford when, in 1929 at age 31, he was converted, not at first to Christianity, but to theism. This came about largely through his contemplation of Samuel Alexander's *Space, Time, and Deity*, and his study of the writings of the philosopher Bishop George Berkeley. It was two years later that he took the major step of identifying with the Church of England. However, during his earlier period, when he was the master of literary criticism, he, like Eliot and Auden, constantly warned, as in his major essay, "Christianity and Literature," against substituting aesthetics for ethics and religion.

Lewis thus combined three careers, being at once the brilliant scholar of English literature, the instigator of philosophical inquiry and public discussion of philosophy—he was President of the Oxford Socratic Club from 1942-1954—and the popular religious writer. In all these areas he avoided extremes; he was conservative, but not reactionary, in his religious, political, and personal life. Not at all the joyless Puritan, he was a humanist, not of the American, secular variety but of a deeply Christian sort. Philosophically active all his life, he nonetheless disparaged "schools"—e.g., the reigning idealism of his time. Strenuously advocating rational and personal belief, he at the same time avoided standard dogmatic and exegetical theology and ecclesiastically dominated movements and causes. Lewis's international fame was based on his witty, brilliant, highly imaginative yet common sense discussion of basic Christian belief and practices. He opposed the abstractions of concepts and laws and favored clear particulars. He wrote in a letter: " 'Our Father which art in heaven' means something to the minds who use it, but 'The supreme being transcends space and time,' though possibly clear to the philosopher, really says nothing."

The surprising fact is that in his radio talks, e.g., *The Case for Christianity*, and books, e.g., *The Problem of Pain* and *The Screwtape Letters*, he was far tougher, more original, and acute than most readers and critics credited him with being. His insight into human nature, for example in his B.B.C. lectures, *Beyond Personality*, and his subtle apologetics, *Mere Christianity*, evidenced the skill with which he dealt in lively, winsome fashion with issues which others smothered in obscure technicalities. Lewis's religious literature is elatingly different from most writing in this century because it is not like what he called "straw dust" theology, i.e., attempts to adjust to contemporary thought, prove the relevance of theology to psychological and social problems, and the like. Lewis, on the contrary, forthrightly asked what Christian insights we could clearly identify, what grounds we have for believing them to be true accounts of objective reality. Like a master teacher, he captured profound truths in short, simple, imaginative prose. His writing, in short, has the dynamic clarity of the New Testament literature and the reported teaching of the Master teacher. He addressed us as we experience our joys and sorrows, pleasures and griefs, sustaining beliefs and honest doubts.

—Charles W. Kegley

LEWIS, Gilbert Newton. American chemist. Born in Weymouth, Massachusetts, 23 October 1875. Studied at the University of Nebraska, Lincoln, 1890-93; Harvard University, Cambridge, Massachusetts, B.A. 1896, M.A. 1898, Ph.D. 1899; University of Leipzig and University of Göttingen, 1900-01. Served in the United States Army, 1918-19: Lt.-Colonel; Distinguished Service Medal. Married Mary Hinckley Sheldon in 1912; 3 children. Instructor in Chemistry, Harvard University, 1899-1906; Assistant Professor, 1907-08, and Associate Professor, 1911-12, Massachusetts Institute of Technology, Cambridge; Professor of Physical Chemistry, University of California, Berkeley, 1912-46. Silliman Lecturer, Yale University, New Haven, Connecticut, 1925. Recipient: Nichols Medal, 1929; Gibbs Medal, 1929; Davy Medal, 1929; Society of Arts and Sciences Medal, 1930; Richards Medal, 1938; Arrhenius Medal, 1939. Honorary doctorate: University of Liverpool, 1923; University of Wisconsin, Madison,1928; University of Chicago, 1929; University of Madrid, 1934; University of Pennsylvania, Philadelphia, 1938. Fellow, American Academy of Arts and Sciences. Honorary Member, Swedish Academy; Danish Academy; Franklin Institute; and Royal Society; Honorary Fellow, London Chemical Society; Royal Institution; and Indian Academy of Sciences. Chevalier, Légion d'Honneur. *Died 23 March 1946.*

PUBLICATIONS

Sciences

Thermodynamics and the Free Energy of Chemical Substances, with Merle Randall. New York, McGraw Hill, 1923.
Valence and the Structure of Atoms and Molecules. New York, Chemical Catalog Company, 1923.
The Anatomy of Science (lectures). New Haven, Connecticut, Yale University Press, and London, Oxford University Press, 1926.

*

Critical Study: *Borderline of the Unknown: The Life Story of Gilbert Newton Lewis, One of the World's Great Scientists* by Arthur Lachman, New York, Pageant Press, 1955.

*   *   *

Gilbert Newton Lewis's scientific interests extended over a number of fields and included both experimental research and theoretical speculation. The first subject to which he turned his attention was chemical thermodynamics. Two problems in this field were of special concern to Lewis. First, the fledgling science was still somewhat in a state of disorganization. A good many concepts had been established, but they had not yet been tied together by any grand theory. Lewis developed the notion of *fugacity* or *escaping tendency* in an effort to achieve this synthesis. He defined fugacity as the tendency of a substance to pass from one chemical phase to another. He attempted to apply the concept to a wide variety of known thermodynamic phenomena. His expectations, however, were not realized. Nonetheless, the concept of fugacity has been retained and has proved useful in understanding the deviation of many real-world events from ideal models. For example, Lewis was able to show how fugacity, or "activity," was a more useful measure in the solution of mass-law problems than was the older variable, "concentration."

Lewis also recognized the ignorance of chemists about the power of thermodynamics. By the early 1900's, most physicists were familiar and comfortable with thermodynamic concepts like free energy and entropy. Chemists had yet to learn, however, how these ideas related to their own work. From his position at Berkeley, Lewis was able to introduce some of the nation's most promising chemistry students to this previously neglected field of study. In addition, his textbook, *Thermodynamics and the Free Energy of Chemical Substances* (with Merle Randall, 1923) soon became the "bible" in the field for chemistry students. It opened the door for these students to a powerful tool from physics for the solution of chemical problems.

Lewis's second field of interest was the nature of chemical bonds. Rutherford's discovery of the nuclear atom and Bohr's "planetary" model for the atom appeared to resolve questions about the fundamental character of elements and the atoms of which they were made. But what is the process by which these elements (atoms) combine with each other to form more complex substances (compounds; molecules)? A young German chemist, Richard Abegg, had suggested in 1899 that the stable configuration of inert elements provided a clue to this problem. Might not, he asked, atoms give away and take on electrons in such a way as to achieve the electronic configuration of inert gases? This concept was the germ from which our present notion of ionic bonding eventually developed.

By the late 1910's, Lewis had recognized that other forms of bonding between atoms were possible. He suggested that two atoms might share pairs of electrons between them. Lewis proposed that atoms had a cubic structure with an electron located—or possible—at each of the eight vertices of the cube. A bond between a carbon atom and a hydrogen atom, then, occurred when the cubes representing the two atoms shared a side between them. The electron at one end of the shared side had come from the carbon atom; the electron at the other end, from the hydrogen atom.

The model described here is essentially our modern view of covalent bonding. The difficulty with Lewis's model, however, was its static view of electronic structure. Rutherford, Bohr, and most other physicists were committed to a dynamic model of the atom, in which electrons were traveling in some kinds of orbits outside the nucleus. How this model could be adapted to Lewis's cubic atom was not at all clear, and the debate between the two schools raged until Schrödinger's wave mechanical model of the atom resolved the issue some years later.

In the last portion of his career, Lewis eschewed theoretical analysis and returned to laboratory research. The subject he chose was "heavy hydrogen," or deuterium, the isotope of hydrogen with mass number two. Chemists had long suspected the existence of an isotope of hydrogen whose atoms contained a neutron as well as a proton. The race to discover that isotope was won by Harold Urey in 1931. Urey carried out a long series of successive evaporations of a sample of liquid hydrogen. In each stage, the concentration of heavy hydrogen increased in the evaporate until, after many repetitions of the process, sufficient numbers of heavy hydrogen atoms existed to be measured by the spectroscope. He found that natural hydrogen contains only 0.015% of the heavy isotope.

Questions remained, however, about the physical and chemical properties of compounds—especially water—made from deuterium. Lewis hoped and speculated that deutero-hydrogen compounds would have significantly different properties and a variety of useful applications. To test his hypothesis, he prepared in 1933 a sample of nearly pure "heavy" water, that is, water in which the hydrogen atoms consist almost entirely of deuterium. This achievement did not result in the realization of Lewis's fond hopes for other unique and useful deutero-hydrogen compounds, however.

—David Newton

LEWIS, Oscar. American anthropologist. Born in New York City, 25 December 1914. Studied at City College of New York, B.S.S. 1936; Columbia University, New York, Ph.D. 1940. Married Ruth Maslow in 1937; 2 children. Research Associate, Yale University, New Haven, Connecticut, 1942-43; propaganda analyst, Department of Justice, 1943; social scientist, Department of Agriculture, 1944-45; Department of State Visiting Professor, Havana, 1945-46; Associate Professor of Anthropology, Washington University, St. Louis, 1946-48; Professor of Anthropology, University of Illinois, Urbana, 1948-70. Ford Foundation Consultant in India, 1952-54. Recipient: Social Science Research Council Fellowship, 1952; Ford grant, 1952; National Book Award, 1967; Saturday Review-Anisfield Wolf Award, 1967. Fellow, American Academy of Arts and Sciences. Died 16 December 1970.

PUBLICATIONS

Anthropology

The Effects of White Contact upon Blackfoot Culture, with Special Reference to the Role of the Fur Trade. New York, Augustin, 1942.
On the Edge of the Black Waxy: A Cultural Survey of Bell County, Texas. St. Louis, Washington University, 1948.
Life in a Mexican Village: Tepoztlán Restudied. Urbana, University of Illinois Press, 1951.
Group Dynamics in a North-Indian Village: A Study of Factions, with Harvant Singh Dhillon. New Delhi, Programme Evaluation Organization Planning Commission, 1954.
Village Life in Northern India: Studies in a Delhi Village, with Victor Barnouw. Urbana, University of Illinois Press, 1958.
Five Families: Mexican Case Studies in the Culture of Poverty. New York, Basic Books, 1959.
Tepoztlán: Village in Mexico. New York, Holt, 1960.
The Children of Sánchez: Autobiography of a Mexican Family. New York, Random House, 1961; London, Secker and Warburg, 1962.
Pedro Martínez: A Mexican Peasant and His Family. New York, Random House, and London, Secker and Warburg, 1964.
La Vida: A Puerto Rican Family in the Culture of Poverty—San Juan and New York. New York, Random House, 1966; London, Secker and Warburg, 1967.
A Study of Slum Culture: Backgrounds for "La Vida," with Douglas Butterworth. New York, Random House, 1968.
A Death in the Sánchez Family. New York, Random House, 1969; London, Secker and Warburg, 1970.
Anthropological Essays. New York, Random House, 1970.
Four Men: Living the Revolution: An Oral History of Contemporary Cuba, with Ruth M. Lewis and Susan B. Rigdon. Urbana, University of Illinois Press, 1977.

*

Critical Study: Culture and Poverty: Critique and Counter-Proposals by Charles A. Valentine, Chicago, University of Chicago Press, 1968.

*   *   *

Both in his method and in the substance of his work, Oscar Lewis exemplifies the shift that took place in American anthropology in the 1950's and 1960's. He believed that the function of the modern anthropologist was to serve as the mouthpiece for the world's downtrodden—at times to suspend critical analysis and allow members of the "third world" to present themselves in their own words. He was centrally concerned with the masses of peasants and ex-peasants on the margins of "underdeveloped" societies, rather than with the "traditional" or tribal peoples who have been the customary domain of anthropologists. This focus on the contemporary poor led to his theory of the international "culture of poverty," a persistent source of controversy in the social sciences.

Much of Lewis's early work is a challenge to the folk/urban dichotomy as seen in the work of Georg Simmel, Louis Wirth, and particularly that of the anthropologist Robert Redfield. In this provocative spirit, he undertook an ethnography of "Tepoztlán," the tiny Mexican village that had served as Redfield's ideal type of a "folk" community. Redfield had described the village as an isolated, simple society, with minimal division of labor and a strong sense of social solidarity. Society was sacred, he found, and individual consciousness was uncritical. Lewis maintained that while this description might have fit some pre-agricultural societies, it was inappropriate for contemporary Tepoztlán. The villagers there had been involved in cash crop agriculture since pre-Columbian days. This "folk" society exhibited social stratification and status rivalries, and had been involved in a national war. In short, it manifested many characteristics usually attributed to "urban" societies.

Lewis later turned his attention to the "urban" side of the folk/urban dichotomy and found that ideal type equally inadequate. He followed Tepoztlán villagers as they migrated to Mexico City. By focusing on families rather than individuals or institutions, Lewis demonstrated that urbanization was not the wrenching, disorganizing experience that the Redfield, Wirth, and Simmel typologies would have suggested. Kinship did not break down; village beliefs were maintained, as were personal ties to the village. Religious life was actually strengthened. As he extended his studies to slum families from all over Mexico, Lewis came to the conclusion that, in general, rural peasants were not as well integrated, nor were poor urbanites as atomized and alienated, as previous research would suggest. Lewis suggested that the urban/folk dichotomy was ethnocentric (based on a European model), and was more true of the rich than of the poor, whose lives were lived not in the city as a whole, but in isolated slum communities similar to peasant villages.

Starting with *Five Families*, Lewis's work entered a new phase, theoretically and methodologically. Until this point, while his works had focused on family life, they had been more or less conventional ethnographies in which he provided detailed descriptions of economic and social conditions. Starting with *Five Families*, Lewis focuses on family life and individual life histories almost exclusively. He attempts to portray slum families in their own words. To do this, he employs a "day in the life" approach, near biography, and finally, in *La Vida*, autobiography. Except for his lengthy introductions, the anthropologist moves into the background in these works, and the poor speak in their own voices. The later books have been criticized for reading like raw data (or novels) and have been praised for the same reason. On the one hand, these works provide unique insights into the lives of the poor. On the other hand, the reader has no real way of knowing, outside of Lewis's assurances, that the persons presented are in any way typical of Mexican (and later Puerto Rican) slum dwellers. In addition, while the anthropologist becomes less visible in these works, he is, of course, still there, asking questions, editing transcripts, possibly directing the narrative. Despite Lewis's detailed descriptions of *how* he worked on these books, exactly *what* he did, where his contribution ends and the respondents' begins, is unclear.

It is in the introductions to these works and in articles of the same period that the notion of the "culture of poverty" is fully developed. Lewis maintained that under certain conditions—a market economy, persistent high rates of unemployment, a lack of social and political organization among the poor, and a dominant value system that sees economic failure as evidence of personal inadequacy—the very poor develop a subculture that, despite national differences, exhibits similar characteristics in many nations. Principal among these are: a lack of participation in larger society, a minimum of organization beyond the family, an absence of childhood and an early initiation into sexuality, low self-esteem, and strong feelings of personal worthlessness. Despite these characteristics, Lewis emphasized that the "culture of poverty" was more than simply the absence of a culture. It was, he maintained, an adaptation to a situation. Further, while it originated in material deprivation, once entrenched as a value system it would require not only material improvements, but also changes in value systems and in consciousness, to end the "culture of poverty." Lewis was careful to note the positive features of the subculture as a survival mechanism. He was also quick to point out that excluded ethnic minority groups, pariah sects, tribal peoples, and the poor in socialist societies, are less likely to exhibit the characteristics of a "culture of poverty."

Many critics have charged that Lewis simply restated social disorganization theory, despite his protests about the adaptive features of the culture of poverty. Others have questioned the use of the concept of "culture" in this context, stating that Lewis merely described the results of material deprivation. Still others maintain that Lewis's own data, based almost entirely on individual perceptions and on family life, does not support his far-reaching conclusions about the value system and beliefs of entire social classes. Nevertheless, Lewis's description of both the lively *esprit de corps* and the tragic feelings of worthlessness and inadequacy that the poor exhibit remains a poignant and insightful comment on the nature of poverty in the modern world. His central contribution is the extension of the notions of poverty and underdevelopment into the realms of family life and individual psychology. He therefore uses the notion of "culture" as a bridge between biography and socio-economic structure.

—Philip Kasinitz

LIPPMANN, Walter. American political philosopher and journalist. Born in New York City, 23 September 1889. Educated at Dr. Julius Sachs's School for Boys, New York, 1896-1906; studied at Harvard University, Cambridge, Massachusetts, 1906-09, A.B. (cum laude) 1910 (Phi Beta Kappa), graduate study, as assistant to George Santayana, 1909-10. Served in the United States Army Military Intelligence, 1918-19: attached to the American Commission to Negotiate the Peace: Captain. Married Faye Albertson in 1917 (divorced, 1938); Helen Byrne Armstrong in 1938. Reporter, *Boston Common*, 1910; assistant to Lincoln Steffens, 1910, and Associate Editor, 1910-12, *Everybody's Magazine*; executive secretary to George R. Lunn, mayor of Schenectady, New York, 1912; Founder, with Herbert Croly, and Associate Editor, 1914-21, *New Republic*; assistant to Newton D. Baker, Secretary of War, 1917; Secretary, Colonel Edward House Inquiry, 1917-18; staff member, 1922-29, and Editor, 1929-31, New York *World*; U.S. Correspondent, Manchester *Guardian* from 1920; syndicated Columnist ("Here and Now"), New York *Herald Tribune*, 1931-67; TV interviewer, *CBS Reports*, from 1960; columnist, *Newsweek*, from 1963. Member of the Board of Directors, Fund for the Advancement of Education, 1951-74. Recipient: Overseas Press Club Award, 1953, 1955, 1959; Pulitzer Prize, 1958; George Foster Peabody Award, 1962; Medal of Freedom, 1964; American Academy Gold Medal, 1965. LL.D.: Wake Forest College, Winston-Salem, North Carolina, 1926; University of Wisconsin, Madison, 1927; University of California, Berkeley, 1933; Union College, Schenectady, 1933; Wesleyan University, Middletown, Connecticut, 1934; University of Michigan, Ann Arbor, 1934; George Washington University, Washington, D.C., 1935; Amherst College, Massachusetts, 1935; University of Rochester, New York, 1936; College of William and Mary, Williamsburg, Virginia, 1937; Drake University, Des Moines, Iowa, 1937; University of Chicago, 1955; New School for Social Research, New York, 1959; Litt.D.: Dartmouth College, Hanover, New Hampshire, 1932; Columbia University, New York, 1932; Oglethorpe College, Atlanta, 1934; Harvard University, 1944. Member of the Board of Overseers, Harvard University, 1933-39; Senator, Phi Beta Kappa, 1934-40; Fellow, Sigma Delta Chi, 1950. Commander, Legion of Honor; Officer, Order of Crown of Leopold; Commander, Order of Orange-Nassau; Knight Cross First Class, Order of St. Olaf. Member, American Academy. *Died 14 December 1974.*

PUBLICATIONS

Political Philosophy

A Preface to Politics. New York, Kennerley, and London, Unwin, 1913.
Drift and Mastery; An Attempt to Diagnose the Current Unrest. New York, Kennerley, and London, Unwin, 1914.
The Stakes of Diplomacy. New York, Holt, 1915.
The Political Scene: An Essay on the Victory of 1918. New York, Holt, and London, Allen and Unwin, 1919.
The Basic Problem of Democracy. Boston, Atlantic Monthly Press, 1919.
The Fourteen Points and the League of Nations (address). New York, League of Free Nations Association, 1919.
Liberty and the News. New York, Harcourt Brace, 1920.

France and the European Settlement (address). New York, Foreign Policy Association, 1922.

Public Opinion. New York, Harcourt Brace, and London, Allen and Unwin, 1922.

Mr. Kahn Would Like to Know. New York, Foreign Policy Association, 1924.

The Phantom Public. New York, Harcourt Brace, 1925.

Men of Destiny. New York, Macmillan, 1927.

American Inquisitors: A Commentary on Dayton and Chicago (lectures). New York, Macmillan, 1928.

A Preface to Morals. New York, Macmillan, and London, Allen and Unwin, 1929.

Notes on the Crisis. New York, Doubleday, 1931.

The United States in World Affairs: An Account of American Foreign Relations, 1931. New York, Harper, 2 vols., 1932-33.

The Scholar in a Troubled World (address). New York, Press of the Woolly Whale, 1932.

Interpretations, 1931-32, edited by Allan Nevins. New York, Macmillan, 1932; London, Allen and Unwin, 1933.

Poverty and Plenty (address). New York, Press of the Woolly Whale, 1932.

A New Social Order (address). New York, Day, 1933.

The Method of Freedom (lectures). New York, Macmillan, and London, Allen and Unwin, 1934.

The New Imperative. New York, Macmillan, 1935.

Interpretations, 1933-1935, edited by Allan Nevins. New York, Macmillan, 1936.

An Inquiry into the Principles of the Good Society. Boston, Little Brown, 1937; as *The Good Society*, London, Allen and Unwin, 1938.

The Supreme Court: Independent or Controlled? New York, Harper, 1937.

Some Notes on War and Peace. New York, Macmillan, 1940.

What Is Wanted from France (address). New York, France Forever, 1942.

The Foreign Policy of the United States (address). Chicago, Republican Postwar Policy Association, 1943.

U.S. Foreign Policy: Shield of the Republic. Boston, Little Brown, and London, Hamish Hamilton, 1943.

U.S. War Aims. Boston, Little Brown, and London, Hamish Hamilton, 1944.

In the Service of Freedom (address). New York, Freedom House, 1945(?).

The Cold War: A Study in U.S. Foreign Policy. New York, Harper, and London, Hamish Hamilton, 1947.

Commentaries on American Far Eastern Policy. New York, American Institute of Pacific Relations, 1950.

Public Opinion and Foreign Policy in the United States (lectures). London, Allen and Unwin, 1952; as *Isolation and Alliances: An American Speaks to the British*, Boston, Little Brown, 1952.

Education for Leadership (address). New York, National Citizens Commission for the Public Schools, 1955.

Essays in the Public Philosophy. Boston, Little Brown, 1955; as *The Public Philosophy*, London, Hamish Hamilton, 1955.

America in the World Today (lecture). Minneapolis, University of Minnesota Press, 1957.

The Communist World and Ours. Boston, Little Brown, and London, Hamish Hamilton, 1959.

The Coming Tests with Russia. Boston, Little Brown, 1961.

The Nuclear Era: A Profound Struggle (address). Chicago, University of Chicago Press, 1962.

Western Unity and the Common Market. Boston, Little Brown, and London, Hamish Hamilton, 1962.

The Essential Lippmann: A Political Philosophy for Liberal Democracy, edited by Clinton Rossiter and James Lare. New York, Random House, 1963.

A Free Press (lecture). Copenhagen, Berlingske Bogtrykkeri, 1965(?).

Conversations with Walter Lippmann. Boston, Little Brown, 1965.

Early Writings, edited by Arthur Schlesinger, Jr. New York, Liveright, 1970.

Other

Editor, *The Poems of Paul Mariett.* New York, Kennerley, 1913.

Editor, with Allan Nevins, *A Modern Reader: Essays on Present-Day Life and Culture.* New York, Heath, 1936; revised edition, Boston, Heath, 1946.

*

Critical Studies: *Walter Lippmann: A Study in Personal Journalism* by David E. Weingart, New Brusnwick, New Jersey, Rutgers University Press, 1949; *Walter Lippmann and His Times* edited by Marquis Childs and James Reston, New York, Harcourt Brace, 1959; *The Crossroads of Liberalism: Croly, Weyl, Lippmann, and the Progressive Era 1900-1925* by Charles B. Forcey, New York, Oxford University Press, 1961; *Walter Lippmann's Philosophy of International Politics* by Anwar H. Syed, Philadelphia, University of Pennsylvania Press, 1964; *The Influence of Walter Lippmann 1914-1944* by F.C. Cary, Madison, State Historical Society of Wisconsin, 1967; *Walter Lippmann, Philosopher, Journalist* by Edward L. and Frederick H. Schapsmeier, Washington, D.C., Public Affairs Press, 1969; *Twentieth Century Pilgrimage: Walter Lippmann and the Public Philosophy* by Charles Wellborn, Baton Rouge, Louisiana State University Press, 1969; *Lippmann, Liberty, and the Press* by John Luskin, University, University of Alabama Press, 1972; *The Intellectual Odyssey of Walter Lippmann* by Hari N. Dam, New York, Gordon Press, 1973; *5 Public Philosophies of Walter Lippmann* by Benjamin F. Wright, Austin, University of Texas Press, 1973; *Walter Lippmann* by Larry L. Adams, Boston, Twayne, 1977; *Walter Lippmann and the American Century* by Ronald Steel, London, Bodley Head, 1980.

*   *   *

Walter Lippmann was a political philosopher and journalist whose writings constitute a sustained and close commentary on American public affairs for a period of nearly six decades. He brought to the discussion and analysis of current social and political problems a degree of learning unprecedented in American journalism. Throughout his career he retained an independent, critical stance on foreign and domestic issues and combined a rigorous commitment to democratic principles with a deep sense of the pragmatic limitations of real political situations. He is certainly among the most thoughtful and cultured newspaper men of all times.

Lippmann was educated at Harvard—he graduated in the same class as T.S. Eliot and John Reed—where he excelled in philosophy and came under the influence of William James, George Santayana, and, more decisively, that of the visiting English Fabian Socialist Graham Wallas. After Harvard, Lippmann worked for several progressive magazines (*Boston Common* and *Everybody's Magazine*) and served briefly as secretary to the socialist mayor of Schenectady, New York, Rev. George R. Lunn. His first book, *A Preface to Politics*, received a lot of attention for its argument that the science of politics and the practice of statecraft need to be based on an understanding of the irrational, unconscious sources of human behaviour. Drawing on Sorel and Nietzsche, and especially on Freud, Lippmann stressed that problems of political order could not be solved, or even usefully thought about, without considering peoples' psychological needs and the vital structure of the will. *Drift and Mastery*, a year later, emphasized that a democratic society must, through science, exercise conscious regulation of the irrational components of human nature in order to cope with "the chaos of new freedom."

Herbert Croly asked Lippmann to work with him in founding the *New Republic* in 1914. This liberal magazine came to be read as the semi-official organ of the Wilson administration, and Lippmann himself frequently consulted the president on questions of international diplomacy. Lippmann was criticized at this time by some of his friends for moving away from his earlier socialism. At the close of World War I he served on the American Commission to Negotiate the Peace and assisted directly in drafting President Wilson's Fourteen Points. Disillusioned by the Allied intervention in the Bolshevik Revolution, Lippmann resigned from federal service and resumed his editorship at the *New Republic*.

The main focus of Lippmann's thinking in the 1920's was on the relation of knowledge to public opinion in mass society. He was one of the first social thinkers to become aware of the growing distance between peoples' stereotyped impressions of their political environment and the complex realities of modern society. The news media increased this gap, according to Lippmann, by disseminating selected, simplified, and dramatized episodes of political life instead of explaining the facts and connections that lay behind these events. Lippmann became doubtful whether citizens *could* be adequately and objectively informed of the knowledge required for self-government, conceived along Jeffersonian lines. Lippmann proposed that there should be a system of collaboration between administrators, policy-makers, and fact-finding experts. The role of the citizenry would be to maintain surveillance over the decision-making procedures of these knowledgeable rulers. *Liberty and the News*, *Public Opinion*, and *The Phantom Public* express Lippmann's pessimism concerning the compatibility of democracy with the social conditions of modern society. *An Inquiry into the Principles of the Good Society* advanced the principle of disinterestedness on the part of statesmen as a cure to the excesses of majority rule and as an antidote to the dangers of elitism.

In 1922 Lippmann took a position at the New York *World* and in 1929 became editor. The *World* was a liberal newspaper that exposed the Jess Smith-Daugherty scandals, vehemently opposed the Ku Klux Klan, drew attention to the working conditions of West Virginian coal miners, promoted international trade, and supported the League of Nations. When the *World* ceased publication in 1931, Lippmann began his column, in the New York *Herald Tribune*, and with this he achieved a tremendously wide audience, both within the United States and throughout the world, and secured his position as the most influential publicist of his day. Although Lippmann thought very highly of Roosevelt as a strong national leader he was opposed to New Deal financial policies because they seemed to aim at the implementation of a planned economy. This, for Lippmann, was incompatible with democratic political principles.

In *U.S. Foreign Policy: Shield of the Republic* and *U.S. War Aims* Lippmann warned against an isolationist policy following the war. He followed closely the course of diplomatic efforts during the war and was in frequent contact with the Roosevelt administration. He strongly favored the creation of the Atlantic Alliance because he believed that international diplomacy must involve balanced relations of power between regionally allied groups of nations. He foresaw that the interests and security of the West would depend on realistic negotiations with Russia conducted from a position of military strength. Lippmann was one of the many political thinkers of this century who'd been disillusioned by the failure of Wilsonian idealism and the League of Nations. *U.S. War Aims* closes with a list of guidelines for post-war American foreign policy:

1. Consolidate the strategical and diplomatic connections...of the Atlantic Community.
2. Recognize as valid and proper the strategical system of the Russian orbit....
3. Recognize that China will be another center of a third strategic center.
4. Recognize that in time the Moslem and the Hindu

nations of North Africa, the Middle East, and Southern Asia will form regional systems of their own.
5. Make the cardinal principle...[be] that Japan shall not hold the balance of power in the Far East [and] Germany shall not hold the balance of power between the Atlantic Community and the Russian Orbit.
6. Recognize that the general aim of any lasting settlement of a war of aggression is to extinguish the war party and to protect the peace party, by making the defeat irrevocable and the peace acceptable.

Lippmann criticized the Cold War foreign policies of Truman—he supported Dewey in the 1948 election—on the grounds that attempting to stamp out communism all over the globe could lead neither to peaceful co-existence with Russia nor to a strengthening of U.S. partnership in Atlantic Community. He saw the Korean War as an unrealistic and over-zealous crusade against communism for merely ideological reasons.

Lippmann formulated the principles that underlay his specific political analyses in *Essays in the Public Philosophy*. An enfeeblement of government and a breakdown of political structures has characterized the fate of liberal democracies in this century, according to Lippmann. The purpose of his reflections in this work is to account for this and to prescribe a remedy. "The central and critical condition of...Western society," Lippmann writes, is "that the democracies are ceasing to receive the traditions of civility in which the good society, the liberal democratic way of life at its best, originated and developed. They are cut off from the public philosophy and the political arts which are needed to govern the liberal democratic society." The main tenet of the public philosophy is that rational enquiry is capable of uncovering objective and universally binding principles by which people may regulate their collective life. The concept of a universal rational order has been the premise of Western political institutions since classical times, and its eclipse in the modern period explains our disfunctional political life. Lippmann insisted that ideas have efficacy, and that a belief in "the laws of a rational order of human society" could reorient both people's private expectations and the conduct of public officials. Lippmann is squarely within the tradition of liberal political philosophy when he writes:

The rational order consists of the terms which must be met in order to fulfill men's capacity for the good life in this world. They are the terms of the widest consensus of rational men in a plural society. They are the propositions to which all men concerned, if they are sincerely and lucidly rational, can be expected to converge.

Our ability to salvage freedom from within the chaos of modern history, for Lippmann, was a question of whether such principles could be made socially actual and operative once again.

—Alan Waters

LIPSET, Seymour M(artin). American political scientist and sociologist. Born in New York City, 18 March 1922. Studied at City College of New York, B.S. 1943; Columbia University, New York, Ph.D. 1949. Married Elsie Braun in 1944; 3 children. Lecturer in Sociology, University of Toronto, 1946-48; Assistant Professor, University of California, Berkeley, 1948-50; Assistant, then Associate Professor, 1950-56, and Assistant Director, Bureau of Applied Social Research, 1954-56, Columbia University; Professor, 1956-66, and Director of the Institute of International Studies, 1962-66, University of California, Berkeley. Visiting Professor, 1965-66, amd since 1966, Professor of Government and Sociology, Harvard University, Cambridge, Massachusetts; since 1975. Professor of Political Science and

Sociology, and Senior Fellow, Hoover Institution, Stanford, California. Henry Ford Visiting Research Professor, Yale University, New Haven, Connecticut, 1960-61; Paley Lecturer, Hebrew University of Jerusalem, 1973; George Markham Professor, Center for International Affairs, 1974-75. Co-Editor, *Public Opinion*, since 1978. Member of the Council, American Sociological Association, 1959-62; Chairman of the Committee on Political Sociology, International Sociological Association, 1959-71; Member of the Executive Committee, Center for International Affairs, 1966-75; Member of the Council, American Political Science Association, 1972-74; Member of the Board of International Science Exchange, National Academy of Science, from 1974; National Chairman, B'nai B'rith Hillel Foundation, from 1975; President, International Society of Political Psychology, 1979-80. Recipient: Social Science Research Council fellowship, 1945; Center for Advanced Study in the Behavioral Sciences fellowship, 1955, 1972; MacIver Award, 1962; Gunnar Myrdal Prize, 1970; Townsend Harris Medal, 1971; Guggenheim Fellowship, 1971; College of the City of New York Medal, 1973. M.A.: Harvard University, 1966; LL.D.: Villanova University, Pennsylvania, 1973. Fellow, Vice-President, 1974-78, and Chairman, Economic and Social Science section, 1975-76, American Academy of Arts and Sciences. Honorary Fellow, Institute of Political Studies (Spain), and Finnish Academy of Science. Address: Hoover Institution, Stanford University, Stanford, California 94305, U.S.A.

PUBLICATIONS

Political Science and Sociology

Agrarian Socialism: The Coöperative Commonwealth Federation in Saskatchewan: A Study in Political Sociology. Berkeley, University of California Press, 1950; revised edition, New York, Doubleday, 1968.

Union Democracy: The Internal Politics of the International Typographers Union, with Martin A. Trow and James S. Coleman. Glencoe, Illinois, Free Press, 1956.

Social Mobility in Industrial Society, with Reinhard Bendix. Berkeley, University of California Press, and London, Heinemann, 1959.

Political Man: The Social Basis of Politics. New York, Doubleday, and London, Heinemann, 1960; revised edition, Baltimore, Johns Hopkins University Press, 1981.

The First New Nation: The United States in Historical and Comparative Perspective. New York, Basic Books, 1963; London, Heinemann, 1964.

Revolution and Counterrevolution. New York, Basic Books, 1968; London, Heinemann, 1969; revised edition, New York, Doubleday, 1970.

"The Socialism of Fools": The Left, The Jews, and Israel. New York, Anti-Defamation League, 1969.

The Politics of Unreason: Right-wing Extremism in America 1790-1970, with Earl Raab. New York, Harper, 1970; London, Heinemann, 1971.

Passion and Politics: Student Activism in America, with Gerald M. Schaflander. Boston, Little Brown, 1971; section reprinted, as *Rebellion in the University*, Little Brown, and London, Routledge, 1972.

Academics, Politics, and the 1972 Election, with Everett Ladd, Jr. Washington, D.C., American Enterprise Institute for Public Policy Research, 1973.

Professors, Unions, and American Higher Education. Washington, D.C., American Enterprise Institute for Public Policy Research, 1973.

Opportunity and Welfare in the First New Nation. Washington, D.C., American Enterprise Institute for Public Policy Research, 1974.

The Divided Academy: Professors and Politics, with Everett Ladd, Jr. New York, McGraw Hill, 1975.

Education and Politics at Harvard, with David Riesman. New York, McGraw Hill, 1975.

Dialogues on American Politics, with Irving Louis Horowitz. New York, Oxford University Press, 1978.

Other

Editor, with Reinhard Bendix, *Class, Status, and Power: A Reader in Social Stratification.* Glencoe, Illinois, Free Press, 1953; revised edition, 1966.

Editor, with Walter Galenson, *Labor and Trade Unionism: An Interdisciplinary Reader.* New York, Wiley, 1960.

Editor, with Leo Lowenthal, *Culture and Social Character: The Works of David Riesman Reviewed.* New York, Free Press, 1961.

Editor, with Neil J. Smelser, *Sociology: The Progress of a Decade: A Collection of Articles.* Englewood Cliffs, New Jersey Prentice Hall, 1961.

Editor, *Society in America*, by Harriet Martineau. New York, Doubleday, 1962.

Editor, *Democracy and the Organization of Political Parties*, by M. Ostrogorski. Chicago, Quadrangle, 2 vols., 1964.

Editor, with Sheldon S. Wolin, *The Berkeley Student Revolt: Facts and Interpretations.* New York, Doubleday, 1965.

Editor, with Neil J. Smelser, *Social Structure and Social Mobility in Economic Development.* Chicago, Aldine, and London, Routledge, 1966.

Editor, with Aldo Solari, *Elites in Latin America.* New York, Oxford University Press, 1967.

Editor, *Student Politics.* New York, Basic Books, 1967.

Editor, with Stein Rokkan, *Party Systems and Voter Alignments: Cross-National Perspectives.* New York, Free Press, 1967.

Editor, with Richard Hofstadter, *Sociology and History: Methods.* New York, Basic Books, 1968.

Editor, with Richard Hofstadter, *Turner and the Sociology of the Frontier.* New York, Basic Books, 1968.

Editor, *Politics and Social Science.* New York, Oxford University Press, 1969.

Editor, with Philip G. Altbach, *Students in Revolt.* Boston, Houghton Mifflin, 1969.

Editor, with David Victor John Bell, *Issues in Politics and Government.* Boston, Houghton Mifflin, 1970.

Editor, with J.H.M. Laslett, *Failure of a Dream? Essays in the History of American Socialism.* New York, Doubleday, 1974.

Editor, *Emerging Coalitions in American Politics.* San Francisco, Institute for Contemporary Studies, 1978.

Editor, *The Third Century: America as a Post-Industrial Society.* Stanford, California, Hoover Institution Press, 1979.

Editor, *Party Coalitions in the 1980's.* San Fransisco, Institute for Contemporary Studies, 1981.

* * *

A prolific social scientist, Seymour M. Lipset, in almost four decades of research and writing, has addressed a number of significant topics, ranging from the rise to power of the Cooperative Commonwealth Federation in Saskatchewan, the processes of social mobility in industrial societies, the politics of young people and academics, the American right wing, the role of political elites in Latin America, to the formation of party systems in Western Europe. Much of this work is seminal.

Not only has Lipset received considerable scholarly attention and reputation, he has attracted many critical commentaries, perhaps most notably for his interpretations of the "end of ideology" and the political development of the United States, and, more generally, other liberal-democratic political systems.

If any single sentence summarizes Lipset's work, it is found in *Political Man*, where he wrote "democracy is not only or even primarily a means through which different groups can attain their ends or seek the good society: it is the good society itself in operation."

Democracy is seen not just in terms of political institutions and procedures, but also as a social system requiring two conditions: consensus and cleavage. The potentiality for conflict within society necessitates that there is widespread agreement, not only about the rules of the game, but the goals and values of the society at large, so that at any particular time issues are not so overwhelming in their divisiveness that people resort to violence or secession to solve their problems, or that the system itself falls into immobilism. Cleavages are necessary because they constitute the structural basis for on-going processes of political competition, which, among other things, allows different parts of society, at various times, to hold authority, and, further, increases the impact of non-elite groups upon elites and the processes of decision-making. The goodness of democracy, then, is found in the generation of consensus through non-coercive means, the balancing of the competing forces of consensus and cleavage, and the broadening of political participation and influence, in the context of a stable, but changing, system.

The interrelationships between consensus and cleavage, while strikingly developed in *Political Man*, are also seen clearly in the essay, co-authored with Stein Rokkan, dealing with the development of Western European party systems, for party, in democratic political systems, is the primary vehicle for the establishment and maintenance of consensus, on the one hand, and the representation of cleavages within society, on the other. The great variety of party labels in Europe, on the face of it, seems to mitigate against the utility of comparative analysis. Indeed, the lack of a comprehensive theoretical schema for understanding the general process of the development of party systems meant that there was in the traditional literature a strong preoccupation with unique and "national" attributes of parties and systems. The strength of this essay is that it treats the development of various systems as being subject to the impact of a few factors and being underlain by similar relationships, even though the "national" characteristics of these systems are so clearly different.

Cleavage structures are marked territorial (regional conflicts or differences between elite groups) and functional (ideological interpretations of economic interests) dimensions. The character of each society's cleavage structure will be determined by how two critical societal revolutions—the national and the industrial—are embodied in each society's structures and processes: the national revolution generates conflicts along centre-periphery lines and also between the claims of the state and the traditional prerogatives of established churches; the industrial revolution creates conflicts, firstly between traditional land owners and industrialists and, secondly, between capitalists and owners versus workers and renters.

The development of cleavage structures into particular party systems is a function of four variables, namely legitimation (the extent to which issues raised by challenging groups are deemed acceptable by established groups); representation (patterns of coalition-building; did old parties reject new social forces, thus forcing the establishment of new parties, or did they absorb them?); incorporation (extent to which members of society are granted equal political rights); and majority-power (extent to which majorities are checked by constitutional rules). Societies vary in the threshold levels for each variable, and the particular pattern of threshold levels creates a certain kind of party system. For example, Great Britain's system since 1918 is interpreted as being a function of low threshold levels for legitimation and incorporation, a high level for representation, and a medium level for majority-power. It also was argued that party systems in Western Europe, for the most part, had been firmly established by the 1920's, and the exceptions—Italy, Spain, France, and Germany—are characterized by basic polarities from that period. Conditions of consensus and cleavage—thus, the nature and operation of various forms of democracy—were reflections of unique historical events and personalities subtly woven into cleavage structures and threshold levels.

Lipset's basic concern with the interaction between consensus and cleavage is also evident in his work on the political development of the United States, as contrasted with the other English-speaking democracies.

American political development has taken place within the context of two primary values—equality and achievement—which are interrelated but not fully congruent. These values not only formed the normative basis of the American revolution, but also are the polar points around which subsequent political debate has revolved. Equality is the belief that "persons must be given respect simply because they are human beings." The belief in achievement—producing the best in people through competitive processes—is related to equality in that it requires a system of equality of opportunity to be adopted widely in the society in order to erase disadvantages caused by one's race, class, or birth.

Two characteristics of American politics—the absence of a strong socialist party and the fact that "...egalitarianism is, of course, for white men only..."—exemplify well the logic of Lipset's analysis. The absence of socialism is explained by the fact that egalitarianism is such a pervasive force in American society there has been no need for a strong socialist party. The position of blacks is a result of the American South being more ascriptive and elitist than are other parts of the United States, in terms of both white-black and white-white social, economic, and political relationships.

Lipset, amongst other things, has argued that the United States is primarily a leftist nation (though, it should be emphasized, not in terms of movements oriented towards equality of conditions). Internationally and domestically, instead of being resistant to change, the United States is portrayed as being fundamentally moved by values supportive of drives for equality. These kinds of judgements give occasion to much critical commentary from an academic community that so often sees the United States as a bastion of reaction. Whatever the merits of that debate, it is to be noted that Lipset's work is characterized by careful consideration of evidence drawn from many different times and places. His work as well is often a model for the lucid expression of difficult and abstract matters. And in the course of that work Lipset has made a number of significant contributions, not only to the understanding of the social bases of democratic political systems, but also to the field of political sociology.

—Peter Woolstencroft

LORENZ, Konrad (Zacharias). German ethologist. Born in Vienna, 7 November 1903. Studied at Columbia University, New York, 1922, and at the University of Vienna, M.D. 1928, Ph.D. in Zoology 1933. Served in the German Army as a physician, 1942-44. Married Margarethe Gebhardt in 1927; 3 children. Assistant, Anatomical Institute, 1928-35, Lecturer in Comparitive Anatomy and Animal Psychology, 1937-40, and University Lecturer, 1940, University of Vienna; Professor of Psychology and Head of Department, University of Königsberg, 1940-42; Director, Institute of Comparative Ethology, Altenberg, 1949-51; Head of Research Station for Physiology of Behavior, Institute of Marine Biology, Max Planck Society for the Advancement of Science, Buldern, 1951-58; Co-Founder, 1958, Co-Director, 1958-61, and Director, 1961-73, Institute for Behavior Physiology, Seewiesen. Since 1973, Director of Department of Animal Sociology, Institute of Comparative Ethology, Austrian Academy of Science. Since 1953, Honorary Professor, University of Münster, since 1957, Honorary Professor, University of Munich, and since 1974, Honorary Professor, University of Vienna and University of Salzburg. Recipient: Gold Medal, Zoological Society of New York, 1955; City of Vienna Prize, 1959; Gold Bölsche Medal, 1962; Austrian Distinction for Science and Art, 1964; Prix Mondial, Cino de Duca, 1969;

Kalinga Prize, Unesco, 1970; Nobel Prize for Physiology and Medicine, with Karl von Frisch and Nikolaas Tinbergen, 1973; Humboldt Medal, 1973; Grosses Verdienstkreuz der Bundesrepublik Deutschland, 1974; Bayerischer Verdienstorden, 1974; International Umwelt-Preis, 1980. Honorary doctorate: University of Leeds, 1962; University of Basel, 1966; Yale University, New Haven, Connecticut, 1967; Oxford University, 1968; University of Chicago, 1970; University of Durham, 1972; University of Birmingham, 1974; University of Vienna, 1980. Member, Austrian Academy of Science; Bavarian Academy of Science; Deutsche Akademie der Naturforscher Leopoldina; Orden Pour le Mérite. Foreign Associate, U.S. National Academy of Sciences; Foreign Member, Royal Society, London. Address: Institut für Vergleichende Verhaltensforschung, Adolf-Lorenzgasse 2, 3422 Altenberg, Austria.

PUBLICATIONS

Ethology

Er redete mit dem Vieh, den Vögeln, und den Fischen. Vienna, Borotha Schoeler, 1949; as *King Solomon's Ring*, New York, Crowell, 1952.

So kam der Mensch auf den Hund. Vienna, Borotha Schoeler, 1950; as *Man Meets Dog*, London, Methuen, 1954; Boston, Houghton Mifflin, 1955.

Das sogenannte Böse: Zur Naturgeschichte der Aggression. Vienna, Borotha Schoeler, 1963; as *On Aggression*, London, Methuen, and New York, Harcourt Brace, 1966.

Gestaltwahrnehmung als Quelle wissenschaftlicher Erkenntnis. Darmstadt, Wissenschaftlicher Buchgesellschaft, 1964.

Darwin hat recht gesehen. Pfullingen, Neske, 1964.

Über tierisches und menschliches Verhalten. Munich, Piper, 2 vols., 1965; as *Studies in Animal and Human Behavior*, Cambridge, Massachusetts, Harvard University Press, 2 vols., 1970-71.

Evolution and the Modification of Behavior. Chicago, University of Chicago Press, 1965.

Der Vogelflug. Pfullingen, Neske, 1965.

Antriebe tierischen und menschlichen Verhaltens, with Paul Leyhausen. Munich, Piper, 1969; as *Motivation of Human and Animal Behavior: An Ethological View*, New York, Van Nostrand, 1973.

Die acht Todsünden der zivilisierten Menschheit. Munich, Piper, 1973; as *Civilized Man's Eight Deadly Sins*, New York, Harcourt Brace, 1974.

Haben Tiere ein subjektives Erleben? Berlin, Die Arche, 1971.

Der Rückseite des Spiegels: Versuch einer Naturgeschichte menschlichen Erkennens. Munich, Piper, 1973; as *Behind the Mirror: A Search for a Natural History of Human Knowledge*, London, Methuen, and New York, Harcourt Brace, 1977.

Vergleichende Verhaltensforschung. Berlin, Springer, 1978; as *The Foundations of Ethology*, New York, Springer, 1981.

Die Wirkungsfüge der Natur und das Schicksal des Menschen: Gesammelte Arbeiten. Munich, Piper, 1978.

Das Jahr der Graugans. Munich, Piper, 1979; as *The Year of the Greylag Goose*, London, Eyre Methuen, 1979.

*

Critical Studies: *Konrad Lorenz: The Man and His Ideas* by Richard I. Evans, New York, Harcourt Brace, 1975 (includes bibliography); *Konrad Lorenz* by Alex Nisbett, London, Dent, 1976; *Konrad Lorenz und seine Kritiker* by Wolfgang Wieser, Munich, Piper, 1976.

* * *

Konrad Lorenz's great scientific contribution to ethology was made possible by applying the accepted methods of observation and objective description used in anatomy and physiology to the world of animal behavior. Before the 1930's animal behavior was studied either by conducting experiments under conditions unrelated to the animal's natural environment or through field studies concentrating on one species with no attempt at establishing rules and laws that govern behavior. In the late 1930's Lorenz and Nikolaas Tinbergen wrote a series of theoretical papers laying the foundation for modern ethology. Lorenz, the acknowledged "father of ethology," can be credited with carrying ethology past the "natural history phase" of fascination with behavioral adaptations to the belief that there are general principles and laws of behavior. In addition, Lorenz helped to make us realize the significance of phylogenetic adaptations in understanding behavioral processes.

While growing up Lorenz developed a passion for hand-raising wild and domestic animals. There were always ample animals living in and around his father's home in Altenberg, Austria, and it was here that Lorenz sharpened his ability to observe animals with remarkable insight. His father was a well-known orthopedist and, therefore, it was not surprising that Lorenz first pursued a career in medicine. Strongly drawn to the study of comparative ethology he added a Ph.D. in Zoology to his M.D. degree.

Perhaps the most famous paper written in ethology is on the egg retrieval response in the greylag goose. Lorenz and Tinbergen described how a brooding goose will retrieve an egg that has rolled out of its nest. The goose rises, extends its neck, places its bill over the egg and rolls the egg back into the nest. The "motor program" is innate, highly stereotyped, and will continue to completion even if the egg is removed from under the bill in mid-journey. They called the goose's behavior a "fixed-action pattern" (FAP). Triggering the FAP they hypothesized an "innate releasing mechanism" (IRM) within the animal which acts in response to stimuli or "releasers" from the environment. Because only one aspect of the stimulus leads to a response the term "sign-stimulus" often is used.

From this conceptual framework Konrad Lorenz developed his famous "psycho-hydraulic" model. "Motivational" water called "action-specific energy" fills a reservoir or tank. A behavior is performed when a "sign-stimulus" acting as a weight triggers a mechanism releasing the water. As the interval between performance of the same behavior increases the amount of the water in the reservoir increases and when released leads to graded behavioral responses. The hydraulic model has been the subject of much criticism, in part, becuase it works in a fashion similar to the flushing of a toilet, an analogy not fully appreciated by the scientific community. Most objections to the model, however, concern Lorenz's attempt to describe a complex phenomenon like motivation with such a simple model.

Following up an observation made by Oskar Heinroth, Lorenz discovered a dramatic example of programmed learning, imprinting. Orphaned geese or ducks under two days old would follow Lorenz as if he was their parent. This "parental imprinting" was a rapid and relatively irreversible learning process during an optimal "critical" or "sensitive" period. Furthermore, when the geese became adults they would court humans instead of other geese. Lorenz concluded that sexual preferences were established very early in the animal's life and that most often sexual imprinting has a critical period lasting for a number of weeks beginning when the animal is a few months old. The concept of a critical period is a crucial one to ethology. It indicates that there are innate dispositions to learn with not every animal being able to learn everything at all ages. Conceptually imprinting has proven valuable for psychologists and psychiatrists in the understanding of human behavior.

Early in his career Lorenz comfirmed that closely related species have similar behavior patterns reflecting their close phylogenetic origins. Observing courtship patterns in ducks Lorenz found that in species believed to be closely related there were ethological correlates just as strong morphological ones. Through observations mainly on fish and birds he also noted that there were "instinctive activities" which were as clearly defined as anatomical structures. These findings suggested to him a large genetic component to behavior. In his book *On Aggression* Lorenz suggests that some animals, including man, are innately motivated to seek out opportunities to fight—needless to say, a controversial viewpoint. Even though Lorenz spent a great deal of time defending his views on the importance of genetically programmed behavior, his early writings clearly indicate the importance of learning in providing for flexibility in a variable environment.

The *Foundations of Ethology*, published in 1981, provides us with Lorenz's view of ethology as a whole. The first draft was written almost 40 years ago when Lorenz was a prisoner in a Russian POW camp in Armenia. In the book he defines ethology as "the discipline which applies to the behavior of animals and humans all those questions asked and those methodologies used as a matter of course in all other branches of biology since Charles Darwin's time." This definition for ethology can be found in the literature as early as the turn of this century; however, not until Lorenz made his contribution did the study of behavior gain momentum, momentum which it has not since lost.

—Fred E. Wasserman

LOVEJOY, Arthur O(ncken Schauffler). American philosopher and historian of ideas. Born in Berlin, Germany, 10 October 1873. Studied at the University of California, Berkeley, B.A. 1895; Harvard University, Cambridge, Massachusetts, M.A. 1897. Associate Professor, Stanford University, California, 1899-1901; Professor, Washington University, St. Louis, 1901-07; Columbia University, New York, 1907-08; University of Missouri, Columbia, 1908-10; and Johns Hopkins University, Baltimore, 1910-38. Howison Lecturer, University of California, Berkeley, 1924; Carus Lecturer, American Philosophical Association, 1928; Visiting Professor, Harvard University, 1932-33 (William James Lecturer, 1932), 1937-38; Visiting Lecturer, Princeton University, New Jersey, 1939; and Swarthmore College, Pennsylvania, 1941. Founder, with John Dewey and others, American Association of University Professors, 1913; *Journal of the History of Ideas*, 1940. Died (in Baltimore) 30 December 1962.

PUBLICATIONS

Philosophy

Three Studies in Current Philosophical Questions, with others. Baltimore, Johns Hopkins University Press, 1914.
The Revolt Against Dualism: An Inquiry Concerning the Existence of Ideas. La Salle, Illinois, Open Court, 1930.
The Great Chain of Being: A Study of the History of an Idea. Cambridge, Massachusetts, Harvard University Press, 1936.
Essays in the History of Ideas. Baltimore, Johns Hopkins University Press, 1948.
The Reason, The Understanding, and Time. Baltimore, Johns Hopkins University Press, 1961.
Reflections on Human Nature. Baltimore, Johns Hopkins University Press, 1961.
The Thirteen Pragmatisms and Other Essays. Baltimore, Johns Hopkins University Press, 1963.

Other

Hitler as Pacifist. Baltimore, American Jewish Conference, 1933.

Should There Be an International Organization for General Security Against Military Aggression, and Should the United States Participate in Such An Organization? Boston, Universities Committee on Post-War International Problems, 1943.
Can We Prevent Future Wars? Washington, D.C., Government Printing Office, 1944.
The Dumbarton Oaks Proposals: The Enforcement of Peace. Boston, Universities Committee on Post-War International Problems, 1944.
What Shall Be Done About Germany after the War? Washington, D.C., Government Printing Office, 1944.

Editor, with others, *Primitivism and Related Ideas in Antiquity: A Documentary History of Primitivism and Related Ideas.* Baltimore, Johns Hopkins University Press, 1933.

*

Bibliography: *Arthur O. Lovejoy: An Annotated Bibliography* by Daniel J. Wilson, New York, Garland, 1982.

Critical Studies: "Lovejoy's Role in American Philosophy" by Philip P. Wiener, in *Studies in Intellectual History*, Baltimore, Johns Hopkins University Press, 1953; *Arthur O. Lovejoy and the Quest for Intelligibility* by Daniel J. Wilson, Chapel Hill, University of North Carolina Press, 1980.

* * *

Arthur O. Lovejoy was one of America's foremost philosophers in the early 20th century, the chief proponent of the history of ideas, and an articulate defender of academic freedom. His diverse works were marked by an acute critical mind, dedication to rigorous standards of scholarship, and a search for intelligibility in a pluralistic world.

Philosophy formed the basis of Lovejoy's thought because it promised intelligibility based on reason. Adopting philosophy to escape the evangelical religion of his father, Lovejoy found the prevalent idealism of the late 19th century too static and absolutistic, and turned to the revived currents of realism and dualism. He was a sharp critic of Josiah Royce's absolute idealism, which denied diversity, and William James's pragmatism, which in its extreme forms threatened reason and understanding. Lovejoy enunciated his mature philosophy, critical realism, most fully in *The Revolt Against Dualism*. Critical realism was based upon both epistemological and psychophysical dualism. The first held that all knowing was indirect and mediated by ideas while the second asserted that both minds, with their ideas, and material objects were equally real. Although a participant in the revival of realism in this century, Lovejoy is probably best known today as a critic of idealism, pragmatism, and all forms of absolutism and monism.

In addition to his substantive work, Lovejoy helped establish philosophy as an academic profession. He worked within the American Philosophical Association to encourage the adoption of scientific methods and standards to foster philosophic intelligibility and utility. Though Lovejoy was a significant philosopher in the first half of this century, his importance has declined as philosophers have moved in new directions.

Lovejoy's studies in the history of ideas were closely linked to his philosophical interests. In his early studies in the history of religious thought he first discovered certain seminal ideas, later called unit-ideas, that had persisted over the centuries and had shaped our thought. Lovejoy's interests later broadened to include pre-Darwinian evolutionary thought and Enlightenment and Romantic thinkers. His essays in the history of ideas were marked by careful discrimination, extensive tracing of the roots and influence of ideas, and wide learning in languages, religion, philosophy, literature, and history. *The Great Chain of Being* marked the culmination of Lovejoy's historical studies. In it he traced the ideas of plenitude, continuity, and gradation from their Platonic origins, to their embodiment in the idea of the Great Chain of Being in the 17th century, and to the decline of the idea under the impact of Enlightenment and Romantic thought. The idea of the chain, which postulated the linkage of all beings from lowest to highest in one absolute structure, was overthrown by the rise of evolutionary ideas. From this Lovejoy drew the moral that no absolute, static conception of the universe was either possible of intelligible. Lovejoy's essays and books helped establish the history of ideas, and *The Journal of the History of Ideas*, which he founded, has continued to encourage the careful study of ideas and their influence.

As a life-long academic Lovejoy was deeply concerned about the profession of college teaching. An early experience at Stanford University made him acutely sensitive to the need to protect the rights of academics. He was a central figure in the establishment of the American Association of University Professors and the major author of its early statements on academic freedom in 1915 and 1918. Lovejoy insisted that the freedom to teach, research, and publish in all areas without outside interference was central to scholarship. Only the standards of the discipline and the judgement of peers placed limits on scholarship. Lovejoy later modified his views during both World War I and the communist scare of the 1950's to exclude from protection those acts and individuals threatening national security. Despite such lapses, Lovejoy devoted himself tirelessly over a long career to defend the academic freedom of American scholars.

Lovejoy's search for intelligibility united the three aspects of his thought and career. His dualistic philosophy offered an explanation of how we understand the world, the history of ideas uncovered the development of the idea that the world was changing and evolving, and his defense of academic freedom helped provide the intellectual climate in which he and others could continue their quest to understand rationally the universe in which they lived. Many of Lovejoy's philosophical and historical ideas are no longer in fashion, but his career continues to provide an example of reasoned thought, rigorous inquiry, and spirited defense of the freedom of ideas.

—Daniel J. Wilson

LUKÁCS, Georg. Hungarian philosopher. Born György Szegedy von Lukács in Budapest, 13 April 1885. Studied at the University of Budapest, Ph.D. 1906, and privately with Heinrich Rickert in Heidelberg, 1912-15. Married Gertrud Bortstieber in 1919. Served as Commissar for Public Education under Béla Kun, 1919. Affiliated with the Marx-Engels-Lenin Institute, Moscow, 1929-30; researcher, Institute of Philosophy, Soviet Academy of Sciences, Moscow, 1933-44; Professor of Aesthetics and Cultural Philosophy, University of Budapest, 1945-56. Minister of Culture under Imre Nagy, 1956. Recipient: Goethe Prize, 1970. *Died* (in Budapest) *4 June 1971.*

PUBLICATIONS

Collections

Werke. Neuwied, West Germany, Luchterhand, 1967-.

Literary Criticism and Social Philosophy

Megjegyzések az irodalomentörténet elméletéhez [The Methodology of Literary History]. Budapest, Franklin Társulat Nyomda, 1910.
A lélék és a formák (Kisérletek). Budapest, Franklin Társulat Nyomda, 1910; as *Soul and Form,* Cambridge, Massachu-

setts, M.I.T. Press, 1974.
A modern dráma fejlő désének története. Budapest, Kisfaludy Társaság, Franklin, 2 vols., 1911; abridged version as *The Sociology of Modern Drama,* Oshkosh, Wisconsin, Green Mountain Editions, 1965.
Esztétikai kultúra [Aesthetic Culture]. Budapest, Atheneum, 1913.
Balázs Béla és akiknek nem kell [Béla Balázs and His Enemies]. Gyoma, Kner, 1918.
Taktika és ethika. Budapest, Közoktatasügyi Népbiztosság Kiadasa, 1919; selections as *The Question of Parliamentarianism and Other Essays,* London, New Left Books, 1972; as *Tactics and Ethics: Political Essays, 1919-1929,* New York, Harper, 1975.
Die Theorie des Romans: Ein geschichtsphilosophischer Versuch über die Formen der grossen Epik. Berlin, Cassirer, 1920; as *The Theory of the Novel: A Historico-Philosophical Essay on the Form of Great Epic Literature,* Cambridge, Massachusetts, M.I.T. Press, 1971.
Geschichte und Klassenbewusstsein: Studien über marxistische Dialektik. Berlin, Malik, 1923; as *History and Class Consciousness: Studies in Marxist Dialectics,* Cambridge, Massachusetts, M.I.T. Press, 1971.
Lenin: Studie über den Zusammenhang seiner Gedanken. Vienna, Malik, 1924; as *Lenin: A Study on the Unity of His Thought,* London, New Left Books, 1970; Cambridge, Massachusetts, M.I.T. Press, 1971.
Moses Hess und die Probleme der idealistischen Dialektik. Leipzig, Hirschfeld, 1926.
Literaturnye teorii XIX veka i marksizm [Marxism and 19th Century Literary Theory]. Moscow, Khudozhestvennaja Literatura, 1937.
K istorii realizma [History of Realism]. Moscow, Khudozhestvennaja Literatura, 1939.
Gottfried Keller. Kiev, Staatsverlag der nationalen Minderheit der USSR, 1940.
Írástudók felelő ssége [The Responsibility of the Man of Letters]. Moscow, Idegennyelvü Irodalmi Kiadó, 1944.
Balzac, Stendhal, Zola. Budapest, Hungária, 1945.
Deutsche Literatur während des Imperialismus: Eine Übersicht ihrer Hauptströmungen. Berlin, Aufbau, 1945.
Fortschritt und Reaktion in der deutschen Literatur. Berlin, Aufbau, 1945.
Lenin és a kultúra kérdései [Lenin and the Problem of Culture]. Budapest, Magyar-Szovjet Müvelő dési Tárasasság, 1946.
Nagy orosz realisták [The Great Russian Realists]. Budapest, Szikra, 1946.
Goethe és kora. Budapest, Hungária, 1946; as *Goethe and His Time,* London, Merlin Press, 1965; New York, Grosset and Dunlap, 1969.
Nietzsche és a fasizmus [Nietzsche and Fascism]. Budapest, Hungária, 1946.
Irodalom és demokrácia [Literature and Democracy]. Budapest, Szikra, 1947.
A történelmi regény. Budapest, Hungária, 1947; as *The Historical Novel,* London, Merlin Press, 1962; New York, Humanities Press, 1965.
A marxi esztétika alapjai [Fundamentals of Marxist Aesthetics]. Budapest, Szikra, 1947.
A polgári filozófia válsága [The Crisis in Bourgeois Philosophy]. Budapest, Hungária, 1947.
Der junge Hegel: Über die Beziehungen von Dialektik und Ökonomie. Zurich, Europa, 1948; as *The Young Hegel: Studies in the Relations Between Dialectics and Economics,* London, Merlin Press, 1975; Cambridge, Massachusetts, M.I.T. Press, 1976.
Essays über Realismus. Berlin, Aufbau, 1948; as *Studies in European Realism: A Sociological Survey of the Writings of Balzac, Stendhal, Zola, Tolstoy, Gorki and Others,* London, Hillway, 1950.
Schicksalwende: Beiträge zu einer neuen deutschen Ideologie.

Berlin, Aufbau, 1948.

Karl Marx und Friedrich Engels als Literaturhistoriker. Berlin, Aufbau, 1948.

Új magyar kultúráért [For a New Hungarian Culture]. Budapest, Szikra, 1948.

Thomas Mann. Budapest, Hungária, 1948; as *Essays on Thomas Mann*, London, Merlin Press, and New York, Grosset and Dunlap, 1965.

A marxista filozófia feladatai az új demokráciában [The Tasks of Marxist Philosophy in the New Democracy]. Budapest, "Budapest" Irodalmi Intézet, 1948.

Marx és Engels irodalomelmélete [The Literary Theories of Marx and Engels]. Budapest, Szikra, 1949.

Existentialismus oder Marxismus? Berlin, Aufbau, 1951.

Deutsche Realisten des 19. Jahrhunderts. Berlin, Aufbau, 1951.

Balzac und der französische Realismus. Berlin, Aufbau, 1952.

Puschkin-Gorki (Zwei Essays). Leipzig, Reclam, 1952.

Der russische Realismus in der Weltliteratur. Berlin, Aufbau, 1952.

Die Zerstörung der Vernunft. Berlin, Aufbau, 1954.

Beiträge zur Geschichte der Ästhetik. Berlin, Aufbau, 1954.

A különösség mint esztétikai kategória [Individuality as an Aesthetic Category]. Budapest, Akadémiai kiadó, 1957.

Wider den missverstandenen Realismus. Hamburg, Claasen, 1958; as *The Meaning of Contemporary Realism*, London, Merlin Press, 1963; and as *Realism in Our Time: Literature and the Class Struggle*, New York, Harper, 1964.

Schriften zur Literatursoziologie, edited by Peter Ludz. Neuwied, Luchterhand, 1961.

Die Eigenart des Ästhetischen. Neuwied, Luchterhand, 2 vols., 1963.

Deutsche Literatur in zwei Jahrhunderten. Neuwied, Luchterhand, 1964.

Der junge Marx: Seine philosophische Entwicklung von 1840 bis 1844. Pfullingen, Neske, 1965.

Schriften zur Ideologie und Politik. Neuwied, Luchterhand, 1967.

Die Grablegung des alten Deutschland: Essays zur deutschen Literatur des 19. Jahrhunderts. Hamburg, Rowohlt, 1967.

Früheschriften. Neuwied, Luchterhand, 1967.

Probleme des Realismus. Neuwied, Luchterhand, 3 vols., 1967-71.

Russische Literatur, russische Revolution: Puschkin, Tolstoi, Dostojewskij, Fadejew, Makarenko, Scholochow, Solschenizyn. Neuwied, Luchterhand, 1969.

Probleme der Ästhetik. Neuwied, Luchterhand, 1969.

Solschenizyn. Neuwied, Luchterhand, 1970; as *Solzhenitsyn*, London, Merlin Press, 1970; Cambridge, Massachusetts, M.I.T. Press, 1971.

Die ontologischen Grundlagen des menschlichen Denkens und Handelns. Vienna, n.p., 1970.

Marxismus und Stalinismus. Hamburg, Rowohlt, 1970.

Writer and Critic and Other Essays. New York, Grosset and Dunlap, 1971; London, Merlin Press, 1978.

Zur Ontologie des gesellschaftlichen Seins: Vol 1, *Die ontologischen Grundprinzipien von Marx*. Neuwied, Luchterhand, 1971; as *Marx's Basic Ontological Principles*, London, Merlin Press, 1978. Vol 2, *Hegels falsche und echte Ontologie*. Neuwied, Luchterhand, 1972; as *Hegel's False and Genuine Ontology*, London, Merlin Press, 1979.

Ästhetik. Neuwied, Luchterhand, 4 vols., 1972.

Marxism and Human Liberation: Essays on History, Culture, and Revolution. New York, Dell, 1973.

Frühe Schriften zur Ästhetik. Neuwied, Luchterhand, 2 vols., 1974, 1975.

Politische Aufsätze. Neuwied, Luchterhand, 1975.

Kurz Skizze einer Geschichte der neuen deutschen Literatur, edited by Frank Benseler. Neuwied, Luchterhand, 1975.

Kunst und objektiv Wahrheit: Essays zur Literaturtheorie und Geschichte. Stuttgart, Reclam, 1977.

Other

Levelezese [Selected Correspondence]. Budapest, Magveto Kiado, 1981.

*

Bibliography: in *Festschrift zum achtigsten Geburtstag von Georg Lukacs* edited by Frank Benseler, Neuwied, Luchterhand, 1965.

Critical Studies: *Georg Lukács' Marxism: Alienation, Dialectics, Revolution: A Study in Utopia and Ideology* by Victor Zitta, The Hague, Nijhoff, 1961; *Lukács* by George Luchtheim, London, Collins, and New York, Viking Press, 1970; *Georg Lukács: The Man, His Work, and His Ideas* edited by G.H.R. Parkinson, London, Weidenfield and Nicolson, 1970; *Georg Lukács* by Erhard Bahr and Ruth Goldschmidt Kunzer, New York, Ungar, 1972; *The Aesthetics of Georg Lukács* by Béla Kiralyfalvi, Princeton, New Jersey, Princeton University Press, 1975.

*   *   *

While Georg Lukács's contribution to modern thought is complex and diverse, it is convenient to examine his work under two broad categories, namely literary criticism and social philosophy. In his analysis of literary forms, Lukács was primarily concerned with the development of the novel in relation to bourgeois culture. For Lukács, great art had to grasp the nature of the modern world realistically, but also develop an awareness of how that social reality might be transcended by the historical process. On these grounds, he has been consistently critical of aestheticism and romanticism in art. In *The Theory of the Novel* Lukács argued that in traditional literature, the hero was intimately tied in an organic relationship to the community, but in bourgeois society the autonomous individual is separated from the community. The novel expresses this isolation of the individual by idealism (in Cervantes), realism (in Flaubert) or utopianism (in Tolstoy). This interpretation of literary works was more sharply stated in *The Historical Novel*, where Lukács argued that the bourgeois author can, often unwittingly and unintentionally, gain some insight into the historical process by generating literary types which transcend imaginatively their own narrow social class basis. The works of Walter Scott, Thomas Mann, Dostoevsky, Balzac, and Flaubert achieved, albeit with contradiction and uncertainty, some purchase on the nature of historical change in modern society. Lukács's positive evaluation of literary realism was thus part of a general hostility to the notion of "art for art's sake" in his critical perspective on bourgeois culture. The greatness of a work of art had to be seen in terms of its realistic grasp of the concrete social world. This critique of aestheticism was closely associated with his rejection of relativism in social thought; both represented a dangerous movement towards irrationalism in Western culture. In *The Destruction of Reason* Lukács gave a comprehensive account of the growth of irrationalism in literature, philosophy and social science. European culture, especially German high culture, was tragically self-destructive. Paradoxically, rationality in the form of modern science appears to foster irrationality. Science destroys any certainty in absolute values and universal codes of behaviour. Because anything is valid in a relativistic culture, anything is permitted. Relativism leads to irrationalism, since it becomes impossible to choose a way of life which has intrinsic merit. This nihilistic theme, according to Lukács, provided the clear linkage between Nietzsche and the founders of German sociology—Georg Simmel and Max Weber.

While Lukács is well known for his literary analysis and more recently for his treatment of ontology and aesthetics in *Zur Ontologie des Gesellschaftlichen Seins* and *Die Eigenart des Aesthetischen*, his reputation rests basically upon eight essays (written between 1919 and 1922) and published as *History and Class Consciousness*. In order to understand these essays, we have to consider the diverse traditions which influenced Lukács's view of Marxism. These diverse influences included the revolutionary tradition of Ervin Szabo, the neo-Hegelianism of Wilhelm Dilthey, and the neo-Kantianism of Max Weber and Georg Simmel. Furthermore, Lukács's turn towards Marxism in 1918 took place after he was thoroughly steeped in German *Lebensphilosophie*. The main issues of the book reflect this unusual mixture of revolutionary romanticism, neo-Kantian epistemology, and Marxist philosophy. Following the central tradition of neo-Kantianism, Lukács argued that natural science does not provide a model for the analysis of society. The essential characteristic of human behaviour is that it is conscious. Because society involves human action which is conscious and involves the exercise of choice between alternative courses of action, the study of human action requires an approach which is clearly different from the natural sciences. Lukács saw that the problem for Marxism was that, in regarding itself as a science of society which could discover the laws of human behaviour and social development, it had denied the conscious intentionality of human action. He thus rejected all forms of economic determinism and reductionism. Marx's dialectical materialism was not a dogmatic body of eternal laws, but a method of inquiry.

In *History and Class Consciousness* Lukács argued that Marx's dialectical method emphasised the historicity of human consciousness, the self-reflective nature of the dialectic, the notion of social totality, and the importance of transcending all forms of reified consciousness. The clue to Marx's thought was to be found in the notion of the "fetishism of commodities" in volume one of *Capital*. While the social world has the appearance of objective, external autonomy, we in fact live in a world created and shaped by human agency. The social world has a thing-like quality in which human products are fetishised. In Lukács's view, this insight into the commodity-structure provides the basis for a critique of both bourgeois and Marxist thought. Thus, the antinomies of bourgeois thought—objectivity, versus subjectivity, will versus law, society versus nature—are products of the contradictions of capitalist relations based on commodity production. However, the Marxist emphasis on objective laws controlling human society is also an instance of reification. The antinomies of bourgeois consciousness, especially the rigid separation of fact and value (is/ought), could not be solved by contemplative philosophy, but only by human action or revolutionary *praxis*. The class which was historically determined to break down the reified consciousness of bourgeois capitalism was the class that had no vested interest in its survival, namely the revolutionary proletariat. The working class would simultaneously resolve the riddle of German philosophy and conclude the logic of history through the destruction of capitalism.

History and Class Consciousness is often treated as a remarkable anticipation of the rediscovery of the philosophy of praxis in the Young Marx which took place in the 1960's. The book prefigured the theoretical recovery of the Young Marx by reconstructing the Hegelian theme of alienation in Marx's so-called "Paris Manuscripts." For this reason, Lukács's analysis of the concept of reification has been at the forefront of debates between humanistic and scientific Marxism. Lukács has thus provided a particular strong criticism of deterministic thought in modern Marxism. He has also been especially influential in such areas of the sociology of literature where his perspective has been prominent in the work of, for example, Lucien Goldmann. Despite this influence, Lukács has also been subject to a number of important criticisms. Since he holds a teleological view of history in which the proletariat is the vehicle of truth which will shatter capitalism and bring about an epoch which is free from false consciousness, there can be no role for critical thought in a post-revolutionary society. Dialectical thought will be obsolete in such a society. Another criticism is that, by regarding Marxism as a method, he tends to put its conclusions beyond criticism.

Dialectical thought need not defend any particular propositions about society, since it is simply a method. Dialectical Marxism could never be false. A third criticism is that Lukács's view of knowledge is elitist. The problem is that the actual consciousness of the working class is not necessarily revolutionary and so this consciousness has to be interpreted, developed, and orchestrated by the Party. The role of Party intellectuals is to recognise the true knowledge which corresponds to the "real interests" of the working class. Finally Lukács has also been charged with providing a justification for political cynicism. Because the Party has a monopoly of truth, there is a moral imperative to lie and dissimulate, if necessary, for the Party's cause. There is thus a form of irrationalism in Lukács's philosophy, because, even when the Party contradicts itself, it is still correct. Lukács's own life provided tragic evidence for this very paradox.

—Bryan S. Turner

LURIA, Alexander R(omanovich). Russian psychologist. Born in Kazan, 16 July 1902. Studied at the University of Kazan, degree in humanities, 1921; First Medical Institute, Moscow, Ph.D. 1936, M.D. 1943. Married Lana P. Lipchina in 1933; 1 daughter. Worked at the Institute of Psychology, Moscow University, 1923-31, and the Center of Psychology, Ukrainian Psychoneurological Academy, 1931-34 (Co-Founder, 1931); Head, Psychology Section, Moscow Medical Institute of Genetics, 1934-36; founded the Laboratory of Neuropsychology, Institute of Neurosurgery, Moscow, 1936; after 1945, Professor of Neuropsychology and head of department, University of Moscow. Editor of *Neuropsychology, Cortex, Cognition*, and other journals. Recipient: Order of Lenin, 1955; Lomonosov Award, 1968. Honorary doctorate: University of Leicester, 1967; University of Nejmegen, 1969; University of Lubin, 1973; University of Brussels, 1975; University of Tampere, 1975. Member, Academy of Pedagogical Sciences of the U.S.S.R. Foreign Member, American Academy of Arts and Sciences, and American Academy of Education; Honorary Member, Swiss Psychological Society, and the French Neurological Society; Honorary Fellow, Colombian Psychological Society, and the British Psychological Society. *Died* (in Moscow) *in 1977*.

PUBLICATIONS

Psychology

Rech i intellekt v razvitii rebenka [Speech and Intellect in the Development of the Child]. Moscow, Poligrafshkola imeni A.V. Lunacharskogo, 1927.
Etiudy po istorii povedeniia [Studies in History of Behavior], with Lev Vygotsky. Moscow, Gosizdat, 1930.
The Nature of Human Conflicts; or, Emotion, Conflict and Will: An Objective Study of Disorganization and Control of Human Behavior. New York, Liveright, 1932.
Vnutreniaia kartina boleznei i iatrogennye zabolevaniia [An Internal Picture of Illnesses and Diseases]. Moscow, Medgiz, 1944.
Travmaticheskaia afaziia: Klinika, semiotika, i vosstanovitel'naia terapiia. Moscow, Medical Academy Press, 1947; as *Traumatic Aphasia, Its Symptoms, Psychology and Treatment*. The Hague, Mouton, 1970.
Vosstanovlenie funktsii mozga posle voennoi travmy. Moscow, Medical Academy Press, 1948; as *The Restoration of Functions after Brain Injury*. Oxford and New York, Pergamon Press, 1963.
Ocherki psikhofiziologii pisma [Essays on the Psycho-physiology of Writing]. Moscow, Pedagogical Academy Press, 1950.

Rol' slova v formirovanii vremennykh sviazei v normal'nom i anomal'nom razvitii (detei). Moscow, Pedagogical Academy Press, 1955; as *The Role of Speech in the Regulation of Normal and Abnormal Behavior,* New York, Pergamon Press, 1961.

Rech' i razvitie psikhicheskikh protsessov u rebenka: eksperimental'noe issledovanie, with F. Ia. Iudovich. Moscow, Pedagogical Academy Press, 1956; as *Speech and the Development of Mental Processes in the Child: An Experimental Investigation,* London, Staples Press, 1959.

Problemy vysstei nervnoi deiatel'nosti normal'nego i anomal'-nogo rebenka [Problems of Higher Nervous Activity in the Normal and Abnormal Child]. Moscow, Pedagogical Academy Press, 2 vols., 1956-58.

Vysshie korkovye funktsii cheloveka i ikh narusheniia pri lokal'-nykh porazheniiakh mozga. Moscow, Moscow University Press, 1962; as *Higher Cortical Functions in Men,* New York, Basic Books, and London, Tavistock Publications, 1966.

Mozg cheloveka i psikhicheskie protsessy. Moscow, Pedagogical Academy Press, 2 vols., 1963-70; vol. 1 as *The Human Brain and Psychological Processes,* New York, Harper, 1966.

Metody issledovaniia detei pri otbore vo vspomogatel'nye shkoly [Methods of Research on Children During Selection for Auxiliary School], with V.I. Luboskii. Moscow, Proveshchenie, 1964.

Lobnye doli i reguliatsiia psikhicheskikh protsessov i neiropsikhologicheskie issledovaniia [The Frontal Lobes and the Regulation of the Mental Processes: Neuropsychological Investigations], with E.D. Khomskaia. Moscow, Moscow University Press, 1966.

Neiropsikhologicheskii analiz resheniia zadach: Narusheniia protsessa resheniia zadach pri lokal'nykh porazheniiakh mozga [A Neuropsychological Analysis of Problem-Solving: Disturbances of the Problem-Solving Process from Localized injuries of the Brain], with L.S. Tsvetkova. Moscow, Prosveshchenie, 1966.

Malen'kaia knizhka o bol'shoi pamiati (Um mnemonista). Moscow, Moscow University Press, 1968; as *The Mind of a Mnemonist: A Little Book about a Vast Memory,* New York, Basic Books, 1968; London, Cape, 1969.

Rasstroistva pamiati v klinike anevrism perednei soedinitel'noi arterii [Memory Disorders in the Clinic from Aneurisms of the Frontal Connective Artery], with others. Moscow, Moscow University Press, 1970.

Poteriannyi i vozvrashchennyi mir (Istoriia odnogo raneniia). Moscow, Moscow University Press, 1971; as *The Man with a Shattered World: The History of a Brain Wound,* New York, Basic Books, 1972.

Psikhologiia vospriiatiia (uchebnoe posobie) [The Psychology of Perception: A Textbook], with others. Moscow, Moscow University Press, 1973.

Osnovy neiropsikhologii. Moscow, Moscow University Press, 1973; as *The Working Brain: An Introduction to Neuropsychology,* London, Penquin, and New York, Basic Books, 1973.

Neiropsikhologiie pamiati. Moscow, Pedagogical Academy Press, 2 vols., 1972-76; as *The Neuropsychology of Memory,* New York, Halsted Press, 1976.

Ob istoricheskom razvitii poznavatel'nykh protsessov. Moscow, Nauka, 1974; as *Cognitive Development, Its Cultural and Social Foundations,* Cambridge, Massachusetts, Harvard University Press, 1976.

Osnovnye problemy neirolingvistiki. Moscow, Moscow University Press, 1975; as *Basic Problems of Neurolinguistics,* The Hague, Mouton, 1976.

Materialy k kursu lektsii po obshchei psikhologii [Material for a Course of Lectures on Common Psychology]. Moscow, Moscow University Press, 1975.

The Selected Writings of A.R. Luria. White Plains, New York, Sharpe, 1978.

Iazyk i soznanie. Moscow, Izdatel'stvo MGU, 1979; as *Language and Cognition,* Washington, D.C., Winston, 1982.

The Making of Mind: A Personal Account of Soviet Psychology. Cambridge, Massachusetts, Harvard University Press, 1979.

*   *   *

Young Alexander Luria was substantially involved in psychoanalytic studies, both as a theorist and experimenter; he also tried himself as a practicing analyst, but the latter role was not his forte. Theoretically Luria advocated psychoanalysis as a "monistic" system capable of unifying the lower drives and higher mental functions. He believed that psychoanalysis together with a study of human reflexes would establish a solid base for the new materialist psychology. Such a belief had been quite fashionable in the Soviet psychology of the 1920's. The experimental work of Luria was much more original. He developed a special methodology that combined a psychoanalytic analysis of free associations with a study of motor responses of a subject. This so-called "combined motor method" helped Luria in detecting hidden emotional complexes of neurotics, suspected criminals, and individuals in emotional states. Although this episode has little in common with the rest of Luria's career, Luria himself emphasized that it was a highly important research experience that provided him with an idea of a close relationship between verbal and motor behavior.

In the late 1920's Luria abandoned the problem of unconscious psychodynamics becoming totally absorbed by a new research project suggested by Lev Vygotsky. According to Vygotsky's cultural-historical theory, which was wholeheartedly accepted and further developed by Luria, language and other symbolic systems play a role of psychological instruments helping individuals to develop their natural processes of perception, attention, and memory into socially structured cognitive functions. It was assumed that in so far as symbolic organization is weak human thinking is limited by a context of immediate practical experience. With the development of symbolic operations, such as reading, writing, and solving mathematical problems, situational reasoning yields to more complex forms of thought that reflect a symbolic character of higher mental functions.

In order to find experimental proofs for this hypothesis Luria undertook an expedition to remote regions of Soviet Central Asia where he was able to test subjects belonging to different cultural groups. He found that illiterate peasants are unable to accomplish tests of abstract classification of ordinary objects. Practical, situational experience completely dominates their mentality. It was shown, however, that a few years of schooling were enough to change this attitude and to subject immediate experience to the control of abstract logical and linguistic categories of thought. Critics hastily accused Luria of insulting the national minorities of Soviet Asia whom he, ostensibly, depicted as an inferior race unable to behave reasonably. The very theme of cultural development became forbidden. Only in 1974 did Luria manage to publish his material and thus to state the problem once again.

In the mid-1930's Luria turned to the problem of the disturbances in brain function. It was especially this field of research that brought him world-wide fame and established him as a leader of Soviet neuropsychology. Observations of aphasics (subjects with speech disorders), patients suffering from Parkinson disease, and other neurological cases led him to the concept of brain functions as functional systems. Functional systems involve different areas of the brain and cannot be attributed to one particular zone or group of nerve cells. Each area of the brain enters into the functional systems in terms of its own particular role and makes its specific contribution to the work of the whole system. Therefore, disturbance of one particular area of the brain may lead to a loss of the entire functional system, but each disturbed center excludes a special factor from a given functional system. Luria elaborated a complex system of testing that attributed a given neuropsychological symptom to an appropriate functional system and further indicated a brain structure that is involved in a particular disturbance in the functional system. Examining different zones of the brain, Luria discovered that the frontal lobes play an especially important role in those complex acts that distinguish human from animal behavior. Subjects with frontal lobe lesions could retain a capability of performing simple behavioral acts, but they become helpless when they approach a problem that requires planning and executive control over performance. In these subjects there is a disintegration of internal planning according to which a complex action should be carried out.

Luria was especially interested in what role language plays in establishing new connections between independent functional centers of the brain. Pursuing this problem he met strong opposition from the orthodox Pavlovians who saw language as a mere extension of a system of conditional reflexes. In the late 1940's the controversy exceeded the limits of academic discussion—Luria was fired from the Institute of Neurosurgery where he had been the Head of the neuropsychological laboratory. In the early 1950's he was forced to accept the Pavlovian terminology which marks his works of that period.

In the 1960's Luria ventured to establish a synthetic theory that combines cultural-historical concepts of Vygotsky and his own findings in the field of neuropsychology. The final result of this synthesis was a thesis that higher psychological processes represent complex functional systems, social in their genesis, mediated in their structure, and carried out by whole complexes of jointly working zones on the brain with certain applications of social ("extracerebral") tool- and sign-using mechanisms.

—Alex Kozulin

LURIA, Salvador (Edward). American biologist. Born in Turin, Italy, 13 August 1912; emigrated to the United States in 1940: naturalized, 1947. Studied at the University of Turin, M.D. 1935. Married Zella Hurwitz in 1945; 1 son. Research Fellow, Curie Laboratory, Institute of Radium, Paris, 1938-40; Research Assistant, Columbia University, New York, 1940-42; Instructor to Associate Professor, Indiana University, Bloomington, 1943-50; Professor of Bacteriology, University of Illinois, Urbana, 1950-59; Professor of Microbiology, 1959-64, Sedgwick Professor, 1964-70, and since 1970 Institute Professor and Director of the Center for Cancer Research, Massachusetts Institute of Technology, Cambridge; since 1965, Non-Resident Fellow, Salk Institute for Biological Studies, San Diego, California. Jessup Lecturer, Columbia University, 1950; Nieuwland Lecturer, University of Notre Dame, Indiana, 1959; Dyer Lecturer, National Institutes of Health, 1963. Associate Editor, *Journal of Microbiology*, 1950-55. Since 1955, Editor, *Virology*. President, American Society for Microbiology, 1967-68. Recipient: Guggenheim Fellowship, 1942, 1963; Lenghi Prize, Accademia dei Lincei, Rome, 1965; Nobel Prize for Medicine (jointly), 1969. Honorary doctorate: University of Chicago, 1967; Rutgers University, New Brunswick, New Jersey, 1970; Indiana University, 1970. Member, National Academy of Sciences; American Academy of Arts and Sciences. Address: Department of Biology, Massachusetts Institute of Technology, Cambridge, Massachusetts 02139, U.S.A.

PUBLICATIONS

Biology

General Virology, with James E. Darnell, Jr. New York, Wiley, 1953.
Life: The Unfinished Experiment. New York, Scribner, 1973.

36 Lectures in Biology. Cambridge, Massachusetts Institute of Technology, 1975.

*   *   *

Salvador Luria's first scientific contributions as a young doctor were in the field of neuro-anatomy of the eye. He left Italy during the rise of fascism, and in Paris was introduced to the scientific problem of the nature of the agent known as "the bacteriophage" (bacterial viruses, or phage). Bacteriology at that time was, in his words, "the last stronghold of Lamarckianism"; it was widely believed that bacteria did not undergo mutation. Alterations in characteristics of a strain of bacteria were attributed to a change in "phase," or the cells were said to have undergone an "adaptation." Luria's work in the early 1940's forever altered the ideas that biologists hold concerning genetics in procaryotic organisms, and paved the way for the revolution known as molecular biology.

In 1940, Luria emigrated to the United States where he continued his investigations at a number of different universities (most recently at MIT). He collaborated with T.F. Anderson to examine several phage strains using the electron microscope at the RCA laboratory in Camden. These studies revealed that what had previously been considered a single agent in fact consisted of distinctly different morphological types that bred true, and could be distinguished also by other characteristics such as host range and plaque appearance.

Luria's collaboration with Max Delbrück (results published in 1943) had an enormous impact, because this study demonstrated that bacterial "variants" were in fact mutants, and the origin of such variants corresponded quantitatively to mutational processes in the higher organisms studied by classical geneticists. Luria had noticed that he could not obtain a reproducible number of bacterial variants from small cultures. The notion that a random event might account for this fluctuation occurred to him, according to his account, while playing slot machines. Luria and Delbrück approached the problem of heritable variation in bacteria as a population study, amenable to statistical analysis. They considered the growing population of wild-type bacterial cells as a substrate of increasing size in which a correspondingly greater frequency of random mutations might occur. Experiments were used to show that the number of mutations that appear in each of a large number of small bacterial cultures can be described by the Poisson distribution. Mutation rates were calculated from the proportion of small cultures showing no mutations, i.e., a lower mutation rate is deduced from the observation of a greater number of cultures containing no mutants. This "fluctuation analysis" was applied by Luria and Delbrück and their colleagues to many other microbiological phenomena, as a tool to distinguish mutations from physiological processes. It has remained the standard technique for this purpose, and for calculating mutation rates.

Luria's subsequent work in microbial genetics has embraced a wide range of pioneering studies. Alfred Hershey, who shared the Nobel Prize in Physiology and Medicine with Delbrück and Luria in 1969, has credited Luria with a main role during the 1940's in perceiving a phage particle as a dual structure consisting of DNA and protein, with corresponding dual functionality of genetic and vegetative roles. Luria studied ultra-violet sensitivity of phage, and quantitated the effects of ultra-violet radiation during phage growth in order to determine the number of sensitive targets. In 1952, Luria described host-induced modification of phages, i.e., the restriction of phage growth that one bacterial host exerts on phage grown previously in a different host. He demonstrated that the characteristic was not due to genetic modification of the phage. Subsequent study of this phenomenon led to the discovery of bacterial restriction enzymes. In the past twenty years Luria has turned his attention to studies on the mechanisms of colicins, a class of bacterial proteins. He remains an active investigator and Director of the Cancer Center at MIT.

Words like teacher or mentor are inadequate to describe the role that Luria plays in leading those around him along the paths of scientific discovery and the highest levels of rational behavior. James Watson, Luria's first doctoral student, recalls his concerns about the choice of graduate advisor because "many students were afraid of Luria who had the reputation of being arrogant toward people who were wrong." At Cold Spring Harbor, Luria " boycotted talks on extra-sensory perception...and on the correlation of human body shapes with disease and personality," that were included in part of a Thursday evening of invited seminars. Time has supported his opinions: what is now surprising is that a gathering of eminent scientists would choose to invite speakers involved with these subjects. Luria's "arrogance" contains within it the dialectical trait: immediate and effortless discarding of an opinion that is subsequently disproved. An unusually large proportion of his students have been women, among them myself. As I continue to learn about variations in types of graduate education, I appreciate to an increasing degree Luria's strict habit of not making allowances for "female" personality traits, and his expectations for the greatest degree of commitment and professionalism from his students. He can truly be said to be a scientific father to a large segment of the molecular biology community.

—Sonia K. Guterman

LUXEMBURG, Rosa. German political and social activist. Born in Zamość, Poland, 5 March 1871. Educated at a school in Warsaw; studied at University of Zurich, from 1889, Ph.D. 1897. Joined Proletariat revolutionary party, subsequently Social Democratic Party, of the Kingdom of Poland (SDKPL), 1894; recognized as theoretical leader, and main contributor of party paper, *Sprawa Rabotnicza*; drawn to center of the International Labour Movement, in Germany, 1898: became primary contributor to *Die Neue Zeit* Marxist theoretical journal, under editor Karl Kautsky; held polemic with Lenin, 1903-04; sentenced to imprisonment for insulting the Kaiser, but served only one month, 1904; developed idea of permanent revolution during Russian Revolution, and smuggled herself into Russian Poland, 1905: arrested and sent to prison, released because of ill health, and expelled from Poland; participated in Congress of Socialist International, speaking in name of Russian and Polish parties, Stuttgart, 1907; lecturer at Central Party School, Berlin, from 1907; widening gap between Luxemburg and centrist leadership of SPD resulted in complete political break between Kautsky and Luxemburg on question of "workers' road to power," 1910; arrested for inciting soldiers to mutiny, 1914; Founder, with Karl Liebknecht, Franz Mehring, and Klara Zetkin, Spartakus League, 1914; imprisoned for most of next four years; from prison followed Russian Revolution and wrote tracts urging German workers and soldiers to emulate Russian counterparts; freed from prison and devoted her energies to the revolution until her death. *Died* (in Berlin) *15 January 1919.*

PUBLICATIONS

Collections

Gesammelte Werke, edited by Paul Frölich.   Berlin, Vereinigung Internationaler Verlagsanstalten, vol. 6, *Die Akkumulation des Kapitals*, 1923; vol. 3, *Gegen den Reformismus*, 1925; vol. 4, *Gewerkschaftskampf und Massenstreik*, 1928 (only vols. to appear).
Gesammelte Werke.   Berlin, Dietz, 3 vols., 1970-73.

Political and Social Theory

Die industrielle Entwicklung Polens.   Leipzig, Duncker und

Humblot, 1899.
Sozialreform oder Revolution; Mit einem Anhang: Miliz und Militarismus.   Leipzig, Leipziger Buchdruckerei, 1899; revised edition, 1908; as *Reform or Revolution*, New York, Three Arrows, 1937.
Die Akkumulation des Kapitals: Ein Beitrag zur ökonomischen Erklärung des Imperialismus.   Berlin, Singer, 1913.
Die Krise der Sozialdemokratie.   Zurich, Verlagsdruckerei, 1916; as *The Crisis in the German Social Democracy*, New York, Socialist Publication Society, 1918.
Die Akkumulation des Kapitals oder was die Epigonen aus der Marxchen Theorie gemacht haben: Eine Antikritik.   Leipzig, Frankes, 1921; as *The Accumulation of Capital*, London, Routledge, and New Haven, Connecticut, Yale University Press, 1951.
Die russische Revolution: Eine kritische Würdigung, edited by Paul Levi.   Berlin, Verlag Gesellschaft, 1922; as *The Russian Revolution*, New York, Workers Age, 1940.
Einführung in die Nationalökonomie, edited by Paul Levi.   Berlin, E. Laub, 1925.
Rosa Luxemburg (speeches), edited by Paul Frölich.   Berlin, Neuer Deutscher Verlag, 1928.
Ausgewählte Reden und Schriften.   Berlin, Dietz, 2 vols., 1951.
Ich war, ich bin, ich werde sein (selection of articles from the *Rote Fahne*, November 1918-January 1919.   Berlin, Dietz, 1958.
Rosa Luxemburg im Kampf gegen den deutschen Militarismus (selection of articles and speeches of 1913-14).   Berlin, Dietz, 1960.
Leninism or Marxism: The Russian Revolution, edited by Bertram D. Wolfe.   Ann Arbor, University of Michigan Press, 1961.
Politische Schriften, edited by Ossip K. Flechtheim.   Frankfurt, Europäische Verlagsanstalt, 1966.
Rosa Luxemburg Speaks, edited by Mary-Alice Waters.   New York, Pathfinder Press, 1970.
Selected Political Writings, edited by Robert Looker.   London, Cape, 1972.
The National Question: Selected Writings, edited by Horace B. Davis.   New York, Monthly Review Press, 1976.

Other

Briefe aus dem Gefängnis (to Sophie Liebknecht, 1914-18).   Berlin, Verlag Junge Garde, 1920.
Briefe an Karl und Luise Kautsky (1896-1918).   Berlin, E. Laub, 1923; as *Letters to Karl and Luise Kautsky*, New York, McBride, 1923.
Briefe an Freunde, edited by Benedikt Kautsky.   Hamburg, Europäische Verlagsanstalt, 1950.
The Letters of Rosa Luxemburg, edited by Stephen Eric Bronner.   Boulder, Colorado, Westview Press, 1978.
Comrade and Lover: Rosa Luxemburg's Letters to Leo Jogiches, edited by Elzbieta Ettinger.   Cambridge, Massachusetts, MIT Press, 1979; London, Pluto Press, 1981.

Translator, *W.G. Korolenko: Die Geschichte meines Zeitgenossen.*   Berlin, Cassirer, 2 vols., 1919-20.

*

Critical Studies: *Rosa Luxemburg: Gedanke und Tat* by Paul Fröhlich, Paris, Editions Nouvelles Internationales, 1939; as *Rosa Luxemburg: Her Life and Work*, London, Gollancz, 1940, revised edition, 1972; *Rosa Luxemburg* by J.P. Nettl, London, Oxford University Press, 2 vols., 1966 (includes bibliography); *Rosa Luxemburg* by Lelio Basso, London, Deutsch, 1975; *The Legacy of Rosa Luxemburg* edited by Norman Geras, London, New Left Books, 1976.

*   *   *

Rosa Luxemburg, the Polish-German revolutionary socialist and Marxist theoretician, was born in Russian Poland. Her parents were assimilated middle-class Jews, and she absorbed both Polish and Western culture. After attending a secondary school in Warsaw, where she was attracted to revolutionary politics, she emigrated to Switzerland in 1889 to avoid arrest. She enrolled at the University of Zürich and studied mathematics and science, later shifting to public law. In 1897 she received a doctorate, presenting a dissertation on the industrial development of Poland. A gifted student, she combined intellectual and political interests and became involved in the émigré socialist movement. Rejecting Polish nationalism as retrogressive and "bourgeois," she consistently stressed the internationalism of socialist doctrine, thus diverging from those Marxists, such as V.I. Lenin, the Russian Bolshevik leader, who advocated self-determination as a solution to the nationality question.

In 1898, after contracting a marriage of convenience to gain entry to Germany, Luxemburg moved to Berlin. There she launched a new career as a revolutionary militant in the German Social Democratic Party and became a regular contributor to the prestigious journal *Neue Zeit* edited by Karl Kautsky. In her pamphlet *Social Reform or Revolution* and various articles she attacked the revision of orthodox Marxism espoused by Eduard Bernstein and consistently denied that the parliamentary charade could do more than ameliorate the harsh realities of capitalist rule. Her uncompromising and often dogmatic zeal on behalf of the proletarian revolution was not well received by many "practicals" within the party, especially those affiliated with the trade unions.

In December 1905, spurred by the revolutionary outburst within the Russian empire, she left for Warsaw to participate first hand in the struggle against Tsarist autocracy. Her arrival was ill-timed, for the spirit of rebellion had waned, and she made preparations to return to Berlin. Early in March 1906, however, she was arrested and spent four months in prison. Upon her release she made her way to Finland, where she renewed her acquaintance with Lenin and began work on a pamphlet on the revolution in Russia and the efficacy of the political strike as a means of radicalizing the proletariat. Published in 1906, it convinced few of the party elite that the Russian example—or her interpretation of it—contained valuable lessons for German socialism.

Reestablished in Berlin by the fall of 1906, Luxemburg resumed her contributions to *Neue Zeit*. But she needed additional income and in 1907 accepted, at first rather grudgingly, a post as lecturer at the central party school. She taught political economy and economic history and soon came to enjoy the experience, especially the intellectual rigor that required her to organize and refine her ideas. Her major theoretical work, *The Accumulation of Capital*, grew out of her lectures. In seeking the roots of imperialism in the nature of Western industrial society, she came to the conclusion that the growth of capitalism hinged upon its ability to expand into underdeveloped areas of the world. Although seriously flawed—some chapters are turgid and abstruse, others unduly polemical—the book is one of the few significant examples of original thought in the Marxist canon. It was virtually ignored by most of the party leaders, a development she probably anticipated because of her open break by this time with the major oracles of German socialism, Kautsky in particular.

In 1914 Luxemburg observed with dismay the outbreak of a general European conflict and the party's capitulation to the patriotic frenzy of the German war effort. Together with Karl Liebknecht, she attempted to organize the tiny minority of anti-war socialists in what became the Spartacus League and scornfully attacked the majority Social Democrats. She spent most of the war years in prison but did manage to publish her views under the pseudonym Junius. Only the collapse of the monarchy in November 1918 freed her from confinement. The success of the Bolshevik revolution in Russia had meanwhile inspired radical socialists throughout Europe. Luxemburg sympathized with the new Soviet regime but did not hesitate to criticize its repressive features in her pamphlet, *The Russian Revolution* (published posthumously in 1922). Late in December 1918 the Spartacists merged with a splinter group of radical socialists to form the German Communist Party, and she reluctantly acquiesced in the provocative tactics of the majority. A poorly organized Communist uprising in Berlin during the second week in January 1919 was drowned in blood. Arrested by paramilitary troops on the 15th, Luxemburg was beaten and then killed by a shot in the head.

A martyr to the cause of revolutionary socialism, Luxemburg became a herioc legend to her supporters. To her enemies "Red Rosa" was a symbol of radicalism run amuck. To Communists of the Lenin tradition she became a respected but somewhat suspect figure because of her strictures on the Soviet dictatorship. As a Marxist theoretician her influence has been somewhat exaggerated. Despite her brilliance and erudition she was chiefly a journalist and political activist, and with the exception of *The Accumulation of Capital* she never aspired to scholarly or intellectual profundity.

—Robert D. Warth

LYSENKO, Trofim (Denisovich). Russian biologist. Born in Karlovka, Ukraine, 29 September 1898. Studied at the Poltava Horticultural School, the Uman Institute, and at the Kiev Agricultural Institute, 1921-25. Married. Worked at the Belotserkov Experimental Station, 1921-25, and at the Experimental Station at Gandzha, Azerbaidzhan, 1925-29. Founded the Vernalization Division, Odessa Agricultural Genetics Institute in 1929 (Director of the Institute, 1934-38); Director, Institute of Genetics of the Academy of Sciences, 1940-65 (removed). Editor, *Bulletin of Vernalization*, Odessa Institute, 1930-32; *Yarovisatsiia*, 1935-46; *Agrobiology*, 1945-65. President, Lenin Academy of Agricultural Sciences, 1938-56, 1961-62. Recipient: Stalin Prize, 1941, 1943, 1947. Member, Ukrainian Academy of Sciences. Hero of Socialist Labor, 1945. *Died 20 November 1976.*

PUBLICATIONS

Biology

Agrogramota [Agricultural Literacy]. Kharkov, Derzhsil'hospvydav, 1934.

Teoreticheskie osnovy iarovizatsii [Theoretical Questions of Jarovization]. Moscow, Gos. izd-vo kolkhoznoi i sovkhoznoi lit-ry, 1935.

Stat'i po selektsi i genetike [Articles on Genetics and Selection]. Voronezh, Oblizdat, 1939.

Biologiia razvitiia rastenii: sbornik statei po voprosam genetiki, selektsii i semenovodstva [The Biology of Plant Development: A Collection of Articles on Problems of Genetics, Selection, and Seed Breeding]. Kiev, Gos. izd-vo kolkhoznoi i sovkhoznoi lit-ry, 1940.

Uvlichit' prodovol'stvennye resursy Sovetskogo gosudarstva [To Increase the Food Resources of the Soviet Union]. Moscow, NKZ SSSR, 1942.

Agrobiologiia: sbornik rabot po voprosam genetiki, selektsii i semenvodstva [Agrobiology: A Collection of Works on Genetics, Selection, and Seed Breeding]. Moscow, Sel'khozgiz, 1943.

Raboty v dni Velikhoi Otechestvennoi voiny [Work During World War II]. Moscow, Sel'khozgiz, 1943.

O nasledstvennosti i ee izmenchivosti. Moscow, NKZ SSSR, 1943; as *Heredity and Its Variability*, New York, King's Crown Press, 1946.

Agrobiologicheskaia nauka v sel'skom khoziaistve voennogo vremeni [Agrobiological Sciences in War-Time Agriculture]. Frunze, Kirgizgosizdat, 1943.

Kul'tura ozimykh v stepi Sibiri[Winter Crops in the Siberian Steppes]. Moscow, Sel'khozgiz, 1945.

O polozhenii v biologicheskoi nauke: doklad na sessii Akademii s.-zh nauk im V.I. Lenina 31 iiulia 1948 goda. Moscow, Sil'khozgiz, 1948; as *Soviet Biology: Report to the Lenin Academy of Agricultural Sciences*, London, Birch Books, 1948.

Vliianie termicheskogo faktora na prodolzhitel'nost' faz razvitiia rastenii: opty so zlakami i klopchatnikom [The Influence of the Thermal Factor on the Length of Phases in Plant Growth] Moscow, Sel'khozgiz, 1949.

Stadiinoe razvitie rastenii: raboty po teorii stadiinogo razvitiia i iarovizatsii sel'skokhoziais tvennykh rastenii [Stadial Development of Plants]. Moscow, Sel'khozgiz, 1952.

O biologicheskom vide i vidoobrazovanii[On Biological Species and Their Formation]. Moscow, Sel'khozgiz, 1957.

Izbrannye sochineniia [Selected works]. Moscow, Sel'khozgiz, 2 vols., 1958-59.

Nekotorye vazhneishie voprosy zemledeliia tselinnykh raionov [Some Most Important Problems of the Virgin Lands Agriculture]. Novosibirsk, Knizhnoe izd-vo, 1960.

*

Critical Studies: *Heredity, East and West: Lysenko and World Science* by Julian Huxley, New York, Schuman, and London, Chatto and Windus, 1949; *The Rise and Fall of T.D. Lysenko* by Zhores A. Medvedev, New York, Columbia University Press, 1969; *The Lysenko Affair* by David Joravsky, Cambridge, Massachusetts, Harvard University Press, 1970.

*   *   *

Trofim Lysenko, Soviet agronomist and virtual dictator of Soviet biology in the Stalin era, was born to peasant parents in the Ukraine. After earning a diploma from the Uman Institute of Horticulture in 1920, he completed his doctorate at the Kiev Agricultural Institute and worked at Gandzha (now Kirovabad) Experimental Station in Azerbaidzhan until 1929. He then accepted a position with the Institute of Plant Breeding in Odessa, where he experimented with "vernalization," a technique of germinating winter wheat that allegedly brought higher grain yields. Although the test plantings mandated by the Ukrainian Commissariat of Agriculture failed to validate Lysenko's theory, he gained favorable publicity and was granted funds to publish his own scientific journal, the *Bulletin of Vernalization*. By 1933, however, the *Bulletin* ceased publication and official support for vernalization became less enthusiastic.

Lysenko's unexpected return to favor in 1935 was due in large part to his ingenuity in adapting the principle of vernalization to a wide range of agricultural problems. He aroused expectations of vast production increases in cotton, potatoes, and wheat while boldly claiming the whole spectrum of plant physiology as the proper domain of vernalization. His method, as applied to spring wheat, involved soaking and turning the seeds in a shed for several days with proper temperature and humidity controls. Specialists, unable to test his theory, were reluctant to attack him and weakened their own case by conceding that he had achieved practical results. They were also intimidated by his gift for political demagogy. In his speech to the Second Congress of Collective Farmers in 1935, for example, he warned of "kulak and saboteur deceptions...[accomplishing] their destructive business, both in the scientific world and out of it; a class enemy is always an enemy whether he is a scientist or not." At the close of the year he was clearly the Soviet Union's most illustrious agronomist, yet he failed to secure the public endorsement of Stalin, the Communist Party chief, whose pronouncement on any question, political or otherwise, was sufficient to cut off further debate.

Emboldened by his success, Lysenko broadened his area of expertise to include the whole field of biology. His friend and collaborator, Isaak Prezent, hailed Lysenkoism for corroborating the Marxist philosophy of dialectical materialism and as a validation of the theory of the inheritance of acquired characteristics. Heredity, therefore, was the result of environmental changes assimilated from past generations, a view directly contrary to the orthodox school of genetics established by Gregor Mendel's experiments in the 19th century and accepted by virtually all biologists. Lysenko and his followers did not seek to refute the chromosome theory of heredity by the normal procedure of scientific investigation but by denouncing it as "reactionary" and substituting their own. Party officials, ill-equipped to detect genuine science from quackery, were interested only in practical achievements. *Pravda* thus placed its seal of approval on Lysenko in February 1936 by lauding his discovery of "the real laws of plant life, which make it possible to solve a number of the most important scientific and practical problems of agriculture quickly, on the basis of new principles." Critics of Lysenkoism were not silenced by fiat, but only a courageous few openly defied the emergent Party line. The Stalinist terror, then gaining momentum, furnished an ominous backdrop to the controversy, though Stalin himself refrained from more than implied support of the Lysenkoists. Most Soviet biologists declined to take a public stand while demonstrating their distaste for the new ideology by passive resistance.

A conference in October 1939 arranged by the Party's ideological guardians sought a compromise. Scientists were directed to abandon their arrogant disdain for agrobiology, and the Lysenkoists were requested to cease their anti-intellectual attempts to suppress classical genetics. But neither side proved conciliatory. The Lysenkoists controlled the agricultural institutes, and the academic biologists held their own in the universities. Prezent, among others, attacked Lysenko's opponents as anti-Darwinian and, more absurdly, linked them to "Trotskyism." The chief target, Nikolai Vavilov, had achieved an international reputation as a plant geneticist, but he was arrested in 1940, charged with various political offenses, and died in prison in 1943. A number of colleagues were also caught up in the purge, though evidence is lacking that the Lysenkoists intended—or indeed were able—to mount a reign of terror against their adversaries. Even a few Lysenko supporters were victimized, suggesting a random quality to the purge rather than a concerted attempt to wipe our the proponents of traditional genetics. Lysenko nevertheless profited from the Stalinist repression, not so much ideologically as in the rewards of power and prestige that accompanied his rise in the hierarchy of official Soviet biology. He was director of the Institute in Odessa (1934-1938), president of the Lenin Academy of Agricultural Sciences (1938-1956, 1961-1962), a member of Academy of Sciences (from 1939), and director of the latter's Institute of Genetics (1940-1965). Named a Hero of Socialist Labor, he also received the Order of Lenin eight times and the Stalin Prize three times.

During World Was II the quarrel among the biologists was muted. Lysenko busied himself with practical tasks to aid the war effort, chiefly a campaign to increase potato production among urban gardeners. Several months after the war he lent his name to an attack on cytology (the study of cells) and sought to undermine the Darwinian theory of natural selection, though he launched his offensive in the name of protecting true Darwinism from its enemies. His critics counter-attacked, and Lysenko reverted in 1947 to his demagogic pre-war tactics by associating his critics with "bourgeois biology" and with American scientists, "the servants of capitalism." But even this blatant appeal to political prejudice—the cold war with the United States was well under way—failed to silence his detractors. He decided to play his trump card—a mandate from Stalin. At a meeting of the Lenin Academy of Agricultural Sciences in August 1948 he delivered the principal address, essentially a political statement that had no relevance to science but did, in effect, outlaw the study of genetics and launch an apparently bloodless but nevertheless drastic purge of his opponents. Hundreds of the most distinguished scholars in Soviet biology were dismissed or demoted, and the Academy was transformed into a servile claque for Lysenkoism. Several years later Lysenko revealed that Stalin had "personally edited the draft of the [August] report...explained to me in detail his corrections, and gave me instructions on delivery."

The triumph of Lysenkoism was relatively brief. Stalin himself indicated in the summer of 1950 that science without the freedom to criticize was undesirable, but biology was not mentioned, and no one in that field ventured to test the limits of toleration. Within a year, however, there were signs that agricultural officials, heretofore Lysenko's staunchest backers, had become skeptical about this theories. The failure of his grandiose tree planting campaign may have been decisive. By October 1952 the Party signaled the scientific community that Lysenkoism was no longer sacrosanct. The leading Soviet botanical journal mounted an attack, and the Lysenkoists responded in their publications with polemical arguments devoid of scientific content. Stalin's death in 1953 and a less repressive regime encouraged a bolder discussion. Slowly the study of genetics and suspect allied sciences revived. Lysenko nevertheless retained much of his influence in the Party and characteristically sought to label his opponents "reactionaries in science," implying that they were lackeys of Western imperialism. Nikita Khrushchev, the new Party leader, admitted that he did not understand the issues involved but maintained that "theoretical and scientific disputes should be settled in the fields." Yet he frequently endorsed Lysenko as an agronomist while carefully avoiding the controversy in genetics. Although his fall from power in 1964 allowed the anti-Lysenkoists a freer hand, the Party itself remained noncommittal. In 1965, however, an official investigation of Lysenko's experimental farm near Moscow resulted in a devastating public report that effectively destroyed his reputation. His journal, *Agrobiology*, ceased publication, and the Institute of Genetics was closed, replaced by a scientifically respectable establishment. But a clean sweep of Lysenkoists from the educational system was not immediately forthcoming. Lysenko himself was demoted to laboratory director of the experimental farm and died in relative obscurity on November 20, 1976. His career represents a tragic example of pseudo-science and politics run amuck.

—Robert D. Warth

MAITLAND, Frederic William. British historian. Born in London, 28 May 1850. Educated at Eton College, 1863-69; studied at Trinity College, Cambridge (Whewell International Law Scholar, 1873), B.A. 1873; M.A. 1876; Lincoln's Inn, London, from 1872; called to the bar, 1876. Married Florence Henrietta Fisher in 1886; 2 daughters. Practiced law, 1876-84; Reader, from 1884, and Downing Professor of English Law, from 1888, Cambridge University. Founder, 1887, and Literary Director, from 1895, Selden Society. Honorary doctorate: Cambridge University, 1891; Oxford University, 1899; University of Glasgow; Cracow University; University of Moscow. Bencher, Lincoln's Inn, London, 1902. Fellow, British Academy. Corresponding Member, Royal Prussian Academy and Royal Bavarian Academy. Honorary Fellow, Trinity College, Cambridge. *Died* (in Las Palmas, Canary Islands) *19 December 1906.*

PUBLICATIONS

History

Justice and Police. London, Macmillan, 1885; New York, Russell and Russell, 1972.

Why the History of English Law Is Not Written (lecture). London, Clay, 1888.

The History of English Law Before the Time of Edward I, with Sir Frederick Pollock. London, Cambridge University Press, 2 vols., 1895; revised edition, 1898.

Domesday Book and Beyond: Three Essays in the Early History of England. London, Cambridge University Press, 1897; New York, Hain, 1970.

Roman Canon Law in the Church of England: Six Essays. London, Methuen, 1898; New York, B. Franklin, 1968.

Township and Borough (lecture). London, Cambridge University Press, 1898.

English Law and the Renaissance (lecture). London, Cambridge University Press, 1901.

The Life and Letters of Leslie Stephen. London, Duckworth, and New York, Putnam, 1906.

The Constitutional History of England (lectures), edited by H.A.L. Fisher. London, Cambridge University Press, 1908.

Equity; Also, The Forms of Action at Common Law (lectures). London, Cambridge University Press, 1909.

The Collected Papers of Frederic William Maitland, edited by H.A.L. Fisher. London, Cambridge University Press, 3 vols., 1911.

A Sketch of English Legal History, with Francis C. Montague, edited by James F. Colby. London, Putnam, 1915.

Selected Essays, edited by H.D. Hazeltine and others. London, Cambridge University Press, 1936; Freeport, New York, Books for Libraries Press, 1968.

Frederic William Maitland Reader, edited by Vincent Thomas Hyginus Delaney. New York, Oceana, 1957.

Selected Historical Essays, edited by Helen M. Cam. Cambridge, Cambridge University Press, and Boston, Beacon Press, 1957.

Frederic William Maitland, Historian: Selections from His Writings, edited by Robert Livingston Schuyler. Berkeley, University of California Press, 1960.

Other

Letters, edited by C.H.S. Fifoot. Cambridge, Massachusetts, Harvard University Press, and London, Selden Society, 1965.

Letters to George Neilson, edited by E.L.G. Stones. Glasgow, University of Glasgow Press, 1976.

Editor, *Pleas of the Crown for the County of Gloucester...1221.* London, Macmillan, 1884.

Editor, *Bracton's Note Book.* London, Clay, 3 vols., 1887.

Editor, *Select Pleas of the Crown: Vol. I: 1200-1225.* London, Quaritch, 1888.

Editor, *Select Pleas in Manorial and Other Seignorial Courts: Vol. I: Reigns of Henry III and Edward I.* London, Quaritch, 1889.

Editor, *The Court Baron*, with W.P. Baildon. London, Quaritch, 1891.

Editor, *Three Rolls of the King's Court...1194-1195.* London, Wyman, 1891.

Editor, *Records of the Parliament Holden at Westminster...28 February 1305.* London, Eyre and Spottiswoode, 1893.

Editor, *Select Passages from the Works of Bracton and Azo.* London, Quaritch, 1895.

Editor, *Magistri Vacarii Summa de Matrimonio.* London, Stevens, 1898.

Editor, with Mary Bateson, *The Charters of the Borough of Cambridge.* Cambridge, Cambridge University Press, 1901.

Editor, *Year Books of Edward II.* London, Selden Society, 3 vols., 1903-05; vol. 4 completed by G.J. Turner, 1907.

Editor, *Hobbes*, by Sir Leslie Stephen. London and New York, Macmillan, 1904.

Translator, *Political Theories of the Middle Ages*, by Otto Gierke.

London, Cambridge University Press, 1900.

*

Critical Studies: *Frederic William Maitland: Two Lectures and a Bibliography* by Arthur Lionel Smith, Oxford, Clarendon Press, 1908; *Frederic William Maitland: A Biographical Sketch* by H.A.L. Fisher, Cambridge, Cambridge University Press, 1910; *The Canon Law of Medieval England: An Examination of William Lynwood's "Provincale," in Reply to F.W. Maitland* by Arthur Ogle, London, Murray, 1912; *Frederic William Maitland, 1850-1906* by Henry A. Hollond, London, Quaritch, 1953; *Frederic William Maitland: A Life* by C.H.S. Fifoot, Cambridge, Massachusetts, Harvard University Press, 1971.

*   *   *

Frederic William Maitland has bequeathed as his legacy to lawyers and historians an approach to legal history and to a wider reading public his elegant studies of our ancestors' development of common law, institutions, and public life, important both in the establishment and preservation of civilization. The guideline which informed Maitland's prodigious and exacting scholarship is human nature itself. In his wisdom, Maitland gave profound expression to the values of human civilization as nurtured by the law through the frequent use of metaphors and similes, constantly reminding us that the science of the law is a product of human imagination.

In Maitland's works we see the technical obscurities of a prior age as the reflection of individuals solving the problems which confronted them and their society. In short, Maitland took the raw materials of the law of earlier ages and gave them a meaningful shape that makes us care about the people and problems of earlier ages and realize that those people were creating the foundation of our civilization as well as their own. Maitland leaves as his living memorial to the founders of English common law the Selden Society, which carries on his works of scholarship by editing and publishing as yet unprinted legal materials from prior centuries, in the process interpreting earlier ages to the present.

More specifically, Maitland traced the development of the common law, brought by English-speaking people as their legal heritage to far-flung parts of the world. The law reports, begun at the end of the 13th century, provided Maitland with much material for discerning the shape of the law. These early reports, known as Year Books, were written in the obscure Anglo-Norman French used in the English courts. In 1903, Maitland published an Anglo-Norman grammar and glossary in his introduction to the Year Books for the first and second years of the reign of King Edward II (1307-9). In commenting on the value of the Year Books to civilization and jurisprudence, Maitland looked beyond the highly technical aspects displayed on the face of the reports without condemning the medieval version of "high tech." "[A]ll this high technique, this mastery of technical phrase and technical thought has its place in the history of the English people.... The qualities that saved English law when the day of trial came in the Tudor age were not vulgar common sense and the reflection of the layman's unanalysed instincts: rather they were strict logic and high technique, rooted in the Inns of Court, rooted in the Year Books, rooted in the centuries."

Maitland's specific genius in substantive legal doctrine was the land law, the most sophisticated branch of medieval common law, dealing as it did with the transmission of the most important kind of wealth. He described the concepts of feudal tenures and estates in land, treating the English notion of ownership of land as a right to time on the land under the rubric of the "calculus" of estates in land. As a historian, he realized very keenly how the ancient and outmoded real property laws which suited prior ages needed reform in his own day. Maitland discerned the accumulated rubbish of the ages in the effect of the Statute of Uses (1535), "that marvellous monument of legislative futility," on title to freehold. In 1879 ("The Law of Real Property," in *Col-lected Papers*), he urged that the primogeniture, the heir-at-law, and the distinction between realty and personalty in intestate succession be abolished. Enriching Bentham's argument from first principles with the erudition of historical scholarship, Maitland advocated that the heir-at-law be consigned to the Society of Antiquaries, with the eulogy to be spoken by Dr. Pangloss, LL.D., A.S.S. Parliament, however, did not act until 1925.

Civil procedure and the jurisdiction of the central and itinerant royal courts of justice came under Maitland's purview. In *Forms of Action at Common Law*, published posthumously in 1909, Maitland presented the old writ system, which had been abolished during the half century before he lectured to the law students at Cambridge. He looked at the fully developed writ system of 1830 as providing the plaintiff with a choice of games, the rules of which, once chosen, were immutable because the form chosen mandated the method of procedure to be followed in the case. The importance of that choice was still felt in Maitland's day: "The forms of action we have buried, but they still rule us from their graves." From that perspective Maitland looked back to Bracton's 13th-century treatise on writs. Milsom, in his act of self-proclaimed heretical departure from Maitland's view, directs our attention from Bracton to *Brevia Placitata*, the practitioner's form book written by Bracton's less scholarly contemporaries. The form books focus our view of jurisdiction not on the royal courts but on the role of feudal lordship (introduction to *The History of English Law*, 1968).

In the field of public institutions and constitutional law, Maitland studied medieval townships, borough municipal corporations, and manors. He stimulated the interest and work of future generations of scholars in institutional studies and popularized constitutional law by lecturing on constitutional history at Cambridge in 1887 and 1888. His lectures were published posthumously in 1909 as an exposition of the English constitution. There Maitland defined constitutional history as encompassing institutions, laws, and results. In short, he suggested that the law and constitution are a whole, living body, which ultimately defies compartmentalization.

The corpus of Maitland's work was itself similarly vast, ranging from a historical sketch of liberty and equality (1875) and the early history of malice aforethought (1883) to editing the *Pleas of the Crown for Gloucester in 1221* (1884) and *Bracton's Note Book* (1887) to *Domesday Book and Beyond* (1897). In *The History of English Law*, Maitland presented his picture of a legal world that works. Maitland's picture reflects those sources and portions of life that he examined. Modern institutional studies built on Maitland's coherent picture and in the process outmoded his institutional studies for the professional historian. Similarly, the history of public law and the constitution has received much modern scholarly attention. The history of substantive law and the life of the legal profession remains to our eyes much as Maitland saw them. His coherent picture lays the foundation for another legal historian to represent prior ages to the 21st century.

—C.M.A. McCauliff

MALCOLM, Norman (Adrian). American philosopher. Born in Selden, Kansas, 11 June 1911. Studied at the University of Nebraska, Lincoln, B.A. 1933; Harvard University, Cambridge, Massachusetts, M.A. 1938, Ph.D. 1940; and at Cambridge University, 1938-40. Served in the United States Navy, 1942-45. Married Leonida Morosova in 1944 (divorced), 3-children; married Ruth Riesenberg in 1976. Instructor in Philosophy, Princeton University, New Jersey, 1940-42, 1946; Assistant Professor, 1947-50, Associate Professor, 1950-55, Professor, 1955-65, and Susan Linn Sage Professor of Philosophy, 1965-79, Cornell University, Ithaca, New York. Visiting Professor, University of

California at Los Angeles, 1964; Fellow, Center for Advanced Studies in the Behavioral Sciences, Palo Alto, California, 1968-69. President, Eastern Division, American Philosophical Association, 1972. Recipient: Guggenheim Fellowship, 1946-47; Hibben Fellowship, Princeton University, 1952; Fulbright Fellowship, University of Helsinki, Finland, 1960-61. Member, American Academy of Arts and Sciences. Address: Department of Philosophy, Cornell University, Ithaca, New York 14850, U.S.A.

PUBLICATIONS

Philosophy

Ludwig Wittgenstein: A Memoir. London, Oxford University Press, 1958.

Dreaming. New York, Humanities Press, and London, Routledge, 1959.

Knowledge and Certainty: Essays and Lectures. Englewood Cliffs, New Jersey, Prentice Hall, 1963.

Studies in the Theory of Knowledge, with others. Oxford, Blackwell, 1970.

Problems of Mind: Descartes to Wittgenstein. New York, Harper, 1971.

Memory and Mind. Ithaca, New York, Cornell University Press, 1977.

Thought and Knowledge. Ithaca, New York, Cornell University Press, 1977.

Wittgenstein: The Relation of Language to Instinctive Behavior (lecture). Swansea, University College of Swansea, 1981.

*   *   *

Much of Norman Malcolm's philosophical thinking revolves around the themes treated by Ludwig Wittgenstein, but it would not be accurate to say that his writings are merely concerned with disseminating Wittgenstein's views. It is true that he thought of his teacher as a philosophical genius who made profound contributions to the subject. He was also deeply impressed by his friend's extraordinary personality, and gave a moving account of it in the highly acclaimed memoir. Convinced that Wittgenstein's views, expressed in a condensed, cryptic style, contain far-reaching philosophical implications, Malcolm employed his special gift for patient and clear elucidation to bring these implications to light in concrete, amply illustrated detail and to give them applicability and scope not immediately evident in Wittgenstein's writings. Malcolm's intent in part is to show how by following Wittgenstein's lead we can be liberated from the errors injected into our philosophical tradition by such eminent thinkers as Aristotle, Descartes, Locke, John Stuart Mill, William James, Bertrand Russell, Rudolf Carnap, and many others. Infected by these errors, our thinking today still suffers from avoidable mental cramps and confusions. To be liberated from them is no small gain.

In a book entitled *Problems of Mind* (and in many articles published in journals and reprinted in two collections) Malcolm shows how philosophical theories about such concepts as knowledge, certainty, thinking, understanding, sensation, perception, and memory can result in distorted accounts of what it means to have a mind or to be a human being. By characterizing mental life as special psychic inner processes accessible only by introspection we land in scepticism about the reality of other people's minds. By claiming that all mental events are identical with certain brain processes we are driven to deny that mental life is based on human form, facial expressions, bodily movements and actions, including the use of language. By ignoring the asymmetry between first-person and third-person statements we reduce mental life to external behavior, which in effect amounts to a denial that there is such a thing as mental life. The corrective in all these cases is to preserve all the important distinctions language enables us to make and to refrain from reductionist philosophical moves.

On the other hand, attracted by certain analogies, we may be inclined to claim more than we are entitled to claim. Concerning dreaming, Malcolm argues in a book on this topic that dreaming is not "the activity of the mind during sleep" and denies that it is correlated with some bodily phenomena such as rapid eye movement. He rejects as unfounded the received theories that purport to tell us what dreaming *is* in itself. If a person tells a dream in sincerity, we have all the evidence for claiming that he dreamt. The recollection of a dream is a criterion of its occurrence.

Another mental concept, that of remembering, was a focus of Malcolm's philosophical investigations, resulting at first in a distinction between three kinds of memory—perpetual, personal, and factual, with the last occupying a special position in this family of concepts. In a subsequent book-length study, *Memory and Mind,* Malcolm criticizes a whole array of theories purporting to describe in what memory consists. His own view is that although remembering does not consist in anything and cannot be accounted for in terms of pictures, memory traces, storing, or isomorphism with neural processes, none of these denials undermine the fact that remembering is a natural human power.

In 1960, Malcolm published an article on Anselm's ontological arguments, which caused a lively debate on this ancient topic. Malcolm defended one version of the argument and argued that the sentence "God is the greatest of all beings" expresses a logically necessary truth. He also claimed that this conception of God is reflected in the Judeo-Christian religion and intrinsically belongs to its language. The belief in God has no grounds other than the "form of life" which the believer finds in religion. Groundlessness of religious belief, argued Malcolm in later articles, parallels the groundlessness of principles which underlie all our testing, verification, and justification in every sphere of human life. Religion, like science, is language embedded in action. "Neither stands in need of justification, the one no more than the other."

Norman Malcolm's powerful arguments in the areas of his interest have secured for him an eminent place in contemporary philosophy.

—Konstantin Kolenda

MALINOWSKI, Bronisław (Kasper). British anthropologist. Born in Poland, 7 April 1884; naturalized British citizen. Educated at King Jan Sobieski School; studied at the University of Cracow, Ph.D. in physics and mathematics 1908; University of Leipzig, 1908-10; London School of Economics, 1910-14. Married Elsie Rosaline Masson in 1919 (died, 1935), 3 daughters; married Anna Valetta Hayman-Joyce in 1940. Field expeditions to Melanesia, 1914-18, East Africa, 1934, and Mexico, 1939-41. Reader, 1924-27, and Professor of Social Anthropology, 1927-42, University of London. Laura Spelman Rockefeller Memorial Visitor, 1926; Messenger Lecturer, Cornell University, Ithaca, New York, 1933; Phi Beta Kappa Lecturer, Harvard University, Cambridge, Massachusetts, 1936; Lecturer, Oslo Institute for the Comparative Study of Cultures, 1936; Visiting Professor, Yale University, New Haven, Connecticut, from 1939. D.Sc.: Harvard University, 1936. Corresponding Member, 1930, and Full Member, 1938, Polish Academy of Science; Member, Royal Academy of Science of the Netherlands, 1933; Honorary Member, Royal Society of New Zealand, 1936. *Died 16 May 1942.*

PUBLICATIONS

Anthropology

The Family among the Australian Aborigines: A Sociological Study. London, University of London Press, 1913.

*Argonauts of the Western Pacific: An Account of Native Enterprise and Adventure in the Archipelagoes of Melanesian New
Guinea.* London, Routledge, and New York, Dutton, 1922.

Crime and Custom in Savage Society. London, Kegan Paul,
and New York, Harcourt Brace, 1926.

Myth in Primitive Psychology. London, Kegan Paul, and New
York, Norton, 1926.

Sex and Repression in Savage Society. London, Kegan Paul,
and New York, Harcourt Brace, 1927.

The Father in Primitive Psychology. London, Kegan Paul, and
New York, Norton, 1927.

*The Sexual Life of Savages in North-Western Melanesia: An
Ethnographic Account of Courtship, Marriage, and Family
Life among the Natives of the Trobriand Islands, British New
Guinea.* London, Routledge, 1929; New York, Liveright, 2
vols., 1929.

*Coral Gardens and Their Magic: A Study of the Methods of
Tilling the Soil and of Agricultural Rites in the Trobriand
Islands.* London, Allen and Unwin, 2 vols., 1935; New York,
American Book Company, 2 vols., 1935; as *Soil-Tilling and
Agricultural Rites in the Trobriand Islands*, Bloomington,
Indiana University Press, 1965.

*The Foundation of Faith and Morals: An Anthropological
Analysis of Primitive Beliefs and Conduct with Special Reference to the Fundamental Problems of Religion and Ethics.*
London, Oxford University Press, 1936.

Freedom and Civilization, edited by A.V. Malinowska. New
York, Roy, 1944; London, Allen and Unwin, 1947.

A Scientific Theory of Culture and Other Essays. Chapel Hill,
University of North Carolina Press, 1944.

The Dynamics of Culture Change: An Inquiry into Race Relations in Africa, edited by Phyllis M. Kaberry. New Haven,
Connecticut, Yale University Press, 1945.

Magic, Science, and Religion, and Other Essays, edited by
Robert Redfield. Boston, Beacon Press, 1948.

*Marriage, Past and Present: A Debate Between Robert Briffault
and Bronisław Malinowski*, edited by M.F. Ashley Montagu.
Boston, Sargent, 1956.

Sex, Culture, and Myth. New York, Harcourt Brace, 1962;
London, Davies, 1963.

*The Ethnography of Malinowski: The Trobriand Islands 1915-
18*, edited by Michael W. Young. London, Routledge, 1979.

*Malinowski in Mexico: The Economics of a Mexican Market
System: Bronisław Malinowski and Julio de la Fuente*, edited
by Susan Drucker-Brown. London, Routledge, 1982.

Other

A Diary in the Strict Sense of the Word. London, Routledge,
and New York, Harcourt Brace, 1967.

Editor, with others, *Essays Presented to C.G. Seligman.* London, Kegan Paul, 1934.

*

Critical Studies: *Man and Culture: An Evaluation of the Work
of Bronisław Malinowski* edited by Raymond Firth, London,
Routledge, 1957; *The Politics of the Kula Ring: An Analysis of
the Findings of Bronisław Malinowski* by Jitendra P.S. Uberoi,
Manchester, Manchester University Press, 1962; *Bronisław
Malinowski* by Michel Panoff, Paris, Payot, 1972.

*   *   *

Bronisław Malinowski was above all a pioneer and exemplary
practitioner of descriptive ethnography. Of his series of monographs on the culture of the Trobriand Islands off the northeast
coast of New Guinea, based on fieldwork during the years 1914-
18, one by no means slavishly admiring commentator (Marvin
Harris) wrote in 1968 that they "still constitute the greatest

ethnographic description ever achieved".

Until the 1890's, most academic anthropology was an armchair study carried out on the basis of reports and artefacts
brought back from the primitive world by missionaries, colonial
administrators, and others having no special scholarly qualifications. When anthropologists did begin to venture into the field,
they retained a large measure of social and psychological detachment from the peoples they investigated, living apart from
them and getting their data through interviews with paid informants (often chosen because of their knowledge of a European
language) who inevitably reported their society's "official" view
of their institutions and behaviour-patterns when these diverged
from the realities of what actually happened. Malinowski, by
contrast, spent years rather than weeks living on the Trobriands
far from contact with other whites, pitching his tent among the
natives' huts, speaking their language, and going as far as was
possible towards the psychologically very demanding and ultimately impossible goal of becoming a genuine participant in the
alien culture. Malinowski was a highly passionate and sensitive
as well as an educated man, whose feelings towards his savage
neighbours veered between protectiveness and hatred; as a result
of his emotional engagement, Malinowski's books succeed in
portraying the bizarre way of life of the Trobrianders "in the
round and not in the flat," with the eye of a novelist rather than a
bloodless, abstract scientist.

Anthropologists of the 19th century had tended to pay attention chiefly to the material trappings of culture, and to see the
culture of a society as a collection of disparate traits which would
"diffuse" between tribe and tribe independently of one another.
Malinowski stressed that any individual artefact must be seen as
playing a role in a culture taken as a whole, as a complex and
interrelated set of institutions which between them functioned to
satisfy certain primary biological needs of members of the society
in question. For instance, the importance of two characteristic
Trobriand artefacts, *mwali* (bracelets made of white *Conus millepunctatus* shells) and *soulava* (necklaces of red spondylus
shells), can be understood only by reference to their role in *kula*,
a system of reciprocal present-giving between individual members
of alien societies. The *kula* involves the Trobrianders and several
other politically and ethnically separate peoples who inhabit a
ring of islands several hundred miles in circumference. At intervals members of each group undertake a long and dangerous
voyage to the next archipelago on one side or the other in order
to solicit gifts; the things given are always *soulava* (which travel
clockwise round the circuit) or *mwali* (which travel anticlockwise), and though these objects are very highly valued by the
participants they serve little other purpose—they are rarely
worn, and are received only to be given away again. Yet much of
the energy of the Trobrianders is expended on matters connected
directly or indirectly with *kula*.

For Malinowski the *kula* system served as an antidote to the
naive evolutionist theories of the 19th century, according to
which men's actions are governed by straightforward economic
motives and their societies are located at different rungs on a
universal ladder of cultural development rising from savagery
through barbarism to civilization—a development which was
often held to correlate with a progression from inferior to superior powers of independent thought. Malinowski insisted that the
Trobrianders were as individual and rational as ourselves, and
that their actions were just as tenuously connected with the
simple motive of economic gain.

However, Malinowski's strength lay in method rather than
theory. He regarded himself as the founder of a "functional"
school of anthropology; but he did little to link his substantial
ethnographic achievements to his theory of cultures as systems
for serving primary biological functions. Nowhere, for instance—and Malinowski himself eventually admitted this—does
he explain what function the *kula* serves in the life of its participants, though he offers several conflicting hints. Furthermore
the idea of a culture as an interconnected, self-regulating whole,
while a useful corrective to the earlier approach in terms of

separately diffusing traits, led Malinowski to what some regard as an exaggeratedly static view of society. He tried to ignore recent changes induced by contacts with Europeans in the Trobriand way of life, regarding them as an untypical disturbance to a fixed traditional pattern. Yet our own cultures are constantly modified by the interplay of interests and forces which do not naturally harmonize with one another. Malinowski gives us little reason to suppose that the same may not be true of primitive communities. (Ironically, Edmund Leach suggests that there is evidence that the "traditional" pattern of Trobriand life reported by Malinowski may have been a recent innovation when he encountered it.)

Malinowski's chief theoretical contribution may have lain in his account of language. He stressed that the language of an alien society cannot be understood apart from the cultural background in which it is embedded, and he argued that, for primitives—and possibly even for ourselves—language is best seen not as a medium for communicating thought but as a tool for achieving concrete results. Malinowski pioneered the notion that the meaning of a term is its use (a notion which was later given wider currency by Ludwig Wittgenstein). However, this view of language, though influential for a time, could not survive the collapse of the logical-positivist movement in philosophy after the Second World War.

Even Malinowski's fieldwork techniques have been attacked, notably by the "structuralist" school of anthropologists who hold that ethnography in the Malinowskian style actually provides *too many* factual data, and that one can make interesting comparisons between different cultures only by ruthlessly abstracting away from the rich complexity of individual behavior. Many of Malinowski's successors, while accepting that what individual members of a society actually do is more important than the society's received theories of what its members are supposed to do, have felt that the solution lies in statistical studies of quantities of individuals rather than in detailed but necessarily anecdotal accounts of a few intimate acquaintances. For a period after the Second World War, British anthropology reacted rather strongly against the dominance of Malinowski's approach. More recently, however, he has regained his rightful position as one of the giants among the founding fathers of the modern discipline.

—Geoffrey Sampson

MALRAUX, (Georges-) André. French novelist and aesthetician. Born in Paris, 3 November 1901. Educated at the École Turgot, Paris, 1915-18. Married Clara Goldschmidt in 1921 (divorced), 1 daughter; married Marie-Madeleine Lioux in 1948; had 2 sons by Josette Clotis. Worked for the book dealer and publisher René-Louis Doyon, 1919, and for the publisher Kra, Paris. Travelled to Indochina, 1923-24; arrested and imprisoned for the appropriation of ancient art works; later released but returned to Indochina in 1925 and organized, with others, the nationalist "Jeune-Annam" group and worked on the newspaper *L'Indochine*; returned to Paris in 1927 and became artistic director for the publisher Gallimard in 1928; organized, headed, and fought with the Escuadrilla España during the Spanish Civil War: Colonel of the Spanish Republic, 1936; volunteered as a private in the tank corps, 1939; captured by the Germans at Sens, escaped, and worked with the Resistance as "Colonel Berger," 1943-44: Officier de la Légion d'Honneur; Compagnon de la Libération; Médaille de la Résistance; Croix de Guerre. In charge of propaganda for the Rassemblement du Peuple Français, 1947-52. Under De Gaulle, Minister for Information, 1958, and Minister of State in Charge of Cultural Affairs, 1959-62. President, Institut Charles De Gaulle, 1971. Recipient: Prix Goncourt, 1933; Prix Louis-Delluc, 1945; Nehru Peace Prize,

1974. Honorary doctorate: Oxford University, 1967; Jyvacskylae University, Finland, 1969; Rajshahi University, Bangladesh, 1973. *Died 3 November 1976.*

PUBLICATIONS

Collections

Oeuvres (fiction).   Paris, Gallimard, 4 vols., 1970.

Art

Esquisse d'une psychologie du cinéma.   Paris, Gallimard, 1946; as "Sketch for a Psychology of Film," in *Reflections on Art*, edited by Susanne Langer, Baltimore, Johns Hopkins University Press, 1958.
La Psychologie de l'art: Vol. 1, *Le Musée imaginaire*, Geneva, Skira, 1946; as *Museum Without Walls*, New York, Pantheon, and London, Zwemmer, 1949; Vol. 2, *La Création artistique*, Geneva, Skira, 1948; as *The Creative Act*, London, Zwemmer, 1949; New York, Pantheon, 1950; Vol. 3, *La Monnaie de l'absolu*, Geneva, Skira, 1949; as *The Twilight of the Absolute*, New York, Pantheon, 1951.
Les Voix de silence (revised version of *La Psychologie de l'art*). Paris, Gallimard, 1951; as *The Voices of Silence*, New York, Doubleday, 4 vols., 1953 (*Museum Without Walls, The Metamorphoses of Apollo, The Creative Process,* and *The Aftermath of the Absolute*).
Saturne: essai sur Goya.   Paris, Gallimard, 1950; as *Saturn: An Essay on Goya*, New York and London, Phaidon, 1957.
Le Musée imaginaire de la sculpture mondiale: Vol. 1, Paris, Gallimard, 1952. Vol. 2, *Des Bas-reliefs aux grottes sacrées*, Paris, Gallimard, 1954. Vol. 3, *Le Monde Chrétien*, Paris, Gallimard, 1954.
La Métamorphose des dieux: Vol. 1, *Le Surnaturel*, Paris, Gallimard, 1957; as *The Metamorphosis of the Gods*, New York, Doubleday, and London, Secker and Warburg, 1960. Vol. 2, *L'Irréel*, Paris, Gallimard, 1974. Vol. 3, *L'Intemporal*, Paris, Gallimard, 1976.
Le Triangle noir.   Paris, Gallimard, 1970.
La Tête d'obsidienne.   Paris, Gallimard, 1974; as *Picasso's Mask*, New York, Holt Rinehart, 1976.
L'Homme précaire et la littérature.   Paris, Gallimard, 1977.

Fiction

Lunes en papier.   Paris, Galerie Simon, 1921.
La Tentation de l'occident.   Paris, Grasset, 1926; as *The Temptation of the West*, New York, Vintage Books, 1961.
Le Royaume du farfelu.   Paris, Gallimard, 1928.
Les Conquérants.   Paris, Grasset, 1928; as *The Conquerors*, New York, Harcourt Brace, and London, Cape, 1929.
La Voie royale.   Paris, Grasset, 1930; as *The Royal Way*, New York, Smith and Haas, and London, Methuen, 1935.
La Condition humaine.   Paris, Gallimard, 1933; as *Man's Fate*, New York, Smith and Haas, 1934; as *Storm in Shanghai*, London, Methuen, 1934.
Le Temps du mépris.   Paris, Gallimard, 1935; as *Days of Wrath*, New York, Random House, 1936; as *Days of Contempt*, London, Gollancz, 1936.
L'Espoir.   Paris, Gallimard, 1937; as *Man's Hope*, New York, Random House, 1938; as *Days of Hope*, London, Routledge, 1938.
Les Noyers de l'Altenburg.   Lausanne, Éditions du Haut-Pays, 1943; as *The Walnut Trees of Altenburg*, London, Lehmann, 1952.

Political Commentary

The Case for De Gaulle (conversation with James Burnham).

New York, Random House, 1949.
Brasilia, la capitale de l'espoir.   Presidencia de Republicia, Servico de Documentacao, 1959.
Discours, 1958-1965.   Paris, Action Etudiante Gaullistes, 1966.
Les Chênes qu'on abat...   Paris, Gallimard, 1971; as *Fallen Oaks: Conversations with De Gaulle*, London, Hamish Hamilton, 1972; as *Felled Oaks: Conversations with De Gaulle*, New York, Holt Rinehart, 1972.
Oraisons funèbres.   Paris, Gallimard, 1971.
Paroles et écrits politiques, 1947-1972.   Paris, Plon, 1973.

Autobiography

Antimémoires.   Paris, Gallimard, 1967; as *Anti-Memoirs*, New York, Holt Rinehart and London, Hamish Hamilton, 1968.
Lazare.   Paris, Gallimard, 1974; as *Lazarus*, New York, Holt Rinehart, and London, Macdonald and Jane's, 1977.
Le Miroir des limbes: Vol. 1, *Antimémoires I*, Paris, Gallimard, 1976. Vol. 2, *La Corde et les souris*, part 1, *Les Hôtes de passage*, Paris, Gallimard, 1976. Vol. 3, *La Corde et les souris*, part 2, *Les Chênes qu'on abat...*, Paris, Gallimard, 1976. Vol. 4, *La Corde et les souris*, part 3, *La Tête d'obsidienne*, Paris, Gallimard, 1976. Vol. 5, *La Corde et les souris*, part 4, *Lazare*, Paris, Gallimard, 1976.

*

Critical Studies: *André Malraux and the Tragic Imagination* by W.M. Frohock, Stanford, California, Stanford University Press, 1952; *Malraux* by Geoffrey H. Hartman, London, Bowes and Bowes, and New York, Hillary House, 1960; *L'Humanisme de Malraux* by Joseph Hoffmann, Paris, Klinsieck, 1963; *André Malraux* by Denis Boak, Oxford, Clarendon Press, 1968; *André Malraux: Une Vie dans la siècle* by Jean Lacouture, Paris, Seuil, 1973, as *André Malraux*, London, Deutsch, 1975; *Malraux's Heroes and History* by James W. Greenlee, DeKalb, Northern Illinois University Press, 1975; *Malraux: Life and Work* edited by Martine de Courcel, New York, Harcourt Brace, and London, Weidenfeld and Nicolson, 1976; *Malraux: A Biography* by Axel Madsen, London, W.H. Allen, 1977; *André Malraux* by James Robert Hewitt, New York, Ungar, 1978.

*   *   *

André Malraux once explained why he had given his best and best-known novel the title of *La Condition humaine*. It was, he said, because it contained a character who did not recognise his own voice when he heard it played back to him on a tape-recorder; and, added Malraux, "it is because we hear other people's voices with our ears but our own through our throat that I called my book *Man's Fate*." It was a symbol of the alienation which Malraux saw as characterizing the whole of human life now that Nietzsche's prophecy had been more than fulfilled, with the death of God—as Malraux put it—being followed by that of man. For it was no longer possible, in Malraux's view, to believe in the classical humanist view which saw man as the measure of all things and especially of himself. Since the First World War had revealed man's total inability to control his own creations, and since the new philosophies called the very possibility of rational thought into question, all human life was afflicted with the same essential absurdity.

Malraux tried to transcend this absurdity first of all through political action and then through artistic creation. *Man's Fate* gave a sympathetic but ultimately ambiguous portrait of how Marxism enabled men to make sense of their experience, since the account which it provided of the Chinese revolution also showed the betrayal of the Chinese Communists in 1927 by a Russia eager to protect her own revolution at all costs. Malraux nevertheless remained a committed anti-fascist, and in 1936 organized the Spanish Republican air force in the civil war against Franco. He described the Republican struggle with great

eloquence in *L'Espoir*, but like many other left-wing activists of the 1930's, he was profoundly disillusioned by the Nazi-Soviet pact of August 1939. This led him to link his fortunes to those of Charles de Gaulle, whom he twice served as Minister, and to become one of the most persuasive advocates of Western democratic values against Marxist totalitarianism during the Cold War. This political move to the Right coincided with Malraux's giving up the novel in favour of an essentially philosophical and even at times metaphysical presentation of the history of art, *Les Voix du silence*, like the three volumes of *La Métamorphose des dieux*, presents art as the supremely human activity in which the changing forms of artistic creativity enable man to understand and transcend the absurdity of his own condition and the otherwise incomprehensible nature of the universe.

—Philip Thody

MANNHEIM, Karl.   German sociologist.   Born in Budapest, Hungary, 27 March 1893. Studied at the universities of Budapest, Berlin, Paris, Freiburg, and Heidelberg, Ph.D. 1922. Married Juliska Lang in 1921. Lecturer in Sociology, University of Heidelberg, 1926-30; Professor and Head of the Department of Sociology, University of Frankfurt, 1930 until dismissed by Nazi government, 1933; Lecturer in Sociology, London School of Economics, University of London, 1933-45; also Lecturer in the Sociology of Education, 1941-44, and Professor of Education and Sociology, 1944-47, Institute of Education, University of London. *Died* (in London) *9 January 1947.*

PUBLICATIONS

Sociology

Lélek és Kultura [Soul and Culture].   Budapest, Benkô, 1918.
Die Strukturanalyse der Erkenntnistheorie.   Berlin, Reuther und Reichard, 1922.
Ideologie und Utopie.   Bonn, Cohen, 1929; expanded edition, as *Ideology and Utopia*, London, Routledge, and New York, Harcourt Brace, 1936.
Die Gegenwartsaufgaben der Soziologie: Ihre Lehrgestalt.   Tübingen, Mohr, 1932.
Rational and Irrational Elements in Contemporary Society.   London, Oxford University Press, 1934; expanded in *Man and Society in an Age of Reconstruction*, 1940.
Mensch und Gesellschaft im Zeitalter des Umbaus (essays).   Leiden, Sijthoff, 1935; revised edition, as *Man and Society in an Age of Reconstruction*, London, Routledge, 1940.
Diagnosis of Our Time: Wartime Essays of a Sociologist.   London, Routledge, 1943.
Freedom, Power, and Democratic Planning, edited by Ernest K. Bramstead and Hans Gerth.   London, Routledge, 1950.
Essays on the Sociology of Knowledge, edited by Paul Kecskemeti.   London, Routledge, and New York, Oxford University Press, 1952.
Essays on Sociology and Social Psychology, edited by Paul Kecskemeti.   London, Routledge, and New York, Oxford University Press, 1953.
Essays on the Sociology of Culture, edited by Ernest Manheim and Paul Kecskemeti.   London, Routledge, and New York, Oxford University Press, 1956.
Systematic Sociology: An Introduction to the Study of Society, edited by J.S. Erös and W.A.C. Stewart.   New York, Grove Press, 1957.
An Introduction to the Sociology of Education, with W.A.C.

Stewart. London, Routledge, 1962.
From Karl Mannheim, edited by Kurt H. Wolff. New York,
Oxford University Press, 1971.

*

Critical Studies: *Karl Mannheim's Sociology of Knowledge* by
A.P. Simonds, Oxford, Clarendon Press, 1978 (includes bibliography); *The Concept of Ideology and Political Analysis: A Critical Examination of Its Usage by Marx, Lenin, and Mannheim*
by Walter Carlsnaes, Westport, Connecticut, Greenwood Press,
1981.

*   *   *

Karl Mannheim was a sociologist whose major achievement
was to define and elaborate the discipline of the sociology of
knowledge. He contributed also to political sociology, the sociology of education, and the study of social structure in modern
society. His work synthesizes much of 19th-century German
philosophy and social science and follows a trajectory that is
itself not without social and historical significance.

Mannheim, born in Budapest, was the only child of a Hungarian father and a German mother. He left Hungary for Germany
in 1919, after the fall of the Hungarian Republic of Councils. His
earliest interest was philosophy, and particularly epistemology.
Indeed, questions of cognition would occupy Mannheim
throughout the first period of his career, that is, until he moved to
Great Britain to avoid Nazism in 1933. His shift from philosophy
to sociology was essentially the adoption of a new framework in
which to consider the nature and limits of knowledge. After
attending the universities of Budapest, Freiburg, Paris, and Berlin, he moved to Heidelberg in the 1920's. The intellectual climate
there was dominated by Heinrich Rickert, Friedrich Gundolf,
Emil Lederer, and by the recent memory of Max Weber. Between
1910 and 1916 Mannheim had corresponded with Georg Lukács
and was deeply influenced by his early aesthetic writings and his
Theory of the Novel (1916). Mannheim's writings during the
1920's draw on phenomenology, neo-Kantianism, Marxism, and
historicism. They show the development of a sociological
approach to thinking and to culture in general, and they exhibit
an acute awareness of the methodological problems involved in
such an approach.

19th-century idealism had given prominence to the idea that
concepts, systems of beliefs, cultural forms, artistic creations,
and scientific theories evolve in an autonomous realm of spirit
("Geist") according to rules of their own. Mannheim's project of
a sociological investigation of mental phenomena was a reaction
to this idea. In his essay "On the Interpretation of Weltanschauung" (1921-22) Mannheim argued that interpretation (or
understanding), as opposed to causal explanation, is the proper
way to grasp intellectual creations. He supposes that they are
parts or expressions of something larger and other than themselves. This pre-theoretical layer of experience that forms their
under-pinning can become an object of investigation only by way
of its objectifications. These objectifications "document" the
Weltanschauung from which they emerge; they are not caused by
it, but participate in its "style."

Lukács's *History and Class Consciousness* (1923) proposed a
theory of the dependence of thought on social life that Mannheim found agreeable but which he rejected for its inherent
political partisanship. Social life, according to Lukács, consisted
primarily of class relations of material production, and consciousness was seen as always *class* consciousness. Even the
aporias of modern academic philosophy (e.g., Kant's antinomies) could be traced to the conditions of productive activity
within society. But for Lukács the proletariat, by virtue of its
increasing estrangement within the socio-economic sphere,
occupied a unique historical position from which it could achieve
universal consciousness. This is where Mannheim's view of the
relation between thought and society goes its own way. Mann-

heim's main work, *Ideology and Utopia*, can be read as an
adoption of Lukács's position that cognition—at all levels—is
ultimately a function of conditions that are not themselves mental, but which rather pertain to the social existence of the thinking subject. At the same time it can be read as a rejection of the
attribution of true, reflexive consciousness to the proletariat. For
Mannheim, intellectuals occupied the optimal standpoint for
understanding the conditioning of thought by social structures,
practices, and expectations.

Mannheim's non-polemical concept of ideology restores
something of the meaning originally given to the term in the 18th
century by Destutt de Tracy, Condorcet, and the Institut de
France. At this time it meant simply the theory or science of
ideas, and was not tied to notions of false consciousness or
self-deception. A pair of distinctions is central to Mannheim's
neutralized definition of ideology, that between the "particular"
and the "total" concepts of ideology, and that between its "special" and "general" senses. The particular conception of ideology
designates only isolated portions of the mental experience of the
other (whether a group or an individual) as distortions of their
life in society; it assumes that only the content of thought is
socially produced, and not its forms and categories as well; it sees
what takes place in consciousness as motivated or caused by an
unadmitted interest on the part of the subject, as in the case of a
more or less conscious lie. The general conception of ideology
recognizes that whole *structures* of thought and feeling express
social existence and shape social experience, and that the distortions of consciousness needn't be deliberately achieved, but can
be connected by broad, formal correspondences to the social
situation of the subject. The distinction between the special and
the general senses of the term has to do with the inclusion of one's
own thinking (i.e., the social analyst's) within the expanded, total
conception. Mannheim believed objectivity could be attained by
subjecting the conceptual apparatus of social science to the same
analysis as other elements of consciousness:

With the emergence of the general formulation of the
total conception of ideology, the simple theory of ideology develops into the sociology of knowledge. What was
once the intellectual armament of a party is transformed
into a method of research in social and intellectual history
generally. To begin with, a given social group discovers
the "situational determination" (Seinsgebundenheit) of
its opponents' ideas. Subsequently the recognition of this
fact is elaborated into an all-inclusive principle according
to which the thought of every group is seen as arising out
of its life conditions. Thus, it becomes the task of the
sociological history of thought to analyse without regard
for party biases all the factors in the actually existing
social situation which may influence thought. This sociologically oriented history of ideas is destined to provide
modern men with a revised view of the whole of the
historical process (*Ideology and Utopia*).

The all-inclusive analysis of the social influences of thought leads
Mannheim to advance a relational (as opposed to a relativistic)
theory of knowledge for which even analytical truths could not
be understood as being experienceable as true unless the life-
situation of the knower were taken into account. Mannheim
applied this sociological epistemology in his essays on "Conservative Thought" (1927), "A Note on '...the State as an Organism'"
(1927), "The Problem of Generations" (1927), and "Competition
as a Cultural Phenomenon" (1928).

When Mannheim moved to the London School of Economics
in 1933 his attention switched from the sociology of knowledge
to a diagnosis of the contemporary social crisis. He viewed his
own era as one in which, due to the modern democratization of
culture, both the individual and society were undergoing an
abrupt and radical transformation. Social planning and a sociologically inspired education would be necessary to preserve
democracy in the face of totalitarianism. Although Mannheim

never adopted a natural science model of social research, in Great Britain he became familiar with empirical methods in psychology and sociology and with the discipline of psychoanalysis. Mannheim came to think of social research as an indispensable component of the attempt to cure society through the establishment of a stable consensus of beliefs and expectations among its members. In a lecture from 1941, "Education, Sociology, and the Problem of Social Awareness," Mannheim wrote: "A sound knowledge of the obstacles to individual adjustment and of collective demands which are based upon the functional needs of society as a whole, will gradually lead us to redraft our moral codes. The educationist and the representatives of the new social services have the special opportunity of standing at the crossroads where they can gain insight both into the working of the individual psyche and of society. They, more than others, have the power to link up the regeneration of man with the regeneration of society." In his final years Mannheim believed that planned religious institutions would add a unity of spiritual purpose to the beneficial social arrangements presciently laid out by the intelligentsia.

The study of ideologies has come to hold the central place that it does within social science largely as a result of Mannheim's work; and his attention to the social role of the intellectual and of intellectual institutions has influenced the work of Robert K. Merton, Talcott Parsons, and Edward Shils. In directing sociological thought to the problems of liberal, mass society Mannheim's work connects with the Weberian themes of the bureaucratization and rationalization of the capitalist social structure.

—Alan Waters

MAO Tse-tung (Mao Zedong). Chinese revolutionary, statesman and political theorist. Born in Shao Shan, Hunan, 26 December 1893. Studied at the Xiang Tan High Middle School, 1910-11; Xiang Xiang Middle School, 1911; Hunan First Middle School, 1912-13; First Teachers Training School, Changsha, 1913-18, graduated 1918. Arranged marriage at age 14; married Yang Kaihui c. 1920 (died, 1930), 2 (possibly 3) sons; married He Zizhen in 1930, 3 daughters; married Kiang Qing c. 1938, 2 daughters. Assistant in Library, Peking University, 1918-19; taught at a Hunan primary school, 1919; editor, *Xiang River Review*, 1919, and *New Hunan*, 1919; Director, First Teachers Training School, 1920-21; editor, *Popular Daily*, 1920-21; one of the original 12 delegates to First Congress of Chinese Communist Party, 1921; organized labor unions, and peasant party membership; Editor, *Political Weekly*, 1925; led Hunan peasants in Autumn Harvest Uprising, 1927; remained in mountain base until forced into the Long March to Shensi Province, 1935; civil war with Chiang Kai-shek, 1946-49, eventually forcing Chiang into exile on Taiwan, 1949: elected Chairman of People's Government, 1949, Chairman of People's Republic, 1954: held many offices in Chinese Government. *Died 9 September 1976.*

PUBLICATIONS in English

Collections

Selected Works. New York, International Publishers, 5 vols., 1954-62.
Selected Works. London, Lawrence and Wishart, 4 vols., 1954-56.
Selected Works. Peking, Foreign Languages Press, 4 vols., 1965.

Political Theory and Commentary

Red China, Being the Report on the Progress and Achievement

of the Chinese Soviet Republic (speech). London, Lawrence, 1934; New York, International Publishers, 1934(?).
On Practice. New York, International Publishers, 1937(?); as *Concerning Practice: On the Connection Between Cognition and Practice, the Connection Between Knowledge and Deeds,* Bombay, People's Publishing House, and London, Trinity Trust, 1951.
The New Stage: Report to the Sixth Enlarged Plenum of the Central Committee of the Communist Party of China. Chungking, New China Information Committee, 1938(?).
China and the Second Imperialist World War. Chungking, New China Information Committee, 1939.
The Chinese Revolution and the Chinese Communist Party. New York, Committee for a Democratic Far Eastern Policy, 1939.
China's New Democracy. New York, Committee for a Democratic Far Eastern Policy, 1943.
On Coalition Government. N.p., China News Agency, 1945.
The Fight for a New China. New York, New Century, 1945.
China's Strategy for Victory. Bombay, People's Publishing House, 1945.
Our Task in 1945. N.p., New China News Agency, 1945.
The Way Out of China's Civil War. Bombay, People's Publishing House, 1946.
Mao Tse-tung's "Democracy": A Digest of the Bible of Chinese Communism, commentary by Lin Yutang. New York, Chinese News Service, 1947.
Aspects of China's Anti-Japanese Struggle. Bombay, People's Publishing House, 1948.
Turning Point in China. New York, New Century, 1948.
Unbreakable China, with Hsia Zoh-tsung. Singapore, Low Phay Hock, 2 vols., 1949.
The Dictatorship of the People's Democracy. New York, Committee for a Democratic Far Eastern Policy, 1949.
New Democracy, Basis of Social, Political, and Economic Structure of New China. Shanghai, Chinese-American Publishing Company, 1949; as *On New Democracy,* Peking, Foreign Languages Press, 1954.
On People's Democratic Dictatorship, and Speech at the Preparatory Meeting of the New PCC. Peking, New China News Agency, 1949; augmented edition (additional speech), Peking, Foreign Languages Press, 1950; first item reprinted, as *On People's Democratic Rule,* New York, New Century, 1950; as *People's Democratic Dictatorship,* London, Lawrence and Wishart, 1950.
On Literature and Art. Chefoo, Chefoo News, n.d.; 3rd edition, Peking, Foreign Languages Press, 1967.
Lessons of the Chinese Revolution, with Liu Shao-chi. Bombay, People's Publishing House, 1950.
Problems of Art and Literature. New York, International Publishers, 1950.
Significance of Agrarian Reforms in China, with Liu Shaochi. Bombay, People's Publishing House, 1950.
Strategic Problems of China's Revolutionary War. Bombay, People's Publishing House, 1951.
On Contradiction. Peking, Foreign Languages Press, 1952; New York, International Publishers, 1953.
Maoism: A Sourcebook: Selections from the Writings of Mao Tse-tung, edited by H. Arthur Steiner. Los Angeles, University of California, 1952.
Report of an Investigation into the Peasant Movement in Hunan. Peking, Foreign Languages Press, 1953.
Mind the Living Conditions of the Masses and Attend to the Methods of Work. Peking, Foreign Languages Press, 1953.
Introductory Remarks to "The Communist." Peking, Foreign Languages Press, 1953.
On the Rectification of Incorrect Ideas in the Party. Peking, Foreign Languages Press, 1953.
On the Tactics of Fighting Japanese Imperialism. Peking, Foreign Languages Press, 1953.
A Single Spark Can Start a Prairie Fire. Peking, Foreign Lan-

guages Press, 1953.

Why Can China's Red Political Power Exist? Peking, Foreign Languages Press, 1953.

Strategic Problems in the Anti-Japanese Guerrilla War. Peking, Foreign Languages Press, 1954; as *Problems of Strategy in Guerrilla War Against Japan*, 1965.

On the Protracted War. Peking, Foreign Languages Press, 1954.

Conquest of China, commentary by Sita Ram Goel. Calcutta, Society for Defence of Freedom in Asia, 1954.

The Policies, Measures, and Perspectives of Combating Japanese Invasion. Peking, Foreign Languages Press, 1954.

Problems of War and Strategy. Peking, Foreign Languages Press, 1954.

The Question of Independence and Autonomy Within the United Front. Peking, Foreign Languages Press, 1954.

Questions of Tactics in the Current Anti-Japanese United Front; On Policy. Peking, Foreign Languages Press, 1954.

Combat Liberalism. Peking, Foreign Languages Press, 1954.

Our Study and the Current Situation. Peking, Foreign Languages Press, 1955.

Economic and Financial Problems During the Anti-Japanese War and Other Articles. Peking, Foreign Languages Press, 1955.

On Methods of Leadership. Peking, Foreign Languages Press, 1955.

Preface and Postscript to "Rural Survey." Peking, Foreign Languages Press, 1955.

Rectify the Party's Style of Work. Peking, Foreign Languages Press, 1955.

Reform Our Study. Peking, Foreign Languages Press, 1955.

Oppose the Party "Eight-Legged Essay." Peking, Foreign Languages Press, 1955; as *Oppose Stereotyped Party Writing*, 1962.

Talks at the Yenan Forum on Art and Literature. Peking, Foreign Languages Press, 1956.

Analysis of the Classes in Chinese Society. Peking, Foreign Languages Press, 1956.

The Question of Agricultural Co-operation. Peking, Foreign Languages Press, 1956.

The Role of the Chinese Communist Party in the National War. Peking, Foreign Languages Press, 1956.

The Situation and Tasks in the Anti-Japanese War after the Fall of Shanghai and Taiyuan. Peking, Foreign Languages Press, 1956.

The Tasks of the Chinese Communist Party in the Period of Resistance to Japan. Peking, Foreign Languages Press, 1956.

On the Correct Handling of Contradictions among the People. Peking, Foreign Languages Press, 1957; as *Let a Hundred Flowers Bloom*, New York, Tamiment Institute, 1957.

Imperialism and All Reactionaries Are Paper Tigers. Peking, Foreign Languages Press, 1958.

On Art and Literature. Peking, Foreign Languages Press, 1960.

Guerrilla Warfare in China. N.p., Marine Corps Institute, 1960.

New-Democratic Constitutionalism. Peking, Foreign Languages Press, 1960.

On Guerrilla Warfare. New York, Praeger, 1961; with *Guerrilla Warfare*, by Che Guevara, London, Cassell, 1962.

On Some Important Problems of the Party's Present Policy. Peking, Foreign Languages Press, 1961.

On the U.S. White Paper. Peking, Foreign Languages Press, 1961.

The Present Situation and Our Tasks. Peking, Foreign Languages Press, 1961.

Speech at Conference of Cadres in the Shansi-Suiyuan Liberated Area. Peking, Foreign Languages Press, 1961.

Talk with the American Correspondent Anna Louise Strong. Peking, Foreign Languages Press, 1961.

Chinese Communist Revolutionary Strategy 1945-49, edited by S.M. Chiu. Princeton, New Jersey, Princeton University Center of International Studies, 1961.

On the Chungking Negotiations. Peking, Foreign Languages Press, 1961.

Mao Tse-tung: An Anthology of His Writings, edited by Anne Fremantle. New York, New American Library, 1962; revised edition, 1971.

Selected Military Writings. Peking, Foreign Languages Press, 1963.

The Political Thought of Mao Tse-tung, edited by Stuart R. Schram. New York, Praeger, and London, Pall Mall Press, 1963; revised edition, Praeger, and London, Penguin, 1969.

Statement Calling on the People of the World to Unite. Peking, Foreign Languages Press, 1964.

We Must Learn to Do Economic Work. Peking, Foreign Languages Press, 1965.

Four Essays on Philosophy. Peking, Foreign Languages Press, 1966.

Quotations from Chairman Mao Tse-tung. Peking, Foreign Languages Press, 1966; edited by Stuart R. Schram, New York, Bantam, 1967.

On War. Dehra Dun, English Book Depot, 1966.

Basic Tactics, edited by Stuart R. Schram. New York, Praeger, 1966; London, Pall Mall Press, 1967.

Selected Readings. Peking, Foreign Languages Press, 1966.

The Thoughts of Chairman Mao Tse-tung. London, Gibbs, 1967.

A Definitive Translation of Mao Tse-tung on Literature and Art: The Cultural Revolution in Context, edited by Theodore N. White. Washington, D.C., Alwhite Publications, 1967.

On People's War. Peking, Foreign Languages Press, 1967.

Five Articles: Serve the People. N.p., China Books, 1968.

The Wisdom of Mao Tse-tung. New York, Philosophical Library, 1968.

Greet the New High Tide of the Chinese Revolution. Peking, Foreign Languages Press, 1968.

On Revolution and War, edited by M. Rejai. New York, Doubleday, 1969.

(Selections), edited by Jerome Ch'en. Englewood Cliffs, New Jersey, Prentice Hall, 1969.

Supplement to Quotations from Chairman Mao. Hong Kong, Chih Luen Press, 1969.

The Concept of Operations for the Liaoshi-Shenyang Campaign (September and October 1948). Peking, Foreign Languages Press, 1969.

Collection of Statements 1956-1967. Hong Kong, American Consulate General, 1969.

Long Live Mao Tse-tung Thought: A Collection of Statements. Hong Kong, American Consulate General, 1969.

Supreme Instructions. Hong Kong, American Consulate General, 1969.

Mao Papers: Anthology and Bibliography, edited by Jerome Ch'en. London, Oxford University Press, 1970.

Selected Works, edited by Bruno Shaw. New York, Harper, 1970.

Selections from Chairman Mao. Washington, D.C., Joint Publications Research Service, 2 vols., 1970.

Six Essays on Military Affairs. Peking, Foreign Languages Press, 1971.

Post-Revolutionary Writings, with Lin Piao, edited by K. Fan. New York, Doubleday, 1972.

Four Essays on China and World Communism. New York, Lancer, 1972.

Mao Tse-tung Unrehearsed: Talks and Letters 1956-71, edited by Stuart R. Schram. London, Penguin, 1974.

Miscellany of Mao Tse-tung Thought. Arlington, Virginia, Joint Publications Research Service, 2 vols., 1974.

Chairman Mao Talks to the People: Talks and Letters 1956-1971, edited by Stuart R. Schram. New York, Pantheon, 1975.

Annotated Quotations from Chairman Mao, edited by John
   DeFrancis. New Haven, Connecticut, Yale University Press,
   1975.
A Critique of Soviet Economics, edited by Richard Levy. New
   York, Monthly Review Press, 1977.
On the Ten Major Relationships. Peking, Foreign Languages
   Press, 1977.

OTHER PUBLICATIONS

Verse

Nineteen Poems. Peking, Foreign Languages Press, 1958.
Poems. Hong Kong, Eastern Horizon Press, 1966.
Ten More Poems. Hong Kong, Eastern Horizon Press, 1967.
Poems. New York, Simon and Schuster, 1972; London, Wild-
   wood Press, 1973.
The Poems, edited by Willis Barnstone and Ko Ching-Po. New
   York, Harper, and London, Barrie and Jenkins, 1972.
Ten Poems and Lyrics. Amherst, University of Massachusetts
   Press, 1975; London, Cape, 1976.
Poems (39 poems). Peking, Foreign Languages Press, 1976.

Other

The Autobiography of Mao Tse-tung (dictated to Edgar Snow).
   Canton, China Truth, 1949.

*

Critical Studies: *Red Star over China*, London, Gollancz, 1937,
New York, Random House, 1938, and *The Other Side of the
River*, New York, Random House, 1962, both by Edgar Snow;
Mao and the Chinese Revolution by Jerome Ch'en, New York,
Oxford University Press, 1965; *Mao Tse-tung* by Stuart R.
Schram, New York, Simon and Schuster, 1966; *Mao Tse-tung
and the Chinese Revolution: The Morning Deluge, Wind in the
Tower* by Han Suyin, London, Cape, 2 vols., 1972-76; *Mao
Tse-tung and China* by Charles Patrick FitzGerald, London,
Hodder and Stoughton, 1976, revised edition, London, Penguin,
1977; *Mao Tse-tung: The Man in the Leader* by Lucian W. Pye,
New York, Basic Books, 1977; *Continuing the Revolution: The
Political Thought of Mao* by John Bryan Starr, Princeton, New
Jersey, Princeton University Press, 1979.

*   *   *

Mao Tse-tung was the principal architect of the Communist
seizure of power in mainland China and the first leader of the
People's Republic of China. From 1921, when he participated in
founding the Chinese Communist Party, through 1949, when the
Red Army completed its conquest of China under his leadership,
Mao had an important though not always a primary role.
Between 1949, when he became chairman of the new Chinese
People's Republic and the time of his death, Mao led Communist
China and became personally identified with certain internal
policies and with strategies of international revolution. Many
have pointed out the failures of his economic policies. Others
have deplored the immense numbers of deaths (estimated up to
100 million) under his regime due to starvation, execution, and
torture. Even so, everyone acknowledges Mao's key role as a
military leader and revolutionary thinker.
   Prior to Mao, Communism had been primarily an urban
doctrine, based on observations of industrial society. Marx and
Lenin believed that city workers were the key to revolution.
Communism was expected to flourish in urban areas, to seize
power there, and then to proceed to the countryside. In 1923,
Mao recognized the revolutionary potential of the Chinese peasantry after witnessing disturbances in his native village of Shao

Shan. He soon began to organize simple peasant protests, channeling their energy toward Communist goals. Eventually, he led
the Red Army to take over the Chinese countryside, encircle the
cities, and drive out the forces of Chiang Kai-shek.
   Basing a revolutionary insurgency in the countryside is an
effective way to take over an agrarian country like China. Mao's
strategy, which he described as a "people's war," has been
imitated by Communists throughout the Third World. Fidel
Castro, for example, took control of Cuba by operating from a
base in the mountains, waging guerrilla warfare to expand his
control of the countryside, and finally marching with a conventional army into Havana, the Cuban capital. Mao had recognized that power in underdeveloped countries lies in rural areas,
not in the city. Furthermore, it is much easier—and cheaper—to
overthrow a government by this kind of insurgency than by a
city-based revolution. Underdeveloped countries have very little
industry and thus a very small industrial proletariat. Since
Communism has been far more successful in poor countries than
in industrial nations, Mao's strategies of revolution are pertinent
to contemporary conditions.
   Mao's Chinese insurgency began in the late 1920's and continued through numerous changes until 1949. He fought many
years and was to write of the "long war" as a path to Communist
victory. This doctrine was followed with success by Communists
in Southeast Asia who fought for more than 15 years as rural
guerillas and in conventional military battles to conquer the
peninsula that contains Vietnam, Laos, and Cambodia.
   Mao's internal policies were far less successful. In the first
years that followed the Communist ascent to power in China,
that nation attempted to develop by following the Soviet model.
Mao emphasized heavy industry and collective farming. The
Soviet Union provided substantial sums to assist in Chinese
industrialization. During the mid-1950's, the Soviets began to
cut back their aid. At the same time, it became apparent that
China was not progressing as planned. In order to accelerate
development, Mao evolved a policy called the Great Leap Forward. In 1958, he decentralized economic planning, emphasizing
small labor-intensive operations throughout the countryside at
the expense of the capital-intensive programs. "Peoples' communes," led by local Communists, were abruptly set up everywhere, disrupting both agricultural and industrial production,
and leading to famine and industrial retreat. The Great Leap
Forward was a disaster for China. Mao's successors have criticized this policy harshly.
   Between 1966 and 1969, Mao started a huge upheaval in China
which is now called the Cultural Revolution. His objective was to
reform what he saw as a bureaucratized and elitist Chinese
Communist party and government. The Cultural Revolution
was characterized by an hysterical hero worship of Mao's personality and thinking. Organized bands of Communist youth,
loyal to Mao and called the Red Guards attacked, humiliated,
and often tortured or murdered senior party officials and
government functionaries who were thought to be corrupt in
some way or simply lacking in revolutionary zeal. Symbols of the
past and of Chinese traditions were destroyed. The Red Guards
wrecked the birthplace of Confucius, for example. When this
violent phase ended, the Red Guards collaborated with other
Communists at the local level to reorganize and presumably to
revivify the party. In actual fact, the Cultural Revolution was a
time of utter madness and constant terror in China. There was
lunatic violence everywhere and utter disregard of human rights.
Industry and agriculture were completely disrupted while China
went through a nightmarish kind of war against its own people.
   Mao was a tenacious fighter and an excellent military strate-
gist who fought a long war to conquer the world's most populous
nation for Communism. He made major additions to Communist doctrine. As a national leader, in spite of some economic
achievements, Mao must be pronounced a failure. His best-
known policies—the Great Leap Forward and the Cultural
Revolution—were fundamentally reactionary and did great
damage. Still, Mao must be considered the most important

figure in 20th-century Chinese history.

—Victor Cassidy

MARCEL, Gabriel (Honoré). French philosopher and dramatist. Born in Paris, 7 December 1889. Educated at the Lycée Carnot, Paris; studied at the Sorbonne, Paris, agrégation de philosophie, 1910. Served in the Red Cross during World War I. Married Jacqueline Boegner in 1919; 1 child. Converted to Catholicism in 1929. Taught at various lycées in Vendôme, Paris, Sens, and Montpellier, 1912-1941. Reader for the publishers Grasset and Plon; drama and music critic for *Nouvelles Littéraires*, 1945-68. Gifford Lecturer, University of Aberdeen, Scotland, 1949; William James Lecturer, Harvard University, Cambridge, Massachusetts, 1951. Recipient: Grand Prix de Littérature, French Academy, 1948; Goethe Hanseatic Prize, Hamburg University, 1956; Prix National des Lettres, 1958; Frankfurt Peace Prize, 1964; European Erasmus Prize, 1969; West German Booksellers Peace Prize. Honorary doctorate: University of Tokyo; University of Chicago. Member, Académie des Sciences Morales et Politiques, 1952. Officer, Légion d'Honneur; Commandeur, Ordre des Arts et des Lettres; Grand-Croix, Ordre National du Mérite. *Died* (in Paris) *8 October 1973.*

PUBLICATIONS

Philosophy and Theology

Journal métaphysique (1914-1923). Paris, Gallimard, 1927; as *Metaphysical Journal*, Chicago, Regnery, 1950; London, Barrie and Rockliff, 1952.
Être et avoir. Paris, Aubier, 1935; as *Being and Having*, London, Dacre Press, 1949; Boston, Beacon Press, 1951.
Du refus à l'invocation. Paris, Gallimard, 1940; as *Creative Fidelity*, New York, Noonday Press, 1964.
Homo Viator: Prolégomènes à une métaphysique de l'espérance. Paris, Aubier, 1945; as *Homo Viator: Introduction to a Metaphysic of Hope*, London, Gollancz, and Chicago, Regnery, 1951.
La Métaphysique de Royce. Paris, Aubier, 1945; as *Royce's Metaphysics*, Chicago, Regnery, 1956.
Position et approches concrètes du mystère ontologique. Paris, Vrin, 1949; as *The Philosophy of Existence*, London, Harvill Press, and New York, Philosophical Library, 1949.
Le Mystère de l'être I: Réflexion et mystère. Paris, Aubier, 1951; as *The Mystery of Being I: Reflection and Mystery*, London, Harvill Press, 1950; Chicago, Regnery, 1960.
Le Mystère de l'être II: Foi et réalité. Paris, Aubier, 1951; as *Mystery of Being*, London, Harvill Press, 1951; Chicago, Regnery, 1960.
Les Hommes contre l'humain. Paris, La Colombe, 1951; as *Man Against Humanity*, London, Harvill Press, 1952; as *Man Against Mass Society*, Chicago, Regnery, 1952.
Le Déclin de la sagesse. Paris, Plon, 1954; as *Decline of Wisdom*, London, Harvill Press, 1954; Chicago, Regnery, 1955.
L'Homme problématique. Paris, Aubier, 1955; as *Problematic Man*, New York, Herder, 1967.
The Influence of Psychic Phenomena on My Philosophy. London, London Society for Psychic Research, 1956.
Théâtre et religion. Lyons, Vitte, 1959.
Présence et immortalité: Journal métaphysique (1938-1943) et autres textes. Paris, Flammarion, 1959; as *Presence and Immortality*, Pittsburgh, Duquesne University Press, 1967.
Fragments philosophiques, 1909-1914. Louvain, Nauwelaerts, 1962; as *Philosophical Fragments, 1909-1914, and The Philos-*

opher and Peace, Notre Dame, Indiana, University of Notre Dame Press, 1965.
The Existential Background of Human Dignity (lectures). Cambridge, Massachusetts, Harvard University Press, 1963.
Paix sur la terre: Deux Discours, une tragédie. Paris, Aubier, 1965.
Gabriel Marcel et les niveaux de l'expérience (selections), edited by Jeanne Parain-Vial. Paris, Seghers, 1966.
Searchings (selected essays). New York, Newman Press, 1967.
Pour une sagesse tragique. Paris, Plon, 1968; as *Tragic Wisdom and Beyond*, Evanston, Illinois, Northwestern University Press, 1973.
Coleridge et Schelling. Paris, Aubier-Montaigne, 1971.
En chemin, vers quel éveil? Paris, Gallimard, 1971.

Plays

Le Seuil invisible (includes *La Grâce* and *Le Palais de sable*). Paris, Grasset, 1914.
Le Coeur des autres. Paris, Grasset, 1921.
L'Iconoclaste. Paris, Stock, 1923.
Un Homme de Dieu. Paris, Grasset, 1925; as *A Man of God*, in *Three Plays*, 1952.
Le Quatour en fa dièse. Paris, Plon, 1925.
Trois Pièces: Le Regard neuf, Le Mort de demain, La Chapelle ardente. Paris, Plon, 1931.
Le Monde cassé. Paris, Desclée De Brouwer, 1933.
Ariadne: Le Chemin de Crête. Paris, Grasset, 1936; as *Ariadne*, in *Three Plays*, 1952.
Le Dard. Paris, Plon, 1936.
La Soif. Paris, Desclée De Brouwer, 1938; revised version, as *Les Coeurs avides*, Paris, La Table Ronde, 1952.
L'Horizon. Paris, Aux Etudiants de France, 1945.
Théâtre comique (includes *Colimbyre; ou, Le Brasier de la paix; La Double expertise; Les Points sur les i.; Le Divertissement posthume*). Paris, Albin Michel, 1947.
Vers un autre royaume (includes *L'Emissaire* and *Le Signe de la croix*). Paris, Plon, 1949.
La Fin des temps. Paris, Realités, 1950.
Rome n'est plus dans Rome. Paris, La Table Ronde, 1951.
Three Plays: A Man of God, Ariadne, The Funeral Pyre. London, Secker and Warburg, 1952; New York, Hill and Wang, 1958.
La Dimension Florestan. Paris, Plon, 1956.

Other

Recherche de la famille, essai sur "l'être familial," with others. Paris, Editions Familiales de France, 1949.
Un Changement d'espérance à la reconte du Réarmement moral: Des témoignages, des faits. Paris, Plon, 1958; as *Fresh Hope for the World: Moral Rearmament in Action*, New York, Longman, 1960.
L'Heure théâtrale: Croniques dramatiques: De Giraudoux à Jean-Paul Sartre. Paris, Plon, 1959.
Entretiens (Paul Ricoeur & G. Marcel). Paris, Aubier, 1968.

*

Bibliography: *Gabriel Marcel and His Critics: An International Bibliography (1928-1976)* by François H. LaPointe and Claire C. LaPointe, New York, Garland, 1977.

Critical Studies: *Gabriel Marcel et Karl Jaspers, deux maîtres de l'existentialisme*, by Paul Ricoeur, Paris, Éditions du Temps Present, 1948; *Gabriel Marcel* by Seymour Cain, London, Bowes and Bowes, and New York, Hillary House, 1963; *The Existentialist Drama of Gabriel Marcel*, edited by Francis J. Lascoe, West Hartford, Connecticut, St. Joseph's College McAuley Institute of Religious Studies, 1974.

*   *   *

Gabriel Marcel, a pioneer of existential and phenomenological thought in France, is notable for his sensitive and illuminating exploration of the trials and depths of human existence, with a specifically religious orientation.

Among the early significant influences on Marcel's personality and thought was the sudden death of his mother when he was four, an experience of irreplaceable loss and abiding presence. Also important were his isolation as an only child, which led him to invent imaginary siblings with whom to converse (he wrote his first play at eight); his subjection to a Gradgrind type of education, which evoked a lifelong repugnance for forced rote methods of learning; and boyhood travels to foreign parts, which provided the impressive experience of becoming at home in the alien and unknown. Quite early he began his immersion in music, as a pianist and a composer, an activity that constituted for him communion with transcendent reality.

Already in his lycée days philosophy became Marcel's main intellectual vocation, culminating in a thesis relating Coleridge's metaphysical ideas with Schelling's philosophy. Later he studied philosophy at the Sorbonne, but never completed his doctoral dissertation (on the necessary conditions for the intelligibility of religious thought). Although he taught philosophy in lycées from time to time, his regular occupation became that of a free-lance writer and thinker, noted not only for his philosophical writings, but also for his literary and dramatic criticism. Moreover, he was the prolific author of intense dramas about spiritual crises, personal relations and disrelations, and various themes later illuminated in his philosophical writings.

In World War I his work for the French Red Cross in seeking to trace soldiers missing in action converted him from a rarified, abstract idealism to a philosophy arising out of intimate personal experience. His investigations of "metapsychical" phenomena (telepathy, clairvoyance, etc.) put him at odds with the prevailing exclusion of such matters from serious philosophical consideration. In 1929 he became converted to Roman Catholicism in a crucial decision that grew out of a long intellectual and spiritual search. Yet he remained an independent thinker, following interests and taking positions sometimes opposed to official or conventional Catholic stances.

As noted, his early philosophical background was idealist. Hegel and Schelling were important early influences, as were also Bradley and Bosanquet, and later Royce and Hocking. He learned from all these thinkers, accepting or rejecting selectively their major concerns and thrusts, as he moved away from abstract idealism toward a concrete philosophy. Undoubtedly Henri Bergson (along with Hocking) was a major influence in this philosophical trajectory from idealism to a new kind of realism.

In his early master work, *Metaphysical Journal* (1927), Marcel used the notion of "participation," borrowed from Hocking, to probe key philosophical questions of existence, sensation, incarnation (being in a body), knowledge of others, memory, and religious belief. "Participation" here has a basically ontological, not the traditionally noetic or fusionist-mystical, sense. It has to do with the primary experience of being with other beings, as notably in sensation, and of the experience of one's own body—the searching discussion of "my body" in *Metaphysical Journal* antedates later considerations of this subject in French philosophy. Breaking with the traditional subject-object mode of predicating existence, Marcel opposed existence, known immediately through sensation, to objectivity, known through abstract thought. His earlier expression of this viewpoint in the essay "Existence and Objectivity" (1925) marked the first use by a French thinker of the terms "existence" and "existential" in the Kierkegaardian sense. And in applying the idea of "participation" in *Metaphysical Journal* to personal relations, he was a pioneer, along with Martin Buber, in elucidating the *I-Thou* relation, including the relation to the Eternal or Absolute *Thou*. He applied it to the whole range of religious experience. It is noteworthy that at the time these journal entries were written they were the explorations of a secular thinker, uncommitted to any particular religious faith.

In the luminous, probing essays and journals that filled his later works, Marcel applied his fundamental notions to concrete instances of human existence, to trust, love, hope, faith, despair, suicide, to the primary existential situations that elicit the will to negation and self-destruction, as well as to the affirmation of being and being-with. "Participation" became more precisely discerned as "engagement" (involvement with other beings) and "availability" (opening up to them). The human mode of being, for Marcel, is no mere brute fact, but a decisive act, an affirmation—not merely of "I am," but of "We are." The former distinction between existence and objectivity was later expressed as one between being and having—between what can be related to, existed with, "coessed," and what can be located, defined, possessed (physically or mentally). The ontological communion adumbrated in his early work is fully fleshed out in the later essays and journals, notably in *Being and Having, Homo Viator*, and the salient "Concrete Approaches to the Ontological Mystery," as well as in his Gifford Lectures, *The Mystery of Being*. And at the same time there was the evocative foreshadowing or accompaniment provided by his plays.

Marcel's work constituted a reclaiming of whole areas of human experience—religious, aesthetic, deeply personal and interpersonal—that had been neglected or excluded as trivial or meaningless by the conventional philosophy of his youth and early manhood. Against the fashionable dogmas of verifiability, universality and normality, he summoned the full range of human experience, calling on the philosopher to begin with the fathoming of his own experience in its fullness and depths to arrive at an awareness of the human condition and of man's relation to transcendent reality. Not a solipsistic subjectivity, but a communal intersubjectivity was the goal, for the philosopher's personal search was to be attended and complemented by the calls and responses of other persons and their experiences.

—Seymour Cain

MARCUSE, Herbert. American political philosopher. Born in Berlin, Germany, 19 July 1898; emigrated to the United States in 1934; naturalized, 1940. Educated at Augusta Gymnasium, Berlin; studied at the universities of Berlin and Freiburg, Ph.D. 1922. Married Sophie Marcuse (died, 1951), 1 son; married Inge Werner in 1955 (died, 1973), 2 step-sons; married Erica Sherova in 1977. Devoted himself to research, at Freiburg, at Frankfurt Institute for Social Research, 1922-33, and at Institut de Recherches Sociales, Geneva, 1933-34; staff member, Institute for Social Research, Columbia University, New York, 1934-40; served with the Office of Strategic Services, 1941-44; Chief of Central European Section, Office of Intelligence Research, 1946-50; member of the Russian Institute, Columbia University, 1951-52, and Russian Research Center, Harvard University, Cambridge, Massachusetts, 1952-53; Professor of Politics and Philosophy, Brandeis University, Waltham, Massachusetts, 1954-65; Professor of Philosophy, University of California at San Diego, 1965-79. Reviewer, *Zeitschrift für Sozialforschung*, 1933-38. Honorary degree: New England Conservatory of Music, Boston. *Died 29 July 1979.*

PUBLICATIONS

Collections

Schriften. Frankfurt, Suhrkamp, 1978-.

Political and Social Theory

Schiller-Bibliographie unter Benutzung der Trämelschen

Schiller-Bibliothek (1865). Berlin, Fraenkel, 1925.

Hegels Ontologie und die Grundlegung einer Theorie der Geschichtlichkeit. Frankfurt, Klostermann, 1932.

Reason and Revolution: Hegel and the Rise of Social Theory. London, Oxford University Press, 1941; augmented edition, New York, Humanities Press, 1954; London, Routledge, 1955.

Eros and Civilization: A Philosophical Inquiry into Freud. Boston, Beacon Press, 1955; London, Routledge, 1966.

Soviet Marxism: A Critical Analysis. New York, Columbia University Press, and London, Routledge, 1958.

One-Dimensional Man: Studies in the Ideology of Advanced Industrial Society. Boston, Beacon Press, and London, Routledge, 1964.

Kultur und Gesellschaft. Frankfurt, Suhrkamp, 2 vols., 1965.

Negations: Essays in Critical Theory. Boston, Beacon Press, and London, Allen Lane, 1968.

Psychoanalyse und Politik. Frankfurt, Europäische Verlagsanstalt, 1968; as *Five Lectures: Psychoanalysis, Politics, and Utopia*, Boston, Beacon Press, and London, Allen Lane, 1970.

An Essay on Liberation. Boston, Beacon Press, and London, Allen Lane, 1969.

Ideen zu einer kritischen Theorie der Gesellschaft. Frankfurt, Suhrkamp, 1969.

Studies in Critical Philosophy. Boston, Beacon Press, and London, New Left, 1972.

Counterrevolution and Revolt. Boston, Beacon Press, and London, Allen Lane, 1972.

Die Permanenz der Kunst: Wider eine bestimmte Marxistische Aesthetik. Munich, Hanser, 1977; as *The Aesthetic Dimension: Toward a Critique of Marxist Aesthetics*, Boston, Beacon Press, 1978; London, Macmillan, 1979.

Other

Editor, *The Democratic and the Authoritarian State*, by Franz Neumann. Glencoe, Illinois, Free Press, 1957.

Editor, with Robert Paul Wolff and Barrington Moore, *A Critique of Pure Tolerance*. Boston, Beacon Press, 1965; London, Cape, 1969.

*

Critical Studies: *The Critical Spirit: Essays in Honor of Herbert Marcuse* edited by Kurt H. Wolff and Barrington Moore, Boston, Beacon Press, 1967; *The Freudian Left: Wilhelm Reich, Geza Roheim, Herbert Marcuse* by Paul A. Robinson, New York, Harper, 1969; *Herbert Marcuse* by Alasdair C. MacIntyre, London, Fontana, 1970; *Contra Marcuse* by Elisio Vivas, New Rochelle, New York, Arlington House, 1971; *Critique of Marcuse* by Paul Mattick, New York, Herder, and London, Merlin, 1972; *Critical Interruptions: New Left Perspectives on Herbert Marcuse* edited by P. Breines, New York, Herder, 1972; *The Party of Eros: Radical Socialist Thought and the Realm of Freedom* (on Marcuse, Paul Goodman, and Norman O. Brown) by Richard King, Chapel Hill, University of North Carolina Press, 1972; *New Theories of Revolution: A Commentary on the Views of Frantz Fanon, Régis Debray, and Herbert Marcuse* by Jack Woddis, London, Lawrence and Wishart, 1972; *The Meaning of Marcuse* by R.W. Marks, New York, Ballantine, 1972; *Marcuse—Dilemma and Liberation: A Critical Analysis* by John Fry, Stockholm, Almqvist & Wiksell, 1974, Atlantic Highlands, New Jersey, Humanities Press, and Hassocks, Sussex, Harvester Press, 1978; *Herbert Marcuse: From Marx to Freud and Beyond* by S.S. Lipshires, Cambridge, Massachusetts, Schenkmann, 1974; *The Imaginary Witness: The Critical Theory of Herbert Marcuse* by Morton Schoolman, New York, Free Press, 1980; *Reason and Eros: The Social Theory of Herbert Marcuse* by Vincent Geoghegan, London, Pluto Press, 1981.

* * *

Herbert Marcuse experienced the failure of the Marxist left to come to power in Europe after the Soviet Revolution and the end of World War I. Furthermore, he and his generation lived through the coming to power of fascism/nazism, and the totalitarianism of the right which took over Europe. Marcuse's Marxist analysis had to be formulated outside of his native Germany after 1933; moreover, it was developed against the background of the Stalinization of Marxist thought. After 1945 he and many other Western Marxists attempted to analyze the seeming stability of consumer capitalism in America and Europe. Marcuse's greatest contribution may be his attempt to keep Marxist thought alive and uncorrupted as a tool with which to analyze, and eventually change, society.

This contribution to the understanding of Marcuse's work will focus upon his: (1) description and analysis of one-dimensional society in the post-1945 affluent West; (2) interpretation of Hegel as a critical thinker; (3) attempt to sketch a society beyond one-dimensionality, through a synthesis of Marx and Freud; and finally, (4) a brief assessment of the man as a serious critical thinker.

Marcuse's term, one-dimensional, became famous after his book *One-Dimensional Man* was published in 1964. Central to a one-dimensional society is capitalist hegemony which is based upon monopoly capitalism's power to control production, distribution, and the formulation of desire for commodities itself. Although this class-stratified society is non-democratic, it has delivered a plethora of consumer goods to people in Western society. Marcuse asserts that such a society is both democratic and unfree. The contemporary status quo is totalitarian by virtue of its economic organization: the range of choices in the merchandise mart of consumer capitalism may be great, but this is not as crucial as what can, or cannot, be chosen.

The atomizing power of monopoly/consumer capitalism creates a marketable mass man who is told by the advertising media what he needs. The problem is that within a one-dimensional society, dominated by a capitalist agenda, man develops a distorted second nature which ties him to the commodity market; moreover, it is within this realm of consumption where gratification is to occur. The rhetoric of individualism is a subterfuge for the imposition of patterns which feature collective imitation. The consumers of the one-dimensional society are, in fact, well-dressed, manipulated objects within a non-democratically administered whole.

Marcuse and his neo-Marxist colleagues of the Frankfurt School have formulated a way which allows the critic to get outside of any status quo in order to analyze and evaluate the whole. Because the one-dimensional society is totalitarian, according to Marcuse, this ability to get outside becomes crucial. In his book *Reason and Revolution*, Marcuse tells us that Hegel insisted on man being rational, and a person need not be at the mercy of the so-called facts that surround him. Instead, man is capable of subjecting the facts of common sense to a higher standard, viz., the standard of reason. Hegel's rational/critical philosophy, armed with the dialectic method, came to be known as negative philosophy because it criticized the descriptive *is* in the name of the normative *ought*. According to Marcuse, Hegel sought to develop an outside point of reference from which to pass judgement on any status quo. Marx learned from Hegel that what meets the eye is not likely to be immutable; instead, it represents what man has made historically.

For Hegel, Marx, and Marcuse, a rational man is one who tests human activity by a standard of truth which goes beyond the status quo. A rationalist, as well as a materialist who subscribes to a unified theory of mind and phenomena (unified by the dialectical process), looks toward a social order which does not yet exist. Marcuse believed, with Hegel, that a free and intelligent person does not accept the given order of things just because it is given, because man possesses reason, imagination, and the analytic ability which allow him to compare the particular given, e.g., contemporary one-dimensional society, to the universal normative ought. What is ultimately considered real comes to mean that which exists in concordance with the standards of reason. For Marcuse, what exists is not immediately and already rational, but must instead be brought into reason.

Marcuse examined the psychological obstacles which lay in the path of meaningful social change. His *Eros and Civilization* speaks of work becoming play within a democratic community, where even necessary labor can be organized in harmony with liberated, and authentic, individual needs. A transformed society which is no longer based on the repressive performance principle would eliminate the need for surplus repression, thus freeing the person from alienating labor. Marcuse attempted to envision what the new post-revolutionary society would be like. He supported the idea of personal happiness as a necessary complement to rationalism.

The cessation of the exploitation of man in the work-place is the *sine qua non* of the Marxist left's definition of the good society. Marcuse was committed to that idea; furthermore, he agreed with Freud that some postponement of gratification is necessary if civilization were to last; however, there exists evidence of massive surplus repression within the one-dimensional society of contemporary capitalism. Marcuse thought that instinctual repression had already fulfilled its historical function, and that Western man has mastered the problem of building a technology capable of allowing everyone to live in freedom and dignity. Renunciation has gained for the species, and specifically for Western man, freedom from mere necessity; consequently, men and women have the ability to go beyond violence and anarchy. They have the ability to change the society in accordance with historical reason.

What Marcuse attempts to formulate in *Eros and Civilization* is a new theory of man: a person who is free from surplus repression, and who is able to make the revolution, and then to construct a new society in which rational men and women are able to be happy. The young Marx had speculated that man might hunt in the morning, fish in the afternoon, raise cattle in the evening, and criticize after dinner. Marcuse's version reads as follows: a state in which productivity no longer results from renunciation and alienation; a situation where socially owned mechanization allows instinctual energy to return to its original form; and a place where alienated labor time would be reduced to a minimum, and eventually be made to disappear, so that life could consist of free time. Marcuse's interpretation of Freud allows for a new kind of man to emerge in this idyllic state—however, only after the Hegelian dialectic allows for an analysis, and then a smashing of the one-dimensional society of capitalism.

Marcuse died in the summer of 1979 after more than a half century of intellectual labor. Except for the most ideologically opposed (to Marcuse) polemicists, there are few, if any, who do not admit that Marcuse is a man of great importance as a serious and profound critical thinker. The following points are typical of serious criticism raised against him in the West. It has been said that Marcuse's description of fascism as an extension of capitalism and bourgeois liberalism is simplistic. Many have faulted him for not engaging in empirical work. The question of his epistemological position has been raised, especially because he contrasts truth to what is merely appearance. Marcuse's view concerning the possibility of happiness for man has been criticized by those who believe that to be human is to suffer because of the permanent gap between aspiration and achievement. Marcuse's sketching of a possible social order in which human relations are enriched by libidinal release and gratification is said to violate Freud's caveat that such a release would mean the destruction of civilization. Some have said that Marcuse is limited by a vision which is pre-Marxist, a nostalgic view held by the Left Hegelians in Germany.

One of the most often heard criticisms of Marcuse is that he, other Western neo-Marxists, and especially members of the Frankfurt School, have lost faith in the revolutionary potential and capabilities of the proletariat. Can one still be a Marxist if the proletariat is not seen as the agency for revolutionary transformation? Marcuse has also been charged with being an elitist because he has argued that the mass of people in the one-dimensional society cannot themselves be arbiters of what they truly need. Marcuse's critics ask: how does he have the right to say what others' needs are? Finally, Marcuse's critics score him for saying that there may be a period featuring a "dictatorship" by a minority of those who have not been fooled by capitalist hegemony in the one-dimensional society. Marcuse is portrayed as one who is not authentically a democrat, but one who sees the alternatives as being among elites. In a word, Marcuse is castigated as one who underrates most men as they are.

There are many who think that Marcuse's great contribution is his insistence upon keeping Marxist analysis free from loyalty to a particular nation's or group's version of Marxian orthodoxy. The subtlety of Marcuse's analysis of contemporary society includes a mastery of many of the West's greatest thinkers: Plato, Aristotle, Kant, Hegel, Marx, Freud. Because of his exile it was difficult for Marcuse to be both an intellectual and a political leader. As a result of the proletariat's historical failure to fulfill Marx's role for it as a class, both in Russia and the West, Marcuse had to deal with that failure in his analysis.

Marcuse and his fellow Critical Theoreticians sought dialectically to overcome the dichotomy between idealism and materialism. This attempt places Marcuse centrally within the Marxist tradition. Marcuse and his colleagues did abandon certain tenets of Marxism (such as the revolutionary potential of the working class); however, he helped to preserve the integrity of Marx's libertarian impulse. By systematically questioning the underlying assumptions upon which Marxist theory rested, Marcuse helped make Marxism stronger, and a legitimate form of inquiry for non-Marxists. While in the United States, Marcuse and his colleagues of the Frankfurt School have profoundly challenged the conventional wisdom of American social thought; however, the position taken against positivism has not arrested its seemingly strengthened position.

—Richard A. Brosio

MARITAIN, Jacques. French philosopher and theologian. Born in Paris, 18 November 1882. Educated at the Lycée Henri IV, Paris; studied at the Sorbonne, Paris, Docteur-en-philosophie, 1905, and at the University of Heidelberg, 1905-08. Married Raïssa Oumansoff in 1904. Converted to Catholicism, 1906; worked for the publisher Hachette, Paris, 1908-11; taught at the Collège Stanislas, Paris, 1912-14, 1915-16; Professor of Philosophy and Modern History, Institut Catholique, Paris, 1913-39; Professor, Institute for Mediaeval Studies, Toronto, 1940-44; French Ambassador to the Vatican, 1945-48; Professor of Philosophy, 1948-53, and Professor Emeritus, 1953-73, Princeton University, New Jersey. Terry Lecturer, Yale University, New Haven, Connecticut, 1943; Walgreen Lecturer, University of Chicago, 1949; Mellon Lecturer, National Gallery, Washington, D.C., 1952. Recipient: Annual Christian Culture Award, 1942; Cardinal Spellman Aquinas Medal, 1951; Grand Prix de Littérature, Académie Française, 1961; Grand Prix National des Lettres, 1963. Honorary degree: Sacred Congregation for Seminaries and Universities, Rome, 1917; honorary doctorate: Manhattan College, New York, 1951; Boston College, 1958. Member, Brazilian Academy of Letters, 1937. Commandeur, Légion d'Honneur; Order of St. Gregory the Great. *Died* (in Toulouse) *28 April 1973.*

PUBLICATIONS

Collections

Oeuvres, edited by Henry Bars. Paris, Desclée De Brouwer, 2 vols., 1975-78.

Philosophy and Theology

La Philosophie Bergsonienne: Études critiques. Paris, Rivière, 1914; as *Bergsonian Philosophy and Thomism,* New York, Philosophical Library, 1955.

Art et scholastique. Paris, Librairie de l'Art Catholique, 1920; as *The Philosophy of Art,* London, Humphries, 1923; as *Art and Scholasticism,* New York, Scribner, 1930.

Éléments de philosophie: I. Introduction générale à la philosophie. Paris, Téqui, 1921; as *An Introduction to Philosophy,* London and New York, Sheed and Ward, 1930.

Théonas; ou, Les Entretiens d'un sage et deux philosophes sur diverses matières inégalement actuelles. Paris, Nouvelle Librairie Nationale, 1921; as *Théonas: Conversations of a Sage,* London and New York, Sheed and Ward, 1935.

Antimoderne. Paris, Desclée, 1922.

De la vie d'oraison, with Raïssa Maritain. Paris, À l'Art Catholique, 1922; as *Prayer and Intelligence,* New York, Sheed and Ward, 1928; London, Sheed and Ward, 1929.

Éléments de Philosophie: II. L'Orde des concepts: Petite logique. Paris, Téqui, 1923; as *An Introduction to Logic,* London and New York, Sheed and Ward, 1937.

Saint Thomas D'Aquin, apôtre des temps modernes. Paris, Éditions de la Revue des Jeunes, 1923.

Réflexions sur l'intelligence et sur sa vie propre. Paris, Nouvelle Librairie Nationale, 1924.

Trois Réformateurs: Luther, Descartes, Rousseau. Paris, Plon, 1925; as *Three Reformers: Luther, Descartes, Rousseau,* London, Sheed and Ward, 1928; New York, Scribner, 1929.

Réponse à Jean Cocteau. Paris, Stock, 1926; as *Art and Faith: Letters Between Jacques Maritain and Jean Cocteau,* New York, Philosophical Library, 1948.

Une Opinion sur Charles Maurras et le devoir des catholiques. Paris, Plon, 1926.

Primauté du spirituel. Paris, Plon, 1927; as *The Things That Are Not Caesar's,* London, Sheed and Ward, and New York, Scribner, 1930.

Quelques Pages sur Léon Bloy. Paris, L'Artisan du Livre, 1927.

Le Docteur angélique. Paris, Desclée De Brouwer, 1930; as *The Angelic Doctor: The Life and Thought of Saint Thomas Aquinas,* New York, Dial Press, 1931; as *St. Thomas Aquinas: Angel of the Schools,* London, Sheed and Ward, 1931.

Religion et culture. Paris, Desclée De Brouwer, 1930; as *Religion and Culture (Essays In Order I),* London, Sheed and Ward, 1931.

Distinguer pour unir; Ou, les Degrés du savoir. Paris, Desclée De Brouwer, 1932; as *The Degrees of Knowledge,* London, Bles, 1937; New York, Scribner, 1938.

Le Songe de Descartes, suivi de quelques essais. Paris, Corrêa, 1932; as *The Dream of Descartes, Together With Some Other Essays,* New York, Philosophical Library, 1944; London, Editions Poetry London, 1946.

De la philosophie chrétienne. Paris, Desclée De Brouwer, 1933; as *An Essay on Christian Philosophy,* New York, Philosophical Library, 1955.

Du régime temporel et de la liberté. Paris, Desclée De Brouwer, 1933; as *Freedom in the Modern World,* London, Sheed and Ward, and New York, Scribner, 1936.

Some Reflections on Culture and Liberty (lecture). Chicago, University of Chicago Press, 1933 (bilingual edition).

Sept Leçons sur l'être et les premiers principes de la raison spéculative. Paris, Téqui, 1934; as *A Preface to Metaphysics: Seven Lectures on Being,* New York and London, Sheed and Ward, 1939.

Frontières de la poésie et autre essais. Paris, Rouart, 1935; as *Art and Poetry,* New York, Philosophical Library, 1943; London, Editions Poetry London, 1945.

La Philosophie de la nature: Essai critique sur ses frontières et son objet. Paris, Téqui, 1935; as *Philosophy of Nature,* New York, Philosophical Library, 1951.

Lettre sur l'indépendance. Paris, Desclée De Brouwer, 1935.

Science et sagesse, suivi d'éclaircissements sur la philosophie morale. Paris, Labergerie, 1935; as *Science and Wisdom,* New York, Scribner, and London, Bles, 1940.

Humanisme intégral: Problèmes temporels et spirituels d'une nouvelle chrétienté. Paris, Aubier, 1936; as *True Humanism,* London, Bles, and New York, Scribner, 1938.

Para una filosofia de la persona humana. Buenos Aires, Cursos de Cultura Catolica, 1937.

Les Juifs parmi les nations. Paris, Éditions du Cerf, 1938; as *A Christian Looks at the Jewish Question,* New York, Longman, 1939; as *Antisemitism,* London, Bles, 1939.

Questions de conscience: Essais et allocutions. Paris, Desclée De Brouwer, 1938.

Situation de la poésie, with Raïssa Maritain. Paris, Desclée De Brouwer, 1938; as *The Situation of Poetry,* New York, Philosophical Library, 1955.

Le Crépuscule de la civilisation. Paris, Éditions Les Nouvelles Lettres, 1939; as *The Twilight of Civilization,* New York, Sheed and Ward, 1943; London, Sheed and Ward, 1946.

Quatre Essais sur l'esprit dans sa condition charnelle. Paris, Desclée De Brouwer, 1939.

De la justice politique: Notes sur la présente guerre. Paris, Plon, 1940.

Scholasticism and Politics. New York, Macmillan, 1940; London, Bles, 1954.

À travers le désastre. New York, Éditions de la Maison Française, 1941; as *France, My Country, Through Disaster,* New York, Longman, 1941.

Confession de foi. New York, Éditions de la Maison Française, 1941.

Ransoming the Time. New York, Scribner, 1941; as *Redeeming the Time,* London, Bles, 1943.

Les Droits de l'homme et la loi naturelle. New York, Éditions de la Maison Française, 1942; as *The Rights of Man and Natural Law,* New York, Scribner, 1943; London, Bles, 1944.

Saint Thomas and the Problem of Evil (lecture). Milwaukee, Wisconsin, Marquette University Press, 1942.

Christianisme et démocratie. New York, Éditions de la Maison Française, 1943; as *Christianity and Democracy,* New York, Scribner, 1944; London, Bles, 1945.

Education at the Crossroads. New Haven, Connecticut, Yale University Press, and London, Oxford University Press, 1943.

Sort de l'homme. Neuchâtel, Éditions de la Baconnière, 1943.

De Bergson à Thomas D'Aquin: Essais de métaphysique et de morale. New York, Éditions de la Maison Française, 1944.

Principes d'une politique humaniste. New York, Éditions de la Maison Française, 1944.

À travers la victoire. Paris, Hartmann, 1945.

Messages, 1941-1945. New York, Éditions de la Maison Française, 1945.

Pour la justice: Articles et discours (1940-1945). New York, Éditions de la Maison Française, 1945.

Court Traité de l'existence et de l'existant. Paris, Hartmann, 1947; as *Existence and the Existent,* New York, Pantheon, 1948.

La Personne et le bien commun. Paris, Desclée De Brouwer, 1947; as *The Person and the Common Good,* New York, Scribner, 1947; London, Bles, 1948.

La Voie de la paix (lecture). Mexico City, Librairie Française, 1947.

Raison et raisons: Essais détachés. Paris, Egloff, 1947; as *The Range of Reason,* New York, Scribner, 1952; London, Bles, 1953.

La Signification de l'athéisme contemporain. Paris, Desclée De Brouwer, 1949.

Man and the State. Chicago, University of Chicago Press, 1951.

Neuf Leçons sur les notions premières de la philosophie morale. Paris, Téqui, 1951.

Approches de Dieu. Paris, Alsatia, 1953; as *Approaches to*

God, New York, Harper, 1954; London, Allen and Unwin, 1955.

Creative Intuition in Art and Poetry. New York, Pantheon, 1953; London, Harvill Press, 1954.

The Social and Political Philosophy of Jacques Maritain: Selected Readings, edited by Joseph W. Evans and Leo R. Ward. New York, Scribner, 1955.

On the Philosophy of History, edited by Joseph W. Evans. New York, Scribner, 1957; London, Bles, 1959.

Truth and Human Fellowship. Princeton, New Jersey, Princeton University Press, 1957.

Reflections on America. New York, Scribner, 1958.

Pour une philosophie de l'éducation. Paris, Fayard, 1959.

The Sin of the Angel: An Essay on a Re-Introduction of Some Thomist Positions. Westminster, Maryland, Newman Press, 1959.

Liturgie et contemplation, with Raïssa Maritain. Paris, Desclée De Brouwer, 1959; as *Liturgy and Contemplation*, New York, P.J. Kenedy, 1960.

La Philosophie dans le cité. Paris, Alsatia, 1960.

La Philosophie morale: Examen historique et critique des grands systèmes. Paris, Gallimard, 1960; as *Moral Philosophy: An Historical and Critical Survey of the Great Systems*, New York, Scribner, and London, Bles, 1964.

Man's Approach to God (lecture). Latrobe, Pennsylvania, Archabbey Press, 1960.

On the Use of Philosophy: Three Essays. Princeton, New Jersey, Princeton University Press, 1961.

The Education of Man: The Educational Philosophy of Jacques Maritain, edited by Donald and Idella Gallagher. New York, Doubleday, 1962.

Dieu et la permission du mal. Paris, Desclée De Brouwer, 1963; as *God and the Permission of Evil*, Milwaukee, Wisconsin, Bruce, 1966.

Carnet de notes. Paris, Desclée De Brouwer, 1965.

Le Mystère d'Israël et autres essais. Paris, Desclée De Brouwer, 1965.

Challenges and Renewals: Selected Writings, edited by Joseph W. Evans and Leo R. Ward. Notre Dame, Indiana, University of Notre Dame Press, 1966.

A Maritain Reader, edited by Donald and Idella Gallagher. New York, Doubleday, 1966.

Le Paysan de la Garonne: Un Vieux Laïc s'interroge à propos du temps présent. Paris, Desclée De Brouwer, 1966; as *The Peasant of the Garonne: An Old Layman Questions Himself about the Present Time*, London, Chapman and Hall, 1968.

De la grâce et de l'humanité de Jesus. Paris, Desclée De Brouwer, 1967; as *On the Grace and Humanity of Jesus*, London, Oates, 1967; New York, Herder, 1969.

De l'église du Christ: La Personne de l'église et son personnel. Paris, Desclée De Brouwer, 1970; as *On the Church of Christ and Her Personnel*, Notre Dame, Indiana, University of Notre Dame Press, 1973.

Approches sans entraves. Paris, Fayard, 1973.

Other

Georges Rouault: Peintre et lithographe. Paris, Frapier, 1926.

Gino Severini. Paris, Gallimard, 1927.

Jacques Maritain: Emmanuel Mounier: 1922-1939 (letters). Paris, Desclée De Brouwer, 1973.

Editor, *The Living Thoughts of Saint Paul*. New York, Longman, 1941.

Editor, *Journal de Raïssa*. Paris, Desclée De Brouwer, 1964; as *Raïssa's Journal*, Albany, New York, Magi, 1975.

*

Bibliography: *The Achievement of Jacques and Raïssa Maritain: A Bibliography 1906-1961* by Donald and Idella Gallagher, New York, Doubleday, 1962.

Critical Studies: *Les Grandes Amitiés: Souvenirs* and *Les Aventures de la grâce*, by Raïssa Maritain, New York, Éditions de la Maison Française, 2 vols., 1941-44, as *We Have Been Friends Together* and *Adventures in Grace*, New York, Longman, 2 vols., 1942-45; *The Philosophy of Jacques Maritain* by Charles A. Fecher, Westminster, Maryland, Newman Press, 1953; *Jacques Maritain: The Man and His Achievement* edited by Joseph W. Evans, New York, Sheed and Ward, 1963; *Jacques Maritain, Antimodern or Ultramodern: An Historical Analysis of His Critics, His Thought, and His Life* by Brooke Williams Smith, New York, Elsevier, 1976.

*   *   *

Jacques Maritain is one of the 20th century's most well-known and influential Thomists. In importance to that branch of philosophy he ranks with Etienne Gilson. However, Maritain is quite a different sort of Thomist from Gilson and one who has set for himself a very different kind of task. Gilson's major undertaking on behalf of Thomism consisted in his clearing away misconceptions about and prejudices towards it and in removing too various other intellectual obstructions standing in the way of a clear view and fair-minded appraisal, by contemporary thinkers, of Thomism. The Thomism of interest to Gilson is Thomism in its 13th-century form, that is to say that the presentation of the actual historical reality of the thought of Thomas Aquinas is his dominant interest. Now, if the Thomism of Gilson is primarily a scholar's and historian's Thomism, that of Maritain is the Thomism of a man whose foremost occupation is that of debating and arguing with his philosophical contemporaries. In Maritain's writings we find him addressing, through the eyes and in light of Thomistic philosophy, major contemporary issues—issues raised by and in philosophy, science, technology, art, politics, and morality. His primary service to Thomism is that of placing it, at least to a degree greater than before, in the hustle and bustle of the contemporary marketplace of ideas and of arguing for its having a legitimate and important role to play therein.

Maritain's writing spans a wide range of topics. He has contributed books and essays on metaphysics, epistemology, moral theory, political theory, the theory and practice of art, and mysticism, to name only the major philosophical areas. Not only did he work in more than one field of philosophy, but he drew inspiration and ideas from more than a single source; from the work of Thomas Aquinas certainly and primordially, but also from the writings of the mystic John of St. Thomas, from that other noted Thomistic commentator, Cardinal Cajetan, and from the teaching (at the Sorbonne) and writings of Henri Bergson.

As I have said, the major focus of Maritain's thought is to be found in his career-long effort to earn for Thomism a central role in contemporary philosophy and, indeed, in present-day culture generally. This is a culture in which the place and influence of science and technology are enormous, hence a culture which, in that very considerable respect, is vastly different from the medieval culture reflected in historical Thomism. A central facet of Maritain's address to the contemporary intellectual world is his claim that, at the heart of this century's intellectual life, there is a malaise, a malaise reflecting primarily a lack of certainty in our own ability to discover the truth regarding the large questions about reality, morality, and politics which confront us. To overcome this Maritain-diagnosed malaise, he aims for a Christian renaissance, at the core of which is to be the thought of Thomas Aquinas.

Maritain traces the lack of certainty in question back to the 17th century, in particular to the work of René Descartes. This was the time of the advent of science in the form that we have come to know, the period when science took on the role of understanding and definitively explaining the nature of the universe. However, this was also the period in which a profound challenge, initiated in the previous century by a renewed interest in Sextus Empiricus, to science's self-conception as the vehicle of truth and knowledge about reality emerged, that is, the challenge of skepticism. Descartes took it upon himself to refute skepticism and thereby to defend and sustain the conception of science as *the* avenue to sure and certain knowledge of reality. Now, in Descartes's approach to skepticism and to philosophy generally—an approach which has exerted a profound influence upon the subsequent development of philosophy—Maritain argues that there is a metaphysical presupposition which, basic both to Descartes's own thought and to much of philosophy since the time of Descartes, is quite false. Indeed, Maritain characterizes the presupposition in question as "the original sin of modern philosophy." What is it? In a phrase: the theory of ideas. This is the theory that the whole of what is given directly to the mind in experience consists of separate, discrete contents of consciousness—ideas—for example, single units of sight, sound, taste, feeling, and so on. In an important break from the Thomistic and, behind that, Aristotelian views, and indeed from what one presumes is the ordinary layman's view of the matter, the theory of ideas holds that there is no direct contact in experience with what we tend ordinarily to regard as things, for example, pens, paper, houses and so on. There is, on this theory, a gap between mind and thing, a gap to be bridged epistemologically by the correspondence of ideas held in the mind to the objects outside which are said to be the source of (some of) those ideas. This theory of correspondence, however, when exploded in a manner such as that formulated first by Berkeley, and then later by Hume, seems—if the immaterialist antidote prescribed by Berkeley himself be rejected—to result in a skepticism more formidable than that which Descartes first set out to defeat. Maritain's tracing of what he believes to be the metaphysical, epistemological, and ethical indecisiveness of contemporary philosophy to the 17th century can be seen to arrive at two main points: one, the concession, by Descartes and others, to science of the task of discovering the ultimate nature of the universe, and, two, the attempt to combat skepticism on the strength of the theory of ideas. Regarding each of those steps as both contributing importantly to the formation of contemporary philosophy and as fundamentally misguided, Maritain proposes a Thomism which, while geared to address contemporary minds, will itself take neither.

In order adequately to understand and appraise what Maritain has to say to his fellow philosophers of this century, we need to have a working account of what contemporary philosophy is like. As one would expect, there is no adequate simple picture, but, nevertheless, in the complex, multi-faceted association of thinkers and ideas which is present-day philosophy, some central strands can be identified. These are, restricting ourselves to those influential in Maritain's heyday, analysis, phenomenology-existentialism, pragmatism, process philosophy (notably the thought of Whitehead and Bergson), Marxism, and a vestige of idealism. Within each of these there is to be found a variety of sub-fields, for example in the case of the dominant current of contemporary philosophy—analysis—there was, during the period in question here, neo-realism, positivism, logicism, to mention only three, and a corresponding manifold could be listed for each of the other areas of philosophy given above. Furthermore, not only is there dispute and argument between the various types of approach to philosophy mentioned but also, and often more vehemently, within each category and sub-category. In short, the philosophical scene which Maritain addresses does not present any single face and that multifariousness is a central characteristic of contemporary philosophy.

Not having the space even to touch upon Maritain's dealings with all aspects of this century's philosophical work, I will concentrate upon two areas, analysis and Marxism. This choice will enable me to focus upon Maritain's address to two crucial areas in contemporary philosophy and, in so doing, to cover the major facets of Maritain's own thought, too, namely, his theory of knowledge and metaphysics on the one hand and his social-political philosophy on the other.

Within analytical philosophy I have chosen to concentrate upon positivism, for that thrusts immediately to the fore an issue of great interest to Maritain, namely, the place of science in the theory of knowledge and the relations between philosophy and science. And in addition to bringing up such issues, positivism presents a set of views on those questions very different from Maritain's own. The positivist concedes to science sole jurisdiction in investigating the huge cluster of puzzles which have as their general motivation the question, What is the ultimate nature of reality? The positivist maintains that inquiry into the nature of reality cannot be done *a priori*, that it is a factual endeavour and consequently that the proper approach to it is empirical. Now science is the discipline (or, more accurately, the group of disciplines) which is suited to handle empirical investigations and, cumulatively, the sciences do indeed answer the focal question presented above. Finally, the traditional claims made by metaphysicians and theologians on behalf of their respective rights of access to, and proposing solutions for, those problems about the nature of the world are brushed aside by the positivist. Once more to berate Descartes, Maritain identifies *his* work as the beginning of this kind of displacement of theology, and of philosophy too, from the *problematik* called "the nature of reality." Now, of course, not all analytical philosophers adopt a position as extreme as that of the positivists on the status of philosophy, but, by and large, the belief that philosophy has no business dealing with factual matters and its sphere is conceptual is accepted by them.

Such a view, whether in the extreme positivistic version, or in the milder and, in other ways too, different view of other analysts, is totally rejected by Maritain. Dismissing the claim that the hypothetico-empirical methodology characteristic of the sciences is *the* method by which to unlock the secrets of the universe, Maritain elaborates his own account of knowledge and, associated closely with it, of metaphysics. The primary error of the positivist, and of the typical scientist too, Maritain argues, is that of supposing that the two expressions "knowledge" and "empirical knowledge" are synonymous. Maritain does not deny that there is empirical knowledge or that its major locus is the empirical sciences. Rather, he maintains that in order properly to understand the relation between science and philosophy and then between each of those and culture generally, we must recognize that empirical knowledge is but one type of knowledge and an occupant of but one place in a larger and wider cognitional framework within which there is room even for mysticism. In his most important book, *The Degrees of Knowledge*, Maritain argues for the view that there is a hierarchy of kinds of knowledge, each one of which reflects a different type of perspective upon reality. Essentially, the hierarchy in question consists of

1) empirical knowledge of material things,

2) mathematical knowledge, the focus of which is upon quantity and shape and

3) metaphysical knowledge, whose concern is with reality under no specialized heading as that of "matter" or "quantity" but in term of what he regards as the very being of things.

Maritain rejects the view, stemming from Plato, that to each kind of knowledge there corresponds a separate category of things in the world. His own position, by contrast, is that each is the articulation of a specific type of curiosity, that far from each investigating its own separate world, they examine the same world through different eyes, with different frames of reference. For example, the natural scientist investigates things insofar as they are material, the geometer insofar as they have surfaces and are shaped, and so on.

But there is more to Maritain's attack upon the typical 20th-century view of science and upon analytical philosophy's having largely abandoned the field of metaphysics as traditionally conceived. This other, and also radical, line of criticism of the post-Cartesian and, specifically, the contemporary analytical movements in philosophy can best be approached thus: Not all analytical philosophers believe that metaphysics is a lost cause or one that ought never to have been taken up in the first place. For some of these thinkers there is a valuable philosophical role for one kind of metaphysics, provided it is recognized that that metaphysics is through and through a conceptual affair. As a leading spokesman for such a view, P.F. Strawson, puts it, such a metaphysics' work is to "describe the actual structure of our thought about the world." To Maritain, however, such a metaphysics as this is impoverished and not worthwhile. In his eyes, and here the influence of Aquinas is unmistakable, metaphysics deals not with the structure of our thought but with reality itself. For Maritain, as we have seen, there is no Descartes-initiated screen of ideas standing between mind and reality. To Maritain's way of thinking, metaphysics is the study of reality itself, of being considered under no such lesser rubric as, say, matter or consciousness, but considered instead in terms of the unrestricted depth and comprehensiveness that he believes appropriate to being. As such a general undertaking, then, metaphysics must be seen as, for Maritain, the systematic expression of that pre-thematic and pre-conscious curiosity to which Aristotle refers in his *Metaphysics*. It is the fully comprehensive articulation of what another influential Thomist of this century, Bernard Lonergan, has called the "pure, unrestricted desire to know" the whole truth about the whole of reality. However, following Aquinas, Maritain does not believe that metaphysics, that is to say inquiry through ratiocination alone, can satisfy this unrestricted desire for knowledge. Only in theology, he argues, can satisfaction in the form of appropriate knowledge be found. In effect, therefore, not only is Maritain rejecting the positivist-championed banishment of philosophy (metaphysics especially) from the field of knowledge but he is maintaining that a fuller, deeper understanding of reality is to be found in philosophy—at least in what is often called the *philosophia perennis*—than in science, and that a still further and fuller level of understanding awaits us in theology.

Can Maritain defend this, or is it to remain only the re-proclamation of an ancient dream? At the center of Maritain's proposed charter for metaphysics is his view of the concept of existence. Put in the terminology of traditional Thomism, his is a metaphysics of *esse*, of existence, not a metaphysics, such as has been typical after Kant and recently postulated again by Strawson, of essences or concepts. This is to say that, therefore, the linchpin of the Thomistic metaphysics that Maritain is advocating is the proposition that, in addition to the viewpoint of the theorist who considers things insofar as they are living (the biologist) and the viewpoint of the theorist who considers things insofar as they have a molecular structure (the chemist) and so on for the whole gamut of the sciences, there is also, and in fact far more basic than any possible scientific perspective, the viewpoint of the theorist who considers things insofar as they are existing. For this to be defended it will require success on the following issue, namely, the justification of the belief that the word "existence" refers to a property or attribute of things, just as legitimately as words like "size" and "weight" and "volume" do. It is a metaphysics built on the presupposition that existence is meaningfully predicated of the things in the world, that, for example, a genuine and substantive contribution is made to our understanding when it is maintained that, in addition to being yellow, ruled, rectangular, smooth-surfaced, of such-and-such dimensions and weight, the paper upon which I am now writing *exists*. Without independent justification of the view that existence is a property of things, a metaphysics of *esse* is devoid of content. Now, formidable obstacles confront him who would undertake this task, obstacles in the form of arguments offered in the 18th century by Hume and Kant and, subsequently, by many other philosophers. Indeed if any single proposition could be said to enjoy near-universal endorsement in the philosophical heritage coming down to us from Hume and Kant—roughly, analytical philosophy—it is the proposition: Existence is not a predicate. However, it is not a necessary proposition and hence there is no *a priori* reason for its having to be true. But, even with its contingent status noted, if Maritain or any other philosopher is to be successful in instituting a renaissance of Thomistic metaphysics, in the sense of providing for such a metaphysics a prominent place on the center-stage of contemporary philosophy, he must defeat, or at least successfully block, the Hume- and Kant-inspired arguments for the non-predicability of existence. It seems to me that neither of these has yet been done.

In the overlapping areas of moral, social, and political theory, Maritain is an advocate of a natural law system. This, in its essence, is the view that certain kinds of actions are, given the nature of human beings, right for man to do while others, judged by the same yardstick, are not. Furthermore, natural law theory maintains that each person is intuitively aware of these moral distinctions, or, at least, becomes so aware, and can recognize their applicability to certain specific courses of action which might arise or be contemplated. In regard to Marxism and other totalitarian political systems, Maritain argues for their being mistaken and unjustified, on the grounds of their neglecting a key distinction between two facets of human nature: on the one hand, the concept of man's being an individual and, on the other, the concept of his being a person. (This distinction, as worked out by Maritain, amounts to his application to the social-political sphere of his mind-body theory.) Both facets, he argues, are legitimate but they are not equal. Following Aquinas, he argues for the dominance, in the life of the individual, of the latter. The concept of being an individual involves adaptation to political theory of the maxim from Aristotle's *Physics* that matter (as opposed to form, or shape) individualizes, that is, renders something to be the particular member of a type or species that it actually is. Being an instance of a type or a member of a species makes the individual conceptually secondary to that type or species itself. Applied to political theory, then, Maritain argues that it follows that the rights of the political community, considered as the natural group to which the individual belongs, outrank those of the man himself, insofar, that is, as he is viewed under the guise of his individuality, as defined above. But, while this subservience seems to be an integral part of any (natural) community-subject relationship, it is, Maritain argues, not itself the whole truth of the matter and to suppose otherwise would be false and a serious distortion of the relation between man and community. But it is of precisely this falsehood and this distortion that he believes totalitarian political regimes justly stand accused. The necessary counterpoint, the concept of man's being a person, is, for Maritain, essentially a theological notion, for it is the idea of man's being ensouled, with the word "soul" understood as having the spiritual connotations associated with it in Christianity. As a soul, a person essentially, one is not subservient to the political community, Maritain argues; one is not a means to some outside end but rather an end in oneself. And, Maritain continues, a just political system, one in accordance with the natural law, will accommodate this dimension of human nature, a dimension which it is an important part of Maritain's Thomistic metaphysics to demonstrate and defend.

It will have been evident at many points in this essay that, as a philosopher, Maritain is a traditionalist. However, it would be quite mistaken to suppose that those contemporary philosophers with whom he is in profound disagreement, the analysts for instance, are, therefore, non-traditionalists. On the contrary, it seems to me that, while perhaps innovative in their methods and techniques of tackling philosophical puzzles and while believing certain segments of their predecessors' work not properly to be the business of philosophy at all, analytical philosophers—with the exception, perhaps, of Wittgenstein and Dewey and a few others—are traditionalists in, by and large, taking for their problems many of the issues which have vexed the philosophers of the past. Hence it would be wrong to view Maritain's place in 20th-century philosophy as that of one calling his contemporaries, in analytical philosophy say, back to the tradition, or even to the mainstream of the tradition. This is for the reason that it is, in epistemological and metaphysical matters at any rate, down to those very analysts that the tradition has come. Maritain's recall is, rather, to a very specific portion of the tradition, the philosophy of Thomas Aquinas. And, to be sure, while Maritain advocates a dynamic Thomism and not one congealed in certain 13th-century texts, yet, nevertheless, as regards the substantive content of Aquinas's philosophy, what Maritain is ultimately committed to is an ahistoricist view of it as the pinnacle of philosophy's achievement and, furthermore, as an achievement to be passed on, without substantive change and certainly without dismemberment, to all future generations. And that is a very large claim, implying as it does that, through the course of the Western philosophical tradition, no substantial change on doctrinal matters can rightly take place.

—David O'Connor

MASLOW, A(braham) H(arold). American psychologist. Born in Brooklyn, New York, 1 April 1908. Educated at the University of Wisconsin, Madison, B.A. 1930, M.A. 1931, Ph.D. 1934. Married Bertha Goodman in 1928; 2 daughters. Assistant, University of Wisconsin, 1930-35; Carnegie Teaching Fellow, Columbia Teachers College, New York, 1935-37; Instructor to Associate Professor of Psychology, Brooklyn College, 1937-51; Associate Professor and Professor of Psychology, Brandeis University, Waltham, Massachusetts, 1951-69 (Chairman of the Department, 1951-61). Resident Fellow, Laughlin Foundation, 1969-70. President, Massachusetts Psychological Association, 1960-62, New England Psychological Association, 1962-63, and American Psychological Association, 1967. Named Humanist of the Year by the American Humanist Association in 1967. Honorary doctorate: Xavier University, Cincinnati. *Died 8 June 1970.*

PUBLICATIONS

Psychology

Principles of Abnormal Psychology: The Dynamics of Psychic Illness, with Béla Mittelmann. New York, Harper, 1941.
The Social Personality Inventory: A Test for Self-Esteem in Women. Palo Alto, California, Consulting Psychologists Press, 1942.
The S-I Test (A Measure of Psychological Security-Insecurity). Palo Alto, California, Consulting Psychologists Press, 1951.
Motivation and Personality. New York, Harper, 1954.
Toward a Psychology of Being. Princeton, New Jersey, Van Nostrand, 1962.
Religion, Values, and Peak-Experiences (lectures). Columbus, Ohio State University Press, 1964; London, Penguin, 1976.
Eupsychian Management: A Journal. Homewood, Illinois, R.D. Irwin, 1965.
The Psychology of Science: A Reconnaissance. New York, Harper, 1966.
The Farther Reaches of Human Nature. New York, Viking Press, 1971; London, Penguin, 1976.
Humanistic Psychology: Interviews with Maslow, Murphy, and Rogers, with Willard B. Frick. Columbus, Ohio, Merrill, 1971.
Dominance, Self-Esteem, Self-Actualization: Germinal Papers of A.H. Maslow, edited by Richard J. Lowry. Monterey, California, Brooks Cole, 1973.

Other

The Journals of A.H. Maslow, edited by Richard J. Lowry. Monterey, California, Brooks Cole, 2 vols., 1979. (contains a bibliography).

Editor, *New Knowledge in Human Values.* New York, Harper, 1959.
Editor, with Hung-Min Chiang, *The Healthy Personality: Readings.* New York, Van Nostrand and Reinhold, 1969.

*

Bibliography: in *The Journals of A.H. Maslow,* 1979.

Critical Studies: *The Third Force: The Psychology of Abraham Maslow* by Frank J. Goble, New York, Grossman, 1970; *Humanism in Personology: Allport, Maslow, and Murray* by Salvatore R. Maddi, Chicago, Aldine, 1972; *A.H. Maslow: An Intellectual Portrait* by Richard J. Lowry, Monterey, California, Brooks Cole, 1973.

*   *   *

The remarkably broad range of A.H. Maslow's clinical, experimental, and theoretical interests reveals a central and persisting concern: the emancipation of science and especially psychology from proclivities to narrowness, rigidity, and monotonous triviality. To take a familiar analogy from architecture, it is as if an architect pondered the needs of a group of human beings engaged in some work and then designed a building that sensibly housed them in a way that helped them to execute their tasks efficiently in a congenial atmosphere. As this group grows and alters over time, enlarging its functions and encountering new needs, the building begins to stifle further growth. Concepts, categories, and theories which were initially provocative often became obsessive dogmas and obstacles to fuller understanding. Maslow's writings resist the facile reduction of human experience to a few set theories (as shown in the more rigid behavioral procedures) or to ossified categories (rampant in schools derived from Freudian manuals). He welcomed and espoused a "Third Force" in psychology which is willing to explore wider perspectives and more dynamic models of human conduct.

While studying comparative animal behavior in the 1930's, Maslow became interested in psychological problems which could not be clarified or tackled by the traditional scientific tools. He began to formulate a fundamental standpoint that evolved into an expansive *Weltanschauung.* He cautioned that behavioral studies of animals can be applied to human behavior only with great circumspection. The human being has no explicit animal instincts, though he has "tags and remnants" which Maslow called "instinctoid." Furthermore, anthropology enhanced cultural relativism in two ways: psychological concepts of normality, pathology, abnormality, and deviance are culture-bound partly because the task of disentangling biological bases from cultural superstructure is well-nigh impossible; and the present state of social psychology does not allow speaking of the "generalized human"—there are only particular men and women. All this suggested the need for more creative co-operation between disciplines if genuinely scientific judgments are to become possible.

Maslow's mature thinking first appeared in his *theory of motivation* (1943). He set forth 13 propositions upon which a sound motivation theory must be based. These include the recognition that the individual is an organized unity, that desires are usually means to ends and not ends in themselves, that "ultimate desires" differ less between humans than their conscious expressions indicate, and that any conscious desire may be a channel for a variety of purposes. Thus any act is likely to show multiple motivation. Since one desire rapidly replaces its satisfied predecessor, the human being is seldom completely satisfied and at motivational rest. Desires not only succeed one another but tend to arrange themselves into a "hierarch of prepotency." This undermines attempts to devise an atomistic list of drives, requiring instead that motivation be understood in terms of goals or needs which are characteristically human. According to Maslow, the *hierarchical prepotency of basic needs* falls readily into five sets: physiological, safety, love, esteem, and self-actualization. These goals are prepotent roughly in this order though varying with each individual. The most prepotent goal will tend to monopolize consciousness and the capacities of the organism until it is fulfilled to some degree. As it is satisfied, the next desire in the prepotent hierarchy will begin to emerge by degrees. If these goals are thwarted by external agency, internal confusion, or socio-cultural conditioning, emergency reactions set in and, when sufficiently acute, manifest themselves as psychopathologies.

A characteristic example of Maslow's application of his motivation theory is his consideration of *the authoritarian personality*. In accepting the Platonic view that much so-called irrational behavior can be understood as rational when one notices the assumptions upon which it is based, Maslow saw the authoritarian as a person who pictures the world as a jungle in which every condition and actor is dangerous and threatening. Hence, for the authoritarian, the alternatives are to fear or be feared. Others are seen in negative terms and ranked along a spectrum from inferior to superior. Seen in this one-dimensional way, the logical responses of the authoritarian are slave-like and masochistic in respect to superiors (since he appreciates why they are harsh) and cold or even brutal towards inferiors (since love, kindness, or sympathy is a sign of weakness). Those with other scales of values, and especially democratic individuals who respect others and rely less on external tokens of power, are threatening to the authoritarian. For Maslow, the facts that the satisfactions sought by the authoritarian are unattainable (he cannot manage the whole world) and that humans cannot be accommodated within his simplistic spectrum demonstrate that his world-view is false. Nevertheless, his "sickness" can be cured only if he wants it, most alleged cures being little more than the removal of specific neurotic or psychosomatic symptoms.

In *Toward a Psychology of Being*, Maslow set out the major conclusions and implications of his thought. As a participant in "Third Force" psychology, Maslow accepted the assumptions that each human being has an essential human nature, in part species-bound and in part unique to the individual, that an expanded science can discover this nature, and that this nature is what we could generally recognize as intrinsically good. Evil is most often the frustration of the expression of this nature. Science, in revealing this nature, can show what aids its actualization, and this means that authentic science (as distinguished from crude reductionism and simplistic model-building) can eventually supply an ethics or a set of values for human beings. To do so, however, science must move away from "means-centering" to "problem-centering," from research developed with the aid of techniques already available to research based on important problems to be solved—in a phrase, from means to ends. Psychopathology alone cannot tell human beings how to think and act, but the careful study of individuals who are basically healthy can uncover mankind's essential humanness. If human nature is at root neutral or good, Maslow maintained, it ought to be possible to give direction to humans, to provide a *naturalistic ethics of goal-fulfillment*. Such a project requires the abandonment of orthodox psycho-social categories, such as "sickness" and "health", in favor of expanded concepts of "human diminution" and "self-actualization" or "full-humanness." Thus, "if you tell me you have a personality problem I am not certain until I know you better whether to say 'Good!' or 'I'm sorry.' It depends on the reasons."

Maslow divided hierarchically organized needs or goals into two general classes: *deficiency needs* and *being needs*. Human beings function much of the time out of a sense of inadequacy. They seek to supply what they think they lack from the external world. Psychopathology originates in repeated frustration in every attempt to repair the initial feeling of deficiency. When deficiency needs are fulfilled to some degree through their satisfaction or through a change of perception, being needs emerge to be satisfied through self-actualization of potentialities, capacities, talents, and fulfillment of a sense of mission, call, or destiny. A crucial feature of Maslow's distinction between deficiency needs and being needs is that the same need could function at different times as an expression of a sense of deficiency or of a sense of being. It is in his way of coping with both his sense of deficiency and his sense of being that a self-actualizing man reveals his enormous capacity for self-dependence. The self-actualizing individual is marked by an acute perception of reality, increased acceptance of self and of others, problem-centering, greater spontaneity and detachment, heightened enjoyment of privacy, freshness of appreciation and creativity, and effortless identity with humanity.

The self-actualizing individual has more *peak-experiences*, intense awareness of self and the world that may manifest themselves as creative excitement or Taoist calm in which "perception can be relatively ego-transcending, self-forgetful, egoless." Such individuals are metamotivated, i.e., beyond striving. For Maslow, most religions have received their original impulse from Founders who lived out extended peak-experiences. While the organizational side of religious traditions serves to share the fruits of such experiences with others, it often loses vitality through repressive dogmas and ritualism that may restrict the actualizing tendency of human beings. At the same time, the dichotomy between science and religion, in which the former is allegedly value-free and the latter the exclusive custodian of values (and thus science-free), harms both science and religion while inhibiting the intrinsic process of *self-actualization*.

In *The Farther Reaches of Human Nature*, Maslow set out a theory of *metamotivation* in which he hypothesized that self-actualizing individuals are motivated in profounder ways than the mere gratification of basic needs. Such individuals are devoted to a task or vocation, often feeling fortunate and perhaps unworthy in performing it, though at this level the dichotomy between work and play dissolves, for this "work" is a defining characteristic of these individuals and so instantiates intrinsic, self-validating values. The distinctions between self and not-self, between internal and external, are transcended. Self-actualization is more a means than an end, for human nature is dynamic, not static. Maslow's attempt to elucidate this elusive nature led him to reconsider the premisses of traditional psychologies, the compartmentalization of disciplines, and even the distinction between science and religion.

Maslow held that many of his insights were not new but could be found in Pythagoras and Plato, in Indian philosophies and Taoism. But he thought that while philosophers, poets and mystics had uttered many truths, in the 20th century they spoke only to the converted. "Science is the only way we have of shoving truth down the reluctant throat." He sought to substitute dynamic concepts for static models and to return the ethical dimension to an expanded science. He repeatedly called his work preliminary and even premature because insufficiently tested, and he tried to formulate his intuitions as testable theses. All of Maslow's work showed a tenacious concern to learn from self-actualizing people, to base psychology and its cognate disciplines on human health, not sickness, on potentiality, not limitation, asserting that the latter in each case must be understood in terms of the former. Maslow believed essentially that: "Self-actualizing people, those who have come to a high level of maturation, health, and self-fulfillment, have so much to teach us that sometimes they seem almost like a different breed of human beings" (*Toward a Psychology of Being*).

—R.N. Iyer

MATTINGLY, Garrett. American historian. Born in Washington, D.C., 6 May 1900. Educated at Harvard University, Cambridge, Massachusetts, B.A. 1923, M.A., 1926, Ph.D., 1935 (Sheldon Fellow, 1922-24). Served with the 43rd Infantry, United States Army, 1918-19; United States Naval Reserves, 1942-

45. Married Gertrude McCollum in 1928. Taught at Northwestern University, Evanston, Illinois, 1926-28, and Long Island University, New York, 1928-42; Professor and Head, Division of Social Philosophy, Cooper Union, New York, 1946-48; Professor, from 1948, and William R. Shepherd Professor of European History, 1959-62, Columbia University, New York. Recipient: Guggenheim Fellowship, 1937, 1946, 1960; Special Pulitzer Citation, 1960. Fellow, Royal Society of Literature, London. *Died 18 December 1962.*

PUBLICATIONS

History

Bernard De Voto: A Preliminary Appraisal. Boston, Little Brown, 1938.
Catherine of Aragon. Boston, Little Brown, 1941; London, Cape, 1942.
Renaissance Diplomacy. Boston, Houghton Mifflin, and London, Cape, 1955.
The Armada. Boston, Houghton Mifflin, 1959; as *The Defeat of the Spanish Armada,* London, Cape, 1959.
The Invincible Armada and Elizabethan England. Ithaca, New York, Cornell University Press, 1963.
Renaissance Profiles, with others, edited by J.H. Plumb. New York, Harper, n.d.

Other

Editor, *Further Supplement* to *Calendar of Letters, Despatches, and State Papers, Relating to the Negotiations between England an Spain, Preserved in the Archives at Simancas and Elsewhere.* London, Longman, 1940.

*

Bibliography: in *From the Renaissance to the Counter-Reformation: Essays in Honor of Garrett Mattingly* edited by Charles Howard Carter, New York, Random House, 1965; London, Cape, 1966.

* * *

Garrett Mattingly wrote history as literature, a distinction that might be lost on those who have not witnessed the periodic battles historians engage in concerning the nature of their discipline. As practiced by Mattingly, history was part of the humanities, not the social sciences; it was important to the learning of all men, not just a closed circle of scholars. The best history, he felt, should thus have a broad popular appeal, and to this end he stressed the narrative style of history over the analytical.

Mattingly's prose was exceedingly fine and popular. *The Armada* was a best seller, winning a special citation from the Pulitzer Prize Committee, and *Catherine of Aragon* was only slightly less charming as a piece of literature. Both are also fine history, for Mattingly was a careful scholar, but his determination to bring history to the general public led him to the avoidance of some academic conventions that serve legitimate scholarly purpose. Footnotes were not allowed to blemish the pages of *The Armada;* those of *Catherine of Aragon* are concealed at the back and banished altogether from the paperback edition. And few modern historians draw from their sources passages like the following from *Catherine of Aragon:* "The big youngster, Francis of Angouleme—Francis I, now of France—was ready to comfort the widow. His long sharp nose, like a humorous fox's nose, poked into her darkened bedroom, his bold, sly eyes appraised the form huddled under the counterpane while the skillful tongue mingled jest and irony with admiring wooing."

At times Mattingly's subject did not lend itself to the charming narrative style possible in treatments of single events or persons.

Such occurred with *Renaissance Diplomacy,* of necessity a scholarly analysis because of the complexity and difficulty of the ideas studied. Yet here, too, Mattingly chose to make alterations in his original, cutting its length in order to make it acceptable to a commercial press. The alternative of publication by a university press would have meant, in his view, cloistering the work in academia and suffering it to remain unread. Nevertheless, *Renaissance Diplomacy* demonstrated that Mattingly never sacrificed scholarly analysis, indeed never believed that good narrative and good analysis were mutually exclusive. He had always preferred to ground his work in primary sources, and his careful research and mastery of a subject were the preconditions of his striving to make his prose pleasant.

All of Mattingly's work deals with the Renaissance, for him the critical period of transition from the ordered, hierarchical, and spiritually oriented medieval society to the more heterogeneous, secularly oriented modern society fragmented into autonomous sovereign states. In *Renaissance Diplomacy* Mattingly showed the convergence in medieval society of three currents of tradition—ecclesiastical, feudal, and imperial—described as the collaboration of revelation, custom, and reason. The Renaissance revival of classical scholarship, the religious revolution, and the idea of national sovereignty all served to undermine this collaboration and the universality of the Roman and Catholic heritages. Mattingly analyzed the legal and diplomatic changes in this transformation centering on the appearance of the resident ambassador and the beginning of modern diplomacy.

As Mattingly could be analytical without overwhelming his narrative, so he could, as in the compelling literature of *The Armada,* give details on stores of biscuit and dried fish and the effects of green barrel staves without obscuring his characters. He was always chiefly concerned with individuals, with human character being tested by adversity. His favorite characters appear to be the losers in the historical drama, the defenders of the Spanish, Catholic order against the emerging English, Protestant dominance. This generalization can be contradicted by his admiration for Elizabeth I and distaste for Henry Guise, but it holds true in the affection he showed for Catherine, his generosity towards Philip II, and the great warmth and respect with which he treated Medina Sidonia. If this did not mean sympathy for the Catholic, medieval order, it did show that Mattingly was drawn to the men and women who inherited and defended that order for the way they accepted their duty and the honor, courage, and dedication they showed in the face of defeat.

Mattingly never worshipped success or used his craft to advance fashionable themes, whether they be the march of progress and democracy or dialectical materialism. In the patterns of the past one might detect the irresistible or determined, but Mattingly always left room in the scheme for chance or accident, for human will or knowledge to play their role in shaping human destiny. Because of this he felt it was important for man to enrich his knowledge through the study of history. He advocated the study of world history as the means of understanding the culture of all peoples, and he was concerned that American historians, by failing to appreciate the importance of connecting American history to Western civilization and its European background, lacked knowledge of the forces and ideas linking America to a common Western destiny.

—Frank M. Baglione

———————

MAURRAS, Charles (Marie Photius). French political philosopher, poet and critic. Born in Martigues, 20 April 1868. Educated at a Roman Catholic college in Aix-en-Provence, graduated 1885; studied in Paris. Critic and journalist: correspondent in Athens for the Olympic Games for *La Gazette de France,* 1896; Co-Founding Editor, *Action Française* newspaper, 1908-

44; welcomed the Vichy government, but jailed for treason in 1945: released, 1952, for ill health. Member Académie Française, 1938. *Died 16 November 1952.*

PUBLICATIONS

Collections

Oeuvres capitales. Paris, Flammarion, 4 vols., 1954.

Political Philosophy

Le Chemin de Paradis. Paris, Flammarion, 1895.
Trois idées politiques. Paris, Crès, 1898.
Décentralisation. Paris, Revue Encyclopédique, 1898.
Enquête sur la monarchie. Paris, Bibliothèque des Oeuvres Politiques, 1901.
Anthinéa, d'Athènes à Florence. Paris, Flammarion, 1901.
L'Avenir de l'intelligence. Paris, Flammarion, 1905.
Un Débat nouveau sur la République et la décentralisation. Toulouse, Société Provinciale d'Éditions, 1905.
Libéralisme et Liberté, démocratie, et peuple. Paris, Librairie d'Action Française, 1905.
Le Dilemme de Marc Sangnier. Paris, Nouvelle Librairie Nationale, 1906.
Si le coupe de force est possible. Paris, Nouvelle Librairie Nationale, 1910.
Idées royalistes. Paris, Librairie d'Action Française, 1910.
Kiel et Tanger. Paris, Bibliothèque des Oeuvres Politiques, 1910.
Une Campagne royaliste au "Figaro." Paris, Nouvelle Librairie Nationale, 1911.
La Politique religieuse. Paris, Nouvelle Librairie Nationale, 1912.
Athènes antique. Paris, Boccard, 1913.
L'Action Française et la religion catholique; Les Éléments d'une imposture; Agressions libérales, démocratiques, sillonistes; Les Maîtres de "L'Action Française"; L'Action Française et la morale. Paris, Nouvelle Librairie Nationale, 1913.
Quand les Française ne s'aimaient pas. Paris, Bibliothèque des Oeuvres Politiques, 1913.
Les Conditions de la victoire. Paris, Nouvelle Librairie Nationale, 4 vols., 1916-18.
Le Pape, la guerre, et la paix. Paris, Nouvelle Librairie Nationale, 1917.
Aux Républicains de Russie. Paris, Librairie d'Action Française, 1917.
La Part du combattant. Paris, Nouvelle Librairie Nationale, 1917.
La Paix de sang. Paris, Librairie d'Action Française, 1918.
Les Chefs socialistes pendant la guerre. Paris, Nouvelle Librairie Nationale, 1918.
Les Trois aspects du Président Wilson. Paris, Nouvelle Librairie Nationale, 1920.
Romantisme et révolution. Paris, Nouvelle Librairie Nationale, 1922.
L'Allée des philosophes. Paris, Crès, 1923.
Les Nuits d'epreuve et la mémoire de l'état. Paris, Nouvelle Librairie Nationale, 1924.
La Violence et le mesure. Paris, Librairie d'Action Française, 1924.
Pour en sortir. Paris, Librairie d'Action Française, 1925.
Le Mauvais traité. Paris, Capitole, 1926.
Réflexions sur l'ordre en France. Paris, Au Pigeonnier, 1927.
Le Tombeau du prince. Paris, Bibliothèque des Oeuvres Politiques, 1927.
La Politique 1926-1927. Paris, Bibliothèque des Oeuvres Politiques, 1927.
Petit manuel de l'"Enquête sur la monarchie.". Paris, Bibliothèque des Oeuvres Politiques, 1928.

Les Princes des Nuées. Paris, Taillandier, 1928.
Corps glorieux; ou, Vertu de la perfection. Paris, Pichou, 1928.
Napoléon avec ou contre la France. Paris, Flammarion, 1929.
Le "Bibliophile" Barthou. Paris, Capitole, 1929.
Lettre à Schramek. Paris, Capitole, 1929.
De Demos à César. Paris, Capitole, 1930.
Meditation sur la politique de Jeanne d'Arc. Paris, Cadran, 1931.
Pour la défense nationale. Paris, Capitole, 1931.
Casier judiciaire d'A. Briand. Paris, Capitole, 1931.
Le Quadrilatère. Paris, Flammarion, 1931.
Au Signe de Flore (selections). Paris, Les Oeuvres Representatives, 1931.
Nos raisons. Paris, Librairie d'Action Française, 1933.
Dictionnaire politique et critique. Paris, Cité des Livres, 5 vols., 1934.
Louis XIV et la France. Paris, Cadran, 1936.
L'Amitié de Platon. Paris, Cadran, 1937.
Les Vergers sur la mer. Paris, Flammarion, 1937.
Mes Idées politiques. Paris, Fayard, 1937.
Devant l'Allemagne éternelle. Paris, L'Étoile, 1937.
Jeanne d'Arc, Louis XIV, Napoléon. Paris, Flammarion, 1937.
La Dentelle du rempart. Paris, Grasset, 1937.
Louis XIV ou l'homme-roi. Paris, Cadran, 1939.
Pages africaines. Paris, Sorlot, 1940.
La Seule France. Paris, Lardanchet, 1941.
Sans la muraille des cyprès. Arles, Gilbert, 1941.
De la colère à la justice. Geneva, Milieu du Monde, 1942.
Avenir de l'intelligence française. Paris, Vox, 1943.
Vers l'Espagne de Franco. Paris, Le Livre Moderne, 1943.
Pour un réveil français. Arles, À l'Ombre des Cyprès, 1943.
L'Allemagne et nous. Paris, Verités Françaises, 1945.
Réponse à Paul Claudel. Paris, Éditions de Midi, 1945.
Quelques pensées de Charles Maurras. Paris, Éditions de Midi, 1945.
Procès de Charles Maurras et de Maurice Pujo devant la Cour de Justice du Rhône. Paris, Verités Françaises, 1945.
La Patriotisme ne doit pas tuer la patrie. Paris, Éditions de la Seule France, 1946.
Les Deux Justices; ou, Notre "J'accuse." Paris, Éditions de la Seule France, 1947.
Le Parapluie de Marianne. Paris, Éditions de la Seule France, 1948.
L'Ordre et le désordre. Geneva, Troix Anneaux, 1948.
Reflexions sur la révolution de 1789. Paris, Plon, 1948.
Inscriptions sur nos ruines. Paris, Éditions de la Girouette, 1949.
Au grand juge de France, with Maurice Pujo. Paris, Éditions de la Seule France, 1949.
Pour réveiller le grand juge. Paris, Éditions de la Seule France, 1951.
Les Mensonges de l' "Expert" Verdenal au procès de Lyon. Paris, Éditions de la Seule France, 1951.
Jarres de Biot. Paris, Lanauve de Tartas, 1951.
Le Guignon français. Paris, Amis des Chemin de Paradis, 1952.
Votre bel aujourd'hui. Paris, Flammarion, 1953.
Le Bienheureux Pie X, sauveur de France. Paris, Plon, 1953.
The French Right (from De Maistre to Maurras), edited by J.S. McClelland. London, Cape, 1970.
(Selections), edited by Jacques Vier. Paris, Nouvelles Éditions Latines, 1978.

Verse

Pour Psyché. Paris, Champion, 1911.
Inscriptions. Paris, Librairie de France, 1921; revised edition, 1931.
Le Mystère d'Ulysse. Paris, Nouvelle Revue Française, 1923.
La Bataille de la Marne: Ode historique. Paris, Champion,

1923.

La Musique intérieure.   Paris, Grasset, 1925.

Quatre poèmes de Eurydice.   Paris, Trident, 1937.

Où suis-je?   Geneva, Anglore, 1945.

Au'devant de la nuit (as Léon Rameau).   Lyons, Lardanchet, 1946.

Le Cintre de Riom.   Geneva, Trois Anneaux, 1946.

Music Within Me.   London, Right Review, 1946.

Prière à deux voix; Le Lai d'Arioste.   Arles, Gilbert, 1950.

Pour l'honneur d'un fleuve "apostat."   Roanne, Amis des Chemin de Paradis, 1950.

À Mes vieux oliviers.   Roanne, Amis du Chemin de Paradis, 1951.

Ni Peste ni colère.   Roanne, Amis du Chemin de Paradis, 1951.

La Balance intérieure.   Lyons, Lardanchet, 1952.

Dear Garment.   Plush, Dorset, Mélissa Press, 1965.

Other

Théodore Aubanel.   Paris, Savine, 1889.

Jean Moréas.   Paris, Plon, 1891.

Les Amants de Venise, George Sand et Musset.   Paris, Flammarion, 1902.

L'Etang de Berre.   Paris, Flammarion, 1915.

Le Conseil du Dante.   Paris, Bibliothèque des Grands Auteurs, 1920.

Tombeaux.   Paris, Nouvelle Librairie Nationale, 1921.

Poètes.   Paris, Le Divan, 1923.

Ironie et poésie.   Paris, Au Pigeonnier, 1923.

Anatole France, politique et poète.   Paris, Plon, 1924.

Barbarie et poésie.   Paris, Bibliothèque des Grands Auteurs, 1926.

Gaulois, Germains, et Latins.   Paris, Bibliothèque des Grands Auteurs, 1926.

Lorsque Hugo eut les cent ans.   Paris, Lesage, 1926.

Un Débat sur le romantisme avec Raymond de la Tailhède.   Paris, Flammarion, 1928.

Mar e Lono.   Paris, Cadran, 1930.

Mistralismes.   Paris, Nouvelle Revue Française, 1930.

Quatres nuits de Provence.   Paris, Flammarion, 1931.

Tryptique de Paul Bourget.   Paris, Redier, 1931.

Paysages et cités de Provence.   Paris, Didier et Richard, 1932.

Prologue d'un essai sur la critique.   Paris, La Porte Étroite, 1932.

Le Long du Rhône et de la mer.   Paris, Cadran, 1934.

Dans Arles au temps des fées.   Paris, Cadran, 1937.

Jacques Bainville et Paul Bourget.   Paris, Cadran, 1937.

La Montagne provençale.   Paris, Cadran, 1938.

Discours de réception a l'Académie.   Paris, Plon, 1939.

Aux Mânes d'un maitre.   Paris, Lardanchet, 1941.

Mistral.   Paris, Aubier, 1941.

La Contre-Révolution spontanée.   Paris, Lardanchet, 1943.

Paysages mistraliens.   Paris, Didier et Richard, 1944.

Poésie et vérité.   Paris, Lardanchet, 1944.

Marseille en Provence.   Paris, Lardanchet, 1946.

Une Promotion de Judas.   Paris, Éditions de la Seule France, 1948.

Maurice Barrès.   Paris, Éditions de la Seule France, 1948.

Pour un jeune français.   Paris, Amiot-Dumont, 1949.

Mon jardin qui s'est souvenu.   Paris, Lanauve de Tartas, 1949.

Tragi-comédie de ma surdité.   Paris, Lanauve de Tartas, 1951.

Le Beau jeu des reviviscences.   Paris, Stanislas Rey, 1952.

Pascal puni: Conte infernal.   Paris, Flammarion, 1953.

Lettres de Prison.   Paris, Flammarion, 1958.

Maurice Barrès, Charles Maurras: La République ou le roi: Correspondance inédite 1888-1923, edited by Hélène and Nicole Maurras.   Paris, Plon, 1970.

*

Critical Studies: *Maurras jusqu'à l'Action Française* by Léon S.

Rodiez, Paris, Bonne, 1957; *Three Against the Third Republic: Sorel, Barrès, and Maurras* by Michael Curtis, Princeton, New Jersey, Princeton University Press, 1959; *Maurras et notre temps* by H. Massis, Paris, Plon, 2 vols., 1961; *Action Française: Royalism and Reaction in Twentieth Century France* by Eugen Weber, Stanford, California, Stanford University Press, 1962; *Maurras: L'Église et l'ordre* by Pol Vandromme, Paris, Centurion, 1965; *Maurras et son temps* by James McCearney, Paris, Michel, 1977; *Charles Maurras: Un Itinéraire spirituel* by Eric Vatré, Paris, Nouvelles Éditions Latines, 1978.

*   *   *

T.S. Eliot once wrote that the most attractive ideas in fascism were found in the works of Charles Maurras. This affinity is understandable since Maurras, advocate of "integral nationalism" and the man who defined the doctrines of the Action Française, was a critic of liberalism who had come to politics by way of his literary interests.

Maurras, who began his career as a classical scholar, came to see the problems of French society in terms of a classic-romantic dichotomy. He saw as the greatest period of French history that time when as the leader of European civilization she had embodied the classical spirit. This period ended when classicism was overthrown by the romanticism of the French Revolution which had introduced anarchy and liberalism into politics, foreign standards and tastes into art, and superficial, fashionable ideas in place of traditional values. It followed, then, that the solution to the anarchy, decadence, and weakness, introduced by the Revolution and institutionalized in the Third French Republic which Maurras despised, was to be found in a revival of the thought and style of classical France.

In Maurras's analysis the chief intellectual threat to a unified and strong France came from romanticism and Protestantism, both of which placed individual conscience above society and unrestrained expression over the classical virtues of form and discipline. Maurras saw both as un-French and largely German in origin, making Germany France's intellectual as well as her political enemy.

On romanticism Maurras laid the blame for the anarchy in society and politics that made mankind cowardly, weak, and effeminate. It had exalted the worst in woman's character, her weakness and sentimentality, while the womanly virtues of sweetness, patience, and resignation were swept away before the new woman—crude, unabashed, claiming sexual freedom, imitating men—living outside the order of nature and abdicating her responsibilities to it. Romanticism's effect on men had been to make them effeminate, soft, and decadent so that the society as a whole had become too willing to submit, too ready to accept foreign ideas and ways, too weak in spirit to resist the nation's enemies.

In Protestantism Maurras also saw a Teutonic misstep responsible for reversing the traditional Latin, Catholic order which had subordinated the individual to society. The result was a climate favorable to liberalism and democracy which leads to a society of barbarians where the best are subject to the worst and the destruction of honor and traditional values disrupts the harmony of community interests.

Maurras believed that a strong French society could again be created if the nation rediscovered her classical heritage of order, discipline, hierarchy, and tradition, best symbolized in the monarchy and Catholic unity. As the errors of romanticism had led to a flaccid literature and a weak state, so the virility of classicism would restore order and style to the state and the authority to define and enforce its form. It was "man's only guarantee against the world of darkness he carries in him."

Politically this would first mean restricting or expelling those who had not been fully assimilated into French society, those without the shared values of a common French heritage, whom Maurras called *métèques.* The term, coined by Maurras in 1894 and later officially accepted into the French language, was taken from the Athenian *metics*—the alien population of the city who had no political rights and could not acquire property. Among those classified as *métèques* by Maurras were Protestants and unassimilated Jews.

Maurras's anti-semitism was not religious or racial since he would accept any Jew, or other foreigner for that matter, who converted to Catholicism and accepted French culture. But Maurras was a political anti-semite. He saw the Jews as a large, united, powerful group occupying influential positions in banking, education, the press, and the arts from which they could shape public opinion and government policy. If unassimilated they formed a state within the state, allied to other Jewish "states," and thus were likely to have conflicting national loyalties and encourage cosmopolitanism. And since Jews emphasized their cultural differences they could hardly be expected to support the classical ideas and traditions needed for strong national unity.

It was not surprising to Maurras that the government of the French Revolution had given the Jews political freedom and had attempted to replace organic national unity with a rigid centralization characterized by these artificial creations, the departments. As Maurras's "integral nationalism" would require revoking the political rights of Jews, so would it abolish the departments and restore the provinces whose sovereign assemblies would control local administration, education, justice, and public works. This provincial federalism would restore organic French society, a sense of community, and something real and living that the population could defend as Frenchmen.

Along with this federalism Maurras envisioned a corporatism that would end the chaos and division of liberalism and socialism. Paralleling the basic social unit of the family, corporatism would serve to balance the interests of the social classes and restore the function of each in a hierarchical society. Trade and professional corporations would have autonomy over their own affairs and a voice in local assemblies. Maurras would also see the equal division of property among heirs be abolished in order to recreate the powerful patrimonies from which an aristocracy of talent and service would spring. This principle would also hold among the workers who would be encouraged to become property owners with state assistance.

The revival of the classical tradition, control of the *métèques*, and decentralization would, Maurras believed, lead to the restoration of the monarchy as a logical necessity. Though not originally a royalist, just as he had long not been a Catholic, Maurras adopted both into his system out of the need for some accepted principle of authority and some symbols of national unity. Royalism and Catholicism were instruments for the nationalists; they provided the authority for the discipline and order the nationalist reformers desired. Unfortunately for Maurras, they were also the most anachronistic parts of his system. Unlike German fascism which was truly revolutionary, Maurras's attempt to restore not merely the spirit, but also the form of the 17th-century French monarchy, made his system reactionary and futile.

—Frank M. Baglione

McDOUGALL, William. British psychologist. Born in Chadderton, Lancashire, 22 June 1871. Educated at Owens College, Manchester; St. John's College, Cambridge University; St. Thomas's Hospital, London, M.B. 1898; Göttingen University. Served in the Royal Army Medical Corps, 1915-19: Major. Married Anne Hickmore in 1900; 5 children. Fellow, St. John's College, 1898; member of anthropological expedition to Torres Straits, 1898; Reader in Experimental Psychology, University College, London, 1902-04; Wilde Reader in Mental Philosophy, Oxford University, 1904-19 (Fellow of Corpus Christi College, 1912); Professor of Psychology, Harvard University, Cambridge, Massachusetts, 1920-27; Professor of Psychology, Duke University, Durham, North Carolina, 1927-38. Visiting Lecturer, University College, London, 1935. Co-founder, British Psychological Society, 1901. D.Sc.: University of Manchester, 1919. Honorary Fellow, St. John's College, 1938. Fellow, Royal Society, London, 1912. *Died* (in Durham) *28 November 1938.*

PUBLICATIONS

Psychology and Social Commentary

Physiological Psychology. London, Dent, 1905.
An Introduction to Social Psychology. London, Methuen, 1908.
Body and Mind: A History and Defense of Animism. London, Methuen, 1911.
Psychology: The Study of Behavior. London, Williams and Norgate, 1912.
The Pagan Tribes of Borneo: A Description of their Physical, Moral, and Intellectual Condition with Some Discussion of their Ethnic Relations, with Charles Hose. London, Macmillan, 2 vols., 1912.
Anthropology and History (lecture). London, Oxford University Press, 1920.
The Group Mind: A Sketch of the Principles of Collective Psychology with Some Attempt to Apply Them to the Interpretation of National Life and Character. Cambridge, Cambridge University Press, 1920.
Is America Safe for Democracy? (lectures). New York, Scribner, 1921; as *National Welfare and National Decay,* London, Methuen, 1921.
An Outline of Psychology. London, Methuen, 1923.
Ethics and Some Modern World Problems. London, Methuen, 1927.
The Indestructible Union: Rudiments of Political Science for the American Citizen. Boston, Little Brown, 1925; as *The American Nation: Its Problems and Psychology,* London, Allen and Unwin, 1926.
Outline of Abnormal Psychology. New York, Scribner, and London, Methuen, 1926.
Character and the Conduct of Life: Practical Psychology for Everyman. London, Methuen, 1927.
Janus, The Conquest of War: A Psychological Inquiry. London, Kegan Paul, 1927.
The Battle of Behaviourism: An Exposition and an Exposure, with John B. Watson. London, Kegan Paul, 1928.
Modern Materialism and Emergent Evolution. London, Methuen, and New York, Van Nostrand, 1929.
Love and Hate: A Study of the Energies of Men and Nations (lectures). London, British Broadcasting Corporation, 1931.
World Chaos: The Responsibility of Science. London, Kegan Paul, 1931.
The Energies of Men: A Study of the Fundamentals of Dynamic Psychology. London, Methuen, 1932.
Religion and the Sciences of Life, with Other Essays on Allied Topics. London, Methuen, 1934.
The Frontiers of Psychology. London, Nisbet-Cambridge University Press, 1934.
Psycho-Analysis and Social Psychology. London, Methuen, 1936.
The Riddle of Life: A Survey of Theories. London, Methuen, 1938.
William McDougall: Explorer of the Mind: Studies in Psychical Research, edited by Raymond Van Over and Laura Oteri. New York, Garrett, 1967.

Other

"Autobiography," in *A History of Psychology in Autobiography, Volume I,* edited by Carl Murchison. Worcester, Massachusetts, Clark University Press, 1930.

Editor, with others, *Problems of Personality: Studies Presented to Dr. Morton Prince, Pioneer in American Psychology.* London, Kegan Paul, 1925.

*

Bibliography: *William McDougall: A Bibliography Together with a Brief Outline of His Life* by Anthony Lewin Robinson, Durham, North Carolina, Duke University Press, 1943.

Critical Studies: "William McDougall" by Harold G. McCurdy, in *Historical Roots of Contemporary Psychology* edited by Benjamin B. Wolman, New York, Harper, 1968; *Purposive Explanation in Psychology* by Margaret A. Boden, Cambridge, Massachusetts, Harvard University Press, 1972.

*   *   *

The British psychologist William McDougall, born in the year of publication of Charles Darwin's *Descent of Man,* was in important ways a follower and developer of Darwin's thought but with more stress on the activity of mind, to which he assigned a degree of independence most unusual in post-Darwinian science.

Like Darwin, McDougall stressed the kinship between men and the other animals; and, like Darwin, he postulated an instinctive basis for their behavior. In his view, animal behavior was innately purposive, an active striving for the attainment of certain goals, and, at all levels from amoeba to man, expressive of some degree of consciousness of these goals, from very dim to very clear. Briefly put, he conceived of purpose as the very basis of life (he could have said with Augustine that we are nothing but wills), and purpose was for him, therefore, absolutely primary in any theory of human nature. Those psychological theories that denied or played down the role of purpose, as did Watsonian behaviorism or the more elegant formulations of Gestalt psychology, he criticized severely. Those theories that admitted the purposive element, as did Freud's psychoanalysis, he welcomed as working in the right direction even if not acceptable in every detail.

This unwavering position of the mature McDougall was, according to his own statement, not the one with which he started. He confesses that in his youth as a scientist—and he had a very broad and deep scientific education—he was for a while something of a mechanist, like that hardboiled disciple of Darwin, Thomas Huxley, who regarded consciousness and conscious striving as no more relevant to the activities of any biological organism, including man, than is the whistle of a locomotive to its forward motion along the rails: such matters of experience were to Huxley a sort of illusion, unworthy of scientific attention. Having wrestled himself free of the Huxley view, which is only one of the many manifestations of the mechanistic thesis in psychology from Descartes and La Mettrie through Hartley and Hume down to the present, McDougall became a strenuous advocate of the relevance, indeed the centrality, of consciousness and purpose in the psychological realm.

McDougall put forward a list of instincts as a way of cataloguing the basic varieties of purpose. These he later called propensities, to lessen the implication of rigid patterning. Each instinct (or propensity) has, according to his analysis, three closely related aspects: perception or imagination of a goal object, a distinctive emotional arousal, and an urge to action with reference to that object. At any given moment the accent may fall unequally on these three aspects; consciousness of the instinctive tendency (or an outside observer's judgment of what is going on)

may concentrate on the goal object, or on the emotional perturbation, or on the action itself. Emotion is, so to speak, the middle term between perception and action. For example, hunger is the emotional state of an animal ready to notice or search for food but it rises to prominence with awareness of the goal object and wanes when the food is eaten. Or again, lust or sexual longing is the distinctive emotional state at the primitive level of one ready to search for and unite sexually with an appropriate partner. McDougall thought that, in the main, each of the several instincts was best identified by the emotional aspect—hunger, lust, fear, anger, and other conditions harder to name by a single word such as the tender feeling of a nurturing parent.

Clearly McDougall could not have catalogued the instincts if they lacked all firmness of outline, but he insisted that they were always modifiable in the individual case, and in all three aspects. Thus, as the individual organism interacts with the environment, preferences develop with respect to the goal object (e.g., food, sexual mate), refinements and complexities enter into the emotional state, and the particular kinds of actions entailed undergo their changes too. The mature human being (or other animal, for that matter) is by no means a rigid programmed automaton following out a crude pattern. The instinctive life becomes variegated, modulated, and organized by the development of what McDougall called sentiments.

The sentiments (and notice here again in the term itself McDougall's emphasis on the emotions) are the outcome of instinctive interactions with particular environments, in consequence of which a single object can become the focus of any number of different instincts and their blended sequels. Thus, the initial relatively simple desire of a man for sexual union with some unspecified woman becomes radically modified on accomplishing its aim with a particular woman. Continued interaction between them builds up a complex sentiment as other purposes besides the sexual come into play—curiosity, anger, nurturing tendencies, fear, etc., which combine to give her a quality and significance that were not there before and cannot afterwards, even by separation and divorce, be wholly eliminated. Sentiments persist and overshadow the instincts out of which they arose. They are like the "complexes" of the psychoanalysts, except that they are not necessarily pathological. Quite the contrary, for the most part. A mature and healthy personality is constituted of many sentiments in harmonious relationship with each other arranged in a hierarchy of power ruled by some master sentiment, such as the sentiment of self-regard, i.e., the self as the focus of positive feelings growing out of a history of steady mastery of the possibilities of failure and conflict presented by the instincts. Obviously, a personality so organized might fall into disarray and the subordinate components become more independent or even displace the once regnant self. That is apparently what happens in the case of multiple personalities, of which Stevenson's famous Dr. Jekyll and Mr. Hyde are fictionalized examples. A personality, then, is potentially or actually not just a single self but a society of selves in a relationship ranging from very harmonious to very disharmonious; that is, in this view of the matter, the sentiments constituting a personality are analogous to the persons constituting a cohesive society: they are independent (though interdependent) powers, selves, or, to adopt the term borrowed by McDougall from Leibniz, monads. McDougall's monadic theory grew out of his sentiment theory as he contemplated the phenomena of multiple personality and the alleged phenomena of parapsychology; but it was never quite completed, perhaps because his open-minded but critical approach to parapsychology left him with too many unresolved questions.

Science for McDougall was a matter of courageous inquiry and open debate. Some of the opposition he encountered from other psychologists was due to the boldness of his entry into shadowy territory, such as parapsychology and the Lamarckian theory of the inheritance of acquired characteristics (to which he devoted a long, painstaking experiment); but it must also not be overlooked that his advocacy of conscious purpose as the very heart of psychology ran counter to strong trends in our technological age. The title of one of his lectures, "Men or Robots?" must have haunted him increasingly as the political and scientific movements of his period seemed to favor the second alternative over the first. It appears that men, at least some men, may make the extraordinary choice of becoming robots in order to fit into a mechanicalized environment created by human imagination and human engineering in generations of effort to cope with the demands of the instincts. Against this dehumanizing tendency William McDougall was the most stalwart of humanists while continuing to be a true scientist, carrying on experimental work and objective self-observation to the end.

—Harold G. McCurdy

McILWAIN, C(harles) H(oward). American historian. Born in Saltsburg, Pennsylvania, 15 March 1871. Studied at College of New Jersey, now Princeton, B.A. 1894, M.A. 1898; Harvard University, Cambridge, Massachusetts, M.A. 1903, Ph.D. 1911; admitted to bar of Allegheny County, Pennsylvania, 1897. Married Mary B. Irwin in 1899 (died 1906); 2 children; married Kathleen Thompson in 1916; 3 children. Teacher, Kiskiminetas School, 1898-1901; Professor, Miami University, Oxford, Ohio, 1903-05; Preceptor, Princeton University, 1905-10; Thomas Brackett Reed Professor of History and Political Science, Bowdoin College, Brunswick, Maine, 1910-11; Assistant Professor, 1911-16, Professor, 1916-26, and Eaton Professor of Science of Government, Harvard University, 1926-46. George Eastman Visiting Professor, Oxford University, 1944; Lecturer, Princeton University, 1948-49. President, American Historical Association, 1935-36. Honorary M.A.: Oxford University, 1944; Honorary doctorate: College of Wooster, Ohio, 1927; Williams College, Williamstown, Massachusetts, 1937; Harvard University, 1938; University of Chicago, 1941; Rutgers University, New Brunswick, New Jersey, 1941; Princeton University, 1946; Yale University, New Haven, Connecticut, 1952. Corresponding Member, Royal Historical Society, London; Corresponding Fellow, British Academy, London; Fellow, American Academy of Arts and Sciences, and Medieval Academy of America. Honorary Fellow, Balliol College, Oxford. *Died in 1968.*

PUBLICATIONS

History

The High Court of Parliament and its Supremacy: An Historical Essay on the Boundaries Between Legislation and Adjudication in England. New Haven, Connecticut, Yale University Press, and London, Henry Frowde, 1910.
The American Revolution: A Constitutional Interpretation. New York, Macmillan, 1923.
The Growth of Political Thought in the West, from the Greeks to the End of the Middle Ages. New York and London, Macmillan, 1932.
Constitutionalism and the Changing World: Collected Papers. New York, Macmillan, and Cambridge, University Press, 1939.
Constitutionalism, Ancient and Modern. Ithaca, New York, Cornell University Press, 1940.

Other

Editor, *An Abridgement of the Indian Affairs Contained in Four-Folio Volumes, Transacted in the Colony of New York, from the Year 1678 to the Year 1751,* by Peter Wraxall. Cambridge, Massachusetts, Harvard University Press, 1915.
Editor, *The Political Works of James I, Reprinted from the Edition of 1616.* Cambridge, Massachusetts, Harvard University Press, 1918.
Editor, *How Superior Powers Oght to be Obeyed, reproduced from the Edition of 1558,* by Christopher Goodman. New York, Columbia University Press, 1931.
Editor, with Paul L. Ward, *Archeion; or, a Discourse upon the High Courts of Justice in England,* by William Lambarde. Cambridge, Massachusetts, Harvard University Press, 1957.

*   *   *

C.H. McIlwain's style of thought was notable for the vividness of his attention to the details of significant past statements. This was what his students found most impressive, and his intellectual influence has been chiefly through them. A reliance on long quotations, lovingly elucidated, characterizes his writings. The penetration of his thinking was thus of a piece with his effectiveness as teacher. He most naturally presented himself, after intense study, as a man thinking rather than as an authority. The preface to his first book, for example, stresses that it is an "essay," an attempt. The preface to his last collection of papers expresses satisfaction at reproducing unaltered an outdated article on Magna Carta because it "may possibly have had something to do with the appearance since 1917 of a number of more thorough studies of the same general subject."

As historian, McIlwain above all valued the ongoing enterprise of inquiry. At the same time, he felt poignantly the present relevance of proper historical inquiries. Some recent readers of his 1936 address as President of the American Historical Association have too hastily concluded that he was concerned only over finding out "what really happened." His two *Foreign Affairs* articles which bracketed that address, the first provoked by Hitlerism and the second by Roosevelt's court-packing effort, show by the passion of their language how keenly he felt the value of the lessons he had helped extract from the past, which however he could urge on others only in his capacity as citizen. His presidential critique of fellow historians who championed relativist "New History," in short, was as heartfelt as it was precisely because he believed as they did, that guidelines from history influence importantly our efforts at social and political reform.

The sharpness of his eye under such impulses led him to two ventures that have been faulted by subsequent scholarship. His championing in 1924 of pre-revolutionary claims by colonial leaders, to the effect that Parliament had no constitutional right to legislate for King George's overseas dominions, won him a Pulitzer Prize but was decisively rebutted soon thereafter. Nearly a half-century later, a new study makes clear the element of rightness in McIlwain's contention, with an accompanying admiring comment that he was "an unabashed libertarian as well as a superb scholar." In the second instance, an ingenious argument he advanced in 1940, that Bracton's use of the words *gubernaculum* and *jurisdiction* embodied the central constitutional distinction between governmental procedures and subjects' rights, led only to scholarly controversy until 1964, when the matter was ably set straight by use of accumulated scholarship.

Both episodes represent McIlwain's continuing effort to make clear the inadequacy of modern one-sided doctrines, whether of law as essentially positive command or of law as embodying general will, to explain mainstream European styles of government. Bracton's aphorism, that "the king ought to be not under man but under God and the law," stands as a perennial paradox of legislative sovereignty that since McIlwain's time, and partly to his credit, has been much clarified within medieval history, especially through attention to books of canon law.

McIlwain's loyalties and expertise lay indeed in traditional Anglo-American law: he had been admitted to the bar even before his first teaching experience in private school. His first book began with insistence on the concept of fundamental law which originated in early medieval customs. An incisive critique of this strand of his thinking, which appeared shortly after his final incapacitation, may have helpfully exposed the anachronism of some over-clear distinctions that he despite himself had carried back to earlier days from 13th-century lawbooks. Yet more comprehensive examination of the early records now vindicates McIlwain's picture of the immanence of right and the authority of custom as the matrix out of which European governments emerged.

McIlwain as theorist held to the belief, so well-accepted during his early years, that feebleness is the great disease of constitutional governments, typically arising out of "an overextension of checks and balances." Hence his admiration for Bodin, however much he insisted on Bodin's errors in judging England. As late as 1950 he could argue (in the journal *History*) that Bodin's doctrine of the state is not to be faulted for contributing in practice to France's decline into absolutism. The strength and justness of McIlwain's insights into the contributions of law to constitutional practice owed much to his confidence in the importance of legal theory quite apart from questions of enforcement. Witness as key example his success by 1940 in elucidating the legal principles of republican Rome that in fact survived centuries of absolutism and anarchy to shape European governments, in the High Middle Ages and subsequently, in the direction of our Western constitutionalism.

—Paul L. Ward

McKEON, Richard (Peter).   American philosopher.   Born in Union Hill, New Jersey, 26 April 1900. Studied at Columbia University, New York, B.A. and M.A. 1920, Ph.D. 1928; University of Paris, diplôme, 1923; École des Hautes Études, Paris, 1924. Served as an apprentice seaman, United States Navy, 1918. Married Clarice Muriel Thier in 1930; 3 children. Instructor in Philosophy, 1925-27, and Assistant Professor, 1927-35, Columbia University; Visiting Professor of History, 1934-35, Professor of Greek, Professor of Philosophy, Dean of the Division of the Humanities, 1935-47, Grey Distinguished Service Professor, 1947-76, and since 1976 Distinguished Service Emeritus Professor of Greek and Philosophy, University of Chicago. Fellow, Center for Advanced Study in the Behavioral Sciences, Stanford, California, 1959-60. U.S. Counselor, Unesco Affairs, Paris, 1945-46; Member, U.S. Delegation, Unesco Conference, Paris, 1945-46, Mexico City, 1947, and Beirut, 1948. Vice-Chairman, American Council of Learned Societies, 1939; President, American Philosophical Society, 1952, and International Institute of Philosophy, 1953-57. Honorary doctorate: Jewish Theological Seminary, New York, 1942; University of Aix-Marseilles, 1951; University of Washington, Seattle, 1963. Fellow, Medieval Academy of America, and American Academy of Arts and Sciences. Address: 5632 South Blackstone Avenue, Chicago, Illinois 60637, U.S.A.

PUBLICATIONS

Philosophy

The Philosophy of Spinoza: The Unity of His Thought.   New York, Longman, 1928.
Freedom and History: The Semantics of Philosophical Controversies and Ideological Conflicts.   New York, Noonday Press, 1952.
Critics and Criticism: Ancient and Modern, with others.   Chicago, University of Chicago Press, 1952.
Thought, Action, and Passion.   Chicago, University of Chicago Press, 1954.
The Freedom to Read: Programs and Perspectives, with others. New York, Bowker, 1957.

Other

Editor and translator, *Selections from Medieval Philosophers.* New York, Scribner, 2 vols., 1929-30.
Editor, *The Basic Works of Aristotle.*   New York, Random House, 1941.
Editor, *Introduction to Aristotle.*   New York, Modern Library, 1947.
Editor, with Stein Kokkan, *Democracy in a World of Tensions: A Symposium Prepared by UNESCO.*   Chicago, University of Chicago Press, 1951.
Editor, with others, *Freedom and Authority in Our Time.*   New York, Harper, 1953.
Editor, *Symbols and Values: An Initial Study.*   New York, Harper, 1954.
Editor, with N.A. Nikam, *The Edicts of Aśoka.*   Chicago, University of Chicago Press, 1959.
Editor, with Blanche B. Boyer, *Sic et Non,* by Pierre Abailard. Chicago, University of Chicago Press, 7 vols., 1976-77.

*   *   *

Richard McKeon's intellectual contributions have addressed problems of education, political and social relations, and philosophical analysis as these problems are manifested under conditions of pluralism. His work reflects a conviction that each philosophical school, political belief structure, social system, or educational curriculum reflects the specific formulations by different groups or during different ages to common concerns. The disputes that are conducted between apparently opposed schools of thought and systems of governance stem from characterizations of alternative perspectives in terms of the framework receiving positive statement. Such expressions ignore underlying unities that permeate apparent diversities, leading to distortions of positions and a beclouding of similarities differently formulated.

Early in his published works McKeon embarked on developing a framework which would permit articulation of unities amid diversities. He has continued to refine and apply this framework throughout his career. In education he sought curricular reforms that brought the physical sciences, biological sciences, social sciences, and humanities into relationship through underlying unities of method applied to shared problems. He attempted to reformulate analysis and practice in social and political relations through an architectonic art of communication. In philosophy he attempted to reconcile perspectival direction by advancing a philosophic semantics that intersected philosophical inquiry. Each of these transformations reflects McKeon's radical shift from grounding the transcendental bases of knowledge and action in consciousness or reason to grounding them in a transcendental conception of discourse. McKeon's published writings elaborate this framework in a variety of ways, each adapted to the specific problem he was addressing. However, its most general statement is contained in his analysis of philosophic semantics in terms of dialectic, logistic, problematic, and operational methods.

McKeon's early work examined the history of philosophy. His studies led him to classify all philosophical expression into four categories, which he regarded as mutually exclusive and exhaustive. First, there were philosophies of the "whole." These shared the assumption that the whole, however conceived, could not be treated adequately in terms of its parts; it rested on an ontological unifying principle. Philosophers working in this mode frequently professed the method of *dialectic*, employing dialogue that proceeded analogically to assimilate similarities and provide exemplifications dependent on a changeless model of a unifying principle.

At the opposite extreme were philosophies of atomic division. These shared the assumption that available existence and experience could be known only insofar as they were composed of discovered least parts. Dialecticians have criticized such philosophies as *logistic.* McKeon retained the label to refer to the method of proving by composition and decomposition in terms of indivisible elements.

Between these extremes were philosophies dubious about such ontological or atomic assumptions because they lacked probity when inquiry was directed toward human problems. McKeon classified philosophies of problems in the middle region as *problematic*. Philosophers using this mode assumed that problems were caused and therefore used a method of inquiry into causes that, once discovered, might resolve problems and answer questions.

Finally; there were philosophies that opposed all theoretic construction. They assumed that all formulations were initially arbitrary, standing as theses to be tested by the criteria of particular and practical consequences in action. McKeon labeled these philosophies *operational*. Their method was debate among perspectives with interlocutors advancing discriminations and postulations resting on theses and accompanying rules.

The four modes of thought characterized in McKeon's philosophic semantic have each had periods of pre-eminence in the history of western thought. During these periods each provided an architectonic for theory and practice with respect to things, thoughts, actions, and statements. The particular philosophical, political, and educational manifestations of the four semantic modes have enjoyed architectonic power to the degree that they accounted for each of these features of existence and experience. However, systems of analysis and action vary extensively as they alter basic assumptions about and principles of truth and method. These variances, when butted against one another, pose significant problems for inquiry and action. McKeon's middle and late writings were devoted to resolving these problems. His major contribution, in this respect, has been his intersection of the philosophic semantic with problems of inquiry and action, especially in the contemporary period where pluralism prevents any single mode from enjoying universal or even widespread endorsement.

McKeon saw two dangers posed by pluralism: an intolerance of divergent perspectives, producing dogmatism and error; and an uncritical acceptance of all views as legitimate, producing irenicism. He sought a conceptual, pedagogical, and practical framework which would overcome these obstacles to understanding and cooperation. He resolved this problem by abandoning all *a priori* assumptions regarding methods, problems, or truths and by embracing the operational commonplaces of all systems of thought and action. His elucidation of this method drew heavily from the ancient arts of discourse: rhetoric, grammar, logic, and dialectic.

McKeon's discussions of the operations (*topoi*), ends (*utilia, justa, honesta*), and places (*controversia*) indigenous to the arts of discourse themselves radically transformed discourse into an architectonic art. His conception transcended those views which held such arts to be instrumentalities in the establishment of being and knowledge or the conduct of inquiry. Similarly it avoided the rigidities of those views which isolated such arts from one another in method and matter. He contended that rhetoric, grammar, logic, and dialectic borrowed methods and subject matters from one another. Each of them contained the basic statement of the principles of all knowledge; and analysis revealed that their interrelations contained all the problems of philosophy and science. Each was an art of unification as well as of transformation of knowledge. An architectonic art of discourse avoided the fixed orientations of the four semantic modes by providing interdisciplinary methods necessary to integrating theory and practice, methods which provided a holistic system for discovering, testing, interrelating, and using knowledge. Finally, the use of discourse as an architectonic avoided the assumptive and methodological biases of the four semantic modes because discourse thought of in this way was *universal* in its application, *neutral* with respect to assumptive biases, and *transformational* in its ability to express problems of one mode in terms of any other. This final contention highlights McKeon's conviction that a transcendental conception of discourse applied to the productive ambiguities of pluralistic expressions can make humankind of one mind in the truth without being of one opinion.

—Gerard A. Hauser

McLUHAN, (Herbert) Marshall. Canadian theorist of the media. Born in Edmonton, Alberta, 21 July 1911. Studied at the University of Manitoba, Winnipeg, B.A. 1932, M.A. 1934; Trinity Hall, Cambridge, B.A. 1936, M.A. 1939, Ph.D. 1942. Married Corinne Keller Lewis in 1939; 6 children. Instructor, University of Wisconsin, Madison, 1936-37, and St. Louis University, 1937-44; Associate Professor of English, Assumption College, Windsor, Ontario, 1944-46; Instructor, 1946-52, and Professor of English, 1952-80, St. Michael's College, University of Toronto; also, Founding Director, Centre for Culture and Technology, 1963-80. Albert Schweitzer Professor in the Humanities, Fordham University, New York, 1967-68; Eugene McDermott Professor, University of Dallas, 1975; Pound Lecturer, 1978. Founding Editor, with Edmund Carpenter, *Explorations*, 1954-59. Editor, Patterns of Literary Criticism series, 1965-69. Chairman, Ford Foundation Seminar on Culture and Communications, 1953-55; Director of media project, U.S. Office of Education and National Association of Educational Broadcasters, 1959-60; Consultant, Johnson McCormick and Johnson, public relations, Toronto, 1966-80, and Responsive Environments Corporation, New York, 1968-80; Consultant, Vatican Pontifical Commission for Social Communications, 1973. Recipient: Governor-General's Award, 1963; Fordham University award, 1964; Molson Prize, 1967; Niagara University award, 1967; Carl Einstein Prize (Germany), 1967; Institute of Public Relations President's Award (UK), 1970; Assumption University Christian Culture Award, 1971; President's Gold Medal (Italy), 1971; University of Detroit President's Cabinet Award, 1972. D.Litt.: University of Windsor, Ontario, 1965; Assumption University, 1966; University of Manitoba, 1967; Grinnell College, Iowa, 1967; University of Western Ontario, London, 1972; University of Toronto, 1977; LL.D.: Simon Fraser University, Burnaby, British Columbia, 1967; L.H.: St. John Fisher College, Rochester, New York, 1969; LL.D.: University of Alberta, Edmonton, 1972; Niagara University, New York, 1978. Fellow, Royal Society of Canada, 1964. C.C. (Companion, Order of Canada), 1970. *Died 31 December 1980.*

PUBLICATIONS

Media

The Mechanical Bride: Folklore of Industrial Man. New York, Vanguard Press, 1951; London, Routledge, 1967.
The Gutenberg Galaxy: The Making of Typographic Man. Toronto, University of Toronto Press, and London, Routledge, 1962.
Understanding Media: The Extensions of Man. New York, McGraw Hill, and London, Routledge, 1964.
The Medium Is the Massage: An Inventory of Effects, with Quentin Fiore. New York, Bantam, and London, Allen Lane, 1967.
War and Peace in the Global Village: An Inventory of Some of the Current Spastic Situations That Could Be Eliminated by More Feedforward, with Quentin Fiore. New York, McGraw Hill, 1968.
Through the Vanishing Point: Space in Poetry and Painting, with Harley Parker. New York, Harper, 1968.
Counter Blast. Toronto, McClelland and Stewart, and New

York, Harcourt Brace, 1969; London, Rapp and Whiting, 1970.

The Interior Landscape: The Literary Criticism of Marshall McLuhan, 1943-1962, edited by Eugene McNamara. New York, McGraw Hill, 1969.

Culture Is Our Business. New York, McGraw Hill, 1970.

From Cliché to Archetype, with Wilfred Watson. New York, Viking Press, 1970.

Take Today: The Executive as Dropout, with Barrington Nevitt. New York, Harcourt Brace, 1972.

The City as Classroom: Understanding Language and Media, with Eric McLuhan and Kathy Hutchon. Agincourt, Ontario, Book Society of Canada, 1977.

Other

Editor, *Selected Poetry*, by Tennyson. New York, Rinehart, 1956.

Editor, with Edmund Carpenter, *Explorations in Communication*. Boston, Beacon Press, 1960; London, Cape, 1970.

Editor, with Richard J. Schoek, *Voices of Literature*. New York, Holt, 4 vols., 1964-70.

*

Bibliography: *The Writings of Marshall McLuhan Listed in Chronological Order from 1934 to 1975*, Fort Lauderdale, Florida, Wake-Brook House, 1975.

Critical Studies: *McLuhan: Hot and Cool* edited by Gerald Emanuel Stearns, New York, Dial Press, 1967, London, Penguin, 1968; *The Message of Marshall McLuhan* by Barry Day, London, Lintas, 1967; *Sense and Nonsense of McLuhan* by Sidney W. Finkelstein, New York, International Publishers, 1968; *McLuhan: Pro and Con* edited by Raymond Rosenthal, New York, Funk and Wagnalls, 1968; *The McLuhan Explosion* edited by Harry H. Crosby and George R. Bond, New York, American Book Company 1968; *Marshall McLuhan* by Dennis Duffy, Toronto, McClelland and Stewart, 1969; *Marshall McLuhan* by Jonathan Miller, London, Fontana, and New York, Viking Press, 1971; *The Medium Is the Rear View Mirror: Understanding McLuhan* by Donald F. Theall, Montreal, McGill-Queen's University Press, 1971; *Culture as Polyphony: An Essay on the Nature of Paradigms* by James M. Curtis, Columbia, University of Missouri Press, 1978.

*   *   *

Marshall McLuhan was one of the most controversial thinkers of the 1960's. With the publication of *The Gutenberg Galaxy* in 1962 and *Understanding Media* two years later, McLuhan catapulted from the obscurity of a respectable academic post in Canada to international fame. His ideas were celebrated by the media, execrated by the intelligentsia, and assimilated by the young. Though by no means the first or most perceptive theorist of mass communications, McLuhan captured public attention in part because he eschewed the conventional snobberies about popular culture. With the certainty of a prophet and the slogans of an advertising man, he articulated theories which gave the newer electronic media a privileged place in the history of communication.

McLuhan believed that the prevailing mode of communication in a society determined the nature and extent of human knowledge. Borrowing from his Canadian colleague Harold Innis and others, he argued that the introduction of any new technology of communication vitally altered the configuration of sense data whereby humans come to know each other and the outside world. In primitive societies, for example, people communicated by speaking to one another face to face. Through sound, gesture, touch, and a host of unconscious signals, they conveyed a message rich in sensual experience. With the advent of the alphabet, language transcended space and time, but words were robbed of their sensual richness when reduced to symbols on a page. To McLuhan, reading one another's words remained a fundamentally different and impoverished event from hearing the writer convey the message in person. The mode of communication shaped the experience of the information, or, as McLuhan put it with characteristic inscrutability, "the medium is the message."

It was not literacy, however, but the printing press which radically transformed Western thought and society. To McLuhan, Gutenberg initiated a technology that converted words into detached, uniform, infinitely repeatable commodities which demanded a trained visual sense for interpretation. Indeed, by forcing knowledge into the linear and sequential segments of words on a page, the printing press inaugurated many of the major intellectual and social movements of modern times. McLuhan suggested but did not prove, for example, that the portability of books contributed to individualism. Since reading and writing were private, solitary experiences, the individual could withdraw from the community in pursuit of his own aims. Then, too, since the linear point of view required a strict, mechanistic relationship between cause and effect, the printing press helped create the scientific revolution. Even capitalism and industrialism, McLuhan argued, stemmed from typography since the assembly-line and mass production shared the linear and sequential logic of the printed page. Clearly, the technology of Gutenberg resulted in an explosion of knowledge with profound implications for the organization of society. Yet, McLuhan maintained that, for all its triumphs, the printing press distorted the human psyche by depleting it of the collective, communal, mythic experience of primitive communication. Only in recent years has health been restored.

To McLuhan, the invention and wide diffusion of the telegraph, telephone, cinema, radio, television and other electronic media recreated an environment for communication not unlike that of primitive societies. Taken individually, a medium like the printed word appealed only to a single faculty. In a confusing distinction which he applied inconsistently, McLuhan discriminated between a "hot" medium which extended a single sense in high definition and a "cool" medium which compelled participation and sensual completion by the audience. Thus, for example, he argued that television was a cool medium since its undetailed picture, like a cartoon, demanded active involvement by the viewer. Yet, McLuhan claimed that in the contemporary world the media should not be evaluated separately but as an integrated phenomenon. By extending the entire nervous system, electronic media involved all the senses and, like the encounter of two people on a village street, restored a harmonious "ratio of the senses" to the act of communication. This ability to grasp messages as a whole and not from a linear, fixed point of view was anticipated by a number of Modernists, such as the Cubists, whom McLuhan invoked as part of his intellectual pedigree. Above all, he asserted the almost mystical claim that instantaneous electronic communications united humanity into a new "global village."

Critics levelled a number of complaints against McLuhan. His method of presenting his ideas in a mosaic rather than a linear pattern, thus paralleling the electronic media he described, struck many observers as ingenious but inept. Like a modern advertiser, McLuhan endlessly repeated himself. Unlike an advertiser, however, he wrote opaque, often gnomic prose which untutored readers associated with profundity. Many of his propositions could not sustain prolonged scrutiny, in part because he used evidence in a cavalier fashion. Some observers found McLuhan's faith in the mystic unity of the global village to be simply a reflection of his Catholicism rather than a statement of fact. Yet, despite the criticism, McLuhan remains an important, even seminal thinker. He forced a generation to re-examine the role of technology in shaping perception, and few who have assimilated his ideas ever look at a newspaper or view a television program with quite the same complacency.

—D.L. LeMahieu

McNEILL, William H(ardy). American historian. Born in Vancouver, British Columbia, Canada, 31 October 1917; emigrated to the United States; later naturalized. Studied at the University of Chicago, B.A. 1938, M.A. 1939; Cornell University, Ithaca, New York, Ph.D., 1947. Served with the United States Army, 1941-46. Married Elizabeth Darbishire in 1946; 4 children. Instructor, 1947-49, Assistant Professor, 1949-55, Associate Professor, 1955-57, Professor, 1957-69, and since 1969 Robert A. Millikan Distinguished Service Professor, University of Chicago; Acting Director, Morris Fishbein Center for Study of the History of Science and Medicine, Chicago, 1977-78. Fulbright Research Scholar, Royal Institute of International Affairs, London, 1950-51; Ford Teaching Fellow, 1954-55; Exchange Professor, University of Frankfurt, 1956. Editor, *Journal of Modern History*, since 1971. Recipient: Rockefeller Grant, 1951; Carnegie Foundation Grant, 1957-62, 1963; National Book Award, 1963; Guggenheim Fellowship, 1971. Honorary doctorate: Washington College, Chestertown, Maryland, 1975; Lawrence University, Appleton, Wisconsin, 1977; Chicago Medical College, 1977. Fellow, American Philosophical Society, and American Academy of Arts and Sciences. Address: Department of History, University of Chicago, 1126 East 59th Street, Chicago, Illinois 60637, U.S.A.

PUBLICATIONS

History

The Greek Dilemma: War and Aftermath. Philadelphia, Lippincott, and London, Gollancz, 1947.
Report on the Greeks: Findings of a Twentieth-Century Fund Team Which Surveyed Conditions in Greece in 1947, with others. New York, Twentieth Century Fund, 1948.
America, Britain, and Russia: Their Cooperation and Conflict, 1941-46. London, Oxford University Press, 1953; New York, Johnson Reprint, 1970.
History Handbook of Western Civilization. Chicago, University of Chicago Press, 1953; revised edition, 1969.
Past and Future. Chicago, University of Chicago Press, 1954.
Greece: American Aid in Action, 1947-1956. New York, Twentieth Century Fund, 1957.
World History in Maps: A Teachers' Manual for Use with Denoyer-Geppert World History Series, with others. Chicago, Denoyer-Geppert, 1960; revised edition as *The World: Its History in Maps*, 1963.
The Rise of the West: A History of the Human Community. Chicago, University of Chicago Press, 1963.
Europe's Steppe Frontier, 1500-1800. Chicago, University of Chicago Press, 1964.
The Contemporary World, 1914/Present. Glenview, Illinois, Scott Foresman, 1967.
A World History. New York, Oxford University Press, 1967.
Sir Herbert Butterfield, Cho Yun Hsu, William H. McNeill on Chinese and World History, edited by Noah Edward Fehl. Hong Kong, Chinese University of Hong Kong, 1971.
The Ecumene: Story of Humanity. New York, Harper, 1973.
The Shape of European History. New York, Oxford University Press, 1974.
Venice: The Hinge of Europe, 1081-1797. Chicago, University of Chicago Press, 1974.
Plagues and People. New York, Doubleday, 1976; Oxford,

Blackwell, 1977.
Modern Europe and America, with Schuyler O. Houser. New York, Oxford University Press, 1977.
The Metamorphosis of Greece since World War II. Chicago, University of Chicago Press, 1978; Oxford, Blackwell, 1979.
The Human Condition: An Ecological and Historical View (lectures). Princeton, New Jersey, Princeton University Press, 1980.
The Pursuit of Power: Technology, Armed Force, and Society since A.D. 1000. Chicago, University of Chicago Press, 1982.

Editor, *Essays in the Liberal Interpretation of History: Selected Papers by Lord Acton*. Chicago, University of Chicago Press, 1967.
Editor, with others, *Readings in World History*. New York, Oxford University Press, 9 vols., 1968-73.
Editor, with Ruth S. Adams, *Human Migrations: Patterns and Policies*. Bloomington, Indiana University Press, 1978.

*   *   *

Wiliam H. McNeill has earned an international reputation as a writer of world history and as a gadfly for a more ecumenical approach to the writing and teaching of history. The inspiration for his global vision came quite early in his career during his undergraduate years at the University of Chicago. Stimulated by Robert Redfield's anthropological studies of civilization, McNeill conceived of a sweeping history of the patterns of contact among civilized communities. At Cornell, work with Philip E. Mosely in Eastern European history further affected his outlook. The relationship between Western and Eastern Europe became the focus of McNeill's global vision, and he became a specialist in the "hinge" and frontier areas of European civilization. The publication of *The Rise of the West* in 1963 established him as a major historian, and in 1976, when *Plagues and People* appeared, McNeill added a new and highly original dimension to the study of world history—an ecological dimension.

In McNeill's global studies he shows how cultural contacts occurred across the Eurasian cultural ecumene and beyond. It is a story of the rise of Western Europe during "the commercial transmutation" of the modern era. He often uses hydraulic images of cultural diffusion and circulation, of ebb and flow, of waves, and in his latest ecological-historical works, of "disease pools." An ecological point of view permits him to connect a great variety of historical phenomena, from the decline of empires to the spread of religions, with biological relationships of micro- and macro-parasitism. He has no peer in the historical profession in his use of epidemiology in the study of history. For example, in *The Rise of the West* McNeill developed the idea of a Eurasian cultural ecumene connecting the Roman Empire with the Han Chinese Empire in the 2nd century AD. In *Plagues and People* and two lectures delivered at Clark University in 1979 and published in 1980 under the title, *The Human Condition*, he showed how separate disease pools in the ecumene flowed together with devastating effect—causing vast die-offs in the Roman Empire and China in the 2nd century AD. After such die-offs, human macro-parasitism, organized in political forms, bureaucratic command systems, and socio-economic relationships, could not be sustained in its earlier forms. Momentous rearrangements ensued over a long period of time across the entire ecumene. A similar moment occurred in the 14th century, when the Mongol Empire linked Asia with Europe and carried the bubonic plague to the West. Human population change and migrations are central to McNeill's view of history. Die-offs and folk wanderings are placed in complex historical contexts and related to such diverse phenomena as warfare, trade, and ideological change. To give another example, McNeill connects the rise and spread of world religions with the psychological impact of die-offs.

The changing balance between bureaucratic command systems and civilizations dominated by the regulation of the market-place is another central theme in McNeill's work. He traces the growth and changing patterns over several millenia of both methods for organizing the materials needed to sustain the life and culture of expanding communities. He posits the dominance of bureaucratic command systems in both the Old and New World and traces the commercial transmutation, beginning in the Christian era, when commercial growth linked the Mediterranean world with China. After the die-offs of the 2nd and 3rd centuries, trade across the Eurasian ecumene slowed, but nomadic migrations and invasions eventually yielded the Mongol Empire and renewed trade links. But the new links caused the die-off of the 14th century and another set-back to commercial development. The commercial transmutation, after a precocious revival in Sung China, took hold in Mediterranean Europe, but only with the shift of initiative in commerce and manufacturing to northwestern Europe did the global balance of wealth and power shift decisively to the market-regulated civilization of Europe. In the 20th century, there has been a trend toward the revival of bureaucratic command and control systems in both states and vast corporations.

McNeill's approach to the human condition is strikingly dispassionate. His broadest vision is naturalistic and ecological and leads to the following neo-Malthusian conclusion: "Like all other forms of life, humankind remains inextricably tangled in flows of matter and energy that result from eating and being eaten. However clever we have been in finding new niches...the enveloping microparasitic-macroparasitic balances limiting human access to food and energy have not been abolished, and never will be." McNeill's vision of precarious balances, disturbed in unforeseen ways when human communities with their attendant microparasites come into contact with each other, provides little hope for painless or steady progress in human development. However, he does not view the human condition reductionistically or pessimistically, despite the apparently gloomy naturalism of his ecological approach to the human condition. As a thinker and educator, McNeill belongs to the broad enlightenment tradition. He believes that the discovery of universal laws and new perspectives on human history alters the human symbolic world, and adds to the fund of knowledge which might permit us to improve the human condition. This is the other side of an unsentimental challenge-and-response vision of historical change, which is more Darwinian and naturalistic than that of most contemporary historians. Through his own scholarship and vigorous activity as editor and promoter of projects for the spread of a many-sided and ecumenical view of the human condition, McNeill has taken up the challenge. He joins those contemporary thinkers whose unsentimental approach to the human condition and the larger patterns of human history might give us some leverage against an uncertain future.

—Philip Pomper

McTAGGART, J(ohn) McT(aggart) E(llis). British philosopher. Born in London, 3 September 1866. Studied at Clifton College, Bristol; Trinity College, Cambridge, B.A. 1888. Married Mary Elizabeth Bird in 1898. Fellow, 1891-1923, and Lecturer, 1897-1923, Trinity College. Honorary doctorate: Cambridge University, 1902; University of St. Andrews, Scotland, 1911. Fellow, British Academy, 1906. *Died 18 January 1925.*

PUBLICATIONS

Philosophy

Studies in Hegelian Dialectic. London, Cambridge University Press, 1896.
The Further Determination of the Absolute. Privately printed, 1896(?).
Studies in Hegelian Cosmology. London, Cambridge University Press, 1901.
Some Dogmas of Religion. London, Arnold, 1906.
A Commentary on Hegel's Logic. London, Cambridge University Press, and Philadelphia, Russell, 1910.
Human Immortality and Pre-Existence. New York and London, Longman, 1915.
The Nature of Existence. London, Cambridge University Press, 2 vols., 1921-27 (vol. 2 edited by C.D. Broad).
Philosophical Studies, edited by S.V. Keeling. London, Arnold, and New York, Longman, 1934.

*

Critical Studies: *J. McT. E. McTaggart* by Goldsworthy Lowes Dickinson, Basil Williams, and S.V. Keeling, London, Cambridge University Press, 1931; *Examination of McTaggart's Philosophy* by C.D. Broad, London, Cambridge University Press, 2 vols., 1933-38; *Truth, Love, and Immortality: An Introduction to McTaggart's Philosophy* by Peter Geach, Berkeley, University of California Press, and London, Hutchinson, 1979.

*   *   *

J. McT. E. McTaggart figures in that general movement in Europe and America in the late 19th century, the Idealist reaction to science and determinism. This reaction took many forms. There were attempts to anchor religious faith in philosophy, or to substitute philosophy for religious faith, or to re-explore the Kantian realm of the beautiful ("free," "independent of natural determinations") and to exalt aesthetic intuition and form over exteriority and representational elements. For a time neo-Hegelianism established itself solidly in British philosophy with F.H. Bradley, Bernard Bosanquet, T.H. Green and McTaggart, and with the Idealist Josiah Royce in America. Within a generation, however, the native concern for empiricism and science reasserted itself. McTaggart saw his influence challenged (not without having had certain effects) by two of his foremost students Bertrand Russell and G.E. Moore, both initially Idealist in sympathy. Yet, until his death in 1925 he remained a considerable presence at Cambridge University, like a lofty mountain, the more splendid without tributary slopes.

With many Idealist philosophers McTaggart shares the assumption that we radically misperceive the world about us. The veil of Maya is rarely, if ever, lifted to reveal ultimate reality. Lives, he felt, are so strewn with error and "so fragmentary that, in trying to explain them, we are almost tied down to two alternatives—either they mean nothing, or they are episodes in a long chain." Then he read Hegel whose description of the self-determining movement of the Absolute Spirit through time revealed the deep pattern of meaning to him. His three books on Hegel and dialectic set forth a new conception of the Absolute which he spent his life expounding with increasing certainty and subtlety. His *magnum opus* is *The Nature of Existence.*

McTaggart's Hegelianism was deeply colored by an emphasis on personhood and love, and this would play a significant role in the development of Cambridge Humanism, the Apostles, and eventually on the Bloomsbury Circle. By love we have the first dim perceptions that enable us to grasp the only really important knowledge we ever have of reality. Man began with these awakened perceptions; he followed their directive, and now strives onward under the forms of time and imperfection through successive, even opposing stages of incarnation, towards the final state of the Absolute, which is "a timeless and endless state of love—love so direct, so intimate, and so powerful that even the deepest mystic rapture gives us but the slightest foretaste of its perfection." The Absolute is a long way off and "between the present and that fruition there stretches a future which may well need courage." However, here and now we can grasp and enjoy something of the Absolute through love. This was his key point: the Absolute was a differentiated unity of finite selves or individuals for each of whom the unity exists. Parts, selves, do not lose themselves in the Whole like drops in the ocean. Selves are timeless, perfect portions of the Absolute.

Every human being, then, is identical with an immortal person in the heavenly company, contains a spark of love, and is eternal. By personalizing the Absolute in this way McTaggart relocated that single, self-subsistent category of Hegel's Absolute in a transcendental idealization of his own existence, his love for his wife, friends, his institutions: Clifton, Trinity, England. He was a member of the Cambridge Apostles. Friends, he believed, would meet again in future lives, and "Love at first sight" was an acknowledgement of the fact that two souls had loved one another in a previous life. McTaggart delivered his mystical insight in *The Further Determination of the Absolute* and *Human Immortality and Pre-Existence* which he gave to his friends who lost members of their families in the First World War. Travelling alone on the train to London, crossing a blighted district, McTaggart would cast his eye and discover a soul for whom he had an inborn affinity, whose soul he shared.

The dialectical method led McTaggart to extravagant conclusions. Although he believed in immortality and retained membership in the Church of England he was either an atheist or had reduced God to a non-creative and non-omnipotent person, more or less like the rest of mankind. He disparaged the sciences and history—strange notions for an Hegelian. Matter, he wrote, is "a bare possibility to which it would be foolish to attach the least importance, since there is nothing to make it at all preferable to any other hypothesis however wild," including belief in "the Gorgons and the Harpies." Physical objects like mountains, tables, and chairs had souls that communicated with one another but go unperceived by man's deceptive senses. Most notoriously, McTaggart denied the existence of Time. The new generation of Cambridge Realists, hunting for the most glaring metaphysical absurdities of the Idealists, liked to attack McTaggart on Time.

—John Paul Russo

MEAD, George Herbert. American philosopher. Born in South Hadley, Massachusetts, 27 February 1863. Studied at Oberlin College, Ohio, 1879-83, graduated 1883; Harvard University, Cambridge, Massachusetts, 1887-88; universities of Berlin and Leipzig, 1888-91. Married Helen Kingsbury Castle in 1891. School teacher, tutor, and surveyor, 1883-87; taught philosophy at the University of Michigan, Ann Arbor, 1891-94; Assistant Professor, 1894-1902, Associate Professor, 1902-07, and Professor of Philosophy, 1907-31, University of Chicago. *Died 26 April 1931.*

PUBLICATIONS

Philosophy

The Philosophy of the Present, edited by Arthur E. Murphy. Chicago, Open Court, 1932.
Mind, Self, and Society from the Standpoint of a Social Behaviorist, edited by Charles W. Morris. Chicago, University of Chicago Press, 1934.
Movements of Thought in the Nineteenth Century, edited by Merritt H. Moore. Chicago, University of Chicago Press, 1936.
The Philosophy of the Act, edited by Charles W. Morris and others. Chicago, University of Chicago Press, 1938.

The Social Psychology of George Herbert Mead (selections), edited by Anselm Strauss. Chicago, University of Chicago Press, 1956; revised edition, as *On Social Psychology*, 1964.
Selected Writings, edited by Andrew J. Reck. Indianapolis, Bobbs Merrill, 1964.

*

Critical Studies: *Self, Society, Existence: Human Nature and Dialogue in the Thought of George Herbert Mead and Martin Buber* by Paul Pfuetze, New York, Harper, 1954; *The Social Dynamics of George Herbert Mead* by Maurice Natanson, Washington, D.C., Public Affairs Press, 1956; *George Herbert Mead: Essays on His Social Philosophy* edited by John W. Petras, New York, Teachers College Press, 1968; *George Herbert Mead: Self, Language, and the World* by David L. Miller, Austin, University of Texas Press, 1973; *The Philosophy of George Herbert Mead* edited by Walter Robert Corti, Winterthur, Switzerland, Amriswiler, 1973; *Four Pragmatists: A Critical Introduction to Peirce, James, Mead, and Dewey* by Israel Scheffler, New York, Humanities Press, and London, Routledge, 1974; *George Herbert Mead's Concept of Rationality: A Study of the Use of Symbols and Other Implements* by W. Kang, The Hague, Mouton, 1976; *Masters of Social Psychology: Freud, Mead, Lewin, and Skinner* by James A. Schellenberg, New York, Oxford University Press, 1979; *Marx and Mead: Contributions to a Sociology of Knowledge* by Tom W. Goff, London, Routledge, 1980.

*   *   *

George Herbert Mead was once a leading figure in American pragmatism and the philosophical pragmatist whose formulations have been most important in the social sciences. Mead had undergraduate degrees from Oberlin and Harvard, and had studied at the universities of Leipzig and Berlin from 1888-1891. He began teaching in philosophy at the University of Michigan in 1891, and was brought to the University of Chicago in philosophy in 1894 by John Dewey. He remained at Chicago after Dewey went to Columbia in 1904. He accepted an appointment at Columbia University in 1931-32, but died before he could assume it. The date of his death is, for all practical purposes, also the date of the dissolution of the important and distinctive school of "Chicago pragmatism."

Mead was not an active writer. His ideas are preserved chiefly through posthumous publications of his lecture notes, which he had been constantly revising and updating, and through transcriptions of his lectures by his students who had anticipated that his ideas might otherwise be lost. Despite these sources, his basic ideas are so often repeated and so closely interwoven and consistent that there is no real reason to doubt what they were.

Recent writers on Mead have tended to stress his analysis of "the act" and his analysis of "the self," which when taken in isolation allow him to be seen as closely paralleling German sociology. But his own major stress was on a concept that underlay these both, and that clearly distinguished his view from that of those of sociologists and associated him clearly with a series of Kantian traditions in German ethnology and psychology—especially with the experimental psychology and "folk-psychology" of Wilhelm Wundt. This was his "emergent evolutionism." It was both a social psychological theory and an epistemology, concerned with both the development of human thought over the history of the human species and the development of each individual's mentality over the course of his life. Mead took as his starting point the Kantian position that the actual individual was the basis of both social and rational order. Given this, he described "the problem of society" as the problem of providing for individual order in a social context that was constantly undergoing evolutionary change. Then, following Wundt, he saw language as an evolutionary device to meet this problem, and "the field of mind" as emerging from language in turn. Thus Mead's system begins with a view of language, which, again following Wundt, he saw not as a set of noises to which significations were attached but rather as a system of ideas. Accordingly, in contrast to the positivists who had based their schemes on a distinction between terms which were particular and those which were general, Mead maintained that "you cannot say anything that is absolutely particular;" anything you say that has a meaning at all is universal." The surface point is that all concepts in a language, whether they appear to name the most encompassing things or the tiniest particulars, are equally shared, equally part of the common legacy. The point beneath this is that all are therefore equally important to communication, and the final point beneath both is that one has to begin by realizing that language as a whole, not just certain parts of language, is an evolved means of communication and is inherently both shared and classificatory. Thus, whenever you use language, "you are saying something that calls out a specific response in anybody else as it does for you" (this and following quotations are from *Social Psychology*, edited by Strauss). Thus the act of using language is an inherently social act; knowing language is knowing that others share one's own knowledge.

Given this, "mind," or consciousness, takes the status of the next organizational level above language: it is in a sense self-awareness of the use of language. It is the way we perceive thought or knowledge when we are forced into becoming aware of it consciously: "Mind, as constructive or reflective or problem solving thinking, is the socially acquired means of mechanism or apparatus whereby the human individual solves the various problems of environmental adjustment which arise to confront him in the course of his experience and which prevent his conduct from proceeding harmoniously on its way until they have thus been dealt." (Strauss: 268). Thus mind is not just an internal state. It too is an evolved device, a social creature. "The locus of mind is not in the individual. Mental processes are fragments of the complex conduct of the individual in and on his environment."

Mead's concepts of the "self" and of society were entities that appeared as aspects of mind. Under some circumstances, one who is aware of knowing things, of thinking, becomes reflexively aware of this knowledge—one actively knows that one knows something, and the "self" is the entity to which such knowledge is attributed, not more or less. "Society" is what the self is set off from, what is considered to surround it, and the two concepts are logically complementary: "A self can arise only where there is a social process within which this self has had its initiation. It arises within that process. For that process, the communication and participation to which I have referred is essential." The "self" in this sense is not something one has but rather more something one does, a process an individual engages in as part of acting in a larger social process, with others: "After all, what we mean by self-consciousness is an awakening in ourselves of the group of attitudes which we are arousing in others, especially when it is an important set of responses which go to make up the members of the community. It is unfortunate to fuse or mix up consciousness, as we ordinarily use the term, and self-consciousness."

Mead's concept of society was closely related to his concept that had been publicised under the label "the generalized other." Society was not a type of objective entity, but rather a framework for interaction that was presupposed by the nature of self and of minds. As the self arose only in a social process, so "society" was the generalized setting within which selves could arise. Specifically, it was the general setting for social institutions.

A social institution, in turn, was a specific set of roles that were interrelated in that they allowed a person taking any one role to see himself from the perspective of any one of the others. An institution was a set of "organized forms of group or social activities—forms so organized that the individual members of society can act adequately and socially by taking the attitudes of others towards those activities." Thus any one using such forms of behavior can see it from the perspective of other potential users, while anyone witnessing such a form of behavior can imagine himself enacting it. A very simple and common example

is the role of "I" vis-à-vis "you" in normal English speech. A more complex example is a role of a policeman vis-à-vis citizen, where even though most citizens may not in fact act as policemen any citizen can still in principle say "if I were a policeman, I would...." He has conventional and standardized assurances of how a policeman should act, and can imagine himself acting as a policeman given any set of circumstances. Similarly there are well-established public ways for a policeman and a judge to imagine themselves in each other's position; knowing what these are is part of the knowledge that each actor has in carrying out his particular role in the relationship. On the other hand, there are no such clear understandings defining the role of policeman and anthropologist, for example. A policeman, in order to be a policeman, does not need to know how he would act if he was an anthropologist, nor does he have to know how any specific act of his own would appear to an anthropologist. By the same token, in order to be an anthropologist, a person does not need to know how to put himself in the place of a policeman, nor does he have to know how any given act on his part would appear to a policeman. Policeman and anthropologist are not, therefore, roles defined in the same institution.

Mead's basic ideas of mind, self, and society supported a wide variety of activities and interests, from linguistics through experimental psychology to educational theory and practice. He exchanged students with, among others, Edward Sapir. These ideas were radically opposed, however, to the new interests and trends in positivistic philosophy of science, social, and cultural determinism in ethnology and sociology, and Freudian and related types of reductionisms in psychology. In the short run, these latter frameworks gained an ascendancy that seemed almost complete by the decade after World War II, and sociologists like Talcott Parsons and Robert Merton could claim to have subsumed Mead's ideas in their own systems of analysis. More recently, however, interest in pragmatism has re-emerged, especially in Peirce and Mead. Pragmatic assumptions underlie the cyberneticists, the psychology of Jean Piaget, the phenomenology of Erving Goffman and several lines of thought in anthropology and sociology concerned with symbolism and the dialectic of subject and object.

—Murray J. Leaf

MEAD, Margaret. American anthropologist. Born in Philadelphia, Pennsylvania, 16 December 1901. Educated at Doylestown High School, Pennsylvania, and New Hope School for Girls, Pennsylvania; studied at DePauw University, Greencastle, Indiana, 1919-20; Barnard College, New York, B.A. 1923 (Phi Beta Kappa); Columbia University, New York, M.A. 1924, Ph.D. 1929. Married Luther Cressman in 1923 (divorced); married Reo Franklin Fortune in 1928 (divorced); married Gregory Bateson in 1936 (divorced, 1950), 1 daughter. Field study of adolescent girls in Samoa (National Research Council fellowship); associate of Bishop Museum, Honolulu, 1925; Assistant Curator, 1926-42, Associate Curator, 1942-53, and Curator of Ethnology, 1964-69, then Emeritus, American Museum of Natural History, New York; also Lecturer, 1947-51, Director of Research in Contemporary Cultures, 1948-50, and Adjunct Professor of Anthropology, 1954-78, Columbia University. Field study of young children in the Admiralty Islands (Social Science Research Council Fellowship), 1928-29, and subsequent field work in New Guinea, 1931-33, 1953, 1964, 1967, 1971, 1973, and Bali, 1936-38, 1957-58. Visiting Lecturer in Child Study, Vassar College, Poughkeepsie, New York, 1939-41; Director, Wellesley School of Community Affairs, Cambridge, Massachusetts, 1943; Jacob Gimbel Lecturer, Stanford University and University of California, 1946; Lecturer, Salzburg Seminar on American Studies, 1947, and Unesco Workshop, Sèvres, 1947; Mason Lecturer,

University of Birmingham, 1949; Inglis Lecturer, Harvard University, Cambridge, Massachusetts, 1950; Jubilee Lecturer for New Education Fellowship, Australia, 1951; Philips Lecturer, Haverford College, Pennsylvania, 1955; Visiting Professor in psychiatry department, University of Cincinnati, 1957-58; Sloan Professor, Menninger School of Psychiatry, 1959-63; Reynolds Lecturer, University of Colorado, Boulder, 1960; Visiting Professor, Yale University, New Haven, Connecticut, 1966; Consultant, 1968, and Professor of Anthropology and Chairman of Social Science Division, 1969-71, Fordham University, New York; Alumni Association Distinguished Professor, University of Rhode Island, Providence, 1970-71; Fogarty Scholar-in-Residence, National Institute of Mental Health, 1973. Executive Secretary, Commission on Food Habits, National Research Council, 1942-45. President, Society of Applied Anthropology, 1940; Member of the Board, 1954-63, and Chairman of the Board, 1976, American Association for Advancement of Science; President, World Federation for Mental Health, 1956-57; President, American Anthropological Association, 1960; President, Scientists Institute for Public Information, 1970-73; President, World Society for Ekistics, 1972-73. Recipient: Society of Women Geographers Gold Medal, 1942; Viking Medal, 1958; Rice University Medal of Honor, 1962; Arches of Science Award, 1971; Kalinga Prize, 1971; Wilder Penfield Award, 1972; New York Academy of Sciences Lehmann Award, 1973; Medal of Freedom, 1979. Honorary doctorate: Wilson College, Chambersburg, Pennsylvania, 1940; Rutgers University, New Brunswick, New Jersey, 1941; Elmira College, New York, 1947; Western College for Women, 1955; University of Leeds, 1957; Kalamazoo College, Michigan, 1957; Skidmore College, Saratoga Springs, New York, 1958; Goucher College, Baltimore, 1960; Temple University, Philadelphia, 1962; Lincoln University, Pennsylvania, 1963; Columbia University, 1964; University of Cincinnati, 1965. Fellow, Society of Women Geographers, and American Orthopsychiatric Association; Member, National Academy of Sciences, 1975. *Died 15 November 1978.*

PUBLICATIONS

Anthropology

An Inquiry into the Question of Cultural Stability in Polynesia. New York, Columbia University Press, 1928.
Coming of Age in Samoa: A Psychological Study of Primitive Youth for Western Civilization. New York, Morrow, 1928; London, Cape, 1929.
Social Organization of Manu'a. Honolulu, Bishop Museum, 1930.
Growing Up in New Guinea: A Comparative Study of Primitive Education. New York, Morrow, 1930; London, Routledge, 1931.
The Changing Culture of an Indian Tribe. New York, Columbia University Press, 1932.
Sex and Temperament in Three Primitive Societies. New York, Morrow, and London, Routledge, 1935.
From the South Seas: Studies of Adolescence and Sex in Primitive Societies. New York, Morrow, 1939.
Balinese Character: A Photographic Analysis, with Gregory Bateson. New York, New York Academy of Sciences, 1942.
The American Troops and the British Community. London, Hutchinson, 1944.
Social Anthropology. Pasadena, California, Western Personnel Service, 1945.
The Family's Food. London, Bureau of Current Affairs, 1949.
Male and Female: A Study of the Sexes in a Changing World. New York, Morrow, and London, Gollancz, 1949.
Soviet Attitudes Toward Authority. New York, McGraw Hill, 1951.
The School in American Culture (lecture). Cambridge, Massachusetts, Harvard University Press, 1951.

Growth and Culture: A Photographic Study of Balinese Childhood, with Francis Cooke MacGregor. New York, Putnam, 1951.
Themes in French Culture: A Preface to a Study of French Community, with Rhoda Metraux. Stanford, California, Stanford University Press, 1954.
New Lives for Old: Cultural Transformation, Manus, 1928-1953. New York, Morrow, and London, Gollancz, 1956.
Israel and Problems of Identity. New York, Herzl Foundation, 1958.
A Creative Life for Your Child. Washington, D.C., Department of Health, Education, and Welfare, 1962.
Food Habits Research: Problems of the 1960's. Washington, D.C., National Academy of Sciences-National Research Council, 1964.
Anthropology, A Human Science: Selected Papers. Princeton, New Jersey, Van Nostrand, 1964.
Continuities in Cultural Evolution. New Haven, Connecticut, Yale University Press, 1964.
Family, with Ken Heyman. New York, Macmillan, 1965.
The Wagon and the Star: A Study of American Community Initiative, with Muriel Brown. St. Paul, Curriculum Resources, 1966.
Culture and Commitment: A Study of the Generation Gap. New York, Doubleday, and London, Bodley Head, 1970.
A Way of Seeing with Rhoda Metraux. New York, McCall, 1970.
A Rap on Race, with James Baldwin. Philadelphia, Lippincott, and London, Joseph, 1971.
World Enough: Rethinking the Future, with Ken Heyman. Boston, Little Brown, 1975.
Some Personal Views, edited by Rhoda Metraux. New York, Walker, and London, Angus and Robertson, 1979.

Other

And Keep Your Powder Dry: An Anthropologist Looks at America. New York, Morrow, 1942; as *The American Character,* London, Penguin, 1944.
A Bread and Butter Letter from a Lecturer. Los Angeles, Occidental College, 1944.
People and Places (juvenile). Cleveland, World, 1959.
Anthropologists and What They Do (juvenile). New York, Watts, 1965.
The Small Conference: An Innovation in Communication, with Paul Byers. The Hague, Mouton, 1968.
Blackberry Winter: My Earlier Years. New York, Morrow, 1972; London, Angus and Robertson, 1973.
Ruth Benedict. New York, Columbia University Press, 1974.
Twentieth Century Faith: Hope and Survival. New York, Harper, 1974.
Letters from the Field 1925-1975. New York, Harper, 1977.
An Interview with Santa Claus, with Rhoda Metraux. New York, Walker, 1978.
Aspects of the Present, with Rhoda Metraux. New York, Morrow, 1980.

Editor, *Cooperation and Competition among Primitive Peoples.* New York, McGraw Hill, 1937.
Editor, *Cultural Patterns and Technical Changes: A Manual Prepared by the World Federation for Mental Health.* Paris, Unesco, 1953.
Editor, with Nicolas Calas, *Primitive Heritage: An Anthropological Anthology.* New York, Random House, 1953; London, Gollancz, 1954.
Editor, with Rhoda Metraux, *The Study of Culture at a Distance.* Chicago, University of Chicago Press, 1953
Editor, with Martha Wolfenstein, *Childhood in Contemporary Cultures.* Chicago, University of Chicago Press, 1955.
Editor, *An Anthropologist at Work: Writings of Ruth Benedict.* Boston, Houghton Mifflin, 1959.

Editor, with Ruth L. Bunzel, *The Golden Age of American Anthropology.* New York, Braziller, 1960.

Editor, with Francis B. Kaplan, *American Women.* New York, Scribner, 1965.

Editor, with others, *Science and the Concept of Race.* New York, Columbia University Press, 1968.

Editor, with others, *To Love or to Perish: The Technological Crisis and the Churches.* New York, Friendship Press, 1972.

*

Bibliography: *Margaret Mead: The Complete Bibliography 1925-1975* by Joan Gordan, The Hague, Mouton, 1976.

Critical Studies: *Margaret Mead: A Voice for the Century* by Robert Cassidy, New York, Universe, 1982; *Margaret Mead and Samoa: The Making and Unmaking of an Anthropological Myth* by Derek Freeman, Cambridge, Massachusetts, Harvard University Press, 1983.

* * *

Margaret Mead was perhaps the only anthropologist ever to become a household word in America. Through her films, best-selling books, her column in *Redbook* magazine, and her counsel to world figures, she attained truly international stature. To the American public, she was synonomous with anthropology. Mead was an innovator in that she consistently tried to point out the relevance of studies of "primitives" for understanding our own society. She applied anthropological insights directly to modern social problems such as sex roles (*Male and Female*), culture change (*Culture and Commitment*), and race relations (*A Rap on Race*, with James Baldwin). Such "popular" concerns did not always win her the respect of colleagues within anthropology. In her later years, Mead's scholarly contributions were overshadowed by her status as a public figure, and her leadership within the discipline was more personal than theoretical. Her daughter has written of her: "much of her contribution will turn out to be the way in which she stimulated and supported the work of others."

Theoretically, Mead's work falls under the rubric of "culture and personality" or "psychological anthropology." Like her long-time friend and colleague, Ruth Benedict, she followed up the theme of psychologism in the work of their mentor, Franz Boas. The legacy of Boasian historical-particularism is evident in Mead's emphasis on the diversity of cultures. Again and again in her books, she brings home the lesson of cultural relativism: that our way is not the only way, that other cultures may do things differently, that they are not inferior, merely different. Following Boas and Benedict, Mead stresses the arbitrary, non-biological nature of the culture. In *Sex and Temperament* she demonstrated that gender-linked temperamental expectations are culturally defined, and relative to particular societies. Her conclusion that the definitions of normal and abnormal vary cross-culturally presaged later sociological theories of deviance such as "labeling" and symbolic interactionism.

Mead's works reflect three major areas of interest: socialization and childrearing, the nature of sex roles, and typical personality or "cultural character." Quite early in her career, she became fascinated with the thought processes of children, and particularly of primitive children. In *Growing Up in New Guinea* Mead was one of the first to question Piaget's thesis that the "savage" and the child think alike, and Freud's theory that the child, the "savage," and the neurotic think alike. She was probably the first ethnographer to use projective psychological techniques in the field, including her own ink-blot test (which she improvised in Manus after reading about the Rorschach test), Chinese glass chimes, and Japanese paper flowers that unfold in water. In Manus, she elicited thousands of drawings by children who had never used a paper and pencil.

Mead's ability to write for a general audience should not overshadow her technical competence. Her first book, *Coming of Age in Samoa*, was a popular as well as scholarly success, but her academic treatise on Samoa, *Social Organization of Manu'a*, remains an essential reference work for students of Polynesian societies. *Coming of Age*, a study of the adolescence of Samoan girls, posed the question: "Are the disturbances which vex our adolescents due to the nature of adolescence itself or to the civilisation? Under different conditions does adolescence present a different picture?" Mead concludes that the period of crisis faced by many adolescents in our own society is not biologically determined, but is due to the cultural milieu: "the main lesson" of the Samoan work is "that adolescence is not necessarily a time of stress and strain, but that cultural conditions make it so." While demonstrating this fact, Mead also described the character of Samoan culture and compared it to our own:

> The Samoan background which makes growing up so easy, so simple a matter, is the general casualness of the whole society. For Samoa is a place where no one plays for very high stakes, no one pays very heavy prices, no one suffers for his convictions or fights to the death for special ends.... No one is hurried along in life or punished harshly for slowness of development. Instead the gifted, the precocious, are held back, until the slowest among them have caught the pace. And in personal relations, caring is as slight. Love and hate, jealousy and revenge, sorrow and bereavement, are all matters of weeks.... In this casual attitude towards life, in this avoidance of conflict, of poignant situations, Samoa contrasts strongly not only with America but also with most primitive civilisations. And however much we may deplore such an attitude and feel that important personalities and great art are not born in such a shallow society, we must recognize that here is a strong factor in the painless development from childhood to womanhood. For where no one feels very strongly, the adolescent will not be tortured by poignant situations.

This was the first of Mead's vivid, holistic portrayals of cultural styles. Along with Ruth Benedict's *Patterns of Culture*, Mead's three early studies of oceanic societies (*Coming of Age*, *Growing Up in New Guinea*, and *Sex and Temperament*) ushered in the configurational approach in psychological anthropology. Mead did not follow Benedict's method of "typing" whole societies, but, like Benedict, she assumed that different societies encourage certain personality traits to flourish, while discouraging others. Mead focused particularly on child-rearing as the means by which a culture "molds and shapes" individuals to fit its approved temperamental type. Her work whittles away at the notion of "human nature" as a core of psychic characteristics shared by all men, and proves rather man's near-infinite plasticity in the face of culture. In *Sex and Temperament* Mead demonstrated that our stereotypic ideas of "masculine" and "feminine" behavior are not universal. She went to New Guinea to study "the conditioning of the social personalities of the two sexes." Her general finding was that "the potentialities which different societies label as either masculine or feminine are really potentialities of some members of each sex, and not sex-linked at all." Within a hundred-mile radius, she found three tribes, the Arapesh, Mundugumor, and Tchambuli, that exemplified the range of possible ways in which societies can standardize sex-role behavior: "In one, both men and women act as we expect women to act—in a mild parental responsive way: in the second, both act as we expect men to act—in a fierce initiating fashion; and in the third, the men act according to our stereotype for women—are catty, wear curls, and go shopping, while the women are energetic, managerial, unadorned partners."

"Temperament" in Mead's formulation is innate individual endowment, the individual's inborn character. Mead's central point in *Sex and Temperament* is that one sex does not have an innate temperament that contrasts with that of the opposite sex.

By nature, certain *people* may be aggressive, dominating, managerial, while others may be passive, sensitive, and nurturing; it is our society that links such temperamental contrasts to gender, and the differentiation we make is merely one of a range of possibilities. "Our own society" makes much of the "theme" of sex difference in its "cultural plot." But neither the "maternal" Arapesh nor the "virile" Mundugumor assume the sexes to be temperamentally different on the order of active vs. passive, rough vs. gentle, unemotional vs. emotional. This is not to say that men and women do the same things, or have the same social status. Women are jurally and ritually inferior to men in all three societies described in *Sex and Temperament*, and Mead has been criticized for ignoring the extreme structural differentiation of the sexes that is widespread in New Guinea. Critics have pointed to evidence in Mead's own work that Arapesh men are more active and aggressive than Arapesh women. But Mead's point is that "Men and Women do different things for the same reasons" among the Arapesh and Mundugumor: "men are not expected to respond to one set of motivations and women to another."

Mead recognized that, although most people are "malleable" enough to conform to their society's expectations, there will always be a minority of individuals who are uncomfortable with their own culture. With Ruth Benedict, she developed the concept of the "deviant" as a cultural misfit, an individual who is "at variance with the values of his society." The deviant is a misplaced temperament, stuck in the wrong pattern, the wrong set of expectations. Among the Arapesh, for example, the deviant is the violent and aggressive person:

> Wabe...was the man who naturally gravitated to the service of the white man, an ideal boss boy in a hierarchical scheme. In his own culture, he was a loss both to himself and to his community. Of all the men in the locality of Alitoa, he was the one who approached most strongly to a western-European ideal of the male, well-built, with a handsome face with fine lines, a well-integrated body, violent, possessive, arbitrary, dictatorial, positively and aggressively sexed. Among the Arapesh, he was a pathetic figure.

The holistic treatment of the three cultures in *Sex and Temperament* strongly reflects the influence of Ruth Benedict's concept of "pattern." Mead was attracted to Benedict's notion of culture as "personality writ large." Mead developed her own configuration theory under the rubric of "cultural character," which she defined as "the regularities in the intrapsychic organization of the individual members of a given society that are to be attributed to these individuals' having been reared within that culture." "Cultural character" is similar to other concepts in psychological anthropology, such as "typical," "basic," and "modal" personality, that presume the "replication of uniformity," to use Anthony Wallace's phrase: the premise that individuals brought up within a culture share a common core of psychological traits. Mead's cultural character derives from the notion that a personality type may be characteristic of a culture as a whole, but she shifts the emphasis from the individual to the level of the whole: to the character of the culture, rather than the character of the individual personalities within. The descriptions in *Sex and Temperament* presage this development; Mead uses details of social organization and even material culture to support her characterizations. She moves from the Arapesh lack of aggression to the absence of private property, from their lack of initiative to dispersed residence and land tenure. The Arapesh "lack of structure, their lack of strict and formal ways of dealing with the interrelations between human beings," extends to all aspects of their culture: even their houses "are carelessly and asymmetrically built." Most anthropologists prefer to analyze kinship and marriage as systems or structures in their own right. Mead's attempt to portray them as reflections of Arapesh character have been criticized as reductionist.

Clearly, this mode of ethnographic description is a very literary undertaking. To anthropologists concerned with scientific rigor and objective proof, Mead's work sometimes seems intolerably subjective. Critics questioned whether the temperamental contrasts described in *Sex and Temperament* were not too "neat" to have occurred within Mead's fieldwork radius, but she always insisted that the differences "lay in these three cultures themselves." Mead left a legacy of vivid ethnography; her descriptions are compelling, rich, and humanistic. Her interpretive, "subjective" ethnographic style nonetheless manages to capture certain essential truths about a culture—truths that elude more "objective" accounts.

Under the guidance of Mead and Benedict, the cultural character concept was applied to contemporary societies in the Columbia University Research in Contemporary Cultures project, also referred to as the study of national character and the study of culture at a distance. The R.C.C. project was perhaps the largest and most organized application of a particular paradigm in anthropology, and bore the stamp of Mead's interests in child development and the cross-cultural use of projective techniques. Mead felt that blind spots were dangerous—that the Russians were a threat to us in the nuclear age only to the extent that we did not understand them. The R.C.C. project included studies of several societies in which direct fieldwork was impossible—Japan, the U.S.S.R., the Eastern European Jewish community. Statements about national character were derived intuitively from qualitative cultural data—norms, ideology, texts, and interviews with expatriates.

In her later years, Mead's theoretical position, and particularly the cultural character concept, represented to many of her colleagues a paradigm that anthropology had transcended. At least, the prevailing theoretical fashion had shifted from psychological anthropology to the opposing paradigms of ecological/biological determinism and structural/symbolic anthropology. Even within psychological anthropology, most scholars came to believe that society represented the "organization of diversity" rather than the replication of uniformity. But Mead's identification with a theory that some felt to be outmoded should not overshadow her scholarly breadth and, particularly, her brilliance as a fieldworker. In the latter area, Mead pioneered the use of photography in fieldwork with Gregory Bateson in Bali. Their use of film and still photographs to document Balinese culture represented a major methodological advance in ethnography.

Mead's most enduring legacy may be her work on sex roles, which foreshadowed many of the arguments advanced by feminists in the 1970's. In *Sex and Temperament* and *Male and Female* she argued that women's—and man's—destiny need not be limited by stereotypic cultural expectations—a principle that she lived, as well as proved. She demonstrated empirically that our rigid gender dichotomization is artificial, and argued convincingly that it produces "unplaced" individuals and wastes human potentialities:

> ...a sex stereotype that decrees the interests and occupations of each sex is usually not completely without a basis. The idea of the male in a given society may conform very closely to the temperament of some of one type of male. The idea of the female *may* conform to the female who belongs to the same type, or instead to the female of some other type. For the children who do not belong to these preferred types, only the primary sex characters will be definitive in helping them to classify themselves. Their impulses, their preferences, and later much of their physique will be aberrant. They will be doomed throughout life to sit among the other members of their sex feeling less a man, or less a woman, simply because the cultural idea is based on a different set of clues, a set of clues no less valid, but different.

With the conviction, perhaps, of experience, she outlines the difficulties faced by the achieving woman in our society:

Just so the New Guinea native tells the story of the woman who hands to men the symbols by which they can compensate themselves for their inferiority to her, and then adds that they had better kill her...there is built into the girl in America a conflict of another order.... If she learns the rules well, if she gets good marks, wins scholarships, gets the cub reporter's job, by so much she has done an unforgivable thing, in her own eyes and in the eyes of all those around her. Each step forward in work as a successful American regardless of sex means a step back as a woman, and also, inferentially, a step back imposed on some male. For maleness in America is not absolutely defined, it has to be kept and re-earned every day, and one essential element in the definition is beating women in every game that both sexes play, in every activity in which both sexes engage.

Male and Female attempts to answer the question: what *are* the innate differences between men and women? But most of the book is a compendium of ethnographic examples, illustrating the almost limitless cultural elaborations on limited biological givens. Yet givens there are; Mead links the division of labor in the family to certain inescapable "biological regularities." The "fundamental regularity" that *some* difference is always recognized between male and female "is of course tied up with lactation, and with the carry-over into social patterns that because women breast-feed children, they are also the ones to care for them." She also emphasizes the imperatives of "natural" female rhythms: "When human beings view their biological inheritance and consider to what extent they are bound by it, women appear at once as the more intractable material. Conception and birth are as stubborn conditions of life as death itself."

Mead's emphasis on biological imperatives as underlying the stereotypic division of labor seems to undercut the conclusions of *Sex and Temperament*. Nonetheless, *Male and Female* ends with a plea for choice, for a society in which *both* sexes might realize their full potential:

Just as for endless ages men's mathematical gifts were neglected...so women's intuitive gifts have lain fallow, uncultivated, uncivilized. Once it is possible to say it is as important to take women's gifts and make them available to both men and women, in transmittable form, as it was to take men's gifts and make the civilization built upon them available to both men and women, we shall have enriched our society.... We can build a whole society only by using both the gifts special to each sex and those shared by both sexes—by using the gifts of the whole of humanity.

—Jocelyn Linnekin

MEINECKE, Friedrich. German historian. Born in Salzwedel, Prussia, 30 October 1862. Studied at the universities of Bonn and Berlin, 1882-86. Archivist, German Secret State Archives, 1887-1901; Professor, University of Berlin, 1896-1901, University of Strasbourg, 1901-06, University of Freiburg, 1906-14, and again at University of Berlin, 1914-28; Head, Historische Reichskommission, 1930-35; Rector, 1948-49, and Honorary Rector, 1949-54, Free University of Berlin. Editor, *Historische Zeitschrift*, 1893-1935. Honorary doctorate: Harvard University, Cambridge, Massachusetts. Senator, German Academy of Science. Member, Prussian Academy of Sciences; Bavarian Academy of Sciences; and Heidelberg Academy of Sciences. Member, Danish Academy of Sciences, and Accademia dei Lincei, Rome; Honorary Member, Vienna Academy, and Boston Academy. *Died 6 February 1954.*

PUBLICATIONS

Collections

Werke, edited by Hans Herzfeld, Carl Hinrichs, and Walther Hofer. Stuttgart, Koehler, 8 vols., 1957-79.

History

Das Stralendorffsche Gutachten und der Jülicher Erbfolgestreit. Potsdam, n.p., 1886.
Die deutschen Gesellschaften und der Hoffmannsche Bund: Ein Beitrag zur Geschichte der politischen Bewegungen in Deutschland im Zeitalter der Befreiungskriege. Stuttgart, Cotta, 1891.
Das Leben des Generalfeldmarschalls Hermann von Boyen. Stuttgart, Cotta, 2 vols., 1896-99.
Das Zeitalter der deutschen Erhebung 1795-1815. Bielefeld, Velhagen und Klasing, 1906; as *The Age of German Liberation 1795-1815*, edited by Peter Paret, Berkeley, University of California Press, 1977.
Von Stein zu Bismarck: Historische Aufsätze. Berlin, Koobs, 1907.
Weltbürgertum und Nationalstaat: Studian zur Genesis des deutschen Nationalstaats. Munich, Oldenbourg, 1908; as *Cosmopolitanism and the National State*, Princeton, New Jersey, Princeton University Press, 1970.
Radowitz und die deutsche Revolution. Berlin, Mittler, 1913.
Die deutsche Erhebung von 1914: Vorträge und Aufsätze. Stuttgart, Cotta, 1914; as *The Warfare of a Nation: Lectures and Essays*, Worcester, Massachusetts, Davis Press, 1915.
Probleme des Weltkriegs: Aufsätze. Munich, Oldenbourg, 1917.
Die Bedeutung der geschichtlichen Welt und des Geschichtsunterrichts für die Bildung der Einzelpersönlichkeit (lecture). Berlin, Mittler, 1918; as *Persönlichkeit und geschichtliche Welt*, 1923.
Für welche Güter zog Deutschland 1914 sein Schwert? Berlin, Siegismund, 1918.
Preussen und Deutschland im 19. und 20. Jahrhundert: Historische und politische Aufsätze. Munich, Oldenbourg, 1918.
Nach der Revolution: Geschichtliche Betrachtungen über unsere Lage. Munich, Oldenbourg, 1919.
Die Idee der Staatsräson in der neueren Geschichte. Munich, Oldenbourg, 1924; as *Machiavellism: The Doctrine of Raison d'Etat and Its Place in Modern History*, New York, Praeger, 1957.
Geschichte des deutsch-englischen Bündnisproblems 1890-1901. Munich, Oldenbourg, 1927.
Staat und Persönlichkeit: Studien. Berlin, Mittler, 1933.
Die Entstehung des Historismus. Munich, Oldenbourg, 2 vols. 1936; as *Historicism: The Rise of a New Historical Outlook*, London, Routledge, and New York, Herder, 1972.
Schiller und der Individualitätsgedanke: Eine Studie zur Entstehungsgeschichte des Historismus. Leipzig, Meiner, 1937.
Vom Geschichtlichen Sinn und vom Sinn der Geschichte (selected essays). Leipzig, Koehler und Amelang, 1939.
Preussisch-deutsche Gestalten und Probleme (selected essays). Leipzig, Koehler und Amelang, 1940.
Aphorismen und Skizzen zur Geschichte. Leipzig, Koehler und Amelang, 1942.
Die deutsche Katastrophe: Betrachtungen und Erinnerungen. Wiesbaden, E. Brockhaus, 1946; as *The German Catastrophe: Reflections and Recollections*, Cambridge, Massachusetts, Harvard University Press, 1950.
1848: Eine Säkularbetrachtung. Berlin, Blanvalet, 1948; as "Year 1848 in German History: Reflections of a Centenary," in *Making of Modern Europe: Waterloo to the Atomic Age*, edited by Herman Ausubel, New York, Dryden, 1951.
Ranke und Burckhardt: Ein Vortrag. Berlin, Akademie, 1948; in *German History: Some New Views*, edited by Hans Hokn,

Boston, Beacon Press, and London, Allen and Unwin, 1954.
Schaffender Spiegel: Studien zur deutschen Geschichtschreibung und Geschichtsauffassung. Stuttgart, Koehler, 1948.

Other

Erlebtes 1862-1901 (autobiography). Leipzig, Koehler und Amelang, 1941.
Strassburg, Freiburg, Berlin 1901-1919: Erinnerungen (autobiography). Stuttgart, Koehler, 1949.

*

Bibliography: *Friedrich Meinecke Bibliographie* by Anne-Marie Reinhold, Munich, Oldenbourg, 1952.

Critical Studies: *Geschichtschreibung und Weltanschauung: Betrachtungen zum Werk Friedrich Meineckes* by Walther Hofer, Munich, Oldenbourg, 1950; *Ethics in a World of Power: The Political Ideas of Friedrich Meinecke* by Richard W. Sterling, Princeton, New Jersey, Princeton University Press, 1958; *From History to Sociology: The Transition in German Historical Thinking* by Carlo Antoni, Detroit, Wayne State University Press, 1959; *The German Conception of History: The National Tradition of Historical Thought from Herder to the Present* by Georg Iggers, Middletown, Connecticut, Wesleyan University Press, 1968; *Frederico Meinecke e la crisi d'ello stata nazionale tedesco* by Sergio Pistone, Turin, Giappichelli, 1969; *Friedrich Meinecke and German Politics in the Twentieth Century* by Robert A. Pois, Berkeley, University of California Press, 1972; *Ideologie des deutschen Weges: Die deutsche Geschichte in der Historiographie zwischen Kaiserreich und Nationalsozialismus* by Bernd Faulenbach, Munich, Beck, 1980.

*   *   *

Friedrich Meinecke was born in Salzwedel, in Prussian Saxony in 1862, the son of a minor civil servant. Meinecke attended the University of Berlin which, during the last decades of the 19th century, probably had the most distinguished history faculty in Germany, if not Europe, and Meinecke was exposed to the influences of Johann Gustav Droysen, Heinrich von Treitschke, and Heinrich von Sybel, representatives of the appropriately named "Prussian School" of historiography. Meinecke was also acquainted with, and sympathetic to, the work of Wilhelm Dilthey.

The Prussian School was informed by the doctrine known as "historicism," and Meinecke, along with the Italian philosopher and historian, Benedetto Croce, would be its last significant representative. Basically, historicism, to which several generations of German philosophers and historians had made substantial contributions, held that the so-called "historical individuality," be it a person, philosophical idea, battle, or state, was *the* unit upon which the reflective, intuitive energies of historians ought to be directed. Inductive generalizations could be made, and there might well be a pattern to historical events; but, the "historical individuality" subsisted as the center, the guiding principle, of historical research. While each individuality was important, the state was the most important one of all and, according to Ranke and to the members of the Prussian School, it was charged with ethical purpose. Historicism, with its belief in the ethical nature of the state and in its general emphasis upon political history and the ideational substructure underlying the emergence of the modern state, was essentially an optimistic doctrine, reflecting the sense of political well-being enjoyed by large sectors of the German bourgeoisie in the heady days following German unification.

Meinecke, who, after serving as an archivist in Berlin, held posts at the universities of Strassburg, Freiburg, and eventually Berlin, was not quite as simplistic as Ranke and his Prussian School mentors. He too thought, however, that a reconciliation between power and culture was possible and that the German state was well on its way towards achieving this goal. Such views found expression in his 1908 work, *Weltbürgertum und Nationalstaat.* Strongly influenced by the ideas of Friedrich Naumann and, to a lesser extent, Max Weber, Meinecke thought that the state could be substantially strengthened by integrating more of Germany's liberal bourgeoisie and working class into it, thus providing these elements with a stronger sense of citizenship and feeling of duty. Before and during the First World War, Meinecke was a champion of reform, calling for a weakening of the powers of the superannuated *Junker* class and a greatly strengthened *Reichstag*. Until Wilhelm II's abdication, however, he remained a strong supporter of the monarchy, albeit longing for a more constitutional one.

Meinecke, like all Germans, was stunned by the toll taken by the First World War, and, more importantly, Germany's defeat in the conflict. Very grudgingly, he accepted the fact that the monarchy was gone, and, along with many liberal academics, joined the newly formed German Democratic Party, the only non-confessional bourgeois party to support the Weimar Republic. In doing this, he was following the lead of his political mentor Friedrich Naumann, who saw a well-established republican government as a means of assuring the continued existence and strengthening of the German state. At the same time, though, World War I caused him to question the presumed ethical character of that state so central to historicism, and this questioning found expression in the 1924 work *Die Idee der Staatsräson in der neueren Geschichte* and in an increasing tendency to try to identify "historical individualities" with cultural rather than power-grounded historical forms. In the interwar period, Meinecke displayed a good deal of intellectual confusion. On the level of practical politics, he continued to call for a strong state, one above political parties, and, in so doing, revealed an increasing tendency towards political romanticism. With regard to historical hypothesyzing, however, he called into question some of the basic assumptions of historicism. Yet, in his two-volume 1936 work, *Die Entstehung des Historismus*, he seemed to praise historicism as a uniquely German, inherently spiritual, doctrine which represented an apotheosis of historical thought. In this work, he had much praise for Ranke, but ended the work by extolling the cosmopolitan Goethe, whose fundamental distaste for the historical discipline was well-known.

When the Nazis, to whom Meinecke was opposed, largely for power-political reasons, came to power, he was distressed but evidenced a certain willingness to accommodate himself to them. Accommodation, however, was not enough, and in 1935 Meinecke was removed from the Historical Commission and, the following year, from the board of the *Historische Zeitschrift*, which he had edited since 1894. He was replaced by the party hack Alexander von Müller. After the Second World War and another, even more crushing, German defeat, Meinecke, now 85 years old and almost blind, wrote *The German Catastrophe* (1946). In this work, and in later essays, Meinecke rejected historicism altogether. He further declared that it was now necessary for Germans to turn back to the hallowed cosmopolitanism of Goethe. However, while condemning those excesses of power which he saw as responsible for the emergence and initial success of National Socialism, Meinecke spent very little time considering Nazi excesses, particularly those singular ones directed against the Jews. Nevertheless, his at least formal opposition to Nazism and his apparent rejection of that nationalism which underlay the historicist position, were primarily responsible for his being appointed first rector of the newly established and presumably democratic Free University of Berlin. He died in Berlin in 1954, the confused intellectual and emotional legacy left behind serving as testimony to that of modern Germany.

—Robert A. Pois

MERLEAU-PONTY, Maurice.   French philosopher and psychologist. Born in Rochefort-sur-Mer, 14 March 1908. Educated at the Lycée Janson-de-Sailly and the Lycée Louis-le-Grand, Paris; studied at the École Normal Supérieure, agregation in philosophy, 1930; Ph.D. 1945. Served as an officer in the French infantry, 1939-40. Taught at the Lycée de Beauvais, 1931-33, and at the Lycée de Chartres, 1934-35; Professor of Philosophy, Lycée Carnot, Paris, 1940-44, and University of Lyons, 1945-48; Professor of Child Psychology and Pedagogy, Sorbonne, Paris, 1949-52; Professor, Collège de France, Paris, 1952-61. Co-Founder, with Jean-Paul Sartre and Simone de Beauvoir, *Les Temps Modernes. Died* (in Paris) *3 May 1961.*

PUBLICATIONS

Philosophy and Psychology

La Structure du comportement.   Paris, Presses Universitaires de France, 1942; as *The Structure of Behavior*, Boston, Beacon Press, 1963.
Phénoménologie de la perception.   Paris, Gallimard, 1945; as *Phenomenology of Perception*, New York, Humanities Press, and London, Routledge, 1962.
Humanisme et terreur: Essai sur le problème communiste. Paris, Gallimard, 1947; as *Humanism and Terror: An Essay on the Communist Problem*, Boston, Beacon Press, 1969.
Sens et non-sens.   Paris, Nagel, 1948; as *Sense and Non-sense*, Evanston, Illinois, Northwestern University Press, 1964.
Éloge de la philosophie (lecture).   Paris, Gallimard, 1953; as *In Praise of Philosophy*, Evanston, Illinois, Northwestern University Press, 1963.
Les Aventures de la dialectique.   Paris, Gallimard, 1955; as *Adventures of the Dialectic*, Evanston, Illinois, Northwestern University Press, 1973.
Les Philosophes célèbres (selected essays).   Paris, Mazenod, 1956.
Signes.   Paris, Gallimard, 1960; as *Signs*, Evanston, Illinois, Northwestern University Press, 1964.
Éloge de la philosophie et autres essais.   Paris, Gallimard, 1960.
The Primacy of Perception and Other Essays, edited by James M. Edie.   Evanston, Illinois, Northwestern University Press, 1964.
L'Œil et l'esprit.   Paris, Gallimard, 1964.
Le Visible et l'invisible suivi de notes de travail, edited by Claude Lefort.   Paris, Gallimard, 1964; as *The Visible and the Invisible, followed by Working Notes*, Evanston, Illinois, Northwestern University Press, 1968.
L'Union de l'âme et du corps chez Malebranche, Biran, et Bergson (lecture).   Paris, Vrin, 1968.
Résumés de cours: Collège de France, 1952-1960.   Paris, Gallimard, 1968; as *Themes from the Lectures at the Collège de France, 1952-1960*, Evanston, Illinois, Northwestern University Press, 1970.
Le Prose du monde, edited by Claude Lefort.   Paris, Gallimard, 1969; as *The Prose of the World*, Evanston, Illinois, Northwestern University Press, 1973.
The Essential Writings of Merleau-Ponty, edited by Alden L. Fischer.   New York, Harcourt Brace, 1969.
Consciousness and the Acquisition of Language (student notes from Merleau-Ponty's Sorbonne lectures).   Evanston, Illinois, Northwestern University Press, 1973.
Phenomenology, Language, and Sociology: Selected Essays, edited by John O'Neill.   London, Heinemann, 1974.

*

Bibliography: *Maurice Merleau-Ponty and His Critics: An International Bibliography (1942-1976), Preceded by a Bibliography of Merleau-Ponty's Writings* by François H. LaPointe, New York, Garland, 1976.

Critical Studies: *The Philosophy of Merleau-Ponty* by John F. Bannon, New York, Harcourt Brace, 1967; *Merleau-Ponty's Critique of Reason*, New Haven, Connecticut, Yale University Press, 1966, and *Speaking and Semiology: Maurice Merleau-Ponty's Phenomenological Theory of Existential Communication*, The Hague, Mouton, 1972, both by Thomas Langan; *Merleau-Ponty's Philosophy* by Samuel B. Mallin, New Haven, Connecticut, Yale University Press, 1979; *Sartre and Merleau-Ponty* by David Archard, Belfast, Blackstaff Press, 1980; *The Political Philosophy of Merleau-Ponty* by Sonia Kruks, Brighton, Harvester, 1981.

*   *   *

Maurice Merleau-Ponty was one of the leading philosophers in France during the postwar period. Although he was less known than Sartre, he was in France in strictly philosophical matters ranked by many higher than any of his contemporaries. It is not easy to characterize the nature of Merleau-Ponty's philosophy because his thought continued to develop gradually without ever reaching a definitive point between 1930, when he received his Ph.D., and 1961, the year of his death. Shortly after completing his formal education at the École Normale Supérieure in Paris, he became dissatisfied with the idealist philosophy in which he had been educated. He first turned to Scheler, then to Marcel, and finally, upon the advice of Sartre, to Husserl. At the same time he became more and more interested in psychology, and he made a careful study of Gestalt psychology and psychoanalysis in particular. The influence of all of this is quite clear in his first major works, *The Structure of Behavior* and *Phenomenology of Perception.* In the latter work, which is still considered to be his masterwork, it becomes clear that Heidegger's *Being and Time* (1927) and Husserl's *Crisis* (1936) finally helped Merleau-Ponty find his own position within the phenomenological movement.

It is now generally accepted that Merleau-Ponty's work constitutes an essential moment in the development of modern phenomenology as a whole. Merleau-Ponty was undoubtedly most deeply inspired by Husserl, the father of phenomenology; yet this does not mean that he did not take distance from Husserl's original conception in several important respects. With Husserl Merleau-Ponty defined the subject matter of philosophy as meaning or sense (*sens*); yet where Husserl conceived of meaning from a transcendental, idealist perspective, Merleau-Ponty maintained that meaning is always interwoven with lack of meaning (*non-sens*), and that the idea of reason can never forget the experience of un-reason. He admitted to have been inspired here by Hegel; yet where Hegel had sublime confidence in the inevitable victory of reason, Merleau-Ponty held that there is not so much question of an intelligible world here as of "focal points of light, separated by panels of night and darkness." Thus Merleau-Ponty also rejected Husserl's transcendental ego and the claim that the philosopher is to be a disinterested spectator; philosophy can never forget its own origin, and the phenomenologist cannot be changed into a disincarnated regard turned toward a world of essences. He equally rejected the idea of a consciousness that is completely transparent to itself and he, thus, conceived of man in terms of ek-sistence as Heidegger had done in *Being and Time.* But contrary to Heidegger, Merleau-Ponty gave a privileged position to perception and re-interpreted the concepts of intentionality and ek-sistence as essentially implying body or flesh as an original source of meaning. For Heidegger reflections on man as Being-in-the-world were oriented toward an ontology that is to focus on the question concerning the meaning of Being; Merleau-Ponty on the other hand was concerned mainly with a philosophical anthropology and even in his last work, where he came much closer to Heidegger than in his earlier works and where he often spoke about Being, the concern with ontology was never primary. Merleau-Ponty agreed with Heidegger that the history of man is the history of the comprehension of Being; yet in his view this does not mean that this comprehension has no ground or source outside itself; on the contrary, this comprehension is intimately related to ontic relations in regard to different types of entities. Thus it is quite possible that in a certain sense one will have to give primacy to the biological and the economic dimensions in man, so that the "absolute" autonomy of Being to which Heidegger seems to subscribe, is to be given up.

One sees here the growing influence of both Marx and Freud even though Merleau-Ponty always remained critical of many basic ideas of both Marxism and psychoanalysis. In both instances Merleau-Ponty was convinced that it is impossible to solve basic philosophical issues simply by an appeal to the sciences, be they physiology, biology, economics, or sociology. As for Marx Merleau-Ponty never accepted the theory according to which man would be able to overcome all problems inherent in man's ek-sistence, once he would have overcome all forms of alienation by means of a full recognition of man by man. Even if man were to be able to overcome all economic, social, and political forms of alienation, even then he would still never be able to suppress himself as an historical idea in favor of a natural species. Man will never cease to question himself, and that is the main reason why human history has no end.

In 1960, a few months before his untimely death, Merleau-Ponty completed an article, "Eye and Mind," which according to many is one of his most important publications and contains a preliminary statement of ideas which he intended to develop systematically in the second part of *The Visible and Invisible* on which he was working at the time, and which was meant to be a new synthesis of the fundamental ideas of his philosophy. Both the article and the posthumously published book clearly reveal that Merleau-Ponty, while adopting an ever more critical attitude in regard to Husserl's transcendental idealism, had simultaneously become more positively drawn toward ideas of Hegel and Heidegger and that these ideas were, in fact, beginning to occupy a central position in his philosophy.

—Joseph Kockelmans

MERTON, Robert K(ing). American sociologist. Born in Philadelphia, Pennsylvania, 5 July 1910. Educated at South Philadelphia High School for Boys, graduated 1927; studied at Temple University, Philadelphia, A.B. 1931; Harvard University, Cambridge, Massachusetts, M.A. 1932, Ph.D. 1936. Married Suzanne M. Carhart in 1934; 3 children. Tutor and Instructor in Sociology, Harvard University, 1936-39; Associate Professor, 1939-40, and Professor and Chairman of the Department of Sociology, 1940-41, Tulane University, New Orleans. Assistant Professor, 1941-44, Associate Director of Bureau of Applied Social Research, 1942-71, Associate Professor, 1944-47, Professor, 1947-63, Giddings Professor of Sociology, 1963-74, and since 1974 University Professor, Columbia University, New York. Lecturer, Princeton University, New Jersey, 1946, Claremont College, California, 1960, and University of Pennsylvania, Philadelphia, 1961; Gilman Lecturer, Johns Hopkins University, Baltimore, 1962; Lecturer, Baylor University, Waco, Texas, 1962, and University of California at Los Angeles, 1962; National Institutes of Health lecturer, 1964; Fulbright Lecturer, University of Kyoto, 1967; Phi Beta Kappa-Sigma Xi Lecturer, 1968; Lecturer, Economic and Social Research Institute, Dublin, 1975, Cornell University Medical School, New York, 1975, Yale University, New Haven, Connecticut, 1976, and Washington University, St. Louis, 1976. Consulting Editor, Harcourt Brace Jovanovich, and History, Philosophy, and Sociology of Sciences series and, with Aron Halberstam, Perspectives in Social Inquiry series, Arno publishers. Trustee, Center for Advanced Study in the Behavioral Sciences, 1953-75, and American Nurses Foundation, 1969-71; Trustee, since 1963, and Chairman, 1971, Guggenheim Foundation Educational Advisory Board, and since 1969, Institute for Scientific Information. Delegate USSR Academy of Sciences, 1961; Vice-President, National Commission for the Study of Nursing and Nursing Education, 1967-69; Chairman, Committee on the Social Organization of Sciences, Social Science Research Council, 1968-70. President, American Sociological Association, 1957, Sociological Research Association, 1968, Eastern Sociological Society, 1969, and Society for Social Studies of Science, 1975-76; Past President, Community Service Council; Member of the Council, Authors Guild, 1974-77. Recipient: American Council of Learned Societies prize, 1962; Guggenheim Fellowship, 1962; Temple University Distinguished Alumni Award, 1964; Center for Advanced Study in the Behavioral Sciences fellowship, 1973; National Academy of Sciences Institute of Medicine fellowship, 1973. LL.D.: Temple University, 1956; Western Reserve University, now Case Western Reserve University, Cleveland, 1966; University of Chicago, 1968; Tulane University, 1971; L.H.: Emory University, Atlanta, 1965; Loyola University, Chicago, 1970; Kalamazoo College, Michigan, 1970; Cleveland State University, 1977; honorary degree: University of Leyden, 1965; Litt.D.: Colgate University, Hamilton, New York, 1967; Dr. Social Sci.: Yale University, 1968; D.Sc. in Econ.: University of Wales, 1968. Member, National Academy of Sciences, National Academy of Education, American Academy of Arts and Sciences, and Royal Swedish Academy of Sciences. Address: Fayerweather Hall, Columbia University, New York, New York 10027, U.S.A.

PUBLICATIONS

Sociology

Science, Technology, and Society in Seventeenth-Century England, in *Osiris: Studies on the History and Philosophy of Sciences, and on the History of Learning and Culture*, edited by George Sarton. Bruges, St. Catherine Press, 1938; published separately, New York, Harper, 1970.

Mass Persuasion: The Social Psychology of a War Bond Drive, with Marjorie Fiske and Alberta Curtis. New York, Harper, 1946.

The Expert and Research in Applied Social Science: Notes for Discussion. New York, Columbia University Bureau of Applied Social Research, 1947.

Social Theory and Social Structure: Toward the Codification of Theory and Research. Glencoe, Illinois, Free Press, 1949; 3rd edition, 1968.

The Focused Interview: A Manual of Problems and Procedures, with Marjorie Fiske and Patricia L. Kendall. New York, Columbia University Bureau of Applied Social Research, 1952.

The Role of Social Research in Business Administration: A Case Study Based Primarily upon the 1930-1949 Experience of the Opinion Research Section of the Chief Statistician's Division of AT&T, with Edward C. Devereaux, Jr. New York, Columbia University Bureau of Applied Social Research, 2 vols., 1956.

The Freedom to Read: Perspective and Program, with Richard McKeon and Walter Gellhorn. New York, Bowker, 1957.

Some Thoughts on the Professions in American Society (address). Boston, Boston University, 1960.

On Theoretical Sociology: Five Essays, Old and New. New York, Free Press, 1967.

Social Theory and Functionl Analysis (in Japanese). Tokyo, Aoki Shoten, 1969.

Varieties of Political Expression in Sociology, with others. Chicago, University of Chicago Press, 1972.

The Sociology of Science: Theoretical and Empirical Investigations, edited by Norman W. Storer. Chicago University of Chicago Press, 1973.

Sociological Ambivalence and Other Essays. New York, Free Press, 1976.

Other

On the Shoulders of Giants: A Shandean Postscript. New York, Free Press, 1965.

The Sociology of Science: An Episodic Memoir. Carbondale, Southern Illinois University Press, 1979.

Editor, *Sociological Analysis: An Introductory Text and Case Book,* by Logan Wilson and William L. Kolb. New York, Harcourt Brace, 1949.

Editor, with Paul F. Lazarsfeld, *Continuities in Social Research: Studies in the Scope and Methods of "The American Soldier."* Glencoe, Illinois, Free Press, 1950.

Editor, with others, *Reader in Bureaucracy.* Glencoe, Illinois, Free Press, 1952.

Editor, with George G. Reader and Patricia L. Kendall, *The Student-Physician: Introductory Studies in the Sociology of Medical Education.* Cambridge, Massachusetts, Harvard University Press, 1957.

Editor, with Leonard Broom and Leonard S. Cottrell, Jr., *Sociology Today: Problems and Prospects.* New York, Basic Books, 1959.

Editor, with Robert A. Nisbet, *Contemporary Social Problems: An Introduction to the Sociology of Deviant Behavior and Social Disorganization.* New York, Harcourt Brace, 1961; London, Davies, 1963; 4th edition, Harcourt Brace, 1976.

Editor, with Jerry Gaston and Adam Podgorecki, The Sociology of Science in Europe. Carbondale, Southern Illinois University Press, 1977.

Editor, with others, *Toward a Metric of Science: Thoughts Occasioned by the Advent of Science Indicators.* New York, Wiley, 1978.

Editor, with James S. Coleman and Peter H. Rossi, *Qualitative and Quantitative Social Research: Essays in Honor of Paul F. Lazarsfeld.* New York, Free Press, 1979.

Editor, with Thaddeus J. Trenn, *Genesis and Development of a Scientific Fact,* by Ludwik Fleck. Chicago, University of Chicago Press, 1979.

Editor, with Matilda W. Riley, *Sociological Traditions from Generation to Generation: Glimpses of the American Experience.* Norwood, New Jersey, Ablex, 1980.

Editor, with Peter M. Blau, *Continuities in Structural Inquiry.* London and Beverly Hills, California, Sage, 1981.

*

Bibliography: in *The Ideas of Social Structure: Papers in Honor of Robert K. Merton,* edited by Lewis A. Coser. New York, Harcourt Brace, 1975.

* * *

Robert K. Merton, the American sociologist, is a founder of the sociology of science. Merton sees science as a distinctive social activity, and has attempted to analyze its growth and development from a sociological point of view, focusing upon the scientific community itself rather than upon the results of the scientific work and their implications. Among other things, Merton wanted to know how scientists perceive each other and their personal roles in the scientific community, and why scientists choose the work they do.

At an early time in his career, Merton teamed with a collaborator to study Arab intellectual development from 700 to 1300 A.D. Though the data on scientific development that the two scholars generated in the course of this work were perfectly adequate, Merton concluded that he could not use them to best advantage without systematic theoretical knowledge of the social structure of science. Merton accordingly focused on this problem. In "A Note on Science and Democracy" (1942), he declared that scientists are united by shared norms: universalism, communism, organized skepticism, and disinterestedness. Though

many have since pointed out that scientists frequently violate these norms, no one has proposed satisfactory alternatives.

The norms are often violated. Individual scientists with controversial opinions have occasionally received harsh treatment from the scientific community, an apparent rejection of universalism and disinterestedness. This and similar departures from norms does not make them irrelevant, however. They continue to operate, and the sociologist's problem is to identify the conditions under which scientists observe the norms and those under which they ignore them.

Merton believes that scientists are most likely to follow the norms when they know that their colleagues observe them and when the norms appear to be convenient and generally accepted "rules of the game." He uses the word "paradigm" to describe this situation. Violations generally occur when the paradigm is in the early stages of development (as when a new branch of science is opening up and norms are relatively weak and ill-defined) or when loyalties outside science exert an unusually strong influence for some reason.

At a later time, Merton began to wonder why scientists did their work. He had already outlined the normative structure showing how universalism, communism, organized skepticism, and disinterestedness interacted and when and why these norms were violated. But what, he asked, made the system go? Why should a scientist hasten to publish the results of experimental investigations? Wouldn't truth eventually be found anyway? Merton concluded that scientists want professional recognition. They receive this in the institutions where they work by being first to make some discovery. The highest form of recognition is eponymy—having one's name attached to a field of science or advance. Newton is eponymously recognized as the father of Newtonian physics while Euler is the author of Euler's theorem. Eponymy, in Merton's view, is thus the accepted reward for great scientific achievement and the thing that all scientists strive for.

Merton's formulation of eponymy as the scientist's ultimate goal was the missing piece of his theoretical structure. Once he had put it in place, he had the model of the social structure of science that he had been groping toward for twenty years. His colleagues and successors could move forward with research. Merton opened the door to them and so is justly termed a founder of the sociology of science.

Merton and his successors were later to distinguish between "normal" science and scientific revolution. Normal science consists of the advances made when the elements of a field are generally understood and accepted, leading to a stable, strong paradigm. As new questions are asked, new theories are proposed, and new data are presented, this paradigm breaks down and there is a scientific revolution. Newtonian physics, for example, was normal science up to about 1900 when numerous investigations began to question them. At that time, there was a scientific revolution in physics with accompanying breakdown of the paradigm and development of a new one. Normal science is far more common than revolution, according to Merton.

—Victor Cassidy

MILLS, C(harles) Wright. American sociologist. Born in Waco, Texas, 28 August 1916. Educated at public schools; studied at A & M College, College Station, 1934-35; University of Texas, Austin (Oldright fellow in philosophy, 1937-38; departmental fellow in logic, 1938-39), B.A. 1939 (Phi Beta Kappa), M.A. in philosophy and sociology 1939; University of Wisconsin, Madison, Ph.D. in sociology 1941. Married Ruth Harper; Yaroslava Surmach in 1959. Associate Professor of Sociology, University of Maryland, College Park, 1941-45; special business consultant to Small War Plants Corporation, 1945; Director of Labor Research Division of Bureau of Applied Social Research,

1945-48, Assistant Professor, 1946-50, Associate Professor, 1950-56, and Professor of Sociology, 1956-62, Columbia University, New York. Visiting Professor, University of Chicago, 1949, and Brandeis University, Waltham, Massachusetts, 1953; Lecturer, William Alanson White Institute of Psychiatry, 1954-56; Fulbright Lecturer, University of Copenhagen, 1956-57. Also a farmer. Vice-President, Industrial Relations Research Association, 1947-48. Recipient: Guggenheim fellowship, 1945. *Died 20 March 1962.*

PUBLICATIONS

Sociology

Small Business and Social Welfare. Washington, D.C., United States Senate, 1946.
The New Men of Power: America's Labor Leaders, with Helen Schneider. New York, Harcourt Brace, 1948.
The Puerto Rican Journey: New York's Newest Migrants, with Clarence Senior and Rose Kohn Goldsen. New York, Harper, 1950.
White Collar: America's Middle Classes. New York, Oxford University Press, 1951.
Character and Social Structure: The Psychology of Social Institutions, with Hans Gerth. New York, Harcourt Brace, 1953; London, Routledge, 1961.
Mass Society and Liberal Education. Chicago, Center for the Study of Liberal Education for Adults, 1954.
The Power Elite. New York, Oxford University Press, 1956.
The Causes of World War Three. New York, Simon and Schuster, 1958; London, Secker and Warburg, 1959.
The Sociological Imagination. New York, Oxford University Press, 1959; London, Oxford University Press, 1967.
Listen Yankee: The Revolution in Cuba. New York, McGraw Hill, 1960; as *Castro's Cuba: The Revolution in Cuba,* London, Secker and Warburg, 1961.
The Marxists. New York, Dell, 1962; London, Penguin, 1963.
Power, Politics, and People: The Collected Essays of C. Wright Mills, edited by Irving Louis Horowitz. New York, Oxford University Press, 1963.
Sociology and Pragmatism: The Higher Learning in America, edited by Irving Louis Horowitz. New York, Paine Whitman, 1964.

Other

Editor and Translator, with Hans Gerth, *From Max Weber: Essays in Sociology.* New York, Oxford University Press, 1946.
Editor, *Images of Man: The Classic Tradition in Sociological Thinking.* New York, Braziller, 1960.

*

Critical Studies: *The World of C. Wright Mills* by Herbert Aptheker, New York, Marzani and Munsell, 1960; *The New Sociology: Essays in Social Science and Social Theory in Honor of C. Wright Mills* edited by Irving Louis Horowitz, New York, Oxford University Press, 1964, and *C. Wright Mills, An American Utopian* by Horowitz, New York, Free Press, 1983; *The Incoherence of the Intellectual: C. Wright Mills's Struggle to Unite Knowledge and Action* by Fredy Perlman, Detroit, Black and Red, 1973.

*   *   *

C. Wright Mills drew apart from contemporary sociological schools he dubbed the Scientists and the Grand Theorists, and remained a compelling advocate for radical humanism in sociology. For Mills, the former vainly sought to reduce society to objective phenomena similar to those studied in classical physics, while the latter speculated at such a level of vacuous generality that they evaded empirical observation. Mills identified himself with a "third camp" of sociologists willing to raise fundamental questions about their subject of study: its meaning for society as a whole and for individual men and women, its relevance to historical trends and to future directions. He fostered a lively search for deeper meanings against the prevailing tendency to trivialize, reinforced by professional and bureaucratic timidity. He ventured to replace methodological pretensions by a sharp sense of social reality and an authentic humanist concern. "IBM Plus Reality Plus Humanism = Sociology." He contended that conservatism had become the preserve of provincialism and inertia, while liberalism was emasculated to the extent it ingratiated itself with any establishment. Marxism is vital to sociological investigation, not because it is valid (for Mills much of it is not) but because it is politically and socially important, quite apart from its scientific rationality.

His methodology was that of sociological biography, a deft combination of statistical studies and personally conducted field interviews (he had an aversion to hordes of assistants charged with mechanically administering questionnaires), together with a sound grasp of social history and the history of ideas. He tried to compose a biographical picture of the kind of individual under study—the immigrant, the elite, the white-collar worker. The pivotal concept around which Mills sketched his complex portrayals of society was that of power. He spurned as "metaphysical" any elaborate disquisition on whether political, economic or other manifestations of power are primary. Forms of power may vary with societies and epochs, but the centrality of power is a constant. In all human interactions, there are elites and proletarians, insiders and outsiders, superiors and subordinates, everyone exhibiting the gathering, nurture, and exercise of power. Systems collect it, strategies channel it, yet power ultimately resides in individuals who cannot, therefore, be ignored in sociological investigation.

In his first major work, *The New Men of Power,* Mills characterized labour union leaders in terms of their backgrounds and the historical context of the emergence of unions. Union leaders are new men of power because unions have become a new power-structure. By analogy, the labour leader can be likened to a generalissimo, a parliamentary debater, the boss of a political machine, an entrepreneur contracting labor for a price, a regulator of the working man's discontent, "a secularized technician of animosity," an economist, but he is also none of these things. He is really a new man of power, who must be understood with the help of new categories. He does not operate in a vacuum, however, for trade unionism presupposes capitalism. Trade unions are bound to private property, and should utopian or state socialism dissolve private property, the trade union will disappear. The labour leader's fate is bound up with the fate of the entrepreneur. In delineating the new man who exercises power in a new form, Mills discerned the division in labour leadership between the old guard (older, less educated, more experienced, and operating largely in the AFL) and the new leaders (younger, more educated, less experienced, more frequently found in the CIO). He showed how these groups would have to learn to co-operate to manage labour effectively through the periodic crises of the American economy. He analyzed the fascination of labour with Communism, and concluded that labour leaders would remain anti-Communist for ideological reasons, because it posed a threat to their power and because acting otherwise resulted in bad public relations. Mills warned of the increasing futility of post-New Deal establishment liberalism, the hollowness of negative conservatism, and the disinclination of labour leaders to found a labour party. He also pointed to the augmented if ambivalent role of the intellectual in the politics of labour unions.

In *The Puerto Rican Journey* (with Clarence Senior and Rose Kohn Goldsen), Mills used the same composite biographical method with Puerto Ricans migrating to New York City. He then employed his refined approach to examine the new American middle class. In *White Collar* Mills held that the traditional middle classes—merchant, farmer, and professional—are rapidly disappearing with the onrush of the giant corporation and of managerial bureaucracy. The new middle classes are composed of white-collar workers whose lives are controlled by enormous forces outside themselves: "Whatever history they have had is a history without events; whatever common interests they have do not lead to unity; whatever future they have will not be of their own making." While they are almost faceless in the massive "managerial demiurge," alienated from work, without authentic values, hardly comprehending ideals like "integrity" and "creativity," power does accrue to those who rise in the white-collar pyramid, so that the highest managerial technicians are replacing the old entrepreneurs and changing the nature of business and the professions. Thus the intellectual becomes a technician of bureaucracy, the worker a salesperson in a society that increasingly resembles a bazaar in which success in the personality market is critical to survival, and managers are surrounded by ever expanding numbers of specialized clerks.

The emergence of a new (or radically transformed) class is manifest in new and different styles of life. With the white-collar worker, alienation from craft and robotic work routines are reflected in a life without values, for the workplace does not function as a lever for self-testing, responsibility, or individual growth. Politically, this shows up as apathy (a mask for uncertainty and insecurity) and a false consciousness of who one is. The pseudo-consciousness, nurtured by the mass media, misleads the middle classes into a delusive view of the world. Thus, the new middle classes are up for sale; whoever seems respectable enough, strong enough, can probably have them. In a short paper, Mills conveyed his concern that gains in leisure time, hard-won over many years, are cancelled by the debilitating nature of work, and what remains is used up through distractions generated by the mass media. Though work cannot satisfy, leisure produces mindless restlessness.

Almost as a companion volume to *White Collar, The Power Elite* contended that not all people are part of the middle classes, that some individuals wield great power, largely through the ability to alter the daily lives of ordinary human beings, not merely by meeting the demands of the time but even by creating those demands. They occupy "the strategic command posts of the social structure," and most of these are located in the major institutional hierarchies of state, corporation, and the military. Dominating the economy through relatively few giant corporations, transforming the political order into an executive establishment, and making the military the most expensive feature of government, the power elite constitutes a self-conscious class with mutual understanding, toleration, and co-operation. By manipulating and creating images and postures, the elite is seen in every way as superior, not only in wealth and prestige, but also in character. While romantics portray this superclass as impotent because of self-cancelling competition and the check-mate of the electorate, Mills maintained that it has the strength of durability. The structure implied by a power elite is such that the masses are distracted by status and petty, if lurid, immoralities, and many are absorbed into a new gentility. The result is that those with power have no ideology and feel no need for any, are barren of ideas, and manipulate without the semblance of justification. This mindlessness constitutes the "higher immorality" which encourages the organized irresponsibility of contemporary American corporate power.

Mills applied his basic thinking to *The Causes of World War Three* in which he attacked the "military metaphysicians" who foster the notion that war is inevitable. Noting that we are not all in this together because the power elite makes decisions that ordinary men do not, he urged the abandonment of illusions, including the inevitability doctrine, and acceptance of the necessity of co-existence along with substantial disarmament. In calling for a more realistic assessment of the human condition and the release of the human imagination, he pleaded that democracy should be taken seriously. In "A Pagan Sermon" he excoriated the Christian clergy for preaching the very illusions that lead to

irresponsibility in human affairs. *Listen Yankee* attempted a dispassionate analysis of revolutionary events in Cuba accompanied by a plea for an enlightened attitude toward Cuba on the part of the American government.

Mills provided an elaborate critique of sociology in *The Sociological Imagination*. Holding that neither the life of an individual nor the history of a society can be grasped without comprehending both, he thought that many human beings do not define their troubles in sufficiently inclusive terms. They lack a "quality of mind" essential to understanding the interplay of forces and the meshing of biography and history. Yet that lack is felt, and all too often attempts to fill it consist of gathering more "facts" even though one cannot absorb the facts available. Only by distilling the essentials and locating oneself in the social context can one transcend a false (because too particularized and personalized) consciousness of one's place in the scheme of things. Individuals need to cultivate the sociological imagination which negated the dichotomy between abstract and particular, social and personal, so that the intimate personal realities are linked to larger social realities. For the sociologically minded, he recommended as initial steps the juxtaposition of available material, playfulness in concepts, attempts to generate whole new sets of categories, thinking of extremes, and free-wheeling comparisons.

Mills advocated a lucid descriptive sociology that did not fear to prescribe, and though his analyses were sometimes pessimistic regarding contemporary society, he was a firm believer in human potentiality and the power of sociology to coax it into potency. "Know that the problems of social science, when adequately formulated, must include both troubles and issues, both biography and history, and the range of their intricate relations. Within that range the life of the individual and the making of societies occur: and within that range the sociological imagination has its chance to make a difference in the quality of human life in our time" (*The Sociological Imagination*).

—R.N. Iyer

MITCHELL, Wesley C(lair). American economist. Born in Rushville, Illinois, 5 August 1874. Studied at the University of Chicago, B.A. 1896, Ph.D. 1899; Oxford University, M.A.; universities of Halle and Vienna, 1897-98. Chief, War Industries Board, Price Section, 1918-19. Married Lucy Sprague in 1912; 4 children. Worked in Census Office, Washington, D.C., 1899-1900; Instructor, University of Chicago, 1900-02; Assistant Professor, 1902-08, Professor, 1902-12, and Hitchcock Professor, 1934, University of California, Berkeley; Lecturer, 1913-14, and Professor, 1914-19 and 1922-44, Columbia University, New York; Lecturer, New School for Social Research, New York, 1919-21. Visiting Lecturer, Harvard University, Cambridge, Massachusetts, 1908-09; George Eastman Visiting Professor, Oxford University, 1930-31; Messenger Lecturer, Cornell University, Ithaca, New York, 1935. Director of Research, National Bureau of Economic Research, 1920-45. Director, New School for Social Research, 1919-31. Chairman, Social Sciences Research Council, 1927-30, and President's Research Committee on Social Trends, 1929-33. President, Academy of Political Science, 1935-38, and Section K, American Academy of Arts and Sciences, 1938. Recipient: Francis A. Walker Medal, American Economic Association, 1947. Honorary doctorate: University of Chicago; Columbia University; University of California; Princeton University, New Jersey; Harvard University; University of Pennsylvania, Philadelphia; University of Paris; New School for Social Research. Member, Institut International de Statistique; Fellow, Royal Economic Society; Corresponding Member, Manchester Statistics Society, and Institut de Science Economique Appliquée; Honorary Fellow, Royal Statistical Society. *Died 29 October 1948.*

PUBLICATIONS

Economics

A History of the Greenbacks, with Special Reference to the Economic Consequences of Their Issue: 1862-65. Chicago, University of Chicago Press, 1903; selections, as *History of the Legal-Tender Acts,* Chicago, University of Chicago Press, 1903.

Gold, Prices, and Wages under the Greenback Standard. Berkeley, University of California Press, 1908.

Business Cycles. Berkeley, University of California Press, 1913.

History of Prices During the War: Summary. Washington, D.C., Government Printing Office, 1919.

International Price Comparisons, with others. Washington, D.C., Government Printing Office, 1919.

A Bold Experiment: The Story of the National Bureau of Economic Research. New York, National Bureau of Economic Research, 1921.

Income in the United States: Its Amount and Distribution, 1909-1919, with others. New York, National Bureau of Economic Research, 1922.

Business Cycles: The Problem and Its Setting. New York, National Bureau of Economic Research, 1927.

Current Problems in Measurement of National Income, with Simon Kuznets. The Hague, Institut International de Statistique, 1934.

Recent Social Trends in the United States: Report of the President's Research Committee on Social Trends. New York and London, McGraw Hill, 1934.

A Preliminary Draft of Chapters I, II and III of Business Cycles. Volume II: Analysis of Cyclical Behavior, with Arthur F. Burns. New York, National Bureau of Economic Research, 1936.

The Backward Art of Spending Money and Other Essays. New York and London, McGraw Hill, 1937.

The Making and Using of Index Numbers. Washington, D.C., U.S. Government Printing Office, 1938.

Statistical Indicators of Cyclical Revivals, with Arthur F. Burns. New York, National Bureau of Economic Research, 1938.

Methods of Measuring Cyclical Behavior, with Arthur F. Burns. New York, National Bureau of Economic Research, 4 vols., 1939.

The National Bureau Enters Its Twentieth Year. New York, National Bureau of Economic Research, 1939.

Studies in Economics and Industrial Relations, with others. Philadelphia, University of Pennsylvania Press, 1941.

Wartime "Prosperity" and the Future. New York, National Bureau of Economic Research, 1943.

Economic Research and the Needs of the Time. New York, National Bureau of Economic Research, 1944.

Measuring Business Cycles, with Arthur F. Burns. New York, National Bureau of Economic Research, 1946.

What Happens During Business Cycles: A Progress Report. New York, National Bureau of Economic Research, 1951.

Lecture Notes on Types of Economic Theory, as Delivered by Wesley C. Mitchell, edited by Joseph Dorfman. New York, A.M. Kelley, 2 vols., 1967.

Other

The Text Books of Harold Rugg: An Analysis, with others. New York, American Committee for Democracy and Intellectual Freedom, 1942.

Editor, *What Veblen Taught: Selected Writings of Thorstein Veblen.* New York, Viking Press, 1936.

*

Critical Study: *Two Lives* by Lucy Sprague Mitchell, New York, Simon and Schuster, 1953.

*   *   *

Wesley Mitchell was the premier empirical analyst of business cycles in the first half of the 20th century, a major contibutor to the development of institutional economics, and a principal interpreter of the externalist or relativist approach to the history of economic thought. The work of the National Bureau of Economic Research, which he helped found, is an institutional monument to his vision and work.

As an institutionalist, Mitchell attempted to explain to his more conventional colleagues the complex and recondite ideas of John R. Commons on the legal foundations and holistic and behavioral elements of the modern economic system. But it was largely as a disciple of Thorstein Veblen, and also of John Dewey, that Mitchell attempted to interpret and especially to develop the institutionalist paradigm. Mitchell, like Veblen, emphasized the complex psychological, cultural, systemic, and evolutionary dimensions of the modern economic system. This system he understood to be distinguished by its use of money, thus constituting a pecuniary, as well as an industrial, economy. Veblen's distinction between making goods and making money became a principal source of Mitchell's insight into cyclical developments. He also argued that, in light (in part) of what he called the backward art of consumer spending, the behavioral assumptions of conventional economic theory were unrealistic and misdirected. Mitchell argued for a plurality of approaches to the study of economic organization, for a variety of types of economic theory.

Business cycle analysis was important to Mitchell as both an independent topic of practical consequence and an avenue to comprehend the nature and operation of a pecuniary economy. The problem of the generation of business cycles, he thought, was inseparable from the problem of how a capitalist economy operates. Rather than being aberations, business cycles manifested to Mitchell the inherent instability of a market economy. Business cycles were self-generating, involving the operation of continuing—if changing—destabilizing factors and obstacles to hypothetical perfect automatic adjustment. In his view, the study of business cycles required the detailed statistical analysis of price-cost-profit structures and especially the critical role of the factors governing expectations of profits. Within the multiplicity of his statistical series resided the data giving substance to what later economists were to emphasize as the multiplier, accelerator, liquidity preference, and, especially, the marginal efficiency of capital. The basic model of the business cycle used by late 20th century macro-economists grew directly from the work of Mitchell and his associates and successors. He literally described what happens during business cycles.

Two characteristics marked Mitchell's general approach to questions of policy. First, he continually cautioned against the fallacy of wishful thinking in making economic policy. Second, he was an early and strong advocate of macro-economic stabilization planning by government in which economics, as a collection of insights into and instruments of control, would be made useful for making public policy.

Although he was criticized for practicing empiricism without theory, Mitchell's approach was more subtle. Faced with an inconclusive array of mechanistic business cycle theories each providing a single-factor explanation, he preferred to analyze empirical data, using the theories as guides to research and the production of empirically warranted conclusions rather than self-contained topics of debate. Mitchell's statistical work later was readily integrated with the macro-economic theory of Keynes and other writers.

As an interpreter of the history of economic thought Mitchell emphasized that the development of economic theory was conditioned by environmental institutions, policies, ideology, and other circumstantial factors. His substantive work gave effect to this view and also to his appreciation that the scope of economic thought encompasses ideas and theorizing on the organization and control of the economic system as well as on price, resource allocation, and other topics.

—Warren J. Samuels

MONOD, Jacques (Lucien). French biologist. Born in Paris, 9 February 1910. Studied at the University of Paris, B.A. 1931, D.Sc. 1941. Served as an officer with the French Resistance and in the French Army during World War II: Bronze Star, Croix de Guerre, Legion of Honor. Married Odette Bruhl in 1938; 2 children. Assistant Professor of Zoology, University of Paris, 1933-44; Head of Microbic Physiology Department, 1945-54, Head of Cellular Biochemistry Department, 1954-71, and Director, 1971-76, Pasteur Institute, Paris; Professor of Science, University of Paris, 1959-67; Professor of Molecular Biology, Collège de France, Paris, 1967-72. Fellow, Salk Institute for Biological Studies, San Diego, California, 1968-76. Recipient: Rockefeller Fellowship, California Institute of Technology, Pasadena, 1936-37; Léopold Mayer Prize, French Academy of Sciences, 1962; Nobel Prize in Physiology and Medicine, with François Jacob and André Lwoff, 1965. Honorary doctorate: University of Chicago, 1965. Member, American Academy of Arts and Sciences; Washington Academy of Science; Royal Society, London; U.S. National Academy of Sciences; Czechoslovak Academy of Science. Commandeur de l'Ordre National du Mérite. *Died* (in Cannes) *31 May 1976.*

PUBLICATIONS

Biology

Recherches sur la croissance de cultures bactériennes. Paris, Hermann, 1942.
From Biology to Ethics. San Diego, Salk Institute for Biological Studies, 1969.
Le Hasard et la nécessité: Essai sur la philosophie naturelle de la biologie moderne. Paris, Seuil, 1970; as *Chance and Necessity: An Essay on the Natural Philosophy of Modern Biology,* New York, Knopf, 1971.
Selected Papers in Molecular Biology, edited by André Lwoff and Agnes Ullman. New York, Academic Press, 1978.

Other

Épistémologie et Marxisme, with others. Paris, Union Générale d'Éditions, 1972.

Editor, with Ernest Borek, *Of Microbes and Life.* New York, Columbia University Press, 1971.

*

Critical Studies: *The Necessity of Being* by Joseph Chiari, London, Elek, 1973.

*   *   *

Jacques Monod's Nobel Prize in 1965 was awarded for his work with André Lwoff and François Jacob on the chemical basis of protein synthesis in cells. The problem to which the three men addressed themselves was an obvious one. The genes located along a DNA molecule are present at all times. They do not appear and disappear from time to time. Yet, not all genes on all DNA molecules in a cell function at all times. This is simply to

say that a cell never manufactures the maximum amount of every compound it is capable of producing at all times. Instead, the amount of any particular substance produced by a cell varies over time. At one time, a protein may be manufactured at some maximum rate, while at other times there may be little or none of it produced. The chemical composition of a cell, to put it still another way, is constantly changing with the kind and amount of all possible cell products in constant flux. The fundamental question, then, is how a constant structural entity (an unchanging sequence of genes on a DNA molecule) can result in a variable production of cellular products.

Monod's research on the bacterial enzyme β-galactosidase led him to propose a model in which gene action is regulated by portions of the DNA molecule adjacent to and somewhat more distant from the gene itself. The model contains two distinct parts: the "operon" and the regulator gene. The operon, in turn, consists of two parts: an operator gene and a sequence of structural genes. The latter entities, the structural genes, are the portions of the DNA molecule actually responsible for the synthesis of RNA molecules which, in turn, act as the template for new protein molecules. The operator gene is found immediately adjacent to one of more structural genes. In most cases studied so far, a single operator gene controls the operation of a series of structural genes whose function it is to manufacture the enzymes necessary for a sequence of biochemical reactions. Thus, if a substance is metabolized in the cell by the series of reactions, $A \xrightarrow{W} B \xrightarrow{X} C \xrightarrow{Y} D \xrightarrow{Z} E$, then the genes responsible for the manufacture of enzymes w, x, y, and z are adjacent to each other on the DNA molecule. Further, the function of these genes is under the control of a single operator gene.

The final question is how the operator itself is controlled. Monod and his colleagues suggested that this function was supplied by a regulator gene, located on the same DNA molecule, but at some distance from the operon. This regulator gene releases a "repressor" which binds to the operator gene and switches it to an "off" position. In this position, the operator gene prevents the structural genes from manufacturing RNA molecules. The regulator gene is, itself, controlled by cell constituents. An excess of certain cell products will cause the regulator gene to release a repressor which turns off the operator gene, while an excess of other cell products will bind to the repressor itself, allowing the operator gene to switch to the "on" position. Logically, the end products of a biochemical process might be expected to satisfy the first condition. This would provide a way to stop the manufacture of some cell constituent after its concentration had reached some necessary level. The raw materials of that same process might satisfy the latter conditions, since their presence at high concentrations would signal the necessity for the process by which they are used up to begin. Although the basic principles of this theory have now been confirmed, a number of modifications have been proposed, particularly for more complex cells than those originally studied by Monod, Jacob, and Lwoff.

Monod's scientific discoveries have led him to consider broader philosophical questions of the nature of life. This analysis led to his widely popular *Le Hasard et la nécessité.* In this book, Monod argues for the development of a new philosophical system, based on, but transcending, the epistemology of modern science. He suggests that "blind faith" which lies at the basis of historical religion and some philosophies will be inadequate for humans to deal with the profound problems created by developments of modern science. Instead, he believes that a new philosophical system, inspired by and created on the model of modern science, will be needed to understand and resolve these problems.

—David Newton

MONTESSORI, Maria. Italian educationist. Born in Chiaravalle, Ancona, 31 August 1870. Studied at the University of Rome, M.D. 1896; later studied in philosophy and psychology. One son. Instructor in psychiatric clinic, and lecturer, 1900-07, University of Rome; Director of the Scuola Ortofrenica, 1898-1900; in charge of children's home of Istituto di Beni Stabili, Rome, 1907-11; gave training courses in London regularly from 1913, and elsewhere; lived in Spain, and later in the Netherlands and India; government inspector of schools, Italy, from 1922; interned in India during World War II. D.Litt.: University of Durham, 1923; honorary doctorate: University of Amsterdam, 1950. Honorary Member, Academy of Science, Chicago, and Pedagogical Academy of Budapest; Fellow, Educational Institute of Scotland. *Died 6 May 1952.*

PUBLICATIONS

Collections

Opera Montessori. Milan, Garzanti, 1950-.

Education

Caraterri fisici delle giovani donne del lazio. Rome, La Sede delle Società, 1905.
Il metodo della pedogogia scientifica applicato all'educazione infantile nelle case dei bambini. Castello, Lapi, 1909; as *The Montessori Method,* New York, Stokes, and London, Heinemann, 1912; revised edition, as *The Discovery of the Child,* Madras, Theosophical Publishing House, 1948; as *La scoperta del bambino,* Milan, Garzanti, 1950.
Antropologia pedagogica. Milan, Vallardi, 1910; as *Pedagogical Anthropology,* New York, Stokes, 1913.
Dr. Maria Montessori's Own Handbook. New York, Stokes, and London, Heinemann, 1914.
My System of Education, Education in Relation to the Imagination of the Little Child, The Organization of Intellectual Work in School, The Mother and the Child (lectures). New York, House of Childhood, 4 vols., 1915.
L'autoeducazione nelle scuole elementari. Rome, Loescher, 1916.
The Advanced Montessori Method (Spontaneous Activity in Education, The Montessori Elementary Material). New York, Stokes, 2 vols., 1917; London, Heinemann, 2 vols., 1919.
Manuale di pedagogica scientifica. Naples, Morano, 1921.
The Montessori Didactic Apparatus. New York, House of Childhood, 1926.
The Child in the Church: Essays on the Religious Education of Children and the Training of Character, edited by E.M. Standing. St. Louis, Herder, and London, Sands, 1929.
The Mass Explained to Children. London, Sheed and Ward, 1932; as *The Mass Explained to Boys and Girls,* Chicago, Sadlier, 1934; as *La santa messa spiegate ai bambini,* Milan, Garzanti, 1949.
Peace and Education. Geneva, International Bureau of Education, 1932.
Psico aritmética. Barcelona, Araluce, 1934.
Psico geometría. Barcelona, Araluce, 1934.
The Secret of Childhood, edited by Barbara Barclay Carter. London, Longman, 1936; New York, Stokes, 1939; as *Il segreto dell'infanzia,* Milan, Garzanti, 1950.
The Reform of Education During and after Adolescence. Amsterdam, Association Montessori Internationale, 1939.
The Erlkinder, and The Functions of the University. London, Montessori Society of England, 1939(?).
Education for a New World. Madras, Kalakshetra, 1946.
Das Kind in der Familie. Vienna, Montessorischule, 1946(?); as *The Child in the Family,* Chicago, Regnery, 1970.
De l'Enfant à l'adolescent. Bruges, Desclee, 1948.

The Child. Madras, Theosophical Publishing House, 1948.
Child Training (radio talks). Delhi, Ministry of Information and Broadcasting, 1948.
Reconstruction in Education. Madras, Theosophical Publishing House, 1948.
To Educate the Human Potential. Madras, Kalakshetra, 1948.
What You Should Know about Your Child. Colombo, Bennet, 1948.
The Absorbent Mind. Madras, Theosophical Publishing House, 1949; revised edition, as *La mente del bambini,* Milan, Garzanti, 1953; as *The Absorbent Mind,* Madras, Theosophical Publishing House, 1959; New York, Holt Rinehart, 1967.
Formazione dell'uomo. Milan, Garzanti, 1949; as *The Formation of Man,* Madras, Theosophical Publishing House, 1955.
Educazione e pace. Milan, Garzanti, 1949.
La vita in Cristo. Milan, Garzanti, 1949.
Educazione alla Libertà, edited by Maria Luisa Leccese. Bari, Laterza, 1950.
From Childhood to Adolescence. New York, Schocken, 1975.

*

Critical Studies: *Maria Montessori: Her Life and Work* by E.M. Standing, Fresno, California, Academy Guild Press, 1959; *Learning How to Learn: An American Approach to Montessori* by Nancy McCormick Rambusch, Baltimore, Helicon, 1962; *Maria Montessori: A Biography* by Rita Kramer, New York, Putnam, 1976, Oxford, Blackwell, 1978.

*   *   *

Maria Montessori was a feminist long before it was admirable to be such. Throughout her life, Montessori determinedly followed her ambitions into male-dominated institutions and professions. Fortunately for the world of education, Montessori's indomitable spirit never gave way to the fashion of the day concerning the woman's role in society.

The first barrier that Montessori had to overcome was put up by her father, Allesandro, a conservative man who was a former army officer turned government finance officer. While her father greatly disapproved of his daughter's headstrong desire to pursue higher education in the field of engineering, her mother, Renilde, who came from an academic background, was supportive and helpful to Montessori. After Montessori's first 12 years of education in the province of Ancona, the family moved to Rome. It was here that the self-willed woman overcame her father's opposition to her attending a technical school in preparation for an engineering career. Following this training, Montessori again upset tradition, and also her father, by entering the University of Rome. Here Montessori, finding the study of biology particularly appealing, decided to study medicine rather than engineering. In 1896, Montessori became the first woman to be graduated from the University of Rome school of medicine. Soon after this, Montessori's work at the University's psychiatric clinic put her in contact with patients in insane asylums—a bridge on her way to teaching mentally retarded children.

Montessori's first opportunity to work with children came in 1900 when she became director of a demonstration school established by the National League for Retarded Children. It was here that the seeds which would grow into the Montessori Method were planted. In preparation for her own teaching, Montessori drew upon her studies of such educators as Jean Itard, Edouard Seguin, Jacques Rousseau, and Friedrich Froebel, the German who introduced kindergartens to education. Like Itard, who believed that observation of children was the key to their education, Montessori also put the teacher in the background as an observer and guide, rather than a dictator of the day's lesson. She also approached the children who were labeled "mentally retarded," with Seguin's belief that mental deficiency was not a medical problem, but rather a pedagogical one. Montessori took these beliefs along with her knowledge of scientific investigation to the classroom where she set up a "prepared environment" of child-sized tables and chairs in an orderly room in which materials of Montessori's own design replaced the usual learning tools. Amazingly, the children, previously deemed incapable of learning, learned so well that they passed exams that were designed for normally educable children.

Impressed herself with these achievements, Montessori went on to teach "normal" but culturally deprived children in the slums of Rome. The 1907 opening of Casa dei Bambini gave Montessori another chance to show educators how her developing method worked not only for mentally deficient children but also for children who were considered unwilling to learn because of their lives on the streets and the lack of education in their families. Again Montessori succeeded where success was not expected. The children of the streets came to school gladly, left regretfully, and while in school worked as Montessori expected children would, not for reward, but for the joy of learning. Word spread about the achievements at Casa dei Bambini; visitors came to observe; and in 1909 Montessori gave her first training course along with a statement of her philosophy, which was later to become known as the Montessori Method. In 1911, the first Montessori school was established in the United States at Tarrytown, New York. In 1913, her first International Teacher Training course was given in London. Soon Montessori schools were being established all over Europe and in the United States.

Throughout her life of promoting the Montessori Method, the founder, like many a pioneer into a new area, was regarded by some as a gift to education, a woman to be revered. Others saw Montessori as an arrogant, self-willed promoter who believed that only her way was right, a woman who did not tolerate contradiction. Despite how she was perceived, Montessori made an undeniable contribution to education. Many of her ideas have been incorporated into even traditionally run schools. Open classrooms, readiness programs, and team teaching are only a few adaptations which can be traced back to Montessori. Though Montessori's Method was for a long time overshadowed by Freudianism and behaviorism, today Montessori schools are flourishing throughout the world along with teacher training centers.

—Patricia Devine

MOORE, G(eorge) E(dward). British philosopher. Born in London, 4 November 1873. Educated at Dulwich College, London; studied at Trinity College, Cambridge. Married Dorothy Ely in 1916; 2 sons. Fellow, Trinity College, 1898-1904; Lecturer in Moral Sciences, 1911-25, and Professor of Mental Philosophy and Logic, 1925-39, Cambridge University. Visiting Professor, Smith College, Northampton, Massachusetts, 1940-41, and Columbia University, New York, 1942. Editor of *Mind*, 1921-47. Honorary doctorate: Cambridge University, 1913; University of St. Andrews, Scotland, 1918. Fellow, British Academy, 1918. O.M. (Order of Merit), 1951. *Died 24 October 1958.*

PUBLICATIONS

Philosophy

Principia Ethica. London, Cambridge University Press, 1903.
Ethics. London, Williams and Norgate, and New York, Holt, 1912.
Philosophical Studies. London, Routledge, and New York, Harcourt Brace, 1922.
The Philosophy of G.E. Moore, edited by Paul Arthur Schilpp. Evanston, Illinois, Northwestern University Press, 1942.
Some Main Problems of Philosophy. London, Allen and

Unwin, and New York, Macmillan, 1953.
Philosophical Papers. London, Allen and Unwin, and New York, Macmillan, 1959.
Commonplace Book 1919-1935, edited by Casmir Lewy. London, Allen and Unwin, and New York, Humanities Press, 1967.

*

Critical Studies: *The Philosophy of G.E. Moore* edited by Paul Arthur Schilpp, Evanston, Illinois, Northwestern University Press, 1942; "G.E. Moore" by Norman Malcolm, in *Knowledge and Certainty*, Englewood Cliffs, New Jersey, Prentice Hall, 1963; *The Epistemology of G.E. Moore* by E.D. Klemke, Evanston, Illinois, Northwestern University Press, 1969, and *Studies in the Philosophy of G.E. Moore* edited by Klemke, New York, Quadrangle, 1969; *G.E. Moore and the Apostles* by Paul Levy, New York, Holt Rinehart, 1979, London, Oxford University Press, 1981; *The Metaphysics of G.E. Moore* by David O'Connor, Dordrecht, Reidel, 1982.

*   *   *

G.E. Moore was one of the most important and most influential philosophers of the first several decades of the 20th century. The most widespread philosophical movement of the 19th century was (Hegelian) idealism. To some extent, Hegelianism had begun to collapse in Germany by the latter part of the 19th century, as neo-Kantianism became predominant. But in England there was a new interest in Hegel and a resurgence of idealism. Some of the main theses of most forms of idealism were: (1) Reality is one, a single, unified whole; (2) In this whole everything is logically connected with everything else; (3) What is known is in some ways dependent on its being known; (4) Reality is spiritual or mental; (5) Reality is organic—a process rather than something static; (6) The world is fully known only through philosophical reason.

So pervasive was this philosophy that even Moore and Bertrand Russell started out as idealists of a sort. But both revolted and leveled devastating blows at idealism. As Russell put it (in "My Mental Development"):

> G.E. Moore took the lead in the rebellion, and I followed, with a sense of emancipation. Bradley [one of the British idealists] argued that everything common sense believes in is mere appearance. We reverted to the opposite extreme, and thought that *everything* is real that common sense, uninfluenced by philosophy or theology, supposes real. With a sense of escaping from prison, we allowed ourselves to think that grass is green, and that the sun and stars would exist if no one was aware of them; and also that there is a pluralistic, timeless world of Platonic ideas. The world, which had been thin and logical, suddenly became rich and varied and solid.

Let us look at some of Moore's main philosophical contributions.

In his important essay "The Refutation of Idealism," Moore undertook to prove that the main conclusion of idealism—that reality is spiritual or mental—can never be proved to be true by any idealistic argument. He maintains that every such argument must contain an essential premise which, under every non-tautological interpretation of it, is false. That premise is: To be is to be perceived (i.e., to be is to be the object of sensation or thought). Under certain interpretations, this premise, Moore shows, is self-contradictory. In all others it is also false (but not self-contradictory). Hence the idealist conclusion can never be shown to be true. And Moore presents arguments to show that the premise is in fact false.

Moore's positive views on behalf of realism were presented in a number of other essays. One of the most important of these is his "A Defense of Common Sense." In this essay he claims that the common-sense view of the world is wholly true and can be known with certainty. He also argues for what he takes to be the chief tenet of realism, namely, that there is no good reason to hold either (a) that every physical fact is logically dependent on some mental fact or (b) that every physical fact is causally dependent on some mental fact. In this essay Moore also stresses the role of analysis in philosophy. He claims that philosophers must begin by accepting as true certain common-sense statements—which everyone would admit as being true when they are not engaged in doing philosophy. It is not the business of philosophy to deny the truth of those statements. Rather it is the task of philosophy to analyze these true statements. Moore maintains: (1) We know many such commensensical propositions to be true; (2) We understand them perfectly well in their ordinary sense; (3) But such understanding is not equivalent to our being able to give a correct analysis of their meaning. Hence the task of philosophy is precisely to provide such an analysis. In section IV of "A Defense of Common Sense," Moore illustrates this with regard to the proposition "material things exist." He goes through four stages of analysis. In many other works Moore also held or implied that philosophy is (in part) concerned with analysis. And in various works he distinguishes several forms of analysis.

It should be mentioned that Moore wrote many works in the theory of perception—and theory of knowledge in general—and in the area of ethics. In his major work on ethics, *Principia Ethica*, Moore maintains that the main question of ethics is "What is good (and bad)?" That is: "How is 'good' to be defined?" He argues that the only answer can be: Good is indefinable. "Good," he insists, denotes a unique simple object of thought which is indefinable and unanalyzable. To identify *good* with some other object, i.e., to define "good," is to commit the "naturalistic fallacy"; Moore also distinguishes between good in itself and good as means. Judgments about good as means are causal propositions, but judgments about good in itself are self-evident truths.

Almost all of those who knew Moore have acknowledged that he was an exciting teacher, a brilliant critic, and a delightful and charming person.

—E.D. Klemke

MORGAN, Thomas Hunt. American biologist. Born in Lexington, Kentucky, 25 September 1866. Studied at the State College of Kentucky, Lexington, B.S. 1886, M.S. 1888; Johns Hopkins University, Baltimore, Ph.D. 1890. Married Lillian Sampson in 1904; 4 children. Professor of Biology, Bryn Mawr College, Pennsylvania, 1891-1904; Professor of Experimental Zoology, Columbia University, New York, 1904-28; Director, William G. Kerckhoff Laboratories of Biological Science, California Institute of Technology, Pasadena, 1928-1945. President, American Morphological Society, 1900, American Society of Naturalists, 1909, Society for Experimental Biology and Medicine, 1910-12, National Academy of Sciences, 1927-31, and American Association for the Advancement of Science, 1929-30. Recipient: Darwin Medal, Royal Society, London, 1924; Nobel Prize for Medicine and Physiology, 1933; Copley Medal, Royal Society, 1939. Honorary doctorate: McGill University, Montreal, 1921; University of Edinburgh, 1922; University of California, Berkeley, 1930; University of Michigan, Ann Arbor, 1924; University of Heidelberg, 1932; University of Zurich, 1933; University of Paris, 1935. Foreign Member, Royal Society. Fellow, American Association for the Advancement of Science. *Died 4 December 1945.*

PUBLICATIONS

Biology

The Development of the Frog's Egg: An Introduction to Experimental Embryology. New York, Macmillan, 1897.
Regeneration. New York, Macmillan, 1901.
Evolution and Adaptation. New York, Macmillan, 1903.
Experimental Zoology. New York, Macmillan, 1907.
Heredity and Sex (lectures). New York, Columbia University Press, 1913.
The Mechanism of Mendelian Heredity, with others. New York, Holt, 1915.
A Critique of the Theory of Evolution (lectures). Princeton, New Jersey, Princeton University Press, 1916.
Sex-linked Inheritance in Drosophila, with C.B. Bridges. Washington, D.C., Carnegie Institute, 1916.
The Physical Basis of Heredity. Philadelphia, Lippincott, 1919.
Some Possible Bearings of Genetics on Pathology (lecture). Lancaster, Pennsylvania, New Era, 1922.
Laboratory Directions for an Elementary Course in Genetics, with others. New York, Holt, 1923.
Human Inheritance (lecture). Pittsburgh, University of Pittsburgh School of Medicine, 1924.
Evolution and Genetics. Princeton, New Jersey, Princeton University Press, 1925.
The Theory of the Gene (lectures). New Haven, Connecticut, Yale University Press, 1926.
Experimental Embryology. New York, Columbia University Press, 1927.
What is Darwinism? New York, Norton, 1929.
The Scientific Basis of Evolution (lectures). Ithaca, New York, Cornell University Press, 1932.
Embryology and Genetics. New York, Columbia University Press, 1934.
The Relation of Genetics to Physiology and Medicine (Nobel Lecture). Stockholm, Norstedt och Söner, 1935.

*

Critical Studies: *Thomas Hunt Morgan, Pioneer of Genetics* by Ian Shine and Sylvia Wrobel, Lexington, University of Kentucky Press, 1976; *Thomas Hunt Morgan: The Man and His Science* by Garland E. Allen, Princeton, New Jersey, Princeton University Press, 1978.

*   *   *

Thomas Hunt Morgan was born in Kentucky of a distinguished southern family. Educated at Johns Hopkins, he worked at Bryn Mawr, Columbia, and the California Institute of Technology, remaining active right up to the time of his death. He made distinguished contributions to many areas of biology. But his chief work was in leading and directing the team which articulated and established the modern biological picture of heredity: the "classical theory of the gene." For this work, Morgan received the Nobel Prize in medicine in 1933.

Morgan's first scientific work was for his doctoral dissertation. It involved a comparative study of four species of marine invertebrate, the Pycnogonida (sea spiders). However, Morgan soon tired of such comparative work—contrasting one group against another—and he turned more and more to experimental studies, particularly those involving problems of embryology. The end of the century found him fully immersed in questions to do with development, concentrating particularly on the study of factors which influence normal embryonic development. Which of the currently contesting positions was truer: that of Hans Driesch, which stressed the internal hereditary forces working on organisms, or that of Wilhelm Roux's *Entwicklungsmechanik* School, which emphasized external environmental forces? Morgan's own experiments on the sea urchin, frogs, and other animals convinced him that internal factors are causally crucial in development.

Morgan turned next to problems of sex determination. Today

it is known that such determination is a function of chromosome type. For instance, in humans possession of an XY chromosome pair makes for a male, whereas possession of an XX pair makes for a female. Interestingly, given that Morgan was shortly to establish definitively the important causal role of the chromosomes in heredity, at this time (first decade of this century) Morgan rather downplayed the importance of the chromosomes. He saw the difference in chromosome type as something of an epiphenomenon, concealing the deeper, true causal factors. Although Morgan was no environmentalist, as an embryologist he saw organic development as an unfolding according to certain natural laws, rather than as something fixed right at the beginning by immutable factors.

Just before 1910, Morgan began work with the so-called "vinegar fruit-fly," *Drosophila melanogaster*. It was his study of this animal, done together with a group of students at Columbia (A.H. Sturtevant, C.B. Bridges, H.J. Muller, and others), that was to lead to Morgan's most important work. By this time, Mendelian genetics was rediscovered and being articulated in ever greater detail. This is a theory of heredity which supposes that the units of inheritance are discrete, passed on unchanged from generation to generation. It is a theory relying on the indirect evidence of the results of breeding experiments. In this it differs from "cytology," the study of the cell, which works directly by microscopic study of the elements of the organism. This latter also was rushing ahead, and it was known in some detail how the chromosomes, those string-like objects in the nucleus of the cell, get duplicated and passed on down through the generations.

Through its work on Drosophila, the Morgan group showed that these two stories—genetics and cytology—are different sides of the same coin. The group showed that the genes, the units of heredity, sit on the chromosomes, and thus are replicated and transmitted to every cell of the body. Moreover, via the sex cells, the genes are passed on to form new organisms. A major step forward in the development of the theory of heredity came from a realization by Sturtevant, which the Morgan group then exploited to the full. Genes on the same chromosome are "linked" together, tending therefore to be transmitted together. However, in the process of sex-cell production, the chromosomes can break, rejoining with other bits of broken chromosomes. This breakage gave Sturtevant a clue to the "mapping" of the order of genes on a chromosome. The further the genes are apart, the more chance there is of breakage and consequent separation of two genes in sex cell formation. Hence, by considering how frequently same-chromosome genes get separated, one can tell how close they are together.

Before long, Morgan and his associates had carried out a full survey of the chromosomes of *Drosophila melanogaster*, thus giving additional weight to the overall assumption that the genes in a cell are arranged in linear fashion—which, of course, is precisely what one would expect, if the genes are arrayed on the chromosomes. The results of this and other work were collected and published in a definitive study, *The Mechanism of Mendelian Heredity* co-authored by Morgan, Bridges, Sturtevant, and Muller. A new complete science of heredity was in existence.

Not surprisingly, as an active inquiring biologist, Morgan had a life-long interest in evolutionary hypotheses and theories. The time during which he was most active was not a happy time for pure Darwinism, and Morgan himself reflected this fact. This is somewhat paradoxical, for now, looking back, we see that Morgan's classical theory of the gene filled a missing place, which makes Darwinism work! Moreover, one of Morgan's later students was the young Russian geneticist Theodosius Dobzhansky, who was to effect the marriage of Darwin and genetics, so brilliantly in the 1930's, in the "synthetic theory of evolution."

Pure Darwinism emphasizes natural selection—the differential reproduction of the fittest—as the major mechanism of evolutionary change. However, one must have—what Darwin did not have—an adequate theory of heredity. If the units of heredity are not discrete, new changes get "blended" out of existence in

just a generation or two.

Geneticists at the beginning of this century concentrated—naturally enough—on fairly major variations. After all, pioneering in a new field, they needed to work with the simplest features possible. Unfortunately, this led them to think that large discrete variations are the "raw stuff" of evolution: one goes by jumps from one form to another. Thus, natural selection has, at most, a minor role of mopping up after change. It is not the key causal feature in evolution.

We know now that changes can be very small, that the crucial changes in nature are indeed small, and that therefore natural selection has a full evolutionary role as it sorts and selects these small variations. This was not seen by Morgan, either when he worked as an embryologist or when he later worked as a geneticist. He never questioned evolution. However, although Morgan did come to accept that the changes in evolution may not always be drastically large, he was always inclined to think that the crucial changes must be significantly bigger than anything envisioned or allowed by Darwin.

Posterity often judges that great scientists were mistaken, even reactionary, in some respects. Galileo always accepted circular planetary motion, even though Kepler had shown that the planets really go in ellipses. But blind spots should not lead us to play down real scientific merits and advances. Today, we may think Morgan misguided on evolution—although, in fact, there are still those who agree with the early geneticists that natural selection is not really as all-powerful as supposed by Darwinians. What no one would deny is the crucial importance of Morgan's studies in putting the theory of the gene on a firm theoretical and empirical base.

—Michael Ruse

MORISON, Samuel Eliot. American historian. Born in Boston, Massachusetts, 9 July 1887. Studied at Harvard University, Cambridge, Massachusetts, B.A. 1908, Ph.D. 1912; at École des Sciences Politiques, Paris, 1908-09; Oxford University, M.A. 1922. Served in the United States Army Infantry, 1918-19: Private; attached to Russian Division, American Commission to Negotiate the Peace, Paris, 1919; American Delegate, Baltic Commission of Peace Conference, 1919; Historian, U.S. Naval Operations, World War II; Naval Reserve, 1942-51: Rear Admiral; Legion of Merit. Instructor, University of California, Berkeley, 1914; Instructor, Lecturer, and Professor, Harvard University, 1915-55. Harmsworth Professor of American History, Oxford University, 1922-25. Co-Founder, *New England Quarterly*. Recipient: Pulitzer Prize, 1942, 1960; Bancroft Prize, 1949, 1972; Theodore Roosevelt Medal, 1956; Edison Award, 1957; Alfred Thayer Mahan Award, Navy League, 1961; Emerson-Thoreau Medal, American Academy of Arts and Sciences, 1961; Gold Medal in History, National Institute of Arts and Letters, 1962; Balzan Foundation Award in History, 1963; Presidential Medal of Freedom, 1964. Honorary doctorate: Amherst College, Massachusetts, 1936; Harvard University, 1936; Union College, Schenectady, New York, 1939; Yale University, New Haven, Connecticut, 1949; Williams College, Williamstown, Massachusetts, 1950; Oxford University, 1951; Notre Dame University, Indiana, 1954; Boston College, Massachusetts, 1960; Bucknell University, Lewisburg, Pennsylvania, 1960; Holy Cross College, Worcester, Massachusetts, 1962; University of Maine, Orono, 1968. Fellow, Society of Antiquaries; American Philosophical Society; American Academy of Arts and Sciences; and the British Academy. Member, Real Academia de la Historia (Madrid), and American Academy of Arts and Letters. *Died 15 May 1976.*

PUBLICATIONS

History

The Life and Letters of Harrison Gray Otis, Federalist, 1765-1848. Boston, Houghton Mifflin, 1913.

Texts of the Finland "Peace". Washington, D.C., Government Printing Office, 1918.

A Prologue to American History (lecture). Oxford, Clarendon Press, 1922.

The Oxford History of the United States, 1783-1917. New York, Oxford University Press, 2 vols. 1927.

Historical Background for the Massachusetts Bay Tercentenary in 1930. Boston, Massachusetts Bay Tercentenary, 1928.

An Hour of American History, from Columbus to Coolidge. Philadelphia, Lippincott, 1929.

Builders of the Bay Colony. Boston, Houghton Mifflin, and London, Oxford University Press, 1930.

The Growth of the American Republic, with Henry Steele Commager. New York and London, Oxford University Press, 1930; revised edition, 1939, 1952; abridged edition, as *A Concise History of the American Republic*, with others, New York, Oxford University Press, 1977.

Historical Markers Erected by Massachusetts Bay Colony Tercentenary Commission: Text of Inscriptions as Revised by Samuel Eliot Morison. Boston, Commonwealth of Massachusetts, 1930.

Massachusettensis de Conditoribus; or, The Builders of the Bay Colony. Boston, Houghton Mifflin, 1930; revised edition, 1964.

Massachusetts on the Sea, 1630-1930, with others. Boston, Massachusetts Bay Colony Tercentenary Committee, 1930.

The Proprietors of Peterborough, New Hampshire, with Some Consideration on the Origin of the Name. Peterborough, New Hampshire, Peterborough Historical Society, 1930.

The Young Man Washington (lecture). Cambridge, Massachusetts, Harvard University Press, 1932.

The Founding of Harvard College. Cambridge, Massachusetts, Harvard University Press, 1935.

Harvard College in the Seventeenth Century. Cambridge, Massachusetts, Harvard University Press, 2 vols., 1936.

The Puritan Pronaos: Studies in the Intellectual Life of New England in the Seventeenth Century. New York, New York University Press, and London, Oxford University Press, 1936; as *The Intellectual Life of Colonial New England*, New York, New York University Press, 1956.

Three Centuries of Harvard, 1636-1936. Cambridge, Massachusetts, Harvard University Press, 1936.

The Pilgrim Fathers: Their Significance in History (lecture). Boston, Merrymount Press, 1937.

The Ancient Classics in a Modern Democracy (lecture). London and New York, Oxford University Press, 1939.

The Second Voyage of Christopher Columbus from Cadiz to Hispaniola and the Discovery of the Lesser Antilles. Oxford, Clarendon Press, 1939.

Portuguese Voyages to America in the Fifteenth Century. Cambridge, Massachusetts, Harvard University Press, 1940.

Admiral of the Ocean Sea: A Life of Christopher Columbus. Boston, Little Brown, 2 vols., 1942.

History of United States Naval Operations in World War II. Boston, Little Brown, 15 vols., 1947-62; London, Oxford University Press, 15 vols., 1948-62.

History as a Literary Art: An Appeal to Young Historians. Boston, Old South Association, 1948.

The Ropemakers of Plymouth: A History of the Plymouth Cordage Company, 1824-1949. Boston, Houghton Mifflin, 1950.

By Land and by Sea: Essays and Addresses. New York, Knopf, 1953.

Christopher Columbus, Mariner. Boston, Little Brown, 1955; London, Faber, 1956.

Freedom in Contemporary Society (lecture). Boston, Little Brown, 1956.

The Story of the "Old Colony" of New Plymouth, 1620-1692. New York, Knopf, 1956.

Nathaniel Holmes Morison, 1815-1890 (lecture). Baltimore, Peabody Institute, 1957.

American Contibutions to the Strategy of World War II (lectures). London, Oxford University Press, 1958.

Strategy and Compromise. Boston, Little Brown, 1958.

William Hickling Prescott, 1796-1859. Boston, Massachusetts Historical Society, 1958.

John Paul Jones: A Sailor's Biography. Boston, Little Brown, 1959; London, Faber, 1960.

A New and Fresh English Translation of the Letter of Columbus Announcing the Discovery of America. Madrid, Graficas Yagües, 1959.

The Story of Mount Desert Island, Maine. Boston, Little Brown, 1960.

The Maritime History of Massachusetts, 1783-1860. Boston, Houghton Mifflin, 1961.

The Scholar in America: Past, Present, and Future. New York, Oxford University Press, 1961.

The Reconstruction and the Passing of the Frontier, with Henry Steele Commager. New York, Oxford University Press, 1962.

Introduction to Whaler Out of New Bedford. A Film Based on the Purrington-Russell Panorama of a Whaling Voyage round the World, 1841-1845. New Bedford, Massachusetts, Old Dartmouth Historical, 1962.

A History of the Constitution of Massachusetts. Boston, Special Commission on Revision of the Constitution, 1963.

The Two-Ocean War: A Short History of the United States Navy in the Second World War. Boston, Little Brown, 1963.

The Caribbean as Columbus Saw It, with Maurice Obregón. Boston, Little Brown, 1964.

The Oxford History of the American People. New York, Oxford University Press, 1965.

"Old Bruin": Commodore Matthew C. Perry, 1794-1858: The American Naval Officer Who Helped Found Liberia. Boston, Little Brown, 1967; London, Oxford University Press, 1968.

Life in Washington a Century and a Half Ago: Letters of a Federalist Congressman and Senator, and His Wife, 1800-1822. Washington, Cosmos Club, 1968.

Harrison Gray Otis, 1765-1848: The Urbane Federalist. Boston, Houghton Mifflin, 1969.

The European Discovery of America: The Northern Voyages A.D. 500-1600. New York, Oxford University Press, 2 vols., 1971-74.

History as a Literary Art. Hyderabad, American Studies Research Centre, 1971.

Samuel de Champlain, Father of New France. Boston, Little Brown, 1972.

Francis Parkman (1823-1893). Boston, Massachusetts Historical Society, 1973.

The Conservative American Revolution. Washington, D.C., Society of the Cincinnati, 1976.

Sailor Historian: The Best of Samuel Eliot Morison, edited by Emily Morison Beck. Boston, Houghton Mifflin, 1977.

Other

The Class Lives of Samuel Eliot and Nathaniel Holmes Morison. Boston, McGrath Sherrill, 1926.

Fullness of Life: A Memoir of Elizabeth Shaw Morison, 1866-1945. Boston, Merrymount Press, 1945.

One Boy's Boston, 1887-1901. Boston, Houghton Mifflin, 1962.

Spring Tides. Boston, Houghton Mifflin, 1965.

Vita Nuova: A Memoir of Priscilla Barton Morison. Northeast Harbor, Maine, Morison, 1975.

Editor, *The Treaty of Ghent and Negotiations That Followed,*

1814-1818. Boston, Old South Association, n.d.

Editor, *The Humble Request of the Massachusetts Puritans, and A Modell of Christian Charity by John Winthrop, 1630*. Boston, Old South Association, 1916.

Editor, *William Knox on American Taxation, 1769*. Boston, Old South Association, 1917(?).

Editor, *Selections from John Locke's Second Treatise of Government, 1690*. Boston, Old South Association, n.d.

Editor, *The Key of Liberty, Shewing the Causes Why a Free Government Has Always Failed, and a Remidy Against It: Written in the Year 1798 by William Manning*. Billerica, Massachusetts, Manning Association, 1922.

Editor, *Sources and Documents Illustrating the American Revolution, 1764-1788, and the Formation of the Federal Constitution*. Oxford, Clarendon Press, 1923.

Editor, *The Development of Harvard University Since the Inauguration of President Eliot, 1869-1929*. Cambridge, Massachusetts, Harvard University Press, 1930.

Editor, *Records of the Suffolk County Court, 1671-1680*. Boston, The Society, 1933.

Editor, *The Log Cabin Myth: A Study of the Early Dwellings of the English Colonists in North America*, by Harold E. Shurtleff. Cambridge, Massachusetts, Harvard University Press, 1939.

Editor, *Of Plymouth Plantation, 1620-1647*, by William Bradford. New York, Knopf, 1952.

Editor, *France and England in North America*, by Francis Parkman. London, Faber, 1956.

Editor and Translator, *Journals and Other Documents on the Life and Voyages of Christopher Columbus*. New York, Heritage Press, 1963.

Editor, with John S. Rowe, *The Ships and Aircraft of the U.S. Fleet*. Annapolis, Naval Institute Press, 1972.

*   *   *

At his death in 1976, Samuel Eliot Morison was considered the "Grand Old Man of American Historians." His distinguished teaching career at Harvard University, with interruptions for military service in two world wars, had lasted from 1915 until his retirement in 1955. His scholarly achievements in writing spanned an even lengthier duration. These had commenced in 1913 with the publication of his two volume book, *The Life and Letters of Harrison Gray Otis, Federalist*, which was based upon his Harvard doctoral dissertation and in turn the family papers of a noted ancestor. Succeeding years saw Morison's authorship of innumerable books, monographs, and other historical works including his writing of a biography of Samuel de Champlain at age 82 and the publication of his second volume on the European discovery of America during his 87th year.

There were several works during this lengthy and prodigiously productive career that brought Morison to his eminent status among 20th-century American historians. His masterful volumes *The Maritime History of Massachusetts* and *Builders of the Bay Colony* became classics for their brilliant and incisive descriptions of the origins and prominence of the Puritan Commonwealth within early American history. His textbook *The Growth of the American Republic*, written in collaboration with Professor Henry S. Commager, appeared in numerous editions and was one of the most popular American history schoolbooks. His works concerning the founding and early development of Harvard College have had exemplary value to historians of American higher education. Morison's monumental 15-volume *History of Naval Operations in World War II* stemmed from his service as an admiral during this conflict, and it still remains the finest and most complete narrative on this maritime topic. His shorter, though equally respected, *Oxford History of the American People*, was more wide-ranging in scope, as it included observations on athletics, art, literature, music, science, technology, and social customs as well as political, diplomatic, and military developments. His two-volume

study of the European discovery and exploration of the Western Hemisphere was a masterpiece of writing and first-hand research that earned him the noted Bancroft prize for history. Perhaps, though, the most prestigious personal honors he received were two Pulitzer prizes (for his splendid biographies of Christopher Columbus and John Paul Jones) and the first Balzan Foundation Award in History.

Morison's writings followed the narrative or descriptive form of exciting historical scholarship. Within this category, he followed in the tradition of previous eminent historians including Francis Parkman and William Ellery Channing, though with greater dramatic and absorbing prose. Unlike historians such as Charles Beard, William H. McNeill, Frederick Jackson Turner, or Oscar Handlin, Morison placed less emphasis on analyzing the powerful intellectual concepts or processes that led to social change. Instead, he chose to describe with impeccable research and absorbing portraits the prominent individuals and events that have shaped the American past. His consummate search for historical accuracy is particularly evident in his writings on naval matters where he himself made voyages in sailing ships that retraced the journeys and bravery of explorers such as Christopher Columbus. Similar exactitude for detail was also evident in his eyewitness coverage of several combat zones and naval operations during World War II.

The erudite, forceful, and often amusing vignettes of historical personages and events that fill the pages of Professor Morison's writings provide further justification for his prestige and eminence among American historians. For example, he assessed the New Deal as having "saved twentieth century American capitalism by purging it of gross abuses and forcing accommodation to the larger public interest." He regarded Franklin D. Roosevelt as "the most successful democrat since Lincoln." Calvin Coolidge was viewed as "a mean thin-lipped little man, a respectable mediocrity, lived parsimoniously but admired men of wealth and his political principles were those current in 1901."

In earlier periods of American history Morison wrote that George Washington's "superiority lay in character not talents," and although our first President was a Virginia aristocrat, Morison regarded him as "more nationalist and less provincial than any other American of his generation." Morison was somewhat critical of Thomas Jefferson, who he noted "was no social democrat, but a slave holding country gentleman of exquisite taste, lively curiosity and a belief in the perfectability of man." Jacksonian Democracy was regarded with even less enthusiasm; he declared that it "catered to mediocrity, diluted politics with the incompetent and corrupt and made conditions increasingly unpleasant for gentlemen in public life." Morison found Abraham Lincoln's writing filled with "sustained dignity and magnanimity," noting also that during the Civil War he held greater power "than any other President of the United States prior to Franklin D. Roosevelt." One of the best examples of Morison's eloquent prose appeared in his historical eulogy to President Kennedy: "With the death of John Fitzgerald Kennedy something seemed to die in each one of us. Yet the memory of that bright vivid personality, that great gentleman whose every act and appearance appealed to our pride and gave us fresh confidence in ourselves and our country, will live in us for a long, long time."

Besides his masterful and voluminous writing, Morison made other inestimable contributions to the study and appreciation of American history. Throughout his teaching career of four decades, he was among Harvard's most popular instructors. His lectures were renowned for their refinement, insight, and gentle humor, and he often complemented classroom work with excursions to historic sites. The graduate history students that he nurtured with diligence, skill, and benevolence comprised many prominent scholars including Perry Miller, Edmund S. Morgan, and Bernard Bailyn. He also lent his expertise to numerous scholarly journals, including *The New England Quarterly*, of which he was the principal founder, and in its early years its leading book reviewer. In all these influential roles, Morison's lifetime work left a monumental legacy to those who study, research, or write within the field of American history.

—Sheldon S. Cohen

MORRIS, Charles (William). American philosopher. Born in Denver, Colorado, 23 May 1901. Studied at the University of Wisconsin, Madison, 1918-20; Northwestern University, Evanston, Illinois, B.S. 1922; University of Chicago, Ph.D. 1925. Served in the United States Naval Reserve, 1918. Married Gertrude E. Thompson in 1925 (divorced), 1 daughter; married Ellen Ruth Allen in 1951. Instructor in Philosophy, Rice University, Houston, 1925-30; Associate Professor, University of Chicago, 1931-47; Lecturer, 1947-58, Research Professor, 1958-71, and since 1971 Professor Emeritus, University of Florida, Gainesville. Visiting Professor in Social Relations, Harvard University, Cambridge, Massachusetts, 1951-53; Fellow, Center for Advanced Study in the Behavioral Sciences, Stanford, California, 1956-57. President, Western Division, American Philosophical Association, 1937. Recipient: Guggenheim Fellowship, 1942; Rockefeller Fellowship, 1943. Fellow, American Academy for the Advancement of Science, and American Adademy of Arts and Sciences. Address: Post Office Box 14245, University Station, Gainesville, Florida 32601, U.S.A.

PUBLICATIONS

Philosophy

Six Theories of Mind.   Chicago, University of Chicago Press, 1932.
Pragmatism and the Crisis of Democracy.   Chicago, University of Chicago Press, 1934.
Logical Positivism, Pragmatism, and Scientific Empiricism.   Paris, Hermann, 1937.
Foundations of the Theory of Signs.   Chicago, University of Chicago Press, 1938.
Paths of Life: Preface to a World Religion.   New York and London, Harper, 1942.
Signs, Language, and Behavior.   New York, Prentice Hall, 1946.
The Open Self.   New York, Prentice Hall, 1948.
Varieties of Human Value.   Chicago, University of Chicago Press, 1956.
Signification and Significance: A Study of the Relations of Signs and Values.   Cambridge, Massachusetts, M.I.T. Press, 1964.
The Pragmatic Movement in American Philosophy.   New York, Braziller, 1970.
Writings on the General Theory of Signs.   The Hague, Mouton, 1971.

Other

Festival (poems).   New York, Braziller, 1966.

Editor, *Mind, Self, and Society from the Standpoint of a Social Behaviorist,* by George Herbert Mead.   Chicago, University of Chicago Press, 1934.
Editor, with others, *The Philosophy of the Act,* by George Herbert Mead.   Chicago, University of Chicago Press, 1938.

*

Critical Studies: *Charles Morris and the Criticism of Discourse* by Richard A. Fiordo, Bloomington, Indiana University, 1977; *Psycholinguistics Matrices: Investigation into Osgood and Mor-* *ris* by Richard League, The Hague, Mouton, 1977.

*   *   *

Charles Morris's work is primarily in the philosophy of language. Within that field his major interest has been in laying the theoretical groundwork preparatory to the development of a fully comprehensive science of signs and sign-behavior. The subject-matter of this projected science has been of considerable interest to investigators from many different disciplines in the humanities and social sciences, for example, linguistics, psychology, anthropology, philosophy, and so on. This wide spectrum of interest is clear evidence to Morris of the great importance, to an adequate understanding of human nature, culture, and society, of the investigation of sign-behavior. It speaks also, he believes, of the need for a comprehensive science of signs, capable of providing to theorists in those various fields listed above both a general conceptual framework and an adequate terminology for use in their own specific studies of meaning, language, and language-use. Because of the ways in which such a large number of other disciplines touch upon its subject matter, and because, too, of the ways in which he anticipates those disciplines drawing upon the work of the projected science, Morris envisions for the new science a role in its own field—broadly, that of the humanities and social sciences—comparable to that of physics in natural science, that is to say, the role of pivotal science. Morris, borrowing a term first used by John Locke to classify work on the topics in question, calls the projected theory of signs semiotic.

Semiotic may be seen as a composite of three major parts, syntactics, semantics, and pragmatics. The first of these deals with the relations, wholly within a given language, between the various signs and expressions of that language. For example, in a natural language, the syntactical content is to be found in that language's grammar. The second, semantics, deals not so much with intra-language sign relationships but rather with the relations between signs on the one hand and their *significata* on the other; that is to say, semantics is the theory of sign-meaning. In pragmatics the focus of interest is upon the relations between sign-use and user and upon the various kinds of uses to which signs are put. Among philosophers of language it is the third which is the least developed, and one valuable contribution of Morris's to the advancement of pragmatics was his success in convincing Rudolf Carnap, arguably the most influential semanticist since the middle years of this century, of the importance of pragmatics to the philosophy of language.

As Morris visualizes semiotic, syntactics, semantics, and pragmatics become, without loss of their respective identities, integrated into a comprehensive theory of signs. But semiotic, conceived of as comprehensive in the ways mentioned, is a fledgling discipline, yet at the stage of initial development. Fundamental questions about its nature and methodology remain open and subject to no general consensus. It is upon his, often leadtaking, contributions to the debates about fundamental issues in this field that Morris's reputation stands.

In Morris's view, and in this there is clearly reflected his own philosophical training in the theory of pragmatism, especially as formulated by George Herbert Mead, semiotic should have a pronounced bio-behavioral flavor. This is to say that, in his eyes, the new science should be rooted in biology and operate within the orbit of behaviorism. In the words of Otto Neurath, it should draw primarily upon the theory of behavioristics. But behavioristics, especially in regard to the study of human behavior, is itself a fledgling, indeed often controversial, discipline and so its ability adequately to ground and orient semiotic is open to serious question. Furthermore, it is by no means acceptable to all semioticians that their discipline *should* be guided by the canons of behaviorism, even if the latter were capable of providing a base and a set of operating procedures. The primary focus of this opposition to behaviorism in semiotic has been directed against the stimulus-response psychology which Morris's program presupposes and which he takes for the most important key to the understanding of human sign-behavior.

In Morris's efforts at laying down an adequate working terminology for semiotic, the basic terms he uses are those employed in describing the overt behavior of lower organisms, for example, such words, in addition to "stimulus" and "response," as "need," "goal-object," "cause," "disposition," "influence," and so on. But, even if the language of stimuli, influences, needs, and the others mentioned were indeed to be pressed into the service of semiotic, it has been argued against Morris's program by Max Black and others that, in his use of these as basic terms, he fails to abide by his own stated objective of "[providing] a set of terms [for] talk about signs...[and]...to reduce, for scientific purposes, their *vagueness* and *ambiguity*." (*Signs, Language, and Behavior*; italics mine). That is to say, against Morris's behavioristic approach to the theory of signs, the charge has been made that he fails to define adequately some key elements of the terminology that he proposes for semiotic and that he appears to regard the terms in question as univocal and unproblematic in their application to the description of human sign-behavior.

The study of meaning and of language, fed by the seminal works of Russell, Frege, and Peirce in the early years of this century, is a dominant interest of contemporary philosophers, especially of those in the analytic tradition. Two movements which have contributed greatly to giving analytic philosophy its present character, logical positivism (or empiricism) and pragmatism, owe much to the influence of these thinkers, and it is within the framework of those movements that Morris's own work developed and belongs. Among members of the second generation of American pragmatists, Morris was in the vanguard of those who were receptive to logical empiricism, particularly as that position was formulated by Carnap. Indeed a notable contribution of Morris's to the development of the two movements just mentioned was his arguing for the proximity of many of their respective central concerns and approaches and he articulated a position, scientific empiricism, upon which he claimed that the bio-social orientation of the pragmatists and the logico-analytic orientation of the positivists would converge.

—David O'Connor

MOSCA, Gaetano. Italian political theorist. Born 1 April 1858. Lecturer on law, University of Palermo, 1885 to 1890's; taught at the University of Rome in the 1890's; Professor of Constitutional Law, University of Turin, 1898-1923, and University of Rome, 1923-33. Editor of Chamber of Deputies journal in 1890's; regular contributor, *Il Corriere della Sera*, 1901-25. Member of the Italian Chamber of Deputies, 1908-19, and Senator, 1919-28; Undersecretary of the Colonies, 1914-16. *Died 9 November 1941.*

PUBLICATIONS

Political Theory

Sulla teorica dei governi e sul governo parlamentare: Studi storici e sociali. Turin, Loescher, 1884; as *Teorica dei governi e governo parlamentare*, 1925; edited by Rodolfo De Mattei, Milan, Giuffrè, 1968.
Sulla libertà di stampa: Appunti. Turin, Loescher, 1885.
Questioni costituzionali. Palermo, Amenta, 1885.
Le costituzioni moderne: Saggio. Palermo, Amenta, 1887.
Elementi di scienza politica. Turin, Bocca, 1896; revised edition, 1923; as *The Ruling Class*, edited by Arthur Livingston, New York, McGraw Hill, 1939; as *La classe politica*, edited by Norberto Bobbio, Bari, Laterza, 1966.
Questioni pratiche di diretto costituzionale. Turin, Bocca, 1898.

Il principio aristocratico ed il democratico nel passato e nell'avvenire (lecture). Turin, Stamperia Reale della Ditta Paravia, 1903.
Appunti di diritto costituzionale. Milan, Societa ed Libraria, 1908.
Sui provvedimenti per l'istruzione superiore. Rome, Tip. della Camera dei Deputati, 1909.
Italia e Libia: Considerazioni politiche. Milan, Treves, 1912.
Sulla riforma elettorale politica. Rome, Tip. della Camera dei Deputati, 1912.
Sul Trattato di Losanna. Rome, Colombo, 1912.
Sulla riforma della legge elettorale politica. Rome, Iip. della Camera dei Deputati, 1919.
Per l'assetto della Tripolitania. Rome, Tip. del Senato, 1920.
Sulle comunicazioni del governo. Rome, Tip. del Senato, 1920.
Sulle cause degli ultimi fatti avvenuti in Tripolitania. Rome, Tip. del Senato, 1920.
Sui disegno di legge relativo alle "Attribuzioni del Capo del Governo." Rome, Tip. del Senato del Dott. G. Bardi, 1925.
Sul bilancio delle colonie. Rome, Tip. del Senato dell Dott. G. Bardi, 1926.
Saggi di storia della scienza politica. Rome, Anonima Romana Editoriale, 1927.
Lezioni di storia della istituzioni e delle dottrine politiche. Rome, Castellani, 1933; revised edition, as *Storia delle dottrine politiche*, Bari, Laterza, 1937; as *A Short History of Political Philosophy*, New York, Crowell, 1972.
Histoire des doctrines politiques depuis l'antiquité jusq'à nos jours. Paris, Payot, 1936; revised edition, 1966.
Partiti e sindacati nella crisi del regime parlamentare. Bari, Laterza, 1949.
Ciò che la storia protebbe insegnare: Scritti di scienza politica. Milan, Giuffrè, 1958.
Il tramonto della stato liberale, edited by Antonio Lombardo. Catania, Bonanno, 1971.
Scritti sui sindacati, edited by Francesco Perfetti and Maurizio Ortolani. Rome, Bulzoni, 1974.

Other

Carteggio 1896-1934, with Guglielmo Ferrero, edited by Carlo Mongardini. Milan, Giuffrè, 1980.

*

Bibliography: *Bibliografia di Gaetano Mosca* by Mario delle Piane, Florence, La Nuova Italia, 1949.

Critical Studies: *The Myth of the Ruling Class: Gaetano Mosca and the "Elite"* by James H. Meisel, Ann Arbor, University of Mighigan Press, 1962, and *Pareto and Mosca* edited by Meisel, Englewood Cliffs, New Jersey, Prentice Hall, 1965; *On Mosca and Pareto* by Norberto Bobbio, Geneva, Droz, 1972; *The Anti-Democratic Sources of Elite Theory: Pareto, Mosca, Michels* by Robert A. Nye, London and Beverly Hills, California, Sage, 1977.

*   *   *

As a political theorist and active politician, Gaetano Mosca sought to establish an objective method of portraying and examining the varieties of political organization of developed societies. Like Saint-Simon, Mosca made a broad distinction between intellectual and moral social forces—comprising fundamental ideas and beliefs concerning religion, traditional allegiances, and group membership—and material social forces acting through hierarchies of functionaries capable of exerting power to achieve desired ends. He contended that human beings prefer submission to abstract principles rather than to persons. Therefore, social control or power is effectively embodied in political organization. Individuals with power over the mental and material forces of a particular society coalesce into a *classe politica* or "ruling class" which maintains authority through an articulated "political formula" or specific principle of sovereignty suited to social conditions. Mosca developed a complex account of the crucial factors affecting the dynamic balance of social forces. He identified criteria for depicting the structural integrity or "juridical defense," and the liberal merit or "level of civilization," of different regimes.

Mosca's methodology was somewhat positivist in its assumptions and essentially political rather than sociological in its focus, but he disavowed any ideological interest in historiography and offered no overall theory of history. His aim was chiefly to discern general tendencies and laws of political organization by investigating the political history of divergent societies. While he rejected theories of evolutionary political development for implying a doctrine of automatic progress, he insisted that the interplay of social forces involves a struggle for pre-eminence, not mere survival. He hoped that an objective approach to the interdependence of political ideas and conduct could have a salutary effect on politics by reducing the irrational excesses of ideology in formulating institutional practices. Employing his concept of the legitimating "political formula," Mosca deplored unreflective enthusiasm for the devices of mass democracy and popular sovereignty. Sceptical of the politics of heroic acts and symbolic gestures, dubious about radical innovations, he favoured a realistic and prosaic approach to the theory of practice based on cumulative historical criticism.

Mosca's conception of *the ruling class* stems from the observation that in every developed society a minority rules the majority through an organizational structure which derives power from the control of social forces. Mosca repudiated the view that any particular social force is primary in all societies, but instead stressed the importance of maintaining a fluid balance of forces. While considering the usual array of mental and material forces, he left it open that human potentiality can give rise to new social forces and fresh versions of older forces which could not have been foreseen. The stability of the ruling class of a particular society would be affected by the ratio of controlled to uncontrolled forces channelled through its organizational structure. Although Mosca recognized that political organization is itself a significant basis of power, it is also capable of creating or provoking other social forces beyond its powers of control or assimilation. Hence Mosca distinguished, among the members of the ruling class, between politicians, skilled in securing and holding known varieties of power, and statesmen capable of sensing changing forces in society and responding with novel visualizations of political organization. The matrix of social forces mobilized through political organization, together with the means of responding to the open texture of society to maintain authority as well as power, determines different types of ruling class and political systems.

Through the relation and content of *social type* and *political formula*, varying versions of the ruling class may be readily identified. The wide varieties of economic, religious, dynastic, military, racial, aesthetic, and other patterns of significance in a society yield a mass of common conscious experience, which evolves over time and determines a social type. From this assemblage of experience and its internal values, the leaders of different segments of society formulate a moral or legal principle justifying or legitimating their joint pre-eminence. The *political formula* conveys an accepted principle of sovereignty in a society, giving authority and rulership to social pre-eminence and affecting the structure of government. Whether the formula is the divine right of kings, the spiritual prerogative of priests, the natural rights of man, or the might of wealth and conquerors, the critical factor is the intelligibility and acceptability of the formula among the rulers and the ruled. Mosca classed all such formulae (and also their denials) as myths without objective validity. They are metaphysical constructs with meaning relative to given social realities. But they are essential to political society, both in shap-

ing the nature of rule and in shaping the society subject to the maxims of that rule. Political formulae vary in their degrees of universality and narrowness, and correspondingly in the extent of social cohesion or antagonistic fragmentation which they foster. When absolutized, they lead to an oversimplification of issues and structures, but when they are too pluralistic they lead to *ennui*. Whilst Mosca acknowledges the propaganda value of political formulae for reactionaries and radicals alike, there is a definite limit to cynicism since they are integral to the political order and limited in their social malleability.

Mosca based his critical assessment of political organizations upon the concept of *juridical defense*. Through the system of formal and informal, legal and administrative, devices of government, including the processes of selection of officials, a specific political organization offers diverse modes of due process for the adjustment of active social forces. Owing to this system of due process, the power and authority of the members of the ruling class are more (or less) limited, and the moral sensitivities of the ruled are given more (or less) satisfaction. The degree to which the system accommodates and offers orderly articulation to the entire congeries of forces operative in any society is the degree of juridical defense of the system. In effect, it is a measure of the moral coherence of the political order. Using this criterion of adjudication, Mosca criticized a variety of historical regimes and modes of political organization. For example, he held that the lack of church-state differentiation in Islamic institutions permitted the development of militarily fanatic provincial officials, leading to a breakdown of cohesion. He argued that the maintenance of an economic middle class promotes the development of talent and independent opinion, thus providing a pool of potential entrants to the ruling class capable of articulating emergent social forces. He proposed that the institution of standing armies serves to police random social violence as well as to control organized violence by offering its exponents reputable employment. He held that overgrown bureaucracy is more likely than political malfeasance to lead to revolt. He also contended that universal suffrage and numerical schemes of proportional representation tend to make parliamentary institutions the victims of irresponsible and self-serving interests.

Mosca pleaded for the representation in government of as large an array as feasible of the active forces of society. Through a high degree of juridical defense, capable of meeting society's needs for adjudication, it is possible for a people to attain a higher *level of civilization*. This net level is made up of the grades and qualities of achievement within the different areas of social endeavour, and represents an aggregate assessment of the scale of cohesive diversity in a society. In order to sustain or elevate its level of civilization, a political society must coordinate alterations in its social type with alterations in its ruling class. To this end, Mosca recommended a fluid balance between the "aristocratic" tendency of the ruling class to perpetuate itself from within and the "democratic" tendency to replenish itself from without. He similarly recommended a fluid balance between the "autocratic" principle of transmitting authority from above below and the "liberal" principle of transmitting authority from below above. Mosca held that much political wisdom rests in the ability to discern when and how to shift these balances in response to social need. The objective recognition of the existence of "ruling class" was, for Mosca, the perception of a spinal fact of the body politic, vitally important to rulers and ruled alike. "Every generation produces a certain number of generous spirits who are capable of loving all that is, or seems to be, noble and beautiful, and of devoting large parts of their activity to improving the society in which they live, or at least to saving it from getting worse. Such individuals make up a small moral and intellectual aristocracy, which keep humanity from rotting in the slough of selfishness and material appetites" (*The Ruling Class*).

—R.N. Iyer

MOWRER, O(rval) Hobart. American psychologist. Born in Unionville, Missouri, 23 June 1907. Studied at the University of Missouri, Columbia, B.A. 1929; Johns Hopkins University, Baltimore, Ph.D. 1932. Served as a clinical psychologist, Office of Strategic Services, 1944-45. Married Willa Mae Cook in 1931; 3 children. National Research Council Fellow, Northwestern University, Evanston, Illinois, 1932-33, and Princeton University, New Jersey, 1933-34; Sterling Fellow, 1934-36, and Instructor in Psychology and Member of Research Staff, Institute of Human Relations, Yale University, New Haven, Connecticut, 1936-40; Assistant Professor, 1940-43, and Associate Professor, 1943-48, Harvard University, Cambridge, Massachusetts; Research Professor, 1948-75, and since 1975 Professor Emeritus, University of Illinois, Urbana. President, American Psychological Association, 1954, and American Psychological Foundation, 1959-60. Recipient: Certificate of Merit, University of Missouri, 1956; Distinguished Contribution Award, Illinois Psychological Association, 1975. Fellow, American Psychological Association. *Died in June 1982.*

PUBLICATIONS

Psychology

The Modification of Vestibular Nystagmus by Means of Repeated Elicitation. Baltimore, Johns Hopkins University Press, 1934.
Frustration and Aggression, with others. New Haven, Connecticut, Yale University Press, 1939; London, Kegan Paul, 1944.
Preparatory Set (Expectancy)—Some Methods of Measurement. Columbus, Ohio, American Psychological Association, 1940.
Avoidance Conditioning and Signal Duration: A Study of Secondary Motivation and Reward, with R.R. Lamoreaux. Evanston, Illinois, American Psychological Association, 1942.
Learning Theory and Personality Dynamics: Selected Papers. New York, Ronald Press, 1950.
Psychotherapy: Theory and Research, with others. New York, Ronald Press, 1953.
Learning Theory and the Symbolic Process. New York, Wiley, 1960.
Learning Theory and Behavior. New York, Wiley, 1960.
The Crisis in Psychiatry and Religion. Princeton, New Jersey, Van Nostrand, 1961.
The Quest for Community. Rockford, Illinois, Augustana College Library, 1962.
The New Group Therapy. Princeton, New Jersey, Van Nostrand, 1964.

Other

Editor, *Morality and Mental Health.* Chicago, Rand McNally, 1967.
Editor, with Ronald Charles Johnson, *Conscience, Contract, and Social Reality.* New York, Holt Rinehart, 1972.
Editor, *Psychology of Language and Learning.* New York, Plenum Press, 1980.

*   *   *

O. Hobart Mowrer was in many ways a psychologist of all seasons. One of the factors that made Mowrer such a maverick in the field is that he managed to bridge the gap between experimental psychology and applied psychology without detriment to either field. He is among the five psychologists most often cited in the literature for their scientific contributions. From the time he retired until his recent death, Mowrer remained an active author and speaker within the fields he worked in.

Mowrer studied as an undergraduate at the University of Missouri, graduating in 1929. Following this, he began his grad-

uate work at Johns Hopkins University. During this time Mowrer became interested in vestibulo-ocular functions and spatial orientation, and he published extensively on this subject between 1929 and 1934, when he joined the Yale Institute of Human Relations.

In the mid-1940's, Mowrer's work led him into the field of language and learning. One of the results of these studies was one of his most important contributions to the field of language and thought, the Autism Theory of Speech Development. This theory arose out of Mowrer's work with talking birds (as opposed to laboratory animals such as rats) such as the mynah bird. In this theory Mowrer developed the idea of subjective utility as secondary reinforcement in the process of the bird's learning to "talk."

According to Mowrer, the use of certain words or phrases in intimate connection with the process of caring for the bird results in a positive conditioning of the bird; that is, the bird comes to consider them *good sounds*. In the course of its own, at first random, vocalizations, the bird will make somewhat similar sounds. Writing in the *Journal of Speech and Hearing Disorder,* Mowrer had this to say: "By the principle of generalization, some of the derived satisfaction of pleasure which has become attached to the trainer's sounds will now be experienced when the bird itself makes and hears like sounds; and when this begins to happen the stage is set for the bird's learning to 'talk.' " Essentially this means that when the bird hears itself making sounds like the trainer's, it is encouraged to continue making the same sounds. Further, the bird soon learns that he can use these sounds instrumentally, as a means of indicating some need or simply to attract an admiring crowd. Mowrer ascribes such an action to a desire in the bird to be like its trainer, which results from the development of a positive relationship between the bird and the human being.

From this Mowrer extrapolated a theory of language development in human infants. The child first identifies certain sounds as being good because his parents use them in connection with actions that provide the child with pleasure. He begins imitating them and perfecting his imitations; this provides him with a sense of gratification and attracts attention from his parents, which encourages him to continue. Finally he discovers the use of words in communicating by learning to use them to control his parents and other people, and to get what he wants. In his 1952 paper, Mowrer concludes that:

> By the procedures indicated, the response is, so to speak, *baited* in advance with secondary reinforcement so that whenever a closely related response occurs, a satisfying experience is assured, without our necessarily being present to reward it. The autistic satisfaction is, of course, likely to be relatively weak and ephemeral, but it is often strong enough to carry the desired response along until it can occur in the presence of another organism and thus elicit a more powerful, external reinforcement. Then its stability can be assured.

In the early 1960's, Mowrer became interested in psychopathology and this led him, through the "back door" as he describes it, to become interested in deception and its effects on personality. One of the first pieces he wrote on deception was for the Alcoholics Anonymous newsletter, *The Grapevine,* in 1962. Mowrer was impressed at the time with the axiom among members of AA that every alcoholic is a "liar" and that he can't get sober until he gets honest. While Mowrer recognizes the role heredity plays in causing mental illness, he feels that the stress created by deception can play an enormous part in triggering otherwise inert physiological troubles. In his paper for *The Grapevine* Mowrer quotes Sir Walter Scott, who says in "Lochinvar," "Oh what a tangled web we weave, when first we practice to deceive." It is the stress caused by becoming tangled in this web of deception that Mowrer believes is responsible for much of the mental anguish that people suffer. It is not just the deception of others that Mowrer cites too; it is also self-deception.

Few psychologists have contributed more to the advancement of psychology, and particularly the psychology of language and thought, than Mowrer. His work has been both imaginative and practical, as well as very often being candid and outspoken in its direction.

—R.W. Rieber

MULLER, Hermann Joseph. American geneticist. Born in New York City, 2 December 1890. Studied at Columbia University, New York, B.A. 1910, M.A. 1911, Ph.D. 1916; Cornell Medical School, New York. Married Jessie M. Jacobs in 1923, 1 son; married Dorothea J. Kantorowicz in 1939, 1 daughter. Instructor in Biology, Rice Institute, Houston, 1915-18; Instructor in Zoology, Columbia University, 1918-20; Associate Professor, 1920-25, and Professor, 1925-36, University of Texas, Austin; Senior Geneticist, Institute of Genetics, Leningrad, 1933-34, and Moscow, 1934-37; Research Associate, Institute of Animal Genetics, University of Edinburgh, 1937-40; Research Associate, 1940-42, and Visiting Professor, 1942-45, Amherst College, Massachusetts; Professor of Zoology, 1945-64, Distinguished Service Professor, 1953-64, and Professor Emeritus, 1964-67, Indiana University, Bloomington. Visiting Professor, University of Wisconsin, Madison, 1965-66. President, American Humanist Association, 1955-59. Recipient: Nobel Prize in Medicine and Physiology, 1946; Kimber Genetics Award, 1955; Darwin Medal, Linnean Society, 1959; Alexander Hamilton Award, Columbia University, 1960. Honorary doctorate: University of Edinburgh, 1940; Cornell University, Ithaca, New York, 1949; University of Chicago, 1959; Jefferson Medical College, Philadelphia, 1963; Swarthmore College, Pennsylvania, 1964. Member: American Academy of Arts and Sciences; Institute for Advanced Learning in Medicine; Royal Danish Academy of Science; Royal Swedish Academy of Science; Royal Society, London; Japanese Academy of Science; Genetical Society of Japan; National Institute of Science, India. Foreign Member, Mendelian Society, Lund, Sweden; Accademia Nazionale dei Lincei, Rome. Honorary Member, American Philosophical Society. *Died 5 April 1967.*

PUBLICATIONS

Biology

The Mechanism of Mendelian Heredity, with others. New York, Holt, 1915.
Out of the Night: A Biologist's View of the Future. New York, Vanguard Press, 1935.
Bibliography on the Genetics of Drosophila. Edinburgh, Oliver and Boyd, 1939.
Genetics, Medicine, and Man, with others (lectures). Ithaca, New York, Cornell University Press, 1947.
Studies in Genetics: The Selected Papers of H.J. Muller. Bloomington, Indiana University Press, 1962.
The Modern Concept of Nature: Essays on Theoretical Biology and Evolution, edited by Elof Axel Carlson. Albany, State University Press of New York, 1973.
Man's Future Birthright: Essays on Science and Humanity, edited by Elof Axel Carlson. Albany, State University Press of New York, 1973.

*   *   *

Hermann Joseph Muller was one of the greatest biologists of this century. His research career in genetics was crowned by the Nobel Prize in 1946 specifically for his work demonstrating the relationship between ionizing radiation and mutation. However,

Muller's reputation was not solely as a brilliant research scientist, but also as a humanist, deeply caring about the future of mankind. His research interests and humanitarian efforts were deeply fused.

Muller attributed his early interests in both science and the condition of humanity to his father, a manufacturer of metal art objects, who died when Muller was nine. His interests in genetics began early when he first saw models of the development of horses through geologic history. This interest was to be a broad-based one, concerning not only the physiological mechanisms of genetics, but also the evolutionary implications of genetic changes to organisms. It was an understanding of the evolutionary implication of deleterious genetic mutants that encouraged this sensitive young man to try to find an acceptable way for society to deal with the consequences of these mutations. As Muller said, "Scientists have the responsibility of seeing to it that their efforts are used for the benefit, not disadvantage, of their fellow humans".

Muller began his scientific career as a graduate student at Columbia University in 1910. After a Master's degree in 1911 and a one year study at the Medical College of Cornell University, he resumed study at Columbia working with two giants, the developmental biologist E.B. Wilson and Thomas Hunt Morgan, the first geneticist to win the Nobel Prize (in 1933). This was the dawn of genetics as a science, as Mendel's work had only been "rediscovered" in 1900. While Muller was a collaborator with and colleague of the Morgan "fly-lab" group (Morgan's group, which included Sturtevant, Bridges, and others, worked almost exclusively on *Drosophila*), he felt his strongest ties and allegiance with Wilson whom he considered his mentor. While Morgan's group, among other things, proceeded to map the fruit fly chromosomes, locating genes for various traits along the four chromosomes of *Drosophila*, Muller concerned himself more with the nature of the gene and the way it changed, or mutated.

Remembered primarily for his work demonstrating that ionizing radiation caused mutation, Muller had numerous other scientific accomplishments of great significance. He was the first to locate a gene on the fourth, and last chromosome of *Drosophila*. He had the first demonstration, in 1916, of a balanced lethal system. He demonstrated multiple crossing over in fruit flies. And he demonstrated that much of the evolutionary change in organisms was due to modifier genes. Throughout his research career, the role of mutation in gene expression and the nature of the gene itself were the major foci of his research.

In his work with radiation, Muller came to realize that we were increasing our rate of mutations by nuclear weapons testing and medical and industrial applications of radiation technology. Muller knew that the overwhelming majority of mutations were deleterious to living things. He forcefully, and shockingly, used to point this out in his evolution course which he taught at Indiana University. Prior to class, he would purchase a very inexpensive pocket watch. During his lecture he would point out that mutation is change and most changes to a well-adapted organism, like a change to a fine piece of machinery, would be deleterious. With that, he would take out his pocket watch and smash it down on the table top, demonstrating what a "random" change would do to a fine piece of machinery, or by analogy, what a mutation might do to an organism. No biology education at Indiana was complete without Professor Muller's course.

Muller felt the need to let everyone know that a build-up of radiation induced mutations, a "biological time-bomb," would be a terrible legacy to leave our future generations. Improvements in medicine only exacerbated this situation since modern medicine allows individuals to survive and reproduce who would normally not have been able to do so earlier. To counter this "mutational load," Muller suggested positive eugenics. In other words, he felt that the parents of each new generation should be carefully chosen from those who had proven themselves superior by either their accomplishments or good health. Always against a police state approach, he felt that people would freely choose this course if the technology of storage of germinal material and artificial insemination were well developed. Although we currently have a non-too-successful Nobel Laureate's Sperm Bank in California, his ideas have never been met with enthusiasm. Presumably the overwhelming majority of people simply want to produce their own children regardless of the potential consequences.

However, Muller persisted in this view that he considered of the utmost importance to future generations. Tolerated by some, offensive to others, the weight of his intellectual brilliance could not persuade Americans to agree with his views. This inability to be persuasive in his point of view was partly responsible for a period in Muller's life when he travelled, taught, and did research outside the United States.

In 1932 Muller left a professorship at the University of Texas for a Guggenheim Fellowship to work with the well known geneticist, Timofeeff-Ressovsky, in Berlin. With Hitler's rise to power, Muller ventured to Russia at the request of Vavilov. Muller hoped that in a Communist society he could apply his ideas in eugenics. However, he was frustrated by the rise of Lysenkoism, a movement that eventually drove him from Russia. Lysenko preached the inheritance of acquired characteristics which, while disputed by Western geneticists, was declared State doctrine in the Soviet Union where it was hoped Lysenko's ideas could vastly improve agricultural output. From Moscow, Muller travelled to Edinburgh and Amherst College, Massachusetts before securing a permanent position at Indiana University. He served there from 1945 until his death.

—Robert H. Tamarin

MUMFORD, Lewis. American theorist of planning, and social and literary critic. Born in Flushing, New York, 19 October 1895. Studied at Stuyvesant Technical High School, New York, 1909-12; City College of New York, 1912-17; Columbia University, New York, 1915-16; New School for Social Research, New York, 1919. Served in the United States Navy, 1918-19: Radio Electrician, second class. Married Sophia Wittenberg in 1921; 1 child. Investigator in dress and waist industry, 1916; laboratory assistant, U.S. Bureau of Standards, New York, 1917; special investigator, New York Housing and Planning Commission, 1924; Lecturer, New School for Social Research, 1925, and Geneva School of International Studies, 1925, 1929; Visiting Professor, Dartmouth College, Hanover, New Hampshire, 1929-35; Lecturer, Columbia University 1931-35; Professor, Stanford University, California, 1942-44; Earle Lecturer, Pacific Institute of Religion, 1947; Visiting Professor, North Carolina State University, Raleigh, 1948-52; Bampton Lecturer, Columbia University, 1951; Professor of City Planning, 1951-56, and Ford Professor, 1959-61, University of Pennsylvania, Philadelphia; Visiting Professor, Massachusetts Institute of Technology, Cambridge, 1957-61, and University of California, Berkeley, 1961-62; Saposnekow Lecturer, City College of New York, 1962; Senior Fellow, Wesleyan University Center for Advanced Studies, Middletown, Connecticut, 1962-64; Visiting Lecturer, 1973-74, and Charles Abrams Professor, 1975, Massachusetts Institute of Technology. Associate Editor, *Fortnightly Dial*, 1919; Acting Editor, *Sociological Review*, London, 1920; Contributing Editor, *New Republic*, 1927-40; Columnist ("The Sky Line"), *The New Yorker*, 1932. Founding Member, Regional Planning Association of America, 1923; Member of the Board of Higher Education, New York, 1935-37; Member of the American Council on Education Commission on Teacher Education, 1938-44; Vice-President, Société Européenne de Culture. Recipient: Guggenheim fellowship, 1932, 1938, 1956; Townsend Harris Medal, 1939; Ebenezer Howard Memorial Medal, 1946; Fairmount Park Art Association Medal of Honour, 1953; Town-Planning Institute Gold Medal, 1957; Royal Institute of British

Architects Royal Gold Medal, 1961; American Institute of Architects Award of Merit, 1962; National Book Award, 1962; Medal of Freedom, 1964; American Society of Planning Officials Silver Medal, 1965; Emerson-Thoreau Medal, 1965; Kaufman International Design Award, 1965; Society for the History of Technology Leonardo da Vinci Medal, 1969; American Academy Gold Medal, 1970; Smithsonian Institution Hodgkins Medal, 1971; Thomas Jefferson Memorial Foundation Medal, 1972; National Medal for Literature, 1972; Prix Mondial del Duca, 1976. LL.D.: University of Edinburgh, 1965; Dr.Arch.: University of Rome, 1967. Member, American Academy of Arts and Sciences; President, American Academy of Arts and Letters, 1963-65. Honorary Fellow, Stanford University, 1941; Honorary Member, Phi Beta Kappa, 1957; Honorary Member, Town Planning Institute, 1946, American Institute of Planners, 1955, Town Planning Institute of Canada, 1960, American Institute of Architects, and Colegio del Arquitectas del Peru; Honorary Associate, 1942, and Fellow, Royal Institute of British Architects. Honorary K.B.E. (Knight Commander, Order of the British Empire), 1975. Address: R.D. 1, Amenia, New York 12501, U.S.A.

PUBLICATIONS

Planning and Social and Literary Criticism

The Story of Utopias. New York, Boni and Liveright, 1922; London, Harrap, 1923.
Sticks and Stones: A Study of American Architecture and Civilization. New York, Boni and Liveright, 1924.
Aesthetics: A Dialogue. Privately printed, 1925.
The Golden Day: A Study in American Experience and Culture. New York, Boni and Liveright, 1926; as *The Golden Day: A Study in American Literature and Culture*, New York, Norton, 1933.
Architecture. Chicago, American Library Association, 1926.
American Taste. San Francisco, Westgate Press, 1929.
Herman Melville. New York, Harcourt Brace, and London, Cape, 1929; revised edition, as *Herman Melville: A Study of His Life and Vision*, Harcourt Brace, 1962; London, Secker and Warburg, 1963.
The Brown Decades: A Study of the Arts in America 1865-1895. New York, Harcourt Brace, 1931.
Technics and Civilization. New York, Harcourt Brace, and London, Routledge, 1934.
Whither Honolulu? Privately printed, 1938.
The Culture of Cities. New York, Harcourt Brace, and London, Secker and Warburg, 1938.
Men Must Act. New York, Harcourt Brace, and London, Secker and Warburg, 1939.
Regional Planning in the Pacific Northwest: A Memorandum. Portland, Oregon, Northwest Regional Council, 1939.
Faith for Living. New York, Harcourt Brace, 1940; London, Secker and Warburg, 1941.
The South in Architecture (lectures). New York, Harcourt Brace, 1941.
World-Wide Civil War, with Herbert Agar and Frank Kingdon. New York, Freedom House, 1942.
The School of Humanities: A Description. Stanford, California, Stanford University, 1942.
New World Theme, with Henry A. Wallace and Jay Allen. Stanford, California, J.L. Delkin, 1943.
The Social Foundations of Post-War Building. London, Faber, 1943.
The Condition of Man. New York, Harcourt Brace, and London, Secker and Warburg, 1944.
The Plan of London County. London, Faber, 1945.
City Development: Studies in Disintegration and Renewal. New York, Harcourt Brace, 1945; London, Secker and Warburg, 1946.

Values for Survival: Essays, Addresses, and Letters on Politics and Education. New York, Harcourt Brace, 1946; as *Programme for Survival,* London, Secker and Warburg, 1946.

Atomic War—The Way Out. London, National Peace Council, 1948(?).

Man As Interpreter. New York, Harcourt Brace, 1950.

The Conduct of Life. New York, Harcourt Brace, 1951; London, Secker and Warburg, 1952.

Art and Technics (lectures). New York, Columbia University Press, and London, Oxford University Press, 1952.

Towards a Free World: Long-Range Planning under Democratic Control (address). New York, Church Peace Union, 1952.

In the Name of Sanity. New York, Harcourt Brace, and London, Secker and Warburg, 1954.

The Human Prospect (selections), edited by Harry T. Moore and Karl W. Deutsch. Boston, Beacon Press, 1955; London, Secker and Warburg, 1956.

From the Ground Up: Observations on Contemporary Architecture, Housing, Highway Building, and Civic Design. New York, Harcourt Brace, 1956.

The Transformations of Man. New York, Harper, 1956; London, Allen and Unwin, 1957.

The Human Way Out (lecture). Wallingford, Pennsylvania, Pendle Hill, 1958; London, Friends Peace Committee, 1962.

The Role of the Creative Arts in Contemporary Society (lecture). Durham, University of New Hampshire, 1958.

The City in History: Its Origins, Its Transformations, and Its Prospects. New York, Harcourt Brace, and London, Secker and Warburg, 1961.

Social Responsibility in the Business Community (lecture). Baltimore, Baltimore Life Insurance Company, 1961.

The Highway and the City. New York, Harcourt Brace, 1963; London, Secker and Warburg, 1964.

Myth of the Machine:

1. *Technics and Human Development.* New York, Harcourt Brace, and London, Secker and Warburg, 1967.
2. *The Pentagon of Power.* New York, Harcourt Brace, 1970; London, Secker and Warburg, 1971.

The Urban Prospect. New York, Harcourt Brace, and London, Secker and Warburg, 1968.

Interpretations and Forecasts 1922-1972: Studies in Literature, History, Biography, Technics, and Contemporary Society. New York, Harcourt Brace, and London, Secker and Warburg, 1973.

Architecture as a Home for Man: Essays for "Architectural Record", edited by Jeanne M. Davern. New York, Architectural Record, 1975.

Other

Thomas Beer, Aristocrat of Letters. Privately printed, 1944.

Green Memories: The Story of Geddes Mumford. New York, Harcourt Brace, 1947.

The Letters of Lewis Mumford and Frederic J. Osborn: A Transatlantic Dialogue, edited by Michael R. Hughes. Bath, Adams and Dart, 1971; as *Lewis Mumford and Frederic J. Osborn: A Transatlantic Dialogue,* New York, Praeger, 1972.

Findings and Keepings 1914-1936 (Analects for an Autobiography). New York, Harcourt Brace, 1975; London, Secker and Warburg, 1976.

My Works and Days: A Personal Chronicle 1895-1975. New York, Harcourt Brace, 1979.

Editor, with others, *The American Caravan: A Yearbook of American Literature* (and *The Second* and *The New American Caravan, American Caravan IV,* and *The New Caravan*). New York, Macaulay, 5 vols., 1927-36.

Editor, with others, *America and Alfred Stieglitz: A Collective Portrait.* New York, Doubleday, 1934.

Editor, *Roots of Contemporary American Architecture.* New York, Reinhold, 1952.

Editor, *Essays and Journals,* by Ralph Waldo Emerson. New York, Doubleday, 1968.

Editor, *The Ecological Basis of Planning,* by Artur Glikson. The Hague, Nijhoff, 1971.

*

Bibliography: *Lewis Mumford: A Bibliography 1914-1970* by Elmer S. Newman. New York, Harcourt Brace, 1971.

*   *   *

For over sixty years Lewis Mumford's ideas have provoked and challenged philosophers, historians, sociologists, architects, city planners, and critics around the world. Most of his major books remain in print and much of his writing remains as relevant today as it did when first completed. Mumford is a distinguished 20th-century thinker whose ideas make sense for the approaching 21st-century.

Virtually every problem which Mumford warned about since the 1920's deserves serious attention today. Problems like environmental pollution, nuclear proliferation, and urban deterioration have intensified rather than faded since he first wrote about them. Dehumanization and alienation have grown more severe while a rational world order committed to life-affirming values seems more elusive than ever.

Mumford has been called an "American Prophet" by literary critic Van Wyck Brooks and indeed he is. Mumford retains a vision which is unique, powerful, and timely. He was prophetic in the 1930's when writing about unchecked technological growth occurring at the expense of human needs. Since his early books, he has supported a global perspective which acknowledges a world community composed of diverse individuals and cultures. He has always stressed the idea of thinking globally but acting locally in neighborhoods, communities, and regions.

Self-renewal and personal/social transformation are important elements in Mumford's philosophy. A strong believer in the potentiality and creativity of human beings, he strives for synthesis between rational and unrational processes, stability and change, participation and contemplation, self-renewal and cultural renewal. He supports development of a new social order centering on life-needs and a technology which respects rather than denies organic demands. Mumford's "biotechnic" economy and culture rejects corporate capitalism in favor of a democratic socialism which strives for justice and equality in deed as well as word. In his vision, communities control and distribute their own resources with the vital needs of everyone provided, but an economy of super-abundance is rejected.

Mumford argues for a technology sensitive to organic, biological, and aesthetic needs and desires. Long a critic of technological faddism and mechanistic schemes which lead to alienation and depersonalization, he neither condemns technology outright nor credits it with the power to save humanity. Mumford poses a central question about technological projects and proposals: "What essential human need, viewed in historic perspective, is being fulfilled or is being sacrificed?" He challenges the popular overemphasis on early humans as tool makers and tool users, stressing the key role of ritual, language, and social development. Dreams, images, sounds, and symbols played a central role in the evolution of human cultures, he maintains.

One of Mumford's most valuable concepts is that of the megamachine. Seen in pyramid building in ancient times and construction of giant submarines and missiles with lethal nuclear warheads in our own time, the megamachine is characterized by predominance of order, regularity, predictability, and centralized power. War is "the body and soul of the megamachine" with the tremendous waste in planning for war (in the name of "national defense") leading to huge profits for a few and great losses for the many who happen to be poor, elderly, and unemployed.

Mass civilian bombing in World War II revealed the mega-machine at its worst, Mumford asserts. Nuclear weapons development since the 1940's has brought fragmented parts of the megamachine together and threatens the globe with omnicide. The contemporary military megamachine is especially dangerous because it is commanded by these who remain physically and emotionally detached, flying high above the clouds in B-52 bombers, cruising deep beneath the seas in nuclear submarines or sitting rigidly in front of buttons ready to launch World War III. The terrible destruction of human life at the target of these weapons is well hidden from those who carry out orders. All is automated; all is impersonal and devoid of feeling.

As an alternative to the megamachine, Mumford calls for a "democratic technics" which places human beings in charge of technological processes and brings them in closer contact with fellow workers and with products of their labor. He supports technology that helps eliminate degrading work or unwilling drudgery. At the same time, Mumford is a strong advocate of work which is creative or fulfilling and technology which is small scale and human-controlled.

Mumford's interest in architecture as well as technology has never wavered. The total environment in which architecture plays both a symbolic and functional part concerns him most. The community should be treated as a major element in design, he maintains. Good architecture combines form and function, symbolic meaning and functional integrity; his chief interest lies in buildings "as a many-sided expression of the human mind: not just its intelligence and practical mastery, but its feelings, its prophetic aspirations, its transcendental purposes." Mumford should be credited with bringing three great American architects to popular attention: Henry Hobson Richardson, Louis Sullivan, and Frank Lloyd Wright. His early books on American architecture and art remain outstanding contributions to the field.

One of the foremost living historians and critics of the city, Lewis Mumford has been disturbed for years about anti-urban trends like the proliferation of sky-scrapers and automobiles, suburban sprawl, and the lack of any organic limits to growth in the modern city. He was heavily influenced by the Scot Patrick Geddes whose interest in surveying and evaluating every aspect of cities led Mumford to describe Geddes as a philosopher of life in its fullness and unity. Though Mumford himself has been criticized for being anti-urban, he affirms that "...it is in and through the city, with all the responses it offers for the mind, that man has created a symbolic counterpart to nature's creativity, variety and exuberance." Mumford stresses integrated neighborhoods in cities and is also fascinated by the idea of creating balanced new communities on a human scale. He was active in the "New Towns" movement in the 1920's and 1930's based upon Ebenezer Howard's ideas.

A world citizen in every sense, Mumford remains committed to the utopian goal of a world order which guarantees peace and justice for all. The emergence of a new world society, he argues, will not result from a series of minor modifications but rather from a radical leap from one plane to another. He dares to dream of "One World" civilization while also envisioning invigorated local communities and a renewed sense of individual purpose. Mumford is a great American scholar in the tradition of Emerson, Thoreau, and Whitman. But he is also a "prophet-father of the coming world civilization," in the words of historian W. Warren Wagar.

—David R. Conrad

MURDOCH, (Jean) Iris. British philosopher and novelist. Born in Dublin, Ireland, 15 July 1919. Educated at Froebel Education Institute, London, and Badminton School, Bristol; studied at Somerville College, Oxford, B.A. 1942 (honours), and Newnham College, Cambridge (Sarah Smithson Student in philosophy), 1947-48. Married the writer John Bayley in 1956. Assistant Principal in the Treasury, London, 1942-44; Administrative Officer with the United Nations Relief and Rehabilitation Administration (UNRRA) in London, Belgium, and Austria, 1944-46; Fellow, St. Anne's College, Oxford, and University Lecturer in Philosophy, Oxford University, 1948-63; since 1963, Honorary Fellow, St. Anne's College; Lecturer, Royal College of Art, London, 1963-67. Recipient: Black Memorial Award, 1974; Whitbread Literary Award, 1974; Booker Prize, 1978. Member, Irish Academy, 1970. Honorary Member, American Academy of Arts and Letters, 1975. Honorary Fellow, Somerville College, 1977. C.B.E. (Commander, Order of the British Empire), 1976. Address: Cedar Lodge, Steeple Aston, Oxford, England.

PUBLICATIONS

Philosophy

Sartre, Romantic Rationalist. Cambridge, Bowes and Bowes, and New Haven, Connecticut, Yale University Press, 1953.
The Sovereignty of Good over Other Concepts (lecture). Cambridge, University Press, 1967.
The Sovereignty of Good (essays). London, Routledge, 1970; New York, Schocken, 1971.
The Fire and the Sun: Why Plato Banished the Artists. London and New York, Oxford University Press, 1977.

Novels

Under the Net. London, Chatto and Windus, and New York, Viking Press, 1954.
The Flight from the Enchanter. London, Chatto and Windus, and New York, Viking Press, 1956.
The Sandcastle. London, Chatto and Windus, and New York, Viking Press, 1957.
The Bell. London, Chatto and Windus, and New York, Viking Press, 1958.
A Severed Head. London, Chatto and Windus, and New York, Viking Press, 1961.
An Unofficial Rose. London, Chatto and Windus, and New York, Viking Press, 1962.
The Unicorn. London, Chatto and Windus, and New York, Viking Press, 1963.
The Italian Girl. London, Chatto and Windus, and New York, Viking Press, 1964.
The Red and the Green. London, Chatto and Windus, and New York, Viking Press, 1965.
The Time of the Angels. London, Chatto and Windus, and New York, Viking Press, 1966.
The Nice and the Good. London, Chatto and Windus, and New York, Viking Press, 1968.
Bruno's Dream. London, Chatto and Windus, and New York, Viking Press, 1969.
A Fairly Honourable Defeat. London, Chatto and Windus, and New York, Viking Press, 1970.
An Accidental Man. London, Chatto and Windus, 1971; New York, Viking Press, 1972.
The Black Prince. London, Chatto and Windus, and New York, Viking Press, 1973.
The Sacred and Profane Love Machine. London, Chatto and Windus, and New York, Viking Press, 1974.
A Word Child. London, Chatto and Windus, and New York, Viking Press, 1975.
Henry and Cato. London, Chatto and Windus, 1976; New York, Viking Press, 1977.
The Sea, The Sea. London, Chatto and Windus, and New York, Viking Press, 1978.

Nuns and Soldiers.   London, Chatto and Windus, 1980; New York, Viking Press, 1981.
The Philosopher's Pupil.   London, Chatto and Windus, and New York, Viking Press, 1983.

Plays

A Severed Head, with J.B. Priestley.   London, Chatto and Windus, 1964.
The Italisn Girl, with James Saunders.   London, French, 1969.
The Three Arrows, and The Servant and the Snow: Two Plays.   London, Chatto and Windus, 1973; New York, Viking Press, 1974.

Verse

A Year of Birds.   Tisbury, Wiltshire, Compton Press, 1978.

*

Bibliography: *Iris Murdoch and Muriel Spark: A Bibliography* by Thomas T. Tominaga and Wilma Schneidermeyer, Metuchen, New Jersey, Scarecrow Press, 1976.

Critical Studies: *Degrees of Freedom: The Novels of Iris Murdoch*, London, Chatto and Windus, and New York, Barnes and Noble, 1965, and *Iris Murdoch*, London, Longman, 1976, both by A.S. Byatt; *The Disciplined Heart: Iris Murdoch and Her Novels* by Peter Wolfe, Columbia, University of Missouri Press, 1966; *Iris Murdoch* by Rubin Rabinovitz, New York, Columbia University Press, 1968; *Iris Murdoch* by Frank Baldanza, New York, Twayne, 1974; *Iris Murdoch* by Donna Gerstenberger, Lewisburg, Pennsylvania, Bucknell University Press, 1974; *Iris Murdoch: The Shakespearian Interest* by Richard Todd, New York, Barnes and Noble, 1979; *Iris Murdoch: Work for the Spirit* by Elizabeth Dipple, London, Methuen, and Chicago, University of Chicago Press, 1982.

*   *   *

From solid Anglo-Irish origins and an Oxford education, Iris Murdoch became a professional moral philosopher and then a prolific witty novelist. After early fascination with Marxism and then existentialism (critically in her first small book, on Sartre, and as a continuing demonic counterforce in her fictions), she staked out in a number of essays a qualified modern Platonism (*The Sovereignty of Good*). Apparently agnostic—"I assume that human beings are naturally selfish and that human life has no external point or [purpose]"—she yet holds to a Christian fellow-travelling transcendent "Good," or at least the quest for it.

Even the True and the Beautiful are finally subordinate to the Good. Modern science ("so interesting and so dangerous") and modern philosophy (so trapped in positivistic, utilitarian, and existentialist falsities) stand inferior to the best of literature and art for wisdom. Literature, though often morally distorted into consoling fantasy (see the discussion of art and Plato in *The Fire and the Sun*), provides "the most essential and fundamental aspect of culture," thus the proper study of how to reach beyond egotism into the moral sympathy in human situations. It also provides senses of human love, which may give intimations of Love of the Good. Yet love and goodness are so mysterious that the unexamined life may be the most worth living and the simplest people sometimes the best. A paradoxically claimed moral democracy.

Though sometimes suggestive, and a rationale for her art, Murdoch's philosophical essays are neither exceptionally rigorous nor rich, hence not persuasive. But her twenty novels often are, not least in that the Good becomes far more ambiguous and peculiar than the Platonizing mandates. She puts an endlessly ironic modern consciousness, and a sophisticatedly self-conscious

fictional gaming, into traditional forms—the novel of manners, the realistic comedy, the philosophical farce, the gothic romance, the family saga, and the moral fable. All are ballasted, often surprisingly but delightfully, with much "realistic" observation of scenes (especially London), highly individualized eccentrics, and sharp wit about human relationships.

Her usual subject is the moral "muddler," most often an English upper-middle-class intellectual male in the sexual and moral perplexities of middle age. The ironic gaming of morality with such both proposes and undercuts a transcendent Good which is rarely confirmed but often dissolved into a conventional love-ethic—the higher muddle. More exalted ethical claims usually reveal egotistic self-delusions. She most often uses the ironist's art of transcendence by intellectually defeating intellect, thus pyrrhically falling back on the affirmation of ordinary decencies.

While some admire her philosophical gothic melodramas—*The Unicorn, The Italian Girl, The Time of the Angels*—and they do emphatically present some of her arguments (egotism vs. goodness, Luciferian existentialism vs. compassionate decency, etc.), I would argue for the superiority among the early fictions of the polished *A Severed Head*. This Laclos comedy uses erotic musical chairs and double-played Freudian dialectics perceptively to reveal reversing motivations. Psycholanalysis in Murdoch's deft analysis exposes itself as glibly closed postulates which are really infinite regresses (the most neurotic seduces the analyst, his disease his trade). The will to discover motivations may defeat the will to be motivated, which is to be one's self. But Murdoch does not counter with the old moral will since right and wrong also too easily reverse and obscure a possible larger good, the fusion of desire and self in a new destiny. The muddler-hero, finally accepting a more dangerous self and the shocking head-severing "dark gods" (less defineable, thus less objectionable than the Christian God responsible for this cruel world), may have reached beyond irony. A rather Lawrencean passional transformation reinvigorates the man, and the world, giving not the Good but at least a "truth" beyond the ordinary complacencies of "what you call civilization."

This romantic dialectic by an anti-romanticist considerably turns into moral sentimentality, though often with some wit and perception and metaphoric flair, in the family sagas, such as *An Unofficial Rose* and *The Nice and the Good*. Harsher, and more allegorical, are *Bruno's Dream, Henry and Cato, The Sea, The Sea*, and—perhaps the mocking best of them with its evil-muddler psychotherapist—*The Sacred and Profane Love Machine*. The richer *A Fairly Honorable Defeat* and, especially, *An Accidental Man*, with their complex contingency and some saintly muddlers, have more than the usual mockeries. Murdoch's contemporary English version of the Dostoevskian underground man, *A Word Child*, explores the failure of guilt and remorse and envy in the attempt to reach the moral that "Forgiving equals being forgiven." *The Black Prince*, a Nabokovian labyrinth of obsession and of redone *Hamlet* as black comedy, may be read as Murdoch's dramatized aesthetic that "all art deals with the absurd and aims at the simple."

In using comic and dark eros to show that "all morality is ultimately mysticism," a sometimes too clever Murdoch deploys labyrinthine egotism masked as virtue, ingenious loadings of demonic complications and strange forces such as father-enchanter dieties, bizarrely intriguing mixtures of chance and necessity, and a humane sensitivity to varied eccentrics—all to discover gleamings of goodness in an absurd universe. In some crucial senses a very contemporary novelist of existential cast (however that righteously be mocked), she nonetheless pursues old-fashioned moral verities for loving humanity. But in the later fictions the overcoming of proper pessimism takes more and more intellectual bravado. Perhaps the artful intelligence for an audience of intellectual muddlers turns the works into self-consuming fictional machines. The daring mind is returned to the traditional, after all is said and done—a pyrrhonistic faith. The intellectual ironist has found the witty yet sentimental catharsis which finally confirms conventional decencies amidst the wryly sad yearning for some larger Good.

—Kingsley Widmer

MURPHY, Gardner. American psychologist. Born in Chillicothe, Ohio, 8 July 1895. Studied at Yale University, New Haven, Connecticut, B.A. 1916; Harvard University, Cambridge, Massachusetts, M.A. 1917; Columbia University, New York, Ph.D. 1923. Served in the United States Army as a medical corpsman, 1917-19. Married Lois Barclay in 1926; 2 children. Lecturer, 1921-25, Instructor, 1925-29, and Assistant Professor of Psychology, 1929-40, Columbia University; Professor of Psychology and Chairman of the Department, 1940-52, City College of New York; Director of Research, Menninger Foundation, Topeka, Kansas, 1952-68; Professor of Psychology, George Washington University, Washington, D.C., 1968-73. Unesco Consultant, Ministry of Information, 1950. President, Eastern Psychological Association, 1941-42, American Psychological Association, 1943-44, and American Society for Psychical Research, 1961-71. Recipient: Butler Medal, Columbia University, 1932; Gold Medal, American Psychological Association, 1972. Member, American Academy of Arts and Sciences. *Died* (in Washington, D.C.) *18 March 1979.*

PUBLICATIONS

Psychology

An Historical Introduction to Psychology. New York, Harcourt Brace, and London, Kegan Paul, 1929.
Experimental Social Psychology: An Interpretation of Research Upon the Socialization of the Individual, with others. New York, Harper, 1931.
Approaches to Personality: Some Contemporary Conceptions Used in Psychology with Psychiatry, with Friedrich Jensen. New York, Coward McCann, 1932.
General Psychology. New York, Harper, 1933; abridged version as *A Briefer General Psychology,* New York, Harper, 1953.
Public Opinion and the Individual: A Psychological Study of Student Attitudes on Public Questions, with a Retest Five Years Later, with Rensis Likert. New York, Harper, 1938.
Personality: A Biosocial Approach to Origins and Structure. New York, Harper, 1947.
An Introduction to Psychology, with Herbert Spohn. New York, Harper, 1951.
In the Minds of Men: The Study of Human Behavior and Social Tensions in India. New York, Basic Books, 1953.
Human Potentialities. New York, Basic Books, 1958.
Development of the Perceptual World, with Charles Marion Solley. New York, Basic Books, 1960.
The Challenge of Psychical Research: A Primer of Parapsychology, with Laura A. Dale. New York, Harper, 1961.
Freeing Intelligence Through Teaching: A Dialectic of the Rational and the Personal. New York, Harper, 1961.
Encounter with Reality: New Forms for an Old Quest, with Herbert Spohn. Boston, Houghton Mifflin, 1968.
Psychological Thought from Pythagoras to Freud: An Informal Introduction. New York, Harcourt Brace, 1968.
Outgrowing Self-Deception, with Morton Leeds. New York, Basic Books, 1975.

Other

Editor, *An Outline of Abnormal Psychology.* New York,

Modern Library, 1929.
Editor, *Human Nature and Enduring Peace.* Boston, Houghton Mifflin, 1945.
Editor, *An Outline of Social Psychology,* by Muzafer Sheriff. New York, Harper, 1948.
Editor, *Industrial Psychology and Its Social Foundations,* by Milton L. Blum. New York, Harper, 1949.
Editor, *William James on Pyschical Research.* New York, Viking Press, 1961.
Editor, with Lois B. Murphy, *Asian Psychology.* New York, Basic Books, 1968.
Editor, with Lois B. Murphy, *Western Psychology: From the Greeks to William James.* New York, Basic Books, 1969.

*   *   *

It was as a notable teacher and textbook author that Gardner Murphy throughout his career served the community of empirical psychologists. His guidance is most apparent in his successful survey tests: *Historical Introduction to Modern Psychology, Experimental Social Psychology, Approaches to Personality, A Briefer General Psychology, Personality,* and *An Introduction to Psychology.* Murphy was a synthesizer with staunch adherence to positivism and a general systems analysis, and as such he provided the rapidly expanding discipline of psychology, especially the subfields of social psychology and personality, with a potential model for disciplinary coherence. Thus, while he conducted experimental research in perception, attitudes, and public opinion, his primary contributions must be seen as the synthetic appraisals and directives offered in his textbooks.

Whether describing the structure of the discipline or of personality, Murphy contemplated an expansive and eclectic systemization and confirmed his commitment to these overriding principles through an avowed lifetime devotion to the works of William James. He typically posed the ideal system for an integrative view of human nature as one melding the knowledge of biological tendencies which he recognized as motives, impulses, and desires; an assessment of the plasticity of these tendencies and their canalization into social habits; and analysis of the architectonics of attitudes and values in the socialized individual. Knowledge of the biological substrates, the learning or molding processes, and the cultural structures was held as the basis of any adequate social psychology. While his conviction that "almost every problem in social psychology is in some sense a problem of the relation between unique gene-patterns and endlessly shifting personal environments" did not differ from most social psychologists' conception of their mission, Murphy stood apart in insisting that attention be given to the dynamics of historical change and the necessity of anthropological studies. Further, despite the fact that he published the first explicitly experimental text on social psychology, he candidly commented on the limitations of social psychological experimentation.

Murphy's vision of psychology also resembled those of his contemporaries in a firm belief in a rather naive positivism, a belief that was demonstrated in several ways. His historical analysis of psychology provides an inductive account of the refinement of scientific methods and the accumulation of knowledge yielded from use of these methods: *Historical Introduction to Psychology* presents "in rough chronological order the conquest by scientific methods of one research field after another." When writing on personality and social psychology Murphy frequently looked toward the more refined science of biology as a hierarchically superior realm upon which psychologists must undertake their inquiries. Finally, in keeping with positivism of the period, he argued repeatedly that the scientific method was the sole means by which psychologists could achieve their obligations to better public life for only that method would yield the reliable knowledge for enlightened social planning.

Murphy's texts attained prominence for their coherent integration of the multiple and sometimes discordant ideals of a scientific psychology and for fusing the plethora of research ventures into a plausible model of human nature as well as of research programs. Murphy served as an alacritous and elucidating guide through a period when psychology was undergoing seemingly haphazard specialization, when, as one psychologist put it, psychologists were learning more and more about less and less.

—J.G. Morawski

———————

MURRAY, Henry A(lexander). American psychologist. Born in New York City, 13 May 1893. Studied at Harvard University, Cambridge, Massachusetts, B.A. 1915; Columbia University College of Physicians and Surgeons, M.D. 1919; Cambridge University, Ph.D. in biochemistry, 1927. Served in the Office of Strategic Services, 1942-46: Lieutenant Colonel. Married Josephine Rantoul in 1916, 1 daughter; married Caroline C. Fish in 1969. Surgical Intern, Presbyterian Hospital, New York, 1924-26; did research work in embryology at the Rockefeller Institute for Medical Research, New York, 1926-27; Instructor, 1927-29, Assistant Professor, 1929-37, Associate Professor, 1937-48, Professor of Clinical Psychology, 1948-62, and since 1962 Professor Emeritus, Harvard University (after 1929, Director of the Psychological Clinic). Recipient: Distinguished Science Contribution Award, American Psychological Association, 1961. Honorary doctorate: Lawrence College, Appleton, Wisconsin, 1964; University of Louvain, Belgium, 1966. Member, American Academy of Arts and Sciences. Address: 22 Francis Avenue, Cambridge, Massachusetts 02138, U.S.A.

PUBLICATIONS

Psychology

Explorations in Personality: A Clinical and Experimental Study of Fifty Men of College Age, with others. New York, Oxford University Press, 1938.
Thematic Apperception Test Manual, with others. Cambridge, Massachusetts, Harvard University Press, 1943.
A Clinical Study of Sentiments, with Christina D. Morgan. Provincetown, Massachusetts, Journal Press, 1945.
Assessment of Men, with others. New York, Rinehart, 1948.
Endeavors in Psychology: Selections from the Personology of Henry A. Murray, edited by Edwin S. Shneidman. New York, Harper, 1981 (contains a bibliography).

Other

Melville and Hawthorne and the Berkshires, with others. Kent, Ohio, Kent State University Press, 1968.

Editor, *Pierre; or, The Ambiguities*, by Herman Melville. New York, Hendricks House, 1949.

*

Critical Study: *Humanism in Personology: Allport, Maslow, and Murray* by Salvatore R. Maddi, Chicago, Aldine, 1972.

*   *   *

The focus of Henry A. Murray's work has been the study of human personality for which he has coined the word "personology," defining it as "the branch of psychology which principally concerns itself with the study of human lives and the factors that influence their course." The ultimate aim of the personologist is threefold: to construct a theory of personality, to devise suitable techniques for studying its more important attributes, and to discover its basic facts through careful and extensive studies of actual human lives. Since personology is the science of men, Murray considers it the most inclusive field of psychology, other branches being essentially special areas within it.

Murray has always been an advocate of interdisciplinary personality studies, accepting a wide range of approaches as useful in personology. Biological, historical, cultural, social, and evolutionary concepts, as well as those in all areas of psychology, are important to personality as Murray sees it. He is concerned with interpersonal, intrapersonal, and impersonal psychological forces, and, while recognizing the value of subjective material, he does not neglect objective observation. He has formulated a number of special evaluation techniques to study both conscious and unconscious psychological processes. Among the most well-known of these are the Thematic Apperception Test, a projective technique through which data can be analyzed to permit inferences about the dominant psychological forces affecting the subject's thought and behavior. This is done through the intermediary device of heroes or central figures in the TAT pictures, about which the subject is asked to make up stories. The ways he handles the issues he projects into the pictures are assumed to indicate his own characteristic problem-solving approaches, and the endings he envisions are assumed to embody the endings he desires for his own conflicts.

Murray defines personality as "the hypothetical structure of the mind, the consistent establishments and processes of which are manifested over and over again...in the internal and external proceedings which constitute a person's life. In speaking of personality Murray uses a number of terms. The term "proceedings" refers to the units of time during which the person attends to either the internal or external circumstances of his life. Serials, a series of proceedings, are related to each other but separate in time and permit the pursuit of long-range goals. Murray sees the person as continually planning schedules for achieving these goals by setting up serial programs, sequences of subgoals, which serve as steps along the way. All of these processes constantly arise, shift, and give way to others as circumstances change, and personality changes with them. He sees the person as constantly under pressure by conflicting internal and external demands so that throughout his life he must give up things as well as take for himself.

Murray's views on personality contain a strong Freudian emphasis, stressing the role of the past as the seed of the present. At the same time, however, he does not neglect either present or future states and their influence on personality. Murray uses Freudian concepts to describe the stages of childhood. The id, as he conceives it, remains the source of energy and the reservoir of unacceptable impulses as it was for Freud. However, Murray also sees the id as containing positive and constructive impulses. The ego is not merely a repressor and inhibitor for him; it has energies of its own which direct id drives toward a suitable expression. The super-ego, although still the internal regulator of behavior derived from early experiences, can be significantly changed later by peer-group and other influences, including those associated with literary, historiocal, and mythological characters with whom the person identifies. Murray's concept of the ego ideal, which is associated with the superego, consists of the various self-images representing the person at his very best, helping him to maintain goal directed living.

Murray also identifies certain temporal sequences in childhood that represent their Freudian counterparts, although they are a bit more widely interpreted. To the oral, anal, and phallic stages, Murray introduces two further stages, the claustral and the urethral. The cluastral involved the tranquil state of prenatal existence, while the urethral, falling between the oral and anal stages, involves the pleasurable sensations associated with urethral erotism. In Murray's view these can naturally lead to complexes of their own, the claustral producing a passive, dependent personality with prominent withdrawal tendencies, and the urethral complex producing an overly ambitious, strongly narcissistic adult with a prominent concern for achieving immortality and a strong attachment to fire. The urethral complex is also known as the Icarus complex. The extremely detailed case history called "An American Icarus" is one of Murray's best-known works.

Murray has also developed a theory of motivation, one of the main concepts of which is that of "need," which he regards as a force in the brain which can be aroused by either internal or external stimulation. Once stimulated it produces continued activity until it is reduced or satisfied. Murray has worked out a number of classifications of needs in a continuing effort at greater precision. In one such system he distinguishes between activity and effect needs, activity needs being directed towards activity for its own sake and effect needs being directed towards some goal. Another of his classifications involves mental, viscerogenic, and sociorelational needs. These arise respectively from the character of the human mind, from properties of physiological tissues, and from man's inherent social nature. He also adds creative needs which promote novel and productive activities, as opposed to negative needs, which induce avoidance of the undesirable. Another distinction he makes is between proactive needs, which arise from within the person, and reactive needs, those induced by environment. This emphasis on proactive needs removes man from being merely acted on and gives him some control of his destiny.

Although he has insisted that he has never made more than a beginning in the work which he set out to do, Henry Murray's contribution to personality study has been described in a book of essays published in his honor as "a unique and inexhaustible house of treasures."

—R.W. Rieber

MYRDAL, (Karl) Gunnar. Swedish economist. Born in Gustafs Dalecarlia, 6 December 1898. Studied at Stockholm University, J.D. 1923, Ph.D. 1927. Married Alva Reimer in 1924; 3 children. Lecturer, 1927, Professor, 1931, Lars Hierta Professor of Political Economy and Finance, 1933-50 and 1960-67, and since 1967 Professor Emeritus, Stockholm University. Rockefeller Fellow, United States, 1929-30; Assistant Professor, Geneva Institut Universitaire de Hautes Etudes Internales, 1930-31; Godkin Lecturer, Harvard University, Cambridge, Massachusetts, 1938; Visiting Research Fellow, Center for the Study of Democratic Institutions, Santa Barbara, California, 1973-74; Distinguished Visiting Professor, City University of New York, 1974-75; Regents Professor, University of California at Irvine, 1977; Distinguished Visiting Professor, University of Wisconsin, Madison, 1977; Glick Professor of Peace, Lyndon B. Johnson School of Public Affairs, University of Texas at Austin, 1978. Government Advisor, 1933, Senator, 1934, and Minister of Trade and Commerce, 1945-47, Sweden. Director, Study of American Negro Problem, Carnegie Corporation, 1938-43; Executive Secretary, U.N. Economic Commission for Europe, 1947-57; Founder, Institute for International Economic Studies, Stockholm University, 1961; Former Chairman, Board of Stockholm International Peace Research Institute. Recipient: Peace Prize of Federal Republic of Germany, 1970; Nobel Prize in Economics, with Friedrich von Hayek, 1974; Nitti Prize, 1976. Honorary doctorate: Harvard University, Cambridge, Massachusetts, 1938; Fisk University, Nashville, Tennessee, 1947; University of Nancy, 1950; Columbia University, New York, 1954; New School for Social Research, New York, 1956; University of Leeds, 1957; Yale University, New Haven, 1959; University of Birmingham, 1961; Brandeis University, Waltham, Massachusetts, 1962; Howard University, Washington, D.C., 1962; Wayne State University, Detroit, 1963; University of Edinburgh, 1964; Lincoln University, Pennsylvania, 1964; Swarthmore College, Pennsylvania, 1964; Stockholm University, 1966; Sir George

Williams University, Montreal, 1967; University of Michigan, Ann Arbor, 1967; Lehigh University, Bethlehem, Pennsylvania, 1967; Temple University, Philadelphia, 1968; University of Louisville, Kentucky, 1968; University of Jyväskyla, Finland, 1969; Upsala College, East Orange, New Jersey, 1969; Oslo University, 1969; Atlanta University, 1970; Dartmouth College, Hanover, New Hampshire, 1971; University of Philippines, 1971; Gustavus Adolphus College, St. Peter, Minnesota, 1971; Helsinki University, 1971; Heriot-Watt University, Glasgow, 1979. Member, Royal Swedish Academy of Sciences, Hungarian Academy of Sciences, American Academy of Arts and Sciences, and the British Academy. Fellow, Econometric Society. Honorary Member, American Economics Association, and Americans for Democratic Action. Address: Svalnäs Allé 12B, 18263 Djursholm, Sweden.

PUBLICATIONS

Economics

Prisbildningsproblemet och föränderligheten [The Problem of Price Formation and Changeability]. Uppsala, Almqvist och Wiksell, 1927.

Vetenskap och politik i nationalekonomien. Stockholm, Norstedt, 1930; as *The Political Element in the Development of Economic Theory,* London, Kegan Paul, 1953; Cambridge, Massachusetts, Harvard University Press, 1954.

Sveriges väg genom penningkrisen [Sweden's Path Through the Monetary Crisis]. Stockholm, Natur och Kultur, 1931.

Wages, Cost of Living, and National Income in Sweden 1860-1931. London, P.S. King, 1933.

Bostadsfrågan såsom socialt planläggninsproblem under krisen och på längre sikt [The Question of Housing as a Social Planning Problem During the Crisis and in the Long Run]. Stockholm, Kooperativa Förbundets Bokförlag, 1933.

Konjunktur och offentlig hushållning: En utredning [Conjuncture and Public Budgeting: An Explanation]. Stockholm, Kooperativa Förbundets Bokförlag, 1933.

Undersökning rörande behovet av en utvidgning av bostadsstatistiken jämte vissa därmed förbundna bostadspolitiska frågor [An Examination of the Need for an Enlarged Housing Statistics and other Related Political Questions]. Stockholm, Marcus, 1933.

Finanspolitikens ekonomiska verkningar [The Financial Policy's Economic Effects]. Stockholm, Norstedt, 1934.

Kris i befolkningsfrågan [Crisis in the Population Question]. Stockholm, Bonnier, 1934.

Befolkningsproblemet i Sverige: Radioforedrag den 27 Jan. 1935 [The Population Problem in Sweden: Radio lecture]. Stockholm, Arbetarnes Bildningsforbunds Centralbyra, 1935.

Samhällskrisen och socialvetenskaperna [The Crisis in Society and the Social Sciences]. Stockholm, Kooperativa Förbundets Bokförlag, 1935.

Vad gäller striden i befolkningsfrågan? [What is the Controversey about in Regard to the Population Question?]. Stockholm, Frihets Förlag, 1936.

Jordbrukspolitiken under omläggning [The Agricultural Policy During Reorganization]. Stockholm, Kooperativa Förbundets Bokförlag, 1938.

Monetary Equilibrium. London, Hodge, 1939; New York, Kelley, 1962.

Population: A Problem for Democracy (lecture). Cambridge, Massachusetts, Harvard University Press, 1940.

Kontakt med Amerika [In Touch with America], with Alva Myrdal. Stockholm, Bonnier, 1941.

Amerika mitt i världen [America in the Middle of the World]. Stockholm, Kooperativa Förbundets Bokförlag, 1943.

An American Dilemma: The Negro Problem and Modern Democracy. New York and London, Harper, 2 vols., 1944.

Economic Developments and Prospects in America (lecture).

Washington, D.C., National Planning Association, 1944.

De internationella förhandlingarna i Washington om ekonomiska efterkrigsproblem [The International Negotiations in Washington Regarding Post-War Economic Problems] (lecture). Stockholm, Svenska Bankföreningen, 1944.

Varning för fredsoptimism [Warning Against Peace Optimism]. Stockholm, Bonnier, 1944.

Psychological Impediments to Effective International Cooperation. New York, Society for Psychological Study of Social Issues, 1952.

Realities and Illusions in Regard to Inter-Governmental Organizations (lecture). London, Oxford University Press, 1955.

Development and Under-Development: A Note on the Mechanism of National and International Economic Inequality (lecture). Cairo, 1956; revised edition as *Economic Theory and Under-Developed Regions*, London, Duckworth, 1957; as *Rich Lands and Poor: The Road to World Prosperity*, New York, Harper, 1958.

Världsekonomin. Stockholm, Tidens Förlag, 1956; as *An International Economy: Problems and Prospects*, New York, Harper, 1956.

Economic Nationalism and Internationalism (lecture). Melbourne, Australian Institute of International Affairs, 1957.

Value in Social Theory: A Selection of Essays on Methodology, edited by Paul Streeten. London, Routledge, and New York, Harper, 1958.

Beyond the Welfare State: Economic Planning and Its International Implications. London, Duckworth, and New Haven, Connecticut, Yale University Press, 1960.

Problemet Sverige hjälper [The Problem Which Sweden Aids]. Stockholm, Rabén och Sjögren, 1961.

Vi och Västeuropa [We and Western Europe], with Tord Ekström. Stockholm, Rabén och Sjögren, 1962.

Challenge to Affluence. London, Gollancz, and New York, Pantheon, 1963.

Vår onda värld [Our Evil World]. Stockholm, Rabén och Sjögren, 1964.

USA och Vietnamkriget [USA and the Vietnam War]. Stockholm, Vietnam Press, 1967.

Objektivitetsproblemet i samhällsforskningen. Stockholm, Rabén och Sjögren, 1968; as *Objectivity in Social Research*, New York, Pantheon, 1969; London, Duckworth, 1970.

Asian Drama: An Inquiry into the Poverty of Nations. London, Penguin, and New York, Patheon, 3 vols., 1968; abridged edition as *An Approach to the Asian Drama: Methodological and Theoretical*, New York, Vintage, 1970.

The Challenge of World Poverty: A World Anti-Poverty Program in Outline. New York, Vintage, 1970.

Vi och Västeuropa: Andra ronden [We and Western Europe: Another Round]. Stockholm, Rabén och Sjögren, 1971.

Världsfattigdomen [World Poverty]. Stockholm, Utrikespolitiska Institutet, 1972.

Against the Stream: Critical Essays on Economics. New York, Pantheon, 1973; London, Macmillan, 1974.

Essays and Lectures, edited by Mutsumi Okada. Kyoto, Keibunsha, 1973.

Miljö och ekonomisk tillväxt [Environment and Economic Growth]. Stockholm, Utrikespolitiska Institutet, 1976.

*

Bibliography: *Gunnar Myrdal: A Bibliography 1919-1976* by Harald Bohrn, Stockholm, Kungliga Biblioteket, 1976.

Critical Study: *Asian Dilemma: A Soviet View and Myrdal's Concept* by R.A. Ul'ianovskii and V. Pavlov, Moscow, Progress, 1974.

*   *   *

A leading figure of the early Stockholm School and a self-described institutionalist, perhaps the latter school's leading modern theorist and analyst, Gunnar Myrdal received the Nobel Prize in economic science, jointly with Friedrich von Hayek, in 1974.

Myrdal's institutionalism is evident in both his methodological position and his substantive research. Methodologically, Myrdal emphasizes the limits of equilibrium analysis and of monocausation models, especially in a world of cumulative causation, disequilibrium, interdependence, and vicious (and virtuous) circles. He also is well known for his stress on the importance of, and of recognizing, the inextricable valuational-political elements or premises found in economic theory and, more obviously, in policy conclusions, and for his prescription that value premises be made explicit and a strategic part of analysis. He stresses realism, with emphasis on non-economic variables, especially the institutions of economic systems; although willing to theorize, he wants abstraction to follow relevant, and not narrowly preconceived, lines. Finally, he follows a multidisciplinary, vis-à-vis a narrowly defined economic, approach to problems (which he perceives as totally social rather than simply economic in nature).

Much of Myrdal's early work was in pure theory and in both (of what is now called) microeconomics and macroeconomics. He explored the roles of uncertainty and of anticipations of the future which operate within and on price and income formation processes. He identified the *ex ante-ex post* distinction in points of view and in constructions of economic concepts, models, and relationships (especially with regard to saving and investment). From one perspective, he developed Wicksell's analysis regarding price formation and monetary equilibrium; from another, he contributed to the Keynesian revolution in macroeconomics by participating in the developments which led to it and by contributing and/or emphasizing certain critical points.

Myrdal's later work focused on the deepest levels of social-economic development through his analysis of the American negro and economic development in South Asia. In *An American Dilemma*, he focused on economic and non-economic but interdependent (mutually reinforcing) variables, on cumulative causation, and on the specific factors governing the improvement or worsening of the conditions of the American negro. He also pinpointed the conflict between the U.S. ideology of equal opportunity and the reality of discrimination against blacks. The book is a premier example of non-ideological and non-mythological social science, with the author's value premises made explicit.

In *Asian Drama* he again focused on the interdependent and cumulatively causal, often systemic, variables governing economic development, such as population, health, education, politics, administration, labor force utilization, and attitudes toward life and work, as well as such conventional economic variables as output, income, and consumption. His analysis is characterized by emphases on cultural, institutional, and personal inertia; the great length of the time lags involved in development; underemployment; and (to some extent in this book but especially in other works) the reality of both development-promoting and inhibiting consequences of international (and interregional) trade, as well as the limits of organizing activity ("planning" in some form) in so-called "soft states." He also was critical of the overemphasis by conventional Western economists on capital accumulation alone as the mode of fomenting development, a facet of their application of the perceptions and preconceptions of Western culture to the problems of the less developed countries.

—Warren J. Samuels

NAGEL, Ernest. American philosopher of science. Born in Novemesto, Czechoslovakia, 16 November 1901; emigrated to the United States in 1911; naturalized, 1919. Studied at the City College of New York, B.S. 1923; Columbia University, New York, M.A. 1925, Ph.D. 1931. Married Edith Haggstrom in 1935; 2 sons. Taught in the New York public schools, 1923-29; Instructor in Philosophy, City College of New York, 1930-31; Instructor, 1931-37, Assistant Professor, 1937-39, Associate Professor, 1939-46, Professor, 1946-55, John Dewey Professor of Philosophy, 1955-66, University Professor, 1967-70, and since 1970 Professor Emeritus, Columbia University; Distinguished Professor, New York University, 1972. Vanuxem Lecturer, Princeton University, New Jersey, 1954; Howison Lecturer, University of California, Berkeley, 1960; Carus Lecturer, American Philosophical Association, 1963; Fellow, Center for Advanced Study in Behavioral Sciences, Stanford, California, 1959-60. Editor, *Journal of Philosophy*, 1939-56 and *Journal of Symbolic Logic*, 1940-46. President, Association for Symbolic Logic, 1947-49, Eastern Division of the American Philosophical Association, 1954, and Philosophy of Science Association, 1961-63. Recipient: Guggenheim Fellowship, 1934, 1950; Butler Silver Medal, Columbia University, 1954; American Council of Learned Societies Prize, 1959. Honorary doctorate: Bard College, Annandale-on-Hudson, New York, 1964; Brandeis University, Waltham, Massachusetts, 1965; Rutgers University, New Brunswick, New Jersey, 1967; Case Western Reserve University, Cleveland, 1970; Columbia University, 1971; City University of New York, 1972; University of Guelph, Ontario, 1979. Member, National Academy of Sciences. Corresponding Fellow, British Academy. Fellow, American Academy of Arts and Sciences; American Philosophical Society; and American Association for the Advancement of Science. Address: 25 Claremont Avenue, New York, New York 10027, U.S.A.

PUBLICATIONS

Philosophy of Science

On the Logic of Measurement. Privately printed, 1932.
An Introduction to Logic and Scientific Method, with Morris R. Cohen. New York, Harcourt Brace, 1934; London, Routledge, 1972.
Principles of the Theory of Probability. Chicago, University of Chicago Press, 1939.
Sovereign Reason. Glencoe, Illinois, Free Press, 1954.
Logic Without Metaphysics, and Other Essays in the Philosophy of Science. Glencoe, Illinois, Free Press, 1957.
Gödel's Proof, with James R. Newman. New York, New York University Press, 1958.
The Structure of Science: Problems in the Logic of Scientific Explanation. New York, Harcourt Brace, 1961; London, Routledge, 1979.
Observation and Theory in Science, with others. Baltimore, Johns Hopkins University Press, 1971.
Teleology Revisited and Other Essays in the Philosophy and History of Science. New York, Columbia University Press, 1979.

Other

Editor, with others, *Logic, Methodology, and the Philosophy of Science.* Stanford, California, Stanford University Press, 1962.
Editor, with Henry E. Kyburg, Jr., *Induction: Some Current Issues.* Middletown, Connecticut, Wesleyan University Press, 1963.
Editor, with Richard B. Brandt, *Meaning and Knowledge: Systematic Readings in Epistemology.* New York, Harcourt Brace, 1965.

*

Bibliography: in *Philosophy, Science and Method: Essays in Honor of Ernest Nagel*, edited by Sidney Morgenbesser, Patrick Suppes, and Morton White, New York, St. Martin's Press, 1969.

*   *   *

Ernest Nagel was born in Czechoslovakia, but has lived in America since the age of 10. He received his Ph.D. in philosophy at Columbia University, and spent his whole academic career teaching at the university, being John Dewey professor of philosophy for many years. Major influences on Nagel were his teachers, Morris R. Cohen, John Dewey, and Frederick J.E. Woodbridge, and the writings of Charles S. Peirce, Bertrand Russell, and George Santayana.

Although Nagel was not a full-time formal logician, many generations of philosophy students thanked Nagel for his first major publication (written with Cohen) *An Introduction to Logic and Scientific Method*, in which he conveyed the basic principles of modern logic in a more illuminating and profound manner than any author previously (or most authors subsequently). Nagel showed in full convincing detail the power of modern logical techniques, and the extent to which they uncover the major principles of science, and indeed of all sound thought.

It is, however, less as an expositer of others' ideas, and more for his own innovative philosophical work that Nagel will be remembered by posterity. Together with a number of other thinkers, primarily naturalized Americans of European origin, Nagel was a creator and expositer of the school of philosophy of science known as "logical empiricism." Drawing on the advances in logic due to such intellectual giants as Russell, Nagel produced a view of science deeply rooted in the British empiricist tradition, yet flavoured with a dash of American pragmatism. The school flourished from about 1940 to 1970, and Nagel produced perhaps *the* leading work, certainly the most accessible: *The Structure of Science*.

Logical empiricists like Nagel see the ideal of science as completed "hypothetico-deductive" systems. A scientific theory starts with a number of general claims, "hypotheses," which are unproven within the system, and then from these "axioms," lower level claims can be deduced. Nagel, like other logical empiricists, took physics as his paradigm of a good science. An excellent exemplar of a Nagelian theory would be Newtonian dynamics, which starts with Newton's laws of motion and of gravitational attraction as axioms, and which concludes with the derived Keplerian laws of planetary motion and Galilean mechanics of terrestrial motion.

The statements of science Nagel believed to be general, universal, and in some sense necessary. We feel that planets *must* go in ellipses, in a way that we do not feel that all the students in my class must be under 30 (even though both statements may be true). As an empiricist, however, Nagel denied that the statements of science are logically necessary. He thought rather that the necessity was some kind of physical necessity, and he spoke of it as "nomic" necessary (from the Greek work for law).

Nagel drew a distinction between the upper and lower level statements of a scientific system. The former (which rather confusingly he spoke of as "theories," using the same term as one uses for the whole system) refer only to unseen entities, like electrons and genes. The latter ("empirical laws") refer to the tangible, the seen, like planets, prisms, and pendulums. This means that, somewhere in the middle of scientific theories, one has to translate from talk of objects of one kind to talk of objects of another kind. This entails that one has "correspondence rules," as, for instance, one has in the kinetic theory of gases, going from talk of the kinetic energy of microscopic bouncing balls to talk of the temperature of macroscopic gases.

Logical empiricism proved a powerful tool in the hands of one as adroit as Nagel. He used it to construct a comprehensive view of the development of science, seeing the progress of knowledge essentially as one of accumulation. In particular, Nagel argued that older theories of science (like Newton's) are rarely rejected when newer theories (like Einstein's) arrive. Rather, the old is "reduced" to the new, that is to say, the old is shown to be a special limited deductive consequence of the new. Hence, Nagel did not see science as constantly "starting again," but as something which builds on the past, while getting ever more powerful and ever more general.

Criticisms were always levelled against logical empiricism. One was that logical empiricism was really just a philosophy of physics, rather than a philosophy for all science. Nevertheless, although this criticism has some truth it is not entirely fair, for Nagel (more than other logical empiricists) did go beyond physics. Specifically, while Nagel thought that living matter was essentially similar to inanimate matter, he did agree that there is a forward-looking "teleological" element to much biology and social science (as in "The function of the heart is to circulate the blood"). In this, these sciences differ from the physical sciences. Nagel argued that function-talk is a reflection of the "goal-directed" nature of organisms: they are mechanically directed to ends, as are torpedoes. This claim has led to lively discourse. Most today would probably agree with Nagel that there is something distinctive about biology, although few would accept his solution.

More serious, perhaps, is the criticism that logical empiricism overplays the extent to which science forms a cumulative, rational enterprise. Following Thomas Kuhn (as articulated in his *Structure of Scientific Revolutions*), many today would argue that in science, as the old is replaced by the new, we see a distinct break. There is no genuine process of reduction. A new theory or "paradigm" gives a whole new way of thinking. Without adopting a somewhat relativistic view of science like this, it is argued, we cannot explain why the history of science shows so many controversies. Reduction is a rational process, and yet at times of change, scientists are anything but rational. They shout as they pass each other.

Philosophy of science, like women's clothes, goes in styles. Logical empiricism is today a little unfashionable. It will return, and Nagel's seminal contributions will endure. Probably, however, what will be necessary is a logical empiricism which does pay more respect to our ever-increasing knowledge of the history of science.

—Michael Ruse

NAMIER, L(ewis) B(ernstein). British historian. Born Ludvik Beĭnsztajn-Niemirowski in Warsaw, Poland, 27 June 1888; emigrated to England, 1907; naturalized, 1913. Studied at the University of Lausanne, 1906-07; London School of Economics, 1907-08; Balliol College, Oxford, B.A. in modern history 1911, M.A. 1914. Served with the 20th Royal Fusiliers, 1914-15; attached to the British Propaganda Department, 1915-17, British Department of Information, 1917-18, and Political Intelligence Department, British Foreign Office, 1918-20. Married Clara Sophia Edeleff-Poniatowska in 1917 (died, 1945); married Julia de Beausobre in 1947. Lecturer, Balliol College, 1920-21; Political Secretary, Jewish Agency for Palestine, 1929-31; Professor, University of Manchester, 1931-53. Honorary doctorate: University of Durham, 1952; Oxford University, 1955; University of Rome, 1956; Cambridge University, 1957. Honorary Fellow, Balliol College, 1948. Fellow, British Academy, 1952. Knighted 1952. *Died 19 August 1960*.

PUBLICATIONS

History

Germany and Eastern Europe. London, Duckworth, 1915.

The Case of Bohemia. London, Czech National Alliance in Great Britain, 1917.

The Czecho-Slovaks, An Oppressed Nationality. London and New York, Hodder and Stoughton, 1917.

The Structure of Politics at the Accession of George III. London, Macmillan, 1929.

England in the Age of the American Revolution. London, Macmillan, 1930; New York, St. Martin's Press, 1961.

Skyscrapers and Other Essays. London, Macmillan, 1931; Freeport, New York, Books for Libraries Press, 1968.

Additions and Corrections to Sir John Fortescue's Edition of the Correspondence of King George the Third (vol. 1). Manchester, Manchester University Press, 1937.

In the Margin of History. London, Macmillan, 1939; Freeport, New York, Books for Libraries Press, 1969.

Conflicts: Studies in Contemporary History. London, Macmillan, 1942; New York, Macmillan, 1943.

1848: The Revolution of the Intellectuals. London, Cumberlege, 1944; New York, Anchor, 1964.

Diplomatic Prelude, 1938-1939. London, Macmillan, 1948; New York, H. Fertig, 1971.

Facing East. London, Hamish Hamilton, 1947; New York, Harper, 1948.

Nationality and Liberty (lecture). Rome, Fondazione Alessandro Volta, 1948.

Europe in Decay: A Study in Disintegration, 1936-1940. London, Macmillan, 1950; Gloucester, Massachusetts, P. Smith, 1963.

Avenues of History. London, Hamish Hamilton, and New York, Macmillan, 1952.

In the Nazi Era. London, Macmillan, 1952.

Monarchy and the Party System (lecture). Oxford, Clarendon Press, 1952.

Basic Factors in Nineteenth-Century European History (lecture). London, University of London, 1953.

Personalities and Powers. London, Hamish Hamilton, and New York, Macmillan, 1955.

Collected Essays, Vol. 1. London, Hamish Hamilton, 1958; as *Vanished Supremacies: Essays on European History, 1812-1918*, New York, Macmillan, 1958.

Charles Townshend: His Character and Career, with John Brooke. London, Cambridge University Press, 1959; New York, St. Martin's Press, 1964.

Crossroads of Power: Essays on Eighteenth-Century England. London, Hamish Hamilton, 1962; New York, Macmillan, 1963.

The House of Commons, 1754-1790, with John Brooke. London and New York, History of Parliament Trust, 1964.

*

Critical Studies: *Lewis Namier: A Biography* by Lady Julia Namier, London and New York, Oxford University Press, 1971; *Lewis Namier and Zionism* by Norman Rose, Oxford, Clarendon Press, 1980.

*   *   *

L.B. Namier was called "the greatest British historian since the First World War" by E.H. Carr in the early 1960's, at which time his reputation stood very high; he had been knighted in 1952, not only for his many distinguished works on British and European (contemporary) history but for his services to the British Government and to Zionism. It was strange that this "British" historian had been born in Poland—of Jewish parents, though his father, a wealthy landowner, converted to Catholicism. Born Niemirowski, Lewis changed his name to Namier when he became a British citizen in 1913 after coming to England in 1907 at the age of 19, where he studied history at the London School of Economics and then at Balliol College, Oxford. Later he became Professor of Modern History at Manchester University. At Balliol a fellow student who became a lifelong friend, despite disagreements, was Arnold J. Toynbee.

It is difficult to separate the extraordinary personality of Sir Lewis from his work. As an alien twice removed, as it were, he suffered some severe emotional problems, including a psychological paralysis of his right arm. He quarreled with his father and was eventually disinherited. His first marriage ended disastrously. His intense research interest in the intricacies of British politics has been interpreted as an attempt to find roots by identifying with his adopted community. A friend of Chaim Weizmann, he also became a dedicated Zionist. He was a driven, dynamic individual.

As a historian, Namier first made his reputation by *The Structure of Politics at the Accession of George III* (1929) and *England in the Age of the American Revolution* (1930), works which upset numerous conventional notions about the role of the King, the origin of political parties, and the relationship of English politics to the American Revolution. In general, Namier saw politics as far less rational and far less ideologically tidy than superficial accounts supposed; he stressed the actualities of behind-the-scene politics where secondary figures might be more important than the nominal leaders. (He once defined "Namierist" history as "finding out who the guys were.") Asked once by a prominent peer why a Polish Jew should devote his energies to the study of British politics, Namier replied that modern Jewish history, purely a tragedy, had too little subtlety for him. He loved the ambiguities and paradoxes.

He was condemned to be involved in the totalitarian violence of his own century, however; his second wife, who wrote a memoir of his life, had spent time in a Soviet concentration camp in the early 1930's. In the post-World War II years (1948-52), Namier published a number of essays about the approach of the war, the Appeasement era, and Nazism, based on the documentation then available, writings which were typically vigorous, powerfully written, and very influential at the time; they have somewhat dated, inevitably (*Europe in Decay*; *In the Nazi Era*; *Diplomatic Prelude*).

His research somewhat anticipated trends in historical methods which later became more fashionable: his keen interest in the irrational side of politics was psycho-historical, while his organization of a research team to do a massive collective biography ("prosopography") of the House of Commons suggests the trend toward quantification. Namier exerted a strong influence on young British historians of the immediate post-war era. The influence was greater, perhaps, because ideologically his disabused realism, aware of the ironies and tragedies of human affairs, fitted the mood of the 1950's. Namier's preoccupation with minor figures and minute details of politics—he was sometimes reproached for having wasted his enormous talents on the less than great—suited the new professionalism of historical studies, though it differed from the French *Annales* school and others of the "new social history" in lacking their scorn for "event" history and court politics. But he was not much interested in narrative history, preferring analysis of a structuralist sort. Thus in some ways he intersected with the changes in historiography that included more sophisticated methods, less familiar subjects, more searching re-interpretations, and a greater interest in structure than continuity.

But Namier's essays on historical subjects and history in general, collected in *Avenues of History*, *Personalities and Powers*, and *Conflicts*, reveal him as a historian in the grand manner, a writer of striking power with a gift for the vivid phrase and the arresting paradox. He was a dynamic person, not always liked but respected as a giant, about whom legends have clustered. He was a historian's historian, in his thirst for specific reality, yet the force of his more popular essays and lectures earned him a considerable recognition in wider circles.

—Roland Stromberg

NEURATH, Otto. Austrian social scientist. Born in Vienna, 10 December 1882. Studied at the University of Vienna; University of Berlin, Ph.D. 1905; Habilitation, University of Heidelberg, 1918. Served in the German Army, 1906; war service at Eastern front and in Vienna, 1914-18. Married Anna Schapire in 1907 (died, 1911); 1 son; married Olga Hahn in 1912 (died, 1937); married Marie Reidemeister in 1941. Teacher, Neue Wiener Handelsakademie, Vienna, 1907-14; travelled in Eastern Europe and Balkan Islands under contract with Carnegie Endowment for International Peace, 1911-13; Worked briefly in Central Planning Office, Munich, before returning to Vienna, 1919; active participation in housing movement in Vienna, and Founder, Museum for Housing and Town Planning, 1919-24; Founder and Director, Social and Economic Museum, Vienna, 1924-34; worked on Vienna Circle manifesto, 1929; Founder, International Foundation for Visual Education, The Hague, 1933; lived in The Hague and continued visual education work (ISOTYPE) while organizing the International Unity of Science movement, 1934-40; fled to England and interned, 1940; lived in Oxford, 1941-45. *Died* (in Oxford) *22 December 1945.*

PUBLICATIONS

Social Sciences

Antike Wirtschaftsgeschichte IV. Leipzig, Teubner, 1909.
Lehrbuch der Volkswirtschaftslehre VIII. Vienna, Alfred Hölder, 1910.
Serbiens Erfolge im Balkankriege: Eine wirtschaftliche und soziale Studie. Vienna, Manzche Hofbuchhandlung, 1913.
Die Wirtschaftsordnung der Zukunft und die Wirtschaftswissenschaften. Berlin and Vienna, Verlag für Fachliteratur, 1917.
Grossvorratswirtschaft und Notenbankpolitik. Berlin, Verlag für Fachliteratur, 1918.
Der Kompensationsverkehr im zwischenstaatlichen Warenhandel, with Wilhelm Heilpern. Berlin, Verlag für Fachliteratur, 1918.
Können wir heute sozialisieren? Eine Darstellung der sozialistischen Lebensordnung und ihres Werdens, with Wolfgang Schumann. Leipzig, Werner Klinkhardt, 1919.
Die Sozialisierung Sachsens: Drei Vorträge. Chemnitz, Verlag des Arbeiter- und Soldatenrats im Industriebezirk Chemnitz, 1919.
Wesen und Weg der Sozialisierung: Gesellschaftliches Gutachten (lecture). Munich, G.D.W. Callwey, 1919.
Technik und Wirtschaftsordnung. Vienna, Verlag Deutsches Wirtschaftsmuseum, 1919.
Durch die Kriegswirtschaft zur Naturalwirtschaft (collection of articles). Munich, Callwey, 1919.
Vollsozialisierung und Arbeiterorganisation (lecture). Reichenberg, Runge, 1920.
Anti-Spengler. Munich, Callwey, 1921.
Gildensozialismus, Klassenkampf, Vollsozialisierung. Dresden, Kaden, 1922.
Österreichs Kleingärtner- und Siedler-Organisation. Vienna, Wiener Volksbuchhandlung, 1923.
Wirtschaftsplan und Naturalrechnung. Berlin, Laub, 1925.
Lebensgestaltung und Klassenkampf. Berlin, Laub, 1928.
Wissenschaftliche Weltauffassung: Der Wiener Kreis. Vienna, Arthur Wolf, 1929.
Die Bunte Welt. Vienna, Arthur Wolf, 1929.
Empirische Soziologie: Der Wissenschaftliche Gehalt der Geschichte und Nationalökonomie. Vienna, J. Springer, 1931.
Bildstatistik nach Wiener Methode in der Schule. Vienna, Deutscher Verlag für Jugend und Volk, 1933.
Einheitswissenschaft und Psychologie. Vienna, Gerold, 1933.
Was bedeutet rationale Wirtschaftsbetrachtung? Vienna, Gerold, 1935.
Le développement du Cercle de Vienne et l'avenir de l'empirisme logique. Paris, Hermann, 1936.

International Picture Language. London, Kegan Paul, 1936.
Basic by Isotype. London, Kegan Paul, 1937.
Health Education by Isotype, with H.E. Kleinschmidt. New York, American Public Health Association, 1938.
Modern Man in the Making. New York, Knopf, and London, Secker and Warburg, 1939.
Visual History of Mankind: Living in Early Times; Living in Villages and Towns; Living in the World; Notes for the Teacher, with Marie Neurath and H.A. Lauwerys. London, Parrish, 4 vols., 1948-49.
Empiricism and Sociology, edited by Marie Neurath and Robert S. Cohen. Dordrecht, Reidel, 1973.
Graphic Communication Through Isotype. Reading, Berkshire, University of Reading, Department of Typography, and New York, State Mutual, 1981.
International Picture Language. Reading, Berkshire, University of Reading, Department of Typography, and New York, State Mutual, 1981.

Other

Editor, *Faust: Ein dramatisches Gedicht in drei Abschnitten von F. Marlow* (Ludwig Hermann Wolfram). Berlin, Ernst Frensdorff, 1906.
Editor, with Anna Schapire-Neurath, *Lesebuch der Volkswirtschaftslehre.* Leipzig, Werner Klinkhardt, 1910.

Translator, with Anna Schapire-Neurath, *Genie und Vererbung,* by Francis Galton. Leipzig, Werner Klinkhardt, 1910.

*

Bibliography: in *Empiricism and Sociology,* 1973.

*   *   *

Otto Neurath, born in 1882, was an Austrian philosopher and sociologist. His major work was in scientific methodology, sociology, economic and social planning, and visual education, the latter by means in particular of an international language of simplified pictures ("isotypes"). He was an energetic organizer of academic, educational, and social affairs. During 1919 Neurath served in the Central Planning office of the Social Democratic Republic of Bavaria and of its short-lived successor, the Bavarian Social Republic. When the latter fell, Neurath, although a civil servant and not a member of the Communist Party, was briefly imprisoned. Upon his release he went to Vienna where, as an independent Marxist socialist, he resumed a career as a publicist for social reform. He was among the first socialists to argue for a centrally planned rational economy based on Marxist concepts but deriving its policy recommendations from considerations of social welfare and from empirical statistical analyses of production and distribution of goods and of standards of living. Less clear to Neurath than equitable distribution of material goods was how a spirit of community and cooperation could be established among workers still overwhelmed by the hegemony of the established culture and the competitive spirit of capitalism.

While in Vienna, Neurath was an active participant, with Schlick, Carnap, and others, in the Vienna Circle. This group of positivist thinkers vigorously defended science and the rationalism of the Enlightenment against the irrationalism into which Europe was then quickly falling. In particular, their aim was to use the tools of the New Logic of Frege, and of Russell and Whitehead, to separate science from the non-science and metaphysics that so often hindered its progress, and as an aid to that progress, to clarify the logic of science: philosophy was to be replaced by the logic of science. Value judgments were statements neither of fact nor of logic, and therefore part of neither science nor philosophy. They were not therefore to be abandoned, however: Neurath's own social commitments make that

clear, as does the commitment of the Vienna Circle to the Enlightenment ideals. What was abandoned was traditional metaphysics aiming to "solve" such "problems" as the "riddle of death": these "problems" were argued to be pseudo-problems, that is, questions of values and of practical goals disguised, in the self-deception of traditional philosophy, as empirical and cognitive issues.

Some members of the Vienna Circle argued that the basic terms of the language of science should be taken as referring to phenomenal entities. Neurath, in contrast, vigorously defended physicalism: the basic terms ought to refer to publicly observable physical objects. This can be seen as Neurath's attempt to express, in epistemological terms, the Marxist idea of a material basis for knowledge. The source of his anti-phenomenalism was his emphasis upon the importance of socially intersubjective agreement. A consequence of his physicalism was a recognition of the essential uncertainty of all scientific description, and of the probabilistic nature of all scientific prediction. He rejected the absolute certainty aimed at by both traditional metaphysics and phenomenalists like Schlick. The physicalistic language was to provide a common standard for confirmation of verification for skeptical enquirers. The standard for confirmation was coherence: Neurath was committed to a coherence theory of verification (though not, as with Hegel, Feyerabend, and others, to a coherence theory of meaning).

Neurath's stress upon the unification of the sciences by means of a unity of language and method led him to recurrent efforts to create a new encyclopedism. He planned the *International Encyclopedia of Unified Science.* The Nazis, from whom Neurath fled first to Holland and then to England, and the War disrupted the work, however, as did Neurath's death, and only two introductory volumes were to appear.

—Fred Wilson

NIEBUHR, H(elmut) Richard. American theologian. Born in Wright City, Missouri, 3 September 1894; brother of the theologian Reinhold Niebuhr, *q.v.* Studied at Elmhurst College, Illinois, B.A. 1912; Eden Theological Seminary, St. Louis, 1915; Washington University, St. Louis, M.A. 1917; Yale University, New Haven, Connecticut, B.D. 1923, Ph.D. 1924; ordained, 1916. Married Marie Mittendorf in 1920; 2 children. Pastor, St. Louis, 1916-18; Professor, Eden Theological Seminary, 1919-22, 1927-31; President, Elmhurst College, 1924-27; Associate Professor, 1931-38, Professor, 1938-54, and Sterling Professor of Theology and Christian Ethics, 1954-62, Yale University. Honorary doctorate: University of Chicago, 1954; Franklin and Marshall College, Lancaster, Pennsylvania, 1955; Wesleyan University, Middletown, Connecticut, 1956; University of Bonn, 1960. *Died 5 July 1962.*

PUBLICATIONS

Theology

The Social Sources of Denominationalism. New York, Holt, 1929.
Moral Relativism and the Christian Ethic. New York, International Missionary Council, 1929.
The Church Against the World, with others. Chicago, Willett Clark, 1935.
The Kingdom of God in America. Chicago, Willett Clark, 1937.
The Meaning of Revelation. New York, Macmillan, 1941.
The Gospel for a Time of Fears (lectures). Washington, D.C.,

Henderson Services, 1950.

Christ and Culture.   New York, Harper, 1951; London, Faber, 1952.

The Churches and the Body of Christ (lecture).   Philadelphia, Young Friends Movement of the Philadelphia Yearly Meeting, 1953.

The Advancement of Theological Education, with others.   New York, Harper, 1957.

Radical Monotheism and Western Culture, with Supplementary Essays.   New York, Harper, and London, Faber, 1960.

The Responsible Self: An Essay in Christian Moral Philosophy.   New York, Harper, 1963.

Other

Editor, with Waldo Beach, *Christian Ethics: Sources of the Living Tradition.*   New York, Ronald Press, 1955.

Editor, with Daniel Day Williams, *The Ministry in Historical Perspectives.*   New York, Harper, 1956.

Translator, *The Religious Situation,* by Paul Tillich.   New York, Holt, 1932.

*

Critical Studies: *The Promise of H. Richard Niebuhr* by John D. Godsey, Philadelphia, Lippincott, 1970; *The Theology of H. Richard Niebuhr* by Libertus A. Hoedemaker, Philadelphia, Pilgrim Press, 1970; *To See the Kingdom: The Theological Vision of H. Richard Niebuhr* by James W. Fowler, Nashville, Abingdon Press, 1974; *The Responsible God: A Study of the Christian Philosophy of H. Richard Niebuhr* by Donald Edward Fecher, Missoula, Montana, Scholars Press, 1975; *H. Richard Niebuhr* by Lonnie D. Kliever, Waco, Texas, Word, 1977.

*   *   *

During a distinguished career H. Richard Niebuhr taught at Eden Theological Seminary, served as president of Elmhurst College, and was professor of Christian ethics at the Divinity School, Yale University. He was an ordained minister of the Evangelical and Reformed Church and of the United Church of Christ after the merger in 1959. In 1954-56, assisted by Daniel Day Williams and James M. Gustafson, he directed the American Association of Theological Schools study of theological education in the United States and Canada. It seems safe to say that Niebuhr, in his writings and teaching, contributed to the preparation of more persons who today are influential as professors, heads of departments of religion, deans, and pastors, than any other American theologian of the 20th century.

Niebuhr's first book, *The Social Sources of Denominationalism,* demonstrated that differences in the beliefs and practice of Christian denominations and groups have to do more with ethnic, social class, racial, and economic factors than with dogmatic convictions. Under the influence of Max Weber, Ernst Troeltsch, and the emerging discipline of the sociology of religion, Niebuhr exposed the scandal and moral impotence of a divided church. As would be characteristic of his later work, Niebuhr kept his use of sociological and historical methods under theological control. While making original and lasting contributions to the sociological study of American religion, *Social Sources* was an act of prophetic enquiry aimed at helping the churches gain faithful freedom from their divided loyalties to temporal values.

While adept at analyzing the sources of their divisions, Niebuhr did not, in 1930, have a theological alternative to offer of sufficient power to re-orient and unify the ethical witness of the churches. The years from 1930 to 1937 mark a crucial period in Niebuhr's career and theological development. In these years, through a series of bold articles and monographs, we can trace a theological revolution occurring. Through a variety of personal experiences and intellectual influences Niebuhr formed a new

and centering conviction of the *reality* and *sovereignty* of God. He came to see and believe that the first and most crucial fact about human life is that of our utter dependence upon and responsibility to the Author of all being. Writing retrospectively in 1960 Niebuhr said, "The thirties were for me as for many of my generation in the church the decisive period in the formation of basic personal convictions and in the establishment of theological formulations of those convictions. The fundamental certainty given to me then (sad to say, not in such a way that my unconscious as well as my conscious mind has been wholly permeated by it) was that of God's sovereignty.... I came to understand that unless being itself, the constitution of things, the One beyond all the many, the ground of my being, and of all being, ...was trustworthy—could be counted on by what had proceeded from it—I had no God at all" (in *How My Mind Has Changed,* edited by Harold E. Fey, 1961).

The specific phrase "sovereignty of God" did not find frequent use in Niebuhr's writings. To grasp the shape and direction of his theological-ethical position, however, we must understand what he meant by it. First, it named an epistemological realization: the being and character of "the ground of all being" is not directly or comprehensively accessible to finite knowing. All our apprehensions of God are partial, limited, and inevitably relative to our particular times and places in history, and the traditions of revelation and interpretation in which we stand. For Niebuhr this realization did not lead to *relativism*—the doctrine that in the plurality of theological interpretations no position has any foundation for claiming more adequate truthfulness than another. Rather, Niebuhr thought in terms of "relationism." Theological interpretations are necessarily relativized by the transcendence of the reality they try to apprehend, but this realization neither negates the possibility of criteria for determining their greater or lesser adequacy, nor does it render theological work merely the subjective projection of personal or group consciousness.

Secondly, Niebuhr formulated the meaning of the conviction of God's sovereignty in three central metaphors—metaphors for depicting and clarifying God-in-relation-to-humanity, and humanity-in-relation-to-God. These three metaphors and their elaboration underlie much of Niebuhr's later theological writing, and constitute the backbone of his year-long course in Christian ethics at Yale.

The first metaphor can be characterized as *God the Creator.* Under this rubric Niebuhr dealt with his theory of value. From the theocentric perspective of Niebuhr's theological ethics, *whatever is (has being) is good.* If God, as creator, is the source and center of all being (whatever is), then all being has value because of the creator's investment in and care for it. This means a break with anthropocentric value systems of all kinds. In the light of understanding God as the source and center of value all other value centers are relativized and dethroned from their claims to ultimacy. Niebuhr's book *Radical Monotheism and Western Culture* develops this theme powerfully with its account of polytheistic, henotheistic, and radical monotheistic patterns of faith and valuing.

The second metaphor Niebuhr employed in his theological-ethical expression of the conviction of God's sovereignty is *God the Judge* and *Ruler.* To use these anthropomorphic terms for this metaphor is misleading. For Niebuhr meant to indicate by them a *structure-intending-righteousness* at the heart of the process of life. While acknowledging limited human freedom, Niebuhr affirmed the presence and involvement of the pattern of divine love, power, and righteousness in human history. Not a simple theory of God acting in history, Niebuhr's view affirms God's capacity and commitment to incorporate human sinfulness and self-assertion into the realization of the divine purposes. We humans are called to respond to God's action in and upon history and to enter into partnership with divine purposes. Niebuhr's agonized writings in *Christian Century* during World War II and his posthumously published *The Responsible Self* bring this aspect of his teaching to the most complete published expression.

Niebuhr's third major metaphor for expressing the conviction of God's sovereignty centered in *God the Redeemer* and *Liberator*. Under this rubric Niebuhr dealt with God's self-disclosure and initiatives toward reconciliation with sinful humankind. Sin, for Niebuhr, ultimately consisted in wrong love—the attachment of the heart and will to finite centers of value; the reliance upon finite sources of power and security; and the effort to overcome our restless lostness by projects of our own construction. His christology centers on the amazing fact that Jesus as the Christ, by submitting to death on the cross, could show forth both the impoverished destructiveness of human sinfulness, and the loving, faithful heart of a God seeking reconciliation with alienated humanity. Human response in faith to this self-giving of God is what brings about the transformation in our valuing and responding that aligns our wills and action with God-ruling. Niebuhr's work with this metaphor can be found in a sermon, "The Logic of the Cross," in *The Meaning of Revelation*, in *Christ and Culture*, and in an as yet unpublished manuscript called *Faith on Earth*. (The Appendix to *The Responsible Self* is important in this regard as well.)

Niebuhr is remembered as a sociologist of religion and historian as well as a theologian and ethicist. No slavish observer of disciplinary lines, he made fundamental contributions in each of these areas. Niebuhr's teaching and writing are marked by the maintenance of several creative tensions, which may help explain why his influence lives on in vital ways, and why all seven of his major published books remain in print: First, he was a catholic thinker and student of the Christian and Biblical traditions. He drew knowledgeably on thinkers from many centuries and eras. Second, he refused dichotomous thinking and defensiveness in intellectual work. Following F.D. Maurice in this respect, Niebuhr recognized that most theological figures and traditions grasp essential truth in their central affirmations. It is in what they deny or neglect that their errors lie. Niebuhr's thought grasps polarities in thought and experience and seeks to hold them together: subjectivity and objectivity, relativity and absoluteness, power and powerlessness, form and spontaneity, revelation and reason, doubt and faith. Third, Niebuhr refused to opt either for a theology that began with human experience and consciousness and tried to work from it toward the conceptualization of God, or for one which started with the absolutizing of particular moments of revelation. Niebuhr's central affirmation of the sovereignty of God enabled him to develop a theological approach I have called *confessional-phenomenology*. From his beginning point in the conviction that God, as Creator, Ruler, and Redeemer, is the fundamental reality with which we have to deal, Niebuhr could provide powerfully illuminative descriptions of the relative, variegated patterns of the human struggle of faith. In bringing these two together Niebuhr offers dynamic accounts of the possibility and pattern of transformation worked in personal and group life when God's reconciling work in Christ meets us at the points of breakdown and failure of our finite "gods." Finally, Niebuhr's thought is durably exciting because of the depth of engagement it exhibits and elicits. As notorious at Yale for his facial contortions and agonizing struggles in lecturing as for his fidelity in attending chapel, Niebuhr's theological work clearly had its roots in his own struggle of faith. Though he would have been uncomfortable with the comparison, some words he once spoke (transcribed Cole Lectures) about Luther also apply to him:

> He found freshly minted parables. He brought forth new symbols because he wrestled with, he encountered, he experienced, he heard, he searched out himself before God and God before himself. What he communicated was not the word of God in scriptures but the word he had heard God speaking to him, Martin Luther, in scriptures. It was...the word which came to the ears of an agonized listener, of one who was fighting for his life, who was crying for help and heard the distant answer of the helper.

Niebuhr's theology is clearly the work of one who "meant it," and who kept submitting his understandings and expressions of faith to the tests and validations of the Biblical tradition and experience.

—James W. Fowler

NIEBUHR, Reinhold. American theologian. Born in Wright, City, Missouri, 21 June 1892; brother of the theologian H. Richard Niebuhr, *q.v.*. Studied at Elmhurst College, Illinois, 1910; Eden Theological Seminary, St. Louis, 1910-13; Yale University, New Haven, Connecticut, B.D. 1914, M.A. 1915; ordained, 1915. Married Ursula Mary Keppel-Compton in 1931; 2 children. Pastor, Bethel Evangelical Church, Detroit, 1915-28; Associate Professor of the Philosophy of Religion, 1928-30, William E. Dodge Jr. Professor of Applied Christianity, 1930-55, Charles A. Briggs Graduate Professor of Ethics and Theology, 1955-60, and Professor Emeritus, 1960-71, Union Theological Seminary, New York (Vice-President, 1955-60). Gifford Lecturer, University of Edinburgh, 1939. Research Associate, Institute of War and Peace Studies, Columbia University, New York. Co-Founder, Americans for Democratic Action, and Fellowship of Socialist Christians. Consultant for the British publisher Gollancz's Christian Faith series; Contributing Editor, *Christian Century, Nation,* and *New Leader;* Editor, *Christianity and Crisis,* 1941-66. Recipient: Presidential Medal of Freedom, 1964. Honorary doctorate: Eden Theological Seminary, 1930; Grinnell College, Iowa, 1936; Wesleyan University, Middletown, Connecticut, 1937; University of Pennsylvania, Philadelphia, 1938; Amherst College, Massachusetts, 1941; Yale University, 1942; Oxford University, 1943; Harvard University, Cambridge, Massachusetts, 1944; Occidental College, Los Angeles, 1945; Princeton University, New Jersey, 1946; University of Glasgow, 1947; New York University, 1947; Hobart College, Geneva, New York, 1948; Dartmouth College, Hanover, New Hampshire, 1951; New School for Social Research, New York, 1951; University of Manchester, 1954; Columbia University, New York, 1954; Hebrew University of Jerusalem, 1964. *Died 1 June 1971.*

PUBLICATIONS

Theology and Social Commentary

Does Civilization Need Religion? A Study of the Social Resources and Limitations of Religion in Modern Life. New York, Macmillan, 1927.
Leaves from the Notebook of a Tamed Critic. New York, Willett Clark, 1929.
The Contribution of Religion to Social Work. New York, Columbia University Press, 1932.
Moral Man and Immoral Society: A Study in Ethics and Politics. New York, Scribner, 1932.
Reflections on the End of an Era. New York, Scribner, 1934.
An Interpretation of Christian Ethics. New York, Harper, 1935.
Beyond Tragedy: Essays on the Christian Interpretation of History. New York, Scribner, 1937.
Christianity and Power Politics. New York, Scribner, 1940.
The Nature and Destiny of Man. New York, Scribner, 2 vols., 1941-43.
The Children of Light and the Children of Darkness: A Vindication of Democracy and a Critique of Its Traditional Defense. New York, Scribner, 1944.

Discerning the Signs of the Times: Sermons for Today and Tomorrow. New York, Scribner, 1946.

Faith and History: A Comparison of Christian and Modern Views of History. New York, Scribner, 1949.

The Irony of American History. New York, Scribner, 1952.

Christian Realism and Political Problems. New York, Scribner, 1953.

The Self and the Dramas of History. New York, Scribner, 1955.

Love and Justice: Selections from the Shorter Writings of Reinhold Niebuhr, edited by D.B. Robertson. Philadelphia, Westminster Press, 1957.

The World Crisis and American Responsibility, edited by Ernest W. Lefever. New York, Association Press, 1958.

Pious and Secular America. New York, Scribner, 1958; as *The Godly and the Ungodly,* London, Faber, 1958.

Essays in Applied Christianity, The Church, and the World, edited by D.B. Robertson. New York, Meridian, 1959.

The Structure of Nations and Empires: A Study of the Recurring Patterns and Problems of the Political Order in Relation to the Unique Problems of the Nuclear Age. New York, Scribner, 1959.

Reinhold Niebuhr on Politics: His Political Philosophy and Its Application to Our Age as Expressed in His Writings, edited by H.R. Davis and R.C. Good. New York, Scribner, 1960.

A Nation So Conceived: Reflections on the History of America from Its Early Visions to Its Present Power, with Alan Heimert. New York, Scribner, 1963.

Man's Nature and His Communities: Essays on the Dynamics and Enigmas of Man's Personal and Social Existence. New York, Scribner, 1965.

Faith and Politics: A Commentary on Religious, Social, and Political Thought in a Technological Age, edited by Ronald H. Stone. New York, Braziller, 1968.

The Democratic Experience, Past and Prospects, with Paul E. Sigmund. New York, Praeger, 1969.

Justice and Mercy, edited by Ursula M. Niebuhr. New York, Harper, 1974.

Young Reinhold Niebuhr: His Early Writings, 1911-1931, edited by William G. Chrystal. St. Louis, Eden, 1977.

*

Bibliography: *Reinhold Niebuhr's Works: A Bibliography* by D.B. Robertson, Boston, Hall, 1979.

Critical Studies: *The Thought of Reinhold Niebuhr* by Gordon Harland, New York, Oxford University Press, 1960; *Reinhold Niebuhr, Prophet to Politicians* by Ronald H. Stone, Nashville, Abingdon Press, 1972; *The Legacy of Reinhold Niebuhr* edited by Nathan Scott, Jr., Chicago, University of Chicago Press, 1972; *Reinhold Niebuhr: A Political Account* by Paul Merkley, Montreal, McGill-Queen's University Press, 1980; *Christian Realism and Liberation Theology* by Dennis P. McCann, Maryknoll, New York, Orbis, 1981.

* * *

Reinhold Niebuhr's vocation was teaching theological students. His major contribution to the health of the church in the world was preparing students of theology to be socially responsible. For four decades he taught Christian social philosophy at Union Theological Seminary in New York City. He avoided the sectarian and utopian tradition in Christian social philosophy and taught the students to be social reformers in the tradition of Christian realism. That meant that while protecting the American tradition of the separation of church and state he expected his students to be actively engaged through their church or secular vocations in the continual process of applying Christian insight into the nature of humanity and history to social problems. Through his teaching, writing, and organizational work he

came to have a far-reaching impact on the culture and thought of the Western world.

Early as a pastor in Detroit from 1915-1928, he became involved in three major issues, those of economics, race relations, and international relations. His lasting contribution was in the area of Christian social thought and international relations. His Christian realism came to dominate the World Council of Churches, the National Council of Churches, and American denominational thought in social concerns. Recently, particularly in the World Council of Churches, his thought has been significantly challenged by liberation theology from the developing world. In the National Council of Churches and in many major denominational bodies his thought is still foundational to Christian social thinking.

In international relations, particularly in the area of American foreign policy, his thought became influential among philosophers of foreign policy in the period after World War II. George Kennan has noted this contribution in commenting on the school of foreign policy thought known as realism: "He was the father of us all." He criticized illusions of U.S. omnipotence and innocence while urging the U.S. to exercise power responsibly in the post-war world. As a delegate to UNESCO and as adviser to the Policy Planning Staff of the State Department, he urged the development of international cooperation and realistic competition with the U.S.S.R.. His view which he articulated in books, e.g., *The Structure of Nations and Empires* and *The Democratic Experience,* was that of long-range competition between the U.S. and the U.S.S.R. dominated by the need for cooperation in containing the dangers of nuclear weapons. The role of the U.S. was to avoid isolation or imperialism in seeking to use its power in a responsible way.

He saw the process of managing the competitive co-existence between the U.S. and the U.S.S.R. as necessary to maintaining peace. War between the super powers would mean mutual annihilation. War had to be avoided. The competition would probably stretch on for decades. There could be no resolution through war, but neither partner in the competition could be expected to surrender its respective myths and ideologies. Wise statecraft was the most important element in maintaining the uneasy partnership in preventing nuclear war. He had little confidence that education, cultural exchanges, religious impulses, or disarmament plans would eliminate the competition of the two continental empires competing for influence in the world. He did not like to see the world as two nuclear armed scorpions locked in a small bottle, but it was the dangerous world he perceived. It was also a world subject to the winds of revolutionary demands arising from within the undeveloped world, and a world made more dangerous and unified by technological development.

He warned of the danger of the U.S. overreliance on military power. The tendency to build defense pacts in Asia revealed little understanding of the political complexities there. Military force could be effective in crises, but without political forces of cohesion military force could accomplish little as demonstrated in both Vietnam and China. Over-reliance on military power was a temptation to a nation as wealthy as the U.S., but it could contribute to our political embarrassment. Military force for Niebuhr was a means of last resort, but the American temptation was to use it as a meat-axe where subtlety was called for. The understanding of the needs of a population required wise statecraft, not primarily military power.

The real task of preserving the nuclear stalemate rested in the political sphere. He noted that technical miscalculation might bring about the nuclear catastrophe, but his primary concern was in political miscalculation. A defeat in some vital area of competition he reasoned might tempt one side or the other in hysteria to resort to nuclear weapons. This was the central reason for his continued reference to the "balance of power" in the post-World War II situation. He often described it as a "nuclear umbrella"; competition could go on, but it must be limited so not as to threaten the vital interests of the other party. Of course, it was not balance of power in an pre-nuclear meaning of the term, but an arrangement, ironically stumbled into which now was securing not peace in any deep sense, but at least the avoidance of the nuclear holocaust.

The cold war was not to be won. Nor was it in the foreseeable future to be abandoned. It was to be endured. The management required shrewd statecraft which could build ties of mutuality with the Soviet Union while resisting Soviet attempts to dominate. He hoped that firm and patient resistance to Soviet expansionism would provide time for some of the revolutionary ardor of Marxism to wane. He himself joined in the ideological struggle, writing essays polemically critical of Marxist thought. At the same time he continued to puncture American illusions of omnipotence and innocence.

As the ideological struggle spread to the poor countries of the world, he saw the U.S. at a disadvantage. The U.S., with its ties to previous colonial powers, its own problems of social injustice and race problems, was not an attractive or relevant model. However, the creed and actual accomplishments of Marxism were so badly flawed that he believed that patient resistance would eventually encourage other governments to find their own solutions without succumbing to alliances with Communist powers. The U.S. would be tested, he reasoned, by its capacity to provide generous aid to the poor countries. Technological development, particularly, depending on transfers of capital and knowledge, was central to overcoming poverty.

His writings are full of opposition to directions of U.S. foreign policy, particularly the Vietnam policies. Also, he frequently opposed armament policies and wrote supporting the banning of atmospheric weapons testing and opposing the antiballistic missile program. Disarmament, however, he thought had to be preceded by trust and community, and those qualities were not available in significant amounts in the cold war.

Niebuhr's sobriety about what could be accomplished in international relations was grounded in empirical observation, his view of history and his understanding of human nature. His major field of teaching in the theological curriculum was Christian ethics. His courses ranged from the ethics and values of non-Christian religions and movements to detailed studies in Christian ethics. The study of ethics revealed the importance but also the weakness of moral norms in regulating human life. His two most important books, *Moral Man and Immoral Society* and *The Nature and Destiny of Man*, both examined the relevance and the irrelevance of norms in the face of egoistic humanity. The earlier volume, *Moral Man and Immoral Society*, studied how human norms derived from the regulation of individual life were violated in all forms of social organization and interaction. Social institutions lacked the function of conscience, and they magnified the egoism of insecure human beings. Conflict between social groups organized into institutions was inevitable. Humanity could not look forward to the diminution of conflict or to moral progress in the regulation of its institutions. Human social relations were dominated by self-seeking interest groups and classes to the extent that the achievement of a rough, tolerable social justice adjudicating claims was the most that could be expected. Socialist allies and friends and pacifist allies found his critique of their plans and hopes too devastating. Eventually his critique of utopianism and his acceptance of the need for force in human relations would lead him out of the Socialist Party of which he had been Vice-Chairman and out of the pacifist organization, the Fellowship of Reconciliation, of which he had served as President. Looking back on the title of this book from a perspective of thirty years he was to agree with a student critic that perhaps the title should have been *Immoral Man and More Immoral Society*. The book became a primer for students of morality and social relations for decades of students here and abroad in both universities and theological schools.

The Nature and Destiny of Man was the text of his Gifford Lectures delivered in Edinburgh in the opening years of World War II. Here his analysis pushed beyond social disorder into an examination of disorder in human nature. Humanity in his theological perspective had the theoretical perspective of accepting its security in a trust in God as the source of all life. However, inevitably human beings chose to rebel against God, the source of their freedom, and against human freedom itself. The fundamental problem was the fear of being free and trusting God. They either denied their freedom through surrendering their freedom to the inordinate love of aspects of human life or they tried to become like God through pride. The first group of disorders or sin he discussed under the rubric of sensuality. Through narcissism, lust, drunkenness, dependence on drugs, etc., humanity gave up its freedom to transcend natural limitations into a human life. The second group of sins he discussed as pride. In pride humanity forgot its dependence on God and strove for an absoluteness that humanity could not possess. Pride corrupted social life through pride of possessing power and through the struggle for power. It also corrupted the life of the spirit in its expression in religion as spiritual pride, in morality through moral pride, and in education through pride of knowledge. All human institutions, therefore, were influenced by corrupting influences rooted in the very meaning of what it meant to be human. The root of human disorder rested in the anxiety caused by human freedom. The anxious conditions of human life produced great works but also the distortions of those works. As long as human history continued, it would be this mixture of great works of freedom and great corruption of freedom.

The divine remedy for the agony of history was not the victory of a country or the victory of a righteous remnant. The revelation of God in Christ was that the source of all life took human failure into the divine nature and suffered. God's victory was in a forgiving love. People could live by acceptance of divine love and a response of responsible love to the revelation and their human comparisons. As a theologian in the tradition of the reformation, grace not works would provide the support for human life. As one inclined to the Calvinist aspect of the reformation, that grace was then to be exhibited in all of life by a continued engagement to create just conditions of life where people could live freely.

Niebuhr's great achievement was to present a theological interpretation of human life where the full squalor of human existence was evident and the magnificent grace of the source of life was seen. The consequences of such a view was intended as a realistic contribution to the Christian's pursuit of social justice. From the analysis also followed other projects, e.g., *The Children of Light and the Children of Darkness*, which would join a realistic analysis of democratic political life with a commitment to struggle for its maintenance and reform. Likewise, in race relations and economics his goal was to conjoin realistic analysis of the injustices with the struggle for more equality and freedom.

—Ronald Stone

NOETHER, (Amalie) Emmy. German mathematician. Born in Erlangen, 23 March 1882; emigrated to the United States, 1933. Studied at the University of Erlangen, Ph.D. 1907. Unofficial lecturer, under David Hilbert, 1915-19, then named Unofficial Associate Professor, University of Göttingen, Germany, 1922-33; Faculty Member, Bryn Mawr College, Pennsylvania, 1933-35; also, Member, Institute for Advanced Study, Princeton, New Jersey, 1933-35. Visiting Professor, University of Moscow, 1928-29, and University of Frankfurt, 1930. Recipient: Ackermann-Teubner award, 1932. *Died* (in Bryn Mawr, Pennsylvania) *14 April 1935.*

PUBLICATIONS

Mathematics

Über die Bildung des Formensystems der ternären biquadratischen Form. Berlin, G. Reimer, 1908.
Zerfallende verschränkte Produkte und ihre Maximalordnungen. Paris, Hermann, 1934.

Other

Editor, with Robert Fricke and Öystein Ore, *Gesammelte mathematische Werke*, by Richard Dedekind. Braunschweig, Germany, F. Vieweg, 1930-.

*

Critical Studies: *The Nature and Growth of Modern Mathematics* by E.E. Kramer, New York, Hawthorn, 1970; "Emmy Noether" by C.H. Kimberling, in *American Mathematical Monthly 79*, 1972.

* * *

Emmy Noether, a leading 20th-century algebraist, was the daughter of Max Noether, professor (*ordinarius*) of mathematics at the University of Erlangen. Sexual discrimination limited her early educational opportunities and later her career advancement. From 1900 to 1904 she studied languages and mathematics as a nonmatriculated auditor at Göttingen and Erlangen. Following enactment of a law sanctioning matriculation of women, Noether formally enrolled at the latter university, from which she obtained a Ph.D. in mathematics in 1907. Her doctoral dissertation on algebraic invariants was filled with formulae and calculations, the marks of Paul Gordan, her advisor. In 1911, however, Gordan's successor at Erlangen, Ernst Fischer, introduced Noether to the abstract approach to mathematics. The application of this new approach to algebra became her lifework.

In 1915 Noether began an 18-year association with the University of Göttingen and with David Hilbert, a leading Göttingen mathematician and an original advocate of the abstract approach. She was initially brought to the University by Hilbert and Felix Klein to apply her invariant theoretic knowledge to Einstein's general theory of relativity. Despite Hilbert's early persistent efforts to secure a formal position for her, Noether was allowed to habilitate as a *Privatdozentin* (unsalaried lecturer) only in 1919. Until then she delivered lectures under Hilbert's name. In 1922 she was named an *ausserordentlicher Professor* (honorary professor) and finally in 1923 she received a *Lehrauftrag* (salaried teaching appointment) in algebra. Despite an international reputation as an algebraist and recognition by Hermann Weyl, a Göttingen colleague, as "the strongest center of mathematical activity" at the University in the early 1930's, Noether never attained an ordinary professorial rank. In 1933, a victim of Hitler's anti-Semitism, she was dismissed from Göttingen and emigrated to the United States where she taught as a visiting professor at Bryn Mawr until her death in 1935.

The fine reputation enjoyed by Noether in her lifetime (and lasting to the present) was based on her creative and fertile use of the abstract approach to mathematics. Rejecting the formal, algorithmic approach of Gordan, she tried to isolate the major concepts of algebra, relate them to one another, and thereby explore algebra's inner structure. For example, she delved far into the structure of the commutative ring (a set of elements which form a commutative group with respect to one operation (addition) and which are closed under a second operation (multiplication) which is associative and commutative, as well as distributive with respect to the first operation). Here she used Richard Dedekind's concept of an ideal (a nonempty subset C of a commutative ring R such that for any a and b in C, a-b is in C, and for any a in C and r in R, ra is in C) and her special ascending chain condition. (A ring meets the ascending chain condition if every sequence of ideals C_1, C_2, C_3, ...in the ring—such that each ideal is a proper subset of its successor in the chain—has a finite number of terms.) Included among her many penetrating results on rings was the proof that in commutative rings with an identity in the ascending chain condition is equivalent to the property that every ideal in the ring has a finite basis.

Noether not only used ideals to probe the structure of rings but established a general axiomatic theory of ideals as well. This theory was important beyond algebra because it subsumed the known properties of the polynomial ideals of algebraic geometry as well as those of Dedekind's algebraic ideals, and even offered new insights into the former. Thus Noether's work on ideals resulted in a unified, fertile theory basic to both algebra and algebraic geometry.

From roughly 1927 on, Noether concentrated on noncommutative rings and algebras. Building on the ideas of F. Georg Frobenius, Theodor Molien, and others, she developed a unified theory of noncommutative algebras and their representations.

Noether's algebraic methods were as important as her specific results. Her conceptual, axiomatic approach became a model for her contemporary and later mathematicians. Noether herself seems to have carried the conceptual (abstract) approach to the extreme. She shunned specific examples, visualization, and calculation (at which she was nevertheless adept, as her dissertation proved). She chose rather to move from idea to idea—determining important concepts, exploring them, and then unifying them in grand conceptual schemes.

Noether reached the peak of her mathematical powers and her public recognition on the eve of her departure from Germany. In 1932, in collaboration with Richard Brauer and Helmut Hasse, she proved that every simple algebra over an ordinary algebraic number field is cyclic. In the same year she delivered one of the major lectures at the international congress of mathematics in Zurich, Switzerland, and shared (with Emil Artin) the Ackermann-Teubner award for arithmetic and algebra.

Noether's ideas survived her in the over forty research articles which she published between 1907 and 1934, in the *Mathematische Annalen* for which she served as an unofficial editor, in B.L. van der Waerden's once-standard *Algebra* which was "in part based on lectures by E. Artin and E. Noether," and in the mathematics of her many graduate students including Grete Hermann, Heinrich Grell, Werner Weber, Jakob Levitzki, Max Deuring, Hans Fitting, and Otto Schilling.

—Helena M. Pycior

OPARIN, A(leksandr) I(vanovich). Russian biochemist. Born 3 March 1894. Studied in the Natural Sciences Department, Physico-Mathematical Faculty, Moscow University, graduated 1917. Specialized in biological chemistry under A.N. Bakh, 1917-29; after 1929, Professor and Head Chair of Plant Biochemistry, Moscow University. Co-Founder, Institute of Biochemistry, 1935 (Director, 1946). Recipient: A.N. Bakh Prize, 1950; I.I. Mechnikov Prize, 1950; Order of Lenin. Corresponding Member, 1939, and Academician, 1946, U.S.S.R. Academy of Sciences. Member, Soviet Committee in Defense of Peace; International Federation of Scientists (Vice-President, 1952, 1962). *Died 21 April 1980.*

PUBLICATIONS

Biochemistry

Fermenty, ikh rol' znachenie v zhizni organizmov [Ferments, Their Role and Significance for Living Organisms]. Petrograd, Izd. Frenkelia, 1923.
Proizkhozhdenie zhizni. Moscow, Moskovskii rabochii, 1924; as *The Origin of Life,* New York, Macmillan, 1938.
Vozniknovenie zhizni na Zemle [The Beginning of Life on Earth]. Moscow, Biomedgiz, 1936.
Biokhimiia vinodeliia: Sbornik 1 [The Biochemistry of Wine Making]. Moscow, Izd-vo AN SSSR, 1947.
Kak zarodilas' zhizhn' na Zemle [How Life Started on Earth]. Moscow, Goskul'tprosvetizdat, 1949.
Zhizhn' vo Vselennoi, with V.G. Fresenkov. Moscow, Izd-vo AN SSSR, 1956; as *Life in the Universe,* New York, Twayne, 1961.
Zhizn', ee priroda, proiskhozhdenie, i razvitie. Moscow, Izd-vo AN SSSR, 1960; as *Life, Its Nature, Origin, and Development,* New York, Academic Press, 1961.
Biokhimiia i fiziologiia immuniteta tastenii [Biochemistry and Physiology of Immunity in Plants], with others. Moscow, Izd-vo AN SSSR, 1960.
Zhizn' kak forma dvizheniia materii [Life as a Form of Matter-Movement]. Moscow, Izd-vo, AN SSSR, 1963.
The Chemical Origin of Life. Springfield, Illinois, C.C. Thomas, 1964.
Vozniknovenie i nachal'noe razvitie zhizni [The Origin and Initial Development of Life]. Moscow, Meditsina, 1966.
Genesis and Evolutionary Development of Life. New York, Academic Press, 1968.
Materiia-zhizn'-Intellekt [Matter-Life-Intellect]. Moscow, Nauka, 1977.

Other

Aleksei Nikolaevich Bakh: Biograficheskii ocherk K 100-letiiu so dnia rozhdeniia [Aleksei Nikolaevich Bakh: A Biographical Sketch], with L.A. Bakh. Moscow, Izd-vo AN SSSR, 1957.

Editor, *Biokhimiia khlebopecheniia* [Biochemistry of Bread-making]. Moscow, Izd.-vo AN SSSR, 1938.
Editor, *Biokhemicheskie osnovy khraneniia ovoshchei* [Biochemical Foundations of the Storage of Vegetables], by B.A. Rubin. Moscow, Izd-vo AN SSSR, 1939.
Editor, *Khranenie sakharnoi svekly* [The Storage of Sugar Beets], by B.A. Rubin. Moscow, Pishchepromizdat, 1939.
Editor, *Sobranie trudov po khimii i biokhimiia* [Collected Works on Chemistry and Biochemistry], by A.N. Bakh. Moscow, Izd-vo AN SSSR, 1950.
Editor, *Deistvie izluchenii i primenenie izotopov v biologii* [Radiation and the Use of Isotopes in Biology]. Moscow, Izd-vo inostr. lit-ry, 1950.
Editor, with others, *Biokhimiia zerna i produktov ego pererabotki* [Biochemistry of Grain and Its Products]. Moscow, Gos. idz-vo tekh. i ekonom. lit-ry po voprosam zagotovok, 1950.
Editor, *Osnovy biokhimii rastenii* [Foundations of Plant Biochemistry], by V.L. Kretovich. Moscow, Sovetskaia nauka, 1956.
Editor, *Razvitie ucheniia o biologicheskom okislenii* [History of the Theory of Biological Oxidation], by D.M. Mikhlin. Moscow, Izd-vo AN SSSR, 1956.
Editor, *Fiziologiia rastenii* [Plant Physiology], by B.A. Rubin. Moscow, Sovetskaia nauka, 1956.
Editor, *Virusy* [Viruses], by K.S. Sukhov. Moscow, Izd-vo AN SSSR, 1956.
Editor, *Glavnye puti assimiliatsii i dissimiliatsii azota u zhivotnikh* [The Main Routes of Assimilation and Dissimilation of Nitrogen in Animals], by A.E. Braunshtein. Moscow, Izd-

vo AN SSSR, 1957.
Editor, *Vozkinovenie zhizni na Zemle: Sbornik dokladov na Mezhdunarodnom soveshchanii, 1957* [The Origin of Life on Earth: Papers Presented to the International Symposium, 1957]. Moscow, Izd-vo AN SSSR, 1957.
Editor, *Biokhimiia chaia i chainogo proizvodstva* [Biochemistry of Tea and Tea Manufacturing], by M.A. Bokuchava. Moscow, Izd-vo AN SSSR, 1958.
Editor, *Osnovy biologicheskogo kontrolia chainogo proizvodstva* [Biological Control of Tea Manufacturing], by K.M. Dzhemukhadze. Moscow, Izd-vo AN SSSR, 1958.
Editor, *Biokhimiia zerna i khleba* [Biochemistry of Grain and Bread], by V.L. Kretovich. Moscow, Izd-vo AN SSSR, 1958.
Editor, *Biokhimiia kletochnogo dykhaniia* [Biochemistry of Cell Breathing], by D.M. Mikhlin. Moscow, Izd-vo AN SSSR, 1960.
Editor, *Nekotorye problemy makromolekuliarnoi struktury ribonukleinovykh kislot* [Some Problems of Macromolecular Structure of RNA], by A.S. Spirin. Moscow, Izd-vo AN SSSR, 1963.
Editor, *Abiogenez i nachal'nye stadii evoliutsii zhizni* [Abiogenesis and Initial Stages in the Evolution of Life]. Moscow, Nauka, 1968.
Editor, *Vozniknovenie zhizni* [The Origin of Life], by D. Bernal. Moscow, Nauka, 1969.
Editor, Russian translation of *Biological Predetermination,* by D. Canyon and G. Steinman. Moscow, Mir, 1972.
Editor, *Molecular Evolution: Prebiological and Biological.* New York, Plenum Press, 1972.
Editor, *Fitoaleksini* [Phytoalexines], by L.V. Metlitskii and others. Moscow, Nauka, 1973.
Editor, *Problemy voznikoveniia i sushchnosti zhizni* [Problems of the Origin and Development of Life]. Moscow, Nauka, 1973.
Editor, *Proiskhozhdenie zhizni (estestvennym putem)* [The Natural Origin of Life], by M. Rutten. Moscow, Mir, 1973.
Editor, *Fermenty obmena folievoi kisloty* [Ferments of the folic acid metabolism], by N.A. Andreeva. Moscow, Nauka, 1974.
Editor, Russian translation of *Molecular Evolution and the Origin of Life,* by S. Fox and K. Doze. Moscow, Mir, 1975.
Editor, *Fitoimmunitet* [Phytoimmunity], by L.V. Metlitskii. Moscow, Nauka, 1976.
Editor, *Kul'tura chaia v Demokraticheskoi Respublike V'etnam* [Tea Culture in the Democratic Republic of Vietnam]. Moscow, Nauka, 1976.
Editor, Russian translation of *Evolution of Bioenergetic Processes,* by E. Broda. Moscow, Mir, 1978.
Editor, *Problema pishchevoi polnotsennosti khleba* [Problem of Alimentary Usefulness of Bread], by V.L. Kretovich and R.R. Tokareva. Moscow, Nauka, 1978.

*   *   *

The question of how life originally formed on earth has been ignored by scientists to a rather surprising extent. One reason for this may have been the basic dictum under which biologists have operated, at least since the death of theories of spontaneous generation, namely that "life begets life." To work within the mainstream of biology, then, it is not necessary to ask the fundamental question of how and when life arose.

Second, the questions of the origin of life clearly carry with themselves profound philosophical and religious issues. The force of religious thought and dogma has been strong enough until recently to give scientists pause before attacking such obviously controversial issues.

Yet few issues in biology are as fundamental as the question of the way life began on the earth. Furthermore, it has long been clear that the relationship between animate and inanimate matter is one of degree and not kind. Since the fall of the Vitalistic Theory in the 19th century, it has been apparent that no spiritual force is required to explain the fact that some forms of matter move, reproduce, react to stimuli...that is, "live," while others do not. The fundamental nature of life now seems completely amenable to explanation in chemical and physical terms.

By the early 1920's, A.I. Oparin had begun to examine the circumstances under which life might have arisen in the primitive conditions on earth some three billion years ago or more. He recognized that this event must have occurred some time between the earth's creation (about 4.7 billion years ago) and the age of the oldest known fossils of living organisms (about 3.2 billion years ago). He concluded that the earth's atmosphere at that time consisted of methane, hydrogen, ammonia, and water vapor. Then, by applying chemical reactions which were already well-known, he demonstrated how these molecules might combine with each other to form amino acids and other simple organic molecules. The energy required to bring about these syntheses, Oparin suggested, came from electrical storms and ultraviolet radiation from sunlight.

Oparin's theory was first tested empirically in 1953 by S.L. Miller, a graduate student of Harold Urey's. A mixture simulating the primordial atmosphere postulated by Oparin was subjected to electric discharges for a period of days. At the conclusion of the test period, the reaction mixture was analyzed and found to contain amino acids, the building blocks from which proteins are made. Oparin's ideas have received additional confirmation from the discovery of amino acids in rocks more than three billion years old.

Late in his career, Oparin was successful in carrying Miller's demonstration one step further. He polymerized the nucleotide adenine, producing a material that will clump together and form tiny droplets in water solutions. These droplets are called *protobionts*. They are capable of carrying out, in a greatly simplified form, many of the processes we associate with the process of life itself. They have the ability, for example, to absorb small molecules from their environment, change the composition of these molecules, and then incorporate the products of this change into their own molecular structure.

Oparin suggested that a type of natural selection might have taken place in the primordial atmosphere, with those molecules most efficient at capturing and utilizing simpler molecules having an evolutionary advantage. From among these protobionts, the first self-replicating molecules may, by some processes still not understood, have been produced. At this point, two crucial conditions of life—the ability to reproduce and ability to take in and utilize "food" would have been achieved.

—David Newton

OPPENHEIMER, J(ulius) Robert. American physicist. Born in New York City, 22 April 1904. Studied at Harvard University, Cambridge, Massachusetts, B.A. 1925; Cambridge University, 1925-26; University of Göttingen, Ph.D. 1927. Married Katherine Harrison in 1940; 2 children. National Research Fellow, 1927-28; International Board of Education Fellow, University of Leyden and University of Zurich, 1928-29; Assistant Professor, 1929-31; Associate Professor, 1931-36, and Professor of Physics, 1936-47, University of California, Berkeley, and California Institute of Technology, Pasadena; Director, Los Alamos Scientific Laboratory, New Mexico, 1943-45; Director and Professor of Physics, Institute for Advanced Study, Princeton, New Jersey, 1947-67. Chairman, General Advisory Committee, Atomic Energy Commission, 1946-52. Recipient: Enrico Fermi Award, Atomic Fellow, American Academy of Arts and Sciences. Foreign Member, Royal Danish Academy of Science; Brazilian Academy of Science; Japanese Academy of Science. *Died 18 February 1967.*

PUBLICATIONS

Physics

The Scientific Foundations for World Order (lecture). Denver, University of Denver Social Science Foundation, 1947.
Physics in the Contemporary World (lecture). Cambridge, Massachusetts Institute of Technology, 1947.
Science and the Common Understanding (lectures). New York, Simon and Schuster, 1954.
The Open Mind (lectures). New York, Simon and Schuster, 1955.
The Constitution of Matter (lectures). Eugene, Oregon State System of Higher Education, 1956.
Some Reflections on Science and Culture (lecture). Chapel Hill, University of North Carolina Press, 1960.
The Flying Trapeze: Three Crises for Physicists (lectures). London and New York, Oxford University Press, 1964.
Lectures on Electrodynamics, edited by S. Kusaka and B.S. DeWitt. New York, Gordon and Breach, 1970.

Other

Robert Oppenheimer: Letters and Recollections, edited by Alice Kimball Smith. Cambridge, Massachusetts, Harvard University Press, 1980.

*

Critical Studies: *J. Robert Oppenheimer and the Atomic Theory* by Alvin Kugelmass, New York, Messner, 1953; *Robert Oppenheimer: The Man and His Theories* by Michel Rouzé, London, Souvenir Press, 1964; *The Swift Years: The Robert Oppenheimer Story* by Peter Michelmore, New York, Dodd Mead, 1969; *The Oppenheimer Case: Security on Trial* by Phillip M. Stern and Harold P. Green, New York, Harper, 1969; *J. Robert Oppenheimer, Shatterer of Worlds* by Peter Goodchild, London, BBC Publications, 1980.

* * *

J. Robert Oppenheimer's career was divided into two fairly distinct episodes. The first began in about 1926, with the publication of his first paper, dealing with a quantum mechanical analysis of molecular spectra. The paper was only the first in a series that attempted to use quantum mechanics to analyze a large variety of physical phenomena.

The preceding years had seen a number of efforts to interweave the concepts of classical Newtonian physics and the fledgling science of quantum mechanics. In too many instances, these efforts were only marginally successful or totally unsuccessful. By 1925, however, the formulations of Dirac, Heisenberg, Schrödinger, and others had provided theoretical physicists with a new option: the challenge of setting Newtonian physics aside and trying to interpret physical phenomena solely on the basis of quantum mechanical principles.

Oppenheimer was only one of many physicists who attacked this problem. But he was probably one of the keenest, most incisive, and most successful. In rapid order, he used quantum theory to analyze questions such as the structure of the hydrogen atom, the emission of X-rays, and the degrees of freedom in molecular motion. In addition, he provided the best early understanding of the nature of anti-particles, and essentially predicted the existence of the positron (positive electron) discovered in 1932 by Carl Anderson.

The discovery of apparent anomalies in the behavior of cosmic rays, observed from the early 1930's on, gave Oppenheimer yet another problem to sort out. His analysis helped to explain the phenomenon of a "cosmic ray shower" in which a single cosmic ray in the upper atmosphere produces a secondary particle which, in turn, produces other secondaries, resulting in a "shower" of particles in the lower atmosphere.

Yet Oppenheimer's name is almost certainly associated in the layperson's mind primarily with the subject of nuclear fission, the Manhattan Project, and the construction of the first atomic bomb. Oppenheimer's experience, expertise, and interest in nuclear physics made him an inevitable candidate for an administrative position in the project to build the first nuclear weapon. And, in 1943, he was appointed director of the Los Alamos (New Mexico) laboratories of the project. The choice proved to be a wise one. Although a theoretician rather than an experimentalist, Oppenheimer brought some valuable skills to the very practical task of making a bomb. His sound reputation helped attract a research team whose members were stars of the first magnitude in nuclear physics. The decision to locate the laboratory in the remote New Mexico desert made possible ideal working conditions for the Oppenheimer team. The essential flow of information and interaction among researchers could continue without fear of breaches of security.

The successful completion of the Manhattan Project was realized on July 16, 1945, when the first atomic bomb was tested near Alamogordo, New Mexico. The event was a mixed blessing for Oppenheimer and his colleagues. The successful solution of a challenging intellectual problem was, of course, a source of great personal satisfaction. The consequences of the weapon they had unleashed, however, raised issues of social and moral responsibility which were to torment the scientific community for years thereafter.

The dramatic political imbroglio in which Oppenheimer was involved a decade later far outshadows, probably unfortunately, almost any other chapter in his life. The mass hysteria of the McCarthy era called into question the loyalty of anyone who could not demonstrate a pure, intense, and unquestioning patriotism. Oppenheimer's earlier association with left-wing groups and his resistance to plans for developing a thermonuclear ("hydrogen") bomb were the only "crimes" needed to convict him in the government's eyes. Although acknowledged by the review board to be a "loyal citizen," his security clearance was withdrawn. The act was one of the darkest days in American political and scientific history.

—David Newton

ORTEGA y GASSET, José. Spanish philosopher. Born in Madrid, 9 May 1883. Studied at the University of Madrid, 1898-1902, Ph.D. 1904; universities of Berlin, Leipzig, and Marburg, 1905-07. Married Rosa Spottorno in 1910; 3 children. Professor of Metaphysics, University of Madrid, 1910-36. Co-Founder Liga de Educación Política Española, 1914, and the review *España*, 1915; Founder *El Sol*, 1917, and *Revista de Occidente*, 1923. Deputy for the province of León, Constitutional Assembly, Second Spanish Republic, and Civil Governor of Madrid, 1931-36. Lived abroad, 1936-46. Returned to Spain and with Julián Marías founded the Instituto de Humanidades, 1948. Member, Real Academia de Ciencias Morales y Políticas, 1914. Honorary President, PEN, 1935. *Died* (in Madrid) *17 October 1955*.

PUBLICATIONS

Collections

Obras completas. Madrid, Revista de Occidente, 11 vols., 1946-69.

Philosophy and Spanish Life and Culture

Los terrores del año mil (Crítica de una leyenda). Madrid, n.p., 1909.
Descartes y el método transcendental. Madrid, Asociación España para el Progreso de las Ciencias, 1910.
Sensación, construcción, e intuición. Madrid, Asociación España para el Progreso de las Ciencias, 1913.
Meditaciones del Quijote. Madrid, Ediciones de la Residencia de Estudiantes, 1914; as *Meditations on Quixote*, New York, Norton, 1961.
El Espectador, I-II. Madrid, Renacimiento, 2 vols., 1916.
Personas, obras, cosas. Madrid, Renacimiento, 1916.
El Espectador, III. Madrid, Calpe, 1921.
España invertebrada. Madrid, Calpe, 1921; as *Invertebrate Spain*, London, Allen and Unwin, and New York, Norton, 1937.
El tema de nuestro tiempo. Madrid, Calpe, 1923; as *The Modern Theme*, London, C.W. Daniel, 1931; New York, Norton, 1933.
Las Atlántidas. Madrid, Revista de Occidente, 1924.
La deshumanización del arte: Ideas sobre la novela. Madrid, Revista de Occidente, 1925; as *The Dehumanization of Art and Notes on the Novel*, Princeton, New Jersey, Princeton University Press, 1948.
El Espectador, IV-VIII. Madrid, Revista de Occidente, 5 vols., 1925-34.
Espíritu de la letra. Madrid, Revista de Occidente, 1927.
Tríptico I: Mirabeau o el político. Madrid, Revista de Occidente, 1927.
Kant. Madrid, Revista de Occidente, 1929.
La rebelión de las masas. Madrid, Revista de Occidente, 1929; as *The Revolt of the Masses*, London, Allen and Unwin, and New York, Norton, 1932.
Misión de la universidad. Madrid, Revista de Occidente, 1930; as *The Mission of the University*, Princeton, New Jersey, Princeton University Press, 1944; London, Kegan Paul, 1946.
La redención de las provincias y la decencia nacional. Madrid, Revista de Occidente, 1931.
Rectificación de la República. Madrid, Revista de Occidente, 1931.
La reforma agraria y el Estatuto catalán. Madrid, Revista de Occidente, 1932.
Goethe desde dentro. Madrid, Revista de Occidente, 1932.
Notas. Madrid, Calpe, 1938.
Historia como sistema; Del Imperio Romano. Madrid, Revista de Occidente, 1941; as *History as a System and Other Essays* and *Concord and Liberty*, New York, Norton, 2 vols., 1946-61.
Castilla y sus castillos. Madrid, Aguado, 1942.
Ideas y creencias. Madrid, Revista de Occidente, 1942.
Teoría de Andalucía. Madrid, Revista de Occidente, 1942.
Esquema de las crisis. Madrid, Revista de Occidente, 1942.
Dos prólogos. Madrid, Revista de Occidente, 1944.
Introducción a Velázquez. San Sebastián, Publicaciones de la Real Sociedad Vascongada de Amigos del País, 1947; as *Velásquez*, New York, Random House, 1953.
Del optimismo en Leibniz. Madrid, Asociación Española para el Progreso de las Ciencias, 1948.
De la aventura y la caza. Madrid, Aguado, 1949.
Papeles sobre Velázquez y Goya. Madrid, Revista de Occidente, 1950.
Estudios sobre el amor. Madrid, Aguilar, 1950; as *On Love: Aspects of a Single Theme*, New York, Meridian, 1957; Lon-

don, Gollancz, 1959.

Al pie de las letras. Madrid, Hernando, 1956.

En torno a Galileo. Madrid, Revista de Occidente, 1956; as *Man and Crisis*, New York, Norton, 1958; London, Allen and Unwin, 1959.

Caracteres y circunstancias. Madrid, Aguado, 1957.

Viajes y países. Madrid, Revista de Occidente, 1957.

El hombre y la gente. Madrid, Revista de Occidente, 1957; as *Man and People*, New York, Norton, 1957.

Ensayos escogidos. Madrid, Aguilar, 1957.

Meditación de la técnica. Madrid, Revista de Occidente, 1957.

Meditación del pueblo joven. Madrid, Revista de Occidente, 1958.

Prólogos para alemanes. Madrid, Taurus, 1958.

La idea de principio en Leibniz. Madrid, Revista de Occidente, 1958; as *The Idea of Principle in Leibniz and the Evolution of Deductive Theory*, New York, Norton, 1971.

Idea del teatro. Madrid, Revista de Occidente, 1958.

Kant; Hegel, Dilthey. Madrid, Revista de Occidente, 1958.

¿Que es filosofía? Madrid, Revista de Occidente, 1958; as *What is Philosophy?* New York, Norton, 1961.

Goya. Madrid, Revista de Occidente, 1958.

Velázquez. Madrid, Revista de Occidente, 1959.

Apuntes sobre el pensamiento. Madrid, Revista de Occidente, 1959.

Una interpretación de la historia universal: en torno a Toynbee. Madrid, Revista de Occidente, 1959; as *An Interpretation of Universal History*, New York, Norton, 1973.

Meditación de Europa. Madrid, Revista de Occidente, 1960.

La caza y los toros. Madrid, Revista de Occidente, 1959.

Origen y epílogo de la filosofía. Mexico City, Fondo de Cultura Económica, 1960; as *The Origin of Philosophy*, New York, Norton, 1967.

Vives-Goethe. Madrid, Revista de Occidente, 1961.

Pasado y porvenir para el hombre actual. Madrid, Revista de Occidente, 1962.

Misión del bibliotecario (y otros ensayos afines). Madrid, Revista de Occidente, 1962; selection as *The Mission of the Librarian*, Boston, Hall, 1961.

Meditación de la técnica. Vicisitudes en las ciencias. Bronca en la física. Madrid, Calpe, 1965.

Unas lecciones de metafísica. Madrid, Alianza Editorial, 1966; as *Some Lessons in Metaphysics*, New York, Norton, 1970.

Tres ensayos sobre la mujer. Barcelona, Almacenes Generales de Papel, 1972.

Escritos políticos. Madrid, Revista de Occidente, 1973.

Discursos políticos. Madrid, Alianza Editorial, 1974.

Phenomenology and Art (selections). New York, Norton, 1975.

Other

Epistolario. Madrid, Revista de Occidente, 1974.

*

Bibliography: *Bibliografía de Ortega: Estudios Orteguianos 3* by Udo Rukser, Madrid, Revista de Occidente, 1971.

Critical Studies: *Ortega y Gasset: An Outline of His Philosophy* by José Ferrater-More, Cambridge, Bowes and Bowes, and New Haven, Connecticut, Yale University Press, 1957; *Human Reality and the Social World: Ortega's Philosophy of History* by Oliver W. Holmes, Amherst, University of Massachusetts Press, 1975.

*   *   *

The most important Spanish philosopher since the 17th century, José Ortega y Gasset was born in Madrid; his father was a man of letters and his mother came from a family of newspaper publishers. Indeed, a good deal of the philosopher's work was written for dailies and magazines, some of which—especially the very prestigious *Revista de Occidente* (1923-36)—were founded by him. His mission, he felt, was to enlighten as wide a public as possible, and, in addition to philosophy, he wrote on a variety of subjects such as politics, sociology, literary theory, art, love, play, linguistics, education, in a style sparkling with simile, metaphor, and anecdote, all enhancing a natural elegance meant to "seduce" his public into reading, and characterized by a clarity he claimed to be the courtesy of the thinker. He completed his doctorate in 1904, and from 1905-07 he went to Leipzig, Berlin, and then to Marburg where he studied with the eminent neo-Kantian, Herman Cohen, and where he became convinced of the superiority of German over Latin culture, but came away with a deep sense of the wrongness of purely abstract cloistered philosophy divorced from the vitality of life.

As against Unamuno's cry for the Hispanization of Europe, Ortega saw the need for the introduction of the formula Europe = science into a "tibetanized" Spain short on laboratories, learned journals, and, above all, precise, rigorous thinking. Ortega held his mission to be a double one: to re-introduce into Spain the study of philosophy as a strict discipline, and to disseminate culture from the podium and the press. This he was able to do as Professor of Metaphysics at the University of Madrid, a chair he occupied from 1910 to 1936, when he left Spain to live in Portugal, France, Holland, and Argentina; he returned in 1945 when, with his disciple and literary executor, Julián Marías, he founded the Institute of Humanities, whose classes and lectures were popular and exceedingly well attended.

From Cohen, Ortega claims to have learned the drama inherent in intellectual problems, but his work is also impelled by a sense of the drama of life, the primordial or "radical" (from "root") reality of all lucubration. Indeed, in his first major book, *Meditations on Quixote* (1914), he established the formula which may be called the matrix of his subsequent work: "I am I and my circumstances," or, put into simpler terms, the "I" exists only in interaction with the surroundings in which it lives.

In *The Modern Theme* he reacts against the divinization of culture by expounding his philosophy of *ratio-vitalism*, or vital reason. Reason, like locomotion, is a function of life and when it severs its relation to its origins, it becomes de-vitalized, abstract: from Socrates through Descartes and Kant, the truth, to be truth, has to be rational, "Platonic," acceptable for all and at all times, "one and invariable," independent of the changes of history, exempt from mutability, a product of pure intellection, the *mos geometricus* of Spinoza, the pure reason of Kant. Thus we are boxed into the "external" truths of doctrines, of "democracy" and of Marxist dialectical materialism. Truth as pure abstraction is a utopianism which leads to revolutions. Abstract thinking keeps us tied to antiquated beliefs without considering their historical roots, and perpetuates the dichotomy of the Cartesian *res cogitans* and *res extensa*. The theme of our time is the need for a synthesis of culture and life. But life is never static nor does it have an essence, for as we are born into a context of beliefs (creencias) or accepted notions, as each belief fails, we replace it with an idea. Thus life is always pointed towards a future; it is always "a doing something," and the choice of what to do makes man an uneasy creature, a shipwreck constantly seeking something to hold on to; life presents him at every step with options, which pose the agonizing question, not only of choice but of personal authenticity.

History as a System is the definitive development of what is, a thing without static being, without essence. Following Dilthey's distinction between *Naturwissenshaft* and *Geisteswissenshaft*, Ortega emphasizes that unlike scientific truth which establishes the nature or essence of things, life has no fixed essence; it is not a *factum* but instead a gerundive, a *faciendum*. Life is given to us but not given to us *made*: we, ourselves, must make it. The tiger today is the same as the tiger since creation, but man is his own novelist or dramatist, creating himself as he acts and changes. Everything changes except change itself: Nietzsche had called man an incomplete animal. Man is accumulation and not an Adam, always beginning from the beginning.

Europe which, in the philosopher's words, is the "protagonist" of world drama is facing the danger of being relegated to a secondary role, and Ortega attempts to explain why. Already in 1921, in *Invertebrate Spain*, he attributed the so-called decadence of his country to the absence of a select minority, the consequence of a deficient feudal system. This historical weakness he lays at the door of the Visigoths who, with the collapse of the Roman empire, had invaded the Iberian peninsula, only after having been debilitated by extensive contact with Rome. No effective social structure is possible without a strong minority to give direction to the masses.

In his best known book, *The Revolt of the Masses*, Ortega extends his theory of the "select man" and the "mass man," none of which has to do with economic status or birth, but is a matter of individual psychology. The noble or select man is the one who ever makes further demands upon himself (*noblesse oblige* means that nobility is defined by obligations) while the mass man reaches a level of self-satisfaction; contrary to general belief, it is the noble man who is enslaved—enslaved always to higher standards. The select man is active, the mass man, reactive. But the disease of our times, deriving from the 19th century which introduced universal suffrage and a technology which reduced the impediments of life, is that the mass man, very cognizant of his legal powers, the ease of his existence, and especially of his numbers, imposes his vulgarity in taste, comportment, and other norms upon the more limited elite. A truly healthy society is not only led by a select minority, but can boast of a majority disposed to recognize and emulate superiority wherever it exists.

The Dehumanization of Art, which has given a shorthand description to so many vanguard movements, could easily have been named the De-realization or The De-sentimentalization of the Arts. Ortega's thrust in this little book is that the most "aristocratic" elements in modern art are the pure spontaneous play of the aesthetic as against the more traditional and anecdotal art, where the majority of ordinary people is most at ease, for they wish not only to recognize themselves physically but also emotionally in the mirror of what they see, read, or hear. The vanguard disdains the human figure and sentiments and is only open to a special audience willing to make a special effort to understand anti-realism, and is, therefore, repugnant to the mass mentality. Thus, Ortega is the prophet of abstract expressionism, atonalism, the *nouveau roman*, and all manner of contemporary experimentation in the arts.

—Martin Nozick

ORWELL, George. Pseudonym for Eric Arthur Blair. British novelist, and political and social commentator. Born in Motihari, Bengal, India, 25 June 1903. Educated at Eton College (King's Scholar), 1917-21. Served with the Republicans in the Spanish Civil War, 1936: wounded in action. Married Eileen O'Shaughnessy in 1936 (died, 1945); married Sonia Mary Brownell in 1949; 1 adopted son. Served in the Indian Imperial Police, in Burma, 1922-27; returned to Europe, and lived in Paris, then in London, working as a dishwasher, tutor, bookshop assistant, etc., 1928-34; full-time writer from 1935; settled in Hertfordshire, 1935, and ran a general store until 1936; Correspondent for the BBC and *The Observer*, and columnist and literary editor, *The Tribune*, London. *Died 21 January 1950.*

PUBLICATIONS

Political and Social Commentary

Down and Out in Paris and London.   London, Gollancz, and

New York, Harper, 1933.
The Road to Wigan Pier.   London, Gollancz, 1937; New York, Harcourt Brace, 1958.
Homage to Catalonia.   London, Secker and Warburg, 1938; New York, Harcourt Brace, 1952.
Inside the Whale and Other Essays.   London, Gollancz, 1940.
The Lion and the Unicorn: Socialism and the English Genius.   London, Secker and Warburg, 1941; New York, AMS Press, 1976.
Critical Essays.   London, Secker and Warburg, 1946; as *Dickens, Dali and Others: Studies in Popular Culture*, New York, Reynal, 1946.
James Burnham and the Managerial Revolution.   London, Socialist Book Centre, 1946.
The English People.   London, Collins, 1947; New York, Haskell House, 1974.
Shooting an Elephant and Other Essays.   London, Secker and Warburg, and New York, Harcourt Brace, 1950.
Such, Such Were the Joys.   New York, Harcourt Brace, 1953; as *England, Your England and Other Essays*, London, Secker and Warburg, 1953.
A Collection of Essays.   New York, Doubleday, 1954.
The Orwell Reader, edited by Richard H. Rovere.   New York, Harcourt Brace, 1956.
Selected Essays.   London, Penquin, 1957; as *Inside the Whale and Other Essays*, 1975.
Selected Writings, edited by George Bott.   London, Heinemann, 1958.
Collected Essays.   London, Secker and Warburg, 1961.
Decline of English Murder and Other Essays.   London, Penquin, 1965.
The Collected Essays, Journalism, and Letters of George Orwell, edited by Sonia Orwell and Ian Angus.   London, Secker and Warburg, 4 vols., 1968.

Novels

Burmese Days.   New York, Harper, 1934; London, Gollancz, 1935.
A Clergyman's Daughter.   London, Gollancz, and New York, Harper, 1935.
Keep the Aspidistra Flying.   London, Gollancz, 1936; New York, Harcourt Brace, 1954.
Coming Up for Air.   London, Gollancz, 1939; New York, Harcourt Brace, 1950.
Animal Farm: A Fairy Story.   London, Secker and Warburg, 1945; New York, Harcourt Brace, 1946.
Nineteen Eighty-Four.   London, Secker and Warburg, and New York, Harcourt Brace, 1949.

Other

Editor, *Talking to India: A Selection of English Language Broadcasts to India.*   London, Allen and Unwin, 1943.
Editor, with Reginald Reynolds, *British Pamphleteers I: From the Sixteenth Century to the French Revolution.*   London, Wingate, 1948.

*

Bibliography: "George Orwell: A Selected Bibliography" by Zoltan G. Zeke and William White, in *Bulletin of Bibliography 23* (Boston), May-August 1961; *George Orwell: An Annotated Bibliography of Criticism* by Jeffrey and Valerie Meyers, New York, Garland, 1977.

Critical Studies: *Chronicles of Conscience: A Study of George Orwell and Arthur Koestler* by Jenni Calder, London, Secker and Warburg, and Pittsburgh, University of Pittsburgh Press, 1968; *Outside the Whale: George Orwell's Art and Politics* by

David L. Kubal, Notre Dame, Indiana, University of Notre Dame Press, 1972; *The Unknown Orwell*, New York, Knopf, 1972, and *Orwell: The Transformation*, London, Constable, 1979, Chicago, Academy, 1981, both by Peter Stansky and William Abrahams; *Orwell and the Left* by Alex Zwerdling, New Haven, Connecticut, Yale University Press, 1974; *The Last Man in Europe: An Essay on George Orwell* by Alan Sandison, London, Macmillan, 1974; *A Reader's Guide to George Orwell* by Jeffrey Meyers, London, Thames and Hudson, 1975, and *George Orwell: The Critical Heritage* edited by Meyers, London, Routledge, 1975; *The Road to Miniluv: George Orwell, The State, and God* by Christopher Small, London, Gollancz, 1975, Pittsburgh, University of Pittsburgh Press, 1976; *George Orwell: A Life* by Bernard Crick, London, Secker and Warburg, 1981, revised edition, 1981; *George Orwell: The Ethical Imagination* by Sant S. Bal, Atlantic Highlands, New Jersey, Humanities Press, 1981.

* * *

George Orwell, the pen name of Eric Arthur Blair, wrote essays, semi-documentary novels, and political fables or satires, as one might describe his best-known works *Animal Farm* and *Nineteen Eighty-Four*. He was very much a writer of the 1930's and 1940's; born in 1903, he died long before his time, of TB, in 1950, just when world fame had come to him. That fame was based on the quality of his prose and the courageous honesty of his message. Orwell participated in the movement to the Left which characterized British literature in the depression-ridden, fascist-haunted 1930's. But his most significant, and controversial, stance was that of left-wing critic of Marxist Communism.

Of "lower-upper middle class" family, Orwell was educated at Eton, but failed to win a university scholarship and did not go to Oxford. Returning to England after a period in Burma during the 1920's, where he worked for the Indian Imperial Police, Orwell struggled to become a writer. *Burmese Days, Down and Out in Paris and London*, and especially *The Road to Wigan Pier* marked him as a keenly observant literary craftsman whose forte was a kind of fictionalized journalism; his "novels" never departed much from his personal experiences and social reportage, but were etched sharply and stamped with a distinctive point of view. They gave an authentic picture of lower-class life, so often sought and so rarely achieved by the proletarian-conscious leftist writers of the 1930's.

Orwell's hard-headed respect for real working-class values (values with which, as a typically conscience-ridden middle-class person, he sought hard to identify) led him to disparage intellectuals and intellectualism and deplore abstract doctrinal ideas. His independent socialism reminds us of a British tradition reaching back to William Cobbett and Robert Blatchford, a tradition essentially populist and somewhat reactionary in cherishing folk customs against modern "progress." He shared with D.H. Lawrence, one of his contemporaries whom he admired, a dislike of the whole modern industrial society.

Nevertheless Orwell was close to Communist circles early in the 1930's; *Wigan Pier* was commissioned by the Left Book Club; Orwell expressed the prevailing intellectual hatred of a class-ridden English society and fear of a coming Fascism. It was his experience as a soldier in the Spanish Civil War, recorded in *Homage to Catalonia*, that soured him on the Communists, primarily because of the ruthlessness with which the Moscow-directed Party told lies about and destroyed other leftist groups like the "Trotskyist" P.O.U.M. At a time when it was not fashionable in intellectual circles to think so, and indeed during World War II when it was politically most inexpedient to say so, Orwell came to believe and write that Stalinist Russia was quite as disgusting a "totalitarian" regime as Hitler's Germany. He expressed such views in his columns written for the Labour newspaper *Tribune* 1943-45, and in the two political parables. "For the past ten years I have been convinced that the destruction of the Soviet myth was essential if we wanted a revival of the

Socialist movement," he wrote in 1947.

Animal Farm, rejected by a number of publishers in 1945 because of its attack on Soviet Russia, proved to be an immediate best-seller when finally printed. To many it was the most amusing political fable since *Gulliver's Travels. Nineteen Eighty-Four* soon surpassed it. That "we are in danger of the centralised slave state, ruled over by a small clique who are in effect a new ruling class," as Orwell thought, was a fate not to be avoided if the intellectuals "worship power and successful cruelty"; and "the countless English intellectuals who kiss the arse of Stalin are not different from the minority who give their allegiance to Hitler or Mussolini." Orwell's famous picture of the Totalitarianism-to-come, conceived in 1943 and published in 1948, along with Zamyatin's *We* (which influenced Orwell) and Aldous Huxley's *Brave New World* (from which as a vision of future nightmare his differs significantly) is one of the classic "dystopias," as Chad Walsh has named them: utopia in reverse, the future as the *hideous* triumph of science and technology and organization. Characteristically Orwellian is the locating of the evil's source in intellectual dishonesty: lies, propaganda, "Newspeak" in which war is peace, ignorance is strength, freedom is slavery. And the abstract-ideological foundations of persecution: one cannot hate real human beings, but one can decree the extermination of whole classes or races.

If the contours of the future did not entirely follow Orwell's vision, that does not detract from his qualities of intellectual honesty, the courage to dissent from fashionable orthodoxies, his robust common sense and shrewd realism. Orwell's writings, including some perceptive essays on literary and political themes, survive because of the superb style in which the insights of a vigorous and unconventional intelligence were expressed. They are among the most important documents of the era *entre deux querres*, and rightfully claim their place in the long tradition of British nonconformity.

—Roland Stromberg

OSGOOD, Charles E(gerton). American psychologist. Born in Somerville, Massachusetts, 20 November 1916. Studied at Dartmouth College, Hanover, New Hampshire, B.A. 1939; Yale University, New Haven, Connecticut, Ph.D. 1945. Married Cynthia Thornton in 1939; 2 children. Research Associate, Yale University, 1945-46; Assistant Professor of Psychology, University of Connecticut, Storrs, 1946-49; Associate Professor, 1949-52, and since 1952 Professor of Psychology and Communications, University of Illinois, Urbana (Director of the Institute of Communications Research, 1957-65; since 1965, Director of the Center for Advanced Study). Fellow, Institute for Advanced Study in the Behavioral Sciences, Stanford, California, 1958. Visiting Professor, University of Hawaii, Honolulu, 1964-65. President, American Psychological Association, 1962-63. Recipient: Guggenheim Fellowship, 1955; Distinguished Science Contribution Award, American Psychological Association, 1961; Kurt Lewin Award, Society for the Psychological Study of Social Issues, 1971. Honorary doctorate: Dartmouth College, 1962. Member, National Academy of Sciences, and the American Academy of Arts and Sciences. Address: 304 East Mumford Drive, Urbana, Illinois 61801, U.S.A.

PUBLICATIONS

Psychology

Method and Theory in Experimental Psychology. New York, Oxford University Press, 1953.
The Measurement of Meaning, with others. Urbana, Univer-

sity of Illinois Press, 1957.

Graduated Reciprocation in Tension-Reduction: A Key to Initiative in Foreign Policy., Urbana, Illinois, Institute of Communications Research, 1960.

The Human Side of Policy in a Nuclear Age. Urbana, Illinois, Institute of Communications Research, 1961.

Some Terms and Associated Measures for Talking About Human Communication, with Kellogg V. Wilson. Urbana, Illinois, Institute of Communications Research, 1961.

Studies on the Generality of Affective Meaning Systems. Urbana, Illinois, Institute of Communications Research, 1961.

An Alternative to War or Surrender. Urbana, University of Illinois Press, 1962.

Perspective in Foreign Policy. Palo Alto, California, Pacific Books, 1966.

Conservative Words and Radical Sentences in the Semantics of International Politics. Urbana, University of Illinois Press, 1968.

Interpersonal Verbs and Interpersonal Behavior. Urbana, Illinois, Group Effectiveness Research Laboratory, 1968.

Cross-Cultural Universals of Affective Meaning, with others. Urbana, University of Illinois Press, 1975.

Focus on Meaning. The Hague, Mouton, 1980.

Lectures on Language Performance. New York, Springer, 1980.

Other

Editor, with Thomas A. Sebeok, *Psycholinguistics: A Survey of Theory and Research Problems.* Baltimore, Waverly Press, 1954.

Editor, with James G. Snider, *Semantic Differential Technique: A Sourcebook.* Chicago, Aldine, 1958.

Editor, with M.S. Miron, *Approaches to the Study of Aphasia.* Urbana, University of Illinois Press, 1963.

*   *   *

Charles E. Osgood has, during his life, developed three major "themes" in psychology. The unifying strain in these themes has been the idea of "meaning." The tentative title of Osgood's autobiography, *Focus on Meaning: In Individual Humans, Across Human Cultures, and for Survival of the Human Species,* gives a good overview of the areas in which he has made a major effort.

The first theme Osgood engaged was a behavioral theory of meaning. Osgood disagreed with the Hullian two-stage behaviorism and formulated his own theory of three-stage behaviorism which postulated an extra integration level to account for more complex levels of behavioral organization. By simply changing one component at the integration level, entirely new "meanings" could be recognized by the organism. In order to analyze this theory Osgood developed the "semantic differential technique" for measuring meaning. Subjects are asked to rate a number of concepts on several different scales, indicating the intensity of meaning. According to Osgood: "all three major factor analyses yielded nearly identical evidence for three massive factors easily identifiable as Evaluation (good, nice, beautiful, honest, etc.), Potency (strong, big, thick, tough, etc.) and Activity (active, quick, excitable, hot, etc.)." Thus Osgood has developed a method to evaluate and compare the meanings of various words. This work was published in 1957 in *The Measurement of Meaning.*

Osgood's second theme is in reality an extension of the first. In order to evaluate more fully his theory of meaning (also now extending into the field of psycholinguistics) Osgood believed it was necessary to use his semantic differential technique (SD) to evaluate meaning in other cultures. Using teenage males and many colleagues in the cultures to be studied, he generated a list of qualifier types, and the subjects rated 100 nouns against 50

scales. Analysis of this led to the selection of 620 concepts for the development of an Atlas of Affective Meaning. These concepts were then rated (again using teenage males) against the SD and evaluation/potency/activity (EPA) structure. An analysis was also made of familiarity, meaningfulness, polarization, and cultural instability. Osgood is also developing a "semantic interaction technique" (SI) in order to evaluate more exactly the usage and meaning of certain words. The aim of these methods of meaning and evaluation is the formulation of an Abstract Performance Grammer (APG) which would differentiate the way in which the mind innately expresses meaning from the "competence grammar" which is the structure of a language. Data has been collected for the Atlas of Affective Meaning from thirty different language/culture groups with the hope that it will provide insight into the "dynamics of human societies."

A final "theme" of Osgood's work has been in the area of "meaning and survival of the human species." His interest in this area was stimulated by the McCarthy era and the development of the atomic bomb. He has studied psychological factors in human relations and developed the GRIT (Graduated and Reciprocated Initiations in Tension-reduction) strategy with regard to disarmament. The book *An Alternative to War or Surrender* (1962) gives an explanation of Osgood's GRIT strategy. Osgood believes that: "the gap between word and thing increases with the remoteness of things from immediate experience, that the words of international politics are typically analogic, that the power of words lies in the way they abstract from reality...and that we are being led by old men using antiquated semantic maps to guide us through the wonderland of the twentieth century." Osgood has propounded this theory at many levels, to scientists and members of the government, in an effort to promote de-escalation of the military.

Osgood, in addition to his work in psychology, has also made many contributions to the field of psycholinguistics. In connection with this Osgood, in an address entitled "A Dinosaur Caper" given at the New York Academy of Sciences, spoke of the nature of scientific revolutions and their relation to modern psycholinguistics. In his book *The Structure of Scientific Revolutions,* Thomas Kuhn argued that a scientific revolution occurs when anomalies or "counterinstances" accumulate that resist attempts at explanation in terms of the prevailing paradigm of "normal science." Does this description of paradigm clash fit the recent or current circumstances in psycholinguistics? Osgood does not believe it does. Although he acknowledges the revolutionary impact of Noam Chomsky's work on the field of psycholinguistics, he questions whether we are witnessing in psycholinguistics a true Kuhnian "crisis" or merely a pendulum swing between visible paradigms. As Osgood sees it, the effect of Chomsky's contributions upon psycholinguistics fails to meet the criteria that distinguish a true scientific revolution because: 1) There has been no attempt to incorporate solutions to problems handled successfully by the old paradigm; 2) The old paradigm has not been shown to be insufficient *in principle*; 3) There has been no new paradigm to shift *to*—in the sense of a well-motivated, internally coherent alternative theory of language performance. There has been a shift *away from* behaviorism in any form, but in the absence of any alternative paradigm this would be better termed "revulsion" than "revolution."

At any rate, having ruled out the probability of an imminent revolution in psycholinguistics, Osgood concludes "A Dinosaur Caper" by venturing a few predictions concerning the future of psycholinguistic theory and research as we approach the year 2000: 1) There will be a complete shift away from emphasis on Competence to emphasis on Performance; 2) As part of this shift, there will be an increasing avoidance of dealing with sentences-in-isolation (whether in linguistic or psychological methodologies) and increasing dependence upon sentence-in-context (in discourse, in ordinary conversation, and so on); 3) Semantics will be moving into the foreground as syntax moves, reciprocally, into the background; 4) As already hinted, logical, rationalist models of language will be shown to be inappropriate for ordinary speakers and will be superseded by more gutsy, dynamic psycho-logical models; 5) There will be a shift from ethno-linguo-centrism toward what might be called anthropo-linguo-centrism.

Charles E. Osgood has made many varied contributions both to psychology (and psycholinguistics) and to the effort for world peace. In his own words, the old dinosaur is now "trying to drive a balanced three-theme wagon into the 1980's."

—R.W. Rieber

OTTO, Rudolf. German theologian. Born in Peine, 25 September 1869. Studied at the University of Erlangen, 1888; University of Göttingen, Licenciate in Theology, 1898. Lecturer, University of Göttingen, 1899-1914; Professor of Theology, University of Breslau, 1914-17; Professor of Theology, University of Marburg, 1917-29. Travelled extensively in India and Japan, 1911-12. Visiting Lecturer, Oberlin College, Ohio, 1924. *Died* (in Marburg) *7 March 1937*.

PUBLICATIONS

Theology

Geist und Wort nach Luther. Göttingen, n.p., 1898.
Die Anschauung vom Heiligen Geiste bei Luther: Eine historisch-dogmatisch Untersuchung. Göttingen, Vandenhoeck und Ruprecht, 1898.
Leben und Werken Jesu nach historisch-kritischer Auffassung. Göttingen, Vandenhoeck und Ruprecht, 1902; as *The Life and Ministry of Jesus According to the Historical and Critical Method*, Chicago, Open Court, 1908.
Naturalistische und religiöse Weltansicht. Tübingen, Mohr, 1904; as *Naturalism and Religion*, London, Williams and Norgate, and New York, Putnam, 1907.
Kantisch-Fries'sche Religionsphilosophie und ihre Anwendung auf die Theologie. Tübingen, Mohr, 1909; as *The Philosophy of Religion, Based on Kant and Fries*, London, Williams and Norgate, 1931.
Goethe und Darwin; Darwinismus und Religion. Göttingen, Vandenhoeck und Ruprecht, 1909.
Das Heilige: Über das Irrationale in der Idee des Göttlichen und sein Verhältnis zum Rationalen. Breslau, Trewendt und Granier, 1917; as *The Idea of the Holy: An Inquiry into the Non-rational Factor in the Idea of the Divine and Its Relation to the Rational*, London, Oxford University Press, 1923.
Aufsätze, das Numinose betreffend. Gotha, Klotz, 1923; selections with added material as *Sünde und Urschuld*, 1932, and as *Das Gefühl des Überweltlichen (Sensus Numinis)*, 1932; selections as *Religious Essays: A Supplement to "The Idea of the Holy,"* London, Oxford University Press, 1931.
Zur Erneuerung und Ausgestaltung des Gottesdienstes. Giessen, Töpelmann, 1925.
West-Östliche Mystik: Vergleich und Unterscheidung zur Wesensdeutung. Gotha, Klotz, 1926; as *Mysticism East and West: A Comparative Analysis of the Nature of Mysticism*, New York, Macmillan, 1932.
Christianity and the Indian Religion of Grace (lecture). Madras, Christian Literature Society for India, 1929.
Die Gnadenreligion Indiens und das Christentum. Gotha, Klotz, 1930.
Gottheit und Gottheiten der Arier. Giessen, Töpelmann, 1932.
Reich Gottes und Menschensohn: Ein religionsgeschichtlicher Versuch. Munich, Beck, 1934; as *The Kingdom of God and the Son of Man*, Grand Rapids, Michigan, Zondervan, and London, Lutterworth, 1938.
Freiheit und Notwendigkeit: Ein Gespräch mit Nikolai Hartmann über Antonomie und Theonomie der Werte. Tübin-

gen, Mohr, 1940.
Verantwortliche Lebensgestaltung: Gespräche mit Rudolf Otto über Fragen der Ethik, edited by Karl Küssner. Stuttgart, Kohlhammer, 1943.

Other

Chorgebete für Kirche, Schule und Hausandacht, with G. Mensching. Giessen, Töpelmann, 1925.
Das Jahr der Kirche in Lesungen und Gebeten. Munich, Beck, 1927.
Eingangspsalmen für die Sonntage des Kirchenjahres. Munich, Beck, 1927.

Editor and translator, *Dipika des Nivasa: Eine indische Heilslehre*. Tübingen, Mohr, 1916.
Editor and translator, *Vischnu-Narayana*. Jena, Diederichs, 1917.
Editor and translator, *Siddharta des Ramanuja*. Tübingen, Mohr, 1923.
Editor, *Grundlegung zur Metaphysik der Sitten*, by Kant. Gotha, Klotz, 1930.
Editor, *Rabindranath Tagores Bekenntnis*. Tübingen, Mohr, 1931.
Editor and translator, *Die Urgestalt der Bhagavad-Gita*. Tübingen, Mohr, 1934; as *The Original Gita: The Song of the Supreme Exalted One*, London, Allen and Unwin, 1939.
Editor and translator, *Der Sang des Hehr-Erhabenen*. Stuttgart, Kohlhammer, 1935.
Editor and translator, *Die Lehrtraktate der Bhagavad-Gita*. Tübingen, Mohr, 1940.
Editor and translator, *Die Katha Upanashad*. Berlin, Töpelmann, 1936.

*

Critical Studies: *Rudolf Otto's Interpretation of Religion* by R.F. Davidson, Princeton, New Jersey, Princeton University Press, 1947; *Rudolf Ottos Bedeutung für die Religionwissenschaft und die Theologie heute* edited by Ernst Benx, Leiden, Brill, 1971; *Möglichkeiten und Grenzen einer Theologie der Religionen* by Michael von Brück, Berlin, Evangelische Verlagsanstalt, 1979.

*   *   *

Rudolf Otto was a German philosopher of religion and theologian who gained worldwide influence among academic and religious circles with the publication in 1917 of his book *Das Heilige* (*The Idea of the Holy*, 1923). In this and his many other works, Otto depicted the religious experience as a unique and powerful subjective apprehension of a mysterious, impelling, and ultimate objective reality that is completely different (*ganz andere*) from the mundane world. Arguing that religion is constituted of intuitive and emotional, rather than intellectual, events, Otto's works were highly appealing to those Europeans who, at the end of the First World War, felt a widespread disillusionment with the rational and secular pre-war cultural ethos. People from other parts of the world found in Otto's writings an appreciative and respectful depiction of certain elements of their own religious traditions.

While Otto's publications were welcomed by pietistic Protestant Christians who longed to experience the world in its "dimensions of depth," they were perhaps more widely read in the first decades of this century by philosophers and historians of religions. Philosophers saw in Otto's thought an attempt to develop Immanuel Kant's critique of reason. Historians of religions found in his works the assertion that the experience of the *numinous* (a word he coined, from the Latin *numen*, "divine," "spiritual") is an awareness of a transcendent reality that at once inspires awe and fear and yet is undeniably attractive (*mysterium tremendum et fascinosum*). Otto insisted that this apprehension of the numinous is an experience that cannot be reduced to or interpreted by other modes of thought or patterns of cognition. Otto maintained, furthermore, that the experience of the numen lies at the core of all of the world's religions. Accordingly, historians of religions who agree with Otto have used his notion of the numinous experience as a methodological category with which they approach their comparative studies.

Describing himself as a "pietistic Lutheran," Otto followed Martin Luther's theological position that religion is basically a personal inner experience, rather than a system of philosophical or doctrinal assertions. He never deviated from this position, and it influenced all of his studies. His early work *Die Anschauung vom Heiligen Geiste bei Luther* stressed the Lutheran notion that the Holy Spirit serves as the personal inner teacher (*inter docer*) of one's religious experience. He did not confine this understanding to Protestant Christianity alone. Having travelled in 1911-12 to North Africa, Egypt, Palestine, India, China, and Japan (and to India, again, in 1925 and 1927-28), Otto developed a lasting appreciation for Islam, Hinduism, and Buddhism. Of these three religions, Otto was most attracted to Hinduism. He learned Sanskrit and published several original translations of Sanskrit texts. In all of his translations and studies, he stressed the mystical or devotional qualities of the works. For example, in *West-Östliche Mystik* he compared the thought of the German mystic Meister Eckhart and the Śaiva philosopher Śankara; and in his work *Die Gnadenreligion Indiens und das Christentum* Otto described the writings of the medieval Śri Vaisnava theologian Ramanuja in pietistic terms. Otto was similarly touched by Daisetz Teitaro Suzuki's teachings on the non-rational character of Zen Buddhism, and writes with deep appreciation of Zen in *Das Gefühl des Überweltlichen*. Otto's interest in cross-cultural and interreligious understanding is exemplified by his advocacy of the programs of the Religious League of Mankind and of a museum of comparative religion, which he founded in Marburg.

Otto's understanding of religion owed much to the intellectual climate in Germany in his time. With Luther, Otto stressed the inner significance of the religious experience. From Kant and the Neo-Kantian philosopher Friedrich Fries, Otto took the notion that the transcendent sphere of reality is unknowable by means of reason and rationality but, rather, is made available through the epistemological process of what Fries called "intuition" (*Ahndung* [*Ahnung*]). Despite his debt to these thinkers, Otto was not wholly a philosophical idealist nor a psychological subjectivist. He avoided some of the possible criticism by the followers of Ludwig Feuerbach and Sigmund Freud—both of whom held that religion is an illusion—by saying that while the religious feelings of *tremendum* and *fascinosum* are subjective states of being, the religious experience itself is a response to an objective and external *mysterium*. Otto argued against the social psychological teachings of Wilhelm Wundt, who felt that religion develops out of non-religious experiences and evolves from lower into higher forms. In this regard, Otto owed a great deal to Friedrich Schleiermacher's depiction of religion as a unique and independent mode of experience that is irreducible to any other state of being.

Even though Otto was highly influential in the early decades of this century, he has not been without his critics. Some people think that his definition of religion as a personal and pietistic experience is too narrow, as they argue that religion also includes communal, social, and theoretical aspects. Other people, particularly Indologists, feel that Otto was somewhat ideologically biased in his selection of Sanskrit texts with which he characterized Hinduism. Still others hold philosophical and psychological disagreements with Otto, who they sense did not fully distinguish the difference between subjective experience and objective reality.

Despite these criticisms, Otto's influence on 20th-century thought should not be underestimated. *Das Heilige* was the most widely read theological work of his time, matched in its influence perhaps only by Karl Barth's *The Epistle to the Romans*. In his attention to the emotional and devotional depth of the major Asian religious systems, Otto served as a corrective to the philosophical and linquistic approaches to Asian religions that dominated German studies at his time. His Religous League of Mankind fostered international understanding. Perhaps his most lasting impact lies in his contributions to the academic discipline of History of Religions. His *Mysticism East and West* and *India's Religion of Grace*—as well as his less well-known but equally important last book, *Reich Gottes und Menschensohn*, a work in which he presented the Iranian influence on Jesus's teachings—served as methodological models for many historians of religions in the decades following his death.

—Joseph M. Kitagawa / W. Mahoney

PANOFSKY, Erwin. American art critic and art historian. Born in Hannover, Germany, 30 March 1892; emigrated to the United States in 1934: later naturalized. Studied at the University of Berlin; University of Munich; University of Freiburg, Ph.D. 1914. Married Dora Moss in 1916; 2 sons; married Gerda Soergel in 1965. Privat Dozent, then Professor of Art History, University of Hamburg, 1921-33; Visiting Professor of Fine Arts, New York University, 1931-35; Member, then Professor, Institute for Advanced Study, Princeton, New Jersey, 1935-62; Samuel F.B. Morse Professor, New York University, 1962-68. Charles Eliot Norton Professor, Harvard University, Cambridge, Massachusetts, 1947-48; Gottesman Lecturer, Uppsala University, 1952; Flexner Lecturer, Bryn Mawr College, Pennsylvania. Recipient: Haskins Medal, Mediaeval Academy of America 1962. Honorary doctorate: University of Utrecht, 1936; Princeton University, New Jersey, 1947; Oberlin College, Ohio, 1950; Uppsala University, 1953; Rutgers University, New Brunswick, New Jersey, 1954; Bard College, Annandale-on-Hudson, New York, 1956; Harvard University, 1957; University of Berlin, 1962; New York University, 1962. Member, American Academy of Arts and Sciences. Corresponding Fellow, Mediaeval Academy of America. Member, British Academy, and Royal Academy of Belgium. *Died 14 March 1968.*

PUBLICATIONS

Art and Art History

Dürers Kunsttheorie, vornehmlich in ihrem Verhältnis zur Kunsttheorie der Italiener.   Berlin, Reimer, 1915.
Dürers "Melencolia I": Eine quellen- und typengeschichtliche Untersuchung, with Fritz Saxl.   Leipzig, Tübner, 1923.
"Idee": Ein Beitrag zur Begriffsgeschichte der älteren Kunsttheorie.   Leipzig, Tübner, 1924; as *Idea: A Conception in Art History,* Columbia, University of South Carolina Press, 1968.
Die deutsche Plastik des elften bis dreizehnten Jahrhunderts.   Munich, Wolff, 2 vols., 1924.
Hercules am Scheidewege und andere antik Bildstoffe in der neueren Kunst.   Berlin, Tübner, 1930.
The Meaning of the Humanities, with others (lectures).   Princeton, New Jersey, Princeton University Press, and London, Oxford University Press, 1938.
Studies in Iconography: Humanistic Themes in the Art of the Renaissance (lectures).   New York, Oxford University Press, 1939.
The Codex Huygens and Leonardo da Vinci's Art Theory: The Pierpont Morgan Library, Codex M.A. 1139.   London, Warburg Institute, 1940.
Albrecht Dürer.   Princeton, New Jersey, Princeton University

Press, 1943; as *The Life and Art of Albrecht Dürer*, 1955.

Gothic Architecture and Scholasticism (lecture). Latrobe, Pennsylvania, Archabbey Press, 1951.

Early Netherlandish Painting: Its Origins and Character (lecture). Cambridge, Massachusetts, Harvard University Press, 1953.

Galileo as a Critic of the Arts. The Hague, Nijhoff, 1954.

Meaning in the Visual Arts: Papers in and on Art History. New York, Doubleday, 1955.

Pandora's Box: The Changing Aspects of a Mythical Symbol, with Dora Panofsky. New York, Pantheon, and London, Routledge, 1956.

Renaissance and Renascences in Western Art. Stockholm, Almqvist and Wiksell, 1960; New York, Harper, 1972.

The Iconography of Correggio's Camera di Sao Paolo. London, Warburg Institute, 1961.

Aufsätze zu Grundfragen der Kunstwissenheit, edited by Hariolf Oberer and Egon Verheyen. Berlin, Hessling, 1964.

Tomb Sculpture: Four Lectures on Its Changing Aspects from Ancient Egypt to Bernini, edited by H.W. Janson. New York, Abrams, 1964.

Problems in Titian, Mostly Iconographical (lecture). New York, New York University Press, 1969.

Other

Editor and translator, *Abbot Suger on the Abbey School of St.-Denis and Its Art Treasures.* Princeton, New Jersey, Princeton University Press, 1946.

*

Bibliography: in *Essays in Honor of Erwin Panofsky*, Zurich, Büchler Buchdruck, 2 vols., 1960.

*   *   *

Erwin Panofsky was a lecturer, teacher, and scholar in the field of art history. His influence through his lectures on the intellectual community in general, and, through his academic training, on a generation of graduate students in particular, was profound. His contributions, through his scholarship and publications, to the understanding of the history and theory of art were original and far-reaching.

Panofsky's scholarship was distinguished by a wide-reaching humanistic knowledge that included a thorough-going command of classical languages, an intimate familiarity with European history and literature, and an understanding of the philosophical and religious outlooks of the west. Over 155 published articles, monographs, and books, which include detailed studies of Dürer, Michelangelo, Jan van Eyck, Poussin, and Titian as well as broader treatments of medieval, Italian Renaissance, and Netherlandish art, attest to the breadth of his learning. However, Panofsky's writings are never merely pedagogical displays but evidence of a mind that was curious, analytical, and synthesizing.

The problem that was to determine his research throughout his career was first outlined by Panofsky in his doctoral dissertation on Dürer's Theory of Art. Panofsky sought to establish the link between thoughts and ideas, between philosophies and styles. Often considered an iconographer, Panofsky was concerned with far more profound questions than the identification of symbols and subjects. He tried to discern the ways that stylistic changes, as well as subject choices, could be seen as reflections of a changing cultural outlook or mode of thought. Influenced by Hegel, Panofsky rejected Wölfflin's concept of an autonomous art that had a life independent of its content and cultural context. While he never reduced the individual artist to a mere instrument of the will-to-form, nevertheless he interpreted stylistic developments as occurring in harmony with philosophical, intellectual, and cultural changes. He considered that the study of stylistic innovation was impossible without the interpretation of the subjects of specific works of art, but he considered the investigation of the links between styles of art and philosophies to be more deeply revealing of the meaning of art works, the intentions of artists, and the understanding of a culture. In contrast to iconography, Panofsky called this type of analysis iconology. His concern for iconology is especially evident in his works, *Studies in Iconology*, *Albrecht Dürer*, *Abbot Suger*, *Gothic Architecture and Scholasticism*, *Early Netherlandish Painting*, and *Renaissance and Renascences in Western Art*.

The richness of Panofsky's scholarship was complemented by his effectiveness as a teacher. Panofsky enjoyed the classroom which, he once said, provided him with the relief he needed from the ardors of research. He utilized seminars and public lecture series as occasions to enlighten and enliven the minds of his audience and also to explore new areas of interest. His interests were broad and various, but were united by his deep belief that the essential business of the historian was both to preserve the heritage of the past and to endow the present with wisdom and moral significance.

—Linnea Wren

PARETO, Vilfredo (Federigo Damaso, Marquis). Italian sociologist and economist. Born in Paris, France, 15 August 1848. Studied at the Polytechnic Institute, Turin, graduated 1870. Married Alessandra Bakunin in 1889; married Jeanne Régis in 1923. A director of the national railways in Rome, and superintendent of iron mines near Florence; lecturer in mathematics and engineering in Florence and Fiesole, 1882-92; lecturer in economics, University of Lausanne, 1893-1900; then retired to write. Delegate to Disarmament Conference, Geneva; appointed a Senator by Mussolini. *Died 19 August 1923.*

PUBLICATIONS

Collections

Oeuvres complètes, edited by Giovanni Busino. Geneva, Droz, 1964-.

Sociology and Economics

Il protezionismo in Italia ed i suoi effetti. Florence, Ricci, 1891.

Programme d'économie politique. Lausanne, Vallotton, 1892.

Théorie mathématique des changes étrangers. Paris, Secrétariat de l'Association Française pour l'Avancement des Sciences, 1895.

Cours de économie politique.... Lausanne, Rouge, 2 vols., 1896-97.

La Liberté économique et les événements d'Italie. Lausanne, Rouge, 1898.

Les Systèmes socialistes. Paris, Giard et Brière, 2 vols., 1901-02.

Manuale di economica politica. Milan, Società Editrice Libraria, 1906; as *Manual of Political Economy*, New York, Kelley, 1971; London, Macmillan, 1972.

La Mythe vertuiste et la littérature immorale. Paris, Rivière, 1911.

Trattato de sociologica generale. Florence, Barbera, 2 vols., 1916; revised edition, edited by Giulio Farina, 3 vols., 1923; as *The Mind and Society*, New York, Harcourt Brace, 4 vols., and London, Cape, 4 vols., 1935.

I sistemi socialisti. Milan, Istituto Editoriale Italiano, 6 vols., 1917-20.

Fatti e teorie.   Florence, Vallecchi, 1920.

Il problema dei cambi e l'industria nazionale.   Rome, Eraristo Armani, 1920.

Compendio di sociologica generale, edited by Giulio Farina. Florence, Barbera, 1920.

Transformazione della democrazia.   Milan, Corbaccio, 1921.

The Ruling Class in Italy Before 1900.   New York, Vanni, 1950.

Scritti teorici, edited by Giovanni Demaria.   Milan, Malfasi, 1952.

Cronache italiane, edited by Carlo Mongardini.   Brescia, Morcelliana, 1965.

(Selections), edited by Joseph Lopreato.   New York, Crowell, 1965.

Sociological Writings, edited by S.E. Finer.   New York, Praeger, and London, Pall Mall Press, 1966.

Socialismo e democrazia nel pensiero di Vilfredo Pareto, edited by Paola Maria Arcari.   Rome, Volpe, 1966.

Scritti sociologici, edited by Giovanni Busino.   Turin, Unione Tipografica-Editrice Torinese, 1966.

The Rise and Fall of the Elites, edited by Hans L. Zetterberg. Totowa, New Jersey, Bedminster Press, 1968.

Scritti politici, edited by Giovanni Busino.   Turin, Tipografica-Editrice Torinese, 1974.

Lo sviluppo economico italiano, edited by Lucio Avagliano. Salerno, Società Editrice Salernitana, 1975.

Battaglie liberiste: Raccolta di articoli e saggi comparsi sulla stampa italiana, edited by Lucio Avagliano.   Salerno, Società Editrice Salernitana, 1975.

Guida a Pareto: Un'antologia: Per una teoria critica delle scienza della società, edited by Giovanni Busino.   Milan, Rizzoli, 1975.

The Other Pareto, edited by Placido Bucolo.   London, Scholar, 1980.

Other

Principi fondamentali della teoria della elasticità de corpi solidi e ricerche sulla integrazione differenziali che ne definiscono l'equi-librio.   Florence, Pellas, 1969.

Istanza al R. Ispettore delle Ferrovie.   Florence, Società delle Ferriere Italiane, 1886.

Alcune lettere di Vilfredo Pareto, edited by A. Antonucci. Rome, Maglione, 1938.

Corrispondenza, edited by Guido Sensini.   Padua, Cedam, 1948.

Vilfredo Pareto dal carteggio con Carlo Placci, edited by T. Giacalone-Monaco.   Padua, Cedam, 1957.

Pareto-Walras da un carteggio inedito (1891-1901), edited by J. Giacalone-Monaco.   Padua, Cedam, 1957.

Mon journal, edited by Tulio Bagiotti.   Padua, Cedam, 1958.

Pareto-Walras da un carteggio inedito (1891-1901), edited by T. Giacalone-Monaco.   Padua, Cedam, 1960.

Lettere a Maffeo Panteleoni 1890-1923, edited by Gabriele De Rosa.   Rome, Edizioni di Storia e Letteratura, 3 vols., 1960.

Carteggi paretiani 1892-1923, edited by Gabriele De Rosa. Rome, Edizioni di Storia e Letteratura, 1962.

Lettere ai Peruzzi 1872-1900, edited by T. Giocalone-Monaco. Rome, Edizioni di Storia e Letteratura, 2 vols., 1968.

Lettere ad Arturo Linaker 1885-1923, edited by Marcello Luchetti.   Rome, Edizioni di Storia e Letteratura, 1972.

*

Bibliography: in *Oeuvres complètes 20*, 1975.

Critical Studies: *The Works of Vilfredo Pareto* by G.H. Bousquet, Hanover, New Hampshire, Sociological Press, 1928; *An Introduction to Pareto: His Sociology* by George C. Homans and Charles P. Curtis, New York, Knopf, 1934; *The Structure of Social Action* by Talcott Parsons, New York, McGraw Hill,

1937; *Pareto and Mosca* edited by James H. Meisel, Englewood Cliffs, New Jersey, Prentice Hall, 1965; *On Mosca and Pareto* by Norberto Bobbio, Geneva, Droz, 1972; *Pareto on Policy* by Warren J. Samuels, Amsterdam, Elsevier, 1974; *The Anti-Democratic Sources of Elite Theory: Pareto, Mosca, Michels* by Robert A. Nye, London and Beverly Hills, California, Sage, 1977; *The Economics of Vilfredo Pareto* by R. Cirillo, London, Cass, 1979.

*   *   *

Wilfredo Pareto, born in France, was an Italian sociologist and economist. His father had been exiled from Genoa in 1836 by the ruling house of Savoy and had taken a French wife. When Pareto was ten years old the family returned to Italy where he continued his secondary studies, which were mostly in mathematics and classics. He studied engineering at the Polytechnic Institute in Turin, where he completed his degree with a thesis on the theory of elasticity. Then he worked for the Italian national railways and as a superintendent of iron mines. During this time Pareto developed an interest in economic problems, and he began his career as a social scientist at the age of 45 by becoming professor of political economy at Lausanne. He inherited a sizeable fortune in 1898 and moved to Céligny, Switzerland where he lived and wrote as a recluse. Shortly before his death Pareto accepted briefly a position as senator in the Mussolini dictatorship. The direction of his social scientific work was largely determined by a vast knowledge of ancient history, by his training in mathematics and physical science, and by an interest in the concrete economic questions of his day. Pareto was fluent in French and Italian and wrote in both languages throughout his life.

Pareto's main contributions to economics are contained in the *Cours de économie politique* (1896-97), in the *Manuale di economica politica* (1906), and in his article for the *Encyclopédie des sciences mathématiques* entitled "Économie mathématique" (1911). Pareto stressed that economics is but a part of the social sciences and that its conclusions need to be integrated into a total theory of social action. Economic phenomena, for Pareto, always include other elements which it is the province of a broader sociology to investigate. He considered the study of society to be methodologically akin to the physical sciences of nature, although he avoided adopting their substantive doctrines of the ultimately material nature of reality. The logico-experimental method prescribes that theory take its point of departure from what is observed and that it recognize that it can only partially and approximately account for even the delimited segment of reality in which the concrete phenomena have occurred. Pareto's methodological modesty distinguishes his work from the extreme empiricism of Alfred Marshall. The purpose of social science, including economics, is to discover laws, and these laws formulate the uniformities in what is observed. They only achieve probability in relation to their data, they cannot serve to predict future behaviour, and a single law is never the only law relevant to a given phenomenon.

Pareto was the first to devise a general theory of economic demand incorporating the factors of variable psychological satisfaction involved in consumption. He was able to define theoretically a situation of maximally efficient resource use in which supply and demand would be equalized and no individual consumer would lessen the amount of goods available to all others. "Pareto's law" of the distribution of wealth established that inequalities in income vary systematically in relation to the number of incomes above a certain fixed value within the confines of a specific socio-economic system. Pareto's law has been subject to a great deal of analysis and criticism. Socialist economists in particular have found fault with the implication that if economic inequality is independent of the economic system then the only way to diminish it would be through greater efficiency in production. Pareto placed great importance on what he took to be the discovery of an invariant factor in the structure of human societies. Pareto's economic thinking has had little acknowledged influence outside Italy and France.

Pareto's main and lasting contributions to sociology (cf. *Trattato de sociologica generale*, 1916) were the theory of non-logical action and the idea of the circulation of elites. Sociology, for Pareto, deals with all the forms of human action not covered by some special branch of social science, such as economics, military strategy, or technology. These focus on discrete realms of activity in which agents' means are logically related to their ends, not only for the subject in question but for the scientific onlooker with more extensive knowledge. Non-logical action—not the same as illogical action, for Pareto—deviates from this ideal by being influenced either by organic factors or by belief systems that are not part of the logico-experimental knowledge attributable to the agent. Pareto referred to the patterns of belief that determine action as "theories," and he divided them into two groups according to their way of deviating from the logico-experimental standard. Agents' non-logical theories may be pseudo-scientific, in which case they try but fail to meet the scientific standard; or they may be beyond the scope of the scientific orientation and hence be immune to demonstration or refutation by evidence. The first class of non-logical theories covers irrational forces such as instincts, and the second class includes cultural meanings, symbols, and values.

A fundamental task of sociology, for Pareto, was to analyze the capacity of this second class of non-logical "theories" to determine social action. He discovered what he called "residues" at the center of such theories. The residual component of a non-logical theory is the "sentiment" that operates in an agent's self-understanding and which is detachable, by the social scientist, from the explanations or expositions of that non-logical theory provided by the actor. It is residual in that it is left over when the actor's elaboration of it is removed. It is the component of the "theory" that can be clearly seen to surpass experience. It is the non-empirical core (or premise) of the agent's non-logical theory. In many ways Pareto's theory of non-logical action, his pre-figuring of the subject according to the model of the investigator's methodology, can be read as an attempt to speak about the subjective constituents of action without possessing the concept of transcendental reflection bequeathed to German social science by Kant.

Pareto's theory of the circulation of elites remains the most discussed and most controversial part of his sociology. The basis of this theory is a formal division of society into a lower, non-elite stratum and a higher, elite stratum. The theory describes a regular pattern of movement of individuals (and individual families) from the lower to the higher stratum. The elite includes both a governing and a non-governing section. People move upward and into it according to their ability in their profession. This theory both implies the necessity of social hierarchy and domination, and hypothesizes an incessant aspiration for upward mobility. Many have thought that it uncritically translates an historically specific authoritarian social structure into a theory of the inherent nature of social life.

The desire for a systematic theoretical construct of a total social system lay behind nearly all of Pareto's work. He was relentlessly consistent in his methodology. Talcott Parsons has written: "His procedure follows the best traditions of theory construction and, with all its substantive limitations, can serve as an important model today."

—Alan Waters

PARK, Robert E(zra). American sociologist. Born in Harveyville, Pennsylvania, 14 February 1864. Educated at Red Wing High School, Minnesota; studied at the University of Minnesota, Minneapolis, 1 year; University of Michigan, Ann Arbor, 4 years, Ph.B. 1887; Harvard University, Cambridge, Massachusetts, 1898-99, M.A. 1899; Friedrich-Wilhem University, Berlin, University of Strasbourg, and University of Heidelberg, 1899-1904, Ph.D. 1904. Married Clara Cahill in 1894; 4 children. Journalist: reporter, Minneapolis *Journal*, 1887-90, and worked for Detroit *Times*, 1891, Denver *Times*, 1891-92, and New York *Morning Journal*, 1892-93; reporter and city editor, Detroit *Tribune*, 1893-94, and Detroit *News*, 1894-96; reporter and drama critic, Chicago *Journal*, 1897-98. Assistant in philosophy, Harvard University, 1903-05; Secretary, Congo Reform Association, and associated with Booker T. Washington in work on race relations; Lecturer, 1914-23, and Professor of Sociology, 1923-33, University of Chicago; Guest Professor, University of Hawaii, Honolulu, 1931-33, and Yenching University, Peking, 1932; Lecturer, Fisk University, Nashville, 1936-44. President, National Community Center Association, 1922-24, and American Sociological Association, 1925-26. Honorary degree: University of Michigan, 1937. *Died 7 February 1944.*

PUBLICATIONS

Sociology

Masse und Publikum: Eine methodologische und soziologische Untersuchung. Bern, Lack und Grunau, 1904; in *The Crowd and the Public*, 1972.
The Man Farthest Down: A Record of Observation and Study in Europe, with Booker T. Washington. New York, Doubleday, 1912.
The Principles of Human Behavior. Chicago, Zalaz, 1915.
Old World Traits Transplanted, with W.I. Thomas and Herbert A. Miller. New York, Harper, 1921.
Introduction to the Science of Sociology, with Ernest W. Burgess. Chicago, University of Chicago Press, 1921.
The Immigrant Press and Its Control. New York, Harper, 1922.
The City, with Ernest W. Burgess and Roderick D. McKenzie. Chicago, University of Chicago Press, 1925.
The Problems of Cultural Differences. New York, Institute of Pacific Relations, 1931.
The Collected Papers of Robert E. Park, edited by Everett C. Hughes and others
  1. *Race and Culture 1913-1944*. Glencoe, Illinois, Free Press, 1950.
  2. *Human Communities, The City, and Human Ecology 1916-1939*. Glencoe, Illinois, Free Press, 1952.
  3. *Society, Collective Behavior, News and Opinion, Sociology and Modern Society 1918-1942*. Glencoe, Illinois, Free Press, 1955.
On Social Control and Collective Behavior: Selected Papers, edited by Ralph H. Turner. Chicago, University of Chicago Press, 1967.
The Crowd and the Public, and Other Essays, edited by Henry Elsner, Jr. Chicago, University of Chicago Press, 1972.

Other

Editor, *An Outline of the Principles of Sociology*. New York, Barnes and Noble, 1939.

*

Critical Studies: *Quest for an American Sociology: Robert E. Park and the Chicago School* by Fred H. Matthews, Montreal, McGill-Queen's University Press, 1977; *Robert E. Park: Biography of a Sociologist* by Winifred Raushenbush, Durham, North Carolina, Duke University Press, 1979.

*   *   *

Robert E. Park was the leading figure of the Chicago School of Sociology in the period after the First World War, and as such crucially important in the creation of an American sociology—American both in its topics and its intellectual style. His vision was shaped by the American experience; he saw society not as a system ideally stable (although threatened by conflict and deviance) but rather as an open system constituted and constantly renewed by the emergence of new groups, by tensions between separatism and assimilation, communication and confrontation. The social sphere which most interested him was the American city, seen as a kind of inner frontier where the thematic American tensions of race, class, and ethnicity became most acute and clear.

Park did his doctoral work in Germany under the philosopher Wilhelm Windelband; his German thesis, *Masse und Publikum*, set the program for his later work. In contrast to those continental theorists who saw the crowd as constantly tending to degenerate into an irrational mob, Park saw in structureless masses a potentiality for developing common purposes and a sense of common interests. What makes the difference, he said, is discussion and the exchange of ideas; even when social structure breaks down individuals retain the capacity for thought.

Later Park developed a related contrast between "culture" and "civilization." Culture refers to those norms and traditions which define particular groups; it is relatively separatist and unreflective. "Civilization," he wrote, "is the term we apply to those aspects of culture which have been generalised, rationalised, and are generally intelligible." Persons of diverse cultures could share a common civilization to the extent that they recognised overarching common interests, and submitted their differences to discussion and agreed procedural rules.

One of Park's most important concepts was that of the "marginal man," the person on the border between mutually hostile or competitive groups. He substituted this term for such pejorative expressions as "halfbreed" or "rootless cosmopolite" because he saw marginality as a positive condition. "The marginal man," he wrote, is "the individual with a wider horizon, the keener intelligence, the more detached and rational viewpoint...always relatively the more civilized human being." Park also saw himself as marginal, particularly in relation to the academic community. He did not become a teacher until he was nearly fifty, and had no established academic post until he was appointed Professor at the University of Chicago in 1923. His preparation was equally atypical. His formal education was by his own choice intermittent, and although he studied with many of the great figures of his day—with John Dewey (*q.v.*) at Ann Arbor, with William James (*q.v.*) at Harvard, with Georg Simmel (*q.v.*) in Germany—he never signed on as a career academic. He was a newspaperman for some years, and later became Booker T. Washington's secretary and ghostwriter. He thus brought to sociology a sense of concrete experience and involvement—while at the same time, perhaps paradoxically, perhaps of necessity (given his closeness to events), he cultivated an ironic detachment from ideologies and "causes." In stimulating and shaping discussion of the realities of social difference he was contributing to the creation of a realistic civilization.

Park was called by his biographer Fred H. Matthews an "entrepreneur of research"; his most important work was done by his collaborators and students—who included Ernest Burgess (*q.v.*), Robert Redfield (*q.v.*), W.I. Thomas (*q.v.*), and Louis Wirth (*q.v.*). He was more important as a teacher than as a writer (although he wrote a great deal), as an informal observer than as a practitioner of formal research (although he stimulated the creation of research instruments), as an inquirer than as a theoretician (although he was constantly sketching theoretical frameworks around his inquiries). Park opened a field by revealing much that was interesting, important, and potentially intelligible; his vocation was suggestions, not conclusions. He set a tone which has survived him by insisting that those who wish to understand some aspect of society must go and look. He brought to the work a restless energetic curiosity, not a finished method;

he was indeed the founder of a science who distrusted the pretensions of science. At the end of his life he wrote: "According to my earliest conception...a sociologist...was to be a kind of superreporter. He was to report a little more accurately, and in a manner more detached than the average...the 'Big News'...the long-time trends...what is actually going on rather than what, on the surface of things, merely seems to be going on."

—James Redfield

PARSONS, Talcott. American sociologist. Born in Colorado Springs, Colorado, 13 December 1902. Educated at Colorado Springs High School; Horace Mann School, New York, graduated 1920; Amherst College, Massachusetts, A.B. 1924 (Phi Beta Kappa); London School of Economics, 1924-25; University of Heidelberg, 1925-26, Dr. of Phil. 1927. Consultant, Foreign Economic Administration, 1944-46. Married Helen Bancroft Walker in 1927; 3 children. Instructor in Economics, Amherst College, 1926-27; Instructor of Economics, 1927-31, and of Sociology, 1931-36, Assistant Professor, 1936-39, Associate Professor, 1939-44, staff member of School for Overseas Administration, 1943-46, Professor of Sociology, 1944-73, then Emeritus, Chairman of the Department, 1944-46, and Chairman of the Department of Social Relations, 1946-56, all at Harvard University, Cambridge, Massachusetts. Visiting Professor, Columbia University, New York, summers 1933, 1935, University of Chicago, 1937, 1971, 1972, Cambridge University, 1953-54, and University of Pennsylvania, Philadelphia, 1973-74; Fellow, Center for Advanced Study in the Behavioral Sciences, Stanford, California, 1957-58. President, Eastern Sociological Society, 1941-42, and American Sociological Association, 1949. Recipient: Guggenheim fellowship, 1966. L.H.D.: Amherst College, 1949; Dr.rev.pol.: University of Cologne, 1963; LL.D.: University of Chicago, 1967; University of Pennsylvania, 1974; D.Social Sci.: Boston College, 1968; D.Phil.: Hebrew University of Jerusalem, 1972; D.Arts: Stonehill College, North Easton, Massachusetts, 1974. Honorary Fellow, Trinity Hall, Cambridge, 1974, and London School of Economics; Corresponding Member, British Academy. President, American Academy of Arts and Sciences, 1967-71. *Died 8 May 1979.*

PUBLICATIONS

Sociology

The Structure of a Social Action: A Study in Social Theory with Special Reference to a Group of Recent European Writers. New York, McGraw Hill, 1937.
Social Science: A Basic National Resource. New York, Social Science Research Council, 1948.
Essays in Sociological Theory, Pure and Applied. Glencoe, Illinois, Free Press, 1949; revised edition, 1954.
Religious Perspectives of College Teaching in Sociology and Social Psychology. New Haven, Connecticut, Hazan Foundation, 1951(?).
The Social System. Glencoe, Illinois, Free Press, 1951; London, Tavistock, 1952.
Working Papers in the Theory of Action, with Robert F. Bales and Edward A. Shils. Glencoe, Illinois, Free Press, 1953.
Family, Socialization, and Interaction Process, with others. Glencoe, Illinois, Free Press, 1955; London, Routledge, 1956.
Economy and Society: A Study in the Integration of Economic and Social Theory, with Neil J. Smelser. Glencoe, Illinois, Free Press, and London, Routledge, 1956.
Structure and Process in Modern Societies. Glencoe, Illinois, Free Press, 1960.

Social Structure and Personality. New York, Free Press, 1964.

Societies: Evolutionary and Comparative Perspectives. Englewood Cliffs, New Jersey, Prentice Hall, 1966.

Sociological Theory and Modern Society. New York, Free Press, 1967.

Politics and Social Structure. New York, Free Press, 1969.

The System of Modern Societies. Englewood Cliffs, New Jersey, Prentice Hall, 1971.

The American University, with Gerald Platt. Cambridge, Massachusetts, Harvard University Press, 1973.

The Evolution of Societies, edited by Jackson Toby. Englewood Cliffs, New Jersey, Prentice Hall, 1977.

Social Systems and the Evolution of Action Theory. New York, Free Press, 1977.

Zur Theorie sozialen Handelns: Ein Briefwechsel, with Alfred Schütz, edited by Walter M. Sprondel: Frankfurt, Suhrkamp, 1977; as *The Theory of Social Action: The Correspondence of Alfred Schütz and Talcott Parsons*, edited by Richard Grathoff, Bloomington, Indiana University Press, 1978.

Action Theory and the Human Condition. New York, Free Press, 1978.

Other

Editor, and Translator with A.M. Henderson, *The Theory of Social and Economic Organization*, by Max Weber. New York, Oxford University Press, 1947.

Editor, with Edward A. Shils, *Toward a General Theory of Action.* Cambridge, Massachusetts, Harvard University Press, 1951.

Editor, with others, *Theories of Society: Foundations of Modern Sociological Theory.* New York, Free Press, 2 vols., 1961.

Editor, with Kenneth B. Clark, *The Negro American.* Boston, Houghton Mifflin, 1966.

Editor, *American Sociology: Perspectives, Problems, Methods.* New York, Basic Books, 1968.

Editor, with Victor Lidz, *Readings on Premodern Societies.* Englewood Cliffs, New Jersey, Prentice Hall, 1972.

Translator, *The Protestant Ethic and the Spirit of Capitalism*, by Max Weber. New York, Scribner, and London, Allen and Unwin, 1930.

*

Critical Studies: *The Social Theories of Talcott Parsons* edited by Max Black, Englewood Cliffs, New Jersey, Prentice Hall, 1961; *Sociological Analysis and Politics: The Theories of Talcott Parsons* by William C. Mitchell, Englewood Cliffs, New Jersey, Prentice Hall, 1967; *Institutions and Social Exchange: The Sociologies of Talcott Parsons and George C. Homans* edited by Herman Turk and Richard L. Simpson, Indianapolis, Bobbs Merrill, 1971; *Stability and Social Change* (essays in honor of Parsons) edited by Bernard Barber and Alex Inkeles, Boston, Little Brown, 1971; *Talcott Parsons and American Sociology* by Guy Rocher, London, Nelson, 1974; *Functionalism in Modern Sociology: Understanding Talcott Parsons* by Benton Johnson, Morristown, New Jersey, General Learning Press, 1975; *Explorations in General Theory in Social Science: Essays in Honor of Talcott Parsons* edited by Jan J. Loubser, New York, Free Press, 2 vols., 1976; *The Social Theories of Talcott Parsons: A Critical Examination* edited by Max Black, Carbondale, Southern Illinois University Press, 1976; *Talcott Parsons and the Social Image of Man* by Ken Menzies, London, Routledge, 1977; *Talcott Parsons and the Conceptual Dilemma* by Hans P.M. Adriaansens, London, Routledge, 1980; *The Sociology of Talcott Parsons* by François Bourricaud, Chicago, University of Chicago Press, 1981; *The Theories of Talcott Parsons: The Social Relations of Action* by Stephen P. Savage, London, Macmillan, 1981.

*   *   *

Talcott Parsons was a major American sociological theorist and teacher, and a principal adaptor of German sociology to American social science. Parsons has described his theoretical ideas as refining, integrating, and incorporating major themes from Max Weber, Emile Durkheim, Immanuel Kant, George Herbert Mead, Alfred Marshall, Vilfredo Pareto, and Sigmund Freud, among others. But such a lengthy list is in a sense misleading. His most basic ideas come mainly from Weber, Pareto, and the Vienna Circle positivists and their American successors including W.V.O. Quine.

By his own account, Parsons moved from economics to sociology after almost accidentally encountering the work of Max Weber. He translated the first of three books of Weber's *Economy and Community* into English in 1930 as *The Protestant Ethic and the Spirit of Capitalism.* Weber's aim had been to provide an anti-Marxist synthesis of sociology and neo-classical economics. He described his theoretical focus as "action," individual and collective, that was meaningful to those who engaged in it. His approach to this action was based on two basic dominant ideas: religious determinism and the concept of the "ideal type." The religious determinism was based on the idea that a religious creed engendered an "ethic" or general outlook toward oneself and others, that in turn shaped the economic ideas and behaviors of the believers. Calvin's theology generated a "Protestant ethic" that in turn generated a rational, disciplined, self-reliant attitude that Weber considered "the spirit of capitalism." Judaism, by contrast, generated "pariah capitalism" and Catholicism produced "anticipatory capitalism." The "ideal type" was an ambiguous notion. It meant both such a set of ideas that people accepted, but at the same time it meant the analyst's own *hypothetical* conception or model. As a hypothesis, ideal types were consistently defended as logical or scientific necessities, even though they were not literally accurate descriptions in fact. Yet they were still held to be what other people accepted, a fundamental paradox that runs throughout Weber's arguments. All these ideas, and their problems, were taken over by Parsons. But Parsons rephrased Weber's concept of ideal types and the need for them in the language of legal positivism, and this let him abstract the core of Weber's theory while putting more distance between himself and Weber's factual claims, and while claiming even more generality than Weber had himself.

The broad plan of Parsons's work, a sociological theory framed and justified by a positivistic philosophy of science, evidently owes much to Pareto, but Parsons's explicitly philosophical assumptions were drawn more from the logical positivist's plan for the reconstruction of science by means of the "logical integration" of its statements. Parsons accepted the positivist's dichotomous distinction between statements which were purely abstract and "analytic" and those which were "synthetic" and descriptive. Only the former (following an old argument of Locke) could be true in general, by virtue of the meaning of the terms themselves, although they had no empirical content. On this basis, the positivists construed the sciences as sets of statements, and proposed to improve and integrate science by providing a still more general language, from which all the various present sciences might be derived as more particular cases by logical implication. Parsons's aim was to integrate social science following the same plan. The concept of theory itself was set out in an essay titled "The Present Position and Future Prospects of Systematic Theory in Sociology" (1945; collected in *Essays in Sociological Theory*, 1949):

"Theory" is a term which covers a wide variety of different things which have in common only the element of generalized conceptualization.... A theoretical system in the present sense is a body of logically interdependent generalized concepts of empirical reference. Such a system tends, ideally, to become "logically closed," to reach such a state of logical integration that every logical implication of any combination of propositions in the system is explicitly stated in some other proposition in the same system.

Parsons's method was to survey existing theories and provide a more abstract phrasing of those he approved of within which to rephrase them. His theory thus consisted of a progressively more elaborate "conceptual scheme" logically circular in its very nature. His revised and abstracted version of Weber's concept of socially formed action was the heart of the system: "In the nature of the case, within the frame of reference of action, such a conceptual scheme must focus on the delineation of the system of institutionalized roles and the motivational process organized around them" (*The Social System*). In *Toward a General Theory of Action*, edited with Edward Shils, the social system was conversely said to consist "in actions of individuals." Yet again, action is not organized around the physical individual but rather around the social role as an idea. It is "the conceptual unit of the social system," and consists in a "complementary set of expectations and the actions to be performed in accordance with these expectations." The values attached to the roles were also the values of collectivities. In effect, collectivities were defined only as coordinated sets of roles. Thus, "the primary integration of the social system is based on an integrated system of generalized patterns of value orientation."

Defining collectivities only through value orientations, given the rest of the system, suggested that they did not exist when no one was acting out their roles, as though, for example, a court system existed only when an actual judge was actually sitting or a family existed only when its members were enacting their perspective roles. This problem was partially addressed by Parsons's concept of a "boundary," which was apparently a role differentiation between insiders and outsiders invoked when action was underway: "The concept of a boundary is of crucial significance in the definition of a collectivity. The boundary of a collectivity is that criterion whereby some persons are included as members and others excluded as non-members.... Thus the boundary is defined in terms of membership roles." For the times when action was not underway, Parsons adapted the psychoanalytic distinction between latent and manifest symptoms: "The solidarity of a collectivity may, therefore, be latent as long as certain types of situations which would activate them fail to arise." Whether it makes sense to speak of a court system as "latent" after hours is of course debatable.

The concepts of actor, value, and collectivity are exceedingly vague. The largest portion of Parsons's written work, often in collaboration with others, was devoted to classifying types of collectivities, roles, situations, values, and motives without losing generality. The qualifications inserted in these specifications to save the scheme from empirical attack create consistent interpretive problems, and ultimately drive it to a kind of solipsism reminiscent of Alice's caterpillar: the words mean what one wants them to mean. The classifications used two major devices: the distinction of "analytic levels" and the distinction of "functional categories" of values, needs, or goals. The segregation of levels mainly reflected the common-sense idea that organizations that encompassed others were "higher," as were those that involved relatively many people compared to those that involved few. Thus at the lowest level, one had the individual personality. At higher levels one had the family, "the economy" or "the political system," and finally "a society."

Applying the idea of the theoretical necessity of logically closed systems of definitions, goals were classified by the repeated use of paired dichotomies, creating four-way categories. There were two major dichotomies, called "pattern variables," each supposedly representing a universal or logical dilemma in the choice of possible goal orientations. These were universalism versus particularism and performance versus ascription. In combination, they defined the four "functional problems" for any system, which in turn defined four "functional subsystems" of any system. For example, the "adaptive" problem of any system in adjusting to its external environment was met by action on the basis of universal and performance oriented criteria; the problem of ordering behavior internally with respect to the goals of the collectivity required universal ascriptive action, and so on. The dichotomies were vague, and their combinations were much more vague still. The cloudiness was further compounded by the consistent assertion that the scheme applied both to whole institutions and to aspects of institutions: the economy was the adaptive portion of society, yet within economic institutions one could still discern all four functions.

Parsons's overall scheme, as it developed over time, was much too complex to review here in its entirety, but the most important point is that to defend it he constantly fell back not on evidence but on his philosophy of science itself, and its major historical impact was to publicize and promulgate this philosophy far more widely than its philosophical proponents had ever been able to do. It was very largely through Parsons that the positivists' conception of science became the basic intellectual foundation for the Harvard School of Social Relations, and through its graduates in the 1950's and 1960's it became virtually the received wisdom for the dominant section of sociology and for a very important segment of anthropology.

—Murray J. Leaf

PAULI, Wolfgang (Ernst). German physicist. Born in Vienna, 25 April 1900. Studied at the University of Munich, Ph.D. 1921. Married Franciska Bertram in 1934. Assistant, University of Göttingen, 1921-22, and University of Copenhagen, 1922-23; Lecturer, University of Hamburg, 1923-28; Professor of Theoretical Physics, Eidgenössliche Technische Hochschule, Zurich, 1928-58; Visiting Professor of Theoretical Physics, Institute for Advanced Study, Princeton, New Jersey, 1935-36, 1940-45, 1949-50, 1954. Recipient: Lorentz Medal, 1930; Nobel Prize in Physics, 1945; Franklin Medal, Franklin Institute, Philadelphia, 1952; Max Planck Medal, 1958. Member, American Academy of Arts and Sciences. Foreign Member, Royal Society, London. *Died 15 December 1958.*

PUBLICATIONS

Physics

"Relativitätstheorie," in *Encyklopädie der mathematischen Wissenschaft.* Leipzig, 1921; as *Theory of Relativity*, Oxford and New York, Pergamon Press, 1958.
Meson Theory of Nuclear Forces. New York, Interscience, 1947.
Exclusion Principle and Quantum Mechanics (Nobel Lecture). Neuchâtel, Editions du Griffon, 1947.
Vorlesung über Optik und Elektromentheorie. Zurich, ETH, 1948; as *Optics and the Theory of Electrons*, edited by Charles P. Enz, Cambridge, Massachusetts Institute of Technology, 1973.
Ausgewahlte Kapitel aus der Feldquantisierung. Zurich, H. Maag, 1951; as *Selected Topics in Field Quantization*, edited by Charles P. Enz, Cambridge, Massachusetts Institute of Technology, 1973.
Gekürtzte Vorlesung über statistische Mechanik. Zurich, ETH, 1951.
Vorlesung über statistische Mechanik. Zurich, ETH, 1951; as *Statistical Mechanics*, edited by Charles P. Enz, Cambridge, Massachusetts Institute of Technology, 1973.
On the Mathematical Structure of T.D. Lee's Model of a Renormalizable Field Theory, with Gunnar Källén. Copenhagen, I Kommission hos Munksgaard, 1955.
Lectures on Continuous and Reflections in Quantum Mechanics.

Berkeley, University of California Radiation Laboratory, 1958.

Vorlesung über Elektrodynamik. Zurich, ETH, 1958; as *Electrodynamics*, edited by Charles Enz, Cambridge, Massachusetts Institute of Technology, 1973.

Prinzipien der Quantentheorie, with Gunnar Källén. Berlin, Springer, 1958.

Vorlesung über Thermodynamik und kinetische Gastheorie. Zurich, ETH, 1958; as *Thermodynamics and the Kinetic Theory of Gases*, edited by Charles P. Enz, Cambridge, Massachusetts Institute of Technology, 1973.

Vorlesung über Wellenmechanik. Zurich, ETH, 1959; as *Wave Mechanics*, edited by Charles P. Enz, Cambridge, Massachusetts Institute of Technology, 1973.

Ausätze und Vorträge über Physik und Erkenntnistheorie. Braunschweig, Vieweg, 1961.

Collected Scientific Papers. New York, Interscience, 2 vols., 1964.

Vierpoltheorie und ihre Anwendung auf elektronische Schaltengen. Berlin, Akademie Verlag, 1974.

Fünf Arbeiten zum Ausschliessungsprinzip und zum Neutrino. Darmstadt, Wissenschaftliche Buchgesellschaft, 1977.

Scientific Correspondence with Bohr, Einstein, Heisenberg and Others, edited by A. Hermann. New York, Springer, 1979.

Other

Editor, *Niels Bohr and the Development of Physics*. London, Pergamon Press, and New York, McGraw Hill, 1955.

*   *   *

Wolfgang Pauli's first post-doctoral experimental work involved a study of the Zeeman effect. This phenomenon, observed when light is passed through strong magnetic fields, provides evidence about the nature of electrons within an atom. For Pauli, the research threw him into the most exciting and fundamental issue in contemporary physical science: What is the nature of the electrons in an atom?

That question had become a primary issue upon Rutherford's discovery of the nuclear atom. His model, Rutherford admitted, corresponded to the results of his "gold foil" experiment, but raised difficult questions about the location of electrons in an atom. According to the nuclear model he proposed, electrons in an atom should radiate energy continuously and fall into the nucleus. The laws of classical physics seemed to offer no alternative to this self-destructive character of his newly discovered nuclear atom.

Niels Bohr's bold attempt to apply quantum theory to the Rutherford model "worked" in the sense that it provided an answer to the Rutherford dilemma. If there exist specified "orbits" in an atom in which electrons can move *without* radiating energy, then the nuclear atom can exist. But how do electrons assign themselves to these "permitted" orbits?

Bohr answered that question on a purely empirical basis. Noting that elements within the same family in the periodic table had similar chemical properties, he assumed that the atoms of which those elements are composed would also have similar electronic structures. On this basis, he assigned certain maximum numbers of electrons to each of his "permitted" orbits: two to the first, eight to the second, and so on. He had no theoretical basis for making these assignments, but, as with the concept of "permitted orbits" itself, was gratified to find that the concept "worked."

Within a decade, a sound theoretical basis for Bohr's model was evolving. By the early 1920's, it was apparent that each electron in an atom possessed at least three characteristic properties: (1) a distinct radial distance from the nucleus, (2) an orbit with a particular elliptical shape, and (3) a particular orientation within the weak magnetic field of the atom. These three properties were identified by three quantum numbers: n (principal quantum number), l (orbital quantum number), and m (magnetic quantum number), respectively.

The three quantum numbers were not randomly available to an electron, but were related to each other in specified, mathematical ways. Any electron in the first shell of an atom ($n = 1$), for example, could also have l and m quantum numbers of zero only. An electron in the second shell ($n = 2$) could have quantum numbers $l = 1$ or 0 and $m = +1, -1,$ or 0 (for $l = 1$) or $m = 0$ (for $l = 0$).

Pauli's contribution to the evolving concept of the electron was to recognize the existence of yet a fourth property of electrons. His studies of the Zeeman effect led him to conclude that each electron also possessed the property of *spin*. To electrons with clockwise spin, he assigned a *spin quantum number* of $+\frac{1}{2}$; to those with a counter-clockwise spin, he assigned a spin quantum number of $-\frac{1}{2}$.

Thus, any electron could be described by listing its four quantum numbers: n, its distance from the nucleus; l, the shape of its orbit; m, its orientation in the magnetic field of the atom; and s, the direction of its spin. Pauli next offered a bold theoretical proposal. The set of quantum numbers for any one electron in an atom, he said, is *unique*. No two electrons in an atom may have the same set of quantum numbers. This proposal came to be called the Pauli Exclusion Principle.

The Exclusion Principle made possible a truly rational explanation of the ordering of electrons in various atoms. Consider the case of lithium, with three electrons. Two of these electrons may be assigned to the first shell, with quantum numbers $n = 1$ (first shell), $l = 0$, $m = 0$, $s = \pm\frac{1}{2}$. These are the only possible quantum number combinations for $n = 1$. The third electron *must*, therefore, appear in the second orbit, with principal quantum number, $n, = 2$. The Exclusion Principle prohibits the repeat of any of the $n = 1$ combinations given above, and no other combinations are mathematically permissible.

By the logical application of the Exclusion Principle to atoms with successively greater numbers of electrons, the electronic configurations of these atoms can be determined. When that has been done, atomic structures that correspond to empirical evidence and to Bohr models result. The Pauli Exclusion Principle provides, that is, a theoretical explanation for the periodic law.

Pauli's work was linked with that of Bohr again within the decade. On this occasion, the subject was the beta decay of radioactive materials. Careful studies of energy changes in this process had produced disturbing results. The energy carried away by beta particles during radioactive decay was consistently less than that which had been predicted on the basis of conservation laws. No explanation for this "missing energy" had been offered and some physicists, Bohr among them, were almost willing to give up on conservation laws for this form of radioactivity. That concession was no small one for Bohr to make since conservation of mass, energy and charge lie at the very foundations of modern science. But, for a while, there seemed to be no option.

Then, in 1930, Pauli suggested that the laws could be saved by assuming that a second particle, later named the *neutrino* by Enrico Fermi, was emitted along with a beta particle during decay. The particle could have no mass and no charge, but by postulating its existence, Pauli was able to show where the "missing energy" had gone.

The hypothesis was a bold one, and many physicists preferred to consider abandoning the conservation laws rather than admitting to a massless, chargeless particle which, conceivably, one could never actually find. Yet the preponderance of opinion finally fell on Pauli's side and, for the next generation, the presence of neutrinos in beta decay was customarily assumed. The actual discovery of the neutrino in an elaborate experiment in 1956, two years before Pauli's death, was a satisfying justification of this 25 year old prediction.

—David Newton

PAULING, Linus (Carl). American chemist. Born in Portland, Oregon, 28 February 1901. Studied at Oregon State Agricultural College, Corvallis, B.S. 1922; California Institute of Technology, Pasadena, Ph.D. 1925. Married Ava Helen Miller in 1923; 4 children. Teaching Fellow, 1922-25, Research Fellow, 1925-27, Assistant Professor, 1927-29, Associate Professor, 1929-31, and Professor of Chemistry, 1931-64, California Institute of Technology (Chairman, Division of Chemistry and Chemical Engineering, and Director of Gates and Crellin Laboratories of Chemistry, 1936-58; Member, Executive Council, Board of Trustees, 1945-48); Research Professor, Center for the Study of Democratic Institutions, Santa Barbara, California, 1963-67; Professor of Chemistry, University of California at San Diego, 1967-69; Professor of Chemistry, Stanford University, California, 1969-74. Since 1973, President and Research Professor, Linus Pauling Institute of Science and Medicine, Palo Alto, California. George Eastman Professor, Oxford University, 1948. Recipient: National Research Council Fellowship, 1925; Guggenheim Fellowship, 1926; United States Presidential Medal for Merit, 1948; Nobel Prize in Chemistry, 1954; Nobel Peace Prize, 1962; International Lenin Peace Prize, 1972; Medal with Laurel Wreath, International Grotius Foundation, 1975; Lomonosov Medal, 1978; National Academy of Sciences Medal in Chemical Science, 1979. Honorary doctorate: Oregon State Agricultural College, 1933; University of Chicago, 1941; Princeton University, New Jersey, 1946; Cambridge University, 1947; University of London, 1947; Yale University, New Haven, Connecticut, 1947; Oxford University, 1948; University of Paris, 1948; University of New Brunswick, Fredericton, 1959; University of Tampa, Florida, 1950; Brooklyn Polytechnic Institute, 1955; University of Montpellier, 1958; Humboldt University, Arcata, California, 1959; Reed College, Portland, Oregon, 1959; University of Melbourne, 1964; Jagiellonian University, 1964; University of Delhi, 1967; Adelphi University, Garden City, New York, 1967; Marquette University School of Medicine, Milwaukee, 1969. Fellow, Balliol College, Oxford, 1948. Address: Linus Pauling Institute of Science and Medicine, 44 Page Mill Road, Palo Alto, California 94306, U.S.A.

PUBLICATIONS

Chemistry

The Structure of Line Spectra, with Samuel Goudsmit. New York, McGraw Hill, 1930.
Introduction to Quantum Mechanics, with Applications to Chemistry, with E. Bright Wilson, Jr. New York, McGraw Hill, 1935.
The Nature of the Chemical Bond and the Structure of Molecules and Crystals: An Introduction to Modern Structural Chemistry. Ithaca, New York, Cornell University Press, 1940.
General Chemistry: An Introduction to Descriptive Chemistry and Modern Chemical Theory. San Francisco, Freeman, 1947.
College Chemistry: An Introductory Textbook of General Chemistry. San Francisco, Freeman, 1950.
The Architecture of Molecules, with Roger Hayward. San Francisco, Freeman, 1964.
Science and Peace: The Nobel Peace Prize Lecture. Santa Barbara, California, Center for the Study of Democratic Institutions, 1964.
The Challenge of Scientific Discovery (lecture). Los Angeles, City College Press, 1967.
Science and World Peace (lectures). New Delhi, Indian Council for Cultural Relations, 1967.
The Chemical Bond: A Brief Introduction to Modern Structural Chemistry. Ithaca, New York, Cornell University Press, 1967.
Structural Chemistry and Molecular Biology, edited by Alexander Rich and Norman Davidson, 1968.
Vitamin C and the Common Cold. San Francisco, Freeman, 1970.
Chemistry, with Peter Pauling. San Francisco, Freeman, 1975.
Cancer and Vitamin C: A Discussion of the Nature, Causes, Prevention, and Treatment of Cancer, with Special Reference to the Value of Vitamin C, with Ewan Cameron. Menlo Park, California, Linus Pauling Institute of Science and Medicine, 1979.

Other

No More War! New York, Dodd Mead, and London, Gollancz, 1958.
The Greatest Experience: The Abolition of War. Boston, Department of Adult Programs for the Unitarian Universalist Association, 1964.

Editor, with Harvey A. Itano, *Molecular Structure and Biological Specificity.* Washington, D.C., American Institute of Biological Sciences, 1957.
Editor, with David Hawkins, *Orthomolecular Psychiatry: Treatment of Schizophrenia.* San Francisco, Freeman, 1973.

*   *   *

The theoretical basis for chemical science, to which Linus Pauling turned his attention in 1926, was in a state of flux at some crucial points. The work of Rutherford, Bohr, Soddy, Schrödinger, Chadwick, and others had provided a reasonably satisfactory model of the atom itself. The quantum mechanics of Pauli, Planck, de Broglie, and Dirac promised an even sounder understanding of atomic structure in the near future. But a second fundamental question in chemistry—how do atoms combine with each other?—had been addressed with only moderate success. G.N. Lewis had recently proposed a model for chemical bonding in which two atoms shared a pair of electrons between them. This notion of covalent bonding offered an alternative to the older model of ionic bonding originally developed by Abegg in 1904.

The problem with both the Lewis and Abegg models, however, was their static character. Atoms were treated in both theories as essentially stationary systems, with electrons at rest in specific locations outside the atomic nucleus. As attractive and/or successful as these models appeared, they were obviously (1) out of touch with the current understanding of atoms which was then being developed by physicists, and, more to the point, (2) wrong.

Pauling's greatest contribution to chemical theory was his resolution of the problem of chemical bonding. He brought together incomplete and previously unrelated ideas from chemistry and quantum mechanics to fashion the basic ideas behind our modern theories of chemical bonding.

Pauling's technique was to examine the ways in which electron waves in two interacting atoms might combine with each other. He found that the overlapping wave patterns of some combinations result in a molecular structure that contains less energy than do the atomic structures of the reactants themselves. The molecule formed in this way is, therefore, energetically more stable than the combination of atoms of which it is formed. The synthesis of the molecule from its component atoms results in the release of energy (the excess of molecular energy less energy of reactant atoms). This provides a simple explanation of the well-known empirical observation that most chemical reactions in which compounds are formed from elements are exothermic reactions.

Pauling went further to point out that the wave patterns used to describe electrons in a neutral atom are not necessarily (or even probably) the patterns they assume during the process of bonding. Instead, the electrons are likely to rearrange themselves in an energetically more favorable way as bonding (that is, the overlap with electron waves from other atoms) takes place. Pauling called this process *hybridization*, highlighting its analogy with the cross-breeding of farm animals of different types.

Finally, Pauling suggested that the formation of even the simplest chemical bond is a far more complex process than had hitherto been imagined. The overlap of electron orbitals might, in any specific instance, occur in a number of different ways. The bond which actually formed in such a case represents some "weighted average" of all these conceivable cases. This concept is known as *resonance*. Its most striking success has probably been in explaining the structure of the benzene molecule. Benzene possesses a molecular structure that corresponds poorly with its chemical properties, and chemists had been singularly unsuccessful in explaining this anomaly for over a century. Pauling showed that describing benzene in terms of traditional single and double bonds was not effective. Instead, he suggested that the electrons provided by carbon and hydrogen atoms in the benzene molecule are shared more or less equally by all atoms in the molecule. He adapted the concept of resonance to describe hybrid bonds that were neither single nor double bonds in the benzene structure.

The latter part of Pauling's career has been devoted to studies of complex biochemical molecules. He has been particularly interested in the three-dimensional configuration of these macromolecules. In 1950, he and Robert B. Corey showed that the "alpha" form characteristic of a great many protein molecules actually corresponds to a helical structure in which portions of the helix are held in place by hydrogen bonds. This discovery led Pauling to suspect that other biochemical molecules—most particularly, those of nucleic acids—might also exist in helical forms. Confirmation of this hypothesis was obtained in 1953 by Watson and Crick. It seems that inadequate X-ray diffraction data may have been all that stood between Pauling and his making this most momentous discovery.

Pauling's interest in biochemical molecules led to the recognition, in 1949, of the molecular basis of the disease known as sickle-cell anemia. Pauling found that patients with the disease carried hemoglobin molecules that differ from those of normal individuals in only a single amino acid in the complex protein molecule. This discovery was an important step in recognizing the chemical basis for certain genetic diseases.

In recent years, Pauling has been especially interested in the therapeutic use of vitamin C in treating the common cold. Politely ignored by most of the scientific community, Pauling has nonetheless contiued to argue for the benefits of massive doses of the vitamin in the treatment of this ailment.

—David Newton

PEIRCE, Charles (Santiago) Sanders. American philosopher. Born in Cambridge, Massachusetts, 10 September 1839; son of the mathematician Benjamin Peirce. Studied at Harvard University, Cambridge, Massachusetts, B.A. 1859, M.A. 1862, Sc.B. 1863. Married Harriet Melusina Fay in 1862 (divorced, 1883); married Juliette Froissy in 1884. Worked for the United States Coastal and Geodetic Service, 1861-91 (special assistant in gravity research, 1884-91). Lecturer in Logic, Johns Hopkins University, Baltimore, 1879-84. Reviewer for the *Nation*. Died (in Milford, Pennsylvania) *19 April 1914*.

PUBLICATIONS

Collections

Collected Papers of Charles Sanders Peirce, edited by Charles Hartshorne and Paul Weiss (vols. 1-6) and Arthur W. Burks (vols. 7-8). Cambridge, Massachusetts, Harvard University

Press, 8 vols., 1931-58.
The Writings of Charles S. Peirce: A Chronological Edition, edited by Max Fisch. Bloomington, Indiana University Press, 1982-.

Philosophy and Philosophy of Science

Photometric Researches, Made in the Years 1872-1875. Cambridge, Massachusetts, Annals of the Astronomical Observatory of Harvard College, 1878.
Chance, Love, and Logic: Philosophical Essays by the Late Charles S. Peirce, the Founder of Pragmatism, edited by Morris R. Cohen. New York, Harcourt Brace, and London, Kegan Paul, 1923.
The Philosophy of Peirce: Selected Writings, edited by Justus Buchler. New York, Harcourt Brace, and London, Kegan Paul, 1940.
Charles S. Peirce's Letters to Lady Welby, edited by Irwin C. Lieb. New Haven, Connecticut, Whitlock's, 1953.
Essays in the Philosophy of Science, edited by Vincent Tomas. New York, Liberal Arts Press, 1957.
Values in a Universe of Chance: Selected Writings of Charles Sanders Peirce, edited by Philip Wiener. Stanford, California, Stanford University Press, 1958.
Semiotics and Significs: The Correspondence Between Charles S. Peirce and Victoria Lady Welby, edited by Charles S. Hardwick and James Cook. Bloomington, Indiana University Press, 1977.

*

Bibliography: *Annotated Catalogue of the Papers of Charles S. Peirce* by Richard Robin, Amherst, University of Massachusetts Press, 1967; *A Comprehensive Bibliography and Index of the Published Works of Charles Sanders Peirce, with a Bibliography of Secondary Sources* by Keith Laine Ketner and others, Greenwich, Connecticut, Johnson Associates, 1977.

Critical Studies: *The Thought of C.S. Peirce* by Thomas Goudge, Toronto, University of Toronto Press, 1950; *Studies in the Philosophy of Charles Sanders Peirce* edited by Philip P. Wiener and Frederick H. Young, Cambridge, Massachusetts, Harvard University Press, 1952, *Second Series* edited by Edward C. Moore and Richard S. Rubin, Amherst, University of Massachusetts Press, 1964; *Peirce and Pragmatism* by W.B. Gallie, London, Penguin, 1952; *The Pragmatic Philosophy of C.S. Peirce* by Manley Thompson, Chicago, University of Chicago Press, 1953; *The Development of Peirce's Philosophy* by Murray Murphy, Cambridge, Massachusetts, Harvard University Press, 1961; *Peirce's Philosophy of Science* by Nicholas Rescher, Notre Dame, Indiana, University of Notre Dame Press, 1978; *The Road of Inquiry* by Peter Skagestad, New York, Columbia University Press, 1981; *Charles S. Peirce: From Pragmatism to Pragmatism* by Karl-Otto Apee, Amherst, University of Massachusetts Press, 1981.

*   *   *

Charles Sanders Peirce was probably the most significant American philosopher and, more generally, one of the most creative philosophers of the post-Kantian era. His work was systematic in nature (although not in form) and ranged over all the areas of philosophy from logic to aesthetics. Although most of Peirce's work was unpublished in his life-time, a partial edition of his collected papers was published in eight volumes by Harvard University Press from 1931 to 1958. There is presently underway a more complete chronological edition of his papers (projected at 22 volumes) under the general editorship of Max Fisch from Indiana University Press.

Although there has been much discussion of the internal inconsistency of Peirce's various philosophical views and their changing development throughout his life, there are two themes (one negative, one positive) that remain constant in Peirce's thought and provide the key to his distinctive philosophical perspective. On the negative side there is his critique of Cartesianism. From the earliest papers to the latest there is a sustained critique of foundationalism in epistemology, internalism in the philosophy of mind, and dualism in metaphysics. On the positive side there is his attempt to replace this Cartesian picture of knowledge and the world by a construal of human inquiry which is through and through fallible in its particulars but yet is marked by a continual progression toward a true understanding of the world.

The *locus classicus* for Peirce's critique of Cartesianism are his 1868 papers on cogniton (*Collected Papers* 5). Epistemologically, these papers contain an attack on the foundational picture of knowledge, namely, the view that in order for there to be any genuine knowledge at all there must be some self-authenticating, non-inferential instances of knowledge (called "intuitions") which epistemically ground the whole cognitive edifice. Peirce saw this view as involving three distinct claims: (1) there are self-authenticating, non-inferential units of knowledge; (2) these privileged instances can be infallibly recognized as such so as to be able to function in grounding other knowledge claims; and (3) without some instances functioning in this way, knowledge would have no foundation and skepticism would ensue.

Peirce objected to all three theses. Focusing on the second one first, he argued that even if we have these alleged "intuitions," we seem to have no intuitive power of distinguishing such intuitions from other cognitions with the result that they can not be reliably identified so as to play their distinctive role in grounding our other beliefs. Moreover, moving on to the first thesis of the foundationalist, he argued that we don't in fact have any intuitions. All instances of knowledge have an inferential structure. To dislodge foundationalism all that remains for Peirce is to come to grips with the third thesis, namely, the transcendental argument that there must be such intuitions if we are to avoid total skepticism. He argues against this that coming to know is a continuous process whose reliability does not depend on the epistemic status of the starting point but rather on the self-corrective character of the process itself.

These same papers contain a sustained critique of a related facet of Cartesianism, namely, its internalism (or introspectivism) in the philosophy of mind. The Cartesian alleges a direct introspective access to mental processes such that his understanding of them need not be conceptually tied to any reference to the external world. Accordingly, taking thinking as a paradigmatic mental activity, thought can be understood directly and language understood as an expression of thought with the mentalistic features of language such as intentionality seen as analogical extensions outward of properties more directly understood to be features of thoughts.

Peirce took the opposite tack: any account of the internal (mental activity) must be in terms of the external (publicly accessible objects). Again, focusing on thinking as our example, it is public thinking (language) which is the direct object of human understanding and which is the direct referent of the categories in terms of which we are to understand our mental life. Thoughts are to be understood by an analogical extension inward of a system of categories whose primary analogate is language. Thus our understanding of even our own mental activity is conceptually mediated by reference to external public objects. Given this externalist strategy, Peirce proceeded to develop an account of all mental activity on the model of a sign process whose formal structure was logical.

In later papers Peirce explicitly attends to the third feature of Cartesianism, namely, its dualism in metaphysics (*Collected Papers* 6). He argues against this in favor of an objective idealism wherein all reality is conceived as ultimately mental in nature as a condition of its knowability. This view would not only enable him to overcome the latent skepticism in the Cartesian view of man's relation to the world but would also render possible a unified and progressive account of scientific understanding.

This brings us to Peirce's positive programme. Just as strong as his negative reaction to Descartes was his positive reaction to Kant. Given the fact that during his formative years as an undergraduate at Harvard Peirce "devoted two hours a day to the study of Kant's *Critique of Pure Reason* for more than three years until I knew almost the whole book by heart," it is not surprising that the positive projects (if not the conclusions) of the First Critique would become central to his own philosophical investigations. Such was clearly the case with regard to the project of exhibiting the conditions of possibility of science. There was a marked difference between Kant and Peirce, however, a difference which had its ultimate ground in the centrality of the notions of "history" and "community" in Peirce's overall philosophical orientation. This general orientation disposed Peirce to what might be termed a concrete as opposed to an abstract conception of science. In contrast to the conception of science as a state set of propositions, he conceived of it as a socio-historical process of inquiry. This fundamental shift in perspective gave a quite different tonality to his project of exhibiting its conditions of possibility.

Peirce generally characterized the scientific process as involving an abductive phase, a deductive phase, and an inductive phase. The abductive stage of the inquiry process is concerned with the original generation and recommendation of explanatory hypotheses; the deductive phase has to do with the logical elaboration of the hypothesis and the derivation from it of specific predictions; and the inductive stage bears on the confirmation or falsification of the hypothesis by future experience. The movement of thought is from experience, through rational elaboration, back to experience. Peirce's most distinctive insights are found in his accounts of the abductive and inductive phases of scientific inquiry.

In his more fine-grained account of the abductive phase of scientific inquiry Peirce distinguishes two moments. The first moment is simply the origination of those conjectures which will make up the list of possible explanations of the phenomena under consideration. This "discovery" moment is a function of the creative imagination of some people. Peirce talks of it in terms of natural instinct and does not think that it can be reduced to strict formulae or rules of inference. The second moment takes its rise from the fact that there may well emerge many suggested hypotheses that equally "explain" the facts. Accordingly, if we are to get on with the task of scientific explanation we must single out from the list of possible explanations those we are seriously to consider, and, furthermore, effect a preference ordering of these. This moment of the abductive process is rule-governed, and it is with regard to this moment that Peirce develops a general theory of the economics of research.

In this general theory of the economics of research Peirce clearly conceives the criteria of antecedent theory choice both historically and socially. One hypothesis is to be preferred over another not in terms of its intrinsic merits or its likelihood of being true but in terms of the role it can play in a process of inquiry which is aimed toward truth in the long run. An hypothesis is recommended to the degree that its pursuance at this point in time would move the inquiry along most effectively. Peirce's invocation of the game of Twenty Questions is instructive. In playing this parlor game a line of questioning recommends itself not in terms of the likelihood it will "hit upon" the correct answer immediately but in terms of the role this line of questioning will play in hastening the convergence on truth of the line of inquiry in general. Secondly, the justification of these abductive "we" rules is not in terms of the individual investigator but in terms of the community of investigators of which he is a member. The hypothesis recommended to any individual may not at all be the one most likely to enable *him* to attain the truth but rather the one which will most efficiently ensure the eventual attainment of truth. Given the state of the inquiry, an individual investigator may be rationally constrained to spend his days eliminating some unlikely possibilities. It seems that in the cognitive order the individual's good is secondary to the good of the community. Accordingly, even in his account of the abductive phase of inquiry, Peirce moves from an abstract propositional conception of scientific theory toward a construal of science as a concrete socio-historical process of inquiry.

This shift in emphasis is even more pronounced in his account of the inductive phase of the inquiry process. "Induction," as Peirce uses the term, is not to be understood simply in terms of the relation of individual cases to a general law but in terms of the role such a relationship plays in the inquiry process. The role of the relationship between propositions describing individual instances to the relevant laws or theories is not that of the latter being derived from them, but rather of these instances, having been predicted by the theory, functioning either to confirm or falsify it. It is through this inductive phase that the speculative flights of inquiry are continually monitored by experience, and it is because of this "monitoring" that Peirce sees himself as able to construe science as a self-regulating and self-corrective process.

When we commit ourselves to the program of testing our hypotheses by the deliverances of experience, we are aware of the fact that any given hypothesis will range over many more cases than can possibly come under our scrutiny. Peirce's contention is that so long as we are careful to predesignate the cases that will count and follow the procedures of fair sampling we can be assured that the continued application of the inductive procedure will reliably eliminate the false theories and thus by indirection recommend the true one. We will eventually discover whether or not reality has those characteristics our theory ascribes to it. And the "we" here does not refer to any specific individual. The logical subject of the inquiry is the scientific community over time and it is in its ultimate success that Peirce has confidence. The self-corrective feature of its method ensures its convergence on the truth. Reality must have some character; so, given that new hypotheses are forthcoming, the continued application of this process of elimination must lead to a result indefinitely approximating to the truth in the long run. The ultimate justification for this conviction that the process of scientific inquiry is self-monitoring and, consequently, truth-guaranteeing in this way involves Peirce's broader metaphysical theories of truth and reality.

Peirce ends up defining "truth" in terms of the settled outcome of such a process of inquiry and "reality" in terms of what is represented in the true opinion. Peirce's reasoning on this issue amounts to asking us to consider the alternative. Inductive inference, the monitoring moment of the process of inquiry, is basically an inference from part to whole, and its validity depends simply on the fact that the parts do make up and constitute the whole. We are involved in drawing samples from a population, and if the frequency with which some relevant property is distributed over the individuals of the sample does not correspond to its frequency of distribution over the population, the discrepancy is sure to become apparent as the sampling process is extended over the long run. To resist this line of thinking is to entertain a conception of the population or the whole which will never manifest itself in the samples or the parts. But to entertain this is to conceive of reality as possibly incognizable, as a thing-in-itself; and this Peirce thinks he has good reason to reject.

—C.F. Delaney

PERUTZ, Max (Ferdinand). British molecular biologist. Born in Vienna, Austria, 19 May 1914; emigrated to England after 1936; later naturalized. Studied at the University of Vienna, 1932-36; Cambridge University, Ph.D. 1940. Married Gisela Peiser in 1942; 2 children. Director, Unit for Molecular Biology, Medical Research Council, Cambridge, 1947-62; Reader, Davy-Faraday Laboratory, Cambridge, 1954-68; Chairman, European Molecular Biology Organization, 1963-69; Fullerian Professor of Physiology, Royal Institution, London, 1973-79; Chairman, 1962-69, and since 1972 Member of the Scientific Staff, Medical Research Council Laboratory of Molecular Biology, Cambridge. Recipient: Nobel Prize for Chemistry, with Sir John Kendrew, 1962; Royal Medal, 1971, and Copley Medal, 1979, Royal Society, London. Honorary doctorate: University of Vienna, 1965; University of Edinburgh, 1965; University of East Anglia, Norwich, 1967; University of Salzburg, 1972; Cambridge University, 1981. Member, Akademie Leopoldina, Halle, and Pontifical Academy of Sciences, Rome; Foreign Associate, U.S. National Academy of Sciences; Corresponding Member, Austrian Academy of Sciences; Foreign Member, American Philosophical Society, French Academy of Sciences, and Royal Netherlands Academy; Honorary Member, American Academy of Arts and Sciences. Fellow of the Royal Society, 1976. Honorary Fellow, Peterhouse, Cambridge, 1962. C.B.E. (Commander, Order of the British Empire), 1963; C.H. (Companion of Honour), 1975. Address: Laboratory of Molecular Biology, Hills Road, Cambridge, England.

PUBLICATIONS

Molecular Biology

Proteins and Nucleic Acids: Structure and Function (lectures). New York and Amsterdam, Elsevier, 1962.
Atlas of Molecular Structures in Biology 2: Haemoglobin and Myoglobin, with G. Fermi. Oxford, Clarendon Press, 1981.

*   *   *

The last four decades have seen the birth and explosive growth of a new scientific discipline, molecular biology. This science employs the tools and concepts of chemistry and physics to the interpretation of biological structures and phenomena. Max Perutz has been a pioneer in the development of molecular biology.

His approach has been to apply the methods of X-ray diffraction analysis to the determination of molecular structure for complex biochemical molecules such as proteins. The biological properties of proteins, nucleic acids, and other complex molecules are a function of two factors: their chemical composition and their three-dimensional structure. The former is described, in the case of proteins, as the molecule's primary structure; the latter, its secondary, tertiary, and quaternary structure.

Primary structure can be determined by traditional chemical techniques although the size and complexity of biochemical molecules make this a significant research task. The elucidation of the amino acid sequence in insulin, the first molecule for which primary structure was determined, required seven years of effort by Frederick Sanger's research team.

Unraveling higher levels of structure proved to be at least as much of a challenge. This task was compounded by the lack of suitable investigatory techniques, a handicap which was not, at least, encountered by groups such as Sanger's. To be sure, methods for looking at the geometric structure of small molecules had long been available. The Braggs had demonstrated in 1915 the possibility of determining molecular architecture by using X-ray diffraction analysis. In this technique, a beam of X-rays is caused to impinge on crystals of a substance. The arrangement of atoms within the crystals causes the X-rays to be diffracted in a characteristic pattern. The exact details of the pattern permit calculations of the positions of atoms in the crystal.

This method had been extraordinarily successful with molecules of small and moderate size. But efforts to use the technique with macromolecules like proteins met with only modest success. The diffraction patterns were blurred and ambiguous. In 1953, Perutz found a way of improving the clarity of diffraction patterns. He inserted individual atoms of heavy metals, such as gold, into biochemical molecules. This modification caused an increased resolution of the diffraction pattern. Changing the heavy atom used and the position of insertion resulted in a series of diffraction pictures. Repeated exposures of a molecule using this technique produced a large number of photographs. By comparing these with each other, it was eventually possible to map the three-dimensional structure of a protein molecule. The method developed by Perutz is known as isomorphous replacement.

By 1959, Perutz had been able to utilize the technique of isomorphous replacement to determine the structure of hemoglobin, the molecule which transports oxygen to the cells and carbon dioxide from cells to the lungs. He found that the molecule consists of four sub-units, each of which is a long, complexly folded helical chain.

Later work on the same molecule led to the discovery that the molecule changes its structure when it combines with oxygen. This result was of interest not only in and of itself, but because of its application to the theory of enzyme action. Prior to this time, the Lock-and-Key theory of enzyme action had proposed that enzymes act on substrates because of the close fit of the molecular architectures of the two substances. The implication from Perutz's work was that the enzyme might actually alter its shape in order to fit around the substrate. This "induced fit" theory of enzyme action has proved to be useful in explaining many types of enzymatic action.

—David Newton

PIAGET, Jean. Swiss psychologist. Born in Neuchâtel, 9 August 1896. Studied at the University of Neuchâtel, Ph.D. 1918; University of Zurich and Alfred Binet Institute, Paris, 1919-21. Married Valentine Châtenay in 1923; 3 children. Director of Studies, 1921-25, and after 1933 Co-Director, Jean-Jacques Rousseau Institute, Geneva. Professor of Psychology, Sociology, and the Philosophy of Science, University of Neuchâtel, 1925-29; Associate Professor of the History of Scientific Thought, 1929-39, Professor of Sociology, 1939-52, Professor of Experimental Psychology, 1940-71, and Professor Emeritus, 1971-80, University of Geneva; Professor of Psychology and Sociology, University of Lausanne, 1938-51; Professor of Developmental Psychology, the Sorbonne, Paris, 1952-63. Director, International Bureau of Education, 1929-67; Institute for Educational Sciences, University of Geneva, 1955-80. Recipient: Prix de la Ville de Geneve, 1963; American Research Association Award, 1967; American Psychological Association Award, 1969; Prix Foneme, 1970; Prix de l'Institut de la Vie, 1973. Honorary doctorate: Harvard University, Cambridge, Massachusetts, 1936; the Sorbonne, 1946; University of Oslo, 1960; Cambridge University, 1960; University of Moscow, 1966; Yale University, New Haven, Connecticut, 1970. Member, Accademia dei Lincei, Rome; Academy of Sciences, Bucharest; New York Academy of Science; Boston Academy of Arts and Sciences; Académie des Sciences et Lettres de Montpellier; Royal Academy of Belgium; Académie Internationale de Philosophie des Sciences; Institut Internationale de Philosophie; Union Internationale de Psychologie Scientifique; Association de Psychologie Scientifique de Langue Française; Société Suisse de Logique et de Philosophie des Sciences; Société de Psychologie de Espagne; Société Suisse de Psychologie; Société Neuchâteloise des Sciences Naturelles; and Federacion Colombia de Psicologia. Died (in Geneva) 16 September 1980.

PUBLICATIONS

Psychology

Le Langage et la pensée chez l'enfant.   Neuchâtel, Delachaux

and Niestlé, 1923; as The Language and Thought of the Child, London, Kegan Paul, and New York, Harcourt Brace, 1926.
Le Jugement et la raisonnement chez l'enfant.   Neuchâtel, Delachaux and Niestlé, 1924; as The Judgment and Reasoning in the Child, London, Kegan Paul, and New York, Harcourt Brace, 1928.
La Représentation du monde chez l'enfant.   Paris, Alcan, 1926; as The Child's Conception of the World, London, Kegan Paul, and New York, Harcourt Brace, 1929.
La Causalité physique chez l'enfant.   Paris, Alcan, 1930; as The Child's Conception of Physical Causality, London, Kegan Paul, and New York, Harcourt Brace, 1930.
Le Jugement moral chez l'enfant.   Paris, Alcan, 1932; as The Moral Judgment of the Child, London, Kegan Paul, and New York, Harcourt Brace, 1932.
La Naissance de l'intelligence chez l'enfant.   Neuchâtel, Delachaux and Niestlé, 1936; as The Origins of Intelligence in Children, New York, International Universities Press, 1952; as The Origin of Intelligence in Children, London, Kegan Paul, 1953.
La Construction du réel chez l'enfant.   Neuchâtel, Delachaux and Niestlé, 1937; as The Construction of Reality in the Child, New York, Basic Books, 1954; as The Child's Construction of Reality, London, Routledge, 1955.
Le Développement des quantités chez l'enfant: Conservation et Atomisme, with Bärbel Inhelder.   Neuchâtel, Delachaux and Niestlé, 1940; as The Child's Construction of Quantities: Conservation and Atomism, London, Routledge, 1974.
La Genèse du nombre chez l'enfant, with Alina Szeminska. Neuchâtel, Delachaux and Niestlé, 1941; as The Child's Concept of Number, London, Routledge, and New York, Humanities Press, 1952.
Classes, relations et nombres: Essai sur les groupements de la logistique et sur la réversibilité de la pensée.   Paris, Vrin, 1942.
Introduction à la étude des perceptions chez l'enfant et analyse d'une illusion relative à la perception visuelle de cercles concentriques, with others.   Neuchâtel, Delachaux and Niestlé, 1942.
La Comparaison visuelle des hateurs à distances variables dans la plan frontoparellele, with Marc Lambercier.   Neuchâtel, Delachaux and Niestlé, 1943.
Essai d'interprétation probabliste de la loi de Weber et de celles concentrations relatives, with others.   Neuchâtel, Delachaux and Niestlé, 1945.
La Formation du symbole chez l'enfant: Imitation, jeu et rêve, image et représentation.   Neuchâtel, Delachaux and Niestlé, 1945; as Play, Dreams, and Imitation in Childhood, London, Heinemann, and New York, Norton, 1951.
Expériences sur la construction projective de la ligne droite chez les enfants de 2 a 8 ans, with Bärbel Inhelder.   Neuchâtel, Delachaux and Niestlé, 1946.
Les Notions de mouvement et de vitesse chez l'enfant, with others.   Paris, Presses Universitaires de France, 1946; as The Child's Conception of Motion and Speed, New York, Basic Books, 1970.
Le Développement de la notion de temps chez l'enfant, with others.   Paris, Presses Universitaires de France, 1946; as The Child's Conception of Time, London, Routledge, and New York, Basic Books, 1970.
Étude sur la psychologie d'Edouard Claparede.   Neuchâtel, Delachaux and Niestlé, 1946.
La Psychologie de l'intelligence.   Paris, Colin, 1947; as The Psychology of Intelligence, London, Routledge, and New York, Harcourt Brace, 1950.
La Représentation de l'espace chez l'enfant, with Bärbel Inhelder.   Paris, Presses Universitaires de France, 1948; as The Child's Conception of Space, London, Routledge, and New York, Humanities Press, 1956.
Le Géométrie sponanée de l'enfant, with others.   Paris, Presses Universitaires de France, 1948; as The Child's Conception of

Geometry, London, Routledge, and New York, Basic Books, 1960.

Le Droit à l'éducation dans le monde actuel. Paris, Unesco, 1949; included in *To Understand Is to Invent: The Future of Education*, New York, Grossman, 1973.

L'Initiation au calcul: Enfants des 4 à 7 ans, with M. Boscher. Paris, Bourrelier, 1949.

Traité de logique: Essai de logistique opératoire. Paris, Colin, 1949.

Introduction à l'épistémologie génétique. Paris, Presses Universitaires de France, 3 vols., 1950.

Le Genèse de l'idée de hasard chez l'enfant, with Bärbel Inhelder. Paris, Presses Universitaires de France, 1951; as *The Origin of the Idea of Chance in Children*, London, Routledge, and New York, Norton, 1975.

Essai sur les transformations des opérations logiques: Les 256 opérations ternaires de la logique bivalente des propositions. Paris, Presses Universitaires de France, 1952.

Logic and Psychology (lectures). Manchester, Manchester University Press, 1953; New York, Basic Books, 1957.

Les Relations entre l'affectivité et l'intelligence dans le développement mental d'enfant. Paris, Centre de Documentation Universitaire, 1954.

L'Enseignement des mathématiques: Essai sur la construction des opératoires, with others. Neuchâtel, Delachaux and Niestlé, 1955.

La Logique de l'enfant à la logique de l'adolescent: Essai sur la construction des opératoires, with Bärbel Inhelder. Paris, Presses Universitaires de France, 1955; as *The Growth of Logical Thinking from Childhood to Adolescence: An Essay on the Construction of Formal Operational Structures*, London, Routledge, and New York, Basic Books, 1958.

Logique et perception, with others. Paris, Presses Universitaires de France, 1958.

La Genèse des structures logique élémentaire: Classifications et sériations, with Bärbel Inhelder. Neuchâtel, Delachaux and Niestlé, 1958; as *The Early Growth of Logic in the Child: Classification and Seriation*, London, Routledge, and New York, Harper, 1964.

Les Mécanismes perceptifs. Paris, Presses Universitaires de France, 1961; as *The Mechanism of Perception*, London, Routledge, and New York, Basic Books, 1969.

Comments on Vigotsky's Critical Remarks Concerning "The Language and Thought of the Child" and "Judgment and Reasoning in the Child." Cambridge, Massachusetts, M.I.T. Press, 1961.

Épistémologie mathématique et psychologie: Essai sur les relations entre la logique formelle et la pensée réel, with E. Beth. Paris, Presses Universitaires de France, 1961; as *Mathematical Epistemology and Psychology*, New York, Gordon and Beech, 1966.

Le Développement des quantités physiques chez l'enfant, with Bärbel Inhelder. Neuchâtel, Delachaux and Niestlé, 1962.

Histoire et méthode, with others. Paris, Presses Universitaires de France, 1963; as *History and Method*, New York, Basic Books, 1968.

La Perception, with others. Paris, Presses Universitaires de France, 1963.

Six Études de psychologie. Geneva, Gonthier, 1964; as *Six Psychological Studies*, New York, Random House, 1967; London, University of London Press, 1968.

Études sociologiques. Paris, Droz, 1965.

Sagesse et Illusions. Paris, Presses Universitaires de France, 1965; as *Insights and Illusions of Philosophy*, Cleveland, World, 1971; London, Routledge, 1977.

L'Image mentale chez l'enfant: Essai sur le développement des représentations imagées, with Bärbel Inhelder. Paris, Presses Universitaires de France, 1966; as *Mental Imagery in the Child: A Study of the Development of Imaginal Representation*, London, Routledge, and New York, Basic Books, 1971.

La Psychologie de l'enfant, with Bärbel Inhelder. Paris, Presses Universitaires de France, 1966; as *The Psychology of the Child*, London, Routledge, and New York, Basic Books, 1971.

Biologie et connaissance: Essai sur les relations entre les régulations organiques et les processus cognitifs. Paris, Gallimard, 1966; as *Biology and Knowledge: An Essay on the Relations between Organic Regulations and Cognitive Responses*, Chicago, University of Chicago Press, and Edinburgh, Edinburgh University Press, 1971.

On the Development of Memory and Identity (lectures). Worcester, Massachusets, Clark University Press, 1968.

Le Structuralisme. Paris, Presses Universitaires de France, 1968; as *Structuralism*, New York, Basic Books, 1970; London, Routledge, 1971.

Épistémologie et psychologie de la fonction, with others. Paris, Presses Universitaires de France, 1968; as *Epistemology and Psychology of Functions*, Dordrecht, Reidel, 1977.

Mémoire et intelligence, with Bärbel Inhelder. Paris, Presses Universitaires de France, 1968; as *Memory and Intelligence*, London, Routledge, and New York, Basic Books, 1973.

Épistémologie des sciences de l'homme. Paris, Gallimard, 1970.

Science of Education and the Psychology of the Child. New York, Orion Press, 1970; London, Longman, 1971.

L'Épistémologie génétique. Paris, Presses Universitaires de France, 1970; as *Genetic Epistemology*, New York, Columbia University Press, 1970.

Psychologie et épistémologie. Paris, Denöel-Gonthier, 1970; as *Psychology and Epistemology*, New York, Grossman, 1971; and as *Psychology and Epistemology: Towards a Theory of Knowledge*, London, Penguin Books, 1971.

Les Explications causales, with R. Garcia. Paris, Presses Universitaires de France, 1971; as *Understanding Causality*, New York, Norton, 1974.

Les Théories de la causalité, with others. Paris, Presses Universitaires de France, 1971.

Les Directions des mobiles lors de chocs et de poussées, with J. Bliss. Paris, Presses Universitaires de France, 1972.

La Transmission des mouvements, with J. Bliss. Paris, Presses Universitaires de France, 1972.

Ou va l'éducation? Paris, Denöel-Gonthier, 1973; as *To Understand Is to Invent: The Future of Education*, New York, Grossman, 1973; London, Penguin, 1976.

La Composition des forces et le problème des vecteurs, with J. Bliss. Paris, Presses Universitaires de France, 1973.

La Formation de la notion de force. Paris, Presses Universitaires de France, 1973.

La Prise de conscience, with A. Blanchet. Paris, Presses Universitaires de France, 1974; as *The Grasp of Consciousness: Action and Concept in the Young Child*, Cambridge, Massachusetts, Harvard University Press, 1976.

Recherches sur la contradiction, with C. Bonnet. Paris, Presses Universitaires de France, 2 vols., 1974; as *Experiments in Contradiction*, Chicago, University of Chicago Press, 1980.

Réussir et comprendre, with M. Amann. Paris, Presses Universitaires de France, 1978; as *Success and Understanding*, Cambridge, Massachusetts, Harvard University Press, 1978.

Adaptation vitale et psychologie de l'intelligence: Sélection organique et Phénocopie. Paris, Hermann, 1974; as *Adaptation and Intelligence: Organic Selection Phenocopie*, Chicago, University of Chicago Press, 1980.

L'Équilibration des structures cognitifs: problème central du développement. Paris, Presses Universitaires de France, 1975; as *The Development of Thought: Equilibration and Cognitive Structures*, New York, Viking Press, 1977.

Le Comportement, moteur de l'évolution. Paris, Gallimard, 1976; as *Behavior and Evolution*, New York, Pantheon, 1978.

Recherches sur la généralisation. Paris, Presses Universitaires de France, 1978.

Recherches sur les correspondances. Paris, Presses Universitaires de France, 1980.

Other

Recherche (novel).   Lausanne, Édition la Concorde, 1918.

Editor, *Études d'épistémologie génétique*.   Paris, Presses Universitaires de France, 1957-.
Editor, with Paul Fraisse, *Traité de psychologie expérimentale*. Paris, Presses Universitaires de France, 1963; as *Experimental Psychology: Its Scope and Method*, New York, Basic Books, 1968.
Editor, with others, *Entretiens sur les notions de genèse et de structure*, The Hague, Mouton, 1965.
Editor, *Logique et connaissance scientifique*.   Paris, Gallimard, 1967.

*

Bibliography: *Catalogue of the Jean Piaget Archives, University of Geneva, Switzerland*, Boston, Hall, 1975.

Critical Studies: *The Developmental Psychology of Jean Piaget* by John H. Flavell, Princeton, New Jersey, Van Nostrand, 1963; *Piaget and Knowledge: Theoretical Foundations* by Han Furth, Englewood Cliffs, New Jersey, Prentice Hall, 1969; *Piaget: The Man and His Ideas* by Richard Isadore Evans, New York, Dutton, 1973; *Piaget's Theory of Intelligence* by J. Brainerd, Englewood Cliffs, New Jersey, Prentice Hall, 1978; *Jean Piaget* by Margaret A. Boden, London, Collins, and New York, Viking Press, 1980; *A Piagetian Model of Character Structure* by A.J. Malerstein and M. Ahern, New York, Human Sciences Press, 1982.

*   *   *

Jean Piaget's training as a natural scientist and his fascination for philosophy and logic led him to concentrate upon research which is logically sound and psychologically consistent. For him, only the most logical questions could lead to the most valid response. He pointed to the subject's response (the individual's conception of an event) as an authentic guide to the investigative inquiry rather than the researcher's set of questions. For Piaget, "in the beginning was the response"; and learning builds upon development.

Piaget can be classed as an early systems thinker; questions pertaining to the part-whole problem permeate all of his inquiries. Cognitive structure (schema of reasoning) grows and changes as an outcome of two basic processes of development; these are organization and adaptation. Piaget submits that new structures, organizational shifts, and equilibration occur in at least four periods of a person's development, creating decisively different forms of thinking patterns. Each new structure demands a new and different human interaction by which the world is experienced and then acted upon with a new and advanced comprehension.

In Piagetian formulations, equilibration involves the adaptive processes of assimilation and accommodation. A process of feedback and forecasting leads to an advancement in thinking. To put it in another way, events are understood or adjusted at first within the context of ongoing comprehension in order to make sense out of one's experience. Assimilation occurs at the expense of the input. Accommodation, in contrast, changes a person's understanding (and eventually the structure of comprehending) in order to adapt more fully and potentially reorganize one's conception of the world. Assimilation and accommodation are always in tandem; they occur as a dual process in every minute adaptive process as well as in the overall process of equilibration—that is, organizing one's thinking.

Cognitive development, most important in Piagetian theory, occurs always in the same transformational sequential progression, although the actual chronological age reference points may vary from individual to individual, or from cultural experience to cultural experience. Development occurs along coherent and discernible patterns. Intelligence doesn't develop at random; rather every act of cognition is related to every other act of cognition. Within the developmental progression, qualitative, transformational changes establish at least four culturally universal overall phases. In each phase, new and different schemes of thinking occur: Phase I: Sensori-motor Phase (infancy). Basic reflex movements evolve into action-sequences with a constant increment of cognition in the use of overt behavior. Phase II: Pre-operational Phase (pre-school years). Internalized (representative or symbolic) thought evolves but remains essentially intuitive. Thought structures emerge without a cognitive awareness of their existence or a conscious use of them. Active thinking is involved without actual mediation. Phase III: Concrete Operational Phase (childhood). Thinking occurs by means of logical mental operations, by "figuring out" on the basis of concrete informational observations and mental representation. "Figuring out" proceeds, dependent on concrete images without resource to basic abstractions. Phase IV: Formal Operational Phase (adolescence and beyond). Advancement to adult thought is achieved. Thinking can now depend fully upon abstraction, symbolization of data, hypothesis formation, and the manipulation of concepts without the necessity for having actually experienced them. Ideas can be applied to ideas. Cognition has achieved a full equilibrium with no further structural changes ahead.

Piaget's theory was essentially conceived and tested within the walls of his Geneva Institute. His concepts and data have been accepted and validated by scholars throughout the academic world. Piagetian formulations have been verified in cross-cultural studies in the dry bushland of Australia and the Eskimo villages at the windy North Slope of Alaska as well as in the studies of Arabic, Hindu, Japanese, Thai, and Ugandian children within their own homelands. The work of Piaget, the giant of psychology, was probably best appraised by Albert Einstein, another giant of the 20th century, when he observed: "The ideas of a genius, such simplicity."

—Henry W. Maier

PIRENNE, (Jean) Henri (Otto Lucien Marie).   Belgian historian.   Born at Verviers, 23 December 1862. Studied at the University of Liège, Ph.D. 1883; École Pratique des Hautes Études, Paris, and École des Chartes, Paris, 1883-84; universities of Leipzig and Berlin, 1884-85. Married Jenny-Laure Vanderhaegen in 1887; 4 sons. Chargé de cours, University of Liège, 1885; Professeur Extraordinaire, 1888-89, Professeur Ordinaire, 1889-1930, and Professeur Emeritus, 1930-35, University of Ghent, Belgium (Rector 1919-21). Visiting Professor, Sorbonne, Paris, 1922, 1924; University of Algiers, 1931. Secretary, Royal Commission of History, 1907-35; Vice President, Society of History and Archaeology of Ghent, 1916, and Comité International des Sciences Historiques, 1926; President, Royal Academy of Belgium, 1918, Union Académique Internationale, 1920-22, Commission des Sciences Historiques du Fonds National de Recherche Scientifique, 1928-33, and Council of the Royal Library, 1931; Honorary President, Society of Modern History, Paris, 1921. Recipient: Prix Raymond, Académie Française, 1919; Prix Francqui, 1933. Honorary doctorate: University of Leipzig, 1909; University of Tübingen, 1911; University of Groningen, 1914; Oxford University, 1919; University of Strasbourg, 1919; University of Brussels, 1919; University of Paris, 1922; University of Bordeaux, 1924; St. Andrews University, Scotland, 1926; Cambridge University, 1930; University of Algiers, 1931; University of Dijon, 1931; University of Montpellier, 1932; University of Toulouse, 1934. Member, Royal Academy of Belgium, 1898; Academy of Sciences of Petrograd, 1918; British Academy, 1918; Polish Academy of Cracow, 1924; Czechoslovakian

Academy, 1926; Associate Member, Society of Antiquarians of France, 1909; Corresponding Member, Royal Society of Sciences of Göttingen, 1906; Royal Society of Sciences of Bohemia, 1907; Imperial Academy of Sciences of Vienna, 1908; Institute of France, 1910; Royal Academy of Bavaria, 1912; Royal Historical Society, London, 1913; Academy of History, Spain, 1917; Foreign Member, Royal Academy of the Low Countries, 1904; Academy of Stockholm, 1931; Honorary Member, Maatschappij der Nederlandsche Letterkunde, Leiden, 1894; Historisch Genootschap, Utrecht, 1906; Royal Society of Sciences, Copenhagen, 1920; Massachusetts Historical Society, 1923; Romanian Academy, 1924. Chevalier, 1899, Officer, 1910, Commander, 1918, and Grand Officer, 1921, Order of Leopold; Grand Croix de l'Ordre de la Couronne, 1926. *Died* (in Ukkel, Belgium) *24 October 1935.*

PUBLICATIONS

History

Sedulius de Liège: Avec un appendice contenant les poésies inédites de cet auteur. Brussels, Académie Royale de Belgique, 1882.
Histoire de la constitution de la ville Dinant au moyen âge. Ghent, Clemm, 1889.
La Version Flamande et la version Française de la bataille de Coutrai. Brussels, Hayez, 1890.
Bibliographie de l'histoire de Belgique: Catalogue méthodique et chronologique des sources et des ouvrages principaux relatifs à l'histoire de tous les Pays-Bas jusqu'en 1598, et à l'histoire de Belgique jusqu'en 1830. Ghent, Engelcke, 1893.
Documents relatifs à l'histoire de Flandre pendant la première moité du XIVe siècle. Brussels, Hayez, 1897.
La Hanse flamande de Londres. Brussels, Hayez, 1899.
La Nation Belge (lecture). Brussels, Guyot, 1899.
Note sur un passage de van Velthem relatif à la bataille de Courtrai. Brussels, Hayez, 1899.
Histoire de Belgique. Brussels, Lamertin, 7 vols., 1900-32.
Une crise industrielle au XVIe siècle: La Draperie urbaine et la "nouvelle draperie" en Flandre (lecture). Brussels, Hayez, 1905.
Les Anciennes Démocraties des Pays-Bas. Paris, Flammarion, 1910; as *Belgian Democracy: Its Early History*, Manchester, University Press, 1915; as *Early Democracies in the Low Countries: Urban Society and Political Conflict in the Middle Ages and the Renaissance*, New York, Harper, 1963.
La Nation Belge et l'Allemagne: Quelques réflexions historiques (lecture). Ghent, Hoste, 1920.
Les Périodes de l'histoire sociale du capitalisme (lecture). Brussels, Librairie du "Peuple," 1922.
Notice sur Godefroid Kurth. Brussels, Hayez, 1923.
Medieval Cities: Their Origins and the Revival of Trade. Princeton, Princeton University Press, 1925; as *Les villes du moyen âge: Essai d'histoire économique et sociale*, Brussels, Lamertin, 1927.
La Belgique et la guerre mondiale. Paris, Presses Universitaires de France, and New Haven, Connecticut, Yale University Press, 1928.
La Place du Hainaut dans l'histoire de Belgique. Frameries and Mons, Belgium, Union des Imprimeries, 1929.
La Fin du moyen âge, with others. Paris, Alcan, 2 vols., 1931.
Suite d'études exposant les diverses activités de la Belgique et de son roi, with others. Antwerp, Buschmann, 1932.
La Civilisation occidentale au moyen âge du XIe au milieu du XVe siècle, with others. Paris, Presses Universitaires de France, 1933; as *Economic and Social History of Medieval Europe*, London, Kegan Paul, 1936; New York, Harcourt Brace, 1937.
La Commission Royale d'Histoire depuis sa fondation (1834-1934). Brussels, 1934.

Histoire de l'Europe des invasions au XVIe siècle. Paris, Alcan, 1936; as *A History of Europe from the Invasions to the XVI Century*, London, Allen and Unwin, and New York, Norton, 1939.
Mahomet et Charlemagne. Paris, Alcan, 1937; as *Mohammed and Charlemagne*, London, Allen and Unwin, and New York, Norton, 1939.
Les Villes et les institutions urbaines. Paris, Alcan, 2 vols., 1939.
The "Journal de Guerre" of Henri Pirenne, edited by Bryce and Mary Lyon. Amsterdam and New York, North Holland, 1976.

Other

Editor, *Histoire de meutre de Charles le Bon, comte de Flandre (1127-1128) par Galbert de Bruges, suivie de poésies latines contemporaines.* Paris, Picard, 1891.
Editor, *Le Livre de l'abbé Guillaume de Ryckel (1249-1272): Polyptique et comptes de l'abbaye de Saint-Trond au milieu du XIIIe siècle.* Brussels, Hayez, 1896.
Editor, *La Soulèvement de la Flandre maritime de 1323-1328: Documents inédits.* Brussels, Kiessling, 1900.
Editor, *Cronique rimée des troubles de Flandre en 1379-1380.* Ghent, Siffer, 1902.
Editor, with Georges Espinas, *Recueil de documents relatifs à l'histoire de l'industrie drapière en Flandre.* Brussels, Imbreghts, 4 vols., 1906-24.
Editor, *Album belge de diplomatique: Recueil de fac-similés pour servir à l'étude de la diplomatique des provinces belges au moyen âge.* Jette-Brussels, Vandamne et Rossignol, 1909.

*

Bibliography: in *Henri Pirenne: Hommages et souvenirs* edited by Jules Duesberg, Brussels, Nouvelle Société d'Éditions, 2 vols., 1938.

Critical Studies: *The Pirenne Thesis: Analysis, Criticism, and Revision* edited by Alfred F. Havighurst, Boston, Heath, 1958; *Henri Pirenne* by François Drion du Chapois, Brussels, 1964; *The Origins of the Middle Ages: Pirenne's Challenge to Gibbon*, New York, Norton, 1972, and *Henri Pirenne: A Biographical and Intellectual Study*, Ghent, Story-Scientia, 1974, both by Bryce D. Lyon.

*   *   *

Henri Pirenne, after graduating from the University of Liège, became a professor of history at the University of Ghent until his retirement in 1930. Although his international fame rested upon a revolutionary interpretation of the origins of medieval civilization, he was celebrated in his native country as the author of the monumental and scholarly 7-volume *Histoire de Belgique.* Historians prior to Pirenne had been divided in their interpretation of the origin of medieval institutions. Most had accepted the view that there was a distinct break with the Roman world in the 5th century AD and that the origins of medieval civilization were to be traced to developments in the Germanic kingdoms established after the barbarian invasions. Some historians, however, argued that the roots of medieval civilization could be seen in gradual alterations which took place in the institutions of the late Roman Empire under the impact of the barbarian invasions. To this Romanist-Germanist controversy Pirenne brought an entirely new insight resulting from his intensive study of medieval cities whose beginnings he traced to developments of the 10th and 11th centuries. Pirenne's hypothesis was first advanced in various papers and in a series of lectures given in America in 1922 and published under the title of *Medieval Cities: Their Origins and the Revival of Trade* (1925). His thesis was given a more extensive treatment in *Mohammed and Charlemagne*, published shortly after his death.

According to Pirenne the collapse of the old Roman order, which persisted through the barbarian invasions, did not take place until the 7th and 8th centuries. The collapse was the direct result of the Islamic invasions which destroyed the unity of the Mediterranean world around which the Roman Empire had centered and which had constituted the essential channel of trade and communication necessary for its preservation. The destruction of international trade had its most marked impact upon the interior of Europe. As depicted by Pirenne the last years of Merovingian rule in France were years of chaos. It was at this point that the Carolingians emerged creating an empire which stretched from the Elbe to the Po. In effect the center of gravity of Europe had shifted from the Mediterranean to the north. It was within this empire that new institutions were created laying the foundation for the social and political order of the Middle Ages. Deprived of the revenue from the impost upon which the Merovingians had relied, the Carolingians had to find new sources of support for the armed forces needed to repel the Moslems and expand their possessions. They also needed to establish political machinery to give stability to the empire. It was in these circumstances and to meet this need that the feudal institutions developed. The kings now depended upon the feudal bond and their own demesnes for support. In contrast to the Merovingians, who had been secular rulers, the Carolingians were Holy Roman Emporors linked in an alliance with the church. It was at this point that cities emerged as merchants now engaged in purely local trade clustered around castles and abbeys for protection.

The Pirenne thesis has been widely challenged but his interpretation has been a major influence on medieval studies. Byzantine studies have since taken on a greater significance as the extension of the Roman Empire. Historians have shifted from the long prevailing stress on periodized political and juridical aspects of the middle ages to turn to social, economic, and demographic studies. Extensive research has subsequently confirmed Pirenne's study of city origins, although most historians are not in agreement with his conclusions about the destruction of international trade, for it has been shown that trade with the Orient through Venice persisted throughout the Carolingian era.

—Harry Ammon

PLAMENATZ, John (Petrov). British political theorist. Born in Cetinje, Montenegro, now Yugoslavia, 16 May 1912; emigrated to Great Britain, 1919. Educated at Clayesmore School; Oriel College, Oxford, B.A. 1934, M.A. 1937. Married Marjorie Hunter in 1943. Fellow of All Souls College, Oxford, 1936-51; University Lecturer in social and political theory, 1950-67, and Fellow of Nuffield College, Oxford, 1951-67; Fellow of All Souls College, 1967-75, and Chichele Professor of Social and Political Theory, Oxford, 1967-75. Fellow, British Academy. *Died 19 February 1975.*

PUBLICATIONS

Political Theory

Consent, Freedom, and Political Obligation. London, Oxford University Press, 1938.
What is Communism? London, National News-Letter, 1947.
Mill's Utilitarianism Reprinted, with a Study of the English Utilitarians. Oxford, Blackwell, 1949; revised edition, as *The English Utilitarians,* 1958.
The Revolutionary Movement in France 1815-71. London and New York, Longman, 1952.
From Marx to Stalin. London, Batchworth Press, 1953.

German Marxism and Russian Communism. London, Longman, 1954; New York, Harper, 1965.
On Alien Rule and Self-Government. London, Longman, 1960.
Man and Society: A Critical Examination of Some Important Social and Political Theories from Machiavelli to Marx. London, Longman, 2 vols., 1963; New York, McGraw Hill, 2 vols., 1963.
Ideology. London, Pall Mall Press, and New York, Praeger, 1970.
Democracy and Illusion: An Examination of Certain Aspects of Modern Democratic Theory. London, Longman, 1973.
Karl Marx's Philosophy of Man. Oxford, Clarendon Press, 1975.

Other

The Case of General Mahailovic. Privately printed, 1944.

Editor, *Leviathan,* by Hobbes. London, Fontana, 1962.
Editor, *Readings from Liberal Writers: English and French.* London, Allen and Unwin, and New York, Barnes and Noble, 1965.
Editor, *The Prince, Selections from the Discourses, and Other Writings,* by Machiavelli. London, Fontana, 1972.

*   *   *

John Plamenatz was a perceptive political theorist with a comprehensive grasp of the intellectual history of modern Europe. He respected the contemporary contributions of linguistic philosophy without being intimidated by it. Great political thinkers have focussed upon problems that are partially dispelled by conceptual analysis, but their fundamental insights are nonetheless significant and valuable. Political theory, systematic thinking about the goals and purposes of government (not explanations concerning how governments function), is practical philosophy as it relates to society. In his well-known paper "The Use of Political Theory," Plamenatz contended that current philosophical trends as well as the enhanced self-consciousness facilitated by psychology and sociology have rendered political theory more relevant than ever. Competing political doctrines have profoundly affected the images human beings hold about themselves, and these images subtly influence the complex attitudes and conduct of individuals. While practical philosophy today cannot be derived from traditional religion and rationalist metaphysics, political thinkers must still do more than set out theoretical systems: they must establish hierarchies of ethical principles and explain why individuals should make choices according to them. They are influential purveyors of ideas, and they are also social preachers and moral propagandists. A human being is not what he aspires to be, but his image of himself (and how he judges what he is) is influenced by his aspirations. Political theory elaborates those aspirations and images in order to understand them better, and to help individuals make effective choices and experience a sense of fulfillment in contemporary society.

Consent, Freedom, and Political Obligation was an impressive if inconclusive effort to engage in a sustained analysis of basic concepts and their complex interrelationships. Plamenatz, a stern critic of his own work, turned with relief from strict philosophical analysis to broader ventures in the history of ideas. In *The English Utilitarians* he traced the emergence of English utilitarianism from Hobbesian self-interest to the notion of self-improvement in Hume, Bentham, James Mill, and John Stuart Mill. Although the utilitarians were simplistic and unsatisfactory, they helped to clear the murky air of political and moral philosophy. Unable to recognize the role of faith, the power of belief to affect human conduct, utilitarianism was left with the hidden claim that individual hedonism is productive of social welfare. Partly because G.E. Moore showed that "good" could not be equated with "pleasant," utilitarianism passed out of English political life, though no movement of such scope and power has replaced it.

The Revolutionary Movement in France 1815-71 was a brave attempt to depict the "spiritual posterity" of the French Revolution, a congeries of competing groups with shifting alliances that did what the ambitious revolutionaries had failed to do: they made France republican and democratic. Repudiating what he saw as the Marxist error of seeking underlying causes before carefully examining the facts, Plamenatz also warned against using facile epithets like "success" and "failure" in respect to dynamic social movements initiated by revolutions. In a similar vein, his *German Marxism and Russian Communism* showed the value of a historical understanding of Lenin, a practical politician and revolutionary leader but not a great thinker. German Marxism, however, would have to be considered on its intrinsic merit, even if it had never been part of German political life, for not since Plato and Aristotle had philosophy and empirical knowledge been so closely allied. Marxism diverges from other varieties of socialism precisely because it is anchored to a wide-ranging philosophy of history and insists it can only be understood within that context. Marx, like the liberal John Stuart Mill, raised fundamental questions that cannot be ignored by the social theorist.

On Alien Rule and Self-Government elaborately and courageously examined the muddled arguments surrounding alien vs. self-rule. Plamenatz addressed the book only to those who already cherished political and social freedom, and he was concerned to show that much colonial justification and anti-imperial rhetoric obscure the real problems. If most subject peoples seeking political independence aspire to democracy and individual freedom, great responsibilities are involved. New nations seeking independence have a history markedly different from older societies in which democracy and freedom have slowly emerged over a long time. The latter are more likely to value patriotism, the former nationalism. Nationalism posits enemies, while patriotism does not. Educating for freedom is as much a discipline as anything else. Just as it is philosophically dubious to assume that the colonial masters are intrinsically superior, so too it is unphilosophical to assume that decolonization under all circumstances is good. Plamenatz cautioned alien rulers against putting down opposition that tended to nurture constitutionalism because it might foster opposition that did not, and he warned against replacing one alien ruler (e.g., a foreign power) with another (e.g., a dominating tribe or indigenous class). He reminded nationalist leaders not to expect independence itself to guarantee either freedom or democracy, or to confuse the waning of alien rule with the emergence of national strength.

Man and Society (in two volumes) is a comprehensive and critical examination of major political theories from Machiavelli to Marx. Plamenatz held that the political theorist must not only seek connections between the ruling political concepts of different times and show the historical contexts out of which they evolved, but also must elucidate their essential meanings for those who held them; otherwise human beings today would not appreciate the contrasting images man has had of himself and their significance in human development. Plamenatz brought the full rigour of his approach to bear upon prevailing doctrines of contemporary democracy. In *Democracy and Illusion* he carefully analyzed the different lines of reasoning used to defend democracy (including criteria assumed by various thinkers to identify a "true" vs. a "sham" democracy) and the arguments of sceptics who doubt that any existing system of government is really democratic. The book sought to remain neutral while pleading for a clarity of thought concerning issues on which individuals should be committed.

In his last book, *Karl Marx's Philosophy of Man*, Plamenatz wished to take Marx seriously, not as a systematic writer (which he was not), but as an original thinker who expounded fundamental ideas about human nature. For Plamenatz, man is a self-conscious being who is "self-creative" in that he strives to develop his powers in social intercourse. Therefore, Marx's concept of alienated life—beginning in alienation from labor but including alienation from religion, morality, and the state—is essential to any understanding of self-realization, freedom, equality, harmony, and the connections between them. Plamenatz was invariably a painstaking sifter of ideas who sharply discriminated the wheat from the chaff. He castigated prejudice (whatever is assumed without critical examination) yet he did not conclude that scholarly impartiality can by itself provide sufficient understanding. He continually tried to clarify lines of reasoning so that human beings could commit themselves to values with greater insight and better hope for the future. "The more men differ, and the longer they have been accustomed to differing, the more likely they are to accept principles which make it possible for those who differ to live peacefully together" ("The Use of Political Theory").

—R.N. Iyer

PLANCK, Max (Karl Ernst Ludwig). German physicist. Born in Kiel, 28 April 1858. Studied at the University of Munich, 1874-77; University of Berlin, Ph.D. 1879. Married Marie Merck in 1887, 4 children; married Marga von Hoesslin in 1911, 1 son. Lecturer, University of Munich, 1880-85; Professor of Theoretical Physics, University of Kiel, 1885-89; Professor of Theoretical Physics, University of Berlin, 1889-1928. Permanent Secretary, Prussian Academy of Sciences, 1912-43; President, 1930, and Honorary President, 1946, Kaiser Wilhelm Society, later the Max Planck Society. Recipient: Nobel Prize in Physics, 1918; Copley Medal, Royal Society, London, 1929. Foreign Member, Royal Society; Honorary Member, Royal Society of Edinburgh. Chancellor of Merit, 1930. *Died* (in Göttingen) *4 October 1947.*

PUBLICATIONS

Physics

Über den zweiten Hauptsatz der mechanischen Wärmetheorie. Munich, Ackermann, 1879.

Gleichgewichtszustände isotroper Körper in verscheidenen Temperaturen. Munich, Ackermann, 1880.

Das Prinzip der Erhaltung der Energie. Leipzig, Teubner, 1887.

Grundriss der allgemeinen Thermochemie. Breslau, Trewendt, 1893.

Vorlesunger über Thermodynamik. Leipzig, Veit, 1897.

Vorlesunger über die Theorie der Wärmestrahlung. Leipzig, Barth, 1906.

Die Einheit des physikalischen Weltbildes (lecture). Leipzig, Hirzel, 1909.

Die Stellung der neueren Physik zur mechanischen Naturanschauung (lecture). Leipzig, Hirzel, 1910.

Acht Vorlesungen über theoretische Physik (lectures). Leipzig, Hirzel, 1910; as *Eight Lectures on Theoretical Physics*, New York, Columbia University Press, 1915.

Über neuere thermodynamische Theorien (lecture). Leipzig, Akademische Verlagsgesellschaft, 1912.

Dynamische und statistische Gesetzmässigkeit (lecture). Leipzig, Barth, 1914.

Einführung in die allgemeine Mechanik. Leipzig, Hirzel, 1916.

Das Wesen des Lichtes (lecture). Berlin, Springer, 1920.

Die Entstehung und bisherige Entwicklung der Quententheorie (Nobel Lecture). Leipzig, Barth, 1920; as *The Origin and Development of the Quantum Theory*, New York, Oxford University Press, 1920.

Physikalische Rundblicke: Gesammelte Reden und Aufsätze.

Leipzig, Hirzel, 1922; as *A Survey of Physics: A Collection of Lectures and Essays*, New York, Dutton, 1923; London, Methuen, 1925.

Kausalgesetze und Willensfreiheit (lecture).   Berlin, Springer, 1923.

Vom Relativen zum Absoluten (lecture).   Leipzig, Hirzel, 1925.

Physikalische Gesetzlichkeit im Lichte neuerer Forschung (lecture).   Leipzig, Barth, 1926.

Das Weltbild der neuen Physik.   Leipzig, Barth, 1929.

Positivismus und reale Aussenwelt.   Leipzig, Akademische Verlagsgesellschaft, 1931.

The Universe in the Light of Modern Physics.   London, Allen and Unwin, and New York, Norton, 1931.

Der Kausalbegriff in der Physik (lecture).   Leipzig, Barth, 1932.

Where Is Science Going?   New York, Norton, 1932; London, Allen and Unwin, 1933.

Wege zur physikalischen Erkenntnis: Reden und Vorträge. Leipzig, Hirzel, 1933.

Die Physik im Kampf um die Weltanschauung (lecture).   Leipzig, Barth, 1934.

Vom Wesen der Willensfreiheit (lecture).   Leipzig, Barth, 1936.

The Philosophy of Physics.   London, Allen and Unwin, 1936.

Determinismus oder Indeterminismus? (lecture).   Leipzig, Barth, 1938.

Religion und Naturwissenschaft (lecture).   Leipzig, Barth, 1938.

Sinn und Grenzen der exakten Wissenschaft (lecture).   Leipzig, Barth, 1942.

Scheinprobleme der Wissenschaft (lecture).   Leipzig, Barth, 1947.

Wissenschaftliche Selbstbiographie.   Leipzig, Barth, 1948; as "Scientific Autobiography," in *Scientific Autobiography and Other Papers*, New York, Philosophical Library, 1949; as *Scientific Autobiography*, London, Williams and Norgate, 1950.

Physikalische Abhandlungen und Vorträge.   Braunschweig, Vieweg, 3 vols., 1958.

The New Science (selections).   New York, Meridian, 1959.

Other

Editor, with C. Pulfrich, *Die mechanische Wärmetheorie, III*, by Rudolf Clausius.   Braunschweig, Vieweg, 1889.

Editor, *Vorlesungen über mathematische Physik, III-IV*, by Gustav Kirchhoff.   Leipzig, Teubner, 2 vols., 1891-94.

Editor, *Über die bewegende Kraft der Wärme*, by Rudolf Clausius.   Leipzig, Englemann, 1898.

Editor, *Abhandlungen über Emission und Absorption*, by Gustav Kirchhoff.   Leipzig, Englemann, 1898.

Editor, *Abhandlungen über mechanische Wärmetheorie*, by Gustav Kirchhoff.   Leipzig, Englemann, 1898.

Editor, *Abhandlungen zur Thermodynamik*, by H. Helmholtz.   Leipzig, Englemann, 1902.

Editor, *25 Jahre Kaiser-Wilhelm-Gesellschaft zur Förderung der Wissenschaften.*   Berlin, Springer, 3 vols., 1936-37.

*

Bibliography: by Max Born, in *Obituary Notices of the Fellows of the Royal Society 6*, London, Morrison and Gibb, 1948; *Max Planck: A Bibliography of his Non-Technical Writings*, Berkeley, University of California Office for History of Science and Technology, 1977.

Critical Studies: *Max Planck als Philosoph* by Hermann Kretzschmar, Munich, Reinhardt, 1967; *Max Planck in Selbstzeugnissen und Bilddokumenten* by Armin Hermann, Hamburg, Rowohlt, 1973; *Early History of Planck's Radiation Law* by Hans Kangro, London, Taylor and Francis, 1976.

*   *   *

The state of physics in which the newly graduated Max Planck found himself in 1879 hardly seemed ripe for revolution. A number of fundamental problems in physics had recently been resolved or were nearing resolution. Maxwell's monumental theory of electromagnetic radiation was but a dozen years old, but it already seemed to be fulfilling its promise as the "new Newtonian synthesis" in physics. Within a decade, Hertz was to provide experimental verification of Maxwell's theory, and the explanatory power of the theory was becoming more and more evident. In this and other areas of physics, a common belief seemed to be that the fundamental questions of physics had all been solved.

Yet, some nagging questions remained, and from one of these, the problem of black-body radiation, was to come one of the great revolutions in the history of science. Superficially, the problem seemed simple. A "black body" is an object which absorbs all the radiation that falls on it. Conversely, the same black body should, when heated, emit a continuous band of radiation (a continuous spectrum), including radiation of every possible frequency. The *specific* type of spectrum produced is dependent only on the temperature of the black body and not on its physical or chemical properties. At lower temperatures, the spectrum of emitted light contains a larger proportion of low-frequency radiation; at higher temperatures, high-frequency radiation predominates.

All of this can be predicted from classical physics. Further, it should be possible to predict the actual shape of emission curves at various temperatures. Knowing the fraction of particles radiating at each frequency, one should be able to predict the total radiation for each frequency, and then to draw a frequency distribution curve for emitted frequencies corresponding to the observed spectrum for any given temperature. In fact, no one had been able to achieve this apparently straightforward task. Predictions based on classical assumptions always produced emission curves that deviated from observed measurements by greater or lesser amounts. It was to the resolution of this problem that Planck devoted himself in the late 1890's. Initially, he was able to find an empirical formula which adequately predicted the relative amounts of radiation produced at each frequency for any given temperature. He found this achievement unsatisfying, however, since it was based purely on observed data and represented no theoretical model of black-body radiation.

The realization of that model came about only when Planck took a bold and revolutionary step in his analysis of radiation. Planck wrote in late 1900 of seeing "the darkness lifted and a new unimagined prospect [begin] to dawn." That "new prospect" was the possibility that energy did not occur as a continuous stream, but that it existed in discrete "packages" to which Planck gave the name *quanta*. A beam of energy, Planck suggested, may not be comparable to a geometric line, infinitely divisible into ever smaller units, but instead to a stream of very small units of energy. The quantum represented the smallest possible unit of energy which cannot itself be subdivided into anything simpler. Each quantum of energy, Planck hypothesized, is a function of only one variable, the frequency of that energy. Specifically, the energy (E) of a quantum is given by: $E = h\nu$, where ν = the frequency of the radiation and h is a constant now known as Planck's constant.

What this tells us is that energy may exist in discrete quanta, with magnitudes $1\,h\nu$, $2\,h\nu$, $3\,h\nu$, etc., but not in fractional quanta of $1/2\,h\nu$, $2/3\,h\nu$, or $3/4\,h\nu$. The quantum is, therefore, comparable to an "atom" of energy.

Planck now applied the notion of quanta to the problem of black-body radiation. In addition to possessing only certain quanta of energy, Planck said, a radiating body emits that energy only when it changes from one energy state to another. A body may go from an energy state of $4\,h\nu$ to $3\,h\nu$ and emit a quantum of $1\,h\nu$ energy. While in a particular energy state, however, the radiator emits no energy at all. The loss of radiation from a body occurs, when it does, only in discrete jumps from one energy level to another. Based on these ideas, Planck was able to predict emission curves for black-body radiators at various temperatures within an acceptable range of experimental error.

The community of physicists in general was amazed, intrigued, and puzzled by Planck's proposal, but hardly more so than Planck himself! The notion of discreteness in radiation violates all our common sense experience with this phenomenon. It is difficult in the extreme to imagine that a beam of light "really" consists of untold numbers of very small packages of light energy. For some time, Planck was concerned that the idea of quanta was little other than a mathematical gimmick that helped resolve a difficult problem in physics. How could the theory be so at variance with everyday experience?

One explanation lies in the character of the constant h itself. The numerical value of the constant is very small: 6.625×10^{-34} joule•seconds. This means that the size of quanta is extraordinarily small. Changes from one quantum level to another on a macroscopic level are so small as to be unobservable. It is only when we deal with atomic-sized phenomena that changes of this order of magnitude become significant.

In any case, the proof of any scientific theory is in the testing. And Planck's quantum theory has been remarkably successful in that respect. Within five years, Albert Einstein had applied the quantum theory to the explanation of the photo-electric effect. This remarkable achievement was soon followed by equally successful applications of quantum theory to the analysis of atomic spectra, the Compton effect, wave mechanics, and other physical phenomena. The 1900 paper on quantum theory by Planck can justly be called a watershed in the development of modern physics.

—David Newton

POINCARÉ, (Jules) Henri. French mathematician. Born in Nancy, 29 April 1854. Studied at the École Polytechnique, Paris, from 1873; École des Mines, Ph.D. 1879. Professor, University of Caen, 1879-81, and University of Paris, 1881-1912. Member, Académie des Sciences, from 1887 (President, 1906), and Académie Française, from 1909. Foreign Member, Royal Society, London, 1894. *Died* (in Paris) *17 July 1912.*

PUBLICATIONS

Collections

Oeuvres. Paris, Gauthier-Villars.
   1. Edited by Jules Drach (Analyse pure. Equations différentielles). 1928.
   2. Edited by N.E. Nörlund and Ernest Lebon (Analyse pure. Fonctions fuchsiennes; groupes fuchsiens et kleinéens). 1916.
   3. Edited by Jules Drach (Analyse pure. Equations différentielles. Theorie des fonctions. Integrales simples et multiples). 1934.
   4. Edited by Georges Valiron (Analyse pure: deuxième partie: Théorie des fonctions). 1950.
   5. Edited by Albert Châtelet (Arithmétique et algébre). 1950.
   6. Edited by Jean Leray. 1952.
   7. Edited by Jules Lévy (Mécanique céleste et astronomie). 1952.
   8. Edited by Pierre Sémirot (Mécanique céleste et astronomie). 1952.
   9-10. Edited by Gérard Petiau (Physique mathématique). 1954.
   11. Edited by Gérard Petiau (Mémoires divers). 1956.

Mathematics

Sur les propriétés des fonctions définies par les équations aux différences partielles (thesis). Paris, Gauthier-Villars, 1879.
Sur la théorie des fonctions fuchsiennes. Caen, Le Blanc-Hardel, 1881.
Memoire sur la réduction simultanée d'une forme quadratique et d'une forme linéaire. Paris, Gauthier-Villars, n.d.
Lectures on mathematical physics:
   Cours de Mr. H. Poincaré, professé pendant l'année 1885-1886: Cinématique pure; Potentiel, Mécanique des fluides. Paris, Association Amicale des Elèves et Anciens Elèves de la Faculté des Sciences de Paris, 2 vols., 1886.
   Leçons sur la théorie mathématique de la lumière, professées pendant le premier semestre 1887-1888, edited by J. Blondin. Paris, G. Carré, 1889.
   Electricité et optique: Cours de physique mathématique: Les Théories de Maxwell et la théorie électromagnétique de la lumière (edited by J. Blondin); *Les Théories de Helmholtz et les expériences de Hertz* (edited by Bernard Brunhes). Paris, G. Carre, 2 vols., 1890-91.
   Leçons sur la théorie de l'élasticité, edited by Émile Borel and Jules Drach. Paris, G. Carre, 1892.
   Les Méthodes nouvelles de la mécanique céleste. Paris, Gauthier-Villars, 3 vols., 1892-99; as *New Methods of Celestial Mechanics,* Washington, D.C., National Aeronautics and Space Administration, n.d.
   Théories mathématiques de la lumière II: Leçons professées pendant le premier semestre 1891-1892: Nouvelles études sur la diffraction, Théorie de la dispersion de Helmholtz, edited by M. Lamotte and D. Hurmuzescu. Paris, G. Carré, 1892.
   Thermodynamique: Leçons professées pendant le premier semestre 1888-89, edited by J. Blondin. Paris, G. Carré, 3 vols., 1892-1923.
   Théorie des tourbillons: Leçons professées pendant le premier deuxième semestre 1891-92, edited by M. Lamotte. Paris, G. Carré, 1893.
   Les Oscillations électriques: Leçons professées pendant le premier trimestre 1892-93, edited by C. Maurain. Paris, G. Carré, 1894.
   Capillarité: Leçons professées pendant le deuxième semestre 1888-89, edited by J. Blondin. Paris, G. Carré, 1895.
   Théorie analytique de la propagation de la chaleur: Leçons professées pendant le premier semestre 1893-1894, edited by Rouyer and Baire. Paris, G. Carré, 1895.
   Calcul des probabilitiés: Leçons professées pendant le deuxième semestre 1893-1894, edited by A. Quiquet. Paris, G. Carré, 1896; revised edition, Paris, Gauthier-Villars, 1912.
   Cinématique et mécanismes: Potentiel et mécanique des fluides, edited by A. Guillet. Paris, G. Carré and C. Naud, 1899.
   La Théorie de Maxwell et les oscillations hertziennes. Paris, C. Naud, 1899; as *Maxwell's Theory and Wireless Telegraphy, Part I,* New York, McGraw Hill, 1904.
   Théorie du potentiel Newtonien: Leçons professées à la Sorbonne pendant le premier semestre 1894-1895, edited by Édouard Le Roy and Georges Vincent. Paris, G. Carré and C. Naud, 1899.
   Figures d'équilibre d'une masse fluide: Leçons professées à la Sorbonne en 1900, edited by L. Dreyfus. Paris, C. Naud, 1902.
   Leçons de mécanique céleste professées à la Sorbonne. Paris, Gauthier-Villars, 3 vols., 1905-10.
   Conférences sur la télégraphie sans fils. Paris, La Lumière Electrique, 1909.
   Leçons sur les hypothèses cosmogoniques professées à la Sorbonne, edited by Henri Vergne. Paris, A. Hermann, 1911.
   La Dynamique de l'électron. Paris, A. Dumas, 1913.
   La Mécanique nouvelle: Conférence, mémoire, et note sur la

théorie de la relativité.   Paris, Gauthier-Villars, 1923.

Other

La Science et l'hypothèse.   Paris, Flammarion, 1902; as *Science and Hypothesis*, London, Walter Scott, 1905.
La Valeur de la Science.   Paris, Flammarion, 1905; as *The Value of Science*, New York, Science Press, 1907.
Science et méthode.   Paris, Flammarion, 1908; as *Science and Method*, London and New York, Nelson, 1914.
Savants et écrivains.   Paris, Flammarion, 1910.
Les Sciences et les humanités.   Paris, A. Fayard, 1911.
Questions du temps présent, with others.   Paris, Foi et Vie, 1911.
Ce que disent les choses, with others.   Paris, Hachette, 1912.
Dernières pensées.   Paris, Flammarion, 1913; as *Mathematics and Science: Last Essays*, New York, Dover, 1963.
Des Fondements de la géometrie.   Paris, Chiron, 1921.

*

Critical Studies: *Henri Poincaré: Biographie, bibliographie analytique des écrits* by Ernest Lebon, Paris, Gauthier-Villars, 1912; *Henri Poincaré: L'Oeuvre scientifique, l'oeuvre philosophique* by Vito Volterra and others, Paris, Alcan, 1914; *La Philosophie géométrique de Henri Poincaré* by Louis Rougier, Paris, Alcan, 1920; *Henri Poincaré* by Paul Appell, Paris, Plon, 1925; *La Principe de relativité selon Poincaré et la mécanique invariante de Le Roux* by Pierre Dive, Paris, Dunod, 1937; *Variations sur un thème de H. Poincaré* by F. Châtelet, Paris, Gauthier-Villars, 1945; *Henri Poincaré, Critic of Crisis: Reflections on His Universe of Discourse* by Tobias Dantzig, New York, Scribner, 1954; *La Philosophie des mathématiques de Henri Poincaré* by J.-J.A. Mooij, Paris, Gauthier-Villars, 1966; *La filosofia de la matematica de Jules Henri Poincaré* by Javier de Lorenzo, Madrid, Tecnos, 1974; *Une Philosophie de savant: Henri Poincaré et la logique mathématique* by Anne-Françoise Schmid, Paris, Maspero, 1978.

*   *   *

The French mathematician and physicist born in Nancy to a great Lorrainese bourgeois family, Henri Poincaré distinguished himself in mathematics at an early stage, coming first at the École Polytechnique. His scientific works, amounting to some five hundred papers, touch on so many essential problems of the day that his oeuvre is almost identical with the mathematics of the time. The papers are short and to the point, frequently using specially produced methods, constantly revealing unexpected links in the fields of research: as far as was possible Poincaré dealt with problems in a general sense. It is therefore impossible to summarize here his scientific works of which he himself made *Analyses* reproduced in part in the eleven volumes of his *Oeuvres*. His most important works concern the study of the properties of definite functions on differential equations—he constructed at that time the Fuchsian and Kleinian groups—and qualitatively on that of curves defined by these equations, which would lead him to the construction of *Analysis situs*, and become algebraic topology, a result which he immediately applied to the study of the movement of celestial bodies (the three body problem, the stability of the solar system). In the theory of functions he reduced the study of non-uniform functions by a variable to that of uniform functions; he showed that a meromorph function of two variables is the quotient of two whole functions. He extended the application of Dirichlet's principle which he professed not to know. In algebra he first studied the methods of solution of n equations to n unknown; in arithmetic he studied substitution groups which do not change ternary quadratic forms. He used throughout the theory of discontinuous or continuous groups (particularly Lie's groups) whether he worked on Fuchsian functions or on questions of Euclidean or non-

Euclidean geometry. From 1886 until his death he held the chair of mathematical physics, then that of celestial mechanics and astronomy at the Sorbonne; his published lectures touch on most of the important problems of physics of the time (probability, theory of potential, thermodynamics, electricity and optics, mathematical theory of light, analytical theory of the propagation of heat, wireless, etc.). We owe to him a theory on tides. His best-known contributions are on celestial mechanics (there are three volumes and various papers) where he studied the conditions of convergence of the series used in the forecasting of astronomic phenomena, and a study on the electrodynamics of bodies in movement where he reveals his conception of the theory of relativity starting with the works of Lorentz; he established the group in physics known as "Poincaré's group."

Taken in isolation Poincaré's truly philosophic ideas do not always demonstrate originality—they particularly over-simplify the Kantian contribution—but the functioning of his thought is remarkable in the constantly controlled tension between general principles and the meticulous specification of particular cases. It is the systematic separation which Poincaré maintains between fact and scientific theory which ensures the coherence of his thought; as a matter of fact, if Poincaré has a clear notion of scientific theory, he accepts the notion of fact without criticism. Any scientific theory is evaluated in relation to the facts that it co-ordinates. The perception we have of fact is "a constant link in our sensations," and this link is at the same time the subject, the content, and the truth of science; scientific theory is thus seen as inductive, integrating these constant links by successive generalisations into a system of relations—a language. Theory is thus an interpretation, even at the level closest to "raw fact," as he calls it contrary to the conventionalists. Interpretation is built up by the use of various methods, all hypothetical in regard to fact. If we ignore the very general hypotheses controlling in particular the application of mathematics to physical phenomena, we first of all find systematic extrapolations (smoothing of curves) which are already hypotheses suggested by the theory or an outline of it; these extrapolations, applied to a larger number of phenomena, serve as approximate laws. The arrangement of these laws is then ensured by a choice among them, erecting some of them as principles; this choice takes place during appropriately theoretical work and is controlled by the supra-theoretical ideal of simplicity. The transition from law to principle takes place, in all disciplines, by decomposition of the law: we see in this either a purely geometric phenomenon which precisely obeys the law (this is the principle) and a very small perturbatory phenomenon, or a definition (non-arbitrary conventional link within the theory) and a verifiable law; principles are thus beyond the control of experience, although applicable to reality since they are constructed inductively. But the theory does not affect reality itself; it is used *as if* reality conformed to principles, *as if* solid bodies were invariable and rigid. In other words, theory is metaphorical. This conception of theory, which loses its meaning in the necessary process of generalisation, gives place to philosophy: it is built up inductively, starting in particular from theories of physics where equations are omitted: in Poincaré there are constant transitions between his theories of physics and his philosophy. It is understandable that he has regularly revealed a false attitude towards theories: they are the source of invention but they are dangerous, for they modify individual facts by integrating them into a hypothetical language. And Poincaré has manifested this duplicity in many new situations: he was one of the first to recognise the importance of G. Cantor's works, to use them, and he even appears to have translated one of his papers. But he expressed a growing mistrust of the theory of sets which exceeds—and therefore generalises beyond measure—the power of natural numbers (aleph zero). He appreciated Hilbert's axiomatic works while remaining reserved about the value of works too far removed from the sources of invention. He was among the first to demonstrate the possibility of applying in physics mathematical models other than analytical, but he kept as far as possible to mechanical models whose conditions he had moreover

established. He preferred to treat relativity as experimental truth, verifiable in relation to the mechanical properties of ether, rather than, as Einstein, to pose the principle and examine the consequences.

This conception of theory as inductive had effects in each of the disciplines of exact science that Poincaré dealt with: these epistemological effects are determinable in each case through the specific combination of the relation between fact and interpretation. This is why Poincaré himself dealt with these questions, from case to case and always in the same order, in the three books devoted during his life to the philosophy of the sciences (*Science and Hypothesis, The Value of Science, Science and Method*, to which should be added *Last Thoughts*); this order is determined by the two sources that Poincaré attributes to facts: mind for facts *a priori*, experience for facts *a posteriori*. This is why Poincaré, aware more than any other that a scientific fact has already been interpreted, nevertheless made it function, in his philosophy, as raw fact.

In the same way he assimilated arithmetic into the sphere of facts of the mind, then experimental physics into that of the facts of experience; "convention" ("a rough area between our love of simplicity and the desire not to distance ourselves too much from that which our instruments teach us") shows then the distancing of the enunciations of a discipline from the two sources of fact, facts which sometimes only provide the opportunity for a theory (geometry) or which form the subject of it (mechanics): but at the same time, these conventions are also the necessary internal ingredients of theories: definitions and hypotheses. Poincaré is at the junction of two conceptions, one which creates from theory an image of the world, a reflection of reality, and one which sees in it an instrument for understanding a certain kind of reality. One sees that the false conventionalism often attributed to Poincaré is only a consequence of his positive confidence in fact ("a fact is a fact").

We now understand that, although Poincaré's philosophic direction was always the same—research into the origin of fact—each time he drew different conclusions.

In *Arithmetic*, the raw fact is the faculty possessed by our mind to repeat an operation indefinitely as soon as it is possible. Poincaré thus refused any conceptual distinction between the finite and the infinite (which was to him the indefinite), this transition being operated according to him by the principle of total induction: not that he confused, as has been wrongly claimed, mathematical induction with physical induction, for he based the former on an "a priori synthetic intuition"; technically that means that one can not demonstrate that *reasoning* by induction can be applied to a *definite* set by induction. He did not want to see that Peano and Russell, whom he criticised very sharply, outlined the idea of final clause, permitting use of the induction principle as algorithm deciding if a number is finite or not. His epistemology of repeated fact finally made him refuse the notion of algorithm. In the circumstances Poincaré's opposition was not an anticipation of Godel's theorem. We also understand how Poincaré was able to inspire the intuitionism of Brouwer.

In *Analysis*, Poincaré dealt mainly with the notion of continuity; faithful to his constructivist conception of theories starting from facts, he treated continuity as a progressive creation: when the sensations of physical continuity lead us to mathematical contradictions, we create an intermediary mathematical entity which, if it has suitable properties, will be called a real number. Poincaré did not like Dedekind's definition of the break, which did not take into account the origin of the notion of continuity.

In *Geometry*, Poincaré's philosophy was liberating. Geometry is the discipline which ensures the link between mathematics and the experimental sciences; *a priori* non-revisable in the sense of a physical law, it was built with regard to the exterior world. He tried to describe its psychomotor formation, a work which inspired J. Piaget; it is thus so far removed from the two sources of facts that neither mind nor experience are adequate to determine uniquely the notion of distance; this notion will be defined

each time by a special postulate. Euclid's fifth postulate is thus a convention, the "disguised definition" of Euclidean law. In this way Poincaré established the validity of the non-Euclidean geometries. He showed that Euclid's geometry is a model for that of Lobatchevsky. In its application to physical reality one geometry is not therefore more true than another, but more convenient.

Poincaré saw a structural analogy between mechanics and geometry: the first differs from the second in that it is an experimental science, and in its subject which is no longer the study of groups, but that of the movements of solid bodies, yet it draws nearer to it in the function of the conventions. This analogy establishes the applicability of mathematics to the physical world. This central position between mathematics and experience has earned for mechanics the role of philosophical interpretation for physics, and Poincaré saw as a crisis the questioning of the universal validity of the principles of mechanics.

The important philosophic problem in *Physics* evidently concerns the status of mathematical physics, since "experience is all"; it is a necessary guide, but it prompts the multiplication of hypotheses. This is why Poincaré reminds us on several occasions that one must "free the vault of its arches": a prevision realised in an experiment is not only the verification of a consequence of the theory, but in certain cases is the experimental demonstration of a law; one can then abstract the theory that suggested the experiment. In principle this point of view is progressive since it does not cling to a particular theory. Poincaré was also mindful of new ideas in physics; he judged rather favourably Planck's theory of quanta and followed the work on radioactivity. But his conception of fact obliged a prudent attitude. We can see how far we are from Einstein's conception which poses principles and seeks to verify their consequences: perhaps it is also for that reason that Poincaré who made discoveries more or less in every direction did not give his name to a complete theory.

Despite the interest that Poincaré's philosophy has, in that it takes to its furthest limit a classic philosophy of the sciences, it finally earned him an undeserved bad reputation. It is true that in opposing new ideas with facts it created an obstacle in the path of certain of the former. That these obstacles became political, blocking the study in particular of mathematical logic in France, is due however to the centralisation of French scientific and university politics which, for a long time, employed Poincaré's immense scientific influence to justify its conservatism, forgetting that its most important factor was its invention.

—Anne-Françoise Schmid

POLANYI, Michael. British chemist and philosopher. Born in Budapest, Hungary, 12 March 1891; emigrated to England in 1933. Studied at the Technische Hochschule, Karlsruhe; University of Budapest, M.D. 1913, Ph.D. 1917. Served as a Medical Officer in the Austro-Hungarian Army, 1914-17. Married Magda Kemeny in 1921; 2 sons. Worked at the Kaiser Wilhelm Institute of Fibre Chemistry, Berlin, 1920-23, and the Institute of Physical and Electro-Chemistry, Berlin, 1923-33; Chair of Physical Chemistry, 1933-48, and Professor of Social Studies, 1948-58, University of Manchester; Senior Research Fellow, Merton College, Oxford, 1958-76. Visiting Professor, University of Chicago, 1950, 1954, 1967, 1968, 1979, 1970, Duke University, Durham, North Carolina, 1964, and University of Texas, Austin, 1968, 1969, 1971; Distinguished Research Fellow, University of Virginia, Charlottesville, 1961; Fellow, Center for Advanced Study in the Behavioral Sciences, Stanford, California, 1962-63; Senior Fellow, Center for Advanced Studies, Wesleyan University, Middletown, Connecticut, 1965. Riddell Lecturer, University of London, 1945; Lloyd Roberts Lecturer. University of Manchester, 1946; Gifford Lecturer, University of Aberdeen, 1951; Lindsay Lecturer, University of Keele, 1958; Eddington Lecturer, Cambridge University, 1960; Gunning Lecturer, University of Edinburgh, 1960; Bose Lecturer, University of Calcutta, 1960; McEnnerny Lecturer, University of California, Berkeley, 1961; Terry Lecturer, Yale University, New Haven, Connecticut, 1962. Recipient: Nuffield Gold Medal, Royal Society of Medicine, London, 1970. Honorary doctorate: Princeton University, New Jersey, 1946; University of Leeds, 1947; University of Aberdeen, 1959; University of Notre Dame, Indiana, 1965; Wesleyan University, 1965; University of Manchester, 1966; University of Toronto, 1967; Cambridge University, 1969. Fellow of the Royal Society, 1944. Member, International Academy of Philosophy of Science; Life Member, Kaiser Wilhelm Gesellschaft, later the Max-Planck-Gesellschaft, 1929. Foreign Member, Society of Science, Letters, and Arts, Naples, 1933; Foreign Life Member, Max-Planck-Gesellschaft, 1949; Foreign Honorary Member, American Academy of Arts and Sciences, 1962. *Died 22 February 1976.*

PUBLICATIONS

Science, Sociology and Philosophy

Atomic Reactions. London, Williams and Norgate, 1932.
U.S.S.R. Economics: Fundamental Data, System and Spirit. Manchester, Manchester University Press, 1935.
The Contempt of Freedom. London, Watts, 1940.
Full Employment and Free Trade. London, Cambridge University Press, 1945.
Science, Faith, and Society (lectures). London, Oxford University Press, and Chicago, University of Chicago Press, 1946.
The Logic of Liberty: Reflections and Rejoinders. London, Routledge, and Chicago, University of Chicago Press, 1951.
Personal Knowledge: Toward a Post-Critical Philosophy. London, Routledge, and Chicago, University of Chicago Press, 1958.
Tyranny and Freedom, Ancient and Modern. Calcutta, Quest, 1958.
The Study of Man. London, Routledge, and Chicago, University of Chicago Press, 1959.
Beyond Nihilism (lecture). London, Cambridge University Press, 1960.
The Tacit Dimension. New York, Doubleday, 1966.
Toward a Unity of Knowledge, edited by Marjorie Grene. New York, International University Presses, 1969.
Knowing and Being: Essays by Michael Polanyi, edited by Marjorie Grene. London, Routledge, 1969.
Scientific Thought and Social Reality: Essays by Michael Polanyi, edited by Fred Schwartz. New York, International University Presses, 1974.
Meaning, with Harry Prosch. Chicago, University of Chicago Press, 1975.

*

Critical Studies: *Intellect and Hope: Essays in the Thought of Michael Polanyi* edited by Thomas A. Langford and William H. Poteat, Durham, North Carolina, Duke University Press, 1968 (includes bibliography); *The Way of Discovery: An Introduction to the Thought of Michael Polanyi* by Richard Gelwick, New York, Oxford University Press, 1977; "Michael Polanyi," by E.P. Wigner and R.A. Hodgkin, in *Biographical Memoirs of Fellows of the Royal Society 23* (London), 1977 (includes bibliography).

*   *   *

Michael Polanyi was successively a medical doctor, a physical chemist, a social scientist, and a philosopher. Out of his background of avant-garde Hungarian liberalism and personal acquaintance with the tragedies of the first World War and the

Soviet revolution, he was moved to take on the fundamental problem of the 20th century: the ubiquity of wide-spread moral aspirations for truth, justice, and brotherhood, the collapse of any transcendent faith that could uphold these aspirations, and the consequent distortion of moral imperatives into unprecedented destructiveness.

The first great period of Polanyi's creativity was in the field of physical chemistry. His first success was on the adsorption isotherm for gases and solids, introducing the conception of a condensation without change of state, under the control of the potential field in multilayered regions on surfaces. In fiber studies he developed with Weissenberg the rotating-crystal x-ray method, went part way to the structure of cellulose, and studied cold-working on long metal crystals, from which he discovered the influence of dislocations. He is best known for his discovery of the highly dilute flame method for elucidating steps in gas reactions, but his initiation of the modern potential-surface approach to reaction rates is of more far-reaching importance. Polanyi experienced from within the character of science as involving a community of scholars immersed in a vital tradition centering its attention on innovation for the purpose of learning more truths about nature, and this formed the ground out of which he could speak with authority on the basis of human knowledge and the organization of society.

Moved by the contrast of actual science with Marxist proposals for the planning of scientific research by political bodies concerned with socially valuable applications, Polanyi proposed his theory of the operations of any cultural circle, of science or art or literature or sport. Every circle has its traditions and rules of rightness, its influential authorities, its framework for recognizing and encouraging innovation, and its mode of introducing new members by apprenticeship. Every person engaged in a group that practices and develops a special portion of culture makes a commitment to the traditions and standards of the group and comes to have a conscience concerned with right action within it—one can even say that he or she has a particular self that has some identity with the group. Polanyi pursues his theory of such circles of thought all the way to the necessary background of faith in the fundamental principles of a free society: loyalty to truth and the power of thought, loyalty to justice and the use of legal reasoning, tolerance for dissent, and charity for all. The problems of governance focus for Polanyi on the essential impossibility of any central agency being able to predict where any creative circle will go in its innovation, or being able to furnish or even to obtain the knowledge needed to direct decision-making. On the other hand, he stresses the fundamental need for authoritative and influential opinion in every separate area of thought. Only the members of all the circles—and all those who take the roles of producers and consumers—acting from their consciences can carry out the huge number of decisions needed daily in a modern society.

In his brief excursion into economics, he wrote in favor of the free market economy as being the only way that economic and financial decisions can adequately be made. At the same time, however, he was concerned deeply with governmental channeling of free enterprise for the sake of social equity. The Keynesian scheme of monetary control to maintain full employment was the example he championed most strongly.

Polanyi's social theory requires a philosophy that can account for the recognition of achievements, for trust in authority and tradition, and for the expansion of the self both by participation in a tradition and by the irreversible changes brought about by every acceptance of novelty. His way of affirming our belief in our ability to recognize meanings, to find truths about nature, or to achieve right actions, rests on his description of perception as an active, integrative process in which perceiving creatures try to see what is there by integrating subsidiary clues into a whole. This way of looking at perception leads to a description of the whole range of unspecifiable arts and acts of judgment by which we make our way about the world, use tools by assimilating them into our bodies, learn and use language, and develop human thought and culture. It has the consequence that all explicit knowledge rests on the tacit awareness of clues, things that we know but cannot tell because we rely on them for focussing attention on other things. Polanyi's conception of tacit knowing constitutes a sweeping rejection of the critical spirit with which linguistic philosophers and logical positivists attempt to find a wholly explicit rationale for propositional language and scientific theory-construction. At the same time, tacit knowing provides new answers to old philosophical problems, such as the relation of sense data to the actual world, the conception of a class in relation to its members, and meaning in relation to words and sentences.

Polanyi shows that values and emotions are essential aspects of all knowledge. The efforts to know, to be rational, to find beauty, and to relate lovingly and ethically with others are all driven by our basic passions for seeking reality and entering into relationships. Rather than distinguishing between reason and emotion, he sorts out with care the distinctions between the personal motivations for objectivity and universality that underlie rationality in science and indeed all scholarship, and motivations that are directed toward ourselves for which he used the term "subjective" as contrasted with the term "personal."

Polanyi's view is decidedly anti-reductionistic, both in the logical sense that the parts never can explain the whole (a given set of parts are equally compatible with many different wholes) and in the epistemological sense that the world we perceive and live in is indeed a world of many levels of being and organization. We grant reality to any entity—and there are many kinds—which we anticipate meeting anew in unexpected ways. In particular, he stresses that persons cannot be reduced to impersonal machine-like creatures. We know persons only in I-Thou relationships or as consequences of them, and the entire knowing process is self-contradictory if described in terms of deterministic reactions rather than in terms of persons committing themselves to responsible judgments within trusting communities of thought and observation.

The consequences of Polanyi's views for the social sciences are particularly important, both for the light thrown by his philosophy on their basic operations and outlooks and also for the fundamental changes he has made in the models of physical science they have borrowed. In fact, Polanyi puts all of our academic disciplines into relationships along a continuum rather than sharply distinguishing them by method.

Polanyi develops his affirmation of religious faith out of his account of the elements of faith and commitment underlying all of our culture, from the most objective science to the implicit values of a free society. His ontology of transcendent realities is based on the transitive nature of tacit knowing whereby any set of entities can become the clues to the intuition of higher entities: persons, communities, ideas, ideals, and values, with clues to God as the highest spiritual entity.

—William T. Scott

POPPER, Karl (Raimund). British philosopher. Born in Vienna, Austria, 28 July 1902; emigrated to New Zealand in 1937 and to England in 1945: later naturalized. Studied at the University of Vienna, Ph.D. 1928; University of New Zealand, Christchurch, M.A. 1938. Married Josefine Anna Henninger in 1930. Senior Lecturer in Philosophy, Canterbury University College, Christchurch, 1937-45; Reader, 1945-49, Professor of Logic and Scientific Method, 1949-69, and since 1969 Professor Emeritus, London School of Economics, University of London. Visiting Professor, University of California, Berkeley, 1962; University of Minnesota, Minneapolis, 1962; Indiana University, Bloomington, 1963; New York University, 1963; Massachusetts Institute of Technology, Cambridge, 1963; Institute for Advanced Studies, Vienna, 1964; and University of Denver, 1966; Kenan Visiting Professor, Emory University, Atlanta, 1969; Ziskind Profes-

sor, Brandeis University, Waltham, Massachusetts, 1969; Visiting Professor, University of Otago, Dunedin, New Zealand, 1973. Visiting Fellow, Center for Advanced Study in the Behavioral Sciences, Stanford, California, 1956-57; Salk Institute for the Biological Sciences, San Diego, California, 1966-67; Visiting Erskine Fellow, Canterbury University College, 1973. William James Lecturer, Harvard University, Cambridge, Massachusetts, 1950; Rathbone Lecturer, University of Bristol, 1956; since 1960, Annual Philosophical Lecturer, British Academy; Herbert Spencer Lecturer, Oxford University, 1961, 1973; Shearman Lecturer, University College London, 1961; Farnum Lecturer, Princeton University, New Jersey, 1963; Arthur Holly Compton Lecturer, Washington University, St. Louis, 1965; Romanes Lecturer, Oxford University, 1972; Henry D. Broadhead Memorial Lecturer, University of Canterbury, Kent, 1973; Darwin Lecturer, Cambridge University, 1977; Tarner Lecturer, University of Michigan, Ann Arbor, 1978; Doubleday Lecturer, Smithsonian Institution, Washington, D.C., 1979; Morrell Memorial Lecturer, University of York, 1981. Member of the Council, Association for Symbolic Logic, 1951-55; President, Aristotelian Society, 1958-59, and British Society for the Philosophy of Science, 1959-61. Recipient: Prize of the City of Vienna, 1965; James Scott Prize, Royal Society of Edinburgh, 1970; Sonning Prize, University of Copenhagen, 1973; Lippincott Award, American Political Science Association, 1976; Renner-Prize, Vienna, 1978; Gold Medal, American Museum of Natural History, New York, 1979; Lucas Prize, University of Tübingen, 1980; Grand Decoration of Honor in Gold, Austria, 1976; Ehrenzeichen für Wissenschaft und Kunst, Austria, 1980; Order Pour le Mérite, 1980. Honorary doctorate: University of London, 1948; University of Chicago, 1962; University of Denver, 1966; University of Warwick, 1971; University of Canterbury, Kent, 1973; City University, London, 1976; University of Salford, 1976; University of Guelph, Ontario, 1978; University of Vienna, 1978; University of Mannheim, 1978; University of Salzburg, 1979; Cambridge University, 1980; Gustavus Adolphus College, St. Peter, Minnesota, 1981. Member, Institut de France; Associate Member, Royal Academy of Belgium, and Accademia dei Lincei, Rome; Honorary Member, American Academy of Arts and Sciences, 1966; Académie Internationale d'Histoire des Sciences, 1977; Allgemeine Gesellschaft für Philosophie in Deutschland, 1979; and Deutsche Akademie für Sprache und Dichtung, 1979. Fellow, International Academy for the Philosophy of Science, 1949; British Academy, 1958; and the Royal Society, London, 1976. Honorary Fellow, London School of Economics and Political Science; Darwin College, Cambridge. Knighted, 1965. Address: London School of Economics, Houghton Street, London WC2, England.

PUBLICATIONS

Philosophy

Logik der Forschung: Zur Erkenntnistheorie der modernen Naturwissenschaft, edited by Philipp Frank and Moritz Schlick, Berlin, Springer, 1934; as *The Logic of Scientific Discovery*, London, Hutchinson, and New York, Basic Books, 1959.

The Open Society and Its Enemies. London, Routledge, 2 vols., 1945; revised edition, Princeton, New Jersey, Princeton University Press, 1950.

The Poverty of Historicism. London, Routledge, and Boston, Beacon Press, 1957.

On the Sources of Knowledge and of Ignorance (lecture). London, Oxford University Press, 1960.

Conjectures and Refutations: The Growth of Scientific Knowledge. London, Routledge, and New York, Basic Books, 1963.

Of Clouds and Clocks (lecture). St. Louis, Washington University Press, 1966.

Objective Knowledge: An Evolutionary Approach. Oxford, Clarendon Press, 1972.

Philosophy and Physics: Essays in Defense of the Objectivity of Physical Science. Oxford, Clarendon Press, 1974.

The Self and Its Brain: An Argument for Interactionism, with John C. Eccles. New York, Springer, 1977.

Die beiden Probleme der Erkenntnistheorie (1930-33), edited by von Troels Eggers Hansen. Tübingen, Mohr, 1979.

Postscript to The Logic of Scientific Discovery (1957), edited by W.W. Bartley. London, Hutchinson, and Totowa, New Jersey, Rowman and Littlefield, 3 vols., 1982.

Other

"Intellectual Autobiography," in *The Philosophy of Karl Popper*, edited by Paul Arthur Schilpp. La Salle, Illinois, Open Court, 2 vols., 1974; as *Unended Quest: An Intellectual Autobiography*, London, Collins, 1976.

*

Critical Studies: *Karl Popper* by Bryan Magee, London, Collins, and New York, Viking Press, 1973; *The Philosophy of Karl Popper* edited by Paul Arthur Schilpp, La Salle, Illinois, Open Court, 2 vols., 1974 (includes bibliography); *The Philosophy of Karl Popper* by Robert J. Ackerman, Amherst, University of Massachusetts Press, 1976; *Karl Popper* by Anthony O'Hear, London and Boston, Routledge, 1980.

*   *   *

Like George Orwell's *Animal Farm* (1945), Karl Popper's *The Open Society and Its Enemies* (1945) had some difficulty in finding a publisher. When the first volume, "The Spell of Plato," was read by an eminent American philosopher, he declared that it was too irreverent even to be submitted to a publisher, while Popper's attack on totalitarianism of the Left as well as of the Right in the second volume, "The High Tide of Prophecy: Hegel, Marx and the Aftermath" ran just as counter as did the political message of Orwell's fable to the worship of Soviet Russia which was endemic in the Great Britain of the mid-1940's. Albert Camus nevertheless kept a copy of *The Open Society and Its Enemies* on his bookshelf; and Popper's recommendation that all "final solutions" in politics and economics should be replaced by what he called "piecemeal social engineering" is in fact a summary of what the Western democracies have done since the end of the Second World War. Insofar as this has made Western society more attractive, both to its own members and to anyone who manages to escape from the Russian Empire, it has also proved how justified Popper was in applying to the study of politics the same criteria of verifiability by experience on which he insisted in his writings on science, especially *The Logic of Scientific Discovery* and *Objective Knowledge: An Evolutionary Approach.* For although Popper, in spite of his Viennese origins, was not a logical positivist, his thinking both in science and politics had the same suspicion of metaphysics and respect for empirical data. What he did in philosophy was to replace the logical positivists' view that all scientific and other theories had to be verifiable by experience by the insistence that, in order to be meaningful, some process should exist whereby they could be falsified. For, he argued, unless one could somehow make observations or devise an experiment which would show a particular theory to be wrong, then it ought indeed to be relegated to the meaningless realm of metaphysics. Where Popper also goes further than the logical positivists is in seeing a link between faith in abstract theories and political intolerance. He dedicated *The Open Society and Its Enemies* to "the millions who have been sacrificed to the doctrine of Historical Inevitability"; and his defence of democracy against its totalitarian opponents involves not only a respect for facts and a determination to discover them but also a determination to recognise that human beings cannot

be made perfect by decree of a society invented from which conflict is absent.

—Philip Thody

POUND, Roscoe. American jurist. Born in Lincoln, Nebraska, 17 October 1870. Studied at University of Nebraska, Lincoln, B.A. 1888, M.A. 1889, Ph.D. 1897; Harvard Law School, Cambridge, Massachusetts, 1889-90: admitted to the bar, 1890. Married Grace Gerard in 1899 (died, 1928); married Lucy Miller in 1931 (died 1959). Practiced law in Lincoln, 1890-1901, 1903-07; Assistant Professor, 1899-1903, and Dean of the Law Department, 1903-07, University of Nebraska; Professor, Northwestern University, Evanston, Illinois, 1907-09, and University of Chicago, 1909-10; Story Professor of Law, 1910-13, Dean of the Law School, 1916-36, Professor, 1937-47, and Professor Emeritus, 1947-64, Harvard University. Tagore Professor of Law, University of Calcutta, India, 1948; Visiting Professor, University of California Law School, Los Angeles, 1949-53. Director, Botany Survey of Nebraska, 1892-1903; Commissioner of Appeals, Supreme Court of Nebraska, 1901-03; Nebraska Commissioner on Uniform State Laws, 1904-07; Director, Survey of Criminal Justice, Cleveland, 1922, and National Conference of Judicial Councils, from 1938; Legal Adviser to Chinese Ministry of Justice, 1946-49. President, American Academy of Arts and Sciences, 1935-37, and International Academy of Comparative Law, 1950-56. Recipient: American Bar Association Medal, 1940; Gourgas Medal, Scottish Rite of Freemasonry, 1952. Honorary Master of Laws: Northwestern University, 1908; honorary doctorate: University of Michigan, Ann Arbor, 1913; University of Nebraska, 1913; University of Missouri, Columbia, 1916; University of Chicago, 1916; Brown University, Providence, Rhode Island, 1919; Harvard University, 1920; Cambridge University, 1922; Union College, Schenectady, New York, 1923; University of Pittsburgh, 1926; University of Colorado, Boulder, 1927; George Washington University, Washington, D.C., 1928; University of California, Berkeley, 1929; Boston University, 1933; University of Cincinnati, 1933; University of Berlin, 1934; Rutgers University, New Brunswick, New Jersey, 1941. Honorary Fellow, Stanford University, California, 1941. Fellow, American Academy of Arts and Sciences. Died 1 July 1964.

PUBLICATIONS

Law

Evolution of Legal Education (lecture). Lincoln, Nebraska, North, 1903.

Outlines of Lectures on Jurisprudence, Chiefly from the Analytical Standpoint. Lincoln, Nebraska, North, 1903; revised edition, Cambridge, Massachusetts, Harvard University Press, 1914, 1920, 1928, 1943.

Cases on Practice: Select Cases and Other Authorities on Procedure in Civil Causes with Reference to the Code and Decisions of Nebraska, Vol. I. Lincoln, Nebraska, North, 1904.

Report upon Uniformity of Laws Governing the Establishment and Regulation of Corporations and Joint Stock Companies in the American Republics. Washington, D.C., Government Printing Office, 1915.

Cases on Equitable Relief against Defamation and Injuries to Personality: Supplementary to Ames's Cases in Equity Jurisdiction, Vol. I. Privately printed, 1916.

The Spirit of the Common Law (lectures). Boston, Marshall Jones, 1921.

An Introduction to the Philosophy of Law (lectures). New

Haven, Connecticut, Yale University Press, 1922; revised edition, 1954.

Interpretations of Legal History (lectures). Cambridge, University Press, and New York, Macmillan, 1923.

Law and Morals (lectures). Chapel Hill, University of North Carolina Press, 1924.

Criminal Justice in 19th Century America (lecture). Los Angeles, Chimes Press, 1926.

Culture and Population (lecture). Pittsburgh, University of Pittsburgh, 1926.

The Harvard Law School: Its History, Its Development, Its Needs. New York, Harvard University Law School Endowment Fund Committee, 1926.

The Problem of Criminal Justice (lecture). Los Angeles, Chimes Press, 1926.

Criminal Justice in America (lectures). New York, Holt, 1930.

Cases on Equitable Relief Against Torts, Including Defamation and Injuries to Personality, with Zechariah Chafee, Jr. Privately printed, 1933.

Fashions in Juristic Thinking (lecture). Birmingham, Holdsworth Club of the University of Birmingham, 1937.

The Formative Era of American Law (lectures). Boston, Little Brown, 1938.

American Juristic Thinking in the Twentieth Century. Durham, North Carolina, Duke University Press, 1939.

The History and System of the Common Law. New York, P.F. Collier, 1939.

Contemporary Juristic Theory (lectures). Claremont, California, Claremont Colleges, 1940.

Organization of Courts. Boston, Little Brown, 1940.

Appellate Procedure in Civil Cases. Boston, Little Brown, 1941.

The Task of Law (lectures). Lancaster, Pennsylvania, Franklin and Marshall College, 1941.

Social Control Through Law (lectures). New Haven, Connecticut, Yale University Press, 1942.

The Development of Constitutional Guarantees of Liberty (lectures). Notre Dame, Indiana, University of Notre Dame, 1945.

Public Policy Formation and Administration in a Democracy, with John W. Ford. New Wilmington, Pennsylvania, Economic and Business Foundation, 1945.

Administrative Agencies and the Law. New York, National Industrial Conference Board, 1946.

Sources and Forms of Law. Notre Dame, Indiana, University of Notre Dame, 1946.

Law and the Administration of Justice (lectures). Nanking, Sino-American Cultural Service, 1947.

Some Problems of the Administration of Justice in China (lectures). Nanking, National Chengchi University, 1948.

New Paths of the Law (lectures). Lincoln, University of Nebraska Press, 1950.

Justice According to Law (lectures). New Haven, Connecticut, Yale University Press, 1951.

The Lawyer from Antiquity to Modern Times, with Particular Reference to the Development of Bar Associations in the United States. St. Paul, Minnesota, West, 1953.

Legal Immunities of Labor Unions. Washington, D.C., American Enterprise Association, 1957.

The Ideal Element in Law (lectures). Calcutta, University of Calcutta, 1958.

Jurisprudence. St. Paul, Minnesota, West, 5 vols., 1959.

Labor Unions and the Concept of Public Service. Washington, D.C., American Enterprise Association, 1959.

A World Legal Order: Law and Laws in Relation to World Law (lecture). Medford, Massachusetts, Fletcher School of Law and Diplomacy, 1959.

Law Finding Through Experience and Reason. Athens, University of Georgia Press, 1960.

The Foundation of Law (lecture). Washington, D.C., Washington College of Law, 1961.

Threescore and Ten Years of the Harvard Law School (lecture). Cambridge, Massachusetts, Harvard Law School, 1961.

The Tort Claims Act: Reason or History. Watertown, Massachusetts, Roscoe Pound-NACCA Foundation, 1963.

Roscoe Pound and Criminal Justice, edited by Sheldon Glueck. Dobbs Ferry, New York, Oceana, 1965.

Other

The Phytogeography of Nebraska. I: General Survey, with Frederic E. Clements. Lincoln, Nebraska, North, 1898; revised edition, Lincoln, Nebraska, University of Nebraska Botanical Seminar, 1900.

Lectures on the Philosophy of Freemasonry. Anamosa, Iowa, National Masonic Research Society, 1915; as *Lectures on Masonic Jurisprudence*, Washington, D.C., Masonic Service Organization, 1924.

Masonic Addresses and Writings. New York, Macoy and Masonic Supply, 1953.

Editor and translator, *Readings in Roman Law*. Lincoln, Nebraska, North, 1906.

Editor, *Readings on the History and System of Common Law*. Lincoln, Nebraska, North, 1904; revised edition, with Theodore Pluncknett, Rochester, New York, Lawyers Co-operative, 1927.

Editor, *Cases on the Law of Torts*, by James Barr Ames and Jeremiah Smith. Privately printed, 1916.

Editor, with Felix Frankfurter, *Criminal Justice in Cleveland*. Cleveland, Cleveland Foundation, 1922.

Editor, *Twentieth Century Ideas as to the End of Law: Harvard Legal Essays, Written in Honor of, and Presented to Joseph Henry Beale and Samuel Williston*. Cambridge, Massachusetts, Harvard University Press, 1934.

Editor, *The National Law Library*. New York, P.F. Collier, 6 vols., 1939.

Editor, with others, *Perspectives of Law: Essays for Austin Wakeman Scott*. Boston, Little Brown, 1964.

Translator, *Laws of France, 1919: Town Planning and Reparation of Damages Caused by the Events of the War*. New York, National Civic Federation, 1919.

*

Bibliography: *A Bibliography of the Writings of Roscoe Pound* by F.C. Setaro, Cambridge, Massachusetts, Harvard University Press, 1942; supplement by George A. Strait, 1960.

Critical Studies: *Social Engineering: The Legal Philosophy of Roscoe Pound* by Linus J. McManaman, Atchison, Kansas, Abbey Student Press, 1956 (?); *The Administration of Justice in Retrospect: Roscoe Pound's 1906 Address in a Half-Century of Experience* edited by Arthur Leon Harding, Dallas, Southern Methodist University Press, 1957; *The Pound Conference: Perspectives on Justice in the Future*, St. Paul, Minnesota, West, 1979.

*   *   *

The name of Roscoe Pound is invariably linked with those of Supreme Court Justices Oliver Wendell Holmes, Jr., Louis Brandeis, and Benjamin Cardozo. Together, they were instrumental in transforming early 20th-century American legal thinking. Unlike the others, Pound never served as a judge on any court, and therefore never had the opportunity to express his views through the medium of judicial decision or dissent. His contributions came through his long tenure in academe, and through writing and lecturing.

Pound's law career began unconventionally. Although he was

THINKERS OF THE TWENTIETH CENTURY

PRAZ 457

a precocious scholar and the son of a judge, his first interests and publications were in botany. He did enter law school, but never completed his studies. However, his astute writings about the law led to his appointment as professor, and later dean, at several major midwestern universities. With only an honorary law degree, he became dean of the nation's most prestigious law school, at Harvard University, a position he held until 1936.

At Harvard, Pound was able to build on the curricular reforms instituted by his predecessor, Christopher Langdell. These centered on the "case method," which provided law students with a realistic apprenticeship in dealing with trial situations, replacing the traditional lecture-and-discussion system. Like Langdell and also like his contemporary Holmes, Pound was a close student of the Common Law; that complex field of legal activity, which demanded continual judicial creativity, made the "case method" seem an ideal training ground for budding attorneys.

His studies of legal history and theory had already shaped his beliefs about how the law should work. Beginning in 1906 with a highly controversial address to the American Bar Association, Pound took issue with all the traditional theories of jurisprudence: Cartesian rationalism, the empiricism rooted in Locke and Hume, idealism, positivism, and, most crucially, the influential *a priori* approach set forth by Kant. In their place, Pound outlined what he called "sociological jurisprudence"; since society itself was in constant flux, the law must manifest flexibility, adjusting and adapting familiar principles to ever-changing social realities. Skeptical of any absolutes, Pound found it difficult even to define "justice."

The parallels between Pound's ideas and those of Holmes are clear enough. This is not surprising since both, together with the pragmatic philosophers John Dewey and William James, arose out of the same late 19th-century evolutionary climate of opinion. But Pound probably was less abstract in his thinking than the somewhat remote Holmes. In 1905, when the Supreme Court invalidated a New York law that limited the working hours of bakers, Holmes had dissented: "This case is decided upon an economic theory which a large part of the country does not entertain." Pound praised that dissent; in commenting upon an analogous case a few years later, when the Court again decided in favor of "liberty of contract," he wondered: "Why do we find a great and learned court...taking the long step into the past of dealing with the relation between employer and employee...as if the parties were individuals—as if they were farmers haggling over the sale of a horse?"

Pound called for social realism, for the "adjustment of principles and doctrines to the human conditions they are to govern rather than to assumed first principles." In 1921 he presented his "theory of interests," which held that the law's function is to enable people to live together, not to uphold "justice" in some disembodied, abstract form.

On more than one occasion, Pound insisted that courts must have *facts* to buttress their understanding of actual social conditions. He seems to have underestimated the strength of John Marshall Harlan's dissent in the 1905 Lochner case, which was more solidly factual than Holmes's. And he apparently never quite recognized the significance of Louis Brandeis's achievement in *Muller v. Oregon*, 1908. In that classic case Brandeis, then an attorney practicing before the Court, adduced a mass of factual data for judicial consideration, and triumphed. In truth, Pound was far closer in temperament to the more discursive Holmes than to the crisp realist Brandeis. Pound and Holmes were social libertarians, while Brandeis was an activist for whom the law was an instrument for helping to achieve social ends.

Yet Pound could be highly visible on many public issues. He served on a number of important committees and commissions: in 1920, for example, he joined with Zechariah Chafee, Felix Frankfurter and others in sharply criticizing the government's role in the "Red Scare." In 1931 he was on the Wickersham Commission, that effectively pronounced Prohibition to be unenforceable—paving the way for Repeal.

By the time the New Deal was underway, Pound's version of sociological jurisprudence seemed mild, even conservative. The brand of idealism pioneered by him and Holmes, who died in 1935, was being transformed into "legal realism" by such younger scholars as Thurman Arnold and William O. Douglas. Even the "case method" in legal education, which had become the dominant mode, was losing ground.

Retired from the Deanship at Harvard, Pound spoke out opposing the emergence of the "welfare state." He said he could not accept the "Good Samaritan" tendencies of the government, which help every citizen "out of the ditch, bind up his wounds, set him on his way, and pay his hotel bill." The nation, he felt, was losing "the claim to liberty—to free self-assertion or self-determination." These accents were reminiscent of the liberal mood of the Progressive period. But at mid-century they seemed out of touch with the changing directions of the nation.

—Don Hausdorff

PRAZ, Mario (Alcibiade, Giano di Guisa). Italian critic, translator and literary historian. Born in Rome, 6 September 1896. Studied at the University of Rome, Dr.Juris. 1918; University of Florence, D.Litt. 1920. Married Vivian Eyles in 1934 (divorced, 1947); 1 daughter. Free-lance journalist and translator, 1915-23. Senior Lecturer in Italian, University of Liverpool, 1924-32; Professor of Italian Studies, University of Manchester, 1932-34; Professor of English, 1934-66, and Professor Emeritus, 1966-82, University of Rome. Recipient: British Academy Gold Medal for Anglo-Italian Studies, 1935; Premio Marzotto, 1952; Italian Gold Medal for Cultural Merit, 1958. Honorary doctorate: Cambridge University, 1957; Aix-Marseille University, 1964; Sorbonne, University of Paris, 1964; University of Uppsala, 1977. Member, Accademia Nazionale dei Lincei, Rome; American Academy of Arts and Letters; Accademia Letteraria Italiana; Sezione Artistica e Culturale de Cenacolo Triestino. Honorary Member, Modern Language Association of America. Grande Ufficiale della Repubblica Italiana, 1972. *Died* (in Rome) *23 March 1982.*

PUBLICATIONS

Literature and Art

La fortuna di Byron in Inghilterra. Florence, La Voce, 1925.
Secentismo e marinismo in Inghilterra: John Donne, Richard Crashaw. Florence, La Voce, 1925; enlarged editions as *Richard Crashaw,* Brescia, Morcelliana, 1945, and as *La poesia metafisica inglese del Seicento: John Donne,* Rome, Documento, 1945.
La carne, la morte, e il diavolo nella letteratura romantica. Milan, La Cultura, 1930; as *The Romantic Agony,* London, Oxford University Press, 1933; New York, Meridian, 1956.
Studi sul concettismo. Milan, La Cultura, 1934; as *Studies in Seventeenth-Century Imagery* and *A Bibliography of Emblem Books,* London, Warburg Institute, 2 vols., 1939-47.
Storia della letteratura inglese. Florence, Sansoni, 1937.
Studi e svaghi inglesi. Florence, Sansoni, 1937.
Gusto neoclassico. Florence, Sansoni, 1940; as *On Neoclassicism,* Evanston, Illinois, Northwestern University Press, 1969.
Machiavelli in Inghilterra ed altri saggi. Rome, Tumminelli, 1942; revised edition, Florence, Sansoni, 1962.
Outline of English Literature. Milan, Principato, 1943.
Ricerche anglo-italiane. Rome, Edizioni di Storia e Letteratura, 1944.
La filosofia dell'arredamento. Rome, Documento, 1945; revised edition, Milan, Longanesi, 1964; as *An Illustrated History of Interior Decoration from Pompeii to Art Nouveau,* London,

Thames and Hudson, and New York, Braziller, 1964.

Motivi e figure. Turin, Einaudi, 1945.

Il dramma elisabettiano: Webster-Ford. Rome, Edizioni Italiane, 1946.

La poesia di Pope e le sue origini. Rome, Edizioni dell'Ateneo, 1948.

Cronache letterarie anglosassoni. Rome, Edizioni di Storia e Letteratura, 4 vols., 1951-66.

La casa della fama: Saggi di letteratura e d'arte. Milan, Ricciardi, 1952.

La crisi dell'eroe nel romanzo vittoriano. Florence, Sansoni, 1952; as *The Hero in Eclipse in Victorian Literature,* London, Oxford University Press, 1956.

The Flaming Heart: Essays on Crashaw, Machiavelli and Other Studies of the Relations between Italian and English Literature. New York, Doubleday, 1958.

John Donne. Turin, Editrice S.A.I.E., 1959.

Le bizzarre sculture di Francesco Pianta. Venice, Sodalizio del Libro, 1959.

Bellezza e bizzarria. Milan, Mondadori, 1960.

Il volt del tempo. Naples, Edizioni Scientifiche Italiane, 1964.

James Joyce, Thomas Stearns Eliot, due maestri dei moderni. Turin, ERI, 1967.

Caleidoscopio Shakespeariano. Bari, Adriatica, 1969.

Scene di conversazione. Rome, U. Bozzi, 1969; as *Conversation Pieces: A Survey of the Informal Group Portrait in Europe and America,* London, Methuen, and University Park, Pennsylvania State University Press, 1971.

Mnemosyne: The Parallel Between Literature and the Visual Arts. Princeton, New Jersey, Princeton University Press, 1970.

Il patto col serpente: Paralipomeni de La carne, la morte e il diavolo nella letteratura romantica. Milan, Mondadori, 1972.

Il giardino dei sensi: Studi sul manierismo e il barocco. Milan, Mondadori, 1975.

Perseo e la Medusa: Dal romanticismo all'avanguardia. Milan, Mondadori, 1979.

Other

Penisola pentagonale. Milan, Alpes, 1928; as *Unromantic Spain,* New York, Knopf, 1929.

Viaggio in Grecia: Diario del 1931. Edizioni di Lettere d'oggi, 1943.

Fiori freschi. Florence, Sansoni, 1943.

Lettrice notturna. Rome, Casini, 1952.

Il mondo che ho visto: II. Viaggi in Occidente. Florence, Sansoni, 1955.

Panopticon romano. Milan, Ricciardi, 2 vols., 1967-78.

La casa della vita (autobiography). Milan, Mondadori, 1958; as *The House of Life,* London, Methuen, and New York, Oxford University Press, 1964.

Toscana, with Folco Quilici. Rome, Ufficio Pubbliche Relazioni della Esso Italiana, 1971.

Lazio, with Folco Quilici. Rome, Ufficio Pubbliche Relazioni della Esso Italiana, 1975.

Editor, *Antologia della letteratura inglese.* Messina, Principato, 1936.

Editor, *Lettera sopra i buccheri con l'aggiunta di lettere contro l'ateismo, scientifiche, ed erudite e di relazioni varie,* by Lorenzo Magalotti. Florence, Le Monnier, 1945.

Editor, *Prospettiva della letteratura inglese da Chaucer a V. Woolf.* Milan, Bompiani, 1947.

Editor, with E. Lo Gatto, *Antologia delle letterature straniere.* Florence, 1947.

Editor, *Il libro della poesia inglese.* Messina, D'Anna, 1951.

Editor, *Tre drammi Elisabetiani.* Naples, Edizioni Scientifiche Italiane, 1958.

Editor, *Shakespeare: Tutte le opere.* Florence, Sansoni, 1964.

Editor, with Ferdinando Gerra, *Poesie, Teatro, Prose,* by D'Annunzio. Milan, Ricciardi, 1966.

Translator, *I saggi di Elia,* by Charles Lamb. Lanciano, Carabba, 1924.

Translator, *Poeti inglesi dell'ottocento.* Florence, Bemporad, 1925.

Translator, *Esther Waters,* by George Moore. Milan, La Cultura, 1934.

Translator, *Misura per misura,* by Shakespeare. Florence, Sansoni, 1939.

Translator, *Troilo e Cressida,* by Shakespeare. Florence, Sansoni, 1939.

Translator, *Lo spettatore,* by Joseph Addison. Turin, Einaudi, 1943.

Translator, *Volpone,* by Ben Jonson. Florence, Sansoni, 1943.

Translator, *Riccardo III,* by Shakespeare, in *Teatro I.* Florence, Sansoni, 1943.

Translator, *Ritratti imaginari,* by Walter Pater. Rome, Donatello De Luigi, 1944.

Translator, *Walter Pater* (selections). Milan, Garzanti, 1944.

Translator, *La ballata del vecchio marinaio,* by S.T. Coleridge. Florence, Fussi, 1947.

Translator, *Estetica, etica e storia nelle arti della rappresentazione visiva,* by Bernard Berenson. Florence, Electa Editrice, 1948.

Translator, *La Terra desolata, Frammento di un agone, Marcia trionfale,* by T.S. Eliot. Florence, Fussi, 1949.

Translator, *Elogio dell'uomo politico,* by Frederick S. Oliver. Naples, Ricciardi, 1950.

Translator, *La duchessa di Amalfi,* by John Webster, in *Teatro elisabettiano,* edited by A. Orbertello. Milan, Bompiani, vol. 2, 1951.

Translator, *Emma,* by Jane Austen. Milan, Garzanti, 1951.

*

Bibliography: *Bibliografia degli scritti di Mario Praz* by Vittorio and Mariuma Gabrieli, Rome, Edizione di Storia e Letteratura, 1967.

*   *   *

Mario Praz was an Italian critic, scholar, and autobiographer distinguished for his great erudition and cultivation. He wrote brilliantly on European comparative literature, the history of culture and taste, and on the relations among the high arts. His studies of furniture, fashion, porcelain, and other minor arts reflect his wide and varied sensibility. His memoir, *The House of Life,* is a work of rare stylistic delicacy and perception.

Praz is concerned repeatedly with the interrelation of the pictorial and verbal arts. His compendious *Seventeenth-Century Imagery* examines the origin of emblems and devices in Alexandrian culture, their key role in 17th-century English poetry, mainly in the elaborate metaphors and conceits of Donne, Herbert, Crashaw, and Vaughan, and their decline in popularity after the Romantic period. Praz also explores repeatedly the parallelism of literature and poetry as expressed in the idea of *ut pictura poesis.* Although he acknowledges the danger and possible triviality of drawing parallels between the arts, particularly when these involve no more than facile thematic similarities, and even though he recognizes the finally irreducible individuality of every artist, Praz finds the "same forces at work in artists belonging to the same phases of history": each epoch has a "general likeness" among its manifestations, its own particular "handwriting" or *ductus.* In *On Neoclassicism* Praz finds similar qualities in Milton and Poussin, who embody in different media such neoclassical aesthetic ideals as unity, gravity, "colorless" serenity, balance, generalization, and sublime simplicity. For Praz, a key moment in neoclassicism was the unearthing of Herculaneum, in 1739, which influenced not only the high arts but the arts of furniture, interior decoration, ornamentation, fashion, and dance. Later versions of neoclassicism reveal two basic types. The "frozen" is typified by Winckelmann, whose ideal of "tranquil grandeur" merges finally into the "rigidity of death," and the under-appreciated Canova, in whom Praz discerns a spiritual and thematic affinity with the "adolescent sexuality" and "repressed eroticism" of Keats, Poe, and Baudelaire. "Revolutionary classicism," on the other hand, emerges in Piranesi, Ledoux, and the Adam brothers, who represent variously a sublime "geometrical functionalism" and an heroic Plutarchian ideal.

In *Mnemosyne* the arts "remember" each other, and architecture and fashion are the "main guide[s]" in pursuing the parallels among them. During the Renaissance the golden section influenced both pictorial and literary composition, which reveal a common emphasis on symmetry, proportion, balance, and unity. In mannerism the *figura serpentinata* provides the key to the qualities common to visual and literary art: tension, counterpoint, tortuous movement, disorientation of normal expectations, bizarre conceits, unsteady perspective—these characterize Lyly's rhetoric as much as Pontormo's compositions. Subsequently in Baroque painting and architecture one finds an obsession with curves, folds, fluctuating movement, while in literature appears analogously the varied movement of the renovated Pindaric ode. Finally, with the rise of Romantic subjectivity and eccentricity, architecture no longer serves as a guide to the parallelism among the arts.

The best known and perhaps the least successful of Praz's explorations of *ut pictura poesis* is *The Hero in Eclipse in Victorian Fiction*, where the 19th-century English novel is the culmination of a "bourgeois realism" originating in Brueghel, Steen, Hogarth, Chardin, and Greuze. For Praz, Victorian painting and culture are pervaded by a "Biedermeier" aesthetic first evident in England in Lamb and de Quincey. In its subject matter painting favors the realistic detailing of social environment, objects, furniture, and clothing, but in feeling embraces sentimentality, prudishness, moral simplicity. In literature, meanwhile, the "golden rule" is *ut pictura poesis*, the imitation of these values as represented in pictorial art. Scott emerges dubiously as a writer of static "fashion book[s]," with "second-hand medieval scenery"; Dickens no less dubiously as an "essential bourgeois type," who admires amiability and lacks psychological depth; Trollope more convincingly as an "accumulator," in the manner of Dutch genre painters, of "little pictures of ordinary life"; Eliot, as a Vermeer-like illuminist of the "dull landscape," the "humble interior," the "not beautiful face." Thus in the Victorian novel the hero disappears amid the furniture; the novel becomes the "epic of the everyday."

The Romantic Agony, Praz's most noted and influential work, is probably the first extended examination of the "pathology" and "erotic sensibility" of European Romanticism. Praz resists Croce's argument for the complexity of Romanticism and finds in sex the "mainspring" of the Romantic imagination. In Romanticism the "transhistorical link between pleasure and suffering becomes intensified," while beauty is enhanced by those qualities which seem to deny it: the Horrible and the Terrible. Anticipated in mannerism, the Baroque, Elizabethan tragedy, and Gothic fiction, the Romantic delights in the abnormal, the sadistic and necrophiliac (algolagnia), in incest, deformity, satanism, and in the indissolubility of Eros and Thanatos. Among its key figures are Shelley, Keats, Byron, Sade, Swinburne, Poe, Baudelaire, Flaubert, Wilds, Pater, D'Annunzio. Although the book distorts Romanticism as a whole, it illuminates one of its crucial aspects and its thesis is now a critical commonplace. More than a mere academic classic, *The Romantic Agony*, to quote Frank Kermode, has "the power to alter a reader's understanding of the history of his society, and perhaps of his own history."

Another of Praz's recurrent interests is the interrelation of Italian and English culture, which he treats in his essay collection *The Flaming Heart*. Besides tracing the influence on English letters of Dante, Petrarch, Ariosto, and Tasso, Praz explores the Elizabethan conception of the diabolical "Machiavel," the extent of Shakespeare's knowledge of Italy, and, in the title essay, Crashaw's debt to Italian Baroque models. In this work, as elsewhere, Praz is the father of the systematic study of English literature and culture within the Italian academy.

Praz's finest work is probably his memoir, *The House of Life*. This illustrated tour of his apartment in Rome evokes in Proustian fashion a theater of memory. Each room, and the objects it contains, distil the flavor or essence of the author's past moments. Life is thus fixed and "preserved" in a series of static images which form a "partial picture" of life's "puzzle"; Praz's apartment becomes a refuge from an ersatz and transitory modern world, whose "foundations" are tottering. In its representation of Praz's life through a series of emblem-like pictures, this work confirms his repeated notion that life imitates art. It also suggests a constant intersection between his scholarly interests and his life and sensibility. Like the bourgeois realists of *The Hero in Eclipse*, he pursues a "cult of things." And, while Praz's personal taste runs generally to the Baroque, the neoclassical, and especially the Empire style, his Romantic and even Decadent strain appears in his treatment of Diamante, a beauty in the *fin du siècle* mode, beneath whose pallid "mask of youth" the "skull betrayed itself," and who bore the "scar of suffering." In the beautiful last chapter Praz views his bedroom through a convex mirror reminiscent of that in Jan Van Eyck's portrait of Arnolfini and his bride: this gesture perfectly captures the oblique and mannered sensibility which Praz shares with some of his favorite artists.

Praz's works are generally unsystematic and untheoretical and even to a certain extent lacking an adequate grounding in history. His method is to research and illustrate exhaustively the "characteristic aspects" and categories of various periods. Thus in *The Romantic Agony*, a "monograph" rather than a "synthesis" of Romantic sexual pathology, Praz eschews Freudianism. In *The Hero in Eclipse*, a study of the increasing meterialism of modern culture, he makes no reference to historically based concepts such as alienation and reification. Praz's "loving punctiliousness" was noted by Croce's student Giulio Marzot, who admired Praz's erudition but considered his lack of system to be a flaw. In spite of such strictures, Praz was undoubtedly one of the truly learned and cultured scholars of this century.

—Robert Cassilo

QUINE, W(illard) V(an) (Orman). American philosopher. Born in Akron, Ohio, 25 June 1908. Studied at Oberlin College, Ohio, B.A. 1930; Harvard University, Cambridge, Massachusetts, M.A. 1931, Ph.D. 1932; Oxford University, M.A. 1953. Sheldon Traveling Fellow, 1932-33, Junior Fellow, Society of Fellows, 1933-36, Instructor, 1936-41, Associate Professor, 1941-48, Professor, 1948-56, Peirce Professor of Philosophy, 1956-78, and since 1978 Professor Emeritus, Harvard University. G.D. Young Lecturer, University of Adelaide, Australia, 1959. Visiting Professor, University of São Paulo, Brazil, 1942; Tokyo University, 1959; Rockefeller University, New York, 1968; and College of France, 1969; Eastman Visiting Professor, Oxford University, 1973-74 (Saville Fellow, Merton College); Hägerström Lecturer, University of Uppsala, 1973. Consultant, Rand Corporation, 1949. Member, Institute for Advanced Study, Princeton, New Jersey, 1956-57; Fellow, Institute for Advanced Study in the Behavioral Sciences, Stanford, California, 1958-59, and Center for Advanced Studies, Wesleyan University, Middletown, Connecticut, 1965. President, Association for Symbolic Logic, 1953-56, and Eastern Division of the American Philosophical Association, 1957. Recipient: Butler Gold Medal, Columbia University, New York, 1970. Honorary doctorate: Oberlin

College, 1955; University of Lille, 1956; Ohio State University, Columbus, 1957; University of Akron, Ohio, 1965; Washington University, St. Louis, 1966; University of Chicago, 1967; Temple University, Philadelphia, 1970; Oxford University, 1970; Cambridge University, 1978; Harvard University, 1979; University of Uppsala. Member, National Academy of Sciences, and American Academy of Arts and Sciences. Fellow, British Academy; Member, Institut de France. Address: Department of Philosophy, Harvard University, Cambridge, Massachusetts 02138, U.S.A.

PUBLICATIONS

Philosophy

A System of Logic. Cambridge, Massachusetts, Harvard University Press, 1934.
Mathematical Logic. New York, Norton, 1940.
Elementary Logic. Boston, Ginn, 1941.
O sentido da nova lógica. São Paulo, Brazil, Martins, 1944.
Methods of Logic. New York, Holt, 1950; London, Routledge, 1962.
From a Logical Point of View: 9 Logico-Philosophical Essays. Cambridge, Massachusetts, Harvard University Press, 1953.
Word and Object. Cambridge, Massachusetts, M.I.T. Press, 1960.
Set Theory and Its Logic. Cambridge, Massachusetts, Harvard University Press, 1963.
The Ways of Paradox and Other Essays. New York, Random House, 1966; revised edition, Cambridge, Massachusetts, Harvard University Press, 1976.
Selected Logic Papers. New York, Random House, 1966.
Ontological Relativity and Other Essays. New York, Columbia University Press, 1969.
The Web of Belief, with J.S. Ullian. New York, Random House, 1970.
Philosophy of Logic. Englewood Cliffs, New Jersey, Prentice Hall, 1970.
The Roots of Reference. La Salle, Illinois, Open Court, 1974.

*

Critical Studies: *Words and Objections: Essays on the Philosophy of W.V.O. Quine* edited by D. Davidson and J. Hintikka, Dordrecht, Reidel, 1969; *Essays on the Philosophy of W.V. Quine* edited by Robert W. Shahan and Chris Swoyer, Norman, University of Oklahoma Press, and Hassocks, Sussex, Harvester, 1979 (includes bibliography).

*   *   *

There is little doubt that W.V. Quine is the most influential living philosopher in the English-speaking world. Although much of his writings have been concerned with comparatively technical topics in mathematical logic, two texts in particular are justly celebrated.

The first, "Two Dogmas of Empiricism" (1951), involves the deconstruction of logical positivism, one of the major philosophical influences on Quine, who studied with the Vienna Circle in the 1930's. Although he agrees with Carnap that natural language is defective, and requires "regimentation" to be brought into line with the perspicuous structures of formal logic, Quine rejects his philosophy of language, as stated by the two dogmas. The first is the claim that meaningful sentences are either analytic, statements such as "All bachelors are unmarried" which are true by virtue of the meaning of their constituent words, or synthetic, asserting matters of empirical fact. Quine argues that the concept of analyticity can be reduced only to such equally obscure notions as synonymy. He concludes that no sharp distinction can be drawn between analytic and synthetic. The meanings of the words we use are inseparable from our empirical beliefs. The second dogma concerns the manner in which we determine these meanings. Quine accepts the logical positivists' verificationist criterion of meaning, according to which the sense of a sentence consists in the means by which we determine its truth or falsity. He denies, however, that sentences can be verified individually, invoking Duhem to show that the truth or falsity of each sentence can be established only in conjunction with our entire system of beliefs.

One implication of this argument is a holist theory of meaning, such that the sense of an individual sentence is determined by its place in the network of sentences constituting a given language. Another is that theories are underdetermined by the empirical evidence for them. For if the truth or falsity of a sentence depends on that of all the other sentences of a language, then we may well choose to protect a favoured hypothesis from refutation by an inconvenient observation, provided that we are prepared to make the necessary adjustments elsewhere in our beliefs to explain the apparent refutation away. The underdetermination of theory by evidence reappears in the first chapter of *Word and Object* (1960), in support of a thesis Quine calls the indeterminacy of radical translation. He argues that we cannot assign meanings to an alien's utterances on the basis of his observed behaviour, because this will admit of more than one interpretation. Moreover, we cannot assume the alien will share our apparatus of individuation (pronouns, numerals, etc.); his language may divide up the world in a way fundamentally different to our own, and therefore we can have no guarantee that the objects he refers to are the same as those picked out by our own utterances.

These arguments would seem to support a radical conventionalism, which would deny any objectivity to our theories about the world. However, in Quine's case they are part of a distinctive philosophical approach, one that treats philosophy as a branch of natural science concerned to explain the capacity of certain primates to construct very complex conceptual structures on the basis of the sensory inputs they receive from their environment. This naturalism, drawn from such sources as the later Dewey, helps to explain his profound hostility to any attempt to account for linguistic behaviour by attributing to speakers inner and unobservable mental states. The data on which our theories of language are built can only be behavioural—speakers' overt dispositions to assent to or dissent from sentences. Hence Quine's suspicion of such occult properties as synonymy and analyticity, and of intensional discourse. His naturalism may also help to explain Quine's residual empiricism, as evidenced by his exemption of observation sentences, those "on which all the speakers of the language give the same verdict when given the same concurrent stimulation," from the indeterminacy of radical translation. This move is open to question, but there can be no doubting the force and elegance of Quine's arguments.

—Alex Callinicos

RADCLIFFE-BROWN, A(lfred) R(eginald). British social anthropologist. Born 17 January 1881. Educated at King Edward's High School, Birmingham; Trinity College, Oxford. Married Winifred Lyon (marriage dissolved, 1933); 1 daughter. Fellow of Trinity College, Cambridge, 1908-14; Lecturer in Ethnology, University of London, 1909-10; Professor of Social Anthropology, University of Cape Town, 1921-25; Professor of Anthropology, University of Sydney, 1925-31, and University of Chicago, 1931-37; Fellow of All Souls College, and Professor of Social Anthropology, Oxford, 1937-46; Professor of Social Science, Farouk I University, Alexandria, 1947-49; taught at Rhodes University, Grahamstown, South Africa, 1952-55. Frazer Lecturer, Cambridge University, 1939; Huxley Lecturer, Royal Anthropological Institute, London, 1951; Mason Lecturer, University of Birmingham, 1952. Editor, *Oceania* magazine, from 1930. President, Royal Anthropological Institute, 1939-40. Member, Royal Academy of Science, Amsterdam; Honorary Member, New York Academy of Science. *Died 24 October 1955.*

PUBLICATIONS

Social Anthropology

The Andaman Islanders: A Study in Social Anthropology. Cambridge, University Press, 1922; revised edition, 1933; Glencoe, Illinois, Free Press, 1948.
The Australian Aborigines. Honolulu, Institute of Pacific Relations, 1927.
The Social Organization of Australian Tribes. Melbourne, Macmillan, 1931.
Taboo (lecture). Cambridge, University Press, 1939.
Religion and Society (lecture). London, Royal Anthropological Institute of Great Britain, 1945 (?).
Structure and Function in Primitive Society: Essays and Addresses. Glencoe, Illinois, Free Press, and London, Cohen and West, 1952.
A Natural Science of Society. Glencoe, Illinois, Free Press, 1957.
Method in Social Anthropology: Selected Essays, edited by M.N. Srinivas. Chicago, University of Chicago Press, 1958.
The Social Anthropology of A. R. Radcliffe-Brown, edited by Adam Kuper. London, Routledge, 1977.

Other

Editor, with Daryll Forde, *African Systems of Kinship and Marriage.* London, Oxford University Press, 1950.

*

Critical Studies: "Radcliffe-Brown's Contributions to the Study of Social Organisation" by M. Fortes, in *British Journal of Sociology 6* (London), March 1955; "A.R. Radcliffe-Brown 1881-1955" by R. Firth, in *Proceedings of the British Academy 42*, London, Oxford University Press, 1957; *Sozialwissenschaft und Gesellschaft bei Durkheim und Radcliffe-Brown* by Gisela Dombrowski, Berlin, Duncker und Bunblot, 1976.

*   *   *

A.R. Radcliffe-Brown is, more than anyone else, the founder of modern social anthropology. His theoretical orientation is generally called "structural-functionalism" to distinguish it from the pragmatic functionalism of Bronislaw Malinowski.

Radcliffe-Brown was educated at Trinity College, Cambridge. He began reading for his A.B. in "Mental and Moral Science" with W.H.R. Rivers just about the time that Rivers shifted his interests from psychology to ethnology. In 1906-08 he undertook field research on the Andaman islanders, working mainly through interpreters at the British penal colony on Big Andaman. The results were presented in his doctoral dissertation, rewritten in 1913-14, published in 1922, and republished with a new Preface in 1933—his only large-scale work.

In 1921 he founded a new department of social anthropology at Cape Town, and collected information that led to important articles on the mother's brother and on joking relationships. In 1926-31 he held the first Chair in Social Anthropology at the Australian National University, and collected information that led to important articles on the relationship between aboriginal kinship terminology and the clan/section system. From 1931 to 1937 he taught at the University of Chicago, and was apparently influenced by the logical positivists' Unity of Science Movement. In 1937, he became the first Professor of Social Anthropology at Oxford University.

Radcliffe-Brown's main arguments appear only in article-length writings. The original *Andaman Islanders* did not conform to his later program, and the subsequent revisions injected them only partially.

Radcliffe-Brown's basic idea was that behavior, or at least social behavior, was to be explained by its social function, which meant its contribution to the total integration of the society.

Function, the first of Radcliffe-Brown's two key ideas, was defined first. The 1933 Preface to *The Andaman Islanders* discussed it specifically in connection with the interpretation of rituals. It defined "meaning" as the significance of the ritual according to the ideas of those in the community under study, rather than the ideas of the analyst, and concluded with the relatively modest position that "Thus 'meaning' and 'function' are two different but related things." Despite this, "The Sociological Theory of Totemism" (1929) extended function (ignoring meaning) to account for the "ritual attitude" associated with totemic observances, and in "Taboo" (1939) function was further held to explain both "ritual value" and "ritual objects." Ritual objects were any objects represented in ritual, from health to animal species. Values, positive and negative, were equated with interests in the objects. The argument, stripped of digressions, was that rituals (not people) harmonized those interests and thereby created an ordered system of interpersonal relations in the society.

Structure, the second half of the scheme, was described in a series of articles that began about 1940 and carried through the very important (and unusually clear) introduction to *Structure and Function in Primitive Society* in 1952. Borrowing heavily from the literature of the logical positivists, the argument is cast as a discussion of definitions. After arguing that theory had to be "nomothetic" (concerned with laws) and therefore could not be either historical or simply descriptive, it holds that "Comparative sociology, of which social anthropology is a branch, is ... a theoretical or nomothetic study of which the aim is to provide acceptable generalization. The theoretical understanding of a particular institution is its intepretation in the light of such generalizations." Where then do such generalizations come from?

> Amidst the diversity of the particular events there are discoverable regularities, so that it is possible to give statements or descriptions of certain *general features* of social life of the selected region. A statement of such significant general features...constitutes a description of what may be called a *form of social life*. My conception of social anthropology is as the comparative theoretical study of forms of social life among primitive peoples.

Social structure is either such a form, or a collection of such forms. Since they result only from comparison by the analyst of patterns he selects, there is no logical way such structures can correspond to ideas current in the populations under study. Theory is thus the analyst's substantive model of society, and theoretical understanding of behavior is interpreting behavior in the light of it—if what he says is taken literally it is more exactly interpreting behavior by showing how it contributes to the discerned patterns.

Radcliffe-Brown's conception of social anthropology as "comparative sociology" in this sense is still widely accepted, although his attempt to construe forms of behavior and meanings in strictly materialistic terms ("objects," "interests") is not.

—Murray J. Leaf

RADHAKRISHNAN, Sarvepalli. Indian philosopher and statesman. Born in Tirutani, 5 September 1888. Educated at Vorhees College, Madras Christian College, M.A. 1909. Married

Sivakamama Ama in 1903; 6 children. Assistant Professor, 1911-16, and Professor of Philosophy, 1916-17, Presidency College, Madras; University Professor of Philosophy, Mysore University, 1918-21; George V Professor of Philosophy, University of Calcutta, 1921-31, 1937-41; Vice-Chancellor, Andhra University, Walthair, 1931-36, and Benares Hindu University, 1939-48; Spalding Professor of Eastern Religions and Ethics, Oxford University, 1936-52. Upton Lecturer, Manchester College, Oxford University, 1926, 1929-30; Haskell Lecturer, University of Chicago, 1926; Hibbert Lecturer, University of London, 1929. Chairman, Indian Philosophical Congress, 1925-37; Leader, Indian Delegation to Unesco, 1946-52; Indian Ambassador to the U.S.S.R., 1949-52; President, General Conference of Unesco, 1952-54; Vice-President, 1952-62, and President, 1962-67, Republic of India. Recipient: German Order pour la Mérite, 1954; Goethe Plakette, 1959; German Booksellers' Peace Prize, 1961; Templeton Prize for Religion, 1975. Honorary doctorate: Cambridge University, 1948; Oxford University, 1952. Honorary Member, Rumanian Academy of Science. Fellow, Royal Society of Literature, London, 1953. Honorary Fellow, All Souls College, Oxford; British Academy, 1962. Knighted, 1931. Honorary Member, Order of Merit, 1963. *Died* (in Madras) *17 April 1975.*

PUBLICATIONS

Religion and Philosophy

The Ethics of the Vedenta and Its Metaphysical Presuppositions. Madras, Guardian Press, 1908.
The Philosophy of Rabindranath Tagore. London, Macmillan, 1918.
The Reign of Religion in Contemporary Philosophy. London, Macmillan, 1920.
Indian Philosophy. London, Allen and Unwin, and New York, Macmillan, 2 vols., 1923, 1927.
The Hindu View of Life (lectures). London, Allen and Unwin, and New York, Macmillan, 1927.
The Religion We Need. London, Benn, 1928.
Kalki—Or the Future of Civilisation. London, Kegan Paul, 1929.
An Idealist View of Life (lectures). London, Allen and Unwin, and New York, Macmillan, 1929.
East and West in Religion. London, Allen and Unwin, 1933.
The Philosophy of the Upanishads. London, Allen and Unwin, and New York, Macmillan, 1935.
The Heart of Hindusthan: On Indian Religions and Philosophy. Madras, Natesan, 1936.
Gautama—The Buddha (lecture). London, Oxford University Press, 1938.
Eastern Religions and Western Thought. London, Oxford University Press, 1939.
Religion and Society. London, Allen and Unwin, 1947.
Radhakrishnan: An Anthology, edited by A.N. Marlow. London, Allen and Unwin, 1952.
Recovery of Faith. New York, Harper, 1955; London, Allen and Unwin, 1956.
Fellowship of the Spirit. Cambridge, Massachusetts, Harvard University Press, 1961.
Religion in a Changing World. London, Allen and Unwin, and New York, Humanities Press, 1967.
The Present Crisis of Faith. Delhi, Hind, 1970.
Selected Writings on Philosophy, Religion and Culture, edited by Robert A. McDermott. New York, Dutton, 1970.

Other

The Essentials of Psychology. Oxford, Oxford University Press, and New York, Frowde, 1912.
Freedom and Culture (addresses). Madras, Natesan, 1936.

India and China. Bombay, Hind Kitabs, 1944.
Education, Politics and War. Poona, International Book Service, 1944.
Is This Peace? Bombay, Hind Kitabs, 1945.
Great Indians. Bombay, Hind Kitabs, 1949.
Report of the University Education Commission, with others. New Delhi, Government of India Manager of Publications, 1949.
East and West: Some Reflections. London, Allen and Unwin, 1955.
Occasional Speeches and Writings. Delhi, Ministry of Education and Broadcasting, 3 vols., 1956-63.
President Radhakrishnan's Speeches and Addresses. Delhi, Ministry of Education and Broadcasting, 1965.
On Nehru. Delhi, Ministry of Education and Broadcasting, 1965.

Editor, with J.M. Muirhead, *Contemporary Indian Philosophy.* London, Allen and Unwin, 1936.
Editor, *Mahatma Ghandi: Essays and Reflections on His Work.* London, Allen and Unwin, 1939.
Editor and translator, *The Bhagavadgita.* London, Allen and Unwin, and New York, Harper, 1948.
Editor and translator, *The Dhammapada.* London, Oxford University Press, 1950.
Editor, *The Principal Upanishads.* London, Allen and Unwin, and New York, Harper, 1953.
Editor, with Charles A. Moore, *A Source Book in Indian Philosophy.* Princeton, Princeton University Press, 1957.
Editor and translator, *The Brahama Sutra.* London, Allen and Unwin, and New York, Harper, 1960.
Editor, with P.T. Raju, *The Concept of Man: A Study in Comparative Philosophy.* London, Allen and Unwin, and Lincoln, Nebraska, Johnsen, 1960.

*

Critical Studies: *The Philosophy of Sarvepalli Radhakrishnan* edited by Paul Arthur Schilpp, New York, Tudor, 1952 (contains a bibliography).

*   *   *

Sarvepalli Radhakrishnan is probably the only person in recent history, who, from being a professional philosopher, came to be the head of a state, President of India; and I might add, without being unnecessarily reticent about my own country, that India is probably the only place where this could happen. A man does not have to devote his entire life to politics and public work in order to be the head of the state. Plato's idea of a philosopher-king could be a distinct possibility in the case of India.

Radhakrishnan was primarily a philosopher concerned with such broader issues as whether the task of philosophy should be only *interpreting* life or *changing* it as well; what role, if any, religion should play in contemporary philosophy, and what is the meaning of life, spirit, and freedom. By his own admission, he was mostly influenced by Sánkara, Ramanuja, and Madhva of classical India, as well as by Plato, Plotinus, and Kant in the West. In spite of his abiding interest in classical India, he was more a creative thinker than a classical scholar. He used the comparative method, being well aware of its limitations as well as the difficulties involved in any adequate historical interpretation of Indian thought. But he realized, as most of us often do when we become well-acquainted with the classical philosophical texts of India, that this could not be simply an antiquarian's pursuit. He wrote: "Ancient Indians do not belong to a different species from ourselves. An actual study of their views shows that they ask questions and find answers analogous in their diversity to some of the more important currents in modern thought."

Radhakrishnan participated in the rather persistent debate about whether the Buddha was inclined towards the metaphysics of the Upanishadic soul, although the Buddha openly repudiated the notion of the empirical soul. Here he disagreed with his pupil, T.R.V. Murti, and gave a positive answer. With regard to the *bodhi* of Buddhism, he raised the question, which often seems pertinent: what can it be, if it is not the universal self? A tentative answer may be that it is exactly what the universal self is NOT.

With regard to the broader questions of philosophy and religion, Radhakrishnan held several distinct views. He believed that the human consciousness has three levels, that of perceptions, that of reason, and that of intuitive insight. The first helps us to collect observed data, the second to exercise rational reflection, and the third to add meaning, value, and character to the observed reality. He defined the third as *nanda*, a spiritual insight, and (using Sri Aurobindo's term) as "integral consciousness." He believed that scientific knowledge, where the first two first two levels are dominant, is "inadequate, partial, and fragmentary, but not false." Our intuitive insight, he claims, is what gives fullness to man as a man, leads to his spiritual joy, which is akin to aesthetic satisfaction, and brings about the fulfilment of his inner being.

The last point brings us to two other components of Radhakrishnan's thought: his idealistic view of life and his idea of a universal religion, i.e., a universal spiritual life for everybody. Regarding the first, he contributed to a world-view which he called "idealism," but refused to identify it with the usual meaning of "idealism," a sort of pan-psychism or a pan-fictional approach to the world. The use of this term was perhaps unfortunate and confusing, as his critics pointed out. But his meaning was not entirely unclear. His "idealism" has to do with the third level of human consciousness, what he described as the integral insight. It is what tries to make our life on this world neither "an irrational blind striving" nor "an irremediably miserable blunder." It is what is supposed to add meaning, value, and worth to our life. Without it, it is believed, our civilization would be bankrupt. "It finds life significant and purposeful." We may rightly disagree about what worth, if any, we should assign to our life, but we cannot deny the presence of a worth-assigning component in human awareness. Radhakrishnan, I believe, referred to this component by his use of the term "idealism." Further, he believed that this part of human awareness, when properly cultivated, will take us away from the pursuit of materialistic pleasure towards the quest for infinite joy of the absolute. In this respect he was an optimist.

Radhakrishnan's idea of a universal religion has been criticized by many. Religions, if anything, encourage dogmas and intensify prejudices about others' religious beliefs. A true believer in one particular religion invariably and necessarily claims monopoly over truth and ultimate values. In the face of this state of affairs, how can one even hope to see common ties and underlying unity in different conflicting religious traditions? Radhakrishnan thought that this could be countered, for we can find a basis, the discovery of "the World of Spirit," as he called it, which will enable us to ignore the concrete formulations of the Divine in different traditions and work towards a unity. For, according to Radhakrishnan, the Divine is "formless and nameless and yet capable of manifesting all forms and names."

Whether this optimism or "idealism" is justified or not, it certainly has a perennial charm for the humans in all ages. Radhakrishnan was, however, well-aware that his use of the term "philosophy" would not agree with that of others, especially in the Anglo-American analytic tradition. He was also far from being an Indianist, who would claim that India, and India alone, can save the world from disaster. For his search was for a universal religion (he called it philosophy, too) which would be found in all lands and cultures, in the meeting point of Upanishadic seers and Plato, Plotinus and Philo, Jesus and Paul. He believed that such a meeting point exists, and at it resides the spirit which alone can save us from the meaninglessness of the present situation.

—B.K. Matilal

RAHNER, Karl (Carolus). German theologian. Born in Freiburg, 5 March 1904. Educated in Jesuit Schools in Feldkirch and Pullach, 1924-27, and in Valkenberg, Holland, 1929-33; studied under Heidegger, University of Freiburg, 1934-36; University of Innsbruck, Ph.D. 1936; ordained as a Jesuit priest, 1932. Professor of Theology, University of Innsbruck, 1937-39, 1948-54 (did pastoral work in Vienna and elsewhere during World War II); Professor of Theology, University of Munich, 1964-67; Professor of Dogmatic Theology, 1967-71, and since 1971 Professor Emeritus, University of Münster. Co-Founder, *Concilium*, 1965, and *Dialog*, 1968. Appointed theological consultant for Vatican II by Pope John XXIII. Recipient: Reuchlin Prize, 1965; German Orden Pour le Mérite, 1968; Medal of Helsinki University, 1968; Romano-Guardini Prize, 1973; Sigmund Freud Prize, 1973; Bundesverdienstkreuz mit Stern, 1979; Kultureller Ehrenpreis, Munich, 1979; Discovery Prize, Marquette University, 1979. Honorary doctorate: University of Münster; University of Strasbourg; University of Notre Dame, Indiana; St. Louis University; Yale University, New Haven, Connecticut; University of Louvain; University of Innsbruck; University of Pittsburgh; University of Chicago. Address: Kaulbachstrasse 33, 8000 Munich 22, Germany.

PUBLICATIONS

Collections

Schriften zur Theologie.   Einsiedeln, Benziger, 1954—.

Theology

Worte ins Schweigen.   Innsbruck, Rauch, 1938; as *Encounters with Silence*, London, Sands, and Baltimore, Westminster Press, 1960.
Geist in Welt: Zur Metaphysik der enlichen Erkenntnis bei Thomas von Aquin.   Innsbruck, Rauch, 1939; as *Spirit in the World*, London and New York, Sheed and Ward, 1968.
Hörer des Wortes: Zur Grundlegung einer Religionsphilosophie.   Munich, Kösel-Pustet, 1941; as *Hearers of the Word*, New York, Herder, 1969.
Der Pfarrer.   Vienna, Herder, 1948.
Die Kirche der Sünder.   Freiburg, Herder, 1948.
Helige Stunde und Passionsandacht (as Anselm Trescher).   Innsbruck, Rauch, 1949; as *Watch and Pray with Me*, New York, Herder, 1966.
Von der Not und dem Segen des Gebetes.   Innsbruck, Rauch, 1949.
Gefahren im heutigen Katholizismus.   Einsiedeln, Benziger, 1950.
Die Vielen Messen und das eine Opfer.   Freiburg, Herder, 1951; as *The Celebration of the Eucharist*, London, Burns Oates, and New York, Herder, 1968.
Das "neue" Dogma.   Vienna, Herder, 1951.
Visionen und Prophezeiungen.   Innsbruck, Tyrolia, 1952; as *Visions and Prophecies*, New York, Herder, 1964.
Das freie Wort in der Kirche; Die Chancen des Christentums.   Einsiedeln, Benziger, 1953; first essay as *Free Speech in the Church*, London and New York, Sheed and Ward, 1959.
Kleines Kirchenjahr.   Munich, Ars Sacra, 1954; as *The Eternal Year*, Baltimore, Helicon Press, 1964.
Maria, Mutter des Herrn.   Freiburg, Herder, 1956; as *Mary, Mother of the Lord*, New York, Herder, and London, Nelson, 1963.
Die Gnade wird es vollenden.   Munich, Ars Sacra, 1957.
Gott liebt dieses Kind.   Munich, Ars Sacra, 1957.
Glaubend und liebend.   Munich, Ars Sacra, 1957.
Über die Schriftinspiration.   Freiburg, Herder, 1957; as *Inspiration in the Bible*, New York, Herder, 1964.
Gebete der Einkehr, with Hugo Rahner.   Salzburg, Müller,

1958.

Zur Theologie des Todes. Freiburg, Herder, 1958; as *On the Theology of Death*, New York, Herder, 1961.

Ewiges Ja. Munich, Ars Sacra, 1958; as *The Eternal Yes*, Denville, New Jersey, Dimension, 1958.

Happiness Through Prayer. Dublin, Clonmore and Reynolds, and Baltimore, Westminster Press, 1958.

Das Dynamische in der Kirche. Freiburg, Herder, 1958; as *The Dynamic Element in the Church*, New York, Herder, 1964.

Sendung und Gnade: Pastoraltheologische Beiträge. Innsbruck, Rauch, 1959; selections as *The Christian Commitment: Essays in Pastoral Theology*, New York, Sheed and Ward, 1963; as *Mission and Grace: Essays in Pastoral Theology*, London, Sheed and Ward, 1963; as *Theology for Renewal: Bishops, Priests, Laity*, New York, Sheed and Ward, 1964; as *Christian in the Marketplace*, New York, Sheed and Ward, 1966.

Das Geheimnis unseres Christ. Munich, Ars Sacra, 1959.

Vom Glauben inmitten der Welt. Freiburg, Herder, 1961.

Kirche und Sakramente. Freiburg, Herder, 1961; as *The Church and The Sacraments*, New York, Herder, 1963.

Kleines theologisches Wörterbuch, with H. Vorgrimler. Freiburg, Herder, 1961; as *Concise Theological Dictionary*, Freiburg, Herder, 1965.

The Bible in a New Age. London, Sheed and Ward, 1965.

Episkopat und Primat, with J. Ratzinger. Freiburg, Herder, 1961; as *The Episcopate and the Primacy*, New York, Herder, 1962; London, Burns Oates, 1966.

Das Problem der Hominisation, with Paul Overhage. Freiburg, Herder, 1961; selections as *Hominisation: The Evolutionary Origin of Man as a Theological Problem*, New York, Herder, 1965.

Auferstehung des Fleisches. Krevelaer, Butzon and Bercker, 1962.

Zur Theologie des Buches. Leipzig, Benno, 1962.

Gegenwart des Christentums. Freiburg, Herder, 1963.

Nature and Grace and Other Essays. London and New York, Sheed and Ward, 1963.

Die Antwort der Religionen, with G. Szczesny. Munich, Ars Sacra, 1964.

Bishops: Their Status and Function. London, Burns Oates, 1964.

On Heresy. Freiburg, Herder, 1964.

Man in the Church. Baltimore, Helicon, 1964.

Alltägliche Dinge. Einsiedeln, Benziger, 1964; as *Everyday Things*, London, Sheed and Ward, 1965.

Inquiries. New York, Herder, 1964.

Nature and Grace: Dilemmas in the Modern Church. London, Sheed and Ward, 1964.

Betrachtungen zum ignatianischen Exerzitienbuch. Munich, Kösel, 1965; as *Spiritual Exercises*, New York, Herder, 1965; London, Sheed and Ward, 1967.

Biblische Predigten. Freiburg, Herder, 1965; as *Biblical Homilies*, New York, Herder, 1966.

Bergend und Heilend: Über das Sakrament der Kranken. Munich, Ars Sacra, 1965.

Studies in Modern Theology. New York, Herder, 1965.

God, Christ, Mary, and Grace. New York, Herder, 1965.

Kirche im Wandel: Nach dem Zweiten Vatikanischen Konzil. Krevelaer, Butzon and Bercker, 1965.

Offenbarung und Überlieferung, with J. Ratziger. Freiburg, Herder, 1965; as *Revelation and Tradition*, London, Burns Oates, and New York, Herder, 1966.

Im Heute glauben. Einsiedeln, Benziger, 1965.

Kleines Konzilskompendium, with H. Vorgrimler. Einsiedeln, Benziger, 1966.

More Recent Writings. Baltimore, Helicon Press, 1966.

Das Konzil—ein neuer Beginn. Munich, Kösel, 1966.

Intellektuelle Redlichkeit und christlicher Glaube; Glaube und Wissenschaft, with M. Dantine. Freiburg, Herder, 1966.

Glaube, der die Ende liebt: Christliche Besinnung im Alltag der Welt. Freiburg, Herder, 1966.

Von Sinn des Kirklichen Amtes. Freiburg, Herder, 1966.

Later Writings. Baltimore, Helicon Press, 1966.

Sind die Erwartungen erfüllt? with others. Munich, Hüber, 1966.

Knechte Christi: Meditationen zum Priestertum. Freiburg, Herder, 1967; as *Servants of the Lord*, London, Burns Oates, and New York, Herder, 1968.

The Theology of the Spiritual Life. Baltimore, Helicon, 1967.

Glaubst du an Gott?, edited by O. Karrer. Munich, Ars Sacra, 1967; as *Do You Believe in God?*, New York, Newman Press, 1969.

Belief Today. New York, Sheed and Ward, 1967.

The Christian of the Future. London, Burns Oates, and New York, Herder, 1967.

Meditationen zum Kirchenjahr. Freiburg, Herder, 1967.

Faith Today. London, Sheed and Ward, 1967.

Der eine Mittler und die Vielfalt der Vermittlungen. Wiesbaden, Steiner, 1967.

Demokratie in der Kirche? Freiburg, Herder, 1968.

Gnade als Freiheit: Kleine theologisches Beiträge. Freiburg, Herder, 1968; as *Grace in Freedom*, New York, Herder, 1969.

Theology of Pastoral Action. New York, Herder, 1968.

On Prayer. New York, Paulist Press, 1968.

Ich glaube an Jesus Christus. Einsiedeln, Benziger, 1968.

Zur Reform des Theologiestudiums. Freiburg, Herder, 1969.

Kerygma and Dogma, with Karl Lehmann. New York, Herder, 1969.

Concerning Vatican II. Baltimore, Helicon Press, 1969.

Einübung priesterlicher Existenz. Freiburg, Herder, 1970; as *Meditations on Priestly Life*, London, Sheed and Ward, 1973.

Kritisches Wort: Aktuelle Probleme in Kirche und Welt. Freiburg, Herder, 1970.

Freiheit und Manipulation in Gesellschaft und Kirche. Munich, Kösel, 1970.

The Trinity. New York, Herder, 1970.

Chancen des Glaubens. Freiburg, Herder, 1971; as *Opportunities for Faith*, London, SPCK, 1974; New York, Seabury Press, 1975.

Unfehlbarkeit: Antworten auf die Aufrage von Hans Küng. Freiburg, Herder, 1971.

Further Theology of the Spiritual Life. London, Darton Longman and Todd, and New York, Herder, 1971.

Christologie, systematisch und exegetisch, with Wilhelm Thüssing. Freiburg, Herder, 1972; as *A New Christianity*, New York, Seabury, 1980.

Strukturwandel des Kirches als Aufgabe und Chance. Freiburg, Herder, 1972; as *The Shape of the Church to Come*, London, SPCK, and New York, Seabury Press, 1974.

Belief Today: Three Theological Meditations. London, Sheed and Ward, 1973.

Ist Gott noch gefragt? Dusseldorf, Patmos, 1973.

The Priesthood. New York, Seabury Press, 1973.

Writings of 1965-67. New York, Herder, 1972; London, Darton Longman and Todd, 1973.

Auch heute weht der Geist. Munich, Ars Sacra, 1974; as *A New Baptism in the Spirit*, Denville, New Jersey, Dimension, 1975.

Die siebenfältige Gabe. Munich, Ars Sacra, 1974.

Vorfragen zu eines ökumenischen Amtsverständnis. Freiburg, Herder, 1974.

Wagnis des Christen. Freiburg, Herder, 1974; as *Christian at the Crossroads Today*, New York, Seabury Press, 1975; as *The Religious Life Today*, London, Burns Oates, 1976.

Herausforderung des Christen. Freiburg, Herder, 1975.

Was sollen wir jetzt tun? Freiburg, Herder, 1975.

A Rahner Reader, edited by Gerald McCool. London, Darton Longman and Todd, and New York, Seabury Press, 1975.

Allow Yourself to be Forgiven. Denville, New Jersey, Dimension, 1975.

Glaube als Mut. Einsiedeln, Benziger, 1976.

Grundkurs des Glaubens: Einführung in den Begriff des Christentums. Freiburg, Herder, 1976; as *Foundations of Chris-*

tian Faith: An Introduction to the Idea of Christianity, New York, Crossroad, 1982.
Meditations on Hope and Love. London, Burns Oates, 1978.
Meditations on Freedom and the Spirit. London, Burns Oates, 1977; New York, Seabury Press, 1978.
Befreiende Theologie. Berlin, Kohlhammer, 1977.
The Spirit in the Church. New York, Seabury Press, 1979.

Other (For a full listing of the series edited by Rahner, see the bibliography listed below)

Editor, *Der Glaube der Kirche in den Urkunden der Lehrverkündigung*, by J. Neuner and H. Roos. Regensburg, Pustet, 1948; as *The Teaching of the Christian Church as Contained in Her Documents*, New York, Alba House, 1967.
Editor, *Enchiridion Symbolorum*, by H. Denzinger. Freiburg, Herder, 1952.
Editor, with J. Höfer, *Lexicon fur Theologie und Kirche.* Freiburg, Herder, 10 vols., 1957-67.
Editor, *Diaconia in Christo*, with H. Vorgrimler. Freiburg, Herder, 1962.
Editor, with others, *Handbuch der Pastoraltheologie: Praktische Theologie in der Gegenwart.* Freiburg, Herder, 4 vols., 1964-69.
Editor, with others, *The Pastoral Approach to Atheism.* New York, Paulist Press, 1967.
Editor, *Encyclopedia of Theology: The Concise Sacramentum Mundi.* London, Burns Oates, 1975.

*

Bibliography: *Bibliographie Karl Rahner 1924-1969* by Roman Bleistein and Elmar Klinger, Freiburg, Herder, 1969, supplement, 1974.

Critical Studies: *The Achievement of Karl Rahner* by Louis Roberts, New York, Herder, 1967; *A World of Grace: An Introduction to the Themes and Foundations of Karl Rahner's Theology* edited by Leo J. O'Donovan, New York, Seabury Press, 1980; *Karl Rahner: An Introduction to His Theology* by Karl-Heinz Weger, London, Burns Oates, 1980; *Karl Rahner: The Philosophical Foundation* by Thomas Sheehan, Athens, Ohio University Press, forthcoming.

*   *   *

The uniqueness of Karl Rahner's work lies in his life-long effort to put Catholic theology on a transcendental footing. He has carried out this enterprise in two stages, the first being philosophical and the second theological.

The first stage occupied Rahner from 1935-1941 and found expression in his two early books *Geist in Welt* and *Hörer des Wortes.* In these works Rahner reformulated Thomistic philosophy—specifically its epistemology (theory of knowledge) and metaphysics (theory of being)—as *transcendental philosophy.* In the second stage of the undertaking, which has occupied him since 1941, Rahner has used the "transcendental Thomism" of the first stage as a foundation on which he has rebuilt Catholic theology as *transcendental theology.*

Transcendental philosophy, as Rahner understands it, focuses its questions not on the object to be known but on the subject who does the knowing. "The inquiring subject," as Rahner says, "becomes the subject of the inquiry." More specifically, transcendental questioning focuses on the subject insofar as he *transcends* himself towards the object and establishes the necessary and universal conditions that must obtain if the object is to be known. Thus philosophy becomes a transcendental epistemology at the service of a transcendental metaphysics: a delimitation of the subject's knowing powers for the sake of delimiting the range of objects that the subject can possibly know.

The transcendental epistemology and metaphysics that Rahner elaborated in *Geist in Welt* consist in a reinterpretation of Thomas Aquinas's medieval theory of knowledge and being in the light of the philosophies of Immanuel Kant and Martin Heidegger. Aquinas had insisted on the inseparability of intellect and sense in the knowing process. Following Heidegger, Rahner reinterpreted intellect as man's projectivity towards being as such, and, going beyond Heidegger, he insisted that the goal of this projection was absolute being. On the other hand, Rahner reinterpreted sense knowledge (or "conversion to the phantasm") in terms of Heidegger's notion of man's situatedness in the world. The unity of this bivalence of projectivity towards the infinite (intellect) and situatedness in the world (senses) *is man*, the ever unfinished act of self-transcendence who, by anticipating the absolute without ever reaching it, renders the world of things humanly intelligible. The metaphysics correlative to this epistemology demonstrates that the only entities man can grasp are worldly entities, but that the condition which makes that grasp possible is man's anticipation ("pre-grasp") of an ever elusive ultimate reality, which is usually called God.

In carrying out the second, or theological, stage of his project, Rahner insists that traditional dogmatic theology must today become theological anthropology—a study of man insofar as he is oriented towards God—and specifically, it must become *transcendental* anthropology. In other words, all theological issues must be raised from the subject's point of view and reinterpreted in a way that shows how the structure of human existence makes possible and necessary man's personal knowledge and appropriation of the doctrine or object of faith in question. Rahner believes this transcendental turn in theology is required in order to show the correlation between man's existential understanding of himself and the otherwise largely unintelligible doctrines of Christianity.

Rahner begins his theology with the principle that the created order is universally and necessarily within the dispensation of supernatural Christic grace, quite apart from the question of Adam's fall. Hence, all human beings are "anonymous Christians" (that is, caught up in God's universal saving grace) by the very fact that they exist and regardless of whether or not they are baptized. Therefore, the anticipation or pre-grasp of absolute being, which goes to make up man's very existence, is directed *a priori* to God's supernatural revelation of Himself. Thus man has a "supernatural existential" structure. In fact, this self-transcending anticipation already constitutes supernatural revelation, so much so that to accept one's own existence in its fullness is to accept the self-communicating God and therefore to be saved. Throughout these reinterpretations, the transcendental turn is at work: Rahner is attempting to show that man learns about God not by trying to peer ahead into the divine mystery (the object), but rather by experiencing himself (the subject) as the constant process of self-transcendence which is directed into the supernatural order.

To be sure, Rahner says, this transcendental revelation requires historical and categorical mediation in the concrete history of salvation of the Jewish covenant and the Christian dispensation centered on Jesus of Nazareth. But even when studying Jesus, Rahner employs the transcendental approach. He begins with a "Christology from below" or an "ascending Christology," rather than with a Christology from above or a descending Christology. That is, rather than beginning his reflections on Jesus with the doctrine of the Incarnation of the Divine Word, he attempts to show, from analyses of evolution and of human existence, that the need for an "absolute savior" is intrinsic to the human condition. The same method holds for all his analyses of Christian doctrine.

While his theological orientation is occasionally controversial, Rahner is certainly the most influential Roman Catholic theologian of the century and, some would claim, the most important since Thomas Aquinas. The impact of his theological writings on the Second Vatican Council was so great and the diffusion of his teachings in Catholic seminaries and universities is now so widespread that it can be said without exaggeration that, as regards its systematic theology, the post-Conciliar Church has been fundamentally and radically shaped by Karl Rahner.

—Thomas Sheehan

RAUSCHENBUSCH, Walter. American theologian. Born in Rochester, New York, 4 October 1861. Educated at the Free Academy, Rochester; Evangelical Gymnasium, Gütersloh, Westphalia, 1879-80; University of Rochester, B.A. 1884; Rochester Theological Seminary, 1884-86. Married Pauline Rother in 1893; 4 children. Pastor, Second German Church, New York, 1883-97; Professor of New Testament Interpretation and later Professor of Church History, Rochester Theological Seminary, 1897-1918. Earl Lecturer, Pacific School of Religion, Berkeley, California, 1910; Merrick Lecturer, Ohio Wesleyan University, Delaware, 1911; Gates Lecturer, Grinnell College, Iowa, 1914; Taylor Lecturer, Yale University, New Haven, Connecticut, 1917. Founded the workers' newspaper *For the Right* in New York, 1889; Co-Founder of the Brotherhood of the Kingdom, 1892, and of the Federal Council of the Churches of Christ, 1908. Honorary doctorate: University of Rochester, 1902; Oberlin College, Ohio, 1916. *Died 25 July 1918.*

PUBLICATIONS

Religion and Society

Das Leben Jesu: Ein systematischer Studiengang für Jugendverein und Bibelklassen. Cleveland, Ritter, 1895.
Christianity and the Social Crisis. New York and London, Macmillan, 1907.
For God and the People: Prayers of Social Awakening. Boston, Pilgrim Press, 1910.
Christianizing the Social Order. New York, Macmillan, 1912.
Dare We Be Christians? Boston, Pilgrim Press, 1914.
The Social Principles of Jesus. New York, Association Press, 1916.
A Theology for the Social Gospel (lectures). New York, Macmillan, 1917.
A Rauschenbusch Reader, compiled by Benson Y. Landis. New York, Harper, 1957.
The Righteousness of the Kingdom, edited by Max Stackhouse. Nashville, Abingdon Press, 1968.

Other

Leben und Werken von August Rauschenbusch zu Ende geführt von seinem Sohn Walter Rauschenbusch. Cleveland, Ritter, 1901.
Die politische Verfassung unseres Landes. Cleveland, Ritter, 1902.

Editor, with Ira D. Sankey, *Evangeliums-Lieder.* Chicago, Bigelow and Main, 1890.
Editor, *Evangeliums-Lieder Number 2.* New York, Bigelow and Main, 1894.
Translator, *The Charm of Jesus*, by Gustav Zart. New York, Crowell, 1899.

*

Critical Studies: *Walter Rauschenbusch* by Dores Robinson Sharpe, New York, Macmillan, 1942; *The Social Gospel of Walter Rauschenbusch and Its Relation to Religious Education* by Vernon Bodein, New Haven, Connecticut, Yale University Press, and London, Oxford University Press, 1944; *The Great*

Tradition of the American Churches by Winthrop S. Hudson, New York, Harper, 1953; "Walter Rauschenbusch in Historical Perspective" by Reinhold Niebhur, in *Religion in Life*, Autumn 1958; *The Fatherhood of God and the Victorian Family: The Social Gospel in America* by Janet Forsythe Fishburn, Philadelphia, Fortress Press, 1981.

*   *   *

Walter Rauschenbusch, the German-American prophet of the "social gospel," challenged the conscience of "the people" and "the Church" through pulpit, press, and platform. Born of immigrant parents in Rochester, New York, in 1860, Rauschenbusch was educated in Germany and at Rochester Theological Seminary before being ordained a Baptist minister in 1886. Much of his interest in labor-related social issues and in socialism came from an intimate knowledge of "the working class" acquired during his 11-year pastorate to German immigrants in the Hell's Kitchen area of New York's west side. During those years a new interest in the social sciences led Rauschenbusch back to Germany in 1891 for a year of study in sociology and biblical "higher criticism."

Although Rauschenbusch wrote regularly for periodicals— including *For the Right*, a paper he helped found for "workers"—his enduring contribution to social ethics and social philosophy is found in six books published between 1907-17. A professor of church history at Rochester Theological Seminary from 1902 until his death in 1918, Rauschenbusch thought of himself more as a pastor and prophet than as a scholar and theologian. Choosing to address his books to the "religious spirit" of the people and to "the Church" rather than to the intellectual community, he was one of many pastors and professors who influenced public opinion during the turbulent early years of the 20th century before the advent of political columnists like Walter Lippmann.

The social gospel movement, pastors concerned with social injustice related to industrialization, began in the post-Civil War period. The movement rapidly lost credibility at the time of World War I because of the undue optimism about human nature and progress in history of many of its leaders. In the two decades before American entry into "the Great War" the movement reached its culmination as Rauschenbusch addressed "the social principles of Jesus" and the "spirit of love" of Christianity to "the social problem." In all his books, Rauschenbusch presented all social issues, from rising divorce rates to labor disputes, in relation to "the lust for easy and unearned gain." Social Christianity, the application of Christian ethics to social problems, has been a lasting impulse in American religion. The theology of the movement is considered by some church historians to be the only indigenous American theology.

During his lifetime, the most widely read of the Rauschenbusch books were *Prayers of Social Awakening* and *The Social Principles of Jesus*, both written as study guides for young adults. However, his work in social ethics influenced new generations of pastor ethicists and seminary professors in the 1930's and again during the 1960's. *Christianity and the Social Crisis, Christianizing the Social Order*, and *A Theology for the Social Gospel* have been published in multiple editions in English and in translation. Despite his own critique of Rauschenbusch, Reinhold Niebuhr considered the writing of this "founder of social Christianity" to be a seminal influence in laying a foundation for later Christian ethicists. When Max Stackhouse edited a newly discovered Rauschenbusch manuscript for publication as *The Righteousness of the Kingdom* in 1968, he noted that the "old Social Gospel" of Rauschenbusch contains themes of continuing relevance for "the new Social Gospel."

It was with "fear and trembling" that Rauschenbusch committed himself to the task of introducing a modified socialism to American Christians in a time when socialism was identified with "anarchism." His corpus includes a sustained critique of the inequities that accompany capitalism, with emphasis on the evils of class conflict and competition. He was the only leader of the "old Social Gospel" to condemn the unlimited accumulation of wealth and the absolute sanctity of private property. Rauschenbusch advocated relatively little governmental intervention in the social process through legislation. Because he believed that all men would work if fairly compensated, he believed that "the right to property is a corollary of the right to life...." Among the few legislative solutions that he did support were the land tax proposal of Henry George and the abolition of inheritance. He viewed the land tax as a viable means for the redistribution of property which would give all persons an equal opportunity to work. If inheritance was prohibited by law, then all persons would begin their work without an accumulation of capital and no one would begin with an automatic advantage. Rauschenbusch looked to a time in history when social solidarity between persons would lead to a spirit of "each for all and all for each."

The Rauschenbusch vision of the "good society" in which the democratic ideals of fraternity, equality, and freedom might become reality was linked to a version of evolutionary progress. Although he considered it unrealistic to believe that progress in history was automatic, Rauschenbusch did write his books in the hope that the Kingdom of God might emerge out of the present social revolution "unparalleled in history for scope and power." Because his interpretation of history included the possibility of social modification forward or backward, in each book he analysed contemporary signs of progress—and regress. Each time he called on Christians to live out the revolutionary love seen in Jesus that would characterize a co-operative society characterized by "the love-motive" insead of selfishness and violence. Because he believed that "the religious spirit is an incalculable power in the making of history" he saw his life work as the stimulation of high ideals and a social spirit in the people. Insofar as love was a natural "faculty" his appeal was not limited to Christians.

The writing of Rauschenbusch continues to be compelling because of the passion with which he catalogued the human suffering caused by the inequitable distribution of wealth that he saw around him in Victorian America. A man of great sympathy, he portrayed "the worker," the tenement family, the materialistic middle-class "society" woman, the degraded prostitute primarily as victims of their social environment. "Outward opportunity and inward inclination" worked together to produce "sin." Because he believed that love experienced in the family circle could naturally radiate outward to transform other social institutions he appeals to the family sentiments of his readers in his vivid portrayals of the effects of capitalism on family units.

Rauschenbusch can be considered an apologetic theologian in his attempt to express the "truth" of Christianity in the language and thought categories of his time. The revelation of Christian "truth" had its roots in the Bible but continues in human history. Rauschenbusch used scripture on the basis of the utility of a passage or book to interpret and inspire revelatory acts and events in the present. His writing style is more often polemical and rich in metaphor than it is logical or systematic. Because he believed that legislation properly embodied the "truth" of public opinion he wrote and spoke to touch the heart—to inspire the "social spirit" necessary to correct the idleness, greed, and violence that seem to accompany capitalism. He hoped that the spiritual power of Christianity would transform the high democratic ideals of an "almost Christianized America" to overcome the transitory evils of capitalism: "We need a Christian ethics of property, more perhaps than anything else.... On the one hand property is indispensable to personal freedom, to all higher individuality, and to self-realization; the right to property is a corollary to the right of life; without property men are at the mercy of nature and in bondage to those who have property" (*The Social Principles of Jesus*).

Rauschenbusch intentionally wrote for men because he observed that the church failed to offer men "a religious ideal...capable of enlisting to the full the masculine faculties." The social

regeneration he considered possible depended on the civic virtue of men in the masculine spheres of property and politics. Although the church functions to inspire and empower social love and civic virtue in individuals it should not make political pronouncements or become involved in politics. American separation of church and state was a sign of progress insofar as moral behavior was voluntary and not coerced by either church or state. The role of pastors and prophets as "the people who give direction to the forces of religion" is therefore magnified because Rauschenbusch denied the church as a social institution access to the political arena. In part, the continuing appeal of the writing of Walter Rauschenbusch is related to his emphasis on the importance of the family to the health and future of society, and to the role of religious men in seeking and achieving social justice and equality in America.

—Janet F. Fishburn

RAWLS, John (Boardley). American philosopher. Born in Baltimore, Maryland, 21 February 1921. Studied at Princeton University, New Jersey, Ph.D. 1950. Married; 3 children. Instructor, Princeton University, 1950-52; Assistant Professor, Cornell University, Ithaca, New York, 1953-62; Professor, 1962-76, and since 1976 John Cowles Professor, Harvard University, Cambridge, Massachusetts. Recipient: Fulbright Fellowship, Oxford University, 1952-53. Address: Department of Philosophy, Harvard University, Cambridge, Massachusetts 02138, U.S.A.

PUBLICATIONS

Philosophy

A Theory of Justice. Cambridge, Massachusetts, Harvard University Press, 1971.

*

Critical Studies: *The Liberal Theory of Justice: A Critical Examination of the Principle Doctrines in "A Theory of Justice" by John Rawls* by Brian M. Berry, Oxford, Clarendon Press, 1973; *Reading Rawls* edited by Norman Daniels, Oxford, Blackwell, 1975; *New Essays in Contract Theory* edited by K. Nelsen and R. Shiner, Guelph, Ontario, Canadian Association for Publishing in Philosophy, 1977; *Understanding Rawls: A Reconstruction and Critique of "A Theory of Justice"* by Robert Paul Wolff, Princeton, New Jersey, Princeton University Press, 1977; *Judging Justice* by Philip Pettit, London, Routledge, 1980; *Liberal Equality* by Amy Gutmann, Cambridge, Cambridge University Press, 1980.

*   *   *

It is probably fair to say that no single work has had as profound an impact on Anglo-American philosophy in the second half of the 20th century as John Rawls's *A Theory of Justice*. This single work re-vitalized the long dormant field of political philosophy, and, more generally, gave new direction and respectability to normative moral theory. Its way was prepared by several very influential earlier papers by Rawls and in its wake came a spate of treatises by others providing extensions of or alternatives to Rawls's theory of justice.

The expressed aim of *A Theory of Justice* is to present a fully elaborated alternative to the various utilitarian-inspired conceptions of justice that have been dominant in this century. The core of the project (contained in the first part of the book) is his derivation of the two principles of justice and his technique for deriving them. It is in his technique for deriving the principles that Rawls identifies himself with the contract tradition (Locke, Rousseau, and Kant). We are to imagine an hypothetical choice situation wherein a group of people gather together to agree upon a set of principles of justice to govern their conduct. The correct principles are the ones that will be chosen under certain conditions bearing specifically on knowledge and motivation. The conditions on knowledge are to guarantee fairness: these hypothetical choosers are assumed to know general scientific principles and to know that conflicting interests and moderate scarcity obtain, but they are shielded by a "veil of ignorance" from a knowledge of their own conception of the good, their own talents, their own social position, and the stage of development of their particular society. In short, the parties to the decision do not know the contingencies that would be the source of prejudice and would put them in opposition. The conditions on motivation are to guarantee the fruitfulness of the derivation. The hypothetical choosers are construed as mutually disinterested and characterized by no substantive moral sentiments at all. The reason for this is methodological. If the choosers were characterized as altruistic or as having other specific moral sentiments, the "deduction" of the principles of justice would have considerably less impact for it would be rationally compelling only on antecedently moral men. As it stands, however, if the deduction is sound, the principles would be compelling on all who met the minimal conditions of prudential rationality.

The normative principles that Rawls in fact argues for are the following:

First Principle. Each person is to have an equal right to the most extensive total system of basic liberties compatible with a similar system of liberty for all.
Second Principle. Social and economic inequalities are to be arranged so that they are both (a) to the greatest benefit to the least advantaged consistent with the just savings principle and (b) attached to offices and positions open to all under conditions of fair equality of opportunity.

Moreover, there is a lexical order to the principles such that the first always takes priority over the second. The basic liberties referred to in the first principle are the traditional ones of political liberty, freedom of speech and assembly, freedom of thought and conscience, and freedom from arbitrary arrest and seizure. Although this principle has not been uncontroversial, the second principle has been the more controversial. It is not strongly egalitarian (as is the first principle) inasmuch as it provides for unequal distribution, but it is egalitarian in spirit for it implies that inequalities are to be justified and specifies rather stringent conditions which alone would justify them. The nub of the principle is what Rawls calls "the difference principle" which directs us to distribute all social primary goods so as to maximize the expectations of the least advantaged. Rawls argues that this conservative principle of distribution would be chosen in the original position over less conservative principles such as average utility which would allow us to take greater risks in return for the probability of higher gains.

In the second part of the book Rawls draws out the specific implications of his theory for social institutions. Given the principles of justice as established, the strategy is to extend the contract model so that it applies to more and more specific situations. The institutionalized structure for which he argues is a constitutional democracy with a competitive economy, but he allows for the possibility that a liberal socialist regime might be so formulated as to answer to the two principles of justice.

In the third part of the book Rawls completes his theory of justice by exploring its grounding in human feeling and its ties with our ends and aspirations. This excursion into the realm of moral psychology is an essential part of the general argument because Rawls feels that the final acceptability of any theory of justice is not indepedent of its ability to account for our de facto

sense of justice and thus its ability to explain that stability of social cooperation we actually do have. Hence, an important feature of a conception of justice is that it should generate its own support; its principles should be such that when they are embodied in the basic structure of society men tend to develop a desire to act in accord with them. The argument of part three is that his theory has these concrete characteristics.

It is difficult to overemphaize the impact of Rawls's work on contemporary philosophy. His A Theory of Justice is an instance of philosophy in the grand manner. While it may be premature to list it among our philosophical classics, it is clearly the case that it represents the "state of the art" in contemporary political philosophy.

—C.F.Delaney

READ, Herbert (Edward). British art critic and poet. Born in Muscoates Grange, Kirbymoorside, Yorkshire, 4 December 1893. Educated at Crossley's School, Halifax, Yorkshire; studied at the University of Leeds. Commissioned in the Green Howards, 1915, and fought in France and Belgium, 1915-18: Captain; Military Cross, Distinguished Service Order, 1918; mentioned in despatches. Married Evelyn Roff; married Margaret Ludwig; 5 children. Assistant Principal, The Treasury, London, 1919-22; Assistant Keeper. Victoria and Albert Museum, London, 1922-31; Watson Gordon Professor of Fine Arts, University of Edinburgh, 1931-33; Editor, Burlington Magazine, London, 1933-39; Sydney Jones Lecturer in Art, University of Liverpool, 1935-36; Editor, English Master Painters series, from 1940. Leon Fellow, University of London, 1940-42; Charles Eliot Norton Professor of Poetry, Harvard University, Cambridge, Massachusetts, 1953-54; A.W. Mellon Lecturer in Fine Arts, Washington, D.C., 1954; Senior Fellow, Royal College of Art, London, 1962; Fellow, Center for Advanced Studies, Wesleyan University, Middletown, Connecticut, 1964-65. Trustee, Tate Gallery, London, 1965-68. President, Society for Education Through Art, Yorkshire Philosophical Society, Institute of Contemporary Arts, and British Society of Aesthetics. Recipient: Erasmus Prize, 1966. Honorary Professorship, University of Cordoba, Argentina, 1962. Honorary doctorate: State University of New York, Buffalo, 1962; Boston University, 1965; University of York, 1966. Honorary Fellow, Society of Industrial Artists; Foreign Corresponding Fellow, Académie Flamande des Beaux Arts, 1953; Foreign Member, Royal Academy of Fine Arts, Stockholm, 1960; Honorary Member, American Academy of Arts and Letters, 1966. Knighted, 1953. Died 12 June 1968.

PUBLICATIONS

Art and Society

English Pottery: Its Development from Early Times to the End of the Eighteenth Century, with Bernard Rackham. London, Benn, 1924.
English Stained Glass. London, Putnam, 1926.
Staffordshire Pottery Figures. London, Duckworth, and Boston, Houghton Mifflin, 1929.
The Place of Art in a University (lecture). Edinburgh, Oliver and Boyd, 1931.
The Meaning of Art. London, Faber, 1931; as The Anatomy of Art: An Introduction to the Problems of Art and Aesthetics, New York, Dodd Mead, 1932.
Art Now: An Introduction to the Theory of Modern Painting and Sculpture. London, Faber, and New York, Harcourt Brace, 1933.
Henry Moore, Sculptor: An Appreciation. London, Zwemmer, 1934.

Art and Industry: The Principles of Industrial Design. London, Faber, 1934; New York, Harcourt Brace, 1935.

Art and Society. London, Heinemann, and New York, Macmillan, 1937.

Education Through Art. London, Faber, 1943; New York, Pantheon, 1948.

Paul Nash. London, Penguin, 1944.

The Grass Roots of Art: Four Lectures on Social Aspects of Art in an Industrial Age. London, Drummond, and New York, Wittenborn, 1947.

Culture and Education in World Order (lecture). New York, Museum of Modern Art, 1948.

The Psychopathology of Reaction in the Arts. London, Institute of Contemporary Arts, 1948.

Contemporary British Art. London, Faber, 1951.

Art and the Evolution of Man (lecture). London, Freedom Press, 1951.

The Philosophy of Modern Art: Collected Essays. London, Faber, 1952; New York, Meridian Books, 1955.

Icon and Idea: The Function of Art in the Development of Human Consciousness (lectures). Cambridge, Massachusetts, Harvard University Press, and London, Faber, 1955.

The Art of Sculpture (lectures). London, Faber, and New York, Pantheon, 1956.

The Significance of Children's Art: Art as a Symbolic Language. Vancouver, University of British Columbia Press, 1957.

A Concise History of Modern Painting. London, Thames and Hudson, and New York, Praeger, 1959.

The Forms of Things Unknown: Essays Towards an Aesthetic Philosophy. London, Faber, and New York, Horizon Press, 1960.

A Letter to a Young Painter. London, Thames and Hudson, and New York, Horizon Press, 1962.

To Hell with Culture and Other Essays on Art and Society. London, Routledge, 1963.

Art and Education. Melbourne, Cheshire, 1964.

Henry Moore: A Study of His Life and Work. London, Thames and Hudson, and New York, Praeger, 1965.

The Origins of Form in Art. London, Thames and Hudson, and New York, Horizon Press, 1965.

The Redemption of the Robot: My Encounter wih Education Through Art. New York, Trident Press, 1966; London, Faber, 1970.

Art and Alienation: The Role of the Artist in Society (lectures). London, Thames and Hudson, and New York, Horizon Press, 1967.

Henry Moore: Mother and Child. London, Collins, and New York, New American Library, 1967.

Arp. London, Thames and Hudson, 1968; as *The Art of Jean Arp*, New York, Abrams, 1968.

Literary Criticism

Reason and Romanticism. London, Faber, 1926; New York, Russell and Russell, 1963.

English Prose Style. London, Bell, and New York, Holt, 1928.

Phases of English Poetry. London, Hogarth Press, and New York, Harcourt Brace, 1928.

The Sense of Glory: Essays in Criticism. Cambridge, Cambridge University Press, and New York, Harcourt Brace, 1929.

Wordsworth: The Clark Lectures 1929-1930. London, Cape, 1932.

Form in Modern Poetry. London, Sheed and Ward, 1932.

In Defence of Shelley and Other Essays. London, Heinemann, 1936.

Collected Essays in Literary Cricitism. London, Faber, 1938; as *The Nature of Literature*, New York, Horizon Press, 1956.

Poetry and Anarchism. London, Faber, 1938; New York, Macmillan, 1939.

Coleridge as Critic. London, Faber, 1949.

Byron. London, Longman, 1951.

The True Voice of Feeling: Studies in English Romantic Poetry. London, Faber, and New York, Pantheon, 1953.

The Tenth Muse: Essays in Criticism. London, Routledge, 1957.

Truth Is Most Sacred: A Cultural Exchange on Modern Literature, with Edward Dahlberg. London, Routledge, and New York, Horizon Press, 1961.

Selected Writings: Poetry and Criticism. London, Faber, 1963; New York, Horizon Press, 1964.

T.S.E.: A Memoir (on T.S. Eliot). Middletown, Connecticut, Wesleyan Center for Advanced Studies, 1966.

Poetry and Experience. London, Vision Press, and New York, Horizon Press, 1967.

Politics

Julian Benda and the New Humanism. Seattle, University of Washington Bookstore, 1930.

Essential Communism. London, Nott, 1935.

The Philosophy of Anarchism. London, Freedom Press, 1940.

To Hell with Culture: Democratic Values Are New Values. London, Kegan Paul, 1941.

The Politics of the Unpolitical. London, Routledge, 1943.

The Education of Free Men. London, Freedom Press, 1944.

Freedom Is a Crime? London, Freedom Press, 1945.

Education for Peace. New York, Scribner, 1949; London, Routledge, 1950.

Existentialism, Marxism, and Anarchism: Chains of Freedom. London, Freedom Press, 1949.

Anarchy and Order: Essays in Politics. London, Faber, 1945.

Verse

Songs of Chaos. London, Elkin Mathews, 1915.

Eclogues: A Book of Poems. London, Beaumont Press, 1919.

Naked Warriors. London, Arts and Letters, 1919.

Mutations of the Phoenix. London, Hogarth Press, 1923.

Collected Poems 1913-1925. London, Faber, 1926; Norfolk, Connecticut, New Directions, 1951; revised edition, Faber, 1953, 1966.

The End of a War. London, Faber, 1933.

Poems 1914-1934. London, Faber, and New York, Harcourt Brace, 1935.

Thirty-Five Poems. London, Faber, 1940.

A World Within a War. London, Faber, 1944.

Moon's Farm, and Other Poems, Mostly Elegiac. London, Faber, 1955; New York, Horizon Press, 1956.

Selected Writings: Poetry and Criticism. London, Faber, 1963; New York, Horizon Press, 1964.

Other

In Retreat (autobiographical). London, Hogarth Press, 1925.

Ambush (autobiographical). London, Faber, 1930.

The Innocent Eye: Recollections of Childhood. London, Faber, 1933; New York, Holt, 1947.

The Green Child: A Romance. London, Heinemann, 1935; New York, New Directions, 1948.

Annals of Innocence and Experience (autobiographical). London, Faber, 1940.

A Coat of Many Colours: Occasional Essays. London, Routledge, 1945; New York, Horizon Press, 1956.

A Parliament of Women (play). Huntingdon, England, Vine Press, 1960.

Lord Byron at the Opera: A Play for Broadcasting. London, Ward, 1963.

The Contrary Experience: Autobiographies. London, Faber, and New York, Horizon Press, 1963.

The Cult of Sincerity. London, Faber, and New York, Horizon Press, 1968.

Editor, *Speculations: Essays on Humanism and the Philosophy of Art*, by T.E. Hulme. London, Kegan Paul, and New York, Harcourt Brace, 1923.

Editor, *Form in Gothic*, by W. Worringer. London, Putnam, 1927.

Editor, *Notes on Language and Style*, by T.E. Hulme. Seattle, University of Washington Bookstore, 1929.

Editor, *A Sentimental Journey*, by Sterne. London, Scholartis Press, 1929.

Editor, with Bonamy Dobree, *The London Book of English Prose*. London, Eyre and Spottiswoode, and New York, Viking Press, 1931.

Editor, *The English Vision*. London, Eyre and Spottiswoode, 1933.

Editor, *Unit I: The Modern Movement in English Architecture, Painting, and Sculpture*. London, Cassell, 1934.

Editor, with Denis Saurat, *Selected Essays and Critical Writings*, by A.R. Orage. London, Nott, 1935.

Editor, *Surrealism*. London, Faber, 1936.

Editor, *The Knapsack: A Pocket-Book of Prose and Verse*. London, Routledge, 1939.

Editor, *Kropotkin: Selections from His Writings*. London, Freedom Press, 1942.

Editor, *The Practice of Design*. London, Lund Humphries, 1946.

Editor, with Bonamy Dobree, *The London Book of English Verse*. London, Eyre and Spottiswoode, and New York, Macmillan, 1949.

Editor, *Outline: An Autobiography, and Other Writings*, by Paul Nash. London, Faber, 1949.

Editor, with Michael Fordham and Gerhard Adler, *The Collected Works of C.G. Jung*. New York, Pantheon, 17 vols., 1953-73.

Editor, *This Way Delight: A Book of Poetry for the Young*. New York, Pantheon, 1956; London, Faber, 1957.

Editor, *Origins of Western Art*. New York, Grolier, 1965.

Translator, with Margaret Ludwig, *Radio*, by Rudolf Arnheim. London, Faber, 1936.

*

Critical Studies: *Herbert Read* by Francis Berry, London, Longman, 1953, revised edition, 1961; *Herbert Read: A Memorial Symposium* edited by Robin Skelton, London, Methuen, 1971; *Herbert Read: The Stream and the Source* by George Woodcock, London, Faber, 1972.

*   *   *

Broad English Man of Letters, Herbert Read was a cultural figure of considerable influence for the generation from the 1930's on. His happy childhood in an antique and solid North England farming family, an "organic" order with which he always retained a romantic identification, was broken by orphaning and a harsh boarding school. Then came several years of clerking, a short stay in a university, and more than four years as a junior infantry officer in the Great War. Following a dozen postwar years in the civil service, his writing gave him a reputation not only as a literary figure (memoirs, poems, essays, studies) but as probably the leading British interpreter of the visual arts. For more than three decades, he was not only a widely recognized critic and lecturer but an energetic organizer, editor, and spokesman for part of cultural modernism.

Various parts of his life were recounted in four short autobiographical works of pleasant modesty and reflectiveness (most of them eventually combined as *The Contrary Experience*). Read also published one novel, *The Green Child*, an odd combination of fantasy and several utopias, which has its admirers. A life-long minor lyric poet, he wrote competently in various manners—

Imagist, Wordsworthian nature contemplation, and mythic monologues. While he was the progenitor of a small movement of romantic revivalism in the 1940's (partly because of his apologetics for romanticism), his poetry remains slight, often forced and portentously poetical, and without a distinctive voice.

His discussions of literature were rather more important, ranging from a sensible handbook on rhetoric, *English Prose Style*, through his longest critical study, *Wordsworth*, to apologetics for Surrealism and other modernist experiments. While he wrote enthusiastically of varied English writers from Traherne through James to Eliot, his preferences from his earliest critical book (*Reason and Romanticism*) to his last (*The Cult of Sincerity*) were for the romantics (especially Wordsworth, Coleridge, Shelley, more briefly Byron, the Brontës, Blake, and others). His most usual focus was on the issue of relating romantic sensibility to modernism and coherent forms, hence his adaption of psychoanalytic criticism, then Surrealist doctrines, various organicist aesthetics (Whitehead, Croce, etc.) and finally enthusiastic Jungianism. Most of his criticism took the form of occasional essays, and many of them are little anthologies of apt quotations. They strikingly include a broad learning (psychology, anthropology, social criticism, philosophy) not usual in genteel *belle lettres* or in the often narrow New Criticism which Read partly attempted to enlarge.

Part of Read's larger concern was a libertarian ethic. From his early romanticism, he had identified with anarchist views. Though for long muted (his 17 years as an army officer and civil servant—and later unpersuasive after he incongruously accepted a knighthood), he published a number of anarchist essays (*Anarchy and Order, The Politics of the Unpolitical*, etc.) lucidly summarizing what were essentially Kropotkinesque positions (though, as usual, there are also other elements—Stirner and Nietzsche, Morris and Guild Socialism, Bakuninist Spanish syndicalism, and the religious anarchism of Tolstoy, Gandhi, and Simone Weil). The arguments are for equality, pacifism, decentralization, workers' control, resistance to the State, full individual liberty, communal forms, and other usual anarchist themes. He was positive about human nature, negative about modern institutions. Perhaps his distinctive emphasis was to see the arts as libertarian education, and as central to anarchist sensibility. While not an extensive or unique libertarian thinker, in the frequently conservative or reactionary politics linked with much cultural modernism, Read's anarchism had a large resonance.

So did his art criticism. As a museum civil servant, Read early developed a visual art expertise—early books on English stained glass and pottery—which he soon typically combined with a large philosophic concern, such as genetic aesthetics (Worringer). Though wide ranging in his interests, his main concentration was on modernist painting and sculpture, post-Cezanne. A "high popularizer," he wrote histories of modern painting and modern sculpture as well as other responsive expositions (*Art Now, The Meaning of Art*). Besides essays on major European modernists, such as Kandinsky, Klee, Gabo, Picasso, Arp, and others, he was a strong advocate of his British contemporaries—Hepworth, Nash, Nicholson, etc.—and especially of his friend Henry Moore, on whom he did several books. The postmodernist styles of the 1960's (Pop Art, and others) with their lack of romantic aspiration and subservience to the technocratic ordering drew his negative responses.

For Read had a large positive social view of the arts, deployed in a series of books (*Art and Society, Art and Industry, Grass Roots of Art*), of which probably the most influential was *Education Through Art*. Revolting against over-mechanization (à la the Ruskin-Morris tradition) and technocratic functionalism, Read held that all schooling—and much more—should center on acquiring a deeply aesthetic sense of experience. This was essential as counter-knowledge to science, and as a humanization of the technological disorder. Work and art needed to be fused. All needed aesthetically organic living. In several late books (*Icon and Idea, The Forms of Things Unknown*), his Platonist-Jungian aesthetic aimed at art as a social substitute for religion.

Art is nothing less than "spirit informing matter," and the "education of sensibilities" in the deep "perception of form" is one of our few redemptive possibilities.

Though not a thinker or writer of great originality, Read was a suggestive critic of wide learning, responsiveness, sensitivity, earnestness. In a positive sense, he was the Man of Letters as cultural broker, distributing the romantic side of modernism. His liberating senses of aesthetic experience expressed high humane aspiration against a confining English society and a declining civilization.

—Kingsley Widmer

REDFIELD, Robert. American anthropologist. Born in Chicago, Illinois, 4 December 1897. Educated privately, and at Laboratory School of University of Chicago, 1910-15; studied at the University of Chicago, Ph.B. 1920 (Phi Beta Kappa), J.D. 1921, Ph.D. 1928; studied biology briefly at Harvard University, Cambridge, Massachusetts, 1918. Served as an ambulance driver, American Field Service in France, 1917; worked in military intelligence, 1918. Married Margaret Lucy Park in 1920; 4 children. Lawyer: admitted to the Illinois bar, 1922, and practiced in his father's firm of Holeman Redfield and Handler, Chicago, 1921-24; Instructor in Sociology and Anthropology, University of Colorado, Boulder, 1925-26; field work in Tepoztlán, Mexico (Social Science Research Council Fellowship), 1926; Instructor, 1927-28, Assistant Professor, 1928-30, Associate Professor, 1930-32, Professor of Anthropology, 1934-53, Dean of Graduate Division of Social Sciences, 1934-46, Chairman of the Anthropology Department, 1947-49, and Robert Maynard Hutchins Distinguished Service Professor, 1953-58, University of Chicago. Research Associate, Carnegie Institution, Washington, D.C., 1930-46. Visiting Professor, Tsinghua University, Peking, 1948, and University of Frankfurt, 1949; Messenger Lecturer, Cornell University, Ithaca, New York, 1952; Gottesman Lecturer, Uppsala University, 1954. Consultant, Fund for the Republic. President, American Anthropological Association, 1944; Director, American Council on Race Relations, 1947-50; Member of the Executive Council, United World Federalists; Member of the Board of Directors, American Council of Learned Societies, 1952-55. Recipient: American Anthropological Association Viking Fund Medal, 1954; Royal Anthropological Institute Huxley Memorial Medal (UK), 1955. L.H.D.: Fisk University, Nashville, 1946. Fellow, American Association for the Advancement of Science, and American Philosophical Society. Died 16 October 1958.

PUBLICATIONS

Anthropology

Tepoztlán, A Mexican Village: A Study of Folk Life. Chicago, University of Chicago Press, 1930.
Culture of the Maya (lectures). Washington, D.C., Carnegie Institution, 1933.
The Maya and Modern Civilization. Washington, D.C., Carnegie Institution, 1933.
Chan Kom, A Maya Village, with Alfonso Villa Rojas. Washington, D.C., Carnegie Institution, 1934.
Designs for Living (lecture). Chicago, University of Chicago, 1935.
What Is an Education? Chicago, University of Chicago, 1936.
On Maya Research (lecture). Washington, D.C., Carnegie Institution, 1937.
The Folk Culture of Yucatan. Chicago, University of Chicago Press, 1941.

The Village That Chose Progress: Chan Kom Revisited. Chicago, University of Chicago Press, 1950.
The Primitive World and Its Transformations. Ithaca, New York, Cornell University Press, 1953; London, Penguin, 1968.
The Educational Experience (lecture). Pasadena, California, Fund for Adult Education, 1955.
The Little Community: Viewpoints for the Study of a Human Whole (lectures). Uppsala, Almqvist & Wiksells, and Chicago, University of Chicago Press, 1955.
Peasant Society and Culture: An Anthropological Approach to Sociology. Chicago, University of Chicago Press, 1956.
The Genius of the University (lecture). Eugene, University of Oregon, 1956.
Talk with a Stranger. New York, Fund for the Republic, 1958.
Aspects of Primitive Art (lectures), with Melville J. Herskovits and Gordon F. Ekholm. New York, Museum of Primitive Art, 1959.
The Papers of Robert Redfield, edited by Margaret Park Redfield. Chicago, University of Chicago Press, 2 vols., 1962-63.

Other

Editor, Levels of Integration in Biological and Social Systems. Lancaster, Pennsylvania, Jaques Cattell Press, 1942.
Editor, Magic, Science, and Religion, and Other Essays, by Bronislaw Malinowski. Boston, Beacon Press, 1948.

*

Critical Study: "Robert Redfield" by Fay-Cooper Cole and Fred Eggan, in American Anthropologist (Menasha, Wisconsin), n.s. 61, 1959.

*   *   *

Robert Redfield was one of those who, in the mid-20th century, defined the profession and the discipline of anthropology, both for the professionals and for the public. His intellectual career had two phases; in the first, longer, phase he worked toward a definition of anthropology as a science of man; in the later phase he worked away from this definition toward a more humanistic, philosophical understanding of the anthropologist's art. Throughout his career, further, he looked for occasions to put his ideas to use, since for him social action was a proper use of social science and the anthropologist had a special obligation to speak to the dilemmas of race and war.

Redfield's first fieldwork was done in central Mexico; it was, indeed, the attraction of the field which drew him to the science. He and his wife Margaret, who became his lifelong collaborator, travelled to Mexico while Redfield was still a young lawyer, and their private discovery of the villages converted Redfield to social science. In his studies of village life Redfield filled a gap in the science, which had up to this time largely been concerned with the sociology of cities (his wife's father, Robert Park, q.v., was important here) or else, in the ethnographic tradition dominated in America by Franz Boas (q.v.), with more primitive communities. Redfield's own teachers at the University of Chicago (where he spent his whole career) were Edwin Sapir (q.v.) and Fay Cooper Cole; the first phase of his work was concerned with the peasantry, defined as peoples living in small self-contained communities which are nevertheless in cultural and economic contact with cities, and whose cultural life is defined in part by their resistance to urbanization.

In his Ph.D. thesis and first book, on Tepoztlán in Morelos in central Mexico, Redfield began his exploration of the "folk society," defined as a pattern of life which, in contrast to the urban pattern, is dominated by face-to-face interaction, inherited roles and relationships, and traditional values. It was said of him later that his genius enabled him to discover the folk society where it did not exist; a later re-study of Tepoztlán by Oscar Lewis (q.v.) found it to be less of a village than Redfield had reported, more of a town, less culturally coherent and more torn by conflict and cultural incoherence. Thus challenged, Redfield responded that it is appropriate for different investigators to perceive different dimensions in the life of a given community, and that both reports can be scientifically valid. His own ethnographic work throughout his career involved an identification with the center of the society studied, rather than its periphery, and sought out the local sources of cultural coherence and continuity. This tendency was called by some critics "romantic" since it seemed to idealize non-urban life; it should perhaps rather be called "classic" since Redfield tended to see culture not as an arena for conflict but as a source of social order and solidarity from generation to generation.

The problems of the peasantry brought Redfield to Yucatan, where he made a special study of the agricultural Maya village of Chan Kom, and at the same time, in collaboration with Alfonso Villa Rojas, placed this community within the whole range of societies inhabiting the peninsula, from the urban capital, Merida, through the provincial town of Tzetas, and including the savage hunting-and-collecting Maya of Quintana Roo. These inquiries were published in *The Folk Culture of Yucatan*, where the notion of folk culture was developed into an understanding of the "folk-urban continuum."

A gap in Redfield's intellectual career was made by his ten years as Dean of Social Sciences at Chicago, as a close associate of Robert Hutchins; these years roughly corresponded with the Second World War. During this period he continued his fieldwork, now in the highlands of Guatemala, but published next to nothing of the results. The next phase was announced (and the first phase completed) by his own re-study of Chan Kom; published as *A Village That Chose Progress*, this is a study of the process of rural modernization and of a village transformed by history. In his later work, particularly in *The Primitive World and Its Transformations*, Redfield began to develop an anthropologist's vision of human history, particularly in terms of the interaction between the "great tradition," the literate culture of the cities and the intelligentsia, and the "little tradition," largely oral and maintained by small communities. When his final illness overtook him he had just begun a field study of this interaction in India; this work has been continued by some of his collaborators, particularly Milton Singer.

Redfield's most-read book, also from his later years, is *The Little Community*, which is a distillation of his fieldwork expento a general theory of the problems of small community studies.

Redfield was noted for the calm elegance of his style and the clarity of his ideas. This drive toward clarity produces a certain intellectual modesty and sometimes seems almost a limitation; Redfield avoids grand theoretical syntheses in the manner of Talcott Parsons (*q.v.*) or Claude Lévi-Strauss (*q.v.*). In reading his work, however, we are always in contact with a cultivated subtle mind; he tells us exactly what he knows and how he knows it. His capacity for lucid plain talk, and his passionate concern for social justice and the future of our species, made him one of those social scientists who had the ear of the public, and who made a difference—as an expert witness in the desegregation cases of the 1950's, as a founding member of the Committee on Social Thought, and in such enterprises as the Commission on the Freedom of the Press, the Committee to Draft a World Constitution, and the *Bulletin of the Atomic Scientists*.

—James Redfield

REICH, Wilhelm. American psychoanalyst. Born in Galicia in 1897; emigrated to Denmark and Sweden, 1934, and to the United States in 1939; naturalized, 1946. Studied at the University of Vienna, M.D. 1922. Served in the German Army, 1915-18;

Lieutenant. Married four times. Assistant at the Wagner-Jauregg Clinic, Vienna; entered private practice in 1919; joined the Vienna Psycho-Analytic Society in 1921 and organized the Vienna Seminar for Psycho-Analytic Therapy in 1922; broke with the Society in 1934; practiced in Scandinavia, 1934-38: founded the International Institute for Sex-Economy in 1936; founded the Orgone Institute in Forest Hills, New York, in 1939. Sentenced to two years in prison in 1956 for Food and Drug Administration violations. *Died* (in the Lewisburg Penitentiary, Pennsylvania) *23 November 1957*.

PUBLICATIONS

Psychology

Der triebhafte Charakter: Eine psychoanalytische Studie zur Pathologie des Ich. Vienna, Internationaler Psychoanalytischer Verlag, 1925; as "The Impulsive Character," in *The Impulsive Character and Other Writings*, New York, New American Library, 1974.

Die Funktion des Orgasmus. Vienna, Internationaler Psychoanalytischer Verlag, 1927; revised version as *The Discovery of the Orgone, I: The Function of the Orgasm*, New York, Orgone Institute Press, 1942; London, Panther, 1966.

Sexualerregung und Sexualbefreidigung. Vienna, Münster Verlag, 1929.

Geschlechtsreife, Enthaltsamkeit, Ehemoral. Vienna, Münster Verlag, 1930; revised version as *Die Sexualität im Kultukampf: Zur charakterlichen Selbsteuerung des Menschen*, Copenhagen, Sexpol, 1936; as *The Sexual Revolution: Toward a Self-Governing Character Structure*, New York, Orgone Institute Press, 1945; London, Vision Press, 1952.

Die Sexuelle Kampf der Jugend. Berlin, Verlag für Sexualpolitik, 1932; as *The Sexual Struggle of Youth*, London, Socialist Reproduction, 1972.

Der Einbruch der Sexualmoral. Berlin, Verlag für Sexualpolitik, 1932; as *The Invasion of Compulsory Sex-Morality*, London, Souvenir Press, 1972.

Charakteranalyse. Privately printed, 1933; as *Character Analysis*, New York, Orgone Institute Press, 1949; London, Vision Press, 1950.

Massenpsychologie des Faschismus. Copenhagen, Verlag für Sexualpolitik, 1933; as *The Mass Psychology of Fascism*, New York, Orgone Institute Press, 1946; London, Souvenir Press, 1972.

Der Orgasmus als Elektro-physiologische Entladung. Copenhagen, Sexpol, 1934; as "The Orgasm as an Electrophysiological Discharge," in *The Bioelectrical Investigation of Sexuality and Anxiety*, New York, Farrar Straus, 1982.

Der Urgegensatz des vegetatives Lebens. Copenhagen, Sexpol, 1934.

Was ist Klassenbewusstsein? Copenhagen, Verlag für Sexualpolitik, 1934; as *What Is Class-Consciousness?*, London, Socialist Reproduction, and New York, Liberation, 1971.

Psychischer Kontakt und vegetative Stromung. Copenhagen, Sexpol, 1935.

Experimentelle Ergebnisse über die elektrische Funktion von Sexualität und Angst. Copenhagen, Sexpol Verlag, 1937.

Orgasmusreflex, Muskelhaltung und Korperausdruck. Copenhagen, Sexpol, 1937.

Der dialektische Materialismus in Lebensforschung. Copenhagen, Sexpol, 1937.

Die natürliche Organisation der Arbeit in der Arbeitsdemokratie. Copenhagen, Sexpol, 1937.

Die Bione. Oslo, Sexpol, 1938.

Bion Experiments on the Cancer Problem and Drei Versuche am statischen Elektroscop. Oslo, Sexpol, 1939.

Weitere Probleme der Arbeitsdemokratie. Rotterdam, Sexpol, 1941.

The Discovery of the Orgone, II: The Cancer Biopathy. New

York, Orgone Institute, 1948.

Listen, Little Man!.   New York, Orgone Institute Press, 1948; London, Souvenir Press, 1972.

Ether, God and Devil.   New York, Orgone Institute Press, 1949.

Cosmic Superimposition.   Rangerley, Maine, Orgone Institute Press, 1951.

The Oranur Experiment: First Report.   Rangerley, Maine, Orgone Institute Press, 1951.

The Murder of Christ: Emotional Plague of Mankind.   Rangerley, Maine, Orgone Institute Press, 1953; London, Souvenir Press, 1975.

People in Trouble.   Rangerley, Maine, Orgone Institute Press, 1953.

The Einstein Affair.   Rangerley, Maine, Orgone Institute Press, 1953.

Conspiracy: An Emotional Chain Reaction.   Rangerley, Maine, Orgone Institute Press, 2 vols., 1955.

Contact with Space: The Second Oranur Report.   New York, Core Pilot Press, 1957.

Legal Writings.   Rangerley, Maine, Orgone Institute Press, 1957.

Selected Writings: An Introduction to Orgonomy.   New York, Farrar Straus, 1960; London, Vision Press, 1961.

Reich Speaks of Freud: Wilhelm Reich Discusses His Work and His Relationship with Sigmund Freud, edited by Mary Higgens and Chester M. Raphael.   New York, Farrar Straus, 1967; London, Souvenir Press, 1972.

Sex-pol Essays, 1929-1934, edited by Lee Baxandall.   New York, Random House, 1972.

Selected Sex-pol Essays, 1934-1937.   London, Socialist Reproduction, 1972.

Early Writings, edited by Philip Schmitz.   New York, Farrar Straus, 1975.

Other

Record of a Friendship: The Correspondence of Wilhelm Reich and A.S. Neill, 1936-1957, edited by Beverley R. Placzek. New York, Farrar Straus, 1981.

*

Critical Studies: *Reich* by Charles Rycroft, London, Collins, 1971; *Wilhelm Reich: The Evolution of His Work* by David Boadella, London, Vision Press, 1973 (includes bibliography); *Ideology and Unconsciousness: Reich, Freud, and Marx* by Ira H. Cohen, New York, New York University Press, 1982.

*   *   *

The life and career of Wilhelm Reich constitute one of the strangest chapters in the history of psychoanalysis. At one time he was one of the most creative thinkers in Sigmund Freud's exclusive Vienna circle. Later in life, after having embraced a long string of controversial, sometimes bizarre, ideas, he was dismissed as a messianic crank. He died in a federal prison.

As a physician and psychoanalyst in Austria and Germany in the 1920's, Reich accepted Freud's "libido" theory that repressed sexual energy was instrumental in generating neuroses. Now, he wondered, why did patients exhibit stern resistance, even hostility, toward therapy? From his clinical experience Reich concluded that patients had developed a "protective armor" to shield themselves from the outside world; that "armor" was derived in part from the same outside world. From this idea Reich went on to formulate a theory of "social character," the process whereby an individual absorbs characteristics from his enveloping society.

Freud had noted that "all psychology is social psychology," but he never fully transcended his own cultural biases. Reich, in trying to assess "how social existence is transformed into psychic structure," could not come up with all the answers, but he raised

excellent questions: how do political and economic systems, and codes of social and moral behavior, interact with and shape the individual psyche? The scope of psychoanalytic investigation was dramatically widened; henceforth, cultural forces, as well as the familiar instinctual and narrowly interpersonal ones, had to be considered. In different ways, the Neo-Freudians all built on this insight.

Reich next took a long leap. Freud had argued that "civilization," even while it caused frustrations by repressing sexual drives, nevertheless was essential because it forestalled anarchy. Reich turned this notion on its head. Re-direct energies, he advised, into healthy orgasmic experiences, and the neuroses would be dissipated. Liberated sexuality would bring about both pleasure and profound self-knowledge. (Parenthetically, it might be mentioned that Reich, like Freud, never understood the role of culture in shaping female sexuality.)

Of course, Reich reasoned, society opposed any genuine individual liberation. The enemy therefore was society itself, especially as it assumed authoritarian forms. In 1927 he joined the Communist Party. He also became active in social medicine: he established mental health clinics where he promoted natural childbirth, breast-feeding, and sexual freedoms for children and adults alike. All of these ideas ultimately developed their own lines of influence. In addition, his attempts to fuse ideas from Marx and Freud into a unified sociopsychoanalytic structure anticipated efforts by such other cross-disciplinary theorists as Erich Fromm and Herbert Marcuse. Reich's seminal works in this period were *The Mass Psychology of Fascism* and *Character Analysis*, both published in 1933.

With the advent of Naziism in 1933 Reich left Germany and commenced an odyssey that carried him to several countries, all the while advocating his theories in a tone that became increasingly zealous and self-righteous. His sexual determinism became so extreme that he antagonized most of his psychoanalytic and political associates; eventually he severed all of his professional connections.

By the late 1930's Reich became intrigued by a concept that would remain central to his thinking for the rest of his life. He came to believe that sexual energy was governed by electrochemical particles, and shortly announced that he had discovered the "bion," a fundamental unit of life energy. Next he postulated a universal life force that he called "orgone energy." His goal was to collect and control this energy, and thereby cleanse the body, cure cancer and other diseases, and ultimately lead the way to universal health and happiness.

In 1939 Reich emigrated to the United States. His arcane biophysical theories and intellectual arrogance had effectively cut him off from all but a tiny fringe of followers and fellow-believers. In a series of strident polemics, which later included such titles as *Listen, Little Man!* and *The Murder of Christ*, he denounced his critics together with a wide range of existing political and social institutions and the mass public which refused to recognize his greatness.

In the final decade of his life Reich's writings and activities began to border on the hallucinatory. He thought that alien forces from outer space were interfering with his latest experiments in "orgonic weather control." Perhaps, he wondered, he himself was a spaceman? The Unidentified Flying Objects did not capture him, but agents from the Federal Drug Administration did. They accused him of quackery for promoting and transporting his orgonic "cancer cure" (the orgone-box). When Reich ignored a federal restraining order, he was imprisoned. He died in a penitentiary a year and a half later, in 1957.

During the late 1960's and early 1970's, in the heyday of the "counterculture," some of Reich's ideas—especially those concerned with sexual freedom and authoritarian repression—found favor among "radical psychologists" and others hostile to the "establishment." At a time when the public was being bombarded with tales of UFO's and with accounts of the revelations to be gleaned from parapsychology and astrology, Reich's theories did not (to some) seem so arcane.

But the curious amalgam of imaginative thinking, social awareness, and gibberish that ran through so much of his work made the sorting-out process difficult. Recent attempts to salvage what is valuable and humane in Reich's analysis of character formation have run into the same obstacles.

—Don Hausdorff

RICHARDS, I(vor) A(rmstrong). British philosopher and literary critic. Born in Sandbach, Cheshire, 26 February 1893. Educated at Clifton College; studied at Magdalene College, Cambridge, B.A. 1915, Married Dorothy Eleanor Pilley in 1926. Lecturer in English and Moral Sciences, Cambridge University, 1922; Fellow, Magdalene College, 1926; Visiting Professor, Tsing Hua University, Peking, 1929-30; Visiting Lecturer, 1931, University Professor, 1943-63, and Professor Emeritus, 1963-79, Harvard University, Cambridge, Massachusetts. Director, Orthological Institute of China, 1936-38. Recipient: Loines Award, 1962; American Academy of Arts and Sciences Emerson-Thoreau Medal, 1970; Brandeis University Creative Arts Award, 1972. Honorary Member, American Academy of Arts and Sciences. Corresponding Fellow, British Academy, 1959. Honorary Fellow, Magdalene College, 1964. C.H. (Companion of Honour), 1964. *Died 7 September 1979.*

PUBLICATIONS

Literary Criticism and Language Theory

The Foundations of Aesthetics, with C.K. Ogden and James Wood. London, Allen and Unwin, 1922; New York, Lear, 1925.
The Meaning of Meaning, with C.K. Ogden. London, Kegan Paul, 1923; New York, Harcourt Brace, 1926.
Principles of Literary Criticism. London, Kegan Paul, 1924; New York, Harcourt Brace, 1925.
Science and Poetry. London, Kegan Paul, 1926; revised edition, 1935; as *Poetries and Sciences*, London, Routledge, and New York, Norton, 1970.
Practical Criticism: A Study of Literary Judgment. London, Kegan Paul, 1929; New York, Harcourt Brace, 1930.
Mencius on the Mind: Experiments in Multiple Definition. London, Kegan Paul, and New York, Harcourt Brace, 1932.
Basic Rules of Reason. London, Kegan Paul, 1933.
Coleridge on Imagination. London, Kegan Paul, 1934; New York, Harcourt Brace, 1935.
Basic in Teaching: East and West. London, Kegan Paul, 1935.
The Philosophy of Rhetoric. London and New York, Oxford University Press, 1936.
Interpretation in Teaching. London, Kegan Paul, and New York, Harcourt Brace, 1938.
How to Read a Page: A Course in Effective Reading, with an Introduction to a Hundred Great Words. New York, Norton, 1942; London, Paul Trench Trubner, 1943.
A World Language: An Address. New York, New York Herald Tribune, 1942.
Basic English and Its Uses. London, Kegan Paul, and New York, Norton, 1943.
Speculative Instruments. London, Routledge, and Chicago, University of Chicago Press, 1955.
Design for Escape: World Education Through Modern Media. New York, Harcourt Brace, 1968.
So Much Nearer: Essays Towards a World English. New York, Harcourt Brace, 1968.
Coleridge's Minor Poems (lecture). Missoula, Montana State University Press, 1960.

Poetries: Their Media and Ends, edited by Trevor Eaton. The Hague, Mouton, 1974.
Beyond. New York, Harcourt Brace, 1974.
Complementarities: Uncollected Essays and Reviews, edited by John Paul Russo. Cambridge, Massachusetts, Harvard University Press, 1976; Manchester, Carcanet Press, 1977.
Verse v. Prose (lecture). London, English Association, 1978.

Verse

Goodbye Earth and Other Poems. New York, Harcourt Brace, 1958; London, Routledge, 1959.
The Screens and Other Poems. New York, Harcourt Brace, 1960; London, Routledge, 1961.
Internal Colloquies: Poems and Plays. New York, Harcourt Brace, 1971; London, Routledge, 1972.
New and Selected Poems. Manchester, Carcanet Press, 1978.

Other

The Pocket Book of Basic English: A Self-Teaching Way into English with Directions in Spanish, French, Italian, Portuguese, German, with Christine Gibson. New York, Pocket Books, 1945; revised edition, 1946; as *English Through Pictures*, 1952.
Learning Basic English: A Practical Handbook for English-Speaking People, with Christine Gibson. New York, Norton, 1945.
Nations and Peace. New York, Simon and Schuster, 1947.
The Republic of Plato: A Version in Simplified English. London, Paul Trench Trubner, 1948.
French Self-Taught with Pictures, with M.H. Ilsley and Christine Gibson. New York, 1950.
Spanish Self-Taught Through Pictures, with Ruth C. Metcalf Romero and Christine Gibson. New York, Pocket Books, 1950.
The Wrath of Achilles: The Iliad of Homer, Shortened. New York, Norton, 1950; London, Routledge, 1951.
German Through Pictures, with others. New York, Pocket Books, 1953.
Hebrew Through Pictures, with David Weinstein and Christine Gibson. New York, Pocket Books, 1954.
Italian Through Pictures, with Italo Evangelista and Christine Gibson. New York, Pocket Books, 1955.
First Steps in Reading English, with Christine Gibson. New York, Pocket Books, 1957.
French Through Pictures, with M.H. Ilsley and Christine Gibson. New York, Pocket Books, 1959.
A First Workbook of French, with M.H. Ilsley and Christine Gibson. New York, Washington Square Press, 1960.
Russian Through Pictures, with Evelyn Jasiulko Harden and Christine Gibson. New York, Pocket Books, 1961.
Tomorrow Morning, Faustus! An Infernal Comedy. New York, Harcourt Brace, and London, Routledge, 1962.
Why So, Socrates? A Dramatic Version of Plato's Dialogues: Euthyphro, Apology, Crito, Phaedo. New York, Harcourt Brace, and London, Cambridge University Press, 1964.

Editor, with C.K. Ogden, *The Times of India Guide to Basic English.* Bombay, Times of India Press, 1938.
Editor, *The Portable Coleridge.* New York, Viking Press, 1950; London, Penguin, 1977.
Editor and translator, *Republic*, by Plato. London, Cambridge University Press, 1966.

*

Bibliography: by John Paul Russo, in *I.A. Richards: Essays in His Honor* edited by Helen Vendler, Reuben A. Brower, and John Hollander, New York, Oxford University Press, 1973.

Critical Studies: *Language, Thought and Comprehension: A Case Study of the Writings of I.A. Richards* by W.H.N. Hotopf, London, Routledge, and Bloomington, Indiana University Press, 1965; *I.A. Richards' Theory of Literature* by Jerome P. Schiller, New Haven, Connecticut, Yale University Press, 1969 (includes bibliography); "Richards and the Search for Critical Instruments," in *Twentieth-Century Literature in Retrospect* edited by Reuben A. Brower, Cambridge, Massachusetts, Harvard University Press, 1971, and "I.A. Richards in Retrospect," in *Critical Inquiry* (Chicago), 8, 1982, both by John Paul Russo.

*   *   *

Beginning in the 1920's, I.A. Richards exerted a profound influence in literary criticism, semantics, and education. The influence in criticism has been largely in methodology and psychological aesthetics; the influence in semantics, in a functional theory of language; and in education, in the teaching of English as a second language, or at the primary level, and with the aid of various media. Richards's ideas and terms—close reading, context, pseudo-statement, attitude, tone, tension, equilibrium, irony, stock response, tenor and vehicle of metaphor, emotive and referential language—entered the critical stream and remained there for so long that they eventually became part of the way students asked how a poem works. Historically, his name is connected inseparably with the formalistic movement of New Criticism of which, according to John Crowe Ransom, he was virtual founder. Yet Richards's work, while it has a formalistic component, has marked differences from the New Criticism. His criticism is in fact Janus-faced: centered in the linguistic object, it looks out in one direction to the reader's response, to memory, judgment, sincerity, and modifications of the self; and in the other, looks toward the imagination and "normality" of the artist, values in society, and the state of culture.

Practical Criticism is Richards's major methodological work. Half of this book consists of student responses, and Richards's comments on these responses, to poems that he had set for them without revealing title or author. Richards was confirming in the laboratory, so to speak, the common view that poetry was widely misread, but the impact of the experiment was enormous. And Richards went on to argue that their misreadings were part of a larger failure both of the teaching of literature and of society itself, in a situation likely to worsen. Many students in the experiment blamed their faulty readings on the poems. In the second half of the book, Richards diagnosed and categorized ten types of error in reading (stock response, doctrinal adhesions, inhibition, irrelevant or too personal association, sentimentality, etc.) and formulated corrective procedures for reading poetry or artistic prose. He borrowed from his own semantic theories in *The Meaning of Meaning*, co-written with C.K. Ogden. This book combined nominalism and behaviorism, and anticipated certain developments in philosophy and the linguistics, e.g., the General Semantics movement; it has been called "perhaps the best-known book ever written on semantics."

According to Richards, language has numerous functions; the exact number of functions is not important compared with the assignment of an appropriate and clearly distinguishable job to each. Although he eventually distinguished seven functions (1955), in *Practical Criticism* he proposed just four: (1) sense, or the symbolizing of reference, e.g., the factual content of what is being said or asserted, (2) tone, expression of attitude toward a reader or listener, (3) feeling, or expression of an attitude toward the object spoken of or written about, (4) intention, or the promotion of effects through the statement. Besides the functions, there are two overall uses or "principles of structuring or organization" to which the various functions could be put: the referential (or scientific) and the emotive. In referential language, characterizing or descriptive aspects of language are foremost; this is pure expository prose, scrubbed clean of the subjective element. With emotive language, however, functions governing tone, feeling, and valuing dominate, though not to the exclusion

of the others. In later years, Richards retained the concept of the functions but did not insist very strenuously on the emotive and referential distinction.

No one followed the method of *Practical Criticism* to the letter, and, in fact, it is an open-ended set of strategies rather than fixed procedures. Richards, always empirically minded, was more interested in using theory to protect criticism from worse theory, and maintained that the immediate response to great poetry was, in itself, inviolable and a challenge to the very capaciousness of the theory. "No theory, no description, of poetry can be trusted which is not too intricate to be applied." When Richards performed practical criticism, he pursued the interrelations of the various functions in their poetic context. Thus, a poet might question or qualify on one level what he implied on another. Tone itself is multiple: that of the author, the narrator, and their separate attitudes to each other as well as to the audience. Intention produces effects irreducible to the effects of other functions. Richards was extremely cautious of visualization of imagery, believing that in many cases it only led readers astray. He was an adept at teasing out the nuances of sense and "more important...the further thoughts caused by the sense, the network of interpretation and conjecture which arise therefrom." Most of his best practical criticism was accomplished in the lecture hall. He was a "spellbinding" lecturer, as William Empson has said, and many students have attested to his unrivaled ability to read poetry aloud, one of the truly lost arts, and to render a version of his method applied to English or classical poetry.

The method of close reading was designed to deal with poetry and artistic prose of any period. But it proved especially helpful with works in the high modernist mode with their intellectual complexity, ambiguity, allusiveness, irony, and experiments in consciousness, time, and tone. Although Richards's tastes in poetry were broad, he prized the poem that moved in and around the themes that it raised, that set one group of attitudes against another without premature suppression, and led to an "equilibrium of opposed impulses" or "balanced poise." He defined irony as "the bringing in of the opposite, the complementary impulses." The greater the poem, the wider is the area of "inclusion." The vastest oppositions of attitude occurred in tragedy, and catharsis is their resolution "in an ordered single response": in tragedy "the mind does not shy away from anything, it does not protect itself with any illusion, it stands uncomforted, unintimidated, alone and self-reliant." Tragedy is "unmitigated experience" (*Principles of Literary Criticism*).

Richards's greatest critical difficulties came from his introduction of a psychological model, derived eclectically from William James, C.S. Sherrington's neurophysiology, J.B. Watson's behaviorism, and Pavlov's environmentalism. Richards hoped to bring criticism into touch with disciplines that were having an impact in modern society. Also, for purposes of evaluation he placed experiences of art on a continuum with experiences that come to us in other ways. Poetry provided finer, subtler organizations of the mind's experience and powers. The poet's imagination "outwits the force of habit" and presents "conciliations of impulses which in most minds are still confused, intertrammelled, and conflicting." Invoking Coleridge as a forerunner, Richards stated that "a growing order is the principle of the mind." But, arguing as a Benthamite in *Principles of Literary Criticism*, he considered the question of value in terms of greater organization of mental powers, readiness, lack of waste. His psychological model could not adequately support the weight of his argument and he did not bother reconstructing it. (The deployment of scientific concepts, however, was never abandoned and he became particularly interested in N. Bohr's complementarity principle in his later years.) His claims for value were subsequently made through a concept of sincerity, which he borrowed from Confucian thought, though Richards was much influenced by G.E. Moore, Coleridge, and Romantic theory too; sincerity is the moral truthfulness one brings to the response to a work of art when it is measured against one's complete ethically relevant experience. That might mean to reject what the response is doing.

With respect to his social criticism, Richards thought that "badness" in art, literature, the press, and the cinema, posed "an influence of the first importance in fixing immature and actually inapplicable attitudes to most things." The very extent of the influence was the clearest rebuke to the opinion that the arts were powerless to effect the direction of culture. What Richards deduced from his studies in misreading was that the crude or "stock" responses of his subjects were a "withdrawal from experience." These responses pointed to the fact that "the average adult is worse, not better adjusted to the possibilities of his existence than the child." The discovery was a turning point in Richards's career. Having spent half of his career on the upper levels of educational training, after the mid-1930's Richards directed his attention increasingly to language training and education on the lower levels. He wanted to design programs in language learning that would prepare students for scientific and humanistic culture. He worked in experimental programs in China for several years (1936-38), then taught at Harvard (1939-63), returning permanently to Cambridge (England) in 1974. Mostly he spent his efforts developing Basic English, an experimentally reduced version of English designed to be an international auxiliary language based on 850 words, the invention of C.K. Ogden. With the close collaboration of Christine M. Gibson, Richards created the Language Through Pictures series in many languages and kept abreast of developments in media technology for teaching language by slide, film, videotape, and cassette. To ensure the best reading for newcomers to the language, Richards translated the *Iliad*, five dialogues by Plato including *The Republic*, and the Book of Job into an expanded version of Basic known as Everyman's English. He also turned to writing poetry and drama: his style is metaphysical, Hardyesque, and metrically diverse. His last major work was *Beyond* (1974), a humanistic study of man's dialectic relation to his images of godhead in Homer, Job, Dante, and Shelley.

Looking back on both careers in 1968, Richards said: "I think we have a better way of teaching English, but while you're teaching beginning English, you might as well teach everything else. That is to say, a world position, what's needed for living, a philosophy of religion, how to find things out, and the whole works—mental and moral seed for the planet. In this way the two-thirds of the planet that doesn't yet know how to read and write would learn in learning how to read and write English, the things that would help them in their answers to 'Where should man go?'"

—John Paul Russo

RICOEUR, Paul. French philosopher. Born in Valence, 27 February 1913. Studied at the University of Rennes; University of Paris, agrégation de philosophie 1935, Docteur-ès-lettres 1950. Married Simone Lejas in 1935; 5 children. Taught at various lycées, 1933-39; affiliated with the Centre National de la Recherche Scientifique, 1945-48; Professor of the History of Philosophy, University of Strasbourg, 1948-56. Since 1956, Professor of Philosophy, University of Paris-Nanterre; since 1970, John Nuveen Professor of the History of Philosophy, University of Chicago. Visiting Professor, Yale University, New Haven, Connecticut, 1964; University of Montreal, 1965; and University of Louvain, 1970. Honorary doctorate: University of Basel, 1964; University of Montreal, 1968; University of Chicago, 1969; Ohio State University, Columbus, 1970; DePaul University, Chicago, 1973; University of Zurich, 1975; and Boston University, 1975. Member, Institut International de Philosophie. Address: Department of Philosophy, University of Paris, Nanterre, France.

PUBLICATIONS

Philosophy

Karl Jaspers et la philosophie de l'existence, with Mikel Dufrenne. Paris, Seuil, 1947.
Gabriel Marcel et Karl Jaspers: Philosophie du mystère et philosophie du paradoxe. Paris, Temps Présent, 1947.
Philosophie de la volonté: I. Le Volontaire et l'involontaire. Paris, Aubier, 1950; as *Freedom and Nature: The Voluntary and the Involuntary*, Evanston, Illinois, Northwestern University Press, 1966.
Histoire et vérité. Paris, Seuil, 1955; as *History and Truth*, Evanston, Illinois, Northwestern University Press, 1965.
Philosophie de la volonté: Finitude et culpabilité: I. L'Homme fallible. Paris, Aubier, 1960; as *Fallible Man*, Chicago, Regnery, 1965. *II. La Symbolique du mal.* Paris, Aubier, 1960; as *The Symbolism of Evil*, New York, Harper, 1967.
Être: Essence et substance chez Platon et Aristotle. Paris, Centre de Documentation Universitaire, 1960.
De l'interprétation: Essai sur Freud. Paris, Seuil, 1965; as *Freud and Philosophy: An Essay on Interpretation*, New Haven, Connecticut, Yale University Press, 1970.
Husserl: An Analysis of His Phenomenology. Evanston, Illinois, Northwestern University Press, 1967.
Pourquoi la philosophie? with others. Montreal, Éditions de Sainte-Marie, 1968.
Entretiens Paul Ricoeur-Gabriel Marcel. Paris, Aubier, 1969; as *Tragic Wisdom and Beyond, Including Conversations between Paul Ricoeur and Gabriel Marcel*, Evanston, Illinois, Northwestern University Press, 1973.
Le Conflit des interprétations: Essais d'herméneutique. Paris, Seuil, 1969; as *The Conflict of Interpretations: Essays in Hermeneutics*, Evanston, Illinois, Northwestern University Press, 1974.
Political and Social Essays. Athens, Ohio University Press, 1974.
La Métaphore vive. Paris, Seuil, 1975; as *The Rule of Metaphor: Multi-disciplinary Studies in the Creation of Meaning in Language*, Toronto, University of Toronto Press, 1977.
Interpretation Theory: Discourse and the Surplus of Meaning. Fort Worth, Texas Christian University Press, 1976.
The Philosophy of Paul Ricoeur: An Anthology of His Work, edited by Chärles E. Reagan and David Stewart. Boston, Beacon Press, 1978.
Main Trends in Philosophy. New York, Holmes and Meier, 1979.

Other

Editor, *Histoire de la philosophie allemande*, by E. Brehier. Paris, Vrin, 1954.
Editor, *L'Homme et sa raison*, by Pierre Thevenaz. Paris, Baconnière, 2 vols., 1956.
Editor, with A. MacIntyre, *Religion, Atheism, and Faith.* New York, Columbia University Press, 1969.
Translator, *Der Tod des Sokrates*, by R. Guardini. Paris, Seuil, 1956.
Translator, with E. Sacre, *Wahrheit und Methode*, by Hans-Georg Gadamer. Paris, Seuil, 1976.

*

Critical Studies: *Hermeneutic Phenomenology: The Philosophy of Paul Ricoeur* by Don Ihde, Evanston, Illinois, Northwestern University Press, 1971; *Extension of Ricoeur's Hermeneutics* by Patrick L. Bourgeois, The Hague, Nijhoff, 1975; *Studies in the Philosophy of Paul Ricoeur* edited by Charles E. Reagan, Athens, Ohio University Press, 1979 (includes bibliography); *The Question of Belief in Literary Criticism: An Introduction to the Hermeneutical Theory of Paul Ricoeur* by Mary Gerhart,

Stuttgart, Heinz, 1979; *The Surplus of Meaning: Ontology and Eschatology in the Philosophy of Paul Ricoeur* by Theodoor Marius van Leeuwen, Amsterdam, Rodopi, 1981.

*   *   *

For most of his career, Paul Ricoeur has attempted to "graft" structural and hermeneutical thought in order to create what might be called a critical hermeneutics. The problem of speech and language can be approached validly both from a fundamental ontology, as exemplified by Heidegger and Gadamer, and through contemporary epistemology, especially semiotics. However, considered by themselves, neither of these can adequately describe or explain the actual processes of interpretation and the significance of full speech.

Ricoeur has strongly criticized Heidegger and Gadamer for avoiding discussions of method and for going directly to the level of the ontology of finite being. As he once put it, "Instead of asking: On what condition can a knowing subject understand a text or history? one asks: What kind of being is it whose being consists of understanding?" Although Ricoeur accepts Heidegger's basic claims about the relationship between Being and the anticipatory nature of all understanding, he claims that Heidegger inadequately observes the "distinction between anticipation according to the things themselves and an anticipation which comes from fancies (*Einfallë*) and popular conceptions (*Volksbegriffe*). More important, the leap to fundamental ontology precludes "any return from ontology to the epistemological question about the status of the human sciences."

Accordingly, Ricoeur insists that interpretation theory must retain a certain "objectivism" against Gadamer's and Heidegger's apparently inescapable subjectivism. By positing the text as a mediator belonging neither to its author nor its reader, Ricoeur can hold that a sufficient distanciation exists to allow the development of interpretive methods. The semiotic approach to language as such, however, presents as many problems as the ontological. A certain reductivism is inevitable. Any definition of structure must presuppose that language is closed in order to establish the text as an object, thus suppressing the historical, dynamic characteristics of language in favor of the synchronic. More important, structural analysis cannot provide an answer to this overriding question: "what motive does the analyst have in looking for the signs of the narrator and listener *in* the text of the story itself, if not the understanding which envelops all of the analytic steps and places the narrative back into a movement of transmission, into a living tradition, as a story told by someone to someone?" Thus, although a purely structural approach is legitimate at the lower levels of language (such as the phonetic level, where there are limited and closed entities), progression to the level of the sentence "represents a break, a mutation, in the hierarchy of levels" requiring a change of method adequate to the sentence's character as an event, an act of saying.

In order to rectify the inadequacies of that hermeneutics which attends to the historicized force or existential meaning of a text while ignoring its inner sense, and of structural analysis, which can explain a text but cannot interpret it, Ricoeur abandons both the circularity of the former and the linearity of the latter in favor of what he has called the "hermeneutic arc." This arc represents an ongoing dialectic between distanciation and appropriation: an "objectified and dehistoricized" text of ideal sense is appropriated meaningfully by the reading subject. Ricoeur emphasizes that "To 'make one's own' what was previously 'foreign' remains the ultimate aim of all hermeneutics." Yet he warns that this version of appropriation is quite different from the Romantic version. Like Gadamer, he insists that an understanding of or empathy with the author's original intention or his audience's receptivity will not establish any interpretive norms. What is "made one's own" is not the psychic interior of the other, but the "project of a world": "If the reference of the text is the project of a world, then it is not the reader who primarily projects himself. The reader is rather enlarged in his capacity of self-projection by

receiving a new mode of being from the text itself." Unlike Gadamer, however, Ricoeur insists that we can have no appropriative understanding of "foreign" texts except insofar as understanding is a non-methodic moment in a dialectic with methods of explanation. Through understanding in this sense, our understanding in the larger sense—as our apprehension "of our belonging to the whole of what is"—escapes the confines of our present.

—Stephen R. Yarbrough

RIESMAN, David (Jr.). American sociologist. Born in Philadelphia. Pennsylvania. 22 September 1909. Educated at Penn Charter School, Philadelphia, 1919-26; studied at Harvard University, Cambridge, Massachusetts, A.B. 1931 (Phi Beta Kappa); Harvard Law School (Editor, *Harvard Law Review*), LL.B. 1934, and research fellow, 1934-35. Married Evelyn Hastings Thompson in 1936; 4 children. Law clerk in office of Justice Brandeis, U.S. Supreme Court, 1935-36; Lawyer, Lyne Woodworth and Evarts, Boston, 1936-37; Professor of Law, University of Buffalo, New York, 1937-41; Visiting Research Fellow, Columbia University Law School, New York, 1941-42; Deputy Assistant Attorney, New York County, 1942-43; war contract termination director, and assistant to the treasurer, Sperry Gyroscope Company, Lake Success, New York, 1943-46; Visiting Associate Professor, University of Chicago, 1946-47; director of research projects on mass communications, Committee on National Policy, Yale University, New Haven, Connecticut, 1948-49; Professor of Social Sciences, University of Chicago, 1949-58. Since 1958, Professor, now Henry Ford II Professor of Social Sciences, Harvard University. Visiting Professor, University of Kansas City, 1953; Deiches Lecturer, Johns Hopkins University, Baltimore, 1954. Member, National Advisory Council, Peace Corps; Member, Advisory Council, Marlboro College, Vermont, and Hampshire College, Amherst, Massachusetts; Member of the Council, American Studies Association, 1953-60, and American Sociological Association, 1956-57; Member of the Executive Committee, Society for the Study of Social Problems, 1961-62; Member, Carnegie Commission for Study of Higher Education, from 1967, and Institute for Advanced Study, Princeton, New Jersey, 1971-72. Recipient: American Academy award, 1954. LL.D.: Marlboro College, 1954; Grinnell College, Iowa, 1957; Temple University, Philadelphia, 1962; University of Sussex, Brighton, 1965; Muhlenberg College, Allentown, Pennsylvania, 1967; University of California, Berkeley, 1968; Ed.D.: Rhode Island University, Providence, 1959; D.Litt.: Wesleyan University, Middletown, Connecticut, 1960; D.C.L.: Lincoln University, 1962; L.H.D.: St. Ambrose College, Davenport, Iowa, 1966; D.H.L.: Oakland University, California. Honorary Fellow, New College, Sarasota, Florida, and Cowell College, University of California at Santa Cruz. Address: 49 Linnaean Street, Cambridge, Massachusetts 02138, U.S.A.

PUBLICATIONS

Sociology

The Lonely Crowd: A Study of the Changing American Character, with Nathan Glazer and Reuel Denney. New Haven, Connecticut, Yale University Press, 1950.
Faces in the Crowd: Individual Studies in Character and Politics, with Nathan Glazer. New Haven, Connecticut, Yale University Press, 1952.
Thorstein Veblen: A Critical Interpretation. New York, Scribner, 1953.

Individualism Reconsidered and Other Essays. Glencoe, Illinois, Free Press, 1954; excerpts, as *Selected Essays from Individualism Reconsidered*, New York, Doubleday, 1955.

Constraint and Variety in American Education. Lincoln, University of Nebraska Press, 1956.

The Oral Tradition, The Written Word, and the Screen Image (address). Yellow Springs, Ohio, Antioch Press, 1956.

Some Continuities and Discontinuities in the Education of Women (address). Bennington, Vermont, Bennington College, 1956.

The Academic Mind: Social Scientists in a Time of Crisis, with Paul F. Lazarsfeld and Wagner Thielens. Glencoe, Illinois, Free Press, 1958.

Cultural and Social Factors in National Strength. Washington, D.C., Industrial College of the Armed Forces, 1958.

Abundance for What? and Other Essays. New York, Doubleday, and London, Chatto and Windus, 1964.

Conversations in Japan: Modernization, Politics, and Culture, with Evelyn Thompson Riesman, edited by Irving Kristol. New York, Basic Books, and London, Allen Lane, 1967.

The Academic Revolution, with Christopher Jencks. New York, Doubleday, 1968.

Academic Values and Mass Education: The Early Years of Oakland and Monteith, with Joseph Gusfield and Zelda Gamson. New York, Doubleday, 1970.

Education and Politics at Harvard, with Seymour M. Lipset. New York, McGraw Hill, 1975.

The Perpetual Dream: Reform and Experiment in the American College, with Gerald Grant. Chicago, University of Chicago Press, 1978.

On Higher Education: The Academic Enterprise in an Age of Rising Student Consumerism. San Francisco, Jossey Bass, 1980.

Other

Editor, with others, *Institutions and the Person: Papers Presented to Everett C. Hughes.* Chicago, Aldine, 1968.

Editor, with Verne A. Stadtman, *Academic Transformation: Seventeen Institutions under Pressure.* New York, McGraw Hill, 1973.

*

Critical Studies: *Culture and Social Character: The Work of David Riesman Reviewed*, edited by Seymour M. Lipset and L. Lowenthal, New York, Free Press, 1961.

*			*			*

David Riesman, the sociologist and author, is best known for *The Lonely Crowd* (1950), his study of American social behavior. In this book, Riesman asserts that national character changed as population grew. "Other-directed" and "inner-directed," two terms originated by Riesman in *The Lonely Crowd*, have passed into common speech. The phrase "lonely crowd" is associated in the minds of many with 20th-century social alienation.

In 1948, Riesman, who was then Professor of Social Sciences at the University of Chicago, took a leave of absence to direct research on mass communications for the Yale University Committee on National Policy. Two years later, the results of this project were published as *The Lonely Crowd: A Study of the Changing American Character*. Riesman's collaborators on this book were Reuel Denny and Nathan Glazer. *The Lonely Crowd* connects changing human character with socioeconomic differences between historic periods. Riesman identifies three major eras: those with potentiality for rapid population growth such as the Middle Ages in the West or less-developed areas of the world today; those of transitional population growth (e.g., the Renaissance-Reformation); and those of low population growth or actual decline (today's highly industrialized nations).

For each of these eras, Riesman describes a typical social person. During the first period, people are "tradition-directed." Their world is largely defined "by power relations among the various age and sex groups, the clans, castes, professions . . . relations which have endured for centuries and are modified but slightly, if at all, by successive generations." Typical people during the second period are termed "inner-directed." These persons' outlooks are established early in life by elders and "directed toward generalized but nonetheless inescapable destined goals." Thus inner direction is the principal means by which conformity is secured. Such people, Riesman declares, are like gyroscopes rather than the tradition-directed types of the earlier period. Men and women of the third period—contemporary times, that is—are "other-directed" according to Riesman. "Peer-groups" consisting of the individual's contemporaries of similar age, class, and status, direct the individual. The direction of the peer group is internalized: "dependence on it for guidance is implanted early. The goals toward which the other-directed person strives shift with that guidance; it is only the process of striving itself and the process of playing close attention to the signals from others that remain unaltered throughout life." Such people are more like radar than the inner-directed gyroscope types of an earlier period, says Riesman.

Riesman next characterizes the individual according to his/her manner of social adjustment. "Adjusted" persons remain passive to the social forces that come to bear upon them, he says, while those who cannot adjust are "anomic." Certain "autonomous" men and women are capable of picking and choosing by themselves.

Critics of *The Lonely Crowd* have questioned Riesman's conclusions, claiming that he gathered most of his data from middle-class respondents in metropolitan areas, especially New York City, all but ignoring smaller towns and farming areas. Russell Kirk, a well-known conservative author, has cast doubt upon some of Riesman's assumptions. Kirk writes that "this facile analysis of social change is interesting; but it is undemonstrable, and one is almost astonished that [Riesman] should venture to build the elaborate structure of *The Lonely Crowd* upon it."

In 1952, Riesman and Nathan Glazer wrote *Faces in the Crowd: Individual Studies in Character and Politics*, a successor volume to *The Lonely Crowd*. Here the two scholars interviewed 21 Americans: students, housewives, a business executive, and others. The discussions in this book center around issues treated in *The Lonely Crowd*. Riesman writes in his preface that the profiles "may indicate the possible usefulness of my typology in the understanding of individual character in its social setting."

Individual alienation in modern urban society is a major theme in essays by David Riesman published by numerous scholarly quarterlies and journals of serious commentary. In 1954, Riesman gathered many of these shorter writings into *Individualism Reconsidered and Other Essays*. "What is feared as failure in American society is, above all, aloneness," he writes there. "And aloneness is terrifying because it means that there is no one, no group, no approved cause to submit to. Even success . . . often becomes impossible to bear when it is not socially approved or even known." To escape this painful condition, the individual must have the "nerve to be oneself when that self is not approved of by the dominant ethic of a society." Ten years later, Riesman published *Abundance for What? and Other Essays*, a second anthology that continued his treatment of earlier themes and also addressed the sociological effects of the Cold War.

Riesman's third major book was an analysis of the work of Thorstein Veblen, the pioneer sociologist. In *Thorstein Veblen: A Critical Interpretation* (1953) Riesman analyzes and evaluates both the work and the influence of his subject. Critics found parallels between Veblen and his interpreter; both were given to imaginative, stimulating speculation. Said the *New York Times*, Riesman's ideas "may be debatable, but they are never dull."

David Riesman brought an unusually broad background to his studies of society. He trained to become a lawyer and served as clerk to U.S. Supreme Court justice Louis D. Brandeis before teaching law in a university. He left the academic world to serve as an assistant district attorney and subsequently as an executive for a firm that manufactured gyroscopes. At the end of World War II, Riesman returned to teaching but chose social sciences rather than law.

—Victor M. Cassidy

ROBBINS, Lionel Charles; Baron Robbins of Clare Market. British economist. Born 22 November 1898. Studied at University College, London; London School of Economics. Served in First World War, 1916-19; Director, Economic Section, War Cabinet, 1941-45. Married Iris Elizabeth Gardiner in 1924; 2 children. Lecturer, 1924, and Fellow and Lecturer, 1927-29, New College, Oxford; Lecturer, 1925-27, Professor, 1929-61, Chairman of the Court of Governors, 1968-74, and Member of the Court of Governors, from 1974, London School of Economics; Chairman, *Financial Times*, London, 1961-70. Chairman, Committee on Higher Education, 1961-64. President, Royal Economic Society, 1954-55, and British Academy, 1962-67. Trustee, National Gallery, 1952-59, 1960-74, and Tate Gallery, 1953-59, 1962-67. Director, Royal Opera House, Covent Garden, from 1956. Chancellor, Stirling University, 1968-78. Honorary doctorate: University of Durham; University of Exeter; University of Strathclyde, Glasgow; University of Sheffield; Heriot-Watt University, Glasgow; Columbia University, New York; Cambridge University; University of Leicester; University of Strasbourg; University of California, Berkeley; Technical University of Lisbon; University of London; University of York; Stirling University; University of Pennsylvania, Philadelphia; and Oxford University. Member, Accademia dei Lincei, Rome; American Philosophical Society; American Academy of Arts and Sciences. Foreign Associate, American National Academy of Education. Honorary Fellow, University College, London; Manchester College of Science and Technology; London School of Economics; London Graduate School of Business Studies; and the Courtauld Institute, London. C.B. (Companion of the Order of Bath), 1944; C.H. (Companion of Honor), 1968; created Life Peer in 1959. Address: 10 Meadway Close, London NW11, England.

PUBLICATIONS

Economics

Wages: An Introductory Analysis of the Wage System under Modern Capitalism. London, Jarrolds, 1926.
An Essay on the Nature and Significance of Economic Science. London, Macmillan, 1932; revised edition, 1935, 1962; New York, St. Martin's Press, 1962.
The Great Depression. London, Macmillan, 1934.
Economic Planning and International Order. London, Macmillan, 1937.
The Economic Basis of Class Conflict and Other Essays in Political Economy. London, Macmillan, 1939.
The Economic Causes of War (lectures). London, Cape, 1939; New York, Macmillan, 1940.
Economic Aspects of Federation. London, Macmillan, 1941.
The Economic Problem in Peace and War: Some Reflections on Objectives and Mechanisms. London, Macmillan, 1947.
The Balance of Payments (lecture). London, Athlone Press, 1951.
The Theory of Economic Policy in English Classical Political Economy. London, Macmillan, 1952.
The Economist in the Twentieth Century and Other Lectures in Political Economy. London, Macmillan, and New York, St.

Martin's Press, 1954.
Robert Torrens and the Evolution of Classical Economics. London, Macmillan, and New York, St. Martin's Press, 1958.
Politics and Economics: Papers in Political Economy. London, Macmillan, and New York, St. Martin's Press, 1963.
Bentham in the Twentieth Century (lecture). London, Athlone Press, 1965.
The Theory of Economic Development in the History of Economic Thought (lecture). London, Macmillan, and New York, St. Martin's Press, 1968.
The Evolution of Modern Economic Theory and Other Papers on the History of Economic Thought. London, Macmillan, and Chicago, Aldine, 1970.
Technology and Social Welfare (lecture). Haifa, Israel Institute of Technology, 1972.
The International Monetary Problem (lecture). London, Oxford University Press, 1973.
Aspects of Post-War Economic Policy (lecture). London, Institute of Economic Affairs, 1974.
Political Economy, Past and Present: A Review of Leading Theories of Economic Policy. London, Macmillan, and New York, Columbia University Press, 1976.
Against Inflation. London, Macmillan, 1979.

Other

Of Academic Freedom (lecture). London, Oxford University Press, 1966.
The University in the Modern World and Other Papers on Higher Education. London, Macmillan, and New York, St. Martin's Press, 1966.
Address Delivered by Lord Robbins on the Occasion of His Installation as Chancellor of the University of Stirling. Stirling, University of Stirling, 1968.
Jacob Viner: A Tribute. Princeton, New Jersey, Princeton University Press, 1970.
Autobiography of an Economist. London, Macmillan, 1971.
Higher Education Revisited. London and New York, Macmillan, 1980.

Editor, *The Common Sense of Political Economy, and Selected Papers and Reviews on Economic Theory*, by Philip H. Wicksteed. London, Routledge, 1933.
Editor, *Lectures on Political Economy*, by J.G.K. Wicksell. London, Routledge, 1934.

*

Bibliography: in *Essays in Honour of Lord Robbins* edited by Morris Peston and Bernard Corry, London, Weidenfield and Nicolson, 1972; White Plains, New York, International Arts and Sciences Press, 1973.

Critical Studies: "Lionel Robbins: Methodology, Policy, and Modern Theory" by Morris Peston, in *Twelve Contemporary Economists* edited by J. Shackleton and G. Locksley, London, Macmillan, 1981.

*   *   *

In well over 50 years in active academic and public life Lionel (now Lord) Robbins has made many contributions to economic and social thought and has also been influential in the formulation of public policy, especially in education and the arts.

After an early, and remarkably brief, flirtation with socialist ideas, his intellectual development has proceeded along what would now be considered conservative and individualistic lines, especially in relation to the role of the state in economic and social life. However, an examination of his work shows him to be no simple advocate of *laissez-faire*: indeed, his philosophy may be viewed as a subtle attempt to accomodate the values of traditional economic liberalism within a slightly more statist framework than is normally associated with that system of thought. Although he has made no original discovery in economic theory the bulk of his work, which ranges over the fundamentals of economic methodology, political economy, macroeconomics, the history of economic thought and the political organization of a free society, constitutes an impressive restatement of the principles of classical liberalism.

In the economic profession he is remembered chiefly for his *Essay on the Nature and Significance of Economic Science*. Here he defined economics as the "science which studies human behaviour as a relationship between ends and scarce means which have alternative uses." Economics is not limited merely to the study of wealth-creation but is appropriate to *any* human activity in which humanly chosen ends compete for necessarily limited resources. The content of economic theory, the laws of supply and demand, the theory of value, the laws of return, and the explanation of money, are not derived inductively from observation, history, or psychology, but are universally true statements of those constraints to which human action is subject. In this he was heavily influenced by the Austrian *a priori* tradition which maintains that economic theorems are necessarily true statements about the nature of things and therefore impervious to verification, or even falsification. In the second edition, Robbins modified this essentialism and suggested that the laws of economics are derived introspectively from "indisputable facts of experience" (such as the fact that individuals *order* their preferences and that there is more than one factor of production).

Robbins makes a distinction between economic science, which is abstract and value-free, and political economy, which is concerned with ethics and politics, although it does make use of the findings of pure theory. In his early writings Robbins was particularly critical of those versions of utilitarian welfare economics which tried to evaluate scientifically various social states. However, since such evaluations depended on illegitimate interpersonal comparisons of utility they could not be objective.

Nevertheless, this does not imply a lack of interest in normative questions on Robbins's part. In much of his own work he has been eager to demonstrate the virtues, in the sense of the maximization of liberty and efficiency, of the decentralized market economy and capitalist property system subject to the minimum of central direction and control. However, this general statement is subject to an important qualification; for Lord Robbins now maintains that at the "macro" or aggregative level, a market economy, if left entirely to itself, may not be self-equilibriating. An unhampered market may occasionally generate such a deflation that the consequent fall in aggregate demand produces mass involuntary unemployment. Robbins's present views were formed out of his experience of the 1930's when he opposed (mistakenly, he now thinks) Keyne's argument that increases in public spending would alleviate unemployment. In his *Autobiography* (1971) he says that he was "the slave of theoretical constructions which, if not intrinsically invalid as regards logical consistency, were inappropriate to the total situation which had then developed." The mistaken theory was the Austrian theory of money and the trade cycle, which Robbins himself had adopted in *The Great Depression* (1934).

None of this, however, should be taken as an endorsement of post-war "full employment" policies since in his opinion these have been used, erroneously, to cure unemployment generated by the monopoly powers of labour unions. According to Robbins, such policies can only lead to never-ending inflation and economic dislocation.

In another area of controversy with Keynes, Robbins has not changed his mind at all. This is his unwavering commitment to free trade. His attitude springs not only from the economic view that protectionism leads to a serious misallocation of resources but also from his belief that the survival of free societies depends on international monetary and political arrangements.

In the history of economic thought Lord Robbins's most scholarly work is undoubtedly *Robert Torrens and the Evolution of Classical Economics*. However, his most influential work is probably his re-evaluation of the English Classical economists. In his *Theory of Economic Policy in English Classical Economics* he successfully dispelled the illusion that those writers were ideological advocates of *laissez-faire* who saw no function for the state beyond the maintenance of law and order. Robbins showed that they saw a positive role for the state in the supply of public goods (i.e., goods that are not produced by the private market) and in the provision of minimum levels of education and welfare.

It is the cautious utilitarianism of the classical economists that informs Lord Robbins's social philosophy, lucidly expressed in *The Economic Problem in Peace and War* and *Political Economy, Past and Present*. He has repeatedly rejected the extreme libertarian appeal to immutable natural rights as the foundation of anti-statist economics and ethics, and has been criticized from that quarter for his apparent acquiescence in some of the collectivist tendencies of the contemporary world. However, irrespective of the arguments that surround his normative economics, his status in the methodology and history of economics is assured.

—Norman Barry

ROBERTSON, D(ennis) H(olme). British economist. Born in Lowestoft, Suffolk, 23 May 1890. Educated at Eton College, 1902-08; studied at Trinity College, Cambridge, B.A. 1911, M.A. 1915. Lieutenant, 11th Battalion, London Regiment, in Egypt and Palestine, 1914-18. Fellow, Trinity College, 1914-38, 1944-63; Reader in Economics, Cambridge University, 1930-38; Cassel Professor of Economics, University of London, 1938-44. Adviser to British Treasury, 1939-44; Member, United Kingdom Delegation to Bretton Woods Financial Conference, and Royal Commission on Equal Pay, 1944. President, Royal Economic Society. Honorary doctorate: University of Amsterdam, 1932; Harvard University, Cambridge, Massachusetts, 1936; University of Louvain, 1947; University of Durham, 1951; and University of London, 1952. Fellow, Eton College, 1948-57. Fellow, British Academy. Honorary Member, American Academy of Arts and Sciences. C.M.G. (Companion, Order of St. Michael and St. George), 1944; Knighted, 1953. *Died 21 April 1963.*

PUBLICATIONS

Economics

A Study of Industrial Fluctuation. London, King, 1915.
Money. London, Nisbet, and New York, Harcourt Brace, 1922.
The Control of Industry. London, Nisbet, and New York, Harcourt Brace, 1923.
The Ebb and Flow of Unemployment. London, Daily News, 1923.
Banking Policy and the Price Level. London, King, 1926; New York, Kelley, 1949.
Economic Fragments. London, King, 1931.
Economic Essays and Addresses, with A.C. Pigou. London, King, 1931.
A Scheme for an Economic Census of India, with A.L. Bowley. New Delhi, Government of India Press, 1934.
Essays in Monetary Theory. London, King, and New York, Staples Press, 1940.
Utility and All That and Other Essays. London, Allen and Unwin, and New York, Macmillan, 1952.
Britain in the World Economy (lectures). London, Allen and Unwin, 1954.
Wages (lecture). London, Athlone Press, 1954; New York, J. de Graff, 1955.
The Role of Persuasion in Economic Affairs (lecture). Newcas-

tle upon Tyne, Andrew Reid, 1955(?).
Economic Commentaries.   London, Staples Press, 1956; West-
port, Connecticut Greenwood Press, 1978.
Lectures on Economic Principles.   London, Staples Press, 3
vols., 1957-59.
Growth, Wages, Money (lectures).   London, Cambridge Uni-
versity Press, 1961.
*A Memorandum Submitted to the Canadian Royal Commission
on Banking and Finance.*   Princeton, New Jersey, Princeton
University, 1963.
Essays in Money and Interest, edited by Sir John Hicks.
London, Collins, 1966.

*

Critical Study: *Robertsonian Economics: An Examination of
the Work of Sir D.H. Robertson on Industrial Fluctuation* by
John R. Presley, London, Macmillan, 1979.

*   *   *

D.H. Robertson's major contribution to economics was made
early in his career. The theory of the trade cycle he put forward in
1915 remained at the heart of all his later writings in macroeconomics. This theory was the first proposed by a British economist to emphasize real forces operating on industrial fluctuations—what textbooks would now classify as a non-monetary,
over investment explanation of the cycle. He was influenced in
his approach by Marcel Labordère, A. Aftalion, and M. Tugan-
Baranowski. His later work, particularly that in the 1920's and
1930's, was an attempt to explain how monetary forces acted on
industrial fluctuation.

It was during the 1920's that Robertson worked closely with
J.M. Keynes. The fruits of their collaborations are not only to be
seen in Robertson's books of 1921 and 1926 but also in Keynes's
major works titled *Tract on Monetary Reform* and *Treatise on
Money,* although none of these titles appeared under joint
authorship. Robertson became the keeper of Keynes's conscience. If Keynes could persuade Robertson of his views on
theory and policy, he felt content.

In the 1920's they studied closely the relationship between
saving and investment, but neither, at that time, was satisfied
with the conclusions reached. Robertson took little part in the
working out of the *General Theory* and remained the main critic
of Keynesian economics for the rest of his life despite supporting
many of its conclusions—in particular, the importance of
investment, the possibility of under full employment equilibrium, and the belief in the effectiveness of fiscal policy.

Robertson was always anxious to stress the evolutionary
nature of his work, following on from the Marshallian tradition
in Cambridge. He was upset by what he saw as Keynes's attempt
to undervalue classical and neoclassical economics in order to
create a revolution in economics. He vociferously attacked the
multiplier process and the liquidity preference theory of interest,
remaining faithful to the quantity theory approach, the loanable
funds theory of interest, and economic dynamics rather than the
comparative statics of the *General Theory.*

The major cause of recovery was the occurrence of invention
and innovation, a view shared with J. Schumpeter; but Robertson also saw industrial fluctuation resulting from agricultural
variations and from the need for replacement investment in
major industries. The downturn was caused by over-investment,
the result of imperfections in the investment process—the time
lag in setting up capital equipment, imperfect knowledge on the
part of businessmen, and the "imperfect divisibility and intract-
ability" of capital. In proposing this explanation of the cycle
Robertson could claim some originality for this theory; his
insistence on period analysis, what he called a step-by-step
approach, from 1915 onwards has encouraged some economists
to regard him as the father of economic dynamics; monetary and
psychological forces were not the cause of the cycle, but they

could exaggerate the amplitude of fluctuation and had to be
counteracted through monetary and fiscal policies.

Robertson did not claim to have made any other substantial
contributions to economics other than in relation to the cycle
theory. He did enter into debate on the theory of competition,
especially in the 1930's. He was active in the establishment of the
International Monetary Fund at Bretton Woods after the
Second World War and had some impact upon economic policy
in Britain through the Cohen Council. Interestingly, he persis-
tently, in the 1950's, warned against pushing employment to too
high a level for fear of fuelling inflation. This was a policy
pronouncement scorned at the time but currently in great favour
in Western economies. Much of his work in the post-war period
was devoted to policy issues and to teaching in Cambridge as well
as to the continuing controversies surrounding the *General
Theory.*

—John R. Presley

ROBINSON, Joan (Violet). British economist. Born 31
October 1903. Educated at St. Paul's Girls' School, London;
studied at Girton College, Cambridge, B.A. in economics 1925.
Married Sir Austin Robinson in 1926; 2 daughters. Assistant
Lecturer, 1931, University Lecturer, 1937-49, Reader, 1949-65,
and Professor of Economics, 1965-71, Cambridge University.
Visiting Professor, Stanford University, California, 1969. Fel-
low, British Academy, 1958. *Died 5 August 1983.*

PUBLICATIONS

Economics

*Economics is a Serious Subject: The Apologia of an Economist
to the Mathematician, the Scientist, and the Plain Man.*
Cambridge, Heffer, 1932.
The Economics of Imperfect Competition.   London, Macmil-
lan, 1933; New York, St. Martin's Press, 1972.
Essays in the Theory of Employment.   London and New York,
Macmillan, 1937.
Introduction to the Theory of Employment.   London and New
York, Macmillan, 1937.
An Essay on Marxian Economics.   London, Macmillan, 1942;
New York, St. Martin's Press, 1957.
Private Enterprise or Public Control.   London, English Uni-
versities Press, 1942.
The Future of Industry.   London, Muller, 1943.
*Budgeting in the Post-War World: Can Planning Be Democra-
tic?* London, Fabian Society, 1944.
The Problem of Full Employment: An Outline for Study Circles.
London, Workers Educational Association and Workers
Educational Trade Union Committee, 1944.
Collected Economic Papers.   Oxford, Blackwell, 5 vols.,
1951-79.
Conference Sketch Book, Moscow.   Cambridge, Heffer, 1952.
The Rate of Interest and Other Essays.   London, Macmillan,
1952; as *The Generalisation of the General Theory, and Other
Essays,* New York, St. Martin's Press, 1979.
On Re-Reading Marx.   Cambridge, Students' Bookshops,
1953.
Marx, Marshall, and Keynes.   Delhi, University of Delhi, 1955.
The Accumulation of Capital.   London, Macmillan, and
Homewood, Illinois, R.D. Irwin, 1956.
China: An Economic Perspective, with Sol Adler.   London,
Fabian Society, 1958.
Exercises in Economic Analysis.   London, Macmillan, 1960;
New York, St. Martin's Press, 1961.

Economic Philosophy. London, Watts, and Chicago, Aldine, 1962.

Essays in the Theory of Economic Growth. London, Macmillan, and New York, St. Martin's Press, 1962.

Notes from China. Oxford, Blackwell, and New York, Monthly Review Press, 1964.

Economics: An Awkward Corner. London, Allen and Unwin, 1966; New York, Pantheon, 1967.

The New Mercantilism (lecture). Cambridge, University Press, 1966.

Economics Today (lecture). Zurich, Polygraphischer Verlag, 1970.

Freedom and Necessity: An Introduction to the Study of Society. London, Allen and Unwin, and New York, Pantheon, 1970.

Economic Heresies: Some Old-Fashioned Questions in Economic Theory. London, Macmillan, and New York, Basic Books, 1971.

Economic Management: China, 1972. London, Anglo-Chinese Educational Institute, 1973.

An Introduction to Modern Economics, with John Eatwell. London and New York, McGraw Hill, 1973.

Reflections on the Theory of International Trade (lectures). Manchester, Manchester University Press, 1974.

Aspects of Development and Underdevelopment. Cambridge and New York, Cambridge University Press, 1979.

Further Contributions to Modern Economics. Oxford, Blackwell, 1980; as *What Are the Questions and Other Essays,* Armonk, New York, M.E. Sharpe, 1981.

Other

Letters From a Visitor to China. Cambridge, Students' Bookshops, 1954.

Editor, *The Cultural Revolution in China.* London, Penguin, 1969.

Editor, *After Keynes.* Oxford, Blackwell, and New York, Barnes and Noble, 1973.

*   *   *

Joan Robinson may be the world's leading heterodox economist. She has pioneered important developments within mainstream neoclassical economics. She has considered seriously the content and significance of Marxian economics and policy. She has nurtured and advanced the development of macroeconomics as produced initially by John Maynard Keynes and Michael Kalecki. She has, with Piero Sraffa and others, helped generate a critique of neoclassicism which augurs the possibility of a new, less deterministic but more realistic paradigm. She has generally and pointedly challenged the complacency of conventional economists more concerned with analytical and professional respectability and career and less with the exigent problems of distribution, poverty, and injustice and oppression resident, for example, in class use of government. She also has been a deep analyst of the inevitability and operation of ideology in economic theory, most notably its social control function and its inadvertent service in generating hypotheses for truly objective scientific analysis.

Her first major contribution was to solve a problem lurking in Alfred Marshall's *Principles of Economics* (1890; 8th ed., 1920) and pointed out by Sraffa in 1926, namely, the conflict between competition and a decreasing revenue function for the firm. Her solution, embodied in a theory of imperfect competition, advanced the mathematics of marginalism by establishing the optimization rule of marginal cost equal to marginal revenue. The theory of the firm was rescued, at least insofar as the elegant analytics of equilibrium analysis was concerned, although the problems of competition and of distribution in accordance with marginal productivity largely remained.

As a later student of Marx's work, Robinson came to empha-

size history and social and institutional structure, and therefore the distributional issue, *vis-à-vis* static resource allocation and equilibrium. She did this without accepting the labour theory of value. In many respects she was influenced by Kalecki's reformulation of Marxian economics with regard to capital accumulation and growth.

Robinson played a significant role in the early 1930's in helping Keynes work out and clarify the analysis eventually presented in his *General Theory* (1936). She subsequently presented an early exposition of Keynes's ideas and remained a leading Keynesian. Robinson also came to stress the simultaneous and independent development by Kalecki of ideas similar to those of Keynes.

Perhaps her most important contribution, as yet still problematic, may consist in having helped generate a new approach to political economy, one incorporating Ricardian, Marxian, Keynesian, and even neoclassical elements. The focus of the Cambridge, England, approach is on growth and distribution. It is premised on a questioning of the coherence and completeness (for the theories of production, growth, and distribution) of neoclassical understanding of the quantity of capital in relation to the rate of growth, in a world of disequilibrium, uncertainty, capital accumulation, growth, alternative production functions and (re)switching from one to another, and power structure factors underlying the operation of markets. Some of this analysis is predicated on her understanding of a dual relationship between profitability and growth: growth is a function of profits (actual and expected), and profitability is a function of growth; a complexity not readily handled by conventional neoclassical or Keynesian economics. In her hands, the theory of production and of distribution is shown to be far more complex and, especially, open-ended than standard neoclassical economics has thus far portrayed, a showing strongly resisted by neoclassicists. If her theory of imperfect competition was felt to threaten neoclassical economics, as it was, perhaps mistakenly, by John R. Hicks, the threat from this post-Keynesian counter-revolution may be far greater.

—Warren J. Samuels

* * *

ROGERS, Carl (Ransom). American psychologist. Born in Oak Park, Illinois, 8 January 1902. Studied at the University of Wisconsin, Madison, B.A. 1924; Union Theological Seminary, New York, 1924-26; Columbia University, New York, M.A. 1928, Ph.D. 1931. Psychological Consultant, United States Air Force, 1944; Director, Counseling Services, United Service Organizations, 1944-45. Married Helen Elliot in 1928; 2 children. Fellow in Psychology, Institute for Child Guidance, New York, 1927-28; Psychologist, 1928-30, and Director of the Child Study Department, 1930-38, Society for the Prevention of Cruelty to Children, Rochester, New York; Director, Rochester Guidance Center, 1939; Professor of Clinical Psychology, Ohio State University, Columbus, 1940-45; Professor of Psychology and Director of the Counseling Center, University of Chicago, 1945-57; Professor, Department of Psychology and Department of Psychiatry, University of Wisconsin, 1957-63; Fellow, Center for Advanced Study in the Behavioral Sciences, Stanford, California, 1962-63; Resident Fellow, Western Behavioral Sciences Institute, La Jolla, California, 1964-68. Since 1968, Resident Fellow, Center for Studies of the Person, La Jolla. Vice-President, American Orthopsychiatric Association, 1944-45; President, American Association for Applied Psychology, 1944-45, American Psychological Association, 1946-47, and American Academy of Psychotherapists, 1957-58. Recipient: Distinguished Science Contribution Award, 1957, and Distinguished Professional Contribution Award, 1972, American Psychological Association; Butler Medal, Columbia University, 1955;

Humanist of the Year Award, Humanist Association, 1964; Distinguished Contribution Award, American Pastoral Counselors Association, 1967; Professional Award, American Board of Professional Psychologists, 1968. Honorary doctorate: Lawrence College, Appleton, Wisconsin, 1956; Gonzaga University, Spokane, Washington, 1968; University of Santa Clara, California, 1971; University of Cincinnati, 1974; University of Hamburg, 1975; University of Leiden, 1975; Northwestern University, Evanston, Illinois, 1978. Fellow, American Psychological Association, and American Academy of Arts and Sciences. Address: 2311 Via Siena, La Jolla, California 97037, U.S.A.

PUBLICATIONS

Psychology

Measuring Personality Adjustment in Children Nine to Thirteen Years of Age. New York, Columbia University Teachers College, 1931.
The Clinical Treatment of the Problem Child. Boston, Houghton Mifflin, 1939.
Counseling and Psychotherapy: Newer Concepts in Practice. Boston, Houghton Mifflin, 1942.
Counseling with Returned Servicemen, with others. New York, McGraw Hill, 1946.
Client-Centered Therapy: Its Current Practice, Implications, and Theory. Boston, Houghton Mifflin, 1951.
On Becoming a Person: A Therapeutic View of Psychotherapy. Boston, Houghton Mifflin, 1961.
Person to Person: The Problem of Being Human: A New Trend in Psychology, with others. Walnut Creek, California, Real People Press, 1967.
The Interpersonal Relationship in the Facilitation of Learning (lecture). Columbus, Ohio, Merrill, 1968.
Freedom to Learn: A View of What Education Might Become. Columbus, Ohio, Merrill, 1969.
Carl Rogers on Encounter Groups. New York, Harper, 1970.
Humanistic Psychology: Interviews with Maslow, Murphy, and Rogers, with Willard B. Fish. Columbus, Ohio, Merrill, 1971.
Becoming Partners: Marriage and Its Alternatives. New York, Delacorte, 1972.
Carl Rogers on Personal Power. New York, Delacorte, 1977; London, Constable, 1978.

Other

Editor, with Rosalind F. Dymand, *Psychotherapy and Personality Change.* Chicago, University of Chicago Press, 1954.
Editor, with others, *The Therapeutic Relationship and Its Impact.* Madison, University of Wisconsin Press, 1967.
Editor, *The Therapeutic Relationship with Schizophrenics.* Madison, University of Wisconsin Press, 1967.
Editor, with William R. Coulson, *Man and the Science of Man.* Columbus, Ohio, Merrill, 1968.

*

Critical Study: *Carl Rogers: The Man and His Ideas* by Richard I. Evans, New York, Dutton, 1975.

*   *   *

Carl Rogers has developed an important theory of personality and a widely used approach to psychotherapy. The latter is loosely based on the former, so they will be discussed more or less together.

According to Rogers, the person has a tendency to grow in a basically healthy direction. The person possesses what Rogers calls the "organismic valuing process," which experiences what the person does and can tell if it is good or not good. Implicit in Rogers's theory is the assumption that none of our organismic valuing processes condone or enjoy murder. However, Rogers's theory is not completely helpless when it comes to the problem of man's constant and extreme inhumanity to man. When the developing personality has imposed upon it "conditions of worth," that is, when, for example, parents do not grant the child "unconditional positive regard," but instead give it praise and affection when it does only what *they* approve of, then the organismic valuing process is not able to operate, and the person, developing along lines suggested by others rather than by himself, loses touch with himself and may become neurotic. It is not clear from Rogers himself whether the person becomes neurotic (or even just plain bad) because those who impose conditions of worth upon him guide him towards neurosis or evil; or because blocking the organismic valuing process causes a buildup of dangerous tensions. In any event, in his approach to therapy, Rogers stresses the importance of granting the patient—or "client," to use the term preferred by Rogers and now widely adopted in psychology—unconditional positive regard. That is, the client must know that the therapist cares for him regardless, and does not impose conditions of worth. This allows the client to get back in touch with his organismic valuing process.

Critics of Rogers wonder how one can grant a vicious psychopath unconditional positive regard, or what possible good it will do. They are also puzzled about what a parent should do when little Johnny starts beating up his sister Mary and reports that his organismic valuing process likes what he's doing. According to Rogers's theory of personality, the parents should not impose conditions of worth. That is, they should not tell Johnny they will not love him if he kills his sister. Perhaps they must count on Johnny's organismic valuing process. This makes some sense. Blake's Proverb of Hell is wise: "The road of excess leads to the palace of wisdom." Perhaps Johnny will soon come to experience self-loathing when he beats up Mary. But recall another of Blake's Proverbs of Hell: "Sooner murder an infant in its cradle than nurse unacted desires." Will Johnny's parents have enough faith in Rogers's theory to hope he needn't go that far—or doesn't want to?

In Rogers's defense, Freud is the only theorist of human behavior who has made a coherent attempt to explain evil. The others deny evil or ignore it; the best of the others, and Rogers belongs in this group, deal with it feebly.

In Rogers's further defense, it may be pointed out that his theory was developed in the context of therapeutic situations with neurotics. Neurotics are not prone to evil or even to the more minor forms of inhumanity. They *are* prone to self-loathing, to excessive concern with the opinions and directives of others, and to ignorance of their own desires and needs. For such people, a warm supportive environment may well be helpful. And in fact, research conducted by Rogers and his associates has found that during the course of therapy, many clients' perception of themselves as they actually are grow closer to their image of what they would ideally be. This may simply reflect an abandonment of unrealistic ideals during the course of therapy; it could also indicate an inflated and false image of the self as it actually is; but it may indicate that clients are in fact coming closer to being what they themselves want to be rather than what others want them to be.

Rogers's approach to therapy is called "client-centered" or "nondirective." One would expect a lack of directiveness from his theory—he would want to allow the client to go in the client's own direction. (There is an interesting analysis of one of Rogers's own therapy sessions which shows, however, that he is really very directive in the sense that he steers the client in certain ways and not in others.) Perhaps the most well known aspect of Rogers's approach to therapy is "reflection." The therapist emphasizes—reflects back—the emotional portion of what the client says, in an attempt to make the client aware of that aspect of his existence that has been neglected due to conditions of worth. Reflection lends itself to burlesque, e.g., Client: "I was very mad at my wife today." Therapist: "I feel that you were angry at your wife today." Those who burlesque Rogers, however, assume, without question grossly incorrectly, that people—therapy clients especially—are able to and habitually do make direct statements about their emotions.

In summary, Roger's theory of personality seems sensible within a rather limited range of applicability—neurotic clients—and problematic outside that range. His approach to therapy also seems sensible, and there is some research supporting its efficacy. It has not been shown to be more successful than other approaches, but neither has it been shown to be less.

—George W. Kelling

ROSENBERG, Harold. American art critic. Born in Brooklyn, New York, 2 February 1906. Studied at City College of New York, 1923-24; St. Lawrence University, Canton, New York, LL.B. 1927. Married May Natalie Tabak in 1932; 1 daughter. Art Editor, *American Guide* series, Works Progress Administration, 1938-42; Department Chief, Domestic Radio Bureau, New York, Office of War Information, 1944-45; Director, Longview Foundation, 1944-78. Program Consultant, Advertising Council, 1943-73; Consultant, United States Treasury, 1945-46; Commissioner, National Collection of Fine Arts; Member, Advertising Council, Smithsonian Institution, Washington, D.C. Lecturer, New School for Social Research, New York, 1953-54; Regents Lecturer, University of California, Berkeley, 1962; Christian Gauss Lecturer, Princeton University, New Jersey, 1963; Visiting Professor, Southern Illinois University, Carbondale, 1963; Professor, Department of Art and Committee on Social Thought, University of Chicago, 1966-78. Art Critic, *The New Yorker* magazine, 1967-78. Recipient: Frank Jewett Mather Award, College Art Association of America, 1964; Morton Dauwen Zabel Award, American Academy of Arts and Letters, 1976. Honorary doctorate: Lake Forest College, Illinois, 1971; Parsons College, Kansas, 1975. *Died 11 July 1978.*

PUBLICATIONS

Art

The Tradition of the New. New York, Horizon Press, 1959; London, Thames and Hudson, 1962.
Arshile Gorky: The Man, The Time, The Idea. New York, Horizon Press, 1962.
The Anxious Object: Art Today and Its Audience. New York, Horizon Press, 1964; London, Thames and Hudson, 1965.
Artworks and Packages. New York, Horizon Press, 1968; London, Thames and Hudson, 1969.
Act and the Actor: Making the Self. Cleveland, World, 1970.
Barnett Newman: Broken Obelisk and Other Sculptures. Seattle, University of Washington Press, 1971.
The De-Definition of Art: Action Art to Pop to Earthworks. New York, Horizon Press, 1972.
Discovering the Present: Three Decades in Art, Culture, and Politics. Chicago, University of Chicago Press, 1973.
Willem De Kooning. New York, Abrams, 1974.
Art on the Edge: Creators and Situations. New York, Macmillan, 1975.
Saul Steinberg. New York, Knopf, 1978.
Barnett Newman. New York, Abrams, 1978.

Other

Trance Above the Streets (poems). New York, Gotham Book Mart, 1943.

Translator, *I Accuse De Gaulle*, by Henri de Kerillis. New York, Harcourt Brace, 1946.

*

Critical Studies: "On Harold Rosenberg" by Dore Ashton, in *Critical Inquiry* (Chicago), 6, 1980.

* * *

As probably the most influential New York art critic from the 1960's to his death, Harold Rosenberg had a strong role in the public acceptance of some of the styles, and ideologies, of contemporary visual arts. His directions, and writings, need to be recognized as part of the matrix of what has often been described as the "New York intellectual." He typified much of it (along with such friends as Paul Goodman, Irving Howe): secularized Jewish-American, raised and educated in the city, strongly identifying with its marginal political leftism and cultural bohemianism, marked by a ranging sophistication, ideological bellicosity, and energetically self-conscious (and somewhat parochial) assertion of the dialectical role of the New York Man of Letters.

A literary radical out of the 1930's, Rosenberg, as with a number of journals he wrote for, combined European cultural modernism with social-political polemics of a Marxist cast (see his anti-Stalinist essays and other disenchanted Marxism in *Act and the Actor*, and other rather arch polemics in *Discovering the Present*). He published verses and rather abstract essays around literary issues (mostly uninteresting because of a lack of a sense of texture), but more of his writing was intellectual high journalism, reviews and diagnostic ruminations on fashions in cultural ideology, including many ambivalent pieces on Jewish identity and on the role of the independent (as against academic) intellectual.

But his more significant role came from his relatively late identification with what has been called the "New York school of painting" following World War II. From his first art-criticism monograph, *Arshile Gorky*, to his posthumously published *Barnett Newman*, he interpreted and defended many of the artists usually lumped as Abstract Expressionists. Propounding the somewhat tenuous nomenclature of "Action Painting," he held that the key to such abstraction was the very process of painting with its rituals of creative self-discovery, rather than the autonomous art objects. Bluntly put, he expounded the aesthetic value of drippings, the metaphysics of a zipped line of color across a large monochromatic field, and the spiritual values of the spontaneous (but profoundly prepared for) slash and swirl of paint on an idiosyncratically prepared canvas. His was the rationale for radical American art.

Besides Gorky and Newman, he included as heroes of the artist-metaphysical vanguard Willem de Kooning and Hans Hoffman. He was less emphatic on some of the related (and visually more interesting) painters, such as Pollock, Rothko, Baziotes, Gottlieb, and others. His strong exposition of the ingenious draftsman Saul Steinberg seemed a bit afield. He thoughtfully interpreted, though rather avoided judging, those who more coldly continued some of the experiments in visual logic, such as Stella and Johns. He dialectically placed the Pop Art of the 1960's as a reactive continuation of the vanguardist experiments, though merging with the commercial, with apt comments on Oldenburg, rather cutting analysis of Warhol, and perhaps rather inadequate responses to the satiric Keinholz and Segal. Over the years, he extended his interpretive dialectics coolly to characterize photorealism, earthworks, brutalism, Christo's megalomaniac packaging, and other of the alternately frenzied and banal novel art manners of the 1960's and 1970's. He came to realize historically that the emphasis on intellectual development rather than crafted artifact had to lead dialectically to the explosive expansion of the limits of art and to "happenings," purely Conceptual Art, and other "post-object" frontiers of artistic activity. "Art is what is viewed as art." And as he also aptly noted, "The integration of art and non-art is the essence of twentieth century vanguardism."

Well aware that he was dealing with a "late stage of modernism," and quite possibly its "final phase," he related New York painting to, and more generally discussed, the preceding experiments of Cubism, Dada, Picasso, Duchamp, Surrealism, Klee, Constructivism, Miro, Fauvism, Mondrian, Futurism, Giacometti, and others. He maneuvered only briefly into post-World War II European art (such as his rather negative commentary on Dubuffet), a bias based on the insistence that New York was setting the global styles, the new forms of the great modernist quest.

Rosenberg almost always pursued the art context in his essays—"comment on the current human condition"—including anxious cultural instability, the manipulative fashions of museums, the frenzied twists of the art markets, the ambiguous careerisms of artists no longer essentially craftsmen and iconmakers. All were part of the ideological drama. He insisted that contemporary paintings and sculptures have "need of being filled out with the thought and will of their creators." Impersonally. To understand them requires focusing on their "intellectual origins." Hence he was strongly anti-formalist, "pure" art often being the most expressionistic (Mondrian's theosophy, Newman's metaphysics). Art always takes a "social position," and the critic should less "judge it" than "locate it" in the dialectics of both art and history and social-cultural reaction. "Seeing" and visual analysis should be subordinate to intellectual understanding— and the critic's use of disciplined metaphor of meaning.

Not only did he hold that "thought cannot be separated from form"—perhaps his most crucial intellectual emphasis, contra much criticism—but that all art must be related to the "intellectual situation." Early on, he exalted "the new," avant-gardist "continuous experiment," as *the* tradition of modernism. Painting was "one of the powers giving form to the unknown." The argument was somewhat incoherent, as with art predicting the unpredictable, and endless innovation becoming shallow novelty as well as radical redefinition of the human. His 1970's essays implicitly renounced part of his major "tradition of the new," with the cultural warfare of styles media-processed into an artistic "De-Militarized Zone." Some art, he reluctantly admitted, was more decorative than the precarious quest for a truer human identity: "It may be unwise for art today to try to assume the burden of man's future—at least to try to assume it alone." Which suggests how radical the underlying conception of art had been.

Rosenberg's dialectical advancement of mid-20th century art styles, especially Abstract Expressionism, is historically important. But perhaps most valuable remains his insistence on understanding visual art as sophisticatedly large intellectual experience.

—Kingsley Widmer

RUSSELL, Bertrand (Arthur William); 3rd Earl Russell, Viscount Amberley. British philosopher and social critic. Born in Trelleck, Monmouthshire, 18 May 1872. Studied at Trinity College, Cambridge, first-class honours, Mathematical and Moral Tripos, 1894. Married Alys Whitall Pearsall Smith in 1894 (divorced, 1921); married Dora Winifred Black in 1921 (divorced, 1935), 2 children; married Patricia Helen Spence in 1936 (divorced, 1952), 1 son; married Edith Finch in 1952. Honorary Attaché, British Embassy, Paris, 1894; Fellow, 1895-1901, and Lecturer, 1901-16, Trinity College (removed by Trinity Council in 1916 for opposing British entry into World War I). Visiting Professor, Harvard University, Cambridge, Massachusetts, 1914. Founding Member, Union for Democratic Control, 1914. Joined the No-Conscription Fellowship in 1915 (fined, 1916, and sentenced to six months imprisonment, 1918). Visited Russia and China, 1920. Founded and directed the experimental Beacon Hill School, Sussex, 1927-32. Lecturer, University of Chicago, 1938; Visiting Professor, University of California at Los Angeles, 1939-40; received and then denied appointment, City College of New York, 1940; William James Lecturer, Harvard University, 1940; Barnes Foundation Lecturer, Merion, Pennsylvania, 1941-42. Fellow of Trinity College after 1944. Reith Lecturer, British Broadcasting Corporation, 1948. President, Campaign for Nuclear Disarmament, 1958-60; fined and imprisoned for inciting the public to civil disobedience, 1961; Founder, Bertrand Russell Peace Foundation, 1963; Co-Organizer, International War Crimes Tribunal, 1966. Recipient: Nicholas Murray Butler Medal, New York, 1915; Sylvester Medal of the Royal Society, London, 1934; Nobel Prize for Literature, 1950; Unesco Kalinga Prize, 1957; Sonning Foundation Prize, Denmark, 1960. Fellow, Royal Society of Literature, London, 1908. O.M. (Order of Merit), 1949. *Died 20 February 1970.*

PUBLICATIONS

Philosophy and Social Comment

German Social Democracy.   London and New York, Longman, 1896.
An Essay on the Foundations of Geometry.   Cambridge, Cambridge University Press, 1897; New York, Dover Books, 1956.
A Critical Exposition of the Philosophy of Leibnitz.   Cambridge, Cambridge University Press, 1900.
The Principles of Mathematics, Volume I.   Cambridge, Cambridge University Press, 1903; New York, Norton, 1937.
Principia Mathematica, with Alfred North Whitehead.   Cambridge, Cambridge University Press, 3 vols., 1910-13.
Philosophical Essays.   London, Allen and Unwin, and New York, Longman, 1910.
Anti-Suffragist Anxieties.   London, People's Suffrage Federation, 1910.
The Problems of Philosophy.   London, Williams and Norgate, and New York, Holt, 1912.
Our Knowledge of the External World as a Field for Scientific Method in Philosophy.   London, Allen and Unwin, and Chicago, Open Court, 1914.
The Philosophy of Bergson.   London, Macmillan, 1914.
Scientific Method in Philosophy (lecture).   Oxford, Clarendon Press, 1914.
War, The Offspring of Fear.   London, Union of Democratic Control, 1915.
Principles of Social Reconstruction.   London, Allen and Unwin, 1916; as *Why Men Fight: A Method of Abolishing the International Duel,* New York, Century, 1916.
The Policy of the Entente, 1904-1914.   Manchester, National Labour Press, 1916.
Justice in War-time.   London, Allen and Unwin, and Chicago, Open Court, 1916.
Mysticism and Logic and Other Essays.   London, Allen and Unwin, and New York, Doubleday, 1917.
Roads to Freedom: Socialism, Anarchism, and Syndicalism.   London, Allen and Unwin, 1918; as *Proposed Roads to Freedom: Socialism, Anarchism, and Syndicalism.* New York, Holt, 1919.
Introduction to Mathematical Philosophy.   London, Allen and Unwin, and New York, Macmillan, 1919.
The Theory and Practice of Bolshevism.   London, Allen and Unwin, 1920; as *Bolshevism: Theory and Practice,* New York, Harcourt Brace, 1920.
The Analysis of Mind.   London and New York, Macmillan, 1921.
The Problem of China.   London, Allen and Unwin, and New York, Century, 1922.

Free Thought and Official Propaganda. London, Allen and Unwin, and New York, Huebsch, 1922.

The Prospects of Industrial Civilization, with Dora Russell. London, Allen and Unwin, and New York, Century, 1923.

The ABC of Atoms. London, Kegan Paul, and New York, Dutton, 1923.

Icarus or the Future of Science. London, Kegan Paul and New York, Dutton, 1924.

Bolshevism and the West, with Scott Nearing. London, Macmillan, 1924.

How to Be Free and Happy (lecture). New York, Rand School of Social Science, 1924.

The ABC of Relativity. New York and London, Harper, 1925.

What I Believe. London, Kegan Paul, and New York, Dutton, 1925.

On Education Especially in Early Childhood. London, Allen and Unwin, 1926; as *Education and the Good Life*, New York, Boni and Liveright, 1926.

Why I Am Not a Christian (lecture). London, Watts, and Girard, Kansas, Haldeman-Julius, 1927.

The Analysis of Matter. London, Kegan Paul, and New York, Harcourt Brace, 1927.

An Outline of Philosophy. London, Allen and Unwin, 1927; as *Philosophy*, New York, Norton, 1927.

Selected Papers of Bertrand Russell. New York, Modern Library, 1927.

Skeptical Essays. London, Allen and Unwin, and New York, Norton, 1928.

Marriage and Morals. London, Allen and Unwin, and New York, Liveright, 1929.

A Liberal View of Divorce. Girard, Kansas, Haldeman-Julius, 1929.

The Conquest of Happiness. London, Allen and Unwin, and New York, Liveright, 1930.

Has Religion Made Useful Contributions to Civilization? London, Watts, and Girard, Kansas, Haldeman-Julius, 1930.

Divorce as I See It. London, Douglas, 1930.

Is Modern Marriage a Failure? with John Cowper Powys. New York, Discussion Guild, 1930.

The Scientific Outlook. London, Allen and Unwin, and New York, Norton, 1931.

Education and the Social Order. London, Allen and Unwin, 1932; as *Education and the Modern World*, New York, Norton, 1932.

Freedom and Organization, 1814-1914. London, Allen and Unwin, 1934; as *Freedom Versus Organization, 1814-1914*, New York, 1934.

In Praise of Idleness and Other Essays. London, Allen and Unwin, and New York, Norton, 1935.

Religion and Science. London, T. Butterworth-Nelson, and New York, Holt, 1935.

Determinism and Physics (lecture). Newcastle-upon-Tyne, Armstrong College, 1936.

Which Way to Peace? London, Michael Joseph, 1936.

Power: A Social Analysis. London, Allen and Unwin, and New York, Norton, 1938.

An Inquiry into Meaning and Truth. London, Allen and Unwin, and New York, Norton, 1940.

Let the People Think: A Selection of Essays. London, Watts, 1941.

How to Become a Philosopher: The Art of Rational Conjecture. Girard, Kansas, Haldeman-Julius, 1942.

How to Become a Logician: The Art of Drawing Inferences. Girard, Kansas, Haldeman-Julius, 1942.

How to Become a Mathematician: The Art of Reckoning. Girard, Kansas, Haldeman-Julius, 1942.

An Outline of Intellectual Rubbish: A Hilarious Catalogue of Organized and Individual Stupidity. Girard, Kansas, Haldeman-Julius, 1943.

How to Read and Understand History. Girard, Kansas, Haldeman-Julius, 1943.

A History of Western Philosophy: Its Connection with Political and Social Circumstances from the Earliest Times to the Present Day. New York, Simon and Schuster, 1945; London, Allen and Unwin, 1946.

Physics and Experience (lecture). London, Cambridge University Press, 1946.

Ideas that Have Helped Mankind. Girard, Kansas, Haldeman-Julius, 1946.

Ideas that Have Harmed Mankind. Girard, Kansas, Haldeman-Julius, 1946.

Is Materialism Bankrupt? Girard, Kansas, Haldeman-Julius, 1946.

Philosophy and Politics (lecture). London, Cambridge University Press, 1947.

Human Knowledge: Its Scope and Limits. London, Allen and Unwin, and New York, Simon and Schuster, 1948.

Authority and the Individual. London, Allen and Unwin, and New York, Simon and Schuster, 1949.

Unpopular Essays. London, Allen and Unwin, 1950; New York, Simon and Schuster, 1966.

New Hopes for a Changing World. London, Allen and Unwin, and New York, Simon and Schuster, 1951.

The Impact of Science on Society. London, Allen and Unwin, 1952.

Bertrand Russell's Dictionary of Mind, Matter, and Morals. New York, Philosophical Library, 1952.

What is Democracy? London, Batchworth Press, 1953.

The Good Citizen's Alphabet. London, Gaberbocchus Press, 1953; New York, Philosophical Library, 1958.

History as Art. Aldington, Kent, Hand and Flower Press, 1954.

Human Society in Ethics and Politics. London, Allen and Unwin, 1954; New York, Simon and Schuster, 1955.

John Stuart Mill (lecture). London, Oxford University Press, 1956.

Logic and Knowledge: Essays, 1901-1950. London, Allen and Unwin, and New York, Macmillan, 1956.

Why I Am Not a Christian and Other Essays on Religion and Related Subjects, edited by Paul Edwards. London, Allen and Unwin, and New York, Simon and Schuster, 1957.

Understanding History, and Other Essays. New York, Philosophical Library, 1957.

The Will to Doubt. London, Allen and Unwin, and New York, Philosophical Library, 1958.

Wisdom of the West: A Historical Survey of Western Philosophy in Its Social and Political Setting. London, Macdonald, and New York, Doubleday, 1959.

My Philosophical Development. London, Allen and Unwin, and New York, Simon and Schuster, 1959.

Common Sense and Nuclear Warfare. London, Allen and Unwin, 1959; New York, Simon and Schuster, 1960.

Bertrand Russell Speaks His Mind. London, Barker, and Cleveland, World, 1960.

The Basic Writings of Bertrand Russell 1903-1959, edited by Robert E. Egner and Lester E. Denonn. London, Allen and Unwin, and New York, Simon and Schuster, 1961.

Education and Character. New York, Philosophical Library, 1961.

Fact and Fiction. London, Allen and Unwin, 1961; New York, Simon and Schuster, 1962.

Has Man a Future? London, Allen and Unwin, 1961; New York, Simon and Schuster, 1962.

Unarmed Victory. London, Allen and Unwin, and New York, Simon and Schuster, 1963.

War and Atrocity in Vietnam. London, Bertrand Russell Peace Foundation, 1965.

Appeal to the American Conscience. London, Bertrand Russell Peace Foundation, 1966.

War Crimes in Vietnam. London, Allen and Unwin, and New York, Monthly Review Press, 1967.

The Art of Philosophizing and Other Essays. New York, Philosophical Library, 1968.

The Good Citizen's Alphabet: And, History of the World in Epitome.   London, Gaberbocchus Press, 1970.

Atheism: Collected Essays 1943-1949.   New York, Arno Press, 1972.

My Own Philosophy.   Hamilton, Ontario, McMaster University Press, 1972.

Russell's Logical Atomism, edited by David Pears.   London, Collins, 1972.

Essays in Analysis, edited by Douglas Lackey.   London, Allen and Unwin, and New York, Simon and Schuster, 1973.

Other

Satan in the Suburbs, and Other Stories.   London, Bodley Head, and New York, Simon and Schuster, 1953.

Nightmares of Eminent Persons, and Other Stories.   London, Bodley Head, and New York, Simon and Schuster, 1954.

Portraits from Memory.   London, Allen and Unwin, and New York, Simon and Schuster, 1956.

The Vital Letters of Russell, Khruschev, Dulles.   London, McGibbon and Kee, 1958.

The Autobiography of Bertrand Russell.   London, Allen and Unwin, 3 vols., 1967-69; Boston, Little Brown, 2 vols., and New York, Simon and Schuster, 1 vol., 1967-69.

Dear Bertrand Russell: A Selection of His Correspondence with the General Public, edited by B. Feinberg and R. Kasrils.   London, Allen and Unwin, and Boston, Houghton Mifflin, 1969.

The Collected Stories of Bertrand Russell.   London, Allen and Unwin, and New York, Simon and Schuster, 1972.

Bertrand Russell's America: His Transatlantic Travels and Writings: A Documented Account by B. Feinberg and R. Kasrils. Volume I: 1896-1945.   London, Allen and Unwin, 1973; as *Bertrand Russell's America*, New York, Viking Press, 1974.

Mortals and Others: Bertrand Russell's American Essays 1931-1935, edited by Harry Ruja.   London, Allen and Unwin, 1975.

Editor, with Patricia Russell, *The Amberley Papers: The Letters and Diaries of Bertrand Russell's Parents.*   London, Hogarth Press, and New York, Norton, 1937.

*

Bibliography: *Bertrand Russell: A Bibliography of His Writings 1895-1976* by Werner Martin, Hamden, Connecticut, Linnet, 1981.

Critical Studies: *The Philosophy of Bertrand Russell* edited by Paul Arthur Schilpp, LaSalle, Illinois, Open Court, 1944; *Bertrand Russell and the British Tradition in Philosophy* by David Pears, London, Collins, and New York, Random House, 1967; *Essays on Bertrand Russell* edited by E.D. Klemke, Urbana, University of Illinois Press, 1970; *Russell* by A.J. Ayer, London, Collins, and New York, Viking Press, 1972; *The Life of Bertrand Russell* by Ronald W. Clark, London, Cape-Weidenfeld and Nicolson, and New York, Knopf, 1975; *Russell* by Mark Sainsbury, London, Routledge, 1979.

*   *   *

Bertrand Russell is one of the most widely known and perhaps widely read philosophers of the 20th century. He is also one of the most important philosophers and logicians of this era—and one of the most prolific. Due to the enormous range of his thought, the vast number of his books and articles, and the frequent changes of his philosophical position, any attempt briefly to summarize his philosophy is impossible. Hence, in what follows only a bare sketch can be given. (For a more detailed and readable account, the reader is advised to consult

Russell's *My Philosophical Development*.) My discussion here will focus on some of the main areas of his thought.

In his early (1903) book *The Principles of Mathematics*, Russell defends the thesis known as logicism—the claim that all mathematical concepts are definable via a small number of primitive logical concepts, and that all mathematical propositions are deducible from a small number of fundamental logical principles. In so doing, he also develops a philosophy of logic according to which logic has metaphysical or ontological status. The ontology which he introduces for this purpose is highly Platonic in character. Russell maintains that fundamental logical concepts are not merely verbal; rather these terms refer to (non-verbal) entities with which the mind may have acquaintance. Indeed, Russell broadens this thesis to refer to all terms. Thus his "fundamental principle" is: "Every word occurring in a sentence must have *some* meaning." He introduces the misleading word "term" to refer to anything that has being, that is an entity. Anything that can be mentioned, whether it be a man, a moment, a number, a class, or even a chimaera, is such an entity. And furthermore, each is immutable and indestructible.

The logistic thesis—without the extreme Platonism of the earlier version—is further developed and exemplified in Russell and Whitehead's monumental three-volume work, *Principia Mathematica*. This is perhaps the most important and influential treatise in logic (and to some extent, the philosophy of logic) of the 20th century, and one of the most important of all times. Since it is highly technical, no effort will be made to summarize it here. It should also be mentioned that many other issues in these areas of philosophy are discussed not only in the above-mentioned works, but in a large number of journal articles. (Several of these are reprinted in Russell's *Logic and Knowledge*.)

The Problems of Philosophy, which is one of Russell's most accessible books for the ordinary reader, deals with a number of epistemological and metaphysical problems. In it he is concerned to refute the main thesis of idealism and to establish that of realism (in one of its forms), the view that an external world of matter exists. But he also argues for the central thesis of another form of realism, that abstract entities (or universals) are real. He maintains that they must have being in order to answer the question of how *a priori* knowledge is possible.

But in "The Philosophy of Logical Atomism" he advocates a very different metaphysics. He characterizes logical atomism as the view that there are many separate things, or that the world can be analyzed into a number of separate things. These are known as logical atoms (in contrast to physical atoms) and consist of particulars, predicates (or properties), and relations. All of these are momentary entities—such things as patches of color, sounds, etc. Thus Russell defends a phenomenalist metaphysics in this work. Indeed, such things as tables, chairs, streets (physical objects) are said to be series of classes of sense-data and hence "logical fictions."

At various times, Russell was very much interested in the position known as neutral monism, the view that the world consists of only one kind of "stuff," and that what we call mind and matter are merely different arrangements of the one underlying reality.

In *The Problems of Philosophy*, Russell presents a systematic account of almost all of the main problems of epistemology. He begins with the question as to whether there is any knowledge in the world so certain that no reasonable person could doubt it. He maintains that there are several main classes of such knowledge: knowledge of things by acquaintance, knowledge of a priori principles (such as the laws of logic), and other intuitive knowledge of truths. This book is an interesting effort to synthesize rationalism (of a Platonic variety) and empiricism (reminiscent of Hume). In later works, Russell's approach is a more thorough-going empiricist one, supplemented by emphases upon semantics and science. Among the most important of these are: *An Inquiry Into Meaning and Truth* in which he departs from his earlier strict phenomenalism; and *Human Knowledge: Its Scope and Limits*. But again, many problems and issues are discussed in a large number of books and papers, too numerous to mention.

Although Russell's contributions to ethics are not as significant or extensive as those in other areas of philosophy, they are deserving of mention. In his early "The Elements of Ethics," and more briefly in *The Problems of Philosophy*, he advocates an objectivist and to some degree rationalist approach to the problems of ethics. However, somewhat later, in one chapter of *Religion and Science*, Russell articulates one of the first versions of the emotivist theory of ethics, according to which ethical statements merely express the feelings of those who assert them. This more empirical and subjectivist approach to ethics is found in several of his more popular works, some of which appear in *Why I Am Not a Christian*. Some of these are very moving and convey a humanitarian and deeply social concern. His book *Marriage and Morals* created somewhat of a scandal when it appeared.

Russell wrote several essays in the philosophy of religion which, due to their appearance in more popular works, aroused great controversy when they were published. Some of these essays are found in *Why I Am Not a Christian*, but also in many other works as well. In the title essay of that volume Russell maintains that, in most forms, there are two requisites for being a Christian: (1) You must believe in the existence of God (and in immortality). (2) You must believe that Christ was, if not divine, at least the best and wisest among men. With regard to (1), Russell maintains that there are no grounds for this belief, since all of the known arguments are fallacious. With regard to (2) he cites passages from *The New Testament* which indicate that Christ (if he existed at all) was niether the best nor wisest of men. He holds that religious belief is based on fear and the need to have a sort of "big brother" watching over one.

It should be mentioned that throughout his life Russell was actively involved in many issues of social and political concern. To cite only one example, he participated in many demonstrations against the Vietnam War and wrote and spoke extensively on this and other matters. He was imprisoned several times because of his public utterances on such matters. But he never gave up his hope that men, through reason and compassion, could bring about a better world of peace, justice, and cooperation.

—E.D. Klemke

RUTHERFORD, Ernest. British physicist. Born in Spring Grove, later Brightwater, near Nelson, New Zealand, 30 August 1871. Educated at Nelson College, 1887-89; Canterbury College, Christchurch, New Zealand, B.A. 1892, M.A. 1893, B.Sc. 1894; Trinity College, Cambridge (Coutts Trotter Studentship), B.A., Research Degree, 1897. Married Mary Georgina Newton in 1900; 1 daughter. Macdonald Research Professor of Physics, McGill University, Montreal, 1898-1907; Langworthy Professor of Physics and Director, Physics Laboratories, University of Manchester, 1907-19; Fellow, Trinity College, 1919-37, and Cavendish Professor of Experimental Physics and Director of the Cavendish Laboratory, 1919-37, and Director of Mond Laboratory, 1936-37, Cambridge University. Chairman, Advisory Council of Department of Scientific and Industrial Research, 1930-37. President, Royal Society, London, 1925-30. Recipient: Rumford Medal, Royal Society, 1905; Bressa Prize, Turin Academy of Science, 1908; Nobel Prize for Chemistry, 1908; Barnard Medal, Columbia University, New York, 1910; Copley Medal, Royal Society, 1922; Franklin Medal, Franklin Institute, Philadelphia, 1924; Albert Medal, Royal Society of Arts, London, 1928; Faraday Medal, Institution of Electrical Engineers, London, 1930. Honorary doctorate: University of New Zealand; University of Pennsylvania, Philadelphia; University of Wisconsin, Madison; McGill University, Montreal; University of Birmingham; University of Edinburgh; University of Melbourne; Yale University, New Haven, Connecticut; University of Glasgow; University of Giessen; Cambridge University; University of

Dublin; University of Durham; Oxford University; University of Liverpool; University of Toronto; University of Bristol; University of Cape Town; University of London; University of Leeds; and Clark University, Worcester, Massachusetts. Fellow of the Royal Society. Member, French Academy of Science. Honorary Member, Royal College of Physicians, London. Knighted, 1914. O.M. (Order of Merit), 1925. Created 1st Baron of Nelson, 1931. *Died* (in Cambridge) *19 October 1937.*

PUBLICATIONS

Physics

Radio-activity. London, Cambridge University Press, 1904.
Radioactive Transformations. New York, Scribner, 1906.
Radioactive Substances and Their Radiations. London, Cambridge University Press, and New York, Dutton, 1913.
The Natural and Artificial Disintegration of the Elements (lecture). Philadelphia, Franklin Institute, 1924.
Electricity and Matter (lecture). Nelson, New Zealand, Stiles, 1928.
Radiation from Radioactive Substances. London, Cambridge University Press, 1930.
The Artificial Transmutation of the Elements (lecture). London, Oxford University Press, 1933.
The Newer Alchemy (lecture). London, Cambridge University Press, 1937.
Science in Development (lecture). London, British Association for the Advancement of Science, 1937.
The Collected Papers of Lord Rutherford of Nelson, edited by Sir James Chadwick. London, Allen and Unwin, and New York, Interscience, 1962-.
Rutherford and Boltwood: Letters on Radioactivity, edited by Lawrence Badash. New Haven, Connecticut, Yale University Press, 1969.

*

Critical Studies: *Rutherford, Being the Life and Letters of the Rt. Hon. Lord Rutherford* by Arthur Stewart Eve, London, Cambridge University Press, and New York, Macmillan, 1939; *Rutherford and the Nature of the Atom* by Edward Neville da Costa Andrade, New York, Doubleday, 1964; *The Self-Splitting Atom: The History of the Rutherford-Soddy Collaboration* by Thaddeus J. Trenn, London, Taylor and Francis, 1977.

*   *   *

For many scientists, a single outstanding achievement is sufficient to earn life-long acclaim. Many famous names are remembered for a key discovery or invention. Less commonly, we encounter the genius who follows one great discovery with another, and yet another. He or she appears to be a bottomless well of ideas, explanations, research designs, and understandings. Such a man was Ernest Rutherford.

Rutherford arrived at the Cavendish Laboratory at a pivotal moment in the history of science, just a year before Becquerel's discovery of radioactivity. He was to spend the remaining forty years of his working life attempting to understand the nature of radiation and of radioactive materials.

Becquerel's discovery immediately raised two fundamental questions about the nature of radioactivity: (1) What is the nature of the radiations emitted by radioactive materials? and (2) What is the nature of the radioactive materials themselves? Rutherford addressed the first of these questions in the historic "lead block" experiment in 1898. In the experiment, a small sample of pitchblende, a radioactive ore of uranium, is placed at the bottom of a long, narrow hole drilled in a large block of lead. Radioactive emanations from the pitchblende in every direction are absorbed by the lead block, except those which escape upward through the hole. This apparatus provided Rutherford with a clearly defined, collimated beam of radiation for analysis.

In order to identify the nature of the emissions leaving the block, Rutherford placed the poles of a magnet on either side of the escaping beam. He observed that the magnetic field caused the beam to separate into two parts, one of which he called the *alpha rays*, the other of which he named the *beta rays*. In a similar experiment in 1900, the French physicist Paul Villard was able to show the existence of yet a third segment of the emanations, a group of rays unaffected by the magnetic field. Rutherford names these rays *gamma rays*.

The identity of beta rays and gamma rays was quickly and rather easily recognized as streams of electrons and a very high energy form of electromagnetic radiation, respectively. The alpha rays proved more difficult to analyze and were not identified as streams of helium nuclei until 1908. Again it was Rutherford, working in collaboration with Hans Geiger, who made this determination.

The alpha particle was to become a key research tool in future Rutherford experiments. Between 1906 and 1911 he studied the effects of firing alpha particles through very thin sheets of metals. His work produced two rather startling results. First, the great majority of alpha particles passed directly through the thin sheets, without experiencing any deviation. To Rutherford, this suggested that the atoms of which the metal sheets were made were primarily empty space.

The second result was that a few alpha particles were deflected through large angles, some actually being reflected, through 180°. This was a totally unexpected event, prompting Rutherford to observe that "It was quite the most incredible event that has ever happened to me in my life. It was almost as incredible as if you fired a 15-inch shell at a piece of tissue paper and it came back and hit you."

Rutherford's interpretation of this remarkable observation was that the positive charge of the atom must be concentrated in a very small space in the core—or nucleus, as he called it—of the atom. Only a concentration of charge like this would exert enough force on the positively charged alpha particle to cause it to be reflected back upon itself. Some time later, Rutherford also showed that the positive charge on the nucleus was due to the presence of positively charged "hydrogen nuclei," for which he suggested the name *proton* in 1919.

Even after the nature of radioactive emissions was clarified, scientists continued to be puzzled about the event itself. What was it that actually took place during the process of radioactive decay? What was the source of the alpha, beta, and gamma radiations? What change, if any, took place in the radioactive material itself? An answer for these questions was posed by Rutherford and Frederick Soddy in 1902. According to their theory of nuclear disintegration, radioactivity is the process by which a particular nucleus breaks apart, changes into a new nucleus of a new atom, and emits an alpha particle, beta particle, and/or gamma ray in the process.

This theory was very difficult for Rutherford's fellow scientists to accept. The indestructibility of matter was a basic concept that lay at the very heart of physics and chemistry. The notion that matter might spontaneously change into something new was profoundly disturbing. It required some years of accumulated evidence before the Rutherford-Soddy interpretation of radioactive decay was accepted generally by the scientific community.

Rutherford's research on naturally radioactive materials raised in his mind an obvious related question. If some materials in nature undergo spontaneous radioactive decay, is it possible that a comparable change can be brought about artificially? That is, would it be possible artificially to induce the transformation of one atom into another in a radioactive-like transition? Rutherford answered that question in 1919 when he reported the results of an experiment in which he once more employed his favorite experimental tool, alpha particles. The alpha particles were used to bombard nitrogen gas contained within a glass tube. After a certain period of exposure to the alpha radiation, the gas within the tube was analyzed and found to contain not only nitrogen, but also oxygen and hydrogen.

From these results, Rutherford inferred that an artificial transmutation had occurred. Some alpha particles had struck nitrogen nuclei and become embedded in them, he surmised. This created unstable nuclei which decayed with the emission of protons (the nuclei of hydrogen atoms), leaving atoms of oxygen behind. The experiment became a model for other researchers, and within a short time literally thousands of comparable nuclear transformations had been achieved.

Yet another Rutherford discovery in the field of radioactivity concerned the rate at which radioactive decay occurs. In his studies of thorium emanation in 1906, Rutherford noted that the rate of decay of the sample decreased over time. He further recognized that this property—rate of decay—was useful in distinguishing various types of radioactive materials from each other. The property Rutherford identified was half life. Today we recognize that half life is a universal and identifying characteristic of all types of radioactive isotypes.

—David Newton

RYLE, Gilbert. British philosopher. Born in Brighton, 19 August 1900. Educated at Brighton College; studied at Queen's College, Oxford, B.A. Served in the Welsh Guards, 1939-45; Major. Lecturer in Philosophy, 1924-25, and Tutor in Philosophy, 1925-44 (and sometime Junior and Senior Censor of Christ Church and Junior Proctor of the University), Christ Church, Oxford; Waynflete Professor of Metaphysical Philosophy, Oxford University, 1945-68. Editor of *Mind*, 1947-71. Honorary doctorate: University of Warwick, 1969; University of Sussex, Brighton, 1971; University of Hull, 1972; University of Birmingham; University of Keele; Trinity College, Dublin; and Trent University, Peterborough, Ontario. Honorary Fellow, Queen's College and Magdalen College, Oxford. Foreign Honorary Member, American Academy of Arts and Sciences. *Died 15 October 1976.*

PUBLICATIONS

Philosophy

John Locke on the Human Understanding (lecture). London, Oxford University Press, 1933.

Philosophical Arguments (lecture). Oxford, Clarendon Press, 1945.

The Concept of Mind. London and New York, Hutchinson, 1949.

Essays on Logic and Language, with others, edited by Anthony Flew. Oxford, Blackwell, 1951.

Dilemmas: The Tarner Lectures. London, Cambridge University Press, 1954.

A Rational Animal (lecture). London, Athlone Press, 1962.

Plato's Progress. London, Cambridge University Press, 1966.

Studies in the Philosophy of Thought and Action, with others, edited by P.F Strawson. London, Oxford University Press, 1968.

Collected Papers: Critical Essays; Collected Essays, 1929-1968. London, Hutchinson, 2 vols., and New York, Barnes and Noble, 2 vols., 1971.

On Thinking, edited by Konstantin Kolenda. Oxford, Blackwell, and Totowa, New Jersey, Rowman and Littlefield, 1979.

Other

Editor, *Proceedings of the Seventh International Congress of*

Philosophy Held at Oxford, England, September 1-6, 1930. London, Oxford University Press, 1931.

Editor, *Contemporary Aspects of Philosophy.* Boston, Oriel Press, 1977.

*

Critical Studies: *Moore and Ryle: Two Ontologists* by Laird Addis and Douglas Lewis, Iowa City, University of Iowa Press, 1968; *Ryle: A Collection of Critical Essays* edited by Oscar P. Wood and George Pitcher, New York, Doubleday, 1970 (includes bibliography); *Studies in Philosophy: A Symposium on Gilbert Ryle* edited by Konstantin Kolenda, Houston, Rice University, 1972; *Gilbert Ryle: An Introduction to His Philosophy* by William Lyons, Brighton, Harvester, 1980.

*   *   *

Gilbert Ryle's contributions to philosophy can be conveniently summarized under four headings.

Philosophy as Conceptual Cartography. Ryle first expressed the view that the task of philosophy was to clarify the content and inter-relationships of our concepts, in particular those whose use could easily mislead philosophers into error, in his early paper "Systematically Misleading Expressions." This view he continued to hold in slightly varying forms all his life. In his book *Dilemmas* a very special version of this view emerged according to which philosophical problems arose because of the apparent clash of obvious truths which one cannot abandon, such as that between the truth that we are responsible for our actions and the truth that we are moulded by heredity and environment. A careful examination of the concepts involved would reveal that the conflict was not real but arose from fundamental misunderstandings of a kind which Ryle called "category mistakes." To believe that fictitious persons were a class of persons alongside official persons would be to commit such a mistake.

Empiricist Reductionism. Ryle believed that philosophers were particularly liable to be misled by forms of speech into an over-inflated ontology. Thus philosophers talked of a realm of universals, of timelessly true propositions, of fictional entities, as though they were irreducible elements in the world. The techniques of conceptual cartography were particularly valuable in showing that discourse on such topics did not involve paradoxical ontological commitments.

Philosophical Psychology. The two elements in Ryle's thought already mentioned display themselves very evidently in Ryle's work in philosophical psychology, especially in *The Concept of Mind.* There Ryle claimed that talk about the mind, the soul, the self, mental activity and the like had seriously misled philosophers. By a "category mistake" they had construed as talk about a special kind of object, the mind, what should be understood as sometimes talk about the manner and skill of witnessable behavior, sometimes talk about the dispositions to behave in certain ways. To this "category mistake" Ryle gave the often copied name "the dogma of the ghost in the machine." We do not need a duality of mind and body as ultimate entities in some obscure relationship, the one observable, the other hidden. But Ryle's philosophical psychology is not all pursued at this high level of metaphysical generality. There are also many close and detailed studies of various aspects of mental life. Ryle's doctrine that knowing how to do things is independent of and more fundamental than knowing certain things are the case was particularly influential. He also produced a number of studies on the nature of thinking, but never succeeded in satisfying himself that he had solved all the problems he had tackled.

History of Philosophy. Ryle regarded the history of philosophy as a part of history, not of philosophy. His philosophical works are notable for a lack of historical reference. But Ryle was very interested in certain areas of the history of philosophy, and particularly in Plato. Ryle's treatment of Plato as a serious philosopher whose works, especially such later ones as the

Theaetus, Parmenides, and *Sophist,* contained mature contributions to problems still vexing philosophers and had a profound effect on all subsequent work in ancient philosophy.

No account of Ryle can be complete without a reference to his prose style. The syntax and semantics are impeccably orthodox, but the style is so personal that almost every sentence bears an individual stamp that cannot be counterfeited.

—J.O. Urmson

———————

SAHLINS, Marshall (David). American anthropologist. Born in Chicago, Illinois, 27 December 1930. Studied at the University of Michigan, Ann Arbor, M.A. 1952; Columbia University, New York, Ph.D. 1954. Lecturer in Anthropology, Columbia University, 1955-57; Assistant Professor of Anthropology, 1957-61, Associate Professor, 1961-64, and Professor from 1964, University of Michigan, Ann Arbor. Currently Professor of Anthropology, University of Chicago. Fellow, Center for Advanced Study in the Behavioral Sciences, Stanford, California, 1963-64. Recipient: Guggenheim Fellowship, 1967. Address: Department of Anthropology, University of Chicago, Chicago, Illinois 60637, U.S.A.

PUBLICATIONS

Anthropology

Social Stratification in Polynesia. Seattle, University of Washington Press, 1958.
Maola: Culture and Nature on a Fijian Island. Ann Arbor, University of Michigan Press, 1962.
Tribesmen. Englewood Cliffs, New Jersey, Prentice Hall, 1968.
Stone Age Economics. Chicago, Aldine, 1972.
The Use and Abuse of Biology: An Anthropological Critique of Sociobiology. Ann Arbor, University of Michigan Press, 1976; London, Tavistock, 1977.
Culture and Practical Reason. Chicago, University of Chicago Press, 1977.
Historical Metaphors and Mythical Realities: Structure in the Early History of the Sandwich Islands Kingdom. Ann Arbor, University of Michigan Press, 1981.

Other

Editor, with Elman R. Service, *Evolution and Culture.* Ann Arbor, University of Michigan Press, 1960.

*   *   *

A new Ph. D. introduced himself to an older colleague as a student of Marshall Sahlins, and met with the reply, "Which Marshall Sahlins?" Theoretical adversaries perceive Sahlins as a talented but mercurial thinker; supporters counter that, unlike most scholars, Sahlins is not afraid to change his mind. In the course of his intellectual career, Sahlins has made a transition from materialism to idealism. Today he is one of anthropology's foremost theoreticians, with a reputation that is truly worldwide. The frequency with which he is cited in the pages of *American Anthropologist* alone indicates that Sahlins is enormously influential: irritatingly provocative to some of his colleagues, inspiring to others. The hallmark of his work is that he suggests creative and original solutions to difficult theoretical problems. A reviewer called him "one of the finest synthesizing minds in anthropology." Sahlins's analytic procedure is akin to rationalism rather than the "on-the-ground" empiricism that many anthropologists hold sacred. In a prose that is elegant and literary, if occasionally obscure, he freely discusses areas where anthropology and philosophy intersect, underscoring his points with citations from such diverse sources as Kant and Joseph Heller, Hobbes and Gilbert and Sullivan.

At the most general level, Sahlins's career has been dedicated to investigating the relationship between nature and culture, and specifically their order of determinacy: is culture constituted out of practical action, or is it arbitrary (in the linguistic sense) and logically prior to nature? In his early work, Sahlins presumed that nature came first in the equation, reflecting the tutelage of his mentor Leslie White. His dissertation investigated a Whitean hypothesis relating social stratification in Polynesian societies to differential energy-capture: "the degree of stratification varies directly with productivity." In this work, Sahlins adopted White's "layer-cake" model of culture, with the "technoenvironmental base" as prior and determinant, and social stratification relegated to the dependent "superstratum." An impressive piece of library research, *Social Stratification in Polynesia* is still an indispensable reference work for students of Polynesia, whether or not one agrees with its theoretical conclusions (which Sahlins himself has disavowed). Sahlins has since pointed out that stratification, far from being a dependent variable of energy-capture, is itself a spur to production, forcing the population to produce more than is needed to support the domestic group: "the political life is a stimulus to production."

After *Moala*, Sahlins broke decisively with the materialist paradigm, and has become one of its most articulate critics. The essays in *Stone Age Economics* stress the fundamental differences between modern and primitive societies, and warn against applying concepts such as scarcity, supply-and-demand, and maximization to non-Western economies: "Economic Man is a bourgeois construction...." Influenced by the work of Karl Polanyi, Sahlins takes the "substantivist" position in opposition to economic "formalism," which holds that Western economic concepts are appropriate for the study of primitive societies. In an oft-quoted essay, Sahlins refutes anthropology's conventional understanding of hunters and gatherers as preoccupied with the food quest and living on the edge of starvation. Field studies have revealed that hunters and gatherers do have "leisure" as well as an adequate diet. Sahlins draws on this material to assert that hunters and gatherers are "the original affluent society."

Sahlins's current theoretical position has more in common with French structuralism and "semiotics," the theory of signs derived from the work of Ferdinand de Saussure, than with American symbolic anthropology. His association with Claude Lévi-Strauss is well known. Sahlins is one of the few American anthropologists to work through the implications of Lévi-Strauss's concept of structure. *Culture and Practical Reason*, a brilliant and sweeping essay in intellectual history, documents Sahlins's passage from materialism to idealism. Here he examines the work of major social theorists in light of two paradigms, the "cultural" and the "practical." In the turning point of the book, he asserts that the "practical" construction of culture reflects the ideology of Western society:

> ...this conclusion from "experience" that culture does not exist is an illusion doubly compounded. For it takes as the model of all social life not the reality of bourgeois society but the self-conception of the society. It credits the appearance of Western culture as its truth, thus conspiring in the illusion that it really is the socialized product of practical activity by ignoring the symbolic constitution of the practical activity.

As an alternative to a view of culture as Western society, Sahlins offers "some semiotic dimensions of our economy" to illustrate "Western Society as Culture." In this discussion he skillfully deciphers some of the "cultural codes" that order seemingly "practical" behavior in our own society.

Sahlins is at his best when exploring apparent dichotomies and paradoxes. In *Historical Metaphors and Mythical Realities* he attempts to resolve the "radical opposition" between structural anthropology and history by showing how history is ordered by prior categories and cultural precedents: "...all structural transformation involves structural reproduction, if not the other way around." *Historical Metaphors* is a first installment in Sahlins's analysis of the encounter between Hawaiians and Europeans in the early contact period. Displaying an unusual enthusiasm for foreign goods and customs, the Hawaiian chiefs accelerated the destruction of their own culture. Sahlins explains that their behavior followed from certain well-established cultural precedents:

> This apparently headlong rush to their own culture doom on the chiefs' part, this kind of "acculturation," can be shown to reflect basic Hawaiian principles, and, by virtue of these principles, to be selective rather than indiscriminate. For in realizing themselves as European chiefs, the Hawaiian nobility reproduced a customary distinction between themselves and the underlying population.... The Hawaiian symbolic proportion—chiefs are to people as the Europeans were to Hawaiians in general—entered into relationship with corresponding distinctions within European culture to render these historically salient....A basic intercultural agreement was reached about the value of the differences between Europeans and Hawaiians.... The chiefs were differentiated from the common people (*maka'ainana*) by a higher degree of culture, just as the British thought themselves distinguished from the Hawaiians.

Against those who would subordinate culture to biological or material determinants, Sahlins asserts the uniqueness of humankind and the priority of the symbolic faculty. Yet critics have questioned whether, in rejecting a crude materialism, Sahlins has merely inverted the order of determinations between nature and culture, without achieving a true dialectical understanding. In spite of his stature within the discipline, Sahlins eschews disciples, and has no interest in heading a "theoretical school." He is that rare scholar who is capable of challenging his own preconceptions. For this reason, one can learn from him, but not follow him. For this reason also, anthropologists eagerly await publication of his latest theoretical forays.

—Jocelyn Linnekin

SAMUELSON, Paul A(nthony). American economist. Born in Gary, Indiana, 15 May 1915. Studied at the University of Chicago, B.S. 1935; Harvard University, Cambridge, Massachusetts, M.A. 1936, Ph.D. 1941 (David A. Wells Prize, 1941). Married Marion Crawford in 1938 (died, 1978); 6 children. Assistant Professor, 1940-44, Associate Professor, 1944-47, since 1947 Professor, and since 1966, Institute Professor, Massachusetts Institute of Technology, Cambridge, Massachusetts. Stamp Memorial Lecturer, London, 1961; Wicksell Lecturer, Stockholm, 1962; Franklin Lecturer, Detroit, 1962; Hoyt Visiting Fellow, Calhoun College, Yale University, New Haven, Connecticut, 1962; John von Neumann Lecturer, University of Wisconsin, Madison, 1971; Gerhard Colm Lecturer, New School for Social Research, New York, 1971; Davidson Lecturer, University of New Hampshire, Durham, 1971; Sultzbacher Memorial Lecturer, Columbia Law School, New York, 1974; John Diebold Lecturer, Harvard University, 1976. Member, Radiation Laboratory Staff, 1944-45. Consultant, National Resources Planning Board, 1941-43; War Production Board, 1945; U.S. Treasury, 1945-52 and from 1961; Rand Corporation, 1949-75; Council of Economic Advisors, 1960-68; Federal Reserve Board, from 1965; Loomis Sayles and Co., Boston, and Burden Investors

Services. Member, Editorial Board, *Econometrica*. President, Econometric Society, 1951; American Economic Association, 1961; and International Economic Association, 1965-68 (Lifetime Honorary President). Recipient: John Bates Clark Medal, American Economic Association, 1947; Guggenheim Fellowship, 1948; Ford Research Fellowship, 1958; Nobel Prize in Economics, 1970; Albert Einstein Commemorative Award, 1971; Distinguished Service Award, Investment Education Institute, National Association of Investment Clubs, 1974. Honorary doctorate: University of Chicago, 1961; Oberlin College, Ohio, 1961; Ripon College, Wisconsin, 1962; Boston College, 1964; University of Indiana, Bloomington, 1966; East Anglia University, Norwich, 1966; University of Michigan, Ann Arbor, 1967; Claremont Graduate School, California, 1970; University of New Hampshire, Durham, 1971; Keyo University, Tokyo, 1971; Seton Hall University, South Orange, New Jersey, 1971; Williams College, Williamstown, Massachusetts, 1971; University of Massachusetts, Amherst, 1972; University of Rhode Island, Kingston, 1972; Harvard University, Cambridge, Massachusetts, 1972; Gustavus Adolphus College, St. Peter, Minnesota, 1974; University of Southern California, Los Angeles, 1975; University of Pennsylvania, Philadelphia, 1976; University of Rochester, 1976; Catholic University of Louvain, 1976; Emmanuel College, Boston, 1977; Stonehill College, North Easton, Massachusetts, 1978; University of London, 1980. Member, American Academy of Arts and Sciences, and National Academy of Sciences. Corresponding Fellow, British Academy. Address: 75 Clairemont Road, Belmont, Massachusetts 02178, U.S.A.

PUBLICATIONS

Economics

After the War, 1918-1920: Military and Economic Demobilization of the United States: Its Effect Upon Employment and Income. Washington, D.C., Government Printing Office, 1943.

Economic Analysis of Guaranteed Wages, with Alvin H. Hansen. Washington, D.C., Bureau of Labor Statistics, 1947.

Foundations of Economic Analysis. Cambridge, Massachusetts, Harvard University Press, 1947.

Economics: An Introductory Analysis. New York, McGraw Hill, 1948; 11th edition, 1980.

Equilibrium Points in Game Theory. Santa Monica, California, Rand Corporation, 1951.

Notes on the Dynamic Approach to Saddlepoints and Extremum Points. Santa Monica, California, Rand Corporation, 1951.

Linear Programming and Economic Analysis, with Robert Dorfman and Robert Solow. New York, McGraw Hill, 1958.

Problems of the American Economy: An Economist's View (lecture). London, Athlone Press, and New York, Oxford University Press, 1962.

Stability and Growth in the American Economy. Stockholm, Almquist and Wiksell, 1963.

The Collected Scientific Papers of Paul A. Samuelson, edited by Joseph F. Stiglitz. Cambridge, Massachusetts, M.I.T. Press, 4 vols., 1966-77.

Full Employment: Guideposts and Economic Stability, with Arthur F. Burns. Washington, D.C., American Enterprise Institute for Public Policy Research, 1967.

Foundations of Economic Analysis. Cambridge, Massachusetts, Harvard University Press, 1971.

International Trade for a Rich Country (lecture). Stockholm, Federation of Swedish Industries, 1972.

The Samuelson Sampler. Glen Ridge, New Jersey, Horton, 1973.

Other

Editor, with others, *Readings in Economics*. New York,

McGraw Hill, 1952.

Editor, *International Economic Relations: Proceedings of the Third Congress of the International Economic Association*. London, Macmillan, and New York, St. Martin's Press, 1969.

Editor, with James L. Bicksler, *Investment Portfolio Decision-Making*. Lexington, Massachusetts, Lexington Books, 1974.

Editor, *Trade, Stability, and Macroeconomics: Essays in Honor of Lloyd A. Metzler*. New York, Academic Press, 1974.

*

Critical Studies: *Anti-Sammy: Des Nobel Presitragers Paul A. Samuelson*, Cologne, R. Horst, 1974; *The Anti-Samuelson* by Marc Linder and Julius Sensat, New York, Urizen, and London, Pluto Press, 2 vols., 1977; *The Foundations of Paul Samuelson's Revealed Preference Theory* by Stanley Wong, London, Routledge, 1978; *Samuelson and Neoclassical Economics*, edited by George R. Feiwel, Boston, Kluwer, 1982.

* * *

It is difficult to overestimate the direct and indirect impact of Paul A. Samuelson on the development of economics in this century.

His thesis, written in 1937 at the age of 22, presented a general framework for economic analysis which revealed fundamental common elements in aspects of economic behavior which had until that time been investigated separately. Since then, he has made major contributions to every area of economic research. His collected works (through 1976) comprise some 3700 pages in four volumes, with no end in sight.

His indirect influence is equally important. His introductory textbook has dominated the market since 1948. Economists commonly indicate their vintage in terms of just which edition of Samuelson's *Economics* was used in their own principles of economics class. More than one graduate student has prepared for a theory prelim by working through the footnotes of *Economics*.

This would be enough to make Samuelson the economist's economist. So he is. But he is not just the economist's economist. Throughout his career—whether advising Presidents or discussing economic aspects of current events in the popular press—he has been the noneconomist's economist as well.

A detailed treatment of Samuelson's research contributions is inappropriate (and impossible) here. However, it is possible to outline several major themes which have characterized his work.

Many of his early contributions (including *Foundations of Economic Analysis*) involved a formal description of the activities of economic agents as the consequences of optimization processes. The hiring and production decisions of firms can be analyzed under the assumption that firms act to maximize profit. The behavior of individuals, as consumers (or, as suppliers of labor), can be understood if it is supposed that individuals act to maximize their own well-being. Use of the optimization framework revealed formal similarities in the theories of firm and individual economic behavior which had not previously been recognized.

Although the way a consumer evaluates his own welfare cannot be observed directly (in contrast to the profit of a firm), Samuelson's concept of "revealed preference" shows that in principle a sufficient description of individual preferences can be inferred from observable consumption behavior.

These optimizing models of individual consumption and firm production (and investment) decisions can be combined to yield a framework within which the consequences of economic growth can be explored. Samuelson's contributions in this area have been made individually and in collaboration with Robert Solow and others. Optimizing models can be applied to the analysis of international trade (outlining, for example, the circumstances under which international trade will equalize wages and other factor returns across countries). The same sort of framework can be used to analyze the production and joint consumption of public goods (such as a school system or a force for national defense). Samuelson's work has touched on all of these areas.

In the macroeconomic arena, Samuelson has made basic contributions to the analysis of government monetary and fiscal policy. He was one of several researchers to develop independently the "balanced budget multiplier" theorem (which shows that an increase in government spending matched by a corresponding increase in taxes will generate an identical increase in national income, under some circumstances). His "multiplier-accelerator" model clarified the short-run and long-run impact of changes in (for example, government) spending on investment and national output.

In addition, Samuelson has made fundamental contributions to the history of economic thought. He has developed formal versions of the "world views" inherent in the writings of several classical economists, including Adam Smith, David Ricardo, and Karl Marx.

Samuelson has applied linear programming to the analysis of economic problems, explored the economics of natural resources, and made major contributions to the development of mathematical economics.

Samuelson's influence on the development of modern economics extends beyond the substantial impact of the content of his own research. It extends to the standards of scholarship which he has set for himself and for the profession. Although his own work has furthered the use of mathematics as a framework for the exposition of economic theory, he has always had the purpose of the analysis in view: "Part of the beauty of any applied mathematics lies in its applicability to some reality. Extra zest comes from following the rules of the game; and it is part of the rules of the game of economic theory that your deductive creations be of *empirical relevance.* Who wants easy victories?"

He has always been careful to relate his work to the results of other economists, saying "for myself, it was a matter of pride to try to do justice to the literature. Not only did equity require this, but also the efficiency of building up the edifice of scientific knowledge called for integrating new findings with old. He who goes out each morning to invent the wheel furthers his vanity more than his locomotion."

If a single characteristic can be said to be typical of such a large body of work over such a long period of time, it is perhaps his consistent refusal to oversell the nature of the results. Typical is the care with which a fundamental economic doctrine is expressed:

> Properly formulated, the correct version of the Invisible Hand doctrine does not allege that dollar votes are distributed by the competitive regime of laissez faire so as to have equal ethical value. Its correct versions say...that once the initial distribution of wealth and economic voting power has been ethically rectified by non-laissez faire forces, the algorithm of perfect market competition, if you could attain it, could *efficiently* achieve production and allocation of economic goods and services...so that it will never be possible to better the condition of some without sacrificing the well-being of others.

Samuelson's research contributions will remain forever an integral part of economic thought. But his influence on current economic thinking is greater than that of his research alone, as illustrated by the following story. A classmate of mine at M.I.T., seeking academic employment in the 1970's, was interviewed by the chairman of the department of economics at a small college which will remain nameless. They discussed various people from whom my friend had taken classes. When my friend named Paul Samuelson, the reply was "A fine economist; we use his textbook. Has he ever done anything else?" The distinctive (in 1948) nature of this textbook is best illustrated by quotation from the preface to the first edition:

> With the needs of the intelligent layman in mind, the

author has been ruthless in omitting completely many of the usual textbook topics and in reducing to more appropriate emphasis the conventional "marginal" analysis of "value and distribution" theory. This has released space for an extended presentation of the rich array of quantitative material about economic institutions that has become available for the first time only within the past half-dozen years.

There are today many fine introductory textbooks which share this same emphasis; they must be counted as "fellow travelers" on the path charted by Samuelson. John Maynard Keynes (1972) wrote of Alfred Marshall:

> ...the master-economist must possess a rare *combination* of gifts. He must reach a high standard in several different directions and must combine talents not often found together. He must understand symbols and speak in words. He must contemplate the particular in terms of the general, and touch abstract and concrete in the same flight of thought. He must study the present in the light of the past for the purposes of the future. No part of man's nature or his institutions must lie entirely outside his regard. He must be purposeful and disinterested in a simultaneous mood; as aloof and incorruptible as an artist, yet sometimes as near the earth as a politician.

Paul Samuelson is the quintessential master economist.

—Stephen Martin

SANTAYANA, George (Agustin de). Spanish-American philosopher and poet. Born in Madrid, 16 December 1863; emigrated to American in 1872. Educated at the Latin School, Boston; studied at Harvard University, Cambridge, Massachusetts, B.A. 1886, M.A. (Walker Fellowship, Germany and England, 1886-88), 1888, Ph.D. 1889; Trinity College, Cambridge, 1896-97. Instructor, 1889-98, Assistant Professor, 1898-1907, and Professor of Philosophy, 1907-12, Harvard University; resigned in 1912 to devote himself entirely to philosophy and lived abroad in England, France, and Rome, 1912-52. Hyde Lecturer, Sorbonne, 1905-06; Spencer Lecturer, Oxford, 1923. Honorary doctorate: University of Wisconsin, Madison, 1911. Member, National Institute of Arts and Letters. *Died* (in Rome) *26 September 1952.*

PUBLICATIONS

Collections

The Works of George Santayana: Triton Edition. New York, Scribner, 15 vols., 1936-40.

Philosophy

The Sense of Beauty: Being the Outlines of Aesthetic Theory. New York, Scribner, and London, Black, 1896.
Interpretations of Poetry and Religion. New York, Scribner, and London, Black, 1900.
The Life of Reason; or, The Phases of Human Progress: Introduction and Reason in Common Sense, Reason in Society, Reason in Religion, Reason in Art, Reason in Science. New York, Scribner, 5 vols., and London, Constable, 5 vols., 1905-06; revised and abridged version, as *The Life of Reason,* with Daniel Cory, New York, Scribner, and London, Constable, 1954.

Three Philosophical Poets: Lucretius, Dante, and Goethe. Cambridge, Massachusetts, Harvard University Press, and London, Oxford University Press, 1910.

Winds of Doctrine: Studies in Contemporary Opinion. New York, Scribner, and London, Dent, 1913.

Egotism in German Philosophy. New York, Scribner, 1915; London, Dent, 1916; as *The German Mind: A Philosophical Analysis,* New York, Crowell, 1968.

Character and Opinion in the United States, with Reminiscences of William James and Josiah Royce and Academic Life in America. New York, Scribner, and London, Dent, 1920.

Little Essays: Drawn from the Writings of George Santayana by Logan Pearsall Smith, with the Collaboration of the Author. New York, Scribner, and London, Dent, 1920.

Soliloquies in England and Later Soliloquies. New York, Scribner, and London, Constable, 1922.

Scepticism and Animal Faith: Introduction to a System of Philosophy. New York, Scribner, and London, Constable, 1923.

The Unknowable (lecture). Oxford, Clarendon Press, 1923.

Dialogues in Limbo. London, Constable, 1925; New York, Scribner, 1926.

Realms of Being: The Realm of Essence, The Realm of Matter, The Realm of Truth, The Realm of Spirit. New York, Scribner, 4 vols., and London, Constable, 4 vols., 1927-40.

Platonism and the Spiritual Life. New York, Scribner, and London, Constable, 1927.

The Genteel Tradition at Bay. New York, Scribner, and London, Adelphi, 1931.

Some Turns of Thought in Modern Philosophy: Five Essays. New York, Scribner, and London, Cambridge University Press, 1933.

Obiter Scripta: Lectures, Essays and Reviews, edited by Justus Buchler and Benjamin Schwartz. New York, Scribner, and London, Constable, 1936.

Philosophy of George Santayana (selections), edited by Irwin Edman. New York, Scribner, 1936; revised edition, 1953.

The Idea of Christ in the Gospels; or, God in Man: A Critical Essay. New York, Scribner, 1946.

Atoms of Thought: An Anthology of Thoughts, edited by Ira D. Cardiff. New York, Philosophical Library, 1950.

Dominations and Powers. New York, Scribner, and London, Constable, 1951.

Essays in Literary Criticism, edited by Irving Singer . New York, Scribner, 1956.

The Idler and His Works, edited by Daniel Cory. New York, Scribner, 1957.

Ten Letters and a Foreword. Turin, Edizioni di Filosofia, 1960.

Animal Faith and Spiritual Life: Previously Unpublished and Uncollected Essays by George Santayana, edited by John Lachs. New York, Appleton Century, 1967.

George Santayana's America: Essays on Literature and Culture, edited by James Ballowe. Urbana, University of Illinois Press, 1967.

The Birth of Reason and Other Essays, edited by Daniel Cory. New York, Columbia University Press, 1968.

Santayana on America: Essays, Notes, and Letters on American Life, edited by Richard Calton Lyon. New York, Harcourt Brace, 1968.

Selected Critical Writings, edited by Norman Henfrey . London, Cambridge University Press, 2 vols., 1968.

Physical Order and Moral Liberty: Previously Unpublished Essays by George Santayana, edited by John and Shirley Lachs. Nashville, Vanderbilt University Press, 1969.

Lotze's System of Philosophy (1889 doctoral dissertation), edited by Paul Kurtz. Bloomington, Indiana University Press, 1977.

Verse

Sonnets and Other Verses. Cambridge, Massachusetts, Stone

and Kimball, 1894; revised edition, New York, Stone and Kimball, 1896.

Lucifer: A Theological Tragedy. Chicago, Stone, 1899; revised edition, as *Lucifer; or, The Heavenly Truce: A Theological Tragedy,* Cambridge, Massachusetts, Dunster House, 1924.

A Hermit of Carmel and Other Poems. New York, Scribner, 1901; London, Johnson, 1902.

Poems. New York, Scribner, and London, Constable, 1923.

The Poet's Testament: Poems and Two Plays. New York, Scribner, 1953.

The Complete Poems of George Santayana: A Critical Edition, edited by William Holzberger. Lewisburg, Pennsylvania, Bucknell University Press, 1979.

Other

The Last Puritan: A Memoir in the Form of a Novel. London, Constable, 1935; New York, Scribner, 1936.

Persons and Places: Memories of Childhood and Early Youth, The Middle Span, My Host the World. New York, Scribner, 3 vols., 1943-53; London, Constable, 2 vols., 1944-47; and Cresset Press, 1 vol., 1953.

Letters, edited by Daniel Cory. New York, Scribner, 1955.

*

Critical Studies: *The Philosophy of George Santayana* edited by Paul Arthur Schilpp, Evanston, Illinois, Northwestern University Press, 1940 (includes bibliography); *Santayana: The Later Years: A Portrait with Letters* by Daniel Cory, New York, Braziller, 1963; *George Santayana* by Willard E. Arnett, New York, Washington Square Press, 1968; *Santayana: An Examination of His Philosophy* by Timothy L.S. Sprigge, London and Boston, Routledge, 1974.

*   *   *

Although George Santayana is not generally regarded as a shaper of current philosophical trends, he had a great deal of influence during the first half of the 20th century on the philosophical movement called naturalism. This movement, with roots in the thought of such ancient thinkers as Democritus and Aristotle, was inspired most directly by the Darwinian view that there can be a "natural" explanation for every event, including human life, thought, and action, although no doubt Santayana regarded his own naturalism as independent of Darwinism. For Santayana, to say that there is a "natural" explanation was in effect to say (as Democritus had but Aristotle had not) that there is a "material" explanation, and that what we feel, think, and do depends primarily on the complex mechanisms—the neurology—of the body under the influence of a particular environment. In other words, and in spite of the fact that he said much that is inconsistent with it, Santayana claimed to be a thoroughgoing materialist, convinced that every form of existence must be ultimately a product of the "dark fertility" of matter.

It is a bit odd that Santayana took this turn in philosophy, for he was also the most Platonist of modern philosophers in so far as Platonism is a matter of temperament and an attitude towards life and the world. He led a detached, contemplative life, and found his own life valuable primarily, he said, because of the world of ideas in which he chose to live. His fondest ambition, he claimed, was "to be able to despise fortune and to live simply in some beautiful place." Consistent with this attitude, his earliest interest was in the philosophy of beauty. He developed a naturalistic theory of beauty as a form of subjective pleasure which nonetheless attempted to explain the sense of moral and intellectual importance which the experience of beauty seems to bear. He admitted the "apparent objectivity" and the "moral dignity" of beauty as experienced, and observed that "if we look at things teleologically, and as they ultimately justify themselves to the heart, beauty is of all things what least calls for explanation." He found no puzzle in the fact that beauty is called *divine* because "the perception of beauty exemplifies that adequacy and perfection which in general we objectify in an idea of God." Descriptively, then, the Platonist account of beauty is correct. Beauty seems objective in his account, however, only because a pleasure not obviously related to any organ of perception or bodily function is nonetheless inseparable from a perceived object. The moral dignity of beauty has a similar natural explanation. Because the experience of beauty does not call attention to the body and its organs, the result is an illusion of disembodiment which is exhilarating in contrast to the sense of "grossness and selfishness" which accompanies those pleasures which call attention to some part of the body. Thus the extraordinary attributes of beauty can, he thought, be understood as "products" of perceptual processes. Beauty is in the eye or the brain of the beholder; it is an epiphenomenon, an unsubstantial phase in the life of a perceiving creature, not itself something to be sought and found or missed.

In his later works Santayana distinguished four *realms of being*: matter, essence, spirit, and truth. Only two of these, matter and spirit, he said, exist, and the existence of spirit (or mind) is not only inseparable from but completely dependent upon the complexities and processes of matter. Spirit or mind is an epiphenomenal result of material processes, an ephemeral witness to the parade of essences (forms, images, appearances) which its fleeting existence generates. And truth is simply the faith that some of these essences are reliable clues to the structures and processes of the material world out of which they arise.

Santayana recognized that his materialism and theory of mind implied that knowledge in a strict sense is impossible. Sense experience and ideas, pleasure and pain as well as poems and scientific theories, are products of "our innocent organs under the stimulus of things." What we experience are essences which do not exist and what exists is never experienced. Even our most critical reconstructions and anticipations of experiences, as in the sciences, are at best only guides to the regularities in experience which the future may repeat, and which may seem to enable us to avoid certain dangers. But scientific as well as practical knowledge is only indirectly related to the values of life. The distinctive values are products of the imagination: poetry, the arts, and religion. None of these, however, is a source of truth or knowledge. They give us other worlds to live in imaginative landscapes which are intrinsically valuable because the ideals they express may delight the spirit without misleading it. Religion is poetry but a poetry that fails to deceive only when it is not regarded as the source of metaphysical and moral truth.

The main thrust of Santayana's philosophy is, then, that human life and history began, as Bertrand Russell suggested, in an "accidental collocation of atoms," and that existence is justified—in the sense of being made worthwhile—only by the life of the spirit in contemplation of the brief beauties which its existence calls into being. No one, he thought, is in any degree the master of his fate; everyone is at all times in the clutch of circumstance. It is vanity, then, to suppose that one's own efforts can affect the inevitable course of events, and only frustration or disappointment await those who make such efforts. The spiritual man, however, recognizes his helplessness and is content to be a witness to events, including his own actions, which he cannot alter. Indeed, a genuine spiritual life is possible only to the extent that one is reconciled to the fact that his life and destiny are determined in every particular by circumstances over which he has no control, including sometimes the unpredictable quirks of chance. The spirit or mind is then free to observe without commitment, to understand without seeking to determine, to delight in the unending parade of essences without regret or guilt or fear.

—Willard E. Arnett

SAPIR, Edward. American anthropologist and linguist. Born in Lauenburg, Pomerania, now Poland, 26 January 1884; emigrated to the United States with parents in 1889. Studied at Columbia University, New York, B.A. 1904, M.A. 1905, Ph.D. 1909. Married Florence Delson in 1911 (deceased, 1924), 3 children; married Jean V. Mc Clenaghan in 1926, 2 children. Research Assistant in Anthropology, University of California, Berkeley, 1907-08; Instructor in Anthropology, University of Pennsylvania, Philadelphia, 1908-10; Chief, Division of Anthropology, Canadian National Museum, 1910-25; Associate Professor of Anthropology, 1925-27, and Professor of Anthropology and General Linguistics, 1927-31, University of Chicago; Sterling Professor of Anthropology and General Linguistics, Yale University, New Haven, Connecticut, 1931-39. Editor, Yale University Publications in Anthropology, 1936-39. President, American Anthropological Association. Honorary doctorate: Columbia University, 1929. Member, American Academy of Arts and Sciences. *Died 4 February 1939*.

PUBLICATIONS

Linguistics and Anthropology

Takelma Texts. Philadelphia, University Museum, 1909.
Wishram Texts: Together with Wasco Tales and Myths, collected by Jeremiah Curtin and edited by Edward Sapir. Leyden, E.J. Brill, 1909.
Yana Texts. Berkeley, University of California Press, 1910.
The Takelma Language of Southwestern Oregon. Washington, D.C., Government Printing Office, 1912.
Abnormal Types of Speech in Nootka. Ottawa, Government Printing Bureau, 1915.
Noun Reduplication in Comox, a Salish Language of Vancouver Island. Ottawa, Government Printing Bureau, 1915.
A Sketch of the Social Organization of the Nass River Indians. Ottawa, Government Printing Bureau, 1915.
Time Perspective in Aboriginal American Culture. A Study in Method. Ottawa, Government Printing Bureau, 1916.
Dreams and Gibes. Boston, Poet Lore, 1917.
The Position of Yana in the Hokan Stock. Berkeley, University of California Press, 1917.
Yana Terms of Relationship. Berkeley, University of California Press, 1918.
Language: An Introduction to the Study of Speech. New York, Harcourt Brace, 1921; London, H. Milford, 1922.
The Fundamental Elements of Northern Yana. Berkeley, University of California Press, 1922.
Religious Life, with others. New York, Van Nostrand, 1929.
Totality. Baltimore, Waverly Press, 1930.
Wishram Ethnography, with Leslie Spier. Seattle, University of Washington Press, 1930.
International Communication: A Symposium on the Language Problem, with others. London, Kegan Paul, 1931.
The Southern Paiute Language. Boston, American Academy of Arts and Sciences, 1931(?).
The Expression of the Ending-Point Relation in English, French, and German, with Morris Swadesh, edited by Alice V. Morris. Baltimore, Waverly Press, 1932.
Songs for a Comox Dancing Mask, edited by Leslie Spier. Stockholm, Ethnographical Museum of Sweden, 1939.
Culture, Language, and Personality: Selected Essays, edited by David G. Mandlebaum. Berkeley, University of California Press, 1949.
Selected Writings in Language, Culture, and Personality, edited by David G. Mandlebaum. Berkeley, University of California Press, 1949; selections as *Culture, Language, and Personality: Selected Essays*, 1949.
Native Accounts of Nootka Ethnography, with Morris Swadesh. Bloomington, Indiana University Research Center in Anthropology, Folklore, and Linguistics, 1955.

Yana Dictionary, with Morris Swadesh, edited by Mary R. Haas. Berkeley, University of California Press, 1960.

The Phonology and Morphology of the Navaho Language, with Harry Hoijer. Berkeley, University of California Press, 1967.

Linguistic Convergence: An Ethnography of Speaking at Fort Chipewyan, Alberta, edited by Ronald Scollon and Suzanne B.K. Scollon. New York, Academic Press, 1979.

Other

Letters from Edward Sapir to Robert H. Lowie, edited by Luella Cole Lowie. Privately printed, 1965.

Editor and translator, with Marius Barbeau, *Folk Songs of French Canada*. New Haven, Connecticut, Yale University Press, 1925.

Editor, with Morris Swadesh, *Nootka Texts: Tales and Ethnological Narratives, with Grammatical Notes and Lexical Materials*. Philadelphia, University of Pennsylvania, 1939.

Editor with Harry Hoijer, *Navaho Texts, with Supplementary Texts by Harry Hoijer*. Iowa City, University of Iowa, 1942.

*

Bibliography: in *Language, Culture, and Personality: Essays in Memory of Edward Sapir* edited by Leslie Spier and others, Menasha, Wisconsin, Sapir Memorial Publication Fund, 1941.

Critical Studies: *Universalism vs. Relativism in Language and Thought: Proceedings of a Colloquium on the Sapir-Whorf Hypotheses* edited by Rix Pinxten, The Hague, Mouton, 1975; *Ethnolinguistics: Boas, Sapir, and Whorf Revisited* edited by Madeleine Mathiot, The Hague, Mouton, 1979.

*   *   *

Edward Sapir was a distinguished linguist of the early part of this century, specializing in American Indian languages. He will be remembered for the famous Sapir-Whorf hypothesis of linguistic relativity, which will be the major subject of this essay. However, it should be pointed out that Sapir, Whorf's teacher, was in general concerned with the relationship of language and behavior. This concern was reflected in a variety of explorations and in the pursuits of his many well-known students, most of whom emulated their teacher in pursuing a multi-disciplinary approach to linguistics and related fields.

In its most general form, the Sapir-Whorf hypothesis holds that the nature of a language dictates the thought, perception, and behavior of its speakers. By "nature of a language" is meant its syntax and lexicon. Claims about the influence of syntax are often called the strong version of the hypothesis; claims about the influence of the lexicon are often called the weak version. We shall discuss the latter first.

We will start with a standard example. The Eskimo have a variety of words for what we call "snow." What does this mean? Undoubtably, the Eskimo *see* the varieties of snow codified by their language with a directness that we cannot muster (just as an Eskimo would undoubtably be unable to see the differences among the scores of varieties of automobiles being driven around our streets). This is not to say that we could not learn to see the different varieties of snow, for we clearly could. It is to say, at most, that we do not. Why not? It seems likely that we do not need to. Skiers have several terms for varieties of snow; a non-skier learns these as he learns to ski because he needs to know how to respond to these different varieties of snow. In fact, part of what it means to learn to ski is to learn the language of skiing. Similarly, while in their daily lives the Eskimo do not need to know the names of our many varieties of automobiles, if they wanted to live here, they would have to. In some cases, it would not be important to survival—you do not need to know the difference between a Cobra and a Rattler. But in other cases it would—knowing the difference betweeen a stick shift and an automatic or between power brakes and normal brakes is very important.

The version of the Sapir-Whorf hypothesis that finds a correlation between the words in a lexicon and the culture and cultural practices of a people is often considered trivial, and with some reason. While interesting, it is not earth-shaking. We codify important differences and don't bother to codify unimportant differences. Thought and perception are not involved to any great extent. The snow-Eskimo example is given in dozens of brief textbook accounts of the Sapir-Whorf hypothesis, and no mention is made of the fact that we do in fact have more than one word for "snow"—"slush" for example. That nobody thinks of this demonstrates that we do not think of slush as a variety of snow, that we think of it as sufficiently different to deserve a completely different name. But we all know that slush was once snow, even that in some sense it is a variety of snow.

Sapir and Whorf did in fact suggest a link between language and behavior, thought, and perception that is stronger, more causal, and less easily changed by experience. This stronger link is found on the level of syntax. For example, the Hopi do not, Sapir and Whorf maintained, conjugate their verbs according to the time when the action took place. Rather, they specify the validity the speaker intends his utterance to have. For example: "Dick and Jane of first grade reader fame, now adults, married but not to each other, were/are/will have an affair (and this statement was/is/will be malicious gossip I made up/make up/ will make up because I hated/hate/will hate Jane)." The speakers of such a language are hypothesized to have a particular preoccupation with validity, whereas we English speakers presumably have a preoccupation with time. Unfortunately, this claim overlooks the fact that there are a variety of ways of specifying time and validity. We are perfectly able to specify—or request—statements of validity, and we could get along quite well with a tenseless verb, for example, "I happy in past" and "I happy in future." If that was the way our language worked, as a matter of fact, it would be a moot point whether the phrases "in past" and "in future" belonged to the verb or not.

Proponents of the Sapir-Whorf hypothesis have made much of the fact that English has nouns and verbs, while certain American Indian languages do not. If this is a legitimate analysis (and there is considerable debate about it), what difference would it make? According to Whorf, it means that "we are constantly reading into nature fictional acting entities, simply because our verbs must have substantives in front of them." But consider the sentence, "It rains." Is it really the case, as Whorf maintains, that we English speakers believe that there is something, for example a god, who is involved in the production of rain? Certainly not. (The American Indians are a good deal more prone to pantheism than Christians and Jews, by the way.) In this case, the Sapir-Whorf hypothesis confuses syntax with reality. In order to speak grammatical English, we do often add words that are unnecessary, especially in context. But that does not mean we add entities, fictional or otherwise, in addition. The obvious can be pointed out in defense of this criticism—that imperfectly grammatical English is common and usually quite comprehensible. If I say "Raining" while looking out the window, I will be understood. And I will not be considered to have briefly abandoned belief in the fictional entity, "It."

On the whole, the Sapir-Whorf hypothesis does not hold up well to conceptual criticisms, largely because the examples advanced in its support take too rigid a view of what language can do. Nor has the theory held up well to empirical tests. These, however, have failed to do justice to the theory—their operational definitions of the theory's concepts have been trivial. Still, some of them addressed themselves adequately to the weak version of the theory and failed to show that lexical differences mean anything more than this essay has suggested they do.

The Sapir-Whorf hypothesis is, however, still alive and well, even if only in its descendents. The hypothesis has been—as has psychoanalysis, another controversial theory which threatened man's ego and received harsh criticism—unquestionably heuristic. The attempt to understand schizophrenia has been enriched by a large amount of research attempting to find and describe the differences in the verbal behavior of schizophrenics. This research is based on the notion, very much a part of the Sapir-Whorf hypothesis, that language reflects non-linguistic factors, in this case mental disorders. For another of several examples that could be given, the centuries-old attempt to isolate or even to describe style has been enlightened by attempts to find out by close, usually computer-assisted analysis what it is about the language of a writer that makes him so strongly and undeniably him.

Finally, the hypothesis will survive because it puts in formal terms an interest many of us come naturally to have. No matter how poorly the theory has fared as an academic theory, it is fortunate that the academic atmosphere of the social sciences once allowed the free production of broad general theories and multi-disciplinary approaches to problems so typical of Edward Sapir.

—George W. Kelling

SARTRE, Jean-Paul (-Charles-Aymard). French philosopher, dramatist and novelist. Born in Paris, 21 June 1905. Educated at the Lycée Montaigne and at the Lycée Henry-IV, Paris; studied at the École Supérieure, Paris, agrégation in philosophy 1929. Served in the French Army during World War II; captured at Padoux, 1940; escaped 1941. Began life-long association with the writer Simone de Beauvoir in 1929; adopted Arlette El Kaïm in 1965. Professor, Lycée du Havre, 1931-32, 1934-36; Lycée de Laon, 1936-37; Lycée Pasteur, Paris, 1937-39; and Lycée Condorcet, Paris, 1941-44. Co-Founder, *Les Temps Modernes*, Paris, in 1944. Travelled and lectured extensively during the 1950's and 1960's. Member of Bertrand Russell's International War Crimes Tribunal, 1966. Editor, *La Cause du peuple* after 1970; editor, *Tout*, 1970-74, and *Révolution*, 1971-74. With Maurice Clavel founded the news agency Libération in 1971 (editor of the daily *Libération*, 1973-74). Recipient: Research grant, French Institute, 1933-34; French Popular Novel Prize, 1940; Légion d'honneur, 1945 (refused); New York Drama Critics Award, for play, 1947; French Grand Novel Prize, 1950; Novel Prize for Literature, 1964 (refused); Omegna Prize, Italy, 1960. Foreign Member, American Academy of Arts and Sciences. *Died* (in Paris) *15 April 1980.*

PUBLICATIONS

Philosophy and Literature

L'Imagination. Paris, Alcan, 1936; as *Imagination: A Psychological Critique*, London, Cresset Press, and Ann Arbor, University of Michigan Press, 1962.

"La Transcendance de l'ego: Esquisse d'une description phénoménologique," in *Recherches Philosophiques.* (Paris), 6, 1936-37; as *The Transcendence of the Ego: An Existentialist Theory of Consciousness*, New York, Farrar Straus, 1957; London, Vision Press, 1958.

Esquisse d'une théorie des émotions. Paris, Hermann, 1939; as *The Emotions: Outline of a Theory*, New York, Philosophical Library, 1948; as *Sketch for a Theory of the Emotions*, London, Methuen, 1962.

L'Etre et le néant: Essai d'ontologie phénoménologique. Paris, Gallimard, 1943; as *Being and Nothingness*, New York, Philosophical Library, 1956; London, Methuen, 1957.

L'Existentialisme et un humanisme. Paris, Nagel, 1946; as *Existentialism*, New York, Philosophical Library, 1947; as *Existentialism and Humanism*, London, Methuen, 1948.

Explication de "L'Étranger." Sceaux, Le Palimugre, 1946.

Réflexions sur la question juive. Paris, Morihien, 1946; as *Anti-Semite and Jew*, New York, Schocken, 1948; as *Portrait of an Anti-Semite*, London, Secker and Warburg, 1948.

Baudelaire. Paris, Gallimard, 1947; as *Baudelaire*, London, Horizon Press, 1949; New York, New Directions, 1950.

Situations I. Paris, Gallimard, 1947; selections in *Literary and Philosophical Essays*, London, Rider, and New York, Criterion, 1955.

Situations II. Paris, Gallimard, 1948; selection as *What Is Literature?* New York, Philosophical Library, 1949; London, Methuen, 1950.

"Qu'est-ce que la littérature?" in *Situations II* . Paris, Gallimard, 1948; as *What is Literature?* New York, Philosophical Library, 1949; London, Methuen, 1950.

Situations III. Paris, Gallimard, 1949; selections in *Literary and Philosophical Essays*, London, Rider, and New York, Criterion, 1955.

Saint Genet, Comédien et martyr. Paris, Gallimard, 1952; as *Saint Genet, Actor and Martyr*, New York, Braziller, 1963; London, W.H. Allen, 1964.

Critique de la raison dialectique: Vol. 1, *Théorie des ensembles pratiques.* Paris, Gallimard, 1960; as *Critique of Dialectical Reason: Theory of Practical Ensembles*, London, New Left, and Highlands, New Jersey, Humanities Press, 1976.

Essays in Aesthetics, edited by Wade Baskin. New York, Philosophical Library, 1963.

Que peut la littérature? with others. Paris, Union Générale d'Éditions, 1965.

The Philosophy of Jean-Paul Sartre, edited by Robert Denoon Cumming. New York, Random House, 1966.

Of Human Freedom, edited by Wade Baskin. New York, Philosophical Library, 1967.

Essays in Existentialism, edited by Wade Baskin. New York, Philosophical Library, 1967.

L'Idiot de la famille: Gustave Flaubert de 1821 à 1857. Paris, Gallimard, 3 vols., 1971-72; as *The Family Idiot: Gustave Flaubert 1821-1857*, Chicago, University of Chicago Press, 1981.

Situations VIII: Autour de 68. Paris, Gallimard, 1971; selections in *Between Existentialism and Marxism*, London, New Left, 1974; New York, Pantheon, 1975.

Situations IX: Mélanges. Paris, Gallimard, 1971; selections in *Between Existentialism and Marxism*, London, New Left, 1974; New York, Pantheon, 1975.

Un Théâtre de situations, edited by Michel Contat and Michel Rybalka. Paris, Gallimard, 1973; as *Sartre on Theater*, New York, Pantheon, 1976.

Politics and Literature. London, Calder and Boyars, 1973.

Fiction

La Nausée. Paris, Gallimard, 1938; as *The Diary of Antoine Roquentin*, London, Lehmann, 1949; as *Nausea*, New York, New Directions, 1949.

Le Mur. Paris, Gallimard, 1939; as *The Wall and Other Stories*, New York, New Directions, 1949; as *Intimacy and Other Stories*, London, Nevill, 1949.

Les Chemins de la liberté: vol. 1, *L'Âge de raison.* Paris, Gallimard, 1945; as *The Age of Reason*, London, Hamish Hamilton, and New York, Knopf, 1947; vol. 2, *Le Sursis*, Paris, Gallimard, 1945; as *The Reprieve*, London, Hamish Hamilton, and New York, Knopf, 1947; vol. 3, *La Mort dans l'âme*, Paris, Gallimard, 1949; as *Iron in the Soul*, London, Hamish Hamilton, 1950; as *Troubled Sleep*, New York, Knopf, 1951.

Plays

Les Mouches. Paris, Gallimard, 1943; as *The Flies*, in *The Flies and In Camera*, London, Hamish Hamilton, 1946; in *No Exit and The Flies*, New York, Knopf, 1947.

Huis Clos: Pièce en un acte. Paris, Gallimard, 1945; as *In Camera*, in *The Flies and In Camera*, London, Hamish Hamilton, 1946; as *No Exit*, in *No Exit and the Flies*, New York, Knopf, 1947.

Morts sans sépulture. Lausanne, Marguerat, 1946; as *Men Without Shadows*, in *Three Plays*, London, Hamish Hamilton, 1949; as *The Victors*, in *Three Plays*, Knopf, 1949.

La Putain respectueuse. Paris, Nagel, 1946; as *The Respectable Prostitute*, in *Three Plays*, London, Hamish Hamilton, 1949; as *The Respectable Prostitute*, in *Three Plays*, New York, Knopf, 1949.

Les Jeux sont faits (film script). Paris, Nagel, 1947; as *The Chips Are Down*, New York, Lear, 1948; London, Rider, 1951.

Les Mains sales. Paris, Gallimard, 1948; as *Crime Passionnel*, in *Three Plays*, London, Hamish Hamilton, 1949; as *Dirty Hands*, in *Three Plays*, New York, Knopf, 1949.

L'Engrenage (film script). Paris, Nagel, 1948; as *In the Mesh*, London, Dakers, 1954.

Le Diable et le bon dieu. Paris, Gallimard, 1951; as *Lucifer and the Lord*, London, Hamish Hamilton, 1953; as *The Devil and the Good Lord, and Two Other Plays*, New York, Knopf, 1960.

Kean, adaptation of the play by Alexandre Dumas, père. Paris, Gallimard, 1954; as *Kean*, London, Hamish Hamilton, 1954; in *The Devil and the Good Lord, and Two Other Plays*, New York, Knopf, 1960.

Nekrassov. Paris, Gallimard, 1956; as *Nekrassov*, London, Hamish Hamilton, 1956; in *The Devil and the Good Lord, and Two Other Plays*, New York, Knopf, 1960.

Les Séquestrés d'Altona. Paris, Gallimard, 1960; as *Loser Wins*, London, Hamish Hamilton, 1960; as *The Condemned of Altona*, New York, Knopf, 1961.

Bariona; ou, Le Fils du tonnerre. Paris, Atelier-Anjour, 1962; as *Bariona; or, The Son of Thunder*, in *The Writings of Jean-Paul Sartre 2*, Evanston, Illinois, Northwestern University Press, 1974.

Les Troyennes (adaptation of *The Trojan Women* by Euripides). Paris, Théâtre National Populaire, 1965; as *The Trojan Women*, London, Hamish Hamilton, and New York, Knopf, 1967.

Other

Entretiens sur la politique, with others. Paris, Gallimard, 1949.

L'Affaire Henri Martin, with others. Paris, Gallimard, 1953.

Sartre on Cuba. New York, Ballantine, 1961.

Les Mots (autobiography). Paris, Gallimard, 1963; as *Words*, London, Hamish Hamilton, 1964; as *The Words*, New York, Braziller, 1964.

Situations IV: Portraits. Paris, Gallimard, 1964; selections in *Situations*, London, Hamish Hamilton, and New York, Braziller, 1965.

Situations V: Colonialisme et néo-colonialisme. Paris, Gallimard, 1964.

Situations VI: Problèmes du marxisme, 1. Paris, Gallimard, 1964; selections as *The Communists and Peace*, New York, Braziller, 1965; London, Hamish Hamilton, 1969.

Situations VII: Problèmes du marxisme, 2. Paris, Gallimard, 1965; selection as *The Ghost of Stalin*, New York, Braziller, 1968; as *The Specter of Stalin*, London, Hamish Hamilton, 1969.

On Genocide. Boston, Beacon Press, 1968.

Les Communistes ont peur de la révolution. Paris, Didier, 1969.

War Crimes in Vietnam, with others. London, Bertrand Russell Peace Foundation, 1971.

On a raison de se révolter, with Philippe Ravi and Pierre Victor. Paris, Gallimard, 1974.

Situations X: Politique et autobiographie. Paris, Gallimard, 1976; as *Life/Situations: Essays Written and Spoken*, New York, Pantheon, 1977.

Sartre in the Seventies: Interviews and Essays. London, Deutsch, 1978.

*

Bibliography: *The Writings of Jean-Paul Sartre: A Bibliographical Life* by Michel Contat and Michel Rybalka, Evanston, Illinois, Northwestern University Press, 1974; *Jean-Paul Sartre: A Bibliography of International Criticism* by Robert Wilcocks, Edmonton, University of Alberta Press, 1975; *Jean-Paul Sartre and His Critics: An International Bibliography (1938-1980)* by François and Claire Lapointe, Bowling Green, Ohio, Bowling Green State University Press, revised edition, 1981.

Critical Studies: *Sartre, Romantic Rationalist* by Iris Murdoch, Cambridge, Bowes and Bowes, 1953; *Jean-Paul Sartre: A Literary and Political Study* by Philip Thody, London, Hamish Hamilton, 1960; *The Philosophy of Sartre* by Mary Warnock, London, Hutchinson, 1965; *Sartre* by Peter Caws, London and Boston, Routledge, 1979; *The Philosophy of Jean-Paul Sartre* edited by Paul Arthur Schilpp, La Salle, Illinois, Open Court, 1981.

*   *   *

Author, playwright, social critic, and existentialist philosopher, Jean-Paul Sartre personifies French letters for fully a third of the 20th century. Reacting against the philosophical idealism of his formal education, he adapts the phenomenologies of Husserl and Heidegger to his own existentialist ontology developed in his master work, *Being and Nothingness*. From Husserl he accepts the notion of eidetic reduction, the attempt to lay bare the essential structure of any object of consciousness by rigorous descriptions, as well as the idea that consciousness itself is essentially intentional. Sartre gives "intentionality" a robustly realist interpretation to avoid the problems of inside/outside epistemologies. Consciousness is ecstatic and vectorial; it is dynamically directed toward an other-than-consciousness. But Sartre "historicizes" consciousness by ascribing to it Heidegger's three temporal "ekstases," viz., facticity or the givens in one's situation, presence-to or the inner distance which prohibits the self-identity of consciousness, and possibility or the futural dimension.

Unlike those of his German mentors, Sartre's concerns are anthropological and moral. They find ready expression in his many ventures into imaginative literature as well as in two phenomenological studies of the imagination and one of the emotions. Indeed, imaging consciousness is paradigmatic of Sartrean consciousness in general. It is the locus of possibility, of negativity, and of lack. The apparent "idealism" of this claim is tempered by his realist reading of "intentionality." When it imagines, consciousness does not produce inner pictures of an external world; rather, it "derealizes" that perceptual world, grasping it as present-absent, as a "no-thing." This thesis yields two major conclusions, one for Sartre's aesthetic theory and the other for his ontology.

It follows for Sartre that the aesthetic object is an "unreality" which "visits" the physical artifact which, in turn, serves as an analogue to direct our attention as we adopt the aesthetic attitude. Here too Sartre adapts the phenomenological act-object relationship characteristic of all consciousness to further his anthropological and moral concerns. Since our imaging power presumes the radical freedom to hold the real at bay, aesthetic experience is read both as a communication between freedoms (the artist's and the public's) and by the politicized Sartre as an implicit demand for a disalienated community of freedoms.

Extended to consciousness in general, the paradigm of imaging consciousness issues in Sartre's basic ontology of being-in-itself (nonconsciousness, thingness, inertia) and being-for-itself (consciousness, no-thingness, spontaneity). His "dualism" is a functional one of inertia and spontaneity, not of substances, since consciousness is by definition nonsubstantial. Here lies the ontological root of Sartrean freedom: "Man is free because he is no self [substance] but self-presence [consciousness as internal negation of the nonconscious]."

Consciousness-imagination enables the agent to experience his own contingency and possibility: no state of affairs need be what it is; anything can be otherwise. Sartre expresses this graphically in the famous meditation on a tree root from his novel *Nausea*. This same awareness of nonnecessity fosters the "philosophy of revolution" that he calls for in the late 1940's and 1950's. Then it is the socio-economic system whose contingency is underscored. The political utopian use of this concept of consciousness finds expression in the student uprising in Paris, 1968, with its cry of "all power to the imagination." By this time the philosopher of the imagination has joined the moralist in projecting a vision of the disalienated society in which "freedoms recognize one another" in a life free from political authority or material scarcity.

One can distinguish three stages in Sartre's evolving ethical theory. The first is the well-known existentialist ethic of authenticity, defined as the willingness to get clear on one's choices, to make them with full consciousness, and to accept their consequences. Negatively, this entails criticism of "bad faith," the "truncated ignorance" which conceals an unwillingness to live with the anguish of freedom, creative choice, and responsibility. Sartre's plays, novels, and short stories dramatize this conflict between the authentic and the inauthentic. His "bibliographies" of Baudelaire, Tintoretto, Genet, and Flaubert, themselves imaginative reconstructions, likewise serve as object lessons in the ethics of authenticity. But this existentialist ethic proffers more style than content. As Simone de Beauvoir remarks: "Ethics does not furnish recipes."

We may term the next phase of Sartre's development his ethic of disalienation. This matures along with his politicization after the war and his close association with the French Communist Party in the early 1950's. Its aim is to transform those socio-economic "bases and structures of choice" which leave the oppressed no option but submission or death. This ethic is much more sensitive to what Marx, Weber, and Lukács call "objective possibility" than the ethic of authenticity. And its underlying concept of freedom expands beyond the ontological notion of consciousness as self-presence to include the positive freedom promised by the socialist revolution. Expressed in the "committed literature" of this same period, this ethic allies itself with political movements to liberate the exploited and oppressed everywhere.

Guiding this principally negative ethic of disalienation is a positive vision which can be termed Sartre's ethic of freedom. It fosters as values fraternity and mutuality, firytic spirit of capitalism as atomistic, deterministic, and antihumanistic, with the dialectical spirit of socialism, which he takes to be holistic, libertarian, and humanistic.

The motto of Sartre's humanism is that "you can always make something out of what others have made of you." His classic existentialism stresses the radical freedom and concomitant responsibility of the first part of that claim; his later philosophy delves into what others, especially by family mediation and socio-economic conditioning, "have made" of you.

He pursues the matter of family upbringing in the existential psychoanalyses of his "biographies," including his autobiography *The Words*. His method, which he later calls "progressive-regressive" once it is conjoined to historical materialism, moves from the givens in a person's life to that project by which he "personalizes" himself in terms of those givens. For example, Sartre argues from a hermeneutic of Flaubert's juvenilia, from a phenomenological description of young Gustave's perception of his place in sibling rivalry and the family romance, and from a social analysis of the tensions plaguing a provincial bourgeois family in Louis-Philippard society to Flaubert's "existential choice" of the imaginary in dedicating himself to the life of a novelist and specifically in writing *Madame Bovary*. Applied exhaustively in nearly three thousand pages of *The Family Idiot*, this method addresses "what we can know about a man in the present state of our knowledge."

Sartre incorporates socio-economic conditioning into his thought via the *Critique of Dialectical Reason* and its prefatory *Search for a Method*. Here he develops an existentialist social philosophy. Its pivotal concepts are "praxis," "practico-inert," and "mediating third." Each is formulated to guarantee the "existentialist" values of individual freedom and moral responsibility within a neo-Marxian context. The result is a highly original social theory which is more existentialist than Marxist, but whose significance is clouded by the badly written text of the *Critique*.

"Praxis," defined roughly as "purposive human activity in its material environment," replaces "consciousness" as the ground concept of Sartrean thought. It enjoys a threefold primacy in his social thought, namely, ontological, epistemological, and ethical. All social relations are practical, being the immediate or mediated actions of individuals. Correspondingly, we are able, Sartre believes, to understand the self comprehension (the underlying praxes) of the most foreign societies sustaining whatever structures we may discover there. Consequently, we can ascribe moral responsibility to individuals for the "impersonal" laws/structures of any institution or society. Beneath every exploitative system, Sartre the moralist insists, rest oppressive praxes for which moral responsibility can be attributed.

The "practico-inert" constitutes "fundamental sociality." All social forms to the extent that they are social have a basis in the practico-inert, i.e., in the relation among agents mediated by such "worked matter" as natural languages, rituals of exchange, and physical artifacts. But even here praxis is primary, for it is the *practico*-inert that mediates. As modified by material scarcity, the practico-inert contorts human relations, subjecting actions to counterfinalities and turning society into a Hobbesian war of all against all. Only material abundance offers lasting deliverance from the tyranny of *practico*-inert mediation where, in Marx's phrase, we are the product of our products.

Still, a momentary relief from this dehumanizing state and a taste of the "reign of freedom" occur in the revolutionary group of all-for-one and one-for-all. The ontology of the group, which must respect individual existence while warranting collective action, turns on the concept of the mediating third person. This functional concept denotes the agent who is transformed from alienating Other (the looking/looked-at relations of *Being and Nothingness*) to cooperating "same" by the practical internalization of multiplicity in a common project. This is the apex of Sartre's social ontology—the freedoms mutually recognizing one another of his earlier existentialism. But whether it can perdure even in material abundance, Sartre is unable to promise. For the abiding ontological freedom of self-presence can just as easily betray as cooperate.

The career of Sartre's thought displays a certain permanence throughout its changes. His functional dualism is a constant as is the corresponding tension that marks the inner life of the individual and of the group—total integration of either is impossible. A kind of rationalist urge to explain every facet of a human's or a society's life, save the brute fact of its existence, leads Sartre to humanize the universe. The primacy of praxis merely translates this project into the social realm. Finally, he remains committed to individual freedom and responsibility, to the moral dimension of every human relation, and to unmasking the hypocrisy and injustice of his own bourgeois class at every turn. These constitute respectively the ontological, the methodological, and the moral legacy of Sartrean existentialism. Couched in powerfully imaginative language and displayed in arresting psychological descriptions, they have earned Sartre a unique and lasting place in the history of Western thought.

—Thomas R. Flynn

SCHAPIRO, Meyer. American art historian and critic. Born in Shavly, Lithuania, 23 September 1904; emigrated to the United States in 1907: naturalized, 1914. Studied at Columbia University, New York, B.A. 1924, M.A 1926, Ph.D. 1929. Married Lillian Milgrim in 1928; 2 children. Lecturer, 1928-36, Assistant Professor, 1936-46, Associate Professor, 1946-52, Professor of Art History and Archaeology, 1952-65, University Professor, 1965-73, and since 1973 Professor Emeritus of Fine Art, Columbia University. Visiting Lecturer or Professor, New York University, 1932-36, New School for Social Research, New York, 1938-52, Warburg Institute, University of London, 1947, 1957; Messenger Lecturer, Cornell University, Ithaca, New York, 1960; Patten Lecturer, Indiana University, Bloomington, 1961; Visiting Professor, Hebrew University of Jerusalem, 1961; Weil Lecturer, Hebrew Union College, Cincinnati, 1965; Charles Eliot Norton Professor, Harvard University, Cambridge, Massachusetts, 1966-67; Slade Professor, Oxford University, 1968; Gottesman Lecturer, Yeshiva University, New York, 1973; Lecturer, Collège de France, Paris, 1974. Fellow, Center for Advanced Study in the Behavioral Sciences, Palo Alto, California, 1962-63. Recipient: Guggenheim Fellowship, 1939, 1953; American Council of Learned Societies award, 1960; Creative Arts award, Brandeis University, 1966; Art Dealers Association award, 1973; Alexander Hamilton Medal, Columbia University Alumni Association, 1975. Honorary M.A.: Oxford University, 1968; honorary doctorate, Yale University, New Haven, Connecticut, 1978. Member, National Institute of Arts and Letters. Fellow, Mediaeval Academy of America, and American Academy of Arts and Sciences. Commandeur de l'ordre des Arts et des Lettres, Paris, 1976. Address: Press Relations, George Braziller, 1 Park Avenue, New York, New York 10016, U.S.A.

PUBLICATIONS

Art

Van Gogh. New York, Abrams, 1950.
Paul Cézanne. New York, Abrams, 1952.
Style. Chicago, University of Chicago Press, 1963.
The Parma Ildefonsus: A Romanesque Illuminated Manuscript from Cluny and Related Work. New York, College Art Association of America, 1964.
Alexander Calder. Paris, Maeght, 1966.
Romanesque Art. New York, Braziller, and London, Chatto and Windus, 1977.
Modern Art: 19th and 20th Centuries. New York, Braziller, and London, Chatto and Windus, 1978.
Late Antique, Early Christian, and Mediaeval Art. New York, Braziller, 1979.

*   *   *

Meyer Schapiro's international reputation as a humanist rests upon a rich variety of scholarly achievement. His thoughts on medieval, early Christian and modern art, on aesthetics and essential problems of the creative process, are admired by scholars not only of the history of art but by those who have an interest in the history of ideas. He also enjoys almost legendary renown as a lecturer, and, by virtue of his generosity and receptiveness to new ideas, is, for many, the exemplar of the modern scholar-teacher.

The many subjects treated by Schapiro are all rooted in underlying, human concerns. Whether he is writing on the 12th-century sculpture of Moissac or on such diverse modern painters as Van Gogh, Cézanne, or Mondrian, his approach reflects a deep interest in the way the external forms of art reveal the spirit and intentions of a society or an individual. Throughout his clear, elegant prose there are numerous relevant references to the art and cultures of other times as well as to other social phenomena that direct the reader to a deeper and broader conception of a given problem than he may at first have expected. It is in his writings on medieval art that we find illuminating remarks on modern painting, and we respond to his modern studies through the communication of his awareness of that level of art that is universal. Schapiro's early, pioneering work in semiotics is an expression of his abiding interest in visual art as fundamental human expression and communication.

Schapiro's knowledge of the history of art, its countless monuments, its stylistic and iconographical development, is vast, and his sense for isolating the right problems, for those likely to be the richest mines of multiple strata of information, is unusually keen. His method of investigation is empirical, and his conclusions do not actually exceed the possibilities of the evidence he presents. That the conclusions are profoundly revealing, often in surprising ways, is due to his broad general knowledge of other disciplines and, ultimately, to his gift for analogy. In his study of the church of Saint Gilles, his attention to sculptural style is matched by his knowledge of paleography and his awareness of the abstract elements of style presented by an inscription. The two together lead to a convincing dating of the monument, and that dating, in turn, is essential to the understanding of the order of development of a style and its cultural significance.

In discussions of art historical problems, Schapiro has had recourse to the concepts and methods of Freudian analysis, Gestalt psychology, and other socio-cultural disciplines. He works comfortably with them, uses them with discretion and relevance. They serve to illuminate points and intuitions which arise from the most rigorous investigation of objects and problems of the art historian. Some of Schapiro's most persuasive argumentation, in fact, is to be found in his criticism of scholars who in their own disciplines, whether psychology or philosophy, have, as he demonstrates, made inappropriate use of art historical considerations, due to inadequate knowledge or erroneous conceptions. Freud and Heidegger, both of whom he respects, have been corrected on this count.

A cornerstone of Schapiro's achievement is his definitive characterization of the Romanesque style as a discrete and complete one whose practitioners were cognizant of its own internal, anti-classical order and remarkable vitality. He has done this by means of a rigorously systematic and minute analysis of the sculpture of Moissac and other monuments. Subsequently, Schapiro has been able to demonstrate that the medieval viewer experienced an aesthetic response to the work of art as well as an intellectual one to its iconographic meaning.

—George Mauner

SCHELER, Max. German philosopher and sociologist. Born in Munich, 22 August 1874. Studied at the University of Munich; University of Berlin; University of Jena, Ph.D. 1897. Married Amélie von Dewitz-Krebs in 1899 (divorced, 1912), 1 son; married Märit Furtwängler in 1912 (divorced, 1924); married Maria Scheu in 1924, 1 son. Lecturer, University of Jena, 1900-06; lecturer and free-lance writer in Munich, Göttingen, and Berlin, 1907-17; Professor of Philosophy and Sociology, and Director of the Sociological Institute, University of Cologne, 1919-27; appointed Professor of Philosophy and Sociology, University of Frankfurt, 1928. *Died* (in Frankfurt) *19 May 1928.*

PUBLICATIONS

Collections

Gesammelte Werke, edited by Maria Scheler and Manfred S. Frings. Bern, Francke, 13 vols., 1954.

Philosophy and Sociology

Beiträge zur Feststellung der Beziehungen zwischen den logischen und ethischen Prinzipien. Jena, Vopelius, 1899.
Die transzendentale und die psychologische Methode: Eine grundsätzliche Erörterung zur philosophischen Methodik. Leipzig, Dürr, 1900.
Über Ressentiment und moralisches Werturteil: Ein Beitrag zur Pathologie der Kultur. Leipzig, Englemann, 1912; as *Ressentiment*, New York, Free Press, 1961.
Zur Phänomenologie und Theorie der Sympathiegefühle und von Liebe und Hass, mit einem Anhang über den Grund zur Annahme der Existenz des fremden Ich. Halle, Niemeyer, 1913.
Der Formalismus in der Ethik und die materiale Werkethik, mit besonderer Berücksichtigung der Ethik I: Kants. Halle, Niemeyer, 1913; as *Formalism in Ethics and Non-Formal Ethics of Values*, Evanston, Illinois, Northwestern University Press, 1973.
Der Genius des Krieges und der deutsche Krieg. Leipzig, Verlag der Weissen Bücher, 1915.
Abhandlungen und Aufsätze. Leipzig, Verlag der Weissen Bücher, 2 vols., 1915.
Krieg und Aufbau. Leipzig, Verlag der Weissen Bücher, 1916.
Die Ursachen des Deutschenhasses: Eine nationalpädagogische Erörterung. Leipzig, Wolff, 1917.
Deutschlands Sendung und der katholische Gedanke. Berlin, Germania, 1918.
Vom Ewigen im Menschen: Religiöse Erneuerurg. Leipzig, Der Neue Geist, 1921; as *On the Eternal in Man*, London, SCM Press, 1960; New York, Harper, 1961.
Die Sinngesetze des emotionalen Lebens: Wesen und Formen der Sympathie: Der "Phänomenologie der Sympathiegefühle". Bonn, Cohen, 1923; as *The Nature of Sympathy*, London, Routledge, and New Haven, Connecticut, Yale University Press, 1954.
Schriften zur Soziologie und Weltanschauungslehre. Leipzig, Der Neue Geist, 4 vols., 1923-24.
Die Formen des Wissens und die Bildung. Bonn, Cohen, 1925.
Die Wissensformen und die Gesellschaft. Leipzig, Der Neue Geist, 1926; as *Problems of a Sociology of Knowledge*, London, Routledge, 1979.
Die Stellung des Menschen im Kosmos. Darmstadt, Reichl, 1928; as *Man's Place in Nature*, Boston, Beacon Press, 1961.
Der Mensch im Weltalter des Ausgleichs. Berlin, Rothschild, 1929.
Philosophische Weltanschauung. Berlin, Cohen, 1929; as *Philosophical Perspectives*, Boston, Beacon Press, 1958.
Die Idee des Friedens und der Pazifismus. Berlin, Der Neue Geist, 1931.
Schriften aus dem Nachlass: Zur Ethik und Erkenntnislehre. Berlin, Der Neue Geist, 1933.
Zur Rehabilitierung der Tugend. Zurich, Arche, 1950.
Liebe und Erkenntnis. Bern, Francke, 1955.
Selected Philosophical Essays. Evanston, Illinois, Northwestern University Press, 1973.
Gedanken zu Politik und Moral. Bern, Francke, 1973.

*

Bibliography: *Max Scheler: Bibliographie* by Wilfried Hartmann, Stuttgart, Frommann, 1963.

Critical Studies: *La Philosophie de Max Scheler* by Maurice Depuy, Paris, Presses Universitaires de France, 2 vols., 1959; *Max Scheler: A Concise Introduction to the World of a Great Thinker* by Manfred S. Frings, Pittsburgh, Duquesne University Press, 1965; *Max Scheler 1874-1928: An Intellectual Portrait* by John Raphael Staude, New York, Free Press, 1967; *Max Scheler im Gegenwartsgeschehen der Philosophie* edited by Paul Good, Bern, Francke, 1975.

*   *   *

Max Scheler, the German philosopher, was born in Munich in 1874. After his doctorate at Jena University in 1887 and his habilitation-thesis in 1899 he began teaching first at Jena, then at the predominantly Catholic University of Munich. Due to the dissolution of his first marriage and subsequent controversies between his University and political parties and the press he lost his position in Munich in 1910. It was only in 1919 that he could continue lecturing at the University of Cologne which had offered him a chair in both philosophy and sociology.

Scheler's mother was of Jewish extraction; his father was protestant. Already as an adolescent he became a Catholic, until about 1921 when he became non-committal in favor of a metaphysical, strenuous attempt to explicate the Divine as "becoming" in and through history. Scheler's thought can, therefore, be divided up into these two periods of his equally productive and dramatic life.

His thought covered the following areas: 1) phenomenology (in which he set himself off from E. Husserl), 2) ethics, 3) philosophy of religion, 4) sociology and metaphysics, 5) philosophical anthropology. In all of his thought the being of the human person remained central.

In his first two major works, *The Nature of Sympathy* and *Formalism in Ethics and Non-Formal Ethics of Values*, Scheler investigated the emotive side of the person, saying that the human "heart" rather than will, sensibility, or reason constitutes man's essence. In the former work he distinguished among various pre-logical feelings in relation to the core of the person, love; in the latter work he investigated the being of values. Values resemble colors in that they represent themselves only in whatever things, goods, etc., just as colors do only on whatever surfaces. Just as colors are given only in seeing, values are given only in feeling them. Just as there are a few spectral colors so also there are a few spectral values in all possible values. Spectral or "ideal" values are, however, unhistorical and hidden in practice much as they are necessary for the coming about of all real values which, like colors, are independent of the things they realize themselves on. The seat of such ideal values is the human heart as the Topos of Love. There are five such essential or "objective" value ranks given in feeling, each of them having particular "material" contents comparable to the gradations of spectral colors. These range from the value of the Holy down to mental (cultural) values, life values, utilitarian values, and those felt only in an organism. All values have respective negative values in each rank. Values are, therefore, also relative to either the person or to life. This led Scheler to the contention that if a person in lived experience emotively "prefers" higher values than those given, the tenor of his heart realizes moral goodness. Moral goodness, therefore, "rides on the back" of value-preferring. It is not an object to be willed or reasoned, since a value is first felt. Also moral oughtness presupposes the value of that which ought to be done or of what I ought to be. The determination of the "order of the heart," i.e., of Love, (ordo amoris), remained central to all of Scheler's early writings.

The second period is mainly characterized by the concept of the "becoming" Deity in history. Divine existence is structured like human existence. It has two poles: 1) the uncreated vital, energy of self-activation, "urge," whose form is life, and 2) "spirit," whose form is person. Ideas of spirit must be in simultaneous conjunction with urge in order to become historical, real, and effective. This point made Scheler the father of Sociology of Knowledge: ideas in "ideal factors" such as in art, law, religion, etc., require drive-conditioned "real factors" such as distributions of population, races, powers, economy, etc., for their realization. All reality, then, including the Divine, is constituted by "resistance" between at least two discordant factors, ultimately those of urge and spirit. Inasmuch as this vital urge, both pre-spatio-temporal and four-dimensional and, like spirit, an attribute of God, is itself gauged toward increasing spiritualization, the human person appears to be the "transition" between a universal urge and cosmic Divinization, i.e., a "bridge"between them as *Man's Place in Nature* in which God realizes his own Becoming.

Scheler's thought fell victim to Nazi suppression and post World War II European trends toward existentialism, Marxism, etc. Ortega y Gasset and Heidegger, among others, considered him to be the most germinal thinker in this century.

—Manfred S. Frings

SCHILLEBEECKX, Edward. Belgian theologian. Born in Antwerp, 12 November 1914. Educated at the Studium Generale Dominican Fathers, Ghent and Louvain; Studied at École des Hautes Études, Paris; Le Saulchoir, Paris, Doctor of Divinity. Entered the Dominican Order in 1934 and ordained as a priest, 1941. Professor of Dogmatic Theology, Dominicum Studium, Louvain, 1943-57; Professor, Higher Institute for Religious Studies, Louvain, 1956-57; after 1957, Professor of Dogmatic Theology and the History of Theology, Roman Catholic University of Nijmegen, Netherlands (now retired). Founder and Editor of *Tijdschrift voor Theologie*; Chairman, Board of Editors, *Concilium*. Recipient: Erasmus Prize, 1982.

PUBLICATIONS

Theology

De sacramentele heilseconomie: Theologische bezinnigen op S. Thomas' sacramentenleer in licht van de traditie en van de hedendaagse sacraments problematik [Theological Reflections on St. Thomas' Teachings on the Sacraments and on Contemporary Problems Concerning the Sacraments]. Antwerp, Nelissen, 1952.

Maria Moeder van der verlossing. Antwerp, Apostalaat van de Rozenkrans, 1955; as *Mary, Mother of the Redemption*, New York, Sheed and Ward, 1964.

De christusonmoeting als sacrament van de Godsontmoeting. Antwerp, 'L Groeit, 1958; later editions as *Christus, sacrament van de Godsontmoeting*, Bilthoven, Nelissen; as *Christ the Sacrament of Encounter with God*, New York, Sheed and Ward, 1963.

The Layman in the Church and Other Essays. Staten Island, New York, Alba House, 1963.

Het huwelijk, aardse werkelijkheid en heilsmysterie. Antwerp, Nelissen, 1963; as *Marriage: Secular Reality and Saving Mystery*, London, Sheed and Ward, 1965.

Het tweede Vaticans Concilie. Tielt, Lannoo, 2 vols., 1964-66; translated in part as *Vatican II: The Real Achievement*, New York, Sheed and Ward, 1965.

Theologische Peilingen. Bilthoven, Nelissen, 5 vols., 1964-72; vol. 1 as *Revelation and Theology* and *The Concept of Truth and Theological Renewal*, London, Sheed and Ward, 1965-

68; vol. 2 as *God and Man*, New York, Sheed and Ward, 1969; vol. 3 as *World and Church*, London, Sheed and Ward, 1967; vol. 4 as *The Mission of the Church*, New York, Sheed and Ward, 1973; vol. 5 as *The Understanding of Faith: Interpretation and Criticism*, London, Sheed and Ward, 1974.

Het ambtscelibaat in de branding. Bilthoven, Nelissen, 1966; as *Clerical Celibacy Under Fire: A Critical Appraisal*, London, Sheed and Ward, 1968.

Christus Tegenwoordigheid in de eucharistie. Bilthoven, Nelissen, 1967; as *The Eucharist*, New York, Sheed and Ward, 1968.

God the Future of Man. London, Sheed and Ward, 1968.

Gerechtigheid en liefde: Genade en bevrijding. Bloemendaal, Nelissen, 1970; as *Christ: The Experience of Jesus as Lord*, New York, Seabury Press, 1980.

Edward Schillebeeckx, O. P. (selections), edited by Martin Redfern. London and New York, Sheed and Ward, 1972.

Jesus, het verhaal ven een levende. Bloemendaal, Nelissen, 1975; as *Jesus: An Experiment in Christology*, London, Collins, 1979; New York, Crossroad, 1981.

Tussentijds verhaal over twee Jesus boeken. Bloemendaal, Nelissen, 1978; as *Interim Report on the Books Jesus and Christ*, New York, Sheed and Ward, 1981.

Kerkelijk Ambt: Voorgangers in de gemeente van Jesus Christus. Bloemendaal, Nelissen, 1980; as *Ministry: Leadership in the Community of Jesus Christ*, New York, Crossroad, 1981.

Evangelieverhalen [Gospel Stories]. Baarn, Nelissen, 1982.

Other

Editor, with Boniface Willems, *The Sacraments in General*. New York, Paulist Press, 1968.

Editor, with Boniface Willems, *The Problem of Eschatology*. New York, Paulist Press, 1969.

Editor, *Dogma and Pluralism*. New York, Herder, 1970.

Editor, *Sacramental Reconciliation*. New York, Herder, 1971.

Editor, *The Unifying Role of the Bishop*. New York, Herder, 1972.

Editor, with Bas van Iersel, *Truth and Certainty*. New York, Herder, 1973.

Editor, with Bas van Iersel, *Jesus Christ and Human Freedom*. New York, Herder, 1974.

Editor, with Bas van Iersel, *A Personal God?* New York, Seabury Press, 1977.

Editor, with Bas van Iersel, *Revelation and Experience*. New York, Seabury Press, 1979.

Editor, with Johannes Metz, *The Right of a Community to a Priest*. New York, Seabury Press, 1980.

Editor, with Johannes Metz, *God as Father?* New York, Seabury Press, 1981.

Editor, with Johannes Metz, *Jesus as Son of God?* New York, Seabury Press, 1982.

*

Bibliography: "Bibliogradie van E. Schillebeeckx" by T.M. Schoof, in *Tijdschrift voor Theologie 14*, 1974; supplement, in *Meedenken met Edward Schillebeeckx bij zijn afscheid als hoogleraar te Nijmegen* edited by H. Häring and others, Baarn, Nelissen, 1983.

*   *   *

Edward Schillebeeckx has been one of the most influential Roman Catholic theologians in the 20th century. The amount of his publication, and the breadth of topics which he has been willing to undertake, have manifested the depth of his erudition and incisive character of his thought. Recognition of this came in 1982 when he was awarded the Erasmus Prize for his contribution to European civilization, the first time the prize had ever been given to a theologian.

Two important intellectual influences have shaped the style of his theology. The first was the work of his philosophical mentor in Leuven, D. De Petter. De Petter's neo-Thomism concentrated on the role of experience and intuition in epistemology. Rather than beginning with conceptual thought as the basis for a theory of knowing, De Petter held that a basic intuition into reality lay at the heart of knowing, which in turn led to a need for conceptualization. De Petter tried to combine personalist concerns for human experience with Thomist notions of conceptualization as the foundation of knowing. De Petter's concerns helped shape Schillebeeckx's appropriation of Thomism.

The second major influence was the thoroughgoing historical approach of the *nouvelle theologie* in France, represented especially by Schillebeeckx's doctoral mentor at Le Saulchoir, M.D. Chenu. The *ressourcement* of scholastic theology with the range of patristic and medieval thought led to a greater appreciation of the wealth and breadth of the Christian tradition, allowing theology to develop new alternatives.

These two influences have affected not only Schillebeeckx's style of theology, but its substance as well. Human experience, and the unfolding of divine revelation in the divine-human encounter in history, serve as a leitmotif running through the entirety of his work. A contemporary understanding of Christian faith has been his constant concern.

For convenience, the development of Schillebeeckx's thought can be divided into roughly three periods.

In the first period, spanning the completion of his doctoral work in 1951 into the mid-1960's, Schillebeeckx took up many of the classical themes of Christian theology. Building upon the epistemology elaborated by De Petter, and combining it with the resources of Christian history as taught at Le Saulchoir, Schillebeeckx took up questions on the sacraments, mariology, and marriage. In each of these instances, he tried to rethink classical formulations in light of personalist approaches to human experience. Thus, in his treatment of the sacraments, he emphasized how Christ was the primordial sacrament (as revelation from God) from which the several sacraments flowed. The human encounter with Christ was the source of salvation in the sacrament.

The second period, from the mid-1960's to the early 1970's, coincided with Schillebeeckx's growing international reputation. His travels brought him into contact even more with the existential situations many Christians were facing. The theme of secularization recurs in those years, best represented by his *God the Future of Man*. The need to address secularization led him beyond the epistemology of De Petter in a number of ways, as he explored German hermeneutics, French structuralist thought, Anglo-American analytic and linguistic philosophy, and neo-Marxist social criticism. Out of these studies emerged a highly refined sense of hermeneutics more adequate to the pluralism of the contemporary world than was the neo-Thomist epistemology of his earlier work. The results of this are best exemplified in his *Understanding of Faith*, and in a general hermeneutics to be published in 1984. The hermeneutics is eclectic in base, but criticizes the German romanticist assumptions of Gadamer and others, and shows some predilection for the Frankfurt School, notably Habermas. If rethinking the Christian tradition marked the first period of Schillebeeckx's work, a refinement of tools for understanding experience marked the second period.

The third and current period has seen a return to great dogmatic themes, now aided by the tools of a critical hermeneutic. His three volume christology, *Jesus* (vol. 1), *Christ* (vol. 2), with a third volume projected for 1983, stands as a monument to erudition and reflection. Starting from a concern for the experience of salvation today, Schillebeeckx returns to the beginnings of Christianity to understand how early Christians came to confess Jesus as Lord, and moves in the third volume toward understanding how the reality of Christ is active today in the church and in the world. His work has aroused a great deal of interest and not a little controversy. The first volume has been especially widely read and debated (the *Christian Century* considered it one

of the ten best religious books of the 1970's), and led to an investigation of Schillebeeckx's methods and conclusions by Vatican authorities in 1976-80. His project of understanding the experience of salvation in the early church provides a correlate against which to measure contemporary experience.

The attempt to understand the religious experience of Christians has stood at the center of Schillebeeckx's enterprise. His sensitivity, both to belief and to unbelief, has made it widely appreciated in Western circles. His concern remains faith: the response that grows out of the encounter of human experience with the divine reality, especially in the person and work of Christ.

—Robert J. Schreiter

SCHLICK, Moritz. German philosopher. Born in Berlin, 14 April 1882. Studied at the University of Heidelberg; University of Lausanne; University of Berlin, Ph.D. 1904. Married Blanche Gay Hardy in 1907; 2 children. Lecturer and Associate Professor, University of Rostock, 1911-17; Professor, University of Kiel, 1921-22; Professor, University of Vienna, 1922-36. Visiting Professor, Stanford University, California, 1929. *Died* (in Vienna) *22 June 1936.*

PUBLICATIONS

Philosophy

Über die Reflexion des Lichtes in einer unhomogenen Schicht. Berlin, Francke, 1904.
Lebensweisheit: Versuch einer Glückseligkeitslehre. Munich, Beck, 1908.
Raum und Zeit in der gegenwärtigen Physik: Zur Einführung in der Verständnis der Relativitäts-und Gravitationstheorie. Berlin, Springer, 1919; revised edition, 1919, 1920; as *Space and Time in Contemporary Physics: An Introduction to the Theory of Relativity and Gravitation.* Oxford and New York, Oxford University Press, 1920.
Allgemeine Erkenntnislehre. Berlin, Springer, 1918; as *General Theory of Knowledge,* Vienna and New York, Springer, 1974.
Fragen der Ethik. Vienna, Springer, 1930; as *Problems of Ethics.* New York, Prentice Hall, 1939.
Gesammelte Aufsätze 1926-1936. Vienna, Gerold, 1938.
Gesetz, Kausalität, und Wahrscheinlichkeit. Vienna, Gerold, 1948.
Grundzüge der Naturphilosophie, edited by W. Hollitscher and J. Rauscher. Vienna, Gerold, 1948; as *Philosophy of Nature,* New York, Philosophical Library, 1949.
Kultur und Natur. Vienna, Humboldt, 1952.
Aphorismen. Vienna, n.p., 1962.
Philosophical Papers, edited by Henk L. Mulder and Barbara F.B. van de Velde-Schlick. Dordrecht, Reidel, 2 vols., 1978-79.

Other

Editor, with Paul Hertz, *Schriften zur Erkenntnistheorie,* by Hermann von Helmholtz. Berlin, Springer, 1921.

*

Bibliography: in *Philosophical Papers,* 1978-79.

*   *   *

A small number of thinkers, mostly trained in the physical sciences, with strong tendencies to take seriously only empirical and verifiable reasoning, gathered in Vienna in the 1920's. They included Otto Neurath, Rudolph Carnap, Friedrich Waismann, Hans Hahn, Kurt Gödel, Herbert Feigl, and others. Moritz Schlick had recently come from Kiel to be professor of philosophy, and it was around him that the group gathered. In 1922 this group constituted themselves "Logical Positivists"; and therewith they became, no longer just a club, but a major movement in European culture. Schlick had begun to write in his twenties and his *Allgemeine Erkenntnislehre* mapped in 1918 the limits of knowledge. His thought was firm and declaratory, and it argued on erstwhile new logical grounds, provided by an assessment of the physical sciences, that the metaphysics of old was an immature predecessor of science.

When Wittgenstein's *Tractatus* was published in 1921, this group tried to assimilate its teachings. In contrast to Schlick, Wittgenstein argued that metaphysics was excluded by the essential nature of language itself. But it was probably true that Schlick's work, both as editor, mentor, and theorist of knowledge, was more formative of the positivistic attitudes than was Wittgenstein's, which though more dramatic and powerful, hinted at something else. Furthermore, Schlick was an organizer of thoughts and enthusiasms. A manifesto in 1929 (*The Vienna Circle: Its Scientific Outlook*) declared a position and a program of problems to be resolved; an international congress was organized in 1929 in Prague followed by others in Königsberg, Copenhagen, Paris, etc.; a journal was rejuvenated under the title *Erkenntnis*; then a series of monographs under the provocative title *Unified Science* began to appear. All of these owed a great deal to Schlick. Schlick's unfortunate death in 1936 by the hands of a student plus the enforced exile of the majority of the group during the late 1930's led to a dissipating of the logical positivism movement.

Schlick was a bold thinker. He believed that an end had come to the fruitless conflict of philosophical systems, that there is no domain of philosophical truths, that philosophy is an activity through which the meaning of statements is revealed, that meaning depends upon there being a verifiable difference, that "protocol statements" (stating with certainty the facts, and with absolute simplicity) are the only "foundations" we need for knowledge. When all of that is put together with moral concerns, then we find Schlick saying that ethics is a factual science, that we must discover the causes of human actions, that the methods of ethics now have to be those of an empirical kind of psychological behaviorism.

Little wonder, then, that Schlick forged both a scheme of programmatic ideas and a group-spirit that made positivism anti-clerical and anti-tradition, but also revivified philosophy for America, Great Britain, and Scandinavia as well as Germany and Austria.

—Paul Holmer

SCHOENBERG, Arnold (Franz Walter). American composer and musical theorist. Born in Vienna, Austria, 3 September 1874; emigrated to the United States in 1933; naturalized, 1941. Largely self-educated. Served in the Austrian Army in 1916. Married Mathilde Zemlinsky in 1901, 2 children; married Gertrud Kolisch in 1923, 3 children. Taught composition at the Stern Conservatory, Berlin, 1902-03 and 1911-14. With Alexander von Zemlinsky founded the Vereinigung Schaffender Tonkünstler in Vienna, 1904; founded the Society for Private Musical Performances in 1919. Taught composition at the Prussian Academy of Arts, Berlin, 1925-32, and at the Malkin Conservatory, Boston, 1933; taught privately in Hollywood, California, 1934-36; Lec-

turer, University of Southern California, Los Angeles; Professor of Composition, University of California, Los Angeles, 1936-44. President, International Mahler League, 1920-21. Honorary President, Israel Academy of Music, 1951. *Died* (in Los Angeles) *13 July 1951.*

PUBLICATIONS

Music

Harmonielehre. Vienna, Universal, 1911; abridged version as *Theory of Harmony*, New York, Philosophical Library, 1948; complete version, Los Angeles, University of California Press, and London, Faber, 1978.
Models for Beginners in Composition. New York, Schirmer, 1943; revised version, edited by Leonard Stein, Los Angeles, Belmont, 1972.
Style and Idea. New York, Philosophical Library, 1950; London, Williams and Norgate, 1951; revised edition, New York, St. Martin's Press, and London, Faber, 1975.
Structural Functions of Harmony, edited by Humphrey Searle. London, Williams and Norgate, and New York, Norton, 1954; revised version, Norton, and London, Benn, 1969.
Preliminary Exercises in Counterpoint, edited by Leonard Stein. London, Faber, 1963; New York, St. Martin's Press, 1964.
Schöpferische Konfessionen, edited by Willi Reich. Zurich, Arche, 1964.
Fundamentals of Musical Composition, edited by Gerald Strange. London, Faber, and New York, St. Martin's Press, 1964.
Gesammelte Schriften, edited by I. Vojtech. Frankfurt, Fischer, 1976-.

Other

Briefe, edited by Erwin Stein. Mainz, Schott, 1958; enlarged edition as *Letters*, New York, St. Martin's Press, and London, Faber, 1964.
Testi poetici e drammatical, edited by L. Rognoni. Milan, Feltrinelli, 1967.
Arnold Schönberg-Franz Schreker Briefwechsel, edited by F.C. Heller. Tutzing, Schneider, 1974.
Berliner Tagebuch, edited by Josef Rufer. Frankfurt, Propyläen, 1974.
Arnold Schönberg-Wassily Kandinsky: Briefe, Bilder und Dokumente, edited by Jelena Hahl-Koch. Vienna, Residenz, 1980.

*

Critical Studies: *Schönberg and His School* by Rene Leibowitz, New York, Philosophical Library, 1949; *Schoenberg: A Critical Biography* by Willi Reich, New York, Praeger, 1971; *Schönberg* by Charles Rosen, New York, Viking Press, and London, Collins, 1976; *Schoenberg* by Malcolm MacDonald, London, Dent, 1976; *Schönberg: His Life, World, and Work* by Hans Stuckenschmidt, New York, Schirmer, 1978; *Schoenberg Remembered: Diaries and Recollections (1938-1976)* by Dika Newlin, New York, Pendragon, 1980.

*

Schoenberg's major compositions include the opera *Moses und Aron* (1932); *Five Orchestral Pieces* (1909); *Pierrot Lunaire* (1912); *Concerto for Violin and Orchestra* (1935), and four string quartets (1905-36). For a full list of his compositions, see the bibliography which follows O.W. Neighbour's essay in *The New Grove Dictionary of Music and Musicians*, London, Macmillan, vol. 16, 1980.

*   *   *

Arnold Schoenberg, whose "Method of Composing with Twelve Tones related only to one another" consummated the liquidation of the tonal system that had governed the texture and structure of Western music for some three hundred years, was also an incisive author, accomplished painter, and, above all, imaginative teacher who counted among his devoted students some of this century's finest composers, including Anton von Webern and Alban Berg, often grouped with him as the Second or New Viennese School to distinguish them from their "classical" predecessors. The son of small-time Jewish merchants of Hungarian and Bohemian origins, Schoenberg, though converted to Protestantism in 1898, professed his life-long deep attachment to the Old Testament and the Jewish people well before he did so officially as a refugee in Paris in a ceremony witnessed by, among others, the painter Marc Chagall. Religious motives inspired an abortive symphonic project as early as 1912, just ahead of the surrealistic melodramas of *Pierrot Lunaire* and the theosophically inspired opera *Die Glückliche Hand* (The Golden Hand). The unfinished oratorio *Die Jakobsleiter* (Jacob's Ladder), written for the most part in 1917 after his medical discharge from the Austrian army, then initiated that central group of sacred works which reached its apogee with the equally unfinished opera *Moses und Aron* and ended with the choral pieces gathered shortly before his death in the final Opus 50.

Meanwhile, the as-yet-unperformed spoken drama *Der Biblische Weg* (The Biblical Road), which occupied Schoenberg primarily in 1926-27, served to crystallize his rather personal position with regard to Jewish nationhood. He had grown up in the Vienna of Theodor Herzl, on the one hand, and of Karl Kraus on the other and, like the latter, had at first chosen the path of assimilation. The year 1923, however, brought not only Hitler's Munich Putsch attempt but also largely unfounded rumors of anti-Semitic remarks by his close friend, the painter Wassily Kandinsky, who had urged him to join the *Bauhaus* circle in Dessau. In a remarkably prophetic letter addressed to Kandinsky on May 4, 1923, Schoenberg as much as predicted the deluge that was to engulf European Jewry a decade later, when in fact he decided to put aside all artistic projects and devoted himself for a while full-time to political activity on behalf of his fellow Nazi victims. *A Survivor from Warsaw*, for speaker, male chorus, and orchestra, composed in 1947 after the destruction of European Jewry at the hands of the Nazis, stands in a class by itself as the only musical work which, in its explosive brevity, has managed to come to grips with modern man's unprecedented inhumanity to man.

Schoenberg has been called "the conservative revolutionary" by one of his best informed biographers. Yet, in historical perspective, the 20th century's most original musician-thinker has little of the conservative or, for that matter, the revolutionary. He was, rather, an unreformed radical whose uniquely diverse oeuvre marks an extended evolutionary stage in the millenial tradition of Western art music, triggered by post-Wagnerian harmonic excesses that had begun to threaten its very existence. Schoenberg grasped his historical mandate, which he conceived as given by "the Supreme Commander," at first instinctively but soon with rare intellectual insight and proceeded to act accordingly with unswerving consistency, determined to renew the tradition to which he felt so deeply indebted by restoring melodic-rhythmic forces to their once-preponderant position from which they had been displaced by the early 19th-century tyranny of the square phrase no less than the subsequent reign of chromatic harmony. Largely self-taught under the aegis of practicing musician-philosophers like Oscar Adler and composer-conductors like his eventual brother-in-law, Alexander von Zemlinsky, Schoenberg never suffered from academic inhibitions, let alone the taboos that so seriously interfered with dynamic change in music at the leading conservatories.

His celebrated or, as the case may be, notorious Method of Composing with Twelve Tones, revealed first about 1923 in a number of keyboard and chamber works, before it was subjected to various verbal elaborations for the benefit of his growing circle of students both in Vienna and Berlin, merely systematizes his own compositional practice in the light of long-held views concerning the importance of logic and coherence in the projection of musical thoughts, whatever the style in question. As his ubiquitous references to "musical thought" amply suggest, Schoenberg adamantly refused to distinguish between creative inspiration and mere craftsmanship in the conventional sense. Instead, he liked to cite his favorite author Balzac to the effect that "the heart belongs to the domain of the head." And it was this, his allegedly "Jewish intellectualism," concealed in many a tightly written programmatic statement, that incurred the wrath of racially biased conservative opponents like Hans Pfitzner, the composer of the cantata *Von deutscher Seele* (Of the German Soul).

The customary historical classification of Schoenberg as a musical expressionist has only limited applicability, at most to his atonal works so-called, which belong for the most part to the 15-year period preceding the formulation of the Method of Composing with Twelve Tones. Thus in 1909, at a time when Sigmund Freud's stress on deep-seated psychological impulses had begun to leave profound imprints on verbal and pictorial art, at the inevitable expense of supposedly immutable formal principles, Schoenberg's "monodrama" *Erwartung* was designed so as "to represent in *slow motion* everything that occurs during a single second of maximum spiritual excitement, stretching it out to half an hour, whereas in *Die glückliche Hand* a major drama is compressed into about 20 minutes, as if photographed with a time-exposure." Even then, however, *Pierrot Lunaire*, those 21 short pieces for "speaking voice" and chamber ensemble, in which his arch-rival Igor Stravinsky saw the "solar plexus" of modern music, thrives on that overriding concern for melodic "line" over harmonic "mass" which spoke so directly to painters like Kandinsky and Marc, to whose *Blaue Reiter* group Schoenberg was drawn during the immediate pre-World War I period, contributing music and essays as well as paintings to its publications, concerts and exhibits. The Method of Composing with Twelve Tones, in turn, evokes ready associations with contemporaneous theories of relativity, since it recognizes no essential difference between time and space, based, as it is, on the virtual interchangeability of original motivic forms and their retrogrades, mirror inversions, and pitch transpositions. In so doing, of course, Schoenberg merely reasserted in 20th-century terms what had been taken for granted in truly polyphonic music from its late-medieval beginnings on. The unfaltering consistency of his fundamental insights, moreover, received dramatic confirmation in the surprising conclusion of his *Theory of Harmony* of 1911. After exploring every possible avenue left to tonal harmony, this remarkable book, "learned from my students" and dedicated to the memory of Gustav Mahler, ends with a plea for "Farben-Melodie" (Color Melody) as the logical way of the future.

Schoenberg was a prolific author, providing his own texts for most of his important vocal works and writing poetry of considerable merit, like the "Moderne Psalmen" of his last years. In addition, he addressed a broad range of artistic, philosophical, and political issues in numerous cogent essays produced over a period of nearly half a century, not to speak of a lifetime reflected in hundreds of remarkable letters exchanged with contemporaries all over the world. Finally, though little known as such, he was the inventor of a variety of ingenious games and devices, quite in keeping with a mind that left no possible stone unturned when challenged by a problem the solution of which he felt was well within his reach. In short, Arnold Schoenberg was a many-faceted, indomitably individualistic artist-philosopher whose position in 20th-century culture exceeds the conventional limits of any vocation and/or profession, a genuinely original thinker who, as his friend Kandinsky recognized as early as 1910, combined "great freedom with profound faith in the lawful development of the human spirit."

—Alexander L. Ringer

SCHOLEM, Gershom (Gerhard). Israeli historian of religion. Born in Berlin, 5 December 1897; emigrated to Palestine in 1923. Studied at the University of Berlin, 1915-17; University of Jena, 1917-18; University of Bern, 1918-19; University of Munich, Ph.D. 1922. Married Fania Freud in 1936. Head of Department of Hebraica and Judaica, University Library, Hebrew University of Jerusalem, 1923-27; Lecturer, 1925-33, Professor of Jewish Mysticism, 1933-65, and since 1965 Professor Emeritus, Hebrew University of Jerusalem. Visiting Professor, Jewish Institute of Religion, New York, 1938, 1949; Brown University, Providence, Rhode Island, 1956-57. Vice-President, 1962-68, and since 1968 President, Israel National Academy of Science and Humanities. Recipient: State Prize of Israel, 1958; Rothschild Prize, 1962. Honorary doctorate: Hebrew Union College and Jewish Institute of Religion, New York. *Died* (in Jerusalem) *20 February 1982.*

PUBLICATIONS

Theology

Bibliografia Kabbalistica: Verzeichnis der Gedruckten die jüdische Mystik (Gnosis, Kabbala, Sabbatianismus, Frankismus, Chassidismus) behandelnden Bücher und Aufsätze von Reuchlin bis zur Gegenwart. Leipzig, Drugulin, 1927.
Halomotav shel ha-Shabtai R. Mordekhai Ashkenazi [The Dreams of R. Mordecai Ashkenazi, a Follower of Shabbetai Zevi]. Jerusalem, Shocken, 1938.
Major Trends in Jewish Mysticism. Jerusalem, Schocken, 1941; New York, Schocken, 1946; London, Thames and Hudson, 1955.
Reshit ha-Kabbala [The Beginning of Kabbala]. Jerusalem, Schocken, 1948.
Parashat ha-Shabta'ut: harsa'a ba 'arikhat Rivka Shin [The Case of Sabbetianism]. Jerusalem, Hebrew University, 1955.
Shabta'i Tsvi veha-tenu 'a ha-Shabta'it bi-ymei hayyav. Tel-Aviv, 'Am 'Oved, 1957; as *Sabbatai Sevi: The Mystical Messiah, 1626-1676,* London, Routledge, and Princeton, New Jersey, Princeton University Press, 1973.
Zur Kabbala und ihrer Symbolik. Zurich, Rhein-Verlag, 1960; as *On the Kabbalah and Its Symbolism,* London, Routledge, and New York, Schocken, 1965.
Reshit ha-Kabbala ve-Sefer ha-Bahir [The Beginning of the Kabbalah and Sefer ha-Bahir]. Jerusalem, Mif'al ha-Shikhpul, 1962.
Ursprung und Anfänge der Kabbala. Berlin, De Gruyter, 1962.
Von der mystischen Gestalt der Gottheit: Studien zur Grundbegriffen der Kabbala. Zurich, Rhein-Verlag, 1962.
Ha-Kabbala be-Provans [The Kabbala in Provence]. Jerusalem, Hebrew University, 1963.
Ha-Kabbala be-Geronah [The Kabbala in Ger ona]. Jerusalem, Mif'al ha-Shikhpul, 1964.
Ha-Kabbalah shel Sefer ha-Temuna ve-shel Avraham Abul 'afiyah...'arakh Y Ben-Shlomo [The Kabbala of Sefer ha-Temura and of Avraham Abul-afiah]. Jerusalem, Akademon, 1965.
Jewish Gnosticism, Merkabah Mysticism, and Talmudic Tradition. New York, Jewish Theological Seminary of America, 1968.
Über einige Grundbegriffe des Judentums. Frankfurt, Suhrkamp, 1970.
The Messianic Idea in Judaism and Other Essays on Jewish Spirituality. London, Allen and Unwin, and New York, Schocken, 1971.
Kabbalah. Jerusalem, Keter, and New York, Quadrangle, 1974.
Meh karim u-mekorot le-toldot ha-Shabta'ut ve-gilguleyha [Studies and Texts Concerning the History of Sabbetianism and Its Metamorphoses]. Jerusalem, Mosad Bialik, 1974.
Devarim be-go: Pirkei morasha u-tehiyya [Explications and

Implications]. Tel-Aviv, Am Over, 1975.
On Jews and Judaism in Crisis: Selected Essays. New York, Schocken, 1976.

Other

Walter Benjamin: Die Geschichte einer Freundschaft. Frankfurt, Suhrkamp, 1975; as *Walter Benjamin: The Story of a Friendship,* Philadelphia, Jewish Publishing Society of America, 1981.
Von Berlin nach Jerusalem: Jugenderinnerungen. Frankfurt, Suhrkamp, 1977; as *From Berlin to Jerusalem: Memories of My Youth,* New York, Schocken, 1980.
Avraham Kohen Herera, ba'al "Sha 'ar ha-Shamayin" [Abraham Cohen Herrera]. Jerusalem, Mosad Bialik, 1978.
Briefwechsel 1933-1940: Walter Benjamin, Gershom Scholem. Frankfurt, Suhrkamp, 1980.

Editor, *Das Buch Bahir: Ein Schriftdenkmal aus der Frühzeit der Kabbala auf Grund der kritischen Neuausgabe.* Leipzig, Drugulin, 1923.

Editor, *Das Buch Bahir, Sepher ha-Bahir: Ein Text aus der Frühzeit, auf Grund eines kritischen Textes ins Deutsche übersetzt und kommentiert.* Berlin, Scholem, 1923.
Editor, *Kitvei ha-yad ha-'ivriyim ha-nimtsa'im be-Veit ha-Sefarim ha-Le'umi veha Universita' i bi-Yrushalayim* [The Hebrew Manuscripts Found in the National and University Library of Jerusalem]. Jerusalem, Hevrah le-hosa'at sefarim 'al-yad ha-Universita ha-'Ivrit, 1934.
Editor, *Die Geheimnisse der Schöpfung: Ein Kapitel aus dem Sohar.* Berlin, Suhrkamp, 1935.
Editor, *Be-'ikov mashiah, 'osef mekorot me-reshit hitpathut ha-'emuna ha-Shabta'it: Melukkatim mittokh ketavav shel R. Avraham Binyamin Natan ben Elisha'Hayyim Ashkenazi he-mekhunne Natan Ha-'Azzati* [In the Footsteps of Messiah: A Collection of Sources from the Beginning of the Development of the Shabtaian Belief]. Jerusalem, Sifrei Tarshish, 1944.
Editor, *Zohar, the Book of Splendor.* New York, Schocken, 1949.
Editor, *Mysticism and Society.* Cincinnati, Hebrew Union College and Jewish Institute of Religion, 1966.
Editor, *Kabbalistes chrétiens.* Paris, Michel, 1979.

Translator, *In der Gemeinschaft der Frommen: Sechs Erzählungen aus dem hebräischen,* by Samuel Joseph Agnon. Berlin, Schocken, 1933.

*

Bibliography: *Bibliografya shel kitvei Gershom Scholem* by Mochè Catane, Jerusalem, Magnes, 1977.

Critical Study: *Gershom Scholem: Kabbalah and Counter-History* by David Biale, Cambridge, Massachusetts, Harvard University Press, 1979.

*   *   *

Gershom Scholem, founder of the modern critical-historical study of Jewish mysticism, was noted especially for his knowledge, elucidation, and interpretation of Kaballah. He brought to his researches a keen philosophical and theological mind, a mastery of modern critical-historical methods, and a facility in the languages of the basic documents. When Scholem began his studies in Jewish mysticism he found that generally it had not been taken seriously as a subject for sound critical scholarship. He discovered an astounding amount of ignorance, even among those who professed to be experts in the field, and a good deal of prejudice, especially among Jewish scholars wedded to Enlightenment rationalism. On the other hand, there were enthusiastic protagonists of Kaballah, inspired by various Romantic, visionary, or mystical aspirations, but lacking critical scholarly criteria or concerns.

Scholem's approach was entirely different from that of the passionate detractors and admirers of Jewish mysticism. He set out first to master the texts, using careful philological methods to ascertain their authenticity, provenance, dating, etc., then moved toward an interpretation and understanding of them as expressions of significant religious experiences and ideas, and finally to the history of the various phases and movements in their interconnections with one another and with the surrounding non-Jewish religious culture. The title of probably his best-known work, *Major Trends in Jewish Mysticism*, indicates what he was accomplishing—nothing less than a history of Jewish mysticism, based on close textual studies and a remarkably creative interpretation and synthesis.

Scholem's was no merely narrow specialized interest, nor was his motivating concern a merely spectatorial one. He was at home in the Biblical and Rabbinic strands of the Judaic tradition, a master of Talmud and Midrash as well as of the mystical writings. His view of Judaism was a very broad, pluralistic one, open to all the phenomena and movements in the actual living history of the Jewish people, no matter how anomalous or repellent they might seem to what had become established points of view. Thus he held that Kaballah and the heretical Sabbatian and Frankist movements (17th and 18th centuries) constituted an essential, vital factor in the development of Judaism, an authentic element of the ongoing Jewish tradition. Although Gnosticism had long been generally considered a non-Judaic or anti-Judaic phenomenon, Scholem held that there was an original, authentic Jewish Gnosticism, with some probable links to certain Rabbinic texts. So also with myth, also conventionally labeled non-Judaic or anti-Judaic, which he found to be a central, vital factor in Judaism. And he even found a place for magic, especially in its theurgical form, in the Judaic tradition, against the conventional doctrine that, along with *gnosis*, it was the enemy of Judaism.

Not content merely with a careful critical-historical interpretation of Kaballah as basically a speculative theosophical system based on Gnostic mythical themes, Scholem went on to a daring linkage of 16th-century Lurianic Kaballah and the later heretical Sabbatian movement to modern Jewish reform and revolutionary movements. Thus Lurianic Kaballah's emphasis on human action—specifically the action of the Jewish people through Torah observances—to restore man, the universe, and God to wholeness is viewed as a constructive symbolistic response to the traumatic situation of Jewry following the expulsion of the Jews from Spain. And the Sabbatian movement, centered on the apostate false Messiah, Sabbatai Zevi, despite its radically destructive stance toward traditional Jewish values, is viewed as a significant pre-intimation of the Jewish Enlightenment, Reform Judaism and even Zionism—as signaling the re-entry of the Jews and Judaism into the larger historical world. Despite the repellent and assimilationist aspects of Sabbatianism and its offshoots, such as Frankism, Scholem saw positive and constructive elements in them, which could more easily be grasped by a 20th-century Zionist than by the typical 19th-century Jewish bourgeois mind.

Scholem's scholarly achievement was not only the product of his great intellectual gifts, but was motivated by a passionate concern for the national, spiritual, and cultural regeneration of the Jewish people. His originality in scholarship and thought proceeded out of an early independence of spirit that took him from the assimilated Germanic atmosphere of his familial home to a lifelong commitment to Jewish tradition, culture, and nationhood. At an early age he became an adherent of Zionism as the vehicle of Jewish national renewal, and he emigrated to Palestine shortly after he received his Ph.D. There he established a world-famous center for the study of Jewish mysticism and Kaballah at Hebrew University of Jerusalem. At no time did he become a narrowly ideological or chauvinistic historian, for his Zionism was basically spiritual, cultural, and non-political. With such figures as Judah Magnes and Martin Buber, he was an adherent of the movement for Arab-Jewish rapprochement.

Something of the richness, complexity and provocative paradoxes of Scholem's thought may be gained from his treatment of Jewish Messianism, to which he devoted decades of searching studies (collected in his *The Messianic Idea in Judaism*). There he asserts that the essential and distinguishing tenet of Jewish Messianism is that redemption must occur in empirical, publicly visible, historical actuality, not as an inner spiritual event to be grasped through recondite symbolical interpretation. Yet that sweeping assertion becomes qualified as he recognizes the utopian element in Apocalyptic and later forms of Messianism, which are emphatically ahistorical and transhistorical. But then Scholem insists that utopian Messianism aims at a totality that includes both the inner/spiritual and the outer/historical realms. So also with the quite different Messianism of medieval rationalism (e.g., Maimonides), which stresses historical restoration rather than a uniquely new state of things, as in utopian Messianism, but yet paradoxically ahistorical in its basic thought. And in Lurianic Kaballah, as noted, the historical and transhistorical are linked through a symbolical interpretation of the exile and sufferings of the Jewish people. But in 18th-century Hasidism the emphasis on individual salvation here and now led to an allegorization of basic Judaic concepts, in which historical and national terms became images for inward states, abandoning the essential national-historical element of Jewish Messianism.

Scholem had his own problems and paradoxes in responding to the fact and spirit of Jewish Messianism. It exerted an enormous attraction on him, and he found an especial value in its "totalistic" combination of emphases on this-worldly fulfillment and transhistorical spirituality. Moreover, he discerned a vital, energizing factor even in the most extreme forms of utopian-apocalyptic Messianism, which he saw as letting fresh air into the musty house of Rabbinic Judaism. Yet, as he considered the long history of the Jewish people in exile, he saw the grandeurs and splendors of Jewish Messianism being paid for by an enormous price: historical powerlessness, the devaluation of the present moment, a state of constant incompletion, "a life lived in deferment." And he saw in modern Zionism obvious traces of the Messianic tradition, but with a concentration on historical fulfillment and a foregoing of the metahistorical aspect of Messianism. Yet he was deeply concerned about the spiritual danger of viewing political and military developments as signs of divine redemption, noxiously confusing the political and theological realms.

—Seymour Cain

SCHRÖDINGER, Erwin. Austrian physicist. Born in Vienna, 12 August 1887. Studied at the University of Vienna, 1906-10. Served as an artillery officer in World War I. Married Annamarie Bertel in 1920. Lecturer, University of Vienna, 1914-20; Professor, universities of Jena, Stuttgart, and Breslau, 1920-21; Professor, University of Zurich, 1921-27; Professor, University of Berlin, 1927-33; Fellow of Magdalen College, Oxford, 1936-38; Director, School of Theoretical Physics, Dublin Institute for Advanced Study, 1940-56; Professor Emeritus of Theoretical Physics, University of Vienna, 1956-61. Recipient: Nobel Prize in Physics, with P.A.M. Dirac, 1933; Matteucci Medal; Max Planck Medal. Honorary doctorate: University of Ghent; University of Dublin; University of Edinburgh. Member Academy of Science, Berlin; Academy of Science, Vienna; Academy of Science, Dublin; Academy of Science, Madrid; U.S.S.R. Academy of Science, Flemish Academy of Science; Academy of Science, Vatican City; Academy of Science, Lima, Peru; Accademia dei Lincei, Rome; Accademia dei Quaranta, Rome. Foreign Member,

Royal Society, London, 1949. Litteria et Artibus, Austria. Order of Merit, Germany. *Died 4 January 1961.*

PUBLICATIONS

Physics

Abhandlungen zur Wellenmechanik. Leipzig, Barth, 1927; as *Collected Papers on Wave Mechanics*, London, Blackie, 1928.
Four Lectures on Wave Mechanics. London, Blackie, 1928.
Über Indeterminismus in der Physik; Ist die Naturwissenschaft milieubedingt? Zwei Vorträge zur Kritik der naturwissenschaftlichen Erkenntnis. Leipzig, Barth, 1932.
Science and the Human Temperament. London, Allen and Unwin, and New York, Norton, 1935; enlarged edition as *Science, Theory, and Man*, New York, Dover, 1957; Allen and Unwin, 1958.
What Is Life? The Physical Aspect of the Living Cell. London, Cambridge University Press, 1944.
Statistical Thermodynamics (lectures). London, Cambridge University Press, 1946.
Space-Time Structure. London, Cambridge University Press, 1950.
Science and Humanism: Physics in Our Time. London, Cambridge University Press, 1951.
Nature and the Greeks. London, Cambridge University Press, 1954.
Expanding Universes. London, Cambridge University Press, 1956.
What Is Life? and Other Scientific Essays. New York, Doubleday, 1956.
Mind and Matter. London, Cambridge University Press, 1958.
Was ist ein Naturgesetz? Beiträge zum naturwissenschaftlichen Weltbild. Munich, Oldenbourg, 1962.
Briefe zur Wellenmechanik. Vienna, Springer, 1963.

Other

Gedichte. Godesberg, Kupper, 1949.
Meine Weltansicht. Hamburg, Zsolnay, 1961; as *My View of the World*, London, Cambridge University Press, 1964.

*

Critical Study: *Erwin Schrödinger: An Introduction to His Writings*, by William T. Scott, Amherst, University of Massachusetts Press, 1967 (includes bibliography).

*   *   *

Erwin Schrödinger's wave mechanics is the heart of modern quantum theory, and has served as the pattern for our current theories of elementary particles and basic universal forces. Quantum theory has revolutionized the physicist's conception of the world, but wave mechanics itself was created in an attempt to turn back this revolution. Schrödinger's understanding of the purpose and method of physics was rooted in the classic 19th-century descriptive tradition: the purpose is to describe the way that physical objects move and interact in space and time, the method, to construct mechanical models of these objects and processes and to uncover the laws that govern these motions and interactions. During and immediately following the First World War, physics had begun to move away from this descriptive tradition. Niels Bohr's theory of atomic structure said that electrons make apparently uncaused and instantaneous leaps from one orbit to another in the atom. In the early 1920's, as it became clear that Bohr's theory was inadequate to explain certain atomic phenomena, many of Bohr's followers began to argue that the way to find a better theory of the atom was to make an even more radical break with the classic tradition. One must give up entirely the aim of describing motions in the atom, urged Max Born, Werner Heisenberg, and Wolfgang Pauli, since such motions are forever unobservable. Rather, one must retreat to a search for a theory involving only the "observable properties" of the atom. For Schrödinger, however, to give up the idea that "atomic events can even be described in the space-time form of thought... [is] equivalent to a complete surrender." (This statement is from the second of Schrödinger's original papers on wave mechanics.) Taking his cue from the young Louis de Broglie, Schrödinger began to explore the possibility of obtaining a descriptive account of atomic processes by supposing that matter consists not of tiny bits of mass and charge, but of widely spread and continually pulsating waves. In his search for a mathematical characterisation of these matter waves, Schrödinger adopted the typical 19th-century method of constructing a wave equation. Just as one solves for the unknown x in an algebraic equation, one solves for the unknown ψ in a wave equation. The solution is not a number, as in algebra, but a function $\psi(x, y, z)$ whose value at each point (x, y, z) is the height or "amplitude" of the wave at that point. It was on the basis of his wave equation for matter that Schrödinger developed, in early 1926, a wave mechanics for the atom. (See Schrödinger's Nobel Prize address, reprinted in *Science, Theory, and Man*, for a very readable account of his original vision of matter as waves, and of the way that wave mechanics was meant to capture that vision.)

The revolutionary character of Schrödinger's theory was not immediately apparent. As might be expected, Bohr's followers were the first to argue that wave mechanics can only be understood as a quantum theory that fails to provide any spatio-temporal description of the atomic and subatomic domains. For several years Schrödinger fought to save his interpretation of the theory as a description of wave motions. The difficulties he faced were formidable, however. For example, once he had tailored his wave mechanics so that it gave correct experimental predictions, he found that the ψ function will not have just real numbers as its values, but must also be allowed to take imaginary numbers as values. What sense can one make of a physical wave with an amplitude measured in imaginary numbers? Just when Schrödinger thought he had found a way of getting around this problem by taking the square of the ψ function as the amplitude of the physical wave (when properly defined, the square will always be real), another problem arose. Recognizing that at times (e.g., when not in an atom) an electron can be observed to behave very much like a small particle, Schrödinger had proposed that at such times the electron wave "bunches up" so that it has negligibly small amplitude everywhere except in a small particle-sized region. The small region is called a wave packet. Schrödinger was even able to show mathematically that a wave packet of just the right sort to simulate a classical particulate electron can occur. In mid-1926, however, it was further shown that a wave packet formed from ψ waves will never stay very small for very long. The wave will unbunch and the packet spread out in a time period much shorter than the periods for which the electron is known to retain its small particulate size. At about the same time other difficulties for Schrödinger's wave picture began to emerge, and, in addition, Max Born developed an alternative interpretation of Schrödinger's ψ function. According to Born, ψ does not represent a physical thing but is only a device for calculating probabilities. The square of $\psi(x, y, z)$ is not the amplitude at point (x, y, z) of an electron wave, but gives the probability of finding the electron at point (x, y, z). Further elaboration of this statistical interpretation by Bohr and Heisenberg in 1927 led to the now generally accepted Copenhagen interpretation of quantum mechanics (the more general form of wave mechanics): quantum mechanics never gives precisely both position and momentum of an object, but always contains some uncertainty in its predictions; neither the wave model nor the particle model is applicable to matter, but these are alternative and complementary modes of description; no object can have both a position and a momentum at the same time, but these concepts too must be used in a complementary way; indeed none of the spatio-temporal properties attributed to bits of matter in the classic descriptive tradition can be attributed in the usual way to the small objects of quantum theory—when atomic-sized objects are not being observed, they cannot be said to have any spatio-temporal properties; when they are being observed the spatio-temporal concepts apply, but only in the complementary way mentioned above.

It is not surprising that Schrödinger was reluctant to accept the revolutionary break from the classical world view that was apparently required by this transformed version of his own theory. In the period from 1930 to 1950, while Bohr, Born, Heisenberg, Pauli and others were extending the ideas of quantum theory to cover the nucleus, the behavior of light, and finally elementary particles, Schrödinger turned his attention to other things. The several papers he wrote on issues related to quantum theory during this time were aimed not at furthering the applicability of the theory, but at criticising the Copenhagen interpretation of the theory. Several of the years in this period were given over to the practical problems of several relocations, forced by the rise and spread of Nazi power. Schrödinger left Berlin in 1933 out of disgust and as a gesture of protest when one of his young assistants was accosted on the streets because he was Jewish. Schrödinger was able to return to his native Austria in 1937, only to be labeled *persona non grata* after Anschluss. No longer allowed to hold a university position nor legally to emigrate, Schrödinger spirited his family out of Austria, leaving behind all of his money, personal possessions, and scientific papers and library. Settled finally in Dublin, he was able to concentrate again on physics. Much of Schrödinger's research in the rest of this period was devoted to the search for a unified field theory. Few physicists of that time besides Schrödinger and Einstein thought that a unified field theory was even worth pursuing. Like Einstein, Schrödinger sought such a theory because it promised a way of bypassing the rejection of the descriptive tradition apparently required by quantum theory. In a unified field theory one might be able to portray electrons and other subatomic "particles" as regions of extreme concentration in traditionally conceived undulating fields that fill all of space. Neither Schrödinger nor Einstein (nor anyone else) succeeded in finding such a theory. (The "unified field theories" being developed today are very different in conception from those that Einstein and Schrödinger envisioned.)

By 1950 Schrödinger had given up his search for a descriptive alternative to quantum theory. He turned then to the task of convincing others to pick up the search where he had left off. In the last decade of his life Schrödinger published a series of papers containing his arguments against the Copenhagen interpretation of quantum mechanics and his own intuitive ideas on how to replace it with something like the wave interpretation with which he had begun.

It is in his work on quantum theory and unified field theory that one sees most clearly the way that Schrödinger's approach to physics was shaped by his commitment to the classic descriptive tradition. He also made significant contributions in other areas of physics, particularly in the areas of statistical mechanics and thermodynamics, and of relativity theory. Much of this work too was guided by that commitment. For example, his early work in statistical mechanics was aimed, in part, toward uncovering ways that theory and experiment could be used to determine the size and characteristics of motion of atoms and molecules. Some of his first work on Bohr's theory of the atom focused on difficulties that seem to arise when the precise orbits of atomic electrons are sought. The problem that led Schrödinger to a first successful application of de Broglie's concept of matter waves was that of finding a physical descriptive explanation of a mysterious molecular interaction that seemed to be implied by a new way of calculating the statistics of gas molecules introduced by Einstein and S.N. Bose in 1924. The mere calculation of correct experiment and predictions was only part of what physics is about, in Schrödinger's view. Equally important is the understanding of our observations that physics provides, an understanding that comes from having a full spatio-temporal description of the objects and processes that lie behind and give rise to the observable phenomena.

Schrödinger's search for understanding was not limited to physics. He wrote several volumes on the history of the very notion of scientific understanding. His investigation of what quantum mechanics might say about genetic structure and genetic mutation and stability (*What Is Life?*) had a significant impact on the development of molecular biology right after the Second World War. Schrödinger read widely in both ancient and modern literature, often in the original language. Besides English he read Greek, Latin, French, and Spanish, and while in Dublin attempted Celtic. He wrote poetry in several different languages. (Schrödinger's *Gedichte* is a collection of some of his own poems and his translations of the poetry of others.) In addition, Schrödinger read and wrote extensively on philosophy.

An insight into Schrödinger's world view and the place of science in it can be gained by looking briefly at his philosophy. Schrödinger's *My View of the World* contains two essays. One was written in 1925, shortly before he began the work on de Broglie's matter waves that led him to wave mechanics. The other was written in 1958, three years before his death. These essays are remarkably similar in style and content, and they (as well as other published and unpublished writings of Schrödinger) testify to the strong influence that Ernst Mach had on Schrödinger's thought. Early in his life Schrödinger adopted Mach's theory of neutral monism, a theory based on the assumption that the world is made up neither of physical entities, like chunks of matter or fields of energy, nor of mental entities like sensations or ideas. Rather, at bottom there are only neutral (neither physical nor mental) "elements": "the same elements go to make up both the self and the external world," wrote Schrödinger in 1925, "and in various complex forms are sometimes described as constituents of the world—things—and sometimes as constituents of the self—sensations, perceptions." The spatio-temporal descriptions which he took to be the aim in physics are not to be sought because they reflect the true and ultimate structure of reality, but because they represent a way of organizing the neutral elements that has always been the basis of communicable agreement among individuals. "The so called external world," he explained in his 1925 essay, "is built up exclusively of constituents of the ego [i.e., the neutral elements]. It is characterized by what is common to all.... This 'being-shared-by-everybody,' this community, is the one and only hall-mark of physical reality." Both Mach and Schrödinger were captivated by the similarities between this way of looking at the world and that offered by East Indian mysticism. The "idea of Mach," explained Schrödinger in 1925, "comes as near to the orthodox dogma of the Upanishads as it could possibly do without stating it *expressis verbis*. The external world and consciousness are one and the same thing, in so far as they are constituted by the same primitive elements. We are hardly using a different formula whether we express [this]... by saying that there is only *one* external world or that there is only *one* consciousness."

The man who insisted that physics give spatio-temporal descriptions of the sub-microscopic world was also the man who insisted that such spatio-temporal descriptions are nothing more than a convenient way of imposing an order on the true constituents of reality, the neutral elements. He was also the same man whose search for such spatio-temporal descriptions led to wave mechanics, one of the major advances taken by physics in this century. The complexity of Schrödinger's world view is undeniable, and equally undeniable is the significance of the contribution to science that it engendered.

—Linda Wessels

SCHUMPETER, Joseph (Alois). Czech economist. Born in Triesch, Moravia, now Czechoslovakia, 8 February 1883; emigrated to the United States, 1932. Studied at the University of Vienna, Dr. Juris. 1906; Columbia University, New York, Ph.D. 1913; University of Sofia, Ph.D. 1939. Married Elizabeth Boody in 1937. Lecturer, University of Vienna; Professor, University of Czernowitz, Ukraine; Professor, University of Graz, Austria, 1911-14; Austrian Exchange Professor, Columbia University, 1913; Austrian Minister of Finance, 1919-20; Professor, University of Bonn, 1925-32, and Harvard University, Cambridge, Massachusetts, from 1932. President, Econometric Society, 1939-41. Member, Royal Economic Society, London. *Died 8 January 1950.*

PUBLICATIONS

Economics and Sociology

Das Wesen und der Hauptinhalt der theoretischen Nationalökonomie. Leipzig, Duncker und Humblot, 1908.

Wie studiert man Sozialwissenschaften. Czernowitz, Ukraine, Kommissionsverlag H. Pardini, 1910.

Theorie der Wirtschaftlichen Entwicklung. Leipzig, Duncker und Humblot, 1912, as *The Theory of Economic Development: An Inquiry into Profits, Capital, Interest, and the Business Cycle,* Cambridge, Massachusetts, Harvard University Press, 1934.

"Epochen der Dogmen—und Methodengeschichte," in *Grundriss der Sozialökonomie.* Tübingen, Mohr, 1914; as *Economic Doctrine and Method: An Historical Sketch,* New York, Oxford University Press, and London, Allen and Unwin, 1954.

Vergangenheit und Zukunft der Sozialwissenschaften. Munich and Leipzig, Duncker und Humblot, 1915.

Zur Soziologie der Imperialismen. Tübingen, Mohr, 1919; with "Die sozialen Klassen im ethnisch homogenen Milieu" as *Imperialism and the Social Classes,* New York, A.M. Kelley, and Oxford, Blackwell, 1951.

Das deutsche Finanzproblem: Reich, Länder, Gemeinden. Berlin, Der Deutsche Volkswirt, 1928.

Business Cycles: A Theoretical, Historical, and Statistical Analysis of the Capitalist Process. New York and London, McGraw Hill, 2 vols., 1939.

Capitalism, Socialism, and Democracy. New York, Harper, 1942; London, Allen and Unwin, 1943.

Rudimentary Mathematics for Economists and Statisticians, with W.L. Crum. New York and London, McGraw Hill, 1946.

Ten Great Economists, from Marx to Keynes. New York, Oxford University Press, 1951.

Aufsätze zur ökonomischen Theorie (selected essays). Tübingen, Mohr, 1952.

Aufsätze zur Soziologie (selected essays), edited by Erich Schneider and Arthur Spiethoff. Tübingen, Mohr, 1953.

History of Economic Analysis, edited by Elizabeth Boody Schumpeter. New York, Oxford University Press, and London, Allen and Unwin, 1954.

Dogmenhistorische und biographische Aufsätze (selected essays). Tübingen, Mohr, 1954.

Das Wesen des Geldes, edited by Fritz Karl Mann. Göttingen Vandenhoeck und Ruprecht, 1970.

Other

Editor, with K. Bücher and Friedrich Freiherr von Wieser, *Wirtschaft und Wirtschaftswissenschaft.* Tübingen, Mohr, 1914.

*

Critical Studies: *Essays,* edited by Richard V. Clemence, Cambridge, Massachusetts, Addison Wesley, 1951; *Schumpeter, Social Scientist,* edited by Seymour E. Harris, Cambridge, Massachusetts, Harvard University Press, 1951; *Joseph A. Schumpeter: Leben und Werk eines grossen Sozialökonomen,* by Erich Schneider, Tübingen, Mohr, 1970.

* * *

Joseph Schumpeter's major economic and social theories are presented in three works, *The Theory of Economic Development, Business Cycles,* and *Capitalism, Socialism and Democracy.* Although he published other significant material, in particular his essay on imperialism, this trilogy set out and developed his chief ideas on capitalism and capitalist society.

The consistent concern of the Schumpeterian System was to explain the economic growth of capitalism, the cyclical nature of that growth, and the transformation of capitalist society to socialist society. In the latter area, and in his writings on imperialism, he did not approach problems exclusively in economic terms. Rather, aware that economic reality is only a part of total reality, Schumpeter often considered phenomena from a sociological or historical point of view, thus expanding and enriching his thought.

When Schumpeter began his academic career equilibrium theory dominated the field of economics, and there is no doubt that the "general" theory of the French economist L. Walras provided the point of departure for his work. Schumpeter began work on dynamic theory to explain what static theory could not—what happens when equilibrium is broken by radical changes in the method of production? Excluding disruptions of equilibrium occurring as the result of forces outside the economy, like war, his *Theory of Economic Development* concentrated on spontaneous changes in the industrial and commercial aspects of a circular flow static economy.

Economic development in this sense occurs in the following five cases set out by Schumpeter: (1) The introduction of a new good unfamiliar to consumers, or a new type of good; (2) The introduction of a new method of production, including application of a known method to another branch of manufacture or simply a new way of handling a commodity commercially; (3) The opening of a new market, including one to which a particular industry did not previously have access although that market may have already existed; (4) The opening of a new source of raw materials or half-manufactured goods, again irrespective of whether the source existed previously or is newly created; (5) The carrying out of a reorganization of an industry, as in the creation or breaking up of a monopoly or trust situation.

These five activities Schumpeter called innovations, their introduction the "entrepreneurial act," and their originator the entrepreneur, the central figure of capitalism. The innovations of the entrepreneur, which create new plants and equipment, are peculiar to development, and hence completely unknown in the state of equilibrium characterized by simple management and routine.

Profit, in this system, is the result of innovation, as when a new method allows a firm to produce a commodity more cheaply or a new market offers high prices for a previously unavailable product. Once innovations become generalized throughout an industry, however, and competition reduces the disparity between cost and price, they no longer produce profit. Even if an innovation is not generalized or competition malfunctions, allowing profit to be kept within one firm, it ceases to be a profit because no longer the result of innovation and becomes monopoly rent.

Another fundamental characteristic of economic development according to Schumpeter is credit, the entrepreneur's use of resources or savings to finance innovations embodied in new plants. Depending on the stages of capitalism such credit would be found in the accumulated savings of small firms, the development of the banking system, or from sources within large-scale firms. The presence of innovations also determined Schumpeter's definition of competition in the capitalist system, which, for him, was not the struggle between firms manufacturing the same product, but between firms in which entrepreneurial acititvty is present and those where it is not. Called "creative destruction" by Schumpeter, this competition is the effect of innovations on existing companies.

Schumpeter's ideas were amplified in *Business Cycles*, which uses a good deal of historical material and some mathematical models to demonstrate his theories. It is, he explained, the bunching together of innovations at certain times that accounts for the cyclical nature of capitalist development and the alternating periods of equilibrium and disruption of equilibrium. For certain periods dominant methods of production and "social resistances" block the introduction of innovations. But once these resistances are broken and traditional patterns of manufacture are changed, successive innovations find less resistence and there is a flood of change.

Eventually the wave of innovations spends itself as the market attempts to cope with the mass of new goods, and the increased level of debt repayments lessens profits and savings. There is then a return to equilibrium during which the economy adapts to the changes caused by innovations and reestablishes the conditions for entrepreneurial activity.

It was the time relationship between the introduction of innovation and its effect on the economy which produced, according to Schumpeter, business cycles of varying frequencies. He distinguished three cycles, each bearing the name of the economist who first identified the cycle. The longest of these cycles or waves, 54 to 60 years in duration, was named for Kondratieff. They occurred as a result of the appearance of major innovations like steam power, railroads, or electrification. Schumpeter noted that the first identifiable Kondratieff began in 1787 and lasted to 1842. His choice was determined by a combination of statistical and industrial facts mainly centering on the cotton textile and iron trades, commonly referred to as the industrial revolution. A second Kondratieff, which Schumpeter associated with railroads, began in 1842 and lasted until 1897, when the third Kondratieff associated with the innovation of electrification began.

Within the Kondratieff there are two other cycles, the medium-length Juglar cycle and the shorter Kitchin cycle. The Juglar cycle referred to the effects of individual innovations like the introduction of new machinery, such as Crompton's mule, or new products. There would be about six Juglars of about nine to ten years in each Kondratieff. In each Juglar there would be a series of three to four year Kitchin cycles associated chiefly with the accumulation and disposal of inventories.

Within each cycle Schumpeter also identified four phases—the prosperity and recession phases which were essential to capitalist development, and the depression and recovery phases. In Schumpeter's definition, the prosperity phase was a period of abstaining from consumption for the sake of investment, while the recession period was one of consuming the harvest. Since depression and recovery were phases brought on by unsound speculation and poor economic policies they could be eliminated by careful planning and policy decisions.

The bulk of Schumpeter's theories concern only the growth and functioning of capitalist economy from the late 18th century into the 20th, and he acknowledged that his theory might be rendered obsolete by trust-dominated capitalism or socialist planning. Still, he has been criticized for his misunderstanding of econometrics, his hostility to Keynesian theory as "short run" economics, and his failure to deal adequately with monopolistic competition. Thus his work is seen as "historical" with little relevance for present economies. Such criticism fails to recognize, however, that Schumpeter's attempt to construct a "model of the process of economic change in time" and "to answer the question of how the economic system generates the force which incessantly transforms it" retains its usefulness for participants and planners of economies which are responsible for the entrepreneurial-type activities that lead to self-sustaining growth.

Schumpeter was also well aware that the matter of which he spoke—capitalism—would like all other social phenomena pass from history. His theories on the decline of capitalism in *Capitalism, Socialism, and Democracy* make up a brilliant economic and sociological treatise. Schumpeter rejected the notion that contradictions in capitalism would lead to the increasing misery of the masses, or that capitalism was the cause of war and imperialism, and he believed that Marx's reduction of capitalist society to two classes defined by ownership of the means of production distorted reality and was "next to valueless for purposes of analysis."

Rather, Schumpeter credited capitalism with concentrating human energy on economic tasks, creating the rational attitude favorable to technological development, and greatly improving the condition of human society. That it would pass and be followed by socialism was not to be the result of its weaknesses, but of its success and achievements which have created the political and social climate to which it must eventually succumb.

First of all, as large-scale firms become dominant, the role of the entrepreneur whose innovations created new plants and equipment would be reduced in relation to that of the administrator of existing plants. More important, the success of capitalism creates a hostile social and intellectual environment in which its own spirit of rational egalitarianism, which earlier undermined the spiritual and political sanctions for the authority of the feudal system in order to liberate the bourgeoisie, is now turned against itself undermining the sanctions for private property, corporations, and inheritance. As the small businessmen and farmers supporting traditional, conservative ways are reduced in numbers, the protective social layers of capitalist society are stripped away and it becomes prey to that other peculiar product of its society, the intellectual, hostile and openly subversive of the social and political order. But the socialism Schumpeter saw as heir was not that of the "Gosplan" or the liberal welfare state. He felt a workable socialism must wait until the concentration of business had proceeded further and public attitudes were adjusted to it. This socialism would be democratic, although the state might have to restrict freedom and enforce social discipline, and it would be a class society operating under a centralized government which would control the economic process through a huge bureaucracy. As such, according to Schumpeter, socialism when it comes might resemble aspects of fascism.

The provocative nature of Schumpeter's thought is also apparent in his treatment of imperialism in his essay "Zur Soziologie der Imperialismen" (1919). The instinct for expansion, according to Schumpeter, developed in early warrior societies where it was necessary to survival. It is totally out of place in capitalist society which provides other means for venting aggressive tendencies and is essentially democratic, cooperative, and peaceful. Thus he felt it was a fallacy to describe imperialism as a necessary phase or development of capitalism. Rather it was an atavism, an eruption from the past. In this Schumpeter echoes Benjamin Kidd's unhappy recognition of the stirring of the "fighting pagan male of the West," and Oswald Spengler's celebration of the eternal, warlike beast-of-prey man.

Eventually Schumpeter became dissatisfied with this explanation and came to accept that even in the rational capitalist society fundamental volition arises from impulses that appear from the economic point of view to be nonrational. This opened the way to the recognition of an imperialism of a whole people such as Schumpeter had once assumed existed only among ancient peoples constantly fighting for survival.

In its early form Schumpeter's social-psychological interpretation of imperialism suggests that economic systems can condition behavior. His later amendment, unpublished, implies that rational ends do not always motivate human behavior, certain aspects of which are beyond the control of any economic or social system.

—Frank M. Baglione

SCHWEITZER, Albert. German theologian and humanitarian. Born in Kaysersberg, Haute Alsace, 14 January 1875. Studied at the University of Strasbourg, Ph.D. in philosophy, 1899, licenciate in theology, 1900, Ph.D. in theology, 1901, Ph.D. in music 1905, Doctor of Medicine, 1911. Married Helene Bresslau in 1912; 1 daughter. Vicar, St. Nicholas, Strasbourg, 1900-12; Lecturer, University of Strasbourg, 1902-12; Principal, Protestant Theological Seminary, Strasbourg, 1906; founded the hospital of the Paris Missionary Society at Lambaréné, Africa, in 1913 (between 1913 and 1959 Schweitzer made fourteen trips to Lambaréné, enlarging the hospital and working as a doctor there for periods ranging from a few months to nine years). Hibbert Lecturer, Oxford University, 1934; Gifford Lecturer, University of Edinburgh, 1934-35. Honorary doctorate: University of Zurich, 1920; University of Prague, 1925; University of Edinburgh, 1931; Oxford University, 1932; University of St. Andrews, Scotland, 1932; University of Chicago, 1949; Cambridge University, 1955. Recipient: Goethe Peace Prize, Frankfurt, 1928; German Bookdealers Peace Prize, 1951; Prince Charles Medal, Sweden, 1952; Nobel Peace Prize, 1953; German Order pour le Mérite, 1955; Sonning Prize, Denmark, 1959; Joseph-Lemaire Prize, 1959. Member, French Academy of Moral and Political Sciences, 1951. Foreign Honorary Member, American Academy of Arts and Sciences, 1954. Chevalier, Légion d'Honneur, 1950. Honorary Member, Order of Merit, 1955. *Died* (in Lambaréné) *4 September 1965.*

PUBLICATIONS

Collections

Chosakushu [Collected Works]. Tokyo, Hakasuisha, 20 vols., 1956-62.
Ausgewählte Werke. Berlin, Union Verlag, 5 vols., 1971.

Philosophy and Theology

Die Religionsphilosophie Kants von der Kritik der reinen Vernunft bis zur Religion innerhalb der Grenzen der blossen Vernunft. Freiburg, Mohr, 1899; as *The Essence of Faith: Philosophy of Religion*, New York, Philosophical Library, 1966.
Das Abendmal im Zusammenhang mit dem Leben Jesu und der Geschichte des Urchristentums. Tübingen, Mohr, 1901; selection as *The Mystery of the Kingdom of God* and *The Secret of Jesus' Messiahship and Passion*, London, Black, and New York, Dodd Mead, 1914.
Von Reimarus zu Wrede: Eine Geschichte der Leben-Jesu Forschung. Tübingen, Mohr, 1906; as *The Quest for the Historical Jesus: A Critical Study of Its Progress from Reimarus to Wrede*, London, Black, and New York, Macmillan, 1910.
Geschichte der Paulinischen Forschung von der Reformation bis auf die Gegenwart. Tübingen, Mohr, 1911; as *Paul and His Interpreters: A Critical History*, London, Black, and New York, Macmillan, 1912.
Die psychiatrische Beurteilung Jesu. Tübingen, Mohr, 1913; as *The Psychiatric Study of Jesus: Exposition and Criticism*, Boston, Beacon Press, 1948.
Christianity and the Religions of the World (lectures). London, Allen and Unwin, 1922.
Verfall und Wiederaufbau der Kultur: Kulturphilosophie. Munich, Beck, 1923; as *The Philosophy of Civilization: The Decay and Restoration of Civilization; Civilization and Ethics*, London, Black, 2 vols., 1923; New York, Macmillan, 2 vols., 1933.
Die Mystik des Apostels Paulus. Tübingen, Mohr, 1930; as *The Mysticism of the Apostle Paul*, London, Black, and New York, Holt, 1931.
Goethe (lecture). Munich, Beck, 1932.
Die Weltanschauung der indischen Denker (Mystik und Ethik).

Munich, Beck, 1934; as *Indian Thought and Its Development*, London, Hodder and Stoughton, and New York, Holt, 1935.
Goethe: Drei Reden, edited by C.H. Beck. Munich, Biederstein, 1949; as *Goethe*, London, 1949.
Goethe: Five Studies. Boston, Beacon Press, 1951.
Die Lehre der Ehrfurcht vor dem Leben. Berlin, Union Verlag, 1963; as *The Teaching of Reverence for Life*, New York, Holt Reinhart, 1965.
Die Lehre von der Ehrfurcht vor dem Leben: Gundtexte aus fünf Jahrzehnten. Munich, Beck, 1966.
Strassburger Predigten, edited by Ulrich Neuenschwander. Munich, Beck, 1966; as *Reverence for Life*, New York, Harper, 1969; London, SPCK, 1970.
Reich Gottes und Christentum, edited by Ulrich Neuenschwander. Tübingen, Mohr, 1967; as *The Kingdom of God and Primitive Christianity*, London, Black, and New York, Seabury Press, 1968.
Was sollen wir tun?, edited by Martin Strege and Lothar Stiehm (sermons). Heidelberg, Schneider, 1974.

Other

Eugène Munch, 1857-1895. Milhausen, Brinkmann, 1898.
J.S. Bach le musicien-poète, with Hubert Gillot. Leipzig, Breitkopf and Härtel, 1905; as *Johann Sebastian Bach* (in English), London, Breitkopf and Hartel, 1911.
Deutsche und französische Orgelbaukunst und Orgelkunst. Leipzig, Breitkopf and Härtel, 1906.
J.S. Bach. Leipzig, Breitkopf and Härtel, 1908.
Mitteilungen von Prof. Dr. Albert Schweitzer aus Lambaréné. Strasbourg, Schauberg, 1913.
Zwischen Wasser und Urwelt: Erlebnisse und Beobachtungen eines Arztes im Urwalde Äquatorialafrikas. Berne, Haupt, 1921; as *On the Edge of the Primeval Forest: The Experiences and Observations of a Doctor in Equatorial Africa*, London, Black, and New York, Macmillian, 1922.
Aus meiner Kindheit und Jugendzeit. Munich, Beck, 1924; as *Memoirs of Childhood and Youth*, London, Allen and Unwin, 1924; New York, Macmillan, 1925.
Mitteilungen aus Lambaréné: Früjahr bis Herbst 1924, Herbst 1924 bis Herbst 1925. Munich, Beck, 2 vols., 1925-26; as *More from the Primeval Forest*, London, Black, 1931; as *The Forest Hospital at Lambaréné*, New York, Holt, 1931.
Selbstdarstellung. Leipzig, Meiner, 1929.
Aus meinem Leben und Denken. Leipzig, Meiner, 1931; as *My Life and Thought: An Autobiography*, London, Allen and Unwin, and as *Out of My Life and Thought: An Autobiography*, New York, Holt, 1933.
Afrikanische Jagdgeschichten; Ojembo, der Urwaldschulmeister. Strasbourg, Edition des Sources, 1936.
Afrikanische Geschichten. Leipzig, Meiner, 1938; as *From My African Notebook*, London, Allen and Unwin, 1938; as *African Notebook*, New York, Holt, 1939.
Albert Schweitzer: An Anthology, edited by Charles R. Joy. New York, Harper, 1947; London, Black, 1952.
Das Spital im Urwald. Berne, Haupt, 1948.
Ojimbo, der Urwaldschulmeister. Stuttgart, Salzer, 1948.
Ein Pelikan erzahlt aus seinem Leben. Hamburg, Meiner, 1950; as *The Story of My Pelican*, London, Souvenir Press, 1964.
The Problem of Peace in the World of Today. London, Black, and New York, Harper, 1955.
Peace or Atomic War? New York, Holt, 1958.

Editor, *J.S. Bachs Präluden und Fugen für Orgel*. New York, Schirmer, 5 vols., 1911 (3 later volumes were published posthumously).

*

Bibliography: *Albert Schweitzer: An International Bibliography* by Nancy Snell Griffith and Laura Person, Boston, Hall, 1981.

Critical Studies: *Albert Schweitzer: His Work and His Philosophy* by Oskar Kraus, London, A. and C. Black, 1944; *Albert Schweitzer: The Man and His Mind* by George Seaver, New York, Harper, 1947; *Albert Schweitzer: A Study of His Philosophy of Life* by Gabriel Langfeld, London, Allen and Unwin, 1960; *Dr. Schweitzer of Lambaréné* by Norman Cousins, New York, Harper, 1960; *Schweitzer: Prophet of Radical Theology* by Jackson Lee Ice, Philadelphia, Westminster Press, 1971; *Albert Schweitzer: A Biography* by James Brabazon, New York, Putnam, 1975.

*   *   *

To religious scholars, Albert Schweitzer is known primarily as the author of *The Quest for the Historical Jesus*, a landmark book which irrevocably altered the direction of historical studies of Jesus. It maintains that previous lives of Jesus reflected more the theological orientation of the writers—orthodox and liberal alike—than the actual historical situation, and that although *spiritually* each age can and must, in its own way, discover "who He is," the facts in the Gospels are so meager and interpolated that *historically* Jesus remains to us as "One unknown." Yet, in spite of the difficulties which confront the researcher of historical facts in inspirational literature, certain objective features emerge from the New Testament, which, according to Schweitzer, consistently support the following conclusions: the life and teachings of Jesus cannot be correctly understood except in the light of late Jewish eschatology, i.e., the imminent, supernatural transformation of the world; Jesus believed himself to be the Anointed One delegated to help initiate the Kingdom's appearance by his sacrificial suffering (the full secret of which he kept from himself and his disciples until after Caesarea Philippi); and his call for moral perfection made sense only because it was an "interim ethics," the necessary preparation, in the last few days, for entrance into the world to come (and not an ethic for the long-range realization of God's reign in history). It aroused strong opposition at its inception; and although partially eclipsed by various theological trends over the years, present-day scholarship bears testimony to its influence and the validity of its insights. Schweitzer applied the same "consistent eschatology" in his quest of the historical Paul (*Paul and His Interpreters*) and the same profound erudition in *The Mysticism of the Apostle Paul* (which some believe to be his major theological work).

To the music world, Schweitzer is known as the young prodigy who became a concert organist, an authority on organ building, and one of the foremost interpreters of J.S. Bach, who authored a definitive, two-volume work which challenged the world for the first time with the "Schweitzerian heresy" that Bach was not, as traditionally held, a composer of "pure music," but a musical poet, a tone-painter, who developed a precise musical language to express his deepest religious passions. First and foremost, Schweitzer contends, Bach was a church organist nurtured in scriptural texts who dramaticized, particularly in his cantatas and chorals, the presence of the divine. Indeed, he was one of the great Christian mystics. Schweitzer also edited the complete organ works of Bach in eight volumes, a laborious task which took most of his life to finish.

In social philosophy, Schweitzer is recognized as one of the few thinkers at the turn of the century to foresee the coming time of troubles for the West and to undertake independently a serious study of the causes underlying its decline. He states, in *The Decay and Restoration of Civilization*, that the signal reason for the collapse was the overall waning of an optimistic, viable world-view and the loss of an ethical conception of civilization. He also cites decisive subsequent causes which include: dominance of the market-oriented way of life; exploitation of workers; over-specialization; over-organization and control of public life; loss of individual freedoms; and the increase of aggressive nationalism. Among other things, Schweitzer tried to restore to the term "civilization" its ideal connotations, since it had fallen into a mere descriptive designation for whatever *is* the state of the world's peoples. His dark predictions which appeared far-fetched indeed a half-century ago reflect a prophetic insight into the cultural shocks we are experiencing today. Because his ideas bear a resemblance to those of Spengler, whose major work appeared six years prior, many conclude that Spengler's was the original, and Schweitzer's smaller volume only a variation on the theme. But this is not so; it was an accident of war that his book was not published the same year. Also the differences are notable. For example, instead of stopping with the causes of decay, Schweitzer went on to suggest possible steps toward restoration, abjuring deterministic fatalism, as held by Spengler and others, and stressing humanity's ability to make, and not merely suffer, history.

Ethical philosophers know Schweitzer by his *Civilization and Ethics*, which is his ardent search for "the basic principle of the moral" and contains his solution for reestablishing an ethical world-view, something which European thought had lost with its preoccupation with science and its regard of nature as an indifferent force devoid of nurturing power. It was an ambitious undertaking. The major portion of the work is a sweeping review of all the ethical theories of both East and West. Each theory in turn proves inadequate to his demands. A complete ethic must be related to the world as a whole, be world- as well as life-affirming, be active (altruistic) as well as passive (self-realizationist), combine these two in a natural way, be universal, i.e., applicable to all forms of life, be grounded ontologically and not historically, be absolute, i.e., unlimited and unyielding in its responsibility. Employing a kind of phenomenological analysis of what he calls the "will-to-live," Schweitzer arrives at his ethic of "reverence for life," which he maintains logically unites ethics and nature, life and world, value and fact.

Despite its Schopenhauerian overtone, Schweitzer uniquely employs "will-to-live" to include, besides the will to survive, the urge-to-self-realization and the urge-to-relatedness (both social and cosmic), which are proto-ethical proclivities. Even though it may attain to the highest spirituality, Schweitzer states, ethics is given to us physically. We have an instinctive reverence for life. His primary axiom of consciousness is "I am life that wills-to-live in the midst of life that wills-to-live." Reflection on this fact leads to the awe-ful, demanding experience of the interdependency and unity of all Life—we, and all things, are "in the grasp of the inexplicable forward-urging Will in which all Being is grounded." Our felt duty is to raise our instinctive reverence for life to its highest level of reflective, ethical concern, where we will arrive at the basic principle, "it is good to maintain and to encourage life, it is bad to destroy or obstruct it." This includes all life whatsoever, hence it is a truly ecological ethic. Since it also signifies a veneration for the universal Will in which all life is grounded, it is an ethical mysticism. "Reverence for Life," then, is a descriptive statement of general fact, as well as a prescriptive maxim of conduct, and contains subtle meanings which critics often overlook. For example, it means having the proper love of oneself; and since the will-to-live exhibits the power of reason, it means having reverence for truth. It is obvious that it is not just an ethic, it is a *Humanitätsphilosophie*, Schweitzer's ultimate goal, which unites both the mystical-sacramental and the ethical-social elements of our lives. "And this ethic, profound, universal, has the significance of a religion. It *is* religion." Schweitzer's book demonstrates that deep religious convictions are not incompatible with rational thought, and that ethical values are not incompatible with facts.

To scientists and world leaders, Schweitzer is known for his humanitarian peace efforts, his sober warnings about the perils of nuclear war (*Peace or Atomic War?*), and for his being awarded the 1964 Nobel Peace Prize.

To the general public, Schweitzer is the symbol of humane service, the medical doctor who for fifty years dedicated his life to the underprivileged peoples of Africa at his jungle hospital in Gabon.

These are some of the various facets which go to make up certainly one of the 20th century's outstanding and unique individuals.

—Jackson Lee Ice

SCHWINGER, Julian. American physicist. Born in New York City, 12 February 1918. Studied at Columbia University, New York, B.A. 1936, Ph.D 1939. Married Clarice Carrol in 1947. National Research Council Fellow, 1939-40; Research Associate, University of California at Berkeley, 1940-41; Instructor and Assistant Professor, Purdue University, Lafayette, Indiana, 1941-43; Staff Member, Radiation Laboratory, Massachusetts Institute of Technology, Cambridge, 1943-46; Staff Member, Metallurgy Laboratory, University of Chicago, 1943; Associate Professor, 1945-47, Professor, 1947-62, and Higgens Professor of Physics, 1966-72, Harvard University, Cambridge, Massachusetts. Since 1972, Professor of Physics, University of California at Los Angeles. J.W. Gibbs Honorary Lecturer, American Mathematical Society, 1960. Recipient: C.L. Mayer Nature of Light Award, 1949; University Medal, Columbia University, 1951; Einstein Peace Award, 1951; National Medal of Science Award, 1964; Nobel Prize in Physics (jointly), 1965; Guggenheim Fellowship, 1970. Honorary doctorate: Purdue University, 1961; Harvard University, 1962; Brandeis University, Waltham, Massachusetts, 1963; Columbia University, 1966; City College of New York, 1972; Gustavus Adolphus College, St. Peter, Minnesota, 1975. Member, National Academy of Sciences; American Academy of Arts and Sciences; New York Academy of Sciences. Address: Department of Physics, University of California, Los Angeles, California 90024, U.S.A.

PUBLICATIONS

Physics

Differential Equations of Quantum Field Theory (lecture notes). Menlo Park, California, Stanford Research Institute, 1956.
The Theory of Fundamental Interactions. Alberta, Canadian Association of Physicists, 1957.
Lectures on Quantum Field Theory. Coral Gables, University of Miami Center for Theoretical Studies, 1967.
Discontinuities in Waveguides, with David Saxon. New York, Gordon and Breach, 1968.
Particles and Sources. New York, Gordon and Breach, 1969.
Particles, Sources, and Fields. Reading, Massachusetts, Addison Wesley, 2 vols., 1970-73.
Quantum Kinematics and Dynamics. New York, Benjamin, 1970.
Selected Papers (1937-1976), edited by M. Flato and others. Dordrecht, Reidel, 1979.

Other

Editor, *Quantum Electrodynamics.* New York, Dover, 1958.

*   *   *

Julian Schwinger, Sin-itiro Tomonaga, and Richard Feynman shared the 1965 Nobel Prize in Physics "for their fundamental work in quantum electrodynamics, with deep-ploughing consequences for the physics of elementary particles." Quantum electrodynamics is the physical theory which incorporates two of the principal advances of 20th-century physics, Einstein's Special

Theory of Relativity and quantum mechanics, into a description of the electric and magnetic interactions between charged particles. In such a quantum field theory, the classical waves of electric and magnetic fields become particle-like quanta, known as photons.

The quantum-mechanical theory of the electron proposed by Dirac in 1928 (which contained some features of relativity) brilliantly predicted the intrinsic electron spin and the existence of the electron's anti-particle, the positron (discovered in 1932). But during the 1930's, it was realized that the existing relativistic quantum theories were plagued with theoretical difficulties. In quantum electrodynamics the self energy of the electron and the quantum zero-point fluctuations of the electromagnetic field led to "divergences," i.e., infinite answers, for many calculations. It was realized that these difficulties were due in part to the fact that the "vacuum"—so called empty space—is not a simple entity, but really has the properties of a polarizable medium. In addition to these theoretical problems, what provided real urgency to the search for a new quantum electrodynamics were observations starting in the late 1930's and culminating in the experiments of Lamb, Retherford, Foley, and Kusch in 1947 which indicated that the Dirac theory incorrectly predicted the details of the energy level spectrum of the hydrogen atom and did not give a precisely accurate value for the magnetic moment of the electron.

Working independently, Schwinger developed (in 1948-53) a coherent and systematic formal machinery for handling the divergences due to self-energy effects and vacuum fluctuations by the procedure of mass and charge renormalization, and thus was able to do relativistically invariant field-theoretical calculations of observable physical quantities. Both Schwinger's and Feynman's approaches to relativistic quantum mechanics employ the action as a fundamental ingredient, but Feynman's final formulation is a global (integral) viewpoint while Schwinger's is a local (differential) one. Feynman's techniques are more intuitive and non-rigorous but generally easier to use in practical computations.

Schwinger is a mathematical formalist of incredible originality, power, and elegance. In his Nobel Prize lecture, he wrote, "Mathematics is the natural language of theoretical physics. It is the irreplaceable instrument for the penetration of realms of physical phenomena far beyond the ordinary experience upon which conventional language is based."

Schwinger has produced a prodigious amount of significant research, much of it of extreme technical difficulty not easily accessible because of its idiosyncratic formal viewpoint. Although he has collaborated with other physicists and supervised a sizeable number of Ph.D. students, he has tended to work in isolation on problems or approaches not currently in vogue. In this way, he has often proposed ideas which become successfully implemented quite a bit later.

In addition to his famous work on quantum electrodynamics and the structure of quantum field theories, Schwinger has made major contributions to many areas of physics (starting with his first scientific paper at age 16!). Since his work on waveguide theory and devices during World War II (at the MIT Radiation Laboratory) he has continued to publish on classical electromagnetic theory—including diffraction problems and radiation from charges accelerated in electric and magnetic fields. Among his earliest interests was low energy nuclear scattering, and in 1950 he presented the first published effective range derivation. In 1957, in a paper entitled "A Theory of the Fundamental Interactions," Schwinger made several speculations which were brilliantly confirmed by research over the next twenty years. These included: the vector-axial vector theory of the weak interactions, the existence of two different neutrinos associated with the electron and muon (found experimentally in 1962-63), the existence of charged intermediate massive mesons which transmit the weak force just as the neutral massless photon transmits the electromagnetic force, and the possibility that the weak and electromagnetic interactions can be dynamically unified into a single gauge theory.

Since the mid-1960's, Schwinger has examined the role of

magnetic charge (which has never been observed experimentally) in quantum field theory, and he has presented a highly speculative theory of strong interactions in which dyons—particles carrying both electric and magnetic charge—play a fundamental role in the internal structure of matter.

Beginning in 1966, Schwinger has passionately advocated a method which he calls "Source Theory." This phenomenological viewpoint was originally stimulated by the situation in strong interaction physics, where there are many unstable particles differing in no fundamental way from stable ones. Source theory is an attempt to give a useful characterization of the particle concept based on the physical possiblity of creating or annihilating any particle in a suitable collision. It remains to be seen whether this approach will be widely adopted and will lead to deep new ways of thinking about the nature of matter.

—Harvey Shepard

SEARLE, John R(ogers). American philosopher. Born in Denver, Colorado, 31 July 1932. Studied at the University of Wisconsin, Madison, 1949-52; Oxford University, England (Rhodes Scholar), B.A. 1955, M.A. and D.Phil. 1959. Married Dagmar Carboch in 1959; 2 sons. Lecturer in Philosophy, Christ Church, Oxford, 1956-59; Assistant Professor, 1959-64, Associate Professor, 1964-66, and since 1966 Professor of Philosophy, University of California, Berkeley (Special Assistant to the Chancellor, 1965-67). Visiting Professor, University of Michigan, Ann Arbor, 1961-62, and University of Washington, Seattle, 1963; Visiting Fellow, Brasenose College, Oxford, 1968-69. Recipient: American Council of Learned Societies grant, 1963; Guggenheim Fellowship, 1975. Member, American Academy of Arts and Sciences. Address: Department of Philosophy, University of California, Berkeley, California 94720, U.S.A.

PUBLICATIONS

Philosophy

Speech Acts: An Essay in the Philosophy of Language. London, Cambridge University Press, 1969.
Expression and Meaning: Studies in the Theory of Speech Acts. London, Cambridge University Press, 1979.

Other

The Campus War: A Sympathetic Look at the University in Agony. New York, World, 1971.

Editor, *The Philosophy of Language.* London, Oxford University Press, 1971.
Editor, with others, *Speech Act Theory and Pragmatics.* Dordrecht, Reidel, 1980.

*   *   *

John R. Searle's main contributions to philosophy have been in philosophy of language, although his attention has turned recently, and increasingly, to philosophy of mind. The key concept in the former area for Searle is the speech (or elocutionary) act, a concept which he gets directly from his mentor John Austin ("How To Do Things With Words"). Although Searle thinks of the speech act as the minimal unit of language communication, he allows that it can be analyzed in terms of its elocutionary force

and its propositional content. The content of a speech act is what is shared by the following speech act representations: (1) "I order you to shut the door"; (2) "I ask you to shut the door"; (3) "I plead with you to shut the door"; (4) "I predict that you will shut the door." The force pertains to what in the speech act is said about, or is done with, the content (e.g., whether it is an order, a request, a plea or a prediction).

In his thinking about speech acts, Searle has been anxious to find some order among the almost indefinite number of speech-act types which Austin thought exist. Toward this end, he has developed a sophisticated taxonomy of elocutionary acts which is based upon the point (or purpose), the direction of fit, and the expressed psychological state of speech acts. Thus the point of saying that it is raining outside is to commit the speaker to the truth of his assertion; the direction of fit is to match his words with the world (the fact that it is raining); and the expressed psychological state is the belief presupposed in the assertion that it is raining. In contrast, the purpose of uttering "Please shut the door" is to attempt to get the hearer to shut the door and not, as with the former example, to state something which is true. Likewise, the direction of fit is different here, since the speaker is attempting to match the world (i.e., to change it) to fit his words. As to the expressed psychological state, instead of being a belief, it is now a wish or a want (that the door be shut). Using these three speech-act dimensions, plus nine other less important ones, Searle argues that there are only five basic types of elocutionary acts and one derivative type. First, there are assertives of various kinds (e.g., hypotheses, conjectures, flat assertions, predictions) which are all assessable as either true or false. Second, there are directives (e.g., pleadings, commands, requests) whose aims are to get the hearers in the communicative setting to do something, or to change their beliefs or attitudes. Third, there are commissives (e.g., promises, contracts) which bind speakers to do something in the future. Fourth, there are expressives, a mixed bag which includes apologies, congratulations, condolences and welcomings. These speech acts focus attention more than the others on the expressed psychological state of the speaker and, in a sense, do little else. Fifth, there are declarations which have the peculiar property of making things happen simply by utterance. For example, a declaration of war uttered in the proper circumstances by the President of the United States makes it true that the United States is at war. The derivative category, assertive-declarations, are declarations which require some reference to the fact before they can be issued (e.g., as when the umpire declares the runner out in baseball after carefully watching the runner and the tag made on him).

Although Searle insists that all speech-act issuing comes down to one or another of these basic types, he is sensitive to the fact that we do not always use our language literally and, therefore, cannot always easily identify the type of speech act being issued. Thus with what he calls indirect speech acts, we mean more than what we say (e.g., I'm sorry I hurt you" not only asserts something about the speaker but, indirectly, and more importantly, expresses an apology), while with metaphor we mean something other than what we say (e.g., "Sam is a pig" when we mean that he eats too much. In analyzing indirect speech acts, metaphors, other non-literal uses, and even literal uses, Searle takes account of the context of the utterance and the mental state (especially the intentions) of the speaker. Indeed he argues that philosophy of language and philosophy of mind are closely related since the mind imposes intentionality (in the spirit of Brentano) upon certain sounds and markings, and, thereby, gives them meaning. Because it is mind which does the imposing, Searle considers philosophy of language to be a branch of philosophy of mind.

—N. Fotion

SEILLIÈRE, (Baron) Ernest (Antoine Aimé Léon). French man of letters. Born in Paris, 1 January 1866. Studied at the Collège Stanlislas and École Polytechnique, Paris, and at the University of Heidelberg. Married Germaine Demachy in 1895; 3 children. Recipient: Grand Prize, Institut de France, 1951. Member, Société des Gens de Lettres; Académie des Sciences Morales et Politiques, Institut de France, 1914 (Permanent Secretary after 1934); Académie Française, 1946. Officer, Order of Leopold, Belgium, 1937. Commandeur, Légion d'Honneur, 1952. *Died 15 March 1955.*

PUBLICATIONS

Literature and Culture

Études sur Ferdinand Lasalle, fondateur du parti socialiste allemand. Paris, Plon, 1897.
Littérature et morale dans le parti socialiste allemand: Essais. Paris, Plon Nourrit, 1898.
Le Comte de Gobineau et l'aryanisme historique. Paris, Plon Nourrit, 1903.
La Philosophie de l'impérialisme. Paris, Plon Nourrit, 4 vols., 1903-08.
Apollôn ou Dionysos: Étude critique sue Frédéric Nietzsche et l'utilitarisme impérialiste. Paris, Plon Nourrit, 1905.
L'Impérialisme démocratique. Paris, Plon Nourrit, 1907.
Le Mal romantique: Essai sur l'impérialisme irrationnel. Paris, Plon Nourrit, 1908.
Une Tragédie d'amour au temps du romantisme: Henri et Charlotte Stieglitz. Paris, Plon Nourrit, 1909.
Barbey d'Aurevilly: Ses idées et son oeuvre. Paris, Bloud, 1910.
Les Mystiques du néo-romantisme: Évolution contemporaine de l'appétit mystique. Paris, Plon Nourrit, 1911.
Introduction à la philosophie de l'impérialisme. Paris, Alcan, 1911.
Arthur Schopenhauer. Paris, Bloud, 1911.
Diderot. Paris, Les Éditions de France, 1911.
Mysticisme et domination: Essai de critique impérialiste. Paris, Alcan, 1913.
Le Romantisme des réalistes: Gustave Flaubert. Paris, Plon Nourrit, 1914.
Houston-Stewart Chamberlain, le plus récent philosophe du pangermanisme mystique. Paris, La Renaissance du Livre, 1917.
L'Avenir de la philosophie bergsonienne. Paris, Alcan, 1917.
Un Artisan d'énergie française, Pierre de Goubertin. Paris, Didier, 1917.
Le Péril mystique dans l'inspiration des démocraties contemporaines: Rousseau, visionnaire et révélateur. Paris, La Renaissance du Livre, 1918.
Madame Guyon et Fenelon, précurseurs de Rousseau. Paris, Alcan, 1918.
Edgar Quinet et le mysticisme démocratique. Paris, Société d'Économie Sociale, 1919.
George Sand: Mystique de la passion, de la politique, et de l'art. Paris, Alcan, 1920.
Les Origines romanesques de la morale et de la politique romantiques. Paris, La Renaissance du Livre, 1920.
Jean-Jacques Rousseau. Paris, Garnier, 1921.
Balzac et la morale romantique. Paris, Alcan, 1921.
La Morale de Dumas fils. Paris, Alcan, 1921.
Le Romancier du Grand Condé, Gauthier de Coste, sieur de La Calprenède. Paris, Émile Paul, 1921.
Sainte-Beuve, agent, juge, et complice de l'évolution romantique. Paris, Société d'Économie Sociale, 1921.
Emile Zola. Paris, Grasset, 1923.
Nouveaux Portraits de femmes. Paris, Émile Paul, 1923.
Vers le socialisme rationnel. Paris, Alcan, 1923.
Auguste Comte. Paris, Alcan, 1924.
Les Pangermanistes d'après guerre. Paris, Alcan, 1924.
Le Coeur et le raison de Madame Swetchine. Paris, Perrin, 1924.
Alexandre Vinet, historien de la pensée française, suivi d'un appendice sur Henri-Frédéric Amiel. Paris, Payot, 1925.
Christianisme et romantisme. Paris, Payot, 1925.
Du Quiétisme au socialisme romantique. Paris, Alcan, 1925.
Le Romantisme. Paris, Stock, 1925; as *Romanticism*, New York, Columbia University Press, 1929.
Une Académie à l'époque romantique. Paris, Leroux, 1926.
La Grâce du romantisme sage: Armand de Malun et Sophie Swetchine. Abbeville, Faillart, 1927.
Les Goncourts moralistes. Paris, Nouvelle Revue Critique, 1927.
Morales et religions nouvelles en Allemagne. Paris, Payot, 1927.
Pour le centenaire du romantisme: Un Examen de conscience. Paris, Champion, 1927.
Psychanalyse freudienne ou psychologie impérialiste? Paris, Alcan, 1928.
La Sagesse de Darmstadt. Paris, Alcan, 1929.
Un Poète parnassien: André de Guerne, 1853-1912. Paris, J. de Gigord, 1930.
La Religion romantiques et ses conquêtes, 1830-1930. Paris, Champion, 1930.
Romantisme et démocratie romantique. Paris, Nouvelle Revue Critique, 1930.
Baudelaire. Paris, Colin, 1931.
De la déesse natur à la déesse vie (naturalisme et vitalisme mystiques). Paris, Alcan, 1931.
J.-K. Huysmans. Paris, Grasset, 1931.
Marcel Proust. Paris, Nouvelle Revue Critique, 1931.
Le Romantisme et la morale (essai sur le mysticisme esthétique et le mysticisme passionel). Paris, Nouvelle Revue Critique, 1932.
Sur la psychologie du romantisme allemand. Paris, Nouvelle Revue Critique, 1933.
Anatole France, critique de son temps. Paris, Nouvelle Revue Critique, 1934.
La Jeunesse d'Anatole France. Paris, Nouvelle Revue Critique, 1934.
Jules Lemaître, historien d'évolution naturiste. Paris, Nouvelle Revue Critique, 1935.
L'Évolution morale dans le théâtre d'Henri Bataille. Paris, Boivin, 1936.
David Herbert Lawrence et les récentes idéologies allemandes. Paris, Boivin, 1936.
Léon Bloy: Psychologie d'un mystique. Paris, Nouvelle Revue Critique, 1936.
Paul Bourget, psychologue et sociologue. Paris, Nouvelle Revue Critique, 1937.
Émile Faguet, historien des idées. Paris, Nouvelle Revue Critique, 1938.
Le Naturisme de Montaigne, et autres essais. Paris, Nouvelle Revue Critique, 1938.
Un Précurseur du national-socialisme: L'Actualité de Carlyle. Paris, Nouvelle Revue Critique, 1939.
Un Familier des doctrinaires: Ximénès Doudan. Paris, Sirey, 1940.
L'Histoire et nous: avertissements et conseils. Bordeaux, Picquot, 1942.

*

Critical Studies: *The Challenge of Humanism: An Essay in Comparative Criticism* by Louis J. Mercier, New York, Oxford University Press, 1933; *Humanism and Naturalism: A Comparative Study of Ernest Seillière, Irving Babbitt, and Paul Elmer More* by Folke Leander, Göteborg, Sweden, Elanders, 1937.

*   *   *

Ernest Seillière's system of thought was built upon the central idea that all human activity was the expression of a basic instinct for expansion. This human imperialism, much like Schopenhauer's concept of Will, appeared as a wild aggressiveness serving the deeper purpose of self-preservation and, similar to Nietzsche's formulation, reflected the reality that as one's power was increased so were chances for survival.

In *La Philosophie de l'Impérialisme* and subsequent works, man's imperialist activity was viewed as guided by mysticism—spiritual alliances with forces encountered in the struggle for existence—and reason—the application of human experience and intelligence to the problems of survival. Mysticism provided the blind confidence and certainty of success needed in the battle for survival, while reason served to restrain fanaticism and excessive aggressiveness which might become counterproductive to the aim of self-preservation.

Seillière believed that man had only gradually learned to use experience to control the natural alliance of mysticism and imperialism. The best example of this was found in the Christian church which for centuries had been able to restrain the irrational aspirations characteristic of mystical imperialism by channeling its expansive forces to the profit of society. But as European society had become increasingly secularized in the 19th century he saw man's desire for conquest being served by a new mysticism identified with the romanticism of Rousseau.

Seillière cautioned against this "modern alliance" of romanticism and imperialism, based on Rousseau's idea of the natural goodness of man, which exalted emotion over reason. This type of romantic mysticism seemed a rejection of acquired "reason-experience" in a regression to the emotional, impulsive side of human nature where imperialism was unchecked.

Seillière distinguished four forms of romantic mysticism. Passional mysticism, which placed sexual desire over conventional morality, and aesthetic mysticism, which assumed artistic expression was intimately connected with inner truths, fed the imperialism of the individual. The imperialist drive of groups was served by social (or democratic) mysticism, which found the lower classes more pure and closer to nature and thus entitled to rule, and racial (or national) mysticism, which claimed the same right for groups endowed with superior racial qualities.

Since all these forms presented a danger for 20th-century society, Seillière intended to reinforce a historical pessimism that would curb the belief in man's natural goodness, while at the same time softening the bleaker aspects of this pessimism by offering the possibility of future progress through the use of reason-experience. Much like Christianity, this system combined a gloomy estimate of human nature with the expectation of improvement in the future. Therefore the modern alliance of mysticism and imperialism could prove beneficial if properly channeled. If passional mysticism was limited to marriage for procreation, if aesthetic mysticism meant free expression with proper style and form, if social mysticism produced gradual reform within established society, and if racial mysticism translated into patriotism and sacrifice for the national interest, all would serve to aid individuals and groups in the struggle for existence. This would not mean the disappearance of imperialism, which was impossible, but its increasing rationality and the elimination of its more violent aspects.

That this was the ideal and not the reality of the modern age Seillière recognized in his treatment of race mysticism, which in *La Philosophie* he traced to the historical Aryanism of Arthur Gobineau. The adoption of the ideal of Aryan superiority by the Germans, Seillière wrote, had gone beyond the reasonable aims of national unification in the 19th century to become the most dangerous illusion of the 20th century.

It would seem that Seillière, writing in the first three decades of the 20th century, would have had ample material in the Russian and Fascist revolutions to demonstrate his theories. Yet he never gave systematic treatment to either phenomenon, nor did he ever fully draw out the implications of his theory for political life. Preferring to study the literary and philosophical expressions of imperialistic ideas instead, he insisted that expansion was a psychological necessity before it was a political device, and therefore the political forms it adopted were not necessarily those it was condemned to in the future.

—Frank M. Baglione

SHAW, George Bernard. Irish political and social commentator, and playwright. Born in Dublin, 26 July 1856. Educated privately and at the Wesleyan Connexional School and elsewhere in Dublin. Married Charlotte Payne-Townshend in 1898 (died, 1943). Office boy and cashier for Charles Townshend, estate agent, Dublin, 1871-76; settled in London, 1876; worked briefly for the Edison Telephone Company, 1879; became a socialist in 1882; speaker for the Social Democratic Federation; joined the Fabian Society in 1884; Member of the Executive Committee for many years; Music Critic (as "Corno di Bassetto"), *The Star*, 1888-1890, and *The World*, 1890-94; began writing for the stage in the 1890's; Drama Critic, *The Saturday Review*, 1895-98; Member of the Borough Council of St. Pancras, London, 1900-03. Recipient: Nobel Prize for Literature, 1925; Irish Academy of Letters medal, 1934; Oscar, for screenplay, 1939. Declined a peerage and the Order of Merit. *Died 2 November 1950.*

PUBLICATIONS

Political and Social Commentary

The Fabian Society: What It Has Done, and How It has Done It. London, Fabian Society, 1892.
The Irresponsibilities of Anarchism (lecture). London, Fabian Society, 1893.
A Plan of Campaign for Labour. London, Fabian Society, 1894.
Report on Fabian Policy and Resolutions. London, Fabian Society, 1896.
Socialism for Millionaires. London, Fabian Society, 1901.
The Common Sense of Municipal Trading. London, Constable, 1904.
Fabianism and the Fiscal Question. London, Fabian Society, 1904.
Is Free Trade Alive or Dead? (lecture). Privately printed, 1906.
Socialism and Superior Brains. London, Fabian Society, 1909.
Common Sense about the War. London, Statesman, 1914.
How to Settle the Irish Question. Dublin, Talbot Press, 1917.
Peace Conference Hints. London, Constable, 1919.
Irish Nationalism and Labour Internationalism. London, Labour Party, 1920.
Ruskin's Politics. London, Christophers, 1921.
Bernard Shaw and Fascism. London, Favil Press, 1927.
G. B. Shaw—Do We Agree? A Debate Between G.K. Chesterton and Bernard Shaw. London, Palmer, 1928.
The Intelligent Woman's Guide to Socialism and Capitalism. London, Constable, and New York, Brentano's, 1928; revised edition, 1937.
The League of Nations. London, Fabian Society, 1929.
Socialism: Principles and Outlook, and Fabianism. London, Fabian Society, 1930.
What I Really Wrote about the War. London, Constable, 1930.

What Bernard Shaw Told the Americans about Russia! London, Friends of the Soviet Union, 1932.

Essays in Fabian Socialism, in *Works*. London, Constable, 1932.

The Future of Political Science in America (address). New York, Dodd Mead, 1933; as *The Political Madhouse in America and Nearer Home*, London, Constable, 1933.

Are We Heading for War? (broadcast). London, Labour Party, 1934.

What I Said in New Zealand. Wellington, Commercial, 1934.

Everybody's Political What's What. London, Constable, and New York, Dodd Mead, 1944.

The Rationalism of Russia, edited by H.M. Geduld. Bloomington, Indiana University Press, 1964.

The Road to Equality: 10 Unpublished Lectures and Essays 1884-1918, edited by Louis Crompton. Boston, Beacon Press, 1971.

Practical Politics: Twentieth Century Views on Politics and Economics, edited by Lloyd J. Hubenka. Lincoln, University of Nebraska Press, 1976.

Novels

Cashel Byron's Profession. London, Modern Press, 1886; revised edition, London, Scott, 1889; revised edition, London, Richards, and Chicago, Stone, 1901.

An Unsocial Socialist. London, Sonnenschein, 1887; New York, Brentano's, 1900.

Love among the Artists. Chicago, Stone, 1900; London, Constable, 1914.

The Irrational Knot. London, Constable, and New York, Brentano's, 1905.

Immaturity, in *Works*. London, Constable, 1930.

The Adventures of the Black Girl in Her Search for God. London, Constable, 1932; New York, Dodd Mead, 1933.

My Dear Dorothea: A Practical Guide of Moral Education for Females, edited by Stephen Winsten. London, Phoenix House, 1956; New York, Vanguard Press, 1957.

An Unfinished Novel, edited by Stanley Weintraub. London, Constable, and New York, Dodd Mead, 1958.

Plays

Widowers' Houses. London, Henry, 1893; revised edition, in *Plays Unpleasant*, 1898.

Plays: Pleasant and Unpleasant (includes *Arms and the Man, Candida, The Man of Destiny, You Never Can Tell; Widowers' Houses, Mrs. Warren's Profession, The Philanderer*). London, Richards, 2 vols, 1898; Chicago, Stone, 2 vols., 1898.

Three Plays for Puritans (includes *The Devil's Disciple, Captain Brassbound's Conversion, Caesar and Cleopatra*). London, Richards, and New York, Stone, 1901.

The Admirable Bashville; or, Constancy Rewarded, from his novel *Cashel Byron's Profession*, in *Cashel Byron's Profession*. London, Richards, and Chicago, Stone, 1901.

Man and Superman. London, Constable, and New York, Brentano's, 1903.

How He Lied to Her Husband, John Bull's Other Island, Major Barbara. London, Constable, and New York, Brentano's, 1907; screenplay version of *Major Barbara*, London, Penguin, 1946.

Press Cuttings. London, Constable, and New York, Brentano's, 1909.

The Shewing Up of Blanco Posnet. London, Constable, and New York, Brentano's, 1909.

The Doctor's Dilemma, Getting Married, The Shewing Up of Blanco Posnet. London, Constable, and New York, Brentano's, 1911.

Great Catherine. London, Constable, 1914.

Misalliance, The Dark Lady of the Sonnets, Fanny's First Play. London, Constable, and New York, Brentano's, 1914.

Pygmalion, Androcles and the Lion, Overruled. London, Constable, and New York, Brentano's, 1916; screenplay version of *Pygmalion*, London, Penguin, 1941.

Great Catherine, Heartbreak House, Playlets of the War. London, Constable, and New York, Brentano's, 1919.

Back to Methuselah. London, Constable, and New York, Brentano's, 1921.

Saint Joan. London, Constable, and New York, Brentano's, 1924; screenplay version, edited by Bernard F. Dukore, Seattle, University of Washington Press, 1968.

Translations and Tomfooleries. London, Constable, and New York, Brentano's, 1926.

The Apple Cart. London, Constable, and New York, Brentano's, 1930.

Complete Plays. London, Constable, 1931; 6th revised edition, 1965.

Too True to Be Good, Village Wooing, On the Rocks. London, Constable, and New York, Dodd Mead, 1934.

The Six of Calais, The Millionairess, The Simpleton of the Unexpected Isles. London, Constable, and New York, Dodd Mead, 1936.

Geneva. London, Constable, 1939.

In Good King Charles's Golden Days. London, Constable, 1939.

Cymbeline Refinished, Geneva, In Good King Charles's Golden Days. London, Constable, and New York, Dodd Mead, 1946.

Buoyant Billions. London, Constable, 1949.

Shakes Versus Shaw: A Puppet Play, Buoyant Billions, Far-Fetched Fables. London, Constable, and New York, Dodd Mead, 1951.

Ten Short Plays. New York, Dodd Mead, 1960.

The Bodley Head Shaw (plays and prefaces), edited by Dan H. Laurence. London, Reinhardt, 7 vols., 1970-74.

Passion Play: A Dramatic Fragment, 1878, edited by Jerald E. Bringle. London, Rota, 1971.

Collected Screenplays, edited by Bernard F. Dukore. London, Prior, 1980.

Screenplays: *Pygmalion*, with others, 1938; *Major Barbara*, with Anatole de Grunwald, 1941; *Caesar and Cleopatra*, with Marjorie Deans and W.P. Lipscomb, 1946.

Other

The Quintessence of Ibsenism. London, Scott, and Boston, Tucker, 1891; revised edition, London, Constable, and New York, Brentano's, 1913.

The Perfect Wagnerite: A Commentary on the Ring of the Nibelungs. London, Richards, 1898; New York, Stone, 1899.

The Author's Apology to "Mrs. Warren's Profession." London, Richards, 1902.

Dramatic Opinions and Essays, edited by James Huneker. New York, Brentano's, 2 vols., 1906; London, Constable, 2 vols., 1907.

The Sanity of Art. London, New Age Press, and New York, Tucker, 1908.

A Discarded Defence of Roger Casement. Privately printed, 1922.

Table Talk of G.B.S.: Conversations Between Bernard Shaw and His Biographer, by Archibald Henderson. London, Chapman and Hall, 1925.

Letters to Miss Alma Murray (and *More Letters*). Privately printed, 2 vols., 1927-32.

Ellen Terry and Bernard Shaw: A Correspondence, edited by Christopher Saint-John. New York, Fountain Press, and London, Constable, 1932.

Works. London, Constable, 34 vols., 1931-51.

Music in London 1890-94. London, Constable, 3 vols., 1932.

Nine Answers. Privately printed, 1932.

Prefaces. London, Constable, 1934; 3rd revised edition, 1965.

William Morris As I Knew Him. New York, Dodd Mead, 1936.

Shaw Gives Himself Away: An Autobiographical Miscellany. Newton, Montgomeryshire, Gregynog Press, 1939.

Florence Farr, Bernard Shaw, and W.B. Yeats Letters, edited by Clifford Bax. Dublin, Cuala Press, and New York, Dodd Mead, 1942.

Shaw on Vivisection, edited by G.H. Bowker. London, National Anti-Vivisection Society, 1949.

Rhyming Picture Guide to Ayot Saint Lawrence. Luton, Bedfordshire, Leagrave Press, 1950.

Plays and Players: Theatre Essays, edited by A.C. Ward. London, Oxford University Press, 1952.

The Voice: An Autobiographical Explanation. Privately printed, 1952.

Shaw and Mrs. Patrick Campbell: Their Correspondence, edited by Alan Dent. London, Gollancz, and New York, Knopf, 1952.

Advice to a Young Critic and Other Letters, edited by E.J. West. New York, Crown, 1955; London, Owen, 1956.

Letters to Granville Barker, edited by C.B. Purdom. London, Phoenix House, and New York, Theatre Arts, 1957.

Shaw on Theatre: Sixty Years of Letters, Speeches, and Articles..., edited by E.J. West. New York, Hill and Wang, 1958.

To A Young Actress: Letters to Molly Tompkins, edited by Peter Tompkins. London, Constable, and New York, Potter, 1960.

The Matter with Ireland, edited by Dan H. Laurence and D.H. Green. London, Hart Davis, and New York, Hill and Wang, 1962.

The Religious Speeches of Bernard Shaw, edited by W.S. Smith. University Park, Pennsylvania State University Press, 1963.

Collected Letters, edited by Dan H. Laurence. London, Reinhardt, 2 vols. only, 1965-72.

An Autobiography, edited by Stanley Weintraub. London, Reinhardt, 2 vols., 1969-70.

Non-Dramatic Literary Criticism, edited by Stanley Weintraub. Lincoln, University of Nebraska Press, 1972.

Shaw 1914-1918: Journey to Heartbreak (from Shaw's journals), edited by Stanley Weintraub. London, Routledge, 1973.

The Portable Shaw, edited by Stanley Weintraub. New York, Viking Press, and London, Penguin, 1977.

Flyleaves, edited by Dan H. Laurence and Daniel J. Leary. Austin, Texas, Taylor, 1977.

Shaw's Music: The Complete Music Criticism, edited by Dan H. Laurence. London, Bodley Head, 3 vols., 1981.

Bernard Shaw and Alfred Douglas: A Correspondence, edited by Mary Hyde. New Haven, Connecticut, Ticknor and Fields, and London, Murray, 1982.

Editor, *Fabian Essays on Socialism.* London, Fabian Society, 1889; revised edition, 1908; revised edition, as *Fabian Essays Forty Years Later,* 1931.

Editor, *The Co-operative Commonwealth,* by L. Gronlund. London, Reeves, 1892.

Editor, *Fabianism and the Empire: A Manifesto.* London, Fabian Society, 1900.

*

Bibliography: in *Bernard Shaw* by Jean-Claude Amalric, 1977.

Critical Studies: *Revolutionists in London: A Study in Five Unorthodox Socialists* by James W. Hulse, Oxford, Clarendon Press, 1970; *A Good Man Fallen among Fabians* by Alick West, London, Lawrence and Wishart, 1974; *Shaw: The Critical Heritage* edited by T.F. Evans, London, Routledge, 1976; *Fabian Feminist: Bernard Shaw and Women* edited by Rodelle Weintraub, University Park, Pennsylvania State University Press, 1977; *Bernard Shaw: Du Reformateur victorien au prophète edouardien* by Jean-Claude Amalric, Paris, Didier, 1977.

*   *   *

George Bernard Shaw, dramatist, critic, and social thinker, has been described as the greatest British playwright since William Shakespeare, and of some of his major stage works, including *Caesar and Cleopatra, Man and Superman, Major Barbara, Heartbreak House, and Saint Joan,* it has been commented that they have a beauty and seriousness unmatched by any of his contemporaries.

It has been said, too, that perhaps no man since Voltaire has had so great an influence on his time as Shaw, dealing as he did with a very wide range of subjects so wittily and entertainingly that people began to think about things which they had previously dismissed as either incomprehensible or plain boring. People were stimulated, too, when—as he did on occasion—he treated serious matters with levity.

Almost every topic about which there was discussion at the time became the subject of Shaw's tracts and lectures. They included subjects as wide apart as Christianity, marriage, the British empire, and the family. And it can hardly be doubted that Shaw's irreverence for tradition and contempt of current morality helped to explode some of the conventions and illusions of the Victorian age. And it is generally agreed, too, that as a dramatic critic he had no rival.

Heartbreak House and *Saint Joan* are considered by many to be Shaw's best plays from the middle years of his life, he himself describing the latter as an historical tragi-comedy, being anxious to illustrate his theme of Joan as an early symbol and example of nationalism and protestantism.

Crime, adultery, and sentimental romance were the usual themes of serious plays before Shaw started writing. He shocked the critics and startled the public by dealing with such subjects as landlordism and prostitution and by going on to preach the folly of punishment and revenge. And he substituted witty dialogue for a repetition of stale situations.

While Shaw's wit and observations "sugar the critical pill" it is generally accepted that perhaps the most valuable parts of his plays are where he challenged the social and moral values of the time. And in dealing with historical subjects he initiated a natural and humorous treatment of famous figures.

When Shaw came to London in 1876, he set to work as a novelist, and although that form of authorship proved not to be his medium, his efforts in that field were an apprenticeship for the dramatic writing at which he was later to excel. Perhaps the best known of his five novels are *Cashel Byron's Profession* and *The Admirable Bashville.*

Long after he had achieved success with his plays Shaw continued to be a prolific and enthusiastic writer on a wide range of political and economic subjects, particularly socialism, his political works including *The Intelligent Woman's Guide to Socialism.* Very active in the Fabian Society, he was a leading spirit in the group that created a new Parliamentary Party and it was partly as a result of its propaganda and enthusiasm that the British Labour Party first appeared in the House of Commons in 1906.

Shaw's influence on the drama was more strongly felt and has had a more beneficial effect than his teaching in other spheres, and by ridiculing the (to him) absurd fashion of dramaturgy he doubtless created a public receptive to the play of ideas. When he started to write for the theatre it was largely dependent on third-rate melodramas and adaptations from inferior continental pieces. *Androcles and the Lion* was at once hailed as a masterpiece, and this was followed by perhaps his greatest financial success, *Pygmalion.*

During the years immediately before the turn of the century Shaw had attacked the popular kind of play in his weekly articles, praised Ibsen, and laid the foundations for a new drama unrestricted by 19th-century conventions. And it is generally conceded that as a dramatic critic Shaw had no rival, Max Beerbohm saying of him that "the best of us are pygmies in comparison."

Some of Shaw's early plays were rejected for performance because they were thought unactable or because of their—at the time—controversial subject matter. Consequently, he published a readers' volume of six *Plays Pleasant and Unpleasant* in 1898 with prefaces that pithily drive home the intellectural substance of the drama. This marked a precedent in a tradition of prefaces to the published plays that were often longer than the plays themselves.

Plays Unpleasant contained *Widowers' Houses*, an attack on housing conditions; *The Philanderer*, dealing with the concept of the developing role of women in society; and *Mrs. Warren's Profession*, which is about prostitution. *Plays Pleasant* included *Arms and the Man*, a satire on the military world; a farce, *You Never Can Tell;* and *Candida*, the story of a vicar's wife and her love for a young artist.

Pygmalion (already referred to as Shaw's greatest financial success) portrays Henry Higgins creating a society lady from a flower-girl, Eliza Doolittle, by means of the science of phonetics. And it caused a sensation when the well-schooled Eliza, in a moment of stress, reverted to the expressive use of the phrase "not bloody likely."

The massive work *Man and Superman* deals at one level with the pursuit and capture of a man, John Tanner, by an intelligent and typically scheming Shavian woman, Ann Whitefield. At another level it sets out Shaw's view of a life-force which is central to the evolution of man.

Shaw himself has explained why he wrote plays: "I am not an ordinary playwright in the general sense. I am a specialist in immoral and heretical plays. My reputation has been gained by my persistent struggle to force the public to reconsider its morals. In particular I regard much current morality as to economic and sexual relations as disastrously wrong; and I regard certain doctrines of the Christian religion as understood in England today with abhorrence. I write plays with the deliberate object of converting the nation to my opinions in these matters."

—Granville Eastwood

SIEGFRIED, André. French political and social commentator. Born in Le Havre, 21 April 1875. Educated at the Lycée Condorcet, Paris; studied at the Sorbonne, Paris, D. ès Let. Married Paule Lareche in 1907; 1 daughter. Professor of Economic Geography, École Libre des Sciences Politiques, Paris, from 1911, and the Collège de France, Paris, from 1933. Chief of the Economic Section, League of Nations, 1920-22. Recipient: Académie Française Prix Montyon, 1927; Rumford Medal, Royal Society, London, 1940. Fellow, All Souls, Oxford, 1927; Officer, 1919, and Grand Officer, 1955, Légion d'Honneur; Member, Académie Française, 1944. *Died 28 March 1959.*

PUBLICATIONS

Political and Social Commentary

La Démocratie en Nouvelle-Zeland. Paris, Colin, 1904; as *Democracy in New Zealand*, London, Bell, 1914.
Edward Gibbon Wakefield et sa doctrine de colonisation systématique. Paris, Colin, 1904.
La Canada: Les Deux races. Paris, Colin, 1906; as *The Race Question in Canada*, London, Nash, 1907.
Tableau politique de la France de l'ouest sous ca Troisième République. Paris, Colin, 1913.
Deux mois en Amérique du Nord à la veille de la guerre, juin-juillet 1914. Paris, Colin, 1916.
L'Angleterre d'aujourd'hui: Son evolution économique et politique. Paris, Crès, 1924; as *Post-War Britain*, London, Cape, 1924; New York, Dutton, 1925.
Les États-Unis d'aujourd'hui. Paris, Colin, 1927; as *America Comes of Age*, London, Cape, and New York, Harcourt Brace, 1927.
France: A Study in Nationality. New Haven, Connecticut, Yale University Press, 1930.
Tableau des partis en France. Paris, Grasset, 1930.
La Crise britannique au XXe siècle. Paris, Colin, 1931; as *England's Crisis*, London, Cape, and New York, Harcourt Brace, 1931.
Amérique Latine. Paris, Colin, 1933; as *Impressions of South America*, London, Cape, and New York, Harcourt Brace, 1933.
La Crise de l'Europe. Paris, Calmann-Lévy, 1935; as *Europe's Crisis*, London, Cape, 1935.
Le Canada, puissance internationale. Paris, Colin, 1937; as *Canada*, London, Cape, and New York, Harcourt Brace, 1937; revised edition, Cape, and New York, Duell, 1949.
Qu'est-ce que l'Amérique? Paris, Flammarion, 1938.
What the British Empire Means to Western Civilization. Toronto, Oxford University Press, and New York, Farrar and Rinehart, 1940.
Suez, Panama, et les routes maritimes mondiales. Paris, Colin, 1940; as *Suez and Panama*, London, Cape, and New York, Harcourt Brace, 1940.
Vue générale de la Méditerranée. Paris, Gallimard, 1943; as *The Mediterranean*, New York, Duell, 1947; London, Cape, 1948.
Quelques maximes. Paris, Haumont, 1943.
La Civilisation occidentale (lecture). Oxford, Clarendon Press, 1945.
France, Angleterre, États-Unis, Canada. Paris, Émile-Paul, 1946.
Mes Souvenirs de la IIIe République: Mon père et son temps, Jules Siegfried 1836-1922. Paris, Éditions du Grand Siècle, 1946.
La Suisse, démocratie-témoin. Neuchâtel, Baconnière, 1948; revised edition, 1969; as *Switzerland: A Democratic Way of Life*, London, Cape, and New York, Duell, 1950.
Afrique du Sud: Notes de voyage. Paris, Colin, 1949; as *African Journey*, London, Cape, 1950.
L'Âme des peuples. Paris, Hachette, 1949; as *The Character of Peoples*, London, Cape, 1952; as *Nations Have Souls*, New York, Putnam, 1952.
Géographie électorale de l'Ardèche sous la IIIe République. Paris, Colin, 1949.
Savoir parler en public. Paris, Michel, 1950.
La Fontaine, Machiavel français. Paris, Fragrance, 1950.
Voyage aux Indes. Paris, Colin, 1951.
Géographie humoristique de Paris. Paris, La Passerelle, 1952.
Géographie poetique des cinq continents. Paris, La Passerelle, 1953.
Tableau des États-Unis. Paris, Colin, 1954; as *America at Mid-Century*, London, Cape, and New York, Harcourt Brace, 1955.
Aspects du XXe siècle. Paris, Hachette, 1955.
Édouard Le Roy et son fauteuil, with Henry Daniel-Rops. Paris, Fayard, 1956.
De la IIIe à la IVe République. Paris, Grasset, 1956.
De la IVe à la Ve République au jour, le jour. Paris, Grasset, 1958.
Les Voies d'Israël: Essai d'interprétation de la religion juive. Paris, Hachette, 1958.
Itinéraire de contagions: Épidémies et idéologies. Paris, Colin, 1960; as *Germs and Ideas: Routes of Epidemics and Ideologies*, Edinburgh, Oliver and Boyd, 1965; as *Routes of Contagion*, New York, Harcourt Brace, 1965.
La Langue française et les conditions de la vie moderne, edited by

Josef Felixberger.   Munich, Hueber, 1968.

Other

Jules Siegfried 1837-1922.   Paris, Firmin-Didot, 1942.
L'Alsace, photographs by Michel Nicolas.   Paris, Del Duca, 1954.
Normandie, photographs by Noël Le Boyer.   Paris, Hachette, 1957.

*

Critical Study: *L'Oeuvre scientifique d'Andre Siegfried*, Paris, Presses de la Fondation Nationale des Sciences Politiques, 1977.

*   *   *

André Siegfried's work and intellectual contributions can be divided into three types, though undoubtedly some themes—such as the impact of religion upon social, economic, and political life, and the development of Anglo-American and French conceptions and practices of democratic political life—are found in each.

The first type (which is primarily represented by the works dealing with the United States, Latin America, France, the Mediterranean, Africa, and England) is for the most part of limited interest, though each represents the considered and informed judgments of a man who approached his tasks with care and diligence. They suffer, however, from one critical weakness: the reliance on over-arching generalizations about social attitudes, patterns of behaviour, and orientations to economic and political questions. These interpretations are buttressed, to be sure, by references to cases and instances, but the evidence for what is said, unfortunately, is not much above the anecdotal. This weakness is the hallmark of the "national character" school of social analysis, to which André Siegfried must be admitted. The problem with this approach—even if limited to economics and politics as it was for the most part in Siegfried's case—is that the boundaries between the most noticeable and the most representative of institutions and attitudes are not easily discerned. Nor are such works easily replicated, which, in part, explains the decline in the popularity of such pieces. Another part of the explanation is that the advent of survey research forced social analysts to focus on actual patterns of behaviours and attitudes at the mass level rather than relying on inferences from social, economic, and political elites. As well, in the latter part of the 20th century, those who follow public affairs are reluctant to appreciate—even granting the pleasures of hyberbole—phrases such as the "personality of continents" and the "individuality of states" and the attribution of certain characteristics to "race" and "blood."

Siegfried's second contribution was the development of the field of "electoral geography," to which he made seminal contributions, models of attentive work, scrupulous recording of detail, and subtle analyses. The importance of his influence is seen in the sustained popularity of this method of electoral analysis, particularly in France. The method is simple in conception and involved in execution. It requires the analysis of maps depicting the spatial distribution of social, economic, geographic, and political variables in order to delineate the factors associated with party preference and voter turnout. Given this format, it is easy to fall prey to crude environmental determinism, but Siegfried's analyses were acute and sophisticated, reflecting the assumption that the interaction of varied geographical factors and human forms produced environments supportive of varying political tendencies.

Most electoral analysts outside of France have eschewed the cartographic technique, attracted by more sophisticated statistical ones. In North America, in particular, there was a downplaying of the utility of this form of research because of its inability to produce individual-level statements or test propositions concern-

ing the psychological correlates of behaviour. In recent years, however, electoral geography has attracted renewed interest, a reflection of the field's stress upon historical continuities and environmental factors, matters which are not easily incorporated into survey research. Siegfried's work, long passed by, is now the basis for awakened interest in the geographical dimensions of political behaviour.

Siegfried's third contribution is represented by his works on Canada (for which he has been titled Canada's Tocqueville, though he lacks his majesty of phrase and scope of interpretation) and, to a lesser extent, his works on the United States. Here we find two signal interpretations.

The first is contained in his discussion of the difficulties of bringing together two disparate peoples—the French and the English—into one society and one political system in the northern half of North America. Siegfried described in careful and sensitive terms two forms of social organization—as manifested in religion and language—so divergent that "an open warfare is in progress, the bitterness of which it were useless to seek to disguise." Retrospectively, from the vantage point of an age when social analysts have tended to interpret conflict in material terms, Siegfried's account is instructive and salutary in its reminder that the appeals and ties of ethnicity and language are strong and enduring. Although Siegfried's image of the degree of accommodation between the French and the English may have been too sanguine, it is also prophetic in its vision of a bilingual and bicultural society.

The other significant contribution by Siegfried is found in his treatment of the role of political parties and politicians in a complex, pluralistic society. In 1906 Siegfried acutely described political parties as organizations attempting to act as brokers between contending interests and values in an effort to maximize their electoral standing. In the course of doing so they also perform the important function of integrating otherwise incompatible social forces. This perspective is in contradistinction to that of many others who have assumed that the solutions to Canada's problems are located in the nature and operation of political institutions, especially the federal system. This latter assumption led to the great proliferation of studies dealing with the constitutional development of the system, to the neglect of non-legal political entities and values. Siegfried in his 1955 study of the United States continued this portrayal of political parties as central components of the process of brokerage politics. Politicians are seen as "parasitical" but nonetheless vital for the proper functioning of a liberal democratic political system.

For over half a century, then, André Siegfried produced an extraordinary number of diverse works, all of which, to varying degrees, can be read with profit, appreciated for their insights and many prescient analyses, and, in some instances, for their innovative contributions to political science in particular and to social thought in general.

—Peter Woolstencroft

SIMMEL, Georg.   German sociologist.   Born in Berlin, 1 March 1858. Studied at the University of Berlin, Ph.D. 1881. Privatdozent in Philosophy, 1885-1900, and Professor Extraordinary, 1900-14, University of Berlin; Professor of Philosophy, University of Strasbourg, 1914-18; retired to complete his last book, 1918. *Died 26 September 1918.*

PUBLICATIONS

Sociology and Philosophy

Das Wesen der Materie nach Kants physischer Monadologie.

Berlin, Druck der Norddeutschen Buchdruckerei, 1881.

Über sociale Differenzierung: Sociologische und psychologische Untersuchungen. Leipzig, Duncker und Humblot, 1890.

Die Probleme der Geschichtsphilosophie: Eine erkenntnistheoretische Studie. Leipzig, Duncker und Humblot, 1892; revised edition, 1905; as *The Problems of the Philosophy of History,* edited by Guy Oakes, New York, Free Press, 1977.

Einleitung in die Moralwissenschaft: Eine Kritik der ethischen Grundbegriffe. Berlin, Hertz, 2 vols., 1892-93.

Philosophie des Geldes. Leipzig, Duncker und Humblot, 1900; as *The Philosophy of Money,* edited by David Frisby, London, Routledge, 1978.

Kant: Sechzehn Vorlesungen gehalten an der Berliner Universität. Leipzig, Duncker und Humbolt, 1904; revised edition, 1913.

Philosophie der Mode. Berlin, Pan-Verlag, 1905; revised edition, as "Die Mode" in *Philosophische Kultur: Gesammelte Essays,* 1911.

Kant und Goethe. Berlin, Marquardt, 1906; revised edition, 1916.

Die Religion. Frankfurt, Rütten und Loening, 1906; revised edition, 1912.

Schopenhauer und Nietzche: Ein Vortragszyklus. Leipzig, Duncker und Humblot, 1907.

Soziologie: Untersuchungen Über die Formen der Vergesellschaftung. Leipzig, Duncker und Humblot, 1908; third edition, 1923; chapters 2,3, and 5, with *Grundfragen der Soziologie (Individuum und Gesellschaft)* as *The Sociology of Georg Simmel,* edited by Kurt H. Wolff, Glencoe, Illinois, Free Press, 1950; chapters 4 and 6 as *Conflict and the Web of Group-Affiliations,* Glencoe, Illinois, Free Press, 1955.

Hauptprobleme der Philosophie. Leipzig, Göschen, 1910.

Philosophische Kultur: Gesammelte Essays. Leipzig, Kröner, 1911; revised edition, 1919.

Goethe. Leipzig, Klinkhardt und Biermann, 1913.

Deutschlands innere Wandlung (lecture). Strasbourg, Trübner, 1914.

Das Problem der historischen Zeit. Berlin, Reuther und Reichard, 1916.

Rembrandt: Ein Kunstphilosophischer Versuch. Leipzig, Wolff, 1916.

Grundfragen der Soziologie (Individuum und Gesellschaft). Berlin, de Gruyter, 1917; as "Fundamental Problems of Sociology (Individual and Society)," in *The Sociology of Georg Simmel,* 1950.

Der Krieg und die geistigen Entscheidungen: Reden und Aufsätze. Munich, Duncker und Humblot, 1917.

Der Konflikt der modernen Kultur: Ein Vortrag. Munich, Duncker und Humblot, 1918.

Lebensanschauung: Vier metaphysische Kapitel. Munich, Duncker und Humblot, 1918.

Vom Wesen des historischen Verstehens. Berlin, Mittler, 1918.

Zur Philosophie der Kunst: Philosophische und kunstphilosophische Aufsätze, edited by Gertrud Simmel. Potsdam, Kiepenheuer, 1922.

Schulpädagogik (lectures), edited by Karl Hauter. Osterwieck, Zickfeldt, 1922.

Fragmente und Aufsätze aus dem Nachlass und Veröffentlichungen der letzten Jahre, edited by Gertrud Kantorowicz. Munich, Drei Masken Verlag, 1923.

Rembrandtstudien. Basle, Schwabe, 1953.

Brücke und Tür: Essays des Philosophen zur Geschichte, Religion, Kunst, und Gesellschaft, edited by Michael Landmann. Stuttgart, Koehler, 1957.

Georg Simmel 1858-1918: A Collection of Essays, edited by Kurt H. Wolff. Columbus, Ohio State University Press, 1959.

On Individuality and Social Forms: Selected Writings, edited by Donald N. Levine. Chicago, University of Chicago Press, 1971.

Georg Simmel: Sociologist and European (selections), edited by P. Lawrence. New York, Barnes and Noble, and London, Nelson, 1976.

*

Bibliography: in *Georg Simmel 1858-1918,* 1959.

Critical Studies: *Buch des Dankes an Georg Simmel: Briefe, Erinnerungen, Bibliographie* edited by Kurt Gassen and Michael Landmann, Berlin, Duncker und Humblot, 1958; *Die soziologische Gesamtkonzeption* George Simmel by P.E. Schnabel, Stuttgart, Fischer, 1974; *Asthetik und Soziologie um die Jahrhundertwende: Georg Simmel* edited by Hannes Böhringer and Karlfried Gründer, Frankfurt, Klostermann, 1976 (includes bibliography); *Georg Simmel, Sociologist and European* by P.A. Lawrence, London, Nelson, 1976; *Sociological Impressionism: A Reassessment of Georg Simmel's Social Theory* by David Frisby, London, Heinemann, 1981.

*   *   *

Although Georg Simmel was an important figure in the intellectual life of Germany in his own lifetime, he has been somewhat neglected in sociology, being overshadowed by, for example, Max Weber. In the Anglo-Saxon context, Simmel has suffered from late and partial translation of his major works as well as his minor essays, and as a result he has often been interpreted in a one-sided manner. Having been defined as the founder of "formal sociology," Simmel has been seen as the precursor of social psychology and symbolic interactionism. He is thus narrowly identified with the sociology of interpersonal relations and small groups. To some extent, the nature of Simmel's work has encouraged these limited and uneven evaluations of his position in sociology. Much of his most innovative and significant work in sociology appeared in essay form, was highly impressionistic, and precluded any systematic treatment of social relationships. Many of his essays were, to use the title of his contributions to the *Jugend,* "Snapshots *subspecie aeternitatis*"; they aimed to catch the detail of fleeting relationships from "the perspective of eternity." The translation into English in 1978 of his major work—*Philosophie des Geldes*—will provide a more comprehensive view of the importance of Simmel's thought and dispel existing misconceptions.

To refer to Simmel as a "sociologist" is itself misleading. His early work, in the period 1880-90, was primarily concerned with philosophical issues, especially in the philosophy of Kant. His publications in social science span the period from 1890 to 1908, when he wrote on social differentiation, money, religion, and the character of sociology. Simmel then returned to his philosophical interests, publishing *Schopenhauer und Nietzsche* and *Hauptprobleme der Philosophie.* In his final years, he was primarily concerned with the philosophy of culture as the area within which he chose to discuss the fragmentation of human experience in a society where the division of labour produced specialised individuals. These phases in his work are, to some extent, linked together by a pessimistic view of human existence in which external forms of social life inevitably limit human creativity and personal development.

Simmel laid the foundations for the discipline of sociology long before Max Weber turned to the problem of sociology as a special subject. In establishing sociology as a discipline within the university system, Simmel sought to identify sociology as a special approach to social phenomena and to differentiate it from history and psychology. The aim of sociology was to describe the forms of social interaction or sociation and the rules of sociation between individuals and groups. Sociation involved the complex web of interactions, both co-operative and conflictual, between socialised individuals. In this respect "society" was not a collective entity nor merely the sum of individuals, but the effect of the ongoing process of sociation between social individuals. The task of sociology was to identify the more or less stable forms of sociation, irrespective of their variable content. For example, the structure of interaction in dyadic forms of interaction will be very different from that of triadic forms. Triadic situations allow for complex strategies of alliance regardless of the particular people involved. Forms or structures of interaction can be studied without reference to their particular content. This, in general terms, is what is meant by "formal sociology." Formal sociology is a-historical in the sense that illustrations of form can be taken from any period or context in order to illustrate a specific issue. These snapshots of the particular, fleeting detail of interaction, were meant to illustrate some universal form of human sociation. The selection of any given item of interaction was not a problem since, in Simmel's sociology, all phenomena are related. One aspect of culture can be separated from the total context within which it is situated; the ephemeral gestures of interaction are clues to the nature of the total social structure. However, Simmel was not prepared to offer any firm generalisations about social life on the basis of these social vignettes. In this respect, Simmel's sociology is often described as social impressionism. Against this interpretation, it can be argued that Simmel's work represents a sociological interpretation of the problems raised in Kantian philosophy. In this interpretation, the forms of sociation are seen to intervene between the transcendental ego and the raw materiality of the natural world.

One important theme in Simmel's sociology and social philosophy was "the tragedy of culture." While the forms of sociation are human constructs, they quickly become the boundaries of interaction which limit individual expression. He thus metaphorically argued that the forms of life were created as "dwelling places," but they have become "its prisons." This pessimistic view of culture provided much of the metatheoretical basis for his main single publication, *The Philosophy of Money*. For Simmel, Marxists had missed the significance of money by treating it as simply an economic category, thereby neglecting its symbolic importance. Money was symbolic of a more basic process of human interaction, namely the conversion of subjectivity into objectivity. Money was simply part of a growing calculation of personal qualities and quantification of human relationships in modern society. Simmel was thus concerned to examine the effect of the money economy, exchange relations, and the division of labour on the individual. These effects included the fragmentation of experience, the atomisation of the individual, the standardisation of differences, and the reification of consciousness. The debate about the symbolic nature of money raised the question of the relationship between the individual and society. The individual and individuality were progressively undermined by the growing impact of the calculation of performances which money made possible. Simmel did not see the tragedy of culture as specific to capitalist society. On the contrary, Simmel anticipated Max Weber's criticism of socialism as an extension of the process of rationalisation and calculation. Socialism would involve an even greater extension of quantification into human relationships, resulting in a profound estrangement from personal life. This theme continued beyond the analysis of money and the money economy into Simmel's later period when he came to see the tragedy of culture as part of an inevitable and universal struggle between form and content.

Simmel's sociology has been regarded by some as simply the glittering product of German bourgeois society before the First World War. His lack of overt political commitment, his apparent detachment from the social settings he observes, his use of the essay form, and his reluctance to provide a systematic statement of his work have been taken as reflecting the transitory superficiality of a *fin de siècle* culture. Many of Simmel's essays—on urban life, the stranger, conversations, or the dinner table—reflect the character of urban life in which strangers are herded into intimacy. Simmel's ability to write on such a diversity of subjects—from women's rights to Goethe, from urbanism to Rembrandt—suggests a brilliant mind which could not settle on any central issue. These features of Simmel's work may suggest why until recently he was not taken as seriously as, for example, Émile Durkheim or Karl Marx.

Despite these frequently negative evaluations of Simmel's own work, his influence on sociology has been considerable. Simmel in 1912 belonged to a discussion group which included Georg Lukács and Max Weber; it is perhaps not surprising, therefore, that Simmel's view of the tragedy of culture should also come to exercise a powerful influence on these two social theorists. Weber's conception of capitalism as an "iron cage" in which the individual would become overwhelmed by the minute calculation of actions which rational-technical thought made possible appears to be a direct application of Simmel's pessimistic contrast between form and content. The impact of Simmel on Lukács, who criticised what he saw as Simmel's irrationalism, is perhaps even more striking. Lukács's employment of the alienation theme in the work of Karl Marx was thus mediated by Simmel's critique of the money economy and economic fetishism. Simmel's influence has, however, extended much further outside the European context. In America, for example, social exchange theory and conflict theory have been especially dependent on the Simmelian tradition. More recently, there has been a growing appreciation of the centrality of Simmel to any discussion of the concepts of individuality, the individual, and individualism because Simmel's concept of sociation offers a fruitful position for approaching the relationship of the individual and society, individuality and sociability.

Simmel provided an approach to social phenomena which was highly original and distinctive, offering in sociology a clear alternative to the positivistic approaches of Herbert Spencer and Émile Durkheim; his criticisms of historical materialism anticipated and laid the basis for much recent work on the concept of alienation.

—Bryan S. Turner

SIMON, Herbert A(lexander). American social scientist. Born in Milwaukee, Wisconsin, 15 June 1916. Studied at the University of Chicago, B.A. 1936, Ph.D. 1943. Married Dorothea Pye in 1937; 4 children. Research Assistant, University of Chicago, 1937; Staff Member, International City Managers' Association, 1938-39; Director, Administrative Measurement Studies, Bureau of Public Administration, University of California, 1936-42; Assistant Professor of Political Science, Illinois Institute of Technology, Chicago, 1942-45; Associate Professor, 1945-47, Professor, 1947-49, Professor of Administration and Psychology, 1949-65, and since 1965 Richard King Mellon University Professor of Computer Sciences and Psychology, Carnegie-Mellon University, Pittsburgh (Trustee since 1972). Ford Distinguished Lecturer, New York University, 1959; Vanuxem Lecturer, Princeton University, New Jersey, 1961; William James Lecturer, Harvard University, Cambridge, Massachusetts, 1963; Sigma Xi Lecturer, 1964, 1976-78; Harris Lecturer, Northwestern University, Evanston, Illinois, 1967; Karl Taylor Compton Lecturer, Massachusetts Institute of Technology, Cambridge, 1968; Wolfgang Koehler Lecturer, Dartmouth College, Hanover, New Hampshire, 1975; Katz-Newcombe Memorial Lecturer, University of Michigan, Ann Arbor, 1976; Carl Howland Lecturer, Yale University, New Haven, Connecticut, 1976; Ueno Lecturer, University of Tokyo, 1977; Ely Lecturer, American Economics Association, 1977; Gaither Lecturer, University of California, Berkeley, 1980; Honorary Professor, Tianjin University, China, 1980. Consultant, International City Managers' Association, 1942-49; United States Bureau of the Budget, 1946-49; United States Census Bureau, 1947; and Cowles Foundation for Research in Economics, 1947-60. Member, Board of Directors, Social Science Research Council, 1961-65; Chairman, Division of Behavioral Sciences, National Research Council, 1968-

70; Member, President's Science Advisory Committee, 1968-71. Recipient: American College Hospital Administrators Award, 1957; Distinguished Science Contribution Award, American Psychological Association, 1969; Frederick Mosher Award, American Society of Public Administrators, 1974; A.M. Turing Award, American Association for Computing Machinery, 1975; Nobel Prize in Economics, 1978; Proctor Prize, Sigma Xi, 1980. Honorary doctorate: Case Institute of Technology, Cleveland, 1963; Yale University, 1963; University of Chicago, 1964; University of Lund, 1968; McGill University, Montreal, 1970; Erasmus University, Rotterdam, 1973; University of Michigan, 1978; University of Pittsburgh, 1979; Marquette University, Milwaukee, 1981. Member, National Academy of Sciences, and the National Science Foundation. Fellow, Econometrics Society; American Academy of Arts and Sciences; and the American Philosophical Association; Distinguished Fellow, American Economics Association. Foreign Member, Royal Society of Letters, University of Lund; Organization of the Social Sciences, Japan; Yugoslav Academy of Sciences. Address: Department of Psychology, Carnegie-Mellon University, Pittsburgh, Pennsylvania 15213, U.S.A.

PUBLICATIONS

Psychology, Economics and Administration

Measuring Municipal Activities, with C.E. Ridley. Chicago, International City Managers' Association, 1938.
Determining Work Loads for Professional Staff in a Public Welfare Agency, with others. Berkeley, California, Bureau of Public Administration, 1941.
Fiscal Aspects of Metropolitan Administration. Berkeley, California, Bureau of Public Administration, 1943.
Fire Losses and Fire Risks, with others. Berkeley, California, Bureau of Public Administration, 1943.
Administrative Behavior: A Study of Decision-Making Processes in Administrative Organization. New York, Macmillan, 1947.
Techniques of Municipal Administration. Chicago, International City Managers' Association, 1947.
Public Administration, with others. New York, Knopf, 1950.
Centralization vs. Decentralization in Organizing the Controller's Department, with others. New York, Controllership Foundation, 1954.
Models of Man, Social and Rational: Mathematical Essays on Rational Human Behavior in a Social Setting. New York, Wiley, 1957.
Organizations, with John G. March. New York, Wiley, 1958.
The New Science of Management Decision. New York, Harper, 1960; as *The Shape of Automation for Men and Management*. New York, Harper, 1965.
The Sciences of the Artificial. Cambridge, Massachusetts Institute of Technology, 1969.
Human Problem Solving, with W.A. Newell. Englewood Cliffs, New Jersey, Prentice Hall, 1972.
Skew Distributions and the Sizes of Business Firms, with others. Amsterdam, North Holland, 1977.
Models of Discovery and Other Topics in the Methods of Science. Dordrecht, Reidel, 1977.
Models of Thought. New Haven, Connecticut, Yale University Press, 1979.
Models of Bounded Rationality. Cambridge, Massachusetts Institute of Technology, 2 vols., 1982.

*   *   *

Herbert A. Simon is an American economist, psychologist, and computer scientist who received the 1978 Nobel Prize in economics. The citation noted Simon's "pioneering research into the decision-making process within economic organizations"

and declared that "modern business economics and administrative research are largely based on Simon's ideas."

Classical economic theory says that entrepreneurs maximize business profits. It tells how they do this and examines the short and long-range effects of their behavior. Simon challenges this view, asserting that real world business managers do not have enough information to maximize. All they can hope is to reach acceptable goals.

Simon's influential work can be said to have begun in 1947 with publication of *Administrative Behavior: A Study of Decision-Making Processes in Administrative Organization*. This book, which grew out of research that Simon did toward a doctorate in political science, attacked current administrative theory and proposed a new way of looking at the workings of an administrative organization. Simon's major beliefs, as he put them, were "that decision-making is the heart of administration, and that the vocabulary of administrative theory must be derived from the logic and psychology of human choice."

Though his original research had pertained largely to public administration, Simon soon expanded his interests toward business organizations. With associates, he extensively studied decision-making in ten business firms and replicated the corporate environment under controlled experimental conditions. Simon ultimately concluded that it was impossible for any human being in the real world to obtain or process all the information needed to make the maximizing decisions of classical economic theory. Companies, therefore, try to do the best they can under their circumstances—to work toward acceptable goals. This Simon termed "satisficing" behavior. He then proposed to replace "economic man" and his "maximizing" decisions with a more realistic "administrative man" and "satisficing" decisions. Though many classical economists have rejected Simon's conclusions, his ideas have found acceptance among economists whose special interest is business operations and among teachers in business schools.

Problem-solving is central to decision-making. During the course of his work on corporations, Simon reached this conclusion and teamed with Allen Newell of the Rand Corporation to simulate the problem-solving process with computer programs. The two men began by presenting human beings with problems of logical analysis and asking them to describe what steps they took to solve the problems. The elements of reasoning were then translated into computer language and put into a program which made no reference to the original problem. The completed program made it possible for the computer to "reason" its way through simple problems of logical analysis.

Simon and Newell completed their program late in 1955. It enabled the computer to solve many problems that humans could. This kind of program was to be called "artificial intelligence." Simon later expanded upon this work, developing routines that enabled computers to cope with much more complex problems, and to define problems that were poorly structured at the outset and then to solve them. By using the computer to simulate human intelligence, Simon, without abandoning his original interest in decision-making, had moved from pure economics into computer science and psychology.

Some people call Herbert Simon a "technological radical" for his views on psychology and the computer. Since he has demonstrated that computers can "think," like people, Simon declares that the human mind, both its conscious and subconscious portions, is like a data processor. He has stated that his mind "works according to laws and mechanisms, not some mysterious mind fluid." Simon believes that the computer will soon be able to "do anything a man can do. They can already read, think, learn, create." With help from associates, Simon has programmed computers to play chess, to solve abstruse mathematical equations, and to discriminate among shapes. He believes that the day is near when some of the higher-status jobs in society, such as those of the doctor, corporate manager, and college teacher, will be computerized.

According to one associate, Herbert Simon is "the one man in the world who comes closest to the ideal of Aristotle or a Renaissance man." He has spent most of his life in the academic world, teaching courses in political science (his original field of study), economics, psychology, and computer science. At one time, he even taught a course on the French Revolution to a group of undergraduate students.

—Victor Cassidy

SKINNER, B(urrhus) F(rederic). American psychologist. Born in Susquehanna, Pennsylvania, 20 March 1904. Studied at Hamilton College, Clinton, New York, B.A. 1929; Harvard University, Cambridge, Massachusetts, M.A. 1930, Ph.D. 1931. Conducted war research for the Office of Scientific Research and Development, 1942-43. Married Yvonne Blue in 1936; 2 children. Research Fellow, National Research Council, 1931-32; Junior Fellow, Harvard Society of Fellows, 1933-36; Instructor in Psychology, 1936-37, Assistant Professor, 1937-39, and Associate Professor, 1939-45, University of Minnesota, Minneapolis; Professor and Chairman of the Department of Psychology, Indiana University, Bloomington, 1945-48; Professor of Psychology, 1948-57, Edgar Pierce Professor, 1958-74, and since 1974 Professor Emeritus, Harvard University. William James Lecturer, Harvard University, 1947. Recipient: Harry Crosby Warren Medal, 1942; Guggenheim Fellowship, 1944; Career Grant, National Institute of Mental Health; Distinguished Science Contribution Award, American Psychological Association, 1958; National Medal of Science, 1971; Joseph P. Kennedy Jr. Foundation Award, 1971. Honorary doctorate: Ripon College, Wisconsin, 1957; North Carolina State University, Greensboro, 1960; University of Chicago, 1967; University of Michigan, Ann Arbor, 1968; Alfred University, New York, 1969; University of Exeter, England, 1969; Indiana University, Bloomington, 1970; McGill University, Montreal, 1970; Ohio Wesleyan University, Delaware, 1971; C.W. Post Center, Long Island University, New York, 1971; Rockford College, Illinois, 1971; Hobart and William Smith Colleges, Geneva, New York, 1972; Dickinson College, Carlisle, Pennsylvania, 1972; Framingham State College, Massachusetts, 1972; University of Baltimore, 1973; Lowell Technological Institute, Massachusetts, 1974; New College, Hofstra University, Hempstead, New York, 1974; Nasson College, Springvale, Maine, 1976; Western Michigan University, Kalamazoo, 1976; University of Louisville, Kentucky, 1977; Tufts University, Medford, Massachusetts, 1977; Johns Hopkins University, Baltimore, 1979; Keio University, Tokyo, 1979. Member, National Academy of Sciences, and the American Academy of Arts and Sciences. Fellow, Royal Society of Arts, London. Address: 13 Old Dee Road, Cambridge, Massachusetts 02138, U.S.A.

PUBLICATIONS

Psychology

The Behavior of Organisms: An Experimental Analysis. New York, Appleton Century, 1938.
Science and Human Behavior. New York, Macmillan, 1953; London, Collier Macmillan, 1965.
Verbal Behavior (lectures). New York, Appleton Century, 1957; London, Methuen, 1979.
Schedules of Reinforcement, with C.B. Ferster. New York, Appleton Century, 1957.
Cumulative Record (essays). New York, Appleton Century, 1959; revised edition, 1961, 1972.
The Analysis of Behavior: A Program for Self-Instruction, with James G. Holland. New York, McGraw Hill, 1961.
The Technology of Teaching. New York, Appleton Century, 1968.
Contingencies of Reinforcement: A Theoretical Analysis. New York, Appleton Century, 1969.
Beyond Freedom and Dignity. New York, Knopf, 1971; London, Cape, 1972.
About Behaviorism. New York, Knopf, and London, Cape, 1974.
Reflections on Behaviorism and Society. Englewood Cliffs, New Jersey, Prentice Hall, 1978.

Other

Walden Two (novel). New York, Macmillan, 1948; London, Macmillan, 1969.
Particulars of My Life. New York, Knopf, and London, Cape, 1976.
The Shaping of a Behaviorist: Part Two of an Autobiography. New York, Knopf, and London, Holdan Books, 1979.
Notebooks, edited by Robert Epstein. Englewood Cliffs, New Jersey, Prentice Hall, 1980.

Editor, with William A. Skinner, *A Digest of Opinions of the Anthracite Board of Conciliation.* Scranton, Pennsylvania, n.p., 1928.

*

Bibliography: "A Listing of the Published Works of B.F. Skinner with Notes and Comments" by Robert Epstein, in *Behaviorism* (Reno, Nevada), 5, 1977.

Critical Studies: *The Skinner Primer: Behind Freedom and Dignity* by Finley Carpenter, New York, Free Press, 1974; *B.F. Skinner: The Man and His Ideas* by Richard I. Evans, New York, Dutton, 1978; *What Is Skinner Really Saying?* by Robert D. Nye, Englewood Cliffs, New Jersey, Prentice Hall, 1979.

* * *

For the past four decades the dean of behavioral psychologists has been B.F. Skinner. Both influential and controversial, Skinner has pioneered techniques to analyze and modify animal and human behavior, and he has contributed to both the theory and the technology of learning. He has also sought to formulate a philosophy of "the science of human behavior."

In the beginning of behavioral psychology was René Descartes, who theorized that animal behavior was purely "reflex action," mechanical cause-and-effect relationships. Between the Cartesian reflexologists and Skinner were the "classical" behaviorists at the turn of the 20th century, most notably the Russian Ivan Pavlov and the American John Watson.

Pavlov, of course, remains most famous for his experiments with dogs. He discovered they would salivate at the smell of food, even at the sound of attendants bringing the food. These "stimuli" elicited the "response" of salivating. When Pavlov rang a bell at the same time that food was delivered, the dogs salivated. Eventually, the bell was rung in the total absence of food; the dogs' nervous systems responded with salivation anyway. The bell stimulus had substituted for the food stimulus and now constituted a "conditioned stimulus."

Pavlov's disciple John Watson extended the theory of conditioned reflexes to human habits. "Different kinds of habits," he declared, "are nothing but a long chain of conditioned reflexes." A number of other American psychologists, including E.L. Thorndike, incorporated or adapted aspects of conditioning or "behavioral" methods into their own work.

Building on this early research, Skinner's first major publication was *The Behavior of Organisms: An Experimental Analysis*, in 1938. Then and since, the distinction between his work and that of the "classical" conditioners has been marked. Where Skinner's predecessors concentrated on varying stimuli, Skinner's efforts were directed toward building and changing responses.

For purposes of environmental control, he invented the Skinner Box. In it, a rat, after wandering around haphazardly, accidentally pressed a lever. This action caused a pellet of food to be delivered. The food was the rat's inadvertent reward, or as Skinner termed it, "positive reinforcement" for its behavior. More lever-pressing, more food-reinforcement; the rat "learned." In the Pavlov-Watson model, an animal's response was elicited by an experimenter's action. Now the rat (or later, a pigeon or person) was an active contributor, acting on, "operating" on, its environment. With subsequent variations and refinements, this was the foundation of "operant conditioning"—the heart and soul (to employ a most non-Skinnerian metaphor) of Skinner's behavioral psychology.

A few of Skinner's basic terms should be defined. "The word 'operant,' " he says, "is used to emphasize the fact that behavior operates upon the environment to produce consequences, certain kinds of which 'reinforce' the behavior they are contingent upon, in the sense that they make it more likely to occur again." A "positive reinforcer" strengthens the behavior that produces it; a "negative reinforcer" strengthens the behavior that reduces it. And when reinforcement is no longer forthcoming the tendency to continue the behavior disappears; it is "extinguished."

Skinner's essentially simple techniques lent themselves both to replication and quantification, and in these respects at least could be classified as scientific experimentation. But Skinner saw implications for his experiments that transcended the laboratory. In his view, behavioral psychology was the counterpart of Darwinian biology. "The process of operant behavior supplements natural selection," he argued. "Important consequences of behavior which could not play a role in evolution because they were not sufficiently stable features of the environment are made effective through operant conditioning during the lifetime of the individual."

Now, according to Skinner, all of the "pre-scientific" theories in psychology could be discarded. We are in a position, he said, to abandon the elaborate and unprovable "mentalistic" explanations of behavior theorized by Freud and all of Freud's successors. Furthermore, the findings based on overt, observable behavior in response to environmental stimuli made it possible to bury, once and for all, the myth that we are "autonomous" beings who can freely choose what we are and what we do.

These heady ideas he developed in a controversial book, *Beyond Freedom and Dignity*, in 1971. "Autonomous man" who acted on his "own" volition was, said Skinner, a romantic illusion perpetuated by well-meaning poets and philosophers. In actuality, man was always and necessarily controlled by his environment. He argued cogently that the controls exercised through language, media, customs, and institutions were often capricious, inconsistent, and destructive. The one realistic alternative, since "freedom" from environmental control was impossible, was behaviorism. By recognizing that environment was the prime shaping force and then exercising responsible control, we could modify behavior to insure survival and satisfaction.

Paradoxically, Skinner was arguing that in order to achieve the benefits we would like to derive from "freedom," we need to systematize controlling mechanisms. This argument seems more than vaguely reminiscent of Puritan John Winthrop's 17th century definition of "true liberty": "It is maintained and exercised in a way of subjection to authority." In some matters, such as when he deals with sexual freedoms, Skinner does sound a trifle Puritanical. But the parallels stop abruptly at the mention of religion. "Faith" was defined by the skeptical Skinner as "a matter of the strength of behavior resulting from contingencies which have not been analyzed."

Incidentally, the absence of substantive content in Skinner's definition is typical—virtually all of his definitions are literal restatements from his own tightly regulated, laboratory-bound vocabulary. Language itself, as he explained in detail in *Verbal Behavior* (1957), exemplifies reinforcement techniques.

Beyond Freedom and Dignity was a curious amalgam. It was a survey, and attempted demolition, of pre-behavioral attempts to understand and guide man. It contained bleak warnings about the anti-social trends of our time. And it was a cautiously optimistic polemic about the potential blessings of behaviorism. The book's principal force came from its insistence that the exalted ideas of "freedom" and "dignity" were hollow constructs.

Earlier in his career, Skinner had written a novel to illustrate his theories and objectives. This was *Walden Two*, published in 1948. As Edward Bellamy had done in *Looking Backward* (1888), novelist Skinner created a flimsy story line and bloodless characters for the purpose of describing a utopian society. Skinner's fictional hero, Prof. Burris (the author's own first name is Burrhus) was introduced to a cheerful, egalitarian, and efficient community, and he came to love it; that was the entire plot. The dialogue was little more than explanation of how things worked.

The fictional community was Walden Two (an ironic nod to the reclusive Thoreau, a great believer in "freedom"). It was small and self-sufficient, and its workings were adapted from the behavioral principles of operant conditioning and positive reinforcement. Baby care, education, work selection and routines, family life and recreation were all constructed with "schedules of reinforcement," with continual re-tinkering to insure proper "behavior modification." The governmental system, like everything else, was "based upon a science of human behavior."

Since all members of the community were totally integrated into the system of positive reinforcement through their behavior, there was no need to praise anyone for what they did. "We are grateful to all and to none," said a community leader. "We feel a sort of generalized gratitude toward the whole community." The little world of Walden Two may have seemed an unexciting place to many of the book's readers, but unquestionably its denizens were very well behaved.

Reactions to the book were, as usual with Skinner's work, mixed. Was this a sensible blueprint for survival? Or was it an Orwellian nightmare vision of a robotized future? At least one group of people took the conception seriously enough to try it. In Twin Oaks, Virginia, a small community, modeled roughly on Skinner's ideas, was established. It enjoyed some modest success and duration.

By 1982, Skinner had published many books and articles. Behavioral psychologists (not all of them Skinnerians) were active at many institutions, as teachers, researchers, and consultants. And selected applications of behavioral methods were being used by many mental health practitioners who were not, strictly speaking, behaviorists. Reinforcement techniques were credited with some notable successes in treating the mentally retarded; in enabling some psychotic patients to cope better with everyday tasks; in "curing" phobias; in aiding many students to learn some kinds of materials through programmed texts and teaching machines.

Many psychologists believed, however, that more significant advances in the study of human behavior were coming from two other directions. "Cognitive" psychologists, whose number and body of theory have increased dramatically, stress that a comprehensive psychology must deal with a complete "person"; they find severe limitations in the behavioral approach to conditioning "organisms" (Skinner's first book title was *The Behavior of Organisms*).

Perhaps even more consequential for psychology has been the impact of scientific brain research, leading to, among other things, the discovery of endorphins and hitherto unknown neuro-transmitters. Skinner has taken an insulated position in regard to physiology, holding that such research is outside the province of (and apparently irrelevant to) research in operant conditioning. Skinner's insularity here seems quite out of touch with modern attitudes in *all* of the sciences.

Now a Professor Emeritus of Psychology at Harvard University, Skinner continues to believe that the experimental analysis of behavior "may offer a solution" to the most pressing problems of our time. And, as has been the case throughout his career, he remains convinced that behaviorism's principal problem is that it is "misunderstood." People still connect his work, he recently remarked, with "Pavlovian conditioning using shock or vomit-inducing drugs."

—Don Hausdorff

SOMBART, Werner. German economist and sociologist. Born in Ermsleben, Germany, 19 January 1863. Educated at Pisa; studied at the University of Berlin, Ph.D. 1888. Secretary, Bremen Chamber of Commerce, 1888-90. Professor Extraordinary of Economics, University of Breslau, 1890-1905; taught at the Handelshochschule, Berlin, 1905-17; Professor of Economics, University of Berlin, 1917-31. Editor, with Max Weber, *Archiv für Sozialwissenschaft und Sozialpolitik*, 1903-33. *Died (in Berlin) 13 May 1941.*

PUBLICATIONS

Economics and Sociology

Die römische Campagna: Eine sozialökonomische Studie. Leipzig, Duncker und Humblot, 1888.
Sozialismus und soziale Bewegung im 19. Jahrhundert; nebst einem Anhang: Chronik der sozialen Bewegung von 1750-1896. Jena, Fischer, 1896; as *Socialism and the Social Movement in the 19th Century; with a Chronicle of the Social Movement, 1750-1896,* New York and London, Putnam, 1898.
Der moderne Kapitalismus. Leipzig, Duncker und Humblot, 3 vols. in 4, 1902-27.
Wirtschaft und Mode Ein Beitrag zur Theorie der modernen Bedarfgestaltung. Wiesbaden, Bergmann, 1902.
Die deutsche Volkswirtschaft im neunzehnten Jahrhundert. Berlin, Bondi, 1903.
Die gewerbliche Arbeiterfrage. Leipzig, Göschen, 1904.
Das Proletariat: Bilder und Studien. Frankfurt, Rütten und Loening, 1906.
Warum gibt es in den Vereinigten Staaten keinen Sozialismus? Tübingen, Mohr, 1906; as *Why Is There No Socialism in the United States?,* edited by C.T. Husbands, London, Macmillan, and White Plains, New York, International Arts and Sciences Press, 1976.
Kunstgewerbe und Kultur. Berlin, Marquardt, 1908.
"Dennoch!": Aus Theorie und Geschichte der gewerkschaftlichen Arbeiterbewegung. Jena, Fischer, 1909.
Das Lebenswerk von Karl Marx. Jena, Fischer, 1909.
Die Juden und das Wirtschaftsleben. Leipzig, Duncker und Humblot, 1911; as *The Jews and Modern Capitalism,* London, Unwin, 1913; New York, Dutton, 1914.
Die Zukunft der Juden. Leipzig, Duncker und Humblot, 1912.
Judentaufen, with others. Munich, Müller, 1912.
Der Bourgeois: Zur Geistesgeschichte des modernen Wirtschaftsmenschen. Munich, Duncker und Humblot, 1913; as *The Quintessence of Capitalism: A Study in the History and Psychology of the Modern Business Man,* edited by M. Epstein, London, Unwin, 1915.
Studien zur Entwicklungsgeschichte des modernen Kapitalismus: Luxus und Kapitalismus; Krieg und Kapitalismus. Munich, Duncker und Humblot, 2 vols., 1913; vol. 1 as *Luxury and Capitalism,* Ann Arbor, University of Michigan Press, 1967.

Händler und Helden: Patriotische Besinnungen. Munich, Duncker und Humblot, 1915.
Die Ordnung des Wirtschaftslebens. Leipzig, Springer, 1924.
Beamtenschaft und Wirtschaft (lecture). Berlin, Verlagsanstalt des Deutschen Beamtenbundes, 1927.
Volk und Raum: Eine Sammlung von Gutachten zur Beantwortung der Frage: "Kann Deutschland innerhalb der bestehenden Grenzen eine wachsende Bevölkerung Erhalten?" Hamburg, Hanseatische Verlagsanstalt, 1928.
Die Rationalisierung in der Wirtschaft (speech). Leipzig, Scholl, 1928.
Gewerbewesen. Berlin, de Gruyter, 2 vols., 1929.
Die drei Nationalökonomien: Geschichte und System der Lehre von der Wirtschaft. Munich, Duncker und Humblot, 1930.
Nationalökonomie und Soziologie (lecture). Jena, Fischer, 1930.
Die zukunft des Kapitalismus. Berlin, Buchholz und Weisswange, 1932.
Bilder aus dem deutschen Wirtschaftsleben des 19. und 20. Jahrhunderts. Bielefeld, Velhagen und Klasing, 1932.
Deutscher Sozialismus. Berlin, Buchholz und Weisswange, 1934.
Soziologie: Was sie ist und was sie sein sollte. Berlin, Akademie der Wissenschaften, 1936.
A Help to the Reading of the German/Einleitung zu dem Werke "Sozialismus und soziale Bewegung." Oxford, Blackwell, 1936.
A New Social Philosophy, edited by Karl Geiser. Princeton, New Jersey, Princeton University Press, and London, Oxford University Press, 1937.
Vom Menschen: Versuch einer geisteswissenschaftlichen Anthropologie. Berlin, Buchholz und Weisswange, 1938.
Weltanschauung, Wissenschaft und Wirtschaft. Berlin, Buccholz und Weisswange, 1938; as *Weltanschauung, Science, and Economy,* New York, Veritas, 1939.

Other

Editor, *Grundlagen und Kritik des Sozialismus.* Berlin, Askanischer Verlag, 1919.
Editor, *Soziologie.* Berlin, Heise, 1923.

*

Critical Studies: *Social Conservatism and the Middle Classes in Germany 1914-1933* by Herman Lebovics, Princeton, New Jersey, Princeton University Press, 1969 (includes bibliography); *Sociology and Estrangement: Three Sociologists of Imperial Germany* by Arthur Mitzman, New York, Knopf, 1973.

*   *   *

The economist and social theorist Werner Sombart is probably best known for his work on the spirit and origins of capitalism, which in one study he attributed to Judaism and in another to woman's sensuality and desire for luxury. Sombart also worked from various ideological positions during his career, beginning as an evolutionary socialist and ending as a national socialist.

Sombart's early ideas on capitalism showed the influence of the works of Karl Marx. In a series of lectures first presented in 1896 Sombart had drawn the conclusion that capitalism's destruction of the old social order had been inevitable and progressive, and that the continuing growth of industrial capitalism would result in an evolutionary, peaceful advance to socialism. The first two volumes of *Der moderne Kapitalismus* (1902), in which Sombart attempted to explain how and why the victory of capitalism over the handicraft system had occurred, repeated the theme that the development of capitalism carried with it the higher level of civilization and prosperity of the modern age whose moving force was the capitalist "spirit."

Sombart did not retain his enthusiasm for socialism or the productive capacities of capitalism and his ideas changed considerably in the next few years, although subsequent writings often presented old and new ideas fearless of the contradictions. As his faith in industrialism and socialism faded, his lectures of 1896, periodically revised and enlarged over the next thirty years, became increasingly critical of socialism and Marxism. On issuing the third volume of *Der moderne Kapitalismus* in 1927 Sombart claimed his work was a continuation and in some sense a completion of the work of Marx, although the claim was hardly credible by that time and, even in the earliest editions of the book, Sombart's slackening faith in the progress of industrial society and nostalgia for the Middle Ages were occasionally evident.

These changes were clearly coming about as early as 1903 when in a study on German economic life, reissued in 1927, Sombart brought out a new hero—the artisan, whose demise had once been acclaimed as a sign of progress. And in time Sombart would conclude that Marx's failure to complete *Das Kapital*, a work he had praised in 1894, was not due to Marx's illness and death, but to the inadequacy of his theory. By the 1930's Sombart was amending his own works "from the national socialist way of thinking."

These shifts of position, which embroiled Sombart in countless controversies and polemics, were not capricious. They followed, rather, from clear modifications of his social thought, not the least bit uncommon for the generation of the 1890's, that reflected a loss of faith in the progress of a mechanistic and materialistic world, alienation from modern industrial society, and a rejection of its civilization.

Like Max Weber, Sombart maintained that the development of capitalism could not be explained in purely economic terms, and like Weber, Ernst Troeltsch, and Max Scheler, he was interested in the connection between religious morality and the capitalist spirit. However, Sombart argued against the view of these writers that Protestant Christianity was associated with the morality of capitalism. In *Der Bourgeois* (1913) Sombart presented Protestantism as the foe of capitalism. Against Weber's thesis that Calvinism, and Puritanism in particular, had played a key role in creating the spirit of modern capitalism, Sombart argued that Puritanism was actually hostile to the middle-class values, worldliness, and manifestation of wealth in capitalism.

It was, Sombart admitted, Weber's ideas that led him to consider the importance of Judaism for capitalist development. This theme was treated in a separate work, *Der Juden und das Wirtschaftsleben* (1911), in which Sombart argued that Judaism's legalism, rationalism, genius for commerciality, and differing moral and commercial codes of behavior for relations between Jews and non-Jews had nourished the spirit of capitalism. In addition, he claimed that the dispersion of the Jewish people, in particular their expulsion from Spain and resettlement in northern Europe, had resulted in a shift of economic activity to the northwestern European states in the 16th century. Further, Sombart discovered "an almost unique identity of view between Judaism and Puritanism on the question of divine rewards and punishments, the close relationship between business and religion, and the rationalization of life." He therefore concluded, "Puritanism is Judaism."

Sombart had brought himself to the position of having argued that Protestantism was hostile to capitalism while also maintaining that Puritanism was indistinguishable from the aspects of Judaism vital to the growth of capitalism. He explained this apparent contradiction in the chronological priority of Judaism which had shaped the spirit of capitalism as early as the 16th century. Puritanism, confronted by an established capitalist spirit and thus unable to organize its economic life according to its otherworldly beliefs, had to adjust and adopt the moral justification of Judaism. Rather than Puritanism having shaped the spirit of capitalism, the reverse had occurred as those parts of Puritanism which appear most important for the development of the capitalist spirit were borrowed from Judaism.

In the period from 1911 to 1913 Sombart also wrote *Luxus und Kapitalismus* on the growth of early capitalism. Its general theme was that from various economic and cultural phenomena, including the great trading fortunes of 13th- and 14th-century Italy, the princely courts of the 15th century with their studied refinement and grace, and the new middle-class fortunes and alliances with the old nobility in the 17th century, there had emerged a new society. Crucial to the development of this capitalist society were the concentration of consumers in growing urban centers, the expansion of business and industry to supply consumer goods, and the growth of credit banking for state and business debt.

In the emergence of this new society women had played a central role, according to Sombart. He claimed that the secularization of love from the 11th century onwards had loosened the former religious and institutional restraints, and by changing attitudes towards sexuality, produced a hedonistic aesthetic conception of woman. A new type of liberated woman began to appear at court and her presence influenced the measure of artifice, conformity to social graces, and passion for luxury goods. Women began to set the standards for the display of wealth and conspicuous consumption. As the bourgeoisie came to adopt the tastes and styles of the nobility, the formally thrifty middle-class wife developed an appetite for extravagance and luxury.

Sombart exposed the psychological meaning of this transition. "All personal luxury springs purely from sensuous pleasure," he wrote. Therefore the taste for luxury stemmed from the desire to refine and multiply the means of stimulating the senses. And since sensual and erotic pleasure were essentially the same, when a society became wealthy and sexuality was freely expressed, one found luxury in the ascendent. "Luxury, then, itself a legitimate child of illicit love...gave birth to capitalism."

Sombart never attempted to coordinate his theory of the origins of capitalism in luxury and sensuality with that of the special role of religion in forming the capitalist spirit. It may have been a difficult task for a thinker so often ambiguous, who left the special properties of capitalism so poorly defined and whose concepts were so promiscuous and omnipresent that for many they lost their usefulness. Yet Sombart's work was still compelling and interesting for the possibilities for understanding that it offered.

—Frank M. Baglione

SONTAG, Susan. American essayist and novelist. Born in New York City, 16 January 1933. Studied at the University of California, Berkeley, 1948-49; University of Chicago, B.A. 1951; Harvard University, Cambridge, Massachusetts, 1954-57, M.A. 1955; St. Anne's College, Oxford, 1957. Married the sociologist Philip Rieff in 1950 (divorced, 1957); 1 son. Instructor in English, University of Connecticut, Storrs, 1953-54; Teaching Fellow in Philosophy, Harvard University, 1955-57; Editor, *Commentary*, New York, 1959; Lecturer in Philosophy, City College of New York, and Sarah Lawrence College, Bronxville, New York, 1959-60; Instructor, Department of Religion, Columbia University, New York, 1960-64; Writer-in-Residence, Rutgers University, New Brunswick, New Jersey, 1964-65. Recipient: American Association of University Women Fellowship, 1957; Rockefeller Fellowship, 1965, 1974; Guggenheim Fellowship, 1966, 1975; American Academy Award, 1976; Brandeis University Creative Arts Award, 1976. Address: c/o Farrar Straus and Giroux, 19 Union Square West, New York, New York 10003, U.S.A.

PUBLICATIONS

Literature, Politics and the Arts

Against Interpretation and Other Essays. New York, Farrar Straus, 1966; London, Eyre and Spottiswoode, 1967.
Styles of Radical Will. New York, Farrar Straus, and London, Secker and Warburg, 1969.
On Photography. New York, Farrar Straus, 1977; as *Susan Sontag on Photography*, London, Allen Lane, 1978.
Under the Sign of Saturn (essays). New York, Farrar Straus, 1980.

Other

The Benefactor (novel). New York, Farrar Straus, 1963; London, Eyre and Spottiswoode, 1964.
Death Kit (novel). New York, Farrar Straus, 1967; London, Secker and Warburg, 1968.
Trip to Hanoi. New York, Farrar Straus, and London, Panther, 1969.
Duet for Cannibals (screenplay). New York, Farrar Straus, 1970; London, Allen Lane, 1974.
Brother Carl (screenplay). New York, Farrar Straus, 1974.
Illness as Metaphor. New York, Farrar Straus, 1978; London, Allen Lane, 1979.
I, Etcetera (short stories). New York, Farrar Straus, 1978; London, Gollancz, 1979.
A Susan Sontag Reader. New York, Farrar Straus, 1982.

Editor, *Selected Writings of Artaud.* New York, Farrar Straus, 1976.
Editor, *A Barthes Reader.* New York, Hill and Wang, and London, Cape, 1982.

*

Critical Studies: "Susan Sontag's 'New Left' Pastoral: Notes on Revolutionary Pastoralism in America" by Leo Marx, in *Tri-Quarterly* (Evanston, Illinois), 23-24, 1972; "Soliciting Self-Knowledge: The Rhetoric of Susan Sontag's Criticism" by Cary Nelson, in *Critical Inquiry* (Chicago), 6, 1980; *Beautiful Theories: The Spectacle of Discourse in Contemporary Criticism* by Elizabeth W. Bruss, Baltimore, Johns Hopkins University Press, 1982.

*   *   *

Susan Sontag has regularly declared that she thinks of herself primarily as a writer of fiction. She has, indeed, published two novels and a collection of short stories and written and directed two narrative films. Yet it is not as a fiction writer that she has become a widely known, read, publicized, and debated figure; it is rather as a writer of non-fiction essays. How that non-fiction is viewed in the future is likely to determine her place in the thought of the second half of the 20th century.

Sontag's essays fall roughly into two categories—treatments of individual works and figures, often emphasizing the heroic difficulty of individual creation, and basic efforts of definition, the latter ranging from studies of particular genres or concepts to treatments of entire art forms. The studies of individual figures form a major part of *Against Interpretation, Styles of Radical Will*, and *Under the Sign of Saturn*. The ambitious efforts to define whole art forms or basic aesthetic and cultural concepts include, among others, "On Style," "The Aesthetics of Silence," and "Theatre and Film" in her first two books and the entirety of *On Photography* and *Illness as Metaphor*.

Although her work has clearly developed over the course of writing five non-fiction books and a number of uncollected essays, Sontag's concerns and style show more consistency than comments about her sometimes suggest. She has remained devoted throughout, on the one hand, to resisting the conservative pressure of received opinion *(Doxa)*, and, on the other, to explicating the special lure and burden of post-modern art. Like Roland Barthes, about whom she has written, there is always a reactionary culture present as an antagonist in her work. Unlike Barthes, she is rarely drawn to claim an irreducible plurality of interpretations; her mode is more assertive and declamatory, even though her sentences are often impacted with qualification.

If it is fair to characterize her work in a phrase, then one may say that for Sontag the artist is an existential hero viewed with a certain post-modern irony. The difficulty of this paradoxical stance infects her writing as well; indeed, to the extent that the difficulties of writing provide her with a continuing self-reflexive subject, the phrase also describes her own intellectual project. The hortatory tone of her cultural analysis conflicts with its inner sense of futility; her essays manage at once to assert the universality of her definitions of "theatre," "silence," "interpretation," and "photography," and to insist on the complete historicity of those concepts and art forms. The contradiction, of course, must apply equally to her own work: it too will be superceded by more pertinent intellectual crises.

Understood in this context, we may more easily recognize that her work has always been simultaneously pervaded by moral urgency and camp theatricality. The relative dominance of these moods has varied but their constitutive role in her work has been continuous. Early reviewers noted only the advocacy of a certain cultural stance, not her uneasiness with it or her tendency to valorize radical art forms in terms of their capacity to nourish us and increase our capacity for moral choice. Recent reviewers note the supposedly "new" moral urgency and ignore the inner attraction to the tawdry theatricality of the very cultural images she criticizes. In time, her contribution must be assessed in terms of the value of the display of these tensions in her work.

I would argue that she has made several important contributions to our cultural understanding. Should we ever choose to write a general history of interpretive theory and practice, her polemical positions, because of their cold urgency and the almost aphoristic economy of their claims, will have an important place. Similarly, any analysis of a number of basic cultural concepts and art forms will have to take account of her powerful readings. We may not, in other words, agree with her reading of photography, but we can hardly ignore it. In addition, a number of her readings of individual works are likely to survive: her analyses of Bergman's *Persona* and Syberberg's *Hitler: A Film from Germany*, for example, are among the most effective essay-length readings of individual films we have; her essay on Artaud is one of the major statements on his work.

None of this, however, addresses the place of her work as a whole, a question that may require some thought about how critical and aesthetic writing can be evaluated. The answer may be suggested by Sontag's political and cultural writing, some of which she has chosen not to reprint in her book-length collections. The conclusion, of course, is that those pieces were topical and ephemeral, limited by and to the moment of their first publication. To some extent, this harsh critique must be applied to all of her work and, moreover, to all writing on culture and art: it contributes to and epitomizes its moment in time; at its best it shows us what was possible and necessary for that age to write.

Sontag's special contribution has been to display with exceptional elegance the necessary difficulty in defining aesthetic, philosophical, and political convictions in a post-apocalyptic age. She writes about the heroism of artistic production in a period that no longer believes in the Romantic image of individual creativity and no longer assumes its own accomplishments will survive. Her unifying aesthetic, repeated in the guise of many different figures and numerous works and key concepts, has been the pursuit of absence, silence, and emptiness in the carnival diversity of contemporary culture. Her success in that project makes her work exemplary and essential reading.

—Cary Nelson

SOREL, Georges. French political and social theorist. Born in Cherbourg, 2 November 1847. Educated at private school; Collège Rollin, Paris; studied at the École Polytechnique, graduated 1866. Engineer in Department of Roads and Bridges from 1866: in Corsica, 1867-71, Albi, Gap, Algeria (3 years), and Perpignan, 1879-92: retired as Chief Engineer, 1892; then writer: Co-Founder, *Le Devenir Social*, 1895. Légion d'Honneur, 1891. *Died 28 August 1922.*

PUBLICATIONS

Political and Social Theory

Contribution a l'étude profane de la Bible. Paris, Ghio, 1889.
Le Procès de Socrate. Paris, Alcan, 1889.
L'Avenir socialiste des syndicats. Paris, Jacques, 1901.
La Ruine du monde antique: Conception materialiste de l'histoire. Paris, Jacques, 1901.
Introduction à l'économie moderne. Paris, Jacques, 1902.
Essai du l'état et l'église. Paris, Jacques, 1902.
Saggi di critica del marxismo. Palermo, Sandron, 1902.
Le Système historique de Renan. Paris, Jacques, 1905.
Insegnamenti sociale della economica contemporanea. Palermo, Sandron, 1906.
Les Illusions de progrès. Paris, Rivière, 1908; as *The Illusions of Progress*, Berkeley, University of California Press, 1969.
Réflexions sur la violence. Paris, Librairie des "Pages Libres," 1908; as *Reflections on Violence*, New York, Huebsch, 1914; London, Allen and Unwin, 1916.
La Décomposition du marxisme. Paris, Rivière, 1908; as *Decomposition of Marxism*, in *Radicalism and the Revolt Against Reason* by Irving Louis Horowitz, New York, Humanities Press, and London, Routledge, 1961.
La Révolution dreyfusienne. Paris, Rivière, 1909.
Matériaux d'une théorie du prolétariat. Paris, Rivière, 1919.
De l'Utilité du pragmatisme. Paris, Rivière, 1921.
D'Aristote à Marx, edited by Édouard Berth. Paris, Rivière, 1935.
Propos de Georges Sorel, edited by Jean Variot. Paris, Gallimard, 1935.
"Da Proudhon a Lenin" e "L'Europa sotto la tormenta," edited by Gabriele De Rosa. Rome, Edizioni di Storia e Letteratura, 1974.
From Georges Sorel: Essays in Socialism and Philosophy, edited by John Stanley. New York, Oxford University Press, 1976.

Other

Lettres à Paul Delesalle, edited by André Prudhommeaux. Paris, Grasset, 1947.

*

Bibliography: "Bibliographie Sorélienne" in *International Review for Social History 4*, Leiden, Brill, 1939; in *The Sociology of Virtue* by John Stanley, 1981.

Critical Studies: *The Genesis of Georges Sorel* by James H. Meisel, Ann Arbor, Michigan, Wahr, 1951; *Georges Sorel: Prophet Without Honor* by Richard Humphrey, Cambridge, Massachusetts, Harvard University Press, 1951; *Three Against the Third Republic: Sorel, Barrès, and Maurras* by Michael Curtis, Princeton, New Jersey, Princeton University Press, 1959; *Radicalism and the Revolt Against Reason: The Social Theories of Georges Sorel* by Irving Louis Horowitz, New York, Humanities Press, and London, Routledge, 1961; *Commitment and Change: Georges Sorel and the Idea of Revolution* by Richard Vernon, Toronto, University of Toronto Press, 1978; *The Cult of Violence: Sorel and the Sorelians* by Jack J. Roth, Berkeley, University of California Press, 1980; *The Sociology of Virtue:*

The Political and Social Theories of Georges Sorel by John Stanley, Berkeley, University of California Press, 1981; *Georges Sorel and the Sociology of Virtue* by Arthur L. Greil, Washington, D.C., University Press of America, 1982.

* * *

Georges Sorel was a powerful force in French intellectual life, with influences extending abroad, especially into Italy, between about 1895 and 1914. He is usually considered one of the top few political thinkers of the era of the Third Republic—a republic which he heartily despised. He left an ambiguous but potent legacy, influencing Italian Fascism but also left-wing radicalism; his books such as *The Illusions of Progress* and *Reflections on Violence* were favorites of the 1960's New Left, offering as they did a radically personalist critique of capitalist society. Sorel is also of much interest as a representative figure of the early modernist period, eclectically uniting many of its leading strains of thought and feeling.

Retiring from a career as government engineer in his forties, Sorel was an auto-didact who read widely in the ideas of his time. "He knows everything, he has read everything," a young disciple wrote. Holding forth in the offices of Charles Péguy's *Cahiers de la Quinzaine*, the liveliest intellectual journal of the time, Sorel exerted influence as conversationalist as well as writer. On principle, he was the author of no dogma—a position itself characteristic of this Nietzschean era. He disliked the *esprit de système, le petit science* which he associated with both academic pedants and fanatical ideologists of the Left. So his writings cannot be reduced to any formula, but they are, as Isaiah Berlin observed in a notable essay on Sorel, informed by a consistent spirit. The deepest influence on Sorel was an irrationalism, ultimately deriving from Darwin and Schopenhauer, which he learned from his contemporary Henri Bergson (whose popular Sorbonne lectures Sorel attended) and found confirmed in Friedrich Nietzsche. Thought is a product of the struggle for existence, ideas are tools, truth is thus only the human will to power, and science itself is not objective truth but an affirmation of man's creativity. This creative energy is a matter of intuition rather than logic. Sorel joined Nietzsche in thinking that modern European man was over-intellectualized, this being an aspect of his decadence, his loss of energy and spontaneity.

Such insights were abundant at the end of the 19th century, coming not only from Nietzsche and Bergson but from the American Pragmatists and others. Sorel absorbed and popularized these ideas. He applied them particularly to politics. A reader of Marx, he became a considerable revisionist, and joined his friend the Italian philosopher Benedetto Croce in believing that "scientific" Marxism as purveyed by the organized disciples was a fraud. Nevertheless, as an energizing myth the doctrine of the exploited proletariat's class struggle against capitalism could rescue modern man from sterility. Sorel betrayed Proudhon's influence in scorning materialism as the basis for socialism; rather it was human dignity, honor, belief in justice that counted. Sorel hated the machine age and sneered at the whole notion of modern "progress." Though he stood apart from any organized movement, Sorel contributed to what was known as Syndicalism, a faith in the spontaneous revolutionary action of the working class. Akin to Anarchism, this outlook was anti-Marxist (Marxism being too systematizing, an ideology of the intellectuals) but also anti-liberal, anti-capitalist, anti-parliamentary. (Representative democracy is an order in which each voter is one ten-millionth a tyrant and every bit a slave!) And it was of course hostile to the state, favoring the government by local worker organizations.

About 1909, however, Sorel lost faith in the working class, believing rather like Lenin that trade unionism was incapable of a revolutionary consciousness, and he turned toward nationalism. *Sorelismo* gained a particular following in Italy where syndicalists became a left wing of Mussolini's Fascism; the statism that the Italian dictator eventually followed, was, however, a betrayal of this element. Sorel also admired Lenin and the Russian Revolution. Revolutionary energy as such attracted him. His polemical role as gadfly and catalyst of new ideas was probably Sorel's leading contribution. His key ideas—heroic violence, myth-making, irrationalism—may seem as repellent as his admiration for Fascist and Bolshevik terror. But his mordant criticisms of politics and society have kept their interest and relevance. One of these was his contribution to the elitist theory of democracy, where he joined Pareto and Mosca in seeing that political democracy only substitutes one sort of elite for another.

—Roland Stromberg

SOROKIN, Pitirim (Alexandrovitch). American sociologist. Born in Touria, Russia, 21 January 1889; emigrated to the United States in 1923: naturalized, 1930. Studied at the Teachers College, Kostroma Province, 1903-06; Psycho-Neurological Institute, St. Petersburg, 1909-10; University of St. Petersburg, Bachelor LL.M. 1914, Magister of Criminal Law 1916, Dr. of Sociology 1922. Married Elena Petrovina Baratynskaya in 1917; 2 sons. Taught from 1916, and first Professor of Sociology, and Chairman of the Department, 1919-22, University of St. Petersburg; Visiting Professor, 1923, and Professor of Sociology, 1924-30, University of Minnesota, Minneapolis; Professor of Sociology, 1930-59, Chairman of the Department, 1930-42, and Director of Research Center in Creative Altruism, 1949-68, Harvard University, Cambridge, Massachusetts. Political activist: Co-Founder, Russian Peasant Soviet; Member of Council of Russian Republic, and Secretary to Prime Minister Alexander Kerensky, 1917; member of Russian Constituent Assembly, 1918; banished by the Soviet government, 1922. Co-Editor, *New Ideas in Sociology*, 1913-15; Editor-in-Chief, *Vollia Naroda* (Will of the People), Petrograd, 1917. President, International Institute and Congress of Sociology, 1936-37, International Society for Comparative Study of Civilizations, 1960-63, and American Sociological Society, 1965. A.M.: Harvard University; Ph.D.: National University of Mexico, 1950. Fellow, American Academy of Arts and Sciences, Royal Academy of Arts and Sciences of Belgium, Royal Academy of Romania, and Czecho-Slovak Academy of Agriculture; Honorary Member, International Institute for Social Reform. *Died 10 February 1968.*

PUBLICATIONS

Sociology

Prestuplenie i kara, podvig i nagrada (Crime and Punishment). St. Petersburg, Dolbyshev, 1914.
L.N. Tolstoy, kak filosof (Leo Tolstoy as a Philosopher). Moscow, Posrednik, 1915.
Problema sotsialnago ravenstva (The Problem of Social Equality). St. Petersburg, Revoluzionnaia Mysl, 1917.
Uchebnik obschey teorii prava (General Theory of Law). Yaroslavl, Yaroslavskago Soyuza, 1919.
Obschedostupnuy uchebnik soziologii (Elements of Sociology). Yaroslavl, Yaroslavskago Soyuza Kooperativov, 1920.
Sistema soziologii (System of Sociology). St. Petersburg, Kolos, 2 vols., 1920.
Golod kak factor (Hunger as a Factor). St. Petersburg, Kolos, 1921 (destroyed by Soviet government); as *Hunger as a Factor in World Affairs*, edited by T. Lynn Smith, Gainesville, University Presses of Florida, 1975.
Sovremennoe sostoianie Rossii (The Contemporary Possibility of Russia). Prague, Kooperativnoie Isdatelstvo, 1922.
Popularnuye ocherki sotsialnoi pedagogiki i politiki (Popular Notes About Pedagogy and Politics). Ujgorod, Isdane

Komiteta Delovodchikov i Narodnonprosvetitelnukh rad Podkarpatskoi Rusi, 1923.
The Sociology of Revolution. Philadelphia, Lippincott, 1925.
Social Mobility. New York, Harper, 1927; augmented edition, as *Social and Cultural Mobility*, Glencoe, Illinois, Free Press, 1959.
Contemporary Sociological Theories. New York, Harper, 1928.
Principles of Rural-Urban Sociology, with Carle C. Zimmerman. New York, Holt, 1929.
Social and Cultural Dynamics. New York, American BOok Company, 4 vols., and London, Allen and Unwin, 4 vols., 1937-41; abridged edition, Boston, Sargent, 1 vol., 1957; London, Owen, 1 vol., 1959.
Time-Budgets of Human Behavior, with Clarence Q. Berger. Cambridge, Massachusetts, Harvard University Press, 1939.
The Crisis of Our Age: The Social and Cultural Outlook. New York, Dutton, 1941.
Man and Society in Calamity: The Effects of War, Revolution, Famine, Pestilence upon Human Mind, Behavior, Social Organization, and Cultural Life. New York, Dutton, 1942.
Sociocultural Causality, Space, Time: A Study of Referential Principles of Sociology and Social Science. Durham, North Carolina, Duke University Press, 1943.
Russia and the United States. New York, Dutton, 1944; London, Stevens, 1950.
Society, Culture, and Personality: Their Structure and Dynamics: A System of General Sociology. New York, Harper, 1947.
The Reconstruction of Humanity. Boston, Beacon Press, 1948.
Altruistic Love: A Study of American "Good Neighbors" and Christian Saints. Boston, Beacon Press, 1950.
Social Philosophies in an Age of Crisis. Boston, Beacon Press, 1950; London, A. and C. Black, 1952; as *Modern Historical and Social Philosophies*, New York, Dover, 1963.
S.O.S.: The Meaning of Our Crisis. Boston, Beacon Press, 1951.
The Ways and Power of Love: Types, Factors, and Techniques of Moral Transformation. Boston, Beacon Press, 1954.
Fads and Foibles in Modern Sociology and Related Sciences. Chicago, Regnery, 1956; London, Vision Press, 1958.
The American Sex Revolution. Boston, Sargent, 1956; as *Sane Sex Order*, Bombay, Bharatiya Vidya Bhavan, 1961.
Power and Morality: Who Shall Guard the Guardians?, with Walter A. Lunden. Boston, Sargent, 1959.
The Basic Trends of Our Times (essays). New Haven, Connecticut, College and University Press, 1964.
Sociological Theories of Today. New York, Harper, 1966.
Sociology of Yesterday, Today, and Tomorrow. New York, Harper, 1969.

Other

Prachesnaia tchelovecheskikh dush (science fiction). St. Petersburg, Ejemesiachnyi Journal, 1917.
Leaves from a Russian Diary. New York, Dutton, 1924; London, Hurst and Blackett, 1925; augmented edition, as *Leaves from a Russian Diary, and Thirty Years After*, Boston, Beacon Press, 1950.
A Long Journey: The Autobiography of Pitirim A. Sorokin. New Haven, Connecticut, College and University Press, 1963.

Editor, with Carle C. Zimmerman and Charles J. Galpin, *A Systematic Source Book in Rural Sociology.* Minneapolis, University of Minnesota Press, 3 vols., 1930-32.
Editor, *Explorations in Altruistic Love and Behavior.* Boston, Beacon Press, 1950.
Editor, *Forms and Techniques of Altruistic and Spiritual Growth.* Boston, Beacon Press, 1954.

*

Critical Studies: *History, Civilization, and Culture: An Introduction to the Historical and Social Philosophy of Pitirim A. Sorokin* by Frank R. Cowell, Boston, Beacon Press, 1952; *The Sociology of Knowledge: Essays in Honor of Pitirim A. Sorokin* edited by J. Maquet, New York, Free Press, 1963; *Pitirim A. Sorokin in Review* edited by Philip J. Allen, Durham, North Carolina, Duke University Press, 1963; *Sociological Theory, Values, and Sociological Changes: Essays in Honor of Pitirim A. Sorokin* edited by Edward A. Tiryakian, New York, Harper, 1967 (includes bibliography); *Sorokin and Sociology: Essays in Honour of Professor Pitirim A. Sorokin* edited by G.C. Hallen and Rajeshwar Prasad, Agra, Satish, 1972; *Sociological Theories of Pitirim A. Sorokin* by Carle C. Zimmerman, edited by T.K.N. Unnithan, Bombay, Thacker, 1973.

*   *   *

Pitirim Sorokin, an encyclopaedic sociologist, wrote profusely and provocatively over almost half a century. His widely ranging work may be assigned to five categories.

1) His initial works on specific themes sought to elicit theories about social change from the vast data he assembled to show the recurrent crises and irreversible developments of the early decades of the 20th century. *Hunger as a Factor in World Affairs* and *The Sociology of Revolution* were written to convey the distinctive consequences of the social crisis he witnessed during the Russian Revolution. He then delineated the complex implications of social transformation in the United States in his classic treatment of *Social Mobility*.

2) His systematic surveys of social systems were elaborated in support of fundamental principles of coherence and change. *Principles of Rural-Urban Sociology* anticipated his monumental work *Social and Cultural Dynamics*. Together with its popular abridgement in *The Crisis of Our Age*, it provided an elaborate appraisal of European cultures to buttress a broad framework of socio-cultural transformation. In a similar vein, *Society, Culture, and Personality* was written as a basic text on general sociology.

3) His more philosophical works considered conceptual schemes and analytical classifications which were germane to the future development of alternative social systems. He was especially prodigious in his varied studies as in *The Ways and Power of Love*. Although confident of the empirical evidence supporting the efficacy of his essential concepts, he was a tireless exponent of his architectonic vision of moral reformation. This is powerfully expressed in his volume *The Reconstruction of Humanity*.

4) He also wrote on a variety of current issues for the general public. Such works dealt with the symptoms of social disintegration and cultural crisis. *The American Sex Revolution* was a bold and pioneering statement on a controversial theme. Similarly, he wrote *Power and Morality* to warn against the increasing inflation of government authority and activity.

5) He composed general surveys of contemporary sociological theories. He examined the distinctive social philosophies of writers like Spengler and Toynbee. He also wrote extensively on diverse theoretical frameworks in academic sociology (*Contemporary Sociological Theories, Social Philosophies in an Age of Crisis, Sociological Theories of Today*).

The crisis of social disintegration was a central theme in the entire corpus of Sorokin's writings. His own research as well as his personal experience in Russia convinced him that revolutions are far from being ideological panaceas. They are explosive consequences of cultural failure in the fulfillment of basic human needs. Such crises exhibit perversions in human conduct, accentuate egotism and dogmatism, and demonstrate the appalling cynicism of revolutionary leaders. In societies wherein social disintegration is accompanied by enormous increase of individual freedom, as in the United States, institutions are faced with moral challenges that they cannot meet. While socially mobile persons are more flexible and innovative, they also suffer from acute mental strain, loneliness, and moral anarchy, resulting from rapid changes in their social location.

Social space differs from geometrical space in that physical proximity is not an index of social proximity. Social space is the universe of humanity, and locus is determined by social relationships with other human beings, the basis for defining social mobility in respect to direction and velocity. Social stratification, which includes economic, political, and occupational strata, is subject to fluctuations that affect individual and collective social mobility. Individuals shift social strata through institutions like the school and the church, which test, select, and distribute them according to desired qualities. When the strata fluctuate or are disturbed by turbulent events, mobility increases, profoundly affecting the individuals involved. They tend to become more plastic and versatile in behaviour, inventive, intellectually active and less parochial in thought, but the accompanying loss of intimacy and increase of psycho-social isolation are manifested in mental disorders, decreased sensitivity to self and others and the environment, and pervasive superficiality. Thus mobility encourages scepticism and even cynicism while intensifying loneliness, all of which fosters restlessness and a search for sensate pleasures. By any widely accepted standard, increased social mobility facilitates the disintegration of moral values. Nonetheless, mobility aids in a more adequate social distribution of individuals, atomizing and diffusing both antagonism and solidarity. Even while heightening individualism, it increases a vague cosmopolitanism and collectivism.

Any society or culture, according to Sorokin, reflects a socio-cultural reality that transcends physical perception of specific objects or a constellation of institutions. Social reality is both created and sustained by the meanings assigned by individuals to shared ideas, and the values they perceive in their separate and common experience. Social phenomena are invariably integrated in "coherent aggregates" which give expression to a veiled mental reality. Society is not a random distribution of social events, although not every phenomena is necessarily linked to the prevailing system of social values. Integration may be developed hierarchically and establishes an indivisible unity between cultural systems (religion, art, science, ethics, law, and philosophy), social relationships (familial, contractual, and compulsory), and individual behaviour. Institutions represent the highest level of integration, and are existentially organized around a major premise or fundamental principle. It may take centuries for this major premise to create a complex and cohesive structure. Growth and transformation are as much a part of society as continuity and persistence. In the course of time, the creative principle will lose its power in accordance with a "principle of limits." Growth is not governed by fixed or regular cycles, as Spengler suggested, but is rather dependent upon the faith and capacity which individuals develop to apply and sustain the constructive power of guiding cultural principles.

Three levels of cognition, the sensory, the rational, and the supersensory or intuitive, are available to human beings for the discovery and use of socio-cultural reality. Specific cultures will collectively reflect the dominant level of cognition used to create each. No individual perception of value or statement of truth can convey the total reality. Corresponding to the three powers of cognition are three types of major premises, culminating in three basic types of societies. Sensory perception produces a sensate culture, supersensory intuition creates an Ideational culture, and, from the mixing of the two, an idealistic gestalt may emerge through rational methods of thought. In later works, in which Sorokin's religious faith was strongly expressed, he wrote with feeling about the Infinite Manifold and the spontaneous forces emanating from it. He was concerned to give distinct importance to supersensory experience and its refined cultural expression. He showed a lively awareness of Eastern religions and philosophies, tried to correct Western misconceptions, and stressed the relevance of Patanjali's text on yoga to moral growth, self-transformation, and spiritual transcendence.

One of the chief aims of Sorokin, in his massive study *Social* and *Cultural Dynamics*, was to show that Western or European culture over the past several centuries had replaced the ideational principle of medieval society by a sensate culture. The widespread belief that true reality is sensory is revealed in art, in social relations, and in personal expectations. Sensory values reduce all perceptions to material things and excessively relativate everything. Egotistic and nihilistic attitudes feed upon contractual concreteness. The result is an immense exhaustion of dynamism in the sensory gestalt and the inevitable disintegration of society. The contemporary crisis is the product of a long and painful process of social disintegration, with a traumatic dissolution of a cultural gestalt which no government or economic plan, no ideology or charismatic leader, can prevent. Sorokin had predicted forthcoming wars and economic depression to deaf ears during the "Golden Twenties," but after the Second World War ushered in the "Age of Calamity" he felt constrained to devote the rest of his life to prophesies, exhortations, and agendas for social salvation.

Sorokin's passionate plea for a radical transformation of social institutions and normative patterns of interaction was based upon his lifelong preoccupation with social change. He had already set forth three main sources of change: the principle of immanence bringing change from within society, the principle of mis-integration, and the principle of limits. Spatial, temporal, and causal dimensions produce cyclical fluctuations, suggesting some sort of dialectical process in which the crucial role must be assigned to the countervailing influence of the ideational or idealistic principle. Since altruistic love is the purest expression of the Infinite Manifold, what is needed is the replacement of the sensate principle by the broader, deeper, richer, and more valid premise that true reality is an Infinite Manifold possessing not only sensory but also supersensory, rational, and superrational aspects, all harmoniously reflecting its infinity. It is, therefore, essential that individuals embark upon the radical restructuring of their selves. Moral transformation alone would make them eventual masters of altruistic energies.

Sorokin recognized that there are degrees of altruism already expressed by individuals and groups and that no society could survive without minimal levels of mutual aid and sacrifice. But the highest, purest, and most powerful love is that state of universal and spontaneous benevolence displayed by the great teachers and spiritual leaders of mankind. While appealing for even a modest effort by each and all to improve their conduct towards others in everyday encounters, he elaborated an extensive programme for restructuring the personality in a manner corresponding to the monastic modes of spiritual aspirants. A triple organization of one's ego, one's values, and one's group affiliations is required, and four steps are suggested by him.

1) Development of the supraconscious to its maximum, corresponding with a focus on the supreme value of creative love as the centre of a culture and the organization of altruistic, creative groups to replace aggressive groups and selfish affiliations.

2) Development of the conscious mind to its possible maximum, with a dedication of conscious energy to the service of love, truth, and beauty, and the denial of hate and enmity. This aim corresponds to the rational rearrangement of all secondary cultural values into one unified system subordinated to the supreme values of truth, love, and beauty. Group affiliations must also be reorganized to define the functions, duties, and roles of each member.

3) Vertical control of one's lower energies by higher energies, of the unconscious by the conscious and supraconscious, is needed, but with an increase of spontaneous expression rather than rigid control. Cooperation through self-control would replace the coercive and violent tendencies in social patterns.

4) Subsequent elimination of friction between all egos, drives, and activities in each and all levels of mental reality. Unification of all conscious egos and unconscious drives into one harmonious unity, sublimated to the egoless, suprapersonal, and supraconscious "self." Friction between individual and cultural values and among social groups would be similarly eliminated.

Those who undertake this demanding discipline could become creative agents in the conscious development of a new social reality.

If the possibility of altruistic changes seems somewhat remote, Sorokin pleaded that social change had been achieved many times before. Most of his later writings were intended to alert his contemporaries about the depth and magnitude of the crisis of the age, and its almost irrevocable consequences. The path of creative altruism is a dire necessity for individual and social survival in the compelling context of persisting disintegration and increasing social anarchy. He also contended that the outlined plan of rearrangement of social affiliations is the ideal and maximal plan. "It goes without saying that this ideal plan can be reached only by a small fraction of human beings. The majority can climb only to the lower ridges of this towering peak. In spite of this, each step towards it represents the moral progress of humanity" (*The Ways and Power of Love*).

—R.N. Iyer

SPEARMAN, Charles E(dward). British psychologist. Born in London, 10 September 1863. Educated at Leamington College; studied at the University of Leipzig, Ph.D. 1905; University of Würzburg, 1906; University of Göttingen, 1907. Served in the British Army during the Burmese War (Medal and 2 Clasps), the Boer War (Deputy Assistant Adjutant General, Guernsey), and World War I (General Staff, Tyne Defences). Married Fanny Aikman in 1901; 1 son. Reader in Psychology, 1907-11, Grote Professor of Mind and Logic, 1911-28, Professor of Psychology, 1928-31, and Professor Emeritus, 1931-45, University College, London. Honorary Member, British Psychological Society (President, 1923-26); Deutsche Gesellschaft für Psychologie; Kaiserlich Deutsche Akademie der Naturforscher; Kentucky Academy of Science; Psychotechnical Club, Prague. Foreign Associate, United States Academy of Sciences; Foreign Associate Member, French Psychological Society. *Died 17 September 1945.*

PUBLICATIONS

Psychology

The Nature of "Intelligence" and the Principles of Cognition. London, Macmillan, 1923.
A Measure of "Intelligence" for Use in Schools. London, Macmillan, 1925.
The Abilities of Man: Their Nature and Measurement. London, Macmillan, 1927.
Creative Mind. London, Nisbet-Cambridge University Press, 1930.
Psychology Down the Ages. London, Macmillan, 2 vols., 1937.
Human Ability: A Continuation of "The Abilities of Man," with L. Wynn Jones. London, Macmillan, 1950.

*   *   *

Charles E. Spearman was a leading British psychologist during the first half of the 20th century, mainly notable for his researches on human abilities, particularly intelligence, and for the method of factor analysis of which he was the founding father. His influence has been extensive on both sides of the Atlantic.

Spearman's background was an unusual one. He commenced his adult life as an army officer, and he was in his middle thirties before he left the army and took up the systematic study of psychology in Germany, which in the closing years of the 19th century was world leader in the subject. Spearman first studied in Leipzig under Wilhelm Wundt, the eminent founder of the first psychological laboratory, and then at various other German universities. It was during this period that his interest in intelligence was aroused, in spite of the fact that German psychologists were not prepared to give him much encouragement. Intelligence, indeed, was a topic much more in line with British modes of thought, following the tradition of Spencer, Darwin, and Galton. Nevertheless it was from Germany that Spearman in 1904 sent to the *American Journal of Psychology* his epoch-making article "General Intelligence Objectively Determined and Measured," in which he first enunciated the idea of factor analysis.

Intelligence tests had been developed by various continental, British, and American workers in the last decades of the 19th century, but what these tests were measuring was far from clearly defined. By employing the technique of factor analysis Spearman hoped to be able to clarify precisely what abilities the tests were tapping. Just as the chemist by an experimental analysis determines the chemical elements from which compounds are derived, so the statistical method of factor analysis aimed at determining the elementary abilities which might account for performances on intelligence and other psychological tests. Spearman came to the conclusion that every test performance could be accounted for by two types of factor, hence his theory has been termed "the two-factor theory." These two types of factors he termed the "general" factor (symbolized by "g") and "specific" factors (symbolized by "s"). The general factor was common to all test and other performances, and was broadly equivalent to what is commonly termed general intelligence, though later Spearman preferred to equate it with "mental energy"; the specific factors were peculiar to performances of a particular type (verbal, mathematical, mechanical, artistic, etc.).

Though Spearman's two-factor theory has been drastically modified, if not abandoned, by subsequent workers, and his laborious methods of computation wholly superseded, the birth of factor analysis was a momentous development in psychology, and has had a wide impact on theories of ability and personality. Particularly in the United States Spearman has had many eminent successors, such as Thurstone, Guilford, and R.B. Cattell, who have developed factorization far beyond its original simple foundations, though still acknowledging Spearman as the fountainhead. The method has, of course, also had its critics. It has been argued that the solutions provided by factor analysis are not unique, that alternative solutions are possible and indeed the disagreements among factorists seem to lend support to such an argument. The choice between solutions, therefore, to some extent depends on the personal choice of the factorist. Spearman, it is said, showed an undue proclivity towards a "monarchical" view of intelligence, regarding general intelligence as the supreme ability which directed and controlled all human performances other than those of a purely reflex and mechanical nature. American psychologists, more democratic in their outlook, have commonly denied the existence of any such general factor of intelligence, and defended the existence of numerous broad "group" factors. The issue must still be regarded as an open one, possibly to be decided on the grounds of practical convenience rather than purely theoretical considerations.

Spearman's further contributions to the elucidation of *The Nature of "Intelligence" and the Principles of Cognition*, as he entitled his first major book, proved less fruitful, but were interesting in that they recognized the creative nature of the mind. His so-called "neogenetic" laws, which reduced all cognitive processes to the "eduction of relations and correlates," were a gross over-simplification of the complex intellectual life of man, and have played almost no part in the revival of cognitive psychology which has occurred since the 1950's. Equally sterile were the quantitative laws of cognition (tendency to recurrence, perseveration, oscillation, fatigue, etc.) which Spearman set out in *The Abilities of Man*. Several of his other contributions to statistical

methodology were, however, of some importance; and in Great Britain he established in London University the first really effective school of psychological research in the country, attracting pupils from many parts of the world. But it is primarily as the founder of factor analysis that he will be remembered.

—Leslie Hearnshaw

SPENGLER, Oswald (Arnold Gottfried). German historian and philosopher. Born in Blankenburg am Hars, 29 May 1880. Studied mathematics, natural science, and philosophy, University of Hamburg; University of Berlin; University of Halle, Ph.D., 1904. Teacher in secondary schools in Düsseldorf, 1906-07, and in Hamburg, 1908-11. Private scholar, writer, and lecturer, devoting himself to the study of history, in Munich, from 1911. Recipient: Stiftung Nietzsche-Archiv Prize, 1919. *Died* (in Munich) *8 May 1936.*

PUBLICATIONS

History and Philosophy

Der Metaphysische Grundgedanke der Heraklitischen Philosophie. Halle, Kaemmerer, 1904.
Der Untergang des Abendlandes: Umrisse einer Morphologie der Weltgeschichte: vol. 1, *Gestalt und Wirklichkeit,* Vienna, Braumüller, 1917; vol. 2, *Welthistorische Perspektiven,* Munich, Beck, 1922; as *The Decline of the West; Form and Actuality; Perspectives of World History,* London, Allen and Unwin, and New York, Knopf, 2 vols., 1926-28.
Preussentum und Sozialismus. Munich, Beck, 1919.
Neubau des deutschen Reiches. Munich, Beck, 1924.
Der Mensch und die Technik: Beitrag zu einer Philosophie des Lebens. Munich, Beck, 1931; as *Man and Technics: A Contribution to the Philosophy of Life,* London, Allen and Unwin, and New York, Knopf, 1932.
Politische Schriften. Munich, Beck, 1932.
Die Revolution ist nicht zu Ende. Oldenburg, Germany, Stalling, 1932.
Jahre der Entscheidung: Deutschland und die weltgeschichtliche Entwicklung. Munich, Beck, 1933; as *The Hour of Decision,* London, Allen and Unwin, and New York, Knopf, 1934.
Reden und Aufsätze, edited by Hildegard Kornhardt. Munich, Beck, 1937; as *Selected Essays,* Chicago, Regnery, 1967.
Gedanken, selected by Hildegard Kornhardt. Munich, Beck, 1941; as *Aphorisms,* Chicago, Regnery, 1967.
Urfragen: Fragmente aus dem Nachlass, edited by Anton Mirko Koktanek and Manfred Schröter. Munich, Beck, 1965.
Frühzeit der Weltgeschichte: Fragmente aus dem Nachlass, edited by Anton Mirko Koktanek and Manfred Schröter. Munich, Beck, 1966.

Other

Briefe 1913-1936, edited by Anton Mirko Koktanek and Manfred Schröter. Munich, Beck, 1963; as *Spengler Letters 1913-1936,* abridged and edited by Arthur Helps, London, Allen and Unwin, and New York, Knopf, 1966.

*

Critical Studies: *Metaphysik des Untergangs: Eine kulturkritische Studie über Oswald Spengler* by Manfred Schröter, Munich, Leibniz, 1949; *Oswald Spengler: A Critical Estimate* by H. Stuart Hughes, New York, Scribner, 1952; *Philosoph oder Prophet: Oswald Spengler Vermächtnis und Voraussagen* by

Arnim Baltzer, Neheim-Hüsten, Verlag für Kulturwissenschaften, 1962; *Oswald Spengler in Seiner Zeit* by Anton Mirko Koktanek, Munich, Beck, 1968 (includes bibliography); *Twilight of the European Lands: Oswald Spengler—A Half Century Later* by John F. Fennelly, New York, Brookdale, 1972; *Spengler Heute: 6 Essays* edited by Peter Christian Ludz, Munich, Beck, 1980.

*   *   *

Oswald Spengler who, along with Arnold Toynbee, was one of the last of the so-called "speculative" historians, was born in Blankenburg, Prussia in 1880. The son of a postal official, he attended the universities of Munich, Berlin, and Halle. His primary training was in mathematics, but he obtained an impressive background in the natural sciences as well, something that would find reflection in his major work, *The Decline of the West*. At first, Spengler was a school teacher. Quite early, however, in 1911, he gave up this career and, from that point on, devoted his time to studying history, a subject in which he had some background (although not as much as that held by him in the natural sciences), and, eventually, to writing it.

Contrary to some popular opinion, his *Decline of the West* was *not* a product of World War I. Indeed, the first volume of the work appeared in 1917. To be sure, the second volume came out in 1922 and was, to some extent, influenced by the war. Basically, though, Spengler was influenced by what Fritz Stern has called that sense of "cultural despair" endemic in pre-World War I educated bourgeois circles in Germany and, perhaps to a less extreme extent, in Western Europe in general. This was the feeling, a word which is appropriate in this context, that there was something radically wrong with modern, urbanized, industrial civilization, that rich values of an older, more noble period had been lost. It was out of this feeling, and out of his obvious contempt for the "aimless, striving masses," that Spengler wrote a work in which the decline and fall of Western civilization was predicted and, one must say, even with a certain degree of thinly concealed enthusiasm. As Spengler saw it, each of the great world cultures, Egyptian, Chinese, Semitic, Indian, Magian (roughly, Muslim), Apollonian (Greek and Roman), and Western, went through a life cycle analogous to that of a living organism. The life cycle was informed by the birth, flowering, maturation, and eventual degeneration of a particular "idea" which the historian (or at least Spengler) could grasp intuitively, utilizing that sense of understanding designated by some philosophers of history, such as Wilhelm Dilthey—a person of whom Spengler had little knowledge—as *verstehen*. For Spengler, here sounding very much like Benedetto Croce, the historian's mind was similar to that of an artist, and his own rather singular, synoptic vision enabled him to grasp the very essence, i.e., the "idea" of all eight cultures. For example, the idea that informed Classical culture was the drive for finitude, the desire somehow to delimit an otherwise threatening world. This found reflection in classical conceptions of philosophy, aesthetics, mathematics, and politics. In contrast to this, modern Western civilization was characterized by a bold, almost ruthless, thrust towards the infinite, something which Spengler designated as "Faustian," and this also found reflection in mathematical, philosophical, aesthetic, and political misconceptions.

Spengler's Faust was not that of the mature Goethe who, as is well known, allowed his hero to be saved by sublimating his drive for the infinitude into the more innocuous tasks of a civil engineer. Rather, Spengler's variation bore more of a resemblance to the Faust of German legend and of Marlowe. Faustian culture of the West was doomed. As in the previously considered seven other cultures, the Western variety saw its "idea," i.e., the striving for infinitude, go through four stages: birth and infancy (the "spring season") of the culture; youth ("summer"); maturity ("fall"); and old age and decay ("winter"). Naturally, as all cultural pessimists since Hesiod have had it, Spengler saw himself as living in the final, unhappy stage. Modern industrial mass culture, whose crowning achievement was the metropolis, had become rootless and thoroughly materialistic. In *Decline of the West* and later works, Spengler attacked those phenomena, e.g., atonal music, which he saw as representative of cultural decay. In short, Western man, in the truest Faustian sense, had overreached himself, and was now heading towards the triumph of a sort of gloomy—but to Spengler, almost welcome—"Caesarism," a universal dictatorship similar to that which later would be described in more theological terms by Toynbee.

Particularly after World War I, Spengler's neo-romantic musings obtained a wide appeal in humiliated Germany; but, it must be noted, his cultural pessimism corresponded to the needs of many in the West in general. After all, this was a time of questioning of modern values, of increasing despair regarding the future, and rising racism. *The Decline of the West* became a fashionable book to own and even if, as in the case of the Bible or the collected works of Sigmund Freud, few had the spiritual energy to read it through, many of those disturbed by 20th-century developments often *referred* to it, albeit usually in vague ways.

As might be expected, Spengler was not pleased by the Weimar Republic, an institution which seemed to confirm all his worst fears. Its at times anarchcial political pluralism and seeming cultural degeneracy (particularly in Berlin) pointed to that degenerative stage of historical development characterized by Spengler as rootless, overly sophisticated "civilization." In various post-World War I works, Spengler decried the triumph of materialistic values and loss of idealism, events which surely had to lead to the partially unwanted but certainly necessary "new Caesarism."

The decline and fall of the West seemed to be something which was predestined. After all, the previous seven major cultures had been condemned to extinction by a "law" (i.e., the playing out of the cultural "idea" had to prove to be fatal), which operated with a cruelly dispassionate biological necessity. Yet, as in the case of Arnold Toynbee, Spengler seemed to be ill at ease with his own disquieting prognostications. In the end, there was perhaps a way out, a means by which Western civilization—in many ways, the most heroic venture undertaken by human beings against the unknown—could save itself. At least the German portion of it might have been able to do so, thus providing an example to others. This was through adherence to what Spengler referred to as "Prussian Socialism," and, as the Weimar Republic slid to its doom, he became ever more enamoured of this solution. Prussian Socialism was rooted in a well-established German political tradition—the tendency to seek out the political solution which, in the end, was comfortably "above politics." Prussian Socialism was, after all, nothing else but the blending together of a sense of duty towards the fatherland and a willingness to accept the necessity of serving the interests of every member of the "Folk Community" (*Volksgemeinschaft*). As indicated earlier, such an idea had a well-established pedigree in German intellectual history. At least one socialist, Lassalle, came close to accepting this notion *in toto* during the course of his peregrinations around the concept of "state socialism." The liberal, Friedrich Naumann, had espoused a similar idea around the turn of the century. For Spengler, though, the notion of Prussian Socialism was infused with an almost mystical purpose. In its blending together of duty and societal altruism, it represented a veritable apotheosis of that idealism which, battered and torn as it might have been by those crude materialistic forces unleashed by a civilization in the latter stage of spiritual decay, found its noblest embodiment in Germany.

Prussian Socialism, for Spengler, represented a way out for a culture seemingly doomed to spiritual and physical extinction. The idealism which subsisted at the base of Western man's striving for infinity remained. At the same time, though, discipline and a sense of order—the historically nurtured alter-egos of this striving—were present as regulatory principles. There might very well have to be "new Caesarism" but, at the very least, it could be grounded in or informed by a variety of socialism resonant with those characteristics which had made Germany the spiritual heart of Europe.

In various essays and speeches, Spengler called for the emergence of this Prussian Socialism as well as for new leaders who could translate axiological hypothesis into reality. As can well be imagined—most particularly, if we bear in mind Spengler's tendency towards neo-romanticism and his rebellion against modern, mechanized, urban civilization—National Socialism seemed to offer distinct possibilities. In its anti-Enlightenment, anti-positivistic quasi-mysticism, it appealed to Spengler not only on the political level, but also on that of his own methodology. As we have seen, intuitionalism and mysticism played great roles in Spengler's conception of history and the historian's task. Thus, Spengler lent some support to the National Socialist movement.

With the movement's coming to power, however, he experienced a great disappointment. For Spengler, the elitist, Hitler came increasingly to represent much of what he despised. The latter's playing upon mass emotionalism and his apparent ability to adjust all too well to certain—to Spengler—vulgar aspects of mass, industrial society bothered him greatly. Further, he increasingly came to view Hitler as an opportunistic, lazy dilettante. With some courage, Spengler made public statements critical of the Führer, a man who no longer seemed destined to save at least German culture from the ravages of modern society, but rather, appeared to be more of an exponent of it. In 1936, Oswald Spengler died of a heart attack. For all of his seeming right-wing radicalism and ideational cynicism, Hitler's ability to fuse bureaucratic Caesarism and that idealism which Spengler thought subsisted at the spiritual basis of Faustian man would no doubt have baffled, and probably horrified, him had he lived to see it in its full, hideous articulation.

As it was, Spengler lived long enough to contribute to that intellectual tradition—that informed by the "cultural despair" emphasized by Fritz Stern—which provided spiritual ammunition for those opposed to the Weimar Republic in particular and republicanism in general. Both his cultural pessimism, and the way in which he strove to overcome it, were of immense value for individuals who, even if they ultimately did not support Nazism, nonetheless made substantial contributions to that ideational atmosphere which was of great importance in helping to bring the movement to power. Spengler's work, imaginative and, in some cases, incisive as it might have been, stands as a warning to those who, in despair, seek out that common and perversely pleasing synthesis of cultural pessimism and teleologically grounded elitism.

—Robert A. Pois

SPITZER, Leo. American philologist. Born in Austria in 1887; emigrated to the United States in 1936; naturalized, 1945. Studied at the universities of Vienna, Paris, and Leipzig. Lecturer, University of Vienna, from 1913, and University of Bonn, from 1918; Professor, Marburg University, from 1925; University of Cologne, from 1930; University of Istanbul, 1933-36; and Johns Hopkins University, Baltimore, 1936-60. *Died* (in Forte dei Marmi, Italy) *18 September 1960*.

PUBLICATIONS

Philology

Die Wortbildung als stilistisches Mittel exemplifiziert an Rabelais, nebst einem Anhang über die Wortbildung bei Balzac in seinen "Contes drolatiques." Halle, Niemeyer, 1910.
Die Bezeichnungen der Klette im galloromanischen, with Ernst Gamillschleg. Halle, Niemeyer, 1915.

Anti-Chamberlain: Betrachtungen eines Linguisten über Houston Stewart Chamberlains "Kriegsaufsätze" und die Sprachbewertung im allgemeinen. Leipzig, Reisland, 1918.
Aufsätze zur romanischen Syntax und Stilistik. Halle, Niemeyer, 1918.
Fremdwörterhatz und Fremdvölkerhass: Eine Streitschrift gegen die Sprachreinigung. Vienna, Manz, 1918.
Katalanische Etymologien. Hamburg, Meissner, 1918.
Über einige Wörter der Liebessprache: Vier Aufsätze. Leipzig, Reisland, 1918.
Während der Militärdienstzeit: Aufsätze. Leipzig, Reisland, 1918.
Studien zu Henri Barbusse. Bonn, Cohen, 1920.
Die Umschreibungen des Begriffes "Hunger" im italienischen: Stilistisch onomasiologische Studie auf Grund von unveröffentlichtem Zensurmaterial. Halle, Karras Kröber und Nietschmann, 1920.
Beiträge zur romanischen Wortbildungslehre, with Ernst Gamillscheg. Geneva, Olschki, 1921.
Italienische Kriegsgefangenenbriefe: Materialien zu einer Charakteristik der volkstümlichen italienischen Korrespondenz. Bonn, Hanstein, 1921.
Lexikalisches aus dem katalanischen und den übrigen iberoromanischen Sprachen. Geneva, Olschki, 1921.
Italienische Umgangssprache. Bonn, Schroeder, 1922.
Puxi: Eine kleine Studie zur Sprache einer Mutter. Munich, Hueber, 1927.
Stilstudien. Munich, Hueber, 2 vols., 1928.
Marie de France, Dichterin von Problem-Märchen. Halle, Karras Kröber und Nietschmann, 1929.
Romanische Stil-und Literaturstudien. Marburg, Elwert, 1931.
Die Literarisierung des Lebens in Lope's Dorotea. Bonn, Röhrscheid, 1932.
Essays in Historical Semantics. New York, Vanni, 1948.
Linguistics and Literary History: Essays in Stylistics. Princeton, New Jersey, Princeton University Press, 1948.
A Method of Interpreting Literature (lectures). Northampton, Massachusetts, Smith College, 1949.
Romanische Literaturstudien 1936-1956. Tübingen, Niemeyer, 1959.
Interpretation zur Geschichte der französischen Lyrik, edited by Helga Jauss-Meyer and Peter Schunck. Heidelberg, Heidelberg University, 1961.
Essays on English and American Literature, edited by Anna Hatcher. Princeton, Princeton University Press, 1962.
Classical and Christian Ideas of World Harmony: Prolegomena to an Interpretation of the Word "Stimmung," edited by Anna Granville Hatcher. Baltimore, Johns Hopkins University Press, 1963.

Other

Editor, *Hugo Schuchardt-brevier: Ein Vademekum der allgemeinen Sprachwissenschaft, als Festgabe zum 80. Geburtstag des Mesiters.* Halle, Niemery, 1922.
Editor, *Meisterwerke der romanischen Sprachwissenschaft.* Munich, Hueber, 2 vols., 1929-30.

*   *   *

As one might imagine, emigration from Europe to the United States embraces both change and continuity. For a humanistic Romance philologist such as Leo Spitzer, the move had far-reaching implications. Whereas Erich Auerbach arrived in America only after the war (and thus was never able to balance adequately his desire to function in his new country with his sense that all life had been ineluctably altered by that great watershed between cultural differentiation and undifferentiation), Spitzer assumed residence in 1936 at the age of 49; thus, he spent fully a third of his productive professional life as an American scholar. The United States was envisioned not as temporary refuge or as a purely professional domicile but as a new and permanent haven—a context within which the philologist strives to search for the inward form.

Rooted in Geistesgeschichte, Spitzer adhered to the notion (as expressed in *Linguistics and Literary History*) that "language is only one outward crystallization of the 'inward form,' or, to use another metaphor: the lifeblood of the poetic creation is everywhere the same, whether we tap the organism at 'language' or 'ideas,' at 'plot' or at 'composition.' " Once in America, this was extended to the assertion that since "the best document of a nation is its literature, and since the latter is nothing but its language as this is written down by elect speakers," it is possible to "grasp the spirit of a nation in the language of its outstanding works of literature." Thus, Spitzer the mature practitioner asserted that the philological circle and its accompanying methodology which he had utilized in Europe could be exploited as well in his new home to penetrate to the historical "spirit" and "soul" of America.

But the United States was not the same as Europe. In his essay "American Advertising Explained as Popular Art," Spitzer noted that "of all the peoples among whom I have lived, the Americans seem to me most jealously insistent on the right of being addressed as individuals. It is an interesting paradox that the same civilization that has perfected standardization to such a degree is also characterized by this intense need for the recognition of one's personal existence" (*A Method of Interpreting Literature*). Further, he confided in an interview that the average American resident is "a linguistic isolationist [for whom] there exists no inner urge to study ways of expression not his own. The American way of life seems to admit no relativism, linguistic or otherwise" (*Johns Hopkins Magazine*, April 1952).

But how does one disclose the humanistic spirit of the American nation through its literature when that collective entity is comprised of "jealously insistent" individuals who are "linguistic isolationist[s]"? For Spitzer, it was necessary to modify his Old World humanism in order to view himself in America as a humanist "devoted to man and to an understanding of man. The humanist should live among his fellow-men. He should not lose contact with them, for then he would be no longer humane himself; but he should live somewhat removed from them." Thus, Spitzer the American critic saw himself as exerting a dual function: he must "live among" his countrymen as a fellow citizen, but at the same time he must transcend that level of existence and perception—"somewhat remove" himself—in order to penetrate through to cultural and linguistic truth. In practice, Spitzer was both a man eager to be assimilated within the American soul and spirit and a philologist for whom "the idea *and* the word are, at every moment of the reading, *seen* together" (*Classical and Christian Ideas of World Harmony*)—in short, a philologist for whom the writing of literary criticism carried a moral imperative which ought to be disseminated among the American peoples.

It is this dichotomy—between man in time, in language, in culture, and scholar removed from these realms—which animates the best and most enduring of Spitzer's American works. We may examine it most dramatically in such pieces as "American Advertising Explained as Popular Art" (where he embraces commercial advertising as a positive cultural force), "*Explication de Texte* Applied to Walt Whitman's Poem 'Out of the Cradle Endlessly Rocking' " (where he speaks of Whitman's poem which refers to the "low and delicious word death...the sweetest song and all songs, that strong and delicious word" as signifying Whitman's peculiarly "American *optimism* and love of life" as opposed to the *Weltschmerz* of 19th-century Europe), and in his address to the Modern Language Association on "The Formation of the American Humanist" (where he calls for a formal European-derived intellectual elite to be integrated within American democratic society). Evidenced in dramatic form here, the polarity is to be found in all of Spitzer's work—as a dramatic and poignant reminder of his aspiration which in large measure we share: to achieve objective critical understanding of an enterprise of which we are in the midst.

Perhaps because he believed that "it is not the letter of any idea...[but] the total system of ideas charged with emotion" that produces explicative results, Spitzer's work continues to be a living force among us. For in the flux and turbulence of our contemporary critical environment, it is edifying to consider Leo Spitzer, who sought truth unhesitantly in a variety of literary controversies and from a multitude of historical contexts and who yet would fit his own words as "a harmonious and poised man [who] is apt, by nature, to see everywhere himself, and the things connected with himself, as being 'embraced' and caressed: to feel that he is the center of a whole—the embryo in the egg, the tree within the bark, the earth wrapped around by ether. This is an inner form, a living pattern of thought, which must reproduce itself unceasingly..." (*Essays in Historical Semantics*).

—Geoffrey Green

STANISLAVSKY. Stage-name of Konstantin Sergevich Alexeyev, Russian actor, director and theorist of the drama. Born in Moscow, 18 January 1863. Educated privately. Married Maria Lilina in 1889; 2 children. Director, Moscow Branch of the Russian Musical Society and Moscow Conservatory, 1885; founded the Society of Art and Literature, 1888, and began producing plays in 1895; with Nemirovich-Danchenko founded the Moscow Art Theatre in 1898; founded the First Studio (improvisatory theatre and theatre training program) in 1913, and the Opera Studio of the Moscow Bolshoy Theatre in 1918; toured extensively with the company in Europe and America, 1922 and 1924. Recipient: Order of the Red Banner, 1933. *Died 7 August 1938.*

PUBLICATIONS

Collections

Sobranie sochinenii [Collected Works].   Moscow, Iskusstvo, 8 vols., 1954-61.

Theatrical Arts and Techniques

My Life in Art (first published in English).   London, Bles, and Boston, Little Brown, 1924.
Rabota aktera nad soboi, rabota nad soboi v tvorcheskom protsesse perezhivaniia dnevnik uchenika.   Moscow, Khudozhestvennaia literatura, 1938; part 1 as *An Actor Prepares*, New York, Theatre Arts, 1936, London, Bles, 1938; part 2 as *Building a Character*, New York, Theatre Arts, 1949, London, Reinhard and Evans, 1950.
Besedy K.S. Stanislavskogo v Studii Bol'shogo teatra v 1918-1922 g.g. zapisannye K.E. Antarovoi.   Moscow, n.p., 1939; as *Stanislavsky on the Art of the Stage*, London, Faber, 1950; New York, Hill and Wang, 1961.
Khudozhestvennye zapisi 1877-1892 [Artistic Notes 1877-1892].   Moscow, Iskusstvo, 1939.
A.P. Chekhov v Moskovskom khudozhestvennom teatre [A.P. Chekhov in the Moscow Artistic Theater].   Moscow, Izd. Muzeia Moskovskogo Khudozh. akademicheskogo teatra, 1947.
Etika [Ethics].   Moscow, Izd. Muzeia Moskovskogo ordenov Lenina i Trudovogo Krasnogo Znameni Khudozh. akademicheskogo teatra SSSR, 1947; selections in *Discipline or Corruption*, London, Fact and Fiction, 1966.
Stanislavsky Produces Othello.   London, Bles, and New York, Theatre Arts, 1948.
The Seagull, Produced by Stanislavsky: Production Score for

the Moscow Art Theatre. London, Dobson, 1952.

Stati, rechi, besedy, pisma [Articles, Speeches, Talks, Letters]. Moscow, Iskusstvo, 1953.

Stanislavsky's Legacy: A Collection of Comments on a Variety of Aspects on an Actor's Life and Art. New York, Theatre Arts, 1958; London, Reinhard, 1959; revised edition, London, Eyre Methuen, 1981.

Creating a Role. New York, Theatre Arts, 1961; London, Bles, 1963.

An Actor's Handbook. New York, Theatre Arts, 1963.

Stanislavskii i Nemerovich-Danchenko ob iskusstve aktera pevtsa [Stanislavsky and Nemirovich-Danchenko about the Art of the Actor-Singer]. Moscow, Iskusstvo, 1973.

Stanislavsky on Opera. New York, Theatre Arts, 1975.

*

Critical Studies: *Stanislavsky: A Life*, by David Magarshack, London, MacGibbon and Kee, 1950; *The Stanislavski System*, by Sonia Moore, New York, Viking Press, 1965.

*   *   *

Stanislavsky's significance as an important figure in cultural history is secured by his co-founding and direction of the Moscow Art Theatre with Nemirovich-Danchenko in 1898. But what keeps his fame alive today is his working out of a system of acting technique which, though originally formulated for his own company to accomodate the productions of the realistic drama of Anton Chekhov, has been promulgated throughout the world.

In his autobiography, *My Life in Art*, Stanislavsky purported to have begun work on his "System" at age 44, in 1906, during a period of depression following the death of Chekhov. Actually, the System was a codification of the fruits of a lifetime of experimentation, the seeds of which were sown in his early childhood. His first stage appearance, which in his biography he claimed to recall vividly, was in a holiday tableaux at the age of two or three. In fact, the very nature of his technique requires the recreation of child-like naivety, the kind of belief seldom found outside of children's play—which Stanislavsky himself termed the "magical if." With its game-like quality of make-believe, the "if" allows the actor to place himself in the given circumstances of the character he is playing and thus react naturally. Stanislavsky described it as "the lever to lift us out of everyday life onto the plane of imagination."

Stanislavsky provided the actor with a practical textbook. Yet the seeming paradox, that of applying a scientific approach to an art which is dependent upon instinct and freedom of spirit, was not designed to be restrictive, but rather to induce a favorable condition for the all-important "creative mood." It was a method of courting inspiration by means of the will. As an actor himself, Stanislavsky was no mere theoretition; he became his own laboratory. Dissatisfaction with his own work was the spur for his using each of his roles to search for the elusive key to what he called "the feeling of true measure."

The basic tenets of the System are outlined in *An Actor Prepares*, which is written in the form of a journal kept by an eager young student recording lessons with a famous acting teacher. One can see Stanislavsky in both personae—the sage, old mentor and the ever-inquisitive pupil. The true measure Stanislavsky was seeking was not literal reality but the "inner truth" of the imagination. "The actor must first of all believe in everything that takes place on the stage, and most of all he must believe in what he himself is doing. And one can believe only in the truth." He delved into the subconscious, the source of emotion. "True art must teach him [the actor] how to awaken consciously his subconscious creative self for its superconscious organic creativeness."

Some of the means of achieving this state were: motivated action; relaxation of the muscles; concentration of attention;

memory of emotion. The play script was analyzed and literally translated into a psychological subtext consisting of "actions" suggested by the dialogue and stage directions. These actions diagrammed what was actually happening beneath the surface of the dialogue. The through-line of action, or "super-objective," was broken down into individual units of actions or objectives. What the characters were striving for, and how they achieved their goals, became the basis of the breakdown. The subtext was always expressed in the infinitive verb form, as opposed to a state of emotion or passive mood. Emotion was not to be pursued for its own sake, but would result out of action. Of course, all this hinged on the "magical if."

With all his emphasis upon inner truth, that was never Stanislavsky's entire rubric. He planned three volumes. *Building a Character* concentrates on the vocal and body techniques essential for projecting the stage truth beyond the footlights to the audience. Stanislavsky died before completing the third book, but his drafts and notes were later reconstructed. *Creating a Role* deals with the actual construction of a character in its final form, using specific roles from great plays as examples.

As a thinker, Stanislavsky was not original; his method was drawn from observation and experience. He never claimed to have invented realistic acting, evidence of which has been documented from the Roman pantomimists to Shakespeare, Molière and onwards to his own time. He merely set out to codify what he had gleaned from his life in the art.

As a mature man, the tall, distinguished looking Stanislavsky was an imposing figure, striking awe, if not fear, into the hearts of his students. Yet those who interviewed him in his later years found him to be simple, direct, gracious, and even self-effacing. The American director Harold Clurman, who adapted Stanislavsky's System to the Group Theatre in the 1930's, effecting a pervasive influence on the American theatre to the present time, interviewed Stanislavsky at length in 1934. Clurman puzzled over the aging master's parting statement: "After all my years of study and work in the theatre, I have come to the conclusion that I know nothing about it."

—Constance Clark

STEINER, Rudolf. German anthroposophist. Born in Kraljevec, Hungary, 27 February 1861. Educated at the Technische Hochschule, Vienna. Married Anna Eunicke in 1898; married Marie von Sievers in 1914. Worked as a tutor in Vienna, and edited Goethe's scientific papers at the Goethe Archives, Wiemar, 1888-97; editor, *Magazin für Literatur*, 1897-1900; Leader of the German section of the Theosophical Society, 1902-13; founded the Anthroposophical Society and its cultural center, the Goetheanum, Dornach, Switzerland, 1913. *Died 30 March 1925.*

PUBLICATIONS

Collections

Gesamtausgabe. Dornach, Steiner Verlag, 1955-.

Theosophy and Anthroposophy (For a full listing of Steiner's separately published lectures and pamphlets see the bibliographies listed below. Titles in the present bibliography refer to works and collections published in English)

Goethe the Scientist (1883). New York, Anthroposophical Press, 1950.
The Theory of Knowledge Implicit in Goethe's World-Conception

(1886).   New York, Anthroposophical Press, 1940.

Goethe as the Founder of a New Science of Aesthetics (1889). London, Steiner Press, n.d.

Goethe's Standard of the Soul (1902).   London, Anthroposophical Publishing Company, n.d.

Atlantis and Lemuria (1904).   London, Anthroposophical Publishing Company, 1923.

Schiller and Our Times (1905).   London, Anthroposophical Publishing Company, 1933.

The Gates of Knowledge (1906).   Chicago, Anthroposophical Literature Concern, 1922.

The Education of the Child in the Light of Anthroposophy (1907).   London, Steiner Press, 1947.

Christianity as Mystical Fact and the Mysteries of Antiquity (1910).   London, Steiner Press, 1938.

Spiritual Guidance of Man and Humanity (1911).   New York, Anthroposophical Press, 1950.

A Road to Self-Knowledge (1912); *The Threshold of the Spiritual World* (1913).   London, Steiner Press, 1938.

Calendar 1912/13—The Calendar of the Soul.   London, Steiner Press, n.d.

Spiritual Science: A Review of Its Aims and the Attacks of Its Opponents (1914).   London, Steiner Press, 1914.

The Mission of Spiritual Science and Its Building at Dornach, Switzerland (1916).   London, H.J. Heywood-Smith, 1917.

Human Life in the Light of Spiritual Science—Anthroposophy (1916).   New York, Anthroposophic Press, 1933.

The Philosophy of Spiritual Activity (Freedom) (1918).   London, Steiner Press, 1949.

Goethe's Conception of the World (1918).   London, Anthroposophical Publishing Company, 1928.

Knowledge of Higher Worlds and Its Attainment (1918).   New York, Anthroposophic Press, 1947.

The Threefold Commonwealth (1919).   London, New York, Threefold Commonwealth, 1922.

Theosophy: An Introduction to the Supersensible Knowledge of the World and the Destination of Man (1922).   New York, Anthroposophic Press, 1946.

Cosmology, Religion, and Philosophy (1922).   London, Steiner Press, 1943.

Lectures to Teachers—Christmas, 1921.   London, Anthroposophical Publishing Company, 1923.

The Life of the Soul (1923).   London, Steiner Press, 1941.

Mysticism and Modern Thought (1923).   London, Steiner Press, 1928.

To the Members: Volume I.   Dornach, Anthroposophischer Verlag, 1931.

To the Members: Volume II.   London, Steiner Press, n.d.

Occult Science: An Outline (1925).   New York, Anthroposophical Press, 1938.

Fundamentals of Therapy, with Ita Wegman (1925).   New York, Anthroposophical Press, 1938.

Anthroposophical Leading Thoughts (1925).   London, Anthroposophical Publishing Company, 1927.

*

Bibliography: *The Writings and Lectures of Rudolf Steiner: A Chronological Bibliography of His Books, Lectures, Addresses, Courses, Cycles, Essays and Reports As Published in English Translation*, by Paul Marshall Allen, New York, Whittier, 1956.
Rudolf Steiner: Das Literarische und Künstlerische Werk: Eine Bibliographische Übericsht, Dornach, Steiner Verlag, 1961.

Critical Studies: *The Life and Work of Rudolf Steiner from the Turn of the Century to His Death* by Guenther Wachsmuth, New York, Whittier, 1955; *A Scientist of the Invisible: An Introduction to the Life and Work of Rudolf Steiner* by A.P. Shepherd, New York, British Book Centre, 1959.

*   *   *

Rudolf Steiner was born in Hungary of German parents. Educated in Vienna he worked in Germany, finally moving to Dornach, near Basel, Switzerland. He left behind him a thriving movement—"anthroposophy"—dedicated to the promulgation of his ideas, which extend all the way from a distinctive form of dance to a version of organic gardening.

A crucial influence on Steiner was the thought of the German polymath Goethe, whose scientific writings Steiner spent some seven years editing at the Goethe-Archiv in Weimar. Combining "organic" ideas of Goethe with other notions then prevalent, especially the evolutionism of Ernst Haeckel, Steiner produced his first and probably major work, *Philosophie der Freiheit* (1896). He argued that mechanistic science (i.e., the kind of science most scientists produce) gives only limited abstract knowledge of some of nature's uniform relations. To science, to attain full knowledge, one must add intuitive thinking, such as is revealed to us through art and philosophy. Drawing on Goethe's notion of life as a self-evolving, self-directing phenomenon, Steiner advocated a "monism of thought": as individuals live in the world, an ever-more-valid world picture is being produced.

At the beginning of this century, Steiner became more and more involved with the movement known as "theosophy." This led him to take an intense interest in Indian thought, an interest also spurred by his reading of Nietzsche and the attraction of Nietzsche's doctrine of "eternal recurrence" (itself an idea coming from the East). A key concept for Steiner was the notion of reincarnation, and together with this he adopted the Eastern view that humans are constructed from several parts, including the physical, the ethereal, and the astral.

In 1907 Steiner broke from theosophy, particularly on account of the pro-Hindu policies of Annie Besant. However, he continued to develop his own thought more and more in esoteric directions, finally in 1913 giving his system the name "anthroposophy." He argued that we have had a progression of physical bodies, with spirits being incarnated over and over again, aiming ultimately to achieve some sort of supreme self-consciousness. At the practical level, this has resulted in the dangers of 19th-century individualism, as, for instance, one finds typified in the writings of Nietzsche.

Steiner's solution was not the collectivism of totalitarianism. In fact, his ideas were suppressed during the period of Nazi rule in Germany. Rather, Steiner wanted a three-part social organism, in which one has autonomous, yet functioning in harmony, spheres of the juridical, spiritual, and economic. Somewhat idealistically, Steiner thought that economic society could be based primarily on voluntary co-operation. This is an interesting reversal of the usual reactions to evolutionary ideas, where the emphasis tends to be on struggle and selfish strife.

Steiner's own interests lay in the spiritual sphere, and his later thought became distinctly esoteric, as he explored through a series of visions and special insights what he took to be the ultimate nature of reality. He believed that spirit had (through the evolutionary process of incarnation) become more and more material. However, thanks to the anti-Lucifer impressions left in the cosmic ether by Buddha, Zarathustra, Plato, and Christ (especially through the regenerative solar influence of the blood shed in the Crucifixion), spirit can once again move back up to its pure self. Ultimately, one will have both self-consciousness and the knowledge of universal cosmic relations.

In the latter part of his life, Steiner founded a cultural centre, the Goetheanum in Dornach. The ideas of anthroposophy spread from Germany to England and the U.S.. Steiner developed a whole world system, governing art, architecture, science, farming, and so on, emphasizing the organic, growing nature of reality. Followers could therefore participate in Steinerism at various levels, from the fairly uncritical to the deepest participation in the mysteries. One of Steiner's most important legacies is so-called "Waldorf" education. Started in order to cater to children of the employees of one of Steiner's richer followers, the Waldorf School in Stuttgart is now copied all over the world. In such schools, teachers try to achieve Steiner's hopes of developing spiritual insight and a proper harmony between dispositions of excess and defect. Naturally, there tends to be a gap between reality and the ideal. Outsiders are struck by the extent to which Waldorf schools achieve excellence in the arts. Unfortunately, this tends to be done at the expense of the sciences—a feature which Steiner himself would regret. Also, there tends to be confusion between the true aims of Steiner himself, and the inessential trappings of the culture in which Steiner lived. Habits of early 20th-century Germany are taken to be a necessary part of spiritual regeneration in late 20th-century America.

But, of course, this is a problem of a kind that any movement faces. What cannot be denied is that an increasing number of people find inspiring Steiner's emphasis on the spiritual in an age of increasing materialism.

—Michael Ruse

STERN, (Louis) William. German psychologist. Born in Berlin, 29 April 1871; emigrated to the United States in 1933. Studied at the University of Berlin, habilitation 1897. Married Clara Joseephy in 1899; 3 children. Instructor, 1897-1907, and Associate Professor, 1907-16, University of Breslau; Professor, Colonial Institute and Lecture Fund, Hamburg, 1916-18; Co-Founder and Professor of Psychology, Hamburg Institute, 1919-33; Professor of Psychology, Duke University, Durham, North Carolina, 1934-38. Honorary doctorate: University of Wittenberg; Clark University, Worcester, Massachusetts. *Died* (in Durham) *28 March 1938.*

PUBLICATIONS

Psychology

Die Analogie im Volkstümlichen Denken: Eine psychologische Untersuchung. Berlin, Salinger, 1893.
Psychologie der Veränderungsauffassung. Breslau, Preuss and Junger, 1898.
Über Psychologie der individuellen Differenzen (Ideen zu einer "Differentiellen Psychologie"). Leipzig, Barth, 1900.
Die Aussage als geistige Leistung und als Verhörsprodukt. Leipzig, Barth, 1904.
Helen Keller: Die Entwicklung und Erziehung einer Taubstummblinden. Berlin, Reuther and Reichard, 1905.
Person und Sache. Leipzig, Barth, 3 vols., 1906-24.
Die Kindersprache: Eine theoretische und sprachtheoretische Untersuchung, with Clara Stern. Leipzig, Barth, 1907.
Die differentielle Psychologie in ihren methodischen Grundlagen. Leipzig, Barth, 1911.
Die psychologischen Methoden der Intelligenzprüfung und deren Anwendung an Schulkindern. Leipzig, Barth, 1912; as *The Psychological Methods of Testing Intelligence,* Baltimore, Warwick and York, 1914.
Der Student und die pädagogischen Bestrebungen der Gegenwart. Leipzig, Teubner, 1913.
Psychologie der frühen Kindheit bis zum sechsten Lebensjahre. Leipzig, Quelle and Meyer, 1914; as *Psychology of Early Childhood Up to the Sixth Year of Age,* London, Allen and Unwin, and New York, Holt, 1924.
Vorgedanken zur Weltanschauung. Leipzig, Barth, 1915.
Die Intelligenzprüfung an Kindern und Jugendlichen: Methoden, Ergebnisse, Ausblicke. Leipzig, Barth, 1916.
Grundgedanken der personalistischen Philosophie. Berlin, Reuther and Reichard, 1918.
Über eine psychologische Eignungsprüfung für Strassenbahnfahrerinnen. Leipzig, Barth, 1918.
Methodensammlung zur Intelligenzprüfung von Kindern und

Jugendlichen, with Otto Wiegmann. Leipzig, Barth, 1920.
Die Psychologie und die Schülerauslese. Leipzig, Barth, 1920.
Anfänge der Reifezeit: Ein Knabentagebuch in psychologischer Bearbeitung. Leipzig, Quelle and Meyer, 1925.
Probleme der Schülerauslese. Leipzig, Barth, 1926.
Studien zur Personwissenschaft. Leipzig, Barth, 1930.
Erinnerung, Aussage, und Lüge in der ersten Kindheit, with Clara Stern. Leipzig, Barth, 1931.
Prinzipienfragen der Psychotechnik, with others. Leipzig, Barth, 1933.
Allgemeine Psychologie auf personalistischen Grundlage. The Hague, Nijhoff, 1935; as *General Psychology from the Personalistic Standpoint,* New York, Macmillan, 1938.

Other

Editor, *Beiträge zur Psychologie der Aussage.* Leipzig, Barth, 2 vols., 1903-06
Editor, with Otto Lipmann, *Forschung und Unterricht in der Jugendkunde.* Berlin, Teubner, 1913.
Editor, *Die Ausstellung zu vergleichenden Jugendkunde der Geschlechter auf dritten Kongress fur Jugendbildung und Jugundkunde in Breslau Oktober 1913.* Leipzig, Teubner, 1913.
Editor, *Jugendliches Seelenleben und Krieg: Materialien und Berichte.* Leipzig, Barth, 1915.
Editor, *Untersuchung über die Intelligenz von Kindern und Jugendlichen,* by Walther Minkus. Leipzig, Barth, 1919.
Editor, with Otto Lipmann, *Vorträge über angewandte Psychologie gehalten beim 7. Kongress fur experimentelle Psychologie.* Leipzig, Barth, 1921.
Editor, *Neue Beitrage zur Theorie und Praxis der Intelligenzprüfung.* Leipzig, Barth, 1925.

* * *

William Stern was born of Jewish parents in Berlin in 1871, and studied psychology at the University of Berlin under the eminent psychologist Hermann Ebbinghaus, famous for his pioneering experiments on memory. Stern was among the most distinguished of his pupils, and became one of the most versatile and most profound psychologists of the 20th-century. In 1933 he had to leave Hitler's Germany, and he settled in the United States, where he died in 1938.

Probably Stern is best known for his devising of the Intelligence Quotient (I.Q.) in 1912. Previously intelligence had been measured in terms of Mental Age. The I.Q. was obviously a more convenient index, but later, particularly after settling in America, Stern came to deplore its abuse, and, in fact, it was of far less significance than many of his other contributions to psychology, which were of seminal importance in a number of quite different fields—experimental psychology, child psychology, differential psychology, applied psychology, and the theory of personality, or "personalistics," as he termed it.

Stern was a talented experimental psychologist, and early in his career made studies of the perception of change. In the course of these experiments he devised an instrument for investigating changes in auditory pitch, his "Tonvariator," which was extensively used before the days of electronic equipment. He also carried out important pioneering experiments on the reliability of witnesses' reports. These were carried out in the early years of the century, but Stern maintained his interest on this topic, and his last public lecture delivered in New York shortly before his death was concerned with testimony in relation to legal procedure.

His studies of childhood, many of them carried out together with his wife, were among the most thorough of the early studies. They were largely based on the observation of his own three children, but also involved studies in schools. He was among the first to report on the case of Helen Keller, the American blind and deaf child. The Sterns' work on children's language is still something of a classic.

Stern was intensely interested in the applications of psychology to problems of real life. He founded the Berlin Institute for Applied Psychology in 1906, and shortly after, in 1907, the *Journal for Applied Psychology*. When he moved to Hamburg in 1916, he established the famous Hamburg Institute, which flourished until his flight from Germany in 1933. His book on applied psychology (1903) was among the first formal surveys of the subject.

The field of individual, or differential, psychology, which is concerned with individuality and the psychological differences between people, was also a major interest of Stern's. His first book on the subject was published in 1900, and his second in 1911. It was in an endeavour to bring greater precision into the measurement of individual differences that he developed the I.Q. index.

Stern's work on "personalistics" has not been widely appreciated, though it greatly influenced the work of Gordon Allport in America; but it is arguably his most significant, and likely to be his most enduring, contribution to psychology. It was an endeavour to provide a synoptic conceptual framework for the whole of psychology, broad enough to embrace all that was valuable in the different schools of thought ranging from behaviourism and psychoanalysis to the highest levels of human personality. Stern embodied his proposals in his last important book, which was translated into English in the year of his death under the title *General Psychology from the Personalistic Standpoint*. The positive core of Stern's system was the "person-world relation." The person he defined as "a living whole, individual, unique, striving towards goals, self-contained and yet open to the world around him." The person lived at three levels: at the level of a biological organism, at the level of an experiencing subject, and as a member of the world of values. Within this broad framework, which he filled with much subtle detail and factual material, Stern was able to include the whole field of psychology, theoretical and applied. Unfortunately the book, which was not altogether easy reading, appeared just prior to the outbreak of war, and before its merits were recognized it was swamped by wartime preoccupations. Although now dated in some matters of detail, its general theoretical orientation is coming back into favour, and Stern may well come to be recognized as one of the most able and balanced of 20th-century psychologists.

—Leslie Hearnshaw

STEVENS, S(tanley) S(mith). American psychologist. Born in Ogden, Utah, 4 November 1906. Studied at the University of Utah, Provo, 1927-29; Stanford University, California, B.A. 1931; Harvard University, Cambridge, Massachusetts, Ph.D. 1933. Married Maxine Leonard in 1930, 1 son; married Geraldine Stone in 1963. Assistant in Psychology, 1932-34, Research Fellow, Medical School, 1934-35, Research Fellow in Physics, 1935-36, Member of the faculty, 1936-46, Professor of Psychology, 1946-62, and Professor of Psychophysics, 1962-73, Harvard University (Director, Psychoacoustic Laboratory, 1944-62, Psychology Laboratory, 1949-62, and Psychophysics Laboratory, 1962-73). Chairman, Division of Anthropology and Psychology, National Research Council, 1949-52; Member, Sensory Diseases Study Section, National Institutes of Health, 1956-58. Recipient: Howard Crosby Warren Medal, Society of Experimental Psychologists, 1943; Distinguished Scientific Contribution Award, American Psychological Association, 1960; Award for Distinguished Accomplishment, Beltone Institute, 1966; Rayleigh Gold Medal, British Acoustical Society, 1972. Member, National Academy of Sciences, and American Academy of Arts and Sciences; Fellow, Acoustical Society of America. *Died 18 January 1973*.

PUBLICATIONS

Psychology

Hearing: Its Psychology and Physiology, with Hallowell Davis. New York, Wiley, 1938.
The Varieties of Human Physique: An Introduction to Constitutional Psychology, with W.H. Sheldon and W.B. Tucker. New York, Harper, 1940.
The Varieties of Temperament: A Psychology of Constitutional Differences, with W.H. Sheldon. New York, Harper, 1942.
Hearing Aids: An Experimental Study of Design Objectives, with others. Cambridge, Massachusetts, Harvard University Press, 1947.
Sound and Hearing, with others. New York, Time Incorporated, 1965.
Psychophysics and Social Scaling. Morristown, New Jersey, General Learning Press, 1972.
Psychophysics: Introduction to Its Perceptual, Neural, and Social Prospects, edited by Geraldine Stevens. New York, Wiley, 1975.

Other

Bibliography on Hearing, with others. Cambridge, Massachusetts, Harvard University Press, 1955.

Editor, *Handbook of Experimental Psychology*. New York, Wiley, 1951.

*

Bibliography: in *Sensation and Measurement: Papers in Honor of S.S. Stevens* edited by Howard K. Moskowitz and others, Dordrecht, Reidel, 1974.

*   *   *

In 1974, shortly after S.S. Stevens's death, some forty colleagues and former students contributed articles for a volume to honor his memory. Significantly the volume took on the title *Sensation and Measurement* because these two terms best typify his interests from his first year in graduate school at Harvard to his untimely death in 1973.

From the start he took a deep interest in the fundamental nature of scientific measurement. He was much influenced by the positivism of the Vienna Circle, newly transplanted to America, and the operational thinking of P.W. Bridgman at Harvard. He sought to instill the austere epistemology of operationism into the domain of psychology. In other words, the truth or falsity of a psychological proposition can be determined only in terms of the operations used to build up the proposition.

During the 1930's he took a burning interest in the nature of scales of measurement because he felt that the quantification of sensory attributes was impossible without a better understanding of measurement in general. After a couple of false starts he finally constructed a classification of scales of measurement that was satisfactory to him and came to have widespread acceptance not only within the discipline of psychology (especially psychophysics) but throughout the natural sciences and statistics ("On the Theory of Scales in Measurement," *Science*, 1946). For whatever reason, the classification often appears in textbooks curiously detached from his name.

There are four types of scales of measurement—nominal, ordinal, interval, and ratio. The scales are hierarchically arranged such that a ratio scale contains the information sufficient to generate interval, ordinal, and nominal scales; interval scales can generate ordinal and nominal scales but not ratio scales, etc. The scales are defined by the mathematical operations that leave the form of the scale invariant.

Nominal scales are empirically constructed by the determination of equality, such as the numbering of football players. The only permissible mathematical operation on these scales is one-to-one substitution. Ordinal scales, such as scales of quality of leather or pleasantness of odors, are constructed by the determination of greater or less, and the scale value can be transformed by any increasing monotonic function without loss of empirical information. Interval scales are constructed by determination of equality of intervals or differences (e.g., calendar time, Fahrenheit and Celsius scales of temperature), and the only permissible mathematical transformation is $x' = ax + b$ as in going from, say, $°F(x)$ to $°C(x')$. Finally ratio scales are constructed from the determination of equal ratios (e.g., length, weight) and the only permissible transformation is $x' = ax$ as in going, say, from inches to centimeters.

A striking feature of the classification is the way in which it limits the logically permissible statistical treatments of data measured on the various scale types. For example, statistics such as means and standard deviations are permissible for interval and ratio data but inappropriate for ordinal and nominal data; geometric statistics are appropriate for ratio scales alone, etc. The general conclusion is that the nature of the scale is determined by the operations used to construct it and that the scale type determines the permissible mathematical transformations and statistical analyses of a data set.

There was a kind of Linnean bent to Stevens's mind that sought to bring simplicity where diversity prevailed. In addition to the classification of scales he constructed a useful classification of the problems and methods of psychophysics ("Problems and Methods in Psychophysics," *Psychological Bulletin*, 1958). He also collaborated with W.H. Sheldon in the construction of classificatory scales of human somatotypes and temperaments.

From the start of his career to the finish Stevens was also a laboratory scientist whose work touched on a great variety of sensory problems: sound localization, visual saturation, tonal pitch, density and volume, aural harmonics, electrical stimulation of hearing, the neural quantum, hearing aids, speech spectra, and auditory masking, to name some of them. Chief among his empirical inquiries, especially after about 1952, was the area of measurement of scales of sensory magnitude. This effort had commenced in the 1930's when it became evident that perceived loudness failed to accord with the logarithmic function postulated by G.T. Fechner on the basis of integration of just-noticeable differences of stimulus intensities. Although Stevens established a scale (called the sone scale), based on fractionation (subjects adjust one tone to sound half as loud as another), the formula chosen to relate loudness to sound pressure was formidably complex.

With the pressure of wartime research over and after the production of an influential *Handbook of Experimental Psychology*, Stevens returned to the problem of loudness measurement. New procedures emerged, including the famous "magnitude estimation," which calls upon subjects to match numbers to perceived intensity. This and other methods helped to explain the biases that account for the apparent complexity of the early sone scale. More important, application of these methods by Stevens and others, including the undersigned (no relation), led to a startling and simple generalization. On a great variety of sensory dimensions—e.g., loudness, brightness, taste and odor intensity, warmth, cold, apparent weight, vibration magnitude—apparent intensity appeared to grow as a power function of the physical stimulus (often called Stevens's Power Law). The exponent varies greatly from one sense modality to another and can be smaller than unity (indicating slow growth of sensation as a function of stimulus intensity) or larger than unity (indicating fast growth). Its size also depends on many other conditions such as state of adaptation of the sense organ.

By 1970 he was able to claim:

In the 17 years since 1953, research in psychophysics has disclosed important but unsuspected human capacities. The normal sentient observer turns out to be a marvelous

matching instrument. With surprising consistency he can assign numbers to any aspect of nature that appears to him to vary in degree, and he can make the numbers proportional to the strength of his subjective impressions. Already more than 40 perceptual continua have been scaled by simple number matching—magnitude estimation, as it is called. Equally important, the human subject can match any variable to any other variable, such as apparent loudness to apparent brightness, or force of handgrip to warmth on the skin, or apparent duration to apparent area, and so on. The demonstrated success of such cros-modality matching means that the interrelations among all subjective variables can be quantified. Definitive descriptions of the operating characteristics of all the sensory systems are placed within reach.

Despite the high degree of internal consistency displayed by the matching data and widespread acceptance of the Power Law, there remain those who are skeptical that sensations can truly be measured on a ratio scale. Nevertheless, Stevens's Power Law marked the end of any general acceptance of its 19th-century precursor, Fechner's Logarithmic Law, it served to generate research on sensory processes in laboratories round the world, and it will continue to help shape the thought and research of the psychophysicist into the future.

—Joseph C. Stevens

STEVENSON, Charles L(eslie). American philosopher. Born in Cincinnati, Ohio, 27 June 1908. Studied at Yale University, New Haven, Connecticut, B.A. 1930; Cambridge University, B.A. 1933; Harvard University, Cambridge, Massachusetts, Ph.D. 1935. Married Ellen Distler in 1930, 3 children; married Nora Carroll Cary in 1965, 1 son. Instructor, Harvard University, 1937-39; Assistant Professor, Yale University, 1939-46; Associate Professor, 1946-49, and Professor of Philosophy, 1949-77, University of Michigan, Ann Arbor; Professor of Philosophy, Bennington College, Vermont, 1977-78. Recipient: Guggenheim Fellowship, 1945. *Died 19 March 1978.*

PUBLICATIONS

Philosophy

Ethics and Language. New Haven, Connecticut, Yale University Press, 1944.
Facts and Values. New Haven, Connecticut, Yale University Press, 1963.

*

Bibliography: in *Values and Morals: Essays in Honor of William Frankena, Charles Stevenson and Richard Brandt* edited by A.I. Goldman and J. Kim, Dordrecht, Reidel, 1978.

*   *   *

Charles L. Stevenson, the American philosopher, is the premiere figure in America in the development of the theory of emotive meaning and the emotive theory of ethics. These theories were articulated at a time when, in philosophical circles, it had become difficult to regard sentences containing value terms (such as good, bad, obligatory, right, wrong, beautiful, and ugly) as factual reports about the subjects of sentences containing them. Beginning at least in 1936 with the publication of A.J. Ayer's *Language, Truth, and Logic*, and increasingly after World War II, the view that all discourse can be divided into two broad categories came to dominate philosophy in England and America. This view held that all discourse was either cognitive or noncognitive, i.e., it either contained sentences in the declarative form which asserted the existence of facts and which were thus either true or false, or it did not. Scientific theory and simple statements of fact whose truth can be directly tested (e.g., "This house is white.") are cognitive. Moral judgments, however, even though they might look to be in the declarative form, were regarded by the emotive theory as noncognitive. This theory held that there were no moral facts to which these statements referred and, so, they were neither true nor false. The emotive theory of meaning was developed to explain the meaning of these statements. It became the centerpiece of the emotive theory of ethics, both of which were fully developed by Stevenson in his book *Ethics and Language*, published in 1944.

The emotive theory of meaning and ethics was able to flourish, although briefly, because of alleged fatal defects in the naturalistic and nonnaturalistic cognitive theories which opposed it. Ethical naturalism is the view that value terms describe the subjects of the sentences in which they appear as possessing certain natural property. A natural property was conceived of very broadly as any property which could conceivably be detected and measured by empirical means. These theories cover a wide spectrum. They typically begin with a definition of (morally) good and proceed to define our duty in terms of the good, i.e., it is our duty to do what is good and to avoid what is bad. Theories which tell us that happiness, or consideration of others, or knowledge, or a life of service, or money, or power is the good are all naturalistic theories. On the other hand, nonnaturalistic, but still cognitive, theories contend that moral terms correspond to nonnatural properties possessed by the subjects of sentences which contain them. The presence of a nonnatural property is determined not by one of the physical senses (thus the designation "nonnatural") but by a moral sense or sensibility sometimes called intuition. Nonnatural properties are simple properties like red, and, like red, their presence is immediately sensed by intuition. Typically nonnaturalistic theories begin with a perception of what is right or what is our duty and then define what is (morally) good in terms of rightness or duty.

The fatal defect in nonnaturalism is said to be its implausibility. In light of the existence of widely divergent views about what behavior is morally acceptable, it seems very, very unlikely, so the argument goes, that nonnatural properties exist. This impression is reinforced by the circumstance that even nonnaturalists are unable to agree among themselves about basic issues in morality. On the other hand, the difficulty with naturalism is more subtle because many of the naturalistic theories offer very plausible definitions of moral terms. However, naturalism fails successfully to define moral terms because no matter what the particular definition, it contains an incomplete connection between definiendum and definiens. To illustrate the problem, consider this example. If one knows that Jones is a male who is over 30 years old and who has never been married, then one can say that Jones is a bachelor. If one has this information about Jones and still wonders whether he is a bachelor, then one reveals a lack of understanding of the meaning of "bachelor." On the other hand, if one knows, for example, a certain act promotes the greatest good for the greatest number one does not know "by definition" (as in the bachelor case) that the act is morally good. According to the critics of naturalism, no set of natural conditions can successfully replace the word good in "X is (morally) good" in the way that a set of natural conditions can replace bachelor in "X is a bachelor." Yet, this is exactly what would have to happen if naturalism were correct.

Stevenson offers an explanation for this failure of naturalism. It is that ethical terms such as "good" have emotive meaning which is not captured in naturalistic definitions. The emotive meaning of ethical terms is an expressive and an imperative or prescriptive force. Rather than describing their object, ethical terms are used to mold attitudes toward it, and to indicate the speaker's attitude as well. For Stevenson "X is (morally) good"

has the same meaning as "I like X. Do so as well." Such statements tell us little or nothing about X, but do express the speaker's attitude—which can range from approval or commitment or preference through disapprobation to hate or guilt—and indicate what the speaker desires for his or her audience. Because "X is good" is not a cognitive statement of fact, it does not report but rather expresses the speaker's attitude. According to Stevenson, an utterance expresses an attitude when it does not explicitly state that the speaker has the attitude, when a hearer of the speaker's culture world, upon hearing the speaker, form a belief that the speaker has the attitude, when the utterance arises spontaneously from the speaker's attitude, and when the hearer comes spontaneously to a belief about the speaker's attitude.

In addition to being expressive, ethical discourse molds attitudes. According to Stevenson this molding takes place as a result of our language training. Regardless of what beliefs may arise when we hear ethical utterances, there is always a tendency to develop a positive attitude toward that which we hear praised and a negative attitude toward what is condemned. "Murder is wrong" causes one to be inclined to disapprove of murder, not because of any reasons which are offered, but because we have become conditioned to feel almost automatically negatively toward anything which is labeled "wrong," and, of course, automatically positively and warmly toward anything which is labeled "good" or "right."

For Stevenson reasons in ethics operate quite differently from those in logic or science. Reasons in ethics do not entail or logically demonstrate any conclusion, nor do they inductively establish a conclusion as they might in science. In ethical discourse reasons are causally related to moral utterances. If statement S causes a hearer to adopt a certain moral attitude A, then S is a reason for A. It follows that anything which a speaker can use to effect those hearer attitudes which a speaker wants to effect is a reason. What gets called a reason depends upon what changes a person's attitudes. However, what is acceptable as a reason may also depend upon other attitudes, according to Stevenson. We may have negative attitudes toward the use of appeals to authority or of threats in moral discourse. We, thus, do not use them even though they would prove effective in changing attitudes.

The emotive theory of meaning, viz., the theory that certain words express attitudes rather than report facts, becomes central to Stevenson's emotive theory of ethics when it is applied to moral discourse. Both the theories have come under considerable criticism and exist today in philosophy in a much modified, many would say a much more sophisticated, form than Stevenson's early formulation. The absolute distinction between cognitive and noncognitive uses of language has been shown to be simplistic. Moral discourse is now seen to be a shifting and delicate balance of the interactions of fact and attitude. Moral terms sometimes express attitudes and sometimes they do not. Reasons in ethical discourse are sometimes identified with that which is persuasive, but most of the time we employ other criteria for determining what is reasonable and what is not. Stevenson's work on meaning and ethical theory brought about, beginning in the decade of the 1950's, a host of publications by philosophers in England and America which greatly deepen our sensitivity toward moral discourse.

—William Bywater

STOKES, Adrian (Durham). British art critic and poet. Born in London, 27 October 1902. Educated at Rugby School; studied at Magdalen College, Oxford, B.A. 1923. Married Margaret Mellis in 1936; married Ann Mellis in 1947; 3 children. Trustee, Tate Gallery, London, 1960-67. *Died* (in London) *15 December 1972.*

PUBLICATIONS

Art and Culture

The Thread of Ariadne. London, Kegan Paul, 1925.

Sunrise in the West: A Modern Interpretation of Past and Present. London, Kegan Paul, 1926.

The Quattro Cento. London, Faber, 1934; New York, Schocken, 1969.

The Stones of Rimini. London, Faber, 1934; New York, Schocken, 1969.

Tonight the Ballet. London, Faber, 1934; revised edition, 1935; New York, Dutton, 1935.

Russian Ballets. London, Faber, 1935; New York, Dutton, 1936.

Colour and Form. London, Faber, 1937; revised edition, 1950.

Venice: An Aspect of Art. London, Faber, 1945.

Cézanne. London, Faber, 1947; New York, Pitman, 1950.

Inside Out. London, Faber, 1947.

Art and Science. London, Faber, 1949.

Smooth and Rough. London, Faber, 1951.

Michelangelo: A Study in the Nature of Art. London, Tavistock, 1955; New York, Philosophical Library, 1956.

Raphael, 1483-1520. London, Faber, 1956.

Greek Culture and the Eye. London, Tavistock, 1958.

Monet, 1840-1926. London, Faber, and New York, Wittenborn, 1958.

Three Essays on the Painting of Our Time. London, Tavistock, 1961.

Painting and the Inner World. London, Tavistock, 1963.

The Invitation in Art. London, Tavistock, 1965; New York, Chilmark Press, 1966.

Venice. London, Duckworth, 1965.

Reflections on the Nude. London, Tavistock, and New York, Barnes and Noble, 1967.

The Image in Form: Selected Writings of Adrian Stokes, edited by Richard Wollheim. London, Penguin, and New York, Harper, 1972.

A Game That Must Be Lost: Collected Papers. Manchester, Carcanet Press, 1973.

The Critical Writings of Adrian Stokes. London, Thames and Hudson, 3 vols., 1978.

Verse

Penguin Modern Poets 23: Geoffrey Grigson, Edwin Muir, Adrian Stokes. London, Penguin, 1973.

With All the Views: Collected Poems. London, Black Swan, 1980.

*   *   *

Adrian Stokes was one of the most vigorous of the "non-technical" and "non-academic" art critics and historians in Great Britain during the middle third of the 20th century. He has wielded, through a set of writings of astounding range and virtuosity, an enormous influence on such people as John Berger, Lawrence Gowing, and the philosopher Richard Wollheim, and he has a small, but extremely devoted and well-deserved, readership. Stokes was one of the few writers on art and aesthetics in the 20th century—though he did have some important forerunners such as Ruskin and Pater and contemporaries such as the Marxist-inspired critic Walter Benjamin—whose writings had as their deepest intention to mime the lived structures of the experiences with which they were intimately connected. All of his major themes, as well as the principles which governed his later work, were limned in two seminal, hard, and highly contentious books written when he was in his early thirties, *The Stones of Rimini* and *The Quattro Cento.* In these books Stokes argued passionately for the paradigmatic place of the perceptual structures of the Mediterranean world in general, and of its architec-

ture and part of its sculpture in particular. Stokes was drunk with love of the Mediterranean world's, more specifically Italy's, distinctive perceptual physiognomy, which was so different, Stokes thought, from the northern types. Its compound of stone, light, and water resonated in him unceasingly from the time of his first trips to Italy, which utterly transformed him. Although psychoanalysis, deriving from the writings of Melanie Klein, later influenced him deeply, there was really no transformation in his fundamental insights nor in the value, both heuristic and otherwise, that he, and others, saw in them.

Stokes's work centered around some key categories and manifested as well some overriding biases. The categories give his thought a marvelous coherence and perspicacity, while his biases force us, without necessarily coercing total agreement, to re-examine the very grounds of our response to art, particularly architecture, sculpture, and painting, with which he was primarily concerned. Stokes argued constantly—with examples ranging from Greek art to modern "abstract" painting and sculpture—for the primacy of "carving" values in art as opposed to "plastic" or "molding" values. Carving values, he thought, were instantiated in their most substantial form in certain examples of the art of the 15th century, though they were also present in the classic Greek achievement. When Stokes spoke of "quattro cento" art he did not refer to the particular historical period itself but rather to what was essential and distinctive to the art of that period. Stokes believed that in the best and most revolutionary art of the 15th century stone was made to "bloom like a rose" through the "carving" powers of those who worked with it. Carving, resolutely opposed by Stokes to molding, especially in the domains of architecture, sculpture, and painting, elicited the inner forms of the materials themselves which gave no hint of being "stuck on" to the surface, being rather a part or manifestation of the stone's inner reality. Thus the paeans to "stone blossom" throughout the whole range of Stokes's writings. Stokes both applied this distinction between carving and molding to, and derived it from, a meditation on what he thought was most distinctive in quattro cento art as a whole. Carving values emphasized the all-at-onceness of the perceptual form, its simultaneity in space without any evocation of development or "musical" rhythm. Stokes wanted to develop a position directly in opposition to Pater's dictum that ultimately all art strives to attain the condition of music. In his dense and percipient descriptions and analyses of paradigmatic carving forms such as the Tempio Malatestiano in Rimini, the quattro cento architecture of Venice (about which he differed profoundly with Ruskin), the paintings of Piero della Francesca (whom he considered the greatest of painters), and the magnificent courtyard of Luciano Laurana at Urbino, Stokes arrived at analytical and poetic utterances the power and ringing character of which he never surpassed in his later work.

For Stokes the height of existence was reached in the immersion of subjectivity in the structures of the external world. The original empty self was filled with forms. His explicitly autobiographical writings, *Inside Out* and *Smooth and Rough,* are replete with descriptions and arguments for the necessity of building the self through opening oneself completely to the play of appearance and surface which marked the perceptual world. *Inside Out* idiosyncratically charts part of Stokes's extraordinary voyage of self-discovery through love of the external world. The inside is truly to be found on the outside, in the realm of simultaneity, of laid-out massive presence. As he said in his essay on Giorgione's *Tempestà,* art's task is to show the "utmost drama of the soul as laid-out things."

Stokes was nevertheless no lover of mere immediacy. The built world, the habitat wrought by men's hands, was his first love, and for him "architecture, building, is truly the mother of the arts." It displayed the power of sustaining presence without the twistings and turnings of false reflection or hyperconsciousness, to which a consciousness attracted to psychoanalysis could have all too easily succumbed, though Stokes never thought of psychoanalysis as supplanting his earlier insights but rather as deepening and confirming them. Indeed, the unbiased reader will perhaps ask himself whether Stokes's overriding aesthetic categories do not actually explain his adoption of the Kleinian psychoanalytic framework, with its central notions of projection and substitution, since Stokes wanted in his deepest being to explore all those dimensions in which "life within, fire within, is projected entirely upon a surface." Still, Klein's framework, with its central categories of projection and substitution, gave him, it must be admitted, sharper tools for understanding the bodily bases of art and the dialectic of projection and absorption which governed the genesis of artistic forms. It also furnished him with an instrument, still not adequately wielded, for engaging in a critique, on aesthetic principles, of the modern world with its insistence on molding and plastic values rather than the more "humanistic" values of carving.

Stokes's lifelong project, and the themes permeating all his analyses, was to show "the way that a work of art concentrates and solidifies mental process in the guise of the spatial world," through a process of projection and of substitutioin, which, for Stokes, was the essence of life. In this way he could make as one of his central theses that "to live is to substitute. Art is the symbol of human process," a principle instantiated in his own life preeminently. By immersing ourselves by projection and substitution in those laid-out things we come to know ourselves through the distinctively "visually" aesthetic, a domain to which Stokes was extraordinarily sensitive. Stokes's great insight, which guided his writings from the very beginning and his painting at the end of his life and also governed his life as a whole, can be described in his own words: "When objects of the senses compel in the percipient the profoundest of emotions of the contemplative state, the soul is at peace." It is this peace that Stokes's own writings are so successful in evoking.

—Robert E. Innis

STONE, Lawrence. American historian. Born in Epsom, Surrey, England, 4 December 1919; emigrated to the United States, 1963: naturalized, 1970. Educated at Charterhouse School, London, 1933-38; studied at the Sorbonne, Paris, 1938; Christ Church, Oxford, 1938-40, B.A., M.A. 1946 (Bryce Research Student, 1946-47). Served in Royal Naval Volunteer Reserves, 1940-45. Married Jeanne Caecilia Fawtier in 1943; 2 children. Joint Lecturer, University College and Corpus Christi College, Oxford, 1947-50; Fellow, Wadham College, Oxford, 1950-63. Since 1963, Dodge Professor of History, and since 1968, Director of the Shelby Cullom Davis Center for Historical Studies, Princeton University, New Jersey. Honorary doctorate: University of Chicago, 1979. Fellow, American Academy of Arts and Sciences, 1968. Address: 266 Moore Street, Princeton, New Jersey 08540, U.S.A.

PUBLICATIONS

History

Sculpture in Britain: The Middle Ages. Baltimore and London, Penguin, 1955.
An Elizabethan: Sir Horatio Palavicino. Oxford, Clarendon Press, 1956.
The Crisis of the Aristocracy, 1558-1641. Oxford, Clarendon Press, 1965; abridged edition, London and New York, Oxford University Press, 1967.
The Causes of the English Revolution, 1529-1642. London, Routledge, 1972.
Family and Fortune: Studies in Aristocratic Finance in the Sixteenth and Seventeenth Centuries. Oxford, Clarendon Press, 1973.
The Family, Sex, and Marriage in England, 1500-1800. London, Weidenfeld and Nicholson, and New York, Harper, 1977.
The Past and the Present. London and Boston, Routledge, 1981.

Other

Editor, *Social Change and Revolution in England, 1540-1640.* London, Longman, and New York, Barnes and Noble, 1965.
Editor, *The University in Society.* Princeton, New Jersey, Princeton University Press, 2 vols., 1974.
Editor, *Schooling and Society: Studies in the History of Education.* Baltimore, Johns Hopkins University Press, 1976.

*

Critical Studies: "Crisis of the Aristocracy, 1558-1641" by E.E. Aylmer, in *Past and Present 32*, 1965; "The Early Modern Family" by F.O. Dow, in *History 63*, 1978; "Lawrence Stone and the English Aristocracy" by J.H. Hexter, in *On Historians*, Cambridge, Massachusetts, Harvard University Press, 1979.

*   *   *

Lawrence Stone published in 1965 *The Crisis of the Aristocracy, 1558-1641*, a work considered both as one of the most important modern books on the background of the Puritan rebellion as well as one of the most remarkable works of contemporary historical writing on any period. It is remarkable not only in the originality of its interpretation but in its masterly combination of extensive quantification with traditional methods of historical research. Stone's object was to seek an answer to the question why the aristocracy (peers and upper gentry) were supplanted as political leaders in the first half of the 17th century by the middle and lower gentry, who constituted the backbone of the resistance to the crown. He attributed this shift in the center of power to a decline of confidence in the aristocracy which began at the end of the reign of Elizabeth I and continued until the Restoration. He began with the assumption that there had been a decline in the wealth of the peers during this era. However, his investigation established that while the wealth of the peers had been substantially reduced early in the century, by 1610 their real income was as great, if not greater than under the Tudors. The evidence he presented for the decline in confidence was complex. Among the many factors he singled out as particularly important was the inflation of honors under James I, giving precedence and status to men whose claims were not justified by birth. Moreover, the increased real income of the peers was obtained through court patronage, thus identifying them with an increasingly unpopular monarchy. The peers, no longer allowed to maintain large bodies of armed retainers, steadily lost power, nor were they able to exercise the personal influence in the country and among their tenants which they had once enjoyed. The rise of Puritanism and the increased education of the lower gentry introduced new forces into the social and political scene, thus further eroding the position of the aristocracy. Certainly one of the most significant achievements of Stone's work was to establish beyond all doubt that the aristocracy in the early 17th century had ceased to be feudal in character.

In 1977 Stone published a second major work—*The Family, Sex, and Marriage in England, 1500-1800*. Drawing upon sociology, economics, psychology, and historical methodology he attempted a synthesis between demographical studies and those concerned with cultural changes and emotional attitudes. Quantification played a significant, though lesser role than in his earlier work, because the data revelant to sexual mores was truly sparse for this period. Stone traced the family through three notable stages since 1500. In the 16th century, although the family was nuclear in character, its most important bond was that of kinship, and relations between parent and child were distant. In the 17th century a patriarchal family prevailed: the husband's authority over the wife and children was absolute, the education of children was rigidly supervised, but affective bonds were still limited. These two structures are best seen in relation to the upper classes, for the data on the family life of the workers and farmers is scanty. Among the aristocracy, vestiges of both these early structures persisted until the 20th century. The most modern development appeared among the well-to-do middle class in the mid-18th century—the affective individual family—a family bound by emotional ties with a close parent-child relationship. For the first time the personal autonomy of its members was recognized, permitting privacy and individual choice in the selection of mates. It was this form of the family whose spread could be traced through all classes of society as the general standard of living and education improved in the 19th century. As a pioneer work Stone's book offers fruitful suggestions for more intensive investigation.

—Harry Ammon

STRAUSS, Leo. American political theorist. Born in Kirchhain, Germany, 20 September 1899; emigrated to the United States in 1938. Studied at the University of Hamburg, Ph.D. 1921. Served in the German Army during World War I. Married Miriam Bernson in 1933; 2 children. Research Assistant, Academy for Jewish Research, Berlin, 1925-32; Professor, New School for Social Research, New York, 1938-49; Robert Maynard Hutchins Distinguished Service Professor of Political Science, University of Chicago, 1949-68; Professor of Political Science, Claremont Men's College, California, 1968-69; Scott Buchanan Scholar-in-Residence, St. John's College, Annapolis, Maryland, 1969-73. *Died 18 October 1973.*

PUBLICATIONS

Political Theory

Die Religionskritik Spinosas als Grundlage seiner Bibelwissenschaft. Berlin, Akademie-Verlag, 1930; as *Spinoza's Critique of Religion,* New York, Schocken, 1965.
Philosophie und Gesetz: Beiträge zum Verständnis Maimunis und seiner Vorläufer. Berlin, Schocken, 1935.
The Political Philosophy of Hobbes: Its Basis and Its Genesis. Oxford, Clarendon Press, 1936; Chicago, University of Chicago Press, 1962.
On Tyranny: An Interpretation of Xenophon's "Hiero." New York, Political Science Classics, 1948; revised edition, as *Tyranny and Wisdom,* Glencoe Illinios, Free Press, 1963.
Natural Right and History. Chicago, University of Chicago Press, 1950.
Persecution and the Art of Writing. Glencoe, Illinois, Free Press, 1952.
What is Political Philosophy? (lecture). Jerusalem, Magnes Press, 1955.
Thoughts on Machiavelli. Glencoe, Illinois, Free Press, 1958.
What Is Political Philosophy? and Other Studies. Glencoe, Illinois, Free Press, 1959.
The City and Man. Chicago, Rand McNally, 1964.
Socrates and Aristophanes. New York, Basic Books, 1966.
Jerusalem and Athens: Some Preliminary Reflections (lecture). New York, City College, 1967.
Liberalism, Ancient and Modern. New York, Basic Books, 1968.
Xenophon's Socratic Discourse: An Interpretation of the Oeconomicus. Ithaca, New York, Cornell University Press, 1970.

Xenophon's Socrates. Ithaca, New York, Cornell University Press, 1972.
The Argument and Action of Plato's Laws. Chicago, University of Chicago Press, 1975.
Political Philosophy: Six Essays, edited by Hilail Gilden. Indianapolis, Pegasus, 1975.

Other

Editor, with others, *Gesammelte Schriften,* by Moses Mendelssohn. Berlin, Akademie-Verlag, 1929.
Editor, with Milton C. Nahm, *Philosophical Essays, Ancient, Mediaeval, and Modern,* by Isaac Husik. New York, Macmillan, and Oxford, Blackwell, 1952.
Editor, with Joseph Cropsey, *History of Political Philosophy.* Chicago, Rand McNally, 1963.

*

Bibliography: in *Ancients and Moderns: Essays on the Tradition of Political Philosophy in Honor of Leo Strauss* edited by Joseph Cropsey, New York, Basic Books, 1964.

Critical Studies: "Leo Strauss's Conception of Political Philosophy," in *Review of Politics,* October 1967; "Two Critiques of Scientism: Leo Strauss and Edmund Husserl," in *Independent Journal of Philosophy 2,* 1978; "The Life-World, Historicity, and Truth: Reflections on Leo Strauss's Encounter with Heidegger and Husserl," in *Journal of the British Society for Phenomenology,* 9, 2, 1978; and "A Hermeneutic Accent on the Conduct of Political Inquiry," in *Human Studies 1,* 1978, all by Haw Yol Jung.

*   *   *

Leo Strauss's work in political philosophy is devoted to re-examining the quarrel between the ancients and the moderns. This examination principally consists of a critique of modern liberalism and egalitarian democracy, a critique of modern political science, and a critique of historicist hermeneutics.

Although he embraced Western liberal democracy as the only viable alternative to Soviet-styled communism, Strauss contended that the former is fraught with intrinsic difficulties that may well be irremedial. According to Strauss, egalitarian democracy invariably fosters mass culture, the mediocrity and conformism of which has the effect of producing morally bankrupt leadership. Public education contributes to this malaise by abjuring the traditional task of molding moral character through exposure to culture (the one-time privilege of the aristocracy) in favor of providing uniformly accessible, vocationally oriented training in the technical arts and sciences. The liberal defense of tolerance is correspondingly reflected in its acceptance of a relativity of values—a tendency which ironically undermines any supreme estimation of its own worth. As a remedy to these problems, Strauss advocates the restoration of the humanities to their once prominent position in education. He also promotes the fostering of a healthy deference to authority based upon the recognition of superior character and its concomitant nurturance of an aristocracy—the classical model of government by the best (not to be confused with technocracy)—within the framework of representative government.

Strauss's critique of modern political science is really a vindication of classical political theory against positivist and historicist attacks on universal moral truth. Positivism and historicism are symptomatic of the "scientistic" dismemberment of concrete political life into empty abstractions and artificial dichotomies, such as those between facts and values and nature and society. Modern political thought beginning with Machiavelli eschews the classical quest for substantive moral ideals (one of which is the contemplative ideal of philosophy) for the more modest pursuit of recommending political goals which can be more easily implemented. The narrowing of the political horizon to expectations which conform to minimal models of moral agency initiated by Hobbes, Locke, and other modern natural law theorists (the "first wave of modernity") is accompanied by the strictly secular project of devising institutions which are designed for no other purpose than to mitigate the worst effects of human nature as it is, i.e., egoistic, economistic, amoral man "in the state of nature." The attempt to reconcile the formal "ought" of Kantian ethics with actuality that informs German idealism (the second wave) does not preserve classical idealism as intended, but rather ends up by reducing morality to positive law and folk custom. The ascendence of historicism, positivism, and existentialism in the 20th century (the third wave) finds its most dangerous embodiment in value-neutral political science, which offers itself to various and sundry purposes, be they worthy or otherwise, for the sole aim of manipulating human behavior.

Strauss maintained that classical political philosophy is superior to modern political science because it depicts the totality of political life in its concrete richness. Following the example of the later Husserl's phenomenological critique of scientism, Strauss argued that classical political philosophy exhibits political life with more pristine clarity and authenticity because its own language and method (dialectic) are themselves directly rooted in the pre-scientific experience of everyday politics. By transcending the variability of transient parochial prejudices, however, the philosopher is capable of discerning permanent, immutable moral truths (classical natural law), which, though seldom capable of realization, at least serve to illuminate the essential limits of political practice in general.

Strauss's theory of interpretation is chiefly predicated on reproducing the author's own self-understanding of his work—a canon which is directed against the historicist demand to understand the author's intended meaning better than he himself did. Methodologically speaking, Strauss emphasized a need to restore a naive respect for the potential truth value of the text's intrinsic message in opposition to the historicist tendency to relate textual meaning to extrinsic psycho-sociological considerations. He also strenuously protested against the importation of alien categories (such as modern notions of natural law, natural rights, liberalism, etc.) into the interpretation of classical texts. In his treatment of esoteric writing in which a deeper, hidden meaning is indirectly communicated, Strauss recommended that kind of meticulously detailed exegesis and interpolative "reading between the lines" that characterizes much of his own dense scholarship.

Like that of all deep thinkers, Strauss's attempt to come to grips with fundamental questions led to fruitful tensions and not so fruitful inconsistencies. His conservative appreciation for the diversity of particular cultures and traditions is curiously juxtaposed to his critique of cultural relativism and liberal tolerance, which he thought renounced a belief in universal truth. This tension, manifested in the conflict between reason and religious revelation and reflected in his own dual loyalty to Greek idealism on the one hand and orthodox Judaism on the other, was openly acknowledged by him. Not so understandable was his intransigent antipathy toward historicity. As H.Y. Jung observes, because Strauss ignored the historicity of the political life world, he found a need to engage in "hypothetical anthropological studies" concerning primitive or prehistoric societies whose understanding is not yet encumbered by scientific sophistication. Again, in his correspondence with the Heideggerian H.G. Gadamer, he betrayed an unwillingness to recognize the historicity of human interpretation which always mediates the past with the present. Indeed, his identification of interpretation with the activity of reproducing the author's original self-understanding and his conception of truth as an ahistorical essence is precisely indicative of the very "naturalization" and "objectification" of human reality and knowledge which he himself found to be so reprehensible in the case of scientism.

—David Ingram

STRAVINSKY, Igor (Fyodorovich). Russian-American composer and music commentator. Born in Oranienbaum, now Lomonosov, Russia, 17 June 1882; emigrated to the United States in 1939; naturalized, 1945. Educated at the Gurevich School and St. Petersburg University, 1903-05; also studied privately with Rimsky-Korsakov, 1902-08. Married Katerina Nossenko in 1906, 4 children; married Vera de Bosset Sudeikin in 1940. Worked with the Ballets Russes, 1910-29, and as a conductor and pianist during the 1920's and 1930's. Charles Eliot Norton Professor, Harvard University, Cambridge, Massachusetts, 1939-40. Works commissioned by the Boston Symphony Orchestra, Chicago Symphony Orchestra and other major organizations. Recipient: State Department Medal, 1962. *Died (in New York City) 6 April 1971.*

PUBLICATIONS

Music

Poétique musicale sous forme de six leçons. Cambridge, Massachusetts, Harvard University Press, 1942; as *Poetics of Music in the Form of Six Lessons*, London, Oxford University Press, 1947.
Conversations with Igor Stravinsky, with Robert Craft. New York, Doubleday, and London, Faber, 1959.
Memories and Commentaries, with Robert Craft. New York, Doubleday, and London, Faber, 1960.
Expositions and Developments, with Robert Craft. New York, Doubleday, and London, Faber, 1962.
Dialogues and a Diary, with Robert Craft. New York, Doubleday, 1963; London, Faber, 1968.
Themes and Episodes, with Robert Craft. New York, Knopf, 1966; with *Retrospectives and Conclusions*, as *Themes and Conclusions*, London, Faber, 1972.
Retrospectives and Conclusions, with Robert Craft. New York, Knopf, 1969; with *Themes and Episodes*, as *Themes and Conclusions*, London, Faber, 1972.

Other

Chroniques de ma vie, with W. Nouvel. Paris, Denoël and Steele, 1935; as *An Autobiography*, London, Gollancz, and New York, Simon and Schuster, 1936.
Selected Correspondence, edited by Robert Craft. New York, Knopf, 1982-.

Stravinsky's major compositions include the ballets *The Firebird* (1910), *Petrouchka* (1911), *The Rite of Spring* (1913), *Histoire du Soldat* (1918), *Orpheus* (1947), and *Agon* (1957); the opera-oratorio *Oedipus Rex* (1927); the opera *The Rake's Progress* (1951); and the *Symphony of Psalms* for chorus and orchestra (1930). For a full listing of Stravinsky's compositions, see Dominique-Rene De Lerma, *Igor Fyodorovich Stravinsky: A Practical Guide to Publications of His Music*, Kent, Ohio, Kent State University Press, 1974.

*

Critical Studies: *Stravinsky: A New Appraisal of His Work* edited by Paul Henry Lang, New York, Norton, 1963; *Stravinsky: The Composer and His Works*, Berkeley, University of California Press, and London, Faber, 1966, revised edition, 1979; *Stravinsky: Chronicle of a Friendship 1948-1971* by Robert Craft, New York, Knopf, 1972; *Stravinsky* by Kenneth McLeish, London, Heinemann, 1978.

*   *   *

Igor Stravinsky spent much of his critical energy denying criticism. "How misleading," he was to insist throughout his career, "are all literary descriptions of musical form." Music expresses nothing but itself; the composer works to discharge "a daily function," and speaks with the sole authority of a craftsman investigating his craft. The style of commentary becomes one of anecdote, epigram, local insight, explicitly refusing aesthetic systems: Stravinsky the anti-Romantic chastizes Wagner for his contamination of music with literary and philosophical pretensions. The key to Stravinsky's thought is a profound historical anxiety. A constant, uneasy dialogue between the universal and the historically relative informs his writing: the impulse to assert the former checked and defined by an acute perception of the latter. Stravinsky's most extended commentaries, as in *Poetics of Music*, are concerned with investing music with an ontology, by the discrimination of the absolute from the historically conditioned. Music is defined as "a form of speculation in terms of sound and time," owing its existence to a necessary "transcendental appetite." Form is the *a priori* which allows music to occupy its saving metahistorical space. Specific forms—the local instances of the modal, diatonic, serial, etc.—may be relative and arbitrary, but form itself is the condition of all music as "a succession of impulses that converge towards a definite point of repose," a resolution or plenitude based on categorical "poles of attraction." Form organizes epistemological principles of similarity and contrast; form answers the Kantian proposition that "the One precedes the Many": that variety is the phenomenal texture of things, and form enacts the movement towards revelation of a deep, hidden, generative Unity. Stravinsky is ready to translate these post-Kantian terms into the 20th century: he explicitly argues, in the conclusion to *Poetics*, that desire must be enclosed, dissemination bound: else dispersion induces a "false hunger" that can never be satisfied. "How much more natural and more salutary it is to strive towards a single, limited reality than towards endless division." Stravinsky's aesthetic model is explicitly that of a "closed cycle," or rather of a spiral, the enactment of formal closure raising one to a higher plane of integration: participation, indeed, of the human with "the Supreme Being." *Poetics* asserts a strong positivist-humanist stance: music proceeds from and affirms "integral man," and the historical determinisms of both Marx and Freud are rejected. In these terms, subjection to tradition follows as a condition of subjection to form. Stravinsky's idea of tradition is close to T.S. Eliot's: no "archeological" conservation of relics, but voluntary subscription to a signifying community of culture. Stravinsky denies that he was ever "revolutionary" in *Le Sacre*: he has no time for Wagnerian exaltation of the inchoate flux of becoming, for submission to the random vectors of historical discontinuity. Stravinsky's historical imagination is exceptionally acute: it is at the center of his importance as a thinker, and defines the quality of his perceptions: an imaginative consciousness of the historical specificities of musical practice, of period and convention, informs, for example, his commentaries on the Renaissance Venetian school, Gesualdo, Webern and Boulez and the new music trends of the 1960's, and Russian music (an interestingly political synopsis, in *Poetics*.) The humanism remains: in 1969, Stravinsky celebrates Beethoven for his "unpredictability, rising above period, style, context, historical circumstance," describes the quartets as "a charter of human rights...a measure of man, and part of the description of the quality of man." Nevertheless, from the evidence of the Craft conversation books, the discourse of the last decade grows more threatened: on the one hand, Stravinsky will assert that his activity "was conditioned not by concepts of history but by music itself" (1967), on the other admit a bleaker, more defensive awareness of historical conditionality:

> My processes are determined by aesthetic accidents—the accidents are not accidents, of course, until we recognize them as such, giving the word to those we catch, not to those we accept, so that in this sense our accidents are also determined.... I have no confidence in the justice of posterity.... To me all histories are deterministic. They offer not "what was," but a choice governed by the determina-

tions, conscious and unconscious, of the choosers. (1966)

It is tempting to relate all of this to Stravinsky's own career, uniquely subject to the tremendous historical displacements that have characterized the 20th century. There is evidence that Stravinsky invested in the post-war serialism of Schoenberg and Webern as the dominant musical language, at least for a while, and was disconcerted by its brief life. So central a figure to the age remains one of its most formidable adversaries.

—Ian Duncan

STRAWSON, P(eter) F(rederick). British philosopher. Born 23 November 1919. Educated at Christ's College, London; studied at St. John's College, Oxford (scholar, 1937-40). Served in the Royal Artillery, 1940-42, and the Royal Electrical and Mechanical Engineers, 1942-46: Captain. Married Grace Martin in 1945; 4 children. Assistant Lecturer in Philosophy, University College of North Wales, Bangor, 1946-47; John Locke Scholar, 1946, Lecturer in Philosophy, 1947-48, and Fellow and Praelector, 1948-66, New College, Oxford. Since 1965, Fellow, Magdalen College, Oxford, and since 1968 Waynflete Professor of Metaphysical Philosophy, Oxford University. Visiting Professor, Duke University, Durham, North Carolina, 1955-56; Princeton University, New Jersey, 1960-61, and 1972. Fellow, British Academy, 1965. Foreign Honorary Member, American Academy of Arts and Sciences. Knighted, 1977. Address: Magdalen College, Oxford, England.

PUBLICATIONS

Philosophy

Introduction to Logical Theory. London, Methuen, and New York, Wiley, 1952.
Individuals: An Essay in Descriptive Metaphysics. London, Methuen, and New York, Doubleday, 1959.
The Bounds of Sense: An Essay on Kant's "Critique of Pure Reason." London, Methuen, 1966.
Meaning and Truth (lecture). Oxford, Clarendon Press, 1970.
Logico-linguistic Papers. London, Methuen, 1971.
Freedom and Resentment, and Other Essays. London, Methuen, and New York, Harper, 1974.
Subject and Predicate in Logic and Grammar. London, Methuen, 1974.

Other

Editor, *Philosophical Logic*. London, Oxford University Press, 1967.
Editor, *Studies in the Philosophy of Thought and Action*. London, Oxford University Press, 1968.

*

Bibliography: in *Philosophical Subjects: Essays Presented to P.F. Strawson* edited by Zak van Straaten. Oxford, Clarendon Press, 1980.

*   *   *

P.F. Strawson has been called a philosopher's philosopher both for the significant content and consistent method of his subtle philosophical thought. An independent pathfinder in the contemporary Oxford mode of linguistic philosophy, he has been less concerned to develop a systematic world-view or methodology than to re-examine central philosophical issues, to extend his approach to neglected and unexplored arenas, and to offer fresh insights and perspectives. Others have supplemented, elaborated, and disputed his observations, and an entire corpus of derivative philosophical literature testifies to his broad and continuing influence. In a symposium on "Truth," Strawson pointed out that "true" cannot describe semantic properties (as implied in semantic theories of truth) because "true" does not describe. "True" grants something, agrees with, supports, or accedes to something uttered or utterable. This proposal that "true" is usually employed in a manner analogous to performatives (in which the utterance *is* the act) stimulated an interesting interchange with J.L. Austin, who supported a sophisticated version of the correspondence theory of truth (in which true statements refer to facts). Strawson argued that true statements cannot refer to facts because notions such as facts already have the "word-world relationship" built into them. Facts are what statements state, if true.

Strawson also took exception to Bertrand Russell's Theory of Descriptions in which Russell held that statements like "The king of France is bald" are meaningful but false. In his celebrated essay "On Referring," following the lead given much earlier by Frege, Strawson showed that Russell's analysis confuses mentioning with meaning. Russell did not distinguish between an expression or a sentence and its use. While such statements as Russell cited generally presuppose the existence of an entity, they do not assert it. Sentences can be meaningful or meaningless, but only statements making use of sentences in particular contexts can be true or false. The meaning of a sentence cannot be identified with the assertion it is used, on a particular occasion, to make. Thus, in "The king of France is wise," the sentence is meaningful, but the statement which the sentence is used to make fails to say anything true or false because the expression "The king of France" fails to refer to anybody. One of the presuppositions of the statement—that there is a king of France—is false.

In *Introduction of Logical Theory* Strawson examined the connections between ordinary language and formal logic, showing that when the actual use of ordinary words and the textbook operations of logical symbols are compared, propositional logic fails to reflect the "logic" of ordinary language to a greater degree than had been realized. He also criticized attempts to "justify" the reasonableness of inductive procedures by pointing out that to call a belief or hypothesis reasonable or unreasonable is to apply inductive standards. The search for a justification of induction arises from a failure to notice a fundamental feature of rationality. Induction is the only rational mode of discerning what has happened in the past or will happen in the future. The demand for a general justification of induction is in effect a demand that induction must be shown to be really a kind of deduction—which is absurd.

Individuals: An Essay in Descriptive Metaphysics partially rescued metaphysics from the undiscriminating disrepute cast upon it by the heavy-handed critiques made by logical positivism and linguistic analysis. Distinguishing between *descriptive metaphysics* which describes the actual structure of our thought about the world (Aristotle and Kant) and *revisionary metaphysics* which tries to create a better structure (Descartes, Leibniz, Berkeley), Strawson held that the latter is useful chiefly because it rests upon the former. Descriptive metaphysics differs from conceptual analysis only in scope and generality. Though concepts change over time, there remains an ahistorical core of human thinking in which the concepts and categories of thought exhibit no change. This core with all its interconnections is the subject of descriptive metaphysics. Even if the entire structure were laid out, descriptive metaphysics would have to be undertaken again and again, for the permanence of its subject is rendered in impermanent idioms. Strawson's major contribution to descriptive metaphysics is deliberately confined to considering material bodies and persons and showing the connection between the general idea of a particular and the notion of an object of reference. He argued that material objects are basic particulars in

the sense that they are a necessary condition of knowledge of all objective particulars and of language, and other classes of particulars cannot be identified without ultimate reference to material objects. This is because identification (which includes both referential identification and reidentification) has as a precondition observable entities that endure in space and time, and the material universe is a system of such entities.

From a descriptive metaphysical standpoint, Strawson offered a solution to the traditional mind-body problem. Some philosophers want to ascribe states of consciousness to minds (or Cartesian mental substances) different from, but closely associated with, bodies, and other philosophers support what he calls the "no-ownership" theory in which states of consciousness are not ascribed to anything at all. Both views assume that the concept of a person is complex or derivative when, in fact, it is primitive. The logically primitive concept is such that both material *and* mental predicates are equally applicable to it, and being primitive, it cannot be broken down into components of which one can reduce one component to the other. Person-predicates are unique because of the primitiveness of the concept of a person, for they may be ascribed to oneself on a basis other than that upon which they are ascribed to oneself by others. It follows from the concept of person that one thinks of oneself as both conscious and embodied, as "having" a mind and a body.

"Freedom and Resentment" considered determinism, without reference to indeterminist metaphysics, by looking to "reactive attitudes" and their presupposed moral sentiments as a part of human nature. If reactions are expressions of moral attitudes and not just calculated regulatory devices, then our practices do not merely exploit our natures, they express them. A determinism which implies that such attitudes could (or worse, should) be wiped away fails to acknowledge the nature of the human being. Moral responses are not rendered insignificant by determinism, and recognizing this should considerably cool the debate between determinism and champions of free will.

In *The Bounds of Sense*, Strawson's extended commentary on Kant's *Critique of Pure Reason*, he sorted out viable parts of its structure from parts he felt he had to reject, and supplied a unified interpretation of the whole. For Strawson, Kant sought to argue that a minimum structure is essential to any intelligible conception of experience (and here classical empiricism fails), though ranging beyond the limits of experience results in conceptual claims devoid of meaning (the pitfall of dogmatic rationalism). Kant's arguments, however, violate his own principles in attempting to establish the limits of coherent thinking from within (which is sufficient) *and* from without (which is impossible). While distinguishing the valuable from the problematic in Kant's effort to establish the parameters of thought, Strawson concluded that no philosopher in any book had come nearer to achieving this strenuous aim than Kant himself in the *Critique of Pure Reason*.

Strawson's seminal essays have stimulated many philosophers in several countries. He has been less concerned to declare sides than to understand divergent points of view, discern what underlies them, distill the valuable insights embedded in them, and suggest ways in which to reconcile positions and to search in new directions. The grace and skill he has shown in his philosophical commitment may be seen in his "Replies" to contributions presented to him in *Philosophical Subjects* as well as in his constructive appraisals of recent works by younger contemporaries. Singularly free from the affections, intransigence, or triviality of more strident practitioners of linguistic analysis, he has remained a luminous witness to the integrity and fertility of post-war Oxford philosophy.

—R.N. Iyer

SULLIVAN, Harry Stack. American psychoanalyst. Born in Norwich, New York, 21 February 1892. Studied at Cornell University, Ithaca, New York, 1908; Chicago College of Medicine and Surgery, M.D. 1917. Served as a Captain in the United States Army Medical Corps, 1918-19 (Assistant District Medical Officer and later Medical Executive Officer, Eighth District Office of the Division of Rehabilitation for Disabled Soldiers, Sailors, and Marines); Liaison Officer, Veterans Bureau and St. Elizabeth's Hospital, Washington, D.C., 1921-22; Staff Member, Sheppard and Enoch Pratt Hospital, Towson, Maryland, 1922-30; in private practice as a psychoanalyst in New York, 1930-39; taught at the Washington School of Psychiatry, 1939-49. Co-Founder, William Alanson White Psychiatric Foundation, Washington, D.C., 1933; Co-Founding Editor, *Psychiatry*, 1938-49; participant in Unesco Tensions Project, Paris, 1948. *Died* (in Paris) *14 January 1949*.

PUBLICATIONS

Collections

Collected Works. New York, Norton, 2 vols., 1940-64.

Psychology

Conceptions of Modern Psychiatry. Washington, D.C., William Alanson White Psychiatric Foundation, 1945; London, Tavistock, 1955.
The Study of Psychiatry: Three Orienting Lectures. Washington, D.C., Washington School of Psychiatry, 1947.
The Meaning of Anxiety in Psychiatry and Life. New York, William Alanson White Psychiatric Foundation, 1948.
The Interpersonal Theory of Psychiatry, edited by Helen Swick Perry and Mary Ladd Gavell. New York, Norton, 1953; London, Tavistock, 1955.
The Psychiatric Interview, edited by Helen Swick Perry and Mary Ladd Gavell. New York, Norton, 1954.
Schizophrenia as a Human Process. New York, Norton, 1962.
The Fusion of Psychiatry and Social Science. New York, Norton, 1964.
Personal Psychopathology: Early Formulations. New York, Norton, 1972.
A Harry Stack Sullivan Case Seminar: Treatment of a Young Male Schizophrenic, edited by Robert G. Kvarnes. New York, Norton, 1976.

*

Critical Studies: *Psychoanalysis and Interpersonal Psychiatry: The Contributions of Harry Stack Sullivan* by Patrick Mullahy, New York, Science House, 1970; *Harry Stack Sullivan: His Life and His Work* by A.H. Chapman, New York, Putnam, 1976; *Interpersonal Approach to Psychoanalysis: Contemporary Views of Harry Stack Sullivan* by Gerard Chrzanowski, New York, Gardner Press, 1977; *Psychiatrist of America: The Life of Harry Stack Sullivan* by Helen Swick Perry, Cambridge, Massachusetts, Belknap Press, 1982.

* * *

Harry Stack Sullivan rose to prominence in the 1930's and 1940's as a neo-Freudian psychoanalyst who challenged, and sometimes drastically altered, many of the tenets of orthodox Freudian theory and therapy. Together with Karen Horney and Erich Fromm, with whom he collaborated for a while, he is considered one of the key figures in "socializing" psychoanalysis.

Horney and Fromm were German emigrés, educated in the European tradition. Sullivan was American-born, trained under William Alanson White· and Adolf Meyer, and influenced by contemporary currents in American philosophy and the social sciences. His emerging theories, far more than those of Horney or Fromm, reflected a deep immersion in clinical practice, with a resulting heavy reliance on abstract, specialized terminology that was frequently impenetrable to the layman. Sullivan's language, it was remarked, "breathes the odor of the clinic."

It was in the clinical situation that Sullivan first established his reputation, when he found he was able to reach schizophrenic patients. Freud had believed that fruitful therapy with schizophrenics was impossible, but Sullivan persisted, on the premise that we all share a "common humanity." His breakthrough into useful dialogue with his patients was achieved by a profound empathy, a passion for "facts, events, and reactions," and what was then a novel technique—group therapy in less formal settings than a doctor's office.

From his clinical experience, Sullivan gradually constructed his own psychiatric theories, all centering on "interpersonal relations." He argued that from birth onward, every individual is continually interacting with, absorbing attitudes from, reacting to, other people. These multiple experiences were the shaping force of life. In an important sense, said Sullivan, people *are* their experience.

The child's earliest and most crucial relationships are with parents; Sullivan had no quarrel with Freud on that point. But while the parents may be the first "significant others" to a child, Sullivan held, they are not necessarily the last. As a person develops from infancy through childhood and adolescence to adulthood, other relationships of a profound nature may be established. These newer significant others also may have powerful influence by what they do, or appear to do.

Because a person is so enmeshed in relationships, Sullivan concluded that the term "self"—referring to an autonomous entity that exists as a permanent core of personality—is deceptive. It is more accurate, he said, to conceive of the self as an "envelope," that encloses one's total experience and that originates and functions interpersonally.

Here, Sullivan's ideas ran parallel to those of social psychologist George Herbert Mead, who described "mind" as a continually changing dynamism, or to the many modern philosophers who have rejected the concept of self, considering it only a vestigial remnant of old-fashioned mind-body dualism. But fellow neo-Freudian Erich Fromm sharply disagreed: he felt that Sullivan had been so captivated by the "socialization" obsession of American life that he had abandoned the individual altogether.

That charge could hardly be levelled against Sullivan in his day-to-day therapeutic activity. With ordinary troubled people (his clientele were rarely from the rich or privileged class) he sought to prevent the "splintering" of personality. With the deeply disturbed his goal was to restore the personality's "wholeness." To see the genesis of these conceptions, it may be useful to summarize Sullivan's notions about how personality is formed.

People, he held, have two major purposes, or "strivings." These are the pursuit of satisfactions and the pursuit of security. Both kinds of strivings are basically biological in origin; but they are shaped, immediately and continually, by parental teachings, examples, and judgments. So the raw biological material is culturally conditioned, creating an indissoluble fusion of heredity and environment.

He believed that physiology was always linked with social psychology. As childhood conflicts develop between personal strivings and culturally approved patterns of behavior, anxieties appear (here he is roughly paralleling Freud's theory of neurosis). Anxieties generate somatic manifestations. Conversely, purely physiological needs—stomach contractions and hunger for example—breed anxieties. So the body is inextricably entwined with culture and its derivatives: we are fully biosocial creatures.

Anxiety, from whatever source it originally springs, thus became the focus of Sullivan's attention. It was both the key to the developing personality and the source of personality breakdowns. And it always functioned in an interpersonal context. Sullivan's own life, with his professional ambitions, personal and financial disappointments (as well as a sprinkling of schizophrenic episodes), gives this focus added pathos. It may also help explain his deep feeling for the commonality of human experience.

Believing as he did that instinct plays only a minor role in human life, Sullivan jettisoned Freud's instinctual theories. Similarly, he shared with the other neo-Freudians the belief that Freud had overemphasized the importance of erotic drives. For Freud's anal, oral, and genital stages of development, Sullivan substituted a series of stages of growth, called "modes of experience." He particularly emphasized the infant's increasing awareness of "differentiation," that is, distinguishing oneself from others, and developing an orientation in space and time.

In advanced mode, differentiation becomes clear and distinct. Then, said Sullivan, "fairly exact communication" can begin. One can start to draw useful inferences, to test reactions. In sum, one can start to participate more fully in the complex web of relationships that makes us human.

At any point in this lifelong humanizing process, breakdowns and distortions can occur. A relationship can be damaged and, when it involves a significant other, a personality can suffer. Here we are back at the anxieties and the struggles to understand and surmount them. Frequently we bury guilty or unwanted feelings; the Freudian term was "repression." Sullivan substitutes "selective inattention," which presumably is a phrase that makes the behavior more accessible to clinical investigation and therapy. The therapist, who is part of the current interpersonal relationship with the patient, must function in a dual role—both observer and participant.

The kinds of clinical methods employed by Sullivan have become widely disseminated, used even by many therapists who adhere to traditional psychoanalytic theory. It is also true that some mental health practitioners feel that many of Sullivan's observations and conclusions (excluding the terminology) have become commonplace. Some of the ideas that Sullivan proposed have been expanded and amplified so that the original is barely recognizable; it might be argued, for example, that "anxiety" has been subsumed, by the psychosomatic theorist Hans Seyle, under the more complex concept of "stress."

According to Clara Thompson, a long-time colleague of Sullivan, his principal contribution to psychiatry was really a very simple idea: Sullivan's "ever present awareness of the need to convey respect for the patient and to maintain the patient's own self-esteem."

—Don Hausdorff

SULLIVAN, Louis (Henry). American architect and theorist. Born in Boston, Massachusetts, 3 September 1856. Educated at Boston District Grammar School, 1860-63; Patrick Sullivan Academy, Newburyport, Massachusetts, 1863, and Halifax, Nova Scotia, 1863-64; Brimmer School, Boston, 1864-65; Rice School, Boston, 1865-70; English High School, Boston, 1870-72; studied architecture at the Massachusetts Institute of Technology, Cambridge, under William Ware and Eugene Letang, 1872-73; École des Beaux-Arts, Paris, under Emile Vaudremer, 1874-76. Married Margaret Hattabough in 1899 (divorced, 1917). Draftsman in the office of Frank Furness and George Hewitt, Philadelphia, 1873; Assistant in the office of William LeBaron Jenney, Chicago, 1874, 1876-79, and in the office of Dankmar Adler, Chicago, 1879-81; Partner, Adler and Sullivan, Chicago, 1881-95. Travelled extensively throughout the United States after 1895, but maintained his Chicago office until 1909. Recipient: Gold Medal, American Institute of Architects, 1946. *Died* (in Chicago) *14 April 1924.*

PUBLICATIONS

Architecture

Essay on Imagination.   Chicago, Inland Architect Press, 1886.
The Autobiography of an Idea.   New York, American Institute of Architects, 1924.
A System of Architectural Ornament According with a Philosophy of Man's Powers.   New York, American Institute of Architects, 1924.
Kindergarten Chats on Architecture, Education, and Democracy, edited by Claude F. Bragdon.   Lawrence, Kansas, Scarab Fraternity Press, 1934.
What is Architecture: A Study in the American People of Today.   Milwaukee, Wisconsin, Bruce, 1944.
The Testament of Stone: Themes of Idealism and Indignation from the Writings of Louis Sullivan, edited by Maurice English.   Evanston, Illinois, Northwestern University Press, 1963.
Architectural Essays from the Chicago School: Thomas Tallmadge, Louis H. Sullivan, Jens Jensen, and Frank Lloyd Wright.   Park Forest, Illinois, Prairie School Press, 1967.

Other

Paul E. Sprague, *The Drawings of Louis Henry Sullivan: A Catalogue of the Frank Lloyd Wright Collection at the Avery Architectural Library.*   Princeton, New Jersey, Princeton University Press, 1978.

*

Critical Studies: *Genius and the Mobocracy* by Frank Lloyd Wright, New York, Duell, 1949, London, Secker and Warburg, 1972; *Louis Sullivan* by Albert Bush-Brown, New York, Braziller, 1960; *Louis Sullivan as He Lived: The Shaping of American Architecture: A Biography* by Willard Connely, New York, Horizon Press, 1960; *Architecture as Nature: The Transcendental Idea of Louis Sullivan* by Narciso G. Menocal, Madison, University of Wisconsin Press, 1981.

*

For a complete listing of Sullivan's buildings, see *Contemporary Architects,* edited by Muriel Emmanuel, London, Macmillan, and New York, St. Martin's Press, 1980.

*   *   *

Architect, ornamentalist, and critic, Louis Sullivan was one of the most influential figures in the development of early modern architecture. Although not an engineering innovator, Sullivan recognized the visual potentiality of steel frame construction and gave aesthetic shape to the skyscraper. His preparation as an architect consisted in study at the Massachusetts Institute of Technology and the École des Beaux Arts in Paris, as well as brief periods of employment in several firms, including that of William LeBaron Jenney. In 1879, Sullivan joined the firm of Dankmar Adler where he became a full partner in 1881 and where his gifts as a designer were complemented by Adler's ability as a skilled engineer. The partnership was dissolved in 1895 after which Sullivan practiced alone until his death in 1924.

Adler and Sullivan's first major work was the Auditorium Building in Chicago (1886-89). Awarded to the firm because of Adler's reputation as an acoustical engineer, the complex multiple-use building was designed as a large civic theater wrapped by a ten-story shell of hotel rooms with business offices located in a 17-story tower above the theater entrance. Structurally traditional, the Auditorium building employed massive masonry bearing walls on the exterior and an iron and steel frame to support the interior. The exterior facades with their rough masonry textures and arcaded openings clearly reveal

Sullivan's early indebtedness to the neo-Romanesque style of H.H. Richardson as exemplified by the Marshall Field Warehouse in Chicago. The interior embellishment of the theater, with richly varied patterns of curvilinear foliate motifs demonstrates Sullivan's originality as an ornamentalist.

Aesthetic form appropriate to the skyscraper first appeared in Sullivan's design for the Wainwright Building in St. Louis (1890-91). A ten-story commercial structure, the Wainwright Building is carried on a steel frame fireproofed by brick and terra cotta sheathing. Sullivan organized the external elements of the structure into three horizontal units: a two-storied granite base of ashlar masonry occupied by shops; a seven-storied shaft of red brick piers containing offices; and an attic and overhanging cornice slab housing mechanical equipment. The exterior tripartite division reflects the multiple functions performed by the interior spaces and recalls the traditional compositional schemes of the classical column and of Renaissance architectural practices. However the articulation of the building in its scale and proportion and its lavish ornament applied to the spandrels and cornice is stripped of any specific reference to the past. The upward thrust of the structure is emphasized by the recessed spandrels, by the addition of non-structural mullions that alternate with structural steel members and by the simplified geometric shape of the building. In the Guaranty Building in Buffalo, New York (1894-95), a 13-story skyscraper, Sullivan again achieved a fusion of external form that expresses the building's steel frame and internal uses with organic ornament that suggests its structural energies.

The Schlesinger and Mayer Department Store in Chicago (1899-1904), executed without Adler, was Sullivan's last major work. In this building, which consists of a stack of open floor spaces, Sullivan retained the tripartite compositional format while creating a system of narrow mouldings that permit the exterior walls to be read simultaneously as a tier of horizontal layers and as a grid of structural members. White terra cotta sheathing forms a continuous membrane around the windows of the upper floors; a casing of ornamental iron worked into dense serpentine patterns frames the display windows of the two-storied base.

During the remaining two decades of Sullivan's life, commissions dwindled in number and became modest in scope. Nonetheless, the buildings of the final year, such as the National Farmers' Bank in Owatonna, Minnesota (1908), and the Merchants' National Bank in Grinnell, Iowa (1914), merit high regard for their integration of strong simple shapes with exuberant ornamental designs.

Sullivan is credited with the creation of an aesthetic approach to the steel frame structure that openly recognized the structural nature and functional purposes of the modern commercial building. His much quoted dictum, "form follows function," helped popularize functional attitudes toward architecture. Yet Sullivan was not a functionalist. In his writings as in his practice, Sullivan insisted that buildings must interpret the imaginative and emotional life of a people as well as provide physical structures. A master designer of ornamental schemes, Sullivan sought architectural forms which were consonant with the technological means of the age and were expressive of the spiritual aspirations of a society.

—Linnea Wren

SUZUKI, D(aisetz) T(eitaro). Japanese Zen philosopher. Born in Kanagawa, 18 October 1870. Educated at Tokyo Imperial University, studied Zen under Shaku Soyen. Married Beatrice Erskine Lane in 1911. Worked as an editor and translator at Paul Carus's Open Court Publishing Company, LaSalle, Illinois, 1897-1908. Lecturer, Tokyo Imperial University, 1909-14; Pro-

fessor at Gakushu-in, 1910-21; Professor of Buddhist Philosophy, Otani University, Kyoto, after 1921. Visiting Professor of Zen Buddhist Philosophy, Columbia University, New York, 1952-57. Editor, *Zendo*; Founder *Eastern Buddhist*, 1921, and *Cultural East*, 1946. Recipient: Cultural Medal, Japan, 1949; Asahi Cultural Award, Japan, 1955; Senior Grade of the Third Court rank, 1966. Honorary doctorate: Otani University, 1933; University of Hawaii, 1959. Member, Japan Academy, 1949. *Died* (in Tokyo) 12 July 1966.

PUBLICATIONS

Buddhism

Outlines of Mahayana Buddhism. London, Luzac, 1907; Chicago, Open Court, 1908.
A Brief History of Early Chinese Philosophy. London, Probsthain, 1914.
Essays in Zen Buddhism. London, Luzac, 3 vols., 1927-34; New York, Harper, 1 vol., 1949, and New York, Weiser, 2 vols., 1971.
Studies in the Lankavatara Sutra. Kyoto, Eastern Buddhist Society, 1933.
An Index to the Lankavatara Sutra. Kyoto, Eastern Buddhist Society, 1933.
An Introduction to Zen Buddhism. Kyoto, Eastern Buddhist Society, 1934.
The Training of the Zen Buddhist Monk. Kyoto, Eastern Buddhist Society, 1934.
Manual of Zen Buddhism. Kyoto, Eastern Buddhist Society, 1935; London, Rider, 1950; New York, Grove Press, 1960.
Buddhist Philosophy and Its Effects on the Life and Thought of the Japanese People. Tokyo, Kokusai Bunka Shinkokai, 1936; revised edition as *Buddhism in the Life and Thought of Japan*, London, Buddhist Lodge, 1937.
Zen Buddhism and Its Influence on Japanese Culture. Kyoto, Eastern Buddhist Society, 1938; as *Zen and Japanese Culture*, London, Routledge, and New York, Pantheon, 1959.
Japanese Buddhism. Tokyo, Board of Tourist Industry, 1938.
The Essence of Buddhism. London, Buddhist Society, 1947.
The Zen Doctrine of No-Mind. London, Rider, 1949.
Living by Zen. Tokyo, Sanseido, 1949; London, Rider, 1950.
A Miscellany on the Shin Teachings of Buddhism. Tokyo, Higashi-hongwanji, 1949.
Studies in Zen. London, Rider, and New York, Philosophical Library, 1955.
Zen Buddhism, edited by William Barrett. New York, Doubleday, 1956.
Mysticism: Christian and Buddhist. London, Allen and Unwin, and New York, Harper, 1957.
Zen Buddhism and Psychoanalysis, with Erich Fromm and Richard DeMartino. New York, Harper, 1960.
The Essentials of Zen Buddhism, edited by Bernard Phillips. New York, Dutton, 1962.
The Chain of Compassion. Cambridge, Massachusetts, Cambridge Buddhist Association, 1966.
On Indian Mahayana Buddhism. New York, Harper, 1968.
The Field of Zen. London, Eastern Buddhist Society, 1969; New York, Harper, 1970.
Shin Buddhism. London, Allen and Unwin, and New York, Harper, 1970.
Sengai, the Zen Master. London, Faber, and New York, New York Graphic Society, 1971.
What is Zen? New York, Harper, 1972.
Japanese Spirituality. Kyoto, Japanese Society for the Promotion of Science, 1972.
Collected Writings on Shin Buddhism. Kyoto, Shinshu Otaniiha, 1973.
The Awakening of Zen. Boulder, Colorado, Prajñá Press, 1980.

Other

Editor, with H. Idzumi, *The Gandavyuha Sutra*. Tokyo, Sanskrit Buddhist Text Publishing Society, 4 vols., 1934-36.

Translator, with Paul Carus, *Lao-Tze's Tao-Teh King*. Chicago, Open Court, 1898.
Translator, *Açvaghosha's Discourse on the Awakening of the Faith in the Mahayana*. Chicago, Open Court, 1900.
Translator, *Sermons of a Buddhist Abbot*, by Shaku Soyen. Chicago, Open Court, 1906.
Translator, with Paul Carus, *T'ai-Shang Kan-Ying P'ien*. Chicago, Open Court, 1906.
Translator, with Paul Carus, *Yin Chin Wen*. Chicago, Open Court, 1906.
Translator, with Ghesso Sasaki, *The Life of Shomin Shinran*. Tokyo, Buddhist Text Translation Society, 1911.
Translator, *The Lankavatara Sutra*. London, Routledge, 1932.
Translator, *The Sengai Calendar 1960-67*. Tokyo, Idemitsu Kosan, 1960.

*

Critical Studies: "Suzuki Issue" of *The Eastern Buddhist* (Kyoto), n.s. 2, 1967 (includes bibliography).

*   *   *

D.T. Suzuki was a Japanese Buddhist scholar who made significant contributions to the understanding of Zen (Ch'an in Chinese) Buddhism in the Western world. Since his thought underwent some changes in his lifetime (which covered nearly a century), we might profitably divide his life and thought into several phases.

Suzuki was born in the city of Kanazawa during the unsettling period of transition from feudal to modern Japan. During his college days studying English literature in Tokyo, Suzuki was influenced by the writings of Ralph Waldo Emerson. At the same time, his spiritual restlessness led him to practice Zen Buddhism. In 1867, Suzuki established an academic collaboration in La Salle, Illinois, with Paul Carus, a free-lance German-American editor and philosopher whom one of Suzuki's teachers had met at the 1893 World Parliament of Religions in Chicago. This affiliation with Carus marks the first phase of Suzuki's scholarly career in the West.

During the time he spent with Carus (1897-1909), Suzuki energetically worked on translations into English of Chinese Buddhist and Taoist works. But it was the publication of his own *Outlines of Mahayana Buddhism* (1907) that established his reputation not only as a translator but also as a scholar. It is interesting to note that, like Carus, Suzuki at the time was interested in finding a scientific foundation of religion and came to be influenced by the writings of William James and Emmanuel Swedenborg.

Upon his return to Japan in 1909, Suzuki taught English literature at the Peer's School in Tokyo. His continued interest in Swedenborg was such that not only did he visit England two years later by the invitation of the Swedenborg Society, but also translated Swedenborg's four major works into Japanese and wrote a biography of Swedenborg. At the same time, Suzuki became interested in the doctrine of the True Pure-Land School of Buddhism, which he saw to be a necessary complement to Zen. In 1914, he began publishing a series of English articles on Zen in *New East* magazine, and also started writing works in Japanese on Zen.

Suzuki's reputation as a Zen scholar and interpreter of Zen for Western readers grew steadily during the 1920's and 1930's. In 1921, Suzuki accepted a chair at Otani University in Kyoto which, inspite of its affiliation with the True Pure-Land School, offered him considerable academic freedom. He founded and edited an English journal, *Eastern Buddhist*, and regularly contributed to it lengthy articles on Zen and related subjects. Suzuki's scholarly agenda at this time was divided into two main areas. One area was technical Buddhological scholarship. He contributed *An Index to the Lankavatara Sutra* and an edition of *The Gandavyuha Sutra*. Secondly, in the area of Zen, he published his three-volume *Essays in Zen Buddhism, An Introduction to Zen Buddhism*, and *Manual of Zen Buddhism*. In all these works on Zen, which were obviously addressed to Western readers, Suzuki affirmed that Zen must be understood on its own terms and not through categories of Western philosophy, religion, mysticism, or science.

It has often been pointed out that Suzuki's writings prior to 1945 were different in ethos from his post-war works. Before the war, Suzuki assiduously combed through important Chinese and Japanese Zen literatures, especially those of Rinzai (Lin-chi) tradition, and presented them without too much theorizing to contemporary Western as well as Japanese readers. His primary concern was with Ch'an (Zen), which became the most thoroughly Chinese form of Buddhism during the period between the middle of the T'ang (618-907 A.D.) and the end of the Sung (979-1279) dynasties. While Ch'an practices and insights came to be neglected in China after the Sung period, they were kept alive in Japàn, where Zen became thoroughly indigenized and has exerted a decisive influence on Japanese religion, culture, and art. In retrospect, Suzuki's followers and critics agree that there was a strong psychological bent in Suzuki's pre-war writings on the Zen experience. Suzuki repeatedly stated that Zen had no philosophical system of its own, nor did it affirm any dogma or any objects of worship. According to Suzuki, the aim of Zen is the attainment of a certain kind of "experience," which must be supported by Zen-consciousness and expressions.

At the end of World War II, Suzuki planned to retire to his Matsu-ga-oka ("Pine Hill") Library at Kamakura. However, after attending the second "Philosophy East and West" conference in Honolulu in 1949, Suzuki, then 80 years old, began a second career in America. Based at New York's Columbia University, he lectured at various American universities until 1958. During this time, he became increasingly interested in metaphysical and philosophical issues which previously had not concerned him. He read the works of Eckhart, Berdyaev, Tillich, Fromm, and various existentialists (although there is much truth in critics' comments that he read metaphysics in order to refute it from a Zen perspective). Suzuki was fond of using two Japanese expressions—*kono-mama* or *sono-mama*—which imply the "is-ness" of a thing, or reality in its "is-ness." From his Zen perspective, everything exists by its own right and does not point to any reality other than itself. In other words, being is meaning. Only our intellect bifurcates being and meaning, and thus fails to discern the "such-ness" of things. *Satori* is a discovery in our concrete experience of this simple truth. As Suzuki was fond of saying, Zen is "being itself, in becoming itself, in living itself." Suzuki returned to Japan in 1958, presumably to "retire," but true to his Zen principles—he continued to work until his death in 1966.

Opinions vary greatly regarding Suzuki's scholarship and his understanding of Zen and its relation to other religions. Some historians feel that he was too narrow when he confined his attention only to the Rinzai Zen tradition at the expense of the equally important Soto (Ts'ao-tung) tradition. Others criticize him for stressing the use of *koan* (enigmatic problems posed by Zen masters to their pupils) while giving little reference to meditation. Still others feel that he was too open-ended when he freely allowed the Zen experience to be interpreted indiscriminately by various psychological and philosophical insights, thus unwittingly misleading people into thinking that Zen could be divorced from historic Buddhism or its Mahayana tradition and could develop new forms, both lofty and bizarre, in any cultural situation. Be that as it may, no one would disagree that without Suzuki's dedicated lifelong endeavor, the Western world would not know as much as it does of the great Eastern spiritual legacy

of Zen and its religious significance to our understanding of
humanity.

—Joseph M. Kitagawa

———————

TAWNEY, R(ichard) H(enry). British historian. Born in
Calcutta, India, 30 November 1880. Educated at Rugby School;
studied at Balliol College, Oxford (scholar), B.A. 1903. Served
with the 22nd Manchester Regiment during World War I. Married Annette Jeanie Beveridge in 1909. Lecturer, Glasgow University, 1906-08; Teacher, Oxford University Tutorial Classes
Committee, 1908-14; Fellow, Balliol College, 1918-21; Reader,
1920-31, Professor 1931-49, and Professor Emeritus, 1949-62,
London School of Economics. Ford Lecturer, Oxford University, 1936; Visiting Professor, University of Chicago, 1948. Editor, *Economic History Review*, from 1927. Founder, and President, 1928-44, Workers' Educational Association; Director,
Ratan Tata Foundation, University of London, 1913-14; Adviser,
British Embassy, Washington, D.C., 1941-42. Honorary doctorate: University of Manchester, 1930; University of Chicago,
1941; University of Paris, 1945; Oxford University, 1950; Uni-
versity of Birmingham, 1951; University of London, 1951; Uni-
versity of Sheffield, 1953; University of Melbourne, 1955; Uni-
versity of Glasgow, 1961. Honorary Fellow, Balliol College,
Oxford, 1938, and Peterhouse, Cambridge, 1946. Fellow, British
Academy, 1935. *Died* (in London) *16 January 1962.*

PUBLICATIONS

History and Social Philosophy

The Agrarian Problem in the Sixteenth Century. London and
New York, Longman, 1912.
Poverty as an Industrial Problem (lecture). London, Ratan
Tata Foundation, 1913.
*The Establishment of Minimum Rates in the Chain-Making
Industry under the Trade Boards Act of 1909.* London, Bell,
1914.
*The Establishment of Minimum Rates in the Tailoring Industry
under the Trade Boards Act of 1909.* London, Bell, 1915.
The Nationalization of the Coal Industry. London, Labour
Party, 1919.
The Acquisitive Society. London, Bell, and New York, Har-
court Brace, 1920.
Recent Thoughts on the Government of Industry (lecture).
Manchester, Manchester University Press, 1920.
The Sickness of an Acquisitive Society. London, Allen and
Unwin, 1920.
Education: The Socialist Policy. London, Independent
Labour Party, 1924.
The British Labour Movement. New Haven, Connecticut,
Yale University Press, 1925.
Religion and the Rise of Capitalism: A Historical Study.
London, Murray, and New York, Harcourt Brace, 1926.
The Possible Cost of Raising the School Leaving Age (lecture).
London, National Union of Teachers and Workers' Educa-
tional Association, 1927.
Equality (lectures). London, Allen and Unwin, and New York,
Harcourt Brace, 1931; revised edition, 1952.
A Memorandum on Agriculture and Industry in China. Hono-
lulu, Institute of Pacific Relations, 1931.
Land and Labour in China. London, Allen and Unwin, and
New York, Harcourt Brace, 1932.
The Reorganisation of Education in China, with others. Paris,
League of Nations' Institute of Intellectual Co-operation,
1932.

The Choice Before the Labour Party. London, Socialist
League, 1933(?).
The Condition of China (lecture). Newcastle upon Tyne, Arm-
strong College, 1933(?).
Juvenile Employment and Education (lecture). London, Ox-
ford University Press, 1934.
The School Leaving Age and Juvenile Unemployment. Lon-
don, Workers' Educational Association, 1934.
Labour and Education. London, Labour Party, 1934.
The School Age and Exemptions. London, Workers' Educa-
tional Association, 1936.
Some Thoughts on the Economics of Public Education. Lon-
don, Oxford University Press, 1938.
Why the British People Fight. New York, Workers' Education
Bureau Press, 1940; as *Why Britain Fights*, London, Macmil-
lan, 1941.
Harrington's Interpretation of His Age (lecture). London, H.
Milford, 1941; New York, Haskell House, n.d.
Education, the Task Before Us (lecture). London, Workers'
Educational Association, 1943.
The Problem of the Public Schools. London, Workers' Educa-
tional Association, 1944.
The Webbs and Their Work (lecture). London, Fabian Society,
1945.
The Western Political Tradition (lecture). London, SCM
Press, 1949.
Social History and Literature (lecture). London, Cambridge
University Press, 1950; Folcroft, Pennsylvania, Folcroft
Library Editions, 1977.
The Attack, and Other Papers. London, Allen and Unwin, and
New York, Harcourt Brace, 1953.
The W.E.A. and Adult Education (lecture). London, Athlone
Press, 1953.
The Webbs in Perspective (lecture). London, Athlone Press,
1953.
*Business and Politics under James I: Lionel Cranfield as Mer-
chant and Minister.* London, Cambridge University Press,
1958; New York, Russell and Russell, 1976.
British Socialism Today. London, Metcalfe and Cooper, 1960.
The Radical Tradition: Twelve Essays on Politics, edited by Rita
Hinden. London, Allen and Unwin, and New York, Pan-
theon, 1964.
Commonplace Book, edited by J.M. Winter and D.M. Joslin.
London, Cambridge University Press, 1972.
Wage Regulation in Pre-Industrial England, with others, edited
by W.E. Minchinton. Newton Abbot, Devon, David and
Charles, 1972.
History and Society: Essays by R.H. Tawney, edited by J.M.
Winter. London and Boston, Routledge, 1978.
The American Labour Movement and Other Essays edited by
J.M. Winter. Brighton, Harvester, and New York, St. Mar-
tin's Press, 1979.

Other

Editor, with others, *English Economic History: Select Docu-
ments.* London, Bell, 1914.
Editor, *Secondary Education for All: A Policy for Labour.*
London, Labour Party, 1922.
Editor, with Eileen Power, *Tudor Economic Documents: Being
Select Documents Illustrating the Economic and Social His-
tory of Tudor England.* London and New York, Longman, 3
vols., 1924.
Editor, *A Discourse upon Usury, by Way of Dialogues and
Orations, for the Better Variety and More Delight of All
Those that Shall Read This Treatise (1572)*, by Thomas Wil-
son. London, Bell, 1925; New York, A.M. Kelley, 1963.
Editor, *Studies in Economic History: The Collected Papers of
George Unwin.* London, Macmillan, 1927.
Editor, with Eileen Power, *Studies in Economic and Social
History.* London, London School of Economics and Politi-

cal Science, from 1929.

*

Critical Studies: *R.H. Tawney and His Times: Socialism as Fellowship* by Ross Terrill, Cambridge, Massachusetts, Harvard University Press, 1973 (includes bibliography); *States and Welfare: Tawney, Galbraith, and Adam Smith* by David Reismann, London, Macmillan, 1982.

* * *

Throughout his influential work in social philosophy and history, R.H. Tawney illuminated fundamental relationships between values and institutions, ideas and events, presuppositions and consequences. At the same time he always looked for insight into available means for realizing the larger ends of individual and collective life. As a social philosopher, Tawney held that there is no creative force outside the ideas which control men in their ordinary conduct, and hence no amount of detailed research into social conditions could reveal the underlying directions of social change determined by quite other moral and intellectual causes whose springs lie deeper. Just as no amount of conjuring will turn a fact into a principle, so too for Tawney there is no alchemy whereby force can be transmuted into right. The futile unreality of modern politics and social theory, for scholars and reformers alike, arises from an absence of philosophic understanding. Lacking this, the tendency is to think in terms of surface difficulties and mechanical remedies, to collect vast accumulations of facts and make calculations of forces, forgetting that the human mind demands not explanation only but justification of all established orders and all schemes of progress.

"The problem of modern society is a problem of proportions, not of quantities; of justice, not of material well-being." This cannot be understood or resolved until people recognize that the external arrangements of society are based on principles which they feel to correspond with their subjective ideas of justice. When this correspondence is weak or faltering, the unseen foundations of a society begin to shift or crumble, setting a fresh stage for collective life, with new intricacies and lessons to be learned. Tawney thought that the primary social task of the present century was the elaboration of an economic order consistent with the principles of equality and liberty.

Tawney's scholarly researches as an economic historian and his political labours as a democratic socialist were complementary aspects of a single endeavour. Inquiry into the history of the 16th and 17th centuries was a means of access to the life of a society experiencing the first disturbing impact of industrial urban civilization. While he argued that principles of justice and equity had been essential to European culture throughout the Christian era, and also that the necessities of material livelihood were an essential consideration of any historical study, he also held that applications of moral principles must vary with changing conditions and that the living fabric of a society was too elusive to allow any grand theory of history, either sacred or secular. He saw the 20th century struggle toward economic liberty and social equality as the successor to earlier struggles for political rights and religious freedom, but he did not consider these as separable stages of any inevitable, or irreversible, progress.

Just as consideration for the needs of the governed is no substitute for political freedom, no amount of material progress or compensation is a substitute for the liberty or power to control the material and spiritual conditions of one's own life and the choice of those conditions. As a reform-minded social critic, Tawney placed primary emphasis upon the principle of equality. Acknowledgement of equality—the identity of nature of human beings, and the negligibility of their differences before the infinite—is the basis of human obligation, and hence the foundation of human subordination, of order, authority, and justice. "A belief in equality means that because men are men they are bound to acknowledge that man has claims upon man." No social structure or revolutionary scheme can justifiably treat men as means, or pretend that compulsion is essential for maintaining or improving the social order. With his strong convictions Tawney worked tirelessly on behalf of social and economic reform through Labour Party politics, the Workers' Education Association, and the University Grants Commttee. At the same time, he influenced generations of students at the London School of Economics and wrote voluminously, patiently expounding the principles of socialist democracy.

His historical writings ranged over the period from Richard of York's defeat at Bosworth Field (1485) down to the Stuart Restoration (1660), with primary emphasis upon the Elizabethan era. He characterized Elizabethan England as "the child of that happy interlude between two worlds—between the meaningless ferocities of a feudalism turned senile...and the demure austerities of the first, pious, phase of capitalism." In *The Agrarian Problem in the Sixteenth Century* he traced the gradual reversal of attitudes towards land-holding which changed England from a country of numerous freeholders, customary tenants sharing common tillages under manorial authority, and village guild craftsmen, all protected theoretically by the Crown, to a system of large leasehold farms used for pasture, depopulated villages, enclosed commons, and swelling ranks of urban wage labourers, all presided over by City capital. Here, as in his studies of the assessment of wages and a census of occupations, Tawney provided the portrait of a society wherein individuals could choose between being farmers, small masters in crafts, or wages labourers. He did not romanticize the era, but emphasized the element of choice open to husbandmen, yeomen, and craftsmen. He argued that since the allegiance of men had been crucial to the feudal system, there was a tendency in both Crown and Clergy to uphold the status of peasants. Then, with the decline of the political power of the Crown, the dissolution of the monasteries, and the development of continental trade through the City, the balance of economic life shifted.

In his introduction to Wilson's *Discourse Upon Usury*, Tawney examined the stages by which the role of finance capital and credit expanded to the point where interest became as dominant a form of income as rents, despite traditional objections to usury. As he argued in *Religion and the Rise of Capitalism*, the worldly individualism of later Calvinists and Puritans provided a rationale for the unrestrained acquisition of property by identifying the thrifty, industrious, and materially successful as the most likely candidates for salvation. Unlike Weber, Tawney did not take this as a one-sided influence of religion upon economics, but rather as a complex interaction of both with political changes as well as the geographical and intellectual discoveries of the age. Nonetheless, Tawney found that, by the time of the Long Parliament, England was prepared in mind, if not yet entirely in practice, for the era of mass industry and mass labour, and was also armed with the assurance that proverty is wicked, wealth virtuous.

Tawney thought that the lamp of history should shine ahead, as well as behind, and if his writings regarding the 20th century were more topical than historical, they were all amply linked with his larger vision of ideas and events. Indeed, in *The British Labour Movement, The Acquisitive Society, and Equality*, he explored the 18th and 19th-century development of capitalism, along with the rise of socialist opposition to its depredations and hypocrisy. Beneath the horrors of child labour, sweating, workhouses, and debtor's prisons, he discerned a fundamental corruption in the utilitarian attitude. In the notion that no man is to be blamed for business actions compatible with law, Tawney saw the denial of responsibility; in the notion that a man may legitimately be employed to realize an end which he would not pursue, except under fear of starvation, he found the denial of personal worth; in the notion that economic transactions have their justification simply in the fact that they are made, he saw the denial of social morality; and in the assumption that as long as men are well-fed and housed the nature of the social relations which they enter into to earn food and housing does not matter, he found the denial of freedom. The Benthamite principle itself was chiefly a justification for oppression of minorities, illusory in its claimed simplicity and decisiveness, and incapable of reconciling conflicting interests. It confused a method of making judgments with the standard by which judgments are to be made. In short, no argument for utility, convenience, and efficiency, even on behalf of a majority, could justify the oppression or destruction of minorities.

As Tawney clearly showed, the actual situation is one whereby a minority chokes off the life and opportunities of the majority. Through a series of inversions, industries are identified as "private" which control the lives of millions, schools are identified as "public" which are accessible only through hereditary privilege, and men are said to have an "independent" income precisely when they are entirely dependent upon the work of others. Tawney sought the rectification of these conditions by advocating the nationalization of certain industries, the universalization of access to at least secondary education, and the imposition of effective death and income taxes to provide social services to working people. While he never advocated the abolition of property, he drew a sharp distinction between creative property—which is actively productive through the efforts of its holder—and functionless property, which merely yields monetary income without work. Broadly, Tawney advocated elimination of property in the second sense, and its redistribution to private and public productive agencies. He acknowledged the vices of bureaucracy and indolence, but countered that plutocratic nepotism is more likely to waste human talent and enthrone lazy ineptitude than will an equitable distribution of wealth. He found the saccharine charity of the upper classes insulting to human dignity, and in the system of poor relief he recognized a persistent refusal to admit that poverty was a deliberate consequence of industrial capitalism.

Although Tawney addressed most of his analyses to England, he recognized that they had a much wider relevance. In *Land and Labour in China* he was able to apply his expertise with regard to pre-industrial England to the similar context of post-imperial China. In *The American Labour Movement* he contrasted the strong social and political values of the English labour movement with the more narrowly economic goals of its American counterpart. More generally, Tawney argued for the strengthening of democracy throughout the world, rejecting collectivist dictatorships of the right and left as inconsistent with social justice whatever their claims. He also warned that equality of civil and political rights, which is the essence of political democracy, could not long be reconciled with violent inequalities of social condition and economic power. Either democracy must reject capitalism and extend its authority to economics, or it must experience a moral paralysis and decline. He held that the greatest asset of democracy should be the sense of human dignity felt by common men, and the devotion to freedom and equality which that feeling inspired. Between nations, the need was to protect common values and national individualities by preventing forced artificial unity from crushing diversity while preventing divergences from degenerating into anarchy. He considered the nation state as the symbol of internal order and external anarchy, and felt that once the full logic of its pretensions were clear, it would be the task of the future to bury once and for all the monstrous doctrine of national sovereignty whose principle is murder.

Fundamentally, Tawney was an optimist, both as a historian and a social critic, because he reposed a deep faith in human possibilities. He held that since the essential fact about human beings is that they are human, the discoveries which thought makes are of permanent significance. These discoveries, though they are clothed in the relativities of time and place, do reflect elements of human nature and necessity. They involve both facts and the values by which facts are appraised, and concern the forms of association by which men unite to avert common perils and serve collective ends. In times of crises, when wide gulfs open

between inward needs, ideals, and values and outward practices and institutions, old truths require an exacting reformulation, lest they invert their meanings and poison social and political morality at the source. It is shocking, but not fatal, when oppression becomes a vested interest in a society which pays lip service to freedom, but it signals the approach of spiritual death when such crimes are claimed to be virtues if committed for the advantage of nation, race, or religion. "In the collective affairs of mankind, bad doctrines are always and everywhere more deadly than bad actions. The latter are the sins of the wicked, the former of the good. The latter destroy life; the former make it not worth while to live" (Introduction to Mayer's *Political Thought*).

—R.N. Iyer

TEILHARD DE CHARDIN, Pierre. French philosopher and paleontologist. Born in Sarcenat, 1 May 1881. Educated in Jesuit schools in Villefranche-sur-Saône, the Isle of Jersey, and Hastings, Sussex, 1893-1911; studied at the Institut Catholique, Paris; Paris Museum of Natural History, 1912-22; University of Paris, Sc.D. 1922; ordained as a Jesuit priest in 1911. Served as a stretcher-bearer during World War I. Professor of Geology, Institut Catholique, 1920-23; assigned to the Jesuit Collège des Hautes Études, Tientsin, China, 1923-46. Conducted paleontological expeditions in China and Africa; President, French Geological Society, 1920; Director, Laboratory for Advanced Studies in Geology and Paletontology, Paris, 1938; worked with the Wenner-Gren Foundation, New York City, 1951-55. Corresponding Member, Académie des Sciences, Paris. Member, Institut de France. Chevalier, Légion d'Honneur, 1923. *Died* (in New York) *10 April 1955.*

PUBLICATIONS

Collections

L'Oeuvre scientifique 1905-1955, edited by Nicole and Karl Schmitz-Moormann (French and English texts). Freiburg, Walter, 10 vols., 1971.

Theology and Philosophy

Le Phénomène humain. Paris, Seuil, 1955; as *The Phenomenon of Man*, New York, Harper, 1959; London, Collins, 1960; revised edition, Harper, 1965.
Science et Christ. Paris, Seuil, 1955; as *Science and Christ*, London, Collins, and New York, Harper, 1968.
L'Apparition de l'homme. Paris, Seuil, 1956; as *The Appearance of Man*, London, Collins, and New York, Harper, 1965.
La Vision du passé. Paris, Seuil, 1957; as *The Vision of the Past*, London, Collins, and New York, Harper, 1966.
Le Milieu divin: Essai de vie intérieure. Paris, Seuil, 1957; as *The Divine Milieu: An Essay on the Inner Life*, London, Collins, and New York, Harper, 1960.
Construire la terre. Paris, Seuil, 1958; as *Building the Earth*, London, Chapman, and Wilkes-Barre, Pennsylvania, Dimension, 1965.
L'Avenir de l'homme. Paris, Seuil, 1959; as *The Future of Man*, London, Collins, and New York, Harper, 1964.
Pensées, edited by Fernande Tardivel. Paris, Seuil, 1961.
L'Énergie humaine. Paris, Seuil, 1962; as *Human Energy*, London, Collins, and New York, Harper, 1969.
Hymne de l'univers. Paris, Seuil, 1962; as *Hymn of the Universe*, London, Collins, and New York, Harper, 1965.
La Messe sur le monde. Paris, Desclée DeBrouwer, 1962.

L'Activation de l'énergie.   Paris, Seuil, 1963; as *Activation of Energy*, London, Collins, and New York, Harper, 1970.
Le Christ évoluteur: Socialisation et religion: Carrière scientifique.   Paris, Seuil, 1965.
Mon Univers.   Paris, Seuil, 1965.
Le Prêtre.   Paris, Seuil, 1965.
Sur le bonheur.   Paris, Seuil, 1966; as *On Happiness*, London, Collins, 1973.
Je m'explique, edited by Jean-Pierre Demoulin.   Paris, Seuil, 1966; as *Let Me Explain*, London, Collins, and New York, Harper, 1970.
Sur l'amour.   Paris, Seuil, 1967; as *On Love*, London, Collins, 1972.
Comment je crois.   Paris, Seuil, 1969; as *Christianity and Evolution*, London, Collins, and New York, Harper, 1971.
Toujours en avant, edited by Charlotte Engles.   Paris, Desclée, 1970.
Réflexions et prières dans l'espace-temps, edited by Édouard and Suzanne Bret.   Paris, Seuil, 1972.
Les Directions de l'avenir.   Paris, Seuil, 1973; as *Towards the Future*, London, Collins, and New York, Harper, 1975.
Sur la souffrance.   Paris, Seuil, 1974; as *On Suffering*, London, Collins, and New York, Harper, 1975.
Le Coeur de la matière.   Paris, Seuil, 1976; as *The Heart of Matter*, London, Collins, 1978; New York, Harper, 1979.

Paleontology

Les Mammifères de l'éocène inférieur français et leurs gisements.   Paris, Masson, 1922.
Étude géologique sur la région du Dalai-Noor.   Paris, Geological Society of France, 1926.
Les Mammifères de l'éocène inférieur de la Belgique.   Brussels, Royal Museum of Natural History, 1927.
Les Mammifères fossiles de Nihowan (Chine), with Jean Piveteau.   Paris, Masson, 1930.
Études géologiques en Éthiopie, Somalie, et Arabie méridionale, with others.   Paris, Geological Society of France, 1930.
Fossil Mammals from the Late Cenozoic of Northern China, with C.C. Young.   Peking, Geological Survey of China, 1931.
Fossil Man in China, with others.   Peking, Geological Survey of China, 1933.
Fossil Mammals from Locality 9 of Choukoutien.   Nanking, Geological Survey of China, 1936.
On the Mammalian Remains from the Archaeological Site of Anyang, with C.C. Young.   Nanking, Geological Survey of China, 1936.
The Fossils from Locality 12 of Choukoutien.   Nanking, Geological Survey of China, 1938.
Cavicornia of South-Eastern Shansi, with M. Trassaert.   Nanking, Geological Survey of China, 1938.
The Fossils from Locality 18, Near Peking.   Chungking, Geological Survey of China, 1940.
The Fossil Mammals from Locality 13 of Choukoutien, with W.C. Pei.   Peking, Geological Survey of China, 1941.
Early Man in China.   Peking, Institute of Geo-Biology, 1941.
New Rodents of the Pliocene and Lower Pleistocene.   Peking, Institute of Geo-Biology, 1942.
Chinese Fossil Mammals, with Pierre Leroy.   Peking, Institute of Geo-Biology, 1942.
Fossil Men: Recent Discoveries and Present Problems (lecture).   Peking, Vetch, 1943.
Le Néolithique de la Chine, with Pei Wen-Ching.   Peking, Institute of Geo-Biology, 1944.
Les Félides de Chine, with Pierre Leroy.   Peking, Institute of Geo-Biology, 1945.
Les Mustélidés de Chine, with Pierre Leroy.   Peking, Institute of Geo-Biology, 1945.
Le Groupe zoologique: Structure et directions évolutives.   Paris, Michel, 1956; as *Man's Place in Nature: The Human Zoo-*

logical Group, London, Collins, and New York, Harper, 1966.

Other

Lettres de voyage (1923-1939), Nouvelles Lettres de voyage (1939-1955), edited by Claude Aragonnès.   Paris, Grasset, 2 vols., 1956-57; as *Letters from a Traveller*, London, Collins, 1962.
Genèse d'une pensée: Lettres 1914-1919, edited by Alice Teilhard-Chambon and Max Henri Begouen.   Paris, Grasset, 1961; as *The Making of a Mind: Letters from a Soldier-Priest, 1914-1919*, London, Collins, and New York, Harper, 1965.
Lettres d'Égypte, 1905-1908.   Paris, Aubier, 1963; as *Letters from Egypt, 1905-1908*, New York, Herder, 1965.
Écrits du temps de la guerre (1916-1919).   Paris, Grasset, 1965; as *Writings in Time of War*, London, Collins, and New York, Harper, 1968.
Lettres à Léontine Zanta.   Paris, Desclée De Brouwer, 1965; as *Letters to Léontine Zanta*, London, Collins, and New York, Harper, 1969.
Lettres d'Hastings et de Paris 1908-1914.   Paris, Montaigne, 1965; as *Letters from Paris 1912-1914* and *Letters from Hastings 1908-1912*, New York, Herder, 2 vols., 1967-68.
Pierre Teilhard de Chardin and Maurice Blondel: Correspondence.   New York, Herder, 1967.
Être Plus: Directives extraites des écrits publiés ou inédits du père de sa correspondance et des ses notes.   Paris, Seuil, 1968.
Letters to Two Friends, 1926-1952.   New York, New American Library, 1968; London, Collins, 1972.
Dans le silage des sinanthropes: Lettres inédites de Pierre Teilhard de Chardin et Johan Gunnar Andersson, 1926-1934.   Paris, Fayard, 1971.
Lettres intimes à Auguste Valentin, Bruno de Solages, Henri de Lubac, 1919-1955.   Paris, Montaigne, 1972.
Journal, edited by Nicole and Karl Schmitz-Moormann.   Paris, Fayard, 1975.
Lettres familières de Pierre Teilhard de Chardin, mon ami: Les Dernières Années, 1948-1955 (to Pierre Leroy).   Paris, Centurion, 1976; as *Letters from My Friend, Pierre Teilhard de Chardin, 1948-1955, Including Letters Written During His Final Years in America*, New York, Paulist Press, 1980.

*

Critical Studies: *Teilhard de Chardin: A Biographical Study* by Claude Cuénot, Baltimore, Helicon Press, 1965 (includes bibliography); *The Religion of Teilhard de Chardin* by Henri de Lubac, New York, Desclée De Brouwer, 1967; *From Science to Theology: The Evolutionary Design of Teilhard de Chardin* by Georges Crespy, New York, Abingdon Press, 1968; *The One and the Many: Teilhard de Chardin's Vision of Unity* by Donald P. Gray, New York, Herder, 1970; *Towards a New Mysticism: Teilhard de Chardin and Eastern Religions* by Ursula King, New York, Seabury Press, and London, Collins, 1980; *Teilhard's Mysticism of Knowing* by Thomas M. King, New York, Seabury Press, 1981.

*   *   *

At the time of his death in 1955 Pierre Teilhard de Chardin's religious vision of the world was little known outside a small circle of friends and colleagues. Although he had written extensively on philosophical and theological questions during his long and successful career as a paleontologist, his Jesuit superiors had consistently denied him permission to publish the material, given the inimical climate to evolutionary ideas in the Roman Catholic Church of his day. With the posthumous publication of his masterwork, *The Phenomenon of Man*, however, together with a long succession of occasional essays, both the man and the work aroused a storm of controversy. Understandably a symbolic focus for the liberalizing tendencies then at work in the Catholic Church, Teilhard was reviled by traditionalist elements. In 1962, on the eve of the Second Vatican Council, the Vatican issued a cautionary warning directed at the "ambiguities and indeed even serious errors" in Teilhard's writings which were viewed as "offensive to Catholic doctrine". This did not prevent the Council itself from incorporating significant teilhardian perspectives into its final documents. Teilhard has remained a sign of contradiction in the post-conciliar era. His influence has been incalculable both within the church and outside of it.

Fundamental for the French Jesuit is the act of seeing. He had undergone a striking shift of standpoint himself in his intellectual and spiritual development, and it is essentially this vision of an evolving world in relation to the divine creative presence and activity that he seeks to communicate to the reader. He writes with both Christians and humanists in mind. He invites each to see the world anew, as he sees it. The world is neither a mere passageway to the next world (as the Christian might be tempted to believe) nor is it a self-contained system intelligible without reference to a divine Center or an ultimate divine purpose (as the humanist believes). The world is a process, of immense temporal and spatial proportions, moving ineluctably towards a grand and magnificent conclusion in the divine goal and ground. It is one of Teilhard's most cherished convictions that the world process has a meaning and that without such a meaning both hope and action would be quite impossible to sustain in the long run.

Meaning comes to expression throughout Teilhard's writings in his law of complexity and consciousness which enables the observer to see the evolutionary development of the world in terms of increasingly complex forms of matter accompanied by increased capacity for consciousness (or spirit). This correlation between complexity (the without of things) and consciousness (the within of things) is especially evident in human beings but it can also be discerned in less complex life forms as well. Even for the pre-life phase of evolution this law remains valid although the dimension of spirit is not yet apparent owing to the diminished complexity of matter. With the appearance of the human phenomenon, however, it seems that the law of complexity and consciousness ceases to be operative any longer. The accelerated history of expanding capacity for consciousness in human evolution can hardly be accounted for on the basis of a similarly accentuated complexification of the biological organism, especially the brain and nervous system. Appearances are deceiving in this case as in many others. Complexification has indeed continued but a shift of emphasis, from the biological dimension to the social, has occurred. The more complex the society, the larger the capacity for consciousness in the personal realm.

With the advent of modern times the varied human cultures which have formed in the course of history begin to interact in quite new ways, giving rise to an enormously complex international (or planetary) community of peoples bound together, however loosely and uncomfortably, by increasingly powerful and inevitable ties of interdependence. It was Teilhard's view that the divergent phase of human evolution, characterized by cultural differentiation, is gradually coming to a close only to be replaced by a convergent phase in which all human traditions will be drawn together and upwards towards an ultimate point of unanimity and community which will make possible an unparalleled and unsurpassable realization of consciousness. The history of spirit will at last, after billions of years of effort, have achieved its final goal. This goal, this point of unity up ahead, he called Omega. It is this exalted destiny for which we are today responsible even if it still lies at a considerable distance from us. Having indicated the goal, he likewise suggested the means to it: an all-embracing, indeed cosmic love which simultaneously personalizes as it socializes. Nothing less than such a universal love can bring the vast evolutionary development of the world to a successful conclusion.

Clearly, Teilhard asks a great deal of his reader by way of revision of conventional standpoints. Nonetheless, he asks that the reader go even further still, for he is by no means content with the utopian humanism just described. His vision is at heart a religious one; more precisely, one that is deeply Christian. It is necessary to see the world in the light of a revelation, of God's revelation in Jesus of Nazareth. By virtue of his death and resurrection he has become the commanding center of an evolving creation, leading and directing the march towards Omega. He is in fact Omega Himself, the ultimate goal and unitive principle of a convergent humanity. Cosmogenesis (the world in process of becoming an ordered whole) is now seen to be a Christogenesis (the world in process of becoming the Body of Christ). The incarnation of God's Word in Jesus possesses a creative and redemptive meaning not only for humanity but also for the entire cosmos. In him the divine, the human, and the cosmic meet and are made one; in him "all things hold together" (Colossians 1:17); through him "God will be all in all" (I Corinthians 15:28). Teilhard's vision is thoroughly Christocentric. His re-vision of modern evolutionary thinking in terms of the law of complexity and consciousness is matched by an equally radical re-vision of classical Christian thinking in terms of a cosmic Christology.

The power of Teilhard's visionary interpretation of the world process resides only partly in the argumentation employed to support it, for it is ultimately founded upon an intuitive sense, indeed a mystical experience, of meaning and purpose at work everywhere in cosmogenesis. This meaning and purpose is for him at once divine and personal, ever active in pursuit of creative and redemptive goals. It has been decisively revealed in Jesus of Nazareth and in the stream of tradition and community to which his life, death and resurrection gave rise. However, it is manifest throughout the whole movement if one knows where to look for it, even if it will only be fully exposed at the end point. "Nothing here below is profane," Teilhard maintains in *The Divine Milieu*, "for those who know how to see." This is the voice of a believer inviting anyone who is willing to share a faith with him, to "come and see."

—Donald P. Gray

TEMPLE, William. British theologian. Born in Exeter, 15 October 1881. Educated at Rugby School (Scholar, 1895); studied at Balliol College, Oxford, B.A. 1904, M.A. 1907; ordained, 1909. Married Frances Anson in 1916. Fellow and Lecturer in Philosophy, Queen's College, Oxford, 1904-10; Headmaster, Repton School, 1910-14; Rector, St. James's, London, 1914-17; Honorary Chaplain to the King, 1915-21; Canon of Westminster, 1919-21; Bishop of Manchester, 1921-29; Archbishop of York, 1929-42; Archbishop of Canterbury, 1942-44. President, Workers' Educational Association, 1908-24; Editor, *The Pilgrim*, 1920-27; Chairman, B.B.C. Advisory Council, 1935; Chairman, Governing Body, Rugby School. Paddock Lecturer, General Theological Seminary, New York, 1915; Gifford Lecturer, University of Glasgow, 1932-34; Noble Lecturer, Harvard University, Cambridge, Massachusettes, 1936; Moody Lecturer, University of Chicago, 1936. Honorary doctorate: Oxford University, 1918 and 1934; University of Manchester, 1929; University of Durham, 1929; University of Leeds, 1930; University of Sheffield, 1931; Cambridge University, 1933; University of Dublin, 1934; Princeton University, New Jersey, 1936; Columbia University, New York, 1936. Honorary Fellow, Queen's College, Oxford, 1925. *Died 26 October 1944.*

PUBLICATIONS

Religion and Society

Faith and Modern Thought.   London, Macmillan, 1910.

Principles of Social Progress.   Melbourne, Australian Student Christian Union, 1910.

The Nature of Personality (lectures).   London, Macmillan, 1911.

The Kingdom of God.   London, Macmillan, 1912.

Repton School Sermons.   London, Macmillan, 1913.

Studies in the Spirit and Truth of Christianity.   London, Macmillan, 1914.

Church and Nation.   London, Macmillan, 1915.

Plato and Christianity (lectures).   London, Macmillan, 1916.

Challenge to the Church.   London, SPCK, 1917.

Issues of Faith.   London, Macmillan, 1917.

Mens Creatrix: An Essay.   London, Macmillan, 1917.

Fellowship with God.   London, Macmillan, 1920.

The Universality of Christ.   London, SCM Press, 1921.

Christ and His Church.   London, Macmillan, 1924.

Christus Veritas.   London, Macmillan, 1924; as *Christ the Truth*, New York, Macmillan, 1924.

Christ's Revelation of God.   London, SCM Press, 1925.

Personal Religion and the Life of Fellowship.   London, Longman, 1926.

Essays in Christian Politics and Kindred Subjects.   London, Longman, 1927.

Christianity and the State (lectures).   London, Macmillan, 1928.

Christian Faith and Life.   London, SCM Press, 1931.

Basic Convictions.   New York and London, Harper, 1936.

The Preacher's Theme Today.   London, SPCK, 1936; as *The Centrality of Christ*, New York, Morehouse-Gorham, 1936.

Christianity in Thought and Practice (lectures).   New York, Morehouse Gorham, 1936.

The Church and Its Teaching Today (lectures).   London, Macmillan, 1936.

Readings in St. John's Gospel.   London, Macmillan, 2 vols., 1939-40.

Thoughts in Wartime.   London, Macmillan, 1940.

The Citizen and Churchman.   London, Eyre and Spottiswoode, 1941.

Hope of a New World (addresses).   New York, Macmillan, 1941.

Christianity and Social Order.   New York, Penguin, 1942; London, SCM Press, 1950.

The Church Looks Forward.   New York, Macmillan, 1944.

Religious Experience, and Other Essays and Addresses, edited by A.E. Baker.   London, Clarke, 1958.

About Christ (lectures).   London, SCM Press, 1962.

Some Lambeth Letters, edited by F.S. Temple.   London and New York, Oxford University Press, 1963.

What Christians Stand For in the Secular World.   Philadelphia, Fortress Press, 1965.

Other

The Life of Bishop Percival.   London, SCM Press, 1924.

*

Critical Studies: *William Temple, Archbishop of Canterbury: His Life and Letters* by Frederic Iremonger, London and New York, Oxford University Press, 1948; *The Christian Philosophy of William Temple* by Jack F. Padgett, The Hague, Nijhoff, 1974.

*   *   *

Although William Temple was at the pinnacle of his career as Archbishop of Canterbury for only two years, he achieved an international reputation. When he died, during the closing months of the 1939-45 war, world-wide tributes were the measure of the recognition of his thought, message, and work. President Franklin Roosevelt in a message to King George VI said: "He was rightly considered a good friend of the United States and his efforts to promote Anglo-American understanding and co-operation were unceasing. As an advocate of international co-operation based on Christian principles he exercised profound influence thoughout the world". And from Pretoria, Field Marshall Smuts cabled: "A great man passed. Church, nation and the world have suffered an irreparable loss".

The understanding among ordinary people of Temple's work, thought, and message to the world had been such that when inmates of a Japanese prison-camp in Singapore heard of his death "very many men," in the words of one of them, "British, Australian and Dutch spoke with love and affection of one whom they had never seen and the whole camp drooped with the shock." And, to give just another example, in the dressing-room of a London theatre her dresser told the distinguished actress Sibyl Thorndike: "The poor man has lost a friend."

At different times in his life Temple stressed that he believed a better social order would include both control by the state and enterprise through competition. He advocated housing that would provide for family life in privacy and urged universal education up to the age of 18. And he wanted workers to have a voice in the control of the enterprise in which they were employed, to have a five-day working week and holidays with pay. These things were only a dream to countless workers at the time they were advocated by Temple. A major contribution of Temple's to social progress was his share in the passing of the 1944 Education Act, one of its features being that every school day should begin with an act of worship. He considered it important, too, that the school-leaving age should be raised to 16, a measure he advocated both in the House of Lords and the Country.

Temple felt that through music, art, and religion man's mind apprehended the beautiful goodness of the world. He urged that men and women should come together believing that their relations with others formed and deepened their ethical values "so that the supreme activity of the mind was its judgment of rightness."

Deeply concerned with the massacres and starvation of Jews and others in enemy and enemy-occupied countries during the war, Temple never ceased to call for active intervention. The horrors which culminated in the Buchenwald massacres of 1944 inspired him to repeat his vigorous protest and it is not surprising that the World Jewish Congress deeply mourned his passing, declaring: "Lamented by Christian world, the premature death of Dr. Temple will be particularly mourned by Jewish people whose champion he was. His maintained interest in the welfare of our much persecuted brethren was not rooted, as in the case of many theologians, in an attitude of sanctimonious pity. He approached the overwhelming problem of the destiny of the Jews in a mood more positive, more comprehensive, more liberal, and, above all, more human.... He was at all times ready to make every contribution to the alleviation of the great tragedy that had befallen a great people."

It has been said that the peak of Temple's evangelical appeal was reached in his introduction to a book published in the year of his death. In it he wrote: "Our need is a new integration of life: religion, art, science, politics, education, industry, commerce, finance. All these need to-be brought into a unity as agents of a single purpose. That purpose can hardly be found in human aspirations; it must be the divine purpose. That divine purpose is presented to us in the Bible under the name of the Kingdom of God, or as the summing-up of all things in Christ, or as the coming down out of heaven of the holy city, the New Jerusalem.... All nations are to walk in the light of the holy city but it comes down out of heaven from God. The Kingdom of God is the goal of human history but it is His kingdom, not man's."

It was during the dark days of the war that Temple, as Primate, asked if the clergy were doing all they could in the leading of special prayers to show that regard was being paid to what was uppermost in people's minds. He wrote: "If people come to Church with hearts filled with either anxiety or gratitude and find the service conducted without reference to the occasion of their feeling, they learn to think of the Church as something aloof and unsympathetic, and without any message for their needs. By meeting those needs we may lead people increasingly to make their requests known to God and to cast their care upon Him—a lesson which once learnt, will be a permanent source of spiritual strength."

Temple's biographer, F.A. Iremonger, one-time chaplain to the King and Honorary Chaplain to Temple when he was Archbishop of York, has said: "Many primates have ruled the church with vigour and distinction. One or two have helped to determine the course of its history, and a few have wielded an appreciable influence over one section or another of the life of England. But of none, except Temple, since the Reformation, can it be said that the *world* was the poorer for his passing."

—Granville Eastwood

TERMAN, Lewis M(adison). American psychologist. Born in Johnson County, Indiana, 15 January 1877. Studied at Central Normal College, Danville, Indiana, B.A. 1898; University of Indiana, Bloomington, M.A. 1903; Clark University, Worcester, Massachusetts, Ph.D. 1905. Served as a psychologist in the United States Army, 1918-19: Major. Married Anna Belle Minton in 1899; 2 children. High School Principal, Smiths Valley, Indiana, 1898-1901, and San Bernadino, California, 1905-06; Professor of Psychology and Pedagogy, Normal State School, Los Angeles, 1906-10; Assistant Professor of Education, 1910-12, Associate Professor, 1912-16, Professor, 1916-42, and Professor Emeritus, 1942-56, Stanford University, California. President, American School Hygiene Association, 1917, and American Psychological Association, 1923. Recipient: Award of Merit, American Vocational Guidance Association, 1956; Gold Medal, Distinguished Psychologist Award, American Psychological Foundation, 1956. Honorary doctorate: University of Indiana, 1929; University of California, Berkeley, 1946; University of Pennsylvania, Philadelphia, 1946; University of Southern California, Los Angeles, 1949. Member, National Academy of Sciences; Fellow, American Academy of Arts and Sciences. Honorary Fellow, American Psychological Association; Educational Institute, Scotland, 1947; and the British Psychological Society, 1950. *Died 21 December 1956.*

PUBLICATIONS

Psychology

The Teacher's Health: A Study in the Hygiene of a Vocation. Boston, Houghton Mifflin, 1913.
Health Work in the Schools, with E.B. Hoag. Boston, Houghton Mifflin, 1914.
Medical Inspection, Hygiene Teaching, Physical Training, and Special Schools for Defectives in Portland, Oregon. Yonkers, New York, World Book, 1914.
Whittier State School Biennial Report, with J.H. Williams. Whittier, California, Whittier State School, 1914.
Relation of Delinquency and Criminality to Mental Deficiency, with J.H. Williams. Whittier, California, Whittier State School, 1915.
Research in Mental Deviation Among Children. Stanford, California, Stanford University Press, 1915.

The Measurement of Intelligence. Boston, Houghton Mifflin, 1916.
The Stanford Revision of the Binet-Simon Tests. Boston, Houghton Mifflin, 1916.
The Intelligence of School Children. Boston, Houghton Mifflin, 1919.
National Intelligence Tests, with Manual of Directions, with others. Yonkers, New York, World Book, 1920.
Terman Group Test of Mental Ability. Yonkers, New York, World Book, 1920.
Suggestions for Children's Reading, with others. Stanford, California, Stanford University Press, 1921.
Suggestions for the Education and Training of Gifted Children. Stanford, California, Stanford University Press, 1921.
Intelligence Tests and School Reorganization, with others. Yonkers, New York, World Book, 1922.
Report of Subcommittee of Leland Stanford Junior University Committee on Scholarship and Student Ability. Stanford, California, Stanford University Press, 1923.
School Organization and Administration, with others. Yonkers, New York, World Book, 1923.
Stanford Achievement Test: Manual of Directions for Primary Examination and Advanced Examination, with others. Yonkers, New York, World Book, 1923.
Genetic Studies of Genius, I: Mental and Physical Traits of a Thousand Gifted Children, with others. Stanford, California, Stanford University Press, 1925.
Children's Reading: A Guide for Parents and Teachers, with Margaret Lima. New York, Appleton Century, 1926.
Genetic Studies of Genius, II: The Early Mental Traits of 300 Geniuses, with others. Stanford, California, Stanford University Press, 1926.
New Stanford Achievement Test. Yonkers, New York, World Book, 1929.
Genetic Studies of Genius, III: The Promise of Youth: Follow-up Studies of a Thousand Gifted Children, with others. Stanford, California, Stanford University Press, 1930.
Attitude-Interest Analysis Test, with C.C. Miles. New York, McGraw Hill, 1936.
Sex and Personality: Studies in Masculinity and Femininity, with C.C. Miles. New York, McGraw Hill, 1936.
Measuring Intelligence, with M.A. Merrill. Boston, Houghton Mifflin, 1937.
Revised Stanford-Binet Scale, with M.A. Merrill. Boston, Houghton Mifflin, 1937.
Manual of Information and Directions for Use of Attitude-Interest Analysis Test, with C.C. Miles. New York, McGraw Hill, 1938.
Psychological Factors in Marital Happiness. New York, McGraw Hill, 1938.
Terman-McNemar Test of Mental Ability, with Quinn McNemar. Yonkers, New York, World Book, 1941.
The Stanford Study of Gifted Children: Condensed Summary 1921-1946. Stanford, California, Stanford University Press, 1946.
Genetic Studies of Genius, IV: The Gifted Child Grows Up: Twenty-five Years Follow-up of a Superior Group, with Melita H. Oden. Stanford, California, Stanford University Press, 1947.
Scientists and Nonscientists in a Group of 800 Gifted Men. Washington, D.C., American Psychological Association, 1954.
Concept Mastery Test. New York, Psychological Corporation, 1956.
Genetic Studies of Genius, V: The Gifted Group at Mid-life: Thirty-five Years Follow-up of the Superior Child, with Melita H. Oden. Stanford, California, Stanford University Press, 1959.
Genius and Stupidity (1906 Dissertation). New York, Arno Press, 1975.

*

Critical Study: *Terman and the Gifted* by May V. Seague, Los Altos, California, William Kaufmann, 1975 (includes bibliography).

*   *   *

With the construction of a standardized device for measuring intelligence, a revision of the Binet-Simon scale developed in France, Lewis M. Terman introduced what was to become perhaps both the most controversial and the most prosperous venture in American psychology. Considering the widescale use of intelligence tests in education, immigration, and personnel management, he also might be credited with initiating an unprecedented use of scientific psychology in social policy. Terman's theoretical interests were clearly those of understanding individual differences in the human personality, and the intelligence test enabled him to investigate two aspects of these individual differences: the extent to which differences are innate rather than acquired and the particular patterns of variation in differences across the population. On the former issue Terman was to conclude that his extensive testing of thousands of school children unequivocally indicated a substantial innate component of intelligence and the relative stability of an individual's intelligence quotient throughout childhood. When these results were coordinated with longitudinal studies of extreme variations in a population, from the "feebleminded" to the "genius," Terman became more convinced of the fixedness of intellectual abilities. Terman's autobiographical statement that even as a child he was "impressed by those who differed in some respect from the common run," and his dissertation, *Genius and Stupidity*, attest to an enduring enchantment with the variability of outstanding personality characteristics. For these reasons Terman became a major target of criticism for the environmentalists who rapidly grew in number during the same period, 1912-40, in which Terman produced revised scales and related research on human abilities.

Terman's prominence in the nature-nurture controversies and in the field of mental testing is undeniable yet has obscured several other areas in which he influenced American psychology. First, he committed considerable effort to establishing American psychology as a practical, applied profession in addition to a scientific one. He did so not simply through production of usable measuring instruments but also through active promotion of those instruments, notably in the examination of soldiers during World War I, and through repeated appeals that American psychologists should apply their knowledge to the problems of everyday life. He argued that practical applications of psychology would benefit humanity and promote the support of scientific research. Second, Terman extended his interests in individual differences beyond the issue of intelligence. In 1936 he published, with Sarah Cox Miles, the first scale to measure the personality dimensions of masculinity and femininity. Having found no sex differences in intelligence, Terman sought to locate what he believed were deep psychological differences between the sexes. The Terman-Miles Masculinity-Femininity scale was the first of a host of tests to ascertain the deep psychology of the sexes which they thought presented continual confusion to the ordinary person and was a source of deviant behavior and marital problems. Two years later he published a scale for assessing marital happiness in the hopes of being able to forecast successful marriages.

These activities make Terman exemplary of the scientific ideals of early 20th-century psychologists. As others, he was influenced by the tenets of evolutionary theory which posited an identifiable order to the variety of human personalities and a biological bases of these variations, and was convinced of the possibility of creating a science of psychology by striving for objectivity and control through quantitative and experimental methods. He devoted his career to identifying the dimensions of these human variations and to doing so by being an exacting, analytical, and methodical scientist.

—J.G. Morawski

THOMAS, W(illiam) I(saac). American sociologist. Born in Russell County, Virginia, 13 August 1863. Educated at public schools in Virginia and Tennessee; studied at the University of Tennessee, Nashville, B.A. 1884, Ph.D. in Literature 1886; Universities of Berlin and Göttingen, 1888-89; University of Chicago, 1893-96, Ph.D. in sociology 1896. Married Harriet Park in 1888 (divorced, 1934), 5 children; married Dorothy Swaine in 1935. Instructor in English, Greek, and Latin, University of Tennessee, 1884-88; Professor of English and Comparative Literature, 1889-94, and Professor of Sociology, 1894, Oberlin College, Ohio; Instructor, 1895-1900, Assistant and Associate Professor, 1900-10, and Professor of Sociology, 1910-18, University of Chicago. Lecturer, New School for Social Research, New York, 1923-28, and Harvard University, Cambridge, Massachusetts, 1936-37. Director, Helen Culver Fund for Race Psychology, Chicago, 1908-18. President, American Sociological Society, 1927. Member, American Academy of Arts and Sciences. *Died 5 December 1947.*

PUBLICATIONS

Sociology

Sex and Society: Studies in the Social Psychology of Sex. Chicago, University of Chicago Press, 1907.

The Origin of Society and the State. Chicago, Zalaz, 1915.

The Polish Peasant in Europe and America, with Florian Znaniecki. Boston, Badger, 5 vols., 1918-20.

Old World Traits Transplanted, with Robert E. Park and Herbert A. Miller. New York, Harper, 1921.

The Unadjusted Girl, with Cases and Standpoint for Behavior Analysis. Boston, Little Brown, 1923; London, Routledge, 1924.

The Child in America: Behavior Problems and Programs, with Dorothy Swaine Thomas. New York, Knopf, 1928.

Primitive Behavior: An Introduction to the 'Social Sciences. New York, McGraw Hill, 1937.

Social Behavior and Personality: Contributions of W.I. Thomas to Theory and Social Research, edited by Edmund H. Volkart. New York, Social Science Research Council, 1951.

On Social Organization and Social Personality: Selected Papers, edited by Morris Janowitz. Chicago, University of Chicago Press, 1966.

*

Critical Study: *An Appraisal of Thomas and Znaniecki's "The Polish Peasant in Europe and America"* by Herbert Blumer, New York, Social Science Research Council, 1939.

*   *   *

W.I. Thomas is associated with sociological "symbolic interactionism" and is especially known for two major theoretical concepts: the "four wishes" and the "definition of the situation."

Thomas completed his undergraduate work at the University of Tennessee, studied at Berlin and Gottingen, and eventually took his doctorate at the University of Chicago in 1896 under Albion Small (1854-1926), whose background and program were similar.

Thomas defined sociology as the comparative study of the evolution of society, and repeatedly described the basic problem of social analysis as tracing the influence of culture and society on the individual, and of the individual on culture and society. The implication was that each shapes the other but neither is determinant of the other.

The concept of the "four wishes" developed from a basic problem in pragmatic epistemology. If "mind" is a process of consciousness that emerged as an aspect of problem-solving behavior, then what generated "problems?" Thomas's first formulation of the answer was "interests," or general desires that were based upon physiological instincts but not reducible to them, and that were independent of the social goals given by external conditions. When achievement of these desires by habitual (unconscious) means was frustrated, one was forced into conscious, reflective behavior. "Interest" was broadened into "attitudes" in the famous "Methodological Note" at the beginning of *The Polish Peasant* (1918). An attitude was an inclination to move toward or away from some object, to try to obtain it or try to avoid it. It was at once a desire, an evaluation, and a "wish." The four wishes were attitudes that were especially important and prominent cross-culturally: "(1) the desire for new experience...; (2) the desire for recognition...; (3) the desire for mastery...; (4) the desire for security." Each could be expressed in ways that were socially desirable or socially undesirable. It was the de facto task of society, and the proposed task of rational "social technique," to encourage the desirable forms and "repress" the undesirable.

Attitudes were channeled by "social values." A social value was "any datum having an empirical content accessible to members of some social group and a meaning with regard to which it is or may be an object of activity." Social values include actual valued objects (like houses, wealth), social groups (like the family), cultural and social traditions, and rules.

Thomas stressed that attitudes called for by social values were not necessarily the same as the attitudes *provoked* by them. In the ordinary state of social organization, values and attitudes were generally concordant. At times of change, they became discordant. Then, in the normal course of events, it would be necessary to reform social values and/or attitudes, to restore the harmony. It was the aim of social theory to find the values and attitudes and state their relation to behavior as general and invariant causal laws; it was the aim of social "technique" informed by such theory to aid in the reformulations that lead to harmony by rational means. A causal law always had, as a minimum, to have three elements: a value, and attitude, and a behavior.

The conception of the definition of the situation arose directly in response to a problem in these formulations in *The Polish Peasant*. Often the value and the attitude were still not enough to explain behavior: one had to say what the circumstances were. The concept of the definition of the situation developed this concept of "circumstances" in a way that did not vitiate the initial stress on values and attitudes. The definition of the situation (but perhaps not the situation per se) was not itself objectively given, but was rather set up and negotiated by those who were in it, on the basis of attitudes and with a view to values.

The Polish Peasant was narrowly focussed on relations between Polish immigrants in the United States and their kin and friends in Poland. *Primitive Behavior* applied Thomas's perspective on a larger scale. This owed much to the ethnological work of Franz Boas and those associated with him. In it, he held that "diversities in behavior and culture are the result of different interpretations of experience, resulting in characteristic reactions and habit systems, and that a uniform course of cultural and behavioral evolution is consequently out of the question."

To explain cultural differences, "emphasis should be placed on the culture area rather than the natural environment." Cultural differences were to be described by the ways in which each culture emphasised the definitions of certain situations and ignored others, out of the range of all possible definitions of all possible situations.

Thomas's conceptions, more than any others, mark the boundary between modern sociological theory and the earlier formulations of the French and German schools. Before he wrote, sociology had none of the ability to recognize relativity of perspective and dynamism in human communication and interpretation that was found in contemporary pragmatic theory. His formulations simplified the pragmatic ideas to the point of distortion, but in so doing allowed them to be inserted into the sociological theories and narrowed the gap between the two traditions.

—Murray J. Leaf

THORNDIKE, E(dward) L(ee). American psychologist. Born in Williamsburg, Massachusetts, 31 August 1874. Studied at Wesleyan University, Middletown, Connecticut, B.A. 1895; Harvard University, Cambridge, Massachusetts, B.A. 1896, M.A. 1897; Columbia University, New York, Ph.D. 1898. Served in the United States Army as Chairman, Committee on Classification of Personnel and Member of Advisory Board, Division of Psychology, Office of the Surgeon General, 1917-18. Married Elizabeth Moulton in 1900; 4 children. Instructor in Education, Western Reserve University, Cleveland, 1898-99; Instructor in Genetic Psychology, 1899-1901, Adjunct Professor, 1901-04, Professor of Educational Psychology, 1904-40, and Professor Emeritus, 1940-49, Columbia University; also Head, Department of Comparative Psychology, Marine Biological Laboratory, Woods Hole, Massachusetts, 1900-02. Visiting Professor, Johns Hopkins University, Baltimore, 1931-32. Messenger Lecturer, Cornell University, Ithaca, New York, 1928-29; William James Lecturer, Harvard University, 1942-43. President, American Psychological Association, 1912, New York Academy of Sciences, 1919-20, American Association for the Advancement of Science, 1934, American Association for Adult Education, 1934-35, and the Psychometric Society, 1936-37. Honorary doctorate: Wesleyan University, 1919; University of Iowa, Iowa City, 1923; Columbia University, 1929; University of Chicago, 1932; Harvard University, 1934; University of Edinburgh, 1937; University of Athens, 1937. Member, National Academy of Sciences; Fellow, American Academy of Arts and Sciences. Honorary Member, British Psychological Society; Leningrad Scientific-Medical Pedological Society; and Comenius Educational Association of Czechoslovakia. *Died* (in Montrose, New York) *9 August 1949.*

PUBLICATIONS

Psychology

Educational Psychology. New York, Lemcke and Buechner, 1903.
An Introduction to the Theory of Mental and Social Measurements. New York, Science Press, 1904.
The Elements of Psychology. New York, Seiler, 1905.
Principles of Teaching. New York, Seiler, 1906.
Animal Intelligence: Experimental Studies. New York, Macmillan, 1911.
Individuality. Boston, Houghton Mifflin, 1911.
Education: A First Book. New York, Macmillan, 1912.
Educational Administration, with G.D. Strayer. New York, Macmillan, 1913.
Educational Psychology: Vol. I: The Original Nature of Man; Vol. 2: The Psychology of Learning; Vol. 3: Mental Work and Fatigue, and Individual Differences and Their Causes. New York, Columbia University Teachers College, 1913-14.
Educational Psychology: Briefer Course. New York, Columbia University Teachers College, 1914.

Ventilation in Relation to Mental Work, with others. New York, Columbia University Teachers College, 1916.

English Composition: 150 Specimens Arranged for Use in Psychological and Educational Experiments. New York, Columbia University Teachers College, 1916.

Plan for Rating and Classification of Soldiers in the Students' Army Training Corps. Washington, D.C., War Department Committee on Education and Special Training, 1918.

Reading Scales. New York, Columbia University Teachers College, 1919.

Thorndike Extension of the Hillegas English Composition Scale. New York, Columbia University, Teachers College, 1919.

Intelligence Examination for High School Graduates: Instructions for Giving, Scoring, and Interpreting Scores: Series 1919-1924. New York, Columbia University Teachers College, 1919.

The Teacher's Word Book New York, Columbia University Teachers College, 1921.

Thorndike-McCall Reading Scales for Grades 2-12, with W.A. McCall. New York, Columbia University Teachers College, 1921.

The New Methods in Arithmetic. Chicago, Rand McNally, 1921.

The Thorndike Test of Word Knowledge, Forms A,B,C,D. New York, Columbia University Teachers College, 1922.

The Psychology of Arithmetic. New York, Macmillan, 1922.

The Psychology of Algebra. New York, Macmillan, 1923.

Intelligence Examination for High School Graduates: Instructions for Giving, Scoring, and Interpreting Scores: Series 1925-1930. New York, Columbia University Teachers College, 1924.

I.E.R. Intelligence Scale CAVD Levels A to Q. New York, Columbia University Teachers College, 1925.

The Measurement of Intelligence, with others. New York, Columbia University Teachers College, 1926.

Adult Learning: Studies in Adult Education, with others. New York, Macmillan, 1928.

Elementary Principles of Education, with A.I. Gates. New York, Macmillan, 1929.

Human Learning. New York, Century, 1931.

A Teacher's Word Book of the Twenty Thousand Words Found Most Frequently and Widely in General Reading for Children and Young People. New York, Columbia University Teachers College, 1931.

The Fundamentals of Learning, with others. New York, Columbia University Teachers College, 1932.

An Experimental Study of Rewards. New York, Columbia University Teachers College, 1933.

Prediction of Vocational Success. New York, Commonwealth Fund, 1934.

Adult Interests, with others. New York, Macmillan, 1935.

The Psychology of Wants, Interests, and Attitudes. New York, Appleton Century, 1935.

Thorndike-Century Junior Dictionary. Chicago, Scott Foresman, 1935.

The Teaching of Controversial Subjects. Cambridge, Massachusetts, Harvard University Press, 1937.

Your City. New York, Harcourt Brace, 1939.

Education as Cause and Symptom. New York, Macmillan, 1939.

Human Nature and the Social Order. New York, Macmillan, 1949.

144 Smaller Cities. New York, Harcourt Brace, 1940.

Teaching of English Suffixes. New York, Columbia University Teachers College, 1941.

Thorndike-Century Senior Dictionary. Chicago, Scott Foresman, 1941.

Man and His Works. Cambridge, Massachusetts, Harvard University Press, 1943.

The Teacher's Word Book of 30,000 Words, with I. Lorge. New York, Columbia University Teachers College, 1944.

Thorndike-Century Beginning Dictionary. Chicago, Scott Foresman, 1945.

Thorndike-Lorge Reading Test for Grades 7 to 9: Forms 1 and 2. New York, Columbia University Teachers College, 1945.

Selected Writings from a Connectionist's Psychology. New York, Appleton Century, 1949.

Psychology and the Science of Education: Selected Writings, edited by Geraldine M. Joncich. New York, Columbia University Teachers College, 1962.

*

Critical Study: *The Sane Positivist: A Biography of Edward L. Thorndike* by Geraldine M. Joncich, Middletown, Connecticut, Wesleyan University Press, 1968.

*   *   *

Few scientists have had as great an influence on their disciplines as the psychologist E.L. Thorndike. His pioneering work of rewards and punishments in learning and problem solving served as a starting point for the stimulus-response (S-R) learning theories which followed, and his enduring interest in extending his findings to educational practice stands as a model for how basic research can help generate solutions to problems of applied significance.

Because he was an avowed Darwinian who believed in the continuity between animal and human behavior, Thorndike's early work focused on the actions of cats, dogs, and chicks in puzzle boxes and mazes. The puzzle box allowed an animal to escape from an enclosure in order to obtain food placed in view outside the apparatus. Such simple acts as pulling on a cord or pressing a lever caused a door to open permitting the animal to reach the food. The behaviors observed in such situations provided the data from which several basic laws of learning were formulated.

Thorndike believed that the interior of the box constituted a stimulus situation to which the animal brought a number of behaviors, such as biting, clawing, pulling, etc. Through trial-and-error those behaviors which did not lead to escape were "stamped out," while those behaviors which did lead to solution were "stamped in." This automatic "stamping in" of correct responses by their satisfying after-effects increased the probability of repeating the response when the situation next recurred, i.e., when the animal was placed back in the box on a succeeding trial. The strengthening or weakening of connections as a result of their satisfying (e.g., food when hungry) or annoying (e.g., pain) properties became known as the law of effect and firmly established Thorndike as a reinforcement theorist.

As a result of later experiments with humans, the law of effect became a law of reward only. One reason for the modification was the finding that subjects given a multiple choice vocabulary test with Spanish words tended to repeat not only choices followed by reward (the experimenter saying "Right"), but also choices followed by punishment (the experimenter saying "Wrong"). Thorndike's revised view was that punishment acted only to increase response variability, thereby causing the learner to try different responses until one was subsequently rewarded.

A second basic law of learning was the law of exercise. According to this law, connections were strengthened by their use and weakened by disuse. The emphasis here was on strengthening by mere frequency of occurrence, a notion akin to the principle of learning by doing or to the belief that practice makes perfect. As with the law of effect, this law was questioned by later findings. In one study, people were asked to draw lines of a given length while blindfolded. When information as to whether the product was too long or too short was withheld, no improvement occurred over repeated attempts. Mere frequency, then, had little effect on learning in the absence of reward.

A number of subordinate laws were also formulated, one of

the most important being the principle of associative shifting. The notion here is that responses can become attached to new stimulus situations by appropriate training. Thorndike gives the example of trying to get a cat to stand up by dangling a fish in front of it. After repeatedly pairing the words "stand up" (S1) with the sight of the fish (S2), followed by the placement of the fish into the mouth (unconditioned stimulus or UCS) when the animal actually stands up, the cat will eventually stand up to S1 in the absence of S2. The similarity of this idea to Pavlovian conditioning was obvious to Thorndike but he believed that the latter was a special case of his own principle.

Thorndike's experimental attack on the doctrine of formal discipline was another significant contribution. According to this doctrine, the "faculties" of the mind (e.g., memory, reasoning) can be improved by exercising them with difficult lessons. The early educational belief that the learning of Latin and geometry could help students master science and other subject matters was largely based on such thinking. Thorndike (with Woodworth in one study) presented evidence which seriously questioned this view. In the first study, it was shown that improvement in estimating rectangular areas depended mainly on practice in the same task and not on practice in different tasks (e.g., estimating the areas of triangles). In the second study, Thorndike reported that mental test scores showed no differential improvement in high school students taking practical courses as contrasted with other students taking courses presumably having disciplinary value. Thorndike concluded that transfer of training was always specific, depending only on the number of "identical elements" present in two situations.

Thorndike had many critics, most of whom assailed his work on epistemological grounds. He was attacked for being restrictive in his choice of experimental situations and variables, and for generally ignoring the complexities of behavior when formulating his laws of learning. Although the same criticisms of later behaviorists produced a decided shift in recent years toward studying "cognitive behavior," Thorndike's research in the areas of animal and human learning, as well as his contributions to the field of educational psychology, have had a fundamental influence on learning theory in the 20th-century.

—Seymore Simon

THURSTONE, L(ouis) L(eon). American psychologist. Born in Chicago, Illinois, 28 May 1887. Studied at Cornell University, Ithaca, New York, M.E. 1912; University of Chicago, Ph.D. 1917. Married Thelma Gwinn in 1924; 3 children. Professor of Psychology, Carnegie Institute of Technology, Pittsburgh, 1915-23; Professor of Psychology, 1924-38, and Charles F. Grey Distinguished Service Professor, 1938-52, University of Chicago; Research Professor and Director of the Psychometric Laboratory, University of North Carolina, Chapel Hill, 1952-55. Visiting Professor, University of Frankfurt, 1948; University of Stockholm, 1954. Co-Founder, Psychometric Society and its journal Psychometrika. Member, Committee on Classification of Military Personnel, Adjutant General's Office, World War II. President, American Psychological Association, 1932-33. Recipient: Centennial Award, Northwestern University, Evanston, Illinois, 1951. Honorary doctorate: University of Gothenburg, 1954. Member, National Academy of Sciences. Honorary Fellow, British Psychological Society; and Swedish Psychological Society. Died (in Chapel Hill, North Carolina) 29 September 1955.

PUBLICATIONS

Psychology

The Learning Curve Equation. Princeton, New Jersey, Psychological Review Corporation, 1919.
Thurstone Employment Tests. Yonkers, New York, World Book, 1922.
The Nature of Intelligence. New York, Harcourt Brace, and London, Kegan Paul, 1924.
The Fundamentals of Statistics. New York, Macmillan, 1925.
Vocational Guidance for College Students, with Charles R. Mann. Washington, D.C., National Research Council, 1925.
The Measurement of Attitude: A Psychological Method and Some Experiments with a Scale for Measuring Attitude Toward the Church, with E.J. Chave. Chicago, University of Chicago Press, 1929.
Order of Birth, Parent-Age, and Intelligence, with Richard L. Jenkins. Chicago, University of Chicago Press, 1931.
The Reliability and Validity of Tests. Ann Arbor, Michigan, Edwards, 1931.
Computing Diagrams for the Tetrachoric Correlation Coefficient, with others. Chicago, University of Chicago Bookstore, 1933.
Motion Pictures and Social Attitudes of Children. with Ruth C. Peterson. New York, Macmillan, 1933.
The Theory of Multiple Factors. Ann Arbor, Michigan, Edwards, 1933.
Penmanship and Psychological Tests, with others. Scranton, Pennsylvania, International Textbook Company, 1934.
The Vectors of the Mind: Multiple-factor Analysis for the Isolation of Primary Traits. Chicago, University of Chicago Press, 1935.
Safe-Driving: Human Limitations in Automobile Driving, with J.R. Hamilton. New York, Doubleday, 1937.
Primary Mental Abilities. Chicago, University of Chicago Press, 1938.
Factorial Studies of Intelligence, with Thelma Gwinn Thurstone. Chicago, University of Chicago Press, 1941.
A Factorial Study of Perception. Chicago, University of Chicago Press, 1944.
Multiple-factor Analysis: A Development and Expansion of the Vectors of the Mind. Chicago, University of Chicago Press, 1947.
SRA Primary Mental Abilities, with Thelma Gwinn Thurstone. Chicago, Science Research Associates, 1947.
The Measurement of Values (selected papers). Chicago, University of Chicago Press, 1959.

Other

Freehand Lettering. Chicago, B.D. Berry, 1915.

Editor, with Thelma Gwinn Thurstone, Personality Schedule. Chicago, University of Chicago Press, 1929.
Editor, The Measurement of Social Attitudes. Chicago, University of Chicago Press, 1933.
Editor, Applications of Psychology: Essays to Honor Walter V. Bingham. New York, Harper, 1952.

*

Critical Study: Louis Leon Thurstone, Creative Thinker, Dedicated Teacher, Eminent Psychologist by Dorothy Adkins Wood, Princeton, New Jersey, Educational Testing Service, 1962.

*   *   *

L.L. Thurstone was a foremost contributor to the development of psychology as a quantitative, rational science. His contributions fall into several interrelated areas: theories of psychological scaling, the theory of psychological tests, and factor analysis. Factor analysis is a mathematical technique for isolating the basic dimensions in which any set of variables lie and by which they can be described in terms of a series of linear equations.

Although Thurstone was pre-eminent in the development of mathematical and statistical procedures in psychology, his work had many practical applications. His theories of psychological scaling addressed the problem of quantifying subjective judgments and resulted in the construction of scales for measuring social attitudes. He brought order to the theory of psychological tests and inspired the further development of this field. His major contribution, however, was in the development of the theory of multiple factor analysis, which was a major advance over the simpler "two-factor" theory of Charles Spearman that postulated the predominance of a general factor "g" of intelligence. He worked out the concepts of communality and of factorial invariance, and developed procedures for rotation of the reference frame to what he called "simple structure." Applying these ideas to the study of abilities, he discovered a series of "primary abilities" or factors of intelligence—chief of which were verbal, word fluency, spatial, numerical, reasoning, memory, and perceptual speed abilities. His tests of these primary abilities have been influential in programs of personnel selection and educational and vacational guidance. Thurstone's methods of factor analysis have been applied in many other fields of psychology, such as the analysis of dimensions of personality and emotion, and in fact in other disciplines such as economics and demography. His studies of fluency factors in abilities have led to much research on the measurement of creativity.

Thurstone was interested in the application of quantitative methods in many fields of psychology. He was well known for his derivation of a method for the absolute scaling of mental development; he applied quantitative methods to such diverse problems as the analysis of voting records of members of the Supreme Court and the prediction of food preferences. Collecting data on similarities of the mental profiles of twins, he contributed to the study of the genetic determination of abilities.

In collaboration with his wife, Thelma Gwinn Thurstone, over 24 years he prepared successive annual editions of the *American Council on Education Psychological Examination*, a precursor of widely used scholastic aptitude tests. His work in the study of abilities was aided by his ingenuity in the construction of novel forms of testing. His lasting achievements, however, were in the realm of quantitative theory and methodology, especially in psychophysical scaling and factor analysis.

—J.B. Carroll

TILLICH, Paul (Johannes Oskar). American theologian. Born in Starzeddel, Kreis Guben, Prussia, 20 August 1886; emigrated to the United States in 1933; naturalized, 1940. Studied at the University of Berlin, 1904-05; University of Tübingen, 1905; University of Halle, 1905-07; University of Berlin, 1908; University of Breslau, Ph.D. 1911; Licenciate in Theology, 1912; Ordained, 1912. Served as a chaplain in the German Army in World War I: Iron Cross. Married Hannah Werner in 1924; 2 children. Lecturer, University of Berlin, 1919-24; Professor of Theology, University of Marburg, 1924-25, University of Dresden, 1925-28, University of Leipzig, 1928-29, and University of Frankfurt, 1929-33 (expelled by the Nazis); Professor of Philosophy and Theology, Union Theological Seminary, New York, 1933-55; Professor of Theology, Harvard University, Cambridge, Massachusetts, 1955-62; John Nuveen Professor of Theology, University of Chicago, 1962-65. Taylor Lecturer, 1935, and Terry Lecturer, 1950, Yale University, New Haven, Connecticut; Richard Lecturer, University of Virginia, Charlot-

tesville, 1951; Firth Lecturer, University of Nottingham, 1952; Gifford Lecturer, University of Edinburgh, 1953; Foerster Lecturer, University of California, Berkeley, 1960; Bampton Lecturer, Columbia University, New York, 1962; Ingersoll Lecturer, Harvard University, 1962. Co-Founder and later Honorary President, Self-Help for Emigrés from Central Europe; Provisional Chairman, Council for a Democratic Germany. Recipient: Grosses Verdienstkreuz, West Germany, 1956; Goethe Plakette, Frankfurt, 1956; Hanseatic Goethe Prize, Hamburg, 1958; Stern zum Grossen Verdienstkreuz, West Germany, 1961; German Publishers Association Peace Prize, 1962; Academy of Religion and Mental Health award, 1962. Honorary doctorate: University of Halle, 1926; Yale University, 1940; University of Glasgow, 1951; Princeton University, New Jersey, 1953; Harvard University, 1954; University of Chicago, 1955; Clark University, Worcester, Massachusetts, 1955; Colby College, Waterville, Maine, 1955; New School for Social Research, New York, 1955; Brandeis University, Waltham, Massachusetts, 1955; Free University of Berlin, 1956; Franklin and Marshall College, Lancaster, Pennsylvania, 1956; Wesleyan University, Middletown, Connecticut, 1957; Huron College, South Dakota, 1960; Bucknell University, Lewisburg, Pennsylvania, 1960. *Died 22 October 1965.*

PUBLICATIONS

Collections

Gesammelte Werke.   Stuttgart, Evangelisches Verlagswerk, 14 vols., 1959-75.

Theology and Society

Die religionsgeschichtliche Konstruktion in Schellings positiver Philosophie, ihre Voraussetzungen und Prinzipien.   Breslau, Fleischmann, 1910; as *The Construction of the History of Religion in Schelling's Positive Philosophy: Its Presuppositions and Principles,* Lewisburg, Pennsylvania, Bucknell University Press, 1978.

Mystik und Schuldbewusstsein in Schellings philosophischer Entwicklung.   Gütersloh, Bertelsmann, 1912; as *Mysticism and Guilt Consciousness in Schelling's Philosophical Development,* Lewisburg, Pennsylvania, Bucknell University Press, 1974.

Der Begriff des Übernatürlichen, sein dialektischer Charakter und das Prinzip der Identät, dargestellt an der supernaturalistischen Theologie vor Schleiermacher.   Königsberg, Madrasch, 1915.

Der Sozialismus als Kirchenfrage.   Berlin, Gracht, 1919.

Masse und Geist: Studien zur Philosophie der Masse.   Berlin, Verlag der Arbeitsgemeinschaft, 1922.

Das System der Wissenschaften nach Gegenständen und Methoden.   Göttingen, Vandenhoeck and Ruprecht, 1923; as *The System of the Sciences According to Objects and Methods,* Lewisburg, Pennsylvania, Bucknell University Press, 1981.

Kirche und Kultur (lecture).   Tübingen, Mohr, 1924.

Die religiöse Lage der Gegenwart.   Berlin, Ullstein, 1925; as *The Religious Situation,* New York, Holt, 1932.

Das Dämonische: Ein Beitrag zur Sinndeutung der Geschichte.   Tübingen, Mohr, 1926.

Religiöse Verwicklichung.   Berlin, Furche, 1929.

Protestantisches Prinzip und proletarische Situation.   Bonn, Cohen, 1931.

Hegel und Goethe: Zwei Gedenkreden.   Tübingen, Mohr, 1932.

Die sozialistische Entscheidung.   Potsdam, Protte, 1933; as *The Socialist Decision,* New York, Harper, 1971.

The Interpretation of History.   New York and London, Scribner, 1936.

The Protestant Era.   Chicago, University of Chicago Press, 1947; London, Nisbet, 1951; as *Der Protestantismus,* Stuttgart, Steingrüben, 1950.

The Shaking of the Foundations (sermons). New York, Scribner, 1948; London, SCM Press, 1949.

Systematic Theology. Chicago, University of Chicago Press, and London, Nisbet, 3 vols., 1953-63.

The Courage to Be (lectures). New Haven, Connecticut, Yale University Press, and London, Nisbet, 1952.

Die Judenfrage, ein christliches und ein deutsches Problem (lectures). Berlin, Weiss, 1953.

Love, Power, and Justice (lectures). New York and London, Oxford University Press, 1954.

Biblical Religion and the Search for Ultimate Reality (lectures). Chicago, University of Chicago Press, 1955; London, Nisbet, 1956.

The New Being (sermons). New York, Scribner, 1955; London, SCM Press, 1956.

Die Philosophie der Macht. Berlin, Colloquium, 1956.

Dynamics of Faith. New York, Harper, 1957; London, Allen and Unwin, 1958.

Theology of Culture. New York, Oxford University Press, 1959.

Auf der Grenze: aus dem Lebenswerk Paul Tillichs. Stuttgart, Evangelisches Verlagswerke, 1962.

Symbol und Wirklichkeit. Göttingen, Vandenhoeck and Ruprecht, 1962.

Die verlorene Dimension: Not und Hoffnung unserer Zeit. Hamburg, Furche, 1962.

Morality and Beyond. New York, Harper, 1963; London, Routledge, 1964.

The Eternal Now (sermons). New York, Scribner, and London, SCM Press, 1963.

Christianity and the Encounter of the World Religions. New York, Columbia University Press, 1963.

The World Situation. Philadelphia, Fortress Press, 1965.

Ultimate Concern: Tillich in Dialogue, edited by D. Mackenzie Brown. New York, Harper, and London, SCM Press, 1965.

The Future of Religions. New York, Harper, 1966.

My Search for Absolutes. New York, Simon and Schuster, 1967.

Perspectives on 19th and 20th Century Protestant Theology, edited by Carl E. Braaten. New York, Harper, and London, SCM Press, 1967.

A History of Christian Thought. New York, Harper, and London, SCM Press, 1968.

What Is Religion?, Political Expectation (selections), edited by James L. Adams. New York, Harper, 2 vols., 1969-71.

Other

On the Boundary: An Autobiographical Sketch. New York, Scribner, 1966.

My Travel Diary: 1936: Between Two Worlds, edited by Jerald C. Brauer. New York, Harper, 1970.

Editor, *Kairos: Zur Geisteslage und Geisteswendung.* Darmstadt, Reichl, 1926.

Editor, *Protestantismus als Kritik und Gestaltung.* Darmstadt, Reichl, 1929.

*

Bibliography: in *Gesammelte Werk 14,* 1975.

Critical Studies: *Paul Tillich's Philosophy of Culture, Science, and Religion* by James L. Adams, New York, Harper, 1965; *From Time to Time* by Hannah Tillich, New York, Stein and Day, 1973; *Paul Tillich: His Life and Thought* by Wilhelm and Marion Pauck, New York, Harper, 1976; *Paul Tillich* by Carl Heinz Tatschow, Iowa City, North American Paul Tillich Society, 1980; *The Theology of Paul Tillich* edited by Charles W. Kegley, New York, Pilgrim, 2nd edition, 1982 (includes bibliography).

*   *   *

An imposing person as well as a penetrating thinker, Paul Tillich is best known for his philosophical theology, which not only introduced, into the United States, aspects of existentialist philosophy (especially its analysis of the experience of the abyss of meaninglessness) but also stands as one of the major systematic statements of Christian theology. It is based on a principle (called "the Protestant principle" or, alternatively, "the prophetic principle") which he regarded as an adaptation and expansion of the Lutheran principle of "justification by grace through faith" and on a method (called "the method of correlation") in which religious symbols are interpreted as containing answers to existential questions. In addition, he was the inaugurator of what is known as "theology of culture," that is, an interpretation of the culture of a given time with a view to formulating the theology that it indirectly expresses. This was made possible by his conception of religion as "ultimate concern," that is, the state of being unconditionally concerned about something that concerns one unconditionally (because it has to do with one's being anyone or anything at all), a definition to which the Supreme Court of the United States also appealed (*United States v. Seeger*) as the basis for exempting from military service during the Vietnam war, on grounds of conscientious objection, some persons who had no affiliation with a traditionally pacifist religious institution or with an identifiable religious community at all.

It was in philosophical theology, especially as a systematic discipline, that Tillich wrote his essays and books. His concepts and questions were taken, in large measure, from the tradition of philosophical and theological thought that begins with Immanuel Kant and Friedrich Schleiermacher. But he was especially influenced by the work of F.W.J. Schelling, whom he regarded, throughout his life, as his philosophical mentor. (By chance, the month and day of his birth—August 20—were the same as those of Schelling's death.) Nevertheless, Tillich's appropriation of such influences was original, and it is all but impossible to trace any direct lines of thought from previous thinkers in Tillich's synthesis. Fundamental to this philosophical theology is a theory of symbols, according to which symbols have a status intermediate between ideas and things—symbols are objects, persons, images, and the like, when these are spontaneously connected with meanings ("they participate in the reality to which they refer" was Tillich's characteristic way of stating the relation). Symbols thus differ, on one side, from conventional signs (in which we arbitrarily assign a meaning to a figure) and, on the other side, from mere objects (with which we do not associate any meaning at all). Equally fundamental to this theology is the conception of human existence as a "question," that is, as an existence which, by its openness (its exposure to its limits: experienced in anxiety at the prospect of having to come to an end) and by its "predicament" (its involvement in apparently self-defeating situations), points away from itself to something else to give it meaning. An existential question of this sort is like an empty symbol, because it points to a meaning but does not convey that meaning; it is then filled when it is brought into correlation with the religious symbol that conveys the meaning sought. Thus, the symbol of creation (the word and image of the world as brought into being by another, a Creator) answers the question of finitude ("What meaning makes it possible to accept the insecurity of human existence?"), and the symbol of salvation answers the question of estrangement ("What meaning makes it possible to overcome the guilt of not being what one could and should be?"). The most important symbol, corresponding to the Protestant principle, is the symbol of the cross, which bears the meaning that the unconditional (unconditional truth, unconditional virtue, and so on) can never be grasped as such: the one absolute truth is that no one possesses the absolute truth.

The idea of a theology of culture, which Tillich first set forth in detail in an essay of 1919 ("The Idea of a Theology of Culture"), was occasioned by observations that, for large numbers of people, traditional religious symbols had lost their symbolic power, not only because of literalistic misunderstanding but also because of cultural changes, and that, at the same time, works of art could evoke the responses of religious symbols. These observations indicated that, as Tillich formulated it, religion is the substance (or depth) of culture and culture is the form of religion. This formulation was intended to express a number of interrelated points: (1) there are no religious forms as such—forms of knowledge, forms of art, forms of law, forms of community are all cultural forms; (2) traced to their roots, all such forms contain something of unconditional importance, which they express indirectly—that is the religious element in them; (3) out of the whole number of forms, some can also be used to express that unconditional meaning directly—these forms constitute the religious expressions in the narrower sense of "religion." (For example, there is no moral law that is distinguished from other moral laws through being given directly by a divine being; all moral laws are on a par with respect to their morality. But in some cultures, or at some times, particular moral laws may also possess the power of expressing directly the unconditional meaning of all moral laws. When they do so, they are "religious" as well as "moral" laws, expressing the "divine will" as well as the "human good" or "human obligation.") Interpreting culture from the standpoint of the unconditional meaning it expresses as a whole is the task of a theology of culture. The method for doing so Tillich formulated in the statement that the unconditional depth, or substance, "is grasped in the content by means of the form." This statement is intended to express the fact that the way in which unconditional meaning (German: *Gehalt*) is made known in the work of art is that the content of the work becomes indifferent because what the form (that is, the esthetic work itself as well as its particular subject matter) is seeking to shape is not the ordinary esthetic content but the unconditional meaning (or what Tillich later called "ultimate concern") which is "breaking into" the form even though it cannot be contained by the form. Tillich did not think of this kind of analysis as applicable to cultural works in isolation, but he thought that, when applied to the ensemble of works typical of a given culture, it could yield a formulation of the theology indirectly expressed by the culture.

Besides the idea of a theology of culture, there are several concepts that Tillich worked out and made current. Two of them pertain to the philosophy of history: "kairos" and "the demonic." (1) "Kairos" (the Greek word for "ripe time," in contrast to *Chronos*, or sequential time) refers to the fact that new things are possible only when the time is ripe for them. Tillich first applied this notion to the German situation in the 1920's, when he thought that the time was ripe for creating a new social order (called "religious socialism" and opposed to "national socialism") to replace the mixture of feudal and capitalist orders then coming to an end. Beyond this application, however, Tillich also introduced the idea into epistemological theory, by analyzing how, even in objective science, there is an element of timing involved, an element which is recognized in such professions as politics and counseling but a fact which hitherto had not been systematically incorporated into a theory of knowledge. Tillich undertook to incorporate it into that theory as the "third dimension" of knowledge—knowledge, then, has form and content but also "time." (2) "The demonic" was a category applied to certain actual powers which are characterized by their having a creativity that in the end is destructive. Tillich subsumed both the divine and the demonic under the category of the holy: both are creative (hence the demonic can be confused with the divine, as happened in the early years of National Socialism in Germany) and both are destructive, but the difference is that the demonic creates forms only for the purpose of destroying, whereas the divine destroys existing forms for the purpose of creating new ones.

—Robert P. Scharlemann

TINBERGEN, Jan. Dutch economist. Born in The Hague, 12 April 1903. Studied at the University of Leiden, Ph.D. 1929. Married Tine Johanna De Wit in 1929; 4 children. Business Cycle Statistician, Central Bureau of Statistics, The Hague, 1929-36, 1938-45, and the League of Nations, Geneva, 1936-38; Director, Netherlands Economic Institute, Rotterdam, 1933-68; Director, Central Planning Office, The Hague, 1944-45. Since 1955, Professor of Development Planning, Netherlands School of Economics, Rotterdam. Chairman, United Nations Development Planning Committee, 1965-72. Recipient: Erasmus Prize, 1967; Nobel Prize in Economics (jointly), 1969. Member, Netherlands Academy of Sciences; Econometric Society; American Economic Association; American Statistical Association. Officer, Order of the Lion. Commander, Order of Orange Nassau. Address: Haviklaan 31, 2566XD The Hague, Netherlands.

PUBLICATIONS

Economics

Minimumproblemen in de natuurkunde en de ekonomie [Minimal Problems in the Natural Sciences and Economics]. Amsterdam, J.H. Paris, 1929.
De konjuktuur [The Business Situation]. Amsterdam, Arbeiderspers, 1934.
Grondproblemen der theoretische statistiek [Basic Problems of Theoretical Statistics]. Haarlem, Bohn, 1936.
An Economic Approach to Business Cycle Problems. Paris, Hermann, 1937.
Les Fondements mathématiques de la stabilisation du mouvement des affaires. Paris, Hermann, 1938.
Statistical Testing of Business Cycle Theories: vol. 1: *A Method and Its Application to Investment Activity*; vol. 2: *Business Cycles in the United States of America 1919-1932.* Geneva, League of Nations, 1939.
Technische ontwikkeling en werkgelegenheid [Technical Developments in Employment Opportunities]. Amsterdam, North Holland, 1940.
Econometrie. Gorinchem, Noorduijn, 1941; as *Econometrics*, London, Allen and Unwin, and New York, Blakiston, 1951.
Economische bewegingsleer. Amsterdam, North Holland, 1943; as *The Dynamics of Business Cycles: A Study in Economic Fluctuations*, adapted by J.J. Polak, London, Routledge, and Chicago, University of Chicago Press, 1950.
De las van dertig jaar: Economische evaringen en mogelijkheden [The Lesson of Thirty Years: Economic Experiences and Opportunities]. Amsterdam, Elsevier, 1944.
International Economic Co-operation. Amsterdam and New York, Elsevier, 1945; revised edition, as *International Economic Integration*, 1954.
Redelijke inkonstenverdeling [Reasonable Income-distribution]. Haarlem, De Gulden Pers, 1946.
Beperkte concurrentie [Limited Competition]. Leiden, Kroese, 1946.
Business Cycles in the United Kingdom, 1870-1914. Amsterdam, North Holland, 1951.
On the Theory of Economic Policy. Amsterdam, North Holland, 1952.
The Design of Development. Baltimore, Johns Hopkins University Press, 1953.
Centralization and Decentralization in Economic Policy. Amsterdam, North Holland, 1954.
Economic Policy: Principles and Design. Amsterdam, North Holland, 1956.
Selected Papers, edited by L.H. Klaassen and others. Amsterdam, North Holland, 1959 (contains a bibliography).
De optimale organisatie der economische beslissingen [The Optimal Organization of Decisions]. Amsterdam, North Holland, 1961.
Shaping the World Economy: Suggestions for an International

Economic Policy. New York, Twentieth Century Fund, 1962.

Mathematical Models of Economic Growth, with Hendricus C. Bos. New York, McGraw Hill, 1962.

Lessons from the Past. Amsterdam and New York, Elsevier, 1963.

Central Planning. New Haven, Connecticut, Yale University Press, 1964.

Essays in Regional and World Planning. New Delhi, National Council of Applied Economic Research, 1966.

Ontwikkelingsplannen. Amsterdam, Meulenhoff, 1967; as *Developmental Planning,* London, Weidenfeld and Nicolson, and New York, McGraw Hill, 1967.

The Element of Space in Development Planning, with L.B.M. Mennes. Amsterdam, North Holland, 1969.

Een leefbares aarde [A Liveable Way]. Amsterdam, Elsevier, 1970.

Meten in de menswetenschappen [Measurements in Anthropology]. Assen, Van Gorcum, 1971.

Politique économique et optimum social (selected essays). Paris, Economica, 1972.

Possible Futures of European Education: Numerical and System's Forecasts, with Stefan Jensen. The Hague, Nijhoff, 1972.

Income Distribution: Analysis and Policies. Amsterdam, North Holland, 1975.

Income Differences: Recent Research. Amsterdam, North Holland, 1975.

Maatschappelijke alternatievan [Corporate Alternatives], with C.J. Cramwinckel-Weeda. Meppel, Boom, 1977.

Other

Editor, *Recueil international de statistiques économiques, 1919-1930.* The Hague, International Statistical Institute, 1934.
Editor, with others, *Contributions to Economic Analysis.* Amsterdam, North Holland, 1952.
Editor, with Kurt Dopfer, *Economics in the Future: Towards a New Paradigm.* Boulder, Colorado, Westview Press, 1972.

*

Bibliography: in *Selected Papers,* 1959.

Critical Study: *Jan Tinbergen, de eerste Nobelprijswinnaar Economie* by E. van Rompuy, Antwerp, Nederlandsche Boekhandel, 1974.

*   *   *

Jan Tinbergen, co-winner (with Ragnar Frisch) of the first Nobel Prize in economics, has contributed to the development of economic science in an uncommonly broad range of areas. These include international trade, economic development, econometrics, macroeconomic modelling, the theory of economic policy, and the distribution of income, among others. The unifying themes running through this vast body of work are his concern with important real world economic problems, his insistence on formulating his theories in a way that would make them empirically testable and useful, and his determination actually to confront theory with empirical data. Though well versed in the tools of mathematics, statistics, and economic theory, Tinbergen is little impressed with theoretical elegance for its own sake. Never content to prove neat theorems with limited practical relevance, or to postpone study of a problem until an ideal data set became available, he has boldly attacked problems others viewed as intractable, and frequently made giant strides toward their solutions. The discussion that follows attempts to summarize some of his most important contributions.

Tinbergen is probably best known for his pioneering work in developing statistical models of the macroeconomy. This work began in the world-wide depression of the 1930's, and aimed ultimately at improving policy-making by providing a basis for quantitative predictions of the effects of policy. His initial contribution came in a paper on the hog cycle, explaining the tendency of prices and quantities to fluctuate in opposite directions in this market. Tinbergen pointed out that this finding, seemingly inconsistent with the theory of supply, could be readily explained if supply was treated as a function of the price *in the previous year.* Though initially applied to this relatively simple case, the type of analysis—in which current economic variables are treated as functions of past values of other variables—has had profound implications for models of business cycles. Previous cycle theories had generally looked for separate explanations for each phase of the cycle. Tinbergen's work showed the possibility of explaining the complete cycle as a consequence of the natural workings of a dynamic economic model.

His approach was applied most innovatively and influentially in his 1939 study done for the League of Nations, *Business Cycles in the United States of America 1919-32.* This study set out, estimated, and analyzed a complete 48 equation model of the United States economy. Along with its companion volume, *A Method and its Application to Investment Activity,* it has been called "the undisputed monument of early empirical macroeconomic model building and theory testing." Although statistical techniques, data gathering, and economic theory have improved considerably in the time since, all current macroeconomic models owe a tremendous debt to Tinbergen's work.

During his term as director of the Dutch Central Planning Bureau, Tinbergen continued to work on the problem of macroeconomic modelling, concentrating even more on the use of such models for forecasting and analyzing the effects of policies. At the same time he became interested in the question of what optimal government policies are in a world of multiple objectives and multiple policy instruments. Drawing on the work of Frisch, Tinbergen developed the "theory of economic policy," in which he explored the implications of variations in the relative numbers of objectives (targets) and instruments, the possibilities for decentralization of policy decisions, and other matters. Though perhaps less elegant than theoretical welfare economics, this theory has proven more readily applicable to actual policy problems, and has stimulated considerable further work by other researchers.

Throughout his career, and particularly since he retired from the Central Planning Bureau in 1955, Tinbergen has taken a special interest in the problems of the poor. His efforts in this regard have not been limited to scientific research, but have included writing and lecturing to more general audiences, and consulting work for international organizations and developing countries. He has, however, also contributed significantly to the study of income distribution and development planning. In the latter area, Tinbergen has once again been a pioneer in the development of quantitative techniques suited to empirical implementation.

—John Goddeeris

TITCHENER, Edward Bradford. British psychologist. Born in Chichester, 11 January 1867; emigrated to the United States in 1892. Studied at Brasenose College, Oxford, B.A. 1890, M.A. 1895; University of Leipzig, Ph.D. 1892. Married Sophie Kellogg Bedlow in 1894; 4 children. Research Student in physiology, 1889-90, and Extension Lecturer in biology, 1892, Oxford University; Assistant Professor, 1892-95, Sage Professor, 1895-1910, and Sage Professor of Psychology, Graduate School, 1910-27, Cornell University, Ithaca, New York. Visiting Lecturer, Columbia University, New York, 1907-08; University of Illinois, Urbana, 1909; Lowell Institute, Massachusetts, 1911. American editor of *Mind,* 1894-1920; Associate Editor, 1895-1921, and

Editor, 1921-25, *American Journal of Psychology*. Foreign Member, Polish Academy of Arts and Sciences. Fellow, Zoological Society of London; Royal Society of Medicine, London; and American Academy of Arts and Sciences. *Died 3 August 1927.*

PUBLICATIONS

Psychology

An Outline of Psychology.   New York, Macmillan, 1896.
A Primer of Psychology.   New York, Macmillan, 1898.
Experimental Psychology: A Manual of Laboratory Practice. New York, Macmillan, 2 vols., 1901-05.
Lectures on the Elementary Psychology of Feeling and Attention. New York, Macmillan, 1908.
A Text-book of Psychology.   New York, Macmillan, 2 vols., 1909-10.
Lectures on the Experimental Psychology of Thought Processes. New York, Macmillan, 1909.
A Beginner's Psychology.   New York, Macmillan, 1915.
Systematic Psychology: Prolegomena.   New York, Macmillan, 1929.

Other

Translator, with J.E. Creighton, *Lectures on Human and Animal Psychology*, by Wilhelm Wundt.   New York, Macmillan, and London, Sonnenschein, 1894.
Translator, *Ethics*, by Wilhelm Wundt.   New York, Macmillan, and London, Sonnenschein, 1901.
Translator, with W. Pillsbury, *Introduction to Philosophy*, by Oswald Külpe.   New York, Macmillan, and London, Sonnenschein, 1901.
Translator, *Outlines of Psychology*, by Oswald Külpe.   New York, Macmillan, and London, Sonnenschein, 1901.
Translator, *Principles of Physiological Psychology*, by Wilhelm Wundt.   New York, Macmillan, and London, Sonnenschein, 1910.

*   *   *

Edward Bradford Titchener studied philosophy and classics at Oxford, working there as a research assistant in physiology before moving to Leipzig, where he studied psychology under the direction of Wilhelm Wundt. Wundt's impression upon Titchener would be carried throughout Titchener's professional life. He remained committed to Wundt's principles of empiricism (experimentation) and introspection and moved beyond Wundt's psychology to develop his own structural psychology, often interjecting his own interpretations of Wundt which others questioned.

Earning his degree in 1892, Titchener returned to Oxford where he lectured briefly in biology before accepting a position in psychology at Cornell University, where he was to remain until his death. At Cornell he replaced his friend from Leipzig, James Angell (who moved to Stanford University), and took over his laboratory, fashioning it into a major center of psychological research in the United States. During his most productive years, the first two decades of his residence, he presented in his own work and that of his students what he considered the "psychological point of view," what others were later to critique as a structuralist or existentialist psychology. The behavioralist and functionalist currents which came to dominate American psychological research hastened Titchener's alienation from the emerging discipline. Social and professional isolation marked his later years. His productivity declined as well, although he continued to be revered as a pioneer in American psychology and became a legend at Cornell.

Titchener's accomplishents were numerous and major: he represented a conduit of European developments to work in the United States, translating several editions of Wundt's books on psychology. His *Outline of Psychology, A Primer of Psychology*, and the four volumes of *Experimental Psychology* established his own positions concerning the realm of psychology vis-à-vis other areas of scientific inquiry. During the same years he participated personally in the extensive research undertakings in his laboratory (including several dozen doctorates) and wrote, or influenced the publication of, numerous articles, mainly concerned with sensation, perception, memory, and attention. In later years he advanced his point of view in *A Text-book of Psychology* and attempted to systemize his approach in a new work which was never finished, though published posthumously as *Systematic Psychology* (1929).

Titchener's professional posture was consistent and provocative. Though he formed a group called the "experimentalists" in 1904 he kept it as his own. Elected an associate editor of the *American Journal of Psychology* in 1895, he became its sole editor in 1921 and the *Journal* became his platform. Elected to the American Psychological Association upon his arrival in the United States, he resigned almost immediately in a dispute over professional ethics and was never again close to the association.

Titchener's "psychological point of view" held that the rigorous analysis of conscious experience was the sole legitimate arena of psychological research. He admitted the charge of being a structuralist in the sense that he felt the study of the structure of mental processes should precede functional questions. However, the major juxtaposition in his thought was between the study of experience (i.e., "psychology") and the mounting attention of American psychology to "behavior," which he felt was outside the arena of psychology. In methodology Titchener stressed experimentation in the analysis of conscious experience and introspection as the experimental framework where experience was dependent on the experiencing individual to the exclusion of outside interference. Psychology dealt with questions of "what" and "why." Sensation represented the core of perception within the unconscious context. Titchener also stressed the duality of sensation and perception. The study of images as the elements of ideas and emotions was a central aspect of this system.

It was Titchener's belief that introspection was the proper research method and that it took trained observers to perform this task. He thought that psychology should be the study of three elements which form the basic structure of consciousness: images, thoughts, and feelings. He did not believe that learning, intelligence, motivation, personality, or abnormal or social behavior were part of psychology. He attacked Robert S. Woodworth and others who thought that thinking could occur without images and sensations. Titchener maintained the view that conscious attitudes, feelings of relationship, and mental sets were not new types of thought elements but were actually kinesthetic (muscular) sensations or images. Today, most psychologists have decided against Titchener and believe that thinking is a process based on many different types of cues from previous experience.

Like William James, Titchener stressed the contrast between focal and marginal consciousness. That is, when we "pay attention" to anything we bring it to the focus of our consciousness. All other information is relegated to the fringe. The focus then demands a high level of attention while the fringe is at a low level. One of his pupils, Ludwig R. Geissler, believed that many individuals had more than two levels: some of his subjects actually claimed that they could distinguish three or more.

Titchener also extended Wundt's "tri-dimensional theory of emotions." Wundt proposed that all feelings had three aspects: pleasantness or unpleasantness; excitement or quiet; and tension or relaxation. A feeling could be pleasant, relaxed, and quiet, or it could be unpleasant, excited, and tense. In experimenting with his subjects, Titchener found that they had difficulty identifying these "dimensions" of feeling and instead proposed that the only real dimension was that traditional classification of pleasant-unpleasant. Other experience such as "excitement" he attributed to romantic phenomena and not feelings.

Although Titchener held the opinion that all scientists are concerned with some aspect of human experience, he felt that psychologists were unique in that they were able to view it as though they were a part of it. Elements of nature are, to most, experienced as a set of datum in consciousness. From Titchener's point of view the datum was not important; what was important was the process of experiencing the datum. If a subject describes an object in "ordinary" terminology he has committed what Titchener termed a "stimulus error," that is, the subject has failed introspectively to report the conscious content of the experience.

It has been argued that Titchener refused to reconcile himself to the broadening of his field, but his posture would seem to have been more one of principle than professional attachment. Clearly he strengthened the roots of psychology as it developed into new areas in the United States.

—R.W. Rieber

TOLMAN, E(dward) C(hace). American psychologist. Born in West Newton, Massachusetts, 14 April, 1886. Studied at the Massachusetts Institute of Technology, Cambridge, B.S. 1911; Harvard University, Cambridge, Massachusetts, M.A. 1912, Ph.D. 1915. Married Kathleen Drew in 1915; 3 children. Instructor, Northwestern University, Evanston, Illinois, 1915-18; Instructor, 1918-20, Assistant Professor, 1920-23, Associate Professor, 1923-28, Professor of Psychology, 1928-54, and Professor Emeritus, 1954-59, University of California, Berkeley. President, American Psychological Association, 1937; Chairman, Society for the Psychological Study of Social Issues, 1940. Honorary doctorate: Yale University, New Haven, Connecticut, 1951; McGill University, Montreal, 1954; University of California, 1959. Member, National Academy of Sciences; Fellow, American Academy of Arts and Sciences. Honorary Fellow, British Psychological Society. *Died 19 November 1959.*

PUBLICATIONS

Psychology

Retroactive Inhibition as Affected by Conditions of Learning. Princeton, New Jersey, Psychological Review Company, 1917.
Purposive Behavior in Animals and Men. New York, Century, 1932.
Drives Toward War. New York, Appleton Century, 1942.
The Wants of Men. Berkeley, University of California Press, 1948.
The Psychology of Learning. New York, Association Press, 1949.
Behavior and Psychological Man: Collected Papers in Psychology. Berkeley, University of California Press, 1951.

*   *   *

E.C. Tolman's most important contribution to 20th-century psychology derives from his purposive behavior approach to learning. Tolman's theory was an attempt to synthesize the ideas of behavioristic and Gestalt psychologists. With others such as Hull and Guthrie, Tolman considered himself a behaviorist because of his rejection of the introspective method, his use of measurable stimulus and response terms, and his willingness to formulate principles of learning from research conducted mainly with animals. However, by adopting the data language of Gestalt theory to interpret animal and human experiments, Tolman placed himself in direct opposition to the mainstream behavioristic theorizing of the time which took the writings of Thorndike and Watson as its foundation. Yet, the rivalry which ensued eventually led to the clarification of important theoretical and empirical issues, and became a major impetus for the later development of cognitive psychology as an experimental science.

Major statements of Tolman's position are contained in his 1932 book, *Purposive Behavior in Animals and Men,* and in a later (1938) paper titled "The Determiners of Behavior at a Choice Point." In these works, Tolman introduced his new terminology and set forth a theoretical account of animal learning research. Tolman believed that because behavior was purposive or goal-directed, the behavior act itself (e.g., a rat running a maze, a person driving a car) was the proper unit of analysis and not the sequence of muscle, glandular, or neural processes which comprised the act. This emphasis on the behavior act and its docility (teachableness) constituted the basis for his distinction between molar vs molecular behaviorism. Tolman also believed that organisms learn central (sign-significate or S-S) and not peripheral (stimulus-response or S-R) relations; they learn "what leads to what." These expectations are cognitive events which are organized into a map of the environment, and it is this map which eventually determines the responses the animal will make.

For Tolman, a theory was simply a set of intervening variables or behavior determinants which helped a theorist relate interdependent (manipulated) and dependent (measured) variables. For example, to predict whether a rat will turn left at a choice point in a maze, we need to understand (1) how certain independent variables (e.g., previous experience with similar situations, maintenance schedule, appropriateness of goal object) relate to their corresponding intervening variables (e.g., hypotheses, demands, appetites), and (2) how these hypotheses, demands, and appetites are then translated into overt behavior. In attempting to understand this translation, Tolman was not afraid to anthropomorphise: "...I in my future work intend to go ahead imagining how, if I were a rat, I would behave as a result of such and such demand combined with such and such an appetite..." ("The Determiners of Behavior at a Choice Point," *Psychological Review,* 1938).

Several kinds of investigations were derived from the theory. In one series of studies, Tolman demonstrated that maze learning could occur in the absence of food reward, a finding that presumably contradicted the early S-R assumption that reinforcement was necessary for learning. In one variation of these so-called latent learning experiments, rats were first allowed to explore a maze without food being present. When food was later introduced, the rats found the shortest path to the reward faster than a second group who had no prior experience with the maze. According to Tolman, the rats in the first group gained knowledge of the maze (i.e., learned) during the exploration trials, and such learning was later observed when a motivator was introduced. These studies led Tolman to make the important distinction between learning and performance, the former being a function of contiguity alone and the latter dependent upon the presence of reinforcement.

A second series of investigations, referred to as tests of place vs. response learning, showed that rats learned the location of rewards and not the sequence of movements leading to rewards. For example, in a variation of the so-called "spatial orientation" experiment, a familiarized path to a goal was blocked and a series of radiating paths were added. After briefly exploring the initial segments of the new paths, the rats displayed a strong tendency to choose the path which led to the vicinity of the original food box. Tolman believed that such results implied that the rats had initially acquired a broad spatial map of the food environment which subsequently allowed them to select an alternate path to the goal.

Tolman also must be credited with having played a significant role in other areas of research, including vicarious trial and error (VTE) behavior and hypothesis testing. The first of these refers to various responses displayed by a rat at a choice point in a maze, such as hesitation and vacillation. Tolman showed that VTEing always aided learning, and he believed that such behavior lent support to his views that animals were always active and selective during the course of acquisition. Tolman further believed that animals had provisional expectancies about a learning problem and that such hypotheses were revealed in systematic patterns of responding prior to solution. Since shifts in these patterns appeared to be abrupt, Tolman interpreted the data as providing evidence for a discontinuity (one-trial) as opposed to a continuity (gradual) view of learning.

Tolman had many critics, most of whom objected to his use of mentalistic terms and pointed to his unsuccessful attempt to develop a logically integrated system. Yet, many of Tolman's ideas have outlived those of his critics. Certainly, Tolman would have been pleased with the meteoric rise of "cognitive psychology" in the last two decades and its dominant influence on contemporary experimental psychology.

—Seymore Simon

TOULMIN, Stephen E(delston). British philosopher and historian of ideas. Born in London, 25 March 1922. Studied at Cambridge University, B.A., M.A. 1946, Ph.D. 1948 (Research Fellow, King's College, 1947-51). Junior Scientific Officer, British Ministry of Aircraft Production, 1942-45. Lecturer in the philosophy of science, Oxford University, 1949-55; Professor of Philosophy, University of Leeds, 1955-59; Director, Unit for the History of Ideas, Nuffield Foundation, London, 1960-64; Professor of History of Ideas and Philosophy, Brandeis University, Waltham, Massachusetts, 1965-69; Professor of Philosophy, Michigan State University, East Lansing, 1969-72; Provost of Crown College and Professor of Philosophy, University of California at Santa Cruz, 1972-73. Since 1973, Professor, Committee on Social Thought, University of Chicago. Visiting Lecturer, University of Melbourne, 1954-55; Visiting Professor, New York University, 1959, and Columbia University, New York, 1959-60; Phi Beta Kappa Lecturer, 1978. Councillor, Smithsonian Institution, Washington, D.C. 1967-76. Recipient: Guggenheim Fellowship, 1975. Address: Committee on Social Thought, University of Chicago, Chicago, Illinois, 60637, U.S.A.

PUBLICATIONS

Philosophy

An Examination of the Place of Reason in Ethics. London, Cambridge University Press, 1950.
The Philosophy of Science: An Introduction. London, Hutchinson, and New York, Rinehart, 1953.
Metaphysical Beliefs: Three Essays, with others. London, SCM Press, 1957.
The Uses of Argument. London, Cambridge University Press, 1958.
Foresight and Understanding: An Enquiry into the Aims of Science. Bloomington, Indiana University Press, 1961.
Seventeenth-Century Science and the Arts, with others. Princeton, New Jersey, Princeton University Press, 1961.
The Ancestry of Science, with June Goodfield: vol. 1, *The Fabric of the Heavens: The Development of Astronomy and Dynamics,* London, Hutchinson, 1961; New York, Harper, 1962; vol. 2, *The Architecture of Matter,* London, Hutchinson, 1962; New York, Harper, 1963; vol. 3, *The Discovery of Time,* New York, Harper, 1965.
Human Understanding: vol. 1, *The Collective Use and Development of Concepts.* Princeton, New Jersey, Princeton University Press, 1972.
Wittgenstein's Vienna, with Allan Janik. New York, Simon and Schuster, 1973.
Knowing and Acting: An Introduction to Philosophy. New York, Macmillan, 1976.
An Introduction to Reasoning, with Allan Janik and R. Rieke. New York, Macmillan, 1979.
The Inwardness of Mental Life (lecture). Chicago, Center for Policy Study, 1979.

Other

Night Sky at Rhodes. London, Methuen, 1963; New York, Harcourt Brace, 1964.

Editor, *Physical Reality: Philosophical Papers on Twentieth-Century Physics.* New York, Harper, 1970.
Editor, *What I Do Not Believe, and Other Essays,* by Norwood Russell Hanson. Dordrecht, Reidel, 1972.

*

Critical Study: *Moral Reasoning: A Study in the Moral Philosophy of Stephen E. Toulmin* by Tore Nilstun, Lund, Studentlitteratur, 1979.

*   *   *

Throughout his philosophical career, Stephen E. Toulmin has shown remarkable breadth of interest, independence of thought, an almost preternatural foresight. Never precisely in step with his colleagues, he has in retrospect typically been *ahead* of them, pointing the way for future thought in such disparate areas as ethics, logic, epistemology, history of ideas, and especially philosophy of science. Though in matters of detail his many works have encountered their fair share of criticism, as regards general themes they have consistently foreshadowed the movement of recent Anglo-American philosophical thought. Although Toulmin himself has generously disavowed credit for some of the influence attributed to his work, particularly as regards the eclipse of logical positivist philosophy of science, it is quite possible that future historians will count him among the prototypic thinkers of the mid-20th century.

The central thrust of Toulmin's thought has been *against* the formal, axiomatic, purely "analytic" methods that have dominated much of 20th century philosophy (and thought in general) and *towards* more empirical, historical, "substantive" concerns. The central problem situation within which he has worked is succinctly expressed by his own reference to "the end of the Parmenidean era"—that is, the downfall of belief (and of the intellectual and emotional conditions of belief) in a static, unchanging universe which can (at least potentially) be understood once and for all by means of necessary and universal laws. Confronted by this downfall, Toulmin has attempted to establish a new conceptual and methodological framework within which it will be possible "to make sense of" the post-Rankean, post-Darwinian, post-Einsteinian world in which dynamics is "of the essence." In trying to fulfill this task, he has had to redefine such basic concepts as rationality itself, and to make room for modes of thought that defy traditional philosophical criteria for inductive and deductive propriety. Indeed, in his estimation, innumerable patterns of thought deserve to be designated as "rational" even though they cannot yield certain or even final conclusions. At the core, for Toulmin, human understanding—whether in ethics, science, medicine, law, or any other realm—is simply, but marvelously, a finite, on-going process of cognitive adjustment to the ever-new "demands" placed upon individuals by their changing life-situations (which may or may not include "situations" in "intellectual disciplines").

Toulmin's elaboration of this viewpoint has been creative and original, but he has always acknowledged his indebtedness to other philosophers and scholars. Two of these debts—to R.G. Collingwood and Ludwig Wittgenstein—deserve particular attention. Toulmin encountered both of these philosophers firsthand during his years of education at Cambridge University in the 1940's, and the trajectory of his own thinking has reflected their joint impact ever since. Collingwood, whom Toulmin has described as "a philosopher of talent and enthusiasm who also wrote first-class professional history," impressed upon Toulmin both the basic historicity of human thought and the basic danger inherent in historical analysis. At the same time that he convinced Toulmin that historically situated conceptual "presuppositions" underlie all instances of human understanding, he also illustrated in his own work what for Toulmin is an unwarranted epistemological relativism that can result from such an historicist pattern. In this way Collingwood provoked Toulmin's own long-range task, which can be restated as the quest for an historical view of human understanding which admits conceptual change (relativity) without sanctioning intellectual anarchism (relativism). Although Collingwood himself wrote at a time when historicism of any sort was anathema to philosophers, Toulmin could claim in 1958—a bit before the actual flowering of the new historical sensitivity among philosophers—that "we can now look with new sympathy on Collingwood's vision of philosophy as a study of the methods of argument which at any historical moment have served as the ultimate Court of Appeal in different intellectual disciplines." That is precisely the vision of philosophy that had been guiding Toulmin since the early 1950's, and that he is still following—with notable amendations—to this day.

Wittgenstein not only corroborated with Collingwood's influence on Toulmin, he also provided the intellectual framework within which Toulmin has striven to fulfill his task. In the most important respect, then, he served as Toulmin's mentor, though he never acted as his primary academic advisor. At the time of his contact with Toulmin, Wittgenstein was in his celebrated (and controversial) "later period" during which he had turned his attention to the contextual factors bearing upon the meaning and use of language, broadly conceived. Having given up his earlier, simpler view of language-meaning as based upon direct "pictorial representations," he was then pondering the complex relations between the tangible "forms of life" and the particular "language games" of distinctive linguistic communities. In this new "functional" analysis of language, Wittgenstein was arguing that the intelligibility of any language depended upon enculturation within the particular mode of life that had been the occasion of that language's existence. However, he also maintained, as in his "earlier" phase, that the realm of ethics lay beyond the reach of any "linguistic," or rational interpretation. Showing indebtedness and independence at the same time, Toulmin's doctoral thesis presented a "Wittgensteinian" analysis of ethical arguments, asserting that "good" and "bad" reasoning (if not formal induction and deduction) characterize the area of ethics as much as any other realm.

After publishing this thesis, entitled *An Examination of the Place of Reason in Ethics*, Toulmin turned his attention to the realm of science. One former student of Wittgenstein, W.H. Watson, had already applied Wittgenstein's "later" view of language in an analysis of scientific language, or more precisely, scientific "methods of representation." Toulmin extended this application, thus setting the foundation for all his subsequent work in the philosophy of science. The following, more recent quotation provides a glimpse of this foundation:

> when I began lecturing at Oxford in 1950...I sought...to extend and reapply Wittgenstein's analysis of "language games" and "methods of representation" to the life and work of natural science: showing, as best I could, how the actual "language games" operative in that life are in fact played, and so indicating how—and why—the more formal "inductive logic" approach presupposed by English logicians since the time of J.S. Mill missed the serious philosophical points that arise in the course of scientific work. Scientific theories and scientific explanations (I argued) in practice employ "representations" of many different kinds, and they can be usefully analyzed as

deductive or axiomatic systems only in special cases and on special conditions. Rather than allowing the axiomatic method of analysis any monopoly, what was most needed was a functional taxonomy of explanatory procedures and techniques which would relate these procedures to the problematics of different kinds of scientific inquiry.

This initial excursion into the philosophy of science resulted in *The Philosophy of Science: An Introduction*. Soon thereafter, in *The Uses of Argument*, Toulmin applied the same "linguistic" approach directly to the discipline of logic and, by implication and brief discussion, to the discipline of epistemology. In both areas Toulmin argued for the primacy and relevance of an analysis of the actual *use* of reason in place of the typical theoretical analysis of the ideal nature of "proper" reasoning. As a prototype of human reasoning, he proposed "the common law, or jurisprudence, model" in which empirical evidence and precedents are used as the basis for reasoning and argumentation. Neither inductive nor deductive in a strict sense, legal reasoning and courtroom argumentation proceed from "facts" and "principles" without any pretense that some algorithmic formula of justice exists. The goal in jurisprudence is the presentation and acceptance of the *best possible* argument, given the facts, precedents, and principles at hand and the ultimate goal of justice. Optimally, all human understanding, according to Toulmin, comes to be in this way, as a result of the best reasoning possible at a given time, and often with the truth (rather than justice) as its ultimate goal.

All of this fitted well with Collingwood's historicist thesis, except that it left out any real historical analysis of the actual *development* of "languages" and language communities (such as scientific disciplines). In essence, Toulmin's more recent work in the philosophy of science has been an extension of Wittgenstein's late thought in a direction influenced by his contact with Collingwood. Although Wittgenstein himself was uninterested in such analyses, Toulmin believes that "we are now entitled to pursue, further than Wittgenstein himself ever did, the functional considerations underlying the *historical* development of our rational methods and modes of thought, in different fields of life and inquiry." Based upon preliminary sketches presented in *Foresight and Understanding: An Inquiry into the Aims of Science* and in various articles, and based upon more than a decade of historical research (which is reflected in three co-authored books on the history of science), Toulmin published the first volume of his major work, *Human Understanding*, in 1972. Described by Toulmin himself as a work "moving by the way of the history of science into the borderland between epistemology and the sociology of knowledge," this volume presents Toulmin's seasoned analysis of the historical development of the procedures and concepts that guide human understanding, particularly but not exclusively in the scientific disciplines. The central features of this analysis are Toulmin's continued focus upon the actual *use* of concepts and his articulation of an explicitly "Darwinian" analysis of the evolution of concepts. The term "intellectual ecology" captures the thrust of Toulmin's analytic approach, according to which certain concepts in any given "population" of concepts (say, in a scientific discipline) are better "adapted" to the current "demands" of the intellectual and social environment and are therefore used more often and thus perpetuated; but as the "demands" (problem situation) of the given area change, the survival value of these concepts may decrease and that of others increase. Thus occurs conceptual evolution, which is guided throughout by "rationality," defined simply as the adaptation of the procedures and patterns of argument to the "demands" of changing problems.

In future installments to *Human Understanding*, Toulmin plans to extend his treatment of conceptual "growth" to include analyses of the "grasp" of concepts by individuals (concept acquisition) and the "worth" of concepts (judgements of value). When completed, Toulmin's work promises to be one of the major contemporary statements on the nature of human understanding. Whatever its flaws in detail (e.g., regarding the specifics of Toulmin's evolutionary model of conceptual change), *Human Understanding* will certainly provide a platform for future conceptual development in a variety of disciplines.

—David E. Leary

TOWNES, Charles H(ard). American physicist. Born in Greenville, South Carolina, 28 July, 1915. Studied at Furman University, Greenville, B.S. 1935; Duke University, Durham, North Carolina, M.A. 1937; California Institute of Technology, Pasadena, Ph.D. 1939. Married Frances H. Brown in 1941; 4 children. Staff Member, Bell Telephone Laboratory, 1939-47; Associate Professor, 1948-50, and Professor of Physics, 1950-61, Columbia University, New York (Executive Director, Columbia Radiation Laboratory, 1950-52, and Chairman of the Physics Department, 1952-55); Provost and Professor of Physics, 1961-66, and Institute Professor, 1966-67, Massachusetts Institute of Technology, Cambridge. Since 1967, University Professor, University of California, Berkeley. Fulbright Lecturer, University of Paris, 1955-56, and University of Tokyo, 1956; Lecturer, 1950, 1955, and Director, 1963, Enrico Fermi International School of Physics; Scott Lecturer, Cambridge University, 1963; Centennial Lecturer, University of Toronto, 1967; Lincoln Lecturer, 1972-73; Halley Lecturer, 1976. Vice-President and Director of Research, Institute of Defense Analyses, Washington, D.C., 1959-61; Chairman, Science and Technology Advisory Committee for Manned Space Flight, NASA, 1964-69; Member, President's Science Advisory Commission, 1966-69 (Vice-Chairman, 1967-69); Member, President's Commission on Science and Technology, 1976. Trustee, California Institute of Technology and Carnegie Institution of Washington. President, American Physics Society, 1967. Recipient: Guggenheim Fellowship, 1955; Comstock Award, National Academy of Sciences, 1959; Stuart Ballantine Medal, Franklin Institute, 1959, 1962; Thomas Young Medal and Prize, Institute of Physics and Physics Society, England, 1963; Nobel Prize in Physics, 1964; Mees Medal, Optical Society of America, 1968; Distinguished Public Service Medal, NASA, 1969; Wilhelm Exner Award, Austria, 1970; Plyler Prize, American Physics Society, 1977; Niels Bohr International Gold Medal, 1979. Named to National Inventors Hall of Fame, 1976. Fellow, Optical Society of America, and American Physics Society. Member, American Academy of Arts and Sciences, and National Academy of Sciences. Foreign Member, Royal Society, London; Member, Société Francaise de Physique. Address: Department of Physics, University of California, Berkeley, California 94720 U.S.A.

PUBLICATIONS

Physics

Molecular Microwave Spectra Tables, with Paul Kisliuk. Washington, D.C., Government Printing Office, 1952.
Microwave Spectroscopy, with A.L. Schawlow. New York and London, McGraw Hill, 1955.
Masers, Lasers, and Instrumentation. N.p., 1964.

Other

Editor, *International Conference on Quantum Electronics.* New York, Columbia University Press, 1960.

*   *   *

As with untold numbers of scientists before him and since,

Charles H. Townes's research efforts were strongly influenced by his early military associations. During World War Two, he worked in the Bell Telephone Research Laboratory on problems of navigation, radar bombing systems, and airborne electronic computing systems. After the war, Townes pursued his studies of radar technology and related issues at Columbia.

The spectacular successes of radar in wartime situations suggested to Townes and other researchers a number of possible theoretical and practical applications for this tool. The specific problem Townes considered was how to construct microwave generators that would produce radiation with wavelengths of less than a millimeter. Wartime research had produced devices that could emit radiation in the radio and far microwave (e.g., greater than a millimeter) range. But the production of radiation with wavelengths shorter than that posed seemingly insoluble problems. The oscillator required in such a device would have to have dimensions comparable to those of a molecule.

In fact, it was precisely this realization that suggested a possible solution to Townes. His reasoning was as follows. Molecules which have been excited by heat, electricity, or some other source of energy vibrate in a variety of ways. If these excited molecules are exposed to an external source of radiation, they are stimulated to give off their excess energy as radiation. Furthermore, the wavelength of the emitted radiation will be identical to the wavelength of the applied radiation. Even a very weak beam of applied radiation is enough to cause the excited molecules to release all of their excess energy. The intensity of the incoming radiation can, therefore, be *amplified* by the *stimulation* of the excited molecules. From this, the name MASER (*m*icrowave *a*mplification by *s*timulated *e*mission of *r*adiation) was given to Townes's discovery.

Townes and his colleagues constructed and tested the first practical maser in 1954. They used ammonia gas which, when excited and exposed to external radiation, emitted microwaves of wavelength equal to about one centimeter. Later developments showed that a more useful maser could be constructed from paramagnetic solids rather than gases. By the late 1950's, solid state masers had become the most common instruments of this kind.

Townes carried his analysis one step further by considering the conditions under which molecules could be used to stimulate radiation in the near microwave, infrared, optical, and ultraviolet regions. The instrument he proposed in a theoretical paper co-authored by him and his brother-in-law, A.L. Schawlow, in 1958, was first constructed by T.H. Maiman in 1960. Because of its emission of radiation in the visible region, it is referred to as a LASER (*l*ight *a*mplification by *s*timulated *e*mission of *r*adiation).

The radiation emitted by lasers and masers has a number of useful properties. The path in which it travels is, first of all, coherent, meaning that it is restricted to a very narrow beam that does not spread out over very long distances. As a consequence, the energy carried by the radiation is intense since the radiation produced during emission does not spread out in all directions, but focuses in a single, highly defined region of space. Finally, the beam is essentially monochromatic. All of the radiation released has essentially the same wavelength.

These characteristics have made possible a number of valuable applications of masers and lasers. The coherence of their beams means that they can be used to transmit signals over very great distances. One of their earliest applications was in planetary astronomy. Maser beams reflected off the moon and nearby planets provided precise measurements of many surface features on these bodies. The ability of masers and lasers to amplify incoming radiation has made them useful, also, in detecting and analyzing very weak radiation from extraterrestrial sources.

Many medical and industrial applications of masers and lasers depend on the intensity of the radiation they product. They can be used, for example, to make highly precise microwelds in metals and to perform very exact surgical procedures on the eye.

—David Newton

TOYNBEE, Arnold. British historian. Born in London, 14 April 1889. Educated at Winchester College, Hampshire, 1902-07; studied at Balliol College, Oxford, 1907-11; British Archeological School, Athens, 1911-12. Married Rosalind Murray in 1912 (divorced, 1945), 2 sons; married Veronica Boulter in 1946. Fellow and Tutor, Balliol College, 1912-15; Koraes Professor of Byzantine and Modern Greek Language, Literature, and History, 1919-24, Professor, 1925-55, and Professor Emeritus, 1955-75, University of London; also, Director of Studies, Royal Institute of International Affairs, London, 1925-55. Assigned to Political Intelligence Department, British Foreign Office, 1918; Member, Middle Eastern Section, British Delegation to Peace Conference, Paris, 1919; Director, Research Department, British Foreign Office, 1943-46; Member, British Delegation to Peace Conference, Paris, 1946. Honorary doctorate: Oxford University; Cambridge University; University of Birmingham; University of Birmingham, Alabama; Princeton University, New Jersey; Columbia University, New York. Associate Member, Institute of France. Fellow, British Academy, 1937. C.H. (Companion of Honor), 1956. *Died 22 October 1975.*

PUBLICATIONS

History

Greek Policy since 1882. London, Oxford University Press, 1914.
Armenian Atrocities: The Murder of a Nation. London, Hodder and Stoughton, 1915.
Nationality and the War. London, Dent, 1915.
The New Europe: Some Essays in Reconstruction. London, Dent, 1915.
British View of the Ukranian Question: The Ukraine—A Problem of Nationality. New York, Ukranian Federation of the U.S.A., 1916.
The Destruction of Poland: A Study in German Efficiency. London, Allen and Unwin, 1916(?).
Annexation. The Hague, Nijhoff, 1917.
The Belgian Deportations. London, Unwin, 1917(?).
The German Terror in Belgium. London, Hodder and Stoughton, 1917.
The German Terror in France. London, Hodder and Stoughton, and New York, Doran, 1917.
The Murderous Tyranny of the Turks. London, Hodder and Stoughton, and New York, Doran, 1917.
Turkey: A Past and a Future. London, Hodder and Stoughton, and New York, Doran, 1917.
The Place of Mediaeval and Modern Greece in History (lecture). London, Vellonis, 1919.
The League in the East. London, British Periodicals, 1920.
The Tragedy of Greece (lecture). Oxford, Clarendon Press, 1921.
The Western Question in Greece and Turkey: A Study in the Contact of Civilisations. London, Constable, 1922.
Survey of International Affairs, 1920-23 [to *1938*], with others. London, Oxford University Press, 16 vols., 1925-41.
The World after the Peace Conference. London, Oxford University Press, 1925.
Turkey, with Kenneth P. Kirkwood. London, Benn, and New York, Scribner, 1926.
The Conduct of British Empire Foreign Relations since the Peace Settlement. London, Oxford University Press, 1928.
Economics and Politics in International Life (lecture). Nottingham, University College, 1930.
World Order or Downfall? Six Broadcast Talks. London, British Broadcasting Corporation, 1930.
Britain and the Modern World Order. London, British Broadcasting Corporation, 1932.
A Study of History. London and New York, Oxford University Press, 12 vols., 1934-61; abridged edition by D.C. Somer-

vell, 2 vols., 1946-57; abridged edition by Arnold Toynbee and Jane Caplan, 1972.
British Interests in the Far East (lecture). Nottingham, University College, 1938.
Christianity and Civilization (lecture). London, Student Christian Movement Press, 1940.
Civilization on Trial. London and New York, Oxford University Press, 1948.
An Historian's View of American Foreign Policy (lecture). Chicago, Chicago Council on Foreign Relations, 1949.
The Prospects of Western Civilization (lecture). New York, Columbia University Press, 1949.
Russian Catfish and Western Herring (lecture). New York, Oxford University Press, 1949.
Recovering Europe's Sovereignty. Strasbourg, Council of Europe, 1953.
The World and the West (lectures). London, Oxford University Press, 1953.
The Concentration of Power and the Alternatives Before Us (lecture). Sheffield, J.W. Northend, 1954.
"Counsels of Hope": The Toynbee-Jerrold Controversy: Letters to the Editor of the Times Literary Supplement, with Leading Articles, Reprinted. London, Times Publishing Company, 1954.
Man at Work in God's World in the Light of History (lecture). Albany, New York, 1955?
An Historian's Approach to Religion (lectures). London, Oxford University Press, 1956.
The New Opportunity for Historians (lecture). Minneapolis, University of Minnesota Press, 1956.
The Resurrection of Asia and the Role of the Commonwealth (lecture). 1956?
Christianity Among the Religions of the World (lectures). New York, Scribner, 1957.
Democracy in the Atomic Age (lectures). Melbourne, Oxford University Press, 1957.
Hellenism: The History of a Civilization. New York, Oxford University Press, 1959.
Population and Food Supply (lecture). Rome, Food and Agriculture Organization of the United Nations, 1959.
Civilization on Trial and The World and the West. New York, Meridan Books, 1960.
One World and India (lectures). New Delhi, Indian Council for Cultural Relations, 1960.
The Continuing Effect of the American Revolution (lecture). Williamsburg, Virginia, Colonial Williamsburg, 1961.
The Future of Judaism in Western Countries. New York, American Council for Judaism, 1961.
America and the World Revolution and Other Lectures. New York, Oxford University Press, 1962.
The Economy of the Western Hemisphere (lectures). London, Oxford University Press, 1962.
The Importance of the Arab World (lectures). Cairo, National Publications House Press, 1962.
The Present-Day Experiment in Western Civilization (lectures). London, Oxford University Press, 1962.
The Toynbee Lectures on the Middle East and Problems of Underdeveloped Countries. Cairo, National Publications House Press, 1962.
Four Lectures. Cairo, National Publications House for the United Arab Republic, 1965.
Hannibal's Legacy: The Hannibalic War's Effects on Roman Life. London, Oxford University Press, 1966.
On the Role of Creativity in History; And, Is America Neglecting Her Creative Talents? Salt Lake City, University of Utah Press, 1967.
Some Problems of Greek History. London and New York, Oxford University Press, 1969.
An Ekistical Study of the Hellenic City-State. Athens, Athens Center of Ekistics, 1971.
Surviving the Future. London, Oxford University Press, 1971.

Constantine Porphyrogenitus and His World. London, Oxford University Press, 1973.

Mankind and Mother Earth: A Narrative History of the World. New York and London, Oxford University Press, 1976.

The Greeks and Their Heritages. New York, Oxford University Press, 1981.

Other

A Journey to China; or, Things Which Are Seen. London, Constable, 1931.

East to West: A Journey round the World. London, Oxford University Press, 1958.

Between Oxus and Jumna. London, Oxford University Press, 1961.

Comparing Notes: A Dialogue across a Generation, with Philip Toynbee. London, Weidenfeld and Nicolson, 1963.

Janus at Seventy-Five. London, Oxford University Press, 1964.

Between Niger and Nile. London, Oxford University Press, 1965.

Acquaintances. London, Oxford University Press, 1967.

Between Maule and Amazon. London, Oxford University Press, 1967.

Cities of Destiny. London, Thames and Hudson, and New York, McGraw Hill, 1967.

Higher Educatin in a Time of Accelerating Change. New York, Academy for Educational Development, 1968.

Impressions of Japan (lecture). Tokyo, Kinseido, 1968.

Experiences. London, Oxford University Press, 1969.

Cities on the Move. London, Oxford University Press, 1970.

Toynbee on Toynbee: A Conversation Between Arnold J. Toynbee and G.R. Urban. New York, Oxford University Press, 1974.

The Toynbee-Ikeda Dialogue: Man Himself Must Choose, with Daisaku Ikeda. Tokyo and New York, Kodansha International, 1976.

Editor, *The Treatment of Armenians in the Ottoman Empire, 1915-1916.* London, His Majesty's Stationary Office, 1916.

Editor, *British Commonwealth Relations.* London, Oxford University Press, 1934.

Editor, *The Crucible of Christianity: Judaism, Hellenism, and the Historical Background to the Christian Faith*, by Abraham Schalit and others. London, Thames and Hudson, and New York, World, 1969.

Editor, *Half the World: The History and Culture of China and Japan.* London, Thames and Hudson, and New York, Holt Rinehart, 1973.

Translator, *Greek Civilisation and Character: The Self-Revelation of Ancient Greek Society.* London, Dent, and New York, Dutton, 1924.

Translator, *Greek Historical Thought from Homer to the Age of Heraclitus.* New York, Dutton, 1924.

*

Bibliography: *A Bibliography of Arnold J. Toynbee* by S. Fiona Morton, London and New York, Oxford University Press, 1980.

Critical Studies: *Social Philosophies for an Age of Crisis* by Pitirim A. Sorokin, London, A.&C. Black, 1952; *The Lie about the West: A Response to Professor Toynbee's Challenge* by Douglas Jerrold, New York, Sheed and Ward, 1953, London, Dent, 1954; *Toynbee and History: Critical Essays and Reviews* edited by Ashley Montagu, Boston, Sargent, 1956; *The Intent of Toynbee's History: A Historical Appraisal* edited by Edward T. Gargan, Chicago, Loyola University Press, 1961; *Arnold J. Toynbee: Historian for an Age of Crisis* by Roland N. Stromberg, Carbondale, Southern Illinois University Press, 1972;

Arnold Toynbee: The Ecumenical Vision by Kenneth Winetrout, Boston, Twayne, 1975.

*   *   *

Arnold Toynbee is a problem for those who would comment on him. Shall one approach him as a civilizationist, a moralist, or yet as a philosopher? Toynbee is the ultimate polymath of our era. We may group his published works under: wartime work with the British Intelligence; *A Study of History*; Graeco-Roman studies; publications for the Royal Institute of International Affairs; books with a religious dimension; travel books; autobiography and biography; and discussions of contemporary affairs.

But no less is he a problem for those who would read him. The sheer mass is sufficient to scare off many. Then among those brave and diligent who do read him, there is the temptation on the part of the expert to note errors and assumed errors from the perspective of a special discipline, and so miss the wonderful insights, the large visions. The general reader is likely to be overwhelmed by marvelous philosophical and near-poetic observations that he is quite oblivious to the particularities Toynbee may or may not address. At whatever level, it seems that Toynbee has a peculiar talent to turn on or to turn off the scholarly reader, the casual reader. The reader should begin by reading Toynbee before turning to his critics.

Whatever his failings, his strengths, Toynbee has assured and deserved place among the most eminent who have taken civilization in the large sense as their subject. In one grouping we conventionally find three names: Sorokin, Spengler, and Toynbee. However much we may extend this list, Toynbee's name is a sure bet to appear on it. He can't be ignored: friend and foe alike feel compelled to discuss him.

There is a sense in which Toynbee may be seen as a very busy mortician: busy signing death certificates, picking out the caskets, arranging the flowers, writing epitaphs for civilizations. One thing is consistent at the Toynbee mortuary: all these civilizations have died of self-inflicted wounds: suicides every one. But Toynbee is no careless mortician. He engages in repeated disinternments to perform post mortems seriatim to make sure his diagnosis was indeed correct.

The progression of civilizations to their deaths is in each case pretty much the same: 1. An Age of Growth. During the phase a civilization masters its physical environment. 2. Time of Troubles. The breakdown comes on not as a result of floods, famines, invasions, or yet acts of Gods, but by self-destructive acts. (See list below.) 3. Universal States. Growth comes to an end. A tremendous effort is made to cover over the troubles. This is a conservative stage; the civilization is frozen. 4. The Interregnum, Disintegration, the End. Once a universal state is in place, the end is at hand. There may be a rally or two, but sooner or later we have the end. Toynbee allows that the West might survive; but this is very much a question.

Whatever shortcomings one may wish to assign to Toynbee's stages, this pattern is surely as useful as Spengler's organicism: Spring, Summer, Fall, and Winter, and likewise as helpful as Sorokin's cultural typology: Ideational, Sensate, and Idealistic. For example, one may find the Universal State construct useful in evaluating the work of the Trilateral Commission or the direction of multinational corporate diplomacy.

The primary terminal diseases for civilizations are these: 1. The effort to escape the present via two routes: archaism, an excessive respect for the past; futurism, an excessive concern for the future. 2. Loss of self-determination. 3. Mimesis: a civilization tries to imitate what worked for another people at another time and place. 4. Idolization: to place on a pedestal a person, an institution, a technique. The military phalanx is an example. 5. Resting on one's oars: plain smugness over an accomplishment and thus overlooking the challenges at the gate. 6. Failure to act. 7. War. 8. Nationalism. 9. Petrification: the loss of creativity. 10. Failure to relate to "the ultimate spiritual reality" behind all phenomena. This is the religious dimension in Toynbee. One of the above or some combination brings the end, this suicide.

Toynbee is fond of saying that he has a "binocular" view of humankind. His classical education and the decades of work on *A Study of History* represent his profound involvement with the past. His work at the Royal Institute of International Affairs meant writing an annual survey of the relationships among nations. "I have always had one foot in the present and one in the past."

This foot in the present makes Toynbee very sensitive to the perils facing Western civilization. Suicidal civilizational tendencies in the West are 1. Atomic war. 2. Technology. 3. Space Exploration. The problems are on earth. 4. Extreme consumerism. Toynbee feels that only austerity can save us. 5. Greed. 6. Overpopulation. 7. Pollution. 8. Chaos. Just more confusion than mankind can take. 9. The morality gap: the gap between our technological power and our ethical standards. 10. Self-centredness. A civilization may escape this sin by a proper relationship to that "ultimate spiritual reality."

The rise and decline of civilizations is the great theme in Toynbee. But he is much more than his massive 12-volume *A Study of History*. (Fortunately shortly before his death he completed his one-volume version in 1972, better than, say, B.C. Somervell's two-volume abridgement, and ever so much more manageable than that original work.) He is many other things, and we should be remiss if we were not unmindful of these other Toynbees. There is the Toynbee of *Hannibal's Legacy, Constantine Porphyrogenitus*, and *The Greeks and Their Heritages*. Unless one is a scholar's scholar and has a patience beyond that of Job, the first two can only be seen as massive monuments to the virtuosity of compulsive erudition. The first dumps some 1600 pages on the reader.

Toynbee also comes in small packages now and then. Two volumes are devoted to putting the West into a perspective that comes only from the pen of a person with an "ecumenical vision," of a man who tried to "look at Mankind's history as a whole." *The World and the West* gives us a glimpse of how the non-West world sees the West: "the arch-aggressor of modern times."

In *America and the World Revolution* Toynbee lectures an upstart United States. "Today America is no longer the inspirer and leader of World Revolution....America is today the leader of a world-wide anti-revolutionary movement in defence of vested interests. She now stands for what Rome stood for." America suffers from the "penalty of affluence" and so is cut off from the rest of the world.

Two dialogue books might easily get overlooked: *The Toynbee-Ikeda Dialogue* and *Toynbee on Toynbee*, with G.R. Urban. In these two books Toynbee makes exciting observations on an amazing array of topics. Perhaps here we get the clearest notion of just where Toynbee stands on current issues. In the Ikeda book: "The level of man's ethical performance has been low, and it has not risen. The level of technological performance has risen in an ascending curve. Our present situation ought to make us feel humble." No longer can we trust our future to an occasional saint. Now each of us must be a saint. In Urban: "It would be a useful type of spiritual discipline and a humbling thought for people acting, say, on armament or pollution, to imagine what their great-grandchildren will think of their activities." And: "We have the power to put an end to history and, indeed, to life." Thus we find the prophet-moralist-historian playing back and forth between the past and present, and the future.

Nor should we overlook Toynbee as the author of travel books. At Chichen Itza in Yucatan: "They [Yucatan priests] used to take human lives by the hundreds with their obsidian blades. We take them by the hundred thousand with our bombs. Murder does not cease to be murder when it is committed at long range. Our modern technology has enabled us to commit murder on a scale that was beyond the capacity of the most blood-thirsty pre-Columbian murderer." Toynbee ever takes the larger view that at times he strikes us as non-Western: "Europeans have a saying that 'all roads lead to Rome.' From a European standpoint they may look as if they do. But Europe is one of the fringes

of the Old World....Plant yourself, not in Europe, but in Iraq, which is the historic centre of our Oikoumene. Seen from this central position, the road-map of the Old World will assume a very different pattern....half the roads will lead to Aleppo, and half to Begram."

Thus we see that there are many Toynbees, and each one illustrates that remarkable facility Toynbee has to give a certain Toynbee stamp to whatever is under discussion. And always we seem to encounter a certain ambiguity: there is the Toynbee who boasts of his "empirical methods" and withal sees history as a "revelation of God," as a "vision of God's creation on the move, from God its source toward God its goal." Yet no one, it seems, took such pains to declare himself an agnostic, an ex-believer for more than 50 years. No ordinary man, this Arnold Toynbee.

Toynbee was fond of quoting Quintus Aurelius Symmachus: "The heart of so great a mystery cannot ever be reached by following one road only." Perhaps the finest contribution of Toynbee is that he encouraged each one of us to keep on with the search for ever new roads to that great mystery, and not to dismiss out of hand the roads that others have traveled.

—Kenneth Winetrout

TROELTSCH, Ernst. German theologian and historian. Born in Haunstetten, 17 February 1865. Studied at the University of Erlangen; University of Berlin, 1883-88; University of Göttingen, license in theology, 1892. Married Marta Fick in 1901; 1 son. Lutheran curate, Munich, 1887-90; Lecturer, University of Göttingen, 1890-92; Professor of Theology, Bonn University, 1892-94, and University of Heidelberg, 1894-1914; Philosophical Chair, University of Berlin, 1915-23. Member, Prussian Landtag and Bavarian Upper Legislative House; Under-Secretary of State, Ministry of Public Worship, 1919-21. Honorary doctorate: University of Griefswald; University of Heidelberg; University of Breslau, 1911; University of Berlin, 1915. *Died* (in Berlin) *1 February 1923*.

PUBLICATIONS

Religion and Culture

Vernunft und Offenbarung bei Johann Gerhard und Melanchton. Göttingen, Vandenhoeck and Ruprecht, 1891.
Richard Rothe (lecture). Freiburg, Mohr, 1899.
Die Wissenschaftliche Lage und ihre Anforderung an die Theologie. Tübingen, Mohr, 1900.
Die Absolutheit des Christentums und die Heiliglongeschichte. Tübingen, Mohr, 1902; as *The Absoluteness of Christianity and the History of Religions*, Richmond, Virginia, Knox, 1971.
Das Historische in Kants Religionsphilosophie. Berlin, Reuther and Reichard, 1904.
Politische Ethik and Christentum. Göttingen, Vandenhoeck and Ruprecht, 1904.
Psychologie und Erkenntnistheorie in der Religionswissenschaft. Tübingen, Mohr, 1905.
Die Bedeutung des Protestantismus für die Entstehung der Modernen Welt. Munich, Oldenbourg, 1906; as *Protestantism and Progress: A Historical Study of the Relations of Protestantism to the Modern World.* London, Williams and Norgate, and New York, Putnam, 1912.
Die Trennung von Staat und Kirche, der staatliche Religionsunterricht und die theologischen Fakultäten. Heidelberg, Hörning, 1906.
Die Bedeutung der Geschichtlichkeit Jesu für den Glauben.

Tübingen, Mohr, 1911.

Die Soziallehren der christlichen Kirchen und Gruppen. Tübingen, Mohr, 1912; as *The Social Teachings of the Christian Churches,* New York, Macmillan, 1931; London, Allen and Unwin, 1949.

Religion und Wirtschaft. Leipzig, Teubner, 1913.

Zur religiösen Lage, Religionsphilosophie und Ethik. Tübingen, Mohr, 1913.

Nach Erklärung der Mobilmachung. Heidelberg, Winter, 1914.

Unser Volksheer. Heidelberg, Winter, 1914.

Deutscher Glaube und deutsche Sitte in unserem grossen Kriege. Berlin, Kameradschaft, 1915.

Augustin, die christliche Antike, und das Mittelalter. Munich, Oldenbourg, 1915.

Das Wesen des Deutschen. Heidelberg, Winter, 1915.

Deutsche Zukunft. Berlin, Fischer, 1916.

Humanismus und Nationalismus in unserem Bildungswesen. Berlin, Weldmann, 1917.

Die Dynamik der Geschicht nach der Geschichtsphilosophie den Positivismus. Berlin, Reuther and Reichard, 1919.

Der Berg der Läuterung. Berlin, Mittler, 1921.

Der Historismus und seine Probleme. Tübingen, Mohr, 1922; as *History and Its Problems,* Tübingen, Mohr, 1922.

Protestantisches Christentum und Kirche in der Neuzeit: Die Kultur der Gegenwart, edited by Paul Heineberg. Berlin, Teubner, 1922.

Der Historismus und seine Uberwendung. Berlin, Teubner, 1923; as *Christian Thought: Its History and Application,* London, University of London Press, 1923.

Spektatorbriefe: Aufsätze über die deutsche Revolution und die Weltpolitik. Tübingen, Mohr, 1923.

Glaubenslehre. Munich, Duncker und Homblot, 1925.

Aufsätze zue Geistesgeschicht und Religionssoziologie. Tübingen, Mohr, 1925.

Deutscher Geist und Westeuropa, edited by Hans Baron. Tübingen, Mohr, 1925.

Writings on Theology and Religion, edited by Robert Morgan and Michael Pye. Atlanta, Knox, 1977.

Other

Briefe an Friedrich von Hügel 1901-1923, edited by Karl-Ernst Apfelbacher and Peter Neuner. Paderborn, Bonifacus, 1974.

*

Critical Studies: *Towards a Theory of Involvement: The Thought of Ernst Troeltsch* by Benjamin A. Reist, Philadelphia, Westminster Press, 1966; *Ernst Troeltsch and the Future of Theology* edited by John P. Clayton, London, Cambridge University Press, 1976; *Frömmigkeit und Wissenschaft: Ernst Troeltsch und sein theologisches Programm* by Karl Ernst Apfelbacher, Munich, Schöningh, 1978; *The Concept of Glaubenslehre: Ernst Troeltsch and the Theological Heritage of Schleiermacher* by Walter E. Wyman, Jr., Chico, California, Scholar's Press, 1983.

*   *   *

It is difficult to fit Ernst Troeltsch into a tidy classification. He has been called both the "systematic theologian of the history of religions school" and an "indifferent philosopher of our culture." His published writings span a wide range of areas. He is probably best known in the English speaking world for *The Social Teachings of the Christian Churches.* Influenced by the work of Max Weber, Troeltsch employs sociological methods and categories to study the development of institutional forms and ethical teachings of Christianity. His sociological typology of church, sect, and mysticism remains influential. But Troeltsch's thought and influence extend beyond the sociology of religion; other works, many of which have never been published in English translation,

deal with intellectual history, the history of Protestantism in the modern period, the philosophy of history, Christian theology and ethics, and the philosophy of religion. His historical writings are well known for the controversial thesis that the Enlightenment, rather than the Reformation, marks the beginning of the modern world; the Reformation was in Troeltsch's view a medieval phenomenon. Less well known are his essays commenting on the political and social situation in Germany during World War I and the Weimar Republic.

This diverse intellectual work revolves around a central problem: that of normative values in a historically conscious age. Troeltsch probes deeply the nature of historical thinking and its impact both on Christianity and on Western culture generally. The central issue is historical relativism (sometimes called "historicism"): the awareness that all cultural values are products of the past which undergo change and development over time. Accordingly, this historical consciousness holds all phenomena to be relative to their historical context; it excludes all absolutes from the stream of history. Even Christianity is seen to be a human and historical phenomenon, conditioned by social and historical circumstances, and subject to change and development. Neither Jesus, the Bible, the Church, nor Christian dogmas and doctrines can be considered absolute, that is, valid for all times and places. Troeltsch argues that this relativization of all thought, values, and institutional forms is the inescapable consequence of the modern historical consciousness.

Troeltsch not only analyzed this state of affairs; he sought to provide a constructive solution to the problem of historicism. Are there values that we can still affirm? How can we take a stand in the shifting sands of historical existence? In his philosophy of religion, Troeltsch seeks to demonstrate the irreducible validity of the religious consciousness through his famous theory of the "religious a priori." Human beings are necessarily religious; human religion cannot be reduced to non-religous causes. Although cast in the language of a Kantian a priori of consciousness (alongside the categorical imperative and the a priori elements of knowledge there is a religious a priori), Troeltsch's argument in fact rests on a metaphysics of spirit stemming from Absolute Idealism (the human, finite spirit is everywhere entwined with the Divine Spirit). Having thus defined the place of religion generally in human culture, he attempts to demonstrate the highest value of Christianity in particular for Western culture in *The Absoluteness of Christianity and the History of Religion.* Here the argument rests finally upon an axiomatic decision that the Christian form of salvation, which grounds the value of the human personality in a personal God, is of higher value for us than Eastern forms, with their ultimate dissolution of personality. In systematic theology, he argues for a liberal Protestant reinterpretation of the Christian tradition that, while not ascribing divinity to Christ, sees forces of redemption proceeding from him which lead to the formation of ethical persons. Naturally, he acknowledges that his reinterpretation cannot pretend to dogmatic finality; it is, he thought, a formulation of the "essence of Christianity" which is adequate for his time and place. Finally, in his philosophy of history and ethics he calls for a synthesis of cultural values that once again rests on a decision in favor of the highest value of the human personality.

Troeltsch's work spans the concluding decade of the 19th century and the opening decades of the 20th. In a sense he belongs to both epochs. His own constructive thinking is influenced by the classic figures of the 19th-century German philosophy and theology (Kant, Hegel, and Schleiermacher), as well as by some important thinkers at the end of the century (Ritschl, Windelband, Dilthey, Rickert). 20th-century theology is launched by a movement (Neo-orthodoxy) that rejected many of the characteristic emphases of 19th-century thought; neo-orthodox theologians such as Barth include Troeltsch in their sharp criticisms of 19th-century theology. Generally, his critics have held that Troeltsch concedes too much to the historical consciousness; in particular, they argue that in giving up the absoluteness of Jesus Christ and the Christian faith he undercuts, indeed dissolves, Christian theology. In addition, they find his position subordinates theology to a problematic philosophy (Absolute Idealism). Recently, however, there has been a renewed interest among theologians in Troeltsch's work. Troeltsch addresses a number of problems which, with the declining popularity of neo-orthodox theologies, are once again on the agenda of many theologians: historical and ethical relativism; the sociological conditioning of ideas; the plurality of religions and Christianity's place and value among the world's religions; the impact of historical modes of thought on both the content and the method of Christian theology. While few would argue that Troeltsch has the definitive answers to the problems he addresses, many are finding that, after nearly 50 years of neglect, Troeltsch's thought is worth a second look. A conception of Christian theology that starts with Christianity as a religion among religions and takes seriously the relativity of all historical phenomena is, in the view of many, of contemporary relevance.

—Walter E. Wyman, Jr.

TROTSKY, Leon. Russian revolutionary, theorist and political leader. Born Lev Davidovich Bronstein in Yanovka, 26 October 1879; assumed the name Leon Trotsky while escaping from Siberia in 1902. Educated in Odessa and Nikolayev; studied mathematics at the University of Odessa, 1897. Married Alexandra Sokolovskaya in 1900, 2 daughters; married Natalya Sedova in 1903, 2 sons. Worked with the South Russian Workers' Union; arrested and imprisoned in Odessa, 1898-99; sentenced to 4 years in Siberia, 1899; escaped, 1902. Worked with Lenin in London, 1902. Returned to Russia, 1905; arrested, 1906, and sentenced to life-exile in Siberia; escaped, 1907. Lived abroad, and returned to Russia in 1917; Chairman, Petrograd Soviet, Commissar for Foreign Affairs, and Commissar of War, 1917-19. Leader of the Left Opposition after 1923; deported by Stalin in 1929. Lived in Turkey, France, Norway, and Mexico, 1929-40. *Died* (murdered by G.P.U. agents in Coyoacan, Mexico) *20 August 1940.*

PUBLICATIONS

Collections

Sochineniia [Works]. Moscow, Gosizdat, 1924-27 (discontinued).
The Trotsky Papers, 1917-1922 (Russian and English texts). The Hague, Mouton, 2 vols., 1964-70.

Society and Politics

Nashi politicheskiia zadachi [Our Political Tasks]. Geneva, Tip. Partii, 1904.
Do deviatago ianvaria [Before January 9th]. Geneva, Tip. Partii, 1905.
Nasha revoliutsiia. St. Petersburg, Izd. Glagoleva, 1906; as *Our Revolution,* New York, Holt, 1918.
Iz istorii odnogo goda: Intelligentsiia [The History of One Year: The Intelligentsia]. St. Petersburg, Novyi mir, 1906.
Istoriia Soveta Rabochikh Deputatov g. S.-Petersburga [History of the St. Petersburg Soviet of Workers Deputies]. St. Petersburg, Izd. Glagoleva, 1906.
Gospodin Petr Struve v politike [The Politics of Mr. Peter Struve]. St. Petersburg, Noyyi mir, 1906.
V zashchitu partii [In Defense of the Party]. St. Petersburg, Tip. partii, 1907.
Tuda i obratno. St. Petersburg, Shipovnik, 1907; as *My Flight from Siberia,* New York, American Library Service, 1925.
O germanskoi sotsial-demokratii [On German Social-Demo-crats]. Moscow, n.p., 1908.
Perspektivy russkoi revoliutsii [Perspectives of the Russian Revolution]. Berlin, Ladyzhnikov, 1917.
Na bor'bu s golodom! [Fight the Famine!]. Moscow, Kommunist, 1918.
Itogi i perspektivy: dvizhushchie sily revoliutsii [Results and Prospects: The Motive Forces of the Revolution]. Moscow, Sovetskii mir, 1919.
Gody velikogo pereloma [The Years of the Great Upheaval]. Moscow, Kommunist, 1910.
Liudi staroi i novoi epokh [People of the Old and New Epochs]. Moscow, Kommunist, 1919.
Bel'giia i Serbiia v voine [Belgium and Serbia in the War]. Moscow, Kommunist, 1919.
Voina i tekhnika [War and Technology]. Moscow, Kommunist, 1919.
Ot Oktiabr'skoi revoliutsii do Brestkogo mira. Kremenchug, Proletarii, 1919; as *From October to Brest-Litvosk,* New York, Socialist Publishing Society, 1919.
Bor'ba za Petrograd, with others. [Struggle for Petrograd]. Petrograd, Gosizdat, 1920.
Noyvi etap: mirovoe polozhenie i nashi zadachi [A New Stage: The World Situation and Our Tasks]. Moscow, Gosizdat, 1921.
O roli professional'nykh soiuzov. Moscow, l-ia obratztsovaia tip. MSNKh, 1921; as *On the Trade Unions,* New York, Merit, 1969.
Mezhdu imperializmom i revoliutsiei: osnovnye voprosy revoliutsii na chastnom premere Gruzii. Moscow, Gosizdat, 1922; as *Between Red and White: A Study of Some Fundamental Questions for Revolution, with Particular Reference to Georgia,* London, Communist Party of Great Britain, 1922.
Osnovnaia voennaia zadacha momenta [The Main Military Task of the Moment]. Moscow, Vysshii Voennyi Redaksionnyi Sovet, 1922.
Voina i revoliutsiia: Krushenie Vtorogo Internatsionala i podgotovka Tret'ego [War and Revolution: The Collapse of the Second International and the Preparation to Establish the Third]. Petrograd, Gosizdat, 1922.
1905. Moscow, Gosizdat, 1922.
Voprosy byta: eopkha "kul'turnichestva" i ee zadachi. Moscow, Krasnaia nov', 1923; as *Problems of Life,* London, Methuen, 1924.
Literatura i revoliutsiia. Moscow, Krasnaia nov', 1923; as *Literature and Revolution,* New York, International Publishers, 1925.
Novaia ekonomicheskaia politika Sovetskoi Rossii i perspektivy mirovoi revoliutsii [The New Economic Policy of Soviet Russia and the Perspectives of World Revolution]. Moscow, Moskovskii rabochii, 1923.
Kommunisticheskoe dvizhenie vo Frantsii. Moscow, Moskovskii rabochii, 1923; as *Whither France?* New York, Pioneer, 1936.
Kak vooruzhalas' revoliutsiia [How the Revolution Was Armed]. Moscow, Vysshii Voennyi Redaktsionnyi Sovet, 5 vols., 1923-25.
Osnovyne vopsory revoliutsii [Fundamental Problems of Revolution]. Moscow, n.p., 1923.
Osnovnye voprosy promyshlennosti [Fundamental Problems of Production]. Moscow, Krasnaia nov', 1923.
O Lenine: materialy dlia biografia. Moscow, Gosizdat, 1924; as *Lenin,* New York, Minton, Balch, 1925.
Novyi kurs. Moscow, Krasnaia nov', 1924; as *The New Course,* New York, International, 1943.
Zapad i Vostok [The East and the West]. Moscow, Krasnaia nov', 1924.
Uroki Oktiabria. Berlin, Berlinskoe knigoizdatel'stvo, 1924; as *Lessons in October,* New York, Pioneer, 1937.
Leninizm i bibliotechnaia rabota [Leninism and the Work of Libraries]. Moscow, Krasnaia nov', 1924.
Piat' let Kominterna. Moscow, Gosizdat, 1924.

Pokolenie Oktiabria [The October Generation].   Petrograd.
Molodaia gvardiia, 1924.
O deviatom ianvairia [January 9th].   Moscow, Gosizdat, 1925.
Kuda idet Angliia?   Moscow, Gosizdat, 2 vols., 1925, 1926; as
Whither England?, New York, International, 1925; as *Where
Is Britain Going?*, London, Allen and Unwin, 1926.
K sotsializmu ili kapitalizmu?   Moscow, Planovoe khoziaistvo
Gosplan SSSR, 1925; as *Towards Socialism or Capitalism?*,
London, Methuen, 1926.
Terrorizm i kommunizm.   Moscow, Gosizdat, 1925; as *Dicta-
torship vs. Democracy (Terrorism and Communism): A
Reply to Karl Kautsky*, New York, Workers Party of Amer-
ica, 1922; as *The Defense of Terrorism: A Reply to K.
Kautsky*, London, Allen and Unwin, 1935.
Bor'ba za kachestvo [Struggle for Quality].   Leningrad, Plano-
voe khoziaistvo, 1926.
Delo bylo v Ispanii [What Happened in Spain].   Moscow,
Artel' pisatelei "Krug," 1926.
Evropa i Amerika [Europe and America].   Moscow, Gosizdat,
1926.
Chto i kak proizoshlo? Shest' statei dlia burzhuaznoi pechati
[What Happened and How].   Paris, Navarre, 1929.
Moia zizhn': opyt avtobiografii.   Berlin, Granit, 2 vols., 1930; as
My Life, New York, Scribner, 1931.
Permanentnaia revoliutsiia.   Berlin, Granit, 1930; as *The Per-
manent Revolution*. New York, Pioneer, 1931.
De einzige Weg.   Berlin, Links Opposition der KPD, 1931; as
The Only Road, New York, Pioneer, 1933.
Istoriia russkoi revoliutsii.   Berlin, Granit, 1933; as *The History
of the Russian Revolution*, New York, Simon and Shuster,
1932.
K istorii Oktiabr'skoi revoliutsii [On the History of the October
Revolution].   New York, Russkaia Sotsialisticheskaia
Federatsiia, 1932.
Nemetskaia revoliutsiia i stalinskaia biurokratiia.   Berlin,
Grylewicz, 1932; as *What Next?* New York, Pioneer, 1932.
Stalinskaia shkola fal'sifikatsii.   Berlin, Granit, 1932; as *The
Stalin School of Falsification*, New York, Pioneer, 1937.
The Diary in Exile, 1935.   Cambridge, Massachusetts, Harvard
University Press, 1958.

*

Critical Studies: *The Prophet Armed: Trotsky 1879-1921, The
Prophet Unarmed: Trotsky 1921-1929, The Prophet Outcast:
Trotsky 1929-1940* by Isaac Deutscher, London and New York,
Oxford University Press, 3 vols., 1954-63; *The Life and Death of
Leon Trotsky* by Victor Serge and Natalya Sedova Trotsky, New
York, Basic Books, 1975; *Leon Trotsky* by Irving Howe, Lon-
don, Collins, and New York, Viking Press, 1978; *The Social and
Political Thought of Leon Trotsky* by Baruch Knei-Paz, Oxford,
Clarendon Press, 1978.

*   *   *

The cornerstone of Leon Trotsky's thought is the theory of
permanent revolution. Not only is it his most distinctive intellectual contribution to Marxism, but it provided a clearly stated
analytical foundation to his political opposition to Stalin's dictatorship in the lonely and tragic years after Lenin's death in 1924.
   The theory originated as an analysis of the Russian social
formation at the turn of the 19th century. As expounded in such
works as *Results and Prospects*, it represented a radically heterodox contribution to Russian socialist debate. The two main
Marxist tendencies, the Bolsheviks and Mensheviks, were agreed
that revolution in Russia, given the backward and agrarian
nature of the country, would confine itself to "bourgeois-
democratic" tasks such as the abolition of the monarchy, the
expropriation of the gentry, and the convocation of a constituent
assembly; socialism would have to wait upon the further development of capitalism. They differed on the question of who

would carry out the revolution: would it be the liberal bourgeoisie, as Plekhanov and the Mensheviks believed, or Lenin's
"revolutionary-democratic" alliance of workers and peasants.
   Trotsky rejected the premisses of this debate. He argued that
the peculiar development of the Russian social formation had led
to the creation of an industrial working class whose socio-
political weight far exceeded that of its numbers. Only the Russian proletariat, even though it was a small minority of the
largely rural population, could lead a successful revolution
against Tsarism. The small-holding peasantry's horizons were
too narrow and parochial to provide the focus of a national
movement; they could only follow the lead of an urban class. But
such a coalition of workers and peasants, once installed in power,
would suffer from the differing class-interests of the partners, of
socialist workers and petty-bourgeois peasants. Either the working class would apply a self-denying ordinance and eventually
succumb to the power of capital, or it would take power and
initiate a transition to socialism, with the support of the poorer
peasants. In the latter case, Trotsky argued, a workers' and
peasants' government in Russia could survive only if it acted as a
stimulus to socialist revolutions in the advanced industrial countries. There were thus two levels to the analysis: the class-
structure of Russian society, and the capitalist world-system of
which it was part. It was the latter dimension which Trotsky
would make more explicit in later years.
   It is well known that Lenin accepted the essentials of this
analysis in April 1917 when he adopted the slogan of "All power
to the soviets." Previously the two men had differed not only over
their perspectives for the Russian revolution, but also in their
views on socialist organization. During and after the second
congress of the Russian Social-Democratic Labour Party in
1903, Trotsky had bitterly opposed Lenin's conception of a
centralized revolutionary party, arguing that socialist consciousness would arise spontaneously from workers' mass struggles;
the task of organization was merely to articulate and clarify this
consciousness. By 1917 Trotsky was prepared to concede that the
revolutionary party should play a more active role in transforming working-class consciousness. His admission that, in this matter, Lenin had been right and he wrong, led Trotsky temporarily
to abandon the theory of permanent revolution. It was only the
controversy with Stalin after Lenin's death over "socialism in one
country" and the Chinese revolution of 1925-27 which stimulated
Trotsky to revive and generalize the theory.
   His starting point was to stress that capitalism was a world-
system, of which different economies were merely component
parts. Socialism could not be constructed in one such economy,
but only on an international scale. Therefore, "socialism in one
country" was, as Trotsky put it, a "bureaucratic utopia" whose
effect would be to legitimize the power of the elite party officials
gathering around Stalin, and to subordinate the interests of
world revolution to those of the Soviet state.
   Trotsky did not advocate simultaneous working-class uprisings across the globe. By virtue of what he called "the law of
uneven and combined development," socialist revolutions would
break out in those countries where circumstances were especially
favourable. Such a conjunction could occur even in countries
such as Russia and China that were in the early stages of industrialization. The effect of imperialism was to create hybrid and
unstable class structures in which old land-owners coalesced with
new capitalists, and peasants found themselves proletarianized.
Revolution in such circumstances could succeed only if, as in
Russia, they came under working-class leadership, and made
their goal, not merely national independence and democracy, but
socialism. Their survival, however, would depend ultimately on
socialist revolutions in the advanced capitalist countries, which
would liberate the resources of the world economy, and place
them under rational and collective control.
   Trotsky's critique of the Stalin regime flowed from this perspective. The Bolshevik revolution's basic failure had been that it
had not spread—first, because of the defeat of the postwar
revolutionary wave in central Europe, then because of the

nationalist foreign policy pursued by Stalin. Confined to a single, backward country, the revolution inevitably degenerated. Classes could not be abolished where material scarcity still existed. Where there was not enough to go round, coercion was necessary to police the distribution of resouces. It was this situation which gave rise to the Stalinist bureaucracy, alienated from the working class but dependent for its power on such gains of the revolution as state ownership of the means of production. The only escape from this impasse lay in the forcible overthrow of the regime by the Soviet working class, in conjunction with socialist revolutions in the West.

In his last years, after the foundation of the Fourth International in 1938, Trotsky often fell victim to the belief that such a revolutionary denouement was inevitable, predetermined by the iron laws of history. Within a few years of his death it became clear that capitalism was not on the verge of collapse, while the achievements of the Soviet regime in defeating Hitler and reproducing itself from the Elbe to the Pacific revealed that the bureaucracy was more than the parasitic excrescence Trotsky had believed it to be. Nevertheless, his heroic and isolated struggle helped to preserve the authentic Marxist tradition for later generations.

—Alex Callinicos

TURING, A(lan) M(athison). British mathematician. Born in London, 23 June 1912. Educated at Sherborne School; studied at King's College, Cambridge, B.A. 1934, Fellow, 1933-36 (Smith's Prize, 1936); Princeton University, New Jersey, Ph.D. 1938. Served in the British Foreign Office, 1939-45: O.B.E. (Officer, Order of the British Empire), 1946. Staff Member, National Physical Laboratory, 1945-48; Reader, and Assistant Director, Manchester Automatic Digital Machine, University of Manchester, from 1948. Fellow, Royal Society, 1951. *Died* (in Wilmslow) *7 June 1954.*

PUBLICATIONS

Mathematics

Systems of Logic Based on Ordinals. London, C.F. Hodgson, 1939.

*

Bibliography: in *Biographical Memoirs of Fellows of the Royal Society 1955* (London), 1, 1955.

Critical Studies: *Alan M. Turing* by Sara Turing, Cambridge, Heffer, 1959.

*   *   *

A.M. Turing did fundamental work in logic, computer science, and applied mathematics. This latter work included seminal work in mathematical biology. His research was often marked by a strong preference for self-sufficiency, i.e., he often carried out his work with whatever materials or references were immediately at hand. This is particularly true of his biological work where, to quote M.H.A. Newman, "This sort of self-sufficiency stood him in good stead in starting on his theory of morphogenesis where the preliminary reading would have drowned out a more orthodox approach." This tendency probably slowed his research output but clearly did not effect its quality.

Turing demonstrated his unique mental abilities at an early age and entered Cambridge University fully prepared to take advantage of both the University environment and his own instincts for research. His first published work, "On the Gaussian Error Function," was the basis for his being elected a fellow of King's College. In this paper he gave a new proof of the central limit theorem of probability apparently in ignorance that it had previously been proved by others. At about the same time he began his work in mathematical logic which eventually resulted in his landmark paper "On Computable Numbers" (1937).

The paper on computable numbers would have made a reputation for Turing even if he had published nothing else. Although he and Alonzo Church arrived at the same results by different means, it is Turing's approach that has prevailed. The question about the possibility of finding a mechanical process for deciding whether a statement A, or not-A, or neither, was provable in a given system, was answered in the negative by the hypothetical machine to which Turing submitted the problem. This "Turing Machine" has received widespread adoption and makes this type of analysis accessible to many who find they cannot cope with the usual logical apparatus.

Turing spent the years 1936-38 at Princeton University. Several additional papers on logic resulted from this period. He had also published two other mathematical papers. These few papers were sufficient to mark him as a researcher of great power and insight. He received a Princeton Ph.D. for the paper "Systems of Logic Based on Ordinals."

In 1939 Turing became involved in war work in Great Britain. For the next six years little is known about the nature of the work he did. He evidently did this work very well since he was awarded an O.B.E. at the end of the war. This interruption undoubtedly had a great effect on his research output but the extent of this can only be conjectured.

Following the war he continued working in logic. One paper was a collaboration with M.H.A. Newman, while others are individual efforts. The paper "Practical Forms of Type-Theory" (1948) dealt with Russell's theory of types in a form that could be used in ordinary mathematics. These papers were of a high order but did not have the impact of the paper on computable numbers.

In addition to the above work, Turing now became fascinated with the development of the electronic computer. His pioneering efforts in the development of the logic of the modern computer place him in the company of notables like von Neumann. His first computer work was done at the National Physical Laboratory with the computer ACE (Automatic Computing Engine). While engaged in this work he became interested in certain problems of numerical analysis. The problem of using the computer to locate zeros of the Riemann zeta function which do not lie on the critical line impressed him as a good application of the computer. He wrote two papers on this topic. The second paper was written after he had transferred his efforts to Manchester University to work on the Manchester Electronic Computer. A brief quote from the introduction to this paper gives the flavor of a still young and struggling technology as expressed in Turing's open and frank style. "The calculations had been planned some time in advance, but had in fact to be carried out in great haste. If it had not been for the fact that the computer remained in serviceable condition for an unusually long period from 3 p.m. one afternoon to 8 a.m. the following morning it is probable that the calculations would never have been done at all ("Some Calculations of the Riemann Zeta-Function," 1953). Turing turned his hand to various tasks including writing the *Programmers' Handbook for the Manchester Electronic Computer.*

During this period he also wrote some papers in a more popular vein. One ("Computing Machinery and Intelligence") should be particularly noted in which he argues quite cogently the affirmative side of the question, can a machine think? This paper has been reprinted in the *World of Mathematics IV* (New York, 1956).

All during the latter part of his computer work Turing was

becoming interested in the biological problems of growth and development. His initial efforts on the topic are contained in "The Chemical Basis of Morphogenesis" (1952). He was concerned about how initially uniform biological growth became specialized and non-uniform. Unfortunately the theory was not fully developed by him before his death, and the state of his research was such as to make it difficult for others to follow it up. Some people, including his collaborator, M.H.A. Newman, feel that this research was potentially more important than anything that he had done to date.

The recollections of co-workers and friends are contained in the book written by his mother, Sara Turing, indicate the high regard in which they all held him. Even when he was fully engaged in his work in morphogenesis he did not hesitate to stop and solve problems originating out of the computer projects with which he was formerly associated. A letter to Turing's mother from Professor J.Z. Young, F.R.S., commenting on Turing's approach to biological problems, is an illustration of what a distinguished scientist thought of his abilities. "I have always felt that his insight into the significance of morphogenesis was one of the best signs that he really understood the biological problems. So many mathematicians who attack these problems seek only to understand the adult organism. Every biologist knows that a proper understanding can only come by studying how the tissues were formed and how they were maintained. Your son seemed to grasp this better than any other mathematician that I know." It is indeed tragic that this research was never completed.

Turing's research is both profound and lasting. M.H.A. Newman expressed very well the feelings of many at Turing's premature death, "The sudden death of Alan Turing on 7 June 1954 deprived mathematics and science of a great original mind at the height of its power." There is no question that this is so.

—Richard C. Roberts

TURNER, Frederick Jackson. American historian. Born in Portage, Wisconsin, 14 November 1861. Studied at the University of Wisconsin, Madison, B.A. 1884, M.A. 1888; Johns Hopkins University, Baltimore, Ph.D. 1890. Married Caroline Mae Sherwood in 1889; 3 children. Tutor in Rhetoric and Oratory, 1885-88, Assistant Professor of History, 1889-91, and Professor, 1891-1910, University of Wisconsin; Professor, 1910-24, and Professor Emeritus, 1924-32, Harvard University, Cambridge, Massachusetts. Research Associate, Carnegie Institute, Pittsburgh, 1916-17, and Henry E. Huntington Library, San Marino, California, 1927-30. Member, Board of Editors, *American Historical Review*, 1910-15. President, American Historical Association, 1910-11, and Colonial Society of Massachusetts, 1914-16. Honorary doctorate: University of Illinois, Urbana, 1908; Harvard University, 1909; Royal Frederic University, Christiana, Norway, 1911; University of Wisconsin, 1921. Fellow, American Academy of Arts and Sciences. *Died 14 March 1932.*

PUBLICATIONS

History

Outline Studies in the History of the Northwest. Chicago, Kerr, 1888.
The Character and Influence of the Fur Trade in Wisconsin (lecture). Baltimore, Johns Hopkins Press, 1891.
The Significance of the Frontier in American History (lecture). Madison, State Historical Society of Wisconsin, 1894.
The Rise of the New West, 1819-1829. New York and London, Harper, 1906.
Reuben Gold Thwaites (lecture). Madison, State Historical

Society of Wisconsin, 1914.
The Frontier in American History. New York, Holt, 1920.
The Significance of Sections in American History. New York, Holt, 1932.
The Early Writings of Frederick Jackson Turner, with a List of All His Works. Madison, University of Wisconsin Press, 1938.
The United States, 1830-1850: The Nation and Its Sections, edited by M.Y. Crissey, Max Farrand, and Avery Craven. New York, Holt, 1935.
Frontier and Section: Selected Essays. Englewood Cliffs, New Jersey, Prentice Hall, 1961.
Frederick Jackson Turner's Legacy: Unpublished Writings in American History, edited by Wilbur R. Jacobs. San Marino, California, Huntington Library, 1965; as *Frederick Jackson Turner's Unpublished Essays*, Lincoln, University of Nebraska Press, 1969.

Other

"Dear Lady": The Letters of Frederick Jackson Turner and Alice Forbes Perkins Hooper, 1910-1932, edited by Ray Allen Billington, with Walter Muir Whitehill. San Marino, California, Huntington Library, 1970.

Editor, *Correspondence of the French Ministers to the United States, 1791-1797.* Washington, Government Printing Office, 1904.
Editor, *List of References on the History of the West.* Cambridge, Harvard University Press, 1913; enlarged editions, 1915-1938.

*

Critical Studies: *Turner and Beard: American Historical Writing Reconsidered* by Lee Benson, Glencoe, Illinois, Free Press, 1960; *Turner, Bolton, and Webb: Three Historians of the American Frontier*, Seattle, University of Washington Press, 1965, and *The Historical World of Frederick Jackson Turner, with Selections from his Correspondence*, New Haven, Connecticut, Yale University Press, 1968, both by Wilbur R. Jacobs; *The Progressive Historians: Turner, Beard, Parrington* by Richard Hofstadter, New York, Knopf, and London, Cape, 1968, and *Turner and the Sociology of the Frontier* edited by Hofstadter and Seymour Martin Lipset, New York, Basic Books, 1968; *Frederick Jackson Turner, Historian, Scholar, Teacher* by Ray Billington, New York, Oxford University Press, 1973; *Frederick Jackson Turner* by James D. Bennett, Boston, Twayne, 1975.

*   *   *

Frederick Jackson Turner, along with Charles A. Beard, exercised a greater influence upon the interpretation of the American past than any other historians in the first half of the 20th century. Born in Portage, Wisconsin, in 1861, Turner attended the University of Wisconsin and then John Hopkins where he obtained his doctorate under the direction of Herbert Baxter Adams, a leading exponent of the germ theory of the evolution of social institutions.

His primary influence stemmed from his essay *The Significance of the Frontier in American History*, first read prior to publication at a meeting of the American Historical Association in 1893. In this paper he formulated what has become known as the "Frontier thesis"—an interpretation of the evolution of American democracy. America was depicted as unique in the continuous existence of a frontier zone of free land that had lasted until 1890. This frontier, a constantly moving zone of settlement, was viewed as a process which deeply affected all who lived there and which in turn affected all aspects of American life. The frontier had created distinct national characteristics—individualism, democracy, inventiveness, egalitarianism, self-reliance, and adventuresomeness. In this process, old institutions were replaced by new and better ones. The frontier, in his terms, represented progress.

Turner also regarded the frontier as a form of safety valve which enabled workers to escape from the oppressive conditions of urban life. The fact that the frontier of free land was closed in 1890 meant the beginning of a new epoch in American history.

In developing his thesis, Turner was not only reacting against the rigidity of the Darwinian postulates involved in the germ theory with its stress on Teutonic origins in the remote past; he was also deeply influenced by the writings of Achille Loria, an Italian economist whose theories were widely discussed among American scholars in the 1880's. Loria had postulated that the presence or absence of free land had been a fundamental factor in the evolution of European societies. In its simplist terms, Loria's theories were a form of geographical determinism.

Turner's long-term influence on American thought came largely from his role as a teacher, for apart from essays he published only two books: *The Rise of the New West, 1819-1829* (1906) in the widely read *American National Series*, and *The United States, 1830-1850*, published posthumously in 1935. In contrast to the romantic sweep of his essays, these volumes were highly factual presenting much detail about the west but not in a way that substantiated his thesis. He tended to repeat earlier generalizations without giving them a firmer substance. Not surprisingly, he was one of the first American historians to praise Andrew Jackson and his role as a democratic leader. The most significant original contribution of these volumes was his stress upon the sectional character of the American past and the importance of sectional rivalry. Turner's pupils did little to give solidity to his thesis, compiling monographs of a purely descriptive character.

Turner's thesis reigned supreme until the 1930's—its very simplicity and vagueness, its patriotic character giving it a ready acceptance. Beginning in the 1930's historians, some Turner's students, began to raise fundamental questions, for it was apparent that Turner had relied almost exclusively for his data on the 19th-century trans-Allegheny frontier. He had given little attention to the Southwest and seemed unconcerned about the application of his thesis to the colonial frontier. Scholars now pointed out that the frontier, while it may have promoted individualism and self-reliance, had in fact been anti-intellectual, conformist in social organization, lawless and violent, and, in many ways, anti-democratic. In the Southwestern frontier both aristocracy and slavery had flourished.

Although Turner's thesis is no longer accepted in its simple form, his work has had an enduring value. He turned the attention of historians from an excessive emphasis upon the Teutonic and English background of American institutions to an awareness that the conditions of American life had had a profound effect upon European institutions. As other frontier regions were studied by a new generation of historians, they discovered new clues to the American character which could indeed be related to frontier conditions, although not in the optimistic and idealistic terms employed by Turner. While it was now recognized that the safety valve theory was invalid in terms of an escape for the urban worker, it is now understood that the frontier did offer an opportunity for farmers to better themselves and thus indirectly affected wages in urban areas.

—Harry Ammon

TURNER, Victor (Witter). British social anthropologist. Born in Glasgow, Scotland, 28 May 1920. Studied at University College, London, B.A. (honours) 1949; University of Manchester, Ph.D. 1955. Served in the British Army, 1941-46. Married Edith Lucy Brocklesby Davie in 1943; 5 children. Research Officer, Rhodes-Livingstone Institute, Lusaka, Northern Rhodesia,

1950-54; Lecturer, then Senior Lecturer, University of Manchester, 1943-63; Professor of Anthropology, 1963-68, and Chairman of Committee on African Studies, 1964-68, Cornell University, Ithaca, New York; Professor of Anthropology and Social Thought, University of Chicago, 1968-77. Since 1977, William R. Kenan Professor of Anthropology, University of Virginia, Charlottesville. Simon Research Fellow, University of Manchester, 1956-58; Fellow, Center for Advanced Study in the Behavioral Sciences, Stanford, California, 1961-62; Chairman of Advisory Council to the Department of Anthropology, Princeton University, New Jersey, 1975-77. General Editor, Symbol, Myth, and Ritual series, Cornell University Press. Address: Department of Anthropology, University of Virginia, Charlottesville, Virginia 22903, U.S.A..

PUBLICATIONS

Anthropology

Lunda Rites and Ceremonies. Livingstone, Northern Rhodesia, Rhodes-Livingstone Museum, 1953.
The Lozi People of North-Western Rhodesia. London, International African Institute, 1953.
Schism and Continuity in an African Society: A Study of Ndembu Village Life. Manchester, Manchester University Press, 1957.
Ndembu Divination: Its Symbolism and Techniques. Manchester, Manchester University Press, 1961.
Chihamba the White Spirit: A Ritual Drama of the Ndembu. Manchester, Manchester University Press, 1962.
Lunda Medicine and the Treatment of Disease. Livingstone, Northern Rhodesia, Rhodes-Livingstone Museum, 1964.
The Forest of Symbols: Aspects of Ndembu Ritual. Ithaca, New York, Cornell University Press, 1967.
The Drums of Affliction: A Study of Religious Processes among the Ndembu of Zambia. Oxford, Clarendon Press, 1968.
The Ritual Process: Structure and Anti-Structure. Chicago, Aldine, and London, Routledge, 1969.
Drama, Fields, and Metaphors: Symbolic Action in Human Society. Ithaca, New York, Cornell University Press, 1974.
Revelation and Divination in Ndembu Ritual. Ithaca, New York, Cornell University Press, 1975.
Image and Pilgrimage in Christian Culture: Anthropological Perspectives, with Edith Turner. New York, Columbia University Press, and Oxford, Blackwell, 1978.
Process, Performance, and Pilgrimage. Atlantic Highlands, New Jersey, Humanities Press, 1979.

Other

Editor, with Marc J. Swartz and Arthur Tuden, *Political Anthropology.* Chicago, Aldine, 1966.
Editor, *Profiles of Changes: African Society and Colonial rule.* London, Cambridge University Press, 1971.

*   *   *

To write about Victor Turner's work is to write about the people he studied, the Ndembu of Zambia: for Turner, perhaps more than any other contemporary social anthropologist, has provided a multifaceted, "thick description" (in Clifford Geertz's term) of one particular group of people. From an initial interest in the Ndembu's tribal political organization, Turner went on to provide ethnographic narratives that increasingly focussed on ritual practices and religious beliefs. Taking his analysis of the Ndembu as a point of departure, Turner has made some illuminating suggestions about rites of passage in general. Most recently, he has begun research on the dramatic and ceremonial activities of large-scale European and American cultures.

The Ndembu, according to Turner, number some 18,000 people. They live in highly mobile and dispersed villages, interspersed and inter-married with people from other tribal groups. Turner went to the Ndembu well trained in the orthodoxy of British structuralist-functionalism. At the center of this paradigm there rests an image of social stability manifested in the stability of local level social organization: in brief, stable villages and stable homes. The Ndembu had neither. Viewing the Ndembu from this perspective, Turner's primary concern was to demonstrate that "although the majority of local groups in Ndembu society are relatively transient and unstable, the organizational principles on which they are formed and re-formed are persistent and enduring." Thus, in *Schism and Continuity in an African Society*, Turner argued that the diversity and apparent disorder of Ndembu social life could be understood in terms of the inherent contradictions between two principles: matrilineal descent and virilocal marriage. A Ndembu man, according to Turner, has the right to reside in the village of his matrilineal kin, and it is in this village that a man can fill political offices. At marriage a Ndembu women frequently leaves her own village to reside with her husband. Though this allows the husband to stay where he has matrilineal relatives and political status, it separates the wife and her children from the village of their lineage—and the village in which her male children have political status. Given this structural contradiction there are a number of possible outcomes. This conflict could be "reduced," says Turner, if Ndembu boys went to live with their mothers' brothers while they were growing-up, a practice found among some other African tribes. The Ndembu, however, lack such a practice. Men have strong ties to their sons and discourage them from returning to their matrilineal village; by contrast, maternal uncles try to win the presence of their sisters' children by encouraging their sisters to leave their husbands and return with their children to their own matrilineal village.

Turner argues that the contradiction between matrilineal tendencies, on the one hand, and virilocal and patrifocal tendencies, on the other, manifests itself both in a high rate of mobility and divorce, and also in numerous personal and psychological conflicts. In *The Drums of Affliction* and *Revelation and Divination in Ndembu Ritual*, Turner argues that a wide variety of Ndembu rituals can be understood as attempts to redress social and psychological rifts caused by the underlying contradiction between the principles of matrilineality and patrifocality. Turner develops a Freudian approach to these religious-healing rites, arguing that the rituals provide a routinized and separate domain for dealing with issues that are essentially "too hot to handle" consciously in everyday life. Thus, Turner attributes an intentional subjectivity to the unconscious features of ritual—a view that contrasts strongly with Lévi-Strauss's vision of underlying structuring principles that are prior to individual intentions and affects.

In his analyses of the symbolic components of ritual, Turner emphasizes the multivocality of symbolic features. He argues that by bringing together a multiplicity of associations, rituals express a fundamentally religious vision of the unity of things in the world, and, furthermore, that Ndembu rituals offer this vision in response to particular manifestations of the recurring structural contradictions of Ndembu society. On the basis of numerous detailed interpretations of the symbolic components of Ndembu rituals, Turner concludes that the most powerful symbols are those that combine a physical or organic feature, such as red tree sap that coagulates like blood, with a fundamental principle of the Ndembu social order, such as the unity of matrilines.

In his examination of Ndembu rituals, Turner pays particular attention to rites of passage, which, in his view, are rituals that seek to provide a bridge between two separated social identities. Following Van Gennep, Turner argues that rites of passage are universally marked by three phases: a period of separation, a period of transition or a "liminal" period, and a period of reintegration. Turner's work, such as his analysis of *Mukanda*, the Ndembu Rite of Circumcision, focuses on the second of these

phases. Males pass through *Mukunda* at any age from late childhood to early adulthood. Following their circumcision, the initiates leave their homes to live in a special hut while their circumcision wounds heal. Building both upon Van Gennep's work and upon Mary Douglas's *Purity and Danger*, Turner argues that during this liminal period the initiates are "betwixt and between" childhood and adulthood, and thus they have an "unclear and contradictory" position in the social order. Because their ambiguity is contrary to the rules of social order, they are kept separated from the rest of society, and the initiates' separation from the social order places them outside the confines of its rules. The symbolic expressions of liminal periods, such as masks and songs, typically show a freedom from social taboos, according to Turner. Furthermore, liminal periods are marked by a removal of social distinctions between initiates, and the concomitant presence of what Turner calls "*communitas*," or a general feeling of egalitarian harmony. In brief, in Turner's theory, liminal periods are periods of "anti-structure" in which individuals experience a unity with others normally precluded by established social roles, and in which individuals have an unusual opportunity to act as free and willful agents independent of social determinants. Turner's discussion of liminality has been extremely influential, not only in anthropology, but in history and comparative literature as well. As Turner recognized, his theory has the great strength of offering a systematic account of creative and transforming moments in human history without vulgar reductionism.

As Turner extended his work beyond Ndembu rites of passage, he introduced the term "social drama" to refer more generally to periods of social transition and disharmony. Social dramas, according to Turner, occur because of a breach of the "norm-governed" rules of social life. If a breach escalates, it becomes a social crisis, a period in which the previous social order has, at least temporarily, been destroyed and in which no new order yet reigns. Such periods, Turner argues, are liminal, for they fall "betwixt and between" periods of social order, and thus allow men to operate free of the determining structures of social rules.

Turner's analysis of "Thomas Becket at the Council of Northampton" (in *Drama, Fields, and Metaphors*) provides an impressive demonstration of the insights that the concept of liminality allows beyond the forests of the Ndembu. Nonetheless, Turner's attempt to use "liminality" as a universally valid, cross-cultural term has not been entirely satisfactory. For one thing, Turner has never recognized the distinction between the inversion of social rules and freedom from social rules. Furthermore, as Turner has extended his concepts they have lost a substantial amount of their analytic rigor—for instance in *Drama, Fields, and Metaphors* Turner writes: "I extend" the use of liminality "to refer to any condition outside or on the peripheries of everyday life." In brief, Turner's great contribution lies not in his articulation of theoretical programs, but in the strength of his rich accounts of social life, most particularly, in his success at bridging the long *liminal* passage between the Ndembu and his Western readers.

—Daniel Alan Segal

VAIHINGER, Hans. German philosopher. Born in Nehren, 25 September 1852. Studied at the University of Tübingen; University of Leipzig, Ph.D. 1876. Married Elizabeth Schweigger in 1889; 2 children. Professor, University of Halle, 1884-1906 (retired because of poor health). Founder *Kant-Studien*, 1896, and the Kant Gesellschaft in 1904; with Raymund Schmidt, Founder, *Annalen der Philosophie und philosophischen Kritik*, 1919. Honorary doctorate: University of Königsberg; University of Dresden. *Died 17 December 1933.*

PUBLICATIONS

Philosophy

Göthe als ideal universeller Bildung (lecture).   Stuttgart, Meyer,
   1875.
*Hartmann, Dühring, und Lange: Zur Geschichte der deutschen
   Philosophie im XIX Jahrhunderts.*   Iserholm, Baedeker,
   1876.
Commentar zu Kants Kritik der reinen Vernunft.   Stuttgart,
   Spemann, 2 vols., 1881-92.
Die transcendentale Deduktion der Kategorien.   Halle, Nie-
   meyer, 1902.
Nietzsche als Philosoph.   Berlin, Reuther und Reichard, 1902.
Die Philosophie in der Staatsprüfung.   Berlin, Reuther and
   Reichard, 1906.
*Die Philosophie des Als-Ob: System der theoretischen, prakti-
   schen, und religiösen Fiktionen der Menschheit auf Grund
   eines idealistischen Positivismus.*   Berlin, Reuther and Rei-
   chard, 1911; as *The Philosophy of "As If": A System of the
   Theoretical, Practical, and Religious Fictions of Mankind*,
   London, Kegan Paul, and New York, Harcourt Brace, 1925.
*Der Atheismusstreit gegen die Philosophie des Als Obs und das
   Kantische System.*   Berlin, Reuther and Reichard, 1916.

Other

Editor, with B. Bauch, *Zu Kants Gedächtnis.*   Berlin, Reuther
   and Reichard, 1904.

*   *   *

Hans Vaihinger was a German philosopher best known for his
discussion of "as if" fictions (*Die Philosophie des Als-Ob*, 1911).
Although fictions often are similar in form to hypotheses and
may be confused with them in practice, methodologically the two
are fundamentally different. Hypotheses are "directed toward
reality" and verifiable in principle, but fictions are known to be
false and hence are unverifiable. Humans, according to Vaihinger, need to supplement reality by an idealized and often simplified world. Fictions help to cope with problems in science, metaphysics, theology, social ideals, and morality; they can work *as if*
true, even though they are known to be false. What is untenable
as an hypothesis, therefore, can be useful and even necessary as a
fiction.
   To illustrate, although the Virgin Birth is a myth, Vaihinger
believed that it has been useful symbolically in helping mankind
to resist evil and to raise itself above temptation. An atom is "a
group of contradictory concepts...necessary in order to deal with
reality." Goethe's notion that all known animal species are modifications of a single animal archetype is not to be confused with a
biological hypothesis. Although Goethe's archetypical animal
never existed, that fiction was useful in suggesting biological
classificatory systems and had heuristic value for later evolutionary thought.
   Fictions have four general characteristics. (1) They either fail
to conform to reality or are self-contradictory. (2) They are used
provisionally and later disappear through time or through logical operations. A fiction "is a mere auxiliary construct, a circuitous approach, a scaffolding afterwards to be demolished." (3)
Although the original users of a fiction may confuse it with an
hypothesis, in general a user of a fiction is aware that the fiction is
false. (4) Fictions are means to a specific end; when not so
restricted they are mere subjective fancies.
   Vaihinger emphasized the "law of the preponderance of the
means over the end." Means that are well adapted to a specific
end have a tendency to become independent and to turn into
ends. When that happens, senseless problems arise, such as questions about the origin of the world, its meaning, the purpose of
life, etc. Such world-riddles cannot be solved rationally, but they
can be solved through experience and intuition, which supply a

harmonious unity that reason cannot.
   In addition to his work on fictions, Vaihinger achieved renown
as a Kant scholar. He was interested in the theory of evolution
and the biological function of thought. Although certain of his
views were similar to those of some pragmatists, Vaihinger differentiated his position from any view that links usefulness to
truth. For Vaihinger, false statements can be expedient and
important. Nor should fictionalism be confused with skepticism;
the fictionalist does not doubt the truth of fictions, but knows
them to be false.
   Vaihinger saw much to approve in Schopenhauer's pessimism
and irrationalism. Vaihinger believed that often nature and history are irrational and that pessimism may help one to endure life
and to develop a more objective view of the world. When quite
young, he defined mankind as "a species of monkey suffering
from megalomania," a statement that engendered considerable
controversy. The later Vaihinger regretted his youthful definition but continued to find some merit in it, which suggests
something of his general view of humanity.

—Rollo Handy

VALÉRY, Paul (-Ambroise).   French poet and aesthetician.
Born in Cette (now Sète), 30 October 1871. Educated at the
Lycée, Montpellier; studied at the University of Montpellier,
license in law, 1892. Married Jeannie Gobillard in 1900; 3 children. Worked for the War Office, 1897-99; private secretary to
Edouard Lebey, Director of the press association Agence Havas,
Paris, 1900-22. Co-Editor, with Valery Larbaud and Léon-Paul
Fargue, of the literary review *Commerce*, 1924-32. Administrator, Centre Universitaire Mediterranéen, Nice, after 1933. Chair
of Poetics, Collège de France, Paris, 1937-45. Honorary doctorate: Oxford University, 1931. Chevalier, 1923, Officier, 1926,
and Commandeur, 1931, Légion d'Honneur. Member, Académie Française, 1925. *Died* (in Paris) *20 July 1945*.

PUBLICATIONS (The references given here are usually to the first
commercial editions rather than to the limited editions in which
many of Valéry's works first appeared)

Collections

Oeuvres.   Paris, 12 vols.: vols. A and B, Le Sagittaire, 1931;
   vols. C through L, Gallimard, 1933-50.
Oeuvres, edited by Jean Hytier.   Paris, Gallimard, 2 vols.,
   1957-60.
The Collected Works of Paul Valéry, edited by Jackson
   Mathews.   New York, Pantheon, 15 vols., 1956-75.

Philosophy, Art and Literature

La Soirée avec Monsieur Teste.   Paris, Gallimard, 1919; as *An
   Evening with Mr. Teste*, Paris, Ronald Davis, 1925; revised
   edition as *Monsieur Teste*, Paris, Gallimard, 1946; as *Monsieur Teste*, New York, Knopf, 1947; London, Peter Owen,
   1951.
Introduction à la méthode de Léonard de Vinci.   Paris, Nouvelle Revue Française, 1919; as *Introduction to the Method of
   Leonardo da Vinci*, London, Rodker, 1929.
Eupalinos; ou, L'Architecte, précédé de L'Âme et la danse.   Paris, Gallimard, 1923; as *Eupalinos; or, The Architect*, London
   and New York, Oxford University Press, 1932; as *Dance and
   the Soul*, London, John Lehmann, 1951.
Fragments sur Mallarmé.   Paris, Ronald Davis, 1924.
Situation de Baudelaire.   Paris, Madame Lesage, 1924.
Variété.   Paris, Gallimard, 5 vols., 1924-44; vols. 1-2, as *Var-*

iety, New York, Harcourt Brace, 1927-38.

Durtal.   Paris, Champion, 1925.

Études et fragments sur le rêve.   Paris, Claude Aveline, 1925.

Le Retour de Hollande, Descartes et Rembrandt.   Maestricht, Stols, 1926.

Petit recueil de paroles de circonstance.   Paris, Plaisir de Bibliophile, 1926.

Discours de la diction des vers.   Paris, Le Livre, 1926.

Maitres et amis.   Paris, Beltrand, 1927.

Discours sur Émile Verhaeren.   Paris, Champion, 1927.

Discours de réception a l'Académie Française.   Paris, Gallimard, 1927.

Lettre à Madame C....   Paris, Grasset, 1928.

Poésie: Essais sur la poétique et le poète.   Paris, Bertrand Guégan, 1928.

Variation sur une "Pensée, " annotée par l'auteur.   Liège, Balancier, 1930.

Littérature.   Paris, Gallimard, 1930.

Discours en l'honneur de Goethe.   Paris, Gallimard, 1932.

L'Idée fixe.   Paris, Gallimard, 1934.

Pièces sur l'art.   Paris, Gallimard, 1934.

Villon et Verlaine.   Maestricht, Stols, 1937.

Essai sur Stendhal.   Paris, Schiffren, 1937.

L'Homme et la coquille.   Paris, Nouvelle Revue Française, 1937.

Discours aux chirurgiens.   Paris, Nouvelle Revue Française, 1938.

Introduction à la poétique.   Paris, Gallimard, 1938.

Degas, Danse, Dessin.   Paris, Gallimard, 1938; as *Degas, Dance, Drawing*, London, Fama, and New York, Lear, 1948.

Existence de symbolisme.   Maestricht, Stols, 1939.

Poésie et pensée abstraite (lecture).   Oxford, Clarendon Press, 1939.

Mélange.   Paris, Gallimard, 1941.

Dialogue de l'arbre.   Paris, Firmin-Didot, 1943.

Au sujet de Nerval.   Paris, Textes Prétextes, 1944.

Voltaire (lecture).   Paris, Domat-Montchrestien, 1945.

Henri Bergson.   Paris, Domat Montchrestien, 1945.

Souvenirs Poétiques.   Paris, Le Prat, 1947.

Vues.   Paris, La Table Ronde, 1948.

Ecrits divers sur Stéphane Mallarmé.   Paris, Gallimard, 1950.

Verse and Prose Poems

La Jeune Parque.   Paris, Nouvelle Revue Française, 1917.

Album de vers anciens 1890-1900.   Paris, Monnier, 1920.

Charmes ou poèmes.   Paris, Nouvelle Revue Française, 1922.

Amphion: Mélodrame.   Paris, Rouart Lerolle, 1931.

Séramis (poetic drama).   Paris, Nouvelle Revue Française, 1934.

Paraboles.   Paris, Editions du Raisin, 1935.

Mélange (poetry and prose).   Paris, Gallimard, 1941.

L'Ange.   Paris, Nouvelle Revue Française, 1946.

Other

Une conquête méthodique.   Paris, Champion, 1924.

Propos sur l'intelligence.   Paris, À L'Enseigne de la Porte Étroite, 1926.

Rhumbs.   Paris, Gallimard, 1926.

Autre Rhumbs.   Paris, Gallimard, 1927.

Discours de l'histoire.   Paris, Les Presses Modernes, 1932.

Choses tues.   Paris, Gallimard, 1932.

Moralités.   Paris, Gallimard, 1932.

Suite.   Paris, Gallimard, 1934.

Analecta.   Paris, Gallimard, 1935.

Tel quel.   Paris, Gallimard, 2 vols., 1941-43.

Mauvaises Pensées et autres.   Paris, Gallimard, 1942.

Mon Faust (ébauches).   Paris, Gallimard, 1946.

Histoires brisées.   Paris, Gallimard, 1950.

Lettres à quelques-uns.   Paris, Gallimard, 1952.

Correspondance d'André Gide et de Paul Valéry.   Paris, Gallimard, 1955.

Correspondance de Paul Valéry et Gustave Fourment.   Paris, Gallimard, 1957.

Cahiers.   Paris, Centre National de la Recherche Scientifique, 29 vols., 1957-61.

Translator, *Les Bucoliques de Virgile.*   Paris, Scripta et Picta, 1956.

*

Bibliography: *Bibliographie des oeuvres de Paul Valéry* (1895-1925) by Ronald Davis and Raoul Simonson, Paris, Plaisir de Bibliophile, 1926; in *Oeuvres 2*, 1960.

Critical Studies: *Paul Valéry and the Civilized Mind* by Norman Sutcliffe, London, Oxford University Press, 1955; *Valéry* by André Berne-Joffroy, Paris, Gallimard, 1960; *The Universal Self: A Study of Paul Valéry* by Agnes E. Mackay, Toronto, University of Toronto Press, 1961; *Paul Valéry* by Henry Grubbs, New York, Twayne, 1968; *Paul Valéry and the Poetry of Voice* by Christine M. Crow, Cambridge, Cambridge University Press, 1982.

*   *   *

Paul Valéry's poetry, criticism, essays, and dialogues mark the culminating point of several traditions in French literature. As a poet, he rejected both the romantic concept of inspiration and the equally romantic idea that poetry expressed the author's own emotions. Instead, he saw the poem as a linguistic device for arousing emotions in the mind of the reader, and this cult of impersonality links him with the classicism of the 17th-century. So, too, does his cult of form, and desire to dominate instead of being led by language. At the same time, his interest in the workings of his own mind links him with the philosophical introspectives who form part of the French Cartesian tradition. So, too, does his interest in the mathematical sciences, reflected in detail in the 29 volumes of his posthumously published *Cahiers*.

Like his great contemporary, Marcel Proust, Valéry was preoccupied by the same problem of trying to find, in an age dominated by analysis, some steady and defining core to his own personality; and, again like Proust, he found it in physical sensation and in the act of literary creation, remarking that he constructed himself at the same time as he perfected his poems. In his cult of pure poetry, he followed the tradition exemplified by his acknowledged master, Stéphane Mallarmé. However, his best and best-known poem, "Le Cimetière Marin," combines a Mallarmean concern for precise poetic diction with a meditation on the great philosophical issues of life, death, and immortality which makes it perhaps the most immediately accessible poem in the French symbolist tradition. Technically, the poem offers the unusual quality of being written in ten syllable lines and not in the traditional Alexandrine; while its celebration of an essentially pagan attitude to nature and religious belief looks forward to the passionate agnosticism of the early Camus.

Valéry's creative period as a poet did not extend beyond the early 1920's. Instead, he became a kind of official *homme de lettres*, publishing the literary criticism and social or philosophical commentaries collected in the five volumes of *Variété* (1924-1945). His ideal self-image as a writer capable of totally dominating language led him to write one of his best works, the dialogue on architecture, *Eupalinos* (1924) in exactly the number of words needed to fit into a book of diagrams and illustrations. In 1967, this and other dialogues won him an unexpected, posthumous glory by being very successful on the Parisian stage. The National Funeral awarded to him in 1945 recognised his position as almost the official poet of the now defunct Third Republic, as well as his hostility to the even more defunct Vichy régime. In

1936, it had been his words which were graven upon the outer walls of the Palais de Chaillot, built to celebrate the International Exhibition. They read: "Every man creates, as he breathes, without knowing what he does. But the artist feels himself creating. His act commits the whole of himself. His beloved travail fortifies him."

—Philip Thody

VEBLEN, Thorstein (Bunde). American economist. Born in Cato Township, Wisconsin, 30 July 1857. Educated at Carleton College Academy and Carleton College, Northfield, Minnesota, 1874-80, B.A. in philosophy 1880; Johns Hopkins University, Baltimore, 1881; Yale University, New Haven, Connecticut (Porter Prize, 1884), Ph.D. 1884; studied economics at Cornell University, Ithaca, New York, 1891. Married Ellen May Rolfe in 1888 (divorced); married Anne Fessenden in 1914 (died, 1920), 2 step-daughters. Taught at Monoma Academy, Madison, Wisconsin, 1880-81; Fellow, 1892-93, Reader, 1893-94, Associate, 1894-96, Instructor, 1896-1900, and Assistant Professor of Economics, 1900-06, University of Chicago; Associate Professor of Economics, Stanford University, California, 1906-09; Lecturer in Economics, University of Missouri, Columbia, 1911-18, and New School for Social Research, New York, 1919-26. Managing Editor, Journal of Political Economy, 1896-1905; Co-Editor, Dial, New York, 1918. Died 3 August 1929.

PUBLICATIONS

Economics

The Theory of the Leisure Class: An Economic Study in the Evolution of Institutions. New York, Macmillan, 1899; London, Allen and Unwin, 1924.
The Theory of Business Enterprise. New York, Scribner, 1904.
The Instinct of Workmanship, and the State of the Industrial Arts. New York, Macmillan, 1914.
Imperial Germany and the Industrial Revolution. New York, Macmillan, 1915.
An Inquiry into the Nature of Peace and the Terms of Its Perpetuation. New York, Macmillan, 1917.
The Higher Learning in America: A Memorandum on the Conduct of Universities by Business Men. New York, Huebsch, 1918.
The Vested Interests and the State of the Industrial Arts ("The Modern Point of View and the New Order"). New York, Huebsch, 1919; London, Allen and Unwin, 1924.
The Place of Science in Modern Civilization and Other Essays. New York, Huebsch, 1919; as Veblen on Marx, Race, Science, and Economics, New York, Capricorn, 1969.
The Engineers and the Price System. New York, Huebsch, 1921.
Absentee Ownership and Business Enterprise in Recent Times: The Case of America. New York, Huebsch, 1923; London, Allen and Unwin, 1924.
Essays in Our Changing Order, edited by Leon Ardzrooni. New York, Viking Press, 1934.
What Veblen Taught: Selected Writings, edited by Wesley C. Mitchell. New York, Viking Press, 1936.
The Portable Veblen, edited by Max Lerner. New York, Viking Press, 1948; London, Penguin, 1976.
Selections, edited by Bernard Rosenberg. New York, Crowell, 1963.

Other

Translator, The Science of Finance, by Gustav Cohn. Chicago, University of Chicago Press, 1895.
Translator, Science and the Workingmen, by Ferdinand Lassalle. New York, International Library, 1900.
Translator, The Laxdaela Saga. New York, Huebsch, 1925.

*

Critical Studies: Thorstein Veblen: A Chapter in American Economic Thought by Richard Victor Teggart, Berkeley, University of California Press, 1932; Thorstein Veblen and His America by Joseph Dorfman, New York, Viking Press, 1934; Thorstein Veblen: A Critical Interpretation by David Riesman, New York, Scribner, 1953; The Values of Veblen by Bernard Rosenberg, Washington, D.C., Public Affairs Press, 1956; Thorstein Veblen: A Critical Reappraisal edited by Douglas F. Dowd, Ithaca, New York, Cornell University Press, 1958; The Technical Elite by Jay M. Gould, New York, Kelley, 1966; The Carleton College Veblen Seminar Essays edited by Carlton C. Qualey, New York, Columbia University Press, 1968; The Political Economy of Thorstein Veblen and John Kenneth Galbraith by Jonathan Kahn, Stanford, California, Stanford University, 1974; Thorstein Veblen and the Institutionalists: A Study in the Social Philosophy of Economics by David Seckler, London, Macmillan, 1975; The Bard of Savagery: Thorstein Veblen and Modern Social Theory by John P. Diggins, Hassocks, Sussex, Harvester Press, 1978.

*   *   *

Thorstein Veblen, an enigmatic and eclectic social thinker, has been classified as an economist, sociologist, anthropologist, psychologist, and philosopher. He was a relentless critic of both radical and reactionary social practices and theories but he never became involved in activist social movements. Dewey noted that Veblen's phrases—"conspicuous consumption," "the leisure class," "predatory society," "the discipline of the machine," and many others—have been better remembered than the concepts which Veblen elaborated. Among post-Darwinian thinkers he must be counted as one of the most forthright exponents of the theory of social evolution. He recognized the severity of the demands this theory placed upon dominant conceptions in many arenas of modern thought.

In his first published work, an essay entitled "Kant's Critique of Judgement," Veblen explored the process of judgment whereby a free agent acts intelligently in a sphere of cause and effect. The free person must be able to exert a casuality on things, or else his freedom is only an absurdity. The agent must know what will be the effect of this or that action, if his activity is not to be nugatory or deleterious. Since the immediate data of experience do not tell what the effect of an action will be, rational judgment must mediate between theoretical knowledge of casuality and intelligent action in the phenomenal realm. Veblen was concerned with the passage of judgment beyond the simple data of experience as it seeks a universal not given in empirical cognition. Since human choice presupposes a teleology of action, and since reasoned experience presupposes universal casuality, reflective judgment must think things through in a system as though they were made by an intelligent cause, but one must not suppose that this is ultimately true.

Veblen outlined two stages of inductive judgement. Initially, the simple data of apprehension are assessed by subjective aesthetic judgment. The judgment of taste is not logical, and in it feeling is its own activity. Next, such data of cognition and also concepts may be logically considered as entering into a system in which they must stand in relation to other data. Given the nature of the faculties of reason and action, the relations under which the world of reality is conceived are those of universal interaction and interdependence within a unitary whole, "made by an intelligent cause, and made with intention and purpose." Such an approach yields only an imputed finality and intelligent cause to the things of the world.

Veblen objected to claims that final causes have been proved to operate in history, economics, politics, and evolution, and also to claims that definitive normative laws have been discovered therein. Each individual carries a vast accumulation of unreflective phenomenal data as well as the abstract principles of choice and casuality. Each individual is, in his own apprehension, a centre of unfolding activity—"teleological activity"—an agent seeking in every act the accomplishment of some objective impersonal end (*The Place of Science in Modern Civilization*). For Veblen, the most fundamental fact in man's psychology is that he continually attempts to alter his life and the conditions of his living, that individually and collectively men always and everywhere seek to do something (*The Theory of the Leisure Class*). Thus Veblen rejected hedonism and utilitarianism on the ground that they fail to conceive man as the bearer of a process of living, except in the sense that he is subject to a series of permutations enforced upon him by external circumstances alien to him. A simplistic conception of man as a self-contained sphere of desire, oscillating and equilibrizing with the parallelogram of forces, leaves him isolated and without antecedent or consequent.

What all such theories lack, according to Veblen, is the ability to locate human activity in a context of cumulative understanding and ubiquitous interactions extending through time. In addition to raw data and the constitutive principles of reason and action, each individual retains a cumulative body of tentative testimony regarding the quality of past inductive reflections and attempts to embody such intentions. The principle of reflective judgement acts as a constant impetus to further formulations of means to carry out human ends in fresh circumstances. The life history of the individual is a cumulative process of adaptation of means to ends that cumulatively change as the process goes on, both the agent and the environment being at any point the outcome of the previous process. The methods of life today derive from the habits of life carried over from yesterday, along with the residue of circumstances produced by that life. Veblen referred to the coherent structure of propensities and habits which seeks expression in an unfolding activity as the "temperament" of an individual, and as displaying an overall theory of life, a specific "spiritual attitude" (*Essays in Our Changing Order*.) The same process in a society makes up its institutions. There is an inherent natural process of change in the form of active human intelligence taken collectively. This evolution of society is substantially a process of mental adaptation on the part of individuals under the stress of circumstances, a mutual adjustment of internal and external relations. "The same physical mechanism that expresses itself in one direction as conduct expresses itself in another direction as knowledge." Thus, there is a high degree of interdependence between the cultural situation and the state of theoretical enquiry which affects the methods and canons of truth-seeking moral and aesthetic evaluation, and the legitimation of institutions and habits of thought.

Veblen placed this overall evolution of active, or teleological, human intellect within the broader framework of evolving intelligent life, but he argued that this teleological aptitude is a product of unteleological natural selection. The foundations of pragmatic intelligence are not pragmatic, nor even personal or sensible. On the human plane, not only is the agent's intelligent response of a teleological character, it may also involve a non-motor, non-pragmatic element of irrelevant attention, or idle curiosity which formulates interpretations of the sequence of activities occurring in observed phenomena. Idle curiosity nurtures continued advance toward a more and more comprehensive system of knowledge. Threading his way between mechanistic determinism and behavioural reductionism on the one side, and transcendental idealism on the other, Veblen found that the facility of collective life establishes a code of action, habits of thought, and discernible intentions.

In the light of this fundamental framework of a theory of social evolution, it is possible to set in perspective the major elements of Veblen's far-reaching criticism of the contemporary social structure. He loosely differentiated a series of states of society in terms of their primary economic modalities. For him, economics is essentially an evolving expression of human teleological activity with regard to the material means of life. As such, its root factors include human knowledge, skills, and habits of thought (institutions) as well as the mass of external materials and resources involved in the production of goods and services. The series of economically differentiated societies set out by Veblen express not only economic attitudes, but cognitive and communal attitudes as well. He described these in terms of three genetic instincts. First of all, directly connected with economic activity is the *instinct of workmanship*, a taste for or sense of efficiency, merit, and serviceability in purposive effort, coupled with a distaste for waste, futility, and incapacity. Secondly, connected with knowledge of causality and means, is the *instinct of idle curiosity* which, in its broadest aspect, envisages a spiritually consistent theory of life. Thirdly, connected with the legitimation of social institutions in relation to an ideal of manhood, is the *instinct of race solidarity*, which is called conscience and includes the sense of truthfulness and equity. These three instincts correspond to the elements of efficacy, interdependence, and unity in Veblen's analysis of free action based upon reflective judgement about causes. They are, in effect, normative principles.

The sequence of societies depicted by Veblen begins with the primitive society and passes to the predatory "lower barbarian" or feudal society, and then to the equally predatory "higher barbarian" or pecuniary society, which itself has two stages, the handicraft age and the machine age. This last is contemporary industrial civilization. According to Veblen, the dominant spiritual feature of neolithic culture was an unreflecting, unformulated sense of group solidarity, largely expressing itself in a complacent, but by no means strenuous, sympathy with the facility of human life, and an uneasy revulsion against apprehended inhibition or the futility of life. In primitive society the instinct of workmanship finds its play in providing basic sustenance and the habit of emulation operates within the sense of solidarity. The primitive society is essentially displaced by the lower barbarian society, which is characterized by its predatory restless nature. Eventually, primitive societies accumulate sufficient matter-of-fact knowledge regarding the production of goods to devise technologies capable of generating excess wealth. The availability of excess wealth creates the possibility of its exclusive acquisition and a relative release from the need to work at all. Particularly in societies where hunting becomes established, those able to inflict injury and death upon animate nature become the objects of emulation and the exemplars of worthiness. Veblen suggested that women were the most efficacious and earliest form of property for the predatory barbarian.

With the development of predatory society, the instinct of workmanship is contaminated through displacement from industry or work to fighting and exploitation. The instinct of idle curiosity is also affected, first through concern with hunting magic and ceremony and then through a pragmatic anthromorphic reworking of myths and cosmologies to reflect the principles of divine authority and moral subservience. The instinct of solidarity is pressed into the scheme of feudal status hierarchies based upon obligations of humility and the recognition of inferiority. Through invidious comparison based upon envy, those most able to exercise ferocity, force, and fraud are judged most successful: they became the lords, warriors, priests, sportsmen, and schoolmen constituting the barbarian leisure class.

The transition from the lower barbarian society to the higher barbarian is marked by the competitive seizure of power by those skilled in pecuniary force and fraud from those skilled in merely physical rapine. Skill in the manipulation of markets includes the establishment of vested property rights. Workmanship comes to be measured in profits and production, not quality, and superiority begins to find its measure in conspicuous consumption and waste as well as leisure. Idle curiosity and learning are set to work converting the theory of divine right into natural rights of property, and exchanging the blessings of the sacriments and Inquisition for inviolability to contracts and the poorhouse. Social solidarity is adapted into the theory of political rights. To Veblen, the machine age of pecuniary society presents a major tension or paradox, comparable to the crises that brought about earlier evolutionary social changes. The vested interests of the age continue to develop their instrumentalities of predatory behaviour. They are able to sabotage or waste productivity through imperialistic wars and cycles of depression, thereby maintaining their superior status and self-regard. While there are concessions in wages and social services, any loss of status is made up through inflation of currency and profits from greater consumer consumption stimulated by advertising.

The discipline of the machine for the industrial worker is one of close attention to impersonal matters of fact, contributing to the development of a vast body of mechanistic knowledge or empirical science. The institution of empirical science is marked by impersonality and probability, sharply at odds with the personalism and absolutism of the pecuniary metaphysics of higher barbarism. The machine discipline breeds a scepticism towards the received habits of thought of the business culture. To Veblen, writing in 1914, new habits of thought connected with the machine age had consolidated to the point where a crisis of confidence in the old order was likely. To these new ways of thinking, the waste and futility of business methods was an affront to the instinct of workmanship; the scheme of business metaphysics was either unintelligible or hopelessly incomplete; and the claims to equity and honesty made by the pecuniary culture for its distribution of approval, self-regard, and work were losing all legitimacy before the instinct of solidarity.

During and after World War I Veblen saw in dynastic Germany a lower, more feudal form of barbarism enjoying the advantage of borrowing the technology of the machine age, while England, the originator of machine industry, had to pay the penalty of going first. In 1915 he pointed out Japan's similar opportunity to gain the advantage of borrowing and wrote: "If the Japanese are to utilize these newfound gains for dynastic aggrandizement in Asia, they must strike within the effective lifetime of the generation now coming to maturity" (*Essays in Our Changing Order*). Although for a moment he held out some hope for the possibilities of the League of Nations, after Versailles he held that through political chicanery the vested interests had succeeded in making the world safe for war. He characterized the American red scare of the twenties as a form of *dementia praecox*, formented the redirect to attention of the passive population away from the disembowelling of the country's natural resources by a system of absentee owners. Although he held that America's abundance of resources gave it a deeper capacity for self-deception, he contended that the magic of overvalued capital stock and credit expansion would eventually lead to "bread lines and movies"—an apt description of the 1930's. Eventually, he thought, the issue would come to a head, in America and throughout the global business civilization, when the proponents of social reform would either prevail through abolition of ownership of industry, or yield in their efforts and spill their strength on the sands of patriotism.

Veblen was convinced that the machine process and discipline, mechanistic empirical science, technology and engineering had rooted themselves as the dominant circumstances and habits of thought of the century. He argued that life and material well-being were already in the hands of the technological industrial system, whose character is not merely international, but cosmopolitan. Yet, Veblen argued, if the metaphysics of the machine is apparently on the ascendant, there are other, older grounds of finality that may conceivably be better, nobler, worthier, more profound, more beautiful. He concluded that the race reached the human plane with little of our modern knowledge of facts; throughout the greater part of its life-history it has been accustomed to make its higher generalizations and to formulate its larger principles in other terms than those of passionless matters

of fact. "This manner of knowledge has occupied an increasing share of men's attention in the past, since it bears in a decisive way upon the minor affairs of the workaday life; but it has never until now been put in the first place, as the dominant note of human culture. The normal man, such as his inheritance·has made him, has therefore good cause to be restive under its dominion" (*The Place of Science in Modern Civilization*).

—R.N. Iyer

VERNANT, Jean-Pierre. French classicist. Born in Provins, 4 January 1914. Educated at the Lycées Carnot and Louis-le-Grand, Paris; studied at the Sorbonne, Paris, Agrégé de Philosophie. Married Lida Nahimovitch in 1939. Professor of Philosophy, Lycée de Toulouse, 1940, and Lycée Jacques Decour, Paris, 1946. Since 1948, Associate, then Director of Research, Centre National de la Recherche Scientifiques. Director of Studies, of 6th Section, then 5th Section, École Pratique des Hautes Études, 1958-75. Since 1975, Professor, Collège de France, Paris. Associate Member, Royal Academy of Belgium; Officer, Légion d'Honneur. Address: Collège de France, 11 Place Marcelin-Berthelot, Paris 5, France.

PUBLICATIONS

Classics

Les Origines de la pensée grecque. Paris, P.U.F., 1962.
Mythe et pensée chez les Grecs: Études de psychologie historique. Paris, Maspero, 1965; revised edition, 2 vols., 1971.
Mythe et tragédie en Grèce ancienne, with Pierre Vidal-Naquet. Paris, Maspero, 1972; as *Tragedy and Myth in Ancient Greece*, Brighton, Harvester, and Atlantic Highlands, New Jersey, Humanities Press, 1981.
Mythe et société en Grèce ancienne. Paris, Maspero, 1974; as *Myth and Society in Ancient Greece*, Brighton, Harvester, 1979; Atlantic Highlands, New Jersey, Humanities Press, 1980.
Les Ruses de l'intelligence: La Métis des Grecs, with M. Detienne. Paris, Flammarion, 1974; as *Cunning Intelligence in Greek Culture and Society*, Hassocks, Sussex, Harvester Press, and Atlantic Highlands, New Jersey, Humanities Press, 1978.
Religion grecque, religions antiques. Paris, Maspero, 1976.
Oedipe et Prométhée: La Conception mythique de l'homme en Grece (in Japanese). Tokyo, Misuzu Shobo, 1978.
Religions, histoires, raisons. Paris, Maspero, 1979.
La Cuisine du sacrifice en pays grec, with M. Detienne. Paris, Gallimard, 1979.

Other

Editor, *Problèmes de la guerre en Grèce ancienne.* Paris, Mouton, 1968.
Editor, with Gherardo Gnoli, *La Mort, les morts dans les sociétés anciennes.* Cambridge, Cambridge University Press, 1982.

*

Critical Studies: "Jean-Pierre Vernant Issue" of *Arethusa* (Buffalo), Spring and Fall, 1982.

*   *   *

Jean-Pierre Vernant is probably the most influential living classical scholar. Over a twenty-year period his effect on his collaborators, younger colleagues, and students has been such as to create a whole school of Greek studies in Paris, and his influence on the work of scholars elsewhere, particularly in Italy and America, has been extensive and radical, often shaping the orientation of a whole scholarly career, even for those who have never met him and know him only through his work. At the same time, Vernant is not, in the ordinary sense, a classicist, and his influence has often been negative, in that he for some represents a path not to be taken. Precisely because he proposes a radical re-orientation of the field, he is, for many classicists, a scholar to be glanced at and then carefully ignored.

The field of classics traditionally has defined itself by its commitment to texts: to editions, commentaries, and explication of the great works of the ancients. Vernant is not much interested in literature, however; he is rather interested in culture. He looks through the text, as it were, to the underlying categories and concepts which were presumed as common ground by the poet and his audience, and thereby made possible communication between them. Because his analysis is on so general a level it often seems rather abstract; he writes on Greek conceptions of space, of time, of the community and the individual, of gods, men, and animals, of the living and the dead. All of these categories, for him, stand to be investigated because the Greek way of thinking about them, of defining the boundaries and relating the contrasted elements, was very different from our own. In his work we encounter always the otherness of the ancients; their works may be "our" classics, but the people who made them, and for whom they were made, were, it seems, very different from us.

Vernant is often classed as a structuralist, and his work does have certain affinities with the structuralisms (very different from each other) of Georges Damézil and Claude Lévi-Strauss. Vernant is, however, much more of a culture historian than either of these; whereas Lévi-Strauss is in search of human nature or universal truths about mankind, whereas Dumézil discerns patterns which, while historically conditioned, remain suitable for millenia, Vernant is concerned to discover facts which, although general and abstract, are still particular facts about the Greeks, especially the Greeks of the late archaic and classical periods. Furthermore Vernant is interested in historical change, and also in the way in which change is perceived by those who undergo it. His discussions of Greek tragedy, in particular, see it as an art expressive of and responsive to historical change, as each poet in each work dramatises the contradictions and ambiguities of a culture in transition, unsure of itself, and engaged in a continuing argument with itself.

Vernant has grown away from the narower ideological Marxism of his youth; nevertheless he remains, in a sense, a populist. He investigates classical culture, not as the creation of a few geniuses, but as the common possession of a whole people. He resists any tendency to idealize these Greeks; for him they are (like us) violent, sexual, and often anxious. Particularly in his studies of *metis*, the crafty, playful, disingenuous gift of the trickster, he shows us the underside of Greek intellectuality.

Vernant's first book, *Les Origines de la pensée grecque*, argued that the origins of Greek intellectualism were to be found in the peculiarly political character of Greek social life; the Greeks handled conflict and distributed resources by submitting questions to open debate, and they learned how to think because they were forced to talk. This placing of intellectual history in a firm context of concrete social institutions has also characterized his later work.

Lévi-Strauss says somewhere of himself that he has a "neolithic mind"; Vernant's work is more accessible to us, perhaps because his sympathies are not with the primitive, but with the pre-classical, the archaic. In his work the language of mythology and ritual, of contests between opposing gods, of daemonic forces, threatening impurity, and ritual purification, seems a natural way to talk about the constitution of the human world. Vernant's love of abstraction and paradox is typically French, but in the "ancient quarrel between the philosophers and the poets" of which Plato's Socrates speaks, Vernant has taken the side of the poets. He has been a master teacher, generous with his

time and his thought; many of his best ideas appear in print in the work of others. These others are drawn to him by his generosity, his gifts, and his vitality; he seems at home in this early Greek world, and communicates his joy in what he finds there.

—James Redfield

VOEGELIN, Eric (Herman Wilhelm).   American historian and political philosopher.   Born in Cologne, Germany, 3 January 1901; emigrated to the United States, 1938: naturalized, 1944. Studied at the University of Vienna, Ph.D. 1922. Married Lissy Onken in 1932. Assistant in Law Faculty, 1923-24, 1928-29, Privat-Dozent, 1929, and Associate Professor until dismissed by the Nazi Government, 1936, University of Vienna; Instructor, Harvard University, Cambridge, Massachusetts, 1938-39; Instructor, Bennington College, Vermont, 1939; Assistant Professor, University of Alabama, Tuscaloosa, 1939-42; Associate Professor, 1942-46, Professor, 1946, and Boyd Professor, from 1952, Louisiana State University, Baton Rouge: now emeritus. Professor of Political Science, University of Munich, 1958. Henry Salvatori Distinguished Scholar, Hoover Institution, Stanford, California. Member, Administrative Board, Volkshochschule, Vienna, and Austrian Commission of Civil Service Examiners, both 1936-38. Address: 839 Sonoma Terrace, Stanford, California 94305, U.S.A.

PUBLICATIONS

History and Political Philosophy

Über die Form des amerikanischen Geistes.   Tübingen, Mohr, 1928.
Rasse und Staat.   Tübingen, Mohr, 1933.
Die Rassenidee in der Geistesgeschichte von Ray bis Carus. Berlin, Junker and Dünnhaupt, 1933.
Der autoritäre Staat: Ein Versuch über das österreichische Staatsproblem.   Vienna, Springer, 1936.
Die politischen Religionen.   Vienna, Bermann-Fischer, 1938.
The New Science of Politics: An Introduction (lectures).   Chicago, University of Chicago Press, 1952.
Order and History: Israel and Revolution; The World of the Polis; Plato, and Aristotle; The Ecumenic Age.   Baton Rouge, Louisiana State University Press, 4. vols., 1956-74.
Wissenschaft, Politik, und Gnosis.   Munich, Kösel, 1959; as *Science, Politics, and Gnosticism* (includes the essay "Ersatz Religion"), Chicago, Regnery, 1968.
Anamnesis: Zur Theorie der Geschichte und Politik.   Munich, R. Piper, 1966; abridged edition as *Anamnesis*, edited by Gerhart Niemeyer, Notre Dame, Indiana, University of Notre Dame Press, 1978.
From Enlightenment to Revolution, edited by John H. Hallowell.   Durham, North Carolina, Duke University Press, 1975.
Conversations with Eric Voegelin (lectures and discussions), edited by Eric O'Connor.   Montreal, Thomas More Institute, 1980.

Other

Editor, *Zwischen Revolution und Restauration: Politisches Denken in England im 17. Jahrhundert.*   Munich, List Verlag, 1968.

*

Bibliography: in *The History of Order: Essays on History, Con-

sciousness, and Politics edited by Peter J. Opitz and Gregor Sebba, Stuttgart, Klett Cotta, 1981.

Critical Studies: *Eric Voegelin's Search for Order in History* edited by Stephen A. McKnight, Baton Rouge, Louisiana State University Press, 1978; *The Voegelinian Revolution: A Biographical Introduction* by Ellis Sandoz, Baton Rouge, Louisiana State University Press, 1981, and *Eric Voegelin's Thought: A Critical Appraisal* edited by Sandoz, Durham, North Carolina, Duke University Press, 1982; *Eric Voegelin, Philosopher of History* by Eugene Webb, Seattle, University of Washington Press, 1982.

*   *   *

Eric Voegelin is a political philosopher and a philosopher of history. In both connections he has been centrally concerned with the nature and sources of order, both in society and in the individual. Like Plato, who has been probably the greatest single influence on his thought, Voegelin believes that order and disorder in society and history are rooted in the order or disorder embodied in persons according to their success or failure in the pursuit of authentic existence, which Voegelin refers to as an "open" existence or "existence in truth." This makes Voegelin's thought fundamentally philosophical in the classical sense, since it is more than just a speculation about objects, their metaphysical structure, and their place in a universal system, but is rather a "way" or quest for true being.

The starting point of Voegelin's reflection is therefore not an analysis of speculative constructions or a history of ideas, but an exploration of historical human experience. Experience, as he conceives it, is always concrete and becomes in each individual the starting point for a process in which one may develop critical self-awareness by way of a reflection on the symbols in which experience articulates itself in consciousness. Historically the modes and patterns of symbolization take shape and change over time. For example, the civilizations of ancient Mesopotamia and Egypt, with which Voegelin's major study, *Order and History*, commences, developed cosmological myths to represent their experience of participation in the creation of order in this world and of their striving for attunement to a transcendent source of order. Some subsequent cultures (e.g., Israelite, Greek, and Christian), Voegelin suggests, have developed different symbols to express further insights into the radical difference, within experience, between the world and what transcends it. Or else, as in the case of such modern ideologies as Fascism or Marxism, other symbols have been developed to express distorted conceptions growing out of the experience of what Voegelin calls "closed" existence. The difference between existence in the mode of openness and in that of closure, according to Voegelin, lies in the willingness or unwillingness of a person to notice the significant features of his experience and to accept its essential structure, which he believes involves an awareness both of human limitedness and fallibility and of an inescapable longing for the perfection of being represented by such symbols as "God," the "Beyond" (Plato's *epekeina*), etc. Voegelin's special term for this fundamental longing as a characteristic feature of human experience is "tension" (*Spannung* in his German writings), and he believes that this "tension of existence" or "tension toward the beyond" is the central dynamism of human thought and activity. When it is interpreted inadequately, its energy can become virtually demonic. In the Marxist case, for example, Voegelin believes the mistake of supposing that the perfection represented by the beyond can be realized within a transfigured humanity in this world has given rise to coercive efforts to force such a development. This is essentially the mistake, which is shared, Voegelin believes, among many false ideologies, of supposing that the experience of tension might be overcome in a possible tension-free existence. Voegelin's own belief is that existential tension is fundamental to human being and that in acknowledging and submitting to its demands, such as the pursuit of truth and justice, one may discover the possibility of authentic humanity

and aspire to genuinely philosophical existence. Socrates and Christ, thinks Voegelin, as well as certain other seminal figures in a variety of civilizations, offer examples of such realization, and history, philosophically understood, finds its fulfillment in the movement both of individuals and of the societies they constitute toward the "open existence" such figures have manifested.

—Eugene Webb

---

von FRISCH, Karl (Ritter). German zoologist. Born in Vienna, 20 November 1886. Studied at the University of Munich; University of Vienna, Ph.D. 1910. Married Margarete Mohr in 1917; 4 children. Teaching Assistant and Lecturer, University of Vienna, 1910-21; Assistant Professor, University of Rostock, 1921-23; Professor, University of Breslau, 1923-25; Professor of Zoology, and Director of the Zoological Institute, University of Munich, 1925-46; Professor of Zoology, University of Graz, 1946-50; Professor of Zoology, 1950-58, and since 1958 Professor Emeritus, University of Munich. Recipient: Ritter Orden Pour le Mérite, Friedenski, 1952; Magellan Prize, American Philosophical Society, 1956; Kalinga Prize, Unesco, 1959; Balzan Prize for Biology, 1963; Nobel Prize for Medicine and Physiology (jointly), 1973; Grand Federal Cross of Merit with Star and Sash, 1974. Honorary doctorate: University of Bern, 1940; Technische Hochschule, Zurich, 1955; University of Graz, 1957; Harvard University, Cambridge, Massachusetts, 1963; University of Tübingen, 1964. Member, Academy of Science, Munich, 1926; Academy of Science, Copenhagen, 1931; Akademie der Naturforscher (Leopoldina); Academy of Science, Halle; Academy of Science, Helsinki, 1937; Academy of Science, Vienna, 1938; Academy of Science, Göttingen, 1947; U.S. National Academy of Sciences, 1949; Academy of Science, Uppsala, 1952; American Academy of Arts and Sciences, 1952; Royal Swedish Academy, 1952; Royal Society of London, 1954; American Entomological Society, 1955; Linnaean Society, London, 1956; Academy of Science, the Netherlands, 1959; French Psychological Society, 1959; Academy of Science, Bologna, 1963. Honorary Member, Royal Entomological Society, 1949; American Physiological Society, 1952. Address: Über der Klause 10, 8000 Munich 90, West Germany.

PUBLICATIONS

Zoology

Sechs Vorträge über Bakteriologie für Krankenschwestern. Vienna, Hölder, 1918.
Aus dem Leben der Bienen. Berlin, Springer, 1927; as *The Dancing Bees: An Account of the Life and Senses of the Honey Bee*, London, Methuen, 1954; New York, Harcourt Brace, 1955.
Du und das Leben: Eine moderne Biologie für Jedermann. Berlin, Ullstein, 1936; as *You and Life*, London, Scientific Book Club, 1939, and as *Man and the Living World*, New York, Harcourt Brace, 1963.
Zehn kleine Hausgenossen. Munich, Heimeran, 1940; as *Ten Little Housemates*, New York and Oxford, Pergamon Press, 1960.
Duftgelenkte Bienen im Dienst der Landwirtschaft und Imkerei. Vienna, Springer, 1947.
Medizinstudium und Biologienunterricht. Graz, Keinreich, 1947.
Bees: Their Vision, Chemical Sense, and Language. Ithaca, New York, Cornell University Press, 1950.
Biologie. Munich, Bayerischer Schulbuch Verlag, 2 vols.,

1952-53; as *Biology*, New York, Harper, 1965.

Bienenfiebel.   Munich, Bruckmann, 1954.

Tanzsprache und Orientierung der Bienen.   Berlin, Springer, 1965; as *The Dance Language and Orientation of Bees*, Cambridge, Massachusetts, Belknap Press, 1967.

Ausgewählte Vorträge, 1911-1969.   Munich, BLV, 1970.

Tiere als Baumeister, with Otto von Frisch.   Frankfurt, Ullstein, 1974; as *Animal Architecture*, New York, Harcourt Brace, 1974.

Other

Erinnerungen eines Biologen.   Berlin, Springer, 1957; as *A Biologist Remembers*, New York and Oxford, Pergamon Press, 1967.

Editor, *Ergebnisse der Biologie*.   Berlin, Springer, 1926.

*   *   *

Karl von Frisch began his research in animal behavior in the early 1900's. At that time bees, and insects in general, were thought to be "simple" animals quite unaware of their environment. Through his carefully designed experiments and dedication to research he was one of the first to make man realize that these animals look through sensory windows unavailable to us and their behavior was anything but simple.

Despite prevailing scientific opinion von Frisch set out to prove bees were capable of distinguishing color. His experiments not only confirmed his hypothesis but also demonstrated that bees see ultraviolet (UV) light as a separate color, a color to which we are blind. In von Frisch's experiment one colored card and an array of cards of various shades of gray were set out on a table. On each card was placed a foraging dish but only the dish on the colored card contained a sugar solution. After removing the food the bees searched exclusively on the colored card trying to find the missing sugar solution; proving that bees can discriminate colors. Reasoning that there must be a purpose to the bees' color vision von Frisch decided to take a closer look at flowers which depend on bees for pollination. He found that when placed under UV light these flowers display a pattern designed to lead a bee to a nectar reward; justifying the bees' sensitivity to UV light.

After World War I von Frisch began investigating fine olfactory discrimination in bees and hearing in fish. In 1923 he discovered a phenomenon with which he will always be associated; the language of the bee. For more than 2000 years man had known that if food is placed near a beehive it might go unnoticed for days but when discovered many more bees soon arrive. The first bee to find the food has been called a "forager" and the ones to come later "recruits." Von Frisch's initial observations suggested that foragers performed two types of dances in the hive to attract recruits; one a *round dance* implying sugar was available and the other a figure-eight or *waggle dance* when pollen was in the area of the hive. This interpretation of the bee dances remained unchallenged for over 20 years when von Frisch, himself, unraveled the true secret behind the language of the bee. Grateful for the opportunity to correct his own "mistake" von Frisch's careful experiments determined the round dance actually meant food was nearby and the waggle dance that food was at some distance. More remarkably, von Frisch found that the duration of the waggle dance indicated distance to the food and the straight portion of the dance direction. On a vertical hive "straight up" corresponded to the direction of the sun. The angle of the straight portion of the waggle dance from the "straight up" direction of the dance indicated the angle of the food source from the sun. In the mid-1960's a controversy developed. Adrian Wenner and his colleagues believed that the recruits were not using the information conveyed by the forager's dance and instead depended on odors alone to forage. In 1975 James Gould devised an elegant experiment in which foragers were induced to give accurate information in the dance but the recruits were deceived into misinterpreting the information in a predictable fashion. The misguided recruits could be directed to forage in any direction; confirming that bees must be communicating with their dance language.

For decades to follow von Frisch and his students continued to fill in the pieces of the bee language puzzle. One notable finding was that on partly cloudy days bees use the plane of polarization of light from patches of blue sky to navigate. Once again von Frisch had made us realize that these "simple" creatures had sensory capabilities unknown to man.

In 1973 the Nobel Prize for medicine and physiology was awarded jointly to von Frisch, Konrad Lorenz, and Nikolaas Tinbergen. The award recognized for the first time the importance of their work in the understanding of what animals do, and how and why they do it. Karl von Frisch, in particular, will be remembered for altering our view of the "lower" animals and for making us realize that honey bees have a language and are capable of communicating with fellow members of their closely integrated society.

—Fred E. Wasserman

---

von HARNACK, (Karl Gustav) Adolf.   German theologian. Born in Dorpat, Livonia, Russia, 7 May 1851. Studied at the University of Leipzig, Ph.D. 1873. Married Amalie Thiersch in 1879; 7 children. Lecturer, 1874-76, and Assistant Professor, 1876-79, University of Leipzig; Professor, University of Geissen, 1879-86; Professor, University of Marburg, 1886-88; Professor, 1888-1921, and Professor Emeritus, 1921-30, University of Berlin. After 1906, Director-General, Royal Library, Berlin (later the Prussian State Library); President, Kaiser Wilhelm Gesellschaft, 1911-30. Founder, and Chairman of the Editorial Board, *Critical Edition of the Greek Christian Authors of the First Three Centuries*. Member, Prussian Academy of Sciences, Berlin, 1890. Knight, Vice-Chancellor, and later Chancellor, Orden Pour le Mérite. Raised by Kaiser Wilhelm II to the rank of hereditary nobility in 1914. *Died* (in Heidelberg) *10 June 1930.*

PUBLICATIONS

Theology

Zur Quellenkritik der Geschicht des Gnosticismus.   Leipzig, Bidder, 1873.

De Apellis Gnosi Monarchia: Commentario Historica.   Leipzig, Bidder, 1874.

Die Zeit der Ignatius und die Chronologie der Antiochenischen Bischöfe bis Tyrannus nach Julius Africanus und den späteren Historiker. Nebst einer Untersuchung über die Verbreitung der Passio S. Polycarpi im Abendlande.   Leipzig, Hinrichs, 1878.

Das Mönchthum: Seine Ideale und seine Geschichte.   Giessen, Ricker, 1881; as *Monasticism: Its Ideals and Its History*, New York, Christian Literature Company, 1895; London, Williams and Norgate, 1901.

Die Überlieferung der griechischen Apologeten des zweiten Jahrhunderts in der alten Kirche und im Mittelalter.   Leipzig, Hinrichs, 1882.

Die Apostellehre und die jüdische Wege.   Leipzig, Hinrichs, 1886.

Die Quellen der sogenannten Apostolischen Kirchenordnung, nebst einer Untersuchung über des Lectorats und der anderen niederen Weihen.   Leipzig, Hinrichs, 1886; as *Sources of the Apostolic Canons, with a Treatise on the Origin of the Readership and other Lower Orders*.   London, Black, 1895.

Grundriss der Dogmengeschichte.   Freiburg, Mohr, 2 vols.,

1889-91; as *Outline of the History of Dogma*, New York, Funk and Wagnalls, 1893.

Lehrbuch der Dogmengeschichte. Freiburg, Mohr, 3 vols., 1896-99; as *History of Dogma*, London, Williams and Norgate, 1896-99; Boston, Little Brown, 1899-1903.

Das Neue Testament und das Jahr 200: Theodor Zahns Geschichte des neutestamentlichen Kanons (1 bd., 1 hälfte) geprüft. Freiburg, Mohr, 1889.

Über das gnostische Buch Pistis-sophia; Brod und Wasser: Die eucharistischen Elemente bei Justin: Zwei Untersuchungen. Leipzig, Hinrichs, 1891.

Dogmengeschichte. Freiburg, Mohr, 1891.

Das apostolische Glaubensbekenntnis: Ein geschichtlicher Bericht nebst einem Nachwort. Berlin, Haack, 1892; as *The Apostles' Creed*, London, Black, 1901.

Die griechische Übersetzung der Apologeticus Tertullians; Medizinisches aus der ältesten Kirchengeschichte. Leipzig, Hinrichs, 1892.

Geschichte der altchristlichen Litteratur bis Eusebius. Leipzig, Hinrichs, 2 vols., 1903-04.

Das Christentum und die Geschichte (lecture). Leipzig, 1895; as *Christianity and History*, London, Black, 1896.

Evangelisch-sozial, with Hans Delbrück. Berlin, Walther, 1896.

Thoughts on the Present Position of Protestantism. London, Black, 1899.

Die Pfaff'schen Irenäus-fragmente als fälschungen Pfaffs nachgewissen: Miscellen zu den Apostolischen Vätern, den Acts Pauli, Apelles, dem Muratorischen Fragment, den pseudocyprianischen Schriften, und Claudianus Marmertus. Leipzig, Hinrichs, 1900.

Das Wesen des Christentums: Sechzehn Vorlesungen. Leipzig, Hinrichs, 1900; as *What is Christianity?*, London, Williams and Norgate, and New York, Putnam, 1901.

Diodor von Tarsus: Vier pseudojustinische Schriften als eigentum Diodors Nachgewiesen. Leipzig, Hinrichs, 1901.

Die Mission und Ausbreitung des Christentums in den ersten drei Jahrhunderten. Leipzig, Hinrichs, 1902; as *The Expansion of Christianity in the First Three Centuries*, London, Williams and Norgate, and New York, Putnam, 2 vols., 1904-05.

Reden und Aufsätze. Giessen, Ricker, 2 vols., 1904; revised edition, Giessen, Töpelmann, 5 vols., 1911-30.

Militia Christi: Die christliche Religion und der Soldatenstand in den ersten drei Jahrhunderten. Tübingen, Mohr, 1905.

Beiträge zur Einleitung in das Neue Testament. Leipzig, Hinrichs, 7 vols., 1906-16; selections as *New Testament Studies*, London, Williams and Norgate, and New York, Putnam, 6 vols., 1907-25 (*Luke the Physician, the Author of the Third Gospel and the Acts of the Apostles; The Sayings of Jesus, the Second Source of St. Matthew and St. Luke; The Acts of the Apostles; The Date of the Acts and the Synoptic Gospels; Bible Reading in the Early Church; The Origin of the New Testament and the Most Important Consequences of the New Creation*).

Essays on the Social Gospel, with Wilhelm Herrmann. London, Williams and Norgate, and New York, Putnam, 1907.

Entstehung und Entwickelung der Kirchenverfassung und des Kirchenrechts in den zwei ersten Jahrhunderten. Leipzig, Hinrichs, 1910; as *The Constitution and Law of the Church in the First Two Centuries*, London, Williams and Norgate, and New York, Putnam, 1910.

Neue Untersuchungen zur Apostelgeschichte und zur Abfassungszeit der synoptischen Evangelien. Leipzig, Hinrichs, 1911.

Aus Wissenschaft und Leben. Giessen, Töpelmann, 1911.

Ist die Rede des Paulus in Athen ein ursprünglicher Bestandteil der Apostelgeschichte?; Judentum und judenchristum in Justins dialog mit Typho, nebst einer Collation der Pariser Handschrift nr. 450. ˙ Leipzig, Hinrichs, 1913.

Aus der Friedens- und Kriegsarbeit. Giessen, Töpelmann,

1916.

Martin Luther und die Grundlegung der Reformation (lecture). Berlin, Wiedmannsche Buchhandlung, 1917.

Die Teminologie der Wiedergeburt und verwandter Erlebnisse in der ältesten Kirche. Leipzig, Hinrichs, 1918.

Kirchengeschichtliche Ertrag der exegetischen Arbeiten des Origines. Leipzig, Hinrichs, 2 vols., 1918-19.

Marcion: Das Evangelium vom fremden Gott: Eine Monographie zur Geschichte der Grundlegung der katholischen Kirche. Leipzig, Hinrichs, 1921.

Erforschtes und Erlebtes. Giessen, Töpelmann, 1923.

Die Briefsammlung des Apostels Paul und die anderen vorkonstantinischen christlichen Briefsammlungen (lectures). Leipzig, Hinrichs, 1926.

Die Entstehung der christlichen Theologie und des kirchlichen Dogmas (lectures). Gotha, Klotz, 1927.

Aus der Werkstatt des Vollendeten: Als Abschluss seiner Reden und Aufsätze, edited by Axel von Harnack. Giessen, Töpelmann, 1930.

Vom inwedigen Leben: Betrachtungen über Bibelworte und freie Texte. Heilbronn, Salzer, 1931; as *A Scholar's Testament: Meditations*, London, Nicholson and Watson, 1933.

Ausgewählte Reden und Aufsätze, edited by Agnes von Zahn-Harnack and Axel von Harnack. Berlin, De Gruyter, 1951.

Other (For a full listing of von Harnack's separately published lectures and editions and translations in the series *Critical Edition of the Greek Christian Authors of the First Three Centuries*, see the bibliography cited below)

Editor and translator, *Bruchstücke des Evangeliums und der Apokalypse des Petrus*. Leipzig, Hinrichs, 1893.

Editor, *Der Ketzer-katalog des Bischofs Maruta von Maipherat*. Leipzig, Hinrichs, 1899.

Editor, with others, *Patrum apostolicorum opera, textum ad fidem codicum et graecorum et latinorum adhibitis praestantissimis editionibus*. Leipzig, Hinrichs, 1902.

Editor, *Kritik des Neuen Testaments von einem griechischen Philosophen des 3. Jahrhunderts*. Leipzig, Hinrichs, 1911.

Editor and translator, *Das Leben Cyprians, von Paulus: Die erste christliche Biographie*. Leipzig, Hinrichs, 1913.

Editor and translator, *Augustin: Reflexionen und Maximen*. Tübingen, Mohr, 1922.

Editor and translator, *Einführung in die Kirchengeschichten: Das Schreiben der romischen Kirche an die Korinthische aus der Zeit Domitians: I. Clemensbrief*. Leipzig, Hinrichs, 1929.

*

Bibliography: *Verzeichnis der Schriften Adolf von Harnack* by Friedrich Smend, Leipzig, Hinrichs, 1927.

Critical Studies: *Adolf von Harnack* by Agnes von Zahn-Harnack, Berlin, De Gruyter, 1936; *The Reality of Christianity: A Study of Adolf von Harnack as Historian and Theologian* by Garland Wayne Glick, New York, Harper, 1967.

*　　　*　　　*

The life of Adolf von Harnack spanned the last half of the 19th and the first third of the 20th century, and Harnack was at the center of most of the theological and cultural storms which shook the world in the latter half of his life. Indeed, it is a defensible thesis that the heritage he enjoyed and the work he performed made him, as theological liberalism's "representative," the lightning rod for these storms.

The heir of Kant and Schleiermacher, of Hegel and Baur, the child of a tradition of biblical orthodoxy (Dorpat and Erlangen), Harnack found a way of resolution in Ritschl. But in a way not true of Ritschl he faced an emerging cultural materialism, spawned by a particular understanding of and devotion to science, challenging any religious interpretation of human life. Harnack tried to act as mediator, first between his orthodox upbringing and the "new" historical-critical approach, and, after 1900 and the appearance of his famous *Das Wesen des Christentums*, between religion and the culture.

No interpretation of Harnack, however, dare forget the prodigious and specifically scholarly output of his life. Friedrich Smend, his bibliographer, lists 1611 entries—and the variety of Harnack's interests is astounding. If he is seen only as apologist to the culture, his significance is denigrated; he was the greatest church historian of his time, the mentor to a generation of church historians throughout the world.

In his historiography, Harnack sought to be faithful to *Wissenschaft*, defining the object of this science as the very life of humanity, past and present. He wrote repeatedly on the meaning of "scientific knowledge," analyzed its "stages," faced its complexities, and argued for a more than "natural" standard to which all activity is held accountable.

As his view of science informed his historical practice, Harnack's method was, not surprisingly, complex and thorough. In summary, historical knowledge is knowledge of the material and spiritual structure of past life, to be seen as the progressive concretion of the spirit and its mastery of material circumstances. Such progression is undoubtedly present, but it is not inevitable. The historian should proceed to the task with a frank admission of the limits of historical knowledge, and should seek insofar as possible to root out all preconceptions and prejudices; he or she would further be well-advised to seek the truth in the "mean" rather than the extreme. History is to be studied in order to intervene in the course of history and prepare for the future in a responsible way. Before one can engage in that responsible action which is the purpose of historical study, certain requirements must be fulfilled. These are: (1) the requirement that the historian possess a "practical wisdom" which can grasp the inner relationships between facts, and a "rich, deep, and many-sided wisdom of life" which contributes to and is continually strengthened by historical investigation; (2) source-work; (3) the analysis of the elementary, cultural, and individual factors as embodied in the memorials, events, and institutions which constitute the backbone of history; (4) the identification of the *Geist* of an epoch, made possible by the fact that "the same mind is at work in history and in us;" and (5) the representation of the facts, which is dependent upon all of the preceding steps, and also requires an analysis of the power, the direction, and the result characteristic of a given epoch. This analysis in turn is based upon the source-study, and centers upon the institutions produced by the ideas of the great people of an epoch. It is eminently clear that the method is highly contextual, the total framework being well-nigh presupposed in each part.

These assumptions and aims, rich and convoluted as they are, run throughout Harnack's practice. Yet, as he did his work, he did not avoid the problem raised by what he called the "special character" of church history. On the one hand he argued that there is only *one* history, of which church history is a part; on the other, religion is "a definite state of feeling and will, basing itself on inner experience." On the one hand, there is the involved theory of historical knowledge, demanding a scientific procedure; but on the other hand there is the appeal to an inner experience "which cannot be simply explained as the product of something else." This experience is identified as "that inner, moral, new creation which transmutes all values" but in itself remains an inviolate mystery. On the one hand, "everything that happens enters into one stream of events;" but on the other, there is the claim of a "special character" to church history, which, when identified, raises the puzzling question of Harnack's own presuppositions.

The fact that everyone carries presuppositional baggage may not have been recognized as vividly in the heady days of early 20th-century scientific, historical, and cultural optimism as it is today. Indeed, Harnack contributed to this understanding, albeit

unwittingly. His staking out a vocational claim and working that claim, his attempt at universality and his fidelity to its canons demonstrated "thus far historical, scientific effort can go." Troeltsch identified his *Blick*, arguing that however great he was, because of his insistence on bringing to history a standard of worth which did not necessarily arise out of the history itself, the result was "an ideological-dogmatic representation of history."

Compressing Harnack's grand vision into a formula, one would say that History (Tradition) is overcome by History (Responsible Acts), when Tradition and Responsibility are understood by a method which combines scientific fidelity and a rich wisdom about life. The judgment of fact and the judgment of value thus merge to bring forth, in given historical situations, creative activity.

But it is just at this point that the basic problem becomes evident. Whether it be expressed by the use of the categories of "scientific knowledge" and "life," or "judgment of fact" and "judgment of value," or "fact" and "interpretation," or "history" and "axiology," the problem is always present, as Troeltsch understood when he characterized Harnack's history as "ideological-dogmatic." To be sure, Harnack seems to have believed that he had overcome the tensions and achieved the certainty and unity which he so ardently sought.

Conceding the brilliance of his understanding and the protean character of his achievement, it must be judged (1) that his attempt to understand Christianity historically is dominated throughout by his concern to isolate a value essence and this a priori norm shapes his historiographical theory throughout; (2) that the commitment to historical procedure, issuing in a *Dogmengeschichte* or a *Marcion*, was under the influence of this a priori; and (3) that the methodological principle, "the same mind is at work in history and in us," is interpreted in such a way that the mind "in us," i.e., the 19th-century culturally conditioned mind, is made determinative in a too simple way.

—G. Wayne Glick

von HAYEK, Friedrich (August). British economist. Born in Vienna, Austria, 8 May 1899; emigrated to England, 1931: naturalized, 1938. Studied at the University of Vienna, Dr. Juris. and Ph.D.; University of London, D.Sc. Married Hella von Fritsch (died 1960); 2 children; married Helene Bitterlich. Served in Austrian Civil Service, 1921-26; Director, Austrian Institute for Economic Research, Vienna, 1927-31; Lecturer, University of Vienna, 1929-31; Tooke Professor of Economic Science and Statistics, University of London, 1931-50; Professor of Social and Moral Science, University of Chicago, 1950-62; Professor, University of Freiburg in Breisgau, 1962-70. Recipient: Nobel Prize in Economics, (jointly), 1974; Austrian Distinction for Science and Art, 1975. Honorary doctorate: Rikkyo University, Tokyo, 1964; University of Salzburg, 1974; University of Dallas, 1975; Marroquin University, Guatemala, 1977; Santa Maria University, Valparaiso, Chile, 1977; University of Buenos Aires, 1977. Fellow, British Academy, 1944. Honorary Fellow, London School of Economics; Austrian Academy of Science; American Economic Association; Hoover Institution; and Argentine Academy of Economic Science. Member, Orden pour le Mérite, 1977. Address: Urachstrasse 27, D-7800 Freiburg im Breisgau, Federal Republic of Germany.

PUBLICATIONS

Collections

Freiburger Studien: Gesammelte Aufsätze (includes bibliography). Tübingen, Mohr, 1969.

Social and Economic Philosophy

Hermann Heinrich Gossen: Eine Darstellung seines Lebens und seiner Schrift. Berlin, Prager, 1928.

Das Mieterschutzproblem: Nationalökonomische Betrachtungen. Vienna, Steyermühl, 1928(?).

Geldtheorie und Konjunkturtheorie. Vienna and Leipzig, Hölder, Pichler, and Tempsky, 1929; as *Monetary Theory and the Trade Cycle,* New York, Harcourt Brace, 1933.

Preise und Produktion. Vienna, Springer, 1931; as *Prices and Production,* London, Routledge, 1931; New York, Macmillan, 1932.

Monetary Nationalism and International Stability. London and New York, Longman, 1937.

Freedom and the Economic System. Chicago, University of Chicago Press, 1939.

Profits, Interest, and Investment, and Other Essays on the Theory of Industrial Fluctuations. London, Routledge, 1939.

The Pure Theory of Capital. London, Macmillan, 1941; Chicago, University of Chicago Press, 1942.

The Road to Serfdom. Chicago, University of Chicago Press, and London, Routledge, 1944.

Individualism: True and False (lecture). Dublin, Hodges, 1946.

Individualism and Economic Order (essays). Chicago, University of Chicago Press, 1948; London, Routledge, 1949.

John Stuart Mill and Harriet Taylor: Their Correspondence and Subsequent Marriage. London, Routledge, 1951.

The Counter-Revolution of Science: Studies on the Abuse of Reason. Glencoe, Illinois, Free Press, 1952.

The Sensory Order: An Inquiry into the Foundations of Theoretical Psychology. Chicago, University of Chicago Press, and London, Routledge, 1952.

The Political Ideal of the Rule of Law. Cairo, n.p., 1955.

The Constitution of Liberty. Chicago, University of Chicago Press, and London, Routledge, 1960.

Wirtschaft, Wissenschaft, und Politik (lecture). Freiburg, Schulz, 1963.

Was der Goldwährung geschehen ist: Ein Bericht aus dem Jahre 1932 mit zwei Ergänzungen. Tübingen, Mohr, 1965.

Studies in Philosophy, Politics, and Economics. Chicago, University of Chicago Press, and London, Routledge, 1967.

The Confusion of Language in Political Thought, with Some Suggestions for Remedying It. London, Institute of Economic Affairs, 1968.

Der Wettbewerb als Entdeckungsverfahren. Kiel, University of Kiel, 1968.

Die Irrtümer des Konstruktivismus und die Grundlagen legitimer Kritik gesellschaftlicher Gebilde (lecture). Munich, Fink, 1970.

A Tiger by the Tail: A 40-Years' Running Commentary on Keynsianism, with a New Essay on the Outlook for the 1970's: Open or Repressed Inflation, edited by Sudha R. Shenoy. London, Institute of Economic Affairs, 1972.

Economic Freedom and Representative Government (lecture). London, Institute of Economic Affairs, 1973.

Law, Legislation and Liberty: Rules and Order; The Mirage of Social Justice; The Political Order of a Free Society. Chicago, University of Chicago Press, and London, Routledge, 3 vols., 1973-79.

A Discussion with Friedrich A. von Hayek. Washington, American Enterprise Institute for Public Policy Research, 1975.

Full Employment at Any Price? London, Institute of Economic Affairs, 1975.

Choice in Currency: A Way to Stop Inflation. London, Institute of Economic Affairs, 1976.

Denationalisation of Money: An Analysis of the Theory and Practice of Concurrent Currencies. London, Institute of Economic Affairs, 1976.

Drei Vorlesungen über 'Demokratie, Gerechtigkeit, und Sozialismus. Tübingen, Mohr, 1977.

A Conversation with Friedrich A. von Hayek: Science and Socialism. Washington, D.C., American Enterprise Institute for Public Policy Research, 1979.

New Studies in Philosophy, Politics, Economics, and the History of Ideas. Chicago, University of Chicago Press, and London, Routledge, 1978.

Other

Editor, *Friedrich Freiherr von Wieser: Gesammelte Abhandlungen.* Tübingen, Mohr, 1929.

Editor, *Beiträge zur Geldtheorie,* by Marco Fanno and others. Vienna, Springer, 1933.

Editor, *Collectivist Economic Planning: Critical Studies on the Possibilities of Socialism,* by N.G. Pierson and others. London, Routledge, 1935.

Editor, *An Enquiry into the Nature and Effects of the Paper Credit of Great Britain (1802),* by Henry Thornton. London, Allen and Unwin, 1939.

Editor, *Capitalism and the Historians* (essays). Chicago, University of Chicago Press, and London, Routledge, 1954.

*

Bibliography: in *Roads to Freedom: Essays in Honour of Friedrich A. von Hayek* edited by Erich Streissler and others, London, Routledge, and New York, A.M. Kelley, 1969.

Critical Studies: *Road to Reaction* by Herman Finer, Boston, Little Brown, 1946; *Essays on Hayek* edited by Fritz Machlup, New York, New York University Press, 1976 (includes bibliography); *Hayek's Social and Economic Philosophy* by Norman P. Barry, London, Macmillan, 1979.

*   *   *

The significance of Friedrich von Hayek's work is twofold. He is the chief channel through which the Austrian tradition of economics, the main alternative to the British school founded by Adam Smith and David Ricardo, entered the mainstream of discussion in the English-speaking world; and he has created a system of thought which extends far beyond economics to embrace sociology, politics, and even cognitive psychology in a single coherent, unified account which has become increasingly influential in recent years.

A keynote of Austrian economics is that it presents a dynamic rather than static picture of economic life. The classical British approach suggested that movements of prices or levels of production away from "equilibrium" will be unusual, self-righting aberrations. For the Austrians, equilibria are purely hypothetical constructs: demand and supply schedules alter so constantly, in response to changing tastes and technical innovations, that the equilibrium-points where they meet are likely to move more rapidly than economic activity can adapt to them.

Hayek emphasizes the corollary that economic life is a process of discovery, offering many parallels to the process of scientific discovery described by his friend and colleague Karl Popper. Any society must try to discover how best to use its multifarious means of production in order to satisfy the wants of its members. The potential uses of any particular good, and the goals of different individuals, are so diverse, ever-changing, and inscrutable that any hope of deducing an ideal solution from first principles is out of the question. Instead, economic life must advance by experimentation. Prices, wages, profits, and losses are the means by which information is distributed among the network of economic agents. From the unmanageable ocean of particular economically relevant facts these figures abstract just enough information to enable people to support successful economic experiments and abandon those which fail; but success in this domain is always provisional. We can discover that some productive arrangement is more satisfactory than others tried to date, but we can never know that it will not be made obsolete by an alternative that someone will think up tomorrow.

The notion that human problems are too complex, subjective, and mutable to be resolved by human intelligence applies not merely to economic life but more generally. Hayek's master-idea is that social institutions, in many cases, are "the result of human action but not of human design." Hayek rejects, as dangerously misleading, the Aristotelean dichotomy between the "natural" and the "artificial." Many of our most useful institutions—language is one example, the English Common Law is another—have emerged from a process of cultural evolution lasting over very many generations. They are not "natural" in the sense of being biologically determined, but at the same time they are clearly not "artificial" in the sense of being planned by a guiding intelligence. Hayek argues that such institutions are likely to be far superior in practice to any alternatives that might be created by conscious planning, because they will have been shaped through confrontation with a much wider range of practical considerations than a planner could hope to foresee, and the impact of which he would in any case be unable to assess.

Hayek thinks it dangerous to overlook the existence of such institutions, because this oversight encourages us to mutilate the subtle fabric of society in the attempt to realize simplistic theoretical ideals. Social practices which were not introduced by conscious decision will seem to be mere arbitrary traditional accretions; because we cannot see the point of inherited social conventions we will suppose that they have no point and should be swept away in favour of streamlined, rational alternatives. To ignore the role of cultural evolution is to encourage a kind of "social engineering" which Hayek sees as having emerged in Revolutionary France and spread throughout the 20th-century Western world.

Hayek is hostile to state intervention in the detailed arrangements of society. In the economic field, interventionist policies damage the process of knowledge-generation in two ways. By draining capital away from many private hands towards the central state machine, such policies tend to reduce the incidence of economic experimentation. Economic progress will be most successful when many entrepreneurs are trying out different money-making propositions, just as science advances most successfully when many scientists try out rival theories: competition is crucial in both domains. Perhaps more important, state intervention causes the information-network constituted by the price system to give false signals, so that the results of those economic experiments which are conducted cannot be correctly assessed. To give a simple example: a high marginal rate of income tax will "tell" the possessor of a rare and valuable expertise that society prefers him to spend Saturdays on do-it-yourself work at home, rather than putting in an extra day at his profession and paying from taxed income for his odd jobs to be done by someone less skilled. This may be directly contrary to the true interests of society.

Many defenders of intervention would justify it in terms not of economic efficiency but of morality. Material equality ought to be promoted by political action, if necessary at some cost in terms of material progress. But for Hayek the notion of material equality as a *possible* (let alone desirable) goal of political action is a delusion: the interventionist policies which would have to be applied in order to approach equality themselves destroy the only yardstick by which inequality can be meaningfully measured. There can be no special virtue in equal money incomes, if the relative prices of the goods which money can buy are influenced by arbitrary State action.

But, while Hayek strongly defends individual freedom against state interference, he is no friend of the anarchic, self-willed approach to life. For Hayek, the advantages of civilization depend crucially on the acceptance by individuals of rules whose rationale will often be obscure and whose consequences in particular situations may be adverse. Hayek condemns Freud for having "destroyed culture" by encouraging people to liberate themselves from traditional emotional shackles. A society must have rules, and some at least of these will need to be state-enforced; but a good framework of rules will be general, will apply to all individuals equally, and will not aim at achieving specific outcomes (as contemporary state action often does)—because a society as a whole is not the kind of entity which can have goals, and the goals of its members are more diverse than a government can reckon with.

Hayek insists that his social philosophy is not conservative but liberal, in the classical sense. The social arrangements produced by cultural evolution should not be seen as unsurpassably excellent: further evolution must be allowed to improve on them, but successful evolution requires competition between alternative practices rather than the imposition of uniform innovation. At the individual level, though, Hayek does not make it wholly clear how one should distinguish a legitimate social experiment from the culture-destroying abandonment of a vital rule of behaviour. Furthermore, the idea of competition between variants leading to selection of the fittest is not wholly unproblematical in the biological field, and Hayek fails to consider problems (e.g., concerning small populations) which seem likely to be particularly troublesome when the units of selection are not individual traits but social institutions.

Hayek's reputation has fluctuated in accordance with the changing temper of the times. He first attracted widespread attention when *The Road to Serfdom* (1944) argued that the welfare state then being planned was not a continuation into peacetime of the battle for individual freedom but, rather, a step towards tyranny which Britain, of all countries, should have known better than to take. In the 1950's and 1960's the virtues of a mild, "mixed economy" type of socialism were so universally accepted that Hayek's social and political views simply ceased to be taken seriously (though his standing as an economist was always secure); in 1967 Anthony Quinton described the discipline of political philosophy as extinct, and dismissed Hayek's *The Constitution of Liberty* (1960) as a "magnificent dinosaur." In the mid-1970's, as revulsion against the practical results of welfare-state policies spread, Hayek began to come into his own. In the USA he became the guru of the growing "libertarian" movement; in Britain Margaret Thatcher, arguably the most doctrine-minded, unpragmatic Prime Minister for many decades, acknowledged herself as Hayek's disciple. In his eighties Hayek is probably more influential than at any earlier period of his life.

—Geoffrey Sampson

---

von HÜGEL, Friedrich. British theologian. Born in Florence, Italy, 5 May 1852; succeeded his father as Baron von Hügel in 1870; emigrated to England in 1867: naturalized, 1914. Privately educated. Married Lady Mary Herbert in 1873; 3 daughters. Lived and wrote in London, 1876-1925. Honorary doctorate: University of St. Andrews, Scotland, 1919; Oxford University, 1920. *Died* (in London) *27 January 1925.*

PUBLICATIONS

Theology

Notes Addressed to the Very Reverend H.I.D.R. Upon the Subject of Biblical Inspiration and Inerrancy.   Privately printed, 1891.
The Papal Commission and the Pentatuch.   London, Longman, 1906.
The Mystical Element of Religion as Studied in St. Catherine of Genoa and Her Friends.   London, Dent, 2 vols., 1908.
Eternal Life: A Study of Its Implications and Applications.

Edinburgh, Clark, 1912.

The German Soul in Its Attitude Towards Ethics and Christianity. London, Dent, 1916.

Essays and Addresses on the Philosophy of Religion. London, Dent, 2 vols., 1921-26.

Readings from Friedrich von Hügel, edited by Algar Thorold. London, Dent, 1928.

Some Notes on the Petrine Claims (1893). London, Sheed and Ward, 1930.

The Reality of God, and Religion and Agnosticism, Being the Literary Remains of Baron Friedrich von Hügel, edited by Edmund G. Gardner. London, Dent, 1931.

Other

Some Letters from Baron von Hügel. Privately printed, 1925.
Selected Letters, edited by Bernard Holland. London, Dent, 1927.
Letters from Friedrich von Hügel to a Niece, edited by Gwendolen Greene. London, Dent, 1928.

Editor, *Christian Thought: Its History and Application,* by Ernst Troeltsch. London, University of London Press, 1923.

*

Critical Studies: *Von Hügel and the Supernatural* by A. Hazard Dakin, London, SPCK, 1934; *The Life of Baron von Hügel* by Michael de la Bedoyere, London, Dent, 1954; *Baron Friedrich von Hügel and the Modernist Crisis in England* by Lawrence Barmann, London, Cambridge University Press, 1972.

* * *

In 1925, when Baron von Hügel died, there seemed to be a wide consensus that he and John Henry Newman had been the Roman Catholic thinkers who had left the most enduring and deepest mark on Catholicism in England in the past two centuries. Protestants as well as Catholics seemed of the same mind. This is all the more remarkable when one realizes that the Baron was born of an Austrian father and a Scottish mother, that he was a layman all his life, that he never had gone to a school or university, that he never had an official position, that he was English but with all kinds of qualifications, and that he was strictly an amateur. Besides all of that he had no platform and no audience, except that which he created by his own efforts.

Von Hügel made himself a force in English life and thought chiefly through his writings. With a modest patrimony he never held a job. Instead he made for himself a happy home and married life, but he included in that home a magnificent private library. From that home study, he began a correspondence that in later years was truly vast. He regularly wrote to: Alfred Loisy, the Scripture critic who subsequently left the Catholic Church; Father George Tyrrell, around whom the Modernist Movement swirled; Norman Kemp Smith, the renowned scholar and translator of Kant; A.E. Taylor, the distinguished Protestant philosopher of Edinburgh; Ernst Troeltsch, the historian of social thought and Germanic Lutheran theologian; and countless others on matters philosophical, theological, spiritual, and historical. He began writing to others for enlightenment and help on matters often very personal. Within a few years, he was increasingly being asked for his wisdom and succor on this ever larger range of issues.

This would not have happened except for a stream of articles and reviews that also began to come from his pen. But his influence did not reach widely until 1908 with his *The Mystical Element of Religion.* From then until his death, with *Essays and Addresses, Eternal Life,* and other books and essays (most of this being published in book form after his sixtieth birthday), von Hügel was a major force in English religious life. Dean Inge, Evelyn Underhill, and Clement C.J. Webb were but a few of his Protestant and typically renowned admirers.

What did he say or do that made him powerful? First, von Hügel dared to probe into both science and history with integrity and patience. It was not that he sought there new proofs for God's existence, but he dispatched with his life-time of careful inquiry the notion that these two areas of learning were likely to dislodge the foundations of Catholic belief. Instead, he found that the more he knew about the world and people the more he knew about the setting for God's action. Thus, he examined in a fresh way the Gospels, the historicity of the traditions, the dependence upon miracles. He seemed, then, to suggest something new, that all Christians, but especially Catholics, were life-long debtors to all the evidence, all of history, and all of experience. He articulated a kind of robust confidence, that learning, even evolution, historical criticism of documents, geology, etc., were not harmful at all to religious belief. He gave a picture of a tough faith, resilient and responsible.

Secondly, he made a case, both by his devoted life and by his writings, for the idea that liberty and authority, especially of the Church, were not incompatible. His enthusiasm for institutional religion made him a critic of English popular thought while also making him an advocate of the thought that the personal choice of the individual could only be made rich within a social organism that promised certainty and surety. He offered a new look at an old context, a life guided and guarded by the search for the good life within the limits laid down by tradition and Papal governance.

Thirdly, he gave credence to Catholicism for intellectuals, not by praising St. Thomas Aquinas and begging for a neo-scholastic synthesis, but rather by describing an organism in history, the Christian Church, nurturing its adherents by liturgical worship, by sacraments, as well as by doctrine. That church began to loom up in his pages as the very matrix for self-realization and deepening of seriousness. Such a positive evaluation of an institution made von Hügel's pages look like a restoration of earlier Catholic belief and a subtle correction of Protestant and secular extravagances.

Lastly, none of this would probably have had a wide appeal if it had not been linked so firmly with a deep strand of piety. Von Hügel's letters are the very stuff of classical spirituality, but never naive, always helping his reader to that moral and Christian secret, of winning by losing, of gaining the self by losing it to God. Much of this he summarizes under the rubrical title, *The Mystical Element of Religion.* He was an expert on qualifying a person's life so that conscience, goodwill, and the Christian fruits of the Spirit could triumph. That this was possible for a sophisticated person of letters and science was shown by his life and argued by his literature.

—Paul Holmer

---

von NEUMANN, John. American mathematician. Born in Budapest, Hungary, 28 December 1903; emigrated to the United States in 1931; naturalized, 1937. Studied at the University of Berlin, 1921-23; Technische Hochschule, Zurich, Ph.D. 1926; University of Budapest, Ph.D. 1926. Married Marietta Kövesi in 1930 (divorced), 1 daughter; married Klári Dán in 1938. Rockefeller Fellow, University of Göttingen, Germany, 1926-27; taught at the University of Berlin, 1927-29, and the University of Hamburg, 1929; Visiting Professor, 1930, and Professor, 1931-33, Princeton University, New Jersey; Member, Institute for Advanced Study, Princeton, New Jersey, 1933-57 (Director, Electronic Computer Project, 1945-55). Member, Technical Advisory Panel on Atomic Energy, Department of Defense, and Chairman, Nuclear Weapons Committee, U.S. Air Force Scientific Panel, from 1940; served in group developing the atomic bomb, Los Alamos, New Mexico, 1943-45. Member, U.S.

Atomic Energy Commission, 1954-57. *Died* (in Washington, D.C.) *8 February 1957.*

PUBLICATIONS

Collections

Collected Works, edited by A.H. Taub.   New York, Macmillan, 6 vols., 1961-63.

Mathematics

Mathematische Grundlagen der Quantenmechanik.   Berlin, Springer, 1932; as *Mathematical Foundations of Quantum Mechanics,* Princeton, New Jersey, Princeton University Press, 1955.
Charakterisierung des Spektrums eines Integraloperators.   Paris, Hermann, 1935.
Functional Operators.   Princeton, New Jersey, Institute for Advanced Study, 1935.
Continuous Geometry.   Princeton, New Jersey, Institute for Advanced Study, 2 vols., 1936-37.
Theory of Games and Economic Behavior, with Oskar Morgenstern.   Princeton, New Jersey, Princeton University Press, 1944.
Entwicklung und Ausnutzung neuerer mathematischer Maschinen.   Cologne, Westdeutscher Verlag, 1955.
The Computer and the Brain.   New Haven, Connecticut, Yale University Press, 1958.
Theory of Self-Producing Automata, completed by Arthur W. Burks.   Urbana, University of Illinois Press, 1966.

*

Critical Studies: "Von Neumann Issue" of *Bulletin of the American Mathematical Society,* 64, no.3, part 2, 1958; *John von Neumann and Norbert Wiener: From Mathematics to the Technologies of Life and Death* by Steve J. Heims, Cambridge, Massachusetts, MIT Press, 1980.

*   *   *

John von Neumann evidenced his gift for mathematics as a high-school student in Budapest, and already then was brought into contact with mathematicians Fejér, Kürschak, and especially Fekete, who became his tutor. In his university student days he was particularly receptive to the influence of Erhard Schmidt, Hermann Weyl, and David Hilbert as mentors. He himself became a Privatdozent in Berlin in 1927.

Von Neumann appreciated a link between the ideas of pure mathematics, which are freely invented mental constructs, and the facts of the material world. In an essay on "The Mathematician" he wrote:

> At a great distance from its empirical source, or after much "abstract" inbreeding, a mathematical subject is in danger of degeneration. At the inception the style is usually classical; when it shows signs of becoming baroque, then the danger signal is up.... In any event, whenever this stage is reached, the only remedy seems to me to be the rejuvenating return to the source: the reinjection of more or less directly empirical ideas. I am convinced that this was a necessary condition to conserve the freshness and vitality of the subject and that this will remain equally true in the future.

But the relation between mathematics and empirical fields is a symbiotic one. Thus von Neumann's forays into mathematical physics and mathematical economics also constituted important contributions to 20th-century theoretical physics and economics,

not only a stimulus to guide mathematics away from the baroque. During World War II von Neumann became active in applications of mathematics to high technology, especially the development of atom bombs and that of high-speed general purpose computers. A concomitant of his work in computer development was his logical theory of automata, which invited attempts to compare the patterns of organization of the central nervous system with those of computers. After the war he was instrumental in developing and promoting weather prediction by means of numerical solutions of the dynamical equations describing the earth's atmosphere. However, he became increasingly occupied as a U.S. government expert on atomic and thermonuclear weapons and missiles, and finally, as a full-time government official, had little time for mathematics or science.

In view of the broad scope and diversity of von Neumann's work only some portions of it can be indicated even briefly here. (The areas in pure mathematics on which von Neumann wrote in the 1920's and 1930's include ergodic theory, measure theory, lattice theory, algebras, operator theory, rings of operators, and topological groups.)

By the 1920's serious doubts had been raised concerning the internal consistency of mathematics, and in response to these threats to mathematics von Neumann joined Hilbert in a meta-mathematical effort to use purely formal methods to prove mathematics to be free from contradiction. Von Neumann succeeded in setting up a clear and concise axiomatic formulation for set theory, a fundamental branch of mathematics, and went just about as far as was possible toward proving it free from contradiction. Gödel subsequently demonstrated the inherent limitations on such proofs of self-consistency, but Gödel's work did not invalidate any of von Neumann's proofs. A general approach concerned with logics, axiomatic formulations, and formal structure also characterizes much of von Neumann's later mathematical work.

At Hilbert's instigation von Neumann undertook to formulate the empirical theories of atomic physics, viz., quantum theory, in a unified mathematical language and put the whole theory into axiomatic form. In von Neumann's formulation the two seemingly disparate, but in fact equivalent, descriptions of atomic phenomena, the Schrödinger wave theory and the Heisenberg matrix theory, appeared naturally as two different representations of unifying abstract equations. The language von Neumann found suitable for quantum theory is that of "abstract Hilbert space," wherein formal analogs to the concepts of a vector and rotation in ordinary three-dimensional space are constructed in a complex space of arbitrarily large dimensionality. A different unified formulation of quantum theory had been devised by the physicist P.A.M. Dirac, and both formulations have survived side by side for half a century of subsequent developments in theoretical physics. Von Neumann continued to ponder the logic of quantum theory, and together with Garrett Birkhoff was able to distinguish clearly the logical structure of the propositional calculus for quantum mechanics from that of classical mechanics in terms of lattice theory. The question of the appropriateness of the Birkhoff-von Neumann viewpoint has provoked still unsettled controversy concerning quantum logics. Von Neumann's formulation of quantum mechanics also includes a general mathematical description of the process of measurement, but this description is epistemologically strained and strange, and is, similarly, the subject of unresolved philosophical controversy. His proof that the probabilistic nature of quantum theory does not hide any unknown variables (Einstein believed it does) was widely admired and for many years inhibited the search for hidden variables. However, relatively recent re-examination of von Neumann's proof showed that it prohibits only particular types and not all hidden variables.

Émile Borel had introduced the mathematical description of parlor games in 1921 and had posed the general problem of defining the criteria under which a player has a "best" strategy for winning (or at least not losing) on the average, but in 1928 von Neumann gave a solution to the problem. He returned to "game theory" in the early 1940's, especially as he and the economist Oskar Morgenstern shared the belief that the theory of games "is the proper instrument with which to develop a theory of economic behavior." Together they embarked on such a development. Unlike the mere calculation of odds in a game of pure chance, game theory postulated that each player must reckon with clever opponents pursuing their own self-interest. Game theory was at first taken up with overly high expectations by economists and other social scientists, but the limitations of the theory in practical applications led to disillusionment with it among many of them after about a decade. Its serious application to military strategy and tactics, although fashionable for a time among U.S. government strategic analysts, is full of booby-traps because the structure of game theory and the unstated premises underlying the theory tend grossly to prejudice the conclusions reached by means of it. However, von Neumann's fundamental work laid the foundation for game theory as a new mathematical discipline.

Von Neumann's participation in the rapid improvement of computers during the 1940's on the one hand, and his development of the formal theory of automata on the other, encompassed a remarkable variety of his interests. In the automata theory, which utilized earlier work of Turing, Pitts, and McCulloch, von Neumann formulated axioms and proved theorems about assemblies of simple elements that might in an idealized way represent possible circuits in artifacts or structures and processes in organic systems. He constructed formal models of automata capable of reproducing themselves; he also concerned himself with formal models of unreliable elements composing an automaton, but organized in such a way that the output of the automaton is nevertheless reliable. Automata theory has now become a well-established branch of mathematics, for which von Neumann's work has been seminal. He also worked directly with engineers to advance computer design beyond the ENIAC, the fastest then available. His special contribution lay in improving the logical organization of computers, which was then translated into hardware at the Princeton Institute for Advanced Study under his overall direction. The team-work of computer groups and acrimonious patent-suits becloud the issue of precisely which innovations are to be credited to von Neumann.

He also played an historically important role in the development of the Nagasaki atom bomb, hydrogen bombs, and intercontinental ballistic missiles: In the first of these von Neumann, through elaborate numerical computation, was able to work out the arrangements needed to implement the implosion method for detonating it. For the hydrogen bomb he performed the crucial task of bringing the most advanced computers to bear. In the early 1950's he became (to use Herbert York's words) the "dominant advisory figure in nuclear missilery" in the United States and promoted a crash program for ICBM development. Throughout the period from World War II until his health failed he worked actively, both on the scientific-technical level and politically, in the race (in which the U.S. was leading the Soviet Union) to innovate in nuclear weapons technology. During his last years he was a full-time U.S. Atomic Energy Commissioner, but spent many an evening on the preparation of a manuscript to elucidate analogies and differences between computers and the human brain.

Colleagues have described von Neumann's impressive intellectual power in various ways. We quote Eugene Wigner:

> Only an extraordinary mind could have made the unusual contributions to science which von Neumann made. The accuracy of his logic was, perhaps, the most decisive character of his mind. One had the impression of a perfect instrument whose gears were machined to mesh accurately to a thousandth of an inch. "If one listens to von Neumann, one understands how the human mind should work," was the verdict of one of our perceptive colleagues. Brilliance was the second, perhaps even more striking characteristic of von Neumann's mind. This

property was clearly evident in the youth of fifteen. The third characteristic of his mind was its retentiveness. It was his exceptional memory which enabled him to pursue a host of hobbies, in addition to his scientific endeavors. He was an amateur historian as intimately familiar with long stretches of history as any professional. He spoke five languages well....He had read and remembered innumerable books...(*Symmetries and Reflections*, 1967).

However, his fascination with progress in weapons during the last decade of his life, it seems to me, exposed his Achilles' heel.

—Steve Heims

VYGOTSKY, L(ev) S(emenovich). Russian psychologist. Born 5 November 1896. Graduated from Shaniavskii University and the Department of History and Philosophy, Moscow University, 1917. Taught at Gomel, Byelorussia; Professor, Moscow University. *Died 11 June 1934.*

PUBLICATIONS

Collections

Sobranie sochinenii [Collected Works]. Moscow, Pedagogika, 1892-.

Psychology

Pedagogicheskaia psikhologiia [Pedagogical Psychology]. Moscow, Rabotnik Prosveshcheniia, 1926.
Grafika A. Bykhovskogo [A. Bykhovskii's Drawings]. Moscow, n.p., 1926.
Trudnoe detstvo [Difficult Childhood]. Moscow, Izd. TSIPKNO, 1929.
Pedologiia iunosheskogo vozrasta [Teenage Pedology]. Moscow, Izd. TSIPKNO, 1929.
Pedologiia shkol'nogo vozrasta [Pedology of the School Age]. Moscow, Izd. BZO 2-go MGU, 1929.
Pedologiia podrostka [Pedology of the Adolescent]. Moscow, Izd. BZO 2-go MGU, 1929.
Etiudy po istorii povendeniia: obez'iana primitiv, rebenok [Studies in the History of Behavior], with A.R. Luria. Moscow, Gosizdat, 1930.
Voobrazhenie i tvorchestvo v detskom vozraste: Psikhologicheskii ocherk [Imagination and Creativity in Childhood]. Moscow, Izd. Akademii im. N.K. Krupskoi, 1930.
Psikhologicheskii slovar' [Dictionary of Psychology], with B.E. Varshava. Moscow, Gosuchpedgiz, 1931.
Myshlenie i rech': Psikhologicheskie issledovaniia. Moscow, Sotsekgiz, 1934; as *Thought and Language*, Cambridge, Massachusetts, Institute of Technology Press, 1962.
Umstvennoe razvitie detei v protsesse obucheniia [Intellectual Development in Children During the Learning Process]. Moscow, n.p., 1935.
Izbrannye psikhologicheskie issledovaniia [Selected Works]. Moscow, Izd-vo Akademii Pedagogicheskikh Nauk, 1956.
Razvitie vysshikh psikhicheskikh funktsii: Iz neopublikovannykh trudov. Moscow, Izd-vo Akademii Pedagogicheskikh Nauk, 1960; as *Mind in Society: The Development of Higher Psychological Processes*, Cambridge, Massachusetts, Harvard University Press, 1978.
Psikhologiia iskusstva. Moscow, Iskusstvo, 1965; as *The Psychology of Art*, Cambridge, Massachusetts Institute of Technology Press, 1971.

*   *   *

L.S. Vygotsky came to prominence in the Soviet Union just after the Russian Revolution. This time-frame had a major influence on his work; one of the goals of his work was the study and integration of psychology into a Marxist framework. Vygotsky wanted to analyze higher forms of human behavior. He disagreed with the popular idea that such behavior could be understood in terms of multiplication and concentration of segments of behavior which had been studied in animals. He believed that in order to achieve an understanding of complex behavior it was important to observe the process of learning rather than the performance of tasks which have already been learned.

One of Vygotsky's greatest contributions to developmental psychology was the method originated to analyze the process of learning in children. Vygotsky used three major principles in designing his experiments. First, it is important to analyze the process of development, which requires an "experimental" method which provokes development in the laboratory where it can be observed in detail. The second principle is that an attempt must be made to explain the behavior, not just describe it. This is because "though two types of activity can have the same external manifestation, whether in origin or essence, their nature may differ most profoundly." Vygotsky termed these two categories of analysis as phenotypic (descriptive) and genotypic (explanatory). The third principle had to do with the problem of "fossilized behavior": processes that have "gone through a very long stage of historical development and become fossilized." In order to analyze this type of behavior, it must be altered and "turned back to its source through experiment." Vygotsky believed that method was the base of developmental study: "The search for method becomes one of the most important problems of the entire enterprise of understanding the uniquely human forms of psychological activity. In this case, the method is simultaneously prerequisite and product, the tool and the result of the study."

The major area in which Vygostsky worked was child development. He believed that one of the behaviors that distinguished higher forms from lower forms was the creation and use of signs as a memory aid. Both signs and tools are a form of mediation, the distinction being that a tool is externally oriented (leading to changes in objects) whereas signs are internally oriented, aimed at mastering oneself. Internal reconstruction of a formerly external operation is called internalization. Three major steps are involved in internalization: 1) "an operation that initially represents an external activity is reconstructed and begins to occur internally"; 2) "an interpersonal process is transformed into an intrapersonal one"; 3) "The transformation of an internal process into an external one is the result of a long series of developmental events."

Vygotsky also studied the role of play in child development. He believed that, in play, action is subordinated to meaning. This is in contrast to a child's real-life situation, in which meaning is subordinated to action. This subordination can take the form of rules, which must be strictly obeyed in play. In young children play often takes the form of imaginary imitations of real-life situations, but as the child gets older, rules become more and more important as an aspect of play activity.

Vygotsky also did work in the development of written language in children. He believed that writing should be taught to young children and that it should be taught as a natural process. An intrinsic need should be developed in the child for writing so that it becomes, in effect, another form of speech. Vygotsky believed that, in time, the learning process precedes the developmental process, and leads to further development. The two processes do not occur in parallel.

Vygotsky believed that development was "a complex dialectic process, characterized by periodicity, unevenness in the development of different functions, metamorphosis or qualitative transformation of one form into another, intertwining of external and internal factors and adaptive processes." He was greatly influenced by Marx and the revolutionary situation in Russia at the time. His contributions, just recently translated, have had a great impact on the field of developmental psychology.

—R.W. Rieber

WALLAS, Graham. British political scientist. Born in Bishopwearmouth, Sunderland, 31 May 1858. Educated at Shrewsbury School, 1871-77; studied at Corpus Christi College, Oxford, 1877-81, B.A. 1881. Married Ada Radford in 1897; 1 daughter. Schoolmaster, at Highgate School, London, 1881-85, and elsewhere, 1885-90; university extension lecturer, 1890-95; Lecturer, London School of Economics, 1895-1923; University Professor of Political Science, University of London, 1914-23, then Emeritus. Lowell Lecturer, Boston, 1914; Dodge Lecturer, Yale University, New Haven, Connecticut, 1919. Founding Member, 1886-1904, and Member of the Executive Board, 1888-95, Fabian Society, resigned 1904. Member, London School Board, 1894-1904; Chairman, School Management Committee, 1897-1904; Member of the Technical Education Board, 1898-1904, and the Education Committee, 1908-10, London County Council; Member of the London County Council, 1904-07; Member of the Senate, University of London, 1908-28; Member of the Royal Commission on Civil Service, 1912-15. D. Litt.: University of Manchester, 1922; Oxford University, 1931. *Died 9 August 1932.*

PUBLICATIONS

Political Science

What to Read: A list of Books for Social Reformers. London, Fabian Society, 1891; 4th edition, 1901.
The Case Against Diggleism, with Harold Spender. Privately printed, 1894.
The Life of Francis Place, 1771-1854. London, Longman, 1898; revised edition, 1918; New York, Knopf, 1919.
Human Nature in Politics. London, Constable, 1908; Boston, Houghton Mifflin, 1909.
The Great Society: A Psychological Analysis. London and New York, Macmillan, 1914.
Our Social Heritage. London, Allen and Unwin, and New Haven, Connecticut, Yale University Press, 1921.
Jeremy Bentham (lecture). London, University College, 1922.
William Johnson Fox (1786-1864) (lecture). London, Watts, 1924.
The Art of Thought. London, Cape, and New York, Harcourt Brace, 1926.
Physical and Social Science (lecture). London, Macmillan, 1930.
Social Judgment, edited by May Wallas. London, Allen and Unwin, 1934; New York, Harcourt Brace, 1935.
Men and Ideas: Essays, edited by May Wallas. London, Allen and Unwin, 1940; Freeport, New York, Books for Libraries, 1971.

Other

Editor, *Social Peace: A Study of the Trade Union Movement in England,* by G. von Schulze-Gaevernitz, translated by C.M. Wicksteed. London, Sonnenschein, and New York, Scribner, 1893.

*

Critical Studies: *Between Two Worlds: The Political Thought of*

Graham Wallas by Martin J. Wiener, Oxford, Clarendon Press, 1971; *Graham Wallas and The Great Society*, by Terence H. Qualter, London, Macmillan, 1980.

*   *   *

Graham Wallas's historical reputation is strangely paradoxical. Almost everywhere he is remembered for two things: his status as one of the founders of Fabian socialism and contributor to the *Fabian Essays in Socialism*; and his imaginative concepts of a "behavioral" political science. Yet both these memories are at odds with the central thrust of Wallas's own life work.

Most writings on the historical development of modern political science make some reference to Wallas's pioneering work. The one book most commonly coupled with his name is *Human Nature in Politics* (1908), with its warnings about the dangers of exaggerating the intellectuality of mankind. Yet in a sense this was the least representative of Wallas's works, and he spent much of the rest of his life trying to correct the misleading impressions arising from an over-hasty reading of its first chapters. Graham Wallas was, in fact, much more appalled and frightened by the anti-intellectualism of the 20th-century than by the naive over-intellectualism of the 19th. A dominant mood of anti-intellectualism, whether manifested in the deliberate defence of irrationalism by the fascists, or in overly rigid deterministic psychologies, would deny even the possibility of a rational free will, and so would make nonsense of any dream of a new *polis*, the Good Society recreated in the setting of the urban-industrial Great Society.

Wallas had attacked the 19th-century's unrealistic assumptions about the ways in which men reasoned, and the connections between reason and behavior, simply in order to teach mankind how to think more clearly, and to apply their reason to the improvement of the human condition. He had no wish to deny them the capacity to think at all. And so his attacks on the anti-intellectualism of the 20th-century were much more important to him than his criticisms of earlier excessive rationalism. This assumed socialist critic of intellectualism spent the greater part of his life, and devoted most of his later writings, to refuting the critics of liberal democracy, and to seeking ways to increase the role of individual rational free will in human social behavior. Wallas was not a behavioral political scientist at all, but a moral reformer who looked to a new science of politics and government, not as an end in itself, but as a means to a more democratic political order, offering more effective challenges to the self-confident assurances of the old ruling classes.

His own enthusiasm for a science of politics gradually faded. He remained convinced of the value of more quantitative data in the social sciences, but confidence in the relevance of biology and psychology waned. In particular he was soon out of sympathy with a new generation of political scientists. Those who assiduously set out to create a value-free social science were not interested in a pioneer who suggested that the reason for studying human behavior was to overcome the obstacles to the emergence of ultimate moral values. Wallas was never "value-free."

The socialism and collectivism, too, is misleading. He had joined the Fabian Society in 1886, becoming a member of what Beatrice Webb referred to as the Fabian Junta, but he gradually drifted away from it, formally resigning in 1904. Wallas's socialism is unintelligible out of the context of his own evangelical upbringing. It owed little to Marxist economic determinism, or to any systematic economic theory. It was instead an outburst of moral outrage at the effects of capitalism. Capitalism was to be condemned because its materialistic and competitive values demoralized and degraded its peoples. The only way to the Good Life lay in a collectivist society in which all could come to understand that the good of each depended upon the co-operative pursuit of the good of all. The ultimate object of his political thinking was still the liberal goal of the maximum individual liberty and dignity, but it was a goal to be accomplished through collective social action rather than through the

competitive machinery of the market place, which so inequitably distributed its rewards. As Wallas grew older the individual good took ever greater prominence in his mind and he increasingly distrusted institutionalized socialism.

These are the major components of Wallas's thought. He attacked older assumptions about the basis of human social behavior, and the established political and economic institutions for dealing with selfish individualism, but always he had as his vision of the purpose of political activity the recreation of the *Polis*, the communal Good Life. In time the scientific criticisms faded and the moral passions which inspired them came to the front.

—Terence H. Qualter

WATSON, James D(ewey).   American molecular biologist. Born in Chicago, Illinois, 6 April 1928. Studied at the University of Chicago, B.S. 1947; Indiana University, Bloomington, Ph.D. 1950. Married Elizabeth Lewis in 1968; 2 children. National Research Council Fellow, University of Copenhagen, 1950-51; National Foundation for Infantile Paralysis Fellow, Cavendish Laboratory, Cambridge University, 1951-53; Senior Research Felllow in Biology, California Institute of Technology, Pasadena, 1953-55; Assistant Professor, 1955-58, Associate Professor, 1958-61, and Professor of Biology, 1961-76, Harvard University, Cambridge, Massachusetts. Since 1968, Director, Cold Spring Harbor Laboratory, Cold Spring Harbor, New York. Recipient: John Collins Warren Prize, with F.H.C. Crick, Massachusetts General Hospital, Boston, 1959; Eli Lilly Award in Biochemistry, American Chemical Society, 1959; Albert Lasker Prize, American Public Health Association, 1962; Nobel Prize in Medicine, with F.H.C. Crick and M.H.F. Wilkins, 1962; Research Corporation Prize, with F.H.C. Crick, 1962; Carty Medal, National Academy of Sciences, 1971; Presidential Medal of Freedom, 1977. Honorary doctorate: University of Chicago, 1961; Indiana University, 1963; University of Notre Dame, Indiana, 1965; Long Island University, 1970; Adelphi University, Garden City, New York, 1972; Brandeis University, Waltham, Massachusetts, 1973; Albert Einstein College of Medicine, New York, 1974; Hofstra University, Hempstead, New York, 1976; Harvard University, 1978; Rockefeller Institute, New York, 1980. Member, National Academy of Sciences. Address: Cold Spring Harbor Laboratory, Cold Spring Harbor, New York 11724, U.S.A.

PUBLICATIONS

Molecular Biology

Molecular Biology of the Gene.   New York, Benjamin, 1965, revised edition, 1970, 1976.
The Double Helix: A Personal Account of the Discovery of the Structure of DNA.   New York, Atheneum, 1968.
The DNA Story: A Documentary History of Gene Cloning, with John Tooze.   San Fransisco, Freeman, 1981.

Other

Editor, with others, *Origins of Human Cancer.*   Cold Spring Harbor, New York, Cold Spring Harbor Laboratory, 1977.

*   *   *

Some historians of biology have called the discovery of the structure of DNA molecules the greatest scientific achievement of the 20th century. A bold statement, perhaps, but clearly an indication of the profound significance of Watson and Crick's accomplishment. There was a feeling of anticipation among many researchers at the end of World War Two that some truly revolutionary discoveries in biology were about to occur. The role of nucleic acids as the hereditary material had recently been confirmed by the studies of Oswald Avery. It had become obvious that the convenient but ambiguous concept of the "gene" in biology was about to be replaced by specific physical entities, i.e., chemical (that is, nucleic acid) molecules. The question of how hereditary characteristics are transmitted had been shifted from recognizing the carriers of those traits (they were now acknowledged to be molecules of nucleic acids, rather than "genes") to unraveling the mechanism by which transmission occurs (what the structure of DNA molecules is which permits the encoding and transmission of genetic information).

The team of Watson and Crick was uniquely well suited to the resolution of this problem. Watson was a geneticist with a firm commitment to finding chemical explanations for biological (i.e., genetic) phenomena. Crick was a physicist eager to find structural explanations for chemical and biological behaviors. The two attacked the problem of DNA structure as a trial-and-error exercise in model-building. Their task was to construct a molecule whose structure and function would explain the ability of cells to (1) reproduce and, in the process, pass on their genetic history virtually unaltered to all daughter cells, and (2) manufacture without significant error the vast number and variety of biochemical compounds which living organisms need to live and develop.

Watson and Crick began with certain fundamental information about the DNA molecule. They knew, first of all, that the molecule is composed of three fundamental building blocks: a sugar, deoxyribose; phosphate groups; and nitrogen-containing heterocyclic compounds known as "bases." The sugar and phosphate groups are bonded to each other (-S-P-S-P-S-P-S-P-) in a very long chain. The bases are joined to the sugar-phosphate backbone in apparently random fashion. Finally, some structural data about the geometry of the DNA molecule, such as intramolecular spacing, had been determined by X-ray diffraction analysis.

The task confronting Watson and Crick was to use these data to construct a molecule that could perform all the biological functions associated with DNA. Many possible structures presented themselves. Diffraction studies had shown that the molecule almost certainly consists of more than one chain. But were there two, three, or more chains involved? Second, the nitrogen bases were certainly attached to the sugar-phosphate chain. But was the molecule constructed with the backbone inside the molecule and the bases extending outward or, vice-versa, with the sugar-phosphate chain on the outside and the bases projected inward from it? Also, what was the relationship of the nitrogen bases attached to one chain to those on other parts of the same chain or on other chains?

These and many other questions were approached by the construction of molecular models and the testing of those models against X-ray diffraction pictures. In this effort, Watson and Crick were enormously aided by the work of Maurice Wilkins and Rosalind Franklin. In fact, the somewhat dubious way in which Watson and Crick obtained Franklin's diffraction photographs has become something of a cause celebre in the history of molecular biology, with some scholars suggesting that Franklin's contribution to this effort well qualified her for a share of the Nobel Prize with Watson, Crick, and Wilkins.

In any case, the final solution to this problem was reached early in 1953. Watson and Crick determined that the most likely structure of the DNA molecule was a double helix—a pair of chains wrapped around each other—in which the sugar-phosphate backbones are on the outside of the molecule and the nitrogen bases are projected inward from them. The bases are arranged in such a way, furthermore, that two of them—adenine and thymine—are always paired with each other, and the other two—cytosine and guanine—are paired with each other.

This model effectively fits the processes of both replication and transcription. In the process of replication, the double helix separates, as the two chains of the double helix uncoil and move away from each other. Each chain then acts as a template on which an exact, but reversed, copy of itself is synthesized. The old and new chains then rejoin and reform two new double helices. In this way, two exact copies of the original molecule are produced.

In the process of transcription, the double helix first uncoils and separates, much as in the case of replication. In this case, however, only one chain acts as a template on which an exact, but reversed, copy of the base sequence is made. The molecule produced in this way is a single-stranded nucleic acid, ribonucleic acid (RNA), which contains the sugar ribose rather than deoxyribose and the nitrogen base uracil instead of thymine. The RNA thus formed carries in its molecular structure the genetic message originally stored in DNA. The RNA migrates out of the cell nucleus to the ribosomes, where it directs the synthesis of proteins according to these genetic instructions.

Shortly after, the exact way in which a genetic "message" is stored in DNA molecules was elucidated. The sequence of any triplet of bases (a *codon*) was found to represent a single amino acid. The codon TAC, for example, codes for the amino acid methionine. The concept of a codon allows us, then, to provide a precise, chemical definition for the "gene." A gene is nothing other than a certain segment of a DNA molecule containing many thousands of nitrogen bases. This sequence of bases corresponds to a particular sequence of amino acids. The type and order of these amino acids corresponds, in turn, to a particular protein. The chemical constitution of the DNA molecule, that is, dictates the type of protein molecule the cell is to make. This chemical constitution is protected within the three-dimensional structure of the DNA molecule and is transmitted from generation to generation in the process of replication. The century-old biological concept of "genes" and "chromosomes" can be seen, therefore, to be completely explicable in terms of chemical molecules.

—David Newton

WATSON, J(ohn) B(roadus). American psychologist. Born in Greenville, South Carolina, 9 January 1878. Studied at Furman University, Greenville, B.A. 1898, M.A. 1899; University of Chicago, Ph.D. 1903. Served as a psychologist in the United States Army, 1917-19: Major. Married Mary Ickes in 1904, 2 children; married Rosalie Rayner in 1920, 2 children. Principal, Batesburg Institute, Greenville, 1899-1900; Assistant in Experimental Psychology, University of Chicago, 1903-04; Instructor, 1904-08; and Professor of Experimental and Comparative Psychology and Director of the Psychology Laboratory, 1908-20, Johns Hopkins University, Baltimore; worked for the J. Walter Thompson Company, New York, 1920-35 (Vice-President, 1924-35) and William Esty and Company, New York, 1935-47 (Vice-President). Editor, *Psychological Review*, 1908-15, and *Journal of Experimenatl Psychology*, 1915-27. President, American Psychological Association, 1915. Honorary doctorate: Furman University, 1919. Fellow, American Academy of Arts and Sciences. *Died 25 September 1958.*

PUBLICATIONS

Psychology

Animal Education: An Experimental Study on the Psychological Development of the White Rat. Chicago, University of Chicago Press, 1903.

Methods of Studying Vision in Animals, with Robert M. Yerkes. New York, Holt, 1911.

Behavior: An Introduction to Comparative Psychology. New York, Holt, 1914.

Psychology from the Standpoint of a Behaviorist. Philadelphia, Lippincott, 1919.

Behaviorism. New York, Norton, and London, Kegan Paul, 1925.

The Battle of Behaviorism: An Exposition and an Attack, with William McDougall. London, Kegan Paul, 1928; New York, Norton, 1929.

The Psychological Care of the Infant and Child. New York, Norton, and London, Allen and Unwin, 1928.

The Ways of Behaviorism. New York, Harper, 1928.

*

Critical Studies: *J.B. Watson, The Founder of Behaviorism: A Biography* by David Cohen, London and Boston, Routledge, 1979 (includes bibliography).

*   *   *

At 16, J.B. Watson entered Furman University in his hometown of Greenville, S.C., where his first interests were more in the area of philosophy than psychology. Pursuing the prescribed requirements of Latin, Greek, mathematics, and philosophy, he graduated with a Master's degree. He became interested in the philosophy of John Dewey and enrolled as a graduate student at the University of Chicago where Dewey taught. Finding Dewey to be "incomprehensible" he became disillusioned with the field of philosophy, although he continued to minor in the subject. As philosophy at this time included the study of psychology, it so happened that he was exposed to the functionalist James R. Angell, who stimulated his interest in psychology as a career.

In the neurological laboratory of H.H. Donaldson, where he became acquainted with techniques of study using white rats, and in the biology and physiology classes of Jacques Loeb his interest in psychology continued. In his doctoral dissertation, using both neurological and behavioral techniques, he wrote about his study of the correlation of growth and behavior of medullation in the central nervous system. He felt that Loeb, Angell, and Donaldson were his most influential teachers, and it was to the latter two that he dedicated his first book.

In the year of his graduation, 1903, Watson suffered a breakdown accompanied by anxiety attacks. He recovered within a few weeks and was later to view his illness as a valuable lesson in understanding his own limitations. He went to work as an assistant for Angell for a year and was then made an instructor teaching mostly Jamesian psychology in the classroom, although his primary interest was animal research in a lab which he constructed in the university basement.

Watson's interest in animal psychology was stimulated by the work of the American psychologist Lloyd Morgan and Edward Thorndike, as the details of Pavlov's experiment were still unknown in this country. It would remain so until 1909 when another Russian, Vlademir M. Bekhterev, published his book *Objective Psychology* and introduced the concept of conditioning to America. Watson became the most diligent sponsor of this new "reflexology," enthusiastically welcoming Pavlov's and Bekhterev's work and utilizing the concept of the conditioned reflex to explain learning and habit formation. Watson concluded that it was kinesthetic sense (or muscle sense) that was most essential in the learning process for rats.

In the tradition of the physical sciences, Watson believed that the goal of psychology should be to study observable behavior and not consciousness. He therefore opposed introspection as a basic approach to the study of the human mind. Real scientific evidence, he felt, could only be found by exposing animal or human to a stimulus and then objectively recording the responses or resulting behavior. He believed thought to be nothing more

than talking to ourselves; that is, he felt it occurred as subvocal speech resulting from almost imperceptible movements of the muscles in the throat, tongue, and larynx. He extended his approach to incorporate any muscle action, giving the example of deaf and dumb individuals who, he said, "think just as they talk, in hand movements". Most psychologists have not accepted Watson's theory correlating thinking and hand movements.

In 1908 Watson accepted a full scholarship in experimental and comparative psychology at Johns Hopkins University in Baltimore, where he was to remain until 1920. It was there that he did his most important work. Because he was given the directorship of the laboratory as well, one of his first priorities was establishing an animal research section within it.

In 1913 Watson published his famous article "Psychology as the Behaviorist Views It" in *The Psychological Review*, marking the beginning of a new psychology. Stemming from years of hard work which led to a series of lectures at Columbia, at the invitation of Cattell, the article announced behavioralism and its goals. A year later he published *Behavior: An Introduction to Comparative Psychology* in which he declared that animal psychology should be declared a special branch of psychology. In this book he presented evidence to demonstrate his claims, showing how animals could contribute significantly to the field of psychology as they offered better experimental control conditions than those available when experimenting with humans.

In conjunction with the Phipps Clinic in Baltimore, Watson, in 1918, began his research with young children. Until this time the primary research tools had been biographies, questionaires, and some testing; little experimentation had been attempted. Watson introduced the manipulation of stimulation variables which he felt was necessary for objective experimental research. From research where he observed hand movements in young infants, he proposed that right-handedness was a result of conditioning caused by social pressure. One of Watson's most popular works, *Psychology from the Standpoint of a Behaviorist* (1919), extended methods and principles of his research with animals into the realm of human psychology.

His academic career at Johns Hopkins came to an end in 1920 as a result of a divorce and the senational publicity surrounding it. He remarried that same year and went to work for the J. Walter Thompson advertising agency, maintaining contact with psychology by writing articles for various popular magazines. Watson published his book *The Psychological Care of the Infant and Child* in 1928 in which, in style and language intended for the general public, he attempted to show the practical value of psychology in its application towards child-rearing practices. In it, he tried to show how faulty or adverse conditioning could hamper a child's upbringing. He firmly committed himself to a disciplined rather than a permissive stance. In 1930 Watson decided to leave the field of psychology and spend the rest of his life in the business world. His name is now synonymous with behaviorism, a school of psychology which is still influential in the profession today.

—R.W. Rieber

WEBB, Sidney and Beatrice.   British social and political philosophers.   **WEBB, Sidney (James); 1st Baron Passfield:** born in London, 13 July 1859. Educated in private schools in Switzerland and Macklenburg-Schwerin; studied at Birkbeck Institute; City of London College; LL.B. (London) 1886; Barrister, Gray's Inn, London, 1885. Married Beatrice Potter in 1892. Clerk in a colonial brokers office, London, 1875-78; civil servant, in War Office, 1878-79, Surveyor of Taxes Office, 1879-81, and Colonial Office, 1881-91; Member for Deptford, London County Council, 1892-1910; lecturer on political economy, City of London

College and Working Men's College; Professor of Public Administration, London School of Economics, 1912-27; Member of
Parliament (Labour), for Seaham Division, County Durham,
1922-29: President of the Board of Trade, 1924; Secretary of
State for Dominian Affairs, 1929-30, and for the colonies, 1929-
31. Member of Faculty and Board of Studies in Economics,
University of London. Member of Royal Commission under
Development Act, 1910-22. Member, Fabian Society, from
1885. Member, Royal Commission on Trade and Union Law,
1903-06, on Coal Industry Commission, 1919, and on Departmental Committees on Technological Institute at South Ken-
sington, 1904-05, Agricultural Settlements and Emigration,
1905-06, Territorial Army, 1906-07, Census of Production, 1907-
08, Intelligence as to Distress in London, 1914-15, Economic
Conditions of Industrial Discovery, 1915-16, Railways, 1917-18,
Trusts, 1918-20, Fertilisers, 1919-20, and on Central Committee
of Profiteering Act, 1919-20. Member of the Senate, London
University, 1900-09. D.Sc.: University of London; Litt. D.: University of Wales; D. in Pol. Econ.: University of Munich. P.C.,
(Privy Councillor), 1924; O.M. (Order of Merit), 1944; created
Baron Passfield of Passfield Corner, 1929. *Died 13 October
1947.* **WEBB, (Martha) Beatrice (née Potter):** Born at Standish
House, near Gloucester, 22 January 1858. Educated privately.
Married Sidney Webb in 1892. Social worker, as assistant to
Charles Booth: Member of the Royal Commission on Poor Law
and Unemployment, 1905-09, and joint author of minority
report; member of government committee upon Grants in Aid of
Distress in London, 1914-15, of Statutory War Pensions Com-
mittee, 1916-17, of Reconstruction Committee, 1917-18, of
Committee on National Registration, 1917-18, of Committee on
the Machinery of Government, 1918-19, of War Cabinet Com-
mittee on Women in Industry, 1918-19, and of Lord Chancellor's
Advisory Committee for Women Justices, 1919-20. Justice of the
Peace for London, 1919-27. D.Litt.: University of Manchester;
LL.D.: University of Edinburgh; D. in Pol. Econ.: University of
Munich. Fellow, British Academy, 1931. *Died 30 April 1943.*

Publications

Political Writings by Sidney and Beatrice Webb

The History of Trade Unionism. London and New York,
   Longman, 1894; revised edition, 1920.
Industrial Democracy. London and New York, Longman, 2
   vols., 1897; revised edition, 1920.
Problems of Modern Industry. London and New York,
   Longman, 1898.
*The History of Liquor Licensing in England, Principally from
   1700 to 1830.* London and New York, Longman, 1903; as
   English Local Government 11, 1963.
English Local Government:
   The Parish and the Country. London and New York,
      Longman, 1906.
   The Manor and the Borough. London and New York,
      Longman, 2 vols., 1908.
   English Poor Law Policy. London and New York, Long-
      man, 1910.
   The Story of the King's Highway. London and New York,
      Longman, 1913.
   Statutory Authorities for Special Purposes. London and
      New York, Longman, 1922; excerpt, as *The Development
      of English Local Government 1689-1835,* London, Oxford
      University Press, 1963.
   English Prisons under Local Government. London and New
      York, Longman, 1922.
   English Poor Law History. London and New York, Long-
      man, 3 vols., 1927-29.
The State and the Doctor. London and New York, Longman,
   1910.
The Prevention of Destitution. London and New York,

Longman, 1911; excerpt, as *The Sphere of Voluntary Agen-
   cies in the Prevention of Destitution,* London, National
   Committee for the Prevention of Destitution, 1911.
A Constitution for the Socialist Commonwealth of Great Britain.
   London and New York, Longman, 1920.
The Consumers Co-operative Movement. London and New
   York, Longman, 1921.
The Decay of Capitalist Civilisation. London, Fabian Society,
   and New York, Harcourt Brace, 1923.
Methods of Social Study. London and New York, Longman,
   1932.
Soviet Communism: A New Civilisation? London, Longman,
   2 vols., 1935; New York, Scribner, 2 vols., 1936; excerpt, as *Is
   Soviet Communism a New Civilisation?,* London, Left Review,
   1936.
Soviet Communism: Dictatorship or Democracy?. London,
   Left Review, 1936.
The Truth about Soviet Russia. London and New York,
   Longman, 1942.
Constitution of the U.S.S.R. Cape Town, Stewart, 1942.

Political Writings by Sidney Webb

The Difficulties of Individualism. London, Fabian Society,
   1884.
Facts for Socialists. London, Fabian Society, 1887; 14th edi-
   tion, 1937.
A Plea for the Taxation of Ground Rents. London, "United
   Committee" for the Taxation of Ground Rents and Values,
   1887.
The Progress of Socialism (lecture). London, Modern Press,
   1888.
Wanted: A Programme: An Appeal to the Liberal Party. Pri-
   vately printed, 1888.
What Socialism Means: A Call to the Unconverted (lecture).
   London, Leaflet Press, 1888; New York, International Pub-
   lishing Company, 1889.
Facts for Londoners. London, Fabian Society, 1889.
An Eight Hours Bill. London, Fabian Society, 1889; revised
   edition, 1890.
Socialism in England. Baltimore, American Economic Associ-
   ation, 1889; London, Sonnenschein, 1890.
English Progress Towards Social Democracy (lecture). Lon-
   don, Fabian Society, 1890.
The Workers' Political Programme. London, Fabian Society,
   1890.
The Eight Hours Day, with Harold Cox. London, Scott, 1891.
The London Programme. London, Sonnenschein, 1891.
*The Best Method of Bringing Co-operation Within the Reach of
   the Poorest of the Population.* Manchester, Co-operative
   Union, 1891.
The Fabian Society: Its Objects and Methods (lecture).
   Netherfield, Nottinghamshire, Stafford, 1891.
The Case for an Eight Hours Bill. London, Fabian Society,
   1891.
*Fabian Municipal Program (The Unearned Increment, Lon-
   don's Heritage in the City Guilds, The Municipalisation of the
   Gas Supply, Municipal Tramways, London's Water Tribute,
   The Municipalization of the London Docks, The Scandal of
   London's Markets, A Labour Policy for Public Authorities).*
   London, Fabian Society, 8 vols., 1891.
The Reform of the Poor Law. London, Fabian Society, 1891.
The Reform of London. London, Eighty Club, 1892.
The London Vestries: What They are and What They Do.
   London, Fabian Society, 1894.
Socialism: True or False. London, Fabian Society, 1894.
The Economic Heresies of the London County Council (address).
   London, Office of "London," 1894.
The Work of the London County Council. London, London
   Reform Union, 1895.
Three Years Work on the London County Council: A Letter to

the Electors of Deptford. London, May, 1895.

Labour in the Longest Reign 1837-1897. London, Fabian Society, 1897.

Six Years' Work on the London County Council: A Letter to the Electors of Deptford. London, May and Goulding, 1898.

The London County Council Election. London, The Echo, 1898.

The Economics of Direct Employment, with an Account of the Fair Wages Policy. London, Fabian Society, 1898.

Nine Years' Work on the London County Council: A Letter to the Electors of Deptford. Privately printed, 1901.

The Education Muddle and the Way Out. London, Fabian Society, 1901.

Five Years' Fruit of the Parish Councils Act. London, Fabian Society, 1901; revised edition, as *Parish Councils and Village Life*, 1908.

Twentieth Century Politics: A Policy of National Efficiency. London, Fabian Society, 1901.

The Education Act, 1902: How to Make the Best of It. London, Fabian Society, 1903.

London Education. London, Longman, 1904.

The London Education Act, 1903: How to Make the Best of It. London, Fabian Society, 1904.

Fifteen Years' Work of the London County Council: A Letter to the Electors of Deptford, with R.C. Phillimore. Privately printed, 1907.

The Decline in the Birth-Rate. London, Fabian Society, 1907.

Paupers and Old Age Pensions. London, Fabian Society, 1907.

The Necessary Basis of Society (address). London, The League, 1908.

The Basis and Policy of Socialism, with the Fabian Society. London, Fabian Society, 1908.

Socialism and Individualism, with others. London, Fabian Society, 1909.

Poor Law Reform. London, Political Committee of the National Liberal Club, 1909.

The Place of Co-operation in the State of To-morrow. London, Co-operative Union, 1910.

The Work of the Local Education Authority, and the Part to Be Played by Voluntary Organisation (address). Manchester, The Union, 1910.

Grants in Aid: A Criticism and a Proposal. London and New York, Longman, 1911; revised edition, 1920.

How the Government Can Prevent Unemployment. London, National Committee for the Prevention of Destitution, 1912.

The Legal Minimum Wage. London, National Committee for the Prevention of Destitution, 1912.

The Economic Theory of a Legal Minimum Wage. New York, National Consumers' League, 1912.

What about the Rates? or, Municipal Finance and Municipal Autonomy. London, Fabian Society, 1913.

The Cost of Living. Brussels, International Socialist Bureau, 1914.

The War and the Workers. London, Fabian Society, 1914.

Towards Social Democracy? A Study of Social Evolution During the Past Three-Quarters of a Century. London, Fabian Society, 1916.

Great Britain after the War, with Arnold Freeman. London, Allen and Unwin, 1916.

When Peace Comes: The Way of Industrial Reconstruction. London, Fabian Society, 1916.

The Reform of the House of Lords. London, Fabian Society, 1917.

The Restoration of Trade Union Conditions. London, Nisbet, and New York, Huebsch, 1917.

The Works Manager To-day (address). London and New York, Longman, 1917.

The Teacher in Politics. London, Fabian Society, 1918.

To the Men and Women Graduates of the University of London: An Open Letter. London, St. Clement's Press, 1918.

Ministry of Health: What the Bill Must Be If It Is Really Going to Save People. London, Association of Approved Societies, 1918.

National Finance and a Levy on Capital: What the Labour Party Intends. London, Fabian Society, 1919.

The Root of Labour Unrest (address). London, Fabian Society, 1920.

The Story of the Durham Miners, 1662-1921. London, Fabian Society, 1921.

The Constitutional Problems of a Co-operative Society. London, Fabian Society, 1923.

The Labour Party on the Threshold (address). London, Fabian Society, 1923.

The Need for Federal Reorganisation in the Co-operative Movement. London, Fabian Society, 1933.

The Local Government Act, 1929— How to Make the Best of It. London, Fabian Society, 1929.

What Happened in 1931: A Record. London, Fabian Society, 1932.

Political Writings by Beatrice Webb

The Co-operative Movement in Great Britain. London, Sonnenschein, and New York, Scribner, 1891.

How Best to Do Away with the Sweating System. Manchester, Co-operative Union, 1892.

The Relationship Between Co-operation and Trade Unionism (lecture). Manchester, Co-operative Union, 1892.

Women and the Factory Acts. London, Fabian Society, 1896.

The Relation of Poor-Law Medical Relief to the Public Health Authorities. Bristol, Wright, 1906.

Socialism and the National Minimum, with B.L. Hutchins and the Fabian Society. London, Fabian Society, 1909.

The Minority Report in Its Relation to Public Health and the Medical Profession. London, National Committee to Promote the Break-Up of the Poor Law, 1910.

The New Crusade Against Destitution. Manchester, National Labour Press, 1910.

Complete National Provision for Sickness: How to Amend the Insurance Act. London, National Committee for the Prevention of Destitution, 1912.

A Woman's Appeal:... Personal Expenditure in Wartimes. London, National War Savings Committee, 1916.

The Abolition of the Poor Law. London, Fabian Society, 1918.

The Wages of Men and Women: Should They Be Equal?. London, Fabian Society, 1919.

The Discovery of the Consumer. London, Benn, 1928; New York, Cooperative League, 1934 (?).

The English Poor Law: Will It Endure? (lecture). London, Oxford University Press, 1928.

A New Reform Bill. London, Fabian Society, 1931.

Other Writings by Sidney and Beatrice Webb

Visit to New Zealand in 1898: Beatrice Webb's Diary, with Entries by Sidney Webb. Wellington, Price Milburn, 1959.

The Webbs' Australian Diary, 1898, edited by A.G. Austin. Melbourne, Pitman, 1965.

The Letters of Sidney and Beatrice Webb, edited by Norman MacKenzie. London, Oxford University Press, 3 vols., 1978.

Editor (Beatrice alone), *The Case for the Factory Acts.* London, Richards, and New York, Dutton, 1901.

Editor, *The Break-Up of the Poor Law, and The Public Organisation of the Labour Market* (minority report of the poor law commission). London and New York, Longman, 2 vols., 1909.

Editor (Sidney alone), with Arnold Freeman, *Seasonal Trades.* London, London School of Economics, 1912.

Editor (Sidney alone), *How to Pay for the War*. London, Fabian Society, 1916.

Other Writings by Beatrice Webb

My Apprenticeship.   London and New York, Longman, 1926.
Our Partnership, edited by Barbara Drake and Margaret I. Cole.   London and New York, Longman, 1948.
Diaries, 1912-1932, edited by Margaret I. Cole.   London and New York, 2 vols., Longman, 1952-56.
American Diary, 1898, edited by David A. Shannon.   Madison, University of Wisconsin Press, 1963.
The Diary of Beatrice Webb, vol. 1, 1873-1892, edited by Norman and Jeanne MacKenzie.   London, Virago-London School of Economics, 1982.

*

Bibliography: *Publications of Sidney and Beatrice Webb: An Interim Check List*, London, British Library of Political and Economic Science, 1973.

Critical Studies: *Sidney and Beatrice Webb* by Mary A. Hamilton, London, Sampson Low, 1933; *Beatrice Webb*; London, Longman, 1945, New York, Harcourt Brace, 1946, *Beatrice and Sidney Webb*, London, Fabian Society, 1955, both by Margaret I. Cole, and *The Webbs and Their Work* edited by Cole, London, Muller, 1949, New York, Barnes and Noble, 1974; *The Pursuit of Certainty: David Hume, Jeremy Bentham, John Stuart Mill, Beatrice Webb* by Shirley R. Letwin, Cambridge, University Press, 1967; *Education for National Efficiency: The Contribution of Sidney and Beatrice Webb* edited by J.T. Brennan, London, Athlone Press, 1975; *Socialism and Society: A New View of the Webb Partnership* by Norman MacKenzie, London, London School of Economics, 1978; *A Victorian Courtship: The Story of Beatrice Potter and Sidney Webb* by Jeanne MacKenzie, London, Weidenfeld and Nicolson, 1979.

*   *   *

It can be said, in a phrase, that Beatrice and Sidney Webb were social philosophers, almost all the books volumes they wrote (twenty of them written in combination) being about the history, structure, and function of some kind of social organisation. They were both deeply interested, indeed fascinated, in the forms it might take and the functions it had performed and could perform. It can be said, too, that they regarded themselves as "social scientists," and just as the biologist studies the living organism they studied the social organisation.

In her book *Our Partnership* Beatrice Webb has described their joint motives and methods thus: "Like other scientists, we were obsessed by scientific curiosity about the universe and its working. But, unlike the astronomers and the physicists, the chemists and the biologists, we turned our curiosity to the phenomena that were being less frequently investigated, namely those connected with the social institutions characteristic of *homo sapiens* or what is called sociology. We accordingly devoted ourselves as scientists to the study of social institutions, from trade unions to Cabinets, from family relationships to churches, from economics to literature." She readily admitted that it was "a field in itself so extensive that we have never been able to compass more than a few selected fragments of it."

The Webbs always made a clear distinction between their work as practical politicians and as writers of social science. Throughout their long lives together they knew exactly what they wanted to do—and why they were doing it. And it was readily recognised that no one who knew and worked with them could fail to appreciate their complete personal disinterestedness.

While their influence on the Labour Party, the trade unions, and the co-operative movement was immense it was not limited to what could be called the "Labour" side of British politics. It permeated the Conservative and Liberal parties and the machinery of local government. And when advocating greater municipal educational facilities, Sidney said, "I want no class of hewers of wood and drawers of water; no class destined to remain there, and prevented from rising because we do not provide for it."

There is hardly an area of social thought and practice in which they did not leave an important mark. The Webbs were great historians. Their *History of Trade Unionism* made it recognised that the life of the nation was not seriously capable of effective interpretation without a full grasp of the place in its working of the important institutions trade unions had built up in self-defence from the first days of the Industrial Revolution. And that volume, with its sequel, *Industrial Democracy*, has been the model of all subsequent work.

Although the general opinion of the Webbs' written work might not now be as favourable as when it was first published—with their comparatively heavy literary style—they broke fresh ground and set new standards. Indeed, there can be no doubt about the Webbs' tremendous impact on social study and method.

Fascinating accounts of the Webb's lives and habits have been preserved for posterity by their own literary portraits, principally in Beatrice's *My Apprenticeship* (written in 1921) which tells the story of her life up to marriage, and *Our Partnership*. And later there came—published posthumously—further volumes of diaries.

At the time of Sidney's death it was said that there was no area of social thought and practice in which, during the last 60 years of life, he did not leave an important mark. It was commented that he brought to the service of the Labour movement not only the mind of a great scholar but the practical gifts of a remarkable organiser with something akin to genius in his power to realise what was required to meet the mental climate of his time. With his wife, it was declared, no other partnership in the intellectual life of Great Britain had so remarkably combined happiness and creative accomplishment.

Beatrice's biographer, Margaret Cole, has said that never in all their lives did she or Sidney have any personal axe to grind. There was never any promotion of public political ends or search for personal prestige or aggrandisement. No malice was born, either, for insults and attacks that would have rankled in lesser minds. Never before had there been a married partnership so complete and so equal in its achievement. And, as Bernard Shaw once said, no one can completely separate their contributions or judge which was the more dominant or the more gifted partner.

Reviewers of their lives have stressed the point that while neither Beatrice or Sidney ever wielded political power they helped to build up institutions and initiate social changes of importance and permanence, the Fabian Society, the London School of Economics, State education, the *New Statesman*, and social security being given as examples. Of Sidney it has been said that he gave the best years of his life with selfless devotion to the cause of social justice, that he saw with clear and steady vision "that only a socialist society could end the exploitation of man by man. Not only did he make that vision clear to his own day and age but he made that age happier by his own constructive work, combining in himself the insight of a great historian with the practical ability of a great reformer."

—Granville Eastwood

WEBER, Max.   German social scientist.   Born in Erfaut, Thuringia, 21 April 1864. Studied at the universities of Heidelberg, Berlin, and Göttingen, passed bar examination 1886, Ph.D. 1889. Served in the German Army, 1883. Married Marianne Schnitger in 1893. Professor of Economics, Freiburg University, 1894-96; Professor, Heidelberg University, 1896-97; Professor,

Munich University, 1918-20. Incapacitated by psychic disturbance, 1897-1902. Editor, with Werner Sombart, *Archiv für
Sozialwissenschaft und Sozialpolitik*, from 1903; Editor, *Outline
of Social Economics*, from 1909; Co-Founder, Deutsche Soziologische Gesellschaft, 1910; devoted most of his time to his
studies of China, India, and ancient Judaism. *Died* (Munich) *14
June 1920.*

PUBLICATIONS

Collections

Max Weber-Gesamtausgabe. Tübingen, Mohr, 1982-.

Social Sciences

*Entwicklung des Solidarhaftprinzips und des Sondervermögens
    der offenen Handelsgesellschaft aus den Haushalts- und
    Gewerbegemeinschaften in den italienischen Städte.* Stutt-
    gart, Kröner, 1889.
*Zur Geschichte der handelsgesellschaften im mittelalter: Nach
    südeuropäischen Quellen.* Stuttgart, Enke, 1889.
*Die römische agrargeschichte in ihrer bedeutung für das staats-
    und privatrecht.* Stuttgart, Enke, 1891; as *The Agrarian
    Sociology of Ancient Civilizations*, London, New Left Books,
    1976.
Die Verhältnisse der Landarbeiter im ostelbischen Deutschland.
    Leipzig, Duncker und Humblot, 1892.
Die Börse. Göttingen, Vandenhoeck und Ruprecht, 1894.
Der Nationalstaat und die Volkswirtschaftspolitik (lecture).
    Freiburg, Mohr, 1895.
*Die "Objektivität" sozialwissenschaftlicher und sozialpolitischer
    Erkenntnis.* Tübingen, Mohr, 1904.
*Parlament und Regierung im neugeordneten Deutschland: Zur
    politischen Kritik des Beamtentums und Parteiwesens.* Mu-
    nich, Duncker und Humblot, 1918.
Wissenschaft als Beruf (lecture). Munich, Duncker und Hum-
    blot, 1919; as "Science as a Vocation," in *Essays in Sociology*,
    1946.
Politik als Beruf (lecture). Munich, Duncker und Humblot,
    1919; as "Politics as a Vocation," in *Essays in Sociology*, 1946.
Gesammelte Aufsätze zur Religionssoziologie. Tübingen, Mohr,
    3 vols., 1920-21; "Die protestantische Ethik und der Geist des
    Kapitalismus" as *The Protestant Ethic and the Spirit of Capi-
    talism*, London, Allen and Unwin, and New York, Scribner,
    1930; "Konfuzianismus und Taoismus" as *The Religion of
    China: Confucianism and Taoism*, edited by Hans Gerth,
    Glencoe, Illinois, Free Press, 1951; vol.2, *Hinduismus und
    Buddhismus* as *The Religion of India: The Sociology of Hin-
    duism and Buddhism*, edited by Hans Gerth and Don Martin-
    dale, Glencoe, Illinois, Free Press, 1958; vol. 3, *Das antike
    Judentum* as *Ancient Judaism*, edited by Hans Gerth and Don
    Martindale, Glencoe, Illinois, Free Press, 1952.
Gesammelte politische Schriften. Munich, Drei Masken, 1921;
    expanded edition, edited by Johannes Winkelmann, Tübin-
    gen, Mohr, 1958.
Die rationalen und soziologischen Grundlagen der Musik.
    Munich, Drei Masken, 1921; as *The Rational and Social
    Foundations of Music*, edited by Don Martindale and others,
    Carbondale, Southern Illinois University Press, 1958.
Wirtschaft und Gesellschaft. Tübingen, Mohr, 1922; revised
    edition, 1925; part 1 translated as *The Theory of Social and
    Economic Organization*, edited by Talcott Parsons, New
    York, Oxford University Press, and London, Hodge, 1947;
    selection translated as *Max Weber on Law in Economy and
    Society*, edited by Max Rheinstein, Cambridge, Massachu-
    setts, Harvard University Press, 1954; 4th German edition
    revised as *Wirtschaft und Gesellschaft: Grundriss der verste-
    henden Soziologie* (includes "Die rationalen und soziologi-
    schen Grundlagen der Musik"), 1956; as *Economy and*

Society: An Outline of Interpretive Sociology, edited by
    Günther Roth and Claus Wittich, New York, Bedminster
    Press, 3 vols., 1968; selections translated separately as *Basic
    Concepts in Sociology*, New York, Philosophical Library,
    1962; "Religionssoziologie" translated separately as *The
    Sociology of Religion*, Boston, Beacon, 1963; London,
    Methuen, 1965.
Gesammelte Aufsätze zur Wissenschaftslehre. Tübingen, Mohr,
    1922; expanded edition, 1951.
*Wirtschaftsgeschichte: Abriss der universalen Sozial- und Wirt-
    schaftsgeschichte*, edited by S. Hellmann and M. Palyi.
    Munich, Duncker und Humblot, 1923; as *General Economic
    History*, Glencoe, Illinois, Free Press, and London, Allen and
    Unwin, 1927.
Gesammelte Aufsätze zur Sozial- und Wirtschaftsgeschichte.
    Tübingen, Mohr, 1924.
Gesammelte Aufsätze zur Soziologie und Sozialpolitik. Tübin-
    gen, Mohr, 1924.
Essays in Sociology, edited by Hans Gerth and C. Wright Mills.
    New York, Oxford University Press, 1946; London, Kegan
    Paul, 1947.
*Schriften zur theoretischen Soziologie, zur Soziologie der Politik
    und Verfassung.* Frankfurt, Schauer, 1947.
Aus den Schriften zur Religionssoziologie: Auswahl, edited by
    Ernst Graf zu Solms. Frankfurt, Schauer, 1948.
The Methodology of the Social Sciences, edited by Edward A.
    Shils and Henry A. Finch. Glencoe, Illinois, Free Press,
    1949.
Soziologie, weltgeschichtliche Analysen, Politik (selections), edited
    by Johannes Winckelmann. Stuttgart, Kröner, 1955; revised
    and expanded edition, 1960.
Staatssoziologie, edited by Johannes Winckelmann. Berlin,
    Duncker und Humblot, 1956.
The City, edited by Don Martindale and Gertrud Neuwirth.
    Glencoe, Illinois, Free Press, 1958; London, Heinemann,
    1960.
Rechtssoziologie, edited by Johannes Winckelmann. Neuwied,
    Luchterhand, 1960.
Max Weber (selections). New York, Crowell, 1963.
Max Weber: Werk und Person: Dokumente, edited by Eduard
    Baumgarten. Tübingen, Mohr, 1964.
*Staat, Gesellschaft, Wirtschaft: Quellentexte zur politischen Bil-
    dung von Max Webers gesammelten Schriften*, edited by
    Ludwig Heieck. Heidelberg, Meyer, 1966.
*Max Weber on Charisma and Institution Building: Selected
    Papers*, edited by S.N. Eisenstadt. Chicago, University of
    Chicago Press, 1968.
The Interpretation of Social Reality, edited by J.E.T. Eldridge.
    London, Joseph, 1970.
*Max Weber on Universities: The Power of the State and the
    Dignity of the Academic Calling in Imperial Germany*, edited
    by Edward Shils. Chicago, University of Chicago Press,
    1973.
*Roscher and Knies: The Logical Problems of Historical Econo-
    mics.* New York, Free Press, 1975.
Critique of Stammler. New York, Free Press, 1977.
Weber: Selections in Translation, edited by W.G. Runciman.
    Cambridge, Cambridge University Press, 1978.

Other

Jugendbriefe. Tübingen, Mohr, 1936.

*

Bibliography: *Max Weber Bibliographie: Eine Dokumentation
der Sekundär-literatur* by Constans Seyfarth and Gert Schmidt,
Stuttgart, Enke, 1977; by Martin Riesebrodt, in *Prospekt der
Max Weber-Gesamtausgabe*, Tübingen, Mohr, 1981.

Critical Studies: *The Legacy of Max Weber* by L.M. Lachmann,

San Francisco, Boyd and Fraser, 1971; *Capitalism and Modern Theory: An Analysis of the Writings of Marx, Durkheim, and Max Weber* by Anthony Giddens, Cambridge, Cambridge University Press, 1971; *Value and Politics in Max Weber's Methodology* by H.H. Brunn, Atlantic Highlands, New Jersey, Humanities Press, 1972; *The Rise of Western Rationalism: Max Weber's Developmental History* by Wolfgang Schlucter, Berkeley, University of California Press, 1981; *Max Weber* by Frank Parkin, London, Methuen, 1982; *Max Weber and Karl Marx* by Karl Lowith, London, Allen and Unwin, 1982.

*   *   *

Though Max Weber died more than sixty years ago, his importance to social and political theory, comparative religion, the sociology of law, and the philosophy and method of the social sciences refuses to diminish. Each year scholarly studies and applications of his work appear in greater numbers than before, so that over 3,000 items now occupy the latest bibliography of Weberian analysis, and in the last several years a half-dozen major monographs exclusively on Weber have appeared in English alone. The three fathers of modern sociology—Durkheim, Weber, and Marx—are all essential to its overall project, yet one would be hard-pressed today to decide whether Weber or Marx remains the more vital. While Marx's influence in social theory and political sociology certainly predominates abroad, within the U.S. Weber still holds the upper hand. It is impossible to discuss American sociology without coming quickly to the terms "rationalization," "ideal-type," "unintended consequences of social action," "charismatic authority," "the iron cage of bureaucratic life," and "the Protestant ethic," to name only a few. All of these were originated or greatly augmented by Weber, and when tied to his "nominalistic" and "value-free" approach to social research, they go a long way toward defining the self-understanding of today's non-Marxist sociology.

Though it is possible to separate Weber's life from his work in considering the latter, it is not advisable, for the same "tensions" about which he constantly wrote, whether emanating from ancient civilizations or his own, affected his private life profoundly. It was largely in response to these overwhelming sensations of powerlessness, displacement, and pervasive meaninglessness which he believed saturated modern life for most "social actors," that Weber began the single largest research task ever undertaken by a social scientist, and carried it remarkably far toward completion in a short life. He sought to answer several large, interrelated questions, and found that only through rigorous comparative research could he attempt probable answers. Marx's challenge to conventional historical methods posed itself to all social scientists of Weber's generation and forced him from the outset to consider the causal relation of ideas to societal change. For the Left ideas held somewhat epiphenomenal status in relation to events in the infrastructural (economic) realm. Weber expressed repeatedly his agreement that in the last instance economic interests do guide "consciousness," and not vice-versa. Yet his unrivalled historical knowledge and his accompanying sensitivity to the subtleties of historical explanation forced him to accede to the importance of the opposing, "idealist" view. This antinomy, which irreconcilably divided Marxist from "bourgeois" social science, Weber went further than anyone before him in mitigating, specifically through his studies in the "economic ethics of world religions." And it was in carrying out these works that he developed his most famous analytic, substantive, and methodological approaches to the problem of world history.

Yet he had begun much differently, and with smaller aims. He had been excellently educated in history and languages prior to university training. Early essays on ancient history and political economy already displayed remarkable analytic ability. After the obligatory law degree he published a dissertation (1889) on medieval trading companies in Italy and Spain, and his habilitation on Roman agrarian history and law (1891) won him instant esteem among senior colleagues in the field, notably Theodor Mommsen. This early recognition led him to oversee in 1892 an elaborate empirical study of agrarian workers in Prussia. Though only 28 when this 900-page report appeared, Weber had already adopted a style of conceptualization that stayed with him throughout his career. The specific concern of the sponsoring research organization was to learn what effect Slavic workers would have upon indigenous culture east of the Elbe. But Weber, wishing always to bridge structure and process, to identify the altering power of ideas within political-economic constraints, focussed instead on the pull urban "individualism" exercised on traditionally inert rural workers. He combined this social-psychological perspective with treatment of grosser issues concerning the transformation of the Prussian political economy due to revised circumstances and practices of the ruling *(Junker)* class in their new pursuit of capitalist profit. As their private fortunes grew, their commitment to the commonwealth declined. This ordering of priorities was long in evidence among the bourgeoisie, who meanwhile "ennobled" themselves by purchasing landed titles. Taken together these new behavior patterns imperilled Prussian social structure. Weber analytically thrived on just this sort of phenomena, since their explanation demanded the shrewd connecting of micro (psychological) with macro (structural) events and processes.

Even more importantly, however, it prompted Weber to reflect upon the antinomic relation of ethics peculiar to "pre-capitalist" life and the totally different focus of action suited to capitalist social organization. Though published much later, after his death (in the chaotic masterpiece, *Economy and Society*), his theory or typology of fundamental social action originated here, as he assessed the behavior of social actors moving from one historical structure to the next. And with this structural transformation necessarily came rearrangements of personality. This type of linking is Weber's major contribution to social theory and general sociology, and at the same time the most difficult to understand easily. Many modern practitioners see Weber as principally a "structuralist," yet the classical Weberian analysis, of the Protestant capitalist, turns more upon social-psychological than organizational dynamics. (This could be said *tout court* for his theory of "charisma.") For Weber the sociologist must attend not only to character types (the traditional mode of explanation), nor only to the frozen givenness of structure *à la* crude Marxism, but to an heuristic synthesis of both. This he did by dividing action into the famous typology: traditional, affectual (emotional), value-rational, and purpose-rational. The subtleties of this arrangement cannot be pursued here, but his intention was clear. To the first two types he allocated pre-rational, pre-modern social action, though circumspectly noting—as he habitually did—that his "ideal-types" were never purely found in social life, and that all four types played their roles in modern existence. Yet the *homo oeconomicus* evident within the last type (*zweckrationalische*) served Weber not only as an empirical reference for comparison with the others, but also as a normative goal toward which contemporary social actors, and the collectivities they constituted, should sometimes aspire. This is an important avenue toward understanding Weber's mature work, since it was as a rigorous, even ascetic proponent of rationality in all social arrangements, and especially politics, that he most fully recognized the dimensions of irrational or non-rationalizable aspects of social life. To say he was the Freud of *collective* nonrationality is only minor exaggeration.

He always pursued solutions to large questions through comparative research. When he wanted to disentangle the basic ingredients of the earliest capitalism, he turned to the Orient, rapidly producing masterful analyses of Hinduism, Confucianism, Buddhism, Judaism, and unfinished notes on Islam. His purpose was to discover why sheer business acumen, even greed, had not produced within these cultures capitalist social organization as found in northern Europe. Likewise in assessing modern bureaucracy and its tendency toward ethical and practical "universalism"—the systematic elimination of nonrationalizable categories of knowledge, advancement, and control—he studied bureaucracies in ancient Rome, China, India, and his own Prussia. One should not conclude that because he studied the course of rationalization through history, noting its advances and retreats with equal care, he embraced a rational model of action as an unequivocal good. He was not a Benthamite. But neither was he Hegelian enough to overvalue the "organic" pre-rationality of social life prior to industrialism. There were aspects of the latter—personal honor and integrity, historical sensitivity, individual sacrifice for collective well-being—that he admired strongly. But he refused to join the massive chorus of protest against modernity and its values which sounded then from many German intellectuals. Though not an evolutionist, he recognized the irresistible power of rationality as it turned from one social institution to another, creating sometimes irritating uniformity and predictability where before had been some measure of uniqueness and chance. The logic of modernization demanded predictability in mechanical as well as personal relations, in addition to consistency of approach, record keeping, and uniform action toward a specified goal. The fruits of this regimenting were obvious to all the celebrants of Victorian, imperialistic Europe, but Weber (along with Nietzsche and few others) also saw the debilitating nature of profound rationalization. What had begun as a "light cloak" had evolved into "an iron cage," and in some of Weber's most famous lines, he warns: "No one knows who will live in this cage in the future.... For of the last stage of this cultural development, it might well be truly said: Specialists without spirit, sensualists without heart; this nullity imagines that it has attained a level of civilization never before achieved" (*The Protestant Ethic and the Spirit of Capitalism*).

Certain German scholars today argue that Weber was predominantly a moral and political philosopher, and that his summary essays on the sociology of religion should be viewed as his Archimedian point. Yet whether one takes his theory of bureaucracy, his analyses of classical religious dogmas and their social structures, his work on Roman and modern law, or his abstract typologies of economic, political, and legal relations as the central achievement of the man, the reason he continues to lead social theorists and researchers into new paths is because of his moral vision and his courage in stating it boldly. What Nietzsche did for philosophy, Weber did for social science, but without the bravado and inaccuracy of Spengler. He continued to believe that rationality, in creating the iron cage, at the same time proved its ability to melt the bars when guided wisely. What he could not find in 1920 was the social group skilled enough, powerful enough, or faithful enough to do it.

—Alan Sica

WEIL, Simone (Adolphine). French religious thinker. Born in Paris, 3 February 1909. Educated at the Lycée Henri IV, Paris, agrégation, 1931. Taught at lycées in Le Puy, Auxerre, Roanne, Bourges and Saint-Quentin, 1931-37. Factory worker, 1934-35, and farm worker, 1941; served briefly in the Spanish Republican Army, 1936; left France in 1942 to join the Free French Forces in London. *Died* (in Ashford, Kent) *24 August 1943.*

PUBLICATIONS

Religion and Society

"L'lliade; ou, Le Poème de la force" (as Émile Novis), in *Les Cahiers du Sud* (Marseilles) 26, 1947; as *The Iliad; or, The Poem of Force.* Wallingford, Pennsylvania, Pendle Hill Pamphlets, 1956.

La Pesanteur et la Grâce. Paris, Plon, 1947; as *Gravity and Grace,* London, Routledge, 1952.
L'Enracinement: Prelude à une déclaration des devoirs envers l'être humain. Paris, Gallimard, 1949; as *The Need for Roots,* London, Kegan Paul, 1952; New York, Putnam, 1953.
La Connaissance surnaturelle. Paris, Gallimard, 1950.
Attente de Dieu. Paris, La Colombe, 1950; as *Waiting for God,* London, Kegan Paul, and New York, Putnam, 1951.
La Condition ouvrière. Paris, Gallimard, 1951.
Lettre à un religieux. Paris, Gallimard, 1951; as *Letter to a Priest,* London, Routledge, 1953; New York, Putnam, 1954.
Intuitions pré-chrétiennes. Paris, La Colombe, 1951; as *Intimations of Christianity,* London, Routledge, 1957; Boston, Beacon Press, 1958.
La Source grecque. Paris, Gallimard, 1953; selections in *Intimations of Christianity,* 1957.
Oppression et Liberté. Paris, Gallimard, 1955; as *Oppression and Liberty,* London, Routledge, 1958.
Écrits de Londres et dernières lettres. Paris, Gallimard, 1957.
Leçons de philosophie (Roanne 1933-1934), edited by Anne Reynaud. Paris, Plon, 1959; as *Lectures on Philosophy,* London, Cambridge University Press, 1978.
Écrits historiques et politiques. Paris, Gallimard, 1960.
Pensées sans ordre concernant l'amour de Dieu. Paris, Gallimard, 1962.
Selected Essays. London, Oxford University Press, 1962.
On Science, Necessity, and the Love of God (Collected Essays), edited by Richard Rees. London and New York, Oxford University Press, 1967.
The Simone Weil Reader, edited by George A. Panichas. New York, McKay, 1977.

Other

Cahiers. Paris, Plon, 3 vols., 1951-56; as *The Notebooks of Simone Weil,* London, Kegan Paul, and New York, Putnam, 2 vols., 1956.
Venise sauvée: Tragédie en trois actes. Paris, Gallimard, 1955.
Seventy Letters, edited by Richard Rees. London and New York, Oxford University Press, 1965.
Poèmes, suivis de Venise sauvée. Paris, Gallimard, 1968.

*

Critical Studies: *Simone Weil as We Knew Her* by J.M. Perrin and Gustave Thibon, London, Routledge, 1952; *Simone Weil* by E.W.F. Tomlin, Cambridge, Bowes and Bowes, and New Haven, Connecticut, Yale University Press, 1954; *Simone Weil: A Fellowship in Love* by Jacques Cabaud, New York, Channel Press, 1964 (includes bibliography); *Simone Weil: A Life* by Simone Pétrement, New York, Pantheon, 1976, London, Mowbrays, 1977; *Simone Weil: Interpretations* edited by George Abbott White, Amherst, University of Massachusetts Press, 1981.

*   *   *

Simone Weil came out of a cultivated middle-class French-Jewish background and an elite education in classics and moral thought (especially Alain). In her short life, she was a striking philosophy teacher, a dedicated left-militant, a provocative essayist on social and religious issues, and a quite exceptional afflicted mystic personality. In her student days she had some notoriety as the "Red Virgin." In her last years, and posthumously for a much larger audience (when her essays, notes, and letters were first published in book form), she gained an even more paradoxical notoriety as a "Catholic saint outside the church." An unsettling figure, her extreme moral scrupulosity and anguished social and religious intensity have for two generations appealed, not without considerable perplexity, to diverse intellectuals.

For most of her life, she had an overwhelming identification with the oppressed and "humiliated"—factory workers and peasants, colonized and other exploited peoples, refugees from red and black fascism. Part of her later commitment to Christianity was explicitly because she saw its authentic form as "pre-eminently the religion of slaves," and herself as at one with them. Far more quickly than most left-intellectuals, she perceptively and courageously moved to a radicalism independent of revolutionary Marxism. This was not just away from the deception, tyranny, and cruelty of the Stalinism of her time but from its base in the ruthless opportunism of Leninism, and in the contradictions of Marxist dogma. Her rigorous analytic polemics of the mid-1930's argued for a militant democratic unionism, anticolonialism, pacifism, and a compassionate and libertarian social re-ordering (see *Oppression and Liberty*).

Though frail, awkward and sickly (including anorexia), her scrupulous dedication to the exploited drove her to painful personal engagements in learning and purification as a field laborer and factory hand. Her probing essays on her laboring ("Factory Journal"; *La Condition ouvrière*) argued not for the conventional leftist change in ownership and political power but for a more profound transformation of modern work itself. The hierarchical domination and the rest of the managerial-efficency ordering, and even the very machine designs and system of technology, should be radically humanized to meet the needs of intelligent and sensitive beings. Her still pertinent responses, including what is now called "Worker's Control" and "libertarian decentralization," were those of a pessimistic utopian.

While her later social thought, such as her programmatic abstract moralizing on post-war society done under the aegis of the Gaullists while a war-refugee in London (*The Need for Roots*), still emphasized the centrality of work justice, it shows less of her earlier insight. The anti-politics, and the libertarianism, egalitarianism, and pacifism, had partly submerged in a hierarchical, exclusionary, and patriotic ordering. As so often, a heightened spiritual quest had undercut merely human social goods.

Her political disenchantment as Popular Front hopes waned in the later 1930's, under the violence of red and black fascism, had encouraged her religious emphasis. Repeated mystical experiences (from 1938 on) brought her to close relations with Catholicism. This included rejection of her secular-Jewish identity (and both Zionism and Jewish separatism). Ironically, her Platonist revulsion to the Old Testament and its cruel deity perplexed her relation to Christianity. Just as in her philosophy teaching she emphasized the moral explication of literary texts, so some of her most cogent religious reflections took the form of a commentary on Homer. Her rather unilaterally tendentious *The Iliad: or, The Poem of Force* deploys a tragic insistence on the pervasive negative effects of violent power, a compassionate bitterness.

Along with its intensely personal and ascetic qualities, Weil's Christianity was elaborately and learnedly syncretistic. It included not only Greek avatars of Christ (*Intimations of Christianity*), but the Buddhistic (Krishna), the far-flung folkloristic, and the literary. The religious aesthetic included a love of Romanesque architecture, the iconography of the high art periods, Gregorian music, the writings of the saints, the traditional mass, and some range of literature. She wrote Catholic poetry. Yet her intimately devout Catholicism dialectically joined with a very critical view of the church as a bureaucratic establishment, especially in its inquisitorial intolerance, ambiquous morality, anti-intellectualism, and other-worldly impurity. She never joined it, and was never baptized. This was not just the modern intellectual's characteristic "pride" of dialectical stance (though that is undoubtedly some of Weil's present appeal) but a consciously deeper heresy, Gnosticism.

Her love for the Provençal Cathers (victims of extreme state and church persecution), her hatred of all Roman-style imperialisms, and her immersion in Greek idealism and later neoplatonism led to extreme dualism. This drastic heretical spiritualism achieved unusual tones because of her lucid analytical style and toughly argumentative scrupulosity around metaphysics of the absent deity of absolute goodness whose realization requires of one contemplative perfection (*Waiting for God* and *Gravity and Grace*). Perhaps most striking are her paradoxical demands for "the gift of affliction" (an envy of the crucifixion) and for utter purity. "The root of evil...is daydreaming," for its egotistic inattention to the suffering world and corrupting of attention to a transcendent good.

Her revulsion to the fallen material world, which had always included sexuality and comfort and other human desires, not least for food, culminated in her death at 34 in an English tuberculosis sanitarium of self-starvation and the need for total personal affliction in the suffering world to which she was so sensitive. Her remarkable intensity and impassioned earnestness, unusually combined with sophisticated philosophical and historical abilities (indeed, a harshly contentious intellectual manner), made her, if not a saint without God and church, a poignant witness to the possible social-religious transcendence of unmerited human suffering.

—Kingsley Widmer

WERTHEIMER, Max. German psychologist. Born in Prague, Czechoslovakia, 15 April 1908; emigrated to the United States in 1934. Studied at the University of Prague; University of Berlin; University of Würzburg, Ph.D. 1904. Married Anni Caro; 4 children. Lecturer, University of Frankfurt, 1912-18; Lecturer, 1918-21, and Professor of Psychology, 1921-33, University of Berlin; Professor of Psychology and Philosophy, Graduate Faculty, New School for Social Research, New York, 1934-43. Editor, *Psychologische Forschung*, 1921-35. *Died* (in New Rochelle, New York) *12 October 1943*.

PUBLICATIONS

Psychology

Expreimentelle Studien über das Sehen von Bewegung. Leipzig, Barth, 1912.
Über Schlussprozesse in produktiven Denken. Berlin, De Gruyter, 1920.
Über Gestalttheorie (lecture). Erlangen, Philosophische Akademie, 1925.
Drei Abhandlungen zur Gestalttheorie. Erlangen, Philosophische Akademie, 1925.
Productive Thinking. New York, Harper, 1945; enlarged edition, 1959 (contains a bibliography).
Wertheimer's Seminars Revisited: Problem Solving and Thinking, reconstructed by Abraham S. Luchins and Edith H. Luchins. State University of New York at Albany, Faculty-Student Association, 3 vols., 1970.
Revisiting Wertheimer's Seminars: Value, Social Influences and Power; Problems in Social Psychology, reconstructed by Abraham S. Luchins and Edith H. Luchins. Lewisburg, Pennsylvania, Bucknell University Press, 2 vols, 1978.

*   *   *

Gestalt theory developed as an answer to a crisis in 20th-century intellectual thought, manifested by discontent with what science had to offer. Confronted with problems of everyday life, science in general and psychology in particular provided trivial answers or dismissed the problems, as not proper subjects of scientific investigation. Max Wertheimer spoke on this issue to the Kantgesellschaft in Berlin in 1924: "we come from the full reality of living events to science of which we seek clarification, deeper penetration into the core of what is happening...we often find, information...yet at the end we feel poorer than before.

Somehow what we considered the most crucial, the most essential and the most vital [feature of the phenomenon] has...been lost. For example, when we ask psychologists what happened when a pupil grasps the point of what is being taught...[we are] shocked at the poverty, aridity, unreality, the utter triviality of what is said." Wertheimer noted that the hostility to science contributed to anti-scientific movements, e.g., toward mysticism and vitalism. He went on to suggest how the neglected psychological phenomenon could be dealt with in an exact scientific manner.

It seemed to him that one reason that science did not deal adequately with the "actual spectacle of human life" was its fundamental assumption that the only scientific method was that of traditional analysis. Wertheimer characterized this method as working "from below upwards," i.e., as attempting to divide complexes into their component parts or elements, isolating them and deriving their laws, and then combining or reconstructing them for comprehension of the phenomena. That this approach was not appropriate for all wholes was the fundamental formula (*Grundproblem*) of Gestalt theory: "There are wholes, the behavior of which is not determined by that of their individual elements, but where the part-processes are themselves determined by the intrinsic nature of the whole."

Characteristically, Wertheimer ended his 1924 speech with an example of structure in music. Music provided him with a lifelong source of illustrations, ideas, and entertainment. His research on music confirmed what had been pointed out by Christian von Ehrenfels, his teacher in Prague, namely, that a melody cannot be understood merely in terms of its individual notes. Wertheimer went beyond this formulation to demonstrate that the recognition of an altered melody depends not on the number of notes changed but on the notes' place, role, and function in the melody's structure. His research at the Berlin Phonogram Archives had shown that the music of a primitive tribe, the Wedda, was not an and-summation but a whole structure. He also found that this was characteristic of various numerical structures of primitive people. The importance of Gestalten had become evident even earlier (1905-08) when Wertheimer was doing research in Vienna on diagnosing alexia and testing feeble-minded children.

To establish his ideas about Gestalten in a more precise manner, which might more readily convince German psychologists, Wertheimer sought for scientific exactness. On a train trip in 1910 he thought of a suitable optical phenomenon. He got off the train at Frankfurt and bought a toy stroboscope. In a hotel room he substituted for the pictures in the toy strips of papers on which he had drawn lines. By varying the time interval between the exposure of the lines, he could see one line and then another line, two lines standing side by side, or a line moving from one position to another. This movement came to be known as the Phi phenomenon.

Wertheimer asked Friedrich Schumann, his former teacher at Berlin, and then at the Frankfurt Psychological Institute, if he could provide someone to serve as a subject. Schumann's laboratory assistant, Wolfgang Köhler, came. For the next session Köhler brought his friend Kurt Koffka, who also served as a subject. Schumann visited Wertheimer and invited him to conduct the experiment at the Frankfurt Institute. A simple apparatus was constructed and the now classical experiment on the Phi phenomenon was conducted.

Through experimental variations, Wertheimer demonstrated that movement was not an arbitrary and-summation of events, that it was not an inference from static sensations, but that it was a genuine dynamic event. As a model for such events, Wertheimer hypothesized a physiological process: "The motion is due to a field of activity among cells,...not excitation in isolated cells but field effects." Although Wertheimer has been accredited with anticipating neurophysiological models of movement, his aim was only to show how a dynamic event may take place. It was Köhler who later offered a more refined neurophysiological model. Wertheimer continued throughout his life to search for

mathematical or logical models of Gestalten. The study of Phi movement launched gestalt psychology. Its importance is attested not only by the excitement it aroused when Wertheimer reported on it at the 1911 Psychological Congress, but by the brilliant collaborative research it engendered with Köhler and Koffka. Much of their work was in perception because it offered "the best scientific techniques." For the same reason Wertheimer used visual forms to illustrate principles of organization. When Kurt Lewin joined the trio, the approach broadened to the study of human motivation and group dynamics.

Wertheimer directed students' research projects that were classics in experimentation, e.g., Kurt Denker on problem solving. Wertheimer studied productive thinking, e.g., in 1916 the thinking that led Einstein to relativity theory; an account of it was not published until 1945 (posthumously). On the whole, Wertheimer published little. But it has been said that the "claw of the lion" showed in the writings of his associates and students with whom he generously shared his time.

When Wertheimer came to the New School for Social Research, after the rise of the Nazis, he did not have the facilities to continue the investigations on perceptual phenomena. There followed a period of ten years in which his long-standing interest in other phenomena came to the fore. In the United States he published papers on truth, ethics, democracy, and freedom. The discussions in his seminars attracted many young instructors of psychology who, in a sort of informal post-doctoral program, produced work that transformed social psychology into an experimental science and yet kept its concepts and work in close touch with daily life. Attempts to constuct aspects of the social psychology seminars in the New School were made by Asch and more recently by the Luchins.

In post-World War II psychology, his influence is seen in the work in perception (e.g., Gibson, Witkin) cognitive psychology (e.g., Niessen), humanistic psychology (e.g., Maslow), social psychology (e.g., Sherif, Asch, Luchins) and clinical diagnostic testing (e.g., Rapaport, Wolfe).

Wertheimer's work and teaching have been admired by those who love clarity of thinking, penetrating anlysis, and systematic experimentation, and who appreciate his humanness and his respect for what was being studied. As the writer noted elsewhere (1968): His greatness lay in his ability to fire the imagination and creativity of two generations of psychologists in America and abroad.

—Abraham S. Luchins

WESTERMARCK, Edvard (Alexander). Finnish philosopher and sociologist. Born in Helsinki, Finland, 20 November 1862. Educated at Böök's Lyceum, and Svenska Normallyceum, Helsinki; studied at the University of Finland, B.A., M.A., Ph.D. 1889. Married; 1 son. Docent, University of Helsinki, 1894; taught at Academy of Abo: Emeritus Professor of Philosophy; Professor of Sociology, University of London, 1907-30. Field work in Morocco, 1898-1902. LL.D.: universities of Aberdeen and Glasgow. *Died 3 September 1939.*

PUBLICATIONS

Philosophy and Sociology

The Origin of Human Marriage. Helsinki, Frenckell, 1889.
The History of Human Marriage. London, Macmillan, 1891; revised edition, 3 vols., 1921; New York, Allerton, 3 vols., 1922.
The Origin and Development of the Moral Ideas. London, Macmillan, 1906-08.

Kristendom och moral [Christianity and Morality]. Stockholm, Bonnier, 1907; Minneapolis, Forskaren, 1910.

Religion och magi [Religion and Magic]. Stockholm, Bonnier, 1907; Minneapolis, Forskaren, 1910.

Der Krieg: Soziologische Studie. Leipzig, Dietrich, 1909.

Ur sedernas historia [From the History of Mores]. Stockholm, Bonnier, 1912.

Ceremonies and Beliefs Connected with Agriculture, Certain Dates of the Solar Year, and the Weather in Morocco. Helsinki, Akademiska Bokhandeln, 1913.

Marriage Ceremonies in Morocco. London, Macmillan, 1914.

Nomina im status absolutus und status annexus in der Südmarokkanischen Berbersprache. Helsinki, Akademiska Bokhandeln, 1914.

The Moorish Conception of Holiness (Baraka). Helsinki, Akademiska Bokhandeln, 1916.

Sex ar i Marocko [Sexual Maturity in Morocco]. Stockholm, Bonnier, 1918.

The Belief of Spirits in Morocco. Abo, Abo Akademi, 1920.

The Origins of Sexual Modesty. London, Francis, 1921.

Ritual and Belief in Morocco. London, Macmillan, 2 vols., 1926.

A Short History of Marriage. London and New York, Macmillan, 1926; abridged edition, as *Marriage*, London, Benn and New York, Cape and Smith, 1929.

The Goodness of Gods. London, Watts, 1926.

Wit and Wisdom in Morocco: A Study of Native Proverbs. London, Routledge, 1930; New York, Liveright, 1931.

Blodshämnd bland marockanska berber [Blood-Feud among Moroccan Berbers]. Abo, Abo Akademi, 1931.

Ethical Relativity. London, Kegan Paul, and New York, Harcourt Brace, 1932.

Early Beliefs and Their Social Influence. London, Macmillan, 1932.

Pagan Survivals in Mohammedan Civilisation. London, Macmillan, 1933.

Freuds teori om Oedipuskomplexen: I sociologisk belysning [Freud's Theory of the Oedipus Complex]. Stockholm, Bonnier, 1934.

Three Essays on Sex and Marriage. London, Macmillan, 1934.

The Future of Marriage in Western Civilisation. London and New York, Macmillan, 1936.

Christianity and Morals. London, Kegan Paul, and New York, Macmillan, 1939.

Other

Minnen ur Mitt Liv. Helsinki, H. Schildt, 1927; as *Memories of My Life*, London, Allen and Unwin, and New York, Macaulay, 1929.

*

Critical Studies: *Edvard Westermarck as Anthropologist and Sociologist* (lecture) by Karl R.V. Wikman, Copenhagen, Munksgaard, 1962; *Kristinuskon moraalikritiikki Edvard Westermarckin elämässä ja ajattelussa* (with English summary) by Matti Luoma, Tampere, Finland, Tampereen Yliopisto, 1967.

*   *   *

In order to avoid the mistake of treating Edvard Westermarck as a specialist in either philosophy or social science who dabbled in one field in order to support a position taken in another, it is necessary to take account of two primary aspects of his work. The first has to do with his decision as a philosopher to replace the construction of ethical rules with the study of moral consciousness as such. This position (which has been called "ethical relativism" by some and "ethical subjectivism" by others) constitutes a search for the facts which underlie the seeming self-evidence of moral principles. This aspect of his work constitutes

a philosophical defense of the grounding of ethics in consciousness. What follows is an anthropological investigation into the nature of "consciousness" designed to isolate the social origins of morality and to see institutions such as the family as the social manifestation of morals. Thus, the second aspect of Westermarck's work is necessitated by the position taken in the first. His argument against more objective or normative moral philosophies rests on the claim that they fail to account for the way people actually distinguish between right and wrong; empirical verification, then, is obviously the next step.

Of course, the separation of Westermarck's work into "philosophy" and "social science" is artificial. Aside from the more specialized works such as *Ethical Relativity*, much of Westermarck's writing tends to be philosophically "informed"; his arguments and assumptions guide his research and are built into his concepts and the organization of his findings. With this in mind, the remainder of this essay is devoted to presenting some of the more interesting applications of his thesis regarding ethics and social life. First of all, there are the ostensible subjects of the institutionalization of morals and the family, the connections among causality, biology and social facts and the conjoining of Morality and Reason within a history of progressive development and increasing complexity. Secondly, and equally important, is the unspoken (that is, not systematically developed) issue of methodology. Stripped of its substantive content, his research agenda provides excellent clues to Westermarck's theory of scientific knowledge.

Ethical subjectivism questions the objective validity of moral judgements; it does not deny the existence of morality itself. The possibility remains that subjective notions of right or wrong are not arbitrary. Westermarck observes that moral principles which are "truly self evident" are unlikely, but then shifts attention to the interplay of morality, instinct, and emotion in the context of social life. An anthropological study of emotions and instincts may uncover invariant psychological, sociological, or biological facts which underlie a variable set of moral codes.

The stand against ethical objectivism provides the background for an empirical investigation designed to describe and explain the presence of social institutions characterized by sanctions. Why are there rules concerning how one ought to behave? How did these rules originate? How can one account for the seemingly contradictory observations of the universality of morality on the one hand, and the incredibly diverse forms that moral judgements take on the other? Westermarck, then, was not concerned with merely enumerating the patterned differences and similarities that empirical work inevitably uncovers. His ambitions were to *explain* these patterns, to *account* for them in terms of biology and psychology and to *predict* future patterns on the basis of assumptions about the origin of morals and the evolution of reason and knowledge.

Westermarck studied the institution of marriage, searching for the biological and psychological facts that "cause" its appearance. He begins with such antecedent biological conditions as the relatively low number of offspring, their dependence on adults for protection, and an "instinct acquired through the process of natural selection" to produce "normal" human familial arrangement in which the female protects and nurses the children (a "maternal instinct") while the male protects and provides for the entire family. Following the establishment of these instincts, a "habit" of constructing stable family relationships arises within which emotions such as "approval" are encouraged. At this point, there is a transition from biology to psychology as "sentiments" (in this case, "conjugal and parental") develop out of a combination of these retributive emotions and biological facts. Two of the former, approval and disapproval, are what Westermarck calls "moral emotions." They constitute the broad parameters of what will later become custom and law. At this stage, however, emotions serve only to distinguish the members of one's immediate family (however that is defined) from all others. It is what separates the moral from the non-moral emotions (gratitude and anger or revenge)—their "more comprehensive qualities" such as disinterestedness, impartiality, and generality—that makes possible the major transition from sentiments extended toward the significant others of one's immediate family to the sympathy extended to a general class of persons.

"Marriage," then, is the effect of a complex set of causes. By describing its genesis and thus enumerating these causes, Westermarck accounts for the universality of marriage along with similar kinds of institutions. But how does he explain the diverse *forms* they take? Here, Westermarck shifts the level of analysis again, this time from the psychological level of emotion, sentiment, and sympathy to the sociological level of morality and moral judgements. This leap accomplishes two things. First, he clarifies the notion of moral judgements by locating their "birthplace" in society, thus giving them a public rather than a private character. Second, the differences among groups are now brought into focus, explaining why the evolution of moral systems has occurred at different rates and along different paths. The different forms that institutions such as marriage take are the result of three variables, each of which can be used to distinguish one society from another. The first has to do with external conditions—hardship, general economic conditions, and the like. For example, the accepted ways of treating the older, weaker, or less healthy members of society are likely to be affected when resources such as food are difficult to obtain. The second and third variables contribute to Westermarck's effort to predict the future forms of sanctioning institutions by providing the basis upon which to rank societies. All societies differ to the degree in which altruism is encouraged and "enlightened" attitudes prevail.

Ironically, this last area of Westermarck's work, with its not so subtle Eurocentric bias, prefigures an approach which is very much alive in contemporary social theory. Although he wrote from within an evolutionary framework which has generally been discredited today (at least in its cruder forms), Westermarck's central point is significant: moral condemnation may change to tolerance or even acceptance as knowledge about the act or the identity of the actor increases.

—Martin Rouse

WEYL, Hermann. German mathematician. Born in Elmshorn, 9 November 1885. Studied at the University of Göttingen, Ph.D. 1908. Served in the German Army, 1915. Married Helene Joseph in 1913 (died, 1948), 2 children; married Ellen Baer in 1950. Privatdozent, University of Göttingen, 1910-13; Professor of Mathematics, Technische Hochschule, Zurich, 1913-30; Professor of Mathematics, University of Göttingen, 1930-33; Professor of Mathematics, 1933-50, and from 1950 Professor Emeritus, Institute for Advanced Study, Princeton, New Jersey. Visiting Lecturer, Institut d'Estudis Catalans, Barcelona, and University of Madrid, 1922; Jones Research Professor of Mathematical Physics, Princeton University, New Jersey, 1928-29. Honorary Doctorate: University of Oslo, 1929; Technische Hochschule, Stuttgart, 1929; D.Sc.: University of Pennsylvania, 1940; Columbia University, New York, 1954; Technische Hochschule, Zurich, 1945; Université de Paris, 1952. Member, American Academy of Arts and Sciences; Fellow, Royal Society of London. *Died* (in Zurich) *8 December 1955.*

PUBLICATIONS

Collections

Gesammelte Abhandlungen, edited by K. Chandrasekharan. Berlin, Springer, 4 vols., 1968.

Mathematics

Singuläre Integralgleichungen mit besonderer Berücksichtigung des Fourierschen Integraltheorems. Göttingen, Kaestner, 1908.

Die Idee der Riemannschen Fläche. Stuttgart, Teubner, 1913; revised edition, 1955; as *Concept of a Riemann Surface,* Reading, Massachusetts, Addison Wesley, 1964.

Das Kontinuum: Kritische Untersuchungen über die Grundlagen der Analysis. Leipzig, Veit, 1918.

Raum, Zeit, Materie: Vorlesungen über allgemeine Relativitätstheorie. Berlin, Springer, 1918; revised edition, 1919, 1921; as *Space, Time, Matter,* New York, Dutton, 1921; London, Methuen, 1922.

Mathematische Analyse des Raumproblems: Vorlesungen gehalten in Barcelona und Madrid. Berlin, Springer, 1923.

Was ist Materie? Zwei Aufsätze zur Naturphilosophie. Berlin, Springer, 1924.

Die heutige Erkenntnislage in der Mathematik. Erlangen, Weltkreis, 1926.

Philosophie der Mathematik und Naturwissenschaft. Munich, Oldenbourg, 1927; as *Philosphy of Mathematics and Natural Science,* Princeton, New Jersey, Princeton University Press, 1949.

Gruppentheorie und Ouantenmechanik. Leipzig, Hirzel, 1928; revised edition 1929; as *The Theory of Groups and Quantum Mechanics,* London, Methuen, and New York, Dutton, 1931.

Die Stufen des Unendlichen (lecture). Jena, Fischer, 1931.

The Open World: Three Lectures on the Metaphysical Implications of Science. New Haven, Connecticut, Yale University Press, and London, Oxford University Press, 1932.

Mind and Nature (lecture). Philadelphia, University of Pennsylvania Press, 1934.

The Structure and Representation of Continuous Groups (lectures). Princeton, New Jersey, Institute for Advanced Study, 2 vols., 1934-35.

Elementary Theory of Invariants. Princeton, New Jersey, Institute for Advanced Study, 1936.

Lectures on the Theory of Invariants. Princeton, New Jersey, Institute for Advanced Study, 1936.

The Classical Groups: Their Invariants and Representations. Princeton, New Jersey, Princeton University Press, and London, Oxford University Press, 1939; revised edition, 1946.

Algebraic Theory of Numbers. Princeton, New Jersey, Princeton University Press, and London, Oxford University Press, 1940.

Metamorphic Functions and Analytic Curves. Princeton, New Jersey, Princeton University Press, and London, Oxford University Press, 1943.

Symmetry. Princeton, New Jersey, Princeton University Press, 1952.

Other

Der Epileptiker: Erzählung. Ems, Kircheberger Presse, 1927.

Editor, with Andreas Speiser, *Gesammelte Abhandlungen von Hermann Minkowski.* Leipzig and Berlin, Teubner, 1911.

*

Bibliography: in *Gesammelte Abhandlungen,* 1968.

*   *   *

Hermann Weyl was a German mathematician whom his colleagues called a man with a universal mind, meaning that he could unite previously unrelated subjects. He made significant contributions to many fields of mathematics. The work of Weyl that would be most quickly recognized by the public consists of his long exploration of the mathematical framework of the general theory of relativity.

The term relativity, as used by scientists, relates to measurements made by persons moving relative to one another. Classical physics states that all space and time measurements are the same, regardless of one's location in the universe and regardless of whether one is moving or stationary. Relativity theory denies this assertion, declaring instead that space and time measurements will vary, depending on the relative motions of the observers. Albert Einstein, the German physicist and mathematician, originated the special theory of relativity in 1905 and the general theory eleven years later. Weyl's mathematical investigations of the general theory began in 1916, the year he worked with Einstein in Zurich. The general theory deals with gravitation, advancing views of space and time that differ radically from those the general public holds. The theory of relativity underlies contemporary scientific thinking on a wide range of phenomena in physics starting at the atomic level and proceeding to the universe itself. The general theory is based on the special theory, which supplanted the classical tenets of physics advanced during the 18th century by Isaac Newton and employed by scientists for 200 years thereafter. The special theory deals with electricity and magnetism while the general theory is concerned with gravitation. The general theory became necessary because it was impossible to use classical and relativistic notions of space and time for different kinds of interactions, particularly when scientists knew that particles may interact electromagnetically, gravitationally, and according to nuclear forces.

It was Newton who advanced the classical theory of gravitation in the solar system. His ideas accounted remarkably well for the motions of the planets. Newton did assume, however, that heavenly bodies exert an instantaneous gravitational pull upon each other, even over the immense distances of interplanetary space. Since the special theory of relativity states that nothing can move faster than the speed of light, some adjustment became necessary.

Einstein began applying his special theory, suggesting that gravitation spreads at the speed of light. He quickly concluded that a gravitation theory was mathematically more complex than one of electricity and magnetism. The sources of an electric field are the electric charges of particles. These particles have values which are independent of the state of motion of the instruments that measure them. The mass of particles, which is the source of gravitational fields, varies with the speed of the particles relative to the frames of reference in which they are determined. Thus, particle mass will differ, depending upon the frame of reference. Einstein went on to say that there was no clear way to separate the effects of the frame of reference from those of gravitational pull. For this reason, gravity was different from all other force fields found in nature.

Einstein proceeded through elaborate reasoning to the conclusion that the presence of a gravitational field causes space and time to be curved. The path of a particle in space is thus curved rather than straight. But it is the straightest, the most economical curve possible in curved space-time.

The mathematical expression of gravity's role in curved space-time is based upon calculations originated for purposes of pure mathematics in the 19th century by the German mathematician Bernhard Reimann. He was interested in the fact that it is impossible to fit a simple grid onto a sphere. In the course of his investigations, Reimann developed abstract quantities called curvature tensors. These function in a coordinate system like a grid and have a definite number of components which change when the coordinate system changes. In his work on the mathematics of relativity theory, Hermann Weyl built upon Reimann's discoveries to develop Weyl's tensor.

At each point of space-time, Einstein defined 20 distinct and independent components of curvature. Mathematically, these are the 20 components of Reimann's curvature tensor. Of these 20 components, ten can be related to the sources of the gravitational field by following Newton's classical formulas. These are called Ricci's tensor. At the same time, it is necessary to create

laws which take the same form, regardless of the frame of reference. The remaining ten components, called Weyl's tensor, may be arbitrarily selected at one point but are then systematically related to each other and to neighboring points according to a specific partial differential equation. This equation, combined with the rule that a freely falling body moves along a geodesic (the shortest curved line described above) together form Einstein's general theory of relativity.

Weyl also made major contributions to the theory of Lie Groups. These are concepts in topology, the branch of mathematics that investigates the properties retained by an object under deformation (e.g., bending, squeezing, stretching) but not breaking, tearing, or pasting parts together. He also was very active in spectral theory, another area of topology.

—Victor M. Cassidy

WHITEHEAD, Alfred North.   British mathematician and philosopher.   Born in Ramsgate, Kent, 15 February 1861. Studied at Trinity College, Cambridge, B.A. 1884, M.A., 1887, D.Sc. 1905. Married Evelyn Wade in 1890; 3 children. Lecturer, and Senior Lecturer in Mathematics, Trinity College, 1885-1910; Lecturer in Applied Mathematics and Mechanics and Later Reader in Geometry, 1911-14, University College, and Professor of Applied Mathematics and later Chief Professor of Mathematics, 1914-24, Imperial College of Science and Technology, University of London; Professor of Philosophy, 1924-37, and Professor Emeritus, 1937-47, Harvard University, Cambridge, Massachusetts. President, Mathematical Association, 1915-16. Recipient: James Scott Prize, Royal Society of Edinburgh, 1922; Sylvester Medal, Royal Society, London, 1925; Butler Medal Columbia University, New York, 1930. Honorary doctorate: University of Manchester, 1920; St. Andrews University, Scotland, 1921; Harvard University, 1925; University of Wisconsin, Madison, 1925; Yale University, New Haven, Connecticut, 1926; McGill University, Montreal, 1931. Fellow, Trinity College: British Academy; Royal Society. O.M. (Order of Merit), 1945. *Died* (in Cambridge, Massachusetts) *30 December 1947.*

PUBLICATIONS

Mathematics and Philosophy

A Treatise on Universal Algebra.   Cambridge, University Press, 1898.

The Axioms of Projective Geometry.   Cambridge, University Press, 1906; New York, Hafner, 1971.

The Axioms of Descriptive Geometry.   Cambridge, University Press, 1907; New York, Hafner, 1971.

Principia Mathematica, with Bertrand Russell.   Cambridge, University Press, 3 vols., 1910-13.

The Organization of Thought, Educational and Scientific.   London, Williams and Norgate, and Philadelphia, Lippincott, 1917.

An Enquiry Concerning the Principles of Natural Knowledge.   Cambridge, University Press, 1919.

The Concept of Nature.   Cambridge, University Press, 1920.

The Principle of Relativity and Applications to Physical Science.   Cambridge, Cambridge University Press, 1922.

Science and the Modern World (lectures).   New York, Macmillan, 1925; Cambridge, University Press, 1926.

Religion in the Making (lectures).   New York, Macmillan, and Cambridge, Cambridge University Press, 1926.

Symbolism: Its Meaning and Effect (lectures).   New York, Macmillan, 1927; Cambridge, University Press, 1928.

The Aims of Education and Other Essays.   New York, Macmillan, and London, Williams and Norgate, 1929.

The Function of Reason (lecture). Princeton, New Jersey, Princeton University Press, 1929.

Process and Reality: An Essay in Cosmology. New York, Macmillan, and Cambridge, University Press, 1929.

Adventures of Ideas. New York, Macmillan, and Cambridge, University Press, 1933.

Nature and Life. Chicago, University of Chicago Press, and Cambridge, University Press, 1934.

Modes of Thought (lectures). New York, Macmillan, and Cambridge, University Press, 1938.

Essays in Science and Philosophy. New York, Philosophical Library, 1947; London, Rider, 1948.

The Wit and Wisdom of Alfred North Whitehead (selections), edited by A.H. Johnson. Boston, Beacon Press, 1947.

Dialogues of Alfred North Whitehead, as Recorded by Lucien Price. Boston, Little Brown, 1954.

*

Bibliography: *Alfred North Whitehead: A Primary-Secondary Bibliography by Barry A. Woodbridge*, Bowling Green, Ohio, Bowling Green Documentation Center, 1977.

Critical Studies: *The Philosophy of Alfred North Whitehead* edited by Paul Arthur Schilpp, Evanston, Illinois, Northwestern University Press, 1941, Cambridge, University Press, 1943, revised edition, New York, Tudor, 1951; *Whitehead's Philosophy: Selected Essays 1935-1970* edited by Charles Hartshorne, Lincoln, University of Nebraska Press, 1972; *Alfred North Whitehead: A Primer of His Philosophy* by Nathaniel Morris Lawrence, New York, Twayne, 1974; *Whitehead's Metaphysics: An Introductory Exposition* by Ivor Leclerc, Bloomington, Indiana University Press, 1975; *An Interpretation of Whitehead's Metaphysics* by William A. Christian, Westport, Connecticut, Greenwood Press, 1977.

*   *   *

Alfred North Whitehead's first book was *A Treatise on Universal Algebra*. In 1910-1913 he published with Bertrand Russell *Principia Mathematica*. His first studies in the philosophy of science were three books published from 1919 to 1922, *An Enquiry Concerning the Principles of Natural Knowledge*, *The Concept of Nature*, and *The Principle of Relativity*. They develop four interrelated themes: (1) Space and time are not primary elements of nature but abstractions from the spatiality and temporality of the real elements of nature, namely, events. Moreover, neither space nor time can be adequately treated without reference to the other. (2) Matter and its properties are also abstractions from events, not distinct elements in it. (3) There is "only one nature which is before us in perception." Thus, nature reveals herself as a passage of events in which the basic stuff is not bits of matter moving or lodged in space or time. In effect, the classical Newtonian elements—space, time, matter, and motion—together with Locke's "secondary qualities" are concepts derived from the real stuff of nature, i.e., processive flow of occurrences. (4) There is a special kind of event, the "percipient event," "the mind's foothold in nature." The elaboration of these basic ideas moves Whitehead's philosophy of science toward philosophy of nature.

Whitehead's most widely read works appeared in 1925-1927: *Science and the Modern World*, *Religion in the Making*, and *Symbolism: Its Meaning and Effect*. Again, several themes bind the three works together.

(1) The "percipient event" of the philosophy of science now becomes in the philosophy of *nature* the model of *all* events. Following a suggestion of Francis Bacon's, Whitehead postulates a fundamental interrelation of all events, exhibited in the spatio-temporal continuum which they concretely share. Every event is percipient, whether or not it is conscious. Events thus "prehend" one another, jointly sharing the same continuum, but selectively sharing the ingredient "objects" which appear in events, as their qualities. When I see a green rock, the rock is out there embodying the "eternal object" "green" in the mode of being present, but also in here, at the locus of my physiological perception, in the mode of being known. Materialism, on the other hand, regards the source of the green as in the object given, but cannot explain how the green as green "gets" to me. It must invent one green "here" and the other "there." True, material objects must have Simple Location—matter can't be in two places at the same time. There is a mistake, however (Whitehead calls it the "Fallacy of Misplaced Concreteness"), in supposing that a material object is a concrete chunk of reality. Material objects are semi-abstractions from the actual flow of events, with the knower left out of the picture. He merely receives, by waves or particles, messages from an external world.

(2) In this period Whitehead deals for the first time with the idea of value. Values comprise the "intrinsic reality" of an event. Ingredient eternal objects, colors, shapes, etc., which, taken by themselves, are mere possibles, are *actualized* by their presence in events, that is, by "ingression" into them. Ingression is generally of several eternal objects under "limitations" and "gradations" of "types of entry," which render them jointly compatible. Every event is an instance of creativity, in which the event fashions itself out of the rest of the world, using it as a resource. "Creativity" and "novelty" were not explicitly present in the early philosophy of science but they were implied by the unique, once-for-all status of the event. Events, he says, can not be repeated; objects, however, can "be again." Now, in the philosophy of nature, Whitehead divides objects into two kinds: (a) eternal objects, like "red" and "triangularity," which exhibit the capacity to "be again," and (b) enduring objects, "this dog," "that daisy," which are complex assemblages of events with persistent characteristics and spatio-temporal specificity; they can't therefore "be again." Enduring objects are not merely possible, but actual. The intrinsic reality of an event, then, arises from the specific way in which the event takes into its self-synthesis "aspects" of the world about it, namely, what other events are *for it*. For example, in some event of my life, the primrose by the river's brim is brief, factual, unimportant. At some moment in your life you consider both the primrose and me and you observe, "A primrose by a river's brim/A yellow primrose was to him/And it was nothing more." In your percipient event it was more.

(3) Whitehead also extends the philosophy of nature to include mentality. The dominant view in this period is that every event is bipolar, both mental and physical. The physical pole of an actual event is embodied in its spatio-temporal extension, through which it prehends the extensive features of other events. The mental pole, complementarily, is that by which the event prehends eternal objects *as eternal objects*, not merely as ingredients in a particular event. An event is thus not necessarily committed to exploiting any eternal object in exactly the same way as did another event which it prehends.

(4) Finally, in this period Whitehead introduces the idea of God. *Religion in the Making* is addressed to the relation between ordinary experience and religious experience. In a break with tradition, he treats creativity as one of three autonomous "formative" elements—the others being God and the eternal objects. Through them events become actual. The creativity provides the raw, protean stuff of an advancing world. It is rendered definite in "the creatures"—namely, events. Eternal objects as such are not causal, save perhaps in analogy to Aristotle's material cause. They merely are the ways in which the creativity becomes definite. There is, however, harmony in the synthesis of larger and more diverse orders of beings than a single event, because of the "actual but non-temporal" entity, God. "Non-temporal" here means "abiding," "non-perishing." God's role is that of a "lure," Much—again—like Aristotle's unmoved Mover, active not as changing, but as attractive.

Whitehead and Mrs. Whitehead (according to a private communication) for many years read religious literature in search of a body of belief they could accept. They were unsuccessful. Whitehead, however, like Augustine, came to the anti-neoplatonic position that evil is real, positive, but destructive, and therefore inherently unstable; and that good is what is real, positive, and constructive, "to be reckoned with," not just an absence of evil.

In this transition period, which develops his "philosophy of organism" and affirms the role of God in the philosophy of nature, Whitehead is reaching back to his student days, saturated as they were with discussions of the bold new, Darwinian theory. He also reaches further back to childhood and ancestry to import an idea he found—to the dismay of many of his enthusiastic friends—philosophically indispensable: God and his role in cosmology.

The stage is now set for Whitehead's masterwork *Process and Reality*, a general cosmology. It deals systematically with the many problems arising from the themes we have considered: prehension and percipience; values and eternal objects; creativity and novelty; mentality (thus subjectivity vs. objectivity—the "primrose" example); and finally Deity and the world order. The first three sets of the above topics are intertwined intricately in the first three parts of *Process and Reality*, following a set of protocol categories to be used throughout the book. Part IV of the book centers on the revision of Whitehead's early "Method of Extensive Abstraction." The revision is called "The Method of Extensive Connection"; it examines the formal assumptions through which we can derive, from roughhewn experience, the precise notions of formal geometry.

In addition to developing, in a coherent metaphysics, the detailed consequences of the primary themes from the philosophy of nature, this cosmology undertakes: (1) to accommodate current physical theory as well as likely developments in the future and (2) to provide an epistemology adequate to the order of nature, examined as a progressively emergent evolution of complex types of existence from simpler ones, while (3) maintaining the primacy of metaphysics considerations over epistemological ones.

The fifth part of *Process and Reality* is a scant 22 pages devoted to God and the World. It is visionary, but not mystical. In it God is revealed as both "primordial," i.e., non-conscious—a kind of permanent "possibility," hence the repositum of eternal objects, and "consequent," an abiding presence, conscious and, as in *Religion in the Making*, an actual but "non-temporal"entity whose task is the leading out of greater value from temporary losses. Whitehead, in *Process and Reality*, touches on nearly all of his earlier interests, including those of the matchless essays on education (not mentioned in this sketch). He reveals a faith beyond sorrow, but not in terms of a creed.

After *Process and Reality* Whitehead published three more books (*The Function of Reason, Adventures of Ideas*, and *Modes of Thought*). All are essays, lectures, or collections on a wide variety of subjects, from teleological reasoning to problems of society, culture, and aesthetics. Many can be read by themselves, but most profit from a prior acquaintance with at least *Science and the Modern World*. They are special reflections from a centrally illuminating mind whose scope may not be duplicated in this century.

—Nathaniel Lawrence

WHORF, Benjamin Lee. American linguist. Born in Winthrop, Massachusetts, 24 April 1897. Studied at Massachusetts Institute of Technology, Cambridge, B.S. 1918. Married Celia Inez Peckham in 1920; 3 children. Engineer, 1918-29, Special Agent, 1929-40, and Assistant Secretary, Hartford Fire Insurance Company, Connecticut. Lecturer in Anthropology, Yale University, New Haven, Connecticut, 1937-38. Recipient: Social Science Research Council of New York Fellowship, 1930;

Honorary Research Fellowship in Anthropology, 1936, and Sterling Fellowship, 1937, Yale University. *Died* (in Wethersfield, Connecticut) *26 July 1941*.

PUBLICATIONS

Linguistics

The Phonetic Value of Certain Characters in Maya Writing. Cambridge, Massachusetts, Peabody Museum, 1933.
Four Articles on Metalinguistics. Washington, D.C., Foreign Service Institute, 1949.
Collected Papers on Metalinguistics. Washington, D.C., Foreign Service Institute, 1952.
Language, Thought, and Reality: Selected Writings, edited by John B. Carroll. Cambridge, Massachusetts, Technology Press, 1956.

*

Critical Studies: *Language: Mirror, Tool, and Weapon* by George W. Kelling, Chicago, Nelson Hall, 1975; *Universalism vs. Relativism in Language and Thought: Proceedings of a Colloquim on the Sapir-Whorf Hypotheses* edited by Rix Pinxten, The Hague, Mouton, 1975; *Sprach and Dasein: Ein Beitrag zur Sprachpsychologie anhand der Schriften von Benjamin Whorf und Medard Boss* by Peter Müller-Locher, Zurich, Juris, 1977; *Ethnolinguistics: Boas, Sapir, and Whorf Revisited* edited by Madeleine Mathiot, The Hague, Mouton, 1979; *Benjamin Lee Whorf: Lost Generation Theories of Mind, Language, and Religion* by Peter C. Rollins, Ann Arbor, Michigan, University Microfilms International, 1979.

*   *   *

Benjamin Lee Whorf was the foremost modern proponent of the idea that the structure of the language used by a person or group—be it English, Arabic, Navaho, or whatever—somehow influences the manner in which that person or group thinks and acts, differently from the way persons or groups using other languages think and act. The influence of language structure was thought by Whorf to extend to the nature of a group's culture and view of the world. This notion of "linguistic relativity" was not original with Whorf; it had been suggested by philosophers and linguists of the 18th and early 19th centuries, for example by the German linguistic philosopher Wilhelm von Humboldt. Whorf did not, however, derive his ideas from von Humboldt; rather, he derived them from his study of a number of American Indian languages and from his association with the noted American linguist Edward Sapir. For this reason, his ideas are frequently referred to as comprising the "Sapir-Whorf hypothesis," but it may be said that the Sapir-Whorf hypothesis is due more to Whorf than to Sapir.

He was born in Winthrop, Massachusetts, the son of a commercial artist and designer who had wide interests. His only higher degree was as Bachelor of Science in chemical engineering at Massachusetts Institute of Technology, in 1918. Throughout his life, his only occupation was as an employee and officer, in Hartford, Connecticut, of a fire insurance company. He specialized in the evaluation of insurance risks at chemical manufacturing companies. His work, however, permitted him to spend a substantial amount of time in linguistic studies, in which he became interested through early avocational curiosity about the Hebrew language of the Old Testament. These studies eventually led him to begin his own investigations of several American Indian languages, especially the indigenous languages of Mexico, including Nahuatl (Aztec) and Maya. He postulated that certain features of these languages represented universal characteristics of human thought that were also to be found in Hebrew and other languages of the old world. With the support of the

Social Science Research Council, Whorf took leave from his company and spent a number of weeks in Mexico in 1930, studying the grammar of Nahuatl. It was at this time, also, that he began an interest in the decipherment of Maya hieroglyphics; although he may have made certain contributions in this field, like other scholars who have been concerned with it, he did not succeed in arriving at any full solution to this problem.

These and other studies, carried out with virtually no advice or supervision from academicians, aroused the attention of several eminent linguists, especially Edward Sapir, with whom he began an association in 1931 when Sapir took a post at Yale University. With the help of Sapir, Whorf became familiar with the then developing science of linguistics, and was later able to make a number of important contributions to its theory and methods. Sapir encouraged Whorf to study the Hopi language, distantly related to Nahuatl, and this he did with the aid of a native Hopi-speaking informant residing in New York City. It was principally as a result of this work that Whorf developed his notion that language structure influences thought and world-view, for in the Hopi language he saw features that emphasized conceptual distinctions not present or prominent in the structures of familiar Western languages, or in what Whorf termed "standard average European" or "SAE" languages.

Whorf's ideas came to the attention of the general public—including psychologists, anthropologists, and others—principally through his publication, in 1940 and 1941, of a series of articles in the *Technology Review* of the Massachusetts Institute of Technology. He died in 1941, before he was able to explore these ideas further or confirm them through any sort of empirical research. His ideas were, however, promoted widely after his death through republication of his writings.

Although appealing and attractive in many respects, it has not as yet been possible to confirm the Sapir-Whorf hypothesis in any complete and satisfactory way, and it cannot be said that it has enjoyed full acceptance among linguists, psychologists, and anthropologists. Nevertheless, Whorf may be credited with bringing the notion of linguistic relativity to the attention of contemporary scholars, and offering a highly original basis for proposing that, rather than thought influencing language, language influences thought.

—J.B. Carroll

WIENER, Norbert. American mathematician. Born in Columbia, Missouri, 26 November 1894. Studied at Tufts University, Medford, Massachusetts, B.A. 1909; Cornell University, Ithaca, New York; Harvard University, Cambridge, Massachusetts, Ph.D. 1913 (Harvard Traveling Fellow); Cambridge University; University of Göttingen, Germany. Married Margaret Engemann; 2 daughters. Instructor, 1919-24, Assistant Professor, 1924-29, Associate Professor, 1929-32, and Professor from 1932, Massachusetts Institute of Technology, Cambridge. Recipient: National Medal of Science, 1964. *Died* (in Stockholm) *18 March 1964.*

PUBLICATIONS

Collections

Collected Works with Commentaries, edited by P. Masani. Cambridge, Massachusetts, MIT Press, 3 vols., 1976-81.

Mathematics

Bilinear Operations Generating All Operations Rational in a Domain. Boston, 1920.

Tauberian Theorems. Hamburg, Luetcke and Wulff, 1932.

The Fourier Integral and Certain of Its Applications. London, Cambridge University Press, 1933; New York, Dover, 1951.

Fourier Transforms in the Complex Domain, with Raymond E.A.C. Paley. New York, American Mathematical Society, 1934.

Extrapolation, Interpolation, and Smoothing of Stationary Time Series, with Engineering Applications. Cambridge, Massachusetts Institute of Technology, 1942; as *Time Series,* Cambridge, Massachusetts, Massachusetts Institute of Technology, 1964.

Cybernetics; or, Control and Communication in the Animal and the Machine. Cambridge, Massachusetts, Technology Press, 1948.

Time and Organization (lecture). Southampton, England, University of Southampton, 1955.

Nonlinear Problems in Random Theory. Cambridge, Massachusetts Institute of Technology, and London, Chapman and Hall, 1958.

Progress in Biocybernetics, with Johannes Petrus Schadé. Amsterdam, Elsevier, 3 vols., 1964-66.

Selected Papers. Cambridge, Massachusetts, M.I.T. Press, 1965.

Differential Space, Quantum Systems, and Prediction, with others. Cambridge, Massachusetts, M.I.T. Press, 1966.

Other

The Human Use of Human Beings: Cybernetics and Society. Boston, Houghton Mifflin, and London, Eyre and Spottiswoode, 1950.

Ex-Prodigy: My Childhood and Youth. New York, Simon and Schuster, 1953.

I Am a Mathematician: The Later Life of a Prodigy. Cambridge, Massachusetts, M.I.T. Press, and London, Victor Gollancz, 1956.

The Tempter. New York, Random House, 1959.

God and Golem, Inc.: A Comment on Certain Points Where Cybernetics Impinges on Religion. Cambridge, Massachusetts, M.I.T. Press, and London, Chapman and Hall, 1964.

Editor, *Nerve, Brain, and Memory Models: Symposium on Cybernetics of the Nervous System.* Amsterdam and New York, Elsevier, 1963.

Editor, with J.P. Schadé, *Cybernetics of the Nervous System.* Amsterdam and New York, Elsevier, 1965.

*

Critical Studies: *Bulletin of the American Mathematical Society,* 72, no. 1, part 2, 1966; *Norbert Wiener* by Jacques Guillaumaud, Paris, Seghers, 1971; *John von Neumann and Norbert Wiener: From Mathematics to the Technologies of Life and Death* by Steve J. Heims, Cambridge, Massachusetts, MIT Press, 1980.

*   *   *

Norbert Wiener was a polymath, who made original contributions to many mathematical, scientific, and technical problems, but also in his philosophic reflections on values and ethics in connection with technology. When a graduate student at Harvard he began working in biology, but when his father objected he switched to philosophy for his doctorate. During his postdoctoral years (1913-14) in Europe, where he was working under Bertrand Russell's guidance, he was also greatly impressed with the clarity of thought and intellectual power of the mathematician G.H. Hardy, and made Hardy his primary mathematical mentor. Wiener was becoming a powerful mathematician himself as he focussed his energies on achievements in that discipline. He joined the mathematics department faculty at M.I.T. at the age of 25 and remained until, upon his retirement, he was termed

Institute Professor. And when he wrote a biographical volume about his adult life, he titled it *I Am a Mathematician*. Indeed, the major corpus of his work is in mathematics, written to be read and understood mostly by mathematicians. Yet he is known outside mathematics for innovations he introduced in other disciplines. To an electrical engineer he might be primarily known as the founder of the modern (statistical) theory of communication and control, to a theoretical physicist for his introduction of the (functional) integral over paths, and to a biologist as the person who had done the most to introduce the fruitful concepts of positive and negative feedback, cybernetic system, message, information, and noise into biology. To opponents of hyper-militarization he is an example of one who renounced weapons work on principle after having engaged in it actively during World War II. To a biographer he is the exceptional mathematician for whom the content of his work and his general outlook on life were of a piece, linked by a conscious philosophy. To a technologist he may be important as the creator of a coherent and humane philosophy of technology (at a time when technology was hardly recognized as worthy of the attention of philosophers). To literary people and historians of science, he is the author of a remarkably candid, interesting, and well-written volume about his own youth, *Ex-Prodigy*. To the general public he was at mid-century the scientist who had given cogent reasons for anticipating an era dominated by concerns with organization, communication, and control in contrast to the 19th-century preoccupation with engines and power. This list omits his relatively minor, yet significant, excursions into special fields such as quantum theory, meteorology, analog computers, and the design of devices to compensate for sensory and motor handicaps.

After his time with Russell—he was barely twenty—Wiener continued to work for a number of years within the general framework of the Russell-Whitehead *Principia Mathematica* and Russell's formal system to contain mathematics and logical reasoning. However, already in 1915 Wiener concluded that "it is highly probable that we can get no certainty that is absolute in the propositions of logic and mathematics, at any rate in those that derive their validity from the postulates of logic." Gödel's famous proof (1931) demonstrating that complex mathematical and logical systems must in a certain sense be incomplete confirmed Wiener in his own understanding of the nature of mathematics, although it came as "an astounding and melancholy revelation" to most mathematicians at the time. Wiener rejected the logical atomism, the analytic philosophy of Russell; nor did he take to the logical positivism so popular in the 1930's and 1940's. He came to define his own outlook as closer to existentialism. Wiener refers to Kierkegaard, and some of his statements remind one of Camus's famous essay on the myth of Sisyphus, but his thinking and language is conditioned by familiarity with the statistical basis for the Second Law of Thermodynamics. Some quotations from Wiener:

> To me, logic and learning and all mental activity have always been incomprehensible as a complete and closed picture and have been understandable only as a process by which man puts himself *en rapport* with his environment.... We are swimming upstream against a great torrent of disorganization.... It is the greatest possible victory to be, to continue to be, and to have been. No defeat can deprive us of the success of having existed for some moment of time in a universe that seems indifferent to us.... The declaration of our own nature and the attempt to build up an enclave of organization in the face of nature's overwhelming tendency to disorder (*I Am a Mathematician*).

A central theme that wends its way through much of Wiener's mathematical work is that of an underlying chaos or randomness, which nevertheless is the foundation for many completely rigorous mathematical statements. Consider for example the seminal development by Wiener, most simply referred to as the introduction of the "Wiener measure" into mathematics or "integration in function space". Wiener devised a generalization from the Lebesgue integral over a space of points, to an integral over a space of curves, in fact over a statistical assembly of curves. He linked the mathematical theory to physical reality by applying it to Brownian motion, the motion of particles (suspended in a liquid such as water) observable under a microscope. One scientific observer (Jean Perrin) described the phenomenon: "Each particle, instead of sinking steadily, is quickened by an extremely lively and wholly haphazard movement.... Each particle spins hither and thither, rises, sinks, rises again without ever tending to rest." Wiener solved the problem of averaging over all possible such "haphazard" trajectories for given endpoints in a completely well-defined and mathematically rigorous way. When Wiener did this work (1920-23) Brownian motion was no longer of particular interest to physicists, but his theory opened up a new field of investigation in mathematics, which ultimately found applications in many branches of physics, engineering, and biology. It initiated the mathematical theory of stochastic processes and solved its central problem; it set a precedent in formulating a problem in probability theory in these terms, a precedent followed by others in formalizing probability theory in terms of measure theory. As Marc Kac wrote in a memorial volume to Wiener in 1966:

> In retrospect one can have nothing but admiration for the vision which Wiener had shown when, almost half a century ago, he had chosen Brownian motion as a subject of study from the point of view of the theory of integration. To have foreseen, at that time, that an impressive edifice could be erected in such an esoteric corner of mathematics was a feat of intuition not easily equalled now or ever.... Integration in function space...gave us not only a new way of looking at problems but actually a new way of *thinking* about them.

Other areas in mathematics to which Wiener made major contributions include generalized harmonic analysis, Tauberian theorems, the theory of Fourier integrals in the complex plane, potential theory, and ergodic theory. (For a survey of this work see the Wiener memorial issue of the *Bulletin of the American Mathematical Society*, 1966).

Wiener's polymathic interests served him well from the 1940's onward. During World War II he was concerned with mathematical aspects of communication and control engineering and left an indelible mark on the field by considering message and noise as statistical phenomena, but he had also maintained contact with biologists and physiologists, especially his Mexican friend Arturo Rosenblueth. Engineer Julian Bigelow and Wiener saw organizational parallels between self-steering engineering devices and homeostatic mechanisms in organisms, and together with Rosenblueth conjectured that these parallels hinted at unifying principles which cut across many disciplines and could be stated mathematically. Within a few years the outlines of such a synthesis became apparent, and was seen to have a substantial empirical basis. In his book *Cybernetics* (a word derived by Wiener from the Greek for "steersman"), Wiener made the case for such a synthesis and introduced a wide cross-disciplinary audience to the ideas. The ideas were picked up by biologists ("among the most fertile ideas introduced into biology in recent years are those of *cybernetics*," P.B. Medawar and J.S. Medawar wrote in 1977), and by some concerned with describing social interactions (e.g. Gregory Bateson, Karl Deutsch). Communication, control, self-regulation, and a strong and ubiquitous probabilistic element (rather than rigid determinism) are the central themes of Wiener's synthesis. The conceptual synthesis was loose and open-ended; it incorporated paradox and contradiction via analogs of Russell's theory of logical types. He urged social theorists not to take it too seriously, for in those fields it is no more than a set of useful concepts, metaphors from engineering. Wiener's social thought was premised on a liberal outlook, expressed by the words of the French Revolution, Liberté, Egalité, Fraternité, as explicated by him:

> The liberty of each human being to develop in his freedom the full measure of the human possibilities embodied in him; the equality by which what is just for A and B remains just when the positions of A and B are interchanged; and a good will between man and man that knows no limits short of humanity. These great principles of justice mean and demand that no person, by virtue of the personal strength of his position, shall enforce a sharp bargain by duress.

With these underlying value premises he used concepts from cybernetics to expose particularly inhuman use of human beings, incidentally criticized the practices of corporate capitalism and of Soviet Communism, and addressed the issue of proper and improper uses of automation, computers, and other recent high technology.

In all, Wiener was not only one of the outstanding mathematicians of the present century, and one who liked and understood sophisticated technical devices, but a man who felt impelled to bring his intellect to bear on the ethical aspect of creating and using technologies and to attempt to translate his insights into his personal life.

—Steve Heims

WIGNER, Eugene Paul. American physicist. Born in Budapest, Hungary, 17 November 1902; emigrated to the United States in 1930: naturalized, 1937. Educated at the Technische Hochschule, Berlin, Dr. Engr. 1925. Married Amelia Z. Frank in 1936; married Annette Wheeler in 1941, 2 children; married Eileen C.P. Hamilton in 1979. Lecturer, 1930, part-time Professor of Mathematical Physics, 1931-36, and Thomas D. Jones Professor of Theoretical Physics, 1938-71, Princeton University, New Jersey; also, Professor of Physics, University of Wisconsin, Madison, 1936-38; at Metallurgy Laboratory, University of Chicago, and Director of Research and Development, Clinton Laboratory, Oak Ridge, Tennessee, 1946-47; Director of Civil Defense Research Project, Oak Ridge, Tennessee, 1964-65. Member, General Advisory Committee, Atomic Energy Commission, 1952-57, 1959-64; Mathematics Section, National Research Council, 1952-54; Physics Panel, National Science Foundation, 1953-56. President, American Physics Society, 1956. Recipient: Medal of Merit, 1946; Franklin Medal, Franklin Institute, 1958; Enrico Fermi Award, Atomic Energy Commission, 1958; Atoms for Peace Award, 1960; Max Planck Medal, German Physics Society, 1961; Nobel Prize in Physics, 1963; George Washington Award, American Hungarian Studies Foundation, 1964; Semmelweiss Medal, American Hungarian Medical Association, 1965; National Science Medal, 1969; Pfizer Award, 1971; Albert Einstein Award, 1972; Wigner Medal, 1978. Honorary doctorage: Case Institute of Technology, Cleveland, 1956; University of Chicago, 1957; University of Alberta, Edmonton, 1957; Colby College, Waterville, Maine, 1959; University of Pennsylvania, Philadelphia, 1961; Yeshiva University, New York, 1963; Thiel College, Greenville, Pennsylvania, 1964; University of Notre Dame, Indiana, 1965; Technische Universität, Berlin, 1966; Swarthmore College, Pennsylvania, 1966; University of Louvain, 1967; University of Liège, 1967; University of Illinois, Urbana, 1968; Seton Hall University, South Orange, New Jersey, 1969; Catholic University of America, Washington, D.C. 1969; Rockefeller University, New York, 1970; Israel Institute of Technology, Haifa, 1973; Lowell University, Massachusetts, 1976; Princeton University, New Jersey, 1976; University of Texas, Austin, 1978; Clarkson College, Pottsdam, New York,

1979; Allegheny College, Pennsylvania, 1979. Member, American Academy of Arts and Sciences, and National Academy of Sciences. Member, Austrian Academy of Science, and German Physics Society; Corresponding Member, Academy of Science, Göttingen; Foreign Member, Royal Society, London; Honorary Member, Hungarian Academy of Science. Address: Palmer Physics Laboratory, Princeton University, Princeton, New Jersey 08540, U.S.A.

PUBLICATIONS

Physics

The Physical Theory of Neutron Chain Reactors, with A.M. Weinberg. Chicago, University of Chicago Press, 1958.
Nuclear Structure, with Leonard Eisenbud. Princeton, New Jersey, Princeton University Press, 1958.
Group Theory and Its Application to the Quantum Mechanics of Atomic Spectra. New York, Academic Press, 1959.
The Growth of Science—Its Promise and Its Dangers (lecture). Ames, Iowa State University, 1964.
Symmetries and Reflections: Scientific Essays. Bloomington, Indiana University Press, 1967.
Science and Society (lecture). Haifa, Israel Institute of Technology, 1973.

Other

Editor, *Dispersion Relations and Their Connection with Causality.* New York, Academic Press, 1964.
Editor, *Who Speaks for Civil Defense?* New York, Scribner, 1968.
Editor, *Survival and the Bomb.* Bloomington, Indiana University Press, 1969.
Editor, *Aspects of Quantum Theory*, with Abdus Salam. London, Cambridge University Press, 1972.

*   *   *

The context in which Eugene Paul Wigner is most likely to be known to the general public is his participation in the Manhattan Project and in issues related to the use of nuclear power following the war. Within the scientific community, however, Wigner had accumulated an impressive reputation long before his involvement with the Project. The breadth of these accomplishments is truly impressive. They include studies of the binding energies and fine structure of nuclei, the mechanics of beta decay, the conservation of parity, reaction mechanisms of chemical changes, and the applications of group theory to quantum mechanics. This diversity of interests and achievements was recognized when Wigner was awarded the Nobel Prize in 1963 not for any single accomplishment, but for the numerous ways in which he improved, extended, and applied the methods of quantum mechanics.

Like many physicists active in the 1930's, Wigner developed a special interest in nuclear fission reactions. His early studies on the mechanics of neutron absorption by nuclei was eventually to be of value in his work at the Project. Along with two other Hungarian-born scientist-emigrés, Leo Szilard and Edward Teller, Wigner was instrumental in convincing Einstein to write his historic letter about atomic power to President Roosevelt in 1939. Wigner's assignment in the Manhattan Project, formed as a result of that letter, was as head of the theoretical physics section of the Metallurgical Laboratory at the University of Chicago. In this position, he was present at the initiation of the first controlled nuclear fission reaction on December 2, 1942.

Wigner's interest during the Manhattan Project was not only in the development of a nuclear weapon, but also in the technology needed for nuclear power plants in the postwar years. Like many of his colleagues, he recognized the potentiality of nuclear power for constructive purposes, as well as for the destructive applications which had first justified the Manhattan Project. His background as a chemical engineer provided him with the rather unusual ability to recognize both theoretical and practical aspects of reactor production potential and problems.

Wigner has consistently maintained an interest in the social and political consequences of nuclear power. He has long argued for a strong defense establishment and has been particularly active in the government's civil defense program.

—David Newton

WILLIAMS, Raymond (Henry). British cultural theorist. Born in Lianfihangel Crocorney, Wales, 31 August 1921. Educated at Abergavenny Grammar School, 1932-39; studied at Trinity College, Cambridge, 1939-41, 1945-46, M.A. 1946, Litt.D. 1969. Served in the Anti-Tank Regiment, Guards Armoured Division, 1941-45: Captain. Married Joy Dalling in 1942; 3 children. Editor, *Politics and Letters*, 1946-47. Extra-Mural Tutor in Literature, Oxford University, 1946-61. Since 1961, Fellow of Jesus College, Cambridge Reader, 1967-74, and since 1974 Professor of Drama, Cambridge University. Visiting Professor of Political Science, Stanford University, California, 1973. General Editor, New Thinkers Library, 1962-70. Reviewer for *The Guardian*, London. D. Univ.: Open University, Milton Keynes, Buckinghamshire, 1975; D.Litt.: University of Wales, Cardiff, 1980. Member of the Welsh Academy. Address: Jesus College, Cambridge CB5 8BL, England.

PUBLICATIONS

Culture, Politics and Society

Culture and Society, 1780-1950. London, Chatto and Windus, and New York, Columbia University Press, 1958.
The Long Revolution. London, Chatto and Windus, and New York, Columbia University Press, 1961.
Communications. London, Penguin, 1962; revised edition, London, Chatto and Windus, 1966; New York, Barnes and Noble, 1967.
The Country and the City. London, Chatto and Windus, 1973; New York, Oxford University Press, 1974.
Television: Technology and Cultural Form. London, Fontana, 1974; New York, Schocken, 1975.
Keywords: A Vocabulary of Culture and Society. London, Croom Helm, and New York, Oxford University Press, 1976.
Marxism and Literature. London and New York, Oxford University Press, 1977.
Politics and Letters: Interviews with New Left Review. London, New Left Books, and New York, Schocken, 1979.
Problems in Materialism and Culture: Selected Essays. London, New Left Books, 1980; New York, Schocken, 1981.
Culture. London, Fontana, 1981.

Novels

Border Country. London, Chatto and Windus, 1960; New York, Horizon Press, 1962.
Second Generation. London, Chatto and Windus, 1964; New York, Horizon Press, 1965.
The Volunteers. London, Eyre Methuen, 1978.
The Fight for Manod. London, Chatto and Windus, 1979.

Plays

Koba, in *Modern Tragedy*. London, Chatto and Windus, and

Stanford, California, Stanford University Press, 1958.

Television Plays: *A Letter from the Country*, 1966; *Public Inquiry*, 1967; *The Country and the City* (documentary, *Where We Live Now* series), 1979.

Other

Reading and Criticism. London, Muller, 1950.
Drama from Ibsen to Eliot. London, Chatto and Windus, 1952; New York, Oxford University Press, 1953; revised and expanded as *Drama from Ibsen to Brecht*, Chatto and Windus, 1968; Oxford University Press, 1969.
Drama in Performance. London, Muller, 1954; Chester Springs, Pennsylvania, Dufour, 1961; revised edition, London, Watts, 1968.
Preface to Film, with Michael Orrom. London, Dobson, 1954.
Modern Tragedy. London, Chatto and Windus, and Stanford, California, Stanford University Press, 1958.
The English Novel from Dickens to Lawrence. London, Chatto and Windus, 1970.
Orwell. London, Fontana, 1971.

Editor, *May Day Manifesto 1968*. London, Penguin, 1968.
Editor, *The Pelican Book of English Prose: From 1780 to the Present Day*. London, Penguin, 1970.
Editor, with Joy Williams, *D.H. Lawrence on Education*. London, Penguin, 1973.
Editor, *George Orwell: A Collection of Critical Essays*. Englewood Cliffs, New Jersey, Prentice Hall, 1974.
Editor, with Marie Axton, *English Drama: Forms and Development: Essays in Honour of Muriel Clara Bradbrook*. London, Cambridge University Press, 1977.

*

Critical Studies: *Criticism and Ideology* by Terry Eagleton, London, New Left Books, 1976; *The Cultural Critics* by Lesley Johnson, London, Routledge, 1979; *Raymond Williams* by J.P. Ward, Cardiff, University of Wales Press, 1981.

* * *

For Raymond Williams, the definition of modern values and their communication has been the thesis of a variety of literary and cultural studies. Whether the subject matter is from his disciplinary field, drama, or film, or television, or the novel—all topics of full-length books—Williams is always interested in the ways in which a medium serves to transmit culture to people. The "masses" and "mass communication" dominate a way of thinking about art which is socialistic and, at times, Marxist, and, consequently, the focus of his historical studies of social values is on the period of the rise of capitalism since the Industrial Revolution.

Williams's fascination with values and social concepts has led him to identify and study the "keywords" of modern society, the most significant of which is "culture," and major themes of his work as an historian of ideas are established in *Culture and Society: 1780 to 1950*. This study clarifies the idea of culture since the Industrial Revolution by studying the thoughts and feelings of various English thinkers and writers in response to changes in their society. Not intended as a general theory of culture (though certainly approaching one), Williams defines the tradition by following the evolution of meaning not only of "culture" but of related value words of a capitalistic society, "industry," "democracy," "class," and "art." (A dictionary with a total of sixty terms originally intended as an appendix was later published with refinement and expansion as *Keywords: A Vocabulary of Culture and Society*.) In *Culture and Society* Williams begins by showing the establishment of this cultural vocabulary of shared meanings in the late 18th and early 19th centuries; he presents a wide-ranging survey of Romantic and Victorian writers, major and minor, and, specifically, shows how their views of art emerge from their society rather than being imposed upon it. Following an interregnum from 1880 to 1920, the opinions on industrialism of such 20th-century writers as Lawrence, Tawney, Eliot, Orwell, and various Marxist thinkers define the issues to be those of developing a common culture in a capitalistic society: problems of social relations in an industrial society, democracy in an era of mass communications, and the function of art in the common life of society.

Throughout Williams's career, he has displayed a Marxist position on how to impart art and culture to the majority of people, and a culminating theme of the progress of ideas traced in *Culture and Society* is the rise of multiple ways of communicating as a means for transmitting culture. His books on the theory of communications and the various media extend this concern in detailed ways. For example, in *Communications*, by tracing the history of book publishing, the theatre, journalism, and film, Williams explores how these changing forms of communication shape social institutions. He concludes that while the audience has been expanded with these developments, the means of communicating has been controlled and oriented to capitalism with an attendant dedication to authoritarian, paternal, and commercial values. He calls for reform of the media to permit true democracy and the achievement of human liberation.

These attitudes emerge in artistic terms in Williams's study of the revival of Marxist thought in recent cultural theory, *Marxism and Literature*. Viewing his own position as one of "radical populism," he continues his fascination with the vocabulary of culture by viewing language as arising from a consciousness of one's social being and as a product of social and economic history. Consequently, he seeks to extend the sense of the literary to a multiplicity of popular forms, and rejects any elitist sense of what is "aesthetic."

Williams's ideological bias and broad knowledge of literature triumphantly unite in *The Country and the City*. Again, as in *Culture and Society*, his method is a broad survey of English writers and an analysis of their historically varied experiences which focuses sharply, in this instance, on the persistent images and associations of country and city. Beginning with a review of the origin of the pastoral ideal in the classical understanding of a "golden age," he shows how the history of the English countryside has centered on problems of property and the consequent affects on social and working relationships. Williams carefully traces in poets like Goldsmith and Cowper and novelists like Austen and Hardy artistic responses to such political and economic events as the enclosure acts,' the decline of rural villages, the disruption of the lives of the landed class, as well as the rise of the city with its complex social relationships and the loss of a sense of a "knowable community." There never has been an ideal time for rural or urban life, according to Williams, because the controlling force for both since the 18th century has been capitalism—which first affected the rural scene, then extended to cities and, eventually, to the colonial system of Great Britain. For Williams, then, tracing the literary images of country and city is a way of comprehending a basic process of economic self-interest and control. This is the essential assumption of all of Williams's cultural studies, and they are successful to the extent that the political theory illuminates the chosen subject matter. In *Culture and Society* and *The Country and the City*, the topics fit the filter of socialist consciousness to which they are subjected, and the results are profound and lasting.

—George H. Gilpin/Hermione de Almeida

WILSON, Edward O(sborne). American zoologist. Born in Birmingham, Alabama, 10 June 1929. Studied at the University of Alabama, University, B.S. 1949, M.S. 1950; Harvard University, Cambridge, Massachusetts, Ph.D. 1955. Married Irene Kelley in 1955; 1 daughter. Fellow, Society of Fellows, 1953-56, from Assistant Professor to Professor of Zoology, 1956-77, since 1971 Curator of Entomology, and since 1977 Frank J. Baird Jr. Professor of Science, Harvard University. Charles and Martha Hitchcock Professor, University of California, Berkeley, 1972. President, Society for the Study of Evolution, 1973. Recipient: Cleveland Prize, American Association for the Advancement of Science; Mercer Award, Ecological Association of America, 1971; Founders Memorial Award, Etomological Society of America, 1972; National Medal of Science, 1976; Distinguished Service Award, American Institute of Biological Sciences, 1976; Guggenheim Fellowship, 1977; Archie Carr Medal, University of Florida, 1978; Pulitzer Prize, 1979; Leidy Medal, Academy of Natural Science, 1979. Honorary doctorate: Duke University, Durham, North Carolina; Grinnell College, Iowa; Lawrence University, Appleton, Wisconsin; University of West Florida, Pensacola; University of Alabama. Member, National Academy of Sciences. Fellow, American Academy of Arts and Sciences; American Philosophical Society; Society for the Study of Evolution, and Deutsche Akademie für Naturforschung. Address: Museum of Comparative Zoology, Harvard University, Cambridge, Massachusetts 02138, U.S.A.

PUBLICATIONS

Zoology and Biology

A Monographic Revision of the Ant Genus Lasius. Cambridge, Harvard Museum of Comparative Zoology, 1955.
The Discovery of Cerapachyine Ants on New Caledonia, with the Description of New Species of Phyracaces and Sphinctomyrmex. Cambridge, Harvard Museum of Comparative Zoology, 1957.
The Tenuis and Selenophora Groups of the Ant Genus Pomera (Hymenoptera: Formicidae). Cambridge, Harvard Museum of Comparative Zoology, 1957.
Studies on the Ant Fauna of Melanesia. Cambridge, Harvard Museum of Comparative Zoology, 1958.
Behavior of Daceton Armigerum (Latreille), with a Classification of Self-Grooming Movements in Ants. Cambridge, Harvard Museum of Comparative Zoology, 1962.
The Ants of Polynesia (Hymenoptera: Formicidae), with Robert W. Taylor. Honolulu, Bernice P. Bishop Museum, 1967.
The Insect Societies. Cambridge, Massachusetts, Belknap Press, 1971.
A Primer of Population Biology, with William H. Bossert. Stamford, Connecticut, Sinauer Associates, 1971.
Life on Earth, with others. Stamford, Connecticut, Sinauer Associates, 1973.
Sociobiology: The New Synthesis. Cambridge, Massachusetts, Belknap Press, 1975.
On Human Nature. Cambridge, Massachusetts, Harvard University Press, 1978.
Caste and Ecology in the Social Insects, with George F. Oster. Princeton, New Jersey, Princeton University Press, 1978.
Genes, Mind, and Culture: The Coevolutionary Process, with Charles J. Lumsden. Cambridge, Massachusetts, Harvard University Press, 1981.

*

Critical Study: *Sociobiology: Sense or Nonsense?* by Michael Ruse, Dordrecht, Reidel, 1979.

*   *   *

Edward O. Wilson, one of the most distinguished albeit controversial figures in modern science, is responsible above all else for showing that traditional biology is a far-from-spent force. Although molecular biologists are breaking the organism into finer and finer parts, Wilson's work demonstrates that there are still rewarding problems posed, and subtle answers to be found, in the study of whole organisms.

The first major contribution to biology produced by Wilson came in collaboration with the late Robert H. MacArthur. Together, they revitalised the study of island biogeography, a topic which has been of keen interest to evolutionary biologists since Charles Darwin conceived of descent with modification, after viewing the birds and reptiles of the Galapagos Archipelago in the Pacific. Essentially, MacArthur and Wilson showed, both theoretically and empirically, that species numbers on islands can be expected to achieve equilibria, with numbers arriving balancing numbers leaving or going extinct. Roughly, the number of species of a taxon on an island increases as the cube root to the fourth root of the area of the island.

This work was an extremely important contribution to biology. But, it was in the 1970's that Wilson really came into his own, with three works which he retroactively sees as a connected trilogy. The first of these works, *The Insect Societies*, looks at the world of the social insects (the bees, the ants, and the wasps); the second, *Sociobiology: The New Synthesis*, at all of the animal world, from insects to man; and the third, *On Human Nature*, exclusively at our own species. It is not too much to say that in these works, although admittedly building on and synthesizing the ideas of others, Wilson created the modern science of animal (including human) social behaviour, considered from a biological viewpoint: so-called "sociobiology."

In the *Origin of Species* (1859) Charles Darwin applied his mechanism of natural selection to many different areas of the organic world, including behaviour. Darwin and his successors were convinced that actions are as much part of the world of evolution as are physical features. However, until recently, the study of behaviour lagged behind other areas of evolutionary investigation. No one really understood how an animal can develop behavioural features which aid other organisms. Fortunately, a major theoretical breakthrough came in 1964 thanks to W.D. Hamilton, who developed the notion of "kin selection," showing that one can evolve by proxy, as it were, when one helps close relatives rather than oneself. Thus, there is scope for the evolution of "altruistic" behaviours, since in help to others one promotes one's own evolution.

Seizing on this and similar notions, Wilson showed that they have wide applicability in the animal world. Why do we find intricate patterns of conduct between members of the same species? Why do we not have an unrestrained free-for-all, "nature red in tooth and claw?" Simply, because it is to an animal's biological self-interest to conceal its ultimate ends beneath a cloak of cooperation. Working through the animal world, especially in *Sociobiology: The New Synthesis*, Wilson showed in magnificent fashion how modern theory illuminates and explains the problems of social behaviour, thus bringing the area firmly up-to-date within the overall Darwinian synthesis.

What makes Wilson such a controversial figure is his application of his biological conclusions to our own species. Like Darwin, Wilson believes that, in important respects, we really are animals. In our behaviour, no less than in our physical makeup, we show the legacy of evolution through natural selection. Thus, for instance, Wilson thinks there are biological foundations to incest taboos: they prevent the deleterious effects of close-inbreeding. More provocatively, Wilson suggests that biology lies behind male/female behavioural and attitudinal differences. Although he admits that the environment (as in family training) does have some impact, Wilson believes that males are innately more aggressive, more domineering, and given to promiscuity and possession of multiple mates. Females, conversely, tend to be more domestic.

Wilson has also embraced a form of evolutionary ethics. He certainly believes that our moral sense is a product of evolution, and is not beyond suggesting even that the very notions of right and wrong are determined by the evolutionary expedient. We do what we do and we think what we think because we have evolved from animals, by a natural process. There is no escape from this, and there is no ultimate objective standard to take us beyond the relativity of our situation.

No one denies Wilson's major contributions to animal biology. The imagination to synthesize a whole new field is a talent not possessed by most, and Wilson deserves full credit. Time alone will tell whether Wilson's speculations about our own species hold true: is he courageously and perceptively pushing forward the boundaries of knowledge (as his supporters claim), or is he the reactionary manifestation of a sexist, capitalist, sick society (as his detractors claim)?

Perhaps, in the end, it will prove unnecessary to answer this last question. Recently, Wilson and other sociobiologists have been moving more towards an understanding of human beings which emphasizes both biology and culture. In the end, perhaps we shall learn that biology is a necessary element in human understanding, but not a sufficient one. If we do learn this, Wilson will take major credit as a teacher.

—Michael Ruse

WIRTH, Louis. American sociologist. Born in Gemünden, Germany, 28 August 1897; emigrated to the United States in 1911: naturalized, 1924. Educated at schools in Germany and Omaha, Nebraska; studied at the University of Chicago, Ph.B. 1919, M.A. 1925, Ph.D. 1926. Married Mary Bolton in 1923; 2 daughters. Director of delinquent boys division, Jewish Charities of Chicago, 1919-22; Instructor of Sociology, University of Chicago, 1926-28; Associate Professor, Tulane University, New Orleans, 1928-29; Assistant Professor, 1930-31, Associate Professor, 1930-40, Professor of Sociology, 1940-51, and Associate Dean of Social Science, 1940-45, University of Chicago Visiting Professor, universities of Michigan, Ann Arbor, Minnesota, Minneapolis, and Iowa, Iowa City, and Stanford University, California. Active in University of Chicago Round Table radio broadcasts, 1938-52 (many published by the University of Chicago Press, 1938-52). Associate Editor, *American Journal of Sociology*, 1926-28, 1931-52. Consultant, 1935-42, and Regional Chairman, 1942-43, National Resources Planning Board; Consultant, Federal Housing Authority, 1942-44; Director, Illinois Postwar Planning Board, 1944. President, American Sociological Society, 1947, American Council on Race Relations, 1947, and International Sociological Association, 1950-52. Recipient: Social Science Research Council fellowship, 1929. *Died 10 May 1952.*

PUBLICATIONS

Sociology

The Ghetto. Chicago, University of Chicago Press, 1928.
Our Cities: Their Role in the National Economy, with others. Washington, D.C., National Resources Committee, 1937.
Urban and Rural Living, with Ray Lussenhop. Washington, D.C., National Council for the Social Studies, 1944.
Community Life and Social Policy: Selected Papers, edited by Elizabeth Wirth Marvick and Albert J. Reiss, Jr. Chicago, University of Chicago Press, 1956.
On Cities and Social Life: Selected Papers, edited by Albert J. Reiss, Jr. Chicago, University of Chicago Press, 1964.

Other

Editor, with Margaret Furez, *Local Community Fact Book 1938*. Chicago, Recreation Commission, 1938.

Editor, with Max Lerner, *Contemporary Social Problems: A Tentative Formulation for Teachers of Social Studies*. Chicago, University of Chicago Press, 1939.

Editor, *Eleven Twenty-Six: A Decade of Social Science Research*. Chicago, University of Chicago Press, 1940.

Editor, *Technology and Society: The Influence of Machines in the United States*, by S. McKee Rosen and Laura Rosen. New York, Macmillan, 1941.

Editor, with Ernest R. Hilgard and I. James Quillen, *Community Planning for Peacetime Living*. Stanford, California, Stanford Workshop on Community Leadership, 1946.

Editor, with Eleanor B. Bernert, *Local Community Fact Book of Chicago*. Chicago, University of Chicago Press, 1949.

Translator, with Edward Shils, *Ideology and Utopia* by Karl Mannheim. New York, Harcourt Brace, 1936.

*

Bibliography: in *On Cities and Social Life*, 1964.

*　　*　　*

Louis Wirth was a key transitional figure in the history of American sociology and particularly in the development of the "Chicago School" of urban studies. Both intellectually and biographically, he served as a connection between his mentors, Robert Park and Georg Simmel, and the highly empirical "urban ecologists" who dominated urban sociology from the 1930's to the 1960's. With the latter he shared an orientation toward pragmatic research and problem solving. Yet he was unusual among his contemporaries in that he never lost sight of the psychic and moral dimensions of social life that were the central concerns of the older generation.

Wirth is generally considered a theoretical sociologist. Yet he did not leave a coherent "Wirthian Theory" of society. He had little interest in building a grand, predictive theory of social life, nor did he believe that the current state of social scientific knowledge made such a theory possible. Nevertheless, he was equally unimpressed with the aimless empiricism that characterized much of the later work of the Chicago School.

Wirth's method of doing sociology was based largely on the use of the "Ideal Types"—a conceptual device by which the observer isolates those characteristics that typify a given social phenomenon. Using this method, Wirth produced not so much theories as masterful typologies. In "Urbanism as a Way of Life" he outlines what is unique about the mental life of the "urban" actor, contrasting (albeit by implication) urbanism with the "Folk" ways of life. In *The Ghetto* he proposes a series of pairs of opposite personality types to be found among residents of the Jewish Ghetto. The "Mensch" type responds to his situation with the opposite attitudes and values from those of the "Schlemiel" type.

These "ideal types" serve two purposes. First, they draw a clear picture of the abstract concept of the "Mensch" or "Schlemiel" mode of personality that real cases may be judged against. Secondly, by using terms used by the ghetto residents themselves, Wirth proposes to make *their* categories clear to the audience, rather than merely to impose the categories of the social scientist.

The Ghetto was Wirth's first major piece of research, and it dealt with the two subjects with which he would be most closely identified throughout his career: urbanism, and race and ethnicity. While Wirth would go on to publish on a huge variety of subjects, from the sociology of knowledge to the rise of the mass media, it would be in these two areas that he would make his lasting contribution.

In *The Ghetto* Wirth explores the inter-relationship between geographic and psychological factors that create the minority community. He traces the history of the Chicago Jewish community as both a product and a producer of social geography. The work stands as a model for urban ethnographic research to this day.

In several essays written in the 1930's, most notably "Urbanism as a Way of Life," Wirth attempts to develop a "sociological" definition of "urbanism." The urban mode of life, he writes, is a human response to distinct demographic factors in human settlements: increases in size, density, and heterogeneity. In such an environment, a person must "segment" his or her life in order to cope with the psychic overload of constant dislocation. While urbanites know many people, their relationships tend to be transitory, limited, immune to personal claims and expectations. As the city typically does not replace its own population, the growing city must constantly draw people from the hinterland, insuring contrasts of personality and culture. Given these contrasts, secular, rational, predictable rules of behavior must replace the traditional understandings of a Folk society.

In the city, no one group has the undivided allegiance of the individual. Hence Wirth, like Simmel, sees urbanism as providing a unique freedom from social restraint. Yet while Simmel's freedom was a mental state—the knowledge that "I" am more than the many segmented tasks that "I" perform—Wirth's is a freedom of behavior, resulting in both innovation and deviance. On the other hand, Wirth notes that urbanites are uniquely susceptible to the manipulation of symbols by mass movements. Since all governmental services must be geared to the "average man," political action in the city often means a loss of individuality.

Wirth's essay is a classic, first because it defines urbanism as a mode of action not limited to politically defined city boundaries, and secondly because his urbanite—relativistic, insulated, sophisticated, and lonely—has been the subject of a tremendous amount of criticism. Among these critiques are that Wirth's ideal type of "urbanism" is in fact only applicable to western, or modern, or capitalistic, urbanism. Others maintain that Wirth was describing the psychological results not of urbanism *per se*, but of geographical mobility. Many have argued that Wirth sees urbanism as a mass phenomenon, while in fact most urbanites live in subcultures or "urban villages" more analogous to traditional communities. Despite all of these objections, Wirth's essays remain the starting point for all serious discussions of the social ecology of modern cities.

Less frequently read today is Wirth's extensive work on race and nationalism. Ironically, while his work on urbanism remains a source of controversy, his other major contribution is often forgotten because his views are now so widely accepted that they are seldom subject to debate. Wirth took as a given that racial and national identities are social, not biological, constructs. Therefore, he explored the question of how and why racial "myths" came about. Today, his critique of Hitler's racial notions would raise few eyebrows. However, in the mid-1930's, many thought this an intrusion of politics into the classroom. Furthermore, Wirth's comparison of the ideological underpinnings of British imperialism and American segregation with those of Hitler's fascism was far from non-controversial at the time. As with urbanism, Wirth's work on race reflects his overall commitment to liberal values.

—Philip Kasinitz

WITTGENSTEIN, Ludwig (Josef Johann). Austrian-British philosopher. Born in Vienna, 26 April 1889; naturalized British citizen, 1939. Studied at the Technische Hochschule, Berlin-Charlottenberg, 1906-08; University of Manchester, 1908-11 (studied aeronautical engineering and mathematics); Trinity College, Cambridge, 1911-13, Ph.D. 1929. Served in the German Army during World War I. Enrolled in one of Otto Glöckel's teacher training colleges, Vienna, and taught at various elementary schools in lower Austria, 1920-26. Returned to Cambridge in 1929; Fellow, Trinity College, 1930-35, and Professor of Philosophy, 1939-47 (also worked as a porter at Guy's Hospital, London, and as a medical technician in Newcastle during World War II). Resigned in 1947 to devote himself entirely to philosophy. *Died* (in Cambridge) *29 April 1951.*

PUBLICATIONS

Collections

Schriften. Frankfurt, Suhrkamp, 7 vols., 1960-78.

Philosophy

Tractatus Logico-Philosophicus (German and English texts). London, Routledge, 1922; New York, Humanities Press, 1961.
Philosophical Investigations (German and English Texts), edited by G.E.M. Anscombe and Rush Rhees. Oxford, Blackwell, and New York, Macmillan, 1953.
Remarks on the Foundations of Mathematics (German and English texts), edited by G.H. von Wright, Rush Rhees, and G.E.M. Anscombe. Oxford, Blackwell, and New York, Macmillan, 1956.
Preliminary Studies for the "Philosophical Investigations," Generally Known as the Blue and Brown Books. Oxford, Blackwell, and New York, Harper, 1958.
Notebooks 1914-1916 (German and English texts), edited by G.E.M. Anscombe and G.H. von Wright. Oxford, Blackwell, and New York, Barnes and Noble, 1961.
Philosophische Bemerkungen, edited by Rush Rhees. Oxford, Blackwell, 1965; as *Philosophical Remarks,* New York, Barnes and Noble, 1968.
Lectures and Conversations on Aesthetics, Psychology, and Religious Beliefs, edited by Cyril Barrett. Oxford, Blackwell, and Berkeley, University of California Press, 1966.
Zettel (German and English texts), edited by G.H. von Wright and G.E.M. Anscombe. Oxford, Blackwell, and Berkeley, University of California Press, 1967.
On Certainty (German and English texts), edited by G.E.M. Anscombe and G.H. von Wright. Oxford, Blackwell, and New York, Harper, 1969.
Philosophische Grammatik, edited by Rush Rhees. Oxford, Blackwell, 1969; as *Philosophical Grammar,* Oxford, Blackwell, and Berkeley, University of California Press, 1974.
Protractatus: An Early Version of the Tractatus Logico-Philosophicus, edited by G.H. von Wright, B.F. MuGuinness, and T. Nyberg. London, Routledge, and Ithaca, New York, Cornell University Press, 1971.
Philosophical Remarks, edited by Rush Rhees. Oxford, Blackwell, and New York, Barnes and Noble, 1975.
Wittgenstein's Lectures on the Foundations of Mathematics, Cambridge, 1939, edited by Cora Diamond. Hassocks, Sussex, Harvester, and Ithaca, New York, Cornell University Press, 1976.
Vermischte Bemerkungen, edited by G.H. von Wright. Frankfurt, Suhrkamp, 1977; as *Culture and Value,* Chicago, University of Chicago Press, 1980; Oxford, Blackwell, 1981.
Remarks on Colour, edited by G.E.M. Anscombe. Berkeley, University of California Press, 1977; Oxford, Blackwell, 1978.
Remarks on Frazier's Golden Bough, edited by Rush Rhees. London, Brynmill Press, and Atlantic Highlands, New Jersey, Humanities Press, 1979.
Remarks on the Philosophy of Psychology, edited by G.E.M. Anscombe and G.H. von Wright. Oxford, Blackwell, and Chicago, University of Chicago Press, 1980.
Wittgenstein's Lectures, Cambridge, 1930-1932, edited by Desmond Lee. Totowa, New Jersy, Rowman and Littlefield, 1980.
Wittgenstein's Lectures, Cambridge, 1932-1935, edited by Alice Ambrose. Totowa, New Jersey, Rowman and Littlefield, 1980.

Other

Wörterbuch für Volksschulen. Vienna, Hölder-Pichler-Tempsky, 1926.
Letters from Ludwig Wittgenstein, with a Memoir by Paul Englemann, edited by B.F. MuGuinness. Oxford, Blackwell, 1967.
Brief an Ludwig von Ficker. Salzburg, Müller, 1969.
Brief und Begegnungen, edited by B.F. McGuinness. Munich, Oldenberg, 1970.
Letters to C.K. Ogden, edited by G.H. von Wright. Oxford, Blackwell, and London and Boston, Routledge, 1973.
Letters to Russell, Keynes, and Moore, edited by G.H. von Wright. Ithaca, New York, Cornell University Press, 1974.

*

Bibliography: "The Wittgenstein Papers" by G.H. von Wright, in *Philosophical Review* (Ithaca, New York), 78, 1969; *Ludwig Wittgenstein: A Comprehensive Bibliography* by Françoise H. LaPointe, Westport, Connecticut, Greenwood Press, 1980.

Critical Studies: *Ludwig Wittgenstein: A Memoir, with a Biographical Sketch by Georg Henrik von Wright* by Norman Malcolm, London, Oxford University Press, 1958; *Ludwig Wittgenstein* by David Pears, London, Collins, and New York, Viking Press, 1969; *Wittgenstein's Conception of Philosophy* by K.T. Fann, Berkeley, University of California Press, 1969; *Wittgenstein's Vienna* by Allen Janik and Stephen Toulmin, New York, Simon and Schuster, 1973; *Wittgenstein* by William Warren Bartley, Philadelphia, Lippincott, 1973; *Perspectives on the Philosophy of Wittgenstein* edited by Irving Block, Oxford, Blackwell, and Cambridge, Massachusetts, MIT Press, 1980; *Wittgenstein* by G.H. von Wright, Oxford, Blackwell, 1982.

* * *

Ludwig Wittgenstein has been called the most influential philosopher of the 20th century. There are two reasons for this. Either one might support this claim and both together make a strong case for its truth.

Wittgenstein fathered not one but two philosophies. What makes this paradoxical is that the second is a sustained criticism of the first. There is no other philosopher of whom it can be said that he fashioned two different antithetical philosophies in his lifetime, each exercising an important influence within its own sphere.

Wittgenstein's earlier philosophy is contained in the only book published in his lifetime, the *Tractatus-Logico Philosophicus,* commonly called the *Tractatus,* which was written while he was serving in the Austrian army in the First World War. He had finished the manuscript in August 1918 and had it in his possession when he was captured a few months later and interned in a prisoner-of-war camp in Cassino, Italy. He managed to get this manuscript to Russell with the help of the British economist, J.M. Keynes, with whom Wittgenstein had established a friendship from his pre-war days in Cambridge. Wittgenstein subsequently received a letter from Russell in which the latter asked a number of questions about the *Tractatus* to which Wittgenstein replied in a letter dated 19.8.19. In it Wittgenstein complains that Russell had not understood the "main contention" of the *Tractatus.* The main contention of the *Tractatus* that Russell failed to grasp was the distinction between what can be said and what can not be said but only shown. Since Wittgenstein himself calls this distinction the "main contention" of the *Tractatus*, let us dwell on it a moment.

What can be said are descriptions of facts of the world that are either true or false. The mechanism of how this is carried out is the well-known picture theory of meaning. Every sentence that has meanings of necessity must describe a fact of the world. If it does this successfully, the proposition is true, otherwise it is false. However, propositions or sentences are not exactly pictures of facts the way photographs are. A photograph of a cat on a mat is a picture of a cat on a mat, but the sentence "the cat is on the mat" is not a picture of a cat on a mat. In what way does a sentence picture a fact? The answer Wittgenstein gave is that they are "logical" pictures. The explication of what a "logical" picture is involved a kind of analysis of propositions that has come to be called "logical atomism." Wittgenstein derived his basic insight on this question from Russell though he added some important modifications of his own. The basic insight of this view is that all significant language (by "significant" is meant all language that purports to describe facts) must be able to be analyzed solely into names that signify simple unanalyzable objects. Since these objects are simple they cannot be described, only named. Description begins when these names are combined to form sentences that describe how objects are combined to form facts. When through analysis one reaches those sentences in which all the words are simple names, then one has reached simple sentences or "elementary" sentences as Wittgenstein called them. In elementary sentences the numerical multiplicity of the names matches the numerical multiplicity of the objects combined in the fact being described. Thus if "The cat is on the mat" were an elementary sentence which for purposes of analysis might be just simply "Cat on mat," then cat would be a simple object in relationship to a mat which would be another simple object. Of course a cat is not a simple object and so "cat" is not a name but a disguised description which stands in need of analysis. The capacity that non-elementary sentences have of picturing facts even though they are not composed of names is derived from the fact that they are ultimately derived from elementary sentences which are the source of the picturing relationship. Thus the claim that sentences picture facts is really a statement about elementary sentences and is applicable to everyday language only in so far as everyday language is completely analyzable into elementary sentences. The picture theory of meaning thus has two theses. One is that an elementary sentence is a picture of fact and the second is that all other meaningful sentences are truth functions of those elementary sentences.

The picture theory as described above is only one aspect of the theory of meaning contained in the *Tractatus*. The picture theory by itself is incomplete, for the picture theory is essentially a theory of truth. It is concerned to say how it is that a sentence can be true or false. The thorny problem of how words can combine to form a meaningful sentence in the first place is not touched by the picture theory *per se*. This is unlike Russell's theory of logical atomism, where meaning and truth of an atomic sentence was determined by the single operation of ostention as in uttering the sentence "This is red" while pointing to a red colour. For this reason Russell's atomic sentences could not be false.

Wittgenstein, however, argued that elementary propositions could be true or false, for ostention was not involved in establishing the meaning or "sense," as he called it, of an elementary proposition. The answer to the question of what *does* establish a string of words as a sentence, if not ostention, is contained in the thesis of "showing" which was that aspect of the *Tractatus* which Russell had difficulty comprehending.

There are a number of features to this doctrine but the most notable for our purposes is that there can be no rules that stipulate how words combine to form sentences. The ordinary rules of grammar give the appearance of doing this, but it is only an appearance. That a sentence is composed of a subject and a predicate does not begin to tell you which subjects combine with which predicates to form meaningful sentences. "Sentences" as

"It is 5 o'clock on the Sun" or "The sum of 5 + 7 is green" appear to be sentences for they are composed of a subject and a predicate, but they are nonsense. What enables us to recognize a string of words as a sentence? There are no rules that can help us here. A sentence "shows" its sense, as Wittgenstein expressed it in the *Tractatus*. There is a "logic" that determines which words can combine to make a sentence, but one can not say what that logic is. It manifests itself in the actual sentences. This realm of logic determines the totality of all possible sentences. Wittgenstein called this logic "logical space." One can not formally set out the rules of logical space for the language in which one would set out the rules itself but must obey them. There is no way of standing outside language and thought so as to be able to give a description of how it operates. Language can be known only from the "inside."

At this point the question arises, which comes first, the name or the sentence? Unlike the chicken or egg question, Wittgenstein gives us a clear and unmistakable answer. Names occur only within the context of sentences (*Tractatus*, 3.3). Names have no meaning isolated by themselves. "(It is impossible for words to appear in two different roles: by themselves, and in propositions)" (*Tractatus*, 2.0122). The sense or meaning of a sentence is prior to the reference or meaning of a word. Here arises incoherence. The reference of words entails sentences in which they occur. However, the sense of sentences is a formal matter, depending on the "logic" of logical space which is seen or "shown" independently of any empirical observations. In elementary sentences, the names necessarily designate simple objects, so it would seem that whether a word is a name in this sense is determined by a formal relation and not an empirical one. This I believe most philosophers would find incoherent.

For over ten years after Wittgenstein had completed his *Tractatus*, he removed himself from philosophy. When he returned to Cambridge in 1930 and took up philosophy as a full-time occupation he evolved a way of viewing language that was essentially a critique of the *Tractatus* described above. Though he published nothing during the course of his remaining career, after his death his work was published in the form of a book called *Philosophical Investigations*.

In this work, the essence of language is no longer that of the picture theory. To be a meaningful sentence it is no longer necessary that it say something about the world that is true or false. What gave language its meaning were not the conditions of its truth or falsity, but the role that it played in human activities. Language is used to describe the world, but it has many other uses and its descriptive use is not its most predominant. Among common uses of language mentioned by Wittgenstein in paragraph 23 of his *Philosophical Investigations* are giving orders and obeying them, making up stories, singing, guessing riddles, making jokes, asking, thanking, cursing, greeting, and playing. Immediately after giving the list of various language uses, Wittgenstein writes "It is interesting to compare the multiplicity of the tools in language and of the ways they are used, the multiplicity of kinds of word and sentence, with what logicians have said about the structure of language. (Including the author of the *Tractatus Logico-Philosophicas*)." One should not theorize about what language should be in order to satisfy certain preconceived philosophical requirements. One should just observe how language is used in actual practice. We have a tendency to over-intellectualize language. We seek a validity for language as we seek the validity of a scientific theory. However, language is a part of a person's normal routine as walking, eating, drinking or playing (see paragraph 25 of *Philosophical Investigations*). The meaning of language is thus derived from its very activities. What does it mean to play a game? Well, this is how one plays the game of hop-scotch and there are many other games that one can play. Similarly, how does one describe the weather? Just look outside and tell me what you see.

This no doubt sounds too simplistic to be illuminating and one may well wonder what the point of saying it could be. In truth this way of viewing language initiated nothing less than a revolution in philosophy. For two thousand or more years it was taken for granted that a theory of language was primarily concerned with explaining how a word or sentence could point to something outside itself be it something in the world or something in one's mind. A word pointed to an object and a sentence to a fact. It was the central problem of the *Tractatus* to explain how this was possible. In his "later philosophy" Wittgenstein rejected any and all such attempts to explain language. Language was not to be understood in terms of how it signified something else. The essence of language was to be understood in terms of the role it played in human activities which he called "language games." It is not possible to produce some anaysis which will describe how a mark on a paper or a sound uttered by a human voice is transformed into language, any more than it is possible to say how the movements of the limbs of a human body dance or play a piano. Dancing and playing the piano are human activities that have their meaning in what they are and can not be explained by a description of the motion of muscles or fingers.

This is a very superficial account of Wittgenstein's later philosophy, but there is something this account shares with his earlier one, and that is that there are no rules that stipulate how language comes about. In the *Tractatus*, the sense of a sentence "showed" itself and in the later philosophy, the meaning of an expression was established by the role it plays in human activities, and no rules can determine what these activities are or should be—"This language game is played" (P.I. 654). In neither case nothing outside language can account for it or "explain it." It is what it is an not another thing.

Interestingly enough, this way of seeing language is succinctly expressed very early in a passage Wittgenstein wrote before he finished the *Tractatus*. On the entry for 29/5/15 in the *Notebooks*, the following remarkable passage occurs.

But is *language* the *only* language?

Why should there not be a mode of expression through which I can talk *about* language in such a way that it can appear to me in co-ordination with something else?

Suppose that music were such a mode of expression: then it is at any rate characteristic of *science* that *no* musical themes can occur in it.

I myself only write *sentences* down here. And why?

How is language unique?

In 1948 Wittgenstein told his friend, M.O'C. McDrury, that "his most fundamental ideas come to him very early in life." This is an intriguing remark, and Drury speculates what these ideas might have been, seeing that Wittgenstein revolutionized his thoughts midway in his career. I would choose the above-quoted words from his *Notebooks*, as the most likely candidate which bridges his earlier and later philosophy. Language is an "organic whole," to use a metaphor. But the metaphor fits, for you can analyze an organism by taking it apart but then it is no longer organic or whole. The pieces are in your hand but the creature is dead. The only way to understand this creature is to let it roam around free, observe its habits, how it lives, what it does, etc. So language can be understood only in its actual functioning and no analysis of its parts can explain it much less justify it, as philosophers throughout the ages have attempted to do. In his early period, the sense of a sentence expressed this organic feature of language for no analysis could say how one recognizes it; and in his later philosophy the sphere of human life and action expressed it, for such context is the well-spring and life of all meaningful language.

—Irving Block

WÖLFFLIN, Heinrich. German art historian and aesthetician. Born in Winterthur, Switzerland, 21 June 1864. Studied at the University of Basel, 1882-86; University of Berlin; University of Munich, Ph.D. 1888. Lecturer, 1888-93, and Professor, 1893-1901, University of Basel; Professor of Art History, University of Berlin, 1901-12; Professor of Art History, University of Munich, 1912-24; and after 1924, Professor of Art History, University of Zurich. *Died 19 July 1945.*

PUBLICATIONS

Art and Art History

Prolegomena zu einer Psychologie des Architektur. Munich, Wolf, 1886.
Renaissance und Barock: Eine Untersuchung über Wesen und Entstehung der Barockstils in Italien. Munich, Ackermann, 1888; as *Renaissance and Baroque*, Ithaca, New York, Cornell University Press, 1966.
Salomon Gessner. Frauenfeld, Switzerland, Huber, 1889.
Die Jugendwerke des Michelangelo. Munich, Ackermann, 1891.
Das klassische Kunst: Eine Einführung in die italienische Renaissance. Munich, Bruckmann, 1899; as *The Art of the Italian Renaissance: A Handbook for Students and Travellers*, London, Heinemann, and New York, Putnam, 1903.
Die Kunst Albrecht Dürers. Munich, Bruckmann, 1905; as *The Art of Albrecht Dürer*, London and New York, Phaidon, 1971.
Kunstgeschichtliche Grundbegriffe: Das Problem der Stilentwicklung in der neueren Kunst. Munich, Bruckmann, 1915; as *Principles of Art History: The Problem of the Development of Style in Later Art*, London, Bell, 1932; New York, Dover, 1950.
Die Bamberger Apokalypse: Eine Reichenauer Bilderhandschrift vom Jahre 1000. Munich, Bavarian Academy, 1918.
Das Erklären von Kunstwerken. Leipzig, Seeman, 1921.
Albrecht Dürer (lecture). Darmstadt, Reichl, 1922.
Die Kunst der Renaissance: Italien und das deutsche Formgefühl. Munich, Bruckmann, 1931; as *The Sense of Form: A Comparative Psychological Study*, New York, Chelsea, 1958.
Gedanken zur Kunstgeschichte, Gedrucktes und Ungedricktes. Basel, Schwabe, 1941.
Kleine Schriften (1886-1933), edited by Joseph Gentner. Basel, Schwabe, 1946.

Other

Jacob Burckhardt und Heinrich Wölfflin: Briefwechsel und andere Dokumente ihrer Begegnung, 1892-1897, edited by Joseph Gantner. Basel, Schwabe, 1948.

Editor, *Albrecht Dürer: Handzeichnungen.* Munich, Piper, 1914.
Editor, *Gesamtausgabe*, by Jacob Burckhardt, vols. 3, 4, 6, 13. Basel, Schwabe, 1932-34.

*

Critical Studies: *Schönheit und Grenzen der klassischen Form: Burckhardt, Croce, Wölfflin: Drei Vörtrage* by Joseph Gantner, Vienna, Schroll, 1949; *Heinrich Wölfflin als Literarhistoriker* by Walther Rehm, Munich, Beck, 1960; *Heinrich Wölfflin: Biographie einer Kunsthistorie* by Meinhold Lurz, Worms, Werner, 1981.

*   *   *

Heinrich Wölfflin deserves to be regarded as one of the great founders of modern art history. Born at Winterthur in Switzerland, Wölfflin was raised in a wealthy and educated household. He studied art history and philosophy at Munich, Basel, and Berlin. His own thought was deeply influenced by the concept of the history of culture espoused by the art historian Burckhardt and by the concept of the history of vision described by the sculptor Hildebrand.

In 1886, after completing his doctoral dissertation, Wölfflin embarked on a two-year stay in Italy. The result of his travels was the publication in 1888 of his first major work, *Renaissance and Baroque*. In this volume, Wölfflin for the first time tackled the problem and outlined the method that was to be the primary concern of his scholarship, the establishment of objective criteria in aesthetics by a system of comparative analysis. Wölfflin considered that art had a life and a history of its own only loosely connected with the general culture. While capable of acute observations about individual works of art, Wölfflin did not share the 20th-century view of style as an intellectual abstraction deduced from the study of individual works of art. Rather, he considered style to be a force existing in its own right, independent of individual works. National and period styles, in his view, were the inescapable channels by which individual artists expressed themselves in their specific art works.

1888 also marked the beginning of Wölfflin's career as a popular and influential teacher. He spent 5 years in Munich as a university lecturer before being appointed in 1893 to the Chair of Art History at Basle. Success as a lecturer led to a subsequent appointment to the Chair at Berlin, a post he vacated when he returned to Munich. His lectures attracted large public audiences; his scholarship drew a generation of students to work on doctoral theses under his direction. His influence, which was enormous in Germany, extended to England and the United States at the same time as art history was gaining recognition as a significant academic discipline.

Renaissance and Baroque was succeeded by a second important volume, *The Art of the Italian Renaissance*, which like its predecessor seeks to elucidate a consistent and objective theory of art as the basis for understanding individual art works. However, it is in *Principles of Art History* that Wölfflin developed his theoretical approach in a fully matured form. Here Wölfflin argued that the transformation of Renaissance into Baroque art in the three major media, painting, sculpture, and architecture, had followed a law of evolution. This law of evolution, which was in his view equally applicable to other periods, was illustrated through the juxtaposition of five contrasting visual schemes, each scheme representing the development from one polarity to its antithetical opposite. These schemes, as described by Wölfflin, were: 1.) the development from the linear to the pictoral, by which was meant the change from the delineation of objects in terms of lines to the apprehension of objects in terms of shifting masses; 2.) the development from the vision of the surface to the vision of depth, by which was meant the change from the definition of space in terms of clearly demarcated planes to the comprehension of space in terms of continuous recession; 3.) the development from closed to open form, by which was meant the definition of a representational area that was complete in itself to the suggestion that the representational area extended beyond the borders of the art work; 4.) the development from multiplicity to unity, by which was meant the change from a concept of unity that consisted in the co-ordination of independent elements to a concept of unity that submerged secondary elements to a principal focus; 5.) the development from absolute clearness to relative clearness of objects, by which was meant the change from the consideration of composition, light, and color as being separate elements to the concern for treating them as a single interpenetrating element.

Never an iconographer, Wölfflin sought to write an art history "without names" and was capable of discussing works without mentioning their subjects. His later works became less dogmatic in their adherence to his five schemes and less determined in maintaining the distinction between form and content. If his concept of style, which was indebted to the Hegelian notion of

the will-to form, now seems rigid and limited in its usefulness, nonetheless Wölfflin performed a great service to his field. He purged art history of the anecdotal approach popular in the 19th century and established art history as an intellectually demanding and exciting discipline of modern scholarship.

—Linnea Wren

WOODWARD, C(omer) Vann. American historian. Born in Vanndale, Arkansas, 13 November 1908. Studied at Emory University, Atlanta, Georgia, Ph.B. 1930; Columbia University, New York, M.A. 1932; University of North Carolina, Durham, Ph.D. 1937. Served as a lieutenant in the United States Naval Reserve, 1943-46. Married Glenn Boyd MacLeod in 1937; 1 son. Instructor of English, Georgia School of Technology, 1930-31, 1932-33; Assistant Professor of History, University of Florida, Gainesville, 1937-39; Associate Professor, Scripps College, Claremont, California, 1940-43; Associate Professor, 1946, and Professor, 1947-61, Johns Hopkins University, Baltimore; Sterling Professor of History, 1961-77, and since 1977, Professor Emeritus, Yale University, New Haven, Connecticut. Visiting Assistant Professor, University of Virginia, Charlottesville, 1939-40; Commonwealth Lecturer, University of London, 1954; Harmsworth Professor of American History, Oxford University, 1954-55; Jefferson Lecturer in the Humanities, Yale University, 1978. President, Southern Historical Association, 1952, American Historical Association, 1968-69, and Organization of American Historians, 1968-69. Recipient: Guggenheim Fellowship, 1946, 1960; Bancroft Prize, 1951; National Institute of Arts and Letters Award, 1954; American Council of Learned Societies Prize, 1962. Honorary doctorate: University of North Carolina, 1959; University of Michigan, Ann Arbor, 1971; Princeton University, New Jersey, 1971; Columbia University, 1972; Northwestern University, Evanston, Illinois, 1977; Cambridge University, 1975. Member, National Institute of Arts and Letters; American Academy of Arts and Sciences; British Academy; Royal Historical Society. Address: Hall of Graduate Studies, Yale University, New Haven, Connecticut 06520, U.S.A.

PUBLICATIONS

History

The South in Search of a Philosophy.   Gainesville, University of Florida Press, 1938.
Tom Watson, Agrarian Rebel.   New York, Macmillan, 1938.
The Battle for Leyte Gulf.   New York, Macmillan, 1947; London, Landsborough, 1958.
The Origins of the New South, 1877-1913.   Baton Rouge, Louisiana State University Press, 1951.
Reunion and Reaction: The Compromise of 1877 and the End of Reconstruction.   Boston, Little Brown, 1951.
American Attitudes Toward History (lecture).   Oxford, Clarendon Press, 1955.
The Strange Career of Jim Crow (lectures).   New York, Oxford University Press, 1955.
The Burden of Southern History.   Baton Rouge, Louisiana State University Press, 1960.
The Age of Reinterpretation (lecture).   Washington, Service Center for Teachers of History, 1961.
American Counterpoint: Slavery and Racism in the North-South Dialogue.   Boston, Little Brown, 1971.

Other

Editor, *Cannibals All! or, Slaves without Masters*, by George Fitzhugh.   Cambridge, Massachusetts, Belknap Press, 1960.

Editor, *A Southern Prophecy*, by Lewis H. Blair.   Boston, Little Brown, 1964.
Editor, *After the War: A Tour of the Southern States, 1865-66*, by Whitelaw Reid.   New York, Harper, 1965.
Editor, *The Comparative Approach to American History*.   New York, Basic Books, 1968.
Editor, *Responses of the Presidents to Charges of Misconduct*.   New York, Delacorte Press, 1974.
Editor, *Mary Chesnut's Civil War*, by Mary Boykin Miller.   New Haven, Connecticut, Yale University Press, 1981.

*

Bibliography: in *Region, Race, and Reconstruction: Essays in Honour of C. Vann Woodward* edited by J. Morgan Konsser and James M. McPherson, New York, Oxford University Press, 1982.

Critical Studies: "Origins of the New South in Retrospect" by Sheldon Hackney, in *Journal of Southern History*, 38, 1972; "Southern Democrats and the Crisis of 1876-1877: A Reconsideration of Reunion and Reaction" by Michael Les Benedict, in *Journal of Southern History*, 46, 1980.

*   *   *

C. Vann Woodward has been responsible for a major reinterpretation of the end of Reconstruction as a central policy of the Republican Party and of the restoration of white rule by the so-called "Redeemer" governments in the Southern states after the Civil War. His conclusions grew out of an earlier work on the career of Tom Watson, a major Populist leader, but did not reach maturity until two books published in 1951. In the first, *The Origins of the New South, 1877-1913*, he demonstrated with solid evidence that the white regimes which supplanted the Reconstruction governments in the South were not the work of die-hard planters seeking to restore the pre-war order. These leaders, the so-called "Bourbons," were, in fact entrepreneurs with pre-war Whig affiliations. Although many were also plantation owners, they fully shared the economic aims of northern capitalists and eagerly sought to utilize the state and national governments as instruments to advance special business interests. Nor were these "Redeemer" governments less prone to the wide-scale political corruption which characterized their northern counterparts in the Gilded Age.

Equally significant was Woodward's revelation that the Southern populist movement—an aspect of Populism almost totally neglected by historians who had studied Populism primarily from a midwestern perspective—had constituted a major threat to the pro-business regimes of the Redeemers. Lacking sympathy for the program of the Populists, the Redeemers succeeded, according to Woodward, in defusing the populist movement by raising the spectre of black domination if the Populists should merge with their black counterparts who were also involved in the agrarian protest movement. In the long run the poor whites of the South were betrayed by special interest groups invoking white supremacy. Racial fears made it possible for an oligarchy unfriendly to agrarian aspirations to entrench itself in power. In this work and in subsequent publications Woodward showed that the alliance between the oligarchs and the poor whites resulted in the legal enactment of an increasingly rigid system of segregation and the total exclusion of the black population from the political life of the South.

In *Reunion and Reaction: The Compromise of 1877 and the End of Reconstruction* Woodward examined in detail the circumstances surrounding the Hayes-Tilden disputed election of 1876. He traced the negotiations between the northern Republicans and southern Democrats by which the Democrats agreed to accede to the election of Hayes in return for specific Republican commitments. According to Woodward, the Republicans agreed to the withdrawal of the last federal troops in the South, to support the construction of a trans-continental railroad with a southern terminus and to rebuild the levees along the Mississippi River. The Republicans were all the more willing to abandon Black Reconstruction and the protection of the rights of free blacks, since it was apparent that the southern Democrats no longer constituted a threat to northern economic interests.

Recent monographs have raised questions about Woodward's delineation of the events of 1876 in terms of a specifically formulated compromise. They have noticed that the northern Democrats, anxious to avoid violence should Hayes be elected, were just as deeply involved in the decision. They have also pointed out that there was no absolute consistency in the Southern voting pattern in Congress fully to substantiate his thesis. Critics, too, have noted that he did not give sufficient credence to the Redeemers' profession of loyalty to the values of the Old South and thus gave too narrow an economic interpretation of the restoration of the white rule. However, what Woodward's work has done is to demonstrate beyond question that the post-war Southern leaders, apart from fixed racial attitudes, were not radically different in their economic aspirations from those of their northern counterparts.

—Harry Ammon

WOODWORTH, Robert S(essions).   American psychologist. Born in Belchertown, Massachusetts, 17 October 1869. Studied at Amherst College, Massachusetts, B.A. 1891; Harvard University, Cambridge, Massachusetts, B.A. 1896, M.A. 1897; Columbia University, New York, Ph.D. 1899; universities of Edinburgh, Bonn, and Liverpool. Married Gabrielle Schjöth in 1903; 4 children. Teacher of mathematics, Watertown High School, New York, 1891-93; Instructor in mathematics, Washburn College, Topeka, Kansas, 1893-95; Assistant in Physiology, Harvard Medical School, 1897-98; Instructor in Physiology, University and Bellevue Hospital Medical College, New York, 1899-1902; Demonstrator in Physiology, University of Liverpool, 1902-03; Instructor in Psychology, 1903-05, Adjunct Professor, 1905-09, Professor, 1909-42, and Professor Emeritus, 1942-62, Columbia University. Assistant Editor, *Psychological Index*, 1898-99; Editor, *Archives of Psychology*, 1906-45. President, American Psychological Association, 1914, Psychological Corporation, 1929, and Social Science Research Council, 1931-32. Recipient: Gold Medal, American Psychological Foundation, 1956. Honorary doctorate: Columbia University, 1929; Lake Erie College, Painesville, Ohio, 1934; University of North Carolina, Chapel Hill, 1946; University of Pennsylvania, Philadelphia, 1946; Amherst College, 1951. Member, National Academy of Sciences, and National Institute of Psychology. Fellow, American Academy for the Advancement of Science; New York Academy of Sciences; American Academy of Arts and Sciences; British Psychological Society. *Died 4 July 1962*.

PUBLICATIONS

Psychology

Le Mouvement.   Paris, Doin, 1903.
Elements of Physiological Psychology, with G.T. Ladd.   New York, Scribner, 1911.
Care of the Body.   New York, Macmillan, 1913.
Dynamic Psychology.   New York, Columbia University Press, 1918.
Psychology: A Study of Mental Life.   New York, Holt, 1921.
Contemporary Schools of Psychology.   New York, Ronald Press, 1931; revised edition, 1948.
Adjustment and Mastery: Problems in Psychology.   Baltimore, Williams and Wilkins, 1933.

Experimental Psychology. New York, Holt, 1938; revised edition, with Harold Schlosberg, 1954.
Psychological Issues: Selected Papers. New York, Columbia University Press, 1939.
Heredity and Environment: A Critical Survey of Recently Published Material on Twins and Foster Parents. New York, Social Science Research Council, 1941.
First Course in Psychology, with Mary R. Sheehan. New York, Holt, 1944.

*

Bibliography: in *Psychological Issues: Selected Papers*, 1939.

*   *   *

Robert S. Woodworth dedicated most of his life to the field of psychology, in which he had a long and distinguished career. After completing his Ph.D. under the direction of James Cattell, they both, along with Edward Thorndike, began what was to be known as the "Columbia School" of functionalism. Along with the "Chicago School" of Dewey, Angell, Carr, and Mead, the early 20th-century functionalists concerned themselves with the adaptive properties of various activities of the mind. Their interest was an outgrowth of the structuralism originating in Germany which was later reinterpreted in the United States by William James.

Early in his career, Woodworth worked with George T. Ladd, revising Ladd's book on physiological psychology which was the first text on the subject. Later, Woodworth wrote his own editions to supplement the earlier work. In 1901, he and Thorndike performed their famous experiment on the transfer of training. They demonstrated that, unlike muscle tissue, mental skills are not "strengthened" by repeated use or training; rather, identical elements are the only properties that can be transferred from one learning activity to another. Building on the older theory of "formal discipline," Woodworth said that "a theory of learning must explain the mechanism of transfer, so far as the transfer occurs, and a theory of thinking must intepret the fact that original thought on a new problem uses past experiences with other problems."

To Woodworth, the element that was transferred was not a single sensory quality or a reflex; rather, it was a transfer of concrete performances. If any improvement was observed in a fore-after-test, it was described by him as being irregular, undependable, and seldom as great as the improvement in the particular function trained.

Woodworth believed that memory training showed a greater transfer effect than memory practice and in 1927 he tested this hypothesis. Results showed that while the practice group was only about equal to the control, the training group surpassed both in every test. This clearly demonstrated that while one kind of training, undirected drill, will produce positive or negative transfer in amounts that are always small, another kind, utilizing the same drill material, results in transference whose effects are uniformly large and positive.

Throughout much of his work, Woodworth's functional orientation led him to what he called a dynamic view of psychology, emphasizing the importance of motivation in the understanding of behavior, with such principles as that well-trained patterns may carry with them their own motivation. Woodworth also argued that psychology must consider the individual's own contribution to his behavior, and changed the behaviorist's stimulus-response (S-R) formula to stimulus-organism-response (S-O-R).

Woodworth granted that psychology should be existential, but by that he meant that "it should be tough-minded in its existence on definitely factual data." He did not believe that psychology should be limited to the study of sensations or of the individual as an experiencer. He felt that studying motor behavior was as important as studying the motivation of individuals in terms of their personal history. He defined psychology so that it showed the individual's relationship to biological as well as sociological variables, attempting to take the best from the behaviorist and introspectionist schools without regard for the taboos they set up against using the other's data. He also stressed the study of animal as well as human behavior, integrating biological and psychological data. He said: "The greatest deficiency of behaviorism is that it minimizes the receptive phase of the organism's activity, the process ordinarily called sensation and perception. Behaviorism has either to regard these as motor processes or else to exclude them altogether from the list of the organism's activities."

Woodworth's basic point of view incorporated the notion that psychology has a responsibility to study the dependence of an event in its relationship to the circumstances in which it takes place. This is what he referred to as his dynamic psychology. He therefore was sympathetic to the gestalt psychological approach; however, he warned that gestalt psychology must eventually show "how it can take up into its system the positive findings of sensory analysis, motor analysis, and the analysis of learning." So long as the gestalt school had a negative attitude to the above-mentioned factors, Woodworth felt that it had not completed its job.

Woodworth's dynamic psychology showed how his framework while using the concepts of stimulus and response, and moreover using the notion of total sensory/motor reaction as consisting of a series of response, leaves room for sensory analysis (introspection) and gestalt psychology. His point of view had great sympathy with the various homric psychologists such as McDougall and Freud. However, the difficulty, as he saw it, was "to bring these concepts down to earth so as to let them work along with stimulus and response, set, association, conditioning, learning, and forgetting." Woodworth was committed to the notion that psychology was free to deal with the data of sensation and emotion, as well as with motivation and motor activities, without any fear of violating the principles of the natural sciences.

In addition to his technical work, Woodworth wrote a number of outstanding texts on psychology. His *Contemporary Schools of Psychology* was a widely read analysis of the various schools of thought in the field; likewise, his text *Experimental Psychology* remained the standard book on the field from the time of its publication in 1938 until the early 1950's and the publication of Osgood's equally outstanding book on the subject. In *Experimental Psychology* the author discussed in great depth the nature of memory, feeling, sensation, and thought, as well as various theories regarding each. As had always been Woodworth's leaning, he continued to pay little attention to various schools. In his introduction he says, "I have felt free to incorporate methods and results from any investigator, without regard to his theoretical leanings. He may have hoped to build up factual support for the tenets of his school, but this hope of his is beside the point when the evidence on a particular problem is under consideration."

Woodworth's first major text was *Psychology: A Study of Mental Life*, published in 1921. For a beginning text in psychology this book is extremely broad, covering such topics as reactions, instinct, emotion, thought, feeling, sensation, and intelligence. One of the longest chapters in the book is on imagination; in it Woodworth discusses imagination in both the child and adult.

Throughout his life, Woodworth moved freely throughout the field of psychology, unafraid of crossing boundaries and moving into new territory.

—R.W. Rieber

WORRINGER, Wilhelm (Robert). German art historian and aesthetician. Born in Aachen, 13 January 1881. Studied at the universities of Freiburg, Munich, Berlin, and Bern. Lecturer,

University of Bern, 1909-13; Lecturer, 1913-20, and Professor, 1920-28, University of Bonn; Professor, University of Königsberg, 1928-46; after 1946, Professor, University of Halle. *Died in 1965.*

PUBLICATIONS

Art

Abstraktion und Einfühlung: Ein Beitrag zur Stilpsychologie. Neuwied, Heuser, 1907; as *Abstraction and Empathy: A Contribution to the Psychology of Style,* London, Routledge, and New York, International Humanities Press, 1953.
Lukas Cranach. Munich, Piper, 1912.
Die altedeusche Buchillustration. Munich, Piper, 1912.
Formprobleme der Gotik. Munich, Piper, 1912; as *Form Problems of the Gothic,* New York, Stechert, 1919; as *Form in Gothic,* London, Putnam, 1927.
Künstlerische Zeitfragen. Munich, Bruckmann, 1921.
Die Anfänge der Tafel-Malerei. Leipzig, Insel, 1924.
Ägyptische Kunst, Probleme ihre Wertung. Munich, Piper, 1927; as *Egyptian Art,* London, Putnam, 1928.
Greichentum und Gotik. Munich, Piper, 1928.
Über den Einfluss der angelsächsischen Buchmalerei auf die frühmittelsalterliche Monumentalplastik des Kontinents. Halle, Niemeyer, 1931.
Problematik der Gegenwartskunst. Munich, Piper, 1948.
Fragen und Gegenfragen: Schriften zum Kunstproblem. Munich, Piper, 1956.

Other

Deutsche Jugend und östlicher Geist. Bonn, Cohen, 1924.

Editor, *Festschrift zum sechzigsten Geburtstag von Paul Clemen 31 October 1926.* Bonn, Cohen, 1926.

*   *   *

Wilhelm Worringer transformed his generation's view of art and art history, and made substantial contributions to the theories and practices of modernist art of his day. His major texts, *Abstraction and Empathy* and *Form in Gothic,* forced a re-evaluation of aesthetic ideals and encouraged a more sympathetic reception of non-realist and non-harmonious distortion and abstraction in Egyptian, Far Eastern, Islamic, Gothic, and Northern European art. Worringer's analysis of abstraction significantly affected and furthered expressionist and other modernist theories and practices, and in fact he became a major theorist of expressionist art himself.

Worringer's writings on art are quite metaphysical and comprehensive, and analyze art in terms of the *aesthetic experience* and its role in social life. He employs a sociological perspective which views art in relation to its social context and he interprets successions of styles in terms of varying psychic needs, world views, and social forms. *Abstraction and Empathy* builds on the concept of empathy developed in hermeneutics by Wilhelm Dilthey and on its later application to art by Theodor Lipps, who explained the aesthetic experience as one in which the viewer, responding to the fundamental human need for "happy" self-activation, projects himself empathically into the naturalistically rendered art object. Worringer adds to this his own opposing concept of abstraction in which the contemplating subject, responding to the caprice and confusion of the natural world, seeks visual satisfaction in abstractly rendered works of art.

Worringer claims that naturalistic art offers satisfaction in the appearances and surfaces of life, while abstract art is motivated by a fear of space and "natural" three-dimensional depth, and seeks escape from the confusion of the natural world in the contemplation of abstract forms. He argues that "whereas the precondition for the urge to empathy is a happy pantheistic relationship of confidence between man and the phenomena of the external world, the urge to abstraction is the outcome of a great inner unrest inspired by the phenomena of the outside world." Abstract art thus seeks the tranquil and eternal as opposed to the eternal flux of the natural three-dimensional world. Worringer insists that "the history of art represents an unceasing disputation" between these two tendencies.

Following in the steps of the 19th century art historian and theoretician Alois Riegl, Worringer also appropriated the concept of "artistic revolution," arguing that "the stylistic peculiarities of past epochs are...not to be explained by lack of ability, but by a differently directed volition." Artistic volition (and the resulting work of art) always directs itself toward the satisfaction of the fundamental psychic needs of the individuals in question; thus every style represents "the maximum bestowal of happiness for the humanity that created it." Attempts by later generations to assess the benefit or value of such creations in terms of their *own* later aesthetic criteria are "from a higher standpoint absurdities and platitudes." Thus Worringer moved the concept of "aesthetic volition" into the center of aesthetic theory.

Worringer's re-evaluation of the importance of abstract art and his insistence that the viewer must widen his/her understanding of the respective psychic needs and values made manifest in the myriad artistic volitions of the culture or individuals involved helped to broaden the viewpoints of his contemporaries "to pass beyond a narrowly European outlook" in which the naturalistic or "classic" style was valued above all else. Realizing the dialectical nature of art production (in terms of its historical and cultural relativity), Worringer asserted "the evolutionary history of art is as spherical as the universe, and no pole exists that does not have its counterpole."

Worringer viewed the art of his day as "a confused, complicated formation," reacting against the confusion of modern life. His championing of aesthetic modernism, and especially Expressionism, was thus an ironic cultural protest against the chaos of modern life that he believed engendered insecurity, unrest, and anxiety. Worringer believed that one could attain refuge from the complexities of modern life in the eternalizing and transcendent forms of abstract art. Thus while his theories of abstraction and form in modern art continue to be relevant as a means of characterizing certain types of modern art that abstract from everyday experience and seek repose and tranquility in pure form, his views are not as useful in describing the nature and function of modern art forms which themselves articulate the flux and dynamism of contemporary society.

—Carolyn Appleton/Douglas Kellner

WRIGHT, Frank Lloyd. American architect and theorist. Born in Richland Center, Wisconsin, 8 June 1867. Educated at Second Ward School, 1879-83; studied at the University of Wisconsin School of Engineering, Madison, 1885-87. Married Catherine Lee Tobin in 1889 (divorced), 6 children; lived with Mrs. Mamah Borthwick Cheney, 1909-14; married Miriam Noel in 1915; married Olgivanna Lazovich in 1925, 1 daughter. Worked as a Junior Draftsman for Allen D. Conover, Madison, 1885-87, and for Lyman Silsbee, Chicago, 1887; Assistant Architect, 1888-89, and Head of the Planning and Design Department, 1889-93, Adler and Sullivan, Chicago; in partnership with Cecil Corwin, Chicago, 1893-96; in private practice, Oak Park, Illinois, 1896, and in Chicago, 1897-1909. Travelled abroad, then resumed practice in Spring Green, Wisconsin, 1911, and reopened his Chicago office in 1912. Established office in Tokyo in 1915; worked in California, 1921-24, and established southwestern headquarters, Ocatillo, at Chandler, Arizona, 1928-29; worked on major theoretical studies for Broadacre City from

1933; built Taliesen West, Paradise Valley, near Scottsdale, Arizona, in 1938, and continued to practice in Wisconsin and Arizona, 1938-1959. Recipient: Kenchiko Ho Citation, Royal Household of Japan, 1919; Royal Gold Medal, Royal Institute of British Architects, 1941; Gold Medal, American Institute of Architects, 1949; Gold Medal, American Institute of Architects, Philadelphia Chapter, 1949; Peter Cooper Award, 1949; Centennial Award, *Popular Mechanics*, 1950; Star of Solidarity, City of Venice, 1951; Medici Medal, City of Florence, 1951; Gold Medal, National Institute of Arts and Letters, 1953; Brown Medal, Franklin Institute, 1954; Freedom of the City, Chicago, 1956. Honorary M.A.: Wesleyan University, Middletown, Connecticut, 1939; honorary doctorate: Princeton University, New Jersey, 1947; Florida Southern College, Lakeland, 1950; Yale University, New Haven, Connecticut, 1954; University of Wisconsin, Madison, 1955; University of Wales, Bangor, 1956. Member, National Institute of Arts and Letters, 1949. Honorary Member, Royal Academy of Fine Arts, Brussels, 1927; Berlin Academy of Art, 1929; National Academy of Brazil, 1932; Royal Institute of British Architects, 1941; National Academy of Architects, Uruguay, 1942; National Academy of Architects, Mexico, 1943; National Academy of Finland, 1946; Royal Academy of Fine Arts, Stockholm, 1953. *Died* (in Phoenix, Arizona) *9 April 1959.*

PUBLICATIONS

Architecture and Art

Ausgefuhrte Bauten (designs).   Berlin, Wasmuth, 1911.
The Japanese Print: An Interpretation.   Chicago, Seymour, 1912.
Experimenting with Human Lives.   Chicago, Seymour, 1923.
Modern Architecture (lecture).   Princeton, New Jersey, Princeton University Press, 1931.
Two Lectures on Architecture.   Chicago, American Institute of Architects, 1931.
The Disappearing City.   New York, Payson, 1932; as *When Democracy Builds*, Chicago, University of Chicago Press, 1945; and as *The Living City*, New York, Horizon Press, 1958.
Architecture and Modern Life, with Baker Brownell.   New York and London, Harper, 1937.
An Organic Architecture: The Architecture of Democracy (lecture).   London, Lund Humphries, 1939.
Frank Lloyd Wright on Architecture: Selected Writings 1894-1940, edited by Frederick Gutheim.   New York, Duell, 1941.
Genius and the Mobocracy.   New York, Duell, 1949; London, Secker and Warburg, 1972.
The Future of Architecture.   New York, Horizon Press, 1953; London, Architectural Press, 1955.
The Natural House.   New York, Horizon Press, 1954.
An American Architecture, edited by Edgar Kaufmann.   New York, Horizon Press, 1955.
The Story of the Tower: The Tree That Escaped the Crowded Forest.   New York, Horizon Press, 1956.
A Testament.   New York, Horizon Press, 1957.
Frank Lloyd Wright: Writings and Buildings, edited by Edgar Kaufmann and Ben Raeburn.   New York, Horizon Press, 1960.
Architectural Essays from the Chicago School: Thomas Tallmadge, Louis H. Sullivan, Jens Jenson, and Frank Lloyd Wright.   Park Forest, Illinois, Prairie School Press, 1967.
In the Cause of Architecture: Essays by Frank Lloyd Wright for the Architectural Review 1908-1952, edited by Frederick Gutheim.   New York, Architectural Record, 1975.

Other

Love and Ethics, with Mamah Boulton Borthwick.   Chicago, Seymour, 1912.

An Autobiography.   New York and London, Longman, 1932; revised edition, New York, Duell Sloan, 1943; London, Faber, 1945.

*

Bibliography: *Frank Lloyd Wright: An Annotated Bibliography* by Robert L. Sweeney, Los Angeles, Hennessey and Ingalls, 1978.

Critical Studies: *Frank Lloyd Wright* by Vincent Joseph Scully, New York, Braziller, 1960; *Frank Lloyd Wright: An Interpretive Biography* New York, Harper, 1973, and *Frank Lloyd Wright: His Life and Architecture*, New York, Wiley, 1979, both by Robert C. Twombly; *Writings on Wright: Selected Comment on Frank Lloyd Wright* edited by H.A. Brooks, Cambridge, MIT Press, 1981.

*

For a full listing of Wright's buildings and projects, see *Contemporary Architects*, edited by Muriel Emanuel, London, Macmillan, and New York, St. Martin's Press, 1980.

*   *   *

The architecture of Frank Lloyd Wright is brilliantly innovative in its structures, materials and styles. Too varied to be typified by any single design, Wright's works can, however, be characterized by a life-long concern to create structures which were geometrically ordered, to define spaces which were rhythmic and continuous, and shape man-made forms which were expressive of natural laws. Throughout a career which spanned almost 75 years, Wright repeatedly enunciated his commitment to an organic theory of architecture in which every element should be exploited so as to reveal its inherent color, shape, and structural properties and in which every part should be related to the whole so as to form a structually complete organism.

Wright's formal training was irregular and brief. In 1885 he began work as a draftsman for A.D. Conover and attended classes at the University of Wisconsin at Madison. In 1887 he moved to Chicago where he first was employed in the office of J.L. Silsbee and subsequently entered the firm of Adler and Sullivan. He remained with Sullivan until 1893 and was involved primarily with the design of domestic structures. Of equal importance to his development as an architect were his childhood play experiences with Froebel building blocks and his adolescent work experiences on his uncle's farm in Spring Green, Wisconsin.

Wright's mature style emerged around 1900 and is evident both in his designs for private residences and public buildings. In the Prairie House, as typified by the Ward Willetts House, Highland Park, Illinois (1902), and the later Robie House in Chicago (1909), Wright opened the house outward towards its environment. Built of brick, unplaned wood, and plaster, these houses consist of interlocking spaces which radiate from a central hearth and which extend under long horizontal roof planes into the surrounding landscape. At the same time, Wright faced the public building inward. In order to foster a sense of community space among the workers, Wright designed the interior of the four-story Larkin building, Buffalo (1904), around a glass-roofed central well, while on the exterior he treated the building segments as abstract geometrical units expressive of the interior spaces. The sense of closure and abstraction is continued in Unity Temple, Oak Park, Illinois (1906), one of the first examples in the United States of the use of exposed reinforced concrete.

In 1909 Wright left for Europe in order to prepare the publication of his designs by Ernst Wasmuth. The resultant folio of 100 plates profoundly influenced European design and established Wright as an internationally known architect. Upon his return, Wright sought new directions in his architectural designs. Large-scale works, such as Midway Gardens, Chicago (1914), with its cubistic profile of turrets and terraces arranged on intersecting levels, and the Imperial Hotel, Tokyo (1922), with its system of concrete posts and jointed building sections designed to resist earthquake shocks, illustrate Wright's increasing complexity in plan and spatial organization and his ingenuity in structural terms. Private residences such as the Millard House, Pasadena, California (1921), and the Ennis House, Los Angeles (1923), combine an innovative use of materials—hollow, pre-cast concrete blocks—with a monumental abstract shape.

During the late 1920's and early 1930's, Wright received few commissions and executed a comparatively small number of buildings. Public prominence returned to Wright with the founding of the Taliesin Fellowship, a community of apprentices, in 1929, with the publication of *An Autobiography* in 1932 and, most importantly, with the completion of two spectacular designs, Fallingwater (Kaufmann House), Bear Run, Pennsylvania (1935), and the Johnson Administration Building, Racine, Wisconsin (1936). The exploration of unorthodox shapes, materials, and structural systems, evident in both these designs, continued throughout the last quarter century of Wright's career and can be seen in structures such as Taliesin West, Scottsdale, Arizona (1938), which incorporated a canvas roof supported on redwood trusses; the Johnson Research Tower, Racine, Wisconsin (1944), which is cantilevered from a central core; the Beth Sholom Synagogue, Elkins Park, Pennsylvania (1959), which is based on a 60/30 degree triangle; and the Guggenheim Museum, New York City (1959), which is built as an expanding spiral. Principles of the Prairie House are simultaneously reaffirmed in the designs of the Usonian houses, such as the Jacobs House, Westmoreland, Wisconsin (1936), and the Winkler-Goetsch House, Okemos, Michigan (1939).

Frank Lloyd Wright died in 1959. In his effort to integrate the spatial, structural, and sculptural principles of the modern age with his traditional love of the landscape, Wright drew on many sources including Pre-Columbian, Japanese, Native American, and 19th-century styles of architecture. But in his reshaping of these sources to serve the physical, psychological, and emotional needs of 20th-century man, Wright invented his own highly personal and extremely prolific architectural language.

—Linnea Wren

ADVISERS
AND
CONTRIBUTORS

AMEND, Edward. Essayist. Associate Professor of Religion and Humanities, University of Northern Iowa, Cedar Falls (Director of Individual Studies, 1971-78). Formerly, Pastor, Ascension Lutheran Church, Tulsa. **Essay:** Auerbach.

AMMON, Harry. Essayist. Professor of History, Southern Illinois University, Carbondale, since 1950. Author of *James Monroe: The Quest for National Identity*, 1971, and *Citizen Genet*, 1974. **Essays:** Beard; Pirenne; Stone; Frederick Jackson Turner; Woodward.

ARNETT, Willard E. Essayist. Gillespie Professor of Philosophy, Chatham College, Pittsburgh. Author of *Santayana and the Sense of Beauty*, 1955, *Religion and Judgement*, 1966, and *George Santayana*, 1968; editor of *A Modern Reader in the Philosophy of Religion*, 1966. **Essays:** Langer; Santayana.

BAGLIONE, Frank M. Essayist. Assistant Professor of History, Centenary College of Louisiana, since 1981. Taught at Bridgewater State College, 1980-81. **Essays:** Kautsky; Mattingly; Maurras; Schumpeter; Sellière; Sombart.

BAROLSKY, Paul. Essayist. Associate Professor of Art History, University of Virginia, Charlottesville, since 1969. Author of *Infinite Jest: Wit and Humor in Italian Renaissance Art*, 1978, and *Daniele da Volterra: A Catalogue Raisonné*, 1979. **Essay:** Berenson.

BARRY, Norman P. Essayist. Reader in Politics, University of Birmingham, since 1983. Lecturer, University of Exeter, 1967-69, Queen's University of Belfast, 1969-71, and the Birmingham Polytechnic, 1972-82. Author of *Hayek's Social and Economic Philosophy*, 1979, and *An Introduction to Modern Political Theory*, 1981. **Essays:** Berlin; Dworkin; Hart; Robbins.

BIRD, Randall Davey. Essayist. Graduate Student, Department of the History of Science, Harvard University, Cambridge, Massachusetts, since 1979. Author, with Garland E. Allen, of *A Source Book in the History of Animal Biology 1860-1950*. **Essays:** Beadle; Bernal; Crick; Fleming, Haldane.

BLOCK, Irving. Essayist. Associate Professor of Philosophy, University of Western Ontario, London, since 1964. Editor of *Perspectives on the Philosophy of Wittgenstein*, 1981. **Essay:** Wittgenstein.

BOTEIN, Stephen. Essayist. Associate Professor of History, Michigan State University, East Lansing, since 1977. Author of *Early American Law and Society*, 1983; co-editor of *Experiments in History Teaching*, 1977. **Essay:** Handlin.

BOUCHARD, Donald F. Essayist. Associate Professor of English, McGill University, Montreal, since 1968. Author of *Milton: A Structural Reading*, 1974; editor and translator of *Language, Counter-Memory, Practice: Selected Essays and Interviews* by Michael Foucault, 1977. **Essay:** Foucault.

BOWLT, John E. Essayist. Professor, Department of Slavic Studies and Department of Art History, University of Texas at Austin, since 1971; also, Director of the Institute of Modern Russian Culture at Blue Lagoon, Texas, and New York. Author of *Russian Art of the Silver Age*, 1979, and *Scenic Innovation: Russian Stage Design 1900-1930*, 1982; author, with R.C. Washton Long, of *The Life of Kandinsky in Russian Art*, 1980; and editor of *The Russian Avant-Garde: Theory and Criticism*, 1976. **Essay:** Kandinsky.

BROOKS, Charles I. Essayist. Chairman, Department of Psychology, King's College, Wilkes-Barre, Pennsylvania, since 1975. Author, with others, *Theories of Learning*, 1980. **Essay:** Hull.

BROSIO, Richard A. Essayist. Associate Professor of Secondary and Foundations of Education, Ball State University, Muncie, Indiana, since 1978 (joined faculty, 1972). Author of the monographs, *The Relationship of Dewey's Pedagogy to His Concept of Community*, 1972, and *The Frankfurt School: An Analysis of the Contradictions and Crises of Liberal Capitalist Societies*, 1980. **Essays:** Gramsci; Marcuse.

BYWATER, William. Essayist. Associate Professor of Philosophy, Allegheny College, Meadville, Pennsylvania, since 1974. Author of *Clive Bell's Eye*, 1975. **Essays:** Clive Bell; Stevenson.

CAIN, Seymour. Essayist. Freelance scholar and critic. Member, Editorial Planning Board and Senior Editor for Religion and Philosophy, *Encyclopaedia Britannica*, 1966-73; Visiting Professor in the Humanities, Religion and Philosophy, Tri-College University, 1974-78; National Endowment for the Humanities Fellow, 1979-80. Author of *Religion and Theology*, 1961; *Imaginative Literature*, 2 vols., 1961-62; and *Ethics: The Study of Moral Values*, 1963; translator of *Selected Essays on Political Economy* by Frederick Bastiat, 1964. **Essays:** Marcel; Scholem.

CALIAN, Carnegie Samuel. Essayist. President and Professor of Theology, Pittsburgh Theology Seminary, since 1981. Professor of Theology, University of Dubuque Theological Seminary, Iowa, 1963-81. President, Midwest Division, American Theological Society, 1979-80. Author of *The Significance of Eschatology in the Thoughts of Nicolas Berdyaev*, 1965; *Berdyaev's Philosophy of Hope: A Contribution to Marxist-Christian Dialogue*, 1968; *Icon and Pulpit: The Protestant-Orthodox Encounter*, 1968; *Grace, Guts and Goods: How to Stay Christian in an Affluent Society*, 1971; *The Gospel According to the Wall Street Journal*, 1975; *Today's Pastor in Tomorrow's World*, 1977, 1982; *For All Your Seasons: Biblical Direction Through Life's Passages*, 1979. **Essay:** Berdyaev.

CALLINICOS, Alex. Essayist. Lecturer in Politics, University of York, since 1981. Author of *Althusser's Marxism*, 1976; *Southern Africa after Soweto*, 1977; with John Rogers, *Southern Africa after Zimbabwe*, 1981; *Is There a Future for Marxism?*, 1982; *Karl Marx*, 1983; and *Marxism and Philosophy*, 1983. **Essays:** Althusser; Lenin; Quine; Trotsky.

CAPPS, Donald. Essayist. Professor of Pastoral Theology, Princeton Theological Seminary, New Jersey, since 1981. Editor, *Journal for the Scientific Study of Religion*. Author of *Pastoral Care: A Thematic Approach*, 1979; *Pastoral Counseling and Preaching*, 1980; *Biblical Approaches to Pastoral Counseling*, 1981; and *Life Cycle Theory and Pastoral Care*, 1983; editor of *The Religious Personality* (with Walter H. Capps), 1970; *Psychology of Religion* (with others), 1976; *The Biographical Process* (with Frank E. Reynolds), 1977; and *Encounter with Erikson* (with Walter H. Capps and M. Gerald Bradford), 1977. **Essay:** Erikson.

CARROLL, J.B. Essayist. Professor Emeritus of Psychology, University of North Carolina, Chapel Hill, since 1982 (Kenan Professor of Psychology, 1974-82). Instructor to Professor of Educational Psychology, Harvard Graduate School of Education, Cambridge, Massachusetts, 1949-67; Senior Research Psychologist, Educational Testing Service, Princeton, New Jersey, 1967-74. Author of *The Study of Language*, 1953; *Modern Language Aptitude Test*, 1959; *Language and Thought*, 1964; and *The American Heritage Word Frequency Book* (with P. Davies and B. Richman), 1971; editor of *Language, Thought, and Reality: Selected Writings of Benjamin Lee Whorf*, 1956. **Essays:** Thurstone, Whorf.

CASSIDY, Victor. Essays. Freelance writer and editor, Chicago.   Senior Editor, *Specifying Engineer*, since 1980.   **Essays:** Bettelheim; Brouwer; Hardy; Mao Tse-tung; Merton; Riesman; Simon; Weyl.

CASSILO, Robert.   Essayist.   Professor of English, University of Miami.   **Essay:** Praz.

CHASE, Myrna.   Essayist.   Associate Professor of History, Baruch College of the City University of New York, since 1971.   Assistant Editor, *The Public Interest*, 1969-71.   Author of *Elie Halévy: An Intellectual Biography*, 1980.   **Essays:** Aron; Daniel Bell; Burnham; Halévy.

CLARK, Constance.   Essayist.   Assistant Coordinator, Theatre History Program, American Theatre Association, since 1983.   Instructor, Hunter College, New York, 1977-81, and Davis Center of Performing Arts, City College, New York, 1981-82.   **Essay:** Stanislavsky.

COHEN, Sheldon S.   Essayist.   Professor of History, Loyola University, Chicago, since 1969.   Author of *A History of Colonial Education 1607-1776*, 1974, and *Connecticut's Loyalist Gadfly, The Reverend Samuel Andrew Peters*, 1977; editor of *Canada Preserved*, 1968.   **Essay:** Morison.

COLEMAN, William H.   Essayist.   Associate Professor of Biology, University of Hartford, Connecticut, since 1981 (Assistant Professor, 1971-81).   **Essay:** Jacob.

CONRAD, David R.   Essayist.   Professor of Foundational Studies, College of Education and Social Services, University of Vermont, Burlington, since 1970; also, Co-Director, University of Vermont Center for World Education.   Author of *Education for Transformation: Implications in Lewis Mumford's Ecohumanism*, 1976.   **Essay:** Mumford.

COTTRELL, Robert D.   Essayist.   Professor of French, Ohio State University, Columbus, since 1978.   Author of *Brantôme: The Writer as Portraitist of His Age*, 1970; *Colette*, 1974; *Simone de Beauvoir*, 1975; and *Sexuality/Textuality: A Study of the Fabric of Montaigne's Essais*, 1981; co-author of *Répondez-Moi!*, 1971.   **Essay:** de Beauvoir.

DAVIS, Philip J.   Adviser.   Professor of Mathematics, Brown University, Providence, Rhode Island.

DAVIS, Robert R.   Essayist.   Vice-President and Economics, Harris Trust and Savings Bank, Chicago, since 1981 (International Economist, 1979-81).   Financial Economist, Federal Deposit Insurance Corporation, Washington, D.C., 1977-79.   **Essays:** Friedman; Knight.

de ALMEIDA, Hermione.   Essayist.   Associate Professor of English, University of Miami, since 1981.   Fellow, American Council of Learned Societies, 1981-82, and National Humanities Center, 1982-83.   Author of *Byron and Joyce Through Homer: "Don Juan" and "Ulysses"*, 1981.   **Essay:** Williams.

DEEDY, John.   Essayist.   Consultant and Editor for Claretian Publications, Chicago; American Correspondent, *The Tablet*, London, and *Information Catholiques Internationales*, Paris.   Founding Editor, *The Catholic Free Press*, Worcester, Massachusetts, 1951-59; Editor, *Pittsburgh Catholic*, 1959-67; Managing Editor, *Commonweal*, 1967-78.   Author of *Apologies, Good Friends: An Interim Biography of Daniel Berrigan, S.J.*, 1981, and *The New Nuns*, 1982.   **Essay:** Küng.

DE GENNARO, Angelo A.   Essayist.   Professor of Romance Languages and Philosophy, Loyola Marymount University, Los Angeles, since 1951.   Author of *The Philosophy of Benedetto Croce*, 1961; editor and translator of *Croce: Essays on Marx and*

Russia, 1966.   **Essay:** Croce.

DELANEY, C.F.   Essayist.   Professor of Philosophy, University of Notre Dame, Indiana (Chairman of the Department, 1972-83).   Member of the Executive Committee, American Philosophical Association, 1983-86; President-Elect, American Catholic Philosophical Association, 1984-85.   Author of *Mind and Nature*, 1969, and co-author of *The Synoptic Vision*, 1977; editor of *Rationality and Religious Belief*, 1979; and co-editor of *The Problems of Philosophy*, 1976.   **Essays:** Cohen; Peirce; Rawls.

DEVINE, Patricia.   Essayist.   Journalist in Chicago.   **Essay:** Montessori.

DEVINE, William.   Essayist.   Lawyer and psychologist, El Cerrito, California.   **Essay:** Hilgard.

DUNCAN, Ian.   Essayist.   Member, Creative Writing Program, University of Denver.   Taught at the universities of Palermo, 1979-80, and Rome, 1980-81.   **Essays:** Eisenstein; Stravinsky.

EASTWOOD, Granville.   Essayist.   Governor, Chelsea School of Art, London, since 1963; Member, Editorial Advisory Board, *Industrial Relations Digest*, 1973.   Assistant General Secretary, 1943-58, and General Secretary, 1958-73, Federation of Printing and Kindred Trades Unions (U.K.).   Author of *George Isaacs*, 1952, and *Harold Laski*, 1977.   **Essays:** Laski; Shaw; Temple; the Webbs.

EHRLICH, Leonard H.   Essayist.   Professor of Philosophy and Chairman of the Judaic Studies Program, University of Massachusetts at Amherst (joined faculty, 1956).   Author of *Karl Jaspers: Philosophy as Faith*, 1975.   **Essay:** Jaspers.

ELEVITCH, Bernard.   Essayist.   Associate Professor of Philosophy, Boston University, since 1968.   **Essay:** Brunschvicg.

FISHBURN, Janet Forsythe.   Essayist.   Assistant Professor of Teaching Ministry and Church History, The Theological and Graduate Schools, Drew University, Madison, New Jersey, since 1978.   Author of *The Fatherhood of God and the Victorian Family: The Social Gospel in America*, 1982.   **Essay:** Rauschenbusch.

FISHER, Ronald C.   Essayist.   Associate Professor of Economics, Michigan State University, East Lansing, since 1981 (Assistant Professor, 1976-81).   **Essay:** Arrow.

FLYNN, Thomas R.   Essayist.   Associate Professor of Philosophy, Emory University, Atlanta, since 1982 (Assistant Professor, 1978-82).   Author of *Sartre and Marxist Existentialism: The Test Case of Collective Responsibility*, 1984.   **Essay:** Sartre.

FOTION, N.   Essayist.   Professor of Philosophy, Emory University, Atlanta, since 1970.   Author of *Moral Situations*, 1968.   **Essay:** Searle.

FOWLER, James W.   Essayist.   Professor of Theology and Human Development, and Director of the Center for Faith Development, Candler School of Theology, Emory University, Atlanta, since 1977.   Associate Professor of Applied Theology, Harvard Divinity School, 1969-76.   Author of *To See the Kingdom: The Theological Vision of H. Richard Niebuhr*, 1974; *Stages of Faith*, 1981; and *Becoming Adult, Becoming Christian*, 1984.   **Essay:** H. Richard Niebuhr.

FRIEDMAN, Maurice.   Essayist.   Professor of Religious Studies, Philosophy, and Comparative Literature, San Diego State University, California, since 1973.   Professor of Religion,

Temple University, Philadelphia, 1967-73. Author of *Martin Buber: The Life of Dialogue*, 1955; *Problematic Rebel: Melville, Dostoievsky, Kafka, Camus*, 1963, 1970; *To Deny Our Nothingness: Contemporary Images of Man*, 1967; *Touchstones of Reality: Existential Trust and the Community of Peace*, 1972; *The Hidden Human Image*, 1974; *Martin Buber's Life and Work*, 2 vols., 1982-83; and *The Human Way: A Dialogical Approach to Religion and Human Experience*, 1982; and editor, with Paul Arthur Schilpp, *The Philosophy of Martin Buber*, 1963. **Essay:** Buber.

FRINGS, Manfred S. Essayist. Professor of Philosophy, DePaul University, Chicago, since 1966. Editor, *The Collected Works of Max Scheler*, since 1970. Professor of Philosophy, University of Detroit, 1958-63, and Duquesne University, Pittsburgh, 1963-66. Author of *Max Scheler*, 1965, and *Person und Dasein*, 1969; editor of *Max Scheler: Centennial Essays*, 1974; *Martin Heidegger: Heraklit*, 1979; and *Martin Heidegger: Parmenides*, 1982. **Essay:** Scheler.

GILPIN, George H. Essayist. Associate Professor of English since 1977, and Associate Provost since 1980, University of Miami. Author of *The Strategy of Joy: An Essay on the Poetry of Samuel Taylor Coleridge*, 1972. **Essay:** Williams.

GLENNON, Robert Jerome. Essayist. Professor of Law, Wayne State University, Detroit, since 1977. Author of *Jerome Frank's Impact on American Law: The Iconoclast as Reformer*. **Essay:** Frank.

GLICK, G. Wayne. Essayist. President and Professor of Church History, Bangor Theological Seminary, Maine, since 1978. President, Keuka College, Keuka Park, New York, 1966-74; Director, Moton Center for Independent Studies, Philadelphia, 1975-78. Author of *The Reality of Christianity*, 1967, and *Long Range Planning for Franklin and Marshall College 1960-1970*, 1980. **Essay:** von Harnack.

GODDEERIS, John. Essayist. Professor of Economics, Michigan State University, East Lansing. **Essay:** Tinbergen.

GODSEY, John D. Essayist. Professor of Systematic Theology, Wesley Theological Seminary, since 1968 (Associate Dean, 1968-71). Author of *The Theology of Dietrich Bonhoeffer*, 1960; *Preface to Bonhoeffer*, 1965; and *The Promise of H. Richard Niebuhr*, 1970; editor of *Karl Barth's Table Talk*, 1963, and *Ethical Responsibility: Bonhoeffer's Legacy to the Churches*, 1981. **Essay:** Barth.

GOUINLOCK, James. Essayist. Associate Professor of Philosophy, Emory University, Atlanta, since 1971. Member of the Executive Committee, 1979-82, and President, 1983-86, Society for the Advancement of American Philosophy. Author of *John Dewey's Philosophy of Value*, 1972; editor of *The Moral Writings of John Dewey*, 1976. **Essays:** Dewey; James.

GRAY, Donald P. Essayist. Professor of Religious Studies, Manhattan College, New York, since 1962. Vice-President, The American Tielhard Association for the Future of Man, since 1975. Author of *Where Is Your God?*, 1965; *The One and the Many: Tielhard de Chardin's Vision of Unity*, 1969; *Finding God Among Us*, 1977; *Jesus, The Way to Freedom*, 1979. **Essay:** Tielhard de Chardin.

GRAY, Walter D. Essayist. Associate Professor since 1969, and Chairman of the Department of History since 1980, Loyola University, Chicago (Dean of the Loyola University Rome Center, 1972-74). Author of *The Opposition of the Notables to Napoleon III 1859-1864*, 1959. **Essays:** Marc Bloch; Braudel; Febvre; Goubert.

GREEN, Geoffrey. Essayist. Assistant Professor of English, University of Southern California, Los Angeles, since 1977. Author of *Literary Criticism and the Structures of History: Erich Auerbach and Leo Spitzer*, 1982; editor, with Jackson I. Cope, of *Novel vs. Fiction: The Contemporary Reformation*, 1981. **Essay:** Spitzer.

GUTERMAN, Sonia K. Essayist. Associate Professor, Boston University, since 1982 (Assistant Professor, 1976-82); Senior Scientist, BioTechnica International Inc., since 1983. **Essays:** Delbrück; S. Luria.

GUTIERREZ, Mauricio. Essayist. Associate Professor of Mathematics, Tufts University, Medford, Massachusetts, since 1978. Member, Institute for Advanced Study, Princeton, New Jersey, 1972-73. **Essay:** Hilbert.

GUTTING, Gary. Essayist. Professor of Philosophy, University of Notre Dame (joined faculty, 1959). Author of *The Synoptic Vision: Essays on the Philosophy of Wilfrid Sellars* (with Delaney, Loux and Solomon), 1977, and *Religious Belief and Religious Skepticism*, 1982; editor of *Problems of Philosophy* (with Delaney, Loux and Moore), 1976, and *Paradigms and Revolutions: Appraisals and Applications of T.S. Kuhn's Philosophy of Science*, 1980. **Essay:** Kuhn.

HANDLER, Richard. Essayist. Assistant Professor, Department of Sociology and Anthropology, Lake Forest College, Illinois, since 1979. **Essays:** Benedict; Geertz.

HANDY, Rollo. Essayist. President, Behavioral Research Council, Great Barrington, Massachusetts, since 1976. From Associate Professor of Philosophy and Acting Chairman to Professor and Chairman, Department of Philosophy, 1962-67, and Provost of the Faculty of Educational Studies and Professor of Philosophy, 1967-76, State University of New York at Buffalo. Author of *Methodology of the Behavioral Sciences*, 1964; *Value Theory and the Behavioral Sciences*, 1969; and *The Measurement of Values*, 1970; co-author of *A Current Appraisal of the Behavioral Sciences*, 1964, 1973, and *Useful Procedures of Inquiry*, 1973; co-editor of *Philosophical Perspectives on Punishment*, 1968, *The Behavioral Sciences*, 1968, and *The Idea of God: Philosophical Perspectives*, 1968. **Essay:** Vaihinger.

HARRIS, Dale B. Adviser and essayist. Professor Emeritus of Psychology and Human Development, Pennsylvania State University, University Park, since 1978 (Prof., 1959-78; Head of the Department of Psychology, 1963-68). Editor of *The Concept of Development* (with Faegre and Anderson), 1957; *Child Care and Training*, 8th ed. 1958; and *Children's Drawings as Measure of Intellectual Maturity*, 1963. **Essay:** Gesell.

HARRIS, H.S. Essayist. Professor of Philosophy and Humanities, Glendon College, York University, Toronto, since 1965. Author of *Social Philosophy of Giovanni Gentile*, 1960, and *Hegel's Development*, 2 vols., 1972, 1982; editor and translator of *Gentile: Genesis and Structure of Society*, 1960. **Essay:** Gentile.

HARVEY, Irene G. Essayist. Doctoral student, Paris. Author of *The Economy of Différance*, and *On Derrida and Heidegger*. **Essay:** Derrida.

HAUSDORFF, Don. Essayist. Professor of History and American Studies, College of Staten Island, City University of New York, since 1972. Author of *Literature in America: A Century of Expansion*, 1971, and *Erich Fromm*, 1972. **Essays:** Hugo L. Black; Cardozo; Holmes; Pound; Reich; Skinner; Henry Stack Sullivan.

HAUSER, Gerard A. Essayist. Associate Professor of Speech

Communication since 1973, and Associate Director of the Inter-disciplinary Graduate Program in Humanities since 1975, Pennsylvania State University, University Park. Associate Editor of *Philosophy and Rhetoric*, since 1976. **Essay:** McKeon.

HEARNSHAW, L.S. Essayist. Emeritus Professor of Psychology, University of Liverpool, since 1975 (Professor, 1947-75). President, British Psychological Society, 1955-56. Author of *A Short History of British Psychology*, 1964, and *Cyril Burt, Psychologist*, 1979. **Essays:** Bartlett; Broadbent; Burt; Eysenck; Spearman; Stern.

HEIMS, Steve J. Essayist. Visiting Professor, University of Massachusetts, Boston. Author of *John von Neumann and Norbert Wiener: From Mathematics to the Technologies of Life and Death*, 1980. **Essays:** Lewin; von Neumann; Wiener.

HENLE, Mary. Essayist. Assistant Professor, 1946-48, Associate Professor, 1948-54, and Professor of Psychology, 1954-83, Graduate Faculty, New School for Social Research, New York. President, Eastern Psychological Association, 1981-82. Editor of *Documents of Gestalt Psychology*, 1961; *The Selected Papers of Wolfgang Köhler*, 1971; and *Vision and Artifact*, 1976; co-editor of *Historical Conceptions of Psychology*, 1973. **Essay:** Koffka.

HEXTER, J.H. Adviser. Professor of History, Washington University, St. Louis.

HOLMER, Paul L. Essayist. Noah Porter Professor of Philosophical Theology, Yale University, since 1960. Professor of Philosophy, University of Minnesota, Minneapolis, 1946-60. Author of *Philosophy and the Common Life*, 1959; *Theology and the Scientific Study of Religion*, 1961; *C.S. Lewis: The Shape of His Life and Thought*, 1976; and *The Grammar of Faith*, 1978; editor of *Edifying Discourses* by Kierkegaard, 1964. **Essays:** Feigl; Hägerström; Schlick; von Hügel.

HORNE, Fred. Adviser. Professor of Chemistry, Michigan State University, East Lansing.

HUTCHINSON, Dennis J. Adviser. Peter B. Ritzma Associate Professor in the College and Associate Professor of Law, The University of Chicago, since 1981. Co-Editor, *The Supreme Court Review*, since 1981.

ICE, Jackson Lee. Essayist. Professor of Religion, Florida State University, Tallahassee, since 1974 (Assistant Professor, 1955-63, and Associate Professor, 1963-74). Author of *The Death of God Debate*, 1967; *Das Gott Auferstehe*, 1970; and *Albert Schweitzer: Prophet of Radical Theology*, 1971. **Essay:** Schweitzer.

INGRAM, David. Essayist. Assistant Professor of Philosophy, University of Northern Iowa, Cedar Falls, since 1980. **Essays:** Arendt; Benjamin; Strauss.

INNIS, Robert E. Essayist. University Professor of Philosophy, University of Lowell, Massachusetts, since 1981 (joined faculty, 1969). Author of *Karl Bühler: Semiotic Foundations of Language Theory*, 1982; translator of *The Essential Wittgenstein* by Gerd Brand, 1979. **Essays:** Bühler; Stokes.

IYER, R.N. Essayist. Professor of Political Thought, University of California at Santa Barbara, since 1965. President, Institute of World Culture, Santa Barbara, since 1976. Fellow, St. Antony's College, Oxford, 1956-63. Author of *The Moral and Political Thought of Mahatma Gandhi*, 1973; *The Society of the Future*, 1977; *Parapolitics: Toward the City of Man*, 1979; and *Novus Ordo Seclorum*, 1980; editor of *The Glass Curtain*, 1965. **Essays:** Adler; Fanon; Fromm; Gandhi; Hohfeld; Hor-

ney; Hulme; Hutchins; Inge; Lecomte du Noüy; Maslow; Mills; Mosca; Plamenatz; Sorokin; Strawson; Tawney; Veblen.

JOHANNES, James M. Essayist. Associate Professor of Economics, Michigan State University, East Lansing, since 1981 (Assistant Professor, 1978-80). **Essay:** Klein.

JOHANSEN, J. Dines. Essayist. Professor of General and Comparative Literature at Odense University, Denmark, since 1976. Author of *Novelleteori efter 1945*, 1970; *Om fortolknings-situationen*, 1972; *Psykoanalyse, litteratur, tekstteori*, 1977; and *Hvalerne venter. Studier i Klaus Rifbjergs forfatterskab*, 1981; editor of *Dansk kortprosa*, 1970-71; *Danish Semiotics* (with M. Nojgaard), 1979; and *Jürgen Habermas: Teorier om samfund og sprog* (with J. Glebe-Moller), 1981. **Essays:** Habermas; Hjelmslev.

JOHNSTON, Jill. Essayist. Freelance writer and journalist, New York City. Critic, *Artnews*, New York, 1959-65; Columnist, *Village Voice*, New York, 1959-80. Author of *Marmalade Me*, 1971; *Lesbian Nation*, 1973; *Gullibles Travels*, 1974; and *Mother Bound*, 1983. **Essay:** Cage.

JORDAN, Michael C. Essayist. Assistant Professor of English, College of St. Thomas, St. Paul, Minnesota, since 1982. **Essays:** Ingarden; Iser.

JORGENSEN, Marian. Essayist. Teacher of academically gifted, Brockton, Massachusetts, since 1973; Professor of English, Massasoit College, Brockton, since 1980. **Essay:** R. Buckminster Fuller.

KAMINSKY, Jack. Essayist. Professor of Philosophy, State University of New York at Binghamton, since 1961 (Assistant Professor, 1953-57; Associate Professor, 1957-61; Chairman of the Department of Philosophy, 1953-65). Author of *Logic and Language* (with B.F. Huppe), 1956; *Hegel on Art*, 1962; *Language and Ontology*, 1969; *Logic: A Philosophical Introduction* (with Alice R. Kaminsky), 1974; *Essays in Linguistic Ontology*, 1982. **Essay:** Max Black.

KASINITZ, Philip. Essayist. Adjunct Instructor in Sociology, New York University. **Essays:** Oscar Lewis; Wirth.

KEGLEY, Charles W. Essayist. Professor of Philosophy, California State College, Bakersfield, since 1970. Founder-Editor, *The Library of Living Philosophy*, since 1956. Author of *Protestantism in Transition*, 1965; *Religion, Politics and Modern Man*, 1969; *Religion in Modern Life*, 1969; *Introduction to Logic* (with Jacquelyn Ann K. Kegley), 1978; *The Theology of Paul Tillich*, 1982; *Reinhold Niebuhr: His Religious, Social and Political Thought*, 1983. **Essay:** C.S. Lewis.

KEGLEY, Jacquelyn Ann K. Essayist. Professor of Philosophy, California State College, Bakersfield, since 1981 (Associate since 1977). Author, with Charles W. Kegley, *Introduction to Logic*, 1978; editor of *The Doctrine of Interpretation*, 1978; *A New Challenge to the Educational Dream: The Handicapped*, 1980; and *The Humanistic Delivery of Services to Families in a Changing and Technological Age*, 1982. **Essay:** Austin.

KELLING, George W. Essayist. Consultant and writer, New York, since 1981. Assistant Professor of Psychology, Barnard College, Columbia University, New York, 1972-81. Author of *Language: Mirror, Tool and Weapon*, 1975, and *Blind Mazes: A Study of Love*, 1979. **Essays:** Allport; Binet; Bruner; Goffman; Laing; Rogers; Sapir.

KELLNER, Douglas. Essayist. Associate Professor of Philosophy, University of Texas at Austin, since 1979 (Assistant Professor, 1973-79). Author of *Karl Korsch: Revolutionary*

Theory, 1977; editor, with Stephen Bronner, of *Passion and Rebellion: The Expressionist Heritage*, 1982. **Essays:** Ernst Bloch; Guevera; Korsch; Worringer.

KITAGAWA, Joseph M. Essayist. Professor of the History of Religions, Divinity School and Department of Far Eastern Languages and Civilizations, University of Chicago, since 1964 (joined faculty, 1951; Dean of the Divinity School, 1970-80). Co-Editor, *History of Religions*, since 1961. President, American Society for the Study of Religion, 1969-72. Author of *Religions of the East*, 1960, 1968; *Gibt es ein Verstehen fremder Religionen*, 1963; and *Religion in Japanese History*, 1966; editor of *The Comparative Study of Religions* by J. Wach, 1958; *The History of Religions: Essays in Methodology* (with M. Eliade), 1959; *The History of Religions: Essays on the Problem of Understanding*, 1967; *Understanding and Believing* by J. Wach, 1968; *Folk Religion in Japan* by I. Hori (with A.L. Miller), 1968; *Myths and Symbols: Studies in Honor of M. Eliade* (with C.H. Long), 1969; and *Understanding Modern China*, 1969. **Essays:** Eliade; Otto; Suzuki.

KLEIN, Philip. Adviser. Professor of Economics, Pennsylvania State University, University Park.

KLEMKE, E.D. Essayist. Professor of Philosophy, Iowa State University, Ames, since 1976 (Associate Dean, 1974-76). Professor and Chairman, Department of Philosophy, Roosevelt University, Chicago, 1964-74. Author of *The Epistemology of G.E. Moore*, 1969; *Reflections and Perspectives: Essays in Philosophy*, 1974; and *Studies in the Philosophy of Kierkegaard*, 1976; editor of *Essays on Frege*, 1968; *Studies in the Philosophy of G.E. Moore*, 1969; *Essays on Bertrand Russell*, 1970; *Essays on Wittgenstein*, 1971; *Readings in Semantics* (with Jacobson and Zabeeh), 1974; *Introductory Readings in the Philosophy of Science* (with Hollinger and Kline), 1980; *The Meaning of Life*, 1981; *Philosophy: The Basic Issues* (with Hollinger and Kline), 1981; and *Contemporary Analytic and Linguistic Philosophies*, 1982. **Essays:** Moore; Russell.

KOCKELMANS, Joseph J. Essayist. Professor of Philosophy since 1968, and Director of the Interdisciplinary Graduate Program in the Humanities since 1973, Pennsylvania State University, University Park. Author of *Martin Heidegger*, 1965; *Phenomenology and Physical Science*, 1966; *Edmund Husserl's Phenomenological Psychology*, 1967; *A First Introduction to Husserl's Phenomenology*, 1967; *The World in Science and Philosophy*, 1969; and *Letter on Humanism: Introduction and Commentary to Heidegger's Text*, 1973; editor of *Phenomenology*, 1967; *Philosophy of Science: The Historical Background*, 1968; *Phenomenology and the Natural Sciences*, 1970; *On Heidegger and Language*, 1972; *Contemporary European Ethics*, 1972; *Interdisciplinarity and Higher Education*, 1979; and *The Challenge of Religion*, 1982. **Essays:** Bachelard; Bonhoeffer; Heidegger; Husserl; Merleau-Ponty.

KOLENDA, Konstantin. Essayist. Carolyn and Fred McManis Professor of Philosophy, Rice University, Houston, since 1975 (Chairman of the Department of Philosophy, 1968-75). Author of *The Freedom of Reason*, 1964; *Ethics for the Young*, 1972; *Philosophy's Journey*, 1974; *Religion Without God*, 1976; and *Philosophy in Literature*, 1981. **Essay:** Malcolm.

KOZULIN, Alex. Essayist. Senior Lecturer, Department of Behavioral Sciences, Ben-Gurion University, Beer-Sheva, Israel, since 1982. Author of *Psychology in Utopia*, 1983. **Essay:** Alexander Luria.

KURTZ, Paul. Essayist. Professor of Philosophy, State University of New York at Buffalo, since 1965. Chairman, Committee for the Scientific Investigation of Claims of the Paranormal, since 1976; Editor, *Free Inquiry* magazine, since 1980. Editor,

The Humanist, 1967-78. Author of *Decision and the Condition of Man*, 1968; *The Fullness of Life*, 1973; and *Exuberance*, 1977; editor of *American Thought Before 1900*, 1966; *American Philosophy in the Twentieth Century*, 1966; *Sidney Hook and the Contemporary World: Essays on the Pragmatic Intelligence*, 1968; and *Sidney Hook: Philosopher of Democracy and Humanism*, 1983. **Essay:** Hook.

LANGE, John. Essayist. Professor of Philosophy, Queens College, City University of New York, since 1974 (joined faculty, 1964). Author of *The Cognitivity Paradox: An Inquiry Concerning the Claims of Philosophy*, 1970; editor of *Values and Imperatives: Studies in Ethics* by C.I. Lewis, 1969. **Essay:** C.I. Lewis.

LAWRENCE, Nathaniel. Essayist. Professor of Philosophy, Williams College, Williamstown, Massachusetts, since 1960. Author of *Whitehead's Philosophical Development*, 1956, and *Alfred North Whitehead: A Primer of His Philosophy*, 1974. **Essay:** Whitehead.

LEAF, Murray J. Essayist. Professor of Anthropology and Political Economy, University of Texas, Richardson, since 1981 (Associate Professor, 1975-81). Author of *Information and Behavior in a Sikh Village*, 1972; and *Man, Mind and Science: A History of Anthropology*, 1979; editor of *Frontiers of Anthropology*, 1974. **Essays:** Boas; Evans-Pritchard; Fortes; Lévy-Bruhl; Kroeber; George Herbert Mead; Parsons; Radcliffe-Brown; W.I. Thomas.

LEARY, David E. Essayist. Co-Director of the History and Theory of Psychology Program since 1977, and Associate Professor of Psychology and the Humanities since 1981, University of New Hampshire, Durham (Assistant Professor, 1977-81). Editor, with Sigmund Koch, of *A Century of Psychology as Science: Retrospections and Assessments*, 1982. **Essay:** Toulmin.

LEHE, Robert T. Essayist. Assistant Professor of Philosophy, North Central College, Naperville, Illinois. **Essay:** Broad.

LeMAHIEU, D.L. Essayist. Associate Professor of History, Lake Forest College, Illinois, since 1974. Author of *The Mind of William Paley: A Philosopher and His Age*, 1976. **Essay:** McLuhan.

LINDSAY, R. Bruce. Essayist. Hazard Professor of Physics Emeritus, Brown University, Providence, Rhode Island, since 1971 (Hazard Professor, 1936-71; Chairman of the Department of Physics, 1934-54; Dean of the Graduate School, 1954-66). Editor-in-Chief, Acoustical Society of America, since 1957. Author of *Acoustics* (with G.W. Stewart), 1930; *Physical Mechanics*, 1933, 3rd ed. 1961; *Foundations in Physics* (with H. Mergenau), 1936; *General Physics for Students of Science*, 1940; *Physical Statistics*, 1941; *Handbook of Elementary Physics*, 1943; *Concepts and Methods of Theoretical Physics*, 1951; *Mechanical Radiation*, 1960; *The Role of Science in Civilization*, 1963; *The Nature of Physics*, 1968; *Lord Rayleigh: The Man and His Work*, 1970; *Basic Concepts of Physics*, 1971; and *Julius Robert Mayer: Prophet of Energy*, 1973; editor of *Acoustics: Its Historical and Philosophical Development*, 1973; *Physical Acoustics*, 1974; *Energy-Historical Development of the Concept*, 1975; *Applications of Energy: Nineteenth Century*, 1976; *The Control of Energy*, 1977; and *Energy in Atomic Physics 1925-1960*, 1983. **Essays:** Bohr; Bridgman; Heisenberg; Kramers.

LINNEKIN, Jocelyn. Essayist. Assistant Professor of Sociology and Anthropology, Lake Forest College, Illinois, since 1982. Instructor in Anthropology, Roosevelt University, Chicago, 1976-81. **Essays:** Raymond Firth; Margaret Mead; Sahlins.

LUCHINS, Abraham S.   Essayist.   Member of the Psychology Faculty, State University of New York at Albany.   **Essay:** Wertheimer.

LYON, Christopher.   Essayist.   Art Critic, *Chicago Sun-Times*, since 1982; Arts Editor, St. James Press, Chicago, since 1982. Editor of *Films and Filmmakers*, 4 vols., 1983-84.   **Essay:** Fry.

MAIER, Henry W.   Essayist.   Professor, School of Social Work, University of Washington, Seattle, since 1963.   Author of *Group Work as Part of Residential Treatment*, 1965, and *Three Theories of Child Development*, 1978.   **Essay:** Piaget.

MARTIN, Stephen.   Essayist.   Assistant Professor of Economics, Michigan State University, East Lansing, since 1977. **Essay:** Samuelson.

MARTY, Martin E.   Adviser.   Fairfax M. Cone Distinguished Service Professor of the History of Modern Christianity, University of Chicago (joined faculty, 1963).   Associate Editor, *The Christian Century*; Editor, *Context*; Co-Editor, *Church History*. Past President, American Society of Church History, and the American Catholic Historical Association.   Author of *Righteous Empire*; *A Cry of Absence*; *Modern American Religion*; etc.

MASSING, J.M.   Essayist.   Fellow, King's College, Cambridge; Lecturer in the History of Art, Cambridge University, since 1977.   **Essay:** Gombrich.

MATILAL, B.K.   Essayist.   Spalding Professor of Eastern Religions and Ethics, Oxford University, and Fellow of All Souls College, Oxford, since 1976.   Associate Professor, 1968-70, and Professor, 1971-76, University of Toronto.   Author of *Epistemology, Logic and Grammar in Indian Philosophical Analysis*, 1971; *Logical and Ethical Issues of Religious Belief*, 1982; etc.   **Essays:** Dasgupta; Radhakrishnan.

MAUNER, George.   Essayist.   Professor of Art History, Pennsylvania State University, University Park.   **Essay:** Schapiro.

McCAULIFF, C.M.A.   Essayist.   Assistant District Attorney of New York County since 1982.   Assistant Professor of Law, Washington and Lee University School of Law, 1979-82.   **Essay:** Maitland.

McCURDY, Harold G.   Essayist.   Kenan Professor of Psychology Emeritus, University of North Carolina at Chapel Hill, since 1971 (Assoc. Prof. to Kenan Professor, 1948-71).   Author of *A Straw Flute* (poetry), 1946; *The Personality of Shakespeare*, 1953; *The Personal World*, 1961; *Personality and Science*, 1965; *Barbara* (with Helen Follett), 1966; *The Chastening of Narcissus* (poetry), 1970; *Novus Ordo Seclorum* (poetry, 1981); and *And Then The Sky Turned Blue* (poetry), 1982.   **Essay:** McDougall.

McMURRIN, Sterling M.   Essayist.   E.E. Erickson Distinguished Professor of Philosophy and History, University of Utah, Salt Lake City, since 1948.   United States Commissioner of Education, 1961-62. Author of *Religion, Reason, and Truth*, 1982, and of a revision of B.A.G. Fuller's *Philosophy of History*, 1954; editor of *Contemporary Philosophy*, 1955; *On the Meaning of the University*, 1976; and *The Tanner Lectures on Human Values*, 4 vols., 1980-83.   **Essay:** Blanshard.

MILNER, Chris.   Essayist.   Lecturer in Economics, Loughborough University of Technology, since 1979.   Lecturer in Economics, Leicester Polytechnic, 1973-78.   Author, with D. Greenaway, of *An Introduction to International Economics*, 1979.   **Essay:** Leontief.

MINK, Louis O.   Essayist.   Professor of Philosophy since 1965, and Kenan Professor of Humanities since 1979, Wesleyan University, Middletown, Connecticut, (Senior Tutor, College of Social Studies, 1959-81; Director of the Center for the Humanities, 1981-83).   Associate Editor, *History and Theory*, since 1965.   Author of *Mind, History and Dialectic: The Philosophy of R.G. Collingwood*, 1969, and *A Finnegans Wake Gazetteer*, 1978.   **Essay:** Collingwood.

MORAWSKI, J.G.   Essayist.   Assistant Professor of Psychology, Wesleyan University, Middletown, Connecticut, since 1980.   **Essays:** Murphy; Terman.

MOSTOW, Joshua S.   Essayist.   Graduate Student, Comparative Literature and Literary Theory Program, University of Pennsylvania, Philadelphia.   Editor and translator of *Language as Process: The Selected Writings of Sergej Karcevskij*, 1983.   **Essay:** Karcevskij.

MUNRO, C. Lynn.   Essayist.   Director of the American Culture Program, University of Missouri, Kansas City, since 1981. Assistant Professor of American Studies, Kendall College, 1977-81.   Author of *The Galbraithian Vision: The Cultural Criticism of John Kenneth Galbraith*, 1977.   **Essay:** Galbraith.

NEISSER, Ulric.   Essayist.   Robert W. Woodruff Professor of Psychology, Emory University, Atlanta, since 1983.   Professor of Psychology, Cornell University, Ithaca, New York, 1967-83.   Author of *Cognitive Psychology*, 1967, and *Cognition and Reality*, 1976; editor of *Memory Observed: Remembering in Natural Contexts*, 1982.   **Essay:** Gibson.

NELSON, Cary.   Essayist.   Director of the Unit for Criticism and Interpretive Theory since 1981, and Professor of English since 1982, University of Illinois, Urbana-Champaign (Assistant Professor, 1970-75, and Associate Professor, 1975-82).   Author of *The Incarnate World: Literature as Verbal Space*, 1973, and *Our Last First Poets: Vision and History in Contemporary American Poetry*, 1981.   **Essay:** Sontag.

NEU, Jerome.   Essayist.   Professor of Philosophy, University of California at Santa Cruz, since 1972.   Author of *Emotion, Thought, and Therapy*, 1977.   **Essay:** Hampshire.

NEWTON, David.   Essayist.   Visiting Professor of Science Education, Western Washington University, Bellingham, since 1980.   Assistant Professor, 1969-72, Associate Professor, 1972-76, and Professor of Chemistry, 1976-83, Salem State College, Massachusetts.   Author of *Man and the Physical World*, 1959; *Science Skills*, 1961; *Chemistry Problems*, 1962; *Guidelines in Chemistry*, 1965; *Nutrition Today*, 1973; *Understanding Venereal Disease*, 1973, 1978; *Science and Society*, 1974; *General Science Casebook*, 1974; *Biological Casebook*, 1974; *Math in Everyday Life*, 1975; *The Chemistry of Carbon*, 1980; etc. **Essays:** Arrhenius; Lawrence and William Bragg; Bronsted; de Broglie; Debye; Eddington; Fermi; Hoyle; Hubble; Jeans; Kendrew; Krebs; Gilbert Newton Lewis; Monod; Oparin; Oppenheimer; Pauli; Pauling; Perutz; Planck; Rutherford; Townes; J.D. Watson; Wigner.

NOZICK, Martin.   Essayist.   Executive Officer, Ph.D. Program in Spanish, Graduate School of the City University of New York (formerly, Professor of Spanish, Queens College, CUNY). Author of *The Generation of 1898 and After*, 1962; *Spanish Literature 1700-1900*, 1972; *Spanish Literature after the Civil War*, 1974; and *Miguel de Unamuno: The Agony of Belief*, 1982; co-editor of *Selected Works of Miguel de Unamuno*, 7 vols. **Essays:** de Unamuno; Ortega y Gasset.

OBST, Norman P.   Essayist.   Associate Professor of Economics, Michigan State University, East Lansing, since 1977 (Assistant Professor, 1973-76).   **Essay:** Fisher.

O'CONNOR, David.   Essayist.   Assistant Professor of Philosophy, Seton Hall University, New Jersey, since 1980.   Author of *The Metaphysics of G.E. Moore*, 1982.   **Essays:** Bergson; Gilson; Maritain; Morris.

PARISER, David A.   Essayist.   Assistant Professor since 1978, and Chairman of the Department of Art Education, Concordia University, Montreal.   **Essay:** Arnheim.

PAULSON, Stanley L.   Essayist.   Associate Professor of Philosophy, Washington University, St. Louis, since 1978.   **Essay:** Kelsen.

PETERS, Eugene H.   Essayist.   Professor of Philosophy, Hiram College, Ohio, since 1962.   Author of *The Creative Advance*, 1966, and *Hartshorne and Neoclassical Metaphysics*, 1970.   **Essay:** Hartshorne.

POIS, Robert A.   Essayist.   Professor of History, University of Colorado, Boulder, since 1975 (Assistant Professor, 1965-71, Associate Professor, 1971-75).   Author of *Friedrich Meinecke and German Politics in the 20th Century*, 1972; *The Bourgeois Democrats of Weimar Germany*, 1976; and *Emil Nolde*, 1982; editor of *Alfred Rosenberg: Selected Writings*, 1970.   **Essays:** Huizinga; Meinecke; Spengler.

POMPER, Philip.   Essayist.   Professor of History since 1976, and Chairman of the Department of History since 1981, Wesleyan University, Middletown, Connecticut (joined faculty, 1964).   Author of *The Russian Revolutionary Intelligentsia*, 1970; *Peter Lavrov and the Russian Revolutionary Movement*, 1972; and *Sergei Nechaev*, 1979.   **Essay:** McNeill.

PRESLEY, John R.   Essayist.   Reader in Economics, Loughborough University (Lecturer, 1969-76, and Senior Lecturer, 1976-81).   Senior Economic Adviser, Saudi Arabia Ministry of Planning, and Consultant Economist, Saudi British Bank, 1979.   Author of *European Monetary Integration* (with P. Colley), 1971; *Currency Areas: Theory and Practice* (with G. Dennis), 1976; and *Robertsonian Economics*, 1978; editor of *Pioneers of Modern Economics in Britain* (with D. O'Brien), 1981.   **Essays:** Hicks; Robertson.

PROCHILO, Michael I.   Essayist.   Associate Professor of English, Salem State College, Massachusetts, since 1965.   **Essay:** Bernstein.

PYCIOR, Helena M.   Essayist.   Associate Professor, Department of History, University of Wisconsin, Milwaukee, since 1982 (Assistant Professor, 1977-82).   **Essays:** Gödel; Noether.

QUALTER, Terence H.   Essayist.   Professor of Political Science, University of Waterloo, Ontario, since 1968 (joined faculty, 1960; Chairman of the Political Science Department, 1963-66, 1966-70).   Author of *Propaganda and Psychological Warfare*, 1962; *The Election Process in Canada*, 1970; and *Graham Wallas and the Great Society*, 1980.   **Essay:** Wallas.

RAJCMAN, John.   Essayist.   Professor, Center for the Humanities, Wesleyan University, Middletown, Connecticut.   **Essay:** Lacan.

REDFIELD, James.   Adviser and essayist.   Professor, Committee on Social Thought, University of Chicago.   **Essays:** Gernet; Lévi-Strauss; Park; Redfield; Vernant.

RIEBER, R.W.   Essayist.   Professor, John Jay College of Criminal Justice, New York.   **Essays:** Boring; Anna Freud; Goldstein; Harlow; Hebb; Jung; Köhler; Lashley; Mowrer; Murray; Osgood; Titchener; Vygotsky; J.B. Watson; Woodworth.

RINGER, Alexander L.   Essayist.   Professor of Musicology, University of Illinois, Urbana-Champaign, since 1963 (Associate Professor, 1958-63).   Founder and First Editor, *Yearbook of the International Folk Music Council*.   Author of *A Language of Feeling: Music in 19th Century Europe*, and *Arnold Schoenberg und seine Zeit*.   **Essay:** Schoenberg.

ROBERTS, Richard C.   Essayist.   Chairman of the Department of Mathematics and Computer Science, University of Maryland Baltimore County, Catonsville, since 1982 (Chairman and Dean, Division of Math and Physics, 1966-79; Professor of Mathematics, 1979-82).   **Essay:** Turing.

ROUSE, Martin F.   Essayist.   Research Associate, Center for Applied Social Science Research, New York, since 1982.   **Essays:** Castaneda, Westermarck.

RUSE, Michael.   Essayist.   Professor, Departments of History and Philosophy, University of Guelph, Ontario, since 1974 (joined faculty, 1965).   Author of *The Philosophy of Biology*, 1973; *Sociobiology: Sense or Nonsense?*, 1979; *The Darwinian Revolution: Science Red in Tooth and Claw*, 1979; *Is Science Sexist? And Other Problems in the Bio-Medical Sciences*, 1981; and *Darwinism Defended: A Guide to the Evolution Controversies*, 1982; editor of *Nature Animated*, 1982.   **Essays:** Dobzhansky; Morgan; Nagel; Steiner; Wilson.

RUSSO, John Paul.   Essayist.   Professor and Chairman, Department of English, University of Miami, since 1982.   Professor, Rutgers University, New Jersey, 1978-82.   Author of *Alexander Pope: Tradition and Identity*; editor of *Complementarities: Uncollected Essays by I.A. Richards*.   **Essays:** Busoni; McTaggart; Richards.

SAMPSON, Geoffrey.   Essayist.   Reader, University of Lancaster, since 1976.   Author of *The Form of Language*, 1975; *Liberty and Language*, 1979; *Making Sense*, 1980; and *Schools of Linguistics*, 1980.   **Essays:** Bloomfield; Chomsky; de Saussure; Einstein; J. Firth; Jesperson; Jakobson; Lakatos; Malinowski; von Hayek.

SAMUELS, Warren J.   Essayist.   Professor of Economics, Michigan State University, East Lansing, since 1968.   Editor, *Research in the History of Economic Thought and Methodology*, since 1982.   Editor, *Journal of Economic Issues*, 1971-81.   President, History of Economics Society, 1981-82.   Author of *The Classical Theory of Economic Policy*, 1966; *Pareto on Policy*, 1974; and *Law and Economics* (with Schmid), 1981; editor of *Taxing and Spending Policy* (with Wade), 1980; *The Methodology of Economic Thought*, 1980; etc.   **Essays:** Frisch; Keynes; Kuznets; Mitchell; Myrdal; Robinson.

SCHARLEMANN, Robert P.   Essayist.   Commonwealth Professor of Religious Studies, University of Virginia, Charlottesville, since 1981.   Associate Professor, 1966-68, and Professor of Religion, 1968-81, University of Iowa, Iowa City.   Author of *Thomas Aquinas and John Gerhart*, 1964; *Reflection and Doubt in the Thought of Paul Tillich*, 1969; and *The Being of God: Theology and the Experience of Truth*, 1981.   **Essay:** Tillich.

SCHMID, Anne-Françoise.   Essayist.   Professor at L'Ecole Polytechnique Fédérale de Lausanne, Switzerland, since 1980.   Author of *Une philosophie de savant: Henri Poincaré et la logique mathématique*, 1978.   **Essay:** Poincaré.

SCHREITER, Robert J.   Essayist.   Dean of the Catholic Theological Union in Chicago, since 1977.   **Essay:** Schillebeeckx.

...ZE, Lark. Essayist. Law Clerk to Federal District ...piegel, Southern District of Ohio, since 1982. Teacher in ...ous Ohio colleges, 1972-82. **Essay:** Frankfurter.

SCOTT, William T. Essayist. Professor Emeritus of Physics, University of Nevada, Reno, since 1981 (Professor, 1961-81). Author of *The Physics of Electricity and Magnetism*, 1959, 3rd ed. 1977, and *Erwin Schrödinger: An Introduction to His Writings*, 1967. **Essay:** Polanyi.

SEBEOK, Thomas F. Adviser. Distinguished Professor of Linguistics and Semiotics, Indiana University, Bloomington, since 1978 (joined faculty, 1943). President, Linguistic Society of America, 1975; President, Semiotic Society of America, 1984.

SEGAL, Daniel Alan. Essayist. Graduate Student, Department of Anthropology, University of Chicago. **Essays:** Bateson; Victor Turner.

SHEEHAN, Thomas. Essayist. Professor of Philosophy, Loyola University, Chicago (joined faculty, 1972). Author of *Karl Rahner: The Philosophical Foundations*, 1983; editor of *Heidegger: The Man and the Thinker*, 1981. **Essay:** Rahner.

SHEPARD, Harvey. Essayist. Professor of Physics, University of New Hampshire, Durham, since 1979 (Assistant and Associate Professor, 1969-79). Member, Institute for Advanced Study, Princeton, New Jersey, 1977. **Essays:** Feynman; Gell-Mann; Schwinger.

SHERMAN, Franklin. Essayist. Professor of Christian Ethics since 1966, and Dean of the Faculty since 1979, Lutheran School of Theology at Chicago. Tutor and Dean of Lutheran Students, Mansfield College, Oxford, 1961-66. Author of *The Promise of Heschel*, 1970; editor of *Christian Hope and the Future of Humanity*, 1969, and the American Edition of *Luther's Works*, vol. 47, 1971; translator of *Paul Tillich: The Socialist Decision*, 1977. **Essay:** Heschel.

SHULL, Ronald K. Essayist. Business Manager, Lexington Children's Theatre, Kentucky, since 1982. Author, with Joachim Lucchesi, *Musik bei Brecht*, 1984. **Essay:** Brecht.

SICA, Alan. Essayist. Associate Professor of Sociology, University of Kansas, Lawrence, since 1982 (Assistant Professor, 1977-82). Editor, with Gary Shapiro, of *Looking for Meaning: Questions and Prospects for Hermeneutics*, 1983. Associate Editor, *Contemporary Sociology*, and *Current Perspectives in Social Theory*. **Essay:** Weber.

SIMON, Seymore. Essayist. Professor of Psychology, Northern Illinois University, DeKalb, since 1971 (joined faculty, 1961). Translator, with John Shybut, *The Psychology of Preschool Children* by Zaporzhets and Elkonin, 1971. **Essays:** Estes; Thorndike; Tolman.

SKOLIMOWSKI, Henryk. Essayist. Professor of Philosophy, University of Michigan, Ann Arbor, since 1971. Author of *Polish Analytical Philosophy*, 1967; *Polish Marxism*, 1969; *Eco-Philosophy: Designing New Tactics for Living*, 1981. **Essay:** Ajdukiewicz.

SLYTHE, R. Margaret. Essayist. Head of the Library, Dulwich College, London, since 1980. Director of Library Studies, Bournemouth and Poole College of Art, 1962-72; Librarian and Researcher to Kenneth Clark, 1962-82. Author of *The Art of Illustration*, 1970. **Essay:** Clark.

SMITH, Charlotte W. Essayist. Lecturer, University of Maryland, College Park, since 1966. Author of *Carl Becker: On History and the Climate of Opinion*, 1956. **Essay:** Becker.

STEVENS, Joseph C. Essayist. Fellow, John B. Pierce Foundation Laboratory, since 1966, and Senior Research Psychologist and Lecturer in Psychology, since 1977, Yale University, New Haven, Connecticut. Author of *Laboratory Experiments in Psychology*, 1965; editor of *Sensation and Measurement: Papers in Honor of S.S. Stevens*, 1974. **Essay:** Stevens.

STONE, Jerome Arthur. Essayist. Member of the faculty, Department of Philosophy, William Rainey Harper College, Palatine, Illinois, since 1981. Chairman, Department of Philosophy, Kendall College, 1967-81. President, Association for the Development of Philosophy Teaching, 1983. **Essay:** Alexander.

STONE, Ronald H. Essayist. Professor of Social Ethics, Pittsburgh Theological Seminary, since 1972 (Associate Professor, 1969-72). Author of *Reinhold Niebuhr: Prophet to Politicians*, 1972; *Realism and Hope*, 1977; and *Paul Tillich's Radical Social Thought*, 1980; editor of *Faith and Politics*, 1968, and *Liberation and Change*, 1977. **Essay:** Reinhold Niebuhr.

STROMBERG, Roland. Essayist. Professor, Department of History, University of Wisconsin, Milwaukee, since 1967. Author of *The Heritage and Challenge of History* (with Conkin), 1971; *After Everything: European Thought since 1945*, 1975; *Europe in the 20th Century*, 1980; *European Intellectual History since 1789*, 3rd ed. 1981; *Redemption by War: The European Intellectuals and the 1914 War*, 1982, etc. **Essays:** Benda; Sigmund Freud; Le Roy Ladurie; Namier; Orwell; Sorel.

TAMARIN, Robert H. Essayist. Associate Professor of Biology, Boston University, since 1977 (Assistant Professor, 1971-77). Author of *Genetics*, 1982; editor of *Population Regulation*, 1978. **Essay:** Müller.

THODY, Philip. Essayist. Professor of French Literature, University of Leeds, since 1975. Author of *Albert Camus: A Study of His Work*, 1957; *Jean-Paul Sartre: A Literary and Political Study*, 1960; *Albert Camus 1913-1960*, 1961; *Jean Genet: A Study of His Novels and Plays*, 1968; *Jean Anouilh*, 1968; *Four Cases of Literary Censorship*, 1968; *Laclos: Les Liaisons dangereuses*, 1970; *Jean-Paul Sartre: A Biographical Introduction*, 1971; *Aldous Huxley: A Biographical Introduction*, 1973; *Roland Barthes: A Conservative Estimate*, 1977; *A True Life Reader for Children and Parents*, 1977; *Dog Days in Babel*, 1979. **Essays:** Artaud; Barthes; Camus; Eliot; Malraux; Popper; Valéry.

TSUGAWA, Albert. Adviser and essayist. Associate Professor of Philosophy, Pennsylvania State University, University Park, since 1959. Author of *Idea of Criticism*, 1967. **Essays:** Beardsley, Grice.

TURNER, Bryan S. Essayist. Professor of Sociology, The Flinders University of South Australia, since 1982. Reader in Sociology, King's College, Aberdeen, Scotland, 1980-82. Author of *Weber and Islam*, 1974; *Marx and the End of Orientalism*, 1978; *The Dominant Ideology Thesis* (with Abercrombie and Hill), 1980; *For Weber*, 1981; *Confession* (with M. Hepworth), 1982. **Essays:** Aries; Durkheim; Gellner; Lukács; Simmel.

UNWIN, Stephen D. Essayist. Senior Scientific Officer, United Kingdom Atomic Energy Authority, since 1982. Research Fellow, Department of Theoretical Physics, University of Newcastle upon Tyne, 1980-82. **Essay:** Dirac.

URMSON, James O. Essayist. Emeritus Fellow, Corpus Christi College, Oxford (Fellow, 1959-78); Emeritus Professor, Stanford University, California (Professor of Philosophy, 1975-80). Author of *Philosophical Analysis*, 1956; *The Emotive Theory of Ethics*, 1968; and *Berkeley*, 1982; editor of *Concise Encyclopedia of Western Philosophy*, 1960; *Philosophical Pa-*

pers by J.L. Austin (with G.J. Warnock), 1962; and *How to Do Things with Words* by J.L. Austin, 1962. **Essays:** Ayer; Ryle.

VERENE, Donald Philip. Essayist. Professor and Chairman of the Department of Philosophy, Emory University, Atlanta, since 1982. Associate Professor, 1971-80, and Professor, 1980-82, Pennsylvania State University, University Park. Editor, *Philosophy and Rhetoric*. Author of *Vico's Science of Imagination*, 1981; editor of *Man and Culture*, 1970; *Sexual Love and Western Morality*, 1972; *Symbol, Myth, and Culture: Essays and Lectures of Ernst Cassirer 1935-1945*, 1979; and *Hegel's Social and Political Thought: The Philosophy of Objective Spirit*, 1980. **Essay:** Cassirer.

WARD, Paul L. Essayist. Head, Department of History, Carnegie Institute of Technology, Pittsburgh, 1953-60; President, Sarah Lawrence College, Bronxville, New York, 1960-65; Executive Secretary, American Historical Association, 1965-74. Author of *Elements of Historical Thinking*, 1971; editor of *Archeion* by William Lambarde (with C.H. McIlwain), 1957, and *William Lambarde's Notes on the Procedures and Privileges of the House of Commons*, 1977. **Essay:** McIlwain.

WARTH, Robert D. Essayist. Professor of History, University of Kentucky, Lexington, since 1968. Author of *The Allies and the Russian Revolution*, 1954; *Soviet Russia in World Politics*, 1963; *Joseph Stalin*, 1969; *Lenin*, 1973; *Leon Trotsky*, 1977. **Essays:** Luxemburg; Lysenko.

WASSERMAN, Fred E. Essayist. Assistant Professor of Biology, Boston University, since 1977. **Essays:** Lorenz; von Frisch.

WATERS, Alan. Essayist. Teacher and writer, Chicago; doctoral candidate, Committee on Social Thought, University of Chicago. **Essays:** Adorno; Horkheimer; Lippmann; Mannheim; Pareto.

WEBB, Eugene. Essayist. Professor of Comparative Religion and Comparative Literature, University of Washington, Seattle, since 1975 (joined faculty, 1967). Author of *Samuel Beckett: A Study of His Novels*, 1970; *The Plays of Samuel Beckett*, 1972; *The Dark Dove: The Sacred and Secular in Modern Literature*, 1975; and *Eric Voegelin: Philosopher of History*, 1981. **Essay:** Voegelin.

WESSELS, Linda. Essayist. Associate Professor, History and Philosophy of Science, Indiana University, Bloomington, since 1981 (Assistant Professor, 1976-81). **Essays:** Born; Schrödinger.

WEST, Lorna Bowlby. Essayist. Marriage and family therapist, since 1976. **Essay:** Bowlby.

WHITEHURST, Carol A. Essayist. Lecturer in Sociology, Humboldt State University, Arcata, California, since 1981. Author of *Women in America: The Oppressed Majority*, 1977. **Essay:** Cooley.

WIDMER, Kingsley. Essayist. Professor of English and Comparative Literature, San Diego State University, California. Author of *The Art of Perversity: D.H. Lawrence*, 1962; *Henry Miller*, 1963; *The Literary Rebel*, 1965; *The Ways of Nihilism: Melville's Short Novels*, 1970; *The End of Culture: Essays on Sensibility in Contemporary Society*, 1975; *Paul Goodman*, 1980; *The Edges of Extremity: Problems of Literary Modernism*, 1980; and *Nathanael West*, 1982. **Essays:** Paul Goodman; Illich; Murdoch; Read; Rosenberg; Weil.

WILSON, Daniel J. Essayist. Assistant Professor of History, Muhlenberg College, Allentown, Pennsylvania. Author

of *Arthur O. Lovejoy and the Quest for Intelligibility*, 1980, and *Arthur O. Lovejoy: An Annotated Bibliography*, 1982; editor, with Paul F. Paskoff, of *The Cause of the South: Selections from De Bow's Review 1846-1867*, 1982. **Essay:** Lovejoy.

WILSON, Fred. Essayist. Professor, Department of Philosophy, University of Toronto, since 1981 (Assistant Professor, 1965). Author of *Carnap and Goodman: Two Formalists* (with A. Hausman), 1967; editor of *Pragmatism and Purpose: Essays in Honour of T.A. Goude* (with L.W. Sumner and J.G. Slater), 1980. **Essays:** Carnap; Neurath.

WINETROUT, Kenneth. Essayist. Margaret C. Ellis Professor of Education Emeritus, American International College, Springfield, Massachusetts (joined faculty, 1948). Author of *F.C.S. Schiller and the Dimensions of Pragmatism*, 1967, and *Arnold Toynbee: The Ecumenical Vision*, 1975. **Essay:** Toynbee.

WINSTON, Kenneth I. Essayist. Professor of Philosophy, Wheaton College, Massachussetts (joined faculty, 1969). Editor of *The Principles of Social Order: Selected Essays of Lon L. Fuller*, 1981. **Essay:** Lon L. Fuller.

WOOLSTENCROFT, Peter. Essayist. Assistant Professor, Department of Political Science, University of Waterloo, Ontario. **Essays:** Lipset; Siegfried.

WREN, David J. Essayist. Associate Professor of Philosophy, The College of St. Catherine, St. Paul, Minnesota. **Essays:** Bronowski; Nelson Goodman.

WREN, Linnea H. Essayist. Associate Professor of Art History, Gustavus Adolphus College, St. Peter, Minnesota, since 1977. **Essays:** Gropius; Le Corbusier; Panofsky; Louis Sullivan; Wölfflin; Wright.

WYMAN, Walter E., Jr. Essayist. Assistant Professor, Department of Religion, Whitman College, since 1982. **Essay:** Troeltsch.

YARBROUGH, Stephen R. Essayist. Assistant Professor of English, Texas A and M University, College Station, since 1982. Editor, with others, *An Annotated Bibliography of American Studies*, 1983. **Essays:** Gadamer; Ricoeur.

ZOHN, Harry. Essayist. Professor of German, and Chairman of the School of Humanities, Brandeis University, Waltham, Massachusetts (joined faculty, 1951). Author of *Weiner Juden in der deutschen Literatur*, 1964, and *Karl Kraus*, 1971; editor of *Liber Amicorum Friderike Maria Zweig*, 1952; *The World Is a Comedy: A Kurt Tucholsky Anthology*, 1957; *Osterreichische Juden in der Literatur*, 1968; *Der farbonvolle Untergang: Osterreichisches Lesebuch*, 1971; *Greatness Revisited* by F.M. Zweig, 1972; *The Saints of Qumran* by Rudolf Kayser, 1976; *Half-Truths and One-and-a-Half Truths: Selected Aphorisms by Karl Kraus*, 1976; *In These Great Times: A Karl Kraus Reader*, 1976; etc. **Essay:** Kraus.